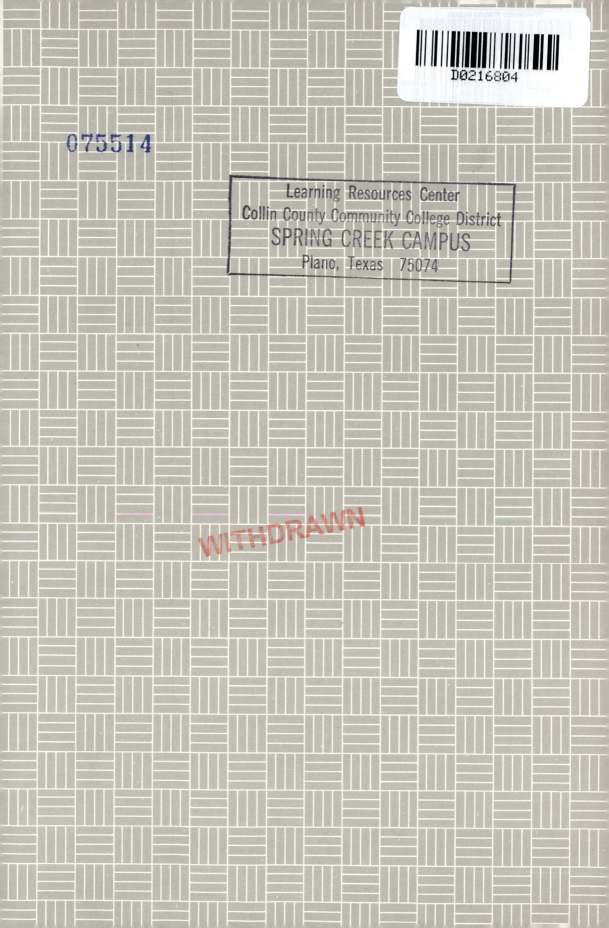

BIOGRAPHICAL DICTIONARY
OF TWENTIETH-CENTURY
PHILOSOPHERS

BIOGRAPHICAL DICTIONARY
OF TWENTIETH-CENTURY
PHILOSOPHERS

Edited by
Stuart Brown
Diané Collinson
Robert Wilkinson

London and New York

First published 1996
by Routledge
11 New Fetter Lane, London EC4P 4EE

Simultaneously published in the USA and Canada
by Routledge
29 West 35th Street, New York, NY 10001

Typeset in Franklin Gothic Demi and Times by Routledge

Printed and bound in England by
Clays Ltd, St Ives plc

British Library Cataloguing in Publication Data

A catalogue record for this book is available from the British Library

Library of Congress Cataloging in Publication Data

A catalogue record for this book is available on request.

ISBN 0-415-06043-5

CONTENTS

INTRODUCTION

This *Dictionary* is composed of information concerning over 1,000 philosophers who have lived all or part of their lives in the twentieth century. The aims, scope and rationale of the work are set out below.

The first point to consider is the sense in which the term 'philosopher' has been used. At present, the very great majority of those would describe themselves as philosophers are academics with posts in various types of educational institution in which they are employed to teach the subject. This is a relatively recent development in philosophical history, more so in the east than in the west, and a little thought will show that it would be wrong to include in this book only those whose claim to be a philosopher rests on a line in their job description. Accordingly, a dominant principle used in compiling the list of entries has been to consider for inclusion those thinkers regarded as philosophers in the communities and cultures to which they belong.

Again, care has been taken to ensure that the scope of the *Dictionary* is worldwide. Manifestly, what counts as philosophy at different times and in different places has differed to a degree; but it is important not to overstress this point. One feature which does emerge in the following pages is an unforced set of family resemblances between philosophers. A consequence of the use of this basic principle has been the inclusion of thinkers from all the major schools and traditions of the period, from analytic philosophy to Marxism and from neo-Hinduism to Zen, though no attempt has been made to massage the selection to produce any artificial equality in the numbers of entries devoted to representatives of schools (etc.) concerned. Though First World philosophers are well represented, the application of this principle has resulted in a very significant number of entries being devoted to thinkers from the Near and Far East and from the non-European Hispanic-language communities. Every area of philosophy, from formal logic to aesthetics, is represented.

The final selection of entries was made using a number of criteria in conjunction with one another in the light of the guiding principles outlined above. These criteria were adopted with the goal of avoiding personal bias on the part of the editors. They rely greatly on the reception of the work of the thinkers concerned in the philosophical community, and so embody the value judgements of many. The criteria are as follows:

i) Inclusion in major reference works

The major figures of the century up to approximately the 1960s are easily identified as those in most of the main histories of the period—Frege, Nietzsche, Husserl, Wittgenstein and so on. Also included are other slightly less important philosophers, mentioned by some but not others, who have exerted some influence and/or have received more than passing critical attention, e.g. W. D. Ross, H. H. Price, H. A. Prichard.

ii) Volume and range of secondary literature

Philosophers who have come to the fore more recently and so are not yet adequately represented in histories and surveys and would be missed by criterion i) alone. Other sources have been used, such as the *Philosopher's Index* (especially its CD-ROM), to identify contemporary philosophers who have been to the fore in journal debates, But people have not been included merely because of frequent citation, e.g. because their name is used in connection with a particular paradox or theorem.

iii) Substantial publication

Major library catalogues and other relevant sources have been used to establish which philosophers have published substantial works, though of course mere bulk of publication has not of itself guaranteed appropriateness for inclusion.

iv) Advice from consultants

In areas outside the expertise of the editors, advice from specialist consultants has been obtained, though final responsibility for the choice of entries has rested with the editors alone.

We believe that no major twentieth-century philosopher is missing from this *Dictionary*. At the same time, it would be impossible to include every worthwhile philosopher in a single volume. We have sought to represent philosophy throughout the world and throughout the century in the light of the different criteria which apply to different countries and different times. We have, of course, reflected the volume of activity to some extent but have thought it important not to allow this to be the only consideration. Not everyone will agree with the balance we have drawn between different categories. We have sought, however, to be consistent in applying our criteria to each category.

Application of the above criteria yields not only a list of names for inclusion but also an indication of the importance of the figures concerned, and these judgements are reflected in the different lengths of entry. Entries fall into five classes from short (*c.*250 words) to long (*c.*1,250 words). Whatever the length of the entry, however, each follows the same basic pattern. Following the name of the philosopher, the entry is arranged in fields as follows: nationality; date of birth and, where appropriate, of death, with places where these can be ascertained (dates are given in terms of the Western/Christian calendar, with Old Style dates indicated for Russian philosophers); brief categorization (e.g. vitalist; phenomenologist, etc.); interests, i.e. fields of major contributions to philosophy (e.g. ethics; metaphysics, etc.); details of higher education; major influences on the entrant; professional and other appointments; list of major works; reference to significant commentaries/secondary works, where these exist at the time of writing; an outline of the philosopher's ideas, with some indication of the reception and influence on others where appropriate; an indication of any additional sources, other than those listed in the primary and secondary material, used by the writer of the entry. Some of the categorizations, where not explained in the entry, are covered in the Index of Schools and Movements. We have additionally introduced one specially defined tern for use in the 'categorization' field, and that is 'systematic philosopher'. For much of the period and in many places, the goal of a philosopher has been to construct a complete world-picture, a description of the whole *rerum natura* and our place in it, and this term has been introduced to indicate such an outlook.

Some of the most innocent-seeming of these fields hold problems, not least as a result of political changes during the time of writing of the book. The collapse of the USSR and emergence of the Russian federation, the civil war in former Yugoslavia and similar events can make an indication of nationality, for example, a more complex undertaking than might at first appear. Where appropriate, the writers have indicated the nationality under which the philosopher would have described him/herself during their lifetime, or have used their discretion to indicate an ethnic origin (e.g. Serbian; Croatian; Ukrainian) where the political map is still fluid. Naturalizations are indicated as appropriate, as are significant emigrations, notably as a result of the Spanish Civil War and the Second World War.

In order to keep the overall word limit for the book within bounds, full bibliographical information is generally given only for works published in or after 1945, and is omitted where individual editions have been replaced by a standard *Works* or *Complete Works*. Full bibliographical information is given for all secondary material, where available. Most titles in the 'sources' field are abbreviated; a list of the full titles can be found on pages xv–xix of this book.

The same need not to swell the overall number of words has determined the principles used in dealing with languages other than English. Titles of works in the Romance languages (except Romanian) and German have been left in the original, though any phrases quoted from these works in the text of entries have been translated. Titles etc. from all other languages have been translated. All titles etc. from languages which are either non-alphabetic or which do not use the roman alphabet have been romanized as well as translated. Quantitative accents on transliterated Japanese have been omitted, as have accents from Indian, Arabic, Turkish and other languages of the Middle and Far East.

In addition to the entries on individual philosophers, we have included a number of general entries dealing with important philosophical groupings (e.g. the Vienna Circle) or currents of thought (e.g. analytic philosophy; vitalism) which provide a complementary approach to the study of twentieth-century philosophy. However, since this book is a dictionary of philosophers not of philosophy we have not introduced articles defining the branches of the subject, or basic technical terms such as a priori/posteriori, and the like. A basic knowledge of philosophy is assumed. A list of the general articles can be found immediately before the main alphabetical sequence of entries (**List of Schools and Movements**), and the general articles themselves are grouped together in the **Guide to Schools and Movements** at the end of the book.

Where the initial basic description of a philosopher appears in inverted commas/italics at the start of an entry, it indicates an idiosyncratic stylization favoured by the philosopher in question and explained in the text of the entry. Where the name of a philosopher appears in bold in the text paragraphs of an entry, this indicates that the philosopher is also the subject of an entry in this book.

Finally, a number of indexes have been included at the end of the book. Philosophers are listed there in a number of different but illuminating ways:

- by nationality;
- by category;
- by interest (e.g. there is a section headed 'Aesthetics' giving the names of all the philosophers listed in the book who have written in that area);
- by major influences on twentieth-century philosophers (i.e. there are lists headed Plato, Kant, Bergson, Ortega y Gasset, Wittgenstein, and so on, to indicate which thinkers have been influenced by these philosophers);
- by people (i.e. all persons significantly mentioned in the text paragraphs of an entry);
- by subject (i.e. all subjects significantly mentioned in the text paragraphs of an entry).

In preparing the *Dictionary* we have benefited from advice from many people, including the following: Professor Leslie Armour; Dr Hugh Bredin; Dr Nicholas Bunnin; Dr Colin Chant; the late Professor F. C. Copleston; Dr Thorild Dahlquist; Dr Anthony Ellis; Dr Ivor Grattan-Guinness; Jean Grimshaw; Professor Rudolf Haller; Dr Oliver Leaman; Mr Peter Lewis; Dr Richard Mason; the late Professor Bimal Matilal; Dr Wolfe Mays; Professor D. J. O'Connor; Anthony, Lord Quinton; Mr Stig Rasmussen; Professor Andrew Reck; Mr Jonathan Ree; Professor Marcus Singer; the late Wim Van Dooren; M. Jean Michel Vienne.

We would like to acknowledge also the extensive help given to the editors by the staff of the Open University Library, notably Tony Coulson and Annette Flynn and the staff of the Inter-library Loans division, and by Ms S. Hodgman at the Memorial Library, University of Wisconsin (Madison).

Despite our best efforts no doubt errors and omissions remain, and we would welcome suggestions for future editions.

PROFESSOR STUART BROWN
DR DIANE COLLINSON
DR ROBERT WILKINSON

HOW TO USE THE DICTIONARY

Structure of an entry

The *Dictionary* comprises signed entries on over 1,000 philosophers. There are three basic elements to each entry.

The opening section gives biographical details and summarizes the philosophical interests of the entrant. The first item of information after the name is nationality. Because of the difficulty of establishing entrants' preferences, English, Welsh and Scottish have been standardized as British. Cases of dual nationality or changes of citizenship have been noted. Following are dates and places of birth (*b:*), and death (*d:*) if appropriate, category (*Cat:*), interests (*Ints:*), higher education (*Educ:*), influences on the entrant (*Infls:*), and professional appointments (*Appts:*). The last are often posts held in higher education institutions, but where appropriate political and other activities are detailed.

A bibliographical section gives titles of major works by the entrant (**Main publications**), and critical or biographical works (**Secondary literature**), with dates, location and publisher where these are available. For books published before 1945, these details may not be so readily available; for political reasons also some works may be difficult to trace. The **Sources** field, at the end of the entry, lists works which were used in researching the entry, and not previously given in the **Secondary literature**. Many of these are reference works or journals, and are abbreviated. A list of the full titles can be found on page xv–xix.

Text paragraphs offer a description of the interests, ideas and work of the philosopher, expanding on the earlier summary. Influences (both on and by the entrant), central works, developments and changes in thought, alignments to schools or movements, may all be elements within this section. Names in bold type within the text are cross-references, indicating other entries that will be found in the book.

Guide to Schools and Movements

This acts as a kind of 'glossary' and consists of short articles, with suggested reading, on 39 major schools and movements of philosophy mentioned in the book. Of the persons named in the article, those in bold type have an entry in the *Dictionary*.

Indexes

The following indexes are in the traditional form, with sub-headings and the names of relevant entrants listed underneath. Surnames only are given for entrants, except where this would lead to ambiguity.

Nationality Index
The nationality for each entrant is given; those of dual nationality are listed under one or the other but not both, i.e. Lévi-Strauss is listed under **Belgian-French**. Changes of citizenship are also given where known.

Category Index
This index is linked to the *Cat:* field in the main entry, and reflects the main 'types' of philosopher, i.e. the main philosophical subject area of an entrant's work. An entrant may be (and often is) listed under more than one category.

Index of Interests
This index is linked to the *Ints:* field in the main entry, and gives the special area(s) of interest for each philosopher.

Index of Influences
This index is linked to the *Infls:* field in the main entry. The persons under each heading have been influenced by the person, subject, movement, work, etc. in bold type.

Index of People
Lists persons mentioned in the text paragraphs of an entry as being of some significance in the life of the entrant. They may be influences on the entrant, admirers, critics (hostile or otherwise), persons influenced by the entrant, etc. and may or may not work or have worked in the field of philosophy (for instance, some are writers).

Index of Subjects
Lists subjects (branches of philosophy, theology, literature, etc.) mentioned in the text paragraphs of an entry as having some impact on the entrant.

NOTES ON CONTRIBUTORS

Ainley, Alison
Lecturer in Philosophy, Anglia Polytechnic
University, Cambridge.

Allaire, E. B.
Department of Philosophy, University of Texas at
Austin.

Armour, Leslie
Professor of Philosophy, University of Ottawa.

Aslan, Adnan
Studying for PhD at University of Lancaster;
affiliated to the Centre for Islamic Studies,
Istanbul.

Barth, Else M.
Professor Emeritus, Rijksuniversiteit Groningen.

Binder, Thomas
Member of the Forschungsstelle für
österreichische Philosophie, Graz.

Borst, Clive
Lecturer in Philosophy (retired), Keele
University.

Brady, Emily
Lecturer in Philosophy, University of Lancaster.

Bredin, Hugh
Senior Lecturer in Scholastic Philosophy, Queen's
University, Belfast.

Brown, Stuart
Professor of Philosophy, Open University.

Bunnin, Nicholas
Fellow, University of Essex, and Director,
Philosophy Project, Centre for Modern Chinese
Studies, University of Oxford.

Bunting, H.
Lecturer in Philosophy, University of Ulster.

Cadwallader, Eva
Professor of Philosophy, Westminster College,
Pennsylvania.

Campanini, Massimo
Teacher of Medieval Islamic Philosophy,
University of Milan.

Carr, Indira Mahalingam
Senior Lecturer in Law, University of Exeter,
Special Lecturer in Philosophy, University of
Nottingham, Director of Exeter University
Centre for Legal Interdisciplinary Development
(EUCLID).

Chant, Colin
Lecturer in History of Science and Technology,
Open University.

Christofidou, Andrea
Worcester College, Oxford.

Collinson, Diané
Senior Lecturer in Philosophy, Open University.

Dahlquist, Thorild
Lecturer (retired), Department of Philosophy,
University of Uppsala, Sweden.

Davey, Nicholas
Lecturer in History and Theory of Art, University
College Llandalb.

Dlugos, Peter
Graduate student and PhD candidate, University
of Virginia.

Dunlop, Francis
Honorary Research Fellow, University of East
Anglia (Lecturer in Philosophy, 1995–6).

Duthie, Jim
Senior Lecturer in Philosophy, University of
London.

Edwards, Jim
Senior Lecturer in Philosophy, University of
Glasgow.

Ellis, Anthony
Professor of Philosophy, Virginia
Commonwealth University.

Emlyn-Jones, Chris
Senior Lecturer in Classical Studies, Department
of Classical Studies, Open University.

Everitt, Nicholas
Lecturer in Philosophy, School of Economic and
Social Studies, University of East Anglia.

Fabian, Reinhard
Managing Director, Forschungsstelle und
Dokumentationszentrum für österreichische
Philosophie, Graz, Austria.

Fellows, Roger
Senior Lecturer in Philosophy and Head of
Department of Interdisciplinary Human Studies,
University of Bradford.

Føllesdal, Dagfinn
Professor of Philosophy, University of Oslo, and
Professor of Philosophy, Stanford University.

Franks, Benjamin
Research Assistant, Institute of Education,
University of London.

Frazier, Robert
Lecturer, Christ Church, Oxford.

Fujimoto, Kiyohiko
Professor, Bukkyo University, Kyoto, Japan.

Fulford, K. W. M.
Professor of Philosophy and Mental Health,
University of Warwick.

Gorner, Paul
Lecturer in Philosophy, Department of
Philosophy, University of Aberdeen.

Gower, Barry
Senior Lecturer in Philosophy of Science,
University of Durham.

Graham, Keith
Reader in Philosophy, University of Bristol.

Grattan-Guinness, Ivor
Professor of the History of Mathematics and
Logic, University of Middlesex.

Gullvåg, Ingemund
Professor of Philosophy, University of
Trondheim, Norway.

Haller, Rudolf
Professor of Philosophy, University of Graz.

Heijerman, Erik
Formerly associated with the International
School for Philosophy, Amersfoort, Netherlands.

Heil, John
Professor of Philosophy, Davidson College,
North Carolina.

Humphreys, Paul
Professor of Philosophy, Corcoran Department
of Philosophy, University of Virginia.

Iannone, A. Pablo
Professor of Philosophy, Central Connecticut
State University.

Jadacki, Jacek Julius
Professor of Philosophy, University of Warsaw.

Jamieson, Dale
Professor of Philosophy, University of Colorado
at Boulder.

Jones, Barry
Formerly research student, University of
Manchester.

Kasher, Asa
Laura Schwarz-Kipp Professor, Department of
Philosophy, University of Tel Aviv.

Kieran, Matthew
Lecturer in Philosophy, University of Leeds.

Kline, George L.
Professor Emeritus of Philosophy, Bryn Mawr
College, Pennsylvania.

Kuehn, Manfred
Associate Professor of Philosophy, Purdue
University, Lafayette, Indiana.

Lacey, A. R.
Senior Lecturer in Philosophy (retired), King's
College, University of London.

Lamarque, Peter
Ferens Professor of Philosophy, University of
Hull.

Lamb, David
Reader in Philosophy, Department of Biomedical
Science and Bioethics, University of Birmingham.

Lancaster, Irene
Part-time Lecturer in Biblical and Modern
Hebrew, Centre for Continuing Education,
University of Liverpool.

Lange, Bettina
Tutor in Philosophy, Open University.

Langenfus, William
Assistant Professor, John Carroll University, Ohio.

Leaman, Oliver
Reader in Philosophy, Liverpool John Moores University.

Lee, Keekok
Reader in Philosophy, University of Manchester; Director of the Centre for Philosophy and the Environment.

Leggatt, Stuart
Research student, University of Reading.

Lewis, Peter
Lecturer in Philosophy, University of Edinburgh.

Lindström, Sten
Associate Professor, University of Umeå.

Lyas, Colin
Senior Lecturer in Philosophy, University of Manchester.

McCulloch, Gregory
Professor of Philosophy, University of Birmingham.

Malachowski, Alan
Teacher of Philosophy, University of Reading.

Martin, R. N. D.
Self-employed; part-time work for the Open University.

Mason, Richard
Fellow of Wolfson College, Cambridge, and Tutor in Philosophy, Madingley Hall.

Masugata, Kinya
Professor, Osaka Kyoiku University.

Matthews, Eric
Professor of Philosophy and Head of Department, University of Aberdeen.

Mills, Stephen
Lecturer in Philosophy, University of Ulster at Coleraine, Northern Ireland.

Moller, Stephen
Lecturer in Philosophy, University of Wales, Cardiff.

Mouralis, Bernard
University of Cergy-Pontoise, France.

Mudimbe, V. Y.
Professor of Philosophy, Stanford University.

Odiari, Sebastien
Lecturer in Philosophy, School of Humanities and Social Sciences, University of Glamorgan.

Oliver, Amy A.
Associate Professor of Spanish and Latin American Studies, American University, Washington, DC.

Outhwaite, William
Professor of Sociology, University of Sussex, Brighton.

Pappas, George S.
Professor of Philosophy, Ohio State University, Columbus.

Plant, Kathryn
Tutor in Philosophy, Open University.

Pollard, Denis
Senior Lecturer in Philosophy, University of Glamorgan.

Poltier, Hugues
Privat-docent, University of Lausanne, and Chargé de cours, University of Fribourg.

Puhl, Klaus
Assistant, Department of Philosophy, University of Graz, Austria.

Pyle, Andrew
Lecturer in Philosophy, University of Bristol.

Quinton, Lord Anthony
Formerly President of Trinity College, Oxford, and Fellow of the British Academy.

Rasmussen, Stig
Teacher of Philosophy, University of Copenhagen.

Reck, Andrew
Professor of Philosophy and Director of Liberal Arts Program, Tulane University, New Orleans; Editor, *History of Philosophy Quarterly*.

Reese, William
Formerly Professor of Philosophy, State University of New York at Albany.

Rickman, H. P.
Visiting Professor in Philosophy, City University, London.

Rockmore, Tom
Professor of Philosophy, Duquesne University, Pittsburgh.

Rosenberg, Jay F.
Taylor Grandy Professor of Philosophy, University of North Carolina at Chapel Hill.

Sakai, Kiyoshi
Professor, Faculty of Letters, Okayama University.

Scaltsas, Patricia
Tutor in Philosophy, Open University.

Scanlan, James
Professor of Philosophy, Ohio State University.

Scott, David
Teacher of Philosophy, Memorial University of Newfoundland, St John's.

Sell, Alan
Professor of Christian Doctrine and Philosophy of Religion, and Director of the Centre for the Study of British Christian Thought, both at the United Theological College, University of Wales.

Shildrick, Margrit
Lecturer in Feminist Theory, Centre for Women's Studies, University of Lancaster.

Sim, Stuart
Professor of English Studies, University of Sunderland.

Singer, Marcus
Professor of Philosophy Emeritus, University of Wisconsin, Madison.

Sosa, Ernest
Romeo Elton Professor of Natural Theology, Department of Philosophy, Brown University.

Spooner, David
Tutor in Philosophy, Open University.

Stickler, Ursula
Researcher, University of Sheffield.

Tayama, Reishi
Assistant Professor in the Faculty of Literature, Bukkyo University, Kyoto, Japan.

Tsinorema, Stavroula
Lecturer in Philosophy, University of Ioannina, Greece.

Tsukahara, Togo
Lecturer, Faculty of Letters, Tokai University, Japan.

Van Dooren, Wim (deceased)
Formerly Teacher of Philosophy, University of Utrecht.

Verburg, M. E.
Historian to the Ministry of Justice in the Netherlands (The Hague).

Walford, David
Lecturer in Philosophy, University of Wales, Lampeter.

Warburton, Nigel
Lecturer in Philosophy, Open University.

Warner, Martin
Senior Lecturer in Philosophy, University of Warwick.

White, John
Professor of Philosophy of Education, Institute of Education, University of London.

Whitford, Margaret
Teacher, Queen Mary and Westfield College, London.

Wilde, Carolyn
Lecturer in Philosophy, University of Bristol.

Wilkinson, Robert
Staff Tutor and Senior Lecturer in Philosophy, Open University.

Williams, James
Lecturer in Philosophy, University of Dundee.

Williams, Mark
Lecturer in Japanese Studies, Department of East Asian Studies, University of Leeds.

Williams, Paul
Reader in Indo-Tibetan Studies, and Co-director of the Centre for Buddhist Studies, University of Bristol.

Wolfskeel, Cornelia W.
University of Utrecht.

Wright, Andrew
Senior Lecturer in Philosophy, School of Historical, Philosophical and Contemporary Studies, University of North London.

LIST OF ABBREVIATED SOURCES

These abbreviations appear in the **Sources** field at the end of an entry, where the author gives the sources used in compilation of the entry. Periodical abbreviations, including indexes, derive from the initial letters of each significant word in the title, and remain in italic. Books, including annuals, use the author's or editor's name(s), or a contraction of the title where this is not possible, and appear in roman.

ADB	*Australian Dictionary of Biography (1891–1939)*, Melbourne: Melbourne University Press, 1981
AHCI	*Arts and Humanities Citation Index*
AHES	*Arch. Hist. Exact Sciences*
AJP	*Australasian Journal of Philosophy*
AmBio	*The National Cyclopaedia of American Biography*
ASCR	*Académie des Sciences Comptes Rendus*
Baruzi	*Philosophes et savants français*, J. Baruzi, Paris: F. Alcan, 1926
BDM	*Biographical Dictionary of Marxism*, ed. Robert A. Gorman, London: Mansell and New York: Greenwood Press, 1986
BDN	*Biographical Dictionary of Neo-Marxism*, ed. Robert A. Gorman, London: Mansell and New York: Greenwood Press, 1986
Becker	*Encyclopedia of Ethics*, ed. Lawrence C. and Charlotte Becker, New York: Garland, 1992
Benrubi	*Contemporary Thought of France*, Isaac Benrubi, trans. Ernest B. Dicker, London: Williams & Norgate, 1926
BJA	*British Journal of Aesthetics*
Blau	*Men and Movements in American Philosophy* by Joseph L. Blau, New York: Prentice-Hall, 1952
BLC	British Library Catalogue
BMFRS	*Biographical Memoirs of Fellows of the Royal Society*
BMMRS	*Biographical Memoirs of Members of the Royal Society*
Bochenski	*Contemporary European Philosophy* by I. M. Bochenski, second edition, 1951 (English translation, Berkeley: University of California Press, 1965, and New York: Greenwood Press, 1982)
BP	*Bibliographica Philosophica*
Brockhaus	*Brockhaus Enzyklopädie*, Wiesbaden: F. A. Brockhaus, 1973 (seventeenth edition, Elsevier Science Ltd, 1981)
BS	*Berkeley Studies*
Bullock & Stallybrass	*The Fontana Dictionary of Modern Thought*, ed. A. Bullock and O. Stallybrass, London: Fontana, 1977
Bullock & Woodings	*The Fontana Dictionary of Modern Thinkers*, ed. A. Bullock and R. B. Woodings, London: Fontana, 1983
Burkhardt	*Handbook of Metaphysics and Ontology*, ed. Hans Burkhardt, Munich: Philosophia Verlag, 2 vols, 1991
Burr	*Handbook of World Philosophy: Contemporary Developments since 1945*, ed. John A. Burr, London: Aldwych Press, 1980
CA	*Contemporary Authors: A Bio-bibliographical Guide to Current Authors and their Works*, Detroit: Gale Research Inc., 1962–present
CA FR	*Contemporary Authors First Revision*
CA NRS	*Contemporary Authors New Revision Series*
CanBio	*Macmillan Dictionary of Canadian Biography*, London: Macmillan, 1963
CAP I & II	*Contemporary American Philosophy*, vols I and II, ed. G. P. Adams and W. P. Montague, New York: Macmillan and St Martin's Press, 1930
CB	*Current Biography*, New York: H. H. Wilson, various editions

CBD	*Chambers Biographical Dictionary*, various editions; 1994 edition ed. Magnus Magnusson
CBP I, II, III	*Contemporary British Philosophy: Personal Statements* (first and second series ed. J. H. Muirhead, third series ed. H. D. Lewis) London: Allen & Unwin, 1924–5 (I and II), 1956 (III)
ChEnc	*Chambers Encyclopedia*, Oxford: Pergamon, various editions
CJE	*Cambridge Journal of Economics*
CollEnc	*Collier's Encyclopedia*, New York: Macmillan, various editions
Cooper	*A Companion to Aesthetics*, ed. David Cooper, Oxford: Blackwell, 1995
Copleston	*History of Philosophy*, vol. 9: *Maine de Biran to Sartre* by F. C. Copleston, London: Search Press, 1975
Corsini	*The Concise Encyclopedia of Psychology*, ed. R. Corsini, New York: John Wiley, 1987
CPBI	*Cumulative Philosophical Book Index*
DA	*Dissertation Abstracts*
DAB	*Dictionary of American Biography*, Oxford: Oxford University Press and New York: Scribner's, various editions
Dancy & Sosa	*A Companion to Epistemology*, ed. J. Dancy and E. Sosa, Oxford: Blackwell, 1992
DAP	*Directory of American Philosophers*, Bowling Green, OH: Philosophy Documentation Center, Bowling Green State University, 1993
DAS	*Directory of American Scholars*, New York: R. R. Bowker, 1942–present
Devine	*Thinkers of the Twentieth Century: A Biographical, Bibliographical and Critical Dictionary*, ed. Elizabeth Devine *et al.*, London: Macmillan, 1983
DFN	*Dizionario dei Filosofi dei Novecento*, Florence: Sansoni, 1976
DH	*Dialectics and Humanism*
DNB	*Dictionary of National Biography*, London: Oxford University Press, various editions
DSB	*Dictionary of Scientific Biography*, ed. G. C. Gillespie, New York: Scribner's, 1970–present
EAB	*Encyclopedia of American Biography*, second edition, ed. J. A. Garraty, HarperCollins (US), 1995
Edwards	*Encyclopedia of Philosophy*, ed. Paul Edwards, New York: Macmillan & Co., 1967
EF	*Enciclopedia Filosofica*, Florence: G. C. Sansoni, 6 vols, 1967
Eisler	*Philosophen-Lexikon: Leben, Werke und Lehren der Denker*, ed. Rudolf Eisler, Berlin, 1912; revised edition, 2 vols, 1937–9
EncAm	*Encyclopedia Americana*, Grolier (US), 1995
EncBrit	*Encyclopaedia Britannica*
EncIslam	*Encyclopaedia of Islam*, ed. H. A. R. Gibb *et al.*, second edition, Leiden: Brill, 6 vols, 1960–
EncJud	*Encyclopaedia Judaica*, Jerusalem: Keter, 1971
FCLE	*The Feminist Companion to Literature in English*, ed. Isobel Grundy, Virginia Blain and Patricia Clements, Batsford, 1993
Ferm	*A History of Philosophical Systems*, ed. V. T. A. Ferm, Freeport, NY: Books for Libraries Press, 1950
Ferrater Mora	*Diccionario de Filosofia*, José Ferrater Mora, Madrid: Alianza Editorial, fifth edition, 1984
Flew	*A Dictionary of Philosophy*, ed. Antony Flew, New York: St Martin's Press, revised second edition, 1984
FranBio	*Dictionnaire de biographie française*, Paris: Librairie Letouzey et Ané, 1985
Goldenson	*Longman Dictionary of Psychology and Psychiatry*, ed. R. M. Goldenson, New York and London: Longman, 1984

Grave	*A History of Philosophy in Australia*, S. A. Grave, St Lucia: University of Queensland Press, 1985
Gregory	*Oxford Companion to the Mind*, R. L. Gregory, Oxford: Oxford University Press, 1987
Harré & Lamb	*The Encyclopedic Dictionary of Psychology*, ed. R. Harré and R. Lamb, Oxford: Basil Blackwell, 1983
HC	*The Human Context*
Hill	*Contemporary Theories of Knowledge*, T. E. Hill, New York: Ronald, 1961
Huisman	*Dictionnaire des Philosophes*, ed. Denis Huisman, Paris: PUF, 2 vols, 1984
IDPP	*International Directory of Philosophy and Philosophers*, Bowling Green, OH: Philosophy Documentation Center, Bowling Green State University, seventh edition, 1992
IWW	*International Who's Who*, London: Europa Publications, various editions
IWWW	*International Who's Who of Women*, London: Europa Publications, 1992
JBAA	*Journal of the British Astronomical Association*
JBSP	*Journal of the British Society for Phenomenology*
JHI	*Journal of the History of Ideas*
JPS	*Journal of Philosophical Studies*
JSL	*Journal of Symbolic Logic*
Kersey	*Women Philosophers: A Biocritical Source Book*, Ethel M. Kersey, New York: Greenwood Press, 1989
Kindler	*Kindlers Literatur Lexikon*, Zurich: Kindler Verlag, 1965 and 1970
Kurtz	*American Philosophy in the Twentieth Century: A Sourcebook*, ed. Paul Kurtz, New York: Macmillan, 1966
Landgrebe	*Philosophie der Gegenwart*, L. Landgrebe, Bonn: Atheneum, 1992
LXXS	*Larousse du XXième siècle*, Paris: Librairie Larousse, 1928–53
MA	*Manuscripts and Archives*
Macquarrie	*Twentieth Century Religious Thought*, John Macquarrie, London: SCM Press, revised edition, 1971
Mercier & Svilar	*Philosophes critiques d'eux memes*, ed. A Mercier and M. Svilar, Bern, Frankfurt and New York: Peter Lang, 1975–
Metz	*A Hundred Years of Philosophy*, Rudolf Metz, trans. J. W. Harvey, T. E Jessop and H. Sturt, ed. J. H. Muirhead, London: Allen & Unwin, 1938 (originally published in German, Heidelberg, 1934)
Metzler	*Metzler Philosophenlexikon*, Stuttgart: J. B. Metzlersche, 1989
Meyer & Vahle	*Philosophinnen Lexion*, ed. Ursula I. Meyer and Heidemarie Bennent Vahle, Aachen: ein-Fach-verlag, 1994
MGP	*Modern German Philosophy*, R. Bubner, Cambridge: Cambridge University Press, 1981
Mittelstrass	*Enzyklopädie Philosophie und Wissenschaftstheorie*, ed. Jürgen Mittelstrass, Mannheim: Bibliographisches Institut AG, 1980–
MSSPNB	*Mémoires, Société des Sciences Physiques et Naturelles de Bourdeaux*
NDB	*Neue Deutsche Biographie*, Berlin, 1953–
Nida	*Philosophie der Gegenwart*, ed. J. Nida-Rümelin, Stuttgart: Alfred Kröner Verlag, 1991
NÖB	*Neue Österreichische Biographie*, Vienna and Munich, Amalthea
NH	*Natural History*
NP	*Natural Philosophy*
NUC	National Union Catalog (US)
NYRB	*New York Review of Books*

PAAPA	*Proceedings and Addresses of the American Philosophical Association*
Parodi	*La Philosophie contemporaine en France*, D.-H. Parodi, Paris: F. Alcan, 1920
PAS	*Proceedings of the Aristotelian Society*
Passmore 1957	*A Hundred Years of Philosophy*, John Passmore, London: Duckworth, 1957
Passmore 1985	*Recent Philosophers*, John Passmore, London: Duckworth, 1985
PBA	*Proceedings of the British Academy*
PCS	*Proceedings of the Chemical Society*
Perry	*Philosophy of the Recent Past*, Ralph Barton Perry, New York: Scribner's, 1926
PEW	*Philosophy East West*
PI	*Philosopher's Index*, Bowling Green, OH: Philosophy Documentation Center, Bowling Green State University, various editions
PInv	*Philosophical Investigations*
PM	*Praxis der Mathematik*
PPR	*Philosophy and Phenomenological Research*
PR	*Philosophical Review*
PSci	*Philosophy of Science*
PSt	*Philosophical Studies*
PT	*Physics Today*
QJRAS	*Quarterly Journal of the Royal Astronomical Society*
RA	*Reader's Adviser*, Bowker (US), fourteenth edition, 1994
Reck 1964	*Recent American Philosophy*, Andrew Reck, New York: Pantheon Books, 1964
Reck 1968	*The New American Philosophers*, Andrew Reck, Baton Rouge: Louisiana State University Press, 1968
Reese	*Dictionary of Philosophy and Religion*, William L. Reese, New Jersey: Humanities Press, 1980
RFR	*Resources for Feminist Research*
von Rintelen	*Contemporary German Philosophy and its Background*, F. J. von Rintelen, Bonn: Bouvier, 1970
RMM	*Revue de Métaphysique et de Morale*
RNP	*Revue Néoscolastique de Philosopique*
RNW	*Repertorium der Nedelandse Wijsbegeerte*, ed. J. J. Poortman, Amsterdam: Wereldbibliothek, 1948 (supplements 1958 1968, 1983)
RPL	*Revue Philosophique de Louvain*
RQS	*Revue des Questions Scientifiques*
Runes	*Twentieth Century Philosophy*, New York: Greenwood Press, 1947
RTP	*Revue de Théologie et de Philosophie*
Sassen	*Wijgerig Leven in Nederland in de twintigste eeuw* [Philosophical Life in the Netherlands in the Twentieth Century], F. Sasssen, Amsterdam: North-Holland, 1941
Schneider	*A History of American Philosophy*, ed. Herbert W. Schneider, New York: Columbia University Press, 1946
Schoeps	*Neues Lexikon des Judentums*, ed. J. H. Schoeps, 1992
Sciacca	*La Filosofia, Oggi*, M. F. Sciacca, Milan: Marzorati, 1958 (English translation, *Philosophical Trends in the Contemporary World*, trans. A. Salerno, Notre Dame, IN: Notre Dame University Press, 1964)
Sell	*The Philosophy of Religion*, Alan P. F. Sell, London: Croom Helm, 1988
Shanker	*Philosophy in Britain Today*, ed. Stuart Shanker, London: Routledge, 1986
Sills	*International Encyclopedia of the Social Sciences*, ed. D. L. Sills, New York: Macmillan, 1968
Spiegelberg	*The Phenomenological Movement: A Historical Introduction*, Herbert Spiegelberg, Dordrecht: Kluwer, 1971; third, revised edition, 1981
SR	*Social Research*
STASMP	*Séances et Travaux de l'Académie des Sciences Morales et Politiques*

Turner	*Thinkers of the Twentieth Century*, ed. Roland Turner, Chicago: St James Press, second edition, 1987
UCDCL	Union Catalogue of Departmental and College Libraries, University of Cambridge
Urmson & Rée	*The Concise Encyclopaedia of Western Philosophy*, ed. J. O. Urmson and J. Rée, London: Hutchinson, 1960
WAB	*Webster's American Biographies*, Springfield, Mass.: Merriam Webster Inc., various editions
WD	*The Writer's Directory*, Chicago: St James Press, biennial
Wer	*Wer is Wer*, Berlin, 1948
Wintle	*Makers of Modern Culture: A Biographical Dictionary*, ed. Justin Wintle, London: Routledge, 1981
WorldBio	*Dictionary of Twentieth Century World Biography*, Oxford University Press, 1992
WW	*Who's Who*, London: A. & C. Black, 1843–present
WW(Am)	*Who's Who in America*, Chicago: Marquis Who's Who, 1899–present
WW(Arab)	*Who's Who in the Arab World*, Publitec (US), eleventh edition, 1992
WW(Aus)	*Who's Who in Australia*, ed. Ann C. Howie, International Publications Service (US), 27th edition, 1991
WW(Can)	*Who's Who in Canada*, International Publications Service, 86th edition, 1995
WW(Eur)	*Who's Who in Europe*, International Publications Service, fifth edition, 1983
WW(Fr)	*Who's Who in France*, Detroit: Gale Research Inc., eighteenth edition, 1986
WW(It)	*Who's Who in Italy*, Sutter's Red Series (US), 2 vols, 1994
WW(Rel)	*Who's Who in Religion*, Chicago: Marquis Who's Who, fourth edition, 1992
WW(Scan)	*Who's Who in Scandinavia*
WWW	*Who Was Who*, London: A. & C. Black, various editions
WWW(Am)	*Who Was Who in America*, Chicago: Marquis Who's Who, 1899–present
WW(West)	*Who's Who in the West*, Chicago: Marquis Who's Who, 24th edition, 1993
WW(World)	*Who's Who in the World*, Chicago: Marquis Who's Who, twelfth edition, 1995
WWWWE	*World Who's Who of Women in Education*, ed. Ernest Kay, Cambridge: International Biographical Centre, 1978.
ZAW	*Zeitschrift für Allgemeine Wissenschaftstheorie*
Ziegenfuss & Jung	*Philosophenlexikon*, ed. W. Ziegenfuss and G. Jung, Berlin: Walther de Gruyter, 1950
ZPF	*Zeitschrift für philosophische Forschung*

LIST OF SCHOOLS AND MOVEMENTS

The **Guide to Schools and Movements** contains short descriptions and bibliographies concerning the major schools of philosophy mentioned in the biographical entries. The guide itself can be found after the main entries, on pp. 876–902. The **Category Index** (p. 909) and the **Index of Interests** (p. 918) list those philosophers connected with particular schools and movements.

Absolute Idealism
Analytical Philosophy
Comtean Positivism
Critical Realism
Empiricism
Evolutionary Philosophers
Existentialism
Frankfurt School
Hegelianism
Hermeneutics
Idealism
Intuitionism
Legal Positivism
Linguistic Philosophy
Logical Positivism
Lvov-Warsaw School
Marxism
Materialism
Munich Circle
Naturalism

Neo-Kantians
Neoscholasticism
New Realism
Personalism
Phenomenology
Philosophical Anthropology
Positivism
Post-Marxism
Postmodernism
Post-structuralism
Pragmatism
Process Philosophy
Realism
Semiology
Structuralism
Uppsala School
Utilitarianism
Vienna Circle
Vitalism

A

Aaron, Richard Ithamar

British. *b:* 6 November 1901, Seven Sisters, Wales. *d:* 29 March 1987, Aberystwyth. *Cat:* Commonsense realist. *Ints:* Epistemology; history of philosophy; metaphysics. *Educ:* University College, Cardiff, and Oriel College, Oxford. *Infls:* John Cook Wilson, H. A. Prichard, W. D. Ross and A. C. Ewing. *Appts:* Lecturer in Philosophy, University College of Swansea; Professor of Philosophy, University College of Wales, Aberystwyth, 1932–69; Visiting Professor of Philosophy, Yale University, 1952–3; Fellow of the British Academy, 1955; Editor of *Efrydiau Athronyddol*, 1938–68.

Main publications:

(1930) *The Nature of Knowing*, London: Williams & Norgate.
(1932) *Hanes Athroniaeth: o Descartes i Hegel* [History of Philosophy: From Descartes to Hegel], Cardiff: University of Wales Press.
(1936) (ed. with J. Gibb) *An Early Draft of Locke's Essay*, Oxford: Clarendon Press.
(1937) *John Locke*, London: Oxford University Press; third, revised edition, Oxford: Clarendon Press, 1971.
(1952) *The Theory of Universals*, Oxford: Clarendon Press; second, revised edition, 1967.
(1971) *Knowing and the Function of Reason*, Oxford: Clarendon Press.

Secondary literature:

There is an incomplete list of Aaron's publications up to 1967 compiled by Sir Ben Bowen Thomas in *Efrydiau Athronyddol* 32, 1969. There is also a list of publications, manuscripts and typescripts, together with a short biography, tribute and a catalogue of Aaron's library, in *The Aaron Philosophy Collection*, with an introduction by I. C. Tipton and D. O. Thomas (Dorking: C. C. Kohler, 1987).

Aaron's reputation rests on his contribution to the study of the philosophy of John Locke through his discovery of an early draft of Locke's *Essay Concerning Human Understanding* and his classic study of Locke's thought, first published in 1937. Aaron's own philosophical preoccupations centred on the topic of universals, where he defended a theory of naturally recurring common qualities, and on the nature of knowledge, where he argued in favour of a form of probable knowledge which is better than fallible opinion, though falling short of infallible knowledge.

Sources: O. R. Jones (1987) obituary notice, *PBA* 73.

PETER LEWIS

Abbagnano, Nicola

Italian. *b:* 15 July 1901, Salerno, Italy. *Cat:* Existentialist. *Appts:* Taught since 1936 at Turin.

Main publications:

(1923) *Le sorgenti irrazionali del pensiero.*
(1925) *Il problema del arte.*
(1927) *Il nuovo idealismo inglese e americano.*
(1934) *La fisica nuova.*
(1936) *Il principio della metafisica.*
(1939) *La stuttura dell'esistenza.*
(1942) *Introduzione all'esistenzialismo.*
(1947) *L'esistenzialismo di Heidegger*, Turin: Taylor.
(1947) *Filosofia, religione, scienza*, Turin: Taylor.
(1948) *Esistenzialismo positivo*, Turin: Taylor.
(1959) *Problemi di sociologia*, second edition, Turin: Taylor, 1967.
(1968) *Per o contro l'uomo*, Milan: Rizzoli.
(1969) *Critical Existentialism*, New York: Anchor.
(1973) *Fra il tutto e il nulla*, Milan: Rizzoli.
(1979) *Questa pazza filosofia, ovvero l'io prigionero*, Milan: Editoriale Nuova.
(1982) *Storia della filosofia*, third edition.
(1990) *Ricordi di un filosofo*, Milan: Rizzoli.
(1990) *L'esercizio della libertà: scritti scelti 1923–1988*, Bologna: Bosi.

Secondary literature:

Bruno, M. (1974) *Bibliografia degli scritti di N. Abbagnano*, Torino: Giaprichelli.
Langiulli, N. (1992) *Possibility, Necessity and Existence: Abbagnano and his predecessors*, Philadelphia: Temple.

In Abbagnano's earliest work we find a disposition to existentialist modes of thought in opposition to the idealism of **Croce** and **Gentile**. This existential impulse was strengthened by the influence of **Husserl**, **Heidegger** and **Jaspers**. A central work is *La struttura dell'esistenza* (1939), in which the involvement of man with being is analysed. Whereas for Heidegger existence lay in anxiety, in Abbagnano the nature of existence lies in the way in which being goes in search of the possible, the undetermined existence of which makes searching itself possible. This possibility of possibility is called 'transcendental possibility'. Once a possibility has been chosen other possibilities then open. We can, by the existential option, accept our situation and, having undertaken this, realize ourselves in a continual transcending of ourselves as we move towards being or, alternatively, we can opt for inauthenticity and fall into an aimless banality. Central to much of Abbagnano's thought is a discussion of the way in which other existentialists contradict themselves in implicity denying possibility. In what he calls 'German existentialism' (with which he associates **Sartre**) possibility is undermined by the belief that all our projects are doomed to failure. The possible simply becomes impossible. In what is called 'theological existentialism' possibilities become potentialities which, being bound to succeed, cease to be genuinely open possibilities. The notion of possibility is further illuminated by Abbagnano in his pioneering study of modality and of the different senses of the term 'possible', an analysis which distinguishes the usually confused notions of logical possibility, the physical 'may be' and Aristotelian potentiality. He further asserts that existentialism requires a *positive* recognition of the necessity of value which has as its norm liberty, where liberty does not, as in Sartre, mean choosing anything whatsoever but, rather, involves a positive choice that underwrites the possibility of choosing. These notions are expressed in a form intended to be more easily accessible in *Introduzione all'esistenzialismo* (1942). Subsequent work developed his earlier writing on science (for example, *La fisica nuova* of 1934), took account of neopositivism, and emphasized connections between his existentialist analysis of possibility and verification as a scientific criterion. In 1947 he showed his interest in religion, arguing that philosophy and religion are two ways of realizing existence in faith without which there is no meaning. Abbagano's work also contains notable contributions to the history of philosophy, culminating in his *Storia della filosofia* (third edition, 1982).

COLIN LYAS

Abbott, Francis Ellingwood

American. *b:* 6 November 1836, Boston, Massachusetts. *d:* 25 October 1903, Beverly, Massachusetts. *Cat:* Scientific realist; philosopher of religion. *Ints:* Philosophy of biology. *Educ:* Harvard College and Meadville Theological Seminary (in Chicago). *Infls:* Sir William Hamilton, Charles Darwin, Herbert Spencer, Kant and Hegel. *Appts:* Unitarian minister in Dover, New Hampshire, and Toledo, Ohio; as editor of *The Index* (1870–80), he argued for a radical and rational theology; Professor of Philosophy, Harvard, 1888, substituting for Josiah Royce.

Main publications:

(1885) *Organic Scientific Philosophy: Scientific Theism*, Boston: Little, Brown & Co.
(1890) *The Way Out of Agnosticism; or, The Philosophy of Free Religion*, Boston: Little, Brown & Co.
(1906) *The Syllogistic Philosophy: A Prolegomenon to Science*, Boston: Little, Brown & Co.

Secondary literature:

Callaghan, W. J. (1952) 'Abbot's syllogistic philosophy', Dissertation, Microfilm, Columbia University Library.
Peden, Creighton M. (1992) *The Philosopher of Free Religion: Francis Ellingwood Abbot*, New York: Lang.
Royce, Josiah (1890-1) 'Dr Abbot's way out of agnosticism', *International Journal of Ethics* 1: 98–113.

Abbott fused ideas from science, especially biology, with philosophy to achieve what he earlier called scientific, or objective, realism and later the syllogistic philosophy. Relations are objective and there is 'a dynamic correlation of object and subject' (1885, p. 39). His realism required the coexistence of experience and reason in all knowledge. This implied, he thought, a union of existence and knowledge both in ourselves and in nature; and thus not only scientific realism but scientific theism. In the end this was 'a unitary and universal system' uniting being, knowing and doing.
Sources: Schneider Blau.

WILLIAM REESE

Abd al-Raziq, Ali

Egyptian. *b:* 1888, village of the province of Minya, Upper Egypt. *d:* 23 September 1966. *Cat:* Islamic modernist and reformer. *Educ:* 1912, graduated Al-Azhar University, Cairo; 1913–14,

University of Oxford. **Appts:** 1915, appointed judge at the religious tribunal of Mansurah but dismissed in retaliation for his bold reformistic ideas; 1925, condemned by the '*ulama*' of al-Azhar, deprived of his titles by Royal decree; after long trips abroad, was partially restored to his position and became member of the Academy of the Arab League, 1947.

Main publications:

(1925) *Al-Islam was Usul al Hukm* [Islam and the Foundations of Power], Cairo: Matba-at Misr (French translation, in *Revue des études islamiques*, L. Bercher, 1933–34).

(1944) *Tamhid li-Tarikh al-Falsafah al-Islamiyyah* [Introduction to the History of Islamic Philosophy] Cairo.

Secondary literature:

Adams, C. (1933) *Islam and Modernism in Egypt*, London.

Colombe, M. (1951) *L'Évolution de l'Egypte*, Paris: Maisonneuve.

Hourani, A. (1970) *Arabic Thought in the Liberal Age*, London: Oxford University Press.

Orient (1964–5) (papers by A. Morabia).

Revue du monde musulman, 1925.

Rosenthal, E. (1965) *Islam in the Modern National State*, Cambridge: Cambridge University Press.

Studi Politici, (1925) (papers by E. Panetta).

The core of Abd al-Raziq's thought is the problem of the caliphate. He starts from an examination of the link between magistrature and politics in which the caliphate appears to be necessary for a correct understanding of the legal basis of power and sovereignty in both past and present Islam. He points out the need for the Arabs to study political science in order to have a more accurate perception of human reality. Concerning the move for the abolition of the caliphate by Mustafa Kemal (1924), he then argues that the caliphate does not have any basis either in the Koran or in the consensus of the community (*Igma*). From these two ideas—that the caliphate is not a necessary part of Muslim religion and that prophetic mission is only spiritual—he argues that religion has nothing to do with government and politics. This secular approach was strongly opposed by traditionalist teachers of Islamic law and contributed to Abd al-Raziq's marginalization and his limited influence.

Sources: Archives of the Pontifical Inst. of Arabic Studies in Rome.

MASSIMO CAMPANINI

Abduh, M(uhammad)

Egyptian. **b:** 1849, Egyptian Delta. **d:** 1905. **Cat:** Islamic rationalist and modernist thinker; Islamic philosopher and social thinker. **Ints:** Politics of Islam. **Educ:** The Ahmadi mosque, Tanta and later al-Azhar. **Infls:** Jamal al-Din al-Afghani. **Appts:** Exiled by the British and moved to Beirut and Tripoli, then Paris, later returning to Egypt eventually to become the Mufti; at various times a teacher, writer and judge.

Main publications:

(1903) *Risa-lat al-waridat* [Treatise on Mysticism], Cairo.

(1948) *Al-Islam wa l-Nasraniyya* [Islam and Christianity], Cairo.

Many works of Tafsir or commentary on the Qur'an.

(1965) *Risalat al-tawhid* [Theology of Unity], trans. I. Musa and K. Cragg, London: Allen & Unwin.

Although Muhammad Abduh started off his philosophical work with a study of Avicenna (ibn Sina), he soon came to concentrate upon political and religious issues. He was very much under the influence of al-Afghani and of the latter's call to the Islamic world to unite in order to resist the West. Part of this policy was to be achieved by returning to a purer form of Islam which is cleansed of the influence of Western thought, and which none the less is based upon an argument for the rational basis of religious thought. Scientific findings will, on close examination, be shown to be similar to the doctrines of Islam, and it is important to defend the role of reason in the understanding of Islam. One should accept the teachings of Islam through the free use of reason and not because they are traditional. Islam is the most rational of religious doctrines and should be applied to the whole of life. Fighting against the pernicious influence of the West is not only a physical struggle but also, and much more importantly, an effort to reform the practice of Islam itself to restore it to its original purity.

Like so many of his contemporaries, Abduh was obsessed with finding a solution to the apparent decline of the Islamic world, and he sought an answer in the construction of a form of Islam which could encompass progress and at the same time control it. The basis of Islam consists of beliefs about the nature of the world and the rules of human morality. For those beliefs to be attained we must employ both reason and revelation, which lead us in exactly the same direction. Reason will inform us that God exists, is omniscient, omnipotent, one; that there is another life after this one, that some things are good and others evil. We can also know rationally of the need for prophets and the nature which prophecy takes. Revelation is important because it fills in those aspects of religion which we cannot grasp entirely rationally. But revelation can only work properly if it is in agreement with rationality. When there is doubt about the direction in which the laws of religion actually go, it is important to use reason to work out how one is to act or what one is to believe. Reason and revelation have to work together if Islam is to be properly embodied in the life of the believer.

Islam is in retreat because the corrupt Muslim governments have encouraged a blind reliance on tradition. They have confused the accidental features of Islam with the essential, demanding, unthinking adherence to a particular version of Islamic law. The way forward to a more Islamic and successful state is by adapting Islam to changing circumstances through examining rationally those aspects of the religion which appear to contradict modernity and seeing whether they might be altered to replicate more faithfully the sort of society which Muhammad created at Medina. The notion that modernity should not be rejected outright but could be partially incorporated into Islam had great influence upon Abduh's followers in this century. Although many of those in the Islamic world came to reject his views, he set the agenda for much of the contemporary discussion concerning the nature of the Islamic state and the role of reason and revelation in religion.

Sources: A. Hourani (1993) *Arabic Thought in the Liberal Age 1798–1939*, Cambridge: CUP.

OLIVER LEAMAN

(1959) 'The philosophy of language in revolutionary France', Dawes Hick Lecture to the British Academy, *Proceedings of the British Academy* 45: 199–219.
(1967) *What Marx Really Said*, London: Macdonald.
(1969) (ed.) *The Philosophy of Punishment*, London: Macmillan.
(1970) *Kant's Moral Philosophy*, London: Macmillan; New York: St Martin's Press.
(1971) *The Morals of the Markets: An Ethical Exploration*, London: Longman; new edition with additional essays, *The Morals of the Market and Related Essays*, ed. David Gordon and Jeremy Shearmur, Indianapolis: Liberty Fund, Inc., 1993.
(1972) (ed.) J. S. Mill, *Utilitarianism, Liberty, and Representative Government*, London: J. M. Dent & Sons Ltd., reset 1984.
(1974) 'The idea of spiritual power', *Auguste Comte Memorial Trust Lecture 1973*, London: Athlone Press.

Acton was a distinguished historian of late eighteenth-century and early nineteenth-century French and German thought. As a political philosopher he maintained that Marxism was (in his own words) 'a philosophical farrago', an inconsistent mixture of positivism and Hegelianism. He also attempted a moral defence of the principles of profit and competition in the free-market economy at a time when this view was intellectually unfashionable.

Sources: WW; Special Minute, Univ. of Edinburgh, *Senatus Minutes*, 26, 1974–5; obituary notice, *Philosophy* 49 (1974): 229; personal communication.

PETER LEWIS

Acton, Harry Burrows

British. *b:* 2 June 1908, London. *d:* 16 June 1974, Edinburgh. *Cat:* Conservative; historian of philosophy; moral and political philosopher. *Educ:* St Olave's Grammar School, London, and Magdalen College, Oxford. *Infls:* F. von Hayek, Karl Popper, J. N. Findlay and John Watkins. *Appts:* Professor of Philosophy, Bedford College, London, 1945–64; Professor of Philosophy, University of Edinburgh, 1964–74; Director of Royal Institute of Philosophy, 1962–4; Editor of *Philosophy*, 1956–72.

Main publications:

(1955) *The Illusion of the Epoch: Marxism–Leninism as a Philosophical Creed*, London: Cohen & West Ltd.

Adams, George Plimpton

American. *b:* 7 October 1882, Northboro, Massachusetts. *d:* 1961, Berkeley, California. *Cat:* Idealist. *Ints:* Metaphysics; theory of knowledge. *Educ:* Lewis Institute, Chicago; PhD, Harvard University, 1911. *Appts:* Taught Biology at the Lewis Institute, 1903; while finishing his doctorate he accepted a post in Philosophy at the University of California in Berkeley, and remained there until his retirement in 1954; periods as Visiting Professor at Cornell and Columbia Universities.

Main publications:

(1910) *The Mystical Element in Hegel's Early Theological Writings*, Berkeley: University of California Publications in Philosophy.

(1919) *Idealism and the Modern Age*, New Haven: Yale University Press.

(1930) (ed. with W. Pepperell Montague) *Contemporary American Philosophy*, London: Allen & Unwin; New York: Macmillan.

(1948) *Man and Metaphysics*, New York: Columbia University Press.

(1955) *Competitive Economic Systems*, New York: Crowell.

Adams believed that philosophers faced a basic paradox: the issues which they do and ought to address are precisely those issues which lie outside the domain of what can be known and understood. Thus the philosopher may either become a critic of philosophy itself or a romantic dependent on his intuitions. If philosophy is not to be abandoned or end in irrationalism, he urged, philosophers must accept what many idealists of Adams's time denied, that reality cannot be simply equated with experience. Equally, however, Adams accepted that it was nonsense to try to return to the Kantian thing in itself. The alternatives are naturalism (which holds that reality consists essentially of the restricted set of properties assignable to the physical world) and idealism, which Adams urged permitted a wider framework of interpretation, allowing as wide a range of characteristics as are necessary for intelligibility. Reality is thus made up of essentially logical characteristics, i.e. those which figure in what must be assumed to make the whole range of initial experiences intelligible. Adams insisted, however, that this does not necessarily imply the kind of unity characteristic of absolute idealism.

Adams was responding to the American realists and pragmatists who attacked the idealism of Josiah **Royce**. In the essentially pluralist atmosphere which developed, he sought to explain why philosophy must necessarily involve a process of constant criticism and why its aim was not to propound final doctrines but to critcally aware of the human situation. The nature of philosophy became his main interest. To this end he devoted much time to such projects as the *Contemporary American Philosophy* volume (1930) which he edited with W. Pepperell **Montague**. Although his work attracted almost no direct commentary, nearly all the essays in that volume show signs of responses to the questions which he raised.
Sources: WWW(Am).

LESLIE ARMOUR

Adickes, Erich
German. *b:* 29 June 1866, Lesum (bei Bremen), Germany. *d:* 8 July 1928, Tübingen. *Cat:* Neo-Kantian; Kant philologist; metaphysician. *Educ:* Theology, Classical Philology and Philosophy at Tübingen and Berlin. *Appts:* At one time a high-school teacher, later became Professor at Kiel, Münster and Tübingen.

Main publications:
Editor of Kant's *Reflexions* in the Kant edition of the Prussian Academy, volumes 14–18 (1911–28).
(1893–6) *German Kantian Bibliography*, New York: Burtt Franklin.
(1895) *Kant-Studien*, Kiel and Leipzig: Lipsius & Tischer.
(1911) *Die Zukunft der Metaphysik* in *Weltanschauung, Philosophie und Religion*, ed. Max Frischeisen-Köhler, Berlin: Reichl.
(1920) *Kants Opus postumum dargestellt und beurteilt*, Berlin: Reuther & Reichard.
(1924) *Kant und das Ding an sich*, Berlin: Reuther & Reichard.
(1927) *Kant und die Als-Ob Philosophie*, Stuttgart: Frommann.
(1924–5) *Kant als Natuforscher*, 2 vols, Berlin, Reuther & Reichard.
(1929) *Kants Lehre von der doppelten Affektion des Ichs*, Tübingen: J. C. B. Mohr.

Secondary literature:
Menzer, Paul (1926) tribute in *Kant-Studien* 33.
Schmidt, Raymund (1928) 'Kant–Vaihinger–Adickes', *Annalen der Philosophie und philosophischen Kritik* 7: 1–16.

In his many articles and books Adickes proved himself to be an independent follower of Kant. While he is sometimes described as a 'Neo-Kantian' who advocated a metaphysical interpretation of Kant, it is perhaps more appropriate to view him as a critic of the neo-Kantian movement. He was also vehemently opposed to Hans **Vaihinger**'s philosophy of the 'As If' or his 'fictionalism' arguing that it is was un-Kantian. Yet Adickes himself was not a strict follower of Kant either. He emphasized a more eudaimonistic ethical theory and a form of spiritualist pantheism that ultimately would be quite foreign to any strict Kantian. Adicke's edition of Kant's *Reflexions* is one of the most important contributions to Kant scholarship. It revolutionized the discussion of Kant's philosophical development by providing a firm temporal framework for dating Kant's handwritten notes. It would be difficult to imagine current Kant scholarship without his careful editorial work. His interpretation still plays a significant role in the discussion of Kant.

MANFRED KUEHN

Adler, Alfred

Austrian. **b:** 1870, Vienna. **d:** 1937, Aberdeen, Scotland. **Cat:** Neo-Freudian psychoanalyst. **Ints:** Child development; family relationships; individual and social psychology; analysis of dreams. **Educ:** Medical School, University of Vienna. **Infls:** Freud and Pierre Janet. **Appts:** Psychoanalyst in private practice; founder of child-guidance centres in schools in Vienna, Berlin and Munich after the First World War; first President of the Vienna branch of the Psychoanalytic Society, 1910.

Main publications:

(1907) *Studie über die Minderwertigkeit von Organen*, Berlin and Vienna: Urban & Schwarzenberg (English translation, *Inferiority and Its Psychical Compensation*, trans. Smith Ely Jelliffe, New York: The Nervous and Mental Disease Publishing Company, 1917).

(1912) *Über den nervösen Charakter*, Wiesbaden: Dodd, Mead & Company (English translation, *The Neurotic Constitution*, trans. Bernard Glueck and John E. Lind, New York: Dodd, Mead & Company, 1926).

(1920) *Praxis und Theorie Individualpsychologie*, Munich and Wiesbaden: J. F. Bergmann (English translation, *Practice and Theory of Individual Psychology*, trans. P. Radin, New York: Harcourt, Brace & World, 1927).

(1927) *Menschenkenntnis*, Leipzig: S. Hirzel (English translation, *Understanding Human Nature*, trans. W. Béran Wolfe, London: Allen & Unwin, 1927).

(1933) *Der Sinn des Lebens*, Vienna and Leipzig: R. Passer (English translation, *Social Interest: A Challenge to Mankind*, trans. John Winton and Richard Vaughan, London: Faber & Faber, 1938).

(1965) *Superiority and Social Interest*, ed. Heinz and Rowena Ansbacher, Evanston, Ill.: Routledge & Kegan Paul (annotated collection of later papers).

Secondary literature:

Ansbacher, H. L. and R. R. (eds) (1956) *The Individual Psychology of Alfred Adler*, New York: Basic Books (contains a full bibliography).

Mosak, H. H. and Birdie, M. (1975) *A Bibliography for Adlerian Psychology*, New York and London: John Wiley.

Munroe, R. L. (1955) *Schools of Psychoanalytic Thought*, New York: Dryden Press.

Orgler, Hertha (1939) *Alfred Adler: The Man and His Work*, London; third edition, London: Sidgwick & Jackson, 1963.

Adler was the second son of Hungarian-Jewish parents. He practised general medicine for several years before developing an interest in psychiatry. Although one of the original members of a small group who met regularly in Freud's house to discuss psychoanalysis, he soon became dissatisfied with the orthodox Freudian view and broke away to establish his own school, called Individual Psychology. The remainder of his life was spent elaborating his psychoanalytic theories, lecturing and publishing.

Adler rejected two of Freud's principal tenets: the pervasive importance of infantile sexuality, and the psychic determinism implicit in Freud's identification of the main causes of behaviour in the unconscious. Individual Psychology shares with Freudian theory a recognition of the significance of unconscious mental processes, but in place of the reductive mental structures of the Freudian model, it emphasizes the importance of the individual person as an indivisible whole: active, self-creating and motivated as much by conscious goals (individual and social) as by unconscious fantasies and wishes. The social context is important to the extent that it triggers self-perceptions.

Adler maintained that feelings of inferiority are universal, but countered by a striving for superiority guided by a 'fictive goal' and modified by the 'antifiction' of social reality. Normal development involves a balanced resolution of these factors. The neurotic adopts rigid or unrealistic ways of adapting to reality; psychotics seek to mould reality to their own fiction. Adler's individual psychology continues to flourish as a distinct discipline. However, his approach to theory-building was speculative rather than scientific and his ideas now have little currency outside his own school. Many of his concepts have none the less become absorbed into common parlance—'inferiority complex', for example, and 'overcompensation'—and important aspects of modern child and family therapy owe much to his influence.

Sources: *Psychlit* journal articles (Silver Platter); Goldenson; UCDCL; Edwards.

K. W. M. FULFORD

Adler, Felix

American (brought to USA from Germany in 1857). **b:** 13 August 1851, Alzey, Germany. **d:** 24

April 1933, New York City. *Cat:* Ethical idealist. *Ints:* Ethics; applied ethics; moral education; Kant's ethics; ethical culture. *Educ:* Columbia University, AB 1870; Universities of Berlin and Heidelberg, PhD Heidelberg, 1873. *Infls:* Literary influences include Humboldt, F. Bacon, M. Arnold, F. A. Lange, Emerson and Kant; personal influences include H. Bonitz, Hermann Cohen, Abraham Geiger, Eduard Zeller, Heymann Steinthal and Thomas Davidson. *Appts:* Professor of Hebrew and Oriental Literature, Cornell University, 1874–6; Founder, Ethical Culture Movement, 1876; Professor of Social and Political Ethics, Columbia University, 1902–18; started *The Ethical Record* (1888) and *The International Journal of Ethics* (1890); organized the New York Philosophy Club, 1900; President, American Philosophical Association, 1928.

Main publications:

(1877) *Creed and Deed*, New York: G. P. Putnam's Sons.
(1892) *The Moral Instruction of Children*, New York: D. Appleton & Co.
(1902) 'A critique of Kant's ethics', *Mind* 11: 162–95.
(1903) *Life and Destiny*, New York: McClure, Philips & Co.
(1915) *The World Crisis and its Meaning*, New York: Appleton.
(1919) *An Ethical Philosophy of Life*, New York: Appleton.
(1924) *The Reconstruction of the Moral Ideal*, New York: Appleton.

Secondary literature:

Guttchen, Robert S. (1973) 'Felix Adler's concept of worth', *Journal of the History of Philosophy* 11, 2: 213–27.
Kraut, Benny (1979) *From Reform Judaism to Ethical Culture: The Religious Evolution of Felix Adler*, Cincinnati: Hebrew Union College Press (contains brief bibliography).
Singer, Marcus G. (1988) 'The place of Felix Adler in American philosophy', *Journal of Humanism and Ethical Religion*, 1, 1: 13–36 (whole issue devoted to Adler).

Felix Adler's thought was dominated by practical ethical concerns to an extent practically unparalleled in the history of philosophy. As an ethical leader, Adler can be ranked with Confucius, Socrates, Jesus, **Tolstoy** and **Gandhi**. Starting from a basis in Kant's ethics, with its emphasis on the intrinsic worth and dignity of the person, Adler rejected Kant's metaphysics and reformulated the categorical imperative so as to emphasize the development of the human personality in relation to human fellowship and communal concerns. Adler combined Kant's emphasis on a supreme moral principle with an ideal of self-realization and also emphasized the essential social nature of humanity and morality. He thus advanced a special form of moral perfectionism. However, unlike the vast majority of philosophers, Adler concerned himself with the actual conditions of human life for people who had to live in conditions of poverty, misery, hunger and disease, and proposed ways for rectifying these conditions in accord with essential human dignity. He also provided fundamental criticisms of the basic institutions and proposals for improving or reconstructing them. Thus, before **Dewey**, Adler was concerning himself with the 'problems of men' rather than just with the problems of philosophers.

Adler's first principle of ethics goes thus: 'A. Act as a member of the ethical manifold (the infinite spiritual universe). B. Act so as to achieve uniqueness ... C. Act so as to elicit in another the distinctive, unique quality characteristic of him as a fellow-member of the infinite whole.' These are summed up in 'the supreme ethical rule: *Act so as to elicit the best in others and thereby in thyself*'. To a greater extent than Kant and the Stoics, Adler emphasized that virtue is and *must be* its own reward. 'A virtuous act is one in which the ends of self and of the other are respected and promoted jointly'. One 'who claims a reward because of his virtue has thereby forfeited his right to ... the claim, since that is not virtue which looks for reward'.

In his attempt to coordinate a Kantian universalistic and imperative ethics with a form of self-realizationism, itself a form of consequentialism, Adler anticipated the attempts in the later twentieth century to combine Kantian ethics with utilitarian-type ethics. Adler, however, rejected utilitarianism: 'The quantitative standard implied in such phrases as "the greatest good of the greatest number" is out of place when we deal with ethical relations, which in their very nature are qualitative.' The critical question is whether Adler could successfully combine a modified Kantian formalism with his own idealistic and spiritualistic, but neither egoistic nor altruistic, form of self-realization. Success in this would indicate that deontological and teleological ethical standards are not necessarily incompatible with each other.
Sources: DAB, 1944, 21, supplt 1, pp. 13–14; WAB; EncAm; CollEnc; WWW(Am) 1892–1942; WWW 1929–40.

MARCUS SINGER

Adorno, Theodor Wiesengrund

German. *b:* 11 September 1903, Frankfurt am Main. *d:* 6 August 1969, Visp, Switzerland. *Cat:* Social philosopher; critical theorist; musicologist. *Ints:* Epistemology. *Educ:* University of Frankfurt, doctorate 1924; studied music with Alban Berg in Vienna, 1925–8. *Infls:* Walter Benjamin, Max Horkheimer, Hegel, Marx and Nietzsche. *Appts:* Editor, *Musikblätter des Anbruchs*, Vienna, 1928–1930; Privatdozent, University of Frankfurt, 1931–3; worked in Oxford, 1934–7; member of the Institute for Social Research, New York, from 1938; Beverly Hills from 1941; also worked with Paul Lazarsfeld on the Princeton Radio Research Project; Professor of Philosophy, University of Frankfurt, 1950–69; Assistant Director, 1950–5, Co-Director with Horkheimer, 1955–8, and Director, 1958–69, Institut für Sozialforschung, Frankfurt.

Main publications:

(1933) *Kierkegaard: Konstruktion des Ästhetischen*, Tünbingen: J. C. B. Mohr; second edition, Frankfurt: Suhrkamp, 1966 (English translation, *Kierkegaard: Construction of the Aesthetic*, trans. and ed. Robert Hullot-Kentor, Minneapolis: University of Minnesota Press, 1989).

(1947) (with Max Horkheimer) *Dialektik der Aufklärung*, Amsterdam: Querido (English translation, *Dialectic of Enlightenment*, trans. John Cumming, New York: Herder & Herder, 1972).

(1949) *Philosophie der neuen Musik*, Tübingen: J. C. B. Mohr (English translation, *Philosophy of Modern Music*, trans. Anne G. Mitchell and Wesley W. Bloomster, London: Sheed & Ward, 1949).

(1950) (with Elke Frenkel-Brunswick, Daniel J. Levinson and R. Nevitt Stanford) *The Authoritarian Personality*, New York: Harper & Brothers.

(1951) *Minima Moralia. Reflexionen aus dem beschädigten Leben*, Frankfurt: Suhrkamp (English translation, *Minima Moralia*, trans. E. F. N. Jephcott, London: New Left Books, 1974).

(1955) *Prismen. Kulturkritik und Gesellschaft*, Berlin and Frankfurt: Suhrkamp (English translation, *Prisms*, trans. Samuel and Shierry Weber, London: Neville Spearman, 1967).

(1956) *Zur Metakritik der Erkenntnistheorie. Studien über Husserl und die phänomenologischen Antinomien*, Stuttgart: W. Kohlhammer (English translation, *Against Epistemology: A Metacritique*, trans. Willis Domigno, Oxford: Blackwell, 1982).

(1956) (with Max Horkheimer) *Soziologische Exkurse*, Europäische Verlagsantalt (English translation, *Aspects of Sociology*, trans. John Viertel, London: Heinemann, 1973).

(1963) *Drei Studien zu Hegel*, Frankfurt: Suhrkamp.

(1963) *Eingriffe. Neun Kritische Modelle*, Frankfurt: Suhrkamp.

(1964) *Jargon der Eigentlichkeit. Zur deutschen Ideologie*, Frankfurt: Suhrkamp (English translation, *Jargon of Authenticity*, trans. Knut Tarnowski and Frederick Will, London: Routledge & Kegan Paul, 1964).

(1966) *Negative Dialektik*, Frankfurt: Suhrkamp (English translation, *Negative Dialectics*, trans. E. B. Ashton, New York: Seabury Press, 1973).

(1967) *Ohne Leitbild. Parva Aesthetika*, Frankfurt: Suhrkamp.

(1969) *Stichworte. Kritische Modelle 2*, Frankfurt: Suhrkamp.

(1969) (Introduction and contributions to) *Der Positivismusstreit in der deutschen Soziologie*, Neuwied and Berlin: Luchterhand (English translation, *The Positivist Dispute in German Sociology*, trans. Glyn Adey and David Frisby, London: Heinemann, 1976).

(1969) (ed.) *Spätkapitalismus oder Industriegesellschaft? Verhandlungen des 16 deutschen Soziologentages vom 8–11 April 1968 in Frankfurt am Main*, Frankfurt: Suhrkamp.

(1970) *Ästhetische Theorie*, ed. Gretel Adorno and Rolf Tiedemann, Frankfurt: Suhrkamp (English translation, *Aesthetic Theory*, trans. C. Lenhardt, London: Routledge & Kegan Paul, 1984).

(1973–4) *Philosophische Terminologie. Zur Einleitung*, 2 vols, ed. Rudolf Zur Lippe, Frankfurt: Suhrkamp.

(1970–86) *Gesammelte Schriften*, 20 vols, ed. Rolf Tiedemann, Frankfurt: Suhrkamp (the Theodor W. Adorno Archive plans to publish a further twenty volumes of posthumous papers).

Secondary literature:

Benjamin, Andrew (ed.) (1989) *The Problems of Modernity: Adorno and Benjamin*, London: Routledge.

Bernstein, J. M. (1992) *The Fate of Art: Aesthetic Alienation from Kant to Adorno*, Cambridge: Polity.

——(1994) *The Politics of Transfiguration*, London: Routledge.

Brunkhorst, Hauke (1990) *Theodor W. Adorno: Dialektik der Moderne*, Munich: Piper.

Buck-Morss, Susan (1977) *The origin of 'negative dialectics': Theodor W. Adorno, Walter Benjamin and the Frankfurt Institute*, Hassocks: Harvester Press.

Friedeburg, Ludwig von and Habermas, Jürgen (eds) (1983) *Adorno-Konferenz 1983*, Frankfurt: Suhrkamp.

Jameson, Fredric (1990) *Late Capitalism: Adorno, or, the Persistence of the Dialectic*, London: Verso.

Jay, Martin (1973) *Adorno*, Glasgow: Collins Fontana.

——(1973) *The Dialectical Imagination: A History of the Frankfurt School and the Institute of Social Research, 1923–1950*, London: Heinemann (includes substantial bibliography).

——(1984) *Marxism and Totality*, Berkeley and Los Angeles: University of California Press.

Löbig, Michael and Schweppenhäuser, Gerhard (eds) (1984) *Hamburger Adorno-Symposium*, Lünneburg: Dietrich zu Klampen Verlag.

Rose, Gillian (1978) *The Melancholy Science: An Introduction to the Work of Theodor W. Adorno*, London: Macmillan (includes substantial bibliography).

Schweppenhauser, Hermann (ed.) (1971) *Theodor W. Adorno zum Gedächtnis*, Frankfurt: Suhrkamp (includes bibliography by Klaus Schultz).

Thyen, Anke (1989) *Negative Dialektik und Erfahrung: Zur Rationalität des nichtidentischen bei Adorno*, Frankfurt: Suhrkamp.

Wiggershaus, Rolf (1986) *Die Frankfurter Schule: Geschichte, theoretische Entwicklung, politische Bedeutung*, Munich: Hanser (English translation, *The Frankfurt School*, trans. Martin Robertson, Cambridge: Polity).

——(1987) *Theodor W. Adorno*, Munich: Beck.

Adorno is without question the most important thinker of the Frankfurt School, where he acted as a crucial mediating force between Marxism and the rest of philosophy, and between philosophy itself and sociology and cultural studies. His studies on Hegel, **Heidegger**, **Husserl**, Kierkegaard and other major philosophers are unequalled in their incisiveness, and are only now beginning to have the impact they deserve outside the German-language area. His critique of Husserl is also a critique of epistemology as traditionally conceived.

Adorno's own conception of 'negative' dialectic, a dialectic which rejects as utopian the possibility of total reconciliation, is central to neo-Marxist philosophy (see Jay 1984), as is the line of cultural criticism expressed throughout his work, notably in *Dialectic of Enlightenment* (1947), one of the central books of the twentieth century, and in his many works in the philosophy and sociology of music. Adorno's aesthetic theory has an importance far outside that field, and has been taken by many contemporary philosophers as a starting-point for reconceptualizing the role of philosophy as a whole. As Bernstein (1994) has shown, the tension between Adorno's speculative theorizing and **Habermas**'s more disciplined or, from this point of view, scientistic approach,

remains a fundamental legacy of the Frankfurt School.

In both philosophy and cultural theory Adorno combined a revolutionary modernism with a deep attachment to what he saw as the best elements of European thought and high culture, threatened by fascist and Stalinist totalitarianism and by commercial philistinism. *Jargon of Authenticity* (1964) is a powerful critique of the abuse of philosophical language. Adorno's own sensitivity to issues of language, including a Nietzschean hostility to terminological definition, comes out clearly in some of his more accessible works, such as his contributions to *Aspects of Sociology* (1956) and the Introductory Lectures published as *Philosophische Terminologie* (1973–4). Although his thought was sceptical, aphoristically formulated and often despairing, he was far from the nihilism and frivolity of later 'post-structuralist' thought, whose insights he may be seen to have anticipated and transcended.

WILLIAM OUTHWAITE

Ahad ha-Am (pseudonym for Asher Ginsberg)

Ukrainian Jew. *b:* 18 August 1856, Skwira, Kiev Province. *d:* 2 January 1927, Tel Aviv, British-mandated Palestine. *Cat:* Cultural Zionist. *Ints:* Judaism. *Educ:* Odessa, Berlin, Vienna, Paris and Brussels; in 1885 he returned to Odessa, moving to London in 1908 and to Tel Aviv in 1922. *Infls:* The Talmud (Code of Jewish Law, *c.* 500 CE), medieval Jewish Philosophy, the Haskalah (Jewish Enlightenment movement), Hasidism, and European literature, philosophy and science.

Main publications:
(1889) *Lo Zeh ha-Derekh*; revised as *The Wrong Way*, 1962.

(1891) *Emet me-erets Yisrael* [Truth from the Land of Israel].

(1895–1913) *Al-Parshat ha-Derakhim* [At the Crossroads], Odessa: Ravnitsky (translation: Yiddish, Berlin 1921; Tel Aviv, Hebrew, *Devir*, 1946, reprinted 1948–9, English, *Ten Essays on Zionism and Judaism*, New York: Arno Press: 1973).

(1917) 'Tehiyyat ha-Ruah' [The Spiritual Revival] (English translation in *The Zionist*, L. Simon, 1917, revised edition, 1962).

(1917) 'Shilton ha-Sekhel' (English translation, 'The supremacy of reason: to the memory of Maimonides', trans. L. Simon, *The Zionist*, London, 1917, and in *Maimonides Octocentennial Series*, i–iv, New York, Arno Press: 1973).

(1917) 'The transvaluation of values', trans. L. Simon, *The Zionist*, London, 1917 and New York, 1935.

(1965) *Complete Writings* (Hebrew), Jerusalem: Jewish Publishing House.

Secondary literature:

Bentwich, Norman (1927) *Ahad Ha-Am and his Philosophy*, Jerusalem: Keren ha-Yesod.

Goldshtain, Yosef (1992) *Ahad Ha'Am* (Hebrew), Jerusalem: Keter.

Simon, Leon (1946) *Ahad Ha-Am. Essays, Letters, Memoirs*, Oxford: East and West Library.

——(1948) *Selected Essays by Ahad Ha-Am*, translated from the Hebrew, Philadelphia: JPSA.

'Ahad ha-Am' means 'one of the people'. He argued that Judaism's cultural identity should not be lost in the contemporary political Zionist debate. He oscillated between positivism and idealism, whilst emphasising the importance of nationhood: the nation has the 'will to live'; i.e. a love for the Jewish nation must be rekindled in European Jewry by equating Judaism with absolute justice and pure morality, as revealed by the Biblical prophets. He held that the essence of Judaism is absolute monotheism. Although not systematic, Ahad ha-Am's philosophy has influenced modern Jewish and Zionist thought, stimulating critical debate.

Sources: EncJud; NUC; Schoeps.

IRENE LANCASTER

Ai Siqi (Ai Ssu-ch'i)

Chinese. *b:* 1910, Tengchong County, Yunnan Province, China. *d:* 1966, Beijing. *Cat:* Marxist. *Ints:* Historical and dialectical materialism. *Educ:* Fukuoka Higher Technical School, Japan. *Infls:* Marx, Engels, Mao and others in the Marxist tradition. *Appts:* From 1937–47, many posts in Yanan, the headquarters of Communist power; after 1949–66, Head of the Philosophy Teaching and Research Section and later Vice President of the Central Higher Party School of the Chinese Communist Party; 1955–66, Vice President of the Chinese Philosophy Society; Member of the Philosophical and Social Sciences Section of the Chinese Academy of Science.

Main publications:

(1934) *Philosophy of the People*, Shanghai: Dushushenghuo Publishers.

(1935) *On How to Think*, Shanghai: Dushushenghuo Publishers.

(1937) *Philosophy and Life*, Shanghai: Dushushenghuo Publishers.

(1939) (with Wu Liping) *Manual of the Scientific Conception of History*, Shanghai: Chenguang Bookstore.

(1939) *Philosophical Selections*, Shanghai: Chenguang Bookstore.

(1939) *Practice and Theory*, Shanghai: Dushushenghuo Publishers.

(1950) *Historical Materialism: History of Social Development*, Guangzhou: Xinhua Bookstore.

(1956) *Critique of the Philosophical Thought of Liang Souming*, Beijing: Renmin Publishing House.

(1957) *The Outlines of Dialectical Materialism*, Beijing: Renmin Publishing House.

(1957) (contributor to) *A Symposium on the Problems of the History of Chinese Philosophy*, Beijing: Kexue Publishing House.

(1961) (main editor) *Dialectical Materialism and Historical Materialism*, Beijing: Renmin Publishing House.

(1977) *Critiques of the Philosophical Thought of Hu Shi and Liang Souming*, Beijing: Renmin Publishing House.

(1979, 1983) *Collected Works of Ai Siqi*, 2 vols, Beijing: Renmin Publishing House.

Secondary literature:

Boorman, H. (ed.) (1970) *Biographical Dictionary of Republican China*, New York and London: Columbia University Press.

Brière, O. (1956) *Fifty Years of Chinese Philosophy 1898–1950*, London: George Allen & Unwin Ltd.

Complete Chinese Encyclopedia (1987), Philosophy Volumes, Beijing: Chinese Encyclopedia Publications.

Fogel, J. (1987) *Ai Ssu-ch'i's Contribution to the Development of Chinese Marxism*, Cambridge, Massachusetts: Council on East Asia Studies/ Harvard University Press.

For three decades Ai Siqi was the most important popularizer of Marxist philosophy in China and a polemicist opposing other philosophical schools. In the disputes about Marxism in the 1930s, he strongly criticized **Zhang Dongsun**'s neo-Kantian views as well as Ye Qing's rival heterodox Marxism. He was a main ideological critic of the New Life Movement and the vitalism and philosophy of action of Jiang Jieshi (Chiang K'ai-shek). After Liberation, he presented **Mao Zedong**'s philosophical thought to a wider public and explained many principles of dialectical and historical materialism, while arguing against idealism and metaphysics.

NICHOLAS BUNNIN

Ajdukiewicz, K(azimierz)

Polish. *b:* 12 December 1890, Tarnopoi. *d:* 12 April 1963, Warsaw. *Cat:* Logician; analytical philosopher. *Ints:* Logic; ontology. *Educ:* John Casimir University, Lvov. *Infls:* K. Twardowski, J. Łukasiewicz, D. Hilbert and A. Reinach. *Appts:* 1922–6, Dozent of Philosophy, John Casimir University, Lvov; 1926–8, Professor of Philosophy, Warsaw University; 1928–39, Professor of Philosophy, John Casimir University, Lvov; 1946–55, Professor of Logic, 1948–52, Rector, Adam Mickiewicz University, Poznan; 1955–61, Professor of Logic, Warsaw University.

Main publications:

(1949) *Problems and Theories of Philosophy*, London: Cambridge University Press, 1973.
(1958) 'On the freedom of science', *Review of the Polish Academy of Science* 2, 1/2: 1–19.
(1961) 'A method of eliminating intensional sentences and sentential formulae', *Atti del XII Congresso Internationale di Filosfia. Firenze* 5: 17–24.
(1965) *Pragmatic Logic*, Dordrecht: D. Reidel, 1974.
(1977) *The Scientific World-Perspective and Other Essays. 1931–1963*, Dordrecht: D. Reidel (with full biobligraphy, 1913–1974).
(1984) 'On definitions', *Dialectics and Humanism* 2/3: 235–56.

Secondary literature:

Czeźowski, T. (1977) 'Bibliography of Ajdukiewicz's works', in K. Ajdukiewicz; *The Scientific World-Perspective*, pp. 363–9.
Küng, G. (1989) 'Ajdukiewicz's contribution to the realism/idealism debate', in K. Szaniawski (ed.), *The Vienna Circle and the Philosophy of the Lvov-Warsaw School*, Dordrecht: Kluwer.
Marciszewski, W. (1991) 'K. Ajdukiewicz and the Polish debate on universals', *Quaderni* 391/30: 7–16.
Poli, R. (1993) 'The dispute over reism: Kotarbiński–Ajdukiewicz–Brentano', in *Polish Scientific Philosophy: The Lvov-Warsaw School*, Amsterdam: Rodopi, pp. 339–54.
Sinisi, V. and Woleński, J. (eds) (1995) *The Heritage of Kazimierz Ajdukiewicz*, Amsterdam: Rodopi.
Steizner, W. (1992) 'Pragmatics and Ajdukiewicz's logical concepts of language', *Ruch Filozoficzny* 49 3/4: 277–87.

Ajdukiewicz is one of the most influential thinkers in Polish philosophy in our century. In logic his contributions rest upon: being the promoter of formalizing deductive systems and outlining the logic of questions; creating the theory of semantic categories and examining the syntactic connexion; explicating the associationist conception of meaning; constructing his own directical and then codenotational theory of meaning; and analyzing the foundations of classifying and defining. Formulating rules of reducing semantic categories of expressions, he initiated the idea of categorial grammars (next developed, for example, by J. Lambek and Y. **Bar-Hillel**).

In epistemology and ontology Ajdukiewicz was the originator of radical and then moderate conventionalism, and in the end a defender of methodological pluralism, an anticipator of radical empiricism and a critic of transcendental idealism and philosophical irrationalism. He evolved the method of semantic paraphrasing in solving metaphysical problems.

The genuine masterpieces are his short articles concerning the problems of ontology (for example, the notions of existence, substance, matter, spirit, time, change and finality) and ethics (on the concepts of life-design, liberty and justice) and his clear and didactically matchless handbooks of logic and philosophy.

Sources: J. J. Jadacki (1980) 'On the sources of contemporary Polish logic', *DH* 4: 163–83; Z. Jordan (1945) *The Development of Mathematical Logic and of Logical Positivism in Poland Between the Two Wars*, London: OUP; H. Skolimowski (1967) *Polish Analytical Philosophy*, London: Routledge & Kegan Paul; J. Woleński (1988) *Logic and Philosophy in the Lvov-Warsaw School*, Dordrecht: Kluwer.

JACEK JULIUS JADACKI

Akselrod, Pavel Borisovich

Russian. *b:* 1850(?), Pochep, Ukraine. *d:* 1928, Berlin. *Cat:* Marxist. *Ints:* Politics. *Infls:* Marx and Engels.

Main publications:

(1923) *Perezhitoe i Peredumannoe* [Experience and Reflection], Berlin (memoirs).
(1932) *Aus dem literarischen Nachlass von Pavel Axelrod*, ed. I. Tsereteli and W. Woytinsky, Jena.

Secondary literature:

Ascher, Abraham (1972) *Pavel Axelrod and the Development of Menshevism*, Cambridge, Mass.: Harvard University Press.

Akselrod as a young man was forced by police repression into early exile, and spent most of his life abroad. Becoming a Marxist in the 1880s, he founded with **Plekhanov** and others the Emancipation of Labour Group in 1883, which in 1898 gave way to the Russian Social-Democratic Party. In 1900 he cofounded with **Lenin** and others the revolutionary paper *Iskra* (Spark), which Lenin then edited with such skill. Akselrod sided with the Mensheviks in the 1903 Bolshevik/Menshevik split, and subsequently became the leading Menshevik ideologue. Returning to Russia at the time of the February revolution in 1917, he was again abroad when the Bolsheviks seized power in October. The rest of his life was spent in exile as a persistent critic of the new revolutionary government. Akselrod's mature thought was heavily influenced by his experience of western social democratic parties, in particular of the German SPD. It reinforced his twin convictions that a properly socialist party *must* adopt democratic procedures, and that the emancipation of the working class must be performed *by* the working class. Both of these convictions lay behind his unremittingly critical stance towards Lenin after 1917.

Sources: Joseph L. Wieczynski (1976) *The Modern Encyclopaedia of Russian and Soviet History*, Academic Intl Press.

NICHOLAS EVERITT

Aksel'rod (pen-name Ortodoks), Liubov' Isaakovna

Russian. *b:* 1868, Dunilovichi, Vilnius province. *d:* 5 February 1946. *Cat:* Marxist. *Educ:* Doctorate in Philosophy, University of Berne, 1900. *Infls:* Marx, Engels and Plekhanov. *Appts:* 1921–3, taught at the Institute of Red Professors; thereafter at the Institute of Scientific Philosophy.

Main publications:

(1906) *Filosofskie ocherki: otvet filosofskim kritikam istoricheskogo materializma* [Philosophical Essays: A Reply to the Philosophical Critics of Historical Materialism], St Petersburg.

(1922) *Protiv idealizma: kritika nekotorykh idealisticheskikh techenii filosofskoi mysli* [Against Idealism: A Critique of some Idealist Trends in Philosophical Thought], Moscow and Petrograd.

(1924) *Karl Marks kak filosof* [Karl Marx as a Philosopher], Khar'kov.

(1934) *Idealisticheskaia dialektika Gegelia i materialisticheskaia dialektika Marksa* [The Idealist Dialectics of Hegel and the Materialist Dialectics of Marx], Moscow and Leningrad.

Secondary literature:

Joravsky, D. (1961) *Soviet Marxism and Natural Science 1917–1932*, London: Routledge & Kegan Paul, pp. 138–42.

Wetter, G. A. (1958) *Dialectical Materialism: A Historical and Systematic Survey of Philosophy in the Soviet Union*, trans. Peter Heath, London: Routledge & Kegan Paul, pp. 149–53.

Aksel'rod (Ortodoks)—a combination helping to distinguish her from the Menshevik leader P. B. Akselrod—joined the Russian revolutionary movement in 1884, and was forced to emigrate to Western Europe in 1887, following a plot to assassinate the Tsar. She joined the Marxist group *Osvobozhdenie Truda* [Liberation of Labour] in 1892, and was a member of the Menshevik faction of the Russian Social-Democratic Labour Party from 1903 to 1917. She returned to Russia in 1906, and after the October Revolution committed herself to the exposition of Marxism–Leninism, albeit not as a member of the Communist Party.

Aksel'rod's pen-name 'Ortodoks' derived from her opposition to the grafting on to Marxist historical materialism of neo-Kantian or Machian epistemologies. She was a supporter of **Plekhanov**, and defended his theory of hieroglyphs in a review of **Lenin**'s *Materialism and Empiriocriticism* (1909) in the journal *Sovremennyi Mir* [Contemporary World]. As well as attacking Lenin's philosophical superficiality and cut-and-paste approach, she rejected his equation of materialism with naive realism. She also dismissed his copy theory of knowledge as 'inverted Platonism', or a form of dualism, whereas the theory of symbols or hieroglyphs was consonant with a monistic, materialistic and scientific worldview in regarding sensation as the outcome of the interaction of two objects.

Although Aksel'rod had (like Lenin) rejected **Bogdanov**'s empiriomonism, she was associated with him in the 1920s among the loose grouping of Mechanists in the debate with the Deborinites. The acrimonious contest was broadly between a positivist and a dialectical interpretation of Marxism. Aksel'rod was more accommodating to the dialectical method than the thoroughgoing scientific reductionists in the Mechanist camp, but objected to the Deborinites' abstract 'formalist' approach, arguing instead that the significance of the dialectic can only be realized in the differing concrete contents of the separate spheres of reality.

COLIN CHANT

Alain, (Chartier, Émile)

French. *b:* 3 March 1868, Perche, France. *d:* 2 June 1951, Vésinet. *Cat:* Humanist; anti-idealist; essayist. *Ints:* Political philosophy; ethics; aesthetics.

Educ: Lycée de Vauves, Paris, 1886–9; École Normale Supérieure, Paris, 1890–3. *Infls:* Jules Lagneau (founder of the Lycée de Vauves), Descartes, Kant and Plato. *Appts:* Taught Philosophy at the Lycée Henri-IV and at the Collège Sévigné, Paris.

Main publications:

Collected *Propos:*
(1926) *Éléments d'une doctrine radicale*, Paris: NRF.
(1927) *Esquisse de l'homme*, Paris: Hellen & Sergent.
(1933) *Propos d'économique*, Paris: Gallimard.
(1937) *Les Saisons de l'esprit*, Paris: Gallimard.
(1942) *Les Vigiles de l'esprit*, Paris: Gallimard.
(1972) *Propos sur le bonheur*, Paris: Gallimard
    (English translation, *Alain on Happiness*, trans. R. and J. Cottrell, New York: Ungar, 1973).

Other philosophical works:
(1920) *Système des beaux-arts*, Paris: Gallimard.
(1931) *Entretiens au bord de la mer*, Paris: Gallimard.
(1934) *Les Dieux*, Paris: Gallimard (English translation, *The Gods*, trans. Richard Pevear, New York: New Direction, 1974).
(1936) *Histoire de mes pensées*, Paris: Gallimard.
(1941) *Éléments de philosophie*, Paris: Gallimard.

Secondary literature:

Bridoux, A. (1964) *Alain*, Paris: PUF.
Gil, D. (1990) *Alain, la république ou le matérialisme*, Paris: Klinksieck.
Maurois, A. (1952) *Alain*, Paris: Domat.
Pascal, G. (1970) *L'Idée de philosophie chez Alain*, Paris: Bordas.
Sernin, A. (1985) *Alain, un sage dans la cité*, Paris: Laffont.

Under the pseudonym 'Alain', Émile Chartier wrote over 5,000 essays on political, moral and aesthetic topics for newspapers and journals ('les *Propos* d'Alain'). His experience at the front during the First World War conditioned his view that philosophy should have a practical moral, social and political application. The expression of philosophy through the diverse, topical and aphoristic essays reflects this view. Alain's philosophy is an anti-idealist and anti-determinist existential humanism; he insists on the function of a fallible human judgement and spirit (*esprit*: spirit, intelligence and wit) in making sense of the chaos of the world. This judgement is based on human conscience and active free will as they encounter and overcome human passions. For Alain, the human spirit unfolds in the history and the present of human activities, above all in religion, philosophy and art.

Sources: Huisman; catalogues of Bibliothèque Nationale, Paris and National Library of Scotland.

JAMES WILLIAMS

Alberini, Coriolano

Argentinian. *b:* 27 November 1886, Buenos Aires. *d:* 18 October 1960, Buenos Aires. *Cat:* Metaphysician; philosopher of science. *Educ:* University of Buenos Aires. *Infls:* Henri Bergson. *Appts:* 1920 to retirement, Professor of Philosophy, University of Buenos Aires; several times Dean of the School of Philosophy and Letters; interim Rector 1940; Professor of Pyschology, University of Buenos Aires; Professor of Metaphysics; University of La Plata; delivered invited lectures at the Universities of Paris, Berlin, Hamburg and Leipzig, and at Columbia University and Harvard University; named Doctor *honoris causa* by University of Leipzig.

Main publications:

(1966) *Problemas de la historia de las ideas filosóficas en la Argentina*, La Plata: Universidad Nacional de La Plata.
(1973) *Escritos de ética*, Mendoza, Argentina: Universidad Nacional del Cuyo.
(1973) *Escritos de filosofía de la educación y pedagogía*, Mendoza, Argentina: Universidad Nacional del Cuyo.
(1981) *Precisiones sobre la evolución del pensamiento argentino*, Buenos Aires: Editorial Docencia-Proyecto CINAE.

Secondary literature:

Capdevila, A. (1973) 'Semblanza de Coriolano Alberini', Prologue to *Escritos de ética*, Mendoza, Argentina: Universidad Nacional del Cuyo.

Alberini was one of the first to introduce German philosophy into Argentina. Early in his career he was an adherent of positivism, but later became an anti-positivist. He sought to develop a synthesis of science and philosophy, two fields which he believed were complementary and essential to a comprehensive understanding of reality.

AMY A. OLIVER

Aleksandrov, Aleksandr Danilovich

Russian. *b:* 22 July (O.S.) 1912, Riazan' province, Russia. *Cat:* Philosopher of science; administrator. *Ints:* Philosophy of physics; dialectical materialism; principles of geometry. *Educ:* University of Lenigrad. *Appts:* 1933–52, University of Leningrad; 1952–64, Rector, University of Leningrad;

from 1964, Professor, Novosibirsk University, and member, Novosibirsk Institute of Mathematics.

Main publications:
(1951) 'Ob idealizme v matematike' [On idealism in mathematics], *Priroda* [Nature] 7: 3–11; 8: 3–9.
(1953) 'Po povodu nekotorykh vzgliadov na teoriiu otnositel'nosti' [Apropos of certain views of the theory of relativity], *Voprosy filosofii* [Problems of Philosophy] 5: 225–45.
(1957) 'Dialektika i nauka' [Dialectics and science], *Vestnik Akademii nauk SSSR* 6: 3–17.
(1959) 'Filosofskoe soderzhanie i znachenie teorii otnositel'nosti' [The philosophical content and significance of the theory of relativity], *Voprosy filosofii* [Problems of Philosphy 1: 67–84].

Secondary literature:
Graham, Loren R. *Science and Philosophy in the Soviet Union*, New York: Alfred A. Knopf; revised second edition, *Science, Philosophy, and Human Behavior in the Soviet Union*, Columbia University Press, 1987 (bibliography and discussion).

An internationally renowned mathematician, Aleksandrov played an influential role in the Soviet debates concerning the relation between dialectical materialism and the sciences in the 1950s. Fully accepting dialectical materialism as the correct worldview and a valuable scientific methodology, he none the less was a leader in the defence of quantum theory and relativity theory against the attacks of Marxist-Leninist dogmatists. He argued that those theories, far from denying the objective reality of the material world, as some claimed, actually confirmed the materialist outlook and established its relevance to science. It was largely through the efforts of Aleksandrov, V. A. **Fock** and others that Soviet theoretical physics survived the ideological assaults of the time. Aleksandrov was also noted for his support of science as Rector of University of Lenigrad, where genetics was reintroduced into the curriculum as early as 1957.

JAMES SCANLAN

Aleksandrov, Georgii Fedorovich
Russian. *b:* 22 March (O.S.) 1908, St Petersburg. *d:* 21 July 1961, Moscow. *Cat:* Marxist historian of philosophy; administrator. *Ints:* Dialectical materialism; history of philosophy. *Educ:* Moscow Institute of History and Philosophy. *Appts:* 1938–41, Head, Department of the History of Philosophy, Moscow Institute of History and Philosophy; 1940–7, Director, Office of Propaganda and Agitation of the Soviet Communist Party; 1947–54, Director, Institute of Philosophy of the Soviet Academy of Sciences; 1954–5, Minister of Culture of the USSR; 1955–61, Head, Section of Dialectical and Historical Materialism, Institute of Philosophy of the Belorussian Academy of Sciences.

Main publications:
(1939) *Filosofskie predshestvenniki Marksizma* [Philosophical Forerunners of Marxism], Moscow.
(1940) *Aristotel'* [Aristotle], Moscow.
(1940) *Formirovanie filosofskikh vzgliadov Marksa i Engelsa* [For Formation of the Philosophical Views of Marx and Engels], Moscow.
(1946) *Istoriia zapadnoevropeiskoi filosofii*, Moscow (English translation, *A History of Western European Philosophy*, trans. Hugh McLean, Yale Institute of International Studies, 1949).
(1954) (ed.) *Dialekticheskii materializm* [Dialectical Materialism], Moscow.
(1959) *Ocherk istorii sotsial'nykh idei v drevnei Indii* [An Essay in the History of Social Ideas in Ancient India], Minsk.

Secondary literature:
Esakov, V. D. (1993) 'K istorii filosofskoi diskussii 1947 goda', *Voprosy filosofii* 2: 83–106 (English translation, 'Toward a history of the philosophical discussion of 1947', *Russian Studies in Philosophy*, spring, pp. 6–47, 1994).
Wetter, Gustav A. (1958) *Dialectical Materialism: A Historical and Systematic Survey of Philosophy in the Soviet Union*, trans. Peter Heath, London: Routledge & Kegan Paul, London.

A dedicated Marxist–Leninist, much honoured in the USSR for his work in the history of philosophy as well as his propaganda activities, Aleksandrov gained international notoriety in 1947 when his *History of Western European Philosophy* provided the occasion for a sweeping attack by Stalin's culture czar, Andrei Zhdanov, on Soviet philosophers for insufficient partisanship and militancy. Aleksandrov himself weathered the storm and remained a prominent figure, rising even to become Minister of Culture in 1954. In 1955, however, after another controversy involving the 1954 textbook on dialectical materialism that he edited, Aleksandrov retired to the semi-obscurity of the Institute of Philosophy in Minsk.

JAMES SCANLAN

Alexander, Hartley Burr

American. *b:* 9 April 1873, Lincoln, Nebraska. *d:* 27 July 1939. *Cat:* Idealist. *Ints:* Art and culture of the Americas; mythology. *Educ:* University of Nebraska, graduating in 1897; after a period at the University of Pennsylvania, he completed his doctorate at Columbia in 1901. *Appts:* For several years he was an encyclopedia and dictionary editor; 1908–27, Professor of Philosophy at the University of Nebraska; 1927–39, Scripps College, California.

Main publications:

(1902) *The Problem of Metaphysics*, New York: Columbia University Press (PhD thesis).

(1906) *Poetry and the Individual*, New York: Putnam.

(1908) *The Lost Pedigree of the Princess Callista: A Philosopher's Fairy Tale*, The Author.

(1910) *Religious Spirit of the American Indian*, Chicago: Open Court.

(1913) *The Mystery of Life. A Poetization of 'The Hako', a Pawnee Ceremony*, Chicago: Open Court.

(1916) *North American Mythology*, Boston: Marshall Jones.

(1918) *Liberty and Democracy*, Boston: Marshall Jones.

(1919) *Letters to Teachers*, Chicago: Open Court.

(1920) *Latin American Mythology*, Boston: Marshall.

(1923) *Nature and Human Nature*, Chicago: Open Court.

(1926) *L'Art et la philosophie des Indiens de l'Amérique du Nord*, Paris: E. Leroux.

(1929) *Truth and the Faith*, New York: Holt.

(1930) 'The great art which is philosophy', in G. P. Adams and W. Pepperell Montague (eds), *Contemporary American Philosophy*, vol. 1, New York: Macmillan.

(1936) *God and Man's Destiny*, New York: Oxford University Press.

Secondary literature:

Cosens, Grayson V. (1957) 'The nature and function of myth in the philosophies of Ernst Cassirer, Susanne Langer, and H. B. Alexander', PhD thesis, University of Southern California (relates his work to others for whom mythology is central).

Alexander had a strong interest in art, literature and the cultures of the native peoples of the Americas. The study of mythology played a large part in his work. He engaged in a constant and wide-ranging search for accounts of human experience from which one could infer the metaphysical underpinnings of the human situation. His metaphysical idealism was predicated less on logic and epistemology than on his belief—strongly expressed in *God and Man's Destiny*—that idealism better fits what we know of the human condition than any other metaphysical doctrine. The real world, he claims, lies at a deeper level than matter, and we are evidently immortal beings. His main interest was in ways of expressing these truths and it was this which made the study of mythology important to him. Of God, he says that there is always an impression of God in human experience and reflection does not suggest that it is an illusion, though God is nowhere seen and has not triumphed over evil. These interests led him to wrestle with the problem of evil, but he claimed later that, if we see the world as a drama within which there is a moral evolution, the apparent contradiction between claims about the existence of God and what we know of the existence of evil can be overcome.

Although Alexander was influenced by the growing interest in the complexity of experience in American philosophy generally—exemplified in many of the writings of John **Dewey**—he was influenced less by any specific philosopher than by his own analyses of philosophical problems which suggested that they would yield only to an understanding of myth and poetry.

Sources: WW(AM); *DA*.

LESLIE ARMOUR

Alexander, Samuel

British. *b:* 6 January 1859, Sydney, Australia. *d:* 13 September 1938, Manchester, England. *Cat:* Realist. *Ints:* Metaphysics; aesthetics; ethics. *Educ:* Wesley College, Melbourne; Balliol College, Oxford. *Infls:* T. H. Green and C. Lloyd Morgan. *Appts:* Fellow of Lincoln College, Oxford, 1882–88, Professor, Manchester 1893–1924.

Main publications:

(1889) *Moral Order and Progress*, London: Trübner.

(1908) *Locke*, London: Constable.

(1920) *Space, Time and Deity* 2 vols, London: Macmillan.

(1933) *Beauty and Other Forms of Value*, London: Macmillan.

(1939) *Philosophical and Literary Pieces* (with bibliography), London: Macmillan.

Secondary literature:

Broad, C. D. (1921) article in *Mind* 30: 25–39 and 129–50.

——(1925) *Mind and its Place in Nature*, pp. 646–50.

Devaux, P. (1929) *Le Système d'Alexander*, Paris.

Laird, J. (1948) Obituary Notice in *Proceedings of the British Academy.*
McCarthy, J. W. (1929) *The Naturalism of Samuel Alexander*, New York.

Samuel Alexander was an interesting person in many ways. Born and brought up in Australia, he was the first Jew to become a fellow of an Oxford or Cambridge college. Leaving Oxford for thirty years' tenure of a Chair in Manchester, he became widely known and loved in that city for his many virtues and his gentle eccentricity. His Oxford studies at the high point of British Hegelianism (at the time of T. H. Green's death and the publication of **Bradley**'s *Principles of Logic*) inspired him with the ideal of a systematic philosophy. But it turned out to be very different from the body of doctrine he had been taught. In the first place, it was naturalistic not spiritualistic. The world as a whole was not, for him, an absolute spirit, but was the totality of things in space and time. It was not contained within an all-encompassing, metaphysically demythologized God, but contained God, or, more precisely, a striving or nisus towards deity, within it. Secondly, his procedure was descriptive rather than argumentative. It was not provoked by a sense of the misconceptions of other philosophers. What led Alexander away from idealism was a profound conviction of the truth of Darwin's evolutionism, which he took in a straightforwardly naturalistic way and extrapolated to cover the whole range of what there is. Thirty years before the publication of his system he applied the evolutionary principle to morality. Historically considered it turns out to be a constant field of conflict between alternative ideals. In part the change can be attributed to recognition of changed circumstances; in part it is a matter of conflicting impulses. Viewed as a whole the process of moral evolution can be understood as an increasingly successful pursuit of equilibrium as between the contending factors.

At the basis of the metaphysics of *Space, Time and Deity* (1926) is a theory of knowledge, a bluntly realistic one which rejects the view that the immediate objects of knowledge are mental or subjective by simple assertion. Knowledge, for Alexander, is a particular version of the relationship of compresence or togetherness between two things, that, specifically, where one of the two is a consciousness. Compresence is not to be interpreted literally as contact, immediate juxtaposition in space. Memory, for example, is a direct awareness of past events. Ordinary perception, unless it is by the sense of touch, is always of objects at a distance. The object of knowledge is not altered or modified by our knowledge of it and is certainly not 'constructed' by our minds. Perception is always selective, it does not tell the whole truth. But it tells some truth. What is given to us are 'perspectives' of things, but these are still parts of the real world, like the cross-sections of a tree. Illusions are the result of misplacing perspectives. The best-known part of Alexander's theory of knowledge is his distinction between the contemplation of objects and the 'enjoyment' we have of our own experiencings and mental acts. This is one of many attempts to get rid of the legacy of Locke's doctrine of reflection, the idea that we have an introspective knowledge of our own mental states which is formally parallel to our perceptual knowledge of things outside us.

Alexander's metaphysics proper is introduced as an empirical study of the a priori features of the world. That is not quite as paradoxical as it sounds since for Alexander the a priori is not the rationally necessary and demonstrable but is the universal and pervasive. *Space, Time and Deity* does contain a theory of the categories, which is of reasonably conventional membership: existence, universality, relation, order, substance, quantity, number and motion. These are all to be found in the fundamental stuff of the universe and go on to pervade everything that develops or emerges from that fundamental stuff. The stuff in question is space–time. There is some distant echo of the new physics of his epoch in this, but the considerations that weighed with **Einstein** and Minkowski played no part in Alexander's thinking. He conceived space and time in a perfectly conventional way but as implying each other since always found together, space and time being, therefore, abstractions from the common matrix. Space–time is composed, in an abstract sort of way, of point-instants; more concretely it proves to be composed of 'pure motions'. These unappetizing ingredients (for how can that whose fixed identity defines the motion of anything itself move?) are held to generate matter by a process of 'emergent evolution'. Alexander derived that idea from the biologist C. Lloyd **Morgan**. Organisms or organic structures come into existence in the course of evolution which are, or appear to be, irreducible to the organic items from which they have developed. Such emergent things show unpredictable novelty. Matter, endowed with primary qualities, is the first new level of existence to emerge from the pure motions of space–time. Next, there is the physicochemical realm and, beyond it, life. From life, in turn, mind or consciousness emerges, specifically from the neural aspect of the living organism. The relation of a mind to its body is put forward as a model for every level of existence in relation to that from which it has emerged. In a particularly bold speculative flight Alexander maintains that time is the mind of space (and, in consequence, that space is the body of time), which seems to imply that there was a time before time had emerged from space. The system is crowned with the account of deity, which is the next highest level of existence of mind and is destined to emerge from it. The world, indeed, is already pregnant with it, or has a nisus towards it. For obvious reasons little positive can be said about it. Alexander acknowledges an ambiguity in his account of God. On the one hand it is the being, not yet in existence, which the world is in process of gestating; on the other, it is the world as a whole, deific, as one might put it, by reason of the premonitory intimations of deity within it. The first is much like the God of Aristotle, an ideal towards which the world directs itself. The second is more like the God of Spinoza. Alexander has an account of values as tertiary qualities of things, different from other qualities in being not intrinsic to their possessors but as being relative to minds and their impulses. Our awareness of them must be a hybrid of contemplation (of the thing's qualities) and enjoyment (of our favourable attitude to them). Linking value to impulse, he attributes the value we attach to art to the satisfaction it provides for our impulse to construct. Alexander had no influence in Britain whatever, but in a curious way was very important for philosophy in the land of his birth. John **Anderson**, a very independent-minded Scottish admirer of Alexander, went to Sydney in the mid-1920s and came to be the very dominant leader of the country's most powerful and distinctive philosophical school, numbering among its members J. A. **Passmore**, J. L. Mackie, D. C. Stove and, at a greater distance, D. M. **Armstrong**. Anderson held, not that space–time is the stuff of the world, but that to exist is to exist in space and time. He is as uncompromisingly realistic about knowledge as Alexander but is totally hostile to the latter's conception of values as relational.

Sources: Copleston; Edwards; Metz; Passmore 1957; DNB.

ANTHONY QUINTON

Ali, S(yed) Ameer

Indian. *b:* 1849, Chinsura, Bengal. *d:* 1928, England. *Cat:* Islamic modernist; Shiite philosopher; historian of religion. *Educ:* Muhsiniyya College; the Inner Temple, London. *Infls:* Karamat Ali, Sayyid Ahmad Khan and Shah Wali

Allah. *Appts:* After being called to the Bar at Inner Temple, he became Chief Magistrate of Calcutta, a member of the Imperial Legislative Council of India, a judge of the High Court in Bengal and a member of the Judicial Committee of the Privy Council in London.

Main publications:

(1921) *A Short History of the Saracens*, London: Darf Publishers Ltd.
(1922) *The Spirit of Islam*; second edition, Lahore, 1974.
(1976) *Mahommedan Law*, ed. R. Khan, Lahore.

Although Ameer Ali was a pillar of the British establishment in India he also sought to defend the principles of Islam as relevant to the modern world. He sees the main contribution which Islam has to make to history as the notion of ethical humanism. The object of religion is to communicate ethical points, and Islam is superior to other religions such as Christianity since the Muslim faith on the whole rejects insularity and exclusiveness, allows liberty of conscience and freedom of belief, and advocates toleration in religion and politics. A strong defender of the Shiite version of history, he none the less takes a fairly tolerant line on the first two caliphs, but argues throughout that Ali was primarily an ethical humanist, emphasizing the rationality of his principles. This humanism is mainly concerned with the nature of the life of the present, and it involves kind and dutiful human relationships based upon physical and moral health. The universal message of Islam is of the necessity of fraternal love and cooperation.

In his political philosophy Ali sees no incompatibility between Islam and the modern constitutional state. The executive side of the state needs to be checked by the consensus (*ijma* of the people and the educated elite, and not just by the *ijma* of the *ulama*, the religious authorities. Ali was convinced that once Islam was presented properly as a rational faith its significance would be more widely acknowledged. Every aspect of Islamic law has a basis in reason, and even the ceremonial practices are to be perceived as rational. For instance, prayer strengthens the feeling of togetherness in the community and is physically beneficial for the person who undertakes it. Fasting is also good for people: it encourages the development of virtues such as self-discipline and promotes social justice. Ali's books went through many editions and were important in communicating a view of Islam as a rational and dynamic faith to the non-Islamic world. He was also influential in the Islamic world, and his approach to the reconciliation of reason and religion was much studied and discussed.

Sources: EncIslam, 2nd edn; A. Ahmad (1970–) *Islamic Modernism in India and Pakistan 1857–1964*, London; K. Aziz (1988) *Ameer Ali: His Life and Work*, Lahore.

OLIVER LEAMAN

Aliotta, Antonio

Italian. *b:* 18 January 1881, Palermo, Sicily. *d:* 1 February 1964, Naples. *Cat:* Experimental and spiritualist philosopher. *Appts:* Professor of Theoretical Philosophy, Padua, 1913–19, and then Naples, 1919–51.

Main publications:

In *Opere complete*, second edition, Rome: Cemonese, 1957:
(1905) *La misura in psicologia sperimentale.*
(1922) *La teoria d'Einstein e le mutevoli prospettive del mondo.*
(1922) *Relativismo e idealismo.*
(1924) *Il problema di Dio e il nuovo pluralismo.*
(1942) *L'estetica di Kant e degli idealisti romantici.*
(1946) *Il sacrificio come significato del mondo.*
(1947) *Scetticismo, misticismo e pessimismo.*
(1948) *Evoluzionismo e spiritualismo.*
(1948) *Il relativismo, l'idealismo e la teoria di Einstein.*
(1950) *L'origini dell'irrazionalismo contemporaneo.*
(1951) *Critica dell'esistenzialismo.*
(1951) *L'estetica dell'Croce e la crisi dell'idealismo italiano.*
((1954) *Il nuovo positivismo e lo sperimentialismo.*

Secondary literature:

Carbonara, C. *et. al.* (1951) *Lo sperimentalismo de Antonio Aliotta*, Naples: Libreria scientifica editrice.
Pallavicini, G. (1968) *Il pensiero di Antonio Aliotta*, Naples: Libreria scientifica editrice.
Petruzzeuis, N. (1970) *Maestri d'ieri*, Naples: Giannini.

After initial work in experimental psychology Aliotta came across the work of **Croce**, rejecting that philosopher's species of idealism with its commitment to the absolute creativity of spirit. Having rejected this form of idealism Aliotta arrived at romantic idealism, where, following Schelling and **Bergson**, he posited an evolutionary process produced at the root of nature by a creative activity. This dynamic concept of being, together with his distrust of pure mechanism, caused him to consider again the cognitive value of science, which he thought to lie in its power to integrate the various intuitively arrived at elements of experience. Firmly opposed to what had become the prevalent orthodoxy of neo-Hegelian idealism he asserted the irreducible objectivity of natural things, while admitting the capacity of humans to integrate things into higher forms of life. He also continually reminded his countrymen of intellectual movements occurring beyond Italy, notably in the philosophy of science and in realism. In the mature phase of his work he envisaged a plurality of centres of consciousness and their progressive harmonization on the road to a unity always approached but never reached. Central to that view is a commitment to experimentation, not just in laboratories but wherever the method of trial and error could be used. Successful experiment eliminates conflict and produces a relatively greater harmony. That harmony widens from agreement over the things of common sense, through the higher harmony and coordination produced as science eliminates the conflicting perspectives of common sense, and finally in philosophical enquiry. The widening harmonization converges on a single end which is God. He none the less defends philosophical relativism, the only measure of truth being the degree of coordination that is realized in the fabric of experience. The quest for truth just is the quest for a superior harmony. In later writings Aliotta moves towards a spiritualist Christianity in which faith, conceived as thought in operation, is the foundation of philosophy. Human progress to unity is facilitated by universal postulates assumed in our acting, for example the postulates that there is a certain constant order in the world and that there is a plurality of persons. The supreme postulate is that of a superior consciousness, God. The existence of God guarantees the perennial character of human values.

COLIN LYAS

Alquié, Ferdinand

French. *b:* 18 December 1906, Carcassonne, France. *d:* 28 February 1985, Montpellier, France. *Cat:* 'Surrealist' philosopher; historian of ideas. *Ints:* Metaphysics; history of 'modern' philosophy. *Educ:* University of Sorbonne. *Infls:* Plato, Descartes and Kant. *Appts:* 1940–7, teacher in various lycées; 1947–52, Professor, University of Montpelier; 1952–76, Professor, Sorbonne, Paris; 1975, elected to the Académie des Sciences; 1979, Emeritat, Sorbonne.

Main publications:

(1943) *Le Désir d'éternité*, Paris: PUF.
(1950a) *La Découverte métaphysique de l'homme chez Descartes*, Paris: PUF.
(1950b) *La Nostalgie de l'être*, Paris: PUF.
(1955) *Philosophie du surréalisme*, Paris: Flammarion.
(1956) *Descartes, l'homme et l'oeuvre*, Paris: Haitien–Boivin.
(1957) *L'Expérience*, Paris: PUF.
(1966) *Solitude de la Raison*, Paris: Losfeld.
(1968) *La Critique kantienne de la métaphysique*, Paris: PUF.
(1971) *Signification de la philosophie*, Paris: Hachette.
(1974) *Le Cartésianisme de Malebranche*, Paris: Vrin.
(1981) *Le Rationalisme de Spinoza*, Paris: PUF.

Secondary literature:

Gouhier, Henri (1974) 'À la memorie de Ferndinand Alquié, *Revue Internationale de Philosophie* 28: 532–9.
Marian, J.-L. (1983) *La Passion de la raison: hommage à Ferdinand Alquié*, Paris: P.U.F.
Riley, Patrick (1986) *The General Will Before Rousseau*, Princeton: Princeton University Press.
Smith, Colin (1984) *Contemporary French Philosophy: A Study in Norms and Values*, London: Methuen, pp. 77–93.

Alquié saw in works such as Plato's *Symposium*, Descartes's *Meditations* and Kant's *Critique of Pure Reason* a recognition both of 'transcendent Being' and at the same time of its non-availability to human experience. He opposed himself to those contemporary philosophers (such as the existentialists and the Marxists) who denied transcendence and recognized only 'man-made truth' (1950b, p. 63). Equally he opposed those who objectified transcendent being and made it into something human beings could, in some sense, possess. The titles of two of his books–*The Desire for Eternity* (1943) and *The Nostalgia of Being* (1950)–indicate both the aspiration of philosophy and the need to restrain its pretensions. The self-styled 'surrealism' of his *Philosophie de surréalisme* (1955) reflects both his concern with transcendence and his rejection of any analogy between the history of philosophy and that of science. According to Alquié: 'Philosophy is analysis and separation. The history of philosophy shows no progress, only a ceaseless recall to being' (1950b, p. 152, quoted from Smith 1964, p. 83). Alquié enjoyed a high reputation as a historian of philosophy, and some of his contributions to the history of ideas have been

influential. His *Le Cartésianisme de Malebranche* (1974) interpreted Malebranche as extending Cartesian thinking about the regularity of nature into the realm of grace. According to Alquié, this proved a powerful stimulus to the Enlightenment deists. Pursuing Alquié's suggestion, Patrick Riley (1986) has suggested that Malebranche's conception of 'volontés générales' influenced Rousseau's idea of 'the general will'.

Sources: Huisman; G. Deledalle and D. Huisman (eds) (1965) *Les Philosophes français d'aujourd'hui*, Paris.

STUART BROWN

Alston, W(illiam) P(ayne)

American. *b:* 1921, Shreveport, Louisiana. *Cat:* Analytic philosopher. *Ints:* Philosophical theology; epistemology; philosophy of language; philosophical psychology; early modern philosophy. *Educ:* Centenary College and University of Chicago. *Infls:* Reid, Hegel, Whitehead, Wittgenstein, J. L. Austin and Wilfrid Sellars. *Appts:* 1949, Instructor, 1952, Assistant Professor, 1956, Associate Professor, 1961, Professor, University of Michigan; 1971–6, Professor of Philosophy, Rutgers University; 1976–80, Professor of Philosophy, University of Illinois, Urbana-Champaign; 1980, Professor of Philosophy, Syracuse University; 1990, Fellow of the American Academy of Arts and Sciences.

Main publications:

(1964) *Philosophy of Language*, Englewood Cliffs: Prentice-Hall.
(1989) *Divine Nature and Human Language*, Ithaca: Cornell University Press.
(1989) *Epistemic Justification*, Ithaca: Cornell University Press.
(1991) *Perceiving God*, Ithaca: Cornell University Press.

Secondary literature:

McCleod, Mark S. (ed.) (1993) *Rationality and Theistic Belief: An Essay in Reformed Epistemology*, Ithaca: Cornell University Press.

Alston's major influence has been in the philosophy of religion and in epistemology. He was the first President of the Society of Christian Philosophers, and the founding editor of *Faith and Philosophy*, a journal which has been a major vehicle for a movement characterized, like his own work, by the rigorous application of modern philosophical and logical techniques to traditional questions in the philosophy of religion. In epistemology, Alston has worked towards a qualified foundationalism and reliabilism, a position which he has used to argue that the direct experience of God can be regarded as a legitimate ground of belief.

Sources: Personal communication.

ANTHONY ELLIS

Althusser, Louis

Algerian-French. *b:* 1918, Birmendreis, Algeria. *d:* 1990, Yvelines, France. *Cat:* Marxist; political philosopher; epistemologist; metaphysician; philosopher of science. *Educ:* Studied at the École Normale Supérieure, Paris. *Infls:* Marx, Lenin, Gramsci, Lévi-Strauss, Gaston Bachelard and Mao Zedong. *Appts:* Professor of Philosophy, École Normale Supérieure.

Main publications:

(1959) *Montesquieu: la politique et l'histoire*, Paris: Presses Universitaires de France (English translation, *Politics and History: Montesquieu, Rousseau, Hegel and Marx*, trans. Ben Brewster, London: NLB, 1972).

(1965) *Pour Marx*, Paris: Maspero (English translation, *For Marx*, trans. Ben Brewster, London: NLB, 1969).

(1965) (with Étienne Balibar, Pierre Macherey, *et al.*), *Lire le Capitale*, Paris: Maspero; revised edition, 1968 (English translation, *Reading Capital*, trans. Ben Brewster, London:NLB,1970)

(1969) *Lénine et la philosophie*, Paris: Maspero (English translation,*Lenin and Philosophy and Other Essays*, trans. Ben Brewster, London: NLB, 1971).

(1974) *Éléments d'autocritique*, Paris: Hachette (English translation,*Essays in Self-Criticism*, trans. G. Lock, London: NLB, 1976).

(1974) *Philosophie et philosophie spontanée des savants*, Paris: Maspero (English translation,*Philosophy and the Spontaneous Philosophy of the Scientists*, trans. Ben Brewster *et al.*, London: NLB, 1990).

Secondary literature:

Assiter, Alison (1990) *Althusser and Feminism*, London: Pluto Press.

Benton, Ted (1984) *The Rise and Fall of Structural Marxism*, London and Basingstoke: Macmillan.

Callinicos, Alex (1976) *Althusser's Marxism*, London: Pluto Press.

Clarke, Simon (1980) *One Dimensional Marxism: Althusser and the Politics of Culture*, London: Allison & Busby.

Elliott, Gregory (1987) *Althusser: The Detour of Theory*, London: Verso.

Smith, Steven B. (1984) *Reading Althusser*, Ithaca, NY, and London: Macmillan.

Thompson, E. P. (1978) *The Poverty of Theory and Other Essays*, London: Cornell University Press.

Althusser is the leading figure in the movement known as structural Marxism, which sought to reinterpret Marx in the light of the work of structuralists like **Lévi-Strauss**. A member of the French Communist Party, Althusser's development as a philosopher is very much tied up with the fortunes of that organization, in particular with the intense policy debates that occurred within the party in the aftermath of the denunciation of Stalin at the 1956 Congress of the Soviet Communist Party, and in the context of the growing rift between Soviet and Chinese Communism. Most of Althusser's major contributions to Marxist theory, such as the theory of the symptomatic reading, the doctrine of the epistemological break, the Overdeterminism Thesis and the insistence on a sharp separation between science and ideology, stem from his interventions in these debates, as does his later interest in the work of **Mao Zedong**. Althusser's earliest intellectual influence was the philosopher of science Gaston **Bachelard**, from whose work he derived the basis for the doctrine of the epistemological break. Althusser also drew heavily on the work of **Lenin** and **Gramsci**, whose doctrine of hegemony and theories of the mutually interactive relationship between the economic base of a society and its cultural superstructure had a profound impact on Althusser's mature thought. The general drift of Althusser's project is to establish Marxism as a 'theoretical anti-humanism'; that is, as a social theory whose concern is with historical process rather than with the actions of individual human beings: 'historical process without a subject' as it is known. Structuralism, with its commitment to independently operating deep structures of thought, and downgrading of the role of human agency within history, is an obvious point of reference here. Althusser's concern in his theoretical interventions was to press the claims for Marx's mature writings, *Capital* for example, over those of his youthful, so-called 'humanist' period of the early 1840s, such as the *Economic and Philosophical Manuscripts* of 1844. To counter the fashion of these largely Hegelian works amongst French humanist Marxists, Althusser posited the existence of a dramatic change in Marx's thought in the mid-1840s, a rupture or 'epistemological break', roughly from *The German Ideology* and

Theses on Feuerbach onwards, which marked his coming of age as a 'scientific' theorist. Before 1845 Marx's thought is constrained by the ideological notions of its time; after 1845 he is conducting a scientific critique of his ideology and pointing out its deficiencies and internal contradictions. The key to identifying this break lies in Althusser's theory of the symptomatic reading, where the objective is to isolate the underlying structure of thought, or 'problematic' as Althusser terms it, which governs the production of the text and moulds its argument. It is in the nature of a problematic, whose family resemblance to **Kuhn**'s notion of 'paradigm' has been noted by several commentators, to set limits on what can be thought or called into question, and a symptomatic reading is concerned precisely to identify what those limits are. A sharp distinction is made in Althusser between ideology, a closed system of belief featuring internal contradictions which most of us are unaware of in everyday lived experience, and science, a system of enquiry open to change from within. Marxism, through its theory of dialectical materialism, is for Althusser a science, and sciences are seen to be beyond the reach of ideology. Theory is in fact an autonomous area of discourse, or 'practice', to Althusser, with Marxism being regarded as a self-validating science. In Althusser's social theory the superstructure of a culture consists of a series of such practices, variously political, ideological or theoretical, which are in a dialectical relationship with the economic base. Taking his cue from Gramsci, Althusser treats the relationship as one of mutual interaction where base and superstructure can affect each other, whereas in a more traditional Marxist thought the base is held to be dominant. Althusser posits a 'relative autonomy' of the superstructure which is only in 'the last instance' (a thesis which remains fairly obscure) under the dominance of the base. Thus events in the superstructure are as capable of triggering a revolutionary situation as those in the base, since the former may well constitute the weak, or 'overdetermined', link in a given social formation: this is Althusser's 'Overdeterminism Thesis'. Such a relationship between base and superstructure actively precludes any possibility of meaningful human action, and historical process without a subject is primarily a matter of 'Repressive State Apparatuses' (instruments of state power such as the police or army) and 'Ideological State Apparatuses' (hegemonic institutions such as the church or universities) working through individuals. Those individuals simply act out the roles assigned to them by ideology, which provides little scope for human agency. Althusser was a major theoretical force in the French Communist Party, and his recasting of the fundamental elements of Marxist thought within a structuralist framework generated vigorous debate in Marxist circles, both inside and outside France. Arguably the most influential voice in Western Marxism during the 1960s and 1970s, Althusser's structural Marxism was much in vogue at the time and had a significant impact across a range of intellectual disciplines, such as political economy, sociology, anthropology, aesthetics and literary theory. Althusser's reputation has declined markedly since the 1970s, partly in the wake of the poststructuralist critique of the metaphysics underpinning structuralist methodology, as well as the postmodernist challenge to 'grand narrative' theories such as Marxism; and structural Marxism no longer commands much support on the left, where notions like the epistemological break are felt to be unhistorical and far too schematic. A common criticism of Althusser's work has been that it lacks a human dimension, and his theory of ideology is now considered to be overly determinist in character. E. P. Thompson, for example, has been particularly scathing of Althusser's denial of the role of human agency in history, and has also been one of a number of commentators to accuse Althusser of having Stalinist tendencies, although others, such as Steven B. Smith, have been just as keen to defend him from this highly emotive charge. Althusser's most committed disciples have been his ex-students Étienne **Balibar** and Pierre **Macherey**; the former being the co-author with Althusser of one of the central texts of structural Marxism, *Reading Capital* (revised edition); the latter having had notable success in the application of Althusserian ideas to literary theory in his widely admired study *A Theory of Literary Production* (1966).

STUART SIM

Ambrose, Alice

American. *b:* 1906, Lexington, Illinois. *Cat:* Analytic philosopher. *Ints:* Philosophy of mathematics. *Educ:* Millikin University, Illinois; University of Wisconsin; and University of Cambridge. *Infls:* Ludwig Wittgenstein, G. E. Moore and Morris Lazerowitz. *Appts:* 1937, Assistant Professor, 1943, Professor, 1951, Sophia and Austin Smith Professor of Philosophy, 1972, Professor Emeritus, Smith College; other visiting positions.

Main publications:
(1966) *Essays in Analysis*, London: George Allen & Unwin.
(1976) (with Morris Lazerowitz) *Philosophical Theories*, The Hague: Mouton.
(1977) 'The Yellow Book Notes in relation to *The Blue Book*', *Crítica* 9.
(1979) (ed.) *Wittgenstein's Lectures: Cambridge, 1932–1935*, Oxford: Basil Blackwell.
(1984) (with Morris Lazerowitz) *Essays in the Unknown Wittgenstein*, Buffalo: Prometheus Books.
(1992) (ed.) *Lectures on Metaphysics, 1934–1935, by G. E. Moore*, New York: P. Lang.

Much influenced by the work of **Wittgenstein**, Ambrose argued that philosophical theories typically consist of disguised linguistic claims. The rival claims of, for instance, Platonists and conventionalists about mathematics consist of concealed revisions of language whose aim is to justify the description of mathematics as discovery, or as creation. Such recommendations are typically supported by misleading analogies between the languages of mathematics and empirical facts. Progress is therefore to be made by detailed attention to the actual grammar of language.

Ambrose was a student of Wittgenstein in Cambridge in the 1930s, and has edited students' notes of lectures by **Moore** and Wittgenstein.
Sources: CA NRS 17; personal communication.

ANTHONY ELLIS

Amin, Ahmad

Egyptian. *b:* 1 October 1886, Cairo. *d:* 30 May 1954, Cairo. *Cat:* Islamic modernist and reformist; historian of Arab and Islamic civilization and thought; historian of philosophy. *Ints:* Methodology. *Educ:* Al-Azhar University, 1900, abandoning his studies in 1904; National State University, Cairo, 1907–11; completed the study of English language in 1916. *Appts:* Teacher of Arabic in elementary schools and journalist; appointed Judge in Qena, Tatah and Cairo, 1921–6; University Professor from 1926; Director of the Cultural Centre of Egyptian Ministry of Education, 1945; Director of the Cultural Section of the Arab League, 1947.

Main publications:
(1918) *Mabadi al-Falsafah* [Principles of Philosophy], Cairo: Lagnat at-Talif wat-Targamah wan-Nashr.

(1929) *Fajr al-Islam* [The Dawn of Islam], Cairo: Matba'at al-Iitimad.
(1933) *Duha al-Islam* [The Morning of Islam], 3 vols, Cairo: Lagnat at-Ta'lif wa't-Targamah wa'n-Nashr.
(1936) *Qissat al-Falsafah al-Hadithah* [A History of Modern Philosophy, in collaboration with Zaki Nagib Mahmud], Cairo: Lagnat at-Talif wat-Targamah wan-Nashr.
(1936) *Qissat al-Falsafah al-Yunaniyyah* [A History of Greek Philosophy, in collaboration with Zaki Nagib Mahmud], Cairo: Lagnat at-Talif wat-Targamah wan-Nashr.
(1945–55) *Zuhr al-Islam* [The Noon of Islam] 4 vols, Cairo: Lagnat at-Ta'lif wa't-Targamah wan Nashr.
(1948) *Zuama al-Islah* [The Leaders of Reformism], Maktabat an-Nahdah al-Misriyyah, Cario.
(1969) *Beirut: Dar al-Kitab al-'Arabi (the complete history of the Islamic intellectual movement)*.

Secondary literature:
Borruso, A. (1980) article in *Oriente Moderno*.
Craig A.J. (1955) 'Middle East Journal', *IBLA* (Algiers).
Mazyad, (1963) *A. A.: Advocate of Social and Literary Reform in Egypt*, Leiden: Brill.
Rizzitano, U. L. (1955) article in *Oriente Moderno*.
Shepard (1982) *The Faith of a Modern Muslim Intellectual: A. A.*, New Dehli.

Despite his traditional training, Amin was an open-minded thinker and recognized the usefulness of Western methodology. His aim was the revival of the Islamic cultural heritage as a means to the intellectual and moral renewal of all Arab-Islamic peoples. He held advanced social ideas and was aware of the necessity to relate religious prescriptions to changing situations. Amin espoused Mutazilite rationalism and logic, preferring Mutazilites to philosophers because of their emphasis on (men of) faith. He acknowledged that a modernist awakening must be grounded on intellect and human free will, without immoderate resort to divine predestination. Amin's thought has exerted a powerful influence on Arab intellectuals.
Sources: G. Anawati (1982) *Tendances et courants de l'Islam arabe contemporain*, Munich: Kaiser & Grünewald; Archives of the Pontifical Inst. of Arabic Studies in Rome.

MASSIMO CAMPANINI

Amor Ruibal, Angel

Spanish. *b:* 1869, San Verismo de Barro (Pontevedra). *d:* 1930, Santiago de Compostela, Spain. *Cat:*

Correlationist; metaphysician. *Ints:* Philosophy of religion; hermeneutics; philology. *Educ:* Santiago de Compostela Seminary; Universities of Barcelona and Gregoriana (Rome). *Infls:* Hegel and Régnaud. *Appts:* 1897–8, Professor of Theology, University of Santiago de Compostela; 1905–30, Canon of the cathedral of Santiago de Compostela; 1898–1930, Professor of Canonical Law, University of Santiago de Compostela.

Main publications:

(1914–22) *Los problemas fundamentales de la Filosofía y del Dogma*, vols I–VI, Santiago de Compostela.

(1933–6) *Los problemas fundamentales de la Filosofía y del Dogma*, vols VII–X, ed. C. Pumar Cornes, Santiago de Compostela.

(1964) *Cuatro manuscritos inéditos*, ed. S. Casas Blanco, Madrid: Gredos.

Secondary literature:

Fraile, G. (1972) *Historia de la filosofía española*, Madrid.

Guy, A. (1983) *Histoire de la philosophie espagnole*, Toulouse: Association des Publications de l'Université de Toulouse-Le Mirail.

López-Quintas, A. (1970) *Filosofía Española Contemporanea*, Madrid.

Amor Ruibal's primary philosophical interest centred, due doubtless to his training and professional position as a canon of the catholic church, on the search for a philosophical foundation for theology, much of which was based on the latest scientific advances, and which sought to integrate the contemporary state of science with the details of faith and its dogmatic systemization. José Luis Abellán considers that this investigation signified the 'arrival at the border' where contemporary philosophy met with postmodernity.

The label of 'correlation' attached to Amor Ruibal's work evades the subjectivity of naming it 'transcendental relativism'. The universe is seen as a system of related beings, a network of organically and systematically related correlative elements, and thus an ontological reality, rather than a simple complex of pure relations. This is supported by a unitary vision of the universe in which the individualized substances are seen not as autonomous but as 'mosaics' or 'links': the universe is a system of correlative primary elements characterized by their being universal, natural, given, ontological, intrinsic, essential and organic, although also relative to that which they constitute and to the cosmic entirety.

These primary elements are conceived of as being essentially and absolutely relative, indivisible, irreducible, incomplete, lacking in 'thingness', indefinable, unintelligible, unexplainable and unknowable. The only access to them is through a simple intuitive notion, or 'understanding', of things that can be described but not defined, belonging to a prelogical order presented as an affirmation: it is elsewhere defined as a 'simple intellectual presentiality'. This type of knowledge is distinguished from two other forms: sensible knowledge, that presented to us by the things themselves; and intellectual knowledge, that exercised on the matter provided by us via the first type of knowledge.

This correlationism is contextualized by what he terms a universal dynamism, or causality, which converts this correlationism into a continuous and universal dynamism with the appearance of evolutionism, although this evolutionism is 'organic' and 'perfective' leading to an imminent finality, and it is this, combined with the notion that the universe in totality being relative is what provides proof of the existence of God: the contradiction between total being and absolute nothingness marks out the contigency that separates these states and, thus, a necessary being is postulated. Alain Guy notes that Amor Ruibal has been likened to A. N. **Whitehead**, and whilst philosophically speaking there may be certain resonances between the two, his thought has been much more linked to a particularly Spanish vein of philosophical enquiry, that of the connections between theology and philosophy. **Zubiri**'s work *Sobre la esencia*, published in 1962, was clear about its influence. Critique has been centred on his critical avoidance of the writings of other philosophers, and his tendency to radicalize those views with which he disagrees.

DAVID SPOONER

Anderson, John

Australian. *b:* 1893, Scotland. *d:* 1962, Sydney, Australia. *Cat:* Naturalist; realist; systematic philosopher. *Ints:* Ethics; aesthetics; social philosophy. *Educ:* University of Glasgow. *Infls:* Influenced by Samuel Alexander's defence of realism in his Gifford Lectures, delivered in Glasgow in 1916–17 and published in 1920 under the title *Space, Time, and Deity*. *Appts:* Lecturer in Philosophy, University of Edinburgh; 1927–58 (retired), Challis Professor of Philosophy, University of Sydney.

Main publications:
Anderson wrote no books, but published a number of philosophical articles, mostly in the *Australasian Journal of Philosophy*. Since his death, the following collections of his articles have appeared:

(1962) *Studies in Empirical Philosophy*, Sydney: Angus & Robertson (contains a valuable introductory essay by John Passmore).

(1980) *Education and Enquiry*, ed. D. Z. Phillips, Oxford: Blackwell.

(1982) *Art and Reality*, ed. Janet Anderson, G. Cullum and K. Lycos, Sydney: Hale & Iremonger.

Secondary literature:
Baker, A. J. (1986 *Australian Realism: The Systematic Philosophy of John Anderson*, Cambridge: Cambridge University Press.

Bogdan, Radu J. (ed.) (1984) *David Armstrong*, Dordrecht: Reidel.

Grave, S. A. (1976) *Philosophy in Australia Since 1958*, Sydney: Sydney University Press.

Mackie, J. (1951) 'Logic and Professor Anderson', *Australasian Journal of Philosophy* 29: 109–13.

Ryle, G. (1950) 'Logic and Professor Anderson', *Australasian Journal of Philosophy* 28: 137–53.

Anderson attempted to develop a systematic philosophy of naturalism and realism, grounded in the view that there is only one realm of being, that of events and processes in space and time. There are no Platonic forms or universals, no souls distinct from bodies, and no God. A healthy-minded philosophy should remorselessly criticize such illusions.

Knowledge, for Anderson, is always based on descriptions of matters of fact (events in space and time). Concering a priori knowledge, he took a strongly empiricist position, denying any sharp distinction between the 'rational sciences' (logic and mathematics) and the natural sciences, and insisting that the former are merely extremely general forms of scientific enquiry. Philosophy is conceived as continuous with science rather than distinct from it, a claim that provoked a critical response from Gilbert **Ryle**.

In ethics Anderson adopted a somewhat idiosyncratic position, dismissing the concepts of 'right', 'ought' and 'duty' as empty and outmoded relics from the Age of Faith. (What is a command without a commander?) 'Good', by contrast, names a straightforwardly descriptive property of certain human activities—those that are free, creative, productive, enterprising, intelligent and risky. Like **Nietzsche**, Anderson regarded Christian ethics as the morality of slaves.

In his social and political philosophy, Anderson opposed atomistic individualism, arguing for the reality of irreducibly social forces and movements. He nevertheless opposed 'solidarism', the view that there is such a thing as the common good. Every society, he argues, is made up of conflicting and opposed forces, with no prospect of reconciliation. In his influential writings on education he develops these ideas further, urging that the aim of education should not be 'socialization' but the development of the child's critical intelligence.

In both ethics and aesthetics Anderson's naturalism led him to reject all forms of relativism. Just as 'good' names a natural property of certain human activities (a property just as objective as temperature), so 'beautiful' names a natural property found in art and nature. It cannot be reduced to 'pleasing', which clearly denotes a relation rather than quality. Although he wrote little, and few of his papers were read outside Australia, Anderson was an enormously influential teacher. He was largely responsible for creating, at Sydney in particular, a distinctive new *style* of Australian philosophy, based on a no-nonsense realism, tending towards materialism, a thoroughgoing naturalism, and a moderate empiricism closer to Locke than to Berkeley and Hume. Although he did not anticipate the identity theory of Place, **Smart** and **Armstrong**, his teaching helped to create a philosophical climate sympathetic to that development. His students at Sydney included such figures as David Stove, John **Mackie**, David **Armstrong** and John **Passmore**.

Sources: Passmore 1957; Passmore's introduction to Anderson's *Studies* 1962; Anthony Quinton's introduction to Baker 1986.

ANDREW PYLE

Andreas-Salomé, Lou
Russian. *b:* 12 February 1861, St Petersburg. *d:* 5 February 1937, Göttingen, Germany. *Cat:* Nietzschean; philosopher of love, sexuality and woman; psychoanalytic writer; philosopher of religion. *Educ:* Philosophy and the History of Religion, with Pastor Hendrik Gillot, in St Petersburg, 1879–80; attended university lectures in Philosophy, Theology and Art History in Zurich, 1880–81; attended Freud's classes in Vienna, 1912–13. *Infls:* Nietzsche, Freud, Rainer Maria Rilke and Spinoza.

Main publications:

(1892) *Hendrik Ibsens Frauengestalten* [Hendrik Ibsen's Female Characters], Jena: Eugen Diederichs.

(1894) *Friedrich Nietzsche in seinen Werken* [Friedrich Nietzsche in his Works], Vienna: Carl Conegen (English translation, *Nietzsche*, ed. and trans. Siegfried Mandel, Redding Ridge: Black Swann Books, 1988).

(1910) *Die Erotik* [The Erotic], Frankfurt: Rutten & Loening.

(1925) *Rainer Maria Rilke* Leipzig: Insel.

(1958) *In der Schule bei Freud* [The Freud Journal], ed. Ernst Pfeiffer, Zurich: Max Niehans (English translation, *The Freud Journal of Lou Andreas-Salomé*, trans. S. A. Leavy, London: The Hogarth Press and The Institute of Psycho-Analysis, 1965).

Secondary literature:

Binion, Rudolf (1968) *Frau Lou, Nietzsche's Wayward Disciple*, Princeton.

Livingstone, Anglea (1984) *Lou Andreas-Salomé*, London: Gordon Fraser.

Martin, Biddy (1991) *Woman and Modernity: The (Life) Styles of Lou Andreas-Salomé*, Ithaca: Cornell University Press.

Peters, H. F. (1962) *My Sister, My Spouse*, New York: Norton.

Pfeiffer, Ernst (ed.) (1951) *Lebensruckblick*, Zurich: Max Niehans (autobiography).

Andreas-Salomé wrote widely in philosophy, literary criticism fiction, and psychoanalysis. She was active and influential in intellectual circles at the turn of the century. In particular, her thought contributed to the ideas of Friedrich **Nietzsche**, Paul Rée, Rainer Maria Rilke and Sigmund **Freud**, all of whom she knew well.

Andreas-Salomé's important study of the stages of Nietzsche's thought, *Friedrich Nietzsche in seinen Werken* (1894), has the central thesis that his outer, intellectual life is an expression of his inner, psychological life. In her critique of his philosophical ideas, she argued that the *Übermensch* is both unattainable and destructive. Despite her critical remarks, she embraced much of his anti-foundationalist thought, including the rejection of universal moral truth.

Andreas-Salomé's psychoanalytic writings bring together her early interest in religion and her later ideas on love, sexuality and femininity. In her theory of narcissism, love and sex are a reunion of the self with its lost half. Love is directed back at ourselves because the lost self is actually an ideal image created from ourselves. But the union of the self and the ideal image also represents a union of the individual self with Spinozan Nature (or God). With Nietzsche, she believed that God is dead, but she added that he has an afterlife in the exalted human feelings that endure after the ideal (God) created by humans is replaced. These life-enhancing feelings are characteristic of narcissistic love which constitutes, especially for women, a progressive expansion of the self.

EMILY BRADY

Androutsos, Christos

Greek. *b:* 1869, Kios (Asia Minor). *d:* 1935, Athens. *Cat:* Philosopher and theologian; Platonic scholar. *Ints:* History of ancient thought; philosophical psychology; ethics; philosophy of religion. *Educ:* Theological School of Halki and University of Leipzig. *Infls:* Plato, Wilhelm Wundt and Greek Orthodox dogmatics. *Appts:* Taught at the Theological School of Halki (1895–7, 1901–5); Marasleion Teachers' Training College, Athens (1906–11); Professor of Dogmatic and Christian Ethics, University of Athens (1912–35).

Main publications:

(1895–97) *The Concept of Evil in Plato* vol. 1 *The Concept of Evil, Athens; vol. 2, The Origin of Evil, Constantinople*).

(1903) *Plato's Theory of Knowledge in Itself and in Relation to the Philosophers Before Him, Athens*.

(1909) *Critique of the Fundamental Dogmas of Stoic Philosophy*, Athens.

(1925) *System of Ethics*, Athens.

(1929) *Dictionary of Philosophy*, Athens.

(1931) *On Freud's Psychoanalysis*, Athens.

(1934) *General psychology*, Athens.

Androutsos criticized the neo-Kantian reading of Plato popular among German philosophers of his times, stressing the ontological significance of the Platonic ideas. Again, Androutsos was the most characteristic representative of the philosophical ideas of the Greek Orthodox Church. An exponent of personalism in ethics, he aimed to provide a religious foundation for philosophical ethics. His *Dictionary of Philosophy* (1929) is a remarkable attempt to establish a philosophical terminology in modern Greek.

STAVROULA TSINOREMA

Anscombe, G(ertrude) E(lizabeth) M(argaret)

British. *b:* 1919. *Cat:* Analytic philosopher. *Ints:* Philosophy of mind; ethics; metaphysics; philosophy of religion; history of philosophy. *Educ:* Universities of Oxford and Cambridge. *Infls:* Aristotle, St Thomas Aquinas and Ludwig Wittgenstein. *Appts:* 1946–64, Research Fellowships, Somerville College, Oxford; 1964–70, Fellow of Somerville College, Oxford; 1970–86, Professor of Philosophy, University of Cambridge; 1970–86, Fellow of New Hall, Cambridge, Honorary Fellow since 1986. 1967, Fellow of the British Academy; 1979, Foreign Honorary Member, American Academy of Arts and Sciences.

Main publications:

(1939) (with Norman Daniel) *The Justice of the Present War Examined*, Oxford: published by the authors.

(1953) (trans.) Ludwig Wittgenstein, *Philosophical Investigations*, Oxford: Basil Blackwell.

(1956) 'Aristotle and the sea battle', *Mind* 65.

(1957) *Intention*, Oxford: Basil Blackwell.

(1957) *Mr Truman's Degree*, Oxford: published by the author.

(1958) 'Modern moral philosophy', *Philosophy* 33.

(1959) *An Introduction to Wittgenstein's 'Tractatus'*, London: Hutchinson.

(1961) (with Peter Geach) *Three Philosophers*, Ithaca: Cornell University Press.

(1971) *Causality and Determination*, Cambridge: Cambridge University Press.

(1975) 'The first person', in Samuel Guttenplan (ed.), *Mind and Language*, Oxford: Clarendon Press.

(1976) 'The question of linguistic idealism', in 'Essays on Wittgenstein in honour of G. H. von Wright', *Acta Philosophica Fennica* 28.

(1979) 'Under a description', *Noûs* 13.

(1981) *The Collected Philosophical Papers of G. E. M. Anscombe* (vol. 1, *From Parmenides to Wittgenstein*; vol. 2, *Metaphysics and the Philosophy of Mind*; vol. 3, *Ethics, Religion and Politics*), Oxford: Basil Blackwell.

Secondary literature:

Diamond, Cora and Teichman, Jenny (eds) (1979) *Intention and Intentionality: Essays in Honour of G. E. M. Anscombe*, Brighton: Harvester Press.

MacDonald, Scott (1991) 'Ultimate ends in practical reasoning: Aquinas's Aristotelian moral psychology and Anscombe's fallacy', *The Philosophical Review* vol. 100.

Anscombe converted to Roman Catholicism in her youth, and a substantial portion of her work on ethics and religion has been devoted to exploring and defending Catholic doctrines. As a research student in Cambridge she became a pupil of **Wittgenstein** and, although she was never a *disciple* of his views, much of her thought shows his influence. Like Wittgenstein's, much of Anscombe's work is devoted to the relation between thought and reality. Unlike Wittgenstein, however, she has a serious interest in the history of philosophy and much of her work has been done through the explicit discussion of such philosophers as Aristotle, Aquinas and Hume.

Her first published article was written in the early weeks of the Second World War. It argued, contrary to the usual assumption, that it was not a just war on the grounds that its aims were unlimited and that it would involve the unjustifiable killing of civilians. In its reliance on the theory of natural law this article foreshadowed much of her later work. It also embodied a conception of human action which she explored and developed in many later writings. According to this conception, actions have an intrinsic nature, which depends upon their direct intention, and this intrinsic nature is at least as relevant to their moral status as are their motives and any consequences they may have. For instance, it may be held that deliberately killing the innocent as a means to one's ends is murder—whatever one's motives and whatever the consequences—and is always wrong. (According to the Doctrine of Double Effect which Anscombe espoused, one may permissibly perform actions that have the deaths of innocents as a consequence only so long as this is not one's 'direct intention'.) So, in *Mr Truman's Degree* (1957) she opposed the University of Oxford granting an honorary degree to President Truman, on the ground that his ordering the use of atom bombs, with the intention of causing the deaths of innocent civilians as a means of wringing total surrender from the Japanese, was an act of mass murder. On this conception, the theory of moral evaluation depends upon the theory of action, and Anscombe argued in 'Modern moral philosophy' (1958)—an article that helped lay the groundwork for the reemergence in analytic ethics of Aristotelian virtue theory and natural law theory—that moral philosophy should be abandoned until we have an adequate philosophical psychology.

Her highly influential monograph *Intention* (1957) discussed at length a major element of this philosophical psychology, the notion of intention, although without overt reference to ethical issues. Most philosophers had thought of intentions as mental events which occurred prior to actions and caused them. Anscombe argued that we should not think of intentional action as behaviour brought about by a certain sort of *cause*, but behaviour for which it is appropriate to give a *reason* in response to the question why it occurred. She also held that one knows what one's intentions are *without observation* (in a way in which one cannot always know what, for instance, one's motives are); and this is possible only because there is a species of knowledge—*practical* knowledge—which has been much underplayed by philosophers, who have been obsessed with *theoretical* knowledge. Practical knowledge, however, could only be adequately understood through an understanding of practical reasoning, and this led Anscombe into an influential discussion of this topic and some of its ramifications.

She also drew attention to the importance of the fact that one and the same action may fall under many different descriptions, for instance 'ending a war', 'killing civilians' and 'displacing molecules of air'. Under some of these descriptions it would be intentional and under others not; and different intentional descriptions would evoke different moral evaluations. Is there, then, one *correct* description? This problem has been extensively discussed ever since.

Many of the positions that Anscombe proposed in *Intention* became, for a considerable time, extremely widely accepted. This cannot be said of much of her work. Her paper 'The first person' (1975), for instance, argues that the word 'I' is not a referring expression. Not understanding this, she held, forces us into postulating a Cartesian ego since, if 'I' were indeed a referring expression, it seems that a Cartesian ego is what it would have to refer to. Like much of Anscombe's work, this difficult paper has been much discussed, but without commanding widespread agreement.

To understand the idea of action one needs to understand causality, and some of Anscombe's most discussed work has been on this topic. In her Inaugural Lecture *Causality and Determination* (1971) (in *Collected Papers*, vol. 3) she attacked two views which, since the eighteenth century, have been widely accepted. First, she argued against what she called 'determinism', the view that every event is completely determined by a prior cause. Contrary to the view of Hume, she held that there are many sorts of cause, and some of them do not *necessitate*, or make inevitable, effects. Second, she attacked the view, deriving from Kant and which had been almost an orthodoxy for fifty years, that determinism would be consistent with freedom of the will.

After Wittgenstein's death Anscombe became one of his literary executors. In this capacity she has translated and edited many of his works. One of her own earliest works (1959) was a difficult, though highly influential, commentary on Wittgenstein's *Tractatus Logico-Philosophicus*, in which she combated the then prevalent interpretation according to which the work was a manifesto of logical empiricism. Anscombe is widely thought to be one of Britain's foremost postwar philosophers—'simply the most distinguished, intellectually formidable, original, and troublesome philosopher in sight' (J. M. Cameron, *The New Republic*, 19 May, 1982, p. 34). Her thought is almost always difficult, in large part because it raises questions at the most fundamental level. Consequently, many of her arguments have been more widely discussed than accepted. Her fierce intelligence has often found expression in a fierceness of style that not everyone has found likeable.

Sources: Passmore 1957; CA 129; WW 1992.

ANTHONY ELLIS

Apel, Karl-Otto

German. *b:* 15 March 1922, Düsseldorf. *Cat:* Social philosopher; critical theorist. *Ints:* Philosophy of language; moral philosophy. *Infls:* Wittgenstein, Peirce and Habermas. *Appts:* Professor of Social Philosophy, University of Frankfurt.

Main publications:

(1963) *Die Idee der Sprache in der Tradition des Humanismus von Dante bis Vico*, Archiv für Begriffsgeschichte, vol. 8; second edition, Bonn: Bouvier, 1975.

(1965) 'Die Entfaltung der "Sprachanalytischen" Philosophie und das Problem der "Geisteswissenschaften"', *Philosophisches Jahrbuch* 72: 239–89 (English translation, *Analytic Philosophy of Language and the Geisteswissenschaften*, trans. Harald Holstelilie, Dordrecht: Reidel, 1967).

(1973) *Transformation der Philosophie*, 2 vols, Frankfurt: Suhrkamp (English translation, *Towards a Transformation of Philosophy* (abridged), trans. Glyn Adey and David Frisby, London: Routledge & Kegan Paul, 1980).

(1975) *Der Denkweg von C. S. Peirce*, Frankfurt: Suhrkamp (English translation, *Charles S. Peirce: From Pragmatism to Pragmaticism*, trans. Michel Krois, Amherst: University of Massachusetts Press, 1981).

(1979) *Die Erklären-Verstehen-Kontroverse in Transzendental-Pragmatischer Sicht*, Frankfurt: Suhrkamp (English translation, *Understanding and Explanation*, trans. Georgia Warnke, Cambridge, Mass.: MIT Press, 1984).

(1988) *Diskurs und Verantwortung: Das Problem des Übergangs zur postkonventionellen Moral* Frankfurt: Suhrkamp.

(1989) (contribution to) Axel Honneth *et al.* (eds) *Zwischenbetrachtungen im Prozeß der Aufklärung. Jürgen Habermas zum 60. Geburtstag*, Frankfurt: Suhrkamp (English translation, *Philosophical Investigations in the Unfinished Project of Enlightenment*, trans. William Rehg, Cambridge, Mass.: MIT Press, 1992).

Secondary literature:

Benhabib, Seyla and Dallmayr, Fred (eds) (1990) *The Communicative Ethics Controversy*, Cambridge, Mass.: MIT Press.

Brown, S. C. (ed.) (1979) *Philosophical Disputes in the Social Sciences*, Sussex: Harvester (contains Apel's paper 'Types of social science in the light of human cognitive interests', a comment by Peter Winch and Apel's reply).

Wellmer, Albrecht (1986) *Ethik und Dialog. Elemente des moralischen Urteils bei Kant und in der Diskursethik*, Frankfurt: Suhrkamp.

Apel's work is less well known than that of Jürgen **Habermas**, but they have worked along parallel lines for many years. Apel's account of the convergence between post-Wittgensteinian analytic philosophy and the German hermeneutic tradition is taken up in Habermas's *On the Logic of the Social Sciences* (1967), and his philosophical anthropology of cognition in Habermas's *Knowledge and Human Interests* (1968). Both thinkers engaged in the 1970s with the idea of a linguistic grounding of the social sciences and then turned to a discourse theory derived from speech pragmatics. Apel plays the philosopher to Habermas's sociologist: he is closer to a traditional Kantian search for transcendental grounds, where Habermas puts more emphasis on the cultural assumptions characteristic of modernity. For Apel's criticism of Habermas, see in particular his article ('Normatively grounding "critical theory" through recourse to the lifeworld?') in the Habermas *Festschrift* (1989).

WILLIAM OUTHWAITE

Al-Aqqad, Abbas Mahmud

Egyptian. *b:* 28 June 1889, village near Aswan, Upper Egypt. *d:* 12 March 1964. *Cat:* Columnist and writer; apologist of Islam. *Educ:* Self taught: studied English language, then French; followed a traditional Muslim way of thought. *Infls:* Literary criticism and Thomas Carlyle. *Appts:* Journalist for *Al-Garidah*, the newspaper founded by Lutfi

as-Sayyed, until 1907; in Alexandria (1915), then in Cairo (1923), edited magazines which echoed Sad Zaghlul's political ideas; engaged in politics in the Wafd Party; imprisoned in the 1930s for his nationalistic utterances, but in 1938 became member of the Royal Academy; Senator, 1944; appointed to the Conseil Supérieur des Artes, Lettres et Sciences Sociales, 1956, contributed to *Al-Muqtataf* until 1953.

Main publications:

(1936) *Sad Zaghlul* (a biography of the famous Egyptian statesman), Cairo: Matba-at al-Higazi.

(1940) *Abqariyyat Muhammad* [The Genius of Muhammad], Cairo: Matba-at al-Istiqamah.

(1945) *Francis Bacon*, Cairo: Dar al-Maarif.

(1946) *Ash-Shaykh ar-Ra-is Ibn Sina* [Avicenna], Cairo: Dar al-Ma-arif.

(1953) *Ibn Rushd* [Averroes], Cairo: Dar al-Maarif.

(1957) *Haqaiq al-Islam wa Abatil Khusumihi* [The Truth of Islam and the Mistakes of its Enemies], Cairo: Matba-at Misr.

(1963) *Al-Falsafah al-Our'aniyyah* [The Philosophy of the Koran], Cairo: Dar al-Hilal.

Wrote several essays about the great figures of Islam (Umar; Khalid Ibn al-Walid, Amr Ibn al-As, and so on) and the modernist thinkers (Muhammad Abduh, al-Kawakibi, etc.).

Al-Aqqad was a traditional thinker. He was a national who viewed Islam as a religion appropriate to modern life. He defended the traditional image of Islam and tried to prove Koranic assumptions by a scholarly historical method. Notwithstanding his moderation, he was charged by the Islamic radical, Sayyed Qutb, with inappropriate recourse to non-Islamic sources in order to explain Islamic thought. In Qutb's opinion he betrayed the progressive reformism of Muhammad Abduh.

Sources: G. Anawati (1982) *Tendances et courants de I'Islam arabe contemporain*, Munich: Kaiser & Grünewald; Archives of the Pontifical Inst. of Arabic Studies in Rome.

MASSIMO CAMPANINI

Ardao, Arturo

Uruguayan. *b:* 27 September 1912. *Cat:* Historian of ideas. *Infls:* Vaz Ferreira. *Appts:* Director of the Institute of Philosophy, University of the Republic, Montevideo; taught in Venezuela after fleeing his native Uruguay for political reasons.

Main publications:
(1950) *Espiritualismo y positivismo en el Uruguay*, Buenos Aires: Fondo de Cultura Económica.
(1951) *Batlle y Ordóñez y el positivismo filosófico*, Montevideo, Uruguay: Número.
(1956) *La filosofía en el Uruguay en el siglo XX*, Buenos Aires: Fondo de Cultura Económica.
(1962) *Racionalismo y liberalismo en el Uruguay*, Montevideo, Uruguay: Universidad de la República.
(1963) *Filosofía de lengua española*, Montevideo: Alfa.
(1970) *Rodó: su americanismo*, Montevideo: Uruguay, Biblioteca de Marcha.
(1971) *Etapas de la inteligencia uruguaya*, Montevideo, Uruguay: Universidad de la República.
(1978) *Estudios latinoamericanos: historia de las ideas*, Caracas, Venezuela: Monte Avila Editores.
(1983) *Espacio e inteligencia*, Caracas, Venezuela: Equinoccio.
(1986) *Andrés Bello, filósofo*, Caracas, Venezuela: Academia Nacional de la Historia.
(1987) *La inteligencia latinoamericana*, Montevideo, Uruguay: Dirección General de Extensión Universitaria, División de Publicaciones y Ediciones.

Secondary literature:
Coloquio Nacional de Filosofía (1976) *La filosofía actual en América Latina*, Mexico: Editorial Grijalbo.

Arturo Ardao is a major scholar of the history of ideas in Latin America. His early work dealt with the opposition between positivism and spiritualism in the latter part of the nineteenth century. Ardao is a leading scholar on the work of Uruguay's most prominent twentieth-century philosopher, Carlos **Vaz Ferreira**, as well as on other influential Latin American thinkers.

AMY A. OLIVER

Ardigò, Roberto

Italian. *b:* 28 January 1928, Casteldione, Cremona, Italy. *d:* 15 September 1920, Mantua. *Cat:* Positivist. *Appts:* Professor of the History of Philosophy, Padua, 1881–1909.

Main publications:
(1870) *Psicologia come scienza positiva.*
(1877) *La formazione naturale del sistema solare.*
(1885) *La morale dei positivisti.*
(1886) *Sociologia.*
(1891) *Il vero.*
(1894) *La ragione.*
(1898) *L'unita della coscienza.*

(1908) *Opere filosofiche*, second edition, Padua: Draghi.

Secondary literature:
Dal Covolo, A (1985) *Roberto Ardigò*, Rome: Citta Nuova.
Gentile, A. (1988) *La religione civile*, Naples: Edizione Scientifiche Italiane.
Mandolf, S. (1966) *I positivisti italiani*, Padua: CEDAM.
Marchesini, G. (1922) *Roberto Ardigò: l'uomo e l'umanista*, Florence: Le Monnier.

After studying classics Ardigò entered the priesthood and taught philosophy at Mantua. Following a long crisis of faith his thinking took a positivistic turn, rejecting every form of transcendence, and he left the priesthood. In the heyday of late nineteenth-century positivism Ardigò was its chief representative in Italy, his thought contrasting, however, with such positivists as **Spencer**. Spencer argued that philosophy does not have its own subject matter but is reducible to the particular sciences. Ardigò thought that philosophy was not merely the collection of these sciences. It was, first, the special disciplines concerned with the phenomena of thought (including logic and ethics). It is also 'peratology', the study of the indistinct which lies outside the subject matter of science, the distinct. Ardigò also used the notion of the indistinct to rework Spencer's evolutionism, claiming that the formation of everything, from the solar system downwards, is a journey from the indistinct to the distinct. The distinct and finite never exhausts the infinitude of the indistinct. Evolution is endless. Ardigò, like many positivists, was sceptical about free will. He wished, however, to mitigate the determinism of many positivists, and believed in a degree of unpredictable chance in sequences of events. The self and natural things are syntheses of sensations and differ only in the nature of the synthesis (a view later to be found in **Mach**). Human freedom, therefore, is an effect of the unpredictability of sequences that constitute our psychic lives. Ardigò's moral philosophy, fiercely critical of religious and rationalist ethics, has—like that of Comte and Spencer—a sociological basis. Society, through judicial norms and sanctions, causally produces the altruistic sentiment of moral obligation and an ever growing hope for justice that far exceeds its causal origins.

COLIN LYAS

Arendt, Hannah

German-American (emigrated to USA in 1941).
b: 14 October 1906, Hannover, Germany. **d:** 4
December 1975, New York. **Cat:** Social critic;
political philosopher. **Educ:** Königsberg, Mar-
burg, Freiburg and Heidelberg Universities. **Infls:**
Husserl and Jaspers. **Appts:** 1946–8, Chief Editor,
Schocken Books, New York; 1949–52, Executive
Director, Jewish Cultural Reconstruction, New
York; 1953–67, Professor, Committee on Social
Thought, University of Chicago; 1967–75, Pro-
fessor, Graduate Faculty, New School for Social
Research, New York.

Main publications:

(1951) *The Origins of Totalitarianism*, New York:
Harcourt, Brace.
(1958) *The Human Condition*, Chicago: University of
Chicago Press.
(1961) *Between Past and Future: Six Exercises in
Political Thought*, New York: Viking Press.
(1963) *Eichmann in Jerusalem: A Report on the
Banality of Evil*, New York: Viking Press.
(1963) *On Revolution*, New York: Viking Press.
(1970) *On Violence*, New York: Harcourt, Brace.
(1978) *The Life of the Mind*, 2 vols, ed. Mary
McCarthy, New York: Harcourt Brace.
(1982) *Lectures on Kant's Political Philosophy*, ed. R.
Beiner, Chicago: University of Chicago Press.

Secondary literature:

Canovan, Margaret (1992) *Hannah Arendt: A
Reinterpretation of Her Political Thought*, New
York: Cambridge University Press.
Hill, Melvyn A. (ed.) (1979) *Hannah Arendt: The
Recovery of the Public World*, New York: St
Martin's Press.
O'Sullivan, Noel (1975) 'Hannah Arendt: Hellenic
nostalgia and industrial society', in Anthony de
Crespigny and Kenneth Minogue (eds), *Contem-
porary Political Philosophers*, New York: Dodd,
Mead & Co.
Tolle, Gordon J. (1982) *Human Nature under Fire:
The Political Philosophy of Hannah Arendt*, Wa-
shington: University Press of America.
Young-Bruehl, Elisabeth (1982) *Hannah Arendt: For
Love of the World*, New Haven, Yale University
Press (bibliography included).

Hannah Arendt was a complex and wide-ranging
thinker whose work cannot easily be summarized.
She was a critic of modern mass society which,
with its tendency to atomization, alienation,
anomie and diffusion of responsibility, was fertile
ground for what she called 'totalitarianism', in
which individual human life becomes meaningless
and freedoms are eroded. To counteract this
tendency she advocated the separation of public
life from social and economic life. She looked
back to the Greek polis and, to a lesser extent, the
early United States of America as models for what
public life should be. In these societies individual
citizens sought to excel in service to the community, and authority was vested in institutions to
which they were committed. Arendt's ideas have
been extensively discussed and they have been
widely influential. Her critics have, however,
doubted their philosophical underpinning. One
commentator (O'Sullivan 1975, p. 251) questions
her identification of the broad notion of 'the
public' with the comparatively narrow notion of
'the political'. Without that identification it is not
so clear that political action is as central a part of a
proper human life as Arendt maintained.
Sources: Derwent, May (1986) *Hannah Arendt* (biography), New York: Penguin; Turner.

STUART BROWN

Arkoun, Mohammed

Algerian. **b:** 1928, Kabylia, Algeria. **Cat:** Islamic
philosopher; historian of philosophy; philoso-
pher of religion. **Ints:** Humanism; semiology. **Educ:**
Oran and Algiers University; doctoral research at
the Sorbonne University, Paris. **Infls:** Contempor-
ary French thought and Islamic humanism. **Appts:**
Professor, Sorbonne University (1961–9), Lyon
University (1970–2), Paris 8 (1973–6), Sorbonne
University (1976–92); Visiting Professor, UCLA,
Princeton, Philadelphia, Louvian-La-Neuve and
Amsterdam; Director of *Arabica*; Member of the
Institute for Advanced Study (1992–3).

Main publications:

(1979) *La Pensée arabe*, Paris: PUF.
(1982) *Contribution à l'étude de l'humanisme arabe au
IV/X siècle: Miskawayh philosophe et historien*,
Paris: Vrin.
(1982) *Lectures du Coran*, Paris: Maisonneuve &
Larose.
(1982) (with L. Gardet) *L'Islam hier, demain*, Paris:
Buchet-Chastel.
(1984) *Pour une critique de la raison islamique*, Paris:
Maisonneuve & Larose.

Arkoun's contribution to Islamic philosophy
takes two distinguishable forms. In the first place
he investigated the thought of Miskawayh, and
argued that he represents an important trend in
Islamic humanism. This tenth-century philosopher was impressed by the way in which philosophy, especially Platonic philosophy, could analyse

aspects of human nature and morality, and he appears to give more weight to the approach of the philosophers as compared with the religious authorities. Arkoun points to a tradition in Islamic philosophy which is both Islamic and humanist in that it derives the most significant principles of humanity from a consideration of the nature of that humanity while at the same time showing that such a notion is in accordance with the basic principles of Islam. The principles of reason are shown to accord with the principles of religion, and to a degree the validity of the latter is based upon the former.

In his approach to the understanding of the Qur'an Arkoun employs the semiotic and semiological ideas current in modern French culture. This enables him to see the various sects in Islam as more than divergences from orthodoxy: that is, as aspects of the development of Islam as a tradition. He argues that it is important for modern approaches to Islam to be employed, since Islam has nothing to fear from such methodologies and it is a great error to allow the religion to become fossilized as a result of a disinclination to use the theoretical techniques available through secular intellectual thought. Arkoun's work emphasizes the links between Islam and modernity, and he has thrown light on an important area of Islamic philosophy which was based upon the principles of humanism and which played an important role in the development of philosophical thought in the Islamic world.

Sources: Personal communication.

OLIVER LEAMAN

Armstrong, David Malet

Australian. *b:* 8 July 1926, Melbourne. *Cat:* Materialist philosopher. *Ints:* Epistemologist; metaphysician; philosopher of mind. *Educ:* Studied at Sydney, 1947–50, BA, 1951, and Oxford, 1952–4, BPhil 1954; PhD, Melbourne, 1959. *Infls:* Berkeley, John Anderson, H. H. Price, C. B. Martin, J. J. C. Smart, Oakeshott, Ayer, N. Fleming, A. Michotte, F. Jackson, W. S. Sellars, Kripke, Tooley, D. K. Lewis and Skyrms. *Appts:* Taught at Birkbeck, London, 1954–5; Melbourne, 1956–63; Sydney (as Challis Professor), 1964–91 (Emeritus afer 1991); Visiting Professor at various universities, including Yale, 1962, and Stanford, 1965.

Main publications:

(1960) *Berkeley's Theory of Vision*, Melbourne: Melbourne University Press.

(1961) *Perception and the Physical World*, London: Routledge & Kegan Paul.
(1962) *Bodily Sensations*, London: Routledge & Kegan Paul.
(1965) (ed. and Introduction) *Berkeley's Philosophical Writings*, New York: Collier–Macmillan.
(1968) *A Materialist Theory of the Mind*, London: Routledge & Kegan Paul; second edition with new preface and updated bibliography, 1993.
(1968) (ed. with C. B. Martin and Introduction to Berkeley section) *Locke and Berkeley: A Collection of Critical Essays*, New York: Doubleday; London: Macmillan.
(1973) *Belief, Truth and Knowledge*, Cambridge: Cambridge University Press.
(1977) 'Naturalism, materialism and first philosophy' in *Ist systematische Philosophie möglich?*, Proceedings of the Stuttgarter Hegel-Kongress, 1975; reprinted in *Philosophia* (Israel) 8, 1978, and in *The Nature of Mind* (1980).
(1978) *Universals and Scientific Realism*: vol. 1, *Nominalism and Realism*, vol. 2, *A Theory of Universals*, Cambridge: Cambridge University Press (roughly, vol. 1 is critical and vol. 2 positive).
(1980) *The Nature of Mind and Other Essays*, Brisbane: Queensland University Press; Ithaca, NY: Cornell University Press, 1981; Brighton: Harvester Press, 1981 (includes 1977 article).
(1983) *What is a Law of Nature?*, Cambridge: Cambridge University Press.
(1984) (with N. Malcolm) *Consciousness and Causality*, Oxford: Blackwell.
(1984) 'Replies', in R. J. Bogdan (ed.), *D. M. Armstrong*, Dordrecht: Reidel.
(1984) 'Self-profile', in R. J. Bogdan (ed.), *D. M. Armstrong*, Dordrecht: Reidel.
(1988) (with C. B. Martin) *Berkeley: A Collection of Critical Essays*, London and New York: Garland Publishing Inc. (partial reissue of *Locke and Berkeley*, 1968).
(1989) *A Combinatorial Theory of Possibility*, Cambridge: Cambridge University Press.
(1989) *Universals: An Opinionated Introduction*, Boulder, Co: Westview Press.
(forthcoming) *A World of States of Affairs*, Cambridge: Cambridge University Press (a summing up of his metaphysical position).

Secondary literature:

Bacon, J., Campbell, K. and Reinhardt, L. (eds) (1993) *Ontology, Causality, and Mind: Essays in Honour of D. M. Armstrong*, Cambridge: Cambridge University Press (includes replies to all papers, and bibliography).
Bogdan, R. J. (ed.) (1984) *D. M. Armstrong*, Dordrecht: Reidel (includes bibliography with

substantial summaries by himself of his main works).

Apart from a BA Honours thesis on Kant and an early interest in Berkeley (which led to his first book (1960), originally intended as a PhD thesis), and two editions of or about Berkeley (1965, 1968), Armstrong's work in philosophy has lain on the positive side. Though born in Melbourne, he is a major representative of the Australian materialist tradition, and is mainly associated with Sydney, where as a student he came under the influence of John **Anderson**.

Armstrong's philosophy can be divided into three main, though overlapping, areas: his early work on perception and sensation; a middle period on the mind, consciousness, intentionality, belief and knowledge, abandoning his early behaviourism (see Bogdan 1984, p. 23); and a later interest in universals, branching off into laws of nature and the study of possibility. A keynote underlying nearly all this work is realism of one sort or another, modified only in his latest work on universals (*Universals*, 1989, p. 120), where he shows more sympathy than previously (though still limited) for a version of nominalism based on 'tropes', i.e. properties regarded as numerically distinct for each object possessing them. However, his realism is moderate and he has no truck with Platonic universals, realist possible worlds or other abstractions that cannot satisfy his 'Eleatic principle' (*Replies*, 1984, p. 255) that only what has causes and effects is real which predicates stand for universals is therefore an empirical question. Like Anderson (see 'Self-profile', 1984, p. 43) and a very different philosopher, **Chisholm**, he makes states of affairs basic, universals (properties and relations) and particulars being abstractions from these but real because things cause by having properties; he rejects **Quine**'s doctrine that only subjects carry ontological commitment (ibid., p. 43). He treats laws of nature as relations of non-logical necessity between universals, known empirically (cf. *A Combinatorial Theory of Possibility*, 1989, p. xi). The 1977 article offers a good summary of much of his later philosophy.

Armstrong's attack on nominalism has perhaps been more controversial than those on representationalism and phenomenalism but, apart from his general materialism, particularly controversial was his early claim that perception is nothing but the acquiring of knowledge or an inclination to believe (1961, p. 105). His materialism is not eliminative, however: the mind is not abolished but is indentical with part of the body (*Consciousness and Causality*, 1984, p. 106).

Sources: PI; personal communication.

A. R. LACEY

Aron, Raymond Claude Ferdinand

French. ***b:*** 14 March 1905, Paris. ***d:*** 17 October 1983, Paris. ***Cat:*** Sociologist; political commentator. ***Ints:*** History and critique of sociological thought; philosophy of history; ideological criticism; French politics; analysis of the industrial order; international relations. ***Educ:*** L'École Normale Supérieure. ***Infls:*** Montesquieu, Alexis de Tocqueville, Marx, Max Weber, Dilthey, Simmel and Rickert. ***Appts:*** 1930–3, Lecturer, University of Cologne, then (1931), the French Institute, Berlin; 1934–9, Secretary, Centre of Social Information, École Normale Supérieure; 1940–4, Editor, *La France libre*, London; 1955–68, Professor of Political Science, Sorbonne; 1970–83, Professor of Sociology, Collège de France.

Main publications:

(1936) *La Sociologie allemande contemporaine*, Paris: PUF (English translation from the second edition (1950), *German Sociology*, trans. Mary and Thomas Bottomore, London: Heinemann, 1957).

(1938) *Introduction à la philosophie de l'histoire*, Paris: Gallimard (English translation, *Introduction to the Philosophy of History*, trans. George J. Irwin, Boston: Beacon Press, 1961).

(1955) *L'Opium des intellectuels*, Paris: Gallimard (English translation, *The Opium of the Intellectuals*, trans. Terence Kilmartin, New York: Doubleday, 1957).

(1964) *La Lutte de classes: Nouvelles leçons sur les sociétés industrielles*, Paris: Gallimard.

(1976) *Penser le guerre, Clausewitz*, 2 vols, Paris: Gallimard: vol. 1, *L'Age européen*, vol. 2, *L'Age planétaire*.

Secondary literature:

Casanova, Jean Claude, Shils, Edward and Sperber, Manes (eds) (1971) *Science et conscience de la société: Melanges en l'honneur de Raymond Aron*, 2 vols, Paris: Calmann-Levy.

Colquhoun, Robert (1986) *Raymond Aron*, 2 vols, London: Sage: vol. 1, *The Philosopher in History*, vol. 2, *The Sociologist in Society*.

Aron's work was thoroughly interdisciplinary in both method and substance, and his contributions are prolific and diverse. As a journalist, for decades Aron wrote for *Le Figaro*, and then, after June 1977, for the more progressive *Express*. He became one of France's leading political commentators.

Although affected by Marx and much inspired by Max **Weber**, Aron was the avowed heir of Montesquieu and de Tocqueville. He regarded historical and political forces, rather than social and economic structures, as ultimately shaping human collectives. Above all Aron sought to defend the value of freedom and to preserve the irreducible subjectivity of human experience and the open-endedness of history from sociological and historical determinism.

Aron's prewar concerns were with epistemological and formal problems in sociological thought and the philosophy of history. After the war his work had a different orientation, addressing the immediate concrete political, economic, social and international problems of twentieth-century life.

In his earlier years Aron was a friend of Jean-Paul **Sartre**, but the two fell out in 1947 with the advent of the Cold War. Cutting his ties with the French Left for its unquestioning support of Stalin, Aron attacked the Marxist assumptions of his former friend in *L'Opium des intellectuels* (1955). He contended that the Marxists had confused Marxist goals with Stalinist practice, that their adherence to the idea of 'historical inevitability' was destroying their critical judgement and turning them into fanatics. A liberal and constitutional pluralist, Aron criticized both right and left for reinforcing centralizing and statist tendencies in their plans and practices. Aron's work was effective in forcing a confrontation between theorizing and public policy. A pioneer in the study of international relations involved in peace and war, he also influenced the development of peace studies.

Sources: Huisman; Bullock & Woodings.

STEPHEN MOLLER

Asmus, Valentin Ferdinandovich

Russian. *b:* 18 December (O.S.) 1894, Kiev. *d:* 4 June 1975, Moscow. *Cat:* Marxist; historian of philosophy; logician. *Ints:* History of Western philosophy; aesthetics; logic. *Educ:* Kiev University. *Infls:* Plato, Kant and Marx. *Appts:* Taught Philosophy at various institutions, first in Kiev and from 1927 in Moscow; Professor at Moscow State University, from 1939; senior scientific associate of the Institute of Philosophy of the Soviet Academy of Sciences, from 1968.

Main publications:
(1924) *Dialekticheskii materializm i logika* [Dialectical Materialism and Logic], Kiev.
(1929) *Dialektika Kanta* [The Dialectics of Kant], Moscow.
(1930) *Ocherki istorii dialektiki v novoi filosofii* [An Essay in the History of Dialectics in Modern Philosophy], Moscow and Leningrad.
(1933) *Marks i burzhuaznyi istorizm* [Marx and Bourgeois Historicism], Moscow and Leningrad.
(1947) *Logika* [Logic], Moscow.
(1954) *Uchenie logiki o dokazatel'stve i oproverzhenii* [The Logical Doctrine of Proof and Refutation], Moscow.
(1956) *Dekart* [Descartes], Moscow.
(1960) *Democrit* [Democritus], Moscow.
(1963) *Problema intuitsii v filosofii i matematike* [The Problem of Intution in Philosophy and Mathematics], Moscow.
(1963) *Nemetskaia estetika XVIII veka* [Eighteenth Century German Aesthetics], Moscow.
(1968) *Voprosy teorii i istorii estetiki* [Problems of the Theory and History of Aesthetics], Moscow.
(1969–71) *Izbrannye filosofskie trudy* [Selected Philosophical Works]; 2 vols, Moscow.
(1973) *Immanuil Kant* [Immanuel Kant], Moscow.
(1975) *Platon* [Plato], Moscow.
(1976) *Antichnaia filosofiia* [Ancient Philosophy], Moscow.

Secondary literature:
Motroshilova, N. V. (1989) 'In memory of a professor', *Soviet Studies in Philosophy*, Fall: 59 -65.

One of the Soviet Union's most distinguished philosophical scholars, a friend of Boris Pasternak and other members of the pre-Stalin Russian intelligentsia, Asmus represented for later generations of Soviet philosophers an inspiring living link with the philosophical traditions and scholarly standards of the past. Although a professed Marxist and materialist, he was accused in the 1930s of 'menshevizing idealism', and he remained ideologically suspect throughout the Stalin era, often narrowly escaping dismissal from Moscow University and imprisonment.

Asmus was instrumental in the rehabilitation of formal logic in the Soviet Union after the Second World War; his 1947 book *Logic* was one of the first Soviet texts on the subject. Selections from his many writings on the theory and history of aesthetics were published in the 1968 volume listed here. His greatest influence, however, was as a historian of ancient and modern Western philosophy. His monographs on Plato, Democritus, Descartes and Kant (his personal philosophical paragon), as well as his many substantial essays in the history of philosophy, demonstrated a breadth of knowledge and a freedom from ideological distortion that were exceptional in Russia during his time.

JAMES SCANLAN

Astrada, Carlos

Argentinian. *b:* 26 February 1894, Córdoba, Argentina. *d:* 1970. *Cat:* Heideggerian existentialist. *Ints:* Heidegger; Marxism; history of modern and contemporary philosophy; ethics; epistemology; metaphysics. *Educ:* Studied Law in Córdoba, Argentina, and Philosophy with Max Scheler, Husserl and Heidegger at the Universities of Cologne and Freiburg (1926–30). *Infls:* Heidegger and Marx. *Appts:* Main professional appointments: Associate Professor of Modern and Contemporary Philosophy, Universidad Nacional de Buenos Aires, 1936–47; Professor of Ethics, Universidad Nacional de La Plata, 1937–47; 1947, Professor of Epistemology and Metaphysics, Universidad Nacional de Buenos Aires, after Francisco Romero's resignation in protest against Péron's government; replaced by Romero in 1956, when Péron's regime fell.

Main publications:

(1933) *Goethe y el panteismo spinoziano*, Santa Fé, Argentina: Instituto Social de la Universidad del Litoral.

(1933) *El juego existencial*, Buenos Aires: Babel.

(1936) *Idealismo fenomenológico y metafisica existencial*, Buenos Aires: Imprenta de la Universidad.

(1938) *La ética formal y los valores*, La Plata: Universidad Nacional de La Plata.

(1942) *El juego metafísico*, Buenos Aires: El Ateneo.

(1943) *Temporalidad*, Buenos Aires: Cultura Viva.

(1948) *Sociología de la guerra y filosofía de la paz*, Buenos Aires: Coni.

(1949) *Ser, humanismo, existencialismo*, Buenos Aires: Kairos.

(1952) *El marxismo y las escatologías*, Buenos Aires: Procyon.

(1957) *La revolución existencialista*, n.p.: Nuevo Destino.

(1960) *Nietzsche y la crisis del irracionalismo*, Buenos Aires: Dédalo.

(1960) *Humanismo y dialéctica de la libertad*, Buenos Aires: Dédalo.

(1962) *La doble faz de la dialéctica*, Buenos Aires: Devenir.

(1963) *Existencialismo y crisis de la filosofía*, Buenos Aires: Devenir.

(1964) *Humanismo y alienación*, Buenos Aires: Devenir.

(1964) *Valoración de la 'Fenomenología del espíritu*, Buenos Aires: Devenir.

(1965) *Trabajo y alienación en la 'Fenomenología' y en los 'Manuscritos'*, Buenos Aires: Siglo Veinte.

(1967) *Fenomenología y praxis*, Buenos Aires: Siglo Veinte.

(1968) *La génesis de la dialéctica*, Buenos Aires: Juárez.

(1969) *Dialéctica e historia*, Buenos Aires: Juárez.

(1970) *Heidegger, de la analítica ontológica a la dimensión dialéctica*, Buenos Aires: Juárez.

Secondary literature:

Grand Ruiz, Beatriz Hilda (1982) *El tiempo en Jean Paul Sartre. Apéndice: El tiempo en Carlos Astrada*, Buenos Aires: Ediciones Clepsidra.

Llanos, Alfredo (1962) *Carlos Astrada*, Buenos Aires: Ediciones Culturales Argentinas.

Astrada's work until the early 1950s was primarily influenced by **Heidegger**'s existentialism. It focused on the notions of game and exisential risk as decisive elements in metaphysical speculation. With the publication of *La revolución existencialista* (1952) Astrada began to adopt a Marxist orientation, giving his primarily Heideggerian conception of the human person a strong social emphasis. His position, however, did not become closer to that of **Sartre**, whose work he criticized as lacking ontological foundation. Towards the end of his life Astrada's work acquired a predominantly rhetorical character, proclaiming the decline of Western culture as a consequence of capitalism's impending collapse.

A. PABLO IANNONE

Aurobindo, Ghose (popularly known as Sri Aurobindo)

Indian. *b:* 15 August 1872, Calcutta. *d:* 5 December 1950, Pondicherry. *Cat:* Metaphysician. *Educ:* St Pauls High School and King's College, Cambridge. *Infls:* Vedanta and evolutionists such as Henri Bergson and John Dewey. *Appts:* Founder of Aurobindo Ashram at Pondicherry, India.

Main publications:

(1947) *The Life Divine*, 2 vols, Calcutta: Arya Publishing House.

(1950) *The Ideal of Human Unity*, New York: Sri Aurobindo Library.

(1970–2) *Sri Aurobindo Birth Centenary Library*, Pondicherry: Sri Aurobindo Ashram (containing *Essays on the Gita*; *The Upanishad Texts, Translations and Commentaries*; *The Secret of the Veda*).

Secondary literature:
Chaudhuri, Haridas and Spiegelberg, Frederic (eds) (1961) *The Internal Philosophy of Sri Aurobindo: A Commemorative Symposium*, London: Allen & Unwin.
Chaudhuri, J. (1954) *The Philosophy of Integralism or the Metaphysical Synthesis Inherent in the Teaching of Sri Aurobindo*, Calcutta: Sri Aurobindo Pathamandir.
Pearson, Nathaniel (1952) *Sri Aurobindo and the Soul Quest of Man*, London: George Allen & Unwin.
Price, Joan (1977) *An Introduction to Sri Aurobindo's Philosophy*, Pondicherry: Sri Aurobindo Ashram.

Aurobindo, like the other twentieth-century Indian philosophers such as Radhakrishnan and Vivekananda, was deeply impressed by the idealism of Shankarite Vedanta. According to Shankara, the ultimate Reality, *Brahman*, is beyond space and time, non-dual, qualityless and indescribable. The world as we know it, that is, as consisting of objects in space and time, is *maya* or illusion. Aurobindo accepted *Brahman* as the ultimate reality:

> [*Brahman*] cannot be summed up in any quantity or quantities, it cannot be composed of any quality or combination of qualities. It is not an aggregate of forms or a formal substratum of forms. If all forms, quantities or qualities were to disappear, this would remain. Existence without quantity, without quality, without form is not only conceivable, but it is the one thing we can conceive beyond these phenomena.
> *The Life Divine* (1947, vol. I, p. 96).

However, he disagreed with Advaita Vedanta, who thought that the phenomenal world was unreal. Aurobindo believed that the truth did not lie either in idealism or in materialism since they both gave one-sided views about the nature of reality. The answer instead lay in integralism, according to which matter and consciousness are connected inseparably. In other words, matter and spirit are two aspects of a single whole; they are both real.

According to Aurobindo, Brahman is *sat* (being), *chit* (consciousness) and *ananda* (bliss, delight)—that is to say, *Braham* is, *Brahman*

knows and *Brahman* is bliss. And all that is in space and time is real and is created by *Brahman* out of delight or *ananda*. *Brahman*, for Aurobindo, manifests itself through a process of transformation or involution as matter, and through a gradual process of evolution unfolds its many powers—life, mind and consciousness. Man is a synthesis of the universe and is comprised of physical matter, vital force, emotive qualities, elementary intellect and soul. His goal is one of realizing *Brahman* through knowledge of himself. In essence, Aurobindo's philosophy is largely influenced by the Advaita Vedanta of Shankara. He is, however, to be regarded as a modern interpreter who has tried to provide some justification for the objective existence of the phenomenal world despite accepting a non-dual *Brahman* as Reality.

INDIRA MAHALINGAM CARR

Austin, J(ohn) L(angshaw)

British. *b:* 1911, Lancaster, England. *d:* 1960, Oxford. *Cat:* Analytic philosopher. *Ints:* Epistemology; philosophy of language; philosophy of mind. *Educ:* Oxford University. *Infls:* Aristotle. *Appts:* Fellow, All Souls College, Oxford, 1933–35; Fellow, Magdalen College, Oxford, 1935–52; White's Professor of Moral Philosophy, Oxford; 1952–60; Visiting Professor, University of California at Berkeley, 1958–9.

Main publications:
(1961) *Philosophical Papers*, Oxford: Clarendon Press; second edition, 1970.
(1962) *How to Do Things with Words*, Oxford: Clarendon Press; second edition, 1975.
(1962) *Sense and Sensibilia*, Oxford: Clarendon Press.

Secondary literature:
Berlin, Isaiah *et al.* (1973) *Essays on J. L. Austin*, Oxford: Clarendon Press.
Fann, K. T. (ed.) (1969) *Symposium on J. L. Austin*, London: Routledge & Kegan Paul.
Warnock, G. J. (1991), *J. L. Austin*, London: Routledge.

After a distinguished undergraduate career as a classical scholar, Austin turned to philosophy. He was a Fellow of All Souls College from 1933 to 1935, and lectured in philosophy at Oxford from 1935 until the outbreak of war in 1939. After a notable career in intelligence, he returned to Oxford in 1945, and became Professor of Moral Philosophy in 1952. He had by then only edited a volume of H. W. B. **Joseph**'s *Lectures on the Philosophy of Leibniz*, translated **Frege**'s *Grundlagen der Arithmetik* and published three papers. His influence rested very largely on his lecturing and seminars in Oxford. A considerable proportion of his work was reconstructed and published posthumously.

Austin thought that much philosophical work was characterized by haste and carelessness—about language, and about well-known facts of our experience—and this concern is clear in, for instance, 'The meaning of a word' (a lecture delivered in 1940 and published in *Philosophical Papers*). It can be seen most famously, however, in the series of lectures that he gave in various forms from 1947 to 1958, which were subsequently published as *Sense and Sensibilia* (1962). These lectures consist very largely of a minutely detailed examination of A. J. **Ayer**'s exposition of the Argument from Illusion, an argument which had widely been taken to show that in perception we are only ever acquainted with sense data and never with material objects. Austin tried to show that the argument was vitiated from beginning to end by the failure to give any clear sense to the central terms.

Some have thought that Austin's best philosophical work is in his papers on the philosophy of action: 'A plea for excuses' (*Proceedings of the Aristotelian Society* 1956–7), 'Ifs and cans' (1956), 'Pretending' (1956–7) and 'Three ways of spilling ink' (1958). He thought that there was no way to understand philosophical puzzles about the nature of action, freedom and responsibility other than to examine in detail particular aspects of our talk about action, and the articles are characterized by an extraordinary sensitivity to the distinctions that we ordinarily make when we talk about action. Austin thought that 'our common stock of words embodies all the distinctions worth drawing, and the connexions worth marking, in the lifetimes of many generations: these surely are likely to be more numerous, more sound, since they have stood up to the long test of survival of the fittest, and more subtle, at least in all ordinary and reasonably practical matters, than any that you or I are likely to think up' ('A plea for excuses').

Probably Austin's most famous and influential contribution was the notion of 'speech acts'. The idea first makes its appearance (incipiently and unnamed) in 'Other minds' (1946), and was given fuller treatment in 'Performative utterances' and *How to Do Things with Words*. Austin seems initially to have been struck by such forms of speech as 'I promise to...', 'I name this ship ...', 'I

hereby bequeath ...'—forms of speech which *look* initially like ordinary indicative statements, but which in fact are not. When I say 'I promise to ...', I do not, according to Austin, thereby state *that* I promise; I *do*, by using that form of words, actually promise: my utterance is itself the *act* of promising. It seems initially tempting to contrast such speech forms, which Austin called 'performatives', with statements: doings as opposed to sayings. But Austin saw that this would be a mistake: after all, stating something is itself doing something, and Austin found no significant way to distinguish that sort of doing from other sorts of verbal doings.

The way forward, he thought, was to recognize that all speech consists of what he called 'speech acts'; and speech acts have different levels. When someone utters a sentence in a language, Austin called that a 'locutionary act'. But in performing a locutionary act one may thereby perform a further act: *in* saying, for instance, 'there is a bull in that field', I may, depending on the circumstances, either be merely *stating* that there is a bull or be *warning* you. Such further acts Austin called 'illocutionary acts'. I may also accomplish some effect by what I say: if I warn you that there is a bull in the field, and you are deterred from going into the field, *by* my warning I deter you. This Austin referred to as the 'perlocutionary effect' of my act.

Austin went on to distinguish five different types of illocutionary act, and he seems to have thought that attention to this variety would have significant philosophical implications. It would, for instance, wean us away from our obsession with the true–false distinction and the fact–value distinction.

There has been much discussion as to what Austin thought was the relevance to philosophy of the study of language. In part, it was no doubt that he thought that philosophers should use more care in the way that they treated an essential tool, and that this would lead to progress with old problems. In part, it was no doubt simply the sense that the phenomena of language raised problems which were interesting in themselves. Austin also toyed with the idea that, just as philosophy had given birth to such disciplines as psychology, it might one day give birth to a 'science of language', and this would no doubt be the home of much that he was interested in.

During the 1970s Austin's influence, which had been enormous in Britain during his lifetime and for some years thereafter, largely waned. However, detailed work was done on the notion of speech acts (by, for instance, J. R. **Searle**) and that notion itself has passed into common philosophical parlance. According to Geoffrey Warnock, Austin's contributions to philosophy 'were not predictable. They opened questions that had seemed closed, and brought in new questions. They followed no tramlines, deepened no dialectical ruts. They brought balloons down to earth—sometimes very visibly much the worse for wear when they got there' (1991, p. 153). Austin was a superb, and hilariously amusing, writer. *Sense and Sensibilia* is one of the funniest books of serious philosophy ever written.

Sources: Flew; Passmore 1957; Isaiah Berlin *et al.* (1973) *Essays on J. L. Austin*, Oxford: Clarendon Press; DNB; *The Times*, 10 Feb 1960, p. 13.

ANTHONY ELLIS

Axelos, Kostas

Greek. *b:* 26 June 1924, Athens. *Cat:* Historian of philosophy. *Ints:* Politics; psychoanalysis. *Educ:* University of Athens and the Sorbonne, Paris. *Infls:* Heraclitus, Hegel, Marx, Nietzsche and Heidegger. *Appts:* Centre National des Recherches Scientifiques (1950–7); École Pratique de Hautes Études (1957–9); taught at the Sorbonne (1962–73); member of the editorial committee and then editor of *Arguments* (1956–62); Editor of the series 'Arguments' of Éditions de Minuit.

Main publications:

I. Le déploiement de l'errance:
   (1961) *Marx penseur de la technique*, Paris: Minuit.
   (1962) *Héraclite et la philosophie*, Paris: Minuit.
   (1964) *Vers la pensée planétaire*, Paris: Minuit.
II. Le déploiement du jeu:
   (1969) *Le jeu du monde*, Paris: Minuit.
   (1972) *Pour une éthique problématique*, Paris: Minuit.
   (1977) *Contribution à la logique*, Paris: Minuit.
III. Le déploiement d'une enquête:
   (1969) *Arguments d'une recherche*, Paris: Minuit.
   (1974) *Horizons du monde*, Paris: Minuit.
   (1979) *Problèmes de l'enjeu*, Paris: Minuit.
(1984) *Systématique ouverte*, Paris: Minuit.
Axelos has published in French, Greek and German; his works have been translated into sixteen languages.

Axelos advocates a 'postphilosophical' approach with poetic and aphoristic tendencies. Its basic concepts are those of 'wandering', 'planetary thought' and 'game of the world'. Planetary thought is engaged not in a quest for truth but a kind of wandering in the world, which is viewed as neither intelligible nor unintelligible but as a constant unfolding of games. The concept of game, which resists rational systematization, characterizes both thought and the world.

STAVROULA TSINOREMA

Ayer, Alfred Jules

British. *b:* 29 October 1910, London. *d:* 27 June 1989, London. *Cat:* Logical positivist. *Ints:* Epistemology; philosophical logic; ethics. *Educ:* Christ Church, Oxford. *Infls:* Russell, Carnap and Ryle. *Appts:* Lecturer, Christ Church, Oxford 1933–40; Professor, University College, London 1946–59; Professor of Logic, Oxford 1959–78.

Main publications:

(1936) *Language, Truth and Logic*, London: Gollancz.
(1940) *Foundations of Empirical Knowledge*, London: Macmillan.
(1947) *Thinking and Meaning*, London: H. K. Lewis.
(1954) *Philosophical Essays*, London: Macmillan.
(1954) *The Problem of Knowledge*, London: Macmillan.
(1963) *The Concept of a Person and Other Essays*, London: Macmillan.
(1968) *The Origins of Pragmatism*, London: Macmillan.
(1969) *Metaphysics and Common Sense*, London: Macmillan.
(1971) *Russell and Moore: the Analytical Heritage*, London: Macmillan.
(1972) *Probability and Evidence*, London: Macmillan.
(1972) *Russell*, London: Fontana.
(1973) *The Central Questions of Philosophy*, London: Weidenfeld.
(1980) *Hume*, Oxford: Oxford University Press.
(1980) *Philosophy in the Twentieth Century*, London: Weidenfeld.
(1981) *Philosophy and Morality and Other Essays*, Oxford: Clarendon Press.

Secondary literature:

Foster, John (1985) *A. J. Ayer*, London: Routledge.
Hahn, L. E. (ed.) (1972) *The Philosophy of A. J. Ayer*, La Salle, Ill.: Open Court.
Joad, C. E. M. (1950) *Critique of Logical Positivism*, London: Gollancz.
Macdonald, G. F. (ed.) (1979) *Perception and Identity*, London: Macmillan.
Phillips Griffiths, A. (ed.) (1991) *A. J. Ayer: Memoral Essays*, Cambridge: Cambridge University Press.

Ayer impressed himself emphatically on the philosophical consciousness of his age with the publication of *Language, Truth and Logic* in 1936.

For the rest of his long career he was largely engaged in developing the ideas it contained, often by attenuating them. Its striking effect was due to a number of factors: the provocative nature and expression of its contents, its notable literary merits (clarity, force, elegance, firmness of outline and solidity of construction), perhaps, even, its refreshing brevity. The ideas it put forward were not without British exponents—**Russell**, **Moore** and the marginally British **Wittgenstein**—and, before them, W. K. Clifford and Karl Pearson. But they had been passed through the Vienna Circle, which had endowed them with a particularly uncompromising character.

The first, and crucial, thesis was that a sentence is significant only if it is verifiable by experience. From this it follows that metaphysics, to the extent that it claims to supply information about what lies beyond or behind experience, is impossible. Metaphysical sentences are without meaning and so neither true nor false. From this elimination of metaphysics it follows, in turn, that the only proper business of philosophy is analysis, the definition, in some sense, of intellectually essential words and types of sentence. The definitions in question will not be explicit definitions of the sort to be found in a dictionary. They will be definitions in use, or 'contextual' definitions, giving rules for translating sentences in which a problematic term occurs into sentences in which only less problematic, epistemologically more elementary, terms are to be found.

There is, however, one kind of non-empirical, a priori, sentence which has an acceptable method of verification. This is the kind of sentence of which logic, mathematics and, it turns out, philosophy proper are composed. These sentences are analytic: true (if true or, if false, false) in virtue of the meaning of the terms they contain. In elementary cases they cannot be understood unless their truth (or falsity), is acknowledged. Others, whose truth is not intuitively obvious, can be derived from them by proofs which rely on rules which themselves correspond to evidently analytic truths. (This account of the matter somewhat idealizes Ayer's too headlong exposition.)

The most disconcerting consequence of the verification principle was the insignificance and emptiness, not of metaphysics, but of moral utterances (indeed, of judgements of value of all kinds) and of the doctrines of religion. Religious creeds are transcendentally metaphysical. The basic terms of morality and evaluation general-ly—*good, right, ought*—are neither natural, that is to say empirical (here Ayer invokes Moore's argument that ethical naturalism is fallacious,

improving its formulation in the process) nor can there be non-empirical properties for them to apply to. The function of value-judgements is to express the emotions, favourable or unfavourable, of the speaker and to arouse, in a way that is neither explained nor evidently explainable, similar emotions in the hearer.

Attempts at the constructive task of analysis are made on material objects, the past, the self and the minds of others. What is empirically given in perception is sense-data, momentary and private to the perceiver (an ancient empiricist dogma Ayer could never bring himself seriously to question), so, Ayer concluded, material objects must be logical constructions out of actual and possible sense-data, Mill's phenomenalism stated in more linguistic terms. The self, equally, is not an underlying substratum of experience, but the series, in each case, of the experiences each of which contains as an element an experience of a particular, identifiable human body. Since experiences can enter into the construction of both bodies and minds they are neither mental nor physical, but neutral, in the style of neutral monism, as in Russell. Past events are startlingly analysed in terms of the future experiences which will verify their occurrence. Other people's minds are analysed in terms of their empirical manifestations in bodily behaviour.

Ayer's next book, *Foundations of Empirical Knowledge* (1940), develops in quite persuasive detail the phenomenalist account of material objects briefly sketched in its predecessor. A wholly original idea—that theories of perception are 'alternative languages', proposals, to be justified by their convenience, for discussing the facts of perception—was soon abandoned without traces. There is further consideration of the problem of other minds, reinstating the argument from analogy by the supposition that it is only a contingent fact that another's experience is his and not mine. Ayer also gives up his earlier thesis that no empirical proposition can be known for certain to be true. He dilutes his phenomenalism by the admission that statements about material objects cannot strictly be translated into statements about sense-data; the two can be correlated only in an indefinite and schematic way.

Further concessions appear in the substantial introduction to the second edition of *Language, Truth and Logic*, ten years after its first publication. The chief of these concern the verification principle. It had originally been stated in a 'weak' form, as requiring, not conclusive verification, but only that observation be relevant to the determination of a statement's truth or falsehood. That, he saw, is weak in another way. The notion of relevance is too indefinite. Ayer proposed various, more precise versions of the principle, but admitted, in the face of criticism, that the aim of exact elucidation had eluded him. His earlier, weird, reductive accounts of statements about future events and the minds of others were rejected. But reductive enthusiasm is evident in his London inaugural lecture of the same year, *Thinking and Meaning*. Here the self that thinks, the process of supposed mental acts in which it does so and the substantive meanings on to which it is alleged to be directed are all analysed into the expression of thought in significant sentences.

In *Philosophical Essays* (1954) topics in philosophical logic receive serious attention. Discussing individuals, he defends the implication of Russell's theory of descriptions that a thing is no more than the sum of its qualities, something he was to reaffirm more forcefully later. Negation is ingeniously investigated. The rest of the collection covers familiar ground in epistemology and ethics, going fully for the first time into the problem of free will, opposing it, not to causation, but to constraint.

In *The Problem of Knowledge* (1954) three major issues with which he had been occupied throughout his career—perception, knowledge of the past and knowledge of other minds—are shown to have a common structure. In each case the only evidence that seems to be available—sense-impressions, current recollections, observed behaviour—falls short of the conclusions drawn about material things, past events and the minds of others. The possible reactions are appraised: scepticism, an a priori principle to bridge the gap, its closure by reducing the inferred items to the evidence for them, non-empirical direct access to the problematic items. Ayer offers a fifth option—roughly that of explaining the gap in detail and then doing nothing about it. The account of memory is excellent, dispelling an inheritance of confusion from Russell. In the opening chapter knowledge is distinguished from true belief by the 'right to be sure', an evaluative notion whose credentials to objectivity are not discussed.

Ayer's later writings do not contain many new ideas. There are two forceful and lucid historical studies: on **Peirce** and **James** and on Russell and Moore. Three more essay collections contain good things but no great surprises. There are small books on Hume, Russell and Wittgenstein and a history of twentieth-century philosophy written very definitely from his point of view. The best and most substantial of his later books is *The Central Questions of Philosophy* (1973) in which a very broad range of topics is treated with admirable liveliness and concision, but in which no new ideas are advanced.

Nearly all Ayer's doctrines were derived very recognizably from others, except for those he soon abandoned. The fact was not recognized at first because in 1936 they were exotic and unfamiliar. Most of his early thinking was fairly direct transcription of **Carnap**, modified, where particularly paradoxical, by infusions of **Schlick**. He was, nevertheless, an exemplary philosophical writer: presenting definite theses for discussion, backing them up with explicit and often ingenious argument and expressing his thoughts in superbly lucid, slightly chilly, prose. He deserved his fame. Ayer became immediately well-known on the publication of his first book and strongly influenced his young contemporaries, perhaps giving them the courage of their own developing convictions. After 1946, at University College, London, both staff and students philosophy of the department revealed the strong impress of his personality. But his self-regard did not take the form of requiring submissive disciples; philosophy to him was more a competitive game than a religious rite focussed on himself. His pupils have his intellectual style, but not usually his opinions. His department, in the early postwar years, was the main effective opposition to the uneasy coalition between Cambridge Wittgensteinianism and the Oxford philosophy of **Ryle** and **Austin**. He came back to Oxford just when the latter, on Austin's death, was disintegrating philosophically. In these years he was a dedicated and effective teacher and animator of philosophical discussion. In the view of the interested public he was gradually transformed from being the prophet of moral nihilism into the paradigm of a philosopher.

Sources: Passmore 1957; Edwards; Hill.

ANTHONY QUINTON

Al-Azm, Sadiq Jalal

Syrian. *b:* 1934, Damascus, Syria. *Cat:* Marxist. *Ints:* Religious and political philosophy. *Educ:* Studied at the American University in Beirut; MA and PhD, Yale University, 1959 and 1961. *Appts:* Taught at the University of Damascus; then Beirut (American University) and Amman.

Main publications:

(1968) *An-Naqd adh-Dhati bad al-Hazimah* [Self-criticism after the Defeat], Beirut.

(1969) *Naqd al-Fikr ad-Dini* [Criticism of Religious Thought], Beirut: Dar at-Talia.

(1973) *Dirasah Naqadiyyah li-Fikr al-Muqawamah al-Filastiniyyah* [A Critical Study of the Thought of the Palestinian Resistance], Beirut.

Secondary literature:

Ajami F. (1981) *The Arab Predicament*, Cambridge: Cambridge University Press.
Khoury, P. (1981) *Tradition et modernité*, Paris.
Lelong (1972) in *Comprendre*.

Al-Azm's thought developed as a reaction to the Six Days War. He claimed that Arab regimes (Nasserism in particular) did not choose a clear path to revolution but wavered between socialism and state capitalism. His arguments led to a critique of all past Islamic heritage, which can be considered responsible for the backwardness of the Arabs. In his view, a mixture of secularism, Baathism and Marxism, Arab progress requires the foundation of a secular and modern state. The main task is the moulding of a scientific and truly advanced frame of mind. On the one hand Arabs have always been too quietist to be really revolutionary; on the other machinery and weapons are not enough to constitute modernism. It is necessary to develop a receptivity permeated by a form of Orientalism in reverse. It is seriously dangerous to confuse the Koranic meaning of science (*ilm*) with contemporary science. A revolution in thought must be preparatory to political resurgence and uprising.

Sources: Abdel Malek (1970) *La Pensée politique arabe contemporaine.*

MASSIMO CAMPANINI

B

Bachelard, Gaston

French. **b:** June 1884, Bar-sur-Aube, France. **d:** October 1962, Paris. **Cat:** Scientist; critic. **Ints:** Philosophy of science and of criticism. **Educ:** Studied for a Mathematics degree, 1912; degree in Philosophy, 1920; agrégation, 1922. **Infls:** Nietzsche, Einstein and Jung. **Appts:** Began adult life as a clerk; served with gallantry during the First World War; Professor of Philosophy, Dijon; Professor of the History and Philosophy of Science, the Sorbonne, retiring 1954; Légion d'Honneur, 1951.

Main publications:

On the philosophy of science:
(1928) *Essai sur la connaissance approchée.*
(1934) *Le Nouvel Esprit scientifique.*
(1940) *La Philosophie du non.*
(1949) *Le Rationalisme appliqué*, Paris: PUF.
(1953) *Le Matérialisme rationnel*, Paris: PUF.
Theory of criticism:
(1938) *La Psychanalyse du feu.*
(1940) *Lautréamont.*
(1942) *L'Eau et les rêves.*
(1943) *L'Air et les songes.*
(1948) *La Terre et les Rêveries de la volonté*, Paris: Corti.
(1948) *La Terre et les Rêveries du repos*, Paris: Corti.
(1957) *La Poétique de l'espace*, Paris: PUF.
(1961) *La Flamme d'une chandelle*, Paris: PUF.

Secondary literature:

Ginestier, P. (1968) *Pour connaître la pensée de Bachelard*, Paris: Bordas.
Lafrance, G. (ed.) (1987) *Gaston Bachelard*, Ottawa: University of Ottawa Press.
Quillet, P. (1964) *Bachelard*, Paris: Seghers.

The features of the world which most concerned Bachelard were change and discontinuity, especially in the working of the mind. Trained as a scientist and deeply impressed by relativity, he began his intellectual career with a sustained attack on the positivistic idea of scientific progress as a neat process of the accretion of truths. Discoveries, he argued, are more accurately regarded as discontinuities. Later in life, turning his attention to artistic creativity, he argued forcibly against the deterministic criticism of the school of Sainte-Beuve, in Bachelard's view false to the real workings of the imagination. Scientific discoveries and works of art are important discontinuities in the world.

The growth of scientific knowledge, Bachelard argues, is not a neat, sequential piling up of new truths, as the positivists have presented it. Discoveries are made not by those who accept current science but by those who say no to it, those who correct errors (cf. 1940), and discoveries frequently involve revisions of concepts at all levels, down to the most fundamental. The assumption, for example, that the notion of reason as enshrined in traditional rationalism is fixed for all time is untenable: 'Reason must obey science ... which is evolving' (1940, p. 144; there is much in Bachelard which is Kuhnian *avant la lettre*). The outmoded assumptions of such rationalism Bachelard replaces by his preferred method, surrationalism: mutable, polymorphic and in principle revisable at all levels of conceptual generality. This method furthers rather than stifles the mental process at the heart of discovery, the sudden intuition which goes beyond currently received belief sets. Everything which presents itself as a final discovery or immutable principle is to be regarded with suspicion: stasis was not a property Bachelard saw around him either in the world or in our knowledge of it; what we call being at rest is merely 'a happy vibration' (*La Dialectique de la durée*, 1936, p. 6).

Partly for emotional reasons and partly as a result of his interest in the psychology of creativity, Bachelard was not content to remain solely a philosopher of science. From 1938 onwards he published a series of works which are centrally concerned with the processes of the artistic imagination, and his views have important consequences for the nature of criticism. The imagination is as valuable and as basic a mental faculty as reason. Its product is the image, irreducible to concepts, imprecise and suggestive. The process of the imagination cannot be predicted, and can be studied only a posteriori. The imagination works best in the state Bachelard calls reverie, by which he means neither a dream nor a dreamy condition but a contemplative state in which the surface ego is in abeyance, time consciousness is modified and the mind follows its own impulsions. Since the imagination is in principle unpredictable, criticism of the kind practised by Sainte-Beuve, further vitiated by its reliance on deterministic principles rejected by science, is a waste of effort. Nothing in the humdrum life of the artist allows us to predict the occurrence and nature of creative acts. It is more appropriate, in Bachelard's view, to classify artistic imaginations into types. His way of doing this was to associate them with one of the elements: hence the reference, in the titles of many of his literary works, to fire, earth, air and water.

ROBERT WILKINSON

Bachelard, Suzanne

Swiss. *b:* 1919, Switzerland. *Cat:* Phenomenologist. *Ints:* Husserlian phenomenology; mathematical physics. *Educ:* Sorbonne, University of Paris: Agrégée de Philosophie; Docteur des lettres: Licenciée des sciences. *Appts:* Professor of Philosophy, Sorbonne, University of Paris.

Main publications:

(1958) *La Conscience de rationalité: Étude phénoménologique sur la physique mathématique*, Paris: PUF.
(1968) *A Study of Husserl's Formal and Transcendental Logic*, trans. Lester E. Embree, Evanston, Ill.: Northwestern University Press.
(1971) *Hommage à Jean Hypolite*, Paris: PUF.
(1988) (ed.) *Fragment d'un poétique de fer*, Paris: PUF.

Suzanne Bachelard's main preoccupation has been with the clarification of the phenomenological dimensions of all branches of knowledge. A dominant theme in her work is the claim that epistemology has two orientations: the subjective and the objective. Her translation of and commentary on **Husserl**'s *Formal and Transcendental Logic* (1968) are exemplars of scholarship in which she examines Husserl's theory of science and clarifies the nature of his anti-psychologism. She emphasizes that although anti-psychologism is an important strand in Husserl's thought, his phenomenology should never be reduced simply to that strand. Rather, her aim is 'to exclude beforehand the hypothesis of a psychologistic interpretation, the danger of which seems to us to be ever renascent' (1968, Preface, p. xxxi). She maintains that when Husserl returned, in 1929, to

the study of logic, his earlier work enabled him not only to find a radical grounding for logic but also, and by means of this radical grounding, to present new aspects of the phenomenological method in an impressively systematic manner.

Bachelard holds that the human *cogito* is never exhausted by descriptions of its *cogita*; that any actual intention has a scope or horizon of potentialities. The transcendental analysis of consciousness, she writes, 'can be a concrete investigation of this entire totality of actualities and potentialities without losing, as a result, its specifically transcendental character' (ibid.).
Sources: Huisman; Kersey.

DIANÉ COLLINSON

Bagu, Sergio

Argentinian. *b:* 1911. *Cat:* Philosopher of the social sciences; Marxist. *Ints:* Political philosophy. *Appts:* 1944–5, University of Illinois; 1944–6, Middlebury College, but taught primarily at the University of Buenos Aires.

Main publications:

(1949) *Economía de la sociedad colonial: Ensayo de historia comparada de America Latina*, Buenos Aires: El Ateneo.
(1952) *Estructura social de la colonia*, Buenos Aires: El Ateneo.
(1959) *Acusación y defensa del intelectual*, Buenos Aires: Editorial Perrot.
(1961) *La sociedad de mases en su historia*, Cordoba: Ciudad Universitaria.
(1967) *El desarrollo cultural en la liberación de America Latina*, Montevideo: Centro de Estudiantes en Derecho.
(1972) *Marx–Engels: diez conceptos fundamentales*, Buenos Aires: Ediciones Nueva Vision.
(1977) *Tiempo, realidad social y conocimiento*, fourth edition, Mexico: Siglo Veintiuno Editores.
(1985) *Evolución historica de la estratificacion social en la Argentina*, Buenos Aires: EUDEBA.
(1989) *La idea de Dios en la sociedad de las hombres*, Mexico: Siglo Veintiuno Editores.

Bagu's primary interests have always centred on the economic structures imposed by the Spanish and Portuguese colonial powers in Latin America. These studies have mainly been done with a firm social science basis, comparing the economies of, for example, the indigenous populations of countries such as Colombia, with the way in which such economies came to be organized and governed after the imposition of colonial power. This said, the novelty of these primarily empirical studies is centred on the analysis of parallels between such colonialisms and those of the Dutch and Anglo-Saxon worlds. Thus Bagu's assertion that the most fruitful way of analysing the history of the Latin American continent is from the 'angle of comparative history'. At this point his studies become light treatises which touch on the philosophy of history and of politics, by informing the reader that a historical revision of the economies of such societies is necessary not in order to analyse how they prolong the 'agonizing feudal cycle', rather in order to examine how such societies gradually integrated themselves into the nascent capitalist economic cycle, an analysis in many ways distinct from the traditional empirical viewings of such societies which give primacy to their particular economic-cultural differences and resist their integration into a wider economic order. To this end, for example, one of the major parts of his main work, *Economía de la sociedad colonial* (1949) examines the structure and nature of social classes during the colonial period. His work has had little echo in either the Iberian or Latin American academies, although the above-mentioned work was reissued to coincide with the recent 'celebrations' regarding the anniversary of the Iberian colonialization of Latin America.

Sources: BDM.

DAVID SPOONER

Baier, Annette C.
New Zealander. *b:* 11 October 1929, Queenstown, New Zealand. *Cat:* Philosopher of mind; philosophy of ethics; philosophy of language. *Educ:* Otago University, 1947–52; University of Oxford, 1952–4. *Infls:* Hume and Wittgenstein. *Appts:* Lecturer, University of Auckland, 1956–8; Lecturer, University of Sydney, 1958–9; part-time Lecturer, Senior Lecturer, then Associate Professor, Carnegie Mellon University, 1963–9; Associate, full Professor, then Distinguished Service Professor, University of Pittsburgh, since 1973.

Main publications:
(1985) *Postures of the Mind: Essays on Mind and Morals*, London: Methuen.
(1991) *A Progress of Sentiments: Reflections on Hume's Treatise*, Cambridge, Mass. and London: Harvard University Press.
(1994) *Moral Prejudices: Essays on Ethics*, Cambridge, Mass. and London: Harvard University Press.

Baier's thought combines a (later) Wittgensteinian perspective in the philosophy of mind with Hume's emphasis on the role of sentiment and our relations to others in shaping human nature and action.

Baier rejects both representational and reductive theories of mind on the grounds that mental phenomena—thought, intentionality, memory, emotions, reason—can only be properly understood as constituents of a social being. Her views on human action reflect her emphasis on the social dimension of the mind. She holds that intentional acts are abilities; they depend for their formation upon the norms and standards of competence within a language community. Reason, too, presupposes a community of connected persons and should be understood not as abstract theorizing, but rather as deliberation aided by particular skills and methods learned through human interaction.

The nature of our mental life is further explored in her writings on Hume's philosophy. She develops his anti-rationalist stance and attacks the theoretical generalizations that lie at the foundation of moral theories such as Kant's. Baier both defends and develops Hume's account of moral deliberation, claiming that caring, conscience, trust, cooperation and a practical understanding grounded in social custom and tradition motivate moral conduct. She extends this in her view that philosophers should resist the urge of moral theorizing that seeks to systematize human action. Moral philosophy, properly done, is not a matter of finding universal rules.

Baier has also made stimulating contributions to Hume scholarship. In *A Progress of Sentiments* (1991), she argues that Hume's philosophical ideas and the relationship between them in Books I, II and III of *A Treatise of Human Nature* can only be properly understood by reading the text as an evolving process of reflexive thought. This approach to the text also reveals the unity of his ideas in it.

Sources: Personal communication.

EMILY BRADY

Baier, Kurt E(rich) M(aria)
Australian (US resident). *b:* 26 January 1917, Vienna, Austria. *Cat:* Ethicist; philosopher of law. *Ints:* Ethical theory; political and social philosophy; business and medical ethics. *Educ:* Law, Vienna, 1935–8; BA, Philosophy, Melbourne (1st Hons, top of class) 1945, and MA (1st Hons, 1947); graduate studies at Oxford, 1949–52 (DPhil 1952). *Infls:* Hobbes, and more recently Stephen Toulmin and Gilbert Ryle. *Appts:* Assistant Lecturer, 1945–7, Lecturer, 1947–9, 1953–5;

Senior Lecturer, 1955–6, Melbourne; Canberra University College (later Australian National University), Foundation Professor, 1957–62; Chairman, Department of Philosophy, 1962–7, Professor of Philosophy, 1967–81, Distinguished Service Professor of Philosophy, 1981–, Pittsburgh; Visiting Professor, Cornell, 1952, and Illinois, 1960; Matchette Lecturer, Brooklyn, 1964; Teaching Member, First Summer Institute (Ethics and Philosophical Psychology) organized by Council for Philosophical Studies; Visiting Professor, Calgary, 1970; Sir Arthur Evans Visiting Professor, Otago, 1971; Distinguished Visiting Professor, Delaware, Florida Atlantic, Lycoming College, W. Florida; Everett Hall Memorial Lecturer, Iowa, 1971; Lecturer, The Philosophical Perspectives Series, Notre Dame, 1978; Visiting Professor, Florida, 1983.

Main publications:

(1957) *The Meaning of Life*, Canberra: Canberra University College.

(1958) *The Moral Point of View: A Rational Basis of Ethics*, Ithaca: Cornell University Press.

(1969) (ed. with N. Rescher) *Values and the Future*, New York: The Free Press.

Secondary literature:

Brown, Curtis (1986) 'Overriding reasons and reasons to be moral', *Southern Journal of Philosophy* 24: 173–87.

Castaneda, H. N. (1962) 'Baier's justification of the rules of reason', *Philosophy and Phenomenological Research* 22: 366–72.

Flynn, J. (1976) 'The realm of the moral', *American Philosophical Quarterly* 13: 273–86.

Gauthier, David (1987) 'Reason to be moral?' *Synthèse* 72: 5–27.

Jack, H. (1969) 'The consistency of ethical egoism', *Dialogue* 8: 475–80.

Johnson, C. D. (1975) 'Moral and legal obligation', *Journal of Philosophy* 72: 315–33.

Kalin, J. (1971) 'Baier's refutation of ethical egoism', *Philosophical Studies* 22: 74–8.

Lahey, J. L. (1971) 'Ethical egoism: can it be refuted?', *Dialogue* (PST) 13: 45–50.

McGrath, P. (1967) *The Nature of Moral Judgement*, London: Sheed & Ward.

Nielsen, Kai (1985) 'Must the immoralist act contrary to reason?', in D. Copp (ed.), *Morality, Reason and Truth*, Totowa: Rowman & Allanheld.

——(1986) 'Some moral mythologies', *Philosophia* (Isr.) 16: 119–35.

Sen, Amartya K. (1977) 'Rationality and morality: a reply to Kurt Baier', *Erkenntnis* 11: 225–32.

Wadia, P. S. (1964) 'Why should I be moral?', *Australasian Journal of Philosophy* 42: 216–26.

Baier argues for a form of objectivity in ethics and for the view that ethical questions have a method of empirical verification and validation. Rejecting the views of Hobbes, Kant and Hume, he forges a socially grounded link between rationality and morality. The partial basis for this is his view that although moral judgments are normative, they are also natural statements of fact and are thus either true or false.

For Baier traditional ethical theories fail to answer the problem of moral knowledge, and particularly against intuitionism he urges that values are neither simple qualities nor intuited. Most notably, Baier holds to the untenability of egoism as moral theory. We move beyond self-interest to 'the moral point of view' partly through recognition that egoism leads to a Hobbesian state of nature in which life is nasty, brutish and short. Baier asserts the rationality of a system of rules for interaction, and it is the specifically ethical requirement of 'interpersonal compatibility' which provides the 'weightiest' reason in any course of action. A legal system is the closest analogue to a moral system for Baier, who outlines the conditions of a robust theory of personal and social obligations and argues that utilitarianism fails adequately to account for obligation and fairness. His view of punishment is that it is by nature retributive. Baier's neo-Hobbesian contractarianism has influenced recent ethicists such as David **Gauthier**.

Related metaethical interests see Baier address questions of logic and ordinary linguistic usage in moral discourse, and questions of the nature and status of pain. He explores issues of individual control and agency, and the broader metaphysical concerns of the meaning of life. Baier has written extensively on such practical ethical issues as moral education, business ethics and culture, technology and value, and he has translated Gilbert **Ryle**'s *The Concept of Mind* into German.
Sources: DAS, 9, 1969; PI.

DAVID SCOTT

Baillie, (Sir) J(ames) B(lack)

Scottish. *b:* 24 October 1872, Haddington, East Lothian, Scotland. *d:* 9 June 1940, Weybridge. *Cat:* Idealist, later realist. *Ints:* Metaphysics: moral philosophy. *Educ:* Edinburgh University and Trinity College, Cambridge. Also studied at Halle, Strasburg and Paris. *Infls:* Personal influences include Fraser, Pringle-Pattison and S. S. Laurie;

Literary influences are Hegel, Balfour, Bradley and Bosanquet. **Appts:** 1902–24, Regius Professor of Moral Philosophy, University of Aberdeen; 1924–38, Vice Chancellor, University of Leeds.

Main publications:

(1901) *The Origin and Significance of Hegel's Logic*, London: Macmillan.
(1906) *An Outline of the Idealistic Construction of Experience*, London: Macmillan.
(1921) *Studies in Human Nature*, London: G. Bell.

Secondary literature:

Creighton, J. E. (1929) Review of *Studies in Human Nature*, in *Philosophical Review* 30: 624–9.
Sciacca, M. F. (1964) *Philosophical Trends in the Contemporary World*, trans. A. Salerno, Notre Dame, Indiana: University of Notre Dame Press, pp. 327–9.

A reviewer of Baillie's second book described him as 'in many respects the most orthodox of present-day Hegelians' (*Mind* 16 (1907): 549). That book was indeed highly derivative from Hegel's *Phenomenology of Mind*, and Baillie's reputation as an idealist was confirmed when he produced a translation of the *Phenomenology* in 1910. In his *Studies in Human Nature* (1921), however, Baillie repudiated idealism for a kind of personalistic pragmatism in which he emphasized individuality and 'critical common sense'. In place of the Hegelian world-reason he now took a more relativistic and anthropocentric view of philosophy and science. Metz attributed this change to a 'deeply felt experience of the tragedy and meaninglessness of the World War' (Metz, p. 318). Baillie's personal statement in CBP II, however, suggests that what had seemed to him 'problems of vital importance' had always included ones to which idealism did not have a satisfactory solution. For instance he accepted, against empiricism, the necessity of interpretation in science but insisted, against **Bosanquet** and 'the idealistic school', on the independence of the reality thus interpreted (CBP II, p. 16). This suggests that, notwithstanding his earlier adherence to idealism, the seeds of his disaffection from it had been sown long before the World War.
Sources: Metz; CBP II; DNB, 1931–40; obituary, *The Times*, 11 Jun 1940.

STUART BROWN

Bakradze, Konstantin Spiridonovich

Georgian. **b:** 24 November (O.S.) 1898, Georgia. **d:** 28 April 1970, Tbilisi. **Cat:** Marxist; historian of philosophy; logician. **Ints:** Logic; history of modern philosophy; contemporary non-Marxist philosophy. **Educ:** Tbilisi University. **Appts:** Taught Philosophy and Logic at Tbilisi University, from 1922; Professor from 1930; Founder and first Dean of the Philosophy Faculty; Head of the Department of Logic from 1940.

Main publications:

(1931) *Problems of Dialectics in German Idealism* [Logic], Tbilisi (in Georgian language).
(1951) *Logika*, Tbilisi.
(1958) *Sistema i metod v filosofii Gegelia* [System and Method in the Philosophy of Hegel], Tbilisi (first published in Georgian in 1936).
(1960) *Ocherki istorii noveishei i sovremennoi burzhuaznoi filosofii* [An Essay in the History of Modern and Contemporary Bourgeois Philosophy], Tbilisi.
(1962) *Ekzistentsializm* [Existentialism], Tbilisi.
(1965) *Pragmatizm* [Pragmatism], Tbilisi.

Secondary literature:

Scanlan, James P. (1985) *Marxism in the USSR: A Critical Survey of Current Soviet Thought*, Cornell University Press.
Wetter, Gustav A. (1958) *Dialectical Materialism: A Historical and Systematic Survey of Philosophy in the Soviet Union*, trans. Peter Heath, London: Routledge & Kegan Paul.

The dominant philosophical figure in the Soviet republic of Georgia, Bakradze gained prominence throughout the USSR in the early 1950s through his defence of formal logic against those who championed dialectical logic as the logic appropriate to Marxism. Contrary to the officially tolerated 'two logics' practice that evolved, Bakradze insisted that there can be only one science of reasoning—formal logic—and that dialectics was intended by the founders of Marxism to be a broad philosophical science combining epistemology with ontology. He authored some of the Soviet Union's first textbooks in formal logic and was influential in developing instruction in the subject throughout the country. Bakradze's early work in the history of philosophy also concentrated on questions of dialectics. He criticized Engels' adoption of the Hegelian view that motion is inherently contradictory, and he argued that one need not deny any of the three traditional laws of thought in order to understand motion and development. He also believed that the Hegelian idea of a system of dialectically developing and interpenetrating categories was the product of figurative and confused thinking;

in his view, philosophical categories must remain conceptually separate and distinct if they are to do their proper job. His later works, which include monographs on existentialism and pragmatism, presented critical analyses of contemporary Western philosophical movements from a Marxist perspective.

JAMES SCANLAN

Baldwin, James Mark

American. *b:* 12 January 1861, Columbia, South Carolina. *d:* 8 November 1934, Paris. *Cat:* Idealist. *Ints:* Evolution; psychology. *Educ:* Princeton, Oxford, Leipzig, Berlin and Tübingen. *Appts:* Instructor of French and German, Princeton, 1886; Professor of Philosophy, Lake Forest, 1887–9; Toronto, 1889–93; Professor of Psychology, Princeton, 1893–1903; Professor of Philosophy and Psychology, Johns Hopkins, 1903-9; ended his career in 1913 at the National University of Mexico; a long interest in France led to many visits there; served for 12 years, beginning in 1894, as editor of the *Psychological Review*; editor of *Baldwin's Dictionary of Philosophy and Psychology*, New York: Macmillan, 1901–5.

Main publications:

(1889–91) *Handbook of Psychology*, New York: Holt.
(1893) *Elements of Psychology*, New York: Holt.
(1894) *Mental Development in the Child and the Race: Methods and Processes*, New York and London: Macmillan; third edition, 1925.
(1894) *Personality-Suggestion*, New York: Macmillan.
(1895–6) *Consciousness and Evolution*, Princeton: The University Press.
(1897) *Determinate Evolution*, Princeton: The University Press.
(1897) *Social and Ethical Interpretations of Mental Development; a Study in Social Psychology*, London: Macmillan.
(1898) *Story of the Mind*, New York: Appleton.
(1902) *Development and Evolution, Including Psychophysical Evolution, Evolution by Orthoplasy, and the Theory of Genetic Modes*, New York: Macmillan.
(1902) *Fragments in Philosophy and Science*, New York: Scribner.
(1906) *The History of Psychology*, New York: Houghton Mifflin.
(1906) *Thought and Things: A Study of the Development of Meaning of the History of Psychology*, New York: Houghton Mifflin.
(1906–11) *Thought or Genetic Logic*, 3 vols, New York: Macmillan.
(1909) *Darwin and the Humanities*, Baltimore: Reivew Publishing.
(1911) *The Individual and Society; or, Psychology and Sociology*, Boston: Badger.
(1913) *History of Psychology: A Sketch and an Interpretation*, 2 vols, London: Watts; New York: G. P. Putnam.
(1913) *French and American Ideals*, London: Sheratt & Hughes (French translation, *L'Idéal américain et l'idéal français*, Paris: Bibliothèque Franco-Américique, 1914).
(1915) *Genetic Theory of Reality*, New York: Putnam.
(1915) *France and the War, as seen by an American*, London: Sheratt & Hughes.
(1916) *American Neutrality, its Cause and Cure*, New York: Putnam.
(1916) *The Super State and the 'Eternal Values'*, London: Oxford University Press, H. Milford (a Herbert Spencer Lecture).
(1919) *Paroles de guerre d'un Américain*, Paris: F. Alcan.

Secondary literature:

Barber Montgomery, Martha (1971) 'The place of ethical disagreement in the ethical theory of emotivism versus the genetic tradition of Baldwin, Piaget and Kohlberg', PhD thesis, University of Pennsylvania.
Holmes, Eugene C. (1942) 'Social philosophy and the social mind: a study of the genetic methods of J. M. Baldwin, G. H. Mead and J. E. Boodin', PhD thesis, Columbia University.

Baldwin was chiefly known for his 'genetic' theses to the effect that the origins and patterns of development of mind, value and culture reveal what is crucial about the nature of these phenomena and about the nature of reality. His philosophical interests were always centred on problems posed by evolutionary theories, on developmental psychology and on the problems associated with the idea of psychology as a discipline, although during and after the First World War he became much more involved in questions of peace and war.

He rejected materialism because, although he thought that the natural sciences could be understood in materialist terms, no such explanations could account for specific human phenomena or for the psychological events which figured in much of his work. Amongst idealists he is nearest to John Elof **Boodin** with whom he shared some ideas about the development of nature and knowledge.

Sources: *Enciclopedia Garzanti di Filosofia*; EF; WWW(Am).

LESLIE ARMOUR

Balfour, Arthur James, first Earl of Balfour

British. *b:* 25 July 1848, Whittingehame, East Lothian, Scotland. *d:* 19 March, 1930, Woking, Surrey. *Cat:* Metaphysician; statesman. *Ints:* Epistemology; philosophy of relgion. *Educ:* Trinity College, Cambridge. *Infls:* His brothers Gerald and Francis Maitland, his sister Eleanor and his brothers-in-law Henry Sidgwick and John, third Lord Rayleigh. *Appts:* Conservative Member of Parliament, 1874–1930; Prime Minister, 1902–5; Leader of the Opposition, 1905–11; President of the British Academy, from 1921.

Main publications:

(1879) *A Defence of Philosophic Doubt*, London: Macmillan.
(1893) *Essays and Addresses*, Edinburgh: David Douglas.
(1895) *The Foundations of Belief*, London: Longmans.
(1915) *Theism and Humanism*, London: Hodder & Stougthon (Gifford Lectures).
(1920) *Essays Speculative and Political*, London: Hodder & Stoughton.
(1923) *Theism and Thought*, London: Hodder & Stoughton (Gifford Lectures).

Secondary literature:

Dudgale, B. E. C. (1936) *Arthur James Balfour*, 2 vols, London: Hutchinson (includes an account of his philosophy by A. S. Pringle-Pattison).
Jones, H. (1904–5) 'Mr. Balfour as sophist', *The Hibbert Journal* 3: 452–77.
Malcolm, I. Z. (1930) *Lord Balfour: A Memory*, London: Macmillan.
Pringle-Pattison, A. S. (1902) *Man's Place in the Cosmos*, Edinburgh: Blackwood, second edition.
Young, K. (1963) *Arthur James Balfour*, London: G. Bell.

Although a mid-Victorian, temperamentally Balfour preferred what he saw as the serenity and order of the eighteenth century to Carlyle's 'windy prophesyings' or Mill's 'thin lucidity'. Yet in his writings his aspiration was to probe the foundations of current thought rather than to indulge in intellectual history. He was especially concerned to endorse modern science against its detractors, and at the same time to shun materialism and evolutionary naturalism. In what might be termed his holistic transcendentalism, reason had its

place, but due heed was also paid to the 'authority' of such non-rational factors which influence human believing as personal circumstances—familial and societal—and cultural inheritance. (Psychical research was among his many interests.) Balfour was convinced that the foundations of theology were at least as secure as those of science, that all intellectual positions rest upon faith, and hence that there was nothing discreditable about the theistic metaphysic which alone satisfied him. Indeed he felt that in order to be properly rational, science itself required the theistic presupposition.

Balfour's critics commonly found him more adept at demolishing naturalism (his familiar targets being Mill and **Spencer**) than at substantiating his own position or employing some of his key concepts with due rigour. From the standpoint of idealism Henry **Jones**, noting Balfour's view that the object of science was a reality which is independent of perception, regretted that he thus set out from 'the conception of reality which it was the main triumph of Idealism to prove impossible'. Balfour thus 'maintains the pure naturalism of science, and by a theological *tour de force* makes it appear to yield spiritual conclusions'.

Sources: DNB.

ALAN SELL

Balibar, Étienne

French. *b:* 1942, Avallon, France. *Cat:* Marxist; metaphysician; political philosopher; social philosopher. *Ints:* Structuralism. *Educ:* École Normal Supérieure. *Infls:* Marx, Lenin, Althusser and others in the Marxist tradition. *Appts:* Lecturer in Philosophy, Paris I.

Main publications:

(1965) (with Louis Althusser, Pierre Macherey, *et al.*), *Lire le Capitale* Paris: Maspero.
(1968) (with Louis Althusser) *Lire le Capitale*, Paris: Maspero (revised edition of 1965; *Reading Capital*, trans. Ben Brewster, London: NLB, 1970).
(1974) *Cinq études du matérialisme historique*, Paris: Maspero.
(1976) *Sur la dictature du prolétariat*, Paris: Maspero (English translation, *On the Dictatorship of the Proletariat*, trans. G. Lock, London: NLB, 1977).
(1979) *Marx et sa critique de la politique*, Paris: Maspero.
(1985) *Spinoza et la politique*, Paris: Presses Universitaires de France.
(1988) (with Immanuel Wallerstein), *Race, nation, classe: les identités ambiguës* Paris: Découverte

(English translation, *Race, Nation, Class: Ambiguous Identities*, trans. Chris Turner, London: NLB, 1991).
(1991) *Écrits pour Althusser*, Paris: Découverte.

Secondary literature:
Benton, Ted (1984) *The Rise and Fall of Structural Marxism*, London and Basingstoke: Macmillan.

Balibar was a student of Louis **Althusser** and has been one of his most important disciples, collaborating with him on *Reading Capital*, one of the central texts of structural Marxism, the Althusser-led movement to reinterpret Marx through structuralist theory. Balibar's contribution to the project, 'The basic concepts of historical materialism', sought to give an account of the supposedly scientific conception of history that followed in the wake of what Althusser called the 'epistemological break' between Marx's early and late work. **Lenin** is another major influence on Balibar's thought, and he has been a keen defender of the former's conception of the 'dictatorship of the proletariat'. As one of the leading theoreticians of the French Communist Party, Balibar's reputation is very much linked to that of Althusser and has suffered from the decline in influence of structural Marxism.
Sources: Ted Benton (1984)–see above.

STUART SIM

Banfi, Antonio
Italian. *b:* 30 September 1886, Vimercate. *d:* 20 July 1957, Milan. *Cat:* Historian of philosophy.

Main publications:
(1922) *La filosofia e la vita spirituale.*
(1926) *Principi di una teoria della ragione.*
(1930) *Vita di G. Galileo.*
(1934) *Nietzsche.*
(1943) *Socrate.*
(1947) *Vita dell' arte.*
(1959) *La ricerca della realtà.*
(1960) *Saggi sul Marxismo.*
(1962) *Filosofia dell'arte.*
(1965) *Studi sulla filosofia del Novecento.*
(1965) *Ricerche sull'amore familiare.*
(1965) *Incontro con Hegel.*
(1986–) *Opere*, Reggio Emilia: Instituto A. Banfi.

Secondary literature:
Erbetta, A. (1978) *L'umanesimo critico di Antonio Banfi*, Milan: Marzorati.
Salemi, R. (1982) *Bibliografia banfiana*, Parma: Pratiche.

Banfi studied in Berlin and his philosophy was influenced by **Husserl**, **Simmel** and German neo-Kantianism. He grafts a critical rationalism onto an ethical-political notion that is Marxist in origin. Reason is not a faculty of the mind nor, as in Hegelianism, the end sought by reason. Rather it is a force which moves in every aspect of experience, both personal and social, in a constant work of universalization and which finds anathema any restriction on liberation from particularity and any partiality to any rigid dogmatism. Reason is made concrete in knowledge, both scientific and philosophical. Science stresses the universal and tries infinitely to widen the connections that can be traced between things. Philosophy cleanses the autonomy of thought of every residue of dogmatism and manifests itself in dialectic, eidectic and phenomenological forms. The dialectical form shows the inadequacy of every conceptual synthesis to capture the infinity of experience. The eidectic form reveals the antinomies in grand theories which reflect on experience. The reflective form completes the two foregoing by systematizing the variety and complexity of experience without mischaracterizations that arise from the use of a priori or any other kind of presuppositions. Using this method Banfi maps the different levels on which cultures attempt to resolve antitheses between the individual and the world, as they reveal themselves in, for example, law (in the clash between individualism and social life) and morality (where there is a clash between the personal and the social). Banfi believed his philosophy to correspond to Marxism since it, too, implied that an awareness of reality and its problems enables humans to act in society as it is in order to resolve its contradictions. Marxist materialism has the merit of having discovered the direction of history and, in the theory of the class struggle, the technical understanding necessary for its completion. It also offered the guarantee of a collective ethic in which personhood would not be thought of as a transcendental self-sufficient state but as a reality to be realized in the whole of humanity in activities which would imply the social responsibilities of all. Banfi at all times confronted dogmatic, closed metaphysics with an open, constructive morality aimed at human liberation. He was a central figure in resistance during the war and after it sat as a Communist senator. In his last years he turned to Chinese civilization and Chinese Marxism, in which he believed himself to have found a humanism that was ethical rather than religious and naturalistic rather than idealistic.

COLIN LYAS

Bar-Hillel, Yehoshua

Israeli born in Austria. *b:* 1915, Vienna. *d:* 1976, Israel. *Cat:* Theoretical linguist; mathematical philosopher; logician. *Ints:* Philosophy of language; mathematics; logic; philosophy of science; mechanization of information and semantics. *Educ:* Germany until 1933; PhD, Hebrew University, Jerusalem, 1947; studied under Rudolph Carnap, University of Chicago, and then at MIT. *Infls:* A. H. Fraenkel, R. Carnap and N. Chomsky. *Appts:* Professor of Logic and Philosophy of Science, Hebrew University, Jerusalem, 1961; member, Israeli Academy of Arts and Sciences, 1963; President, International Union of History and Philosophy of Science, 1967.

Main publications:

(1958) (with A.H. Fraenkel) *Foundations of Set Theory*, Amsterdam: North Holland.

(1964) *Language and Information*, Redding, Mass.: Addison-Wesley.

(1966) *Essays on the Foundations of Mathematics*, Jerusalem: Magnes Press.

(1970–1) *Aspects of Language*: Jerusalem: Magnes Press.

(1976) *Language in Focus*, Dordrecht and Boston: D. Reidel.

Bar-Hillel's early writings depict the connection of mathematics with broader philosophical issues. He argues that mathematical entities have only a pseudo-existence. Under **Carnap**'s influence he worked in the fields of semantics and inductive logic, his later research being concerned with the possibility of machine translation. Like **Chomsky**, he became fascinated with the relationship between grammar, logic and language. In *Language and Information* (1964) he discusses the possibility of developing a science of language.

Sources: EncJud; WorldBio; NUC.

IRENE LANCASTER

Barreto, Luis Filipe

Portuguese. *b:* 1954. *Cat:* Philosopher of history. *Ints:* History of ideas; philosophy of history; hermeneutics. *Infls:* Derrida and Gadamer.

Main publications:

(1983) *Descobrimentos e Renascimento: Formas de ser e pensar nos séculos XV e XVI*, Lisbon: Impr. Nacional-Casa da Moeda.

(1985) *Os descobrimentos e o Renascimento*, Lisbon: Temas Portugeses.

(1989) *Os descobrimentos e o ordem do saber: Uma analise Sociocultural*, second edition, Lisbon: Gradiva.

Barreto's main emphasis is on rewriting the history of Portuguese colonialism from a primarily post-structuralist point of view. There is a 'commonsense' element which asks us, first, to dispense with the mythologies which have grown-up surrounding such exploits, and which are expounded in history texts, in favour of the Derridian concept of *différance*, holding that if we view history as *différance*, as temporalization, as spacing, we can then begin to reappraise it as the handing-down of a series of discourses conditioning both the individual as well as what he calls 'Portugal's destiny' (1985, 1, p. xv), and can thus begin to see how such disciplines as philosophy and science helped to support what he labels 'ideological construction' (ibid.). This is made difficult due to an intellectual and social hermeneutics of inferiority.

This 'complex' is analysed dually: firstly, by looking at the margins of transitivity of the medieval world for the Renaissance and, second, investigating linguistically Renaissance philosophical formulations. Jointly, such an analysis will highlight what he sees as history's ideological status as a way of discursively 'colonizing' the past for presentist purposes.

This historical colonization breeds a false consciousness which often uses historiography as what Barreto calls its 'sounding box'. It is so, he says, due to the fact that the past, that is, the projection of the (historical) other from within the (contemporary) self, forms part of a complex structural anthropology which is projected on the basis of an 'entire sociocultural imaginarium' which endlessly feeds back into itself. Barreto attempts with some success to harness post-structuralist, especially Derridian, concepts in order to critically re-appraise historical writing and history itself, viewing it as primarily a set of ideologically reinforcing discourses which are, therefore, susceptible to analysis under the Derridian notion of *différance*, strangely, though fruitfully, allied to Gadamerian hermeneutics—- Barreto holds that linguisticity is a form of realization of comprehension, and this sits well with a deconstruction of the colonial(izing) subject—and it is this that makes Barreto's work influential, not only in Portugal, but in the Iberian peninsula in general, where the philosophical community has always been receptive to European philosophical research and which, crucially, has shared the historical colonializing tendency and which is now doing so much to reappraise that past.

DAVID SPOONER

Barbusse, Henri

French. *b:* 1873, Asnières. *d:* 1935, Moscow. *Cat:* Marxist; pacifist. *Infls:* Lenin, Stalin and the Soviet cultural commissar A. A. Zhdanov. *Appts:* Served in the French army during the First World War, and wrote two novels, *Le Feu* (1918) and *Clarté* (1920), on the basis of his experience in the trenches; 1919, Cofounder and Editor of the journal *Clarté*; 1923, joined the Parti Communiste Français; 1928, founded the journal *Monde*, precursor of the Committee of Anti-Fascist Intellectuals.

Main publications:

(1920) *La Lueur dans l'abîme*, Paris: Editions Clarté.
(1921) *Le Couteau entre les dents*, Paris: Les Ecrivains Réunis.
(1927) *Manifeste aux intellectuels*, Paris: Les Ecrivains Réunis.
(1930) *Russie*, Paris: Flammarion (English translation, *One Looks at Russia*, London: Dent, 1935).
(1935) *Staline*, Paris: Flammarion (English translation, *Stalin*, London: Bodley Head, 1935).

Secondary literature:

Caute, D. (1964) *Communism and the French Intellectuals 1914–1960*, London: Deutsch.
Duclos, J. and Fréville, J. (1946) *Henri Barbusse*, Paris: Editions Sociales.

Barbusse, like many of the survivors of his generation, emerged from the First World War with his patriotic and nationalistic ideals in ruins. He thought that the war was an outcome of the competition between bourgeois nations inherent in the capitalist system, and wished to replace the capitalist ideology with one based on social justice, equality, popular democracy, republicanism and reason. Immediately after the war his position was one of unqualified pacifism, but this had changed by 1921 to one in which violence was justified provided that it was directed towards the overthrow of the capitalist system.

The journal *Clarté* was an organ for the expression of Barbusse's ideals, and from 1921 to 1925 it was the channel for the PCF, which Barbusse joined after his initial reluctance to become politically affiliated. After control of *Clarté* had been lost to French Trotskyists and surrealists, Barbusse founded *Monde*, whose contributory base was broader than that of official French communist ideology.

Barbusse's eventual aim was the liberation of the working classes from economic exploitation by the bourgeoisie (a goal which he thought had been achieved in the USSR). However, his attitude towards the workers was that they were a reactionary element, who had to be led away from the false values of bourgeois society and towards an understanding of their true interest.

Barbusse thought that intellectuals and artists had a social role and duty to produce art according to socialist realist principles. His own novels, *Le Feu* and *Clarté*, contained many socialist realist passages, but these failed because they were grafted on to, and did not emerge from, the plot.

KATHRYN PLANT

Barth, Karl

Swiss. *b:* 10 May 1886, Basel. *d:* 10 December 1968, Basel. *Cat:* Reformed theologian. *Ints:* Existentialism; philosophy of religion. *Educ:* Universities of Bern, Berlin, Tübingen and Marburg. *Infls:* Anselm, Calvin, Schleiermacher, Kierkegaard, C. G. and J. C. Blumhardt, F. Overbeck, A. von Harnack and W. Herrmann. *Appts:* Assistant Pastor, Geneva, 1909–11; pastor, Safenwil, 1911–21; Professor, Universities of Göttingen (1921–5), Münster (1925–30), Bonn (1930–5) and Basel (1935–62).

Main publications:

(1919) *Der Römerbrief* (English translation, *Romans*, London: Oxford University Press, 1933).
(1927) *Die christliche Dogmatik in Entwurf*, Munich.
(1928) *The Word of God and the Word of Man*, Boston: Pilgrim Press.
(1932) *Church Dogmatics*, Edinburgh: T. & T. Clark.
(1938) *The Knowledge of God and the Service of God according to the Reformation*, London: Hodder & Stoughton (Gifford Lectures).
(1946) 'No!', in *Natural Theology*, London: G. Bles.
(1949) *Dogmatics in Outline*, London: SCM Press.
(1960) *Anselm: Fides Quaerens Intellectum. Anselm's Proof of the Existence of God in the Context of his Theological Scheme*, London: SCM Press.
(1961) *The Humanity of God*, London: Collins.
(1963) *Evangelical Theology: An Introduction*, London: Weidenfeld & Nicolson.

Secondary literature:

Berkouwer, G. C. (1956) *The Triumph of Grace in the Theology of Karl Barth*, London: Paternoster Press.

Bromiley, G. W. (1979) *An Introduction to the Theology of Karl Barth*, Edinburgh: T. & T. Clark.

Busch, E. (1976) *Karl Barth: His Life from Letters and Autobiographical Texts*, London: SCM Press.

Hartwell, H. (1964) *The Theology of Karl Barth: An Introduction*, London: Duckworth.

Hepburn, R. W. (1958) *Christianity and Paradox*, London: Watts.

Hunsinger, G. (1991) *How to Read Karl Barth*, New York: Oxford University Press.

Lewis, H. D. (1947) *Morals and the New Theology*, London: Gollancz.

——(1951) *Morals and Revelation*, London: Allen & Unwin.

MacConnachie, J. (1931) *The Significance of Karl Barth*, London: Hodder & Stoughton.

Meynell, H. A. (1965) *Grace Versus Nature: Studies in Karl Barth's Church Dogmatics*, London: Sheed & Ward.

Sykes, S. W. (ed.) (1979) *Karl Barth: Studies in his Theological Method*, Oxford: The Clarendon Press.

Van Til, C. (1946) *The New Modernism: An Appraisal of the Theology of Barth and Brunner*, Philadelphia: Presbyterian and Reformed; third edition, 1972.

——(1962) *Christianity and Barthianism*, Philadelphia: Presbyterian and Reformed.

Wildi, H. M. (1984) *Bibliographie Karl Barth*, Zurich: Theologischer Verlag.

Nurtured in the Calvinistic tradition, and under the tutelage of Harnack and Herrmann, Barth came to distance himself both from the liberal theology of the early decades of this century and from conservative Protestant theology. The former was unduly anthropocentric, and in its optimism failed to take the measure of the human predicament; the latter was hidebound and 'scholastic'. Both were bankrupt in face of the trauma of the First World War. In company in the early years with E. **Brunner**, R. **Bultmann**, F. Gogarten and E. Thurneysen, Barth developed a (non-Hegelian) 'dialectical theology' according to which the only proper object of theology is God—the God who addresses his Word to humanity: hence the requirement of a 'Yes' to the Word of God, a 'No' to all attempts to translate theology into talk about human beings and their condition. The approach was also characterized as a theology of crisis (judgement); for when God, though wholly other, yet speaks to sinners—as he does supremely in Christ—they are under gracious judgement. In all of this Barth's *Romans* (1919) was a catalyst.

The developing theology was one of practical urgency: Barth regarded dogmatics and ethics as a whole, and for some this is the most enduring aspect of his legacy. We thus find him among the 'religious socialists' (L. Ragaz, H. Kutter) during the First World War, while in the 1930s he was a leader of the German Confessing Church, and the principal author of the Barmen Declaration of 1934. He was deposed from his Chair in Bonn in 1935 for refusing to swear an oath of unconditional loyalty to Hitler. (By now the originators of dialectical theology had gone their separate methodological ways.) After the Second World War Barth was prominent in working for restored relations across Europe. He delivered the opening address at the inauguration of the World Council of Churches in 1948, remaining a not uncritical supporter of the Council to the end of his life.

Having made a self-confessed false start with his *Prolegomena to a Christian Dogmatics* (1927), Barth embarked upon his *Church Dogmatics* (1932 etc.), a corpus at once strongly Christocentric and staunchly trinitarian. There had intervened his study of Anselm (1931; English translation, 1960)—in Barth's view his most significant work. He learned from Anselm that theology does not and cannot have metaphysical underpinnings. Theology is a matter of discerning and responding to God's Word as this bears upon the whole of life. The approximation of theology to preaching is not accidental, for, to Barth, the Church, where the Word is declared, is the proper context of theological activity, and is the place where recourse is had to the criterion of Scripture.

To Barth God's sole revelation is in Jesus Christ—a view rebutted by those more or less favourable to general revelation. Religion is the idolatrous human attempt to appropriate God—hence Barth's contentious denial of common ground between Christianity and other faiths. God's Word is to be heard *in* the Bible, although the words of the latter are not equivalent to the former. This brought the charge from conservative Reformed circles that Barth was repudiating the Bible *qua* supreme rule of faith and order. (More liberal exegetes have deemed some of Barth's exegesis 'fanciful'.) Further doubts were raised concerning Barth's status as Reformed by his Christological amendment of the doctrines of predestination and election, according to which Jesus Christ is both the electing God and the elected Man: both Israel and the Church are called in him. Some adverse critics found incipient universalism here.

Barth's aversion to any attempt to elevate human considerations to a level with God's revealed Word, with the attendant risk of elevating the sociocultural context into the interpetative norm, was prompted by his conviction that the

Fall entails that humanity suffers the noetic effects of sin. Hence his rejection of an independent natural theology (on which issue he had a celebrated joust with E. Brunner in the 1930s): there can be no analogy of being ('the invention of antichrist!'), for between God and creatures there is an impassable gulf. It follows that traditional apologetics are ruled out (although Barth does not deny a correspondence between God and the rationally ordered universe). God gives himself graciously through faith (the *analogia fidei*), and apart from this there is no knowledge of him. Concern at Barth's apparent removal of claims concerning the revelation in Christ from the realm of rational criticism, and puzzlement as to how religious language can be meaningful if there is no human-divine analogy, are being expressed to this day. It has frequently been observed that some of the secular and 'death of God' theologians of the 1960s were students of Barth who agreed with him that human language could not be used of God and, unlike him, opted for the view that theology must therefore be couched exclusively in mundane terms.

Barth's thought was ever on the move. He turned from his earlier existentialism, and the 'crisis' mode of expression; he came to emphasize more the humanity of God, although some still found him weak on the side of the human response to God's grace; and his latter-day claim that the sacraments are signs only, and not means of grace—this in the interests of the supremacy of the Word—likewise caused concern. Relatively few British philosophers paid professional heed to Barth during his lifetime (this is not necessarily an adverse judgement upon him or them), **Lewis** and Hepburn being among those who found him wanting. With theologians he enjoyed greater, though not universal, success: T. F. Torrance is prominent among those influenced by, though not at some points uncritical of, Barth. Such was Barth's general influence, however, that it became common to refer to 'Barthians'—although Barth declared that if there were such a school he did not belong to it! At the same time, his swingeing rebuttals of those who pursued theological directions other than his own could hardly fail to give the impression that a distinctive and strongly fortified position was being established. Perhaps not even those most at odds with Barth would grudge him the title of this century's greatest theologian, even if some of them may feel hard pressed to equate him, as has been done, with Augustine, Aquinas and Calvin. However much he has ruffled their feathers, even those most distant from him have been known to find Barth's simple faith, his humour and his love of Mozart strangely reassuring.

Sources: Obituary notices.

ALAN SELL

Barthes, Roland

French. *b:* 1915, Cherbourg, France. *d:* 1980, Paris. *Cat:* Structuralist; cultural theorist; literary theorist; semiologist. *Educ:* University of Paris. *Infls:* Saussure, Camus, Sartre and Marx. *Appts:* Professor of Literary Semiology, Collège de France.

Main publications:

(1953) *Le Degée zéro de l'écriture, suivi de nouveaux essais critiques*, Paris: Seuil (English translation, *Writing Degree Zero*, trans. Annette Lavers and Colin Smith, London: Jonathan Cape, 1967).

(1957) *Mythologies*, Paris: Seuil (English translation, *Mythologies*, trans. Annette Lavers, London: Jonathan Cape, 1972).

(1963) *Sur Racine*, Paris: Seuil (English translation, *On Racine*, trans. Richard Howard, New York: Hill & Wang, 1964).

(1964) 'Éléments de semiologie', *Communications* 4: 91–135 (English translation, *Elements of Semiology*, trans. Annette Lavers and Colin Smith, London: Jonathan Cape, 1967).

(1970) *S/Z*, Paris: Seuil (*S/Z*, trans. Richard Miller, London: Jonathan Cape, 1975).

(1970) *L'Empire des signes*, Geneva: Skira (English translation, *Empire of Signs*, trans. Richard Howard, London: Jonathan Cape, 1983).

(1970) *Sade, Fourier, Loyola*, Paris: Seuil.

(1973) *Le Plaisir du texte*, Paris: Seuil (English translation, *The Pleasure of the Text*, trans. Richard Miller, London: Jonathan Cape, 1976).

(1977) *Image-Music-Text*, ed. and trans. Stephen Heath, Glasgow: Fontana/Collins.

(1980) *La Chambre claire*, Paris: Seuil (English translation, *Camera Lucida: Reflections on Photography*, trans. Richard Howard, London: Jonathan Cape, 1982).

Secondary literature:

Culler, Jonathan (1983) *Barthes*, London: Collins.

Lavers, Annette (1982) *Roland Barthes: Structuralism and After*, London: Methuen.

Mortimer, Kotin Armine (1989) *The Gentlest Law: Roland Barthes' The Pleasure of the Text*, New York: Peter Lang.

Thody, Philip (1977) *Roland Barthes: A Conservative Estimate*, London: Macmillan.

Ungar, Stephen (1983) *Roland Barthes: The Professor of Desire*, Lincoln, Neb.: University of Nebraska Press.

Wasseman, George R. (1981) *Roland Barthes*, Boston: Twayne.

Barthes is a key figure in the history of structuralism, and has exercised a profound influence on modern aesthetics, particularly through his work on narratology. His earliest intellectual influences were **Sartre** and Marx, although he later came under the spell of modern structural linguistics, the disciplines which formed the basis of his mature work. Initially coming to national prominence in the mid-1960s, Barthes rapidly became a figure of international renown for his semiological analyses of a range of cultural phenomena. Barthes's major theoretical achievements are to be found in his work developing a grammar of narrative, as in his essay 'Introduction to the structural analysis of narratives' (in *Image-Music-Text*, 1977) and the Study *S/Z* (1970). Drawing freely on linguistic theory, the former text establishes criteria by which any narrative can be analysed down into its constituent parts ('functions') the latter expounds a theory of narrative coding which reduces Balzac's novella *Sarrasine* to a series of interactions between five main codes: proairetic, hermeneutic, semic, symbolic and referential. *S/Z* also contains Barthes's theory of the 'readerly' and 'writerly' text. The readerly text imposes the author's meaning on the reader, whereas the writerly is more open and encourages the reader to participate in the construction of textual meaning. In similar vein Barthes put forward the 'death of the author' notion ('The death of the author', in *Image-Music-Text*), which argued that the reader, not the author, was to be considered the crucial figure in the literary process. Barthes's work was generally well received in France and America in the 1960s and 1970s, although it had more limited success in British academic circles. Since the rise of poststructuralism Barthes's reputation has suffered somewhat. For all that he displays poststructuralist tendencies in his later writings, insisting on the infinite plurality of meaning in texts for example, Barthes remains committed to a highly structured and systematic form of textual analysis that is anathema to the more radical poststructuralist theorists such as Jacques **Derrida**.

STUART SIM

Bataille, Georges

French. **b:** September 1897, Billom, Puy-de-Dôme, France. **d:** July 1962, Paris. **Cat:** Nietzschean; illuminist. **Ints:** Development of a method and theory of mystical experience in a Nietzschean context. **Infls:** Hegel and Kojève, but above all Nietzsche. **Appts:** Tempted by the idea of a religious life before losing his faith, he trained as an archivist at the École des Chartes, and was employed as a curator or librarian throughout his life; the progress of his beliefs is marked in his relations with the Surrealists, in his work on literary reviews and in his books.

Main publications:

(This is a tentative list: Bataille had no interest in writing works which conform to recognized genres, and his books are highly resistant to labelling. All in *Oeuvres complètes*, 12 vols, Paris, Gallimard, 1970–87.)

(1943) *L'Expérience intérieure.*
(1944) *Le Coupable.*
(1945) *Sur Nietzsche, volonté de chance.*
(1947) *Méthode de méditation.*
(1955) *Le Littérature et le mal.*

Secondary literature:

Critique (1963) 19, (195–6), Aug.–Sept., Paris: Editions de Minuit (a memorial issue of the periodical founded by Bataille).
Graham, A. C. (1993) *Unreason within Reason*, Chicago: Open Court.
Magazine littéraire (1987) 243, June, Paris (includes a lengthy synoptic perspective on Bataille).
Surya, M. (1987) *Georges Bataille, la mort à l'oeuvre*, Paris: Libraire Séguier.

Bataille took as his starting-point complete agreement with some of **Nietzsche**'s key beliefs, notably the death of God and its consequences for our understanding of the human predicament. We have no certainties on which to lean, and for Bataille it followed that we have a stark choice between inauthentic clinging to beliefs falsified by criticism and saying yes to the only remaining form of intense life, the pursuit of fusion, of disintegration of the ego at the limits of possible experience. There are several paths to the limit: via poetry, love (it is no accident that Bataille wrote some very fine erotica), but chiefly via what Bataille calls 'interior experience' (*l'expérience intérieure*)—in a religious context this would be called mystical experience, but, being an atheist, Bataille wished to avoid the overtones of the term. He describes his experiences and methods for attaining them in the works of 1943, 1944 and

1945. The experiences of an 'ungraspable beyond' he describes have many parallels in mystical literature, though his methods of a simplified yoga without 'metaphysical excrescences' or asceticism is his own. (He would first still the flow of conscious thought by means of basic hatha-yoga breath control, and then visualize scenes of horror, pain or death. When successful, the technique opens a 'rift' in the ego, and the beyond is revealed.)

The works in which these experiences are described are deliberately not sequential expositions, but are designed (as are many other mystical texts) to assist in disrupting the grip of reason. Bataille hoped to break the tyranny of words, the set forms of the intelligence, or previous styles. It is not surprising that he should have written a study of the Lascaux cave paintings (*Lascaux*, Geneva: Skira, 1955). Here is pure genius, free creativity, without the burden of a 'heritage' to be broken or undone.

Sources: J.-P. Sartre (1943) 'Un nouveau mystique' (review of 1943), *Cahiers du Sud*, 260–2, Oct–Dec.

ROBERT WILKINSON

Bauch, Bruno

German. *b:* 19 January 1877, Gross-Nossen, Silesia. *d:* 27 February 1942, Jena. *Cat:* Neo-Kantian; epistemologist. *Educ:* Philosophy at Freiburg, Strassburg and Heidelberg. *Infls:* Wilhelm Windelband, Kuno Fischer and Heinrich Rickert. *Appts:* Professor of Philosophy, University of Jena.

Main publications:

(1902) *Glückseligkeit und Persönlichkeit in der kritischen Ethik*, Stuttgart: Frommann.

(1910) *Das Substanzproblem in der griechischen Philosophie bis zu ihrer Blütezeit*, Heidelberg: C. Winter.

(1911) *Studien zur Philosophie der exakten Wissenschaft*, Heidelberg: C. Winter.

(1917) *Immanuel Kant*, Leipzig, Göschen.

(1923) *Wahrheit, Wert und Wirklichkeit*, Leipzig: Meiner.

(1926) *Die Idee*, Leipzig: Reinicke.

(1935) *Die Grundzüge der Ethik*, Stuttgart: Kohl-hammer.

Secondary literature:

F. Keller, (1965) 'Zusammenfassender Bericht über Bruno Bauchs unveröffentlichtes Nachlasswerk "Natur und Geist"', *Wirklichkeit und Wahrheit* 2: 9–42.

Strasser, J. (1967) *Die Bedeutung des hypothetischen Imperatives in der Ethik Bruno Bauchs, Bonn: Bouvier.*

Like Kroner, Lask, **Rickert** and other members of the so-called 'Heidelberg,' 'Baden' or 'South-western school' of neo-Kantianism, Bauch entirely rejected metaphysics and concentrated on ethical and epistemological questions, arguing for a comprehensive theory of culture. Bauch was especially interested in the relations between 'truth', 'value' and 'reality'. He argued that epistemology cannot dispense with the concept of value. Factually true (*gültige*) judgements have a greater value than those that are not. This value of factually true judgements is ultimately based on transcendental conditions. Therefore the transcendental conditions of judgements constitute themselves pure values. Ethical values and truth values are closely connected. They constitute different perspectives on one and the same whole.

MANFRED KUEHN

Baudrillard, Jean

French. *b:* 1929, Reims, France. *Cat:* Post-structuralist; sociologist; translator (of Brecht, Weiss and Mühlmann into French). *Ints:* Marxism; semiology; postmodernism. *Educ:* Trained as a sociologist. *Infls:* Marx, Saussure and Lévi-Strauss. *Appts:* Professor of Sociology, University of Paris X, Nanterre.

Main publications:

(1968) *Le Système des objets*, Paris: Denoë-Gonthier.

(1970) *La Société de consommation*, Paris: Gallimard.

(1972) *Pour une critique de l'économie politique du signe*, Paris: Gallimard (English translation, *For a Critique of the Political Economy of the Sign*, St Louis: Telos, 1981).

(1973) *Le Miroir de la production: ou, l'illusion critique du matérialisme historique*, Tournai: Casterman (English translation, *The Mirror of Production*, St. Louis: Telos, 1975).

(1976) *L'Échange symbolique et la mort*, Paris: Gallimard.

(1979) *De la séduction*, Paris: Denoël-Gontheir (English translation, *Seduction*, trans. B. Singer, New York: St Martin's Press, 1990).

(1981) *Simulacres et simulation*, Paris: Éditions Galilée.

(1988) *Jean Baudrillard: Selected Writings*, ed. Mark Poster, Cambridge: Polity Press (selected works in English).

Secondary literature:
Kellner, D. (1989) *Jean Baudrillard, from Marxism to Postmodernism and Beyond*, Cambridge: Polity.
Pefanis, J. (1990) *Heterology and the Postmodern: Bataille, Baudrillard and Lyotard*, Durham, NC: Duke University Press.

Jean Baudrillard is a thinker in the Marxist tradition of the critique of political economy. He has, though, gone beyond the Marxist critique of capitalism by applying structuralist theories of the sign to the consumer society. This shift has lead him to a critique of the political economy of the sign: 'All the repressive and reductive strategies of power systems are already present in the internal logic of the sign, as well as those of exchange value and political economy' (1972, trans. p. 163). Baudrillard's later work applies his semiology to studies of the media and how reality comes to be constituted. Here, Baudrillard adopts a postmodern standpoint abandoning any appeals to truth and reality in favour of hyperreality, that is, a world consisting of simulacra. Baudrillard's main influence is as a media analyst and social theorist; his work defines the term postmodern in these fields. The positive reaction to his work in the field of social studies is tempered by a critical reaction to the philosophical basis of his work where Baudrillard is accused of avoiding clear definitions of the main terms in his analyses and of neglecting to consider the logical implications of his critique of capitalism.

Sources: Catalogues of Bibliothèque Nationale, Paris and National Library of Scotland.

JAMES WILLIAMS

Bauer, Otto
Austrian. *b:* 1881, Vienna. *d:* 1938, Paris. *Cat:* Marxist. *Educ:* University of Vienna, Doctorate in Law 1906. *Infls:* Kant and Marx.

Main publications:
(1907) *Die Nationalitätenfrage und die Sozialdemokratie*, Vienna: Wiener Volksbuchhandlung.
(1919) *Der Weg zum Sozialismus*, Vienna: Wiener Volksbuchhandlung.
(1923) *Die österreichische Revolution*, Vienna: Wiener Volksbuchhandlung (English translation and abridgement, *The Austrian Revolution*, trans. H. J. Stenning, New York: Burt Franklin, 1970).
(1931) *Kapitalismus und Sozialismus nach dem Weltkrieg*, Vienna: Wiener Volksbuchhandlung.
(1936) *Zwischen zwei Weltkriegen? Die Krise der Weltwirtschaft, der Demokratie und des Sozialismus*, Bratislava: Prager.

(1975–9) *Werkausgabe*, Vienna: Europa.

Secondary literature:
Bottomore, Tom and Goode, Patrick (1978) *Austro-Marxism*, Oxford: Clarendon Press (translated extracts from Bauer and other AustroMarxists).
Kolakowski, Leszek (1978) *Main Currents in Marxism*, vol. 2 Oxford: Oxford University Press.
Leichter, Otto (1970) *Otto Bauer: Tragodie oder Triumph?*, Vienna: Europa.
Rabinach, Anson (1983) *The Crisis of Austrian Socialism: From Red Vienna to Civil War 1927–1934*, Chicago: University of Chicago Press.

From his student days Bauer contributed regularly to Marxist journals, becoming Secretary to the Social Democratic delegation to the Reichsrat in 1907; in the same year, he cofounded *Der Kampf*, which became under his editorship the leading theoretical journal of Marxism in Austria; conscripted in 1914, he spent 1914–17 as a prisoner of war; after the fall of the Hapsburg monarchy, Bauer was briefly Foreign Minister of the Austrian Republic, resigning when his plans for German–Austrian unification were rejected by the Allies; he continued to serve in the Austrian Parliament 1920–34 as the leading member of the Social Democrats; with the outbreak of fighting in 1934 he was forced into exile in Czechoslovakia; and when the Nazis invaded Austria in 1938, shortly before his death, he moved to Paris.

With Hilferding, Adler and Renner, Bauer was a leading member of the so-called Austro-Marxists, a group distinguished by its concern to develop Marxism as an empirical science, by its interest in questions of ethics and by its openness to new developments in non-Marxist philosophy and economics. Bauer's distinctive contributions included the idea that national differences would increase rather than diminish under socialism; that proletarian interests were by Kantian standards superior to those of other classes; and that even a capitalist state could achieve some degree of autonomy from the capitalist class whose tool it normally was. Although initially critical of Leninism, Bauer came to believe by the 1930s that the USSR was capable of developing towards socialism.

Sources: BDN.

NICHOLAS EVERITT

Beardsley, Monroe Curtis
American. *b:* 10 December 1915, Connecticut. *d:* 18 September 1985, Philadelphia. *Cat:* Analytical philosopher. *Ints:* Aesthetics; philosophy of lan-

guage. *Educ:* Yale University. *Infls:* Kant, E.
Bullough and John Dewey. Personal: W. M.
Urban, W. K. Wimsatt, R. Rudner and R. Brandt.
Appts: Professor of Philosophy, Swarthmore
College, Pennsylvania, 1947–69; Professor of
Philosophy, Temple University, Pennsylvania,
1969–85; Fellow of American Academy of Arts
and Sciences.

Main publications:
(1946) (with W. K. Wimsatt) 'The intentional
  fallacy', *The Sewanee Review* 54, 1: 3–23.
(1949) (with W. K. Wimsatt) 'The affective fallacy',
  The Sewanee Review 57, 1: 3–27.
(1950) *Practical Logic*, New York: Prentice Hall.
(1958) *Aesthetics: Problems in the Philosophy of
  Criticism*, New York: Harcourt Brace; second
  edition, Indianapolis: Hackett, 1981.
(1965) (with Elizabeth Beardsley) *Philosophical
  Thinking*, New York: Harcourt Brace.
(1966) *Aesthetics from Classical Greece to the
  Present: A Short History*, New York: Macmillan;
  second edition, Alabama: University of Alabama
  Press, 1969.
(1967) *(ed. with H. Schueller) Aesthetic Inquiry:
  Essays on Art Criticism and the Philosophy of Art,
  Belmont, CA: Dickenson.*
(1970) *The Possibility of Criticism*, Detroit: Wayne
  State University Press.
(1982) *The Aesthetic Point of View: Selected Essays*,
  ed. Michael J. Wreen and Donald M. Callen,
  Ithaca, NY: Cornell University Press.

Secondary literature:
Aagaard-Mogensen, L. and de Vos, L. (eds) (1986)
  *Text, Literature and Aesthetics: Essays in Honour of
  Monroe Beardsley*, Amsterdam: Rodopi (includes
  full bibliography).
Fisher, John (ed.) (1983) *Esays on Aesthetics:
  Perspectives on the Work of Monroe C. Beardsley*,
  Philadelphia: Temple University Press (includes
  bibliography).

Beardsley was a prolific and highly influential
writer on aesthetics, noted for the rigour and
clarity of his thought. His early essay on 'The
intentional fallacy' (with W. K. Wimsatt, 1946)
was a seminal work, supporting one of the
doctrines of New Criticism: that knowledge of
an artist's intentions is not logically relevant to the
interpretation or evaluation of the work of art. A
guiding theme of his aesthetics is his concern with
the nature of aesthetic experience, which he
identifies in terms of such notions as unity,
coherence and completeness.

Sources: WW(Am); Turner; John Fisher (1986)
obituary notice, *JHI* 47.

PETER LEWIS

Beauvoir, Simone de
French. *b:* 1908, Paris. *d:* 1986, Paris. *Cat:* Moral
philosopher; social philosopher; existentialist;
feminist. *Educ:* Educated at a private girls' school,
Cours Désir, and at the Sorbonne and the École
Normale Supérieure, where she took her *agréga-
tion* in philosophy. *Infls:* Jean-Paul Sartre. *Appts:*
Taught at various lycées until dismissed by the
German authorities in 1943; thereafter earned her
living by writing and lecture tours; 1945–,
Cofounder and Editor, with Sartre, of the journal
Les Temps Modernes; associated with various left-
wing political and feminist movements.

Main publications:
(1944) *Pyrrhus et Cinéas*, Paris: Gallimard.
(1947) *Pour une morale de l'ambiguïté*, Paris:
  Gallimard (English translation, *The Ethics of
  Ambiguity*, New York: Philosopical Library, 1948).
(1948) *L'Existentialisme et la sagesse des nations*,
  Paris: Nagel.
(1949) *Le deuxième sexe*, 2 vols, Paris: Gallimard
  (English translation, *The Second Sex*, London:
  Jonathan Cape, 1953).
(1955) *Privilèges*, Paris: Gallimard (contains an
  essay, 'Faut-il brûler Sade?', translated into English
  as *Must We Burn Sade?*, London: Peter Nevill,
  1953).
(1970) *La Vieillesse*, 2 vols, Paris: Gallimard (English
  translation, *Old Age*, London: André Deutsch,
  1972).

Secondary literature:
The secondary literature on Beauvoir as a philoso-
pher, novelist and essayist is vast. The following are
a selection of commentaries on the philosophical
works, and contain extensive bibliographies:
Evans, R. (ed.) (forthcoming) *On Re-reading The
  Second Sex*, Manchester: Manchester University
  Press.
Keefe, T. (1983) *Simone de Beauvoir: A Study of Her
  Writings*, Part II, London: Harrap.
Marks, E. (ed.) (1987) *Critical Essays on Simone de
  Beauvoir*, Boston: Hall.
Whitmarsh, A. (1981) *Simone de Beauvoir and the
  Limits of Commitment*, Cambridge: Cambridge
  University Press.
Zéphir, J. J. (1982) *Le Néo-féminisme de Simone de
  Beauvoir*, Paris: Denoël/Gonthier.

Beauvoir's two earliest publications were in the field of ethics. Both works were influenced by existentialism and in particular by Jean-Paul **Sartre**'s *Being and Nothingness*. She put forward the view that the situation of human beings within the universe is ambiguous, due to everyone's having both an inner and an outer life. People's inner lives are characterized by consciousness and thus freedom, which is the human essence. Their outer lives are characterized by their being material objects. This means that everyone is limited by other material objects, including other people.

In being free, we have to make choices. Any denial that we do have freedom is self-defeating, as such a position is in itself a result of free choice. Freedom is completed and fixed only by death: throughout life, it has to be constantly renewed, as choices continually have to be made.

Beauvoir is best known as an early feminist, and her views in this area are mainly to be found in *The Second Sex* (1949). Her feminist position is stated in existentialist terminology. The category of the Other, and the consequent marginalization of whatever is assigned to this category, is essential to all human thought. Men have always relegated women to the category of non-essential Otherness, whilst considering themselves (whether consciously or not) as central and essential to society. Men project their feelings onto the Other, and the ambivalence of their feelings is reflected in their creation of myths about women. The myths of motherhood embody both male disgust and tenderness; and the male fear of, and desire for, women is expressed in the inconsistent myths of virginity and sex.

The dominant position of men in society is almost totally self-regenerating because women, who have acquiesced in their own marginalization, have traditionally had no way of rebelling against it. The concept of womanhood is primarily a social, not a biological, psychological or economic one, and is instilled into girls from an early age. Beauvoir saw economic independence and legal rights as necessary, but not sufficient, conditions for the emancipation of women. She regarded some twentieth-century social developments as helpful to the feminist cause, and urged women to take an active role in ensuring that progress towards an equal society initiated by these developments continued, to the benefit of both sexes.

KATHRYN PLANT

Becker, Oskar

German. *b:* 5 September 1889, Leipzig. *d:* 13 November 1964, Bonn. *Cat:* Phenomenological philosopher. *Ints:* Fundamental research in, and history of, mathematics and logic; a founder of modal logic. *Educ:* Studied at Leipzig; habilitated at Freiburg, where he was Husserl's assistant. *Infls:* Husserl and Heidegger. *Appts:* 1923–30, edited Husserl's *Jahrbuch* with Heidegger; 1928–31, Associate Professor, Freiburg; 1931 to retirement Professor Ordinarius of the History of Mathematics, Bonn.

Main publications:

(1923) 'Beiträge zur phänomenologischen Begründung der Geometrie und ihrer physikalischen Andwendungen' *Jahrbuch* 6: 385–560. (English translation, 'Contributions toward the phenomenological foundation of geometry and its physical applications', in J. J. Kockelmans and T. J. Kisiel (eds) *Phenomenology and the Natural Sciences*, Evanston: Northwestern University Press, 1970).

(1927) 'Mathematische Existenz. Untersuchungen zur Logik und Ontologie mathematischer Phänomene' [Mathematical existence. Investigations on logic and the ontology of mathematical phenomena], *Jahrbuch* 8: 441–809 (Tübingen 2, 1973).

(1930) 'Zur Logik der Modalitäten' [On the logic of modalities], *Jahrbuch* 11: 497–548.

(1933–36) [Eudoxos Studies I–IV], *Quellen und Studien zur Geschichte der Mathematik, Astronomie und Physik*, Abt. B. (Studien) 2 (1933), 311–33, 369–87; 3 (1936), 236–44, 370–410, 'Eudoxos-Studien, I–IV'.

(1951) (with J. E. Hofmann) *Geschichte der Mathematik* [History of Mathematics], Bonn: Athanaum.

(1951) *Einführung in die Logistik, vorzüglich in den Modalkalkül* [Introduction to Logistics, especially Modal Calculus], Meisenheim: Hain.

(1952) *Untersuchungen über den Modalkalkül* [Investigations on the Modal Calculus], Meisenheim: Hain.

(1954) *Grundlagen der Mathematik in geschichtlicher Entwicklung* [The Foundations of Mathematics in its Historical Development], Freiburg and Munich: Alber.

(1957) *Das mathematische Denken der Antike* [The Mathematical Thought of Antiquity], Göttingen: Vandenhoek & Ruprecht.

(1957) *Zwei Untersuchungen zur antiken Logik* [Two Investigations on Ancient Logic], Wiesbaden: Harrassowitz.

(1959) *Größe und Grenze der mathematischen Denkweise* [The Greatness and Limit of the Mathematical Way of Thinking], Freiburg and Munich: Alber.

(1963) *Dasein und Dawesen. Gesammelte philoso-phische Aufsätze* [Being-There and Essential Being. Collected Philosophical Essays], Pfullingen: Neske.
(1965((ed.) *Zur Geschichte der griechischen Mathematik* [On the History of Greek Mathematics], Darmstadt: Wissenschaftliche Buchgesellschaft.

Secondary literature:
Pöggeler, O. (1965) 'Hermeneutische und mathematische Phänomenologie', *Philosophische Rundschau*, 13: 1–39.
——(1969) 'Hermeneutische und mantische Phänomenologie', in O. Pöggeler (ed.) *Heidegger*, Cologne: Berlin.
——(1969) 'Oscar Becker als Philosophe', *Kantstudien* 60: 298–311.
Ströker, E. (1987) *Investigations in Philosophy of Space*, trans. Algis Mickunas, Athens: Ohio University Press (originally published in German; 1965).

Husserl hoped that **Heidegger** and Becker would complete his massive research plan—Heidegger the human sciences part and Becker the natural sciences part. Philosophically and politically Heidegger was a great disappointment to Husserl. Initially Becker worked on Husserl's project. Later he was influenced by Heidegger's hermeneutics and finally he developed his own 'mantic phenomenology'. In his later life Becker made only passing references to his phenomenological past.

In his 'Contributions' (1923) he employed Husserl's concept of 'definite multiplicities' in investigating the various fundamental concepts of mathematical continua. Following Hermann **Weyl**, he opted for L. E. J. **Brouwer**'s intuitionism, which guarantees mathematical entities by a step-by-step construction and avoids the paradoxes of formalism. Investigating the phenomenal constitution of spatiality, he demonstrated the rationality of the intuitive foundation of the continuum and Euclidean geometry, idealized the vague morphology of space into an exact metric by a process of 'going to the limit' and demonstrated the transcendental necessity of physical systems and of Euclidean axioms.

Following Heidegger, his 'Mathematical Existence. Investigations on Logic and the Ontology of Mathematical Phenomena' (1927) incorporates mathematical existence within a 'hermeneutic of facticity'. Attempting a synthesis of mathematical-constructivism and hermeneutics, he also investigated lifeworld philosophy and the anthropological foundation of mathematical science. He later redressed the 'one-sided' hermeneutical imbalance and introduced *Dawesen* (ahistorical essence *Para-Existenz*) as a counter-concept to *Dasein* (historical being). As the ahistorical realms of nature, aesthetic existence and the unconscious lie 'before, under and outside' historical factuality, they cannot be hermeneutically interpreted but only 'mantically deciphered'. Like his mathematical works, his aesthetic studies again treat of the ahistorical as a 'parontological' or 'hyperontological' phenomenon.

In his 'On the Logic of Modalities' (1930) he demonstrated that C. I. **Lewis**'s S3 System of 'strict implication' involved—besides Lewis' six modalities—numerous irreducible *complex* modalities. To achieve intuitive understanding, he added a postulate reducing *iterated* modalities, such that 'improper' modalities, resulting from iterated *negation* (~), reduce to two: 'p' and '~p', and 'proper' modalities, resulting from iterated *necessity* ($\square$) and *possibility* ($\Diamond$) reduce to 12. Adding a further postulate, he defined a system of six modalities. By translating A. **Heyting**'s connectives into Lewis's connectives, he gave a modal interpretation of intuitionistic logic and enabled others to find a modal meaning for all of Heyting's theorems. In his *Investigations on the Modal Calculus* (1952) he also created a deontic logical system parallel to modal logic.

Following his influential 'Eudoxos Studies' (1933 and 1936), his succession of mathematical-historical investigations led to his standard work, *The Foundation of Mathematics in its Historical Development* (1954), which covers the history of mathematics from its Egyptian and Babylonian origins to the modern schools of logicism, intuitionism and formalism. He died shortly after editing *On the History of Greek Mathematics* (1965).
Sources: J. E. Hofmann (1965) obituary, *PM* 7: 245; Mittelstrass; Leo, Zimny (1969) 'Oskar Becker-Bibliographie', *Kantstudien* 60: 319–30.

BARRY JONES

Beerling, Reinier Franciscus
Dutch. *b:* 7 April 1905, Gorinchem, The Netherlands. *d:* 29 November 1979, Leyden. *Cat:* Hegelian existentialist. *Ints:* Philosophy of culture and society. *Educ:* Philosophy, University of Amsterdam. *Infls:* Personal influences included Plessner and Pos; philosophical influences included Hegel, Nietzsche and Heidegger. *Appts:* Journalist; Professor of Philosophy, Batavia (Djakarta), 1946–

58; Professor of Social Philosophy and Philosophy of History, Leyden, 1958– 73.

Main publications:
(1935) *Antithesen* [Antitheses], Haarlem: Bohn.
(1938) *Crisis van den mensch* [Crisis of Man], Haarlem: Bohn.
(1945) *Moderne doodsproblematiek* [Modern Problems of Death], Delft: Delftsche Uitg. Mij.
(1949) *Onsocratische gesprekken* [Unsocratic Conversations], Amsterdam: Meulenhoff.
(1956) *Kratos. Mens en macht* [Kratos, Man and Power], Antwerp: Standaard.
(1964–5) *Wijsgerig-sociologische verkenningen* [Philosophical-sociological Investigations], Arnhem: Van Loghum Slaterus.
(1968) *Ideeën en idolen* [Ideas and Idols], Arnhem: Van Loghum Slaterus.
(1972) *Argumenten, sceptisch en anti-sceptisch* [Arguments, Sceptical and Anti-sceptical], Meppel: Boom.
(1979) *Niet te geloven* [Unbelievable], Deventer: Van Loghum Slaterus.

One of the main issues in Beerling's philosophy is the problem of death, not as the end of life, but as an essential part of it. From here a sense of finiteness and of scepticism results. Belief in God is no more than an anthropological fact negating the real *conditio humana*. From this imminent-human viewpoint Beerling analyses social phenomena like alienation, labour and power. He considers them all in a Hegelian-dialectical manner and sees ideology as a necessary tool to handle man's situation, although philosophy has to be very critical of it. Wisdom remains the necessary, but always unattainable, aim of philosophical reflection.

WIM VAN DOOREN

Belaünde, Victor Andrés
Colombian. *b:* 1883, Arequipa, Peru. *d:* 1966, New York. *Cat:* Political philosopher. *Ints:* Political philosophy. *Infls:* Bolivar. *Appts:* 1927–30, Member of the Groupement des Écoles, Paris; 1928–9, Miami University; 1930, Johns Hopkins University; 1931, Deputy in Constituent Assembly; 1957–8, Minister of External Relations; from 1959, Colombian delegate to the UN.

Main publications:
See his *Obras completas*, Lima: Comisión Nacional del Centenario Victor Andrés Belaünde, 1987–.
(1908) *El Peru antiguo y los modernos sociologos.*
(1917) *La vida universitaria.*

(1918) *El idealismo en la politica americana.*
(1931) *La realidad nacional* fifth edition, Lima: Tip. Santa Rosa, 1984.
(1932) *Meditaciones peruanas.*
(1938) *Bolivar y el pensamiento politico de la revolución hispanoamericana* (English translation, *Bolivar and the Political Thought of the Spanish-American Revolution*, New York: Octagon, 1978).

Secondary literature:
Libro jubilar de Victor Andrés Belaünde en su octogesimo anniversario, Lima: Pontifica Universidad Catolica del Peru/Mercurio peruano, 1963.

All of Belaünde's work could be said to be an elaboration of the general ideological panorama of the Bolivarian revolution and an analysis of the thought of Bolivar himself, who he constantly refers to as the 'Liberator'. His work is also a series of comparisons in the sense that he embarks upon studies of the main ideological currents of the eighteenth century and traces their repercussions in the rest of Latin America.

However, his work is by no means a celebration of the 'hero of the people' genre, rather a systematic and detailed analysis of the politico-philosophical background to Bolivar's thought. 'Bolivar embodies the programme of organic, hierarchical and technical democracy or monarchical reaction' (1978, p. x). To this end he elaborates the distinct elements of Bolivar's philosophy as being those of radical, demagogic propagandist, revolutionary leader and creator of strong unitarian government, foreign statesman, victor, statesman for internal democratizaton, together with an element of dictatorship necessary to preserve national unity. This 'democratic Caesarism' (ibid., p. xi) Belaünde places in the context of the conflict of a tradition of absolutism with the democratic ideal of the revolution. His work has been well received in the USA, inside of a certain radical tradition dedicated to reappraising the history of Latin America, and in France, where he was invited to lecture at the Sorbonne in 1927. Elsewhere, however, his writings have had little influence, and this is probably due in part to a certain 'cult of the individual' on Belaünde's part towards Bolivar, exemplified in phrases such as 'historical truth does not diminish his stature' (1938, p. xiii), and whom he treats as a 'vital hero, like Napoleon' (ibid.).

DAVID SPOONER

Bell, (Arthur) Clive (Heward)

British. *b:* 16 September 1881. *d:* 18 September 1964. *Cat:* Critic; writer; aesthetician. *Educ:* Trinity College Cambridge (Exhibitioner and Earl of Derby Student). *Infls:* Schopenhauer, G. E. Moore, Roger Fry, Walter Sickert, the Bloomsbury Group and Cézanne. *Appts:* Art critic, *New Statesman and Nation*, 1933–43.

Main publications:

(1914) *Art*, London: Chatto & Windus.
(1922) 'The creed of an aesthete', *New Republic* 25 (January): 241-2.
(1922) *Since Cézanne*, London: Chatto & Windus.
(1923) *On British Freedom*, London: Chatto & Windus.
(1928) *Civilization: An Essay*, London: Chatto & Windus; New York: Harcourt Brace.
(1928) *Proust*, London: Hogarth Press; New York: Harcourt Press.

Secondary literature:

Cooper, David (ed.) (1992) *A Companion to Aesthetics*, Oxford: Blackwell.
Elliott, R. K. (1965) 'Clive Bell's theory and his critical practice', *The British Journal of Aesthetics*, 2: 5: 111–122.
Meager, Ruby (1965) 'Clive Bell and aesthetic emotion', *The British Journal of Aesthetics*, 2, 5: 123–31.

Bell's most influential book, *Art* (1914), declared for the visual arts a formalist theory of the nature of art and aesthetic. He maintained that it is in virtue of possessing significant form, that is, 'lines and colours combined in a particular way', that a work qualifies as art and stirs emotions that are properly aesthetic. According to Bell, aesthetic emotion is a response to form, not to content: 'we need bring nothing with us from life ... nothing ... but a sense of form and colour and three-dimensional space'. At a metaphysical level he hypothesizes that formal significance is 'the significance of Reality'. The artist's emotion is an emotion felt for the ultimately real and the work of art springs from that emotion. Bell writes: 'Not what he saw but only what he felt will necessarily condition his design'.

The theory of significant form has been criticized on four main counts: first, for its circularity in defining both the aesthetic emotion and significant form in terms of each other; second, for oversimplification in that it nominates a single characteristic (significant form) as the defining property of a work of visual art; third, for its subjectivity in taking a feeling as a criterion of aesthetic significance; fourth, for the way in which its overriding formalism fails to recognize that there are works of art in which form and subject matter are fused. Bell's zestful and vivid writing guaranteed the discussability of his theory of significant form. It has exerted considerable influence on philosophical aesthetics in the twentieth century.

Sources: Herbert Read (1965) 'Clive Bell', *BJA* 5, 2: 107–10.

DIANÉ COLLINSON

Benhabib, Seyla

American. *b:* 9 September 1950, Istanbul. *Cat:* Social and political thinker in area of nineteenth- and twentieth-century continental philosophy; critical theorist; feminist theorist; philosopher of ethics. *Educ:* American College for Girls, Istanbul, 1966–70; Brandeis University, 1970–2; Yale University, 1972–7. *Infls:* Habermas. *Appts:* Lecturer, then Assistant Professor, Yale, 1976–9; Assistant Professor, Boston University, 1981–5; Associate Professor of Political Theory, Harvard, 1987–9; Associate Professor of Philosophy and Women's Studies, State University of New York, Stonybrook, 1989–91; Professor of Political Science and Philosophy, New School for Social Research, 1991–3; 1993–,Professor of Government, Harvard.

Main publications:

(1986) *Critique, Norm, and Utopia: A Study of the Foundations of Critical Theory*, New York: Columbia University Press.
(1987) (trans.) *Herbert Marcuse Hegel's Ontology and the Theory of Historicity*, Cambridge, Mass.: MIT Press.
(1987) (ed. with Drucilla Cornell) *Feminism as Critique: On the Politics of Gender*, Minneapolis: University of Minnesota Press.
(1990) (ed. with Fred Dallmyer) *The Communicative Ethics Controversy*, Cambridge, Mass.: MIT Press.
(1992) *Situating the Self: Gender, Community and Postmodernism in Contemporary Ethics*, Cambridge: Polity Press.
(1993) (ed.) *On Max Horkheimer: New Perspectives*, Studies in Contemporary Social Thought, Cambridge, Mass.: MIT Press.
(1995) (ed.) *Feminist Contentions*, New York: Routledge.

Benhabib is centrally concerned with a reconstruction of the normative foundations of critical theory. She argues that the critical theory of **Horkheimer**, **Marcuse** and **Adorno** has not sufficiently divorced itself from problematic ideas in Hegel and Marx, and she turns to **Habermas**'s communicative ethics as the model for her project. However, she criticizes the version of Kantian universalisation in Habermas's theory of practical discourse. Benhabib develops an alternative theory of communicative ethics based on the concrete relations of the members of a community which are built upon a system of norms that bring together friendship, care and solidarity.

The feminist element in her ideas emerges in her belief that we must reassess traditional moral theory. She calls for a normative ethic that integrates a contextual model of moral judgement (an ethic of care) with a universalizability requirement. Benhabib defends a reformulation of Enlightenment universalism that replaces its metaphysical presupposition of a 'disembedded autonomous male ego' with an interactive social moral subject, the 'situated self'.

Sources: Personal communication.

EMILY BRADY

Benjamin, Walter

German. **b:** 1892, Berlin. **d:** 1940, Port Bou, Franco-Spanish border. **Cat:** Marxist; cultural theorist; literary theorist. **Ints:** Art and society. **Educ:** Universities of Berlin, Freiburg, Munich and Bern. **Infls:** Goethe, Baudelaire, Marx, Lukács and Brecht. **Appts:** Benjamin held no formal academic position, working mainly as a freelance critic and translator, although he was associated with the Institute of Social Research at the University of Frankfurt (later relocated in New York).

Main publications:

(1928) *Der Ursprung des deutschen Trauerspiels*, (English translation, *The Origin of German Tragic Drama*, trans. John Osborne, London: NLB, 1977).

(1966) *Versuche über Brecht*, Frankfurt-am-Main: Suhrkamp Verlag (Englsih translation, *Understanding Brecht*, trans. Anna Bostock, London: NLB, 1973).

(1968) *Illuminations*, ed. Hannah Arendt, trans. Harry Zohn, New York: Harcourt, Brace & World.

(1969) *Charles Baudelaire: Ein Lyriker in Zeitalter des Hochkapitalismus*, ed. Rolf Tiedemann, Frankfurt: Suhrkamp Verlag (English translation, *Charles Baudelaire: A Lyric Poet in the Era of High Capitalism*, trans. Harry Zohn, London: NLB, 1973).

(1970) *Berliner Chronik*, Frankfurt: Suhrkamp Verlag.

(1979) *One-Way Street and Other Writings*, trans. Edmund Jephcott and Kingsley Shorter, London: NLB.

Secondary literature:
Benjamin, Andrew (ed.) (1989) *The Problems of Modernity: Adorno and Benjamin*, London: Routledge.

Bullock, Marcus Paul (1987) *Romanticism and Marxism: The Philosophical Development of Literary Theory and Literary History in Walter Benjamin and Friedrich Schlegel*, New York: Peter Lang.

Eagleton, Terry (1981) *Walter Benjamin*, London: Verso.

Jennings, Michael W. (1987) *Dialectical Images: Walter Benjamin's Theory of Literary Criticism*, Ithaca, NY, and London: Cornell University Press.

Nagele, Rainer (1988) *Benjamin's Ground: New Readings of Walter Benjamin*, Detroit: Wayne State University Press.

Smith, Gray (ed.) (1988) *On Walter Benjamin: Critical Essays and Recollections*, Cambridge, Mass.: MIT Press.

Benjamin was one of the first Marxist theorists to insist that art is a form of social production. A champion of the aesthetic theories of the playwright Bertolt Brecht ('epic theatre'), he argued that the artist should set out to challenge the audience's preconceptions about both art and politics.

STUART SIM

Bennett, Jonathan Francis

New Zealander. **b:** 17 February 1930, Greymouth, New Zealand. **Cat:** Analytical philosopher. **Ints:** History of modern philosophy; philosophy of language. **Educ:** University of New Zealand, MA 1952; Oxford, BPhil 1955. **Appts:** Lecturer, University of Cambridge; Professor, Simon Fraser University, University of British Columbia, Syracuse University.

Main publications:

(1964) *Rationality*, London: Routledge & Kegan Paul.

(1966) *Kant's Analytic*, Cambridge: Cambridge University Press.

(1971) *Locke, Berkeley, Hume: Central Themes*, Oxford.

(1974) *Kant's Dialectic*, Cambridge: Cambridge University Press.

(1976) *Linguistic Behaviour*, Cambridge: Cambridge University Press.

(1984) *A Study of Spinoza's Ethics*, Cambridge: Cambridge University Press.

(1988) *Events and their Names*, Cambridge: Cambridge University Press.

(1995) *The Act 'Itself'*, Oxford: Clarendon Press.

Secondary literature:

Cover, J. A. and Kulstad, M. (eds) (1990) Festschrift: *Central Themes in Early Modern Philosophy*, Indianapolis: Hackett (contains brief bibliography).

Bennett's historical studies are an extreme example of an analytical approach to past philosophy. Historical positions are taken as sets of discrete propositions to be assessed by current criteria with little regard to their context. **Rorty** writes of Bennett's 'conversations with the British Empiricists about phenomenalism', for example: 'we have a fulfillment of the natural desire to talk to people, some of whose ideas are quite like our own, in the hope of getting them to admit that we have gotten those ideas clearer, or in the hope of getting them clearer still in the course of the conversation' ('The historiography of philosophy: four genres', in R. Rorty, J. B. Schneewind and Q. Skinner (eds), *Philosophy in History*, Cambridge: Cambridge University Press, 1988, p. 52). Bennett's *Linguistic Behaviour* (1976) presents a detailed view of language as 'essentially a matter of systematic communicative behaviour' (p. ix). The later *Events and their Names* (1988) continues to exemplify his desire to 'analyse' what he sees as 'our' concepts—in this case 'our event concept' the aim being: 'just to describe how it works and how it relates to its neighbors ... to get the concept, of an event into perspective and to command a whole, clear view of what its strengths and weaknesses are' (p. 20). This typifies Bennett's philosophical approach.

RICHARD MASON

Berdyaev (also Berdiaev, etc.), Nikolai Aleksandrovich

Russian. *b:* 6 (18 N.S.) March 1874, Kiev. *d:* 24 March 1948, Clamart, Paris. *Cat:* Religious philosopher. *Educ:* Military Corps of Cadets, then studied Law at the University of Kiev without graduating; studied under Windelband at University of Heidelberg in 1903. *Infls:* Main influences include Böhme, Kant, Schelling, Schopenhauer, Nietzsche, Dostoevsky, Tolstoy, Fedorov, Solov'ev and Bulgakov. *Appts:* 1920–2, Professor of Philosophy, University of Moscow.

Main publications:

(1916) *Smysl tvorchestva: opyt opravdaniia cheloveka*, Moscow (English translation, *The Meaning of the Creative Act*, trans. Donald A. Lowrie, London: Victor Gollancz, 1955).

(1923) *Smysl istorii: opyt filosofii chelovecheskoi sud'by* Berlin (English translation, *The Meaning of History*, trans. George Reavey, London: Geoffrey Bles, 1936).

(1927–8) *Filosofiia svobodnogo dukha: problematika i apologiia khristianstva*, 2 vols, Paris (English translation, *Freedom and the Spirit*, Oliver Fielding Clarke, London: Geoffrey Bles, 1935).

(1931) *O naznachenii cheloveka: opyt paradoksal'noi etiki*, Paris (English translation, *The Destiny of Man*, trans. Natalie Duddington, London: Geoffrey Bles, 1937).

(1934) *Ya i mir ob'ektov: opyt filosofii odinochestva i obshcheniia*, Paris (English translation, *Solitude and Society*, trans. George Reavey, London: Geoffrey Bles, 1938).

(1938) *Dukh i real'nost': osnovy bogochelovecheskoi dukhovnosti*, Paris (English translation, *Spirit and Reality*, trans. George Reavey, London: Geoffrey Bles, 1939).

(1940) *O rabstve i svobode cheloveka: opyt personalisticheskoi filosofii*, Paris (English translation, *Slavery and Freedom*, trans. R. M. French, London: Geoffrey Bles, 1943).

(1947) *Opyt eskhatologicheskoi metafiziki: tvorchestvo i ob'ektivikatsiia*, Paris: YMCA Press (English translation, *The Beginning and the End*, trans. R. M. French, London: Geoffrey Bles, 1952).

(1949) *Samopoznanie: opyt filosofskoi avtobiografii*, Paris: YMCA Press (English translation, *Dream and Reality: An Essay in Autobiography*, Katharine Lampert, London: Geoffrey Bles, 1950).

Secondary literature:

Clarke, O. F. (1950) *Introduction to Berdyaev*, London: Geoffrey Bles.

Copleston, F. C. (1986) *Philosophy in Russia: From Herzen to Berdyaev*, Tunbridge Wells: Search Press; Notre Dame: University of Notre Dame Press, pp. 370–89.

Lossky, N. O. (1952) *History of Russian Philosophy* London: George Allen & Unwin, ch. 16.

Nucho, F. (1967) *Berdyaev's Philosophy: The Existential Paradox of Freedom and Necessity*, London: Victor Gollancz.

Zenkovsky, V. V. (1953) *A History of Russian Philosophy*, trans. George L. Kline, London: Routledge & Kegan Paul, vol. 2, pp. 760–80.

Born into a noble family, Berdyaev joined the social-democratic movement as a student, and was consequently expelled from the University of Kiev and exiled to Vologda. In company with other 'legal' Marxists of the 1890s, notably **Bulgakov**, S. L. **Frank** and **Struve**, he underwent an ideological and metaphysical crisis around the turn of the century. He embraced idealism and renounced socialism, at least in its existing secular forms; this change of mind and heart found expression in contributions to the collections *Problemy idealizma* [Problems of Idealism] (1902) and *Vekhi* [Landmarks] (1909). He was at this time a leading representative, along with D. S. Merezhkovsky (1865–1941), of the 'new religious consciousness'. Following the October Revolution, he was able to organize a 'Free Academy of Spiritual Culture' and teach at Moscow University; but he was expelled from Russia in 1922 along with many other non-Marxist scholars. He established a Religio-Philosophic Academy in Berlin, and in 1924 moved it to Paris, where he also founded the journal *Put'* [The Way] and directed the YMCA Press.

Despite its variety and approach, there are certain philosophical constants in Berdyaev's mature work, the most fundamental of which is a Kantian distinction between the phenomenal and the noumenal. Unlike Kant, Berdyaev held that noumenal reality, or the realm of the spirit, was knowable, through mystical experience, albeit inexpressible in the categories of human reason. This basic distinction between an evil, fallen world of nature and human society and a spiritual world of eternal values informs all Berdyaev's forays into concrete issues. It underpins his elevation of ethical creativity over passive obedience to society's moral laws as it also underpins his rejection of collectivist socialism, with its preoccupation with economics and disregard for individual freedom, in favour of a 'personalist' socialism or 'aristocracy of freedom' in which each individual ego is able to transcend society and achieve personality. It is only by reference to the meta-historical realm of spiritual values that Berdyaev can assign any meaning to human history; that is to say, the realization outside historical time of the kingdom of God.

One of the labels Berdyaev attached to his metaphysics was 'personalist'. What existed was spirit, the fallen, phenomenal world being an enslaving 'objectification' of spirit; but he rejected absolute idealism, regarding the highest form of reality as universal, self-creating personality (he rejected **Lossky**'s hierarchical personalist monadology). The assertion of freedom was the central concern of his writings. Freedom is given logical priority over existence, and, according to

Berdyaev, cannot be God's creation since it gives rise to evil; it is uncreated, and arises from the *Ungrund* (a notion derived from Böhme and Schelling), a mysterious potentiality for existence which is the necessary condition of God's creative act, the Nothing from which the world was created. In his later writings Berdyaev applied the terms 'existential' and 'existentialist' to his philosophy, although he regarded as pessimistic and degrading the accounts of human freedom in the works of **Heidegger** and **Sartre**.

Berdyaev has been the most widely read of the Russian religious philosophers, partly because of the intensely personal nature of his writings, and also because of their broad religious, ethical, social, political and historiosophical canvas. His unsystematic and inspirational approach and his aphoristic and avowedly paradoxical style have engendered disagreement about his philosophical credentials (see the constrasting judgements of contemporaries Lossky and **Zenkovsky**).

COLIN CHANT

Berger, Gaston

French. *b:* 1 October 1896, Saint-Louis, Senegal. *d:* 13 November 1960, Longjumeau, Seine-et-Oise, France. *Cat:* Phenomenologist. *Ints:* Philosophy of action; the analysis of character and personality; epistemology. *Educ:* Lycée de Marseille and University of Aix-en-Provence. *Infls:* Descartes, Kant, Edmund Husserl, Maurice Blondel and René Le Senne. *Appts:* 1926, Founder of the Société d'Études philosophique de Marseille; 1941–7, Professor of Philosophy, University of Aix-en-Provence; 1945, Founder of *Les Études philosophiques*; 1949, Secretary General of the Commission for French-American Cultural Exchange; 1953–60, Director General of L'Enseignement Supérieur; 1955–60, Professor of Philosophy, Académie des Sciences Morales; 1957, Founder of the Centre d'Études Prospectives and (1958) of the Journal *Prospective*; President of the Comité de l'*Encyclopédie française* (vol. XIX), and of the Société Française de Philosophie; Vice President of the Institut International de Philosophie; also Founder of the *Revue de l'Enseignement supérieur*, and President of the French delegation to Unesco.

Main publications:

(1941) *Le Cogito dans la philosophie de Husserl*, Paris: Aubier.

(1941) *Recherches sur les conditions de la connaissance. Essai d'une théorétique pure*, Paris: PUF.

(1950) *Traité pratique d'analyse du caractère*, Paris: PUF.
(1954) *Caractère et personnalité*, Paris: PUF.

Secondary literature:
Les Études philosophiques 4 (1961) and *Prospective* 7 (1961) are both devoted to Berger and his philosophy.

In the period 1926 to 1960 Berger established himself as one of the most prominent figures of French philosophy. He founded three important philosophical journals (*Les Études philosophiques*, *Revue de l'Enseignement supérieur* and *Prospective*), and was constantly active in organizing or directing many notable societies and institutions that promoted philosophy both nationally (for example, La Société d'Études Philosophiques de Marseille) and internationally (for example, L'Institut International de Philosophie). He was also a pioneer, in France, of the study of the philosophy of Edmund **Husserl**.

Berger's own philosophy was an original synthesis of ideas drawn from Husserl's phenomenology, Maurice **Blondel**'s philosophy of action and René **Le Senne**'s 'caractèrologie'. That he was prepared to posit the difficult concept of a universal or collective transcendental subject as the centre of all significant reference reflected his deep conviction that the role of philosophy in the modern world is one of reconciling diverse standpoints in order to achieve a better cultural and intellectual integration.
Sources: Huisman; EF.

STEPHEN MOLLER

Bergman, Samuel Hugo (also known as Hugo Bergmann)
Israeli. *b:* 25 December 1883, Prague. *d:* 18 June 1975, Jerusalem. *Cat:* Philosopher of religion and politics; translator; librarian; editor. *Ints:* Philosophy of science; philosopy of religion; politic philosophy; perception; epistemology; mysticism. *Educ:* 1900–06, studied Philosophy in Universities of Prague and Berlin. *Infls:* Significant personal influences inlcude Franz Kafka, Max Brod, Emil Utiz, Einstein, Bernard Bolzano, Franz Brentano, Edmund Husserl, Rudolf Steiner and Martin Buber. Philosophically, influenced by Kant and the neo-Kantian school of Hermann Cohen. Religiously he was influenced by Martin Buber, Franz Rosenzweig and Sri Aurobindo. *Appts:* Librarian, Prague University Library, 1907–19; first Director, the National and University Library, Jerusalem, 1920–35; Lecturer, Professor

of Philosophy, then first Rector, Hebrew University, Jersualem, 1928–38; founder and elected member of the executive of the *Histadrut ha-Ovedim* [Israeli Trade Union Party]; founder of journal, *Kiryat Sefer*, editor of the latter and of general philosophy for the *Encyclopaedia Hebraica*, and philosophical quarterly, *Iyyun*; member of Ha Po'el ha-Za'ir and Brit Shalom, left-wing peace organizations, becoming their main spokesman; headed the Jewish delegation from Palestine to the Pan-Asiatic Conference, New Delhi, 1947; awarded Israel Prize for Humanities for his work on logic, *Mavo le-Torat ha-Higgayon* (*Introduction to Logic*, 1953).

Main publications:
(1929) *Der Kampf um das Kausalgesetz in der jüngsten Physik* [The Struggle for the Law of Causality in Early Physics], Braunschweig, (Brunswick): F. Vieweg.
(1940) *Introduction to the Theory of Knowledge* (Hebrew), Jerusalem: Hebrew University.
(1953) *Introduction to Logic* (Hebrew), Jerusalem.
(1961) *Faith and Reason: An Introduction to Modern Jewish Thought*; trans. A. Jospé, New York: Bnai Brith, and Schocken Books, 1963.
(1964) *Schelling on the Source of Eternal Truths*, Jerusalem: Magnes Press.
(1964–5) *Ha-Filosofiah ha-Dialogit mi-Kirkagor ad Buber*, Jerusalem: Akadamon (English translation, *Dialogical Philosophy from Kierkegaard to Buber*, trans. A. A. Gerstein, Albany: SUNY, 1991).
(1967) *Philosophy of Solomon Maimon*, trans. N. J. Jacobs, Jerusalem: Magnes Press.
(1970) *A History of Modern Philosophy from Nicolas Cusanus to the Age of Enlightenment*, Jerusalem, Mosad Bialik.
(1970) *The Quality of Faith: Essays on Judaism and Morality*, trans. Y. Hanegbi, Jerusalem: Youth and Hechalutz Department of World Zionist Organization.
(1983) *Fichte, Johann Gottlieb, 1762–1814* (Hebrew), Jerusalem: Magnes Press.
(1985) *Diaries and Letters*, 2 vols, Königstein: Jüdischer Verlag bei Athenäum.

Secondary literature:
Klüback, W. (1992) *Courageous Universality*, Atlanta, Georgia: Scholars Press: Brown Judiac Studies, no. 245.

Bergman was an ardent Zionist, who espoused peaceful coexistence with the Arabs, as well as being one of the early pioneers of modern Israeli philosophy. As a student he was influenced by anti-Kantian Christian philosophy as well as by

Edmund **Husserl** and Rudolph **Steiner**. Later influences included Kant and the neo-Kantanians, especially Hermann **Cohen** and Ernst **Cassirer**. In his religious philosophy he utilized aspects of Indian and Christian teachings, as well as the anthropomorphic ideas of Steiner. Like Martin **Buber** he saw faith as direct, lived experience, which he called 'dialogic'. His works on the history of philosophy, and his translations into Hebrew of Solomon Maimon, Kant and **Husserl**, have proved of great value and influence.
Sources: EncJud; NUC; Schoeps.

IRENE LANCASTER

Bergmann, Gustav

Austrian-American. **b:** 4 May 1906, Vienna. **d:** 21 April 1987, Iowa City. **Cat:** Ontologist; philosopher of psychology; philosopher of the natural sciences. **Ints:** Philosophy of language. **Educ:** University of Vienna, PhD in mathematics, 1928, law degree, 1935. **Infls:** Vienna Circle, Moore, Russell and Wittgenstein. **Appts:** 1940–77, Instructor-Professor, University of Iowa.

Main publications:

(1954) *The Metaphysics of Logical Positivism*, New York: Longmans, Green & Co.; second edition, Madison: University of Wisconsin Press, 1967.

(1957) *Philosophy of Science*, Madison: University of Wisconsin Press (Spanish translation, *Filosofia de la Ciencia*, Madrid: Tecnos, 1961).

(1959) *Meaning and Existence*, Madison: University of Wisconsin Press.

(1964) *Logic and Reality*, Madison: University of Wisconsin Press.

(1967) *Realism: A Critique of Brentano and Meinong*, Madison: University of Wisconsin Press.

(1992) *New Foundations of Ontology*, ed. William Heald, Madison: University of Wisconsin Press.

Secondary literature:

Gram, M. S. and Klemke, E. D. (eds) (1974) *The Ontological Turn*, Iowa City: University of Iowa Press.

Grossmann, R. (1983) *The Categorial Structure of the World*, Bloomington: Indiana University Press.

Hochberg, H. (1984) *Logic, Ontology, and Language*, Munich and Vienna:Philosophia.

Peterson, J. (1976) *Realism and Logical Atomism*, Mobile: University of Alabama Press.

Bergmann was an ideal-language ontologist. He tried to construct a formalism which could support an analytic—synthetic distinction and into which natural-language statements could be translated. Bergmann was not a mere formalist: the formalism had to be interpreted, its signs anchored in extra-linguistic entities, and the anchoring had to accord with a principle of acquaintance.

The ideal-language method, originating with **Russell** and **Frege**, was brilliantly used and celebrated by the early **Wittgenstein**. By the late 1930s it was under attack however, largely because Wittgenstein himself had come to spurn it. By the late 1940s, Bergmann was the leading proponent of the method, defending it, for example, against the attacks by ordinary-language philosophers, those who thought that the later Wittgenstein had made it safe again to do ontology on the basis of the grammar of ordinary language.

Although trained in mathematics, a member of the Vienna Circle and a prominent apologist for behaviourist psychology, Bergmann never took science as a guide to ontology. He had, indeed, no patience for materialism: direct or immediate experience testified to the *existence* of the mental. The problem was to locate talk of the mental in the formalism such that the intentionality or aboutness of thoughts is reflected, consistent with an analytic—synthetic distinction.

Bergmann also had no patience for nominalism. He attacked it frequently. In the early years of his career, his objections rested mainly on formal considerations. In later years, he became preoccupied with issues having to do with acquaintance. As a result, he began to worry about how words like *universal* and *particular* relate to extra-linguistic entities. Suddenly he was rethinking the nature and limits of ontology.

Bergmann's last work, the posthumous *New Foundations*, shows him struggling to the end to design 'the' ideal language. The work is adventuresome, the formalism novel, but neither the mental nor universals are forsaken.

E. B. ALLAIRE

Bergson, Henri-Louis

French. **b:** 18 October 1859, Paris. **d:** 3 or 4 January 1941, Paris. **Cat:** Metaphysician; process philosopher. **Ints:** Evolution. **Educ:** Studied at École Normale, Paris, graduating in 1881, and taking his doctorate in 1889. **Infls:** Zeno of Elea, Plato, Aristotle, Plotinus, Oriental and Christian mystics, Descartes, Spinoza, Leibniz, Berkeley, Hume, Kant, Claude Bernard, Lachelier, Ravaisson, Spencer, Darwin and Einstein. (See also R. Berthelot, 1913.). **Appts:** Taught at Anger, 1881–3, Clermont-Ferrand, 1883–7, and Paris; Professor, Collège de France, in 1900; main works placed on Vatican's Index, 1914; Nobel Prize for Literature, 1927.

Main publications:

(1889) *Essai sur les données immédiates de la perception*, Paris: Alcan (English translation, *Time and Free Will*, trans. F. L. Pogson, London: Allen & Unwin, 1910).

(1896) *Matière et mémoire*, Paris: Alcan (English translation, *Matter and Memory*, trans. N. M. Paul and W. S. Palmer, London: Allen & Unwin, 1911).

(1900) *Le Rire*, Paris: Alcan (English translation, *Laughter*, trans. C. Brereton and F. Rothwell, London: Macmillan, 1911).

(1903) 'Introduction à la métaphysique', *Revue de Métaphysique et de Morale*, 29 January (see 1912, 1934 for translations).

(1907) *L'Evolution créatrice*, Paris: Alcan (English translation, *Creative Evolution*, A. Mitchell, London: Macmillan, 1911).

(1912) *Introduction to Metaphysics*, New York: Putnam's Sons (trans. by T. E. Hulme of 1903).

(1919) *L'Energie spirituelle: Essais et conférences*, Paris: Alcan (English translation, *Mind-Energy*, trans. H. W. Carr, London: Macmillan, 1920).

(1922) *Dureé et simultanéité: A propos de la théorie d'Einstein*, Paris: Alcan (English translation, *Duration and Simultaneity*, trans. with an introduction by H. Dingle, Indianapolis: Bobbs-Merrill, 1965).

(1932) *Les Deux Sources de la morale et de la réligion*, Paris: Alcan (English translation, *The Two Sources of Morality and Religion*, trans. R. A. Audra and C. Brereton with the assistance of W. H. Carter, London: Macmillan, 1935).

(1934) *La Pensée et le mouvant: Essais et conférences*, Paris: Alcan (English translation, *The Creative Mind*, trans. M. L. Andison, New York: Philosophy Library, 1946).

Collected editions:
(1959) *Oeuvres*, Paris: PUF.
(1972) *Mélanges*, Paris: PUF (includes 1922, which is not in 1959).

Secondary literature:

Barlow, M. (1966) *Henri Bergson*, Paris: Editions universitaires (brief biography linking life and works).

Berthelot, R. (1938) *Un Romantisme utilitaire*, troisième partie, Paris: Alcan (thorough but hostile).

Čapek, M. (1971) *Bergson and Modern Physics*, Dordrecht: Reidel (full, scholarly and largely sympathetic account, seeing Bergson against the intellectual background).

Gunter, P. A. Y. (ed. and trans.) (1969) *Bergson and the Evolution of Physics*, Knoxville, Tenn.: Tennessee University Press (reactions to Bergson by modern physicists and others; often technical).

——(1986) *Henri Bergson: A Bibliography*, Bowling Green, Ohio: Philosophy Documentation Centre (revised edition of 1984 original).

Hanna, T. (ed.) (1962) *The Bergsonian Heritage*, New York: Columbia Univeristy Press.

Husson, L. (1947) *L'Intellectualisme de Bergson*, Paris: PUF (claims Bergson is not anti-intellectualist).

Jankélévitch, V. (1959) *Henri Bergson*, Paris: PUF (much revised version of 1931 original).

Kolakowski, L. (1985) *Bergson*, Oxford: Oxford University Press (brief introduction).

Lacey, A. R. (1989) *Bergson*, London: Routledge (attempts down-to-earth assessment of Bergson's actual arguments, although it has been accused of not bringing out his importance).

Les Études bergsoniennes (1948–76) (periodical in eleven volumes).

Mossé-Bastide, R.-M. (1955) *Bergson éducateur*, Paris: PUF.

Papanicolaou, A. C. and Gunter, P. A. Y. (eds) (1987) *Bergson and Modern Thought*, Chur, Swit.: Harwood Academic Publishers (essays tending to stress anticipations of modern physics and pyschology, and also parapsychology).

Russell, B. (1914) *The Philosophy of Bergson*, Cambridge: Bowes & Bowes (includes H. W. Carr's reply and Russell's further reply).

One of the most striking things about Bergson is perhaps the extraordinary width of his cultural attainments. At 17 he won an open prize for an original solution to a mathematical problem, and in the same year solved a problem Pascal claimed to have solved but left unpublished (1972, pp. 247–55). His graduation thesis (in Latin) was on Aristotle's theory of place and he wrote a short commentary on Lucretius (both reprinted in *Mélanges*, 1972); and he lectured on Plato, Aristotle and Plotinus, among other things. He made a thorough study of the technical literature on the role of the brain in connection with aphasia (1972, p. 1209), quoted detailed scientific evidence when discussing evolution, and in later years took on **Einstein** in public debate on certain paradoxical implications of relativity theory—a debate he is generally regarded as having lost, but several of the leading physicists of the century have devoted articles to his work (see Gunter 1969); Papanicolaou and Gunter 1987).

Bergson is among the regrettably few great stylists in philosophy. His ideas are often intricate and difficult, but his exposition of them ranks with those of **Russell**, Berkeley, the early Plato and his cordial admirer William **James**, and this feature survives in the English translations (all the non-posthumous ones having his imprimatur, as he was bilingual because of his English mother). 'There is nothing in philosophy which could not be said in everyday language', he told an interviewer (1972, p. 939). Like Russell he tried to combine philosophy with action: 'one should act like a man of thought and think like a man of action', as he told a Danish congress in 1937 (1972, p. 1579). In 1917 he helped to bring America into the war, visiting for that purpose, and later helped to set up the educational side of the League of Nations, believing that education and mutual understanding would prevent war. For his last seventeen years he endured crippling arthritis. Fiercely patriotic, he died at the darkest moment of French history, of bronchitis possibly caused by several hours' standing in freezing conditions to register as a Jew, refusing, it is said, to desert his fellow Jews by accepting a presumably face-saving exemption offered by the authorities (he refused for the same reason to join the Catholic Church, to which he had by then became spiritually converted).

Bergson is often regarded as a rather unrigorous, if not hopelessly high-flown, thinker. His sympathy with mysticism, especially in his later writings (see 1932), such rather cloudy notions as the *élan vital* (1907), and his often rather lyrical and picturesque style, do give some countenance to this. The success of style meant that his prewar lectures became so crowded (a photograph shows people straining to listen through the open windows) that they were nearly moved to the Opera. But all this is only one feature of a complex whole, and is far removed from his actual intentions. Twenty years before his book on morality (1932) he explained his silence on that topic by saying he could not there reach results 'as demonstrable or as "presentable" [*montrables*]' as in his other works, adding that philosophy could 'claim an objectivity as great as that of the positive sciences, although of another nature' (1972, p. 964). Not only did he appeal to detailed scientific evidence when relevant, but he reached his main philosophical positions by starting not, as was commonly thought, from the intuitive data of lived experience but by reflecting on the treatment of time by science and mathematics. Like William James, with whose 'stream of consciousness' his own philosophy had so much in common, he insisted on the importance of introspective psychology; but whereas for James it was a

starting-point, for himself it was a point of arrival: for all the similarities of their philosophies, he said, he and James had reached them quite independently (1972, pp. 656–61; 1959, pp. 1541–3): Bergson was rather suspicious of claims to see philosophical influences' (1972, p. 1480). His 1889 work, with its title and its opening chapter on the nature of experience, might seem to belie this; but the latter, at least, although it does of course represent his own view, was added for strategical reasons connected with getting a doctorate (1959, p. 1542).

In the same important autobiographical fragment (ibid., pp. 1541–3), written in 1922, Bergson tells how in his youth he was confronted by two opposing currents of opinion, Kantian orthodoxy and Spencerian evolutionism. He preferred **Spencer** because of the 'concrete character of his mind' and his desire to keep always to the domain of facts. He has often been regarded as anti-intellectualist because of his emphasis on intuition, a faculty which evolved from instinct (and is first treated in 1903). (On the anti-intellectualism charge see Husson 1947.) Although he later abandoned Spencer (because his science was inadequate), and does indeed give pride of place to intuition as the highest human faculty, it is not at the expense of intellect in its own sphere, that of science and mathematics, which he never abandoned. The 'intuition of duration' is indeed the linchpin of Bergson's philosophy (1972, p. 1148), but intuition in general is 'instinct that has become disinterested, self-conscious, capable of reflecting upon its object and of enlarging it indefinitely' (1907, translation, p. 187). It is certainly not a substitute for hard work (1934, translation, p. 103. But Bergsons' treatment of intuition does seem to involve some confusions. Sometimes it seems to mean the getting of bright ideas, which both presupposes and involves intellectual hard work. But it is also a faculty which diverges from intellect, partly by apprehending duration as something essentially unified and continuous (and the qualitative aspects of our experiences in general) and partly as apprehending ineffable metaphysical reality, culminating in mysticism: here intuition is the method of philosophy as intellect is of science and mathematics—but does he distinguish philosophy as an intellectual study *about* intuition? Bergson's most lasting influence has certainly lain in his distinction between time as indivisible, qualitatively heterogeneous and known to experience (duration) and time as divisible, qualitatively homogeneous, and studied by science, which treats it as analogous to space; though from *Matière et*

mémoire (1896) on, both belong in the world itself. He solves Zeno's Achilles paradox by similarly distinguishing Achilles' indivisible motion from the divisible trajectory it covers, a solution which, along with his asymmetrical treatment of time and space, has been much criticized. Not only have these views on time been generally (though not undisputedly) taken to have influenced Proust and many other literary figures (see, for example, Delattre in *Les Études bergsoniennes*, 1948–76, vol. 1), but here and in his 'process philosophy' approach to substance (1896) and his views on determinism (1889) and on the influence of consciousness (1896) he is sometimes claimed to have anticipated features of relativity theory, microindeterminacy and modern scientific theories of the mind (see, for example, Papanicolaou and Gunter 1987).
Sources: Passmore 1957.

A. R. LACEY

Berkovits, Eliezer
American Jew. *b:* 8 September 1908, Oradea, Nagyvarad, Hungarian Transylvania, now Romania. *d:* 25 August 1992, Jerusalem. *Cat:* Philosopher of religion; Orthodox rabbi. *Ints:* Orthodox Jewish philosophical response to non-Orthodox Jewish and anti-Jewish philosophies; Holocaust philosophy; philosophy of *halakhah* (Jewish Law). *Educ:* Ordained, Hildesheimer Rabbinical Seminary, 1934. *Appts:* Rabbi, Berlin, 1934–8; Leeds, 1940–6; Sydney, 1946–50; Boston, 1950–8; Chairman, Department of Jewish Philosophy, Hebrew Theological College, Chicago, 1958–75; emigrated to Israel, 1975.

Main publications:
(1943) *Towards a Historic Judaism*, Oxford: East and West Library.
(1956) *Judaism: Fossil or Ferment*, New York: Philosophical Library.
(1959) *God, Man and History: a Jewish Interpretation*, New York: Jonathan David.
(1962) *Jewish Critique of Martin Buber*, New York: Yeshiva University.
(1969) *Man and God: Studies in Biblical Theology*, Detroit: Wayne State University Press.
(1973) *Faith after the Holocaust*, New York: Ktav (Hebrew translation, Jerusalem, 1987).
(1974) *Major Themes in Modern Philosophies of Judaism*, New York: Ktav.
(1975) *Crisis and Faith*, New York: Sanhedrin Press.
(1979) *With God in Hell*, New York: Sanhedrin Press.
(1983) *Not in Heaven: The Nature and Function of Halakha*, New York: Ktav.

(1990) *The Jewish Woman in Time and Torah*, New York: Ktav.

Secondary literature:
Raffel, C. M. (1993) 'Eliezer Berkovits', in *Interpreters of Judaism in the Late Twentieth Century*, ed. S. T. Katz, Washington, DC: Bnai Brith, pp. 1–15.

In his writings Berkovits contrasts secular Zionism with Jewish religious tradition. He examines the non-Jewish origins of much of Martin **Buber**'s work, as well as defending Judaism against those he considered as unsympathetic, such as Arnold **Toynbee**. His *Faith After the Holocaust* (1973) has been particularly influential, especially among exponents of the Modern Jewish Orthodox position. The fact that much of his work was translated into Hebrew in the last two decades of the twentieth century, and that he has become the subject of PhD theses, confirms Berkovits's importance as a major Holocaust thinker. His concerns with the role of women within the religious tradition and his desire to interpret the *halakhah*, or practice of Jewish Law, generally in a flexible manner have influenced major late twentieth-century thinkers, such as Rabbis Irving Greenberg and David Hartman.
Sources: EncJud, 4, pp. 633–4; NUC; WW(Am).

IRENE LANCASTER

Berlin, (Sir) Isaiah
British (emigrated to England, 1920). *b:* 9 June 1909, Riga, Latvia. *Cat:* Political philosopher; historian of ideas. *Educ:* Corpus Christi College, Oxford. *Infls:* Personal background and 'Oxford Realism'. *Appts:* 1932–8 and 1950–66, Fellow of New College Oxford; 1942–6, First Secretary, British Embassy, Washington; 1945–6, First Secretary, British Embassy, Moscow; 1957–67, Chichele Professor of Social and Political Theory and Fellow, All Souls College, Oxford; 1957, knighted; 1966–75, President of All Souls College, Oxford; 1971, Order of Merit; 1975–, Honorary Fellow, All Souls College, Oxford. Berlin held many visiting appointments in the USA and has received many honorary degrees.

Main publications:
(1948) *Karl Marx: His Life and Environment*, London: Butterworth.
(1953) *Historical Inevitability*, London: Oxford University Press, reprinted in 1969.
(1958) *Two Concepts of Liberty*, Oxford: Clarendon Press; reprinted in 1969.

(1969) *Four Essays on Liberty*, London & New York: Oxford University Press.

(1974) *The Divorce between the Sciences and the Humanities*; reprinted in 1979.

(1976) *Vico and Herder: Two Studies in the History of Ideas*, London: Hogarth Press; New York: Viking Press.

(1978) *Russian Thinkers*, ed. Henry Hardy, London: Hogarth Press; New York: Viking Press.

(1979) *Concepts and Categories: Philosophical Essays*, ed. Henry Hardy, London: Hogarth Press; New York: Viking Press.

(1980) *Against the Current: Essays in the History of Ideas*, ed. Henry Hardy, London: Hogarth Press; New York: Viking Press.

(1991) *The Crooked Timber of Humanity, Chapters in the History of Human Ideas*, London: Fontana.

(1993) *The Magus of the North, J. G. Hamann and the Origins of Modern Irrationalism*, London: Murray.

Secondary literature:
Cohen, M. (1960) 'Berlin and the liberal tradition', *Philosophical Quarterly* 10: 216-27.

Ryan, Alan (ed.) (1979) *In the Idea of Freedom: Essays in Honor of Isaiah Berlin*, Oxford and New York: Oxford University Press.

Trained in the analytic tradition, Berlin is well known for his *Four Essays on Liberty* (1969), in which he distinguished between 'negative liberty'—absence of external constraint, which can be combined with slavery to irrational desires—and 'positive liberty', in which self-mastery is achieved. Berlin attacked the 'despotic vision' behind the utopian hankering after 'positive liberty'. His own thought is permeated by a deep commitment to 'pluralism' and an intense dislike of monistic systems.

Although he joined in the rebellion against idealism in the 1930s and was a colleague of A. J. **Ayer**, Berlin was not at all attracted by positivism and opposed it in his *Concepts and Categories* (1979). His dislike of scientism and his belief in the *sui generis* character of historical understanding made him sympathetic to such anti-Enlightenment figures as Vico and Herder. Amongst his important contributions to the history of philosophy was his work on these two neglected figures. Berlin is perhaps best known for his lectures, in which, with great erudition and broad humanity, he has impressed his audiences with the richness and variety of Europe's philosophical heritage.

Sources: Henry Hardy (ed.) (1981) *Personal Impressions*, London: Hogarth Press and New York: Viking

Press; Ramin Jahanbegloo (1992) *Conversations with Isaiah Berlin*, London: Halban; Turner.

STUART BROWN

Bernstein, Eduard

German. *b:* 1850, Berlin. *d:* 1932. *Cat:* Marxist. *Infls:* Marx and Engels. *Appts:* Bank clerk; Editor of *Der Sozialdemokrat*; writer and journalist.

Main publications:
(1887) *Die Chartisten-Bewegung in England*, Zurich.

(1899) *Die Voraussetzungen des Sozialismus und die Aufgaben der Sozialdemokratie* (English translation, *Evolutionary Socialism*, trans. Edith C. Harvey, London, 1909; reissued, New York, 1963).

(1907–10) *Geschichte der Berliner Arbeiterbewegung*, 3 vols, ed. H. Weber, Berlin: Buchh. Vorwärtse.

(1908) *Sozialismus und Demokratie in der Grossen englischen Revolution*, Stuttgart (English translation, *Cromwell and Communism: Socialism and Democracy in the Great English Revolution*, London, 1930).

Secondary literature:
Gay, Peter (1952) *The Dilemma of Democratic Socialism*, Columbia University Press.

Hulse, James W. (1970) *Revolutionists in London*, Oxford: Clarendon Press.

Kolakowski, Leszek (1978) *Main Currents in Marxism*, vol. 2, Oxford: Oxford University Press.

Laidler, Harry W. (1968) *History of Socialism*, London: Routledge & Kegan Paul.

The son of a railway engineer, Bernstein converted to Marxism in 1878. From 1881 to 1900, he edited the official SDAP (later SPD) newspaper, first from Zurich, then London, where he became a close friend of Engels. In 1891 he drafted with **Kautsky** the Erfurt Programme, founding document of the SPD. With his *Die Voraussetzungen des Sozialismus* of 1899, he became the leading exponent of Marxist revisionism. For most of the First World War, Bernstein, a member of the Reichstag since 1902, was in the minority anti-war faction of the SPD. By 1918, his view that Germany should admit to war guilt, and his severe criticisms of the Bolsheviks, left him an isolated figure, and he remained on the fringes of the Marxist movement for the rest of his life.

A prolific writer, Bernstein is now chiefly remembered for his *Evolutionary Socialism* (1899), whose central claim was that Marx's predictions had largely turned out false. The crises of capitalism were not getting worse; the proletariat was becoming richer not poorer; class divisions were becoming more blurred not more acute; there *was* concentration of capital, but it proceeded very unevenly, and in agriculture hardly at all; bourgeois privileges were not immovable, but instead were being eroded piecemeal and peacefully. Capitalism, in short, was not about to collapse, and the workers had much more to lose than their chains. The socialist moral of this was the importance of continuing with piecemeal reform, and of accepting compromises and alliances with non-socialist parties. In what turned out to be a highly provocative formulation, Bernstein declared: 'Unable to believe in finalities at all, I cannot believe in a final aim to socialism. But I strongly believe in the socialist movement, in the march forward of the working class.' (Preface, *Evolutionary Socialism*, 1909).

In spite of these differences from the prevailing Marxist orthodoxy, Bernstein claimed that his position was still substantively Marxist by distinguishing between the basic principles of Marxism (which he accepted) and specific applications of them by Marx and Engels (which he disputed). Although Bernstein's account of the tasks for socialists matched the actual practice of the SPD, it differed considerably from SPD theory, which still proclaimed the need for a violent overthrow of the capitalist state and its replacement by the dictatorship of the proletariat. Accordingly, he was vigorously attacked by other Marxists such as Kautsky and **Luxemburg**. Bernstein was not a significant contributor to the *theories* of Marxism. Rather, his importance lies in the fact that he provided the first serious attempt to address the tactical implications of the failure of Marx's predictions about the collapse of capitalism.

Sources: T. Bottomore (ed.) (1983) *A Dictionary of Marxist Thought*, Oxford: Blackwell.

NICHOLAS EVERITT

Bertalanffy, Ludwig von

Austrian. *b:* 1901, near Vienna. *d:* 12 June 1972, Buffalo, New York. *Cat:* Philosopher of biology; general systems theorist. *Ints:* Organisms; medicine; culture. *Educ:* Universities of Innsbruck and Vienna. *Infls:* Literary influences: Leibniz, W. Köhler and Jakob von Uexküll. Personal: A. Rapport and Ervin Laszlo. *Appts:* 1934–48, Dozent, then Professor of Biology, University of Vienna; 1949–54, Professor and Director of Biological Research, University of Ottawa; 1955–8, Director of Biological Research, Mount Sinai Hospital; 1961–8, Professor of Theoretical Biology, University of Alberta.

Main publications:

(1928) *Kritische Theorie der Formbildung*, Berlin: Gebrüder Bomtraeger (English translation, *Modern Theories of Development*, trans. J. H. Woodger, Oxford: Oxford University Press, 1933).

(1932) *Theoretische Biologie*, 2 vols, Berlin: Gebrüder Bomtraeger; revised edition, Bern: Francke, 1951 (English translation, *Problems of Life: An Evaluation of Modern Biological Thought*, New York: J. Wiley, 1952).

(1968) *General Systems Theory*, New York: Braziller.

Secondary literature:

Hempel, Carl G. 1951) 'General system theory and the unity of science', *Human Biology* 23: 313–27.

Laszlo, E. (1972) *Introduction to Systems Philosophy*, New York: Gordon & Breach.

Bertalanffy was a theoretical biologist of international reputation. His researches in medicine led him, by 1926, to repudiate both mechanistic and vitalistic views of life and to develop an 'organismic' conception giving scientific meaning to the idea of 'organic wholeness' in terms of a 'dynamic morphology', an 'interpretation of organic forms as the result of an ordered flow of processes' (*Problems of Life* 1952, pp. 185–6). Thus he conceived the organism as a self-regulating 'open system', one which varies its structure and activity relevantly to a constant and overruling pattern of organization.

Bertalanffy subsequently universalized the 'organismic' conception into a 'general systems theory', envisaged both as a 'new realm of science' whose subject matter is the formulation and derivation of those principles which hold for systems in general, and as a comprehensive semantic system including all the various sciences (1968, 139ff.). While Bertalanffy's contributions to philosophical biology were considerable, his programme for the systematic unity of science remains unrealized—and perhaps unrealizable—ideal.

Sources: Edwards; DAS.

STEPHEN MOLLER

Beth, Evert Willem

Dutch. *b:* 7 July 1908, Almelo. *d:* 12 April 1964, Amsterdam. *Cat:* Logician; semanticist; historico-critical philosopher. *Educ:* Universities of Utrecht, Leyden and Brussels. *Infls:* Neo-Kantianism; significist psycholinguistics; set theory; model theory. *Appts:* 1935–45, teacher of mathematics in various schools; 1946, Chair of Logic and its History and the Philosophy of the Exact Sciences,

Amsterdam; Founder of the Institute for Foundations Research and Philosophy of the Exact Sciences.

Main publications:
(1959) *The Foundations of Mathematics: A Study in the Philosophy of Science*, Amsterdam: North Holland Publishing Co.
(1962) *Formal Methods: An Introduction to Symbolic Logic and the Study of Effective Operations in Arithmetic and Logic*, Dordrecht: D. Reidel.
(1965) *Mathematical Thought: An Introduction to the Philosophy of Mathematics*, Dordrecht: D. Reidel.
(1966) (with Jean Piaget) *Mathematical Epistemology and Psychology*, Dordrecht: D. Reidel.
(1968) *Science, a Road to Wisdom*, Dordrecht: D. Reidel
(1970) *Aspects of Modern Logic*, Dordrecht: D. Reidel.

Secondary literature:
Barth, E. M. (1985) 'In the service of human society: formal, informal or anti-logical? The philosophy of the logician Evert Willem Beth', *Informal Logic* XII: 1–10.
Destouches, J. L. (ed.) (1967) *E. W. Beth Memorial Colloquium: Logic and the Functions of Science*, Dordrecht: Reidel.
Heyting, A. (1966) '*In memoriam* Evert Willem Beth', *Notre Dame Journal of Formal Logic* VII: 289–95.
Van Fraassen, B. (1970) 'On the extension of Beth's semantics of physical theories', *Philosophy of Science* 37: 325–34.

Events in occupied Holland in the Second World War generated in Beth an enduring concern to counter the effects of irrational forms of thought. He worked intensively in logic, the foundations of mathematics and theoretical philosophy, dividing his attention between the history of these topics and contemporary theories. Beth's rejection of the logical positivist view that some statements are simply meaningless led him to historical investigations and the identification of an invalid principle, which he called the Principle of the Absolute, in Aristotle's methodology of science and philosophy. He linked the Locke–Berkeley problem concerning general (absolute) terms to pre-Fregean theories of quantification.

From his experiences during the war, and through contacts with Alfred **Tarski** and others, Beth developed a completely new and fundamental orientation in which formal and mathematical logic are supported by a semantical methodology. He now introduced into Dutch philosophy the

category Falsity, on a par with the category Truth, treating the search for counterexamples and countermodels as the core method of logical thought. This method of Semantical Tableaux defines logical validity as the impossibility of ever finding or construing a countermodel to the pair *given class of premises; expected or desired conclusion*. For a two-valued semantics this means that one can speak of a deduction as being valid on logical grounds only if it is impossible to find a model (of the sentences involved) with respect to which all the premises are true whereas the expected/desired conclusion is false. On this account the definitions of logical particles are given as rules for the systematic search for countermodels. Beth applied this semantical method widely: to modal logic, intuitionist mathematics, the theory of definition ('Beth's Theorem'), the history of philosophy, and the foundations of the physical sciences. Beth's influence has been considerable. He wrote 26 books and over 160 articles and papers. His method of Semantical Tableaux is now standard.
Sources: Personal acquaintance.

E. M. BARTH

Bierens de Haan, Johannes Diderik
Dutch. *b:* 14 October 1866, Amsterdam. *d:* 17 September 1943, Haarlem. *Cat:* Spinozist idealist. *Ints:* Philosophy of culture; philosophy of ethics. *Educ:* Theology, University of Utrecht; thesis on the significance of Shaftesbury in the context of English ethics. *Infls:* Personal influences included Van der Wyck, and Van den Bergh van Eysinga; philosophical influences included Plato, Spinoza and Hegel. *Appts:* Minister of the Dutch Reformed Church, 1881–1906, and after 1906 free publicist.

Main publications:
(1891) *De beteekenis van Shaftesbury in de Engelsche ethiek* [The Significance of Shaftesbury within English Ethics], Utrecht: Beyers (dissertation).
(1898) *Idee-studies* [Idea Studies], Amsterdam: Van Looy.
(1900) *Levensleer naar de beginselen van Spinoza* [Moral Conviction According to the Principles of Spinoza], 's-Gravenhage: Nijhoff.
(1909) *De weg tot het inzicht, een inleiding in de wijsbegeerte* [The Way into Insight], Amsterdam: Sijthoff.
(1921–27) *Hoofdfiguren der geschiedenis van het wijsgeerig denken* [Main Personalities of Philosophical Thinking] 2 vols, Haarlem: Bohn.

(1935) *Plato's levensleer* [The Moral Conviction of Plato], Haarlem: Bohn.

(1938) *Het rijk van den geest* [The Reign of Spirit], Zeist: Ploegsma.

(1941) *Amor, caritas en het altruïsme* [Amor, Caritas and Altruism], Assen: Van Gorcum.

(1942) *Ethica, beginselen van het zedelijk zelfbewust-zijn* [Ethics, Principles of Moral Consciousness], 's-Gravenhage: Servire.

Secondary literature:

In memoriam Dr. J. D. Bierens de Haan (1944), Assen.

Van der Bend, J. G. (1970) *Het Spinozisme van Dr J. D. Bierens de Haan*, Assen.

Bierens de Haan was one of the founders of the 'Internationale School voor Wijsbegeerte' (Leusden), an international centre for courses in philosophy, founded in 1916 and still flourishing.

He also founded the first general journal of philosophy in the Netherlands, the *Algemeen Nederlands Tijdschrift voor Wijsbegeerte*, still existing as the leading Dutch philosophical journal.

Bierens de Haan was first of all influenced by the philosophy of Spinoza. He tried to elaborate a contemporary version of Spinozism. In his own development he started with a rationalist interpretation of Spinoza, but changed into a form of mystical Spinozist religion with a strong moral accent. This was combined with a kind of Platonic idealism, aiming at 'inner harmony' in the way of life. In his opinion culture is only able to develop if self-reflection and self-consciousness are present in an idealist manner and if they are accompanied by moral responsibility. The realm of spirit has to reign over the lower human abilities and functions. The 'Idea' is the deepest ground of reality; man has to realize the Idea in his own thinking and acting; religion can offer a helpful way to attain the highest philosophical insight. His popularizing courses, articles and books on philosophy led to a significant influence in the Netherlands.

WIM VAN DOOREN

Binet, Alfred

French. *b:* 1857, Nice, France. *d:* 1911, Paris. *Cat:* Psychologist. *Ints:* Child development; measurement of intelligence quotient and of other individual differences. *Educ:* Studied Law and Science at the Sorbonne; doctorate with the embryologist Edmond Balbiani; studied under Charcot in the Salpêtrière Hospital after becoming interested in psychology. *Infls:* The English

empiricist tradition, including J. S. Mill; Hippolyte Taine in France. *Appts:* Psychologist in schools and hospitals (including the Salpêtrière); 1889, Founder (with Henry Beaunis), of the first psychology laboratory in France at the Sorbonne, and Director in 1894.

Main publications:

(1887) (with C. Fere) *Le Magnetisme animale*, Paris: Alcan.

(1889) *The Physical Life of Micro-organisms: A Study in Experimental Psychology*, trans. T. McCormack, Chicago: Open Court Publishing Company.

(1894) *Psychologie de calculateurs*, Paris: Slatkine.

(1894) *Psychologie de grands calculateurs et joueurs d'échecs*, Paris: Slatkine.

(1896) *Alterations of Personality*, London: Chapman & Hall.

(1898) (with V. Henri) *La Fatigue intellectuelle*, Paris: Schleicher Frères.

(1899) *The Psychology of Reasoning*, Chicago: Open Court Publishing Company.

(1909) (with Théodore Simon) 'L'Intelligence d'imbéciles', *L'Année Psychologique* 15: 1–147.

(1911) 'Qu'est ce qu'une émotion? Qu'est qu'un acte intellectuel?', *L'Année Psychologique* 17: 1–47.

(1916) (with Théodore Simon) *The Development of Intelligence in Children: The Binet-Simon Scale*, Baltimore: William & Wilkins Co.

(1946) *Les Régions Génitales de la femme*, third edition, Paris: Vigot.

Secondary literature:

Reeves, J. W. (1965) *Thinking about Thinking*, London: Secker & Warburg, ch. 7.

Varon, E. J. (1934–5) 'The development of Alfred Binet's psychology', *Psychological Monographs*, New York: American Psychological Association, 46 (207) (this includes a detailed bibliography).

Alfred Binet is best known for his work on the measurement of intelligence, from which the still widely used Stanford–Binet test is derived. The son of an artist and a doctor, Binet had wide-ranging interests and published a philosophical article in *La Revue Philosophique* while still a doctoral student. It was the editor of *La Revue*, Théodore Ribot, who persuaded Binet to concentrate on psychology. His research was always detailed and systematic. He worked in schools and hospitals and with his own daughters. Initially sympathetic to associationism, his results led him to see that, contrary to the associationist theory, unconscious mental processes, the attitude or set of the individual and developmental factors could all exert important influences on thinking.

Binet's work on children's intelligence was carried out with a younger colleague, Théodore Simon. They devised a series of numerical, visuo-spatial and verbal tasks of varying difficulty, and measured the abilities of children of different ages to perform them. The IQ or intelligence quotient for a given child could then be calculated as the child's mental age (measured by the test) divided by his or her chronological age and expressed as a percentage. Thus an above average child scores over 100 per cent, a below average child below 100 per cent, for any particular age group.

Binet's test should be understood against the extensive background of research and clinical experience on which it was based. It was originally commissioned by the French government, following the migration of rural families into the towns, to distinguish those children whose educational failures were due to cultural dislocation from those who were genuinely disadvantaged intellectually. It has often been portrayed as a mechanical measure, allocating children to fixed, dehumanized categories. However, Binet himself emphasized that individual factors could have important influences on test performance, that testing could never be wholly divorced from cultural influences and that his test should be supplemented by other modes of assessment. Binet has had an enduring influence on theories of child development and the standardized measurement of individual differences. The original Binet–Simon scale was restandardized by L. M. Terman and colleagues at Stanford University in 1916 and 1937.

Sources: UCDCL; Goldenson; Edwards.

K. W. M. FULFORD

Binswanger, Ludwig

Swiss. *b:* 1881, Kreuzlingen, Switzerland. *d:* 1966, Kreuzlingen, Switzerland. *Cat:* Psychiatrist; psychoanalyst. *Ints:* Existential analysis; existentialism; phenomenology. *Educ:* Universities of Lausanne, Heidelberg and Zurich; qualified as a doctor, 1907. *Infls:* Husserl, Heidegger, Freud and Jung. *Appts:* 1910–56, Director, Sanatorium Bellevue, Kreuzlingen.

Main publications:

(1922) *Einführung in die Probleme der allgemeinen Psychologie* [Introduction to the Problems of General Psychology], Amsterdam: E. J. Bouset.

(1942) *Grundformen und Erkenntnis menschlichen Daseins* [Basic Forms and Cognition of Human Existence], Zurich: Niehaus; second revised edition, Zurich: Niehaus, 1953.

(1947–55) *Ausgewählte Vorträge und Aufsätze* [Selected Letters and Essays], 2 vols, Bern: Francke.

(1957) *Schizophrenie*, Pfullingen: Neske (contains Binswanger's well-known clinical studies of Ilse, Ellen West, Jurg Zund, Lola Voss and Suzanne Urban).

(1960) *Melancholie und Manie*, Pfullingen: Neske.

English translations of some of Binswanger's work are to be found in:

May, Rollo, Angel, Ernest, and Ellenberger, Henri F. (eds) (1958) *Existence*, New York: Basic Books.

Needleman, J. (1963) *Being-in-the-World*, New York: Basic Books (includes a philosophical critique of Freud and Binswanger, in the context of a background of Kant and Heidegger).

Secondary literature:

Pivnicki-Dimitrije (1979) 'Paradoxes of psychotherapy: in honour and memory of Ludwig Binswanger', Allan Memorial Institute, Montreal, Canada: *Confinia-Psychiatrica* 22 (4): 197–203.

Sahakian, W. S. (1976) 'Philosophical psychotherapy: an existential approach', *Journal of Individual Psychology* 32 (1): 62–8.

Van Den Berg, J. H. (1955) *The Phenomenological Approach to Psychiatry*, Springfield, Ill., and Oxford: Thomas.

Binswanger developed a form of psychotherapy, called *Dasein analyse* or 'existential analysis', based directly on the philosophical work of Edmund **Husserl** and Martin **Heidegger**. He was born into a family of distinguished physicians and psychiatrists, succeeding his father as Director of the Sanatorium Bellevue, founded by his grandfather.

Binswanger sought to counter what he saw as the excessive reductionism both of natural science and of current psychoanalytic accounts of human experience and behaviour. All such accounts, he argued, imposed their own point of view on the patient. Phenomenology and existentialism, on the other hand, could help us to achieve an understanding of the world in terms of the patient's own framework of meaning (his or her own 'transcendental category'), without presupposition, without restructuring. Existential analysis thus seeks to draw out and make explicit the patient's a priori 'being in the world', the phenomena being allowed to 'speak for themselves' rather than being viewed through the lens of this or that theory. This is not to say that natural science is unimportant. On the contrary, in so far as we seek to change or control the patient's experience, science (including traditional psycho-analysis) remains our most effective tool. But scientific explanation needs to be set alongside direct understanding of the patient's worldview. Existential analysis, although for many years restricted to relatively small numbers of practitioners in continental Europe, has experienced something of a revival in recent years. This is partly because of a new meeting of minds between the continental and Anglo-American philosophical traditions. It also reflects a shift of emphasis in health care towards what has become known as patient-centredness, that is clinical decisions being based increasingly on the patient's own values and experience (what Binswanger would have called their worldview or *Weltanschauung*) rather than on the professional's opinion of their needs.

Sources: Edwards; *Psychlit* journal articles (Silver Platter); UCDCL.

K. W. M. FULFORD

Black, Max

British-American. *b:* 24 February 1909, Baku, Russia. *d:* 27 August 1988, Ithaca, New York. *Cat:* Analytical philosopher. *Ints:* Philosophy of language; philosophy of science; philosophy of mathematics; logic. *Educ:* Cambridge University, BA in Mathematics, 1930; University of Göttingen, 1930–1; University of London, PhD 1939, D Litt 1955. *Infls:* Personal influences include Ramsey, Moore, Wittgenstein, Hilbert, Bernays, W. Empson, J. Bronowski, C. K. Ogden, I. A. Richards, L. S. Stebbing and A. E. Murphy; literary influences include Peirce, James, Russell, Frege, Carnap, Keynes, Ryle and Brentano. *Appts:* Mathematics Master, Royal Grammar School, Newcastle-upon-Tyne, 1931–6; Lecturer and Tutor, University of London Institute of Education, 1936–40; Professor of Philosophy, University of Illinois, 1940–6; Professor of Philosophy, 1946–77; and Susan Linn Sage Professor of Philosophy and Humane Letters, 1954–77, Professor Emeritus from 1977; Cornell University, Director, Cornell Society for the Humanities, 1965–70; senior member, Program in Science, Technology and Society, from 1971.

Main publications:

(1933) *The Nature of Mathematics: A Critical Survey*, London: Kegan Paul, Trench, Trubner & Co. Ltd; second edition, 1950.

(1946) *Critical Thinking*, New York: Prentice-Hall, Inc.; revised edition, 1952.

(1949) *Language and Philosophy: Studies in Method*, Ithaca: Cornell University Press.

(1954) *Problems of Analysis: Philosophical Essays*, Ithaca: Cornell University Press.

(1962) *Models and Metaphors: Studies in Language and Philosophy*, Ithaca: Cornell University Press.

(1964) *A Companion to Wittgenstein's 'Tractatus'*, Ithaca: Cornell University Press.

(1968) *The Labyrinth of Language*, New York and London: Frederick A. Praeger.

(1970) *Margins of Precision: Essays in Logic and Language*, Ithaca: Cornell University Press.

(1975) *Caveats and Critiques: Philosophical Essays in Language, Logic, and Art*, Ithaca: Cornell University Press.

(1983) *The Prevalence of Humbug and Other Essays*, Ithaca: Cornell University Press.

(1990) *Perplexities: Rational Choice, the Prisoner's Dilemma, Metaphor, Poetic Ambiguity, and Other Puzzles*, Ithaca and London: Cornell University Press.

Secondary literature:
Black, Max (1985) 'The articulation of concepts', *Philosophers on Their Own Work*, Bern and New York: Verlag Peter Lang, vol. 12, pp. 9–41(provides a brief autobiography and, on pp. 29–41, the most complete bibliography available).

Garver, N. (1967) in Paul Edwards (ed.) *The Encyclopedia of Philosophy*, New York: Macmillan & Co., vol. I, pp. 318–19.

Marcus, Ruth B. (1990) 'Max Black (1909–1988)', *Dialectica* 44: 5–8.

Urmson, J. O. and Rée, J. (1960) *The Concise Encyclopedia of Western Philosophy and Western Philosophers*, London: Hutchinson.

Black's forte was the essay, and most of his published books are collections of his essays. He was fascinated by puzzles of all kinds, and had a special talent for thinking up imaginative examples. He made contributions of importance to a wide range of subjects. These include his work on vagueness; on metaphor, which took him into literary criticism and the understanding of poetry; his contributions to the understanding of scientific method and of the nature of a definition of scientific method; the validation of inductive inference; Zeno's and other paradoxes; the justification of logical axioms and the concept of justification itself.

Black conceived of his work early in his career as linguistic analysis. Forty years later he was speaking of conceptual clarification, which he dubbed 'the articulation of concepts'. There was a change in name, but not much in style or method, and there was also a shift in interest to questions of rationality and reasonableness, conjoined with an attempt to work out the rudiments of a theory of practical reasoning and of the concept of humaneness. Throughout his career he provided incisive critical comment on the work of his best-known contemporaries. On his own interests he said: 'There is work aplenty for semantic hygiene or the clarification of concepts.'

Although he 'never ... belonged to any philosophical school', Black none the less confessed an affinity for the philosophy of common sense of Reid and **Moore**, if with certain demurrers and provisos. He confessed 'to a strong belief that common-sense convictions ... are more likely to be right than the skeptical objections of even the greatest philosophers'. He once said, 'The task of the moral philosopher is to solve the moral problems of his society', and in the latter part of his career he was beginning to turn in this direction. One reviewer characterized him in this way: 'a trenchant intellect and a flawless expository style'. All his life he was in search of clarity and more than once contemplated using that expression as the title of one of his collections. He did not, in the end, do so, but the phrase marks the character of the philosophical enterprise as he engaged in it. Another reviewer said: 'Keen and sound criticism employing arguments which might be used by a philosopher of any school—if he had the acumen to marshal them and the literary skill thus to present them.' This was said about his first collection of essays. It could be said about all of them.

Sources: Obituary notice, *PAAPA*, 64, 1991, pp. 61–2; WW(Am) 1984–5; WWW(Am) 1985–9; biographical data and bibliography supplied by Black in 1963–4; Profs W. H. Hay and F. L. Will; personal communication.

MARCUS SINGER

Blanshard, Brand

American. *b:* 27 August 1892, Fredericksburg, Ohio. *d:* 19 November 1987, New Haven, Connecticut. *Cat:* Idealist; rationalist. *Ints:* Epistemologist; metaphysician; moral philosopher. *Educ:* University of Michigan, AB 1914; Columbia University, AM 1918; Oxford University, Rhodes Scholar, BSc 1919; Harvard University, PhD 1921. *Infls:* Joachim, Bradley, Dewey, H. W. B. Joseph and C. I. Lewis. *Appts:* 1921–5, Assistant Professor of Philosophy, University of Michigan; 1925–45, Associate Professor to full Professor of Philosophy, Swarthmore College; 1945–87, Pro-

fessor of Philosophy, Chairman of Department, 1945–50 and 1959–61, Emeritus Professor, 1961.

Main publications:

(1939) *The Nature of Thought*, 2 vols, London: George Allen & Unwin; reprinted, New York: Macmillan Co., 1940.
(1945) (with C. J. Ducasse, C. W. Hendel, A. E. Murphy and M. C. Otto) *Philosophy in American Education: Its Tasks and Opportunities*, New York and London: Harper & Brothers.
(1954) *On Philosophical Style*, Manchester, England: University of Manchester Press; reprinted, Bloomington and London: Indiana University Press, 1967, and West Port, CT: Greenwood, 1954.
(1961) *Reason and Goodness*, London and New York: George Allen & Unwin and Macmillan Co.
(1962) *Reason and Analysis*, La Salle, Ill., Open Court Publishing Co. and London: George Allen & Unwin; second edition, 1964.
(1973) *The Uses of a Liberal Education and Other Talks to Students*, ed. Eugene Freeman, La Salle, Ill.: Open Court Publishing Co.
(1974) *Reason and Belief*, London: George Allen & Unwin; reprinted, New Haven, CT: Yale University Press, 1975.
(1984) *Four Reasonable Men*, Middletown, CT: Wesleyan University Press.

Secondary literature:

Reck, A. J. (1968) *The New American Philosophers: An Exploration of Thought Since World War II*, Baton Rouge: Louisiana State University Press, pp. 81–119; reprinted, New York: Dell Publishing Co., 1970.
Schilpp, P. A. (ed.) (1980) *The Philosophy of Brand Blanshard*, La Salle, Ill.: Open Court Publishing Co., The Library of Living Philosophers.
Wright, W. E. (ed.) (1990) *Idealistic Studies* 20, 2.

The hallmarks of Blanshard's philosophy are idealism and rationalism. In *The Nature of Thought* (1939) he presented a systematic theory of mind, knowledge and reality. Epistemologically he defined the relation between an idea and its object as teleological, and he advanced a coherence theory of truth. Metaphysically he upheld the theory of the concrete universal, the doctrine that all relations are internal and the thesis of cosmic necessity. He articulated these theories in an elegantly lucid style.

Blanshard responded to the rise of irrationalism in mid-twentieth century with the authorship of an imposing trilogy in defence of reason. His Gifford Lectures at the University of St Andrews in 1951 and 1952 engendered two parts of the trilogy. Presenting a thorough critique of non-cognitivism and relativism in ethics, *Reason and Goodness* (1961) offers constructively a teleological rationalist moral philosophy. Trenchantly criticizing religious pragmatism and existentialism, neo-orthodoxy in theology, and Roman Catholicism, *Reason and Belief* (1974) advocates a religious rationalism. While Blanshard did not reject ontological idealism, he nevertheless denied that God, or absolute reality, is good in the human sense.

Blanshard's 1959 Carus lectures before the American Philosophical Association came to fruition in *Reason and Analysis* (1962). A critical polemic against analytic philosophy, logical positivism and linguistic analysis, it reaffirms the epistemology and metaphysics of *The Nature of Thought*. Blanshard restated the sovereignty of reason, defending it against the strictures of such thinkers as Ernest **Nagel**.

Sources: Edwards; WW(Am); obituary, *New York Times*, 21 Nov 1987.

ANDREW RECK

Blewett, George John

Canadian. *b:* 9 December 1873, St Thomas, Ontario. *d:* 15 August 1912, Go-Home Bay, Ontario. *Cat:* Idealist. *Ints:* Rational religion. *Educ:* Universities of Toronto, Oxford, Wurzburg and Harvard. *Infls:* Josiah Royce and Edmund Caird. *Appts:* Ordained Minister of the Methodist Church, but served only briefly in the western Canadian mission fields before becoming a Lecturer in Philosophy at Wesley College, Winnipeg; he returned to Toronto as Professor of Philosophy at Victoria College in 1906 and remained there until his death despite determined attempts to recruit him as the successor to Borden Parker Bowne at Boston University.

Main publications:

(1907) *The Study of Nature and the Vision of God*, Toronto: William Briggs.

(1912) *The Christian View of the World*, New York: Yale University Press.

Secondary literature:

There is, in the archives of Victoria College, Toronto, an unpublished biography by W. J. Rose, who taught for many years at the London School of Slavonic and East European Studies. This is the only extended study.

Armour, Leslie (1981) *The Idea of Canada and the Crisis of Community*, Ottawa: Steel Rail (suggests that Blewett was perhaps the idealist philosopher most influenced by the Canadian context).

——and Trott, Elizabeth (1981) *The Faces of Reason*, Waterloo, Ontario: Wilfrid Laurier University Press, 1981 (contains a critical chapter).

Blewett was strongly influenced by Josiah **Royce** and Edward **Caird**, but went his own way in important respects. His experiences in the Canadian west convinced him that the natural Canadian environment was very fragile, and he tried to develop a view of nature which lay between the romantic notion of a perfect nature created by God and the pragmatic view that nature exists for us to do with as we please. He insisted that nature is something towards which we have duties and that these duties consist in developing it in a harmonious way while maintaining as much variety as is consistent with the maintenance of basic social values necessary for human survival and intellectual development. His own strongest interest was in the development of rational religion, and he attempted to create an idealism which would permit an integration of God and the world. He thus had strong interests in Spinoza and in John the Scot. But his concern with religious peace and order in the Canadian situation caused him to pay sympathetic attention to Catholic philosophers including Aquinas and Newman.

Sources: CanBio.

LESLIE ARMOUR

Bloch, Ernst

German. *b:* 1885, Ludwigshofen, Germany. *d:* 1977, Stuttgart. *Cat:* Marxist. *Educ:* Psychology, University of Munich; Philosophy, Physics and Music, University of Wurzburg; University of Berlin. *Infls:* Marx.

Main publications:

(1959) *Gesamtausgabe*, 16 vols, Frankfurt: Suhrkamp (includes the three following):

——(1918) *Geist der Utopie* [Spirit of Utopia].

——(1921) *Thomas Munzer als Theologe der Revolution* [Thomas Munzer as Theologian of the Revolution].

(1959) *Das Prinzip Hoffnung* [The Principle of Hope], 3 vols.

(1971) *On Karl Marx*, New York: Herder & Herder.

Secondary literature:

Hudson, Wayne (1982) *The Marxist Philosophy of Ernst Bloch*, London: Macmillan.

Kolakowski, Leszek (1978) *Main Currents of Marxism*, vol. 3, Oxford: Oxford University Press.

After spending the First World War in Switzerland, started his teaching career in Leipzig in 1918, before working as a freelance writer in the 1920s. With the rise of the Nazis he left Germany in 1933, moving ultimately to the USA where he started work on his *magnum opus*, *Das Prinzip Hoffnung* (1959). He returned to Leipzig in 1948 to teach philosophy, and in 1955 won the Nationalpreis of the German Democratic Republic, but the government found his ideas increasingly heterodox, his works were condemned and he was forbidden to publish. In 1961 he defected to the West, becoming a Professor at Tübingen; his final years were spent lecturing and writing, to the acclaim of a number of thinkers in the West.

Although standardly classified as Marxist, Bloch's thinking share little with orthodox Marxism in terms of concepts, methods, interests or even style. With Marx and 'scientific socialism' as only one influence among many on his thought, Bloch was an avowed supporter of utopianism, which he sets in a very specific epistemological and metaphysical context. Reality is not a fixed, stable system but is essentially teleological, the process aiming at and culminating in utopia. This transformation, however, is not brought about by the operation of impersonal objective laws of historical development, but by a transformation within the mind of each individual, a transformation produced by the individual's understanding of the unfolding movement towards the utopian goal. Unsurprisingly, Marxist theoreticians have found such views idealist, unscientific and un-Marxist, but in fields of study beyond Marxism, such as radical theology, he has been much more influential and highly regarded.
Sources: Turner; BDN.

NICHOLAS EVERITT

Blondel, Maurice

French. *b:* 1861, Dijon, France. *d:* 1949, Aix-en-Provence, France. *Cat:* Metaphysician; theologian; philosopher of action. *Ints:* Philosophy of religion. *Educ:* École Normale Supérieure. *Infls:* Léon Ollé-Laprune, Émile Boutroux and Victor Delbos. *Appts:* 1895–6 , University of Lille; 1896–1927, University of Aix-en-Provence.

Main publications:

(1893) *L'Action, essai d'une critique de la vie, et d'une science de la pratique*, Paris: Alcan; republished as *Premiers Écrits*, Paris: PUF, 1950.

(1893) *De Vinculo Substantiali et de Substantia composita apud Leibnitium*, Paris: Alcan.

(1896) 'Lettre sur les exigences de la pensée contemporaine en matière d'apologétique', *Annales de Philosophie Chrétienne*; republished with 'Histoire et dogme', Paris: PUF, 1951.

(1904) 'Histoire et dogme', *La Quinzaine* (Jan–Feb): 1–90.

(1922) (with P. Archambault) *Le Procès de l'intelligence*, Paris: Bloud et Gay.

(1928) *L'Itinéraire philosophique de Maurice Blondel*, Paris: Spes.

(1930) *Une Énigme historique, le vinculum substantiale d'après Leibniz*, Paris: Beauchesne.

(1932) 'Le Problème de la philosophie catholique', *Cahiers de la Nouvelle Journée* XX.

(1934) *La Pensée*, 2 vols, Paris: Alcan.

(1935) *L'Être et les Êtres*, Paris: Alcan.

(1936–7) *L'Action*, 2 vols, Paris: Alcan.

(1939) *Lutte pour la civilisation et philosophie de la paix*, Paris: Flammarion.

(1944–6) *La Philosophie et l'esprit chrétien*, 2 vols, Paris: PUF.

(1950) *Exigences philosophiques du christianisme*, Paris: PUF.

Secondary literature:

Archambault, P. (1938) 'Oeuvre philosophique de Maurice Blondel', *Cahiers de la Nouvelle Journée* XII, Paris: Bloud et Gay.

Borne, E. (1962) *Passion de la vérité*, Paris, Fayard.

Bouillard, H. (1961) *Blondel et le christianisme*, Paris: Seuil.

Cartier, A. (1955) *Existence et vérité*, Paris: PUF.

Duméry, H. (1948) *La Philosophie de l'action*, Paris: Aubier.

——(1954) *Blondel et la religion, Essai critique*, Paris: Aubier.

——(1963) *Raison et religion dans la philosophie de l'action*, Paris: Seuil.

École, J. (1959) *La Métaphysique de l'Être dans la philosophie de Maurice Blondel*, Louvain: E. Nauwelaerts.

Favraux, P. (1987) *Une Philosophie du Médiateur, Maurice Blondel*, Paris: Lethielleux.

Gélinas, J. P. (1959) *La Restauration du thomisme sous Léon XIII et les philosophies nouvelles*, Washington: Catholic University of America Press.

Lavelle, L. (1942) *La Philosophie entre les deux Guerres*, Paris: Aubier, pp. 121–76.

McNeill, J. J. (1966) *The Blondelian Synthesis*, Leiden: E. J. Brill.

Paliard, J. (1950) *Maurice Blondel, ou le dépassement chrétien*, Paris: Julliard.

Poulat, E. (1979) *Histoire, dogme et critique dans la crise moderniste*, second edition, Tournai: Casterman.

Romeyer, B. (1943) *La Philosophie religieuse de Maurice Blondel*, Paris: Aubier.

Saint-Jean, R. (1965) *Genèse de l'action, Maurice Blonde*, Paris and Bruges: Desclée de Brouwer.

Somerville, J. M. (1967) 'Blondel, Maurice', *New Catholic Encyclopedia*, New York: MacGraw Hill, II 617b–618b.

Tres-montant, C. (1963) *Introduction à la métaphysique de Maurice Blondel*, Paris: Seuil.

Virgoulay, R. (1980) *Blondel et le Modernisme*, Paris: Cerf.

With some features in common with later existentialism, the so-called philosophy of action was a quasi-phenomenological approach to a philosophy of concrete experience and moral behaviour based on an analysis of willing and doing that emphasized the ultimate unattainability of the object willed. Blondel's initial aim had been to develop a philosophy of religion, in the sense of religious feeling and living rather than of religious dogmatic systems. In his view human action only made sense if directed towards a transcendent God, an argument not however presented as a proof of God's existence—he hoped rather to offer a critique of religious systems in terms of their ability to make sense of human action. The larger works of the 1930s and 1940s were an attempt to expand the earlier views into a more comprehensive metaphysics, including an account of reason and an ontology claiming to avoid idealism. Although a committed Catholic Blondel advocated an open approach to apologetics involving dialogue with non-believers Léon **Brunschvicg** and resolute opposition to the more authoritarian neoscholastic approaches then in vogue, a policy carried out under the editorship of Laberthonnière by the *Annales de Philosophie Chrétienne*, which he owned from 1905 to 1913 when it was put on the Index. He played a major role in the modernist crisis of early twentieth-century Catholicism (on which see Poulat 1979). He held a weak version of the ontological argument for God's existence. Recently many Catholics have become attracted to his alternative to officially sponsored neoscholasticism.

Sources: J. Lacroix (1963) *Maurice Blondel, sa vie, son oeuvre, avec un exposé de sa philosophie*, Paris: PUF; Edwards; R. Virgoulay (1975–6) *Maurice Blondel bibliographie analytique et critique*, 2 vols, Louvain: Institut Supérieure de Philosophie.

R. N. D. MARTIN

Bloomfield, Leonard

American. **b:** 1 April 1887, Chicago. **d:** 18 April 1949, Connecticut. **Cat:** Philosopher of language; linguist. **Ints:** Linguistics; comparative philology. **Educ:** Universities of Harvard, Wisconsin and Chicago. **Infls:** Eduard Prokosch, W. Wundt, E. Sapir and Albert Paul Weiss. **Appts:** 1910–21, Instructor, then (1913) Assistant Professor of German and Comparative Philology, University of Illinois; 1921–7, Professor of German and Linguistics, Ohio State University; 1927–40, Professor of Germanic Philology, University of Chicago; 1940–9, Professor of Linguistics, Yale University.

Main publications:

(1914) *An Introduction to the Study of Language*, New York: Holt.

(1933) *Language*, New York: Holt.

(1935) 'Linguistic aspects of science', *Philosophy of Science* 2: 499–517.

(1936) 'Language or ideas?', *Language* 12: 89–95.

(1939) *Linguistic Aspects of Science*, Chicago: University of Chicago Press.

Secondary literature:

Bloch, Bernard (1949) 'Leonard Bloomfield', *Language* 25: 87–98.

Dempwolff, Otto (1934–8) 'Vergleichende Laulehre des austronesischen Wortschatzes', *Zeitschrift für eingeborenen Sprachen*, Supplements 15, 17, 19.

Bloomfield did more than anyone else to transform linguistics from a desultory pursuit into a branch of science. Concerned at first with the study of Germanic and Indo-European languages, Bloomfield turned to wider-ranging considerations of language in his *Introduction to the Study of Language* (1914). In 1924 he helped to found the Language Society of America, and in 1925 began its influential journal, *Language*.

In making linguistics 'autonomous and scientific', Bloomfield shunned operationally undefinable mentalistic terms and pursued a 'physicalist' approach which excluded all data that were not directly observable or physically measurable. This led him to formulate the principles of phonological and syntactic analysis largely without reference to semantic considerations, since he believed that a precise definition of most words in terms of a complete 'scientific' description of the objects to which they refer could not yet be given.

In his monumental *Language* (1933) Bloomfield presented his famous 'single-stratum' scheme of language design: 'phonemes' directly observable in the speech signal are the minimum though

meaningless 'units' of a language; sequences of phonemes, called 'morphemes', are the minimum meaningful units; morphemes form words; words form phrases and clauses, and these form sentences. Bloomfield's work defined an epoch in American linguistics. His followers, particularly Zellig **Harris**, carried even further than he did the idea of a linguistics 'without semantics'. However, since the 1960s prominent linguists (for example, **Chomsky**) have become increasingly critical of the 'Bloomfieldian' school and have abandoned many of its original assumptions.
Sources: Bullock & Woodings.

STEPHEN MOLLER

Bocheński, Jozef (also Innocentius Marie)
Polish. *b:* 30 August 1902, Czuszów, Poland. *Cat:* Logician. *Ints:* History of philosophy; Soviet philosophy. *Educ:* University of Lwów and University of Poznań. *Infls:* Jan Łukasiewicz. *Appts:* 1934–40, Professor of Philosophy, Angelicum University, Rome; 1945–72, Professor of Modern and Contemporary Philosophy, University of Freiburg, Switzerland; 1958–75, Director, Institute of East European Studies, Freiburg.

Main publications:

(1947) *Europäische Philosophie der Gegenwart*, second edition, Munich: Lehnen, 1951 (English translation, *Contemporary European Philosophy*, Cambridge: Cambridge University Press, 1956).

(1948) *Précis de logique mathématique*, Bussum: Kroonder (English translation *A Precis of Mathematical Logic*, Dordrecht: D. Reidel, 1959).

(1950) *Der sowjet-russische dialektisch Materialismus*, Bern: Franke (English translation, *Soviet Dialectical Materialism*, Dordrecht: D. Reidel, 1963).

(1956) *Formale Logik*, Freiburg and Munich: Alber (English translation *A History of Formal Logic*, Notre Dame: University of Notre Dame Press, 1961).

(1959) *Die zeitgenössichen Denkmethoden*, Bern: Franke (English translation, *The Methods of Contemporary Thought*, Dordrecht: D. Reidel, 1965).

(1965) *The Logic of Religion*, New York: New York University Press.

Secondary literature:

Heaney, James J. (1971) 'Analogy and "kinds" of things', *The Thomist* 35: 293–304.

McMullan, Ernan (1959) 'Mathematical logic', *Philosophical Studies* (Ireland) 9: 190–9.

Bocheński is one of the most distinguished and prolific contemporary historians of logic, particularly logic in the classical period. His studies of twentieth-century philosophy have focused most sharply upon dialectical materialism, and Soviet philosophy in general, and he has greatly influenced this area of scholarship by founding and editing the journal *Studies in Soviet Thought*, as well as by his own numerous publications. Amongst his work in theoretical philosophy one of the most interesting and innovative is *The Logic of Religion* (1965), which examines the logical character of religious terminology and discourse. He distinguishes three elements in religious discourse: (i) object-linguistic sentences such as 'There is a God', 'Christ is the Son of God', 'Mohammed is the Prophet of Allah'; (ii) a meta-linguistic rule which specifies which sentences are of this type; (iii) a meta-logical rule which states that all such sentences have to be accepted as true. He considers also the manner in which these sentences are axiomatized in a theology, the primitive terms (such as 'God') which they contain, their semantic character, the method of their verification and the methodology of their justification. There is also a useful appendix on the nature of analogy. All of Bocheński's work is well regarded, especially his studies in the history of logic.
Sources: EF; DFN; IWW.

HUGH BREDIN

Boden, Margaret A.
British. *b:* 26 November 1936, London. *Cat:* Philosophical psychologist; philosopher of artificial intelligence; cognitive scientist. *Educ:* Medical Sciences and Philosophy, Newnham College, Cambridge, 1955–9; Social Biology, Harvard University, 1962–8; Biology, Cambridge University, 1990. *Appts:* Assistant Lecturer, then Lecturer, University of Birmingham, 1959–65; 1965–, Lecturer, Reader, then Professor, University of Sussex.

Main publications:

(1972) *Purposive Explanation in Psychology*, Cambridge, Mass.: Harvard University Press.

(1977) *Artificial Intelligence and Natural Man*, Hassocks: Harvester Press.

(1979) *Piaget*, London: Fontana Press; second, revised edition, 1995.

(1981) *Minds and Mechanisms: Philosophical Psychology and Computational Models*, Hassocks: Harvester Press.

(1988) *Computer Models of the Mind: Computational Approaches in Theoretical Psychology*, Cambridge: Cambridge University Press.

(1989) *Artificial Intelligence in Psychology: Interdisciplinary Essays*, Cambridge, Mass.: MIT Press.

(1990) (ed.) *The Philosophy of Artificial Intelligence*, Oxford: Oxford University Press.

(1990) *The Creative Mind: Myths and Mechanisms*, London: Weidenfeld & Nicolson.

(1994) (ed.) *Dimensions of Creativity*, Cambridge, MA: MIT Press.

(forthcoming) (ed.) *Computational Psychology and Artificial Intelligence*, London: Academic Press.

(forthcoming) (ed. with A. Bundy) *Artificial Intelligence and the Mind: New Breakthroughs or Dead Ends?*, London: Royal Society and British Academy.

Boden incorporates philosophy, artifical intelligence and psychology in her approach to understanding the mind. She adopts a functionalist position, taking thoughts, beliefs, intentions, values and emotions to be dependent on causal (neurophysiological) mechanisms, and she argues that the mind operates like a computational system.

In *Purposive Explanation in Psychology* (1972) Boden maintains a position between mechanistic and humanistic psychology, arguing that human purpose cannot be entirely understood through mechanistic language. Although she thinks we can grasp how the mind works in terms of computational processes, psychological explanations are still required to fully explain the nature of mental representations. Boden believes that the computational model of the mind is not incompatible with human autonomy. Minds are mechanisms but freedom depends on deliberation and choice, both of which are possible through the 'computational resources' of the mind—concepts, beliefs, values, preferences and reasoning powers.

In her classic work on artificial intelligence, *Artificial Intelligence and Natural Man* (1977), Boden argues that to simulate human intellectual abilities, computer programmes must operate in an intentional manner, and be able to enhance and extend their capacities without additional human programming. Boden defends the usefulness of artificial intelligence for understanding human intentionality, and argues that even if computer programs ultimately fail to tell us the exact nature of intentions, they offer a strong explanatory analogy.

Sources: Personal communication.

EMILY BRADY

Bogdanov, Aleksandr Aleksandrovich (penname of A. A. Malinovsky)

Russian. *b:* 22 (10 N.S.) August 1873, Tula. *d:* 7 April 1928, Moscow. *Cat:* Marxist. *Educ:* Graduated from the Medical Faculty of Khar'kov University in 1899. *Infls:* Marx, Ostwald, Mach and Avenarius. *Appts:* From 1918, Professor of Economics, University of Moscow, and Director of the Socialist Academy of Social Sciences; from 1926, Director, Institute for Haematology and Blood Transfusions.

Main publications:

(1901) *Poznanie s istoricheskogo tochki zreniia* [Knowledge from a Historical Viewpoint], St Petersburg.

(1904–6) *Empiriomonizm: stat'i po filosofii* [Empiriomonism: Articles on Philosophy], 3 vols, Moscow.

(1912) *Filosofiia zhivogo opyta: populiarnye ocherki* [Philosophy of Living Experience: Popular Essays], St Petersburg.

(1922) *Tektologiia: vseobshchaia organizatsionnaia nauka*, 3 vols, Berlin and Petrograd–Moscow (English translation, *Essays in Tektology: the General Science of Organization*, trans. George Gorelik, Seaside, Cal.: Intersystems Publications, 1980).

Secondary literature:

Jensen, K. M. (1978) *Beyond Marx and Mach: Aleksandr Bogdanov's Philosophy of Living Experience*, Dordrecht: D. Reidel.

Sochor, Z. A. (1988) *Revolution and Culture: The Bogdanov–Lenin Controversy*, Ithaca: Cornell University Press.

Vucinich, A. (1976) *Social Thought in Tsarist Russia: The Quest for a General Science of Society, 1861–1917*, Chicago: University of Chicago Press, ch. 8.

Initially a Populist, Bogdanov joined the Russian Social-Democratic Labour Party in 1896, and sided with the Bolsheviks after the 1903 conference. He was, however, frequently at odds with **Lenin** and the Party on political and theoretical issues, and was expelled from the Party following Lenin's assault on his views in *Materialism and Empiriocriticism* (1909). During the First World War, Bogdanov served as an army surgeon; between 1918 and 1923, he was involved with **Bukharin** and **Lunacharsky** in the Proletkul't organization, and in addition to philosophy produced economics textbooks and works of technocratic science fiction. From 1921 he was preoccupied with scientific experiments, and died as a result of a blood transfusion performed on himself.

Bogdanov was motivated above all by enthusiasm for the contemporary 'scientific and technological revolution' and by dissatisfaction with dialectical materialism as the philosophical basis of Marxism. At the turn of the century, he embraced **Ostwald**'s energeticism, but the critical positivism of Avenarius and **Mach** proved a more lasting basis for his repudiation of materialism, which he regarded as inappropriate for an ideology of the proletariat in the new scientific and technical era. It was his resultant theory of empiriomonism, a synthesis of Avenarius's empiriocriticism and Marxism, which stimulated **Lenin**'s invective. Its fundamental characteristic was an appeal to experience as a neutral category bridging the gulf between the psychic and the physical, the psychic being individually organized experience, and the physical socially organized experience. The theory extended to a model of society in which technical knowledge was seen as the driving force of social progress.

The other dimension of Bogdanov's rejection of dialectical materialism was his attempt to translate the dialectic into contemporary scientific terms, notably the concept of dynamic equilibrium. He contended that the dialectic was not a universal feature of the world but, like the laws of science, a particular way of organizing experience, one which reflected the production relations of a particular historical period. The culmination of Bogdanov's revisionism was 'tectology', his new monistic science which sought to replace philosophy and bring nature and society under a set of general principles of organization. Bogdanov earned himself the opprobrium of the Marxist-Leninist establishment in his lifetime, although he subsequently received accolades for his perceived anticipation of modern cybernetics. It was esteem of science and disregard for dialectics, rather than sympathy with mechanistic materialism, which underlay his tangential association with the Mechanists in their debate with the Deborinites during the 1920s.

COLIN CHANT

Bohm, David Joseph
American. **b:** 20 December 1917, Wilkes-Barre, Pennsylvania. **d:** 27 October 1992, London. **Cat:** Physicist and anti-Cartesian holist. **Ints:** Philosophy of science; metaphysics. **Educ:** 1939, Pennsylvania State College; University of California, Berkeley, PhD 1943. **Infls:** Personal influences include Einstein, Oppenheimer and Basil Hiley; literary influences include Einstein, Bohr, Hegel, Piaget and Whitehead. **Appts:** 1943–7, Radiation Laboratory, University of California; 1947–51, Assistant Professor, Princeton University; 1951–5, Professor, University of São Paulo, Brazil; 1955–7, Professor, The Technion, Haifa, Israel; 1957–61, Research Fellowship, University of Bristol; 1961–92, Professor (1983 Emeritus Professor) of Theoretical Physics, Birkbeck College, University of London.

Main publications:
(1957) *Causality and Chance in Modern Physics*, London: Routledge & Kegan Paul.
(1980) *Wholeness and The Implicate Order*, London: Routledge & Kegan Paul.
(1987) (with F. David Peat) *Science, Order and Creativity*, New York: Bantam.
(1993) (with B. Hiley) *The Undivided Universe: an Ontological Interpretation of Quantum Mechanics*, London: Routledge.

Secondary literature:
Griffin, D. R. (ed.) (1986) *Physics and the Ultimate Significance of Time: Bohm, Prigogine and Process Philosophy*, New York: SUNY Press.
Hiley, B. and Peat, F. D. (eds) (1987) *Quantum Implications: Essays in Honour of David Bohm*, London and New York: Routledge.

David Bohm's most well-known contribution to philosophy is his promotion of a heterodox theory in quantum physics: the (inaptly named) 'hidden variables' view or (better) 'causal interpretation' or 'ontological interpretation', using the notions of 'quantum potential' and 'wholeness'.

Dissatisfied with what he saw as the orthodoxy's too-easy acceptance of von **Neumann**'s Theorem proscribing alternative ontological views, Bohm urged theoreticians to dig deeper in realist vein to provide an explanation of individual quantum processes to make quantum theory more complete. His unorthodox views initially failed to arouse the curiosity of most scientists but this has changed more recently, despite the appeal to non-locality. Recently, Bohm published works which, using quantum physics as a model (particularly for non-locality), promote what he saw as a necessary alteration in metaphysical outlook. Themes include a rejection of Cartesian 'atomism' in favour of a philosophy or 'order' embracing 'wholeness'. Bohm claims that whilst the 'explicate (unfolded) order' may appear a world of fragmented things, each such thing expresses the whole universe ('implicate' or 'enfolded order'). He deploys the metaphor of 'hologram': for Bohm, the world is like a 'holomovement', a dynamic totalilty. It is doubt-

ful that mainstream philosophers have been much influenced by these later works.
Sources: WW 1993.

ANDREW WRIGHT

Bohr, Niels Hendrik David

Danish. **b:** 7 October 1885, Copenhagen. **d:** 18 November 1962, Copenhagen. **Cat:** Physicist; philosopher of science. **Ints:** Foundations of atomic physics; quantum mechanics. **Educ:** Doctorate, Copenhagen, 1911, Cambridge and Manchester. **Infls:** E. Rutherford, J. J. Thomson and Harald Høffding. **Appts:** Copenhagen, 1913–14, Manchester, 1914–16, Copenhagen, 1916–43 and 1945–62, Los Alamos, 1943–5; Nobel Prize for Physics, 1922.

Main publications:

(1934) *Atomic Theory and the Description of Nature*, Cambridge: Cambridge University Press; revised edition, 1961.

(1958) *Atomic Physics and Human Knowledge*, New York: Wiley.

(1963) *Die Kopenhagener Deutung der Quantentheorie*, ed. A. Hermann, Stuttgart: Battenberg (reprints papers by Heisenberg and Bohr).

(1963) *Essays 1958–62 on Atomic Physics and Human Knowledge*, New York: Wiley.

(1972–) *Collected Works*, ed. L. Rosenfeld *et al.*, Amsterdam: North-Holland (particularly vol. III, *The Correspondence Principle 1918–23*, 1976 and and vol. VI, *Foundations of Quantum Physics I 1926–32*, 1985).

Secondary literature:

Aaserud, H. (1990) *Redirecting Science: Niels Bohr*, Oxford: Clarendon.

Favrholdt, D. (1976) 'Niels Bohr and Danish philosophy', *Danish Yearbook of Philosophy*, XIII: 206–220.

——(1991) 'Remarks on the Hohr–Høffding relationship', *Studies in History and Philosophy of Science*, 22: 399–414.

Faye, J. (1979) 'The influence of Harald Høffding's philosophy on Niels Bohr's interpretation of quantum mechanics', *Danish Yearbook of Philosophy*, 16: 37–72.

Folse, H. J. (1985) *The Philosophy of Niels Bohr: The Framework of Complementarity*, Amsterdam: North-Holland.

French, A. P. and Kennedy, P. J. (1985) *Niels Bohr: A Centenary Volume*, Cambridge, Mass.: Harvard University Press.

Honner, J. (1987) *The Description of Nature: Niels Bohr and the Philosophy of Quantum Physics*, Oxford: Clarendon Press.

Jammer, M. (1966) *The Conceptual Development of Quantum Mechanics*, New York: McGraw-Hill.

——(1974) *The Philosophy of Quantum Mechanics*, New York: Wiley.

Meyenn, K. von, *et. al.* (1985) *Niels Bohr 1885–1962, Der Kopenhagener Geist in der Physik*, Braunschweig: Vieweg.

Meyer-Abich, K. M. (1965) *Korrespondenz, Individualität und Komplementarität*, Wiesbaden: Steiner.

Murdoch, D. (1987) *Niels Bohr's Philosophy of Physics*, Cambridge: Cambridge University Press.

Pauli, W. *et. al.* (1955) *Niels Bohr and the Development of Physics*, London: Pergamon.

Petruccioli, S. (1993) *Atoms Metaphors and Paradoxes: Niels Bohr and the Construction of a New Physics*, Cambridge: Cambridge University Press.

Rozental, S. (ed.) (1967) *Niels Bohr, his Life and Work as Seen by his Friends and Colleagues*, New York: Wiley.

Ruhla, C. (1992) *The Physics of Chance from Blaise Pascal to Niels Bohr*, Oxford: Oxford University Press.

Bohr was the main inventor of the quantum theory of atomic structure and of the usual (Copenhagen) interpretation of that theory, with its twin principles of correspondence and complementarity. Starting with his realization that Rutherford's nuclear or 'planetary' model of the atom was unstable, and the discoveries of spectroscopists like Rydberg, he devised methods of applying **Planck**'s quantum of action to it, subject to the condition that as the scale increased the resulting formula should converge on the established classical macroscopic formulae ('correspondence'). Under his guidance, and cooperating principally with the Göttingen school, the quantum approach became statistical. **Heisenberg**'s discovery of indeterminacy, resting on non-commutativity of the matrices used technically in his analyses, was interpreted by Bohr as illustrating a notion he had first conceived in discussions involving his psychologist father in his schooldays. In most fields of inquiry discoverable truth was at best partial and only approachable via complementary ideas which could not be determined simultaneously. In this case these were, for example, the position and momentum of microscopic particles. Complementarity was widely interpreted in an instrumentalist sense (physical theory could only describe experiments and not physical reality) and opposed in particular by **Einstein, de Broglie** and **Schrödinger**, who made considerable but unsuccessful efforts to refute it. (On much of this see Jammer, 1966 and 1974.)

Sources: 'Niels Hendrik David Bohr', *PT*, 16 (1963): 21–64; J. Cockcroft (1963) 'Niels Hendrik David Bohr', *BMFRS* 9: 37–53; J. R. Oppenheimer (1964) 'Niels Bohr and atomic weapons', *NYRB* 3, 9: 6–8; G. P. Thomson (1964) 'Niels Bohr Memorial Lecture', *PCS*, 351–4; R. E. Moore (1966) *Niels Bohr: The Man, his Science, and the World they Changed*, New York: Knopf ; S. Rozental (ed.) *Niels Bohr: His Life and Work*; DSB 1973; S. Rozental 'Bohr, Niels', *Dansk Biografisk Leksikon*, Copenhagen: Gyldendal; Mittelstrass; N. Blaedel (1989) *Harmoni og enhed Niels Bohr en Biografi*, Copenhagen: Carlsbergfondet Rhodos; A. Pais (1991) *Niels Bohr's Times in Physics Philosophy and Polity*, Oxford: Clarendon Press.

R. N. D. MARTIN

Bolland, Gerardus Johannes Petrus Josephus

Dutch. *b:* 9 June 1854, Groningen, The Netherlands. *d:* 11 February 1922, Leyden. *Cat:* Hegelian idealist. *Ints:* Theology; political philosophy; social philosophy. *Educ:* He had an adventurous youth: a military education (1868–73), and was dismissed and imprisoned in a case of insubordination because of his offended sense of justice. *Infls:* E. von Hartmann (in his earlier period) and Kant and Hegel (during his professorship). *Appts:* Taught at a primary school 1876; studied English language and taught at a secondary school in Batavia (Dutch East Indies), 1881–96; Professor of Philosophy, University of Leyden, from 1896.

Main publications:

Most of Bolland's writings are published lecture courses. He edited many works of Hegel (*The Phenomenology of Spirit, The Philosophy of Religion, The Science of Logic*).

(1896) *Het wereldraadsel* [The Cosmic Riddle], Leyden: Adriani.

(1896) *Verandering en tijd* [Change and Time], Leyden: Van Doesburgh (Inaugural Lecture).

(1902) *Alte Vernunft und neuer Verstand*, Leyden: Adriani.

(1904) *Zuivere rede* [Pure Reason], Leyden: Adriani.

(1904–5) *Collegium Logicum* (course of lectures), Leyden: Versluys.

(1921) *De teekenen des tijds* [The Signs of Time], Leyden: Adriani.

Secondary literature:

Pen, K. J. (1922) *Over het onderscheid tusschen de wetenschap van Hegel en de wijsheid van Bolland*, Leyden: Brill (dissertation).

Bolland originated from a Roman-Catholic family, but soon became an atheist. In the field of philosophy he was an autodidact, developing from an adherent of von **Hartmann** to a Hegelian philosopher. He had the ambition to be the Hegel of his time, to teach the real wisdom and he made philosophy speak 'hollands-bollands'. His interpretation of Hegelian philosophy was very systematic, more than historic or dialectical. He saw it as his duty to make the Hegelian system more perfect and in doing so he took part in the ever continuing process of absolute idealism. Bolland used as his tool a higher form of reasoning than the 'low' arguing of the understanding, coming near to a form of philosophical mysticism. He illustrated this 'higher' manner by playing with words and concepts and by using ambiguous terms.

The 'Idea' is the highest unity and reality; in our reasoning we are able to reach this Idea and to understand our world as the explication of the Idea. Negations and dialectical contradictions are reconciled and have lost their power in the all-including synthesis.

This fixed system had its consequences in the socio-political field: it is the most conservative branch of Hegelianism. The existing world is the real world and is understood by means of the Idea. No change is desired, let alone a revolution; the existing powers are fully justified. Bolland strongly attacked all kinds of innovation: he was a declared enemy of socialism and of feminism. Had he lived longer, it is unquestionable that he would have adhered to fascism and Nazism. Many of his pupils later became National Socialists.

In theology his position is to be compared with the German school of Bruno Bauer, who denied the historicity of Jesus and considered Christian faith only as a lower representation of the higher philosophical idea. He also agreed with the 'Dutch radical school' of theologians in their rejection of a historical ground for an eternal idea of divineness. The amount of polemic literature around Bolland's philosophy is enormous; nearly all Dutch philosophers are engaged in these polemics. A pupil of Bolland wrote a dissertation about his philosophy: K. J. Pen (1922). After his death the 'Bolland-Genootschap voor zuivere rede' was founded (1922), a league of Bolland-followers, with its philosophical journal *De Idee*

(1923–45); the 'Bolland-Stichting' was founded in 1932, maintaining a special Chair of Philosophy at the University of Leyden. His followers also took the initiative to found the first international 'Hegel-Bund' (1930).

WIM VAN DOOREN

Bollnow, Otto Friedrich

German. *b:* 14 March 1903, Stettin, Germany. *d:* 7 February 1991, Tübingen. *Cat:* Philosopher and educational theorist; exponent of Dilthey's philosophy of life and hermeneutic approach. *Ints:* Hermeneutics; philosophy of life. *Educ:* After completing his studies in Mathematics and Physics, took up Philosophy in Göttingen and Freiburg. *Appts:* Professor of Philosophy and Pedagogy at Giessen in 1939, Mainz in 1946, Tübingen from 1953.

Main publications:

(Works on education not listed here.)
(1936) *Dilthey*.
(1941) *Das Wesen der Stimmungen* [The Nature of Moods].
(1943) *Existenzphilosophie* [Existentialism].
(1947) *Einfache Sittlichkeit* [Simple Morality].
(1951) *Rilke*, Suttgart: Kolhammer.
(1955) *Neue Geborgenheit. Das Problem einer Überwindung des Existentialismus* [The New Sense of Security: The Problem of Overcoming Existentialism].
(1958) *Die Lebensphilosophie* [The Philosophy of Life].

Secondary literature:

Göbbeler, H. P. (1984) 'Grundlagen hermeneutischen Philosophierens' (a review of Bollnow's *Studien zur Hermeneutic*), in *Dilthey Jahrbuch für Philosophie und Geschichte der Geistewissenschaften*, vol. 2.
—— and Lessing, H. V. (1983) *Bibliographie O. F. Bollnow 1925–82*, Freiburg and Munich: Alber.
Rodi, F. (1983) Introduction to *O. F. Bollnow im Gespräch*, Freiburg and Munich: Alber.
——(1993) *Hermeneutische Philosophie im Spätwerk von O. F. Bollnow*, expanded from Memorial Lecture, 31 January 1992, in *Dilthey Jahrbuch für Philosophie und Geschichte der Geistewissenschaften*, vol. 8.
Schwartländer, Johannes (1984) Symposium on *Die Verantwortung der Vernunft in einer friedlosen Welt*, in honour of Bollnow's 80th birthday, Tübingen.

Bollnow's central achievement lay in preserving (during a period of neglect in the Nazi era),

clarifying and, indeed, carrying forward **Dilthey**'s philosophy of life and thereby inspiring another generation of Dilthey scholars. Focusing specifically on Dilthey's late writings, only made accessible in the 1920s through the work of **Misch** (Bollnow's teacher in Göttingen) and the publication of volume VII of the collected works, Bollnow was to the very end of his life preoccupied with the development of a hermeneutic philosophy—not just a philosophical hermeneutic as methodological basis of the human studies, but the openminded and undogmatic interpretation and spelling out of an already meaningful experience of life. The exploration of poetic uterrances (as those of Rilke) and the exploration of everyday moods and morals were part of the scheme. The fixed starting-points of traditional epistemology, including that of the earlier Dilthey, he considered unnecessary and polemicized against **Heidegger**'s similarly hermeneutic approach for basing itself on highly selected experiences such as dread while ignoring positive moods such as hope or celebration. Since editing Dilthey's lectures on education (volume IX, 1934) he remained dedicated to the development of educational philosophy based on interpretations of life and human relations.

After the war Bollnow encouraged the reissue and continuation of Dilthey's *Collected Works*, which at the end of his life had reached twenty volumes, and actively supported a translation into English of substantial selections from Dilthey's writings.

Sources: Edwards; letters from Prof. F. Rodi, 2 Feb 1993.

H. P. RICKMAN

Boltzmann, Ludwig Eduard

Austrian. *b:* 20 February 1844, Vienna. *d:* 1906, Duino, near Trieste. *Cat:* Physicist; philosopher of science. *Ints:* Epistemology. *Educ:* Doctorate, Linz, Vienna, 1867. *Infls:* Stefan, Loschmidt, Kelvin and Maxwell. *Appts:* 1869 and 1876, Graz; 1873, 1894 and 1902, Vienna; 1889, Munich; 1900, Leipzig;.

Main publications:

(1891–3) *Vorlesungen über Maxwells Theorie der Elektricität und des Lichtes*, 2 vols, Leipzig: J. A. Barth.
(1896–8) *Vorlesungen über Gastheorie*, Leipzig: J. A. Barth.
(1903) *Über die Prinzipien der Mechanik, Zwei akademische Antrittsreden* (Leipzig, November

1900, and Vienna, October 1902), Leipzig: S. Hirzel.

(1905) *Populäre Schriften*, Leipzig: J. A. Barth.

(1909) *Wissenschaftliche Abhandlungen*, 3 vols, Leipzig: 1909.

(1974) *Theoretical Physics and Physical Problems*, Dordrecht: Reidel.

Secondary literature:

Bierhalter, G. (1990) 'Cyclical representation of time', *Centaurus* 33: 345–67.

Broda, E. (1983) *Ludwig Boltzmann: Man, Physicist and Philosopher*, Woodbridge, Conn.: Ox Bow Press.

Curd, M. V. (1978) 'Ludwig Bolzmann's philosophy of science', University of Pittsburgh PhD dissertation.

Dagostino, S. (1990) 'Boltzmann and Hertz on the Bild conception of physical theory', *History of Science* 28: 380–98.

Dilworth, C. (1990) 'Empiricism versus realism', *Studies in History and Philosophy of Science*, 21: 431–62.

Dugas, R. (1959) *La Théorie physique au sens de Boltzmann et ses prolongements modernes*, Neuchâtel: Éditions de Griffon.

Ehrenfest, P. and T. (1959) *The Conceptual Foundations of the Statistical Approach in Mechanics*, Ithaca: Cornell University Press.

Klein, M. J. (1974) *Boltzmann Monocycles and Mechanical Explanation*, Boston: Studies in the Philosophy of Science, II 155–75.

Krüger, L., *et al.*, (1981) *Thermodynamics and Physical Reality II: Probabilistic Thinking*, Dordrecht: Reidel.

Reichenbach, H. (1956) *The Direction of Time*, Berkeley: University of California Press.

Boltzmann was a defender of physical atomism in the face of the instrumentalist and energeticist approaches of the likes of W. **Ostwald** and E. **Mach**, and in the face of the incompatibility of classical molecular theory with the second law of thermodynamics (i.e. hot bodies never spontaneously become hotter, but mechanical equations are always reversible). He did so by extending the statistical approach of Maxwell to the theory of gases in an attempt to explain the successes of classical thermodynamics and to suggest the possibility of fluctuations contrary to the second law. This was soon to be borne out by the theoretical work of **Einstein** and the experimental work of Perrin, but Boltzmann was by then dead. He seems to have held, contrary to many instrumentalists, that experimental facts were all hypothetical, and to a fallibilist epistemology

generally, and used this in arguments with Ostwald.

Sources: Edwards; A. Sommerfeld (1953) 'Boltzmann, Ludwig Erhard', NDB 2: 4436b–4437b; S. G. Brush (1970) DSB, 2: 260a–268a; G. Jäger (1925) 'Ludwig Boltzmann', NöB 1915–8; R. Maiocchi (1988) *La 'Belle Époque dell'Atomo ...* ', Milan: Franco Angeli.

R. N. D. MARTIN

Bonatelli, Francesco

Italian. **b:** 25 April 1830, Iseo, Brescia, Italy. **d:** 13 May 1911, Padua. **Cat:** Christian spiritualist philosopher. **Appts:** Professor at the Universities of Bologna and Padua; Editor of *Filosofia delle scuole italiane*.

Main publications:

(1864) *Pensiero e conoscenza*.

(1872) *La cosicenza e il meccanismo interiore*.

(1892) *Elementi di psicologia e logica*.

Secondary literature:

Alliney, G. (1947) *Francesco Bonatelli*, Brescia.

Crippa, R. (ed.) (1982) *Convengo sui filosofici bresciani*, Brescia: Ateneo di Brescia.

'In onore di Francesco Bonatelli', *La cultura filosofica* 4 (2) (includes bibliography).

Against positivism Bonatelli argued the spiritual character of psychological awareness and its non-reducibility to pure mechanism. Against idealist philosophers opposed to any notion of transcendence Bonatelli further attempted to demonstrate the existence of an ideal order, founded on the divine, which guarantees the objective value of every principle of thought and action. This work involved a subtle reworking of the philosophies of Plato and Rosmini, undertaken in constant awareness of German philosophers such as Herbart, Fechner and Lotze, philosophers who owed their reputation in Italy largely to Bonatelli. Of these philosophers he was closest to Lotze, translating his *Microcosm* in 1911. Bonatelli begins with the belief that psychological observation shows there to be a duality between mere psychological psychic internal mechanisms and consciousness. Consciousness is nothing other than the act of judgement, the simple act in which we say to ourselves that something is or is not the case in some way or other. This act cannot be reduced to sensation. Consciousness is thought turned on itself, creating itself and willingly accepting the laws of logic. Thought is governed not merely by psychological laws concerning the ways in which we in fact think, but by metaphysical and logical laws concerning the contents of our thoughts according to a necessity that has to do with the rights and wrongs of thoughts. The laws of empirical psychology are incomplete and the laws of logic and metaphysics make good what is lacking. By these laws we formulate such concepts as identity, substance, causality, force, matter, spirit and the like, concepts which structure things and our thinking about them and through which thought can become objective knowledge. Thought infinitely turns back on itself. This is not an aimless infinite progression but an advance in self-understanding.

COLIN LYAS

Boodin, John Elof

Swedish. *b:* 14 September 1869, Pjetteryd, Sweden. *d:* 14 November 1950, Los Angeles. *Cat:* Idealist (with overtones of pragmatism and realism). *Ints:* Metaphysics; philosophy of religion. *Educ:* Universities of Colorado and Minnesota, Brown Universities and Harvard. *Infls:* C. S. Peirce, William James and, especially, Josiah Royce. *Appts:* Brown University, 1896–7; Harvard, 1899–1900; Grinnell College, 1900–4; University of Kansas, 1904–13; Carleton College, 1913–28; UCLA, 1928 -39.

Main publications:

(1904) *Time and Reality*, New York: Macmillan.
(1909) 'What pragmatism is and is not', *Journal of Philosophy* 6: 627–35.
(1911) *Truth and Reality* , New York: Macmillan.
(1916) *A Realistic Universe*; revised edition, New York: Macmillan, 1931.
(1925) *Cosmic Evolution: Outlines of Cosmic Idealism*, New York: Macmillan.
(1934) *God and Creation*, 2 vols, New York: Macmillan.
(1934) *Three Interpretations of the Universe*, New York: Macmillan.
(1939) *The Social Mind*, New York: Macmillan.
(1943) *Religion of Tomorrow*, New York: Macmillan.
(1947) *A Cosmic Philosophy*, New York: Philosophical Library.
(1957) *The Posthumous Papers of John Elof Boodin*, Los Angeles: University of California Press.

Secondary literature:

Nelson, Charles N. (1987) *John Elof Boodin: Philosopher Poet*, New York: Philosophical Library.
Reck, Andrew (1961) 'The philosophy of J. E. Boodin (1869–1950)', *Review of Metaphysics* 15: 148–73.

Determined to do justice to the salient features of life and philosophy, Boodin produced a complicated system bringing together fact and value, science and religion, while incorporating portions of classical metaphysical systems with similar objectives. The result was interesting, but then somewhat dated. Boodin came to terms with his contemporaries by subscribing to pragmatism, realism and idealism simultaneously. In his article on pragmatism (1909), he defined it as the application of scientific method to 'philosophical hypotheses'. This also meant finding the human significance of scientific and philosophical concepts. With respect to idealism he wished to retain its emphasis on value, while avoiding its tendency to 'psychologitis'. He endorsed both evolutionary theory and modern physics yet, as with the idealists, the goal of evolution is both in the process of being achieved and already present. He held that his view combined 'empirical realism and cosmic idealism' (1925, p. 7).

He thought of substance as totality, and found it to possess the five attributes of being, time, space, consciousness and form. He thought of the first attribute as 'pragmatic energism'. The other four are 'not-being' in that they are not things although making a difference to things. Consciousness, for example, is energy becoming aware of itself; and form is 'formulation', part of the 'executive constitution' of nature, having to do with direction, order and standards within the process of evolution. At the same time Boodin referred in a single locution to 'form, spirit or God'. He argued that God's existence was not in question since God is 'the quality of the highest level to which we strive to adapt ourselves [at] our best' (1925, p. 129). That might be taken to mean that God is merely a quality of human awareness. In fact, however, the fields of physics, organic life, conscious awareness and society—called forth by the interworking of the attributes of substance—constitute a hierarchy of overlapping levels. God as the highest level and 'field of fields' is both the form evolution must take and an awareness 'stimulating the evolution of every part in the direction of divinity' (1925, p. 123). The inertia of the parts, including human indifference and opposition, limits the divine effectiveness, mingling tragedy with achievement.

The unfinished essay of the *Posthumous Papers* (1957) places the foregoing in a context where metaphysics is the only field remaining to philosophy, and where science and metaphysics are correlative disciplines. The former reduces reality to its simplest, measurable aspects, while the latter takes reality in its concreteness, whole-

ness and individuality. Metaphysics proceeds by discovering the categories necessary to explain experience. The categories, those 'supreme binders of experience', come in two forms. One set—simplicity, economy, consistency and harmony—are 'cosmic feelings' which come to light as humans interact with their environment. Together, the categories explicate a reality which, while richer than, is not inconsistent with, science.
Sources: Edwards; Reck 1964; Reese.

WILLIAM REESE

Boreas, Theophilos

Greek. *b:* 1873, Marousi (near Athens). *d:* 1953, Athens. *Cat:* Positivist. *Ints:* Ancient Greek philosophy; history of philosophy; continental philosophy; psychology. *Educ:* University of Athens, University of Leipzig. *Infls:* Positivist philosophy and Wilhelm Wundt. *Appts:* Taught at teachers' training colleges in Athens and elsewhere (1900–12); Professor of Philosophy, University of Athens (1912–39, 1946–9); founding member of the Academy of Athens (1926).

Main publications:

(1932–57) *Academeica* (I. *Logic*, II. *Psychology*, III. *Introduction to Philosophy*, IV. *Ethics*), Athens.

(1937–41) *Analecta*, 4 vols (topics in the history of philosophy and psychology), Athens.

(1948) *The Problem of Freedom of the Will in Ancient Greece*, 2 vols, Athens.

Boreas was an advocate of scientific philosophy; he viewed philosophy as continuous with the sciences and endorsed empirical methodology; he introduced experimental psychology in Greece and founded the first laboratory of experimental psychology at the University of Athens in 1925.

STAVROULA TSINOREMA

Born, Max

German. *b:* 11 December 1882, Breslau, Poland. *d:* 5 January 1970, Göttingen, Germany. *Cat:* Physicist; Philosopher of science. *Ints:* Foundations of physics; mathematical physics. *Educ:* Breslau 1901–5 (Heidelberg summer 1902 and Zurich summer 1903), Göttingen 1905–7, PhD 1907; Breslau 1908; Göttingen 1909–12; Habilitation 1909. *Infls:* Hilbert (assistant 1905), Minkowski, Schwarzschild, Carathéodory and Einstein. *Appts:* Privatdozent, Göttingen, 1912–14; Professor, Berlin, 1915–19; Frankfurt 1919–21; Göttingen 1922–33; Lecturer, Cambridge and

Bangalore, 1933–6; Professor, Edinburgh, 1936–53; Nobel Prize 1954.

Main publications:

(1924) *Einstein's Theory of Relativity*, London: Methuen; revised edition, New York, 1962.

(1935) *Atomic Physics*, London and Glasgow: Blackie.

(1935) *The Restless Universe*, London: Blackie.

(1943) *Experiment and Theory in Physics*, Cambridge: Cambridge University Press.

(1949) *The Natural Philosophy of Cause and Chance*, Oxford: Clarendon.

(1955) 'Statistical interpretation of quantum mechanics', *Physics Teacher*, 6: 284–90.

(1956) *Physics in my Generation*, London: Pergamon; second revised edition, New York: Springer.

(1962) *Physics and Politics*, Edinburgh: Oliver & Boyd.

(1968) *My Life and Views*, New York: Scribner.

(1969) *Albert Einstein, Hedwig und Max Born, Briefwechsel 1916–55*, Munich: Nymphenburger.

(1971) *The Born-Einstein Letters*, London: Macmillan.

(1978) *My Life Recollections of a Nobel Laureate*, London: Taylor & Francis.

Secondary literature:

Beller, M. (1990) 'Born's probabilistic interpretation', *Studies in History and Philosophy of Science* 21: 563–88.

Klein, M. J. (1970) 'The first phase of the Bohr–Einstein dialogue', *Historical Studies in the Physical Sciences* 2: 1–39.

Konno, H. (1978) 'The historical roots of Born's statistical interpretation', *Japanese Studies in the History of Science* 17: 129–45.

Pais, A. (1982) 'Max Born's statistical interpretation of quantum mechanics', *Science* 118: 1193–8.

Paliglandla, R. (1974) 'Max Born and the problem of objectivity', *Scientia* 109: 499–507.

Vogel, H. (1968) *Physik und Philosophie bei Max Born*, Berlin: Deutscher Verlag der Wissenschaften.

Wessels, L. (1980) 'What was Born's statistical interpretation?', *Philosophy of Science Association Biennial Meeting Proceedings, II, 187–200.*

Born trained as a mathematical physicist in the Göttingen school. After early work in solid state physics (like his contemporary Niels **Bohr**), he played a major role in the development of atomic physics and the quantum theory. In particular he had with **Heisenberg** a decisive role in the development of the statistical interpretation of the quantum theory, being responsible for showing the mathematical equivalence of **Schrödinger**'s wave mechanics to Heisenberg's matrix mechanics—he had earlier been responsible for showing the relevance of matrix mathematics to the development of the theory. He was also a prolific writer of influential textbooks—that on atomic physics was used by generations of students. With **Russell** and **Einstein** he campaigned against the military uses of atomic energy.

Sources: N. Kemmer and R. Schlapp (1971) 'Max Born', *BMFRS* 27: 17–52.

R. N. D. MARTIN

Bosanquet, Bernard

British. *b:* 14 June 1848, Alnwick, Northumberland. *d:* 8 February 1923, Hampstead, London. *Cat:* Idealist. *Ints:* Metaphysics; political philosophy; aesthetics. *Educ:* Harrow School and Balliol College, Oxford. *Infls:* Hegel, T. H. Green and Bradley. *Appts:* Fellow of University College, Oxford 1871–81; Professor of Moral Philosophy, St Andrews 1903–8.

Main publications:

(1885) *Knowledge and Reality*, London.
(1888) *Logic or the Morphology of Knowledge*, London.
(1892) *History of Aesthetics*, London.
(1899) *Philosophical Theory of the State*, London.
(1912) *The Principle of Individuality and Value*, London.
(1913) *The Value and Destiny of the Individual*, London.
(1913) *The Distinction Between Mind and its Objects*, Manchester.
(1920) *Implication and Linear Inference*, London.
(1921) *The Meeting of Extremes in Contemporary Philosophy*, London.

Secondary literature:

Bosanquet, Helen (1924) *Bernard Bosanquet, a Short Account of his Life*.
Bradley, A. C. and Lord Haldane (1923) Obituary in *Proc. Brit. Acad.*
Hobhouse, L. T. (1918) *The Metaphysical Theory of the State*, London.
Houang, F. (1954) *Le Neo-Hegelianisme en Angelterre: la philosophie de Bernard Bosanquet*, Paris.
Muirhead, J. H. (1935) *Bernard Bosanquet and his Friends*, London.

Bosanquet was much influenced by **Bradley** (and, in return, had some influence upon him) but the two men were very different. Bradley spent his entire career in his college, neither teaching nor lecturing. Bosanquet, after ten years as an active college tutor, left for London to work in the organization of charities and in adult education, spending only five of his post-Oxford years in an academic post. Bradley's metaphysics ended in a kind of nebulously hopeful mysticism, in which reason or the intellect is transcended by something called 'absolute experience'. Bosanquet had his feet firmly on the ground of the social and cultural life of mankind. Against Bradley's view that the intellect, the instrument of discursive thought, inevitably misrepresents reality, Bosanquet saw it as the only mode of access to reality. Thought is not, as in Bradley, doomed to traffic in abstractions; it seeks to apprehend the concrete universal or system. Approximate concrete universals are finite selves and, above them, social and cultural institutions: the state, art, religion and philosophy. The only true concrete universal is the absolute, the all-inclusive system. The work of thought is to develop the judgements which are its elements into rationally articulated systems. The inferences by which this is brought about are not the 'linear inferences' of formal logic, but spread out in all directions to take in all its conditions so as to reveal the place of the judgement in a comprehensive system. Every judgement always implicitly refers to reality, so hypothetical judgements embody a categorical assertion about some relation of connectedness. In the same ample spirit he maintains that hypothetical judgements are reciprocal. Less peculiar is his claim that judgement and inference are only superficially distinct: every judgement rests on inference and is the starting-point of further inferences. Bradley accepted much of Bosanquet's criticism of his own account of logic with uncharacteristic meekness. Since the person, or finite self, is only an approximation to the true concrete universal it is not wholly real. The absolute is not the God of theism since it is beyond personality. The finite human self, furthermore, is not the abstract self-sufficient, self-interested individual of traditional liberal and utilitarian doctrine. Human beings are constituted as such by their involvement in society and culture with others. That conception of the essentially social nature of human beings is the basis of Bosanquet's theory of the state. He follows Rousseau in taking it to express the real will of its citizens, who are made what they are by membership of it. Compulsion is the essence of the state; enforcing citizens to obey the law it enables their real natures to overcome their baser impulses. But a residue of Green's more liberal outlook is present in his view that state's main task is the removal of obstacles to human self-perfection. He conceives the state as inevitably national; the human community in general is not sufficiently 'actual' to serve as the domain of a single world-state. Bosanquet's influence was most notable in the field of political theory. It came in for severe criticism from L. T. Hobhouse in 1918 after Hobhouse had lost a son in the war. Hobhouse argues persuasively that Bosanquet fails to distinguish society, which does humanize us, from the state, which has a humbler role. His larger inquiries contributed to the generally edifying and anti-scientific mood of the age. But while his contemporaries were arguing for various forms of personal idealism against the pure doctrine of Hegel, Bosanquet remained loyal to the old faith.

Sources: Metz; Passmore 1957; Edwards.

ANTHONY QUINTON

Bourdieu, Pierre

French. *b:* 1 August 1930. Denguin (Basses-pyrénées). *Cat:* Post-structuralist. *Ints:* Social structures in art, education and culture; sociology. *Educ:* Lycée de Pay; Lycée Louis-Le-Grand; Faculté des lettres de Paris, École Normale Supérieure (Agrégé de philosophie). *Appts:* Professor, Lycée de Moulins, 1955; Assistant à la faculté des lettres d'Alger, 1958–60; Assistant à la faculté des lettres de Paris, 1960–1; Maître de conférences, l'École Pratique des Hautes études, since 1964; Directeur of the revue *Actes de Recherches en Sciences Socialies*, since 1975; Professeur-titulaire de la chaire de sociologie, Collège de France, since 1981.

Main publications:

(1964) (with A. Sayad) *Le Déracinement*, Paris: Minuit.

(1964) (with Jean-Claude Passeron) *Les Héritiers*, Paris: Minuit (English translation, *The Inheritors: French Students and their Relation to the Culture*, trans. Richard Nice, Chicago: University of Chicago Press, 1979).

(1965) *Un art moyen, essai sur les usages sociaux de la photographie*, Paris: Minuit.

(1969) (with Alain Darbel) *L'Armour de l'art, les musées d'art Europeens at leur public*, second revised and augmented edition, Paris: Minuit.

(1970) *Sociologie de L'Algérie*, third edition, Paris: PUF.

(1970) (with Jean-Claude Passeron) *La Réproduction, Paris: Minuit (English translation, Reproduction in Education, Society and Culture*, trans.

Richard Nice, foreword Tom Bottomore, London: Sage, 1990).

(1972) *Esquisse d'une theorie de la pratique, précédé de trois études d'ethnologie kabyle*, Geneva: Librairie Droz.

(1977) *Outline of a theory of Practice*, trans. Richard Nice, Cambridge: Cambridge University Press.

(1988) *L'Ontologie politique de Martin Heidegger*, Paris: Minuit (English translation, *The Political Ontology of Martin Heidegger*, trans. Peter Collier, Oxford: Polity Press, 1991).

(1989) *La Noblesse d'état: grandes écoles et esprit de corps*, Paris: Minuit.

Secondary literature:

Ferry, Luc and Renaut, Alain (1990) *French Philosophy of the Sixties: An Essay on Antihumanism*, trans. Mary Schnackenberg, Amherst: University of Massachusetts Press.

Gorder, Karen L. (1980) 'Understanding school knowledge: a critical appraisal of Basil Bernstein and Pierre Bourdieu', *Educational Theory* 30: 335–46.

Jenkins, Richard (1992) *Pierre Bourdieu*, London: Routledge.

Robbins, Derek (1991) *The Work of Pierre Bourdieu, Recognizing Society*, Milton Keynes: Open University Press.

Schatzki, Theodore (1987) 'Overdue analysis of Bourdieu's theory of practice', *Inquiry* 30: 113–35.

Bourdieu has contributed significantly to the sociology of culture and education. Through his empirical work on art, literature, power and intellectuals (especially relating to the ruling classes) he constructs a theory of practice that constitutes an analysis of the practical intelligibility governing action with a perspective on how the structure of social phenomena determines and is itself perpetuated by action. His sociological methodology is relevant to philosophical questions through his critical studies of the role of philosophy in specific social spheres (see his study of Kantian aethetics in *La Distinction* and of the question of politics in **Heidegger**'s ontology *L'Ontologie politique de Martin Heidegger*). Bourdieu draws philosophy back into a debate about the social ground and impact of any philosophical construction.

JAMES WILLIAMS

Boutroux, Émile

French. *b:* 1845, Montrouge, near Paris. *d:* 1921, Paris. *Cat:* Philosopher of science; philosopher of religion. *Educ:* École Normale Supérieure, and in

Heidelberg. *Infls:* Leibniz, Kant and Jules Lache-lier. *Appts:* Taught at the Universities of Montpellier and Nancy, then (1878) at the École Normale Supérieure, and finally (from 1885) at the Sorbonne; elected to the Académie des Sciences Morales in 1898, and to the Académie Française in 1912.

Main publications:

(1874) *De la contingence des lois de la nature*, Paris: Baillière (English translation, *The Contingency of the Laws of Nature*, London: Open Court, 1916).

(1895) *De l'idée de la loi naturelle dans la science et la philosophie contemporaines*, Paris: Lecène (English translation, *Natural Law in Science and Philosophy*, London: Macmillan, 1914).

(1908) *Science et religion dans la philosophie contemporaine*, Paris: Flammarion (English translation, *Science and Religion in Contemporary Philosophy*, London: Duckworth, 1909).

(1925) *La Morale et la religion*, Paris: Flammarion.

Secondary literature:

Baillot, A.-F. (1957) *Émile Boutroux et la pensée religieuse*, Paris: La Nef de Paris.

Crawford, L. S. (1924) *The Philosophy of Emile Boutroux*, New York: Longmans Green & Co.

Boutroux was concerned with the problems created by the tension between freedom and determinism, and necessity and contingency. His proposed solution tried to do justice to both science and religion. He maintained that, in the natural world, there is no pure or logical necessity, which is confined to areas such as mathematics. Further, within the sciences themselves, there are several different levels: the physical, the biological and the human; or the inorganic, the organic and the thinking, none of which is reducible to any of the other strata. He thus reached the position that there is a qualitative, and not merely a quantitative, element in science. Mechanical laws are progressively less capable of providing a full account of phenomena as one moves from the physical, through the biological, to the human sciences, because there is a greater amount of contingency and lack of uniformity at each level. One example of non-uniformity given by Boutroux was biological evolution, in which there is always an element of novelty, and this is one of the pointers to the possibility of there being a creative act or principle on which everything else depends.

According to Boutroux, scientific understanding can never provide a completely objective view of the world, as data is always selected to form abstractions, instead of an appreciation of the wholeness of concrete existences. A scientific understanding of the world around us is only one aspect of the use of human reason, which can and should also be employed in the spiritual, moral and aesthetic dimensions, to allow for the full development of human beings.

Boutroux thought that science was to be placed in a wider metaphysical framework, and to this end he developed a theory of a hierarchy of perfections, which owes much to Leibniz. At one end of the hierarchy is God, who is absolutely perfect and thus pure act, and at the other are inorganic material things, which are nevertheless endowed with a potential spirituality towards which they are constantly striving. There is no essential difference between the inorganic, the organic and the spiritual, and no purely mechanistic causes, but only teleological ones. The whole of creation is a system imbued with vitalism.

The reason of human beings can degenerate into mere habit, or it can render us capable of belief in God, who is the creative principle of life and who, by analogy with the life of the whole universe, is recognized to be the infinite mind or person. Religion and science should not be viewed as conflicting, but as complementary: both are legitimate areas for the employment of human reason, and both are needed for human development.

Whilst the works of Boutroux rightly stress that scientific explanations are limited, and that even within the sciences there is no one model of explanation, one criticism of his thought is that the attempt to postulate a hierarchy of perfection, and in particular to extend this beyond experience to end in God, is unwarranted speculation.

KATHRYN PLANT

Bouveresse, Jacques

French. *b:* 20 August 1940, Epenoy, Doubs, France. *Cat:* Analytic philosophy. *Ints:* Wittgenstein; philosophy of language; philosophy of mathematics; rapprochement of analytic and continental philosophy (hermeneutics and phenomenology); critique of recent continental philosophy (post-structuralism). *Educ:* École Normale Supérieure. *Infls:* Carnap, Quine, Wittgenstein and Austrian philosophy and literature (Musil, Kraus and Lichtenberg). *Appts:* Taught at the Sorbonne and University of Paris I; Professor, University of Geneva.

Main publications:

(1971) *La Parole malheureuse*, Paris: Minuit.

(1973) *Wittgenstein, la rime et la raison*, Paris: Minuit.

(1976) *Le Mythe de l'intériorité*, Paris: Minuit.

(1981) 'Herméneutique et linguistique', in Panet and Bouveresse (eds), *Meaning and Understanding*, New York and Berlin: De Gruyter.

(1987) *La Force de la règle: Wittgenstein et l'invention de la nécessité*, Paris: Minuit.

(1988) *Le Pays des possibles: Wittgenstein, les mathématiques et le monde*, Paris: Minuit.

(1990) '"The darkness of this time": Wittgenstein and the modern world', *Philosophy* 28, suppl.: 11–39.

(1991) *Philosophie, mythologie et pseudo-science: Wittgenstein lecteur de Freud*, Combas: L'Éclat.

Bouveresse is important in France as the main commentator on and interpreter of **Wittgenstein**'s philosophy. He was also one of the first philosophers to introduce analytic philosophy into France. His work marks a departure in French philosophy towards more analytical approaches to classic philosophical problems. His later work uses the resources of analytic philosophy to criticize the claims of sceptical trends in current French thought. Instead of cynical and irrationalist reactions to the crisis of modernity, Bouveresse defends an ironic rationalism that he traces back to Wittgenstein, Musil, Kraus and Lichtenberg.

JAMES WILLIAMS

Bouwsma, Oets Kolk

American. *b:* 22 November 1898, Muskegon, Michigan. *d:* 1 March 1978, Austin, Texas. *Cat:* Wittgensteinian. *Ints:* Philosophy and language; epistemology; religion; aesthetics. *Educ:* Calvin College and University of Michigan. *Infls:* G. E. Moore and L. Wittgenstein. *Appts:* Professor of Philosophy, University of Nebraska, 1928–65, and University of Texas, Austin, 1965–78; John Locke Lecturer, University of Oxford, 1950–1.

Main publications:

(1965) *Philosophical Essays*, Lincoln: University of Nebraska Press.

(1982) *Toward a New Sensibility*, ed. J. L. Craft and Ronald E. Hustwit, Lincoln: University of Nebraska Press.

(1984) *Without Proof or Evidence*, ed. J. L. Craft and Ronald E. Hustwit, Lincoln: University of Nebraska Press.

(1986) *Wittgenstein: Conversations 1949–51*, ed. J. L. Craft and Ronald E. Hustwit, Indianapolis: Hackett.

Secondary literature:

(1985)'O. K. Bouwsma: philosopher and teacher' a special issue of *Philosophical Investigations*, 8, 3.

Hustwit, Ronald E. (1992) *Something About O. K. Bouwsma*, Lanham, MD: University Press of America.

Bouwsma was a dedicated and inspiring teacher whose work remained largely unpublished in his lifetime. Two collections of essays and a volume of memoirs have been published from the material deposited after his death at the Humanities Research Center, University of Texas at Austin.

After abandoning his early Hegelianism Bouwsma studied the work of G. E. **Moore**, attracted by its anti-idealism and attention to language. His essay 'Moore's theory of sense-data' was published in *The Philosophy of G. E. Moore* (volume IV of *The Library of Living Philosophers*, edited by Paul Arthur Schilpp, Evanston and Chicago: Northwestern University, 1942; reprinted in *Philosophical Essays*, 1965, pp. 1–20), and it led him to be invited to give the John Locke Lectures at the University of Oxford in 1950–1.

During the 1940s some of Bouwsma's postgraduate students, including Norman **Malcolm**, accepted his advice to study with G. E. Moore at Cambridge. It was through them that Bouwsma discovered **Wittgenstein**'s later work, which had a profound effect on his own approach to philosophy. Bouwsma's notes of his conversations with Wittgenstein, whom he met at Cornell University in 1949 and at Oxford, were published under the title *Wittgenstein: Conversations 1949–51* (1986).

In his essay 'The Blue Book' (1965, pp. 175–209) Bouwsma presents his understanding of Wittgenstein's method in philosophy, a method which Bouwsma himself practised in his own distinctive manner. He understood Wittgenstein to be concerned, not with the defence of theories or doctrines, but rather with the cultivation of a skill in the handling of philosophical problems. In a later essay Bouwsma spoke of Wittgenstein helping us towards 'a new sensibility in the matter of language', in particular a sensibility for, or an awareness of, the confusion, the nonsense, endemic in language as used by philosophers. Wittgenstein's interest in language, Bouwsma believed, was an interest in 'saving intelligence—which means us—from the corruption that comes so natural to us'; and in this respect Bouwsma compared Wittgenstein to Kierkegaard and to **Nietzsche** (see 'A new sensibility', in 1982, pp. 1–4).

Bouwsma's writings are characterized by sensitivity to fine shades of linguistic usage which

he exposes through attention to concrete examples, often taking the form of stories exhibiting his
humour and playfulness as well as his love of
language. When discussing a theory or argument
he frequently focuses on a sentence or a phrase
which he takes to be a source of confusion,
showing the unintelligibility 'by pressing the
grammar' or by using analogies as 'reminders of
sense'. (Quotations taken from a note made by
Bouwsma in 1971 and reprinted in Craft and
Hustwit's introduction to *Toward a New Sensibility*, 1982, pp. xviii–xix.) In *Philosophical Essays*
and *Toward a New Sensibility* Bouwsma addresses
questions on the nature of philosophy, on scepticism, on metaphysics and aesthetics. *Without
Proof or Evidence* (1984) is primarily devoted to
problems in religion. But of all this work it may be
fairly said, as Bouwsma said of Wittgenstein: 'He
isn't satisfied with telling the reader something.
He nags. He intends to get under your skin, to get
into your hair, to make you uncomfortable, to
drive you to self-examination and improvement'
('Ryle and Wittgenstein', in *Toward a New
Sensibility*, p. 29).
Sources: WW(Am).

PETER LEWIS

Bowne, Borden Parker

American. *b:* 14 January 1847, Leonardville (now
Atlantic Highlands), New Jersey. *d:* 1 April 1910.
Cat: Personalist. *Ints:* Philosophy of religion. *Educ:*
New York University, Halle, Paris and Göttingen.
Infls: Lotze, Kant and, as a subject of criticism,
Spencer. *Appts:* New York University, 1875–6;
Professor of Philosophy, Boston University,
1876–1910, where he also served as Dean of the
Graduate School of Arts and Sciences, 1888–
1910.

Main publications:

(1874) *The Philosophy of Herbert Spencer*, New York:
Nelson & Phillips.
(1879) *Studies in Theism*, New York: Phillips & Hunt.
(1882) *Metaphysics*, revised edition, New York:
Harper & Bros, 1898.
(1886) *Introduction to Psychological Theory*, New
York: Harper.
(1887) *Philosophy of Theism*, New York: Harper &
Bros.
(1887) *Theism*, New York: Harper & Bros (a revised
and expanded edn. of *Philosophy of Theism*).
(1892) *The Principles of Ethics*, New York: Harper &
Bros.
(1896) *The Christian Revelation*, Cincinnati: Jennings & Pye.

(1897) *Theory of Thought and Knowledge*, New York:
Harper & Bros.
(1899) *The Christian Life*, Cincinnati: Curts &
Jennings.
(1900) *The Atonment*, Cincinnati: Curts & Jennings.
(1905) *The Immanance of God*, Boston: Houghton
Mifflin.
(1908) *Personalism*, Boston: Houghton Mifflin.
(1909) *Studies in Christianity*, Boston: Houghton
Mifflin.
(1910) *The Essence of Religion*, Boston: Houghton
Mifflin (posthumous).
(1912) *Kant and Spencer*, Boston: Houghton Mifflin
(posthumous, edited from student notes).

Secondary literature:

Brightman, Edgar S. (1927) ' Personalism and the
influence of Bowne', in E. S. Brightman (ed.),
*Proceedings of the Sixth International Congress of
Philosophy*, New York and London: Longmans
Green & Co., pp. 161–7.
McConnell, Francis John (1929) *Borden Parker
Bowne: His Life and his Philosophy*, Cincinnati:
Curts & Jennings (includes bibliography).
Steinkraus, Warren E. (1960) 'A century of Bowne's
theism', *Idealist Forum* (Boston) 18: 11–16.

Founder of the Boston School of personalism,
Bowne formulated his position through criticism
of Herbert **Spencer**, whose synthetic philosophy
failed to reach a positive interpretation of God
and whose explanation of persons was cast in
physiological terms. Bowne found a connection
between these two features of Spencer's system.
As a result of them the system was a 'miracle of
confusion and absurdity'. The natural processes
of evolution cannot be explained without teleology: 'Assume a controlling purpose, and all
becomes luminous and intelligible' (1874, p. 254);
and mind cannot be explained by brain processes
since 'a mechanical motion of brain-molecules is
no explanation of a thought' (p. 276). Logic
requires one to go beyond Spencer to the
'postulate of an ever-ruling, ever-active spiritual
power', and to accept experience as qualitative
and normative. These conclusions reflect Lotze's
view that spirit controls mechanism both within
nature and within ourselves, and that reality is
saturated with value.

Bowne drew the conclusion that the controlling purpose within nature and ourselves is best
understood as 'person'. Although he used the
term 'soul', the emphasis on person allowed him
to stress our interactions with each other and with
God. We are directly aware of a reality beyond
finite persons, whose phenomena we categorize

according to our needs. It is more parsimonious to think of this reality as the energy of a cosmic Person than as an independent, material system. Throughout Bowne's work the options are theism or positivism, and theism always wins out, impersonalism giving way to personalism.

Thinking, feeling, willing persons are centres of freedom, and thus cannot be either material constructs or modes of the divine. As early as 1887 Bowne had argued that 'the soul is real' and its continued existence is to be presumed. Without human freedom, he held, knowledge would be impossible. He emphasized the ethical element in religion, showing how the natural instincts, appetites and passions can develop into higher forms. His interpretations of Christianity were for the most part translations of theological positions into their personalistic equivalences.

Brightman (1927) ended his critical appreciation by saying that Bowne's personalism 'is a way of understanding experience which will always have to be reckoned with, and which opposing views will have to consider'. The perspectives of personalism, developed by Bowne and his followers in the first third of the twentieth century, continued to exert influence past mid-century.

Sources: A. C. Knudsen (1949) *The Philosophy of Personalism*, Boston: Boston UP.

WILLIAM REESE

Bradley, Francis Herbert
British. **b:** 1846, London. **d:** 1924, Oxford. **Cat:** Absolute idealist. **Ints:** Ethics; logic; metaphysics. **Educ:** MA, University College, Oxford. **Infls:** T. H. Green, E. Caird, Bosanquet and Hegel. **Appts:** Fellow of Merton College, Oxford, 1870–1924.

Main publications:
(1876) *Ethical Studies*, London; second edition, Oxford, 1927 (1962 edition cited here).

(1883) *Principles of Logic*, Oxford; second edition, Oxford, 1922.

(1893) *Appearance and Reality*, London: Allen & Unwin; second edition, 1897 (1969 edition cited here).

(1914) *Essays on Truth and Reality*, Oxford.

(1935) *Collected Essays*, Oxford.

Secondary literature:
Eliot, T. S. (1964) *Knowledge and Experience in the Philosophy of F. H. Bradley*, London: Faber & Faber.

Mander, W. J. (1994) *An Introduction to Bradley's Metaphysics*, Oxford: Clarendon Press.

Manser, A. (1983) *Bradley's Logic*, Oxford: Blackwell.

——and Stock, G. (eds) (1984) *The Philosophy of F. H. Bradley*, Oxford: Clarendon Press.

Taylor, A. E. (1924–5) Obituary, *Proceedings of the British Academy* 11.

Wollheim, R. (1959) *F. H. Bradley*, Harmondsworth: Penguin.

Bradley's central work in idealist metaphysics was expressed in *Appearance and Reality* (1893), although he did not regard this as a systematic exposition of his thinking. His earlier *Ethical Studies* (1876) and *Principles of Logic* (1883) were also important as critiques of utilitarianism and empiricism. *Ethical Studies* and the chapter on 'goodness' in *Appearance and Reality* stress the importance of *self-realization* as an end for morality, but Bradley was equally anxious to stress that this end could only be understood in a wide metaphysical context, rather than as an appeal to mere self-interest. The 'self to be realized' was not 'the self to be pleased' (1876, Essay V, p. 160). The 'real moral idea' was the community, which provided the only intelligible framework for realization (p. 210): Bradley's famous notion of 'My station and its duties'. 'There is nothing better' than this, he wrote, 'nor anything higher or more truly beautiful' (ibid.). His scorn for utilitarian ethics was almost unlimited: happiness could have nothing at all to do with morality; the idea that any kind of pleasure principle could act as a moral motivation was incoherent. The general strategy of *Ethical Studies* was dialectical in a way that can mislead the unwary reader searching for clear conclusions. Essay VI, on 'Ideal morality', tries to explain how self-realization falls into his wider view: 'The general end is self-realization, the making real of the ideal self; and for morality, in particular, the ideal self is the good will, the identification of my will with the ideal as a universal will' (p. 230). However, none of the necessary superstructure for this was given in *Ethical Studies*. That had to wait for *Appearance and Reality*.

Principles of Logic, like *Appearance and Reality*, opens with a denial that it is a systematic treatise. Bradley also distances himself from Hegel, usually seen as his main source of influence: 'We want no system-making or systems home-grown or imported' (Preface). Although there are obvious differences, Bradley's logic can be appreciated best in contrast with that of **Frege**, his near contemporary (see Manser's paper in Manser & Stock 1984). Like Frege, he totally rejected psychologism in logic, sarcastically referring to Mill as our 'great modern logician' (1876, p. 113). But, also like Frege, he was preoccupied with whatever it was about or within a judgement that held it together, and with the connections between judgements that enabled logical relations to exist between them. Like Frege, but without any supporting symbolism, he repudiated subject—predicate logic and stressed the significance of logical as opposed to superficial forms (1883, pp. 618–19). (All of this may have influenced the early **Russell** far more than he claimed to remember). But extremely unlike Frege, Bradley drew idealist conclusions from his critiques of psychologistic logic: the unity within a statement, and the unity between logically related statements, could only be grasped truly as part of a wider metaphysical unity: 'All judgment is of Reality, and that means that it makes its idea the adjective of the real Universe' (Terminal Essay, 1922, II, p. 628). Again, as with his moral philosophy, the underlying metaphysics of this had to wait to be fully explained.

This explanation came in *Appearance and Reality*, where Bradley expounded his absolute idealism as fully as he ever did anywhere. The object of the book was 'to state merely a general view about Reality, and to defend this view against more obvious and prominent objections' (p. 403). His metaphysical thinking was not based on epistemology. Appearance and reality (as with **McTaggart**) were not aligned with phenomena and noumena (chapter XII). Although the ordinary, perceived world was not *Reality* for Bradley, he was at pains to stress that it was unreal in comparison with a higher ideal and, not in comparison with anything concealed behind the veil of perception inherited from egocentric epistemology: 'The assertion of a reality falling outside knowledge, is quite nonsensical' (p. 114). Experience, he held, was genuine enough in its own terms. Appearance was unreal mainly for logical reasons (see p. 334). The idea that anything could be only accidentally ('externally') related to anything else was a profound error. Deeper reflection would show that all relations were in some way essential or intrinsic ('internal'), and could not, in any event, be considered themselves, apart from the reality within which they existed. 'Reality is one. It must be single, because plurality, taken as real, contradicts itself (p. 460). So a full statement about anything—and hence a fully true statement about anything—could not be made without reference to everything else. Thus: 'There will be no truth which is entirely true, just as there will be no error which is totally false' (pp. 320–1). The repudiation of 'external relations' and the

doctrine of degrees of truth and reality were seen by Bradley's pluralist critics, **Moore** and Russell, as well as by him, as logically fundamental.

The critical side of Bradley's metaphysics is often surprisingly trenchant. The positive characterization of the absolute is more elusive. 'There is but one Reality, and its being consists in experience' (p. 403). Any further categorical statement about it would be bound to be false since: 'any categorical judgment must be false. The subject and the predicate, in the end, cannot either be the other' (p. 319). Nevertheless, in a sense, it may be said that: 'the Absolute is actually good, and throughout the world of goodness it is truly realized in different degrees of satisfaction. Since in ultimate Reality all existence, and all thought and feeling, become one, we may even say that every feature in the universe is thus absolutely good' (p. 365). *Appearance and Reality* ends with what Bradley invokes as 'the essential message of Hegel': 'Outside of spirit there is not, and there cannot be, any reality, and the more that anything is spiritual, so much the more is it veritably real' (p. 489). Bradley, with McTaggart, is normally taken to be the principal figure in British idealism: a movement that now seems peculiar for the speed of its total downfall. Its culmination in Bradley's *Appearance and Reality* (1893) was succeeded, soon after 1898, by its alleged intellectual defeat by Moore and Russell. But its influence lasted longer than that, starting with the earlier work of **Green**, **Bosanquet** and Bradley himself, going on through McTaggart's *Nature of Existence* (1921–7) and lasting for the terms of many later university appointments of idealists in England and Scotland, half a century after their philosophy had been pronounced dead (**Collingwood** and **Joachim** were two notable examples in Oxford).

Russell tended to take Bradley as a main target of his 'revolt into pluralism', although it is striking that he engaged in direct published debate only with Joachim. Bradley scarcely mentioned his pluralist critics. His only sustained response was the posthumous 'Relations' (1923–4, in *Collected Essays*, 1935).

Bradley was a remarkable writer: powerful, allusive and scornful, and wholly undeserving of the charges of woolly unclarity brought against him by his later positivist critics. T. S. Eliot noted in his Preface (1964) to the reissue of his doctoral dissertation on Bradley how closely his own prose style was 'formed on that of Bradley and how little it has changed in all these years' (pp. 10–11). Bradley's colourful use of metaphor may be valued more highly as philosophical rhetoric becomes more appreciated. ('The Absolute has no seasons, but all at once bears its leaves, fruit, and blossoms. Like our globe it always, and it never, has summer and winter' (1893, p. 442).)

RICHARD MASON

Braithwaite, Richard Bevan

British. *b:* 15 January 1900, Banbury, England. *d:* 21 April 1990. *Cat:* Philosopher of science. *Ints:* Ethics; philosophy of religion. *Educ:* Studied at King's College, Cambridge from 1919 (Fellow 1924, MA 1926). *Infls:* J. M. Keynes, Heinrich Hertz, Bain, N. R. Campbell, W. E. Johnson, Peirce, Wittgenstein, M. Arnold, von Neumann, Morgenstern and Raiffa. *Appts:* Lectureship, 1928–34, Sidgwick Lectureship, 1934–53, Knightbridge Professor of Moral Philosophy, 1953–67, University of Cambridge; Visiting Professor at Johns Hopkins University, 1968, at University of Western Ontario, 1969, and at City University of New York, 1970; FBA, 1957; Hon. DLitt, Bristol, 1963; Foreign Honorary Member, American Academy of Arts and Sciences, 1986.

Main publications:

(1927) *The State of Religious Belief: An Inquiry based on 'The Nation and Athenaeum' Questionnaire*, London: L. and V. Woolf.
(1931) (ed.) F. P. Ramsey), *The Foundations of Mathematics and Other Essays*, London: Kegan Paul, Trubner, Trench.
(1953) *Moral Principles and Inductive Policies*, London: Cumberlege (Henrietta Hertz Lecture to British Academy 1950, reprinted from *Proceedings of the British Academy* 36).
(1953) *Scientific Explanation*, Cambridge: Cambridge University Press (his main book, based on Tarner Lectures 1946–7).
(1955) *An Empiricist's View of the Nature of Religious Belief*, Cambridge: Cambridge University Press (ninth A. S. Eddington Memorial Lecture).
(1955) *Theory of Games as a Tool for the Moral Philosopher*, Cambridge: Cambridge University Press (Inaugural Lecture, delivered 1954).
(1962) *Introduction to K. Gödel, On Formally Undecidable Propositions of Principia Mathematica and Related Systems*, trans. B. Meltzer, Edinburgh and London: Oliver & Boyd.

In his contribution to J. Leach, R. Butts and G. Pearce (eds), (1973) *Science, Decision and Value*, Dordrecht: Reidel, p. 55, Braithwaite refers to a book entitled *Pure Theory of Applied Belief*, forthcoming from Cambridge University Press, but this was apparently never published.

Secondary literature:

Mellor, D. H. (ed.) (1980) *Science, Belief and Behaviour*, Cambridge: Cambridge University Press (includes bibliography of Braithwaite's philosophical writings).

Braithwaite's main work lies in the philosophy of science and decision theory, both of which he links with ethics (see *Moral Principles*, 1953, and *Theory of Games*, 1955). In particular he emphasizes the role of deductive systems.

Braithwaite relates models and theories so that a theory and its corresponding model are deductive systems interpreting the same abstract calculus, but in the model the initial formulae, containing theoretical terms for unobservables, are epistemologically prior to the derived formulae, containing terms for observables, while in the theory they are epistemologically posterior (*Scientific Explanation*, 1953, chapters 3 and 4, especially pp. 89–90). We have some choice about which theories to adopt, but theories are true propositions and not mere rules of inference (ibid. pp. 85–7, 110–14).

On probability Braithwaite develops a version of the frequency view, though without appeal to limiting frequencies (ibid., chapters 5 and 6). The meaning of probability statements is given in terms of rules for rejecting them, which involve a complex sampling procedure. But their rejection is always revisable by reference to higher-order sampling procedures applied to the sampling procedures themselves. If the hypothesized probability is in fact correct, and our mistaken rejection of it based on a deviant sample, this fact will show itself when we sample the set of possible samples from which the deviant sample was taken.

Despite this Popperian emphasis on rejections Braithwaite does not share **Popper**'s scepticism about induction, which he thinks, following **Peirce**, can be self-supporting without circularity (ibid., chapter 8). This has not generally convinced later writers, who see more value in his offering a criterion for confirming statistical, and not just universal, hypotheses (ibid., chapter 7), where his introduction of pragmatic or value elements shows the link with ethics but has been criticized (by R. J. Hirst in *Philosophical Quarterly*, 1954).

The emphasis on deductive systems reappears in Braithwaite's analysis of natural laws. These involve only Humean regularities and no 'metaphysical' necessity, but owe their status to the explanatory power they gain from being deduced within a system from premises resting on inductive evidence that goes beyond the direct evidence for the laws themselves. The apparent paradox that the top-level premises are themselves not laws is defused by reflecting that explanation must stop somewhere.

An Empiricist's View (1955) achieved a certain *succès de scandale* by basing on Matthew Arnold an ultra-Wittgenistenian reduction of religious beliefs to certain intentions (including intentions to feel, which distinguishes them from moral beliefs), supported by stories.

Sources: WWW 1981–90; PI; Mittelstrass.

A. R. LACEY

Brandenstein, Bela von

Hungarian. *b:* 1901, Budapest. *Cat:* Systematic philosopher. *Ints:* Ontology/metaphysics. *Infls:* Von Pauler, Plato, Aristotle, Leibniz and Hegel. *Appts:* Succeeded von Pauler as Professor of Philosophy at Peter Pázmány University, Budapest (1934–45); Professor at University of Saarbrüken, from 1948.

Main publications:

(1926–7) *Grundlegung der Philosophie*, revised 1965–70.

(1930) *Metaphysik des organischen Lebens*.

(1930) *Müveszetfilozofia* [Philosophy of the Arts], second edition, 1941.

(1934–6) *Az ember a mindensegben* [Man and his Place in the Whole] (German translation, *Der Mensch und seine Stellung im All*, Switzerland: Benziger, 1947).

(1950) *Der Aufbau des Seins, System der Philosophie*, Saarbrüken: Minerva Verlag.

(1954) *Das Bild des Menschen und die Idee des Humanismus*, Bregenz, Austria: Verlag I. N. Teutsch.

(1954) *Vom Werdegang des Geistes in der Seele*, Saarbrüken: Minerva Verlag.

(1955) *Die Quellen des Seins Einführung in die Metaphysik*, Bonn: H. Bouvier Verlag.

(1957) *Vom Sinn der Philosophie und ihrer Geschichte*, Bonn: H. Bouvier Verlag.

(1960) *Teleologischen Denken Betrachtungen zu dem gleichnamigen Buche Nikolai Hartmanns*, Bonn: H. Bouvier Verlag.

(1963) *Wahrheit und Wirklichkeit*, Meisenheim am Glan: A. Hain Verlag.

(1975) *Bewusstsein und Vergänglichkeit*, Munich: Berchmans Verlag.

(1976) *Logik und Ontologie*, Heidelberg: Winter Verlag.

(1983) *Sein, Welt, Mensch: philosophische Studien*, Munich: Berchmans Verlag.

Secondary literature:

Kovach, S. J. (1957) 'The philosophy of Bela von Brandenstein', *Review of Metaphysics* 11: 315–36.

Brandenstein's work is an attempt to produce a complete and systematic philosophical account of what there is. Although an eclectic, Brandenstein produced an original ontology, and furnished a Christian theodicy of an unusual kind. They key doctrines are set out in his book of 1950. He contends that the goal of philosophy is to unveil the ultimate properties (*Voraussetzungen*) of being, and its method is 'regressive inquiry' (*Rückschluss*). This method reveals that being has three ultimate determinations (*Urbestimmungen*): content (*Gehalt*), what a being is; form (*Form*), its relations, at least that of identity; and formation (*Gestaltung*), the unity of a being. Each of these aspects of being has a branch of philosophy proper to it, which Brandenstein calls Totic (*Gehaltlehre*), Logic and Mathematics. The application of *Rückschluss* to each subject matter reveals in each case 18 fundamental categories, making 54 in all.

Brandenstein distinguishes metaphysics (*Wirklichkeitslehre*) from ontology, and his key assertions in this area concern causality. He contends that an infinite sequence of causes is impossible, and further that, in a finite series, the first member must be intransitive. Again, every real cause he holds to be inexhaustible, intransitive and imperishable, from which it follows that such causes must be spiritual. All causal agency he attributes to finite (non-human) spirits which guide the course of nature. The cause of the spirits and the matter they mould is God, who pre-established a harmony at the moment of creation.

In other works, Brandenstein develops the implications of these views for ethics and aesthetics.

ROBERT WILKINSON

Brandt, R(ichard) B(ooker)

American. *b:* 1910, Wilmington, Ohio. *Cat:* Ethics. *Ints:* Philosophy of mind; legal and political philosophy. *Educ:* Denison University, University of Cambridge, Tübingen University and Yale University. *Infls:* Hume, Adam Smith, G. E. Moore and C. I. Lewis. *Appts:* 1937–64, Professor of Philosophy, Swarthmore College; 1964–81, Professor of Philosophy, University of Michigan; visiting appointments at many universities.

Main publications:

(1941) *The Philosophy of Schleiermacher*, New York: Greenwood Press.

(1954) *Hopi Ethics*, Chicago: University of Chicago Press.

(1959) *Ethical Theory*, Englewood Cliffs: Prentice-Hall.

(1979) *A Theory of the Good and the Right*, Oxford: Clarendon Press.

(1993) *Morality, Utilitarianism and Rules*, Cambridge: Cambridge University Press.

Secondary literature:

Goldman, Alvin I. and Kim, Jaegwon (eds) (1978) *Values and Morals*, Dordrecht: Reidel.

Hooker, Bradford W. (ed.) (1993) *Rationality, Rules, and Utility*, Boulder: Westview Press.

Brandt was initially trained in classics and religion, as well as philosophy, and his study of **Schleiermacher** is a standard work. He has written widely in philosophy, but his most important work is in ethics. In *A Theory of the Good and the Right* (1979) he replaces the question 'What is the right thing to do?' (which he regards as having no clear meaning) with the question 'What is the moral code that a fully rational person would support for a society that he had to live in?' Brandt holds that such a person would support a code that would maximize the expectable happiness of some group (the size of the group depending on the extent of his benevolence). Such a code would be a plural code, rather like the one that we now have. His view is thus a form of rule utilitarianism.

Sources: Personal communication.

ANTHONY ELLIS

Braybrooke, David

American (naturalized Canadian). *b:* 18 October 1924, Hackettstown, New Jersey. *Cat:* Analytical political philosopher; ethicist; social scientist. *Ints:* Ethical theory; political philosophy; philosophy of the social sciences; applied business and economics ethics. *Educ:* Hobart College, New School for Social Research; Downing College, Cambridge, UK; Harvard University BA 1948 and Cornell University, PhD, 1953; New College, Oxford. *Infls:* Brooks Otis, F. R. Leavis, Norman Malcolm, J. L. Austin and C. E. Lindblom. *Appts:* Instructor, History and Literature, Hobart and William Smith Colleges, 1948–50; Teaching Fellow, Economics, Cornell, 1950–2; Instructor, Philosophy, Michigan, 1953–4; Instructor, Philosophy, Bowdoin College, 1954–6; Assistant Professor, Philosophy, Yale, 1956–63; Associate

Professor, Philosophy and Politics, Dalhousie, Nova Scotia, 1963–5, Professor, 1965–88, McCulloch Professor of Philosophy and Politics, 1988–90, Professor Emeritus from 1990; Texas, Austin, from 1990, Centennial Commission in the Liberal Arts (Government and Philosophy).

Main publications:

(1963) (with C. E. Lindblom) *A Strategy of Decision: Policy Evaluation as a Social Process* New York: The Free Press.

(1965) *Philosophical Problems of the Social Sciences*, New York: Macmillan.

(1968) *Three Tests for Democracy*, New York: Random House.

(1974) *Traffic Congestion Goes Through the Issue-Machine*, London: Routledge & Kegan Paul.

(1983) *Ethics in the World of Business*, Totowa: Rowman & Allanfield.

(1987) *Philosophy of Social Science*, Englewood Cliffs: Prentice Hall.

(1987) *Meetings Needs*, Princeton: Princeton University Press.

Secondary literature:

Boenvac, D. (1991) 'Ethical impressionism: a response to Braybrooke', *Social Theory and Practice*, 157–73.

Goldman, Alvin (1974) 'Power, time, and cost', *Philosophical Studies* 26: 263–74.

——(1976) 'Reply to Braybrooke', *Philosophical Studies* 30: 273–6.

Mulholland, L. A. (1971) 'Norm explanations in history', *Dialogue* 10: 96–102.

Phillips Griffiths, A. (1963) 'The generalization argument: a reply to Mr. Braybrooke's "Collective and distributive generalization in ethics"', *Analysis* 23: 113–15.

Braybrooke's early writings address concerns of analytic epistemology and philosophical linguistic analysis, which along with ethical analysis have direct bearing on the social sciences. His general 'unitarian' approach has led him to deal with theoretical considerations involved in effecting a rapprochement between the humanities and social science, and he has explored the project of effecting a similar unification of various schools of social science itself, by attacking the alleged independence of their methods, investigations and explanations. A vision of interdisciplinary unity is reflected in his claim that 'doing philosophy is a way of doing social science', and although his work has suggested a primacy of social science over philosophy, Braybrooke asserts their mutual and fundamental concern with the meaning of human behaviour and action.

Braybrooke's (rule) utilitarianism, which he regards as a premise of democracy, and his arch-concern to coordinate philosophy and social science appear especially in his work with the economist C. E. Lindblom, *A Strategy of Decision* (1963), in which 'social science and philosophy meet'. With Lindblom, Braybrooke aims for an improved strategy of decision-making, involving a reinterpreted felicific calculus of Bentham's utilitarianism, resulting in a policy decision-making strategy of 'disjointed incrementalism'. Braybrooke regards policy evaluation as social process and he advocates the analysis of social policy problems into a series of smaller problems which allows results to develop incrementally. He has also attempted to provide a measure for evaluating the democracy of a state by developing tests for the concepts of personal rights, human welfare and collective preference. An abiding concern with social policy decision-making underscores his examinations of practical issues such as traffic congestion (1974) and of such theoretical concepts as preference and needs.
Sources: IWW 1993–4, p. 202; PI.

DAVID SCOTT

Bréhier, Émile

French. *b:* 12 April 1876, Bar-le-Duc. *d:* 3 February 1952, Paris. *Cat:* Historian of philosophy. *Infls:* Dilthey, Bergson and Émile Boutroux. *Appts:* Taught philosophy at the Universities of Rennes (1909–12), Bordeaux (1912–14 and 1919) and Paris (1919–46); Editor of the *Revue Philosophique* from 1940; elected in 1944 to the Académie des Sciences Morales et Politiques.

Main publications:

(1908) *Les idées philosophiques et religieuses de Philon d'Alexandre*, Paris: Picard.

(1910) *Chrysippe et l'ancien stoïcisme*, Paris: Alcan; revised edition, Paris: Presses Universitaires de France, 1950.

(1921) *Du Sage antique au citoyen moderne*, Paris: Colin.

(1921) *Histoire de la philosophie allemande*, Paris: Payo.

(1926–32) *Histoire de la philosophie*, 7 vols, Paris: Alcan (English translation, *History of Philosophy*, 7 vols, Chicago and London: University of Chicago Press, 1965–8).

(1930) *Les Études de philosophie antique*, Paris: Hermann.

(1937) *La Philosophie du moyen age*, Paris: Michel.

(1940) *La Philosophie et son passé*, Paris: Presses Universitaires de France.

(1947) *Science et humanisme*, Paris: Michel.

(1950) *Transformation de la philosophie française*, Paris: Flammarion.

(1951) *Les Thèmes actuels de philosophie*, Paris: Presses Universitaires de France.

(1965) *Études de philosophie moderne*, Paris: Presses Universitaires de France.

Bréhier's histories of philosophy range over the theory of knowledge, ethics, political philosophy and the philosophy of religion. According to *Transformation de la philosophie française* (1950) there are two basic approaches, which he characterizes as 'internal' and 'external', to the study of the history of philosophy.

The 'external' method is to regard any development in philosophy as a function of changes in social conditions. One example of this is the Marxist approach to philosophy, which regards the discipline as a function of the class war, or of the dominant contemporary social group, and as arising out of the social subconscious. There is, on this 'external' approach, no intrinsic or absolute truth to be found in any period of philosophy: instead, truth is regarded as being relative to a particular era, country or social class.

Bréhier rejects this approach to the history of philosophy and instead adopts what he calls the 'internal' method. Truth is universal and absolute, and the primary quest of any history of philosophy is to determine whether the theories under examination are true. Such theories arise from the reflection or consciousness of particular thinkers, and are attempts to solve the problems of previous philosophical systems. Philosophy arises from, but goes further than, ordinary thought in that it pushes back the boundaries of knowledge and understanding.

In keeping with his methodology, Bréhier's *History of Philosophy* (1926–32) deals with philosophical thought mainly on the basis of individual philosophers: in the fifth volume, which deals with the eighteenth century, 11 out of 15 chapters take this approach.

KATHRYN PLANT

Brentano, Franz

German-Austrian. *b:* 1838, Marienburg, Germany. *d:* 1917, Florence. *Cat:* Philosophical psychology. *Ints:* Intentionality; act psychology. *Educ:* Universtiy of Tübingen. *Infls:* Aristotle, Kant and the post-Kantians. *Appts:* Professor of

Philosophy, first at the Catholic University of Würzburg, later at University of Vienna.

Main publications:

(1874) *Psychologie vom empirischen Standpunkt*, Leipzig: Duncker & Humblot, 1874; second edition in 2 volumes, 1911; third edition, ed. O. Kraus, Leipzig: F. Meiner, 1925 (English translation, *Psychology from an Empirical Standpoint*, ed. L. L. McAlister, London, 1973).

(1889) *Ursprung sittlicher Erkenntnis*, Leipzig: Duncker & Humblot; third edition, ed. Oskar Kraus, 1934 (English translation, *The Origins of Our Knowledge Right and Wrong*, trans. Cecil Hague, London: A. Constable, 1902).

(1893) *The Future of Philosophy*, Vienna: A. Holder

(1895) *Die vier Phasen der Philosophie* [The Four Phases of Philosophy], Stuttgart: J. C. Cott'schen Buchhandlung; ed. Oskar Kraus, Leipzig: F. Meiner, 1926.

(1907) *An Investigation of the Psychology of the Senses*, Leipzig: Duncker & Humblot.

(1925) *Versuch über die Erkenntnis* [Inquiry into the Nature of Knowledge] ed. Alfred Kastil, Leipzig: F. Meiner.

(1929) *Vom Dasein Gottes* [On the Existence of God], ed. Alfred Kastil, Leipzig: F. Meiner.

(1930) *Wahrheit und Evidenz* [Truth and Evidence], ed. Oskar Kraus, Leipzig: F. Meiner.

(1952) *Grundlegung und Aufbau der Ethik* [The Basis and Structure of Ethics], ed. F. Mayer-Hillebrand, Bern: A. Francke.

(1954) *Religion und Philosophie*, ed. F. Mayer-Hillebrand, Bern: Francke.

Secondary literature:

Chisholm, R. M. (ed.) (1960) *Realism and the Background of Phenomenology*, Glencoe, Ill.: Free Press (contains portions of *Psychologie vom empirischen Standpunkt*).

Kastil, A. (1951) *Die Philosophie Franz Brentano: Eine Einführung in seine Lehre*, Bern: A. Francke.

Moore, G. E. (1903) 'Review of Franz Brentano: The origins of the knowledge of right and wrong', *International Journal of Ethics* 14: 115–23.

Spiegelberg, H. (1960) *The Phenomenological Movement: A Historical Introduction*, 2 vols, The Hague: Nijhoff.

A philosopher and psychologist, Franz Brentano has a permanent place in the history of philosophy as the first to give a clear account of the intentionality, or object-relatedness, of mental phenomena. Born in the Rhineland, he became a Roman Catholic priest and Professor of Philosophy at the Catholic University of Würzburg. He resigned both priesthood and Chair after the Declaration of Papal Infallibility in 1871, and was appointed to a Chair of Philosophy at Vienna University. In a voluminous output, his most important work was *Psychology from the Empirical Standpoint*, first published in 1874, the same year as Wundt's *Foundations of Physiological Psychology*.

In the *Psychology* Brentano set out to provide an account of the structure of mind which would serve as a foundation for empirical psychology. He called this 'descriptive psychology' (and sometimes 'descriptive phenomenology'). He considered himself an empiricist: experience, he claimed, was his only teacher. Where **Wundt** was establishing psychology as an empirical science through the experimental investigation of the context of experience, Brentano's primary method was careful observation of the act of experience itself. Taking for granted a broadly dualistic view of the world (as divided into 'psychical' and 'physical' phenomena), he concentrated on two questions: What are the essential or defining characteristics of the mental?; Into what categories can mental phenomena be classified?

It was in attempting to answer the first of these questions that he developed his influential ideas on the intentionality of mind. Mental phenomena, he argued, are distinguished from physical by 'intentional inexistence', that is 'reference to a content' or 'direction upon an object'. Thus a thought is always a thought *about* something, a desire is always a desire *for* something, a perception is always a perception *of* something, and so on. This is more than a merely contingent matter. The 'something' may be some other mental content (an image, say). It may be something that does not exist (for example, a unicorn). Hence the intentionality of mind is not a relation between it and its object (which would entail that the object existed) it is 'relational' or 'relation-like'. But there must (logically must) always be something towards which a mental act is directed. In the absence of this, mental verbs are literally meaningless. Subjective experiences can only be understood as acts of consciousness directed towards objects.

As to the second question, Brentano allowed only three categories, or 'Grand Classes', of mental phenomena: representations, judgements and feelings (including both emotions and volitions). These reflect three ways in which mental phenomena may be directed upon their objects. Thus with a representation an idea is simply before the mind or 'present to consciousness'. But with a judgement we take up a stance towards an idea, an intellectual stance, which may be either of acceptance or rejection. A feeling also involves taking a stance. In this case the stance is emotional, a feeling being broadly either 'for' or 'against' the idea in question. (Brentano used 'love'/'hate' here to mean something along the lines of approach/avoidance.)

In this classification, representations are basic in the sense that we must have an idea before we can take up a stance towards it, intellectual or emotional. However, it is with the epistemological and ethical implications respectively of judgements and feelings that much of the remainder of Brentano's extensive philosophy is concerned. Thus representations, ideas directly present to consciousness, cannot be either correct or incorrect. They are as it were just there. But when we take up one or other of two opposed stances we open up the possibility of being right or wrong. In the case of judgements, then, one or other of the two opposed stances of affirmation or rejection must be correct in a given case: 'This is a pencil', or, 'This is not a pencil'. As to which is correct, we come to understand the difference by contrasting actual cases of judgements which are correct with those which are not. And judgements are objective in the sense that we cannot affirm correctly what anyone else denies correctly, or vice versa. This is a non-propositional theory of judgement. To affirm/deny that there is a pencil is not to affirm/deny the proposition 'my pencil exists'. It is to affirm/deny the existence of a pencil. The object of the affirmation/denial is not a proposition, nor even a state of affairs, but, like the object of the corresponding representation, the pencil. Indeed, terms like 'exist' do not refer: they are 'systematic', allowing us to express our acceptance or rejection of things.

Much the same, Brentano argued, is true of feelings and, hence, since this category includes the ethical stances of good and bad, morals. This is the basis of his moral philosophy. He considered morality, no less than epistemology, to be a branch of descriptive psychology. As with opposed intellectual stances, only one of two opposed emotional stances can be correct in a given case. Again, we grasp the difference between correct and incorrect emotional stances only by experience of contrasting cases, much as we learn what it is for something to be, say, red. Moreover feelings, like judgements, are objective in the sense that we cannot correctly have a pro-emotion towards an object towards which anyone can correctly have an anti-emotion, and vice versa. The correctness of feelings, then, including moral feelings, is, like the correctness of judgements, objective.

Brentano developed his ideas on truth and evidence in the posthumously published *Truth and Evidence* (1930). He distinguished *evident judgements* and *blind judgements*. The former we should perhaps call self-evident: they include judgements of inner awareness ('I seem to see a pencil') and judgements of necessary truth ('two pencils are more than one'). Blind judgements are all those that are not self-evident ('I see a pencil'). Most judgements of the outer world and all judgements of memory are blind; but, to the extent that they confirm each other, we can have confidence in them. The judgement, for instance, that there is a three-dimensional (spatial) world is, Brentano believed, so widely confirmed as to be infinitely more likely than any of its alternatives. Truth is then that which 'pertains to the judgement of one who asserts what the person who judges with evidence would assert' (p. 139).

Besides epistemology and moral philosophy, Brentano wrote on a wide range of other topics. First, on logic, developing a revised syllogism. Second, on the nature of categories, arguing that there are only concrete (as opposed to abstract) things, and that every judgement is an acceptance or rejection of a concrete thing (thus any true sentence which appears to refer to some abstract entity can be translated into a sentence which refers to a concrete thing—for example, 'he believes that there are horses' becomes 'he affirms horses'). Third, on God, whose existence, as a Necessary Being, he derived from the Principle of Sufficient Reason. Fourth, on the nature of chance, rejecting the notion of absolute chance as self-contradictory, and arguing that determinism is incompatible with the fact of freedom of the will. His ideas, though often speculative, were always sharp and challenging. In *Religion and Philosophy* (1954), for instance, he extended his dualistic view of the mind to incorporate a Christian picture of the soul as separate from the body and yet capable of acting through it. He argued that the soul was created *ex nihilo* at the time of conception, defending this idea by claiming that 'psychical' things are created *ex nihilo* every time we call an image to mind. He believed that philosophy went through cycles of flourishing and decline, the latter being marked by three phases: a shift of interest from theory to practice, scepticism, and mysticism. As well as being a prolific writer, Brentano was a charismatic and inspiring teacher. His pupils included Alexius **Meinong**, Karl **Stumpf**, Christian **Ehrenfels** and Edmund **Husserl**. Through the last, his ideas helped to establish the school of phenomenology, from which (though in a much modified form) modern descriptive psychopathology is derived. His picture of the mind as intentional rather than as a receptacle was an important formative idea for Freud in the development of psychoanalysis. Along with others who have sought a philosophical foundation for empirical science, his project failed: the positivist tendencies of scientific psychology owe more to Wundt. His account of the intentionality of subjective experience remains important in the philosophy of mind.

Sources: Goldenson; Reese; Corsini; Edwards; Urmson & Rée.

K. W. M. FULFORD

Brett, George Sidney

Welsh-Canadian. *b:* 5 August 1879, Briton Ferry, Wales. *d:* 27 October 1944, Toronto. *Cat:* History of philosophy; psychology. *Ints:* Science and medicine; history of psychology. *Educ:* University of Oxford, graduating in 1899. *Infls:* James Ward. *Appts:* After some teaching in England, appointed Professor of Philosophy, Government College, Lahore, 1904; 1908, Lecturer in Classics, Trinity College, Toronto; 1921, Professor of Philosophy, 1932, Dean of Graduate Studies; first editor of the *University of Toronto Quarterly.*

Main publications:

(1908) *The Philosophy of Gassendi*, London: Macmillan.

(1912–21) *The History of Psychology*, 3 vols, London: G. Allen; re-edited and abridged with new material by Richard Peters, London: George Allen & Unwin, 1953, 1962.

(1920) *The Government of Man: An Introduction to Ethics and Politics*, second edition, G. Bell.

(1928) *Psychology, Ancient and Modern*, London: Harrap.

Secondary literature:

Armour, Leslie and Trott, Elizabeth (1981) *The Faces of Reason*, Waterloo: Wilfrid Laurier University Press (discusses the history of philosophy).

Irving, John A. (1945) 'The achievement of George Sidney Brett', *University of Toronto Quarterly* 14, 4.

——(1952) contribution in *Philosophy in Canada: A Symposium*, Toronto: The University Press.

Brett was chiefly concerned with the history of philosophy and especially with the history of what he called 'psychology'. His claim was that psychology has a specific subject matter, the immediate experience of human beings. But it is not a subject matter like any other because our conceptualizations of it are part and parcel of the experience itself. Nor can it be easily separated from the subject matters of other disciplines, for other disciplines deal with it in their own ways. Its understanding can only be grasped by a study of the historical development of the relevant conceptualizations. In so far as such an enquiry can be objective it is because we can study its historical development and formulate intelligible theories about what goes into changes of views. Nearly all philosophers have contributed to this field, and so Brett's history of psychology tells the story of one strand of the history of philosophy. Brett also studied closely the development of science and medicine as well as that of philosophy, and so his history of psychology is a history of the philosophy of mind and of its relations to religion and medicine. Only in the later parts is it dominated by the developing science of psychology.

Like many philosophers of his time, he was reacting against what he took to be oversimplifications of the nature of philosophy, though he sympathized with many of the concerns of the British idealists. He was both influenced by and sceptical of the efforts of thinkers like James **Ward** to establish a distinct nature for psychology, and his history devotes considerable space to the reflections of Ward and of T. H. Green and of their battles with the 'associationists'. Richard **Peters**, who abridged and revised Brett's *History of Psychology*, says Brett did succeed in illuminating the nature of psychology as well as its history, and that his account continues to be worth reading. The philosophical curriculum at the University of Toronto became predominantly historical under his leadership. He built one of the largest philosophy departments in the world.

Sources: CanBio.

LESLIE ARMOUR

Bridgman, Percy William

American. *b:* 12 April 1882, Cambridge, Massachusetts. *d:* 20 August 1961, Randolph, New Hampshire. *Cat:* Physicist; philosopher of science. *Ints:* Epistemology; foundations of physics. *Educ:* PhD, Harvard University, 1908. *Infls:* W. Clifford, Einstein, K. Pearson, H. Poincaré and J. Stallo. *Appts:* Harvard University, 1908–54.

Main publications:

(1922) *Dimensional Analysis*, New Haven: Yale University Press.

(1927) *The Logic of Modern Physics*, New York: Macmillan.

(1936) *The Nature of Physical Theory*, Princeton: Princeton University Press.

(1943) *The Nature of Thermodynamics*, Cambridge, Mass.: Harvard University Press.

(1950) *Reflections of a Physicist*, New York: Philosophical Library.

(1959) *The Way Things Are*, Cambridge, Mass.: Harvard University Press.

(1962) *A Sophisticate's Primer of Relativity*, London and Middletown, Conn.: Wesleyan Univeristy Press.

Secondary literature:

Allen, H. J. (1980) 'P. W. Bridgman and B. F. Skinner on private experience', *Behaviourism* 8: 15–29.

Moyer, A. E. (1991) 'Bridgman, P. W., The operational perspective in physics, I, Origins and development', *Studies in History and Philosophy of Science* 22: 237–58.

——(1991) 'Bridgman, P. W., The operational perspective in physics, II, Refinements, publication and reception', *Studies in History and Philosophy of Science* 22: 373–397.

Known in physics for his work on the behaviour of materials at high pressures, Bridgman became noted among philosophers of science for a type of positivist instrumentalism in which the only permissible concepts were to be those reducible to experimental operations. He also allowed for models and constructs which could possess physical reality if they were experimentally correlated with other constructs out of experimental operations. Bridgman rejected any attempt at limiting theoretical development by more general ideas and to content with a thoroughgoing relativism. Explanation for him was the reduction of the unfamiliar to the familiar; and in situations in which that was not possible, because the available ideas were not familiar (true at the time he was writing), the resulting crisis was to be resolved by working with the new ideas until physicists became familiar with them. His system gives the impression of being the response of a working practical physicist to relativity and quantum mechanics. His writing shows scant knowledge of the prolific turn-of-the-century literature on the philosophy of science, and he seems to have read **Poincaré** in German only. Operationism was to enjoy a continued, if minority, vogue among later philosophers of science.

Sources: D. M. Newitt (1962) 'Percy Williams Bridgman, 1882–1961', *BMFRS* 8: 29–40; E. C. Kemble, F. Birch and G. Holton (1970) 'Bridgman, Percy Williams', *DSB* 2: 457a–462b; A. E. Moyer (1981) 'Bridgman, Percy Williams', *DAB*, supplt 7.

R. N. D. MARTIN

Brightman, Edgar Sheffield

American. *b:* 20 September 1884, Holbrook, Massachusetts. *d:* 25 February 1932, Boston. *Cat:* Philosopher of religion; personalist. *Ints:* Philosophy of religion. *Educ:* Brown University, AB 1906, AM 1908; Universities of Berlin and Marburg, 1910–11; Boston University, STB 1910, PhD 1912. *Infls:* Berkeley, Hegel and Bowne. *Appts:* 1906–8, Assistant in Philosophy and Greek, Brown University; 1912–15, Professor of Philosophy and Psychology, Wesleyan University, Nebraska; 1915–19, Associate Professor to Professor, Wesleyan University, Connecticut; 1919–53, Professor, Boston University (Borden Parker Bowne Professor, 1925–53; Chairman, Board of the Graduate School, 1933–53).

Main publications:

(1925) *An Introduction to Philosophy*, New York: Henry Holt & Co.; revised edition, 1951.

(1925) *Immortality in Post-Kantian Idealism*, Cambridge, Mass.: Harvard University Press.

(1925) *Religious Values*, New York: Abingdon Press; reprinted, Milwood, NY: Kraus, 1968.

(1928) *A Philosophy of Ideals*, New York: Henry Holt & Co.

(1930) *The Problem of God*, New York: Abingdon Press; reprinted, New York: AMS Press, 1978.

(1931) *The Finding of God*, New York: Abingdon Press.

(1932) *Is God a Person?*, New York: Association Press.

(1933) *Moral Laws*, New York: Abingdon Press; reprinted, Millwood, NY: Kraus, 1968.

(1934) *Personality and Religion*, New York: Abingdon Press; reprinted, New York: AMS Press, 1981.

(1940) *A Philosophy of Religion*, Englewood Cliffs, NJ: Prentice-Hall, Inc.; reprinted, West Port, CT: Greenwood Press, 1984.

(1942) *The Spiritual Life*, Nashville, Tennessee: Abingdon Press; reprinted, New York: AMS Press, 1981.

(1945) *Nature and Values*, New York: Abingdon Press.

(1952) *Persons and Values*, Boston: Boston University Press.

(1958) *Person and Reality: An Introduction to Metaphysics*, ed. P. A. Bertocci, New York: Ronald Press.

(1988) *Studies in Personalism: Selected Writings of Edgar Sheffield Brightman*, ed. W. E. Steinkraus and R. N. Beck, Utica, NY: Meridian Publishing Co.

Secondary literature:
Bertocci, P. (1993) 'Edgar Sheffield Brightman', in A. J. Reck, T. Horvath, T. Krettek and S. Grean (eds), *American Philosophers' Ideas of Ultimate Reality and Meaning*, Toronto: University of Toronto Press, pp. 195–214.
Flewelling, R. T. (ed.) (1953) *The Personalist* 34 (October): 341–71.
Reck, A. J. (1964) *Recent American Philosophy*, New York: Pantheon Books, pp. 311–35.

Brightman came to philosophy through religion, with expertise in the field of Biblical scholarship, evident in his first book, *The Sources of the Hexateuch* (New York: Abingdon Press, 1918). He won his greatest fame, however, as a leading exponent of personalism in philosophy. As Borden Parker **Bowne** (1847–1910) had founded personalism, a form of pluralistic idealism, at Boston University, it was fit that Brightman was appointed to a Chair that memorialized Bowne there.

Brightman's philosophy centred on three main topics: persons, values and God. Like Bowne, he held that human personality is the key to the understanding of reality, and in the elaboration of his theories he drew upon the resources in British and German idealism. Further, he strove to engage in concrete thinking, relating the most abstract and universal categories to personal experiences in the present.

Brightman's own experience as a young man in the presence of his first wife's early death was the crisis that impelled him to rethink the concept of God. The upshot was his most original contribution to philosophy his concept of God as finite.

Although Brightman, like other personalists, considered religion to be central to human life and esteemed God to be a person not a metaphysical abstraction, he related these personalistic principles to value-centric situations, requiring that every admissible philosophical or theological conception be empirically coherent. Unable to explain away occurrences of evil, such as his young wife's death, or to attribute them to human responsibility, he broke with orthodox belief in an omnipotent, omniscient and omnificent God. He proposed instead the theory of a finite God. Thus he described God as 'a person supremely conscious, supremely valuable, and supremely creative, yet limited by both the free choices of other persons and by restrictions within his own nature' (1930, p. 113).

Sources: Edwards; RA, 4; WW(Am).

ANDREW RECK

Broad, Charlie Dunbar

British. *b:* 1887, Harlesden, Middlesex. *d:* 1971, Cambridge, England. *Cat:* Cambridge empirical philosopher. *Ints:* Philosophy of mind; philosophy of science; psychical research. *Educ:* MA, LittD, Trinity College, Cambridge. *Infls:* Russell, W. E. Johnson, Moore, G. F. Stout and Whitehead. *Appts:* Fellow of Trinity College, Cambridge, 1911–7 and 1923–71; Assistant to Professor, University of St Andrews, 1911–4; Lecturer, Dundee, 1914–20; Professor of Philosophy, University of Bristol, 1920–3; Lecturer, University of Cambridge, 1926–33, Knightbridge Professor of Moral Philosophy, 1933–53.

Main publications:
(1914) *Perception, Physics and Reality*, Cambridge.
(1923) *Scientific Thought*, London: Kegan Paul, Trench, Trubner.
(1925) *The Mind and its Place in Nature*, London: Kegan Paul, Trench, Trubner.
(1930) *Five Types of Ethical Theory*, London: Kegan Paul, Trench, Trubner.
(1933) *An Examination of McTaggart's Philosophy*, Cambridge; reprinted 1938.
(1952) *Ethics and the History of Philosophy*, London: Routledge & Kegan Paul (articles of 1927–50).
(1953) *Religion, Philosophy and Psychical Research*, London: Routledge & Kegan Paul (articles of 1923–50).
(1962) *Lectures on Psychical Research*, London: Routledge & Kegan Paul.
(1975) *Leibniz*, ed. C. Lewy, Cambridge: Cambridge University Press.
(1978) *Kant*, ed. C. Lewy, Cambridge: Cambridge University Press.

Secondary literature:
Schilpp, P. A. (ed.) (1959) *The Philosophy of C. D. Broad*, New York: Tudor (contains an autobiography and a reply to critics by Broad, with full bibliography to 1959). (This *Autobiography* was composed at a time when he felt he had little more to say, and when he placed an unduly low value on his past achievements. It is remarkable in revealing virtually nothing about his motivations in his philosophizing.)

Broad's philosophical writings deserve interest as much for their approach as for their contents or conclusions. They display the merits and disadvantages of what might be seen as reasoned academic common sense: the impartial statement of considerations for and against a set of theories on the topic in hand, a weighing of arguments, a judicious conclusion. He applied this approach painstakingly to scientific method, to ethical theories, to theories of perception and to philosophical methodology. The conclusions he reached are seldom compelling, but his ways of reaching them often contain useful résumés of past arguments.

He now seems unusual in the history of philosophy as a Fellow of Trinity College throughout the active life of **Wittgenstein** in Cambridge, and for much of the life of **Moore**, yet as having no part in the development of analytical philosophy. His own attitudes towards philosophical methods were stated as carefully as his other views (for example in 'Critical and speculative philosophy', in J. H. Muirhead (ed.) *Contemporary British Philosophy*, First Series, London: George Allen & Unwin, 1924). Broad's understanding of the Cambridge tradition, including his own distant view of Wittgenstein, appeared in his essay 'The local historical background of contemporary Cambridge philosophy' (in C. A. Mace (ed.), *British Philosophy in the Mid-Century*, London: George Allen & Unwin, 1957, itself a valuable source of comment on the period).

Broad wrote that his *Examination* of **McTaggart** (1933 and 1938) was 'about the best work' of which he was capable. It typifies his approach in its thoroughness and patience, as well as in its scrupulous fairness towards a philosopher whom Broad admired but whose views he did not share in any way. His works on Kant and Leibniz (edited posthumously from lecture notes) were equally meticulous. Among philosophers of his background he was exceptional in his long interest in psychical research, the more so since this does not seem to have been based on any particular personal convictions or preconceptions.

RICHARD MASON

Brodbeck, May

American. *b:* 26 July 1917, Newark. *d:* 2 August 1983, San Francisco. *Cat:* Philosopher of science; philosopher of the social sciences. *Ints:* History of American philosophy. *Educ:* 1941, BA in Chemistry, New York University; 1945, MA in Philosophy, University of Iowa; 1947, PhD in Philosophy, University of Iowa. *Infls:* John Dewey, Rudolf Carnap, Herbert Feigl and Gustav Bergmann. *Appts:* University of Minnesota: 1947–54, Assistant Professor and Associate Professor; 1954–74, Professor of Philosophy; 1967–70,

Chair, Department of Philosophy; 1972–4, Dean, Graduate School; 1974, Visiting Lecturer, University of Cambridge; 1974–81, Vice-President and Dean of Faculties, 1974–83, Carver Professor of Philosophy, 1983, Professor Emeritus, University of Iowa.

Main publications:
(1949) 'Coherence theory reconsidered: Professor Werkmeister on semantics and on the nature of empirical laws', *Philosophy of Science* 16: 75–85.
(1951) 'Toward a naturalistic "Non-naturalist" ethic', *Philosophical Studies* 2: 7–11.
(1952) *Philosophy in America: 1900–1950*, Chicago: Regnery.
(1952) 'An analytic principle of induction?', *Journal of Philosophy* 49: 747–9.
(1953) (ed. with Herbert Feigl) *Readings in the Philosophy of Science*, New York: Appleton-Century-Crofts.
(1963) 'Meaning and action', *Philosophy of Science* 30: 309-24.
(1966) 'Objectivism and interaction: a reaction to Margolis', *Philosophy of Science* 33: 287–92.
(1968) (ed.) *Readings in the Philosophy of the Social Sciences*, New York: Macmillan.
(1972) 'Descartes and the notion of external reality', in *Reason and Reality*, London: Macmillan.

Secondary literature:
Margolis, Joseph (1966) ' Reply to a reaction: second remarks on Brodbeck's objectivism', *Philosophy of Science* 33: 293–300.
Mayeroff, Milton (1950) 'The nature of propositions in John Dewey's logic: a reply to Miss Brodbeck', *Journal of Philosophy* 47: 353–8.

Brodbeck's broad philosophical aim was to delineate the possibility and conditions of a 'science of man' in the context of a tension between the scientific ideal and intuitive understanding.

Her analysis focuses on the concepts of action, cause, motives, intentions and reasons, and on explanations of human behaviour that draw on theories of interactionism and parallelism. She propounded a thesis of objectivism embodying the view that 'a complete description and causal explanations of human actions can be given *in principle* by means of terms that, like those of physical science, *have reference* only to objectively observable properties of material objects' (1963). This view, she maintained, did not mean that talk of bodily states could replace talk of mental states. Brodbeck's objectivism generated lively debate and was criticized by Joseph **Margolis**, who espoused an interaction of body and mind that did not preclude a 'science of man' but which was, he argued, less vulnerable to criticism than Brodbeck's objectivist account.

Sources: WW(Am); *PS* 33, 1966; Kersey; personal correspondence with Professor Laird Addis; Univ. of Iowa.

DIANÉ COLLINSON

Broglie, Louis Victor Pierre Raymond, Duc de

French. *b:* 15 August 1892, Dieppe, France. *d:* 19 March 1987, Paris. *Cat:* Physicist; philosopher of science. *Educ:* Faculté de Lettres et des Sciences (in History), Paris. *Infls:* Einstein and Schrödinger; introduced to atomic physics by brother, Maurice. *Appts:* Lecturer (1928–30) and Professor (1932–62) at the Paris Faculté des Sciences (Institut Henri Poincaré); Académie des Sciences, 1933 (Secrétaire Perpétuel, 1942–75); Académie Française, 1944; Bureau des Longitudes, 1943; Nobel Prize in Physics, 1932.

Main publications:

(1947) *Physique et microphysique*, Paris: A. Michel.
(1953) *La Physique nouvelle restera-t-elle indéterministe? Exposé du problème suivi de la réproduction de certains documents et d'une contribution de J. P. Vigier*, Les Grands Problèmes de la Science I, Paris: Gauthier-Villars.
(1957) *Nouvelles Perspectives en microphysique*, Paris: A. Michel (English translation, A. J. Pomerans, Edinburgh, 1962).
(1969) *The Revolution in Physics: A Non-mathematical Survey of Quanta*, trans. with additions, R. W. Niemeyer, London and New York.

Secondary literature:

Barut, A. O. (1984) *Quantum Space and Time: The Quest Continues*, Cambridge: Cambridge University Press.
Bohm, D. (1957) *Causality and Chance in Modern Physics*, with a Foreword by Louis de Broglie, London: Routledge.
Flato, M. (ed.) (1976) *Determinism, Causality and Particle: An International Collection of Contributions in Honor of Louis de Broglie on the Occasion of ... his Celebrated Thesis*, Mathematical Physics and Applied Mathematics I, Dordrecht: Reidel.
Synge, J. L. (1954) *Geometrical Mechanics and de Broglie Waves*, Cambridge: Cambridge University Press.

Inventor of wave mechanics, the theory that supposes that elementary particles have wave-like properties, Louis de Broglie was persistently opposed to the **Bohr–Heisenberg** statistical and instrumentalist interpretation of this theory. His own inspiration had been realist, seeing in physics the search for the true nature of reality: to him his discovery was that matter was both wave-like and particle-like. None the less he did initially concede the case for the Bohr–Heisenberg view, but in later life, in agreement with other pioneers like Schrödinger and **Einstein** and in cooperation with Vigier and **Bohm**, he returned to his earlier intuitions. Despite much philosophically minded advocacy, this neorealist programme has found little favour.

Sources: Paul Germain (1987) *Louis de Broglie ou la passion de la vraie physique, Comptes rendus de l'Académie des Sciences*, La Vie des Sciences 4, Série Générale, 6, pp. 569–93; André George (ed.) (1953) *Louis de Broglie, physicien et penseur*, Paris: Albin Michel.

R. N. D. MARTIN

Brouwer, Luitzen Egbertus Jan

Dutch. *b:* 27 February 1881, Overschie, The Netherlands. *d:* 2 December 1966, Blaricum, The Netherlands. *Cat:* Mathematical intuitionist. *Ints:* Philosophy of mathematics. *Educ:* University of Amsterdam. *Appts:* Professor of Mathematics, University of Amsterdam, 1912–51.

Main publications:

(1907) *Over de Gronslagen der wiskunde Maas and van Suchtelen*, Amsterdam.
(1913) 'Intuitionism and formalism', *Bulletin of the American Society* 20: 81–96.
(1929) 'Mathematik, Wissenschaft und Sprache', *Monatshefte für Mathematik* 36: 153–64.
(1949) 'Consciousness, philosophy and mathematics', *Proceedings of the Tenth International Congress of Philosophy*, Amsterdam: North-Holland, pp. 1235–49.
(1952) *Historical background, principles and methods of intuitionism'*, *South African Journal of Science* 49: 139–46.
(1975) *Collected Works*, vol. 1, *Philosophy and Foundations of Mathematics*, ed. A. Heyting, Amsterdam and Oxford: North-Holland.

Secondary literature:

Dummett, M. (1977) *Elements of Intuitionism*, Oxford University Press.
Haack, S. (1974) *Deviant Logic: Some Philosophical Issues*, Cambridge: Cambridge University Press.
Kreisel, G. N. M. (1969) 'Luitzen Egbertus Jan Brouwer (1881–1966)', *Biographical Memoirs of*

Fellows of the Royal Society, 15: 39–68, published by the Royal Society.

Quine, W. V. O. (1980) 'Two dogmas of empiricism', in *From a Logical Point of View*, New York: Harper.

Van Stigt, W. P. (1990) *Brouwer's Intuitionism*, Amsterdam: North Holland.

Brouwer's principal philosophical concern was with the foundations of mathematics. He rejected both Platonism, the view that mathematical statements refer to an external and independent reality, and formalism, the view that they possess no content but are simply sets of formal symbols manipulated according to rules. He adopted the intuitionist perspective in the philosophy of mathematics, one which can be traced back to Aristotle's discussions on infinity.

Brouwer held the view that the foundations of classical mathematics are unsafe, a fact indicated by the presence of the antinomies, and that mathematics needs to be reconstituted on a proper foundation. His diagnosis was that classical mathematics had overextended the use of certain principles of inference and proof, in particular the use of the law of Excluded Middle with respect to infinite classes. According to traditional logic a well-formed statement asserts something true or false and the law of Excluded Middle, sometimes expressed in the formula a $v \neg a$, marks this outlook. Brouwer rejects the law and an associated principle of double negation, ($\neg \neg s \rightarrow a$), which plays an essential role in indirect proof along with principles from the predicate calculus for quantifiers, e.g. $\neg (x)(a) \rightarrow Ex(\neg a)$.

However, Brouwer's critique implies more than a rejection of some procedures. It involves a reinterpretation of certain notions along with a fundamental reconsideration of the relationship between the concepts of truth and meaning as applied to mathematics. The claim, if accepted, leads to radical revision of our understanding of the logical constants, the meanings of which cannot then be given by reference to the classical two valued truth tables as set out in **Wittgenstein**'s *Tractatus Logico-Philosophicus*.

A different foundation for mathematics is explained in a lecture Brouwer gave on 10 March 1928 in Vienna, a lecture attended by Wittgenstein. A Schopenhauerian view of man as a being whose actions may be understood as an expression of the basic will to live is advanced. Mathematics is explained in terms of this conception—it helps him to establish his position of dominance in the world. Two fundamenal kinds of apprehension of the world have been evolved by

man, the temporal and the causal. These make up the basic mathematical structure as grasped by the human agent. However, for Brouwer, unlike Kant, the structure is not objective, being a product of the human will. The fundamental intuition of mathematics is a structure of temporal perceptions whereby the self separates experiences from each other and Brouwer describes this temporal perception as 'the falling apart of a life moment into two qualitatively different things of which the one withdraws before the other and nevertheless is held onto by the memory'. This process of division and synthesis can be continued indefinitely and gives rise to the series of natural numbers. In turn, basic mathematical constructions are created to establish mathematical truths and the existence of mathematical entities. These then are mental constructions created in individual minds. Mathematical knowledge is to be extended by the development of private, constructive proofs. Thus according to Brouwer mathematics is essentially a process which takes place in the mind. Its expression in symbols is logically secondary, cannot be adequately expressed in a formal system and is needed only for purposes of communication. Its content when communicated is imperfect and inprecise. Following **Dummett**, it is useful to distinguish two aspects of intuitionism:

1.)The positive aspect, which involves the claim that the development of intuitionist mathematical theory is a worthwhile and coherent enterprise. To illustrate the nature of this enterprise: in classical mathematics it is sufficient for the proof of the existence of an object that either the necessity of existence or the impossibility of non-existence is demonstrated whereas an intuitionist demands the construction and production of the object in question. Such demands have proved mathematically productive and a branch of mathematics now exists devoted to the development of as much as possible on this basis. However, the philosophical underpinning provided by Brouwer for his mathematical work cannot be accepted, principally because it is provided by a wholly uncritical acceptance of the notion of an intuition. This notion is deployed in an obscure way, but it is clear thatBrouwer assumes the infallibility of basic intuitions. These are experienced by individuals and are hence subjective in origin. An immediate difficulty arises from the possibility that the intuitions of individuals may differ thereby undermining the claim of epistemological infallibility. Brouwer attempts to avoid this difficulty by insisting on the essential privacy of mathematical thinking and the unreliability of communication. However, scepticism concerning intuition as a criterion of knowledge has been a theme of philosophy since the time of Descartes and it is now widely accepted that there are no 'authoritative sources of knowledge'.

This problem is nowhere properly addressed by Brouwer because of his insistence that mathematical thinking is essentially a private enterprise. In a mundane sense this claim is correct. But philosophically understood, especially when with a naive theory of language it leads to philosophical solipsism, making it impossible for Brouwer to address some of the main questions of the philosophy of mathematics, such as how are we to account for the apparent necessity of mathematical propositions or the distinction between pure and applied mathematics. However, the fundamental issue raised by Brouwer's view is whether it is necessary or possible to establish foundations for mathematics. Scepticism concerning this enterprise has been expressed by both **Wittgenstein** and **Quine**. The latter, in particular, encourages us to adopt a holistic view of human knowledge according to which mathematical knowledge would be relatively secure but revisable.

2.)As to the negative thesis, this is prima facie implausible since to most mathematicians classical mathematics is a continuously developing and coherent body of mathematics. It is true that during the latter part of the nineteenth century certain contradictions were developed within mathematics. However, these are well understood and mathematicians have learned to proceed more cautiously, especially in connection with the use of self-reference. It should be noted that these contradictions were discovered by classical logicians and mathematicians and various strategies developed to avoid them before Brouwer's critique was publicized.

More substantial conflict between classical and intuitionist mathematics concerns certain results, in particular the definition of the real number continuum. According to the classical definition its elements are non-countable while according to the intuitionist definition its elements are definable. The appearance of a contradiction might be removed, however, by regarding the definitions as being definitions of different concepts. This possibility, that classical and intuitionist mathematics are dealing with different concepts, is one which can be deployed elsewhere in the controversy. For example, a number of concepts appear different in meaning and hence have different implications in intuitionist mathematics and logic. However the interpretation of Brouwer's views is still not entirely clear. For example, as noted above, Brouwer rejects the Law of Excluded Middle of classical logic but what this rejection amounts to is doubtful and a matter of debate. Brouwer rejects the law on various grounds not all of which are mutually compatible: it is meaningless; it expresses a tautology; its use has not been justified because there exist unsolved problems, e.g. Fermat's Theorem; there exist counterexamples to the theorem.

The creative mathematical work of Brouwer includes theorems, such as the Bar and Fan Theorems, which do not appear in classical mathematics. Such investigations encourage the speculation that intuitionist mathematicians can be seen as putting forward and investigating alternative mathematical systems. Intuitionist mathematics may then be regarded as an alternative to classical mathematics. The question which is the correct mathematics might then be thought of in the same light as the question which is the correct geometry, with the decision being made, if need be, not on philosophical grounds which appeal to a solipsistic mental foundation but on public and practical grounds. Whether or not this is correct, Brouwer's work continues to provoke questioning concerning the nature of meaning and truth, with philosophical implications beyond the province of mathematics and logic.

JIM DUTHIE

Bruggen, Carry van (Carolina Lea de Haan)

Dutch. *b:* 1 January 1881, Smilde, The Netherlands. *d:* 16 November 1932, Laren (NH). *Cat:* Novelist and essayist. *Ints:* Philosophy of language; philosophy of culture. *Infls:* Hegel, Marx and Bolland. *Appts:* Teacher and journalist.

Main publications:

(1916) *Vaderlandsliefde, menschenliefde en opvoeding* [Patriotism, Humanitarianism and Education], Baarn: Hollandia.

(1919) *Prometheus, bijdrage tot het begrip der ontwikkeling van het individualisme* [Prometheus, Contribution to the Concept of the Development of Individualism], Rotterdam: Brusse.

(1924) *De grondgedachten van 'Prometheus'* [The Basic Thoughts of Prometheus], Amsterdam: Querido.

(1925) *Hedendaags fetischisme* [Contemporary Fetishism], Amsterdam: Querido.

Van Bruggen was born in an Orthodox-Jewish family, but struggled a long time to free herself from that background; her novels illustrate this development. Her main philosophical work centres around an analysis of individualism and of its political consequences. For her Prometheus was the symbol of consequent individualism. The Absolute distinguishes itself and creates in this way the different beings. Lust for life is lust for distinction. Lust for unity as its counterpart is lust for death. Man striving towards synthesis strives towards annihilation. Thinking as an instrument for searching unity is therefore self-abolishing. In practice men distinguish themselves from others by means of language and of nation. Nationalism is an instrument of individual survival and has to be overcome. Van Bruggen opposes strongly the Hegelian idea of the state and of man as citizen. In philosophy it is possible for man to lose his individual distinctiveness and to merge into the Absolute. In her philosophy of language Van Bruggen analyses and unmasks many political concepts and expressions and shows how man adheres to fixed meanings and is in need of a kind of fetishism.

WIM VAN DOOREN

Brunner, (Heinrich) Emil

Swiss. *b:* 23 December 1889, Winterthur, Switzerland. *d:* 6 April 1966, Zurich. *Cat:* Reformed theologian. *Ints:* Philosophy of religion. *Educ:* Universities of Zurich and Berlin. *Infls:* Christoph Blumhardt, Herrmann Kutter, Leonhard Ragaz, S. Kierkegaard, M. Buber and Ferdinand Ebner. *Appts:* Pastor at Obstalden, Glarus, 1916–22; Professor, Zurich, 1922–53, with a period at Princeton, 1938–9; Professor, International Christian University, Tokyo, 1953–5.

Main publications:

(1914) *Das Symbolische in der Religiosen Erkenntnis*, Tübingen.
(1928) *Die Mystik und das Wort*, Tübingen.
(1929) *The Theology of Crisis*, New York: Scribner's.
(1934) *The Mediator*, London: Lutterworth.
(1937) *The Divine Imperative*, London: Lutterworth.
(1937) *The Philosophy of Religion from the Standpoint of Protestant Theology*, London: Nicholson & Watson.
(1939) *Man in Revolt*, London: Lutterworth.
(1944) *The Divine-Human Encounter*, London: SCM Press; new enlarged edition, *Truth as Encounter*, 1964.
(1945) *Justice and the Social Order*, London: Lutterworth.
(1946) *Natural Theology*, London: G. Bles.
(1947) *Revelation and Reason*, London: SCM Press.
(1947–8) *Christianity and Civilisation*, London: Nisbet (Gifford Lectures).
(1949–62) *Dogmatics*, 3 vols, London: Lutterworth.
(1953) *The Misunderstanding of the Church*, London: Lutterworth.

Secondary literature:

Barth, K. (1958) 'No!' in *Natural Theology*, London: G. Bles.
Hepburn, R. W. (1958) *Christianity and Paradox*, London: Watts.
Jewett, P. K. (1954) *Emil Brunner's Concept of Revelation*, London: James Clarke.
Kegley, C. (ed.) (1962) *The Theology of Emil Brunner*, New York: Macmillan.
Lewis, H. D. (1947) *Morals and the New Theology*, London: Gollancz.
——(1951) *Morals and Revelation*, London: Allen & Unwin.
Smith, J. J. (1967) *Emil Brunner's Theology of Revelation*, Manila: Loyola House of Studies.

Like **Barth** and **Bultmann** (and earlier P. T. Forsyth), Brunner came to repudiate the optimistic liberal theology in which he had been reared as inadequate in a world which was witnessing the horrors of the First World War, and in which the churches were at once being marginalized and reaching out to one another ecumenically. Was there a Word from God? Brunner and others thought that there was. It was, however, a Word to be distilled from the Bible utilizing the techniques of modern scholarship; it was not literalistically to be identified with the Bible. Where Schleiermacher had elevated human religious experience and regarded revelation as a matter of the enlightened self-consciousness, Brunner's concern was to hold together the objective and subjective aspects of faith, whilst always giving precedence to the former. What was all-important was: 'The revelation and self-communication of God in Jesus Christ, apprehended by obedient faith.' But this subject-object relationship was not on all fours with such relationships within the 'It' world. Rather, we have to do with the encounter of persons with one another. God has supremely and uniquely revealed himself in Jesus Christ, and this revelation encompasses all things from the creation to the eschaton. Originating outside of history, it decisively touches all history. (The language of encounter was subjected to philosophical analysis by Ronald W. Hepburn in *Christianity and Paradox* (1958).)

In fidelity to his objective 'to declare the *Word* of the Bible to the *World*', Brunner was exercised by the missionary obligation of the Church (in which connection his duties as teacher of homiletics and practical theology as well as systematics, and his sojourn in Japan, should not be overlooked), frustrated by the obstacles which organized Christianity had placed in the path of enquirers, and anxious to communicate with all. Hence his insistence upon general revelation—the revelation in creation—as providing common ground between human beings *qua* human, and as attested in Scripture in such passages as Romans 1. Not indeed that he thought that an intellectually coercive natural theology was desirable or possible: (i) because God is not reached by the argumentative route; (ii) because our experience of the world is of a Babel of conflicting views, not of a firm intellectual base for a natural theology; and (iii) because of the noetic effects of sin. Brunner's position horrified Barth (*Nein! Antwort an Emil Brunner*, 1934), but he continued to insist that human beings are and must be addressable by God; he deemed natural theology of 'decisive importance for the dealings of Christians with unbelievers'; and he remained undaunted by 'that terrible book' of Barth's. Many concluded that while Barth won the argument, the truth was on Brunner's side. Some, however, felt that Brunner's insistence upon the uniqueness of Christianity compromised his relatively positive appreciation of natural theology.

Brunner further emphasized the importance for ethics of revelation in creation. Of this revelation the structures of society—supremely the family—are a part. Reinhold **Niebuhr** criticized Brunner's view of the structures of society as inadequately allowing for the sinful forms in which we experience them—a charge which Brunner resisted. Important though societal structures were, Brunner maintained that 'the value of personal life stands above all other structures'. Hence his opposition to totalitarian regimes which, by reducing human beings to functionaries denied their true status as persons.

Perhaps to a greater extent than any of his contemporaries, Brunner was able to reach the person in the pew. This he did through his more popular books, his preaching and his work at the lay academy at Boldern. Towards the end of his life he said of his first appointment: 'I was a pastor with my whole heart and am still that today'.

Sources: Obituary notices.

ALAN SELL

Brunschvicg, Léon

French. *b:* 10 November 1869, Paris. *d:* 18 January 1944, Aix-les-Bains. *Cat:* Idealist metaphysician. *Ints:* Speculative theology; history of philosophy; history of science. *Educ:* École Normale Supérieure 1888–91, PhD 1897. *Infls:* Kant, Descartes, Spinoza, Pascal, Montaigne and Boutroux. *Appts:* Rouen, Paris, 1909 Sorbonne (Académie des Sciences Morales et Politiques 1919).

Main publications:

(1897) *La Modalité du jugement, la vertu métaphysique du syllogisme selon Aristote*, Paris: Alcan.
(1897–1904) (ed. with P. Boutroux) *Oeuvres de Pascal* Paris: Hachette. (1900) *Introduction à la Vie de l'Esprit*, Paris: Alcan.
(1905) *L'Idéalisme contemporain*, Paris: Alcan.
(1912) *Les Étapes de la philosophie mathématique*, Paris: Alcan.
(1921) *Nature et liberté*, Paris: Flammarion.
(1922) *L'Expérience humaine et la causalité physique*, Paris: Alcan.
(1923) *Spinoza et ses contemporains*, Paris: Alcan (third edition of work first published in 1894).
(1927) *Progrès de la conscience dans la philosophie occidentale*, 2 vols, Paris: Alcan.
(1931) *De la connaissance de soi*, Paris: Alcan.
(1932) *Introduction à la vie de l'esprit*, Paris: Alcan.
(1934) *Les Âges de l'intelligence*, Paris: Alcan.
(1936) *La physique du XXe siècle et la philosophie*, Paris: Alcan.
(1939) *La Raison et la religion*, Paris: Alcan.
(1945) *Descartes et Pascal, lecteurs de Montaigne*, Neuchâtel: Baconnière. (1945) *Héritage des mots, héritage des idées*, Paris: PUF.
(1947) *L'Esprit européen*, Neuchâtel: Baconnière.
(1948) *Agenda retrouvé 1892 et 1942*, Paris: Éditions du Minuit.
(1949) *La Philosophie de l'esprit*, Paris: PUF.
(1950) *De la vrai et de la fausse conversion suivie de la querelle de l'athéisme*, Paris: PUF.
(1951–8) *Écrits Philosophiques*, 3 vols, ed. A.-R. Weill-Brunschvieg and C. Lehec, Paris: PUF.
(1953) *Blaise Pascal*, Paris: Vrin.

Secondary literature:

Cochet, M. A. (1937) *Commentaire sur la conversion spirituelle dans la philosophie de Léon Brunschvicg*, Brussels: Lammertin.
Deschoux, M. (1949) *La Philosophie de Léon Brunschvicg*, Paris: PUF.
——(1969) *Léon Brunschvicg ou l'idéalisme à l'hauteur de l'homme*, Paris:
Seghers (extracts from his work with an introduction).

Etcheverry, A. (1934) *L'idéalisme français contemporain*, Paris: Alcan. Hawidy, Y. (1955) 'L'Idée de la transcendance dans la philosophie contemporaine', Paris (thesis).

Messaut, J. (1938) *La Philosophie de Léon Brunschvicg*, Paris: Vrin.

——(1942) *La Philosophie française entre les deux Guerres*, Paris: Aubier, pp. 179–200.

Revue de Métaphysique et de Morale, Jan–Apr 1945 (commemorative pieces on Brunschvieg by E. Bréhier, A. Cresson, A. Reymond, M. Blondel, R. G. Lacombe, G. Bastide, J. Nabert, R. Lenoble, L. De Broglie, G. Bachelard, J. Laporte, C. Seras, G. Berger and R. Aron).

A radically anti-realist idealist rationalist who took something from both Spinoza and Pascal (he followed Pascal in rejecting the pantheism in Spinoza's deism). His final position had something of the Hegelian in it—he held that consciousness tended in history towards a final unity, but in his commitment to individual freedom and spontaneity he rejected the determinism in Hegel's (and Spinoza's) position. Rejecting imputations of atheism advanced by **Blondel** and **Le Roy**, he nevertheless looked for a religion free of anthropomorphic conceptions of God. He maintained a historicist approach according to which the metaphysics of any one period flowed from the science of that period, thus giving a high value to the history of science. He was joint founder (with Xavier **Léon**, his student friend from the Lycée Condorcet) in 1893 of the influential *Revue de Métaphysique et de Morale*, and also of the Société Française de Philosophie in 1903. A very influential figure in French academic life in the first half of the century, there now seems to be little interest in his work.

Sources: BDF 7 (1956): 566b–567a; Edwards; EncJud, 1419a–b.

R. N. D. MARTIN

Buber, Martin

Israeli. *b:* 8 August 1878, Vienna. *d:* 13 June 1965, Jerusalem. *Cat:* Philosopher of religion; social philosopher; editor; philosopher of education; publisher and translator. *Ints:* Hasidism; idealist German philosophy; Protestant philosophy; philosophy of religion; cultural Judaism; Zionist philosophy. *Educ:* Universities of Vienna, Leipzig, Zurich and Berlin, 1896–1904; PhD under Georg Simmel, 1904. *Infls:* Grandfather and midrashic scholar, Solomon Buber; Ahad ha-Am and Franz Rosenzweig, as well as Zionist youth movements and East European Jewry. *Appts:* 1920, Cofounder

(with Rosenzweig), Freies Jüdisches Lehrhaus, Frankfurt; 1925–33, Lecturer, Religion and Ethics, then Professor, Religion, University of Frankfurt; 1933–5, Director, Central Office for Adult Jewish Education; 1935, Lecturer at Quaker meetings until prevented by Nazi policy; 1938–51, Professor of Social Philosophy, Hebrew University, Jerusalem; 1938, Cofounder of Israeli College for Adult Education teachers, of new immigrants; 1960–2, first President, Israeli Academy of Sciences and Humanities; 1964, Hon. Doc., University of Heidelberg; 1951, Hanseatic Goethe Prize; 1953, Peace Prize of the German Book Trade; 1956, Erasmus Prize.

Main publications:

(1906) *Die Geschichten des Rabbi Nachman* Frankfurt: Rütten & Loening (English translation, *The Tales of Rabbi Nachman*, New York: Horizon, 1956; Atlantic Highlands, NJ: Humanities, 1988).

(1908) *Die Legende des Baalschem*, Frankfurt: Rütten & Loening, and Berlin, Schocken (English translation, *Jewish Mysticism and the Legends of the Baal-Schem*, trans. M. Friedman, London: Dent, 1931; *The Legend of the Baal Shem*, London: East and West Library, and New York: Harper, 1955, and New York: Schocken, 1987).

(1923) *Ich und Du*, Leipzig, and Berlin: Schocken, 1936 (English translation, *I and Thou*, trans. W. Kaufmann, Edinburgh: Clark, 1937, and New York, Scribner, 1970).

(1936) *Die Frage an den Einzelnen*, Berlin: Schocken (English translation, *Between Man and Man*, London: Kegan Paul, 1947, and Boston: Beacon, 1955).

(1941) *Gog u-Magog*, (English translation, *For the Sake of Heaven*, trans. L. Lewisohn, Philadelphia: JPSA, 1945, and New York, Atheneum, 1969).

(1942) *Torat ha-Neviim* Jerusalem: Mosad Bialik (English translation, *The Prophetic Faith*, trans. C. Witten-Davies, New York: Macmillan, 1949).

(1943) *Or ha-Ganuz* (English translations, *Tales of the Hasidim*, New York: Schocken, 1947, and Scribner, 1957; *From the Treasure House of the Hasidim*, ed. D. Hardan, Jerusalem: Dept. Education and Culture in the Diaspora, World Zionist Organization, 1969, and Atlantic Highlands, NJ: Humanities, 1988).

(1945) *Pardes ha-Hasidut*, Tel Aviv: Mossad Bialik (English translations, *Hasidism and Modern Man*, 2 vols, trans. M. Friedman, Horizon: New York, 1958; *The Origin and Meaning of Hasidism*, 1960 and Atlantic Highlands, NJ: Humanities, 1988).

(1947) *Netivot be-Utopia* [Paths in Utopia], Tel Aviv: Am Oved, and Boston: Beacon Press, 1958.

(1950) *Good and Evil: Two Interpretations*, trans. R. G. Smith, London: Macmillan, and trans. M. Bullock, New York: Scribner, 1953.

(1952) *Eclipse of God: Studies in the Relation between Religion and Philosophy*, New York: Harper; London, Gollancz, 1953; reprinted, Westport: Greenwood Press, 1977, and Atlantic Highlands, NJ: Humanities, 1988.

(1962–4) *Werke* (Collected Works) 3 vols, Munich: Schneider.

(1963) *Israel and the World*, New York: Schocken.

(1965) *The Knowledge of Man*, ed. Maurice Friedman, London: Allen and Unwin, and New York: Harper & Row.

(1967) *On Judaism*, trans. A. Jospé, ed. N. N. Glatzer, New York: Schocken.

(1973) *On Zion: the History of an Idea*, trans. S. Goldman; foreword N. N. Glatzer, New York: Schocken.

(1990) *A Believing Humanism: My Testament*, Atlantic Highlands, NJ: Humanities.

Secondary literature:

(1991) *Encounter on the Narrow Ridge*, New York: Paragon House.

Bergman, Samuel A. (1956) *Filosofiah ha-Dialogit mi Kirkagor ad Buber*, Jerusalem: Hebrew University Press; Akadamon, 1964/5 (English translation, A. A. Gerstein, *Dialogical Philosophy from Kierkegaard to Buber*, Albany: SUNY, 1991) .

Buber, Martin and Friedman, Maurice (eds) (1957) *Pointing the Way: Collected Essays*, London: Routledge, and New York: Harper, 1957; Atlantic Highlands, NJ: Humanities, 1990.

Friedman, M. (1981–4) *Martin Buber's Life and Work* 3 vols, New York: E. P. Dutton.

——'Buber' in *Thinkers of the Twentieth Century*, second edition, (includes bibliography), 1987.

Gordon, H. and Bloch, J. (eds) (1984) *Martin Buber: A Centenary Volume*, New York: Ktav.

Green, A. (ed.) (1989) *Jewish Spirituality II*, New York: Crossroad, pp. 283–432.

Herberg, Will (ed.) (1956) *The Writings of Martin Buber*, New York: Meridian.

Horwitz, Rivkah (1978) *Buber's Way to I and Thou*, Heidelberg: L. Schneider.

Kaufmann, Walter (1992) *Nietzsche, Heidegger and Buber: Discovering the Mind*, New Brunswick: Transaction Books.

Kohn, H. (1961) *Martin Buber, Sein Werk und seine Zeit*, Cologne: Melzer.

Mendes-Flohr, Paul (1989) *From Mysticism to Dialogue*, Detroit: Wayne State University Press.

Rotenstreich, Nathan (1991) *Immediacy and its Limits: a Study in Martin Buber's Thought*, Philadelphia: Harwood Academic.

Schaeder, Grete (1984) *The Hebrew Humanism of Martin Buber*, trans. N. J. Jacobs, Detroit: Wayne State University Press (German original, 1966).

Schilpp, P. A. and Friedman, M. (eds) (1967) *The Philosophy of Martin Buber*, La Salle: Open Court.

Buber has exerted a powerful influence on twentieth century philosophies of religion, education, sociology and politics. Prevented by Nazism from continuing his academic post at a German university, he initiated deep and far-reaching research into the subject of adult Jewish education, continuing this work, together with his more purely philosophical interests, when he emigrated to mandated Palestine. In his early career he was most famous for his philosophy of 'I and Thou', which appears, superficially, to be grounded in German idealist, or Christian, rather than Jewish philosophy. He has been criticized for this approach, most strongly by Gershom **Scholem**. However, it is possible to trace aspects of traditional Jewish thought, mediated through the *Talmud*, and the medieval thinkers, Rashi and Yehuda Halevi, in this concept of dialogue. As with his work on Hasidism, however, the original teaching has been modernized and dressed in the garb of contemporary idealist, Christian and socialist philosophy. Studies on Buber have dealt with all aspects of his thought, including its relevance for communication, education, ethics, music, psychology, peace studies, sport and linguistics. In additon his work has been compared with that of other contemporary philosophers.

Sources: *Leo Baeck Memorial Conference on Jewish Social Thought*, New York: The Federation, 1973; EncJud; NUC; Schoeps; WorldBio; *CPBI*, 1992.

IRENE LANCASTER

Buchler, Justus

American. *b:* 27 March 1914, New York City. *d:* 19 March 1991, Chambersburg, Pennsylvania. *Cat:* Humanistic naturalist. *Ints:* Metaphysics. *Educ:* City College of New York, BA 1934; Columbia University, MA 1935, PhD 1939. *Infls:* Santayana, Peirce, Dewey and Nagel. *Appts:* 1937–71, Instructor to Professor of Philosophy, Columbia University (Chair of Department, 1964–7); 1971–91, Distinguished Professor of Philosophy (Emeritus Professor 1981), State University of New York at Stony Brook.

Main publications:

(1951) *Toward a General Theory of Human Judgment*, New York: Columbia University Press.

(1955) *Nature and Judgment*, New York: Columbia University Press; reprinted, Lanham, Maryland: University Press of America, 1985.

(1961) *The Concept of Method*, New York: Columbia University Press; reprinted, Lanham, Maryland: University Press of America, 1985.

(1966) *Metaphysics of Natural Complexes*, New York: Columbia University Press; second expanded edition, Albany: SUNY Press, 1990.

(1974) *The Main of Light: On the Concept of Poetry*, New York: Oxford University Press.

Secondary literature:

Singer, B. J. (1983) *Ordinal Naturalism: An Introduction to the Philosophy of Justus Buchler*, Lewisburg, PA: Bucknell University Press.

Buchler's philosophy is a singular expression of humanistic naturalism. Beginning in epistemology he articulated a unique and idiosyncratic categorial philosophy. His investigations led him more deeply into metaphysics, coining new terms or using old terms in novel ways to formulate his system.

Sources: RA, 4: WW(Am); *New York Times*, 22 Mar 1991.

ANDREW RECK

Bühler, Karl

German. *b:* 1879. *d:* 1963, USA. *Cat:* Experimental psychologist. *Ints:* Gestalt theory; systems; psychoanalysis; the psychological problem of the existence of 'imageless thought', of language, perception, and of child development. *Educ:* MD, PhD. *Infls:* Würzburg School of Psychology (directed by Oswald Külpe); experimental psychological studies of Wolfgang Köhler and Kurt Koffka; psychoanalysis. *Appts:* Dozent, University of Berlin; Assistant Professor, University of Würzburg, 1907–8; Professor of Psychology, University of Bonn, 1909–13; Professor of Psychology, University of Munich, 1913–22; Professor and Chairman of Department of Psychology, University of Vienna, 1922–38.

Main publications:

(1907–8) 'Tatsachen und Probleme zu einer Psychologie der Denkvorgänge', in three parts: 'Über Gedanken', *Arch. ges. Psychol.*, 9: 297–305; 'Über Gedankenzusammenhänge', *Arch. ges. Psychol.* 12: 1–23; 'Über Gedankenerinerungen', *Arch. ges. Psychol.*, 12: 24–92.

(1919) 'Kritische Durchmusterung der neueren Theorien des Satzes', *Indogerm. Jahrbuch* VI.

(1922) *Die Erscheinungsweisen der Farben* in *Handbuch der Psychologie*, Jena: Fischer, Heft 1, Teil 1.

(1923) 'Über den Begriff der Sprachlichen Darstellung', *Psychol. Forschung* III.

(1949) *The Mental Development of the Child*, trans. Oskar Oesner, London: Routledge & Kegan Paul (largely a summary of Bühler's *Die geistige Entwicklung des Kindes*).

Bühler was a member of the Würzburg School of experimental psychology (1900–9) that was based at the University of Würzburg. The school specialized in the psychological determination of the existence or non-existence of 'imageless thought'. Bühler joined the school in 1907; it was disbanded in 1909.

Bühler's influence on the psychological community, and especially on the Würzburg School, was radical. Previously the School had adopted the so-called *Aussagemethode* (the method of setting tasks for the observer) in their study of 'imageless thought'—the production of a thought without the mediation of an imaging or sensory element. But the method had a serious disadvantage in that it limited the school to searching for thoughts that lacked any sensory element. When Bühler joined, he quickly introduced a different experimental method, the *Ausfragemethode*. The essence of the new method was that it established a freer and sympathetic relationship between the questioner and the observer, with the former asking the questions and the latter answering as clearly as possible. For example, the observers would be told complicated problems, to which they were asked to answer 'yes' or 'no'. When they reported that they could call to mind the meaning of what they were told, but could not explain how it was done, it proved to Bühler that such non-sensory dimensions were important to thought, and should be investigated. Bühler's results unleashed a controversy that took some time to subside. On the one side were psychologists like **Wundt**, Dürr and Titchener, who doubted his results because of his lack of rigour in distinguishing between what is constitutive of mind and what can be said 'about' mind. On the other side were the defenders of the 'imageless thought', such as R. S. Woodsworth and C. C. Pratt. By the time the controversy subsided, a willingness to accept the existence of 'impalpable materials' as imageless thoughts' was already evident.

Sources: E. G. Boring (1950) *A History of Experimental Psychology*, New York: Appleton-Century-Crofts; E. Hearst (1979) *The First Century of Experimental Psychology*, New Jersey: Lawrence Erlbaum Associates; T. S. Krawiec (ed.) (1972) *The Psycholo-*

gists 2 vols, Oxford: OUP; S. S. Stevens (ed.) (1966) *Handbook of Experimental Psychology*, London: John Wiley & Sons.

SEBASTIEN ODIARI

Bukharin, Nikolai Ivanovich

Russian. *b:* 27 September (O.S.) 1888, Moscow. *d:* 15 March 1938, Moscow. *Cat:* Marxist, social theorist and political figure. *Ints:* Social and political philosophy; dialectic and historial materialism. *Infls:* Marx, Engels, Bogdanov and Lenin. *Appts:* Although Bukharin studied economic theory for a short time at Moscow University and attended the lectures of Böhm-Bawerk in Vienna, these studies were incidental to his life of political engagement, first as a young revolutionary in Russia, then (1911–17) in exile abroad, and subsequently as a leader and the most respected theoretician of the ruling wing of Lenin's Bolshevik party during the 1920s. He served the party and the Soviet government in many prominent capacities, including that of editor of the newspapers *Pravda* (1917–29) and *Izvestiia* (1934–6).

Main publications:

(1918) *Mirovoe khoziastvo i imperializm*, Petrograd (English translation, *Imperialism and World Economy*, London, 1929).

(1919) (with E. A. Preobrazhenskii) *Azbuka kommunizma*, Petrograd (English translation, *The ABC of Communism*, trans. Eden and Cedar Paul, London: Communist Party of Great Britain, 1922).

(1921) *Teoriia istoricheskogo materializma*, Moscow (English translation, *Historical Materialism*, New York, 1925).

(1925) *Put' k sotsializmu i raboche-krest'ianskii soiuz* [The Road to Socialism and the Worker-Peasant Alliance], Moscow and Leningrad.

(1932) *Darvinizm i marksizm* [Darwinism and Marxism], Leningrad.

Secondary literature:

Cohen, Stephen F. (1975) *Bukharin and the Bolshevik Revolution*, New York: Vintage Books.

Joravsky, David (1961) *Soviet Marxism and Natural Science, 1917–1932*, London: Routledge & Kegan Paul.

Wetter, Gustav A. (1958) *Dialectical Materialism*, trans. Peter Heath, London: Routledge & Kegan Paul.

Bukharin's pre-1917 writings influenced **Lenin**'s views on imperialism and the dictatorship of the proletariat, and in 1919–21 he wrote two summaries of Marxist theory that served as textbooks for years to come. The first, *The ABC of Communism*, was designed for a broad popular audience; the second, *Historical Materialism*, was intended for use in Communist Party schools. In his overall philosophical outlook Bukharin was indebted to **Bogdanov** as well as to Engels, and he is known as one of the principal 'mechanists' in Soviet philosophy—that is, Marxist materialists who defended a positivistic rather than a Hegelian version of dialectics and who explained motion as a result of external forces rather than internal 'contradictions'. Bukharin's 'equilibrium theory' postulates a system of opposing forces in which development takes place through the disturbance and reestablishment of equilibrium. Bukharin supported Lenin's New Economic Policy and was opposed to forced collectivization; he envisaged the transition from capitalism to communism as a more gradual process with a mixed economy and a democratic political system. These views aroused Stalin's ire, and in 1938 Bukharin was convicted of counterrevolutionary activity and executed. The same views are responsible for the strong revival of interest in Bukharin among reform-minded communists and socialists in Eastern Europe in recent years.

JAMES SCANLAN

Bulgakov, Sergei Nikolaevich

Russian. *b:* 16 (28 N.S.) June 1871, Livny. *d:* 13 July 1944, Paris. *Cat:* Religious philosopher. *Educ:* Graduated in Law from University of Moscow, 1894. *Infls:* Marx, Kant, Schelling, Solov'ev and Florensky. *Appts:* 1901–6, taught Political Economy, Kiev Polytechnic Institute; 1906–18 taught Political Economy, University of Moscow; 1918–22, Professor of Political Economy and Theology, University of Simferopol'; 1925–44, Dean and Professor of Dogmatic Theology, Russian Theological Institute in Paris.

Main publications:

(1903) *Ot marksizma k idealizmu: sbornik statei (1896–1903)* [From Marxism to Idealism: A Collection of Articles 1896–1903], St Petersburg.

(1911) *Dva grada: issledovaniia o prirode obshchestvennykh idealov* [Two Cities: Investigations into the Nature of Social Ideals], 2 vols, Moscow.

(1917) *Svet nevechernyi: sozertsaniia i umozreniia* [The Unfading Light: Contemplations and Speculations], Moscow.

(1937) *The Wisdom of God: A Brief Summary of Sophiology*, trans. P. J. Thompson, O. F. Clarke and K. Braikevich, London: Williams and Norgate.

(1953) *Filosofiia imeni* [Philosophy of the Name], Paris: YMCA Press.

(1976) (ed. J. Pain and N. Zernov) *A Bulgakov Anthology*, London: SPCK (translated extracts from Bulgakov's philosophical and theological works).

Secondary literature:

Lossky, N. O. (1952) *History of Russian Philosophy*, London: George Allen & Unwin, ch. 15.

Zenkovsky, V. V. (1953) *A History of Russian Philosophy*, trans. George L. Kline, London: Routledge & Kegan Paul, vol. 2, pp. 890–916.

The son of a priest, Bulgakov became a prominent 'legal Marxist' during the 1890s, but, like **Berdyaev**, S. L. **Frank** and **Struve**, renounced Marxism at the turn of the century. He was a contributor to *Vekhi* [Landmarks] (1909), the collection criticizing the revolutionary intelligentsia. Having returned to the Orthodox faith, he was ordained in 1918, and was among the non-Marxist scholars expelled from Russia in 1922. After living in Prague, he settled in Paris.

Bulgakov wrote in the tradition of **Solov'ev**'s metaphysics of total-unity and 'Godmanhood'. He followed **Florensky** in giving prominence to the principle of Sophia as a 'fourth hypostasis' of the Deity and the world-soul of the cosmos. His 'sophiology' was censured by the Orthodox Church in the early 1930s. He was also criticized for implying the consubstantiality of God and the creation; this despite his attempt to steer a course between pantheism and Manichean dualism, partly by positing a reified Nothing from which the cosmos was created and from which evil issues. Unlike Berdyaev's *Ungrund*, this was not a separate entity limiting the Divine Spirit.

Bulgakov's posthumous *Philosophy of the Name* (1953) was, like **Losev**'s work of the same name, inspired by Florensky's philosophical linguistics: he contended that, despite the plurality of languages, the sound of a word is the incarnation of its cosmic soul.

COLIN CHANT

Bullough, Edward

British. *b:* 28 March 1880, Thun, Switzerland. *d:* 17 September 1934, Bath, England. *Cat:* Psychological aesthetician; linguist; translator. *Ints:* Aesthetics. *Educ:* Vitzthum Gymnasium, Dresden, and Trinity College, Cambridge. *Infls:* Goethe, Schiller, Theodor Fechner and T. Lipps. *Appts:* Fellow of Gonville & Caius College, Cambridge, 1912–34; University Lecturer in Modern Languages, Cambridge; Professor of Italian, University of Cambridge, 1933–4.

Main publications:

(1904) 'Matter and form', *Modern Languages Quarterly* 7.

(1907) 'The modern conception of aesthetics'; reprinted in *Aesthetics: Lectures and Essays*, 1957.

(1912) '"Psychical distance" as a factor in art and an aesthetic principle', *British Journal of Pyschology* 5, reprinted in *Aesthetics: Lectures and Essays* (1957).

(1921) 'Recent work in experimental aesthetics', *British Journal of Psychology* 12.

(1957) *Aesthetics: Lectures and Essays*, ed. Elizabeth M. Wilkinson, London: Bowes & Bowes; new edition, Westport: Greenwood Press, 1977.

Secondary literature:

Wilkinson, Elizabeth M. (1957) Introduction to Bullough's *Aesthetics: Lectures and Essays*.

In the early years of the twentieth century Bullough pioneered the application of psychology, both introspective and experimental, to questions in aesthetics. His lectures on psychological aesthetics in 1907 were the first of their kind to be given at Cambridge. Bullough is best known for his influential account of 'psychical distance' as a state of mind purged of concern with practical interests and which he held to be a distinguishing feature of aesthetic consciousness in both artists and spectators.

Sources: Obituary, *The Times*; Michael Oakeshott (1934), Memoir, *The Caian* 46.

PETER LEWIS

Bultmann, Rudolf

German. *b:* 20 August 1884, Wiefelstede, Oldenburg, Germany. *d:* 30 July 1976, Marburg, Germany. *Cat:* Lutheran New Testament scholar. *Ints:* Existentialism. *Educ:* Universities of Tübingen, Berlin and Marburg. *Infls:* K. Müller, H. Gunkel, A. von Harnack, A. Jülicher, J. Weiss, W. Herrmann and M. Heidegger. *Appts:* Lecturer, Marburg, 1912–16; Assistant Professor, Breslau, 1916–20; Professor, Giessen, 1920 -1; Professor, Marburg, 1921–51.

Main publications:

(1934) *Jesus and the Word*, New York: Scribners.

(1955) *Essays: Philosophical and Theological*, London: SCM Press.

(1957) *History and Eschatology*, Edinburgh: University of Edinburgh Press (Gifford Lectures).

(1958) *Jesus Christ and Mythology*, New York: Scribners.
(1960) *Existence and Faith: Shorter Writings of Rudolf Bultmann*, New York: Meridian.
(1969) *Faith and Understanding*, New York: Harper & Row; Philadelphia: Fortress Press, 1987.
(1984) *New Testament and Mythology and Other Basic Writings*, Philadelphia: Fortress Press.

Secondary literature:
Fergusson, David (1992) *Bultmann*, London: Geoffrey Chapman.
——(1949) *Festschrift Rudolf Bultmann zum 65. Geburtstag überreicht*, Stuttgart.
Hobbs, Edward C. (ed.) (1985) *Bultmann, Retrospect and Prospect: The Centenary Symposium at Wellesley*, Philadelphia: Fortress Press.
Kegley, Charles W. (ed.) (1966) *The Theology of Rudolf Bultmann*, New York: Harper & Row (includes bibliography).
Macquarrie, John (1955) *An Existentialist Theology*, London: SCM Press.
——(1960) *The Scope of Demythologising*, London: SCM Press.
Ogden, Schubert (1962) *Christ Without Myth*, London: SCM Press.
Owen, H. P. (1957) *Revelation and Existence*, Cardiff: University of Wales Press.
Schmithals, W. (1968) *An Introduction to the Theology of Rudolf Bultmann*, London: SCM Press.

The work of few twentieth-century theologians has attracted comment from as wide a spectrum of theologians, and from as great a number of philosophers as has that of Bultmann. Dismayed by Bultmann's existentialist approach to the Bible, the conservative theologian Robert L. Reymond declared that 'Bultmann is only listening to a "recording" of his own inner voice'. Helmut Thielicke opposed Bultmann's anthropocentrism, and considered that he had mistakenly elevated the modern scientific worldview into the criterion for interpreting Scripture. The Roman Catholic theologian Karl **Rahner** declared that Bultmann was 'the one theologian in the twentieth century who knew what was going on'. The existentialist philosopher **Jaspers** lamented Bultmann's self-confinement to **Heidegger**, while Ronald Hepburn has raised pertinent queries from the standpoint of British analytical philosophy. It has been claimed that Bultmann's utilization of Heidegger leads to theological reductionism no less than did the dependence of some philosophers of an earlier generation upon post-Hegelian idealism.

Raised under liberal theology, Bultmann never repudiated its concern for the application of the best critical scholarship to the biblical texts. But where the liberals went in earnest quest of the historical Jesus, Bultmann doubted whether much could be known about Jesus's life and work. Where the demeanour of the liberals was frequently optimistic, Bultmann's, though not pessimistic, was—not least as a German Confessing Christian of the 1930s—characterized by due appreciation of the tragic in human existence. Bultmann's qualifications of liberalism go hand in hand with his indebtedness to Heidegger, his Marburg colleague (1922–8). Heidegger's insistence upon the givenness of our own existence, upon our fallenness and upon our sense of not being 'at home' in this world, together with his understanding of authentic existence as that which responds appropriately to our existential situation, seemed to Bultmann to provide the basis for a theology for the contemporary world.

This world was one in which older, supernaturalist, presuppositions had been vanquished by the modern scientific worldview, and the Bible had become a closed book to many because its thought-world seemed *passé*. Bultmann nevertheless believed that God addresses humanity in the Scriptures, but for his voice to be heard today the mythological husk must be removed. Hence Bultmann's programme of demythologization: the attempt to translate the 'mythical' language of the New Testament without remainder into existential terms. The translation made, human beings in their fallenness (for Bultmann, sin) are confronted by the living Word who calls them to new, authentic, life. Against those who argued that he was simply reiterating older theologies of self-consciousness in existentialist language, Bultmann argued that his concern was with self-understanding: we understand ourselves truly only in that encounter with God, the source of which is in God, not us.

The following are among points of discussion which have been raised from a variety of quarters by Bultmann's work: (1) Given that Bultmann demythologizes so much (denying, for example, the historicity of the Virgin Birth and the resurrection of Jesus), on what grounds does he stop short of demythologizing those kerygmatic claims which he deems vital for theology—something which Fritz Buri proceeded subsequently to do? (2) If we are encountered by God, does not this imply that God is ontologically distinct from the world? Why, then, should Bultmann be so wary of ontological claims concerning God, which need not land in the kind of objectification which he fears? (3) If we may properly speak of revelation only in respect of present encounters, have we not bracketed a large number of assertions concerning God's actions in themselves, which many Christians wish to make? (4) On Bultmann's own terms, is not all talk of God's acting in history mythological? Bultmann countered this suggestion by saying that such talk is analogical. However, it was then pointed out that this leaves us with post-demythologization statements of more than an existential kind, and this is not the result Bultmann originally sought. (5) While Bultmann's openness to philosophy is applauded by many, does not his existential approach require him to bypass such philosophically interesting questions as the logic of personal identity and post-mortem survival? 6) Bultmann believes that, whether accepted or rejected, Christ is the schatological event. But does he not come close to saying that Christ becomes incarnate only when received by an individual? Does not this appear to make the Incarnation a human (even if an enabled) work?

Sources: Obituary notices.

ALAN SELL

Bunge, Mario Augusto

Argentinian. *b:* 21 September 1919. *Cat:* Philosopher of science; philosopher of technology; philosopher of mind. *Educ:* Doctorate in Physics and Mathematics, University of La Plata; went on to study Nuclear Physics at the Astronomical Observatory of Cordoba; also studied Law at Simon Frasier University. *Infls:* Analytic philosophy. *Appts:* 1956–8, Professor of Physics, University of Buenos Aires; 1957–62, Professor of Philosophy, University of Buenos Aires; from 1966, Professor of Philosophy, McGill University.

Main publications:

(1974) *Interpretation and Truth*, Dordrecht: Reidel.

(1974) *Semantics*, Dordrecht: Reidel.

(1974) *Sense and Reference*, Dordrecht: Reidel.

(1975) *Intuition and Science*, Westport, CT: Greenwood Press.

(1977) *The Furniture of the World*, Dordrecht: Reidel.

(1979) *A World of Systems*, Dordrecht: Reidel.

(1980) *The Mind-Body Problem: A Psychological Approach*, Oxford and NY: Pergamon Press.

(1981) *Scientific Materialism*, Dordrecht: Reidel.

(1983) *Lingüística y filosofía*, Barcelona: Ariel.

(1989) *Ethics: The Good and the Right*, Dordrecht: Reidel.

Secondary literature:

Agassi, Joseph and Cohen, Robert S. (eds) (1982) *Scientific Philosophy Today: Essays in Honor of Mario Bunge*, Dordrecht: Reidel.

Weingartner, Paul (ed.) (1990) 'Mario Bunge's Life and Work', in *Studies on Mario Bunge's 'Treatise'*, Amsterdam: Rodopi.

Mario Bunge was one of the first to embrace analytic philosophy in Buenos Aires in the mid-1950s. He has sought to develop a 'scientific' philosophy which takes into account both scientific knowledge and the methods of enquiry used by scientists. He posits that metaphysics is the overarching science into which all specific sciences are subsumed. A self-defined 'critical realist', Bunge rejects Marxism and psychoanalysis. He is also a critic of Noam **Chomsky**'s transformational theory.

AMY A. OLIVER

Buonaiuti, Ernesto

Italian. *b:* 24 June 1881, Rome. *d:* 20 April 1946, Rome. *Cat:* Historian of Christianity; critic of modernism.

Main publications:

(1908) *Lettere di un prete modernista* (reprint), Rome: Università di Roma, 1948.

(1922) *L'essenza del cristianesimo*.

(1928) *Misticismo medioevale*.

(1942) *Storia del cristianesimo*.

(1954) *Spirit and Nature*, New York: Pantheon.

Secondary literature:

Anon. (1978) *Ernesto Buonaiuti: storico di cristianesimo*, Rome: Istituto Storico per il Medievo.

Buonaiuti's first period, evidencing some leaning to modernism, affirms a pragmatic conception of religion. Religiosity involves hope for a better collective future which, rising in the soul of the masses, overturns the existing order to create a new society. When this movement succeeds, it, in turn, assumes forms against which a reaction will occur, and a religion can become a superstitious fear that atrophies hope and individual initiative. In his second phase, after the papal condemnation of modernism, the First World War and the influence of di Loisy, he claims that at the centre of religion we find humans devoted to sociality. The human is a function of the collective, but humans feel the social as a limitation and there is an imbalance between the social and the sinfully individualistic. To restore equilibrium we resort, for external things, to politics and, for our internal lives, to religion. In his third period, under the influence of Otto, he develops these ideas stressing the place of original sin. His *History of Christianity* (1942) urges a return to original Christianity and traces the historical disappearance of the Christian message into a monistic idealism which undermines the Kingdom of God. The final period comes to a more moderate notion of original sin and reaffirms the value of Thomism.

COLIN LYAS

Burtt, Edwin Arthur

American. *b:* 11 October 1892, Groton, Massachusetts. *d:* 9 September 1989, Ithaca, New York. *Cat:* Naturalist; philosopher of religion. *Ints:* Philosophy of science; Eastern philosophy; comparative religion and philosophy. *Educ:* Yale, Union Theological Seminary and Columbia University. *Infls:* Dewey and Reinhold Niebuhr. *Appts:* 1921–3, Instructor in Philosophy, Columbia University; 1923–31, Instructor to Professor of Philosophy, University of Chicago; 1932–60, Professor of Philosophy; 1961–89, Susan Linn Sage Emeritus Professor of Philosophy, Cornell University.

Main publications:

(1926) *The Metaphysical Foundations of Modern Physical Science* London: Routledge & Kegan Paul; New York: Harcourt; Brace & Co.; a revision of *The Metaphysics of Sir Isaac Network* (Columbia dissertation).

(1928) *Principles and Problems of Right Thinking*, New York: Harper.

(1929) *Religion in an Age of Science*, New York: Holt.

(1939) *The English Philosophers from Bacon to Mill*, New York: The Modern Library.

(1939) *Types of Religious Philosophy*, New York: Harper.

(1955) (ed.) *The Teachings of the Compassionate Buddha*, New York: New American Library.

(1957) *Man Seeks the Divine: A Study in the History and Comparison of Religions*, New York: Harper & Row.

(1965) *In Search of Philosophic Understanding*, New York: New American Library.

(1981) *The Human Journey*, Calcutta: University of Calcutta Press.

(1986) *Light, Love and Life* privately published under the imprint of the Light, Love and Life Foundation.

Secondary literature:

Bertocci, Peter (1975) 'Love and reality in E. A. Burtt's philosophy: a personalistic critique', *Idealist Studies* 5: 269–89.

Coming to philosophy from a prior interest in religion, Burtt's insights and publications emerged from the undergraduate teaching in which he specialized. His book in logic, oriented to **Dewey**'s analysis of the nature of reflection, provided a valuable exposition of the manner in which that analysis fits problems of many kinds. His book on the foundations of modern science was developed from his Columbia course on the history of British philosophy. Examining scientists from Copernicus to Newton, and philosophers from Descartes to Henry More, he takes us through the transition from the teleological world of Dante into the 'meaningless' world of **Russell**'s 'A free man's worship'. His resolution of the problem of meaninglessness directs us to the many variants of religious philosophy which he considers in both East and West. In *Man Seeks the Divine* (1957, pp. 481–6) he argued that psychotherapy can help religion meet its goal of personal self-fulfilment, while religion can help psychotherapy incorporate ultimate deals which, in his view, include the idea of God. In *The Human Journey* (1981), his 1958 Ghosh Lectures given in Calcutta and published much later, Burtt expresses a 'realistic hope' that humanity, both individually and collectively, is related to 'some vaster destiny than we have in the past dared to glimpse' (p. 188).

Sources: E. A. Burtt (1922) 'My path to philosophy', *PEW* 22: 429–40; P. A. Bertocci (ed.) (1974) *Mid-Twentieth Century American Philosophy*, New York: Humanities Press; Elsie Myers Shinton (1972) 'E. A. Burtt: bibliography', *PEW* 22: 461–5.

WILLIAM REESE

Butler, Judith

American. *b:* 24 February 1956, Cleveland, Ohio. *Cat:* Continental and feminist philosopher. *Ints:* Nineteenth- and twentieth-century continental philosophy; feminist philosophy (especially French feminist theory); poststructuralist social and political philosophy. *Educ:* Yale University (BA, MA, MPhil in Philosophy). *Infls:* Personal influences include Seyla Benhabib, Gadamer and George Schrader; literary influences include Plato, Spinoza, Hegel, Kierkegaard, de Beauvoir, Wittig, Luce Irigaray, Foucault and Derrida. *Appts:* Assistant Professor of Philosophy, George Washington University, 1986–9; Associate Professor (then Professor) of Humanities, Johns Hopkins University, from 1989; Professor of

Rhetoric, University of California, Berkeley, 1993–4; Professor of Rhetoric and Comparative Literature, University of California, Berkeley, from 1994.

Main publications:
(1987) *Subjects of Desire: Hegelian Reflections in Twentieth Century France*, Columbia University Press.
(1990) *Gender Trouble: Feminism and the Subversion of Identity*, London: Routledge.
(1992) (ed. with Joan W. Scott) *Feminists Theorize the Political*, London: Routledge.
(1993) *Bodies that Matter: On the Discursive Limits of 'Sex'*, London: Routledge.
(1994) (ed. with Seyla Benhabib, Drucilla Cornell and Nancy Fraser) *Feminist Contentions: A Philosophical Exchange*, New York: Routledge.

Butler has a powerful and prolific voice that resonates not only within feminist philosophy but in critical legal studies, literary theory, lesbian and gay theory, psychoanalysis and race studies. Her first book, *Subjects of Desire* (1987), concerns the takeup of the Hegelian concept of desire as it comes to be understood as that which contests the stability of the subject. A similar theme reemerges in *Gender Trouble* (1990) where a specifically homosexual desire resists the conventional gendering of subjects. Butler argues that gender is a socially and discursively produced category held in place by a reiterative series of performative acts. Her analysis provides a lucid critique of the 'female', and shows how a presumptive heterosexuality must not only produce but naturalize gender norms. This post-Foucauldian approach has been widely influential in feminist studies, and the notion of gender performativity is a *sine qua non* of postmodernist feminism. More recently, *Bodies that Matter* (1993) has extended Butler's notion of performativity to 'sex', which she sees not as given but as the 'materialization of norms'. In stressing the performativity/productivity of discourse and closing the putative split between the ideal and the material, Butler begins to answer those critics who demand a material basis for feminism. To those who question the tenability of politics without the stability of the foundational subject, Butler's essay 'Contingent foundations' (in Butler and Scott 1992) marks feminist postmodernism as the very possibility of feminist politics.
Sources: Personal communication.

MARGRIT SHILDRICK

C

Cabral, Amilcar Lopes

Guinean. **b:** 12 September 1924, Bafata, Guinea-Bissau. **d:** 20 January 1973, assassinated in Conakry, Guinea. **Cat:** Political theorist. **Ints:** Revolutionary theory; African politics. **Educ:** University of Lisbon, Institute of Agronomy. **Infls:** Guevara. **Appts:** 1950–4, Colonial Agricultural Service; 1956, Founder and General Secretary, Partido Africano da Independencia da Guinée Cabo Verde (PAIGC); initiated a revolutionary war in 1963, which ended in Guinean independence from Portugal.

Main publications:

(1971) *Revolution in Guinea: An African People's Struggle*, ed. and trans. R. Handyside, London: Stage 1.

Secondary literature:

Chaliland, G. (1967) *Armed Struggle in Africa*, Paris: Editions François Maspéro.

Davidson, B. (1969) *The Liberation of Guiné*, London: Penguin.

Fine, S. E. (1974) *Comparative Government*, London: Pelican.

Lobban, R. (1979) *Historical Dictionary of the Republics of Guinea-Bissau and Cape Verde*, Metuchen, NJ: Scarecrow Press.

Cabral's writings have been largely in the form of declarations, communiqués and political conferences, together with the odd radio broadcast. As revolutionary theorist as well as leader of the PAIGC, the party which sought, and succeeded, in gaining independence from Portugese colonial rule in 1973, his theoretical writings were centred largely on the development of a revolutionary strategy based on African, specifically Guinean, conditions, rather than the wholesale importation of other revolutionary experiences. Between 1952 and 1954 he elaborated a study of the social structure of Guinean tribal groups, and it was on the basis of this that he posited the distinction between peasantry as a physical rather than a revolutionary force, differences between them being a 'secondary contradiction' (the 'primary' one being Portuguese colonialism) which a sophisticated party apparatus could deal with. Of wider import, whilst accepting the central role of class struggle at certain historical stages, especially in the fight against 'rationalized imperialism' as he labelled colonialism, he examines the determining elements of class struggle, concluding that the real motive force of history is the mode of production, much more useful in the African colonialist context where, he held, for people without history, positing history as a prime revolutionary mover is a disenfranchising theory. His tackling of the contradictory role of the revolutionary bourgeoisie in the liberation struggles of underdeveloped countries, and his prioritizing of revolutionary theory over its practice (his distinction between 'armed militancy' and 'militarism', and of pan-African unity as a means rather than an end, for example) were radically different revolutionary theories to any hitherto advanced in Africa, though his emphasis on unique, local analyses was taken literally in the sense that his pronouncements, whilst echoing around 'isolated' left regimes such as the Cuban, found little reverberation in Africa itself.

DAVID SPOONER

Cai Yi (Ts'ai I)

Chinese. **b:** 1906, Xiaó County, Huoan Province, China. **d:** 1991, Beijing. **Cat:** Marxist. **Ints:** Aesthetics. **Educ:** University of Beijing and Kyushu Imperial University, Tokyo. **Infls:** N. Chernyshevsky. **Appts:** Research Fellow, Institute of Literature, University of Peking; Research Fellow, Institute of Literature, Chinese Academy of Social Sciences.

Main publications:

(1943) *A New Theory of Art*.

(1948) *The New Aesthetics*, Chun Yi Publishing Company.

(1958) *A Critique of Idealist Aesthetics*.

(1978) *Literary Knowledge*.

(1978) *The Sociology of Art*.

(1984) *Basic Principles of Art*.

Secondary literature:
Briere, O. (1956) *Fifty Years of Chinese Philosophy 1898–1950*, London: George Allen & Unwin Ltd.

Cai came to prominence in 1945 and, in contrast with those providing criticism without an explicit intellectual base, was soon recognized as the leading philosophical theorist of Marxist aesthetics in China. He disputed what he considered to be subjectivist and objectivist aesthetic views, in particular **Zhu Guangqian**'s adaptation of the ideas of Kant and **Croce**. He claimed that existing aesthetics, based on art, could be accepted only if beauty were subjective. Because the beautiful is an objective reality, a new aesthetics was required, recognizing the beautiful in things as the source both of our aesthetic sense and of artistic beauty. Things are beautiful which best typify species through the expression of the reality and truth of those species. He believed that his analysis justified the claim that beauty is life. Because both species and individuals are subject to change, aesthetic judgement is also open to change. Cai thus bound artistic beauty to natural beauty and understood natural beauty to be subject to the development of Marxist dialectics. In later controversies over problems of aesthetics, he was criticized as a 'mechanical materialist' with a naive view of the Marxist context framing his aesthetic analysis. Although his ideas fell out of favour, they did much to establish serious aesthetic theory within Chinese Marxist thought.

NICHOLAS BUNNIN

Cai Yuanbei (Ts'ai Yuan-pei)

Chinese. **b:** 1868, Shanyin, Zhejiang Province, China. **d:** 1940, Hong Kong. **Cat:** Western and Chinese philosophy; educator. **Ints:** Chinese philosophy; aesthetics; philosophy of religion; ethics. **Educ:** Studied Chinese classics, gaining traditional degrees culminating in the highest degree in the imperial examination system and a place at the Hanlin Academy; studied at Berlin (1907) and University of Leipzig (1908–11), with later trips to Western Europe and the USA. **Infls:** Kant and Windelband. **Appts:** 1912, Minister of Education; 1912, Chancellor of the University of Beijing; 1916–26, appointed first President, Academia Sinica in 1928.

Main publications:
(1921) *Chinese Philosophy over the Past Fifty Years.*
(1924) *Outline of Philosophy*, Shanghai: Commercial Press.

(1931) *History of Chinese Ethics*, Shanghai: Commercial Press.
(1959) *Selected Writing of Cai Yuanbei*, Beijing: Zhonghua Book Company.
(1963) *Cai Yuanbei's Works on Morality*, Taipei: Taiwan Bookstore.
(1967) *Complete Works of Cai Yuanbei*, Taipei: Wenxing Bookstore.
(1971) *Cai Yuanbei's Autobiography*, Taipei: Zhuanji Wenxue Publishing House.

Secondary literature:
Boorman, H. (ed.) (1970) *Biographical Dictionary of Republican China*, New York and London: Columbia University Press.
Briere, O. (1956) *Fifty Years of Chinese Philosophy 1898–1950*, London: George Allen & Unwin Ltd.
Complete Chinese Encyclopedia (1987), Philosophy Volumes, Beijing: Chinese Encyclopedia Publications.
Duiker, William J. (1977) *Ts'ai Yuan-p'ei: Educator of Modern China*, Pennsylvania State University Press.

Cai, who began his career as a brilliant scholar of the Chinese classics, became China's leading educator and first modern scholar of aesthetics. His commitment to education grew from his assessment that improving education was a basic element in curing China's weakness. He was active politically, first in anti-Manchu revolutionary organizations and then in republican politics, although he sharply criticized his allies, including the Guomintang, for betraying moral principles or for falling into petty conflict. His decade as Chancellor established the University of Beijing as the main centre of ideas and innovation in Chinese academic life. With liberal values and his own scholarly example, Cai attracted fresh, critical and imaginative scholars and established an academic atmosphere tolerant of unorthodoxy but demanding intellectual rigour. He carried the same values over to the foundation of Academia Sinica as China's main centre for advanced research. In 1919, the May Fourth Movement, which set the ensuing agenda for Chinese politics, had its base in the University of Beijing. Characteristically, Cai showed his support for his arrested students.

Cai's own philosophical work, focusing on aesthetics, religion and moral philosophy, owed much to his studies abroad as well as to his deep and original grasp of the Confucian classics. In addition to his philosophical studies, work on ethnology and comparative civilization contributed to his views. His main thesis was that art could replace religion. He thought that all religion was the product of the imagination and that, in the face of suffering, people accepted confused religious dogma because of the aesthetic attraction of the symbols in which it was expressed. Rather than attempting to make the religious beliefs coherent, he argued that our consolation should derive directly from beauty and that the general decline in religion should not be resisted.

NICHOLAS BUNNIN

Caird, Edward

British. *b:* 22 March 1845, Greenock, Scotland. *d:* 1 November 1908, Oxford. *Cat:* Hegelian idealist. *Ints:* History of philosophy; philosophy of religion. *Educ:* University of Glasgow, University of St Andrews and Balliol College, Oxford. *Infls:* Literary influences include Carlyle, Kant, Hegel and Comte; personal influences include Jowett, T. H. Green and William Wallace. *Appts:* 1866–93, Professor of Moral Philosophy at Glasgow; 1893–1907, Master of Balliol College, Oxford.

Main publications:

(1877) *A Critical Account of the Philosophy of Kant*, 2 vols, Glasgow: J. Maclehose.

(1879) *The Critical Philosophy of Immanuel Kant*, 2 vols, Glasgow: J. Maclehose.

(1883) *Hegel*, Edinburgh and London: W. Blackwood & Sons.

(1885) *The Social Philosophy and Religion of Comte*, Glasgow: J. Maclehose.

(1893) *The Evolution of Religion* (Gifford Lectures), Glasgow: J. Maclehose.

(1904) *The Evolution of Theology in the Greek Philosophers* (Gifford Lectures), Glasgow: J. Maclehose.

Secondary literature:

Bosanquet, B. (1909) 'Edward Caird, 1845–1908', *Proceedings of the British Academy* 3: 379–86.

Jones, H. and Muirhead, J. H. (1921) *The Life and Philosophy of Edward Caird*, Glasgow: Maclehose & Jackson.

Lindsay, A. D. (1926) 'The idealism of Caird and Jones', *Philosophy* 1: 171ff.

Mackenzie, J. S. (1909) 'Edward Caird as a philosophical teacher', *Mind* 18: 509–37.

Sell, A. P. F. (1995) *Philosophical Idealism and Christian Belief*, Cardiff: University of Wales Press and New York: St Martin's Press.

Stout, A. K. (1967) 'Caird, Edward' in Paul Edwards (ed.) *Encyclopedia of Philosophy*, New York: Macmillan.

Watson, J. (1909) 'The idealism of Edward Caird', *Philosophical Review* 18: 147–63, 259–80.

Like his teacher T. H. Green, Edward Caird's Hegelian idealism owed much to Kant. He thought that Kant's meaning could only be understood if his philosophy was seen to lead to Hegel. Caird quickly acquired a reputation as an expositor of the thought of others. His monumental works on Kant established him, according to **Bosanquet**, 'in the first rank of Kantian interpreters' (Bosanquet 1909, p. 383). He wrote only a short work on Hegel but this was rated as 'the best textbook that could be written in the space' (Bosanquet 1909, p. 384).

For Caird, as for Green, critical exposition and constructive philosophy were closely interwoven. Thus his own speculative idealism arose from a conception of philosophy as concerned to reconcile different elements of the spiritual life, such as subject and object, religion and science, freedom and determination. Contrary to Kant, Caird held that 'all opposition is capable of reconciliation' and that there are no antagonisms that 'cannot be reconciled' (1883, p. 138). Thus, although science and religion might appear to be opposed, the apparent opposition between them can be overcome in the higher unity sought by philosophy.

Caird's ethical theory was similar to that of Green. He held that human beings had the power to determine their conduct as satisfactions of their selves, conceived as permanent centres. Human freedom consisted in such self-determination rather than behaviour determined by fragmentary desires. His religious theory emphasized the unity of humankind, including the notion of a common rationality. It also stressed the notion of evolution or development. The historian Metz rated Caird, after Green, as 'the next great Pioneer of Idealism in Britain' (Metz, p. 286). It was thanks to Caird that Glasgow became a 'stronghold' of idealism. He was a dedicated teacher and his personal influence was very considerable. His disciples included some who were to turn out as distinguished philosophers in their own right, such as Henry **Jones**, J. H. Muirhead, J. S. **Mackenzie** and John Watson. Caird's idealism was very influential in Australia, particularly at Sydney, where it was maintained by Francis Anderson.

Although he himself avoided religious controversy, many of his students were destined to be clergymen, and left his hands infused with his thought that Christianity was a revelation of reason. They were disposed to reject 'the principle of authority' and the opposition of faith and reason enshrined in the ultra-Calvinism of the leading Presbyterian denominations in Scotland. Thus, as well as inspiring philosophers with something of a missionary zeal, Caird encouraged a more philosophical spirit in Scottish religion and theology.

Sources: DNB 1901–11; Grave; Metz.

STUART BROWN

Calkins, Mary Whiton

American. *b:* 30 March 1863, Hartford, Connecticut. *d:* 26 February 1930, Newton, Massachusetts. *Cat:* Psychologist; personal idealist. *Ints:* Metaphysics; history of modern philosophy. *Educ:* Smith College and Harvard University. *Infls:* Berkeley, Hume, Hegel and, especially, Royce. *Appts:* 1887–94, Instructor in Greek, later in Psychology, 1894–1929, Associate, then full Professor of Psychology and Philosophy, Wellesley College.

Main publications:

(1907) *The Persistent Problems of Philosophy: An Introduction to Metaphysics through the Study of Modern Systems*, New York: Macmillan.

(1916) *The Good Man and The Good*, New York: Macmillan.

(1919) 'Personalistic conception of nature', *Philosophical Review* 28: 115–46.

(1930) 'The philosophical credo of an absolutistic personalist', in G. P. Adams and W. P. Montague (eds), *Contemporary American Philosophy*, vol. 1, New York: Russell & Russell; London: Allen & Unwin, pp. 197–218.

Secondary literature:

Magg, P. (1947) 'The personalism of Mary Whiton Calkins', *Personalist* 28: 44–53.

A teacher of both subjects, Mary Calkins prepared student texts for psychology and the history of philosophy (Berkeley and Hobbes). She made the self as central to psychology as it was to be in her metaphysics, where her real enthusiasm lay. Strongly influenced by **Royce**, she evolved a position she described as 'absolutistic personalism'. She insisted both on the personal nature of all being and on the unity of all being in the 'Absolute Self'. Her high reputation amongst philosophers was confirmed in 1918 by her election as President of the American Philosophical Association.

Sources: ADB; Kersey, pp. 67–9; obituary, *PR* 39 (1930): 323.

STUART BROWN

Calogero, Guido

Italian. *b:* 4 December 1904, Rome. *Cat:* Philosopher of the self; philosopher of language. *Appts:* Arrested for political reasons in 1942; in prison wrote *Lezioni di filosofia*; sometime Director of the Italian Institute in London.

Main publications:

(1944) *Il metodo dell'economica e il marxismo.*

(1945) *Difesa del liberalsocialismo.*

(1947) *Saggi di etica e di teoria del diritto*, Bari: Laterza.

(1946–8) *Lezioni di filosofia*, 3 vols, Turin: Einaudi.

(1950) *Logo e dialogo*, Milan: Edizioni di Communita.

(1960) *La conclusione della filosofia del conoscere*, Florence: Sansoni.

(1962) *Filosofia del dialogo*, Milan: Edizioni di Communita.

(1962) 'Nessuna regola per il pensiero, solo una regola per il significato', in *Thinking and Meaning*, Entretiens d'Oxford.

(1968) *Le regole della democrazia e le ragioni del socialismo*, Rome: Edizioni di Ateneo.

(1972) *Difesa del liberalsocialismo*, Milan: Marzorati.

Secondary literature:

Genzone, P. (1960) *Nous e dianoia nel pensiero di Guido Calogers*, Turin: Edizione di 'Filosofia'.

——(ed.) (1961) *Guido Calogero*, Turin: Edizione di 'Filosofia'.

Calogero defines his philosophy, which is deeply related to his life, as 'presentialism', a concentration on the self and what actually surrounds it, opposed to any abstract formalistic or a priori dogmatism. The self is not a passive mirror but active, and knowledge is inseparable from action. This account distinguishes egoism from active choice. One can choose egoism but one can also choose altruism, and so issue from the prison of the self. Calogero vigorously opposed the theorizing of Oxford linguistic philosophers. Language communicates our experience. No linguistic rules have any value save as historically contingent rules expressing a 'will for discussion' with others and this 'will for discussion' has no need of discussion.

COLIN LYAS

Campbell, C(harles) A(rthur)

British. *b:* 13 January 1897, Glasgow. *d:* 17 March 1974. *Cat:* Idealist. *Ints:* Metaphysics; moral philosophy. *Educ:* University of Glasgow and Balliol College, Oxford. *Infls:* Kant, T. H. Green,

Bradley, Otto and C. D. Broad. **Appts:** 1924–32, Assistant, then Lecturer in Moral Philosophy at Glasgow; 1932–8, Professor of Philosophy, University College of North Wales, Bangor; 1938–61, Professor of Logic and Rhetoric at Glasgow.

Main publications:

(1931) *Scepticism and Construction: Bradley's Sceptical Principle as the Basis of Constructive Philosophy*, London: Glasgow University Publications.

(1957) *On Selfhood and Godhood*, London: Allen & Unwin.

(1967) *Defence of Free Will* (collected essays), London: Allen & Unwin.

Secondary literature:

Brown, N. (1959) Critical Notice of *On Selfhood and Godhood*, in *Mind* 68: 100–4.

Carmichael, John P. (1977) 'C. A. Campbell's defence of free will', PhD, Marquette University.

Lewis, H. D. (1974) 'Tribute to Professor Charles Arthur Campbell', *The Times*, 20 March 1974, p. 18.

Owen, H. P. (1966) 'The moral and religious philosophy of C.A. Campbell', *Religious Studies* 3: 433–46.

Educated at Britain's leading idealist seminaries, C. A. Campbell offered in his first book a development of a principle of **Bradley**'s, that the Absolute is beyond all relations and so beyond rational knowledge. Although he originally held that the 'suprarational' Absolute 'must remain opaque to the categories of the intellect', he was attracted by **Otto's** doctrine of the numinous. In his Gifford Lectures, he sought to defend a symbolical knowledge of God.

Although Campbell wrote only two substantial books, he was the author of several influential articles and was much respected by his students, who included H. D. **Lewis** and **Macquarrie**. He sought to work out a constructive idealism and to counter the critiques of empiricism and linguistic analysis. He was a prominent defender of the coherence theory, of a substantial self and of libertarianism at a time when these doctrines were commonly assumed to be indefensible. According to Lewis, 'Campbell ... has presented what is far and away the best case we have in our time, perhaps at any time, for a genuinely open freedom of choice, combined with penetrating criticism of freedom as self-determination' (Lewis 1985, p. 296).

Sources: H. D. Lewis (1985) 'The British Idealists', in N. Smart *et al.* (eds) *Nineteenth Century Religious*

Thought in the West, Cambridge: CUP, vol. 2; Macquarrie; WW.

STUART BROWN

Campbell, Norman Robert

British. **b:** 1880, Colgrain, Dumbartonshire, Scotland. **d:** 18 May 1949, Asperly, Nottingham. **Cat:** Physicist; philosopher of science. **Ints:** Structure of scientific theories; theory of measurement; nature and methods of scientific thought. **Educ:** Trinity College, Cambridge. **Infls:** Literary Influence: William Whewell, W. S. Jevons, J. S. Mill and Ernst Mach. Personal: J. J. Thomson. **Appts:** 1904–13, Fellow of Trinity College, Cambridge; 1913–19, Honorary Fellow for Research in Physics, University of Leeds; 1919–44, on research staff of General Electrics Co. Ltd.

Main publications:

(1919) *Physics: The Elements*, Cambridge: Cambridge University Press; reprinted as *Foundations of Science: The Philosophy and Theory of Experiment*, New York: Dover, 1957.

(1921) *What is Science?*, Cambridge: Cambridge University Press; reprinted, New York: Dover, 1952.

Secondary literature:

Hempel, Carl G. (1965) *Aspects of Scientific Explanation and Other Essays in the Philosophy of Science*, New York: Free Press, pp. 206–10, 442–7.

Hesse, Mary B. (1963) *Models and Analogies in Science*, New York: Sheed & Ward, pp. 12-28, 128–9.

Losee, John (1980) *A Historical Introduction to the Philosophy of Science*, second edition, Oxford: Oxford University Press, pp. 131–46.

Campbell's philosophy of science, shaped by his experience and ideas as a physicist assisting J. J. **Thomson** at the Cavendish Laboratory, centred upon the analysis of the logical structure of physical theories. This reflected his working view that the aim of science is the discovery and explanation of laws and that laws can be explained only by reference to their incorporation into theories.

In his monumental *Physics* (1919), Campbell elaborated a non-inductive view of a scientific theory, according to which a theory is defined by means of the formal nature and connection of the propositions of which it consists, namely a 'hypothesis' making assertions about 'hypothetical ideas' characteristic of the theory, and a 'dictionary' relating these ideas to the concepts of the laws explained by the theory. Thus he held that the boundary between the 'hypothesis' and the realm of sense experience is to be bridged by 'dictionary' entries which link certain of the 'hypothetical ideas' with experimentally measurable properties in order to achieve empirical significance for the theory as a whole, a point which he illustrated with reference to the dynamical theory of gases.

Campbell believed that a scientific theory, to be of any value at all, must 'display an analogy': the basic laws that its internal principles specify for theoretical entities must be 'analogous to some known laws', as the laws for the propagation of light waves are analogous to (have the same mathematical form as) thr laws for the propagation of water waves. Campbell also contributed an important discussion of measurement (1919, pp. 267–549).

Campbell's work exerted considerable influence upon the subsequent development of the 'hypothetico-deductive' view of scientific explanation.

Sources: Edwards; WW.

STEPHEN MOLLER

Camus, Albert

French. *b:* 1913, Mondovi, Algeria. *d:* 1960, near Paris (road accident). *Cat:* Philosopher of the absurd. *Ints:* Ethics. *Infls:* Greek thought, Augustine, Nietzsche and Sartre. *Appts:* Camus's student work on philosophy (on Plotinus and Augustine) was interrupted by illness, and up to the outbreak of the Second World War he had a number of theatrical and journalistic jobs in Algiers and Paris; active in the Resistance he became Coeditor (with Sartre) of *Combat*; breaking with Sartre after the war, Camus devoted himself to writing. Nobel Prize for Literature, 1957.

Main publications:

(1942) *Le Mythe de Sisyphe*, Paris: Gallimard; second, expanded edition, 1945.

(1942) *L'Étranger*, Paris: Gallimard.

(1945) *Lettres à un ami allemand*, Paris: Gallimard.

(1947) *La Peste*, Paris: Gallimard.

(1950–3) *Actuelles: I and II*, Paris: Gallimard.

(1951) *L'Homme révolté*, Paris: Gallimard.

(1956) *La Chute*, Paris: Gallimard.

Secondary literature:

Ayer, A. J. (1946) 'Novelist-philosophers', *Horizon* 13: 155–68.

Braun, L. (1974) *Witness of Decline: Albert Camus, Moralist of the Absurd*, Cranbury, NJ: Farleigh Dickinson University Press.

Cruickshank, J. (1960) *Albert Camus and the Literature of Revolt*, London and New York: Oxford University Press.

Karpushin, V. A. (1967–9) 'The concept of the individual in the work of Albert Camus', *Soviet Studies in Philosophy*, 6, Winter, pp. 52–60.

Thody, P. (1957) *Albert Camus: A Study of His Work*, New York and London: Macmillan.

Trundle, R. C. and Puligandla, R. (1986) *Beyond Absurdity: The Philosophy of Albert Camus*, Lanham: University Press of America.

As with **Unamuno**, Camus is not an academic philosopher but rather a thinker concerned to work out a way of making sense of a life threatened with meaninglessness. Thanks to his literary skill, Camus's thought was widely diffused and influential and its embodiment in classics of fiction such as *L'Étranger* (1942) and *La Peste* (1947) continues to make it one of the most approachable of examples of recent French philosophy. His thought has two phases, epitomized in the two philosophical essays *Le Mythe de Sisyphe* (1942) and *L'Homme révolté* (1951). Common to each phase are the presuppositions of atheism, the mortality of the soul and the indifference of the universe to human aspirations. The development lies in the value system for which these views form the basis.

The concept central to the early phase of Camus's thought is the absurd. Absurdity is a feeling which arises from the confrontation of the world, which is irrational, with the hopeless but profound human desire to make sense of our condition. The appropriate response to this situation, Camus argues, is to live in full consciousness of it. He rejects philosophies or courses of action which conjure the problem away, notably religious belief, suicide and existentialism, which in Camus's view deifies the irrational. From a lucid appreciation of the absurdity of our life three consequences flow, which Camus calls revolt, freedom and passion. By 'revolt' (in the early phase of his thought) Camus means defiance in the face of the bleak truth about the human condition, hopeless but not resigned, lending to life a certain grandeur. Again, recognition of absurdity frees us from habit and convention: we see all things anew, and are inwardly liberated. By 'passion' Camus means the resolve to live as intensely as possible, not so as to escape the sense of absurdity but so as to face it with absolute lucidity. The way to do this is to maximize not the quality but the quantity of one's experiences. Sisyphus is the hero who exemplifies these virtues. He is aware of the hopelessness of his task but rises above his destiny by facing it lucidly: we must imagine Sisyphus to be happy.

A further consequence difficult to avoid in such an outlook is that any course of action is permissible (*tout est permis*), provided we make no attempt to escape the consequences of our actions—witness the behaviour of Mersault in the fictional depiction of this philosophy, *L'Étranger*. The experience of war caused Camus to change his mind on this point, since it cannot be seriously advanced in the face of unquantifiable suffering. In *L'Homme révolté* and its fictional counterpart *La Peste* Camus seeks to ground values very close to those of liberal humanism on much the same bases as those of his earlier work. The major philosophical change, a marked break with Sartrean existentialism, is the view that there is such a thing as human nature, the conclusion Camus draws from his analysis of the concept of revolt in life and art. In the concept of human nature he finds a reason and a cause for union between human beings. The detachment of the absurdist is replaced by an ethic of sympathy, community and service to others.

ROBERT WILKINSON

Canguilhem, Georges

French. *b:* 1904. *Cat:* Historian and philosopher of science; epistemologist. *Infls:* Gaston Bachelard. *Appts:* Has held various academic posts, including that of Professor of the History and Philosophy of Science at the Sorbonne.

Main publications:

(1943) *Essai sur quelques problèmes concernant le normal et la pathologique*, Clermont-Ferrand: La Montagne (English translation, *The Normal and the Pathological*, London: MIT Press, 1989).

(1952) *La Connaissance de la vie*, Paris: Hachette.

(1959) *Les Concepts de 'lutte pour l'existence' et de 'sélection naturelle' en 1858*, Paris: La Librairie du Palais de la Découverte.

(1968) *Études d'histoire et de philosophie des sciences*, Paris: Vrin.

(1977) *Idéologie et rationalité dans l'histoire des sciences de la vie*, Paris: Vrin (English translation, *Ideology and Rationality in the History of the Life Sciences*, Mass.: MIT Press, 1988).

Secondary literature:

Bolletina di Storia della Filosofia 6: 239–51.

Foucault, M. (1980) 'Georges Canguilhem, philosopher of error', *Ideology and Consciousness* 7: 51–62.

Quarta, G. (1978) 'Ideologica e storia delle scienze in Canguilhem',

Georges Canguilhem's scientific interests were mainly in the life sciences. Following the recommendations of Gaston **Bachelard**, his predecessor at the Sorbonne, he advocated a historical approach to science and epistemology which took into account the changing nature of the disciplines studied and the different approaches taken by investigators at different historical periods.

Canguilhem took over from Bachelard the notion of an epistemological 'break', which can occur when the problems of a particular discipline are insoluble within its existing conceptual framework. The 'break' consists of the adoption of new concepts which are developed in an attempt to solve the problems raised within the old framework. The new conceptual structure is not an extension of the old, but involves a complete 'perspective shift'. There are no fixed, transhistorical concepts upon which all scientists and investigators, no matter from what historical period they come, can rely. The history of science and of epistemology is thus discontinuous, not evolutionary.

Together with the differing conceptual frameworks and epistemological breaks, Canguilhem advocates the investigation of what has constituted the scope of a science or of epistemology during its history. There have been changes in the content of individual disciplines, as well as constant realignments between them. Present-day science has no superior status: it is not a closed and perfected body of knowledge but is, by contrast, open and subject to the possibility of review and replacement. It is only through a historical approach to science that these crucial features of openness and possible revision are revealed. Histories of science and epistemology thus cannot just be expanded in the light of further discoveries, but have to be constantly rethought and rewritten, to take into account their changing theoretical frameworks and subject matter. In his insistence that it is crucial to study and understand the historical dimensions of science and knowledge, and in his exploration of the normal and the pathological, Canguilhem exercised a great influence on the early career of one of his former students, Michel **Foucault**.

KATHRYN PLANT

Cannabrava, Euryalo

Brazilian. *b:*1908, Cataguazes, Brazil. *d:*1981, São Paulo, Brazil. *Cat:* 'Critical objectivist'. *Ints:* Philosophical logic; philosophy of science. *Infls:* Initially Bergson and Heidegger, but later and more importantly Dewey and Anglo-American philosophy of logic and science from Russell on. *Appts:*Professor, Colegio Pedro II, Rio de Janeiro; a well-respected thinker in Brazil.

Main publications:

(1941) *Seis temas do espiritu moderno.*

(1943) *Descartes e Bergson.*

(1956) *Introdução a filosofia cientifica*, São Paulo: Companhia Editora Nacional.

(1956) *Elementos do metodología filosófica*, São Paulo: Companhia Editora Nacional.

(1957) *Ensaios filosóficos*, Rio de Janeiro: Ministerio da Educação e Cultura.

(1963) *Estética da crítica*, Rio de Janeiro: Ministerio da Educação e Cultura.

(1977) *Teoría da decisão filosófica*, Rio de Janeiro: Forense-Universitaria.

After an early phase in which he was sympathetic to spiritualist thought, Cannabrava fell under the influence of modern Anglo-American positivism (from 1956 on). Speculative metaphysics he thereafter dismissed as sterile. In this class he included Marxism, not worthy even to be called a philosophical method, but as 'religião pura e simples' ('religion pure and simple', 1957, p. 140). His mature positive views are mainly concerned with a method, with which philosophy becomes more or less coextensive. The driving thesis in his methodology is the view that a unification of formal and empirical truth, and of deductive and inductive disciplines, is both possible and desirable, and that the distinctions between them are not absolute. He attempts to show this by arguing that the methods of both deductive and inductive investigations can be reduced to or identified with language. This requires him to assert, for example, that the rules of formal logic are reducible to linguistic structures describable in the disciplines of syntax and semantics. Only when there is a 'completa identificação entre o instrumento metodológico e o instrumento lingüístico' ('a complete identification of methodology and language' 1957, p. 195) will we have achieved a satisfactory 'critical objectivist' philosophical method. Such a method is in principle applicable to all branches of the subject, from logic to politics.

ROBERT WILKINSON

Cantor, Georg

German. *b:*3 April 1845, St Petersburg, Russia. *d:* 6 January 1918, Halle, Germany. *Cat:* Mathematician. *Ints:* Philosophy of mathematics. *Educ:* University of Berlin. *Infls:* K. Weierstrass and the development of mathematical analysis. *Appts:* Professor, University of Halle, 1867–1913.

Main publications:

(1932) *Gesammelte Abhandlungen*, Berlin: Springer.

Secondary literature:

Dauben, J. W. (1979) *Georg Cantor*, Cambridge, Mass.: Harvard University Press.

Fraenkel, A. (1953) *Abstract Set Theory*, Amsterdam: North-Holland.

It is largely due to the work of Cantor that set theory and transfinite arithmetic have come to play such important roles in mathematics, logic and some aspects of philosophy. His own philosophical foundation of his theories, however, was not well received.

Cantor started to develop these theories in the early 1870s, in connection with solving certain problems in mathematical analysis of the time. Over the next twenty-five years he gradually developed them: both point set topology (properties of points on the line, derived sets, and so on), and also general set theory and transfinite arithmetic. He published mainly in mathematical journals, and also in a few philosophical ones.

In 1899 Cantor suffered a severe mental breakdown which largely terminated his researches. However, in sad irony, just at that time, the opposition to his work, which had previously been marked in some quarters, was supplemented by a widespead acceptance of its basic legitimacy and importance. The principal aspects of philosophical interest are as follows.

First, Cantor advocated that set theory could found integers and arithmetic, and thereby serve as a basis for mathematics. His means of procedure by idealistic processes of abstraction from sets to 'define' integers met little favour; but the programme influenced others, most notably the logicism of Bertrand **Russell**.

Second, Cantor found criteria by which finite sets could be put into one–one correspondence, *and especially when this was not possible.* He also made clear the importance of the different ways in which members of an infinite set could be ordered.

Third, Cantor's study of the properties of transfinite numbers was based on an assumption, known as the 'well-ordering principle', which claimed that the members of every set could be laid out in that particular kind of order. In 1904 Ernst Zermelo showed that the proof of this assumption required the axiom of choice; non-constructive character led to an intensive debate among mathematicians and philosophers. In addition, Cantor's 'continuum hypothesis', concerning the order of infinitude of the set of real numbers, led not only to technical results but enriched understanding of set theory and its models.

Fourth, Cantor found that the usual definition of continuity (that between any two members of a continuous set there be at least one more) was necessary but not sufficient for the purpose. His search for additional defining properties led to profound understanding of (dis)continuities.

Finally, Cantor was one of the first to find paradoxes in set theory (namely, those of the greatest cardinal). For him the solution was simple: one should not advance as far as the *absolutely* infinite, that realm of sets large enough to contain 'everything'. When Russell found more paradoxes in the 1900s, the status of paradoxes in set theory was raised, and a wide range of solutions sought which has influenced set theory, logics and philosophy ever since.

IVOR GRATTAN-GUINNESS

Being is the fundamental question of philosophy but is not something which exists as an object set apart from the mind but is that upon which mind depends, the task of the mind being to come, by a never-ending critical reflection, to a proper awareness of the inexhaustible Being which is its foundation. The understanding that is sought will not emerge as a relation between understanding and a separate absolute objectivity such as God, for the objectivity that is sought is the foundation of subjectivity and not an object to be pursued by it. God is not one thing among many. For if God were an existent, God would always be another, whereas God is an intrinsic foundation. Being is composed of the plurality of existent subjects who seek it (a plurality being necessary because the self needs to be reciprocated in others) and constitutes a foundation for those seekers. That plurality of selves believes in a common world, but this is a matter of faith in an absolute which is the ground of our likeness to others. Knowledge is not knowledge of Being but knowledge-in-Being. Human thought takes place in this ambience of Being and is always the attempt to reflect upon its foundation in Being.

COLIN LYAS

Carabellese, Pantaleo

Italian. *b:* 6 July 1877, Molfetta, Italy. *d:* 19 September 1948, Genoa. *Cat:* Critical ontologist. *Infls:* Pupil of Varisco. *Appts:* Professor of the History of Philosophy, University of Rome.

Main publications:

(1914) *L'Essere e il problema religioso.*
(1915) *La coscienza morale.*
(1921) *Critica del concreto.*
(1927) *La filosofia di Kant.*
(1929) *Il problema della filosofia da Kant a Fichte 1781–1801.*
(1931) *Il problema teleologico come filosofia.*
(1938) *L'Idealismo italiano.*
(1942) *Che cos'é la filosofia.*
(1946) *Opere complete*, Florence: Sansoni.

Secondary literature:

(1964) *Giornati di studi carabellesiani*, Milan: Silva.
Semerari, P. (1982) *La sabbia e la roccia*, Baris: De Dalo.
Vicarelli, G. (1952) *Il pensiero di Pantaleo Carabellese*, Rome: Editoriale di Arte e Storia.

Carabellese offers himself as a critical ontologist mediating the extremes of realism and idealism.

Carbonara, Cleto

Italian. *b:* 13 April 1904, Potenza, Italy. *Cat:* Critical reviser of idealism. *Appts:* Taught at Cagliari; Catania; 1949–, Professor of the History of Philosophy, University of Naples.

Main publications:

(1938) *Disegno d'una filosofia critica dell'esperienza pura*; reprinted, Naples: Libreria Scientifica Editrice, 1973.
(1944) *Dell bello e dell'arte.*
(1951) *La filosofia greca*, second edition, Naples: Libreria Scientifica Editrice.
(1958) *L'irrazionale in filosofia*, Naples: Libreria Scientifica Editrice.
(1959) *Persona e libertá*; reprinted, Naples: Libreria Scientifica Editrice, 1973.
(1960) *Ricerche per un'estetica del contenuto*, Naples: Libreria Scientifica Editrice.
(1960) *L'estetica del particolare*, Napoli: Libreria Scientifica Editrice.
(1961) *La filosofia dell'esperienza e la fondazione dell'umanesimo*, Naples: Libreria Scientifica Editrice.
(1967) *Hegel e Marx nella polemica del diritto pubblico*, Naples: Libreria Scientifica Editrice.
(1973) *Discorso empirico delle arte*, Naples: Libreria Scientifica Editrice.

(1974) *Empiricismo come filosofia dell'esperienza*, Naples: Libreria Scientifica Editrice.
(1976) *Auto-bio-bibliographice*, Naples: Giannini.

Secondary literature:
(1976) *Scritti in onore di Cleto Carbonara*, Naples: Giannini.

Carbonara undertakes a critical revision of idealism which traces the steps from ancient metaphysics to later idealism and attempts to construct a correct critical philosophy of pure experience which, in its account of the place of spirit, rejects the distinctions within spirit posited in the work of **Gentile** and **Croce**. Experience is conceived as both objective and subjective and has a value that is made concrete in the historical individual whose interior life is expanded by an immediate embodiment in reality that is mediated by reflection. Embodied in an individual experience is an economic life which incorporates as an internal dialectic the demands of Marxism. Important attention is paid to art as the ideal objectification of experience which preserves the life of spirit and gives it organization and coherence.

COLIN LYAS

Carlini, Armando
Italian. *b:* 9 August 1878, Naples. *d:* 30 September 1959, Pisa. *Cat:* Founder and exponent of Italian Christian spiritualism. *Appts:* 1955–, successor to Gentile, University of Pisa.

Main publications:
(1921) *La vita dello spirito.*
(1934) *La religione dell'arte e della filosofia.*
(1936) *Mito del realismo.*
(1942) *Lineamenti di una concezione realistica della spirito umano.*
(1950) *Perché Credo*, Brescia: Morcelliana.
(1951) *Alla ricerca di me stesso*, Florence: Sansoni.
(1958) *Cattolicesimo e pensiero moderno*, Brescia: Morcelliana.
(1959) *Della vita dello sprito al mito del realismo*, Florence: Sansoni.
(1962) *Che cos'e la metafisica*, Florence: Sansoni.

Secondary literature:
Della Volpe, G. (1949) *Spiritualismo Italiano contemporaneo*, Messina: Ferraro.
Galli, G. (1950) *Studi sul pensiero di Armando Carlini*, Turin: Gheroni.
Sainati, V. (ed.) (1961) *Armando Carlini*, Turin: Edizioni di 'Filosofia'.

Carlini seeks an account of the activity of spirit that captures both **Croce**'s emphasis on the historical and the theologizing actualism that he attributed to **Gentile**. He seeks to transcend attempts, found in idealism, to characterize Spirit as a cosmic principle and speaks, instead, of spirituality, the internal valuative activity of humans. Spirit distinguishes itself from the world by acts which render it, as Croce argued, a concrete existent rather than an abstract notion. These concrete presentations, however, disperse value, so that an integrative principle of value is required, and this gives point to Gentile's theologizing, for the integrative principle cannot lie within spirituality but must be transcendent, and a transcendent God becomes the principle of the integration of values. World and God are, therefore, the twin poles between which the human spirit moves in creating its self and values. His later work deals with specific problems of Catholicism and the concrete value of religion in the modern world.

COLIN LYAS

Carnap, Rudolf
German. *b:* 18 May 1891, Ronsdorf (Wuppertal), Germany. *d:* 1970. *Cat:* Logician. *Ints:* Logic; semantics; philosophy of science; epistemology. *Educ:* University of Freiburg; University of Jena, PhD 1921; Harvard University, ScD(Hons) 1936. *Infls:* Kant, Frege, Russell and Wittgenstein. *Appts:* Professor of Natural Philosophy, German University, Prague, 1931–5; Professor of Philosophy, University of Chicago, 1936–52; subsequently Professor, University of California, Los Angeles from 1954–62; Visiting Professor, Harvard, 1941–2.

Main publications:
(1928) *Der Logische Aufbau der Welt*, Berlin: Weltkreis-Verlag (English translation, *The Logical Structure of the World and Pseudoproblems in Philosophy*, trans. R. George, Berkeley: University of California Press, 1969).
(1934) *Logische Syntax der Sprache*, Vienna: Springer (English translation, *The Logical Syntax of Language*, London: Routledge & Kegan Paul, 1937).
(1950) 'Empiricism, semantics and ontology', *Revue Internationale de Philosophie* 4; reprinted in Carnap (1956).
(1950) *The Logical Foundations of Probability*, University of Chicago Press.
(1956) *Meaning and Necessity*, second edition, University of Chicago Press.

(1959) 'The elimination of metaphysics through the logical analysis of language', in A. J. Ayer (ed.), *Logical Positivism*, Glencoe: Free Press.
(1987) 'On protocol sentences', *Nous* 21.

Secondary literature:
Sarkar, S. (ed.) (1992) 'Carnap: a centenary appraisal', *Synthese*, 93, 1–2.
Schilpp, P. A. (ed.) (1963) *The Philosophy of Rudolf Carnap*, La Salle: Open Court.

Carnap occupies an important position in the evolution of the analytic tradition in philosophy, not least in his appreciation of the significance for philosophy of the major developments in logic due to **Frege** and **Russell**. From the latter's influence he also conceived his own project of constructing material objects (or their concepts) from primitive elementary experiences. One important point of difference from the atomism of Russell, however, is that Carnap takes these basic experiences as states of consciousness, the experiences of an individual, and not sensations or simple impressions in the manner of earlier empiricism. He grew dissatisfied with this project, principally on the ground that scientific, and therefore public, knowledge could not plausibly be constructed on such a subjective base. This abandonment of the phenomenalist perspective was heavily influenced by his fellow positivist **Neurath**, whose commitment to physicalism he came to share. Along with this commitment he espoused the thesis, very characteristic of the positivists, of the unity of method in the sciences.

In the heyday of logical positivism Carnap led the assault on metaphysics. Like many empiricists he espoused a form of the analytic—synthetic distinction, according to which knowledge can be only of two basic kinds: 'necessary' truths or tautologies which hold independently of particular matters of fact and are true in all possible cases; and factual propositions about the world. Consequently there are just two permissible categories of proposition which exhaust what can be meaningfully said. By contrast, the assertions of traditional metaphysicians fail to qualify for either category, being neither tautological not empirically verifiable. Thus, while the sentences of metaphysics might, by virtue of their seductive syntactical appearance, suggest that great profundities were being communicated, they in fact lacked any literal sense at all, although they could have some emotional significance for those using them. Indeed Carnap stigmatized metaphysicians as frustrated poets or musicians, seduced by fundamental confusions about language. The principal source of this confusion is that philosophers have typically used what Carnap calls the 'material mode of speech' or 'thing'-language, and much metaphysics can arise from a failure to distinguish what are really sentences about language ('syntactical sentences') from sentences about objects ('object-sentences'). This produces sentences of a third category, ('pseudo-object sentences') which look as if they are about objects but, insofar as they are meaningful at all, could only be about language. The litmus test for items in this category is that there is no empirical test that could be made to determine their truth. For Carnap, therefore, metaphysical problems were totally spurious and did not admit of resolution. The implication of this for philosophy was far-reaching—philosophy had no business masquerading as a source of knowledge beyond science, and its proper role is to be concerned with the logical syntax of language, especially the language of science. Other disciplines with pretensions to scientific status, like psychology, would need to become thoroughly empirical, shedding discredited metaphysical preoccupations, and abandoning vacuous speculations about the mind.

On this approach syntax is a matter of conventions and the rules which license combinations of linguistic expressions. In his earlier work his concerns were largely of this formal complexion, and it was somewhat later that he took more serious account of substantial semantic issues, principally as a result of the influence of the Polish logician Alfred **Tarski**. The mature statement of his approach, which he called the method of extension and intension, was developed through a modification of more traditional concepts, such as those of class and property. He signalled a departure from a common assumption, that the role of an expression in language is that of naming some entity, whether abstract or concrete, preferring to talk of expressions as each possessing an intension and an extension. The intension is the meaning component which is grasped by anyone who understands the expression, while the extension is what is determined by observation or empirical investigation.

Carnap hoped to provide a basis for the analysis of modal logic, and while acknowledging the existence of the formal systems already available, he none the less felt that the fundamental notions themselves, for example necessity and possibility, had not been sufficiently clarified. He also endeavoured to extend the application of logical rigour to the topic of induction, seeking to provide a basis for measuring the degree of inductive support, and produced substantial work on probability.

In a later paper, 'Empiricism, semantics and ontology' (1950), Carnap delivered his most considered views on ontological questions. Maintaining his anti-metaphysical instinct, he distinguished between what he called 'external' and 'internal' questions. Acceptance of a kind of entity was ultimately a matter of adopting a linguistic framework, not one of belief, still less a commitment to some dubious metaphysical reality. So the question of which linguistic framework to adopt ultimately came down to a choice which was to be made on pragmatic grounds of expediency, fruitfulness or utility. Only once a framework was adopted, did it make sense to ask 'existential' questions. Thus the decision to adopt the mathematical framework of numbers was external, a practical question of whether to accept certain linguistic forms. An internal question say, about whether there exist prime numbers greater than a million was a matter of investigation and justification. This combination of pragmatism and empiricism was very much characteristic of Carnap's whole style of thought. Carnap's views attracted criticism from a number of quarters. Apart from those levelled against logical positivism as such, his stance on induction and probability brought him into conflict with Karl **Popper** who notoriously questioned whether any degree of inductive support or 'confirmation' increased either the probability of a theory being true or one's rational entitlement to believe in its truth. Carnap was also confronted by **Quine** with scepticism about modality and the very idea of analyticity as traditionally conceived. He and Quine additionally parted company on ontological commitment. Where Carnap saw a difference of kind between external and internal questions, Quine saw a difference of degree of generality. Others, on different grounds from Popper, have judged his forays into inductive logic to have been less than successful, albeit a substantial stimulus to subsequent work in the field. In other respects, his contributions to the study of syntax and semantics presaged much of the more recent work on truth-conditional semantics and possible worlds accounts of modality, and even logical pragmatics. Among those influenced by him in addition to Quine, were Hilary **Putnam** and the late R. M. Martin, the latter developing, in idiosyncratic style, a form of the logical pragmatics that Carnap had envisaged.

Sources: WW(Am) 1965.

DENIS POLLARD

Carr, H(erbert) W(ildon)

British. **b:** 16 January 1857, London. **d:** 8 July 1931, Los Angeles. **Cat:** Bergsonian idealist; personal idealist. **Ints:** Philosophy of science; philosophy of religion; evolution. **Educ:** King's College, London. **Infls:** Personal influence: Shadworth Hodgson. Literary influences: Bergson, Einstein, Croce, Gentile and Leibniz. **Appts:** 1918–25, Professor of Philosophy, King's College, London; 1925–31, Visiting Professor, University of Southern California, Los Angeles.

Main publications:

(1912) *Henry Bergson: The Philosophy of Change*: London, T. C. & E. Jack.

(1913) *The Problem of Truth*, London: T. C. & E. Jack.

(1914) *The Philosophy of Change. A Study of the Fundamental Principle of the Philosophy of Bergson*, London: Macmillan.

(1918) *The Philosophy of Benedetto Croce: The Problem of Art and History*, London: Macmillan.

(1920) *The General Principle of Relativity in its Historical and Philosophical Aspect*, London: Macmillan.

(1920) (trans.) Bergson, *L'Energie spirituelle*, published as *Mind-Energy: Lectures and Essays*, London: Macmillan.

(1922) *A Theory of Monads: Outlines of the Philosophy of the Principle of Relativity*, London: Macmillan.

(1922) (trans.) Gentile, *Teoria generale della spirito come atto puro*, third edition, published as *Theory of Mind as Pure Act*, London: Macmillan.

(1924) *The Scientific Approach to Philosophy: Selected Essays and Reviews*, London: Macmillan.

(1927) *Changing Backgrounds in Religion and Ethics*, London: Macmillan.

(1928) *The Freewill Problem*, London: T. C. & E. Jack.

(1929) *Leibniz*, London: E. Benn.

(1930) *Cogitans Cogitata*, London: Favil.

Secondary literature:

Acton, H. B. (1975) 'Carr, Herbert Wildon', *Dictionary of Scientific Biography*, New York: Scribner's, pp. 89–90.

Cunningham, G. Watts (1915) review of *The Philosophy of Change*, in *Philosophical Review* 24: 204–9.

Flewelling, R. T. (1976) 'H.W.C., Christian Stoic', *The Personalist* 37: 117–27.

Leighton, J. A. (1923) review of *A Theory of Monads*, in *Philosophical Review* 32: 544–8.

Schiller, F. C. S. (1931) 'In memoriam: Herbert Wildon Carr', *Mind* 40: 535–6.

H. W. Carr took up philosophy as a mature student, attending evening classes at King's College, London, while still working in the City. Plato, Berkeley and Hume were his early favourites in the history of philosophy but he was profoundly influenced by **Bergson**'s *L'Évolution créatrice* (1907). Carr became the first follower of Bergson in England. His interest was also greatly aroused in the idealism of **Croce** and **Gentile** as well as the physics of **Einstein**. Carr saw in Einstein's theory a retrospective support for the monadology of Leibniz. He claimed his system was idealistic (after the manner of Leibniz and Berkeley) in its metaphysics, voluntaristic in ethics, modernistic in religion and relativistic in reference to science. After his move to California Carr, developed further his conviction that a construction could be put on evolution that was consistent with a religious view of the world. Although, as Metz concluded, Carr was more of an able eclectic than an original thinker, he was influential on British philosophy in at least two different ways. He introduced Bergsonism and Italian idealism into Britain. As Secretary of the Aristotelian Society he was responsible, more than anyone else, for establishing the annual joint session with the Mind Association that became Britain's premier regular philosophy conference.

Sources: CBP II, pp. 102–26; Metz, pp. 440–3.

STUART BROWN

Carritt, Edgar Frederick

British. *b:* 27 February 1876, London. *d:* 19 June 1964, Ascot, Surrey. *Cat:* Ethical intuitionist; aesthetical expressionist. *Ints:* Aesthetics; moral and political philosophy. *Educ:* Hertford College, Oxford. *Infls:* Bishop Butler, Richard Price, G. E. Moore, B. Croce and A. C. Bradley. Personal influences: H. A. Prichard, J. Cook Wilson, H. W. B. Joseph and W. D. Ross. *Appts:* Fellow of University College, and University Lecturer in Philosophy, Oxford, 1898–1945; Visiting Professor, State University of Michigan, 1924–5; Fellow of the British Academy, 1945.

Main publications:

(1914) *The Theory of Beauty*, London: Methuen & Co. Ltd.; enlarged edition, 1923; revised edition, 1962.
(1928) *The Theory of Morals*, London: Oxford University Press.
(1931) (ed.) *Philosophies of Beauty from Socrates to Robert Bridges*, Oxford: Clarendon Press.
(1932) *What Is Beauty?*, London: Oxford University Press.

(1935) *Morals and Politics*, London: Oxford University Press.
(1947) *Ethical and Political Thinking*, Oxford: Clarendon Press.
(1949) *Introduction to Aesthetics*, London: Hutchinson's University Library.
(1949) (trans.) *My Philosophy: Selected Essays of B. Croce*, London: George Allen & Unwin Ltd.

Carritt was an outstanding tutor and lecturer at Oxford for almost fifty years: R. G. **Collingwood**, A. D. Lindsay and E. R. Dodds were tutored by him. Audiences for his lectures on dialectical materialism in 1933 overflowed the College Hall. For many years he was the only Oxford philosopher to give serious attention to the subject of aesthetics. He claimed his principal motive in philosophy was to preserve individual and social life from the harmful effects of bad philosophy. As he wrote, 'For bad philosophy the only cure is better'.

Carritt's reputation was made in the two fields of ethics and aesthetics. He developed **Prichard**'s conception of ethical intuitionism in his own way, arguing in *The Theory of Morals* (1928) that we morally apprehend what we ought to do in particular situations. Only then are we able to generalize rules or principles which, in consequence, are not strictly known to be true. Carritt extended the intuitionist theory to political philosophy in *Ethical and Political Thinking* (1947), arguing that our duties to the state do not differ in kind, but only in degree of complexity, from most of our other duties to our neighbours.

In aesthetics Carritt was an enthusiastic, though not uncritical, follower of **Croce**. He disputed Croce's indentification of expression with intuition but applauded Croce's rejection of the problem of genres in art, and he espoused the thesis that beauty, whether of nature or of art, is the expression of feeling and that all such expression is beautiful. In *What Is Beauty?* (1932) Carritt attempted to combine his account of beauty as a mental experience with his conviction that there is a genuine distinction between good and bad taste. Since, he maintained, bad taste is the tendency to mistake something merely 'agreeable or profitable or edifying' for 'the experience of beauty pure', we all need to be scrupulous about the sincerity and disinterestedness of our experiences.

Sources: WW; D. D. Raphael (1965) obituary notice, *PBA* 51: 439–53.

PETER LEWIS

Cartwright, Nancy

American. *b:* 24 January 1944, Pennsylvania. *Cat:* Philosopher of science; mathematician. *Ints:* Scientific explanation; causal laws; the problems of measurement. *Educ:* Universities of Pittsburgh and Illinois, Chicago. *Infls:* Aristotle, J. S. Mill, Ian Hacking, C. W. F. Everitt, Michael Scriven and David Lewis. *Appts:* 1971–3, Assistant Professor of Philosophy, University of Maryland; 1973–91, Assistant then (1977) Associate, then (1983) full Professor of Philosophy, Stanford University; from 1991, Professor, Department of Philosophy, Logic and Scientific Method, and Director of the Centre for the Philosophy of the Natural and Social Sciences, London School of Economics.

Main publications:

(1983) *How the Laws of Physics Lie*, Oxford: Clarendon Press.
(1989) *Nature's Capacities and their Measurement*, Oxford: Oxford University Press.

Secondary literature:

Braddon-Mitchell, David (1991) review of *Nature's Capacities and their Measurement* (1989), in *Philosophical Books* 32 (October): 201–9.
Hacking, Ian (1983) *Representing and Intervening*, Cambridge: Cambridge University Press, pp. 36–40, 216–19.

Cartwright is a philosopher of science who believes that the essential task of her subject is to make sense of actual scientific practice and to rationalize it convincingly. Her writings are outstanding in their presenting discussion of many examples.

In her *How the Laws of Physics Lie* (1983) she argued that physical laws are idealizations rather than descriptions of the processes that occur in nature. Consequently she denied that the laws of physics state the facts, that the models which play a central role in applied physics are literal representations of how things are (pp. 3–4). But although an anti-realist about theories, Cartwright takes a realist view about entities: there are no exactly true laws 'making things happen'; it is electrons and other such real entities that are producing the effects. This position implies a 'striking reversal of the empiricist tradition going back to Hume' in which only observed regularities of succession or co-occurrence are real (Hacking 1983, p. 38).

Her *Nature's Capacities and their Measurement* (1989) develops this thesis by exploring its implications for the nature of causality in the actual world. She defends a realist view of causality, according to which causes are rooted in the real capacities that things have, and she maintains that fundamental statements about causation are not general but singular in logical form. Thus she thinks it best to interpret 'An aspirin has the capacity to relieve a headache' as a modalized singular claim: 'An aspirin can relieve a headache'. Cartwright's work is widely recognized as making an original and important contribution to the understanding of scientific practice.

Sources: Personal communication.

STEPHEN MOLLER

Caso, Antonio

Mexican. *b:* 1883. *d:* 1946, Mexico City. *Cat:* Personalist. *Ints:* Ethics; politics. *Infls:* Nietzsche, Boutroux, Bergson and *Geistesphilosophie*. *Appts:* Qualified initially as a lawyer, changed early on to the academic philosophical career which was to occupy his entire life; appointed to his first Chair of Philosophy before he was 30, went on to become Under-secretary of State for Education and Rector of the National University of Mexico.

Main publications:

All now included in *Obras completas*, 11 vols, Mexico: Universidad Nacional Autónoma de Mexico, 1971–7:
(1915) *Problemas filosoficos*.
(1919) *La existencia como economía, como disinterés, y como caridad*, revised 1943.
(1923) *El concepto de la historia universal*.
(1933) *El concepto de la historia y la filosofía de los valores*.
(1941) *La persona humana y el estado totalitario*.
(1942) *El peligro del hombre*.

Secondary literature:

Escandon, C. (1968) *La respuesta moral en la filosofía del Maestro Antonio Caso*, Mexico: Editorial Pórrua.
Guandique, J. S. (1976) 'Perfiles sobre Caso y Vasconcelos', *Humanitas* (Mexico) 17: 215–66.
Romanell, P. (1952) *Making of the Mexican Mind*, Lincoln: University of Nebraska Press.
Weinstein, M. A. (1976) *The Polarity of Mexican Thought*, Pennsylvania and London: Pennsylvania State University Press.

Together with **Vasconcelos**, Antonio Caso ranks as one of the founders of Mexican philosophy. He was one of the leaders of the generation of Latin American thinkers which found wanting the Comtean positivism which had prevailed in the nineteenth century. Caso disliked in particular the determinism and epiphenomenalism of positivistic thought, and evolved his own libertarian personalism in opposition to it. In common with other Latin American thinkers of his time, Caso regarded philosophy as something to be lived, and not merely as a recondite, abstract body of knowledge. This view did not change, in contrast to other aspects of his thought: most notably, the orthodox Christian elements in his outlook become more pronounced in works post-dating the Mexican Revolution. Within his own country and to a lesser extent throughout Latin America, Caso's thought continues to be a point of reference. In Mexico itself he was, and is, revered as a thinker.

Caso bases his philosophy on a division of existents into three classes: things, individuals and persons. The class of things is that of inorganic entities, which can be divided without injury or loss of any significant property. Individuals are organisms, life forms destroyed by division, far more highly unified than the merely physical things. The highest class of existent is that of persons. Personhood Caso regards as *sui generis*: it is irreducible to any biological functions, and its distinctive property is to be the creator of values. (Here Caso avowedly follows **Nietzsche**.) Values Caso classes as neither objective nor subjective but have a mode of being he describes as social. In the earlier phase of his thought, in which elements of existentialism are present, Caso contends further that this creation of values, which is the essence of personhood, goes on continuously.

The view of human nature which underpins this theory of value is developed in Caso's best known work, *Existence as Economy, as Disinterest and as Charity* (1919). Under the aspect of *individual* (not person), human beings follow the principle of life as economy, i.e. to achieve the maximum gain with the minimum of effort (*maximum de provecho con minimum de esfuerzo*). This is the egotistical life of the satisfaction of basic drives. Caso is emphatic, however, that this principle does not exhaust human nature. There is in human beings a spontaneous impulse to selflessness which manifests itself in two ways, of which the first is the capacity to take an aesthetic attitude to the world. The aesthetic attitude Caso identifies with disinterest, contending that no biological account of human nature can explain this capacity, which has no survival value whatever. The impulse to selflessness also manifests itself in altruistic behaviour, which Caso identifies with the moral good. Human beings can follow the principle of sacrifice, the maximum effort with the minimum gain (*maximum de esfuerzo con*

minimum de provecho). This principle is not a categorical imperative, a law of reason, but an impulse emerging freely from the centre of the personality.

These views inform Caso's political writings, both general and his works devoted to an analysis of the Mexican system. The only satisfactory form of polity is one which not only treats human beings as persons but also encourages them to be such. Those political systems which stultify creativity and reduce us to consumers or functionaries are to be deplored, and, not unexpectedly, Caso devotes a good deal of time to the analysis of the destructive effects of such systems, notably totalitarianism.

ROBERT WILKINSON

Cassirer, Ernst

German. *b:* 28 July 1874, Breslau. *d:* 13 April 1945, New York. *Cat:* Neo-Kantian (Marburg School); historian of philosophy; epistemologist. *Ints:* Culture. *Educ:* Berlin, Leipzig, Munich, Heidelberg and Marburg. *Infls:* Hermann Cohen, Edmund Husserl and Paul Natorp. *Appts:* Professor at Marburg and then at Hamburg University (Rector from 1930–3); Professor at Columbia University in New York; also taught at Oxford (1933–5), Göteborg, Sweden (1935–41) and Yale (1941–4).

Main publications:

Major editions of the works of Leibniz (1904–15) and Kant (1912).

(1899) 'Descartes, Kritik der Mathematischen und Naturwissenschaftlichen Erkenntnis', Marburg: Inaugural Dissertation.

(1906–20) *Das Erkenntnisproblem in der Philosophie und Wissenschaft der neueren Zeit*, 3 vols, Berlin: Bruno Cassirer (English translation of the third volume, *The Problem of Knowledge*, New Haven: Yale University Press, 1950).

(1910) *Der Substanzbegriff und der Funktionsbegriff*, Berlin: Bruno Cassirer (English translation, *Substance and Function, and Einstein's Theory of Relativity*, New Haven: Yale University Press, 1923).

(1918) *Immanuel Kants Leben und Lehre*, Berlin: Bruno Cassirer (English translation, *Kant's Life and Thought*, New Haven: Yale University Press, 1981).

(1923–9) *Philosophie der symbolischen Formen*, 3 vols, Berlin: Bruno Cassirer (English translation, *The Philosophy of Symbolic Forms*, New Haven: Yale University Press, 1953–7).

(1925) *Sprache und Mythos*, Leipzig: B. G. Teubner (English translation, *Language and Myth*, New York: Harper & Brothers, 1946).

(1927) *Individuum und Kosmos in der Philosophie der Renaissance*, Leipzig: B. G. Teubner (English translation, *The Individual and the Cosmos in Renaissance Philosophy*, Philadelphia: University of Pennsylvania Press, 1963).

(1932) *Die Platonische Renaissance in England und die Schule von Cambridge*, Leipzig: B. G. Teubner.

(1932) *Die Philosophie der Aufklärung*, Tübingen: J. C. B. Mohr (English translation, *The Philosophy of the Enlightenment*, Princeton: Princeton University Press, 1951).

(1936) *Determinismus und Indeterminismus in der modernen Physik*, Göteborg: Högskolas Årskrift.

(1939) *Descartes, Lehre, Persönlichkeit, Wirkung*, Stockholm: Berman Fischer Verlag.

(1942) *Zur Logik der Kulturwissenschaften*, Göteborg: Högskolas Arskrift (English translation: *The Logic of the Humanities*, New Haven: Yale University Press, 1974).

(1944) *An Essay on Man: Introduction to the Philosophy of Human Culture*, New Haven: Yale University Press.

(1946) *The Myth of the State*, New Haven: Yale University Press.

(1970) *Rousseau, Kant, Goethe*, Princeton: Princeton University Press.

(1971) *Idee und Gestalt, Goethe, Schiller, Hölderlin, Kleist*, Darmstadt: Wissenschaftliche Buchgesellschaft.

(1979) *Symbol, Myth, and Culture: Essays and Lectures of Ernst Cassirer, 1935–1945*, ed. Donald Philip Verene. New Haven: Yale University Press.

(1985) *Symbol, Technik, Sprache*, Hamburg: Meiner.

Secondary literature:

Braun, H.-J., Holzhey, H. and Orth, E. W. (1988) *Über Ernst Cassirers Philosophie der symbolischen Formen*, Frankfurt am Main: Suhrkamp.

Cassirer, Toni (1981) *Mein Leben mit Ernst Cassirer*, Hildesheim: Gerstenberg.

Hamburg, Carl H. (1956) *Symbol and Reality: Studies in the Philosophy of Ernst Cassirer*, The Hague: Martinus Nijhoff.

Itzkoff, Seymour W. (1971) *Ernst Cassirer: Scientific Knowledge and the Concept of Man*, Notre Dame: University of Notre Dame Press.

Lipton, David R. (1978) *Ernst Cassirer: The Dilemma of a Liberal Intellectual in Germany, 1914–1933*, Toronto, University of Toronto Press.

Schilpp, Paul (ed.) (1949) *The Philosophy of Ernst Cassirer*, La Salle: Open Court; reprinted 1973.

Cassirer was Hermann **Cohen**'s most important student. His work is often considered to be the final testament of the Marburg school. Yet, there are important differences between him and the earlier Marburg neo-Kantians. Although he devoted himself to a critical and historical study of the problem of knowledge and the logic of the sciences, he was also interested in the problem of culture in general. Thinking of human beings as 'symbolic animals', he argued that all culture was based on our conceptual ability that allows us to invent and use artificial signs and symbols. In many ways Cassirer takes up and develops also the ideas of the Baden (or Southwestern) School of neo-Kantianism as they were exemplified in the works of Wilhelm **Windelband** and Heinrich **Rickert**. Just as they did, he felt that it was necessary to move from a 'critique of reason' to a 'critique of culture'. However, his many historical studies were not only in the service of such a critique of culture. They were also meant to be contributions to the advancement of culture, for he believed that in order 'to possess the world of culture we must incessantly reconquer it by historical recollection'.

Like Kant and the neo-Kantians in general, he argued that our concepts determine the way we experience the world. Our experience does not mirror an objectively existing world or things in themselves. Rather, the world is actively constructed by us in accordance with our conceptual framework. In an important sense, we constitute it, using the materials given to us by the senses. For this reason Cassirer thought that philosophers should concentrate on the conceptual framework that enables us to experience the world in the way we do experience it. In more technical terms, we must employ a transcendental method in showing how these concepts make our experience possible. However, unlike Kant (but like some of his own neo-Kantian predecessors), he rejected the idea that the concepts and principles that make our experience possible are the static and forever fixed furniture of the human mind. He claimed that these concepts and principles constantly develop. Although one may speak of a 'natural symbolism' that characterizes all human consciousness, it can take many different forms. His philosophy started from the presupposition that, if there is a definition of the nature or 'essence' of human beings, it can only be functional. It cannot be substantial. Cassirer also thought that the original Kantian conception of critical philosophy was far too narrow. In particular, he argued that the transcendental investigation must be extended to the humanities and even to forms of representation that are often called primitive, namely mythologies. They also constitute conceptual systems worthy of analysis. Indeed, he argued that every manifestation of culture is an important subject of philosophical study in so far as our symbolizing nature is present in it. Cassirer felt that 'the artist is just as much a discoverer of the forms of nature as the scientist is a discoverer of facts or natural laws'.

This philosophy of culture had, for Cassirer, clear ethical consequences, for he believed that 'human culture taken as a whole may be described as the progress of man's progressive self-liberation. Language, art, religion, sciences, are various phases in this process. In all of them man discovers and proves a new power—the power to build up a world of his own, an 'ideal' world'. Being equally opposed to empiricism, naturalism, positivism and *Lebensphilosophie* (which he thought included the kind of existential thinking advocated by Martin **Heidegger**), he argued for a new kind of idealism and humanism. Indeed, he characterized his philosophy also as a 'humanistic philosophy of culture'. At the same time he was rather pessimistic about the influence of philosophy on politics: 'the role of the individual thinker is a very modest one. As an individual the philosopher has long ago given up all hopes to reform the political world'. And even though he also believed that 'philosophy as a whole' should not give up hope, he thought that all that could be done by philosophy was the debunking of political myths. As he said in one of his last lectures: 'To all of us it has become clear that we have greatly underestimated the strength of political myths. We should not repeat this error'. Cassirer had some followers in the USA during the early years after the Second World War, both among historians of philosophy and among philosophical critics. The best known among these was perhaps Susanne **Langer**. However, his thought was then almost completely ignored in Germany. In the late twentieth century, a real interest in Cassirer's philosophy has developed in Germany. Some of his later essays, written in English, have recently been translated into German, and there is even talk of 'the beginning of a renaissance' of his thinking.

MANFRED KUEHN

Castañeda, Héctor-Neri

Guatemalan-American. **b:** 13 December 1924, Zapaca, Guatemala. **d:** 7 September, 1991, Bloomington, Indiana. **Cat:** Philosopher of mind; philosopher of language. **Educ:** Expelled from high school in Guatemala, Castañeda was educated at the University of Minnesota, where he received a BA, MA and in 1954, PhD; received a Postdoctoral Fellowship to Oxford. **Infls:** Wilfrid Sellars. **Appts:** Duke University, 1956–7, Wayne State University, 1957–74; Mahlon Powell Professor of Philosophy, University of Indiana, 1974; lectured in Heidelberg and in Rotterdam, serving as Tinbergen Professor at Erasmus University for a semester; past President of the American Philosophical Association's Western Division.

Main publications:

(1974) *The Structure of Morality*, Springfield, IL: Thomas.

(1975) *Thinking and Doing*, Dordrecht: Reidel.

(1976) *La teoría de Platón sobre las formas, las relaciones y los particulares en el 'Fedón'*, Mexico.

(1980) *On Philosophical Method*, Bloomington: University of Indiana Press.

(1983) *Agent, Language, and the Structure of the World: Essays Presented to Héctor-Neri Castañeda, with His Replies*, Indianapolis: Hackett.

(1989) *Thinking, Language, and Experience*, Minneapolis: University of Minnesota Press.

Secondary literature:

Tomberlin, James E. (ed.) (1986) *Héctor-Neri Castañeda*, Dordrecht: Reidel.

Castañeda's work extends to such areas as metaphysics, epistemology, ontology, moral philosophy, practical reason, action theory and theory of knowledge. His more than 150 essays and articles have sparked considerable theoretical debate on deontic logic, hierarchy of ethical principles and intentionality.

AMY A. OLIVER

Castelli-Gattinara di Zubiena, Enrico

Italian. **b:** 20 June 1900, Turin. **d:** 10 March 1977, Rome. **Cat:** Philosopher of religion and existence. **Appts:** Professor of the Philosophy of Religion, University of Rome; Founder editor of the *Archivo di filosofia*, journal of the Società filosofia Italiana.

Main publications:

(1929) *Filosofia e apologetica.*

(1933) *Idealismo e solipsismo.*

(1938) *Introduzione alla vita della parole.*

(1939) *Commentario al senso commune.*

(1941) *Preludio all vita di un uomo qualunque.*

(1942) *L'Esperienza commune.*

(1947) *Il tempo esaurito*, second edition, Rome: Bocca, 1954.

(1948) *Existenzialisme théologique*; *Esistenzialismo teologico*: Rome: Abete, 1966.

(1949) *Introduzione ad una fenomenologica della nostra epoca*, Paris: Merman.

(1958) *Il demoniaco dell'arte*, Padua: Vrin.

(1968) *I presupposti di una teologica della storia*, Padua: Cedam.

(1970) *I paradossi del senso commune*, Padua: Cedam.

(1972) *La critica della demitizzazione*, Padua: Cedam.

(1975) *Il tempo inqualificabile*, Padua: Cedam.

Secondary literature:
Kaisserlian, G. (1944) *Castelli*, Padua: Cedam.

Castelli's philosophy explores some of the problems in realism conceived as the affirmation of the reality of *things* and of *subjects* as mistakenly understood on the model of the existence of things. For him idealism is founded upon this reduction to objects set in opposition to the subject. Having freed oneself from a realism of things, the data of a common sense lead also to a critique of rationalism. In part that critique analyses contemporary crises not as crises occurring within modernism but as crises, or rather, catastrophes, of modernism. In his writing on art Castelli traces the prophetic story of contemporary crises in the pictorial theological works of fifteenth- and sixteenth-century Flemish and German artists. In those artists he sees evidence of an irresistible concupiscence that drives us to the substitution of knowledge for faith and speculative dialectics for unity. After Vatican II he turned his attention particularly to the problem of demythicization.

COLIN LYAS

Castoriadis, Cornélius

French (originally Greek). **b:** 11 March 1922, Constantinople. **Cat:** Post-Marxist; economist; psychoanalyst. **Educ:** Law, Economics and Philosophy, Athens. **Infls:** Marx and Freud. **Appts:** Director of the École des Hautes Études en Sciences Sociales; founder with Claude Lefort of the communist party splinter group Socialisme ou Barbarie (associated journal *Socialisme ou Barbarie*, 1948–70, where Castoriadis writes under the pseudonyms Chaulieu, Cardan and Delvaux); economist, OECD, 1948–70; psychoanalyst, since 1973.

Main publications:
(1973) *Les Rapports de la production en Russie*, Paris: 10/18.

(1974) *L'Expérience du mouvement ouvrier I: Comment lutter*, Paris: 10/18.

(1974) *L'Expérience du mouvement ouvrier II: Proletariat et organisation*, Paris: 10/18.

(1975) *L'Institution imaginaire de la société*, Paris: Seuil (English translation, *The Imaginary Institution of Society*, trans. Kathleen Blamey, Cambridge: Polity Press, 1987).

(1975) *La Révolution contre la bureaucratie*, Paris: 10/18.

(1978) *Les Carrefours du labyrinthe*, Paris: Seuil (English translation, *Crossroads in the Labyrinth*, trans. Kate Soper and Martin Ryle, Brighton: Harvester, 1984).

(1979) *Capitalisme moderne et révolution I: L'impérialisme et la guerre*, Paris 10/18.

(1979) *Capitalisme moderne et révolution II: Le mouvement révolutionaire sous le capitalisme moderne*, Paris 10/18.

(1981) *Devant la guerre*, Paris: Fayard.

(1990) *Le Monde morcelé*, Paris: Seuil.

(1991) *Philosophy, Politics, Autonomy: Essays in Political Philosophy*, trans. D. Ames, New York: Oxford Unversity Press.

Secondary literature:
Authier, M. and Hess, R. (1981) *L'Analyse institutionelle*, Paris: Presses Universitaires de France.

Busino, G. *et al.* (1989) *Autonomie et transformation de la société: la philosophie militante de Cornelius Castoriadis*, Paris: Champion.

Guibal, F. (1980) 'Cornelius Castoriadis', *Études*, June.

In his early work (1972–5), Cornélius Castoriadis developed a critique of left- and right-wing bureaucracies and of Marxist economies. This work is anti-totalitarian and anti-bureaucratic, it favours the project of a self-instituting and self-creating society and aspires to individual and collective autonomy. His critical thinking has extended beyond this institutional analysis into psychoanalysis, the critique of war and East-West relations. Thus, his later work seeks to foster people's creative assertion of their autonomy in opposition to the expansion of rational mastery through the technoscientific destruction and transformation of nature and society.

JAMES WILLIAMS

Cavaillès, Jean

French. *b:* 1903, Saint Maixent. *d:* 1944, Arras. *Cat:* Historian and philosopher of mathematics, logic and science. *Appts:* Held various posts in Philosophy at the University of Strasbourg and at the Sorbonne; during the Second World War, a leading member of the French Resistance; captured by the Germans in 1943, and executed the following year.

Main publications:

(1937) *Cantor–Dedekind: Briefwechsel*, Paris: Hermann.

(1938) *Méthode axiomatique et formalisme; essai sur le problème du fondement des mathématiques*, Paris: Hermann.

(1938) *Remarques sur la formation de la théorie abstraite des ensembles*, Paris: Hermann.

(1947) *Sur la logique et la théorie de la science*, Paris: PUF.

(1962) *Philosophie mathématique*, Paris: Hermann.

Secondary literature:

Cavaillès, J. (1962) *Philosophie mathématique* (the introduction provides a useful summary of his philosophical approach).

Ferrières, G. (1950) *Jean Cavaillès, philosophe et combattant*, Paris: PUF.

One of Cavaillès's great contributions to the history of mathematics and logic was to publish the nineteenth-century correspondence between **Cantor** and Dedekind on set theory. The publication of these documents illustrates Cavaillès's view that contemporary problems can only be understood through a study of their origin and evolution, and those of the disciplines to which they belong. No system of mathematics, logic or science consists of a core of discovered truths within a fixed theoretical framework. The boundaries of each discipline are always only provisional and have, historically, had to be redrawn on more than one occasion.

Cavaillès also maintains that the evolution of mathematics, logic and science has not been even. Mathematical discoveries are made in response to pragmatic pressures, or the background of a need to provide solutions to particular problems. Mathematics is an open discipline, in the sense that it responds to demands placed upon it by other subject areas, notably by the requirements of science. The insistence of Cavaillès on the historical dimension of what is and can be known has had enormous influence on subsequent

philosophers of mathematics and science, including Gaston **Bachelard** and Georges **Canguilhem**.

KATHRYN PLANT

Cavarero, Adriana

Italian. *b:* 1947, Cuneo, Italy. *Cat:* Feminist philosopher. *Ints:* Ancient philosophy (Plato, Pre-Socratics); political philosophy. *Educ:* Philosophy, University of Padua. *Infls:* French feminist postmodernist thought (Luce Irigaray) and ancient philosophy. *Appts:* Ricercatrice, Department of Philosophy of the University of Verona, Italy; founding member of Diotima, Group of Women Philosophers in Verona.

Main publications:

(1976) *Dialettica e Politica in Platone* [Dialectics and Politics in Plato], Padua: Cedam.

(1984) *L'interpretazione hegeliana di Parmenide* [Hegelian Interpretation of Parmenides], Trento: Verifiche.

(1984) *La teoria politica di John Locke* [The Political Theory of John Locke].

(1986) 'Plato secondo Voegelin' [Plato according to Voegelin], *Verifiche* 15, 4: 449–62.

(1987) 'L'elaborazione della differenza sessuale' [The elaboration of sexual difference] in A. Rossi Doria and C. Marcuzzo (eds) *La ricerca delle donne*, Turin: Rosenberg & Sellier.

(1987) 'L'ordine dell'uno non è l'ordine del due' [The order of the one is not the order of the two] in *Il genere della rappresentanza*, Materiali e atti di 'Democrazia e diritotto'.

(1988) 'L'emancipazione diffidente' [Diffident emancipation], *Reti* 2, Editori Riuniti.

(1989) 'Ansätze zu einer Theorie der Geschlechterdifferenz' [Approaches towards a theory of gender difference] in Diotima (Philosophinnengruppe aus Verona), *Der Mensch ist zwei. Das Denken der Geschlechterdifferenz*, Vienna: Frauenverlag, pp. 65–102.

(1990) 'Und die Magd lachte' [And the maid laughed] in H. Nagl-Docekal (ed.), *Feministische-Philosophie*, Vienna: Oldenbourg, pp. 95–107.

(1990) 'Die Perspektive der Geschlechterdifferenz' [The perspective of gender difference] in Ute Gerhard, Mechthild Jansen, Andrea Maihofer, Pia Schmid and Irmgard Schultz (eds) *Differenz und Gleichheit. Menschenrechte haben (k)ein Geschlecht* [Difference and Equality. Human Rights do (not) Have a Gender], Frankfurt am Main: Ulrike Helmer Verlag, pp. 95–111.

(1990) *Nonostante Platone* [In Defiance of Plato], Rome: Editori Riuniti.

Adriana Cavarero's feminist philosophy emphasises the significance of difference rather than
equality. She argues that the dual categories of
gender permeate Western thought so that it takes
a conscious philosophical effort (the 'thinking of
gender difference') to reveal their effects. Cavarero
refers to examples and metaphors from the
history of philosophy to show the development
and influence of the gender categories throughout
our Western philosophy.

URSULA STICKLER

Cavell, Stanley

American. **b:** 1 September 1926, Atlanta. **Cat:**
Ordinary language philosophy, distinctively mod-
ified. **Ints:** Scepticism and its modern cultural
analogues in philosophy, literature, film and
psychoanalysis. **Educ:** Cavell studied Music at
Berkeley before turning to Philosophy at UCLA
and then Harvard, where Austin's 1955 visit
profoundly influenced him. **Infls:** Wittgenstein,
Austin, Shakespeare, Kant, Emerson, Thoreau,
Nietzsche, Kierkegaard, Freud and Heidegger.
Appts: University of California, at Berkeley; 1963,
Walter M. Cabot Professor of Aesthetics and the
General Theory of Value, Harvard University.

Main publications:

(1969) *Must We Mean What We Say? A Book of
Essays*, New York: Scribner's.
(1971) *The World Viewed: Reflections on the Ontology of Film*, New York: Viking Press; new edition,
Cambridge, Mass.: Harvard University Press,
1979.
(1972) *The Senses of Walden*, New York: Viking
Press; new edition, San Francisico: North Point
Press, 1981.
(1979) *The Claim of Reason: Wittgenstein, Skepticism, Morality, and Tragedy*, Oxford: Oxford
University Press.
(1981) *Pursuits of Happiness: The Hollywood Co-
medy of Remarriage*, Cambridge, Mass.: Harvard
University Press.
(1984) *Themes Out of School: Effects and Causes*, San
Francisco: North Point Press.
(1987) *Disowning Knowledge: In Six Plays of
Shakespeare*, Cambridge: Cambridge University
Press.
(1988) *In Quest of the Ordinary: Lines of Skepticism
and Romanticism*, Chicago: University of Chicago
Press.
(1989) *This New Yet Unapproachable America:
Lectures after Emerson after Wittgenstein*, Albuquerque: Living Batch Press.
(1990) *Conditions Handsome and Unhandsome: The
Constitution of Emersonian Perfectionism*, Chicago: University of Chicago Press.
(1994) *A Pitch of Philosophy: Autobiographical
Exercises*, Cambridge, Mass.: Harvard University
Press.
(1995) *Philosophical Passages: Wittgenstein, Emerson, Austin, Derrida*, Oxford: Blackwell (includes
Cornell bibliography to 1994).

Secondary literature:

Cohen, J., Guyer, P. and Putnam, H. (eds) (1993)
*Pursuits of Reason: Essays in Honour of Stanley
Cavell*, Texas: Ech. University Press.
Fischer, Michael, *Stanley Cavell and Literary Skep-
ticism*, Chicago: University of Chicago Press.
Fleming, R. and Payne, M. (eds) (1989) *The Senses of
Stanley Cavell*, Bucknell University Press (auto-
biographical interview and bibliography to 1987).
Mulhall, Stephen (1994) *Stanley Cavell: Philosophy's
Recounting of the Ordinary*, Oxford: Clarendon
Press.
Smith, J. H. and Kerrigan, W. (eds) (1987) *Images in
our Souls: Cavell, Psychoanalysis and Cinema*,
Johns Hopkins University Press.

Cavell is centrally concerned with the difficulty of
properly grasping the obvious, associating Emerson's appeal to the 'common' with **Austin**'s to
'ordinary' language and **Wittgenstein**'s to criteria.
The self-knowledge involved in becoming conscious of the criteria governing one's use of words
has non-trivial relations with psychoanalysis,
enabling one to grasp one's relations with fellow
language users and the world of which one speaks,
best thought of in terms not of knowledge but of
sympathy, indifference, avoidance and acknowledgement; **Heidegger**'s phenomenological analyses are relevant here. Philosophical writing
should itself be transformative, with a rigour
sharing the Kantian (and 'modernist') aspiration
to a universal voice' grounded in integrity of
vision. Philosophical scepticism represents a form
of that human aspiration to transcend finitude
mapped by Romanticism whose defeat, as Shakespeare shows, can lead to tragedy. Film as a
medium mimics the sceptical predicament, with
several of its genres engaging with the possibilities
of human acknowledgement. Whether in epistemology, art, morality or politics, criteria do not
confer impersonal certainty. Judgement is required and this may quite properly be in the
service of self-transcending regulative ideals, such
as Emersonian 'perfectionism', which defeat all
appeal to established or self-justifying rules. Until
recently Cavell's influence has been greater in the

related disciplines with which he has engaged than in philosophy itself.

Sources: WW(Am) 1995.

MARTIN WARNER

Cerutti Guldberg, Horacio

Argentinian-Mexican. **b:** 12 November 1950, Mendoza, Argentina. **Cat:** Historian of ideas; philosopher of liberation. **Educ:** National University of Cuyo, Mendoza, Argentina; Cuenca University, Azuay, Ecuador, where he was awarded a PhD; held Postdoctoral Fellowships in Argentina and Germany. **Appts:** Lecturer and Researcher, Universities of Salta (Argentina), Cuenca (Ecuador) and Pedagógica Nacional (Mexico); Professor of Political Philosophy, National Autonomous University of Mexico.

Main publications:

(1981) *Pensamiento idealista ecuatoriano*, Quito, Ecuador.

(1983) *Filosofía de la liberación latinoamericana*, Mexico: Fondo de Cultura Económica.

(1986) *Hacia una metodología de la historia de las ideas (filosóficas) en América Latina*, Guadalajara: University of Guadalajara Press.

(1986) *Ideologías políticas contemporáneas*, Mexico: National Autonomous University of Mexico.

(1988–9) 'Actual situation and perspectives of Latin American philosophy for liberation', *The Philosophical Forum* 20: 43–61.

(1989) *De varia utópica*, Bogotá: Publicaciones Universidad Central.

Secondary literature:

Schutte, Ofelia (1993) *Cultural Identity and Social Liberation in Latin American Thought*, Albany: SUNY Press.

Horacio Cerutti believes that philosophy is a tool which can and should positively transform Latin American society. Structural modifications are inevitable and, he thinks, Latin America will be better off if it changes 'with philosophy'. Cerutti has made significant contributions to the historiography of ideas in Latin America and has challenged the use of inherited, European, historiographical categories. He is perhaps best known for his efforts, detailed in *Filosofía de la liberación latinoamericana* (1983), towards developing a political philosophy intended for Latin American liberation. He served as coeditor of the journal *Prometeo: Revista Latinoamericana de Filosofía*.

AMY A. OLIVER

Chan Wing-tsit (Cantonese) Chen Rongjie (Putonghua)

Chinese. **b:** 1901, Guangdong Province, China. **Cat:** Neo-Confucian. **Ints:** History of Chinese philosophy and religion. **Educ:** Lingnan University, Guangzhou, and Harvard University. **Infls:** Zhuangzi, Zhu Xi and Wang Yangming. **Appts:** Dean of Faculty, Lingnan University; Professor of Philosophy, University of Hawaii; Professor of Philosophy, Dartmouth College; Professor of Philosophy, Chatham College; Adjunct Professor, Columbia University; Cofounder East–West Philosophers Conference, Honolulu; editorial and advisory board member, *Philosophy East and West*.

Main publications:

(1947) (co-editor) Takakusu, *The Essentials of Buddhist Philosophy*, Honolulu: University of Hawaii Press.

(1953) *Religious Trends in Modern China*, New York: Columbia University Press.

(1955) *Historical Charts of Chinese Philosophy*, New Haven: Far Eastern Publications, Yale University.

(1960) (co-editor) *Sources of Chinese Tradition*, New York: Columbia University Press.

(1961) *An Outline and an Annotated Bibliography of Chinese Philosophy*, New Haven: Far Eastern Publications, Yale University.

(1963) *A Source Book in Chinese Philosophy*, Princeton: Princeton University Press.

(1963) (trans. and ed.) Chu Hsi and Lu Tsu-ch'ien, *Reflections on Things at Hand: The Neo-Confucian Anthology*, New York: Columbia University Press.

(1963) (trans. and ed.) Chu Hsi and Lu Tsu-ch'ien, *Reflections on Things at Hand: The Neo-Confucian Anthology*, New York: Columbia University Press.

(1963) (trans. and ed.) Huineng, *The Platform Scripture: The Basic Classic of Zen Buddhism*, New York: St John's University Press.

(1963) (trans. and ed.) *Instructions for Practical Living, and Other Neo-Confucian Writing of Wang Yangming*, New York: Columbia University Press.

(1963) (trans. and ed.) *The Way of Lao Tzu*, New York: Bobbs-Merrill.

(1967) *Chinese Philosophy, 1949–1963: An Annotated Bibliography of Mainland Chinese Publications*, Honolulu: East–West Center.

(1969) (co-compiler) *Great Asian Religions*, London: Macmillan.

(1986) (ed.) *Chu Hsi and Neo-Confucianism*, Honolulu: University of Hawaii Press.

Secondary literature:
Chen, Charles K. H. (1969) Foreword to W. Chan, *Neo-Confucianism, etc.: Essays by Wing-tsit Chan*, Hanover, NH: Oriental Society.

Chan's *Sourcebook in Chinese Philosophy* (1963) and **Feng Youlan**'s famous histories stand as the most significant surveys of Chinese philosophy for English-speaking readers. Their main rival, *Sources of Chinese Tradition* (1960), was edited by Chan with the Columbia University sinologists W. T. De Bary and B. Watson. Although Chan was born and educated in China, from 1936 his academic career was spent in the USA, principally at Dartmouth College. He saw the neo-Confucian traditions of Zhu Xi's rationalism and Wang Yangming's idealism as central to understanding Chinese thought and culture and devoted himself to major annotated translations of their writings, but he also saw the need to raise the study of earlier work, particularly that of the great pre-Qin dynasty schools, to a high scholarly standard of translation and commentary for Western readers. The *Sourcebook*, providing Chan's own translations, aimed at uniform renderings of philosophical terms throughout. Chan recognized the importance of articulating the concepts and doctrines of daoism, Buddhism and other Chinese schools to supplement his exegesis of the main tradition of Confucian humanism and to give a balanced account of Chinese thought as a whole. His scholarly studies of Chinese religion added to his sense of the complexity of Chinese intellectual culture. Chan took an interest in modern Chinese philosophers, such as **Kang Youwei** and **Hu Shi**, and introduced **Xiong Shili** and Feng Youlan to English-speaking readers. His appreciation of Feng's rationalist neo-Confucianism was tempered, however, by his rejection of Feng's construction of tradition from the standpoint of his own creative philosophical work. Chan regularly contributed to encyclopedias and journals, especially *Philosophy East and West*. His journal contributions ranged from broad sketches of Chinese philosophy and religion to detailed historical analyses of key neo-Confucian concepts, such as *ren* (humanity) or *li* (principle), and of Buddhist thought. In his eighties, his work returned to Zhu Xi, the figure inspiring his own deepest philosophical response.

NICHOLAS BUNNIN

Chatterjee, Margaret
Indian. *b:* 13 September 1925. *Cat:* Philosopher of the arts; philosopher of religion; music critic and pianist. *Ints:* Existentialism; phenomenology. *Educ:* 1943–6, Exhibitioner, Somerville College, University of Oxford; 1957–61, PhD, University of Delhi. *Infls:* Greek philosophy, Kant, Hegel and Gandhi. *Appts:* Lecturer then Reader in Philosophy, Delhi University; Professor of Comparative Religion, Visva-Bharati, Santiniketan; Professor of Philosophy, Delhi University; member of governing body, Indian Council for Philosophical Research; 1969, President of the History of Philosophy Section, All India Congress; Vice President, International Society for Metaphysics.

Main publications:
(1963) *Our Knowledge of Other Selves*, Bombay: Asia Publishing.

(1968) *Philosophical Enquiries*, Calcutta: New Age.

(1974) *The Existentialist Outlook*, Delhi: Orient Longman.

(1974) *Contemporary Indian Philosophy*, Series I and II, London: Allen & Unwin; New York: Humanities Press.

(1981) *The Language of Philosophy*, Delhi: Martinus Nijhoff and Allied Publishers.

(1983) *Gandhi's Religious Thought*, London: Macmillan.

Margaret Chatterjee has described her philosophical thought as a reaction not only to 'the absorption of English-speaking philosophers with cognition' but also to 'the *atman–Brahman* equation' that has dominated much Indian philosophy. A major concern of her work is to investigate the grounds of intersubjectivity and what she has seen as close but largely unrecognized relationships between the transcendental, the empirical and the ontological.

In aesthetics, although her starting-point has been her experience as a practising musician, she has drawn attention to the frequently ignored differences of status between the perceptual objects that constitute works of art and to the concomitant differences between the 'sensory cues' they provide.

In the philosophy of religion she has focused on the analysis of the religious language of prayer and worship rather than on propositions such as 'God exists'. Her explorations of existentialism in the 1970s, coupled with an interest in **Dilthey**, fostered the consolidation of her view that the philosopher is as much a writer as the novelist, poet and dramatist, and that imagination as much as reason must be at work in philosophy.

DIANÉ COLLINSON

Chen Duxiu (Ch'en Tu-hsiu)

Chinese. **b:** 1879, Huaining County, Anhui Province, China. **d:** 1942, Jinjiang, Sichuan Province, China. **Cat:** Marxist. **Ints:** Radical democratic thought; later, historical and dialectical materialism. **Educ:** Chinese classics at Qiushi Shuyuan School, Hangzhou; in Japan at the Higher Normal School, Tokyo, 1902–3; was greatly influenced by a period in France from about 1907 to 1910. **Infls:** French democratic and Marxist theorists. **Appts:** 1915–21, Chief Editor of magazine *New Youth* (initially called *Youth*), an influential review and forum for novel and exciting ideas, including those introduced by Chen, Hu Shi, Li Dazhao and Lu Xun; 1918, Founder (with Li Dazhao), *The Weekly Critic*; 1917–9, Dean of the Faculty of Letters, University of Beijing; 1920, established the first Chinese Communist Group in Shanghai; 1921, main founder with Li Dazhao, Chinese Communist Party; led the CCP until dismissed from office in 1927; expelled from the Party in 1929 and led an ineffective Marxist opposition group until imprisoned by the Guomintang government 1932–7; after release he studied ancient Chinese language, especially its philology and phonetics.

Main publications:

(1923) *Chen Duxiu's Collected Speeches*, Guangzhou.
(1925) *Sources of the Meaning of Words*, Shanghai: Yadong Library.
(1927) *The Preserved Works of Duxiu*, 4 vols, Shanghai: Yadong Library.
(1933) *Chen Duxiu's Written Defense Statement*, n.p.
(1942) *A Textbook on Recognising Characters*, Taipei.
(1959) *Chen Duxiu's Last Opinions*, Taipei.
(1967) *Chen Duxiu's Autobiography*, Taipei.

Secondary literature:

Boorman, H. (ed.) (1970) *Biographical Dictonary of Republican China*, New York and London: Columbia University Press.
Briere, O. (1956) *Fifty Years of Chinese Philosophy 1898–1950*, London: George Allen & Unwin Ltd.
Complete Chinese Encyclopedia (1987) Philosophy Volumes, Beijing: Chinese Encyclopedia Publications.
Feigon, L. (1983) *Chen Duxiu: Founder of the Chinese Communist Party*, Princeton: Princeton University Press.

Chen was a major campaigner for the modernization of China and a severe critic of the Confucian tradition. Before the May Fourth incident in 1919, he saw the key to China's advance in Western democracy and science and argued for a new culture based on modern economic life and on individual autonomy in ethics. He was an instigator of the New Culture Movement and supported **Hu Shi**'s campaign for vernacular literary reform. He saw cultural change as a precondition of political reform. After the May Fourth Movement, for which his ideas provided intellectual inspiration, he joined **Li Dazhao** as one of China's first two major Marxist theorists. Chen supported materialism, class struggle, revolution and the inevitability of socialism in China under the dictatorship of the proletariat. He opposed China's earlier radical movement of anarchism. He was open to reformist and pragmatist ideas, and tried to influence Hu Shi towards Marxism. Internal party rivalries as well as his programme of seeking to realize a broadly based democratic revolution led to his political fall.

NICHOLAS BUNNIN

Chicherin, Boris Nikolaevich

Russian. **b:** 26 May (7 June N.S.) 1828, Tambov province. **d:** 3 February (16 N.S.) 1904, Karaul, Tambov Province. **Cat:** Idealist. **Educ:** Graduated in Law at University of Moscow in 1849. **Infls:** Kant, Hegel and the Russian liberal historian T. N. Granovsky. **Appts:** Taught at University of Moscow, Professor of Russian Law from 1861.

Main publications:

(1879) *Nauka i religiia* [Science and Religion], Moscow.
(1880) *Mistitsizm v nauke* [Mysticism in Science], Moscow.
(1892) *Polozhitel'naia filosofiia i edinstvo nauki* [Positive Philosophy and the Unity of Science], Moscow.
(1894) *Osnovaniia logiki i metafiziki* [Foundations of Logic and Metaphysics], Moscow.
(1900) *Filosofiia prava* [Philosophy of Law], Moscow.
(1968) (ed. Louis J. Shein) *Readings in Russian Philosophical Thought*, The Hague: Mouton (includes a brief translated extract from Chicherin's writings on metaphysics).
(1973) (ed. Louis J. Shein) *Readings in Russian Philosophical Thought: Logic and Aesthetics*, The Hague: Mouton (includes brief translated extract *Foundations of Logic and Metaphysics*).

Secondary literature:

Hamburg, G. M. (1992) *Boris Chicherin and Early Russian Liberalism, 1828–1866*, Stanford: Stanford University Press.

Walicki, A. (1987) The Legal Philosopher of Russian Liberalism, Oxford: Clarendon Press.

Born into a wealthy noble family, Chicherin was a noted jurist and historian as well as a philosopher. He was a liberal Westernizer in the 1850s, at the end of which decade he turned decisively against the radical intelligentsia. He resigned his Moscow University Chair in 1868 in protest at a violation of the statutes, and became involved in local liberal politics. He was also made to resign as mayor of Moscow in 1883 after a speech at the coronation of Alexander III commenting favourably on representative government. His liberalism was, however, tempered by a belief in a strong state.

As a philosopher, Chicherin is regarded as the leading Russian exponent of right-wing Hegelianism. Like **Solov'ev**, he translated the absolute into the Christian Trinity, although he was critical in his *Mysticism in Science* (1880) of Solov'ev's mystical conception of total-unity. Chicherin's reworking of Hegel was distinctive, not least his replacement of the triadic dialectic with a tetradic sequence, beginning with an initial unity of universal and particular, followed by analytic or synthetic disintegration into multiplicity, and ending with a higher unity. He also insisted, more consistently with his political liberalism than with Hegel, that, as bearers of the absolute, human individuals were ends in themselves, and not simply organs of historical necessity.

Having swum in the 1860s and 1870s against the positivist tide, Chicherin shared Solov'ev's concern to establish science's proper place in the hierarchy of knowledge leading to the absolute. He rejected the Comtean sequence of religion, metaphysics and science, arguing that science, while necessary for a full understanding of the absolute, was without metaphysics the most superficial kind of knowledge. Late in his life, he devised a theory of the structure of the atom, and opposed Darwinian natural selection with a Hegelian account of the evolution of organisms.

COLIN CHANT

Chisholm, Roderick Milton

American. *b:* 27 November 1916, North Attleborough, Massachusetts. *Cat:* Metaphysician; philosopher of mind. *Ints:* Phenomenology. *Educ:* Studied at Brown University, AB 1938; and Harvard, AM 1940, PhD 1942. *Infls:* Fichte, Reid, Brentano, Meinong, Husserl, Moore, C. I. Lewis, Cardinal Mercier and Ducasse. *Appts:* Taught at University of Pennsylvania, 1946–7; thereafter at Brown University; Andrew W. Mellon Professor of the Humanities, 1972; Visiting Professor at many universities, notably Graz in Austria; Editor of *Philosophy and Phenomenological Research*, 1980.

Main publications:

(1957) *Perceiving*, Ithaca: Cornell University Press.

(1960) (ed.) *Realism and the Background of Phenomenology*, Glencoe, Ill.: Free Press.

(1966) *Theory of Knowledge*, Englewood Cliffs: Prentice-Hall (substantially revised in second (1977) and third (1989) editions).

(1966) (ed., with others, and trans. Franz Brentano) *The True and the Evident*, (English edition (with others) translated by Chisholm).

(1973) (ed. with R. J. Swartz) *Empirical Knowledge: Readings from Contemporary Sources*, Englewood Cliffs, NJ: Prentice-Hall.

(1976) *Person and Object*, London: Allen & Unwin; La Salle: Open Court.

(1976) (ed. with S. Körner) *Philosophische Untersuchungen zu Raum, Zeit und Kontinuum*, Hamburg: F. Meiner.

(1978) (ed. with R. Haller) *Die Philosophie Franz Brentanos*, Amsterdam: Rodopi.

(1981) *The First Person*, Brighton: Harvester and Minneapolis: Minnesota University Press.

(1982) *Brentano and Meinong Studies*, Amsterdam: Rodopi.

(1982) *The Foundations of Knowing*, Brighton: Harvester and Minneapolis: Minnesota University Press.

(1985) (ed. with others) *Philosophie des Geistes, Philosphie der Psychologie: Akten des 9. Internationalen Wittgenstein Symposiums*, Vienna: Hölder-Pichler-Tempsky.

(1986) *Brentano and Intrinsic Value*, Cambridge: Cambridge University Press.

(1989) *On Metaphysics*, Minneapolis: Minnesota University Press.

Secondary literature:

Bogdan, R. J. (ed.) (1986) *Roderick M. Chisholm*, Dordrecht: Reidel (includes intellectual autobiography and full bibliography of his writings to date, partly annotated by himself).

David, M. and Stubenberg, L. (eds) (1986) *Philosophische Aufsätze zur Ehren von Roderick M. Chisholm*, Amsterdam: Rodopi.

Lehrer, K. (ed.) (1975) *Analysis and Metaphysics*, Dordrecht: Reidel.

Philosophia 1978 (special issue).

Sosa, E. (ed.) (1979) *Essays in the Philosophy of Roderick M. Chisholm*, (includes extended reply by Chisholm).

Chisholm stands firmly in the main Anglo-American tradition of analytic philosophy, in a broad sense, but he is unusual in the breadth of the influences that he has brought to bear upon it, ranging from the ancient Greeks (his first published paper, in *Philosophy of Science* for 1941, was on Sextus Empiricus) through Fichte, **Brentano** and **Meinong** to Cardinal **Mercier** and his own teacher C. J. **Ducasse**, as well as the standard sources. His earliest publications include many reviews, on topics covering, as well as central philosophy, symbolic logic, aesthetics, ethics and psychology—his war service was as a clinical psychologist. He has edited and contributed to the translation of works by Fichte, Brentano and Meinong.

Chisholm presents his own work in a direct no-nonsense style, using sets of definitions. These are built up gradually and form the skeleton for the main ideas. Despite this rather formal approach he eschews the technicalities of formal logic in his main works and writes in plain English. Apart from commentaries on writers like Brentano and Meinong his work mainly falls under epistemology, philosophy of mind, metaphysics and ethics.

A key motif throughout Chisholm's philosophy, and one heavily influenced by Brentano and the phenomenologists, is his emphasis on consciousness and on how things appear to one. Among his central concepts is one he develops from Brentano, that of evidence, and one of the central problems he sees for epistemology (one which links him with Sextus Empiricus) is that of the criterion for when we have adequate evidence for something. He distinguishes what is directly evident from what is indirectly evident (*Theory of Knowledge*, 1966), and the problem of the criterion concerns the passage from the indirectly evident to the directly evident. The directly evident is the 'self-presenting' (ibid., p. 28; later he prefers this term: *The Foundations of Knowing*, 1982, p. 26), or what we have when: 'What justifies me in counting it as evident that *a* is *F* is simply the fact that *a* is *F*' (*Theory of Knowledge*, 1966, p. 26). The indirectly evident can then hopefully be reached from this by applying certain epistemic rules or principles (ibid., p. 38). Chapter 3 of *The Foundations of Knowing* uses an elaboration of these ideas to defend a view of knowledge as justified true belief in the face of 'Gettier' counterexamples suggesting that such a belief

may fail to be knowledge because its truth and the basis of its justification for the believer in question are irrelevant to each other (cf. chapter 10 of the third edition (1989) of *Theory of Knowledge*). All this forms part of the foundationalism, in the general tradition of Descartes, to which Chisholm adheres (*Foundations*, chapter 1; cf. Bogdan (ed.) 1986, p. 43). He is an 'internalist' rather than an 'externalist' (cf. *Foundations*, p. 29), claiming that justification must be 'epistemic' and rejecting various other kinds of justification (pp. 27–32). The third edition of *Theory of Knowledge* repeats or develops many of these points.

A further effect of Chisholm's foundationalism is his distinction between 'particularists' and 'methodists' (*Foundations*, p. 66). Particularists, of whom Chisholm is one, start from the question 'What do we know?' and only then go on to the question 'How can we decide whether we know?' Methodists do the reverse, while sceptics claim that neither question can be answered without first answering the other. Empiricism is one type of methodism, and can take two forms, a genetic doctrine about how we actually come by our knowledge, and a doctrine of justification. Chisholm rejects both of these in *Perceiving* (1957), but he shares something with them in that he accepts incorrigible states of mind, as a foundationalist perhaps must. These, however, are not sense-datum statements (he rejects substantial appearances, although he once accepted them: 1957, p. 117), but statements that one is in a certain state of mind, or is being appeared to in a certain way (he does not tell us how he would deal with unconscious beliefs and desires). Later, however, he rejected the view that there are first-person propositions, since this view cannot distinguish '*X* believes *X* is *F*' from '*X* believes he himself is *F*'. Instead he develops a theory of intentional states in terms of direct and indirect attribution, taking the 'he himself' locution as basic (*The First Person*, 1981, chapters 3 and 4; see also Boer's summary in Bogdan (ed.) 1986, p. 87).

Chisholm sees a strong analogy between epistemology and ethics. The first part of *Perceiving* borrows its title from W. K. Clifford: 'The ethics of belief' (cf. also *Theory of Knowledge*, (third edition) 1989, pp. 57–60). Belief, or its withholding, is 'required' of us in certain circumstances, and he is sympathetic to the view that requiredness is the central concept of ethics (e.g. 1986, p. 53). *Brentano and Intrinsic Value* (1986) develops the ethics of Brentano along lines paralleling his own epistemology: we have incorrigible knowledge of our own valuings, and these are prima facie evidence for correct valuings—for emotions, like judgements, can be correct or incorrect. This is then applied to a detailed development of **Moore**'s notion of 'organic unities'. Throughout Chisholm assumes, in Moorean fashion, that 'whatever we are justified in assuming, when we are not doing philosophy, we are also justified in assuming when we *are* doing philosophy' (*Person and Object*, 1976, p. 16).

On the nature and existence of the self Chisholm rejects Hume's 'bundle of perceptions' view. Hume says that in seeking himself he always stumbles on some perception, but bundles don't stumble on their own contents; experiences need a subject just as qualities need a substance. But Kant too goes wrong in saying we can never know the self, since this is like saying we can never know the substance of an object as something distinct from the qualities which give us access to it. We know the self in knowing states of it, i.e. in having experiences (ibid.), although later he rejected the view that we have an individuating concept of ourselves, (1981, pp. 16–17, 86–90; but cf. Sosa (ed.) 1979, pp. 324–5). This same self is the cause of its own actions by 'immanent' as against 'transeunt' causation, a medieval distinction he revives between causation by agents and causation by events. He hopes thus to transcend the determinism–indeterminism impasse, each limb of which seems to make responsibility an illusion. The objection that attributing actions to an agent as cause is empty and tells us nothing beyond the mere sequence of events he dismisses as applying equally to transeunt causation: what does talk of 'causing' add there either? One might wonder, however, if this is fair: believers in transeunt causation need not be mere Humeans, and the question arises how agents manage to decide one way or the other. (Chisholm takes his view further in Bogdan (ed.) 1986: see especially pp. 214–15, 223.)

An important contribution to the philosophy of mind is Chisholm's revival of Brentano's idea of intentionality as a mark of the mental, enabling him to maintain 'the primacy of the intentional' over the semantic (ibid., pp. 222, 231). Chisholm started a debate on the criteria for intentionality, offering three in the *Proceedings of the Aristotelian Society*, 1955–6. Later (in his entry on intentionality in P. Edwards (ed.), *Encyclopedia of Philosophy*, 1967), he added two more, but admitted that together they only provided sufficient conditions and not necessary ones (cf. also Bogdan (ed.) 1987, pp. 36–7, 232.

For all his adherence to Moorean common sense Chisholm is ready to distinguish, with Joseph Butler, 'strict and philosophical' from 'loose and popular' speech, especially when defending mereological essentialism, which he claims is really congenial to common sense (*Person and Object*, 1976, pp. 102–3, Appendix B). The self, however, is a continuant, and is immune to Lockean transfers from one substance to another, but none of this commits us to a doctrine of temporal parts (ibid., Appendix A). Perhaps Chisholm's most lasting influence lies in his revival of the ideas of the earlier Austrian philosophers, especially in the area of intentionality. His foundationalism is perhaps less in tune with modern views, although they would mostly (but not entirely) agree with his rejection of substantial appearances and sense data. His apparatus of direct and indirect evidence, and his epistemic principles, have been criticized as inadequate. The externalism–internalism debate is still in full swing. His views on agent causality have had some influence, and mereological essentialism is a currently debated topic, as are the ontological questions to which he has contributed.

Sources: DAS, 7th edn, 1978; Dancy & Sosa; personal communication.

A. R. LACEY

Chomsky, Avram Noam

American. *b:* 7 December 1928, Philadelphia. *Cat:* Linguist; cognitive scientist; libertarian socialist; philosopher of language; philosopher of mind. *Ints:* Philosophy of language; philosophy of mind. *Educ:* University of Pennsylvania. *Infls:* Zellig Harris, Nelson Goodman and W. V. O. Quine. *Appts:* 1951–5, Junior Fellow, Harvard University; from 1955, Assistant, Associate, then full Professor at the Massachusetts Institute of Technology; Institute Professor in the Department of Linguistics and Philosophy.

Main publications:

(1957) *Syntactic Structures*, The Hague: Mouton.

(1965) *Aspects of the Theory of Syntax*, Cambridge, Mass.: MIT.

(1972) *Language and Mind*, enlarged edition, New York: Harcourt Brace Jovanovich.

(1980) *Rules and Representations*, New York: Columbia University Press.

(1980) 'Rules and representations', with Open Peer Commentary and Author's Response, *Behavioral and Brain Sciences* 3: 1–61.

(1986) *Knowledge of Language: Its Nature, Origin and Use*, New York: Praeger.

(1988) *Language and Problems of Knowledge: The Managua Lectures*, Cambridge: Mass.: MIT Press.
(1993) *Language and Thought*, Wakefield, Rhode Island and London: Moyer Bell.
(1995) 'Language and nature', *Mind* 104: 1–61.

Secondary literature:

George, A. (ed.) (1989) *Reflections on Chomsky*, Oxford: Blackwell.
Harman, G. (ed.) (1974) *On Noam Chomsky: Critical Essays*, New York: Anchor.
Kasher, A. (ed.) (1991) *The Chomskyan Turn*, Oxford: Blackwell.
Koerner, K. and Tajima, M. (1986) *Noam Chomsky: A Personal Bibliography, 1951–1986*, Amsterdam: J. Benjamins.
Salkie, R. (1990) *The Chomsky Update: Linguistics and Politics*, London: Unwin Hyman.
Sgroi, S. C. (1983) *Noam Chomsky: Bibliografia 1949–81*, Padua: CLESP.

Noam Chomsky is both an eminent linguist and a prominent political activist. His creation and constant elaboration of generative grammar has been profoundly influential within linguistics and has contributed significantly to the development of cognitive science. As a libertarian socialist he has trenchantly and tirelessly criticized US foreign policy and sought to correct deception and narrowness of debate within the mainstream media. While Chomsky's politics has philosophical underpinnings and is related very generally to his linguistics, his important philosophical views are located predominantly in the latter.

Chomsky holds that scientific linguistics, his fundamental concern, should focus its attention on questions which can be given clearly formulated and empirically testable answers; further, that there are three basic questions of this type: *What constitutes knowledge of language? How is such knowledge acquired?* and *How is such knowledge put to use?* Since the introduction of generative grammar in *Syntactic Structures* (1957) he has concentrated upon the first two questions.

For Chomsky a rigorous scientific description of the knowledge of language possessed by a mature speaker-listener is possible in the form of a particular generative grammar. In this context such a grammar is a fully explicit formal theory which purports to describe precisely the principles and rules in the mind/brain of a speaker-listener which characterize the grammatical sentences of the speaker-listener's particular language. These principles and rules comprise a grammar. Hence, in a second sense, a grammar is a complex mental

structure. To possess such a structure is to be in a mental state of unconscious knowledge of the principles and rules involved and it is this state which constitutes knowledge of language.

Scientific linguistics, then, is conceived as a part of psychology since its proper object of study is language understood as a psychological structure. This runs wholly counter to the widespread view that the proper object of study is language understood as a public phenomenon and, in fact, Chomsky denies that a clear concept of this alleged object is possible. His account entails a rejection of theories which analyse knowledge of language in terms of use and, more generally, it requires a sharp theoretical distinction between knowledge of language and performance. The latter is made prominently in his distinction between *competence* and *performance*. Reference must be made to performance for certain purposes but it is a theory of competence, that is to say, of tacit knowledge of grammar, which is a viable scientific goal. Major questions can be asked about performance: for example, how are people able to consistently produce utterances appropriate to their changing circumstances? In Chomsky's view, however, these are far beyond the reach of foreseeable scientific investigation.

Granted his account of a speaker-listener's knowledge of his or her language, the second, and for Chomsky the most fundamental, question for scientific linguistics can be asked: how is such knowledge acquired? Chomsky is adamant that all answers which in effect say that knowledge of grammar is learned from experience are mistaken. Crucial to his arguments for this and for his alternative answer is a strong claim, for which he holds there is detailed support, *viz.*, that children acquire principles of language for which there was no evidence in their experience. This phenomenon, often called the poverty of the stimulus, can be explained in only one general way in Chomsky's view: the principles are innate features of the child's mind.

Chomsky offers a more detailed nativist theory. Common to all humans is a genetic language-programme which encodes linguistic principles. It is not the mind/brain as a whole which is thus programmed, rather a distinct subsystem, the language faculty. Prior to a child experiencing language the language faculty is in its *initial state*, which comprise the genetically encoded principles and is called by Chomsky *Universal Grammar*. The language faculty develops until it reaches its *steady state*, the mature speaker-listener's state of knowledge of his or her particular language. In order for this development to take place it is certainly necessary for the child to experience its native language, the experience having such roles as 'triggering' the innate mechanisms and 'shaping' acquisition to the particular language. Nevertheless the contribution of experience is relatively superficial, being severely constrained by the genetically determined principles of Universal Grammar, and the whole process of development is characterized as one of biological growth or maturation rather than learning. Thus, for Chomsky, a proper answer to the second question involves a precise specification of the principles of Universal Grammar and a rigorous account of how these interact with experience so as to yield knowledge of a particular language.

A recent revision in his views is pertinent to such an answer. Chomsky has always been concerned to reduce the number of principles and rules postulated by generative grammar. Transformational rules have this effect and were prominent in his earlier work, but his revised theory suggests that only one highly abstract transformational principle is required. Indeed he now proposes that a very small number of highly abstract simple principles which interact can explain language acquisition. Crucial to this is relaxing the notion of a principle of Universal Grammar so that rather than being a rigid rule it permits a narrow range of options, called parameters, with different languages taking different options. As a child acquires a language it effectively fixes a particular parameter on the basis of a small amount of positive evidence in its linguistic experience. Since each principle applies to every sentence as a licenser and since the principles interact, each instance of fixing a parameter can have widespread grammatical effects. It is therefore possible that rules in the traditional sense do not exist. Since Chomsky's views are both influential and controversial they have been subject to a large number of criticisms, many by philosophers. These include arguments that the theory of an innate grammar is biologically implausible (**Piaget**), that the notion of an internal grammar is threatened by indeterminacy of translation (**Quine**), that the idea that general learning procedures are not involved in language acquisition is implausible (**Putnam**), that language is properly conceived as a social phenomenon (**Dummett**) and that innate knowledge is conceptually impossible. Chomsky has responded to these and other criticisms, often at length—a practice which has enabled him to elaborate his position. For Chomsky philosophy is continuous with science, a view that he holds to be exemplified

in the work of such writers as Descartes and Leibniz in whose rationalist tradition he locates himself.

STEPHEN MILLS

Church, Alonzo

American. *b:* 14 June 1903, Washington, DC. *Cat:* Mathematical logician. *Ints:* Logic; philosophy of language. *Educ:* 1924, Princeton University; BA, PhD 1927, Princeton University. *Infls:* Gottlob Frege and Kurt Gödel. *Appts:* 1929–67, Assistant, then Associate, then full Professor, Princeton University; 1967–90, Professor of Philosophy and Mathematics, UCLA.

Main publications:

(1936) 'A note on the *Entscheidungsproblem*', *Journal of Symbolic Logic*', 1: 40–1 (with corrections, pp. 101–2).

(1936) 'An unsolvable problem of elementary number theory', *American Journal of Mathematics* 58: 345–63.

(1940) 'A formulation of the simple theory of types', *Journal of Symbolic Logic* 5: 56–68.

(1940) 'On the concept of a random sequence', *American Mathematical Society Bulletin*, Series 2, 46: 130–5.

(1941) *The Calculus of Lambda-Conversion*, Princeton: Princeton University Press.

(1950) 'On Carnap's analysis of statements of assertion and belief', *Analysis* 10: 97–9.

(1951) 'The need for abstract entities in semantic analysis', *Proceedings of the American Academy of Arts and Sciences* 80: 100–12.

(1956) *Introduction to Mathematical Logic, Volume 1*, Princeton: Princeton University Press.

Secondary literature:

Davidson, D. (1984) *Inquiries into Truth and Interpretation*, Oxford: Clarendon Press.

Kaplan, D. (1975) 'How to Russell a Frege–Church', *Journal of Philosophy* 72: 716–29.

Mendelson, E. (1987) *Introduction to Mathematical Logic*, third edition, Pacific Grove, Cal.: Wadsworth & Brooks/Cole (a thorough treatment of his work on logic).

Alonzo Church was a central figure in the development of mathematical logic. He was the first to prove the undecidability of first-order logic: that is, that there is no mechanical procedure for deciding whether an arbitrary sentence in first-order logic is a theorem or not. This result is known as Church's Theorem. Church also formulated a statement which, while not capable of formal demonstration, is widely accepted. This is Church's Thesis, which asserts that a number theoretic function is effectively computable if and only if that function is recursive. He thus reduced the informal concept of effective computability to the precisely defined concept of recursiveness. Church's Thesis leads to the important result that there is no effective method for deciding the truth or falsity of an arbitrary sentence in elementary number theory.

Church has also argued in favour of an ontology of abstract objects in any adequate account of language and propositional attitudes. He made an important contribution to the foundations of probability via his refinement of von **Mises**'s theory of random sequences. Church's contributions to logic can be found in any serious textbook; and his own, partially completed, text is itself a classic, despite its cumbersome notation. He was for many years the Editor of *The Journal of Symbolic Logic* and contributed a vast array of review articles to that journal, many of considerable interest in their own right.

PAUL HUMPHREYS

Churchland, Patricia Smith

American. **b:** 1943, Oliver, British Columbia, Canada. **Cat:** Analytic philosopher. **Ints:** Philosophy of mind; philosophy of science; philosophy of neuroscience. **Educ:** BA, University of British Columbia, 1961–5; MA, University of Pittsburgh, 1965–6, BPhil; Oxford University, 1966–9. **Appts:** 1969–77, Assistant Professor, University of Manitoba, then Associate Professor, 1977–82, and Professor, 1983–4; Member of Institute for Advanced Study, Princeton, 1982–3; Professor, University of California, San Diego, from 1984.

Main publications:

(1980) 'A perspective on mind-brain research', *The Journal of Philosophy* 77.

(1986) *Neurophilosophy*, Cambridge, Mass.: MIT Press.

(1988) 'The significance of neuroscience for philosophy', *Trends in Neurosciences* 11.

(1990) 'Is neuroscience relevant to philosophy?', in D. Copp, (ed.) *Canadian Philosophers*, University of Toronto Press.

(1992) (with Terence J. Sejnowski) *The Computational Brain*, Cambridge, Mass.: MIT Press.

(1992) (with Y. Christen) *Neurophilosophy and Alzheimer's Disease*, Spinger-Verlag.

(1993) 'Filling in: why Dennett is wrong', in Bo Dahlbohm and V. S. Ramachandran (eds), *Dennett*

and His Critics, Blackwells; reprinted in S. Davis and K. Akins (eds), *Vancouver Studies in Cognitive Science*, Oxford: Oxford University Press.

Secondary literature:

Akins, Kathleen A. (1990) Critical Notice of *Neurophilosophy* (1986), in *Journal of Philosophy* 87, 2: 93–102.

Hooker, C. A. (1988) Critical Notice of *Neurophilosophy* (1986), in *Australasian Journal of Philosophy* 66: 240–8.

From her earliest writings Churchland has shown a twofold interest in the philosophy of mind and in empirical studies of the brain. These have been essentially complementary concerns, each fertilizing the other. Philosophically, she has become (with Paul **Churchland**) a leading exponent of eliminative materialism, rejecting the view that commonsense talk about the mind provides a more or less reliable guide to its real workings. Such talk, she implies, can survive a scientific understanding of the workings of the brain only in the way in which those who know about the rotation of the earth may still speak of the sun's rising and setting. Her *Neurophilosophy* (1986), revealingly subtitled *Towards a Unified Science of the Mind/Brain*, was intended to build bridges between the philosophical and empirical study of the mind/brain, devoting roughly equal attention to each. But in her later work (see, for example, *The Computational Brain*, 1992) she has moved very much in the empirical direction, and is now probably the philosopher best informed about the detailed workings of the brain.

NICHOLAS EVERITT

Churchland, Paul Montgomery

Canadian. **b:** 1942, Vancouver. **Cat:** Analytic philosopher. **Ints:** Philosophy of mind; philosophy of science; epistemology; philosophy of neuroscience. **Educ:** 1960–4, BA in Philosophy, Physics and Mathematics, University of British Columbia; 1964–7, PhD in Philosophy of Mind/of Science, University of Pittsburgh. **Appts:** Instructor, University of Pittsburgh, 1966; Lecturer, University of Toronto, 1967–9; Assistant Professor, University of Manitoba, 1969–74, Associate Professor, 1974–9, Professor, 1979–84; Member of Institute for Advanced Study, Princeton, NJ, 1982–3; Professor, University of California, San Diego, from 1984.

Main publications:

(1979) *Scientific Realism and The Plasticity of Mind*, Cambridge: Cambridge University Press.

(1984) *Matter and Consciousness*, Cambridge, Mass.: MIT Press; second edition, 1988.

(1985) (ed. with C. A. Hooker) *Images of Science: Scientific Realism versus Constructive Empricism*, Chicago: University of Chicago Press.

(1989) *A Neurocomputational Perspective: The Nature of Mind and the Structure of Science*, Cambridge, Mass.: MIT Press.

(1994) *The Computer That Could: A Neurophilosophical Portrait*, Cambridge, Mass.: MIT Press.

Secondary literature:

Gunderson, Keith (1986) Review of *Matter and Consciousness* (1984), *Philosophy of Science* 53: 145–8.

Sharpe, M. (1991) 'Minds made up', Critical Notice of *A Neurocomputational Perspective* (1989), *Inquiry* 34: 91–106.

Churchland is a leading proponent of so-called eliminative materialism in the philosophy of mind. In contrast to a reductive materialism which claims that mental processes are in some way *identical with* physical (e.g. brain) processes, eliminative materialism claims that mental processes as traditionally conceived do not exist. Churchland defends this thesis by arguing that the network of concepts and principles which common sense relies on in explaining mental processes and behaviour is a *scientific* theory, albeit of a primitive kind. But this network (sometimes called folk psychology) is in fact a *poor* scientific theory when judged by the normal scientific requirements of predictive and explanatory success. In place of folk psychology Churchland proposes a theory (or set of interlocking theories) based on a fusion of neuroscience and artificial intelligence. This naturally requires a fairly detailed consideration of the findings of these disciplines, and Paul Churchland's work here is smoothly complemented by that of his wife Patricia, whose work tends to have a greater empirical emphasis than his. Critics have objected to a number of aspects of this general programme. Some have argued that folk psychology is not a scientific theory at all, or, that if it is one, it is not a bad one (**Wilkes**, Sterelny, McGinn). Other critics have objected that Churchland's version of materialism is unble to provide any convincing account either of the intentional states (believing that, desiring that, etc.) or of mental states with a qualitative 'feel' to them.

NICHOLAS EVERITT

Chwistek, L(eon)

Polish. *b:* 13 June 1884, Zakopane, Poland. *d:* 20 August 1944, Moscow. *Cat:* Logician; analytical philosopher; aesthetician; painter. *Educ:* Jagiellonian University and Academy of Fine Arts, Cracow. *Infls:* S. Pawlicki, W. Heinrich, H. Poincaré and B. Russell. *Appts:* 1930–9, Professor of Logic, John Casimir University, Lvov.

Main publications:

(1924–6) 'The theory of constructive types', *Rocznik Polskiego Towarzystwa Matematycznego* 2: 9–48; 3: 92–141.

(1935) *The Limits of Science*, London: Routledge & Kegan Paul, 1948.

(1938) (with W. Hetper) 'New foundation of formal metamathematics', *The Journal of Symbolic Logic* 3, 1: 1–36.

(1939) 'A formal proof of Gödel's theorem', *The Journal of Symbolic Logic*, 4, 2: 61–8.

(1967) 'Antinomies of formal logic', in Z. Jordan (ed.), *Polish Logic, 1920–1939*, Oxford: Oxford University Press.

Secondary literature:

Estreicher, K. (1971) 'Bibliografia pism L. Chwistka', in *L. Chwistek. Biografia artysty*, Cracow: PWN, pp. 369–80.

Jadacki, J. J. (1984) 'On L. Chwistek's semiotic views', in J. Pelc *et al.* (eds) *Sign, System and Function*, Berlin: Mouton.

Pasenkiewicz, K. (1964) 'L. Chwistek's theory of manifold reality', *Studia Filozoficzne (Selected Articles)* 2: 167–84.

In logic Chwistek proposed a certain simplification of the Russellian theory of types; he also elaborated his own version of the pure theory of types. He made a suggestion of bracketless logical notation (next developed by J. **Łukasiewicz**). He introduced the precision notion of semantics. Using the method of explication by formalization (the so-called *constructive method*) he created an axiomatic system of elementary semantics (the notion of containment of one expression in another being primitive). He also made an exact rendering of rules of definition. In the field of the foundations of mathematics he was the creator of the so-called rational metamathematics. In semiotics he described the peculiarities of natural languages: their indefiniteness, ambiguity and self-contradiction.

His epistemology was founded on broad empiricism and realism. In ontology, his conception of plurality of realities (including natural, physical, phenomenalistic and visional) influenced the further discussion on the idea of possible worlds. In the philosophy of mathematics he was a defender of nominalism.

Sources: J. J. Jadacki, (1986) 'L. Chwistek–B. Russell: scientific correspondence', *DH* 13, 1: 239–63.

JACEK JULIUS JADACKI

Cioran, Emile Michel

Romanian. *b:* 8 April 1911, Rasinari (Carpathia). *d:* 20 June 1995, Paris. *Cat:* Existentialist; ideal moralist. *Educ:* University of Bucharest (thesis on Bergson, 1932); moved to France 1937. *Infls:* Kierkegaard, Lichtenberg, Nietzsche and Wittgenstein.

Main publications:

(1934) *Pe culmile disperarii* [On the Summits of Despair].
(1937) *Lacrimi si sfinti* [Tears of the Saints].
(1949) *Précis de décomposition*, Paris: Éditions Gallimard.
(1952) *Syllogismes de l'Amertume*, Paris: Éditions Gallimard.
(1956) *La Tentation d'exister*, Paris: Éditions Gallimard (English translation, *The Temptation to Exist*, trans. R. Howard, London: Quartet, 1987).
(1957) *Joseph de Maistre*, Paris: Éditions Gallimard.
(1964) *La chute dans le temps*, Paris: Gallimard.
(1969) *Le mauvais demiurge*, Paris: Gallimard.
(1973) *De l'inconvenient d'être né*, Paris: Gallimard.
(1979) *Ecartèlement*, Paris: Gallimard.
(1991) *Le crépuscule des pensées*, Paris: Gallimard.
(1993) *Brévaire des vaincus*, Paris: Gallimard.

Secondary literature:

Jaudeau, F. (1990) *Cioran, ou, le dernier homme*, Paris: Corti.
Savater, F. (1992) *Ensayo sobre Cioran*, Madrid: Espasa Calpe.
Sontag, S. (1968) 'Thinking against oneself: reflections on Cioran'; reprinted in Cioran, *The Temptation to Exist*, trans. R. Howard, London: Quartet, 1987.
Tanner, M. (1990) 'Introduction' to *A Short History of Decay*, trans. R. Howard, London: Quartet.
Tiffreau, P. (1991) *Cioran, ou, La dissection du gouffre*, Paris: Veyrier.

Cioran was a self-styled 'analyst of decadence', whose style of writing Tanner describes as that of 'aphorism and rant'. Having never been a 'professional' philosopher, Cioran's first recognised work, *Précis de décomposition* (1949), is a curious mix of the existential and the Nietzschean barbaric, a tirade, in the ideal moralist tradition,

against living life and in favour of describing it. He describes existence as a temptation, a theme he later returns to in greater depth, but one which he chooses not to fall victim to until he has seen what it is like not to live. Dedicating many pages to the necessity of suicide, the cross-currential influence of **Camus** is seen most clearly. This 'decadence', in *La Tentation d'exister* (1956), turns its attention to Western Thought Consolidated. The temptation to exist is seen as no more than the temporary attainment of relevance in a temporal flux, but a relevance carrying within it its own obsolescence, Western thought being a species of monad, relentlessly developing 'ought' from 'is' in an ahistorical, abstracted narrative which, come Hegel, who presented philosophy as the *history* of philosophy, had usurped 'nature' as the prime framework of human experience. Cioran's own writing mirrors the only available recourse, what Sontag describes as 'mutilated, incomplete discourse'. But *The Temptation to Exist* is more a 'mutilated discourse' on thought, and on discourse, itself. Abstraction *in extremis*, he holds that, in order to escape from the mortal ennui created by thought, we have to push that thought to its limit-points, to make ourselves sick with thought in order to find the cure. This cure is to be found in liberation from action, the only authentic mode of human freedom. Cioran's writings, described by himself as 'abstract biography', have found greater resonance in literature than in philosophy—Beckett's later novels and Sontag's essays are just two examples—although Spanish philosophers have 'championed' his work as contributing to the debate over the health of the national intellectual, the moral philosopher Fernando Savater helping to 'publicize' his work, and the style of Eugenio Trías benefiting much from a reading of Cioran.

DAVID SPOONER

Code, Lorraine

Canadian. *b:* 19 October 1937, Calgary. *Cat:* Epistemologist; feminist theorist; philosopher of language. *Educ:* Queen's University, Ontario, 1954–8; University of Guelph, 1973–8. *Appts:* 1987–, Canada Research Fellow, Associate Professor, then full Professor, York University, Ontario.

Main publications:

(1987) *Epistemic Responsibility*, Hanover, NH and London: University Press of New England.

(1988) (ed. with S. Mullett and C. Overall) *Feminist Perspectives: Philosophical Essays on Method and Morals*, Toronto: University of Toronto Press.

(1988) (ed. with S. Burt and L. Dorney) *Changing Patterns: Women in Canada*, Toronto: McClelland & Stewart.

(1991) *What Can She Know? Feminist Theory and the Construction of Knowledge*, Ithaca, NY and London: Cornell University Press.

(forthcoming) *Rhetorical Spaces: Essays on (Gendered) Locations*, New York: Routledge.

Code is centrally concerned with developing a 'responsibilist epistemology' that conceives of the knower as a particular individual situated in an epistemic community rather than the abstracted knower typical of traditional theories of knowledge. Her revised conception makes the character of the knowing subject integral to epistemic justification.

Although Code's position departs from foundationalism and coherentism, she wishes not to replace standard epistemological analysis, but to broaden its scope to include questions about the intellectual virtue of the knower. The justification of beliefs thus importantly involves an assessment of the cognitive activity of the knower, the relevant considerations being practical wisdom, trust, credibility and reliability.

Code argues that the construction of knowledge is grounded in 'second-person knowing', where interpersonal relationships, friendship, trust, feeling and subjectivity are valued alongside reason, facts and objectivity. As an alternative to the traditional epistemological paradigm of the autonomous reasoner (which she believes has contributed to the oppression of women), Code suggests an ecological model of knowing that recognizes human beings as interdependent, and enables the development of a strategy for a liberating, mutual empowerment through knowledge.

Sources: Personal communication.

EMILY BRADY

Coffey, Peter

Irish. *b:* 9 April 1876, Rathrone, Ireland. *d:* 7 January 1943, Maynooth, Ireland. *Cat:* Neoscholastic. *Ints:* Logic; epistemology; ontology. *Educ:* St Patrick's College, Maynooth, and University of Louvain. *Infls:* Aquinas, Mercier and De Wulf. *Appts:* 1902–43, Professor of Logic and Metaphysics, St Patrick's College, Maynooth.

Main publications:
(1912) *The Science of Logic*, 2 vols, London: Longmans, Green & Co.

(1914) *Ontology*, London: Longmans, Green & Co.

(1917) *Epistemology*, 2 vols, London: Longmans, Green & Co.

Secondary literature:
Macquarrie, John (1963) *Twentieth-Century Religious Thought*, London: SCM Press, pp. 282–3.

Although Coffey was a minor figure in the history of twentieth-century philosophy, he was much read in his day and probably influenced more readers than some of his more important contemporaries. He was one of the first to disseminate Louvain's scholasticism in the English-speaking world, partly through his translations of **De Wulf**, and partly through the excellent textbooks, listed above, which were read and relied upon by generations of students. He was not innovative or controversial, but he was a clear and erudite exponent of the revitalized scholasticism from which later and greater thinkers were to emerge. His steadfast orthodoxy can sometimes disappoint: his *Ontology* (1914) is rather wooden, although the chapter on essence and existence displays considerable subtlety. His heart probably lay in some of the areas covered in his *Epistemology* (1917). The chapters on Kant (an interest which may have been stimulated by **Mercier**) are lucid and vigorous. His works were at one time well regarded as textbooks, but are not read now.
Sources: WWW.

HUGH BREDIN

Cohen, Gerald Alan

Canadian-British. *b:* 1941, Montreal. *Cat:* Analytical Marxist. *Educ:* BA, McGill University, 1961; BPhil, University of Oxford, 1963. *Infls:* Marx. *Appts:* 1963–78, Lecturer, and 1978–84, Reader, University College, London; from 1985, Chichele Professor of Social and Political Theory, and Fellow of All Souls, Oxford.

Main publications:
(1978) *Karl Marx's Theory of History: A Defence*, Oxford: Clarendon Press.

(1988) *History, Labour and Freedom*, Oxford: Clarendon Press.

(forthcoming) *Self-Ownership, World-Ownership and Equality*, Cambridge: Cambridge University Press.

Secondary literature:
Elster, Jon (1980) 'Cohen on Marx's theory of history', *Political Studies* 28.
Holmstrom, N. (1983) 'Marx and Cohen on exploitation and the labour theory of value', *Inquiry* 26.
Miller, R. (1981) 'Productive forces and the forces of change', critical notice of *Karl Marx's Theory of History* (1978), *Philosophical Review* 90: 91–117.

Cohen is a co-founder and leading member of a style of Marxist theorizing which has come to be known as analytical Marxism. One of its characteristics is that it carries the concerns of traditional analytic philosophy (with clarity, with precise and explicit formulations of positions, with detailed argumentation, with very close attention to textual detail, etc.) into the domain of Marxist theory. This combination of traditions is well illustrated in Cohen's first book, *Karl Marx's Theory of History* (1978), which won Cohen the Isaac Deutscher Memorial Prize, and was described by John Roemer as 'arguably the most rigorous work of Marxist scholarship this century'. Taking as his guiding thread a page-long extract from Marx's 1859 Preface (to *A Contribution to a Critique of Political Economy*), Cohen subjects it to a line-by-line analysis to show how Marx's own words contradict some of the views attributed to him, and how he is really expounding a technological version of historical materialism. Cohen then takes a number of Marxist theses and shows how in those cases in which they are not already precise in themselves, they can be rendered precise by plausible additions of detail to Marx's own words. Most famously in this connection, he takes the vague claim that the productive forces determine (in some sense of the word) the productive relations, and gives it a functional interpretation that is both sophisticated and able to meet standard objections. The thought is (briefly) that the explanation for the prevalence of a set of productive relations lies in the capacity of that set of relations to produce the optimum utilization of prevailing productive forces.

This 'analytical' approach to Marxism runs through Cohen's second book (1988), a collection of essays partly refining the claims of *Karl Marx's Theory of History*, and partly carrying the approach into new areas. The later essays are also interesting in that they display a less rigid adherence to the details of Marx's own position than does his earlier work. Cohen's interpretation of Marxism has aroused much interest. Some critics, such as Elster, have insisted that Cohen's

functional explanations are necessarily incomplete, and must be supplemented by microstructural explanations specifying the goals of individual rational agents. Others, such as Miller, have argued that Cohen's conception of a productive force is too narrow, that he thereby misconstrues what historical materialism is, and hence gives a misleading view of Marx's practice as a scientific historian.
Sources: WW.

NICHOLAS EVERITT

Cohen, Hermann
German Jew. *b:* 4 July 1842, Coswig, Anhalt, Germany. *d:* 4 April 1918, Berlin. *Cat:* Neo-Kantian. *Ints:* Kant and Jewish ethics. *Educ:* Studied Rabbinics, and then Philosophy, at Breslaw Jewish Theological Seminary and Berlin University; PhD, Halle, 1865. *Infls:* Kant. *Appts:* First Jewish Lecturer, then Professor, of Philosophy, Marburg, 1873–6; then (with renewed interest in Judaism, due to experience of anti-semitism) Lecturer at Hochschule für die Wissenschaft des Judentums [High School for the Science of Judaism].

Main publications:
(1925) *Kants Theorie der Erfahrung* [Kant's Theory of Empiricism], fourth reprint, Berlin: B. Cassirer (PhD thesis of 1871).
(1902) *Logik der Reinen Erkenntnis* [The Logic of Pure Cognition], Berlin: B. Cassirer; new editions 1914 and 1922.
(1904) *Die Ethik des Reinen Willens* [The Ethic of Pure Will], Berlin: B. Cassirer; new editions, 1907, 1920 and 1921.
(1915) *Der Begriff der Religion im System der Philosophie* [The Concept of Religion in the Philosophical System], Giessen: A. Töpelmann.
(1918) *Die Religion der Vernunft aus den Quellen des Judentums* [The Religion of Reason Taken From Jewish Sources], (English translation, *Religion of Reason*, trans. S. Kaplan, New York: Ungar, 1972).
(1924) *Jüdische Schriften* (collected writings); 3 vols, pref. F. Rosenzweig, New York: Arno, 1980.
(1928) *Schriften zur Philosophie und Zeitgeschichte* [Writings on Philosophy and Contemporary History], Berlin: Adkademie-Verlag, (eulogy by E. Cassirer).

Secondary literature:
Bergman, Samuel H. (1961) *Faith and Reason: An Introduction to Modern Jewish Thought*, trans. A. Jospé, New York: Schocken.

Cohen, A. A. (1979) *The Natural and Supernatural Jew*, New York: Berman House.

Guttmann, Julius (1964) *Philosophies of Judaism*, trans. D. Silverman, London: Routledge & Kegan Paul.

Horwitz, Rivkah (1989) 'Revelation and the Bible according to twentieth-century Jewish philosophy', in A. Green (ed.) *Jewish Spirituality II*, New York: Crossroad, pp. 346–70

Köhnke, K. C. (1992) *The Rise of Neo-Kantianism: German Academic Philosophy between Idealism and Positivism*, New York: Cambridge University Press.

Melber, J. (1968) *Hermann Cohen's Philosophy of Judaism*, New York: J. David.

Proceedings of the Hermann Cohen Exhibition (1992) University of Marburg.

Rotenstreich, Nathan (1968) *Jewish Philosophy in Modern Times: From Mendelssohn to Rosenzweig*, New York: Holt, Rinehart & Winston; based on *Jewish Thought in Modern Times* (Hebrew), Tel Aviv: Am Oved, 1945–60.

Strauss, B. and B. (eds) (1939) *Briefe* (Cohen's letters), Berlin: Schocken.

During the first part of his life, Cohen dealt with Kantian ethics and reason, founding the Marburg School of neo-Kantianism. His experience of anti-semitism and his meeting with Polish Jews who were barred from the university system revolutionized his thought, which turned to questions of religion. He advocated a complete integration of Jews into German society and repudiated Zionism. He defined Judaism as ethical monotheism, based on the biblical prophets. He has been criticized for repudiating Jewish nationalism and ritual practice, and ignoring the non-rational side of religion, but this was typical of many thinkers of his day, who tended to regard Germany as the 'new Jerusalem' for Jews! Nevertheless his influence has been considerable, not only on non-Orthodox philosophers such as Max Wiener, Leo Baeck and Franz **Rosenzweig**, but also on the doyen of new American Orthodoxy, J. D. **Soloveitchik**. His work has been compared to **Natorp**'s and contrasted with Hegel's. He has been translated into and commented on in French and Spanish.

Sources: EncJud; NUC; Schoeps.

IRENE LANCASTER

Cohen, Morris Raphael

American. *b:* 25 July 1880, Minsk, Russia. *d:* 29 January 1947, Washington, DC. *Cat:* Philosopher of law; philosopher of science; logician. *Ints:*

Philosophy of mathematics; metaphysics; philosophy of history and of civilization; social ethics; American philosophy. *Educ:* College of the City of New York (CCNY), BS 1900; attended seminars at Columbia University; Harvard University, 1904–6, PhD 1906. *Infls:* Personal influences include Thomas Davidson, Felix Adler, W. H. Sheldon, F. J. E. Woodbridge, James, Royce, Münsterberg, Felix Frankfurter, Dewey, Justice O. W. Holmes and Einstein; literary influences include Aristotle, Spinoza, Hegel, Marx, Bradley, Peirce, Russell, Whitehead and Russell, Alfred Marshall, Franz Boas, Santayana and Roscoe Pound. *Appts:* Teacher at public schools, New York City, 1901–2; Instructor in Mathematics, CCNY, 1902–4, 1906–12; Lecturer in Philosophy, Columbia, 1906–7, 1914–15; Professor of Philosophy, CCNY, 1912–38, Professor Emeritus from 1938; Professor of Philosophy, University of Chicago, 1938–41.

Main publications:

(1931) *Reason and Nature: An Essay on the Meaning of Scientific Method*, New York: Harcourt, Brace & Co.

(1933) *Law and the Social Order: Essays in Legal Philosophy*, New York: Harcourt, Brace.

(1934) (with Ernest Nagel) *An Introduction to Logic and Scientific Method*, New York: Harcourt, Brace.

(1944) *A Preface to Logic*, New York: Henry Holt & Co.

(1946) *The Faith of a Liberal*, New York: Holt.

(1947) *The Meaning of Human History*, La Salle, Ill.: Open Court.

(1949) *A Dreamer's Journey*, Boston and Glencoe, Ill.: The Beacon Press and The Free Press (autobiography, contains bibliography).

(1949) *Studies in Philosophy and Science*, New York: Holt.

(1950) *Reason and Law: Studies in Juristic Philosophy*, Glencoe, Ill.: The Free Press.

(1954) *American Thought: A Critical Sketch*, Glencoe, Ill.: The Free Press.

Secondary literature:

(1968) *International Encyclopedia of the Social Sciences*, New York: The Macmillan Company and the Free Press, (contains references to some other discussions of Cohen).

Cohen Rosenfield, Leonora (1962) *Portrait of a Philosopher: Morris R. Cohen in Life and Letters*, New York: Harcourt, Brace & World (valuable in containing the Holmes–Cohen correspondence along with the Cohen–Einstein and Cohen–Laski correspondence).

Israel Law Review, (1981) 16, 3, July (devoted to a symposium on 'The philosophy of Morris R. Cohen').

Kuhn, Martin A. (1957) *Morris R. Cohen: A Bibliography*, New York: City College Library (more complete than 1949 and lists some writings about Cohen).

Singer, Marcus G. (1985) 'Two American philosophers: Morris Cohen and Arthur Murphy', in M. G. Singer (ed.), *American Philosophy*, Cambridge: Cambridge University Press, pp. 295–329, esp. pp. 298–309 (contains references to later discussions of Cohen and, on pp. 327–9, a critique of David R. Hollinger, *Morris R. Cohen and the Scientific Ideal*, Cambridge and London: MIT Press, 1975).

It was Morris Cohen's early but unrealized ambition to produce a philosophical encyclopedia on the model of D'Alembert and Diderot. He had extensive and deep knowledge of the sciences, mathematics, law, history of law ... and of science, culture, political theory and intellectual history. He was unable to bring many of his publishing ventures to completion. None the less he wrote in an extraordinary range of fields, in a style that was limpid, engaging and witty if not always very precise, although it sometimes cut like a rapier, and he was also known as an extraordinarily gifted teacher who challenged and inspired generations of students.

Cohen held that the laws of logic are not conventions or merely syntactical rules, but have their basis in the nature of things and constitute the basic laws of being. Cohen conceived of logic as 'an indispensable instrument for the exploration of yet unrealized possibilities' and 'an indispensable element of liberal civilization and free thought'. He argued that abstractions and relations are real, rejected nominalism as a form of irrationalism, and argued that such abstractions as numbers and logical relations exist, though not in space and time. This led him to distinguish different realms and types of existence. His view that science embodies logic, that it provides us with knowledge of the world, and that abstractions are real he called 'realistic rationalism'. He rejected 'a priori rationalism', emphasized that scientific theories must be tested against the facts of observation, that the results of scientific inquiry are fallible and corrigible through further inquiry, and that our knowledge in science, law, and ethics develops through constructive interaction between abstract principle and concrete facts or judgements. Although he emphasized the importance of deductive elaboration in scientific inquiry and in explaining the laws of nature, he maintained that any ultimate premise from which the laws of nature could be derived would be in the end contingent. His philosophical method emphasized 'the principle of polarity': the principle that opposite qualities, such as unity and plurality, necessarily involve each other though they remain distinct. 'No one of these conceptions can exist or have meaning without the other, just as the opposite blades of a scissors or the north and south poles of a magnet cannot function except in pairs, united in opposition. The nature of things depends upon the equilibrium of opposing forces, and ... the way to get at the nature of things is to reason from opposing considerations.'

Cohen was thus led to consider the arguments underlying all sides of standing philosophical disputes to determine the element of truth contained in each. He applied this method in philosophy of law (he was the first American philosopher to pursue 'jurisprudence as a philosophical discipline'), in philosophy of science and in other 'philosophy of' areas, a number of which he pioneered in developing. Perhaps his greatest shortcoming was his tendency to tie his discussions too much to intramural and essentially ephemeral disputes, rather than attempting to work out problems in their own right. This is the source of the feeling so many commentators have expressed that they can find no positive Cohenian philosophy. But the Cohenian practice of engaging in discussion and critique is what generated the dialectic called for by the principle of polarity.

Sources: Edwards; Urmson; Ernest Nagel (1948) obituary, *PR* 57, 4: 373–4; WWW(Am) 1943–50; WAB 1979, p. 212; Harry N. Rosenfield; Profs Abraham Edel and A. R. Turquette.

MARCUS SINGER

Cohn, Jonas

German. *b:* 2 December 1869, Görlitz, Germany. *d:* 12 January 1947, Birmingham. *Cat:* Neo-Kantian; metaphysician; ethical philosopher. *Ints:* Educational theory; value theory. *Educ:* Leipzig, Berlin and Heidelberg received doctorate in Systematic Botany in 1892, but switched to Philosophy and Pedagogy at Freiburg. *Infls:* Wilhelm Windelband and Heinrich Rickert. *Appts:* Professor, Freiburg, 1901–33; emigrated to England in 1933.

Main publications:

(1901) *Allgemeine Ästhetik*, Leipzig: Engelmann.

(1908) *Voraussetzungen und Ziele des Erkennens*, Leipzig: Engelmann.

(1923) *Theorie der Dialektik*, Leipzig: Meiner.
(1932) *Wertwissenschaft*, Stuttgart: Frommann.
(1955) *Wirklichkeit als Aufgabe*, ed. J. V. Kempski,
Stuttgart: Kohlhammer.

Secondary literature:
Marck, S. (1949) 'Am Ausgang des jüngeren Neukantianismus', *Archiv für Philosophie* 3: 144–64.

Cohn's philosophy consists largely in a critique of
a mechanistic conception of nature. He argued for
an independent foundation of such axiological
disciplines as ethics, aesthetics, and pedagogy. He
is regarded as a member of the 'Heidelberg' (also
'Baden' or 'Southwest German') school of Neo-
Kantianism. Like the others, he also is interested
in providing a theory of culture. He argued, in
agreement with Kant, that an object cannot be
comprehended in isolation from its cognition.
Rejecting both naturalism and non-naturalism he
advocated a theory of dialectic which utilized the
overcoming of contradictions as a way of
approaching absolute knowledge. However, his
thought should not be understood as advocating a
philosophy of the absolute so much as a philosophy on the way to the absolute. In his ethics,
aesthetics and pedagogy Cohn opposed Kant's
'formalism', advocating a form of material value
theory. His pedagogical theory is deeply influenced by Schleiermacher. He argued that the goal
of education should be to transform the child into
an autonomous member of the culture he/she
belongs to.

MANFRED KUEHN

Coimbra, Leonardo José
Portugese. *b:* December 1883, Lixa. *d:* January
1936, Serra di Baltar. *Cat:* 'Creationist'. *Ints:*
Metaphysics. *Educ:* University of Lisbon. *Infls:*
Leibniz, Hegel, Bergson and the philosopher-poet
Antero de Quental (1842–91). *Appts:* Professor of
Philosophy, University of Oporto; the most
important Portuguese thinker of his time.

Main publications:
See his *Obras Completas*, 14 vols, Oporto: Livraria
Tavares Martins, 1956–62.
(1912) *O Criacionismo.*
(1913) *A Morte.*
(1914) *O Pensamento Criacionista.*
(1916) *A Alegria, a Dor e a Graça.*
(1918) *A Luta Pela Imortalidade.*
(1920) *Do Amor e da Morte.*
(1922) *O Pensamento Filosófico de Antero de
Quental.*

(1923) *A Razão Experimental.*
(1923) *Jesus.*
(1935) *A Rússia de Hoje e o Homem de Sempre.*

Secondary literature:
Marinho, J. (1945) *O pensamento filosofico de
Leonardo Coimbra*, Oporto: Livraria Figueirinhas.

Although usually categorized as a 'creationist',
this term applies accurately only to the first phase
of Coimbra's thought, set out in 1912, 1913 and
the simpler exposition of 1914. The key work of
this phase is the first, in which Coimbra sets out a
metaphysic with extensive debts to Leibniz and
Hegel, exhibiting, not unexpectedly, strong elements of rationalism. Reality is monadic, manifesting itself as what we see as the mechanistic
system of the world. This mechanism is a means of
action of the monads, and only an absolute
monad (god) can dispense with it. The monads
can be classified as they occur on a scale from
those with a minimum of spontaneity to those
with complete liberty. A monad is the more real
the greater its power of synthesis (in the Hegelian
sense of the unifying of opposites, cf. 1912, p. 297).
Liberty consists in continuous growth, which
Coimbra in turn construes as creation: the
ultimate process of reality, therefore, is creative
thought.

Whilst Coimbra retained the presupposition
that reality is constantly changing, he came to find
this monadism and its accompanying rationalism
unsatisfactory. The change begins in the transi-
tional works of 1916 and 1918. He could not
accommodate within a rationalistic epistemology
certain experiences which he held to be of central
importance: they are those brief moments in
which the dull façade of routine falls away, and
experience is charged instead with sense, meaning
and impregnable serenity. These 'nuclei of reality'
(*nucleas de realidade*) are associated with the
experiences of happiness, pain and grace (hence
1916), and are emotional intuitions, not findings
of reason.

Having accepted such intuitions as a key
means to truth, Coimbra had to abandon his
early rationalism, and a new analysis of reason is
developed in the major later works of 1920, 1922
and 1923, notably the last of these. Reason is no
longer the locus of immutable laws and concepts
and the ultimate arbiter of truth; rather, all its
concepts are provisional and mutable, and Coimbra extends this revisability to the foundations of
mathematics. Again, the analytic–synthetic distinction is on this view held to be only a temporary
conceptual convenience, and has no special

significance. All branches of study, he argues, are revisable in the light of experience, as is reason itself, which he now qualifies as 'experimental reason' (*razão experimental*).

In the works published after 1923, Coimbra turned to religious and moral issues, advocating the ethic which he had proposed throughout his career: acceptance of what there is, accompanied by a responsible use of freedom and belief in the life-enhancing power of love.

ROBERT WILKINSON

Collingwood, Robin George

British. **b:** 22 February 1889, Cartmel Fell, Lancashire. **d:** 9 January 1943, Coniston, Cumbria. **Cat:** Neo-idealist; archaeologist; historian. **Ints:** Metaphysics; epistemology; philosophy of history; aesthetics; ethics; political philosophy; philosophy of mind. **Educ:** Rugby Public School and University College, Oxford. **Infls:** Hegel, Vico, Croce, De Ruggiero, Hobbes and Hume. Personal: J. A. Smith, H. H. Joachim, E. F. Carritt and F. J. Haverfield. **Appts:** Fellow of Pembroke College, Oxford, 1912–34; University Lecturer in Philosophy and Roman History, Oxford, 1912–35: Waynflete Professor of Metaphysical Philosophy, University of Oxford, 1934–41; Fellow of the British Academy, 1934.

Main publications:

(1913) (trans.) B. Croce, *The Philosophy of Giambattista Vico*, London: H. Latimer.

(1916) *Religion and Philosophy*, London: Macmillan; reprinted, Bristol: Thoemmes Press, 1994.

(1923) *Roman Britain*, London: Oxford University Press; revised editions, Oxford: Clarendon Press, 1932, 1934.

(1924) *Speculum Mentis: or, the Map of Knowledge*, Oxford: Clarendon Press.

(1925) *Outlines of a Philosophy of Art*, London: Oxford University Press; reprinted in *Essays in the Philosophy of Art*, 1964; also reprinted, Bristol Thoemmes Press, 1994.

(1927) (trans.) B. Croce, *An Autiobiography*, Oxford: Clarendon Press.

(1933) *An Essay on Philosophical Method*, Oxford: Clarendon Press.

(1936) (with J. N. L. Myres) *Roman Britain and the English Settlements*, Oxford: Clarendon Press; second edition, 1937.

(1938) *The Principles of Art*, Oxford: Clarendon Press.

(1939) *An Autobiography*, London: Oxford University Press.

(1940) *An Essay on Metaphysics*, Oxford: Clarendon Press.

(1942) *The New Leviathan: or, Man, Society, Civilization and Barbarism*, Oxford: Clarendon Press; revised edition, ed. David Boucher, Oxford: Clarendon Press, 1992.

(1945) *The Idea of Nature*, ed. T. M. Knox, Oxford: Clarendon Press.

(1946) *The Idea of History*, ed. T. M. Knox, Oxford: Clarendon Press; revised edition, ed. Jan van der Dussen, Oxford: Clarendon, 1993.

(1964) *Essays in the Philosophy of Art*, ed. Alan B. Donagan, Bloomington: Indiana University Press.

(1965) *Essays in the Philosophy of History*, ed. William Debbins, Austin, Texas: University of Texas Press.

(1968) *Faith and Reason: Essays in the Philosophy of Religion*, ed. Lionel Rubinoff, Chicago: Quadrangle.

(1989) *Essays in Political Philosophy*, ed. David Boucher, Oxford: Clarendon Press.

Secondary literature:

Boucher, David (1989) *The Social and Political Thought of R. G. Collingwood*, Cambridge: Cambridge University Press.

——(ed.) (1992) *Collingwood Studies* (the journal of the Collingwood Society) 1.

Donagan, Alan (1962) *The Later Philosophy of R. G. Collingwood*, Oxford: Clarendon Press; second edition, Chicago and London: University of Chicago Press, 1985.

Krausz, Michael (1972) *Critical Essays on the Philosophy of R. G. Collingwood*, Oxford: Clarendon Press.

Mink, Louis O. (1969) *Mind, History and Dialectic: The Philosophy of R. G. Collingwood*, Bloomington, Indiana: Indiana University Press.

Rubinoff, Lionel (1970) *Collingwood and the Reform of Metaphysics: A Study in the Philosophy of Mind*, Toronto: University of Toronto Press.

Taylor, Donald S. (1988) *R. G. Collingwood: A Bibliography*, New York and London: Garland Publishing Co.

Van der Dussen, W. J. (1981) *History As Science: The Philosophy of R. G. Collingwood*, The Hague: Nijhoff.

Collingwood is distinguished by his outstanding achievements in history as well as philosophy. One of the few students of F. J. Haverfield to survive the First World War, Collingwood was internationally recognized at his death as the leading authority on Roman Britain. In the last decade of his life, despite severe illness, he produced a series of philosophical works which in their scope, depth and scholarship are without parallel in twentieth-century British philosophy. But his work has failed to influence the mainstream of modern philosophy.

In his autiobiography Collingwood explains how his involvement in archaeological fieldwork became the inspiration for his reevaulation of the nature of philosophy. His interests in history linked him with philosophers such as **Croce** in the Italian idealist tradition deriving from Vico and Hegel, but brought him into conflict with Oxford realists such as **Joseph** and **Prichard**. Collingwood justly describes his life's work as 'in the main an attempt to bring about a *rapprochement* between philosophy and history' (1939, p. 77), although scholars dispute his account of the development of his ideas.

Many of the themes of Collingwood's mature work make their appearance in his first two books: in *Religion and Philosophy* (1916) he maintains that philosophy and history are 'the same thing'; in *Speculum Mentis* (1924) he articulates a theory of mental life which system-atically relates 'forms of experience' from pure feeling to rational self-consciousness. In later works such doctrines are reinterpreted in the light of Collingwood's changing conception of history, philosophy and the mind.

In the later philosophy of art he continues to think that art, as an imaginative or non-assertive form of experience, both makes possible and affects the character of rational thought. But, whereas in *Speculum Mentis* imagination is in contradiction with expression, in *The Principles of Art* (1938) art is identified with imaginative expression of feeling. Such expression involves bodily gesture, which is language in its primitive stage, verbal language being a refinement facilitating the expression of intellectual ideas. Through a synthesis of Crocean idealism with Humean phenomenalism Collingwood maintains that artistic activity, by raising feelings to consciousness, is at once the beginning of self-knowledge and the making of the world known in language. Since denial of feeling is corruption of consciousness or bad art, the artist proper bears the responsibility of speaking on behalf of his community. The theory of mind and language is further elaborated in *The New Leviathan* (1942) as the basis of Collingwood's liberal view of freedom as mental maturity attainable within a society of people conscious of one another's freedom.

At the centre of Collingwood's philosophy is his denial of what he saw as the principle of propositional logic, that the proposition is the 'unit of thought' (1939, p. 36). Parallel to **Wittgenstein**'s concern with the role of words in language-games, Collingwood emphasizes the place of a proposition in a complex structure of questions and answers. Every proposition is an answer to a question: the significance and the truth or falsity of a proposition depend on what question it is meant to answer. Every question involves presuppositions, some of which are themselves answers to yet further questions, while those that are not count as absolute presuppositions. In *An Essay on Metaphysics* (1940) Collingwood maintains that the aim of metaphysics is to identify the constellations of absolute presuppositions taken for granted by systematic thinkers in different eras. (*The Idea of Nature*, 1945, is Collingwood's account of the presuppositions of European cosmology). However, since absolute presuppositions cannot be either true or false, metaphysics must forgo assessment of them and is thereby revealed to be—contrary to the conclusion of *An Essay on Philosophical Method* (1933)—a historical discipline.

'The logic of question and answer' emerged from Collingwood's reflection on historical methodology and informs the philosophy of historical understanding presented in *The Idea of History* (1946). Historians study, not sheer events, but past actions, traces of which survive into the present. But actions are performed for particular reasons in specific circumstances. So the historian is obliged to discern the thoughts which determined the actions in question. Thus all history is the history of thought. Furthermore, the historian can understand past thoughts only by rethinking them in his own mind, just as the spectator appreciates a work of art by reconstructing in his own imagination the emotions expressed by the artist. On this account understanding the thoughts of others requires understanding one's own thoughts. Thus historical knowledge is a form of self-knowledge. As such it is the science of history, rather than the pseudoscience of psychology, which can provide the insight needed for control of human affairs. Collingwood's opposition to the divorce between theory and practice culminates in *The New Leviathan*, his analysis of the psychological and ethical foundations of European civilization and of the forces threatening to undermine it.

Sources: ENP; Turner; obituary, R. B. McCallum, T. M. Knox and I. A. Richmond, *PBA* 29 (1943): 463–80.

PETER LEWIS

Colorni, Eugenio

Italian. *b:* 22 April 1909, Milan. *d:* 30 May 1944, Rome. *Cat:* Critic of idealism; philosopher of science; epistemologist. *Appts:* Founder of European federalist movement; a leader of the Italian socialist party and organizer of its troops; confined for anti-fascist political activity in 1938; escaped to Rome and was killed by the Nazis, shortly before the Allies arrived; posthumous Gold Medal for bravery.

Main publications:

(1932) *L'estetica di Benedetto Croce.*
(1947) 'Filosofia e scienza' in *Analysis*, Milan.
(1947) 'Apologo', in *Sigma.*
(1947) 'I'dialoghi di Commodo', in *Sigma.*
(1948) 'Critica filosofia e fisica teoria', in *Sigma.*
(1975) *Scritti*, Florence: La Nuova Italia.

Secondary literature:

Rossi-Landi, F. (1952) 'Sugli scritti di Eugenio Colorni', *Rivista critica di storia della filosofia.*
Solari, L. (1980) *Eugenio Colorni: ieri e oggi*, Venice: Marsilio.

The highly original writings of Colorni's lamentably short life display a capacity for scrupulous analysis. They reject any claim to non-natural suprasensible truths or natural laws pre-existing the human activity of theory making. His manuscripts show *inter alia* an interest in anthropomorphism, reification and the distinction between knowing how and knowing that, and the approach has similarities to the operationalism of Bridgman together with a Kantian legacy. The remarks on the logical status of physical constants, such as the speed of light, are said to be especially perspicacious. His work contains a criticism of the idealist philosophy dominant in the Italy of his time. His studies of Leibniz attempt to show the coherence of that philospher's rationalism. There is some attempt to find in Leibniz an account of the struggle of the spirit to liberate itself from the passions of the body, but, it has been argued, this is not to be found in Leibniz's work, where we find only talk of a struggle between distinct and indistinct ideas, virtue lying in a deepening of understanding. In his last years Corloni assembled the materials for a study of the problem of knowledge in the light of contemporary developments in physics, work which was posthumously published in the journal *Sigma* as the 'Critique of philosophy and physics'. A complete collection of his papers is planned.

COLIN LYAS

Conrad-Martius, Hedwig

German. *b:* 27 February 1888, Berlin. *d:* 15 February 1966, Starnberg, Bavaria. *Cat:* Phenomenologist. *Ints:* Perception; ontology, philosophy of nature; metaphysics. *Educ:* Philosophy at Munich and Göttingen Universities. *Infls:* Husserl, Adolf Reinach and Max Scheler. *Appts:* Unable to follow an academic career, initially because she was a woman and later because she had one Jewish grandparent; but in 1949 she was given a Lectureship at the University of Munich and in 1955 was made an Honorary Professor.

Main publications:

(1916) 'Zur Ontologie und Erscheinungslehre der realen Aussenwelt', *Jahrbuch für Philosophie und phänomenologische Forschung*, vol. 3, Halle.
(1923) 'Realontologie', in *Jahrbuch für Philosophie und phänomenologische Forschung*, vol. 6, Halle.
(1944) *Der Selbstaufbau der Natur*, Hamburg.
(1957) *Das Sein*, Munich.

Like other members of the Göttingen circle of phenomenologists Conrad-Martius rejected what were seen as the idealistic implications of **Husserl**'s phenomenology. This is evident in her 1916 contribution to Husserl's *Yearbook*. Phenomenology is understood as the presuppositionless description and analysis of that which shows itself in consciousness, i.e. phenomena. There is no suggestion that things are in some way dependent on consciousness. Indeed the 'external' world shows itself as being self-standing in its being. However, the principal concern of that work is the sensory component in our experience of the world. Conrad-Martius provides a subtle and impressively rich description of the multiplicity of sensory contents in perception and of how they combine to disclose material objects and their properties. The word 'disclose' is important. Objects are not reducible to sensations. They are disclosed in sensations. As well as describing the essence of perception Conrad-Martius also provides a phenomenological analysis, much praised by Roman **Ingarden**, of the difference between perception and imagination as one of kind rather than degree. As a phenomenologist Conrad-Martius is not concerned with what in fact exists. We are concious of various kinds of things as real. But what is it for something to be real? Conrad-Martius poses this question in her 1923 contribution to the *Yearbook*. To ask such a question about being (*Sein*) is to engage in ontology. However, her method of tackling ontological questions remains phenomenological. The meaning of 'reality' is not constructed but is arrived at by interrogating those modes of consciousness in which something shows itself as real. In later life, as she moved into *Naturphilosophie* and metaphysics, her thinking became less phenomenological and more speculative in character.

PAUL GORNER

Cook Wilson, John

British. *b:* 4 June 1849, Nottingham, England. *d:* 11 August 1915, Oxford, England. *Cat:* Realist. *Ints:* Philosophical logic; epistemology. *Educ:* Balliol College, Oxford. *Infls:* T. H. Green and Lotze. *Appts:* Professor of Logic, Oxford, 1889–1915.

Main publications:

(1926) *Statement and Inference* 2 vols, ed. A. S. L. Farquharson, Oxford: Clarendon Press.

Secondary literature:

Joseph, H. W. B. (1915–16) obituary in *Proceedings of the British Academy*.
Prichard, H. A. (1919) in *Mind*.
Robinson, Richard (1931) *The Province of Logic*, London.

In the period between the death of T. H. Green in 1882 and his own in 1915 Cook Wilson was the dominating figure in Oxford philosophy and his pupils, above all H. A. **Prichard** and H. W. B. **Joseph**, ensured its persistence until well into the 1930s. Its first task was to undermine the authority of the local brand of absolute, or Hegelian, idealism, in whose doctrines Cook Wilson had been brought up. After Green's death, **Bradley** remained a recluse: other idealists had gone already, like **Bosanquet** in 1881, or soon did. Against idealism's loosely edifying style of thought Cook Wilson argued with passionate, literal-minded, grammatically and lexicographically scrupulous tenacity. Where they had held that no statement does more than approximate to truth and certainty, he insisted that the axioms and demonstrated theorems of mathematics were both true and known for certain to be so. Against the idealist account of all intellectual activity as 'judgement', he pointed out that in ordinary speech judgement is the result of inference. More important was what he saw as the damaging representation of knowledge, belief and bare conjecture as a continuum. In his view knowledge is unique, *sui generis*, susceptible of neither analysis nor definition. We cannot, he curiously maintained, know something without knowing that we do so. Since mathematics, in which Cook

Wilson had some expertise, is the prime exemplar of knowledge, he was equally hostile to non-euclidean geometries and to the mathematical logic of Russell which agreed with the objectionable view of Bradley that general statements of the form *all A are B* are really hypotheticals (*if anything is A it is B*). Knowledge requires an independent object, neither changed, let alone created, by the mind of the knower nor, necessarily, itself a state of mind. Cook Wilson, however, qualified his realism by holding that only the primary, spatial qualities of things are known as they are in perception. In a famous lecture which took two evenings to deliver, he argued for the existence of God as the only adequate object for our feelings of awe and reverence. Cook Wilson's influence in Oxford has persisted, often unrecognizedly, until very recent times. **Austin**'s treatment of knowledge has a Cook Wilsonian, or Prichardian, flavour as does his insistence on testing philosophical theses against ordinary language. **Strawson**'s critique of the distortions of the common meaning of the logical words, like *all* and *if*, by formal logic is even closer to Cook Wilson.

Sources: Metz; Passmore 1957; Edwards.

ANTHONY QUINTON

Copleston, Frederick Charles

British. *b:* 10 April 1907, Devon, England. *d:* 3 February 1994, London. *Cat:* Historian of philosophy. *Ints:* History of Western thought; later extended to Russian philosophy and religion, and Oriental thought. *Educ:* Marlborough; St John's, Oxford; and the Gregorian University at Rome. *Infls:* The scholastic tradition. *Appts:* Joined Society of Jesus, 1930; ordained 1937; Professor of History of Philosophy, Heythrop College, Oxford, 1939–70; University of London, 1972–4; Visiting Professor, UCSC, 1974–5, 1977–82; University of Hawaii, 1976; Gregorian University, 1952–68; Gifford Lecturer, 1979–80; numerous honorary degrees; CBE, 1993.

Main publications:

(1942) *Friedrich Nietzsche, Philosopher of Culture*; revised edition, London: Search Press, 1975.
(1946) *Arthur Schopenhauer, Philosopher of Pessimism*, London: Burns, Oates & Washbourne.
(1946–75) *A History of Philosophy*, 9 vols, vols: 1–8, London: Burns & Oates; vol 9, London: Search Press; paperback reprint, Garden City, NY: Image Books.
(1948) *Existentialism and Modern Man*, Oxford: Blackfriars.

(1952) *Mediaeval Philosophy*, London: Methuen.

(1955) *Aquinas*, Harmondsworth: Pelican Books.

(1956) *Contemporary Philosophy*; revised editon, London: Burns & Oates, 1972.

(1972) *A History of Mediaeval Philosophy*, London: Methuen.

(1976) *Philosophers and Philosophies*, London: Search Press.

(1979) *On the History of Philosophy*, London: Search Press.

(1980) *Philosophies and Cultures*, Oxford: Oxford University Press.

(1982) *Religion and The One*, London: Search Press.

(1986) *Philosophy in Russia*, Notre Dame: University of Notre Dame Press.

(1988) *Russian Religious Philosophy*, London: Search Press.

Secondary literature:

Conway, J. I. (1947) 'Reflections on the function of the history of philosophy in liberal education', *New Scholasticism* 21: 419–37.

Heinemann, F. H. and Allen E. L. (1955) 'Survey of recent philosophical and theological literature', *Hibbert Journal*, 54: 397–404.

Frederick Copleston, together with **Feng Youlan** and Surendranath Dasgupta, will probably be remembered as one of the most distinguished historians of philosophy of this century: his nine-volume *History of Philosophy* (1946–75) has no serious English-language rivals as a history of Western thought. Announced, in the Preface to its first volume, as a textbook designed for use in Catholic seminaries for students expected to devote most of their time to studying the *philosophia perennis*, it soon became clear that, despite Copleston's modesty, a major work was in the making. From first volume to last, the *History* is based on a scrupulous and scholarly reading of primary sources. It is written in a uniformly lucid style and, as might have been expected from a Jesuit who could write well on **Nietzsche** and Schopenhauer (in 1942 and 1946), extremely fair-minded. Copleston's own commitment to Thomism does not obtrude itself, and the work is nothing if not free from partisan spirit. Indeed Copleston did not understand by *philosophia perennis* a body of doctrine fixed for all time, but a worldview which, if true in its main lines, is not at any given moment complete and can be revised and improved in certain respects (cf. Introduction to *History*, vol. I).

Later on in his career, Copleston widened his horizons even further, to include some work on Russian thought—hardly dealt with in the *His-tory*—and on the several traditions Westerners lump together under the heading 'Oriental'. He noted the attractions of Eastern systems for those in the West disenchanted with various aspects of our culture, philosophy included. For example, recent English-language ethics has tended to concentrate on the arid technicalities of metaethics, a function of the separation of ethics from philosophical anthropology and metaphysics. The appeal of Eastern systems is precisely that they do place human conduct in a cosmic context, and this is a challenge Western philosophy should take up once more (cf. 1980 and 1982, *passim*; and 1979, chapter 3).

Unsurprisingly, Copleston had developed views on the principles of philosophical historiography, and in his writings in this area consistently rebuts the claims of sceptics, subjectivists and relativists. For example, it has been argued that no sustainable distinction can be drawn between historical data and interpretation, and that therefore there are only perspectives on the past, unassessable with regard to truth. Copleston admits that there are indeed no 'uninterpreted data', but denies that this entails that history is a kind of fiction, since it remains true that the historian does not invent the data, and that not all interpretations are regarded as equally persuasive. Again, Copleston denies the thesis of those cultural relativists who maintain that we are so determined by our own milieu that we are unable to enter into the mentalities of people belonging to other societies. Those who derive their view from the autonomy of language-games can only make their case if they so define the term 'understand' that I can understand only language-games I share: yet there is no reason whatever to accept this definition. A good historian, in Copleston's view, is one who progressively overcomes his or her own milieu, developing the ability to enter fully and sympathetically into other mentalities and outlooks.

Sources: WW 1993; obituary, *Daily Telegraph*, Feb 1994.

ROBERT WILKINSON

Corbin, H(enry)

French. *b:* 14 April 1903, France. *d:* 7 October 1978. *Cat:* Iranian philosophy; gnostic thought; Shi'ite philosophy. *Ints:* History; Shiite philosophy. *Educ:* Studied Philosophy at the Sorbonne University, Paris, in Germany, at the French Institute in Istanbul, and in Tehran. *Infls:* Influenced by Mulla Sadra, Suhrawardi, ibn Arabi and ibn Sina. *Appts:* Founder of the French Institute's

Department of Iranology, Tehran; later at the Section des Sciences Religieuses de l'École Pratique des Hautes Études, Paris.

Main publications:

(1971–3, 1991) *En Islam iranien*, Paris: Gallimard.

(1979) *Avicenne et le récit visionnaire*, Paris: Berg (English translation, *Avicenna and the Visionary Recital*, W. Trask, Princeton: Mythos, 1990).

(1981) *Temple et contemplation*, Paris: Flammarion (English translation, *Temple and Contemplation*, P. Sherrard, London: Routledge, 1986).

(1982) *Temps cyclique et gnose ismaélienne*, Paris: Berg (English translation, *Cyclical Time and Ismaili Gnosis*, London: Routledge, 1983).

(1986) *Histoire de la philosophie islamique*, Paris: Gallimard.

Secondary literature:

Jambet, C. (ed.) (1981) *Henry Corbin*, Paris: L'Herne.

Shayegan, D. (1990) *Henry Corbin–La typographie spirituelle de l'Islam iranien*, Paris: Editions de la différence.

Corbin combined a sound understanding of contemporary European thought with a dedication to Shiite and especially Iranian philosophy. He was particularly interested in uncovering the meaning of religious texts in terms of what is esoteric and what is exoteric. To understand such texts we require a hermeneutic methodology which embodies an intermediary between God and human consciousness. Without such an intermediary one falls into the 'paradox of monotheism', which results in the ascription to God of human qualities and characteristics. This led the Islamic mystics to employ the notion of stages of being between the human level and the divine, which one must traverse in order to appreciate the divine essence. Sometimes these intermediaries are called angelic, but they should not be classified as imaginary even though their apprehension may well involve dreams and visions. Corbin uses the expression 'imaginal' for such visions in order to capture their ontological significance for the metamorphosis of the human soul. The intermediate world of angelic forms plays an essential role in all theosophy. This model is strong in the thought of Avicenna and other thinkers influenced by him, but was attacked by Averroes and so led to a turn in Latin European philosophy which deepened the divide between God and humanity in a way which was to fix that relationship in Western philosophy for a long time afterwards.

Corbin's work is important because of the way in which he transformed the understanding of Islamic philosophy. Criticizing the view that it consists of those works known in the Latin West, more or less finishing with Averroes, he argues that there was an important later tradition which continued in Iran. This tradition was often hostile to peripateticism and concentrated more on myticism, Sufism and theosophy, addressing itself to a different range of problems as compared with the thought of the Peripatetics and linking up with a wider notion of knowledge and understanding. He was concerned not only with philosophy but also with Iran and Shiite Islam. In his writings he did a great deal to link philosophy with pre-Islamic ideas and also with twentieth-century concerns, and the notion of a spirituality which is common to a number of religions across a vast breadth of time emerges in his work. Corbin played a vital role in resuscitating a whole tradition of philosophy which was previously little studied in the West. By treating it as living philosophy he did much to increase interest in it in the Islamic world too.

OLIVER LEAMAN

Cornman, J(ames) W(elton)

American. *b:* 1929, Philadelphia. *d:* 31 May 1978, Philadelphia. *Cat:* Metaphysician; epistemologist. *Ints:* Philosophy of mind. *Educ:* Dartmouth College and Brown University. *Infls:* Quine, Carnap and W. Sellars. *Appts:* 1960–3, Assistant Professor, Ohio State University; 1963 -5, Assistant Professor, University of Rochester; 1964–5, Mellon Fellow, University of Pittsburgh; 1965–7, Associate Professor, University of Rochester; 1967–78, Professor, University of Pennsylvania.

Main publications:

(1966) *Metaphysics, Reference, and Language*, New Haven: Yale University Press.

(1968) (with Keith Lehrer) *Philosophical Problems and Arguments*, second edition, New York: Macmillan, 1974.

(1971) *Materialism and Sensations*, New Haven: Yale University Press.

(1975) *Perception, Common Sense and Science*, New Haven: Yale University Press.

(1980) *Skepticism, Justification and Explanation*, Dordrecht: Reidel.

Secondary literature:

Choy, V. (1982) 'The philosophy of James Cornman', *Philosophical Studies*, 41.

Elugardo, R. (1982) 'Cornman, adverbial material-ism, and phenomenal properties', *Philosophical Studies* 41.

Domotor, Z. and Friedman, M. (1982) 'Cornman and philosophy of science', *Philosophical Studies* 42.

Swain, M. (1982) 'Cornman's theory of justification', *Philosophical Studies* 42.

The bulk of Cornman's published work concerned proposed solutions to the mind-body problem. In *Metaphysics, Reference, and Language* (1966) he began by considering generally how one might solve or dissolve metaphysical problems, typically by one or more forms of linguistic analysis, and he took the mind-body problem as a test case. He rejected the positivists' dismissal of metaphysical problems, and the attempts of various ordinary language analysts to dissolve metaphysical pro-blems, on the grounds that each of these approaches relies upon undefended theories of reference. Instead Cornman takes metaphysical problems to be concerned with external questions, in something very close to **Carnap**'s sense of this term, that is to say, questions which cannot be answered by appealing solely to rules which are internal to a linguistic framework.

Cornman's own theory of mind is adverbial materialism, so-called because it incorporates an analysis of sensations which takes them to be objectless events of sensing. These events he takes to be strictly identical to neural events. Cornman also defended a direct realist theory of perception, and embedded the adverbial account of sensa-tions within it. He defended, too, common sense realism, which takes perceived external objects to be very much as they are perceived to be, although he denied that this thesis faced the problems usually attributed to naive realism.

Cornman's posthumously published work, *Skepticism, Justification and Explanation* (1980), is an extremely detailed treatment of epistemic scepticism and of foundationalist and coherentist theories of justified belief. Cornman defends a most complex version of foundationalism, with the added twist that most non-basic beliefs count as justified only if they help to explain basic, foundational beliefs. In this way, Cornman ends up incorporating coherentist elements into his theory, because non-basic beliefs are justified only if they are members of a maximally coherent set of beliefs which serve to explain the basic beliefs.

GEORGE S. PAPPAS

Corradi Fiumara, Gemma

Italian. *b:* 15 January 1939, Rome. *Cat:* Herme-neuticist; psychoanalyst. *Ints:* Philosophy of language. *Educ:* Barnard College, Columbia Uni-versity, New York, 1958–61; University of Rome, 1961–3. *Infls:* Wittgenstein and Heidegger. *Appts:* Associate Professor of Philosophy, University of Rome, 'La Sapienza'.

Main publications:

(1966) *Philosophy and Coexistence*, Leyden: Sijthoff.
(1990) *The Other Side of Language: A Philosophy of Listening*, London: Routledge.
(1992) *The Symbolic Function: Psychoanalysis and the Philosophy of Language*, Oxford: Blackwell.
(1995) *The Metaphoric Process: Connections Be-tween Language and Life*, London: Routledge.

Although it is not until her third book that Corradi Fiumara explicitly foregrounds psycho-analysis, all her philosophical work is informed by the insights of pscyhoanalysis as a model of the mind ('mentation' is the word she prefers, in order to indicate a process rather than an entity).

Corradi Fiumara puts forward a philosophy of listening, offering a model of philosophy which attempts to take Socrates' maieutics in its most faithful form: philosophy not as adversary meth-od, but as holding the other person's thought in one's mind so as to allow the expression of an as-yet unborn thought.

The stress on dialogue and in particular the function of listening leads to an alternative approach to epistemology which emphasises the role of the listener rather than the fixity of the object to be known, and the transformation of the listener in the process of listening rather than the fixity or stability of the knower. This approach is critical of more traditional epistemologies which Corradi Fiumara describes as predatory, territor-ial and colonizing, a proliferation of competing monologues.

In her most recent work, Corradi Fiumara argues that cognition and effects cannot and should not be separated. Extending **Kuhn**'s notion of the paradigm to symbolization, she argues that what holds us back from communication and growth may be a hypostasis of meaning embodied in symbolic paradigms that we are not aware of using and yet to which we are profoundly attached. *The Symbolic Function* (1992) explores the degradation of our symbolic habitat and considers the ways in which sophisticated sym-bolic systems or languages—such as those devel-oped in philosophy—can be used to destroy, immobilize or prevent communication. Corradi

Fiumara's work is unusual in that it draws on both analytical and continental traditions. It belongs with an increasingly significant move towards incorporating the insights of psychoanalysis into philosophy.
Sources: CV supplied by Gemma Corradi Fiumara.

MARGARET WHITFORD

Courtine, Jean-François

French. *Cat:* Phenomenologist; translator of Heidegger into French. *Ints:* Heideggerian philosophy; German romanticism; deconstruction; metaphysics. *Infls:* Heidegger, Husserl, Schelling, Derrida and Hölderlin (poet). *Appts:* Director, Archives Husserl, École Normale Supérieure, Paris; Researcher, Centre National de Recherches Scientifiques.

Main publications:

(1980) 'Anthropologie et anthropomorphisme (Heidegger lecteur de Schelling)', in *Nachdenken über Heidegger*, Hildesheim: Gerstenberg.

(1983) 'Phénoménologie et science de l'être', in M. Haar (ed.), *Cahiers de l'Herne Martin Heidegger*, Paris: Herne.

(1988) (with others) *Du Sublime*, Paris: Belin (English translation, *Of the Sublime: Presence in Question*, trans. J. Librett, Albany: State University of New York, 1993).

(1989) 'Voice of conscience and call of being', in *Topoi* 7: 101–9.

(1990) *Extase de la raison: essais sur Schelling*, Paris: Galilée.

(1990) *Heidegger et la phénoménologie*, Paris: Vrin.

(1990) *Suarez et le système de la métaphysique*, Paris: Presses Universitaires de France.

Jean-François Courtine is a Heideggerian scholar. He brings a powerful exegesis of **Heidegger**'s work to bear on wider questions in German idealism, phenomenology and metaphysics. Thus, Courtine works through the Heideggerian critique of **Husserl**'s phenomenology as science (1983) to elucidate the prior position of philosophy with respect to science and to counter the definition of philosophy as science in phenomenology and German idealism. A similar close reading of Heidegger is deployed on the question of the metaphysics of subjectivity in order to prepare for a study of the relation of language and death (1989).

JAMES WILLIAMS

Couturat, Louis

French. *b:* 17 January 1868, Paris. *d:* 3 October 1914, Ris-Orangis. *Cat:* Logician; historian of philosophy. *Ints:* Mathematical logic; Leibniz; artificial international languages. *Educ:* École Normale Supérieure, Paris; doctorate, University of Toulouse, 1896. *Infls:* Jules Tannery, E. Picard, C. Jordan and J. H. Poincaré and B. Russell. *Appts:* University of Caen, from October 1897; Paris, from October 1899; Assistant to Bergson at the Collège de France, 1905–6; of independent means.

Main publications:

(1896) *De mythis Platonicis*, Paris: F. Alcan (Latin thesis)

(1896) *De l'infini mathématique*, Paris: F. Alcan (French thesis).

(1901) *La Logique de Leibnitz d'après des documents inédits*, Paris: F. Alcan.

(1901) (trans.) B. Russell, *Essai sur les fondements de géométrie*, Paris: Gauthier-Villars.

(1903) (ed.) *Opuscules et fragments inédits*, Paris: F. Alcan (republished, G. W. Leibniz, Hildesheim: Olms, 1961).

(1905) *L'Algèbre de la logique*, Paris: Gauthier-Villars; second edition, 1914.

(1905) *Les Principes des mathématiques avec une appendice sur la philosophie des mathématiques de Kant*, Paris: F. Alcan.

Secondary literature:

Blanché, R. (1967) 'Couturat, Louis', in Paul Edwards (ed.) *Encyclopedia of Philosophy*, New York: Macmillan, II: 248b–9b.
Cassirer, Ernst (1907) 'Kant und die moderne Mathematik mit Bezug auf Russells und Couturats Werke über die Principien der Mathematik', *Kantstudien*.

Initially trained as a mathematician, Couturat advocated the real existence of infinite numbers when **Cantor**'s theories were widely rejected. He then became an advocate of the logistic programme in mathematics and a supporter of **Russell**'s views on the subject. A year in the Leibniz archives in Hanover revealed to him Leibniz's logical writings, which he went on to publicize, becoming the inventor of the well-known thesis that Leibniz's metaphysics was a consequence of his logic. He later became interested in the universal-language movement, favouring Ido as a supposedly more logical alternative to Esperanto. On Leibniz, Couturat may perhaps have been misled by his own thoroughgoing metaphysical rationalism: it is hard to understand how a content-free logic could supply the premises for a content-full metaphysics. (See, for example, Stuart Brown, *Leibniz*, Harvester, 1984.)

Sources: L. Benaerts (1915) 'Louis Couturat', *Annuaire de l'Association Amicale de Secours des Anciens Élèves de l'ENS*, Paris; DSB 2: 455b–457a; Anreé Lalande (1914) 'L'Oeuvre de Louis Couturat', *RMM* 22: 644–88 (career survey: involvement in international language movement; bibliography); Anne Françoise Schmid (1983) 'La Correspondance inédite entre Bertrand Russell et Louis Couturat', *Dialectica* 37: 75–109; Maurice Loi (1976) 'Couturat méconnu', *Scientia* 111: 683–8.

R. N. D. MARTIN

Crahay, Franz

Belgian. **b:** 26 February 1923, Olne, Belgium. **d:** 4 April 1988. **Cat:** Epistemologist; historian of philosophy; symbolic logician. **Educ:** Louvain University and the University of Paris; diploma in Classics, Louvain, 1943, certificate in Psychophysiology, Paris, 1949; Licence ès Lettres and Diplôme d'Études Supérieures, Paris, 1948 and 1951, DPhil 1954. **Appts:** Fellow of The Belgian Foundation of Scientific Research, 1951–7; Chargé de Cours, University of Liège, 1957; Professor of Philosophy, Universities of Lovainium, Kinshasa, 1957–68 and Liège (Belgium) until his death.

Main publications:

(1951) *Le Problème de la vérité*, Durkheim Prize of the University of Paris.
(1957) *Le Formalisme logico-mathématique et le problème du non-sens*, Paris: Les Belles-Lettres.
(1963) *La Diversité des sciences dan l'unité du savoir* Léopoldville: University of Lovainium.
(1965) 'Le Décollage conceptuel: conditions d'une philosophie bantoue', *Diogenes* 52: 61–84.

Secondary literature:

Mudimbe, V. Y. (1989) *The Invention of Africa*, Bloomington: Indiana University Press.

Crahay is well known in the field of African philosophy for the lecture he gave on 19 March 1965 at the Goethe Institute of Léopoldville. The lecture was published in *Diogenes* 52. It is organized around two main questions. First, is there a Bantu philosophy, in an acceptable meaning of the concept of philosophy? Second, if there is not, what are the conditions for a Bantu philosophy? Crahay responds by suggesting five conditions which could generate a Bantu philosophy: (i) the existence of African philosophers;

(ii) their integration in the philosophical tradition; (iii) an inventory of indigenous values which could provoke thought; (iv) a clear distinction between reflexive consciousness and mythical consciousness; and (v) a critical analysis of African intellectuals' main temptations which, as in the case of Marxism, would seem to respond to concrete and urgent needs for development.

V. Y. MUDIMBE

Creighton, James Edwin

Canadian-American. **b:** 8 April 1861, Pictou, Nova Scotia. **d:** 8 October, 1924, Ithaca, New York. **Cat:** Idealist. **Ints:** History of philosophy. **Educ:** Dalhousie University, Halifax, Nova Scotia; Universities of Leipzig and Berlin; PhD, Cornell University. **Infls:** Schurman. **Appts:** Taught Philosophy at Cornell from 1889; Dean of the Graduate School, 1923; editor of the *Philosophical Review* from 1892 until his death, and served as the American editor of *Kant Studien* from 1893 until his death; first President of the American Philosophical Association; a close associate of Jacob Gould Schurman, he is regarded as one of the two founders of the Cornell school of idealist philosophy.

Main publications:

(1898) *An Introductory Logic*, New York: Macmillan; fourth edition, 1920.
(1925) *Studies in Speculative Philosophy*, ed. Harold R. Smart, New York: Macmillan (contains bibliography).

Secondary literature:

Armour, Leslie and Trott, Elizabeth (1981) *The Faces of Reason*, Waterloo: Wilfrid Laurier University Press (contains a discussion of his work).

Apart from his logic text, Creighton's writings are fragmentary. He exerted his influence chiefly through the *Philosophical Review*, the Cornell philosophy department and the fledgling American Philosophical Association. His logic book, although intended as an introduction, discusses and clarifies some of the central issues in idealist logic. It also contains the interesting suggestion that the forms of development found in biological evolution can be applied to inference processes in such a way as to develop a model of the growth of knowledge. Creighton's philosophical writings are generally dominated by two ideas which mapped out his main interests: first, he believed that the history of philosophy is a part of philosophy itself and, second, he believed that philosophy is a social not an individual process. He was fascinated by the concept of the concrete universal, although his approaches to it from various angles seem incomplete. Although he tended to remain an absolute idealist, he was willing to concede that the various special sciences need to develop individually and not merely in the context of a single unified notion of knowledge. His interest in the history of philosophy led him to translate a number of works, and sustained his lifelong interest in Kant. Although he was revered as a teacher, the tensions in his own thought contributed to the tendency for a number of his pupils to become personal rather than absolute idealists. A friend and protege of Jacob Gould **Schurman**, he shows Schurman's influence. His passion for the history of philosophy is a passion which came to dominate Canadian philosophy in the generation which succeeded him. He figures chiefly in accounts of American philosophy as the first President of the American Philosophical Association and as one of those who, along with Schurman, played a significant part in the professionalization of philosophy in North America.

Sources: WWW(Am).

LESLIE ARMOUR

Croce, Benedetto

Italian. *b:* 25 February 1866, Pescasseroli, Italy. *d:* 20 November 1952, Naples. *Cat:* Philosopher of spirit. *Appts:* Croce held no university appointments,; he was a man of independent means.

Main publications:

The collected works number over 70 volumes; the philosophical core, however, are the works which constitute the philosophy of the spirit:

(1902) *Estetica.*
(1909) *La logica.*
(1909) *La Filosofia della practica.*
(1917) *Teoria e storia della storiografia.*

Also notable are:

(1900) *Materialismo storico ed economia marxista.*
(1910) *Problemi di estetica.*
(1911) *La filosofia di G. B. Vico* (English translation), *Poetry and Literature*, trans. G. Gullace, Southern Illinois University Press, 1981).
(1913) *Saggio sul Hegel.*
(1920) *Brevario di estetica.*
(1925) *Elementi di politica.*
(1928) *Estetica in nuce* (English translation, 'Aesthetics', in *Encyclopaedia Britannica*, fourteenth edition).

(1939) *La poesia.*

English editions of most of these exist; there is also a collection by Cecil Sprigge (1966) *Philosophy, Poetry and History*, Oxford: Oxford University Press.

Secondary literature:

Carr, H. W. (1917) *The Philosophy of Benedetto Croce*, New York: Russell & Russell.

Gullace, G. (1981) *Poetry and Literature*, Southern Illinois University Press (translation of *La Poesia* with a full introduction to Croce's work).

Moss, M. (1987) *Benedetto Croce Reconsidered*, University of New England Press.

Niccolini, Fausto (1960) *L''editio ne varietur' delle opere di B. Croce* (full bibliography).

Orsini, G. (1961) *Benedetto Croce*, Southern Illinois University Press.

Piccoli, R. (1922) *Benedetto Croce*, New York: Harcourt, Brace & Co.

Croce is one of the central figures in the cultural and political life of Italy in the first half of the twentieth century. As founder and editor of *La critica* he exercised an extraordinary influence on Italian letters. He was a practising politician, a government Minister, a Senator, during the long years of fascism a focus of sustained opposition, and a member of the postwar Provisional Government. His enormously erudite writings range over the whole of European and world literature, philosophy, and political and economic theory. He never held a university position, having the means to live an independent life amid his magnificent collection of books in Naples. Most Italian philosophers addressed his work, **Gramsci**, indeed, asserting that a close reading of Croce was a prerequisite for contemporary philosophy. Together with **Gentile**, with whom, before an intellectual and political estrangement, he was friend and cothinker, Croce set the agenda (both for his supporters and opponents) of much Italian philosophizing, and, through R. G. **Collingwood**'s acceptance of many of his doctrines his influence extended into the English-speaking world, most noticeably in aesthetics and the philosophy of history. Croce spent much time on Hegel and was one of the earliest debaters of Marxism (Croce, **Labriola**, who introduced the study of Marx to Italy, and **Sorel** were known as the Holy Trinity of Latin Marxist studies, although Labriola was to condemn the revisionism of the other two). Croce found Marx's views, which he took to be deterministic, at odds with his own categorical commitment to freedom.

Following the tragic death of his family in an earthquake, and after brief periods of study in Rome, Croce returned to Naples and spent the early years of his intellectual life exploring the history and culture of that city. The *Scienza Nuova* of Vico awoke his mind to philosophy and he became interested in the much debated question whether history be an art or a science. This led him in turn to think about the nature of art, a thinking that was to issue in his first major work, and the work by which he is best known in the English-speaking world, *Estetica* (1902). In the course of writing this work what had started as an interest in the particular questions of art and history widened itself into a systematic philosophy, what he was to call the philosophy of spirit. Although that philosophy is elaborated in the four works mentioned above, the best short introduction to it is *Estetica*, for that work came to be not merely an account of art but an account that placed art in an overarching account of all the faculties of the human mind.

The drift of the philosophy of spirit may be grasped by considering a stone warmed by the sun. Here the stone passively receives stimuli. Compare this to the receipt of stimuli by a human being. Here the recipient of the stimuli is active in processing them. The first thing the recipient does is to impose a form on the welter of experience. This is the aesthetic stage, which therefore lies at the root of all that we can subsequently do. In that stage we impose order on chaos by finding a way of expressing (intuiting, representing—the terms are interchangeable) the stimuli. That expression issues in language and art and is something that every human and not merely every artist does. In this activity we find expressed our categorical freedom: nothing can in advance determine the direction our expression will take, for until expression has taken place there is nothing formed to do the determining. Croce's commitment to freedom in the active struggle against fascism has, therefore, a foundation in the core of his philosophy. Having given form to our sensations we can now grasp particulars, this stone, this man, this water. At the next stage, which presupposes and is therefore secondary to the aesthetic, comes the stage at which we extract the general from the particular and talk in general terms of stones, water, men by forming concepts. This is the stage of logic, which is investigated more fully in the second of the volumes of the philosophy of spirit. The aesthetic and the logical stages exhaust the theoretical activities of the mind. But there is also the practical. This, too, has two stages: the economic, in which we try to get

what we have conceptualized (so that the economic depends on the logical, which depends on the aesthetic; for, Croce asks, how could we seek something if we did not have a concept of what we seek?); the final stage is the moral, not merely wanting, but being able to distinguish between what ought and what ought not to be wanted. This is further investigated in the third of the works of the philosophy of spirit, *La filosofia della practica* (1909). In these four stages the whole life of the mind is laid before us.

Two aspects of this philosophy deserve brief further comment: first, the account of aesthetics. Initially Croce had said that art simply is expression or intuition so that any intuition or expression is art. Later he was to further characterize art as a certain kind of intuition, first as lyrical intuition and later as cosmic intuition. These notions are continually applied in the actual study of works of art and literature (although it has been argued that examples that would demonstrate their applicability to the plastic arts and to music are distinctly lacking). Some, including Gentile, found the assertion of the existence of such distinctions somewhat at odds with the unifying impulse of idealism, to which Croce felt an affinity. Second, Croce thought history to be allied with art rather than science, being concerned with the particular rather than the general. That influential view of history is set out in the fourth volume of the philosophy of spirit, *Teoria e storia della storiografia* (1917). An implication is that to attempt to find in history scientific laws of progress is to misconstrue that subject, a conclusion which has obvious implications for Marxism.

COLIN LYAS

Cruz Costa, João

Brazilian. *b:* 13 February 1904, São Paulo, Brazil. *d:* 1978. *Cat:* Historian of ideas. *Educ:* The Sorbonne; both the Medical School and the School of Arts and Sciences, University of São Paulo. *Appts:* Professor of Philosophy, University of São Paulo.

Main publications:

(1942) *Ensaio sobre a vida e a obra de Francisco Sánchez.*

(1945) *O pensamento brasileiro* (Spanish translation, *El pensamiento brasileño*, Mexico: UNAM, 1979).

(1950) *Contribuição à história das idéias no Brasil: o desenvolvimento da filosofia no Brasil no século XIX e a evolução histórica nacional*, second edition, Rio de Janeiro: Civilização Brasileira, 1967.

(1956) *O positivismo na república*, São Paulo: Companhia Editora Nacional.

(1957) *Esbozo de una historia de las ideas en Brasil*, Mexico: Fondo de Cultura Economica.

(1962) *Panorama of the History of Philosophy in Brazil*, trans. Fred G. Sturm, Washington, DC: Pan American Union.

(1964) *A History of Ideas in Brazil; the Development of Philosophy in Brazil, and the Evolution of Natural History*, trans. Suzette Macedo, Berkeley: University of California Press.

Secondary literature:

Francovich, Guillermo (1979) *Filósofos brasileños*, Rio de Janeiro: Presença Edicoes.

Cruz Costa analyses the history of nineteeth- and twentieth-century Brazilian thought in terms of how European ideas were assimilated, adapted or 'deformed' to create a unique intellectual history in Brazil. He rejects the notion that Brazilian thought is necessarily derivative of European thought. Instead, he demonstrates that philosophy in Brazil has usually been linked to action, and that thought in Latin America has not had the luxury of 'ivory towers' where 'extravagant theories' could be developed without regard for social and political situations. Cruz Costa is especially well known for his studies on Brazilian positivism.

AMY A. OLIVER

Cunningham, Gustavus Watts

American. *b:* 14 November 1881, Laurens, South Carolina. *d:* 1986, Laurens, South Carolina. *Cat:* Idealist. *Ints:* Epistemology. *Educ:* Cornell University, under James Edwin Creighton, and received his doctorate there in 1908. *Infls:* James Edwin Creighton. *Appts:* 1902–05, taught English at Howard College, Birmingham, Alabama; taught Philosophy at Middlebury College, 1908–17, at the University of Texas, 1917–27, and at Cornell, 1927–49; Dean of the Cornell Graduate School, 1944–49; and President of the Western Division of the American Philosophical Association in 1930, and of the Eastern Division in 1937.

Main publications:

(1910) *Thought and Reality in Hegel's System*, New York: Longmans Green.

(1916) *A Study in the Philosophy of Bergson*, New York: Longmans Green.

(1924) *Problems of Philosophy: An Introductory Survey*, New York: H. Holt; second edition with a foreword by Viscount Haldane, London: Harrap, 1925.

(1925) *Five Lectures on the Problem of Mind*, New York: Century.

(1933) *The Idealistic Argument in Recent British and American Philosophy*, New York: Century.

(1935) *Perspective and Context in the Meaning-Situation*, The Howison Lecture, Berkeley: University of California Press, (*University of California Publications in Philosophy* 16, 2).

Secondary literature:

Howie, John and Burford, Thomas O. (eds) (1975) *Contemporary Studies in Philosophical Idealism*, Cape Cod: Claude Stark.

Insisting that meaning requires both an intrinsic (mental) and an extrinsic dimension, Cunningham accepted some current critiques of idealism. But he agreed that the object of knowledge cannot be separated *completely* from the object itself without making knowledge impossible. In *The Idealistic Argument in Recent British and American Philosophy* (1933) he reviews most of the contemporary discussions. The one argument for idealism which he accepts is that any conception of nature without mind becomes unintelligible because it ignores the presupposition that nature is conceivable. Although influenced by James Edwin **Creighton** he, like J. A. **Leighton**, rebelled against the idea of the timeless absolute. He was evidently influenced also by various currents of American realism and his interests were mainly in epistemology rather than in ontology. He is described by Andrew Reck (in Howie and Burford 1975) as 'the most creative' of the Cornell idealists, a group which included James Edwin Creighton and Jacob Gould **Schurman**. Certainly he did address the specific objections which were brought against idealist philosophy at the time.

Sources: WWW(Am).

LESLIE ARMOUR

D

Dagognet, François

French. **b:** 1924, near Langres. **Cat:** Philosopher and historian of science; psychiatrist. **Ints:** Foundations of biology and medicine. **Educ:** Lycées de Thionville, Langres, Aix-en-Provence (Agrégé in Philosophy, 1949); Lyceé Ampere, Lyon; University of Lyon (Doctor of Medicine, 1958). **Infls:** Gaston Bachelard, Michel Foucault and G. Canguilhem. **Appts:** From 1953, teacher then Professor of Philosophy (1959), University of Lyon.

Main publications:

(1953) *Sciences de la vie et de la culture*, Paris: Hachette.
(1954) *Philosophie biologique*, Paris: PUF.
(1964) *La Raison et les remèdes*, Paris: PUF.
(1967) *Tableaux et langues de la chimie*, Paris: Le Seuil.
(1970) *Le Catalogue de la vie*, Paris: PUF.
(1972) *Gaston Bachelard*, Paris: PUF.
(1973) *Ecriture et iconographie*, Paris: Vrin.
(1977) *Une épistémologie de l'espace concret*, Paris: Vrin.
(1979) *Mémoire pour l'avenir*, Paris: Vrin.

Secondary literature:

Burr, J. R. (ed.) (1980) *Handbook of World Philosophy: Contemporary Developments Since 1945*, London: Aldwych Press, pp. 61–4.

Dagognet is a psychiatrist and also a philosopher and historian of science (particularly of biology and chemistry) much inspired by Gaston **Bachelard**. Like Bachelard he stresses the discontinuity in rational and scientific thought and regards the scientific rationalization of experience as 'un rationalisme ouvert', involving a dynamic 'rapport' between subject and object. Thus, opposed both to the idea that thought is a mere reproduction of reality and to the idea that reality is an a priori rational construction, he holds that knowledge affects the known object and vice versa. He associates this view with a (non-Marxist) dialectical materialism that repudiates the separation of theory and practice and affirms that we only know what we try to change.

This epistemological position underlies Dagognet's philosophical analyses of medicine and therapeutic practices. According to him normative questions concerning the nature of health are logically inseparable from empirical questions concerning the efficacy of remedies. Concerned to expose the 'illusions of pharmacology', he rejects the commonplace medical belief that there is an 'objectivité curative', an absolute remedy for all or even any illness, presupposing invariant relations between the chemical composition of a substance and its physiological effects. Calling attention to the unpredictability of cures, owing to such factors as the effect of the patient's beliefs and individual differences, he maintains that there is only a 'curative dynamism', a material dialectic between the cure (for example, a certain drug) and the patient's convictions, an interaction modifying both. It is widely recognized that the great achievement of Dagognet's analyses is to have shown that remedies are in part social and cultural products.

Sources: Huisman.

STEPHEN MOLLER

Daly, Mary

American. **b:** 16 October 1928, Schenectady, New York. **Cat:** Feminist theologian and philosopher. **Ints:** Philosophy of value. **Educ:** College of St Rose, Catholic University of America, St Mary's College (Notre Dame) and the University of Freiburg (Switzerland). **Appts:** 1954–9, teaching post in Philosophy and Theology, Cardinal Cushing College; 1959–66, junior year abroad programme, Rosary College, La Salle College, Georgetown University, Freiburg; from 1966, Assistant then Associate Professor of Theology, Boston College.

Main publications:

(1966) *Natural Knowledge of God in the Philosophy of Jacques Maritain*, Rome: Catholic Book Agency.
(1968) *The Church and the Second Sex*, London: G. Chapman; revised edition, 1985.
(1973) *Beyond God the Father*, Boston: Beacon Press; second revised edition, 1985.

(1978) *Gyn/Ecology: The Metaethics of Radical Feminism*, Boston: Beacon Press.

(1984) *Pure Lust: Elemental Feminist Philosophy*, London: Women's Press.

(1987) (with Jane Caputi) *Webster's First New Intergalactic Wickedary of the English Language*, Boston: Beacon Press.

(1992) *Outercourse: The Be-dazzling Voyage*, San Francisco: Harper.

Secondary literature:

Grimshaw, Jean (1988) 'Pure lust: the elemental philosophy of Mary Daly', *Radical Philosophy* 49: 24–30.

Sullivan, Timothy D. (1980) 'Women and ideology', *Philosophical Studies (Ireland)* 27: 94–115.

Finding in the women's revolution a counteragent to the oppressive structures of society, the trajectory of Daly's criticism has moved through four stages: traditional philosophical analysis; social criticism directed to the secondary status of women in the Church; analysis of Christianity as patriarchal and misogynist; extension of the criticism to all culture, along with a deepening of the analysis in various ways. The second stage was energized by Daly's disappointment over the outcome of the Second Vatican Council. The third stage grew out of the second, and is embodied in *Beyond God the Father* (1973). Here the claims of misogyny are documented from the writings of major religious leaders and theologians. No one escapes. Even liberal churches continue to reflect a 'faded authoritarianism', and a shadow hangs over 'the kingdom of God'.

The spiritualized human awareness she seeks is offered by some philosophers (William **James**, **Bergson**, **Whitehead** and **Hartshorne**), whose general approach blends with the language of **Buber** and **Tillich** in her resolution of the problem. One exchanges God the Father for a final cause, the creative drawing power of the Good, not a substance but 'the Verb' supplying motive power for becoming, and understood as an eternal, nonreifiable Thou. Women are a nonbeing seeking being, whose power emerges in facing nothingness. Part of the realignment comes from renaming, mentioned here and developed in the *Wickedary* (1987), whose object is a new and more powerful feminist vocabulary. The becoming of women is of crucial importance. Since women are 'the victims of a planetary caste system', their coming to be is the only hope of altering 'the seemingly doomed course of human evolution'.

WILLIAM REESE

Danto, Arthur Coleman

American. *b:* 1 January 1924, Ann Arbor, Michigan. *Cat:* Analytic philosopher; art critic. *Ints:* Aesthetics; metaphysics; philosophy of mind and action; philosophy of history. *Educ:* Wayne State University and Columbia University, 1949–52; Fulbright Scholar, University of Paris, 1949–50: Fellow, the American Academy of Arts and Sciences. *Infls:* Significant philosophical influences include Hegel, Nietzsche, Wittgenstein and Sartre; personal influences include John Herman Randall, Ernest Nagel and Sidney Morgenbesser. *Appts:* Member of Faculty, Columbia University, since 1952; Johnsonian Professor of Philosophy, Columbia University, from 1975; an editor of *The Journal of Philosophy* from 1965; art critic of *The Nation* since 1984.

Main publications:

(1964) 'The artworld', *Journal of Philosophy* 61.

(1965) *Analytic Philosophy of History*, Cambridge: Cambridge University Press; revised edition published as *Narration and Knowledge*, New York: Columbia University Press, 1985.

(1965) *Nietzsche as Philosopher*, New York: Macmillan; reprinted, New York: Columbia University Press, 1980.

(1968) *Analytic Philosophy of Knowledge*, Cambridge: Cambridge University Press.

(1968) *What Philosophy Is*; New York: Harper & Row; Harmondsworth: Penguin, 1971.

(1972) *Mysticism and Morality*, New York: Basic Books; Harmondsworth: Penguin.

(1973) *Analytic Philosophy of Action*, Cambridge: Cambridge University Press.

(1975) *J.-P. Sartre*, New York: Viking Press; Glasgow: Fontana.

(1981) *The Transfiguration of the Commonplace*, Cambridge, Mass.: Harvard University Press.

(1986) *The Philosophical Disenfranchisement of Art*, New York: Columbia University Press.

(1987) *The State of the Art*, New York: Prentice-Hall.

(1989) *Connections to the World*, New York: Harper Collins.

(1990) *Encounters and Reflections: Art in the Historical Present*, New York: Farrar, Straus, & Giroux.

(1992) *Beyond the Brillo Box: The Visual Arts in Post-Historical Perspective*, New York: Farrar, Straus, & Giroux.

Secondary literature:

Lang, B. (ed.) (1984) *The Death of Art*, New York: Haven Publications.

Rollins, M. (ed.) (1993) *Danto and His Critics*, Oxford: Blackwell.

Danto has extended the methods of analytic philosophy into areas often neglected by the Anglo-American tradition, such as the philosophies of **Nietzsche** and **Sartre**, mysticism and history. It is in the theory of art that his most original and influential work is to be found. In his seminal paper 'The artworld', he declared: 'To see something as art requires something the eye cannot descry—an atmosphere of artistic theory, a knowledge of the history of art: an artworld' (*Journal of Philosophy*, vol. 61, 1964, p. 580). That is to say, works of art, such as, Warhol's *Brillo Boxes* are distinguished from their materially indiscernible counterparts, ordinary Brillo boxes, by the interpretations which constitute them as artworks. Danto has continued to deepen and refine this insight through his prolific writing in philosophy and art criticism. Inspired by his reading of Hegel, he articulates a philosophy of the history of art according to which art, through progressive consciousness of its own nature, transforms itself into philosophy and comes to an end. Danto's theory of art has been criticized for (i) misrepresenting the art/non-art distinction as an ontological distinction; (ii) confusing cultural knowledge presupposed in the recognition of artworks with interpretations involved in the appreciation of particular works, as well as with theories concerning the nature of art; and (iii) inflating parochial features of modernism into a definition of art at the expense of attention to the complexities of artistic practices.
Sources: WW(Am).

PETER LEWIS

D'Arcy, Martin Cyril
British. **b:** 15 June 1888, Bath, England. **d:** 20 November 1976, London. **Cat:** Scholastic. **Ints:** Philosophy of religion. **Educ:** University of Oxford and Gregorian University, Rome. **Infls:** Aquinas and Newman. **Appts:** 1932–45, Lecturer in Oxford, then Master of Campion Hall.

Main publications:
(1930) *Thomas Aquinas*, London: Benn.
(1937) *The Nature of Belief*; second edition, London: Herder; Dublin: Clonmore & Reynolds, 1958.
(1959) *The Sense of History*, London: Faber.
(1962) *No Absent God*, London: Catholic Book Club.
(1969) *Humanism and Christianity*, London: Constable.

Secondary literature:
Copleston, Frederick (1976) 'Father Martin D'Arcy', *The Month*, N.S. 10: 22–4.

Much of D'Arcy's work has theological as well as philosophical roots. However, he was extremely well versed both in the philosophy of his time and in medieval philosophy, and had a sharp analytical mind. His *Thomas Aquinas* (1930), though somewhat dated, is still an excellent introduction for philosophy students. *No Absent God* (1962) is in some ways a typical work. It deals briskly with whether existence is a predicate, proofs for the existence of God, and discussions of the concept of the self in both existentialism and analytical philosophy. Not the least of D'Arcy's merits was the elegance and simplicity of his style, and his deep roots in European literature and culture. His books were well received on publication, and are still read.
Sources: WWW.

HUGH BREDIN

Davidson, Donald Herbert
American. **b:** March 1917, Springfield, Massachusetts. **Cat:** Philosopher of mind; philosopher of language. **Ints:** Casuation; meaning. **Educ:** Harvard University, BA 1939, MA 1941, PhD 1949. **Infls:** Carl Hempel, Hans Reichenbach, Rudolf Carnap, Willard Van Orman Quine and Alfred Tarski. **Appts:** Instructor, Queen's University (NY) College, 1947–56; Stanford University, California, 1951–67; Professor, Princeton University, 1967–70; Professor, Rockefeller University, 1970–6; Professor, University of Chicago, 1976–81; Professor, University of California, Berkeley, from 1981; John Locke Lecturer, University of Oxford, 1970.

Main publications:
(1972) (ed. with Gilbert Harman) *Semantics of Natural Language*, Dordrecht: Reidel.
(1980) *Essays on Actions and Events*, Oxford: Clarendon Press.
(1984) *Inquiries into Meaning and Truth*, Oxford.

Secondary literature:
Evnine, S. (1991) *Donald Davidson*, Polity Press.
Lepore, E. (ed.) (1986) *Truth and Interpretation: Perspectives on the Philosophy of Donald Davidson*, Oxford: Blackwell.
——and McLaughlin, B. (eds) (1985) *Actions and Events: Perspectives on the Philosophy of Donald Davidson*, Oxford: Blackwell.

Donald Davidson is one of the major contributors to contemporary analytic philosophy. Over a period of three decades he has outlined and developed two distinctive and intimately related theoretical perspectives in the philosophy of mind and the philosophy of language. Some of his earliest work was devoted to uncovering the logical form of causal and action statements, already demonstrating the close relation between semantic and other substantive issues. Dissatisfied with standard analyses of such statements, he argued that legitimate inferences, for example from 'Caesar stabbed Brutus with a knife' to 'Caesar stabbed Brutus' were not recoverable unless such statements were analysed in terms of relations between events, where these latter were taken as belonging to an ontological category distinct from things and their properties. Espousing a materialist position, Davidson had to accommodate prima facie conflicting theses: that as human beings we were part of the natural order, but that our mental life and voluntary action failed to fit the requirements of deterministic law. Davidson disputes that there are strict laws connecting the mental and the physical, or connecting mental events with one another, despite being committed to the view that each mental event is a physical event. This controversial view, which he calls 'anomalous monism', itself supplies an interesting twist to the debates between proponents of soft and hard determinism, the point being that it is only under a physical description that mental events instantiate deterministic laws. Yet for Davidson causation is essential to understanding the idea of acting with a reason, and we can make singular causal claims without reference to any laws that they might instantiate. Reasons are not only causes, but also explanatory of what people do. Thus Davidson's strategy is appropriately described as rationalizing one, in that normative principles embody all that we know about mental life and human action. So while we might defer to experts about the nature of copper or quarks, our everyday or 'folk-psychology' requires no such deference.

In his treatment of the mental Davidson concentrates on 'propositional attitudes', states with propositional content as expressed in statements like 'Joan believes that snow is white'. He sees beliefs as explanatory, but also as showing how other beliefs and actions can be reasonable, given those initial beliefs. Being a believer-agent, therefore, amounts to being more or less rational. Not only is this strategy normative, it is holistic in that we cannot ascribe beliefs and other attitudes in isolation, but only as elements in a web of attitudes. This holistic dimension owes much to the influence of **Quine**, and this influence is visible elsewhere in Davidson's work.

Undoubtedly Davidson's most significant and influential work has been in the field of what is known as 'truth-conditional semantics', the theoretical position according to which the meaning of a sentence in a language is given by stating the conditions under which it is true. Furthermore, this type of theory purports to show how the truth-conditions of sentences are determined by the semantic properties of the component expressions such as nouns and verbs. Such a theory might be expected to yield for any sentence S, a sentence of the form 'S means p', in which the meaning of S is given by whatever sentence replaces p. However, again under Quinean influence, Davidson regards any appeal to 'meanings' as opaque and, drawing on the work of Alfred **Tarski**, substitutes locutions of the form 'S is true if, and only if, p', claiming that a theory based on the notion of truth is both more perspicuous and can do all that a theory of meaning is supposed to do. Davidson does, however, depart from Tarski in certain respects: the latter's work was exclusively with formalized technical languages, and was combined with a scepticism about the applicability of formal techniques to natural languages, everyday languages being too messy, changeable and inconsistent. It is precisely these features which pose the most acute problems for Davidson himself, especially indexicality (involving terms like 'I', 'this' and 'now'), attributive adjectives like 'good' and 'large', and indirect speech contexts as instanced by 'Galileo said that the earth moves'. Attempts by Davidson and his followers to deal with these problems, while exhibiting considerable ingenuity and innovation, have met with a mixed reception from critics.

The two main strands of Davidson's work have a wider purport which goes beyond their narrower technical interest. It has to be shown how the theory of meaning can be put to work in interpreting the utterances of speakers of an alien tongue, using the strategy of 'radical interpretation'. Davidson imposes a constraint on this, called the 'principle of charity', by which we seek to maximize agreement between ourselves and the speakers of the other language. We are to assume that most of what those natives say is true by our lights. Davidson sets himself against scepticism and relativism, arguing that there is no sense to be attached to the notion of radically divergent or alternative conceptual schemes. Local untranslatability is unremarkable; wholesale untranslatability between languages is unintelligible. Davidson has influenced many younger philosophers including John McDowell, Colin McGinn and Mark Platts. He has also attracted spirited criticisms from thinkers as diverse as Michael **Dummett** (on the question of the form a theory of meaning should take) and Jerry **Fodor** (on the status of the mental within the natural order). More generally, his anomalous monism has been condemned as an unstable compromise, and theorists otherwise sympathetic to his semantical project have none the less suggested that appeal to truth-conditions is at best necessary but not sufficient to account for how and why people behave and speak as they do. Overall his work has had a conspicuous impact on some major philosophical issues such as relativism, objectivity and rationality, and as such has a relevance to debates in discipline areas outside the traditional boundaries of philosophy.

Sources: WWW(Am).

DENIS POLLARD

Dawes Hicks, George

British. *b:* 14 September 1862, Shrewsbury, England. *d:* 16 February 1941, Cambridge, England. *Cat:* Critical realist. *Ints:* Epistemology; philosophy of religion. *Educ:* Owens College, Manchester and University of Leipzig. *Infls:* Adamson, Wundt, Ward and Meinong. *Appts:* Professor, University College, London, 1904–28.

Main publications:

(1937) *Philosophical Bases of Theism*, London.
(1938) *Critical Realism*, London.

Secondary literature:

De Burgh, W. G. (1941) Obituary in *Proceedings of the British Academy*.

Dawes Hicks became a professional philosopher after some years as a Unitarian minister. He ended his career a disappointed man, unrecognized and undiscussed. Deeply learned and very industrious, he never managed to write a proper book (*Critical Realism* is a selection of articles); he nevertheless had one good idea, which he never succeeded in bringing to serious attention. That idea is that in perception—and, indeed, the acquisition of knowledge, or 'cognition', generally—there is no need to interpose a third entity—idea, presentation or sense-datum—between the mind that knows and the object that is known. To perceive is to become aware of *part* of the content of the object, but that part is still part of the *object*, not a private mental item. To cope with error he developed a theory of the imaginative supplementation of the perceived with reproduced perceptual material. Since this deceptive imagery seems

indiscriminable from the content of veridical perception, and yet is indubitably private and mental, the objectivity he ascribes to veridical content is rendered insecure. His Hibbert lectures on natural theology reject attempts to found religious belief on mystical experience, but are well disposed to the claims of religious experience of a more straightforward and coherently expressible kind. The main bulk of Dawes Hicks' published work consists of careful criticism of the writings of his contemporaries: **Bradley**, **Bosanquet**, **Moore**, **Russell**, **Alexander** and, more favourably, **Ward** and Meinong. His reputed expertise on the philosophy of Kant received no interesting public expression. Dawes Hicks's sense of failure was justified; his ideas have neither been influential nor even rejected. Yet he was a serious thinker and, in retrospect, cuts a better figure than many who pottered imitatively about on the topic of sense-data.

Sources: Metz; Passmore 1957; DNB; Hill.

ANTHONY QUINTON

De Koninck, Charles

Belgian-Canadian. *b:* 29 July 1906, Torhout, Belgium. *d:* 13 February 1965, Rome. *Cat:* Aristotelian. *Ints:* History of religion; philosophy of science; politics. *Educ:* His family emigrated to the United States in 1914, but Charles returned to Belgium where he studied Classics at the Collège Notre Dame in Ostend and studied Chemistry and Physics at the École Normale in Torhout, followed by three years reading Philosophy (1925–8); returned briefly to the United States and studied at the University of Detroit but came back to Belgium to study at Louvain in 1932; received his doctorate in philosophy in 1934 with a thesis on the Philosophy of Sir Arthur Eddington. *Infls:* Eddington and Turing. *Appts:* Invited in 1934 to Laval University, in Quebec City, where he stayed for the remainder of his life; Dean of the Faculté de Philosophie, 1939–56.

Main publications:

(1936) *Le Cosmos*, Quebec: Imprimerie Franciscaine Missionaire.
(1943) *De la primauté du bien commun contre les personnalistes; Le principe de l'ordre nouveau*, Quebec: Éditions de l'Université Laval; Montreal: Fides.
(1943) *Ego sapientia ... La sagesse qui est Marie*, Quebec: Éditions de l'Université Laval.
(1954) *La Confédération, rempart contre le grand état*, Quebec: Royal Commission on Constitutional Problems.

(1954) *Le Piété du fils: études sur l'Assomption*, Quebec: Presses Universitaires Laval.
(1960) *The Hollow Universe*, London: Oxford University Press (The Whidden Lectures, McMaster University, Series IV).
(1964) *Tout homme est mon prochain*, Quebec: Presses de l'Université Laval.

Secondary literature:
Armour, Leslie (1987, 1991) *Laval Théologique et Philosophique*.
Gagné, Armand and De Koninck, Thomas (1968) *Mélanges à la mémoire de Charles de Koninck*, Presses de l'Université Laval (contains complete bibliography).
McInerny, Ralph M. (1965) 'Charles de Koninck, a philosopher of order', *New Scholasticism* 39, 4 (summary).
Smith, Michael A. (1992) 'The dignity of the human person and its relationship to the common good', PhD thesis, Laval University (emphasis on scholastic roots).

Aristotelian and Thomistic ideas were central to De Koninck's work, but he developed them in novel ways to support his view that nature is richer than we tend to think. He believed that there is a core of universal moral truths but its essence is such that it demands wide tolerance of human beliefs and of ways of life.

He was Professor of the Philosophy of Nature at Laval, and his own notions about the theory of knowledge—always the main interest to which he returned—stemmed chiefly from his reflections on science. His view of scientific practice was originally strongly influenced by Sir Arthur **Eddington** and later by Alan **Turing**'s notion of calculation. He believed that science, although soundly based on its own ground, could not give us an adequate concept of nature, and that traditional metaphysical questions remained relevant. Armour (1987, 1991) has found early intimations of the environmental movement in some of De Koninck's work and has explored and tried to explain some seeming conflicts between his philosophy of science and his writings on religion. De Koninck had a considerable impact in English Canada as a philosopher of science and in Quebec as a philosopher of religion and a political thinker. Through his many graduate students his influence spread to the USA. In English Canada his *Hollow Universe* (1960) attracted an audience which wanted to reconcile science and religion, and its main theme—that science is a set of abstractions intelligible and valuable in themselves for pragmatic purposes but inadequate to

the whole range of human experience—drew him a wide audience. He was a staunch defender of federalism, political liberty and pluralism, who nevertheless retained a reputation for religious orthodoxy at a time when the Catholic Church was widely accused of supporting authoritarian government.

Sources: Archives of Laval Univ.; unpublished biography by Thomas De Koninck.

LESLIE ARMOUR

De Laguna, Grace Mead Andrus
American. **b:** 28 September 1878, East Berlin, Conn. **d:** 17 February 1978, Devon, Pa. **Cat:** Eclectic thinker. **Ints:** Philosophical anthropology; philosophy of language; metaphysics; science. **Educ:** Cornell University. **Infls:** Heidegger. **Appts:** 1912–72, Assistant Professor, Associate Professor, Professor of Philosophy, Bryn Mawr College; 1925, Founder, with Theodore de Laguna, of Fullerton Philosophy Club.

Main publications:
(1910) (with Theodore de Laguna) *Dogmatism and Evolution* New York: Macmillan.
(1917) 'The limits of the physical', in *Philosophical Essays in Honour of James Edward Creighton*, New York: Macmillan.
(1927) *Speech: Its Function and Development*, Bloomington: Indiana University Press.
(1930) 'Phenomena and their determination', *Philosophical Review* 26.
(1942) 'Cultural relativism and science', *Philosophical Review* 51.
(1951) 'Speculative philosophy', *Philosophical Review* 60.
(1963) 'The person', *Review of Metaphysics* 17.
(1966) *On Existence and the Human World*, New Haven and London: Yale University Press.

In the Preface to her *On Existence and the Human World* (1966) De Laguna delares her speculative concern with problems relating to 'the temporal existence of nature and its relation to man and his human world'. She develops a metaphysical position in which she uses the term 'teleonomy' to describe the existence in nature of ends that are independent of humankind and its conscious purposes. In an examination of the interaction of metaphysical conceptions and scientific theories, with particular reference to the burgeoning of science in the seventeenth century, she discusses the evolution of problems of determinism, natural law and the ontological status of the individual and of values. In her consideration of anthropology and cultural relativism she maintains that 'while anthropology is justified in regarding the specific and varying moral standards of different cultures as relative to these cultures, its own scientific procedure involves the acceptance of standards which are universal and objective'. De Laguna's work on language is aligned with the thought of behaviourists such as **Watson**, **Holt** and **Mead**.

Sources: Obituary, *New York Times*, 25 Feb 1978, p. 24; Kersey.

DIANÉ COLLINSON

De Raeymaeker, Louis

Belgian. *b:* 18 November 1895, Sint-Pieters Rode. *d:* 25 February 1970, Louvain. *Cat:* Scholastic. *Ints:* Metaphysics. *Educ:* Malines and University of Louvain. *Infls:* Aquinas and Mercier. *Appts:* 1927–35, Professor of Philosophy at Malines; 1948–65, President of the Institut Supérieur de Philosophie, University of Louvain.

Main publications:

(1931–2) *Metaphysica Generalis*, 2 vols, Louvain: Warny.

(1938) *Introduction à la philosophie*, Louvain: Editions de L'Institut Supérieur de Philosophie (English translation, *Introduction to Philosophy*, New York: Wagner, 1948).

(1946) *Philosophie de l'être*, Louvain: Editions de L'Institut Supérieur de Philosophie (English translation, *The Philosophy of Being*, St Louis: Herder, 1954).

Secondary literature:

John, Helen James (1966) 'De Raeymaeker, participation and the absolute value of being', in *The Thomist Spectrum*, New York: Fordham University Press, pp. 123–36.

Van Riet, George (1970) 'In memoriam Monseigneur Louis de Raemaker', *Revue Philosophique de Louvain* 68: 5–10.

One of the most influential members of the Louvain school of Thomism in the middle part of the century, not least through his roles as Director of the Institut Supérieur de Philosophie and editor of the *Revue Philosophique de Louvain*. His most characteristic work is *The Philosophy of Being* (1946), which presents a contemporary version of Aquinas's later metaphysics. De Raeymaeker argues that this is a metaphysics whose central explanatory concept is that of participation, testimony to a strong element of Platonism in Aquinas which is too often overlooked. The

most general of all metaphysical notions is the idea of being (*esse*). Individual beings, in this interpretation of Aquinas, are to be thought of as participating in *esse*, and this participation is the source both of their existence as unique individuals and their essential identity as this or that kind of thing. The concept of participation, therefore, indicates the common foundation of essence and existence in being in general. De Raeymaeker's studies of Aquinas were, and are, well received in Thomistic circles.

Sources: DFN; EF.

HUGH BREDIN

De Vogel, Cornelia Johanna

Dutch. *b:* February 1905, Leeuwarden, Netherlands. *d:* May 1986, Renesse, Zeeland, Netherlands. *Cat:* Platonist; historian of philosophy; philosopher of religion. *Educ:* Classical Philology and Philosophy, University of Utrecht. *Infls:* Plato, neo-Platonism, St Augustine and Cardinal Newman. *Appts:* 1946–74, Professor of Ancient and Patristic Philosophy, 1946–68, Professor of Medieval Philosophy, University of Utrecht.

Main publications:

(1946) *Ecclesia Catholica*, Brussels: Spectrum.

(1948) 'L'Idée de l'unité de Dieu une vérité rationelle', *Mélanges Philosophiques* (presented to the members of the Xth International Congress of Philosophy at Amsterdam) Amsterdam, pp. 24–39.

(1950–7) *Greek Philosophy*, 3 vols, Leiden: E. J. Brill (texts with notes and commentary).

(1954) 'À la recherche des étapes précises entre Platon et le Néoplatonisme', *Mnemosyne* 4, 7, Leiden: E. J. Brill, pp. 111–22.

(1958) 'Antike Seinsphilosophie und Christentum im Wandel der Jahrhunderte', in *Festgabe J. Lorentz*, Baden Baden, pp. 527–48.

(1966) *Pythagoras and Early Pythagoreanism*, Assen: Van Gorcum.

(1970) *Philosophia I*, Assen: Van Gorcum (studies in Greek philosophy).

(1972) *Philosophia II*, Assen: Van Gorcum.

(1985) *Rethinking Plato and Platonism*, Leiden: E. J. Brill.

De Vogel wrote extensively on Greek, patristic and medieval philosophy, but her closest attention was given to Plato and the later pagan and Christian Platonic writers. She held that Platonic Ideas have been understood by many Christian authors, including Augustine, as constituting the Divine Wisdom. She maintained that the doctrine of Ideas is an aspect of a theory of predication since, in Plato's view, all predication of designations involves the assertion of Ideas. At the same time, it is more than a theory of predication, for 'the great', 'the small', 'the beautiful' and so on are not just logical entities but real existents in a transcendent world. Her interpretation of Plato is in sharp contrast with those of the English Platonists **Owen** and Cherniss. In opposition to the theologian Karl **Barth**, she defended the possibility of natural knowledge of God.

De Vogel was a Roman Catholic. She did not espouse feminism in the modern style, but her interpretation of Aquinas's concepts of natural and eternal law enabled her to argue for a woman's right to contraception on the grounds that reason (that is, nature in the highest sense) requires protection from nature. She maintained that there are no theological arguments against the priesthood of women.

Sources: De Vogel's writings; personal acquaintance.

C. W. WOLFSKEEL

De Wulf, Maurice Charles Joseph

Belgian. *b:* 6 April 1867, Poperinghe, Belgium. *d:* 23 December 1947, Poperinghe. *Cat:* Scholastic. *Ints:* History of medieval philosophy. *Educ:* University of Louvain. *Infls:* Aquinas and Mercier. *Appts:* 1894–1939, Professor of Medieval Philosophy, Institut Supérieur de Philosophie at Louvain; 1920–7, Professor of Medieval Philosophy, Harvard University.

Main publications:

(1900) *Histoire de la philosophie médiévale*, sixth edition in 3 vols, Louvain: Institut Supérieur de Philosophie; Paris: Vrin, 1947 (English translation, *History of Medieval Philosophy*, of third edition 1909, of fifth edition in 2 vols 1926, of sixth edition in 3 vols, London, New York and Toronto: Longman, Green & Co., 1951).

(1904) *Introduction à la philosophie néoscolastique*, Louvain: Institut Supérieur de Philosophie (English translation, *Scholasticism Old and New*, Dublin: Gill, 1907).

(1920) *L'Oeuvre d'art et la beauté*, Louvain: Institut Supérieur de Philosophie.

(1922) *Philosophy and Civilization in the Middle Ages*, Princeton: Princeton University Press.

Secondary literature:

Harmignie, Pierre (1934) 'La Carrière scientifique de Monsieur Professeur De Wulf', *Revue Néoscolastique de Philosophie*, 36: 39–66 (which includes a bibliography).

Noël, Léon (1934) 'L'Oeuvre de Monsieur de Wulf', *Revue Néoscolastique de Philosophie* 36: 11–38.

One of the most distinguished historians of medieval philosophy in the early part of the century. In keeping with the character of Louvain's Institut Supérieur de Philosophie, he focused sharply upon medieval philosophy, rather than, say, medieval thought (which would have included theology). He provided his philosophical colleagues, and generations of students of philosophy, with clear and accurate accounts of the medieval texts and the medieval philosophical culture on the basis of which they were attempting to reconstruct Thomistic and scholastic thinking in contemporary language, and for a contemporary readership. He envisaged medieval philosophy as a more or less homogeneous and, from the thirteenth century, more or less Aristotelian enterprise. Later historians, influenced by **Gilson** and others, discern great diversities among medieval philosophers, and have uncovered a much greater element of later neo-Platonism than was hitherto realized. De Wulf was highly regarded in his own time, and his historical studies are still worth reading, but he has to some extent been superseded.

Sources: DFN; EF.

HUGH BREDIN

Deborin, Abram Moiseevich (pen-name of A. M. Ioffe)

Russian. *b:* 16 June (4 N.S.) 1881, Upyna, Lithuania. *d:* 8 March 1963, Moscow. *Cat:* Marxist. *Educ:* Graduated in Philosophy at University of Berne in 1908. *Infls:* Marx, Plekhanov and Hegel. *Appts:* Worked at the Sverdlov Communist University, The Institute of Red Professorship, the Communist Academy and the Marx–Engels Institute.

Main publications:

(1916) *Vvedenie v filosofiiu dialekticheskogo materializma* [Introduction to the Philosophy of Dialectical Materialism], Petrograd.

(1924) *Lenin kak myslitel'* [Lenin as a Thinker], Moscow.

(1926) *Filosofiia i marksizm* [Philosophy and Marxism], Moscow.

(1928) *Dialektika i estestvoznanie* [Dialectics and Science], Moscow and Leningrad.

(1961) *Filosofiia i politika* [Philosophy and Politics], Moscow: Izdatel'stvo Akademii nauk SSSR.

Secondary literature:

Joravsky, D. (1961) *Soviet Marxism and Natural Science 1917–1932*, London: Routledge & Kegan Paul, esp. chs 11–13.

Wetter, G. A. (1958) *Dialectical Materialism: A Historical and Systematic Survey of Philosophy in the Soviet Union*, trans. Peter Heath, London: Routledge & Kegan Paul, pp. 155–66.

Born into a poor Jewish family, Deborin emigrated to Switzerland in 1903, joining the Bolshevik faction of the Russian Social-Democratic Labour Party. Although he went over to the Mensheviks from 1907 until 1917, he became the leading Soviet philosopher of the 1920s, and edited the principal ideological and philosophical journal *Pod znamenem marksizma* [Under the Banner of Marxism] from 1926 to 1930. Despite the victory of the Deborinites over the Mechanists at the 1929 conference of Marxist–Leninist Institutes, the very next year his philosophical position was denounced by Stalin as 'Menshevizing idealism'; He subsequently kept a low profile in the Soviet Academy of Sciences until Stalin's death in 1953.

Before the Revolution, Deborin supported dialectical materialism against the aspirations of Machians and neo-Kantians to furnish the philosophical basis of Marxism. During the 1920s, he and his supporters took on the Mechanists, a loose grouping including **Aksel'rod (Ortodoks)**, **Bogdanov** and **Bukharin**, who adopted a broadly positivist interpretation of dialectical materialism; the more extreme among them either dismissed philosophy out of hand or regarded it as subordinate to the natural sciences. Deborin insisted on the independence of dialectical materialism as a discipline concerned with the methodology and theory of scientific knowledge; a dialectical philosophy is necessary to guide the empirical sciences towards a synthesis of the general and the particular. He opposed the reductionism of the Mechanists, asserting the dialectical emergence of qualitatively distinct stages or discontinuities in the development of matter, the higher forms of which (living and thinking matter) are irreducible to the inorganic matter from which they are ultimately derived.

The debate was often acrimonious, and marked on both sides by the caricature of opposing views. The Deborinites were condemned for taking an insufficiently materialist view of the Hegelian dialectic, and for failing to apply it to concrete issues; they were also charged with holding an idealist conception of matter, and for preferring **Plekhanov** to **Lenin** as a philoso-pher. It was ultimately by political decree that a Stalinist unity was imposed on the dialectical struggle between the opposing camps.

COLIN CHANT

Degenaar, Johan (Johannes Jacobus)

South African. *b:* 7 March 1926, Ladysmith, Natal, South Africa. *Cat:* Existential phenomenologist; analytical philosopher; interpreter of other philosophers' work; phenomenological anthropologist and humanist. *Ints:* Political, aesthetic and literary theory. *Educ:* Studied at the University of Stellenbosch in the Republic of South Africa, 1944–9; Groningen in the Netherlands, under Helmuth Plessner and Gerhardus van der Leeuw, 1949–50; Leiden under C. A. van Peursen, 1961. *Infls:* Husserl, Heidegger, Kierkegaard and Buber. *Appts:* 1949–69, Lecturer at the University of Stellenbosch; 1969–91, Professor of Political Philosophy, Stellenbosch.

Main publications:

(1962) *Exsistensie en Gestalte* [Existence and Form], Johannesburg: Simondium-uitgewers.

(1963) *Die Sterflikheid van die Siel* [The Mortality of the Soul], Johannesburg: Simondium-uitgewers.

(1963) *Op Weg na 'n nuwe politieke lewenshouding*, Capetown: Tafelberg.

(1965) *Evolusie en Christendom* [Evolution and Christendom], Capetown: Simondium-uitgewers.

(1966) *Die Wereld van Albert Camus* [The World of Albert Camus], Johannesburg: Afrikaanse Pers-Boekhandel.

(1967) *Sekularisasie* [Secularization], Pretoria: Academica.

(1969) (with M. Versfeld and W. A. de Klerk) *Beweging Uitwaarts*, Capetown: John Malherbe.

(1976) *Moraliteit en Politiek* [Mortality and Politics], Capetown: Tafelberg.

(1980) *Voortbestaan in Geregtigheid*, Capetown: Tafelberg.

(1982) *Keuse vir die Afrikaner*, Johannesburg: Turus.

(1982) *The Roots of Nationalism*, Societas 15, Capetown: Academica.

(1982) *Marxism–Leninism and its Implications for South Africa*, Societas 14, Capetown: Academica.

(1984) *Death of God: A Secular View of Religion*, Capetown: Dept. of Adult Education and Extramural Studies.

(1986) *Art and the Meaning of Life*, Capetown: Dept. of Adult Education and Extramural Studies.

(1991) 'The myth of a South African nation', *IDASA Occasional Papers* 40: 1–20.

Secondary literature:
Burr, J. R. (ed.) *Handbook of World Philosophy*, London: Aldwych Press.
In Gesprek (1986), a Festschrift dedicated to Johan Degenaar.
Van Niekerk, Anton (ed.) (1991) *South African Journal of Philosophy*, 10, 3 (issue dedicated to Degenaar).

Degenaar writes mainly in Afrikaans and his books, which are relatively short, consist mainly of essays on a common theme. His moral concern with the question of what it means to be a human being forms the basis of a political philosophy propounding justice for all, and in taking ordinary experience seriously he endeavours to make philosophy accessible to all in terms of everyday language and by the exploration of the imaginative play of signs in myths, fairy-tales, stories, novels, plays and films.

One aspect of his work is the assessment and interpretation of other philosophers' writings. His *Evolusie en Christendom* (1965) is a sympathetic treatment of the French Jesuit and palaeontologist, **Teilhard de Chardin**. *Die Wereld van Albert Camus* (1966) treats of absurdity, revolt and solidarity in the thought of the French existentialist writer, Albert **Camus**, and *Exsistensie en Gestalte* (1962) concerns existentialist traits in the poetry of the greatest Afrikaans poet, N. P. van Wyk Louw.

Another aspect of his work has a much wider scope. *Die Sterflikheid van die Siel* (1963) is an introduction to phenomenological anthropology in which Degenaar argues that the 'mortality' of the soul underscores a person's commitment to *this* world and fellow human beings. *Op Weg na 'n nuwe politieke lewenshouding* (1963) is a work profoundly influenced by Kierkegaard, **Buber**, **Husserl** and **Heidegger** in which Degenaar rejects the Cartesian view of the human subject as self-enclosed. Instead he advocates a new humanism based upon the principles that human beings are human through relationships and only through openness and receptivity do they become whole and 'at home in the world. In the important little book, *Sekularisasie* (1967), these ideas are further developed within the framework of the concepts of 'secularization' and 'solidarity'. Degenaar argues that secularization either alienates persons or leads to a growing solidarity amongst them, and he is particularly interested in the latter, which he believes involves a theology of encounter.

In the late 1970s his interest gradually shifted towards aesthetics and literary theory, and many believe that it is in this field that—especially during the 1980s—he made his most valuable philosophical contribution. He was certainly instrumental in the introduction of Jacques **Derrida**'s thought and the deconstructivist/post-modernist tradition to South Africa.

It is likewise in the 1970s and 1980s that most of Degenaar's overtly political writings were published. They include such topics as: morality and politics; the place of ethnicity in politics and the concept of structural violence; the nature and danger of (Afrikaner) nationalism and—in 1991—the idea of a democratic culture in preference to the mystifications of the idea of 'nationhood'. Degenaar's anti-apartheid stance aroused considerable opposition from conservative Afrikaner intellectuals. He nevertheless remains perhaps the most influential South African philosopher to date and continues to be admired for his moral integrity and intellectual honesty.

Sources: Personal communication.

BARRY JONES

Del Vecchio, Giorgio

Italian. *b:* 26 August 1878, Bologna, Italy. *d:* 28 Novmeber 1970, Genoa. *Cat:* Philosopher of law. *Appts:* Professor of Philosophy of Law, Universities of Ferrara, Sassari, Messina, Bologna and Rome.

Main publications:
(1905) *I presupposti filosofici della nozione del diritto*.
(1908) *Il concetto della natura e il principio del diritto*.
(1922–3) *La giudizia* (English translation, *Justice*, A. H. Campbell, Edinburgh: Edinburgh University Press, 1952).
(1945) *Evoluzione e involuzione nel diritto*, Rome: Tumminelli.
(1953) *Lo Stato*, Rome: Editrice Studium.
(1956) *Il diritto internazionale e il problema della pace*, Rome: Editrice Studium.
(1957) *Lezioni di filosofia del diritto*, many editions (English translation, *Philosophy of Law*, Washington: Catholic University of America Press, 1953).
(1958) *Diritto naturale e unita europea*, Milan: Angeli.
(1969) *Man and Nature*, trans. A. H. Campbell, Notre Dame University Press.

Secondary literature:
Quaglio, D. (1984) *G. del Vecchio*, Naples: Edizioni Scientifiche Italiane.
Studi filosofici–giuridici dedicato a G. del Vecchio, Modena: Societa tipografica modenese, 1930.
Vidal, E. (1951) *La filosofia giuridici di G. del Vecchio*, Milan.

Del Vecchio entered with vigour into the movement instituted by Petrone against positivism, promulgating a programme for an idealist theory of law. There are three questions for philosophy of law. The first is *quid jus?*, what law is. The second is phenomenological, how law developed. The third is deontological and asks what the law should be, as opposed to what it is. In the manner of Kant, del Vecchio distinguishes the form and the content of the law. The law, as a historical phenomenon, is mutable, but juridical reality exists immutably and is a universal element within singular data. It is based on the fact that the self needs consciousness of others to be a self, a fact which bases the ideal of justice on respect for persons. Juridical reality is a priori and establishes the limiting conditions of the juridical experience. The fount of law is human nature, and, humans being social by nature, where we have people we have societies. One form of society is the state, where the tie between the individuals is the law, although it is an error to believe that the state is its creator. The state is the supreme organ of the law but the law is an emanation of human nature. The supreme law of justice which gives authority to the state is also the basis of relations between states. In so far as a state itself acts by the law so it will naturally be disposed to participate in the wider system of international law, and no state can, without violating the law of justice, refuse allegiance to international law.

COLIN LYAS

Deleuze, Gilles

French. *b:* 18 January 1925. *Cat:* Poststructuralist. *Ints:* History of modern philosophy; Nietzschean philosophy of difference; psychoanalysis (especially the philosophy of desire, schizoanalysis); language and the production of meaning; politics; art; literature; cinema. *Educ:* Lycée Charnot, Paris; Philosophy, Université de Paris I (Sorbonne), mid-1940s; Agrégé in Philosophy, 1949. *Infls:* Nietzsche, Freud, Marx, Lacan and Foucault. *Appts:* Taught Philosophy, Université de Paris VIII (Vincennes); supported several political causes including the Groupe d'Information sur les Prisons, which Foucault helped organize in 1971.

Main publications:

(1962) *Nietzsche et la philosophie*, Paris: PUF (English translation, *Nietzsche and Philosophy*, trans. Hugh Tomlinson, Minneapolis: University of Minnesota Press, 1983).

(1963) *La Philosophie critique de Kant*, Paris: PUF (English translation, *Critical Philosophy of Kant*, trans. Hugh Tomlinson and Barbara Habberjam, Minneapolis: University of Minnesota Press, 1984).

(1964) *Marcel Proust et les signes*, Paris: PUF; revised edition, *Proust et les signes*, 1976 (English translation, *Proust and Signs*, trans. Richard Howard, New York: G. Braziller, 1972).

(1968) *Différence et répétition*, Paris: PUF.

(1968) *Spinoza et le problème de l'expression*, Paris: PUF (English translation, *Expressionism in philosophy: Spinoza*, trans. Martin Joughin, New York: Zone Books, 1990).

(1969) *Logique du sens*, Paris: Minuit (English translation, *The Logic of Sense*, Mark Lester and Charles Stivale, ed. Constantin V. Boundas, London: Athlone, 1989).

(1972) (with Félix Guattari) *L'Anti-Oedipe: capitalisme et schizophrénie I*, Paris: Minuit (English translation, *Anti-Oedipus*, trans. Robert Hurley *et al.*, Preface by Michel Foucault, New York: Viking, 1977; reprinted, Minneapolis: University of Minnesota Press, 1983).

(1975) (with Félix Guattari) *Kafka: pour une littérature mineure*, Paris: Minuit (English translation, *Kafka: For a Minor Literature*, trans. Dana Polan, Foreword by Réda Bensmïa, Minneapolis: University of Minnesota Press, 1986).

(1980) *Empiricisme et sujectivité*, Paris: PUF (English translation, *Empiricism and subjectivity*, trans. and intro. Constantin V. Boundas, New York: Columbia University Press, 1991).

(1980) (with Félix Guattari) *Mille plateaux: capitalisme et schizophrénie II*, Paris: Minuit (English translation, *A Thousand Plateaus: Capitalism and Schizoprenia*, trans. and Foreword by Brian Massumi, Minneapolis: University of Minnesota Press, 1987).

(1983) *François Bacon: Logique de la sensation*, 2 vols, Paris: Éditions de la différence.

(1983) *Cinéma 1: l'Image-Mouvement*, Paris: Minuit (English translation, *Cinema 1: The Movement-Image*, trans. Hugh Tomlinson and Barbara Habberjam, Minneapolis: University of Minnesota Press, 1986).

(1985) *Cinéma 2: l'Image-Temps*, Paris: Minuit (English translation, *Cinema 2: The Time-Image*, trans. Hugh Tomlinson and Robert Galata, Minneapolis: University of Minnesota Press, 1989).

(1986) *Foucault*, Paris: Minuit (English translation, *Foucault*, trans. Sean Hand, foreword by Paul A. Bové, Minneapolis: University of Minnesota Press, 1988).

(1988) *Le Pli*, Paris: Minuit.

(1991) (with Félix Guattari) *Qu'est-ce que la philosophie?*, Paris: Minuit (English translation,

What is Philosophy?, trans. Graham Burchell and Hugh Tomlinson, London: Verso, 1994).

Secondary literature:
(1972) 'Deleuze', *L'Arc* 49; revised 1980.
(1977) 'Anti-Oedipus', *Semiotext(e)* 2, 3, (includes a translation of Lyotard's essay 'Energumen capitalism', pp. 11–26).
(1984) 'Gilles Deleuze', *Substance* 44/45.
(1991) 'Deleuze and Guattari', *Substance 66* 20, 3, guest ed. Charles J. Stivale, Madison: University of Wisconsin Press.
Bogue, Ronald (1989) *Deleuze and Guattari*, London: Routledge.
Burchell, Graham (1984) 'Introduction to Deleuze', *Economy and Society* 13: 43–51.
Cressole, Michel (1973) *Deleuze*, Paris: Éditions Universitaire, 'Psychothèque'.
Descombes, Vincent (1980) *Modern French Philosophy*, trans. L. Scott-Fox and J. M. Hardin, Cambridge: Cambridge University Press.
Foucault, Michel (1977) 'Theatrum Philosophicum', in *Language, Counter-memory, Practice*, trans. Donald F. Bouchard and Sherry Simon, Ithaca: Cornell University Press (on *The Logic Sense* and *Différence et répétition*).
Jameson, Frederic (1981) *The Political Unconscious*, Ithaca, NY: Cornell University Press.
Lecercle, Jean-Jacques (1985) *Philosophy Through the Looking Glass*, La Salle, Ill.: Open Court, pp. 86–117, 160–97.
Massumi, Brian (1992) *A User's Guide to Capitalism and Schizophrenia: Deviations from Deleuze and Guattari*, Cambridge, Mass.: MIT.

Deleuze began his career by producing introductory studies of Hume, Kant, **Bergson** and Spinoza, authors who were not consonant with the Hegelian academic discourse of postwar French thought but formed an anti-rationalist tradition. With *Nietzsche et la philosophie* (1962), *Différence et répétition* (1968) and *Logique du sens* (1969), he established himself as a major philosopher of desire and difference. From here on he argues against the Hegelian concepts of totality, origin and hierarchy, and challenges the metaphysical presuppositions of traditional philosophy with its representational model of thought.

With the psychoanalyst and political activist Félix **Guattari** he wrote a number of important and challenging works: *L'Anti-Oedipe* (perhaps the best known) provides a synthesis of Marxist and Freudian motifs within an anti-structural, Nietzschean thematics of liberation.

The material of Deleuze's analyses has often come from literature and art and in his later work he has produced an original study of the painter Francis Bacon and written on the theoretical implications of the cinematic image. Deleuze's early work helped establish Nietzsche as a serious philosopher in France. His early book on Kant is still considered by many to be a standard work in the field, and his book on Proust was hailed by some as one of the best studies ever produced on the author. He will probably be best remembered for the impact that *L'Anti-Oedipe* had on a generation of radical thinkers after 1968.

JAMES WILLIAMS

Delfgaauw, Bernardus Maria Ignatius
Dutch. **b:** 24 November 1912, Amsterdam. **d:** 20 August 1993, Harem. **Cat:** Existential philosopher. **Ints:** History of philosophy; philosophy of history. **Educ:** Dutch Philology, Literature and Philosophy, University of Amsterdam. **Infls:** Personal influences included De Bruin, Sassen, Pos and Mounier; philosophical influences included Lavelle, Teilhard de Chardin and Marx. **Appts:** Secondary school teacher, 1939–61; Lecturer of Philosophy, University of Amsterdam, 1947–61; Professor of Philosophy and of the History of Philosophy, 1961–77, Professor of Medieval Philosophy, 1977–82, University of Groningen.

Main publications:
(1947) *Het spiritualistisch existentialisme van Louis Lavelle* [The Spiritualistic Existentialism of Louis Lavelle], Amsterdam: North-Holland Publishing Co.
(1950–2) *Beknopte geschiedenis van de wijsbegeerte* [Short History of Philosophy], 3 vols, Baarn: Wereldvenster.
(1961–4) *Geschiedenis en Vooruitgang* [History and Progress], Baarn: Wereldvenster.
(1984–7) *Filosofie van de grammatica* [Philosophy of Grammar], 3 vols, Bussum: Wereldvenster.
Filosofie van de vervreemding [Philosophy of Alienation] 4 vols, Kampen, Kok-Agora.

Secondary literature:
Bakker, R., Hubbeling, H. G. *et al.* (1982) *De filosofie van Bernard Delfgaauw*, Bussum: Het Wereldvenster.
Boelens, J. (1992) *Filosoferen met Bernard Delfgaauw*, Kampen: Kok-Agora.

The aim of Delfgaauw's philosophy is to treat the problems of everyday life. He thinks it desirable and possible to do so in ordinary language. He gives a realistic approach to the world we live in and opposes radically idealism and neo-positivism. Idealism in a Kantian sense cannot approach the world because the (superfluous) concept of 'phenomenon' is shoved between the knowing subject and the known world. Neopositivism does not consider the problems of human life, but occupies itself only with science and loses grip on reality. As a Roman Catholic philosopher Delfgaauw was very progressive in propagating socialist and Marxist ideas and by taking a left standpoint on such matters as the Algerian and Vietnam wars.

WIM VAN DOOREN

Delgado Espinosa, Honorio

Peruvian. *b:* 1892, Arequipa, Peru. *d:* 1969, *Cat:* 'Objective idealist'. *Ints:* Value theory. *Educ:* Graduated in Medicine, Lima, 1919, PhD 1923. *Infls:* Jaspers, Scheler and Blondel. *Appts:* Professor of Psychology, 1928, Professor of Psychiatry, 1930, University of San Marcos, Lima; Minister for Public Education, 1948.

Main publications:

(1916) *El psicoanálisis.*
(1923) *La rehumanización de la cultura científica por la psicología.*
(1926) *Sigmund Freud.*
(1927) *La filosofía del conde Keyserling.*
(1933) *Stefan George.*
(1934) *Stefan George y Karl Jaspers.*
(1943) *La personalidad y el carácter.*
(1947) *Paracelso*, Buenos Aires: Losada.
(1949) *Ecología, tiempo anímico y existencia*, Buenos Aires: Losada.
(1950) *Compendio de psicología*, Lima: Impr. Santa Maria.
(1951) *Introducción a la psicopatología*, Buenos Aires: Universidad de Buenos Aires.
(1956) *Nicolai Hartmann y el reino del espíritu*, Lima: Editorial Lumen.
(1958) *La formación espiritual del indívidus*, Barcelona: Editorial Cientifico-Medica.

Interested also in psychology and literature, Delgado's central philosophical contention is that there is an objective but non-temporal realm of values (hence his self-description 'objective idealist') by which we can shape our lives, and this assertion is grounded on a phenomenology of time-consciousness which shows a debt to **Jaspers** and **Blondel**. Experience of the realm of values is relatively familiar: when, for example, we understand the meaning of Socrates' words or appreciate the value of his attitudes; or when we apprehend a link of purposiveness between the

living things and the cosmos; or when solitary contemplation reveals the mystery around us; or when we are penetrated by the impact of a definitive separation, such moments do not belong solely to the realm of the temporal. They are (as Kierkegaard put it) atoms of eternity, which is not present only in privileged moments but is an element in our whole existence. Human beings alone can rise above the temporal and ephemeral life of the satisfaction of immediate desire and can act by reference to these non-temporal values.

Delgado was also alive to issues in ecology which became well-known some quarter-century after he wrote about them (cf. Part I of 1949). His ecological views are not independent of his value theory: in the (endangered) fantastic richness of nature, he saw a hint of purpose.

ROBERT WILKINSON

Della Volpe, Galvano

Italian. *b:* 24 September 1895, Imola, Italy. *d:* 14 July 1968, Rome. *Cat:* Marxist philosopher. *Appts:* 1939–, Professor of the History of Philosophy, University of Messina.

Main publications:

(1929) *Hegel romantico e mistico.*
(1933–5) *La filosofia di esperienza di David Hume*, 2 vols.
(1943) *Discorso sull'ineguaglianza.*
(1946) *La libertà comunista.*
(1950) *Logica come scienza positiva.*
(1963) *Critica del gusto*, second edition.
(1972–3) *Opere*, ed. I. Ambrogio, Rome: Editori Riuniti.

Secondary literature:

Fraser, J. (1977) *An Introduction to the thought of Galvano della Volpe*, London: Lawrence & Wishart.
Studi dedicati a Galvano della Volpe, (1989) Rome: Herder.

Della Volpe's early work sought to reconcile the philosophies of **Gentile** and **Croce**, and his early writings on Hegel and Hume reveal an opposition to idealism later to influence his Marxism. Although a controversial member of the Italian Communist Party he made substantial contributions to theory. Della Volpe traced Marx's inheritance from Aristotle, Galileo and Hume, categorically rejecting any attempt to link Marx to Hegelian idealism. Empirical science needs to organize facts and Della Volpe rejects a priori theories in favour of historically determinate ones.

What Marx meant by historical materialism is that theories that explain reality are part of that reality. Della Volpe is, however, critical of materialism considered as objective a priori truth. It is historically determined, emerges from capitalist society and is valid only for the historical period from which it emerges. Marx's great contribution was to see that material phenomena that appear isolated are connected in a grand social totality shaped by the economic base. His was a scientific theory whose theoretical interpretations are hypotheses to be inductively confirmed by empirical sociologists, a confirmation that will fuel the class struggle. Sociology is thus both a materialist and a revolutionary empirical science.

COLIN LYAS

Dennett, Daniel Clement

American. **b:** 1942. **Cat:** Analytic philosopher. **Educ:** Harvard University and University of Oxford. **Infls:** Gilbert Ryle, Willard Van Orman Quine and Ludwig Wittgenstein. **Appts:** Distinguished Professor of Arts and Sciences and Director of the Center for Cognitive Studies, Tufts University, Massachusetts.

Main publications:

(1969) *Content and Consciousness*, London: Routledge & Kegan Paul.
(1978) *Brainstorms: Philosophical Essays on Mind and Psychology*, Sussex: Harvester.
(1981) (ed. with D. R. Hofstadter) *The Mind's I: Fantasies and Reflections on Self and Soul*, New York: Basic Books.
(1984) *Elbow Room: The Varieties of Free Will Worth Wanting*, Oxford: Oxford University Press.
(1987) *The Intentional Stance*, Cambridge, Mass.: Bradford Books/MIT Press.
(1991) *Consciousness Explained*, London: Allen Lane.

Secondary literature:

Dahlbom, B. (ed.) (1993) *Dennett and His Critics*, Oxford: Blackwell.

Dennett's position is one of instrumentalism in the philosophy of mind. According to this view, our everyday or 'folk' psychology explains behaviour by showing how it accords with the needs of the human agent as an organism. This folk psychology does not identify internal cognitive states, and hence the terms which appear in this account, like 'belief', 'hope' and 'desire', are not to be construed as having reference to real entities

somehow located in the individual. Dennett contrasts what he calls the 'intentional stance' with the 'design stance'. The latter takes account of the inner machinery which generates behaviour; the former is the strategy by which we are able to predict the behaviour of the agent. Thus our everyday view is to be construed, not as an account of what there really is, but as a stance which serves a predictive rather than explanatory purpose.

Dennett endorses the view of B. F. **Skinner** that mentalistic or 'intentional' phenomena cannot provide a satisfactory basis for a scientific cognitive psychology. There is also evidence of the influence of W. v. O. Quine here, which sees an indeterminacy in all interpretation of human behaviour. Dennett appeals to evolutionary theory, arguing that natural selection has produced organisms that respond appropriately to their environments. The controversial upshot of the view is that no-one literally has beliefs or desires or other propositional attitudes, and that the temptation to treat such things as objects results from a fallacy of misplaced concreteness. 'Beliefs' and 'desires' are abstractions, not entities with a location.

Some critics have protested that our folk psychology does indeed offer explanations, and explanations of failure as well as success, as in the case of false beliefs leading to manifestly inappropriate behaviour. Futhermore, it quite commonly appeals to causes behind behaviour, even if these might be deemed ill-defined or vague by scientific standards. (However, it has also been pointed out that looseness and indeterminacy can be found in the context of scientific theory, so that even this characterization of folk psychology may be tendentious).

Nowhere is Dennett's position set forth more magisterially than in his *Consciousness Explained* of 1991. Deploying with great panache a rich variety of thought experiments, narratives and analogies ranging over neurophysiology, artificial intelligence and evolution, he endeavours to challenge established conceptions of mind and self. Echoing both Hume and his own mentor Gilbert **Ryle**, he mounts an assault on the myth of the 'Cartesian Theatre' with its assumption of a fixed ego scrutinizing its own inner workings and thoughts. For Dennett, this myth has its roots in our folk psychology which treats reports of mental states on the model of reporting events in the external world. Exploiting the phenomena of dreams and hallucinations, he strives to subvert the idea that such things issue from a determinate self as their author. Drawing on the new connectionist paradigm in artificial intelligence, he proposes what he calls the 'multiple drafts' model of consciousness according to which there is no executive centre in the brain and no single 'stream of consciousness', but a multiplicity of different strands and processes only some of which survive to be manifested publicly in behaviour. On Dennett's view, the 'self' is what he calls the 'narrative centre of gravity' of the individual and, like the more familiar notion of centre of gravity, it is an abstraction, not a concrete entity. Jokingly, one might well say that in his view human beings make themselves up as they go along, subject to evolutionary, social and cultural constraints. Dennett's contribution is distinguished by his pointing up the significance for philosophy of work in other disciplines. He has entered into intense debates with Jerry **Fodor**, Hilary **Putnam** and John **Searle** on these issues. Others have not shared his optimism on the explanation of mind and self, notably Thomas **Nagel** and Colin McGinn.

DENIS POLLARD

Dèr Mouw, Johan Andreas

Dutch. *b:* 24 July 1862, Westervoort. *d:* 8 July 1919, The Hague. *Cat:* Critical idealist; metaphysical poet and philosopher. *Ints:* Metaphysics. *Educ:* Classical Philology, University of Leyden. *Infls:* E. von Hartmann; in his later period, Indian Buddhism and mysticism. *Appts:* Taught Greek and Latin at secondary school, 1890–1903; private teacher and poet from 1903.

Main publications:

(1890) 'Quomodo antiqui naturam mirati sunt?', dissertation, University of Leyden.
(1904) *Het absoluut idealisme* [Absolute Idealism], Leyden: Sythoff.
(1906) *Kritische studies over psychisch monisme en nieuw-Hegelianisme* [Critical Studies on Psychical Monism and Neo-Hegelianism], Leyden: Sythoff.
(1947–51) *Verzamelde werken* [Collected Works], 6 vols, Amsterdam: Van Oirschott (posthumous).

Secondary literature:

Cram-Magré, A. M. (1962) *Dèr Mouw-Adwaita, denker en dichter.*

Dèr Mouw criticized very sharply **Bolland**'s philosophy, especially in its use of language with its ambiguous concepts and its metaphysical speculation. He saw no essential difference between this kind of absolute idealism and solipsism. Dèr Mouw remained a critical idealist,

taking into account the reality of the world outside us, however unknown it may be. Certainty is to be found only in one's own mind, which is related to reality in a certain way; the personal 'I' is not isolated from the world as a whole. In his later development Dèr Mouw elaborated this view in connection with his interest in Buddhism. Especially in his poetry he broadened the scope of the individual mind by experiencing it as a part of the totality of the universe. He called himself 'Adwaita' (i.e. he who is no longer two). His poems are written out of a feeling of unity with the universe, the All-One. He opposed this form of mystic religion strongly to the Christian faith, which he attacked in a sharp manner.

WIM VAN DOOREN

Derrida, Jacques

Algerian-French. *b:* 1930, Algiers. *Cat:* Poststructuralist; phenomenologist; philosopher of language; metaphysician; aesthetician. *Ints:* Deconstruction. *Educ:* École Normale Supérieure and Harvard University. *Infls:* Sartre, Husserl, Heidegger and others in the phenomenological tradition, as well as Saussure and structuralist theorists. *Appts:* Philosophy at the Sorbonne and École Normale Supérieure; Visiting Professor, Johns Hopkins, Yale and the University of California at Irvine; key figure in the development of the International College of Philosophy, Paris.

Main publications:

(1962) (trans. and intro.) *L'Origine de la géométrie*, Paris: Presses Universitaires de France (English translation, *Edmund Husserl's 'Origin of Geometry': An Introduction*, trans. John P. Leavey, Pittsburgh: Duquesne University Press, 1978).
(1967) *La Voix et la phénomène: introduction au problème du signe dans la phénoménologie de Husserl*, Paris: Presses Universitaires de France (English translation, *'Speech and Phenomena' and Other Essays on Husserl's Theory of Signs*, trans. David B. Allinson, Evanston, Ill.: Northwestern University Press, 1973).
(1967) *De la grammatologie*, Paris: Minuit (English translation, *Of Grammatology*, trans. Gayatri Chakravorty Spivak, Baltimore: Johns Hopkins University Press, 1976).
(1967) *L'Écriture et la différance*, Paris: Seuil (English translation, *Writing and Difference*, trans. Alan Bass, London: RKP, 1978).
(1972) *La dissémination*, Paris: Seuil (English translation, *Dissemination*, trans. Barbara Johnson, London: Althone Press, 1981).

(1972) *Positions*, Paris: Minuit (English translation, *Positions*, trans. Alan Bass, London: Althone Press, 1981).

(1972) *Marges de la philosophie*, Paris: Minuit (English translation, *Margins of Philosophy*, trans. Alan Bass, Chicago: Chicago University Press, 1982).

(1974) *Glas*, Paris: Galilée.

(1978) *Éperons: Les styles de Nietzsche*, Paris: Flammarion (English translation, *Spurs: Nietzsche's Styles*, trans. Barbara Harlow, Chicago: Chicago University Press, 1979).

(1978) *La Vérité en peinture*, Paris: Flammarion (English translation, *The Truth in Painting*, trans. Geoffrey Bennington and Ian McLeod, Chicago: Chicago University Press, 1987).

(1980) *La Carte postale de Scorate à Freud et au-delà*, Paris: Aubier-Flammarion (English translation, *The Post Card: From Socrates to Freud and Beyond*, trans. Alan Bass, Chicago: Chicago University Press, 1987).

(1993) *Spectres de Marx*, Paris: Galilée (English translation, *Spectres of Marx*, trans. Peggy Kamuf, London: Routledge, 1994).

Secondary literature:

Gasché, Rodolphe (1986) *The Tain of the Mirror: Derrida and the Philosophy of Reflection*, Cambridge, Mass.: Harvard University Press.

Llewelyn, John (1986) *Derrida on the Threshhold of Sense*, London, Macmillan

Norris, Christopher (1987) *Derrida*, London: Collins.

Ryan, Michael (1982) *Marxism and Deconstruction: A Critical Articulation*, Baltimore: Johns Hopkins University Press.

Sallis, John (ed.) (1987) *Deconstruction and Philosophy: The Texts of Jacques Derrida*, Chicago and London: University of Chicago Press.

Staten, Henry (1984) *Wittgenstein and Derrida* Lincoln, Neb.: University of Nebraska Press.

Wood, David and Bernasconi, Robert (1988) *Derrida and Différance*, Evanston, Ill.: Northwestern University Press.

Derrida is the founder and prime exponent of deconstruction, a method of textual analysis applicable to all writing, philosophy no less than creative literature, which by means of a series of highly controversial strategies seeks to reveal the inherent instability and indeterminacy of meaning. One of his primary objectives is to draw attention to the inescapably *textual* character of all philosophical writing, which he feels that most philosophers try to deny, regarding it as pure argument instead. Deconstruction is best ap-

proached as a form of radical scepticism and antifoundationalism (Derrida's philosophical project has been variously compared to those of Hume, **Nietzsche** and **Wittgenstein**), and Derrida adopts an oppositional stance towards Western philosophy from Plato onwards for its unacknowledged commitment to a 'metaphysics of presence', the belief that meaning *is* essentially stable and determinate and can be grasped in its entirety. Western philosophy is in this sense logocentrist, committed to the idea that words are capable of communicating unambiguously meanings that are present in the individual's mind. It is further to be regarded, Derrida argues, as phonocentrist, believing that speech more authentically communicates meaning than writing, being closer to the original thought than writing is. For Derrida, on the other hand, meaning is marked by the continual play of difference, and his entire oeuvre is designed to show how this calls into question the logocentrist and phonocentrist assumptions underlying philosophical discourse. Derrida's is essentially a linguistic enquiry—he takes his lead from **Saussure**'s identification of the sign as arbitrary—although it has involved excursions into metaphysics, aesthetics, ethics, literary criticism and art criticism over the course of what has been a highly prolific writing career. His roots lie in phenomenology, with his earliest important publications being commentaries on **Husserl**, whose concepts of bracketing, *epoché* and phenomenological reduction all play a crucial part in Derrida's development. He argues that, for all the radicalism of the concepts above, Husserl is still caught up in the metaphysics of presence and that it is not until the work of **Heidegger**, a critical influence on Derrida's thinking and the source of the idea of deconstruction, that presence is subjected to close scrutiny. A major target of Derrida's critique of Western philosophical method has been structuralism, which he feels largely ignores the implications of the arbitrariness of the sign, and he has delivered some devastating attacks on the notion of there being underlying structures to discourse. Derrida is particularly critical of **Lévi-Strauss**'s belief that myths can be reduced to a common structure, since it requires the existence of an originary myth—an indefensibly essentialist line of argument in Derrida's view. Derrida is notorious for deploying a range of concepts in his writing—*différance*, supplement, force, for example—while denying that they have the status of concepts. The practice of erasure, derived in the first instance from Heidegger, is taken to sanction the use of a word minus its metaphysical commitments. *Différance* is probably Derrida's best-known 'concept', and it is designed to illustrate the shifting and indeterminate nature of meaning since it can be heard as either *différence* (difference) or *différance* (deferral), with both meanings being kept in play at any one time. Such cases bear out Derrida's point about the indeterminacy of meaning and the arbitrariness of the sign, as well as enabling him to call into question the law of identity and thus strike a blow at the very foundations of philosophy. Derrida is also notorious for the obscurity and eccentricity of his style, in which punning and word-play, applied examples of Saussure's associative relation, are important parts of a strategy to locate gaps (aporias) in our discourse. The end-result is a form of philosophy which looks closer to game-playing than to traditional philosophical argument; but since it is part of Derrida's concern to problematize the division between philosophy and literature, as well as to insist that philosophy is above all a form of writing as dependent as any other on the operation of figures of speech, such practices have become an integral part of the project to deconstruct Western metaphysics. The general thrust of Derrida's work is antifoundationalist, and he is in fact one of the most uncompromising antifoundationalists in modern philosophy, part of a general trend in this respect which encompasses figures such as fellow French poststructuralists Michel **Foucault** and Jean-François **Lyotard** and the American pragmatist philosopher Richard **Rorty**. Derrida has had an enormous impact on modern thought, with deconstruction proving itself to be one of the most controversial as well as most stimulating developments in late twentieth-century intellectual life. There is now what amounts to a Derrida industry—Christopher Norris has spoken of a 'deconstructive turn' to academic discourse in recent years—and few works in the general field of cultural studies fail to acknowledge Derrida's influence or engage with his ideas. Response to Derrida's theories tends to be highly polarized and he arouses extreme hostility and passionate advocacy in almost equal measure. Perhaps his greatest area of success has been in American academic life, where he has inspired the work of the Yale School of literary critics, Harold Bloom, Paul de Man, J. Hillis Miller and Geoffrey Hartman, and through their writings a whole generation of literary academics. Derrida himself has expressed misgivings about the use made of his ideas in 'American deconstruction', 'disagreeably surprised' being his comment, but there is no denying the extent of his impact. In Britain Derrida's ideas have met with a greater degree of resistance, both from the left, which has persistently criticized the deconstructive enterprise as essentially apolitical in character, and from the British philosophical establishment, which, with a few notable exceptions, hardly considers what Derrida does to count as philosophy at all. Charges of intellectual charlatanism are not uncommon, with Derrida's obsession with such philosophically marginal details as the status of signatures being cited as evidence. The literary theorist Christopher Norris has proved to be Derrida's most able apologist from within British academic life, with the philosophers John Llewelyn and David Wood providing sympathetic defences of Derrida's philosophical credibility. On the whole, however, Derrida has exerted far greater influence among culture theorists and literary critics than amongst the philosophical community.

STUART SIM

Descombes, Vincent

French. *b:* 1943. *Cat:* Philosopher of language. *Ints:* History of recent continental philosophy; structuralism; post-structuralism; analytic philosophy; the language and objects of twentieth-century philosophy; philosophy and literature. *Appts:* Professor of Philosophy, Universities of Nice, Montreal and Paris I; Visiting Professor, Johns Hopkins University, Baltimore; on editorial committee of *Critique*.

Main publications:

(1971) *Le Platonisme*, Paris: PUF.
(1977) *L'inconscient malgré lui*, Paris: Minuit.
(1979) *Le Même et l'autre, quarante-cinq ans de philosophie française (1933–1978)*, Paris: Minuit (English translation, *Modern French Philosophy*, trans. L. Scott-Fox and J. Harding, Cambridge: Cambridge University Press, 1980).
(1983) *Grammaire d'objets en tous genres*, Paris: Minuit (English translation, *Objects of all Sorts*, trans. L. Scott-Fox and J. Harding, Oxford: Blackwell, 1986).
(1985) 'The fabric of subjectivity', in H. Siverman (ed.), *Hermeneutics and Deconstruction*, Albany: State University of New York.
(1987) *Proust*, Paris: Minuit (English translation, *Proust: Philosophy of the Novel*, trans. C. Macksey, Stanford, CA: Stanford University Press, 1992).
(1989) *Philosophie par gros temps*, Paris: Minuit (English translation, *The Barometer of Modern Reason: On the Philosophies of Current Events*, trans. S. A. Schwartz, Oxford: Oxford University Press, 1993).

After his early critique of psychoanalysis (1977), Vincent Descombes has written a series of analytical studies of the twentieth-century French philosophical scene. These studies bring the critical tools of analytic philosophy to the understanding of French philosophy, in terms of central historical movements and contemporary questions (1979) and in terms of an analysis of the objects of philosophies (1983). In a similar approach (1989), Descombes questions the way contemporary French philosophies think about the present and predict the future in terms of metaphysics and ontologies.

JAMES WILLIAMS

Dessoir, Max

German. *b:* 1867, Berlin. *d:* 1947, Königstein, Taunus. *Cat:* Neo-Kantian; aesthetician; philosopher of art; psychologist. *Educ:* Universities of Berlin and Würzburg. *Infls:* Immanuel Kant. *Appts:* 1897–20, Assistant Professor, then full Professor (1920), University of Berlin.

Main publications:

(1889) *Karl Philipp Moritz als Ästhetik*, Berlin: H. Sieling.
(1894) *Geschichte der neueren deutschen Psychologie*, Berlin: C. Duncker.
(1906) *Ästhetik und allgemeine Kunstwissenschaft*, Stuttgart: F. Enke (English translation, *Aesthetics and Theory of Art*, trans. Stephen A. Emery, Detroit: Wayne State University Press, 1970).
(1911) *Abriss einer Geschichte der Psychologie*, Heidelberg: C. Winter (English translation, *Outlines of the History of Psychology*, trans. D. Fisher, New York: Macmillan, 1912).
(1923) *Vom Diesseits der Seele*, Leipzig: Dürr and Weber.
(1936) *Einleitung in die Philosophie*, Stuttgart: F. Enke.
(1940) *Die Rede als Kunst*, Munich: E. Reinhardt.
(1947) *Das Ich, der Traum, der Tod*, Stuttgart: F. Enke.

Secondary literature:

Aster, Ernest and Becher, Erich, *et al.* (1925) *Lehrbuch der Philosophie herausgegeben von Max Dessoir*, 2 vols, Berlin: Ullstein.

Having studied philosophy at Berlin, and then medicine at Würzburg, from 1906 Dessoir founded and edited the *Zeitschrift für Ästhetik und allgemeine Kuntswissenschaft*, becoming Director of the said association in 1909. Renowned as an aesthetician, he mixed with many internationally regarded scholars and artists in Berlin. However, from 1933 he faced increasing interference from the National Socialist government, until Goebbels finally prohibited him from speaking, teaching or publishing. Dessoir and his wife left Berlin in August 1943, settling in Bad Nauheim. Dessoir died four years later.

Dessoir thought critical philosophy should not be wholly dismissive of our ordinary world understandings. Although possibly mistaken, our worldviews may serve basic human needs and yearnings. He most notably brought his psychological interests to bear upon aesthetics and, in particular, towards developing a general science of art. He experimentally investigated aesthetic responses and, partly on the basis of his studies, argued that aesthetic objects, whether artworks, parts of nature or mental or social constructs, are such by virtue of their purposiveness, manifested in the formal elements of harmony, proportion, rhythm, metre, size and degree. According to Dessoir, the artist conceives of some definite form, resulting from emotional excitement, and works it through until a unifying vision is manifested in the execution. It is only when an aesthetic attitude, variable in degree and kind, is brought to bear upon such an aesthetic object that the experience afforded is both pleasurable and aesthetic.

In developing his taxonomy of the arts, Dessoir suggests that all the main classificatory categories of art are significantly related to other fundamental aspects of human culture. Hence, he argues, a merely aesthetic understanding of art must be inadequate. Art possesses a cultural and moral function, in particular, enhancing the sensibilities of the informed appreciator. However, only a relative few may be informed and critical enough to be engaged and thus cultivated. Art's highest moral function is ultimately spiritual: through reconciling our subjective and objective worlds' art may reveal the unified grounding of the human world and the divinely created universe.

Sources: Christian Herrmann (1929) *Max Dessoir: Mensch und Werk*, Stuttgart; Edwards.

MATTHEW KIERAN

Deussen, Paul (Jakob)

German. *b:* 7 January 1845, Oberdreis, Neuwied, Germany. *d:* 7 July 1919, Kiel. *Cat:* Schopenhauerian idealist; historian of Indian philosophy. *Ints:* History of philosophy. *Educ:* Universities of Bonn, Tübingen and Berlin (1864–9, 1873–81). *Infls:* Schopenhauer, Plato, Kant and, personally,

Nietzsche. **Appts:** *Privatdozent* (1881–7) and *Extraordinarius* (1887–9), University of Berlin; *Ordinarius* (1889–1919), University of Kiel.

Main publications:

(1877) *Die Elemente der Metaphysik*, Aachen: J. J. Meyer (English translation, *The Elements of Metaphysics*, trans. C. D. Duff, London and New York: Macmillan, 1894).

(1883) *Das System des Vedanta*, Leipzig: F. A. Brockhaus (English translation, *The System of the Vedanta*, trans. C. Johnston, Chicago: Open Court, 1912).

(1887) *Die Sutras des Vedanta*, Leipzig: F. A. Brockhaus (English translation, *The Sutras of the Vedanta*, trans. J. H. Woods and C. B. Runkle, New York: Macmillan, 1906).

(1894–1908; 1911–17) *Allgemeine Geschichte der Philosophie*, 2 vols, Leipzig: F. A. Brockhaus (English translation of volume 1.2, *The Philosophy of the Upanishads*, trans. A. S. Geden, Edinburgh: T. A. Clarke, 1906).

(1897) *Sechzig Upanishads des Veda*, Leipzig: F. A. Brockhaus.

(1901) *Erinnerungen an Friedrich Nietzsche*, Leipzig: F. A. Brockhaus.

(1904) *Erinnerungen an Indien*, Kiel and Leipzig: Lipsius & Tischer (English translation, *My Indian Reminiscences*, trans. A. King, Madras: G. A. Nateson, 1912).

(1922) *Mein Leben*, ed. Erika Rosenthal-Deussen, Leipzig: F. A. Brockhaus.

Secondary literature:

Mockrauer, F. (1919) 'Paul Deussen als Mensch und Philosoph', *Jahrbuch der Schopenhauer-Gesellschaft* 9.

It was **Nietzsche** (whom Deussen first met when they were pupils at Schulpforta and with whom he formed what was to become a lifelong friendship) who first introduced Deussen to Schopenhauer. After initial reservations he became an enthusiastic, though not entirely orthodox, disciple of Schopenhauer, founding the *Schopenhauer-Gesellschaft* in 1911, editing its *Jahrbuch* until his death and preparing an edition of Schopenhauer's works. Deussen's entire work, both philosophical and historical, was dominated by the thought of Schopenhauer.

Deussen wrote only one genuinely philosophical work, *Die Elemente der Metaphysik* (1877). It is basically a restatement of Schopenhauer's philosophy, albeit stripped of its radical pessimism and given a vaguely Christian, vaguely pantheistic interpretation (the noumenal will being identified with the impersonally divine). The book enjoyed considerable popularity in its time.

Today, however, Deussen is chiefly remembered partly as the friend and correspondent of Nietzsche, partly as an editor and translator of the classical texts of Indian philosophy and partly as a historian of philosophy, especially of Indian philosophy. It is generally agreed that, as a historian and interpreter of Indian thought, he tends to read Schopenhauerian ideas into Hindu philosophy; and even his history of European philosophy, contained in the second half of his *Allgemeine Geschichte*, is dominated by the conviction that Schopenhauer represents the climax of European thought, surpassing even Kant in importance.

Sources: Edwards; EF; Eisler; Huisman; NDB.

DAVID WALFORD

Deústua, Alejandro Octavio

Peruvian. **b:** 1849, Huancayo, Peru. **d:** 1945, Lima, Peru. **Cat:** Anti-positivist; historian of ideas; aesthetician. **Educ:** University of San Marcos, Lima. **Infls:** K. C. F. Krause. **Appts:** Professor, University of San Marcos, Lima; served as Dean of the Faculty of Letters and Rector of the University; Director of the National Library.

Main publications:

(1929) *Estética aplicada: lo bello en la naturaleza.*

(1932) *Estética aplicada: lo bello en el arte; la arquitectura.*

(1935) *Estética aplicada: lo bello en el arte; escultura, pintura, música.*

(1937) *La cultura nacional.*

(1939) *La estética de José Vasconcelos.*

The following English translations of excerpts of the work of Alejandro Deústua by Willard Trask appear in Aníbal Sánchez Reulet (ed.) (1954) *Contemporary Latin American Philosophy*, Albuquerque: University of New Mexico Press:

'Order and freedom', pp. 26–38.

'Beauty and freedom', pp. 38–41.

'Definition of beauty', pp. 41–2.

'Art and morality', pp. 43–6.

'Beauty and truth', pp. 46–8.

'Art and science', pp. 48–50.

Secondary literature:

Himelblau, Jack (1979) *Alejandro Octavio Deústua: Philosophy in Defense of Man*, Gainesville: University Press of Florida.

Deústua is considered one of the 'founders' of Latin American philosophy. Deeply influenced by the thought of Karl Christian Krause (1781–1832), Deústua believed that 'liberty is the essence of grace'. He applied the concept of creative evolution to aesthetics, arguing that only in aesthetic activity is creative liberty fully expressed because only in this phase of existence is the imagination freed from resistance. Deústua had a close affinity with the ideas of the Mexican thinker José **Vasconcelos** and, at age 90, wrote a book on his aesthetics.

AMY A. OLIVER

Dewey, John

American. *b:* 20 October 1859, Burlington, Vermont. *d:* 1 June 1952, New York City. *Cat:* Philosopher of education; pragmatist. *Ints:* Social philosophy. *Educ:* University of Vermont, BA 1879; Johns Hopkins University, PhD 1884. *Infls:* Hegel and James. *Appts:* 1884–8, 1889–94, Professor, University of Michigan, Ann Arbor; 1888–9, Professor, University of Minnesota; 1894–1904, Professor and Head, Department of Philosophy, Psychology and Pedagogy, University of Chicago; 1904–30, Professor, Columbia University.

Main publications:

(1969–90) *The Works of John Dewey*, general editor, J. A. Boydston, Carbondale and Edwardsville: Southern Illinois University Press (divided into three parts: (1967–72) *John Dewey: The Early Works, 1882–1898*, 5 vols, referred to below as *EW*; (1976–83) *John Dewey: The Middle Works, 1899–1924*, 15 vols, referred to below as *MW*; (1981–90) *The Later Works, 1925–53*, 17 vols, referred to below as *LW*).
(1887) *Psychology*, New York: Harper & Brothers; reprinted in *EW* 2.
(1899) *The School and Society*, Chicago: University of Chicago Press; reprinted in *MW* 1.
(1902) *The Child and the Curriculum*, Chicago: University of Chicago Press; reprinted in *MW* 2.
(1903) *Studies in Logical Theory*, Chicago: University of Chicago Press; reprinted in *MW* 2.
(1910) *The Influence of Darwin on Philosophy and Other Essays in Contemporary Thought*, New York: Henry Holt & Company; reprinted in *MW* 4.
(1916) *Democracy and Education: An Introduction to the Philosophy of Education*, New York: Macmillan; reprinted in *MW* 9.
(1916) *Essays in Experimental Logic*, Chicago: University of Chicago Press; reprinted in *MW* 10.
(1920) *Reconstruction in Philosophy*, New York: Henry Holt & Co.; reprinted in an enlarged edition with new introduction by John Dewey, Boston: Beacon Press, 1924; reprinted in *MW* 12.
(1922) *Human Nature and Conduct. An Introduction to Social Psychology*, New York: Henry Holt: reprinted in *MW* 14.
(1925) *Experience and Nature*, Chicago: Open Court; reprinted in a revised edition, New York: W. W. Norton, 1929; reprinted in *LW* 1.
(1927) *The Public and its Problems*, New York: Henry Holt; reprinted in *LW* 2.
(1929) *The Quest for Certainty*, New York: Minton, Balch; reprinted in *LW* 4.
(1932) *Individualism, Old and New*, New York: Minton, Balch; reprinted in *LW* 5.
(1932) (with James Hayden Tufts) *Ethics*, revised edition, New York: Henry Holt; reprinted in *LW* 7.
(1934) *A Common Faith*, New Haven: Yale University Press; reprinted in *LW* 9.
(1934) *Art as Experience*, New York: Minton, Balch; reprinted in *LW* 10.
(1935) *Liberalism and Social Action*, New York: G. P. Putnam; reprinted in *LW* 11.
(1938) *Experience and Education*, New York: Macmillan; reprinted in *LW* 13.
(1938) *Logic: The Theory of Inquiry*, New York: Henry Holt & Company; reprinted in *LW* 12.
(1939) *Freedom and Culture*, New York: G. P. Putnam, reprinted in *LW* 13.
(1939) *Theory of Valuation. International Encyclopedia of Unified Science*, vol. 2, ed. Otto Neurath, Rudolf Carnap and Charles Morris, Chicago: University of Chicago Press; reprinted in *LW* 13.
(1949) (with Arthur F. Bentley) *Knowing and the Known*, Boston: Beacon Press; reprinted in *LW* 16.

Secondary literature:

Boydston, J. A. and Poulos, K. (eds) (1978) *Checklist of Writings about John Dewey, 1877–1977*, second edition, Carbondale: Southern Illinois University Press.
Coughlan, N. (1975) *Young John Dewey: An Essay in American Intellectual History*, Chicago: University of Chicago Press.
Dykhuizen, G. (1973) *The Life and Mind of John Dewey*, ed. J. A. Boydston, Carbondale: Southern Illinois University Press.
Rockefeller, Steven C. (1991) *John Dewey, Religious Faith and Democratic Humanism*, New York: Columbia University Press.
Schilpp, P. A. (ed.) (1939) *The Philosophy of John Dewey*, Evanston, Ill.: Northwestern University Press, The Library of Living Philosophers; second edition, New York: Tudor Publishing Company, 1951.

Thomas, M. H. (1962) *John Dewey: A Centennial Bibliography*, Chicago: University of Chicago Press.

Westbrook, R. B. (1991) *John Dewey and American Democracy*, Ithaca and London: Cornell University Press.

Dewey began his career as a Hegelian idealist. His 1887 textbook on psychology sought to synthesize a Hegelianized faculty psychology with the newly emerging experimental psychology.

At the University of Chicago Dewey had assembled an imposing group of thinkers including G. H. **Mead**, Tufts, Ames and A. W. Moore. He founded the famous laboratory school for education. Further, he participated in numerous social reform organizations, most notably Jane Addams' Hull House. Appearing as a decentennial publication of the university, *Studies in Logical Theory* (1903) contained essays by Dewey and his colleagues William **James** at Harvard hailed it as a sign of the birth of a new school of philosophy, the Chicago School. Dewey's philosophy had evolved from Hegelian absolute idealism to experimental pragmatism, James's *Principles of Psychology* (New York: Henry Holt, 1890) having exerted the decisive influence on his thinking. Evolutionary biology also profoundly shaped Dewey's philosophy. Experimental pragmatism, which Dewey preferred to call 'instrumentalism', grounded cognition in action and noncognitive experiences. Although Dewey abandoned the Hegelian ideal of an absolute whole of experience, and stressed the biological basis of experience and the need to experiment, he retained the Hegelian strategy of overcoming dualism by the dialectical discovery of organic unities.

Because of conflict with the administration over the laboratory school Dewey left the University of Chicago and joined the faculty of Columbia University. Affiliated with Columbia Teachers College, Dewey continued his work in education, rising to the forefront of the educational reform movement. He rejected both the formalistic approach and the romantic approach to the education of children since these approaches reflected false psychological theories. He proposed overhauling the system of education. The interests of children, portrayed as naturally curious and active, had to be captivated and cultivated by means of educational experiences which would foster creativity and independence.

Dewey's conception of human nature, basic to his educational theories, stressed the malleability of human nature. He esteemed growth to be the aim of education and of life, growth that should never end. Dewey's zeal for educational reform was at one with his zeal for social reform.

Dewey's conception of experience is crucial to the understanding of his philosophy. It is active as well as passive, social as well as individual, objective as well as subjective, dynamic and continuous. Dewey's metaphysics is focused on the description of the generic traits of existence. In primary experience he found the polarity of stability and uncertainty and the polarity of the actual and the ideal; he also detected qualities, events, histories. These traits discovered in experience are traits of existence and so of nature. Human beings create the meanings that serve to stabilize the uncertain flux of events. Their political economies, their art, their religion, their science, their philosophy are the human enterprises on behalf of meaningful stability. Dewey distinguished philosophy from metaphysics. Philosophy is wisdom; its task is the criticism of cultural values. Metaphysics, by contrast, is a general empirical science; its task is to present the generic traits of existence to serve as the ground-map for philosophy as cultural criticism.

Dewey's penchant for reform extended to philosophy itself. He held that traditional philosophers, while reacting to the problems in the civilizations in which they arose, flew from practical solutions into imagined domains of certainty. Hence Dewey called for the reconstruction of philosophy to confront what he deemed to be the major crisis of his time—the discrepancy between inherited values and ideals and the new forces of control over nature unleashed by science and technology—and to resolve this crisis by applying the method of enquiry that had succeeded in natural science to social and moral problems.

Committed to democracy and its values, Dewey participated in significant public events: he headed the commission that exonerated Leon **Trotsky** of the Stalinist charges in 1937, and he joined in the defence of Bertrand **Russell** against the denial of his teaching post in New York in 1941. Dewey called for the reform of traditional liberalism. Centred on the self-reliant individual and his rights to *laissez faire*, liberalism had to be reconstructed, since the industrialization and urbanization of society by means of new technologies produced a new social environment which called for a type of individual different from the old type of pioneer in the wilderness.

Dewey condemned fascism and communism because they abandoned democracy and resorted to violence. He advocated the method of enquiry and democratic processes.

Dewey's philosophical labours extended to all the fields of human experience. His philosophy of art reinstates the ideal of organic unity which he had derived from Hegelian thought. It also stresses the primacy of immediately felt quality. Such quality may occur in my experience; it is consummatory. Aesthetic values are consummatory qualities, experienced not merely in the presence of art objects stored in a museum, but encountered every day in ordinary life. In philosophy of religion Dewey's position is that of humanistic naturalism. He interpreted religion, not as a personal experience in the manner of William James, but as a non-sectarian social effort on the march to realize the ideal.

In his closing years Dewey associated with logical empiricism, although he maintained his intellectual autonomy. He never yielded in his naturalistic theory of values and his cognitivist theory of value judgments.

For the professional philosopher and scientist, Dewey's method of enquiry is his most important work. This instrumentalist or pragmatist methodology has won him his distinctive niche in the history of philosophy. Enquiry is defined as the process of moving from an indeterminate situation that blocks action towards a determinate situation in which action may proceed. Four stages are described: (i) defining the problem by observation and analysis; (ii) imaginative construction of hypotheses to explain and resolve the problem; (iii) explication of the meanings of the concepts in the hypotheses, in regard to mathematical formulations, experimental design and further deductions; and (iv) actual testing. The method is instrumentalist, not simply because ideas are construed metaphorically as tools for action, but also because, as any experimental laboratory illustrates, instrumentation is employed in nearly every phase of the process.

Dewey's belief that the method of enquiry, the scientific method, should be applied to practical problems lent philosophical support to the rise and the vogue of the social sciences.
Sources: Edwards; DAB, supplt 5, 1951–5; EAB.

ANDREW RECK

Dickie, George Thomas
American. *b:* 12 August 1936, Palmetto, Florida. *Cat:* Aesthetician. *Ints:* Aesthetic theory and art theory. *Educ:* Florida State University and the University of California, Los Angeles. *Infls:* Literary influences: Francis Hutcheson, Kant

and Alexander Gerrad. Personal: Arthur C. Danto. *Appts:* 1956–64, Instructor, then Associate Professor of Philosophy, Walsh State University; 1964–5, Associate Professor of Philosophy, University of Houston; from 1965, Associate, then (1967) full Professor of Philosophy, University of Illinois, Chicago; 1990, Vice President of the American Society of Aesthetics.

Main publications:
(1971) *Aesthetics: An Introduction*, Indianapolis: Pegasus Books.
(1974) *Art and the Aesthetic: An Institutional Analysis*, Ithaca, NY: Cornell University Press.
(1984) *The Art Circle: A Theory of Art*, New York: Havens.
(1988) *Evaluating Art*, Philadelphia: Temple University Press.

Secondary literature:
Cohen, Ted (1973) 'The possibility of art: remarks on a proposal by Dickie', *Philosophical Review* 82 (January): 69–82.
Davies, Stephen (1991) *Definitions of Art*, Ithaca, NY: Cornell University Press.

Dickie is a major figure in contemporary analytical aesthetics, whose contributions have stimulated much debate. One of his fundamental contentions is that the notion of a distinct 'aesthetic realm' or 'aesthetic faculty' such as taste, is ill founded: no philosophical distinction between ordinary experience and alleged aesthetic experience can be made. As well as rejecting the aesthetic, Dickie opposes the neo-Wittgensteinian identification of art by the 'family-resemblance' method, on the grounds that it forces us to count anything as art since everything resembles something else in some respect.

In 1969 Dickie proposed an 'institutional theory of art', which he later elaborated in *Art and the Aesthetic* (1974). He attempted to define art in terms of the idea that a work of art in the descriptive sense is (i) an artefact (ii) upon which some society or some subgroup of a society has conferred the status of candidate for appreciation. But this definition was criticized as 'circular' and as formally lacking a 'dimension without which it is not acute enough to discriminate art from other things' (Cohen 1973, p. 71).

In order to meet these objections Dickie subsequently modified his view. No longer talking of institutions, he now maintains the idea of an 'art circle', that is to say, of an 'artworld system' understood as a 'framework for the presentation of a work of art by an artist to an artworld public'

(1984, pp. 80–2). The principal achievement of Dickie's theory lies in its having compelled a general recognition of the importance of social context for identifying art.
Sources: DAS.

STEPHEN MOLLER

Dilthey, Wilhelm
German. **b:** 19 November 1833, Biebrich, Germany. **d:** 1 October 1911, Siez (Bozen). **Cat:** Philosopher of culture (close to the neo-Kantians of the Baden school); epistemologist. **Educ:** Theology, Philosophy and History in Heidelberg and Berlin. **Infls:** Kuno Fischer, Edmund Husserl and Friedrich Adolf Trendelenburg. **Appts:** Professor at Basel, Kiel, Breslau and Berlin.

Main publications:
Dilthey's works are available in his *Gesammelte Schriften*, 20 vols. Stuttgart: B. G. Teubner; Göttingen: Vandenhoek & Ruprecht, 1914–90). Many of the essays and reviews found in this edition were scattered in various places, and were difficult to obtain before. Apart from the works published by Dilthey himself, this edition also includes a number of manuscripts that were not available before.

(1870) *Das Leben Schleiermachers* vol. I, vol. II 1922, *Gesammelte Schriften* XIII and XIV.

(1883) *Einleitung in die Geisteswissenschaften*, vol. I, Leipzig, *Gesammelte Schriften* I (English translation, *Introduction to the Human Sciences*, trans. R. J. Bretanzos, Detroit: Wayne State University Press, 1989).

(1894) *Ideen über eine beschreibende und zergliedernde Psychologie*, *Gesammelte Schriften* V, 139–237 (English translation in *Descriptive Psychology and Historical Understanding*, trans. R. H. Zaner and K. L. Heiges, The Hague: Nijhoff, 1977).

(1905) *Erlebnis und Dichtung*, Stuttgart: B. G. Teubner.

(1907) *Das Wesen der Philosophie, Gesammelte Schriften* V, pp. 339–428 (English translation, *The Essence of Philosophy*, trans. S. A. and W. T. Emery, New York: AMS Press, 1969).

(1910) *Der Aufbau der geschichtlichen Welt in den Geisteswissenschaften, Gesammelte Schriften* VII, 79–190.

(1961) *Pattern and Meaning in History. Thoughts on History and Society*, trans. H. P. Rickman, London: Allen & Unwin (represents a collection of translated passages from volume VII of the *Gesammelte Schriften*).

(1989–) *Dilthey's Selected Works*, ed. Rudolf A. Makkreel and Frithjof Rodi, Princeton: Princeton University Press. This edition is projected to have six volumes. Two of these have appeared, including vol. I, *Introduction to the Human Sciences* (1989) which includes a translation of *Einleitung in die Geisteswissenschaften*, vol. I and the drafts for vol. II and vol. V, *Poetry and Experience* 1985).

Secondary literature:
Biemel, Walter (ed.) (1968) 'Der Briefwechsel Dilthey–Husserl', *Man and World* 1: 428–46.
Bollnow, O. F. (1955) *Dilthey: Eine Einführung in seine Philosophie*, second edition, Stuttgart: Kohlhammer; originally Leipzig and Berlin 1936.
Hodges, H. A. (1944) *Wilhelm Dilthey: An Introduction*, London: Kegan Paul, Trubner & Co.
——(1952) *The Philosophy of Wilhelm Dilthey*, London: Routledge & Kegan Paul.
Makkreel, Rudolf A. (1969) 'Wilhelm Dilthey and the Neo-Kantians: the distinction of the Geisteswissenschaften and the Kulturwissenschaften', *Journal of the History of Philosophy* 4: 423–40.
——(1992) *Dilthey: Philosopher of Human Studies*, second edition, Princeton: Princeton University Press.
Misch, Clara (ed.) (1960) *Der junge Dilthey: Ein Lebensbild in Briefen und Tagebüchern, 1852–1870*, Göttingen: Vandenhoek & Ruprecht (first published in 1933).
Misch, Georg (1967) *Lebensphilosophie und Phänomenologie. Eine Auseinandersetzung der Diltheyschen Richtung mit Heidegger und Husserl*, Darmstadt: Wissenschaftliche Buchgesellschaft, originally Berlin 1930).
——(1985) Orth, E. W. (1985) *Dilthey und die Gegenwart der Philosophie*, Freiburg/Munich: K. Alber.
Of interest for Dilthey's life are:
Briefe Wilhelm Dilthey's an Rudolf Haym, 1861–1873, ed. Erich Weiniger, Berlin, 1936.

Dilthey's thinking starts from the philosophy of Kant and Schleiermacher. Although he is often described as an idealist and romantic, this characterization of him is rather misleading. In many ways he might be better described as an empiricist. Yet he rejected that label as well. His stance was thoroughly antimetaphysical, and he was more interested in analysing particular problems than in providing a theory of the nature of reality. Starting from what he thought was 'the standpoint of experience and unprejudiced empirical inquiry', his works constituted a series of attempts at establishing the foundation of the experiential sciences of the mind, called by Dilthey *Geisteswissenschaften*. While the term

'Geisteswissenschaften' is usually translated as 'human sciences' or 'human studies', it was originally closer to what John Stuart Mill designated the 'moral sciences'.

Today Dilthey is mainly known for his epistemological analysis of historiography as involving a special kind of mental operation called 'Verstehen' (understanding). Yet, while history and the problems concerned with the writing of history were extremely important to him, his philosophy was much more broadly conceived than this view suggests. His projected 'Critique of historical reason' was to cover all of the human sciences. Arguing that historical reality was 'truncated' and 'mutilated' by those who were trying to force the human sciences into the same mould as the natural sciences, he attempted to establish a new methodology and foundation for these sciences. He rejected positivism not because he felt that the kind of certainty they were seeking could not be had, but because he thought that they were sacrificing the 'legitimate independence of the particular sciences'. Dilthey's new foundation of the human sciences involved a critique of consciousness in a Kantian sense. Yet, unlike Kant, who believed that his critique could uncover universal conditions of the possibility of experience, i. e. categories, principles, and ideas of the human mind that would hold anywhere and at any time, Dilthey thought of these conditions as being embedded in a consciousness of a particular time and place. He found that no 'real blood flows in the veins of the knowing subject constructed by Locke, Hume, and Kant, but rather the diluted extract of reason as a mere activity of thought'. He wished to explain ôeven knowledge and its concepts ... in terms of the manifold powers of a being that wills, feels, and thinks, and thus rejected, as 'fixed and dead' the rigid a priori epistemology of Kant in favour of a developmental history that started 'from the totality of our being'.

This does not mean that Dilthey believed historians can look merely at the motives and the actions of individuals. For him the individual is always part of a certain culture, and to understand the individual is also to understand that culture. Dilthey's 'philosophy of life' (*Philosophie des Lebens*) is an expression of his belief that we must see and understand ourselves as part of the larger whole that has been created by human beings and that forms our social and historical reality. Furthermore 'every expression of life has meaning insofar as it is a sign which expresses something that is part of life. Life does not mean anything other than itself. There is nothing in it which points to a meaning beyond it.' The expressions of life form the subject matter of the human sciences. It is the realm of the method of understanding in the sense of *Verstehen*.

Although different times and different individuals may belong to cultures quite foreign to ours, we can, according to Dilthey, understand the historical and social processes in them because we are living individuals who know 'the process by which life tends to objectify itself in expressions'. Understanding is a process *sui generis*. We cannot explain it by reducing it to other, more basic processes. Nor should it be confused with 'understanding' in the ordinary sense, which signifies any kind of comprehension. Dilthey describes it as the 'rediscovery of the I in the Thou', or as a form of knowing that is concerned with intellectual processes. It is the comprehension of intentions, motives, feelings or thoughts as they are expressed in gestures, words, works of literature, legal codes, etc.

Dilthey is also famous for his analysis of *Weltanschauungen* or world views. Differentiating between three different types: materialism or positivism, objective idealism, and idealism of freedom, he himself could not identify with any one of them. All three of them appeared to him as honest but one-sided views of reality. Dilthey's greatest influence began only after his death. Thus he has had some influence on the contemporary discussion of the philosophy of history. Although his concept of *Verstehen* is often misunderstood, it has generated a great deal of controversy. Dilthey also had an indirect influence on early sociological theories through the works of Max **Weber** and Talcott Parsons. Most importantly, perhaps, early existentialist thought, such as that of Karl **Jaspers** and Martin **Heidegger**, is unthinkable without Dilthey. Thus Heidegger claimed that his own analysis of temporality and historicity in *Being and Time* was 'solely concerned with preparing the way for the assimilation of the investigations of W. Dilthey'. And Bollnow's introduction to Dilthey was perhaps more an introduction to existential thinking than to Dilthey's theory.

MANFRED KUEHN

Dobb, Maurice Herbert

British. *b:* 1900, London. *d:* 1976, Cambridge, England. *Cat:* Political economist. *Educ:* BA, Pembroke College, Cambridge, 1918–21; PhD, University of London, 1922–4. *Infls:* David Ricardo, Marx, Engels and Sraffa, Piero. *Appts:*

Lecturer (1924–59), then Reader (1959–67) and Fellow of Trinity College (1948–67), Cambridge.

Main publications:

(1937) *Political Economy and Capitalism*, London: Routledge; revised edition, 1940.

(1963) *Studies in the Development of Capitalism*, London: Routledge; revised edition, 1963.

(1948) *Soviet Economic Development since 1917*, London: Routledge; revised edition, 1966.

(1955) *On Economic Theory and Socialism: Collected Papers*, London: Routledge.

(1960) *An Essay On Economic Growth And Planning*, London: Routledge.

(1967) *Papers on Capitalism, Development and Planning*, London: Routledge.

(1973) *Theories of Value and Distribution since Adam Smith*, Cambridge: Cambridge University Press.

Secondary literature:

Feinstein, C. H. (ed.) (1967) *Socialism, Capitalism and Economic Growth: Essays Presented to Maurice Dobb*, Cambridge: Cambridge University Press (includes full bibliography).

Even as a student at Pembroke College Dobb was a committed Marxist, joining the Communist Party in 1922. An early (and abiding) interest was the economic development of the Soviet Union. His later prolific writings also focused on supplying a Marxist critique of current approaches to political economy; on the origins of capitalist industrialization; and on the economic development of pre-industrial countries. His work in these areas made him the leading Marxist economist in Britain in the middle decades of this century. Aside from his academic concerns, he was also active in working for the Labour Research Department, in contributing to the classes of the National Council of Labour Colleges, and in writing some two dozen popular books and pamphlets designed to bring Marxist ideas to a wider audience.

Sources: DNB 1971–80; *CJE* 2, 1978: *PBA* 63, 1977.

NICHOLAS EVERITT

Donagan, Alan

Australian-American. *b:* 10 February 1925, Melbourne. *d:* 29 May 1991, Chicago. *Cat:* Analytic philosopher with strong scholastic sympathies. *Ints:* History of philosophy; metaphysics; moral philosophy. *Educ:* University of Melbourne, BA 1946, MA 1951, and University of Oxford, BPhil 1953. *Infls:* Aristotle, Aquinas, Kant and Collingwood. *Appts:* 1946–8, Lecturer in Philosophy,

University of Western Australia; 1949–55, Lecturer in Philosophy, Canberra University College, Canberra; 1955–61, Assistant Professor, Associate Professor and Chairman, Department of Philosophy, University of Minnesota, Minneapolis; 1961–5, Professor of Philosophy, Indiana University; 1965–9, Professor of Philosophy, University of Illinois, Urbana; 1969–90, Professor of Philosophy, University of Chicago.

Main publications:

(1962) *The Later Philosophy of R. G. Collingwood*, Oxford: Clarendon.

(1963) 'Universals and metaphysical realism', *Monist* 47: 211–46.

(1965) (with B. Donagan) *The Philosophy of History*, London: Macmillan.

(1966) 'The Popper–Hempel Theory', in W. D. Dray (ed.) *Philosophical Analysis and History*, London: Harper & Row.

(1977) *The Theory of Morality*, Chicago: Chicago University Press.

(1985) *Human Ends and Human Actions: An Exploration in St Thomas' Treatment*, Milwaukee: Marquette University Press.

(1987) *Choice: The Essential Element in Human Action*, London: Routledge & Kegan Paul.

(1988) *Spinoza*, Chicago: Chicago University Press.

Secondary literature:

Brand, M. (1991) Review of *Choice* (1989) in *Philosophical Review* 100: 115–18.

Loux, M. (1972) 'Recent work in ontology', *American Philosophical Quarterly* 9: 119-38.

Schwartz, A. (1978) Review of *Theory of Morality* (1977) in *Philosophical Review* 87: 649-51.

Alan Donagan was both a historian of philosophy, having written on Aquinas, Spinoza and **Collingwood**, and a philosopher who made significant contributions to recent debates on metaphysics, rationality and human agency. The fruitful interplay which exists between these different strands of Donagan's work has often been noted: he displays, writes James Montmarquet, 'equal mastery of historical and contemporary sources and a philosophical style which is highly argumentative, but never tediously so' (*Nous* 25: 135–6).

In an 'extremely valuable' (Loux 1972) article (1963) on universals Donagan defended metaphysical realism on the basis of an argument to the best explanation. During this early period, and influenced by **Popper**, Donagan also wrote a series of articles on the philosophy of history in which he criticized the 'covering-law' model in favour of a 'situational-logic' model of historical explanation. The underlying hostility to naturalistic views of human agency revealed in this early work has been a feature of much of Donagan's later work.

Donagan's writings on ethics are in the natural law tradition and are deeply influenced by Aquinas and Kant. In *The Theory of Morality* (1977) he described a moral system against which, he claimed, all other moral theories can be judged, a 'system of laws or precepts, binding upon rational creatures as such, the content of which is ascertainable by human reason' (p. 7). The moral system in question is traditional Hebraic–Christian morality and it is said to rest on the following very Kantian principle: 'It is impermissible not to respect every human being, oneself or any other, as a rational creature' (p. 66).

Donagan argues that a substantial body of moral duties can be derived from this basic principle and that both the falsity of consequentialism and the impossibility of genuine moral conflict follow from it. The book attracted widespread respect, even from those who disagreed with its central thesis. A. Schwartz (1978) concludes that although Donagan's arguments are not convincing, his project 'is philosophically important and interesting'.

As a presupposition of his ethics Donagan argues that there is a fundamental distinction between event-causation and agent-causation and this theme is developed in detail in the book *Choice: The Essential Element in Human Action* (1987). Donagan defends the view that 'actions are events explained by their doer's choices'. The conception is Aristotelian but it is informed, equally, by the work of **Frege**, **Davidson** and **Dummet**. It is a strongly libertarian account: choice is characterized as an ultimate and inexplicable power of agency and as a power which, under identical circumstances, is compatible with choosing differently. Although aspects of the account, especially the account of casual waywardness, have been widely criticized, the boldness and ingenuity of the work have been greatly admired. 'I expect it', writes Myles Brand (1991) 'to occupy a place of esteem among the works on human action written in the past several decades'.

Sources: DAP; CA 5.

H. BUNTING

Donnellan, Keith Sedgwick

American. *b:* 25 June 1931. *Cat:* Philosophical logician. *Ints:* Philosophy of language. *Educ:* Studied at University of Maryland; Cornell University, BA 1953, MA 1954, PhD 1961 (dissertation on 'C. I. Lewis and the Foundations of Necessary Truth'), elected to Phi Beta Kappa. *Infls:* Russell, Strawson, N. Malcolm, Kripke and Kaplan. *Appts:* Taught at Cornell University, 1958–67; Professor of Philosophy, Cornell University, 1967–70; Professor of Philosophy, University of California at Los Angeles, from 1970. Visiting appointments at Harvard, 1961–2, 1968, 1969; UCLA, 1966; Stanford, 1968; MIT, 1968, Michigan, 1972; Galileo lecturer, University of Padua, 1991.

Main publications:
(1966) 'Reference and definite descriptions', *Philosophical Review* (numerous reprints).
(1968) 'Putting Humpty-Dumpty together again', *Philosophical Review* (reply to MacKay 1968).
(1970) 'Proper names and identifying descriptions', *Synthèse* 21, reprinted in D. Davidson and G. Harman (eds), *Semantics of Natural Language*, Dordrect: Reidel, 1972.
(1970) 'Causes, objects and producers of the emotions', *Journal of Philosophy* (abstract).
(1974) 'Speaking of nothing', *Philosophical Review* (numerous reprints).
(1977) 'The contingent *a priori* and rigid designators', *Midwest Studies in Philosophy* 2, (reprinted with 1978 in an expanded version, entitled *Contemporary Perspectives in the Philosophy of Language*, Minneapolis: University of Minnesota Press, 1979).
(1978) 'Speaker reference, descriptions and anaphora', in P. Cole (ed.), *Syntax and Semantics*, vol. 9, New York: Academic Press (see 1977).
(1981) 'Intuitions and presuppositions', in P. Cole (ed.), *Radical Pragmatics*, New York: Academic Press.
(1983) 'Kripke and Putnam on natural kind terms', in C. Ginet and S. Shoemaker (eds), *Knowledge and Mind*, New York: Oxford University Press.
(1989) 'Belief and the identity of reference', *Midwest Studies in Philosophy* 14.
(1990) 'Genuine names and knowledge by acquaintance', *Dialectica*.
(1993) 'There is a word for that kind of thing: an investigation of two kinds of thought', *Philosophical Perspectives*.

Secondary literature:
Bach, K. (1981) 'Referential/attributive', *Synthèse* 49.
Beebe, M. (1977) 'Referential/attributive', *Canadian Journal of Philosophy*.
Bertolet, R. (1980) 'The semantic significance of Donnellan's distinction', *Philosophical Studies*.

——(1986) 'Donnellan's distinctions', *Australasian Journal of Philosophy.*

——(1990) *What Is Said: A Theory of Indirect Speech Reports*, Dordrecht: Norwell Kluwer.

Boer, S. E. (1972) 'Reference and identifying descriptions', *Philosophical Review.*

Brinton, A. (1977) 'Uses of definite descriptions and Russell's Theory', *Philosophical Studies.*

Canfield, J. V. (1977) 'Donnellan's theory of names', *Dialogue* (Canada).

Devitt, M. (1981) 'Donnellan's distinction', *Midwest Studies in Philosophy* 6 (defends Donnellan against Kripke 1977).

Kripke, S. (1977) 'Speaker's reference and semantic reference', *Midwest Studies in Philosophy* 2 (see Donnellan 1977, and compare Devitt 1981).

MacKay, A. F. (1968) 'Mr Donnellan on referring', *Philosophical Review.*

Margolis, J. and Fales, E. (1976) 'Donnellan on definite descriptions', *Philosophia* (Israel).

Oldfield, E. (1981) 'On an argument of Donnellan's', *Philosophical Studies.*

Peterson, P. L. (1976) 'An abuse of terminology: Donnellan's distinction in recent grammar', *Foundations of Language* (criticizes a mistaken extension of the distinction in linguistics).

Ray, R. (1980) 'Transparent and opaque reference', *Philosophical Studies.*

Searle, J. R. (1979) 'Referential and attributive', *The Monist* (reprinted in *Expression and Meaning: Studies in the Theory of Speech Acts*, Cambridge: Cambridge University Press, 1979).

Donnellan's most influential article, 'Reference and definite descriptions' (1966), distinguishes referential and attributive uses of definite descriptions (roughly, expressions beginning with singular 'the' or equivalents). Consider two responses to 'Smith's murderer is insane': 'It was Jones he murdered'; 'Smith wasn't murdered'. The former treats the description 'Smith's murderer' as referential (note the 'he'), the latter as attributive, i.e. as 'whoever murdered Smith ... '. The interpretation determines whether what is said is true-or-false or neither (or, for a question, command, etc., what counts as answering or obeying it), and the two conflicting theories of definite descriptions by **Russell** and **Strawson** both ignore this distinction. Donnellan's other work mainly develops this and related themes, with occasional excursions into epistemology and philosophy of mind. Critics have mainly accepted that some such distinction exists but have disputed its real nature and proper formulation, and consequent significance, asking in particular whether it is really semantic (concerning meaning) or pragmatic (concerning what our utterances *do*), and how far the theories of Russell and Strawson (especially that of Russell) are affected by it.

Sources: *PAAPA*; personal communication.

A. R. LACEY

Dooyeweerd, Herman

Dutch. *b:* 7 October 1984, Amsterdam. *d:* 12 February 1977, Amsterdam. *Cat:* Christian philosopher. *Ints:* Philosophy of religion. *Educ:* The Free University, Amsterdam, doctorate in Law 1917. *Infls:* Kant and Husserl. *Appts:* Professor of Encyclopaedia of Jurisprudence, Philosophy of Law and History of Dutch Law at the Free University, Amsterdam, 1926–65; Rector Magnificus, 1930–1 and 1950–1; Member of the Royal Netherlands Academy of Sciences and Letters, 1948; Secretary/Treasurer, 1954–64.

Main publications:

(1953–8) *A New Critique of Theoretical Thought*, Philadelphia: Presbyterian & Reformed Publishing Co.

(1960) *In the Twilight of Western Thought*, 4 vols, Philadelphia: Presbyterian & Reformed Publishing Co.

(1975) *The Christian Idea of the State*, trans. J. Kraay, Nutley, NJ: Craig Press.

Secondary literature:

Kalsbeek, L. (1975) *Contours of a Christian Philosophy: an Introduction to Herman Dooyeweerd's Thought*, Amsterdam: Buijten & Schipperheijn.

Marlet, M. Fr. J. (1954) *Grundlinien der kalvinistischen 'Philosophie der Gesetzesidee' als christlicher Transzendentalphilosophie*, Munich: Karl Zink Verlag.

Philosophy and Christianity: Philosophical Essays Dedicated to Professor Dr Herman Dooyeweerd (1965) Amsterdam: J. H. Kok, Kampen/North-Holland Publishing Co.

In 1964 the President of the Royal Netherlands Academy of Sciences and Letters rated Dooyeweerd as 'the most original philosopher the Netherlands had ever brought forth'. This was in substance due to Dooyeweerd's creation—from the 1920s onwards—of a genuine Christian philosophy. Dooyeweerd showed that every philosophy proceeds from a non-theoretical (religious) point of view. He made clear that even in humanist philosophy the autonomy of reason could not be *theoretically* proven. Dooyeweerd elaborated this hypothesis in a 'transcendental critique of theoretical thought', first published in 1939.

Another important part of Dooyeweerd's philosophy is formed by his theory of modal spheres (also called modalities or modal aspects). He explained that in theoretical thought (sharply to be distinguished from naive or pre-theoretical thought) one abstracts one aspect from reality to analyze it theoretically. Dooyeweerd distinguished fifteen different modal spheres, which are placed in an irreversible order of cosmic time: the numerical and the spatial aspects, the aspects of movement, of physical energy, of organic life, and of psychical feeling, the analytical-logical, the historical and the linguistic aspect, the aspect of social intercourse, the economic and the aesthetic aspect, the juridical and the moral aspect, and the aspect of faith. In their cosmic coherence every modal aspect supposes all the other aspects, but each modal aspect has its own nature which cannot be reduced to another modal aspect.

During the Second World War Dooyeweerd wrote an extensive work entitled *Reformation and Scholasticism in Philosophy*. Of this work, dealing especially with the history of Western philosophy, only the first volume appeared in Dutch in 1949. The trilogy as a whole is hoped to be published in English in the near future. In this work Dooyeweerd exposed his new insights regarding the *four religious basic motifs of Western thought* that rule Western thought: the Greek motif of form and matter, the Christian basic motif of creation, fall and redemption, the Roman Catholic basic motif of nature and grace, and the Humanist basic motif of nature and freedom.

Sources: M. E. Verburg (1989) *Herman Dooyeweerd: leven en werk van een Nederlands christen-wijsgeer*, Baarn: The Hague.

M. E. VERBURG

D'Ors y Rovira, Eugenio

Spanish. *b:* 1884, Barcelona. *d:* September 1954, Villanueva y Geltrú. *Cat:* 'Spiritualistic vitalist'. *Ints:* Metaphysics; philosophy of mind; philosophical logic. *Educ:* Barcelona, Paris, Brussels, Heidelberg, Geneva and Munich. *Infls:* Influenced (negatively) by pragmatism and (positively) by vitalist thought. *Appts:* Secretary General, Instituto d'Estudis Catalans, 1911; Professor of Science and History of Culture, Escuela Social (Madrid), 1923; Perpetual Secretary, Instituto de España; Professor of Science of Culture, University of Madrid, 1932; one of the most influential Spanish thinkers of this period.

Main publications:

The following is a highly selective list. D'Ors was a voluminous writer in Spanish, Catalan, French and Italian on many aspects of cultural life. This selection is restricted to works of philosophical interest.

(1907–16) *El Glosario*, 5 vols (a sort of intellectual diary).

(1914) *La Filosofía del hombre que trabaja y juega*.

(1916) *Una primera llicó de Filosofía*.

(1918) *Grandeza y servidumbre de la inteligencia*.

(1920–43) *Nuevo Glosario*, 3 vols, Madrid: Aguilar.

(1921) *Introducción a la Filosofía. La doctrina de la inteligencia*.

(1939) *Introducción a la vida angélica*.

(1945) *Estilos de pensar*, Madrid: Epesa.

(1946) *Novísimo Glosario*, Madrid: Aguilar.

(1947) *El secreto de la filosofía*, Barcelona: Iberia.

Secondary literature:

Academia Breve de Crítica de Arte (1955) *Homenaje a Eugenio d'Ors*, Madrid: Altamira.

Academia del Faro de San Cristobal (1968) *Homenaje a Eugenio d'Ors*, Madrid: Editora Nacional.

Aranguren, J. L. (1945) *La filosofía de Eugenio d'Ors*, Madrid: Epesa.

Gonzalez-Cruz, L. F. (1988) *Fervor del metodo: el universo creador de Eugenio d'Ors*, Madrid: Editorial Origenes.

Saenz, P. (1983) *The Life and Works of Eugenio d'Ors*, Troy, Michigan: International Book Publishers.

In 1945 (p.14) d'Ors remarks that every philosophy is governed by 'a central and principal intuition' ('una intuición central y matriz') and this is certainly true of his own thought, at the centre of which is an unchanging vision of a universe which is dynamic, creative and irreducibly complex. The entities which compose the dorsian universe are interrelated in many ways, and often endowed with internal, germinal tensions. He sees everywhere a creative tension between that which is trying to express itself and an ambient medium which is resistant to this expression and so must be moulded if the expression is to come to fruition. This resistive tension, which he regards as beneficial, between will to expression and medium d'Ors calls dialectic (*dialéctica*), and its description forms one of the three major divisions of his thought. The other two correspond to the analysis of the will to expression (which he calls *Poética*) and to the description of the resistive features of the universe (which he calls *Patética*).

An important element in the *Poética* is the dorsian analysis of the self. Unsurprisingly in view of the profoundly dynamistic vision underlying d'Ors's thought, he rejects the view that the self is an unchanging thing (*yo-cosa*). The self is better regarded as a function (*yo-función*) characterized by a dynamic hunger for work and play (*el trabajo y el juego*; hence 1914). Moreover, the human soul includes in its constitution a directing principle which d'Ors calls an angel, and his works on the operations of these angels makes up a large part of his *Poética* (cf., for example, the 'angelic life', *vida angelica*, described in 1939).

D'Ors's irrefragable conviction of the dynamism and sheer complexity of what there is underlies his best-known doctrine concerning philosophy itself. It leads him not only to reject as oversimple all types of mechanistic thought and pragmatism, but also to insist that even vitalism, to which he was in many ways highly sympathetic, could not do justice to the richness of the *rerum natura*. Philosophy is in need of 'Keplerian reform' ('reforma kepleriana'). It must have two key poles, not just one: philosophy must do justice not only to life, but also to the operations of the mind or spirit (i.e. the subject-matter of the *Poética*)—hence the summary description of his thought as spiritualistic vitalism. The aspect of the mind whose function it is to do justice to both d'Ors calls the intelligence (hence, for example, 1918 and 1921), which he distinguishes sharply from reason. The latter operates mechanically, on the basis of the principles of identity, excluded middle and non-contradiction. By contrast the intelligence, in order to do justice to the wealth of the universe, must adopt subtler principles, for example, that of 'necessary function', according to which the world is organized not like a mechanism but like a harmonious syntax.

ROBERT WILKINSON

Drake, Durant

American. *b:* 18 December 1878, Hartford, Connecticut. *d:* 25 November 1933. *Cat:* Critical realist. *Ints:* Philosophy of religion; epistemology. *Educ:* University of Hartford and Columbia University. *Infls:* George Santayana and C. A. Strong. *Appts:* University of Illinois, 1911–12; Wesleyan University, 1912–15; Vassar College, 1915–33.

Main publications:

(1911) *The Problem of Things in Themselves*, Boston: Ellis.

(1914) *Problems of Conduct*, Boston: Houghton Mifflin.

(1916) *Problems of Religion*, Boston: Houghton Mifflin.

(1920) (ed. with others) *Essays in Critical Realism*, London: Macmillan.

(1925) *Mind and its Place in Nature*, New York: Macmillan.

(1928) *The New Morality*, New York: Macmillan.

(1933) *Invitation to Philosophy* Boston: Houghton Mifflin.

Given the lead essay in the movement-forming volume *Essays in Critical Realism* (1920), Drake outlined the contributors' common approach: character complexes (or essences) are taken to be characters of existent outer objects, which they are when perception is veridicial. In the case of perceptual error they are characters of mental states (p. 32). The 'monistic realism' surrounding this conception had been outlined in his first work and was still being developed in the last. There is no legitimate distinction between psychic and material stuff: 'Whether we call that stuff psychic or material is a mere matter of convenience' (1911, p. 35). When an organism 'adjusts itself, however vaguely, to something or other' conciousness appears, actualized from the potentiality of the psychic–material stuff (1925, p. 247).

With respect to ethics and religion, he believed that they make common cause in support of what matters, 'to make good prevail and banish evil' (1914, p. 312), a goal he identifies with bringing in the 'kingdom of God'. Although beyond proof we have nothing to lose and everything to gain by believing 'in God, the eternal power that makes for righteousness' (1916, p. 414). The difference in approach is that where traditional morality was authoritarian, the new morality rests on 'observation of the results of conduct', and can direct itself more effectively towards maximizing attainable happiness (1928, p. v).

WILLIAM REESE

Dray, William H(erbert)

Canadian. *b:* 23 June 1921, Montreal, Canada. *Cat:* Analytic philosopher of history and social studies. *Ints:* Metaphysics and causation; theory of knowledge; moral philosophy; early modern philosophy. *Educ:* Toronto BA, Modern History, 1949; Balliol and Nuffield Colleges, Oxford, BA, PPE, 1951, MA 1955, DPhil 1956. *Infls:* W. H. Walsh and R. G. Collingwood. *Appts:* Lecturer in Philosophy, Toronto, 1953–5, and Assistant Professor to Professor, 1955–68; Professor of Philosophy, Trent, 1968–76, and Chair, Department of Philosophy, 1968–73; Professor of Philosophy cross-appointed to History, Ottawa, 1976–86, and Professor Emeritus, from 1986; Visiting appointments at Ohio State, 1959, Case Institute, 1966, Harvard, 1967 and 1973, Stanford, 1962, Duke, 1973.

Main publications:
(1957) *Laws and Explanation in History*, Oxford: Clarendon.
(1964) *Philosophy of History*, New Jersey: Prentice Hall, Inc.
(1966) *Philosophical Analysis and History*, New York: Harper & Row.
(1980) *Perspectives on History*, London: Routledge & Kegan Paul.
(1981) (ed. with L. Pompa) *Substance and Form in History*, Edinburgh: Edinburgh University Press.
(1989) *On History and Philosophers of History*, Bathhurst, NSW: E. J. Brill.

Secondary literature:
Fell, A. P. (1965) 'Dray's philosophy of history ', *Dialogue* 4: 381–8.
Hempel, C. G. (1962) 'Rational action', *Proceedings of the American Philosophical Association* 35: 5–24.
Lewis, T. T. (1981) 'Karl Popper's situation logic and the covering law model of historical explanation', *Clio* 10: 291–303.
Mandelbaum, M. (1961) 'Historical explanation: the problem of "covering laws"', *History and Theory* 1: 229–42.
Rossmann, N. (1967) 'On rational explanation in history', *Philosophical Studies* (Ireland) 16: 116–36.
Stover, R.C. (1961) 'Dray on historical explanation', *Mind* 70: 540–43.

Dray's early work concentrates on the logic of inference and on models of historical inference and explanation. This interest is central in the influential version of his PhD thesis, *Laws and Explanations in History* (1957), in which he challenges as unnecessary, insufficient and misleading the positivist notion attributed to K. **Popper** and C. G. **Hempel** that historical knowledge follows the model of knowledge of physics, requiring the subsumption of events under general laws (the covering-law model of historical explanation). Opposing a formal logical understanding of historical explanation, and opting for the adequacy of empirically based explanations in terms of 'how possibly' rather than 'why necessarily', Dray advocates the loosely idealistic claim that human action belongs to a special 'rational' category involving reasonable human motives or rationale.

Within the philosophy of history itself Dray highlights the important distinction between its speculative branch, pertaining to meaning in history, and its critical branch, which addresses the discipline of history itself. In the latter instance he sees his humanistic approach to historiography as involving logical parallels to literary narrative rather than to science. His interests range widely from ethical judgment in history to epistemological issues of objectivity, truth and the nature of mind especially as these problems arise in philosophy of history. Nor do the metaphysical issues of the nature of cause-effect relations, actions and events escape his attention. Dray's analyses are often informed by or are developments of theses arising from R. G. **Collingwood**'s works, on which Dray is a noted commentator, and Dray has applied his theoretical findings to the actual historical practice of, for example, O. **Spengler** and A. J. P. Taylor.

Sources: IWW 1993–94, p. 425; PI.

DAVID SCOTT

Dretske, Fred Irwin
American. *b:* 9 December 1932, Waukegan, Illinois. *Cat:* Epistemologist; philosopher of mind; philosopher of science. *Educ:* Purdue University and University of Minnesota. *Infls:* Russell, Broad, Reichenbach and Carnap. *Appts:* 1957–9, Teaching Assistant, University of Minnesota; 1960–90, Instructor, then Assistant, Associate, then full Professor, University of Wisconsin, Madison; 1990–, full Professor of Philosophy, Stanford University.

Main publications:
(1969) *Seeing and Knowing*, Chicago: Chicago University Press; London: Routledge & Kegan Paul.
(1970) 'Epistemic operators', *Journal of Philosophy* 69: 1007–23.
(1971) 'Conclusive reasons', *Australasian Journal of Philosophy* 49: 1–22.
(1972) 'Contrastive statements', *Philosophical Review* 81: 411–37.
(1977) 'Laws of nature', *Philosophy of Science* 44: 248–68.
(1981) *Knowledge and the Flow of Information*, Cambridge, Mass.: MIT Press.
(1986) 'Misrepresentation', in R. Bogdan (ed.), *Belief*, Oxford: Oxford University Press.
(1988) *Explaining Behavior: Reasons in a World of Causes*, Cambridge, Mass.: MIT Press.
(1992) 'The metaphysics of freedom', *Canadian Journal of Philosophy* 22: 1–14.

(1992) 'What isn't wrong with folk psychology', *Metaphilosophy* 23: 1–13.

(1993) 'Conscious experience', *Mind* 102: 1–22.

Secondary literature:

Behavioral and Brain Sciences (1983) 6: 55–89, (precis of *Knowledge and the Flow of Information*, peer reviews and author's responses).

McLaughlin, B. (ed.) (1991) *Fred Dretske and His Critics*, Oxford: Blackwell (contains bibliography of Dretske's publications).

Philosophy and Phenomenological Research (1990) 50: 783–839, (precis of *Explaining Behavior*, reviews and replies).

Fred Dretske's major contributions to philosophy are concentrated in four specific areas: the nature of perception, the nature of knowledge, the explanation of behaviour in terms of reasons and the status of the laws of nature. Almost uniquely, he is a philosopher with an initial background in engineering: a first degree in electrical engineering together with brief work experience in the same field. Some of his illustrations and his general orientation undoubtedly reflect this background. As well as this, Dretske utilizes for his philosophical purposes knowledge of the psychology of perception, learning theory, cognitive science, evolutionary biology and information theory. Via an interest in philosophy of science, he rapidly became immersed in epistemological issues, both early and latterly in perception.

What attracted most attention, and certainly controversy, in Dretske's first book was the distinction therein drawn between epistemic and non-epistemic seeing—the latter, which he has also called simple seeing, involving visual discrimination but free of belief content. To see a cat is not to see that a cat is present; nor is it to see that anything whatever is the case. Epistemic seeing is more sophisticated and presupposes the prior ability to see-without-identifying. In *Knowledge and the Flow of Information* (1981) this distinction was cashed out in terms of a difference in the way in which information can be encoded. In a perceptual experience it is encoded in analog form, whereas with cognitive states like knowledge or belief it is encoded in digital form, with specific propositional content.

Two strands in Dretske's account of knowledge can be separated out. First, as with perception, there is the account in information-theoretic terms. Knowledge is equated with information-caused belief. To know that some source, s, is F, is to have the belief that it is F caused or sustained by the information that it is F. Second, Dretske gave one of the earliest formulations of the now quite popular 'relevant alternatives' account of knowledge (1970, 1971), an important aspect of which is its treatment of sceptical possibilities. A denial is boldly made (in contradistinction to what Descartes supposed) that knowledge is closed under known entailment. Something can be known although the knower does not know that certain sceptical possibilities (which he knows to be incompatible with what he knows) do not obtain. One can know that one is seeing a daffodil while not being in a position to exclude such outlandish alternatives as its being a mass hallucination, a clever facsimile, etc.: only *relevant* alternatives need be excluded, and what these are depends upon the particular context.

As with knowledge so too with explanation of behaviour in terms of reasons (beliefs, desires, intentions) Dretske broadly seeks to safeguard the commonsensical or folk-psychological position. Such explanations do not have to give way to, because they do not clash with, scientific explanations of bodily movements. Nor do beliefs (etc.) have a merely epiphenomenal status (a point on which he came to think his earlier view was inadequate). In *Explaining Behavior* (1988), Dretske ambitiously undertakes to show that human (and some animal) behaviour is to be explained in terms of the causal powers which beliefs and desires possess in virtue of the propositional contents they have, through prior learning. For instance, a's now stroking a cat might be (partly) explained by the occurrence in a of an internal state which is a token of a type of state representing the presence of a cat and tending to produce movements M because earlier tokens of this state had been followed by similar movements which had been rewarded. Hence, explanation in terms of an agent's reasons invokes the idea of a structuring cause where this is a matter of explaining why some belief (say) now produces the particular effect it does produce because of what happened in the past. (A longstanding aim has been to produce a naturalistic account of content).

In philosophy of science, Dretske's name is associated with a view about the laws of nature, sometimes called the Dretske–Armstrong–Tooley view, according to which laws of nature are to be understood not as generalizations about particular instances but as singular statements linking properties or universals.

Sources: DAS, 5, 1982; CA NRS 10, 1983; IWW 1993–4; letter from Dretske and CV.

CLIVE BORST

Driesch, Hans Adolf Eduard

German. *b:* 28 October 1867, Bad Kreuznach, Germany. *d:* 17 April 1941, Leipzig. *Cat:* Biologist; philosopher. *Ints:* Vitalism, philosophy of organism and mind. *Educ:* Universities of Freiburg, Munich and Jena. *Infls:* Personal influences: Ernst Haeckel and A. Weismann. Literary: Aristotle, Kant, Otto Liebmann and Alois Riehl. *Appts:* 1891–1900, experimental embryologist at the Marine Biological Station, Naples; 1909–19, Privatdozent, Heidelberg; 1912, Member of Philosophical Faculty, Heidelberg; 1919–21, Professor of Philosophy, Cologne; 1921–33, Professor of Philosophy, Leipzig.

Main publications:

(1908) *The Science and Philosophy of Organism*, 2 vols, London: A. & C. Black.

(1912) *Ordnungslehre, ein System des nichtmetaphysischen Teiles der Philosophie*, Jena: G. Fischer; revised edition, 1923.

(1914) *The Problem of Individuality*, London: Macmillan.

(1917) *Wirklichkeitslehre, ein Metaphysicher Versuch*, Leipzig: Emmanuel Reinicke; revised edition, 1922.

(1926) *Metaphysik der Natur*, Berlin: Druck & Oldenbourg.

Secondary literature:

Cassirer, Ernst (1950) *The Problem of Knowledge: Philosophy, Science, and History since Hegel*, New Haven: Yale University Press, pp. 151–216.

Morgan, T. H. (1909) review of *The Science and Philosophy of Organism* (1908), in *Journal of Philosophy* 6: 101–5.

Oakeley, Hilda D. (1920–1) 'On Professor Driesch's attempt to combine a philosophy of life and a philosophy of knowledge' *PAS* (new series) 21: 161–79.

Spaulding, E. G. (1906) 'Driesch's theory of vitalism', *Philosophical Review* 15: 518–27.

Driesch was the outstanding proponent of neovitalism and the typical metaphysician of biology. Developmental biology was the main concern of his earliest writings and his vitalist thesis was directly connected with it.

From the first, he had sought to explain 'self-regulation' in the organism in a way which would both accord with known experimental facts and reveal the ultimate causes whose formulation he regarded as the object of philosophy. His experiments with the egg of the sea-urchin (Echinus) provided the point of departure for his vitalist metaphysics and subsequent philosophy.

In these experiments Driesch discovered that the diminutive 'blastula', produced by the severed daughter cell, could be cut in the plane of its polar axis, at any angle, into portions of any size, and provided that each was more than one quarter of the whole it would produce a complete organism. Further experiments confirmed a similar tendency of the whole to reassert itself in the dissevered part and, by 1895, led him to believe that development in organic systems leads beyond all mechanistic interpretation (1908, vol. 1. pp. 66–7.)

Driesch concluded that organic life must be regulated not by physico-chemical processes, but by something immaterial, which he called 'entelechy', that is, a unifying cause which directs the activity of living matter so as to produce an 'organic whole'. The matter, he held, is utilized by entelechy, the influence of which is non-energetic and consists in the release or suspension of potentialities in the material parts to fulfil the requirements of the coherent pattern.

In his later, systematic philosophy (for example, in 1912 and 1917), supposedly a 'critical idealism', Driesch sought epistemological and methodological justification for the idea that there is a whole-making causality operative in the psychological and cultural levels—that is, that entelechy is the unconscious foundation of our conscious experience. In *Wirklichkeitslehre* (1917) he also posited the notion of a supra-personal whole. Thus, for him, entelechy became the *ens realissimus*. Finally, his philosophy reflected his interest in parapsychology. Driesch's neovitalist metaphysics may be scouted as overspeculative, but the significance of his works is that they radically called into doubt the adequacy of a mechanistic interpretation for the phenomena of life and consciousness.

Sources: Edwards; Copleston; Bubner; Metzler; Brockhaus.

STEPHEN MOLLER

Drobnitskii, Oleg Grigor'evich

Russian. *b:* 18 January 1933, Mytishchi, USSR. *d:* 3 March 1973, USSR. *Cat:* Marxist; philosopher of ethics. *Ints:* Ethics; value theory. *Educ:* Moscow University and the Institute of Philosophy of the Soviet Academy of Sciences. *Infls:* Kant, Hegel and Marx. *Appts:* Worked at the Institute of Philosophy of the Soviet Academy of Sciences.

Main publications:

(1963) *Opravdanie beznravstvennosti* [The Justification of Immorality], Moscow.

(1965) *Kratkii slovar' po etike* [Short Dictionary of Ethics], Moscow.

(1967) *Mir ozhivshikh predmetov: Problema tsennosti i marksistskaia filosofiia* [The World of Revivified Objects: The Problem of Value and Marxist Psychology], Moscow.

(1967) (with T. A. Kuz'mina) *Kritika sovremennikh burzhuaznykh eticheskikh kontseptsii* [A Critique of Contemporary Bourgeois Ethical Conceptions], Moscow.

(1974) *Poniatie morali: Istoriko-kriticheskii ocherk* [The Concept of Morality: A Historico-Critical Essay].

(1977) *Problemy nravstvennosti* [Problems of Morality], Moscow.

Secondary literature:

Grier, Philip T. (1978) *Marxist Ethical Theory in the Soviet Union*, Dordrecht: D. Reidel.

Scanlan, James P. (1985) *Marxism in the USSR*, Cornell University Press.

During his short career Drobnitskii came to be regarded as one of the most learned and original contributors to the establishment of ethics—a field once dismissed as 'bourgeois' by doctrinaire Marxist-Leninists—as a legitimate discipline within Soviet philosophy. His writings ranged from abstract metaethical reflections to historical and critical studies, practical considerations of the role of morality as a regulator of behaviour, and the first Russian-language dictionary of ethics. In an enterprise reminiscent of Hegel's *Phenomenology of Spirit*, Drobnitskii attempted to base ethical theory on an examination of the logical structure of moral consciousness, within which he finds conceptual levels corresponding to stages in the historical evolution of ethical thinking. His influential articles on moral consciousness, published in journals over the years from 1968 until his death, are reprinted in the posthumously published *Problemy nravstvennosti* [Problems of Morality]. His developed theory combines a Kantian, deontological interpretation of individual moral obligation with a teleological view of the ultimate justification of ethical standards. In accordance with Marxist principles, such justification can only be grounded historically, Drobnitskii argues. Relying on the conception of an ideal human essence as described by Marx, he contends that objective laws of history establish communism as the fulfilment of the true interests of humanity and thus as the social embodiment of the highest moral values.

JAMES SCANLAN

Ducasse, Curt John

French (naturalized US citizen, 1910). *b:* 7 July 1881, Angouleme, France. *d:* 3 September 1969, Providence, Rhode Island. *Cat:* Dualistic analytic philosopher. *Ints:* General philosophy; philosophy of religion. *Educ:* University of Washington and Harvard University. *Infls:* Schopenhauer, whose philosophy he once held to be 'essentially sound', the Hindu philosopher Bhagavan Das, Josiah Royce and Ralph Barton Perry. *Appts:* University of Washington, 1912–26; Brown University, 1926–58.

Main publications:

(1924) *Causation and the Types of Necessity*, Seattle: University of Washington Press.

(1929) *Philosophy of Art*, New York: Dial Press.

(1941) *Philosophy as a Science*, New York: O. Piest.

(1944) *Art, the Critics and You*, New York: O. Piest.

(1951) *Nature, Mind and Death*, La Salle, Ill.: Open Court.

(1953) *A Philosophical Scrutiny of Religion*, New York: Ronald Press.

(1961) *A Critical Examination of the Belief in Life after Death*, New York: Ronald Press.

(1969) *Paranormal Phenomena*, New York: Parapsychology Foundation.

(1969) *Truth, Knowledge and Causation*, London: Routledge & Kegan Paul.

Secondary literature:

Dommeyer, F. C. (ed.) (1966) *Current Philosophical Issues: Essays in Honor of Curt John Ducasse*, Springfield, Ill.: Thomas (contains bibliography, 1912–65).

'Symposium in honor of C. J. Ducasse', *Philosophy and Phenomenological Research*, 13, 1 (contains bibliography of his writings up to 1951).

Participating in the early development of analytic philosophy, Ducasse held causality to be fundamental, rejected sensa in favour of sensing, provided a feeling-centred analysis of aesthetics, proposed that philosophical analyses were semantic hypotheses concerning the meanings to be accorded basic terms, and believed paranormal phenomena to favour some type of mental survival beyond the body.

Rejecting Hume's definition of causality as failing to conform to actual usage, he centred on Mill's method of difference as both following usage and providing an adequate definition of the term. For Ducasse it was analytic that every event requires a cause, and contradictory that there could be a causeless event. It followed that indeterminism is, likewise, contradictory. Finding mind not to be reducible to matter (the source of his dualism), he accepted causes and effects as either mental or physical, thus distinguishing four types of causal relations: the physicophysical, physicopsychological, psychophysical, and psychopsychical. The second and third relations feature mind–body interaction; the fourth is exemplified by instances of mental telepathy.

Arguing against **Moore**'s sensa, he thought it reasonable to replace sensa with adverbial expressions: sensing bluely in place of blue sensa, for example. In aesthetic experience the auditor senses the feeling objectified in it. He thought of philosophy as a science dealing with values. His reasoning was that every science has 'primitive facts' on which it rests and which test its hypotheses, and 'derivative facts' of less importance which help distinguish it from other enterprises. The goal of each science is to discover the premises from which the primitive facts of the science can be deduced. In the case of philosophy the primitive facts are values and appraisals concerning value; and the method of philosophy is to produce analysans which better reflect the standard appraisals of usage. Non-appraisive terms either fall outside of philosophy or are derivative. Derivative terms in philosophy are not appraisive, but are involved in the analysis of appraisals. 'Causality' is derivative in this sense; while 'reality' is both primitive and derivative, appraisive in itself and involved in other appraisals. Although not a theist, he found the balance of evidence, normal and paranormal, suggesting, even supporting, but not establishing, survival of the mind beyond the body.

Ducasse chaired the committee which organized the Pacific Division of Philosophy, was instrumental in establishing the *Journal of Symbolic Logic* and its publisher, the Association for Symbolic Logic, serving as its first President. He also assumed leading roles in activities as widely diverse as aesthetics and psychical research.

Sources: Reese; Edwards.

WILLIAM REESE

Dufrenne, Mikel

French. *b:* 1910. *Cat:* Phenomenologist. *Ints:* Aesthetics; ethics; politics. *Educ:* Studied under Alain and Souriau. *Infls:* Descartes, Kant, Scheler, Heidegger and Merleau-Ponty. *Appts:* Mobilized in 1939, Dufrenne was captured and spent the war years as a prisoner in the same camp as Ricoeur; later taught at the Universities of Poitiers, Buffalo, Michigan and Delaware; was one of the founding staff of l'Université de Paris X at

Nanterre; Chief Editor of the influential journal *10/18*; retired from teaching 1974.

Main publications:

(1953) *Phénoménologie de l'expérience esthétique*, 2 vols, Paris: PUF.
(1953) *La Personnalité de base*, Paris: PUF.
(1963) *La Póetique*, Paris: PUF.
(1966) *Jalons*, The Hague: Martinus Nijhoff.
(1967/76/81) *Esthétique et philosophie*, 3 vols, Paris: Klincksieck.
(1968) *Pour l'homme*, Paris: Éditions du Seuil.
(1977) *Subversion/Perversion*, Paris: PUF.
(1981) *L'Inventaire des a priori*, Paris: C. Bourgois.

Secondary literature:

Edie, J. M. (ed.) (1970) *Patterns of the Life World*, Evanston: University of Illinois Press.
Feezel, R. M. (1980) 'Mikel Dufrenne and the world of the aesthetic object', *Philosophy Today* 24: 20–32.
Kaelin, E. F. (1962) *An Existentialist Aesthetic*, Madison: University of Wisconsin Press.
Magiola, R. R. (1977) *Phenomenology and Literature*, West Lafayette: Purdue University Press.

Dufrenne was the first French phenomenologist to make aesthetics his central concern, and it was largely as a result of his work that this branch of philosophy underwent a revival of interest in France. Through his writing and teaching, Dufrenne has had a significant impact on French philosophical aesthetics, and also, via translations, on English-speaking phenomenologists. Dufrenne's conception of phenomenology is much closer to that of **Merleau-Ponty** than to that of **Husserl**. In his analysis of aesthetic phenomena he develops two notions of striking originality: first that the aesthetic object is best regarded as a quasi-subject (*quasi-pour-soi*), and second that the field of the a priori in philosophy has been conceived too narrowly. Following a lead from **Scheler**, Dufrenne contends that there are a priori affective categories which constitute the conditions under which a world can be felt.

Dufrenne rejects the view that what there is can be divided into categories of *en-soi* (in-itself) and *pour-soi* (for-itself), i.e. (roughly) non-conscious objects and conscious, purposive human beings. Aesthetic objects, by which Dufrenne means works of art or to a lesser degree of nature as they are experienced by us, refuse to fit into either class. Such objects have four important properties: (i) expressiveness: Dufrenne takes a strongly objectivist line concerning expression, ascribing expressive properties to the object itself;

(ii) meaningfulness: whatever is objectively ex-pressive is meaningful or significant; (iii) self-sufficiency: aesthetic objects are ends and not means to a further end; (iv) profundity: aesthetic objects refuse to be summed up, continually manifest new significances, and this is the core of profundity. It is on the ground of their possession of these four properties that Dufrenne assimilates aesthetic objects to persons, and so feels justified in describing them as quasi-subjects.

The notion of the aesthetic object as quasi-subject is an important ground for Dufrenne's second major contention concerning the extent of the a priori: he contends that an objective a priori notion of 'human being' can be constructed, and so if the aesthetic object is a quasi-subject, the chances of being able to construct an a priori description of the latter are to that extent increased. Dufrenne's conception of the a priori differs from that of Kant in its assertion that although the a priori is anterior to experience it is also discerned in it: the a priori is not merely a condition of experience but is constitutive of it. Further, the Kantian list of categories is not exhaustive. There are a priori affective categories which are the conditions under which world can be felt. A subset of these categories are aesthetic: 'If we can feel the tragic in Racine or pathos in Beethoven or serenity in Bach it is because we have an idea, prior to all feeling *sentiment*, of the tragic, pathetic and serene, i.e. of what we must henceforth call affective categories' (*Phénomén-ologie*, 1953, II, pp. 571–2). To repeat, these a prioris are experienceable, and if we fail to grasp them we misunderstand the works which manifest them. Here, as elsewhere, Dufrenne takes a strongly objectivist line concerning the properties of aesthetic objects, a key presupposition for his view, reminiscent of **Heidegger**, that aesthetic experience is in some sense revelatory of ultimate features of being.

Later in his career, Dufrenne showed an increasing concern with the threat to liberty and creativity presented by overregimented structures, be they institutions, fashions, abstractions or theories. This theme, stated in *Pour l'homme* (issued, significantly, in 1968), is developed in many of his later articles (cf. *Esthétique et philosophie*) in which he analyses with approval works of art which break down genre boundaries and shock the mind into freedom.

Sources: Dr V. L. Lamb, unpublished doctoral thesis on Dufrenne's aesthetics, Univ. of Warwick, 1976.

ROBERT WILKINSON

Duhem, Pierre Maurice Marie

French. *b:* 9 June 1861, Paris. *d:* 14 September 1916, Cabréspine Ande. *Cat:* Physicist. *Ints:* Philosophy and history of science; intellectual history; science and religion. *Educ:* Paris, École Normale Supérieure, 1882–7, PhD 1888. *Infls:* B. Pascal, J. W. Gibbs, H von. Helmholtz, H. St Clair Deville, J. Moutier, J. Tannery and L. Blondel. *Appts:* Lille 1887–93, Rennes 1893–4, Bordeaux 1894–1916; Member of Académie des Sciences (non-resident).

Main publications:

(1886) *Le Potentiel thermodynamique*, Paris: Hermann.

(1892) 'Quelques réflexions au sujet des théories physiques', *Revue des Questions Scientifiques* 31: 139–77.

(1892) 'Notation atomique et hypothèse atomistiques', *Revue des Questions Scientifiques* 31: 391–454.

(1893) 'Physique et métaphysique', *Revue des Questions Scientifiques* 34: 55–83.

(1893) L'École anglaise et les théories physiques, *Revue des Questions Scientifiques* 34: 345–78.

(1894) 'Quelques réflexions au sujet de la physique expérimentale', *Revue des Questions Scientifiques* 36: 179–229.

(1900) *Les Théories électriques de J. Clerk Maxwell*, Paris: Hermann.

(1902) *Le Mixte et la combinaison chimique*, Paris: C. Naud.

(1902) *Thermodynamique et chimie*, Paris: Gauthier-Villars (English translation, *Thermodynamics and Chemistry*, New York: Wiley, 1903).

(1903) 'Analyse de l'ouvrage de Ernst Mach', *Bull. Sci. Math.* 2/27: 261–83.

(1903) 'Étude sur l'oeuvre de George Green', *Bull. Sci. Math.* 2/27: 237–56.

(1903) *L'Évolution de la mécanique*, Paris: A. Joanin (German translation, *Die Wandlunger der Mechanik*, Leipzig: J. A. Barth, 1921).

(1905–6) *Les Origines de la statique*, Paris: Hermann (English translation, *The Origin of Statics*, trans. Leneaux *et al.*, Dordrecht: Kluwer, 1991).

(1906) *La Théorie physique, son objet et sa structure*, Paris: Chevalier et Rivière; second edition, 1913 (English translation, *The Aim and Structure of Physical Theory*, trans. Wiener, Princeton: Princeton University Press, 1954; German translation, *Ziel und Struktur physikalischer Theorien*, trans. Adler, Leipzig: J. A. Barth, 1908, reprinted with introduction and bibliography of secondary literature by L. Schäfer, 1978).

(1906–13) *Études sur Léonard de Vinci*, Paris: Hermann.

(1908) ΣΟΖΕΙΝ ΤΑ ΨΑΙΝΟΜΕΝΑ *Essai sur la notion de théorie physique de Platon à Galilée*, Paris: Hermann (English translation, *To Save the Phenomena*, trans.Dolland and Maschler, Chicago: Univeristy of Chicago Press, 1969).

(1913–58) *Le Système du monde, histoire des doctrines cosmologiques de Platon à Copernic*, 10 vols, Paris: Hermann.

(1915) *La Science allemande*, Paris: Hermann (English translation, *German Science*, La Salle: Open Court, 1991).

(1916) *La Chimie est-elle une science française?*, Paris: Hermann.

(1917) 'Notice sur les travaux scientifiques de Duhem', *Mémoires de la Société des Sciences Physiques et Naturelles de Bordeaux* 7/I: 71–169.

(1985) *Medieval Cosmology*, trans. Ariew, Chicago: University of Chicago Press (partial translation of later volumes of *Le Système du Monde*, 1913–58).

(1987) *Prémices philosophiques*, ed. S. L. Jaki, Leiden: Brill.

Secondary literature:

Ariew, A. and Barker, P. (eds) (1990) 'Pierre Duhem, historian and philosopher of science', *Synthese* 83: 177–453.

Brenner, A. (1990) *Duhem, science, réalité et apparence*, Paris: Vrin.

Harding, S. G. (1976) *Can Theories be Refuted? Essays on the Duhem-Quine Thesis*, Dordrecht: Reidel.

Jaki, S. L. (1984) *Uneasy Genius: The Life and Work of Pierre Duhem*, The Hague, Martinus Nijhoff (fullest bibliography in print to date of Duhem's writings).

Lowinger, A. (1941) *The Methodology of Pierre Duhem*, New York: Columbia.

Maiocchi, R. (1985) *Chimica e filosofia, scienza, epistemologia, storia e religione nell'Opera di Pierre Duhem*, Florence: La Nuova Italia (a good critical account with a full bibliography).

Martin, R. N. D. (1982) 'Darwin and Duhem', *History of Science* 20: 64–74.

——(1987) 'Saving Duhem and Galileo', *History of Science* 25: 302–19.

——(1991) *Pierre Duhem: Philosophy and History in the Work of a Believing Physicist*, La Salle. Ill.: Open Court.

——(1991) 'The trouble with authority: the Galileo affair and one of its historians', *Modern Theology* 7: 269–80.

Paul, H. W. (1979) *The Edge of Contingency: French Catholic Reaction to Scientific Change from Darwin to Duhem*, Gainesville: University Presses of Florida.

Popper, K. R. (1959) *The Logic of Scientific Discovery*, London: Hutchinson.

——(1963) *Conjectures and Refutations*, London: Routledge.

Schäfer, L. (1974) *Erfahrung und Kovention*, Stuttgart-Bad Cannstatt: F. Fromman.

Pierre Duhem was a major physicist at the turn of the nineteenth and twentieth centuries, a prolific contributor to the development of the theories of heat, physical chemistry, hydrodynamics and electrodynamics, but opposed to the atomism that ultimately triumphed. He was also a seminal writer on the philosophy of science and on the history of science—particularly the medieval period. The general character and themes of his work as it evolved have to be understood against the broad background of late nineteenth-century physics and philosophy, as well as his avowed Catholicism. Interpretation of his work is complicated by his habit of reusing earlier work in a new context in ways liable to blind the unwary reader to his changes of point of view. At the outset his views were obvious variations on late nineteenth-century positivist themes. Physical theory was to offer a purely symbolic representation of the facts and to assist the memory by providing a classification of them. It was quite distinct from metaphysics and from common-sense knowledge. How this could have been achieved can perhaps be seen from the much more detailed discussion offered by Moritz **Schlick** in his *Allgemeine Erkenntnislehre*, where the relationships established between different concepts are thought of as a kind of net giving each concept, and therefore the reality it represents, its place in the scheme of things. Duhem supported his approach with an instrumentalist account of atomistic symbolism in chemistry, and by some rationally reconstructed history of a kind already familiar in the work of Eugen **Dühring** and Ernst **Mach**. At this point he showed no sign of any interest in or knowledge of medieval science. The first criticisms were Catholic in origin. Duhem was attacked for allegedly disdaining metaphysics, and for conceding too much to scepticism, an important point for Catholics because of their official commitment to a semi-rationalist apologetic. Duhem's initial response, a quasi-Thomist account of the mutual independence of physics and metaphysics, was never afterwards repeated or referred to. His long-term response was twofold: to draw out of his initial doctrine that physical theories were symbolic systems a fully fledged doctrine of the theoreticity of facts, and to flesh out what he meant by classification into his still controversial doctrine of natural classification. Experimental laws depended on other theoretical commitments to state them, so that the very notion of experimental refutation became logically ambiguous; so that, necessary as logic was to physical theory, it was not all-sufficient and not the ultimate arbiter. Experimental refutation and the response of physicists to it were matters of intuitive judgement. Physicists had to judge whether an experimental result refuted the theory or whether it was merely the effect of some other theory involved in the experimental situation. They also had to judge how to amend their theories in the light of accepted experimental refutations. Duhem also claimed that the goal of physics was the intuitively judged improving classification which increasingly reflected the ontological order. This doctrine of a fallible natural classification plays in Duhem's mature system of the *Théorie physique* a role like **Popper**'s notion of fallible truth in his. As Duhem matured, he came increasingly to cite Pascal's *Pensées* at crucial points in his argument. Prone as he was to suggest in the first part of his career that the natural classification looked for by physicists would have a scholastic form, these suggestions do not reflect his deeply Pascalian temper, made very explicit at the end of his life in his *Science allemande*. His later historical work lends itself to a like conclusion. After a decade of work that denied the existence or relevance of medieval science he was genuinely surprised to discover evidence of it while working on the *Origines de la statique* in the early winter of 1903. Thereafter his historical work changed its character. He did not, though, align himself with the Catholic neoscholasticism of the period, but emphasizes those aspects of the Middle Ages with which it was least compatible, claiming indeed that Thomism was incoherent.

Sources: Edwards; Mittelstrass; E. Jordan (1917) 'Duhem, Pierre', *MSSPNB* 7/I: 3–40; H. Pierre-Duhem (1936) *Un Savant français*, Paris: Plon; DSB 4: 225a–233b (bibliography); P. Brouzeng (1987) *Duhem 1861–1916: Science et Providence*, Paris: Belin; S. L. Jaki (1988) *The Physicist as Artist*, Edinburgh: Scottish Academic Press; S. L. Jaki (1992) *Reluctant Heroine: the Life and Work of Hélène Duhem*, Edinburgh: Scottish Academic Press.

R. N. D. MARTIN

Duhring, Karl Eugen

German. *b:* 1833, Berlin. *d:* 1921, Nowawes, near Potsdam. *Cat:* Scientific materialist. *Ints:* Epistemology; metaphysics; political economy. *Appts:*

Practised law, 1856–9, until an eye disease (that eventually blinded him) ended his career; free-lance student at the University of Berlin, doctorate 1861, taught there as a Privatdozent from 1864; in 1877 problems with his colleagues and his attacks on academic philosophy led to his dismissal; private scholar thereafter.

Main publications:

(1871) *Kritische Geschichte der Nationalökonomie und der Sozialismus*, Berlin.

(1873) *Kursus der National- und Sozialökonomie*, Berlin.

(1875) *Kursus der Philosophie*, Leipzig.

Secondary literature:

Doll, E. (1893) *Eugen Duhring*, Leipzig.

Engels, F. (1878) *Herrn Eugen Duhrings Umwälzung der Wissenschaft*, Leipzig (English translation, *Anti-Duhring*, Moscow: Foreign Languages Publishing House, 1959).

Lamberz, H. (1931) *Carey und Duhring*.

Duhring maintained that the laws of thought and of being are fundamentally coincident, philosophy's task being to provide a thoroughgoing knowledge of reality. Although sharing positivist hostility to metaphysics and religion, Duhring rejected positivism's attempts to reduce matter and cause to patterns in experience. In ethics he held that morality rests on an instinctive sympathy between people, and this led him to oppose Marxist claims about class conflict. His economic writings, influenced by the American, Henry Carey, defended a reformed capitalism in which workers' interests would be protected by powerful trade unions, and in which national economies could flourish behind high tariffs. In the 1870s, Duhring was briefly regarded as a leading social-democratic theorist. But his influence quickly waned, and although the Nazis, attracted by his anti-Semitism, took some interest in his writings, he is now remembered principally as no more than the object of Engels's attack in *Anti-Duhring*.

Sources: EncBrit.

NICHOLAS EVERITT

Dumèry, Henry

French. *b:* 29 February 1920, Auzances, Creuse, France. *Cat:* Philosopher of religion; metaphysician; phenomenologist. *Ints:* The phenomenology of religious experience. *Educ:* University of Paris. *Infls:* Plotinus, Maurice Blondel and Edmund Husserl. *Appts:* Professor, University of Caen, then Faculté des Lettres et Sciences Humaines de Paris-Nanterre (1966).

Main publications:
(1948) *La Philosophie de l'action; L'intellectualisme blondelien*, Paris: Aubier.
(1953) *Foi et interrogation*, Paris: Editions Tequi.
(1954) *Blondel et la religion*, Paris: PUF.
(1957) *Philosophie de la religion. Essai sur la signification du christianisme*, 2 vols, Paris: PUF.
(1960) *Phénoménologie et religion. Structure de l'institution chrétienne*, Paris (English translation, *Phenomenology and Religion: Structures of the Christian Institution*, Berkeley: University of California Press, 1975).
(1963) *Raison et religion dans la philosophie de l'action*, Paris: Editions du Seuil.

Secondary literature:
Bouillard, H. (1964) 'Philosophie de l'action et logique de la foi. A propos d'un ouvrage de M. Henry Duméry', *Archives de Philosophie*: 130–50.
Riet, G. van (1960) 'Philosophie de la religion et théologie', *Revue Philosophique de Louvain*: 415–37.

For several decades Duméry has been one of the leading French Catholic philosophers of religion. His work is also known in Catholic circles outside France, especially in the USA.

The three principal influences on his philosophy are: (i) the phenomenological, descriptive method of Edmund **Husserl**; (ii) the metaphysical system of Plotinus and in particular the principle of its ontological hierarchy, namely, the 'One' or the Good and the Deity; and (iii) Maurice **Blondel**'s philosophy of action, particularly its doctrine of human uneasiness, fed constantly by an unsatisfied will, that finds fulfilment only in surrender to the authority of Catholicism and in accepting the supernatural life in which God appears to be both transcendent and immanent, the source of whatever is infinite in our will and the ideal that satisfies this will. Duméry has not merely combined the three but he has given them a new meaning which gives a new complexion to the philosophy of religion. He has sought to provide a critique of religion without destroying religious faith. This has led him to formulate a religious metaphysic according to which the transcendent activity of God is both the source and goal of all human thought and action. His philosophy, however, has aroused some controversy: on 4 June 1958 four of his works were censured by the Saint-Office.

Sources: Huisman; EF.

STEPHEN MOLLER

Dummett, M(ichael) A(nthony) E(ardley)

British. *b:* 1925, London. *Cat:* Analytic philosopher. *Educ:* University of Oxford. *Infls:* Frege and Wittgenstein. *Appts:* Assistant Lecturer, University of Birmingham, 1950–1; Commonwealth Func Fellow, University of California at Berkeley, 1955–6; Reader in the Philosophy of Mathematics, University of Oxford, 1962–74; Fellow of All Souls College, Oxford, 1950–1979; from 1979, Wykeham Professor of Logic, and Fellow of New College, Oxford; other visiting positions in Europe, the USA and Africa.

Main publications:
(1973) *Frege: Philosophy of Language*, London: Duckworth.
(1977) (with the assistance of Roberto Minio) *Elements of Intuitionism*, Oxford: Clarendon Press.
(1978) *Truth and Other Enigmas*, London: Duckworth.
(1991) *Frege and Other Philosophers*, Oxford: Clarendon Press.
(1991) *Frege: Philosophy of Mathematics*, London: Duckworth.
(1991) *The Logical Basis of Metaphysics*, London: Duckworth.
(1993) *Origins of Analytic Philosophy*.
(1993) *The Seas of Language*, Oxford: Clarendon Press.

Secondary literature:
McGuinness, Brian and Oliveri, Gianluigi (eds) (1993) *The Philosophy of Michael Dummett*, Dordrecht: Reidel.
Wright, Crispin (1986) *Realism, Meaning and Truth*, Oxford: Basil Blackwell.

In his 1959 article 'Truth' (*Proceedings of the Aristotelian Society* 59, 1958–9) Dummett proposed the idea that for a proposition to be true is for it to be correctly assertible, and that no statement can be correctly assertible if it is such as to transcend all possibility of our verifying or falsifying it. If this is correct then the correct analysis of some types of statement might reveal that they do not have what Dummett called a 'realist' meaning; that is to say, they will not be true or false in virtue of a reality independent of our cognitive powers. Indeed, some perfectly clear and precise statements of the given class may turn out to be neither true nor false, and a central thrust of Dummett's philosophy has been to question the Principle of Bivalence.

The issue of anti-realism, as Dummett called it, has been the main focus of Dummett's work. It concerns, in his view, a cluster of problems which, though having different subject matters, none the less have a structural similarity. Are statements about the external world, for instance, statements about a reality that exists independently of our knowledge of it? Or are they merely statements about our actual and possible sense experiences? Are statements about the mind statements about a reality for which observable behaviour is merely evidence? Or are they, for instance, really just statements about that observable behaviour? Again, to take an example that has been central in Dummett's discussion, are mathematical statements to be understood as being about a mathematical realm that exists independently of us? Or are they simply statements about a mental realm constructed by what we regard as mathematical proofs?

Although highly sympathetic to intuitionism in mathematics, a form of anti-realism, and although he holds that the argument for anti-realism in many other areas presents a major challenge, Dummett has never been committed to anti-realism generally; in large part, this has been a response to the difficulty in articulating an acceptable anti-realist view of the past. Much of Dummett's work has been pursued through the study of other major philosophers, and one of his significant achievements has been to make the work of **Frege** central to contemporary philosophy.

Dummett has been particularly influential in Great Britain, especially at Oxford. Some, however, have thought that his anti-realism is, in substance, no more than a reversion to the verificationism of the 1930s. It has also been objected that it is an over-hasty extrapolation from a view that is plausible (though controversial) when applied to the realm of mathematics.

Dummett resigned his Fellowship with the British Academy in protest at its failure, as he saw it, to protest sufficiently effectively against the cuts in university funding instituted by the Thatcher government of the 1980s.

Sources: WW 1992.

ANTHONY ELLIS

Dunan, Charles

French. *b:* 1849, Nantes. *d:* 1931. *Cat:* Idealist. *Ints:* Metaphysics; epistemology; history of philosophy. *Educ:* Dunan was the son of a grocer who worked in his father's store and then took up the study of philosophy during his military service; he prepared for the agrégé competition in Philosophy, and eventually submitted two theses required for the doctorate in letters at the University of Paris. *Infls:* Kant and Hegel. *Appts:* Collège Stanislas and Collège Rollin.

Main publications:

(1884) *Les Arguments de Zénon d'Élée contre le mouvement*, Paris: F. Alcan.

(1884) *Essai sur les formes a priori de la sensibilité*, Paris: F. Alcan.

(1895) *Théorie psychologique de l'espace*, Paris: F. Alcan.

(1898) *Essai de la philosophie générale*, Paris: Delegrave; third edition, 1902.

(1911) *Les Deux Idéalismes*, Paris: F. Alcan.

Dunan was an epistemological idealist who insisted that all thought involves ideas, and an ontological idealist in the sense that he believed that ideas and things cannot ultimately be separated. His philosophy is based on the consequences of his conviction that ideas must not be thought of as separate from things. His main interests were in epistemology and the history of philosophy, and he constantly tried to show how a critical understanding of the history of philosophy led naturally to the next steps in its progress. Like Léon **Brunschsvieg** and other French idealists of the period, he was strongly influenced by Kant but also by the Hegelian critiques of Kant, though not by Hegel's formal dialectic.

Philosophers, he argued, have frequently tried to separate ideas and things and then struggled to synthesize the concept of idea and the concept of thing. He believed that the history of philosophy suggests that we must therefore return to concepts used by Plato and Aristotle which emphasize the relatedness of thought and things. Dunan claims that the split with the ancient philosophers created a whole range of spurious subject matters arising from the separation of the objects of experience, the objects of interpretation and the structure of reality. His career demonstrated that an outsider can breach the intellectual aristocracy of France, and he appears in many standard reference works, but his writings have not attracted extensive study.

Sources: Baruzi; Benrubi; Parodi; EF; LXXS; Fran-Bio.

LESLIE ARMOUR

Dupréel, Eugène

Belgian. *b:* 1879, Malines, Belgium. *d:* 1967. *Cat:*
Pluralist value theorist. *Ints:* Ethics; sociology;
history of ancient philosophy. *Educ:* Changed to
Philosophy after initial studies in History. *Infls:*
René Berthelot and dialectical thought. *Appts:*
Rapidly promoted to the Chair of Logic in the
University of Brussels (1906); regarded as the
leader of the Brussels School and the most
eminent of Belgian thinkers; full member of the
Académie Royale de Belgique from 1939 (*corre-
spondant* from 1927).

Main publications:

(1922) *La légende socratique et les sources de Platon.*
(1932) *Traité de morale*, 2 vols.
(1939) *Esquisse d'une philosophie des valeurs.*
(1948) *Les Sophistes*, Neuchâtel: Editions du Griffon.
(1949) *Essais pluralistes*, Paris: PUF.
(1955) *La Pragmatologie*, Brussels: Institut de
Sociologie Solvay.
(1968) *Similitude et dépassement*, Brussels: Presses
Universitaires de Bruxelles.

Secondary literature:

Barzin, M. and Perelman, Ch. *et al.* (1968) *Eugène
Dupréel: L'homme et l'oeuvre*, Brussels: Editions de
l'Institut de Sociologie.

Underlying Dupréel's philosophy are some principles derived from the Hegelianism of his teacher,
René Berthelot. Most notable are the beliefs (i)
that concepts are always related to their contraries
(e.g. no unity without multiplicity, and vice versa);
(ii) that values are multiple and in tension; (iii)
that progress occurs through the working out of
tension. A notable application of (iii) is his view of
philosophy itself, which he regarded as open
(*ouverte*): by this he means that reason itself may
progress, as a result of trial and error (cf.
Gonseth).
    A second major influence on his thought was
the sociology of the Solvay Institute, with which
he was deeply involved. These two major influences shape the value theory of the major works of
1932 and 1939. Society evolves from highly
conformist primitive groups, in which 'moral'
behaviour is merely custom-following, to a
modern, individualistic social order. Modern
societies are marked by a multiplicity of groups
and individuals with their own value-sets, which
have differing degrees of compatibility. The
natural state of affairs in such societies is one of
continual moral tension, conflict, debate and
accommodation, all of which conditions are

precarious. Unsurprisingly, Dupréel had little
sympathy with philosophies or political systems
which propose a universally valid single value
system, notably Kantianism, pragmatism or
totalitarian systems. However, he clearly did
favour one value above others: reasonableness or
accommodation—the response of a non-fanatic
to the fact of the plurality of values.

ROBERT WILKINSON

Durkheim, (David) Émile

French. *b:* 1858, Épinal. *d:* 1917, Paris. *Cat:*
Sociologist; moral philosopher; social philoso-
pher. *Educ:* Collège d'Épinal, then Lycée Louis-le-
Grand and the École Normale Supérieure, Paris.
Infls: Auguste Comte, Herbert Spencer and Alfred
Espinas. *Appts:* Taught at various lycées; 1887,
appointed, Director of Education, University of
Bordeaux; 1896, Professor of Social Science and
founder of the journal *L'Année Sociologique*;
1902, University of Paris, successively Director
of Education, Professor of Education, and
Professor of Sociology.

Main publications:

(1893) *De la division du travail social*, Paris: Alcan
(English translation, *The Division of Labour in
Society*, London: Macmillan, 1985).
(1895) *Les Règles de la méthode sociologique*, Paris:
Alcan (English translation, *The Rules of Sociological Method*, London: Macmillan, 1950).
(1897) *Suicide*, Paris: Alcan (English translation,
Suicide, London: Routledge & Kegan Paul, 1950).
(1912) *Les Formes élémentaires de la vie religieuse*,
Paris: Alcan (English translation, *Elementary
Forms of the Religious Life*, London: Allen and
Unwin, 1976).
(1924) *Sociologie et philosophie*, Paris: Alcan (English translation, *Sociology and Philosophy*, New
York: Free Press, 1975).
(1925) *L'Éducation morale*, Paris: Alcan (English
translation, *Moral Education*, New York: Free
Press, 1974).

Secondary literature:

Lukes, S. (1975) *Émile Durkheim: His Life and Work*,
London: Penguin (contains an extensive biblio-
graphy).
Pickering, W. S. F. (1984) *Durkheim's Sociology of
Religion: Themes and Theories*, London: Rout-
ledge.

At the outset of his teaching career Durkheim
envisaged the possibility of developing an intellectually rigorous methodology for a science of

society, or sociology, which would include a science of ethics. His basic insight was the assertion that society was an entity greater than, and irreducible to, the sum of its individual members.

Sociology would take as its subject matter social facts, which Durkheim defined as 'facts with very distinctive characteristics: they consist of ways of acting, thinking and feeling, external to the individual, and endowed with a power of coercion, by reason of which they control him' (*Rules of Sociological Method*, p. 3). He went on to say that social facts are recognized by their coercive function, which includes the sanctions, either deliberate or non-intended, imposed on those who try to resist their influence. Examples of one set of social facts, termed 'collective representations', are such disparate social features as language, currency, legal codes and business practices: these phenomena are symbolic of the society or its subgroup in which they operate. Another set is the social trends embodied in the social statistics of the rates of birth, marriage and death.

According to Durkheim, social facts are to be explained not by the factors of individual psychology, but only by social structures and functions. The primary function of society or of any of its subgroups is the need for a sense of social cohesion. Durkheim applied this theory to the problem of suicide in his work of that name. The social fact to be explained is the statistical suicide rate, and there are three basic types of suicide, each with its own explanation in terms of social cohesion or its lack. Egoistic suicide is due to insufficient integration of the suicide into social or family life. Altruistic suicide is found in societies with a strong ideology of religious sacrifice, or total allegiance to or identification with a political cause. Anomic suicide is, in general terms, due to a dislocation of the relationship between an individual and their society. Such a dislocation is often economic: the individual's perception of their needs and the satisfaction of them is given and regulated by society, and there is a maximum risk of anomic suicide when economic conditions create a mismatch between the two. Durkheim's work in this area provides an illustration of the utilitarian application of theory to social policy: his recommendation is that family and social ties should be strengthened, in order to reduce the incidence of anomic and egoistic suicide.

Another important concept for Durkheim was that of the 'collective conscience', which arose from the interrelationship of the various collective representations operative within a society or one of its subgroups. Durkheim thought that a society with just one uniform collective conscience did not usually provide a high level of social cohesion: this could be found in developed social structures which consisted of a well-advanced pattern of a properly constituted division of labour, with a distinct collective conscience for each subgroup formed by such a division. The high degree of interdependence of the subgroups accounted for their social integration. The basis of a true or 'organic' division of labour was a society which functioned on meritocratic principles, not on the accidents of birth or wealth.

One social fact to which Durkheim paid particular attention was that of religion, which he regarded as an activity rather than adherence to a set of dogmas, and as another collective representation of the social group in which it was practised. On Durkheim's account the most fundamental feature of primitive religion is totemism. A totem, in most cases an animal or plant, is regarded as sacred by a particular social group, usually a tribe or clan, as it is a symbol of their object of worship. This object in turn is in reality, but unbeknown to its worshippers, the objectification of the social group itself. The system of beliefs and practices of religion is thus the representation of a society by its own members, and has a functional value as the fulfilment of the needs of that society. These two features led Durkheim to take issue with those previous analyses which considered all religion as false, and to state his theory of truth: he regarded all such systems as true, precisely because they are expressions of a social reality and have a social function.

Durkheim considered that religion provided suitable conditions for the origins and development of all intellectual activity, including science. Scientific activity owed to religion the intellectual categories of space, time, force and necessity which, as religion itself is a coercive social representation, are reflections of the unacknowledged necessities of a social group. The alleged antagonism between the two activities is not, according to Durkheim, a necessary feature of their interrelationship. Since religion, like all other social phenomena, is dynamic, he accepted the possibility that new forms of religion might arise in the future. Although Durkheim was not overtly hostile to religion, his account contains an implicit rejection of the view that the object of at least some religious worship is a transcendent reality.

KATHRYN PLANT

Dworkin, Ronald Myles

American. *b:* 11 December 1931. *Cat:* Liberalist. *Ints:* Legal theory; political theory. *Educ:* Harvard College and University of Oxford. *Appts:* Fellow, University College, Oxford; Associate Professor of Law, Yale Law School; Professor of Law, Yale; Wesley. N. Hohfeld Professor of Jurisprudence, Yale; from 1969, Professor of Jurisprudence, Oxford University.

Main publications:

(1977) (ed.) *The Philosophy of Law*, Oxford: Oxford University Press.

(1977) *Taking Rights Seriously*, London: Duckworth.

(1978) *Taking Rights Seriously*, London: Duckworth (a new impression with a reply to critics).

(1985) *A Matter of Principle*, Cambridge, Mass.: Harvard University Press.

(1986) *Law's Empire*, London: Fontana.

(1993) *Life's Dominion: An Argument about Abortion and Euthanasia*, London: Harper Collins.

Secondary literature:

Cohen, Marshall (1983) *Ronald Dworkin and Contemporary Jurisprudence*, Totowa, NJ: Rowman & Allanheld.

Guest, Stephen (1992) *Ronald Dworkin*, Edinburgh University Press.

Hutchinson, A. C. and Wakefield, J. N. (1982) 'A hard look at "hard cases": the nightmare of a noble dreamer', *Oxford Journal of Legal Studies* 2: 86.

Lyons, D. B. (1977) 'Principles, positivism and legal theory', *Yale Law Journal* 87: 415.

Raz, J. (1978) 'Professor Dworkin's Theory of rights', *Political Studies* 26: 123.

Soper, E. P. (1977) 'Legal theory and the obligation of the judge: the Hart/Dworkin dispute', *Michigan Law Review* 75: 473.

According to Dworkin, an account of law in terms of rules (Hart's positivism) or goals such as economic efficiency (R. Posner, *Economic Analysis of Law*, Boston: Little Brown & Co., 1986) is inadequate because law is concerned with rights—'political trumps held by individuals'. Unlike Hart, Dworkin holds that in the course of the judicial process, judges are engaged in determining the rights of the parties. They apply principles and are not guided by policies that promote the general welfare of society. In other words, judges, for Dworkin, are not lawmakers. In order to establish this viewpoint he uses a number of decided cases as illustrations. Although Dworkin is correct in saying that law is concerned with rights it is highly questionable whether judges really are totally unconcerned with policies or collective goals.

Sources: WW 1991.

INDIRA MAHALINGAM CARR

E

Eaton, Ralph M(onroe)

American. *b:* 14 June 1892, Stockton, California. *d:* 13 April 1932, Cambridge, Massachusetts. *Cat:* Analytical philosopher. *Ints:* Theory of knowledge; logic; metaphysics; philosophy of language; philosophy of science. *Educ:* University of California, BA in Literature, 1914; Harvard University, MA 1915, PhD 1917. *Infls:* Personal influences include Royce, R. B. Perry, R. F. Alfred Hoerne, H. M. Sheffer, Raphael Demos and Whitehead; literary influences include Whitehead and Russell, Broad, Husserl, Peirce and M. R. Cohen. *Appts:* Assistant in Philosophy, Harvard, 1915–16; Instructor in Literary Composition, University of California, Summer 1916; USAEF, 1917–19; Instructor in Philosophy, Harvard, 1919–26, Assistant Professor, 1926–32, Department Chairman, 1926–30.

Main publications:

(1917) 'The method of induction: an examination of its aims and logical presuppositions', Thesis, Harvard University.

(1925) *Symbolism and Truth: An Introduction to the Theory of Knowledge*, Cambridge, Mass.: Harvard University Press.

(1920) 'The logic of probable propositions', *Journal of Philosophy* 17: 44–51.

(1921) 'The value of theories', *Journal of Philosophy* 18: 682–90.

(1921) 'The social unrest of the soldier', *International Journal of Ethics* 31: 279–88.

(1921) 'Social fatalism', *Philosophical Review* 30: 380–92.

(1923) 'What is the problem of knowledge?', *Journal of Philosophy* 20: 178–87.

(1927) (ed. and intro.) Descartes, *Selections*, New York: Scribner's Modern Students Library.

(1931) *General Logic*, New York: Charles Scribner's Sons.

(1932) (trans. and preface) W. M. Kranefeldt, *Secret Ways of the Mind: A Survey of the Psychological Principles of Freud, Adler, and Jung*, New York: Henry Holt & Co.

Secondary literature:

Moreno, Jonathan D. (1980) 'Eaton on the problem of negation', *Transactions of the C. S. Peirce Society*, vol. 16, pp. 59–72.

The range of Eaton's interests is indicated by the titles of his published works. His major work, *Symbolism and Truth* (1925), is about the role of symbols in knowledge and attempts to present a 'positive or descriptive theory of knowledge'; the analysis is organized around the theme of symbols since Eaton held that 'knowledge is inseparable from its expression'. Eaton developed a theory of logical form, and also theories of negation and contradiction—consequently also of 'negative facts'—of truth and falsity, of formal deduction and of belief, and a critique of scepticism. His aim was to provide an account of knowledge independent so far as possible from metaphysics and psychology. However, 'a theory of knowledge must come at last to metaphysics', so there is also a discussion of the metaphysics of knowledge. The conclusion reached is that 'reality is logical in form', and so, therefore, is truth. The book was reviewed favourably and at length by H. T. Costello (*Philosophical Review*, 1926) D. W. Prall (*Journal of Philosophy*, 1927) and L. Susan Stebbing (*Journal of Philosophical Studies*, 1926). None the less, it seems not to have had any extensive influence or a wide readership, though it is often recommended favourably by connoisseurs.

Eaton's *General Logic* (1931) attempted to cover the whole subject, as it existed at that time, and to show 'the continuity of the classical Aristotelian logic with contemporary mathematical logic', of which this is one of the earliest elementary presentations. It makes use of some of the analyses provided by *Symbolism and Truth*, and had for some time wide use as a textbook. It was reviewed very favourably in *The Journal of Philosophy* (1932) by J. W. Mauzey, who judged it 'for the most part, truly admirable. As a text it provides probably the only really "general" logic available'.

In 'What is the problem of knowledge?' (1923), Eaton said that 'the positive theory of knowledge ... does not preclude a metaphysics of knowledge and does not exhaust psychology or logic; nor do psychology, logic, and metaphysics exhaust the theory of knowledge. But the theory of knowledge as it often comes to us, confusedly mingled with metaphysics, bears the same relation to the positive analysis of knowledge as alchemy to chemistry'.

Eaton attempted to show this in detail in *Symbolism and Truth*, and his tragically early death deprived philosophy of the opportunity to learn how this gifted and original mind would have developed further. In 'The value of theories' (1921), Eaton observed that 'paradoxical as it may seem, it is only true propositions which demand explanations', and went on to explain the important role played by deductive systems in explanation. His doctoral dissertation was on induction, and there are interesting suggestions in his writings of how he might have gone on to develop a theory of induction if he had survived to be able to do so. Thus, 'If there is any principle of induction it is this: free the imagination to build a deductive system which will yield the truths we know by experience. This is not a postulate of proof, but a counsel of action'.

Eaton's talents were in some ways analogous to those of F. P. **Ramsey** in England and Jean Nicod in France. All three worked our their talents in different ways and all three died young and for different reasons. Like theirs, his premature death was a tragic loss to philosophy.

Sources: Raphael Demos (1933) obituary notice, *PR* 6: 212–13; Profs J. D. Moreno and A. R. Turquette.

MARCUS SINGER

Eboussi-Boulaga, Fabien

Cameroonian. *b:* 17 January 1934, Bafia, Mbam region, Cameroon. *Cat:* Historian of Christianity in Africa; philosopher of cultural identities. *Educ:* Baccalaureate in Philosophy (1955); entered the Society of Jesus in 1955 to study Philosophy and Theology; ordained to the Roman Catholic priesthood in 1967; PhD at Lyon, France, 1968. *Infls:* Hegel. *Appts:* Professor of Philosophy and Theology, Major Seminary St Francis, Yaounde-Messa, 1968–73; Visiting Lecturer for the Claus Committee, Universities of Holland, 1973–4; Professor of Philosophy, National University, Abidjan, Ivory Coast since 1975.

Main publications:

(1968) 'Le Bantou problématique', *Présence Africaine* (Paris) 66: 4–44.

(1973) 'Métamorphoses africaines', *Christus* (Paris) 77: 29–39.

(1976) 'L'identité négro-africaine', *Présence Africaine* (Paris) 99–100: 3–18.

(1977) *La Crise du Muntu*, Paris: *Présence Africaine*.

(1981) *Christianisme sans fétiche*, Paris: *Présence Africaine* (English translation, *Christianity without Fetishism*, New York: Orbis Books, 1984).

A critic of ethnophilosophy, Eboussi-Boulaga focusses on the shortcomings of Tempel's method, which fails to ask how anthropology can be a source of, or a basis for philosophy. Eboussi-Boulaga elaborates an analysis of Tempel's work, focusing on the ambiguity of the ontological hypothesis which, he maintains, emphasizes the notion of life-force rather than that of being. This hypothesis, he thinks, ultimately reduces the Muntu to the primitiveness of an amoral and absolutely determining order of forces. Finally, Eboussi-Boulaga rethinks the sociohistorical African contexts in order to suggest ways of problematizing both African authenticities and the Christian conversion made possible by the colonial experience.

V. Y. MUDIMBE

Echeverría, José

Chilean. *b:* 1913, Santiago de Chile. *Cat:* 'Social humanist'. *Ints:* Philosophy of action. *Educ:* Chile, France and the UK. *Infls:* Jesus, Dante, Cervantes, Freud and Marx. *Appts:* University of Chile (1952–3); Puerto Rico (1953–76); Professor of Philosophy of Law at the Universidad Católica de Chile from 1971.

Main publications:

(1957) *Réflexions métaphysiques sur la mort et le problème du sujet*, Paris: Vrin.

(1963) (ed.) Maine de Biran, *De l'aperception immédiate*, Paris: Librarie Philosophique.

(1965) *La enseñanza de la filosofía en la universidad hispanoamericana*, Washington Union Panamericana.

(1965) *El Quijote como figura de la vida humana*, Ediciones de la Universidad de Chile.

(1987) *Reflexiones sobre la educacion general en el Puerto Rico de Hoy*, Rio Piedras: Universidad de Puerto Rico.

Plus many articles, notably:

'El Dios hermano: deliberacion personal sobre cristianismo y comunismo' (1976), *Sin Nombre* 2: 18–56.

Echeverría's thought addresses itself to the perennial issues which centre on the topic of death and the immortality or otherwise of the soul. Around this question, he sets out views on time in human experience on, what lends value to life and on the ultimately social nature of the human predicament. These views are worked out largely in the course of meditations on the ideas of the figures listed above as influences on him.

The world of human experience is ineludibly a social world, a world of others and of nature in which we find ourselves: our condition is an 'insertion in the world' ('inserción en el mundo', 1965, p. 75). We achieve our selfhood (*mismidad*) by means of our free acts. The future is open, and each life has value according to the contribution it makes to the history of the world. Human time is not cyclical but has a direction: it develops in a line with a terminus which is death. Death is feared because it is absolute exclusion from the world: because humanity is in its essence social, total isolation is our worst fear. The horror of death can be overcome when we make of it an act of communion with the destiny of humanity and the world. This point of view Echeverría discovers in the words of Jesus and the Apostles, and in Marx, and Cervantes' Don Quixote is their embodiment and exemplar. During the course of his three *salidas*, Quixote constructs a past while attempting to change the world by his voluntary acts. The book is a curative ('novela medicinal') for our cultivated ignorance of death, and teaches us how to die well.

ROBERT WILKINSON

Eco, Umberto

Italian. *b:* 5 January 1932, Alessandria, Italy. *Cat:* Semiotician. *Ints:* Philosophy of language; philosophy of culture; medieval aesthetics. *Educ:* University of Turin. *Infls:* Aquinas, C. S. Peirce and Luigi Pareyson. *Appts:* Universities of Turin (1956–64), Milan (1964–5 and 1970–1) and Florence (1966–9); 1971–, Professor of Semiotics, University of Bologna.

Main publications:

(1976) *A Theory of Semiotics*, Bloomington, Ind.: Indiana University Press.

(1979) *The Role of the Reader*, Bloomington, Ind.: Indiana University Press.

(1984) *Semiotics and the Philosophy of Language*, London: Macmillan.

(1992) *Interpretation and Overinterpretation*, Cambridge: Cambridge University Press.

Secondary literature:

Colapietro, Vincent M. (1987) 'Semiosis and subjectivity: a Peircean critique of Umberto Eco', *Southern Journal of Philosophy* 25: 295–312.

Garcia, Reyes (1980) 'A short critique of the role of the sign in Eco's "A Theory of Semiotics"', *Auslegung* 7: 163–83.

Innis, R. E. (1980) 'Notes on the semiotic model of perception', *Philosophical Inquiry* 2: 496–507.

Ridless, Robin (1984) *Ideology and Art: Theories of Mass Culture from Walter Benjamin to Umberto Eco*, New York: Lang.

Since the 1970s, Umberto Eco has revitalized the study of semiotics, and has shown it to be a new paradigm for philosophy, one in which contemporary philosophies of all traditions are synthesized. His theory of semiotics is many-sided, but can be divided roughly into a theory of how signs are deployed systematically in the articulation of meaning (a theory of codes); and a theory of how signs are produced for the purpose of communicating meaning (a theory of communication). The foundation of both theories is the concept of the sign, which he defines as 'everything that, on the grounds of a previously established social convention, can be taken as something standing for something else' (Eco 1976, p. 16). Every sign, therefore, consists of a sign-vehicle together with the meaning that it expresses. Sometimes a sign-vehicle is itself a sign in another code (thus a pressure gauge may indicate high pressure, and this in turn may then be a sign of danger); in such cases, the logically prior signification is denotation, and the subsequent signification is connotation. Whichever it may be, signification is not the same as reference. The sign-function can operate perfectly well without a 'reality' as its object. It is meaningful to say both that Napoleon was an elephant, and that if Napoleon was an elephant Paris is the capital of France, even though one is false and the other (though valid) is absurd. Semiotics, Eco says, is 'the science of everything subject to the lie: it is also the science of everything subject to comic or tragic distortion' (Eco 1976: 64). Semiotics therefore demands an intensional rather than an extensional semantics.

Something can function as a sign only if it is interpretable, that is, if someone is able to pass from the sign-vehicle to its semantic content. The relation of sign-vehicle to content seems to be of more than one kind, the two most common kinds being equivalence and implication: 'A red flag with a Hammer and Sickle is equivalent to Communism ($p \equiv q$), but if someone carries a red flag with a Hammer and Sickle, then that person is probably a Communist ($p \supset q$)'. (Eco 1984: 18). Eco's examination of the different kinds leads him to the conclusion that all are varieties of a mode of inference which C. S. **Peirce** called 'abduction' (or 'hypothesis'). It is by way of an abductive inference that an interpreter passes from a sign to what it stands for. However, if an interpreter is to make this inference, some other factors, external to the code itself, must also come into play. For instance, the occurrence of the sign takes place in a certain context, which will influence the sign's meaning on this occasion. Also the interpreter must have access to some kind of *interpretant* (another term of Peirce's), which Eco construes as 'another representation which is referred to the same "object"' (Eco 1976: 68). One example of a set of interpretants would be a dictionary internalized by the speaker of a language. Eco examines the idea of a dictionary, whose conceptual ancestry he traces back to Porphyry, and concludes that in fact a dictionary is a disguised encyclopedia, by which he means an unordered and unrestricted compendium of world knowledge. Encyclopedic knowledge is the background for the interpretation of signs, at least as a regulative idea: in ractice, some kind of local representation (such as the French dictionary) is what is proximately used, together with the relevant context and background knowledge. Interpretants, however, are themselves in need of further interpretation, by means of further interpretants, in a process of unlimited semiosis. Eco exploits this theory of unlimited semiosis to establish semiotic explanations of many philosophical and logical concepts such as meaning, reference, truth, speech acts, analytic and synthetic, necessity, implication, and so on. Eco's work on semiotics, though dazzling and original, has so far been more influential in linguistics and literary theory than in mainstream academic philosophy.

Sources: IWW.

HUGH BREDIN

Eddington, Arthur Stanley

British. *b:* 28 December 1882, Kendal, Cumbria. *d:* 22 November 1944, Cambridge, England. *Cat:* Physicist; astronomer; philosopher of physics. *Ints:* Epistemology of physics; idealism. *Educ:* Owen's College, Manchester, and Trinity College, Cambridge. *Appts:* 1913, Plumian Professor of Astronomy, Cambridge; 1914, Fellow of the Royal Society; 1919, led eclipse expeditions to test a consequence of Einstein's General Theory of Relativity that light from a star would be bent as it passed close to the sun; knighted in 1930 and received the Order of Merit in 1938.

Main publications:

(1920) *Space, Time and Gravitation*, Cambridge: Cambridge University Press.
(1928) *The Nature of the Physical World*, Cambridge: Cambridge University Press.
(1935) *New Pathways in Science*, Cambridge: Cambridge University Press.
(1939) *The Philosophy of Physical Science*, Cambridge: Cambridge University Press.

Secondary literature:

Dingle, H. (1954) *The Sources of Eddington's Philosophy*, Cambridge: Cambridge University Press.
Kilmister, C. W. (1966) *Sir Arthur Eddington*, Oxford: Pergamon Press.
Stebbing, S. (1937) *Philosophy and the Physicists*, London: Methuen & Co.
Whittaker, E. T. (1951) *Eddington's Principles in the Philosophy of Science*, Cambridge: Cambridge University Press.

Although a realist about scientific theory, Eddington rejected materialism on the grounds that it was incompatible with relativity and quantum theory. In the Introduction to *The Nature of the Physical World* (1928), he expressed his realist convictions by pointing out that objects such as tables described using our familiar everyday language all have duplicates that are described using the less familiar language of physical theory. An 'everyday' table is coloured and solid whereas its 'scientific' counterpart is colourless and consists mostly of empty space. Of these two tables Eddington claims that it is only the scientific table which really exists. His reasoning is considered and criticized in **Stebbing**'s *Philosophy and the Physicists* (1937).

In the Prelude to his *Space, Time and Gravitation* (1920), Eddington took issue with **Poincaré**'s geometrical conventionalism. He claimed that the choice to be made 'by convention' was not between incompatible geometries but merely between different ways of expressing the same geometry. Real, as opposed to verbal, differences between geometries can only be settled on experimental grounds.

Arising from his idealist view that our understanding of nature is influenced by patterns imposed by the mind, Eddington envisioned a harmonization of quantum theory and relativity. It also led him to take an interest in the cosmological significance of numerical coincidences deriving from calculations of physical constants. His speculations are related to debates about anthropic cosmological principles.

BARRY GOWER

Edwards, Paul

Austrian (naturalized US citizen). *b:* 2 September 1923, Vienna, Austria. *Cat:* Analytic philosopher. *Ints:* Ethics; naturalism. *Educ:* University of Melbourne and Columbia University. *Appts:* University of Melbourne, 1945–7; New York University, 1949–66; Brooklyn College of the City University of New York, from 1966.

Main publications:

(1955) *The Logic of Moral Discourse*, Glencoe, Ill.: The Free Press.
(1967) (ed.) *The Encyclopedia of Philosophy*, 8 vols, New York: Collier Macmillan.
(1969) *Buber and Buberism*, Laurence: University of Kansas.
(1979) *Heidegger and Death*, La Salle, Ill.: Hegeler Inst.

In the area of ethics Edwards developed a position which 'combines features of objective naturalism with features of emotive theories' (1955, p. 47). Defending his version of naturalism/emotivism against intuitionism and all other forms of non-naturalism, he finds the latter to have but one purpose, namely, 'to help support the morality of self-denial and sin'. And he pleads guilty to 'undermining the moralities of the fuddy-duddies and the sour-pusses' (ibid., p. 240). In the Introduction (p. xi) to his great *Encyclopedia* Edwards observed that an unavoidable, but nonpolemical, bias towards 'the empirical and analytic tradition of Anglo-Saxon philosophy' governed the space allotments and selected topics of the text. An absence of neutrality is characteristic of all his work. In his Foreword to still another work, he listed his religion as atheism, asserting that 'all the metaphysical claims of traditional religions are untenable' and that 'the decline of religion will be of incalculable benefit to the human race' *The Encyclopedia of Unbelief*, vol. 1 (1985), p. xiii). Consistent with this attitude he finds many of the key terms of religious thinkers meaningless on analytic grounds. Religious existentialists confuse genetic with logical questions: 'there is something very confused in **Buber**'s notion that God can be "addressed" but not "expressed" (1969, p. 23). **Heidegger**'s diverse statements on death and nonbeing play a 'perverse game' with the word 'possibility' (1979, p.

60). Although his editorial decisions in the *Encyclopedia* were, indeed, nonpolemical the same is not true of his views of religion. Echoing Hume's statement about the 'religious principles' which have prevailed in the world, Edwards writes: 'The sooner these sick dreams are eliminated from the human scene, the better' (*Encyclopedia of Unbelief*, p. xiii).
Sources: CA.

WILLIAM REESE

Ehrenfels, Christian Freiherr von

Austrian. *b:* 1859, Rodaun (near Vienna). *d:* 1932, Prague. *Cat:* Psychologist; philosopher; psychiatrist. *Ints:* Gestalt psychology; ethics; metaphysics. *Educ:* University of Vienna. *Infls:* Franz Brentano, Alexius von Meinong and Ernst Mach. *Appts:* 1888–96, *Privatdozent* at University of Vienna; 1896–1900, Assistant Professor, 1900–29, full Professor, German University of Prague.

Main publications:

(1887) *Melusine: Ein Dramatisches Gedicht*, Vienna: C. Konegen.
(1890) 'Über Gestaltqualitäten', *Vierteljahrsschrift für wissenschaftliche Philosophie* 14: 249–92, Leipzig: O. R. Reisland.
(1893–4) 'Werttheorie und Ethik', *Vierteljahrsschrift für wissenschaftliche Philosophie*, five articles: 17: 26–110, 200–66, 321–63, 413–25; 18: 22–97.
(1897–8) *System der Werttheorie*, 2 vols, Leipzig: O. R. Reisland.
(1903–4) 'Sexuales, Ober- und Unterbewusstsein', *Politisch-anthropologische Revue* 2: 456–76, Leipzig: Thüringische Verlags-anstalt.
(1903–4) 'Die sexuale Reform', *Politisch-anthropologische Revue* 2: 970–94, Leipzig: Thüringische Verlags-anstalt.
(1907) *Sexualethik*, Wiesbaden: J. F. Bergmann.
(1911) 'Leitziele zur Rassenbewertung', *Archiv für Rassen- und Gesellschaftsbiologie* 8: 59–71, Berlin: Verlag der Archi-gesellsohatt.
(1913) *Richard Wagner und seine Apostaten: Ein Beitrag zur Jahrhundertfeier*, Vienna and Leipzig: H. Heller.
(1916) *Kosmogonie*, Jena: E. Diederichs.
(1930) 'Sexualmoral der Zukunft', *Archiv für Rassen- und Gesellschaftsbiologie*, 22: 292–304, Berlin: Verlag der Archi-gesellsohatt.

Secondary literature:

Eaton, H. O. (1930) *The Austrian Philosophy of Values*, Norman, Okla.: University of Oklahoma Press.

Meister, R. (1959) 'Ehrenfels' in *Neue Deutsche Biographie*, Berlin: Duncherd Humblot, IV: 352–3.

'Orestano, Francesco, *I Valori Umani*, vols XII and XIII of his *Opere complete*, 2 vols, Milan: Fratelli Bocca, vol. I, pp. 69–102, 123–6, vol. II, pp. 46–101.

Smith, Barry (1988) *Foundations of Gestalt Theory*, Munich: Philosophia Verlag.

Ehrenfels is known principally as one of the founders of the Gestalt School of psychology. He also made important contributions to philosophical ethics and metaphysics. A man of many accomplishments, he wrote several plays and published essays on Richard Wagner.

In his paper 'Über Gestaltqualitaten' [On Gestalt Qualities] 1890) Ehrenfels, although perhaps more of a theorist than a systematic practical psychologist, was the first to attempt a thorough and comprehensive account of the perception of complex wholes. *Mach* had commented on the significance of our ability to 'sense' complex wholes; and the German word *Gestalt* means 'shape', 'figure' or 'form'. But Ehrenfels was the first to develop a specific and detailed theoretical foundation for a psychology of the Gestalt.

Gestalt psychology starts from the observation that our ability to perceive complex wholes is in important respects independent of moment-by-moment perceptions. Thus the book you are now reading is perceived as 'this book' whether it is seen from one angle or another, in daylight or, say, yellow streetlight, for real or in a photograph, and so on. The same is true of other sensory modalities: a particular tune is perceived as 'this tune' whether played on the piano or by an orchestra, whistled or sung. Moreover in both cases we may perceive the 'whole' even though at the time we are aware only of a part: it is the particular *tune* we perceive even if we have heard only a few notes; it is the particular *book* we perceive, even though we have seen only the spine.

From observations such as these Ehrenfels argued that the perception of a complex whole depends on more than an awareness of its elements. We are of course aware of these elements and of their spatial and temporal associations. The associationist psychologists believed that these were sufficient to explain the perception of the figure as a whole. But Ehrenfels argued that we directly apprehend the whole as an additional quality or attribute, alongside and in addition to apprehending its parts and the associations between them. It is this additional attribute which is the Gestalt in Ehrenfels' theory.

Ehrenfels, who was a considerable musician, was concerned particularly with the perception of musical forms such as melodies. But he showed that his theory of the Gestalt could be applied equally to objects (in each of the sensory modalities) and to geometrical figures, to mathematical and logical forms, and to social 'forms' such as style and taste. He argued that complex Gestalts were related hierarchically to simpler Gestalts, and speculated on the nature of a 'proto-Gestalt', a simple undifferentiated form from which all others were built up (although he regarded Gestalts at every level of complexity as atomistic in the sense that they were not reducible to some combination of their parts).

Ehrenfels' original statement of his theory, although detailed, left many questions unanswered. Is the Gestalt a real entity or an abstract universal? What is the precise relationship between the Gestalt and the complex of elements by which it is carried? Is the Gestalt part of the act of perception or independent of it? Although many of these issues were given coherent treatment by **Meinong**, **Husserl**, **Stumpf** and others, Ehrenfels' theory stimulated a considerable theoretical and empirical literature in its own right. His colleague and teacher, Meinong, built up an influential School of Gestalt Psychology in Padua. One of Ehrenfels' pupils, **Wertheimer**, established the better-known school of experimental psychology in Berlin. The Berlin school differed from Ehrenfels in regarding individual elements of the complex whole as inseparable, the very natures of these elements being determined by their place within the Gestalt. It was this school, too, which emphasized the phenomenal basis of the Gestalt—such as the figure/ground relationship— familiar in experimental Gestalt psychology; and an associated physiological theory of cerebral integration. Ehrenfels' theory also had a wider influence beyond Gestalt psychology. William **James**, for instance, in the *Principles*, described brain processes as giving rise to 'figured consciousness', awareness of definite objects rather than 'mere hodge-podges of elements'.

Ehrenfels' work in ethical theory, although less well-known, is as significant as his Gestalt psychology. Indeed value theory is widely regarded as originating with a celebrated debate between Ehrenfels and Meinong. Ehrenfels noted that the separate theories of value which had been developed for different fields—moral, aesthetic, economic—had certain common features. He sought to bring these together in a detailed account of the relationship between value and desire. Value is taken to be a property of an object (to this extent his theory is naturalistic); but the property in question is that of being desired by someone, or being desirable. Values are thus relativistic but (anticipating moral descriptivism) in practice there is almost universal agreement about the desirability of such things as pain and pleasure. Yet value is not solely instrumental: on the contrary, instrumental value depends on the intrinsic value of certain 'psychic' realities—we value things not merely for their utility, nor is their desirability necessarily connected with a desire for possession of them; value consists rather in a certain fittingness (*Fromen*). Similarly, a desire theory of value does not necessarily lead to individualism. Superior non-individualistic values, transcending even personal survival, emerge through cultural progress and are transmitted by education and good example.

Ehrenfels extended his work on value theory to a number of other areas. He developed a social ethic, for instance, concerned with intrinsic values, those which most individuals embrace. Similarly, combining this with the notion of an intrinsic biological value of survival, he came to question received views on sexual morality (for which he was commended by **Freud**) and, less acceptably nowadays, to advocate selective breeding.

Ehrenfels published his metaphysical theories in *Kosmogonie* (1916). He rejected the idea that the evolution of the universe could be explained as the result of an accumulation of chance events. Instead he postulated two interacting principles: a principle of disorder and a principle of unity. The principle of unity takes the form of a Gestalt which, operating over cosmological periods of time, acts creatively to account for the emergence of non-random structures. Although as a systematic and experimental science Gestalt psychology owes more to the work of Wertheimer, **Koffka** and **Köhler**, Ehrenfels is widely regarded as its philosophical founder. Except in the field of perception, the influence of Gestalt psychology waned during the postwar period with the rise of behaviourism. Renewed philosophical and psychological interest in the phenomena of consciousness and complex cognitive activities resulted in something of a revival of interest in the late twentieth century, and the burgeoning cognitive sciences owe much to Ehrenfels' legacy.

Sources: Reese; Edwards; UCDCL; BLC to 1975; *Psychlit* journal articles (Silver Platter).

K. W. M. FULFORD

Einstein, Albert

German-Swiss-American. *b:* 14 March 1879, Ulm, Barvaria. *d:* 18 April 1955, Princeton, New Jersey. *Cat:* Physicist and philosopher. *Ints:* Epistemology; foundations of physics; natural philosophy. *Educ:* ETH, Zurich, 1896–1900; PhD, University of Zurich, 1905; Habilitation, 1908. *Infls:* D. Hume, J. C. Maxwell, J. H. Poincaré, H. A. Lorentz, E. Mach, M. Planck, P. Duhem and H. Minkowski. *Appts:* Swiss Patent Office, 1902–9; University of Zürich, 1909–11; Prague 1911–12; ETH, Zürich, 1912–14; Kaiser Wilhelm Institut für Physik, Berlin, 1914–33; Princeton, 1933–55; Nobel Prize for Physics, 1921.

Main publications:

(1905) 'Über einen der Erzeugung und Verwandlung des Lichtes betreffenden heuristischen Gesichtspunkt', *Annalen der Physik* 17: 132–48.

(1905) 'Über die von der molekularkinetischen Theorie der Wärme Bewegung von in ruhenden Flüssigkeiten suspendierten Teilchen', *Annalen der Physik* 17: 549–60.

(1905) 'Zur Electrodynamik bewegter Körper', *Annalen der Physik* 17: 891–921.

(1916) 'Grundlagen der allgemeinen Relativitätstheorie', *Annalen der Physik* 40: 769–822.

(1920) *Relativity: The Special and General Theory–A Popular Exposition*, London: Methuen.

(1921) *The Meaning of Relativity*, Princeton: Princeton University Press.

(1923) *The Principle of Relativity*, H. A. Lorentz, H. Minkowski and H. Weyl, London: Methuen.

(1926) *Investigations on the Theory of the Brownian Movement*, ed. R. Fürth, London: Methuen.

(1935) *The World as I See It*, London: John Lane.

(1938) (with L. Infeld) *The Evolution of Physics*, Cambridge: Cambridge University Press.

(1950) *Out of My Later Years*, London: Thames & Hudson.

(1954) *Ideas and Opinions*, New York: Crown.

(1960) *Einstein on Peace*, New York: Simon & Schuster.

(1960) *Collected Writings*, New York: Readex Microprint.

(1967) (with E. Schrödinger, M. Planck and H. A. Lorentz *Letters on Wave Mechanics*, ed. M. J. Klein, New York: Philosophical Library.

(1968) (with A. Sommerfeld) *Briefwechsel*, ed. A. Hermann, Basel and Stuttgart: Schwabe.

(1971) *The Born-Einstein Letters*, ed. M. Born, London: Macmillan.

(1987–9) *Collected Papers*, 2 vols, ed. J. Stachel, Princeton: Princeton University Press.

Secondary literature:

Beller, M., Renn, J. and Cohen, R. S. (eds) (1993) *Einstein in Context*, Cambridge: Cambridge Univeristy Press.

Dijn, H. de (1991) *Einstein en Spinoza*, Delft: Eburon.

Fine, A. (1986) *The Shakey Game: Einstein, Realism and the Quantum Theory*, Chicago and London: University of Chicago Press.

French, A. P. (1979) *Einstein: A Centenary Volume*, London: Heinemann.

Hentschel, K. (1987) 'Einstein, Neokantianismus und Theorienholismus', *Kantstudien* 77: 459–70.

Holton, G. and Elkana, Y. *Albert Einstein: Historical and Cultural Perspectives*, Princeton: Princeton University Press.

Howard, D. (1990) 'Einstein and Duhem', *Synthese* 83: 363–84.

Jammer, M. (1964) *Concepts of Space: The History of Theories of Space in Physics*, Cambridge, Mass.: Harvard University Press; second edition, 1969.

Moszkowski, A. (1972) *Conversations with Einstein*, London: Sidgwick & Jackson.

Nordenson, H. (1969) *Relativity, Time and Reality*, London: Allen & Unwin.

Reichenbach, H. (1956) *Philosophy of Space and Time*, New York: Dover.

Schilpp, P. A. (ed.) (1954) *Albert Einstein, Philosopher-Scientist*, 2 vols, Evanston: Library of Living Philosophers.

Seelig, C. (1960) *Albert Einstein, Leben und Werk eines Genies unserer Zeit*, Zurich: Europa Verlag.

Will, C. M. (1986) *Was Einstein Right?*, New York: Basic Books.

Wolters, G. (1987)*Mach I, Mach II, Einstein und die Relativitätstheorie*, Berlin: Walter de Gruyter.

Zahar, E. G. (1989) *Einstein's Revolution: A Study in Heuristic*, La Salle, Ill.: Open Court.

With a radical cast of mind, to some extent self-taught, Einstein made the unification of physics his first priority and concentrated systematically on the ultimate first principles, seemingly assisted by a holistic epistemology that rejected any attempt at judging the hypotheses of physical theories separately. His early analysis of the Brownian motion served to unite thermodynamics into a statistical particulate view of physics, and his early quantum analysis of light and the photo-electric effect served to give a particulate account of light alongside the now traditional wave one. His encouragement of de **Broglie**'s and **Schrödinger**'s wave mechanical theories served a like end. His later suspicion of the **Bohr–Born–Heisenberg** statistical quantum mechanics derived from his belief that physical

theories should give a complete account of nature, which was in principle available to be so described. The development of relativity saw him on a different tack—the unification of mechanics and electromagnetic theory (special relativity), and these with gravitation (general relativity). His chosen instrument to the latter end, a four-dimensional geometry of space-time, presented itself as a field theory in which the actual content appeared not as a force field added to the geometry but as a modification of the geometry itself. It was thus one fruit of his holistic approach to physical theory and rejection of the analytic-synthetic distinction. Later discussion has focused mainly on the implications of relativity and of his criticisms of the quantum theory.

Sources: Edwards; N. Boni, M. Russ & D. H. Laurence (1960) *A Bibliographical Checklist and Index*, New York: Readex Microprint; W. Weil (1960) *Albert Einstein: A Bibliography*, London: E. P. Goldschmidt; DSB 5: 312a–333b; R. W. Clark (1973) *Einstein: His Life and Times*, London: Hodder & Stoughton; M. J. Klein (1971) *The Making of a Theoretical Physicist*, Amsterdam: North-Holland; J. Bernstein (1973) *Einstein*, London: Fontana Modern Masters; A. Pais (1982) *Subtle is the Lord: The Science and the Life of Albert Einstein*, Oxford: Clarendon Press; R. Maiocchi (1985) *Einstein in Italia*, Milan: Franco Angeli; L. Pyenson (1985) *The Young Einstein*, Bristol and Boston: Adam Hilger; M. White and J. Gribbin (1993) *Einstein: A Life in Science*, London: Simon & Schuster.

R. N. D. MARTIN

Eisler, Rudolf

Austrian. *b:* 7 January 1873, Vienna. *d:* 14 December 1926, Vienna. *Cat:* Neo-Kantian; historian of philosophy. *Ints:* Phenomenalism; philosophical lexicor. *Educ:* Prague and Vienna. *Infls:* Wilhelm Wundt, Hermann Cohen and Edmund Husserl.

Main publications:

(1899/1927/30) *Wörterbuch der philosophischen Begriffe und Ausdrücke* 3 vols, Berlin: Mittler.

(1902) *Nietzsche's Erkenntnistheorie und Metaphysik. Darstellung und Kritik*, Leipzig: H. Haacke.

(1906) *Leib und Seele. Darstellung und Kritik der neueren Theorien des Verhältnisses zwischen physischem und psychischem Dasein*, Leipzig: J. A. Barth.

(1907) *Einführung in die Erkenntnistheorie*, Leipzig: Barth.

(1910) *Geschichte des Monismus*, Leipzig: A. Kroner.

(1901) *Handwörterbuch der Philosophie*, Berlin: Mittler.

(1912) *Philosophen-Lexikon: Leben, Werke und Lehren der Denker*, Berlin: Mittler.

(1930) *Kantlexikon*, Berlin; new edition, Hildesheim: Georg Olms, 1972.

Secondary literature:

Sztern, M. (1927) 'Rudolf Eisler und seine Philosophie. Nachruf und Würdigung', *Kant-Studien* 32: 428–34.

Eisler described his philosophical position as an 'objective phenomenalism'. He understood it as a synthesis of 'empirical realism and transcendental idealism'. He was concerned mainly with three fundamental problems, namely the problem of truth and certainty, the problem of the origin of knowledge, and the problem of reality. In dealing with these problems, Eisler constantly looked back to Kant, arguing that Kant's theory is essentially correct. However, he emphasized transcendental logic, downplaying Kant's psychologistic tendencies. Eisler is important mainly for his philosophical lexica. His *Kantlexikon* is still the best work of its kind.

MANFRED KUEHN

Emmet, Dorothy Mary

British. *b:* 29 September 1904, Oxford. *Cat:* Metaphysician. *Ints:* Social philosophy; political philosophy; philosophy of religion. *Educ:* Lady Margaret Hall, Oxford and Radcliffe College, Cambridge, Massachusetts. *Infls:* Aquinas, Temple, A. D. Lindsay and Whitehead. *Appts:* 1931–8, Lecturer in Philosophy, King's College, Durham; 1938–45, Lecturer in Philosophy of Religion, Manchester; 1946–66, Sir Samuel Hall Professor of Philosophy, Manchester; 1966–, Professor Emeritus, Manchester.

Main publications:

(1932) *Whitehead's Philosophy of Organism*, London: Macmillan.

(1936) *Philosophy and Faith*, London: SCM Press.

(1945) *The Nature of Metaphysical Thinking*, London: Macmillan.

(1958) *Function, Purpose and Powers: Some Concepts in the Study of Individuals and Societies*, London: Macmillan.

(1970) *Sociological Theory and Philosophical Analysis*, London: Macmillan.

(1979) *The Moral Prism*, London: Macmillan; New York: St Martin's Press.

(1984) *The Effectiveness of Causes*, London: Macmillan.

(1992) *The Passage of Nature*, Basingstoke: Macmillan.

(1993) *The Role of the Unrealisable: A Study in Regulative Ideals*, London: Macmillan.

Secondary literature:

Paul, Leslie (1952) *The English Philosophers*, London: Faber & Faber, pp. 348–50.

Whitely, C. H. (1946) 'Can philosophical theories transcend experience?', Part II, *Proceedings of the Aristotelian Society* 20: 210–27.

Dorothy Emmet first made her name as an expositor of Whitehead. She agreed with him, against the mainstream of British analytical philosophy, that metaphysics is not only possible but an important function of philosophy. But she established herself as an independent thinker in her own right, critical alike of idealism and empiricism. In *The Nature of Metaphysical Thinking* (1945) she claimed that metaphysics, like science and religion, can only characterize the external, transcendent reality with which it is concerned by using analogies drawn from familiar fields. In *The Effectiveness of Causes* (1984) she criticized the empiricist view of causation, arguing that sequences in which 'transeunt causation' take place depend on 'immanent causation', that is, on changes in the persisting thing said to be the cause. In her social philosophy Emmet has stressed the concept of a 'role', which has been taken up by other philosophers.

Sources: Kersey; PI; WW.

STUART BROWN

Engel, Passal

French. *b:* 1954, Aix-en-Provence, France. *Cat:* Philosopher of logic; philosopher of mind. *Ints:* Logic and analytic philosophy; philosophy of mind; epistemology. *Educ:* École Normale Supérieure, University of Paris I and University of California, Berkeley. *Infls:* Davidson and Dennett. *Appts:* Lecturer, Grenoble and Caen Universities; Researcher, Centre Nationale de Recherches Scientifiques.

Main publications:

(1984) 'Functionalism, belief and content', in S. Torrance (ed.), *The Mind and the Machine*, Chichester: Horwood.

(1985) *Identité et référence* Paris: Presses de l'École Normale Supérieure.

(1986) 'L'anomalie du mental', in *Critique*: 474.

(1986) 'Un réalisme introuvable', in *Critique*: 464–5.

(1987) 'Continental insularity: contemporary French analytical philosophy', in A. Phillips Griffiths (ed.), *Contemporary French Philosophy*, Cambridge: Cambridge University Press.

(1989) *La norme du vrai*, Paris: Gallimard (English translation, *The Norm of Truth*, trans. Pascal Engel and Miriam Kochan, Hemel Hempstead: Harvester Wheatsheaf).

(1992) *États d'esprit: questions de philosophie de l'esprit*, Aix-en-Provence: Alinéa.

Pascal Engel is one of the main French analytic philosophers of language and of logic. His publications played a key role in introducing philosophy of mind and the works of **Davidson** and **Dennett** to a French audience. His *La norme du vrai* (1989) puts forward an analytic philosophy of logic and defends a realism based upon logical inference and truth and the view that logic determines the ideal normative acceptance conditions of sentences for rational agents.

Sources: Catalogues of Bibliothèque Nationale, Paris and National Library of Scotland.

JAMES WILLIAMS

Éspinas, Alfred-Victor

French. *b:* 23 May 1844, Saint-Florentin, Yonne, France. *d:* 24 February 1922, Paris. *Cat:* Social philosopher; economist. *Ints:* Communal life; social organization. *Educ:* Lycée de Dijon (Agrégé in Philosophy). *Infls:* De Maistre, Auguste Comte, Theodule Ribot and Herbert Spencer. *Appts:* Taught philosophy at the Lycée de Dijon; Professor of Philosophy, then Dean of the Faculté des Lettres, University of Bordeaux; Professor of Economics, then (1904) of the History of Economic Doctrine, Sorbonne (1893–1922); Member of the Institute of France, 1905.

Main publications:

(1877) *Des Sociétés animales*, Paris: G. Baillière.

(1891) *Histoire des doctrines économiques*, Paris: A. Colin.

(1897) *Étude sociologique. Les origines de technologie*, Paris: Alcan.

(1898) *La Philosophie sociale au XVIIième siècle et la révolution*, Paris: A. Colin.

(1914) *L'art économique dans Platon*, Paris: Leroux.

(1925) *Descartes et la morale*, Paris: Bossard (posthumous).

Secondary literature:

Benrubi, I. (1926) *Contemporary Thought of France*, trans. E. B. Dicker, London: Williams & Norgate, pp. 78–80.

Davy, Georges (1934) *Sociologues d'hier et d'aujourd'hui*, Paris: PUF.

Éspinas, P. (1961) 'Influence de la pensée d'Alfred Éspinas sur celle de Durkheim', *Revue Philosophique de la France et de l'Étranger*: 138–9.

Inspired by Auguste Comte and Herbert **Spencer**, Éspinas attempted to establish a systematic sociology on a biological, naturalistic foundation. The essentials of his 'organicism' were first introduced in *Des Sociétés animales* (1877). It was the study of animal colonies which led him to the conviction that bodily organs and individuals belong to the same series and are separated only by a contingent difference of degree, such that we may understand individuals in a society to be equivalent to organs in an organism. Thus Éspinas maintained that in mankind the laws which govern the formation of social organisms are the same as in the whole animal world: individuals, animal societies and human societies are alike in that they are all organisms; and as an assemblage of cells an individual is a society. On the basis of this view he attempted to identify different patterns of organization, beginning with primitive communal life in animals designed to satisfy simple vital needs and extending to sophisticated human societies based on morals and laws. This organic view was taken by some to imply a disparagement of humanity, although this had not been its intention.

The great achievement of Éspinas was to have formulated an original theory of 'conscience collective et de représentations collectives', thereby preparing the ground for the work of Émile Durkheim and the sociological school. A fundamental difference between his sociology and that of Durkheim, however, was that for the latter, but not the former, social processes were something *sui generis*, not simply one with the organic.

Sources: Benrubi; Huisman; EF.

STEPHEN MOLLER

Eucken, Rudolf Christoph

German. *b:* 5 January 1846, Aurich, East Friesland, Germany. *d:* 15 September 1926, Jena, Germany. *Cat:* Philosopher of spirit/life. *Ints:* Philosophy of religion; philosophy of life. *Educ:* Universities of Göttingen and Berlin. *Infls:* W. Reuter, K. C. F. Krause, F. A. Trendelenberg. *Appts:* Teacher at Frankfurt Gymnasium, 1867–

71; Professor of Philosophy, Universities of Basel, 1871–4, and Jena, 1874–1926.

Main publications:

(1878) *Geschichte und Kritik der Grundbegriffe den Gegenwart*, Leipzig.
(1888) *Die Einheit des Geisteslebens in Bewusstsein und Tat der Menschheit*, Leipzig.
(1909) *Christianity and the New Idealism*, New York: Harper.
(1909) *Life in the Spirit*, London: Williams & Norgate.
(1909) *The Meaning and Value of Life*, London: A. & C. Black.
(1911) *Can We Still Be Christians?*, London: A. & C. Black.
(1911) *The Truth of Religion*, London: Williams & Norgate.
(1913) *Knowledge and Life*, London.
(1918) *Life's Basis and Life's Ideal*, London: A. & C. Black.
(1921) *Socialism: An Analysis*, London: T. Fisher Unwin.
(1921) *Rudolf Eucken: His Life, Work and Travels*, London: T. Fisher Unwin.
(1923 *The Individual and Society*, London: Faith Press.

Secondary literature:

Booth, Meyrick (1913) *Rudolf Eucken: His Philosophy and Influence*, London: T. Fisher Unwin.
Gibson, W. R. Boyce (1907) *Rudolf Eucken's Philosophy of Life*, London.
Jones, W. Tudor (1912) *An Interpretation of Rudolf Eucken's Philosophy*, London: Williams & Norgate.
MacGowan, W. S. (1914) *The Religious Philosophy of Rudolf Eucken*, London: David Nutt.

Eucken was a leading representative of that spiritual brand of philosophy which, rejecting intellectualism and abstruse speculation, sought a philosophy of the whole of life. He labelled his result 'activism', and distinguished it from pragmatism, the ends of which were mundane. With natural existence, deemed to be ultimately meaningless and self-frustrating, he contrasted spiritual existence—personal relationship with the supreme reality, Spirit, which, though immanent in nature, transcends it. Only in such a relationship are human interests truly fulfilled, and this in a universal religion (*Geistlichkeit*). The necessary prelude to this relationship is conversion from the sensory realm to the spiritual. This entails constant striving. Christianity is the highest—though, because of the truth grasped by other faiths, not the absolute—religion.

The spiritual quest on which, if we are wise, we are embarked is not pursued in solitariness. Our choosing of one 'system of life' in preference to others, and on the basis of its anticipated benefits, inevitably involves those to whom we are related in society. Through their persistent questioning, human beings, though part of the natural order, rise above it: their souls transcend the spatio-temporal sphere.

It is important to note that for all his emphasis upon spirit, Eucken welcomed the positive contributions of modern science. Science, however, could not introduce us to the realm of spirit; and he lamented that our technical achievements have not 'been accompanied by a corresponding growth in the content of life and the soul of man'. The remedy does not lie in the aesthetic transformation of existence into pleasure or enjoyment. Rather, we must develop the life of the spirit, and do this in opposition to naturalism's constricted view of human nature. Earthbound as it is, naturalism offers no guidance as to how new knowledge and human freedom are to be used, or how a better world of peace and freedom may be established. Hence Eucken's trenchant criticism of socialism, which he regarded as the political expression of naturalism.

Eucken's views were widely disseminated. Windelband hailed him as 'the creator of a new metaphysic'. However, some questioned his optimism concerning the ongoing evolution of the spirit; his understanding of the heart of Christianity as a matter of world-denial and world-renewal was deemed reductionist by some; his view that such metaphysical concepts as the Trinity have been superseded by improved understandings of existence has been contested; his Christology—Jesus is not God but 'merely an incomparable individuality which cannot be directly imitated'—has been repudiated by many, and has been branded a deficiency which deprives his activism of that expemplification of the union of humanity with divinity of which the Incarnation is the supreme instance; he has been faulted for not allowing the miraculous as traditionally conceived, and for not giving due weight to the idea of redemption wrought in one historic act; and his lack of attention to the experiential aspects of faith has been deemed an unfortunate relapse into intellectualism. Widely read though he was, Eucken's fame was short-lived. His approach and proposals have not commanded the attention of many professional philosophers since his death. By itself this does not show that, or how, he was mistaken. It may, however, suggest that in philosophy as elsewhere, those who today

are among the arbiters of fashion may, tomorrow, become the victims of it.
Sources: Obituary notices.

ALAN SELL

Evans, Gareth

British. *b:* 1946, London. *d:* 10 August 1980, London. *Cat:* Philosopher of language; philosopher of mind. *Ints:* Metaphysics; philosophy of psychology. *Educ:* University College, Oxford University, 1964–7; Senior Student of Christ Church, Oxford University, 1967–8. *Infls:* Gottlob Frege and Bertrand Russell. *Appts:* Kennedy Scholar at Harvard University, 1968–9; Fellow of University College, Oxford University, 1968–79; Wilde Reader in Mental Philosophy, Oxford University, 1979–80.

Main publications:

(1973) 'The causal theory of names', *Proceedings of the Aristotelian Society Supplement* 47: 187–208; reprinted in *Collected Papers*, 1985.

(1975) 'Identity and predication', *Journal of Philosophy* 72: 343–63; reprinted in *Collected Papers*, 1985.

(1976) 'Semantic structure and logical form', in Gareth Evans and John McDowell (eds) *Truth and Meaning: Essays in Semantics*, Oxford: Clarendon Press, reprinted in *Collected Papers*, 1985.

(1977) 'Pronouns, quantifiers, and relative clauses', *Canadian Journal of Philosophy* 7: 467–536; reprinted in *Collected Papers*, 1985.

(1980) 'Things without the mind', in Zak van Straaten (ed.) *Philosophical Subjects: Essays Presented to P. F. Strawson*, Oxford: Clarendon Press; reprinted in *Collected Papers*, 1985.

(1981) 'Understanding demonstratives', in Herman Parret and Jacques Bouveresse (eds) *Meaning and Understanding*, Berlin: De Gruyter; reprinted in *Collected Papers*, 1985.

(1982) *The Varieties of Reference*, ed. John McDowell, Oxford: Clarendon Press.

(1985) *Collected Papers*, Oxford: Clarendon Press.

Secondary literature:

Bell, David (1990) 'How "Russellian" was Frege?', *Mind* 99: 267–77.

McDowell, John (1990) 'Peacocke and Evans on demonstrative content', *Mind* 99: 255–66.

Travis, Charles (1994) 'On constraints of generality', *Proceedings of the Aristotelian Society* 94: 165–88.

In his short career Gareth Evans made original and significant contributions to the literature on reference and intentionality. His early work in the philosophy of language can be viewed as an attempt to construct a truth-conditional semantic theory for natural languages. These essays range over topics including proper names, pronouns, predication and indeterminacy, and logical form and entailment. 'The causal theory of names' (1973) is aimed at reconciling description and causal theories of reference. In the essay's analysis of reference change Evans argued that speakers' intentions play a crucial role in determining and transmitting reference.

Evans's work on reference was further developed and combined with his mentalist philosophy of mind in *The Varieties of Reference* (1982), which was unfinished at the time of his death. Much of the book is devoted to the relations between various kinds of 'particular-thoughts', or thoughts about objects, and the ways in which we understand singular terms. The position he developed combines elements from the work of **Frege** and **Russell**. Evans attempted to give an account of the conditions under which a mind can think of an object. He attacked the 'Photograph Model': **Kripke**'s causal theory of linguistic reference extended to encompass the intentionality of thought. On this model a causal connection between a thinker and an object is sufficient for a thought to be about that object, even if the thinker is considerably confused about the identity and nature of the object. He rejected this sufficiency claim, and argued instead for what he calls 'Russell's Principle': thought about an object requires that the subject know *which* object his thought is about.

Sources: 'Tribute to Gareth Evans', *The Times*, 12 Aug 1980, p. 12.

PETER DLUGOS

Ewing, Alfred Cecil

British. *b:* 11 May 1899, Leicester. *d:* 14 May 1973, Manchester. *Cat:* Realist; intuitionist. *Ints:* Epistemology; metaphysics; ethics. *Educ:* University College, Oxford. *Infls:* G. E. Moore, C. D. Broad and H. A. Prichard. *Appts:* Lecturer, University College, Swansea 1927–31; Lecturer and, from 1954 until 1966, Reader, Cambridge University.

Main publications:

(1924) *Kant's Treatment of Causality*, London: Routledge.

(1929) *The Morality of Punishment*, London: Routledge.

(1934) *Idealism: A Critical Survey*, London: Routledge.

(1938) *A Short Commentary on Kant's Critique of
Pure Reason*, London: Routledge.
(1947) *The Individual, The State and World Government*, London: Macmillan.
(1947) *The Definition of Good*, London: Routledge.
(1951) *The Fundamental Questions of Philosophy*,
London: Routledge.
(1959) *Second Thoughts on Moral Philosophy*,
London: Routledge.
(1968) *Non-linguistic Philosophy*, London: Allen &
Unwin.
(1973) *Value and Reality*, London: Allen & Unwin.

Secondary literature:
Grice, G. R. (1973) Obituary in *Proceedings of the
British Academy*.

One of Ewing's great virtues was his determination to defend without apology precisely those
doctrines which the votaries of philosophical
fashion in his time were most eager to attack:
that philosophy is the study of the real nature of
the world (not of 'concepts' or the meaning of
words), that there are synthetic a priori propositions, that there are universals, the representative
theory of perception, causation as a real connection between events, mind–body dualism, the
objectivity of value, the existence of God. He was
also a thinker of the utmost honesty and candour,
a virtue associated in his case with a degree of
simple-mindedness which exposed him to much
more or less kindly ridicule. He hoped that his
mind would survive bodily death so that he could
find out if there really are synthetic a priori truths.
He was no stylist. A not untypical sentence is 'the
sole purpose of language is not to communicate

information'. His attacks on the verification
principle (how well does it comply with itself?)
and on the 'linguistic' theory of a priori propositions were substantial contributions to debate in
the 1930s. His earlier writings suffered from too
persistent an impulse to the reconciliation of
opposed points of view: idealism and realism in
epistemology, retributivism and utilitarianism in
the theory of punishment. Typical of this is the
account in his *Idealism* (1934) of the nature of
physical objects. He takes them to be systems of
'unsensed sensa,' of which the sensa we actually
sense are representative. The unresolved self-
contradiction embodied in the phrase 'unsensed
sensa' is rather characteristic. The ethical doctrine
of his *The Definition of Good* (1947), especially as
amended in his *Second Thoughts* (1959), is a form
of rationalism which nevertheless makes a few
emollient concessions to the anti-rationalism of
the age, to the detriment of its own clarity of
outline. He defines the good as that to which one
ought to have a favourable attitude, 'ought' here
being defined in terms of fittingness. It was as if he
needed the stimulus of a body of thought he found
absolutely mistaken, to be specific the doctrine of
Language, Truth and Logic, to concentrate his
mind effectively. Ewing's arrival in Cambridge
coincided with the return there of **Wittgenstein** by
whose charisma and theatricality his own chances
of shining were altogether obliterated. His work
stands as the most comprehensive representation
of the philosophical opposition to analytic
orthodoxy in Britain in the 1930s, much more
than that of the abler, but more cautious, **Broad**.
Sources: Metz; Passmore 1957; Hill.

ANTHONY QUINTON

F

Fabro, Cornelio

Italian. *b:* 24 August 1911, Flumignano, Italy. *Cat:* Scholastic. *Ints:* Thomism; contemporary philosophy; philosophy of religion. *Educ:* University of Padua and University of Rome. *Infls:* Aquinas, Kierkegaard and Heidegger. *Appts:* 1956–81, Professor of Philosophy, Catholic University of Milan.

Main publications:

(1939) *La nozione metafisica di partecipazione secondo S. Tommaso d'Aquino*, third edition, Turin: Società editrice internazionale, 1963.

(1941) *Percezione e pensiero*, second edition, Brescia: Morcelliana, 1961.

(1955) *L'anima*, Rome: Studium.

(1957) *Dall'essere all'esistente*, Brescia: Morcelliana.

(1964) *Introduzione all'ateismo moderno*, Rome: Studium.

(1983) *Introduzione a San Tommaso*, Milan: Ares.

Secondary literature:

Henle, R. J. (1957) 'A note on certain textual evidence in Fabro's "La nozione metafisica di partecipazione"', *The Modern Schoolman* 34: 265–82.

John, Helen James (1966) 'Fabro, participation and the act of being', in *The Thomist Spectrum*, New York: Fordham University Press, pp. 87–107.

Fabro's vast output includes many studies of recent and contemporary philosophy, in particular of Kierkegaard, some of whose works he has translated into Italian. As a theoretical philosopher and, in particular, as a Thomist, he has been a central figure in the movement to reinstate the notion of participation in Thomistic metaphysics. The neo-Platonist concept of participation, which lies at the heart of Plotinus's *Enneads*, was adopted by the Christian Pseudo-Dionysius to describe and explain the relation between God and his creatures. Thus, all created things were held to participate in being in the sense that being flowed to them from God, and the human intellect, according to Augustine, participated in the light of the divine intellect. Fabro, together with others such as Louis **de Raeymaeker**, argues that the idea of participation survived the Aristotelian revival of the thirteenth century, and was employed by Aquinas in his discussion of essence and existence. Essence, taken in itself, is a potency, which is realized when it acquires existence, and this it does by way of participation in the act of being. It had always been conceded that Aquinas had studied neo-Platonist writings in his early years, for instance in his *Commentary on the Divine Names*. Fabro argues that this survived into his mature works, which, far from being a mere restatement of Aristotle, represented instead an Aristotelianism corrected by, and synthesized with, Platonic notions of participation. Fabro's formidable knowledge of contemporary philosophy makes him one of the most striking and accessible of twentieth-century Thomists, and his reputation is generally high.

Sources: DFN; EF; *Dizionario generale degli autori italiani contemporanei*.

HUGH BREDIN

Fackenheim, Emil L.

Canadian Jew. *b:* 1916, Halle, Germany. *Cat:* Rabbi and theologian. *Ints:* Metaphysics; philosophy of religion; existentialism; history of Jewish thought. *Educ:* Ordained rabbi, Hochschule für die Wissenschaft des Judentums, 1939; emigrated to Canada, 1940; interned as 'enemy alien'; University of Toronto 1943–5; PhD, 1945. *Infls:* German idealist philosophy, history of Jewish philosophy, Martin Buber, and his own experience of Kristallnacht and the Holocaust. *Appts:* Rabbi, Hamilton, Ontario, 1943–8; Lecturer, then Professor of Philosophy, University of Toronto, 1945–; Fellow of Institute of Contemporary Jewry, Hebrew University, Jerusalem, 1992–; various Honorary Degrees, LLD and DD.

Main publications:

(1960) *Paths to Jewish Belief*, New York: Behrman House.

(1961) *Metaphysics and Historicity*, Milwaukee: Marquette University Press.

(1968) *Quest for Past and Future–Essays in Jewish Theology*, Bloomington: Indiana University Press.

(1968) *The Religious Dimension in Hegel's Thought*, Bloomington: Indiana University Press, reprinted, Chicago: University of Chicago Press, 1982.

(1970) *God's Presence in History: Jewish Affirmations and Philosophical Reflections*, New York: New York University Press.

(1973) *Encounters between Judaism and Modern Philosophy*, Philadelphia: JPSA.

(1978) *The Jewish Return into History: Reflections in the Age of Auschwitz and a New Jerusalem*, New York: Schocken.

(1982–9) *To Mend the World: Foundations of Future Jewish Thought*, New York: Schocken.

(1988) *What is Judaism: An Interpretation for the Present Ages*, New York: Collier Macmillan.

Secondary literature:
Greenspan L. and Nicholson G. (eds) (1992) *Fackenheim: German Philosophy and Jewish Thought*, Toronto: University of Toronto Press.

Katz, Steven, T. (1983) *Post-Holocaust Dialogues*, New York.

Morgan M. and Fackenheim E. (eds) (1987) *The Jewish Thought of Emil Fackenheim*, Detroit: Wayne State University Press.

Seeskin, K. (1993) 'Emil Fackenheim', in *Interpreters of Judaism in the Late Twentieth Century*, ed. S. T. Katz, Washington: Bnai Brith Books, pp. 41–57.

Wyschogrod, Michael (1971) 'Faith and the Holocaust', in *Judaism* 20 (Summer): 286–94.

Fackenheim's PhD dealt with Greek influences on medieval Arabic philosophy, but he has a wide range of intellectual and practical interests. He is famous for attempting to come to terms with the Holocaust by positing an extra commandment to the 613 incumbent upon traditional Jews. His 614th commandment is not to give Hitler a posthumous victory. He advocates supporting the Jewish people, and by extension the State of Israel, at all times. Various religious and political criticisms have been levelled at this position. However, Fackenheim continues to draw large audiences wherever he goes, because of his refusal to ignore the philosophical dimensions of the destruction wrought by the Holocaust.

Sources: EncJud; NUC; DAS, 4, 1982, p. 149.

IRENE LANCASTER

Fakhry, M(ajid) F.
American citizen. *b:* 6 January, 1923, Zerarieh, Lebanon. *Cat:* Moral philosopher; historian of Islamic philosophy. *Ints:* Greek philosophy. *Educ:* American University of Beirut and University of Edinburgh. *Infls:* In his interpretation of Islamic

philosophy he was influenced by contemporary trends in analytical philosophy. *Appts:* Posts at the School of Oriental and African Studies, London, Lebanese National University, Georgetown University, American University of Beirut and then Georgetown; visiting posts at Princeton, Kuwait and University of California, Los Angeles.

Main publications:
(1958) *Islamic Occasionalism and its Critique by Averroes and Aquinas*, London.

(1970) *A History of Islamic Philosophy*, New York and London; reprinted in 1983 and 1987 (much translated).

(1978) *Arabic Ethical Thought*; reprinted Beirut, 1986.

(1991) *Ethical Theories in Islam*, Leiden.

Majid Fakhry did a great deal to foster the study of Islamic philosophy both in the Islamic world and in the West. The clarity with which he expounded the ideas of the main philosophers brought a new perspective to the area, and his broad historical grasp enabled him to present their ideas within the appropriate context. His many books on particular Islamic philosophers have made an important contribution to the understanding of the subject and established strict criteria of exposition in a field which up to then was sometimes rather loose. His most important work is undoubtedly his *History of Islamic Philosophy* (1970), which for the first time brought together the very diverse thinkers in the Islamic world and linked them perspicuously to Greek philosophy on the one hand and to Islamic theology on the other. He has made important contributions to the understanding of many aspects of Islamic philosophy, but perhaps his most concentrated work has been in ethics. Here his mastery of Greek philosophy and Islamic theology has enabled him to present the ideas of some of the main ethical philosophers in ways not previously realized. His many contributions to conferences and journals have had an important impact upon the way in which the history of Islamic philosophy is studied today.

Sources: Personal communication.

OLIVER LEAMAN

Fang Dongmei (Fang Tung-mei or Thomé H. Fang)
Chinese. *b:* 1899, Tongchen County, Anhui Province, China. *d:* 1977, Taiwan. *Cat:* Comprehensive systematic philosopher. *Ints:* Metaphysics; philosophy of culture; philosophical

anthropology. **Educ:** Studied at university and with John Dewey in China, and at University of Wisconsin and Ohio State University. **Infls:** Wide-ranging, including ancient, medieval and modern, Western philosophy, the main schools of traditional Chinese philosophy (Confucian, daoist and Buddhist) and Indian philosophy; Nietzsche was an important Western influence. **Appts:** Professor of Philosophy, National Central University, Nanjing and Chongqing; Professor of Philosophy, University of Beijing; Professor of Philosophy, National Taiwan University.

Main publications:

(1936) *Science, Philosophy and the Significance of Human Life.*
(1980) *The Chinese View of Life: The Philosophy of Comprehensive Harmony* (in English), Taipei: Linking Publishing Co.
(1980) *Creativity in Man and Nature* (in English), Taipei: Linking Publishing Co.
(1981) *Chinese Philosophy: Its Spirit and Development* (in English), Taipei: Linking Publishing Co.
(1983) *The Ancient World of Confucian Philosophy*, Taipei.
(1984) *Chinese Great Vehicle Buddhism.*

Secondary literature:

International Symposium on Thomé Fang's Philosophy (1987) Taipei.
Republic of China Yearbook 1989 (1989) Taipei: Kwang Hwa Publishing Company.

Throughout his life Fang sought to articulate a comprehensive philosophical system, eclectically based on Chinese and Western philosophy and integrating different fields of philosophical concern. He based the possibility of individual wisdom, integrating reason and emotion, on distinctive types of common cultural wisdom. Different types of men were possible in different cultural worlds, with each world integrating value and existence. His early Nietzschean preference for Greek culture gave way to a deep appreciation of Chinese values.

Fang's metaphysics saw reality as having many facets, at least including the natural world of physics and biology and the human world of psychology, aesthetics, morality and religion. The facets were seen as organized in terms of a hierarchy of layers. According to a pattern of evolution, a more fundamental layer could develop into the next higher layer without that higher layer being reducible to the lower layer. Thus each facet of existence was granted a legitimate place in his metaphysics. Because higher layers had their

own reality, they could shape lower layers as well as being shaped by them. According to Fang's philosophical anthropology, there was a pathway of human development from craft to creation to knowledge to symbol-making to morality and finally to religion, with cultural or individual movement possible in either ascending or descending direction. On this view, religion was at the pinnacle of human life and also immune from sceptical challenge. Human creativity formed the aesthetic grounding of his philosophical system, with art providing unity and integration for the different aspects of our lives, the different layers of reality and the different cultural traditions which concerned him.

In *Chinese Philosophy: Its Spirit and Development* (1981), Fang gave a complex assessment of Confucianism, daoism, Buddhism and neo-Confucianism, using historical sources to supplement philosophical texts. He praised Confucian 'creative creativity' and comprehensive harmony, moderated nihilistic interpretations of daoism, explored Buddhist idealism and phenomenology, and criticized Zhu Xi's neo-Confucian synthesis as flawed. He saw an ontology based on value as the central feature of Chinese thought. Fang extended his comparative skills in *Creativity in Man and Nature* (1980) to a grand critical assessment of cultures, discussing different patterns of language, value, wisdom, cosmology, human nature, ethics, art and organization, with creativity and spirit as central notions. Fang's poetically expressed speculative philosophy was a highly regarded feature of the intellectual life of Taiwan after the Communist victory on the mainland, and his memory was honoured with an international symposium to mark the tenth anniversary of his death.

NICHOLAS BUNNIN

Fanon, Frantz

Martinican (French). **b:** 20 July 1925, Fort-de-France, Martinique. **d:** 1961. **Cat:** Psychiatrist. **Ints:** Politics. **Educ:** Primary and High School in Fort-de-France, Baccalaureate in 1946; Medicine in Lyon, MD in 1951. **Infls:** Sartre, Hegel, Marx and Lenin. **Appts:** Assistant at the Clinique Saint Alban, Lozère; joined Algeria in 1953 and became Medical Director of the Blida-Joinville Hospital.

Main publications:

(1952) *Peau noire, masques blancs*, Paris: Semil (English translation, *Black Skin, White Masks*, New York: Grove Press, 1967).

(1961) *Les Damnés de la terre*, Paris: Maspéro (English translation, *The Wretched of the Earth*, London: Penguin Books, 1978).

A radical theorist of political liberation, in all its dimensions (physical, psychological, cultural), Fanon, following **Lenin**, elaborated a theory of liberational violence in which the role of the avant-garde well distinguished from those of the lumpenproletariat, the masses and the collaborators. His political philosophy is marked by **Sartre**'s and other existentialists commitment to freedom.

V. Y. MUDIMBE

Farber, Marvin

American. **b:** 14 December 1901, Buffalo, New York. **d:** 24 November 1980, Minneapolis. **Cat:** Non-Hegelian Marxian, scientific materialist; naturalistic descriptive phenomenologist. **Ints:** Phenomenology. **Educ:** Harvard; also Berlin, Freiburg and Heidelberg. **Infls:** Edmund Husserl. **Appts:** Instructor in Philosophy, Ohio State University, 1925–6; Instructor in Philosophy, University of Buffalo, 1927–8; Assistant Professor of Philosophy (1928–30) and Professor (1930–61); Professor and Chairman of the Department of Philosophy, University of Pennsylvania, 1961–4; 1964–74, Distinguished Professor of Philosophy, State University of New York at Buffalo; Emeritus Professor, 1974.

Main publications:

(1928) 'Phenomenology as a Method and as a Philosophical Discipline' (Harvard dissertation).

(1943) *The Foundation of Phenomenology: Edmund Husserl and the Quest for a Rigorous Science of Philosophy*, Cambridge, Mass.: Harvard University Press.

(1959) *Naturalism and Subjectivism*, Springfield, Ill.: Thomas.

(1966) *The Aims of Phenomenology: The Motives, Methods, and Impact of Husserl's Thought*, New York: Harper & Row.

(1967) *Phenomenology and Existence: Toward a Philosophy within Nature*, New York: Harper & Row.

(1967) *Basic Issues of Philosophy: Experience, Reality and Human Values*, New York: Harper & Row.

(1985) *The Search for an Alternative: Philosophical Perspectives of Subjectivism and Marxism*, University of Pennsylvania Press.

Secondary literature:

Cho, Kah Kyung and Rose, Lynn E. (1981) 'Marvin Farber (1901–1980)', Obituary, *Philosophy and Phenomenological Research* 42, 1 (September): 1–4.

Riepe, Dale (ed.) (1973) *Phenomenology and Natural Existence: Essays in Honour of Marvin Farber*, SUNY Press.

Farber was a distinguished philosopher, educator, organizer and editor. Originally a scholar of **Husserl**, he later propounded a sort of Marxian, scientific materialism, became outspokenly critical of Husserl's idealism and condemned what he saw as the pretense and irrationalism of existential philosophy. He trained numerous distinguished students, gave generously of his time and was clearly well loved for it.

During the Nazi onslaught in Europe he worked tirelessly on behalf of refugee scholars and was the principal figure in the establishment of phenomenology in the USA. In 1939 he established The International Phenomenological Society at Buffalo and, in 1940, edited *Philosophical Essays in Memory of Edmund Husserl* and founded the Society's journal, *Philosophy and Phenomenological Research*, which he edited until his death. He struggled against the right-wing and anti-phenomenological bias of American institutions, and also incurred the displeasure of the European phenomenologists on his editorial board due to his outspoken views and his liberal policy of publishing non-phenomenological, Russian and South American, articles. Around 1950, the Society was supplanted by various *national* phenomenological organizations, and Louvain—not Buffalo—became the centre for international phenomenological research.

His *The Foundation of Phenomenology* (1943) contains scholarly reports on Husserl's early writings and paraphrases of his *Logische Untersuchungen*, although it is critical of his later development. In 1949 Farber coedited the collection *Philosophy for the Future: The Quest of Modern Materialism*, which marked his 'turn' to a materialist philosophy and critique of Husserl's transcendental idealism. His materialist views received their fullest treatment particularly in his *Naturalism and Subjectivism* (1959), *Phenomenology and Existence* (1967) and *Basic Issues of Philosophy* (1967). In his last work, *The Search for an Alternative* (1985), he construes Husserl's work as politically disengaged and stresses the pre-eminence of socio-historical conditions for the understanding of any system of thought.

Sources: Correspondence with Professor Riepe; WW(Am); Herbert Spiegelberg (1982) *The Phenomen-*

ological Movement: A Historical Introduction, The Hague: Nijhoff.

BARRY JONES

Farias Brito, Raimondo de

Brazilian. *b:* 1862, São Benedito, Ceará, Brazil. *d:* 1917, Rio de Janeiro. *Cat:* Kantian spiritualist; anti-positivist. *Educ:* Studied Law at the University of Recife. *Infls:* Comte, Haeckel, Hume, Schopenhauer, Spencer and Tobias Barreto. *Appts:* Taught at the Liceo in Ceará, at the School of Law in Recife, and at the Colegio Pedro II in Rio de Janeiro, where he held the Chair of Logic.

Main publications:

(1895) *A filsofia como atividade permanente do espirito humano*, Fortaleza, Brazil, n.p.
(1899) *A filosofia moderna*, Ceará, Brazil.
(1900) *Finalidade do mundo: estudos de filosofia e teleologia naturalista*, Ceará, Brazil: Universal.
(1905) *O mundo como atividade intelectual*, Pará, Brazil.
(1905) *A verdade como regra das acções: ensaio de filosofia moral como tro indução ao estudo do direito*, Pará, Brazil.
(1912) *A base fisica do espirito: historia summaria do problema da mentalidade como preparação para o estudo da filosofia do espirito*, Rio de Janeiro, n.p.
(1914) *O mundo interior: ensaio sobre os dados gerães da filosofia do espiriti*, Rio de Janeiro.
(1951–7) *Obras de Farias Brito*, 6 vols, Rio de Janeiro: Ministerio da Educação e Cultura, Insituto Nacional do Livro.

Secondary literature:

Cruz Costa, João (1962) *Panorama of the History of Philosophy in Brazil*, trans. Fred G. Sturm, Washington, DC: Pan American Union.
Sturm, Fred G. (1962) *Existence in Search of Essence: The Philosophy of Spirit of Raimondo de Farias Brito.*

Although well-versed in the history of philosophy, as evidenced in his early work *Finalidade do mundo* (1960), Farias Brito is considered one of the major forces behind the establishment of an independent Brazilian philosophical tradition. His later work is heavily influenced by modern psychology, as he strives to develop a philosophy of spirit which privileges thought over experience.

AMY A. OLIVER

Farrer, Austin Marsden

British. *b:* 1 October 1904, London. *d:* 29 December 1968, Oxford. *Cat:* Philosophical theologian. *Ints:* Philosophy of religion; metaphysics; moral philosophy. *Educ:* Balliol College, Oxford. *Infls:* Aquinas. *Appts:* 1935–60, Fellow and Chaplain of Trinity College, Oxford; 1960–8, Warden of Keble College, Oxford.

Main publications:

(1943) *Finite and Infinite*, Westminster: Dacre Press.
(1948) *The Glass of Vision*, London: Dacre Press.
(1958) *The Freedom of the Will*, London: A. & C. Black.
(1962) *Love Almighty and Ills Unlimited: An Essay on Providence and Evil*, London: Collins.
(1967) *Faith and Speculation: An Essay in Philosophical Theology*, London: A. & C. Black.

Secondary literature:

Crombie, I. M. (1981) Entry on Farrer in *Dictionary of National Biography* (1961–70).
De Burgh, W. G. (1943) Critical Notice of *Finite and Infinite*, in *Mind* 52: 344–51.
Henderson, E. H. (1990) 'Philosophie et théologie chez Austin Farrer', *Archives de Philosophie* 53: 49-74.
McKinnon, D. M. (1971), in R. Klibansky (ed.), *Contemporary Philosophy: A Survey*, vol. 4, Florence: La Nuova Italia Editrice, pp. 214ff.
Mascall, E. L. (1969) 'Austin Marsden Farrer: 1904–68', *Proceedings of the British Academy* 54: 435–42.

After an early period of pantheistic Spinozism, Austin Farrer became an orthodox High Church Anglican clergyman, being described by some as 'para-Thomist'. He sought to steer a middle course between Thomism and the Oxford philosophy of his time, aiming, as he put it, 'to discern what kind of natural philosophy is most congenial to Christian belief'. In the context of Oxford analytical philosophy this required him, as he saw it, to defend the possibility of metaphysics, as he did in his first book. Farrer's central claim was that, when we examine a finite substance—including human beings—and attend to some of its universal characteristics, we are led to an oblique knowledge of the infinite God. His stress on the obliqueness of the knowledge we have of God led Farrer to give particular attention to the use of analogy and images. D. M. McKinnon, rating this as Farrer's 'major work', described it as 'a refashioning of the Thomistic way of analogy' in order to find 'the means whereby rational theology might be constructed and rendered immune from the positivist critique' (McKinnon 1971, p. 214). Farrer was regarded as one of the philosophically most able Christian philosophers of his generation (Crombie 1981, pp. 349–50.) His influence on the intellectual life of Oxford was 'immense' and extended much further afield (Mascall 1969, p. 440).

STUART BROWN

Fatone, Vicente

Argentinian. *b:* 1903, Buenos Aires. *d:* 1962, Buenos Aries. *Cat:* Indian philosophy; existentialist; historian of religions. *Educ:* Studied Philosophy at the Universidad Nacional de Buenos Aires, and Philosophy of Ancient India in Calcutta. *Appts:* Professor of Logic, and of Cosmology and Metaphysics, Universidad Nacional del Litoral, 1929–30; Professor of Logic, Escuela Normal de Profesores Mariano Acosta, 1932–41; Professor of the History of Religions, Universidad Nacional de La Plata, 1940–6; Professor of Philosophy, Colegio Nacional de Buenos Aires, 1945–52; Professor, Universidad Nacional de Buenos Aires; Argentinian Ambassador to India, after the political changes of 1955.

Main publications:

(1931) *Sacrificio y gracia*, Buenos Aires: Glezier.
(1941) *El budismo nihilista*, Buenos Aires: López.
(1942) *Introducción al conocimiento de la filosofía en la India*, Buenos Aires: Viau.
(1948) *El existencialismo y la libertad creadora*, Buenos Aires: Argos.
(1951) *Lógica y teoría del conocimiento*, Buenos Aires, Kapelusz.
(1953) *La existencia humana y sus filósofos*, Buenos Aires: Raigal.
(1953) *Introducción al existencialismo*, Buenos Aires: Columba.
(1954) *Filosofía y poesía*, Buenos Aires: Emecé.
(1963) *El hombre y Dios*, Buenos Aires: Columba.
(1963) *Temas de la mística*, Bahía Blanca: Universidad Nacional del Sur.
(1963) *Temas de mística y religión*, Buenos Aires: Instituto de Humanidades, Universidad Nacional del Sur.
(1972) *Ensayos sobre hinduíso y budismo*, Buenos Aires: Sudamericana.
(1981) *The Philosophy of Nagarjuna*, Delhi: Motilal Banarsidass.

Secondary literature:

Ferrarter Mora, José (1965) *Diccionario de Filosofía*, Buenos Aires: Sudamericana.
Vázquez, Juan Adolfo (1965) *Antología Filosófica Argentina del Siglo Veinte*, Buenos Aires: EUDEBA.

Fatone studied the nature of mystic experience and held that human reality involves dialogue: through it one liberates oneself and others from irrationality, fear and hate, leading oneself and others towards rationality, effort and love. This has led some—though by no means all—commentators to characterize Fatone's position as rational mysticism. A central notion in Fatone's philosophy is that of freedom, which he conceives in an existentialist fashion. For Fatone, freedom is the basic consistituent of human existence in two respects. First, humans are not simply free: they *must* be free. Second, no human being can be free without everyone else's being free.

A. PABLO IANNONE

Fedorov (also Fyodorov), Nikolai Fedorovich

Russian. *b:* 1828, Tambov province. *d:* 15 December (28 N.S.) 1903, probably in Moscow. *Cat:* Religious philosopher. *Educ:* Studied at the Richelieu Lyceum, Odessa, without graduating. *Appts:* 1854–68, teacher of history and geography at various provincial schools; 1874–98, librarian of the Rumiantsev Museum in Moscow.

Main publications:

(1906–13) *Filosofiia obshchego dela*, 2 vols, ed. V. A. Kozhevnikov and N. P. Peterson, Vernyi; Moscow (selected translations in *What Was Man Created For? The Philosophy of the Common Task*, ed. Elisabeth Koutaissoff and Marilyn Minto, London: Honeyglen Publishing and L'Age d'Homme, 1990).

Secondary literature:

Lukasevich, S. (1977) *N. F. Fedorov (1828–1903): A Study in Russian Eupsychian and Utopian Thought*, London: Associated University Presses.
Young Jr, G. M. (1979) *Nikolai F. Fedorov: an Introduction*, Belmont, Mass.: Nordland.

The illegitimate son of a Russian prince (who died in Fedorov's infancy) and (probably) a peasant woman, Fedorov was related to **Kropotkin**. He was noted for ascetic self-denial and modesty, respect for which led his followers Kozhevnikov and Peterson to distribute the posthumous edition of his works free of charge.

Fedorov is difficult to classify among his practically oriented compatriots, let alone within the categories of Western academic philosophy. His insistence that science and technology could control the weather, harness solar energy, convert the earth into a vessel for the colonization of space, and even reconstitute the bodies of the dead, suggests a secular Enlightenment faith in progress. In fact, he was deeply critical of theories of progress (such as the 'historiosophistry' of **Kareev**) as disrespectful to the dead and dying, and deprecated the roles of science and industry in contemporary society. His identification of humanity's common task—the mastery of the blind, death-dealing forces of nature in order to raise the dead—is set within a Christian context. The 'disrelatedness' and 'unbrotherliness' which he abhorred in nature and society stems from the Fall; the capacity to raise the dead and thereby realize the Kingdom of God is contingent upon Christ's resurrection and redemption. Fedorov's thought frequently infringes on the fantastic, but the 'projective' philosophy of action of this singular, self-appointed spokesman for the unlearned was greatly esteemed by Dostoevsky, **Tolstoy** and **Solov'ev**; his influence is also seen in **Berdyaev**.

COLIN CHANT

Feibleman, James K(ern)

American. **b:** 13 July 1904, New Orleans, Louisiana. **d:** 14 September, 1987, Houston, Texas. **Cat:** Systematic metaphysical realist. **Ints:** Metaphysics. **Educ:** Five months at the University of Virginia. **Infls:** Plato and C. S. Peirce. **Appts:** 1942–5, Lecturer in English and Philosophy, Tulane University; 1945–87, Professor of Philosophy (Department Chairman, 1951–69; W. R. Irby Professor, 1969–74: Andrew W. Mellon Professor, 1974–5; Emeritus Professor from 1975).

Main publications:

(1946) *An Introduction to Peirce's Philosophy Interpreted as a System*, New York: Harper & Brothers; reprinted, London: Allen & Unwin, 1960.

(1949) *Aesthetics: A Study of the Fine Arts in Theory and Practice*, New York: Duell, Sloan & Pearce; reprinted, New York: Humanities Press, 1968.

(1951) *Ontology*, Baltimore: Johns Hopkins University Press; reprinted, New York: Greenwood Press, 1968.

(1956) *Institutions of Society*, London: Allen & Unwin; reprinted, New York: Humanities Press, 1968.

(1962) *Foundations of Empiricism*, The Hague: Martinus Nijhoff Publishers.

Secondary literature:

Reck, A. J. (1968) *The New American Philosophers*, Baton Rouge: Louisiana State University Press, pp.

221–54; reprinted, New York: Dell Publishing Co., 1979.

A prolific author of philosophy books and articles, Feibleman entered academe in an unconventional way—without benefit of a college degree. He began, paradoxically, as a poet and a businessman. While managing his family's department store business, he wrote poetry. The author of numerous collections of poetry, several short stories and two novels, he published his *Collected Poems* in 1974 (New York: Horizon Press).

Feibleman offered his philosophy as a comphensive system of thought. In *Ontology* (1951) he presented his fundamental theory: a contemporary interpretation of classical realism, positing three overarching realms or categories—essence, existence and destiny. The originality of his thought resides in *Foundations of Empiricism* (1962), which maintains that this classical metaphysics is scientific and that its ontological categories are empirical. He strove to articulate this fundamental philosophy in works on every area of human experience and reality.

Sources: J. K. Feibleman (1970) *The Way of a Man*, New York, Horizon Press; WW(Am); *New Orleans Times–Picayune*, 16 Sep 1987.

ANDREW RECK

Feigl, Herbert

Austro-Hungarian. **b:** 14 December 1902, Reichenberg, Czech Republic. **d:** 1 June 1988, Minneapolis. **Cat:** Logical empiricist. **Ints:** Philosophy of science; philosophy of psychology. **Educ:** Munich University and Vienna University; 1922–7, research student at Vienna University. **Infls:** Mach, Einstein, Schlick and Popper. **Appts:** Taught philosophy at Vienna University, Iowa State University, Minnesota University and elsewhere.

Main publications:

(1931) 'Logical positivism', *Journal of Philosophy* 28: 281–96.

(1950) '*De Principiis non Disputandum?* On the meaning and limits of justification', in M. Black (ed.) *Philosophical Analysis*, Ithaca, NY: Cornell University Press.

(1958) 'The "mental" and the "physical"', in H. Feigl, M. Scriven and G. Maxwell (eds), *Minnesota Studies in the Philosophy of Science*, vol. 2, Minneapolis: University of Minnesota Press.

(1981) *Inquiries and Provocations: Selected Writings, 1929–1974*, ed. R. S. Cohen, Dordrecht: D. Reidel.

Secondary literature:
Feyerabend, P. K. and Maxwell, G. (eds) (1966) *Mind, Matter, and Method: Essays in Philosophy and Science in Honor of Herbert Feigl*, Minneapolis: University of Minnesota Press (contains bibliography).
Wade Savage, C. and Anne, B., (1989) 'Herbert Feigl remembered', in A. Fine and J. Leplin (eds) *Proceedings of the 1988 Biennial Meeting of the Philosophy of Science Association*, vol. 2, East Lancing, MI: Philosophy of Science Association.

Feigl, together with Friedrich **Waismann** and Moritz **Schlick**, was a founder member of the Vienna Circle and helped originate and promote the central ideas of logical positivism. Like other members of the Circle, his original training was in the physical sciences. Although he retained a philosophical allegiance to the critical realism of his teacher, Schlick, his participation in the Circle in the late 1920s enabled him to work with such philosophers as Ludwig **Wittgenstein**, Rudolf **Carnap** and Karl **Popper**. After emigrating to the USA in 1930 he became a prominent spokesman for logical positivism, playing a role there like that performed by A. J. **Ayer** in Britain. He taught at the University of Iowa and later at the University of Minnesota, where he established the Centre for Philosophy of Science in 1953.

In his philosophy of psychology Feigl adopted a monistic view by claiming that the mental and the physical are to be identified. His version of monism was physicalist in that, using concepts deriving from the physical sciences, it attempted to provide a comprehensive account of human behaviour. The elaborate essay 'The "mental" and the "physical"' (1958) developed the claim that the private mental states or 'raw feels' we know by sensory acquaintance are, as a matter of empirical fact, identical with states of the central nervous system described by neurophysiology. Consequently, for purposes of prediction and explanation of behaviour, mental concepts can be supplanted by neurophysiological concepts. Feigl resisted, though, the reducibility of mental concepts to physical ones on the grounds that the indexical features of sensations, thoughts and feelings cannot be eliminated.

Among Feigl's contributions to the philosophy of science he provided an influential version of the pragmatic solution to the problem of induction. In *'De Principiis non Disputandum ... ?'* (1950) he argued that attempts to validate principles, such as those governing inductive reasoning, in terms of more general or more basic principles must come to an end, but when they do so it may still be necessary to provide assurance of their legitimacy; pragmatic justification may still be needed even where validation cannot be given. He calls this pragmatic justification 'vindication' and claims that we are vindicated in our use of standard inductive rules because, although we cannot be confident that nature is uniform and that therefore any rules can be used successfully, we can be confident—because it is an analytic truth—that if nature is uniform standard inductive rules will reveal its uniformity.

BARRY GOWER

Feinburg, Joel
American. *b:* 19 October 1926, Detroit. *Cat:* Analytical philosopher. *Ints:* Ethics; social and political philosophy; philosophy of law. *Educ:* University of Illinois and University of Michigan (AB 1949, AM 1951, PhD 1957). *Appts:* 1955–62, Ford Teaching Intern, Instructor then Assistant Professor of Philosophy, Brown University; 1962–6, Assistant then Associate Professor of Philosophy, Princeton University; 1966–7, Professor of Philosophy, University of California at Los Angeles; 1967–77, Professor of Philosophy, Rockefeller University; since 1977, Professor of Philosophy, University of Arizona.

Main publications:

(1965) (ed.) *Reason and Responsibility*, Belmont, CA: Wadsworth; eighth edition, 1992.

(1970) *Doing and Deserving: Essays in the Theory of Responsibility*, Princeton, NJ: Princeton University Press.

(1970) (ed.) *Moral Concepts*, Oxford Studies in Philosophy Series, Oxford: Oxford University Press.

(1973) *Social Philosophy*, Englewood Cliffs, NJ: Prentice-Hall.

(1973) (ed.) *The Problem of Abortion*, Belmont, CA: Wadsworth; second edition, 1983.

(1975) (ed. with Hyman Gross) *Philosophy of Law*, Belmont, CA: Wadsworth; fourth edition, 1990.

(1980) *Rights, Justice, and the Bounds of Liberty*, Princeton, NJ: Princeton University Press.

(1984–9) *The Moral Limits of the Criminal Law*, 4 vols, New York: Oxford University Press (vol. I, *Harm to Others*, 1984; vol. II, *Offense to Others*, 1985; vol. III, *Harm to Self*, 1986; vol. IV, *Harmless Wrongdoing*, 1988).

(1992) *Freedom and Fulfillment*, Princeton, NJ: Princeton University Press.

Secondary literature:
Coleman, Jules L. and Buchanan, Allen (eds) (1994) *In Harm's Way: Essays in Honor of Joel Feinburg*, Cambridge: Cambridge University Press.

Liberalism, the view that individual freedom is of preeminent value, has been the core topic of Feinburg's very influential work. In particular, he has been concerned with liberal justifications for the state's imposing criminal sanctions on individuals' conduct. Feinberg adopts a moderate liberalism. Like strict liberals, he accepts that it is permissible to make it a crime for agents to cause wrongful harm to others, as for example, in rape, but goes further in arguing that the state may also impose criminal sanctions against causing extreme offence to others as, for example in the displaying of Nazi emblems. By contrast, he argues, that it is not permissible to have criminal sanctions against agents' causing harm to themselves or simply acting immorally. Nor should there be criminal sanctions requiring some conduct just because of the benefits, to the agent or others, that arise from it.

In developing his liberalism, Feinberg has also done important work on a large number of related topics, including those of freedom, harm, punishment, responsibility, rights, abortion and pornography.

Sources: WW(Am); DAS.

ROBERT FRAZIER

Feng Youlan (Fung Yu-lan)
Chinese. *b:* 1895, Tangho, Honan Province, China. *d:* 1990, Beijing. *Cat:* Neo-Confucian. *Ints:* History of Chinese philosophy; neo-Confucian rationalism. *Educ:* University of Beijing and Columbia University, USA. *Infls:* John Dewey and Frederick J. E. Woodbridge, Neo-Confucianism, daoism, Buddhism, and Western logic and metaphysics. *Appts:* 1923–5, Professor of Philosophy, Zhongzhou University, Kaifeng; 1926–8, Professor of Philosophy, Yenching University, Beijing; 1933–52, Professor of Philosophy, Qinghua University, Beijing: 1933–52, Dean, College of Arts, and Head of Philosophy Department, Qinghua University; 1939–46, Dean, College of Arts, Southwest Associated University, Kunming; 1952–90, Professor, Peking University; 1954–66, Chief, Division of Chinese Philosophy, Research Institute of Philosophy, Academia Sinica; 1946–7, Visiting Professor, University of Pennsylvania, USA; 1947–8, Visiting Professor, University of Hawaii.

Main publications:
(1924) *A Comparative Study of Life's Ideals: the Way of Decrease and Increase with Interpretations and Illustrations from the Philosophies of the East and West*, Shanghai.
(1924) *A Philosophy of Life*, Shanghai.
(1924) *A View of Life*, Shanghai.
(1930–6) *A History of Chinese Philosophy*, 2 vols, Shanghai: Commercial Press (English translation, Derk Bodde, Princeton: Princeton University Press).
(1931) *Zhuangzi: A New Selected Translation with an Exposition of the Philosophy of Guo Xiang*, Shanghai.
(1934) *A Brief History of Chinese Philosophy*, Shanghai.
(1936) *A Supplement to the History of Chinese Philosophy*, Shanghai.
(1938) *A New Treatise on Neo-Confucianism*, Changsha: Commercial Press.
(1939) *China's Road to Freedom*, Kunming: Commercial Press.
(1939) *A New Treatise on the Way of Living*, Kunming.
(1940) *New Culture and Society*, Kunming: Commercial Press.
(1940) *New Self*, Kunming: Kaiming.
(1942) *New Morality*, Chongqing: Commercial Press.
(1943) *A New Treatise on the Nature of Man*, Shanghai: Commercial Press.
(1944) *The Spirit of Chinese Philosophy*, Chongqing (English translation, E. R. Hughes, London: Kegan Paul).
(1944) *New Philosophy*, Chongqing, Commercial Press.
(1946) *New Scholarship*, Shanghai: Commercial Press.
(1946) *A New Treatise on the Methodology of Metaphysics*, Shanghai.
(1948) *Collected Essays in Wartime*.
(1948) *Short History of Chinese Philosophy*, in English, ed. Derk Bodde, Macmillan: New York.
(1958) *Essays on the History of Chinese Philosophy*, Shanghai: Shanghai Renmin Publishing House.
(1983–90) *A New History of Chinese Philosophy*, 7 vols, Beijing: Renmin Publishing House.
(1984) *My Memoirs*.
(1985–) *The Collected Works of Feng Youlan*, 14 vols.
(1991) *Selected Philosophical Writings of Fung Yu-Lan*, in English, Beijing: Foreign Languages Press.

Secondary literature:
Boorman, H. (ed.) (1970) *Biographical Dictionary of Republican China*, New York and London: Columbia University Press.

Briere, O. (1956) *Fifty Years of Chinese Philosophy 1898–1950*, London: George Allen & Unwin Ltd.

Chan, W. T. (1963) *A Source Book in Chinese Philosophy*, Princeton: Princeton University Press.

Complete Chinese Encyclopedia (1987) Philosophy Volumes, Beijing: Chinese Encyclopedia Publications.

Louie, K. *Inheriting Tradition: Interpretations of the Classical Philosophers in Communist China 1949–1966*, Hong Kong: Oxford University Press.

Masson, M. C. (1985) *Philosophy and Tradition: The Interpretation of China's Philosophical Past Fung Yu-Lan 1929–1949*, Taipei: Institut Ricci.

Feng was a creative philosopher of outstanding ability as well as the century's most important historian of Chinese philosophy. His concern for metaphysics, logical analysis, tradition, culture and morality and his masterly appreciation of Western and Chinese philosophy produced a philosophical system marked by intellectual depth and elegance. Feng was a materialist throughout his career, but after 1949 political pressure and his own desire to place his work in a Marxist context led to repeated self-criticism and to fierce attack by others, not exclusively in the Cultural Revolution. Even during this latter phase his work often displayed subtlety and balance.

Feng's doctoral training at Columbia University under the pragmatist John **Dewey** and the neo-realist Frederick **Woodbridge** led him to demand clear argument and analytical rigour in the statement and defence of philosophical positions. Feng reinterpreted allusive and aphoristic Chinese texts to meet his own high standards of cogency. He sought to determine a great tradition of Chinese philosophy, saving what could contribute to a modern flowering of Chinese thought and rejecting the rest. His rejection of Han and Qing learning and his method of determining what belonged to tradition were the focus of exciting controversies. Some critics complained that his perspective altered from one major historical study to another, while others thought that tradition should be a matter of passive discovery rather than active construction. Many contested his assessment of particular figures or schools or rejected his division between the Period of Philosophers (up to about 100 BC) and the Period of Classical Learning (after 100 BC). China's most serious philosophers, especially those associated with the periodical *Philosophical Review*, admired Feng's deep ingenuity in using sophisticated Western techniques to adapt traditional philosophy to the needs of contemporary China. These philosophers also admired his attempt to resolve crucial controversies over the relative value of Western and Chinese thought which preoccupied Chinese intellectual life in the early part of the century.

The focus of the philosophical system Feng developed in the 1930s and 1940s was *A New Treatise on Neo-Confucianism* (1938), more literally rendered 'A new study of principle'. For this work, Feng drew on the Cheng-Zhu school of rationalist neo-Confucianism, especially the work of Zhu Xi (1130–1200), daoism, Chan Buddhism, and Western logical analysis from Plato and Aristotle to the modern day. He identified four fundamental notions in his metaphysics: *li* (principle), *qi* (matter); *dao di* (the evolution of the *dao* or way); and *da quan* (the Great Whole). All are Chinese philosophical concepts, but they are related to the Western concepts of being, non-being, becoming and the absolute. They differ from their Chinese predecessors and Western counterparts, according to Feng, because of his methodological insistence that his analysis provide 'empty' or formal concepts and that associated principles yield no knowledge of actuality. Philosophy was also useless in shaping practice, yet 'sageness within and kingliness without' from a standpoint of transcendence remained the highest pursuit of man as man.

Much of Feng's thought can be related to his realist understanding of the status of universals and his view that metaphysics derived ultimately from logic. All things or events are what they are in virtue of being things or events of certain kinds. Each thing is actual, but its *li* or principle, which makes it be of its kind, is real and exists abstractly outside space and time. Without the distinction between real and actual Feng thought that formality would be lost and that the criticisms of traditional metaphysics would overwhelm his formal system. In Feng's view the Great Whole, as everything there is, cannot be thought or said. If it could the thinking or saying would stand outside it, and it would lack at least one constituent of everything there is. It is therefore unsayable, like Laozi's *dao* and like that which can be shown but not said in Wittgenstein's *Tractatus*. The metaphysics of the unsayable, for Feng, made room for philosophical appreciation of the sublime.

Feng used his metaphysics as a framework for discussions of morality, culture and art. He considered the moral to be that which is in accord with the *li* of society and the immoral to be that which conflicts with the *li*. By introducing the amoral he placed large areas of life outside the scope of traditional Confucian ethical assessment. He argued that cultures should be understood in terms of types rather than in terms of particular historical instantiations and that types of culture could be explained by underlying material causes. He applied this view to Chinese intellectual history and the problem of inheriting the Chinese past. After the establishment of the People's Republic in 1949 Feng set out a doctrine of abstract inheritance, according to which concepts like the Confucian virtue *ren* (humanity or benevolence) could be abstracted from their concrete class circumstances and used without the taint of past oppression in contemporary society. Some of the most important and bitter philosophical debates of the 1950s and 1960s surrounded this claim. Like most eminent intellectuals Feng was badly treated in the Cultural Revolution. His final major history of Chinese philosophy, although displaying great intellectual power, also showed the effects of his maltreatment.

NICHOLAS BUNNIN

Ferrater Mora, José Maria

Spanish. *b:* 1912, Barcelona. *d:* 1991, Barcelona. *Cat:* 'Integrationist'. *Ints:* Metaphysics; history of philosophy. *Educ:* PhD, Philosophy, University of Barcelona, under Joaquín Xirau, 1931–6. *Infls:* Ortega, Bergson and phenomenology. *Appts:* Left Spain after the Civil War, living first in France, then as a teacher at universities in Havana and Chile (1939–47); last major academic appointments at Bryn Mawr College (from 1949, retired 1981) and at Girona.

Main publications:

(1932) *La filosofia en el mundo de hoy*; second edition, Madrid: Revista de Occidente, 1959.
(1935) *Coctel de verdad*.
(1941) *Diccionario de filosofia*, Mexico: Atlante; fifth edition, 4 vols, Madrid: Alianza, 1984.
(1944) *Unamuno; bosquejo de una filosofia*, Buenos Aires: Editorial Sudamericana.
(1945) *Variaciones sobre el espiritu*, Buenos Aires: Editorial Sudamericana.
(1946) *La ironia, la muerte y la admiración*, Santiago de Chile: Cruz del Sur.
(1947) *El sentido de la muerte*, Buenos Aires: Editorial Sudamericana.
(1952) *El hombre en la encrucijada*; second edition, Buenos Aires: Editorial Sudamericana, 1965.
(1957) (with H. Leblanc) *Lógica matemática*, Mexico: FCE; second edition, 1962.
(1957) *Qué es la lógica*, Buenos Aires: Columba.

(1962) *El ser y la muerte. Bosquejo de una filosofia integracionista*, Madrid: Aguilar.
(1968) *El ser y el sentido*, Madrid: Revista de Occidente.
(1974) *Cambio de Marcha en filosofia*, Madrid: Alianza.
(1979) *De la materia a la razón*, Madrid: Alianza.
(1981) (with Priscilla Cohn) *Etica aplicada*, Madrid: Alianza.

Secondary literature:

Cohn, P. (1981) *Transparencies*, Atlantic Highlands, NJ: Humanities Press (a Festschrift volume).
Fernández Suarez, A. (1963) 'Ser y muerte', *Indice* 171 (April).

Ferrater Mora's place in twentieth-century philosophy rests not only on his own philosophy of integrationism (*integracionismo*), but also on his enormous erudition, put to good use in his role as a cultural mediator. In addition to his works of original philosophy, Ferrater Mora produced single-handed a formidable *Diccionario de filosofia* (1941), and works in which he introduced current English-speaking philosophy to the Hispanic world, e.g. *Cambio de marcha en filosofia* [Change of Gear in Philosophy], a survey of philosophical analysis. Both his circumstances as an émigré and his intellectual tolerance fitted him well for this role, and also inform his integrationism. While given this designation only in the major later works, the spirit behind it appears also in the significant works of his middle period, for example, *El hombre en la encrucijada* [Man at the Crossroads] (1952). Here Ferrater Mora identifies four concepts he held to be ineludible in philosophical discussions of the human condition: God, Nature, Society and Man. The current 'crossroads' consists in the unique modern predicament of being uncertain as to the significance of all of them. Whatever resolution of this difficulty is arrived at, Ferrater Mora insists that it will be successful only if it is flexible, yet does not exclude any of these elements from due consideration.

Integrationism rests on an ontology and epistemology which is set out in *El ser y la muerte* [Being and Death] (1962). The central thesis of this work is that fundamental concepts such as matter, spirit, nature or consciousness, often taken to designate absolutes, do not in fact designate features of reality. Rather, they designate limiting cases (*realidades-límite*). They constitute a categorial framework whose function is to permit experience of the world, which can be grasped only in their terms. This thesis is developed further in *El ser y el sentido* [Being and Meaning] (1968), in which these two concepts are used as the basis of an analysis of all there is. All such frameworks are revisable and replaceable. Here, as elsewhere, Ferrater Mora eschews all dogmatism.

If all major philosophical disjunctions (realism-nominalism, idealism-realism, and so on) are composed of revisable concepts, then perhaps their apparent opposition can be dissolved; such is the belief behind integrationism, which is not a set of doctrines but a method of analysing seemingly contrary concepts, with a view to demonstrating their complementarity. Integrationism is a means of integrating concepts by analysing their functions. By the use of this method, Ferrater Mora hoped to reconcile what he discerned as the major bifurcation in philosophical thought, that between systems in which human concerns are central and systems in which Nature as a whole is central, each of which alone he regarded as at best a partial repository of truth.

The notion of revisability figures strongly in his late work on linguistic analysis. When told by analytical thinkers that such and such a question is unaskable because it figures in no language game or 'breaks the limits of language', Ferrater Mora's response was: which language? Language is flexible and eminently revisable, and no Demiurge has fixed its patterns forever.

Sources: Correspondence with Prof. G. L. Kline (Bryn Mawr).

ROBERT WILKINSON

Feyerabend, Paul Karl

Austrian. *b:* 13 January 1924, Vienna. *d:* 11 February 1994. *Cat:* Anti-empiricist; anti-rationalist. *Ints:* Philosophy of science. *Educ:* Institute for the Methodological Renewal of the German Theatre, Weimar; PhD, University of Vienna. *Infls:* Lakatos, Felix Ehrenhaft, David Bohm, Wittgenstein and (though sometimes denied) Popper. *Appts:* Professor, Yale University; Free University, Berlin; University College, London; University of Auckland; University of California at Berkeley; Federal Institute of Technology, Zurich; many visiting appointments.

Main publications:

(1975) *Against Method*, London: NLB.
(1978) *Science in a Free Society*, London: NLB (contains short intellectual autobiography, section 2.11).
(1981) *Philosophical Papers*, 2 vols, Cambridge.
(1987) *Farewell to Reason*, London: Verso.

(1991) *Three Dialogues on Knowledge*, Oxford: Blackwell.
(1995) *Killing Time*, Chicago: University of Chicago Press (posthumous autobiography).

Secondary literature:
Munévar, Gonzalo (ed.) (1991) *Beyond Reason: Essays in the Philosophy of Paul Feyerabend*, Dordretch: Kluwer.

Feyerabend's work in the 1950s and 1960s, much of it collected in his *Philosophical Papers* (1981), contained detailed studies in the development of the sciences. Along with **Kuhn**, **Lakatos** and **Hesse**, he was associated with the view that a historical perspective on scientific change can be at least as fruitful as any logical analysis of scientific methods. Independently of Kuhn, he was an originator of a historical thesis that there are frameworks of thought which are incommensurable (in the sense that logical relations cannot hold between the contents of different frameworks). He believed that so-called scientific observation terms 'are not merely theory-*laden* ... but *fully theoretical* (observation statements have no "observational core" ... Or, to express it differently: there are only theoretical terms' (1981, Introduction, p. x). This provided one basis for his critique of empiricism, both in the philosophy of science and more widely.

Feyerabend's later work, from *Against Method* (1975), argued that changes in science cannot proceed according to any specific method (and hence any 'rational' method: this step is indistinct). That led him to increasingly strong attacks on what he saw as rationality and rationalism. He shares with **MacIntyre** a belief in 'traditions' which can be defended or criticized appropriately only in their own terms. He wrote in *Science in a Free Society* (1978): 'There is ... hardly any difference between the members of a "primitive" tribe who defend their laws because they are the laws of the gods ... and a rationalist who appeals to "objective" standards, except that the former know what they are doing and the latter does not' (p. 82). He has argued for the democratic control of science against its control by scientists, and took this case as far as its practical consequences in his interest in non-conventional medical treatment.

In his last work he acknowledged that he had relied on concepts such as 'democracy', 'tradition' and 'relative truth' which he had come to see to be as rigid as 'truth', 'reality' and 'objectivity', 'which narrow people's vision and ways of being in the world' (*Killing Time*, 1995, p. 179).

Feyerabend had no wish to be accepted as a respectable, academic, professional philosopher. His arguments against rationality, expressed in a violently polemical style (but with a lively sense of humour), provoked the most extreme reactions. The fact that many of his detractors believe that his later writings cannot be taken seriously did not strike him as altogether negative.

RICHARD MASON

Field, Hartry Hamlin

American. **b:** 1946, Boston, Massachusetts. **Cat:** Logician; philosopher of mathematics. **Ints:** Philosophy of logic; philosophy of language; philosophy of mathematics. **Educ:** University of Wisconsin and Harvard University. **Infls:** Paul Benacceraf, W. V. O. Quine, Hilary Putnam and Alfred Tarski. **Appts:** 1970–6, Associate Professor of Philosophy, Princeton University; 1976–81, Associate Professor of Philosophy, University of Southern California; 1981–, Professor of Philosophy, University of Southern California.

Main publications:

(1972) 'Tarski's theory of truth', *Journal of Philosophy* 69: 347–75.
(1980) *Science Without Numbers: A Defence of Nominalism*, Oxford: Blackwell.
(1984) 'Is mathematical knowledge just logical knowledge?', *Philosophical Review* 93: 509–52.
(1986) 'The deflationary conception of truth', in G. McDonald and C. Wright (eds), *Fact, Science and Value: Essays on A. J. Ayer's Language, Truth and Logic*, Oxford: Blackwell.
(1988) 'Realism, mathematics and modality', *Philosophical Topics* 19: 57–107.
(1989) *Realism, Mathematics and Modality*, Oxford: Blackwell (collected works).

Secondary literature:

Benacceraf, Paul (1983) 'What numbers could not be', in P. Benacceraf and H. Putnam (eds) *Philosophy of Mathematics*, second edition, Cambridge University Press.
McDowell, John (1978) 'Physicalism and primitive denotation: Field on Tarski', *Erkenntnis* 13: 131–52.
Putnam, Hilary (1978) *Meaning and The Moral Sciences*, London: Routledge & Kegan Paul.
Stalnaker, Robert (1987) *Inquiry*, Bradford Books/ MIT Press.

Hartry Field is renowned especially for two things: his substantial modification of Alfred **Tarski**'s theory of truth, and his uncompromis-ingly nominalistic stance in the philosophy of mathematics. His work as a whole is informed by a commitment to physicalism.

Field argued that Tarski's theory needed to be supplemented with a causal theory of what he called 'primitive denotation' (a relation between primitive descriptive expressions of a language and what they denoted). Given his physicalism it was essential that there should be no irreducible semantic concepts any more than there should be any irreducible 'mentalistic' ones. Elsewhere he argued for a naturalistic account of intentional notions like 'belief', analysing them in terms of relations between the individual and sentences, where these might be concrete expressions in a natural language or even expressions in a language of thought encoded in the brain. Field also espouses what is called the 'two-factor' theory of meaning, according to which meaning is determined partly by links between mind and world, and partly by the structure and functioning of that mind, physicalistically construed.

For Field, the problem in mathematics is the prima facie indispensable reference to timeless entities like numbers, which also extends to physical theories. Field's stategy is to undermine this apparent indispensability and show how mathematics can be applied without being true. Scientific theory itself, therefore, would need to be rewritten in nominalistic terms. So on this account mathematics is a sort of fiction, justified insofar as it assists inferences from nominalistic premises to nominalistic conclusions. There is a parallel here with instrumentalism about 'unobservables' posited in scientific theories. Field's work has stimulated a wide variety of responses: from John McDowell and Hilary **Putnam** on his revision of Tarski, to Robert **Stalnaker**'s criticism of the treatment of the belief relation. His stance on mathematics has revived the whole Platonist/ nominalist debate.

Sources: See secondary literature.

DENIS POLLARD

Findlay, John Niemeyer

South African-British. **b:** 25 November 1903, Pretoria, South Africa. **d:** 22 September 1987, Boston, Massachusetts. **Cat:** Phenomenologist; then Wittgensteinian; then transcendental metaphysician. **Ints:** Epistemology; philosophy of mind; metaphysics; ethics. **Educ:** Transvaal University, Balliol College, Oxford and Graz. **Infls:** Meinong, Wittgenstein and Hegel. **Appts:** Lecturer, Transvaal Univeristy, 1927–33; Professor of Philosophy, Otago, New Zealand, 1934–44; Natal

University College; 1944–48; Newcastle-on-Tyne 1948–51; King's College, London 1951–66; Yale 1967–72; Boston University from 1972.

Main publications:

(1933) *Meinong's Theory of Objects*, London: Oxford University Press.

(1958) *Hegel: a Re-examination*, London: Allen & Unwin.

(1961) *Values and Intentions*, London: Allen & Unwin.

(1963) *Language, Mind and Value*, London: Allen & Unwin.

(1965) *The Discipline of the Cave*, London: Allen & Unwin.

(1970) *Ascent to the Absolute*, London: Allen & Unwin.

(1981) *Kant and the Transcendental Object*, Oxford: Clarendon Press.

(1984) *Wittgenstein: a Critique*, London: Routledge.

Secondary literature:

Cohen, Martin and Westphal (eds) (1985) *Studies in the Philosophy of J. N. Findlay.*

Findlay, an imaginatively fertile philosopher with an encyclopedically comprehensive range of interests, successively occupied three very different philosophical positions in the course of his career. He first came to notice as a friendly expositor of the theory of objects of **Meinong**, who, along with **Twardowski** and **Husserl**, developed the 'intentional' account of the nature of experience propounded by **Brentano**, a much more elaborate and theoretically sophisticated correlate of the kind of realism, or objectivism, defended by **Moore** and Russell in Britain. From 1940 onwards, for some years, he revealed the influence of Wittgenstein, to whose teaching he had been exposed in Cambridge around the time of the beginning of the Second World War, in a survey of 'recent Cambridge philosophy' and a Wittgensteinian consideration of problems about time. In this second phase, Findlay wrote an ingenious essay on **Gödel**'s discoveries, in prose, with a bare minimum of symbolization and without reliance on Gödel's technique of 'arithmetization'. An interesting, and highly un-Wittgensteinian oddity of this period was his proof that God's existence is impossible. If God were to exist he would have to exist necessarily; but nothing can exist necessarily; therefore God cannot exist. Given this intellectual history, which corresponds quite closely with that of **Ryle**, it was a surprise when Findlay chose as the topic of his presidential address to the Aristotelian Society in

1955 the merits of Hegelianism, and followed it three years later with a large and enthusiastic book on Hegel. Findlay's Hegel is not the Hegel revived by the ideological convulsions of the 1960s. Findlay had little use for Hegel's political philosophy. He aimed to disentangle Hegel, a thoroughly concrete thinker, from the consolatory abstractness of British idealism and to present him as an experimental philosopher, proposing new ways of thinking, not a rigid, dogmatic system. He went on to turn his attention to Plato and Kant, seeing them to some extent as metaphysical poets, offering imaginatively coherent ways of looking at the world rather than attempts at some kind of scientific finality and conclusiveness about the issues with which they were concerned. In keeping with this conception of philosophy as exploratory and imaginative, rather than argumentatively compulsive, Findlay's writing is often eloquent and colourful.

Sources: Passmore 1957.

ANTHONY QUINTON

Finnis, John Mitchell

British. *b:* 28 July 1940. *Cat:* Natural law theorist. *Ints:* Philosophy of law; ethics. *Educ:* University of Adelaide and University College, Oxford. *Infls:* St Thomas Aquinas. *Appts:* Called to the Bar, Gray's Inn, 1970; Rhodes Reader in Laws of British Commonwealth and United States, University of Oxford, 1972–89; Stowell Civil Law Fellow, University College, from 1973: Professor and Head, Department of Law, University of Malawi, 1976–8; Professor of Law and Legal Philosophy, University of Oxford, from 1989.

Main publications:

(1967) *Legal Theory*, London: Stevens & Sons.

(1980) *Natural Law and Natural Rights*, Oxford: Clarendon Press.

(1983) *The Fundamentals of Ethics*, Oxford: Oxford University Press.

Finnis is a major natural law theorist according to whom there is an ideal higher than positive law in terms of which the legal structure of a society can be appraised. After a survey of anthropological research, he concludes that diverse human societies share common concerns. On the basis of this he posits seven basic goods (1980, pp. 86–9) in terms of which morality, justice and law are understood. These basic goods are (i) life, (ii) knowledge, (iii) play, (iv) aesthetic experience, (v) sociability or friendship, (vi) practical reasonableness and (vii) religion understood as 'recognition of, and concern about an order of things "beyond" each and every man' (ibid., p. 90). These goods are objective, basic, fundamental, premoral and self evident.

They are objective since all human societies exhibit a concern for these goods. They are basic since all other values, such as courage, gentleness and moderation, are means of pursuing the basic goods and hence subordinate to them (ibid., p. 90). They are fundamental in that all goods have equal status: there is no priority of value amongst the goods since each acquires a priority when viewed from a certain perspective.

The goods are premoral since they are not moral obligations or recommendations or pre-scriptions, even though they provoke the 'evalua-tive substratum for all moral judgements' (ibid., p. 62). They are self evident since they are obvious to the questioning mind (p. 65). The premoral basic goods (judgements about human goods) are transformed into a theory of morality (judge-ments about the right things to do here and now) by a set of principles consisting of basic require-ments of practical reasonableness. These princi-ples are: a coherent life plan, no arbitrary preferences among the seven basic goods, no arbitrary preferences among persons, detach-ment, commitment, efficiency within reason, respect for every basic value in every act, fostering the common good of the community, following one's conscience, and to choose real goods to apparent goods (ibid., pp. 103–26; and 1983, p. 75).

Finnis regards law as an aspect of practical reasonableness, that works for the common good of the community (1980, pp. 276–7). The moral authority of the law, for him, 'depends ... on its justice or at least its ability to secure justice' (p. 260).

What status do unjust laws have in Finnis's theory? Are these laws invalid because they are unjust? Is there any obligation on the part of citizens to obey unjust laws?

Finnis is aware that law can, at times, work against the common good. According to him, the laws that are unjust (against the common good) lack moral authority and therefore an unjust law. None the less there may be a moral obligation on the part of the citizens to obey them for practical reasons since disobedience of the law may weaken the authority of the ruler and result in harm to the common good.

A problem with Finnis's natural law theory (as with other natural law theories) is that it commits the fallacy of deriving an 'ought' from an 'is': normative statements (basic goods) are derived from statements of fact lacking value content (observation of human nature). However, accord-ing to Finnis, this is not true of his theory, since what is offered is not based purely on the observance of human nature but is also based on being a human being. The primary grasp of what is good for us is a practical grasp.

Although Finnis provides impressively com-prehensive lists of basic goods and basic require-ments of practical reasonableness it is questionable whether these are sufficient to provide clear guidance in moral dilemmas. Is it not the case that there are situations where, for instance, it may not be possible to respect each basic value in every act, or to follow one's conscience?

Sources: WW 1991.

INDIRA MAHALINGAM CARR

Fischer, Kuno

German. *b:* 23 July 1824, Gross-Sandewaid, Silesia. *d:* 5 July 1907, Heidelberg, Germany. *Cat:* Hegelian idealist; historian of German idealism. *Ints:* History of philosophy. *Educ:* Universities of Leipzig and Halle (1842–7). *Infls:* Hegel, Kant and Schopenhauer. *Appts: Privatdozent*, University of Heidelberg, 1850–3; *Ordinarius*, University of Jena, 1855–72; *Ordinarius*, University of Heidel-berg, 1872–1906.

Main publications:

(1852) *Logik und Metaphysik oder Wissenschaft-slehre*, Stuttgart: Scheitlin.

(1852–92) *Geschichte der neuern Philosophie*, 6 vols, Heidelberg: Carl Winter; new edition in 8 vols, 1889–93; definitive edition in 10 vols, 1897–1904 (translations exist only of the volumes devoted to Descartes (I), Spinoza (II), Kant (IV and V) and Bacon (X); the Kant volumes are by J. Mahaffy, *A Commentary on Kant's Critique of the Pure Reason*, London: Longmans, Green & Co., 1866, and by W. S. Hough, *A Critique of Kant*, London: Swan Sonnenschein Lowrey & Co., 1888).

(1888–98) *Kleine Schriften*, 10 vols, Heidelberg: Carl Winter.

(1891–2) *Philosophische Schriften*, 2 vols, Heidel-berg: Carl Winter.

(1896) *Das Verhältnis zwischen Willen und Verstand*, Heidelberg: Carl Winter.

Secondary literature:

Hoffmann, E. (1924) *Kuno Fischer*, Berlin: Carl Winter.

Windelband, W. (ed.) (1904) *Die Philosophie im Beginn des zwanzigsten Jahrhunderts. Festschrift für*

Kuno Fischer, 2 vols, Heidelberg: Carl Winter; enlarged edition, 1907.

——(1907) *Kuno Fischer*, Heidelberg: Carl Winter.

Fischer wrote a number of philosophical works, among them the 1849 *Diotima* (on aesthetics), the 1852 *Logik* (containing an influential critique of Hegelian logic) and the 1896 *Verhältnis* (a Schopenhauerian account of the relation between understanding and will). Fischer is also remembered for his numerous literary studies, particularly those of Shakespeare, Goethe and Schiller. His greatest achievement, however, was his *Geschichte der neuern Philosophie* (1852–92). The heart of the work is represented by the seven volumes devoted to Leibniz (III), Kant (IV and V), Fichte (VI), Schelling (VII), Hegel (VIII) and Schopenhauer (IX). The volumes on Descartes (I) and Spinoza (II) introduce the main theme, German idealism, and the final volume, on Bacon (X), represents a coda on materialism and empiricism. Celebrated for its lucidity and comprehensiveness, Fischer's *Geschichte* constitutes a marvellous synthesis of the philosophical and the historical (for Fischer, philosophy, being the evolution of the mind's knowledge of itself, *is* the history of philosophy). It succeeds both as a series of individual studies and as a continuous history of the development of German idealism. Fischer's interpretation of Kant, in particular, aroused considerable controversy and precipitated the emergence of neo-Kantainism.

Sources: Edwards; EF; Eisler; Fischer; Huisman; Ziegenfuss & Jung.

DAVID WALFORD

Flew, Antony (Garrard Newton)

British. *b:* 11 February 1923, Cambridge, England. *Cat:* Humanist; analytical philosopher. *Ints:* Philosophy of religion; Hume; evolution; moral philosophy. *Educ:* London School of Oriental and African Studies and St John's College, Oxford. *Infls:* Personal influences include Paul Grice, John Mabbott and Gilbert Ryle; literary influences are Hume, Julian Huxley, C. E. M. Joad, Joseph Needham and Susan Stebbing. *Appts:* 1950–4, Lecturer in Philosophy, University of Aberdeen; 1954–71, Professor of Philosophy, University of Keele; 1972–3, Professor of Philosophy, University of Calgary, Alberta; 1973–82, Professor of Philosophy, University of Reading; 1982–, Professor Emeritus, University of Reading; 1983–91, Distinguished Research Fellow, Social Philosophy and Policy Center, Bowling Green State University.

Main publications:

(1953) *A New Approach to Psychical Research*, London: Watts.
(1955) (ed. with A. C. MacIntyre) *New Essays in Philosophical Theology*, London: SCM Press.
(1956) (ed.) *Essays in Conceptual Analysis*, London: Macmillan.
(1961) *Hume's Philosophy of Belief*, London: Routledge & Kegan Paul.
(1966) *God and Philosophy*, London: Hutchinson.
(1967) *Evolutionary Ethics*, London: Macmillan.
(1971) *An Introduction to Western Philosophy: Ideas and Argument from Plato to Sartre*, London: Thames & Hudson.
(1976) *The Presumption of Atheism and Other Philosophical Essays on God, Freedom and Immortality*, London: Elek for Pemberton.
(1978) *A Rational Animal and Other Philosophical Essays on the Nature of Man*, Oxford: Clarendon Press.
(1984) *Darwinian Evolution*, London: Paladin.
(1985) *Thinking about Social Thinking: The Philosophy of the Social Sciences*, Oxford: Blackwell.
(1986) 'Apologia pro philospohia mea', in Stuart Shanker (ed.), *Philosophy in Britain Today*, London: Routledge.
(1986) *David Hume, Philosopher of Moral Science*, Oxford: Blackwell.
(1987) *The Logic of Mortality*, Oxford: Blackwell.
(1987) (with G. N. A. Vesey) *Agency and Necessity*, Oxford: Blackwell.
(1989) *Equality in Liberty and Justice*, London: Routledge.
(1993) *Atheistic Humanism*, Buffalo, NY: Prometheus Books.

Secondary literature:

Heimbeck, R. S. (1969) *Theology and Meaning: A Critique of Metatheological Scepticism*, Stanford: Stanford University Press.
Klein, K. H. (1974) *Positivism and Christianity: a Study of Theism and Verifiability*, The Hague: Nijhoff.

Although the son of a clergyman, Antony Flew declares that his 'long-standing interests in religion have never been ... anything other than prudential, moral or simply curious' (Flew 1986, p. 75). He is a self-professed 'atheist' and 'mortalist', an enthusiast for Darwin and Hume and a tireless philosophical critic of Christian theism. As a humanist, he has also taken an active interest in social and educational questions, where he has deployed his analytical skills and been a keen critic of the doctrinaire. His controversial writings have produced more than a hundred replies in learned journals.

Flew's interest in debates about immortality led him early into a study of the argument from psychical phenomena. He has written extensively on the debate about free will, holding that people can make free choices which are both free and choices even if they were physically caused to be made. It may have been Flew who brought the term 'compatibilism' into philosophical currency for this point of view. He has, however, subsequently come to deny a total causal determinism, which denial he refers to, with characteristic humour, as a 'defection from full compatabilism' (Flew 1986, p. 81). Although the author of many books, Flew first established his reputation as an editor of several books that are among the classical collections of analytical philosophy. Of his own writings, perhaps best known is a short paper he first published in 1951, called 'Theology and falsification', which has been reprinted or translated more than thirty times. In this paper Flew argued against the meaningfulness of claims about God by an analogy with the claim that there had been an 'invisible gardener'. The claim about the invisible gardener turns out to be meaningless because there is nothing the person who makes it is committed to denying. Many articles and even books have been elicited by Flew's critique of theism.

Sources: WW.

STUART BROWN

Florensky, Pavel Aleksandrovich

Russian. **b:** 19 January (21 N.S.) 1882, Evlakh, Azerbaijan. **d:** 8 December 1937, Solovetskii labour camp (executed). **Cat:** Religious philosopher. **Educ:** Graduated in Physics and Mathematics at University of Moscow in 1904 (also studying Philosophy under Lopatin), and in Philosophy and History of Religion, Moscow Theological Academy in 1908. **Infls:** Influenced by Christian neo-Platonism and Solov'ev. **Appts:** 1908–17, Professor of History of Philosophy at Moscow Theological Academy.

Main publications:

(1914) *Stolp i utverzhdenie istiny: opyt pravoslavnoi teoditsei v dvenadtsati pis'makh* [The Pillar and Ground of Truth: An Essay on Orthodox Theodicy in Twelve Letters], Moscow.

Secondary literature:

Lossky, N. O. (1952) *History of Russian Philosophy*, London: George Allen & Unwin, ch. 14.

Slesinski, R. (1984) *Pavel Florensky: A Metaphysics of Love*, New York: St Vladimir's Seminary Press.
Zenkovsky, V. V. (1953) *A History of Russian Philosophy*, trans. George L. Kline, London: Routledge & Kegan Paul, vol. 2, pp. 875–90.

Apart from his philosophical and theological concerns, Florensky composed symbolist poetry, wrote on art and its history and did significant work in pure mathematics and physics. Although he was exiled in the immediate aftermath of the October Revolution, from 1920 the Soviet regime found a use for his scientific skills, principally as a researcher for the state electrification plan. He edited the *Technical Encyclopedia* from 1927 to 1933. His refusal to renounce the priesthood (he was ordained in 1911) resulted in spells of imprisonment, and finally Siberian exile.

Florensky's principal religio-philosophical work *The Pillar and Ground of Truth* (1914) developed **Solov'ev**'s metaphysics of total-unity, advancing the notion of the consubstantiality of all created beings. Florensky rejected human rationality as vitiated by original sin, and leading inevitably to antinomies; perception of truth was possible only through 'rational intuition', or reason in conjunction with faith. Special emphasis was placed on Solov'ev's ambiguous concept of Sophia as mediating between total-unity, identified with the Christian triune deity, and God's freely created world, which is portrayed in the spirit of neo-Platonism as rooted in a world of concrete universals or ideal prototypes. Sophia in one sense is the unity of these underlying ideas, and is likened to a 'fourth hypostasis' entering into the Trinity, though having no independent existence. Florensky's 'antinomism' and sophiological metaphysics of total-unity were developed by his one-time follower and fellow philosopher–theologian **Bulgakov**, who added religio-philosophical interpretations of the Incarnation and the problem of evil. Florensky's intuitionism influenced **Lossky**.

COLIN CHANT

Flower, Elizabeth Farquhar

American. **b:** 31 October 1914, Atlantic City, New Jersey. **Cat:** Philosopher of education; historian of philosophy. **Ints:** Science; ethics; education; legal and social philosophy; history of philosophy in the Americas. **Educ:** University of Pennsylvania. **Infls:** Literary influences: William James and John Dewey. Personal: Edgar A. Singer, Abraham Edel and Murray G. Murphy. **Appts:** Assistant, then Associate Professor of Philosophy, 1945–76;

Professor, 1976–85; Professor Emeritus, 1985, University of Pennsylvania.

Main publications:

(1949) 'The Mexican revolt against positivism', *Journal of the History of Ideas* 10: 115–29.

(1960) 'Norms and induction', in Roland Houde and Joseph P. Mullaly (eds), *Philosophy of Knowledge*, Philadelphia: Lippincott.

(1965) 'On the language of education', *Studies in Philosophy and Education* 4: 123–133.

(1977) (with Murray G. Murphy) *A History of Philosophy in America* 2 vols, New York: G. P. Putnam's Sons.

(1987) 'A moral agenda for ethical theory', in I. L. Horowitz and H. S. Thayer (eds), *Value, Science and Democracy: The Philosophy of Abraham Edel*, New Brunswick, NJ: Transaction Books.

Secondary literature:

Murphy, Murray G. and Berg, I. (eds) (1988) *Values and Value Theory in Twentieth-Century America: Essays in Honour of Elizabeth Flower*, Philadelphia: Temple University Press.

After obtaining a degree in chemistry Flower was attracted to philosophy by a seminar conducted by Edgar Singer in the philosophy of science at the University of Pennsylvania. Later, she was appointed, as 'E. Flower', to teach at Pennsylvania, at a time when women's classes were segregated and female faculty still unimagined. It is not certain 'whether the trustees were aware that they had appointed a woman (and would have been horrified) or whether they were being socially farsighted' (Murphy and Berg 1988, p. 271).

Flower's teaching was centred upon cooperative courses that joined the humanities and the sciences. Believing that the scientific was value-laden and the normative grounded in scientific understanding, she approached ethics in its relation to psychology and social science, to education and law, and to the larger cultural context. Her ethics 'preserved historical insights ... at a time when American philosophers had largely abandoned historical perspectives' (ibid., p. 272). Flower pioneered intellectual exchanges with Latin America and worked with the Organization of American States, producing a series of monographs tracing the history of philosophy in Mexico, Peru, Colombia and Chile. Out of these studies there emerged the monumental *History of Philosophy in America* (1977), which surveyed American philosophy from its earliest beginnings in the colonies, through the 'wasteland of academic philosophy' that prevailed in American

universities for some 100 years (p. 142), to the major figures and movements of contemporary America. It is for this study, outstanding in its field, that Flower is best known.

Sources: Kersey.

STEPHEN MOLLER

Fock (Fok), Vladimir Aleksandrovich

Russian. **b:** 10 December (O.S.) 1898, St Petersburg. **d:** 27 December 1974, Leningrad. **Cat:** Physicist; philosopher of science. **Ints:** Philosophy of physics; dialectical materialism. **Educ:** Petrograd University. **Appts:** Taught Physics at Leningrad University and worked at various research institutes of the Soviet Academy of Sciences.

Main publications:

(1932) *Nachala kvantovoi mekhaniki*, Leningrad, second edition, 1976 (English translation, *Fundamentals of Quantum Mechanics*, trans. Eugene Yankovsky, Moscow, 1978).

(1955) *Teoriia prostranstva, vremeni, i tiagoteniia*, Moscow (English translation, *The Theory of Space, Time, and Gravitation*, trans. N. Kemmer, New York: Pergamon Press, 1959; second edition, 1964).

Secondary literature:

Graham, Loren R. (1972) *Science and Philosophy in the Soviet Union*, New York: Alfred A. Knopf; revised edition, *Science, Philosophy, and Human Behavior in the Soviet Union*, Columbia University Press, 1987 (contains bibliography).

A distinguished physicist, elected to the Soviet Academy of Sciences in 1939, Fock became one of the country's most authoritative interpreters of Marxist-Leninist philosophy as it applied to modern theories in physics. By effecting accommodations between dialectical materialism and those theories, he defended them against the ideological attacks of Soviet dogmatists.

In the 1930s Fock was one of a number of Soviet physicists who accepted Niels **Bohr**'s principle of complementarity in quantum mechanics. After the Second World War, however, these scientists came under attack by Marxist ideologues who charged that complementarity contravened basic postulates of dialectical materialism—namely, the objective reality and knowability of the material world and universal causal determinism. In the ensuing debate Fock elaborated weakened interpretations of those postulates that removed them from jeopardy and he also secured, in personal conversations with Bohr in 1957, assurances that Bohr himself acknowledged the objective reality of micro-objects and their properties and rejected only Laplacian determinism, not causality in general. In Fock's construction of quantum theory, the microworld is characterized by objective properties that he calls 'potentialities'—that is, capacities to be actualized in certain ways.

Fock also played a major role in Soviet discussions of relativity theory, which faced comparable ideological pressure. He fully accepted the special theory of relativity, arguing that it is not only consistent with dialectical materialism but provides strong support for that philosophy's doctrines of space and time as forms of the existence of matter, of the dialectical interconnectedness of all things, and of the inseparability of matter and motion. He did not believe, however, that **Einstein** was justified in proceeding to the general theory of relativity; Fock's criticisms of that theory sparked controversy in the Soviet Union and abroad.

JAMES SCANLAN

Fodor, Jerry Alan
American. *b:* 1935, New York. *Cat:* Philosopher of mind. *Educ:* Columbia and Princeton Universities. *Infls:* Noam Chomsky, Donald Davidson and Hilary Putnam.

Main publications:
(1968) *Psychological Explanation*, New York: Random House.
(1975) *The Language of Thought*, New York: Thomas Crowell.
(1981) *Representations: Philosophical Essays on the Foundations of Cognitive Science*, Bradford Books/ MIT Press.
(1983) *The Modularity of Mind*, Bradford Books/ MIT Press.
(1987) *Psychosemantics: The Problem of Meaning in the Philosophy of Mind*, Bradford Books/MIT Press.
(1990) *A Theory of Content and Other Essays*, Bradford Books/MIT Press.
(1992) (with Ernest Lepore) *Holism: A Shopper's Guide*, Oxford: Blackwell.
(1994) *The Elm and the Expert: Mentalese and its Semantics*, MIT Press/Bradford Books.

Fodor is best known for his trenchant defence of realism about the mental and for his equally strong adherence to a form of innatism about concepts which owes much to the influence of **Chomsky**.

According to Fodor, cognitive states are to be construed as relations between the agent and representations physically instantiated in the brain; congnitive processes are then computational operations on these internal items. Thus the ordinary concepts of belief, hoping, etc. (propositional attitudes) are real, even though this characterization does not answer to an informal understanding of these notions. Fodor is not, therefore, giving an 'ordinary language' analysis of these, but making a claim about the nature of the things to which they apply. Fodor supplements this Representational Theory of The Mind, with his 'Language of Thought' hypothesis—that the medium of these repesentations is *linguistic* and can be described as having a *syntax*. The crux of the problem is whether there can be anything *more* than syntax, if context and environment are excluded.

Both Fodor and his opponents acknowledge that there is an intra-cranial contribution to the business of meaning, but there remains a problem of how the internal and external elements come together. Fodor's argument for a 'narrow' (internalist) story over a 'wide' (externalist) story is that only the former is adequate to capture the role of the propositional attitudes in relation to behaviour. What matters is not how things are in the world outside the head, but how the world seems to the agent. Fodor embraces the strategy of 'Methodological Solipsism', the aim of which is to assign meanings to 'inner representations' in a way which does not presuppose the existence of anything beyond the individual and his thoughts. Fodor does not deny a place for a 'wide' account taking in truth and reference, but disputes that this can play any part in accounting for behaviour. Nor does he intend his account as defending any idiosyncratic or subjective 'meanings': narrow content of representations is what any two individuals share if their representations play essentially the same cognitive roles in their respective heads. They would be in the same states, narrowly speaking.

Critics have posed the tough question of whether the content of narrow states would really deserve to be called 'semantic' at all. (Even Fodor concedes that narrow content is 'radically inexpressible'!) Fodor has battled with many of the most prominent contemporary analytic philosophers, attacking holism in **Quine** and **Davidson**, instrumentalism about the mental in the work of **Dennett**, and linguistic platonism in Jerrold **Katz**, all the while writing in an engagingly facetious style, with frequent reference to his (mainly fictionalized) aunt and grandmother.

Sources: See secondary literature.

DENIS POLLARD

Fogelin, R(obert) J(ohn)

American. *b:* 24 June 1932, Congers, New York. *Cat:* Epistemologist; philosopher of language. *Ints:* Hume and Wittgenstein. *Educ:* BA, University of Rochester, 1955; MA, Yale, 1957; PhD, Yale, 1960. *Infls:* Multifarious, but one is Hume. *Appts:* 1958–66, Instructor, Assistant Professor and Associate Professor, Pomona College; 1966-70, Associate Professor, Yale University; 1970–80, Professor, Yale University; from 1980, Professor, Dartmouth College; Visiting Professor, University of California, Santa Barbara, 1977, University of California, Berkeley, 1984 and 1991.

Main publications:

(1967) *Evidence and Meaning*, London: Routledge & Kegan Paul.
(1976) *Wittgenstein*, London: Routledge & Kegan Paul; second revised edition, 1987.
(1985) *Hume's Skepticism*, London: Routledge & Kegan Paul.
(1988) *Figuratively Speaking*, New Haven and London: Yale University Press.
(1992) *Philosophical Interpretations*, Oxford: Oxford University Press.
(1994) *Pyrrhonian Reflections on Knowledge and Justification*, Oxford: Oxford University Press.

Through all the years, one of Fogelin's main interests has been general epistemology. Among his contributions are sustained attempts at analysing, and investigating the possibility of defending, various brands of scepticism. He has addressed the so-called Gettier paradox facing the Platonic (or 'standard') account of knowledge as justified, true belief.

Fogelin is the author of an influential book on **Wittgenstein**, notable mainly for its lucid account of the doctrines set forth in the *Tractatus* and for its analysis of Wittgenstein's considerations concerning what it is to follow a rule.

He has presented a neo-Aristotelian account of figurative meaning within a minimal Gricean framework, stressing the speech-act aspect of figurative prediction: (e.g. irony and hyperbole) and 'figurative comparisons' (e.g. simile, allegory and metaphor). He defends a 'comparativist' (or 'eliptical-simile') view of metaphors.

Sources: Personal communication.

STIG RASMUSSEN

Føllesdal, D(agffin)

Norwegian. *b:* 22 June 1932, Askim, Norway. *Cat:* Theorist of reference; Husserlian. *Ints:* Applied ethics. *Educ:* 1950–7, studies in Oslo and Göttingen for the Cand.Mag. and Mag.Art. in Mathematics, Mechanics, Astronomy and Philosophy; 1961, PhD in Philosophy, Harvard. *Infls:* Quine and Husserl. *Appts:* Since 1955, numerous teaching and research posts in Oslo and at Harvard; since 1967, Professor in Oslo; 1968, Professor at Stanford (since 1976, C. I. Lewis Professor); Visiting Professor, University of California, Berkeley, 1971, Collège de France, 1977, and University of Auckland, 1982.

Main publications:

(1965) 'Quantification into causal contexts', in Cohen and Wartofsky (eds), *Boston Studies in the Philosophy of Science*, vol. II, New York: Humanities Press.
(1966) *Referential Opacity and Modal Logic*, Oslo: Oslo University Press (revised PhD Thesis, Harvard 1961).
(1969) 'Husserl's notion of noema', *Journal of Philosophy* 66.
(1986) 'Reference and sense', in Venant Cauchy (ed.), *Philosophy and Culture: Proceedings of the XVth World Congress of Philosophy*, Montreal: Éditions de Beffroi, Éditions Montmorency.
(1989) 'Husserl on evidence and justification', in Robert Sokolwski (ed.), *Edmund Husserl and the Phenomenological Tradition: Essays in Phenomenology*, Washington: The Catholic University of America Press.
(1990) 'Indeterminacy and mental states', in Robert Barrett and Roger Gibson (eds), *Perspectives on Quine*, Oxford: Blackwell.

Føllesdal has consistently argued the need for 'genuine single terms'—akin to **Kripke**'s 'rigid designators'—if we are able to devise a semantics for modal contexts impervious to **Quine**'s objections. But the link between word and reference is not guaranteed by a causal tie. In place of this, Føllesdal argues in favour of a 'normative' theory of reference. In general, he stresses the social nature of language and takes Quinean indeterminacy of translation to arise from this source. Thus indeterminacy does not depend upon physicalism.

As regards **Husserl**, Føllesdal interprets the notion of noema as a generalization of the concept of meaning to the realm of acts. Also, rather than taking Husserl's notion of ultimate justification to betray this philosopher as a foundationalist. He argues that Husserl's notion resembles **Rawls**'s idea of 'reflective equilibria'.

Sources: Personal communication.

STIG RASMUSSEN

Foot, P(hilippa) R(uth)

British. *b:* 1920, Owston Ferry. *Cat:* Analytic philosopher. *Ints:* Ethics; philosophy of mind; Wittgenstein. *Educ:* Somerville College, Oxford. *Infls:* Aristotle, Aquinas, Wittgenstein and G. E. M. Anscombe. *Appts:* 1949–69, Fellow, 1967–9, Vice-Principal, 1969–89, Senior Research Fellow, Honorary Fellow, Somerville College, Oxford; 1976–99, Professor of Philosophy, 1989–present, 1988–91, Griffin Professor of Philosophy, University of California at Los Angeles; other visiting positions in the United States; 1976, Fellow of the British Academy; 1983, Fellow of the American Academy of Arts and Sciences.

Main publications:

(1978) *Virtues and Vices* (articles 1957–76), Oxford: Basil Blackwell.

Secondary literature:

Phillips, D. Z. (1977) 'In search of the moral "must"', *Philosophical Quarterly* 27.
Scheffler, Samuel (1985) 'Agent-centred restrictions, rationality and the virtues', *Mind* 94.

In her early work Foot attacked the anti-naturalism, characteristic of intuitionism, emotivism and prescriptivism, which held that it was impossible to derive moral judgements from factual ones. She argued that moral terms have determinate descriptive meanings, and that this lays down logical limits on what might count as a good or bad moral argument. Whether certain behaviour is courageous or just, for instance—supposedly evaluative judgements—can often be straightforwardly settled by appeal to the facts and to the meanings of terms. Further, given the conditions that, as human beings, we inevitably find ourselves in, it will be impossible for an individual to live a satisfactory life without virtues such as courage and justice. It is possible, then, to mount an argument to show that we should be courageous or just, an argument from which no one could sensibly dissent.

In her later writings Foot came to question one element of this, namely the idea that everyone necessarily has a reason to be moral. She argued against Kantian styles of moral philosophy that morality is not a system of law valid for all rational beings as such. Its requirements stem only from the desires that we actually have (desires for the good of others and for a certain sort of life for ourselves, for instance). It is possible to lack those desires, and moral requirements will simply not hold for anyone who does so. Morality is thus a system of 'hypothetical imperatives'. Foot's early work had considerable impact against the prescriptivism of R. M **Hare**. Her later work has been particularly instrumental in placing the virtues at the centre of moral philosophy.

Sources: WW 1992; personal communication.

ANTHONY ELLIS

Foucault, Michel

French. *b:* 1926, Poitiers, France. *d:* 1984, Paris. *Cat:* Post-structuralist; historian of ideas. *Educ:* École Normale Supérieure, Paris. *Infls:* Marx, Nietzsche, Heidegger, Merleau-Ponty, Jean Hyppolite and Georges Canguilhem. *Appts:* Professor of Philosophy, University of Clermont-Ferrand; Professor of History and Systems of Thought, Collège de France.

Main publications:

(1954) *Maladie mentale et psychologie*, Paris: Presses Universitaires de Frances (English translation, *Mental Illness and Psychology*, trans. Alan Sheridan, New York: Harper Colophon, 1976).
(1961) *Folie et déraison: histoire de la folie à l'âge classique*, Paris: Plon (English translation, *Madness and Civilization: A History of Insanity in the Age of Reason*, trans. Richard Howard, New York: Mentor Books, 1965).
(1963) *Naissance de la clinique: une archéologie du regard medical*, Paris: Presses Universitaires de France (English translation, *The Birth of the Clinic: An Archaeology of Medical Perception*, trans. Alan Sheridan, New York: Vintage Books, 1973).
(1966) *Les Mots et les choses: une archéologie des sciences humaines*, Paris: Gallimard (English translation, *The Order of Things: An Archaeology of the Human Sciences*, trans. Alan Sheridan, New York: Random House, 1970).
(1969) *L'Archéologie du savoir*, Paris: Gallimard (English translation, *The Archaeology of Knowledge*, trans. Alan Sheridan, New York: Harper & Row, 1972).
(1977) *Surveiller et punir: naissance de la prison*, Paris: Gallimard (English translation, *Discipline and Punish: The Birth of the Prison*, trans. Alan Sheridan, New York: Pantheon, 1977).
(1976–84) *Histoire de la sexualité*, I–III, Paris: Gallimard (English translation, *The History of Sexuality*, I–III, trans. Robert Hurley, New York: Pantheon, 1978–85).

(1980) *Power/Knowledge: Selected Interviews and Other Writings 1972–1977*, ed. Colin Gordon, Leo Marshall, John Mepham and Kate Soper.

Secondary literature:
Arac, Jonathan (ed.) (1988) *After Foucault: Humanistic Knowledge, Postmodern Challenges*, New Brunswick, NJ: Rutgers University Press.
Cousins, Mark and Hussain, Athar (1984) *Michel Foucault*, London and Basingstoke: Macmillan.
Diamond, Irene and Quinby, Lee (1988) *Feminism and Foucault: Reflections on Resistance*, Boston: Northeastern University Press.
Dreyfus, Hubert L. and Rabinow, Paul (1982) *Michel Foucault: Beyond Structuralism and Hermeneutics*, New York and London: Harvester.
During, Simon (1992) *Foucault and Literature: Towards a Genealogy of Writing*, London: Routledge.
Sheridan, Alan (1986) *Michel Foucault: The Will to Truth*, London and New York: Tavistock Publications.

Originally trained as a philosopher, Foucault subsequently worked in the fields of psychology and psychopathology, the subject of his first book, *Mental Illness and Psychology* (1954), before returning to philosophy and, more specifically, to the history of ideas. He drew inspiration from Marxist, structuralist and Freudian theory at various points in his career, although he tended to disclaim any lasting influence on his thought from these traditions. The main thrust of Foucault's work is to merge philosophy with history such that large-scale analyses, or 'archaeologies' as he has termed them, can be undertaken of those historical 'discourses' (Foucault's name for thought when it is realized as a social practice) that have led to the present rationality-biased discourse of Western culture. Foucault sets himself the objective of constructing 'a history of the present' by means of these archaeologies, which have encompassed such diverse topics as changing attitudes to insanity in post-Renaissance European society, the development of the prison system within the same society, and the codes governing sexual practice in classical times. In each case Foucault's concern is to trace the mechanisms involved in the development of the various discourses of social control in modern culture. There is a consciously anti-Enlightenment strain in Foucault's enquiries, and somewhat notoriously he proclaims 'the death of man' in *The Order of Things* (1966), arguing, as do so many structuralist and poststructuralist thinkers, that the concept of 'man', in particular 'rational' man,

is a very recent, and in many ways very regrettable, cultural invention. Foucault's archaeologies tend to identify discontinuities in history, and he insists that his cultural analyses are specifically directed against all notions of teleology or assumptions of transcendental vantage points. Thus in *Madness and Civilization* (1961) he traces a radical change in social attitudes towards the phenomenon of madness over a relatively short historical period, whereby behaviour tolerated at one point within civil society was very soon designated as a social 'problem' requiring an institutional response. Foucault describes this cultural phenomenon of the seventeenth and early eighteenth centuries as 'The Great Confinement', and emphasizes the discontinuity involved in such a significant shift in perception. The underlying ideological reason for this change, Foucault claims, is to be located in the growing cult of reason, which led to insanity, or 'unreason', taking on negative connotations that were unthinkable before. A whole new structure of power evolved, as it did also in the rise of the modern prison system with its systematized methods of repression and punishment, and Foucault is a particularly acute analyst of power in its institutionalized forms. The analysis of power is a continuing concern throughout his career, surfacing in all his major works. Foucault's approach to cultural history is fairly broad-brush in style and can involve some questionable generalizations. He adopts a rather cavalier attitude to historical research, much influenced by **Nietzsche**'s iconoclasm about such matters, denying the possibility of historical objectivity and dismissing academic history as being merely 'the history of the historians'. The latter requires a vantage-point outside history in order to make it work, Foucault argues, and he is harshly critical of all such examples of 'transcendental narcissism'. Foucault pursues his archaeological enquiries throughout his oeuvre, culminating in his monumental three-volume history of sexuality in classical times, where the concern is to establish the process whereby the relatively guilt-free view of male sexuality in Greek times, including what is by modern standards a very relaxed attitude towards homosexual practices such as pederasty, evolved into the more repressive, as well as recognizably more modern, codes of behaviour of later Roman society. What Foucault identifies yet again is the development and institutionalization of methods of social control that are unacceptable to his quasi-anarchistic outlook. Like so many other French intellectuals in the post-1968 *événements* period, Foucault comes to display a deep distrust of all institutional power and its tendency towards overt control of individual behaviour. Foucault has been a highly controversial figure and his broadly based inter-disciplinary-minded analyses of culture and the nature of institutional power have made him a difficult thinker to categorize. Purists are only too apt to see his projected merger of philosophy and history as lacking the intellectual rigour required of either discipline. There is no doubt, however, that he qualifies as one of the most influential contributors to the field of history of ideas in the modern era. Discourse theory, one of the liveliest areas of debate in recent cultural theory, largely derives from the work of Foucault, and his project to map out a 'history of the present' through archaeological analyses of past discourses has been enthusiastically followed up by a host of scholars across the humanities and social sciences. Foucault has attracted criticism from various quarters. The left, for example, has denounced his anarchistic tendencies and quasi-Nietzschean outlook as inimical to socialist ideas (Foucault's political and intellectual position might best be summed up as post-Marxist). A more general criticism has been, that his archaeologies, with their sweeping historical generalizations and often highly selective use of sources, have been wildly over-schematic. Rather in the manner of the structuralist and Marxist thinkers he affects to disdain, Foucault has been accused of imposing a model on the past which cannot always be substantiated by the available evidence: 'tall orders largely unsupported by the facts' being one not untypical verdict on his archaeological enquiries (J. G. Merquior). Foucault's self-con-sciously anti-Enlightenment stance has also been the subject of much unfavourable comment, with Jürgen **Habermas**, for example, arguing that the abandonment of any commitment to universal reason on the part of poststructuralist thinkers like Foucault ultimately leads to the end of philosophy, and to any possibility of being able to discriminate between the claims of competing theories or discourses. In common with most poststructuralist theories Foucault espouses anti-foundationalism—he claims that the theories in *The Archaeology of Knowledge* are 'groundless', for example—and this aspect of his thought has come under considerable attack as well, on the fairly predictable grounds that it undermines the validity of his own theories and cultural analyses.

STUART SIM

Fougeyrollas, Pierre

French. *b:* 1922, Pays d'Oc. *Cat:* Marxist; social and political philosopher; sociologist. *Ints:* History of social thought; social and revolutionary processes. *Educ:* Docteur d'État ès lettres et sciences humaines. *Infls:* Hegel, Marx, Leon Trotsky and Georges Labica. *Appts:* Director of the Institut Fondamental d'Afrique Noire, 1968–71; Teacher, then Professor of Sociology, University of Paris VII.

Main publications:
(1959) *Le Marxisme en question*, Paris: Editions du Seuil.
(1960) *La Philosophie en question*, Paris: Denoël.
(1964) *Contradiction et totalité*, Paris: Editions de Minuit.
(1970) *La Révolution freudienne*, Paris: Denoël.
(1972) *Marx, Freud et la révolution totale*, Paris: Anthropos.
(1976) *Contre Lévi-Strauss, Lacan, Althusser*, Paris: Savelli.
(1976) *La Révolution prolétarienne et les impasses petits-bourgeoises*, Paris: Anthropos.
(1980) *Savoirs et idéologie dans les sciences sociales*, 2 vols, Paris: Payot: vol. 1, *Sciences sociales et marxisme*, vol. 2, *Les processus sociaux contemporains*.

Secondary literature:
Ansart, Pierre (1990) *Les Sociologies contemporaines*, Paris: Le Seuil.
Gabaude, Jean-Marc (1981) Review of *Savoirs et idéologie* (1980), in *Revue philosophique* 171: 478–80.

In much of his work, particularly in his monumental *Savoirs et idéologie* (1980), Fougeyrollas has been concerned to offer a Marxist critique of the history of sociological and anthropological thought, from its first stirrings in the precursors of the Enlightenment to more recent developments such as the structural anthropology of Claude **Lévi-Strauss**, the idealist *métapsychanalyse* of Jacques **Lacan** and the *panlinguistique* idealism of Michel **Foucault**. Throughout, he has attempted to disentangle knowledge from ideology in the human sciences, an entanglement that he sees as having prevented a breakthrough to the true, scientific understanding of social and human processes which he associates with Marxism. In his estimation Marxist dialectical materialism is a science and not a philosophy.

In connection with this critique, as its fulfilment in practice, Fougeyrollas has proposed a radical, Trotskyite political view or *pensée-action*. In this, he would resume the movement of the 'révolution mondiale' begun in 1917 with the

Russian Revolution and (so he holds) interrupted and largely perverted after 1923 as a result of the general degeneracy of bureaucratic states pretending to be socialist, and of Communist parties and their theoreticians who allowed themselves to be covert accomplices of capitalism. The socio-political programme of Fougeyrollas, a collective liberation conceived as extending to all aspects of human existence, from technical and scientific rationality to our relations with nature, with one another and ourselves, has been criticized as unrealistic (Gabaude 1981, p. 480). But his Marxist critique of the social sciences is widely regarded as one of the most searching of its kind. Through his many writings Fougeyrollas has established himself as a leading critic of contemporary thought and society.

Sources: Husiman.

STEPHEN MOLLER

Fouillée, Alfred Jules Émile

French. **b:** 1838, La Pouèze, Maine-et-Loire, France. **d:** 1912, Lyon, France. **Cat:** Idealist. **Ints:** Theory of ideas; metaphysics; history of philosophy; ethics. **Educ:** Lycée Laval and afterwards prepared himself for the newly revived agrégé in Philosophy. **Appts:** Taught at lycées in Ernée, Louhans, Dôle and Auxerre before becoming Professor of Philosophy at the lycée in Carcassonne; after winning his agrégé, he taught at more prestigious lycées in Douai, Montpellier and Bordeaux; 1872–5, taught at l'École Normale Supérieure in Paris, but ill-health forced his retirement; went on writing, mostly in the Midi, until his death 37 years later.

Main publications:

(1867) *Les Philosophes de la Gascogne: Montaigne, Montesquieu, Maine de Biran, et leur influence sur le développement de l'esprit moderne*, Bordeaux: impr. de Gounouilhou.
(1869) *La Philosophie de Platon; exposition, histoire et critique de la théorie des idées*, 2 vols, Paris: Ladrange; 4 vols, Paris: Hachette, 1904–9.
(1872) *Platonis Hippias minor, sive socratica contra liberum arbitrium argumenta*, Paris: Ladrange.
(1872) *La Liberté et le déterminisme*, Paris: Ladrange; fifth edition, Paris: F. Alcan, 1907.
(1874) *La Philosophie de Socrate*, 2 vols, Paris: Ladrange.
(1875) *Histoire de la philosophie*, Paris: Delagrave; seven edition, 1893.
(1878) *L'Idée moderne du droit en Allemagne, en Angleterre, et en France*, Paris: Hachette; sixth edition, 1909.

(1880) *La Science sociale contemporaine*, Paris: Hachette; fifth edition, 1910.
(1883) *Critique des systèmes de morale contemporains*, Paris: G. Baillière; fifth edition; 1906.
(1884) *La Propriété sociale et la démocratie*, Paris: Hachette; second edition, 1895, reprinted 1904.
(1889) *L'Avenir de la métaphysique fondée sur l'expérience*, Paris: F. Alcan.
(1891) *L'Enseignement au point de vue national*, Paris: Hachette; second edition, 1909.
(1892) *Education from a National Standpoint*, trans. and ed. W. J. Greenstreet, London: L. Arnold.
(1889) *La Morale, l'art, et la religion d'après M. Guyau*, Paris: F. Alcan; fourth edition, 1901.
(1890) *L'Évolutionnisme des idées-forces*, Paris: F. Alcan.
(1893) *Descartes*, Paris: Hachette.
(1893) *La Psychologie des idées-forces*, 2 vols, Paris: Alcan.
(1895) *Tempérament et caractère selon les individus, les sexes et les races*, Paris: F. Alcan.
(1896) *Le Mouvement idéaliste et la réaction contre la science positive*, Paris: F. Alcan.
(1896) *Le Mouvement positiviste et la conception sociologique du monde*, Paris: F. Alcan.
(1898) *Les Études classiques et la démocratie*, Paris: F. Alcan.
(1898) *Psychologie du peuple français*, Paris: F. Alcan.
(1900) *La France an point de vue morale*, Paris: F. Alcan.
(1901) *La Réforme de l'enseignement par la philosophie*, Paris: A. Colin.
(1902) *Nietzsche et l'immoralisme*, Paris: F. Alcan.
(1903) *Esquisse psychologique des peuples européens*, Paris: F. Alcan.
(1905) *Le Moralisme de Kant et l'amoralisme contemporain*, Paris: F. Alcan.
(1906) *Les Éléments sociologiques de la morale*, Paris: F. Alcan.
(1908) *Morale des idées-forces*, Paris: F. Alcan.
(1910) *La Démocratie politique et sociale en France*, Paris: F. Alcan.
(1911) *La Pensée et les nouvelles écoles anti-intellectualistes*, Paris: F. Alcan.
Also, edited works of Aristotle, Arnuald, Guyau, Leibniz, Pascal and Plato.

Secondary literature:
Beaucoudrey, Elisabeth Ganne de (1936) *La Psychologie et la métaphysique des idées-forces chez Alfred Fouillée*, Paris: J. Vrin.
Biermann, Herman (1911) 'Das Selbstbewusstein nach A. Fouillée' PhD thesis, University of Strasbourg.

Guyau, Augustin (1913) *La Philosophie et la socio-logie d'Alfred Fouillée*, Paris: F. Alcan.

Logue, William (1983) *From Philosophy to Sociology: The Evolution of French Liberalism, 1870–1914*, DeKalb: Northern Illinois University Press.

Pasmanik, Dorothée (1899) *Alfred Fouillées psychischer Monismus*, Bern: C. Sturzenegger.

Pawlicky, Stefan (1893) *Alfred Fouillées neue Theorie der Ideenkräfte*, Vienna: J. Roller.

Shellhaas, Joseph B. (1950) 'Fouillée's ethics of idées-forces; its psychological and metaphysical bases and a critique thereof', PhD thesis, Ohio State University.

Fouillée's philosophy is built around the notion of 'idées-forces' which is found in all his major works. His contention is that ideas are active and that they structure both our lives and the world at large. Since they have a subjective and an objective facet they enable us to understand the interface between our private psychological worlds and the public world of independent objects. Fouillée claimed that this analysis could overcome the traditional central dichotomies of philosophy—rationalism and empiricism, freedom and determinism, materialism and psychical idealism, duty and desire. He applied the same analysis to questions of metaphysics, psychology, politics, morals and the history of philosophy. His discussion of rationalism and empiricism can be used to explain the essence of his contention. Ideas are experienced and enter every experience, however primitive. Even a simple sensation becomes recognizable as a sensation only when it is understood in connection with an idea. Applied to ethics, the same analysis suggests that certain powerful ideas—freedom, love and beauty—have an effect on us. One can examine them simply empirically to find out what is desired and desirable but, again, in the process one becomes involved in the logic of the ideas and one sees that they take on certain universal forms.

Fouillée's metaphysics breaks with all the main traditions of French idealism, although there is a clear sense in which his theory can be connected to certain strands of thought going as far back as Malebranche. He was influenced chiefly not by other thinkers but by the problems of the contemporary social sciences, which had failed to come up with concepts and categories needed to distinguish the inner life and the human condition from the world of things. It can be said that his main interest was in the possibilities for a more human social science and a rational political life, although much of his writing is metaphysical and epistemological. Léon **Brunschvieg** argued that Fouillée's metaphysics is based on a confusion. His 'idées' are psychical particulars which Brunschvieg says amount to 'material spirits' (*Revue de Métaphysique et de Morale*, 1884, p. 483), and the term 'psychical realism' has been suggested as the best description of his position. But some critics think that parts of Fouillée's project are revivable. In his 1983 study of political liberalism, William Logue argues, just as Fouillée's notion of *idées-forces* provided a middle way between most characteristic philosophical disputes, so in politics it makes him a kind of communitarian liberal, standing between the state socialists, who do not understand that in the human sphere ideas work in an individual consciousness, and the right-wing individualists, who do not understand that there is a universal logic and a universal duty implied in the idea of morality itself.

Sources: Benrubi; Parodi; Edwards; EF; LXXS; FranBio.

LESLIE ARMOUR

Fox-Keller, Evelyn

American. *b:* 1936, New York. *Cat:* Philosopher of science. *Educ:* Physics and Molecular Biology, Harvard University. *Infls:* T. S. Kuhn, Barbara McLintock and feminist psychoanalysis. *Appts:* 1987–8, Institute of Advanced Study, Princeton; 1988–92, Professor of Women's Studies in Berkeley; from 1992, Professor, Faculty of Science, Technology and Society, MIT; regarded as an important analyst of science from a feminist perspective; Hon. Doctorate, Amsterdam.

Main publications:

(1983) *A Feeling for the Organism: The Life and Work of Barbara McLintock*; tenth edition, New York: W. H. Freeman, 1993.

(1988) *Reflections on Gender and Science*, New Haven: Yale University Press.

(1989) *Three Cultures: Fifteen Lectures on the Confrontation of Academic Cultures*, Rotterdam: Universitaire Pers.

(1990) *Body/Politics: Women and the Discourse of Science*, New York: Routledge.

(1990) *Conflicts in Feminism*, New York and London: Routledge.

(1992) *Keywords in Evolutionary Biology*, Cambridge, Mass.: Harvard University Press.

(1992) *Secrets of Life, Secrets of Death*, New York: Routledge.

(1993) *Refiguring Life: Metaphors of Twentieth-century Biology*, New York: Columbia University Press.

Secondary literature:
Donini, E. (1991) *Conversazioni con Evelyn Fox-Keller*, Milan: Eleuthera.

Trained as a scientist, Fox-Keller changed direction to a degree to become one of the most respected feminist analysts of scientific concepts. Her thought relies heavily on some ideas drawn from the Nobel Laureate Barbara McLintock and from feminist psychoanalysis.

Western science hitherto (she argues) has had an unacknowledged gender bias which has not only tended until quite recently to exclude women from scientific work but has influenced the basic concepts and paradigms (in the Kuhnian sense of the term) with which scientists work. For example, the traditional association of intellect and objectivity with the male and of subjectivity and feeling with the female has tended to exclude women from scientific discourse. Again, the preference among male scientists for models in which nature is regarded as rigidly determined and law-governed, and the biological sphere as one of competition and conflict for scarce resources, she regards as an unconscious reflection of what she asserts to be standard male conditioning: to grow up a male must stifle his emotional relationship with his mother and deny subjective emotional needs, and this Fox-Keller sees as the root cause of the typical male mental set. She argues further that this mental set prevents a proper understanding of nature. It is more productive to approach nature as a system incorporating spontaneity and cooperation. Again, the relationship of scientist and object of study should be regarded as a dynamic rapport, rather than that of a master attempting to subjugate a recalcitrant nature conceived of as female.
Sources: Meyer & Vahle.

ROBERT WILKINSON

Francovich, Guillermo
Bolivian. *b:* 25 January 1901, Sucre, Bolivia. *d:* 24 November 1990. *Cat:* Diplomat; historian of ideas. *Educ:* Law degree, University of San Francisco Xavier, Sucre, Bolivia, 1920, but never practised; Bolivian foreign service, 1930–43. *Appts:* 1922, Professor of Legal Philosophy, University of San Francisco Xavier; 1944–52, Rector of the University of San Francisco Xavier. Served in the Bolivian foreign service, 1930–43.

Main publications:
(1938) *Los ídolos de Bacon*, Sucre, Bolivia: University of San Francisco Xavier.

(1942) *Pachamama, diálogo sobre el porvenir de la cultura en Bolivia*, Asunción: La Colmena.
(1943) *Filósofos brasileños*, Buenos Aries: Losada.
(1945) *La filosofía en Bolivia*, Buenos Aires: Losada.
(1956) *El pensamiento boliviano en el siglo XX*; second edition, Mexico: Fondo de Cultura Económica, 1985.
(1980) *Los mitos profundos de Bolivia*, La Paz: Los Amigos de Libro.

Secondary literature:
Covarrubias Cárdenas, Juan (1978) *Francovich: Humanismo cultural latinoamericana*, Cochabamba: Universidad Católica Boliviana.
Gómex-Martínez, José Luis (1991) 'Homenaje a Guillermo Francovich (1901–1990), *Cuadernos americanos*, May/June.
Ross, Waldo (1954) *Hijos de la roca: el pensamiento de Guillermo Francovich*, Mexico: Orión.

In *Los ídolos de Bacon* (1938), Francovich identifies with Francis Bacon on the threshold of European modernity and seeks to destroy the 'idols' imposed on Latin Americans by Europeans. Francovich maintains that ideas cannot be entirely understood or appreciated if they are isolated from the environment in which they arose. After passing through a nationalistic phase, Francovich concludes that national groups do not differ from one another on the basis of skin colour or the shapes of their heads, but on the basis of their conception of the world and the life they lead.

AMY A. OLIVER

Frank, Manfred
German. *b:* 22 March 1945, Wuppertal, Germany. *Cat:* Philosopher of literature and literary hermeneutics; scholar of German idealism and romanticism. *Educ:* 1977, *Habilitationschrift*, University of Dusseldorf. *Infls:* Kant, Hegel, Schleiermacher, Schelling, Marx, Sartre, Barthes and Derrida. *Appts:* Chair of Philosophy, University of Tübingen.

Main publications:
(1967) *Die Unhintergehbarkeit von Individualität*, Frankfurt am Main: Suhrkamp.
(1972) *Das Problem 'Zeit' in der deutschen Romantik. Zeitbewusstsein und Bewusstsein von Zeitlichkeit in der frühromantischen Philosophie und in Tiecks Dichtung*, Munich: Winkler.
(1975) *Der unendliche Mangel an Sein. Schellings Hegelkritik und die Anfange der Marxschen Dialektik*, Frankfurt am Main: Suhrkamp.

(1977) *Das individuelle Allgemeine: Textstrukturierung und Interpretation nach Schleiermacher*, Frankfurt am Main: Suhrkamp.

(1979) *Die unendliche Fahrt: ein Motiv und sein Text*, Frankfurt am Main: Surhkamp.

(1980) *Das Sagbare und das Unsagbare: Studien zur neuesten französischen Hermeneutik und Texttheorie*, Frankfurt am Main: Suhrkamp.

(1982) *Der Kommende Gott, Vorlesungen über die neue Mythologie*, Frankfurt am Main: Suhrkamp.

(1983) *Was ist Neostrukturalismus?*, Frankfurt am Main: Suhrkamp.

(1986) *Die Unhintergehbarkeit von Individualität. Reflexionen über Subject, Person und Individuum aus Anlass ihrer 'postmodernen' Toterklarung*, Frankfurt am Main: Suhrkamp.

(1988) *Die Grenzen der Verständigung: ein Geistergespräch zwischen Lyotard und Habermas*, Frankfurt am Main: Suhrkamp.

Secondary literature:
Bowie, Andrew (1990) *Aesthetics and Subjectivity*, Manchester: Manchester University Press.

Ormiston, G. L. and Schrift, A. D. (1990) *Transforming the Hermeneutic Context: From Nietzsche to Nancy*, Albany: State University Press of New York.

For Manfred Frank the meaning of a text neither resides in the intentionality of its author nor is it dispersed into a plurality of different readings. It depends upon the intellectual mobility of the reader, who in collaboration with the text is responsible for the creation of its meaning. Frank's contribution to philosophical and literary hermeneutics consists in his steering a middle course between hermeneutic dogmatism (the unreflected transmission of the received critical canon) and hermeneutic atheism (an unquestioning acceptance of post-structuralist critical orthodoxies). He is as critical of those who defend the *mens auctoris* (Dilthey and Hirsch) as he is of those who advocate either the plurality of the text (Barthes) or the undecidability of its interpretation (Derrida).

Mindful of Nietzsche's axiom that the appearance of something can be accepted as the thing itself, Frank sets out to wrest Schleiermacher's hermeneutics from the established (mis)readings of **Dilthey** and **Gadamer** in order to demonstrate that it can be critically deployed against the hermeneutic nihilism of **Barthes** and **Derrida**. The hermeneutic canon in the form of Schleiermacher is not repeated but reappraised as a means to contemporary critical ends. Using a psychological theory of creative imagination derived from

Sartre and variations of Iser's reception theory, Frank resuscitates Schleiermacher's technical (i.e. psychological) interpretation in order to combat the dehumanizing tendencies of post-structuralist criticism.

His thinking is dominated by the question 'What is a text?' Assuming that writing detaches what is written from the meaning intended by an author, Frank argues that a text is not equivalent to a speech act in which aspects of the world in which it is uttered are revealed, but constitutes with the reader's assistance a literary discourse capable of representing any world independent of authorial intention. The meaningfulness of a text resides in the receptive interpretive act which actualizes it. He contends in the manner of Schleiermacher that 'the hermeneutic operation extends to the psychological side': meaning is not to be divinated in 'author discovered meaning' but in the productivity of the reader's act of personal comprehension.

Following Sartre, Frank suggests that if a reader comprehends a text he does not merely repeat it as a speech act but reshapes the text for himself in an interpretive act which is completely his own. This is no hermeneutic solipsism for it recognizes the objective structures confronted by the reader. It allows the reader to see himself in the otherness of the text or, put in Sartre's words, 'the other in me makes my language, which is my way of being in the other'. This expansion of Schleiermacher's psychological interpretation is subsequently deployed against the hermeneutic nihilism of Derrida and Barthes.

Frank argues that if traditional scholarship has sought to explain the multiplicity of meaning within a text in terms of the fewest structures of signification, Barthes, to the contrary, explodes and multiplies such structures in his notion of the plural text. He diminishes reading as a process of discovering meaning by allowing the alleged 'objectivity' of the text's structures to usurp the role of the interpreting subject. If the plurality of a text's meaning-structures assert themselves independently of the reader, the text is not open to interpretation. For Derrida it is meaning rather than the interpreting subject which is dissolved. Without any foundational anchor in either subject matter or intention, meaning attests to a supposedly infinite text of irreducible mutliplicity. At this juncture, Frank comes into his own.

Resisting the pluralization of both text and meaning, Frank advocates a new model of Schleiermacher's 'technical' (i.e. psychological) interpretation. Combining the argument that meaning always transcends the circumstances of its utterance with Sartre's distinction between regressive analysis and progressive synthesis (the distinction between what literary and discursive structures a text creatively contributes to a literary discourse and what preexistent literary structures a text interpretively embodies) Frank insists that a text calls its interpreter to creative collaboration by reminding us of our ability to interpretively move beyond received structures of meaning, and that we as reading subjects are responsible for actualizing texts as meaningful wholes.

Frank's argument revitalizes the question of style in appraising a philosophical text. His contention that meaning transcends both the circumstances of the written text and the intentions of its author permits a differentiation between the 'subject matter' addressed and the manner of its address. The irreplaceable singularity of an author is exhibited in the style of his or her interpretive rendition of the subject matter. Style lies not in the repetition of expressive modes but in what makes a rendition a unique aesthetic instantiation of a universal (*ein individuelle Allgemeine*).

Frank's assessment of literary meaning and style is not without political importance. Whereas the plural text marginalizes subjectivity with its unquestioning submission to the authority of autonomous literary structures, and the lack of any logical terminus to interpretation deprives hermeneutics of any objective correlative, Frank offers a cooperative model of meaning construction not dissimilar to Gadamer's concept of *Wirkungsgeschichte* (effective history). He reminds us that the freedom to consititute meaning is inseparably bound up with the question of what it is to be human, to take decisions and to act.

Sources: *Kurschners Deutscher Gelehrten-Kalender, 1992*, Berlin: de Gruyter, 1992.

NICHOLAS DAVEY

Frank, Phillip

Austrian, Czech and later American. *b:* 20 March 1884, Vienna. *d:* 21 July 1966, Cambridge, Massachusetts. *Cat:* Logical positivist. *Ints:* Philosophy of science. *Educ:* Universities of Göttingen and Vienna. *Infls:* Mach, Boltzmann and Einstein. *Appts:* 1910–12, Lecuturer in Physics, University of Vienna; 1912–38, Professor of Theoretical Physics, University of Prague; 1938–9, lecturing on quantum theory and the foundations of modern physics at twenty American universities; 1940–66, Half-time Lecturer on Physics and Mathematics, Harvard University.

Main publications:

(1908) 'Kausalgesetz und Erfahrung', *Annalen der Naturphilosophie* 6: 445–50.
(1925) (with R. von Mises) *Die Differential- und Integralgleichungen der Mechanik und Physik*, 2 vols, Brunswick.
(1932) *Das Kausalgesetz und seine Grenzen*, Vienna.
(1941) *Between Physics and Philosophy*, Cambridge, Mass.: Harvard University Press; enlarged and republished as *Modern Science and its Philosophy*, Cambridge, Mass.: Harvard University Press, 1949.
(1950) *Relativity: A Richer Truth*, Boston: Beacon Press.
(1956) (ed.) *The Validation of Scientific Theories: The Link between Science and Philosophy*, Englewood Cliffs, NJ: Prentice-Hall.

Secondary literature:

Cohen, R. S. and Wartofsky, M. W. (eds) (1965) *Boston Studies in the Philosophy of Science II: In Honour of Phillip Frank*, New York: Humanities Press.
Miller, David L. (1959) 'Recent speculations in the positivistic movement', *Review of Metaphysics* 12: 462–74.
Potter, Owen (1951) 'Note on Phillip Frank's interpretation of science', *British Journal for the Philosophy of Science* 2: 58–60.

Frank's first (coauthored) book was a textbook of mathematical physics. But his interest in philosophy of science showed itself in his paper of 1908, in which he extended an idea of Poincaré in suggesting that the law of causality itself was a convention. This paper made a favourable impression on **Einstein**, although he thought its claims exaggerated, and was the beginning of an important association between the two. The paper was later expanded into *Das Kausalgesetz* (1932) and he became Einstein's biographer.

Although one of the founder members of the Vienna Circle, Frank had a liberal view of science and did not share the iconoclasm characteristic of the group. Moreover, his view of philosophy was less narrow. He was, for instance, willing to blur some of the distinctions between philosophy and science. At the same time he was committed to ridding philosophy of its 'traditional ambiguity and obscurity'. He also, for instance in his 1941 book, held that scientists should confine themselves to making statements about experimentally testable facts. Although he was strongly committed to the Unity of Science, this was for him less of a doctrinal position than a commitment to explore the interrelationships between the sciences. He was a major contributor to the *International Encyclopedia of Unified Science* project and was, for many years President of the Philosophy of Science Association. The 1965 Festschrift dedicated to him brought tributes from a number of distinguished philosophers, including W. Van O. Quine.

Sources: DSB; G. Holton *et al.* (1968) 'In memory of Phillip Frank', *PSci* 35: 1–5l; Mittelstrass; *PI*.

STUART BROWN

Frank, Semen Liudvigovich

Russian. *b:* 28 January (16 O.S.) 1877, Moscow. *d:* 10 December 1950, London. *Cat:* Religious philosopher. *Educ:* Studied Law at University of Moscow, 1894–8, and Political Economy and Philosophy at the Universities of Berlin and Munich, 1899–1902. *Infls:* Plotinus, Nicholas of Cusa, Kant, Hegel, Marx, Solov'ev and Lossky. *Appts:* (1912–17), taught philosophy at University of St Petersburg; 1917–21, Professor of Philosophy at the University of Saratov; 1921–2, Professor of Philosophy at University of Moscow; 1930–7, lectured on the History of Russian Culture at the University of Berlin.

Main publications:

(1915) *Predmet znaniia: ob osnovakh i predelakh olvlechennogo znaniia* [The Object of Knowledge: on the Foundations and Limits of Abstract Knowledge]. Petrograd.

(1930) *Dukhovnye osnovy obshchestva: vvedenie v sotsial'noiu filosofiiu*, Paris (English translation, *The Spiritual Foundations of Society: An Introduction to Social Philosophy*, trans. Boris Jakim, Athens: Ohio University Press, 1983).

(1939) *Nepostizhimoe: ontologicheskoe vvedenie v filosofiiu religii*, Paris (English translation, *The Unknowable: An Ontological Introduction to the Philosophy of Religion*, trans. Boris Jakim, Athens: Ohio University Press, 1983).

(1956) *Real'nost' i chelovek: metafizika chelovecheskogo bytiia*, Paris: YMCA-Press (English translation, *Reality and Man: An Essay in the Metaphysics of Human Nature*, trans. Natalie Duddington, London: Faber & Faber, 1965).

Secondary literature:

Lossky, N. O. (1952) *History of Russian Philosophy*, London: George Allen & Unwin, pp. 266–92.

Zenkovsky, V. V. (1953) *A History of Russian Philosophy*, trans. George L. Kline, London: Routledge & Kegan Paul, vol. 2, pp. 852–72.

A 'legal' Marxist from his student days, Frank was arrested and exiled in 1899. At the turn of the century, he joined **Struve**, **Berdyaev** and **Bulgakov** in rejecting Marxism, and, despite his Jewish origins, entered the Russian Orthodox Church in 1912. He contributed to the collections *Problemy idealizma* [Problems of Idealism] (1902) and *Vekhi* [Signposts] (1909), and was among the non-Marxist scholars expelled from the Soviet Union in 1922. He lived in Berlin until 1937, when he was forced to move to France; from 1945, he lived in London.

Frank's religious philosophy was an extension of **Solov'ev**'s critique of Western rationalism and his metaphysics of total-unity and 'Godmanhood'. Frank, following Nicholas of Cusa, envisaged reality (distinguished from the fallen empirical world of actuality) as a transcendent 'metalogical unity'. It is 'unfathomable' by analytical reason alone, but can be directly intuited as mystical or 'living' knowledge (**Lossky** classes Frank along with **Losev** and himself as an 'intuitivist'). He attempted to reconcile an avowedly monistic ontology with Christian dualism through the metalogical, transrational character of his 'antinomic monodualism'. In particular, the existence of evil cannot be rationally explained: its connection with God is 'antinomically transrational'. The mediating role of Sophia or world-soul, so prominent in the writings of **Florensky** and Bulgakov, was rejected by Frank, although he invoked Solov'ev's concept of Godmanhood to capture the groundedness of human beings in the Deity. Frank denied the literal creation of the world out of a hypostatized Nothing (see Berdyaev); the world is eternal in time, but 'created' in its groundedness in the absolute.

COLIN CHANT

Frankena, William Klaus

American. *b:* 21 June 1908, Montana. *d:* October 1994. *Cat:* Moral philosopher; philosopher of education; philosopher of the environment. *Ints:* Theoretical ethics; applied ethics; philosophy of education; philosophy of the environment. *Educ:* 1930, graduated from Calvin College; 1930–3, University of Michigan; 1933–7, Harvard University (studied with C. I. Lewis, R. B. Perry, A. N. Whitehead); 1935–6, University of Cambridge (studied with G. E. Moore, C. D. Broad); 1937, PhD, Harvard University. *Infls:* G. E. Moore, C. D. Broad, R. B. Perry, A. N. Whitehead and C. I. Lewis. *Appts:* 1937, Instructor, University of Michigan; 1947–61, Chair of the Department of Philosophy, Michigan; Visiting Professor at Princeton, Columbia, Harvard and the University of Tokyo; Guggenheim Fellowship; Fellow at the Centre for Advanced Study in Behavioural Sciences; Distinguished Achievement Award, University of Michigan; first Carus Lecturer (1973) in the College of Literature, Science and the Arts, Michigan; 1955–6, President of the American Philosophical Association, Western Division; retired 1977.

Main publications:

(1939) 'The naturalistic fallacy', *Mind*.

(1963) *Ethics*, Englewood Cliffs; second edition, 1973.

(1965) (ed.) *Philosophy of Education*, New York: Macmillan.

(1965) *Three Historical Philosophies of Education*, Chicago: Scott Foresman.

(1966) *Some Beliefs About Justice*, The Lindley Lecture, University of Kansas.

(1973) 'Education', in P. P. Wiener (ed.), *Dictionary of the History of Ideas*, vol. 2, New York: Charles Scribner's Sons.

(1974) *Three Questions About Morality*, The Carus Lectures, La Salle: Open Court.

(1976) *Perspectives on Morality: Essays by William K. Frankena*, ed. K. E. Goodpaster, Notre Dame: University of Notre Dame Press.

(1977) 'Moral philosophy and world hunger', in W. Aiken and H. La Follette (eds), *World Hunger and Moral Obligation*, Englewood Cliffs: Prentice Hall.

(1978) 'G. H. von Wright on the nature of morality', in Paul Schilpp (ed.), *The Philosophy of G. H. von Wright*, La Salle: Open Court.

(1980) *Thinking About Morality*, Ann Arbor: University of Michigan Press.

(1983) 'The ethics of right reason', *The Monist* 66: 3–25.

Secondary literature:

Brandt, Richard B. (1981) 'W. Frankena and ethics of virtue', *The Monist* 64: 271–92.

Foot, Philippa (1981) 'William Frankena's Carus Lectures', *The Monist* 64: 305–12.

Goldman, Alvin I. and Kim, Jaegwon (eds) (1978) *Values and Morals: Essays in Honour of William Frankena, Charles Stevenson and Richard Brandt*, Dordrecht: D. Reidel.

Warnock, G. J. (1985) 'Comments on Frankena's three questions', *The Monist* 63: 85–92.

Frankena had a distinguished career as a gifted teacher and as a philosopher working in the mainstream of twentieth-century moral philosophy. Probably his most influential work has been in the history of moral philosophy and, more generally, through his capacity for analysing and drawing distinctions between important moral concepts such as 'deontological' and 'teleological', 'internalist' and 'externalist', etc. This capacity is equally evident in his writing on environmental ethics, where he distinguishes between types of environmental theories and argues for an ethics of the environment that recognizes right and wrong ways of treating beings other than persons that are conscious and sentient. His 1939 paper is a justly famous analysis of the logical and semantic problems attendant on accusations made by G. E. **Moore** and others concerning the committing by ethical naturalists of the naturalistic fallacy.

In his own treatment of the philosophical problems of ethics Frankena argues for a Humean type of ethical objectivity and for an Aristotelian orientation with regard to the virtues. He maintains that to take the moral point of view is to make normative judgements, to be willing to universalize one's judgements, and to found those judgements on facts about what is good and evil for sentient beings (see *Ethics*, 1963, p. 113). 'Morality', he wrote, 'is made for man, not man for morality' (ibid. p. 116).

Sources: *PI*; DAS: Stephen L. Darwall (1982), review of *Thinking About Morality* (1980), in *PR*, 91, 3, Jul 1982.

DIANÉ COLLINSON

Frankfurt, Harry Gordon

American. *b:* 29 May 1929, Langhorne, Pennsylvania. *Cat:* Metaphysician; philosopher of action. *Ints:* History of philosophy; ethics. *Educ:* Johns Hopkins University and Cornell University. *Infls:* Descartes and Russell. *Appts:* 1956–62, Instructor then Assistant Professor of Philosophy, Ohio State University; 1962–3, Associate Professor, Harper College; 1963–76, Research Associate, Associate Professor, then full Professor, Rockefeller University; 1976–90, Professor of Philosophy, Yale University; 1900–, Professor of Philosophy, Princeton University.

Main publications:

(1969) 'Alternate possibilities and moral responsibility', *Journal of Philosophy* 66: 829–39.

(1970) *Demons, Dreamers and Madmen*, Indianapolis: Bobbs Merrill.

(1971) 'Freedom of the will and the concept of a person', *Journal of Philosophy* 67: 5–20.

(1972) (ed.) *Leibniz*, New York: Anchor.

(1988) *The Importance of What We Care About* (collected essays), Cambridge: Cambridge University Press.

(1991) 'The faintest passion', Presidential Address, Eastern Division, American Philosophical Association.

(1993) 'On God's creation', in Eleonore Stump (ed.), *Reasoned Faith*, Ithaca, NY: Cornell University Press.

(1993) 'On the necessity of ideals', in G. Noam and T. Wren. (ed.), *The Moral Self*, Cambridge, Mass.: MIT Press.

Secondary literature:

Synthese 53: 257–321, 1982.

Apart from his contribution to Cartesian scholarship, Harry Frankfurt's philosophical work has centred on a sustained and original approach to a number of related issues in metaphysics and the philosophy of action, involving the concepts of the human person, free will, moral responsibility, coercion and caring. His contribution has, for many, changed the terms of the debate on free will and moral responsibility. Against a long tradition Frankfurt denies what he calls the Principle of Alternate Possibilities. The impossibility of being able to act otherwise than one did does not of itself impugn free will or responsibility, for the unavailability of alternatives might play no part in (explaining) someone's action. Free will, and indeed personhood, requires, for Frankfurt, the presence of second-order volitions, a species of second-order desires, where a person desires that some first-order desire be effective in action. A creature lacking these second-order volitions is aptly described by Frankfurt as a wanton.

In his book on Descartes Frankfurt advanced the provocative thesis that Descartes's aim in the *Meditations* is not truth, but the lesser aim of coherence or incorrigibility.

Sources: DAS, 4, 1982; CA FR, 41–4; IWW, 57th edn, 1993–4; brief telephone conversation, Clive Borst.

STUART BROWN

Fraser, A(lexander) Campbell

British. *b:* 8 September 1819, Ardchattan, Argyll, Scotland. *d:* 2 December 1914, Edinburgh. *Cat:* Berkeleyan 'spiritual realist'. *Ints:* History of philosophy; philosophy of religion. *Educ:* Edinburgh University. *Infls:* Personal influences include Sir William Hamilton and Thomas Chalmers. *Appts:* 1846–56, Professor of Logic at New College, Edinburgh; 1856–91, Professor of Logic and Metaphysics at Edinburgh.

Main publications:

(1881) *Berkeley*, Edinburgh and London: William Blackwood & Sons.

(1890) *Locke*, Edinburgh and London: William Blackwood & Sons.

(1894–6) *The Philosophy of Theism*, Gifford Lectures, 2 vols, Edinburgh and London: William Blackwood & Sons.

(1908) *Berkeley and Spiritual Realism*, London: Archibald Constable.

(1910) *Selections from Berkeley*, sixth edition, Oxford: Clarendon Press.

Secondary literature:

Pringle-Pattison, A. S. (1915) Memoir in *Proceedings of the British Academy* 6 and *Mind*.

Fraser was at one time a minister in the Scottish Free Church and, although glad to escape from ecclesiastical strife into academic life, he was originally barred from appointment to one of the main Scottish Chairs by the rigid enforcement until the 1860s of a test that bound these Chairs to the Church of Scotland. One of his philosophical concerns was to defend a philosophical theism as 'the true *via media* between atheism and pantheism' (1905, p. 321). Middle ways seem indeed to have been a hallmark of Fraser's style of philosophizing. He sought, in his 'spiritual realism', to steer a middle course between the agnostic scientific naturalism of J. S. Mill, Herbert Spencer and others and the absolute idealism of Hegel and his admirers in Oxford and Glasgow. He was an inheritor of the Scottish common sense school and his own philosophy is interconnected with his interpretation of Berkeley. His 1905 account of Berkeley contains, as A. Seth **Pringle-Pattison** acknowledged, 'at least as much of his own maturer way of putting things as of his favourite philosopher' (Pringle-Pattison 1915, p. 537). Fraser took Berkeley seriously as a common sense philosopher. He was a self-styled 'realist', reluctant to call his or Berkeley's philosophy 'idealist' because each seemed to him quite opposed to the Hegelian idealist view that explained 'the concrete things of sense and their motions by abstract Reason' (1910, p. xlvii). He agreed with Berkeley in taking the 'concrete things of sense' as a starting-point and took himself to have 'expanded Berkeley's divine language of vision into a universal sense-symbolism' 1905, p. 188). Fraser played an important role in the revival of interest in Berkeley's philosophy in the early twentieth century. His editions became the standard ones until superseded in the 1930s by that of **Luce** and Jessop. His annotated *Selections*

from Berkeley was extensively used as a textbook, achieving (according to Fraser himself) sales of 10,000 copies by 1908. In his annotations Fraser presented his 'spiritual realism'. But it was as an editor that Fraser made his most important contribution.
Sources: DNB; A. C. Fraser (1904) *Biographia Philosophica*, Edinburgh and London: Wm Blackwood & Sons.

STUART BROWN

Frege, Friedrich Ludwig Gottlob

German. *b:* 1848, Weimar, Germany. *d:* 1925, Bad Kleinen, Germany. *Cat:* Logicist; Platonist philosopher of mathematics; analytic philosopher. *Ints:* The epistemological foundations and ontology of number theory. *Educ:* Universities of Jena (1869–70) and Göttingen (1871–3); doctorate in Mathematics. *Appts:* 1874–1918, Lecturer, Assistant Professor, then Honorary Ordinary Professor of Mathematics at the University of Jena.

Main publications:

(1879) *Begriffsschrift, eine der arithmetischen nach-gebildete Formelsprache des reinen Denkens*, Halle (English translation in J. van Heijenoort (ed.), *Source Book in Mathematical Logic*, Harvard University Press, 1967; and in *Gottlob Frege: Conceptual Notation and Related Articles*, Terrell Ward Bynum, Oxford: Oxford University Press, 1972).
(1884) *Die Grundlagen der Arithmetik, ein logisch-mathematische Untersuchung über den Begriff der Zahl*, Breslau (reprinted with English translation in *The Foundations of Arithmetic: A Logico-mathematical Enquiry into the Concept of Number*, J. L. Austin, Oxford: Oxford University Press, 1953).
(1891) 'Funktion und Begriff', an Address given to the Jenaische Gesellschaft für Medicin und Naturwissenschaft, 9 January 1891 (English translation in *Translations from the Philosophical Writings of Gottlob Frege*, ed. and trans. P. Geach and M. Black, Oxford: Oxford University Press, 1980).
(1892) 'Über Sinn und Bedeutung', *Zeitschrift für Philosophie und philosophische Kritik* 100 (English translation in *Translations from the Philosophical Writings of Gottlob Frege*, ed. and trans. P. Geach and M. Black, Oxford: Oxford University Press, 1980).
(1893) *Grundgesetze der Arithmetik, Begriffsschriftlich abgeleitet Bd. I*, Jena (English translation of Preface, Introduction and Part 1 in *The Basic Laws of Arithmetic*, trans. and ed. with an introduction by Montgomery Furth, Berkeley and Los Angeles: University of California, 1964).

(1903) *Grundgesetze der Arithmetik, Begriffsschriftlich abgeleitet Bd. II*, Jena (English translation of extracts in *Translations from the Philosophical Writings of Gottlob Frege*, ed. and trans. P. Geach and M. Black, Oxford: Oxford University Press, 1980).
(1918) 'Der Gedanke: eine logische Untersuchung', *Beiträge zur Philosophie des deutschen Idealismus* 1 (English translation in P. F. Strawson (ed.), *Philosophical Logic*, Oxford: Oxford University Press, 1967).
(1979) *Posthumous Writings*, ed. H. Hermes, F. Kambartel and F. Kaulbach, trans. P. Long and R. White, Oxford: Blackwell 1979).

Secondary literature:

Baker, G. P. and Hacker, P. M. S. (1984) *Frege: Logical Investigations*, Oxford: Basil Blackwell.
Bell, D. (1979) *Frege's Theory of Judgement*, Oxford: Clarendon Press.
Benacerraf, P. (1981) 'Frege: the last logicist', in P. French *et al.* (eds), *Midwest Studies in Philosophy VI*, Minneapolis: Minneapolis University Press.
Currie, G. (1982) *Frege: An Introduction to his Philosophy*, Brighton: Harvester.
Dummett, M. A. E. (1981) *Frege: The Philosophy of Language*, London: Duckworth.
——(1982) *The Interpretation of Frege's Philosophy*, London: Duckworth.
——(1991) *Frege: Philosophy of Mathematics*, London: Duckworth.
Mind (1992) 101, 404, October (issue to honour the publication in 1892 of Gottlob Frege's 'Über Sinn und Bedeutung').
Resnik, M. (1980) *Frege and the Philosophy of Mathematics*, Ithaca, NY: McGraw-Hill.
Schirn, Mathias (ed.) (1976) *Studien zu Frege*, 3 vols, Stuttgart-Bad Canstatt.
Sluga, H. (1980) *Gottlob Frege*, London: Routledge & Kegan Paul.
Wright, C. J. G. (1983) *Frege's Conception of Numbers as Objects*, Aberdeen: Aberdeen University Press.
Wright, Crispin (ed.) (1984) *Frege: Tradition and Influence*, Oxford: Basil Blackwell.

Frege was influenced by the technical development of number theory in the nineteenth century combined with, as it seemed to him, the 'scandalous' state of its foundations. He set himself the task of giving epistemologically secure foundations for number theory and a proper delineation of its subject matter. Frege rejected, in particular, attempts to ground mathematics in human psychology. He also rejected attempts, like that of John Stuart Mill, to construe number theory as an empirical science. Further, he rejected attempts to portray mathematics as a subject without a subject matter: that is, as the formal manipulation of empty signs with no intrinsic meaning. He took number theory to be the study of the necessary relations between numbers, and he took numbers to be mind-independent abstract objects. This view is known as Platonism after Plato's own similar view. Frege conceived his task as one of setting out precise and self-evident truths of pure logic in terms of which numerical concepts could be defined, and from which the accepted theorems of number theory could be rigorously deduced. This programme is known as logicism, the grounding of number theory in pure logic. In the course of this enterprise Frege made three momentous contributions to philosophy.

First, he developed a radically new way of treating quantifiers in logic. Quantifiers are expressions like 'something', 'all' and 'everything' which can fill the gap in predicates like '—is red' to form sentences which are true or false—for example, 'Something is red', 'Everything is red'. Frege's technique enables us to see a complex expression like '—is red and—is round' as a unitary predicate, from a logical point of view if not from a grammatical point of view. There is no limit to the complexity of predicates which quantifiers can turn into sentences, for example, 'if — is red then all bulls hate —' is a predicate in Frege's logic, and one which itself embeds the quantifier 'all'. Frege deployed his quantifiers in a novel formal language of his own, the first semantically precise language in which logic and set theory could be rigorously formulated.

Frege's discovery was the most important breakthrough in logic since Aristotle had founded the subject some two millennia before. It provided the first successful treatment of relations, and made possible the explosive development of logic in this century. The development of the theory of proofs, in particular the work of Alfred **Tarski** and Kurt **Gödel**, stems directly from Frege's pioneering work. The logic which Frege invented is now so widely accepted that it is taught as a standard toolkit without attribution to its inventor, like elementary mathematics itself. However some, notably **Brouwer**, **Heyting** and perhaps **Dummett**, accept Frege's formal language but not all of the logic he used it to express.

Second, Frege used his formal language to present, in his *Grundgesetze der Arithmetik Band I*, the first system of axioms and definitions of what we would now call logic and set theory, and he commenced the rigorous deduction of the accepted truths of number theory from those axioms and definitions. This was a programme he intended to continue in volume II. But it was a spectacular failure, since, while the second volume was in press, Bertrand Russell showed that Frege's axioms allowed the rigorous deduction of a contradiction, known to subsequent generations as Russell's Paradox. Frege did not find a way of recasting his axioms which satisfied him, and his private papers show he eventually abandoned logicism, coming round to the view that number theory cannot after all be deduced from the necessary truths of pure logic. The trouble lay not in Frege's logical axioms but in his axioms of set theory. Those axioms combine the view that every predicate can be used to define a set, *viz.* the set of objects of which that predicate is true, and the view that every predicate must be true or false of every object there is. So Russell took the predicate '— is not a member of itself' and defined the set of things which are not members of themselves, and he then asked whether the predicate is true or false of that very set. It's easy to see that if it is then it isn't, and if it isn't then it is, which is paradoxical.

Frege had formulated what we would now call Naive Set Theory. However, it is 'naive' only in the sense that to hold such a set theory is naive given Frege's rigorous formulation of it and Russell's exploitation of that rigorous formulation to develop his paradox. Prior to these developments Naive Set Theory had been the intuitively appealing set theory. Frege's contribution here was to produce a rigorous formulation of Naive Set Theory whose rigour Russell could exploit to develop his paradox, thus, between them, ending an age of innocence and prompting the modern development of set theories.

Frege's Platonism has fared better. His basic idea is generally accepted—*viz.* that once a theory is adequately formulated in Frege's formal language, and supposing the theory is true, then its ontological commitment, whether Platonic or not, can be read off from its syntax. This approach is common to, for example, Crispin **Wright**, who has defended Platonism, and to W. V. O. **Quine** and Nelson **Goodman**, who oppose Platonism by seeking to reformulate number theory in a way which eliminates or minimizes its commitment to abstract objects. It is shared also by Hartry Field, but leads him to conclude that number theory is not true but a useful fiction.

Frege's third great contribution was his theory of meaning. Frege needed a theory of meaning to show that his novel formal language, unlike our natural languages, is ontologically perspicuous. The key notions he used were sense and reference (*Sinn* and *Bedeutung*). Roughly, the sense of an expression is what a mind grasps, and sense mediates the connection between mind and the worldly entity (the referent) which the expression is about. More precisely, the sense of an expression (i) is grasped by a mind, but (ii) is not a psychological entity, since two minds may grasp the very same sense. Further, (iii) sense connects an expression with its referent in the world— Frege calls sense 'the mode of presentation of the referent'. Finally, (iv) the sense of an expression contributes to the truth-conditions of sentences in which that expression occurs. To grasp the sense of a sentence involves knowing its truth-conditions.

On the other hand, the referent of an expression is (i) its semantic role: that is, what that expression contributes to determining the truth-values of sentences in which it occurs. It follows that *all* categories of expression have referents— predicates, logical constants, whole clauses, as well as noun phrases. But (ii) Frege also thinks of reference as analogous to the relation between a name and its bearer. So the world contains, he thinks, entities corresponding to predicates, logical constants and whole clauses, as it contains objects corresponding to noun phrases. These additional entities are concepts, truth-functions and truth-values, respectively.

This theory of Frege's has been immensely influential. Wittgenstein radically reworked it in his *Tractatus*, and rejected it root and branch in his *Philosophical Investigations*. **Davidson** claims a Fregean pedigree for his influential blueprint for a theory of meaning, and Dummett criticizes Davidson from a Fregean point of view.

Frege's entire career was passed quietly at the University of Jena, where he was well thought of. But, to his disappointment, his work did not attract much interest in his own lifetime. However, there were illustrious exceptions: **Peano**, **Husserl**, **Russell**, **Wittgenstein** and **Carnap** all studied Frege. His posthumous recognition and his influence upon analytic philosophy have been enormous.

Sources: M. A. E. Dummett (1982) *The Interpretation of Frege's Philosophy*, London: Duckworth (with bibliography); Terrell Ward Bynum (1993) *Gottlob Frege: Conceptual Notation and Related Articles*, Oxford: OUP (with bibliography).

JIM EDWARDS

Freud, Sigmund

Austrian. *b:* 1856, Freiberg, Moravia (now Pribor, Czechoslovakia). *d:* 1939, London. *Cat:* Psychoanalyst. *Ints:* The unconscious; hysteria and other disorders of mind; dreams; culture and religion. *Educ:* Medical Faculty, University of Vienna. *Infls:* Brentano, Charcot, Breuer and Brücke. *Appts:* Practised psychoanalytic therapy from his home in Vienna until forced to flee to London by Nazi persecution fifteen months before his death.

Main publications:

Collected works available in English translation in *The Standard Edition of the Complete Psychological Works of Sigmund Freud*, ed. James Strachey in collaboration with Anna Freud, 24 vols, London: Hogarth Press, 1953–1964. Many works are also reproduced in the *Pelican Freud Library*, 15 vols, trans. James Strachey, ed. Angela Richards, Hogarth Press, 1973–86. Volume numbers for the Standard Edition are shown below in round brackets, and for the Pelican edition in square brackets.

(1895) *The Origins of Psycho-Analysis* (1); with *A Project for a Scientific Psychology*, London: Hogarth Press, 1954.
(1895) (with Joseph Breuer) *Studies on Hysteria* (2) [3].
(1900) *The Interpretation of Dreams* (4–5) [4].
(1901) *The Psychopathology of Everyday Life* (6) [5].
(1905) *Three Essays on the Theory of Sexuality* (7) [7].
(1905) *Humour and its Relation to the Unconscious* (8) [6].
(1908) *Character and Anal Eroticism* (9).
(1909) *Analysis of a Phobia in a Five-year-old Boy* ('Little Hans') (10) [8].
(1909) *Notes upon a Case of Obsessional Neurosis* ('The Ratman') (10) [9].
(1912) *A Note on the Unconscious in Psychoanalysis* (12) [11].
(1912–13) *Totem and Tabu* (13) [13].
(1915) *Repression* (14) [11].
(1915) *The Unconscious* (14) [11].
(1916–17) *Introductory Lectures on Psychoanalysis* (15–16) [1].
(1917) *Mourning and Melancholia* (14) [11].
(1918) *From the History of an Infantile Neurosis* ('The Wolfman') (17) [9].
(1920) *Beyond the Pleasure Principle* (18) [11].
(1923) *The Ego and the Id* (19) [11].
(1923) *Remarks on the Theory and Practice of Dream-Interpretation* (19).
(1924) *Neurosis and Psychosis* (19) [10].
(1925) *An Autobiographical Study* (20) [15].
(1925) *The Resistances to Psychoanalysis* (19) [15].
(1926) *Inhibitions, Symptoms and Anxiety* (20) [10].
(1927) *The Future of an Illusion*, Vienna: International Psychoanaltischer Verlag.
(1930) *Civilisation and its Discontents* (21) [12].

(1933) *New Introductory Lectures on Psychoanalysis* (22) [2].

(1936) *The Problem of Anxiety*, New York: Psychoanalytic Quarterly Press.

(1937) *Analysis Terminable and Interminable* (23).

(1939) *Moses and Monotheism: Three Essays* (23) [13].

(1940) *An Outline of Psychoanalysis* (23) [15].

(1940) *Splitting of the Ego in the Process of Defence* (23) [11].

Secondary literature:

Clark, P. and Wright, C. (eds) (1988) *Mind, Psychoanalysis and Science*, Oxford: Oxford University Press.

Farrell, B. A. (1981) *The Standing of Psychoanalysis*, Oxford and New York: Oxford University Press.

Freud, Ernst L. (ed.) (1961) *Letters of Sigmund Freud: 1873–1939*, London: Hogarth.

Frosh, S. (1987) *The Politics of Psychoanalysis: An Introduction to Freudian and Post-Freudian Theory*, London: The Macmillan Press.

Gardner, S. (1993) *Irrationality and the Philosophy of Psychoanalysis*, Cambridge: Cambridge University Press.

Grünbaum, A. (1984) *The Foundations of Psychoanalysis: A Philosophical Critique*, Berkeley: Berkeley University Press.

Jones, E. (1961) *The Life and Work of Sigmund Freud*, New York: Basic Books; London: Penguin, 1964.

Kline, P. (1981) *Fact and Fantasy in Freudian Theory*, second edition, London and New York: Methuen.

Lacan, J. (1973) *The Four Fundamental Concepts of Psychoanalysis*, London: Penguin.

McGuire, W. (ed.) (1974) *The Freud-Jung Letters*, London: Hogarth; Princeton, NJ: Princeton University Press.

MacIntyre, A. C. (1958) *The Unconscious: A Conceptual Analysis*, London: Routledge & Kegan Paul.

Ricoeur, P. (1970) *Freud and Philosophy*, New Haven and London: Yale University Press.

Robinson, D. N. (1984) 'Psychobiology and the unconscious', in K. S. Bowers and D. Meichenbaum (eds), *The Unconscious Reconsidered*, New York: John Wiley & Sons.

Storr, A. (1989) *Freud*, Oxford: Oxford University Press.

Wilkes, K. V. (1988) 'Freud's metapsychology', *Proceedings of the Aristotelian Society*, 62: 117–37.

Wollheim, R. and Hopkins, J. (eds) (1982) *Philosophical Essays on Freud*, Cambridge: Cambridge University Press.

Freud is widely acknowledged as the founder of the psychological theory and form of therapy known as psychoanalysis. An exceptional student, his early interests were mainly literary, especially the Greek and Latin classics, but by the time he left school he had become interested in the sciences. He did neuroanatomical research in Ernst Brücke's laboratories and attended Franz **Brentano**'s lectures on the object-relatedness of mental processes. Unable to make a living as a researcher, he qualified as a doctor and obtained a travelling scholarship which enabled him to study under the eminent psychiatrist Jean-Martin Charcot in Paris. It was here that he first became interested in psychological disorders through Charcot's work on hysteria. Returning to Vienna, he collaborated with Joseph Breuer, treating hysterics by hypnosis. Many of the essential features of his psychoanalytic theory emerged from this work, although he continued to develop and elaborate his ideas throughout his long life. He had a large family. His youngest daughter, Anna, became a distinguished psychoanalyst.

The central innovation of Freudian theory is a radical extension of the range of human behaviour and experience which can be understood in intentional rather than causal terms. The second half of the nineteenth century had seen an explosion of knowledge of neuroanatomy and of the relationship between brain pathology and symptomatology. Freud himself contributed to this with important research on aphasia. Through his work with Charcot and Breuer he came to see that at least in the case of hysteria, physical symptoms (including aphasia) should be understood primarily not in terms of brain pathology but as a product of motives, wishes and desires of which the patient was not consciously aware. This was not a dualistic view. In his early work in particular (notably in the *Project for a Scientific Psychology* of 1895) Freud maintained that psychological theories could in principle be reduced to neuroanatomy. But he believed that in the current state of scientific knowledge it was in terms of unconscious motivational structures rather than of brain functioning that hysterical symptoms, and by extension a range of other psychological disorders, were best understood.

Freud's account of hysterical disorders illustrates many of the main features of psychoanalysis. Typically, the patient has suffered an experience, often within a significant personal relationship, which is so traumatic that the memory of it has become repressed from consciousness. However, as a defence this is only partially successful, since the trauma reappears later in the form of a physical symptom. Freud is likely to have been much influenced at this point by the conservationist physics of the time, his theory indeed having a strongly 'hydrodynamic' flavour. Consistently, then, treatment involves releasing the energy of the repressed trauma back into the conscious mind, either by hypnosis or, in Freud's later work, through free association, the interpretation of dreams (the manifest content of which is taken to be a coded representation of unconscious wishes and fantasies), and the reawakening of traumatic emotions by 'projection' on to the analyst within the safe confines of the therapeutic relationship.

Freud and Breuer published their joint *Studies on Hysteria* in 1895, but Freud's increasing emphasis on the essentially sexual nature of repressed material (and a general reluctance on Breuer's part to engage in theorizing) led to a split between them. By the turn of the century Freud had come to believe that sexuality was the motivating force behind all mental processes. The libido, as the main component of the instinctive structures of the id, had the function of driving the organism towards the primary goals of survival, pleasure and the avoidance of pain. (He was later to add a death wish, or thanatos.) The libidinous impulses were constantly checked by the demands and constraints of society which, especially as an internalized representation of the child's parents, became the superego. Early infantile conflicts between the id and the superego produced the Oedipus complex (the boy child's desire to kill his father and replace him in his mother's affections) and the corresponding Electra complex (in the girl child). It was the function of the ego (roughly, the self-aware 'I') to resolve these conflicts by negotiating between the drives of the id and the demands of the superego within the dictates of external reality.

Combined with a theory of child development, Freud's model leads to a number of specific hypotheses about different kinds of mental disorder. Thus the gratification of the libidinous drive is perceived as progressing through a number of stages, oral, anal and genital. Failure to progress may then result in neurotic symptoms: for instance, obsessional disorder arises from developmental arrest at the anal stage. At the other end of the scale the model leads to larger claims about aspects of normal experience. Freud regarded religion, for example, as an attempt to remain at an infantile stage of emotional development by projecting the wish for a perfect father on to a heavenly figure. Similarly, creativity in the arts and sciences arises from the sublimation of a libidinous drive partially repressed by the demands of society.

Although it is not a philosophical theory, psychoanalysis has stimulated considerable philosophical debate, in particular in the philosophy of science, the philosophy of mind and ethics. As a 'theory of everything', it has often been criticized as unscientific. In the 'interpretations' of psychoanalytic therapy, for example, there are no clear criteria to differentiate between denial and disproof. On the other hand, some of Freud's empirical claims have now been disproved (for example, the universal 'penis envy' of female sexual development) and, as **Wilkes** (1988) has pointed out, much philosophical discussion of the scientific status of psychoanalysis has assumed criteria by which even physics would not be a science.

Less obvious, but perhaps more fruitful, is the significance of Freud's postulated unconscious motivational structures for our understanding of the nature of rational behaviour. It is often assumed that rational reflection is essentially conscious in nature and so provides an unambiguous criterion for differentiating reasons from causes. But Freudian theory (whether or not correct in detail) undermines this assumption by showing the possibility of a coherent notion of an unconscious reason.

Third, and least discussed, is the significance of Freudian theory for ethics. The traditional claim has been that freedom of the will, as an essential prerequisite for responsible action, depends on conscious intentions. But Freud's theory seeks to show that the sources of an intention are often inaccessible to conscious reflection, at least by ordinary introspection, thus reinforcing a picture of human action as essentially deterministic and, hence, amoral. During Freud's lifetime the psychoanalytic movement became fractured into a number of different schools: Adlerian, Jungian, Kleinian and so on. In recent years there has been something of what Storr (1989) has called an 'armed truce'. But Freud's central contribution—a recognition of the primary importance of unconscious mental processes in human behaviour and experience—has become so much part of our thinking that it now goes largely unremarked.

Sources: Reese; Edwards; Harré & Lamb; Goldenson; UCDCL.

K. W. M. FULFORD

Frolov, Ivan Timofeevich

Russian. *b:* 1 September 1929, Lipetsk province,

Russia. *Cat:* Marxist philosopher of science; editor; public figure. *Ints:* Philosophy of biology; philosophical anthropology. *Educ:* Moscow State University. *Appts:* Editor-in-chief, *Voprosy filosofi* [Problems of Philosophy], 1968–77; editor-in-chief, *Kommunist*, 1986–7; personal adviser to Gorbachev, 1987–9; editor-in-chief, *Pravda*, 1989–91; member of Poltiburo, Communist Party, 1990; President Russian Philosophical Society, 1991–; Director, Russian Academy of Sciences' Centre for the Human Sciences, 1991–.

Main publications:

(1961) *O prichinnosti i tselesoobraznosti v zhivoi prirode* [On Causality and Purposefulnes in Animate Nature], Moscow.

(1965) *Ocherki metodologii biologicheskogo issledovaniia* [Essays on the Methodology of Biological Research], Moscow.

(1967) *Metodologicheskie problemy genetiki* [Methodological Problems of Genetics], Moscow.

(1968) *Genetika i dialektika* [Genetics and Dialectics], Moscow.

(1972) (with S. A. Pastushnyi) *Mendel', mendelizm, i dialektika* [Mendel, Mendelism and Dialectics], Moscow.

(1975) *Progress nauki i budushchee cheloveka* [The Progress of Science and the Future of Man], Moscow.

(1976) (with S. A. Pastushnyi) *Mendelizm i filosofskie problemy sovremennoi genetiki* [Mendelism and the Philosophical Problems of Contemporary Genetics], Moscow.

(1979) *Perespektivv cheloveka* [The Prospects for Man], Moscow.

(1982) *Global Problems and the Future of Mankind*, Moscow.

(1982) *Chelovek, nauka, gumanizm–novyi sintez*, Moscow (English translation, *Man–Science–Humanism: A New Synthesis*, 1986).

(1988) *Filosofiia i istoriia genetiki* [Philosophy and the History of Genetics], Moscow.

(1990) (principal editor) *Vvedenie v filosofii* [Introduction to Philospohy], Moscow.

Secondary literature:

Frolov, I. T. (1990–1) 'Life and cognition', *Soviet Studies in Philosophy*, Winter, pp. 6–27 (autobiographical essay).

Graham, Loren R. (1987) *Science and Philosophy in the Soviet Union*, New York: Alfred A. Knopf; revised edition, *Science, Philosophy, and Human Behavior in the Soviet Union*, Columbia University Press, 1987.

Although Frolov taught philosophy for some years University of Moscow and was named an Academician in 1987, his chief prominence has been as a prolific writer on controversial topics in the philosophy of science, especially genetics, and as editor of influential mass-circulation publications during the Soviet era.

In his early writings Frolov defended neo-Mendelian theories of heredity against the attacks of Lysenko, drawing much criticism from Marxist-Leninist dogmatists. His anti-Lysenko position was expressed in bowdlerized fashion in his 1961 book and more fully in his book *Genetika i dialektika* (1968), in which he explicitly rejected the concept of 'Party science' and sought to construct a nonreductionistic Marxist philosophy of biology consistent with modern advances in the sciences. Further studies in 1972 and 1976 continued this interest in genetics, and his 1988 book contains a retrospective view of the Lysenko controversy in science and philosophy. In his other books of the 1970s and 1980s, Frolov shifted his attention to questions of philosophical anthropology, calling in *Man–Science–Humanism* (1982) for the development of a Marxist science of man in the service of 'communist humanism'.

From 1968 to 1977 Frolov served as editor-in-chief of the Soviet Union's principal philosophy journal, *Voprosy filosofii*, and subsequently he assumed editorship of the authoritative one-volume dictionary of philosophy, *Filosofskii slovar'* (fourth edition, 1980). Under Gorbachev, Frolov was the Soviet Union's most highly placed philosopher, being named to a succession of exceptionally influential positions: editor-in-chief of the Communist Party's principal theoretical organ, *Kommunist*; personal adviser to Gorbachev in the area of ideology; editor-in-chief of the Communist Party newspaper *Pravda*; and member of the Politburo of the Communist Party. In August 1991, however, *Pravda* supported the coup attempt against Gorbachev, and the newspaper was closed shortly thereafter. When it was subsequently reorganized as a non-party publication, the newspaper's staff deposed Frolov as editor. Since 1991 he has served as President of the Russian Philosophical Society and addressed himself to the analysis of global problems.

JAMES SCANLAN

Frondizi, Risieri
Argentinian. *b:* 1910, Posadas, Argentina. *d:* 23 February 1983, Waco, Texas. *Cat:* Philosopher of value. *Ints:* Ethics; philosophy of liberation;

anthropology. *Educ:* Educated in Buenos Aires; postgraduate work at Harvard University under a scholarship from the Institute of International Education at New York, and at the University of Michigan. *Infls:* Romero. *Appts:* Taught Logic, Aesthetics and the History of Philosophy, University of Tucumán, 1938–; Dean of the Faculty of Philosophy and Letters, University of Buenos Aires; two terms as President, 1957–; taught at Yale, Texas, UCLA, Pennsylvania, Baylor and Southern Illinois.

Main publications:
(1943) 'Tendencies in contemporary Latin American philosophy', *Inter-American Intellectual Cultural Exchange*, Austin, Texas: Institute of Latin American Studies.
(1945) *El punto de partida del filosofar*, Buenos Aires: Losada.
(1948) *¿Qué es la filosofía?*, Guatemala: Imprenta Universitaria.
(1953) *The Nature of the Self: A Functional Interpretation*, New Haven: Yale University Press.
(1963) *What is Value? An Introduction to Axiology*, trans. Solomon Lipp, La Salle, Ill.: Open Court.
(1977) *Introducción a los problemas fundamentales del hombre*, Madrid: Fondo de Cultura Económica.

Secondary literature:
Gracia, Jorge J. E. (ed.) (1980) *Man and His Conduct: Essays in Honor of Risieri Frondizi*, San Juan: University of Puerto Rico Press.
——(ed.) (1986) *Risieri Frondizi: Ensayos filosóficos*, Mexico: Fondo de Cultura Económica.

Frondizi's thought was influenced by that of Francisco **Romero**, under whom he studied. In *Introducción a los problemas fundamentales del hombre* (1977) Frondizi was primarily concerned with philosophical anthropology, ethics and liberty. In addition to his administrative work in Argentina he was instrumental in the development of philosophy departments in Venezuela and Puerto Rico.

AMY A. OLIVER

Fuad, Zakariyya
Egyptian. *b:* 1927, Port Said, Egypt. *Cat:* Theoretical philosopher. *Ints:* Western philosophical tradition. *Appts:* Taught at the University of Ain Shams in Cairo; then at the Department of Philosophy in the University of Kuwait (1987); member of the editorial staff of the magazine *al-Fikr al-Muasir* [Contemporary Thought] in which he published several philosophical studies.

Main publications:
(1991) *Laicité ou Islamisme*, Paris: La Découverte, Cairo: Al-Fikr.

Secondary literature:
M. Chartier (1973) 'La Rencontre Orient–Occident dans la pensée de trois philosophes egyptiens contemporains: Hassan Hanafi, Fu'ad Zakkariya, Zaki Nagib Mahmud'in *Oriente Moderno* 53: 605-42

Fuad Zakariyya first sought to understand the meaning of Arab and Islamic thought in comparison with the Western philosophical tradition. He showed sympathy for socialism, but criticized the doctrinal weaknesses of Marxism. Standing aside from any kind of extremism he exalted the role of reason in interpreting and understanding the world and in contending with intellectual underdevelopment. Subsequently Zakariyya's reliance on reason widened to a more inclusive critical perspective, that of secularism. In his view the problem of secularism is the problem of the adaptation of the Arab and Islamic world to the challenges of modernity. Postmodernism is far from a reality in the Arab world of the late twentieth century because the process of modernization there is not yet complete. Zakariyya stresses the universal values of secularism. He does not reject the Arab-Islamic heritage (*turâth*), but points out that, while European science became a common and social patrimony, the Arab-Islamic heritage failed to develop a mass culture. Accordingly, the problem is not Islam as such but the practice of Muslim rulers (often tyrants). If Islamic renewal is no more than a struggle for formal and external issues, Muslims do not have a defined programme for reconstructing society. A secular state is, he maintains, the best solution.

MASSIMO CAMPANINI

Fuller, Lon Luvois
American. *b:* 15 June 1902, Hereford, Texas. *d:* 8 April 1902. *Cat:* Procedural naturalist. *Ints:* Legal theory. *Educ:* Universities of California and Stanford. *Appts:* Professor of Law, Duke University, Harvard University, Member of American Academy of Arts and Sciences.

Main publications:
(1940) *The Law in Quest of Itself*, Chicago: The Foundation Press.
(1964) *The Morality of Law*, New Haven: Yale University Press.

(1967) *Legal Fictions*, Stanford University Press.
(1968) *Anatomy of the Law*, Harmondsworth: Penguin.
(1969) *The Morality of Law*, revised edition, New Haven: Yale University Press.

Secondary literature:

Summers, Robert S. (1984) *Lon L Fuller*, London: Edward Arnold.

According to Fuller, law, 'the enterprise of subjecting human conduct to the governance of rules' (1969, p. 74), has both an external and an internal morality. And it is the internal mortality that Fuller is largely concerned with in *The Morality of Law*. What is the internal morality of law? According to Fuller, it is concerned with the enterprise of effective lawmaking, an essential precondition of good law and one that does not appeal to external standards. It is what he calls a procedural version of natural law. Fuller lists the eight minimum criteria whose presence indicate failure in lawmaking. These are: (i) failure to establish rules (resulting in absolute uncertainty); (ii) failure to promulgate; (iii) improper use of retroactive lawmaking; (iv) failure to make comprehensible rules, (v) making contradictory rules; (vi) making rules that can not be obeyed; (vii) frequent change of rules; and (viii) no congruence between the declared rules and their administration in practice (ibid., p. 39).

The problem with Fuller's account of law is that even an evil ruler could respect the inner morality of law (by ensuring the absence of the above eight criteria) but enact laws that are brutal, unjust and indifferent to human welfare. Fuller, however, doubts whether it would be possible for a tyrant to follow iniquitous ends and respect inner morality at the same time. 'I have treated what I have called the internal morality of law as itself presenting a variety of natural law. It is, however, a procedural or institutional kind of natural law, though ... it affects and limits the substantive aims that can be achieved through law' (ibid., p. 184).

Fuller's answer is only a half-hearted attempt to meet the criticism. In order to give a satisfactory answer some account of substantive naturalism needs to be provided along with the account of procedural naturalism.

Sources: WWW(Am).

INDIRA MAHALINGAM CARR

G

Gadamer, Hans-Georg

German. *b:* 11 February 1900, Marburg, Germany. *Cat:* Hermeneutic philosopher. *Ints:* Hermeneutic theory; classical thought; technology (especially medicine). *Educ:* University of Marburg. *Infls:* Heidegger. *Appts:* Professor of Philosophy, University of Marburg, 1937–9; Professor of Philosophy, 1939–47, and Rector, 1946–7, University of Leipzig; Professor of Philosophy, University of Frankfurt, 1947–9; Professor of Philosophy, University of Heidelberg, 1949–68.

Main publications:

(1942) *Volk und Geschichte im Denken Herders*, Frankfurt: Klostermann.

(1960) *Wahrheit und Methode. Grundzüge einer philosophischen Hermeneutik*; fourth edition, Tübingen: J. C. B. Mohr, 1975 (English translation, *Truth and Method*, trans. William Glyn-Doepel, New York: Seabury Press).

(1964) (ed.) *Hegel-Tage, Royaumont*, Bonn: Bouvier.

(1967) *Kleine Schriften*, 3 vols, Tübingen: J. C. B. Mohr.

(1968) *Platos Dialektische Ethik*; second edition, Hamburg: Meiner, 1983 (English translation, *Plato's Dialectical Ethic*, trans. Robert M. Wallace, 1983).

(1968) *Um die Begriffswelt der Vorsokratiker.*

(1976) *Hegel's Dialectic: Five Hermeneutical Studies*, trans. P. Christopher Smith, New Haven: Yale University Press.

(1976) *Philosophical Hermeneutics*, trans. David Linge, Berkeley: University of California Press (contains essays from *Kleine Schriften*).

(1976) *Vernunft im Zeitalter der Wissenschaft*, Frankfurt: Suhrkamp (English translation, *Reason in the Age of Science*, trans. Frederick Lawrence, Cambridge, Mass.: MIT Press, 1981).

(1977) *Kleine Schriften*, vol 4, Tübingen: J. C. B. Mohr.

(1977) *Philosophische Lehrjahre*, Frankfurt: Klostermann (English translation, *Philosophical Apprenticeships*, trans. Robert R. Sullivan, Cambridge, Mass: MIT Press, 1985).

(1979) *Das Erbe Hegels: 2 Reden aus Anlass der Verleihung des Hegel-Preises der Stadt Stuttgart an Hans-Georg Gadamer am 13 Juni 1979*, Frankfurt: Suhrkamp.

(1979) (ed. with G. Boehm) *Seminar: Philosophische Hermeneutik*, second edition, Frankfurt: Suhrkamp.

(1980) *Dialogue and Dialectic: Eight Hermeneutical Studies on Plato*, trans. P. Christopher Smith, New Haven: Yale University Press.

(1982) *Heidegger Memorial Lectures*, ed. Werner Marx, trans. Steven W. Davis, Pittsburgh, PA: Duquesne University Press.

(1983) *Heideggers Wege. Studien zum Spätwerk*, Tübingen: J. C. B. Mohr.

(1984) 'Text und Interpretation', in Philippe Forget (ed.), *Text und Interpretation: Deutsch-Französische Debatte*, Munich: Fink.

(1986) *The Idea of the Good.*

(1986) *The Relevance of the Beautiful.*

(1986–) *Gesammelte Werke*, 7 vols, Tübingen: J. C. B. Mohr.

(1989) *Das Erbe Europas. Beiträge*, Frankfurt: Suhrkamp.

(1990) *Gedicht und Gespräch*, Frankfurt: Insel-Verlag.

(1993) *Über die Verborgenheit der Gesundheit. Aufsätze und Vorträge*, Frankfurt: Suhrkamp (English translation, *The Enigma of Health*, Cambridge: Polity, 1995).

Secondary literature:

Bernstein, Richard J. (1983) *Beyond Objectivism and Relativism*, Philadelphia: University of Pennsylvania Press; Oxford: Blackwell.

Bleicher, Josef (ed.) (1980) *Contemporary Hermeneutics*, London: Routledge & Kegan Paul.

——(1982) *The Hermeneutic Imagination*, London: Routledge & Kegan Paul.

Böhler, Dietrich (1977) 'Philosophische Hermeneutik und hermeneutische Methode', in Fuhrmann *et al.*, *Text und Applikation: Theologie, Jurisprudenz und Literaturwissenschaft im hermeneutischen Gespräch*, Poetik und Hermeneutik 9, Munich: Fink.

Buber, R. *et al.* (eds) (1970) *Hermeneutik und Dialektik I. Festschrift für Hans-Georg Gadamer*, Tübingen: J. C. B. Mohr.

Dallmayr, Fred (1987) *Critical Encounters*, Notre Dame: Notre Dame University Press.

——and McCarthy, Thomas (eds) (1977) *Understanding and Social Inquiry*, Notre Dame: Notre Dame University Press.

Grondin, Jean (1982) *Hermeneutische Wahrheit? Zum Wahrheitsbegriff Hans-Georg Gadamers*, Königstein: Forum Academicum.

Habermas, Jürgen (1967) *On the Logic of the Social Sciences*; trans. Shierry Weber Nicholsen and Jerry A. Stark, London: Heinemann, 1989.

——(1979) 'Urbanisierung der heideggerschen Provinz' (English translation, 'Urbanizing the Heideggerian province in Habermas', *Philosophical-Political Profiles*, trans. Frederick G. Lawrence, London: Heinemann, 1983, pp. 189–97).

Henrich, Dieter (ed.) (1960) *Die Gegenwart der Griechen im neueren Denken. Festschrift für Hans-Georg Gadamer zum 60 Geburtstag.*

Hermeneutik und Dialektik I. Festschrift für Hans-Georg Gadamer, (1970) Tübingen: J. C. B. Mohr.

Hermeneutik und Ideologiekritik (1971)(various authors) Frankfurt: Suhrkamp.

Howard, Roy (1981) *Three Faces of Hermeneutics: An Introduction to Current Theories of Understanding*, Berkeley: University of California Press.

Hoy, David (1978) *The Critical Circle*, Berkeley: University of California Press.

Jauss, Hans Robert (1982) *Toward an Aesthetic of Reception*, trans. Timothy Bahti, Minneapolis: University of Minnesota Press.

Lang, Peter Christian (1982) *Hermeneutik, Ideologiekritik, Ästhetik*, Königstein: Forum Academicum.

Linge, D. (ed.) (1976) *Philosophical Hermeneutics*, Berkeley: University of California Press.

MacIntyre, Alasdair (1976) 'Contexts of interpretation: reflections on Hans-Georg Gadamer's *Truth and Method*', *Boston University Journal* 27, 1.

Michaelfelder, Diane P. and Palmer, Richard E. (eds) *Dialogue and Deconstruction: The Gadamer-Derrida Encounter*, Albany: SUNY Press.

Misgeld, Dieter (1977) 'Discourse and conversation: the theory of communicative competence and hermeneutics in light of the debate between Habermas and Gadamer', *Cultural Hermeneutics* 4.

Outhwaite, William (1985) 'Hans-Georg Gadamer', in Quentin Skinner (ed.), *The Return of Grand Theory in the Human Sciences*, Cambridge: Cambridge University Press.

——(1987) *New Philosophies of Social Science: Realism, Hermeneutics and Critical Theory*, London: Macmillan.

Ricoeur, Paul (1973) 'Ethics and culture: Habermas and Gadamer in dialogue', *Philosophy Today*, 17.

Schmidt, Lawrence Kennedy (1985) *The Epistemology of Hans-Georg Gadamer: An Analysis of the Legitimation of the Vorurteile*, Frankfurt: Peter Lang.

Silverman, Hugh J. (ed.) (1991) *Gadamer and Hermeneutics*, New York: Routledge, Chapman & Hall.

Sullivan, Robert R. *Political Hermeneutics: The Earlier Thinking of Hans-Georg Gadamer*, Pennsylvania State University Press.

Thompson, John (1981) *Critical Hermeneutics: A Study in the Thought of Paul Ricoeur and Jürgen Habermas*, Cambridge: Cambridge University Press.

Wachterhauser Brice, (ed.) (1986) *Hermeneutics and Modern Philosophy*, Albany: SUNY Press.

Warnke, Georgia (1987) *Gadamer: Hermeneutics, Tradition and Reason*, Cambridge: Polity.

Weinsheimer, Joel (1985) *Gadamer's Hermeneutics: A Reading of Truth and Method*, New Haven: Yale University Press.

——(1991) *Philosophical Hermeneutics and Literary Theory*, New Haven: Yale University Press.

Wright, Kathleen (ed.) *Festivals of Interpretation: Essays on Hans-Georg Gadamer's Work*, Albany: SUNY Press.

Gadamer's philosophical hermeneutics is conceived in opposition to the methodological emphasis of traditional hermeneutic theories and their concern with the accuracy of interpretation. Gadamer's aim is to describe the underlying process, an existential encounter between two perspectives or horizons of expectation, which makes interpretation possible in the first place. Understanding is not just a matter of immersing oneself imaginatively in the world of the historical actor or text, but a more reflective and practical process which operates with an awareness of the temporal and conceptual distance between text and interpreter and of the ways in which the text has been and continues to be reinterpreted and to exercise an influence over us. This effective history (*Wirkungsgeschichte*), which traditional historicist hermeneutics tends to see as an obstacle, is for Gadamer an essential element which links us to the text. Our prejudgements or prejudices are what make understanding possible.

Although Gadamer has often stressed the distinction between his philosophical hermeneutics, with its origin in **Heidegger**'s hermeneutic ontology, and hermeneutics as a *technique* of interpretation, his approach clearly poses a challenge to more traditional interpretations. These differences are brought out in particular in Gadamer's exchanges in the 1960s with Emilio Betti, whose *General Theory of Interpretation* was published in 1955. The alternative conception of the human sciences or *Geisteswissenschaften* put forward in Gadamer's work also made it central to Jürgen **Habermas**'s reformulation of the *Logic of the Social Sciences*. Habermas welcomed Gadamer's critique of hermeneutic objectivism, which he saw as the equivalent of positivism in the philosophy of the natural sciences, and also his stress on the totalizing character of understanding. For Habermas, however, Gadamer's stress on the fundamental nature of language, expressed in his claim that 'Being that can be understood is language', amounted to a form of linguistic idealism. Together with Gadamer's stress on the importance of tradition and his rehabilitation of the category of prejudice, this suggested an ultimately conservative approach which was unable to deal with the systematic distortion of communicative processes by relations of power and domination. Habermas and Gadamer debated these issues in the late 1960s and early 1970s; more recent theorists have tended to stress the compatibility of hermeneutics and critical theory (notably the Frankfurt School) in a conception of critical hermeneutics (cf. Thompson 1981, Outhwaite 1983). More recently, Gadamer also engaged briefly with the French deconstructionist philosopher Jacques **Derrida** (see Gadamer 1984), whose conception of interpretation is more sceptical.

Gadamer has also published an enormous amount of work on the history of philosophy, notably on Greek thought, scientific rationality and other topics, including, most recently, essays on the history and philosophy of medicine.

WILLIAM OUTHWAITE

Galli, Gallo

Italian. *b:* 26 January 1889, Montecarotto, Ancona, Italy. *d:* 9 September 1974, Senigallia, Ancona. *Cat:* Idealist. *Appts:* University of Calabria, 1933–6; Professor of the History of Philosophy, University of Turin, 1939–59.

Main publications:

(1914) *Kant e Rosmini*.
(1933) *Saggio sulla dialettica della realtà spirituale*; third edition, Turin: Gheroni, 1950.
(1939) *L'uno e i molti*.
(1943) *Studi cartesiani*.
(1944) *Dall'idea dell'essere alla forma della coscienza*.
(1944) *Prime linee d'un idealismo critico*.
(1946) *Studi sulla filosofia di Leibniz*; second edition, Padua: CEDAM, 1961.
(1961) *Linee fondamentale d'una filosofia dello spirito*, Turin: Bottega d'Erasmo.

(1965) *L'uomo nell'assoluto*, Turin: Giappichelli.

Galli refers to himself as a subjective realist and as belonging to the pure line of idealism represented by Bishop Berkeley in which being is being in consciousness. His own investigations focus on the problem of the relation between unity and plurality within being and its bearing on debates between realists and idealists. He rejects **Gentile**'s notion that the object is merely the negativity of thought, finding in Gentile's notion of the universality of the act merely an abstraction. His preferred notion of the structure of being is akin to Kant's transcendental unity. The self is a finite entity, eternally making and doing around the poles of sensible knowledge, reason, voluntary and involuntary action, to which others, which transcend it, reveal themselves. God underpins the possibility of our actually completing the process of self-realization but is not to be conceived as existing in some transcendental realm. Galli's work attempts to do justice both to the notion of human autonomy and to notion of a transcendent absolute that is lodged intrinsically within us.

COLIN LYAS

Gandhi, Mohandas Karamchand

Indian. *b:* 2 October 1869, Porbandar, Gujarat. *d:* 30 January 1948, New Dehli (assassinated). *Cat:* Barrister; political activist in South Africa and India. *Ints:* Political and social reform. *Educ:* Studied Law in London, 1888–91; returned briefly to Bombay, then took up a legal post in South Africa, 1893. *Infls:* Vaishanvism, Jainism and Advaita Vedanta.

Main publications:

(1960) *Discourses on the Gita*, Ahmedabad: Navajivan Publishing House.
(1960–2) *Non-violence in Peace and War*, Ahmedabad, Navajivan Publishing House.
(1961) *In Search of the Supreme*, 3 vols, ed. V. B. Kher, Ahmedabad: Navajivan Publishing House.
(1969) *Ethical Religion*, Ahmedabad: Navajivan Publishing House.
(1969) *Truth is God*, 2 vols, ed. R. K. Prabhu, Ahmedabad, Navajivan Publishing House.
(The above works can also be found in *Gandhi's Collected Works*, Delhi: Government of India Publication Division, 1958.)

Secondary literature:

Datta, Dhirendra Mohan (1953) *The Philosophy of Mahatma Gandhi*, Madison: University of Wisconsin Press.

Fischer, Louis (1950) *Gandhi: His Life and Message for the World*, New York: Harper.

Gandhi, Mohandas Karamchand (1927) *An Autobiography, or the Story of my Experiences with Truth*, trans. Mahadev Desai, Ahmedabad: Navajivan Publishing House.

Richards, Glyn (1991) *The Philosophy of Gandhi*, London: Curzon Press.

Verma, Surendra (1970) *Metaphysical Foundations of Mahatma Gandhi's Thought*, New Delhi: Orient Longman.

Gandhi is well known in modern history as a political activist who used *ahimsa* (non-violence) and *satyagraha* (adherence to truth or non-violent resistance) as his tools. He was not a philosopher in the commonly understood sense of the term. However, the principles of *ahimsa* and *satyagraha* are founded on a metaphysics that owes much to Advaita Vedanta.

The ultimate reality, according to Gandhi, is *satya* (Truth). Like the *Brahman* of Advaita Vedanta, *satya* is non-dual, eternal and non-dependent. *Satya* is God and, for Gandhi, all human activities should be centred in *satya*:

> The word *satya* is derived from *sat*, which means that which is. *Satya* means a state of being, Nothing is or exists in reality except Truth. That is why *sat* or *satya* is the right name for God. In fact it is more true to say that Truth is God than to say that God is Truth. But as we cannot do without a ruler or general, the name God is and will remain more current. Devotion to this Truth is the sole justification for our existence. All our existence should be centred in truth. Truth should be the very breath of our life ... [we] should understand the word *satya* or Truth in a much wider sense. There should be Truth in thought, Truth in speech and Truth in action ... If we once learn how to apply this never-failing test of Truth, we shall at once be able to find out what is worth doing, what is worth seeing, what is worth reading.
>
> (*Collected Works* (vol. 44, pp. 40–1)

Following the general tenor of Hinduism, Gandhi believed that the goal of human life is to serve God or Truth. God could be best served by practising *ahimsa*—non-violence or the law of love—which he thought had immense powers:

> The law of love will work, just as the law of gravitation will work, whether we accept it or not. Just as a scientist will work wonders out of various applications of the law of nature, even so man who applies the law of love with scientific precision can work great wonders. For the force of non-violence is infinitely more wonderful and subtle than the material forces of nature, like, for instance, electricity.
>
> (*Young India*, 1 October 1931)

In practising *ahimisa*, man will inevitably serve others and act for the good of all (*sarvodaya*), which would end the inegalitarian Indian caste system.

For Gandhi, politics and religion were intimately intertwined since both of them were concerned with the welfare of mankind. The best form of government, according to him, is one that interfers least with its citizens. The assumption of course is that the citizens of such a state are morally well developed—that is to say, guided by *ahimisa*, *sarvodaya* and *satyagraha*.

Gandhi, as stated earlier, was not a philosopher, and therefore questions such as the relationship of the non-dual *satya* to the phenomenal world remain unanswered. However, it must be said that the Gandhian principles of *ahimisa* and *satyagraha* were instrumental in bringing about India's independence.

INDIRA MAHALINGAM CARR

Gao Heng (Kao Heng)

Chinese. *b:* 1900, Shuangyang County, Jilin Province, China. *d:* 1986, Beijing. *Cat:* Ancient Chinese philosophy. *Ints:* Logic; science; semantics. *Educ:* Beijing Normal University, University of Beijing and Qinghua University. *Appts:* Professor, Shandong University, Jinan, Northeast University, Henan University, Wuhan University, Qilu University.

Main publications:

(1943) *Revised Collation of the Laozi*; revised editon, Beijing: Guji Publishing House, 1956.

(1957) *A Modern Annotation of the Old Text of the Book of Changes*, Beijing: Zhonghua Book Company.

(1958) *A General Explanation of the Old Text of the Book of Changes*, Beijing: Zhonghua Book Company.

(1958) *The Moist Canon Collated and Explained*, Beijing: Kexue Publishing House.

(1961) *The Book of Lord Shang, translated and annotated*, Jinan: Shandong Renmin Publishing House.

(1961) *A New Annotation of Various Philosophical Works*, Jinan: Shandong Renmin Publishing House.

Secondary literature:

Chan, W. T. (1967) *Chinese Philosophy, 1949–1963: An Annotaed Bibliography of Mainland China Publications*, Honolulu: East–West Center Press.

Louie, K. (1986) *Inheriting Tradition: Interpretations of the Classical Philosophers in Communist China 1949–1966*, Hong Kong: Oxford University Press.

Gao was a leading scholar of classical Chinese philosophy, specializing in meticulously prepared editions of pre-Qin dynasty texts and detailed commentaries upon them. The depth of his learning and the ingenuity of his suggestions for correcting corrupt texts to make them intelligible have had an important influence even on scholars who challenge his interpretations. His famous and widely used commentary on the *Laozi* was published in 1940 and shows his mastery of early daoist philosophy. In its 1956 edition, Gao criticized his own approach to Laozi as possibly entirely wrong because of his ignorance of Marxism, but presented the text itself without change. His work on the *Moist Canon* by followers of Mozi again clarified a difficult text and contributed to the modern revival of interest in the ancient Chinese philosophical school most embodying an interest in logic and science. In his studies of the *Book of Changes* and other ancient works, he used textual criticism incorporating rigorous syntactic, phonetic and semantic study.

NICHOLAS BUNNIN

Gaos y Gonzalez Pola, José

Spanish. *b:* 1900, Gijón, Spain. *d:* 1969, Mexico City. *Cat:* 'Personist' (sic). *Ints:* History of philosophy; analysis of the nature of philosophy. *Educ:* Philosophy under Ortega and Garcia Morente, Madrid (doctorate on Husserl, 1928). *Infls:* Garcia Morente, Ortega, Zubiri, Bergson and Husserl. *Appts:* Held a number of important appointments in Spain before the Civil War, notably Professor at Zaragoza (1930) and Rector of the University of Madrid (1936–9); at the end of the Civil War, moved to Mexico as Professor at UNAM, then at Nuevo León (1941), with other appointments in Cuba and Guatemala.

Main publications:

(1940) *La Filosofía de Maimónides*, Mexico: La Casa de España.

(1940) (with F. Larroyo) *Dos ideas de la filosofía*, Mexico: La Casa de España.

(1945) *Dos exclusivas del hombre: la mano y el tiempo*, Mexico: Universidad de Nuevo León.

(1947) *Filosofía de la filosofía e historia de la filosofía*, Mexico: Stylo.

(1958) *Confesiones profesionales*, Mexico: FCE.

(1959) *Sobre Ortega y Gasset*, Mexico: UNAM.

(1959) *Discurso de filosofía*, Mexico: Universidad Veracruzana.

(1960) *Origines de la filosofía y de su historia*, Mexico: Universidad Veracruzana.

(1962) *De la filosofía*, Mexico: FCE.

(1962) *Filosofía contemporanea*, Caracas: BCE.

(1962) *Las 'Críticas' de Kant*, Caracas: BCE.

(1967) *De antropologia e historiografía*, Yalapa, Mexico: Universidad Veracruzana.

Secondary literature:

Abellán, J. L. (1966) *Filosofía española en América 1936–1966*, Madrid: Guadarrama, pp. 103–22.

Hernández Luna, J. (1964) 'Siete años de labor filosófica de José Gaos en Mexico', *Cuadernos Americanos*, Jan–Feb.

Salmerón, F. (1947) 'La estructura de la filosofía de José Gaos', *Dianoia* 20: 147–71.

——(1990) 'Introducción a la filosofía de Gaos', *Dianoia* 36: 1–16.

José Gaos is regarded as one of the most influential Spanish philosophical scholars of his generation. He translated many volumes of philosophy into Spanish, notably by **Dewey**, **Hartmann, Heidegger, Husserl, Jaspers** and **Wahl**, and compiled a number of anthologies in addition to writing his own historical and philosophical studies. His own views, as he candidly notes (cf. 1958), changed on a number of occasions, from neo-Kantianism to phenomenology to ratio-vitalism and finally to the 'personist' (a term he preferred to 'personalist') relativism of his mature works. His great historical learning is reflected in this outlook, which is largely concerned with the nature of philosophy itself, a subject Gaos calls 'la filosofía de la filosofía'.

Gaos drew a number of conclusions from his studies of the history of Western philosophy, of which the most important was that no philosophical system has yet been devised which does justice to the multifariousness and complexity of phenomena. As he puts it, 'La metafísica ha concluido ... en el fracaso' ('Metaphysics has ended ... in failure', 'Discurso de filosofía',

Cuadernos Americanos 2, 1954). The contradictions of the various worldviews advanced in the twenty centuries of Western thought are a manifestation of human intellectual finitude, the recognition of which, Gaos contends, is the only sound starting-point for philosophy. Further, no philosophy is acceptable which does not recognize the following: that even the most fundamental categories of thought are historical and mutable; that these categories are antinomial in nature, a feature Gaos attributes to their being covertly rooted in the contrary passions of love and hatred; and that the object of philosophy, i.e. existence, is concrete and subjective. Philosophers conceive their ideas in response to their circumstances; hence 'personist'. Unsurprisingly, Gaos holds that there are no absolute values. Rather, values are projections of the life (*proyecciones de la vida*) of the subjects who are human individuals.

Gaos's belief that basic categories reflect passions led him to carry out extensive work in an area he calls philosophical anthropology, and some of his most original work is to be found in the phenomenological and psychological analyses thus generated. Thus he attempts to identify distinguishing properties (*exclusivas*) of human nature, and finds these in the hand and in time (cf. 1945, passim). He spends much time analysing the nature of the caress, finding in it evidence not of a tendency to sensuality but on the contrary of the existence of spirit. Concerning time, Gaos argues that life and time are inseparable concepts. We exist only because we must one day cease to exist. We are oriented towards the future, and mortality lends urgency to our lives. His recognition of intellectual finitude prevents him from giving a view on the existence of god.

ROBERT WILKINSON

García Morente, Manuel

Spanish. *b:* 1886, Arjonilla, Spain. *d:* 1942, Madrid. *Cat:* Phenomenologist. *Educ:* Educated at the Sorbonne and at Marburg, Munich and Berlin, before completing his doctorate in Madrid in 1911. *Infls:* Ortega y Gasset, Gumersindo Azcárate and José de Castro. *Appts:* Taught in Madrid and at the University of Tucumán in Argentina.

Main publications:

(1917) *La filosofía de Kant*.

(1917) *La filosofía de Bergson*.

(1932) *Ensayos sobre el progreso*.

(1937) *Lecciones preliminares de filosofía* (later published as *Introducción a la filosofía* and as *Fundamentos de filosofía*).

(1941) *Idea de la Hispanidad*, Buenos Aires: Espasa-Calpe.

(1945) *Ensayos*, Madrid: Revista de Occidente.

Among the philosophers whose works García Morente translated into Spanish are Kant, **Husserl** and **Brentano**. He collaborated with José **Ortega y Gasset** on the *Revista de Occidente* and is responsible for bringing the term *Erlebnis* into Spanish as *vivencia*. García Morente anguished over questions of God and nothingness for many years, ultimately deciding to leave his family to enter the seminary in 1938. In his *Idea de la Hispanidad* (1941) he outlines his concept of the 'Christian gentleman' as a Hispanic ideal.

AMY A. OLIVER

Garrigou-Lagrange, Réginald

French. *b:* 21 February 1877, Auch. *d:* 15 February 1964, Rome. *Cat:* Scholastic. *Ints:* Neo-Thomism; philosophy of religion. *Educ:* University of Bordeaux and University of Paris, and the Angelicum University, Rome. *Infls:* Aquinas, Cajetan and John of St Thomas. *Appts:* 1909–59, Professor of Dogmatic Theology, Angelicum University, Rome.

Main publications:

(1909) *Le Sens commun*; third edition, Paris: Nouvelle Librairie Nationale, 1922.

(1915) *Dieu, son existence et sa nature*; eleventh edition in 2 vols, Paris: Beauchesne, 1951 (English translation, *God, His Existence and His Nature*, 2 vols, St Louis: Herder, 1934–6).

(1932) *La Réalisme du principe de finalité*, Paris: Desclée de Brouwer.

(1946) *La Synthèse thomiste*, Paris: Desclée de Brouwer, (English translation *Reality: a Synthesis of Thomistic Thought*, St Louis: Herder, 1950).

Secondary literature:

(1964) 'L'Oeuvre du P. Garrigou-Lagrange', *Itinéraires* (Paris) 86: 88–94 (bibliography).

James John, Helen (1966) *The Thomist Spectrum*, New York: Fordham University Press, pp. 3–15.

Lavaud, M.-Benoît (1964) 'Le Père Garrigou-Lagrange', *Revue Thomiste* 64: 181–99.

Zorcolo, B. (1965) 'Bibliografia del P. Garrigou-Lagrange', *Angelicum* (Rome) 42: 200–72.

Garrigou-Lagrange espoused and disseminated an orthodox, and what some would regard as an unbending, version of Thomism, with an occasional hint of Catholic apologetics. In this version of Thomism, it is taken to be an Aristotelianism perfected ('In Aristotle the doctrine is still a child. In Aquinas it has grown to full age'), and even, for some, a perfected mode of philosophical thought; as if, in Thomism, a kind of Aristotelian finality had been realized. This rigidity was soon superseded by the genius of **Maritain** and **Maréchal**, and by the innovative school of Louvain. None the less, Garrigou-Lagrange provided a clear, accessible and well-argued Thomism, and he is useful in establishing the orthodoxy against which subsequent developments must be measured. *God, His Existence and His Nature* (1915) is still a classic in twentieth-century philosophy of religion. However, few leading Thomists would now accept Garrigou-Lagrange's version of Thomism without considerable reservation.

Sources: DFN; EF.

HUGH BREDIN

Gaultier, Jules de

French. *b:* 1856, Paris. *d:* 1942, Boulogne sur Seine, France. *Cat:* Idealist. *Ints:* Aesthetics. *Infls:* Flaubert and Nietzsche. *Appts:* Spent his professional life as a civil servant in the Ministry of Finance and in the department which inspected municipal administrations until his retirement in 1919; an extensive contributor over many years to *Mercure de France*; after retirement in 1919 he devoted all his time to his writing.

Main publications:

(1898) *Le Bovarysme, la psychologie dans l'oeuvre de Flaubert*, Paris: L. Cerf; third edition, 1913.
(1900) *De Kant à Nietzsche*, Paris: Mercure de France.
(1903) *La Fiction universelle, deuxième essai sur le pouvoir d'imaginer*, Paris: Mercure de France.
(1904) *Nietzsche et la réforme philosophique*, Paris: Mercure de France.
(1906) *Les Raisons de l'idéalisme*, Paris: Mercure de France.
(1907) *La Dépendance de la morale et l'indépendance des moeurs*, Paris: Mercure de France.
(1912) *Entretiens avec ceux d'hier et aujourd'hui. Comment naissent les dogmes?*, Paris: Mercure de France.
(1913) *Le Génie de Flaubert*, Paris: Mercure de France.
(1913) *La Sensibilité métaphysique*, Paris: Éditions du Siècle.
(1922) *La Philosophie officielle et la philosophie*, Paris: F. Alcan.

(1923) *La Vie mystique de la nature*, Paris: G. Cry.

Secondary literature:

Barrenechea, Antonio (1911) *Un Idealismo estetico: La filosofia de Jules de Gaultier*, Buenos Aires: Cooperativa ditorial Limitada.
Baruzi, Jean (1926) *Philosophie générale et métaphysique*, Paris: F. Alcan.
Cassères, Benjamin de (*c.* 1936) *Jules de Gaultier and La Rochefoucauld*, New York: Blackstone.
Ellis, Wilmot E. (1928) *Bovaryism: The Art Philosophy of Jules de Gaultier*, Seattle: University of Washington Bookstore (University of Washington Chapbooks, ed. G. Hughes, no. 16).
Palante, George (1924) *La Philosophie du Bovarysme*, Paris: Mercure de France.

In calling his philosophy 'Bovaryism', de Gaultier wanted to emphasize that, like Emma Bovary, we are enticed by an ideal world beyond our immediate experience and we constantly confuse the two. But it is the ability to think of things as other than they are which constitutes the most interesting and important fact about human beings. Although it was his understanding of Flaubert's imagination which most interested him, the influence of **Nietzsche** is clear, and his version of 'idealism' is unique amongst French philosophers. His work attracted interest from literary scholars—he has frequently been cited in studies of Flaubert—but his own main interests were in the reform of moral theory and epistemology. He saw the tendency to think of things as other than they are as the source of art, and he believed that this tendency posed an aesthetic problem and not, in the traditional sense, an ethical problem. He wanted explicitly to substitute aesthetics for ethics.

Consciousness, he claimed, is *necessarily* inadequate to its objects because it is a subjective principle which demands for its intelligibility an objective order. Like Pascal, de Gaultier insisted that the infinity of things outreaches reason. He inferred that relativism must result, and this further underlines his insistence on an aesthetic understanding of the problem. Ultimately, human beings are not responsible for their condition. But they do have the power to represent things in many ways and thus an all-important capacity for art.

The critical appreciations listed above all emphasize his interests in Flaubert, in literature and in aesthetics. It is natural that at least one commentator, Benjamin Cassères, should notice the connection with La Rochefoucauld, the sevententh-century epigrammatist and commen-

tator on the corrupt court life of his time. La Rochefoucauld, in his concern to expose the absurd pretensions of the society around him, makes much of the connection between such pretensions and the tendency of human beings to imagine things other than as they are. But La Rochefoucauld's witty moralizing is closer to **Sartre** than to de Gaultier. Sartre's 2,800-page assault in *L'Idiot dans la famille, Gustave Flaubert, 1821–1857* (Paris: Gallimard; revised edition, 1988) sets out to expose 'Bovaryism' and Flaubert himself as manifestations of a corrupt bourgeoisie, while de Gaultier's rather amiable relativism was combined with an intention to undermine moralizing and to concetrate on aesthetic issues.
Sources: Hector Talvart and Joseph Place (1937) *Bibliographie des auteurs modernes de langue française*, Paris: Chronique des lettres françaises, vol. 6, pp. 296–302; Baruzi; Benrubi; Parodi; EF; FranBio; LXXS.

LESLIE ARMOUR

Gauthier, D(avid) P(eter)

Canadian. *b:* 1932, Toronto. *Cat:* Analytical philosopher. *Ints:* Ethics; political philosophy; decision theory. *Educ:* University of Toronto, Harvard University and University of Oxford. *Infls:* Thomas Hobbes, John Rawls and R. M. Hare. *Appts:* 1958–80, Assistant Professor, Associate Professor, then Professor of Philosophy, University of Toronto; from 1980, Professor of Philosophy, University of Pittsburgh.

Main publications:
(1963) *Practical Reasoning*, Oxford: Clarendon Press.
(1969) *The Logic of Leviathan*, Oxford: Clarendon Press.
(1986) *Morals by Agreement*, Oxford: Clarendon Press.
(1990) *Moral Dealing*, Ithaca: Cornell University Press.

Secondary literature:
Frankel, Ellen *et al.* (eds) (1988) *The New Social Contract*, Oxford: Blackwell.
Vallentyne, Peter (ed.) (1991) *Contractarianism and Rational Choice*, Cambridge: Cambridge University Press.

Gauthier's first book argued, amongst other things, that legitimate practical reasoning must take account of all of the desires of those affected by the action in question. Its roots were in Kant and the work of R. M. **Hare**.

His later work has been much more influenced by the Hobbesian tradition. He holds that the point of morality is to constrain the pursuit of self-interest in a world in which our actions affect others, so as to produce the best outcome. And what is morally right is what would be agreed to by mutually disinterested, amoral, fully informed agents bargaining about the terms of social cooperation. Gauthier holds that much of traditional morality is captured by this approach, and that the parts that are not are best abandoned as rationally unfounded.
Sources: Personal communication.

ANTHONY ELLIS

Geach, P(eter) T(homas)

British. *b:* 1916, London. *Cat:* Analytic philosopher. *Ints:* Logic; metaphysics; philosophy of mind; philosophy of religion; ethics. *Educ:* Balliol College, Oxford and St Deiniol's Library, Hawarden. *Infls:* Aristotle, Aquinas, Gottlob Frege, J. M. E. McTaggart and Ludwig Wittgenstein. *Appts:* 1951–61, Assistant Lecturer, Lecturer, Senior Lecturer, University of Birmingham; 1961–6, Reader in Logic, University of Birmingham; 1966–81, Professor of Logic, University of Leeds; 1985, Visiting Professor, University of Warsaw; 1965, Fellow of the British Academy.

Main publications:
(1956) 'Good and evil', *Analysis*, 17.
(1956) *Mental Acts*, London: Routledge & Kegan Paul.
(1960) (trans. with Max Black) *Translations from the Philosophical Writings of Gottlob Frege*, Oxford: Blackwell.
(1962) *Reference and Generality*, Ithaca: Cornell University Press; amended edition, 1968.
(1969) *God and the Soul*, London: Routledge & Kegan Paul.
(1972) *Logic Matters*, Berkeley: University of California Press.
(1973) (with Elizabeth Anscombe) *Three Philosophers*, Oxford: Basil Blackwell.
(1977) *Providence and Evil*, Cambridge: Cambridge University Press.
(1977) *The Virtues*, Cambridge: Cambridge University Press.
(1977) (trans. with R. H. Stoothoff) Gottlob Frege, *Logical Investigations*, Oxford: Basil Blackwell.
(1979) *Truth, Love, and Immortality: An Introduction to McTaggart's Philosophy*, Berkeley: University of California Press.

Secondary literature:

Evans, Gareth, (1977) 'Pronouns, quantifiers, and relative clauses', *Canadian Journal of Philosophy* 7.

Griffin, Nicholas (1977) *Relative Identity*, Oxford: Clarendon Press.

Geach has written influentially in many of the central areas of philosophy, but his most important contribution has been the application of logical techniques to problems of language and metaphysics. His first book gives a logical analysis of the notion of mental acts. Its greatest influence, however, came from its opposition to the empiricist doctrine of abstractionism, the view that concepts are formed by abstracting them from recurrent features of experience. In general, Geach's view of the mind owes much to both **Wittgenstein** and Aristotle.

Geach was never sympathetic to the 'linguistic philosophy' of the 1950s and 1960s, and *Reference and Generality* (1962) used the techniques of formal logic to understand how referring expressions, and expressions of generality, are used in everyday language and thought. Its most influential view was perhaps the claim that identity claims are meaningless except as relative to some general term: 'x = y' can only ever mean 'x is the same something or other as y'.

Geach's work in ethics has promoted the 'doctrine of the virtues', and part of the groundwork for this was laid in his influential article 'Good and evil' (1956). Here Geach attacked the prescriptivism that was fashionable at the time, arguing that the primary sense of 'good' is in fact descriptive. Goodness is not, however, a *sui generis* property, as the intuitionists had thought: rather, to be good is to be a good *something*, and the nature of the something supplies the standards of goodness.

His work in the philosophy of religion has used the techniques and results of modern logic to defend traditional Roman Catholic doctrines. Geach's work continues to be discussed, although the notion of relative identity, highly influential during the 1960s and 1970s, has now largely been rejected. In ethics, however, the theory of the virtues remains central.

Sources: WW 1992; 'A philosophical autobiography', in Harry A. Lewis (ed.) (1991) *Peter Geach: Philosophical Encounters*, Dordrecht: Kluwer.

ANTHONY ELLIS

Gehlen, Arnold

German. *b:* 29 January 1904, Leipzig, Germany. *d:* 30 January 1976. *Cat:* Philosopher of anthropology; sociologist. *Educ:* Philosophy, in Cologne and Leipzig, with N. Hartmann, M. Scheler and H. Driesch (PhD, 1927). *Infls:* German idealism, Nietzsche, American pragmatism, phenomenology, Vilfredo Pareto and G. H. Mead. *Appts:* Taught Philosophy, Frankfurt am Main (1933), Leipzig (1934–8), Königsberg (1938–40) and Vienna (1940–5) taught Sociology at Speyer (1947–61) and Aachen (1961–9).

Main publications:

(1940) *Der Mensch, seine Natur und Stellung in der Welt*, Lepizig (English translation, *Man: His Nature and Place in the World*, trans. Clare McMillan and Karl Pillemer, New York: Columbia University Press, 1988).

(1956) *Urmensch und Spätkultur*, Bonn.

(1957) *Die Seele im technischen Zeitalter*, Hamburg (English translation, *Man in the Age of Technology*, trans. P. Lipscomb, New York: Columbia University Press, 1980).

(1961) *Anthropologische Forschung*, Hamburg: Rowohlt (a collection of articles).

(1978–94) *Gesammelte Werke*, Frankfurt am Main.

Secondary literature:

Bubner, R. (1981) *Modern German Philosophy*, Cambridge: Cambridge University Press.

Rehberg, Karl-Siegbert (1988) Introduction to 1940.

Gehlen's 'philosophical anthropology' constitutes an important contribution to German philosophy and sociology, and his main works are still considered classics at German universities. Once articulated in 1940, Gehlen's basic tenets remained constant throughout his work. Following **Nietzsche**, he saw man as the 'not yet determined [or 'fixed': *festgestellte*] animal'. Unlike animals, humans are not adapted to a particular natural environment; their *Weltoffenheit* ('openness to the world'—a term Gehlen borrowed from *Scheler*) gives them a breadth of experience and a scope for self-development unknown to, and impossible for, animals. But the lack (or, as the later Gehlen thought, minimal extent) of instinctual guidance also makes life precarious for humans, an existential situation from which we constantly seek relief (or 'disburdening': *Entlastung*) by mastering the world and our own 'excess of impulses'. In this way, and with existential necessity, humans develop culture, i.e. those institutions and procedures which reduce complexity, facilitate decision-making and increase stability: for example marriage as a social institution or, centrally, language as a symbolic shorthand representation of the world (including the inner world of emotions). In the process we transform ourselves from naturally 'deficient' beings (*Mängelwesen*) into cultural beings.

Citing Nietzsche's dictum 'we can only understand what we can do', Gehlen attributed central importance to action (rather than contemplation) for human (self-)knowledge, thus facilitating the reception of American pragmatism in Germany and also rendering his philosophy usable to Nazi ideologues. But while Gehlen probably owed much of his academic career to interventions of the Nazi authorities on his behalf, racism cannot consistently be deduced from his anthropology, given that he saw humans as biologically *under*-determined and the fact that *Zucht* ('breeding') in Gehlen is not a biological process but one of cultural self-determination. However, some of Gehlen's own conclusions do not follow consistently from his premises either. While, for example, the assumed 'excess' of human impulses lends justification to (especially the later) Gehlen's call for a disciplined reinforcement of an existing social order, it is not clear why this—rather than an amorphousness—should be the logical result of our lack of biological determination. Gehlen's philosophical judgement was influenced by his conservative political lookout.

Sources: *ZPF*, 1964 (bibliography); Edwards; A. Gehlen, 'An anthropological model', *HC* 1: 11–20, 1968–9 (Gehlen's own account of his position and philosophical development).

BETTINA LANGE

Geiger, Moritz
German. *b:* 26 June 1880, Frankfurt. *d:* 9 September 1937, Seal Harbor, Maine, USA. *Cat:* Phenomenologist. *Ints:* Aesthetics; psychology. *Educ:* Universities of Munich, Göttingen and Harvard. *Infls:* Edmund Husserl, Theodor Lipps and Karl Jaspers. *Appts:* 1907–15, Privatdozent, University of Munich; 1915–23, Professor, University of Munich; 1923–33, Professor, University of Göttingen; 1933–7, Professor, Vassar College.

Main publications:

(1913) 'Beiträge zur Phänomenologie des ästhetischen Genusses', in *Jahrbuch für Philosophie und phänomenologische Forschung*, vol. 1; reprinted, Tübingen: Max Niemeyer Verlag, 1974.

(1921) 'Das Unbewusste und die psychische Realität, in *Jahrbuch für Philosophie und phänomenologische Forschung*, vol. 4.

Secondary literature:
Spiegelberg, H. (1982) *The Phenomenological Movement*, The Hague: Martinus Nijhoff.

Although Geiger produced some interesting reflections on the nature and limitations of phenomenology and on the relationship between science and metaphysics it is principally for his applied phenomenology that he is remembered. In his phenomenological studies Geiger is concerned both with the objects of intentional experiences (*Erlebnisse*) and with the experiences themselves. But in his most celebrated study ('Contributions to the phenomenology of aesthetic enjoyment', 1913) the principal emphasis is on the experience. By means of a method which is neither inductive nor deductive but intuitive he seeks to lay bare the essence (*Wesen*) of aesthetic enjoyment. He first determines the essential features of enjoyment in general, distinguishing it from simple pleasure, being pleased, joy, evaluation, etc. He then asks what distinguishes *aesthetic* enjoyment from other sorts of enjoyment. His answer, in hopelessly condensed form, is that it is enjoyment in the disinterested contemplation (*Betrachtung*) of the intuitive richness (*Fülle*) of the object.

PAUL GORNER

Gellner, André
British. *b:* 9 December 1925, Paris. *Cat:* He has said he is 'a humble adherent' of 'Enlightenment Rationalist Fundamentalism'. *Ints:* Social anthropology; sociology; theory of knowledge. *Educ:* MA, Balliol College, Oxford; PhD, London. *Infls:* Weber and Russell. *Appts:* London School of Economics, 1949–84; Professor of Social Anthropology, University of Cambridge, 1984–92; Fellow of King's College; University of Central Europe.

Main publications:

(1959) *Words and Things*, London: Gollancz.
(1964) *Thought and Change*, London: Weidenfeld & Nicolson.
(1973) *Cause and Meaning in the Social Sciences*, London: Routledge & Kegan Paul.
(1974) *The Devil in Modern Philosophy*, London: Routledge & Kegan Paul.
(1974) *Legitimation of Belief*, Cambridge: Cambridge University Press.
(1979) *Spectacles and Predicaments*, Cambridge: Cambridge University Press.
(1985) *The Psychoanalytic Movement*, London: Paladin.

(1985) *Relativism and the Social Sciences*, Cambridge: Cambridge University Press.

(1987) *Culture, Identity, and Politics*, Cambridge: Cambridge University Press.

(1988) *Plough, Sword and Book*, London: Collins Harvill.

(1992) *Postmodernism, Reason and Religion*, London: Routledge.

(1992) *Reason and Culture*, Oxford: Blackwell.

(1994) *Conditions of Liberty*, London: Hamish Hamilton.

Gellner has written extensively on the social anthropology of the Islamic world. Within academic philosophy, his *Words and Thing* (1959) created a violent controversy by applying a sociological analysis to the style of what he called linguistic philosophy (see Ved Mehta, *Fly and the Fly-Bottle*, Harmondsworth: Penguin, 1965, for a journalistic account). The book contains a good deal of telling argument that might have been more appreciated in the 1990s than it was in the 1960s. Gellner has been a vigorously polemical opponent of psychoanalysis.

His own positive philosophical writings have addressed issues of rationality, relativism and conceptual legitimation, as well as problems of intercultural understanding in social anthropology. His *Plough, Sword and Book* (1988) contains a case for 'philosophic history' on Weberian lines. He characterizes his position as 'Enlightenment Rationalist Fundamentalist' in terms of a denial of relativism: a commitment to the view that 'there *is* external, objective, culture-transcending knowledge'. 'Truth is independent of the social order ...' (1994, p. 31). On the other hand, his position 'does not allow any culture to validate a part of itself with final authority, to decree some substantive affirmation to be privileged and exempt from scrutiny' (1992, pp. 75–6). Gellner is a prolific and independent-minded writer with an enormous range of reference. Many current philosophical fashions (relativism, postmodernism) appear to him as the statements of problems rather than as solutions. His philosophizing about the cultural dominance of Western rationality has been more thorough than that of almost any other recent thinker.

RICHARD MASON

Gentile, Giovanni

Italian. *b:* 30 May 1875, Castelvetrano, Sicily. *d:* 14 April 1944, Florence. *Cat:* Idealist metaphysician. *Ints:* History of philosophy; moral philosophy; philosophy of education. *Educ:* Pisa 1893–97, PhD

1897. *Infls:* Hegel, D. Jaja and B. Spaventa. *Appts:* Campobasso, 1897–1902; Naples, 1902 -6; Palermo, 1906–13; Pisa, 1914–16; Rome, from 1917; Minister of Education, 1922–4; associated with the Fascist regime until its fall and his death at the hands of Italian partisans in 1944.

Main publications:

(1898) *Rosmini e Gioberti*, Pisa: Fratelli Nistri (PhD thesis).

(1899) *La Filosofia di Marx Studi Critici*, Pisa: Spoerri.

(1903) *Dal Genovesi al Galuppi*, Milan: Treves.

(1908) *Scuola e Filosofia*, Palermo: Sandron.

(1913) *I Problemi della Scolastica e il Pensiero Italiano*, Bari: Laterza.

(1913) *La Riforma della Dialettica Hegeliana*, Messina: Principato.

(1916) *Teoria generale dello Spirito come Atto Puro*, Pisa: Vallecchi (English translation, London, Macmillan, 1922).

(1917) *Sistema di Logica come Teoria del Conoscere*, 2 vols, Pisa: Spoerri.

(1920) *Discorsi di Religione*, Florence: Vallecchi.

(1920) *Giordano Bruno e il Pensiero del Renascimento*, Florence: Vallecchi.

(1920) *La Riforma dell'Educazione* Bari: Laterza (English translation, London: Benn, 1923).

(1920) *La Riforma dell'Educazione*, Bari: Laterza.

(1923) *Dante e Manzone*, Florence: Vallecchi.

(1929) *Origine e dottrina del Fascismo*, Rome: Libreria del Littorio.

(1931) *Filosofia dell'Arte*, Milan: Treves (English translation, Ithaca: Cornell University Press, 1972).

(1933) *Introduzione alla Filosofia*, Milan: Treves.

(1936) *Memorie, Italiane e Problemi*, Florence: Sansoni.

(1945) *Genesi e Struttura della Società*, Florence: Sansoni (English translation, Urbana: University of Illinois Press, 1960).

(1964) *Storia della Filosofia, dalle Origine a Platone*, ed. V. Bellezza, Florence: Sansoni.

(1969) *Storia della Filosofia Italiana*, 2 vols, ed. E. Garin, Florence: Sansoni.

(1973) *Italian Fascism from Pareto to Gentile*, ed. Lyttleton, London: Cape.

Secondary literature:

Agosti, V. (1977) *Filosofia e Religione nell'Attualismo Geniliano*, Brescia: Paideia.

Baraldi, G. (1976) 'Divenire e Trascendenza' (PhD thesis), Fribourg.

Calendra, G. (1987) *Gentile e il Fascismo*, Rome: Laterza.

Crespi, A. (1926) *Contemporary Thought in Italy*, London: Williams & Norgate.

Croce, B. (1981) *Lettere a Giovanni Gentile*, Milan: Mondadori.

Harris, H. S. (1960) *The Social Philosophy of Giovanni Gentile*, Urbana: University of Illinois Press.

Holmes, R. W. (1937) *The Idealism of Giovanni Gentile*, New York: Macmillan.

Janowski, F. (1889) 'Gentile, Giovanni', *Metzler Philosophenlexikon*, Stuttgart: Metzlersche Verlagsbuchhandlung, pp. 284–7.

Lion, A. (1932) *The Idealistic Conception of Religion: Vico, Hegel, Gentile*, Oxford: Clarendon.

Minio-Paluello, L. (1946) *Education in Fascist Italy*, London and New York: Oxford University Press.

Natoli, S. (1989) *Giovanni Gentile Filosofo Europea*, Turin: Bollati Boringheri.

Negri, A. (1975) *Giovanni Gentile*, 2 vols, Florence: La Nuova Italia.

Pardo, F. (1972) *La Filosofia di Giovanni Gentile*, Florence: Sansoni.

Romanell, P. (1938) *The Philosophy of Giovanni Gentile*, New York: S. F. Vianni.

——(1947) *Croce versus Gentile*, New York: S. F. Vianni.

Romano, S. (1984) *Giovanni Gentile la Filosofia al Potere Sergio Romano*, Milan: Bompiani.

Signore, M. (1972) *Impegno Etico e formzione del'uomo nel Pensiero Gentiliano*, Galatina: Editrice Salentina.

Spirito, U. (1969) *Giovanni Gentile*, Florence: Sansoni.

——(1976) *Dal Attualismo al Problematicismo*, Florence: Sansoni.

Gentile propounded a system known as actual idealism, in which thought was held to be pure activity and united with action. For Gentile there was no sense in seeking the cause of experience within the content of experience, and belief in an external world was the product of our attempt to organize our experience in thought, a so-called concrete logic. Sensation was the spontaneous activity of self-affirmation and because thought had to be embodied in language, our individual self-consciousness or moral personality was united into the collective consciousness of what he called the transcendental ego or state, although perhaps it could be interpreted as culture. In the interpretation of **Harris** the state here was not—though some of his wrritings might imply otherwise—necessarily the concrete state to be joyfully obeyed but more the future world of the individual's unrealized ideals but it was at this point that Gentile became, with many of his followers (but in contrast to **Croce**, his one-time collaborator on the *Giornale Critica della Filosofia Italiana*), a supporter of Italian fascism and able to serve it as a Minister of Education while carrying through educational reforms in line with his ideals. Gentile was a dominating influence on Italian intellectual life even after the fall of fascism in the postwar era. He founded and edited the journal *Saggi Critici* and was a principal editor of the *Enciclopedia Italiana* (1925ff, 37 vols).

Sources: Edwards; V. A. Bellezza (1950) *Bibliografia degli Scritti di Giovanni Gentile*, Florence: Sansoni; Höllhuber, I. (1969) *Geschichte der Italienischen Philosophie*, Munich and Basel: Reinhardt; Mittelstrass; G. M. Pozzo (1986) 'Gentile, Giovanni', in *Dizionario Critica della Letteratura Italiana*, Turin: Unione Tipografica-editrice.

R. N. D. MARTIN

Georgoulis, Constantine

Greek. *b:* 1894, Kalamata, Greece. *d:* 1968, Athens. *Cat:* Historian of philosophy; philosopher of language; philosopher of history; aesthetician. *Educ:* University of Athens, University of Berlin and University of Freiburg. *Infls:* Heidegger, Dilthey, Troeltsch, Jaeger and Friedländer. *Appts:* Taught in secondary education (1923–40); head of Teachers College for Secondary Education (1941–64); general secretary in the Ministry of Education (1952–7).

Main publications:

(1935) *Aristotle's First Philosophy (Metaphysics): Introduction and Translation*, Thessalonica: Alexiou & Pikopoulou.

(1938) *Inquiry in the Greek Humanities: Contribution to the Philosophical and Methodological Foundation of Greek Studies*, Thessalonica: Alexiou & Pikopoulou.

(1939) *Plato's Republic: Introduction, Translation and Commentary*, Athens: D. E. Alexiou.

(1949) 'Greek philosophy', *Encyclopaedia of Elios*, Athens, 8: 553–725; published as *History of Greek Philosophy*, 2 vols, Athens: Papadimas, 1975.

(1954) *Contemporary Philosophical Trends*, Athens: Union of Christian Teachers.

(1956) *Views from the Philosophy of our Times*, Athens.

(1962) *Aristotle of Stagira*, Thessalonica: Historical and Folklore Society of Halkidiki.

(1964) *Aesthetic and Philosophical Essays*, Athens: I. Sideris.

In his approach to the texts of ancient Greek thought, Georgoulis used the hermeneutical method of *Verstehen*, and regarded philology as a foundational science for all the humanities. He edited and translated classical texts into demotic modern Greek. Further, Georgoulis was one of the first Greek philosophers in the twentieth century to make language the subject of philosophical inquiry, his themes deriving mostly from the German tradition. Again, he was responsible for introducing European trends, notably phenomenology and existentialism, to Greece.

STAVROULA TSINOREMA

Gewirth, Alan

American. *b:* 1912, Union City, New Jersey. *Cat:* Ethics. *Ints:* Political philosophy; history of philosophy. *Educ:* Columbia University. *Infls:* Kant. *Appts:* 1937, Assistant Professor of Philosophy, University of Chicago; 1957, Edward Carson Waller Distinguished Service Professor of Philosophy, University of Chicago; 1957, Fellow of the American Academy of Arts and Sciences.

Main publications:

(1951, 1956) (trans.) *Marsilius of Padua, The Defender of Peace* 2 vols, New York: Columbia University Press.
(1965) *Political Philosophy*, New York: Macmillan.
(1978) *Reason and Morality*, Chicago: University of Chicago Press.
(1982) *Human Rights*, Chicago: University of Chicago Press.

Secondary literature:

Beyleveld, Deryck (1991) *The Dialectical Necessity of Morality*, Chicago: University of Chicago Press.
Regis, Jr, Edward (ed.) (1984) *Gewirth's Ethical Rationalism*, Chicago: University of Chicago Press.

In an attempt to secure for ethical judgements the objective truth that he thought their authority required, Gewirth argued that it is self-contradictory for any agent to reject what he called the Principle of Generic Consistency—the principle that one should always act with favourable consideration for the freedom and well-being of others as well as of oneself.

Many have held that Gewirth's argument is an illegitimate attempt to bridge the gap between facts and values.

Gewirth also produced a standard translation of *Defendor Pacis* by Marsilius of Padua.
Sources: Becker; personal communication.

ANTHONY ELLIS

Geyser, Joseph

German. *b:* 16 March 1869, Erkelenz, Germany. *d:* 11 April 1948, Siegsdorf. *Cat:* Neo-scholastic philosopher; 'critical realist'. *Ints:* Logic; ontology; epistemology and psychology. *Educ:* University of Bonn. *Infls:* Aristotle, Aquinas, Bernhard Bolzano, Francisco Suárez, Leibniz and O. Külpe. *Appts:* 1904–17, Extraordinary Professor, then (1911) Professor of Philosophy, University of Münster; 1917–24, Professor of Philosophy, University of Freiburg; 1924–35, Professor of Philosophy, University of Munich.

Main publications:

(1899) *Das philosophische Gottesproblem*, Münster: Schöningh.
(1902) *Grundlegung der empirischen Psychologie*, Münster: Schöningh.
(1917) *Die Erkenntnistheorie des Aristotles*, Münster: Schöningh.
(1918) *Ueber Wahrheit und Evidenz*, Münster: Schöningh.
(1919) *Grundlegung der Logik und Erkenntnistheorie*, Münster: Schöningh.
(1921) *Eidologie oder Philosophie als Formerkenntnis*, Münster: Schöningh.
(1922) *Erkenntnistheorie*, Münster: Schöningh.
(1923) *Augustin und die phänomenologische Religionsphilosophie der Gegenwart*, Münster: Schöningh.

Secondary literature:

Gruss, Heribert (1980) *Transzendenzerkenntnis im phänomenologischen Ansatz, zur methodischen Neubegrundung Teistischer Weltsicht*, Paderborn: Schöningh.
Rintelen, Fritz-Joachim von (ed.) (1930) *Philosophia Perennis, Festgabe Joseph Geyser*, Regensburg.
——(1948) 'Joseph Geyser zum Gedächtnis', *Philosophisches Jahrbuch der–Gorres-Gesellschaft*: 307–11.

Geyser was a critical realist attached to the Thomistic tradition. His philosophy was essentially a Christian metaphysics addressing the perennial philosophical questions which theology attempts to answer (truth, existence of the outer world, nature of the soul) and seeking completion in a rationally founded knowledge of God.

As against idealistic Kantianism, Geyser's form of critical realism contended that to stand on firm ground philosophy must be based on the view that reality is independent of consciousness, not its product. He maintained that philosophy aims at a progressive penetration into the realm of possible essences of Being, a rational reconstruction of the 'forms of existence' insofar as they present themselves to experience. Although akin to **Husserl**'s phenomenology in some respects, Geyser's 'logical objectivism' differed from the former in its disavowal of intellectual intuition and its claim that the essences which reveal themselves to discursive thought have a real ontological character.

Geyser's position was exemplified throughout his metaphysics. For him true metaphysics does not proceed speculatively by idealistic construction, but inductively by an interpretation of the 'united facts of experience'. Accordingly, Geyser repudiated any knowledge of God reached by an a priori or immediate encounter with essence and maintained instead that God's existence can only be discovered a posteriori, with reference to experience. Geyser was one of the most thorough systematic metaphysicians of this century. But his philosophy, similar in outlook to that of another Thomist realist, Father **Maréchal**, was never widely known. In Germany, it was perhaps the realist metaphysician Nicolai **Hartmann** who learnt most from Geyser.

Sources: Edwards; Burkhardt; Bochenski; EF.

STEPHEN MOLLER

Giannini, Iniguez Humberto

Chilean. *b:* 1927, San Bernardo, Chile. *Cat:* Ancient and medieval philosopher; historian of ideas. *Educ:* Universities of Rome and Chile. *Infls:* Jorge Millas and Bogumil Jasinowski. *Appts:* Professor of Philosophy, University of Chile and the Catholic University of Chile; affiliated with the Instituto de Humanismo Cristiano and the Sociedad Chilena de Filosofía; involved with the journals *Teoría* and *Escritos de teoría*.

Main publications:

(1968) *El mito de la autenticidad*, Santiago: Ediciones de la Universidad de Chile.

(1982) *Tiempo y espacio en Aristóteles y Kant*, Santiago: Editorial Andres Bello.

(1987) *La 'reflexion' cotidiana: Hacia una arqueología de la experiencia*, Santiago: Editorial Universitaria.

(1988) *Breve historia de la filosofia*, seventh edition, Santiago: Editorial Universitaria.

(1992) *La experiencia moral*, Santiago: Editorial Universitaria.

Secondary literature:

Escobar, Roberto (1976) *La filosofia en Chile*, Santiago: Editorial Universal.

Jaksic, Iván (1989) *Academic Rebels in Chile: The Role of Philosophy in Higher Education and Politics*, Albany: SUNY Press.

Through his contact with Jorge **Millas**, Giannini was influenced by the perspectives of such thinkers as **Ortgega y Gasset**, **Scheler** and **Bergson**. **Heidegger** has also influenced his thought to some degree. Although Giannini is acutely aware of the impact that social and political conditions have had on philosophical activity in Chile, particularly the periods of military intervention and human-rights violations, his philosophy has tended to focus on themes he believes are of universal concern such as individuality and human interaction.

AMY A. OLIVER

Gibson, William Ralph Boyce

British-Australian. *b:* 15 March 1869, Paris. *d:* 3 April 1935, Melbourne. *Cat:* Personal idealist. *Educ:* Queen's College, Oxford, University of Jena, University of Paris and University of Glasgow. *Infls:* Particularly Eucken, but also Spencer, Boutroux and Henry Jones. *Appts:* 1898–1909, Lecturer in Philosophy, London; 1910–11, Lecturer in Philosophy, Liverpool; 1912–34, Professor of Philosophy, Melbourne.

Main publications:

(1904) *A Philosophical Introduction to Ethics: An Advocacy of the Spiritual Principle from the Point of View of Personal Idealism*, London: Swan Sonnenschein.

(1906) *Rudolf Eucken's Philosophy of Life*, London: Black.

(1909) *God With Us: A Study in Religious Idealism*, London: Black.

(1909) *The Problem of Logic*, London: Black.

(1932) *The Philosophy of Descartes*, London: Methuen.

Secondary literature:

Grave, S. I. (1984) *A History of Philosophy in Australia*, University of Queensland Press.

Merrylees, W. A. (1935) 'Obituary: William Ralph Boyce Gibson', *Australasian Journal of Psychology and Philosophy* 13.

Spiegelberg, H. (1971) 'From Husserl to Heidegger', *Journal of the British Society for Phenomenology* 2: 58–62, 77–83.

Gibson established himself partly as a translator and expositor of the work of Rudolf **Eucken**, with whom he had studied and who 'had a remarkable vogue in Australia' (Grave 1984, p. 20). His own later philosophy, published in articles in the *Australasian Journal*, was a development of this Christian idealism. He claimed that Truth, Beauty and Right exist objectively and are, in **Pringle-Pattison**'s phrase, 'the reality of God within us'. Although the Ideal and the individual 'interpenetrate', according to Gibson, they do so 'without fusion'.

Gibson and his colleagues at Melbourne took an interest in continental European philosophy, particularly in the work of **Bergson**. Perhaps he is best remembered for his contributions to the introduction of phenomenology into the English-speaking world—his translation of **Husserl**'s *Ideen zu einer reinen Phänomenologie* and his articles on the ethics of Nicolai **Hartmann**.
Sources: ADB 8; Spiegelberg.

STUART BROWN

Gilbert, Katherine Everett

American. *b:* 29 July 1886, Newport, Rhode Island. *d:* 28 April 1952, Durham, North Carolina. *Cat:* Aesthetician. *Ints:* History of aesthetics; poetry and poetics; philosophy of feeling. *Educ:* Brown and Cornell Universities. *Infls:* Literary influences: Plato, Aristotle, M. Blondel, B. Croce, Virginia Woolf and Ruskin. Personal: Helmut Kuhn and James Edwin Creighton. *Appts:* 1915–19, Editorial Assistant, *Philosophical Review*; 1922–30, Research Fellow then (1928) Acting Professor, then (1929) Lecturer in Philosophy, University of North Carolina; 1930–51, Professor of Philosophy, then (1942) Chair of the Department of Aesthetics, Art and Music, Duke University; 1947–8, President of the American Society for Aesthetics.

Main publications:

(1924) *Maurice Blondel's Philosophy of Action*, Chapel Hill: University of North Carolina Press.

(1927) *Studies in Recent Aesthetics*, Chapel Hill: University of North Carolina Press.

(1939) (with Helmut Kuhn) *A History of Esthetics*, New York: Macmillan.

(1952) *Aesthetic Studies*, Durham: Duke University Press (posthumous).

Secondary literature:

Erwin, LuLu C. (1952) 'Katherine Gilbert: a bibliography', in Katherine Gilbert, *Aesthetic Studies*, Durham: Duke University Press.

New York Times, Obituary, 29 April 1952.

Gilbert was one of the outstanding American aestheticians of the first half of the present century and one of the first women to be a full Professor at an American University.

Her philosophy of art was 'not the result of manipulating abstract relations nor of fixating pure essences, but of the natural wonder about things going on around us in the arts' (1952, p. v). She believed that the philosopher needs the constant aid of the richer and finer analysis of detail of the art critic (1939, p. 290).

In the monumental and acclaimed *History of Esthetics* (1939) Gilbert and Helmut **Kuhn** set out to discover what art and beauty mean, and arrived at the conclusion that their meaning is not 'within any four corners of any one or two propositions', but 'within the dialectic of the whole manifold of philosophical systems and styles' (p. xi). Gilbert wrote on many other subjects, including architecture, poetics and the function of imagination. Like Ruskin she refused to separate any one aspect of life from any other. Neglect of her work in the latter half of the twentieth century was probably due to the development of a general aversion to synoptic philosophies.
Sources: WW: Kersey.

STEPHEN MOLLER

Gilson, Étienne Henri

French. *b:* 13 June 1884, Paris. *d:* 19 September 1978, Auxerre, France. *Cat:* Neoscholastic. *Ints:* History of philosophy; metaphysics; epistemology; aesthetics. *Educ:* University of Paris. *Infls:* Lucien Lévy-Bruhl, Descartes, Aquinas and Bonaventure. *Appts:* 1921–32, University of Sorbonne; 1932–51, Collège de France; 1929–78, Institute of Medieval Studies, University of Toronto.

Main publications:

(1919) *Le Thomisme*, Strasbourg: Vix, sixth edition, Paris: Vrin, 1986 (English translation of fifth edition, *The Christian Philosophy of St. Thomas Aquinas*, London: Gollancz, 1957).

(1937) *The Unity of Philosophical Experience*, New York: Charles Scribner's Sons.

(1948) *L'Etre et l'essence*, Paris: Vrin, second edition, 1962 (English translation, *Being and Some Philosophers*, Toronto: Pontifical Institute of Medieval Studies, 1949; second edition, 1952).

(1960) *Le philosophe et la théologie*, Paris: Fayard (English translation *The Philosopher and Theology*, New York: Random House, 1962).

(1963) *Introduction aux arts de beau*, Paris: Vrin (English version, *The Arts of the Beautiful*, New York: Charles Scribner's Sons, 1965).

McCool, Gerald A. (1989) *From Unity to Pluralism*, New York: Fordham University Press, pp. 161–99.
McGrath, Margaret (1982) *Étienne Gilson: A Bibliography. Une Bibliographie*, Toronto: Pontifical Institute of Medieval Studies (complete bibliography of Gilson's works).
Quinn, John M. (1971) *The Thomism of Étienne Gilson*, Villanova, Pa.: Villanova University Press.
Shook, Laurence K. (1984) *Étienne Gilson*, Toronto: Pontifical Institute of Medieval Studies.
Van Riet, Georges (1965) *Thomistic Epistemology*, 2 vols, St Louis & London: Herder, vol. II, pp. 153–74.
Van Steenberghen, Fernand (1979) 'Étienne Gilson: historien de la pensée médiévale', *Revue Philosophique de Louvain* 77: 487–508.

Gilson was the most influential historian of medieval philosophy in the twentieth century. His historical studies led him to adopt the philosophy of Thomas Aquinas as his own, and to expound a metaphysics and a theory of knowledge which, despite his claim that they were simply the views of Aquinas himself, disturbed, or at least irritated, many advocates of orthodox Thomism.

His studies of the medieval period began by a kind of accident, when it was suggested to him that he should examine the medieval provenance of Descartes's thought. He quickly came to the conclusion not only that Descartes had deep roots in medieval philosophy, but also that Cartesian philosophy was in some ways inferior to it. Thenceforward he immersed himself in medieval philosophy, and argued constantly that the great medieval thinkers attained a level of sophistication and insight superior to any philosophy before or after.

One of the first shocks that Gilson administered to conventional Thomists was to show that medieval philosophy was not a simple homogeneous body of thought, still less a mere reworking of Aristotle. In a number of brilliant studies of Aquinas (1919), Bonaventure (1924), Augustine (1929), St Bernard (1934) and Duns Scotus (1952), as well as shorter pieces on Abelard and Albertus Magnus, and other works on medieval philosophy as a whole, he demonstrated that there were radical differences amongst its greatest figures. He thus permanently changed the map of medieval philosophy, and also indirectly challenged the very conception of a homogeneous 'Scholastic Philosophy', whether conceived of as a medieval phenomenon or as a single tradition surviving intact to the present day.

The only incontestable constant in medieval philosophy, according to Gilson, was that it was practised within the context of a belief in God and an acceptance of Christian revelation. (In the same way, contemporary philosophy is practised in a context of quantum mechanics, evolutionism, biogenetic theory, and the like.) This is why he described it as 'Christian' philosophy. By this he meant, not that philosophy and theology, or reason and faith, were confused with one another, but that faith provided insights and data for philosophy to examine and exploit. Christian revelation was, as he put it, 'an indispensable auxiliary to reason'. Gilson's view that medieval philosophy was Christian philosophy was vigorously contested by several of his scholastic contemporaries, most notably by Fernand **Van Steenberghen**.

One of the most decisive insights borrowed by philosophy from Christian faith, according to Gilson, was found in Exodus 3:14, in the Vulgate *ego sum qui sum*, 'I am who am'. In neo-Platonic thought, the creative source of the universe was regarded as something beyond being, therefore something unknowable and unnameable except as non-being. Augustine was inspired by Exodus, Gilson argued, to transform this creative source from non-being into being, and to identify it with the Christian God. Thus, from Augustine onwards the concept of being came to occupy a central role in metaphysics. For Augustine, however, heavily influenced as he still was by Platonic thought, God's being was an immutable essence, from which created being flowed and in which it participated. Knowledge, for instance, was an illumination by the divine intellect, since there could be no other source of its being than the divine being himself.

Aquinas, whose classical mentor was Aristotle, transformed the concept of being again, according to Gilson, this time into the idea of an activity: being as analogous to kicking or throwing. Being in this sense, Gilson argues, refers primarily to existence, not to essence. For Augustine, God had been an immutable essence; for Aquinas, God was the pure act of existence, He whose entire nature it is to exist. His essence is existence. Furthermore, God is not so much the source as the cause of finite existents. He communicates existence to them; and in them, too, existence is an act-of-being, although one which is limited and determined by the essence whose existence it is.

Gilson's theory of knowledge flows from his metaphysics of existence, although, as Georges Van Riet has shown, it underwent various changes and perhaps was never wholly satisfactory. The problem of knowledge, for Gilson, was the problem of explaining our knowledge of an external reality, which is in large part a world of objects. Finite objects possess both essence and existence. The intellect enables us to know the essence of things, but their existence is not conceptualizable. Neither is their existence a sensible quality. How, then, can really existing objects be known? Gilson's answer is that they can be known in a judgement of existence. This kind of judgement differs from the judgement of attribution, which is the judgement studied in logic. In the judgement of existence, the verb 'to be' is not a copula: it is used, not to affirm a predicate of a subject, but rather to affirm its reality.

In his later years Gilson turned his hand to aesthetics; or rather, to the philosophy of art. The roots of art, he argued, lie in the fecundity and dynamism of being, in being-as-act. In humankind, this dynamism generates the order of factivity, of making as opposed to knowing. There is an infinite variety in human making, much of it for utilitarian ends or else for the sake of knowledge or desire. The fine arts, however, have as their end the production of beautiful objects, that is, objects of which the sensuous apprehension is pleasing. Objects of this kind possess the properties of wholeness, proportion and clarity.

The production of beautiful objects is the only purpose of art. Art is not knowledge, nor intuition, nor expression; nor is it symbolical. Works of art may, of course, contain other elements: dramatic, expressive, cognitive, conative; but in so far as they are works of art, they are simply objects of beauty. Similarly, our experiences of art may have a cognitive element, and in the case of a poet such as Dante this may be powerful and significant. But in so far as we experience Dante's poetry as a work of art, we sensuously perceive it just as a beautiful object made out of language. For Gilson, the order of knowing and the order of making might be mingled in artistic realities, but they were conceptually distinct, and were the product and the object of different mental activities.

Sources: DFN; EF; WWW.

HUGH BREDIN

Giner de los Rios, Francisco

Spanish. *b:* 10 October 1839, Ronda, Málaga, Spain. *d:* 17 February 1915, Madrid. *Cat:* Philosopher of law; personalist. *Educ:* Educated in Law in Barcelona and in Granada, where he earned his degree in 1959. *Infls:* Javier Llorens, Julián Sanz del Río and Fernando de Castro. *Appts:* Professor of Philosophy of Law; Madrid University. Resigned for political reasons in 1875, then founded the Institución Libre de Enseñanzo.

Main publications:

(1875) *Estudios jurídicos y políticos*, Madrid.
(1876) *Estudios filosóficos y religiosos*, Madrid.
(1886) *Estudios sobre la educación*, Madrid.
(1898) *Resumen de la filosofía del derecho*, Madrid: Suárez.
(1899) *Estudios y fragmentos sobre la teoría de la persona social*, Madrid.
(1904) *Filosofía y sociología*, Barcelona.
(1973) *Ensayos*, Madrid: Alianza.
(1977) *Antología pedagógica*, Madrid: Santillana.
(1990) *Escritos sobre la universidad española*, Madrid: Espasa Calpe.

Secondary literature:

(1965) *Ensayso y cartas: Edición de homenaje en el cincuentenario de su muerte*, Mexico: Tezontle.
Gómez Molleda, Dolores (1977) *Unamuno 'agitador de espíritus' y Giner: Correspondencia inédita*, Madrid: Narcea.

Giner de los Ríos is perhaps best known for founding the Institución Libre de Enseñanza in 1876, an organization dedicated to establishing private educational institutions that would not be controlled by the church or the state. Many of Giner's philosophical preoccupations revolved around pedagogical issues. He believed that education would play a vital role in the future of society. He was also a philosopher of law who believed that law was a function of the individual's ability to 'loan' solidarity to the community. Giner's thought was deeply influenced by Krausism and personalism.

AMY A. OLIVER

Goblot, (Léonce Laurent) Edmond

French. *b:* 13 November 1858, Mamers, Sarthe, France. *d:* 9 August 1935, Labaroche, Vosges. *Cat:* Methodologist of science; metaphysician. *Ints:* Logical theory; classification; epistemology; teleology. *Educ:* Paris, École Normale Supérieure, doctorate 1898; 1914, corresponding member of the Académie des Sciences Morales et Politiques.

Infls: Jules Lachelier and Émile Boutroux. *Appts:* 1884, Valenciennes; 1885, Pau; 1886, Angers; 1897, Toulouse; 1901, Caen; 1905–30, Lyon.

Main publications:

(1898) *Essai sur la classification des sciences*, Paris: Alcan.

(1898) *De musicae apud veteres cum philosophia conjunctione*, Paris; Alcan.

(1899) 'Fonction et finalité', *Revue Philosophique*, 47: 495–505.

(1900) 'La Finalité sans intelligence', *Revue de Métaphysique et de Morale* 10: 393–406.

(1901) *Vocabulaire Philosophique*, Paris: Colin.

(1902) *Justice et Liberté*, Paris: Alcan.

(1903–4) 'La Finalité en biologie', *Revue Philosophique* 56: 366–81, and 57: 24–37.

(1918) *Traité de logique*, Paris: Colin.

(1922) *Le Système des sciences*, Paris: Colin.

(1927) *La Logique des jugements de valeur*, Paris: Colin.

Secondary literature:

Maldidier, J. (1899) Review of *Essai sur la classification* (1898), in *Revue Philosophique* 37: 313–20.

Nicod, J. (1919) Review of *Traité de logique* (1918), in *Revue de Métaphysique et de Morale*: 375–85.

Vialatoux, J. (1913) 'La Connaissance de la finalité', *Revue Philosophique* 30: 7–34.

While technical logic is not absent from his work, Goblot's main concern was the philosophy of science, motivated by concerns in political economy and sociology, and his work was freely compared with that of Mill. He made the psychology of the knower and the act of judgement the centre of his thinking in a way popular at the time but now controversial. He attempted to rehabilitate finality in biology.

Sources: Edwards; A. Lalande (1935) 'Allocution', *STASMP* 23; J. Kergomard, P. Salzi and F. Goblot (1937) *Edmond Goblot, la vie, l'oeuvre*, Paris: Alcan; FranBio 1985.

R. N. D. MARTIN

Gödel, Kurt

Austrian-American (American citizen from 1948). *b:* 28 April 1906, Brunn, Austria (now Brno, Czech Republic). *d:* 14 January 1978, Princeton, New Jersey. *Cat:* Mathematical logician and philosopher of mathematics. *Ints:* Platonism in mathematics. *Educ:* 1924, University of Vienna, PhD 1930; associated with Vienna Circle. *Infls:* Plato, Leibniz, and David Hilbert. *Appts:* 1933–40, University of Vienna; 1933–8, Privatdo-

cent; 1953–76, Professor, Institute for Advanced Studies, Princeton; 1951, Einstein Award; 1975, National Medal for Science. Honorary doctorates from Universities of Yale, Harvard, Rockefeller, and from Amherst College, Mass. Member of the National Academy of Sciences, the American Academy of Arts and Sciences, and the Royal Society of London, corresponding member of the Academie de Science Morale et Politique, Paris, and the British Academy.

Main publications:

(1986–) *Collected Works*, ed. S. Feferman, Oxford: Clarendon Press. Includes:

(1930) (thesis) 'Über die Vollständigkeit des Logikalkulas' [On the completeness of the logical calculus].

(1930) 'Die Vollständigkeit der Axiome des logischen Funktionenkalkuls' [The completeness of the axioms of the logical calculus of functions].

(1930) 'Einige metamathematische Resultate über Entscheidungsdefinitheit und Widersprufsfreiheit' [Some metamathematical results concerning completeness and consistency].

(1931) 'Über formal unentscheidbare Sätze der *Principia Mathematica* und verwandter systeme' [On formally undecidable propositions of *Principia Mathematica* and related systems] (published in English, New York: Dover Books, 1992).

(1936) 'Über die Länge von Beweisen' [On the length of proofs].

(1938) 'The consistency of the axioms of choice and of the generalized continuum hypothesis with the axioms of set theory' (reprinted Princeton, NJ: Princeton University Press, 1970).

(1939) 'Consistency-proof for the generalized continuum-hypothesis'.

(1940) 'The consistency of the continuum-hypotheisism' (third edition, corrected, 1953).

(1944) 'Russell's mathematical logic', in P. A. Schilpp, ed., *The Philosophy of Bertrand Russell* (Library of Living Philosophers series).

(1947) 'What is Cantor's continuum problem?'

(1949) 'A remark about the relationship between relativity theory and idealistic philosophy' in P. A. Schilpp (ed.) *A. Einstein: A Philosopher Scientist*.

(1958) 'Über eines bisher noch nicht benutzte Erweiterung des finitem Standpunktes' [On a hitherto unused amplification of the finite point of view].

Secondary literature:

Dawson, J. W. (1969) *The Foundations of Mathematics: Symposium Papers Commemorating the Sixtieth Birthday of Kurt Gödel*, Berlin/Heidelberg/NY: Springer Verlag.

———(1984) *The Papers of Kurt Gödel: An Inventory*, Princeton, NJ: The Institute for Advanced Studies.

Kurt Gödel Colloquium (1989) *Proceedings of the First Kurt Gödel Colloquium Sept 1989*, Vienna: Kurt-Gödel-Gesellschaft.

Lolli, Gabrielle (1992) *Incompletezza: saggio su Kurt Gödel*, Bologna: Il Mulino.

Nagel, E. and Newman, J. R. (1958) *Gödel's Proof*, New York: New York University Press.

Shanker, S. G. (ed.) (1988) *Gödel's Theorem in Focus*, Croom Helm.

Between 1930 and 1940 Gödel was responsible for three significant developments in mathematical logic. These were, first, the completeness proof relating to the first-order functional calculus; second, the theorem known as Gödel's Theorem, (the first incompleteness theorem); and third, a demonstration that the system of **Russell**'s and **Whitehead**'s *Principia Mathematica*, which the incompleteness theorem showed to be apparently inconsistent, could be rendered consistent.

Gödel's Theorem constituted a major challenge not only to the generally-held assumption that basic systems in mathematics are complete in that they contain no statements that can be either proved or disproved, but also to **Hilbert**'s view that proofs of the consistency of such a system can be formulated within the system itself. Briefly, the theorem states that in a formal system S of arithmetic, there will be a sentence P of the language of S such that if S is consistent neither P nor its negation can be proved within S. The impact of this on *Principa Mathematica* was to undermine the latter's project of providing a set of logical axioms from which the whole of pure mathematics, as well as the non-axiomatic residue of logic, were deducible, since the theorem showed that mathematics contains propositions that are neither provable nor disprovable from the axioms. Gödel's ingenious argument revealed that in proving the consistency of the system one would also secure a proof that a particular statement, T, could not be proved, and also a proof of statement T. This shows that a consistency proof of ordinary arithmetic is not possible using finite procedures. In connection with this it has been claimed that Gödel's theorem demonstrates that human beings are superior to machines since they can know to be true propositions that no machine programmed with axioms and rules can prove.

After 1940 Gödel extended his interests in the philosophy of mathematics, working in greater detail on the relationship of the continuum hypothesis and the axiom of choice to set theory. His 1949 paper includes a curious argument for the unreality of time. But it is the famous first incompleteness proof that has generated, and continues to generate, lively debate among philosophers.

Sources: Turner.

DIANÉ COLLINSON

Golaszewska, Maria

Polish. *b:* 29 June 1926, Kurzelolw, Poland. *Cat:* Phenomenologist. *Ints:* Aesthetics; existentialism; value theory. *Educ:* 1945–50, Jagiellonian University, Cracow; 1956, Catholic University of Lublin. *Infls:* Roman Ingarden, existentialism and phenomenology. *Appts:* 1963, Assistant Professor, 1981, Head of the Department of Aesthetics, Jagiellonian University, Cracow.

Main publications:

(1958) *Tworczosc a osobowosc tworcy: Analiza procesu twórczego* [Creativity and the Personality of the Author: Analysis of the Process of Creation], Lublin: KUL (with résumé in French).

(1970) *Swiadomosc piekna: Zagadnienie genezy, structury, funkcji i wartosci w estetyce* [Consciousness of Beauty: Issues of Genesis, Structure, Function and the Value in Aesthetics], Warsaw: PWN.

(1973) *Zarys estetyki: Problematyka, metody, teorie* [Outline of Aesthetics: Problems, Methods, Theories], Cracow: WL; second edition, 1984; third edition, Warsaw: PWN, 1986.

(1984) *Estetyka rzeczywistosci* [The Aesthetics of Reality], Warsaw: PAX.

(1990) *Istota i istnienie wartosci: Studium o wartosciach estetycznych na tle sytuacji aksjologicznej* [The Essence and Existence of Value: Aesthetic Values in the Context of the Axiological Situation], Warsaw: PWN.

(1994) *Fascynacja zlem: Eseje z teorii wartosci* [The Fascination of Evil: Essays on the Theory of Value], Warsaw Cracow: Wydawnictwo Naukowe and PWN.

(1995) *Poetyka idei ogolnych* [The Poetics of General Ideas], Cracow: UJ.

Secondary literature:

Essays on Beauty: Problems of Aesthetics and the Theory of Art (1988), Warsaw and Cracow: PWN (Festschrift).

Starting from the context of Roman **Ingarden**'s philosophy, Golaszewska has examined and developed, in a steady flow of books, papers and articles, a network of concepts relating to aesthetics, axiology and philosophical anthropology.

In particular she has elaborated a concept of the aesthetic situation as constituted by the artist, the work of art, the perceiver and aesthetic value; and a concept of aesthetic value regarded as the expression of extra-rational attitudes towards the world. The unifying purpose of her work, which always has an empirical orientation that takes account of aesthetic and artistic facts, is to clarify the subject matter and methods of aesthetics and to define aesthetic values. In some of her later work she has focused on the specific place of knowledge in aesthetic culture, distinguishing the various cognitive functions that the arts can fulfil, but identifying as central their capacity to transmit, through the direct engagement of the perceiver, truths concerning reality, human consciousness and the self. The full bibliography of her writings contains over 170 items.

Sources: *Aesthetics at Jagellionian University of Cracow*, Cracow: Jagellionian Univ., 1985; letters and papers supplied by Maria Golaszewska.

DIANÉ COLLINSON

Goldman, A(lvin) I(ra)

American. *b:* 1 October 1938, Brooklyn, New York. *Cat:* Analytical philosopher. *Ints:* Philosophy of mind; epistemology; social philosophy; cognitive science. *Educ:* Columbia and Princeton Universities. *Appts:* 1964–73, Assistant then Associate Professor of Philosophy, from 1973, Professor of Philosophy, University of Michigan, Ann Arbor; from 1983, Regents' Professor of Philosophy, University of Arizona.

Main publications:

(1967) 'A causal theory of knowing', *Journal of Philosophy* 64: 357–72.
(1970) *A Theory of Human Action*, Englewood Cliffs, NJ: Prentice-Hall.
(1985) 'The relation between epistemology and psychology, *Synthèse* 64: 29–68.
(1986) *Epistemology and Cognition*, Cambridge, Mass.: Harvard University Press.
(1988) *Empirical Knowledge*, Berkeley: University of California Press.
(1992) *Liaisons: Philosophy Meets the Cognitive and Social Sciences*, Cambridge, Mass.: MIT Press (collection of some of his main papers).
(1993) *Philosophical Applications of Cognitive Science*, Boulder, Col.: Westview Press.

Secondary literature:

Feldman, Richard (1989) 'Goldman on epistemology and cognitive science', *Philosophia* (Israel) 19: 197–207 (includes other commentaries and replies from Goldman).
Gorr, Michael (1979) 'Agency and causation', *Journal for the Theory of Social Behaviour* 9: 114.
Jacobson, Anne Jaap (1992) 'A problem of naturalizing epistemologies', *Southern Journal of Philosophy* 30, 4: 31–49.
Lammenranta, Markus (1992) 'Scepticism and Goldman's naturalism', *Ratio* 5, 1: 38–45.

Goldman first made his mark with a journal article in 1967, in which he offered a novel solution to the much-discussed 'Gettier' problem with the view that knowledge is justified true belief. The problem is that someone might, as certain examples were designed to show, be fully justified in believing something and yet only be right by accident. Goldman proposed that, in the case of all empirical knowledge, it is a necessary condition that there is some sort of causal connection between the knower's belief and the fact known. He offered a similar kind of analysis in his 1970 book, where he put forward a causal theory of human action, according to which it is a necessary condition for an item of behaviour to constitute an intentional action that it has been caused in the right sort of way by certain of the agent's prior mental states. Both Goldman's theories, especially his causal theory of knowledge, have been extensively discussed and have been influential despite the problems commentators have found. His book of 1986 put forward a controversial view of epistemology as partially linked to cognitive psychology, on the ground that certain basic psychological processes have 'truth-conducive' properties. In his 1993 book he went so far as to claim that the potential enrichment of philosophy from its interaction with cognitive science was as great as that produced by the interactions with logic at the beginning of the century.

Sources: CA; DAS; PI.

STUART BROWN

Goldmann, Lucien

Franco-Romanian. *b:* 1913, Bucharest, Romania. *d:* 1970, Paris. *Cat:* Marxist; social philosopher; literary theorist. *Educ:* Universities of Bucharest and Zurich. *Infls:* Marx, Lukács and Piaget. *Appts:* Director of Studies, École Pratique des Hautes Études, Paris.

Main publications:

(1945) *Mensch, Gemeinschaft und Welt in der philosophie Immanuel Kants*, Zurich: Europa Verlag (English translation, *Immanuel Kant*, trans. Robert Black, London: NLB, 1971).

(1952) *Sciences humaines et philosophie*, Paris: Presses Universitaires de France (English translation, *The Human Sciences and Philosophy*, trans. Hayden White and Robert Anchor, London: Jonathan Cape, 1969).

(1956) *Le Dieu caché: étude sur la vision tragique dans les Pensées de Pascal et le théâtre de Racine*, Paris: (English translation, *The Hidden God: A Study of Tragic Vision in the Pensées of Pascal and the Tragedies of Racine*, trans. Philip Thody, London: Routledge & Kegan Paul, 1964).

(1956) *Racine*, Paris: L'Arche (English translation, *Racine*, trans. Alastair Hamilton, Cambridge: Rivers Press, 1972).

(1959) *Recherches dialectiques*, Paris: Gallimard.

(1964) *Pour une sociologie du roman*, Paris: Gallimard (English translation, *Towards a Sociology of the Novel*, trans. Alan Sheridan, London: Tavistock, 1975).

(1968) *Der christliche Bürger und die Aufklärung*, Neuwied: Luchterhand (English translation, *The Philosophy of the Enlightenment*, trans. Henry Maas, London: Routledge & Kegan Paul, 1973).

(1970) *Marxisme et sciences humaines*, Paris: Gallimard.

(1971) *La création culturelle dans la société moderne*, Paris: Denoel (English translation, *Cultural Creation in Modern Society*, trans. Bart Grahl, St Louis: Telos Press, 1976).

(1971) *Situation de la critique racienne*, Paris: L'Arche.

(1973) *Lukács et Heidegger: pour une nouvelle philosophie*, Paris: Denoël (English translation, *Lukács and Heidegger: Towards a New Philosophy*, trans. W. Boelhower, London: RKP, 1977).

Secondary literature:
Eagleton, Terry (1976) *Marxism and Literary Criticism*, London: Methuen.
Evans, Mary (1981) *Lucien Goldmann: An Introduction*, Brighton: Harvester.
Slaughter, Cliff (1980) *Marxism, Ideology and Literature*, London and Basingstoke: Macmillan.

Goldmann's main source of inspiration was the work of the early **Lukács**, in particular the latter's *Theory of the Novel* and *History and Class Consciousness*. An important figure in the development of a Marxist sociology of literature, Goldmann devised the method of literary analysis known as 'genetic structuralism', which sought to identify homologies (or structural parallels) between literary texts and the worldviews of key social groups contemporary with the texts. Thus

in *The Hidden God* (1956) Pascal's philosophical writings and Racine's dramas were analysed with reference to debates within the Jansenist movement during the seventeenth century.
Sources: See secondary literature.

STUART SIM

Goodman, Nelson
American. **b:** 7 August 1906, Somerville, Massachusetts. **Cat:** Analytic philosopher. **Ints:** Philosophy of science; philosophy of language; aesthetics. **Educ:** Harvard University. **Infls:** Carnap and C. I. Lewis. **Appts:** Instructor and Professor, University of Pennsylvania, 1946–64; Professor, Brandeis University, 1964–7; Professor, Harvard, 1967–77.

Main publications:
(1951) *The Structure of Appearance*, Cambridge, Mass.: Harvard University Press.
(1954) *Fact, Fiction and Forecast*, London: Athlone Press.
(1968) *The Languages of Art*, London: Oxford University Press.
(1972) *Problems and Projects*, Indianapolis: Bobbs-Meuil.
(1978) *Ways of World-Making*, Inianapolis: Hachett.
(1984) *Of Mind and other Matters*, Cambridge: Mass.: Harvard University Press.
(1988) *Reconceptions in Philosophy* (with Catherine Z. Elgin), London: Routledge.

Secondary literature:
Ayer, A. J. *Philosophy in the Twentieth Century*, c. ix, 4.

Goodman, after undergraduate study of philosophy, worked for some years as an art dealer and then returned to the subject. After writing a distinguished thesis, which was the core of his first major publication, *The Structure of Appearance* (1951), he entered the academic philosophical profession. Even more than **Quine**, his early collaborator and for many years his colleague at Harvard, Goodman is remarkable for his combination of extreme conceptual austerity with speculative intrepidity. He also has a stylistic likeness to Quine: both combine exquisite concision with a measure of playfulness. In an early article which he wrote with Quine they declared their predilection for nominalism. But it emerged that they understood it in different ways. Quine wanted to countenance only concrete individuals: Goodman had no objection to the abstract, but reserved his hostility for classes, which Quine thought had to be admitted to make sense of mathematics. In that first book he took as his starting-point **Carnap**'s *The Logical Construction of the World*. There Carnap had sought to display the entirety of the linguistic apparatus with which matters of fact are described as reducible by definitions and the instruments of formal logic to the smallest possible undefined basis: the single empirical concept of recollection of similarity. Goodman endorsed Carnap's procedure, contrasting his book as a unique example of serious philosophy with everything else, described as 'amorphous philosophical discourses'. But he was highly critical of its detail, replacing its account of definition, providing it with a formal theory of simplicity and rejecting one of its main purposes, that of basing the whole construction on what is epistemologically primary or fundamental. In constructing a phenomenalistic system, he said, he was not claiming that it was in any way 'closer to the facts' than a physicalistic one. The elements he selects are individuals, but they are abstract ones, sense-qualia such colours and, more disputably, places and times. A concrete phenomenal item is the sum of a colour, a place and a time. Another object of Goodman's distaste, along with classes, is similarity. In an early article on likeness of meaning he argued against the notion of synonymy in a way that to some extent prefigured Quine's 'Two dogmas of empiricism' and the protracted campaign against meaning, intensions, properties and so forth that he developed from that article. Later Goodman generalized his critique of similarity, denying its explanatory power in any application. For him denotation or extension is intelligible and that is all there is to general terms applying to a multiplicity of things. Nothing is added by saying that things to which such a word applies are connected by similarity to each other. Congruous with Goodman's preference for individuals is his actualism, his unwillingness to countenance possibilities over and above what there actually is. These have been invoked by philosophers to explain the difference between laws of nature and merely accidental generalities and also to interpret counterfactual conditionals. Laws of nature, it has been suggested, are those from which we are prepared to infer counterfactuals. A most effectively argued paper on this (now the first chapter of *Fact, Fiction and Forecast* (1955)) concludes that counterfactuals, such as 'if this had been put in water it would have dissolved' (also expressible with the use of 'dispositional predicate this is soluble') amount to ascribing some property, presumably microstructural, which is possessed by all those things that do dissolve in water, to the thing of which the disposition is being predicated. He went on, in *Fact, Fiction and Forecast*, to propound what he called a 'new riddle of induction'. Why do we take 'all emeralds up to now have been green' to confirm 'all emeralds whatever are green' and not 'all emeralds are grue', where 'grue' means 'green up to now and blue from now'? Neatly parrying objections, obvious and subtle, Goodman concludes that we project those predicates into unrestricted generalizations and singular predictions ('the next emerald I come on will be blue') that are *entrenched*, that we have got into the habit of projecting. An early paper with the economical title 'About' foreshadowed the elaborate account of the nature of representation in art in his *Languages of Art* (1968). In it the view that art represents the world mimetically by resembling it is emphatically rejected. Works of art are symbols, like sentences, and, like sentences, they have cognitive value and enlarge our knowledge or understanding of the world. In *Ways of World-Making* (1978) a multitude of world-versions, over and above those of art and science, are countenanced, such as the world (or world-version) of common sense, which is not too disturbing, but also those of particular artists or even musical composers. Analogies of denotation or representation are here stretched, many would feel, to breaking point, while the incompatibility, as contrasted with the different selectivenesses, of the apparently competing versions is overdramatized. Much of Goodman's work has been very widely and actively discussed. His early Carnapian idea of formally systematic philosophy has not been carried on by him or others but his philosophical conscience ('I do not want there to be more things in my philosophy than there are in heaven and earth') has been a valuable example.

Sources: Edwards; Passmore 1985.

ANTHONY QUINTON

Gouhier, Henri

French. *b:* 1898, Auxerre. *Cat:* Historian of philosophy. *Infls:* Paul Janet, Alfred Espinas and Étienne Gilson. *Appts:* Professor, then Emeritus Professor, of Philosophy at the Sorbonne; Member of the Académie Française, the Académie des Sciences Morales et Politiques and various other European intellectual societies.

Main publications:

(1924) *La Pensée religieuse de Descartes*, Paris: Vrin.
(1926) *La Philosophie de Malebranche et son expérience religieuse*, Paris: Vrin.

(1937) *Essais sur Descartes*, Paris: Vrin.
(1943) *La Philosophie et son histoire*, Paris: Vrin.
(1952) *L'Histoire et sa philosophie*, Paris: Vrin.
(1952) *Le Théâtre et l'existence*, Paris: Aubier.
(1958) *Les premières pensées de Descartes*, Paris: Vrin.
(1962) *La Pensée métaphysique de Descartes*, Paris: Vrin.
(1966) *Pascal: commentaires*, Paris: Vrin.
(1977) *Fénelon philosophe*, Paris: Vrin.
(1978) *Cartésianisme et Augustinisme au XVIIe siècle*, Paris: Vrin.
(1980) *Etudes sur l'histoire des idées en France depuis le XVIIe siècle*, Paris: Vrin.
(1988) *Trois Essais sur Étienne Gilson*, Paris: Vrin.

One of Gouhier's main interests in the history of philosophy, as can be seen from the list of his publications, is the metaphysics of Descartes. He and Étienne **Gilson** led the revival in the study of Cartesian metaphysics during the early part of this century. One strong theme which emerges from Gouhier's work is that Descartes was an anti-Renaissance figure: he rejected the weight of authority, classical learning and Aristotelian science, and is rightly regarded as one of the founders of modern philosophy.

In the prefaces to his various works on Descartes, Gouhier sets out the principles by which he thinks that the history of philosophy should be written. He says that the historian should enquire into both the lives of the philosophers studied and their cultural and intellectual background. In tracing the origins and development of their thought the writer should work under a self-imposed amnesia about the completed philosophical position in order to promote understanding of how that position was arrived at. Philosophy must be studied through its history in order to be properly understood. No history of philosophy is definitive: they should all be viewed against the background of their own times and preoccupations.

Gouhier thinks that every work studied by the historian of philosophy is to be regarded as a dialogue between the author of the work and his contemporary and subsequent readers.

KATHRYN PLANT

Gourd, Jean-Jacques
Swiss (naturalized in 1876). *b:* September 1850, Fleix. *d:* May 1909, Geneva. *Cat:* Phenomenalist. *Ints:* Philosophy of religion. *Educ:* Geneva, Leipzig, Berlin, Heidelberg and Tübingen, initially Theology and then Philosophy. *Infls:* Kant and

Renouvier. *Appts:* Entered the ministry, 1879; Professor of the History of Philosophy, University of Geneva, 1881–1909; active on the international scene from the time of the first International Congress of Philosophy, Paris, 1900–; admired by Bergson and Boutroux.

Main publications:
(1888) *Le phénomène, Esquisse de philosophie générale.*
(1897) *Les trois dialectiques.*
(1911) *Philosophie de la religion.*

Secondary literature:
Reymond, M. (1949) *La Philosophie de Jean-Jacques Gourd*, Chambéry: Editions Lire.

Best remembered for his philosophy of religion, this aspect of Gourd's thought rests on a phenomenalist epistemology. The ultimate datum in philosophy is the field of consciousness, in which both reality and the self are given as phenomena—this phenomenalism Gourd regarded as the way to avoid positing an unknowable noumenon. His second major assertion (reminiscent of Pascal, though Gourd hardly ever refers to him) is that the analysis of the field of consciousness reveals that it is not coextensive with reason, but contains an irrational element which Gourd calls the incoordinable, sharply distinguished from the coordinable (the domain of reason).

The use of reason increases knowledge in terms of its extent; the incoordinable is grasped by intuition, and furnishes us with intensive knowledge. Gourd finds incoordinable elements in many areas of experience: society (initiative), morality (sacrifice) and the aesthetic (the sublime)—generally in whatever is unforseeable, individual and creative. The major field of experience, however, in which the incoordinable is most fully manifest is that of religion, where we must use concepts such as mystery, revelation and grace in order to capture the quality of the experiences concerned. The ultimate experience of the incoordinable is the mystical, union with that which is beyond all concepts and laws. In this way Gourd, who was personally a deeply and genuinely religious man, sought to allow for the possibility of religious knowledge within a phenomenalist epistemology.

ROBERT WILKINSON

Gramsci, Antonio
Italian. *b:* 1891, Ales, Sardinia. *d:* 1937, Rome. *Cat:*

Marxist; political philosopher; culture theorist. **Educ:** 1911, University of Turin, but did not complete his degree. **Infls:** Marx, Hegel, Lenin, Croce and Sorel. **Appts:** Gramsci held no formal academic appointments, working as a journalist and politician.

Main publications:

(1948–51) *Quaderni del carcere*, Turin: Einaudi (*Prison Notebooks*, trans. Quintin Hoare and Geoffrey Nowell Smith, London: Lawrence & Wishart, 1971).
(1957) *The Modern Prince* (selection from papers given at Institutio Gramsci, Rome), trans. Louis Marks, New York: International Publishers.
(1965) *Lettere del carcere*, Turin: Einaudi (*Letters from Prison*, trans. Lynne Lawner, New York: Harper & Row, 1973).

Secondary literature:

Adamson, Walter L. (1977) *Hegemony and Revolution: A Study of Antonio Gramsci's Political and Cultural Theory*, Berkeley, Los Angeles and London: University of California Press.
Buci-Glucksmann, Christine (1980) *Gramsci and the State*, London: Lawrence & Wishart.
Cammett, John M. (1967) *Antonio Gramsci and the Origins of Italian Communism*, Stanford, CA: Stanford University Press.
Dombroski, Robert S. (1989) *Antonio Gramsci*, Boston: Twayne.
Joll, James (1977) *Gramsci*, London: Collins.
Pozzolini, A. (1970) *Antonio Gramsci: An Introduction to his Thought*, London: Pluto Press.
Williams, Gwyn A. (1975) *Proletarian Order: Antonio Gramsci, Factory Councils and the Origins of Communism in Italy*, London: Pluto Press.

Generally regarded as one of the most creative and original thinkers within the Marxist philosophical tradition, Gramsci spent most of his career in journalism and politics. He was active in the Turin Factory Council movement (a soviet-style workers' organization) in 1919–20, and after its suppression he edited *L'Ordine Nuovo*, later to become a Communist Party journal, and sat as a Deputy in the Italian Parliament. Gramsci was one of the founders of the Italian Communist Party, and although he was a political prisoner for the last ten years of his life, he went on to become one of the Party's major theorists through his prison writings. The earliest intellectual influence on Gramsci was the Italian idealist philosopher and aesthetician Benedetto **Croce**, whose work formed a lifelong source of inspiration despite the fact that its author ultimately turned fascist

sympathizer. From Croce, Gramsci derives his deeply held belief in the importance of history as an intellectual activity. Another important source of influence for Gramsci's intellectual development was the French syndicalist theorist Georges **Sorel**, whose faith in the working class and admiration for the organizational powers of the Catholic Church throughout history, Gramsci shared. Despite the strong pull of Marx and **Lenin**, Gramsci also retained a distinctly Hegelian bias to his thought, conceiving of the dialectic in primarily Hegelian terms. Gramsci's early concern as a Marxist theorist was to find ways of countering the fairly crude and mechanical forms of dialectical materialism being propounded by such Bolshevik theorists as Nikolai **Bukharin**. Marxism was for Gramsci not so much a sociological as a historical theory, and he differed considerably from Soviet orthodoxy on this issue, with his interest invariably being concentrated on cultural and historical factors rather than on purely economic considerations.

Gramsci can be credited with expounding a more human version of Marxist doctrine than most of his contemporaries, one less driven by the dictates of economic determinism and more committed to keeping the political leadership of a Marxist revolutionary movement in touch with the rank and file of its working-class members. Throughout his life Gramsci remained a firm believer in the use of persuasion to achieve political aims, as opposed to the more widespread Marxist–Lenin method of the imposition of party discipline and policy from above. The vision of the Communist Party put forward by Gramsci was a markedly less authoritarian one than usual, closer perhaps to the model of organization presented by the Catholic Church. Gramsci's major contributions to Marxist theory, including the enormously influential doctrine of hegemony, come mainly from his prison writings, not published until after the Second World War. 'Civil hegemony', to give it its full title, represents Gramsci's attempt to provide an explanation for history's periodic failure to conform to the determinist model of Marxism: if the conditions were ripe for the total collapse of the capitalist system, why did it not occur? A ruling class, Gramsci maintained, could keep control over the masses by means other than brute force or economic power. If it could encourage the masses to share its social, cultural and moral values then its dominant position, or 'hegemony', was assured. Thus the working class could often prove to be a reactionary rather than a revolutionary force, even though it could never be in its long-term interests to be so and despite the presence of the correct economic conditions for revolution, because it had internalized the values of its rulers. The continuing strength of capitalism could be attributed to the prevailing influence of hegemonic factors, hence the need for Marxist theorists to turn their attention to the cultural realm, where the ruling class's values were constructed. Intellectuals were allotted a key role in this process, and Gramsci set great store by education as a political weapon. The emphasis on ideas as a means of bringing about effective change is typical of Gramsci, who did not believe that change would be lasting unless individuals truly desired it and political leadership was based on cultural and moral ascendancy rather than just economic power. In *The Modern Prince* Gramsci reformulated Machiavelli's ideas about leadership so that the Communist Party was seen to be just such an instrument of cultural and moral ascendancy. Throughout the prison writings Gramsci evinces a greater interest in analysing the past and identifying historical laws than in laying down specific rules for future political action. He represents a humanist strain of thought within Marxism which owes much to a long-running tradition of humanism in Italian culture stretching back to the Renaissance period, and he remains one of the least 'economist', as well as least dogmatic, of Marxist theorists. Gramsci's humanistic interpretation of Marxist theory has exerted a considerable appeal amongst those Marxists unhappy with the excesses of Stalinism or the cruder forms of dialectical materialism favoured in Russian Communist circles. His reputation has grown steadily since his death and he is generally considered to be the most approachable of Marxist theorists to non-believers, given his lack of dogmatism. Within Italian political and cultural life since the collapse of fascism Gramsci has been a major force. The Italian Communist Party of the post-war period took much of its lead from Gramsci's example as both theorist and political activist, and showed itself more disposed to compromise than most such organizations. In Marxist circles outside Italy, Gramsci's influence is most clearly seen in the work of the French structural Marxist philosopher Louis Althusser, a great admirer of the Italian's ideas, particularly his analyses of the relationship between economic base and cultural superstructure (Althusser's notion of the relative autonomy of the superstructure echoes Gramsci's insistence on the latter's importance vis-à-vis the base) and his doctrine of hegemony. The latter doctrine has won wide acceptance among theorists and has been used to considerable effect in fields such as political science, sociology and aesthetics. Theorists of popular culture, as a case in point, rely heavily on the notion of hegemony in their analyses, and most Western Marxist aesthetic theorists have adopted the doctrine in order to draw attention to the crucial ideological role played by the arts within culture.

STUART SIM

Grene, Majorie Glicksman

American. *b:* 13 December 1910, Milwaukee, Wisconsin. *Cat:* Historian in philosophy; existentialist; philosopher of biology. *Ints:* Theory of knowledge. *Educ:* Wellesley College and Harvard University; exchange student in Germany, 1931–3. *Infls:* Literary influences include Plato, Aristotle, Kant and Merleau-Ponty; personal influences include Polanyi. *Appts:* 1936–7, Instructor, Monticello College; 1937–44, Assistant then Instructor in Philosophy, University of Chicago; 1957–8, Research Assistant to Michael Polanyi, University of Manchester; 1958–9, Senior Research Fellow in Education, Institute of Education, Leeds; 1959–60, Lecturer in Philosophy, University of Leeds; 1960–5, Lecturer in Philosophy, Queen's University, Belfast; 1965–78, Professor of Philosophy, University of Chicago, Davis, then Professor Emeritus; 1988–, Adjunct Professor of Philosophy and of Science Studies, Virginia Polytechnic Institute.

Main publications:

(1940) (ed. with T. V. Smith) *From Descartes to Kant*, Chicago: Chicago University Press.
(1948) *Dreadful Freedom*, Chicago: Chicago University Press.
(1957) *Martin Heidegger*, London: Bowes & Bowes.
(1963) *A Portrait of Aristotle*, Chicago: Chicago University Press.
(1966) *The Knower and the Known*, New York: Basic Books.
(1969) *Approaches to a Philosophical Biology*, New York: Basic Books.
(1969) (ed.) *The Anatomy of Knowledge*, Boston: University of Massachusetts Press.
(1969) (ed.) Michael Polanyi, *Knowing and Being*, Chicago: Chicago University Press.
(1971) (ed.) *Interpretations of Life and Mind*, New York: Humanities Press.
(1973) *Sartre*, New York: Franklin Watts.
(1973) (ed.) *Spinoza*, Garden City, NY: Doubleday.
(1974) *The Understanding of Nature: Essays in the Philosophy of Biology*, Dordrecht: D. Reidel.
(1975) (ed. with E. Mendelsohn) *Topics in the Philosophy of Biology*, Dordrecht: D. Reidel.

(1976) *Philosophy In and Out of Europe*, Berkeley and Los Angeles: University of California Press.

(1983) (ed.) *Dimensions of Darwinism*, Cambridge: Cambridge University Press.

(1985) *Descartes*, Hassocks: Harvester; Minnesota: Minnesota University Press.

(1986) (ed. with D. Nails) *Spinoza and the Sciences*, Dordrecht: D. Reidel.

(1992) (with Niles Eldredge) *Interactions: The Biological Context of Social Systems*, New York: Columbia University Press.

Secondary literature:

(1992) 'The thought of Marjorie Grene', *Synthese* 92, 1.

Donagan, A., Perovich, A. N. and Wedin, M. V. (eds) (1986) *Human Nature and Natural Knowledge*, Dordrecht: D. Reidel (contains bibliography of publications of Marjorie Grene).

As an exchange student in the early 1930s Marjorie Grene worked under both **Heidegger** and **Jaspers**, but it was not until reading **Merleau-Ponty** in the early 1960s that she came fully to appreciate what she had learnt from them. Partly as a possible antidote to Nazism she had become interested in logical positivism and attended **Carnap**'s seminars at Chicago in 1938–9. These in fact produced a firm rejection of positivist views, partly on account of the inadequacy of extensional logic to account for the field of biology.

The thought of Marjorie Grene unusually combines an intimate knowledge of existentialism and scholarship in classical and seventeenth-century philosophy with a major contribution to the philosophy of biology. Anti-Cartesianism, anti-reductionism and anti-scientism find expression in an emphasis on the biological and social but contingent nature of human being-in-the-world.

Sources: DAS, 5, 1982; CA NRS 25; telephone conversation.

CLIVE BORST

Grice, Herbert Paul

British-American. *b:* 15 March 1913, Birmingham, England. *d:* 28 August 1990, Berkeley, California. *Cat:* Linguistic philosopher. *Ints:* Metaphysics; philosophy of language; ethics; history of philosophy. *Educ:* Corpus Christi College, Oxford. *Infls:* Austin, Quine and Kripke. *Appts:* 1939–67, Fellow of St John's College, Oxford; 1967, presented William James Lectures at Harvard; 1967–80, Professor of Philosophy, Uni-

versity of California, Berkeley; 1980–84, Visiting Professor, University of Washington at Seattle; 1980–90, Emeritus Professor of Philosophy, University of California, Berkeley.

Main publications:

(1941) 'Personal identity', *Mind* 50.

(1956) (with Strawson) 'In defense of a dogma', *Philosophical Review* 65.

(1957) 'Meaning', *Philosophical Review* 66.

(1961) 'The causal theory of perception', *Proceedings of the Aristotelian Society*, Supplementary Volume.

(1968) 'Utterer's meaning, sentence-meaning and word-meaning', in *Foundations of Language* 4 (Dordrecht); reprinted in John Searle (ed.), *The Philosophy of Language*, London: Oxford University Press.

(1969) 'Vacuous names', in Donald Davidson and Jaaco Hintikka (eds), *Words and Objections: Essays on the Work of W. V. Quine*, Dordrecht: Reidel.

(1969) 'Utterer's meaning and intentions', *Philosophical Review* 78.

(1975) 'Logic and conversation', in P. Cole and J. L. Morgan (eds), *Syntax and Semantics*, vol. 3, *Speech Acts*.

(1981) 'Presuppositions and conversational implicature', in P. Cole (ed.), *Radical Pragmatics*, New York: Academic.

(1989) *Studies in the Way of Words*, Cambridge, Mass.: Harvard University Press (includes 1967 William James Lectures and most of the articles that Grice had previously had published).

(1991) *The Conception of Value*, Oxford: Oxford University Press (the Carus Lectures for 1983; posthumous).

Secondary literature:

Armstrong, D. M. (1971) 'Meaning and communication', *Philosophical Review*.

Black, Max (1973) 'Meaning and intention: an examination of Grice's views', *New Literary History* 4.

Cole, P. and Morgan, J. L. (eds) *Syntax and Semantics*, vol. 3, *Speech Acts*.

Davidson, D. and Harman, G. (1975) *The Logic of Grammar*.

Grandy, Richard E. and Warner, Richard (eds) (1986) *Philosophical Grounds of Rationality: Intentions, Categories, Ends*, Oxford: Clarendon Press (includes a list of Grice's 'unpublications' as well as works by then published under his name).

MacKay, A. F. (1972) 'Professor Grice's theory of meaning', *Mind* 81.

Ziff, P. (1967) 'On H. P. Grice's theory of meaning', *Analysis*.

After the death of **Austin** in 1960, Grice came to the fore as a defender of the notion of a 'speech-act' and, in the decades following, he became a significant figure in controversies in the philosophy of language. His William James Lectures, published in schematic form in his 'Utterer's meaning' paper (1967), received much attention in America. Grice stressed the importance of the utterer's intention and, in particular, the intended response of the auditor. When someone calls out 'Fire!' he intends others to try to do certain things as a result of recognizing his intention through his utterance. A language consists of a repertoire of communicative devices that are available to agents. In one of the Lectures, 'Logic and conversation' (separately published in 1975), Grice developed the idea of conversational implication. Conversation, he maintained, is subject to rational principles and implications may correctly be drawn from what someone has said which are quite different from those that appear to be licensed by the rules of formal logic. This idea was developed by **Strawson**. Although he published little when he was at Oxford, he had a considerable influence as a teacher; and through his seminars. Strawson was among his pupils, and through his seminars, which were attended which were attended by sabbatical visitors in Oxford, he influenced many others, including **Searle**. Although Grice was most influential as a philosopher of language, his interests were wide-ranging. Late in life he returned to a study of ethics and was engaged, with Judith Baker, on producing a book on Kant's ethics. When he died his many unpublished manuscripts were deposited as the Paul Grice Archives at the University of California at Berkeley.

Sources: Obituary, *Independent*, 31 Aug 1990.

STUART BROWN

Grünbaum, Adolf

German-American. **b:** 15 May 1923, Cologne, Germany. **Cat:** Philosopher of science (notably physics and psychology). **Ints:** Philosophy of physics; philosophy of psychology. **Educ:** Wesleyan University, Connecticut, and Yale University. **Infls:** Hans Reichenbach and C. G. Hempel. **Appts:** 1955–60, Professor of Philosophy, then Selfridge Professor of Philosophy (1956), Lehigh University, Pennsylvania; 1956 and 1959, Visiting Research Professor, University of Minnesota; 1960–, Andrew Mellon Professor of Philosophy at the University of Pittsburgh; Founder (1960), Director (1960–78) and Chairman (1978–) of the Centre of the Philosophy of Science; Research

Professor of Psychiatry (1979–); 1963, Vice President of the American Association for the Advancement of Science (section L); 1965–70, President of the Philosophy of Science Association; 1982–3, President of the American Philosophical Association (Eastern division); visiting appointments in the USA and Europe; on the editorial board of several journals (including *Philosophy of Science*) and coeditor of the Pittsburgh Series in the Philosophy and History of Science; Fellow of the American Association for the Advancement of Science, the American Philosophical Association, the Philosophy of Science Association, the American Academy of Arts and Sciences, and the Academy of Humanism; prizes in the USA and Italy, and awarded Yale's Wilbur Lucius Cross medal, 1990.

Main publications:

(1963) *Philosophical Problems of Space and Time*, New York: Knopf; second enlarged edition, Boston Studies in the Philosophy of Science 12, Dordrecht and Boston: D. Reidel, 1973.

(1967) *Modern Science and Zeno's Paradoxes*, Middletown, CT: Wesleyan University Press.

(1968) *Geometry and Chronometry in Philosophical Perspective*, Minneapolis: University of Minnesota Press.

(1984) *Foundations of Psychoanalysis: A Philosophical Critique*, Pittsburgh Series in the Philosophy and History of Science 2, University of California Press; new edition, 1986.

(1993) *Validation in the Clinical Theory of Psychoanalysis: A Study in the Philosophy of Psychoanalysis*, Psychological Issues Series 61, Madison, CT: International Universities Press.

Secondary literature:

Cohen, R. S. and Laudan L. (eds) (1983) *Physics, Philosophy and Psychoanalysis: Essays in Honor of Adolf Grünbaum*, Boston Studies in the Philosophy of Science 76, Dordrecht and Boston: D. Reidel (includes bibliography of Grünbaum's publications to 1983).

Earman, J. (ed.) *Philosophical Problems of the Internal and External Worlds: Essays on the Philosophy of A. Gruenbaum*, University of Pittsburgh Press.

Adolf Grünbaum is known for his work in the philosophy of science: his studies in the philosophy of space and time, scientific rationality and the foundations of psychoanalytical theory are complemented on a practical level by his directorship of the Centre of the Philosophy of Science at the University of Pittsburgh, and his concern with science is continued by the work of such of his pupils as W. C. **Salmon** and B. C. **Van Fraassen**. In the area of philosophy of space and time, he follows Hans Reichenbach in arguing for the conventional basis of the relation of simultaneity in Einstein's Special Theory of Relativity (see 1963). Grünbaum's position was criticized by H. **Putnam** (see his paper 'An examination of Grünbaum's philosophy of geometry', in *Philosophical Papers* 1 1963); and a panel discussion in the 1969 volume of *Philosophy of Science* was devoted to this issue.

Against the thesis ascribed to P. **Duhem** and maintained by W. V. O. **Quine** denying the feasibility of crucial experiments in science, Grünbaum has maintained, not without criticism, that 'there are cases in which we can establish a strong presumption of the falsity of a component hypothesis, although we cannot falsify [it] in these cases beyond any and all possibility of subsequent rehabilitation' (*Philosophical Problems*, enlarged edition, 1973, p. 626). His criticisms of **Popper**'s appeal to falsifiability as the criterion demarcating science and non-science (see, for instance, the articles in the *British Journal for the Philosophy of Science*, 1976) underlie his examination of the use of this criterion in Popper's rejection of Freudian psychoanalytic theory as pseudoscience. In *Foundations of Psychoanalysis* (1984) and *Validation* (1993) he argues that Popper's charge of unfalsifiability against psychoanalysis is ill founded. None the less, Grünbaum believes the reasoning upon which **Freud** rested his major hypotheses was fundamentally flawed. Moreover, the clinical tests often put forward as vindicating those hypotheses cannot, in the light of placebo effects and the like, provide a firm evidential base. Grünbaum concludes that 'the validation of Freud's cardinal hypotheses has to come, if at all, mainly from well-designed *extra*-clinical studies' (1984, p. 278).

Sources: R. S. Cohen (1983) 'Adolf Grünbaum: a memoir'; WW(Am); DAS.

STUART LEGGATT

Guang Feng (Kuan Feng)

Chinese. *Cat:* Marxist; historian of Chinese philosophy; political activist. *Appts:* Lecturer at Shandong Party School and subeditor of the party journal *Red Flag*; Member, Institute of Philosophy and Social Science, Chinese Academy of Science, Beijing; Member, Cultural Revolution Group.

Main publications:

(1957) *A Study of Wang Chong's Philosophical Ideas* Shangha: Shanghai Renmin Publishing House.

(1957) (contributor to) *Symposium on Problems of the History of Chinese Philosophy*, Beijing: Kexue Publishing House.

(1958) *Oppose Revisionism in the Methodology of the History of Philosophy*, Beijing: Renmin Publishing House.

(1958) 'Oppose revisionism in the work on the history of philosophy', *Philosophical Research*.

(1961) *Translations, Explanations, and Critiques of Zhuangzi's Inner Chapters*, Beijing: Zhonghua Book Company.

(1962) *Collected Essays on the Search for Learning*, Shanghai: Shanghai People's Publishing House.

(1963) (with Lin Yushi) A Series of Essays on the History of Philosophy of the Spring and Autumn Period, Beijing: Renmin Publishing House.

Secondary literature:

Chan, W. T. (1967) *Chinese Philosophy 1949–1963: An Annotated Bibliography of Mainland China Publications*, Honolulu: East–West Center Press.

Louie, K. (1986) *Inheriting Tradition: Interpretations of the Chinese Philosophers in Communist China 1949–1966*, Hong Kong: Oxford University Press.

Guan's interpretation of ancient Chinese philosophers and their leading concepts contributed significantly to the intellectual ferment leading to the Great Leap Forward and the Cultural Revolution. He provided the most refined expression of radical views based on class analysis and careful textual study. His disputes with **Feng Youlan** over the history of philosophy and the controversies sparked by his articles on individual ancient figures were central to Chinese philosophical life from 1957 to 1967 when, with the withdrawal of political patronage, he was expelled from the powerful Cultural Revolution Group and imprisoned as an ultra-leftist. His influence lasted much longer. Guan argued that there was a sharp distinction between materialism and idealism and, following Zhdanov, claimed that there was no materialism or scientific philosophy before Marx. He therefore argued against Feng Youlan and others who sought to rehabilitate traditional philosophers for post-Liberation China by showing that their thought included some materialist features. This crude dismissal of the tradition, however, was combined with detailed and impressive readings of such texts as the Confucian canon, *Daodejing* and the inner chapters of *Zhuangzi*. His work on *ren* (the central Confucian virtue of humanity), on the complexities of the *dao* (the way), and on the whole system of thought in Laozi, although arguing to preordained conclusions, shows great intellectual skill.

NICHOLAS BUNNIN

Guardini, Romano

Italian. *b:* 17 February 1885, Verona. *d:* 1 October 1968, Monaco. *Cat:* Philosopher of the Catholic religion; theologian. *Educ:* Educated in Magunicia and the University of Freiburg, doctorate in Theology. *Infls:* Freud, Dilthey and Husserl. *Appts:* Professor of the Philosophy of Religion, University of Berlin, from 1923; after being dismissed by the Nazis, Tübingen, 1945–7, and Munich, 1948–64.

Main publications:

(1935) *Christliches Bewusstsein. Versuch über Pascal.*
(1948) *Freiheit, Gnade, Schicksal* (English translation, *Freedom, Grace and Destiny*, trans. J. Murray, New York: Pantheon Books, 1961).
(1950) *Das Ende der Neuzeit* (English translation, *The End of The Modern World*, London: Sheed & Ward, 1957).
(1952) *Die Macht.*
(1957) *Welt und Person*, second edition.
(1958) *Religion und Offenbarung.*
(1959) *Über das Wesen des Kunstwerks*, second edition.
(1959) *Die Sinne und die religöse Erkenntnis*, second edition.
(1962) *Sprache–Dichtung–Deutung.*
(1962–6) *Sorge um der Menschen.*
(1964) *Briefe über Selbstbildung*: Mainz: Matthias Grünewald.
(1978) *Bibliographie Romano Guardini*, ed. H. Mercher, Paderborn: Schoningh.
(1985) *Der Gegensatz Versuche zu einer Philosophie de Lebendig-Konkreten*, third edition.
(1986–) *Werke*, Mainz: Matthias Grünewald.

Secondary literature:

Englemann, H. (1966) *Romano Guardini*, Paris: Fleurus.
Gerl, H.-B. (1985) *Romano Guardini 1885–1968*, Mainz: Matthias Grünewald.
Kuhn, H. (1961) *Romano Guardini: Der Mensch und das Werk*, Munich: Kosel.
——(ed.) (1965) *Interpretation der Welt*, Würzburg: Echter.

Most of Guardini's life was lived in Germany. He was a central figure of the Catholic reform movement which turned from the juridical enactment of canon law to a notion of religion as having an existential basis in the lives of the faithful, in which humanistic everyday life bcomes the sign of the transcendent and for which an emphasis on the humanity of Christ supplants arid dogmatism. Guardini was involved, too, in the consequent reform of the liturgy, a reform that made him an inspiration to the young. Located in Germany, Guardini was influenced by **Dilthey**, **Husserl** and **Freud** and, with a sense of man as a living, deeply ambiguous being with a sense of destiny, he attempted to create a new doctrine of humanity using the most recent phenomenology and metaphysics. Central to his thought is the notion of polar opposites as the basis on which our being is to be analysed, an analysis of which reveals how man and the divine are interwoven.

COLIN LYAS

Guattari, Félix

French. *b:* 30 April 1930, Paris. *d:* 29 August 1992, La Borde clinique near Bois. *Cat:* Poststructuralist; political activist; practising/reforming psychoanalyst. *Ints:* Pscyhoanalysis and politics (especially philosophy of desire and schizoanalysis). *Educ:* Pharmacy and Philosophy, Université de Paris in the early 1950s. *Infls:* Freud, Lacan, Marx, Nietzsche, Deleuze and Foucault. *Appts:* Involved with the project to open the Clinique de la Borde, at Cour-Cheverny, near Bois (under the direction of Jean Oury, a Lacanian), which was fundamentally opposed to widespread repressive psychiatric practices; 1975, helped found Réseau International d'Alternative à la Psychiatrie.

Main publications:

(1972) *Psychanalyse et transversalité*, Preface by Gilles Deleuze, Paris: Maspéro.
(1972) (with Gilles Deleuze) *L'Anti-Oedipe: capitalisme et schizophrénie I*, Paris: Minuit (English translation, *Anti-Oedipus*, trans. Robert Hurley *et al.*, Preface by Michel Foucault, New York: Viking, 1977; reprinted, Minneapolis: University of Minnesota Press, 1983).
(1975) (with Gilles Deleuze) *Kafka: pour une littérature mineure*, Paris: Minuit (English translation, *Kafka: For a Minor Literature*, trans. Dana Polan, Foreword by Réda Bensmïa, Minneapolis: University of Minnesota Press, 1986).
(1976) (with Gilles Deleuze) *Rhizome: Introduction*, Paris: Minuit (English translation, 'Rhizome', trans. Paul Foss and Paul Patton, *I & C* 8 (1981): 49–71).
(1977) (with Gilles Deleuze) *Politique et psychanalyse*, Alençon: des mots perdus.

(1977) *La Révolution moléculaire*, Fontenay-sous-Bois: Éditions Recherches (English translation, *Molecular revolution: Psychiatry and Politics*, trans. Rosemary Sheed, New York: Penguin, 1984; includes material from *Psychanalyse et transversalité* and *La Révolution moléculaire*).
(1978) (with Gilles Deleuze) François Châtelet *et al.*, *Où il est question de la toxicomanie*, Alençon: des mots perdus.
(1979) *L'Inconscient machinique*, Fontenay-sous-Bois: Éditions Recherches.
(1980) (with Gilles Deleuze) *Mille plateux: capitalisme et schizophrénie II*, Paris: Minuit (English translation, *A Thousand Plateaus: Capitalism and Schizophrenia*, trans. and foreword by Brian Massumi, Minneapolis: University of Minnesota Press, 1987).
(1985) (with Toni Negri) *Les nouveaux espaces de liberté*, Paris: Dominique Bedou.
(1986) *Les Années d'hiver 1980–85*, Paris: Barrault.
(1986) (with Jean Oury and François Tosquelles) *Pratique de l'institutionnel et politique*, Vigneux: Matrice éditions.
(1989) *Les Trois Écologies*, Paris: Galilée.
(1991) (with Gilles Deleuze) *Qu'est-ce que la philosophie?*, Paris: Minuit.

Secondary literature:
(1977) 'Anti-Oedipus', *Semiotext(e)* 2, 3 (includes a translation of Lyotard's essay 'Energumen capitalism', pp. 11–26).
Bogue, Ronald (1989) *Deleuze and Guattari*, London: Routledge.
Burger, Christa (1985) 'The reality of "machines": notes on the rhizome-thinking of Deleuze and Guattari', trans. Simon Srebrny, *Telos* 64 (Summer): 33–44.
Lecercle, Jean-Jacques (1985) *Philosophy through the Looking Glass*, La Salle.: Open Court.
Massumi, Brian (1992) *A User's Guide to Capitalism and Schizophrenia: Deviations from Deleuze and Guattari*, Cambridge, Mass.: MIT.
Charles J. Stivale (1991) 'Deleuze and Guattari', *Substance 66* 20, 3, Madison: University of Wisconsin Press.

Guattari worked with Gilles **Deleuze** (whom he met in 1968). He searched for a synthesis of Marx and **Freud** and his collaboration with Deleuze on *L'Anti-Oedipe* (1972) contains a powerful critique of both strands of thought, of the reductionisms which dominate contemporary thought in general and French culture in particular. Thus, against the oedipal reductions of psychoanalysis with its presentation of desire as 'law' and 'lack', desire is celebrated as positive, productive and excessive.

Against the orthodox economic reductionism of Marxism, a picture of the 'social' is given in terms of flows and cuts, semiotic machines rather than structures.

In his later work, *Les trois écologies* (1989), Guattari argues that more than ever before, nature cannot be separated from culture, environmental ecology separated from mental ecology. He calls for an 'ecosophy', a combination of philosophy and ecology, which aims at constituting an all-embracing ecological system, at once practical and speculative, political and aesthetic, to replace the archaic forms of religious, political and associative engagement. There is no doubt that his collaborations with Deleuze have had a profound influence on the development of post-structuralism and its influence on the fields of literary and cultural theory. *L'Anti-Oedipe* is often celebrated as a defining moment in twentieth-century thought, the post-68 embodiment of the hopes and frustrations of a whole generation of radical intellectuals.

JAMES WILLIAMS

Gueroult, Martial
French. *b:* 15 December 1891, Le Havre, France. *d:* 13 August 1976, Paris. *Cat:* Historian of philosophy; idealist. *Ints:* Greek philosophy: seventeenth- and eighteenth-century philosophy; J. G. Fichte. *Educ:* L'École Normale Supérieure, 1913–20. *Infls:* Leibniz, J. G. Fichte, Léon Robin and Ginette Dreyfus. *Appts:* Professor of Philosophy, University of Strasbourg, 1929–45, Sorbonne, 1945–51; the Collège de France, 1951–63.

Main publications:
(1930) *L'Évolution et la structure de la doctrine de la science chez Fichte*, 2 vols, Paris: Les Belles-Lettres.
(1931) *La Philosophie transcendantale de Salomon Maïmon*, Paris: PUF.
(1934) *Dynamique et métaphysique leibniziennes*, Paris: Les Belles-Lettres.
(1939) *Étendue et psychologie chez Malebranche*, Paris: Les Belles-Lettres.
(1953) *Descartes selon l'ordre des raisons*, 2 vols, Paris: Aubier.
(1955) *Nouvelles réflexions sur la preuve ontologique de Descartes*, Paris: Vrin.
(1956) *Berkeley, quatre études sur la perception et sur Dieu*, Paris: Aubier.
(1959) *Malebranche*, 3 vols, Paris: Aubier.

Secondary literature:
Bruch, J. L. (1958) 'La méthode de Martial Gueroult et son application à la philosophie de Male-

branche', *Revue de Métaphysique et Morale*: 358–73.

Brunschwieg, J. (1960) 'La preuve ontologique interprétée par Martial Gueroult', *Revue Philosophique de la France et de l'Étranger* 150: 251–65.

Gueroult was one of the most distinguished and prolific twentieth-century French historians of philosophy. His early interests were in Greek philosophy. After 1926, however, modern philosophy (beginning with Descartes) became and thereafter remained the main focus of his researches.

He introduced an original approach to the history of philosophy which he called *la méthode des structures* ('method of structures'), according to which each particular philosophy (for example, that of Descartes) is ideally represented as a systematic whole unfolding itself like a well-constructed plot in which every phase or step follows from its predecessor with a rational inevitability. Thus Gueroult maintained, in a way reminiscent of Hegel, that the doctrinal content of a particular philosophy is inseparable from its demonstrative procedure. As against Hegel, however, he affirmed the irreducible plurality of philosophical systems. He held that each new philosophy presents a unique construction of reality; each has an independent value of its own and cannot be properly understood simply in terms of the 'dialectical' relations in which it stands to other philosophies.

Gueroult was renowned not only as a historian of philosophy but also as an extraordinarily gifted teacher who could speak extempore in a style that was ready for print.

Sources: Huisman; EF.

STEPHEN MOLLER

Guo Moruo (Kuo Mo-jo)

Chinese. *b:* 1892, Loshan, Sichuan Province, China. *d:* 1978, Beijing. *Cat:* Marxist; historian of Chinese philosophy; novelist, playwright, poet and essayist; historian. *Educ:* Studied Medicine at Kyushu Imperial University, Fukuoka, Japan. *Infls:* Wang Yangming (early sixteenth-century neo-Confucian idealist), Tagore, Goethe, Spinoza, Walt Whitman, Nietzsche, Marx, Engels, Lenin and Stalin. *Appts:* Editor of magazines of the Creation Society; Chairman, Department of Literature, Zhongshan University, Guangzhou; propaganda and political posts attached to Chiang Kai-shek and the National Revolutionary Army; 1928–38, exile in Ichikawa (Japan) as an enemy of the National Government; 1949, Chairman, All-China Federation of Writers and Artists; Member, Chinese People's Political Consultative Conference; President, Chinese Academy of Sciences.

Main publications:

(1929) *Study of Ancient Chinese Society*, Shanghai, Xiandai Book Company.
(1945) *The Bronze Age*, Shenghuo Bookstore.
(1945) *Ten Critiques*, Qunyi Publishing Company.
(1957–63) *Moruo's Collected Writings*, 17 vols, Hong Kong, Sanlian Bookstore.

Secondary literature:

Boorman, H. (ed.) (1970) *Biographical Dictionary of Republican China*, New York and London: Columbia University Press.
Briere, O. (1956) *Fifty Years of Chinese Philosophy 1898–1950*, London: George Allen & Unwin Ltd.
Complete Chinese Encyclopedia (1987), Philosophy Volumes, Beijing: Chinese Encyclopedia Publications.
Louie, K. (1986) *Inheriting Tradition: Interpretations of the Classical Philosophers in Communist China 1949–1966*, Hong Kong: Oxford University Press.
Roy, D. (1971) *Kuo Mo-ro: The Early Years*, Cambridge: Mass.: Harvard University Press.

Although trained in medicine, Guo devoted his life to literature and politics. The breadth of his talents enabled him to make important contributions to many other fields, including philosophy, archaeology, economics, history and sociology. His first intellectual enthusiasm was for romanticism, which infused his writing for the Culture Society in the early 1920s, but in 1925 he became a Marxist, supporting a Leninist theory of imperialism and seeing literature as a political weapon. His subsequent studies of Chinese history and intellectual life employed a materialist method, using forces and relations of production to provide the underlying explanation of cultural developments. Most significantly for later Chinese philosophical studies, he rejected the view that China had a static essence and proposed instead that Chinese history should, like Western history, be broken into periods based on changing modes of production, thus repairing the omission of China from the historical writings of Marx and Engels. Philosophers could be interpreted according to their class position in their historical period as progressive or reactionary, materialist or idealist. Subsequent Marxist history of philosophy in China has been dominated by arguments accepting Guo's basic methodological framework, but questioning his determination of historical periods and assessment of individual figures. Within the framework of his method, the evaluation of an ancient philosopher could change completely from reactionary to progressive, depending on whether his society was dominated by slave-owners or landlords. Guo altered his scheme of historical periods, with his 1950 account 'Slave society in China'. The nearly universal acceptance of this version of his scheme contributed to his position of dominance among post-Liberation Chinese intellectuals. Although his historical work showed brilliance and audacity in the use of archaeological and palaeographic studies, including his own, his extreme conclusions about individual philosophers were often controversial, showing that his universal method left much room for ideosyncratic application. He praised Kongzi as a revolutionary figure and condemned Mozi, the pre-Qin dynasty philosopher closest to the people, as a reactionary supporter of the ruling class. He was less unorthodox in condemning the legalist Han Feizi as the intellectual originator of dictatorship in China.

NICHOLAS BUNNIN

Gurvitch, Georges

French (of Russian origin). *b:* 2 November 1894, Novorossisk. *d:* 11 December 1965, Paris. *Cat:* Sociologist. *Ints:* Philosophy of sociology. *Infls:* Fichte, Proudhon, Scheler and Durkheim. *Appts:* Many distinguished academic appointments, including Professorships of Sociology at the Universities of Strasbourg, Columbia (Gurvitch worked in America during the Second World War) and the Sorbonne (from 1948); regarded as the most important of Durkheim's successors, and the central figure in postwar French sociology.

Main publications:

(1924) *Fichtes System der konkreten Ethik*.
(1930) *Les Tendances actuelles de la philosophie allemande*; reissued, Paris: Vrin, 1949.
(1932) *L'Idée du droit social*; reprinted, Aalen: Scientia-Verlag, 1972.
(1937) *Morale théorique et science des moeurs*; third edition, Paris: PUF, 1961.
(1942) *Sociology of Law*.
(1945) *Twentieth-century Sociology*, New York: Philosophical Library.
(1946) *La Déclaration des droits sociaux*, Paris: Vrin.
(1950) *La Vocation actuelle de la sociologie*; third editon, Paris: PUF, 1963.

(1953) *Déterminismes sociaux et liberté humaine*, Paris: PUF.
(1954) *Le Concept des classes sociales*, Paris: Centre de Documentation Universitaire.
(1957) *Les Cadres sociaux de la connaissance sociologique*, Paris: PUF.
(1962) *Dialectique et sociologie*, Paris: Flammarion.
(1966) *Mon itinéraire intellectuel*, New York: Essay Press.

Secondary literature:

Duvignaud, J. (1969) *Georges Gurvitch, symbolisme social et sociologie dynamique*, Paris: Seghers.
La Rosa, M. (1974) *Sociologia, realta e astrazione in Georges Gurvitch*, Bologna: Cooperativa libraria universitaria editrice.
Stefani, M. A. (1974) *Georges Gurvitch: sociologo del diritto*, Rome: Carucci.
Swedberg, R. (1982) *Sociology as Disenchantment: The Evolution of the Work of Georges Gurvitch*, Atlantic Highlands, NJ: Humanities Press.
Toulement, R. (1953) *Sociologie et pluralisme dialectique: introduction à l'oeuvre de Georges Gurvitch*, Louvain: Nauwelaerts.

The philosophical interest of Gurvitch's work rests on his consistent rejection of static analyses of social reality of the kind to be found, for example, in the work of Talcott Parsons or **Lévi-Strauss**. Gurvitch insists, by contrast, that there is no single set of concepts able to do justice to the complexity and variousness of social phenomena. Pluralism of analytic concepts and an insistence on the reality of 'discontinuity' are accordingly major features of his work. He distinguishes ten levels of depth (*paliers en profondeur*) in the analysis of social phenomena, from the superficial morphology of social reality to the most profound, that of mental states and collective psychological attitudes. Unless sociological analyses are in this way pluri-dimensional, he argues, they risk becoming rigid and insensitive.

The object of sociological study is human action in its ambient circumstances. Actions have many and changing levels, and show multiple and ceaselessly changing interrelations. It follows that sociology cannot be regarded as the study of social laws repeatedly manifesting themselves in different historical circumstances. The social fabric is too discontinuous to allow this. Universalisms in the theory of sociology are simplistic, false and to be avoided.

Sources: *The Social Science Encyclopedia*, Kuper & Kuper, London: RKP, 1985.

ROBERT WILKINSON

Gurwitsch, Aron

Lithuanian (became German 1930, and American 1946). *b:* 17 January 1901, Vilna, Lithuania. *d:* 25 June 1973, Zürich. *Cat:* Phenomenological philosopher. *Ints:* Philosophy of the field of consciousness and perception; philosophy of science; social theory; history of philosophy. *Educ:* Berlin, Freiburg and Frankfurt. *Infls:* Karl Stumpf, Edmund Husserl, Kurt Goldstein, Adhémar Gelb and Alfred Schutz. *Appts:* 1933, Lecturer, L'Institut d'Histoire des Sciences (Sorbonne) on Gestalt theory, Gelb and Goldstein's work and finally constitutive phenomenology; introduced Maurice Merleau-Ponty to Gestalt theory; taught at Johns Hopkins University (1940–2), Harvard (1943–6) and Wheaton College (1947–8); Assistant Professor of Mathematics, 1948–51; Associate Professor of Philosophy, Brandeis University, 1951–9; 1959–72, Professor of Philosophy on the Graduate Faculty of Political and Social Science of the New School for Social Research, New York City, where he was made Distinguished Service Professor in 1972 and Emeritus in 1973.

Main publications:

(1929) 'Phänomenologie der Thematik und des reinen Ich' (dissertation; English translation in 1966).

(1957) *Théorie du champ de la conscience* (originally called *A Sketch of Constitutive Phenomenology*), Paris: Desclée de Brouwer (English translation, *The Field of Consciousness*, Pittsburgh: Duquesne University Press, 1964) (a book based on his Sorbonne lectures).

(1966) *Studies in Phenomenology and Psychology*, Evanston: Northwestern University Press (contains reprints and translations of 18 papers published 1929–61.)

(1974) *Phenomenology and the Theory of Science* Evanston: Northwestern University Press.

(1974) *Leibniz: Philosophie des Panlogismus*, Berlin and New York: Walter de Gruyter.

(1979) *Human Encounters in the Social World*, Pittsburgh: Duquesne University Press.

Secondary literature:

Embree, Lester (ed.) (1972) *Life-World and Consciousness. Essays for Aron Gurwitsch*, Evanston: Northwestern University Press (contains a biographical sketch and a bibliography of 50 items).

——*et al.* (eds) (1981) 'The phenomenology of Gurwitsch', *Journal of the British Society for Phenomenology*, 12, 2, May (contains a bibliography of recent Gurwitsch criticism, 37 items).

——(ed.) *Essays in Memory of Aron Gurwitsch*, University Press of America.

Gurwitsch's work consists of a continuation and expansion of Husserlian phenomenology in the light of Gestalt theory, organismic biology, interpretive sociology, genetic psychology, neo-Kantianism, existentialism and the history of modern philosophy. He was led thereby to transform **Husserl**'s theories of the object, attention, perception, thinking and, especially, the ego (vide his "A non-egological conception of consciousness", in *Studies* ...)

His *Habilitation* thesis, *Human Encounters in the Social World*, which was first published in German in 1977, is his only work on social interaction. It may be that, after 1932, he abandoned social theory to Alfred **Schutz** whose phenomenology, unlike his own, attributes an *essential* social dimension to being human. His major work, *The Field of Consciousness* (1957), is a phenomenological development of the insights of William **James**, Jean **Piaget**, the analytical psychologists, the Gestaltists and Kurt Goldstein's organismic biology. The field of consciousness is shown to be divided into three zones: thematic object (or 'theme'), thematic field (the field of relevance) and marginal field (where such relevance is absent). The marginal field is the subject of his *Marginal Consciousness* (1985), which was originally intended to be a section of *The Field of Consciousness*.

Phenomenology and the Theory of Science (1974) consists of ten essays and compilations from 1937–73. For Gurwitsch, science (*Wissenschaft*) includes natural science, the human sciences (psychology, history and sociology) and the formal sciences (logic and mathematics). The book is the expression of his aim to ground these sciences in constitutive phenomenology. The problem is that of a transition from the protologic of the lifeworld to the strict concepts of science. One of his final works, *Leibniz: Philosophie des Panlogismus* (1974), is the result of decades of interest and research. 'Panlogicism' is the view that logic is somehow realized in the structure of the world, and for Leibniz this means that an intelligible contexture of monadic substances underlies phenomena. For Gurwitsch this involves an irreducible correlation of subject (Divine intellect) and object (intelligible world).

Sources: Lester, Embree (1973) 'Aron Gurwitsch (1901–1973)', obituary, *JBSP* 4: 291.

BARRY JONES

Guzzo, Augusto

Italian. *b:* 24 January 1894, Naples. *d:* Deceased. *Cat:* Idealist philosopher; philosopher of spirit.

Educ: Graduated from University of Naples, 1945 (thesis on Kant's early work). *Infls:* Augustine. *Appts:* Taught at the 'leceo' in Castellamare di Stabia, 1918–24; taught Philosophy in Turin, 1924–32; Professor of Moral Philosophy, Pisa, 1932–9; returned in 1939 to Turin to a Chair in Theoretical Philosophy.

Main publications:

(1925) *Verità e realtà: apologia dell'idealismo.*
(1928) *Giudizio e azione.*
(1936) *Idealismo e cristianesimo.*
(1942) *La filosofia e l'esperienza.*
(1942) *Sic vos non vobis.*
(1947) *L'uomo*, Brescia: Morcelliana.
(1955) *La scienza*, Turin: Edizioni di 'Filosofia'.
(1961) *La filosofia*, Turin: Accademia delle scienze.
(1979) *Analisi dell'umana esperienza*, ed. P. Quarta, Lecce: Milella (anthology).

Secondary literature:

Genzone, P. (1974) *Il pensiero estetico di A. Guzzo*, Naples: Morano.
Quarta, P. (1976) *A. Guzzo e la sua scuola*, Urbino: Argalia.

Guzzo's work falls into three periods. The first, up to 1929, culminates in *Verità e realtà* and *Giudizio e azione.* Guzzo was thought there to subscribe to **Gentile**'s views, but his central problem was normative reason in human experience. The second period, up until 1940, reacts against anti-positivist idealist accounts of religion. The third period attempts a systematization of his thinking. The I is conceived as a transcendental subject of thought that must appear concretely in persons. It is not reason but uses reason in the search for truth. Concepts are not mere thoughts but are actively used in interpreting experience. This grounds morality, which conditions both practical and theoretical activities. Science involves the coordination of pure mathematics with experimentation. Art is spirit in its inventiveness. Language is the enabling condition for art, freeing us from the immediacy of experience. Religion is the aspiration for the divine that comes from God who gives us something of himself. Philosophy is the critical knowledge that accompanies all our activities. Its rationality is in positive harmony with faith.

COLIN LYAS

Gyatso, Tenzin (the Fourteenth Dalai Lama)
Tibetan. *b:* July 1935, Taktser, Tibet. *Cat:* Maayana Buddhist. *Ints:* Ethics; ontology; science and its relationship to traditional Tibetan Buddhist teachings, particularly psychology; philosophy and the spiritual life. *Educ:* Educated as a Buddhist monk from the age of five; trained through the traditional scholastic Tibetan education system to compete for the highest qualification of *geshe*; succeeded in 1959 after examination through rigorous and lengthy public debates. *Infls:* Literary influences include the Indian Buddhists Nagarjuna (*c.* second century CE), Candrakirti (*c.* 600–50); Santideva (*c.*695–743), and also Mahatma Gandhi, the Tibetan Tsong kha pa (1375–1419). Personal influences are mainly those who have enriched and deepened his appreciation of the possibilities of compassion, tolerance and understanding, such as his mother (d. 1981), the Indian Buddhist teacher Kunu Lama Tenzin Gyaltsen (*c.*1885–1977) and the Christian monk Thomas Merton (d. 1968). Interest in the outside world, science and technology was early stimulated by the Austrian mountaineer Heinrich Harrer. *Appts:* Selected as Dalai Lama at four years old; in 1950 the Chinese invaded Tibet, and in 1959 he was forced to flee to India; since 1960 he has headed the Tibetan government-in-exile from India; visited the West on many occasions; 1989, Nobel Peace Prize.

Main publications:

Most of the Dalai Lama's many books are compiled from public lectures etc. Two publications of translations of books originally written in Tibetan are:

(1975) *The Buddhism of Tibet and The Key to the Middle Way*, London: George Allen & Unwin.
(1985) *Opening the Eye of New Awareness*, London: Wisdom.

Also an oral commentary to an Indian philosophical text:

(1988) *Transcendent Wisdom*, Ithaca, NY: Snow Lion.

Philosophically interesting material from talks and interviews can be found in:

(1980) *An Interview with the Dalai Lama*, ed. John F. Avedon, New York: Littlebird.
(1984) *Kindness, Clarity and Insight*, ed. Jeffrey Hopkins, Ithaca, NY: Snow Lion.
(1988) *The Bodhgaya Interviews*, ed. José Cabezón, Ithaca, NY: Snow Lion.
(1988) *The Dalai Lama at Harvard*, ed. Jeffrey Hopkins, Ithaca, NY: Snow Lion.
(1990) *A Policy of Kindness: An Anthology of Writings by and about the Dalai Lama*, Ithaca, NY: Snow Lion.
(1991) *Cultivating a Daily Meditation*, Dharamsala: Library of Tibetan Works and Archives.

(1991) *Mindscience: An East–West Dialogue*, Boston: Wisdom.
Recent autobiography:
(1990) *Freedom in Exile*, London: Hodder & Stoughton.

Tenzin Gyatso was born into a relatively poor family on the northeastern borders of the Tibetan world. At the age of four, he was recognized as the reincarnation of the previous Dalai Lama. Since the seventeenth-century the Dalai Lamas have been heads of the Tibetan state as well as monks and abbots of their own monastery; they are also commonly spoken of as emanations of or identical with the personification of pure compassion, a divine figure called in Tibetan Chenrezik.

To date, the Dalai Lama's main contribution has been to express ideas from a sophisticated tradition in a way which is accessible to the modern West, and to show in his own personality an example of someone who is truly trying to live by that tradition. The final goal is one of Buddhahood for all sentient beings, the perfection of wisdom and compassion, the cessation of all suffering. Suffering is the result of not seeing things the way they really are. Wisdom is the opposite of that ignorance. The fundamental mode of ignorance lies in seeing things as having *inherent* existent i.e. existing intrinsically, from their own side. Things are actually only the intersection points of causal forces, particularly conceptual reification. All things are relative, they are empty of inherent existence. This is the ultimate truth about all things. Things themselves are conventional constructs. Emptiness is the mere absence of inherent, intrinsic, existence and applies to absolutely everything, including itself. There is no inherent absolute reality. Emptiness certainly does not entail complete nonexistence, however. Seeing things as having inherent existence leads to expectations of permanence, etc., which are constantly frustrated. Seeing things the way they really are leads to a letting-go which enhances altruism. Compassionate kindness is also a rational imperative. Central to all this is critical reasoning. The Dalai Lama stresses a spiritual perspective where reasoning has pride of place. This partly explains his interest in scientific research. He has recently offered some counter-arguments to a literal identification of consciousness states with brain processes (*Cultivating*, 1991, pp. 83–4). He has stated that if science shows for certain a traditional Buddhist teaching to be false, then Buddhists should no longer hold it (at least as literally true), and he has applied this to aspects of the traditional Buddhist cosmology. On the other hand he has also drawn a distinction between scientific investigation finding something to be false, and scientific investigation not finding something. In the last analysis the Dalai Lama's concern is the very real practical need to improve life: 'There is no need for temples; no need for complicated philosophy. Our own brain, our own heart is our temple; the philosophy is kindness' (1990, p. 58).

PAUL WILLIAMS

H

Habermas, Jürgen

German. *b:* 18 June 1929, Dusseldorf. *Cat:* Post-Marxist critical theorist. *Ints:* Social philosophy; hermeneutics; modernist (emancipatory) thought; communication (speech-act) theory; historical and socio-political criticism. *Educ:* 1954, doctorate, University of Bonn; 1961, second doctorate (*Habilitation*), University of Mainz. *Infls:* Hegel, Kant, Marxist philosophy, Schelling, Fichte, Dilthey, Weber, Adorno, Horkheimer, Lukács, Searle and Anglo-American linguistic philosophy. *Appts:* 1954, Adorno's assistant, University of Frankfurt's Institute for Social Research; 1961, professorship, University of Heidelberg; 1964, taught philosophy and sociology at Frankfurt; 1971–84, Director of the Max Planck Institute, Starnburg; 1984, Professor of History of Philosophy, University of Frankfurt.

Main publications:

(1962) *Strukturwandel der Öffentlichkeit*, Berlin: Leuchterhand.

(1970) *Zur Logik der Sozialwissenschaften*, Frankfurt am Main: Suhrkamp.

(1971) (with Niklaus Luhmann) *Theorie der Gesellschaft oder Sozialtechnologie: Was leistet die Systemforschung?*, Frankfurt am Main: Suhrkamp.

(1973) *Kultur und Kritik*, Frankfurt am Main: Suhrkamp.

(1975) *Legitimation Crisis*, trans. T. McCarthy, Boston: Beacon Press 1975.

(1977) 'The analytical theory of science and dialectics' and 'A positivistically bisected rationalism', in *The Positivist Dispute in German Sociology*, ed. Adey and Frisby, London: Heinemann.

(1984) *The Theory of Communicative Action and the Rationalisation of Science*, 2 vols, trans. T. McCarthy, London: Heinemann.

(1987) *The Philosophical Discourse of Modernity*, trans. F. Lawrence, London: Blackwell.

Secondary literature:

Adey and Frisby (eds) (1977) *The Positivist Dispute in German Sociology*, London: Heinemann.

Bernstein, R. (1985) *Habermas and Modernity*, Oxford: Polity Press.

Held, D. (1980) *Introduction to Critical Theory*, London: Hutchinson.

White (1990) *Recent Works of Jürgen Habermas*, London: Cambridge University Press.

Jürgen Habermas is the most notable and independent-minded successor to the Frankfurt School of Philosophy, which attempted to retrieve Marxism from Stalinist orthodoxy and remould it into an incisive form of ideological and cultural criticism. Habermas has extended that concern into a broad preoccupation with those cultural and political factors which distort and disrupt the assumed openness of human communication. His distinctive contribution to contemporary European thought is his thesis that perfectible structures of reasoning and cumulatively liberating insights into truth are tangibly accessible as they are embedded within our ordinary communicative practices: they are neither grounded in nor reflections of an alleged external reality, but are to be found within the socially constructed discourses which constitute our 'life-world'.

Habermas's thought ranges through an incisive attack upon positivism and Popperian notions of rationality, an attempt to revitalize Marxism as a culturally critical tool, a critique of the conservative foundations of Gadamerian hermeneutics and a stalwart defence of the enlightening capacities of modernist thought against the critical onslaught of French deconstruction. His thinking is not so much marked by distinct transitions as by a continuous bringing forward of one or other of a cluster of themes that bind his overall position together. These include an intense resistance to scientific, political and philosophical attempts to monopolize knowledge and truth, a passionate commitment to open and undistorted communication as a means to truth and the conviction that vigilant criticism of untruth offers the only route to an intellectually open and politically unrepressive society.

Habermas acquired the basis of his conception of emancipatory truth from his initial deep involvement with the Frankfurt School. Marx's teleological framework commences with an abstract notion of mankind as a *potentia* containing the as yet unrealized creative potential. Although the Frankfurt School abandoned the conviction that only the alienating process of historical labour could actualize this truth, Habermas retained through its influence the Marxist notion of truth as a yet to be realized historical situation in which that which was potentially true could be realized as actually true. The importance of this notion for Habermas is that it offers an ideal facilitating a critique of events as a deviation from the envisaged norm, as well as the basis of an ideological critique the task of which is to unmask the social and political factors which hide the anticipated truth. As the realization of individual creative potential depends upon the extent of social emancipation, cultural critique cannot be dissociated from political critique. In its critical and emancipatory capacities, Habermas's ideal of undistorted communication is a true child of this Marxist motif.

In his antipositivist critique of **Popper**'s and Albert's 'critical rationalism' (see Adley and Frisby, 1977), Habermas refuses to allow the motif of an emancipatory truth to be marginalized by a methodology that refuses sense to all except that which can be explicated through scientific analysis. Decisions and values relevant to moral and political life cannot be replaced or rationalized by scientific calculation (*Zweckrationalität*). Curiously, **Gadamer**, Habermas's next chosen opponent, would concur; but just as Habermas resists the ideologically acquired authority of scientific reasoning to legislate upon questions of social and political value, so he disputes the authority of historical and cultural tradition to be the sole opponent of technological thinking. To resist the one-sidedness of scientific reasoning with the evident partisanship of inherited tradition is merely to replace one distorted truth with another. Habermas supports his claim by arguing for an analogy between the problems posed by tradition and those confronted by psychoanalysis. Just as neurotic behaviour entails the suppression of its causes, so tradition can be unknowingly blind to values not its own and to the ideological presuppositions which underwrite is own truth claims.

In his debate with Gadamer, Habermas's commitment to emancipatory truth was not the sole basis of his opposition. He responded profoundly to Gadamer's dialogical model of understanding, fusing it with aspects of **Searle**'s speech-act theory. His famous essay 'The hermeneutic claim to universality' (1980) argues that 'truth ... measures itself as an idealised consensus achieved in unlimited (and unforced) communications'. That which validates the procedures of a discourse as truthful is not metaphysically or ontologically distinct from the discourse but emerges historically from within it. Thus once questions concerning the truth claims of tradition are raised, the participants of that tradition need not remain passively subject to their received authority but are rationally invited to critically reappropriate them and by means of critical involvement extend their claims. A variation of the argument appears in *Knowledge and Human Interests* (1968), where Habermas argues that all knowledge has a sociological origin, suggesting the possibility of a rational discourse permitting the participants the opportunity to revise or make more adequate the norms underwriting its operating consensus. If discourse about the assumptions underwriting knowledge is possible, it is also possible to anticipate more comprehensive (i.e. emancipatory) assumptions for that discourse. Habermas's central contention is that built into the very notion of rational discourse is the anticipation of acheiving for it more adequate and more open foundations. This intrinsic discursive logic impels all rational discourses towards an ever more open and enlightened stance.

In *The Theory of Communicative Action* (1984), Habermas explores the pretheoretical understandings legitimating speech acts. He argues that in the understanding of something said, understanding occurs not because the interlocutors share the same experiences but because one can grasp the point of what the other is saying despite any expressive idiosyncrasy. This effectively reformulates Habermas's ideal speech situation, for if it is in the nature of discourse to generate intersubjective meanings which can transcend a particular interlocutor, it is possible by means of sound argument to arrive at the emancipatory potential within such meanings and expand them beyond the originating discourse. Whosoever speaks a language both belongs to and aspires to the widening of a universal community grounded upon the openness and free consensus of communication. The argument that such a consensus is neither forced on us nor the result of happenstance but springs from actual everyday linguistic practice—is something that we actually talk ourselves into—is Habermas's profoundest contribution to European philosophy.

Habermas's defence of such ideality has drawn the fire of post-structuralist and deconstructivist criticism on the grounds that both his ideal speech act and his espousal of an as yet to be arrived at historical truth are merely fictive vehicles for the peddling of his particular political commitments.

Not only, it is said, do his arguments perpetrate the fiction of an end truth of discourse—the realization of a truly free communicative society—but they exhibit an authoritarian attempt to straightjacket the direction of history. In *The Philosophical Discourse of Modernity* (1987), Habermas responds by arguing that any empirically rooted ideal as that of the undistorted speech situation cannot be falsified by genealogical reductivism. The claim to truth, just as the claim to meaning, always reaches beyond the empirical circumstances which initially generate it. Exploding the universality of a political truth claim by exposing the particularist interests which might hypocritically nurture it, does nothing, he maintains, to undermine the critical potential that truth might have. Furthermore, if there is difference over an issue there is at least agreement over what the issue is; and if there is that, the logical possibility exists of rationally arriving at a consensus as to how such differences might be resolved. In this respect the notion of emancipatory critique is pehaps one of the last defences against the murderous threat ever present within religious and political bigotry.

Habermas's defence of modernity carries with it a political import of some weight. Post-structuralist criticism may expose the particular wills to power sustaining progressivist notions of philosophical and cultural modernism, but what are the consequences of allowing the idealistic aspirations of modernism to fall completely to such cynicism? Post-structuralist criticism may delight in exposing the alleged elitist authoritarianism of modernism, but is not the dream of every political tyranny to convince those under its subjection that there is no other actuality than the immediate? If any claim to meaning or truth which seeks to transcend the horizons of its sociopolitical origin is disallowed, the claim of the ideal, so necessary for any aspiration to reformulate positions in a more embracing manner, will wither. With that withering comes what Habermas is afraid of. Without an awareness of a responsiveness to the wider claims of rational criticism, capable of reminding us of how a situation or argument might be structured differently from previous or present exemplars, humanity's consciousness will be imprisoned within the horizon of the immediate and its freedom to imagine and act beyond that horizon irredeemably impaired.

NICHOLAS DAVEY

Hacking, I(an)

Canadian. *b:* 18 February 1936, Vancouver. *Cat:* Philosopher and historian of science. *Ints:* Philosophical logic. *Educ:* 1956, BA in Mathematics and Physics, University of British Columbia; 1958, BA in Moral Sciences, Cambridge University; 1962, MA and PhD, Cambridge University; 1958–62, Senior Scholar and Rouse Ball student, Trinity College. *Infls:* R. Fisher and H. Jeffreys. *Appts:* 1960–1, Instructor, Princeton University; 1962–4, Research Fellow, Peterhouse, Cambridge; 1964–9, Assistant Professor, then Associate Professor of Philosophy, University of British Columbia (1967–9, seconded to Makerere University College, Uganda); 1969–74, University Lecturer in Philosophy, University of Cambridge, Fellow of Peterhouse; 1974–5, Fellow, Center for Advanced Studies in the Behavioral Sciences, Stanford; 1975–82, Professor, Stanford University; from 1982, Professor, Institute for the History and Philosophy of Science and Technology, and in Department of Philosophy, University of Toronto (since 1991 'University Professor'); various fellowships, and since 1989 Adjunct Professor, York University.

Main publications:

(1965) *Logic of Statistical Inference*, Cambridge: Cambridge University Press.
(1972) *A Concise Introduction to Logic*, New York: Random House.
(1975) *The Emergence of Probability*, Cambridge: Cambridge University Press.
(1975) *Why Does Language Matter to Philosophy?*, Cambridge: Cambridge University Press.
(1983) *Representing and Intervening*, Cambridge: Cambridge University Press.
(1990) *The Taming of Chance*, Cambridge: Cambridge University Press.
(1993) *Le Plus pur nominalisme. 'Vleu' et ses usages*, Combas: Éditions de l'Éclat.
(1994) *Rewriting the Soul: Multiple Personality and the Politics of Memory*, Princeton, NJ: Princeton University Press.

A considerable amount of Hacking's work is concerned with the concept of probability and the foundations of statistics. He has presented a detailed theory of statistical support, worked out from first principles, which is consistent with neo-Bayesianism. Hacking has also conducted historical research into the concept of probability, inductive logic, the problem of induction and related issues. In a metaphilosophical study he demonstrates, through a series of case studies, the importance of language for philosophical spec-

ulation. In a different area Hacking argues in favour of scientific realism, in the sense that some theoretical entities must be real. The point is not that scientific theories are true or false. Hacking argues on the one hand that experimental science is to some extent independent of theorizing, and on the other that a reasonable account of experimentation presupposes realism, in his sense.
Sources: Personal communication.

STIG RASMUSSEN

Haeckel, Ernst Heinrich Phillip August
German. *b:* 16 February 1834, Potsdam, Germany. *d:* 9 August 1919, Jena, Germany. *Cat:* Monistic philosopher; zoologist; medical practitioner. *Ints:* Biology; evolution; religion. *Educ:* Universities of Würzburg, Berlin and Veinna. *Infls:* Literary influences: C. Darwin, A. R. Wallace, Spinoza and Goethe. Personal: Johannes Muller, Rudolf Virchow and R. A. Kolliker. *Appts:* 1861–1909, Privatdozent, Associate Professor (1862), then (1865) Professor of Zoology, University of Jena.

Main publications:
(1866) *Generelle Morphologie der Organismen*, 2 vols, Berlin: G. Reimer.
(1868) *Naturliche Schöpfungsgeschichte*, Berlin: G. Reimer (English translation, *The History of Creation*, trans. E. Ray Lankester, London: Kegan Paul & Trench, 1883).
(1899) *Die Weltrathsel Gemeinvertandliche. Studien über Monistische Philosophie*, Bonn: E. Strauss (English translation, *The Riddle of the Universe*, trans. Joseph McCabe, London: Watts, 1900).

Secondary literature:
Cassirer, Ernst (1950) *The Problem of Knowledge: Philosophy, Science and History since Hegel*, trans. W. H. Woglom and C. W. Hendel, New Haven: Yale University Press, pp. 160–81.
Lodge, O. (1905) *Life and Matter: A Criticism of Professor Haeckel's Riddle of the Universe*, London: Williams & Norgate.
Macquarrie, John (1971) *Twentieth Century Religious Thought*, London: SCM Press; revised edition, pp. 101–2.

Haeckel was a medical practitioner, zoologist and evolutionist turned monistic philosopher. His *Riddle of the Universe* (1899) in particular 'caught the popular imagination as an expression of the scientific outlook of the time' (Macquarrie 1971, p. 101).
    The turning-point in his thinking came in

1861–2 with his reading of *The Origin of Species*. He began to correspond with Darwin and to elaborate the latter's conception of organic evolution. The Darwinian theory of natural selection, in conjunction with his own 'biogenetic law', namely, that ontogeny recapitulates phylogeny, became for Haeckel the basis for a unified, mechanistic explanation of all nature, furnishing a 'universal point of view' stripped of anthropomorphism. He saw evolution as a 'magical pass word', capable of establishing 'the real efficient causes' of all life and of resolving all the problems of the universe and of human knowledge (1868, Preface).
    Thus Haeckel attempted to draft a comprehensive philosophy based upon the theory of evolution. He expounded a naturalistic monism, inclusive of ethics, theology, politics and psychology. Like Spinoza he envisaged a single substance that manifests itself as both body and mind. He identified God with nature and championed a new monistic religion. The significance of Haeckel's semi-popular and often controversial thought lies in the important biological and cosmological questions that it raised.
Sources: Edwards; Bullock & Woodings; Brockhaus.

STEPHEN MOLLER

Hägerström, Axel Anders Theodor
Swedish. *b:* 6 September 1868, Vireda, Sweden. *d:* 7 July 1939, Uppsala. *Cat:* Analytical philosopher; historian of philosophy and of law. *Ints:* Philosophy of law; philosophy of religion. *Infls:* Kant, Westermack, Meinong and Frazer. *Appts:* 1911–33, Professor of Practical Philosophy, Uppsala University; 1917, Jur. Dr *honoris causa* (Uppsala).

Main publications:
(1902) *Kants Ethik im Verhältnis zu seinen erkenntnistheoretischen Grundgedanken systematisch dargestellt*, Uppsala: Almqvist & Wiksell.
(1908) *Das Prinzip der Wissenschaft. Eine logisch-erkenntnistheoretische Untersuchung. I. Die Realität*, Uppsala: Humanistiska Vetenskapssamfundet.
(1911) (inaugural lecture) *Om moraliska föreställningars sanning*, Stockholm: Bonniers (English translation, 'On the truth of moral propositions', in *On the Truth of Moral Ideas*, trans. T. Mautner, Canberra: Department of Philosophy, The Australian National University, 1971).
(1927–41) *Der römische Obligationsbegriff im Lichte der allgemeinen römischen Rechtsanschauung I–II*, Uppsala: Humanistiska Vetenskapssamfundet.

(1929) 'Axel Hägerström', in R. Schmidt (ed.), *Die Philosophie der Gegenwart in Selbstdarstellungen*, vol. VII, Leipzig: Felix Meiner (English translation in *Philosophy and Religion*, trans. R. Sandin, London: Allen & Unwin).

(1953) *Inquiries into the Nature of Law and Morals*, ed. K. Olivecrona, trans. C. D. Broad, Uppsala: Humanistiska Vetenskapssamfundet.

(1965) *Recht, Pflicht und bindende Kraft des Vertrages nach römischer und naturrechtlicher Anschauung*, Uppsala: Humanistiska Vetenskapssamfundet.

Secondary literature:
Broad, C. D. (1951) 'Hägerström's account of sense of duty and certain allied experiences', *Philosophy*.

Cassirer, E. (1939) *Axel Hägerström*, Gothenburg: Göteborgs Högskolas Årsskrift.

Marc-Wogau, K. (1972) 'Axel Hägerström's ontology', in R. E. Olson and A. M. Paul (eds), *Contemporary Scandinavian Philosophy*, London.

Mautner, T. (1994) *Vägledning till Hägerströmstudict* [Guide to Hägerström Research], Uppsala: Humanistska Vetenskapssamfundet (contains bibliography and catalogue of posthumous manuscripts).

Passmore, J. (1961) 'Hägerström's philosophy of law', *Philosophy*.

Kant's Ethik (1902) is a classic of Kant research: a comprehensive and penetrating exegetical treatise on Kant's ethics (the introductory part dealing with Kant's epistemology and interpreting it in an anti-psychologistic manner). In this work Hägerström does not criticize the fundamental ideas of Kant's ethics, and hardly anything in it anticipates the very radical opinions in moral philosophy and legal philosophy developed by him during the years 1907–39. These radical opinions are partly inspired by **Westermack**'s moral relativism, **Meinong**'s emotionalist theory of value, the criticism of the doctrine of natural law in British philosophy and jurisprudence, Frazer's theory of magic, and to some extent by Marx and **Nietzsche**. However, many of the arguments and theses are original, and Hägerström often criticizes on essential points the authors who have influenced him.

In the inaugural lecture (published in 1911) Hägerström formulates the thesis that moral valuations are neither true nor false: there is no intersubjective criterion for the deciding of ethical questions, and moral philosophy cannot be normative, only descriptive. He represents a special version of the emotive (non-cognitive) theory in metaethics. In the same work Häger-

ström explicitly rejects some fundamental doctrines of Kant's ethics, for example the principle of personality and the idea of *Reich der Zwecke*. In the *Inquiries* (1953) he maintains that moral valuations are very often combined with false, even absurd ideas: the ideas of objective values and duties, of free will, of rights. According to this analysis, our ideas of rights are ideas of spiritual forces, and the existence of such metaphysical forces is incompatible with an empirical view of reality. That the absurd ideas mentioned often lead to fanaticism and aggression is frequently pointed out. In law and jurisprudence, both ancient and modern, ideas of rights in the sense of metaphysical forces are of great importance. The idea that certain rights can be transferred from one person to another (for example, ownership by purchase) is an idea of transferring spiritual forces and, thus, of a magical nature. Many metaphysical and magical ideas of Roman law are analysed in the works of 1927–41 and 1965. In his discussion of modern jurisprudence, for example in the *Inquiries*, Hägerström sharply criticizes not only doctrines of natural law but also, *inter alia*, the will theory and **Kelsen**'s *reine Rechtslehre*. Several Scandinavian jurists were influenced by Hägerström, for example V. Lundstedt, K. Olivecrona, Alf Ross and P. O. Ekelöf. The anti-metaphysical view of law he inspired is often called Scandinavian legal realism (compare **Hedenius** and **Wedberg**).

In *Philosophy and Religion* (1964) Hägerström provides contributions to the philosophy of religion. In the final stage of his philosophical development there is an essential analogy between his philosophy of religion and his philosophy of morals: like moral valuations, genuine religious experiences are neither true nor false, but just as moral valuations are often combined with absurd ideas so genuine religious experiences are often combined with dogmatic beliefs or other absurd conceptions. The psychological mechanisms which result in such combinations are analysed in an original way. In addition the connections between religion and magic are considered.

Hägerström rejects all metaphysical ideas (in the sense of ideas implying the existence of things not belonging to the context of space and time). His ontology is marked by this anti-metaphysical attitude. Further, it is determinist: the principle of causality is a necessary presupposition of all empirical knowledge and, Hägerström urges, a corollary of the logical principle of identity. He examines many of the fundamental concepts of our view of reality, for example the concept of the self and the concept of motion. In epistemology he rejects subjectivism, the thesis that what is immediately given is the subject. His final standpoints in ontology and epistemology are presented in *Axel Hägerström*, his *Selbstdarstellung* of 1929. The relation between these standpoints and the views in his first work on ontological and epistemological matters of 1908 has been a subject of controversy. The group of Swedish philosophers directly influenced by Hägerström or by his independent disciple and colleague **Phalén** is often called the Uppsala school of philosophy or the Uppsala school of conceptual analysis (compare Phalén, **Mac Leod**, Hedenius, **Marc-Wogau** and Wedberg).

THORILD DAHLQUIST

Haldane, J(ohn) S(cott)

British. *b:* 3 May 1860, Edinburgh. *d:* Midnight, 14-15 March 1936, Oxford. *Cat:* Physiologist. *Educ:* University of Edinburgh and University of Jena. *Infls:* Leibniz and Kant. *Appts:* 1884-7, Demonstrator in Physiology, University College, Dundee; 1887-1901, Demonstrator in Physiology, Oxford; 1897, Elected Fellow of the Royal Society; 1901-, Fellow of New College, Oxford; 1907-13, Reader in Physiology, Oxford.

Main publications:

(1913) *Mechanism, Life and Personality: An Examination of the Mechanistic Theory of Life and Mind* London: Murray.
(1919) *The New Physiology and Other Addresses*, London: Griffin.
(1929) *The Sciences and Philosophy*, London: Hodder & Stoughton.
(1930) *The Philosophical Basis of Biology*, London: Hodder & Stoughton.
(1932) *Materialism*, London: Hodder & Stoughton.
(1935) *The Philosophy of a Biologist*, Oxford: Clarendon Press.

Secondary literature:

Cunningham, D. J. P. and Lloyd, B. B. (eds) (1963) *J. S. Haldane Centenary Symposium. The Regulation of Human Respiration*, Oxford: Blackwell Scientific Publications.
McDougall, W. (1936) 'The philosophy of J. S. Haldane', *Philosophy* 11: 419ff.

A brother of R. B. **Haldane**, J. S. Haldane is best known as a pioneer in respiratory physiology. He drew no sharp boundaries between applied and theoretical work, however, and his philosophical interests were of a piece with his concerns as a physical scientist. In the preface to the second edition of his lectures on respiration, he explained his attitude in this way: 'Existing physical science can give no account of the characteristic features of life and conscious experience, or their assumed origin in the course of evolution'. To give such an account we need either 'to modify drastically the axioms on which existing physical science is based' or to recognize that physical science is 'no more than a superficial aspect of philosophical truth' (quoted from DSB entry). In later life Haldane came to the view that physical science was essentially limited in the understanding it could achieve and turned increasingly to philosophy.

Haldane claimed that the mechanistic interpretation of the world, despite its success, involved a process of abstracting and selecting. It therefore could not comprehend the real world in its entirety. To do that, he held, we should need to recognize that some of the distinguishing attributes of living things are to be found in all the constituents of the universe, not only in organic nature. Haldane's stature as a scientist ensured that attention would be given to his more speculative work. But few have pretended to understand it and it has not been influential to the extent of his work in physiology.

Sources: DNB; DSB.

STUART BROWN

Haldane, Richard Burdon (from 1911, 1st Viscount of Cloan)

British. *b:* 30 July 1856, Edinburgh. *d:* 19 August 1928, Cloan. *Cat:* Hegelian idealist; lawyer; statesman. *Ints:* Science; religion; metaphysics. *Educ:* University of Edinburgh and University of Göttingen. *Infls:* Fraser, Pringle-Pattison, Sorley and Lotze. Literary influences include Berkeley, Fichte, Kant and Hegel. *Appts:* 1885-1911, MP for Haddingtonshire; 1905-12, Secretary of State for War; 1912-15, 1924, Lord High Chancellor of Great Britain.

Main publications:

(1903-4) *The Pathway to Reality*, 2 vols, London: John Murray.
(1921) *The Reign of Relativity*, London: John Murray.
(1922) *The Philosophy of Humanism and Other Subjects*, London: John Murray.
(1926) *Human Experience: A Study of its Structure*, London: John Murray.

Secondary literature:

Creighton, J. E. (1922) Review of *The Reign of Relativity*, in *Philosophical Review* 31: 288–93.

Pringle-Pattison, A. Seth (1928) 'Richard Burdon Haldane (Viscount Haldane of Cloan) 1856–1928', *Proceedings of the British Academy* 14: 405–41.

R. B. Haldane was brought up in a strongly evangelical household and was drawn to philosophy as a refuge from theology. His stay in Germany confirmed his interest in German philosophy and he colloborated in a translation of Schopenhauer's *The World as Will and Idea*. But he soon turned to the rational and objective idealism that he and others extracted from Kant as developed by Hegel. As a young man he had co-edited and contributed twice to the volume of *Essays in Philosophical Criticism* of 1883 which was a kind of manifesto of the younger idealists. One of his papers, co-authored with his brother J. S. **Haldane**, showed his keen interest in contemporary science. In these early essays he outlined his idea that there was a scale of modes of existence from those of mathematics and mechanism to those of organic life and finally conscious personality. This thought was developed in his Gifford Lectures, published in 1903. His *Reign of Relativity* (1921) sought to incorporate **Einstein**'s theory within a Hegelian framework. Although he himself insisted that he carried his idealism into every activity, a busy career in public life limited Haldane's output in philosophy and most of his substantial works were published late in life. None the less he influenced **Whitehead**'s conception of philosophy and **Bridgman** acknowledged Haldane's thought that all human knowledge is relative.
Sources: R. B. Haldane (1929) *Autobiography*, London: Hodder & Stoughton; CBP II, pp. 127–48; DNB 1922–30; Metz, pp. 313–17; Passmore 1957.

STUART BROWN

Hamelin, Octave

French. *b:* 22 July 1856, Lion d'Angers, Maine et Loire, France. *d:* 11 September 1907, Huchet (Landes). *Cat:* Idealist. *Ints:* Theory of knowledge; history of philosophy; metaphysics. *Educ:* Lycée Henri-IV and l'École Normale Supérieure, Paris. *Infls:* Aristotle and Renouvier. *Appts:* Taught Philosophy at the Lycée de Pau (1883), l'Université de Bordeaux (1884–1905), the Sorbonne, where he was Professor of Ancient Philosophy, as well as at l'École Normale Supérieure, Paris (1905–7).

Main publications:

All posthumous:

(1907) *Essai sur les éléments principaux de la représentation*, Paris: F. Alcan; second edition with references and notes by M. A. Darbon, Paris: F. Alcan.

(1907) *Physique d'Aristote, Livre II, traduction et commentaire*, Paris: F. Alcan.

(1911) *Le Système de Descartes*, ed. L. Robin, preface by Émile Durkheim, Paris: F. Alcan.

(1920) *Le Système d'Aristote*, ed. L. Robin, Paris: F. Alcan; second, revised edition, 1931.

(1927) *Le Système de Renouvier*, ed. P. Muoy, Paris: J. Vrin.

(1953) *Théorie de l'intellect d'après Aristote et ses commentateurs*, notes by E. Babotin, Paris: J. Vrin.

Secondary literature:

Beck, Leslie John (1935) *La Méthode synthétique d'Hamelin*, La Paris: Aubier.

Deregibus, Arturo (1968) *La metafisica critica di Octave Hamelin*, Turin: G. Giapichelli.

Heitkämper, Peter (1971) *Der Personalitätsbegriff bei Octave Hamelin*, Meisenheim am Glan: A. Hain.

Morresi, Ruggero (1973) *Richerche sulla dialettica Hegel–Hamelin*, Rome: Dets, 1973.

——(1983) *Introduzione a Hamelin*, Naples: Guida.

Sesmat, Augustin (1955) *Dialectique: Hamelin et la philosophie chrétienne*, Paris: Blaud & Gay.

Turlot, Fernand (1976) *Idéalisme dialectique et personnalisme: essai sur la philosophie de Hamelin*, Paris: J. Vrin.

Hamelin's principal ideas centre around the development of a system of categories. There are eleven: relation; number; time; space; movement; quality; alteration; specification; causality; finality; personality. He begins with the simplest notion—relation—which characterizes all that can be or that can be said. Then each successive category is shown by Hamelin's 'synthetic method' to demand the next for its functioning. The system is completed with the category of personality which is found by Hamelin to be logically self-sufficient and adequate to experience. Personality is essentially consciousness, and 'consciousness ... is the highest moment of reality and through knowledge is the heart of being'. Reality is thus seen as a set of representations produced for some knowing being. It is finally rational and intelligible.

The concepts of intelligibility and personality are always Hamelin's main interests. Although his idea of reality has much to do with modern ideas of knowledge, Hamelin was always deeply interested in Aristotle and his categories are really a revision of the Aristotelian ones and are only Hegelian in the sense that a notion of 'personality' which involves the union of knower and known is the highest category. He had his own dialectic based on the notion that concepts always come in systems and that each gains its meaning only from its relations to the others. The exploration of these connections constitutes Hamelin's 'synthetic method'. The connection between Aristotle and Hamelin's idealism lies in his interest in the Aristotelian notion of the active intellect and in his interest in the Aristotelian account of the relation of thought to being. By understanding thought as permeating being, he hoped to be able to accept the Kantian critique of seventeenth- and eighteenth-century metaphysics while still being able to give an account of the way in which objective knowledge of the real is possible, and this constituted his major interest. The philosophy of **Renouvier** provided the most direct influence on him, although there are marked differences between their philosophies. L. J. Beck (1935) has explored the connections between his system of categories and that of Renouvier. Hamelin rivals Léon **Brunschvicg** in scholarly attention and he may well prove to be the most durable of the French idealists. Apart from the books listed here there have been some 50 short studies and, while 25 of them date from the 1920s and 1930s, there has been a steady trickle of them in the scholarly journals up to the present. There have been commentaries in German and Italian as well as in French. The studies have focused on his critiques of Kant and Hegel and his 'synthetic method' rather than on his work on Aristotle. Beck argued that the most important element in his work was his decision to make the category of relation fundamental and nearly all the studies emphasize this theme.

Sources: Benrubi; Parodi; Edwards; EF; LXXS; FranBio.

LESLIE ARMOUR

Hamlyn, D(avid) W(alter)

British. **b:** 1 October 1924, Plymouth, England. **Cat:** Analytic metaphysician, philosopher of mind; philosopher of psychology. **Ints:** History of philosophy; ethics; applied ethics; philosophy of education. **Educ:** Exeter College, Oxford, 1942 - 3 and 1946–50, 1st Hons in Honour Moderations in Classics, 1943, 1st Hons in Literae Humaniores, 1948, 1st Hons in Philosophy and Psychology, PPP, 1950; MA, 1949; John Locke Scholarship, 1949. **Infls:** Ludwig Wittgenstein, W. Kneale and

R. Peters. **Appts:** Research Fellow, Corpus Christi College, Oxford, 1950–3; Lecturer, Jesus College, Oxford, 1953–4; Lecturer, 1954–63, Reader, 1963–4, Professor and Chair of Philosophy, 1964–88, Head, Department of Classics, 1981–6, Vice-Master, 1983–8, Professor Emeritus, 1988–, Birkbeck College, London; Editor of *Mind*, 1972–84; Member of the Council of the Royal Institute of Philosophy since 1968; Executive Committee since 1971; Vice-Chairman since 1991.

Main publications:
(1957) *The Psychology of Perception*, London: Routledge & Kegan Paul.
(1961) *Sensation and Perception*, London: Routledge & Kegan Paul.
(1968) *Aristotle's De Anima, II & III*, Oxford: Clarendon Press.
(1970) *The Theory of Knowledge*, London: Macmillan Press.
(1978) *Experience and the Growth of Understanding*, London: Routledge & Kegan Paul.
(1980) *Schopenhauer*, London: Routledge & Kegan Paul.
(1983) *Perception, Learning and the Self*, Routledge & Kegan Paul.
(1984) *Metaphysics*, Cambridge: Cambridge University Press.
(1987) *A History of Western Philosophy*, New York: Viking.
(1990) *In and Out of the Black Box: On the Philosophy of Cognition*, Oxford: Blackwell.
(1992) *Being a Philosopher*, London and New York: Routledge.

Secondary literature:
Elliot, R. K. (1980) 'D. W. Hamlyn on knowledge and the beginnings of understanding', *Journal of the Philosophy of Education* 14: 109–16.
Gallagher, K. T. (1964) 'Recent Anglo-American views on perception', *International Philosophical Quarterly* 4: 122–41.
Goldman, A. I. (1985) 'The relation between epistemology and psychology', *Synthèse* 64: 29–68.
Jones, M. (1981) 'Innate powers, concepts and knowledge: a critique of D. W. Hamlyn's account of concept possession', *Journal of the Philosophy of Education* 15: 139–45.
Vesey, G. N. A. (1971) *Perception*, Garden City, NY: Anchor Books.

A major concern for Hamlyn has been to disentangle philosophical from psychological questions, and in his early work he criticizes as logically hybrid and inappropriate some of the kinds of explanation employed in Gestalt and derivative schools of psychology. This critique reflects Hamlyn's rejection of scientific reductionism within the field of psychology. He points out the failure of cognitive scientists to pay adequate attention to the concept of perception itself and to the related but—for Hamlyn—logically disparate concepts of sensation and judgment.

Similar approaches are reiterated in Hamlyn's critique of contemporary theorists of knowledge and language acquisition in and through experience. Although sympathetic to some of the 'rationalist' concerns of scientists and linguists such as **Piaget** and **Chomsky**, he is also critical of their work. Hamlyn argues for the requirement of a social context and social experience for concept and knowledge acquisition, and for the recognition of the place of emotions, motives and agency in that experience. Hamlyn's anti-Cartesian thesis that accurate analysis of perception must indicate the social and affective nature of our being steers a course between radical empiricism, rationalism and Piaget's biological, genetic epistemology. These factors of society and agency, he claims, figure in any answer to the problem of the *Meno*, which Hamlyn regards as central to cognitive theory.

Hamlyn's strongest critique is of the behaviourist position of **B. F. Skinner**, whose concept of conditioning Hamlyn regards as a scientific non-starter. The metaphysics of this critique is found in his argument against the behaviourist view of the passivity of the perceiving subject, which is developed at length in *In and Out of the Black Box* (1990). Broadly following Aristotle, he argues that a percipient's agency or activity is fundamental to and presupposed in any adequate account of perception, a fact that vitiates the 'black-box' information-processing model of learning and behaviour.

Hamyln's works also includes examinations of love, hate, self-deception, unconscious intentions and false emotions. Generally his interests range widely and along with a monograph on metaphysics he has written on logic, ethics and the philosophy of education. Aside from authoring a general history of philosophy his particular historical intersts are mainly in ancient philosophy—notably Aristotle's theory of agency and cognition—and in the philosophy of Schopenhauer, where similar concerns guide his study.

Sources: John Haldane (1988) 'Prefatory tribute', *PAS*, supp. vol. 62: 223–4; WW 1993, p. 801; PI.

DAVID SCOTT

Hampshire, Stuart Newton

British. *b:* 10 October 1914, Lincolnshire. *Cat:* Analytic philosopher. *Ints:* Philosophy of mind; moral philosophy. *Educ:* Repton and Balliol College, Oxford. *Infls:* Russell, Wittgenstein and Freud. *Appts:* Fellow, All Souls College, Oxford, 1936–40 and 1955–60; Lecturer, University College, London, 1947–50; Fellow, New College, Oxford, 1950–5; Professor, University College, London, 1960–3; Professor, Princeton University, 1963–70.

Main publications:
(1951) *Spinoza*, Harmondsworth: Penguin.
(1959) *Thought and Action*, London: Chatto.
(1965) *Freedom of the Individual*, London: Chatto.
(1971) *Freedom of Mind*, Oxford: Clarendon Press.
(1983) *Morality and Conflict*, Oxford: Blackwell.
(1989) *Innocence and Experience*, Cambridge: Mass.: Harvard University Press.

Secondary literature:
Williams, B. A. O. (1967) in Paul Edwards (ed.) *Encyclopedia of Philosophy*.

Hampshire is an independent-minded analytic philosopher, more remarkable for the breadth of his cultural range, the distinction of his style and an imaginative power that differentiates him from his more pedestrian philosophical colleagues than for exactness and rigour of argument. His most important book, *Thought and Action* (1959), signalled a return to system from the examination of minute issues at much the same time as, but in a different way from, P. F. **Strawson**'s *Individuals*. Like Strawson, Hampshire sets out the preconditions of articulate discourse, which requires the capacity to identify persisting objects and to assign them to classes. He argues for a conception of the self as essentially an agent, involved in manipulative relationships with the contents of its environment, and, therefore, as necessarily embodied, and not as a mere spectator of its surroundings and of the passing scene of its own stream of consciousness. Hampshire has been much concerned with the question of the freedom of the will. Human beings are decision-making, intention-forming creatures. Self-knowledge empowers agents; it does not reveal them as impotent automata. A person's nature is created by his decisions; to the extent that they are real it does not constrain them. In *Innocence and Experience* (1989), he argues, not altogether persuasively, for a procedural conception of morality, according to which adequate moral judgement requires the case of all those affected to be stated and taken

into account. Hampshire has written some perceptive literary criticism and in a short essay on aesthetics has argued that there can be no general rules of criticism since works of art are intrinsically unique. Hampshire has no obvious disciples but has been quietly influential in humanizing analytic philosophy in opposition to the general tendency of its practitioners to treat human beings as no more than rather complicated natural objects, importing into his work themes from such continental European philosophers as **Merleau-Ponty**. Not surprisingly, the manner and content of his thinking were unwelcome to **Ryle**.
Sources: Passmore 1957.

ANTHONY QUINTON

Hanafi, Hasan

Egyptian. *b:* 13 February 1935, Cairo, Egypt. *Cat:* Phenomenologist; philosopher of religion and politics; Islamic theologian. *Educ:* BA in Philosophy, Cairo University (1956); doctorate at the University of Paris, Sorbonne, with a thesis on 'Les Méthodes d'exégèse. Essai sur la science des fondements de la compréhension Ilm Usul al-fiqh, later published by the Conseil Supérieur des Arts, Lettres et Sciences Sociales du Caire (1965). *Infls:* Modern Islamic thinkers and radicals such as Iqbal, al-Mawdudi and Sayyed Qutb, and by Hegel, Bergson, Husserl and Ricoeur. *Appts:* 1967, Professor of Philosophy, Cairo University (Gizah); subsequently, Visiting Professor in Universities in Europe, Africa and Asia; published many essays on Western philosophers in the magazines *Al-Katib* and *Al-Fikr al-Muasir*; founded a magazine, *Al-Yasar al-Islami* [The Islamic Left].

Main publications:

(1977) *L'Exégèse de la phenomenologie*, Cairo.
(1980) *La Phénomenologie de l'exégèse*, Cairo.
(1980) *At-Turath wa at-Tagdid* [Legacy and Renewal], Cairo: al-Markaz al-Arabi lil-Nahth wa'n-Nashr.
(1982) *Dirasat Islamiyyah* [Islamic Studies], Beirut: Dar at-Tanwir.
(1983) *Fi Fikrina al-Muasir* [Our Contemporary Thought], Beirut: Dar at-Tanwir.
(1988) *Min al-Aqidah ila ath-Thawrah* [From Dogma to Revolution], 5 vols, Cairo: Maktabat Madbuli.
(1988–9) *Religious Dialogue and Revolution*, Cairo: Anglo-Egyptian Bookshop.
(1989) *Ad-Din wa ath-Thawrah fi Misr* [Religion and Revolution in Egypt], 8 vols, Cairo: Maktabat Madbuli.

(1991) *Muqaddimah fi Ilm al-Istighrab* [Introduction to the Science of Westernization], Cairo: Maktabat Madbuli.

Secondary literature:
Allard, M. (1964) 'Langage et théologie musulmane', in *Travaux et jours* 12, Beirut, January–March: 63-81.
——(1970) 'Un essai d'Anthropologie musulmane. Analyse et appréciation du livre de M. H. Hanafi "Les méthodes d'exégèse"' in *Comprendre* 53, Rome, November: 1–10.
Amoretti, B. Scarcia (1985) 'Religione popolare e risveglio islamico', in *Il Santo* 25, Padua: 107–19.
Campanini, M. (1990) 'Islam e rivoluzione in un'opera recente di Hasan Hanafi', in *Islàm. Storia e Civiltà* 9, 33, Rome: 243–51.
——(1992) 'Per una nuova lettura dell'Islam moderno. Intervista ad Hasan Hanafi' in *Islàm. Storia e Civiltà* 9, 39, Rome: 69–79.
Chartier, M. (1972) 'La Pensée religieuse Musulmane à la recherche d'un nouveau langage: l'audacieuse tentative du philosophe Egyptien Hasan Hanifi', in *Comprendre* 111, Rome, April: 1–15.
——(1973) 'La Recontre Orient–Occident dans la pensée de trois philosophes egyptiens contemporains: Hasan Hanafi, Fu'ad Zakariyya, Zaki Nagib Mahmud', in *Oriente Moderno* 53: 605–42.
Nwyia, P. (1971) 'Islam et langage moderne' in *Travaux et jours* 38, Beirut, January–March.

The most significant feature of Hanafi's thought is the attempt to apply phenomenological interpretation to Islam, as a religion and a system of life. Hanafi uses the necessity of intersubjectivity (in the Husserlian sense) to overcome the conflict between the rich and the poor, colonialist and subdued peoples, East and West. A genuine renewal of human—and particularly Islamic—thought and society will occur, he maintained, only when everyone becomes a subject of history, not merely an object of study and/or exploitation. This affirmation of subjectivity invites Eastern and especially Muslim peoples to reappraise their dignity and their cultural and political authority.

In Hanafi's view Islam is a revolutionary religion because it leads individuals to live horizontally, in a community, without vertical oppression. Islam is a religion of justice, too, and God is the universal principle ensuring that all people are equal. The unicity of God (*tawhid*) is essentially *telos* (in phenomenological terminology), will and action. In his doctoral thesis Hanafi wrote that consciousness requires a (human)

reality aiming at (divine) truth. In later works the most important philosophical issue is not the knowledge of God's attributes and essence, but the accomplishment of social justice: theology must be superseded by anthropology. Hanafi argues that freedom means making ourselves free; unicity is mainly the process of unification; religion—and Islam in particular, can be a redeeming force and the foundation of an Islamic 'left' looks unavoidable in order to fight against any kind of wrong and to bear witness to the upheaval implied in the Islamic profession of faith. 'There is no god but God and Muhammad is the Messenger of God' means for Hanafi the establishment of a universal code of ethics and the realization of prophecy by the declaration of the independence of reason and the autonomy of will.
Sources: Personal communication.

MASSIMO CAMPANINI

Hannequin, Arthur Edouard

French. *b:* 27 October 1856, Pargny sur Saulx, Marne, France. *d:* 4 July 1905, Pargny sur Saulx. *Cat:* Metaphysician. *Ints:* History of philosophy; history of science; philosophy of religion. *Educ:* Paris, agrégation 1882, doctorate 1895; corresponding membership of the Académie des Sciences Morales et Politiques, 21 December 1901. *Infls:* Spinoza, Leibniz, Kant, Lotze and Renouvier. *Appts:* Chargé de Cours, Lyon, 1885; Professor of History of Science, Lyon, 1891.

Main publications:

(1890) *Cours de Philosophie. Logique, Psychologie, Morale, Philosophie Générale. Introduction à l'Étude de la Psychologie*, Paris: Masson.

(1895) *Essai critique sur l'hypothèse des atomes*, Paris: Masson (Annales de l'Université de Lyon VII); second edition, Paris: Alcan, 1899.

(1895) *Quae fuerit prior Leibnit philosophia seu de motu de mente de Deo Doctrina ante annum 1672*, Paris: Masson.

(1908) *Études d'histoire des sciences, et d'histoire de philosophie*, Paris: Alcan.

Secondary literature:

Couturat, L. (1896–7) 'L'Hypothèse des atomes', *Revue de Métaphysique et de Morale*, 4: 778–97; 5: 87–113, 221–47.

Duhem, P. (1903) *L'Évolution de la mécanique*, Paris: Hermann, pp. 197ff (Duhem does not mention Hannequin directly at this point but his argument seems to be a reply to Hannequin who is in any case cited on page 16; see also P. Duhem, *La Théorie physique*, 1906, part II, chapter I).

Grosjean, J. (1907) 'Arthur Hannequin', *Revue de Métaphysique et de Morale* 15: 217–55.

Pioneer of philosophical history of science and holder of the first Chair of the subject anywhere, Hannequin held that the atomic hypothesis was the necessary epistemological foundation for the mathematization of physics. His *Essai critique* (1985) argued this thesis on the neo-Kantian grounds that atomism was subjectively necessary, although it contained contradictions which he attempted to repair by substituting a type of metaphysical atomism borrowing something from Leibniz. Unlike most contemporary neo-Kantians he accepted the real existence of things in themselves. Like many of his contemporaries he held that metaphysics should be based on a critical analysis of the philosophy of science. His philosophy seems to be an attempt to reconcile Kant and Leibniz, in **Couturat**'s view (1896–7) to the disadvantage of Kant. His attitude to religion seems to have been heavily influenced by Spinoza, but was influential on younger liberal Catholics among his students. His output was limited by lifelong ill health.

Sources: Edwards; H. W. Paul (1976) 'Scholarship versus ideology: the Chair of the General History of Science at the Collège de France, 1892–1913', *Isis* 67: 376–97; FranBio 1989.

R. N. D. MARTIN

Hanson, Norwood Russell

American. *b:* 17 August 1924, New York. *d:* April 1967. *Cat:* Pragmatist; philosopher of science. *Educ:* Cambridge and Oxford. *Infls:* Peirce, Russell and Wittgenstein. *Appts:* 1952–7, University Lecturer in Philosophy of Science, University of Cambridge; 1957–63, Professor of Philosophy, Indiana University, Bloomington; 1963–7, Professor of Philosophy, Yale.

Main publications:

(1958) *Patterns of Discovery*, Cambridge: Cambridge University Press.

(1963) *The Concept of the Positron: A Philosophical Analysis*, Cambridge: Cambridge University Press.

(1965) *A History of Science*, Dell.

(1969) *Perception and Discovery: An Introduction to Scientific Inquiry*, ed. W. C. Humphrey, Freeman, Cooper.

(1971) *Observation and Explanation: A Guide to the Philosophy of Science*, Harper.

(1972) *Why I do not Believe and Other Essays*, ed. S. Toulim and H. Wolff, Dordrecht: Reidel.

(1973) *Constellations and Conjectures*, ed. W. C. Humphrey, Dordrecht: Reidel.

Secondary literature:
Boyd, R., Gasper, Trout, J. D. (eds) (1991) *The Philosophy of Science*, London: MIT Press.
Suppe, F. (1974) 'The search for philosophic understanding of scientific theories', in *The Structure of Scientific Theories*, ed. F. Suppe, London: University of Illinois Press.

Norwood Russell Hanson was a seminal influence in contemporary philosophy of science. He was one of the earlier philosophers to make applications to the philosophy of science of ideas derived from the later **Wittgenstein** concerning logical relationships between perception and concepts to the philosophy of science. His critical response to a number of leading doctrines of logical positivism and logical empiricism was to set the scene for much of the discussion of the 1960s. In particular with his views on perception and explanation he challenged a number of central doctrines of the tradition of positivism. A standard view of logical positivism is that there exists a public world of sensory experience which is available to all observers. This world is neutral with respect to any individual or social and cultural point of view and its contents can be observed with the senses and reported in neutral observation sentences. Were this so there would be, at least in principle, an observational language available to us to report direct observations and it would always be possible for different percipients to see the same thing, process or property and report its presence in an observation language regardless of differences in conceptual or belief background between the percipients. This language is to be distinguished from the theoretical language, the language in which the content of scientific theories is expressed.

Against this view Hanson argued that the idea of neutral observation and a corresponding observation language are philosophical fictions. He attempts to demonstrate, principally by means of examples drawn from the psychology of perception and the history of science, that in perception whatever we perceive to be the case is influenced by our conceptual and theoretical background. If this is so a critical question then arises for science: is the objectivity and hence authority of science thereby undermined?

While the view that all seeing is 'theory laden' and that 'Observation of x is shaped by prior knowledge of x' (1958, p. 19) leads to substantial revision of the traditional account of the relation between observation and theory, it can be argued that this view implies neither relativism nor subjectivism in science, for in learning to perceive (as distinct, say, from learning to imagine) we are trained in circumstances where stimuli from the external world are publicly available and are partly intended to be the causes of what we see. These external ingredients, though possibly not separable in analysis, are available to anyone with normal sensory faculties and enable us to test and maybe revise current and future theories and in so doing provide a guarantee of the objectivity of science.

A particular application of the above critique of Hanson's concerns a central account of the nature of scientific understanding and theorizing embraced by positivism. The positivist account of these is that theories are axiom systems expressed in the theoretical language and incorporated into hypothetico-deductive structures which are then used to deduce observations. Such structures provide us with either predictions or explanations for particular events depending on the temporal position of the scientist with respect to observation and theoretical statement. This view is summed up in the doctrine of logical symmetry between explanation and prediction. However, if the distinction between observation and theory is not viable then the above account of scientific explanation fails as it is formulated in terms of that distinction.

Further themes pursued in *Patterns of Discovery* include positivist views concerning the viability of the distinction between the context of discovery and the context of justification, the nature of scientific reasoning and the analysis of the concept of a cause. For each Hanson offers an alternative, and for some philosophers, persuasive account.

Sources: CA.

JIM DUTHIE

Haraway, Donna Jeanne
American. *b:* 6 September 1944, Denver, Colorado,. *Cat:* Feminist theorist; philosopher of science. *Ints:* Feminism, constructivism and post-structuralism in studies of technoscience; epistemology; relations among humans, machines and other organisms. *Educ:* MPhil, PhD Biology with History of Science and Philosophy, Yale University; Fulbright Fellowship to Paris to study evolutionary philosophy. *Infls:* Multiple influences from contemporary Marxist, feminist and anti-racist intellectual culture; from reading Aquinas, Heidegger, Whitehead and Foucault;

and especially from 'the collective nature of the crafting of feminist theory', including theorists Braidotti, Harding and Spivak; graduate students. *Appts:* Assistant Professor, History of Science, Johns Hopkins University, 1974–80; Associate Professor (then Professor), History of Consciousness Board, University of California at Santa Cruz, from 1980.

Main publications:
(1985) 'Manifesto for cyborgs: science, technology, and socialist feminism in the 1980s', *Socialist Review* 80: 65–108 (reprinted in 10 other publications).

(1988) 'Situated knowledges: the science question in feminism', *Feminist Studies* 14, 3: 575–99.

(1989) 'The biopolitics of postmodern bodies: determinations of self in immune system discourse', *Differences* 1, 1: 3–43.

(1989) *Primate Visions: Gender, Race and Nature in the World of Modern Science*, London: Routledge.

(1991) *Simians, Cyborgs, and Women: The Reinvention of Nature*, London: Free Association Books.

(1992) 'Ecce Homo, Ain't (Ar'n't) I a Woman, and Inappropriate/d Others: the human in a posthumanist landscape', in J. Scott and J. Butler (eds), *Feminists Theorize the Political*, London: Routledge.

(forthcoming) *Modest Witness@Second Millennium: The Female Manø Meets OncomouseTT.*

One of a small band of women pursuing feminist science studies, Haraway has become increasingly influential in the field of a feminist philosophy that self-consiously erodes the distinctions between disciplines. Using a richly metaphorical style, Haraway addresses questions of ontology and epistemology, and speaks to a deconstruction of those limiting boundaries between self and other that historically have constructed and oppressed women. Her iconoclastic essay 'Manifesto for cyborgs' uses a provocative and complex vision of the half-human, half-machine cyborg being to open up the whole problem of what it is to be a self in a postmodern world. For Haraway, the body, far from being a fixed given, is the place of intervention, the site of possibility, of refiguring and realignments. Her aim is 'denaturalization without dematerialization'; and despite her affinity with postmodernism she remains insistent on the necessity for a situated accountability in knowledge production.
Sources: Personal communication.

MARGRIT SHILDRICK

Harding, Sandra

American. *b:* 29 March 1935, San Francisco. *Cat:* Feminist philosopher. *Ints:* Theories of science; epistemology; feminist critique of philosophy of science. *Educ:* Douglass College (BA 1956); New York University (PhD 1973). *Infls:* American Women's Movement and critique of objectivist theories of science (especially Quine, Kuhn and Feyerabend). *Appts:* Professor of Philosophy and Director of Women's Studies, University of Delaware (USA).

Main publications:
(1973–4) 'Feminism: reform or revolution?' in Carol C. Gould and Marx W. Wartofsky (eds) *Women and Philosophy. Toward a Theory of Liberation*, The Philosophical Forum, vol. V. nos 1–2.

(1976) (ed.) *Can Theories Be Refuted? Essays on the Duhem–Quine Thesis*, Dordrecht: Reidel.

(1982) 'Is gender a variable in conceptions of rationality? A survey of issues', *Dialectica International Review of Philosophy of Knowledge* 36, 2–3: 225–42.

(1983) (ed. with Merril B. Hintikka) *Discovering Reality. Feminist Perspectives on Epistemology, Metaphysics, Methodology, and Philosophy of Science*, Dordrecht: Reidel.

(1986) *The Science Question in Feminism*, Ithaca, NY and London: Cornell University Press.

(1986) 'The instability of the analytical categories of feminist theory', *Signs* 11, 4: 645–64.

(1987) (ed.) *Feminism and Methodology*, Bloomington: Indiana University Press and Milton Keynes: Open University Press.

(1987) 'The curious coincidence of feminine and African moralities: challenges for feminist theory', in Eva Feder Kittay and Diana T. Meyers (eds) *Women and Moral Theory*, Rowman & Littlefield.

(1989) 'How the women's movement benefits science—two views', *Women's Studies International Forum* 12, 3: 271–83.

(1989) 'Women as creators of knowledge—new environments', *American Behavioral Scientist* 32, 6: 700–7.

(1990) 'Feminism, science and the anti-enlightenment critiques', in Linda Nicholson (ed.) *Feminism/Postmodernism*, New York and London: Routledge.

(1991) *Whose Science? Whose Knowledge? Thinking from Women's Lives*, Ithaca, NY and London: Cornell University Press.

(1992) 'After the neutrality ideal—science, politics, and strong objectivity', *Social Research* 59, 3: 567–87.

Secondary literature:
Meyer, Ursula I. and Bennent-Vahle, Heidemarie
(eds) (1994) *Philosophinnen Lexikon*, Aachen: ein-
Fach-verlag.

Sandra Harding's feminist critique of theories of
science is based on a view of science as an
essentially social project, thereby rejecting attempts to give a guarantee for the objectivity of
scientific research.

One of the undeniable influences on the
production of knowledge, identified by Harding,
is gender. On various levels, she maintains, from
the politics of education and employment to the
symbolic representation of gender-categories in
scientific (quasi-objective) theories, the duality of
human gender is mirrored, not only the sexual
categories but in other structures of duality in
modern Western thought: the opposites of 'wild'
and 'civilized', of 'working class' and 'intelligentsia', as well as those of 'female' and 'male'
influence, the epistemology of the 'male', 'white',
'civilized' spectator.

Harding states that scientific endeavours have
their own history and development. Science today
can no longer be regarded as a 'craftsmanlike'
search for truth, but should rather be seen as a
complex enterprise in an industrialized surrounding. A critical feminist perspective can help to
reveal those changes and underlying structures of
scientific practice and theory. Nevertheless, Harding does not adhere to a postmodern rejection of
the power of the concept of truth.

URSULA STICKLER

Hare, R(ichard) M(ervyn)

British. *b:* 1919, Backwell, near Bristol. *Cat:*
Analytic philosopher. *Ints:* Ethics; political phi-
losophy; philosophy of language. *Educ:* University
of Oxford, 1945–7. *Infls:* G. E. Moore, J. L. Austin
and Ludwig Wittgenstein. *Appts:* Fellow of Balliol
College, Oxford, 1947–66; White's Professor of
Moral Philosophy, Oxford, and Fellow of Corpus
Christi College, 1966–83; Graduate Research
Professor, University of Florida at Gainesville,
from 1983; Fellow of the British Academy, 1964.

Main publications:
(1952) *The Language of Morals*, Oxford: Clarendon
Press.
(1963) *Freedom and Reason*, Oxford: Clarendon
Press.
(1971) *Practical Inferences*, London: Macmillan.
(1971) *Essays on Philosophical Method*, London:
Macmillan.

(1972) *Essays on the Moral Concepts*, London:
Macmillan.
(1972) *Applications of Moral Philosophy*, London:
Macmillan.
(1981) *Moral Thinking: Its Levels, Method and Point*,
Oxford: Clarendon Press.
(1982) *Plato*, Oxford: Oxford University Press.
(1989) *Essays in Ethical Theory*, Oxford: Clarendon
Press.
(1989) *Essays on Political Morality*, Oxford: Clarendon Press.
(1992) *Essays on Religion and Education*, Oxford:
Clarendon Press.
(1993) *Essays on Bioethics*, Oxford: Clarendon Press.

Secondary literature:
Hudson, W. D. (1983) *Modern Moral Philosophy*,
London: Macmillan.
Seanor, Douglas and Fotion, N. (eds) (1988) *Hare
and Critics*, with comments by R. M. Hare, Oxford:
Clarendon Press.

Hare's first published work, *The Language of
Morals* (1952), has been one of the most
influential works of moral philosophy in the
English-speaking world since the Second World
War. He argued that moral judgements, though
fundamentally imperative in form, could none the
less be rational. His later works elaborated these
themes and, especially in *Moral Thinking* (1981),
developed the claim that a certain sort of
utilitarianism must be the correct ethical theory.
He has also published a considerable amount of
work in practical ethics, increasingly so in the
latter half of his career.

When Hare started working on ethics, the
emotivism of philosophers such as A. J. **Ayer** and
C. L. **Stevenson** was in the ascendant. Hare's view
was that emotivism was right to deny that moral
judgements were factual, or descriptive, statements of any kind, but wrong to hold that they
were merely expressions of emotion or attempts to
influence the emotions of others. In particular, it
went wrong in not distinguishing clearly the claim
that moral utterances are attempts *to influence* the
actions of others (a claim Hare held to be false)
from the view that moral utterances are an
attempt *to tell people what to do* (which he held
to be true). And this rendered emotivism unable to
give a satisfactory account of how ethics could be
a *rational* endeavour. So Hare wished to propound a theory which would be 'a rationalist kind
of non-descriptivism' (Seanor and Fotion 1988:
210).

According to Hare, moral judgements were
fundamentally imperative in their logical form,

which is why any form of naturalism must be incorrect: it would involve the attempt to derive imperative conclusions from factual, and therefore non-imperative, premises. And this was the fault which G. E. **Moore**, although not properly diagnosing it, had labelled the Naturalistic Fallacy. Moral judgements are not usually, of course, imperative in their *grammatical* form. The nub of Hare's claim that they were logically imperative was this: it is a conceptual truth that sincerely accepting a moral judgement commits the speaker to *acting* upon it on appropriate occasions if it is within his power. Thus, if someone does not act upon a moral judgement on the appropriate occasions, then we may logically conclude that either that he *could not* do so or that he did not accept the moral judgement. This view of ethical judgements came to be known as prescriptivism.

Hare was at pains, however, to show that imperatives are subject to logical constraints, just as factual assertions are, and this is part of what brings morality within the domain of reason.

Hare's second major claim is that a genuine moral judgement, such as that I ought not, for instance, to have my pregnancy aborted, must be based upon some *principles*. Hare's claim is that it is a conceptual truth that moral principles are *universal* in form. This does not mean that they need be wide generalizations; indeed they may be very specific. But they must not contain references to particular individuals. And this in turn generates the thesis of the Universalizability of Moral Judgements. To accept a particular moral judgement, *as* a moral judgement, involves accepting it also as a universal principle. If I really think that it would be morally wrong for me to have an abortion then I must think that it would be morally wrong for anyone relevantly like me, in relevantly similar circumstances, to have an abortion. Hare's theory thus came to be known as Universal Prescriptivism.

The practical force of the marriage of prescriptivism and universalizability became clearer in *Freedom and Reason* (1963) and, in particular, *Moral Thinking* (1981). In these works, Hare developed a form of utilitarianism. Like most modern utilitarians, he thought of the individual good as consisting in one's desires being fulfilled, rather than in happiness, a conception known as preference utilitarianism. Desires, which he claimed were the *subject matter* of morality, could be ordered according to their strength, and independently of whose desires they were or what they were desires for. He then argued that a sympathetic identification with the desires of others would make us come to identify with those desires as we identify with our own. We should thus come to want the satisfaction of desires generally, ranked according to their strength, and with no concern for *whose* desires they were nor what they were desires for; and, Hare argued, this would lead us to desire the maximum satisfaction of desires generally.

In *Moral Thinking* Hare worked more concentratedly towards a theory that combined the advantages of both act utilitarianism and rule utilitarianism. Although, at the level of what he called critical thinking—the level of the utterly impartial, rational and knowledgeable agent—an individual act is right if and only if it maximizes the satisfaction of desire, he argued that in making moral decisions we should not usually consider the consequences of each individual act. Doing so would not in fact produce the desired result, since our judgements would often go wrong. Rather, we should generally follow those rules that have been tried and tested,—for example, rules against lying, cheating, stealing and so forth. We should rest content with what Hare calls our intuitive judgements. Indeed we should try to mould our sentiments, and those of our children, to make it psychologically difficult for us to act against them save in exceptional circumstances. So Hare does not suggest that utilitarian thinking should replace an adherence to many of our ordinary, intuitive moral principles. Indeed the fact that a general adherence to these principles maximizes utility explains, in his view, why they have grown up. Hare's work has been the subject of continuous discussion, and virtually every aspect of it has been criticized. It has been argued, for instance, that the diversity of moral utterances cannot be reduced satisfactorily to the imperative model. Many have argued that there is no fact—value distinction of the sort that is central to his work. Others, again, have held that moral judgements are not essentially universalizable. And many philosophers have thought that his recent work commits Hare to a sort of naturalism which his theory was supposed to reject. Allan Gibbard remarks: 'Perhaps no philosopher since Kant has developed a theory of moral judgement and moral reasoning so ingenious and so carefully worked through as R. M. Hare' (in Seanor and Fotion 1988, p. 57).

Sources: Flew; Becker; WW 1992; personal communication.

ANTHONY ELLIS

Harman, G(ilbert)
American. *b:* 26 May 1938, East Orange, New Jersey. *Cat:* Analytical philosopher. *Ints:* Epistemologist; philosopher of mind; philosopher of ethics; philosopher of language. *Educ:* Swarthmore College and Harvard University. *Infls:* W. v. O. Quine and N. Chomsky. *Appts:* Since 1963, Professor of Philosophy, Princeton University; since 1985, Codirector, Princeton University Cognitive Science Laboratory; since 1991, Chairman of the Princeton Programme in Cognitive Studies; visiting positions at the University of California at Berkeley, New York University, Rockefeller University and The Johns Hopkins University.

Main publications:
(1967) 'Quine on meaning and existence', *Review of Metaphysics* 21: 124–51, 343–67.

(1967) 'Towards a theory of intrinsic value', *Journal of Philosophy* 64: 401–11.

(1968) 'Three levels of meaning', *Journal of Philosophy* 65: 590–602.

(1970) 'Knowledge, reasons and causes', *Journal of Philosophy* 67: 841–55.

(1973) *Thought*, Princeton, NJ: Princeton University Press.

(1977) *The Nature of Morality: An Introduction to Ethics*, New York: Oxford University Press.

(1980) 'Reasoning and explanatory coherence', *American Philosophical Quarterly* 117: 165–82.

(1980) '(Nonsolipsistic) conceptual role semantics', in Ernest LePore (ed.), *New Directions in Semantics*, London: Academic Press.

(1986) *Change in View: Principles of Reasoning*, Cambridge, Mass.: MIT Press/Bradford Books.

(1988) 'Wide functionalism', in Stephen Schiffer and Susan Steele (eds) *Cognition and Representation*, Boulder, CO.: Westview Press.

(1990) 'Immanent and transcendent approaches to the theory of meaning', in Roger Gibson and Robert B. Barrett (eds), *Perspectives on Quine*, Oxford: Blackwell'.

(1990) 'The intrinsic quality of experience', *Philosophical Perspectives* 4: 31–52.

Secondary literature:
Annis, David B. (1976) 'Thought', *Philosophia* 6, 2: 345-9.

Brueckner, Anthony L. (1989) 'Harman's naturalistic study of reasoning', *Metaphilosophy* 20, 3 & 4: 356–70.

Copp, D. (1982) 'Harman on internalism, relativism, and logical form', *Ethics* 92: 227–42.

Fullinwider, Robert K. (1980) 'Harman's *The Nature of Morality*', *Metaphilosophy* 11: 3 & 4: 272–77.

Johnson, Ralph H. (1988) 'Gilbert Harman, *Change in View: Principles of Reasoning*', *Canadian Journal of Philosophy* 18, 1: 163-78.

Levi, I. (1987) 'Change in View: Principles of Reasoning', *The Journal of Philosophy*, 84, 7: 376–84.

Sosa, E. (1977) 'Thought, inference and knowledge: Gilbert Harman's *Thought*', *Nous* 11: 421–30.

Harman believes that philosophy is continuous with science and should not be conceived as part of the humanities. Like **Quine**, he rejects the analytic-synthetic distinction, arguing that those philosophers who embrace it suppose, amongst other things, that there is a difference between dictionaries and encyclopedias, the former giving information about word-meanings and the latter providing factual information. This is a distinction without a difference.

Harman's conception of a person is functionalist: mental states and processes possess representational characteristics by virtue of their role in a functional system, and we understand a person's beliefs and desires when we grasp the programme(s) which describe their interrelationships. Harman is an early exponent of the 'language of thought' hypothesis: mental states have a structure which is paralleled by the corresponding structure of the sentences used to describe them; and sentence-meaning is to be characterized truth-conditionally. In his book *Thought* (1973) Harman also argues that knowledge is based upon inference to the best explanation.

Harman argues that, in ethics, the task of the philosopher is to account for the fact that observational evidence plays a different role in the sphere of moral thought from its role in science. Also, he insists that an adequate ethical theory must explain why an agent should act morally. He proposes a version of the social convention theory: there are moral facts, but they are relational facts about reasons for action and about the acceptance of social conventions. People adhere to moral principles through a tacit process of bargaining and mutual adjustment, because overall, and in the long run, they individually benefit from cooperating. Critics have alleged that Harman's theory entails moral relativism; but it does not simply identify wrong conduct with adverse social pressure within a given society, and it is plausible to think that tacit bargaining will form part of any satisfactory moral theory.

Harman's recent work on change in view is of interest to workers in the field of artificial intelligence, as well as to philosophers. A change in view is a change in one's system of beliefs, desires and intentions. Principles of reasoning—rules of revision—govern changes in view, and Harman contends that deductive logic is not of any special relevance to such rules. Harman argues that deductive logic is a theory of inference, not a theory of reasoning. It is, for instance, an inference in deductive logic that from (A & -A) we may infer any proposition B. But if an agent discovers that his belief-set is inconsistent, he does not thereby feel entitled to believe any proposition whatsoever; rather, he rejects one of his beliefs. Again, given that A is true, we may deductively infer (A v B); but in reasoning we adopt what Harman calls a 'clutter-avoidance' principle: a meta-principle which enjoins one not to clutter one's mind with the trivial consequence of one's beliefs.

Some philosophers have alleged that Harman fails to make it sufficiently clear whether his rules of revision are normative or descriptive, but, since Harman's investigations are within the tradition of naturalized epistemology, these critics need to argue against that tradition rather than against Harman's approach in particular. Other critics take issue with certain of Harman's principles of reasoning. For instance, Isaac Levi has argued that what should be stored in the head is, at least in part, a function of information technology; so the clutter-avoidance principle is undermined.

What can be said in general is that Harman's whole discussion of change in view is tentative and undogmatic, and of great importance for understanding the dynamics of real-time reasoning.

Sources: Personal communication.

ROGER FELLOWS

Harré, Rom(ano) (Horace)

New Zealander. *b:* 18 December 1927, New Zealand. *Cat:* Philosopher of science; philosopher of the social sciences. *Ints:* Realism. *Educ:* University of Auckland and University College, Oxford. *Infls:* Locke and Sir Peter Strawson. *Appts:* 1960–, Lecturer in the Philosophy of Science, University of Oxford; 1963–, Fellow of Linacre College; 1973–, Adjunct Professor, State University of New York, Binghamton; 1989–, Professor of Psychology, Georgetown University, Washington, DC; 1992–3, Royden B. Davis Professor of Interdisciplinary Studies, Georgetown University, Washington, DC.

Main publications:

(1961) *Theories and Things*, London: Sheed & Ward.

(1964) *Matter and Method*, London: Macmillan; reprinted, Los Angeles: Sage, 1979.

(1970) *The Method of Science*, London: Wykeham Press.

(1970) *The Principles of Scientific Thinking*, London: Macmillan; Chicago: Chicago University Press, 1971.

(1972) *The Philosophies of Science*, Oxford: Oxford University Press; second edition, 1986, reprints and translations.

(1973) (with P. F. Secord) *The Explanation of Social Behaviour*, Oxford: Blackwell.

(1975) (with E. H. Madden) *Causal Powers*, Oxford: Blackwell.

(1979) *Social Being: A Theory for Social Psychology*, Oxford: Blackwell; revised edition, 1993.

(1981) *Twenty Great Scientific Experiments*, Oxford: Phaidon Press; American edition, 1982, numerous translations.

(1983) *Personal Being: A Theory for Individual Psychology*, Oxford: Blackwell; Cambridge, Mass.: Harvard University Press, 1985.

(1986) *Varieties of Realism*, Oxford: Blackwell.

(1986) 'Persons and powers', in S. Shanker (ed.), *Philosophy in Britain Today*, London: Croom Helm.

(1989) 'Realism, reference and theory', in A. Phillips Griffiths (ed.), *Key Themes in Philosophy*, Cambridge: Cambridge University Press.

(1991) *Physical Being: A Theory for Corporeal Psychology*, Oxford: Blackwell.

(1991) 'Causality and reality', in D. O. Dahlstrom (ed.), *Nature and Scientific Method*, Washington, DC: Catholic University Press.

(1993) *Laws of Nature*, London: Duckworth.

(1993) (with J. Aronson and E. Way) *Realism, Similarity and Type-Hierarchies*, London: Duckworth.

(1994) (with G. Gillett) *The Discursive Mind*, Newbury Park: Sage Publications.

(1995) (with J. Aronson and E. Way) *Realism Rescued: How Scientific Progress Is Possible*, Chicago: Open Court Publishing Co.

Secondary literature:

Bhaskar, Roy (ed.) (1990) *Harré and His Critics*, Oxford: Blackwell.

Musso, Pado (1993) *Ron Harré e il Problemo del Realismo Scientifico*, Milan: Franco Angeli.

Harré's contribution is in the philosophy not only of the natural but also of the social sciences. In the former, he criticizes the logicistic/deductivist account advocated by **Hempel**, **Popper** and **Nagel**. While rejecting the symmetry between prediction and explanation, he emphasizes the role of models in scientific thinking. More fundamentally, he challenges the Humean legacy with its account of causation in terms of concomitance of events. In his alternative ontology the concomitances are the manifestation of the dispositions of enduring material particulars and their constitutive properties. This ties in with his defence of policy realism according to which it would be rational to search for the referents of (plausibly) hypothesized entities and in which theories are 'sets of direction for manipulating observable and unobservable material things that will bring previously unobserved beings ... to the "light of day"' ('Causality and reality', 1991, p. 7). He is also hospitable to a *weak* convergent realism on the grounds that, while plausible theories permit revision of attribute, natural kind and metaphysical category, that revision is not indefinitely open.

Harré's stance is carried over into the study of the social world via the notion of 'the Conversation', which emabraces the social *Umwelten* of individual human beings but at the same time goes beyond them to 'the open set of possibilities that are (its) affordances' (Bhaskar 1990; pp. 351).
Sources: WD; WW(World); PI; personal communication.

KEEKOK LEE

Harris, William Torrey

American. *b:* 10 September 1835, North Killingly, Connecticut. *d:* 1909, Providence, Rhode Island. *Cat:* Idealist. *Ints:* Theory of knowledge; education. *Educ:* Local schools in Connecticut and then at Yale University, but left after his third year and moved to St Louis. *Infls:* Hegel. *Appts:* Became a school teacher in St Louis and eventually superintendent of schools; Henry Brokmeyer used him as a secretary to record his translation of Hegel's *Phenomenology*; was a prime mover in the St Louis Hegelian Society which founded the *Journal of Speculative Philosophy*, the first regular American philosophy journal; returned to New England in 1880 to work in the Concord Movement, dedicated to developing the heritage of Thoreau, Emerson and Hawthorne; he remained in Concord for nine years before moving to Washington as US Commissioner for Education, a post he retained until 1906.

Main publications:

(1881) *Hegel's Doctrine of Reflection, Being a Paraphrase and Commentary Interpolated Into the Text of the Second Volume of Hegel's Larger Logic, Treating of 'Essence'*, New York: Appleton.
(1883) *Philosophy in Outline*, New York: Appleton.

(1889) *Introduction to the Study of Philosophy*, ed. Marietta Kies, New York: Appleton (contains a selection of Harris's more than 500 articles).
(1890) *Hegel's Logic: A Book on the Genesis of the Categories of the Mind*, Chicago: S. C. Griggs; second edition, 1895.
(1902) *The Difference Between Efficient and Final Causes in Controlling Human Freedom*, Bloomington, Ill.: Public-school Publishing Co.
(1904) *Herbert Spencer and His Influence on Education*, Chicago: University of Chicago Press.

Secondary literature:

Leidecker, Kurt, F. (1936) *Bibliography: William Torrey Harris in Literature*, New York: Philosophical Library.
——(1946) *Yankee Teacher, The Life of William Torrey Harris*, Chicago: Open Court.
Lyons, Richard Gerald (1964) 'The influence of Hegel on the philosophy of education of William Torrey Harris', PhD thesis, Boston University.
Schaub, Edward Leroy (ed.) (1936) *William Torrey Harris*, Chicago: Open Court.

Harris saw philosophy as a unifying science which can provide a picture of the whole of reality. It should be based, in a Kantian way, on the search for what is necessary to any possible experience, but it can achieve Hegel's aim and transcend the merely phenomenal world. This is so because the distinction between what merely seems to be and what reason recognizes as the real can be found *within* the pattern of developing experience.

Although Harris was thoroughly engaged in Hegel's entire worldview, and would have said that his only ultimate philosophical interest was in finding out the truth about the world, his actual work is nearly always strongly oriented to the theory of knowledge and this reflects his practical interests in education. He believed that his philosophical method, which concentrated on developing the experience of the partial and transitory into an ever-widening experience which met the criteria of the real, provided the right basis for educational theory. Beyond that he believed it could even guide *political* practice in showing how the legal and moral come to be unified. He became closely involved with the US federal government as Commissioner for Education. As a founder and editor of the first technical philosophical journal—one to which most major philosophers were later to contribute—and as a public official, Harris exercised a wide influence on American life and philosophy. Lloyd D. Easton, in *Hegel's First American Followers* (Athens, OH: Ohio University Press, 1966), and William H. Goetzmann, in *The American Hegelians* (New York: Knopf, 1973), give him pride of place amongst those who made Hegel an American influence. The secondary literature is not vast and it strongly emphasizes his role as an educator and as a major organizer of philosophical opinion rather than his attempts at original philosophy—though inevitably in trying to make Hegel intelligible to Americans, he gave the Hegelian system a distinct shape, one which made it a tool for education and political reform by emphasizing its function in providing a background for a unified value theory. The Hegelianism of the young John **Dewey** shows the influence of these ideas.

Sources: WWW(Am); Edwards.

LESLIE ARMOUR

Harris, Zellig (Sabbettai)

American. *b:* 23 October 1909, Balta, Ukraine. *Cat:* Structural linguist. *Ints:* Linguistics. *Educ:* University of Pennsylvania. *Appts:* 1931–66, Instructor, later Professor of Linguistics, University of Pennsylvania; from 1966, Benjamin Franklin Professor of Linguistics.

Main publications:

(1951) *Methods in Structural Linguistics*, Chicago: Chicago University Press; reprinted as *Structural Linguistics*, 1961.

(1952) 'Discourse analysis', *Language* 28: 1–30, 474–94.

(1957) 'Co-occurrence and transformation in linguistic structure', *Language* 33: 283–340.

(1962) *String Analysis of Sentence Structure*, The Hague: Mouton.

(1965) 'Transformational theory', *Language* 41: 363–401.

(1970) *Papers in Structural and Transformational Linguistics*, Dordrecht: Reidel.

(1982) *The Grammar of English on Mathematical Principles*, Wiley.

(1989) (co-author) *The Form of Intuition in Science*, Dordrecht: Reidel.

Secondary literature:

Miller, J. (1973) 'A note on so-called "discovery procedures"', *Foundations of Language* 10: 123–39.

Harris was born in the Ukraine to a Jewish family and as a child emigrated to the USA. Later on he joined a kibbutz in Israel, where he regularly spends part of his time. From 1931 until his retirement he served as a Professor at the University of Pennsylvania in Philadelphia. He

has been considered the leading structuralist linguist, after **Sapir** and **Bloomfield**.

Harris has reflected in his linguistic work an empiricist philosophy of language and science. However, no trace of this philosophy is found in the linguistic work of Noam **Chomsky**, his most renowned student. Thus, for example, Harris confined each linguistic analysis to a certain corpus of linguistic data, unlike Chomsky, who has been interested in human linguistic competence. He used formal methods in his linguistic analyses, circumventing any allusion to meaning or similar semantic notions. His formal systems were meant to provide compact descriptions of utterances in a corpus, rather than explain the underlying cognitive competence.

Harris tried to show how different levels of linguistic analysis are related to each other in formal ways: phonemes to morphemes and the latter to utterances. He also introduced a form of discourse analysis, where relations are specified between different sentences. In this context he introduced the notion of 'transformation', later to play a major role, in a related but quite different sense, in Chomsky's work.

Harris thought that a procedure could be formulated which would derive linguistic rules from the corpus itself, on grounds of certain informants' judgements of 'sameness' and 'difference'. Generative linguistics, however, has rejected the linguistic objective of such an empiricist approach on linguistic, methodological and philosophical grounds.

Sources: DAS; *PI*.

ASA KASHER

Harrison, Frederic

British. *b:* 18 October 1831, London. *d:* 14 January 1923, Bath. *Cat:* Comtean positivist. *Educ:* Wadham College, Oxford. *Infls:* Personal influences: J. S. Mill, G. Grote, T. Arnold and R. Congreve. Literary influences: Comte and G. H. Lewes. *Appts:* 1854–6, Fellow of Wadham College, Oxford; 1858, called to Bar; 1880–1905, President of English Positivist Committee; 1899–1923, Honorary Fellow of Wadham College, Oxford.

Main publications:

(1901) 'Positivism: its position, aims and ideals', in *Great Religions of the World*, New York and London: Harper.

(1907) *The Philosophy of Common Sense*, London: Macmillan.

(1908) *Bibliography of Frederic Harrison*, Hawkhurst: F. Williams

(1913) *The Positive Evolution of Religion: Its Moral and Social Reaction*, London: Heinemann.

Secondary literature:
Simon, W. M. (1972) *European Positivism in the Nineteenth Century*, Post Washington, NY: Kennikat Press.

Although he had a High Church Anglican upbringing, Harrison did not take to the liturgical form of positivism; and, in spite of his close connections with Wadham, he seems only to have been indirectly influenced by the 'high priest' of English positivism, Congreve, with whom he later quarrelled. Harrison was a very individualistic philosopher. He had studied and been disillusioned by various systems of metaphysics. He also acquired a distaste for sectarian religion and found his own way to views like those of Comte, with whose view of the historical evolution of religion he came to agree.

In spite of his academic connections Harrison was more of a lay philosopher—a Victorian man of letters who wrote on history, literature and current affairs as well as on philosophical matters. He was involved in the production of many English editions of works by Comte and produced a massive *Calendar of Great Men*—a kind of secular alternative to a Catholic calendar of the saints. Philosophy was, for Harrison, a substitute for religion and he thought that, like religion, philosophy should have a practical outcome. He defended what he called 'the philosophy of common sense', claiming that 'Rational Philosophy... from the time of the early Greek sages down to Auguste Comte, has never been anything but the Common Sense of the best minds systematised and correlated to a righteous life' (1907, p. ix). Harrison belonged to a generation who did not take religious unbelief for granted and, compared with the Logical Positivists, he and other Comptean positivists seemed to have had little influence in the period after the First World War.
Sources: DNB, 1922–30; F. Harrison (1911) *Autobiographic Memoirs*, 2 vols, London: Macmillan; Metz; Martha S. Vogeler (1984) *Frederic Harrison: The Vocations of a Positivist*, Oxford: Clarendon Press.

STUART BROWN

Hart, Herbert Lionel Adolphus
British. *b:* 8 July 1907, Harrogate, Yorkshire. *d:* 19 December 1992. *Cat:* Legal positivist. *Ints:* Legal philosophy. *Educ:* New College, Oxford. *Infls:* Austin, Bentham and Hohfeld. *Appts:* Professor of Jurisprudence, Oxford University; Principal, Brasenose College; Fellow and Tutor in Philosophy, New College; Fellow, University College; Senior Research Fellow, Nuffield Foundation.

Main publications:
(1953) *Definition and Theory in Jurisprudence*, Oxford: Clarendon Press (Inaugural Lecture delivered before the University of Oxford).
(1953) *Essays in Jurisprudence and Philosophy*, Oxford: Clarendon Press.
(1959) (with Tony Honore) *Causation in the Law*, Oxford: Clarendon Press.
(1961) *The Concept of Law*, Oxford: Clarendon Press.
(1962) *Bentham: Lecture on the Master Mind*, Oxford: Oxford University Press.
(1962) *Punishment and the Elimination of Responsibility*, London: Athlone Press (L. T. Hobhouse Memorial Trust Lectures).
(1963) *Law, Liberty and Morality*, Oxford: Oxford University Press.
(1968) *Punishment and Responsibility: Essays in the Philosophy of Law*, Oxford: Clarendon Press.
(1977) (ed. with J. H. Burns) *Jeremy Bentham, A Comment on the Commentaries* and *A Fragment on Government*, London: University of London.
(1982) *Essays on Betham: Studies in Jurisprudence and Political Theory*, Oxford: Clarendon Press.
(1994) *The Concept of Law*, second edition, with a postscript edited by Penelope A. Bulloch and Joseph Raz, Oxford: Clarendon Press.

Secondary literature:
Bayles, Michael D. (1992) *Hart's Legal Philosophy: An Examination* , Dordrecht: Kluwer Academic.
Coval, S. C. and Smith, J. C. (1977) 'The completeness of rules, *Cambridge Law Journal*.
Fuller, L. (1958) 'Positivism and the fidelty to law: a reply to Professor Hart', *Harvard Law Review* 71.
Gavison, Ruth (ed.) (1987) *Issues in Contemporary Legal Philosophy: The Influence of H. L. A. Hart*, Oxford: Clarendon Press.
Hacker, P. M. S. and Raz, J. (eds) (1979) *Law, Morality and Society: Essays in Honour of H. L. A. Hart*, Oxford: Clarendon Press.
Leith, Philip and Ingram, Peter (1988) *The Jurisprudence of Orthodoxy: Queen's University Essays on H. L. A. Hart*, London: Routledge.
MacCormick, Neil (1981) *H. L. A. Hart*, London: Edward Arnold.
Moles, Robert N. (1987) *Definition and Rule in Legal Theory: A Reassessment of H. L. A. Hart and the Positivist Tradition*, Oxford: Basil Blackwell.
Singer, P. (1963) 'Hart's concept of law', *Journal of Philosophy* 60.

Summers, R. S. (1963) 'Hart's concept of mind',
  Duke Law Journal.

Hart offers a positivist account of law that does
not have the shortcomings of **Austin**'s and
Bentham's accounts of law. According to Hart
an account of law as a command backed by
sanction (as held by Austin and Bentham) is
inadequate since: (i) criminal statutes, forbidding
or enjoining certain actions under penalty, equally
apply to those who enact the laws; (ii) there are
laws that are power conferring (for instance, laws
conferring powers to legislate); (iii) not all laws
come into being through explicit prescription (for
instance, laws derived from custom); and (iv) an
analysis of law in terms of the sovereign fails to
account for the continuity of legislative authority
in a modern legal system (1961, p. 70).

For Hart, the central feature of law is rules that
are non-optional and create obligations, supported by great social pressure necessary for the
maintenance of society.

> Rules are conceived and spoken of as imposing
> obligations when the general demand for
> conformity is insistent and the social pressure
> brought to bear upon those who deviate or
> threaten to deivate is so great. Such rules may
> be wholly customary in origin; there may be no
> centrally organised system of punishments for
> breach of the rules; the social pressure may
> take only the form of a general diffused hostile
> or critical reaction which may stop short of
> physical sanctions (ibid., p. 84).

However, a concept of rules of obligation without
any formal rules of adjudication, recognition etc.
(i.e. primary rules) does not fully describe a legal
system. Apart from the primary rules a legal
system consists of secondary rules. According to
Hart, the primary rules suffer from three failings:
(i) the precise scope of the rule is uncertain; (ii) the
rules are static; and (iii) the lack of authoritative
arbiters results in an inefficient maintenance of
primary rules. A society that has primary rules, for
Hart, is in a prelegal state. To enter a legal state
such a society would require secondary rules
whereby (i) the uncertainty of the rules could be
remedied by having a 'rule of recognition' by
which the primary rules can be identified, (ii) the
static rules could be made more mobile by 'rules of
change' that empower an individual or body to
introduce new primary rules, and (iii) the inefficient maintenance of primary rules could be
rectified through the 'rule of adjudication' which
empowers individuals to authoritatively deter-

mine the question of when a primary rule is
broken (ibid., pp. 89–95).

According to Hart, although rules are the
essential feature of law, at some point they fail in
producing solutions to legal problems, due to lack
of clarity in the language. At this point judicidial
discretion comes into play and judges arrive at
decisions based on extra-legal factors.

Hart's account of law is open to many
criticisms (see Singer 1963, p. 197; Fuller 1958,
p. 630; Coral and Smith 1977, p. 364; Summers
1963, p. 629). A commonly held criticism is that
Hart's analysis of a legal system could be equally
applied to clubs. Clubs too prescribe acceptable
codes of conduct for their members and have
mechanisms in place to modify club rules, take
formal disciplinary action against members who
break the code of conduct and so on. How then is
one to distinguish between the law of the club and
the law of the state? Hart does not seem to address
this issue adequately.

One of Hart's well known critics is the
American legal philosopher Ronald **Dworkin**.
According to Dworkin, an account of law in
terms of rules alone is incomplete. For instance, he
says that it is correct to say that judges make law
where rules are unclear. Using various cases as
illustrations (such as *Riggs v Palmer* (1899) 2 NE
188) he suggests that legal principles play an
important role in legal decision making and
judges are not lawmakers as Hart claims.

Sources: WW 1991; obituary, *The Times*, 24 Dec 1992.

INDIRA MAHALINGAM CARR

Hartmann, (Karl Robert) Eduard von

German. *b:* 23 February 1842, Berlin. *d:* 5 June
1906, Gross-Lichterfeld, Berlin. *Cat:* Transcendent realist; speculative metaphysician. *Ints:* Metaphysics; philosophy of religion. *Infls:* Schelling,
Hegel, Schopenhauer, Leibniz, Kant and
Nietzsche. *Appts:* Abandoned a military career
for philosophy as a result of a serious knee injury
suffered in 1862; graduated from the University of
Rostock in 1867; after first book, was offered
professorships at the Universities of Leipzig,
Göttingen and Berlin, but declined in favour of
the independent life of a private scholar.

Main publications:

(1868) *Philosophie des Unbewussten*, Berlin: C.
  Duncker (English translation, *The Philosophy of
  the Unconscious*, 3 vols, London: W. C. Coupland,
  1884).

(1874) *Die Selbstzersetzung des Christenthums und
  die Religion der Zukunft*, Berlin: C. Duncker

(English translation, *The Religion of the Future*, trans. E. Dare, London: W. Stewart & Co., 1886).

(1875) *Wahrheit und Irrthum im Darwinismus*, Berlin: C. Duncker (English translation, 'The true and the false in Darwinism', trans. H. J. Davey, *Journal of Speculative Philosophy* 2, 1877).

(1879) *Phänomenologie des sittlichen Bewusstseins*, Naumburg a/s: C. Duncker (C. Heymons).

(1880) *Zur Geschichte und Begründung des Pessimismus*, Berlin: C. Duncker (C. Heymons).

(1882) *Die Religion des Geistes*, Berlin: C. Duncker (English translation of part A, *The Religion of the Spirit*, trans. E. Dare, London: W. Stewart & Co., 1886; of part B, *Religious Metaphysics*, trans. T. Hitchcock, New York: Macgowan & Slipper, 1883).

(1889) *Das Grundproblem der Erkenntnistheorie*, Leipzig: H. Haacke.

(1896) *Kategorienlehre*, Leipzig: H. Haacke.

Secondary literature:

Caldwell, J. W. (1893) 'The epistemology of Eduard von Hartmann ', *Mind* 2.

——(1899) 'Hartmann's moral and social philosophy', *Philosophical Review* VIII.

Darnoi, N. K. (1967) *The Unconscious and Eduard von Hartmann*, The Hague: Martinus Nijhoff.

Drews, A. (1902) *Eduard von Hartmanns philosophisches System*, Heidelberg: C. Winter.

Hall, G. Stanley (1912) *Founders of Modern Psychology*, New York: D. Appleton & Co., pp. 181–246.

Hartmann, Alma von (1912) 'Chronologische Übersicht der Schriften Eduard von Hartmanns', *Kant-Studien* 17.

Heymons, C. (1882) *Eduard von Hartmann. Erinnerungen aus den Jahren 1868–1881*, Berlin: C. Duncker.

Stäglich, H. (1932) *Verzeichnis der Eduard-von-Hartmann-Literatur*, Leipzig: Stäglich.

Von Hartmann published prolifically throughout his life (in the 1870s elucidating the themes of his 1868 *Philosophie des Unbewussten*, and in the 1880s and 1890s writing on ethical, aesthetic, religious and epistemological themes). But his early success was not to be sustained. Von Hartmann's philosophy, a synthesis of Schelling, Hegel and Schopenhauer, marked by its rejection of mechanistic materialism and its espousal of vitalistic modes of explanation, and fashionably combining the popular themes of pantheism, metaphysical pessimism and evolutionary optimism, was to be overtaken by later philosophical developments, particularly the emergence of phenomenology. He was to exercise little influence on twentieth-century philosophy.

According to von Hartmann, the ground of all Being (the Absolute or God) is the Unconscious. The Unconscious is constituted by two absolutely fundamental and inseparable principles: blind Will (Schopenhauer) and rational Idea (Hegel). The former explains the 'That' of the world (its existence as dynamic process), the latter the 'What' of the world (its essence as purposive order). The world (the corporeal manifestation of the Unconscious or God) as Will is suffering. However, redemption or release from suffering is possible. Such redemption is the purpose of the cosmic process, and its attainment would mark the end of that process. The redemption of the world is only possible through individuals and individual consciousness (the product of the conflict of Will and Idea).

Von Hartmann's Schopenhauerian pessimism forms the foundation of his account of morality, art and religion. The moral life involves acknowledging the impossibility of happiness, and recognizing, accepting and surrendering oneself to the ultimate purpose of the cosmic process—redemption from suffering. The aesthetic experience, understood in terms of the intuitive and disinterested apprehension of Beauty (itself construed as the appearance of the Idea, and thus as a manifestation of the Truth), is a stage in the process of the redemption of the world. Religion, too, is interpreted in terms of the felt need for redemption and release from suffering and from the demands of the individual will. In spite of the outmoded character of much of Hartmann's philosophy, certain aspects of it are of continuing interest today. Mention may, in particular, be made of: (i) his analysis of the unconscious in general, and of the unconscious will as a psychological phenomenon in particular; (ii) the critique of Darwinian evolutionary theory on the grounds that evolution cannot be explained exclusively by natural selection (a merely negative principle serving to eliminate the *non*-functional alone) but requires an additional vitalistic principle of positive purpose; (iii) the attack on Schopenhauer's radical pessimism on the grounds that it fails to distinguish 'eudaimonological' from 'teleological-evolutionary' criteria of value. Von Hartmann's religious and aesthetic writings still attract their admirers; and von Hartmann's estimate of his epistemological works of 1889 and 1896 as his most important is not without its plausibility.

Sources: Edwards; EF; Eisler; Kindler 1964; NDB.

DAVID WALFORD

Hartmann, Nicolai

German. *b:* 20 February 1882, Riga, Lativa. *d:* 9 October 1950, Göttingen, Germany. *Cat:* Metaphysician; ethicist. *Ints:* Ontology; ethics. *Educ:* St Petersburg (gymnasium; Philology), Dorpat, Estonia (Medicine) and University of Marburg (Philosophy PhD). *Infls:* Plato, Kant, Hegel, Aristotle, Hermann Cohen, Husserl and Max Scheler. *Appts:* 1920–5, Professor of Philosophy, University of Marburg; 1925–31, Professor of Philosophy, University of Cologne; 1931–45, Professor of Philosophy, University of Berlin; 1945–50, Professor of Philosophy, University of Göttingen.

Main publications:

(1909) *Platos Logik des Seins* [Plato's Logic of Being], Geissen: A. Thopelmann.

(1921) *Grundzüge einer Metaphysik der Erkenntnis* [Outlines of a Metaphysics of Knowledge], Berlin: W. de Gruyter.

(1923–9) *Die Philosophie des deutschen Idealismus* [The Philosophy of German Idealism], 2 vols: vol. I, *Fichte, Schelling und die Romantik* vol. II, *Hegel*, Berlin: W. de Gruyter.

(1926) *Ethik*, Berlin: W. de Gruyter (English translation, *Ethics*, trans. Stanton Coit, 3 vols, London: Macmillan, 1932).

(1933) *Das Problem des geistigen Seins* [The Problem of Ideal Being], Berlin: W. de Gruyter.

(1935) *Zur Grundlegung der Ontologie* [Foundations of Ontology], Berlin: W. de Gruyter.

(1938) *Möglichkeit und Wirklichkeit* [Possibility and Reality], Berlin: W. de Gruyter.

(1940) *Der Aufbau der realen Welt* [The Structure of the Real World], Berlin: G. A. Hain.

(1940) 'Neue Wege der Ontologie', in *Systematische Philosophie*, Stuttgart: N. W. Kohlhammer. (English translation, *New Ways of Ontology*, trans. Reinhard C. Kuhn, Chicago: Henry Regnery, 1953).

(1953) *Asthetik* [Aesthetics], Berlin: W. de Gruyter.

(1955–58) *Kleinere Schriften* [Shorter Writings], 3 vols, Berlin: W. de Gruyter (includes reprints of journal articles).

Secondary literature:

Cadwallader, Eva H. (1984) 'The continuing relevance of Nicolai Hartmann's theory of value', *Journal of Value Inquiry* 18: 113–21.

——(1984) *Searchlight on Values: Nicolai Hartmann's Twentieth Century Value Platonism*, Lanham, Md.: University Press of America.

Hook, Sidney (1930) 'A critique of ethical realism', *International Journal of Ethics* 40 (Jan.): 179–210.

Kuhn, Helmut (1951) 'Nicolai Hartmann's ontology', *Philosophical Quarterly* 1 (July): 289–318.

Mohanty, Jitendra N. (1957) *Nicolai Hartmann and Alfred North Whitehead: A Study in Recent Platonism*, Calcutta.

Werkmeister, W. H. (1990) *Nicolai Hartmann's New Ontology*, Tallahassee: University of Florida Press, 1990.

Nicolai Hartmann, a major German philosopher of the first half of the twentieth century, was primarily a metaphysician, but is best known in the English-speaking world for his monumental *Ethics*. The most characteristic features of his work are his 'aporetic method', and his insistence on the priority of ontology over epistemology. He saw his aporetic method as continuous with the best in Plato and Aristotle, as consistent with the scientific spirit and as central to productive philosophizing. The aporetic method consists of two phases: first, a careful phenomenology of relevant facts (whether ontological, epistemological, ethical or aesthetic); second, a dialectical clarification of the problems they present. Wherever possible, Hartmann formulated problems as antinomies (paradoxes), assessing each side carefully. Hartmann thus eschewed the German tradition of system-building in favour of his unique aporetic approach.

Hartmann fully ontologized the relation (regarding both being and value) between knower and known. Setting the two 'modes of Being' (particulars and universals) on an equal footing in so far as they are both objective and independent of the knower, he proceeded to articulate them by a method partly phenomenological, partly logical and partly metaphysical. This resulted in 'ontological stratifications', Hartmann's unique metaphysical approach. *New Ways of Ontology* and *Ethics* contain its most important examples.

Hartmann's most enduring contribution to philosophy will undoubtedly be his *Ethics*, the aretaic aspect of which has probably already exerted invisible influences. The *Ethics* comprises both a general theory of value (the Platonism of which is universally rejected today) and a revival of the long-neglected aretaic method of doing ethics, originated by Aristotle. Aretaic ethics is virtue-centred ethics, an alternative to utilitarianism and formalism. Hartmann's phenomenology of virtues is in volume II, written in lucid, sometimes austerely poetic prose, illuminating and inspiring. It is governed, Hartmann says, by a 'logic of the heart', and the influence of **Nietzsche** is as powerful as that of Aristotle. Volume I is an aporetic phenomenology of morality and a history of normative ethics and ethical theory. Fortunately, volume III's unconvincing attempt to solve the problem of freedom does not impair the majesty of the second volume.

Certain aspects of Hartmann's philosophy have been compared with Anglo-American work. His value Platonism has been compared with A. N. **Whitehead**'s (Mohanty 1957) and contrasted with G. E. **Moore**'s (Cadwallader 1984). Several factors in Hartmann's epistemology are reminiscent of C. S. **Peirce**, 'Father of American Pragmatism', namely Peirce's subtle balancing of anti-dogmatic objectivism with non-nihilistic fallibilism. On the other hand, Hartmann's value intuitionism, seemingly incorrigible although radically pluralistic, stands in a paradoxical relation to fallibilism (the view that one can always be mistaken). Hartmann claims to resolve this antinomy with a searchlight metaphor according to which values themselves do not change but rather our perceptions of them.

Although this Kantianized value Platonism runs against the current of the times, Hartmann shares the existentialist conviction that human beings must heroically endow reality with meaning. For, despite the partial intelligibility and orderliness of reality and ideality, neither God nor cosmic purpose exists. Despite his objectivism, Hartmann's interests are not religious. Nevertheless, his 'emotional apriorism' ('logic of the heart') imparts a spiritual tone to the *Ethics* which will always appeal to some. In a century starved of sober inspirational thoughts on the virtues, *Ethics II* towers alone.

Sources: Abdulla K. Badsha (date) 'Nicolai Hartmann', in *Great Lives from History: Twentieth Century Series*, vol. 2, ed. F. Magill, Englewood Cliffs, NJ: Salem Press; Edwards.

EVA CADWALLADER

Hartnack, (Johan) Justus (Daniel Gustav Volmer)

Danish. *b:* 29 May 1912, Copenhagen. *Cat:* Analytical philosopher. *Ints:* History of philosophy; social philosophy. *Educ:* Copenhagen. *Infls:* Kant, Hegel, Wittgenstein and Ryle. *Appts:* 1946–54, Visiting Lecturer, then Assistant Professor of Philosophy, Colgate University, Hamilton, NY; 1954–72, Professor and Head of Department of Philosophy, Aarhus; 1972–8, Professor of Philosophy, then Distinguished Professor, State University of New York at Brockport; 1972, made Knight of Dannebroge, first degree; from 1978, Emeritus Professor of Philosophy, State University of New York at Brockport.

Main publications:
(1950) *Analysis of the Problem of Perception in British Empricism*, Copenhagen: Munksgaard.
(1956) *Filosofiske Problemer og Filosofiske argumentationer* [Philosophical Problems and Philosophical Arguments], Copenhagen: Gyldendal (translated into Swedish and Finnish).
(1957) *Filosofiske essays* [Philosophical Essays], Copenhagen: Gyldendal.
(1958) *Logik, klassisk og moderne* (Logic: Classical and Modern), Copenhagen: Gyldendal; second edition, Copenhagen: Reitzel, 1992.
(1959) *Taenkning og virkelighed* [Thinking and Reality], Copenhagen: Berlingske.
(1960) *Wittgenstein og den moderne filosofi*, Copenhagen: Gyldendal (English translation, *Wittgenstein and Modern Philosophy*, trans. M. Cranston, New York: University Press, 1985).
(1967) *Kant's Theory of Knowledge*, New York: Harcourt, Brace & World (Spanish translation, 1977).
(1971) *Philosophical Problems: A Modern Introduction*, New York: Humanities Press (based on 1959).
(1972) *Language and Philosophy*, The Hague: Mouton.
(1973) *History of Philosophy*, Atlantic Highlands, NJ: Humanities Press.
(1974) *Kant: An Explanation of His Theory of Knowledge and Moral Philosophy*, Atlantic Highlands, NJ: Humanities Press.
(1986) *From Radical Empiricism to Absolute Idealism*, Lewiston: Mellen.
(1990) *Hegels Logic*, Copenhagen; Reitzel (German translation, Frankfurt: Long, 1995).
(1992) *Human Rights, Freedom, Equality and Justice*, Lewiston: Mellen.
(1993) *Erkendelsens Grundlag* [Foundations of Knowledge], Copenhagen: Reitzel.

Secondary literature:
Reviews of English translation of 1960 in *British Journal for the Philosophy of Science* 15 (1967): 166–8 and *Philosophical Review* 76 (1967): 385–7.

After a period in America Hartnack was responsible for introducing analytic philosophy into Denmark and sought to combat the psychologism in philosophy that was the legacy of **Høffding**. His first book argued for naive realism on the basis of linguistic analysis. Philosophical problems, according to *Filosofiske Problemer* (1956), are to be dissolved by considering the logic of concepts. This approach is still present in 1992, when he adapts an idea of **Austin**'s that the negative term often 'wears the trousers', suggesting that this is so with 'justice' and 'equality'. He argues accordingly that, as commonly advocated, egalitarianism and distributive justice are based on misunderstandings of our concepts. Hartnack's most influential book (1960) has served not only as an account of **Wittgenstein** but as an introduction to British linguistic philosophy. Particular attention was given to the work of **Ryle**, **Strawson**, **Hart** and J. O. **Urmson** as developments of Wittgenstein's later way of philosophizing. This book has been widely read and editions of it have been published in many countries, including Germany, Italy, Spain, Japan and South Korea. He later used his gifts as an expositor in writing on the history of philosophy, developing a particular interest in Kant and German idealism.

Sources: CA; personal communication; *Dansk Biografisk Leksikon*; Burr; *PI*; Svend Erik Stybe, (1973) 'Trends in Danish philosophy', *JBSP* 4: 166; WW(Scan).

STUART BROWN

Hartshorne, Charles

American. *b:* 5 June 1897, Kittaning, Pennsylvania. *Cat:* Process metaphysician; panentheist; panpsychist. *Ints:* Philosophy of religion. *Educ:* Haverford College, Harvard University, BA 1921, MA 1922, PhD 1923; the Universities of Freiburg and Marburg, 1923–5. *Infls:* Emerson, Peirce and Whitehead. *Appts:* 1925–8, Instructor and Research Fellow, Harvard University; 1928–55, Instructor to Professor, University of Chicago; 1955–62, Professor, Emory University; from 1962, Ashbel Smith Professor of Philosophy (1962–76) and Emeritus Professor (from 1976), University of Texas at Austin.

Main publications:

(1931–5) (ed. with P. Weiss) *Collected Papers of Charles Sanders Peirce*, 6 vols, Cambridge, Mass.: Harvard University Press.

(1934) *The Philosophy and Psychology of Sensation*, Chicago: University of Chicago Press.

(1937) *Beyond Humanism: Essays in the New Philosophy of Nature*, Chicago: Willet, Clark & Company; reprinted with new Preface, Lincoln: University of Nebraska Press, 1968.

(1941) *Man's Vision of God and the Logic of Theism*, Chicago: Willet, Clark & Company; reprinted, New York: Harper & Brothers, 1948, and Hamden, CT: Archon Books, 1964.

(1947) *The Divine Relativity: A Social Conception of God*, New Have, CT: Yale University Press.

(1953) *Reality as Social Process: Studies in Metaphysics and Religion*, Glencoe and Boston: Free Press; reprinted, New York: Hafner, 1971.

(1953) (with W. L. Reese) *Philosophers Speak of God*, Chicago: University of Chicago Press.

(1962) *The Logic of Perfection and Other Essays in Neoclassical Metaphysics*, La Salle, Ill.: Open Court.

(1965) *Anselm's Discovery*, La Salle, Ill.: Open Court.

(1967) *A Natural Theology of Our Time*, La Salle: Open Court.

(1970) *Creative Synthesis and Philosophic Method*, London: SCM Press Ltd and La Salle, Ill.: Open Court.

(1972) *Whitehead's Philosophy: Selected Essays, 1935–1970*, Lincoln: University of Nebraska Press.

(1976) *Aquinas to Whitehead: Seven Centuries of Metaphysics of Religion. The Aquinas Lecture, 1976*, Milwaukee: Marquette University Publications.

(1983) *Insights and Oversights of Great Thinkers: An Evaluation of Western Philosophy*, Albany: SUNY Press.

(1984) *Omnipotence and Other Theological Mistakes*, Albany: SUNY Press.

(1984) *Creativity in American Philosophy*, Albany: SUNY Press.

(1987) *Wisdom as Moderation: A Philosophy of the Middleway*, Albany: SUNY Press.

(1990) *The Darkness and the Light: A Philosopher Reflects upon his Fortunate Career and Those who Made it Possible*, Albany: SUNY Press.

Secondary literature:

Cobb, Jr, J. B. and Gramwell, F. I. (eds) (1985) *Existence and Actuality: Conversations with Charles Hartshorne*, Chicago: Chicago University Press.

Hahn, L. E. (ed.) (1991) *The Philosophy of Charles Hartshorne*, La Salle: Open Court, The Library of Living Philosophers.

Peters, E. H. (1970) *Hartshorne and Neoclassical Metaphysics: An Interpretation*, Lincoln: University of Nebraska Press.

Reese, W. L. and Freeman, E. (eds) (1964) *Process and Divinity: The Hartshorne Festschrift*, La Salle: Open Court.

Viney, D. W. (1984) *Charles Hartshorne and the Existence of God*, Albany: SUNY Press.

Wood, Jr, F. and De Armey, M. (eds) (1986) *Hartshorne's Neo-Classical Theology*, New Orleans: Tulane Studies in Philosophy.

Second only to **Whitehead** in the leadership of process philosophy, Hartshorne has redirected its course from science to religion and theology. He professedly reached his basic philosophical position before becoming Whitehead's assistant at Harvard and working on the *Collected Papers of*

Charles Sanders Peirce (1931–5). In *The Philosophy and Psychology of Sensation* (1934) he drew upon scientific psychology and philosophy to demonstrate that sensation is an evaluative feeling exhibiting continuity, a thesis he subsequently elaborated into a panpsychist or psychalist philosophy according to which life or feeling permeates the cosmos, concentrated in individualized centres, identical to Whitehead's 'actual entities' or 'occasions of experience'. Hartshorne held, like Whitehead before him, that recent developments in natural science require a radical reconception of nature. Since nature is reconceived as an affective continuum of valuational feelings, furthermore, a new theology replaces the classical conception of God. Hartshorne's speculations came to fruition in his 1946 Terry Lectures at Yale University, published in *The Divine Relativity* (1947). Hartshorne's process deity has a dipolar nature—an abstract, eternal nature and a concrete, temporal nature. It mirrors Whitehead's distinction between the primordial and consequent natures of God. The unity of these two aspects of God embraces the World, God being supreme as the eternal–temporal consciousness, knowing and including the world. Hence Hartshorne has advocated panentheism, the doctrine that God includes the world yet transcends it. Hartshorne has sought to employ the instruments of modal logic to prove the existence of God. Thus he has contributed to the revival of interest in the ontological argument in recent decades. His endeavours to rehabilitate the reputation of Anselm and to resuscitate the ontological argument illustrate the 'neo-classical' turn of his thought. Hartshorne's hobby in birdwatching and listening to birdsong has resulted in his international reputation as an ornithologist. He published a prize-winning work, *Born to Sing: An Interpretation and World Survey of Bird Song* (Bloomington: Indiana University Press, 1973).

Sources: Reck 1968; RA, 4; WW(Am).

ANDREW RECK

Hatano, Seiichi

Japanese. *b:* July 1877, Matsumoto (Nagano Prefecture), Japan. *d:* January 1950, Tokyo. *Cat:* Japanese Christian philosopher. *Ints:* Philosophy of religion; history of Western philosophy. *Educ:* Tokyo Imperial University, BA thesis, 'Hyumu ga Kanto ni oyoboseru eikyo' [Hume's influence on Kant] and then under R. Kaeber at the graduate school. *Infls:* Kant. *Appts:* Taught the history of Western philosophy at Waseda University, Tokyo,

1900–17; christened 1902; visiting scholar, Berlin and Heidelberg, 1904–7; Professor of Philosophy of Religion, Kyoto Imperial University, 1917–37; after retirement, served from 1947 as President of Tamagawa Gakuen University until his death; 1949, Membership of the Japan Academy.

Main publications:

(1901) *Seiyo tetsugaku shi yo* [Outline of the History of Western Philosophy].
(1908) *Kirisutokyo no kigen* [Origin of Christianity].
(1943) *Toki to eien* [Time and Eternity] (English translation by Ichiro Suzuki, Japan National Commission for UNESCO, 1963).
(1968–9) *Hatano-seiichi zenshu* [Complete Works of Hatano Seiichi], 6 vols, Tokyo: Iwanami-shoten.

Secondary literature:

Germany, C. H. (1965) *Protestant Theologies in Modern Japan*, Tokyo: IISR Press.
Hamada, Y. (1949) *Hatano shukyo tetsugaku* [Hatano's Philosophy of Religion], Tokyo: Tamagawa University Press.
Ishihara, K. (1954) *Shukyo to tesugaku tono konpon ni aru mono. Hatano seiichi hakushi no gakugyo ni tsuite* [The Fundamental in Religion and Philosophy: On Dr Hatano's Scholarly Achievements], Tokyo: Iwanami-shoten.
Michalson, C. (1960) *Japanese Contributions to Christian Theology*, London: Westminster Press, especially chapter 4.
Wood, R. (1968) 'Philosophy and theology in "Time and Eternity"', a paper given in the International Department of Waseda University.

The philosophical activity of Hatano consists mainly of three parts, corresponding to the three periods of his scholarship. The first is his early historical study of Western philosophy. With his *Seiyo tetsugaku shi yo* (1901) he contributed to the popularization of philosophical studies, especially of Hegel, in Japan. The second is his middle-period work on the history of western religious thought: his *Kirisutokyo no kigen* (1908) is a unique pioneering contribution to Japanese study of the history of Christianity and ancient Greek philosophy. The third and most original of his scholarly achievements lies in constructing a system of philosophy of religion. While using Kantian and neo-Kantian criticism (especially Windelband's) to distinguish the philosophy of religion from deism or supernaturalism (formalidealism), he insists on distinguishing metaphysics from religious history, religious psychology, etc. (anti-intellectualism). Hatano's representative work from this third period, *Toki to eien* (1943) has its basis in his *jinkaku-shugi* (personalism): that God is neither the object nor the idea of human cognition, but the real other, the essentially loving God, and that the true religion is a personal, endless cooperation of life with such a God. This book makes clear how these aspects of human life, through natural life, cultural life and philosophical meditation, are finally rendered eternal, defeating time and death. Not the endlessness of objective, philosophical time, but love is the proof of the true eternity, by which is meant radical revolution of the whole of one's life. It must be the selfless *agape* donated by the creative God, because *eros* remains mere self-realization, and thus neither stable nor free from the bounds of time. Only at this stage does the subject become free from destruction into the past, where only the future can be conserved and death as a factor gains an entirely new meaning. *Time and Eternity*, translated into English in 1963 at the request of the Japan National Commission for UNESCO, attracted wide attention abroad.

Sources: *Kindai-Shisoka-Jiten* [Lexicon of Modern Thinkers], Tokyo: Tokyo-Shoseki, 1982; EncBrit, 15th edn, 1987.

KIYOSHI SAKAI

Havemann, Robert

German. *b:* 11 March 1910, Munich. *d:* 1982. *Cat:* Neo-Marxist; anti-fascist; scientist. *Ints:* Reform of Marxist socialism; ecology. *Educ:* Kaiser Wilhelm University and University of Berlin. *Infls:* Karl Marx and Laozi. *Appts:* 1950–64, Director of the Institute for Physics and Chemistry, Humboldt University, East Berlin; Member of East German Parliament, the People's Chamber of the German Democratic Republic; 1945, Research Fellow, Kaiser Wilhelm Institute, West Berlin (Max Planck Institute); 1981, founding member of the autonomous peace movement in the German Democratic Republic.

Main publications:

(1964) *Dialektik ohne Dogma?*, Hamburg: Rowohlt.

(1970) *Fragen Antworten Fragen* (English translation, *Questions, Answers, Questions*, trans. Salvator Attanasio, New York: Doubleday, 1972).

(1971) *Ruckantworten an die Hauptverwaltung 'Ewige Wahleiten'*, Munich: R. Piper.

(1976) *Berliner Schriften*, Berlin: Verlag Europaische Ideen.

(1980) *Morgen: die Industriegesellschaft am Scherdeweg*, Munich: R. Piper.

Havemann's critical thought is closely bound up with his political position. In 1943 he received a death sentence for his anti-fascist activities, but was reprieved and kept in prison because of the importance of his scientific research. As a research fellow at the Kaiser Wilhelm Institute after the Second World War he vigorously opposed American nuclear armament. During his time at Humboldt University he was fiercely critical of dogmatic communism, and in 1964 was expelled from the Socialist Union Party and the University.

His early criticisms were directed chiefly at Lysenko's claim that acquired characteristics may be passed on to progeny and at many elements in the doctrine of mechanical materialism. He propounded the view that a 'second step', an overthrowing of 'the critical stagnation, the sclerosis of Marxism' (1970, p. 182), was needed to take communism from a position of public ownership of the means of production to a politically democratic system. Following Laotse, he held that 'the more things there are in the world that one is forbidden to do, the more the people are impoverished' (ibid., p. 68).

Havemann's advocacy of reform developed into a thoroughgoing dissidence. In later life he became deeply concerned with ecological issues, arguing that ecological catastrophe would be averted only by transition to a socialist democracy in the East that would then generate a socialist revolution in the West. Leszek **Kolakowski** has described him as one of the most important of the revisionists. He remained staunchly Marxist throughtout.

Sources: BDN; Robert Havemann (1973) *Questions, Answers, Questions*, Garden City, NY: Doubleday; Leszek Kolakowski (1978) *Main Currents of Marxism*, Oxford: Clarendon Press, vol. 3, p. 470.

DIANÉ COLLINSON

Hayek, F(riedrich) A(ugust) (von)

Austrian (naturalized British). *b:* 8 May 1899, Vienna. *d:* 23 March 1992, Freiburg. *Cat:* Economist; political philosopher. *Ints:* Political philosophy. *Educ:* University of Vienna. *Infls:* Hume, Adam Smith, Ernst Mach, von Mises, Popper and Polanyi. *Appts:* 1927–31, Director, Austrian Institute for Economic Research; 1929–31, Lecturer in Economics, University of Vienna; 1931–50, Tooke Professor of Economic Science and Statistics, University of London; 1950–62, Professor of Social and Moral Science, University of Chicago; 1962–9, Professor of Economics, University of Freiburg.

Main publications:
(1944) *The Road to Serfdom*, London: George Routledge & Sons.

(1948) *Individualism and Economic Order*, London: George Routledge & Sons.

(1951) *John Stuart Mill and Harriet Taylor*, London: Routledge & Kegan Paul.

(1952) *The Counter-Revolution of Science*, Glencoe: Free Press.

(1952) *The Sensory Order*, London: Routledge & Kegan Paul.

(1960) *The Constitution of Liberty*, London: Routledge & Kegan Paul.

(1967) *Studies in Philosophy, Politics and Economics*, London: Routledge & Kegan Paul.

(1973) *Law, Legislation and Liberty, vol. 1: Rules and Order*, London: Routledge & Kegan Paul.

(1976) *Law, Legislation and Liberty, vol. 2: The Mirage of Social Justice*, London: Routledge & Kegan Paul.

(1978) *New Studies in Philosophy, Politics, Economics and the History of Ideas*, London: Routledge & Kegan Paul.

(1979) *Law, Legislation and Liberty, vol. 3: The Political Order of a Free People*, London: Routledge & Kegan Paul.

(1988) *The Fatal Conceit*, London: Routledge.

(1991) *Economic Freedom*, Oxford: Basil Blackwell.

Secondary literature:
Barry, N. P. (1979) *Hayek's Social and Economic Philosophy*, London: Macmillan.

Cody, J. V. (1982) 'Bibliography of Friedrich A. Hayek', *Literature of Liberty* 5, 4: 68–101.

Gray, J. (1984) *Hayek on Liberty*, Oxford: Basil Blackwell; second edition, 1986.

Kukathas, C. (1989) *Hayek and Modern Liberalism*, Oxford: Clarendon.

Streissler, E. (ed.) (1969) *Roads to Freedom*, London: Routledge & Kegan Paul.

Tomlinson, J. (1990) *Hayek and the Market*, London: Pluto.

Hayek's work crosses several disciplines. Originating in economic debates about the appropriateness of controlling market forces, it contains a distinctive philosophical theory. Hayek is sceptical about constructivist rationalism, the idea that human institutions can and should be deliberately designed to meet human purposes. Instead, he argues that a spontaneous order evolves out of particular actions and decisions which could not have any such order as their objective. Hayek acknowledges a debt to thinkers such as Adam Smith, Hume and Ferguson in formulating these ideas. They lead to a specific scepticism about socialism, construed as a system of centralized economic planning which displaces the operation of the market. In his *The Road to Serfdom* (1944) he claims that such comprehensive planning erodes individual liberty and cannot succeed because it would not be possible to centralize all the knowledge required for its operation. In his own favoured system, general welfare flows from individuals acting as they choose, against the background of a system of laws and traditions which embody the wisdom of proven fitness. Hayek's work shows interesting affinities with that of other twentieth-century philosophers. His opposition to comprehensive social reconstruction is close to **Popper**'s. He acknowledges similarities with **Ryle**'s distinction between *knowing how* and *knowing that* in his *The Constitution of Liberty* (1960). Evident throughout his work is a negative conception of liberty of the kind sponsored by Isaiah Berlin, according to which liberty consists in the absence of coercive interference by other human agents. Like Berlin, he urges the distinctness of democratic practice and liberty as so defined, and the possibility of conflict between them.

Hayek's ideas received wider attention in the 1980s as one of the acknowledged influences on the British prime minister Margaret Thatcher. They also provided a sharp contrast to theories of social justice of the kind espoused by philosophers such as **Rawls** and **Dworkin**. For Hayek, it is misconceived to adopt a moralizing attitude towards the result of a market system of distribution which is not the intended consequence of any individuals' actions. More strongly, he argues in his *Law, Legislation and Liberty* (1976) that such redistributive aspirations are actually incompatible with the rule of law, which involves treating individuals impartially. Attempts to rectify material inequalities are held to rest on incoherent notions of desert and need, to threaten liberty through coercive reallocation and to undermine the efficiency of the economic system which provides resources for distribution in the first place.

In specifically philosophical, rather than political, critical reaction there has been interesting discussion of the extent to which Hayek's work does or could improve on the justifications of classical liberalism. Questions have been raised about the extent to which he can consistently *argue* for his favoured system, given the very limited role he assigns to reason in human affairs; about the coherence of the evolutionist grounds for the superiority of surviving institutions; and, more generally, about the extent to which he succeeds in reconciling Hume and Kant—that is, in reconciling the idea of valuing liberal institutions which have emerged undesigned with the idea of valuing them by reference to their role in preserving rationality and autonomy.

Sources: Obituary, *The Times*, 25 Mar 1992, p. 15; WW.

KEITH GRAHAM

He Lin (Ho Lin)

Chinese. *b:* 1902, Qintang, Sichuan Province, China. *d:* 1992, Beijing. *Cat:* Idealist; historian of contemporary Chinese philosophy. *Ints:* Neo-Confucian philosophy; Hegel. *Educ:* Qinghua University; Oberlin College; University of Chicago and Harvard University; University of Berlin in Germany. *Infls:* Wang Yangming (early sixteenth-century neo-Confucian idealist), Hegel and Sun Zhongshan. *Appts:* Professor of Philosophy, University of Beijing; Professor, Institute of Philosophy, Chinese Academy of Social Sciences; Dean, Research Institute of Western Philosophy, Chinese Academy of Social Sciences.

Main publications:

(1942) *A Brief Exposition of Idealism*, Duli Publishing Company.
(1942) (ed.) *New Essays on Confucian Thought*, Zhengzhong Book Company.
(1943) *The Saying 'Knowledge is Difficult, Action is Easy' and the Saying 'Knowledge and Action are One'*, Qingnian Bookstore.
(1945) *Contemporary Chinese Philosophy*, Shengli Publishers.
(1947) *Culture and Life.*
(1957) (contributor to) A Symposium on the Problems of the History of Chinese Philosophy, Beijing: Kexue Publishing House.
(trans.) Hegel, *Logic.*
(trans.) Hegel, *Phenomenology of Spirit.*
(trans.) Spinoza, *The Treatise on the Improvement of the Understanding.*

Secondary literature:

Briere, O. (1956) *Fifty Years of Chinese Philosophy 1898–1950*, London :George Allen & Unwin Ltd.
Complete Chinese Encyclopedia (1987) Philosophy Volumes, Beijing: Chinese Encyclopedia Publications.

In his syncretic approach to questions of morals and culture, He drew on Chinese and Western sources. His main inspiration came from the idealist neo-Confucian Wang Yangming, but he also derived much from studying Hegel and other Western philosophers during his period in the USA and Germany. He was the leading Chinese expert on Hegel's thought. In applying his insights to the problems of China, He was drawn to the theoretical framework of **Sun Zhongshan**, especially regarding the relationship between knowledge and action. As a leading member of the highly professional Chinese Philosophical Society in the 1930s and 1940s, He organized the systematic translation of important Western philosophical texts into Chinese and was himself a gifted translator.

In discussing knowledge and action, He touched on deep questions concerning the nature of theoretical and practical reason and the relation between epistemology and morals. He understood how these questions arose in the Western tradition of Plato, Aristotle, Kant and Hegel, but also saw them deeply embedded in idealist neo-Confucian thought. He wanted to use the this common ground to unite the traditions. He accepted Wang Yangming's theoretical unification of knowledge and action and the primacy of the practical, but accepted the constraints on action, including political action, which Sun Zhongshan understood to arise from the difficulties of knowledge.

Although proficient in technical philosophy, He was also a moralist and critic of culture. He combined a Confucian respect for social hierarchy with a Western cult of heroes and heroic action as a remedy for modern unhappiness. The hero triumphed over reality through self-confident optimistic action aimed at the ideal. Education, unless it was based on awakening a sense of the heroic, could lead to unstable commercial success but not happiness, because it would fail to develop personalities capable of stable happiness.

After Liberation in 1949 He was severely criticized for trying to secure a continuing place for idealism in Chinese philosophy, but maintained his role as an expert on Western philosophy. In the 1957 *Symposium on Chinese Philosophy*, which determined the basis for Chinese philosophical work in later decades, He characterized the relationship between idealism and materialism as a relationship between teacher and student or between friends. Although he cited Marx's debt to Hegel in support of his position, he was again criticized.

NICHOLAS BUNNIN

Hedenius, Per Arvid Ingemar

Swedish. *b:* 5 April 1908, Stockholm. *d:* 30 April 1982, Uppsala. *Cat:* Moral philosopher; historian of philosophy. *Ints:* Philosophy of religion. *Educ:* Universities of Uppsala and Lund. *Appts:* 1947–73, Professor of Practical Philosophy, Uppsala University; 1979, Jur. Dr *honoris causa*, Uppsala University.

Main publications:

(1936) *Sensationalism and Theology in Berkeley's Philosophy*, Oxford: Blackwell; Uppsala: Almqvist & Wiksell.

(1937) *Studies in Hume's Ethics*, Uppsala: Almqvist & Wiksell.

(1941) *Om rätt och moral* [On Law and Morals], Stockholm: Tiden.

(1944) 'Überzeugung und Urteil', *Theoria*.

(1945) *Phaidon, Gorgias och Staten. Anmärkningar till några Platoställen* [The Phaedo, the Gorgias and the Republic: Remarks on some Passages in Plato], Uppsala: Acta Universitatis Upsaliensis.

(1949) *Tro och vetande* [Faith and Knowledge], Stockholm: Albert Bonniers förlag.

(1955) *Fyra dygder* [Four Virtues], Stockholm: Albert Bonniers förlag.

(1971) 'Disproofs of God's existence?', *The Personalist*.

(1972) *Om människans moraliska villkor* [On the Moral Conditions of Man], Uddevalla: Författarförlaget.

(1977) 'Kommentar till Platons Gorgias' [A commentary on Plato's Gorgias], in Plato, *Gorgias*, Copenhagen: Gyldendal.

(1978) *De gamle och lögnen* [Essays on Different Subjects in Ancient Philosophy and Literature], Stockholm: Bonniers.

(1982) *Om människovärde* [On Human Dignity], Stockholm: Bonniers.

Secondary literature:

Henschen-Dahlquist, Ann-Mari (1993) *En Ingemar Hedenius bibliografi*, Stockholm: Thales (bibliography).

In his youth Hedenius was a disciple of **Hägerström** and **Phalén**, but later **Moore** and **Russell** influenced him more strongly. However, he never accepted Moore's objectivist theory of value, but remained an adherent of Hägerström's dictum that moral valuations are neither true nor false.

Two of Hedenius's works in Swedish (1941, 1949) stimulated the intellectual debate in Scandinavia to an exceptional degree. In the former he defended Hägerström's dictum, just mentioned, with new arguments and expounded a theory based upon it about practical syllogisms. On the other hand, he sharply criticized another thesis of Hägerström's: that our common legal concepts imply absurd metaphysics and magic. He also made a constructive contribution to the development of Scandinavian legal realism. In his book of 1941 he also formulated an ethical principle for intellectual decisions ('the morals of intellectualism'). Hedenius returned to these themes in several later writings. He also dealt with many other problems of moral philosophy and philosophy of law: utilitarianism, the dignity of man and free will (for example, in *The Philosophy of C. D. Broad*, ed. P. A. Schilpp, New York: Tudor Publishing Company, 1959); command-sentences and performatives (*Theoria*, 1963); retribution and punishment.

In *Faith and Knowledge* (1949) Hedenius unfolded a criticism of different forms of (Lutheran) Christianity. It is framed in a systematic way and based upon three explicitly stated postulates. He often returned to this and other subjects in the philosophy of religion, for example in 'Disproofs of God's existence?' (1971).

A few minor writings deal with literary or musical aesthetics, for example the problem of tragedy. Hedenius was deeply interested throughout his life in many of the great classics of philosophy, especially Plato, Hume and Kierkegaard. As a Plato researcher he published essays on problems concerning the *Gorgias*, the argumentation in the *Euthyphro*, *eros* and *philia*, Socratic irony, the views on lying in the dialogues, and other themes. His great admiration for Kierkegaard was combined with a negative attitude to contemporary existentialism in philosophy.

THORILD DAHLQUIST

Hegenberg, Leonidas Helmut Baebler

Brazilian. *b:* 1925, Curitiba, Brazil. *Cat:* Logician; mathematician. *Ints:* Philosophy of science. *Infls:* Quine, Popper, Carnap and much contemporary philosophy of science. *Appts:* Director of Humanities, Instituto Tecnológico de Aeronáutica, S. José dos Campos.

Main publications:

(1962) *Logica elementar*, n.p., I.T.A.: Departamento de Humanidades.

(1964) *Explicações científicas*; new edition, São Paulo: Editora Herder, 1969.

(1966) *Logica simbolica*, São Paulo: Editora Herder.

(1975) *Significado e conhecimento*, São Paulo: Editora Pedagogia e Universitaria.

(1976) *Etapas de investigação científica*, 2 vols, São Paulo: Editora Pedagogica e Universitaria.

Hegenberg's work is concentrated in the areas of mathematics, logic and the philosophy of science, although his interest in the meaning of key terms within the context of scientific theories has led him to an interest in the issue of meaning in general, outside formal languages (cf. 1975). With regard to the philosophy of science, he argues that it is better regarded as the 'logic of science' ('logica da ciência'), and in his view its central topics are: the types of result obtained from scientific enquiry; the logical relations obtaining between these results; the types of proposition in which these results are formulated; and the way in which these terms are used systematically, in theories and laws. The logic of science cannot be fruitfully studied, in Hegenberg's view, without a solid grounding in mathematics, notably in the areas of functions and probability.

ROBERT WILKINSON

Heidegger, Martin

German. **b:** 26 September 1889, Messkirch, Germany. **d:** 26 May 1976. **Cat:** Phenomenologist; ontologist. **Ints:** The question of being. **Educ:** Theology and Philosophy, University of Freiburg. **Infls:** The pre-Socratics, Plato, Aristotle, St Paul, Augustine, Aquinas, Duns Scotus, Meister Eckhart, Angelus Silesius, Luther, Leibniz, Kant, Hegel, Hölderlin, Schelling, Kierkegaard, Nietzsche, Brentano, Carl Braig, Dilthey, Husserl and Max Scheler. **Appts:** 1919–23, Privatdozent and Assistant of Husserl, University of Freiburg; 1923–8, Professor, University of Marburg; 1928–46, Professor, University of Freiburg; 1946–51, forbidden to teach; 1952–76, Emeritus Professor, University of Freiburg.

Main publications:

(1927) *Sein und Zeit*, Tübingen (English translation, *Being and Time*, trans. J. Macquarrie and E. Robinson, Oxford: Basil Blackwell, 1962).

(1975) *Grundprobleme der Phänomenologie*, Frankfurt (English translation, *Basic Problems of Phenomenology*, trans. A. Hofstadter, Bloomington: Indiana University Press, 1982).

(1978) *Metaphysische Anfangsgründe der Logik*, Frankfurt (English translation, *Metaphysical Foundations of Logic*, trans. M. Hein, Bloomington: Indiana University Press, 1984).

(1929) *Kant und das Problem der Metaphysik*, Bonn (English translation, *Kant and the Problem of Metaphysics*, trans. R. Taft, Bloomington: Indiana University Press, 1990).

(1929) *Grundbegriffe der Metaphysik*, Frankfurt.

(1929) *Was ist Metaphysik?*, Bonn (English translation, 'What is metaphysics?', D. F. Krell, in *Martin Heidegger: Basic Writings*, ed. D. F. Krell, London: Routledge, 1993).

(1929) *Vom Wesen des Grundes*, Halle (English translation, *The Essence of Reasons*, trans. T. Malick, Evanston: Northwestern University Press, 1969).

(1940) *Über den Humanismus*, Frankfurt (English translation, 'Letter on humanism', trans. F. Capuzzi, in *Basic Writings*, ed. D. F. Krell, London: Routledge, 1993).

(1943) *Vom Wesen der Wahrheit*, Frankfurt (English translation, 'On the essence of truth', trans. John Sallis, in *Basic Writings*, ed. D. F. Krell, London: Routledge, 1993).

(1950) 'Der Urpsrung des Kuntswerks', in *Holzwege*, Frankfurt, (English translation, 'The origin of the work of art', trans. A. Hofstadter, in *Basic Writings*, ed. D. F. Krell, London: Routledge, 1993).

(1953) *Einführung in die Metaphysik*, Tübingen (English translation, *An Introduction to Metaphysics*, trans. R. Manheim, Garden City, NY: Doubleday-Anchor Books, 1961).

(1954) *Was heisst Denken?*, Tübingen (English translation, *What is Called Thinking?*, trans. F. D. Wieck and J. Glenn Gray, New York: Harper & Row, 1968).

(1957) *Der Satz vom Grund*, Pfullingen (English translation, *The Principle of Reason*, trans. R. Lilly, Bloomington: Indiana University Press, 1991).

(1957) *Identität und Differenz*, Pfullingen (English translation, *Identity and Difference*, trans. J. Stambaugh, New York: Harper & Row, 1969).

(1959) *Unterwegs zur Sprache*, Pfullingen (English translation, *On the Way to Language*, trans. P. D. Hertz and J. Stambaugh, New York: Harper & Row, 1971).

(1961) *Nietzsche*, 2 vols, Pfullingen (English translation, *Nietzsche* 4 vols, trans. D. F. Krell, New York: Harper & Row, 1979–87).

(1986) *Beiträge zur Philosophie: vom Ereignis*, Frankfurt.

Secondary literature:

Biemel, Walter (1973) *Martin Heidegger*, Hamburg (English translation, *Martin Heidegger: An Illustrated Study*, London: Routledge, 1977).

Caputo, John D. (1978) *The Mystical Element in Heidegger's Thought*, Athens, Ohio: Ohio University Press.

Dreyfus, H. (1991) *Being-in-the-World: A Commentary on Heidegger's 'Being and Time', Division I*, Cambridge, Mass.: MIT Press.

Dreyfus, H. and Hall, H. (eds) (1992) *Heidegger: A Critical Reader*, Oxford: Blackwell.

Franzen, Winfried (1976) *Martin Heidegger*, Stuttgart.

Gadamer, H.-G. (1983) *Heideggers Wege*, Tübingen.

Guignon, Charles (1993) (ed.) *The Cambridge Companion to Heidegger*, Cambridge: Cambridge University Press.

Macann, Christopher (ed.) (1992) *Martin Heidegger: Critical Assessments*, 4 vols, London: Routledge.

Olafson, F. A. (1987) *Heidegger's Philosophy of Mind*, New Haven: Yale University Press.

Ott, Hugo (1988) *Martin Heidegger: Unterwegs zu einer Biographie*, Frankfurt and New York.

Pöggeler, O. (1990) *Der Denkweg Martin Heideggers*, Pfullingen (English translation, *Martin Heidegger's Path of Thinking*, trans. D. Magurshak and S. Barber, Atlantic Highlands, NJ: Humanities Press International, 1987).

Safranski, Rüdiger (1994) *Ein Meister aus Deutschland: Heidegger und seine Zeit*, Munich.

Stern, P. (trans.) (1986), *Self-consciousness and Self-determination*, Cambridge, Mass.: MIT Press (originally published as *Selbstbewusstsein und Selbstbestimmung*).

Tugendhat, E. (1970) *Der Wahrheitsbegriff bei Husserl und Heidegger*, Berlin, 1979.

Herrmann, F.-W. von (1985) *Subjekt und Dasein*, Frankfurt.

——(1987) *Hermeneutische Phänomenologie des Daseins*, Frankfurt.

For Heidegger there was only one question, *die Seinsfrage* (the question of being). While still at school he read **Brentano**'s *On the Manifold Meaning of Being according to Aristotle* and as a theology student he studied *On Being: An Outline of Ontology* by Carl Braig. At the same time he became acquainted with something called 'phenomenology' through the study of **Husserl**'s *Logical Investigations*, a work which exercised a fascination on him which was to remain for the rest of his life. He never accepted Husserl's phenomenology in its transcendental and idealistic form but in Husserl's early phenomenology he saw a way of *seeing* which could provide the method for ontology. Husserl's devastating critique of psychologistic accounts of logic was put to effective use in Heidegger's doctoral thesis on the theory of judgement. The influence of the early Husserl is still strong in Heidegger's habilitation thesis on Duns Scotus. In 1919 Heidegger became Husserl's assistant. Under the influence of Husserl, but also drawing on such figures as Kierkegaard and **Dilthey**, Heidegger began to develop his own brand of phenomenology which focuses on the facticity of lived existence rather than transcendental consciousness and its pure ego. This culminated in *Sein und Zeit* (in English, *Being and Time*), which appeared in 1927 and confirmed a reputation which Heidegger had already established through his teaching.

In the early 1930s, having previously been unpolitical, Heidegger began to be attracted by the National Socialist movement and its charismatic leader, Adolf Hitler. Like many German intellectuals of the time he saw in the movement a force for renewal and regeneration. This led him to accept the rectorship of his university, Freiburg, in April 1933 and shortly afterwards to join the Nazi Party. He was active in the Nazi cause for ten months, resigning the rectorship in February 1934 after it had become clear that he did not have the support needed to implement his romanticized and rather idiosyncratic version of Nazism. Although Heidegger certainly did some shameful things in the early days of the Third Reich it must also be acknowledged that he was deeply critical of what passed in Nazi circles for 'philosophy' (racism and biologism). In 1942 he resigned from the committee charged with editing the works of **Nietzsche** after the committee had been ordered to remove those passages in which Nietzsche speaks contemptuously of antisemitism. After the war Heidegger paid for what he called his *Dummheit* (stupidity or silliness) by being forbidden to teach. His fate was sealed by a damning report written on him by his former friend Karl **Jaspers** (although in 1933 Jaspers had been enthusiastic about the content of Heidegger's rectoral speech). The rest of his life was like that of Kant: uneventful.

Heidegger's major work, (*Being and Time*) explicitly raises the question which had begun to exercise him even as a student: the question of the meaning or sense (*Sinn*) of being. The method of such ontology he calls phenomenology. In the formal sense this is simply adherence to the maxim made famous by Husserl and his followers: 'To the things themselves!' It is the letting be seen of that which shows itself. But as philosophy phenomenology is the letting be seen of what primarily and for the most part does not show itself, but which is the ground of what does show itself. The phenomenon of philosophical phenomenology is not this or that being or entity but the being of beings or entities (*das Sein des Seienden*). Being is that which determines entities as entities, that on the basis of which entities are always already understood. Understanding of being makes all comportment to entities—both those which I am not and that which I myself am—possible. Being

(*Sein*) is not something laid up in some realm to which the phenomenologist has some mysterious access. It is what is understood in the always understanding of being which already belongs to the being of *Dasein* (Heidegger's term for the being which we ourselves are).

Consider the kind of being of the things with which we have-to-do, things which Heidegger calls *Zeug* (equipment). One gets clear about the mode of being of *Zeug* by making explicit, and conceptualizing, the understanding of being which is already implicit in our circumspective having-to-do-with things. We do not have to put ourselves into this mode of comportment; we are always already in it. Phenomenology, as the letting be seen of being, is the laying bare of the conditions of the possibility of entities showing themselves or of our comportment to entities.

Phenomenology, as understood by Heidegger, is phenomenology of *Dasein*. The absolute prerequisite for doing philosophy, in Heidegger's view, is recognition of what he calls the ontological difference (being is not a being). But *Dasein* is a being, so how can phenomenology which makes being thematic be phenomenology of *Dasein*? *Dasein* is a being, but not just *a* being, occurring among other beings. The being of *Dasein*, what Heidegger calls *existence*, is such that *Dasein* understands its own being, but in understanding its own being it at the same time understands the being of entities other than itself. Heidegger calls the understanding of being disclosedness (*Erschlossenheit*). The *Da* in *Dasein* is disclosedness. *Dasein* is the clearing (*Lichtung*) which makes possible the openness of what is.

It is because *Dasein* is the ontological being that the posing and answering of the question of the meaning of being as such (*überhaupt*) requires an analysis of the fundamental structures of the being of *Dasein*. And this is largely what *Being and Time* provides.

Although *Being and Time* is a very large book it is only part of a much larger projected work. *Being and Time*, one might say, answers the question: how is comportment to entities possible? What makes comportment to entities possible is the understanding of being. But how is the understanding of being possible? The complete work was to have shown how *time* is the 'horizon' by reference to which being is understood. Heidegger's lectures of 1927, *Basic Problems of Phenomenology*, go some way to carrying out this task.

There are two ways of interpreting *Being and Time* which make it seem that there is a complete break between the phenomenological Heidegger

and the later Heidegger who describes his philosophy as *Denken* (thought or thinking). According to the first interpretation Heidegger's phenomenology of *Dasein* is just a modification of Husserl's phenomenology of *consciousness*. Heidegger's *Dasein* is Husserl's consciousness or subject but with a practical twist (practical engagement with things is given greater emphasis than mere perception). But as Heidegger sees it the move from consciousness to *Dasein* is much more radical than this. *Dasein* as the understanding, or disclosedness, of being makes possible *both* theoretical *and* practical modes of comportment to what is. According to the second interpretation Heidegger is an existentialist. It is true that *Being and Time* contains some brilliant analyses of such typically existentialist themes as *Angst*, guilt and death. But these are not examined for their own sake but rather for their specially disclosive function in relation to the being of *Dasein*. Their treatment is subservient to the question of the meaning of being as such.

But even when such misinterpretations have been put aside it can still be difficult to see the continuity between early and late Heidegger. The late Heidegger is still talking about being but in ways which make it more tempting for the English-speaker to write 'Being'. 'There is being only so long as *Dasein* is' ('Nur solange Dasein ist, gibt es Sein') he says in *Being and Time*. Being only 'is' in *Dasein*'s understanding of being. But understanding, it would seem, is something we do, so being is the product of human beings. In his later thought it is made clear that we stand in the truth of being. The truth (or unconcealedness) of being as the clearing (*Lichtung*) in which what is shows itself as what is is not in any sense something which we make or which is at our disposal. But although the truth of being is not at our disposal it is not an *eternal* truth. Heidegger speaks of *Seinsgeschichte*, the history of being. There is a necessity about the elements of this history but, unlike Hegel, Heidegger does not think in terms of an inevitable progression towards *the* truth of being. He does, however, talk as though there had been a falling away from a primordial experience of being had by the pre-Socratics. The truth of being which animates our own technology-dominated age is such that entities are experienced as material for use. Underlying such experience is the metaphysics of subjectivity according to which the being of what is is being an object (*Gegenstand*).

Presenting Heidegger in such abbreviated form inevitably makes him seem more abstract than he is. Although he thinks the question of being is *the* philosophical question this does not mean he talks about nothing else and that those who have difficulty with such talk will find nothing valuable in him. His essay on the work of art, for example, in which he overcomes the subjectivist view that the work of art is the object of 'aesthetic experience', but also the Hegelian view that it merely points to a truth which only philosophy can adequately express, has an immediacy and concreteness and wealth of insight which should impress anyone who approaches it in an unprejudiced way. And similar claims can be made for his essay on technology and some of his writings on language.

The same people who dismiss Heidegger as unintelligible sometimes, in contradictory fashion, deplore the extent of his influence. That he has been influential is undeniable. In philosophy **Sartre** would be unimaginable without Heidegger, and **Merleau-Ponty** clearly owes much to him (although perhaps more to Husserl). Philosophical hemeneutics (**Gadamer**) would not have been possible without Heidegger. But his influence has not been confined to philosophy. For example, a distinctive form of psychotherapy was developed under the influence of Heidegger's analysis of *Dasein* (Ludwig Binswanger). And in theology, both Protestant and Catholic, Heidegger's influence is unmistakable (e.g. Rudolf Bultmann, Paul **Tillich**, Karl **Rahner**). But these are just examples of direct influence. In more subtle ways his thought has had a profound impact in fields as diverse as literary theory, envionmental studies, social science and aesthetics.

PAUL GORNER

Heimsoeth, Heinz

German. *b:* 12 August 1886, Cologne, Germany. *d:* 10 September 1975, Cologne, Germany. *Cat:* Neo-Kantian; metaphysician; historian of philosophy. *Educ:* Philosophy and Mathematics in Heidelberg, Marburg and Berlin. *Infls:* Georg Simmel, Hermann Cohen, Paul Natorp and Nicolai Hartmann. *Appts:* Professor of Philosophy, Marburg, Königsberg and Cologne.

Main publications:

(1912–14) *Die Methode der Erkenntnis bei Descartes und Leibniz*, Giessen: Töpelmann.

(1922) *Die sechs grossen Themen der abendländischen Metaphysik*, Berlin; fifth edition, Darmstadt: Wissenschaftliche Buchgesellschaft, 1965.

(1929) *Metaphysik der Neuzeit*; new edition, Darmstadt: Wissenschaftliche Buchgesellschaft, 1967.

(1966–71) *Transzendentale Dialektik*, Berlin: de Gruyter.

(1971) *Studien zur Philosophie Immanuel Kants. Metaphysische Ursprünge und ontologische Grundlagen*, Bonn: Bouvier Verlag Herbert Grundmann (English translation, 'Metaphysical motives in the development of critical idealism', in Moltke S. Gram, *Kant, Disputed Questions*, Chicago, 1967).

Secondary literature:

Funke, Gerhard (1971) 'Der Weg zur ontologischen Kantinterpretation', *Kant-Studien* 62: 446–66.

Kaulback, Friedrich and Ritter, Joachim (eds) (1966) *Kritik und Metaphysik, Studien für Heinz Heimsoeth zum achtzigsten Geburtstag*, Berlin: de Gruyter.

Heimsoeth advocated a metaphysical reading of Kant's critical philosophy. He tried to show that although Kant's critical philosophy criticized traditional metaphysics, it also owed a great deal to it. For Heimsoeth, Kant's precritical writings were much more important than they were for the neo-Kantians who advocated an epistemological reading of Kant. Heimsoeth also argued that any sharply drawn distinction between the history of philosophy on the one hand and metaphysics on the other is a mistake. He thought that metaphysics is always historical, and the history of the problems of metaphysics is always itself metaphysics. Heimsoeth had a great deal of influence on the postwar German interpretation of Kant. However, his metaphysical or ontological interpretation of Kant has had much less influence in English-speaking countries.

MANFRED KUEHN

Heisenberg, Werner Karl

German. *b:* 5 December 1901, Würzburg. *d:* 1 February 1976, Munich. *Cat:* Physicist; philosopher of physics. *Ints:* Philosophy of quantum mechanics. *Educ:* Studied Physics at the University of Munich under Arnold Sommerfeld, a pioneer in applying quantum theory to the atomic model; awarded doctorate in 1923. *Appts:* First teaching post at Göttingen as assistant to Max Born; invented matrix mechanics, the earliest consistent theory of quantum phenomena, in 1925; collaboration with Niels Bohr in Copenhagen in 1926; 1927, Professor of Physics, Leipzig University; 1932, awarded the Nobel Prize for Physics; 1941–5, Chair of Physics, University of Berlin; after the war, appointed Director of the Max Planck Institute, first at Göttingen and then at Munich.

Main publications:
(1958) *The Physicist's Conception of Nature*, London: Hutchinson & Co.
(1959) *Physics and Philosophy: The Revolution in Modern Science*, London: George Allen & Unwin.
(1971) *Physics and Beyond: Encounters and Conversations*, trans. A. J. Pomerans, London: George Allen & Unwin (contains autobiographical reminiscences).

Secondary literature:
Cassidy, D. C. (1991) *Uncertainty: The Life and Science of Werner Heisenberg*, New York: W. H. Freeman & Co. (contains comprehensive bibliography).

Heisenberg was responsible for what has come to be called the indeterminacy or 'uncertainty' principle in quantum mechanics. This states that in determining, by measurement, the position of a particle such as an electron or photon we make its momentum indeterminate, and that in determining its momentum we make its position indeterminate. In the **Bohr–Heisenberg**—or Copenhagen—interpretation of quantum mechanics this principle is understood to mean not merely that we cannot simultaneously and exactly measure the position and momentum of an electron but rather that an electron does not at any time *have* an exact position and momentum. Positions and momentums are, in effect, produced by the measuring process. The legitimacy of this 'ontological' or 'objective' interpretation of the indeterminacy principle has been questioned, not least because of its connection with the verificationism of logical positivism. It was rejected by **Schrödinger** and by **Einstein**, though it has been adopted as the standard interpretation by most physicists.

Heisenberg's view about the significance of the indeterminacy principle was that it signalled a revolution in our attempts to understand the physical world. It implied a radical dichotomy between, on the one hand, the experimental level at which measurements could be undertaken and where classical physics with its concept of causality was applicable, and on the other hand the submicroscopic level where causal concepts could not be applied and where, therefore, the future is not determined by the past nor the past by the future. The methods which led to the quantum theory are continuous with those used in classical physics, but they lead to an understanding of the concept of reality which is discontinuous with the past. We cannot know what 'really happens' at the quantum level

between observations because, according to the Copenhagen interpretation of the quantum formalism, there is no way of describing what happens. The questions that this raises about the completeness of quantum theory have remained a prominent topic in the philosophy of physics.

BARRY GOWER

Held (née Nott), Virginia

American. *b:* 28 October 1929, New Jersey. *Cat:* Moral and social philosopher. *Ints:* Feminism; politics. *Educ:* Barnard College, NYC AB 1950; Columbia PhD 1968. *Appts:* Barnard College, 1964–6; Hunter College, CUNY, from 1965; Professor of Philosophy, CUNY College Graduate Centre, from 1977; Visiting Professor, Yale 1972, Dartmouth, NH, 1984, UCLA 1986; Truax Visiting Professor, Hamilton College, 1989; Director of NEH Summer Seminar, Stanford Law School, 1981; Visiting Scholar, Harvard Law School, 1981–2; Fulbright Fellow, 1950; Rockefeller Foundation Fellow, 1975 -6; Fellow of Center for Advanced Study in the Behavioral Sciences, Stanford, 1984–5; President, American Section of International Association of Philosophy of Law and Social Philosophy, 1981–3; Executive Committee, Eastern Division, American Philosophical Association, 1979–81; Chair, Society for Philosophy and Public Affairs, 1972; Member of Society for Women in Philosophy; Member of editorial boards, *Ethics*, *Hypatia*, *Philosophy and Phenomenological Research*, *Political Theory*, *Public Affairs Quarterly*, *Social Theory and Practice*, 1982–91; Reporter on the *The Reporter*.

Main publications:
(1970) *The Public Interest and Individual Interest*, New York: Basic Books.
(1972) (ed. with K. Nielson and C. Parsons) *Philosophy and Political Action*, New York: Oxford University Press.
(1974) (ed. with S. Morgenbesser and T. Nagel) *Philosophy, Morality, and International Affairs*, New York: Oxford University Press.
(1980) ed. *Property, Profits, and Economic Justice*, Belmont, CA: Wadsworth.
(1983) (with Hunter College Women's Studies Collective *Women's Realities, Women's Choices: An Introduction to Women's Studies*, Oxford and New York: Oxford University Press.
(1984) *Rights and Goods: Justifying Social Action*, New York: Free Press; reprinted, Chicago: University of Chicago Press, 1989.

(1987) 'Feminism and moral theory', in E. Kittay and D. Meyers (eds), *Women and Moral Theory*, Totowa, NJ: Rowman & Littlefield.

(1989) 'Birth and death', *Ethics* 99.

(1993) *Feminist Morality: Transforming Culture, Society, and Politics*, Chicago: University of Chicago Press.

Secondary literature:

Copp, D. (1988) Review of *Rights and Goods* (1984), *Philosophical Review* 97.

——(1992) *The right to an adequate standard of living–justice, autonomy, and basic needs', Social Philosophy and Policy* 9.

Friedman, M. (1991) 'The social self and the partiality debates', in C. Card (ed.), *Feminist Ethics*, Lawrence: University Press of Kansas.

Schwarzenbach, S. (1990) 'Valuing ideal theory—reflections on Virginia Held's critique of Rawls', *Metaphilosophy* 21.

Held's writings aim to use the tools of philosophical analysis and the actual experiences of life to develop moral and political theories as guidelines for practice. Her first book (1970) critically examines a number of theories of the public interest and suggests an alternative explication of the concept: that the concept lies in an area between the 'is' and the 'ought', that it may be seen from alternative points of view, and that valid judgements applying it can be made. In her second book (1984) Held argues that theories of justice (e.g. **Rawls**) are usually designed for a perfect hypothetical world and hence do not help us in an imperfect world where choices and decisions are seldom clearcut. She criticizes the division between public and private morality as misleading and shows that moral judgement should be contextual by mapping out different approaches and positions for various types of issues.

Recently (1983, 1987, 1989 and 1993) she has been applying specifically women's experience to the understanding of moral theory. Offering a reconceptualization of human birth, she argues (1989) that, like human death, birth is distinctively human rather than merely natural, and that the tradition of describing human birth as a natural event has served the normative purpose of discounting the value of women's experiences and activities. In *Feminist Morality* (1993) Held examines how feminist critiques and reconceptualizations are transforming moral theory by emphasizing the caring emotions and sensitivity and responsiveness to concrete individuals, considering the household as no less relevant to morality and moral theory than the polis, and

developing concepts of the self as relational rather than as either atomistic or communal.

Sources: WW(Am) 1994; PI; *AHCI*.

PATRICIA SCALTSAS

Heller, Agnes

Hungarian. *b:* 1929, Budapest. *Cat:* Neo-Marxist. *Ints:* Marxist theory and philosophical anthropology; ethics; philosophy of history; modernity. *Educ:* Budapest University. *Infls:* Literary influences: Marx, Kant, Hegel, A. Gehlen and Husserl. Personal: Gyorgy Lukács, Ferenc Fehér and György Márkus. *Appts:* 1952–8, Assistant to Georg Lukács at University of Budapest; 1958–63, secondary school teacher in Budapest; 1963–73, Researcher, Hungarian Academy of Sciences; 1973–85, Lecturer in Philosophy and Sociology, La Trobe University, Australia; from 1985, Professor of Philosophy, New School of Social Research, New York.

Main publications:

(1967) *A reneszánsz ember*, Budapest: Akadémiai Kiadò (English translation, *Renaissance Man*, Richard E. Allen, London: Routledge & Kegan Paul, 1978).

(1974) *Bedeutung und Function des Begriffs. Bedürfnis im Denken von Karl Marx*, Milan: Feltrinelli (English translation, *The Theory of Need in Karl Marx*, London: Allison & Busby, 1976).

(1979) *On Instincts*, trans. Marion D. Fenyö, Assen: Van Gorcum.

(1979) *A Theory of Feelings*, trans. Mario D. Fenyö, Assen: Van Gorcum.

(1982) *A Theory of History*, London: Routledge & Kegan Paul.

(1984) *A Radical Philosophy*, Oxford: Blackwell.

(1990) *A Philosophy of Morals*, Oxford: Blackwell.

(1992) *General Ethics*, Oxford: Blackwell.

(1993) *A Philosophy of History in Fragments*, Oxford: Blackwell.

Secondary literature:

Benhabib, Seyla (1980) Review of *On Instincts* (1979) and *A Theory of Feelings* (1979), in *Telos* 44: 211–21.

Rovatti, B. P. A. (1976) 'La nozione della bisogno tra teoria politica e ideologica', in B. P. A. Rovatti *et al.*, *Bisogni e teoria marxista*, Milan: Mazzotta.

A pupil, friend and colleague of **Lukács** at Budapest University, Heller left Hungary in 1973 following continued official attacks upon her 'deviant and revisionist' ideas. She then took up posts at Australian and American universities.

From the first, Heller's philosophy has focused upon the relationship between the individual and society. In the late 1970s she proposed a substantive philosophical anthropology, positing a 'species-essence' realizing itself in human history. Developed initially in order to supply Marxism with the normative, epistemological and ontological basis it hitherto lacked, Heller's ambitious project has unfolded in numerous overlapping volumes dealing with needs, instincts, feelings, ethics, personality and history. In her more recent work the specifically Marxist orientation has receded. The philosophical protagonists of *A Philosophy of History in Fragments* (1993) are now Kant, in his conception of culture, and Hegel, in his philosophy of spirit. While Heller's enterprise has received acclaim, she has been criticized for 'her failure ... to address the epistemological relation between philosophy and the sciences of man' (Benhabib 1980, p. 218).
Sources: BDN.

STEPHEN MOLLER

Hempel, Carl Gustav

German-American. **b:** 8 January 1905, Oranienburg, Germany. **Cat:** Philosopher of science. **Educ:** Göttingen, Heidelberg, Berlin and Vienna, originally Physics and Mathematics, then Philosophy (PhD, Berlin, 1934, with dissertation on 'Beiträge zur logischen Analyse des Wahrheitsbegriff', published in part at Jena, 1934); member of Berlin Gesellschaft für empirische (later: wissenschaftliche) Philosophie (allied to Vienna Circle); research with P. Oppenheim in Brussels and Carnap in Chicago, 1934–9. **Infls:** H. Behmann, Hilbert, P. Oppenheim, Shlick, Carnap, Reichenbach, R. A. Fisher, O. Helmer, Nicod, Goodman, Tarski, Grelling and Dray. **Appts:** Taught at City College, New York, 1939–40; Queen's College, Flushing, New York, 1940–8; Yale, 1948–55; Stuart Professor of Philosophy, Princeton, 1955–73; University Professor of Philosophy, Pittsburgh, 1977; Visiting Professor at Columbia, 1950, at Harvard, 1953–4, at Hebrew University in Jerusalem, 1974, at Berkeley, 1975 and 1977, and at Pittsburgh, 1976; President of APA (Eastern Division), 1961; Member of American Academy of Arts and Sciences; sometime Editor of *Erkenntnis*.

Main publications:

(1936) (with P. Oppenheim) *Der Typusbegriff im Lichte der neuen Logik*, Leiden: A. W. Sijthoff.

(1945) 'Studies in the logic of confirmation', *Mind* (reprinted with some changes and postscript in (1965).

(1952) *Fundamentals of Concept Formation in Empirical Science*, Internat. Encyc. of Unified Science, II, 7, Chicago: Chicago University Press (expanded in German translation, *Grundzüge der Begriffsbildung in der empirischen Wissenschaft*, Düsseldorf, 1934).

(1958) 'The theoretician's dilemma', in H. Feigl, M. Scriven and G. Maxwell (eds), *Minnesota Studies in the Philosophy of Science* II, Minneapolis: Minnesota University Press.

(1962) 'Deductive–nomological vs. statistical explanation', in H. Feigl and G. Maxwell (eds), *Minnesota Studies in the Philosophy of Science III*, Minneapolis: Minnesota University Press.

(1963) (ed. with R. G. Colodny) *Frontiers of Science and Philosophy*, Pittsburgh, PA: Pittsburgh University Press.

(1965) *Aspects of Scientific Explanation and Other Essays in the Philosophy of Science*, New York: The Free Press and London: Collier-Macmillan (includes new title essay and eleven reprinted items, many revised and three with Postscripts; expanded and revised in German translation, *Aspekte der wissenschaftliche Erklärung*, Berlin and New York, 1972).

(1966) *Philosophy of Natural Science*, Englewood Cliffs, NJ: Prentice-Hall.

(1983) (ed. with H. Putnam and W. K. Essler) *Methodology, Epistemology, and Philosophy of Science: Essays in Honour of Wolfgang Stegmüller on the Occasion of his Sixtieth Birthday*, Dordrecht: Reidel (reprinted from *Erkenntnis* 19, 1–3, 1983).

Secondary literature:

Carnap, R. (1950) *Logical Foundations of Probability*, §87-8, Chicago: Chicago University Press.

Dray, W. H. (1957) *Laws and Explanation in History*, London: Oxford University Press.

Essler, W. K., Putnam, H. and Stegmüller, W. (eds) (1985) *Epistemology, Methodology, and Philosophy of Science: Essays in Honour of Carl G. Hempel on the Occasion of His Eightieth Birthday*, Dordrecht: Reidel (includes bibliography; reprinted from *Erkenntnis* 22, 1–3, 1985).

Gunnell, J. G. (1975) *Philosophy, Science, and Political Inquiry*, Morristown, NJ: General Learning Press.

Kyburg, H. E. and Nagel, E. (eds) (1963) *Induction: Some Current Issues*, Middletown, CT: Wesleyan University Press (discussions of Hempel and Carnap with replies).

Mandelbaum, M. (1984) *Philosophy, History, and the Sciences*, Baltimore, MD: Johns Hopkins University Press (especially chapter 7).

Rescher, N. (ed.) (1969) *Essays in Honour of Carl G. Hempel: A Tribute on the Occasion of his Sixty-Fifth Birthday*, Dordrecht: Reidel (includes biographical note, and bibliography).

Scheffler, I. (1963) *The Anatomy of Inquiry*, New York: Knopf; London: Routledge & Kegan Paul, 1964.

Hempel's early work primarily aims at analysing confirmation, considered purely as a 'classificatory' concept and postponing questions of degrees or numerical values. Assuming a universal hypothesis is confirmed by positive instances of it, he insists that whatever confirms a hypothesis must confirm all its logically equivalent formulations. A white shoe therefore (or, better (1965, p. 22), a sentence reporting an observation of one) confirms 'All ravens are black' because (being a non-black non-raven) it confirms 'All non-black things are non-ravens'. Hempel simply accepts this, adding that it sounds odd because we normally come to *know* things about the evidence in one order and not another. Not everyone is so sanguine, and this 'paradox of confirmation' has been extensively discussed (see, for example, Scheffler 1963). After adding some further requirements Hempel claims that, roughly, an observation statement confirms a hypothesis if it entails what the hypothesis would say if only the objects mentioned in the observation statement existed (1965, pp. 36–7); it shows that part of what the hypothesis says is indeed true (1966, p. 64). Confirmation so defined is purely syntactical, holding between sentences; but later, answering **Goodman**'s 'grue' paradox, he admits that confirmation must be partly pragmatic, involving restrictions on the kinds of predicates allowed (1965, pp. 50–1).

Hempel also discusses meaning, rejecting both verifiability and falsifiability as adequate criteria (and also **Popper**'s use of falsifiability to demarcate empirical science), and claims that cognitive significance is a matter of degree and no simple criterion can be given (ibid., p. 117). He also agreed with **Quine** in rejecting the analytic/synthetic distinction (1985, p. 1).

But Hempel's other main contribution that has proved controversial is his account of scientific explanation. He develops a 'covering-law model', where to explain something is basically to infer it from a law plus initial conditions. The law may be universal in form or merely statistical, the inference being deductive in the former case and usually (but not always) inductive in the latter. The laws must not be mere accidental generalizations, and explanation is not mere reduction to a familiar, though the inductive kind, unlike the deductive, is relative to the background of knowledge (1965, pp. 397–403). As with **Braithwaite**, the emphasis is on subsumption into a system. Hempel is concerned with an idealized sort of explanation (ibid., pp. 425–8), but controversy has mainly arisen over his claims to extend it over subjects like history and psychology (pp. 231–43, 463–87).

Sources: PI; Edwards; Mittelstrass; IDPP.

A. R. LACEY

Henríquez Ureña, Pedro

Dominican Republican. *b:* 29 June 1884, Santo Domingo, Dominican Republic. *d:* 11 May 1946, Buenos Aires, Argentina. *Cat:* Critical realist; philologist; historian of ideas. *Educ:* In 1901, Henríquez Ureña began his studies which took him to New York (Columbia University), Havana, Mexico City, Paris, Madrid and Buenos Aires; the University of Minnesota awarded him a doctorate in 1918. *Infls:* Ramón Menéndez Pidal, Alejandro Korn, Eugenio María de Hostos, George Santayana, Enrique José Varona and Alfonso Reyes. *Appts:* Taught at Universities in Santo Domingo, Venezuela, Mexico, Cuba, Argentina, Chile and the USA; 1916–21, University of Minnesota; 1931–3, General Superintendent of Education of the Dominican Republic; 1940–1, Charles Eliot Norton Chair at Harvard University.

Main publications:

(1905) *Ensayos críticos*, Havana.

(1925) *La utopía de América*, La Plata, Argentina.

(1928) *Seis ensayos en busca de nuestra expresion*; new edition, Managua: Nueva Nicaragua, 1986.

(1945) *Literary Currents in Hispanic America*, Cambridge, Mass.: Harvard University Press.

(1947) *Historia de la cultura en la América hispana*; reprinted, Mexico City: Fondo de Cultura Economica, 1986.

(1952) *Ensayos en busca nuestra expresión*, Buenos Aires: Editorial Raigal.

(1966) *A Concise History of Latin American Culture*, trans. Gilbert Chase, New York: Praeger.

Secondary literature:

Carilla, Emilio (1977) 'Pedro Henríquez Ureña: biografía comentada', *Inter-American Review of Bibliography* 27, 3: 227–39.

Lara, Juan Jacobo de (1976) *Pedro Henríquez Ureña: Su vida y su obra*, Santo Domingo, Dominican Republic.

Rama, Angel and Gutiérrez Girardot, Rafael (1978) *La utopía de América/Pedro Henríquez Ureña*, Caracas: Biblioteca Ayacucho.

Henríquez Ureña began his intellectual career under the sway of positivism, particularly that of Auguste Comte. His reading of Kant subsequently attracted him to idealism. In his latter years he described his philosophical position as one of critical realism. Throughout his life he remained committed to the idea that scepticism should not inhibit social action.

AMY A. OLIVER

Herbrand, Jacques

French. *b:* 1908, Paris. *d:* 1931, La Bérarde, Isère, in a climbing accident. *Cat:* Philosopher of mathematics. *Educ:* École Normale Supérieure and in Berlin and Hamburg. *Infls:* Bertrand Russell, A. N. Whitehead and David Hilbert.

Main publications:

(1930) *Recherches sur la théorie de la démonstration*, Warsaw: Dziewulski.

(1936) *Le développement moderne de la théorie des corps algébriques, corps de classes et lois de réciprocité*, Paris: Gauthier-Villars.

(1968) *Écrits logiques*, Paris: Presses Universitaires de France (English translation, *Logical Writings*, Cambridge, Mass.: Harvard University Press, 1971; contains many of Herbrand's articles on mathematics and logic, and a useful summary of his thought).

Jacques Herbrand's approach to mathematics is consistently anti-Platonic. The Platonist conception of mathematics is that it consists of statements about a timeless world of abstract entities and their interrelationships, and its truths are true independently of all minds. By contrast, Herbrand asserts that mathematics and logic are intersubjective human creations. Their objectivity consists of their symbolism being regarded as purely formal. The symbolic formulae of mathematics and logic should not be considered to be about, or to arise from, anything given by the real world. The two disciplines are to be concerned only with the form of arguments, and any application of mathematics and logic should be left to scientists or philosophers.

Following **Hilbert**, Herbrand worked on proof theory, which examines the structure of the proofs which can be constructed from the symbols and rules of a formal system, and which takes such systems as the only objects of mathematics.

Herbrand considers that many mathematical confusions can be solved by invoking Hilbert's distinction between mathematics and metamathematics. The former is concerned only with constructing proofs, whereas the latter is concerned with talking about the constructions. Mathematics is based on assumptions which are to be investigated by metamathematics. Proof theory, with its examination of the proofs within formal systems, lies in the latter area. Since Herbrand's death, developments in proof theory have continued in the works of such thinkers as Leopold Löwenheim and Thoraf Skolem.

KATHRYN PLANT

Hersch, Jeanne

Swiss. *b:* 13 July 1910, Geneva. *Cat:* Philosopher of existence. *Ints:* The philosophy of Karl Jaspers; social and political philosophy; existentialism; literature; history; human rights; medical ethics. *Educ:* Universities of Geneva, Heidelberg, Freiburg and Paris. *Infls:* Karl Jaspers and Kant. *Appts:* 1933–55, Teacher, École Internationale, Geneva; 1956, Professor of Systematic Philosophy, Geneva; 1966–8, Director of Philosophy Department, UNESCO, Paris; 1970–2, Swiss representative, UNESCO Executive Council, Paris; 1973–4, President, Karl Jaspers Foundation, Basel; 1973, Awarded Prize of the Fondation pour les Droits d'Homme; 1977, Honorary Director, Faculty of Theology, University of Basel; 1979, Awarded the Montaigne Prize; 1980, Awarded the Max Schmidheiny Freedomprize; 1994, Awarded the Prix Jaspers.

Main publications:

(1936) *L'Illusion philosophique*, Paris: F. Alcan.

(1946) *L'être et la forme*, Paris: Plon and Neuchatel Éditions de la Baconnière.

(1956) *Idéologies et réalité*, Paris: Plon.

(1957) 'The task of the philosopher', *Philosophy Today* 1: 143–5.

(1975) 'Ordre moral et liberté', *Revue de Théologie et de Philosophie*: 125–8.

(1980) *Karl Jaspers*, Munich: R. Piper.

(1983) 'Karl Jaspers: une philosophe par-dela le nihilisme', *Revue Internationale de Philosophie* 37: 410–22.

(1986) 'The central gesture in Karl Jaspers' philosophy', *Journal of the British Society for Phenomenology* 17: 3-8.

(1989) *Quer zur Zeit*, Zurich: Benziger.

(1990) *Temps et Musique*, Fribourg.
(1992) *Zu Schnittpunkt der Zeit*, Zurich: Benziger.

Secondary literature:
Dufour, Gabrielle and Alfred (1986) *Eclairer L'Obscur*, Lausanne: Éditions L'Age d'Homme; Zurich and Cologne: Benziger Verlag.
Pieper, Annemarie (1990) *Die macht der Freiheit*, Festschrift for the eightieth birthday of Jeanne Hersch, Zurich: Benziger.

Hersch has worked extensively on topics in political and social theory, law, history and education, always relating her enquiries to her broad concern with the human condition and her prevailing interest in existentialism and the nature of Being, an interest first generated by her meeting with Karl **Jaspers** when she was a student in Heidelberg. She developed a sustained enquiry into the varying relationships that can hold between what is 'given' and the specific 'form[a-tions]' imposed by humankind through activities such as art and science. A major aim in all her work was to restore to significance the neglected questions of the *philosophia perennis*, questions to do with self-consciousness, conscience, values, freedom and responsibility, approaching them from a standpoint of philosophical wonder and with the intention of engaging others in a vivid and creative philosophical activity.

Hersch's interests were wide. Her writings encompass literature, morality, ideology and reality, the phenomena of time, history, religion, myth and education. She has been deeply concerned with social issues such as euthanasia, drugs, abortion and the oppression of minorities such as the Jews and people with disabilities. Her reflections on finiteness, freedom and wholeness inform all her thought.
Sources: Meyer & Vahle; correspondence with Professor A. Pieper, Univ. of Basel; Huisman; Kersey.

DIANÉ COLLINSON

Heschel, Abraham, Joshua

American Jew. *b:* 11 January 1907, Warsaw. *d:* 23 December 1972, New York. *Cat:* Religious existentialist and phenomenologist; theologian; educator; linguist; poet. *Ints:* Religious, social and political philosophy; Judaism. *Educ:* 1927–33, Berlin University; 1934, grad. Hochschule für die Wissenschaft des Judentums, Berlin. *Infls:* Hebrew Bible; Rabbinic tradition; Jewish medieval and modern philosophy; Hasidic upbringing; Jewish mysticism; idealist existentialist and phenomenological philosophy. Personal influences include

David Koigen, a sociologist and philosopher of history, Martin Buber, and his own experience of the Holocaust. *Appts:* 1932–3, Instructor, Hochschule für die Wissenschaft des Judentums: 1937, Director, Jewish Adult Education, Frankfurt; 1938–9, Lecturer, Philosophical Institution for Judaistic Studies, Warsaw; 1940, Founder, Institute for Jewish Learning, London; 1940–4, Instructor and Associate Professor in Rabbinics, Hebrew Union College, Cincinnati; 1943–72, Associate Professor, and then Professor, of Jewish Ethics and Mysticism, Jewish Theological Seminary of America; 1961–5, Visiting Professor of Theology, Universities of Iowa, Minnesota and Union Theological Seminary; Fellow or member of various learned bodies.

Main publications:
(1935) *Maimonides. Eine Biographie*, Berlin: Reiss (English translation, J. Neurgroshel, New York: Farrar Straus, 1982 and Doubleday, 1991).
(1936) *Die Prophetie*, Cracow: Polish Academy of Sciences (based on 1933 PhD), revised as *The Prophets*, Philadelphia: JPSA, 1955, and New York: Harper & Row, 1962.
(1951) *The Sabbath: Its Meaning for Modern Man*, New York, Farrar Straus & Young, and Harper Torch, 1966.
(1951) *Man Is Not Alone: A Philosophy of Religion*, new edition, New York: Farrar Straus & Young, 1976, and Harper & Row, 1966.
(1955) *God in Search of Man: A Philosophy of Judaism*, New York: Farrar Straus, and Philadelphia: JPSA; new edition, Farrar Straus, 1959.
(1965) *Who is Man?*, Stanford: Stanford University Press.
(1969) *Israel: An Echo of Eternity*; New York: Farrar Straus & Giroux, 1987.
(1973) *A Passion for Truth*, London: Secker and Warburg, and New York: Farrar, Straus & Giroux.

Secondary literature:
(1985) *Proceedings of the Abraham Joshua Heschel Conference*, New York: Macmillan.
Dresner, S. H. (ed.) (1983) *I Asked for Wonder*, New York: Crossroad.
Friedman, M. S. (1987) *Abraham Joshua Heschel & Elie Wiesel, You Are My Witness*, New York: Farrar Straus & Giroux.
Kaplan, E. K. (1993) 'Abraham Joshua Heschel', in *Interpreters of Judaism in the Late Twentieth Century*, ed. S. T. Katz, Washington, DC: Bnai Brith Books.
Neusner, J. and Neusner, N. (eds) (1989) *To Grow in Wisdom*, Lanham, MD; University Press of America.

Rothschild, F. A. (ed. and intro.) *Between God and Man: An Interpretation of Judaism from the Writings of Abraham J. Heschel*; New York: Harper, 1976.

Sherman, F. (1987) 'Heschel', in *Thinkers of the Twentieth Century*, second edition.

Heschel's main philosophical work is *God in Search of Man* (1955), where he combines a phenomenological approach (already evident in his pioneering work, *Die Prophetie* 1936) with an existential depth theology, dealing with the Jewish religion as an act of faith rather than a concept or representation. In *The Sabbath: Its Meaning for Modern Man* (1951) he emphasizes the time-bound rather than space-bound nature of Judaism. In his later life he became active in many left-wing political causes, which were consonant with his philosophical and ethical beliefs. He also participated in interreligious dialogue, playing a leading role in the Second Vatican Council. He is regarded by some as the greatest exponent of religious Judaism in the twentieth century and his influence on American society has been profound.
Sources: EncJud; NUC; Schoeps; WW(Am) 1972–3, p. 1421.

IRENE LANCASTER

Hesse, Mary Brenda

British. *b:* 15 October 1924. *Cat:* Post-empiricist philosopher of science. *Ints:* Philosophy of science; religion; science. *Educ:* MSc, Imperial College, London; PhD, University College, London. *Infls:* Duhem, Quine, Kuhn and Habermas. *Appts:* University of Leeds, 1951–9; University of Cambridge, 1960–; Professor of Philosophy of Science, 1975–85; Fellow of Wolfson College.

Main publications:

(1954) *Science and the Human Imagination*, London: SCM.
(1961) *Forces and Fields*, London: Nelson.
(1963) *Models and Analogies in Science*, London: Sheed & Ward.
(1974) *The Structure of Scientific Inference*, London: Macmillan.
(1980) *Revolutions and Reconstructions in the Philosophy of Science*, Brighton: Harvester (contains a short review of her thinking, with full bibliography, to 1980).
(1986) (with M. A. Arbib) *The Construction of Reality*, Cambridge.

Hesse has been one of the most important figures in the philosophy of science from the 1960s, particularly because of her emphasis on the place of analogy, models and metaphors in the development of the sciences. She describes herself, with some reservations, as 'a lifelong devotee of the close integration of the study of history and philosophy of science' ('Truth and the growth of scientific knowledge' (1977) , in 1980, p. 162). She shares with **Kuhn** and **Feyerabend** a use of examples from the history of science to undermine empiricist and deductivist theories of scientific development and method. The starting-point for her own critique of empiricism has been the thesis of the underdetermination of (scientific) theories by (observational) data. This had been stated by **Duhem** and understood by **Quine**, but Hesse appreciated its critical significance for truth-as-correspondence as a possible objective for scientific theories (or even as an end-point for their convergence). She has recognized that relativism is a consequence of the thesis, but has said that her aim has been to 'steer a course between the extremes of metaphysical realism and relativism' (ibid., Introduction, p. xiv).

She has suggested an instrumentalist interpretation of truth in so far as it is applied in scientific practice, but she has not given a definitive view on truth in scientific theories. Her discussion of **Habermas**'s consensus theory of truth (see her paper of that title (1978) in *Revolutions and Reconstructions*) has been sympathetic, although the theory has relativistic implications which she cannot wholly accept. Her preference is for some 'value-oriented unification of the claims of all sciences' (p. 230), although the details remain to be filled in.

Hesse has been far more cautious than Feyerabend (for example) about a solely historical or sociological approach to the philosophy of science: 'our understanding of scientific rationality must have a special place in historical study.' She has argued that 'there is a relevant sense of "progress" in which science is absolutely progressive in its understanding of facts' ('Reasons and evaluation in the history of science' (1973), in ibid., p. 27).

Hesse is an Anglican. Her own studies of the roles of analogy and metaphor in the growth of the sciences developed into an understanding of metaphor in religious language. Her later work has included extended studies of the relationships between religions and the sciences (Stanton Lectures at Cambridge 1978–80 and her contributions to *The Construction of Reality* , 1986). She has seen the end of a realistic concept of truth in the sciences as an occasion to underline what can be not held in common to the languages of science and religion.

RICHARD MASON

Heymans, Gerardus

Dutch. **b:** 17 April 1857, Ferwerd, The Netherlands. **d:** 18 February 1930, Groningen. **Cat:** Psychomonist; empiricist. **Ints:** Theoretical philosophy. **Educ:** Law, Economy and Philosophy, University of Leyden; thesis on Economy, 1880; second degree in Philosophy, University of Freiburg under the supervision of Windelband, 1881. **Infls:** Fries and Fechner. **Appts:** Lecturer in Philosophy, University of Leyden, 1883–90; Professor of Philosophy and Psychology, University of Groningen, 1890–1927; Founder of the first psychological laboratory at Groningen, 1892.

Main publications:

(1881) *Zur Kritik des Utilismus*, Freiburg (dissertation.)

(1890) *Schets eener critische geschiedenis van het causaliteitsbegrip in de nieuwere wijsbegeerte* [Outline of a Critical History of the Concept of Causality in Modern Philosophy], Leyden.

(1890–4) *Gesetze und Elemente des wissenschaftlichen Denkens*, Leipzig: Barth.

(1890) *Het experiment in de philosophie* [The Experiment in Psychology], Leyden.

(1905) *Einführung in die Metaphysik auf Grundlage der Erfahrung*, Leipzig: Barth.

(1905) *Einführung in die Ethik*, Leipzig: Barth.

(1915) *Het psychisch Monisme* [Psychical monism], Baarn: Hollandia.

(1927) *Gesammelte kleinere Schriften zur Philosophie und Psychologie*, The Hague (posthumously).

Secondary literature:

Gerritsen, T. C. J. (1938) *La Philosophie de Heymans*, Paris.

Heymans founded his philosophy upon experience. His starting-point is formed by the data in consciousness, but he went beyond empiricism in building a scientific philosophy up on these data. The principle of causality is self-evident, therefore our inner psychical world must be caused by an external world, also of psychical character. The psychical world alone is real and gives the explanation of the so called material world; all processes of the brain are processes of consciousness. Therefore he calls his philosophy 'psychomonism', stressing the ultimate reality of mind and consciousness and opposing each kind of dualism. He could build a metaphysics on empirical foundations, although metaphysics itself is no more than a hypothetical theory. His fundamental work in the field of psychological phenomena is a consequence of this standpoint.

Heymann's ethical theory is based on the principle of objectivity: the norm for each act can be found if one puts oneself in an objective standpoint, leaving aside all personal and subjective desires and emotions.

Sources: J. J. Poortman (ed.) (1958) *Repertorium der Nederlandse Wijsbegeerte*, Amsterdam: Wereldbibliotheek, with supplts, 1958, 1968, 1983; F. Sassen (1941) *Wijgerig Leven in Nederland in de twintigste eeuw* [Philosophical Life in the Netherlands in the Twentieth Century], Amsterdam: North-Holland.

WIM VAN DOOREN

Heyting, Arend

Dutch. **b:** 9 May 1898, Amsterdam. **d:** 9 July 1980, Lugano. **Cat:** Mathematical intuitionism. **Ints:** Philosophy of mathematics. **Educ:** University of Amsterdam. **Infls:** His teacher, L. E. J. Brouwer. **Appts:** Lecturer, University of Amsterdam, 1937; Professor, University of Amsterdam, 1948–68.

Main publications:

(1930) 'Die formalen Regeln der intuitionischen Mathematik III', *Sitzunber. Preuss. Akad. Wiss.*: 158–69.

(1958) 'Intuitionism in mathematics', in R. Klibansky (ed.), *Philosophy in the Mid Century*, vol. 1, Florence: Nuova Italia.

(1959) 'Some remarks on intuitionism', in A. Heyting (ed.), *Constructivity in Mathematics*, Amsterdam: North Holland.

(1966) *Intuitionism: An Introduction*, second edition, Amsterdam: North Holland.

(1974) 'Intuitionistic views on the nature of mathematics', *Synthese* 27: 79–91.

Secondary literature:

Eabbay, D. (1981) 'Semantical investigations', in A. Heyting, *Individualist Logic*, Dordrecht: Reidel.

Haack, S. (1974) *Deviant Logics: Some Philosophical Issues*, Cambridge: Cambridge University Press.

Kneebone, G. T. (1963) *Mathematical Logic and the Foundations of Mathematics*, London: Van Nostrand.

Korner, S. (1960) *The Philosophy of Mathematics*, New York: Dover.

Lehman, H. (1979) *Introduction to the Philosophy of Mathematics*, Oxford University Press.

Heyting embraces an intuitionistic philosophy of mathematics. However, in several important respects his philosophy differs from that of L. E. J. **Brouwer**, the father of modern mathematical empricism. As regards foundations for mathematics Heyting rejects the naive intuitionism of Brouwer, acknowledging that certainty in human thinking is impossible and maybe a meaningless aim. Between 1930 and 1960, while continuing to subscribe to the doctrine of self-evidence, he became convinced that it had 'proved not to be intuitively clear what is intuitively clear to mathematics' and developed the view that intuitionists should accept a 'descending scale of grades of evidence', beginning with assertions such as '2+2=4' which are reports of direct mental constructions.

Such a view faces formidable difficulties in connection with the idea of mental objects whose natures are transparent to us through inspection, difficulties which have been investigated in the later philosophy of **Wittgenstein**. It is doubtful whether any psychological and subjective doctrine can provide an epistemological justification for mathematics.

Heyting was to move away from the radical subjectivism and anti-language stance of Brouwer with his attempt in 1930 at a symbolic formulation of the logical principles of intuitionist propositional logic, and in *Intuitionism* (1966) he provides an account of mathematics and logic which does not start from a philosophical foundation. However, the reader is warned that public and symbolic expression of the content is inadequate. One can only learn what intuitionist mathematics is by practising it, for the symbolic account can only be understood by repeating the mental processes recorded in it. However, Heyting is more sympathetic to the acitivity of expressing intuitionist mathematics symbolically than was Brouwer. He sees symbolization as a support for memory as well as for communication and as essential for understanding between mathematicians. So in Heyting's writing there is increasing acknowledgement of a necessary social dimension in an adequate account of mathematical activity.

In his explanation of the foundations of mathematics Brouwer rejected the logicism of **Russell** and **Whitehead**, that mathematics is based on logic, and claimed that logic is based on mathematics. This implies that the steps of a logical proof are intuitively clear mental acts according to intuitionism rather than symbolic applications of previously laid down and publicly available logical laws. While accepting this philosophical position Heyting nevertheless developed an intuitionistic logic for which he provided an interpretation. The calculus employs four primi-

tive constants $\wedge$, $\vee$, $\neg$, $\rightarrow$, which are independent of each other, and lower-case Latin letters are used for propositional variables. The following eleven axioms are accepted:

1. $p \rightarrow (p \wedge p)$
2. $(p \wedge q) \rightarrow (q \wedge p)$
3. $(p \rightarrow q) \rightarrow [(p \wedge r) \rightarrow (q \wedge r)]$
4. $[(p \rightarrow q) \wedge (q \rightarrow r)] \rightarrow (p \rightarrow r)$
5. $q \rightarrow (p \rightarrow q)$
6. $[p \wedge (p \rightarrow q)] \rightarrow q$
7. $p \rightarrow (p \vee q)$
8. $(p \vee q) \rightarrow (q \vee p)$
9. $[(p \rightarrow r) \wedge (q \rightarrow r)] \rightarrow [(p \vee q) \rightarrow r]$
10. $\neg p \rightarrow (p \rightarrow q)$
11. $[(p \rightarrow q) \wedge (p \rightarrow \neg q)]\neg p$

Rules of derivation are the same as in the classical propositional calculus. From these it is not possible to derive part of the principle of Double Negation, $\neg\neg a \rightarrow a$, nor is the Law of Excluded Middle ($a \vee \neg a$) a theorem of the system. Due to the restriction on Double Negation indirect proof is not available in intuitionistic logic. When extended to the calculus of predicates appropriate limitations are placed on quantifiers; the existential quantifier in, e.g., $(Ex)P(x)$ conveys more information than the use of the universal quantifier in a formula regarded as equivalent in classical predicate logic, namely, $\neg(x)\neg P(x)$. The use of the former is only allowed when an object with the property P has actually been constructed while the use of the latter depends only on the condition that we deduce a contradiction from some particular supposition.

The above calculus admits of various interpretations and in particular has been interpreted by Heyting as a calculus of intended constructions. So understood a theorem expresses the fact that one has succeeded in making a construction. This is expressed in the so-called Principle of Positivity, which requires that every mathematical or logical theorem must express the result of a mathematical construction. For comparison, a classical theorem expresses the fact that a proposition is true. Accordingly Heyting contrasts intuitionist and classical logic as the logics of knowledge and truth respectively. He thereby, as indicated in our remarks on language, takes philosophy of mathematics to the heart of an ongoing debate of general philosophical interest concerning the logical relationships between the concepts of truth and meaning.

Sources: Mittelstrass.

JIM DUTHIE

Hick, John

British. *b:* 1922, Scarborough. *Cat:* Philosopher of religion. *Educ:* Universities of Edinburgh and Oxford. *Infls:* Hume, Kant, Schleiermacher, Wittgenstein, Norman Kemp Smith and H. H. Price. *Appts:* 1956–9, Assistant Professor of Philosophy, Cornell University; 1959–64, Stuart Professor of Christian Philosophy, Princeton Theological Seminary; 1964–7, Lecturer in Philosophy of Religion, University of Cambridge; 1967–79, H. G. Wood Professor of Theology, University of Birmingham; 1979–92, Danforth Professor of Philosophy of Religion, Claremont Graduate School.

Main publications:

(1957) *Faith and Knowledge*, London: Macmillan.
(1966) *Evil and the God of Love*, London: Macmillan.
(1966) *Philosophy of Religion*, Englewood Cliffs: Prentice-Hall.
(1974) *God and the Universe of Faiths*, London: Macmillan.
(1976) *Death and Eternal Life*, London: Macmillan.
(1982) *God Has Many Names*, London: Macmillan.
(1985) *Problems of Religious Pluralism*, London: Macmillan.
(1989) *An Interpretation of Religion*, London: Macmillan.

Secondary literature:

Gillis, Chester (1989) *A Question of Final Truth: John Hick's Theory of Salvation*, London: Macmillan.
Hewitt, Harold (ed.) (1991) *Problems in the Philosophy of Religion: Critical Studies of the Work of John Hick*, London: Macmillan.

Hick, who has been one of the major philosophers of religion of the past thirty years, has written influentially on many important issues in the subject, such as the nature of religious language, the rationality of religious belief, the problem of evil, and death and the idea of an after-life. His most radical proposal has been that the great world religions constitute different human responses, formed by their own conceptual schemas, to a single ultimate reality. He uses a basically Kantian epistemology, distinguishing between, on the one hand, the *noumenal* Real which, transcending all (other than purely formal) human concepts is beyond human experience, and, on the other hand, the range of experienceable divine *phenomena*. These phenomena are the various *personae* of the ultimately Real (such as Jahweh, Allah, the Holy Trinity, and so on) and its *impersonae* (such as Brahman, Tao, and so on). The doctrines of the different religions thus refer to different manifestations of the ultimately Real, formed jointly by the presence of the Real and the varieties of human religious mentalities. Their doctrines may be literally true of the personae or impersonae to which they refer, but only mythologically true of the Real in itself—their mythological truth consisting in their capacity to evoke an appropriate response to that to which they ultimately refer. There is, however, something common to the great religions: the centrality of the salvific transformation of human existence from self-centredness to an orientation centred in the Real.

The practical implication of this is that interfaith dialogue should proceed on the basis of full mutual acceptance in which the traditional separate claims to unique superiority have been abandoned. In the case of Christianity, for instance, Hick recommends that the doctrine of the divine incarnation should be regarded as mythologically rather than literally true. In his work on the 'problem of evil', Hick has argued that the problem can be solved by thinking of the afflictions of this world as necessary if it is to serve as a 'vale of soul making'.

Sources: WW 1992; personal communication.

ANTHONY ELLIS

Hilbert, David

German. *b:* 23 January 1862, Königsberg, Germany. *d:* 14 February 1943, Göttingen. *Cat:* Metamathematician. *Ints:* Philosophy of mathematics. *Educ:* Königsberg University. *Infls:* L. Kronecker, G. Cantor and current tendencies towards axiomatization in mathematics. *Appts:* Professor, University of Königsberg, 1892–5, University of Göttingen, 1895–1930.

Main publications:

(1899) *Die Grundlagen der Geometrie*, Leipzig: Teubner; seventh edition, 1930 (English translation, *The Foundations of Geometry*, Chicago: Open Court, 1902; second edition, 1971).
(1928) (with W. Ackermann) *Grundzüge der theoretischen Logik*, Berlin: Springer; second edition, 1938 (English translation, *The Principles of Mathematical Logic*, New York: Chelsea, 1950).
(1934–9) (with P. Bernays) *Grundlagen der Mathematik*, 2 vols, Berlin: Springer.
(1935) *Gesammelte Abhandlungen*, vol. 3 (contains main philosophical papers).

Secondary literature:

Detlefsen, M. (1986) *Hilbert's Program*, Dodrecht: Reidel.

Peckhaus, V. (1990) *Hilbertprogramm und Kritische Philosophie. Das Göttinger Modell interdiszipli-närer Zusammenarbeit zwischen Mathematik und Philosophie.*

Toepell, M.-M. (1986) *Über die Entstehung von David Hilberts 'Grundlagen der Geometrie'*, Göttingen: Vandenhoeck & Ruprecht.

Webb, J. C. (1984) *Mechanism, Mentalism, Meta-mathematics*, Dordrecht: Reidel.

Hilbert was arguably the leading mathematician of the first 30 years of this century. He outlined a list of 23 problems for mathematics at the International Congress of Mathematicians in 1900, which has remained of permanent value as a guide. His philosophical interests centred upon axiomatization of mathematical theories and related metamathematical questions, such as consistency and completeness. Indeed, he was the chief initial founder of metamathematics.

Hilbert's entry into such matters began in the 1890s with the foundations of Euclidean and projective geometry, culminating in his classic booklet of 1899 in which he gave a (nearly) complete list of axioms needed for the Euclidean branch. He then turned to the foundations of arithmetic, and sketched ways in which properties *of* axiom systems might be demonstrated. These early endeavours were not too satisfactory, although in 1904–5 he gave at Göttingen a magnificent (unpublished) lecture course on foundations.

Resuming these concerns in 1917, Hilbert advanced his theories in the 1920s with detailed explanations of how metamathematical proper-ties of a mathematical theory could be formulated in a symbolic manner. The corollary to **Gödel's** theorem (1931) showed that his (apparent) assumption that the metatheory would be simpler that its parent object theory was mistaken; but he had laid down essential guidelines for finitism in mathematics, and of recursive procedures, and the book written with his former student Bernays is a classic.

However, Hilbert's own mathematical writings rarely bear much stamp of the formal metamathe-matician. His term 'formalism' was meant to signify that mathematical theories would be treated as marks on paper for metamathematical purposes. He granted some sense of reality to the objects of those theories, and got on with their examination.

Hilbert was also very supportive of the set theory of **Cantor**. At Paris he gave the continuum hypothesis and the well-ordering theorem as the first of his 23 problems, and he hoped to find proofs of them. His formalist philosophy was probably partly influenced by its traces in Cantor, who, however, left the metamathematical ques-tions as *self-evidently* answerable. Among philo-sophically minded mathematicians his greatest influence fell upon Ernst Zermelo. He did not write on other aspects of philosophy, but he was in lively contact with his colleagues at Göttingen, holding an especially high opinion of Leonard **Nelson**.

IVOR GRATTAN-GUINNESS

Hirst, P(aul) H(eywood)

British. **b:** 10 November 1927, Yorkshire. **Cat:** Epistemologist; philosopher of education. **Ints:** Epistemology. **Educ:** Trinity College, Cambridge. **Infls:** Ryle, Wittgenstein, Hare, Peters, MacIntyre and Taylor. **Appts:** 1955–9, Lecturer and Tutor, University of Oxford Department of Education; 1959–65, Lecturer, Philosophy of Education, University of London Institute of Education; 1965–71, Professor of Education, King's College, University of London; 1971–88, Professor of Education and Head of Department of Educa-tion, University of Cambridge, and Fellow of Wolfson College.

Main publications:

(1970) (with R. S. Peters) *The Logic of Education*, London: Routledge & Kegan Paul.

(1972) (ed. with R. F. Dearden and R. S. Peters) *Education and the Development of Reason*, London: Routledge & Kegan Paul.

(1974) *Knowledge and the Curriculum*, London: Routledge & Kegan Paul.

(1974) *Moral Education in a Secular Society*, London: University of London Press.

(1983) (ed. and contributor to) *Educational Theory and its Foundation Disciplines*, London: Routledge & Kegan Paul.

Secondary literature:

Barrow, R. and White, P. (1993) (eds) *Beyond Liberal Education: Essays in Honour of Paul H. Hirst*, London: Routledge (contains full bibliographies of writings by and on Hirst).

Elliott, R. K. (1975) 'Education and human being I', in S. C. Brown (ed.), *Philosophers Discuss Educa-tion*, London: Macmillan.

Hirst was the cofounder, with Richard **Peters**, of the British school of analytical philosophy of education in the 1960s and 1970s. He is best known for his account—influenced by **Oakeshott**—of a liberal education based on an initiation into logically distinct 'forms of knowl-edge', each with its own peculiar concepts and tests for truth. Hirst developed specific aspects of this view in writings about education in the arts, morality and religious knowledge. His theory has been extraordinarily influential, both within the discipline and in the world of school curriculum planning.

In the late 1980s Hirst began to go further than many of his critics in rejecting what he then saw as the over-rationalistic emphasis of his earlier theory, constructing a new account of the content of education—influenced by neo-Aristotelian thinking—based on social practices. His rethink-ing has also been reflected in his writings on educational theory, which no longer argue for educational practices derived from work in established theoretical disciplines, but stress the prior importance of practical theories operation-ally developed.

Sources: Personal communication.

JOHN WHITE

Hobhouse, Leonard Trelawny

British. *b:* 8 September 1864, Cornwall. *d:* 21 June 1929, Orne, France. *Cat:* Hegelian liberal. *Ints:* Metaphysics; social philosophy. *Educ:* Corpus Christi College, University of Oxford. *Infls:* H. Spencer, A. Comte, J. S. Mill and T. H. Green. *Appts:* Elected to a prize fellowship at Merton College, Oxford, 1887–94; Fellow of Corpus Christi College, University of Oxford, 1894–7; Leader writer for the *Manchester Guardian*, 1897–1905; Political editor of the *Tribune*, 1905–7; the first Martin White Professor of Sociology, Uni-versity of London (part-time 1907–25; full-time 1925–9).

Main publications:

(1896) *The Theory of Knowledge*, London: Methuen & Co.
(1901) *Mind in Evolution*, London: Macmillan & Co.
(1904) *Democracy and Reaction:* London: T. Fisher Unwin.
(1906) *Morals in Evolution*, New York: Henry Holt & Co.
(1911) *Social Evolution and Political Theory*, New York: Columbia University Press.
(1911) *Liberalism*, London: Home University Press.
(1913–27) *Development and Purpose*, London: Mac-millan & Co.
(1918) *The Metaphysical Theory of the State: a Criticism*, London: Macmillan & Co.
(1921) *The Rational Good*, New York: Henry Holt & Co.

(1922) *The Elements of Social Justice*, New York: Henry Holt & Co.
(1924) *Social Development*, New York: Henry Holt & Co.

Secondary literature:

Barker, E. (1929) 'L. T. Hobhouse', *Proceedings of the British Academy*, vol. 15.
Hobson, J. A. and Ginsberg, M. (1931) *L. T. Hobhouse, His Life and Work*, London: George Allen & Unwin.
Owen, J. E. (1974) *L. T. Hobhouse, Sociologist*, London: Nelson.

L. T. Hobhouse possessed remarkably diverse intellectual talents. A philosopher of distinction, he made important contributions to many other fields of enquiry: to research in the empirical sciences, to comparative psychology, to the foundation of sociology and to the systematiza-tion of a vast body of anthropological data. He was also a man of practical affairs—a journalist and controversialist—whose innate humanitar-ianism inspired many leading social reformers of his day. Of his intellectual contribution R. Fletcher writes: 'Hobhouse remains unquestion-ably the most considerable British sociologist of the twentieth century' (in Owen 1974).

The central motivation of Hobhouse's philo-sophy was the desire to develop a human science which would contribute to a rational reconstruc-tion of society. To this end his distinctively philosophical work begins with an epistemologi-cal enquiry into the nature of rationality, proceeds to empirical investigations into the workings of mind in the organic world and in human society, encompasses a study of ethics and sociology, and returns to metaphysics in a final comprehensive synthesis.

The originality of Hobhouse's epistemology and philosophy of science lay in its distinctive combination of central features of the idealist and empiricist traditions of his time. On the one hand this acceptance of a coherence theory of ration-ality showed a sympathy with idealism. Justifica-tion and explanation must be sought in the interrelations of the parts to the whole; the justification of all judgements, even the most basic, depends on their place in a coherent and comprehensive body of beliefs. On the other hand there are empiricist elements in Hobhouse's epistemology. Each categorical judgement asserts a reality independent of the mind of the judging agent, and perceptual beliefs possess initial credibility although they must support and be supported by other judgements. Although sympathetic to idealism, he was, says Ginsberg, 'one of the founders of modern epistemological realism' (1929).

Hobhouse's account of the nature and significance of minds is central to his philosophy. He viewed the emergence of minds, with the capacity for rational direction, as being a crucial turning-point in the evolutionary process and accordingly rejected the belief that evolution is the outcome of inevitable biological processes. In 1901 he attacked the traditional dichotomy of mental and physical substances, arguing that the crucial issues in the philosophy of mind are those concerning the form of explanation appropriate to human behaviour rather than the ontological issue concerning the nature and existence of mind. Experience reveals three different systems of explanation: mechanical, organic and teleogical. Humans are psychophysical organisms in which mechanical modes of action are qualified by teleological ones. Hobhouse held, therefore, that teleological rather than mechanical explanation is appropriate to human behaviour. Within this context a series of stages of development are mapped out, tracing evolution from elementary forms of life to the self-critical awareness of human personality.

The central idea of Hobhouse's theory of development is the existence of broad correlations between social development and the growth of mind. This development, however, is not automatic: it depends on human activity and ideas. Ultimately social development has as its end the harmonious fulfilment of human potentiality achieved in common with all mankind.

The concept of harmony also played a central role in Hobhouse's moral and social theories. In 1921 he argued that the rational good is a harmony of experience with feeling carried consistently through the entire realm of mind and value. Although abstract and obscure when thus formally stated, this conception of harmony proved to be particularly fruitful and unifying when applied to fundamental problems in value theory. For example, he held that the common good is not merely the aggregate of individual goods, it is a harmony of which individual goods are interrelated elements; rights, specifying conditions requisite for the harmonious fulfilment of personality in society, are claims to the common good.

In 1913 and 1927 we have a comprehensive synthesis of his central philosophical ideas, a synthesis which, according to Ginsberg (1929) 'must win for him a high place amongst the systematic thinkers of the world'. According to

this definitive statement of his views an explanation of reality as a whole and of the development of civilization requires the recognition of an interconnecting force, of a correlating and conative activity, which guides development towards growth and maturity. The unity to which it gives rise cannot be that of a mechanical system, nor can it be completely organic. Hobhouse insists that it must be teleological and he calls the power 'Mind'. Mind is not reality itself but is a part of reality; it is that part of reality which makes for the emerging unity and order to which the empirical sciences bear witness.

Development and Purpose (1913–27) is typical of all of Hobhouse's work. The Comtean conception of a growing and developing humanity is blended with an evolutionary bias derived from **Spencer**; a reconciliation is sought between these and the idealist conception of the growth of objective mind; and the entire account is infused by positivist influences derived from Mill.

Sources: M. Ginsberg 'Leonard Trelawny Hobhouse', *JPS* 4, 1929; Edwards.

H. BUNTING

Hocking, William Ernest

American. *b:* 10 August 1873, Cleveland, Ohio. *d:* 13 June 1966, Madison, New Hampshire. *Cat:* Idealist. *Ints:* Philosophy of religion; philosophy of man; philosophy of politics. *Educ:* Iowa State University of Science, 1897–9; Harvard University, BA 1901, MA 1902, PhD 1904; the Universities of Göttingen, Berlin and Heidelberg. *Infls:* James, Royce and Husserl. *Appts:* 1904–06, Instructor in History and Philosophy, Andover Theological Seminary; 1906–08, Instructor to Assistant Professor of Philosophy, University of California, Berkeley; 1908–14, Assistant Professor to Professor of Philosophy, Yale University; 1914–66, Professor, Afford Professor of Philosophy (1920–43), Emeritus Professor, Harvard University; 1946–7, Visiting Professor, University of Leiden.

Main publications:

(1912) *The Meaning of God in Human Experience: A Philosophic Study of Religion*, New Haven: Yale University Press.

(1918) *Human Nature and its Remaking*, New Haven: Yale University Press; revised editions, 1923 and 1929; reprinted, New York: AMS Press, 1982.

(1926) *Man and the State*, New Haven: Yale University Press; reprinted, Hamden, CT: Shoe String Press, 1968.

(1926) *Present Status of the Philosophy of Law and of Rights*, New Haven: Yale University Press; reprinted, Littleton, Col.: Rothman, 1986.

(1928) *The Self, Its Body and Freedom*, New Haven: Yale University Press; reprinted, New York: AMS Press, 1980.

(1929) *Types of Philosophy*, New York: Charles Scribner's Sons; second edition, 1939; third edition, with R. Hocking, 1959.

(1932) *The Spirit of World Politics. With Special Studies of the Near East*, New York: The Macmillan Company.

(1937) *The Lasting Elements of Individualism*, New Haven: Yale University Press; reprinted, New York: AMS Press, 1980.

(1940) *Living Religions and a World Faith*, New York: The Macmillan Co.; reprinted, New York: AMS Press, 1980.

(1944) *Science and the Idea of God*, Chapel Hill: University of North Carolina Press.

(1956) *The Coming World Civilization*, New York: Harper & Brothers.

(1957) *The Meaning of Immortality in Human Experience including Thoughts on Death and Life*, New York: Harper & Brothers; reprinted, West Port, CT: Greenwood, 1982.

Secondary literature:

Furse, M. L. (1988) *Experience and Certainty: William Ernest Hocking and Philosophical Mysticism*, Atlanta, Georgia: Scholars Press.

Reck, A. J. (1964) *Recent American Philosophy*, New York: Pantheon, pp. 42–83.

Rouner, L. R. (1969) *Within Human Experience: The Philosophy of William Ernest Hocking*, Cambridge, Mass.: Harvard University Press.

Hocking employed the appeal to experience in philosophy, which he derived from William **James**. But his pragmatism was, to use his phrase, 'negative pragmatism'. He held that what does not work cannot be true, invoking an absolute standard, similar to **Royce**'s 'absolute pragmatism'. Although a Roycean idealist, Hocking was wary of the impersonal absolute. He sought and found the absolute in a personal form worthy of worship within the immediacy of personal experience, wherein the individual self mystically encounters God.

In his theory of man Hocking esteemed the will-to-power to be the fundamental core of human nature. Its highest expression is found in the missionary religions, especially in Christianity. Striving not only to control conduct, Chris-tianity seeks also to transform the inner feelings of human beings.

For Hocking religion, speculatively reconceived, is the fundament of morality, politics and civilization. Committed to the principle of individual rights and justice, he further believed that traditional liberalism had to be superseded by the co-agent state and an international political system embracing a plurality of nation states.

Hocking attributed the turmoils of the twentieth century to the metaphysical confusions of modernity—the separation of self, dwelling in isolation, from the world, subject to scientific and technological mastery. In overcoming modernity, Hocking hoped, mankind would inaugurate a new world civilization.

Olympian in literary style and personal manner, Hocking was nevertheless an engaged philosopher. With his wife he founded the Shady Hill School. During the First World War, on assignment from the British Government, he studied military psychology, authoring *Morale and its Enemies* (New Haven: Yale University Press, 1918). A firm internationalist, he was critical of the mandates in Asia and Africa to the major European powers (1932). As Chairman of the Layman's Foreign Missions, he edited its report *Re-thinking Missions: A Laymen's Inquiry After One Hundred Years*, (New York: Harper & Brothers, 1932). A Member of the Commission on the Freedom of the Press, he wrote *Freedom of the Press: A Framework of Principle* (Chicago: University of Chicago Press, 1947). Critical of the Allied occupation of Germany in relation to education, he authored *Experiment in Germany: What we can learn from Teaching German* (Chicago: Henry Regnery Co., 1954). Regarding the Cold War he exhorted Americans to trust the Soviet Union on behalf of coexistence in *Strength of Men and Nations: A Message to the USA Vis-a-vis the USSR* (New York: Harper & Brothers, 1959).

The idealist metaphysics expressed in *The Meaning of God in Human Experience* (1912) Hocking later revised to take account of the realities recognized by contemporary philosophies of process and existence, as his Gifford Lectures, entitled 'Fact and destiny' delivered at the University of Glasgow in 1938, testify.

ANDREW RECK

Hoernlé, Reinhold F(riedrich) A(lfred)

German-born British South African. *b:* 27 November 1880, Bonn. *d:* 21 July 1943, Johannesburg. *Cat:* Idealist; social reformer. *Ints:*

Metaphysics; philosophy of religion. *Educ:* Balliol College, Oxford. *Infls:* Personal influences include Bosanquet, Edward Caird, J. A. Smith, Schiller, R. B. Perry, Royce and Hocking. Literary influences: Bradley, Hegel, Kant and Plato. *Appts:* 1912–14, Professor of Philosophy, Armstrong College (Newcastle-upon-Tyne), University of Durham; 1914–20, Assistant Professor of Philosophy, Harvard; 1920–3, Professor of Philosophy, Armstrong College; 1923–43, Professor of Philosophy, University of Witwatersrand at Johannesburg.

Main publications:

(1920) *Studies in Contemporary Metaphysics*, London: Kegan Paul.
(1923) *Matter, Mind, Life and God*, London: Methuen.
(1925) *Idealism as Philosophical Doctrine*, London: Hodder &Stoughton.
(1927) *Idealism as a Philosophy*, New York: G. K. Doran.
(1939) *South African Native Policy and the Liberal Spirit*, Johannesburg: Witwatersrand University Press.
(1952) *Studies in Philosophy*, ed. D. S. Robinson, London: Allen & Unwin (posthumous).

Secondary literature:

MacCrone, I. D. (1945) Memoir in a collection of contributions by Hoernlé to *Race and Reason*, Johannesburg: Witwatersrand University Press.
Robinson, D. S. (1952) 'A memoir of R. F. A. Hoernlé', in Hoernlé 1952.

Hoernlé was an idealist in the tradition of T. H. Green who considered and carried through the implications of his philosophy for practical life. His willingness to find room for everyone made him an outstanding leader of liberal thinking in South Africa, where he became President of the Institute of Race Relations. His wide interests and 'open-minded responsiveness' made what he called a 'synoptic philosophy' natural to him (CNP II, p. 140). The ideal he sought was that of 'combining a comprehensive survey of the whole of experience with the tracing of a coherent order or pattern within it' (CBP II, p. 143).

Hoernlé set no particular store by the title 'idealist' and recognized the need to adapt his thought to new developments in philosophy. None the less he frequently entered the lists to defend idealist doctrines such as the coherence theory of truth from attacks by pragmatists and others. It had been his intention to publish a volume of essays on 'the present-day issue between realism and idealism' (CBP II, p. 155). By the time these were published after his death, however, the problems with which they dealt were no longer topical.

Sources: CBP II, pp. 129–56; Passmore 1957; WW.

STUART BROWN

Høffding, Harald

Danish. *b:* 11 March 1843, Copenhagen. *d:* 2 July 1931, Copenhagen. *Cat:* Positivist philosopher; historian of philosophy. *Ints:* Ethics; epistemology; philosophy of religion. *Educ:* Copenhagen. *Infls:* Kierkegaard, Comte and Spencer. *Appts:* 1883–1915, Professor of Philosophy, Copenhagen.

Main publications:

(1872) *Philosophien i Tydskland efter Hegel* [Philosophy in Germany after Hegel], Copenhagen.
(1974) *Den engelske Philosophi i vor Tid* [The English Philosophers of our Time], Copenhagen (German translation, 1912).
(1880) *Om Grundlaget for den humane Ethik* [Foundations of Human Ethics], Copenhagen.
(1880 *Oplevelse og Tydning; religionsfilosofiske Studier* [Experience and Interpretation: Studies in the Philosophy of Religion], Copenhagen.
(1881) *Psykologi i Omrida paa Grundlag af Erfaring*, Copenhagen (English translation, *Outlines of Psychology*, trans. M. E. Loundes, London: Macmillan, 1891).
(1887) *Etik, en Fremstilling af de etiske Principer og deres Anvendelse paa de vigtigste Livsforhold* [Ethics: An Account of Ethical Principles and Their Application to the Chief Conditions of Life], Copenhagen (German translation, 1901).
(1892) *Søren Kierkegaard som Filosoph* [Søren Kierkegaard as a Philosopher], Copenhagen (German translation, 1896).
(1894–5) *Den nyere Filosofis Historie, en Fremstilling af Filosofiens Historie fra Renaissancens Slutning til voore Dage*, Copenhagen (English translation, *A History of Modern Philosophy: A Sketch of the History of Philosophy from the Close of the Renaissance to our own Day*, 2 vols, trans. B. E. Meyer, London, 1900; new edition, Dover Publications, 1955).
(1896) *Jean Jacques Rousseau og hans Filosofi*, Copenhagen (English translation, *Jean Jacques Rousseau and his Philosophy*, trans. W. Richards and L. E. Saidla, New Haven: Yale University Press, 1930).
(1898) *Kort Oversigt over den nyere Filosofis Historie*, Copenhagen (English translation, *A Brief History*

of *Modern Philosophy*, trans. C. F. Sanders, New York: Macmillan, 1912).

(1899) *Psykologiske Undersøgelser* [Psychological Inquiry], Copenhagen.

(1901) *Religionsfilosofi*, Copenhagen (English translation from the German edition, *Philosophy of Religion*, B. E. Meyer, New York, 1906).

(1902) *Filosofiske Problemer*, Copenhagen (English translation, *The Problems of Philosophy*, trans. M. Fischer, Galen: New York: Macmillan, 1905).

(1904) *Moderne Filosofi* [Modern Philosophy], Copenhagen.

(1909) *Danske Filosofer* [Danish Philosophers], Copenhagen.

(1910) *Den menneskelige Tanke, dens Former og dens Opgave* [Human Thought: Its Forms and its Problems], Copenhagen.

(1914) *Henri Bergson's Filosofi Karakteristik og Kritik* [Henri Bergson's Philosophy Described and Criticized], Copenhagen.

(1915) *Modern Philosophers* and *Lectures on Bergson*, trans. A. C. Mason, New York: Macmillan.

(1917) *Totalitet som Kategori, en erkendelsesteoretisk undersøgelse* [Everything According to its Category: An Epistemological Inquiry], Copenhagen.

(1918) *Spinoza's Ethica. Analyse og Karakteristik* [Spinoza's *Ethica*: Analysis and Description], Copenhagen.

(1920) *Ledende Tanker i det nittende Aarhundrede* [Leading Thinkers of the Nineteenth Century], Copenhagen.

(1923) *Begrebet Analogi* [Concept of Analogy], Copenhagen.

(1924) *Platon's Bøger om Staten. Analyse og Karakteristik* [Plato's Books on the State: Analysis and Description], Copenhagen.

(1925) *Erkendelsesteorie ok Livsopfattelse* [Epistemology and Outlook on Life], Copenhagen.

(1930) *Bemaerkninger am Erkendelesteoriens nuvuernde Stilling* [Remarks on the Actual Situation of Epistemology], Copenhagen.

Secondary literature:

Faye, Jan (1988) 'The Bohr–Høffding relationship reconsidered', *Studies in the History and Philosophy of Science* 19: 321–46.

Sandelin, Kalle (ed.) (1932) *Harald Høffding in Memoriam*, Copenhagen (contains extensive bibliography).

Høffding initially studied theology but decided not to take religious orders and, after a religious crisis, eventually became a liberal humanist. As a result of a stay in Paris from 1865 to 1869 his philosophical outlook was decisively influenced by French and English positivism. His *Ethics*

(1887) is broadly utilitarian. In *Philosophy of Religion* (1906) he claimed that the basis of all religion is a wish to believe in the existence of values. His most influential work has been his history of modern philosophy from the end of the Renaissance to 1880 (1894–5), in which the 'Romantic speculation' of post-Kantian idealism is represented as giving way to positivism. He gave substantially more space to Comte, J. S. Mill, Darwin and **Spencer** than to Hegel. His history emphasized the contribution of scientists to the development of philosophy. Here, and in his epistemological work of 1910, Høffding showed a particular sympathy for Hume and Kant. He has been criticized, for instance by **Hartnack**, for tending to psychologize epistemology and in this respect his huge influence on Danish philosophy in the period up to the Second World War has been regretted. It has been claimed that he was a significant influence on Niels **Bohr**. Less controversially, he played a major role in turning Danish philosophy away from Hegelianism and moving it in the empirical and positivistic direction taken by pupils such as **Jørgensen**. He had a considerable international reputation and many of his books were translated into German, French, Russian and Italian, as well as English.

Sources: Burr; Schmidt, Raymund (ed.) (1923) *Die Philosophie der Gegenwart in Selbstdarstellungen*, vol. 4, Leipzig (with brief autobiography and summary by Høffding of his philosophical views); Huisman; Edwards.

STUART BROWN

Hollak, Jan (Johannes Hermanus Adrianus)

Dutch. *b:* 20 July 1915, Zwolle, The Netherlands. *Cat:* Hegelian. *Ints:* Metaphysics; social philosophy. *Educ:* Social Sciences, Amsterdam University; Philosophy, Universities of Amsterdam, Ghent and Louvain. *Infls:* Personal influences included H. J. Pos and P. de Bruin; philosophical influences included Hegel, Marx and Nietzsche. *Appts:* Assistant and Lecturer in Philosophy, Amsterdam University, 1946–65; Professor in the History of Modern Philosophy, Catholic University of Nijmegen, 1965–86.

Main publications:

(1962) 'De Structuur van Hegel's Wijsbegeerte' [The structure of Hegel's philosophy], Dissertation, University of Louvain.

(1966) *Van Causa sui tot automatie* [From Causa Sui to Automacy], Hilversum: Brand (Inaugural Lecture).

(1986) *Filosoferen in een hypothetisch wordende samenleving* [Philosophy in a Society that is Becoming Hypothethical], University of Nijmegen.

The metaphysical style of Hollak's philosophy attracted many students and followers. With all his knowledge of the social sciences he applied Hegelian and Marxian ideas to them, and proposed many original ideas in the field of the philosophy of technology and culture. Man is not only a 'being within the world' but also a transcendental being, 'a spirit within the world'. In cybernetics the technical idea and also the Hegelian idea are appearing and becoming objective. Man is forced to consider himself as the transcendental power.

WIM VAN DOOREN

Holt, Edwin Bissett

American. *b:* 1873, Winchester, Massachusetts. *d:* 25 January 1946, Rockland, Maine. *Cat:* Materialist. *Ints:* Philosophy of mind. *Educ:* Harvard University. *Infls:* William James. *Appts:* Lecturer and Professor of Pyschology, Harvard, 1901–18; Professor of Social Psychology, Princeton, 1926–36.

Main publications:

(1914) *The Concept of Consciousness*, London.
(1915) *The Freudian Wish*, New York.
(1931) *Animal Drive and the Learning Process*, London.

Holt was, with R. B. **Perry**, the leader of the group who put out the manifesto *The New Realism* in 1912 and was the most radical and uncompromising of them. He followed William **James**'s neutral monism in his doctrine that 'being' is the basic category, which is neither mental nor material itself, the term denoting everything, but connoting nothing. The simple elements of which everything is composed are of the nature of essences or concepts; they are not, as with James, 'experiences', an identification which made James' neutral monism (as it was to do that of **Russell**) subjective or mentalistic in character. They are the constituents of mental and material complexes.

Thought and representation, the having of ideas, are not any sort of copying or imitation of what there is but a matter of partial identity. An idea is part of what it is an idea of. From this it followed, Holt was ready to admit, that reality as a whole was littered with errors and contradictions. The picking out of a coherent order from the confused array of simples Holt saw as a conventional undertaking of no great ontological significance. He took consciousness in a more or less behaviourist way as the 'interested response of an organism', a notion obviously difficult to reconcile with the doctrine that an idea is part of the thing it is an idea of. Even if the body is the perceiver, rather than some disembodied cognitive soul, it is clearly quite distinct from much of what it perceives. Holt turned away from the theory of knowledge after *The Concept of Consciousness* (1914). He argued that unconscious, Freudian desire is the fundamental topic of psychology, not sensation or any other conscious item, developing his behaviouristic conception of the mind as what the body can do, linking his position to Aristotle's doctrine of the soul as the 'form' of the body. He wound up with a purely materialistic theory of the mind as nerves and muscles. Holt was too uncompromising and unwilling to respond to criticism and difficulties to make any converts. He contributed, however, in his somewhat freebooting way to the general transformation of psychology into a science of behaviour.

Sources: Passmore 1957; Hill.

ANTHONY QUINTON

Hong Qian (Hung Chi'en or Tscha Hung)

Chinese. *b:* 1909, Anhui Province, China. *d:* 1992, Beijing. *Cat:* Logical positivist. *Ints:* Philosophy of science; epistemology. *Educ:* Universities of Berlin and Jena in Germany; University of Vienna in Austria, where he obtained a PhD. *Infls:* Schlick, Neurath, Carnap and Wittgenstein. *Appts:* Lecturer, University of Beijing; Professor, Southwest Associated University; Professor and Head of Department, National Wuhan University; Professor and Head of Department, Yenching University; Professor and Head of Department, University of Beijing; Head of Seminar for History of Foreign Philosophy, University of Beijing; Director, Institute of Foreign Philosophy, University of Beijing; President, Society for the Study of Contemporary Western Philosophy; Research Fellow, New College, Oxford.

Main publications:

(1943) 'The Vienna Circle and metaphysical problems', *Philosophical Review* (China).
(1944) 'Causality and probability in modern physics', *Philosophical Review* (China).
(1945) *The Philosophy of the Vienna Circle*, Shanghai: Commercial Press.

(1948) 'Kant's apriorism and modern natural science', *Campus Scientist*.
(1949) 'Moritz Schlick and modern empiricism', *Philosophy and Phenomenological Research*.
(1981) 'Wittgenstein und Schlick', *Proceedings of the International Wittgenstein Symposium*, Vienna: Verlag Hoeder-Pichler-Tempsky.
(1982) 'Moritz Schlick und der Logische Empiricismus', *Grazer Philosophische Studien*, Amsterdam: Rodopi.
(1991) 'Ayer and the Vienna Circle', in *A. J. Ayer*, Open Court.
(Editor in Chief) Series of Anthologies of Western Philosophical Writings.

Secondary literature:
Briere, O. (1956) *Fifty Years of Chinese Philosophy 1898–1950*, London: George Allen & Unwin Ltd.
Complete Chinese Encyclopedia, Philosophy Volumes, Beijing: Chinese Encyclopedia Publications.

The career of Hong Qian was entirely taken up by those agenda-setting arguments and debates of logical positivism which have shaped analytical philosophy in this century. After preliminary training in Germany he became a student of Moritz **Schlick**. In the Vienna Circle from 1931 to 1936 Hong encountered the ideas of **Wittgenstein**, **Carnap**, **Neurath** and Schlick and those of visiting philosophers, including A. J. **Ayer**. Although he was absorbed by the doctrines and controversies of logical positivism in general, Hong was most drawn to Schlick's own project for a 'consistent empiricism' and its relation to the principles of Berkeley and Hume.

From Schlick and Wittgenstein Hong adopted the view of philosophy as a method of analysis rather than a set of doctrines. This, in turn, provided an influential solution to the question of how philosophy related to science. Philosophy was neither cut off from science nor absorbed within it; rather, it was a method for dealing with the meaning of expressions and statements, especially to exclude those which lacked meaning from any enterprise seeking to give knowledge. The method exercising this discipline was verificationism, the claim that a statement was meaningful only if there were in principle a means of showing it to be true or false. Metaphysical statements were those failing the verificationist test. Hong provided a sensitive history of central debates over the difficulties with verificationism: whether a formulation could be found which avoided excluding too much or too little. He also assessed the various accusations of backsliding into metaphysics or, through Carnap's rejection of

a correspondence theory of truth, of falling into conventionalism or crude rationalism.

Hong adopted Schlick's analysis of how traditional metaphysical questions arose. He distinguished sharply between knowledge and experience: the former logical and communicable, the latter psychological and private. He held that by confusing the two a specious discipline was formed. The distinction between logic and psychology, so important to **Frege** at the very beginning of modern analytical philosophy, was thus crucially retained. This distinction gained central importance in relation to a question Hong considered repeatedly: the foundation of knowledge. He endorsed Schlick's rejection of Carnap's basic or protocol propositions as candidates for the foundation of empirical knowledge on the grounds that they were hypotheses as liable to turn out to be false as any hypotheses, but he was also critical of Schlick's own alternative foundation in affirmations or observation statements. Because of their thoroughly ostensive nature, their meaning and truth can be determined together, like analytic statements and unlike other empirical statements. As a result, they are empirical but not hypotheses, and can function as the foundation of knowledge. Yet Hong saw that their completely ostensive character was incompatible with the logical character of statements. Schlick's own distinction between logic and psychology defeated his attempt to found empirical knowledge and provided grounds for the currently prevailing desire to account for knowledge without foundations.

Hong argued that in his last years Schlick came under Wittgenstein's negative influence and fell back into metaphysical confusion. He greatly admired Wittgenstein's *Tractatus*, but believed that Wittgenstein's later work led to error. Regarding Kant, Hong rejected *a priori* constraints on science but was drawn to Kantian themes in the analysis of experience and knowledge. He could accept a Kantianism shorn of transcendence. Although there is nothing syncretic in Hong's philosophy, his work is extremely important for China. It disciplines and clarifies major discussions of philosophy and science in China in the 1920s. His many students have absorbed his exacting standards of argument, reason and truth. The humane fluency of his prose has also made its mark. Most important, he shows what an honest and adventurous mind can achieve through rigorous and independent thought, and that Chinese scholars could make significant contributions to international philosophy. In addition to his own work, anthologies of

Western philosophical writings edited by Hong have had great influence.

NICHOLAS BUNNIN

Honneth, Axel

German. *b:* 18 July 1949, Essen, Germany. *Cat:* Social philosopher; critical theorist. *Ints:* Philosophical anthropology; critical theory; recognition. *Educ:* Philosophy and Sociology, Universities of Bonn, Bochum and Berlin. *Infls:* Critical theory, especially Habermas and Benjamin. *Appts:* Assistant, Fachbereich Philosophie and Institut für Sozialforschung, Frankfurt and Institut für Soziologie, Free University of Berlin; Professor of Political Philosophy, University of Konstanz, 1990–2; Professor of Politics, Free University of Berlin, from 1992.

Main publications:

(1980) (with Hans Joas) *Soziales Handeln und menschliche Natur*, Frankfurt: Suhrkamp (English translation, *Social Action and Human Nature*, Raymond Meyer, Cambridge: Cambridge University Press, 1988).

(1985) *Kritik der Macht. Reflexionsstufen einer kritischen Gesellschaftstheorie*, Frankfurt: Suhrkamp (English translation, *Critique of Power: Stages of Reflection of a Critical Theory of Society*, Ken Baynes, Cambridge, Mass: MIT Press, 1991).

(1986) (ed. with Albrecht Wellmer) *Die Frankfurter Schule und die Folgen*, Berlin: De Gruyter.

(1989) (ed. with Thomas McCarthy, Claus Offe and Albrecht Wellmer) *Zwischenbetrachtungen im Prozeß der Aufklärung. Jürgen Habermas zum 60. Geburtstag*, Frankfurt: Suhrkamp (English translations, *Philosophical Investigations in the Unfinished Project of Enlightenment*, trans. William Rehg, Cambridge, Mass.: MIT Press, 1992 and *Cultural-Political Interventions in the Unfinished Project of Enlightenment*, trans. William Rehg, Cambridge, Mass.: MIT Press, 1992).

(1990) *Die zerrissene Welt des Sozialen. Sozialphilosophische Aufsätze*, Frankfurt: Suhrkamp (English translation, *The Fragmented World of the Social*, ed. Charles W. Wright, Albany: SUNY Press, 1995).

(1992) *Kampf um Anerkennung. Zur moralischen Grammatik sozialer Konflikte* Frankfurt: Suhrkamp (English translation, *The Struggle for Recognition*, Cambridge: Polity Press.

(1993) *Desintegration. Bruchstücke zu einer soziologischen Zeitdiagnose*, Frankfurt: Fischer.

Honneth's *Critique of Power* (1985) is a systematic reconstruction of critical theory which points to the absence of an adequate social theory in the work of the early Frankfurt School, notably that of Max **Horkheimer** and Theodor **Adorno**. This gap is filled, in very different ways, in Michel **Foucault**'s theory of power and in Jürgen **Habermas**'s theory of communicative action. Both these thinkers can be seen to carry forward the analysis of what Horkheimer and Adorno called the dialectic of enlightenment. More recently, Honneth has developed the Hegelian motif of a struggle for recognition into an ambitious outline of a theory of social conflict. He has written extensively on contemporary critical theory and postmodernism and edited a number of important works.

WILLIAM OUTHWAITE

Hook, Sidney

American. *b:* 20 December 1902, Brooklyn, New York. *d:* 12 July 1989, Stanford, California. *Cat:* Pragmatic naturalist. *Ints:* Social philosophy. *Educ:* City College of New York and Columbia University. *Infls:* John Dewey and Bertrand Russell. *Appts:* New York University, 1927–73; Senior Research Fellow, Hoover Institution, Stanford, 1973–89.

Main publications:

(1927) *The Metaphysics of Pragmatism*, Chicago: Open Court.

(1933) *Towards the Understanding of Karl Marx*, New York: John Day.

(1936) *From Hegel to Marx*, New York: Reynard & Hitchcock.

(1939) *John Dewey: An Intellectual Portrait*, New York: John Day.

(1940) *Reason, Social Myths and Democracy*, New York: John Day.

(1943) *The Hero in History*, New York: John Day.

(1946) *Education for Modern Man*, New York: Dial Press.

(1953) *Heresy, Yes–Conspiracy, No*, New York: John Day.

(1955) *Marx and the Marxists: The Ambiguous Legacy*, Princeton, NJ: Van Nostradt.

(1957) *Common Sense and the Fifth Amendment*, New York: Criteria Books.

(1959) *Political Power and Personal Freedom*, New York: Macmillan.

(1961) *The Quest for Being*, St Martin's Press.

(1962) *The Paradoxes of Freedom*, Berkeley: University of California Press.

(1963) *The Fail-Safe Fallacy*, New York: Stein & Day.

(1967) *Religion in a Free Society*, Lincoln: University of Nebraska Press.

(1970) *Academic Freedom and Academic Anarchy*, New York: Cowles Book Co.

(1973) *Education and the Taming of Power*, La Salle, Ill.: Open Court.

(1974) *Pragmatism and the Tragic Sense of Life*, New York: Basic Books.

(1975) *Revolution, Reform and Social Justice*, New York: New York University Press.

(1980) *Philosophy and Public Philosophy*, Carbondale and Edwardsville: Southern Illinois University Press.

(1983) *Marxism and Beyond*, Totoura, NJ: Bowman & Littfield.

(1987) *Out of Step: An Unquiet Life in the XXth Century*, New York: Harper & Row.

Secondary literature:

Kurtz, Paul (ed.) (1983) *Sidney Hook: Philosopher of Democracy and Humanism*, Buffalo, NY: Prometheus Books (includes complete bibliography from 1922 to 1982).

Levine, Barbara (1989) *Sidney Hook: A Checklist of His Writings*, Carbondale and Edwardsville: Southern Illinois University Press.

An activistic intellectual, Sidney Hook struggled to do justice to both the professional demands of his university commitment and the political demands of his commitment to 'the socialist dream'. The political commitment had emerged first. At a time when the American system was mired in deep depression, Marxism appeared to be a promising alternative. Hook considered himself to have been a 'fellow traveller' until the Moscow treason trials of 1936–7 revealed to him the unethical terror at the heart of the Soviet experiment. Thereafter, his position became that of a 'communism without dogmas', which turned into 'democratic socialism'. Eventually, he would call himself a 'social democrat' and insist upon political democracy above all with 'more or less' socialism or capitalism depending on the situation.

His university orientation was fixed by his discovery of the pragmatism of John **Dewey**, which began in his undergraduate work and was completed by his studying under Dewey at Columbia. Dewey wrote an introductory word commending Hook's first book (1927), and seems to have regarded the younger man as his intellectual heir apparent. In any case they became a kind of social action team with Hook attempting to relieve the great man of some of the tedium of scholarly work while arranging for his participation in various political projects which had engaged the interests of the younger man. In

one of these endeavours, for example, Dewey joined a commission to investigate the Moscow trials, including a trip to Mexico to interview Trotsky.

Initially, Hook saw Dewey as a philosopher who was applying 'the principles of historical materialism' to philosophy in a brilliant manner. However that may be, what Dewey gave Hook intellectually was a framework allowing Hook to defend the principles of democratic liberalism and naturalism against attack from whatever quarter. The initial attacks came from the Stalinist left although, to be sure, the vigour of Hook's counterattack would often leave one in doubt concerning the difference between offence and defence. Hook's inner sense was that his 'polemical exchanges' always came 'in response to criticism or in defense of the causes' to which he was committed (1987, pp. 347–8). The particular issues would change with the times. After fighting the cultural cold war against the Communists, during the McCarthy years he opposed the Senator while arguing that intellectuals had an obligation to testify before Congressional committees. With respect to university education he became embroiled 'for almost twenty years' in 'vigorous educational and political controversy' with Hutchins and Adler over the great books and classical, versus progressive, educational ideals (ibid. p. 450). In the 1960s and early 1970s he criticized university administrators for their ineptitude in controlling student disturbances.

Throughout, he said that his energies were called forth by such disputes against his repeated resolves to devote himself 'to the sweet uses of technical philosophy'. In fact, his early writing was more concerned with these uses, whether pragmatistic or Marxist, than his later work. Upon retirement he promised himself that he would turn to 'a systematic exposition and defense of the thought of John Dewey', but the issues and problems of 'the last forty years' remained 'still as topical and compelling' as ever (ibid. p. 582). Approaching his eighty-fourth year he felt 'just as much embattled' as the day he 'first discovered injustice and unnecessary cruelty in the world'.

His position of pragmatic naturalism coupled the appreciation of science to that of political democracy. 'All human knowledge is scientific knowledge' (1961, p. 216). The logic and ethics of scientific method are applicable to all human affairs, including 'normative social inquiry'. It is not only possible to determine the best means to achieve 'given ends', but also to determine what are the best ends. A corollary to this approach was an 'open minded atheism', joined, however, to the proviso that freedom of religious belief is integral to 'any morally acceptable schedule of human rights' (1987, p. 351). A depth note to all of this is his belief (1975) that the incompossibility of goods, requiring that some be sacrificed, introduces a genuine, inescapable tragedy between betrayal of the greater good and the ideal of justice.

Sources: Nicholas, Capaldi (1982) 'Sidney Hook: a personal portrait', *Free Inquiry* 10–15.

WILLIAM REESE

Horkheimer, Max

German. **b:** 14 February 1895, Stuttgart. **d:** 7 July 1973, Nuremberg, Germany. **Cat:** Social philosopher; critical theorist. **Ints:** Philosophy of history; history of philosophy. **Educ:** Universities of Munich, Freiburg and Frankfurt (where he obtained his doctorate in 1922 and his Habilitation in 1925). **Infls:** Hans Cornelius, Theodor Adorno, Friedrich Pollock, Hegel, Marx and Nietzsche. **Appts:** Privatdozent, 1925, Professor of Social Philosophy, 1929, Rector, 1952–3, University of Frankfurt; Member, from 1923, and Director, 1930–58, Institut für Sozialforschung; Director of Scientific Department of American Jewish Committee, 1943–4.

Main publications:

(1925) *Über Kants 'Kritik der Urteilskraft' als Bindeglied zwischen theoretischer und praktischer Philosophie*, Stuttgart: Kohlhammer.

(1930) *Anfänge der bürgerlichen Geschichtsphilosophie*, Stuttgart: Kohlhammer.

(1932) 'Hegel und das Problem der Metaphysik', *Festschrift für Carl Grünberg: zum 70 Geburtstag*, Stuttgart: Kohlhammer.

(1934) (pseud. Heinrich Regius) *Dämmerung*, Zurich: Oprecht & Helbling; *Notizen 1950 bis 1969 und Dämmerung*, Frankfurt: S. Fischer Verlag, 1974 (English translation, *Dawn and Decline: Notes 1926–1931 and 1951–1969*, trans. Michael Shaw, New York: Seabury Press, 1978).

(1936) (with Erich Fromm and Herbert Marcuse) *Studien über Autorität und Familie*, Paris: Félix Alcan.

(1947) *The Eclipse of Reason*, New York: Oxford University Press; reprinted New York: Seabury, 1974.

(1947) (with Theodor W. Adorno) *Dialektik der Aufklärung*, Amsterdam: Querido (English translation, *Dialectic of Enlightenment* John Cumming, New York: Herder & Herder; London: Allen Lane, The Penguin Press, 1972).

(1967) *Zur Kritik der instrumentellen Vernunft*, Frankfurt: S. Fischer (English translation, *Critique of Instrumental Reason*, trans. Matthew J. O'Connell *et al.*, New York: Seabury Press, 1974).

(1968) *Kritische Theorie*, 2 vols, Frankfurt: S. Fischer Verlag (English translation, *Critical Theory*, trans. Matthew J. O'Connell *et al.*, New York: Herder & Herder, 1972). (Contains some of Horkheimer's essays published in the *Zeitschrift für Sozialforschung*, reprinted Munich: Kösel-Verlag, 1970 and Munich: Deutscher Taschenbuch-Verlag, 1980.)

(1970) (with Otmar Hersche) *Verwaltete Welt. Gespräch zwischen Prof. Dr. Max Horkheimer und Otmar Hersche*, Zurich: Arche.

(1972) *Gesellschaft im Übergang: Aufsätze, Reden und Vorträge, 1942–1970*, ed. Werner Brede, Frankfurt: Athenäum Fischer Taschenbuch Verlag.

(1972) *Sozialphilosophische Studien: Aufsätze, Reden und Vorträge, 1942–1970*, ed. Werner Brede, Frankfurt: Athenäum Fischer Taschenbuch Verlag.

(1972) *Traditionelle und Kritische Theorie. Fünf Aufsätze*, Frankfurt: Fischer.

(1985–) *Gesammelte Schriften in achtzehn Bänden*, ed. Alfred Schmidt and Gunzelin Schmidt-Noerr, Frankfurt: Fischer.

Secondary literature:

Arato, Andrew and Gebhardt, Eike (eds) *The Essential Frankfurt School Reader*, New York: Urizen Books and Oxford: Blackwell.

Dubiel, Helmut (1978) *Wissenschaftsorganisation und Politische Erfahrung*, Frankfurt: Suhrkamp (English translation, *Theory and Politics. Studies in the Development of Critical Theory*, trans. Benjamin Gregg, Cambridge, Mass.: MIT Press, 1985).

Gumnior, Helmut and Ringruth, Rudolf (1973) *Max Horkheimer in Selbstzeugnissen und Bilddokumenten*, Reinbek bei Hamburg: Rowohlt.

Habermas, Jürgen (1993) 'Notes on the developmental history of Horkheimer's work', *Theory, Culture and Society* 10, 2.

Hartmann, Frank *Max Horkheimers materialistischer Skeptizismus. Studien zur frühen Kritischen Theorie*.

Held, David (1980) *Introduction to Critical Theory: Horkheimer to Habermas*, London: Hutchinson.

Jay, Martin (1973) *The Dialectical Imagination: A History of the Frankfurt School and the Institute of Social Research, 1923–1950*, London: Heinemann (includes substantial bibliography).

Korthals, Michael (1985) 'Die kritische Gesellschaftstheorie des frühen Horkheimers', *Zeitschrift für Soziologie* 14: 315–29.

Maor, Maimon (1981) *Max Horkheimer*, Berlin: Colloquium.

Schmidt, Alfred (1974) *Zur Idee der Kritischen Theorie. Elemente der Philosophie Max Horkheimers*, Munich: Hanser.

——and Altwicker, Norbert (1986) *Max Horkheimer Heute. Werke und Wirkung*, Frankfurt: Fischer.

Schnädelbach, Herbert (1985–6) 'Max Horkheimer and the moral philosophy of German idealism', *Telos* 66: 81–101.

Skuhra, Anselm (1974) *Max Horkheimer: eine Einführung in sein Denken*, Stuttgart: Kohlhammer.

Stirk, P. M. R. (1992) *Max Horkheimer. A New Interpretation*, Hemel Hempstead: Harvester.

Wiggershaus, Rolf (1986) *Die Frankfurter Schule: Geschichte, theoretische Entwicklung, politische Bedeutung*, Munich: Hauser (English translation, *The Frankfurt School*, trans. Martin Robertson, Cambridge: Polity, 1994).

Horkheimer's central institutional role as Director of the Institute of Social Research has somewhat overshadowed his own substantial philosophical work. Although he lacked **Adorno**'s brilliance, he had if anything a broader range of expertise, including psychology, which he had studied at university before turning to philosophy, and sociology. Horkheimer's combination of synoptic sweep and pregnant formulation, as displayed in particular in his early book on philosophy of history, his classic essay on 'Traditional and critical theory' (1972) or in *The Eclipse of Reason* (1947), make him a major figure in twentieth-century thought. Horkheimer's antimetaphysical conception of philosophy and reason, his radical revision of Marxism and his conception of interdisciplinary critical theory were guiding principles of the Frankfurt School's activity.

With the catastrophe of Nazism and the experience of exile in New York and California, Horkheimer, like Adorno, became increasingly pessimistic. When the Institute was reestablished in Frankfurt in the 1950s he took pains to play down any connection with its former work, discouraged radical young thinkers such as Jürgen **Habermas** and adopted an increasingly conservative position.

WILLIAM OUTHWAITE

Hou Wailu (Hou Wai-lu)

Chinese. *b:* 1903, Pingyao, Shanxi Province, China. *d:* 1992, Beijing. *Cat:* Marxist; historian of Chinese philosophy. *Educ:* Beijing University of Politics and Law and Beijing Normal University; 1927–30, external student, University of Paris. *Infls:* Marx. *Appts:* Professor, Harbin University of Politics and Law; Chairman, History Department, Beijing Normal University; Principal, Northwest University; Committee Member, Philosophy and Social Science Department, Chinese Academy of Science; Deputy Head, and Head, History Research Institute, Chinese Academy of Social Sciences; and many political appointments.

Main publications:

Ancient Chinese Society and Laozi.

(1942) *History of Thought and Scholarship in Ancient China*, Wenfeng Bookstore.

(1947) *History of Thought and Scholarship in Contemporary China*, 2 vols, Shenghuo Bookstore.

(1956) *A History of Enlightened Thought in Early Modern China*, Beijing: Renmin Publishing House.

(1957) (chief editor & contributor) *A Comprehensive History of Chinese Thought*, 6 vols, Beijing: Renmin Publishing House.

(1958) (co-author) *An Outline History of Chinese Philosophy*, Beijing: Zhongguo Qingniam Publishing House.

Secondary literature:

Brière, O. (1956) *Fifty Years of Chinese Philosophy 1898–1950*, London: George Allen & Unwin Ltd.

Complete Chinese Encyclopedia, Philosophy Volumes, Beijing: Chinese Encyclopedia Publications.

Louie, K. (1986) *Inheriting Tradition: Interpretations of the Classical Philosophers in Communist China 1949–1966*, Hong Kong: Oxford University Press.

From the 1940s Hou Wailu gained widespread respect for his large-scale studies using Marxist methodology to understand ancient Chinese thought and culture, according to the principle that social existence determined the social meaning of political and philosophical thought. His great strength was his ability to integrate excellent historical and philosophical scholarship within his methodological framework. His concern to compare Chinese and European thought produced two major studies. In the first he claimed that from a Marxist perspective the intellectual achievements of ancient China were greater than those of Ancient Greece; in the second he argued that the achievements of Chinese thought since the seventeenth-century were comparable to those of the Renaissance. These claims, supported by imaginative scholarly detail, helped to legitimate the continued study of ancient philosophy after Liberation in 1949 by incorporating Chinese experience within a Marxist historical perspective and by countering claims that the Chinese intellectual inheritance, unlike the thought of ancient Greece and the Renaissance, was an inadequate foundation for entry into the modern world.

Perhaps political involvements led to Hou's participation in the anti-Hu Shi campaign of the 1950s, even though Hu's book on logic in ancient China shared the goal of reviving appreciation of China's intellectual traditions. In other respects, however, Hou's Marxism was sophisticated rather than dogmatic. He criticized the crude employment of Zhdanov's idealist–materialist distinction, noting that an ever increasing number of Chinese thinkers were proposed as materialists in order to allow them to be studied. His individual judgements, however controversial, provided a basis for further serious investigation. His claim that Daodejing was written later than the Confucian *Analects*, rather than in the same period, raised many points of textual interpretation, leading to a changed view of that puzzling work. Hou was capable of complex and balanced judgments. He saw Laozi as an idealist because of his conception of the *dao*, but an idealist who worked for the peasants. He saw Mengzi as favouring the rulers, but also as supporting the common people against the feudal lords who held the real power at the time. Hou was drawn to the ancient conflict between Confucian and Monist schools and analysed Mozi's key concept of universal love with great care and precision. He saw universal and partial love not as a distinction between economically determined class notions, but rather as two moral outlooks held by kinds of people filling roles established by the economic structure of society, thus seeing a certain autonomy for moral notions within a Marxist analysis.

NICHOLAS BUNNIN

Hountondji, Paulin J.

Beninan. *b:* 1942, Abidjan, Ivory Coast. *Cat:* Historian of philosophy; phenomenologist; politician. *Educ:* High school in Dahomey, Baccalaureate (1960), Lycée Henri IV, Paris: École Normale Supérieure, Rue d'Ulm, Agrégé in Philosophy, 1966; third cycle Doctorate on Husserl, 1970. *Infls:* Edmund Husserl and Louis Althusser. *Appts:* Assistant in Philosophy, University of Besançon, 1967–70; chargé de cours, University of Lovainium, Kinshasa, 1970–1; Professor of Philosophy, National University of Zäire, Lubumbashi, 1971–4; chargé d'enseignement, Faculté des Lettres, University of Cotonou,

Benin, 1974–90; Minister of National Education and Culture, 1993–3; General Secretary of the Inter-African Council of Philosophy, 1974.

Main publications:
(1973) *Libertés, contribution à la révolution dahoméenne*, Cotonou: Édition Renaissance.
(1977) *Sur la philosophie africaine*, Paris: Maspéro (English translation, *African Philosophy: Myth or Reality*, Bloomington: Indiana University Press, 1983).

Secondary literature:
Binda, P. *La Philosphie Africaine Contemporaine*, Kinshasa: Facultés Catholiques de Kinshasa.
Irele, Abiola (1983) Introduction and Preface to Hountondji, *African Philosophy: Myth or Reality*, Bloomington: Indiana University Press.
Masolo, D. A. (1994) *African Philosophy in Search of Identity*, Bloomington: Indiana University Press.
Mudimbe, V. Y. (1988) *The Invention of Africa*, Bloomington: Indiana University Press.

A disciple of Louis **Althusser** in his conception of philosophy—which is always a history of philosophy—Hountondji is regarded as the principle critic of the ethnophilosophical trend created by **Tempels** and **Kagame** according to which there is in all sociocultural contexts a latent but organized philosophy expecting a translation. His main position is that philosophy should be distinguished from *Weltanschauungen* (worldviews). In this sense he is very close to Franz **Crahay**, yet critical of his five conditions for the promotion of African philosophy. For Hountondji, the notion of a conceptual take-off makes sense as a general condition of existence of an African philosophy. He thinks that in all civilizations a conceptual take-off is always already accomplished even when human actors use or integrate mythical sequences into their discourse. By virtue of this characteristic, one could compare Parmenides's discourse to those of Confucius, Plato, Hegel, **Nietzsche** or Kagame. On the other hand, he insists that, whether mythical or ideological, language evolves in a social environment, developing its own history and the possibility of its own philosophy.

V. Y. MUDIMBE

Hourani, G(eorge)

American citizen. *b:* 3 June 1913, England. *d:* 19 September 1984, USA. *Cat:* Historian of Islamic philosophy; ethical thinker; historian of Arab seafaring in the Indian Ocean. *Ints:* Analytical philosophy; political philosophy. *Educ:* Oxford and Princeton Universities. *Appts:* Taught at Government Arab College, Jerusalem, University of Michigan, and finally at the State University of New York, Buffalo, as Distinguished Professor of Islamic Thought and Civilization.

Main publications:

(1959) *Ethical Value*, Ann Arbor: University of Michigan Press.

(1961) *Averroes on the Harmony of Religion and Philosophy*, London: Luzac.

(1971) *Islamic Rationalism: The Ethics of Abd al-Jabbar*, London: Oxford University Press.

(1985) *Reason and Tradition in Islamic Ethics*, Cambridge: Cambridge University Press.

Hourani's main philosophical interest was ethics, and he was particularly attracted to the development of ethics in the Islamic world. Most of his work concentrates upon Islamic thinkers such as ibn Rushd (Averroes) and the Mutazilite Abd al-Jabbar, and he was clearly attracted to the rationalist trend in Islamic thought. This did not in any way prevent him from discussing clearly and critically the opponents of this position, which he presented in as attractive a manner as possible. His work on the nature of ethical controversy in the Islamic world is outstanding for its clarity and comprehensiveness.

Hourani played an important role in showing how useful it is to consider the works of Islamic philosophy and theology from an analytical standpoint. Although he did examine the minutiae of the particular controversies, he was able to put them within a broader perspective which made them accessible to philosophers in general, not just Islamicists. His work on Averroes' *Decisive Treatise*, which involved editing, translating and commenting upon the text, brought the nature of the Islamic tradition of philosophy to the notice of a comparatively wide audience. The links which he etablished between earlier Islamic thought and modern developments showed how continuous the discussion is and how relevant apparently obscure theological debates are to modern political and ethical concerns.

Sources: Hourani 1985; personal communication.

OLIVER LEAMAN

Howison, George Holmes

American. *b:* 29 November 1834, Montgomery County, Maryland. *d:* 31 December 1916, Berkeley, California. *Cat:* Personal idealist. *Ints:* Evolution; philosophy of man. *Educ:* Marietta College

and Lane Theological Seminary. *Appts:* Assistant Professor of Mathematics, 1864–6, Professor of Political Economy, 1866–9, Washington University, St Louis; Professor of Logic and Philosophy of Science, MIT, Boston, 1872–8; Lecturer on Ethics, Harvard, 1879–80; several courses of lectures at the Concord School of Philosophy between 1880 and 1883; Lecturer in Philosophy, University of Michigan, 1883–4; Professor of Intellectual and Moral Philosophy and Civil Polity, University of California, 1884–1909.

Main publications:

(1869) *A Treatise on Analytic Geometry*, Cincinnati: Wilson, Hinkle & Co.

(1897) (co-editor) *The Conception of God*, New York: Macmillan.

(1901) *The Limits of Evolution and Other Essays in Philosophy*, New York: Macmillan.

(1904) *Philosophy: Its Fundamental Conceptions and Its Methods*, New York: Macmillan.

Secondary literature:

Bakewell, Charles M. (1949) 'The personalism of George Holmes Howison', *Philosophical Review* 49: 267–76.

Fort, Jr, William E. (1941) 'The personalism of George Holmes Howison', *Personalist* 22: 146–58.

An intellectual of extremely broad scope, intimately related to the St Louis Hegelians, the Concord School of Philosophy, and the Harvard philosophers, Howison found his most sustained connection in founding the Department of Philosophy at the University of California (Berkeley) and its Philosophical Union.

Interpreting the ubiquitous idealism of his day through clues from Aristotle, Leibniz and especially Kant, Howison worked out a position he called Personal Idealism which included the following points: (i) since persons cannot be explained by evolution, persons are eternal; (ii) space-time and its contents (the external world) owe their existence to the 'correlation and coexistence' of minds (1904, p. 128); (iii) evolution is the movement of these external things, empowered by the spontaneous cooperation of the individual minds, towards the goal of a common ideal; (iv) the essential ideal is the attraction of God, influencing all persons by final causation, while the causation of the external world is material, formal and final; (v) harmony with the eternal provides the basis for morality, while the constitutive power of individual minds is the mark of their freedom.

Sources: J. W. Buckham and G. M. Stratton (eds) (1934) *Georges Holmes Howison: Philosopher and Teacher*, Berkeley: Univ. of California Press (biography, bibliography and selections); Reese.

WILLIAM REESE

Hu Shi (Hu Shih)

Chinese. **b:** 1891, Shanghai. **d:** 1962, Nangang, Taiwan. **Cat:** Pragmatist; social, cultural and political thinker; literary historian. **Ints:** Pragmatism; social philosophy. **Educ:** Cornell University and Columbia University, USA. **Infls:** Liang Qichao, John Dewey and Thomas Huxley. **Appts:** 1917–26, Professor of Philosophy, University of Beijing; 1927–30, Professor of Philosophy, Guanghua University, Shanghai; 1928–30, President, China National Institute, Wusong; 1930–1, Head, Compilation and Translation Bureau, China Foundation for the Promotion of Education and Culture, Beijing; 1931–7, Dean, College of Arts, Peking University; 1932–7, Editor, *Independent Critic*; 1938–42, Chinese Ambassador to the United States; 1945, Member, Chinese delegation to the founding United Nations Conference; 1945, Acting Head, Chinese Delegation, first UNESCO Conference; 1945–8, Chancellor, University of Beijing; 1958–62, President, Academia Sinica, Taiwan.

Main publications:

(1919) *An Outline of the History of Chinese Philosophy*, Shanghai: Commercial Press.
(1921) *Collected Essays of Hu Shi*, 2 vols, Shanghai: Yadong Library.
(1922) *The Development of Logical Method in Ancient China*, Shanghai: Oriental Book Company (reprinted New York, Paragon Book Company, 1963).
(1924) *Collected Essays of Hu Shi: Second Collection*, 2 vols, Shanghai: Yadong Library.
(1927) *The Philosophy of Dai Dongyuan*, Shanghai: Commercial Press.
(1928) *A History of Vernacular Literature, I*, Shanghai: Xinyue Bookstore.
(1930) *Selected Works of Hu Shi*, Shanghai: Yadong Library.
(1930) *Collected Essays of Hu Shi: Third Collection*; 4 vols, Shanghai: Yadong Library, 1930.
(1930) *A Collection of Works by the Monk Shenhui*, Shanghai: Yadong Bookstore.
(1930) *Selected Works of Hu Shi*, Shanghai: Yadong Librar.

(1931) *A Book on Huainanzi*, Shanghai: Xinyue Bookstore.
(1933) *A Self-Account at Forty*, Shanghai: Yadong Library.
(1934) *The Chinese Renaissance*, Chicago: University of Chicago Press.
(1935) *Hu Shi's Recent Writings on Scholarship*, Shanghai: Commercial Press.
(1939) *Notebooks of the Hidden Brilliance Study*, 4 vols, Shanghai: Yadong Library.
(1953) *Collected Essays of Hu Shi, Collections: 1–4*, 4 vols, Taipei: Yuandong Publishing Company.
(1953) *Collected Speeches of Hu Shi*, 2 vols, Taipei: Huaguo Publishing House.
(1956) *Biography of Ding Wenjiang*, Taipei: Qiming Book Company.
(1958) *A Short History of China's New Literature Movement*, Taipei: Qiming Book Company.
(1962) *Hu Shi's Correspondence*, Taipei: Shidai Cultural Publishing House.

Secondary literature:

Boorman, H. (ed.) (1970) *Biographical Dictionary of Republican China*, New York and London: Columbia University Press.
Briere, O. (1956) *Fifty Years of Chinese Philosophy 1898–1950*, George Allen & Unwin Ltd.
Chan, W. T. (1956) 'Hu Shih and Chinese philosophy', in *Philosophy East and West* 6, 1.
Complete Chinese Encyclopedia (1987), Philosophy Volumes, Beijing: Chinese Encyclopedia Publications.
Grieder, J. B. (1970) *Hu Shi and the Chinese Renaissance: Liberalism in the Chinese Revolution, 1917–1937*, Cambridge, Mass.: Harvard University Press.
Louie, K. (1986) *Inheriting Tradition: Interpretations of the Classical Philosophers in Communist China, 1949–1966*, Hong Kong: Oxford University Press.

Hu was China's most influential liberal thinker for two decades from 1917, when he returned with a BA from Cornell University and a PhD from Columbia University as a Boxer Indemnity Scholar to become Professor of Philosophy at the University of Beijing. He was drawn to the cautious reformist programme of **Liang Qichao** and to Thomas Huxley's evolutionary viewpoint and sceptical demand for evidence to support any hypothesis. His philosophical, literary and political activities, however, gained their main focus from his commitment to applying the pragmatism or experimentalist methodology of his teacher John **Dewey** to the political and social problems of China. Hu, who interpreted for Dewey when Dewey lectured in China (1919–21), considered that while Huxley taught him to doubt, Dewey taught him to think. Although lacking the depth and originality of some other Chinese philosophers of the century, Hu's integrity and liberal commitment led to great influence.

Hu argued that a proper methodology would lead us to reject any untested dogma or metaphysical claim, however ancient or august its origin or powerful its contemporary advocacy. We should produce bold hypotheses, but every hypothesis should be sceptically tested. We should not be satisfied with vague or abstract claims, but should seek clear definitions of specific concrete problems for experimental solution. Claims could be tested through processes of logical reasoning leading to hypothetical conclusions or solutions. Careful attention to final results would determine whether or not the claims were validated. Soluble problems, therefore, replaced abstract doctrine as the keystone of his method.

In spite of his caution and his resistance to the nationalist and Communist ideological projects which came to dominate China, Hu was an iconoclast who used his scepticism and scientific method to transform the view of China's intellectual and literary past and to construct a framework for political and scholarly activity in the contemporary world. Both aspects were evident in his 1917 article 'Tentative proposals for improvement of literature', which appeared in *New Youth* and initiated the profound and far-reaching *baihua* or vernacular Literary Revolution. Hu argued that the history of Chinese literature was the history of the replacement of outmoded forms by new living forms and that in historical context vernacular literature was the orthodox literature of China. He carried forward his literary studies with later articles, analyses of *The Water Margin* and *The Dream of the Red Chamber* and an unfinished *History of Vernacular Literature*. The Literary Revolution is only the most important feature of Hu's wide-ranging activity as a member of the brilliant and energetic group surrounding *New Youth* at Peking University.

Hu's desire to link analysis of the past with a current agenda is displayed in his doctoral thesis, *The Development of Logical Method in Ancient China* (published in 1922), which formed the basis of his book *An Outline of the History of Chinese Philosophy* (1919). Hu rejected the view that Western scientific civilization was entirely foreign to Chinese intellectual practice. He sought to uncover methodological principles in ancient Chinese philosophical writings to show that at least some aspects of modern experimentalist thought were embodied in Chinese tradition. In

doing so, he rejected standard readings of Confucianism as moralism and daoism as mysticism and elevated Mohist, legalist and logicist writing to the same status as the dominant schools. He argued that *The Book of Changes* was a logical treatise. His own sceptical methodology, using modern Western textual studies for a model, articulated and distinguished a whole range of problems for further debate. In the words of **Chan Wing-tsit**: 'He was the first to give Chinese philosophy a clear outline'. Many later philosophical studies, including those of Qing dynasty thinkers, whom Hu considered to have scientific attitudes, and Buddhists elaborated the thought of these early works.

Hu sought to apply his methodology to the overwhelming problems facing China, but argued that Chinese intellectuals should aim at the gradual improvement of society and culture as a precondition for stable democratic life rather than involve themselves directly in political activity. Tensions with **Chen Duxiu** over the place of politics in *New Youth* led to a rupture of relations when Chen, by then a Communist, moved control of the journal from Beijing. In his article 'Problems and isms' (1919) Hu argued for piecemeal reform dealing with concrete and well-defined problems instead of abstract revolutionary doctrines or reactionary nationalism. His discussions of liberty and individualism, the emancipation of women, the Chinese family system and human rights are examples of his approach.

Hu criticized Liang Qichao, **Liang Souming** and other neotraditionalists who argued that spiritual Chinese civilization was superior to bankrupt Western materialism. In the 1923 debate on 'science versus metaphysics' he supported science and Western culture as necessary for Chinese progress, claiming that the distinction between spiritual and material progress was a false antithesis. He was later a serious critic of the Guomindtang, especially concerning the doctrine of political tutelage and the reactionary party attitude toward reform. In spite of this hostility, Jiang Jieshi appointed him as Chinese Ambassador to the United States (1938–42). Hu returned to China briefly as Chancellor of the University of Beijing, but with Communist victory he returned to the USA and then Taiwan, where he was named President of Academia Sinica. In 1955 he was the object of an organized campaign of denigration in China, incorporating criticism by many leading intellectuals—a negative tribute to his importance. In recent years, Chinese intellectuals could again recognize his seminal role in twentieth-century Chinese thought.

NICHOLAS BUNNIN

Hubbeling, Hubertus Gesinus

Dutch. *b:* 27 November 1925, Djokjakarta, Indonesia. *d:* 7 October 1986, Groningen. *Cat:* Spinozist moral philosopher. *Ints:* Logician; philosopher of religion; ethics. *Educ:* Geography, Groningen University; Theology, Universities of Groningen and Basle. *Infls:* Personal influences included: Van der Leeuw, Jaspers and Brunner; philosophical influences included Spinoza, Wittgenstein and Heymans. *Appts:* Protestant minister, 1954–64; Lecturer in Analytic Philosophy, 1964–67, Professor of Ethics and Philosophy of Religion, 1967, Groningen; President of the society 'Het Spinozahuis', from 1972.

Main publications:

(1957) *Natuur en genade bij Emil Brunner* [Nature and Grace in Emil Brunner], Assen: Van Gorcum (dissertation).

(1964) *Spinoza's Methodology*, Assen: Van Gorcum (second dissertation).

(1966) *Spinoza*, Baarn: Wereldvenster.

(1976) *Denkend geloven* [Thinking Faith], Assen: Van Gorcum.

Hubbeling's philosophy had its starting-point in the conviction that language and logic are more objective than the data of human consciousness, because language and logic are universally accessible. His admiration for Spinoza's philosophy originated in the clear argumentation of this philosopher. He interprets Spinoza as claiming that the laws of logic are the expression of the essence of God. Hubbeling aimed at the explication of the reasonableness of Christian religion and the elaboration of a deontic logic.

WIM VAN DOOREN

Hügel, (Baron) Friedrich von

Austrian-British (from 1914). *b:* 8 May 1852, Florence. *d:* 27 January 1925, London. *Cat:* Philosopher of religion; theologian. *Ints:* Mysticism; Biblical criticism; science. *Educ:* Privately educated. *Infls:* R. Hocking, W. G. Ward, A. Von Reumont, H. Huvelin, L. Duchesne, St Catherine of Genoa and E. Troeltsch. *Appts:* Freelance writer.

Main publications:

(1898) 'La méthode historique en son application à l'étude des documents de l'Hexateuque', *Compte Rendu du IVe Congrès Scientifique Internationale des Catholiques*, II: 231–66.

(1904) *Du Christ Éternel et de nos christologies successives*, La Chapelle-Montigeon: Imprimerie-Librairie de Montligeon.

(1906) *The Papal Commission and the Pentateuch*, C. A. Briggs, London: Longmans.

(1908) *The Mystical Element in Religion as Studied in St Catherine of Genoa and her Friends*, London: Dent.

(1912) *Eternal Life*, Edinburgh: T & T Clark.

(1916) *The German Soul and its Attitudes towards Ethical Christianity*, London: Dent.

(1921–8) *Essays and Addresses on the Philosophy of Religion*, 2 vols, London: Dent.

(1927) *Selected Letters*, ed. B. Holland, London: Dent.

(1928) *Letters from Baron von Hügel to a Niece*, ed. G. Greene, London: Dent (1927).

(1928) *The Life of Prayer*, London: Dent.

(1930) *Some Notes on the Petrine Claims*, London: Sheed & Ward.

(1931) *The Reality of God*, London: Dent.

(1967) (with others) *Au coeur de la crise moderniste*, ed. R. Marlé, Paris: Aubier.

(1981) *The Letters of Baron Friedrich von Hügel and Professor Norman Kemp Smith*, ed. N. K. Smith and L. F. Barman, New York: Fordham University Press.

Secondary literature:

Barmann, L. F. (1972) *Baron Friedrich von Hügel and the Modernist Crisis in England*, Cambridge, Mass.: Cambridge University Press.

Cock, A. A. (1929) 'Friedrich von Hügel and his work', in F. C. Burkitt, *Speculum Religionis*, Oxford: Clarendon.

——(1953) *A Critical Examination of Von Hügel's Philosophy of Religion*, London: H. Rees.

Heaney, J. J. (1969) *The Modernist Crisis: Von Hügel*, London: Chapman.

Dakin, A. H. (1934) *Von Hügel and the Supernatural*, London: SPCK.

Lester-Garland, L. V. (1933) *The Religious Philosophy of Baron F. von Hügel*, London: Dent.

Nédoncelle, M. (1935) *La Pensée religieuse de Friedrich von Hügel*, Paris: Vrin.

O'Connor, F. M. (1967) 'Hügel, Friedrich von', *Catholic Encyclopedia*, New York: McGraw Hill, VII: 187b–188a.

Poulat, E. (1979) *Histoire, dogme et critique dans la crise moderniste*, Tournai: Casterman.

Vidler, A. R. (1970) *A Variety of Catholic Modernists*, Cambridge, Mass.: Cambridge University Press, pp. 110–26.

Whelan, J. P. (1971) *The Spirituality of Friedrich von Hügel*, London: Collins.

An autodidact theologian and philosopher, Hügel was concerned with giving due weight both to modern scholarship and to the transcendence of God. In his early writings his main concern was with modern Biblical scholarship and ecclesiastical handling of it. Although on friendly terms with all the main actors in Catholic and Anglican 'modernism' in the early years of the century, and seen by Vidler (1970) as a principal organizer of the movement, he escaped condemnation by Rome and in later life repudiated modernism. His later writings concerned mysticism and its role in the Christian life, with particular emphasis on the career and ideas of St Catherine of Genoa. He argued for the necessity of a balance between the mystical, the intellectual and the institutional, adhering to the necessity of Papal authority, and possibly to a version of the ontological argument for God's existence. For, him though, God and his existence was given not inferred. Against many of his 'modernist' associates, he insisted on the objective reality of a transcendent God, and on institutional religion as the safeguard of a truly religious temper.

Sources: M. Nédoncelle (1951) *The Life of Baron von Hügel*, London, Dent; M. D. Petr (1937) *Von Hügel and Tyrrell: The Story of a Friendship*, London: Dent; M. de la Bedoyere (1951) *The Life of Baron von Hügel*, London: Dent; DNB 1922–30; A. Houtin and F. Sartiaux (1960) *Alfred Loisy*, Paris: Éditions du CNRS (for E. Poulat's Notice Biobibliographique); J. Steinmann (1962) *Friedrich von Hügel*, Paris: Montaigne.

R. N. D. MARTIN

Husserl, Edmund

German. *b:* 8 April 1859, Prossnitz, Moravia. *d:* 27 April 1938, Freiburg, Germany. *Cat:* Phenomenologist. *Ints:* Epistemology; ontology. *Educ:* Universities of Leipzig, Berlin, Vienna and Halle. *Infls:* Literary influences include Descartes, the British empricists and Kant; personal influences include Franz Brentano and Thomas Masaryk. *Appts:* 1891–1901, Privatdozent, University of Halle; 1906–16, Ordinarius, University of Göttingen; 1916–28, Professor, University of Freiburg.

Main publications:

(1900–1) *Logische Untersuchungen*, Halle (English translation, *Logical Investigations*, trans. J. N. Findlay, London: Routledge, 1970).

(1913) *Ideen zu einer reinen Phänomenologie und phänomenologischen Philosophie*, Tübingen (English translation, *Ideas Pertaining to a Pure Phenomenology and to a Phenomenological Philosophy, First Book*, trans. F. Kersten, Dordrecht: Kluwer, 1982).

(1928) *Phänomenologie des inneren Zeitbewusstseins*, Tübingen (English translation, *The Phenomenology of Internal Time-Consciousness*, trans. J. Churchill, Bloomington: Indiana University Press, 1964).

(1929) *Formale und transzendentale Logik*, Tübingen (English translation, *Formal and Transcendental Logic*, trans. D. Cairns, The Hague: Nijhoff, 1969).

(1950) *Cartesianische Meditationen*, The Hague (English translation, *Cartesian Mediations*, trans. D. Cairns, The Hague: Nijhoff, 1960).

(1954) *Die Krisis der europäischer Wissenschaften und die transzendentale Phänomenologie*, The Hague (English translation, *The Crisis of the European Sciences and Transcendental Phenomenology*, trans. D. Carr, Evanston: Northwestern University Press, 1970).

Secondary literature:

Dreyfus, H. (ed.) (1982) *Husserl, Intentionality and Cognitive Science*, Cambridge: Mass.: MIT Press.

Elliston, F. and McCormack, P. (1977) *Husserl: Expositions and Appraisals*, Notre Dame University Press.

Hammond, M., Howarth, J. and Keat, R. (1991) *Understanding Phenomenology*, Oxford: Blackwell, chapters 1–3.

Heidegger, M. (1985) *History of the Concept of Time*, trans. T. Kisiel, Bloomington: Indiana University Press, pp. 27–126.

Kern, I. (1964) *Husserl und Kant*, The Hague: Nijhoff.

Lauer, Q. (1958) *The Triumph of Subjectivity*, New York: Fordham University Press.

Mohanty, J. N. (1990) *Transcendental Phenomenology*, Oxford: Blackwell.

Smith, D. W. and McIntyre, R. (1982) *Husserl and Intentionality*, Dordrecht: Reidel.

Edmund Husserl, the founder of phenomenology, first came to prominence through the publication of his *Logical Investigations* (1900–1). It was on the basis of this book that the phenomenological movement was formed. The early phenomenologists were most impressed by the call to a return to the things themselves ('Zu den Sachen selbst!') in the sense of giving precedence to how things (material objects but also numbers, institutions, works of art, persons, etc.) present themselves in actual experience over the dictates of some theory or system as to how they must be. Such philosophers were strongly influenced by Husserl's arguments against psychologism, were profoundly realist in outlook and generally exhibited a marked anti-Kantian tendency. It therefore came as something of a shock when Husserl published his next main work, *Ideas Pertaining to a Pure Phenomenology and to a Phenomenological Philosophy* (1913). For this seemed to represent a reversal of all that phenomenology had come to stand for. It was not the idea of arriving at pure consciousness by a process of reduction which was found objectionable. Nor was it the idea of intuiting and describing the essential structures of such consciousness (for according to the phenomenologists everything has its essence). Rather what was found objectionable was the idea that everything else is *constituted* in pure consciousness. This seemed like a capitulation to the neo-Kantians. Thereafter it was no longer possible to speak of a Husserlian school. Husserl himself would continue to insist that the reluctance to follow him in the transcendental direction laid down in his *Ideas* was based on a failure properly to understand the nature of his trancendentalism. In 1916 he moved to Freiburg, where three years later Martin **Heidegger** became his assistant. Husserl had great hopes for Heidegger, seeing in him someone of matchless ability who would continue to develop phenomenology along the lines he, Husserl, had laid down. Although not mistaken about Heidegger's ability, he was mistaken about his identification which his conception of phenomenology. The publication in 1927 of *Being and Time*, and Heidegger's succession to Husserl's Chair a year later, served only to accelerate a process which had been underway for some years: the emergence of Heideggerian phenomenology as the dominant force in German philosophy. As Husserl was Jewish the advent of National Socialism resulted in even greater isolation. But then Husserl always thought of genuine philosophy as an essentially lonely task. He continued to be creative, producing in the last years of his life his monumental *Crisis of the European Sciences* (1954).

In attempting to convey the essential character of Husserl's phenomenology it is perhaps best to begin with the notion of the intentionality of consciousness. Consciousness in its various modes has the property of being 'of' something or being directed towards something. For exam-ple, in thinking something is thought about, in perception something is perceived, in imagining something is imagined, in fear something is feared. Husserl calls these various modes of consciousness intentional experiences or acts. Unlike his teacher **Brentano** he does not regard the object of consciousness as being in all cases an inner mental entity. When I think about a mental image my consciousness is directed towards a mental entity. But when, for example, I see this book on my desk this intentional experience, the seeing, is directed towards a material object. What I am concious of is not an inner mental picture of a book but, precisely, a book. Even when I merely imagine a book it is not the case that my consciousness is directed towards a mental image. Each intentional experience, and not just those which essentially involve the use of language, contains something Husserl calls a sense or meaning (*Sinn*), and it is this which is responsible for the experience's directedness towards its object.

Intentionality is not a property which consciousness just happens to have. Without it consciousness would not be consciousness. It belongs to the *essence* of consciousness. The various modes of consciousness, as well as having the fundamental essential feature of intentionality, also have more specific essential features: for example, perception essentially involves sensation. The sense or meaning of the experience 'animates' sensation in such a way that it becomes an appearance of an object. In perception the object perspectivally adumbrates itself (*schattet sich ab*). The perceptually presented front-side of the object refers beyond itself to the unseen rear-side.

Normally consciousness is directed towards some item in the world and normally this item is regarded as really existing and as really possessing such and such properties. But whether or not the object of consciousness in fact exists, and whether or not it possesses the properties it is intended as having, this mode of consciousness, with this object, exists and can be described by the subject whose consciousness it is. It is possible to describe intentional experiences independently of the question of the real existence and real being-thus of their object. Moreover it is possible to describe the essence of such experiences, the features and structures without which they would not be the experiences they are.

However, even if we disregard the question of the reality of the object of an experience we still regard the experience itself as an event in the world, as belonging to a psycho-physical reality, the human being, which is one item among others in the world. And even when we disregard the question of the reality of a particular object we still take for granted the existence of the world as a whole. This taking-for-granted, which Husserl calls the general thesis of the natural attitude, can be suspended or 'put out of action' in an operation which he calls the transcendental reduction. Consciousness on which this operation has been carried out is not itself an item *in* the world but rather that *for which* there is a world. Phenomenology as the mature Husserl understands it is the description of the essential structures of this transcendental consciousness or subjectivity. These structures are not inferred by any kind of Kantian transcendental argument but are 'seen' by the phenomenological 'observer' in the phenomenological, as opposed to the natural, attitude.

Anything, of whatever ontological type, can be an object of consciousness. In the case of each type of entity phenomenology describes the structures of consciousness *of* such an entity. This includes a description of the entity itself but as object of consciousness, i.e. as phenomenon. In abstraction from questions of real existence and real nature one considers the entity simply as it shows itself to consciousness. Phenomenology also describes the world, as the universal horizon of all that shows itself. The world is not just the totality of objects of consciousness, not just one great big object, but that from within which entities show themselves.

What is the purpose of such description? It is supposed by Husserl to yield ultimate understanding of things. To describe the structures of transcendental consciousness in which something becomes an object of consciousness is to describe the 'constitution' of that thing. The world and everything in it, including human beings, is constituted in transcendental subjectivity. As Husserl uses the term, 'constitution' suggests a kind of making, a bringing into being. It was in this 'creationist' sense that Husserl's transcendental idealism was generally understood—and generally rejected. However, it has recently been argued that such an interpretation is mistaken. What is constituted in consciousness is not things but senses, not the things that consciousness intends but the senses 'through' which it intends them.

In the final phase of his phenomenology Husserl introduces the notion of the lifeworld (*Lebenswelt*), the world of lived experience. What he calls objectivism seeks to eliminate everything subjective from our representation of the world by allowing as real only those aspects of experience which can be represented by means of the concepts of the mathematical natural sciences. Such objectivism dismisses the lifeworld as mere appearance. But this is to call in question the lifeworld from ths standpoint of what is itself a construction formed on the basis of the lifeworld. The properties and structures attributed by the objectifying sciences to the 'objective' world are themselves the product of a process of idealization and mathematization of 'lifeworldly' structures. The task of philosophy is not to downgrade the lifeworld but to remove from it the 'garment of ideas' which science has thrown over it. However, Husserl's emphasis on the lifeworld in his later philosophy does not represent a fundamental change in his conception of phenomenology as transcendental phenomenology. The lifeworld does not represent the ultimate foundation, for it is itself constituted in transcendental subjectivity.

PAUL GORNER

Hyppolite, Jean

French. *b:* 1907. *d:* 1968. *Cat:* Neo-Hegelian. *Infls:* Alexandre Kojève and Jean Wahl. *Appts:* Held various academic posts, including that of Maître de Conférences, Faculty of Letters, University of Strasbourg.

Main publications:

(1939) *Hegel: la Phénoménologie de l'Esprit*, vol. I, Paris: Aubier.
(1941) *Hegel: la Phénoménologie de l'Esprit*, vol. II, Paris: Aubier.
(1947) *Genèse et structure à la Phénoménologie de l'Esprit de Hegel*, Paris: Aubier.
(1948) *Introduction à la philosophie de l'histoire de Hegel*, Paris: Rivière.
(1955) *Études sur Marx et Hegel*, Paris: Rivière (English translation, *Studies on Marx and Hegel*, New York: Basic Books, 1969).

Jean Hyppolite was one of a group of French scholars who contributed to, and worked within, the revival of Hegelian studies in France in the mid-twentieth century. This revival was due to three factors: the rediscovery of some of Hegel's early works, which had been commented on by Wilhelm **Dilthey** and were published in 1907 by Dilthey's former student Herman Nohl; the interest in Marx and his philosophical development; and the courses of lectures given by Alexandre **Kojève** at the École Pratique des Hautes Études between 1933 and 1939. Prior to this renewal of interest, the predominant view of Hegel was, according to Hyppolite, that of a Romantic thinker who merely continued and developed a philosophical tradition begun by Kant and elaborated by Fichte and Schelling. This view was put forward as late as 1946 by R. G. **Collingwood** in *The Idea of History* (Oxford: Clarendon Press). Due partly to the work of Hyppolite and other French Hegelians the dominant interpretation of Hegel is now as the chief philosophical ancestor of Marx, and as one of the seminal influences on existentialism and phenomenology. According to Hyppolite's comparison of Marx and Hegel, Marx's views on labour and alienation are heavily dependent on Hegel's theories.

Hyppolite himself regards Hegel's philosophy of history in both his early and his later works as the key to understanding the whole of his philosophy, and as the reason for his rejection of the tradition of Fichte and Schelling. Hegel sees history as the arena for the progress of objective spirit and reason. He rejected Fichte's theories because of the latter's view that reason was manifested most strongly through the moral life, and Schelling's because he held that the fullest revelation of the absolute was in art.

KATHRYN PLANT

I

Iberico y Rodriguez, Mariano

Peruvian. **b:** 1893. **d:** 1974. **Cat:** Speculative metaphysician. **Ints:** Epistemology; aesthetics. **Infls:** Bergson, Blondel and Klages. **Appts:** Professor of the History of Philosophy, University of San Marcos, Lima (successor there to Deústua).

Main publications:

(1919) *La filosofia de Bergson.*

(1926) *El nuevo absoluto.*

(1929) *El viaje del espíritu.*

(1932) *La unidad dividida.*

(1933) (with Honorio Delgado) *Psicología.*

(1939) *El sentimiento de la vida cósmica.*

(1950) *La aparición. Ensayo sobre el ser y el aparecer*, Lima: Imprenta Santa Maria.

(1958) *Perspectivas sobre 'El Tema del Tiempo'* (essays), Lima: Universidad Nacional Mayor de san Marcos.

(1965) *Estudio sobre la metafora*, Lima: Casa de la Cultura del Peru.

(1969) *El espacio humano*, Lima: Universidad Nacional Mayor de San Marcos.

(1971) *La aparición historica*, Lima: Universidad Nacional Mayor de San Marcos.

Secondary literature:

Homenaje a Mariano Iberico (1973), Lima: Universidad Nacional Mayor de San Marcos.

Iberico's thought is focused on the problems arising from the concepts of one and many, being and appearance. This is evident in his earlier works, where the study of Bergson led him to an endeavour to show the unity of metaphysics and aesthetics, which in his view have a common root. This unity is evident, he argues, in what he terms the sense of cosmic life ('sentimiento de la vida cósmica', cf. 1939). This sense is based on, but transcends, aesthetic experience.

These problems are given their most original treatment in the book of 1950, Iberico's major work. Here he argues that there are three ultimate ontological classes: being, which is being in-itself; appearance; and the reflection of appearance in consciousness. These classes are intimately related in the concrete structure of existence, and mutually imply and give rise to one another. Appearance has generally been regarded as a veil of Maya between the soul and being, an obstacle to be overcome, but for Iberico this view rests on a false understanding of the relation between being and appearance. Appearance is no mere epiphenomenon, but it is itself the mode of being of being, *el modo de ser del ser* (1950, p. 175), the universal language in which being expresses itself. On the question of why being should manifest itself as appearance, Iberico contends that inherent in being is a property of dynamism which has been variously labelled eros or caritas. An understanding of the movement from one to many, however, is not possible for the mind restricted to conceptual thought. Iberico contends that we can achieve an intuitive apprehension of what there is in its primitive authenticity.

ROBERT WILKINSON

Idel, Moshe

Israeli. **b:** 1947, Timisoara, Romania. **Cat:** Philosopher of Jewish mysticism. **Ints:** Kabbalah; comparative religious philosophy; philosophy of language; anthropology. **Educ:** PhD, 1976, Hebrew University. **Infls:** Kabbalistic texts, Renaissance studies, the Jewish mystical tradition, comparative mysticism and Gershom Scholem. **Appts:** Lecturer, Associate Professor, then Professor, of Jewish Mysticism, Hebrew University, Jerusalem; Visiting Professor, Harvard University and the Jewish Theological Seminary of America, 1976.

Main publications:

(1988) *The Mystical Experience in Abraham Abulafia*, trans. J. Chipman, Albany: SUNY Press.

(1988/90) *Kabbalah: New Perspectives*, 2nd ed., New Haven: Yale University Press.

(1988) *Language, Torah and Hermeneutics in Abraham Abulafia*, trans. M. Kallus, Albany: SUNY Press.

(1988) *Studies in Ecstatic Kabbalah*, Albany: SUNY Press.

(1990) *Golem: Jewish Magical and Mystical Traditions on the Artificial Anthropoid*, Albany: SUNY Press.

(1994) *Hasidism: Between Ecstasy and Magic*, Albany: SUNY Press.

Secondary literature:

Handelman, Susan (1991) *Fragments of Redemption: Jewish Thought & Literary Theory in Benjamin, Scholem & Levinas*, Bloomington: Indiana University Press p. 381 (bibliography).

Idel's two books on Abulafia are based on his doctoral thesis. He differs from **Scholem** as to the reasons for the development of mystical and ecstatic traditions within Judaism, emphasising internal and linguistic sources, as well as the political and social. He utilizes every nuance in the Hebrew language, itself possessing a tiny vocabulary and therefore lending itself to multiple interpretations, to explain the sometimes radical attitude to the Jewish tradition of Abulafia. Idel's researches emphasize language-based mysticism and ecstatic Kabbalah. His disagreements with Scholem have led to criticism, especially in Israel, but he is generally highly regarded, especially in America, for his openness to the text itself, utilizing contemporary attitudes to textual analysis rather than the 'dry' German approach inherited by Scholem. Idel also emphasises the importance of the traditional Jewish interpretations, and does not regard research as a purely cerebral activity.

Sources: Moshe Idel.

IRENE LANCASTER

Ilyenkov (Il'enkov), Eval'd Vasil'evich

Russian. *b:* 18 February 1924, Smolensk. *d:* 21 March 1979, Moscow. *Cat:* Marxist dialectical materialist. *Ints:* Dialectics; logic; philosophy of mind; epistemology; history of philosophy. *Educ:* Moscow Institute of Philological and Literary Studies and Moscow University. *Infls:* Hegel, Marx and Lenin. *Appts:* Worked at the Institute of Philosophy of the Soviet Academy of Sciences, 1953–79.

Main publications:

(1960) *Dialektika abstraktnogo i konkretnogo v 'Kapitale' Marksa*, Moscow (English translation, *The Dialectics of the Abstract and the Concrete in Marx's 'Capital'*, trans. Sergei Syrovatkin, Moscow: Progress Publishers, 1982).

(1968) *Ob idolakh i idealakh* [On Idols and Ideals], Moscow.

(1974) *Dialekticheskaia logika: Ocherki istorii i teorii*, Moscow; second, revised edition, 1984 (English translation, *Dialectical Logic: Essays on its History and Theory*, trans. H. Campbell Creighton, Moscow: Progress Publishers, 1977).

(1980) *Leninskaia dialektika i metafizika positivizma*, Moscow (English translation, *Leninist Dialectics and the Metaphysics of Positivism*, London: New Park, 1982).

(1984) *Iskusstvo i kommunistichskii ideal: Izbrannye stat'i po filosofii i estetiki* [Art and the Communist Ideal: Selected Articles in Philosophy and Aesthetics], Moscow.

Secondary literature:

Alekseev, P. V. (ed.) (1993) *Filosofy Rossii xix–xx stoletii* [Russian Philosophers of the 19th–20th Centuries], Moscow, p. 74.

Bakhurst, David (1991) *Consciousness and Revolution in Soviet Philosophy: From the Bolsheviks to Evald Ilyenkov*, Cambridge University Press.

Scanlan, James P. (1985) *Marxism in the USSR: A Critical Survey of Current Soviet Thought*, Cornell University Press.

Ilyenkov was the most influential Soviet interpreter of Marx's dialectical method in the post-Stalin period. His 1960 book *The Dialectics of the Abstract and the Concrete in Marx's 'Capital'* marked a serious return to the writings of Marx (including the young Marx) among Soviet philosophers, and the volume became a kind of handbook for the rising generation.

Ilyenkov regarded Marx's materialist inversion of Hegel's dialectic as constituting a universally valid method of inquiry. Like Hegel, whose thought he greatly admired, he believed that the dialectical method is sound because reality itself has a dialectical structure. Antinomies in thought, such as the paradoxes of motion, reflect genuine contradictions in the dialectical development of being. Hence the law of noncontradiction is false, and formal logic should be replaced by Hegel's more adequate dialectical logic.

Ilyenkov's enthusiasm for the Hegelian dialectic left him open to the charge of idealism, and he devoted considerable attention to developing a supposedly materialist theory of the ideal, based on the Marxian concepts of activity and objectification. This theory did not satisfy his orthodox dialectical materialist critics, however, for it included the thesis that ideal phenomena, although generated by human action, have objective existence once formed, and by accepting interaction between being and consciousness it appeared to reject the Marxian principle that the former determines the latter.

Despite the philosophical sophistication and independence of mind displayed by Ilyenkov in his principal areas of investigation, he accepted the partisan role assigned Soviet philosophers by Marxist–Leninist ideology. Contribution to the communist social ideal was a recurring motif of his writing, expressed least subtly in the posthumously published book, *Leninist Dialectics and the Metaphysics of Positivism* (1980).

JAMES SCANLAN

Ingarden, Roman

Polish. *b:* 5 February 1893, Cracow, Poland. *d:* 14 June 1970, Poronin, near Cracow. *Cat:* Phenomenological philosopher; realist. *Ints:* Ontology, epistemology and philosophy of aesthetics; major contributor to the realism/idealism debate. *Educ:* 1912–17, studied in Germany under Edmund Husserl, first at the University of Göttingen (from 1912) and then at the University of Freiburg im Breisgau (from 1916). *Infls:* Bergson and Husserl. *Appts:* 1924, Privatdozent (unsalaried lecturer), John Casimir University of Lvov (Lemberg) in Poland; 1933, Associate Professor; 1935, Full Professor; 1945–63, Professor, Jagiellonian University, Cracow (from 1949–56, during the Stalinist period, he was forbidden to teach and instead was attached to the Academy of Sciences and Letters where his duties left him considerable free time for his own researches); from 1963, Emeritus Professor at the University of Cracow, and Honorary Professor of the University of Lvov.

Main publications:

(1921) 'Über die Gefahr einer Petitio Principii in der Erkenntnistheorie' [On the danger of a petitio principii in the theory of knowledge], *Jarbuch für Philosophie und Phänomelogische Forschung* 4: 545–68.

(1922) 'Intuition und Intellekt bei Henri Bergson' [Intuition and intellect by Henri Bergson], *Jarhbuch für Philosophie und phänomelogische Forschung* 5: 286–461.

(1925) 'Essentiale Fragen. Ein Beitrag zum Problem des Wesens' [Essential questions. A contribution to the problem of essence], Halle an der Saale: Max Niemeyer.

(1925) *Über die Stellung der Erkenntnistheorie im System der Philosophie* [On the position of theory of knowledge in the system of philosophy], *Jahrbuch für Philosophie und Phänomelogische Forschung* 7.

(1929) 'Bemerkungen zum Problem "Idealismus–Realismus"' [Remarks on the problem 'idealism-realism'], *Jahrbuch für Philosophie und Phänomelogische Forschung* 10.

(1931) *Das literarische Kunstwerk* (original in German), Halle an der Saale: Max Niemeyer (English translation, *The Literary Work of Art*, trans. George G. Grabowicz, Evanston Ill.: Northwest University Press, 1973).

(1937) *The Cognition of the Literary Work of Art* (original in Polish; German translation 1968, English translation, Evanston, Ill.: Northwestern University Press, 1973).

(1946) *O budowie obrazu* [On the Structure of Painting], Cracow: Polish Academy of Sciences.

(1947) *Szkice z filozofii literatury* [Essays on the Philosophical Literature], Lodz.

(1947–8) *Spór o istnienia świata* 2 vols [The Controversy about the Existence of the World] (German translation, 1964/65/74), Cracow: Polish Academy of Sciences.

(1958) *Studia z estetyki* [Studies on Aesthetics] 2 vols, vol. 3, Warsaw: PWN, 1970; reviewed in *Journal of Aesthetics and Art Criticism* (1959) 17 by A.-T. Tymieniecka.

(1962) *Untersuchungen zur Ontologie der Kunst, Musikwerk, Bild, Architektur, Film* [Investigations on the Ontology of Art, Music Work, Pictures, Architecture and Film], Tübingen: Niemeyer.

(1963) *On the Motives which Led Husserl to Transcendental Idealism* (English translation, Dordrecht: Kluwer, 1973–5).

(1966) *Przezycie-dzielo-wartosc* [Experience of Artwork and Value], Cracow: Polish Academy of Sciences. (German translation, 1969).

(1971) *U podstaw teorii poznania* [At the Foundation of the Theory of Knowledge], Cracow: Polish Academy of Sciences.

(1974) *Wstep do fenomenologii Husserla* [Introduction to the Phenomenology of Husserl], Warsaw: PWN.

(1984) *Man and Value*, Washington: Catholic University Press.

(1985) *Roman Ingarden: Selected Papers in Aesthetics*, ed. P. J. McCorkick, Munich: Philosophia, and Washington: Catholic University Press.

(1986) *The Work of Music and the Problem of its Identity*, trans. A. Czerniawski, ed. Jean G. Harrell, Berkeley: University of California Press.

(1986) *Ontology of the Work of Art*, Ohio University Press.

Secondary literature:

'Bibliografia Praz Filosoficznych Romana Ingarden, 1915–1965, Odbitka z Ksiazki R. Ingarden', *Studi z estetyki* T. II, 495–527.

Dzmiemidok, B. and McCormick, P. (eds) (1989) *The Aesthetics of Roman Ingarden: Interpretations and Assessments*, Dordrecht: Kluwer.

Mays, W. *et al.* (eds) *Journal of the British Society for Phenomenology* 6, 2, May (Ingarden issue).

Tymieniecka, A.-T. (1955) 'Le Dessein de la philosophie de Roman Ingarden', in *Revue de Métaphysique et de Morale*: 32–57.

——(1957) *Essence et existence. Étude à propos de la philosophie de Roman Ingarden et Nicolai Hartmann*, Paris.

——(ed.) (1976) *Analecta Husserliana*, vol. 4; 'Ingardeniana', Dordrecht: D. Reidel.

Van Breda, H. L. (1970) 'Professor Roman Ingarden', Obituary, *The Journal of the British Society for Phenomenology* I, 3, October: 100.

Although Ingarden is perhaps best known to English speakers for his philosophy of aesthetics, this needs to be seen within the perspective of his lifelong concern with the problems of epistemology and ontology. In his dissertation on **Bergson**, for example, he interprets such Bergsonian themes as the flux of consciousness and its immediate givens in the light of the phenomenologically based epistemological framework of consciousness, content of consciousness and object of consciousness. His 'Essentiale Fragen' (1925) is likewise a work in which he is concerned to delimit the field of phenomenology by a systematic demonstration of the existence of such objective essences as are implied by 'essential questions' of the type '*What* is x?'. Gilbert **Ryle** reviewed this work sympathetically in *Mind* 36 (1927), although he pointed out that Ingarden admits to being unable to solve the old problem of how an *infima species* (individual essence) can realise itself in concrete individuals.

The alien, neo-Kantian climate of Freiburg brought Ingarden and **Husserl** very close together and, although Ingarden returned to Poland at the end of the First World War and did not see Husserl again until 1927, the two philosophers remained lifelong friends and correspondents. Ingarden perhaps kept in closer touch with Husserl's developing thought than any other of the latter's Göttingen students, but it was always the *objects* of consciousness which preoccupied him and not, as it came to be with Husserl, the intentional analysis of consciousness itself. In his 'Bemerkungen zum Problem "Idealismus–Realismus"' (1929) Ingarden's argument is that it is necessary first to investigate the mode of being of objects before drawing conclusions about their relationship to, and possible dependency upon, consciousness.

Perhaps Ingarden's most original phenomenological work has been in the analysis of various works of art, beginning with his book *The Literary Work of Art* (1931) where, utilizing a theory developed by Alexander Pfänder on the basis of suggestions by Husserl, he first discloses the various strata of intentional constituents which interact to form the 'harmonious polyphony' of each art work. However, Ingarden's interest in the philosophy of art arose out of his concern with the ontological problem of idealism–realism, and *The Literary Work of Art* is actually subtitled *An Investigation on the Borderlines of Ontology, Logic and Theory of Literature*. Ingarden's ontological position in this work is that, since works of art are created by human subjects, they are—and may be perceived to be—ontically *heteronomous* (or dependent) objects. In contradistinction, real objects and the objects of mathematics do not depend upon consciousness. They are self-sufficient or ontically *autonomous*.

Ingarden's *chef-d'oeuvre* is almost certainly his massive, three-volume *Spór o istnienia świata* [The Controversy About the Existence of the World]. Volume I, 'Existential ontology', concerns the modal analysis of real, ideal and possible being. Volume II, 'Formal ontology', has two parts. Part II/1 is called 'Form and Essence' and Part II/2 'World and Consciousness'. These first two volumes are reviewed by Anna-Teresa Tymieniecka in *Mind* 56 (1957). He did not live to complete the culminating Volume III, 'Material ontology', but in 1974 a contribution to it was published posthumously in German called 'On the causal structure of the real world'. The full import of these remarkable volumes has yet to be assessed, but it is clear that Ingarden has done much work towards an ontology based on what is given to consciousness which avoids any recourse to transcendental idealism.

BARRY JONES

Inge, William Ralph

British. *b*: 6 June 1860, Crayke, Yorkshire. *d*: 26 February 1954, Wallingford, Berkshire. *Cat*: Divine; neo-Platonist. *Ints*: Philosophy of religion. *Educ*: King's College, Cambridge. *Infls*: Plotinus. *Appts*: 1888–1905, Fellow and Tutor, Hertford College, Oxford; 1905–11, Vicar of All Saints, Ennismore Gardens, London; 1911–34, Dean of St Paul's Cathedral, London.

Main publications:
(1899) *Christian Mysticism*, London: Methuen.
(1906) *Studies of English Mystics*, London: John Murray.
(1907) *Personal Idealism and Mysticism*, London: Longmans.
(1918) *The Philosophy of Plotinus*, 2 vols, London: Longmans Green.
(1947) *Mysticism in Religion*, London: Hutchinson.

Secondary literature:
Geoghegan, W. D. (1951) *Platonism in Recent Religious Thought*, New York: Columbia University Press.
Helm, R. M. (1962) *The Gloomy Dean: The Thought of William Ralph Inge*, Winston-Salem, NC: Blair.
Matthews, W. R. (1961) in *Dictionary of National Biography*, 1951–60.
Micklem, N. (1963) *Faith and Reason*, London: Duckworth.

Inge made no distinction between philosophy and religion: 'If the perfectly real can alone be perfectly known, and if to know God, the perfectly real Being, is eternal life, the goal of philosophy is the same as the goal of religion—perfect knowledge of the Perfect' (CBP II, p. 191). This perspective explains how he saw in neo-Platonism, and especially in the philosophy of Plotinus, the best way for Christianity to avoid the perils of an arid rationalism, on the one hand, or a flight into irrationalism on the other. Inge's *Christian Mysticism* (1899) was widely read and 'important in that it opened up new ground and had a considerable influence on theological thinking' (Matthews 1971, p. 530). He stimulated a greater interest in mysticism which was reflected in the work of von **Hügel** and Evelyn Underhill.
Sources: A. Fox (1960) *Dean Inge*, London: John Murray; CBP II, pp. 189–211; W. R. Inge (1934) *Vale*, London: Longmans Green.

STUART BROWN

Ingenieros, José
Argentinian. *b:* 1877, Palermo, Sicily. *d:* 1925. *Cat:* Positivist; historian of ideas; moral philosopher; psychiatrist; social psychologist. *Educ:* Began his academic career as a medical student, specializing in psychiatry. *Infls:* Leopoldo Lugones, Manuel Ugarte and José Vasconcelos. *Appts:* Professor of Experimental Psychology, University of Buenos Aires; editor of *Revista de filosofía*, 1915–25.

Main publications:
(1911) *Principios de psicología*.

(1917) *El hombre mediocre*; fifth edition, Buenos Aires: Losada, 1969.
(1917) *Ensayos filosóficos*, Madrid.
(1917) *Hacia una moral sin dogmas: Lecciones sobre Emerson y el eticismo*, Buenos Aires.
(1918–20) *La evolución de las ideas argentinas*, 2 vols.
(1919) *Obras completas*, ed. and annotated by Aníbal Ponce, 21 vols, Buenos Aires.
(1919) *Hacia una moral sin dogmas; lecciones sobre el eticismo*, second edition, Buenos Aires.
(1920) *La psicopatología en el arte*, second edition, Buenos Aires.
(1961) *La evolución de las ideas argentinas*, Buenos Aires: Editorial Futuro.
(1965) *Las fuerzas morales*, second edition, Buenos Aires: Losada.
The following English translations of excerpts of the work of José Ingenieros by Willard Trask appear in Aníbal Sánchez Reulet (ed.) (1954) *Contemporary Latin American Philosophy*, Albuquerque: University of New Mexico Press:
'On an idealism based on experience', pp. 151–2.
'Common sense and good sense', pp. 152–3.
'Virtue and decency', pp. 153–5.
'For a future metaphysics', pp. 156–64.

Secondary literature:
Bagú, Sergio (1936) *Vida ejemplar de José Ingenieros*.
Lipp, Solomon (1969) *Three Argentine Thinkers*.
Van Der Karr, Jane (1977) *José Ingenieros*.

The Ingenieros family, whose original surname was Ingegneros, emigrated to Montevideo and eventually settled in Buenos Aires. Early in his career Ingenieros was attracted to Marxism and joined the Argentine Socialist Party shortly after it was founded. He coedited the socialist journal *La montaña* with writer Leopoldo Lugones in 1897, but the journal was short lived as Ingenieros became more deeply interested in philosophy. He was primarily influenced by positivism and theories of evolution, especially those of **Spencer** and Darwin. In his two-volume history of ideas in Argentina, Ingenieros applies positivist and evolutionary theories to Argentine history in an attempt to explain the tensions between colonial traditions and the forces of progress. His philosophical positions and interests broadened throughout his life. He edited the journal *Revista de filosofía* from 1915 to 1925. Ingenieros remained actively engaged in politics, however, until his death in 1925, the year in which an association called the Unión Latinoamericano was formed with his help to protest against military interventions by the United States in Latin America.

AMY A. OLIVER

Iqbal, M(uhammad)

Indian. *b:* 1876, Sialkot, India. *d:* 1938. *Cat:* Islamic philosopher; poet; politician; Process philosoper; interpreter of Islam. *Ints:* Bergsonianism. *Educ:* Government College, Lahore, then at Cambridge University, completing his doctorate at Munich. *Infls:* Bergson, von Hügel, Nietszche, al-Hallaj and Rumi. *Appts:* Barrister in London; teacher at Government College, Lahore; member of the Punjab Legislative Assembly.

Main publications:

(1908) *The Development of Metaphysics in Iran*, Cambridge.

(1920) *Asrar-i-Khudi*, English translation, *Secrets of the Self*, trans. R. Nicholson, London.

(1934) *Reconstruction of Religious Thought in Islam*, London.

(1948) *Zabur-i Ajam*, English translation, *The Persian Psalms*, trans. A. Arberry, Lahore.

(1953) *Rumuz-i Bi-khudi*, English translation, *Mysteries of Selflessness*, trans. A. Arberry, London.

(1961) *Jawid Nama*, English translation, *Pilgrimage to Eternity*, trans. S. Ahmad, Lahore.

Secondary literature:

Malik, H. (ed.) (1971) *Iqbal: The Poet-Philosopher of Pakistan*, New York.

Muhammad Iqbal played a significant part in developing for Muslims an understanding of their role in the modern world, a role which appeared to many to be one of decline. He listed three reasons for this decline. The first is an excessive concern with mysticism, which he identified with a turning away from contemporary practical and political life. Then there is the loss of the inductive spirirt. The essence of Islam lies in its concentration upon the concrete and the finite, and so long as Islamic science concentrated upon empirical investigation it was successful. Once it abandoned this approach and incorporated the deductive spirit of Greek thought it became static and fell behind European intellectual activity. Finally, the scope for Islam to react to new circumstances and situations had been stultified by the authority of religious law. Islam as a system had become rigid and inelastic, quite out of keeping with the basic principles of the religion which are based upon change and adaptation. What is required, he held, is a philosophy which is capable of restoring

dynamism to the religion, the sort of dynamism which is found in the thought of Jalal al-Din Rumi (1207–73) and Henri **Bergson** (1849–1941). In fact Islam is an essentially dynamic faith, with the emphasis upon actions rather than ideas, and for the religion to be revived it is necessary to reconstruct it along these more appropriate and authentic lines.

Iqbal was attracted to the process philosophers who saw change as the fundamental characteristic of reality, and the universe as unfinished and in need of continual effort to make progress. In line with this approach he does not claim any finality to his particular conclusions, but sees them as part of the process of improvement and emancipation which is so important in the revivification of Islam. Not everything needs to be changed, but what is to remain should not be regarded as rigid or sterile, a mere stubborn rejection of the pressure of other religions and imperial powers. He outlined his thinking using the approach of Hegel and Fichte. God is the supreme self, and human beings attain the highest realms of self of which finite creatures are capable. The world contains a vast variety of different kinds of personalities, which exist in a kind of hierarchy, but the individual self requires the appropriate social environment in which to develop. There is little to be gained by isolation, and it is through participation in society that the self can apprehend and create a notion of purpose in an individual's life.

The self (*khudi*) in Iqbal's thought is the whole of the individual's personality which is receiving and dealing with messages and also responding creatively to them. The construction of the personality is not carried out entirely through the understanding of ideas, but also through continuous practical action. We are free to choose and act, and we can create by directing ourselves to the evolution of moral values through our practice. Movement in history works towards a future which has to be created: there is no point in passively harking back to a distant past.

As a Bergsonian, Iqbal propounded a vitalistic theory in which ultimate reality is neither mental nor physical, but rather a continuous and constantly creative form of activity. Since God is the ultimate reality he is constantly active and creative, and the universe is in a state of everlasting change. As the representatives of God on earth we are provided with infinite responsibilities and possibilities which we must utilize by creating through our efforts a new and better world and fighting against the forces of evil which confront us. The Qur'an emphasizes the ontological reality of change and movement. Existence is life in time, and it is only if we grasp this basic fact about ourselves that we shall be able to orient ourselves properly.

In his political thought Iqbal rejects both capitalism and communism and suggests that Islam represents the ideal state. Such a state has not existed in the past and is not to be identified with any particular region or ethnic group. In such a state the human viceregency of God would be actualized and would acknowledge that the ownership of wealth rests with God, with the implication that our duty is to produce wealth for the benefit of all humanity. Given the absence of the right conditions for such an ideal state, Iqbal agreed with Jinnah on the necessity of the creation of an independent Islamic state such as Pakistan was to be. Iqbal managed to combine action and thought in his own life in the sort of way suggested by his philosophy, and he has come to have considerable influence throughout the Islamic world. In part this is due to the attractive and dramatic style in which he wrote, frequently poetically, in Urdu, Persian and English. His attempt at combining traditional Islamic philosophy with modern European thought produces an interesting and exciting amalgam of ideas, and the emphasis upon practice helps to make his thought more accessible than it might otherwise have become had it been entirely theoretical. His poetry in particular has had a wide effect on those who would not normally respond to philosophy. His connection with the campaign for Pakistan, and his description of the malaise of contemporary Islamic thought, has struck a deep chord throughout the Islamic world, and has continued to be much respected and discussed.

Sources: C. Qadir (1988) *Philosophy and Science in the Islamic World*, London: Routledge; A. Ahmad (1970) *Islamic Modernism in India and Pakistan 1857–1964*, London: OUP; EncIslam, 2nd edn.

OLIVER LEAMAN

Irigaray, Luce

Belgian with French nationality. *b:* Either 1930 or 1932, Blaton, Belgium. *Cat:* Feminist philosopher; psychoanalyst. *Educ:* University of Louvain, the University of Paris and the Paris Institute of Psychology; trained as a psychoanalyst with the École Freudienne de Paris. *Infls:* Freud, Lacan, Derrida, Hegel, Nietzsche and Heidegger. *Appts:* Taught sixth-formers in Belgium, 1956–9; attached to the Centre National de Recherches Scientifiques in Paris since 1964; Lecturer, University of Paris VIII (Vincennes) 1969–74; Lecturer, École des Hautes Études en Sciences Sociales, since 1985; attached to the International College of Philosophy in Paris since 1987.

Main publications:
(1973) *Le Langage des déments*, Paris: Mouton.
(1974) *Speculum of the Other Woman*; Ithaca, NY: Cornell University Press, 1985.
(1977) *This Sex Which Is Not One*; Ithaca, NY: Cornell University Press, 1985.
(1980) *Marine Lover of Friedrich Nietzsche*; Columbia University Press, 1991.
(1981) *Le Corps-à-corps avec la mère*, Éditions de la pleine lune.
(1982) *Elemental Passions*, Athlone.
(1983) *L'Oubli de l'air. Chez Martin Heidegger*, Minuit.
(1984) *An Ethics of Sexual Difference*; Ithaca, NY: Cornell University Press, 1993.
(1985) *Parler n'est jamais neutre*, Minuit.
(1987) *Sexes and Genealogies*; Columbia University Press, 1993.
(1989) *Thinming the Difference: For a Peaceful Revolution*; Athlone, 1994.
(1990) *Je, Tu, Nous: Towards a Culture of Difference*; Routledge, 1993.
(1991) *The Irigaray Reader*, ed. Margaret Whitford, Oxford: Blackwell (provides a selection of extracts).
(1992) *J'aime à toi*, Grasset.
(1994) *Essere due*, Editore Bollati Boringhieri.
(1994) *La Democrazia comincia a due*, Editore Bollati Boringhieri.

Secondary literature:
Burke, Carolyn, Schor, Naomi and Whitford, Margaret (eds) (1994) *Engaging with Irigaray*, Columbia University Press (includes a wide range of critical accounts).
Grosz, Elizabeth (1989) *Sexual Subversions*, Sydney: Allen & Unwin, chapters 4 and 5.
Whitford, Margaret (1991) *Luce Irigaray: Philosophy in the Feminine*, Routledge (includes an ample bibliography of primary and secondary texts).

Irigaray was initially attracted to literature, writing her master's thesis on the poet Paul **Valéry**, whose work privileges consciousness and reflexivity. It was not until she left Belgium for Paris, where she undertook a diploma in psychopathology and began training as a psychoanalyst, that she turned her attention to the unconscious, and in particular to the notion of a cultural unconscious (or cultural 'imaginary' as it has come to be called). She was analysed by Serge Leclaire, one of the original members of **Lacan's**

École Freudienne, and until the publication of *Speculum* in 1974 seems to have been uncontroversially Lacanian.

Speculum fused a psychoanalytic attention to what is repressed by culture with a Derridean-inspired account of the repressions required by metaphysics. In both cases, Irigaray argues, the feminine is excluded. She concludes that 'woman' does not yet exist in the cultural imaginary of the West; that Western culture is founded on an originary matricide more ancient than the parricide of **Freud**'s *Totem and Taboo*. The feminist critique contained in *Speculum* led to Irigaray's expulsion from the Lacanian School of Psycho-analysis at Vincennes and launched her on her public career as feminist and philosopher of sexual difference.

Her subsequent work has explored the question of sexual difference in three areas in particular. First, she has looked for the forgotten woman in the history of philosophy; second, she has examined the sexual bias in language; third, she has considered the issues of women's civil status and rights. Along with Hélène Cixous and Julia **Kristeva**, Irigaray is probably one of the best-known representatives of French feminism in Europe, the USA and Australasia. Her international reputation, however, is often based on a misapprehension of her thought. She has been well understood and influential in countries like Holland and Italy which have a strong tradition in continental philosophy, but has so far had no significant effect on philosophy in Britain, where her work has been appreciated predominantly by literary critics.

Sources: CV supplied by Luce Irigaray.

MARGARET WHITFORD

Ivekovič, Rada

Croatian. *b:* 1945, Zagreb (former Yugoslavia). *Cat:* Feminist philosopher. *Ints:* Indian philosophy; postmodern philosophy; feminist theory and the feminist movement; problems of nationalism. *Educ:* University of Zagreb (Philosophy, Indology and Liteature), and Buddhist philosophy in India (from 1970 to 1973, and again in 1987). *Infls:* Indian thought and philosophy, French postmodern philosophy (Irigaray, Lyotard) and feminist movement in the former Yugoslavia. *Appts:* Professor of Philosophy, University of Zagreb; Lecturer, Université Européenne d'Été, Paris, France; Visiting Lecturer, University of Graz.

Main publications:

(1977) *Rana budistička misao* [Early Buddhist Thought].

(1980) (with Cedomil Veljačic: *Indijska i iranska etica* [Indian and Iranian Ethics].

(1981) *Počeci indijske misli* [The Beginnings of Indian Thought].

(1981) *Pregled indijske filizofije* [A Survey of Indian Philosophy].

(1981) (ed.) *Studije o ženi i ženski pokret* [Women's Studies and the Feminist Movement].

(1982) *Druga Indija* [Another India].

(1986) (with B. Bogdanovic:) *EEJI–Epistolarni eseji* [Essays in Letter-form].

(1986) 'Prazno mjesto drugoga / druge u postmodernoj misli' [The empty place/Space of the other in postmodernist thought] in *Postmoderna, Nova epoha ili zabluda?* [Postmodernism, a New Era or an Error?], Zagreb: Naprijed.

(1986) 'Sudbina "Slabog" subjekta i kritika 'post-ajanja-ženom' [The fate of the 'weak' subject and critique of 'becoming a woman'], *Knjizevnost* 8, 9.

(1986) 'Primijenjena filozofija i prizivanje drugoga' [Applied philosophy and the naming of the other] *Filozofska istraživanja* [Philosophical Research] 16.

(1986/7) 'Jedna filozofska izložba' [A philosophical display], *Gordogan* 20.

(1987) 'Le temps dans la tradition indienne et la conception postmoderne' [Time in the Indian tradition and the postmodern concept], *Synthesis Philosophica* 3.

(1989) *India–Fragmenti osamdesetih. Filozofija i srodne discipline* [India–Fragments of the Eighties. Philosophy and Related Disciplines].

(1990) 'Die Postmoderne und das Weibliche in der Philosophie' [Postmodernism and the feminine in philosophy] in Herta Nagl-Docekal (ed.) *Feministische Philosophie*, Vienna: Oldenbourg.

(1990) 'Benares: Esej iz Indije' [Benares: an Essay from India], Zagreb: Graficki zavod Hrvatske.

(1992) 'Intellektuelle zwischen Nationalismus und Demokratie' [Intellectuals between nationalism and democracy] in *Proceedings of the Conferences 'Nation und Vernunft' (Graz, 6–7 November 1992) and 'Nation et raison' (Ljubljana, 5–7 November 1992)*.

(1993) 'Marginal reflections on war in Europe' *Temps modernes* 49, 563: 166–83.

(1993) 'The European war in 1992: the case of Yugoslavia', *History of European Ideas* 17, 4: 415–26.

(1993) 'Jugoslawischer Salat' [Yugoslavian salad], in *Reihe essay*, no. 19, Graz, Vienna: Verlag Droschl.

(1993) 'Kroatische Freiheit heute' [Croatian freedom today], *Literatur und Kritik* 273–4: 107–8.

Rada Ivekovič: uses her education in Indian philosophy to compare current postmodernist concepts with traditional Indian thought. Her feminist perspective grants a critical distance to both schools of thought. She is critical about a postmodernist rejection of the notion of the 'subject' or the 'devenir femme' project of (male) postmodernist thinkers; in her view, arguing away the subject cannot help feminist intentions.

Currently Ivekovič: is concerned with the issues of nationalism and nationhood, and with violence as a result of nationalistic tendencies in the former Yugoslavia.

URSULA STICKLER

Izmirli, I(smail) Hakk

Turkish. *b:* 1868, Izmir, Turkey. *d:* 1 February, 1946, Ankara. *Cat:* Theologian and philosopher of religion. *Ints: Kalam*; Sufism; logic; Islamic jurisprudence. *Educ:* Educated in a traditional way in *madrasa*, 1880–91, in Izmir; studied at Daru-al-Muallimin Aliye, 1892–4, in Istanbul. *Infls:* Descartes, Malebranche, Ibn al-Taymiyyah, Muhammad al-Ghazzali and Abu Mansur al-Maturidi. *Appts:* Taught Theology, Islamic History, the Methodology of Islamic Jurisprudence, Philosophy and History of Philosophy at Istanbul University, 1915–39.

Main publications:

(1911) *Imi Mantk* [The Science of Logic], Istanbul.
(1913) *Arab Felsefesi* [The Philosophy of Arabs], Istanbul.
(1913) *Philosophie première*, Istanbul.
(1914) *Felsefe Desleri* [Lectures on Philosophy], Istanbul.

(1917) *Mu'htasar Ma Ba'da al-Tabia* [On Metaphysics], Istanbul.
(1922) *Ebu Bakr Razi ve Felsefesi* [Abu Bakr Razi and His Philosophy], Istanbul.
(1922) *Ihvan Safa Felsefesi* [Philosophy of Ihwan al-Safa], Istanbul.
(1923–4) *Yeni Ilmi Kalam* [A New Science of Kalam], 2 vols, Istanbul.
(1924) *Islam Felsefesi Tarihi* [The History of Islamic Philosophy], Istanbul.
(1926) *Arab Filozofu Yakub al-Kindi* [Yaqub-al-Kindi: An Arab Philosopher], Istanbul.
(1936) *Müslüman Türk Filozoflar* [Muslim-Turkish Philosophers], Istanbul.

The collapse of the Ottoman Empire and the hegemony of Western thought in Turkey were two major determinants of Izmirli's philosophy. He was a prominent representative of that group of intellectuals named Islamicists, and endeavoured to confront Western cultural supremacy with the power of Islamic ideas, arguing that Muslims have to develop a new science of *Kalam* (Islamic theology), capable of responding to Western thought from the Islamic point of view. He was fluent in many languages including Arabic, Persian, French, Russian, Greek and Latin. Izmirli was influential in the intellectual resurgence of Islam in Turkey and his writings are important sources for the student of Islam. His book *A New Science of Kalam* (1923–4) was extensively used as a textbook in the theology faculties in Turkey.

Sources: Ismail Kara (1987) *Türkiye'de islamcilik Düsüncesi* [The Thought of 'Islamism' in Turkey], Istanbul: Risale.

ADNAN ASLAN

J

Jabès, Edmond

French, of Italian-Jewish parents. **b:** 1912, Cairo. **d:** 2 January 1991, Paris. **Cat:** Stockbroker; author; existentialist; philosopher of language. **Ints:** Literary theory and Judaisim; the Jew as 'other'. **Educ:** Paris. **Infls:** Surrealism; his own role in the French Resistance and his nomadic life. **Appts:** Participated in French Resistance, 1939; fled to Egypt, working as stockbroker and writing for surrealist periodicals; after Suez Crisis returned to France, 1957.

Main publications:

(1973) *El, ou Le Dernier Livre*, Paris: Gallimard.
(1976–84) *The Book of Questions*, trans. Rosemarie Waldrop, 7 vols, Middeletown: Wesleyan University Press; originally published as *Le livre des questions*, 1963.
(1976) *Le Livre des Ressemblances*, Paris: Gallimard.
(1965; 1965–72) *Le Retour au Livre*, 3 vols, Paris: Gallimard.
(1978) *Le Soupçon, Le Désert*, Paris: Gallimard.
(1991) *From the Book to the Book, an Edmond Jabès Reader*, trans. Rosmarie Waldrop *et al.*, Hanover, NH: University Press of New England.

Secondary literature:

(1989) *Écrire le Livre* (conference proceedings), Seyssel, Champ Vallon.
Blachot, Maurice (1969) *L'entretien infini*, Paris: Gallimard.
Caws, M. A. (1988) *Edmond Jabès*, Amsterdam: Rodopi.
Derrida, Jacques (1978) 'Edmond Jabès and the question of the book', in *Writing and Difference*, trans. A. Bass, Chicago: University of Chicago Press, pp. 64–78 (French original, *L'Écriture et la Différence*).
Handelman, Susan (1991) *Fragments of Redemption*, Bloomington: Indiana University Press (bibliography, p. 370).
Hoffman, A. G. (1991) *Between Exile and Return*, Albany: SUNY Press.
Laifer, M. (1986) *Edmond Jabès*, New York: P. Lang.

The aim of Jabès' work (often written in the form of poems or other non-philosophical genres) is to define Judaism in terms of the written word, or text. He even states that to write is to be Jewish, Judaism being an allegory of the 'difference', or 'exile', experienced by the writer. Like **Derrida** and **Levinas** he combines various literary devices and subjects to form one piece, juxtaposing phrases culled from Jewish tradition with those from literary and philosophical sources. He has been commented on in a variety of countries and languages, two of the most impressive interpretations being by Derrida and Maurice **Blanchot**.
Sources: Schoeps; NUC; *CPBI*.

IRENE LANCASTER

Jackson, Frank Cameron

Australian. **b:** 31 August 1943, Melbourne. **Cat:** Analytic philosopher. **Ints:** Philosophical logic; cognitive science; epistemology; metaphysics; meta-ethics. **Educ:** Melbourne University and La Trobe University. **Infls:** A. C. Jackson, D. M. Armstrong, J. J. C. Smart and M. C. Bradley. **Appts:** 1967, Temporary Lecturer in Philosophy, University of Adelaide; 1968–77, Lecturer, then Senior Lecturer, then Reader, La Trobe University; 1978–86, Professor of Philosophy, Monash University; 1986–90 and 1993–, Professor of Philosophy, Research School of Social Sciences, Australian National University; 1991–2, Professor of Philosophy, Monash University; 1992–, Professor of Philosophy, R.S.S.S., Australian National University, 1994–5, John Locke Lecturer in Philosophy, University of Oxford.

Main publications:

(1974) 'Defining the autonomy of ethics', *Philosophical Review* 83: 89–96.
(1976) 'The existence of mental objects', *American Philosophical Quarterly* 13: 33–40.
(1977) *Perception: A Representative Theory*, Cambridge: Cambridge University Press.
(1982) 'Epiphenomenal qualia', *Philosophical Quarterly* 32: 127–36.
(1986) 'What Mary didn't know', *Journal of Philosophy* 83: 291–5; with Postscript in P. Moser and J. Trout (eds), *Contemporary Materialism*, London: Routledge, 1995.

(1987) *Conditionals*, Oxford: Blackwell.

(1988) (with Philip Pettit) 'Functionalism and broad content', *Mind* 97: 381–400.

(1991) (ed.)*Conditionals*, Oxford: Oxford University Press.

(1991) 'Decision theoretic consequentialism and the nearest and dearest objection', *Ethics* 101: 461–82.

Secondary literature:

Horgan, T. (1984) 'Jackson on physical information and qualia', *Philosophical Quarterly* 34: 147-52.

The son of a philosopher, A. C. Jackson (who attended **Wittgenstein**'s classes in Cambridge), Frank Jackson has been, since the 1970s a leading figure among a band of philosophers who have kept alive the strong philosophical tradition in Australia. His first book put up a characteristically powerful defence of the unfashionable representative theory of perception—and against the adverbial version of a direct theory—without invoking the usual argument from illusion. Physical objects are seen 'in virtue of' the direct seeing of mental objects (sense data). (He has, however, since abandoned the sense-datum theory he there defended.)

Jackson is also widely known as a self-confessed 'qualia freak', advancing the so-called knowledge argument in favour of, for example, colour-qualia, and (potentially) against physicalism. Mary, who has lived all her life in a black-and-white room with a black-and-white TV, has learned all there is to know scientifically about colours, but there is something crucial she does not yet know: what it is like to experience colours.

An interest largely independent of philosophy of mind has been in conditionals, on which Jackson has worked for two decades. He has defended a theory of indicative conditionals which he calls a 'supplemented equivalence theory', whereby the data of ordinary usage is taken to support an explanation in terms of equivalence to material conditionals, together with various conditions of assertion, including the probability of the consequent given the truth of the antecedent.

Sources: IWW, 57th edn, 1993–4; brief letter and CV.

CLIVE BORST

Jaggar (née Hayes), Alison Mary

British. *b:* 23 September 1942, Sheffield. *Cat:* Moral philosopher; social and political philosopher; pioneering feminist philosopher. *Ints:* Feminism. *Educ:* Bedford College, London, BA 1964; Edinburgh, MLitt 1967; State University of New York at Buffalo, PhD 1970. *Infls:* Members of Society for Women in Philosophy. *Appts:* Taught at SUNY at Buffalo (part-time), 1968–70; Miami University, 1970–2; Cincinnati, 1972–91 (Full Professor of Philosophy, 1982, Obed J. Wilson Professor of Ethics and Professor of Philosophy, 1984–91); Professor of Philosophy and Women's Studies, University of Colorado at Boulder, from 1990; Visiting Professor, University of Illinois at Chicago, 1975, and UCLA, 1980; first occupant of the Laurie New Jersey Chair in Women's Studies and Visiting Professor of Philosophy, Rutgers University, 1984–5; many Taft grants-in-aid of research and University Research Council awards, Cincinnati, 1972–90; American Association of University Women Dorothy Bridgman Atkinson Endowed Fellowship, 1976–7; National Endowment for the Huamnities Fellowship, 1980–1; Fellow of Institute for Advanced Studies in the Humanities, Edinburgh, 1989; Rockefeller Foundation Fellow, 1990; Founding Member of the Society for Women in Philosophy (SWIP), USA; Chair of the American Philosophical Association Committee on the Status of Women, 1986–91.

Main publications:

(1977) 'Political philosophies of women's liberation', in M. Vetterling Braggin, F. Elliston and J. English (eds), *Feminism and Philosophy*, Totowa, NJ: Littlefield & Adams; reprinted widely.

(1978) (ed. with Paula Rothenberg) *Feminist Frameworks: Alternative Theoretical Accounts of the Relations between Women and Men*, New York: McGraw-Hill; reprinted 1984, 1993.

(1983) *Feminist Politics and Human Nature*, Totowa, NJ: Rowman & Allanheld; Brighton: Harvester.

(1989) 'Love and knowledge: emotion in feminist epistemology', *Inquiry* 32; reprinted in *Gender/Body/Knowledge: Feminist Reconstructions of Being and Knowing* (with Susan Bordo), New Brunswick, NJ: Rutgers University Press, 1989; reprinted widely.

(1991) 'Feminist ethics: projects, problems, prospects', in C. Card (ed.) *Feminist Ethics*, Lawrence: University Press of Kansas; first published in H. Nagl-Docekal and H. Pauer-Studer (eds), *Denken der Geschlechterdifferenz: Neue Fragen und Perspecktiven der feministischen Philosophie*, Vienna: Wiener Frauenverlag, 1990 (Czech translation, Czechoslovak *Journal of Philosophy*, 1992).

(1992) 'Feminist ethics', in L. C. Becker (ed.), *Encyclopedia of Ethics*, New York and London: Garland.

(1993) (ed.) *Living with Contradictions: Ethical Controversies in Contemporary Feminism*, Boulder: Westview.

Secondary literature:
Grimshaw, J. (1986) *Feminist Philosophers: Women's Perspectives on Philosophical Traditions*, Brighton: Harvester Wheatsheaf; titled *Philosophy and Feminist Thinking*, Minneapolis: University of Minnesota Press, 1986.

Held, V. (1993) *Feminist Morality: Transforming Culture, Society, and Politics*, Chicago: University of Chicago Press.

Okin, S. (1985) Review of *Feminist Politics, Ethics* 95.

Young, I. M. (1985) 'Humanism, gynocentrism and feminist politics', *Women's Studies International Forum* 8.

Jaggar pioneered feminist philosophy in America (teaching the first feminist philosophy course in 1971, and setting the agenda for feminist debate (1977)) and has emerged as one of the leading feminist philosophers today. Her *Feminist Politics and Human Nature* (1983) is a lucid, illuminating and systematic analysis of the development of four strands of contemporary feminist political theory: liberal feminism, traditional Marxism, radical feminism and socialist feminism. Jaggar shows how feminism redefines political philosophy not only by extending its domain, but also by transforming its central questions. The book is a standard resource and text for feminist philosophy courses and an influential, rigorously argued defence of socialist feminism.

Turning her attention to moral philosophy, Jaggar (1991) provides a concise overview of the development of feminist ethics in the USA and a delineation of its main themes. She argues convincingly that a focus on male bias in the philosophical canon rather than on masculinity and femininity will more likely 'produce the results that are not only textually defensible but also philosophically interesting and politically significant' (p. 90). Further, she demonstrates how feminist ethics illuminates with special clarity problems in moral epistemology and suggests theoretical as well as practical parameters for developing a feminist moral epistemology. She is developing her ideas in a book *A Feminist Version of Discourse Ethics* and is coeditor with Iris Young of the Blackwell *Companion to Feminist Philosophy*.
Sources: *PI*; *AHCI*; personal communication.

PATRICIA SCALTSAS

Jakobson, Roman Osipovich

Russian-American. **b:** 11 October 1896, Moscow. **d:** 18 July 1982, Boston, Massachusetts. **Cat:** Linguistic theorist; Slavic-language scholar. **Ints:** Structural linguistics; folklore; ethnology; poetics. **Educ:** Universities of Moscow and Prague. **Infls:** Nikolay S. Trubetskoi, Saussure, E. Sapir, S. I. Karcevskij, Victor Shklovsky and Ernst Cassirer. **Appts:** 1933–9, Professor of Philology and of Czech Medieval Literature, Masaryk University in Brno; 1943–9, Professor of Czechoslovak Studies, Columbia University; 1949–67, Professor of Slavic Languages and Literature and General Linguistics, Harvard University and (from 1957) Massachusetts Institute of Technology.

Main publications:
(1962–82) *Selected Writings*, 6 vols, The Hague: Mouton:
Vol. 1, *Phonological Studies*, 1962, expanded 1971.
Vol. 2, *Word and Language*, 1971.
Vol. 3, *The Grammar of Poetry and the Poetry of Grammar*, 1978.
Vol. 4, *Slavic Epic Studies*, 1966.
Vol. 5, *Verse: Its Masters and Explorers*, 1979.
Vol. 6, *Early Slavic Paths and Crossroads*, 1982.

Secondary literature:
Armstrong, D. and Van Schoonveld, C. H. (eds) (1977) *Roman Jakobson: Echoes of His Scholarship*, Lisse: Peter de Ridder Press.
Holenstein, Elmar (1974) *Jakobson ou le structuralisme phénoménologique*, Paris: Seghers.

Jackobson was one of the most important linguistic theorists and Slavic scholars of the twentieth century. He was a principal founder of the European movement in 'structural' linguistics known as the Moscow Linguistic Circle (1915) and the Prague Linguistic Circle (1926). After the Nazi invasion of Czechoslovakia in 1939 Jakobson fled to Scandinavia then, in 1941, emigrated to the USA on the same boat as another prominent thinker in exile, Ernst Cassirer.

Jakobson was concerned with 'the elucidation of linguistic problems of both practical and poetic language as well as questions of folklore and ethnology' (*Selected Writings*, vol. 2, p. 531). His researches soon led him to conclude, as against the then prevalent doctrine of invariant phonetic laws, that each language has its own system of phonemes (distinct sounds) and cannot be subsumed under a uniform and rigid scheme. Further, again contrary to almost all previous phonetic theories, he contended that a phoneme is not a further undecomposable entity but a complex of binary distinctive features, such that it is the feature composition of the different phonemes that determines their function in different languages (vol. 1, pp. 272–9). Jakobson elaborated and applied these ideas in an extraordinarily wide range of studies. His work was crucial to the development not only of structuralism in linguistics, but also of structuralism in social science (**Lévi-Strauss**) and structuralism in literary criticism. The 'generative phonology' of **Chomsky** and others was also directly influenced by Jakobson.

Sources: Wintle; Huisman; Bullock & Woodings; EF.

STEPHEN MOLLER

James, William

American. *b:* 1 January 1842, New York City. *d:* 26 August 1910, Chocorua, New Hampshire. *Cat:* Psychologist; pragmatist. *Ints:* Philosophy of religion. *Educ:* University of Geneva, 1859–60; Harvard University, 1861–7; University of Berlin, 1867–8; Harvard University, 1868–9, MD 1869. *Infls:* Renouvier and Peirce. *Appts:* 1872–80, Instructor, 1880–5, Assistant Professor, 1885–1907, Professor of Psychology and Philosophy, Harvard University.

Main publications:

(1975–90) *The Works of William James*, ed. F. H. Burkhardt, F. Bowers and I. K. Skrupselis, 21 vols, Cambridge, Mass.: Harvard University Press (cited below as *WWJ*).

(1890) *The Principles of Psychology*, 2 vols, New York: Henry Holt; reprinted in 3 vols in *WWJ*, 1981.

(1892) *Psychology, Briefer Course*, New York: Henry Holt; reprinted in *WWJ*, 1984.

(1897) *The Will to Believe and Other Essays*, New York: Longmans, Green & Co.; reprinted in *WWJ*, 1979.

(1898) *Human Immortality: Two Supposed Objections*; second edition, Boston: Houghton Mifflin, 1899; reprinted in *WWJ*, 1986.

(1899) *Talks to Teachers on Psychology: and to Students on Some of Life's Ideals*, New York: Henry Holt & Company; reprinted in *WWJ*, 1983.

(1903) *The Varieties of Religious Experience: A Study of Human Behaviour*, New York: Longmans, Green & Co.; reprinted in *WWJ*, 1985.

(1907) *Pragmatism*, New York: Longmans, Green & Co.; reprinted in *WWJ*, 1975.

(1909) *The Meaning of Truth: A Sequel to 'Pragmatism'*, New York: Longmans, Green & Co.; reprinted in *WWJ*, 1975.

(1909) *A Pluralistic Universe*, New York: Longmans, Green & Co.; reprinted in *WWJ*, 1975.

(1911) *Some Problems of Philosophy: A Beginning of an Introduction to Philosophy*, prepared for press by H. M. Kallen and edited by H. James, Jr, New York: Longmans, Green & Co.; reprinted in *WWJ*, 1979.

(1912) *Essays in Radical Empiricism*, ed. R. B. Perry, New York: Longmans, Green & Co.; reprinted in *WWJ*, 1979.

Secondary literature:

Allen, G. W. (1967) *William James: A Biography*, New York: Viking.

Myers, G. E. (1987) *William James: His Life and Thought*, New Haven: Yale University Press.

Perry, R. B. (1935) *The Thought and Character of William James*, 2 vols, Boston: Little, Brown.

Reck, A. J. (1967) *Introduction to William James*, Bloomington: Indiana University Press.

Seigfried, C. H. (1990) *William James's Radical Reconstruction of Philosophy*, Albany: SUNY Press.

William James was the son of Henry, an eminent transcendentalist writer and lecturer, and the younger brother of Henry, the famous novelist. Educated informally in Europe as a child, and after a brief period in Newport, Rhode Island, preparing to become a portrait artist, James enrolled in Harvard. He interrupted his formal education to participate in the scientific expedition to the Amazon led by Louis Agassiz and also to study in Europe. Hobbled by poor health and psychological depression in his youth, James credited the writings of the French philosopher Charles **Renouvier** for releasing him from depression by providing the formula of choosing or willing to be free. In 1876 he established one of the first psychology laboratories in the United States at Harvard. His comprehensive work *The Principles of Psychology* (1890) won him international fame. In the Preface James announced the intention of establishing psychology as a natural science. Incorporating the findings and theories of the experimental psychologists, primarily German, the *Principles* also drew upon the entire history of introspective psychology, primarily British. Thus James's psychology contains two strands. One is based in biology, revolutionized by Darwinian evolution; it is amenable to experimental investigations of physiology and behaviour. Consciousness is conceived to be a function of the biological organism dependent on the brain, instrumental to the organism's coping with its environment and struggling to realize its purposes. The other strand, based on the intro- spective method, renovated associationist psy- chology by describing consciousness as a stream of feelings and ideas. The 'stream of conscious- ness' concept spread to literature, manifest in the writings, for example, of Gertrude Stein, who had been James's student. In psychology James's influence was profound; it promoted the estab- lishment of experimental methods. In philosophy it influenced **Dewey**'s shift from Hegelianism to instrumentalism and contributed to **Husserl** some of the terminology and insights for phenomenol- ogy. James's interest in philosophy preceded and paralleled his interest in psychology. His earliest papers discussed the sentiment of rationality, the dilemma of determinism, the moral philosopher and the moral life. In 'The will to believe' (in 1897) James argued for the right to hold religious and moral beliefs even when logical or factual evidence is unavailable. If the option for belief in an hypothesis is live, forced and momen- tous—that is, if believing it will make a major difference in life—then, assuming it is compatible with logic and the facts, our passional, volitional nature should seize belief despite the absence of evidence. Religious belief, James contended, contains two propositions: (i) that God guaran- tees the everlastingness of ideals and values cherished by humans; and (ii) that the belief in (i) encourages humans to make a better world, enhancing the survival and triumph of these ideals and values. James's interest in religion was long- standing. In filial devotion to his father's memory James had edited, with a long introductory essay, *The Literary Remains of the Late Henry James* (Boston: James R. Osgood & Company, 1885). But where the father philosophized, drawing upon transcendentalism and Swedenborg's mys- tical theology, the son psychologized, relying on empirical reports and case studies. On the one hand James lent his name to psychical research and the investigation of occult phenomena, falling into the embrace of the spiritualists while reaping the scorn of the professional psychologists. On the other hand he produced one of the greatest works on the psychology of religion, *The Varieties of Religious Experience* (1903). Based on his Gifford Lectures at Edinburgh, James's *Varieties* exam- ines religion as it occurs in individual cases of experience. Religion is treated as distinctively individual, not social or institutional. James's typology of religious experience—for example, 'the healthy-minded', 'the sick soul'—has per- sisted, but his theory of the common structure of all religious experience remains sketchy. The structural dynamics characteristic of religious

experience involves initially a psychological state in which a need is felt; second, a step into a deeper level of consciousness, itself connected to a cosmic consciousness; and, finally, reparation of the initial state by re-energizing the individual.

In 1898, in his address, 'Philosophical concep- tions and practical results', delivered before the Philosophical Union at the University of Califor- nia in Berkeley, James used the term 'pragma- tism', which he attributed to Charles **Peirce**, to designate his philosophy. It stressed action as the goal of thought and clarified concepts in terms of their practical effects. Thus James unleashed pragmatism to the world. Affiliated with a host of thinkers in America and Europe—**Ostwald** in Berlin, **Papini** in Rome, F. C. S. **Schiller** at Oxford, **Bergson** in Paris and Dewey in Chicago—James's pragmatism, to Peirce's consternation, was also allied with such currents of thought as positivism, utilitarianism, nominalism and anti-intellectual- ism. James dedicated his book *Pragmatism* to J. S. Mill, claiming that it applied to the concept of truth the principle of utility that Mill had used in the analysis of the good. Pragmatism for James was both a method for settling metaphysical disputes and a theory of truth. As a method pragmatism prescribed that rival metaphysical theories be evaluated by reference to the differ- ences they make in the lives of those who hold them. If there are no differences then the controversies over the theories are fruitless. The pragmatist conception of truth is dynamic: it maintains that the truth of a proposition consists in the successful consequences of holding it. James's theory of truth immediately aroused criticisms, and his replies to his critics, along with other essays on the topic, were collected in *The Meaning of Truth* (1909). James also espoused radical empiricism. In contrast to traditional empiricism, radical empiricism found that rela- tions are as immediately given in experience as qualities; this James considered to be a matter of fact. In addition, it postulates methodologically that nothing be admitted as a fact except what some experient can experience at some time. Further, it is the generalized conclusion that the parts of experience hang together by means of experienced relations without resort to any trans- empirical principle. Just as James's pragmatism has had a profound impact on American philo- sophy, especially in the instrumentalism of John Dewey, his radical empiricism contributed to the rise of new realism and subsequently to logical empiricism. James's endeavour to articulate the metaphysics suggested by the generalization of radical empiricism finds expression in the last book he published during this lifetime, *A Pluralistic Universe* (1909). Based on his Hibbert Lectures at Oxford, this work offers a sustained criticism of absolute idealism and intellectualism, and finds in the works of Bergson and Peirce the hope of a temporalist metaphysics of change, chance and pluralism. James had intended to formulate this metaphysics in a comprehensive work comparable to his *Principles of Psychology*. Although James discernibly anticipated the rise of process philosophy, death cut his efforts short. His unfinished manuscript was published posthumously under the title *Some Problems of Philosophy* (1911).

Sources: EAB: Edwards; H. James (ed.) (1920) *Letters of William James*, 2 vols, Boston: Atlantic Monthly Press; DAB.

ANDREW RECK

Jankélévitch, Vladmir

French. *b:* 1903, Bourges, France. *d:* 1980. *Cat:* Existentialist; moral philosopher. *Educ:* Lycée Louis-le-Grand and École Normale Supérieure; doctorate in 1933. *Infls:* Henri Bergson and Kierkegaard. *Appts:* Taught at the French Institute in Prague and at various lycées; 1936, lecturing posts at the University of Toulouse, and 1937, University of Lille; dismissed by the Vichy Government in 1940, but returned to academic life in 1945 as Professor of Moral Philosophy, University of Paris.

Main publications:

(1933) *La Mauvaise Conscience*, Paris: Alcan.
(1935) *L'Ironie ou la bonne conscience*, Paris: Alcan.
(1938) *L'Alternative*, Paris: Alcan.
(1943) *Du mensonge*, Paris: Arthaud.
(1948) *Traité des vertus*, Paris: Bordas.
(1954) *Philosophie première*, Paris: PUF.
(1956) *L'Austerité et la vie morale*, Paris: Flammarion.
(1957) *Le Je-ne-sais-quoi et le presque-rien*, Paris: PUF.
(1960) *Le Pur et l'impur*, Paris: Flammarion.

Secondary literature:

Smith, C. (1964) *Contemporary French Philosophy: A Study in Norms and Values*, London: Methuen, chapter 12.

Jankélévitch maintained that there are three separate areas of philosophy: that of rationality, which consists of analytic truths or logical necessity; that of the relative contingency of natural events describable by the synthetic truths

of science, which is the basis for prediction; and that of radical contingency, in which events are regarded as unique and related only by the free flow of time. The unique events of this third area are sometimes regarded as having sufficient similarity to the events studied by science to be reducible to them.

According to Jankélévitch people have unity of being only at the preconscious stage of innocence. In becoming aware of any or all of the three spheres of philosophy, a gap opens up between themselves and either the world or themselves as objects of knowledge.

This gap of awareness is the origin of pain and evil, which can be dealt with in several ways. One partial remedy is to be found by ignoring the radical contingency of events, and treating the uniqueness of one's own predicament as a particular example of a general truth: in other words, by reducing radical to relative contingency. Another partial solution is by the use of irony, which detaches us from our unique situations, allows us to view events as part of an ongoing temporal process, and enlists other people as our accomplices in irony. But the most therapeutic remedy for pain and evil is to regard them as radically contingent occurrences at a particular moment in time, which do not have to prevent us from continuing to live our unique lives.

On Jankélévitch's view there is a two-tier hierarchy of moral virtues. In the upper tier are to be placed the virtues of courage, love, charity and humility, which require initiative and have their outcome in concrete and thus radically contingent situations. In the lower tier are virtues such as justice, loyalty and friendship, which require calculation, abstraction and continuity, and are thus to be found in the moral equivalent of the area of synthetic scientific truths. It is the person who is virtuous, not the action. Ethics is not reducible to a set of rules, and is to be located primarily in the area of radical contingency.

KATHRYN PLANT

Jaspers, Karl

German. *b:* 23 February 1883, Oldenburg, Germany. *d:* 26 February 1969, Basle, Switzerland. *Cat:* Existentialist; psychologist; philosopher; historian of philosophy. *Ints:* History of philosophy. *Educ:* Studied medicine, Universities of Berlin, Göttingen and Heidelberg (1902–8). *Infls:* Literary influences: Kant, Hegel, Kierkegaard, Nietzsche, Plotinus, Bruno, Spinoza and Schelling. Personal influences: Max Weber and Heidegger. *Appts:* Independent Assistant, Heidelberg

Psychiatric Clinic, 1908–15; (1909–20); University of Heidelberg, Psychology (1915–19), then in Philosophy, initially as *Extraordinarius* (1919–21) and then as *Ordinarius* (1921–37 and 1945–8).

Main publications:
(1913) *Allgemeine Psychopathologie*, Berlin: J. Springer (English translation, *General Psychopathology*, trans. J. Hoenig and M. W. Hamilton, Manchester: Manchester University Press, 1962).
(1914) *Psychologie der Weltanschauungen*, Berlin: J. Springer.
(1932) *Philosophie*, 3 vols, Berlin: J. Springer (English translation, *Philosophy*, trans. E. B. Ashton, 3 vols, Chicago: Chicago University Press, 1969–71).
(1935) *Vernunft und Existenz*, Groningen: J. W. Wolters (English translation, *Reason and Existenz*, trans. W. Earle, London: Routledge & Kegan Paul, 1956).
(1947) *Von der Wahrheit*, Munich: R. Piper.
(1949) *Vom Ursprung und Ziel der Geschichte*, Zurich: Artemis and Munich: R. Piper (English translation, *The Origin and Goal of History*, trans. M. Bullock, New Haven: Yale University Press, 1953).
(1957) *Philosophical Autobiography*, in Schilpp (revised and enlarged, 1981); also in Piper (ed.) 1967.
(1962) *Der philosophische Glaube angesichts der Offenbarung*, Munich: R. Piper (English translation, *Philosophical Faith and Revelation*, trans. E. B. Ashton, New York: Harper & Row, 1967).
(1967) *Karl Jaspers: Schicksal und Wille. Autobiographische Schriften*, ed. H. Saner, Munich: R. Piper.

Secondary literature:
Ehrlich, L. H. (1975) *Karl Jaspers: Philosophy as Faith*, Amherst, Mass.: University of Massachusetts Press.
——and Wisser, R. (eds) (1988) *Karl Jaspers Today: Philosophy at the Threshold of the Future*, Washington: University Press of America.
Gefken, G. and Kunert, K. (1978) *Karl Jaspers. Eine Bibliographie*, Oldenburg.
Olson, A. M. (1979) *Transcendence and Hermeneutics: An Interpretation of the Philosophy of Karl Jaspers*, Amsterdam: Kluwer Academic.
Piper, K. (ed.) (1967) *Karl Jaspers. Werk und Wirkung*, Munich: R. Piper.
Samay, S. (1971) *Reason Revisited: The Philosophy of Karl Jaspers*, Notre Dame, Ind.: Gill & Macmillan.
Saner, H. (1970) *Karl Jaspers in Selbstzeugnissen und Bilddokumenten*, Hamburg: Rowohlt.
Schilpp, P. A. (ed.) (1957) *The Philosophy of Karl Jaspers*, New York: Tudor Publishing; second edition, 1981.

Schragg, O. O. (1971) *Existence, Existenz, and Transcendence: An Introduction to the Philosophy of Karl Jaspers*, Pittsburg, PA: Duquesne University Press and Louvain: Editions E. Nauwelaerts.
Wallraff, C. F. (1970) *Karl Jaspers. An Introduction to his Philosophy*, Princeton, NJ: Princeton University Press.

The prewar years were for Jaspers dominated by his friendship with **Heidegger** during 1920–33 and the publication of his chief philosophical work, *Philosophie* (1932). The war years were spent, stripped of his Chair and silenced by the authorities, in Heidelberg with his Jewish wife, working on his second most important philosophical work, *Von der Wahrheit* (1947). At the end of the war Japsers was restored to his Chair but he declined the Rectorship of the University, although he was actively involved in its reform. In 1948 he left Germany to take up the Chair of Philosophy at the University of Basle, where he spent the rest of his life, continuing to publish prolifically, both on philosophy and, controversially, on sensitive issues of postwar German politics.

Jaspers's earliest major work, his *Allgemeine Psychopathologie* (1913), while containing a classification of psychological abnormalities and diagnostic techniques, foreshadows his later philosophical preoccupations in its concern to formulate a methodology for psychiatric medicine suitable for its 'object', a suffering human being. Fundamental to Jaspers's approach is the adoption of a phenomenological method and the deployment of a distinction, deriving from Dilthey and Max Weber, between causal-explanatory methods (*erklären*) and a method involving an intuitive-sympathetic understanding of the 'patient' as a living whole (*verstehen*). Hence Jaspers's emphasis on biography or 'pathography'. His classic study established the methodology of a phenomenological and existential psychiatric medicine.

His two chief philosophical works are *Philosophie* (1931) and *Von der Wahrheit* (1947). The central theme of his thought may be described as the finitude of human existence and the limits of human experience. Jaspers contrasts the truths of philosophy with those of science and religion. The truths of philosophy are forms of *faith*; the truths of natural science are alone objectively true, and are characterized by their 'compelling certainty' and their 'universal validity'; the truths of religion are symbolic, forms of *chiffre*. Philosophy has many possible starting-points; the starting-point of Jaspers's own philosophy is the ultimate experience of knowing (*erkennen*), and the fundamental question arising therefrom: How does Being manifest itself?

All knowing is referential and intentional. As such it involves the fissuring of subject and object (*die Subjekt–Objekt-Spaltung*). This fissure is the *locus* of all beings, all objects, all knowing. It both marks the limits of objectivity and points beyond itself to the transcendent, to the Unfissured (*das Ungespaltene*), the Encompassing (*das Umgreifende*). Jaspers distinguishes two senses of this last term: (i) the Encompassing as such (*das Umgreifende schlechthin*) or Being in itself (*das Sein an sich*); (ii) the Encompassing which we ourselves are (*das Umgreifende, das wir selbst sind*), this latter splintering into a diversity of the ways in which we are (as existence (*Dasein*), existenz (*Existenz*), understanding, reason, consciousness).

The Encompassing as such transcends the subject–object fissure, and is thus not a possible object of knowledge. Being in itself is absolutely inaccessible to thought; ontology is, accordingly, impossible. Only the modes of Being (*die Weisen des Seins*), which mark the limits and the horizon of our experience, can be illuminated (*erhellt*) and clarified (*geklärt*) but not explained (*erklärt*). Such 'illumination' (*Erhellung*) is contrasted with ontology—a project doomed to failure (*scheitern*) and called 'periechontology' (*Periechontologie*).

Although Being as such is inaccessible to thought, we, as conscious beings, enjoy a kind of immediate access to our own lived and experienced Being, the Being of possibilities. Although not capable of conceptual (categorial) articulation or expression, our Being (*Existenz*) can be illuminated by means of tokens (*signa*). Jaspers, in his 'illumination' of our Being or Existenz (*Existenzerhellung*) distinguishes three such *signa*: (i) *Freedom*, the Being of possibilities of Being, is neither conceptually determinable nor knowable as an object; it can only be lived and experienced in choice and action; (ii) *Communication* (*Kommunikation*) with others springs from the existential ground of our Being, involves recognition of the freedom of the other, manifests itself in loving conflict (*liebender Kampf*), and may save us from the isolation and loneliness, to which our singularity and individuality may seem to condemn us; (iii) *Fundamental situations* (*Grundsituationen*) mark the limits of our finitude, include origin, mortality, guilt, conflict, accident and historicality, and become, when recognized and accepted (lived and experienced), *limiting situations* (*Grenzsituationen*); they then mark the transition from

mere existence (*Dasein*) to authentic existenz (*Existenz*).

Jaspers emphasizes the antinomial character of our Being, which is rooted in our striving to transcend the limits of our Being and in attempting to penetrate the inaccessible realm of the Encompassing. This self-transcending tendency of our finite Being towards the infinite manifests itself in universal symbolic forms (*chiffres*), man's attempt to express the inexpressible and the unknowable, finite 'expressions' of the infinite. Such *chiffres* find their expression in art, poetry, myth, religion and metaphysics, but nowhere more vividly and dramatically than in the failure (*Scheitern*) of ontology itself. Although regarded as one of the three leading exponents of existentialism, Jaspers has been overshadowed by the genius of Heidegger and the celebrity of **Sartre**. The neglect from which Jaspers has suffered, particularly in Anglo-Saxony, has been, in part, due to the fact that, until recently, none of his greatest philosophical works has been available in English (*Von der Wahrheit* remains untranslated). On the other hand, most of his popular and semi-popular writings have been translated. Unfortunately, these works often slide into the vacuous, the vague and the platitudinous, and they have won for Jaspers an unfortunate and undeserved reputation for superficiality and banality. This situation is gradually being remedied as Jaspers's importance is slowly coming to be recognized.

Sources: Edwards; EF; Kindler 1964; Kindler 1988; Saner 1970; Wallraff 1970.

DAVID WALFORD

Jauch, Ursula Pia

Swiss. *b:* 1959, Zurich, Switzerland. *Cat:* Feminist philosopher. *Ints:* Enlightenment philosophy (Kant); seventeenth- and eighteenth-century philosophy; feminist interpretation and consequences of Enlightenment thinking. *Educ:* University of Zürich. *Infls:* Kantian Enlightenment thought. *Appts:* Assistant and Lecturer, Department of Philosophy (Philosophisches Seminar), University of Zürich; editor of the *Schweizerische Arbeitsblätter für ethische Forschung* [Swiss Papers of Ethical Research]; Fellow (wissenschaftliche Mitarbeiterin) at the Arbeits- und Forschungsstelle für Ethik [Centre for Ethical Research], Zürich.

Main publications:

(1988) *Immanuel Kant zur Geschlechterdifferenz. Aufklärerische Vorurteilskritik und bürgerliche*

Geschlechtsvormundschaft [Immanuel Kant on the Difference of Gender], Vienna: Passagen Verlag.

(1988) 'Sittlichkeit zwischen Vernunft und Gefühl [Morality between reason and feeling], H. Kimmerle (ed.) *Hegel-Jahrbuch* pp. 368–74.

(1989) 'Männliches Sittengesetz–weibliche Sitzsamkeit: akute Reflexionen zu einem philosophischen Dauerbrenner' [Male Laws of Ethics–Female Regard for Decorum / Or a Settled Way of Life: Acute Reflections on a Philosophical Evergreen], in A. Deuber-Mankowsky *et al.* (eds) *1789/ 1989: Die Revolution hat nicht stattgefunden* [1789/ 1989: The Revolution has not taken Place], Tübingen: Proceedings of the 5th Symposium of the IAP.

(1989) 'Metaphysik häppchenweise–zur Damenphilosophie im 18. Jahrhundert' [Metaphysics in Morsels–on the Eighteenth Century Women's Philosophy], *Studia Philosophica* 48: 77–95.

(1989) 'Schopenhauer oder Kant: Geschlechterdifferenz zwischen Zeitkritik und Zeitgeist' [Schopenhauer or Kant: Gender Difference Between Critique and Zeitgeist] in 'Schopenhauer in der Postmoderne', *Schopenhauer-Studia* 3: 49–58.

(1990) *Damenphilosophie und Männermoral. Ein Versuch über die lächelnde Vernunft* [Ladies' Philosophy and Men's Moral], Vienna: Passagen Verlag.

(1990) 'Nichts von Sollen, nichts von Müssen, nichts von Schuldigkeit weibliche Renitenz und feministische Kritik' [Feminine refractory behaviour and feminist critique], in H. Nagl-Docekal and H. Pauer-Studer (eds) *Das Denken der Geschlechterdifferenz*, Vienna: Frauenverlag.

Ursula Pia Jauch attempts a feminist interpretation of Kantian Enlightenment thought on gender and seeks the presuppositions of feminist thinking in the Enlightenment critique of prejudices. She validates irony as a philosophical method and defends humour and cunning as tools for feminist critique. In that light she regards the 'Damenphilosophie' (women's philosophy) of the eighteenth century, an alternative to strict and sombre moralism.

Sources: Meyer & Vahle.

URSULA STICKLER

Jaurès, Jean

French. ***b:*** 1859, Castres, France. ***d:*** 1914, Paris (assassinated). ***Cat:*** Socialist theorist and activist. ***Ints:*** Politics. ***Educ:*** École Normale Supérieure (Agrégation de philosophie, 1881). ***Infls:*** Maine de Biran, Marx and Lachelier. ***Appts:*** After a period as a teacher at the lycée d'Albi and as a deputy (1885–9), Jaurès went to the Faculty of Letters at Toulouse; became a socialist, in the early 1890s; re-elected as socialist Deputy 1893, an office he retained, except during 1898–1902, until his murder by a nationalist; Dreyfusard and Republican; founded French Socialist Party, 1901, and the Socialist paper *L'Humanité*, 1904.

Main publications:

The nearest to a 'collected works' is Max Bonnefous (ed.) *Oeuvres de Jean Jaurès*, 9 vols, Paris: Rieder, 1931–9.

(1891) *La Réalité du monde sensible*, second edition, 1902.

(1891) *De Primis Socialismi Germanici Lineamentis* (secondary thesis, in Latin).

(1901–) (ed. and contributor) *Histoire socialiste de la Révolution française* (wrote four of the volumes in this series).

(1910) *L'Armée nouvelle*.

Secondary literature:

Guillemin, H. (1966) *L'Arrière-pensée de Jaurès*, Paris: Gallimard.

Philonenko, A. (1982) 'Autour de Jaurès et de Fichte', in *Études kantiennes*, Paris: Vrin.

Rappoport, C. (1915) *Jean Jaurès, l'homme, le penseur, le socialiste*, Paris: L'Emancipatrice.

Robinet, A. (1964) *Jaurès et l'unité de l'être*, Paris: Seghers.

Jaurès is generally classified as a key figure in the evolution of French socialism, and although this is certainly true it tends to obscure the sophistication of the philosophy on which he based his politics. He was third in the *agrégation* for his year (**Bergson** was second), and in his first work of 1891 he defends a worldview from which he never departed and which is the ground for his socialism.

At the root of his metaphysics is a species of pantheism rooted in intuitions of the unity of being of a quasi-mystical character: thus Jaurès describes moments out walking when he felt as if his soul possessed the whole of nature (*La Réalité*, 1891). The conviction of the unity of being directs his criticisms of other philosophies: he denies, for example, **Lachelier**'s contention that truth is logically prior to being. Since being can only be conceived under the forms of thought, Jaurès concludes that being and reason are identical. Further, he contends that the universe is maintained by an infinite, realized act, since otherwise it would undergo sudden changes at each passage from potency to act, and this infinite act can only be the act of an infinite being or God. Again, Jaurès discerns everywhere a tendency to combination and unity, and regards this as explicable only on the assumption that reality is an infinite unity. As in a number of other one-and-many philosophies, Jaurès's thought is ultimately optimistic: the tendency and goal of history is towards a restoration of unity. Pain and division are not absolutes but relative evils, involved in the effort of the perfect (God) to merit its perfection.

The right form of polity is that which is in accordance with the will of God, i.e. that which promotes maximal unity amongst human beings and between them and the cosmos, and this polity is the socialist state, indistinguishable in Jaurès's thought from the true church. He accepted as definitive Marx's analysis of alienation as the condition of those living in the capitalist state. The only way to end this prevailing species of disunity is to eliminate its cause, and so he identifies socialism with collectivism: only the state would own and distribute goods. The collectivist state is the most libertarian form of polity, and will permit maximal development of individual talents. Unity will be further restored by internationalist policies. Jaurès believed that such was the inevitable course of history. Human beings are not merely puppets of the economic base, but are motivated by the ideal of justice. Ultimately the unity of all being will be restored.

ROBERT WILKINSON

Jeans, (Sir) James Hopwood

British. *b:* 11 September 1877, Birkdale, Lancashire. *d:* 16 September 1946, Dorking, Surrey. *Cat:* Mathematician; theoretical physicist; astronomer; scientific publicist. *Ints:* Cosmology and cosmogony. *Educ:* Trinity College, Cambridge, 1896–1903. *Appts:* University Demonstrator, Cambridge, 1904–5, 1910–12; University of Princeton, 1905–9; freelance writer from 1912; Joint Secretary, Royal Society of London, 1919–29; President, Royal Astronomical Society, 1925–7; President, British Association, 1934; Order of Merit, 1939.

Main publications:

(1928) *Astronomy and Cosmogony*, Cambridge: Cambridge University Press.
(1928) *Eos or the Wider Aspects of Cosmogony*, London: Kegan Paul.
(1929) *The Universe Around Us*, Cambridge: Cambridge University Press.
(1930) *The Mysterious Universe*, Cambridge: Cambridge University Press.
(1931) *The Stars in their Courses*, Cambridge: Cambridge University Press.

(1933) *The New Background of Science*, Cambridge: Cambridge University Press.
(1934) *Through Space and Time*, Cambridge: Cambridge University Press.
(1936) *Man and the Universe, in Scientific Progress*, London: Allen & Unwin.
(1937) *Science and Music*, Cambridge: Cambridge University Press.
(1942) *Physics and Philosophy*, Cambridge: Cambridge University Press.
(1947) *The Growth of Physical Science*, Cambridge: Cambridge University Press.

Secondary literature:
Cohen, C. (1930) *God and the Universe*, London: The Pioneer Press.
Harley, C. (1935) *God and the Universe*, Manchester: New Church Publishing Society.
Stebbing, L. S. (1937) *Philosophy and the Physicists*, London: Methuen.

A mathematical physicist who made his reputation with works developing the kinetic-molecular theory of gases, Jeans's interests later moved into theoretical astronomy, particularly theories of the origins and development of the universe, to which he gave, at the end of his life, a deistic interpretation in popular writings with a wide sale. *The Growth of Physical Science* (1947), written at the end of his life, offers a highly synoptic view of the subject. In epistemology he seems to have concluded that the rise of the quantum theory pointed to a subjectivist phenomenalist approach. Milne (1947) considers that his thinking in this area was naive and precritical.

Sources: Obituary, *Obituary Notices of Fellows of the Royal Society* 15 (1947): 573–89; J. G. Crowther (1952) *British Scientists of the Twentieth Century*, London: Routledge; E. A. Milne & S. C. Roberts (1952) *Sir James Jeans*, Cambridge: CUP; DNB 1941–50; DSB 7, 84a–86b; R. W. Smith (1977) 'Sir James Hopwood Jeans 1877–1946', *JBAA* 88: 8–17; W. H. McCrea (1978) 'Sir James Hopwood Jeans OM FRS 1877–1946', *QJRAS* 19: 190–66.

R. N. D. MARTIN

Jin Yuelin (Chin Yueh-lin)

Chinese. *b:* 1896, Changsha, Hunan Province, China. *d:* 1984, Beijing. *Cat:* Logician. *Ints:* History of logic; metaphysics; theory of knowledge. *Educ:* Studied at Qinghua University, Beijing, University of Pennsylvania, Columbia University (PhD in Politics) and, England, Germany and France. *Infls:* T. H. Green, Bertrand Russell, G. E. Moore, and the neo-Confucian tradition. ***Appts:*** Professor, Qinghua University; Founder, Department of Philosophy, Qinghua University; Professor, Southwest Associated University; Professor and Head of Department, University of Peking; Deputy Head, Department of Philosophy, Chinese Academy of Sciences (later Chinese Academy of Social Sciences); Chairman, Chinese Society of Logic.

Main publications:

(ed.) *Formal Logic*.
Treatise on Knowledge.
(1935) *Logic*, Beijing: Qinghua University.
(1940) *On the Dao*, Shanghai: Commercial Press.
(1988) *Philosophy of Russell*.

Secondary literature:

Briere, O. (1956) *Fifty Years of Chinese Philosophy 1898–1950*, London: George Allen & Unwin Ltd.
Chan, W. (1963) *A Source Book in Chinese Philosophy*, Princeton: Princeton University Press.
Complete Chinese Encyclopedia (1987), Philosophy Volumes, Beijing: Chinese Encyclopedia Publications.

Jin was China's most famous contemporary logician. After a decade of advanced study in the USA, England, Germany and France, Jin returned to Qinghua University to teach the history of European political thought under the influence of T. H. Green. In private study he read widely in logic and contemporary philosophy. His reading of **Russell** and other logicians led to his own logical work, initially expressed in his book *Logic* (1935). His tightly reasoned, symbolically expressed formal arguments would have been impressive anywhere, but were especially remarkable in a country without a tradition of formal logic. Jin had precursors also influenced by Western logic, but he far outstripped them in establishing rigorous, original logical studies as a feature of Chinese intellectual life. His students over many years were trained to the same high standards of careful argument.

Jin developed a system of metaphysics to complement his logical studies. The system, inspired in part by Green's criticism of Hume, rigorously deployed concepts drawn from neo-Confucian philosophy and displayed the constructive originality characterisitic of his logic. Jin built up his account of the structure of reality from the interrelationship of his central concepts of *dao* (way or rule), *shi* (form) and *neng* (possibility). Although it would be difficult to ascribe priority to any one of the concepts, the modal notion of possibility might be considered the most distinctive feature of his system. Without possibility there would be no differentiation of individuals in terms of their form and there would be no logical room for the *dao* to govern processes of the natural world and to guide action in the practical world.

Jin carried his distinction between the changing and various and a common stable set of interrelated concepts from his metaphysics into the theory of knowledge. He never accepted Russell's phenomenalism and was influenced by G. E. **Moore**'s common-sense realism. Jin was a realist who believed in the existence of the natural world independent of our knowledge, but his realism was not an invitation to scepticism. He saw knowledge as a developing process which could reach the natural world and grasp its meaning. Jin's many students have carried on his work in logic and philosophy.

NICHOLAS BUNNIN

Joachim, Harold Henry

British. ***b:*** 1868, London. ***d:*** 1938, Croyde, Devon. ***Cat:*** Idealist. ***Ints:*** Logic; Spinoza; ancient philosophy. ***Educ:*** MA, Balliol College, Oxford. ***Infls:*** F. H. Bradley and J. A. Smith. ***Appts:*** Fellow of Merton College, Oxford; Lecturer, St Andrews; Fellow, Balliol, Merton and New Colleges; Wykeham Professor of Logic, University of Oxford, 1919–35.

Main publications:

(1901) *A Study of the Ethics of Spinoza*, Oxford.
(1906) *The Nature of Truth*, Oxford.
(1940) *A Commentary on the Tractatus de Intellectione Emendatus of Spinoza*, Oxford (posthumous).
(1948) *Logical Studies*, Oxford (posthumous).
(1957) *Descartes's Rules for the Direction of the Mind*, ed. E. E. Harris, London: George Allen & Unwin (posthumous).
Editions of Aristotle.

Secondary literature:

Joseph, H. W. B. (1938) *Proceedings of the British Academy* 26.
Mind,(1906–7), Russell's and Moore's comments on *The Nature of Truth*.

Joachim's only work of creative philosophy was *The Nature of Truth* (1906). This contained a critique of truth as correspondence and a defence of a coherence theory, both of exemplary clarity. It also contained a critique of a view of 'truth as a quality of independent entities' which Joachim ascribed to **Russell** and **Moore**. The subsequent discussion of this critique by Russell and Moore, and Joachim's response (*Mind*, 1906–7), are of great interest as the only close and well-argued point of contact between the idealist logic which Joachim had distilled from **Bradley** and the view of logic (held at that time by Russell and Moore) as an objectivized interrelationship of independent propositions. Although the idealist framework of Joachim's critique had no real effect, his wit and the sharpness of his arguments must have done much to temper some of the extremes of the earliest analytical philosophy. He wrote in caricature of Russell:

'Truth' and Falsity', in the only strict sense of the terms, are characteristics of 'Propositions'. Every Proposition, in itself and in entire independence of mind, is true or false: and *only* Propositions can be true or false. The truth or falsity of a Proposition is, so to speak, its *flavour*, which we must recognize, if we recognize it at all, immediately: much as we appreciate the flavour of pineapple or the taste of gorgonzola. (1906, p. 37)

T. S. Eliot wrote that, of his teachers, 'to Joachim alone am I aware of any debt for instruction in the writing of English … to his criticism of my papers I owe an appreciation of the fact that good writing is impossible without clear and distinct ideas' (*The Times*, 4 August 1938). Russell's view (in *The Monistic Theory of Truth*) was that *The Nature of Truth* was the best statement of an idealist theory of truth. Joachim remains the British idealist whose work is most easily accessible to those who lived through the analytical period.

RICHARD MASON

Joad, Cyril Edwin Mitchinson

British. **b:** 1891, Durham, England. **d:** 1953, Hampstead, London. **Cat:** Objectivist value theorist. **Ints:** Ethics; politics. **Educ:** Balliol College, Oxford (John Locke Scholarship, 1914). **Infls:** Plato and Aristotle. **Appts:** Worked for the Ministry of Labour until 1930; 1930–53, Head of the Philosophy Deptartment at Birkbeck College, London; enjoyed contemporary celebrity as a broadcaster on the Brains Trust (first radio series).

Main publications:

(1929) *Matter, Life and Value.*
(1932) *Philosophical Aspects of Modern Science.*
(1936) *Guide to Philosophy.*

(1936) *Return to Philosophy*; second edition, London: Faber & Faber, 1945.
(1938) *Guide to the Philosophy of Morals and Politics.*
(1940) *Philosophy for Our Times.*
(1942) *Guide to Modern Thought.*
(1944) *Philosophy* (Teach Yourself Series).
(1948) *Decadence*, London: Faber & Faber.
(1952) *The Recovery of Belief*, London: Faber & Faber.

Secondary literature:

Findlay, J. N. 'Dr Joad on the verification principle', *Hibbert Journal* 48: 120–6.
Henle, R. J. 'A note on Professor Joad's "How our minds work"', *Modern Scholasticism* 25: 193–6.

Joad is now better remembered as a teacher and broadcaster than as a philosopher in his own right. He has paid the price for being out of sympathy with the dominant philosophical currents of his time: in the period of logical positivism and existentialism he argued for the possibility of traditional metaphysics, of the objectivity of values and the existence of a *philosophia perennis*. He believed that human life could be meaningful only if lived in the belief that the realm of values is as real as those of mind and of physical objects. He saw around him a civilization in crisis, and saw the root cause of the problem in what he called 'the dropping of the object' (1948), i.e. the embracing of various forms of subjectivism or relativism in epistemology and value theory. Granted the unfashionableness of his views, it is unsurprising that most of his books are polemics in favour of the forms of objectivism he favoured. They are written with lucidity, elegance and wit.

Joad argued that there are four ultimate, real and objective values: truth, beauty, goodness and happiness, and on this basis grounds a set of positive moral recommendations derived from Plato and Aristotle. Appetite is to be subordinated to reason, since this is a precondition for the realization of any of the ultimate values. Reason itself is not merely the instrumental slave of the passions but has goals of its own, namely these same values. The rule reason applies in governing the appetites is the Aristotelian doctrine of the mean. (These beliefs Joad regarded as the core of the *philosophia perennis*.) The political consequence drawn from the conjunction of these beliefs together with a sustained attack on Hegelian-derived views of the state as an absolute is a reasoned support for democracy. The function of the state is to permit maximal flourishing of the virtues, and it is imperative that those who obey the laws are ultimately responsible for the laws they obey.

Concerning philosophy itself, Joad believed that it tends to foster tolerance in its practitioners, based on a freedom from dogmatism whose value cannot be overestimated.

Sources: DNB.

ROBERT WILKINSON

Jones, (Sir) Henry

British. *b:* 30 November 1952, Llangernyw, Denbighshire, Wales. *d:* 4 February 1922, Tighnabruaich, Kyles of Bute. *Cat:* Hegelian idealist; educational reformer. *Ints:* Moral philosophy; social philosophy. *Educ:* Bangor Normal College and Glasgow University. *Infls:* Personal influences: John Nichol and Edward Caird. Literary influences: Plato and Hegel. *Appts:* 1884–91, Professor of Philosophy and Political Economy, University College of North Wales, Bangor; 1891–4, Professor of Logic, Rhetoric and Metaphysics, St Andrews; 1894–1922, Professor of Moral Philosophy, Glasgow.

Main publications:

(1891) *Browning as a Philosophical and Religious Teacher*, Glasgow: Maclehose.
(1895) *A Critical Account of the Philosophy of Lotze*, Glasgow: Maclehose.
(1909) *Idealism as a Practical Creed*, Glasgow: Maclehose.
(1922) *A Faith that Enquires*, London: Macmillan.

Secondary literature:

Boucher, David and Vincent, Andrew (1993) *A Radical Hegelian. The Political and Social Philosophy of Henry Jones*, Cardiff: University of Wales Press.
Hetherington, H. J. W. (1937) Entry in *Dictionary of National Biography* 1922–30.
Lindsay, A. D. (1926) 'The idealism of Caird and Jones', *Philosophy* 1: 171ff.
Muirhead, J. H. (1923) 'Sir Henry Jones, 1852–1922', *Proceedings of the British Academy* 10: 552–62.
Sell, A. P. F. (1995) *Philosophical Idealism and Christian Belief*, Cardiff: University of Wales Press and New York: St Martin's Press.

Henry Jones deplored the 'disease of subjectivity' by which, under the undue influence of Lotze, some contemporary idealist philosophy (including that of **Ward** and **Bradley**) had become infected. In opposition to such a subjective idealism he called himself a 'spiritual realist'— perhaps adopting this phrase from **Fraser**. He also opposed himself to some of the other absolute-idealists, such as **Bosanquet**, who seemed to him to stress the perfection and completeness of reality as a whole at the expense of those finite centres we think of as people. He used the Platonic phrase 'to save the appearances' to describe his project in metaphysics.

Jones was concerned not only with metaphysics but also with moral and social philosophy. At Glasgow he gave lectures on ethics for businessmen and pressed for appointments in what would now be called the social sciences. According to his biographer 'the fundamental groundwork of all his thinking was a faith in the reality and reliability of moral values' (Hetherington 1937, p. 459). Jones was an educational reformer, making an important contribution to the development of the University in his native Wales, in recognition of which he was knighted and made a Companion of Honour. He was a dedicated teacher and this was how he made his 'greatest contribution to contemporary philosophy' (Hetherington 1937, p. 459).

Sources: H. J. W. Hetherington (1924) *Life and Letters of Sir Henry Jones*, London: Hodder & Stoughton.

STUART BROWN

Jørgensen, Jens Jørgen (Frederik Theodor)

Danish. *b:* 1 April 1894, Haderup, Denmark. *d:* 30 July 1969, Copenhagen. *Cat:* Logician; neo-Kantian; later, logical positivist. *Ints:* History of logic. *Educ:* Copenhagen. *Infls:* Høffding and Natorp but, according to Jørgensen himself, mainly Cassirer, Russell and Carnap. *Appts:* 1926–64, Professor of Philosophy, Copenhagen.

Main publications:

(1917) *Henri Bergson's filosofi i omrids* [Henri Bergson's Philosophy in Outline], Copenhagen: Nordiske.
(1918) *Paul Natorp som Repraesentant for den kritiske Idealisme* [Paul Natorp, Representative of Critical Idealism], Copenhagen: Nordiske.
(1926-7) *Filosofiske Forelaesninger som Indledning til videnskabelige Studier* [Philosophical Lectures as a General Introduction to Scientific Study], Copenhagen: Levin & Munksgaard.
(1928) *Filosofiens og Opdragelsens Grundproblemer* [Fundamental Problems of Philosophy of Education], Copenhagen.
(1931) *A Treatise of Formal Logic: Its Evolution and Main Branches, with its Relation to Mathematics and Philosophy*, Copenhagen: Levin & Munksgaard; trans. W. Worster, London: Oxford University Press.

(1935) *Bertrand Russell. En praktisk Idealist og hans Filosofi* [Bertrand Russell: A Practical Idealist and his Philosophy], Copenhagen: Levin & Munksgaard.

(1937) *Traek af Deduktionsteoriens Udvickling in den nyere Tid* [Treatise of the Theory of Logical Deduction in Recent Years], Copenhagen: B. Lunos.

(1942) *Indledning til logikken og metodelaeren* [Introduction to Logic and Scientific Method], Copenhagen: Munksgaard; second edition, 1956.

(1942) *Psykologi paa biologisk grundlag* [Psychology Based on Biology], Copenhagen: Munksgaard.

(1948) *Den logiske empirisismes udvickling*, Copenhagen: B. Lunos (English translation, *The Development of Logical Empiricism*, Chicago: University of Chicago Press, 1951).

(1959) 'Towards a theory of inference', *Theorica* 25: 123–47.

(1962) 'Some remarks concerning languages, calculuses and logic', in Y. Bar-Hillel *et al.* (eds), *Logic and Languages: Studies Dedicated to Professor Rudolph Carnap on the Occasion of his 70th Birthday*, Dordrecht: Reidel.

Secondary literature:
Christensen, Niels Egmont (1976) 'Jørgen Jørgensen as Philosopher of Logic' in *Danish Yearbook of Philosophy* 13: 242–8.

Kaila, Eino (1946) Review (in German) of *Psykologi paa biologisk grundlag*, in *Theoria* 12: 91–109.

Neurath, Otto (1931) 'Encyclopedism as a pedagogical aim: a Danish approach', *Philosophy of Science*.

Witt-Hansen, Johs. (1964) 'Jørgen Jørgensen and the grammar of science', *Danish Yearbook of Philosophy* 1: 159–72.

Although a pupil of **Høffding** and at one time inclined to Neo-Kantianism, Jørgensen developed an interest in logic and the work of the Vienna Circle. He wrote a major survey of the development of modern logic and introduced the study of mathematical logic in Denmark. He was one of the organizers of the *International Encyclopedia of Unified Science* and, in his encyclopedic lectures, he sought to instil in his students a general knowledge of the sciences, with a particular emphasis, according to **Neurath**, on 'the grammar of science'. He was hostile to metaphysics and religion and enthusiastic for the empirical sciences, especially psychology and biology. He has been criticized indeed by **Hartnack**, among others, for taking his preoccupation with pyschology too far and subordinating logic and philosophy to it. His interpretation of Kant's epistemology was as the psychology of knowledge. He even held that the principles of logic were based upon psychology, since the human mind might have been structured differently. Hartnack, criticizing Jørgensen's psychologism, attributes it to the influence of Høffding. It was for his encyclopedic vision of the sciences that Jørgensen was most remembered, both by philosophers internationally and by the huge number of students who attended his introductory lectures during his long period as a teacher at Copenhagen.

Sources: Bibliography in *Danish Yearbook of Philosophy* 1 (1964): 183–96 (volume dedicated to Jørgensen); *Dansk Biografisk Leksikon*; Burr; Svend Erik Stybe (1973) 'Trends in Danish philosophy', *JBSP* 4: 153–70; John Witt-Hansen (1952) 'Some remarks on philosophy in Denmark', *PPR* 12: 377–91.

STUART BROWN

Joseph, H(orace) W(illiam) B(rindley)

British. **b:** 28 September 1867, Chatham. **d:** 13 November 1943, Oxford, England. **Cat:** Oxford (or Cook Wilsonian) realist. **Ints:** Philosophical logic; ethics; history of philosophy. **Educ:** Winchester College and New College, Oxford. **Infls:** J. Cook Wilson, H. A. Prichard and, more remotely, Plato. **Appts:** Fellow and Tutor in Philosophy, New College, Oxford, 1899–1932.

Main publications:
(1906) *Introduction to Logic*, Oxford: Clarendon Press.

(1923) *The Labour Theory of Value in Karl Marx*, Oxford.

(1931) *Some Problems in Ethics*, Oxford.

(1935) *Essays in Ancient and Modern Philosophy*, Oxford.

(1948) *Knowledge and the Good in Plato's Republic*, Oxford: Clarendon Press.

Secondary literature:
Smith, A. H. (1943) Obituary Notice in *Proceedings of the British Academy*.

Joseph was closely associated with **Cook Wilson** and **Prichard** and, with them, made up the school of Oxford realists of the early part of this century. It stood in much the same relation to the Oxford linguistic philosophy of the 1950s as did the simultaneous, and more important, realist school in Cambridge to the analytical philosophy of the 1930s and after. Joseph shared his colleagues' predominantly critical standpoint and their first principles that knowledge is both unanalysable and self-intimating, and that it does not affect or modify its objects. All the same his late admission that he did not believe 'either that there is a real world independent of mind altogether, or that my mind is independent of that mind of which the world is not independent; is really a reassertion of T. H. Green's doctrine of the 'eternal consciousness'. Joseph attacked formalism in logic, particularly in the new logic of **Russell**, and the accompanying idea that mathematics is the model of all thought. He argued hat cause and effect are internally related. He also attacked mechanistic conceptions of evolution. Organisms in general, and minds in particular, are not aggregates but wholes. In the same spirit he repudiated Prichard's atomistic view of morality as a collection of duties. For Joseph it is a comprehensive form of life. Joseph was an assiduous and famously persevering teacher. Generations of students were pulverized by his aggressive ferocity. One who survived it was H. L. A. **Hart**, the delicacy and precision of whose reasoning owes something to his tutor, although his good sense is his own.

Sources: Metz; DNB; Passmore 1957.

ANTHONY QUINTON

Juhos, Belva von

Hungarian. *b:* 1901. *d:* 1971, Vienna. *Cat:* Logical positivist. *Ints:* Epistemology; philosophy of science. *Infls:* Schlick and the Vienna Circle. *Appts:* Constant to the ideas of the Vienna Circle, Juhos was one of its few members to remain in Vienna after Schlick's assassination (1936) and during the Second World War; a man of independent means, he became a lecturer only in 1948.

Main publications:

(1928) *Über die Grundlagen der Gewissheit des reinen Denkens.*

(1940) *Erkenntnisformen in Natur- und Geisteswissenschaften.*

(1950) *Die Erkenntnis und ihre Leistung*, Vienna: Springer Verlag.

(1954) *Elemente der neuen Logik*, Frankfurt: Humboldt Verlag.

(1956) *Das Wertgeschelen und seine Erfassung*, Meisenheim am Glan: Verlag Anton Hein.

(1963) (with Hubert Schleichert) *Die erkenntnislogischen Grundlagen der klassischen Physik*, Berlin: Duncker & Humblot.

(1967) *Die erkenntnislogischen Grundlagen der modernen Physik*, Berlin: Duncker & Humblot.

(1970) (with Wolfgang Katzenberger) *Wahrscheinlichkeit als Erkenntnisform*, Berlin: Duncker & Humblot.

Secondary literature:

Frey, G. (1971) Introduction to an English-language selection of Juhos' *Selected Papers on Epistemology and Physics*, Dordrecht & Boston: Reidel.

Kraft, V. (1971) Obituary in *Zeitschrift für allgemeine Wissenschafts-Theorie* 2: 163–73.

Juhos' central interest was in epistemology, especially in its application of science, viewed from the standpoint of the logical positivism of the Vienna Circle. He referred to his method as 'epistemo-logical' or 'epistemo-analytic', and divided his inquiries into two major classes, formal and material. Formal analysis deals with the logical properties of the concepts and propositions of a science, and the language system to which they belong. Material analysis is concerned to locate the objects denoted by various types of expression. Central among the concepts analysed by Juhos is that of scientific law, a class he divides into two, first- and second-order laws. The first permit predictions only concerning items mentioned in the law; the second permit predictions of a broader kind. Classical physics is analysed as the attempt to bring all phenomena under second-order laws, which are laws of proximate action. Again, Juhos paid special attention to relativity theory, regarding the abolition of the Newtonian absolutes of space and time as progress against 'metaphysical' (i.e. non-empirical) elements in science. He hoped that all such 'metaphysical' elements could be expunged from science, whose propositions are characterized by testability. Concerning probability theory, Juhos sought to reduce probabilistic statements to the classical, bivalent logic he accepted.

ROBERT WILKINSON

Jung, Carl Gustav

Swiss. *b:* 1875, Kesswil, Switzerland. *d:* 1961, Zurich. *Cat:* Analytical psychologist; psychoanalyst. *Ints:* The unconscious, individual and collective; personality; dreams, cultural anthropology and comparative religion. *Educ:* Studied Medicine in Basel and then Psychiatry with Eugene Bleuler (in Zurich) and Pierre Janet (in Paris). *Infls:* Schopenhauer, Freud, Jordan and Gross; literary influences include the alchemical text *Rosarium Philosophorum* (1550) and works on history, religion and cultural anthropology. *Appts:* 1905, Lecturer in Psychiatry at the University of Basel, resigning after a few years to concentrate on private practice (in analytical psychiatry), research and writing; 1942–52, Professor, Federal Polytechnical University of Zurich.

Main publications:

The first complete English edition of Jung's works was published by Routledge & Kegan Paul, Ltd., in England, and by the Bollinger Foundation in the United States. The American edition (number XX in the Bollinger series) has been published since 1967 by Princeton University Press. This edition, under the editorship of Sir Herbert Read, Michael Fordham, Gerhard Adler and W. McGuire, includes extensive revisions (supervised by Jung), new translations (mostly by R. F. C. Hall) and a number of works not previously published in English.

(1912) *Freud and Psychoanalysis*; reprinted in vol. 4 of Jung's *Collected Works*, London: Routledge & Kegan Paul, 1961.

(1912) *Symbols of Transformation*; reprinted in vol. 5 of Jung's *Collected Works*, London: Routledge & Kegan Paul, 1961.

(1913) *The Practice of Pyschotherapy*; reprinted in vol. 16 of Jung's *Collected Works*, London: Routledge & Kegan Paul, 1961.

(1921) *Psychologische Typen* Zurich: Raschne.

(1928) *Two Essays on Analytical Psychology*, authorized translation by H. G. and C. F. Baynes, London: Bailliere, Tindall & Cox.

(1933) *Modern Man in Search of a Soul*, London: K. Paul, Trench, Trubner & Co.

(1934) *Archetypes of the Collective Unconscious*; revised edition, 1954; reprinted in vol. 9, part 1 of Jung's *Collected Works*, London: Routledge & Kegan Paul, 1961.

(1934) *The Development of Personality*; reprinted in vol. 17 of Jung's *Collected Works*, London: Routledge & Kegan Paul, 1961.

(1939) *The Integration of the Personality*, New York: Farrar & Rhinehart Inc.

(1940) *Psychologie und Religion* Zurich: Raschner.

(1963) *Memories, Dreams, Reflections* (autobiography), ed. A. Jaffe, London: Collins and Routledge & Kegan Paul.

(1964) *Man and His Symbols*, London: Arkana.

Secondary literature:

Adler, G. (ed.) (1973–4) *C. G. Jung Letters*, vols 1 and 2, London: Routledge & Kegan Paul.

Eysenck, H. J. (1953) *The Structure of Human Personality*, London: Methuen & Co.; in University Paperback Series, 1970.

Fordham, F. (1953) *An Introduction to Jung's Psychology*, Baltimore: Penguin Books.

Jacobi, J. (1959) *The Psychology of C. G. Jung*, London: Routledge & Kegan Paul.

Samuels, A. (1985) *Jung and the Post-Jungians*, London: Routledge & Kegan Paul.

Storr, A. (1983) *Jung: Selected Writings*, London: Fontana.

Wilmer, H. A. (1987) *Practical Jung: Nuts and Bolts of Jungian Psychotherapy*, Wilmett, Ill.: Chiron Publications.

Along with **Freud** and **Adler**, Jung was one of the founders of psychoanalysis. The son of a Protestant clergyman, he considered archaeology before deciding to qualify as a doctor. He travelled widely in Africa, America and India. Notoriously, when the Nazi party came to power he replaced Ernst Kretschmer as the President of the German Society for Psychotherapy. Jung was impressed by Freud's early writings and the two became friends and collaborators in the opening years of the psychoanalytic movement. By 1914, however, after a series of increasingly bitter (mostly on Freud's side) disputes, Jung had broken away to found his own school of psychoanalysis, Analytical Psychology. Like Freud, Jung was concerned with the significance of the unconscious mind: that is, mental contents to which we do not have direct access by ordinary introspection, yet which may profoundly influence conscious experience and behaviour. However, Jung sought to extend the possible content of the unconscious well beyond the limits set by what was already becoming the Freudian orthodoxy. In his early work Freud restricted unconscious material to repressed experiences, arising especially from infantile sexuality. In Jung's analytical psychology on the other hand, unconscious material could take many different forms and arise both from individual experiences and from racial or collective memories.

The notion of a collective unconscious enabled Jung to combine his interests in anthropology and religion with his clinical work. He noted that his patients often spoke in terms of images and symbols which echoed those he had already found to be common in widely different cultures. It seemed to him wholly implausible that these represented experiences which each of his patients had *individually* repressed. Rather they had to be a reflection of 'archetypes' which had become built into our *collective* unconscious through evolutionary processes. Individual experiences are also significant in Jungian theory, but they are to be understood as interacting with inherited archetypes. In child development, for example, the way parents actually behave towards their children is important. But the child's perception of this behaviour is in part determined also by inherited archetypal structures. In this instance these include the 'animus' (the girl's archetypal image of the male) or the corresponding 'anima' (in a boy).

Jung developed a theory of personality types in which, like Kretschmer, he distinguished extraverts (outgoing, sociable) and introverts (unsociable, self-absorbed). He added to this two dimensions of general cognitive style: a thinking/feeling dimension and a sensation/intuition dimension. The personality of a given individual is determined by their fundamental personality type (on the extraversion/introversion scale) together with their characteristic cognitive style. Thus an extraverted thinking type enjoys facts for their own sake while tending to neglect intuition. Most people are a balance of these different elements with some accentuated and others neglected.

Jung's theory of the collective unconscious is the basis of Jungian analysis. The object of this is not merely the elimination of symptoms but a positive process of personal growth through the progressive harmonization of unconscious and conscious mental life, expressed in the symbol of the 'Mandala' (or will). Jung's analytical psychology has been widely criticized for vagueness and inconsistency: the archetypes, in particular, sometimes appear as theoretical constructs, sometimes as empirical postulates, sometimes as homunculi inhabiting a separate world of the collective unconscious. Jung's earlier more conventional psychological work, developing Kretschmer's distinction between extraversion and introversion as aspects of personality, has had a direct influence on mainstream psychology, as in Eysenck's theory of personality. Jung's work has been influential in the arts, and analytical psychology remains a rich and anthropologically interesting picture of the mind.

Sources: Edwards; Reese; UCDCL; Corsini; Gregory; Goldenson.

K. W. M. FULFORD

K

Kagame, Alexis

Rwandan. **b:** 15 May 1912, Kyanza. **d:** 1980. **Cat:** African philosopher. **Ints:** Ancient philosophy; Thomism; history; linguistics; poetry. **Educ:** Minor Seminary, Kabgayi, 1928–33; Major Seminary, 1933–41; ordained in the Roman Catholic priesthood, 1941; Pontifical Gregorian University, Rome 1955; PhD in Philosophy, 1955; independent research in Bantu linguistics in Switzerland, Germany, Holland and England, 1955–6. **Infls:** Aristotle, Thomas Aquinas and Placide Tempels. **Appts:** Editor, *Kinyamateka*, 1941–51; Professor of Philosphy and History, Groupe Scolaire, Astrida; Professor of Literature, Minor Seminary of Kansi, 1956–70; Professor of African Cultures and Professor of History, Major Seminary of Nyakibanda and the National University of Rwanda, 1971–80.

Main publications:

(1956) *La Philosophie bantu–rwandaise de L'être*, Brussels: ARSOM.

(1976) *La Philosophie bantu comparée*, Paris: Présence Africaine.

For Kagame there is a Bantu philosophy and it is founded on two conditions: (i) the linguistic coherence of Bantu languages; and (ii) the practicality of western philosophical methods. For Kagame the merit of Tempels's philosophical work resides in making available the method. He suggests a going beyond Temples's *Bantu Philosophy* by paying attention to languages. Using an Aristotelian grid, Kagame describes what he calls a Bantu–Rwandan philosophy of being—distinguishing formal logic, anthropology, theodicy, cosmology and ethics. Kagame's basic assumptions are that all the Bantu linguistic categories can be reduced to four basic concepts: (a) *Muntu =* being of intelligence, corresponds to the Aristotelian notion of substance; (b) *Kintu* = being without intelligence or *thing*; (c) *Hantu* expresses the *time* and *place* (presents variants such as *Pa-* in the eastern Bantu languages,*Va-* in the west and*Go-* + lo/ro in the south); (d) *Kuntu* indicates the modality and thus centralizes all the notions related to modifications of the being in itself (quantity or quality) or vis-à-vis other beings (relation, position, disposition, possession, action, passion). As such *kuntu* corresponds to seven different Aristotelian categories.

Bantu ontology in its reality and significance expresses itself through the complementarity and connections existing between these four categories, all of them created from the same root, *ntu*, which refers to being but also, simultaneously, to the idea of force. Kagame insists that the Bantu equivalent of *to be* does not express the notion of existence and therefore cannot translate the Cartesian *cogito*. It is by enunciating *muntu, kintu*, etc., that one is signifying an essence or something in which the notion of existence is not necessarily present.

V. Y. MUDIMBE

Kaila, Eino

Finnish. **b:** 9 August 1890, Alajärvi, Finland. **d:** 31 July 1958, Helsinki. **Cat:** Theorist of knowledge; philosopher of science. **Ints:** Logical positivism; philosophy of physics. **Educ:** PhD, University of Helsinki, 1916; Docent of Psychology, University of Helsinki, 1919. **Appts:** 1921–30, Professor of Philosophy, Turku University; 1930–48, Professor of Philosophy, Helsinki;1948, Member of Finland's Academy.

Main publications:

(1930) *Der logistische Neupositivismus. Eine kritische Studie*, Turku: Annales Universitatis Aboensis, 13.

(1934) *Personlighetens psykologi* [The Psychology of Personality], Helsinki: Otava.

(1934) *Persoonallisuus* [The Human Personality], Helsinki: Otava.

(1936) *Über das System der Wirklichkeitsbegriffe. Ein Beitrag zum logischen Empirismus*, Helsinki: Acta Philosophica Fennica, 2.

(1939) *Inhimillinen Tieto, mitä se on ja mitä se ei ole* [Human Knowledge: What It Is and What It Is Not], Helsinki: Otava (Swedish translation by G. H. von Wright, Helsingfors: Söderström).

(1941) *Über den physikalischen Realitätsbegriff. Zweiter Beitrag zum logischen Empirismus*, Helsinki: Acta Philosophica Fennica, 4.

(1943) *Syvähenkinen elämä. Keskusteluja viimeisistä* [The Depths of Spiritual Life: Discussions on the Ultimate Questions], Helsinki: Otava.

(1944) *Tankens oro. Tre samtal om de yttersta tingen* [The Disquietude of Thought: Three Discussions on the Ultimate Questions], Helsingfors: Söderström.

(1950) *Zur Metatheorie der Quantenmechanik*, Helsinki: Acta Philosophica Fennica, 5.

(1956) *Terminalkausalität als die Grundlage eines unitarischen Naturbegriffs. Eine naturphilosophische Untersuchung. Erster Teil. Terminalkausalität in der Atom-dynamik*, Helsinki: Acta Philosophica Fennica, 10.

(1958) 'Einstein–Minkowskin invarianssiteoria. Tutkimuksia sen loogistietoteoreettisesta luonteesta ja sen luonnonfilosofiesesta merkityksesta' [The Einstein–Minkowski theory of invariance: investigations into its logico-epistemological nature and its significance for the philosophy of nature], *Ajatus* 21: 5–121.

(1960) 'Arkikokemuksen perseptuaalinen ja konseptuaalinen aines' [The perceptual and conceptual components of everyday experience], *Ajatus* 23: 50–115 (posthumous).

Secondary literature:

Hintikka, Jaakko (1970) 'Philosophy of science (Wissenschaftstheorie) in Finland', *Zeitschrift für allgemeine Wissenschaften 1*: 119–32

Regnell, Hans (1958–9) 'Eino Kaila', *Vetenskapssocietetens i Lund årsbok*

Kaila's first book was influenced by Gestalt psychology. Later, he worked mostly in the theory of knowledge and the philosophy of science. He became influenced by the logical positivism of the Vienna Circle and wrote several works in the spirit of this philosophy, including his popular book on what knowledge is and what it is not (1939). The central idea in the latter book is that all human cognition is characterized by a search for invariances, lawlike uniformities. From this point of view he traces the development of sciences from antiquity to Galileo to modern times, outlines the logical empiricist views on formal and empirical truth, and defends the deductive-nomological model of explanation. The last ten years of his life he spent studying problems in the philosophy of science arising from the most recent discoveries in physics, especially quantum mechanics. During this period he modified his previous logical empiricist views and returned to a kind of holism. He claimed that the earlier mechanistic and deterministic approach in physics had to be abandoned and replaced by a kind of field-theoretical or holistic approach considering each individual phenomenon as a function of a totality. He also claimed that processes are not always in their entirety determined by the initial conditions. Kaila spoke of 'terminal causality' in contrast to 'initial causality'. The dialogue *Tankens oro* (1944) was concerned with problems of natural philosophy and worldview.

Sources: R. S. Cohen (ed.) (1979) *Reality and Experience: Four Philosophical Essays*, Dordrecht: Reidel (with substantial introduction by G. H. von Wright and a bibliography).

I. GULLVÅG

Kaneko, Takezo

Japanese. **b:** 1905, Kochi, Japan. **d:** 1987; Tokyo. **Cat:** Hegelian. **Ints:** Hegelian studies; ethics; existentialism. **Educ:** Tokyo University. **Infls:** Hegel, Jaspers and Heidegger. **Appts:** Professor, Tokyo, 1945; Dean of Faculty of Letters, 1957; Dean of Faculty of Letters, Hokkaido University, 1963; Dean of Faculty of Letters, Seikei University, 1965; Professor at International Christian University, Tokyo.

Main publications:

(1932–52) (trans.) *Seishin Genshogaku* (translation of Hegel's *Phenomenology of Spirit*; revised and annotated version in 2 vols, (1976) and (1979), Tokyo: Iwanami Publishing.

(1944) *Hegel no Kokka kan* [Hegel's View of the Nation], Tokyo.

(1953) *Jitsuzon Risei no Tetsugaku* [Philosophy of Existentialistic Reason], Tokyo: Kobundo Publishing.

(1957) *Ronrigaku Gairon* [An Introduction to Ethics], Tokyo: Iwanami Publishing.

Kaneko's father, Kaneko Naokichi (1868–1944), was a pioneer in the formation of the style of Japanese business known as 'Shosha'. He was one of the earliest 'Protestant-like' capitalists in Japan, and this background influenced Takezo's outlook. Kaneko himself was not only a commentator on Hegel but also translated him into Japanese, the *Seishin Genshogaku* (1932–52) being regarded as outstanding. The study of Hegel in Japan has been significantly promoted and enhanced by this work. Kaneko was also a student of **Heidegger** and **Jaspers**, and founded the Jitsuzongshugi Kyokai, an Association for the Study of Existentialism in Japan.

TOGO TSUKAHARA

Kang Youwei (K'ang Yu-wei)

Chinese. *b:* 1858, Nanhai District, Guangdong Province, China. *d:* 1927, Qingdao. *Cat:* Confucian scholar and political reformer. *Ints:* Jinwen (new text) Confucianism. *Educ:* Studied the Chinese classics within his family and with Zhu Jiujiang; later studied daoism and Buddhism, and in Shanghai became acquainted with Western thought. Passed traditional examinations in the Chinese classics. *Infls:* Zhu Jiujiang, Liao Ping, the Confucian classics and idealist neo-Confucianism. *Appts:* Founder of the Wanmu Caotang School, Guangzhou; official in the Board of Works; Founder of the reforming newspaper *Zhongwai Jiwen*; Founder of the Society for the Study of National Strengthening; Founder of the Society for Protecting the Nation; adviser to the Emperor in the Hundred Days Reform; Founder of the Society to Protect the Emperor (later changed to Society for Constitutional Government).

Main publications:

(1897) *A Study of Confucius as a Reformer*, Shanghai: Wanmu Caotang.
(1918) *Studies in the Forged Classics*, 6 vols.
(1931) *New Studies in the Forged Classics* Beijing: Wenhua Xueshe.
(1935) *The Book of the Great Unity*, Zhonghua Book Company (English translation, *Ta T'ung Shu: The One-World Philosophy of K'ang Yu-wei*, trans. L. G. Thompson, London: Allen & Unwin, 1958).

Secondary literature:

Boorman, H. (ed.) (1970) *Biographical Dictionary of Republican China*, New York and London: Columbia University Press.
Briere, O. (1956) *Fifty Years of Chinese Philosophy 1898–1950*, London: George Allen & Unwin Ltd.
Chan, W. (1963) *A Source Book in Chinese Philosophy*, Princeton: Princeton University Press.
Complete Chinese Encyclopedia (1987), Philosophy Volumes, Beijing: Chinese Encyclopedia Publications.
Hsiao, K. (1975) *A Modern China and a New World: K'ang Yu-wei Reformer and Utopian*, Seattle: University of Washington Press.

Kang was the leader of the reform movement which led to the abortive Hundred Days Reform of 1898, China's last hope for political transformation under the Qing dynasty. His studies of Confucian, daoist and Buddhist thought and his understanding of Western civilization (later enhanced by years of exile) shaped his deep political apprehension over China's weakness and corruption, and his utopian and mystical side gave him the courage to send a series of severely critical memorials proposing bold programmes of reform to the Guangxu emperor. These include the famous candidates' memorial signed by several hundred examination candidates in Beijing to protest against a humiliating treaty with Japan in 1895 and the memorials which led to the Hundred Days Reform of 1898.

After conservative court opposition smothered his first reforming initiative, Kang turned to scholarship. His study of calligraphy raised questions of the authenticity of the Confucian classics. Under the influence of Liao Ping, Kang claimed that the traditional old text (*guwen*) versions of the classics—allegedly saved from the book-burning of China's first Emperor—were forged and that the true versions were those of the new text (*jinwen*) school of the Former Han dynasty. In taking up this ancient controversy, Kang argued that Confucius of the authentic classics was a reformer, thus lending legitimacy to his own reforming efforts within the context of tradition.

Through his newspaper *Zhongwai Jiwen*, the Society for the Study of National Strengthening and the Society for Protecting the Nation, Kang, assisted by **Liang Qichao** and other former pupils, gained enthusiastic popular support for reform. He also won over key court officials who at the beginning of the Hundred Days Reform recommended him to the Emperor. Kang's proposals shaped many reforming decrees which might have modernized China under imperial rule. The reform period was aborted, however, by a palace coup led by the empress dowager Cixi, and Kang fled to Hong Kong to save his life. Kang travelled to Japan, Britain and Canada, unsuccessfully seeking support for a campaign to rescue the Emperor and to displace the empress dowager.

Kang again turned to scholarship, writing commentaries on the Confucian classics based on his earlier new text interpretation. He also completed the summary of his syncretic utopian views, *The Book of the Great Unity* (1935), written between the 1880s and 1902 and published in full only after his death. In this book Kang provided a vision of society to be reached in the third age of Confucian social progress. The first age is one of chaos and autocracy, egoism, individualism, nationalism and capitalism; the second age is one of minor peace and constitutional monarchy; and the third age is one of great unity under the Confucian virtue of humanity (*ren*) and the rule of the people. In this final age, nation-states would give way to a world parliament in which small democratic communities would have equal representation. Each community would have communally owned property, classes would be abolished, and there would be equality of economic reward. The family would fall away in favour of sexual freedom, sexual equality and communal child-rearing. In all political, social and economic respects there would be full equality. Clearly this vision can be reconciled with Confucian loyalties only against the background of Kang's reinterpretation of Confucius as a radical reformer, but Kang did retain Confucian themes to shape his vision. In applying his account of Confucius to his own times Kang tested the limits of a Confucian response to an overwhelming Western threat to China's survival.

In continuing exile Kang supported constitutional monarchy and fiercely opposed the republican proposals of **Sun Zhongshan**. His return to China in 1914 led to renewed, but fruitless, attempts to gain Qing dynasty restoration. He feared that Westernization would destroy Chinese traditions and proposed establishing a Confucian state religion, but by this time his influence had ended.

NICHOLAS BUNNIN

Kanger, Stig
Swedish. *b:* 10 July 1924, China. *d:* 13 March 1988, Uppsala. *Cat:* Logician. *Ints:* Ethics; philosophy of law; philosophy of language; philosophy of science. *Educ:* University of Stockholm. *Infls:* Literary influences include Frege, Russell, Carnap, Tarski, Church, Gentzen and Quine; personal influences include Anders Wedberg. *Appts:* Associate Professor (Docent), in Theoretical Philosophy, Stockholm University, 1957–63; Acting Professor, Åbo Academy, Finland, 1963–8; Professor of Theoretical Philosophy, Uppsala University, 1968–88.

Main publications:
(1957) *Provability in Logic*, Stockholm Studies in Philosophy, Stockholm: Stockholm University.
(1957) *New Foundations for Ethical Theory*, Part 1, Stockholm (mimeographed); reprinted in R. Hilpinen (ed.), *Deontic Logic: Introductory and Systematic Readings*, Dordrecht: Reidel, 1972.
(1957) 'The Morning Star paradox', *Theoria* 23: 1–11.
(1963) (with Helle Kanger) 'Rights and parliamentarism', *Theoria*, 32: 85–115.
(1972) 'Measurement: an essay in philosophy of science', *Theoria* 38: 1–63.
(1972) 'Law and logic', *Theoria* 38: 105–32.

Although Kanger's greatest achievements were in pure logic he also made important contributions to philosophy by applying logical techniques within ethical theory, philosophy of law, philosophy of language and philosophy of science. His dissertation, *Provability in Logic* (1957), contains major contributions to two central areas of logic. By combining Gentzen's sequent calculus with the model theory of **Tarski**, he obtains new and simplified proofs of central metalogical results like **Gödel**'s completeness theorem, Löwenheim–Skolem's theorem and Gentzen's Hauptsatz. He also develops a new semantic theory for various modal logics and connects it with sequent calculi for these logics. This work makes Kanger one of the founders of possible-worlds semantics.

STEN LINDSTRÖM

Kaplan, D(avid)
American. *b:* 17 September 1933, Los Angeles, California. *Cat:* Logician; analytic philosopher of language. *Ints:* Philosophy of language. *Educ:* University of California, Los Angeles. *Infls:* Frege, Russell and Quine. *Appts:* From 1961, successively Lecturer, Assistant, Associate and full Professor at the University of California, Los Angeles.

Main publications:
(1968) 'Quantifying in', *Synthèse* 19: 178–214.
(1978) 'Dthat', in P. Cole, (ed.) *Syntax and Semantics*, vol. 9, New York: Academic Press.
(1986) 'Opacity', in L. Hahn and P. Schilpp (eds), *Philosophy of W. v. Quine*, La Salle, Ill.: Open Court.
(1989) 'Demonstratives' and 'Afterthoughts', in J. Almog *et al.*, *Themes from Kaplan*, New York: Oxford University Press.

Secondary literature:
Almog J., Perry, J. and Wettstein, H. (eds) (1989) *Themes from Kaplan*, New York: Oxford University Press.

Kaplan's work concerns intensional logics. In his most influential work (1989) he develops **Russell**'s idea of the *singular proposition*, that is a proposition which contains an extralinguistic object as part of its structure. The impetus comes from an approach to modal logic, according to which the assessment of, say, 'Something is necessarily F' involves enquiring, *of a certain given object*, whether *it* is F in other possible worlds. Kaplan argues that sentences of ordinary language containing words like 'this' and 'that', as used to pick out individual objects, express singular proposi-

tions. All of this involves some departure from a claim made by **Frege**, the founder of modern logic, although the extent of the departure is controversial. Frege claimed that a proposition about an object contains a *mode of presentation* of the object, rather than the object itself, and in his earlier 'Quantifying in' (1968) Kaplan had followed this line. His later change to a view which recognizes singular propositions opens up problems about the relationships between language, thought and the world formerly thought to have been solved by the Fregean approach. Kaplan's later views are part of a general supposedly anti-Fregean movement, whose other chief representatives are Saul **Kripke** and Hilary **Putnam** and whose implications are the subject of strenuous contemporary debate.
Sources: DAS, 4.

GREGORY McCULLOCH

Kaplan, Mordechai Menahem

American.*b:*11June1881,Svencionys,Lithuania.*d:*1983,NewYork.*Cat:*Rabbi;philosopher;historianof Jewishthought;Reconstructionisttheologian.*Ints:*PhilosophyofJudaismascultureratherthanfaithor tradition. *Educ:* Jewish Orthodox; ordained 1909, Conservative Jewish Theological Seminary, New York. *Infls:* Moses Haim Luzzato, the Haskalah (Jewish Enlightenment movement), Nachman Krochmal, Hermann Cohen, Ahad ha-Am, Solomon Schechter, American pragmatism, and social philosophiesandscience.*Appts:*1909,Rabbi,Kehillath Jeshurun Orthodox Synagogue, New York; 1909–63, Lecturer, Principal and Dean, Teachers InstituteofandLecturerinHomiletics,Midrashand Philosophies of Religion, Rabbinical School of JewishTheologicalSeminary,NewYork;1917–22, Founder and Rabbi, Jewish Cultural Centre, New York;1935,Founder,SocietyfortheAdvancementof Judaism, *TheReconstructionist*magazine,andJewishReconstructionistFoundation.

Main publications:

(1934) *Judaism as Civilization*; 2nd edition, New York, 1958 New York: Schocken, 1967, Reconstructionist, 1981; Philadelphia: JPSA, 1981.
(1937) *The Meaning of God in Modern Jewish Religion*, New York: Behrman, later editions 1942, 1945, 1947; New York: Reconstructionist, 1962: Wincote, PA: Reconstructionist, 1975.
(1948–9) *Future of the American Jew*, New York: Macmillan and Wincote, PA: Reconstructionist, 1981.
(1951) *The Faith of America*, New York: H. Schuman.

(1954) *Ha-Emunah ve-ha-Musar* [Faith and Ethics], Jerusalem.
(1956) *Questions Jews Ask*, New York: Reconstructionist; revised edition, 1961.
(1958) *Judaism Without Supernaturalism*;39 New York: Reconstructionist, 1960, 1967 (new eds).
(1967) *Greater Judaism in the Making*, Wincote, PA: Reconstructionist.
(1970) *The Religion of Ethical Nationhood: Judaism's Contribution to World Peace*, New York: Macmillan.
(1985) *Dynamic Judaism*, Wincote, PA: Reconstructionist, and New York: Schocken.

Secondary literature:

Goldsmith, E. S. (ed.) (1990) *The American Judaism of Mordecai M. Kaplan*, New York: New York University Press.
Libowitz (1984) *Mordecai M. Kaplan and the Development of Reconstructionism*, New York: Mellen.
Mordecai M. Kaplan Jubilee Volume, 1953.
Rogers, D. J. (1990) *The American Empirical Movement in Theology*, New York: P. Lang.
Scult, M. (1993) *Judaism Faces the Twentieth Century*, Detroit: Wayne State University Press.
Weinberger, T. (1991) *Strategies for Sustaining Religious Commitment*, New York: Mellen.

Through his teaching at the Jewish Theological Seminary for five decades, Kaplan exerted an influence that was both personal and academic. Reconstructionism became a new movement within American Judaism. It was based on the idea of Judaism as an evolving and self-sufficient religious culture, grounded in social mores as well as belief. Kaplan extended *Ahad ha-Am's* advocacy of Israel as a cultural centre to the diaspora community. He emphasized the importance of secular culture to the ongoing development of Jewish civilization and advocated 'evolution' to prevent petrification. His is a social rather than a metaphysical or textual philosophy of Judaism. Kaplan has been criticized for emphasizing humanism at the expense of the revelationary and historical aspects of Judaism and for reducing the idea of God to that of mere abstract potential. Even those who were influenced by him, such as Milton Steinberg and Will Herberg, rejected his evolutionary theory. Although Reconstructionism was successful in its educational and cultural outreach programme, its followers have diminished, although it continues to attract much academic comment.

Sources: EncJud; NUC; Schoeps; *Mordechai M. Kaplan Jubilee Volume*, 1953.

IRENE LANCASTER

Kareev (also Kareyev), Nikolai Ivanovich

Russian. *b:* 6 December (24 November N.S.) 1850, Moscow. *d:* 18 February 1931, Leningrad. *Cat:* Philosopher of history. *Educ:* Studied History at University of Moscow. *Infls:* Kant, Lavrov and Mikhailovsky. *Appts:* 1879–84, Professor of History at the University of Warsaw; 1885–99 and from 1907, Professor of History, University of St Petersburg; from 1929 Honorary Member of the Soviet Academy of Sciences.

Main publications:

(1883) *Osnovnye voprosy filosofii istorii* [Fundamental Problems of the Philosophy of History], Moscow.

(1890) *Sushchnost' istoricheskogo protsessa i rol' lichnosti v istorii* [The Essence of the Historical Process and the Role of the Individual in History] St Petersburg.

(1895) *Mysli ob osnovakh nravstvennosti* [Thoughts about the Bases of Morality], St Petersburg.

(1968) (ed. Louis J. Shein) *Readings in Russian Philosophical Thought*, The Hague: Mouton (includes a brief translated extracts from Kareev's historico-philosophical works).

(1977) (ed. Louis J. Shein) *Readings in Russian Philosophical Thought: Philosophy of History*, Waterloo, Ontario: Wilfrid Laurier University Press (includes brief translated extracts from Kareev's two main historico-philosophical works).

Kareev was a distinguished historian whose work on the peasantry on the eve of the French Revolution impressed Marx and Engels. Although his own political stance was liberal, he was dismissed from the University of St Petersburg in 1899 following student unrest. He returned after the 1905 Revolution, and represented the Constitutional Democrats (Cadets) in the First Duma.

Kareev's philosophy of history was an extension of the subjectivism of the Populists **Lavrov** and **Mikhailovsky**. He combated any conception of historical development as a wholly objective process governed by universal historical laws; historical events, though subject to biological, psychological and sociological laws, are themselves individual and unrepeatable. His first main target was Hegelian historiosophy, although he went on to criticize Marxist and social-Darwinist approaches. Fundamental to his 'personal prin-

ciple in history' was an insistence that historical events are reducible to the actions and interactions of individuals (he criticized **Tolstoy** for belittling the historical impact of individual wills). He believed that history should offer not only an objective survey of the phenomena of social and spiritual life, but also a subjective ethical evaluation of the meaning of the historical process. Although he rejected fictitious and one-sided notions of historical progress associated with belief in historical laws, the idea of progress in this subjective sense was central to his philosophy of history.

In his work on ethics, Kareev expounded an ethical individualism which stressed the individual's absolute value in the face of its depreciation by utilitarians, Hegelians and Marxists.

COLIN CHANT

Katz, Jerrold

American. *b:* July 1932. *Cat:* Philosopher of language; linguistic theorist. *Educ:* 1954, BA, George Washington University; 1960, PhD, Princeton University. *Infls:* Noam Chomsky, W. V. O. Quine and Ludwig Wittgenstein. *Appts:* 1969, Distinguished Professor in Philosophy and Linguistics, Graduate Center of the City University of New York; Visiting Professor at numerous universities.

Main publications:

(1966) *The Philosophy of Language*, New York: Harper & Row.

(1972) *Semantic Theory*, New York: Harper & Row.

(1976) (with T. G. Bever and D. T. Langendoen) *An Integrated Theory of Linguistic Ability*, New York: T. Y. Crowell, Harper & Row.

(1977) *Propositional Structure and Illocutionary Force*, New York: T. Y. Crowell, Harper & Row.

(1981) *Language and Other Abstract Objects*, Blackwell.

(1985) (ed.) *The Philosophy of Linguistics*, Oxford University Press.

(1990) *The Metaphysics of Meaning*, Bradford Books/MIT Press.

Secondary literature:

Langendoen, D. T. and Postal, P. (1984) *The Vastness of Language*, Oxford: Blackwell.

Soames, S. 'Semantics and psychology', in Katz 1985.

Katz is associated especially with Platonism in linguistics. This stance is best understood against the background of his earlier work on language.

He was concerned to develop a semantic theory which explained the meaning of terms by the device of semantic markers which exhibited the salient semantic features of those terms. Subsequently he endeavoured to build on this theory a further account embracing the speech-act theory originating with John **Austin** and later developed by John **Searle**. He intended to show how the propositional content of sentences is the information which determines the particular speech-acts performed by such sentences in a standard context. Critics questioned how such a theory could do justice to the essentially pragmatic features of speech-acts, i.e. those involving context and particular aims and effects. More than anything else, however, it was his concern with the issue of analyticity and necessary truth which led him to principled disagreement with both behaviourism and cognitivism in linguistics. In respect of the latter view it is Chomsky who provides Katz with his main target for attack. Katz contends that, if there are necessary truths, they cannot be dependent on even the most abstract features of a language-speaker's psychology, since these latter are contingent. Additionally, since the number of possible grammars far outstrips those which are compatible with what we know of human capacities, it would again be illegitimate to make necessary truth 'relative' to just those languages which fall into that more restricted range.

It is his contention that the subject-matter of linguistics is more akin to that of mathematics than it is, say, to that of biology or chemistry. Languages are neither external empirical phenomena nor are they housed in the minds of language users. In this respect they resemble the entities of mathematics such as numbers, sets and functions in that they are (i) perfectly real and mind-independent, and (ii) accessed by a non-sensory 'intuition'. Importantly, Katz distinguishes this intuition from introspection: as traditionally conceived, the latter has to do with the apprehension of an agent's subjective states; the former is a matter of the direct apprehension of something beyond such subjective states. The charge Katz lays against cognitivists is that they conflate the knowledge people have of language with what that knowledge is knowledge of, namely the language itself. With regard to semantics, he argues that the elements of a semantic theory no more refer to the cognitive processes that are involved in linguistic understanding than mathematical theories refer to the cognitive processes involved in understanding mathematics.

The linguistic theorist is, therefore, according to Katz, in just the same case with the theorist of mathematics, investigating an objective world of entities and discovering facts about their properties and relationships. In response to the charge that this makes linguistics unscientific, and consequently of little relevance to the main concerns of linguistic theories, Katz maintains that it is an empirical matter to determine which language is the language a speaker knows and understands. The implications of this for linguistics are uncompromising and direct: linguistics thus characterized is independent of other disciplines, especially those claiming to be empirical, like psychology and sociology, and is therefore not reducible to them. Inevitably, Katz has come into conflict with a number of prominent philosophers of mind and language. His stand on the issue of analyticity is plainly opposed to that of **Quine**, and he has received criticism from his former collaborator **Fodor** on the status of linguistics as a discipline. There are others, however, who have adopted the Platonist standpoint, including Scott Soames, D. T. Langendoen and P. Postal, but given the somewhat intimidating, not to say rebarbative, technicality of some of this other work, Katz himself remains Platonism's most accessible and effective publicist in the field of linguistics and the philosophy of language.

Sources: See secondary literature.

DENIS POLLARD

Kautsky, Karl

Czech-German. *b:* 1854, Prague. *d:* 1938, Amsterdam. *Cat:* Marxist. *Educ:* University of Vienna, left without a degree. *Infls:* Marx.

Main publications:

(1887) *Karl Marx's ökonomische Lehren*, Stuttgart, J. H. W. Dietz (English translation, *The Economic Doctrines of Karl Marx*, London, 1925).

(1892) *Das Erfurter Programme in seinem grundsätzlichen Teil erlautert*, Stuttgart: J. H. W. Dietz.

(1895) *Die Vorlaufer des neuern Sozialismus*, 2 vols, Stuttgart: J. H. W. Dietz.

(1901) *Die soziale Revolution*, Berlin: Buchh. Vorwärtz (English translation, *The Social Revolution*, London, 1909).

(1918) *Die Diktatur des Proletariats*, Vienna: Wiener Volksbuchhandlung. (English translation, *The Dictatorship of the Proletariat*, London, 1918; reissued, New York: W. W. Norton Inc., 1971).

(1919) *Terrorismus und Communismus*, Berlin: Verlag Neues Vaterland (English translation, *Terrorism and Communism*, London, 1920).

Secondary literature:

Geary, Dick (1987) *Karl Kautsky*, Manchester: Manchester University Press.

Kolakowski, Leszek (1978) *Main Currents of Marxism*, vol. 2, Oxford: Oxford University Press.

Salvadori, Massimo (1979) *Karl Kautsky*, trans. Jon Rothschild, London: New Left Books.

Born of a Czech father and German mother, Kautsky joined the German Social Democratic Party as a student. After graduating he worked under **Bernstein** on the official Social Democratic newspaper, travelled to Paris (where he met **Plekhanov**) and to London (where he met Marx and Engels), before founding *Die Neue Zeit*. This became the main theoretical journal of Marxism before the First World War, and Kautsky remained its editor until 1917. He played a major role in the drafting of the SPD party manifesto, the Erfurt Programme, and from 1900 was engaged in polemics with Bernstein on the right of the party and with Luxemburg on the left. For most of the war he was in the minority anti-war faction of the party, and from 1917 was engaged in a long-running polemic against **Lenin** and the Bolsheviks. He played a leading role in drafting the programme of the revived Social Democratic Party at Heidelberg in 1925. Having emigrated to Prague after the Dolfuss coup of 1934 in Austria, he moved to Holland just before the Nazi invasion of Czechoslovakia.

In the two decades that separate the death of Engels (1895) from the outbreak of war in 1914, Kautsky was the leading Marxist theoretician, defending the version of Marxism that had been handed on by Engels. This viewed Marxism as a determinist science of history, devoid of value judgements, committed to no theories about human nature or the nature of human emancipation or fulfilment, and hostile to the idea that the spontaneous will-power of committed individuals can play a significant role in historical development. It attached little weight to Hegel's influence on Marx; and of course Kautsky wrote in ignorance of much of Marx's earlier writings, which had not then been published. But he was prepared to make minor amendments to the Marxist system, for example in his claim (later taken over and made famous by Lenin) that 'socialist consciousness is something introduced into the proletarian class struggle from without' by (often bourgeois) members of the intelligentsia. The success of Lenin and the Bolsheviks in seizing power in 1917 and Kautsky's condemnation of their methods combined to sideline the kind of Marxism he represented in favour of the Leninism–Stalinism that became historically dominant.

Sources: Turner; BDM.

NICHOLAS EVERITT

Kedrov, Bonifatii Mikhailovich

Russian. *b:* 27 November (O.S.) 1903, Iaroslavl', Russia. *d:* 10 September 1985, USSR. *Cat:* Marxist dialectical materialist; chemist. *Ints:* Philosophy of science; dialectical materialism; logic. *Educ:* Moscow State University and the Institute of Chemistry of the Soviet Academy of Sciences. *Appts:* Held appointments for varying periods at the Moscow State University, at Communist Party's Academy of Social Sciences and at the Institute of Philosophy and the Institute of the History of the Natural Sciences and Technology of the Soviet Academy of Sciences.

Main publications:

(1946) *O kolichestvennikh i kachestvennikh izmeneniiakh v prirode* [On Quantitative and Qualitative Changes in Nature], Moscow.

(1954) *Dialeckticheskii materializm i sovremennykh otkrytiiakh v oblasti stroeniia materii* [Dialectical Materialism and Contemporary Discoveries in the Field of the Structures of Matter], Moscow.

(1961–85) *Klassifikatsiia nauk* [The Classification of the Sciences], 3 vols, Moscow.

(1963) *Edinstvo dialektiki, logiki, i teoriia poznaniia* [The Unity of Dialectics, Logic and the Theory of Knowledge], Moscow.

(1969) *Lenin i revoliutsiia v estestvoznanii XX veka* [Lenin and the 20th Century Revolution in the Natural Sciences], Moscow.

(1983) *Kak izuchat' knigu V. I. Lenina 'Materializm i empiriokrititsiz'* [How to Study V. I. Lenin's Book 'Materialism and Empirocriticism'], fourth edition, Moscow.

(1987) (with A. P. Ogurtsov) *Marksistskaia Konseptsiia istorii estestvoznaiiam* [The Marxist Conception of the History of the Natural Sciences], Moscow.

Secondary literature:

Alekseev, P. V. (ed.) (1993) *Filosofy Rossii xix–xx stoletii*, Moscow, p. 84.

Graham, Loren R. (1972) *Science and Philosophy in the Soviet Union*, New York: Alfred A. Knopf; revised edition, *Science, Philosophy, and Human Behavior in the Soviet Union*, Columbia University Press, 1987.

Scanlan, James P. (1985) *Marxism in the USSR: A Critical Survey of Current Soviet Thought*, Cornell University Press.

A Communist Party member since 1918, during the Soviet period Kedrov was a prolific and influential exponent of Marxist–Leninist dialectical materialism. Following Friedrich Engels and Vladimir **Lenin**, Kedrov defined philosophy as the science of the most general laws of the development of nature, society and human thinking—the same formula Engels had used for dialectics. Kedrov advocated dialectical logic as the study of the subjective dimension of the dialectics objectively present in reality.

By calling Marxist philosophy a science, Kedrov was opposing those Soviet thinkers who viewed it as an ideology; and by identifying it with dialectics, he was rejecting what he later called the 'absurd ontologization' imposed on Soviet philosophy by Stalin. His influence thus often countered partisan dogmatism and upheld the independence and objectivity of philosophy and science. As early as 1948 he was dismissed as editor of the journal *Voprosy filosofii* [Problems of Philosophy] for failing to support political strictures on biology and physics. In the Soviet controversy concerning formal logic he defended the 'two logics' policy that granted it legitimacy. He never renounced his allegiance to Engels and Lenin, however, and in later years he deplored the lack of unanimity among Soviet philosophers on questions of dialectics.

JAMES SCANLAN

Kelsen, Hans

American (naturalized in 1945). *b:* 11 October 1881, Prague. *d:* April 1973. *Cat:* Legal positivist. *Ints:* Legal theory. *Infls:* Kant and Hume. *Appts:* Professor of Law, University of Vienna, University of Cologne, University of Prague; Lecturer, Harvard Law School; Professor of Political Science, University of California, Berkeley.

Main publications:

(1944) *Peace Through Law*, Chapel Hill: University of North Carolina Press.
(1949) *General Theory of Law and State*, trans. Anders Wedberg, Cambridge, Mass.: Harvard University Press.
(1950) *The Law of the United Nations: A Critical Analysis of the Fundamental Problems*, London: Stevens.
(1955) *The Communist Theory of Law*, London: Stevens.
(1957) *What is Justice?*, University of California Press.
(1967) *Principles of International Law*, rev. Robert W. Tucker, New York: Rinehart & Winston.

(1967) *Pure Theory of Law*, trans. Max Knight, Chapel Hill: University of Carolina Press.
(1974) *Essays in Legal and Moral Philosophy*, trans. Peter Heath, Dordrecht: Reidel.
(1991) *General Theory of Norms*, trans. Michael Hartney, Oxford: Clarendon Press.

Secondary literature:

Harris, J. W. (1971) 'When and why does the *Grundnorm* change?', *Cambridge Law Journal*: 103.
Lipsky, George A. (ed.) (1953) *Law and Politics in the World Community: Essays on Kelsen's Pure Theory and Related Problems in International Law*, Berkeley: University of California Press.
Salo, Engel and Merall, Rudolf A. (1964) *Law State and International Legal Order, Essays in Honor of Hans Kelsen*, Knoxville: University of Tennessee Press.
Tur, Richard and Twining, William (eds) (1986) *Essays on Kelsen*, Oxford: Clarendon Press.

Often termed a 'positivist of positivists', Kelsen offers a 'pure theory of law' which is devoid of any reference to ethics, politics, sociology, etc. He excludes disciplines such as ethics and politics from his enquiry about law because he wants to avoid an uncritical mixture of different methodologies (what he calls methodological syncretism) that could obscure the science of law (1967, p. 1). His theory offers a structural analysis of law as it is, but is not restricted to a specific legal order.

For Kelsen, a legal system is a hierarchy of norms ('ought' statements which cannot be proved to exist factually) where each norm is validated by another norm which in turn is validated by another, and so on down the hierarchy. Each norm is derived from another norm and this is what gives the norm its validity:

'The legal order is not a system of co-ordinated norms of equal level, but a hierarchy of different levels of legal norms. Its unity is brought about by... the fact that the validity of a norm, created according to another norm, rests in that other norm, whose creation in turn, is determined by a third one' (ibid., pp. 221–2).

If a norm can be derived only from another norm, does this derivation of norms carry on *ad infinitum* or does it come to a stop somewhere? According to Kelsen there is a norm on which all the other norms rest and this is the *Grundnorm* (or the basic norm). He formulates the basic norm as 'Coercive acts sought to be performed under the conditions and in the manner which the historically first constitution and the norms created according to it, prescribe. (In short: One ought to behave as the constitution prescribes)' (pp. 200–1).

This *Grundnorm* is non-positive; that is, it is not a real act of will of a legal organ, but is presupposed in juristic thinking. It is that which gives unity to the legal system. And at the *Grundnorm* level, ethical, sociological and political factors do play a role.

Although Kelsen's 'pure theory of law' provides a commendable self-contained account of a legal system, it can be criticized, first, for being too distant from the 'real' world of law and, second, for allowing moral, social and political considerations, which he strenuously tried to keep out of his legal theory, to enter the picture at the *Grundnorm* level.

Sources: WWW(Am).

INDIRA MAHALINGAM CARR

of Hume plays down the sceptical element in his philosophy and stresses his idea of natural belief, our inescapable reliance on principles which we cannot rationally justify, but do not need to. His direct contribution to philosophy in his one non-historical book is not, despite its title, really idealistic except, as he puts it, in affirming that 'spiritual values have a determining voice in the ordering of the universe'. He holds the data of sense to be objective or non-mental, but in a way that does not rule out their being private. They are, in very much the manner of Kant, conceived as non-extended but ordered by categories and by intuitions of space and time. All students of Descartes, Hume and Kant are in Kemp Smith's debt, but his own doctrines have not been taken up or even much discussed.

Sources: Metz; DNB; Passmore 1957.

ANTHONY QUINTON

Kemp Smith, Norman

British. *b:* 5 May 1872, Dundee. *d:* 3 September 1958, Edinburgh. *Cat:* Realist. *Ints:* History of philosophy; epistemology. *Educ:* St Andrews University. *Infls:* Robert Adamson and Samuel Alexander. *Appts:* Assistant to E. Caird and then to Robert Adamson at Glasgow, 1894–1906; Professor of Philosophy, Princeton, 1906–16; Professor of Logic and Metaphysics, Edinburgh, 1919–45.

Main publications:

(1902) *Studies in the Cartesian Philosophy*, London.
(1918) *Commentary on Kant's Critique of Pure Reason*, London.
(1924) *Prolegomena to an Idealist Theory of Knowledge*, London.
(1941) *The Philosophy of David Hume*, London.
(1952) *New Studies in the Philosophy of Descartes*, London: Macmillan.
(1967) *The Credibility of Divine Existence* (essays with memoir), London: Macmillan.

Secondary literature:

Memoir and discussions in *The Credibility of Divine Existence* (1967), London: Macmillan.

Kemp Smith was without doubt the most distinguished philosophical historian of philosophy in Britain in the twentieth century. Descartes, Kant and Hume were the successive objects of his close and penetrating observation. In the case of Kant he supplemented his commentary with a translation of the *Critique of Pure Reason* better than any that had been made before. His account

Kenny, (Sir) Anthony (John Patrick)

British. *b:* 16 March 1931, Liverpool, England. *Cat:* Analytical philosopher. *Ints:* Philosophy of mind; philosophy of religion; history of philosophy. *Educ:* The Gregorian University, Rome and St Benet's Hall, Oxford. *Infls:* Personal influences: Copleston, Prior, P. Fitzpatrick, C. J. F. Williams, Anscombe, Geach and Ryle. Literary influences: Aristotle, Aquinas, Frege and Wittgenstein. *Appts:* 1959–63, Curate in Liverpool; 1964–78, Fellow of Balliol College, Oxford; 1978–89, Master of Balliol College, Oxford; 1989–93, President of the British Academy; 1989–, Warden of Rhodes House, Oxford and Professorial Fellow, St John's College, Oxford.

Main publications:

(1963) *Action, Emotion and Will*, London: Routledge.
(1968) *Descartes: A Study of His Philosophy*, New York: Random House.
(1969) *The Five Ways: St. Thomas Aquinas' Proofs of God's Existence*, London: Routledge & Kegan Paul.
(1973) *The Anatomy of the Soul: Historical Essays in the Philosophy of Mind*, Oxford: Blackwell.
(1973) *Wittgenstein*, Harmondsworth: Penguin.
(1975) *Will, Freedom and Power*, Oxford: Blackwell.
(1978) *The Aristotelian Ethics, a Study of the Relationship between the 'Eudemian' and 'Nicomachian' Ethics of Aristotle*, Oxford: Clarendon Press.
(1978) *Aristotle's Ethics*, Oxford: Clarendon Press.
(1978) *Freewill and Responsibility*: London: Routledge & Kegan Paul.

(1979) *Aristotle's Theory of the Will*, New Haven: Yale University Press.

(1979) *The God of the Philosophers*, Oxford: Clarendon Press.

(1980) *Aquinas*, Oxford: Oxford University Press.

(1983) *Faith and Reason*, New York: Columbia University Press.

(1983) *Thomas More*, Oxford: Oxford University Press.

(1984) *The Legacy of Wittgenstein*, Oxford: Blackwell.

(1985) *The Ivory Tower: Essays in Philosophy and Public Policy*, Oxford: Blackwell.

(1987) *The Heritage of Wisdom: Essays in the History of Philosophy*, Oxford: Blackwell.

(1989) *The Metaphysics of Mind*, Oxford: Oxford University Press.

(1992) *Aquinas on Mind*, London: Routledge.

(1992) *Aristotle on the Perfect Life*, Oxford: Clarendon Press.

(1992) *What is Faith?*, Oxford: Oxford University Press.

Secondary literature:
Bradley, M. C. (1974) 'Kenny on hard determinism', *AJP* 52: 202–11.

Davies, Brian (1982) 'Kenny on God', *Philosophy* 57: 105–18.

Ellis, Anthony (1978) 'Kenny and the continuity of Wittgenstein's philosophy', *Mind* 87: 270–5.

Wilson, J. R. S. (1972) *Emotion and Object*, London: Cambridge University Press.

Trained in scholastic philosophy and theology, Kenny first studied analytical philosophy from the outside. Under the influence of some leading Catholic philosophers in Oxford, however, he came to regard the thinking of Frege and Wittgenstein as less remote from that of Aristotle and Aquinas than had been supposed. His first book quickly established him as a new and significant contributor to the analytic philosophy of mind. Here, and in his later works, Kenny sought to integrate analytical philosophy with traditional philosophy rather than put them in opposition. *The Metaphysics of Mind* (1989) has some affinities with Ryle's *Concept of Mind*, being also a critique of the Cartesian view of mind. But, in contrast with the iconoclasm of Ryle's 1949 classic, Kenny 'tried to show that an employment of the techniques of linguistic analysis can go hand in hand with a respect for traditional, and indeed ancient, concepts and theses in philosophy' (1989, p. ix). This is reflected in the title *The Metaphysics of Mind* since, as Kenny explains, 'the philosophical system which I try to present is

continuous with that of ... medieval Aristotelianism'.

This stress on continuity is implicit in Kenny's prolific writings in the history of philosophy, which combine analytic and scholarly rigour. His *Wittgenstein* (1973) provoked some controversy by its stress on the continuity between the earlier and the later philosophy of Wittgenstein. In *Aristotle on the Perfect Life* (1992) and other writings on Aristotle he has stressed the importance of the *Eudemian Ethics*.

Kenny's interests in the philosophy of mind have always included moral psychology and were naturally extended in *The Ivory Tower* (1985), which brings together some of his essays in the philosophy of law and of war. He has also contributed considerably to the debate about free will through a careful analysis of notions of 'power', 'intention' and 'will'. Although sceptical of the truth of hard determinism he has argued, against compatibilism, that some forms of determinism are inconsistent with the attribution of free will.

Kenny has written extensively in the philosophy of religion. In his *Faith and Reason* (1983) he commended rationality as the intellectual virtue of 'right belief', involving a mean between the two opposed vices of credulity and scepticism. He has taken a close interest in the arguments of natural theology but has acknowledged that he may appear sceptical from the viewpoint of the theist. His *The Five Ways* (1969) is a sympathetic examination of the arguments for the existence of God advanced by Aquinas, but all were found to be seriously flawed. In *The God of the Philosophers* (1979) Kenny argued that there is a contradiction in the notion of a God who possesses the traditional attributes and who, while forseeing all sins, is the author of none of them.

Sources: Correspondence; Anthony Kenny (1986) *A Path from Rome*, Oxford: OUP; PI; WW 1993.

STUART BROWN

Keynes, John Maynard (from 1942, Baron Keynes of Tilton)

British. *b:* 1883, Cambridge, England. *d:* 1946, Tilton, Sussex. *Cat:* Cambridge political economist. *Ints:* Economics; probability; moral philosophy. *Educ:* MA, King's College, Cambridge. *Infls:* In Preface to his *Treatise on Probability*, Keynes said that he had been 'much influenced by W. E. Johnson, G. E. Moore, and Bertrand Russell, that is to say by Cambridge, which, with great debts to the writers of Continental Europe, yet continues in direct succession the English tradition of Locke and Berkeley and Hume, of Mill and Sidgwick'. His early economic work was started in a context set by Alfred Marshall. **Appts:** Fellow of King's College, Cambridge, 1909–46; innumerable official and government positions.

Main publications:
(1971–89) *Collected Writings*, 30 vols, ed. A. Robinson and D. Moggridge, Macmillan/Cambridge. Of particular philosophical importance or interest are:
(1921) *A Treatise on Probability* (vol. VIII) (mostly written before 1914).
(1931) *Essays in Persuasion* (vol. IX).
(1936) *The General Theory of Employment, Interest and Money* (vol. VII).
(1938) 'My early beliefs', in *Two Memoirs* (vol. X).

Secondary literature:
In economics, the secondary literature is almost everything that has been written since 1936.
Bateman, B. W. and Davis, J. B. (eds) (1991) *Keynes and Philosophy*, Aldershot and Brookfield, VT: Elgar.
Braithwaite, R. B. (1921) Editorial Foreword to *Collected Writings*, vol. VIII.
Carabelli, A. M. (1988) *On Keynes's Method*, London: Macmillan (a philosphical reading).
Davis, J. B. (1994) *The Development of Keynes's Philosophy*, Cambridge.
Fitzgibbons, Athol (1988) *Keynes's Vision: A New Political Economy*, Oxford: Clarendon Press.
Keynes, Milo (ed.) (1975) *Essays on John Maynard Keynes*, Cambridge: Cambridge University Press.
Moggridge, D. E. (1992) *Maynard Keynes: An Economist's Biography*, London and New York: Routledge (contains background).
O'Donnell, R. M. (1989) *Keynes: Philosophy, Economics and Politics*, London: Macmillan.
Ramsey, F. P. (1926) 'Truth and probability', Section 2, much reprinted (for theory of probability).
Skidelsky, R. (1983, 1992) *John Maynard Keynes*, 2 vols so far, 1883–1920 and 1920–37, London: Macmillan.

Keynes was the most important and original economic thinker of the twentieth century. His narrowly-defined philosophical works have been less influential, although there is now a growing recognition of how deeply his thinking on economics was grounded in his wider moral and political beliefs. (This is a central theme of Fitzgibbons's 1988 as well as of O'Donnell 1989 studies.) The final words of the *General Theory* (1936) emphasize the interaction of theory and practice:

the ideas of economists and political philosophers, both when they are right and when they are wrong, are more powerful than is commonly understood. Indeed, the world is ruled by little else ... I am sure that the power of vested interests is vastly exaggerated compared with the gradual encroachment of ideas.

Although this view was modified by some disillusionment in Keynes's final years, it does exemplify a crucial element in his true importance as a philosopher: a belief that theoretical thought can *matter* in a direct, practical sense. This belief was elaborated in a detail seen in few philosophical works since Plato's *Laws*.

Keynes's writings and activities represent a life-long attempt to apply reason to theoretical problems and practical affairs. Just as his early emphasis was on the philosophical basis of reasoning, so his later concern was with various dimensions of rationality in economics and politics
(O'Donnell 1989, p. 331).

The *General Theory* argues that political engagement in an economy is inevitable, either through allegedly neutral *laissez-faire* or in terms of fiscal and monetary intervention. It follows, in Keynes's mind, that a context of political and social values must be adequate to sustain this engagement. The model of interaction between (economic) theory and required (political) action has at least as much philosophical interest as the more widely studied model offered by Marx.

A Treatise on Probability (1921) was a revised version of Keynes's fellowship dissertation for King's College, Cambridge (1909), and was his only solely philosophical work. It contains much of the formal theory underlying all subsequent discussions. It is based on the idea that probabilities can be related logically:

A proposition is not probable because we think it so ... The theory of probability is logical ... because it is concerned with the degree of belief it is *rational* to entertain in given conditions, and not merely with the actual beliefs of particular individuals, which may or may not be rational
(*Collected Works*, vol. VIII, p. 4).

'The originality of Keynes's approach', wrote **Braithwaite**, 'lay in his insistence that probability, in its fundamental sense, is a logical relation holding between propositions which is similar to, although weaker than, that of logical consequence' (ibid., p. xvi). This objective view of probabilities shows an evident influence from the early epistemology of **Moore**. Parts III and IV of the *Treatise* contain discussions of induction and statistical inference. There is some debate on how far Keynes changed his view of probability in the 1930s, following the publication of **Ramsey**'s review of his book. He did not write at length on it again. One fundamental stance of his did not change: a reluctance to assign numerical values to uncertainties underpinned a resistance to econometrics that he maintained to the end of his life. (And Keynes's argument remains a powerful case against excessive quantification in the social sciences.)

Keynes made no claim to originality in moral or political philosophy. In 'My early beliefs' he wrote: 'I see no reason to shift from the fundamental intuitions of *Principia Ethica*; though they are much too few and too narrow to fit actual experience which provides a richer and more various content'; and 'as the years wore on towards 1914, the thinness and superficiality, as well as the falsity, of our view of man's heart became, as it now seems to me, more obvious' (*Collected Writings*, vol. X, pp. 444, 449). In politics, Fitzgibbons writes,

> Keynes was neither a liberal nor a socialist, at least in the first instance, because his politics began from his epistemology. Who should rule depends on the abstract question of what we can know. He believed that the state should exercise a practical wisdom in its affairs, meaning a commitment to truth combined with familiarity with all the details of a case. Beyond this his political beliefs would depend on circumstances rather than political dogma (1988, pp. 163–4).

Keynes's influence on economics and economic philosophy is incalculable, in terms of both theory and practice. More narrowly, within philosophy his views on probability influenced **Russell**, who knew of the contents of the *Treatise* before its publication and who acknowledged a debt to Keynes in the Preface to *The Problems of Philosophy*. Keynes is the founder of any subsequent thinking on probability in logical terms. The philosophical foundations of his thinking have been the subject of rapidly increasingly scholarly reappraisal from the 1980s. The connections in his work between theoretical assump-

tions and their practical applications will remain of great interest to philosophers.

RICHARD MASON

Keynes, John Neville

British. *b:* 1852, Salisbury, England. *d:* 1949, Cambridge, England. *Cat:* Aristotelian logician; classical political economist. *Educ:* BSc, MA, University College, London: MA, Pembroke College, Cambridge. *Infls:* H. Sidgwick, J. Venn, A. Marshall and (mutually) W. E. Johnson. *Appts:* Fellow of Pembroke College, Cambridge, 1876–82; Fellow of University College, London; Lecturer, University of Cambridge, 1883–1911; Registrary, University of Cambridge, 1911–25.

Main publications:

(1884) *Studies and Exercises in Formal Logic*, London: Macmillan.

(1891) *The Scope and Method of Political Economy*, London: Macmillan.

Secondary literature:

Moggridge, D. E. (1992) *Maynard Keynes: An Economist's Biography*, London and New York: Routledge, chapter 1.

C. D. **Broad** wrote that Keyne's *Formal Logic* 'was the text-book in formal logic for many generations of Cambridge moral scientists. It is far and away the best book that exists in English so the old-fashioned formal logic and the earlier stages of the more recent developments' ('The local historical background of contemporary Cambridge philosophy', in C. A. Mace (ed.), *British Philosophy in the Mid-Century*, London: George Allen & Unwin, 1957, p. 21). **Russell**, on the other hand: 'When I was young [J. N. Keynes] taught old-fashioned logic at Cambridge. I do not know how far the new developments in the subject altered his teaching. He was an earnest Nonconformist who put morality first and logic second' (*Autobiography*, London: George Allen & Unwin, 1967, vol. 1, p. 71). Part IV of *Formal Logic* contains an ingenious account of 'logical processes in their application to complex propositions' which can serve as an example of the ptolemaic elaboration required to make orthodox logic work. His book on political economy was influential as a standard text J. A. Schumpeter wrote: 'Its perusal may be recommended even at this distance of time [in 1954] because of its merits as well as its success' (*A History of Economic*

Analysis, New York: Oxford University Press, 1954, p. 824).

RICHARD MASON

Keyserling, Hermann Alexander, Graf von

Livonian-German. *b:* 20 July 1880, Könno, Livonia, Russian Empire. *d:* 26 April 1946, Innsbruck, Austria. *Cat:* Irrationalist; neoromantic; nature-philosopher; social philosopher. *Ints:* Human life; 'sageness'. *Educ:* Universities of Dorpat, Geneva, Heidelberg and Vienna. *Infls:* Literary: Nietzsche, Bergson and Eastern thought. Personal: Houston Stewart Chamberlain.

Main publications:

(1919) *Das Reisetagebuch eines Philosophen*, 2 vols, Darmstadt: Reichl (English translation, *The Travel Diary of a Philosopher*, 2 vols, trans. Mercedes G. Parks, New York: Macmillan, 1925).
(1920) *Philosophie als Kunst*, Darmstadt: Reichl.
(1922) *Shöpferische Erkenntnis*, Darmstadt: Reichl.
(1926) *Menschen als Sinnbilder*, Darmstadt: Reichl.
(1927) *Wiedergeburt*, Darmstadt: Reichl.
(1947) *Das Buch vom Ursprung*, Baden-Baden; reprinted in 3 vols, Munich: Keimer, 1973.

Secondary literature:

Boucher, M. (1926) *La Philosophie de Hermann von Keyserling*, Paris: Alcan.
Bouisson, Anne Marie (1978) *Hermann Keyserling et l'Inde*, Lille: Atelier reproduction des Theses.
Boyer, Jean-Paul (1973) *Hermann von Keyserling: le personnage et l'oeuvre*, Lille: Atelier reproduction des Theses.

Keyserling studied the natural sciences at several universities, obtaining his doctorate in 1902 at Vienna where, inspired by Houston Chamberlain, he took up philosophy. In 1908 he returned to Livonia to inherit his family estate, but in 1911 he began a world tour which provided material for his best-known work (1919). Dispossessed after the Russian Revolution, Keyserling emigrated to Germany where, in 1920, he founded the School of Wisdom at Darmstadt. Subsequent travels took him to the Americas. Keyserling's itineracy and émigré status both reflected and conditioned his basic philosophical conviction that human life is essentially rootless and protean.

Keyserling's philosophy was expressly non-academic. His works centred on the theme of 'spiritual regeneration' and were born of a wish to replace Western intellectualistic philosophy with the intuitive wisdom of the sage. According to Keyserling the highest idea is that of truth. We want to know, because knowledge implies in itself a purposive reaction to the outer world. In correct knowledge the human spirit enters into reciprocal relations with the universe. Life carries within itself its own purposive character, a meaning which may be grasped only intuitively, not discursively. Thus Keyserling held that the foremost duty of our time is to make the wise man into a possible type and give him all necessary scope for his activities. But the sage has no definite and final conception of the world; he has only one which absorbs all others, and is liable to constant alteration for the better. The sage is unalterable only in wishing to live his life in its entirety, in vital union with the universe. Keyserling's reflections enjoyed considerable popularity after the First World War, appealing to a dissatisfied, anxious, apprehensive generation that had received little help from 'academic' philosophies.
Sources: Edwards.

STEPHEN MOLLER

Khalid, Khalid Muhammad

Egyptian. *b:* June 1920, village near Zaqaziq. *Cat:* Islamic thinker and reformer. *Ints:* Sociology; politics; religious philosophy. *Educ:* Graduated at al-Azhar University, Cairo, 1947; studied English language at the British Council, Cairo. *Infls:* Traditional Islamic education, Qasim Amin and other Muslim modernists, as well the Western tradition. *Appts:* Teacher of Arabic in secondary schools until 1951, then journalist and independent writer.

Main publications:

(1950) *Min huna Nabda* [From Here We Begin], first edition; several other editions: Cairo: Maktabat al-Anglu al-Misriyyah, 1969; Beirut: Dar al-Kitab al-Arabi, 1973, etc.
(1953) *Dimuqratiyyah Abadan* [Democracy for Ever], Cairo.
(1964) *Azmat al-Hurriyyah fi alamina* [The Crisis of Freedom in our World], Cairo: Maktabat al-Wahbah.
(1966) *Maan ala at-Tariq: Muhammad wal-Masih* [Together on the Road: Muhammad and Jesus], Cairo: Dar al-Kutub al-Gadidah.
(1972) *La Yazalu'l-Rasul Yatahaddath* [The Prophet Is Always Speaking], Cairo: Dar ash-Sha'b.
(1981) *Ad-Dawlah fil-Islam* [The State in Islam], Cairo: Dar Thabit.

Secondary literature:

Anawati, G. (1982) *Tendaces et courants dans l'Islam arabe contemporain*, München: Kaiser Grünewald.

Branca, P. (1984) Article in *Encounter.*

——(1986) Article in *Islam. Storia e Civiltà.*

Campanini, M. (1987) *La teoria del socialismo in Egitto*, Palermo: al-Farabi.

Chartier, M. (1973) Article in *IBLA* (Algiers).

Encounter, 1984 (paper by Branca).

I.B.L.A, 1973 (paper by Chartier).

Islàm, Storia e Civiltà 1986 (paper by Branca).

Khoury, P. (1981) *Une Lecture de la pensée arabe actuele*, Paris.

Rosenthal, E. (1965) *Islam in the Modern National State*, Cambridge: Cambridge University Press.

Khalid was continually changing his theoretical orientation. In *From Here We Begin* (1950) he took a secular approach, maintaining that, even though Christianity and Islam are both expressions of the true religion of God, priests and doctors of religious law have often sided with oppressive regimes. He drew a distinction between religious and political power and did not conceal his sympathy for socialist ideas. This socialist trend is present in *Democracy for Ever* (1953), particularly in its emphasis on cooperativism in a democratic society. Later, in 1981, after a deeper study of Islamic history and probably influenced by the changed political situation (Anwar as-Sadat was killed in 1981), Khalid maintained that *din* (religion) and *dawlah* (state) are brothers, and that Islam actualized a social covenant involving a power whose main task is to execute that covenant. He argued that the idea of reformation means more a recovery of the original sense of Islam than an innovation. Later, Khalid pointed out that politics and worship must contribute together to the growth of personality and that radical organizations have the right to constitute regular parties and to take part in democratic political struggle. Khalid became a distinguished religious figure in late twentieth-century Egypt.

MASSIMO CAMPANINI

Klages, Ludwig

German. **b:** 1872, Hannover, Germany. **d:** 1956, Kilchberg, near Zurich. **Cat:** Philosopher and psychologist. **Educ:** Chemistry (PhD 1901), Physics and Philosophy at Munich University, where in 1905 he founded the Seminar für Ausdruckskunde, which soon became Germany's leading centre for characterological psychology. **Infls:** Goethe, German Romantic poetry, the poet Stefan George (d. 1933), T. Lipps, the early Nietzsche and Bergson.

Main publications:

(1910) *Prinzipien der Charakterologie*, Leipzig: Verlag von Johann Ambrosius Barth; reprinted in *Sämtliche Werke*, vol. 4 (English translation, *The Science of Character*, trans. W. H. Johnson, London, 1929).

(1913) *Mensch und Erde*; reprinted with additions, Stuttgart: Kröner, 1973.

(1921) *Vom Wesen des Bewusstseins*, Leipzig: Johann Ambrosius Barth; reprinted in *Sämtliche Werke*, vol. 3 (a progammatic summary of Klages' philosophy).

(1922) *Vom kosmogonischen Eros*, reprinted in *Sämtliche Werke*, vol. 3.

(1926) *Die pscyhologischen Errungenschaften Nietzsches*, reprinted in *Sämtliche Werke*, vol. 5.

(1929–33) *Der Geist als Widersacher der Seele*, 3 vols, reprinted in *Sämtliche Werke*, vols 1 and 2.

(1944) *Rhythmen und Runen*, Leipzig: Barth.

(1966–) *Ludwig Klages Sämtliche Werke*, ed. E. Frauchiger *et al.*, Bonn: Bouvier.

Secondary literature:

Bramwell, A. (1989) *Ecology in the Twentieth Century: A History*, Oxford: Oxford University Press, pp. 177–85.

Hammer, S. (ed.) (1992) *Widersacher oder Wegbereiter? Ludwig Klages und die Moderne*, Heidelberg and Berlin: Hüthig.

Kasdorff, H. (1969–74) *Ludwig Klages, Werk und Wirkung. Einführung und kommentierte Bibliographie*, 2 vols, Bonn: Bouvier.

——(1984) *Ludwig Klages gesammelte Aufsätze und Vorträge zu seinem Werk*, Bonn: Bouvier.

Rintelen, J. von (1970) *Contemporary German Philosophy and its Background*, Bonn: Bouvier, pp. 36–45.

Schnädelbach, H. (1984) *Philosophy in German 1831–1933*, Cambridge: Cambridge University Press, pp. 149–51.

Klages is best known as a psychologist who (from around 1900) drew conclusions reaching as far as cosmological principles from human expressions such as handwriting or rhythm and metre, unlike most of contemporary psychology, which relied on either introspection or experiment. In fact Klages, trained as a chemist, soon came to regard experimental science as technocratic: 'we will not solve the mystery [or 'riddle'—*Rätsel*] of the world in this way; at the most, we will reduce the price of artificial butter' (quoted in Schröder 1966, p. 244). Technocratic science lends justification to, and constitutes a form of, the subjugation of life by the (human) will as it reduces knowledge to skills necessary to manipulate isolated aspects of reality ('facts'), and natural diversity to categorized uniformity.

'Numerical science' is superficial and circular because it only allows the description of appearance (*Schein*) or of causes (scientific constructs). Klages claims that his own 'phenomenological science' (*Erscheinungswissenschaft*), by contrast, is capable of genuine holistic insight by allowing the essence of reality (the 'All-Life') to reveal itself in (experiences of) envisionment (*Schau*)—understood as phenomenological emergence rather than mystical revelation. This new science of emergence holds out what little hope there is left to heal the rift that has marred Western culture since in Socratic philosophy *Geist* ('spirit' or 'intellect') inserted itself 'like a wedge' between body and soul, depriving the body of life (*Seele*—literally 'soul') and disembodying the soul. The inner dynamic of *Geist* as intellect leads to human and environmental disaster. In the course of history man, as the 'bearer of the intellect', has 'torn himself apart along with the planet which gave him birth' (Schnädelbach 1984, p. 150). Klages saw this 'rape of nature by humanity' as a consequence of patriarchy and therefore regarded the revival of older, matriarchal forms as a positive alternative. These environmental and gender concerns may account for the recent resurgence of interest in Klages in Germany. Widely read between the wars and denounced as a protofascistic irrationalist after the Second World War, Klages now seems due for a revival given that he used the term 'logocentrism' for Western thinking decades beofore it became the focus of Derridian critiques.

Sources: Edwards; H. E. Schröder (1966, 1972) *Ludwig Klages: Die Geschichte seines Lebens* (supplts to *Sämtliche Werke*).

BETTINA LANGE

Klinger, Cornelia

German. **b:** 22 March 1953, Leipzig, Germany. **Cat:** Feminist philosopher. **Ints:** Aesthetics, aesthetical and political theory of the nineteenth and twentieth centuries; women's studies in philosophy and the history of ideas; feminist theory. **Educ:** University of Köln. **Infls:** German Idealism (Kant), Frankfurt School (Theodor Adorno, Max Horkheimer) and Georg Simmel; the feminist scholars: Caroline Schlegel-Schelling, Caroline von Günderode and Simone de Beauvoir. **Appts:** 1978–1983, Assistant (wis-

senschaftliche Mitarbeiterin), Institute for German Language and Literature, University of Cologne; from 1983, Permanent Fellow, Institute of the Humanities, Vienna; appointments as Lecturer, Universities of Vienna and Klagenfurt, Zürich, Bielefeld, Frankfurt and Tübingen.

Main publications:

(1986) 'Das Bild der Frau in der Philosophie und die Reflexion von Frauen auf die Philosophie' [The image of woman in philosophy and the reflection of women on philosophy], in Karin Hausen and Helga Nowotny (eds) *Wie männlich ist die Wissenschaft?* Frankfurt am Main: Suhrkamp.

(1987) 'Über weiblichen Antifeminismus' [On women's anti-feminism], *Österreichische Zeitschrift für Politikwissenschaft*, 1,4: 379–92.

(1989) (ed. with R. Stäblein) *Identitätskrise und Surrogatidentitäten. Zur Wiederkehr einer romantischen Konstellation* [Identity-crisis and Surrogate Identities. On the Recurrence of a Romantic Constellation], Frankfurt am Main: Campus Verlag.

(1990) 'Frau–Landschaft–Kunstwerk. Gegenwelten oder Reservoire des Patriarchats?' [Woman–landscape–work of art. Alternative worlds or reservoirs of patriarchy?], in Herta Nagl-Docekal (ed.) *Feministische Philosophie*, Vienna: Oldenbourg.

(1990) 'Philosophie, eine Entgegnung' [Philosophy, a reply], *Merkur. Deutsche Zeitschrift für europäisches Denken* 44, 2: 176–80.

(1990) 'Welche Gleichheit und welche Differenz?' [Which equality and which difference?] in Ute Gerhard *et al.* (eds) *Differenz und Gleichheit. Menschenrechte haben (k)ein Geschlecht*, Frankfurt am Main: Ulrike Helmer Verlag.

(1992) 'Ein Gespräch mit Cornelia Klinger' [An interview with Cornelia Klinger], *Die Philosophin* 5: 68–77.

(1992) 'Faschismus als deutsche Form des Fundamentalismus' [Fascism as a German form of fundamentalism], *Merkur. Deutsche Zeitschrift für europäisches Denken*, 46, 9–10: 782–98.

(1995) *Flucht, Trost, Revolte: die Moderne und ihre ästhetischen Gegenwelten* [Flight, Comfort, Revolt], Munich and Vienna: Hanser Verlag.

Secondary literature:

'Gespräch mit C. Klinger und Kurzbiographie' (1992), *Die Philosophin. Forum für feministische Theorie und Philosophie* 5 (April); pp. 68–77 and 118.

Cornelia Klinger began her philosophical research with a thesis on the political function of the transcendental philosophical theory of freedom

('Die politische Funktion der transzendentalphilosophischen Theorie der Freiheit', Dissertation zur Dr. phil., 1981). Her current work is concentrated on aesthetics and feminism. She regards aesthetics and aesthetic theory as one category of the symbolic order that has become more important in the second wave of feminism, with the recognition that not all inequality is material. She holds that to discover and reveal those underlying structures of the relation of gender, structures of difference and duality, is one of the tasks of feminist theory and feminist philosophy. To what extent these structures of duality can be overcome eventually will have to be clarified by future philosophical research.

URSULA STICKLER

Kneale, W(illiam) C(alvert)

British. *b:* 22 June 1906, Liverpool, England. *d:* 24 June 1990, Skipton, Yorkshire. *Cat:* Moderate rationalist. *Ints:* Logic; history of logic induction and probability. *Educ:* Brasenose College, Oxford, Freiburg and Paris. *Infls:* Joseph Prichard. *Appts:* Fellow, Exeter College, Oxford 1932–60; Professor of Moral Philosophy, Oxford, 1960–66.

Main publications:

(1949) *Probability and Induction.*
(1962) (with Martha Kneale) *The Development of Logic.*
(1962) *On Having a Mind.*
(1963) *The Responsibility of Criminals.*

Kneale was a learned and capable philosopher who did not quite achieve what his gifts qualified him to do. He was, perhaps, the last of the **Cook Wilson**ians (unless that was **Austin**) and his position in Oxford, chronological and doctrinal, corresponded pretty much to that of C. D. **Broad** in Cambridge (both, *faute de mieux*, became professors of moral philosophy, a subject remote from their main interests). Like Broad, he rejected the prevailing views of the period from 1930 to 1960: verificationism, the linguistic theory of necessary truth, reductionism (whether phenomenalist about material objects or behaviourist about minds), the frequency theory of probability and the extensionalist account of laws of nature. It could be argued that, as the massive expertise of his book on the history of logic makes clear, he knew too much about logic to suppose that acceptance of it in its modern **Frege–Russell** form implied subscription to the articles of the positivist faith. His book on probability and induction, although not long, combined erudite considera-tion of their history as topics of philosophy with original and carefully argued views of his own. Two main principles of a rationalistic flavour that he affirmed were that laws of nature are modal propositions about natural necessity, not mere universals of fact or open conjunctions, and that what is meant by a probability-statement is that the ranges of the related characteristics, defined in terms of their ultimately specific constituents, coincide in a certain proportion. The first principle relies on the fact that laws of nature cover all possible, and not merely actual, instances of what they apply to. Frequency is called upon to provide the best available evidence we can get of the probabilities he defines in such elusive terms. Kneale believed in intuitive induction, as revealing, for example, incompatibilities of sensible properties; but did not see it as disclosing the equally a priori connections asserted by laws of nature. His interest in and endorsement of modern formal logic was a departure from Cook Wilsonian orthodoxy. His large book on the history of logic—it is about a third of a million words in length—admits only two heroes: Aristotle and Frege. But it covers very fully the logic of the post-Aristotelian classical world and the middle ages, while passing fairly swiftly over the Renaissance and very quickly over the 'logic' of German idealism. The book includes independent discussion of theories of logical truth, summing up the content of many previous articles critical of the conventionalist version of the thesis that all necessary truth is analytic. Curiously, the book's bibliography mentions only one modern general history of logic, that of Bocheński, which is mainly an anthology of texts. There is no reference to the historical work of Jan Łukasiewicz and Heinrich **Scholz**. Kneale came at the end of his particular line of thought and engaged himself at length only with rather marginal parts of philosophy. His history of logic is likely to retain its authority for a long time.
Sources: Passmore 1957.

ANTHONY QUINTON

Koffka, Kurt

German-American. *b:* 1886, Berlin. *d:* 1941, USA. *Cat:* Gestalt psychologist. *Ints:* Perception; child development; world-as-perceived and world-as-revealed by science; meaning and value; the ego. *Educ:* University of Berlin, 1903–8; and for a period at University of Edinburgh, (1904); doctorate in Psychology from University of Berlin, 1908. *Infls:* Kant, Nietzsche and Külpe. *Appts:* Taught psychology at Wurzburg, Frankfurt am

Main and Giessen; Visiting Professor at Cornell, Chicago and Wisconsin; 1927–, Professor of Psychology, Smith College, Massachusetts.

Main publications:

(1912) *On the Analysis of Representations and their Laws*, Leipzig: Quelle & Meyer.

(1924) *The Growth of the Mind: An Introduction to Child Psychology*, trans. R. M. Ogden, London: K. Paul, Trench, Trubner & Co.

(1928) 'Mental development', in Carl Murchison (ed.), *Psychologies of 1925*, Worcester, Mass.: Clark University Press, pp. 129–43.

(1930) 'Some problems of space perception', in Carl Murchison (ed.) *Psychologies of 1930*, Worcester, Mass.: Clark University Press, pp. 161–87.

(1935) *Principles of Gestalt Psychology*, New York: Harcourt, Brace.

Secondary literature:

Hartmann, G. W. (1935) *Gestalt Psychology: A Survey of Facts and Principles*, New York: Ronald Press.

Kurt Koffka was one of the founders of Gestalt psychology along with Max **Wertheimer** and Wolfgang **Köhler**. As a student he was interested in Kant and **Nietzsche**. He enrolled at Berlin University, initially in philosophy, and he remained concerned with the philosophical aspects of psychology throughout his life. His association with Wertheimer and Köhler dated from the period in 1910–11 at the Academy in Frankfurt am Main, and the three remained life long friends. He was for many years the editor of the *Psychologische Forschung*, a journal founded in the early 1920s in which much of the early research on Gestalt psychology was published. Koffka's visit to the International Congress of Psychology in Oxford in 1923 helped to bring Gestalt theory to a wider international audience.

Perhaps more than his collaborators, Koffka placed a particular emphasis on the importance of insight in the perception of *Gestalten*. He was also especially interested in developmental psychology, publishing a comprehensive account of Gestalt child psychology in *The Growth of the Mind* (1924). His central philosophical concern was to find a way of reconciling the importance of meaning and value in human experience with the advances of science. He was deeply opposed to the prevailing hard-line materialism in philosophy and to behaviourism in psychology. These theories, he argued, if taken literally, lead to an impoverishment of the scientific endeavour itself. The alternative, though, was not philosophical idealism, still less Cartesian dualism. It was, rather, the concept of the Gestalt. The essential feature of a Gestalt, that the whole is different from the sum of its parts, provided an avenue for meaning and value to find their proper place in a scientific worldview.

Koffka developed a number of more specific philosophical theses in his *Principles of Gestalt Psychology* (1935). First, he sought to distinguish between two environments in which people exist—the behavioural, broadly the world-as-perceived, and the geographical, corresponding with the world-as-revealed by science. These are not necessarily coextensive: the behavioural environment, for example, contains only a small part of the electromagnetic spectrum revealed by science; conversely, perspective is a feature only of the geographical environment. Second, he tried to clarify the difference between 'things' and 'not-things'. 'Things' include such objects as tables and chairs, which, like *Gestalten*, have definite boundary properties and a degree of constancy; 'not-things' lack these properties (one of his examples of a not-thing is a fog gradually thickening around a ship). Third, he brought these two ideas together in an attempt to clarify the concept of the ego, as a 'thing' with definite if somewhat inconstant boundaries, but existing within the behavioural rather than geographical environment. A kindly and well-liked man, Koffka's interests extended beyond science and philosophy to music and art. Many of his contemporaries in America, under the influence of behavioural psychology, were often impatient with his metaphysical interests. Yet the issues with which he was concerned (the relationship between the world-as-perceived and the world-as-revealed by science, and the place of meaning and value within the world-as-revealed) remain key issues for any discipline which claims to be a human rather than merely natural science.

Sources: Edwards; Goldenson; UCDCL.

K. W. M. FULFORD

Kofman, Sarah

French. *b:* 14 September 1934, Paris. *d:* 15 October 1994, Paris. *Cat:* Philosopher of psychoanalysis; feminist theorist. *Ints:* Psychoanalysis; feminism. *Educ:* University of Paris (Sorbonne). *Infls:* Freud, Nietzsche, Derrida, feminist theory and contemporary European theories of art and literature. *Appts:* Teacher, 1960–70; Senior Lecturer, University of Paris I, 1970–91, becoming Professor in 1991, and Chevalier des Arts et de la Culture in the same year.

Main publications:

(1970) *L'Enfance de l'art, une interprétation de l'esthétique freudienne*, Paris: Payot; new editions, PBP 1975, Galilée 1985 (English translation, *The Childhood of Art: An Interpretation of Freud's Aesthetics*, Winifred Woodhull, New York: Columbia University Press, 1988).

(1972) *Nietzsche et la métaphore*, Paris: Gaililée.

(1974) *Quatre romans analytiques*, Paris: Galilée (English translation, *Freud and Fiction*, trans. Sara Wykes, Cambridge: Polity Press, 1991).

(1979) *Nietzsche et la scène philosophique*, Paris: Galilée.

(1980) *L'énigme de la femme*, Paris: Galilée (English translation, *The Enigma of Woman: Woman in Freud's Writings*, trans. Catherine Porter, Cornell University Press, 1985).

(1982) *Le Respect des femmes*, Paris: Galilée.

(1983) *Un métier impossible*, Paris: Galilée.

(1984) *Lectures de Derrida*, Paris: Galilée.

(1989) *Socrate(s)*, Paris: Galilée.

(1991) *Seductions, de Sartre à Héraclite*, Paris: Galilée.

Psychoanalytic approaches to creativity inform Kofman's readings of **Freud**, **Nietzsche**, Kant and other thinkers. Exploring parallels between writing and dreams in a series of close readings of Freud's texts, Kofman uncovers concealment and distortion; attending to structuring mechanisms or 'theoretical fictions' in the texts allows her to question the authority and status of a text. A similar approach is employed in her analyses of philosophers. From a feminist perspective Kofman examines the trope of 'woman as enigma', showing how this ('irreducible' and 'diabolical') image of woman which casts her as both fearful and fascinating is perpetuated within the discplines of psychoanalysis and philosophy.

Sources: IWWW; Duncan Large, obituary in *The Guardian*, 3 Nov 1994.

ALISON AINLEY

Köhler, Wolfgang

German-American. *b:* 1887, Tallin, Estonia. *d:* 1967, USA. *Cat:* Gestalt psychologist. *Ints:* Gestalt psychology; Philosophy and psychology of perception; animal psychology; physics and psychology; value theory. *Educ:* Universities of Tübingen and Bonn; studied physics (under Max Planck) and psychology (under Karl Stumpf) at University of Berlin; PhD on psychology of hearing. *Infls:* Max Planck, Karl Stumpf, Max Wertheimer and Edmund Husserl. *Appts:* Taught psychology and philosophy, University of Berlin; 1913–20, Director, Anthropoid Research Station, Prussian Academy of Sciences, Canary Islands; 1922, Director, Psychological Institute; Professor of Philosophy, University of Berlin; taught psychology at Swarthmore College and Dartmouth College, USA; 1959, Visiting Research Professor, Dartmouth College.

Main publications:

(1917) *Intelligenzprüfungen an Anthropoiden*, Berlin; second revised edition, *Intelligenzprüfungen an Menschenaffen*, Berlin, 1921 (English translation, *The Mentality of Apes*, trans. Ella Winter, London: Kegan Paul, Trench, Trubner & Co Ltd, 1925).

(1920) *Die physikalischen Gestalten in Ruhe und im Stationaren Zustand*, Brunswick; second edition, Erlangen: Philosophische Akademie, 1924.

(1929) *Gestalt Psychology*, New York and London: H. Liveright.

(1938) *The Place of Value in a World of Fact*, New York: H. Liveright.

(1940) *Dynamics in Psychology*, New York: H. Liveright.

(1941) 'On the nature of associations', *Proceedings of the American Philosophical Society* 84: 489–502.

(1944) 'Figural after-effects: an investigation of visual processes', *Proceedings of the American Philosophical Society* 88: 269–357.

Secondary literature:

Ayer, A. J. (1946) *Language, Truth and Logic*, second edition, New York: Dover, pp. 56–9.

——(1947) *The Foundations of Empirical Knowledge*, London: Macmillan & Co. Ltd, pp. 113–35.

Boring, E. G. (1930) 'The Gestalt pyschology and the Gestalt movement', *American Journal of Psychology*, 42: 308–315, Ithaca; NY: Cornell University.

Ellis, W. D. (1938) *A Source Book of Gestalt Psychology*, New York: Harcourt, Brace, Kegan Paul, Trench, Trubner (contains translations of portions of *Die Physikalischen Gestalten in Ruhe und im Stationaren Zustand*).

Hamlyn, D. W. (1957) *The Psychology of Perception*, New York and London: Routledge & Kegan Paul.

Katz, D. (1950) *Gestalt Psychology: Its Nature and Significance*, trans. Robert Tyson, New York: Ronald.

Nagel, E. (1961) *The Structure of Science*, New York: Routledge & Kegan Paul, pp. 380–97.

Petermann, B. (1929) *Die Wertheimer-Koffka-Köhlersche Gestalt-theory*, Leipzig (English translation, *The Gestalt Theory and the Problem of Configuration*, trans. Meyer Fortes, New York and London: Routledge & Kegan Paul, 1932).

Riser, O. L. (1931) 'The logic of Gestalt psychology', *Psychological Review* 38: 359–68.

Robinson, D. N. (1978) 'Thomas Reid's Gestalt psychology' in T. L. Beauchamp and S. Barker (eds), *Thomas Reid*, Philadelphia: Philosophical Monographs.

Wolfgang Köhler was a leading Gestalt psychologist whose wide-ranging interests included physics, animal intelligence, the philosophy and psychology of perception, linguistic theory, epistemology, value theory and the mind-body problem. He founded with **Wertheimer**, **Koffka** and others the journal *Psychologische Forschung*, which became the major journal of Gestalt psychology for several years. Although not Jewish, he published a letter in a Berlin newspaper strongly criticizing the Nazis after their rise to power. It was shortly after this that he moved to the USA. His William **James** Lectures delivered at Harvard in 1934 were published as *The Place of Value in a World of Fact* (1938).

A controversial character, Köhler was throughout his life a passionate advocate of Gestalt psychology. Influenced both by **Husserl**'s phenomenology and by the insights of physics, he sought to apply the central insight of Gestalt psychology—that the whole is different from the sum of its parts—to a wide range of problems not only in psychology but in physics, biology and philosophy.

Gestalt psychology had been widely criticized on the grounds that, contrary to its key assertion, the whole could never be different from the sum of its parts. Köhler sought to counter this by showing that even in physics many systems are recognized in which the properties of the parts of the system depend on the state of the system as a whole. Such systems range from large-scale entities such as the solar system through to the electrostatic fields of laboratory experiments. They are quite unlike mere machines, the properties of which, in Köhler's philosophy, are indeed rigidly determined by the properties of their parts. Such systems, moreover, have a further property in common with psychological *Gestalten*, that of dynamic self-regulation. Psychological systems, Köhler argued, such as perception, memory and intelligence, are appropriately explored in terms of a dynamical rather than a mechanical model, and it was this which Gestalt psychology supplied.

The holism of Gestalt psychology underpins a number of Köhler's philosophical theories. In *The Place of Values in a World of Fact* he developed a general notion of the 'requiredness' of experienced phenomena. Köhler was not concerned with the nature of value as such (although his whole life, in particular his opposition to the

Nazis, showed his commitment to *values*). 'Requiredness' was the general property of 'tending to completion' by which the Gestalt is characterized: for example, a circle with a small segment missing tends to be seen as a complete circle. Similarly, we are often aware that our recollection of, say, someone's name is incorrect before we recall the correct name. Phenomena such as these are interpretable as instances of the whole being different from the sum of its parts: something is required for completion of the mental phenomenon, something which is not given in the features of the experience itself. Evaluation, Köhler argued, as the direct perception of what *ought* to be, is but a special case of this requiredness of the phenomenal (and hence, on his view, also of the objective) world.

Köhler made no attempt to develop a detailed theory of particular kinds of value, such as moral or aesthetic. He regarded his ideas merely as a general framework for the work of philosophers in these particular fields. However he made larger claims in other philosophical areas. Thus he believed that his notion of requiredness provided a solution for the problems raised by the Humean theory of causality as regularity of connection. In Köhler's view causation is not inferred from observing effects regularly following causes (though it may be 'tested' by such observations). Rather it is a direct perception in which, by analogy with the circle closing, cause (or effect) is *demanded by or required of* effect (or cause) in order to complete the phenomenal experience and hence its objective counterpart.

His account of the mind-body problem illustrates a different element in his thinking, his theory of the 'isomorphism' of the phenomenal and the physical. He distinguished between phenomena (or perceptions) on the one hand, and nature (or things in themselves) on the other. Among the latter we can distinguish states of the brain and other physical things. All three, however—phenomena, brain states and states of the outside world—to the extent that they are related, will be isomorphic or similar in *form*: a white square in a black field in the physical world will appear phenomenally (in experience) as a white square in a black field which in turn will be represented by a corresponding 'white square in black field' state of the brain. The theory of isomorphism does not claim that white square/black field brain states are the same 'kind of thing' as white square/black field states of the world. Its claim is rather that the formal relations obtaining between states of the world is preserved in the corresponding relations between states of the brain.

Köhler acknowledged that phenomena and brain states might one day be shown to be the same; to this extent he was a monist. But in insisting on the distinctness of the physical and phenomenal he was an epistemological dualist. The mind-body problem, though, he regarded as a pseudo-problem. It was a problem about the location of percepts: in one sense these are inside the body (the physical processes on which perception depends take place *inside the brain*); in another sense they are outside the body (I perceive this page *outside my brain*, on the table). But the body is a percept among others. Hence we should speak rather of percepts being located both in the phenomenal space which includes the phenomenal body, and in the physical space which includes the physical brain. According to this way of speaking, Köhler claimed, the sense in which the phenomenal page is outside my phenomenal body is no more problematic than the sense in which it is on the phenomenal table.

Köhler's psychological theories were wide-ranging and complex. He rejected behaviourism as failing to recognize the reality of subjective experience; but he also criticized introspectionism as putting theory before the (subjective) facts—the introspectionist simply denies the reality of such experiences as 'seeing' the circle with a gap in it as a complete circle. Gestalt theory, he believed, linked with his principle of isomorphism, provided an appropriate qualitative psychology within which to explore both the content of phenomenal experience and its physiological basis. Philosophically Köhler has been accused of oversimplification. His account of the mind-brain problem, for instance, begs the key question of the relationship between physical object and percept, a relationship which is in some respects at odds with his principle of isomorphism. As a psychologist, his studies of insight and other richly cognitive performances in apes helped to maintain interest in complex mental operations during the behaviourist period. His ideas stimulated many useful hypotheses and they remain a model for the emergent philosophical psychology of the new cognitive sciences.

Sources: Reese; Edwards; Goldenson; UCDCL; *Psychlit* journal articles (Silver Platter).

K. W. M. FULFORD

Kojève (originally Kozhevnikov), Alexandre

Russian-French. *b:* 28 April (11 May N.S.) 1902, Moscow. *d:* 4 June 1968, Brussels. *Cat:* Neo-

Hegelian. *Ints:* Philosophy of history. *Educ:* University of Heidelberg. *Infls:* Solov'ev, Hegel, Heidegger and Marx. *Appts:* 1930–9, taught at École Pratique des Hautes Études, Paris.

Main publications:

(1947) *Introduction à la lecture de Hegel: leçons sur la phénoménologie de l'esprit*, Paris: Gallimard (English translation, *Introduction to the Reading of Hegel: Lectures on the Phenomenology of Spirit*, Raymond Queneau, ed. Allan Bloom, trans. James H. Nichols, Jr., New York: Basic Books, 1969).

(1968–73) *Essai d'une histoire raisonnée de la philosophie païenne*, 3 vols, Paris: Gallimard.

(1990) *Le Concept, le temps et le discours: introduction au système du savoir*, ed. Bernard Hesbois, Paris: Gallimard.

Secondary literature:

Auffret, D. (1990) *Alexandre Kojève: la philosophie, l'état, la fin de l'histoire*, Paris: Grasset pp. 443–9 (contains bibliography).

Cooper, B. (1984) *The End of History: An Essay on Modern Hegelianism*, Toronto: University of Toronto Press.

Lilla, M. (1991) 'The end of philosophy: how a Russian émigré brought Hegel to the French', *Times Literary Supplement*, 5 April pp. 3–5.

Roth, M. S. (1988) *Knowing and History: Appropriations of Hegel in Twentieth-century France*, Ithaca: Cornell University Press (Kojève bibliography, pp. 233–6).

Strauss, Leo (1991) *On Tyranny*, ed. Victor Gourevitch and Michael S. Roth, New York: Free Press (fully documents the prolonged debate between Strauss and Kojève over the interpretation of Hegel).

Kojève was born Aleksandr Vladimirovich Kozhevnikov into a wealthy and prominent Russian family (the painter Wassily Kandinsky was his uncle). He was arrested after the Russian Revolution and, despite leaving prison a convinced communist, departed Russia in 1920. After completing a dissertation under **Jaspers** at Heidelberg, on the Russian religious philosopher **Solov'ev**, he moved to Paris and eventually took over **Koyré**'s course on Hegel's philosophy of religion at the École Pratique, teaching it from 1933 until 1939. Kojève's seiminars on Hegel during the 1930s proved a landmark in twentieth-century French philosophy: among the parcipants were Raymond **Aron**, Georges **Bataille**, André Breton, Jacques **Lacan**, Maurice **Merleau-Ponty** and Eric **Weil**. Kojève spent his postwar years attempting to actualize his philosophy of history as a government adviser in the finance ministry. He continued writing philosophical works, though most remained unpublished in his lifetime.

Kojève initially shared with Solov'ev a desire to unite Western and Eastern philosophy, but came to reject Solov'ev's total-unity and any other transhistorical measure of human action. Reworking Hegel in the light of Marx's class conflict and Heidegger's encounter with death, Kojève substituted for Hegelian monism a dualism of nature and human history, and identified Hegel's master–slave dialectic as the dynamic of the latter. The dialectic manifested itself in bloody battle, leading first to the reign of the masters; it ended in the triumph of the slaves, through the establishment of the idea of equality during the French Revolution, and the emergence of the modern universal and homogeneous state, in which the fundamental human desire for recognition is satisfied. For Kojève in his militant mode, in contrast with his later ironic stance towards the bestiality or snobbery of the post-historical condition of universal satisfaction, the 'end of history' is nigh, though philosophers must continue to press for its actualization.

For Kojève, the end of history necessarily coincides with the end of philosophy. The publication of *Le Concept, le temps et le discours*, along with his *Essai d'une histoire raisonnée de le philosophie païenne*, makes fully available his unfinished account of the progress of philosophy towards its culmination in Hegelian wisdom.

COLIN CHANT

Kolakowski, Leszek

Polish-British. **b:** 23 October 1927, Radom, Poland. **Cat:** Historian of philosophy; writer and dramatist. **Ints:** Culture; religion; Marxism; metaphysics; literature. **Educ:** 1945–50, University of Lodz, Poland; 1953, PhD, University of Warsaw. **Infls:** Marx and Husserl. **Appts:** 1947–9, Assistant in Logic, University of Lodz; 1950–9, University of Warsaw, Assistant and then Docent; 1959–1968, Chairman and then Professor, History of Philosophy, University of Warsaw (expelled in 1968 for political reasons); Professor, Yale University; 1968–9, Visiting Professor, McGill University, Montreal; 1969–70, University of California, Berkeley; from 1970, Senior Research Fellow, All Souls, Oxford; 1980, Fellow of the British Academy; 1983, awarded Erasmus Prize and McArthur Fellowship; 1984, Jefferson Award.

Main publications:

(1968) *Chrétiens sans église*, Paris: Gallimard (originally published in Polish, 1958).
(1971) *Positivist Philosophy*, Penguin: Harmondsworth.
(1972) *The Presence of Myth*, Chicago: Chicago University Press (originally in Polish; English trans. 1990).
(1975) *Husserl and the Search for Certitude*, Cambridge, Mass.: Yale University Press.
(1978) *Main Currents in Marxism*, 3 vols, Oxford: Oxford University Press (available in eight languages).
(1982) *Religion*, England: Fontana.
(1985) *Bergson*, Oxford: Oxford University Press.
(1988) *Metaphysical Horror*, Oxford: Blackwell.
(1991) *Modernity on Endless Trial*, Chicago: University of Chicago Press.
(1995) *God Owes Us Nothing: A Brief Remark on Pascal's Religion and on the Spirit of Jansenism*, Chicago: University of Chicago Press.

Secondary literature:

(1993) Festschrift: *Obecnosc* [The Presence] Lodz: Honoris Causa.
Mejbaum, Waclaw and Zukrowska, Aleksandra (1980–1) 'Leszek Kolakowski's misinterpretation of Marxism', in *Dialectical Humanism* 7 (1980): 107–188; and 8 (1981): 149–160.
Rainkno, Stanislaw (1986) 'On Leszek Kolakowski's Views on Religion', in *Dialectical Humanism* 13 Winter (1986): 149–55.

Kolakowski was a member of the Polish Communist Party in the 1950s and was closely involved in the movement towards liberation that led, in 1956, to the Polish 'spring'. Subsequently, his vigorous criticisms of Communist doctrine provoked his dismissal from the Party in 1966 and from his professorial Chair at Warsaw in 1968. He moved to the West and began to develop a sustained critique of Communism, working out a coherent form of Marxist humanism. His later work moves away from Marxism and is concerned with issues in ethics and metaphysics.

The three volumes of Kolakowski's *Main Currents in Marxism* (1978) provide a comprehensive overview of the movement and examine not only the origins and development of dialectic but also how 'the original idea came to serve as a rallying-point for so many different and mutually hostile forces' (vol. 1, p. 3). The chronology of the work runs from Plotinus, regarded as foundational in the account of dialectic, to the Marxism of the 1970s and **Mao Zedong**. Towards the end of the Epilogue of the third volume Kolakowski writes: 'At present Marxism neither interprets the world nor changes it: it is merely a repertoire of slogans serving to organize various interests, most of them completely remote from those with which Marxism originally identified itself' (p. 530).

In *Religion* (1982) Kolakowski treats of 'God, the Devil, Sin and other Worries of the so-called Philosophy of Religion'. He critically analyses a wide range of arguments for religious belief, as well as a range of proposals that seek an understanding of them through their historical, anthropological and cultural contexts. He maintains that a rationalistic epistemology alone can neither settle the question of the existence of God nor provide a satisfactory foundation for morality.
Sources: PI; personal communication.

DIANÉ COLLINSON

Kollontai (née Domontovich), Aleksandra Mikhailovna

Russian. *b:* 31 March (19 N.S.) 1872, St Petersburg. *d:* 9 March 1952, Moscow. *Cat:* Marxist; feminist. *Educ:* Studied at the University of Zurich. *Infls:* Marx, Engels, Bebel, Luxemburg, Klara Zetkin, Plekhanov, Lenin and Havelock Ellis.

Main publications:

(1909) *Sotsial'nye osnovy zhenskogo voprosa* [The Social Basis of the Woman Question], St Petersburg.

(1916) *Obshchestvo i materinstvo* [Society and Maternity], Petrograd.

(1918) *Novaia moral' i rabochii klass* [The New Morality and the Working Class], Moscow.

(1919) *Sem'ia i kommunisticheskoe gosudarstvo*, Moscow and Petrograd (English translation, *Communism and the Family*, London: Workers' Socialist Federation, 1920).

(1977) *Selected Writings of Alexandra Kollontai*, trans. Alix Holt, London: Allison & Busby (translated extracts).

(1984) *Selected Articles and Speeches*, New York: International Publishers (translated extracts).

Secondary literature:

Clements, B. E. (1979) *Bolshevik Feminist: The Life of Aleksandra Kollontai*, Bloomington: Indiana University Press (contains bibliography).

Farnsworth, B. (1980) *Aleksandra Kollontai: Socialism, Feminism and the Bolshevik Revolution*, Stanford: Stanford University Press.

Porter, C. (1980) *Alexandra Kollontai: A Biography*, London: Virago (contains bibliography).

Born into an aristocratic family, Kollontai left a conventional marriage in 1898 to study political economy in Zurich, and joined the Russian Social-Democratic Labour Party and the international socialist and socialist women's movements. She became Commissar of Social Welfare after the October Revolution, and later Director of the Party's Women's Department. Disgraced in 1922 for her leading part in the libertarian Workers' Opposition, she turned to fictional explorations of sexual morality (notably the trilogy *Love of Worker Bees*, 1923) and spent the remainder of her working life as a diplomat, becoming the world's first woman ambassador (to Norway).

Kollontai was exceptional among the Bolsheviks in attempting a Marxist account of sexual morality. Although now regarded as an important feminist theorist, she rejected the 'bourgeois' feminism of her day, insisting that the achievement of socialism was a necessary condition of women's emancipation. In *Society and Maternity* (1916) she argued for maternity insurance as a step towards the transfer of responsibility for childcare from the family to the community, and more generally towards a new morality of comradeship based on the economic independence of the sexes. Unfairly accused by political opponents of preaching sexual promiscuity, her advocacy of free love ('winged Eros') was predicated upon a critique of sexual double standards, prostitution, the economic function of the family, and women's psychological and material subordination to men in capitalist society.

COLIN CHANT

Kol'man, Ernst (Arnosht Kolman)

Czech. *b:* 6 January 1892, Prague. *d:* 22 January 1979, Stockholm. *Cat:* Marxist dialectical materialist. *Ints:* Philosophy of physics; philosophy of mathematics; logic; history of philosophy; cybernetics. *Educ:* University of Prague. *Appts:* Institute of Philosophy, Soviet Academy of Sciences, 1939–45; Professor of Philosophy, Charles University, 1945–8; Director, Institute of Philosophy, Czech Academy of Sciences, 1959–64.

Main publications:

1936) *Predmet i metod sovremennoi matematiki* [The Subject and Method of Contemporary Mathematics], Moscow.

(1940) *The Development of Physics since Lenin's 'Materialism and Empiriocriticism'*, New York.

(1941) *Engels i estestvoznanie* [Engels and the Natural Sciences], Moscow.

(1943) *Noveishie otkrytiia sovremennoi fiziki v svete dialekticheskogo materializma* [The Latest Discoveries of Contemporary Physics in the Light of Dialectical Materialism], Moscow.
(1947) *Logika* [Logic], Prague.
(1955) *Bernard Bolzano*, Moscow.
(1956) *Kibernetika* [Cybernetics], Moscow.
(1957) *Filosofskie problemy sovremennoi fiziki* [Philosophical Problems of Contemporary Physics], Moscow.
(1961) *O viie v boha* [On Belief in God], Prague.

Secondary literature:
Graham, Loren R. (1972) *Science and Philosophy in the Soviet Union*, New York: Alfred Knopf; revised edition, *Science, Philosophy and Human Behavior in the Soviet Union*, Columbia University Press, 1987.
Kol'man, E. (1979) *Die verirrte Generation. So hätten wir nicht leben sollen. Eine Biographie*, Frankfurt (autobiographical volume).
Scanlan, James P. (1985) *Marxism in the USSR: A Critical Survey of Current Soviet Thought*, Cornell University Press.

Kol'man's tumultuous life was marked by Marxian revolutionary commitment, devotion to the philosophy of science, and frequent conflict between the two and between both and Communist authorities. A military prisoner in Russia during the First World War, he joined the Bolsheviks and was a political organizer during the Russian Civil War, eventually becoming a Soviet citizen and occupying teaching and administrative positions at various institutions in Moscow, including the Institute of Philosophy of the Soviet Academy of Sciences; in 1945 he returned to his native Czechoslovakia to become Professor of Philosophy at Charles University, but soon fell out with the new Communist government: deported to Russia in 1948, he was imprisoned there until 1952; rehabilitated after Stalin's death, he returned to Prague in 1959 to direct the Institute of Philosophy of the Czech Academy of Sciences, but disputes with the government led him to take refuge in the USSR in 1964. Because of his subsequent support for political liberalization in the socialist countries and for philosophical liberalization in dialectical materialism, he was continually at odds with the Soviet government, and in 1976 he defected to Sweden and resigned his membership of the Communist Party.

A staunch defender of Marxist dialectical materialism, Kol'man devoted much of his philosophical work to expounding that philosophy (analytically and historically) and examining its relation to the sciences. In the early decades of his career he had a much-deserved reputation as a Marxist–Leninist ideologue; he championed the views of Lysenko in the genetics debates, and he vigorously supported the purging of Moscow State University of 'idealists', among whom he counted defenders of Einsteinian physics and the principle of complementarity in quantum theory. Later, however, Kol'man was the first Soviet scholar to promote cybernetics, previously considered a 'bourgeois' science, and he urged Marxist philosophers to interpret dialectical materialism in the light of scientific developments rather than rejecting the latter as incompatible with dogma.

JAMES SCANLAN

Kolnai, Aurel Thomas
Hungarian-British. *b:* 5 December 1900, Budapest. *d:* 28 June 1973, London. *Cat:* Phenomenologist; philosopher of common sense. *Ints:* Ethics; social and political philosophy. *Educ:* Mainly the University of Vienna, but also Universities of Budapest and Freiburg. *Infls:* Literary influences: Chesterton, Scheler, Husserl and the English intuitionists. Personal: Oszkar Jászi and Karl Polanyi. *Appts:* 1945–54, Lectureship at Laval University, Quebec; 1959–72, Visiting Lecturer at Bedford College, University of London.

Main publications:
(1927) *Der ethische Wert und die Wirklichkeit* [Ethical Value and Reality], Freiburg: Herder.
(1930) *Sexualethik: Sinn und Grundlagen der Geschlechtsmoral* [Sexual Ethics: The Meaning and Foundations of Sexual Morality], Paderborn: Schöningh.
(1938) *The War against the West*, London: Gollancz; New York: Viking Press.
(1952) *Errores del Anticomunismo* [Mistakes in the Fight against Communism], Madrid: Rialp.
(1959) *Critica de las Utopias Politicas* [Critique of Political Utopias], Madrid: Ateneo.
(1977) *Ethics, Value and Reality*, London: Athlone Press (a posthumous collection).

Secondary literature:
Beach, John D. (1981) 'The ethical theories of Aurel Kolnai', *The Thomist* 45, 1: 132–43.
Dunlop, Francis (1978) 'The philosophy of Aurel Kolnai', *Journal of the British Society for Phenomenology* 9, 1: 56-8.
——(1995) *The Utopian Mind and Other Papers*, London: Athlone Press.

Manent, Pierre (1982) 'Aurel Thomas Kolnai (1900–1973)', *The Chesterton Review* 8, 2: 162–9.

Williams, Bernard and Wiggins, David (1977) 'Aurel Thomas Kolnai (1900–1973)', Introduction to *Ethics, Value and Reality*, London: Athlone Press (contains an extensive bibliography).

Like many young Hungarian Jewish intellectuals, Kolnai was attracted to Oszkar Jászi's liberalism. But the revolutionary upheavals of postwar Hungary, his reading of G. K. Chesterton and the early phenomenologists, and his gradual conversion to Catholicism brought out his moderate conservatism. As his journalistic campaigns show, Austrian semi-fascism after 1929 temporarily revived his social democratic allegiances, and his mature conservative thought only emerged fully in papers he wrote as an exile in the USA, and then Canada.

Kolnai's early academic publications embrace psychoanalytic and sociological, as well as ethical, topics. His great powers of description and analysis are well apparent in his *Sexualethik* (1930), as in his best phenomenological paper, 'Der Ekel' [Disgust]. But the foundations of his mature thought are already laid in his doctoral thesis *Der ethische Wert* (1927), which is a synthesis of the phenomenological ethics of value and the traditional Catholic and Aristotelian ethics of end. Work on *The War against the West* (1938), his 'exposé' of the deep philosophical currents underlying Nazism, followed by two more unpublished topical books of political thought, quite apart from his nomadic life as a refugee, impeded the development of his main ethical ideas.

After writing a series of anti-communist works in Canada, he went to England to work on 'the utopian mind', the fundamental attitude corrupting Western civilization. Utopian thinking, he argued, subverts our experience of value-reality: we turn from the real but partially improvable world, already charged with value-cum-disvalue, towards a 'reality' which *cannot be thought*, to 'perfection values' which cannot even be imagined.

Kolnai held that the philosopher must always be loyal to ordinary experience, though not uncritically so. He argued that conscience and the intuition of moral principles must be supplemented by 'the moral consensus of mankind'. His anti-utopianism shows itself again in the claim that morality, though not coextensive with practice, is nevertheless importantly related to it. At its heart are the great 'moral taboos', where the 'moral theme' is at its most salient. This then shades off gradually, with decreasing emphasis, into the area of supererogation and the morally indifferent.

FRANCIS DUNLOP

Kook (Kuk), Abraham Isaak (also known as Rav Kook)

Latvia, immigrant to pre-mandate Palestine. *b:* 8 September 1865, Griva, Latvia. *d:* 1 September 1935, Jerusalem. *Cat:* Rabbi; philosopher; mystic; poet. *Ints:* Jewish mysticism; Darwinism; secularism. *Educ:* 1880–8, Lithuanian yeshivot (religious Jewish seminaries). *Infls:* Rabbi Loewe (the Maharal) of Prague, Jewish Orthodoxy, secular and religious Zionism and social utopianism and existentialism. *Appts:* 1888–95, Rabbi, Zoimel, Lithuania; 1895–1904, Boisk, Lithuania; 1917–18, London; 1904–19, Chief Rabbi, Jaffa, Palestine; 1921–35, first Chief Rabbi, Jerusalem, and first Ashkenazi Chief Rabbi, mandated Palestine.

Main publications:

(1920) *Ha-Mahashavah ha-Yisre'elit* [The Thought of Israel], Jerusalem; reprinted, Levi Press, 1966–7.

(1941) *Hazon Hageulah* [The Vision of Redemption], Jerusalem; Agudah Lehotzoat Sifre Harayah Kook.

(1888–1919) *Igrot Harayah* [The Letters of Rabbi Abraham Isaac Ha-Kohen Kook] 3 vols, Jerusalem: respectively, Agudah Lehotzoat Sifre Harayah Kook, 1943; with Mosad Harav Kook 1946; Mosad Harav Kook, 1965; Misrad l'Inyene-Datot, 1984–5.

(1971) *Midot Harayah* [The Moral Principles of Rabbi Abraham Isaac Ha-Kohen Kook], Jerusalem: Mosad Harav Kook.

(1938/50) *Orot Hakodesh* [The Lights of Holiness] 3 vols, Jerusalem: Agudah Lehotzoat Sifre Harayah Kook, vols 1–2, vol. 3; Mosad ha-Rav Kook, 1961, 1975.

(1925) *Orot Hateshuvah*, Jerusalem; revised edition, Yeshivot Bnei Akiva, Or Etzion, and Merkaz Shapiro, 1966 (English translation, *Rabbi Kook's Philosophy of Repentance*, trans. A. B. Z. Metzger, New York: Yeshiva University Press, 1968).

(1925) *Orot* [Lights], Jerusalem: Degel Yerushalayim; revised edition, Mosad Harav Kook, 1963; Northvale, NJ: Aronson, 1993.

Secondary literature:

Agus, Jacob B. (1946) *Banner of Jerusalem*, New York: Bloch; republished as *High Priest of Rebirth*, 1972.

——(1963) 'Rabbi Kook', in *Great Jewish Thinkers of the Twentieth Century*, ed. S. Noveck, Clinton, Mass.: Bnai Brith.

Bergman, Samuel H. (1961) *Faith and Reason: An Introduction to Modern Jewish Thought*, ed. and trans. A. Jospé, Washington, DC: Bnai Brith.

Bokser, Ben Zion (1978) *Abraham Isaac Kook*, London: SPCK (includes bibliography).

Buber, Martin (1952) *Israel and Palestine*, London: East and West Library.

Epstein, I. (1951) *Abraham Yizhak Hacohen Kook: His Life and Times*.

Fridman, M. (1988) *Stories from the Life of Rav Kook*, New York: Woodmere, Beit-Shamai.

Green, A. (ed.) (1989) *Jewish Spirituality II*, New York: Crossroad, pp. 277–401.

Hertzberg, Arthur (1959) *The Zionist Idea*, New York: Doubleday & Herzel.

Rosenstreich, Nathan (1968) *Jewish Philosophy in Modern Times*, New York: Holt, Rinehart & Winston.

Kook endeavoured to reconcile Orthodox Jewish religion with secular scientific and Jewish ethnic aspirations through a mystic fusion. He was unique among traditional Jewish thinkers in regarding the theories of Darwinian evolution and secular Zionism as opportunities for a return to God, and believed in the inevitable progress and perfection of humanity. He argued, against **Bergson**, that evolution had purpose and direction. Just as he endeavoured to attract secular kibbutzniks to religion, so he encouraged the very Orthodox to imbue themselves with secular knowledge and modernize their approach. To this end, as Chief Rabbi of Palestine under the British Mandate, he emended Jewish laws which were causing hardship to a large element in the community. Basing himself on Jewish rabbinical tradition, as well as on more contemporary models, he argued that there need be no dichotomy between the sacred and the profane. Pure spirituality was, he held, a necessary result of the diaspora mentality, which could be changed once Jewish life was normalized in Israel, the true homeland. Kook is of particular significance today for his attack on scientific study for its own sake, divorced from ethical considerations. Politically, he advocated harmony between Jews, Muslims and Christians, a view that was not always heeded by his disciples. Kook's influence can be assessed by the volume of his works that were reissued in Israel and the growth in critical appreciations towards the end of the twentieth century.

Sources: EncJud; Schoeps; NUC.

IRENE LANCASTER

Kopnin, Pavel Vasil'evich

Russian. *b:* 27 January 1922, Moscow province. *d:* 27 June 1971, Moscow. *Cat:* Marxist epistemologist. *Ints:* Epistemology; logic; methodology of science; dialectical materialism. *Educ:* Moscow Institute of Philological and Literary Studies, Moscow State University and Moscow Pedagogical Institute. *Infls:* Marx and Lenin. *Appts:* 1947–62, taught Philosophy at various institutions in Moscow, Tomsk and Kiev; 1962–8, Director, Institute of Philosophy of the Ukrainian Academy of Sciences in Kiev; 1968–71, Director, Institute of Philosophy of the Soviet Academy of Sciences and Professor of Philosophy at Moscow State University.

Main publications:

(1961) *Dialektika kak logika* [Dialectics as Logic], Kiev.

(1962) *Gipoteza i poznanie deistvitel'nosti* [The Hypothesis and the Cognition of Reality], Kiev.

(1963) *Ideia kak forma myshleniia* [The Idea as a Form of Thought], Kiev.

(1966) *Vvedenie v marksistskuiu gnoseologiiu* [Introduction to Marxist epistemology], Kiev.

(1968) *Logicheskie osnovy nauki* [The Logical Foundations of Science], Kiev.

(1969) *Filosofskie idei V. I. Lenina i logika* [The Philosophical Ideas of V. I. Lenin and Logic], Moscow.

(1973) *Dialektika kak logika i teoriia poznaniia* [Dialectics and Logic and the Theory of Knowledge], Moscow.

(1973) *Dialektika, logika, nauka* [Dialectics, Logic, Science], Moscow.

(1974) *Gnoseologicheskie i logicheskie osnovy nauki* [The Epistemological and Logical Foundations of Science], Moscow.

(1982) *Problemy dialektiki kak logiki i teorii poznaniia (Izbrannye filosofskie raboty)* [Problems of Dialectic as Logic and the Theory of Knowledge (Selected Philosophical Works)], Moscow.

Secondary literature:

Aleskeev, P. V. (ed.) (1993) *Filosofy Rossii xix–xx stoletii* [Russian Philosophers of the 19th–20th Centuries], Moscow, p. 92.

'Pavel Vasil'evich Kopnin' (1971) *Voprosy filosofii* [Problems of Philosophy] 8: p. 180–3.

Scanlan, James P. (1985) *Marxism in the USSR*, Cornell University Press.

Kopnin's many original investigations in the theory of knowledge and the methodology of science generated much interest in those fields in the Soviet Union in the 1960s and helped to establish epistemology as an identifiable discipline within dialectical materialism, dealing with the relation between subjective mind and the objective world. Kopnin accepted the Leninist theory of cognition as the mental reflection of an independently existing reality, but he believed that such reflection is not passive but active, even creative: he argues that, because of the mind's ability to synthesize and project, creativity has equal importance with reflection as a principle of Marxist–Leninist epistemology.

Kopnin also accepts **Lenin**'s thesis of the unity of dialectics, logic and the theory of knowledge, interpreting that thesis to mean that a dialectical logic is the proper Marxist epistemology: to deal adequately with the objective dialectical processes in the real world the mind must utilize a corresponding subjective dialectic. Kopnin thus devoted much attention to the elaboration of dialectical logic, particularly in its relation to scientific investigation. He did not, however, reject formal logic, which he regarded as a different but legitimate and valuable approach to the analysis of cognition, complementing dialectical logic.

Kopnin is credited with initiating the serious study of the logic and methodology of science among Soviet philosophers. Although he believed that philosophy should develop a general methodology for scientific investigation, he gave priority to the findings of science over philosophical assumptions and argued that the categories of dialectical materialism require continual adjustment to scientific advances. He was an early defender of the view that dialectical materialism can accommodate finitist models of the universe.

JAMES SCANLAN

Korn, Alejandro

Argentinian. *b:* 1860, San Vicente, Argentina. *d:* 1936. *Cat:* Philosopher; psychiatrist. *Infls:* Bergson, Croce, Dilthey and W. James. *Appts:* Practised medicine in Buenos Aires for many years; read the works of major philosophers in his spare time and eventually abandoned medicine to pursue philosophy; 1906, Professor of Philosophy, University of Buenos Aires; later moved to the University of La Plata.

Main publications:

(See *Obras completas*, Buenos Aires: Editorial Claridad, 1949.)

(n.d.) *Filósofos y sistemas.*

(1936) *Influencias filosóficas en la evolución nacional*, Buenos Aires: Editorial Claridad.

(1961) *El pensamiento argentino*, ed. Gregorio Weinberg, Buenos Aires: Editorial Nova.

The following English translations of excerpts of the work of Alejandro Korn by Willard Trask appear in Aníbal Sánchez Reulet (ed.) (1954) *Contemporary Latin American Philosophy*, Albuquerque: University of New Mexico Press:

'Creative freedom', pp. 54–67.

'Axiology', pp. 68–75.

Secondary literature:

Lipp, Solomon (1969) *Three Argentine Thinkers*, New York: Philosophical Library.

Saénz del Castillo, Olarte (1973) 'Alejandro Korn ante el problema de la metafísca', in *Estudios sobre Alejandro Korn*, La Plata: Universidad Nacional de la Plata.

Torchia Estrada, Juan Carlos (1986) *Alejandro Korn: Profesión y vocación*, Mexico: Universidad Nacional Autónoma de México.

Korn was initially a proponent of positivism, but a concern with 'intellectual probity' led him to critique positivism and consider other kinds of philosophy. He was especially influenced by the thought of Henri **Bergson**, Benedetto **Croce**, Wilhelm **Dilthey** and William **James**. Ultimately, Korn did not adhere to any one school of thought but remained an independent thinker. His critique of nineteenth-century thought from an anti-positivist perspective led him to formulate the following concern: 'Does nineteenth-century philosophy possess some common characteristics, despite being divided into romantic and positivist periods, each with a number of divergent tendencies? In my judgment an affirmative answer is warranted. Allow me to point out two such characteristics: the concept of becoming and the problem of our cognitive capacity'.

AMY A. OLIVER

Körner, Stephan

Czech, later British. *b:* 26 September 1913, Ostrava, Moravia. *Cat:* British philosopher; Kantian. *Ints:* Metaphysics; metaphilosophy; history of philosophy; practical reasoning. *Educ:* JurDr, Charles University, Prague; PhD, Trinity Hall, Cambridge. *Infls:* Kant. *Appts:* University of Bristol, 1946–79, Professor of Philosophy, 1952–

79; Yale University, Professor of Philosophy, 1970–84; many visiting appointments.

Main publications:

(1955) *Conceptual Thinking*, Cambridge.

(1955) *Kant*, Harmondsworth: Penguin.

(1957) (ed.) *Observation and Interpretation*, London: Butterworth.

(1960) *The Philosophy of Mathematics*, London: Hutchinson.

(1966) *Experience and Theory*, London: Routledge & Kegan Paul.

(1969) *What is Philosophy? One Philosopher's Answer*, Harmondsworth: Penguin; later published as *Fundamental Questions in Philosophy*, Brighton: Harvester, 1969.

(1970) *Categorial Frameworks*, Oxford: Blackwell.

(1976) *Experience and Conduct*, Cambridge: Cambridge University Press.

(1984) *Metaphysics: Its Structure and Function*, Cambridge: Cambridge University Press.

Secondary literature:

Grazer Philosophische Studien 20, 1984.

Srzednicki, J. T. J. (ed.) (1987) *Stephan Körner: Philosophical Analysis and Reconstruction*, Dordrecht: Nijhoff (with complete bibliography to 1986).

Körner notes in his Preface to *Metaphysics: Its Structure and Function* (1984) that the book represents a culmination of his thinking over forty years. His view of the scope and nature of philosophy is Kantian. He believes in the possibility of an analysis of a conceptual apparatus through which human experience and action is classified. 'A person's immanent metaphysics', he has written, 'comprises the principles to which every proposition about the public world must conform if it is to be acceptable.' This is contrasted with 'transcendent metaphysics'—'speculative conjectures about the relation between the—private or public—world of experience and the world in itself or transcendent reality' (p. 1). He differs radically from Kant in his attention to conceptual development in the histories of both philosophy and science, but appears to share with him a belief that valid generalizations across human societies can be made about cognitive organization and about practical attitudes.

Körner's notion of a 'categorial framework', he says, consists of 'the supreme principles governing my thinking about what I take to be the world of intersubjective experience' ('Reply to Professor Marciszewski', in Srzednicki 1987, p. 26). His interest in categorial frameworks led him

to some acute studies of the nature of philosophy which have been less doctrinaire than those of more narrowly analytical writers. He has brought a formidable technical expertise to this task. His treatments of ordinary language philosophy of the 1950s were brisk and decisive (for example in *Categorial Frameworks*, pp. 70–1). Körner has a lasting reputation as a teacher and expositor. After many years, his *Kant* (1955), *What is Philosophy?* (1969) and *The Philosophy of Mathematics* (1960) all remain almost unchallenged as standard introductions. His philosophical reputation, like his interests, is wider and more international than an orthodox Oxford–Cambridge British mainstream.

RICHARD MASON

Korsch, Karl

German. ***b:*** 1886, Tolstedt, Germany. ***d:*** 1961, Belmont, Massachusetts. ***Cat:*** Neo-Marxist. ***Educ:*** Korsch studied Law, Economics and Philosophy at several universities, gaining his doctorate from Jena. ***Infls:*** Marx. ***Appts:*** Lecturer, University of Jena; elected to the Thuringian Parliament, 1923; later Minister of Justice.

Main publications:

(1923) *Marxism and Philosophy*, Leipzig: Hirschfield; reprinted, London: New Left Books, 1970, and New York: Monthly Review Press, 1970.

(1938) *Karl Marx*, London: Chapman & Hall; New York: Wiley; revised edition, 1947.

Secondary literature:

Goode, Patrick (1979) *Karl Korsch: A Study in Western Marxism*, London: Macmillan.

Kellner, Douglas (ed.) (1977) *Karl Korsch: Revolutionary Theory*, Austin and London: University of Texas Press (a selection of writings, with extensive comments by the editor).

After a distinguished non-combatant war service, returned to Jena. Active in socialist politics, as a member first of the USPD then of the KPD, he was elected to the Thuringian Parliament in 1923, and became a Minister of Justice. His opposition to **Lenin** led to his expulsion from the KPD in 1926. He fled from the Nazis in 1933, emigrating to the USA in 1938. He taught sociology briefly at Tulane, and continued his Marxist writings. Towards the end of his life, he became increasingly distanced from his earlier Marxist commitments.

Korsch's most original work, *Marxism and Philosophy* (1923), applied Marxist principles to the development of Marxism itself. He distinguished three stages in Marxism: a philosophical stage (1843–8), a stage in which Marxist thought became differentiated into economics, politics and ideology (1848–1900), and finally an unfinished phase in which socialism is regarded as a science divorced from immediate political prescriptions. Although writing before Marx's early Hegelian-inspired works had been published, Korsch (like **Lukács** writing at the same time) invoked a Hegelian conception of the dialectical interplay of base and superstructure, thus implicitly rejecting the prevailing Second International view of Marxism as a value-free science. However, in *Karl Marx*, written some sixteen years later, his thought had shifted. While still insisting that Marxism is essentially a critical theory yielding practical prescriptions, he then stressed in more orthodox manner the priority of the economic base over the superstructure.

In addition to academic works on Marxism, Korsch was also an active polemicist in the debates within Marxism. He defended workers' councils (or soviets); he criticized **Bernstein** on the right, **Kautsky** in the centre and **Lenin** on the left; and he condemned the Stalinist thesis of 'socialism in one country' as a betrayal of the international working-class struggle.

Sources: Turner (good bibliography); BDN.

NICHOLAS EVERITT

Kosík, Karel

Czech. *b:* 1926, Prague. *Cat:* Neo-Marxist. *Ints:* Dialectics; praxis; political philosophy; philosophical anthropology. *Educ:* University of Leningrad and Charles University, Prague. *Infls:* Marx, Hegel, G. V. Plekhanov, N. G. Chernyshevsky, A. Hertsen, G. Lukács, L. Goldmann, Husserl and Heidegger. *Appts:* 1950–63, Researcher, Institute of Philosophy of the Czech Academy of Sciences; 1963–9, Professor of Philosophy, Charles University, Prague.

Main publications:

(1958) *Ceská radikální demokcracie* [Radical Czech Democracy], Prague: Století.
(1964) *Dialektika konkrétního*, Prague: SAV (English translation, *Dialectics of the Concrete: A Study on Problems of Man and World*, trans. Karel Kovavda and James Schmidt, Dordecht: Reidel, 1976).
(1969) *La nostracrisi attuale*, Rome: Riuniti.

Secondary literature:

Albritton, Robert (1980) Review of *Dialectics of the Concrete* (1964), in *Philosophy of the Social Sciences* 10: 233–9.

Gorman, B. Robert A. (1982) *Neo-Marxism: The Meanings of Modern Radicalism*, Westport, Conn.: Greenwood Press.

Kosík is one of the major figures of postwar Czechoslovak philosophy. Prominent in the revisionist movment that generated the 'Prague Spring' of 1968, he was for years thereafter banned from teaching and print.

Influenced by neo-Hegelian dialectics in his *Radical Czech Democracy* (1958), and later by **Husserl**'s and **Heidegger**'s phenomenology as well, Kosík sought humanistic dimensions within Marxist theory itself. This led him to develop a critical position which challenged the limits of orthodox Marxist theory with radical questions concerning the significance of the subject and the role of the idea in history. In his *Dialectics of the Concrete* (1964) Kosík returned to praxis as the fundamental category in the interpretation of history, and correlated praxis with 'totality' by defining praxis as the unity of man and the world, spirit and matter, subject and object, producer and product. He thereby asserted that praxis discloses the essence of man as a self-creative being who produces human and social reality and, consequently, is able to understand and transform reality in all its aspects, human and non-human. Thus, although he still held that praxis presupposes material conditions, that it is one moment of the 'concrete totality' of existence, by stressing the primacy of human freedom and self-constitution Kosík effectively transformed the materialist metaphysics of Marxism into a humanist ontology more akin to Hegelianism and existentialism. Kosík also used these ideas in *La nostracrisi attuale* (1969), a series of essays on political philosophy and history of literature. Kosík's heterodox Marxism notably influenced the Petofi Circle in Hungary, East German thinkers such as R. **Havemann**, and the editors of the American periodical *Telos*. His great achievement was to have broken the hegemony of the conception of Marxism as an uncritical objectivist ideology of coercion.

Sources: Burr; BDN.

STEPHEN MOLLER

Kotarbiński, Tadeusz

Polish. *b:* 31 March 1886. *d:* 3 October 1981. *Cat:* Materialist ('reist', 'concretist'). *Ints:* Epistemology; logic; methodology; ethics. *Educ:* Lvov University. *Infls:* Brentano, Twardowski and Lesniewski. *Appts:* Professor, Warsaw University,

1918–60; President, Polish Academy of Sciences, 1957–63.

Main publications:

(1913) *Szkice praktycze*, Warsaw.

(1915) *Utylitaryzm w etyce Milla i Spencera*, Cracow.

(1929) *Elementy teorii poznania, logiki formalnej i metodologii nauk*, Lvov. (English translation, *Gnosiology*, Olgierd Wojtasiewicz, Oxford: Pergamon 1966).

(1955) *Traktat o dobrej robocie* Lodz Ossolineum. (English translation, *Praxiology: the Science of Efficient Action*, Oxford: Pergamon, 1965).

(1957–8) *Wybór Pism* 2 vols, Warsaw: PWN.

(1957) *Wyklady z dziejow logiki*, Lódź Ossolineum. (French translation, *Leçons sur l'histoire de logique*, Paris: PUF, 1957).

(1986) *Drogi dociekah wlasnych*, Warsaw: PWN.

(1987) *Pisma etyczne*, Wroclaw: Osslineum.

Secondary literature:

Woleński, Jan (1989) *Logic and Philosophy in the Lvov-Warsaw School*, Dordrecht: Kluwer.

——*Kotarbiński: Logic, Semantics, Ontology*, Dordrecht: Kluwer.

Kotarbiński's central idea—he called it 'reism'—is that what really exists is only that which is referred to by genuine names and that only names of objects (i.e., approximately, Aristotelian substances) are genuine. The rest, 'apparent names', figure as the grammatical subjects of sentences for which equivalents whose subjects are genuine names can be found. What is more, all objects are bodies, whether sentient or not: the thesis of 'pansomatism'. Names that appear to refer to properties, universals, numbers, events, etc. are all apparent and, in principle, eliminable from discourse. Kotarbiński has also defended what he calls 'radical realism', the doctrine that material things themselves are directly perceived, and not some mental surrogate. He has put forward an idiosyncratic theory of our knowledge of the mental states of others which he calls 'imitationism'. 'John is sad' means the same as 'John experiences thus: I am sad' where 'I am sad' reports what I would say if I were acting as John is in John's situation. A more or less independent invention of Kotarbiński's is the discipline of praxiology in which the scattered dictates of everyday practical good sense are brought together, their leading concepts analysed and then the whole systematized under general principles. In ethics he advocates—for he does not think basic ethical principles can be proved—what he calls independent ethics, independent, that is to

say, of any institutional moral authority: church or party. Its primary principle is that of acting as the brave protector or guardian of others against suffering or misfortune. The leading philosopher of Poland in its great interwar epoch of logical fertility, Kotarbiński nobly lived up to his own professions, never compromising with the regime of the Colonels, with their even more nationalistic and anti-semitic opponents, or with the Marxist despotism by which they were replaced. He was a philosopher of quite exemplary honour and public spirit. Rational philosophy in Poland survived the Communist episode in which it was oppressed but not extinguished. Most senior figures in Polish philosophy after the limited, and soon further constricted, liberalization of 1956 under Gomulka were Kotarbiński's pupils, if not his disciples. Praxiology led an organized life of its own. Reism, as Woleński's two books (1989) show, is still a subject of discussion and has affinities with various forms of reductionism in the English-speaking philosophical world.

Sources: Edwards; Z. Jordan (1963) *Philosophy and Ideology*, Dordrecht: Reidel.

ANTHONY QUINTON

Kovalevsky, Maksim Maksimovich

Russian. ***b:*** 8 September (27 August N.S.) 1851, Khar'kov. ***d:*** 5 April (23 March N.S.) 1916, Petrograd (St Petersburg). ***Cat:*** Positivist. ***Educ:*** Graduated in Law from the University of Khar'kov in 1873. ***Infls:*** Comte, Marx and Engels. ***Appts:*** 1880–7, Professor of Law, University of Moscow; 1905–16, Professor, University of St Petersburg.

Main publications:

(1905) *Sovremennye sotsiologi* [Contemporary Sociologists], St Petersburg.

(1910) *Sotsiologiia* [Sociology], 2 vols, St Petersburg.

Secondary literature:

Vucinich, A. (1976) *Social Thought in Tsarist Russia: The Quest for a General Science of Society, 1861–1917*, Chicago: University of Chicago Press, ch. 6.

Walicki, A. (1979) *A History of Russian Thought: From the Enlightenment to Marxism*, trans. Hilda Andrews-Rusiecka, Stanford: Stanford University Press, pp. 367–70.

A leading representative of Russian positivism, Kovalevsky was a jurist, sociologist and historian, whose work on the peasant commune influenced **Plekhanov** in his switch from Populism to Marxism. He spent many years in Western Europe, both as a student (when he befriended Marx and Engels in London) and after losing his Chair in 1887 for moderate opposition to the government. Having founded, with the Comtean Eugene de Roberty (1843–1915), the Russian School of Advanced Social Studies in Paris in 1901, he returned to Russia in 1905. He founded the moderate liberal Party of Democratic Reforms and was elected to the First Duma in 1906.

Rejecting the 'subjectivism' of **Lavrov** and **Mikhailovsky**, Kovalevsky predicated his own sociology on a Comtean belief in a universal evolutionary pattern of social development based on the fundamental sociological law of progress. He saw the prospect of a world federation of states as each nation progressed towards democracy, cosmopolitanism and economic interdependence. He described himself once as a disciple of Marx as well as a supporter of Comte, and held a compromise position on their opposing notions of conflict and consensus as the driving forces of social progress. Against Marx, he generally rejected monocausal theories of social change, stressing instead the interaction of many factors, including the economic, demographic, legal, political, scientific and artistic; single factors may, however, dominate particular epochs or social structures. Although opposed to class struggle and pathological revolutionary upheavals, he favoured socialism as a way of organizing the economy, and saw nothing contradictory in also advocating constitutional or 'popular' monarchy as his preferred mode of democratic government.

COLIN CHANT

Koyré, Alexandre André

French. *b:* 1882, Taganrog, Russia. *d:* 1964, Paris. *Cat:* Historian of science; historian of modern philosophy. *Educ:* Became a naturalized French citizen and studied at Göttingen under Edmund Husserl and in Paris with Léon Brunschvieg. *Appts:* Held various posts in Philosophy, including a Professorship, École Pratique des Hautes Études in Paris, and a Visiting Professorship, Princeton University.

Main publications:

(1922) *Essai sur l'idée de Dieu et les preuves de son existence chez Descartes*, Paris: Leroux.

(1929) *La philosophie de Jacob Boehme*, Paris: Vrin.

(1938) *Trois leçons sur Descartes*, Le Caire: Imprimerie Nationale.

(1939) *A l'aube de la science classique*, Paris: Hermann.

(1939) *Études Galiléennes*, Paris: Hermann (English translation, *Galileo Studies*, New York: Harvester Press, 1957).

(1944) *Entretiens sur Descartes*, Paris: Hermann.

(1945) *Introduction à la lecture de Platon*, Paris: Brentano (English translation, *Discovering Plato*, New York: Columbia University Press, 1945).

(1950) *Études sur l'histoire de la pensée philosophique en Russie*, Paris: Vrin.

(1957) *From Closed World to Infinite Universe*, Baltimore: Johns Hopkins University Press.

(1961) *La Révolution astronomique*, Paris: Hermann (English translation, *The Astronomical Revolution*, London: Methuen, 1973).

(1986) *De la mystique à la science*, Paris: École des Hautes Études (edited papers).

Together with Étienne **Gilson** and Henri **Gouhier**, Koyré was in the forefront of the revival of interest in Descartes's thought in France during the early part of this century. Koyré maintained that it is impossible to understand the work of any philosopher without a knowledge of the intellectual background of the time. In the sixteenth and seventeenth centuries, philosophical and scientific thought, including that of Descartes, were so interwoven that advances in one field are incomprehensible without some knowledge of progress in the other. As a background to Descartes's philosophical works, the Aristotelian and scholastic worldview had been discredited, and humanity, instead of having its assigned place in the scheme of things, found itself in an alien and uncertain world. In sixteenth-century French philosophy there was a strong strain of scepticism, typified in Montaigne's philosophical outlook. Descartes's views can be seen as a response to the climate of intellectual uncertainty. His complete split between the realms of mind and matter ensured the acceptance of a mechanistic, not a teleological, theory of causation and the mathematical treatment of the physical world.

In Koyré's research into the history of science can be found the now commonplace view that a pure empiricist approach to science is impossible. The fact that this view is now commonly accepted is due, at least in part, to Koyré's work. In his *Études Galiléennes* (1939) he argued that theory took precedence over experience in Galileo's thought. More generally Koyré's position was that scientists, in 'questioning' nature, must already have decided upon a theoretical framework into which they expect to be able to place the answers. Koyré has made available primary scientific sources which were previously not generally accessible to readers.

KATHRYN PLANT

Kraft, Victor

Austrian. *b:* 4 July 1880, Vienna. *d:* 3 January 1975, Vienna. *Cat:* Member of the Vienna Circle. *Ints:* Philosopher of science; value theorist. *Educ:* Philosophy, Geography and History, Vienna University, PhD 1903; postdoctoral studies in Berlin. *Appts:* Lecturer, 1914–24, until his dismissal by the Nazi regime in 1939; after the Second World War, Associate Professor (1947), Full Professor (1950–1), of Philosophy, University of Vienna; member of the Austrian Academy.

Main publications:

(1912) *Weltbegriff und Erkenntnisbegriff*, Leipzig.
(1925) *Die Grundformen der wissenschaftlichen Methoden*, Vienna.
(1947) *Mathematik, Logik und Erfahrung*, Vienna.
(1953) *The Vienna Circle*, New York: Philosophical Library.
(1960) *Erkenntnislehre*, Vienna.
(1981) *Foundations for a Scientific Analysis of Value* ed. H. Mulder, Boston: Reidel.

Secondary literature:

Topitsch, E. (ed.) (1960) *Probleme der Wissenschaftstheorie*, festschrift (contains bibliography), Vienna: Springer.

Kraft remained an unbiased empiricist throughout his political career. His main fields of work were methodology, epistemology and value theory. He accepted that philosophy should be a science (*Wissenschaft*) provable by experience, but Kraft rejected the sensualistic interpretation of experience stressing his realistic position. All our perception is founded on constructions of thoughts which complement sense impressions. These mental constructions are bound to be tested by experience. Knowledge is defined as a normative concept. Only in connection with other statements can the validity of statements be proved. The possibility of inductive inference is denied. In his book of 1925 Kraft propounds a hypothetic-deductive model of science, thus influencing **Popper**'s *Logic of Discovery* (1935).

In his value theory Kraft emphasizes that value-concepts do also have a cognitive content. They can therefore be justified in connection with other judgements. Perhaps the widest echo of Kraft's work came from his book on the Vienna Circle, which also contains his own critique of physicalism and other positions.

Sources: NDB 12; *Almanach der österreichische Akademie der Wissenschaften*, 1975.

RUDOLF HALLER

Kripke, Saul Aaron

American. *b:* 1940, New York. *Cat:* Logician; philosopher of language. *Ints:* Logic; philosophy of language; philosophy of mind. *Educ:* Harvard University and University of Oxford. *Infls:* S. Kleene, Bertrand Russell, Alfred Tarski and Ludwig Wittgenstein. *Appts:* Rockefeller University, New York; McCosh Professor of Philosophy, Princeton University.

Main publications:

(1959) 'A completeness theorem in modal logic', *Journal of Symbolic Logic* 24: 1–14.
(1963) 'Semantical analysis of modal logic 1', *Zeitschrift für Mathematische Logik und Grundlagen der Mathematik*, 9: 67–96.
(1965) 'Semantical considerations on modal logic', *Acta Philosophica Fennica* 16: 83–94.
(1965) 'Semantic analysis of modal logic 2', in J. Addison, L. Henkin and A. Tarski (eds) *The Theory of Models*, Amsterdam: North Holland, pp. 206–20.
(1975) 'Outline of a theory of truth', *Journal of Philosophy* 72.
(1976) 'Is there a problem about substitutional quantification?' in G. Evans and J. McDowell (eds) *Truth and Meaning: Essays in Semantics*, Oxford: Clarendon Press.
(1980) *Naming and Necessity*, Oxford: Blackwell.
(1982) *Wittgenstein on Rules and Private Language*, Oxford: Blackwell.

Secondary literature:

Forbes, Graeme (1985) *The Metaphysics of Modality*, Oxford: Clarendon Press.
Katz, J. (1990) *The Metaphysics of Meaning*, MIT Press.
Linksy, Leonard (ed.) (1971) *Reference and Modality*, Oxford: Oxford University Press.
Martin, R. M. (ed.) (1984) *Recent Essays on Truth and the Liar Paradox*, Oxford: Clarendon Press.
Salmon, Nathan, U. (1982) *Reference and Essence*, Oxford: Blackwell.

Kripke's remarkable career commenced with the publication of his first paper when he was nineteen years of age. Thereafter his work in logic provided a major impetus to the development of 'possible world' semantics, an approach which has had a wide application in philosophy. Having its origins in the Leibnizian idea of necessary truth as truth in all possible worlds, it provided a systematic framework for clarifying problems arising in relation to the plethora of already existing systems of modal logic. These systems, while formally well developed, had yet to be provided with a satisfactory semantics. Among the other applications in which Kripke has played a leading part are those to do with intuitionistic logic, which is of particular interest and concern for philosophers of mathematics. Such was the potential of this framework, that it took in studies of all manner of notions over and above the basic modalities of necessity and possibility.

This very diversity of modal logics posed problems, for the question immediately arose of whether there was any overall unifying perspective under which modal inferences could be systematically treated. Unfortunately some of the best known of these logical systems delivered different accounts of what qualified as correct inferences. It was all very well to have elegantly presented axiomatic systems, but without proper interpretation it was impossible to supply any definition of validity, and hence any satisfactory proofs of completeness for such systems. At best, logicians managed to give rather informal readings of their logical operators of necessity or possibility. The distinctiveness of Kripke's approach was in his definition of what he described as a 'model-structure', comprising a set of possible worlds with relations of accessibility or 'relative possibility' between those worlds. So, with respect to any given modal logic, the model assigns a truth-value to each atomic formula or proposition. So any given formula is either true or false in, or at, a world in the set. Kripke then defined the notion of validity for the given logic, a formula being valid in this sense if it came out true in all models. He went on to develop quantified modal logic, i.e. that which deals with modalized formulae involving the apparatus of quantification (informally expressed by 'all' and 'some'). In this logic an interpretation is provided for predicate expressions, specifying the sets of objects to be assigned to those expressions. In this way Kripke supplied the desired overall framework for accommodating the different logics—the same fundamental ideas were in play, the individual systems embodying specific restrictions or conditions imposed on the relations between worlds. Subsequently Kripke has gone on to make pioneering contributions to the theory of truth and the analysis of the more recalcitrant of the

logical and semantic paradoxes, as well as further developments in the field of quantification theory.

He made his greatest impact in a series of lectures (1970) which appeared in revised form in 1980. At the centre of his analysis was an assault on the long-cherished distinction between necessary and a posteriori truths. It was here that Kripke introduced his famous idea of the 'rigid designator' in his discussion of proper names, a topic which had already received extensive treatment since **Russell**'s analysis of 1905. Kripke's thesis was that proper names pick out their bearers or referents quite independently of any descriptions that might be associated with them. Additionally, he espoused what is known as the causal theory of meaning, i.e. that speakers' use of names is grounded ultimately in an original 'dubbing' of the object with the name, and subsequent use is sustained by a causal chain reaching back to that original episode in which the name was first assigned to the object. This had the immediate implication that names were not to be construed as in any way equivalent in meaning to any associated description or set of descriptions, and this in turn entailed dispensing with any Fregean-type distinction between the sense and reference of terms. Kripke's view also had the consequence that identity statements featuring only proper names were, if true, necessarily true. There were immediate implications here for the philosophy of mind: some of the proponents of the view known as 'central state' materialism had stressed the contingency of the identity of thoughts and brain processes; now the idea of contingent identity was in question.

Another interesting outcome of Kripke's work was a renewed interest in the issue of essentialism, i.e. in whether a distinction between an entity's essential and its merely contingent properties was sustainable. At an intuitive level it seems quite natural to say that some properties are essential to an object or a person, as Kripke would say that having a specific biological parentage was essential to an individual, whereas their becoming a famous philosopher was not. The distinction, and Kripke's account, continues to be hotly debated. Kripke has not ceased to be controversial. In his 1982 monograph he ventured a provocative, and to some minds totally wrong-headed, interpretation of parts of **Wittgenstein**'s *Philosophical Investigations* according to which he attributes to Wittgenstein a comprehensively sceptical position on meaning and rule-following. His influence on both seniors and contemporaries has been considerable, sharpening up the debates with other and more extravagant possible-worlds theorists like David **Lewis**, and attracting a lengthy chapter of critical appraisal from the pro-Fregean Michael **Dummett**. Others, like Hilary **Putnam**, have applied the notion of rigid designation to kind terms as well as individual terms. Inevitably, the notion of possible worlds has itself come into question despite its utility, and few have been convinced by Kripke's arguments for propositions which can be both necessary and a posteriori.

Sources: See secondary literature.

DENIS POLLARD

Kristeller, Paul Oskar

German-American (moved to USA in 1939). *b:* 22 May 1905, Berlin. *Cat:* Historian of Renaissance philosophy. *Ints:* History of philosophy; historiography of philosophy. *Educ:* Heidelberg University as well as University of Berlin, University of Freiburg and University of Marburg. *Infls:* Influences include Ernst Hoffmann and Ernst Cassirer. *Appts:* 1934–5, Lecturer, German Institute Super Magistero, Florence; 1935–8, Lecturer, German University and Scuola Normale Superiore, Pisa; 1939–48, Lecturer, then Associate Professor of Philosophy, 1948–73, Professor, then F. J. E. Woodbridge Professor, 1973–, then Emeritus F. J. E. Woodbridge Professor, Columbia University, New York.

Main publications:

(1937) (ed.) *Supplementum Ficinianum: Marsillii Ficini Philosophi Platonici Opuscula Inedita et Dispersa*, 2 vols, Florence.

(1943) *The Philosophy of Marsilio Ficino*, trans. Virginia Conant, New York: Columbia University Press.

(1955) *The Classics and Renaissance Thought*, Cambridge, Mass.: Harvard University Press.

(1956) *Studies in Renaissance Thought and Letters*, Oram: Storia Letteratura.

(1960) (ed.) *Catalogu Translationum et Commentariorums Medieval and Renaissance Latin Translations and Commentaries: Annotated Lists and Guides*, Washington: Catholic University of America Press.

(1961) *Renaissance Thought*, New York: Harper.

(1963) *Iter Italicum: A Finding List of Uncatalogued or Incompletely Catalogued Humanistic Manuscripts of the Renaissance in Italian and Other Libraries*; 2 vols, London: Warburg Institute and Leiden: Brill.

(1965) *Renaissance Thought II: Papers on Humanism and the Arts*, New York: Harper & Row.

(1972) *Renaissance Concepts of Man, and Other Essays*, London: Harper & Row.

(1974) *Medieval Aspects of Renaissance Learning*, Duke University Press.

(1985) 'Philosophy and its historiography', *Journal of Philosophy* 82: 618–25.

Secondary literature:

Hankins, J. *et al* (eds) (1987) *Supplementum Festivuum: Studies in Honor of Paul Oskar Kristeller*, Binghampton, NY: Medieval & Renaissance Texts and Studies, vol. 49.

Mahony, E. P. (ed.) (1976) *Philosophy and Humanism: Renaissance Essays in Honor of Paul Oskar Kristeller*, Leiden: Brill; New York: Columbia University Press.

Oberman, H. A., and Brady, T. A. Jr. (eds) (1975) *Itinerarium Italicum: The Profile of the Italian Renaissance in the Mirror of its European Transformations: Dedicated to Paul Oskar Kristeller on Occasion of his 70th Birthday*, Studies in Medieval and Renaissance Thought, vol. 14, Leiden: Brill.

Selig, K.-L. and Somerville, R. (eds) (1987) *Floregium Columbianum: Essays in Honor of Paul Oskar Kristeller*, New York: Ithaca Press.

After completing his doctoral thesis on Plotinus, Kristeller spent five very productive years in Italy, where he worked on manuscripts relating to Ficino. He became aware of the huge number of unpublished writings of philosophers and humanists of the Renaissance period that still existed in libraries in Italy and elsewhere. One of his major contributions was to produce a catalogue of this material and thus make the writings of the Renaissance more available to scholars. In collaboration with others he also produced a catalogue of Latin editions which has clarified the classical inheritance of medieval and Renaissance culture. Kristeller was associated with the best of Renaissance scholarship in the postwar period and set new standards for the history of philosophy, which he thought needed to combine philosophical understanding with tested methods of philological interpretation and historical documentation, as well as being based on the critically edited writings of past thinkers in their original language.

Sources: DAS; P. O. Kristeller (1991) *A Life of Learning*, New York: American Council of Learned Societies; PI; WW(Am).

STUART BROWN

Kristeva, Julia

Bulgarian. *b:* 1941, Bulgaria. *Cat:* Psychoanalyst;

aesthetician; linguist; semiologist; feminist theorist. *Ints:* Cultural history. *Educ:* 1966, University of Paris; École Pratique des Hautes Etudes. *Infls:* Marx, Freud, Lacan, Barthes, Jakobson, Lévi-Strauss, Hegel, Bakhtin and Georges Bataille. *Appts:* Professor of Linguistics, University of Paris VII.

Main publications:

(1969) *Séméiotiké: Recherches pour une sémanalyse*, Paris: Seuil.

(1974) *La Révolution du langage poétique*, Paris: Seuil (English translation, *Revolution in Poetic Language*, trans. Margaret Waller, New York: Columbia University Press, 1984).

(1974) *Des Chinoises*, Paris: Editions des Femmes (English translation, *About Chinese Women*, trans. Anita Burrows, New York and London: Marion Boyars, 1986).

(1977) *Polylogue*, Paris: Seuil.

(1980) *Pouvoirs de l'horreur: essai sur l'abjection*, Paris: Seuil (English translation, *Powers of Horror: An Essay on Abjection*, trans. Leon S. Roudiez, New York: Columbia University Press, 1982).

(1980) *Desire in Language: A Semiotic Approach to Literature and Art*, ed. Leon S. Roudiez, trans. Thomas S. Gora, Alice Jardine and Leon S. Roudiez, New York: Columbia University Press.

(1981) *Le langage, cet inconnu*, Paris: Seuil (English translation, *Language the Unknown: An Initiation into Linguistics*, trans. Anna M. Menke, Hemel Hempstead: Harvester, 1989).

(1983) *Histoires d'amour*, Paris: Deneol (English translation, *Tales of Love*, trans. Leon S. Roudiez, New York: Columbia University Press, 1987).

(1986) *Au commencement était l'amour: psychanalyse et foi*, Paris: Hachette (English translation, *In the Beginning was Love: Psychoanalysis and Faith*, trans. Arthur Goldhammer, New York: Columbia University Press, 1987).

(1988) *Étrangers à nous-mêmes*, Paris: Fayard (English translation, *Strangers to Ourselves*, trans. Leon S. Roudiez, New York: Columbia University Press, 1989).

Secondary literature:

Allen, Jeffner and Young, Marion (eds) (1989) *The Thinking Muse: Feminism and Modern French Philosophy*, Bloomington, Ind.: Indiana University Press.

Benjamin, Andrew (ed.) (1990) *Abjection, Melancholia and Love: The Work of Julia Kristeva*, London and New York: Routledge.

Lechte, John (1990) *Julia Kristeva*, London and New York: Routledge.

Miller, Nancy K. (ed.) (1986) *The Politics of Gender*, New York: Columbia University Press.

Kristeva's original subject was linguistics but she has since branched out to become a major theorist in semiotics, psychoanalysis and feminism. She first came to prominence in the late 1960s through her association with the radical Parisian journal *Tel Quel*. **Barthes** was a key influence on her semiotic enquiries, where her early concern was to develop a semiotic theory capable of describing poetic language, with particular reference to modernism. One of her most important contributions to semiotic theory has been the concept of intertexuality, the idea, derived from her study of Bakhtin, that any text is a 'mosaic of quotations' from other textual sources. Another key Kristevian semiotic concept is *chora*, a kind of disruptive energy operating within the semiotic enterprise. A basically untheorizable entity, *chora*, is identified as a feminine element, a receptacle or womb in its original Greek sense, which for Kristeva corresponds to the poetic in language. From the 1970s onwards, after qualifying as a psychoanalyst (with **Lacan** as a major influence), Kristeva's work becomes increasingly preoccupied with psychoanalysis and its application to problems of feminism. Kristeva is a feminist theorist of less radical disposition than such 'second-generation' feminists as Luce **Irigaray** and Hélène Cixous, with their commitment to a 'feminism of difference' and specifically feminine discourse (*écriture féminine*). Reconciling this second-generation feminism with the first-generation feminism of theorists like de **Beauvoir** has been a particular project of Kristeva in her feminist writings, and she has claimed, in opposition to the second generation's sectarian impulses, that 'the dichotomy man/woman' belongs to metaphysics rather than to biology. Kristeva has been a leading voice in French intellectual life since the 1960s and has had a significant impact in her various chosen fields of enquiry. The concept of intertextuality, for example, has passed into general usage in literary and cultural studies. The most contentious part of Kristeva's work remains her feminist theories, which are almost provocatively reactionary by the standards of recent French feminism and have aroused considerable controversy in feminist circles worldwide.

STUART SIM

Kropotkin, Peter (Petr Alekseevich)
Russian. *b:* 27 November (9 December N.S.) 1842, Moscow. *d:* 8 February 1921, Dmitrov, near

Moscow. *Cat:* Anarchist. *Educ:* St Petersburg Corps of Pages, and from 1867, University of St Petersburg University. *Infls:* Fourier, Proudhon and the Russian noble revolutionaries A. I. Herzen and M. A. Bakunin. *Appts:* 1867, Secretary, Department of Physical Geography, Imperial Russian Geographical Society.

Main publications:

(1885) *Paroles d'un révolté*, Paris (English translation, *Words of a Rebel*, trans. George Woodcock, Montreal and New York: Black Rose Books, 1992).

(1892) *La conquête du pain*, Paris (English translation *The Conquest of Bread*, ed. Paul Avrich, London: Allen Lane).

(1899) *Memoirs of a Revolutionist*, 2 vols, London: Smith, Elder & Co.

(1899) *Fields, Factories and Workshops*, London: Hutchinson & Co.

(1901) *Sovremmenaia nauka i anarkhizm*, London: Russian Free Press Fund (English translation, *Modern Science and Anarchism*, trans. D. A. Modell, Philadelphia: Social Science Club, 1903).

(1902) *Mutual Aid: A Factor of Evolution*, London: William Heinemann.

(1922) *Etika, t.1: proiskhozhdenie i razvitie nravstvennosti*, Moscow (English translation, *Ethics: Origin and Development*, trans. Louis S. Friedland and Joseph R. Piroshnikoff, New York: Lincoln McVeagh, 1924).

Secondary literature:

Cahm, C. (1989) *Kropotkin and the Rise of Revolutionary Anarchism 1872–1886*, Cambridge: Cambridge University Press.

Miller, M. A. (1976) *Kropotkin*, Chicago: University of Chicago Press.

Despite his privileged education and status as chamber page to Tsar Alexander II, Prince Peter Kropotkin opted for state service in Siberia, during which time he undertook geographical and geological research. He then resigned his commission, and from 1867 was Secretary to the Imperial Russian Geographical Society's Department of Physical Geography. After the Paris Commune, he committed himself to revolutionary activity, aligning himself with Bakunin and his faction in the First International. In 1872 he joined the revolutionary populist Chaikovsky circle; two years later, he was arrested and imprisoned. In 1876 he escaped, settling in Switzerland and founding the anarchist journal *Le Révolté*. He was expelled in 1881, and moved to France, where he was imprisoned again. In 1886 he settled in London, and was active both in anarchist groups and in the British scientific community. He returned to Russia only after the March Revolution of 1917.

In his theory of 'anarchist communism', Kropotkin envisaged a global federation of free communities based on unwaged labour. It would emerge through alternating revolutionary leaps and periods of evolutionary change from the historical struggle between natural, autonomous communities and artificial authority, as embodied in the state. It would be marked by the harnessing of modern labour-saving technology and the abolition of the division of labour, especially that between manual and mental, and rural and urban work. Kropotkin's anarchism differed from the 'collectivist' version of Proudhon and Bakunin in its emphasis on the distribution of goods according to needs, rather than of rewards according to hours worked. In his optimistic, benevolent anarchist-communist vision, Kropotkin idealized the peasant commune and the institutions of free medieval cities as the highest point yet of human history. In his later works (notably *Mutual Aid* (1902) and *Modern Science and Anarchism* (1901) Kropotkin sought to develop anarchism as a synthetic philosophy based on the natural sciences. He reinterpreted Darwinism, insisting that intraspecific cooperation, as well as interspecific competition and struggle, was a major factor in the evolution of species. In his final uncompleted work, he attempted to derive a naturalistic ethics of solidarity and self-sacrifice from the instinct for mutual aid implanted by the processes of evolution.

COLIN CHANT

Kuhn, Thomas S(amuel)

American. *b:* 18 July 1922, Cincinnati, Ohio. *Cat:* Historian of science; philosopher of science. *Educ:* 1943, graduated in Physics, Harvard University. *Infls:* Alexandre Koyré, Emile Meyerson, Hélène Metzer, Anneliese Maier, Jean Piaget, B. L. Whorf, W. v. O. Quine and Ludwig Fleck. *Appts:* 1948–56, Junior Fellow, then Assistant Professor, General Education and History of Science, Harvard University; 1961–4, Professor, History of Science, University of California, Berkeley; 1968–79, M. Taylor Pine Professor of the History of Science, Princeton University; 1979–83, Professor, Philosophy and History of Science, Massachusetts Institute of Technology; 1983–91, Laurance S. Rockefeller Professor of Philosophy, MIT; 1991–, Professor Emeritus, MIT.

Main publications:

(1957) *The Copernican Revolution: Planetary Astronomy in the Development of Western Thought*, Cambridge, Mass.: Harvard University Press.

(1962) *The Structure of Scientific Revolutions*, Chicago: Chicago University Press; second enlarged edition, 1970.

(1966) (with John L. Heilbron, Paul L. Forman and Lini Allen) *Sources for History of Quantum Physics: An Inventory and Report*, Philadelphia: Memoires of the American Philosophical Society.

(1977) *The Essential Tension: Selected Studies in Scientific Tradition and Change*, Chicago: University of Chicago Press.

(1978) *Black-Body Theory and the Quantum Discontinuity, 1894–1912*, Oxford: Oxford University Press.

(1983) 'Rationality and theory choice', in *Journal of Philosophy* 80, pp. 563–71.

(1992) 'The natural and the human sciences', in D. Hiley et al. (eds) *The Interpretive Turn: Philosophy, Science and Culture*, Ithaca, NY: Cornell University Press.

(1994) 'Afterwords', in P. Horwich (ed.) *World Changes: Thomas Kuhn and the Nature of Science.*

Secondary literature:

Barnes, Barry (1982) *T. S. Kuhn and Social Science*, New York: Columbia University Press.

Buchdahl, Gerd (1965) Review of *The Structure of Scientific Revolutions*, *British Journal of the History of Science* 4: 55–69.

Gutting, Gary (ed.) (1980) *Paradigms and Revolutions*, Notre Dame: University of Notre Dame Press.

Horwich, Paul (ed.) (1994) *World Changes: Thomas Kuhn and the Nature of Science*, Cambridge, Mass.: MIT Press.

Hoyningen-Huene, Paul (1993) *Reconstructing Scientific Revolutions: Thomas S. Kuhn's Philosophy of Science*, Chicago: University of Chicago Press (published in an earlier version in 1989 as *Die Wissenschaftsphilosophie Thomas S. Kuhns: Rekonstruktion und Grundlagenprobleme*).

Lakatos, Imré and Musgrave, Alan (eds) (1970) *Criticism and the Growth of Knowledge*, Cambridge: Cambridge University Press.

Laudan, Larry (1977) *Progress and Its Problems*, Berkeley: University of California Press.

Putnam, Hilary (1981) 'The corroboration of theories', in I. Hacking (ed.), *Scientific Revolutions*, Oxford: Oxford University Press.

Shapere, Dudley (1964) Review of *The Structure of Scientific Revolutions*, *Philosophical Review* 73: 383–94.

Siegel, Harvey (1987) *Relativism Refuted: A Critique of Contemporary Epistemological Relativism*, Dordrecht: D. Reidel.

Kuhn's work falls into two main categories—his writings as a historian of science and his more controversial contribution to the philosophy and sociology of science. His former preoccupation appears to have influenced the latter domain but not vice versa. His reputation as a historian of science is indisputably solid, but his fame, transcending subject boundaries, rests primarily on *The Structure of Scientific Revolutions*, which admirers and critics tend to concentrate on, often excluding much else which might serve to modify the dominant theme which appears to them to emerge from its initial publication in 1962.

That thesis is perceived to consist of: (i) a paradigm establishing itself constitutes the maturity of a science; (ii) paradigms (embodying exemplars) are scientific achievements universally recognized and accepted by the community of practitioners to provide model problems and solutions, permitting normal science to occur; (iii) paradigm changes involve revolutionary science; (iv) competing paradigms are incommensurable because each selects different problems as significant to solve, using in turn different standards to count as success of solution; furthermore, no common observational data exist that could function as a neutral standard for comparing them, as each involves perceiving different 'facts'; (v) neutral rules and facts cannot, therefore, determine paradigm change; (vi) paradigm change is accounted for by the decisions of the scientific community, namely, justification by authority of persons, not by impersonal criteria like logical or methodological rules.

Philosophers of science tend to conclude irrationalism or relativism from the above. If so, there can be no philosophy but only sociology (and history) of science. On the other hand, historians and sociologists of science, while welcoming the treatment of cognitive beliefs and interests by the ordinary methods of empirical sociology, nevertheless, think that Kuhn has underplayed the influence of external factors, such as political and social ones, on scientific research. Kuhn himself, however, moans that he has been much misunderstood. But he is satisfied that Hoyningen-Huene (1993) has done justice to the complexities of his own position and the controversies surrounding it since the publication of *The Structure of Scientific Revolutions*.

Kuhn shares with **Popper** the honour of laying the agenda, in the main, of (Anglo-American) philosophy of science in the last thirty years. Popper and positivists adhere to **Reichenbach**'s distinction between the context of justification and the context of discovery, thereby defending the thesis of scientific rationality and of progress which is linear and continuous. *The Structure of Scientific Revolutions* is perceived as a thought-provoking seminal work posing a powerful challenge to this 'traditional' view. By decentring the formal logical dimension, the Kuhnian account bears some affinity to the writing of French historians and philosophers of science like Gaston **Bachelard**, as well as that of **Feyerabend**, not to mention Michael **Polanyi**. Kuhn himself explicitly acknowledges the influence of **Koyré**, another historian of science on his thoughts.

Sources: CBD; DAS; Turner; WD; *PI*; personal communication.

KEEKOK LEE

Külpe, Oswald

German. *b:* 3 August 1862, Kandau, Kurland. *d:* 30 December 1915, Munich. *Cat:* Critical realist; psychologist. *Ints:* Epistemology; thought processes. *Educ:* Universities of Leipzig, Berlin, Göttingen and Dorpat. *Infls:* Literary influences: Kant, Husserl and Brentano. Personal: Wilhelm Wundt, Theodor Mommsen and Hermann Diels. *Appts:* 1886–94, Dozent in Psychology, University of Leipzig; 1894–1909, Professor in Psychology, University of Würzburg; 1909 -12, Professor of Psychology, University of Bonn; 1912–15, Professor of Psychology, University of Munich.

Main publications:

(1895) *Einleitung in die Philosophie*, Leipzig: Teubner (English translation, *Introduction to Philosophy*, trans. W. B. Pillsbury and E. B. Titchener, London: Sonnenschein, 1901).

(1910) *Erkenntnistheorie und Naturwissenschaft*, Leipzig: S. Hirzel.

(1912–23) *Die Realisierung: Ein Beitrag zur Grundlegung der Realwissenschaften*, 3 vols (vols 2 and 3 edited by August Messer), Leipzig: S. Hirzel.

(1923) *Vorlesungen uber Logik*, ed. Otto Selz, Leipzig: S. Hirzel.

Secondary literature:

Marbe, Karl (1901) *Experimentell-psychologische Untersuchungen über das Urteil: Eine Einleitung in die Logic*, Leipzig: Engelmann.

Messer, August (1923) *Der Kritische Realismus*, Karlsruhe: Quelle & Meyer.

Ogden, R. M. (1951) 'Oswald Külpe and the Würzburg School', *American Journal of Psychology* 61: 4–19.

Külpe registered at Leipzig in 1881 to study history, but once he was there his interests were directed by Wilhelm **Wundt** towards psychology and philosophy. In 1894 Külpe moved to Würzburg where he founded an institute for psychological experimentation, the Würzburg School, which achieved renown for its work in the study of thought processes, being associated especially with the thesis that thought is 'imageless', that it depends on such conscious attitudes (*Bewusstseinslagen*) as doubt and certainty rather than on images and sensations.

Külpe's philosophy was continuous with his psychology. Opposing idealistic neo-Kantianism, he developed a 'critical realism', a philosophical position which, while respecting the achievements of Kant in the critique of knowledge, undertook to justify the realism of everyday consciousness and the sciences, that is, to refute the idealist interpretation of the world as a 'mere representation'. Starting from the 'given' and taking into account the results of the empirical sciences, Külpe's aim was to demonstrate the possibility of arriving at assertions about the general structures of a reality that was independent of consciousness. In this, Külpe contended that imageless thought is integral to the process through which thought achieves relation to something independent of itself. The critical realism of Külpe and his Würzburg colleagues (for example, A. Messer and K. Marbe) represented an important strand of German philosophy during the early decades of the present century, exerting considerable influence on Joseph **Geyser** and Nicolai **Hartmann** in particular.

Sources: Edwards.

STEPHEN MOLLER

L

La Via, Vincenzo

Italian. *b:* 28 January 1895, Nicosia, Sicily. *d:* Deceased. *Cat:* Theorist of knowledge. *Appts:* Taught theoretical philosophy, University of Catania.

Main publications:

(1925) *L'idealismo attuale di G. Gentile.*

(1941) *Idealismo e filosofia.*

(1941) *Dall'idealismo all'assoluto realismo*, Florence: Sansoni.

(1950) *La filosofia e l'idea di Dio*, Messina: Ferrara.

(1950) *Fundamento e struttura della metafisica*, Messina: Sessa.

(1953) *L'unità del filosofare e la persona.*

(1964) *La risoluzione dell'idealismo in assoluto realismo.*

(1965) *L'idealismo e il conoscere fondante.*

(1966) *Coscienza e metafisica.*

Secondary literature:

Omaggio a Vincenzo la Via, Catania: Tipo dell'Università, 1969.

La Via's work is a meditation on internal tensions in a philosophical tradition that finds its Italian expression in **Gentile**, tensions which stem from a Hegelian drive to resolve differences into unity. He unveils in idealism the constant tension between absolute subjectivism and absolute historicism, between the view that everything is determined by the self and the view of the self as a function of historical forces. Descartes and Kant had claimed truth to be something which the self institutes and into which it enters. But from what point of view is this assertion made? If made by a self that stands outside the process, a kind of transcendentalism results that is at odds with its Kantian origins and which implies an unacceptable duality between the self and what it knows. For La Via truth is not, as it was for idealists, something to be viewed from a transcendental viewpoint. *Etre e avoir* generates from this a criticism of possessiveness (later extended into trenchant remarks on technical utility) and its relation to contemporary decadence and opposes to it an analysis of the experiences that lead us to spirituality.

COLIN LYAS

Laberthonnière, Marie Paul Lucien

French. *b:* 5 October 1860, Chazelet, Indre, France. *d:* 6 October 1932, Paris. *Cat:* Philosophical theologian. *Ints:* Catholic apologetics; philosophy of education. *Educ:* Grand Séminaire of Bourges Cathedral; classes at the Sorbonne. *Infls:* Pascal, Malebranche, Maine de Biran, A. J. A. Gratry, E. Boutroux, Ollé-Laprune and M. Blondel. *Appts:* Collège de Juilly (Paris), 1887; École Massillon, 1886; Rector, Collège de Juilly, 1900.

Main publications:

(1903) *Essais de philosophie religieuse*, Paris: Lethielleux.

(1904) *Le Réalisme chrétien et l'idéalisme grec*, Paris: Lethielleux.

(1905–13) *Annales de philosophie chrétienne*, Paris: Bloud.

(1913) *Théorie de l'éducation*, Paris: Vrin.

(1935) *Études sur Descartes*, 2 vols, ed. L. Canet, Paris: Vrin.

(1937) *Études de philosophie chrétienne et premiers écrits philosophiques*, ed. L. Canet, Paris: Vrin.

(1942) *Esquisse d'une philosophie personnaliste*, Paris, Vrin.

(1945) *Pangermanisme et christianisme*, ed. L. Canet, Paris, Vrin.

(1947) *Sicut Ministrator ou Critique de la notion de souveraineté de la loi*, ed. L. Canet and M. M. d'Hendecourt, Paris: Vrin.

(1948) *Critique de laicisme ou comment se pose le problème de Dieu*, ed. L. Canet, Paris: Vrin.

(1955) *La Notion chrétienne de l'autorité*, ed. L. Canet, Paris: Vrin.

(1961) *Correspondance philosophique* (with M. Blondel), ed. C. Tresmontant, Paris: Seuil.

(1961) *Les Fruits de l'esprit*, ed. M. M. d'Hendecourt, Paris: Montaigne.

(1975) *Laberthonnière et ses amis*, ed. M. T. Perrin, Paris: Beauchesne.

(1983) *Le Dossier Laberthonnière*, ed. M. E. Perrin, Paris: Beauchesne.

Secondary literature:
Beillevert, P. (ed.) (1973) *Laberthonnière, l'homme et l'oeuvre, ... Textes et communications*, Paris: Beauchesne.
Brehier, É. 'Descartes d'après le Père Laberthonnière', *Revue de Métaphysique et de Morale* 42: 533–47.
Castelli, E. (1927) *Laberthonnière*, Milan: Athena (French translation, ed. L. Carnet, Paris: Vrin, 1931).
Eastwood, D. M. (1936) *The Revival of Pascal*, Oxford: Clarendon.
Gelinas, J. P. (1959) *La Restauration du thomisme*, Washington: Catholic University of America Press.
Hendecourt, M. M. d' (1947) *Personne et liberté, essai sur la philosophie du Père Laberthonnière*, Paris: Vrin (thesis).
——(1961) 'Laberthonnière', *Revue de Métaphysique et de Morale* 63.
Pazzaaglia, L. (1973) *Educazione Religiosa e Libertà umana*, Bologna: Il Mulino.
Testore, C. (1951) *Enciclopedia Cattolica, Città del Vaticano, Ente per l'Enciclopedia Cattolica e per il Libro Cattolico*, VII: 775–7.
Vidler, A. R. (1970) *A Variety of Catholic Modernists*, Cambridge: Cambridge University Press.
Virgoulay, R. (1980) *Blondel et le modernisme*, Paris: Cerf.

Laberthonnière first appears as an ally of **Blondel**, with a like emphasis on action in practice and on the primacy of the will over the intellect, and when Blondel bought the *Annales de Philosophie Chrétienne* in 1905 he became its editor. He called his position 'dogmatisme moral', meaning that the foundations of belief, religious or otherwise, were ultimately moral. Resolutely opposed to scholasticism and to positivism of any kind, he was equally opposed to all authoritarian approaches to belief and therefore, unsurprisingly, fell victim to the purges of the Catholic modernist crisis, escaping excommunication but banned from publishing from 1913 for the remainder of his life. In epistemology, his system was a type of pragmatism which claimed to avoid relativism by including the self-criticism of the knower. In metaphysics Laberthonnière shares with Berkeley and Leibniz the view that only active beings or spirits can properly be entities, although he sees their existence in the mutual dependence of these beings, with each other and with God. Resolutely opposed to what he regarded as the abstractions of Greek idealism, Laberthonnière only accepted

individuals, each absolutely unique, their uniqueness being guaranteed by God. Denying that any demonstration or catalogue of facts, whether logical, scientific or historical, could ever bring about faith, Laberthonnière seems to have developed his system as an account of human life in which faith could have its place. In later life he quarrelled with what he saw as Blondel's compromises with scholasticism.
Sources: Edwards; M. T. Perrin (1980) *La Jeunesse de Laberthonnière*, Paris: Beauchesne.

R. N. D. MARTIN

Labriola, Antonio
Italian. *b:* 2 July 1843, Cassino, Italy. *d:* 2 February 1904, Rome. *Cat:* First Italian Marxist philosopher. *Educ:* University of Naples. *Appts:* Professor of Moral Philosophy, University of Rome, 1874–1904.

Main publications:
In *Opere*, Naples: Rossi, 1972:
(1873) *Morale e Religione*.
(1873) *Della libertà morale*.
(1895) *In memoria del Manifesto dei comunisti*.
(1896) *Del materialismo storico*.
(1897) *L'università e la libertà della scienza*.
(1898) *Discorrendo di socialismo e di filosofia*.
(1906) *Scritti vari di filosofia e politica*.
(1949) *Lettere a Engels*, Rome: Rinascita.
(1988) *Lettre inedite (1862–1903)*, Rome: Instituto Storico Italiano.

Secondary literature:
Martinelli, R. (1988) *Antonio Labriola*, Rome: Editori riuniti.
Pane, L. dal (1968) *A. Labriola*, Bologna: Forni.
Poggi, S. (1982) *Introduzione a Labriola*, Bari: Laterza.

Labriola subscribed in his early years to Hegelianism, then to Herbart. He discovered Marxism in about 1890, corresponding at length with Engels. His articles on Marxism, published by **Croce** and **Sorel**, were the first exposition of Marxism as a philosophy by an academic and have a supposed purity of interpretation that has been invoked as a model, as when **Gramsci** advocated 'the return to Labriola'. Labriola wished not so much to develop Marx as to expound the philosophy he found there. He denied that historical materialism is designed to capture the infinite variety of historical events under a philosophy of history, wishing to liberate history from the imposition of any metaphysical structure, so that even the law of progress must be preserved from any taint of teleology. Historical materialism is not philosophy but a new method for researching history. The novelty of Marx consists not in unprecedented ideas but in his clear recognition of the proper method of proceeding. Historical materialism as a method and socialism as a practical activity are not to be distinguished, for historical materialism is the truth of socialism. There are idealistic and voluntarist overtones in Labriola's Marxism, for example in his belief in a cultural and sociological rather than an economic base for the notion of class consciousness. Labriola marks a significant development in the history of Marxism, partly because of his determined efforts to free it from any residue of Hegelian metaphysics, partly because of his influence on Croce and Sorel (later rejected by him as revisionists) and on Gramsci, and partly because he introduced into Italy one of the most pervasive features of its intellectual culture.

COLIN LYAS

Lacan, Jacques

French. *b:* 1901, Paris. *d:* 1981, Paris. *Cat:* Psychoanalyst. *Ints:* Philosophy of mind; philosophy of language. *Educ:* Trained in Medicine and Psychiatry at the Paris Medical Faculty. *Infls:* Sigmund Freud and Ferdinand de Saussure. *Appts:* 1932, Chef de Clinique, Paris Medical Faulty; 1964, founded the École Freudienne, Paris, and became President of the Champ Freudien at the University of Vincennes.

Main publications:

(1966) *Écrits I and II*, Paris: Éditions du Seuil.
(1974) *Télévision*, Paris: Éditions du Seuil.
(1975) *Encore, 1972–3*, Paris: Éditions du Seuil.
(1978) *Le Séminaire, Livre II: Le Moi dans la théorie de Freud*, Paris: Éditions du Seuil (English translation, *The Ego in Freud's Theory*, ed. J.-A. Miller, Cambridge: Cambridge University Press.
(1981) *Le Séminaire, Livre VII: L'Ethique de la psychanalyse*, Paris: Éditions du Seuil.
(1986) *Le Séminaire, Livre VIII: Le Transfert*, Paris: Éditions du Seuil.
(1991) *Le Séminaire, Livre XVII: L'Envers de la psychanalyse*, Paris: Éditions du Seuil.

Secondary literature:

MacCannell, J. (1986) *Figuring Lacan: Criticism and the Cultural Unconscious*, London: Croom Helm.
Schneiderman, S. (1983) *Jacques Lacan: Death of an Intellectual Hero*, Cambridge, Mass.: Harvard University Press.

Sturrock, J. (ed.) (1979) *Structuralism and Since*, Oxford and New York: Oxford University Press (contains a short bibliography).

It is not easy to encapsulate Lacan's work because of his persistent refusal to state and develop any systematic theories, but one approach to his ideas is, first, to consider his views on language, and then to take in other concepts with which these views are closely interrelated.

According to Lacan, language has two aspects. There is the public, rule-governed and syntactical structure, but this is counterbalanced by the alternative level of free association in pun, word-play and dreams. Lacan's views on language owe much to **Saussure**, but he stresses to a much greater extent this second, free-association aspect.

The unconscious is both created by and reflects language. The rule-governed aspect of the latter constricts and suppresses the unconscious, which in its turn asserts its freedom and psychical energy through its persistent attempt to undermine and destabilize syntax and fixed meaning by the use of free association.

The unconscious is also in tension with the ideal ego, or persisting and integrated self. It is at the 'mirror phase' that a child makes the first of lifelong attempts to create a self, or to gain a sense of identity. Such attempts always fail, because the self is merely a constantly shifting, fluidly organized matrix or nexus which projects and objectifies itself into a deceptive and fictitious wholeness. Syntactical language is the ground and agent of this deception: the order found within this level of language both allows and directs such objectification.

What we view as reality is also constructed by and reflected in language and changes with linguistic developments. Reality is given its structure by, and is parasitic on, language. There is no metalanguage to describe any ultimate reality 'behind' what is given to us by the language we use. Lacan thus reverses the traditional order between the symbolic (in this case, language) and what it symbolizes: the former creates the latter.

Lacan was concerned to break down the barriers between different intellectual disciplines, and his work ranges freely over the concepts of such traditionally diverse areas as psychoanalysis, linguistics, the theories of knowledge and mind, and literary and critical theory. His interest in, and application of his work to, the latter two areas can be illustrated by his treatment, in *Écrits* (1966), of Edgar Allan Poe's story 'The purloined letter'. According to Lacan's analysis, the letter of the story's title is a symbol of language: as it passes through the hands of the various characters it takes on a different meaning by playing a different role in each life.

There is a strong feminist interest in Lacan's works. According to one feminist interpretation the public aspect of language is male-oriented and paternalistic, whereas conversely the subversive struggle of the free-association aspect of language is a reflection of the attempts of the feminist principle to assert itself.

Lacan's writings are self-critical: his later works examine and destabilize the conceptual structure of the earlier, thus leading to difficulties in giving an exposition of his views. He deliberately incorporates ambiguity, pun, word-play and multiple meaning into his publications, to highlight his position on the continuous slippage of language. However, there must be some statements, or a metalanguage used about language, which are not subject to such a factor: the meaning of the assertion that there is continuous slippage in language must be fixed, so that we can know this alleged fact about language.

KATHRYN PLANT

Lachance, Louis

Canadian. *b:* 18 February 1899, Saint-Joachim-de-Montmorency, Quebec. *d:* 28 October 1963, Montreal. *Cat:* Thomist; philosopher of history; philosopher of language. *Ints:* Law; politics. *Educ:* Petit Séminaire du Québec, 1912–20; the Dominican College of Philosophy and Theology, Ottawa, 1921–4; and the Université de Montréal, 1925–7. *Appts:* After several years of teaching and study in Rome he returned to the Dominican College, Ottawa, as Professor of Philosophy in 1931; in 1936 he was appointed to the Angelicum University, Rome, but teaching in Latin seemed to him unnaturally restrictive, and he returned to Ottawa in 1938; he moved in 1939 to the Grand Séminaire de Sherbrooke and in 1943 became Professor of Moral and Social Philosophy at the Université de Montréal, where he remained until his death, serving as Dean of the Faculty of Philosophy from 1960 onwards.

Main publications:

(1933) *Le Concept du droit selon Aristote et S. Thomas*, Montreal: Éditions Albert Levesque; second edition, Ottawa: Les Éditions du Lévrier, 1948.
(1936) *Nationalisme et religion*, Ottawa: Collège Dominicaine.
(1939) *L'Humanisme politique de Saint Thomas; individu et état*, 2 vols, Paris: Recueil Sirey.

(1943) *Philosophie du langage*, Ottawa: Éditions du Lévrier.
(1950) *L'Etre et ses propriétés*, Montreal: Éditions du Lévrier.
(1959) *Le Droit et les droits de l'homme*, Paris: Universitaires de France.

Secondary literature:

Armour, Leslie (1981) *The Idea of Canada and the Crisis of Community*, Ottawa: Steel Rail (explores his role in Canadian thought).
Dictionnaire des oeuvres littéraires du Québec, vol. 3, Montreal: Fides, 1982.
Papillon, Antonin (1963) *Notice nécrologique*, Montreal: Couvent Albert Le Grand.

Lachance's main interests were always in law and politics, although his work extended naturally to political philosophy and the philosophy of history. Because of his basic outlook these issues inevitably involved him in questions about metaphysics and the philosophy of language. Although a Thomist by conviction, Lachance took scholastic theory on to new ground in the philosophy of history and the philosophy of language. He is best known as a philosopher of language.

The ideas of law and politics as activities which could be conducted on the basis of reason were always at the forefront of his writings. He was not very much influenced by the various kinds of neo-Thomism which flourished while he wrote but rather by events and currents of thoughts in his native Quebec, and particularly by the need to provide a reasoned alternative to the emotional nationalism of Lionel Groulx.

Le Droit et les droits de l'homme (1959) offers a social justification for individual human rights, arguing that they are intelligible only in the context of a community. Lachance's Thomistic work tends to show St Thomas as a humanist who provided an underlying basis for democratic theory. *Nationalisme et religion* (1936) develops arguments for a limited and rational nationalism, quite unlike the ideology of Lionel Groulx which animated many thinkers—and still animates some—in Quebec. His *Philosophie du langage* (1943) explores the social origins of language and its consequent importance in politics.

LESLIE ARMOUR

Lachelier, Jules

French. *b:* 7 May 1832, Fontainebleau, France. *d:* 26 January 1918, Fontainbleau. *Cat:* Idealist. *Ints:* Theory of knowledge; epistemology. *Educ:* L'École Normale Supérieure, Paris, and eventually taught there (1905–7). He successfully submitted two theses for the doctorat d'état in 1871. ***Appts:*** For most of his career he served as an official in public education, first as an inspector of l'Académie de Paris, and, from 1879–1900, as Inspector General of Public Instruction; taught at L'École Normale Supérieure, 1905–7; after retirement, continued to serve as President of the jury for the Agrégation in Philosophy until 1911.

Main publications:

(1933) *Oeuvres de Jules Lachelier*, Paris: F. Alcan (partially rendered into English, ed. and trans. Edward Ballard, *The Philosophy of Jules Lachelier*, The Hague: Martinus Nijhoff, 1960).

(1933) *Lettres de Jules Lachelier*, Paris: G. Girard (large selection of his correspondence).

(1990) *Cours de logique 1866–67*, ed. Jean-Louis Dumas, Paris: Éditions Universitaires.

Secondary literature:

Jolivet, Regis (1953) *De Rosmini à Lachelier*, Lyon: E. Vitte.

Mauchassat, Gaston (1959) *La Liberté spirituelle*, Paris: Presses Universitaries de France.

——(1961) *l'Idéalisme de Jules Lachelier*, Paris: Presses Universitaires de France.

Millet, Louis (1959) *Le Symbolisme dans la philosophie de Jules Lachelier*, Paris: F. Alcan.

Séailles, Gabrielle (1920) *Philosophie de Jules Lachelier*, Paris: F. Alcan.

Lachelier defined idealism as the doctrine that the world consists of representations. These he thought of as psychological events which have a basic metaphysical status. Thus, as Edward Ballard puts it, 'The universe actually is a single history of thoughts and events continuously being transformed'. In his *Cours de logique* Lachelier offers idealism as a response to scepticism. He says Malebranche is inconsistent because he admits the external world as an article of faith. But idealism must not be given a subjective twist in the manner of Berkeley or a sceptical twist in the manner of Hume. The difference seems to be between representation, which is subjective, and representability, which is not. Logic, especially the logic of induction, is at the heart of Lachelier's philosophy. Indeed, the problem of induction—taken in its widest sense as the problem that we can derive principles of knowledge and explanation from our particular experiences—constitutes Lachelier's main continuing interest.

Induction for Lachelier is the passage from facts to laws. Roughly, his solution to the classical problem of induction is that every representation contains a principle through which it is intelligible. Induction is the finding of this principle. The ultimate principle is that 'intelligence cannot exist except in a world of intelligible objects. We cannot believe in our own intelligence without believing in the intelligibility of things'. Lachelier thus seems involved in the dialectical opposite of **Fouillée**'s position. For Fouillée, ideas are particulars even in a context of activity. This context yields principles. For Lachelier, representations are seen as a manifestation of basic underlying principles. The influences of Kant and of some of Hegel's work can be seen clearly, through Lachelier is deeply critical of both. One can see clearly his interaction with the thought of his contemporary Octave **Hamelin**, and the developing pattern in French thought of a kind of post-Kantian rationalism which, in its turn, becomes a defence of idealism. This line of thought was continued by Léon **Brunschvicg** and others.

Jolivet (1953) has found parallels with Rosmini. Séailles (1920) has noticed that there is a problem of explaining continuity in a philosophy like that of Lachelier. A letter in Ballard's collection of Lachelier's writings calls attention to Lachelier's struggle to grasp the notion of freedom and his suggestion that although the real situation is very different from our idea of freedom. 'God', he says, 'may be at the basis of our consciousness'—suggesting that we are more involved with the deity than we think.

Sources: Baruzi; Benrubi; Parodi; Edwards; EF; LXXS.

LESLIE ARMOUR

Lacoue-Labarthe, Philippe

French. ***b:*** 6 March 1940, Tours, Indre-et-Loire, France. ***Cat:*** Post-structuralist. ***Ints:*** History of modern philosophy; literature; art; politics; psychoanalysis; German romanticism. ***Educ:*** Lycées de Tour, Quimper, Auch, Le Mans, Lycée Michel-Montaigne de Bordeaux, Faculté des lettres et des sciences de Bordeaux (Agrégé in Philosophy). ***Infls:*** Heidegger and Derrida. ***Appts:*** Assistant de philosophie (1967–71) and then Maître assistant de philosophie, Université des Sciences Humains de Strasbourg, since 1971; Chargé de conférences, École Normal Supérieure, 1971–8; Visiting Professor, John Hopkins University, Baltimore, 1976–8; member of the editorial committee, *Poétique*, 1972; member of the Groupe de recherches sur les théories du signe et du texte, Université de Strasbourg; member of the Groupe de recherches politiques de la philosophie, École

Normale Supérieure; formally a member of GREPH.

Main publications:

(1973) (with Jean-Luc Nancy) *Le Titre de la lettre*, Paris: Galilée.

(1978) (with Jean-Luc Nancy) *L'Absolu littéraire*, Paris: Seuil (English translation, *The Literary Absolute*, trans., intro. and additional notes Philip Barnard and Cheryl Lester, Albany: SUNY Press, 1988).

(1979) *Le Sujet de la philosophie, typographies I*, Paris: Aubier-Flammarion.

(1981) (with Jean-Luc Nancy) *Les Fins de l'homme*, Paris: Galilée (essays on Derrida).

(1986) *L'Imitation des modernes, typographies II*, Paris: Aubier-Flammarion (English translation, *Typography*, trans. Christopher Fynsk *et al.*, intro. Jacques Derrida, Cambridge, Mass.: Harvard University Press, 1989; selections from *Typographies I* and *II*).

(1986) *La Poésie comme expérience*, Paris: C. Bourgois.

(1988) *La Fiction du politique*, Paris: C. Bourgois (English translation, *Heidegger, Art and Politics*, trans. Chris Turner, Oxford: Basil Blackwell, 1990).

Secondary literature:

Essay by Derrida prefacing the English translation of *Typography*.

Lyotard, Jean-François (1990) *Heidegger et "les juifs"*, Paris: Galilée (on *La Fiction du politique*).

Translators' introduction to the English translation of *The Literary Absolute* (see 1978).

Lacoue-Labarthe is a post-Heideggerian writing under the influence of **Derrida** and interested in the way in which the concept of 'mimesis' and the philosophical-aesthetic assumptions governing the understanding of art and literature become problematized through the history of modern philosophy, and in the concomitant question of the relationship between philosophy and literature. His collaboration with Jean-Luc **Nancy** in *L'Absolu littéraire* (1978) attempts to map the emergence of the modern concept of 'literature' (in its 'philosophical crisis' back to the work of Schelling and Novalis). They attempt to show that many of the moves made later by poststructuralism are already rehearsed in this version of German romanticism, which thus becomes a 'paradigm of crisis'. Lacoue-Labarthe's later work is more concerned with 'the political', and especially with the philosophical-political con-

sequences of coming to terms with **Heidegger**'s National Socialism.

JAMES WILLIAMS

Ladd-Franklin, Christine

American. *b:* 1847, New York. *d:* 1930, Columbia. *Cat:* Logician; mathematician; psychologist. *Ints:* Boolean logic; colour vision theory; women's suffrage. *Educ:* Vassar College (1866–9) and Johns Hopkins University (1878). *Infls:* C. S. Peirce and Boolean logic. *Appts:* 1870–9, taught science in secondary schools; 1879–82, Fellowship, Johns Hopkins University; 1891–2, worked in laboratories at Göttingen and Berlin; 1901–5, Assistant Editor of James Mark Baldwin's *Dictionary of Philosophy and Psychology*.

Main publications:

(1883) 'On the algebra of logic', in C. S. Peirce (ed.), *Studies in Logic by Members of the Johns Hopkins University*, Boston: Little and Co.

(1889) 'On some characterizations of symbolic logic', *American Journal of Psychology* 2.

(1901) 'The reduction absurdity of the ordinary treatment of the syllogism', *Science* 13 (April).

(1912) 'Implication and existence in logic', *Philosophical Review* 21.

(1929) *Colour and Colour Theories*, New York: Harcourt Brace & Company.

Secondary literature:

Grinstein, Louise S. and Campbell, P. (1987) *Women of Mathematics*, Westport, Conn.: Greenwood Press.

Hurvich, Dorothea Jameson (1971) 'Christine Ladd-Franklin', in *Notable American Women 1607–1950*, vol. 2, Cambridge, Mass.: Harvard University Press.

Shen, Eugene (1927) 'The Ladd-Franklin formula in logic: "The Antilogism"', *Mind* 36: 54–60.

Christine Ladd-Franklin vigorously pursued the life of a professional philosopher at a time when such achievements by women received scant professional recognition. By 1882, having managed to gain admittance as a graduate student to the (then) all-male Johns Hopkins University, she had fulfilled all the requirements for the award of a PhD, but the degree was not conferred until 44 years later, in 1926, when she was 78.

Ladd-Franklin worked in two main philosophical fields: symbolic logic and colour vision theory. By refining the well-known test of syllogistic validity that uses symbols to produce an antilogism (or inconsistent triad), she developed a procedure that provided an extremely efficient principle of recognition for valid forms of syllogism and that revealed the invalidity of four forms of the syllogism that had been considered valid by scholastic logicians, though not by mathematical logicians. This achievement was described by Josiah **Royce** as 'the crowning activity in a field worked over since the days of Aristotle'. In her later work in logic, and to its detriment, she ignored the innovatory ideas of **Frege**, **Peano** and **Russell**. It has been remarked that 'her desire to keep things simple made her reject some of the most fruitful developments in mathematical logic' (Grinstein & Campbell 1987: 126).

In her work on colour vision Ladd-Franklin's logical acumen uncovered inconsistencies in the theories of others. Her own theory sought to embody the best ideas of her predecessors and gave prominence to her views on the evolutionary development of colour vision.

Ladd-Franklin lived a full social and cultural life and was continually active in helping other women to obtain graduate education. The bibliography of her articles and reviews on logic and colour vision alone contains over 100 entries.

Sources: Kersey; *Biographical Cyclopaedia of American Women*, vol. 3, New York: Halvord Publishing Co., 1828, pp. 135–41.

DIANÉ COLLINSON

Lahbabi, Muhammad Aziz

Moroccan. *b:* 25 December 1923, Fes, Morocco. *d:* (n. d.) *Cat:* Theoretical philosopher. *Educ:* University of Caen, France; 1953, CNRS, Paris, first Moroccan to obtain doctorate. *Infls:* Existentialism, Bergson, Mounier and the phenomenological tradition. *Appts:* Professor and Dean of the Faculty of Letters at the University of Mohammed V, Rabat, 1958–74; contributed to the Governmental Projects of Scientific Researches; Member of the Royal Academy of Maroc.

Main publications:

(1954) *De L'Être à la personne*, Paris: PUF.
(1956) *Liberté ou libération?*, Paris: Aubier.
(1964) *Le Personalisme musulman*, Paris: PUF.
(1980) *Le Monde de demain*, Paris.
(1984) *Ibn Khaldun*, Rabat and Paris: Okad-L'Harmattan.

Secondary literature:

Alam (1964) 'Travaux et jours'.
Malek, A. Abdel (1965) *Anthologie de la littérature arabe contemporaine*, Paris: Seuil.

The starting-point of Lahbabi's thought was the crisis of the Muslim intellectual divided between Western and traditional culture. He focused on individual human existence rather than on the concept of being in general, concentrating on the individual's struggle for self-realization and for a role in a natural and social framework. There must, he held, be a development from the concept of a human being in general to that of a human being as a person and he argued that: 'I am a unity of being and person, body and mind, engaged in a world where I am humanizing myself at the same time as by humanization with others'.

Lahbabi's aim was the establishment of personal autonomy within the social framework of the Islamic world, and this leads him to a critical apology of the *Salafi* modernist movement. Philosophy, he believed, will find its role when it becomes something more than learning, namely militancy. He held that there is no knowledge without liberation, nor liberation without knowledge. The future world's destiny will be determined by the degree of universality humanity manages to attain, fully developing transcendental unity. Ibn Khaldun's philosophy was for Lahbabi the reaffirmation of human sociability and a promise of further progress.

Sources: P. Branca (1991) *Voci dell'Islam moderno*, Genova: Marietti; Archives of the Pontifical Inst. of Arabic Studies in Rome.

MASSIMO CAMPANINI

Laín Entralgo, Pedro

Spanish. *b:* 1908, Urrea de Gaén, Teruel, Spain. *d:* Deceased *Cat:* Philosopher and historian of medicine; cultural commentator. *Ints:* Medical ethics. *Educ:* Studied Medicine in Spain, and Clinical Psychiatry in Vienna. *Infls:* Zubiri, Scheler, Husserl and Merleau-Ponty. *Appts:* Various academic appointments in Madrid from 1939, including Chair of the History of Medicine (1942–78) at the Universidad Complutense; member of distinguished Spanish academies; founder and director of the Instituto 'Arnaldo Vilanova' (devoted to the history of medicine, 1964).

Main publications:

Obras, Madrid: Editorial Plenitud, 1965, includes:
(1956) *La espera y la esperanza*.
(1961) *Teoría y realidad del otro*; second edition, 1968.
(1964) *La relación medico-enferme*.
(1968) *El estado de enfermedad. Esbozo de un capitulo de una posible antropología médica*.

Secondary literature:
López Quintas, A. (1970) *Filosofía española contemporanea*, Madrid: BAC, pp. 272–87.
Mermall, T. (1970) 'Spain's philosopher of hope', *Thought* 45 (Spring): 103–20.
Soler Puigorial, P. (1966) *El hombre, ser indigente. El pensamiento antropológico de Pedro Laín Entralgo*, Madrid: Guadarrama.

Laín wrote of himself that he began by studying physics, moved to medicine and ended up a historian. He was also deeply impressed by the philosophical anthropology of Xavier **Zubiri** and by both German and French phenomenology. These interests are variously combined in his works on Spanish cultural history, the history of medicine and medical ethics. His distinctive contribution to modern Spanish philosophical thought lies in the elaboration of views of illness and the doctor-patient relationship developed within the framework of a phenomenological account of the self and its experiences.

Following Zubiri, Laín characterizes human beings as entities with substantivity 'sustantividad'. Human substantivity consists in personhood 'personeidad': to be human is to be formally and structurally 'me'. That being so, Laín next asks: how is community possible? How can two beings whose essence is to be persons communicate or have anything in common? Much of the answer has already been given by **Scheler** (in *Wesen und Formen der Sympathie*): to coexist as human beings is to coexecute acts as persons 'coejecutar actos personales', although Laín does not accept that the same experiences can be had by two discrete persons. Persons are free agents, and as a result the future, in which their actions are major shaping factors, is always uncertain. Human existence therefore always contains an element of uncertainty, and this is one of the major factors which leads Laín to characterize the human condition as one of indigence 'indigencia'.

These ideas (from 1956 and 1961) form the presuppositions of his views on illness and the special form of relationship between selves which obtains between doctor and patient (cf. 1964). Illness he regards as a particular and accidental form of the constitutive indigence of the human condition. The doctor–patient relationship falls between the two poles which characterize the relationships of two selves, the objectifying and the interpersonal. In the former we regard the other as a pure object or spectacle, *natura naturata*; in the latter we treat them as intelligent, free agents, *natura naturans*. The doctor-patient relationship is not, as has sometimes been believed, wholly objectifying. Laín argues that it is better thought of as 'quasi dyadic', like other aid-giving relationships between counsellor and counsellee or teacher and pupil. In the doctor-patient relationship, coexecution of actions is needed as a means to health, and objectification (either as contemplation or as manipulation) is elevated to the status of the proper end of the relationship, because what is sought is a modification of the other.

ROBERT WILKINSON

Laird, John

British. **b:** 17 May 1887, Durris, Kincardshire, Scotland. **d:** 5 August 1946, Aberdeen. **Cat:** Realist. **Ints:** Epistemology; philosophy of mind; philosophy of religion; history of modern philosophy; twentieth century philosophy. **Educ:** Edinburgh University and Trinity College, Cambridge. **Infls:** Thomas Reid, Pringle-Pattison and Moore. **Appts:** 1913–24, Professor of Logic and Metaphysics, Queen's University, Belfast; 1924–46, Regius Professor of Moral Philosophy, University of Abderdeen.

Main publications:
(1917) *Problems of the Self*, London: Macmillan.
(1920) *A Study in Realism*, Cambridge: Cambridge University Press.
(1925) *Our Minds and Our Bodies*, London: H. Milford.
(1926) *A Study in Moral Theory*, London: Allen & Unwin.
(1929) *The Idea of Value*, Cambridge: Cambridge University Press.
(1931) *Knowledge, Belief and Opinion*, New York & London: Century Co.
(1932) *Hume's Philosophy of Human Nature*, London: Methuen.
(1934) *Hobbes*, London: Ernest Benn.
(1935) *An Enquiry into Moral Notions*, London: Allen & Unwin.
(1936) *Recent Philosophy*, London: Butterworth.
(1940) *Theism and Cosmology*, London: Allen & Unwin.
(1941) *Mind and Deity*, London: Allen & Unwin.
(1944) *The Device of Government*, Cambridge: Cambridge University Press.
(1946) *Philosophical Incursions into English Literature*, Cambridge: Cambridge University Press.

Secondary literature:
Aaron, R. I. (1932) Critical Notice of *Knowledge, Belief and Opinion*, in *Mind* 41: 113ff.

Broad, C. D. (1941 and 1942) Critical Notices of *Theism and Cosmology* and *Mind and Deity*, in *Mind* 50: 294–9 and 51: 180–8.

Mackenzie, J. S. (1930) Critical Notice of *The Idea of Value*, in *Mind* 39: 202ff.

Patterson, R. L. (1943) 'Professor Laird and the cosmological argument', *The Personalist* 24: 372–82.

Urquhart, W. S. (1946) in *Proceedings of the British Academy* 32: 415–32.

Laird's realism was articulated and defended in *A Study in Realism* (1920), where he claimed that 'knowledge is a kind of discovery in which things are directly revealed or given to the mind' and that 'the fact of being known does not imply any effect upon the character or existence of the thing which is known'. He thought, no doubt rightly, that his own book had been overshadowed by **Alexander**'s *Space, Time and Deity*. But Laird's defence of realism, which he extended into ethics in *The Idea of Value* (1929), had its own virtues. He was admired for his clear and cautious style of doing philosophy, which contrasted with that of some of his idealist contemporaries. He was also respected as a historian of philosophy.

Theism and Cosmology (1940) and *Mind and Deity* (1941) the two books which comprise his Gifford Lectures found him willing to take a positive view of theism, which he had formerly dismissed as 'a decrepit metaphysical vehicle harnessed to poetry'. He remained sceptical about theological speculation but thought none the less that some conclusions could be drawn in natural theology.

Sources: DNB; Metz.

STUART BROWN

Lakatos, Imre (originally Imre Liposchitz, later Imre Molnar)

Hungarian. ***b:*** 9 November 1922, Debrecen, Hungary. ***d:*** 2 February 1974, London. ***Cat:*** Anti-formalist Popperian. ***Ints:*** Philosophy of physical science; philosophy of mathematics. ***Educ:*** University of Debrecen (graduated 1944); 1945–6, University of Budapest; 1949, University of Moscow; 1956–8, University of Cambridge (PhD 1958). ***Infls:*** Hegel, Braithwaite, Polanyi and LSE colleagues, especially Popper. ***Appts:*** 1947–50, Secretary, Ministry for Education; 1950–3, imprisoned; 1954–6, Translator, Mathematical Research Institute, Hungarian Academy of Science; 1960, Lecturer, 1969–74, Professor of Logic, London School of Economics.

Main publications:

(1976) *Proofs and Refutations: The Logic of Mathematical Discovery*, ed. J. Worrall and E. Zahar, Cambridge: Cambridge University Press.

(1978) *Philosophical Papers, Volume 1: The Methodology of Scientific Research Programmes*, ed. J. Worrall and G. Currie, Cambridge: Cambridge University Press (contains bibliography).

(1978) *Philosophical Papers, Volume 2: Mathematics, Science and Epistemology*, ed. J. Worrall and G. Currie, Cambridge: Cambridge University Press (contains bibliography).

Secondary literature:

Cohen, R., Feyerabend, P. and Wartofksy, M. (eds) (1976) *Essays in Memory of Imre Lakatos*, Dordrecht/Boston: Reidel.

Radnitzky, G. and Andersson, G. (eds) (1978) *Progress and Rationality in Science*, Dordrecht and Boston: Reidel.

Lakatos was a philosopher who, perhaps more than most, left a legacy not only in publications but in the minds of colleagues. He was a forceful person who was clearly more interested in engaging in and furthering debate than in laying down written tablets for others to digest.

His first (and lasting) intellectual interest lay in the philosophy of mathematics and his distinctive views on this found a ready home in the London School of Economics where, deploying a similar approach, he developed a deeper interest in the philosophy of science. 'Criticism', 'heuristic', 'problem', 'conjecture', 'proofs and refutations' (the title of his book on the philosophy of mathematics), were concepts fitting the Popperian model of science (except, importantly, 'proof').

Orthodox accounts and histories of mathematics, according to Lakatos, distort the nature of the subject. Mathematics has been seen by philosophers and by some mathematicians as involving 'certainty', a feature reflecting its supposed deductive structure with theorems being rigorously deduced from indubitable axioms and postulates. Concomitantly, discovery of mathematical truth is seen as either totally rational (deduction) or as blind guessing. Lakatos challenges both these dogmatisms. The 'real' history of mathematics, revealed by case studies, shows the subject to be quasi-empirical and less than purely formal. Furthermore, in criticizing mathematical claims, the mathematician is not necessarily combating a completed deductive system, but helping to articulate it, perhaps by means of 'concept-stretching' or by finding 'counter-examples' which do not stand as falsifications of the theory but as heuristic challenges to it. For example, contemporaries saw Euclid's system, not as an attempt to reach infallible foundations, but as a challenge to Parmenides and Zeno, a challenge itself subject to such quasi-empirical criticism. All mathematics is conjectural and 'the vehicle of progress is bold speculations, criticism, controversy between rival theories, problemshifts' (1978, vol. 2, p. 30).

Holding fast to **Popper**'s belief in a universal criterion of scientific rationality (contrary to contemporaries **Kuhn**, **Feyerabend** and **Polanyi**), he saw himself as developing the Popperian methodological research programme with a greater emphasis on (rationally reconstructed) history, using case studies: 'Philosophy of science without history of science is empty; history of science without philosophy is blind' (1978, vol. 1, p. 102).

Lakatos's lasting achievement in philosophy of science undoubtedly lies in his postulation of 'research programmes' as the key to understanding the progress of (theoretical) science. 'My concept of a "research programme" may be construed as an objective, "third world" reconstruction of Kuhn's socio-psychological concept of "paradigm"' (ibid., p. 91). Whereas Popper had postulated individual theories as the focus for falsification (which made a theory scientific), Lakatos held that research programmes (embracing a series of theories), which contained falsifiable *and* unfalsifiable parts, were a better tool for simultaneously acknowledging both the lastingness of scientific theories and the rationality of their rejection. 'Criticism does not—and must not—kill as fast as Popper imagined' (ibid., p. 92).

A research programme—I will use Lakatos's example of Newtonianism—comprises a 'hard core' (the three Laws of Motion and the Law of Gravitation), an unfalsifiable part to which the 'negative heuristic' forbids challenge, a set of 'problem-solving techniques' (mathematical apparatus) and a 'protective belt' of auxiliary hypotheses and initial conditions (geometrical optics, theory of atmospheric refraction) which is falsifiable and against which the falsity-seeking *modus tollens* of Popper is targeted. The 'positive heuristic' directs a scientist to make progressive modifications in the protective belt. Theory, not data, is primary in the formulation of research programmes. Where, then, is the rationality in scientific change? A research programme is 'theoretically progressive' if each new theory in the programme has excess empirical content over its predecessor, i.e. predicts some novel fact; it is 'empirically progressive' if some of this excess content is corroborated (Newton predicted the return of Halley's comet).

What is important for Lakatos in both mathematics and science, is not falsification but heuristic criticism leading to better theories. True to his Hegelian background, which weakened in influence at the LSE, the notion that a theory was 'born refuted' he regarded with insouciance: what mattered was the heuristic value of a refuted theory. Neither corrobations nor refutations are a clearcut matter of a logical relation between statements, but partly depend on context: 'Important criticism is always constructive: there is no refutation without a better theory' (ibid., p. 6). Research prorgammes have had a mixed reception. Whilst philosophers have responded positively to the attempt to have rationality and history at the same time, seen as advice to scientists research programmes seem to forbid nothing. Seen, as Lakatos preferred, as a rational reconstruction of the history of science, they seem to close to a sociological approach for rational comfort. However, philosophers of science havea deployed Lakatosian thinking in their work and research programmes have become part of the lore of philosophy of science.

Sources: Turner.

ANDREW WRIGHT

Lalande, André

French. *b:* 19 July 1867, Dijon, France. *d:* 15 November 1963, Paris. *Cat:* Rationalist; philosopher of science. *Ints:* Evolutionary theory and its application to philosophy; values; morality; art. *Educ:* L'École Normale Supérieure. *Infls:* Influenced by Herbert Spencer, Bergson and Emile Meyerson. *Appts:* 1904–63, Professor of Philosophy, Sorbonne.

Main publications:

(1899) *L'Idée directrice de dissolution opposée à celle de l'évolution dans la méthode des sciences physiques et morales*, Paris: Alcan; revised and reissued as *Les Illusions évolutionnistes*, 1930.

(1926) *Vocabulaire technique et critique de la philosophie*, 2 vols, Paris: Alcan; ninth edition, 1 vol., Paris: PUF, 1962.

(1929) *Les Théories de l'induction et de l'expérimentation*, Paris: Boivin.

(1948) *La Raison et les normes*, Paris: Hachette.

Secondary literature:
Bertoni, Italo (1965) *Il neo-illuminismo etico di André Lalande*, Milan: Pubblicazioni dell' Universita di Genoa.
Lalande, W. (ed.) (1967) *André Lalande par lui-même*, Paris: Vrin.
Poirier, R. (1965) 'André Lalande', *Revue de Métaphysique et Morale*: 140–64.
Smith, Colin (1964) *Contemporary French Philosophy: A Study in Norms and Values*, London: Methuen, pp. 101–5, 161–70.

Lalande was a rationalist interested in the application of evolutionary theory to philosophy and devoted to the promotion of international communication and an interdependent humanity through his life's work. He produced a naturalistic and normative conception of reason as an 'assimilating force within the world', connecting the idea of evolution with the ideal of the unity of life in a stimulating way (Smith 1964, p. 101). In *L'Idée directrice* (1899) he contended that the tendency of evolution is towards the realization of a more complete homogeneity, not heterogeneity, as **Spencer** and others had held. Even more important, rational activity in all its forms—in sciences, ethics and art—accounts for progress in assimilation, which is opposed to the disordered variations of life. Science assimilates things to mind, making them intelligible; as civilization advances, the diversity of morals and legislation disappears; and art itself exists only in virtue of a rational communion which gradually embraces humanity as a whole. That assimilation indicates the true direction of social development is proved, so Lalande maintained, by facts such as egalitarian trends, dissolution of classes, increasing equality (both legal and moral) of men and women and progress in international relations. Lalande's most influential contributions related to his enduring preoccupation with *Vocabulaire* (1926). The basic model of all subsequent dictionaries of philosophical terms, Lalande's work fostered collective enlightenment and effective communication by providing a unified terminology in philosophy, thereby exemplifying his universalist idea of reason.

Sources: Reese; Edwards; Benrubi; Huisman; EF.

STEPHEN MOLLER

Landgrebe, Ludwig

German. *b:* 9 March 1902, Vienna. *d:* 14 August 1991, *Cat:* Phenomenologist; historian of contemporary German philosophy. *Educ:* Studied at Freiburg, where he became Husserl's assistant.

Infls: Husserl and Dilthey. *Appts:* Left Germany during the Nazi period, and taught in Prague and in Loewen; after the war he held Professorships in Hamburg, Kiel and finally, from 1956, in Cologne, where he was also Director of the Husserl archives; after retirement he became Visiting Professor in Chicago and Washington in 1971.

Main publications:

(1928) 'Wilhelm Dilthey's Theorie der Geisteswissenschaften' [W. Dilthey's Theory of the Human], *Jahrbook der Philosophie und phänomenologische Forschung* 9: 237–366.
(1949) *Phenomenologie und Metaphysik*, Hamburg.
(1952) *Philosophie der Gegenwart* [Contemporary Philosophy], Bonn.
(1968) *Der Weg der Phenomenologie* [The Path of Phenomenology], Gütersloh.
(1968) *Phenomenologie und Geschichte* [Phenomenology and History].
(1981) *The Phenomenology of E. Husserl* (6 essays) Ithaca, NY: Cornell University Press.
(1982) *Faktizität und Individuation, Studien zu den Grundfragen der Phenomenologie* [Facticity and Individuation: Studies of Fundamental Questions of Phenomenology], Hamburg.

Secondary literature:
Phenomenologie Heute, (1974) (memorial volume put together by Landgrebe's Cologne students).

Untainted by complicity with the Nazis, Landgrebe was able to revive, expound and refine *Husserl*'s teaching, which had been generally marginalized in Germany and overshadowed by *Heidegger*'s success. He brought the phenomenological viewpoint to bear on, and confront, both existentialism and **Dilthey**'s heritage. He interpreted these movements, and other contemporary philosophical movements, with scholarly, judicious and subtle understanding. In the intellectual climate of the New Germany in which different schools of philosophy clash and debate, Landgrebe's broadly based, lucid and critical expositions made a distinctive and acknowledged contribution.

Sources: Letter from Prof. Hans Wagner.

H. P. RICKMAN

Langer (née Knauth), Susanne Katerina

American. *b:* 20 December 1895, Manhattan, New York. *d:* 17 July 1985, Old Lyme, Connecticut. *Cat:* Neo-Kantian symbolist. *Ints:* Aesthetics; philosophy of mind; philosophy of language. *Educ:* Radcliffe College, Cambridge, Mass., and the University of Vienna (1921–2). *Infls:* C. S. Peirce, L. Wittgenstein, A. N. Whitehead, Ernst Cassirer and Charles Morris. *Appts:* Tutor in Philosophy, Radcliffe College, Harvard, 1927–42; Lecturer in Philosophy, Columbia University, 1945–50; Professor of Philosophy and Professor Emerita, Connecticut College, New London, 1954–85.

Main publications:

(1930) *The Practice of Philosophy*, New York: Holt.
(1937) *An Introduction to the Study of Symbolic Logic*, Boston: Houghton Mifflin and London: Allen & Unwin.
(1942) *Philosophy in a New Key: A Study in the Symbolism of Reason, Rite and Art*, Cambridge, Mass.: Harvard University Press; third edition, 1957.
(1953) *Feeling and Form: A Theory of Art*, New York: Scribner and London: Routledge.
(1957) *Problems of Art: Ten Philosophical Lectures*, New York: Scribner and London: Routledge.
(1958) (ed.) *Reflections on Art*, Baltimore: Johns Hopkins University Press.
(1962) *Philosophical Sketches*, Baltimore: Johns Hopkins University Press and London: Oxford University Press.
(1967–82) *Mind: An Essay on Human Feeling*, 3 vols, Baltimore: Johns Hopkins University Press.

Secondary literature:

Danto, Arthur, de Sousa, Ronald B. and Morawski, Stefan (1984), essays in *Journal of Philosophy* 81: 641–63.
Gosh, Ranjan K. (1979) *Aesthetic Theory and Art: A Study in Susanne Langer*, Delhi: Ajanta.

Although Susanne Langer is famous as an aesthetician, her work in aesthetics is interwoven with her contributions to the philosophy of mind and the philosophy of language. Like her mentors, A. N. **Whitehead** and Ernst **Cassirer**, she is a systematic thinker. But Langer worked in a period when philosophical systems were unfashionable: in the 1940s and 1950s she set about constructing a theory of art when her contemporaries questioned the very possibility of such a theory. However, Langer's theory of art itself originated in her semantic theory and was in its turn the basis of her theory of mind, the crowning achievement of her long career.

The major themes of Langer's philosophy are sounded in *Philosophy in a New Key* (1942), where she identified the 'keynote' of twentieth-century philosophy as a concern with the nature of symbolism. Langer's interest in art led her to a

conception of the symbol stemming from the Kantian analysis of experience as developed by Cassirer rather than to that current in logic and positivist epistemology. She argues that the symbolic ordering of experience occurs at all levels of sensitive life through the making of abstractions, understood as the perception of form. Consequently, Langer distinguishes two kinds of symbol. Discursive symbols, the paradigm of which is verbal language, are characterized by fixed units of meaning and syntactic relations. Non-discursive symbols, found in sensory experience, ritual, myth and art, are characterized as articulated wholes whose function is the presentation of forms of experience incapable of linguistic expression. It is this expanded notion of symbol which has been the target of criticism from contemporary philosophers (see, for example, the review of *Philosophy in a New Key* by Ernst **Nagel**, *Journal of Philosophy* 40 (1943): 323–9).

Having originally taken music to exemplify her view of art as presentational symbol, Langer proceeds in her next book, *Feeling and Form* (1953), to provide a detailed account of the principles of creation and expression in the great orders of art. Art, for Langer, is significant form, and the arts are unified through the notion of expression. The forms of art are abstracted from their everyday employment to create, in Schiller's terms, a semblance or illusion which presents or symbolizes ideas of feeling, the artist's knowledge of feeling, as opposed to signalling his currently felt emotions. Thus the significance of art is that it enables the beholder to recognize directly the forms of human feeling, 'growth, movement, emotion, and everything that characterizes vital existence' (1953, p. 82). The artistic illusion (not delusion), which is not a mere arrangement of given materials in an aesthetically pleasing pattern but what results from the arrangement, Langer calls 'living form'; and "living form" is the most indubitable product of all good art' (ibid.).

However, 'why must artistic form, to be expressive of feeling, always be so-called "living form"?' Moreover, why need art 'only seem, not actually be, life-like'? That is to say: 'Why is semblance necessary?' These questions, prompted by her theory of art, were the origins of the final phase of Langer's philosophy, culminating in the three volumes of *Mind: An Essay on Human Feeling* (1967–82). Here she investigates 'actual living form as biologists find it ... and the actual phenomena of feeling' in order to show that the fundamental division between human and animal mentality is 'a vast and special evolution of feeling in the hominid stock' (see the Introduction to

Mind, vol. 1). Langer's theory of mind is resolutely naturalistic in its exclusion of assumptions about non-physical ingredients in human life. But at the same time it aims, as with all Langer's philosophical writing, to provide a conceptual structure of sufficient generality to be applicable, to be workable, both within and beyond the natural sciences.
Sources: *New York Times*, 19 Jul 1985; Turner.

PETER LEWIS

Lapoujade, María Noel

Uruguayan-Mexican. *b:* 25 September 1942. *Cat:* Kantian aesthetician. *Educ:* Educated in Uruguay and Mexico; MA in Philosophy, 1984, and doctorate in Philosophy, 1988, Universidad Nacional Autónoma de México. *Appts:* 1975–, Universidad Nacional Autónoma de México.

Main publications:

(1982) 'La noción de síntesis en el pensamiento Kantiano y su función en la estética', *Anuario de filosofía*, Mexico.

(1988) *Filosofía de la imaginación*, Mexico: Siglo XXI.

(1990) 'Notas sobre filosofía surrealista', *Relaciones* 68/69, Montevideo.

(1990) 'Filosofía del Dadá, a pesar del Dadá', *Relaciones* 72, Montevideo.

(1991) 'Van Gogh: lo maravilloso cotidiano', *Utopías*, February/March, Mexico.

(1992) 'La revolución Kantiana del sujeto', *Revista de la Universidad de Costa Rica*, December, Costa Rica.

(1993) 'La filosofía de René Schérer en "Pari sur l'impossible"', *Teoría*, Mexico.

(1994) 'El misterio construido', *Revista de Filosofía de la Universidad de Costa Rica*, XXXII (77) 103–7.

In *Filosofía de la imaginación* (1988) Lapoujade offers a phenomenology of the imagination imbued with healthy doses of linguistics and psychology. She seeks to provide a comprehensive study of the imagination by employing multiple approaches to the subject. She situates the notion of imagination in the context of the history of philosophy. Many of her articles focus on philosophy of art and aesthetics. For instance, in one she establishes a philosophical affinity between Van Gogh and **Nietzsche**. Lapoujade has also written on the philosophy of Dada, a movement which flourished in Zurich from 1916 to 1922, but she argues for its present relevance as a complex response to war, oppression, violence, destruction and corruption.

AMY A. OLIVER

Lapshin, Ivan Ivanovich

Russian. *b:* 1870, Moscow. *d:* November 1952, Prague. *Cat:* Neo-Kantian. *Educ:* Studied under Vvedensky at University of St Petersburg. *Infls:* Kant and Vvedensky. *Appts:* From 1906, Professor of Philosophy, University of St Petersburg.

Main publications:

(1906) *Zakony myshleniia i formy poznaniia* [The Laws of Thought and Forms of Cognition], St Petersburg.

(1910) *Problema chuzhogo 'ya' v noveishei filosofii* [The Problem of the Other Self in Contemporary Philosophy], St Petersburg.

(1922) *Filosofiia izobreteniia i izobretenie v filosofii: vvedenie v istoriiu filosofii* [The Philosophy of Creativity and Creativity in Philosophy: Introduction to the History of Philosophy], 2 vols, Petrograd.

(1973) (ed. Louis J. Shein) *Readings in Russian Philosophical Thought: Logic and Aesthetics*, The Hague: Mouton (includes brief translated extracts from *The Laws of Thought*).

Secondary literature:

Lossky, N. O. (1952) *History of Russian Philosophy*, London: George Allen & Unwin, pp. 166–70.

Zenkovsky, V. V. (1953) *A History of Russian Philosophy*, trans. George L. Kline, London: Routledge & Kegan Paul, vol. 2, pp. 687–95.

Lapshin's principal work on *the laws of thought* (1906), was partly the result of study at the British Museum and other European locations after his graduation from the University of St Petersburg. He was among the Russian philosophers expelled from the Soviet Union in 1922, and spent the rest of his life in Prague. He was a scholar of notable breadth, and wrote extensively on artistic, and especially musical, creativity.

Lapshin followed **Vvedensky** in giving prominence to the 'laws of thought', especially the law of contradiction, in his version of Kant's critical philosophy. Unlike Vvedensky (who contended that time had noumenal existence), Lapshin minimized the distinction between space and time and the categories of the understanding: they are all conditions of experience. And since the law of contradiction applies within spatial and temporal limits, it is necessarily restricted to phenomena. Lapshin was starkly opposed to Vvedensky in his vehement renunciation of metaphysics: things in themselves are unknowable. In particular, he insisted on the subjective character of mystical experience. He gave considerable attention to the problem of other minds and its history, concluding that although the immediate perception of other selves is an illusion, they have an 'immanent reality' for the epistemological subject; they are a hypothetical construct of the same order as the atomic theory.

COLIN CHANT

Laroui, Abdallah

Moroccan. *b:* 7 November 1933, village of Azemmour. *Cat:* Political philosopher; historian of Islamic and Moroccan civilization. *Educ:* After a traditional education in a *kuttab* school, completed his studies in Egypt and at the Sorbonne University in Paris where he obtained a degree in Arabic. *Infls:* French thought and a critical form of Marxism. *Appts:* Government Counsellor of Foreign Affairs, 1960–3; Visiting Professor, UCLA, California, 1967–70; Professor of History, Rabat University, from 1964.

Main publications:

(1967) *L'Idéologie arabe contemporaine*, Paris: Maspero.
(1970) *Histoire du Maghreb*, Paris: Maspero.
(1974) *La Crise des intellectuels arabes (traditionalisme ou historicisme?)*, Paris: Maspero.
(1987) *Islam et modernité*, Paris: La Découverte.

Secondary literature:

Khoury, P. (1981) *Tradition et modernité*, Paris.
Labdaoui, A. (1993) *Les Nouveaux Intellectuels arabes*, Paris: L'Harmattan.

In *L'Idéologie arabe contemporaine* (1967), Laroui compares the Arab world with Western and Oriental cultures, starting from the presupposition that the description of the Arabic 'self' means a historicization of the Western notion of 'self'. He criticizes both the prejudices of Orientalism and the limitations of Arabic and Islamic thought, and argues that Arabic thought posits objective truth that can be grasped by the human intellect. In this way Arabic ideology could be consistent with a Western outlook, especially regarding the finality of history. This will happen when the main problem of Arabic ideology—namely the acquisition of (self-)consciousness—is solved. In his other works Laroui returns to the issues of the Arab intellectual's crisis—the deficiency of the Arab view of the state, the dialectical intercourse

between the Arab world and the West—always defending, however, the specificity of Islam and its irreducibility to external categories. Scientific Marxism, he maintained, can help to trace a historicization of underdeveloped societies. **Sources:** WW(Arab) 1991.

MASSIMO CAMPANINI

Larroyo, Francisco

Mexican. *b:* 1908, Jerez, Zacatecas, Mexico. *Cat:* Neo-Kantian. *Ints:* Value theorist and cultural analyst. *Educ:* Studied in Germany. *Infls:* The Marburg and Baden schools. *Appts:* A number of senior appointments, notably Professor in the Escuela Nacional de Maestros (from 1934), in the Escuela Normal (1945–9) and in the Universidad Nacional Autónoma de Mexico.

Main publications:

(1936) *Los principios de la ética social*; seventh edition, Mexico City: Porrúa, 1951.
(1936) *La filosofía de los valores*, Mexico City: Logos.
(1938) *La lógica de la ciencia*; twelfth edition, Mexico City: Porrúa, 1961.
(1946)*El romanticismo filosófico*, Mexico City: Logos.
(1948) *Historia de la filosofía en Norteamérica*, Mexico City: Stylo.
(1952) *El existencialismo: Fuentes y Direciones*, Mexico City: Stylo.
(1963) *La antropología concreta*, Mexico City: Porrúa.

Secondary literature:

Escobar, E. (1970) *Francisco Larroyo y su personalismo critico*.

At the heart of Larroyo's philosophy is a neo-Kantianism showing a marked sympathy for the approach of the Baden school. He begins from the assertion that consciousness is bidimensional, i.e. it can take two distinct attitudes to objects in the world. An object can be regarded solely with regard to what it is (*que es*), or it can be regarded for its purpose or significance (*para que es*). Each of these forms of consciousness has its own set of categories, those of being and those of preference (*del ser y del preferir*). Preferences are the expressions of values, and so Larroyo concludes that values do not transcend consciousness but are inherent in it. Human culture (in its widest sense, taken to include science, art, religion, economics and morality) is the form in which values are realized. Hence, for Larroyo, philosophy becomes the analysis of cultural forms: 'La filosófia es, así, una doctrina de la cultura' (1936 [1951], p. 36). Via both his books and the journal he founded, *La Gaceta filosófia* (Philosophical Gazette), Larroyo's ideas have had considerable influence in his native country. In collaboration with other philosophers, notably G. H. Rodríguez, he developed detailed neo-Kantian critiques of the other philosophies which were influential in Mexico at the time, notably the ideas of **Dilthey** and **Ortega**, neoscholasticism and existentialism.

ROBERT WILKINSON

Laudan, Laurens L. (Larry)

American. *b:* 16 October 1941, Austin, Texas. *Cat:* Philosopher of science. *Educ:* BA, University of Kansas, 1962; MA, University of Princeton, 1964, PhD 1965; University of Cambridge, Fellow 1964–5. *Infls:* C. S. Pierce, C. C. Gillispie, G. Hempel, T. S. Kuhn, G. Buchdahl, K. R. Popper and I. Lakatos. *Appts:* University College, London, 1965 -9; University of Pittsburgh, 1969–83; Virginia Polytechnic Institute, 1983–6; University of Hawaii at Manoa, from 1986.

Main publications:

(1968) 'Theories of scientific method from Plato to Mach', *History of Science* 7: 1–63.
(1977) *Progress and its Problems: Towards a Theory of Scientific Growth*, London: Routledge.
(1981) *Science and Hypothesis: Historical Essays on Scientific Methodology*, Dordrecht: Reidel.
(1984) *Science and Values: An Essay in the Aims of Science and their Role in Scientific Debate*, Berkeley, CA: University of California Press.
(1988) (ed. with A. Donovan and R. Laudan) *Scrutinizing Science: Empirical Studies of Scientific Change*, Dordrecht and London: Kluwer.
(1990) *Science and Relativism: Some Key Controversies in the Philosophy of Science.*

Secondary literature:

Doppelt, G. (1990) 'The naturalist conception of methodological standards in science, a critique', *Philosophy of Science* 57, 1: 1–19.
Siegel, H. (1990) 'Laudan, normative naturalism, a discussion', *Studies in History and Philosophy of Science* 21, 2: 295–313.
Stump, D. (1991) 'Fallibilism, naturalism and the traditional requirements for knowledge', *Studies in History and Philosophy of Science* 57, 3: 451–69.

After earlier scholarly work on the history of theories of scientific method (bibliography and other unpublished work) Laudan's later work, as he himself acknowledges, has been a response to the crisis in the philosophy of science created by the work of T. S. **Kuhn**, which he took to be the problem of giving a rational account of both scientific change and scientific consensus. His *Progress and its Problems* (1977) gives a pragmatic turn to the type of solution proposed earlier by **Lakatos**. He later sponsored a series of scholarly case studies of the historical role of methodological issues in scientific change, while moving (*Science and Values*, 1984) to a type of methodological naturalism in which theories, methodologies and values are considered to be mutually underdetermined, and adjusted separately in a pragmatic way by scientists in the course of their work. This analysis is used to ground critiques of relativism and scientific realism.

Sources: Personal communication; DAS.

R. N. D. MARTIN

Lavelle, Louis

French. *b:* 1883, Saint-Martin-Le-Villeréal. *d:* 1951, Paris. *Cat:* Philosopher of spirit; existentialist. *Infls:* Henri Bergson, Maurice Blondel and Octave Hamelin. *Appts:* Taught philosophy at the Sorbonne and at the Collège de France; 1934, cofounder and coeditor, with René Le Senne, of the collection of works *La Philosophie de l'Esprit*.

Main publications:

(1928) *De l'Être*, Paris: Alcan.
(1933) *La Conscience de soi*, Paris: Grasset.
(1934) *La Présence totale*, Paris: Aubier.
(1936) *Le Moi et son destin*, Paris: Aubier.
(1940) *Le Mal et la souffrance*, Paris: Plon.
(1945) *Du Temps et de l'éternité*, Paris: Aubier.
(1946) *La Dialectique de l'éternel présent*, Paris: Aubier.

Secondary literature:

Smith, C. (1964) *Contemporary French Philosophy*, London: Methuen, pp. 47–74.

Lavelle's philosophical position can be encapsulated in the phrase 'participation in being'. Our own inadequate and imperfect selves are, according to Lavelle, bounded by both the transcendental realm of the totality of being and the external world which is composed of physical objects and other limited human beings. We insert ourselves into this scheme of things when we become the initiators of acts by which we participate in being. For Lavelle, to be is to act.

Our actions have two aspects, the first of which is their interiority, or the awareness that our own beings are part of the totality of being. The existence of our imperfect selves presupposes that there is such an absolute, or God, on which we and our acts depend and which is itself pure act. Through our acts we present ourselves to the absolute. The totality of being is not static but dynamic, and the creative and existential energy in our own actions is derived from this ceaseless source of dynamism.

The other aspect of our actions is their exteriority, which is externalized or embodied in physical objects. Such objects are not dependent on our minds, but we bring them forth through our acts as entities of which we are aware. Once brought forth the physical world then constitutes the limitation of our imperfect selves. Concentration on the external world or any of its constituents is a distraction which turns our attention away from the spiritual inwardness of our being.

Lavelle rejects the views of those existentialists who promote the fragmentation of human existence and the endless quest for new acts in the pursuit of self-authentication. In the words of one commentator, he 'criticises the conception of a wholly creative existence which leaves in the wake of its acts a trail of debris comprising mere rejected by-products of authentic living' (Smith 1964, p. 50). Instead, Lavelle holds that, by continuous involvement in our acts, we can enrich our spiritual being.

For Lavelle, to act is to be free. The absolute, as pure act, is wholly free, whereas we are only limitedly so. Our acts are rational and reflective, in opposition to the passivity and limitation of our instinct, and we become more fully human and more fully free by reducing the spontaneity of the instinct to the benefit of reflection. The ideal towards which we strive and which is our essence is a communion of fellowship founded on rationality.

KATHRYN PLANT

Lavrov, Petr Lavrovich

Russian. *b:* 1 June (12 N.S.) 1823, Melekhovo, Pskov region. *d:* 25 January (6 February N.S.) 1900, Paris. *Cat:* Populist. *Educ:* St Petersburg Artillery School, 1837–42. *Infls:* Kant, Feuerbach, Marx, Fourier, Proudhon, Comte, Spencer and A. I. Herzen. *Appts:* 1844–66, Professor of Mathematics, St Petersburg Artillery School.

Main publications:

(1870) *Istoricheskie pis'ma*, St Petersburg (English translation of revised edition, Geneva, 1891, *Historical Letters*, trans. James P. Scanlan, Berkeley: University of California Press, 1967).

(1898) *Zadachi ponimaniia istorii: proekt vvedeniia v izuchenie evoliutsiia chelovecheskoi mysli* [Problems in the Understanding of History: Attempt at an Introduction to the Study of the Evolution of Human Thought], Moscow.

Secondary literature:

Pomper, P. (1972) *Peter Lavrov and the Russian Revolutionary Movement*, Chicago: University of Chicago Press.

Walicki, A. (1969) *The Controversy over Capitalism: Studies in the Social Philosophy of the Russian Populists*, Oxford: Clarendon Press.

Lavrov was turned down for Chair of Philosophy at University of St Petersburg in 1861, probably because of his radical affiliations. His participation in a secret revolutionary society led to his arrest in 1866 and then to exile in northern Russia. He escaped to France in 1870, and joined the First International. He was active in the Paris Commune, befriended Marx and Engels, and was prominent among the Russian revolutionary migrés, editing the populist journal *Vpered!* [Forward!] from 1873 to 1876 and the more militant *Vestnik Narodnoi Voli* [Herald of the People's Will] from 1883 to 1886.

Lavrov was the foremost ideologist of Russian populism, the main thesis of which was that the excesses of Western capitalism depicted by Marx could be avoided in Russia if socialism were achieved on the basis of existing popular institutions, notably the peasant commune. Lavrov's *Historical Letters* (1870), composed during his internal exile, posited 'critically thinking individuals' as the driving force of historical progress; their message that the thinking minority was in the debt of the suffering majority inspired the 'to the people' craze among radical youth during 1873–4. Lavrov's political views were underpinned by his philosophical 'anthropologism', which pivoted on the active, goal-seeking, human personality and posited an inescapably subjective dimension to all human knowledge. Kant's influence is evident in his phenomenalist rejection of metaphysics and his belief in human freedom as a necessary idealization in the pursuit of moral and social ideals. How much Lavrov owed to the negative elements of positivism is controversial. Although qualified by Marx's influence during his most radical phase in the 1880s, his subjectivist approach to historical and social phenomena was fully reaffirmed in his final works.

COLIN CHANT

Lazerowitz, Morris

American. **b:** 1907, Lodz. **d:** 1987, Northampton, Massachusetts. **Cat:** Linguistic philosopher. **Ints:** Philosophical methodology; philosophy and psychoanalysis. **Educ:** Universities of Nebraska and Michigan. **Infls:** Freud, Wittgenstein, G. E. Moore, O. K. Bouwsma and C. H. Langford. **Appts:** 1937–8; Rackham Fellow, Harvard University; 1938-73, Professor of Philosophy at Smith College, Massachusetts; 1964-73, Sophia and Austin Smith Chair; other visiting appointments.

Main publications:

(1955) *The Structure of Metaphysics*, London: Routledge & Kegan Paul.

(1964) *Studies in Metaphilosophy*, London: Allen & Unwin.

(1968) *Philosophy and Illusion*, London: Allen & Unwin.

(1976) (with Alice Ambrose) *Philosophical Theories*, The Hague: Mouton.

(1977) *The Language of Philosophy: Freud and Wittgenstein*, Dordrecht: Reidel.

(1984) (with Alice Ambrose) *Essays in the Unknown Wittgenstein*, Buffalo: Prometheus Books.

(1985) (with Alice Ambrose) *Necessity and Language*, London: Croom Helm.

Impressed by the marked lack of agreement amongst philosophers, Lazerowitz argued that philosophical theories are unconsciously engineered semantic deceptions. For instance, in *The Structure of Metaphysics* (1955) he suggested that the proposition that nothing ever changes proposes a linguistic innovation: we should not use the word 'change' in the way that we customarily do. The motivation for this proposal lies not in the arguments that are used to support it: its 'function is to ward off anxiety by strengthening the unconscious belief that threatening changes will not happen in our lives' (pp. 69–70).

Although his work aroused the interest of philosophers influenced by **Wittgenstein**, Lazerowitz's attempt to find unconscious motivations for philosophical proposals was never widely influential.

Sources: Passmore 1957; CA 17; personal communication.

ANTHONY ELLIS

Le Doeuff, Michele

French. **b:** 1948. **Cat:** Feminist philosopher. **Ints:** Literary criticism; post-structuralism; philosophy of science; history of philosophy. **Educ:** Awarded Agrégée de Philosophie. **Infls:** Simone de Beauvoir, Jacques Derrida and Michel Foucault. **Appts:** Teaches Philosophy at L'École Normale Supérieure de Fontenay; researcher in philosophy at the CNRS.

Main publications:

(1977) 'Women and philosophy' *Radical Philosophy* 17.

(1979) 'Operative philosophy: Simone de Beauvoir and existentialism', *I. and C* 6.

(1980) *Recherches sur l'imaginaire philosophique*, Paris: Payot.

(1983) (trans. with Margaret Llansena) Francis Bacon, *La Nouvelle Atlantique suivi de voyage dans la Baroque*, Paris: Payot.

(1986) *Venus et Adonis suivi de genèse d'une catastrophe*, Paris: Alidades Distiques.

(1989) *L'Étude et le rouet*, Paris: Seuil.

(1992) *Hipparchia's Choice: Essays Concerning Women and Philosophy*, Oxford: Blackwell.

Secondary literature:

Gattens, M. (1986) 'Feminism, philosophy and riddles without answers', in Pateman, Carol and Gros, Elizabeth (eds) (1987) *Feminist Challenges*, Sydney: Allen & Unwin.

Grosz, Elizabeth (1989) *Sexual Subversives: Three French Feminists*, Sydney: Allen & Unwin.

Lloyd, G. (1983) 'Masters, slaves and others', *Radical Philosophy* 34.

Morris, M. (1981–2) 'Operative reasoning: Michele le Doeuff, philosophy and feminism', *I. and C.* 9.

Le Doeuff's writings are wide-ranging, covering literary criticism, history of philosophy and the philosophy of science. Her major concern is the analysis of the imaginary in philosophy and its relation to feminist theory. She has also carried out empirical research into the historical role of women in philosophy. Le Doeuff argues (especially in the essays in *Recherches sur l'imaginaire*) that philosophy attempts to purify itself of images and concentrate on concepts, thus distinguishing itself from other activities such as poetic or literary pursuits. She maintains that it is in fact dependent upon metaphors in order to say what it cannot otherwise express. In analysing and assessing types of image, how images are integrated in the text and make the text operate, Le Doeuff has sought to uncover forms of confusion in philosophical thinking and exclusions colluded to in the major canons of philosophy. She shows that the discipline is elitist and sexist. The clarity which marks her work has won acclaim from many authors (such as Margaret Whitford and Elizabeth Grosz) interested in feminist philosophy and women's studies, especially in comparison with the enigmatic Luce **Irigary** and Julia **Kristeva**. Further, by arguing that it is not just women who are excluded by the language and canon of philosophy, Le Doeuff has proposed a more wide-ranging and inclusive response, 'an ethics of solidarity and the obligation to help whoever is in danger' (Le Doeuff, in Whitford, 1991).

Sources: Margaret Whitford (1991) *Luce Irigary: Philosophy in the Feminine*, London: Routledge; Toril Moi (1987) *French Feminist Thought*, Oxford: Blackwell.

BENJAMIN FRANKS

Le Roy, Édouard Louis Emmanuel Julien

French. *b:* 18 June 1870, Paris. *d:* 9 November 1954, Paris. *Cat:* French Catholic mathematician and philosopher. *Ints:* Philosophy of science; philosophy of relgion. *Educ:* École Normale Supérieure, 1892–5; doctorate 1898. *Infls:* H. Bergson, P. Teilhard de Chardin and H. Poincaré. *Appts:* Collège de France, 1914–20 (deputy for H. Bergson); Professor, 1921–42 (in succession to Bergson); Académie des Sciences Morales et Politiques, from 1919; Académie Française, 1945 (successor to Bergson).

Main publications:

(1894) (with G. Vincent) 'Sur la méthode mathématique', *Revue de Métaphysique et de Morale.* 2: 505–39, 676-708.
(1896) (with G. Vincent) 'Sur l'idée de nombre', *Revue de Métaphysique et de Morale.* 4: 738–55.
(1899 -1900) 'Science et philosophie', *Revue de Métaphysique et de Morale.* 7: 375–425, 503–62, 708–31; 8: 37–72.
(1900) 'Réponses aux objections', *Revue de Métaphysique et de Morale.* 8: 223–33.
(1901) 'Un Positivisme nouveau, *Revue de Métaphysique et de Morale.* 9: 138–53.
(1901) 'Réponses aux objections', *Revue de Métaphysique et de Morale.* 9: 292–327, 407–32.
(1905) 'Sur la logique de l'invention', *Revue de Métaphysique et de Morale.* 12: 193–223.
(1906) *Dogme et critique*, Paris: Bloud.
(1907) 'Comment se pose le problème de Dieu', *Revue de Métaphysique et de Morale* 15: 129–70, 470–513.
(1908) 'Philosophie en France', *Philosophical Review* 17: 306–15.
(1912) *Une Philosophie nouvelle, Henri Bergson*, Paris: Alcan (English translation, *A New Philosophy: H. Bergson*, trans. Benson, London: Williams & Norgate, 1913).

(1927) *L'Exigence idéaliste et le fait de l'évolution*, Paris: Boivin.
(1929) *Le Problème de Dieu*, Paris: l'Artisan du Livre.
(1929–30) *La Pensée intuitive*, 2 vols, Paris: Boivin.
(1929) *Les Origines Humaines et le Fait de l'Intelligence*, Paris: Boivin.
(1935) 'Ce que la microphysique apporte ou suggère à la philosophie', *Revue de Métaphysique et de Morale.* 45: 151–84, 319–55.
(1944) *Introduction à l'étude du problème religieux*, Paris: Monflon.
(1947) (with others) *Bergson et Bergsonisme*, Paris: Beauchesne.
(1949) 'Henri Poincaré et la critique des sciences', *Revue [des Deux Mondes]* 3: 397–412.
(1956–8) *Essai d'une philosophie première*, Paris: PUF.
(1960) *La Pensée mathématique pure*, Paris: PUF.

Secondary literature:

Balthasar, N. (1931) 'Le Problème de Dieu d'après M. Édouard le Roy', *Revue Néo-Scholastique* 39 : 340–59.
Brunschvicg, L., 'La Philosophie nouvelle et l'intellectualisme', *Revue de Métaphysique et de Morale* 60: 433–78.
Couturat, L. (1900) 'Contre le nominalisme de M. le Roy', *Revue de Métaphysique et de Morale* 8: 87–93.
Gagnebin, S. (1912) *La Philosophie de l'Intuition*, St Blaise: Foyer Solidariste.
Jolivet, R. (1931) *À la recherche de Dieu*, Paris: Beauchesne.
——(1931) *Essai sur le Bergonisme*, Paris: E. Vitte.
Landormy, P. (1901) 'Remarques sur la philosophie nouvelle', *Revue de Métaphysique et de Morale.* 9: 479–86.
Ménégoz, F. (1931) *Réflexions sur le problème de Dieu*, Paris: Alcan.
Perrin, M. T. (ed.) (1975) *Laberthonnière et ses amis*, Paris: Beauchesne.
Poincaré, H. (1906) *La Valeur de la science*, Paris: Flammarion.
Smith, C. (1967) 'Le Roy, Édouard', in Paul Edwards (ed.) *Encyclopedia of Philosophy*, New York: Macmillan, IV: 429b–440b.
Vidler, A. R. (1965) *Twentieth Century Defenders of the Faith*, London: SCM Press.
——(1970) *A Variety of Catholic Modernists*, Cambridge: Cambridge University Press.
Weber, L. (1932) 'Une philosophie de l'invention', *Revue de Métaphysique et de Morale* 39: 59–86, 253–73.

Originally trained as a mathematician, Le Roy's philosophical interests first found expression in the mid-1890s. After a couple of papers on the philosophy of mathematics written with G. Vincent, he emerged as a defender of Henri **Bergson**'s anti-positivist 'new philosophy' at the end of the decade, drawing fierce criticism from Louis **Couturat**. Initially his concern was to assert the rights of common sense and intuition in parallel with scientific reasoning (in a manner somewhat similar to some of **Duhem**'s views), and at the same time to develop a pragmatic and anti-intellectualist view of knowledge that made theory subordinate to 'life', moves encouraged by the 'critique des sciences' movement of the time. Applied to theology as well as to science, such views led to a denial of the transcendent in Catholic dogma, and attracted criticism from Catholics as fierce as that from positivists. His works were soon being put on the Index. In his later writings he increasingly developed the mystical evolutionist side of Bergsonian philosophy with its pantheistic flavour, interpreting 'life' in spiritual as well as in mental and material terms, the spiritual being what in his opinion distinguished human life from animal. This part of his philosophy was closely connected with that of his intimate friend Pierre **Teilhard de Chardin**. He is reported as saying that he often could not tell whether an idea was his or Teilhard's.

Sources: DSB 8: 256b–258a; Mittelstrass.

R. N. D. MARTIN

Le Senne, René

French. *b:* 1882, Elbeuf, Normandy. *d:* 1954, Paris. *Cat:* Philosopher of spirit; existentialist. *Educ:* École Normale Supérieure. *Infls:* Octave Hamelin and Maine de Biran. *Appts:* Cofounder and coeditor, with Louis Lavelle, of the collection *La Philosophie de l'Esprit*; appointed Lecturer at the Lycée Louis-le-Grand, and then (1942) Professor of Moral Philosophy, University of Paris; 1948, elected to the Académie des Sciences Morales et Politiques.

Main publications:

(1930) *Le Devoir*, Paris: Alcan.
(1930) *Le Mensonge et le caractère*, Paris: Alcan.
(1934) *Obstacle et valeur*, Paris: Aubier.
(1942) *Traité de morale générale*, Paris: PUF.
(1945) *Traité de caractérologie*, Paris: PUF.
(1955) *La Découverte de Dieu*, Paris: Aubier.

Secondary literature:

Paumen, J. (1949) *Le Spiritualisme existentiel de René Le Senne*, Paris: PUF.
Pirlot, J. (1954) *Destinée et valeur: la philosophie de René Le Senne*, Paris: Vrin.

Le Senne developed his philosophical system in opposition to what he saw as the antimetaphysical, positivist and determinist influences which, he alleged, were invading contemporary French thought. He considered himself to be working within the metaphysical tradition which stemmed from Descartes, and he thought that the crucial aspect of the cogito was the will, which led to action.

Le Senne maintained that humanity's place within the scheme of things was bounded by two things: the realm of the absolute or God, on whom we depend and in whom we participate; and the concrete reality of the external world. The essence of the self, according to Le Senne, lies in the consciousness of our own actions. In our preconscious state, there is the continuity of an undirected and dynamic spiritual flow or upsurge, ultimately derived from God. Our self-consciousness is achieved through the 'organ-obstacle' of reality. This 'organ-obstacle' is the instrument of our self-consciousness, as it breaks and crystallizes the undifferentiated spiritual flow into determinate acts of will, but it also limits the self by providing us with the recognition that determinate acts of will are limited. In the obstacle we find the divine will, which intends our self-realization.

As essentially spiritual beings we are in search of value, which Le Senne identifies with divine grace. Our preconscious spiritual flow grasps value in an undifferentiated form, but when the upsurge breaks against the limitations of reality, value crystallizes and becomes determinate in specific values. Thus the 'organ-obstacle', through its resistance to our will, is instrumental in our becoming conscious of values. We are not aware of value in its pure form: we can be conscious only of values in their impure and determinate form, but these are indicative of the absolute value towards which we constantly strive.

Corresponding to this, Le Senne maintained that the self has two aspects. There is the private self which is aware of God as the source of our existence and of absolute value, and is the subject of our feeling of totality in the aesthetic or moral appreciation of an object or situation. By contrast, there is the public self which concentrates on the concrete detail of the object perceived. Our lives are spent in constant oscillation between these two aspects of the self.

Le Senne's philosophical system is ultimately anti-individualistic, because the pure spiritual dynamism of the self merges into the absolute, and has no characteristics which allow us to distinguish one person from another.

KATHRYN PLANT

Lefebvre, Henri

French. *b:* 1901, Hagetmau, Gascony. *d:* 1991. *Cat:* Neo-Marxist philosopher. *Ints:* Revolutionary politics; existentialism. *Educ:* University of Aix-en-Provence; 1954, Doctorat d'état, Sorbonne. *Infls:* Hegel, Marx, Leon Bruns, Maurice Blondel, Sartre, Louis Althusser and Lévi-Strauss. *Appts:* 1961–5, Professor, University of Strasbourg; 1965, Professor, University of Paris, Nanterre; 1970, Founder-editor of journal *Espaces et société*; Lefebvre denounced nationalism in 1937 and Hitler in 1938; in 1928 he had joined the French Communist Party and was expelled from it in 1958; he supported the Republicans in the Spanish Civil War and served in the Resistance.

Main publications:

(Many of Lefebvre's early writings were seized and destroyed by the Nazis.)

(1946) *L'Existentialisme*, Paris: Sagittaire.

(1949–54) *Pascal*, 2 vols, Paris: Nagel.

(1958) *Les Problèmes actuels du Marxisme*, Paris: PUF.

(1959) *La Somme et la reste*, Paris: La Nef.

(1965) *Métaphilosophie*, Paris: Éditions de Minuit.

(1968) *Dialectical Materialism*, London: Jonathan Cape.

(1968) *L'Irruption: de Nanterre au sommet*, Paris: Anthropos (English translation, *The Explosion: Marxism and the French Upheaval*, New York: Monthly Review Press, 1969).

(1969) *The Sociology of Marx*, New York: Vintage Press.

(1971) *Au-delà du Structuralisme*, Paris: Anthropos.

(1971) *Everyday Life in the Modern World*, New York: Harper & Row.

(1975) *Hegel, Marx, Nietzsche ou le royaume des ombres*, Paris: Casterman.

(1980) *La Présence et l'absence*, Paris: Casterman.

Secondary literature:

Kelly, Michael (1982) *Modern French Marxism*, Baltimore: Johns Hopkins University Press.

Kurtzwell, Edith (1980) 'Henri Lefebvre—a Marxist against structuralism', in *The Age of Structuralism*, New York: Columbia University Press.

Schmidt, Alfred (1972) 'Henri Lefebvre and contemporary interpretations of Marx', in D. Howard and K. Clare (eds), *The Unknown Dimension*, New York: Basic Books.

Lefebvre was a key figure in the development of French Marxist philosophy and an influential critic of early structuralism as propounded by **Althusser** and **Lévi-Strauss**. As a student he rebelled against the philosophical orthodoxies as imparted in the French universities of the 1920s, and was a founder member of the 'Philosophies' circle, a radical group functioning between 1929 and 1934, that included Georges Politzer, Norbert Guterman and Paul Nizan among its members. He was responsible for the dissemination of fresh perspectives on Marx and Marxism, regarding Marx as a thinker who saw persons and things as 'totalities' rather than merely from the point of view of economic determinism. In similar vein he developed Marx's account of the inversion of the Hegelian dialectic, maintaining that it should be understood as *aufbegung*, 'a transcendence in the double Hegelian sense of an affirmation and negation at once' (*Biographical Dictionary of Marxism*, ed. Robert A. Gorman, London: Mansell and New York: Greenwood Press 1986, p. 256). In his book *Métaphilosophie* (1965) he advocated a much more open form of philosophical thought, one that expanded and elaborated the Marxian categories and concepts. He proposed that philosophy was itself a type of alienation and that a study of the numerous modern forms of alienation could yield insights and critical understanding of socialist as well as bourgeois societies.

In his analysis of 'everyday life' (1971) Lefebvre descries a passivity and fragmentation in the situations of persons who have become mere consumers and live within what he calls 'a closed circuit' of production–consumption–production. The remedy for this state is, he maintains, to transform the everyday situation rather than the workplace, regenerating the human capacity for creative activity, instigating a new way of life and using technology to effect the cultural and not simply the industrial changes that would inaugurate the conditions required for full human living.

In the 1930s, with Norbert Guterman, Lefebvre translated selections in French of the Marx *1844 Manuscripts* and **Lenin**'s *Philosophical Notebooks*. These works, along with Lefebvre's own *Dialectical Materialism* (1939), became highly influential, although his book was banned during the Nazi occupation of France. After the liberation his political and philosophical life became increasingly stormy. In spite of his loyalty to the Communist Party he was obliged to write and publish a 'self-criticism', repudiating the unorthodox ideas he had propounded. In the late 1950s, after Khrushchev's denunciation of Stalin, he

supported de Stalinization and as a result was expelled from the Party. He regarded the May 1968 rebellions in Paris as having not only the political but the cultural temper he had advocated and fostered in his students.
Sources: BDM: Huisman.

DIANE COLLINSON

Lefort, Claude

French. *b:* 21 April 1924, Paris. *Cat:* Phenomenologist; political philosopher. *Ints:* Political, anthropological and social philosophy; historical and literary essays; psychoanalysis. *Educ:* Lycée Carnot, Lycée Henri IV and the Sorbonne. *Infls:* Merleau-Ponty, Marx, Tocqueville and Machiavelli. *Appts:* Professor, University of Sao Paulo, 1953–4; Chargé de Recherches, CNRS, 1956–66; Head of the Department of Sociology, University of Caen, 1966–71; Maître de Recherches, CNRS, 1971–6; Directeur d'Études, EHESS, 1976–89; Visiting Professor in several universities (Ottawa, Chicago, New York, etc.); collaboration with *Les Temps Modernes*, 1945–54; Founder and coanimator of *Socialisme ou Barbarie*, 1948–58; of *Textures*, 1972–5; of *Libre*, 1975–9; Director of *Passé-Présent*, 1982–5; member of the editorial board of *Le Temps de la réflexion*.

Main publications:

Lefort is author of a very large number of essays published in many journals. Except for his doctoral thesis on Machiavelli (1972) and his essay on Solzhenitsyn (1975), all his books are collections of formerly published essays. They include:

(1971) *Éléments d'une critique de la bureaucratie*, Geneva: Droz; second edition, Paris: Gallimard, 1979.

(1972) *Le Travail de l'oeuvre Machiavel*, Paris: Gallimard.

(1975) *Un homme en trop: Essai sur 'l'Archipel du Goulag'*, Paris: Seuil.

(1978) *Les Formes de l'histoire: Essais d'anthropologie politique*, Paris: Gallimard.

(1978) *Sur une colonne absente: Écrits autour de Merleau-Ponty*, Paris: Gallimard.

(1981) *L'Invention démocratique: Les Limites de la domination totalitaire*, Paris: Fayard (English translation, *The Political Forms of Modern Society*, ed. J. B. Thompson, Cambridge: Polity Press, 1986; contains essays drawn from *Éléments*, *Un homme en trop*, and *L'Invention démocratique*).

(1986) *Essais sur le politique (XIXe–XXe siècles)*, Paris: Seuil (English translation, *Democracy and Political Theory*, Cambridge: Polity Press, 1988).

Secondary literature:

Habib, C. and Mouchard, C. (eds) (1993) *La Démocratie à l'oeuvre: Autour de Claude Lefort*, Paris: Esprit (contains a good collection of critical papers).

Howard, Dick (1988) *The Marxian Legacy*, second edition, London: Macmillan.

Poltier, Hugues (1993) 'La Pensée du politique de Claude Lefort', unpublished doctoral dissertation, Lausanne, 1993.

Thompson, J. B. (1988) Introduction to English translation of Lefort 1986.

The dominant theme in Lefort's work is his extended analysis of the opposition of democracy and totalitarianism. He holds that a proper understanding of this situation presupposes the view that the political regime of a society is not simply a formal device designed to regulate people's relationships: power cannot be reduced to a mere instrumental function. Rather, its role is an essentially symbolic one. It gives a society its particular identity, its style of relationships, its criteria of what can be thought, and so on. To understand a society, Lefort maintains, is to elucidate the set of principles embodied in its power structure.

This conclusion leads Lefort to a comparative study of different forms of society with the aim, first, of discovering the principles that give each one its particular shape and dynamics and, second, of showing that democracy and totalitarianism are *the* two possible and opposite political outcomes of modernity, modernity being construed from a Tocquevillian perspective as the form of society whose dynamic is determined by the equality of conditions and the delegitimization of the hierarchical principle. The equalizing process, Lefort argues, leads democracy to accept that the place of power must be empty; whereas totalitarianism arises through a will to give power a definite figure which makes it possible to legitimize the systematic oppression of social deviation.

Sources: Lefort's CV, his writings and conversations with him.

HUGUES POLTIER

Lehrer, Keith

American. *b:* 10 January 1936, Minneapolis, Minnesota. *Cat:* Analytic philosopher. *Ints:* Freedom and determinism; knowledge; probability; induction; meaning; philosophy of mind. *Educ:* University of Minnesota (BA 1957) and Brown University (AM 1959; PhD 1960). *Infls:* Thomas

Reid, Roderick Chisholm, Richard Taylor and Wilfred Sellars. *Appts:* 1960–3, Instructor and Assistant Professor of Philosophy, Wayne State University, Detroit, Michigan; 1963–73, Assistant Professor, Associate Professor and Professor of Philosophy, University of Rochester, Rochester, New York: from 1974, Professor of Philosophy, University of Arizona.

Main publications:
(1966) (ed.) *Freedom and Determinism*, New York: Random House.
(1968) (with J. Cornman) *Philosophical Problems and Arguments: An Introduction*, New York: Macmillan.
(1970) (ed.) (with A. Lehrer) *Theory and Meaning*, Englewood Cliffs: Prentice-Hall.
(1974) *Knowledge*, Oxford: Clarendon Press.
(1975) (ed.) *Analysis and Metaphysics: Essays in Honor of R. M. Chisholm*, Dordrecht: Reidel.
(1981) (with C. Wagner) *Rational Consensus in Science and Society*, Dordrecht: Reidel.
(1981) 'A self-portrait' and 'Replies', in R. J. Bogdan (ed.) *Keith Lehrer* Dordrecht: Reidel.
(1989) *Thomas Reid*, London: Routledge.
(1990) *Theory of Knowledge*, Boulder, CO: Westview Press.
(1990) *Metamind*, Oxford: Clarendon Press.

Secondary literature:
Adams, T. L. (1991) Review of *Thomas Reid* (1989) in *Review of Metaphysics* 44: 645–6.
Bender, J. W. (ed.) (1989) *The Current State of The Coherence Theory*, Boston: Kluwer.
Lehrer, Keith (ed.) (1981) *R. J. Bogdan*, Dordrecht: D. Reidel.

Lehrer's philosophical development has been greatly influenced by his study of Thomas **Reid** and by his teachers Roderick **Chisholm**, Richard **Taylor** and Wilfred **Sellars**, all of whom also acknowledge a debt to Reid. Lehrer's book on Reid has been described as 'a fine introduction to the thought of a very important philosopher' (Adams 1991, p. 646).

In spite of an early sympathy for scepticism the main body of Lehrer's work involves a qualified acceptance of the validity of common sense. He describes his philosophical method as having proceeded: 'by formulating principles in accord with common sense and deriving conclusions. Some of these principles, the most philosophically enlightening ones, were equivalence principles, analysing such concepts as knowledge and freedom' ('A self portrait', in Bogdan 1981, p. 8).

Lehrer has made significant contributions to debates on freedom and determinism, defending a compatibilism which rejects any conditional construal of freedom; to debates on induction, defending the view that inductive inferences are based on judgements of comparative probability; and has developed an account of rationality in which a formal account of consensus is used to solve problems in the philosophy of science and in the theory of social choice. It is Lehrer's work on epistemology, however, which has received the greatest critical attention. According to Mark Paskin 'Keith Lehrer has advanced understanding of almost every issue in epistemology' (ibid., p. 205).

The traditional view that knowledge is justified true belief has been challenged because of the obscurity of the concept of epistemic justification and the occurrence of ('Gettier-type') cases in which the defining conditions are satisfied but knowledge is ruled out by the presence of false justifying beliefs. Lehrer develops a conception of undefeated justification and argues that this 'defeasibility' theory overcomes both objections to the traditional view of knowledge. It attempts to overcome the Gettier problem through the addition of a fourth condition to the effect that the justified belief does not depend on falsehood, and it features centrally in Lehrer's own account of the nature of justification.

Lehrer's account of justification commences with a sustained attack on foundationalism. Both infallible and fallible basic beliefs are rejected; even if they exist there is no intelligible account of their relation to the beliefs derived from them. Lehrer's own account is coherentist and involves accounts of both subjective and objective justification. Subjective justification is a relationship between the beliefs which a person holds and is determined by the reasonableness of beliefs within the context of the entire belief system. Objective justification, by contrast, involves an external relationship between a person and the world and yields truth and falsity for the belief system. A comprehensive account of justification is neither reliabilist nor can it be analysed in terms of either explanatory or probabilistic coherence. Each of these accounts fails but elements of all of them contribute to form a comprehensive coherentist account of justification. Lehrer's conception of knowledge, therefore, involves a combination of both internal and external factors which together yield undefeated justification.

Lehrer dismisses those who criticize his frequent modifications of central positions. He writes: 'As I conceive of philosophical inquiry, and inquiry generally, all the results that we achieve

represent a tentative solution to a problem. Such solutions are offered for evaluation with the expectation that superior solutions will be found' (Bogdan 1981, p. 96).
Sources: DAP; CA 17.

H. BUNTING

Leibowitz, Yeshayahu (Isaiah)
Israeli. *b:* 28 January 1903, Latvia. *d:* 18 August 1994, Jerusalem. *Cat:* Scientist; man of letters; adult educator; philosopher of religion; philosopher of *halakhah* (Jewish Law); politics. *Ints:* Halakhic existentialism; ethics; science; history; philosophy of science. *Educ:* 1919, Chemistry and Philosophy, University of Berlin; Biochemistry, Kaiser Wilhelm Academy; 1924, Medicine and Chemistry, Cologne; 1934, Medicine, Heidelberg; MD, Basle; doctorates in Medicine, Biochemistry and Philosophy. *Infls:* Personal: Bruno Kisch, the biochemist and *Mizrahi* (religious Zionist Youth) movement. Maimonides and Kant, as well as the relationship between *halakhah* and philosophy in a Jewish state. *Appts:* 1924, Assistant Lecturer, Chemistry, Cologne; 1953, Chief Editor, *Encylopaedia Hebraica*, Jerusalem; 1961–73, Professor, Organic Chemistry, Biochemistry and Neurophysics, Hebrew University, Jerusalem; 1973–94, public lectures about Maimonides and Kant and, controversially, on the political philosophy of various Israeli governments.

Main publications:
(1946) *Torah u-Mitzvot ba-Zman ha-Zeh* [A Contemporary Approach to Torah and Commandments], Tel Aviv, 1953–4.
(1974) *Yesodot ha-Beaiah ha-Psichofizit* [Foundations of the Psycho-Physical Problem], Tel Aviv.
(1975) *Yahadut, Am Yehudi u-Medinat Israel*, Tel Aviv: Schocken (English translation, *Judaism, Jewish People and the State of Israel*, Cambridge, Mass: Harvard University Press, 1992; selected Italian translation, 1980; French translation, 1985).
(1977) *Sefer Yeshayahu Leibowitz* [The Yeshayahu Leibovitz Book], Tel Aviv.
(1979) *Sichot al Pirke Avot* [Conversations on 'The Ethics of the Fathers'], Tel Aviv, German translation, 1984.
(1982) *Emunah, Historiah ve-Arachim* [Faith, History and Values], Jerusalem: Akademon.
(1983) *Guf-va-Nefesh: ha-Baaiah ha-Psichofizit* [Body and Soul: the Psycho-Physical Problem], Tel Aviv.
(1984) *Emunato shel ha-Rambam*, Tel Aviv: Gale-Tsahal, Misrad ha-Bitahon (English translation,

The Faith of Maimonides, New York: Adama, 1987).
(1985) *Sichot al Mada ve-Arachim* [Conversation on Science and Values], Tel Aviv.
(1985) *Bein Mada le-Filosofia* [Between Science and Philosophy], Jerusalem.
(1986) *Sichot al Shmone Prakim la-Rambam* [Conversations on Maimonides' Eight Chapters], Jerusalem: Keter.
(1991) *Am, Erets, Medinah* [People, Land, State], Jerusalem: Keter.

Secondary literature:
Bouganim, A. (1990) *Le Juif Égaré*, Paris: Declée de Brouwer.
Goldman, Eliezer (ed. and trans.) (1992) *Judaism, Human Values and the Jewish State*, Cambridge, Mass: Harvard University Press.
David Hartman (1993) 'Yeshayahu Leibovitz', in *Interpreters of Judaism in the Late Twentieth Century*, ed. S. T. Katz, Washington DC: Bnai Brith, pp 189–204.

Leibowitz was the most well known and controversial of all Israeli philosophers. His public stance against the occupation of areas with a large Arab population, was due to his interpretation of the *halakhah* (Jewish Law) as a pure and goalless service of God. For the same reason, however, he regarded Christianity as a form of paganism, and as the adversary, and even the negation, of Judaism. In his advocacy of strict obedience to *halakhah* and his downgrading of cultural and ethnic definitions of Judaism he was influenced by Maimonides and Kant. He was a strong critic of any alliance between Orthodoxy and secular Zionism in the State of Israel, demanding a separation between the two, whilst remaining a fervent Zionist. He was particularly popular in the secular Israeli community, lecturing widely to large audiences and on the media.

He was the brother of Nehama Leibowitz.
Sources: EncJud; Schoeps; obituary, *The Times*, 24 Aug 1994.

IRENE LANCASTER

Leighton, Joseph Alexander
Canadian-American. *b:* 2 December 1870, Orangeville, Ontario. *d:* 17 June 1954, Worthington, Ohio. *Cat:* Personal idealist. *Ints:* Metaphysics; value theory; philosophy of man. *Educ:* Trinity College, Toronto, and Cornell University, PhD 1894; also studied at an Episcopal (Anglican) theological seminary, and in 1896–7 in Germany in Berlin, Tübingen and Erlingen. *Appts:* Taught

at Hobart College in upstate New York, 1897–1910; Professor and Head of Department of Philosophy, Ohio State University, Columbus, 1910–41.

Main publications:

(1901) *Typical Modern Conceptions of God; or, The Absolute of German Romantic Idealism and of English Evolutionary Agnosticism*, New York: Longmans Green & Co.

(1907) *Jesus Christ and the Civilization of To-day*, New York: Macmillan.

(1922) *Man and the Cosmos: An Introduction to Metaphysics*, New York: Appleton.

(1923) *The Field of Philosophy*, New York and London: Appleton.

(1924) *Religion and the Mind of To-day*, New York: Appleton.

(1926) *The Individual and the Social Order: An Introduction to Ethics and Social Philosophy*, New York: Appleton.

(1928) *Individuality and Education*, New York and London: Appleton.

(1937) *Social Philosophies in Conflict: Fascism & Nazism, Communism, Liberal Democracy*, New York: Appleton.

Secondary literature:

Adams, George P. and Montague, William P. (eds) *Contemporary American Philosophy*, New York: Macmillan.

Howie, John and Burford, Thomas O. (eds) (1975) *Contemporary Studies in Philosophical Idealism*, Cape Cod: Claude Stark.

Leighton was a personal idealist. He had been a pupil and friend of James Edwin **Creighton** and was strongly influenced by the Cornell School of idealists but even more by George Holmes **Howison** and by the philosophers who comprised the 'personalist' movement. He insisted that he could not accept Creighton's 'timeless absolute' and argued that the universe is an organic whole but that it has real constituents which are 'active individual wholes'. Although he put his case in metaphysical terms, his interests were oriented towards problems of value and it was for this reason that he complained of the 'apparent indifference' of absolute idealists to the 'uniqueness and value of the individual person'. He insisted, however, that individuals must be understood in the context of a community. His own views are succinctly summarized in his essay in Adams and Montague (1930). They are discussed sympathetically in Howie and Burford (1975).

Sources: WWW(Am).

LESLIE ARMOUR

Lenin, Vladimir Il'ich (pseudonym of V.I. Ul'ianov)

Russian. **b:** 10 April (22 N.S.) 1870 Simbirsk. **d:** 21 January 1924, Gorki, near Moscow. **Cat:** Marxist. **Educ:** Simbirsk gymnasium, 1879–87; briefly attended University of Kazan' in 1887 until his expulsion and exile; graduated in Law as an external student of the University of St Petersburg in 1891. **Infls:** Influenced by Marx, Engels, A. I. Herzen, N. G. Chernyshevsky, Plekhanov and Bukharin. **Appts:** Professor of Philosophy, University of Moscow, 1883–1920.

Main publications:

(1902) *Chto deliat'? Nabolevshie voprosy nashego dvizheniia*, Stuttgart (English translation, *What is to be Done? Burning Questions of our Movement*, New York: International Publishers, 1929).

(1909) *Materializm i empiriokrititsizm: kriticheskie zametki ob odnoi reaktsionnoi filosofii*, Moscow (English translation, *Materialism and Empirio-Criticism: Critical Notes Concerning a Reactionary Philosophy*, trans. David Kvitko, New York: International Publishers, 1927).

(1916) *Imperializm, kak vysshaia stadiia kapitalizma: populiarnyi ocherk*, Petrograd (English translation, *Imperialism, the Highest Stage of Capitalism: A Popular Outline*, New York: International Publishers, 1933).

(1918) *Gosudarstvo i revoliutsiia: uchenie marksizma o gosudarstve i zadachi proletariata v revoliutsii*, Petrograd (English translation, *State and Revolution: Marxist Teaching on the State and the Task of the Proletariat in the Revolution*, United Communist Party of America, 1917).

(1933) *Filosofskie tetradi* [Philosophical Notebooks], Moscow (first separate edition).

(1960–80), *Collected Works*, 47 vols, Moscow and London: Foreign Languages Publishing House, Progress Publishers and Lawrence and Wishart (English translation of the fourth Russian edition of Lenin's work).

Secondary literature:

Copleston, F. C. (1986) *Philosophy in Russia: From Herzen to Berdyaev*, Tunbridge Wells: Search Press and Notre Dame: University of Notre Dame Press, ch. 11.

Harding, N. (1977–81) *Lenin's Political Thought*, vol. 1: *Theory and Practice in the Democratic Revolution*, vol. 2: *Theory and Practice in the Socialist Revolution*, London and Basingstoke: Macmillan.

Wetter, G. A. (1958) *Dialectical Materialism: A Historical and Systematic Survey of Philosophy in the Soviet Union*, trans. Peter Heath, London Routledge & Kegan Paul, ch. 5.

The son of a school inspector, Lenin was introduced to Marxism by his elder brother Aleksandr, who was executed in 1887 for his part in a revolutionary populist plot to assassinate Tsar Alexander III. From 1893 Lenin practised as a lawyer in St Petersburg, where he became leader of the main Marxist circle. In 1895 he was arrested and imprisoned, and in 1897 exiled to Siberia. In 1900 he emigrated to Western Europe, and led the Bolshevik faction which emerged from the Second Congress of the Russian Social-Democratic Labour Party in 1903. He returned to Russia during the 1905 Revolution but again emigrated to Western Europe in 1907, where he was active in the international socialist movement and again embroiled in party strife and leadership struggles, not least with **Bogdanov** and **Trotsky**. He opposed Russia's participation in the First World War, and returned after the February Revolution, organizing the seizure of power in October 1917 with his former opponent Trotsky. The first head of state of the Soviet Union, he survived the period of civil war and Allied intervention (he was severely wounded by a Social Revolutionary in 1918), and in 1921 replaced the coercive policies of War Communism with the more liberal New Economic Policy. He died in 1924 from a stroke.

Although his earliest works criticized the petit-bourgeois economic romanticism of Russian Populism, affinities arguably remained in the emphases Lenin brought to Marxism as a political theory; notably in his rejection of 'objectivist', determinist and evolutionary versions of Marxism, his belief in the peasants' latent revolutionary potential, and the paramount role accorded in *What is to be Done?* (1902) to a tightly disciplined vanguard of professional activists in leading the masses to revolutionary consciousness and action. In his *Imperialism, the Highest Stage of Capitalism* (1916), he saw the growth of monopolies and the scramble for colonies as morbid symptoms, and justified his activist strategy in the Russian context by appealing to the uneven development of capitalism in different countries. The consequence that socialism would triumph at different times in different countries was part of his argument for the continuing post-revolutionary role of the state as an instrument of class domination (this time of the proletariat). The

Leninist theory of the state was expounded in *State and Revolution* (1918).

Lenin's *Materialism and Empirio-Criticism* (1909), a strikingly polemical work replete with quotations from Russian and Western writers, was conceived in the library of the British Museum and prompted by a leadership struggle among the Bolshevik Émigrés. It defended Engels's dialectical materialism against the attempts of Bogdanov, **Lunacharsky** and other Bolsheviks to modernize Marxism by marrying it to the empiriocriticism of Avenarius and **Mach**. Lenin insisted that in denying that human experience is caused by a reality external to it, the Russian Machists were embracing subjective idealism, which inevitably terminates in solipsism. Bogdanov's conflation of social consciousness and social being also undermined the Marxist distinction between class consciousness and objective social conditions (a distinction which underlay Lenin's emphasis on the role of the revolutionary activist). Lenin, by contrast, predicated his metaphysics and epistemology on the naive realism accepted by 'every healthy person who has not spent some time in a lunatic asylum or studied the science of idealist philosophers'. He equated matter with 'objective reality, which is given to man in his sensations, and which is copied, photographed and reflected by our sensations, while existing independently of them' (author's translations; see *Collected Works*, vol. 14, pp. 69, 130). Through this definition he reasserted materialism in the face of 'physical idealist' interpretations of the contemporary 'crisis in physics'. His effective identification of philosophical materialism with realism and a representationalist theory of perception was of decisive significance in Soviet philosophy and intellectual history. Equally influential was his insistence that all philosophical positions are ultimately either materialist or idealist (the 'agnosticism' of Hume and Kant being concealed idealism), and that these 'two great camps' represent antagonistic social classes. Hence the 'struggle of parties' in philosophy, or its 'partisanship' (*partiinost'*), a quality openly exhibited in Lenin's unrestrained invective against his opponents, to the dismay even of fellow Marxists like **Aksel'rod** (Ortodoks).

Despite the philosophical crudities of Lenin's assault on phenomenalism, he was at pains to distinguish his position from the vulgar or 'mechanical' materialism of Vogt, Büchner and Moleschott. Thought is not secreted from the brain like bile from the liver; the psychical is 'the highest product of matter' but is not reducible to it. The relationship between thought and nature is dialectical, and the dialectic in general was given greater prominence in Lenin's *Philosophical Notebooks*, a collection of notes, summaries and drafts largely dating from 1914–16, when he was in Switzerland, and unpublished until 1929–30, when they were included in a collection of his works. Most striking is the respect paid to Hegel (a full understanding of his *Logic* is held to be necessary for a proper understanding of Marx's *Capital*) and, memorably, Lenin asserts that intelligent idealism is closer than stupid materialism to intelligent materialism. Unlike Engels, he placed the law of the unity and struggle of opposites above the law of the transformation of quality into quantity: it was the heart of the dialectic, which he now considered to be the essence of Marxism; and he found support in the dialectic for his typically activist belief that 'man's consciousness not only reflects the objective world, but creates it' (*Collected Works*, vol. 38, pp. 180, 242, 276). Few Western scholars perceive in Lenin's writings anything of philosophical profundity or originality, but their influence upon and reverential treatment by one of the world's largest communities of professional philosophers is an indelible feature of the history of twentieth-century philosophy.

COLIN CHANT

Léon, Xavier

French. *b:* 20 May 1868, Paris. *d:* 21 October 1935, Paris. *Cat:* Kantian, anti-positivist. *Ints:* J. G. Fichte; philosophy of values; the links between philosophy and science. *Educ:* L'École Normale Supérieure. *Infls:* Kant, J. G. Fichte, Charles Renouvier and André Lalande. *Appts:* Founder of *La Revue de Métaphysique et de Morale*, 1893; original convener of les Congrès Internationaux de Philosophie, first held in April 1900; founder of la Société Française de Philosophie, 1901.

Main publications:

(1902) *La Philosophie de Fichte*, Paris: Alcan.

(1922–7) *Fichte et son temps*, 2 vols, Paris: Colin.

Secondary literature:

Benrubi, I. (1933) *Les Sources et les courants de la philosophie contemporaine en France*, 2 vols, Paris: Alcan, vol. 2, pp. 659ff.

Lalande, A., Gueroult, M., Lavelle, L. *et al.* (1960) 'Xavier Léon: vingt-cinq ans après', *Revue de Métaphysique et de Morale*: 241–5.

Although he never announced an original philosophy of his own Léon was nevertheless a key figure in the development of French philosophy for several decades. In 1893 he founded the *Revue de Métaphysique et de Morale* in reaction against the positivism of the *Revue philosophique* of Théodule **Ribot**. This not only fostered the collaboration of philosophers and scientists but also occasioned the revival of Kantian criticism and the birth of the philosophy of values in France.

In 1900, Léon organized the first of many of the Congrès Internationaux de Philosophie in Paris (the last was held in 1937). The Congrès was effective in promoting the spread of ideas and communication and cooperation among philosophers worldwide. It also inspired and made possible the redaction of André **Lalande**'s celebrated *Vocabulaire technique et critique de la philosophie*.

In 1901 Léon founded the Société Française de Philosophie, whose sessions were often devoted to the discussion of theories proposed by scientists such as Albert **Einstein** and Le Dantec. This, too, helped to forge close links between science and philosophy, which had been separated for many years. Through his important studies of J. G. Fichte (his writings of 1902 and 1922–7) Léon renewed interest in the latter's philosophy, arguing that a great mistake was committed in representing him as sharing in the idea that the mission of Germany was to dominate other nations by force. Like Lalande, Léon was a philosopher who subordinated the claims of his own individuality to an ideal of collective enlightenment.

Sources: Huisman; EF.

STEPHEN MOLLER

Leśniewski, Stanislaw

Polish. *b:* 30 March 1886, Serpukhov, Russia. *d:* 13 May 1939, Warsaw. *Cat:* Nominalist. *Ints:* Logic; philosophy of mathematics. *Educ:* Lvov. *Infls:* Twardowski and Łukasiewicz. *Appts:* Professor of the Philosophy of Mathematics, Warsaw, 1919–39.

Main publications:

(1927, 1930) 'O podstawach matematyki', *Przeglą Filosoficzne*, in Leśniewski (1988).

(1929) *Grundzüge eines neuen systems der grundlagen der mathematik*, in Leśniewski (1988).

(1930) *Ueber die grundlagen der ontologie*, in Leśniewski (1988).

(1988) *Collected Papers*, Dodrecht: Kluwer.

Secondary literature:
Luschei, E. C. (1962) *The Logical Systems of Leśniewski*, Amsterdam: North-Holland.

Woleński, J. (1993) *Logic and Philosophy in the Łwów-Warsaw School*, Dordrecht: Kluwer.

Leśniewski was the most systematically productive member of the great school of Polish logicians of the interwar period. He was to repudiate his early, comparatively informal, writings on logical topics, notably on the analysis of existential propositions, when he first came across the unprecedented formal sophistication of *Principia Mathematica*. His first work in the new style was concerned with the foundations of mathematics and, in particular, with the problems raised by the paradoxes, above all that of the class of classes which are not members of themselves. He tried to solve the problem by distinguishing between the ordinary distributive conception of a class, as an abstract entity whose elements are its members, and a collective interpretation in which a class is a whole whose elements are its parts. He went on to construct, in an extremely rigorous fashion, applying the strict standards of **Frege**, rather than the more casual ones of **Whitehead** and **Russell**, three distinctive logical calculi, two of them corresponding to existing bodies of doctrine, and a third connected with his collective notion of classes. His protothetic corresponds approximately to the ordinary propositional or sentential calculus. His ontology is a calculus of terms or names and corresponds, rather more remotely, to ordinary predicate calculus. The terms or names it handles may be empty, singular or general; no distinction of semantic category is drawn between subject terms and predicates. This reflects the absence of articles which the Polish language shares with Latin. His mereology was wholly original, although a closely similar logic of the part–whole relation was developed in the 1930s by H. S. Leonard and Nelson **Goodman**. Leśniewski interpreted the truths of logic 'ontologically', that is, as assertions about the general structure of the world, and not, as with the logical positivists, as reflecting linguistic conventions. His work has been reasonably criticized as remaining committed to an ideal of the total systematization of mathematics, a goal undermined by the discoveries of **Gödel**. Leśniewski had a great deal of influence on **Łukasiewicz**, his original teacher of logic, and on **Tarski**. In philosophy his ontology, or 'general theory of objects', provide a logical background for **Kotarbiński**'s 'reism'. Logical inquiry in his style was continued in the United States, notably by Sobociński and others at Notre Dame.
Sources: Edwards.

ANTHONY QUINTON

Levi, Primo
Italian, of Spanish-Jewish ancestry. *b:* 31 July 1919, Turin. *d:* 11 April 1987, Turin. *Cat:* Chemist; writer on the Holocaust; poet; children's educator; existentialist. *Educ:* Chemistry, Turin University, 1939, just before introduction of Mussolini's race laws; 1941, gradruated. *Infls:* Jewish tradition, Piedmontese upbringing, scientific studies and experiences in Auschwitz. *Appts:* 1941, industrial chemist with firm prepared to ignore Italian race laws; 1941–3, nomadic work; 1943–4, member of Piedmontese resistance; 1944–5, prison and deportation to Auschwitz, where he survived as an expert in chemistry, and transferred to factory; 1945, traveller in Europe; 1945–77, industrial chemist and writer, 1977–87, writer.

Main publications:
(1947) *Se Questo É Un Uomo*, Turin: F. da Silva (English translation, *Survival in Auschwitz: the Nazi Assault on Humanity*, trans. S. Woolf, New York: Orion, 1959; *If This Is A Man: Survival in Auschwitz*, London: Bodley Head, 1961, and New York: Collier, 1993).

(1963) *La Tregua*, Turin: Einaudi, 1972 (English translation, *Breathing Space/Respite; The Truce*, Boston: Little, Brown, 1965, and London: Bodley Head; *The Reawakening*, S. Woolf, New York: Macmillan, 1993).

(1975) *Il Sistemo Periodico*, Turin: Einaudi (English translation, *The Periodic Table*; trans. R. Rosenthal, New York: Schocken, 1984).

(1982) *Se Non Ora, Quando?*, Turin: Einaudi (English translation, *If Not Now, When?*, trans. W. Weaver, New York: Simon & Schuster, 1985, and London: M. Joseph, 1986).

(1983) (trans.) Kakfa, *Trial*, Turin: Einaudi.

(1986) *I Sommersi E I Salvati*, (English translation, *Drowned and the Saved*, trans. R. Rosenthal, New York: Summit, 1988).

Secondary literature:
Conference, (1990) *Primo Levi as Witness*, Fiesole, Firenze: Casalini, 1990.

Sodi, R. B. (1990) *A Dante of Our Time*, New York: P. Lang.

(There have also been numerous television programmes focusing on the world of Levi.)

Levi's experiences of Auschwitz are contained in the novels *If This is a Man* (1947) and *The Truce* (1963). He survived because his knowledge of chemistry and German made him useful to the Nazis. *The Periodic Table* (1975) examines the human condition in allegorical form, comparing life to a biological and social experiment. Utilizing his expertise in chemistry, and subtly alluding to Jewish self-definitions, as well as to attitudes grounded in anti-semitism, he manages, more perhaps than any other writer on the Holocaust, to transcend the personal, and creates a unique existential and curiously optimistic account of this worst example of human cruelty. His optimism faded in the face of revisionist denials of the Holocaust, and he committed suicide in 1987. Many regard Levi as the greatest of all writers on the Holocaust, not only because of his exquisite style, but because of the existentialist philosophy, based in Jewish teachings, which he created. *If Not Now, When?* (1982) is not an original title as many may have thought. It is a question taken from *The Ethics of the Fathers*, the most popular section of the *Mishnah* (compilation of Jewish Oral Law, written down in about 200 CE, but based on much earlier oral teachings). In this work Rabbi Hillel, a contemporary of Jesus, is reported to have said: 'If I am not for myself, who is for me? If for myself, what am I? And if not now, when?' The ethical content of this aphorism is rendered more meaningful when it is realized that the Hebrew letters for 'I' and 'not' (*ani* and *ain*) are identical. The idea of abnegation of ego is part of Levi's philosophy. He chose this quotation with care, and not simply as a socio-political example of Jewish self-sufficiency. His is the quintessential expression of Jewish suffering and revival as found in the Hebrew Bible and rabbinic tradition. Levi has been accorded the highest acclaim, particularly in literary circles. He has been translated into many languages, including, in 1987, Polish.

Sources: EncJud; Schoeps; obituary, *The Times*, 13 Apr 1987, p 16; NUC; WW(It) 1986, p. 633.

IRENE LANCASTER

Lévi-Strauss, Claude

Belgian-French. *b:* 1908, Brussels. *Cat:* Structuralist; culture theorist; anthropologist. *Educ:* The Sorbonne and University of Paris. *Infls:* Marx, Hegel, Freud, Saussure, Jakobson and the Prague School of structural linguistics, and Rousseau. *Appts:* Professor of Sociology, University of São Paulo, Brazil; Professor of New School for Social Research, New York: Director of Studies, École pratique des Hautes Études, University of Paris; Professor of Social Anthropology at the University of Paris.

Main publications:

(1949) *Les structures élémentaires de la parenté*, Paris: Presses Universitaires de France (English translation, *The Elementary Structures of Kinship*, trans. James Harle Bell, John Richardson, Richard von Sturmer and Rodney Needham, London: Eyre & Spottiswoode, 1969).

(1952) *Race et histoire*, Paris: UNESCO (simultaneously published in English as *Race and History*, no translator given).

(1955) *Tristes Tropiques*, Paris: Plon (English translation, *Tristes Tropiques*, trans. John and Doreen Weightman, London: Jonathan Cape, 1973).

(1958) *Anthropologie structurale*, Paris: Plon (English translation, *Structural Anthropology*, trans. Claire Jacobson and Brooke Grundfest Schoepf, New York: Basic Books, 1963).

(1962) *Le totémisme aujourd'hui*, Paris: Presses Universitaires de France (English translation, *Totemism*, trans. R. Needham, London: Merlin Press, 1964).

(1962) *La pensée sauvage*, Paris: Plon (*The Savage Mind*, no translator given, London: Weidenfeld & Nicolson, 1966).

(1964, 66, 68, 72) *Mythologies*, I–IV (*Le crut et le cuit*, *Du miel aux cendres*, *L'Origine des manières de table*, *L'Homme nu*), Paris: Plon (English translation, *Introduction to a Science of Mythology*, I–IV (*The Raw and the Cooked, From Honey to Ashes, The Origin of Table Manners, The Naked Man*), trans. John and Doreen Weightman, New York: Harper & Row, 1969, 1974, 1978, 1981).

(1979) *La voie des masques*, Paris: Plon (English translation, *The Way of the Masks*, trans. Sylvia Modelski, Seattle: University of Washington Press, 1988).

(1985) *La Potière jalouse*, Paris: Plon (English translation, *The Jealous Potter*, trans. Benedicte Chorier, Chicago: Chicago University Press, 1988).

(1987) *Anthropology and Myth: Lectures 1957–82*, Oxford: Blackwell.

Secondary literature:

Blau, Peter Michael and Merton, Robert K. (eds) (1981) *Continuities in Structural Enquiry*, London: Sage.

Boon, A. (1972) *From Symbolism to Structuralism: Lévi-Strauss in a Literary Tradition*, Oxford: Blackwell.

Clark, Simon (1981) *Foundations of Structuralism: A Critique of Lévi-Strauss and the Structuralist Movement*, Brighton: Harvester.

Gardner, Howard (1972) *The Quest for Mind: Piaget, Lévi-Strauss and the Structuralist Movement*, New York: Alfred A. Knopf.

Kurzweil, Edith (1980) *The Age of Structuralism: Lévi-Strauss to Foucault*, New York and Guildford: Columbia University Press.

Leach, Edmund (1974) *Lévi-Strauss*, London: Collins.

Paz, Octavio (1970) *Claude Lévi-Strauss: An Introduction*, Ithaca, NY, and London: Cornell University Press.

Originally trained in law and philosophy, Lévi-Strauss initially worked as a sociologist before turning to anthropology. Structural anthropology is to be distinguished from the more empiricist-inclined Anglo-American tradition by its reliance on the use of models drawn from linguistics to analyse culture, rather than on a commitment to extensive fieldwork by individual anthropologists. The overall objective of Lévi-Strauss's work is to reveal what he refers to as 'the unconscious nature of collective phenomena', as when he notes a universally operative division of foods into those it is considered appropriate to eat raw and, on the other hand, those it is considered appropriate to eat cooked (such binary oppositions are typical of Lévi-Strauss). Lévi-Strauss's analyses range over various aspects of culture such as kinship systems, culinary habits and myth, but in any given case his concern is to identify common features and universal patterns, with each system being seen to be structured like a language. Thus in studying a group of myths, Lévi-Strauss's method is to assume that they are all variations on a theme and that in each case we are essentially dealing with the same myth. Lévi-Strauss enjoyed a considerable vogue in the 1950s and 1960s when structuralism was at the height of its popularity, although his influence was always greater on cultural and literary theorists than on fellow anthropologists. While acknowledging the elegance of his cultural analyses, the Anglo-American tradition in anthropology has been highly critical of his methodology and lack of fieldwork. The rise of poststructuralism, which stresses the claims of difference over unity, has led to some scathing attacks on Lévi-Strauss's obsession with universality.

STUART SIM

Levinas, Emmanuel

French. *b:* 30 December 1905, Kaunas, Lithuania. *Cat:* Phenomenologist; theologian. *Ints:* Ethics; philosophy of religion; judaism. *Educ:* University of Strasbourg Institute of Philosophy and University of Fribourg. *Infls:* Bergson, Husserl and Heidegger. *Appts:* Professor of Philosophy, University of Paris X; University of Paris IV; Director of the École Normale Israélite Orientale.

Main publications:

(1930) *La Théorie de l'intuition dans la phénoménologie de Husserl*, Paris: Alcan (English translation, *The theory of intuition in Husserl's Phenomenology*, trans. André Orianne, Evanston: Northwestern University Press, 1973).

(1947) *De l'existent à l'existence*, Paris: Fontaine (English translation, *Existence and Existents*, trans. Alphonso Lingis, The Hague: Nijhoff, 1978).

(1949) *En découvrant l'existence avec Husserl et Heidegger*, Paris: Vrin.

(1961) *Totalité et infini*, The Hague: Nijhoff (English translation, *Totality and Infinity*, trans. Alphonso Lingis, The Hague: Nijhoff, 1969).

(1963) *Difficile liberté*, Paris: Albin Michel.

(1974) *Autrement qu'être ou au-delà de l'essence*, The Hague: Nijhoff (English transaltion, *Otherwise than Being or Beyond Essence*, trans. Alphonso Lingis, The Hague: Nijhoff, 1981).

(1982) *Éthique et infini*, Paris: Fayard (English translation, *Ethics and Infinity*, trans. Richard A. Cohen, Pittsburgh: Duquesne University Press, 1985).

Secondary literature:

Bernasconi, R and Wood, D. (1988) *The Provocation of Levinas: Rethinking the Other*, London and New York: Routledge (collection of critical essays by T. Chanter, S. Gans, J. Llewelyn, *et al.*).

Blanchot, M. *et al.* (1980) *Textes pour Emmanuel Levinas*, Paris: J. M. Place.

Cohen, R. (ed.) (1986) *Face to Face with Levinas*, Albany: State University of New York Press (collection of essays by T. de Boer, J.-F. Lyotard, R. Bernasconi, *et al.*).

Derrida, J. (1978) 'Violence and metaphysics', in *Writing and Difference*, trans. Alan Bass, London: Routledge & Kegan Paul and Chicago: Chicago University Press, pp. 79–153.

Lingis, A. (1985) *Libido: the French Existential Theories*, Bloomington: Indiana University Press.

Wyschogrod, E. (1974) *Emmanuel Levinas: the Problem of Ethical Metaphysics*, The Hague: Nijhoff.

Emmanuel Levinas was first to introduce the phenomenology of **Husserl** and the philosophy of **Heidegger** to a French audience. His philosophical method is phenomenological but the central themes of his philosophy are ethical. Through a phenomenological study of the relation of the self to other persons, Levinas argues for the primacy of the good over the true. Phenomenology, as the way to discover meaning from within our lived experience, allows him to study face-to-face human relations such as desire and love. From this point of departure, he argues that man's ethical relation to another person comes before his relation to himself (self-interest) or to the world of things (Being). For Levinas, the other person is absolutely other: beyond knowledge or thought about the being of things. Face-to-face with the other person man is obliged to put responsibility for the other before self; for this reason the relation puts man in the position of hostage. Thus Levinas puts forward an ethics of obligation and self-sacrifice dependent on a relation to the other that is beyond totalization, beyond comprehension and expression: he calls it infinite. In *Totality and Infinity* (1961), his most influential book, this infinity is presented through the perception of the face and through the obligation man is put under when in the presence of the face of another. Levinas has influenced philosophers such as Jacques **Derrida** and Jean-François **Lyotard** and the writer Maurice Blanchot. His thought is a major reference-point when philosophers consider the relation of their thought to ethics, theology and Judaism.

Sources: Catalogues of Bibliothèque Nationale, Paris and National Library of Scotland.

JAMES WILLIAMS

Lévy-Bruhl, Lucien

French. *b:* 1857, Paris. *d:* 1939, Paris. *Cat:* Sociologist; philosopher of the social sciences. *Educ:* University of Paris and the École Normale Supérieure; received his doctorate in 1884. *Infls:* Comte, Durkheim and Théodule Ribot. *Appts:* 1885–95, Professor of Philosophy, Lycée Louis-le-Grand; 1885–1908, various posts at the Sorbonne; 1917, elected to the Académie des Sciences Morales.

Main publications:

(1903) *La Morale et la science des moeurs*, Paris: Alcan (English translation, *Ethics and Moral Science*, London: Constable, 1905).

(1910) *Les Fonctions mentales dans les sociétés inférieures*, Paris: Alcan (English translation, *How Natives Think*, London: Allen & Unwin, 1926).

(1922) *La Mentalité primitive*, Paris: Alcan (English translation, *Primitive Mentality*, London: Allen & Unwin, 1923).

(1927) *L'Âme primitive*, Paris: Alcan (English translation, *The 'Soul' of the Primitive*, London: Allen & Unwin, 1928).

(1931) *Le Surnaturel et la nature dans la mentalité primitive*, Paris: Alcan (English translation, *Primitives and the Supernatural*, London: Allen & Unwin, 1936).

Secondary literature:

Caillet, E. (1938) *Mysticisme et mentalité mystique*, Paris: Alcan.

Revue Philosophique de la France, May–June 1939.

Lévy-Bruhl maintained that ethics was a science, the methodology of which was empirical and descriptive. The descriptions of and explanations in terms of ethical ideas provided by this science were not primarily at the level of the individual, but at that of social groups.

Most of Lévy-Bruhl's work was centred on the study of data about primitive societies provided by anthropologists. Amongst the tools he used in his investigation was the concept of collective representations, derived from the work of **Durkheim**. He described them as being 'common to the members of a given social group ... transmitted from one generation to another' and 'present[ing] themselves in aspects which cannot be accounted for by considering individuals merely as such', and gave natural languages as an example. The collective representations of any society form the framework of its thoughts and beliefs, and the worldview yielded by the representations of primitive societies was one in which everything was controlled by mystical powers.

Lévy-Bruhl's views about collective representations led on to another concept crucial to his analysis: that of prelogical thought. He maintained that the structure of thought of primitive societies was different in some but not all respects from that found in civilized societies. If it were the case that the thought-processes of primitive peoples were totally different from our own, then we would find primitive societies totally incomprehensible. He was concerned to point out that, by the use of the term 'prelogical', he meant neither 'alogical' nor a type of thought which subsequently gave way to the logic of civilized society. Instead, the thought-patterns of primitive peoples operated according to a different logic from that of civilized cultures, one main feature being indifference to self-contradiction and to consistency. Thus the members of a primitive society may well regard themselves as being literally identical with the sacred animal or bird which is symbolic of their culture.

The concept of causality held by primitive peoples is not to be regarded as a more simplistic version of that operative within civilized cultures. Instead of a natural or physical order in which events are interconnected and explicable, primitive peoples believe that causality is due to the occult powers with which anything unusual may be endowed. This belief is not affected by experience and is, according to Lévy-Bruhl, one example of what he calls 'the law of participation', which in turn forms a part of the collective representations of primitive cultures. According to this law, anything can be both itself and something other than itself, thus showing the indifference to self-contradiction which is a feature of prelogical thought; and it can both transfer and retain intact its mystic powers and influences.

Lévy-Bruhl can be criticized on several counts. He regards rigorous logical thought as a feature only of technologically advanced Western cultures, and thus has difficulty in explaining the high degree of sophistication often found in the practices of non-Western societies. He fails to take account of the continuities between what he refers to as 'primitive' and 'civilized' societies, and he has placed an exaggerated estimation on the rational features of the social life of the latter.

KATHRYN PLANT

Lewin, Kurt

German-American. **b:** 1940, Posen, Germany (now Poznaq, Poland). **d:** 1947, Newton, Massachusetts. **Cat:** Gestalt psychologist. **Ints:** Social psychology; topology and field theory. **Educ:** University of Berlin, 1909–14. **Infls:** Karl Stumpf, neo-Kantians, Ernst Cassirer, Wilhelm Windelband and Heinrich Rickert. **Appts:** Taught psychology, University of Berlin, Professor in 1927; emigrated to USA, 1933, working first at Cornell and then Iowa (as Head of the Child Welfare Research Station); after the Second World War, Director, Research Centre for Group Dynamics, Massachusetts Institute of Technology.

Main publications:

(1935) *A Dynamic Theory of Personality*, trans. D. K. Adams and K. E. Zener, New York: McGraw-Hill Book Co.

(1936) *Principles of Topological Psychology*, New York: McGraw-Hill Book Co.

(1942) 'Field theory of learning', in *Forty-first Yearbook of the National Society for the Study of Education* 41, 2, Chicago: University of Chicago Press.

(1948) *Resolving Social Conflict*, New York: Harper.

(1949) 'Cassirer's philosophy of science and the social sciences', in P. A. Schilpp (ed.), *Philosophy of Ernst Cassirer*, Evanston, Ill.: Tudor Publishing Co.

(1951) *Field Theory in Social Science*, New York: Harper.

Secondary literature:

Feigl, Herbert (1951) 'Principles and problems of theory construction in psychology', in Wayne Dennis (ed.), *Current Trends in Psychological Theory*, Pittsburgh: University of Pittsburgh Press.

Leeper, R. W. (1943) *Lewin's Topological and Vector Psychology*, Eugene: University of Oregon Press.

Wolman, Benjamin B. (1960) *Contemporary Theories and Systems in Psychology*, New York: Harper.

——(ed.) (1966) *Historical Roots of Contemporary Psychology*, New York: Harper.

Kurt Lewin was among the most philosophically minded of the psychologists active in the first half of this century. Concerned with the reconciliation of nomothetic (rule-governed) and idiographic (individually unique) accounts of behaviour, he sought to apply concepts derived from physics and geometry to psychology.

The starting-point for Lewin's theory is the distinction, introduced by Wilhelm **Windelband** and Heinrich **Rickert**, between the natural sciences (like physics), which are nomothetic disciplines, and the cultural sciences (like history) which are idiographic. Lewin included psychology among the cultural sciences, placing the unique individual at the centre of enquiry. At the same time he insisted that the assertions made by psychology about an individual case must be capable of being tested by general laws. Psychology had not always had this characteristic: it had been through an 'Aristotelian' stage concerned with psychological essences, and a 'descriptive' stage in which facts were collected and minutely analysed. It now had to move on to a 'Galilean' stage in which psychological laws were framed in terms not of patterns of recurrent activity but of the totality of each individual concrete situation.

Thus far, Lewin's account adds little to the qualitative insight of Gestalt psychology that the whole is different from the sum of its parts. But he went on to develop a quantitative treatment of the Gestalt. He sought to model 'individual psychological situations' mathematically by analogy with the mathematical models of 'individual physical situations' employed in physics. In physics, field theory can be used to describe the sum of the facts relevant to the behaviour of a given physical system, and Lewin sought to apply this to psychology, positing the notion of a psychological field, the 'Life Space', capable of describing the sum of the facts relevant to the behaviour of a given psychological system. It includes the individual's personality and environment, both key determinants of experience and behaviour. In later work he applied geometrical (in particular topological) concepts to the description of the life space, drawing a direct parallel between the unity of the space-time continuum in general relativity and Gestalt holism. He argued that psychological space is a new kind of space, one in which 'moving towards' is mathematically distinct from 'moving away'.

Lewin's mathematical treatment of psychology was an ingenious development of the qualitative *Gestalten*. His theories have not proved capable of unambiguous application. Nor have they generated new hypotheses or experimental work. They remain none the less a remarkable attempt to reconcile the nomothetic and idiographic in psychology.

Sources: Edwards; Reese; UCDCL; Goldenson.

K. W. M. FULFORD

Lewis, C(larence) I(rving)

American. *b:* 12 April 1883, Stoneham, Massachusetts. *d:* 3 February 1964, Menlo Park, California. *Cat:* Conceptualistic pragmatist; symbolic logician; epistemologist; value theorist. *Ints:* Epistemology; value theory. *Educ:* Harvard University, BA 1906, PhD 1910. *Infls:* Kant, Peirce, James, Royce and Perry. *Appts:* 1905–6, Instructor in English, University of Colorado; 1911–20, Instructor to Assistant Professor in Philosophy, University of California; 1920–64, Lecturer to Edgar Peirce Professor of Philosophy, then Emeritus Professor (1953–64), Harvard University; 1953–60, Professor of Philosophy, Stanford University.

Main publications:

(1918) *A Survey of Symbolic Logic*, Berkeley: University of California Press.

(1926) *The Pragmatic Element in Knowledge*, Berkeley: University of California Press.

(1929) *Mind and the World-Order: An Outline of a Theory of Knowledge*, New York: Charles Scribner's Sons.

(1932) (with C. H. Langford) *Symbolic Logic*, New York: The Appleton-Century Company.

(1946) *An Analysis of Knowledge and Valuation*, La Salle: The Open Court Publishing Co.

(1955) *The Ground and Nature of the Right*, New York: Columbia University Press.

(1957) *Our Social Inheritance*, Bloomington: Indiana University Press.

(1969) *Values and Imperatives: Studies in Ethics*, ed. J. Lange, Palo Alto, CA: Stanford University Press.

(1970) *Collected Papers of Clarence Irving Lewis*, eds J. D. Goheen and J. L. Mothershead, Palo Alto, CA: Stanford University Press.

Secondary literature:

Reck, A. J. (1968) *The New American Philosophers*, Baton Rouge: Louisiana State University Press, pp. 3–43; reprinted, New York: Dell Publishing Co., 1970.

Rosenthal, S. (1975) *The Pragmatic A. Priori*, Saint Louis, Missouri: W. H. Green, Inc.

Schilpp, P. A. (1968) *The Philosophy of C. I. Lewis*, La Salle: The Open Court Publishing Co.

From his earliest years Lewis was preoccupied with philosophical questions. His interests were further stimulated by the dialectical oppositions of pragmatism, realism and idealism represented at Harvard by **James**, **Perry** and **Royce**. Although Lewis's philosophical thought eventually developed into a singular form of pragmatism, it is profoundly indebted to Royce's idealism.

When studying **Whitehead** and **Russell**'s *Principia Mathematica*, a copy of which Royce gave him, Lewis rejected its theory of material implication: it seemed absurd that a false proposition could imply a true one. Hence Lewis proposed an intensional logic of strict implication, published in 1918, which also presents the first history of the development of symbolic logic. Corrected and enlarged in 1932, Lewis's system defines implication in terms of the logical modalities of possibility and necessity. A relation of strict implication holds between two propositions if it is impossible for the first proposition to be true and the second to be false.

In his early years on the Harvard faculty Lewis studied the Peirce papers. These papers, along with work for his courses on German philosophy, especially on Kant, led him away from concentration on logic to reflection on fundamental problems in the theory of knowledge. In *The Pragmatic Element in Knowledge* (1926), his Howison Lecture at the University of California, Berkeley, Lewis unveiled his conceptualistic pragmatism, which he elaborated in detail in *Mind and the World Order* (1929). Maintaining the pragmatist conception of mind as an evolved natural instrument, Lewis none the less stressed, like Kant, the formal conceptual aspects of knowledge. Capable of constructing alternative sets of concepts, the mind chooses pragmatically which set it will use to interpret the data.

Lewis's intention to proceed from epistemology to ethics was delayed by the movement of logical positivism, which in its heyday advocated a purely syntactic conception of the a priori and a noncognitivist theory of value judgements. *An Analysis of Knowledge and Valuation* (1946), based on Lewis's Paul Carus Lectures before the American Philosophical Association in December 1945, became the text from which American philosophizing set out in the immediate postwar period. Seeking to reestablish the cognitive character of the value judgement as a foundation for moral theory, Lewis surveyed the entire field of knowledge, distinguishing three kinds: (i) analytic a priori judgements; (ii) empirical beliefs; and (iii) value judgements, which, he held, exhibit the same epistemological structure as empirical beliefs and are equally objective. Applauded as a well-constructed refutation of the major tenets of the logical positivists, Lewis's work actually marked a supersession of logical positivism by a more sophisticated and less reductionist logical empiricism. Its defense of a strict distinction between the analytic a priori and the empirical a posteriori, its foundationalism in epistemology and its use of mentalistic language, however, fell out of favour in later Anglo-American philosophy.

Lewis's cognitivist theory of value judgment located value naturalistically within the context of human experience. Intrinsically value as the good is aesthetic. In *The Ground and Nature of the Right* (1955) Lewis distinguished the good from the right, the former being desirable and the latter imperative.

In *Our Social Inheritance* (1957) Lewis, pressed to take up social philosophy because of the acceleration of social change, emphasized our social heritage, man's social memory, for making possible the civilized conditions of human life.

Sources: Edwards; WW(Am); *New York Times*, 4 Feb 1964.

ANDREW RECK

Lewis, David K(ellogg)

American. **b:** 28 September 1941, Oberlin, Ohio. **Cat:** Analytical philosopher of language; logician. **Ints:** Philosophy of mathematics; philosophy of mind; ethics. **Educ:** St Catherine's Society, Oxford, Swarthmore and Harvard. **Infls:** The analytical tradition, in particular Rudolf Carnap and F. P.

Ramsey. **Appts:** 1966–70, Assistant Professor of Philosophy, UCLA; 1970–3, Associate Professor of Philosophy, 1973–, Professor of Philosophy, Princeton; 1983, elected to American Academy of Arts and Sciences; 1992, elected Corresponding Fellow of the British Academy; visiting appointments and fellowships in Australia, the USA and Britain; editorial consultant to *Philosophical Papers*.

Main publications:

(1969) *Convention: A Philosophical Study*, Cambridge: Harvard University Press.
(1973) *Counterfactuals*, Oxford, Blackwell.
(1983) *Philosophical Papers*, vol. 1, Oxford: Oxford University Press.
(1986) *On the Plurality of Worlds*, Oxford: Blackwell.
(1987) *Philosophical Papers*, vol. 2, Oxford: Oxford University Press (contains bibliography to 1986).
(1991) *Parts of Classes*, Oxford: Blackwell.

Secondary literature:

Elgin, C. Z. (1992) Critical Notice of *Parts of Classes*, in *Philosophical Books* 33: 193–8.
Inwagen, P. van (1986) Critical Notice of *Philosophical Papers I*, in *Mind* 95: 246–57.
Loux, M. J. (ed.) (1979) *The Possible and the Actual: Readings in the Metaphysics of Modality*, Ithaca: Cornell University Press.
Stalnaker, Robert (1988) critical notice of *On the Plurality of Worlds*, in *Mind* 97: 117–28.

David Lewis has written on several areas of philosophy (metaphysics, mind, logic, language), but is best known for his work on counterfactuals (conditionals such as 'If kangaroos had no tails, they would topple over'). Lewis analyses such conditionals in terms of possible worlds, and in so doing espouses 'extreme modal realism'—see Robert **Stalnaker**'s article in Loux 1979. Extreme modal realism—as it emerges from Lewis's *Counterfactuals* (1973) *On the Plurality of Worlds* (1986) and articles in the *Philosophical Papers*—is 'the thesis that the world we are part of is but one of a plurality of worlds, and that we who inhabit this world are only a few out of all the inhabitants of all the worlds' (1986, p. vii). Moreover, the claim that there is a plurality of worlds is, Lewis maintains, an existential one.

The notion of similarity between worlds functions here as a primitive and raises issues concerning, for instance, identity across worlds (Lewis's position on which has been criticized by Saul **Kripke** in 'Identity and necessity': see Moore 1993 below), but it offers Lewis a standpoint from which to treat other matters. Modality on his analysis becomes quantification (what is possible is what is the case at some world, what is necessary is what is the case at all worlds, and so on for 'the impossible' and 'the contingent'). Similarly, the articles 'Causation' and 'Events' (in 1987) analyse both phenomena in terms of counterfactuals as Lewis conceives them. Lewis's version of modal realism has, however, been criticized by, among others, P. Forrest and D. M. **Armstrong** (*Australasian Journal of Philosophy* 62 (1984): 164–8), and moderate modal realists such as Robert Stalnaker (see his contribution in Loux) have instead attempted to interpret 'possible worlds' in terms of states of affairs or possible histories of the world (Lewis rejects 'ersatz modal realism', as he calls this position, in chapter 3 of 1986, and replies to other criticisms in chapter 2).

In the introduction to volume 2 of *Philosophical Papers* (1987) Lewis writes that much of his work seems to advance the thesis of 'Humean supervenience ... the doctrine that all there is to the world is a vast mosaic of local matters of particular fact' (p. ix): the world is the sum of all space-time points and qualities at them—'all else supervenes on that'. Lewis's materialism motivates his contributions to the philosophy of mind (see the articles collected under that heading in volume 1 of *Philosophical Papers*, 1983), in which he has developed 'a broadly functionalist theory of mind, according to which mental states *qua* mental are realizers of roles specified in common-sense psychology' (p. xi).

Lewis's more recent concern has been with the philosophy of mathematics. In *Parts of Classes* (1991) he attempts a mereological reduction of set theory: parts of classes are subclasses (the null set not being a genuine class), and singletons (unit classes) are their mereological atoms; Lewis's axiomatization of set theory makes singletons the primitives of his theory. If, as Lewis believes, 'most of mathematics is into set theory up to its ears' (p. 58), then his structuralist treatment of set theory results in the nominalization of mathematics.

Sources: A. W. Moore (ed.) (1993) *Meaning and Reference*, Oxford; *AJP* 62, 1984; IWW; WW(Am); DAS; Burkhardt.

STUART LEGGATT

Lewis, H(ywell) D(avid)

British. *b:* 21 May 1910, Llandudno, Wales. *d:* 6 April 1992. *Cat:* Philosopher of mind; philosopher of religion. *Educ:* University College of North Wales, Bangor, and Jesus College, Oxford. *Infls:* Personal influences include H. A. Prichard, W. D. Ross and H. H. Price as well as philosophers in the

idealist tradition such as C. A. Campbell and T. M. Knox. Literary influences include Plato, Berkeley and Bradley as well as G. E. Moore. *Appts:* 1947–55, Professor of Philosophy, University College of North Wales, Bangor; 1955–77, Professor of the History and Philosophy of Religion, King's College, London.

Main publications:

(1959) *Our Experience of God*, London: Allen & Unwin.
(1963) (ed.) *Clarity is Not Enough: Essays in Criticism of Linguistic Philosophy*, London: Allen & Unwin.
(1969) *The Elusive Mind*, London: Allen & Unwin.
(1973) *The Self and Immortality*, London: Macmillan.
(1978) *Persons and Life after Death: Essays by Hywel D. Lewis and Some of his Critics*, London: Macmillan.
(1982) *The Elusive Self*, London: Macmillan.
(1985) *Freedom and Alienation*, Edinburgh: Scottish Academic Press.

Secondary literature:

Clark, W. N. (1961) 'Our experience of God', *International Philosophical Quarterly* 1: 168–77.
Sutherland, S. R. and Roberts, T. A. (eds) (1989) *Religion, Reason and the Self: Essays in Honour of Hywel D. Lewis*, Cardiff: University of Wales Press (includes a full bibliography of Lewis's works, in Welsh as well as English).

H. D. Lewis's interests in philosophy reflect, in some measure, his religious upbringing in North Wales. When he was at Oxford he came under the influence of some of the remaining idealists. His reading of Green had interested him in social and political philosophy but he later became especially concerned with questions to do with the nature of the mind and immortality. He admitted that there was much to be said for describing him as an idealist (1978, p. 1) but would not adopt the label because of the strong realist influence he acknowledged of philosophers such as **Moore** and **Cook Wilson** (1978, pp. 3ff).

Lewis's commitment to a metaphysical conception of philosophy isolated him to some extent from the mainstream of British linguistic philosophy. As editor of the Muirhead Library of Philosophy he encouraged alternative views, particularly in his *Clarity Is Not Enough* (1963). If he thought that clarity was not enough, he nonetheless thought it important. Lewis is best known for his defence of a dualist view of mind and body in opposition to the more prevalent behaviourist views advocated by **Ryle** and others. He defended with some success a belief in personal survival against the belief common amongst analytical philosophers that immortality was inconceivable. He acquired a high international reputation, particularly in India and America, where he received and took up many invitations to lecture and accept other honours.

Sources: WW; obituary in the *Guardian*.

STUART BROWN

Lewy, Casimir

Polish-British. **b:** 1919, Warsaw. **d:** 1991, Cambridge, England. **Cat:** Analytical philosopher. **Ints:** Philosophy of logic. **Educ:** Fitzwilliam House; MA and PhD, Trinity College, Cambridge, 1943. **Infls:** G. E. Moore. **Appts:** University of Liverpool, 1945–52; Lecturer, then Sidgwick Lecturer, then Reader, University of Cambridge, 1952–82; Fellow of Trinity College, 1959–91.

Main publications:

(1962) (ed.) G. E. Moore, *Commonplace Book 1919–1953*, London: Allen & Unwin.
(1966) (ed.) G. E. Moore, *Lectures on Philosophy*, London: Allen & Unwin.
(1975) (ed.) C. D. Broad, *Leibniz*, Cambridge.
(1976) *Meaning and Modality*, Cambridge: Cambridge University Press.
(1978) (ed.) C. D. Broad, *Kant*, Cambridge.

Secondary literature:

Hacking, I. (ed.) (1985) *Exercises in Analysis* (Festschrift), Cambridge.

Lewy was a prominent participant in the most celebrated era of Cambridge philosophy, as an interlocutor in **Wittgenstein**'s classes 1938–45 and as editor of the works of **Moore**. Later he was a teacher famed for his painstaking analytical clarity and rigorous honesty. His lectures from 1943 were summed up in his one major work, *Meaning and Modality* (1976), which pursued his concerns with entailment, necessity and the requirement for propositions as logical entities.

RICHARD MASON

Li Dazhao (Li Ta-chao)

Chinese. **b:** 1879. Leting County, Hebei Province, China. **d:** 1927, Beijing. **Cat:** Marxist. **Ints:** Historical and dialectical materialism. **Educ:** Beiyang College of Law and Political Science, Tianjin (1907–12) and Waseda University, Japan (1913–

16). **Infls:** Socialist and Marxist theorists. **Appts:** Director of the University Library and Professor of Economics, University of Beijing, 1920–7; 1918, Founder (with Chen Duxiu), *The Weekly Critic*; joined the editorial board of *New Youth* with Hu Shi in 1918 and replaced Chen as editor from 1921; 1920, founded China's first society to study Marxist theory in the University of Beijing; 1921, with Chen Duxiu, a main founder of the Chinese Communist Party, of which he was a leading member until his arrest and execution by the warlord government of Zhang Zhuolin.

Main publications:

(1926) *Essentials of Historiography*, Shanghai: Commercial Press.
(1939) *The Complete Shouchang*, Shanghai: Bei Xin Bookstore.
(1962) *Selected Works of Li Dazhao*, Beijing: Renmin Publishing House.

Secondary literature:

Boorman, H. (ed.) (1970) *Biographical Dictionary of Republican China*, New York and London: Columbia University Press.
Briere, O. (1956) *Fifty Years of Chinese Philosophy 1898–1950*, London: George Allen & Unwin Ltd.
Complete Chinese Encylcopedia (1987), Philosophy Volumes, Beijing: Chinese Encyclopedia Publications.
Meisner, Maurice (1967) *Li Ta-Chao and the Origins of Chinese Marxism*, Cambridge, Mass.: Harvard East Asia Series, 27.

After early support for the New Culture Movement and criticism of the Confucian tradition, Li responded to the Russian Revolution by writing extensively about Marxism, especially historical materialism. He and **Chen Duxiu** were China's first major Marxist theorists. For Li, the world was not static, and development occurred as a result of struggle between opposites, including those drawn from Chinese tradition, such as yin and yang. Progressive ideology had a role in social change, but he gave primacy to dialectical relations between forces and relations of production and between base and superstructure. He endorsed Marx's theory of revolution, class struggle and the necessity of a dictatorship of the proletariat. In a famous controversy with **Hu Shi** in 1919, Li argued for total revolutionary change in opposition to Hu's proposals for piecemeal reform. Li's work shaped Marxist ethical thinking in China. He argued that morals had to evolve in relation to changing social circumstances and later saw morals as part of the superstructure determined by a developing economic base. He criticized traditional Chinese morality, which he saw as related to the clan system, feudal economy and autocracy. He argued the need for interdependent moral and economic revolutions and held that each was bound to fail without the other.

NICHOLAS BUNNIN

Li Shizen (Li Shih-tsen)

Chinese. *b:* 1892, Lilin County, Hunan Province, China. *d:* 1934, Shanghai. *Cat:* Nietzschean; Bergsonian; Marxist. *Educ:* Studied in Japan, and later travelled to France and Germany (from 1928 to 1930). *Infls:* Nietzsche, Bergson and Confucius. *Appts:* Professor, Jinan University, Daxia University, Shanghai; Zhongshan University, Guangzhou; Editor of *Min Duo* and other important reviews.

Main publications:

(n.d.) *Brief Outline of the Philosophy of the Superman*, Shanghai, Commercial Press.
(n.d.) *Kierkegaard*.
(1924) *Anthology of Li Shizen's Essays*, Shanghai: Commercial Press. (1924) *Anthology of Li Shizen's Lectures*, Shanghai: Commercial Press.
(1926) *Philosophy of Life*, Shanghai: Commercial Press.
(1933) *Principles of Philosophy*, Shijie Book Company.
(1933) *Ten Lectures on Chinese Philosophy*, Shijie Book Company.

Secondary literature:

Briere, O. (1956) *Fifty Years of Chinese Philosophy 1898–1950*, London: George Allen & Unwin Ltd.

Li was an ambitious and restless intellectual drawn to new ideas and to the comparative study of Oriental and Western systems of thought. Although unsystematic in his own writing, he was a gifted and energetic expositor whose critical assessments of **Nietzsche**, **Bergson**, and many other leading figures of the day helped to acquaint Chinese opinion with new European intellectual currents. He also wrote about Chinese thinkers, both historical and contemporary. His first enthusiasm, for Nietzsche and Bergson, issued in an exposition and defence of Nietzsche's philosophy. Li was mainly concerned with questions in the philosophy of life and culture. His method was comparative, with broad surveys of

Eastern and European figures and systems leading to a concluding statement of his own favoured stance. His *Philosophy of Life* (1926) preferred Oriental to Western philosophies of life and showed the influence of Confucian thought. His trip to France and Germany in 1928 to immerse himself in European intellectual culture led to a radical conversion to Marxist dialectical materialism. In *Principles of Philosophy* (1933), Li followed his standard procedure of considering all modern systems of philosophy before declaring dialectical materialism the best. Li's early work, discussing Nietzsche, Bergson and other modern European figures for a Chinese intellectual audience, was his most important.

NICHOLAS BUNNIN

Li Zehou (Li Tse-hou)

Chinese. *b:* 1930, Changsha, Hunan Province, China. *Cat:* Marxist. *Ints:* Aesthetics; ethics; Kant; modern history of Chinese thought. *Educ:* Peking University. *Infls:* Kant and Marx. *Appts:* Professor, Institute of Philosophy, Chinese Academy of Social Sciences; Professor of Philosophy, Hebei University.

Main publications:

(n.d.) *Collection on Aesthetics*.
(n.d.) *A Critique of Philosophical Critique: An Evaluation of Kant*.
(n.d.) *Discussion of Aesthetics*.
(n.d.) *The History of Modern Chinese Thought*.
(1958) *Research into the Thought of Kang Youwei and Tan Sitong*, Shanghai: Shanghai Renmin Publishing House.
(1988) *The Path of Beauty* (in English), Beijing: Morning Glory Publishers.

Li is a creative philosopher who began his career with a detailed assessment of the history of nineteenth-century reformers, including the major figures of the 1898 Hundred Days Reform, **Kang Youwei** and **Tan Sitong**. In his account of their political thought and Tan's metaphysical views, he tried to understand the originality and power of their ideas against the background of their ultimate failure. His account of Kang was unusual for the 1950s in arguing for a transformation in Kang's thought from a materialist to a subjective idealist standpoint.

Li's main achievements are in the study of Kant and aesthetics. His work on Kant, particularly on the *Critique of Pure Reason*, took place when Kant's thought was greatly underestimated in comparison to that of Hegel because of Hegel's importance as an influence on Marx. Partly through Li's writing, Kant currently has greatly increased importance in contemporary Chinese philosophy. In addition to criticism of individual aspects of Kant's thought, Li employed his strategic and methodological capacities to criticize Kant's overall conception of philosophical critique.

In aesthetics Li adapted Marx's method of dealing with the duality of commodities as having use value and exchange value to combine what he considered to be the subjective and objective aspects of the analysis of beauty. He argued that beauty is a social rather than a natural property of things. A thing can be said to be beautiful only if it is created or transformed by human activity. The question of beauty does not arise for things in their natural existence. Because beauty is social rather than individual it cannot be understood in terms of individual subjectivity.

NICHOLAS BUNNIN

Liang Qichao (Liang Ch'i'ch'ao)

Chinese. *b:* 1873, Xinhui, Guangdong Province, China. *d:* 1929, Beijing. *Cat:* Confucian–Buddhist syncretist. *Ints:* Moral, political and social philosophy. *Educ:* Studied under Kang Youwei after passing imperial examinations at the provincial level. *Infls:* Kang Youwei, Confucian and Buddhist thinkers, Charles Darwin, T. H. Huxley and other Western thinkers. *Appts:* 1896, Liang founded the magazine *Chinese Progress*; 1897, lectured at the School of Current Affairs, Hunan; 1898, organized the Translation Press for the Emperor; after the collapse of the Hundred Days of reform with the Empress Dowager's coup in 1898, fled to Japan and started two periodicals, *New People* and *New Fiction*; later devoted himself to political activity and academic research.

Main publications:

(1921) *General Discussion of Qin Dynasty Scholarship* Shanghai: Commercial Press.

(1923, 1925) *Anthology of Liang Rengong's Lectures on Scholarship*, 2 series, Shanghai: Commercial Press.

(1925) *Liang Rengong's Recent Writings*, 3 vols, Shanghai: Commercial Press.

(1926) *History of the Evolution of Chinese Scholarship*, Shanghai: Chun Zhong Bookstore.

(1930) *History of Chinese Political Thought During the Early Tsin Period*, London: Kegan Paul & Co.

(1936) *Collected Works and Essays of the Ice-Drinkers' Studio*, 40 vols, Shanghai: Zhonghua Bookstore.

(1953) *The Great Chinese Philosopher K'ang Yu-wei*, San Francisco: Chinese World.

(1955) *An Intellectual History of China During the Last Three Hundred Years*, Taipei.

(1959) *Intellectual Trends of the Ch'ing Period*, trans. Immanuel C. Y. Hsu, Cambridge: Harvard University Press.

Secondary literature:

Boorman, H. (ed.) (1970) *Biographical Dictionary of Republican China*, New York and London: Columbia University Press.

Briere, O. (1956) *Fifty Years of Chinese Philosophy 1898–1950*, London: George Allen & Unwin Ltd.

Complete Chinese Encyclopedia (1987), Philosophy Volumes, Beijing: Chinese Encyclopedia Publications.

Huang, P. (1972) *Liang Chi'i-ch'ao and Modern Chinese Liberalism*, Seattle: University of Washington Press.

Levenson, J. (1959) *Liang Chi'i-ch'ao and the Mind of Modern China*, Cambridge, Mass.: Harvard University Press.

Liang, schooled in the imperial system and under the Confucian reformer and statesman **Kang Youwei**, was an early modernizing reformer in China. His own life combined political activism in the cause of moderate reform and syncretistic political and social thought. He was famed for his clear modern style as well as for his political thought and scholarly explorations in articles throughout his life. Before 1898, Liang published significant discussions of civil rights, constitutional reform, modernization and equality. He took a prominent role in the Candidates' Memorial of 1895, which initiated the movement leading to the Hundred Days of reform in 1898. He argued that a proper understanding of Confucius' own thought, without later accretions, would show that Confucian and Western ideas coincided. After his flight to Japan when the Hundred Days Reform was crushed, he continued to promote reformist ideas, but from a perspective critical of Confucian reform. He placed great value on patriotism, honour, courage, enterprise and autonomy, defending the preservation of the state and the nation, rather than traditional culture, as the vehicle for modernization. Although he saw the importance of science, he believed religion to be necessary to avoid materialism and to regain greatness for China. From 1903 Liang came into conflict with **Sun Zhongshan**. Liang opposed violent revolution, seeing greater safety for China in an enlightened autocracy or constitutional monarchy than in a republic. In the period of the May Fourth Movement, together with **Zhang Dongsun**, Liang opposed Marxism and socialism. After attending the Paris Peace Conference in 1919, Liang blamed the mechanistic science and materialism of the West for producing the carnage of the Great War and argued for the superiority of spiritual Oriental civilization, concentrating his writing on Chinese intellectual history. To the Confucianism he learned from Kang Youwei, Liang added elements of Buddhist idealism and Darwinian evolutionary thought. He saw history as developing in an ascending spiral, led by a small number of heroes rather than by the great mass of the population. Although Liang's political influence diminished in the 1920s his scholarship and intellectual brilliance continued to gain respect, even after his premature death.

NICHOLAS BUNNIN

Liang Souming (Liang Shu-ming)

Chinese. *b:* 1893, Beijing. *d:* 1988, Beijing. *Cat:* Philosopher of Eastern and Western culture; ethical philosopher. *Ints:* Philosophy and practice of education. *Educ:* Studied at Zhili Public Law School and for three years (1913–16) pursued private study of Consciousness Only Buddhism. *Infls:* Buddhism, Confucianism and Bergson. *Appts:* Professor of Indian and Chinese Philosophy, Peking University; Dean of Shandong Reconstruction Institute; Member, National Defence Council; Founder, Democratic League.

Main publications:

(1919) *General Discussion of Indian Philosophy*, Shanghai: Commercial Press.

(1921) *The Cultures of East and West and their Philosophies*, Shanghai: Commercial Press.

(1930) *Writings of Souming after Thirty*, Shanghai: Commercial Press.

(1932) *The Final Awakening of the Chinese People's Self-Salvation Movement*, Beijing: Cun zhi yue kan she.

(1935) *Theory of Rural Reconstruction*, Beijing: Cun zhi yue kan she.

(1935) *Writings on Education*, Couping, Shandong: Xiangcun Bookstore.

(1963) *Essentials of Chinese Culture*, Kowloon: Zhi cheng Study Company.

Secondary literature:

Alitto, G. (1979) *The Last Confucian: Liang Shuming and the Chinese Dilemma of Modernity*, Berkeley: University of California Press.

Boorman, H. (ed.) (1970) *Biographical Dictionary of Republican China*, New York and London: Columbia University Press.

Briere, O. (1956) *Fifty Years of Chinese Philosophy 1898–1950*, London: George Allen & Unwin Ltd.

Liang sought a solution to the crisis facing China through reinterpreting the Confucian tradition. In response to the Westernizing programme of **Chen Duxiu** and **Hu Shi**, he argued for the superiority of Eastern values in his major work *The Cultures of East and West and their Philosophies*. He distinguished three stages of civilization and three corresponding subjective attitudes. In Western civilization people pursued their desires by grasping objects from others and from nature. In Chinese civilization people moderated their desires to achieve an internal balance and an equilibrium with nature and society. Hindu civilization renounced desires. Of the three Liang argued for the superiority of the Chinese culture and philosophy over the limitless greed of the West and the escapist renunciation of India. He thought that the three types would succeed one another, and that in the present world the age of Western dominance would give way to Chinese moderation and harmony. Western scientific and democratic achievements would be conserved, but in an altered form. Science would be pursued with a moral psychology of unselfishness rather than with utilitarian aggression.

Liang's work provoked great controversy. It encouraged those seeking to reconcile tradition and prosperous stability, but those proposing Western scientific and democratic reform as a solution to China's overwhelming problems were hostile. The hostility was acccentuated by Liang's support of metaphysics in the 'science versus metaphysics' debates of the 1920s. His books also led to exchanges on the nature of culture, tradition and religion.

As a first step to realizing the transformation of society, Liang established rural reconstruction institutes in Henan and Shandong. These would provide the moral education to shape the subjective attitudes necessary for reform. Democracy would be based on rural reconstruction, with the élite returning to the countryside to work with local people to solve local problems. The resulting agricultural prosperity would be the basis on which urban industrial prosperity could be established. Liang saw China as different from other societies and opposed the imposition of Western democracy without moral reform. He also opposed Marxist class analysis as divisive. He sought to lessen social tensions through enlightened local action flowing from moral education. The outbreak of war with Japan brought his experiment to an end.

In the period after the Second World War Liang was active in politics, proposing a third force to maintain a united government with the nationalists and Communists. In the 1950s he maintained his viewpoint in spite of many attempts to persuade him to accept Marxist social analysis and to renouce his acceptance of moral attitudes as fundamental to reform. Ironically Liang was linked with his old antagonist **Hu Shi** as an object of fierce campaigns of denunciation.

NICHOLAS BUNNIN

Liebert, Arthur

German. *b:* 10 November 1878, Berlin. *d:* 5 November 1946, Berlin. *Cat:* Neo-Kantian; historian of philosophy; epistemologist. *Educ:* Philosophy, Economics, and Sociology at Berlin. *Infls:* Wilhelm Dilthey, Alois Riehl and Georg Simmel. *Appts:* Professor of Philosophy in Berlin, Belgrade and Birmingham.

Main publications:

(1914) *Das Problem der Geltung*, Berlin: Reuther & Reichard.
(1915) *Der Geltungswert der Metaphysik*, Berlin: Reuther & Reichard.
(1919) *Wie ist kritische Philosophie überhaupt möglich?*, Leipzig: Meiner.
(1923) *Erkenntnistheorie*, Berlin: Mittler.
(1929) *Geist und Welt der Dialektik* vol. 1, Berlin: Pan Verlag Metzner.
(1935) *Der Liberalismus als Forderung, Gesinnung und Weltanschauung*, Zürich: Rascher.
(1938) *Von der Pflicht der Philosophie in unserer Zeit*, Zürich: Rascher.
(1946) *Der universale Humanismus* vol. 1, Zürich: Rascher.

Secondary literature:

Kropp, G. (1949) 'Arthur Liebert in memoriam', *Zeitschrift für philosophische Forschung* 3: 427–35.

Liebert worked on many historical figures in philosophy. Following **Dilthey** and **Simmel**, he tried to do justice to their unique individuality. After emigrating from Germany, he devoted himself to the fight for 'liberalism' and against

'barbarism' and 'brutalism', trying to bring about a 'renaissance' of the idealistic faith in the moral force of freedom and liberalism. Liebert saw no fundamental contradiction between Kant's critical philosophy and the kind of speculative idealism that can be found in Fichte, Schelling and Hegel.

MANFRED KUEHN

Liebmann, Otto

German. *b:* 25 February 1840, Löwenberg, Silesia. *d:* 14 January 1912, Jena. *Cat:* Neo-Kantian; epistemologist; metaphysician. *Educ:* Philosophy, Mathematics and Natural Sciences in Jena, Halle and Leipzig. *Infls:* William Drobisch, Gustav Fechner, Kuno Fischer and Heinrich von Treitschke. *Appts:* Professor at Strassburg and Jena.

Main publications:

(1865) *Kant und die Epigonen*, Berlin: Reuther & Reinhard.
(1869) *Über den objektiven Anblick*, Stuttgart: Teubner.
(1876) *Zur Analyse der Wirklichkeit*, Strassburg: Trübner.
(1884) *Die Klimax der Theorien*, Strassburg: Trübner.
(1882–1904) *Gedanken und Tatsachen* 2 vols, Strassburg: Trübner.

Secondary literature:

Eucken, R. and Bauch, B. (1912) 'Nachruf', *Kant-Studien* 17: 1–8.

Liebmann attacked Fichte, Schelling, Hegel, Schopenhauer and their followers as speculative dogmatists. His motto was 'Back to Kant'. He believed that the fundamental ideas of Kant's transcendental philosophy are true, and argued that it is important to understand the spirit of Kant's philosophy in order that we may continue to develop it. Yet he did not follow Kant slavishly. For Liebmann, pure experience was nothing but a prejudice. Experience must be understood as dependent on transcendental conditions. The 'original fact' of consciousness forms the basis of any science and its object. Liebmann argued against Darwin that there is a life force. This 'life force' is not an a priori concept for him, but a gap in our conceptual framework (*Begriffslücke*) that ultimately must remain a riddle for us. He understood reason as a product of nature. However, because he saw reason as a procuct of nature he also thought that there must be something analogous to reason in nature itself. Liebmann's *Kant und die Epigonen* (1865) was very important for the origins of the neo-Kantian movement. Wilhelm **Windelband** called him 'the most faithful of all Kantians' and 'the most outstanding among the thinkers' of the second half of the nineteenth century. In the late twentieth century he is almost forgotten.

MANFRED KUEHN

Lipps, Theodor

German. *b:* 28 July 1851, Wallhalben, Rhineland-Palatinate. *d:* 17 October 1914, Munich. *Cat:* Aesthetician; psychologist. *Ints:* Logic; ethics. *Educ:* Theology, Mathematics, Science and Psychology at Erlangen, Tübingen, Utrecht and Bonn (PhD in Philosophy 1874). *Appts:* 1877–90, Bonn University; 1890–4, Breslau University; 1894–1914, Professor of Philosophy, Munich University; Founder of the German Psychological Institute in Munich; 1896, joint President (with Carl Stumpf) of the International Congress of Psychology.

Main publications:

(1890–1928) (ed. with R. M. Werner) *Beiträge zur Ästhetik*, 18 vols, Hamburg and Leipzig.
(1895) (ed.) *David Humes Traktat über die menschliche Natur* (*Treatise of Human Nature*), Hamburg and Leipzig.
(1897) *Raumästhetik und geometrisch–optische Täuschungen*, Leipzig.
(1899) *Die ethischen Grundfragen*, Hamburg.
(1902) *Vom Fühlen, Wollen und Denken*, Leipzig.
(1903–6) *Ästhetik*, 2 vols, Hamburg and Leipzig.
(1923) *Grundzüge der Logik*, third edition, Leipzig.

Secondary literature:

Anschütz, G. (1915) 'Theodor Lipps', *Archiv für die gesamte Psychologie* 34: 1–23 (bibliography of Lipps's writings).
Pfänder, Alexander (ed.) (1911) *Münchner Philosophische Abhandlungen. Theodor Lipps zu seinem sechzigsten Geburtstag gewidmet von früheren Schülern*, Leipzig.
Pilzler, J. (1908) *Über Theodor Lipps Versuch einer Theorie des Willens*, Leipzig.

Often grouped with Austrian 'act' psychologists (F. **Brentano**, A. **Meinong**, E. **Mach**), Lipps is better known as a psychologist than as a philosopher. His main philosophical interests lay in aesthetics, but he also wrote on logic and ethics,

and his *Grundzüge der Logik* [Essentials of Logic] (1923) and *Die ethischen Grundfragen* [The Fundamental Issues in Ethics] (1899) became popular reading on degree courses in Philosophy at German universities.

Lipps's 'empathy' theory, first presented in 1897, has been most influential in the philosophy of art but is also a theory of knowledge. According to Lipps, we gain knowledge of both an object and ourselves through empathy (*Einfühlung*): that is, by responding to the qualities of an object sympathetically and, at the same time, projecting our own qualities into it. Lipps gave epistemological priority to mental perception over sense perception. Consciousness is responsive *and* active in the epistemic process of empathy, alternately 'having' a 'content' received from the object (e.g. a perceptual image) ('content' psychology) and acting of its own accord ('act' psychology). Lipps, in the manner of Husserlian phenomenology, characterizes consciousness as 'intentional': it 'reaches out' (or 'aims at') something distinct from itself. This makes consciousness a dynamic activity, a 'striving' (or 'conation'—*Streben*).

Striving determines aesthetic experience and judgement. An object is judged 'beautiful' to the extent to which its qualities correspond to and are in harmony with the subject's own inner activity ('positive empathy') and 'ugly' if subject and object are in conflict ('negative empathy'). Lipps distinguishes between two kinds of objects, ones that can be classified by the 'mind's eye' in a simple act of 'fixation' and ones, art objects and other persons among them, which invite the very different approach of 'questioning', in response to which they then make claims on the subject. While initially experienced as constraints, these demands are transformed into manifestations of freedom once actively acknowledged ('surrendered to'). Positive empathy here links aesthetics and ethics in Lipps. Lipps presents aesthetic qualities as a function of a dynamic interaction, in which both subject and object are alternately active and receptive. In German dialectical philosophy Lipps's empathy theory has (therefore) been received as an attempt to overcome the subject-object dualism in Western thinking, as can be seen in the early work of Ernst **Bloch**, a student of Lipps at Munich.

Sources: Edwards; Leonard Zusne (1984) *Biographical Dictionary of Psychology*, London: Alwych Press.

BETTINA LANGE

List, Elisabeth

Austrian. *b:* 4 January 1946, St Veit/Glan, Austria. *Cat:* Feminist philosopher. *Ints:* Philosophy of the humanities and social sciences; social theories of modernity; feminist theory and critique of science; social philosophy and sociological theory. *Educ:* Universities of Graz (Austria), Konstanz and Berlin (Germany); 1971, PhD (Dr.phil.) of the Karl-Franzens University of Graz; dissertation on Heinrich Gomperz ('Verstehen und Erfahrungswissenschaft'). *Infls:* The philosophy of the 'Vienna Circle' and Ludwig Wittgenstein; feminist theories and critique of science (Evelyn Fox Keller, Dorothy Smith); Inter-University Centre, Dubrovnik (former Yugoslavia); critical theory and phenomenology (esp. Jürgen Habermas, M. Merleau-Ponty and Alfred Schutz). *Appts:* 1971–81, Lecturer and Assistant Professor, Department of Philosophy, University of Graz; 1981, Habilitation (*venia legendi*) for Philosophy with his 1983 work on theory of social sciences/ethnomethodology; since 1981, Associate Professor at the Department of Philosophy, University of Graz; 1986, Visiting Scholar, University of Bergen; 1984 and 1991; Visiting Lecturer, Universities of Hamburg and Tübingen.

Main publications:

(1983) *Alltagsrationalität und soziologischer Diskurs* [Common Sense Rationality and Sociological Discourse], Frankfurt am Main: Campus Verlag.

(1986) 'Homo politicus—Femina privata? Thesen zur Kritik der politischen Anthropologie' in Judith Conrad and Ursula Konnertz (eds) *Weiblichkeit in der Moderne. Ansätze feministischer Vernunftkritik*, Tübingen: edition diskord.

(1987) (ed. with Beate Frakele and Gertrud Pauritsch) *Über Frauenleben, Männerwelt und Wissenschaft. Österreichische Texte zur Frauenforschung* [On Women's Life, Men's World and Science. Austrian Texts on Women's Studies], Wien: Verlag für Gesellschaftskritik.

(1988) (ed. with Beate Frakele and Gertrud Pauritsch) *Kinder machen. Strategien der Kontrolle weiblicher Fruchtbarkeit* [Making Children. Strategies of Controlling Female Fertility], Vienna: Frauenverlag.

(1988) (ed. with Ilja Srubar) *Alfred Schütz. Neue Beiträge zur Rezeption seines Werks* [A. Schütz. Recent Contributions and Interpretations to his Writings], no. 12 of 'Studien zur österreichischen Philosophie', Amsterdam: Rodopi (German and English).

(1989) (ed. with Herlinde Studer) *Denkverhältnisse. Feminismus und Kritik* [The Engendering of Mind.

Feminism and Critique], Frankfurt am Main: Suhrkamp.

(1990) 'Theorieproduktion und Geschlechterpolitik. Prolegomena zu einer feministischen Theorie der Wissenschaften' [Theory and gender politics. Prolegomena to a feminist theory of science], in Herta Nagl-Docekal (ed.) *Feministische Philosophie*, Vienna: Oldenbourg.

(1991) 'Feministische Philosophie im Spektrum der Gegenwartsphilosophie' [Feminist philosophy in the spectrum of present-day philosophy], *Deutsche Zeitschrift für Philosophie* 39, 5: 514–27.

(1993) *Die Präsenz des Anderen* [The Presence of the Other], Frankfurt am Main: Suhrkamp.

(1994) 'Reason, gender, and the paradox of rationalization', in Inga Bostad and Elin Svenneby (eds) *Gender—An Issue for Philosophy?* (Proceedings of the Second Nordic Symposium of Women in Philosophy), Oslo, pp. 27–44.

Secondary literature:

Meyer, Ursula I. and Bennent-Vahle, Heidermaire (eds) (1994) *Philosophinnen Lexikon*, Aachen: ein-Fach-verlag.

The aim of Elisabeth List's feminist critique of the theory and practice of science is to reveal their androcentric character and to show that there is a male bias already in the epistemological foundations of science. She maintains that the dichotomies of objectivity and subjectivity, body and mind, and so on, are sexualized, that they devalue the female element and depict it as the deviance, as a deviation from an implicitly male norm. The task of her feminist critique is to rid science and its theory from these misogynist tendencies, and to generate a creative thinking that goes beyond gender differences and that encompasses the human experience of existing in a body and as a part of nature.

URSULA STICKLER

Liu Jie (Liu Chieh)

Chinese. *b:* 1901, Jiaxin County, Zhejiang Province, China. *d:* 1977, Guangzhou. *Cat:* Confucian philosophy. *Educ:* Shanghai National University and Qinghua University. *Appts:* Professor of Philosophy, Zhongshan University, Guangzhou.

Main publications:

(1948) *An Essay on History.*

(1958) *Textual Research into Ancient History.*

(1962) 'Kongzi's ren only theory', *Academic Research* 3.

(1962) 'The problem of the "unity between heaven and man" in the history of Chinese thought', *Academic Research* 1.

(1963) 'Mozi's theory of universal love and material benefits', *Academic Research* (Guangzhou) 1.

(1982) *A Manuscript on the History of Chinese Historiography.*

Secondary literature:

Louie, Kam (1966) *Inheriting Tradition: Interpretations of the Classical Philosophers in Communist China 1949–1966*, Hong Kong: Oxford University Press.

As an elderly Professor in Guangzhou in the 1960s, Liu argued strenuously for a traditional alternative to Marxist method in the study of ancient Chinese philosophy. He rejected **Mao Zedong**'s demand for class analysis and the distinction between materialism and idealism in his discussions of the Confucian and daoist tradition. Rather, he saw the search for harmony between human activities and the laws of nature as a key to understanding ancient thought. He rejected class analysis in his appreciation of the central Confucian virtue of *ren* (humanity or benevolence). He saw *ren* as incorporating all human virtues; even though the concept originated in feudal times, it was of compelling modern value and should not be abandoned in guiding society. He thus joined **Feng Youlan** in seeing some traditional values as transcending class and historical period and in seeking to legitimate these values in modern society. He rejected Mozi's 'universal love' as an impossibility and preferred the cultivation and education of an elite to provide stable government for the society as a whole. He praised some of those condemned as exploiters by orthodox Marxist opinion, but, more crucially, challenged the whole framework of analysis and assessment of ancient philosophy in which this condemnation took place.

NICHOLAS BUNNIN

Lodge, Rupert Clendon

British-Canadian. *b:* 1886, Manchester. *d:* 1961, St Petersburg, Florida. *Cat:* Eclectic pluralist. *Ints:* Theory of philosophy; applied philosophy; philosophy of education; Plato. *Educ:* Oxford, Marburg and Berlin. *Infls:* A. W. Wright. *Appts:* Taught at the Universities of Minnesota and Alberta before being appointed Professor of Logic and the History of Philosophy at the University of Manitoba in 1920; shared the headship of the

department with A. W. Wright until 1934 when he became sole head, a post he retained until his retirement in 1947; subsequently taught at Queen's University, Kingston, and at Long Island University; President of the Western Division of the American Philosophical Association in 1926.

Main publications:

(1918) *The Meaning and Function of Simple Modes in the Philosophy of John Locke*, Minneapolis: University of Minnesota Studies in the Social Sciences, no. 12.

(1920) *An Introduction to Modern Logic* Minneapolis: Perine.

(1927) *The Platonic Highest Good*, New York: Longmans, Green.

(1928) *Plato's Theory of Ethics*, London: Routledge & Kegan Paul.

(1937) *The Philosophy of Education*, New York: Harper.

(1937) *The Questioning Mind*, London: Dent.

(1945) *The Philosophy of Business*, Chicago: The University Press.

(1947) *Plato's Theory of Education*, London: Kegan Paul, Trench, Trubner (with an appendix on the education of women according to Plato by Rabbi Solomon Frank).

(1949) *The Great Thinkers*, London: Routledge & Kegan Paul.

(1951) *Applied Philosophy*, London: Routledge & Kegan Paul (American edition entitled *Applying Philosophy*, Boston: Beacon Press, 1951).

(1953) *Plato's Theory of Art*, London: Routledge & Kegan Paul.

(1956) *The Philosophy of Plato*, London: Routledge & Kegan Paul; New York: Humanities Press.

Secondary literature:

Armour, Leslie and Trott, Elizabeth (1981) *The Faces of Reason*, Waterloo: Wilfrid Laurier University Press.

Lodge was a pioneer in the development of the notion of 'applied philosophy', and his work on Plato and Locke was highly regarded. But his central claim to originality is his theory about the nature of philosophy. He believed that idealist, realist and pragmatist theories represented natural responses to the ambiguities and complexities of the human condition and that none could be disposed of. Rather, the serious philosopher should seek to work out the most plausible responses to each problem in terms of all three theories. Pluralism became his main interest. His belief that philosophy was irreducibly pluralistic stemmed in part from his experiences in Manitoba, where the complex relations of many cultures and the successive waves of poor immigrants suggested to him that pluralism was inevitable and that, although temperament and culture inclined individuals to one philosophy or another, their partisans had to come to terms with the fact that there will always be representatives of all three philosophies. Each approach, he argued, has real political consequences and influences many facets of life including theories of education and the practice of business. Lodge wrote a series of books working out problems in these terms. Although he converted few professional philosophers, he exerted a real influence on Canadian political life and on educational theory in the USA as well as in Canada. He admired the philosophy of Bernard **Bosanquet** but he was influenced by disciples of John **Dewey**, especially A. W. **Wright**, his colleague in Manitoba.

Plato was a life-interest and, in terms of his scholarly writing, a dominating interest, but he was stireed not so much by Plato's technical achievements as by his insistence on making philosophy relevant to the day-to-day affairs of life.

Armour and Trott (1981) argue that Lodge is a significant source of the 'philosophical federalism' which has been central to Canadian political thought over the past several decades.
Sources: CanBio.

LESLIE ARMOUR

Loeb, Jacques

German-American. *b:* 17 April 1859, Mayen, Germany. *d:* 11 February 1924, Hamilton, Bermuda. *Cat:* Philosopher of biology; experimental biologist. *Ints:* Nature of the will; mechanistic theory of life. *Educ:* Universities of Munich and Strasburg. *Infls:* Literary influences: Schopenhauer, E. von Hartmann and Mendel. Personal: Julius Sachs. *Appts:* 1886–91, Assistant in Physiology, University of Würzburg, then (1888–90) University of Strasburg and (1889) Naples Marine Biological Station; 1891–1910, Professor in Physiology, Bryn Mawr College, then (1892) University of Chicago, then (1902) University of California, Berkeley; 1910–24, Member of the Rockefeller Institute for Medical Research.

Main publications:

(1890) *Der Heliotropismus der Thiere, und seine Übereinstimmung mit dem Heliotropismus der Planzen*, Würzburg: G. Hertz.
(1906) *Vorlesungen über die Dynamik der Lebenserscheinungen*, Leipzig: Barth (English translation, *The Dynamics of Living Matter*, New York: Macmillan, 1906).
(1911) *Das Leben*, Leipzig: Barth (English translation, *The Mechanistic Theory of Life*, New York: Macmillan, 1912).
(1916) *The Organism as a Whole*, London: Hodder & Stoughton.

Secondary literature:
Nordenskiold, Erik (1929) *The History of Biology*, New York: Knopf, chapter 18, pp. 605ff.
Uexküll, Baron von J. (1930) *Die Lebenslehre*, Potsdam: Müller & Kiepenheuer, pp. 133ff.

Loeb was a philosophically inclined physiologist and biologist noted chiefly for his experimental work on parthenogenesis (reproduction without fertilization) and for his staunch defence of biological mechanism. Popular interest, attended by some controversy, was aroused by Loeb's pioneering experiments, beginning in 1899, when he successfully brought about the development of sea-urchin larvae from unfertilized eggs by exposing them to controlled changes in their environment.

From his scientific researches, which were designed to lay the foundations for a common dynamic of all vital phenomena and to illuminate the nature of volition, Loeb drew wide-ranging philosophical conclusions. He contended that not only vital phenomena, but human phenomena too, realized themselves in a purely mechanical way and were explicable solely in terms of physical and chemical concepts. Thus Loeb believed that we have only to improve our understanding of hereditary conditions in order to grasp the source and condition of all human activity. For him, even moral behaviour was no less the forced or automatic reaction of the organism as a whole than was the movement of a plant. Loeb's rigorous application of his pan-mechanistic or 'tropistic' thesis led him to an extreme, reductive philosophical monism. Nevertheless, his views had considerable influence, for example on Thorstein Veblen.
Sources: Edwards; DFN; EF.

STEPHEN MOLLER

Loen, Arnoldus Ewout

Dutch. *b:* 1896, Herveld. *d:* 8 February 1990, Utrecht. *Cat:* Christian existentialist. *Ints:* Philosophy of religion. *Educ:* Technology, University of Delft; Physics and Philosophy, University of Leyden. *Infls:* Personal influences included De

Sopper; philosophical influences included Husserl, Kierkegaard and N. Hartmann. *Appts:* Taught mathematics and physics at secondary schools; Professor of Philosophy of Religion, University of Utrecht, 1955–66.

Main publications:

(1927) *Wijsbegeerte en Werkelijkheid* [Philosophy and Reality], Utrecht: Honig (dissertation).

(1946) *De vaste grond* [The Solid Ground], Amsterdam and Paris.

(1947) *Inleiding tot de wijsbegeerte*, [Introduction to Philosophy], Den Haag: Boekencentrum.

(1955) *De plaats der wijsbegeerte in de theologische faculteit* [The Place of Philosophy within the faculty of Theology], Utrecht (Inaugural Lecture).

(1963) *Het vooronderstelde* (The Presupposed), Den Haag: Boekencentrum.

(1965) *Säkularisation*, München (English translation, *Secularization, Science without God?*, London, 1967).

(1973) *De geschiedenis, haar plaats, zijn, zin en kenbaarheid* [History, its Place, Being, Sense and Knowability], Assen: Van Gorcum.

Secondary literature:

Doevedans, K. (1989) *Inleiding tot het denken van A. E. Loen*, Assen (with full bibliography).

Loen's main interest was to create a philosophy on a Christian basis. The fullest explication of it is to be found in his fundamental book, *De vaste grond* [The Solid Ground]. He analyses the concept of Being and concludes that reason is insufficient to understand it and needs revelation to reach the truth. Philosophy has no proper subject matter, but is metatheory, the science of the way everything is founded in the foundation. Theology is the science of the foundation itself. Loen's viewpoint is existentialist, since he focuses on human existence, where the truth is revealed. This revelation has a historical character: revelation takes place within human history.

WIM VAN DOOREN

Loisy, Alfred Firmin

French. *b:* 1857, Ambrières, Marne. *d:* 1940, Ceffonds, Haute-Marne. *Cat:* Philosopher of religion; Biblical critic and historian. *Educ:* The seminary in Châlons-sur-Marne and the Institut Catholique de Paris. *Infls:* Ernest Renan and Louis Duchesne. *Appts:* Ordained priest in 1879; 1881–9, Professor of Hebrew, 1890–3, Professor of Scripture, Institut Catholique; 1900–04, Lecturer,

École Pratique des Hautes Études; 1909–30, Professor of the History of Religions, Collège de France.

Main publications:

(1902) *L'Évangile et l'Église*, Paris: Vrin (English translation, *The Gospel and the Church*, New York: Prometheus Books, 1988).

(1903) *Autour d'un petit livre*, Paris: Vrin.

(1903) *Le Quatrième Évangile*, Paris: Vrin.

(1908) *Les Évangiles synoptiques*, Paris: Vrin.

(1910) *Jésus et la tradition évangelique*, Paris: Vrin.

(1917) *La Religion*, Paris: Vrin.

(1920) *La Paix des nations et la religion de l'avenir*, Paris: Vrin.

(1923) *La Morale humaine*, Paris, Vrin.

(1931) *Mémoires pour servir à l'histoire religieuse de notre temps*, Paris: Vrin.

(1933) *La Naissance du christianisme*, Paris: Vrin.

(1937) *La Crise morale du temps présent et l'éducation humaine*, Paris: Vrin.

Secondary literature:

Daly, G. (1980) *Transcendence and Immanence*, Oxford: Clarendon Press, chapters 3 and 4 (chapter 4 contains details of his intellectual skirmish with Maurice Blondel).

Houtin, A. and Sartiaux, F. (1961) *Alfred Loisy: Sa Vie et son oeuvre*, Meudon: CNRS.

Petre, M. D. (1944) *Alfred Loisy: His Religious Significance*, Cambridge: Cambridge University Press.

Ratté, J. (1968) *Three Modernists*, London: Sydney, Sheed & Ward.

Vidler, A. R. (1970) *A Variety of Catholic Modernists*, Cambridge: Cambridge University Press.

Catholic modernism, of which Alfred Loisy was a leading French exponent, applied to the study of the Bible the critical historical methods which had been developed primarily in Germany during the nineteenth century.

Despite Loisy's official disclaimer that he was 'only a poor decipherer of texts' (quoted in Daly 1980, p. 54), his initial preoccupation with the critical study of the Bible, and in particular of the four Gospels, led to his conviction that there was a need to revise the traditional teachings of the Roman Catholic Church, and this in turn resulted in the development of his philosophy of religion.

Loisy's view, as propounded primarily in *L'Évangile et l'Église* (1902), was that the contingent truths about the Jesus of history should be regarded as completely separate from those held by the Christian community about the Christ of faith. In his later work *La Naissance du christia-*

nisme (1933), Loisy returned to these views in his specification that the only historical truths about Jesus were that Jesus was a prophet of Galilee in the first century AD and that he was crucified during the governorship of Pontius Pilate. The remainder of the Gospel accounts, and any later additions to the Christian message, were to be assigned to the realm of myth and symbolism.

In repudiating historical truths as a basis for Christianity he delivered a devastating criticism of the conclusions of the German Protestant theologian Harnack, who had maintained both the desirability and the possibility of cutting through the dogmatic accretions of centuries in order to recover the authentic and historical revelation of God in Jesus Christ.

Although Loisy's attack on a major Protestant theologian did not on its own account alarm the Catholic authorities, this was not the case with his positive contribution to the philosophy of religion. As a continuation of his view that the Christian message was to be regarded as mythical or symbolic, he maintained that the teachings of neither the Catholic church, nor any other movement within Christianity, embodied the full and absolute essence of the truths of faith. Far from being static, these truths were in continuous flux and development, and found their expression in the life of the Christian community as guided by the Holy Spirit.

These views aroused considerable controversy, and Loisy's own account of the dispute was published in 1903 in *Autour d'un petit livre*. The rift between Loisy and the Catholic Church widened over the next five years: five of his books were placed on the Index, and in 1908 he himself was excommunicated by Pope Pius X. From 1910 an anti-modernist oath was required of all clerical ordinands.

The implications of Loisy's position on truth were made explicit in *Autour d'un petit livre*, where he stated: 'truth is in us something necessarily conditioned, relative. Truth does not enter our heads ready-made; it comes about slowly, and one can never say that it is complete ... [it] is no more immutable than man himself. It evolves with him, in him, by him' (pp. 191–2).

Loisy stressed the crucial and creative role of the Christian community. The vitality of the community enabled it to gain a better, but never a complete, understanding of the myths and symbols of Christianity. He saw a tension between critical historical methodology and the traditional doctrines of the Catholic Church, and his refusal to relinquish humanity's ongoing quest for understanding led him to reject the doctrines as a body of absolute and fixed truth.

KATHRYN PLANT

Lombardi, Franco

Italian. *b:* 28 June 1906, Naples. *Cat:* Personalist; realist. *Ints:* Epistemology; history of philosophy. *Infls:* Hegel, Feuerbach, Marx, Kierkegaard, Croce and Gentile. *Appts:* Having worked clandestinely for the Italian Socialist Party (until it split into two factions), Lombardi joined the staff of the University of Rome in 1943, and became Professor of Theoretical Philosophy there in 1949; founder and editor of the journal *De homine* from 1962.

Main publications:

An edition of Lombardi's *Scritti* (Florence: Sansoni) began to appear in 1963 (16 vols).

(1935) *L'esperienza e l'uomo.*
(1935) *Il mondo degli uomini.*
(1935) *Ludwig Feuerbach.*
(1936) *Søren Kierkegaard.*
(1941) *La libertà del volere e l'individuo.*
(1943–6) *La filosofia critica.*
(1953) *Nascita del mondo moderno*, second edition, Florence: Sansoni, 1967.
(1955) *Dopo lo storicismo*, Asti: Arethusa.
(1959) *La filosofia italiana negli ultimi cento anni*, Asti: Arethusa.
(1963) *La posizione dell'uomo nell'universo*, Florence: Sansoni.
(1965) *Il senso della storia ed altri saggi*, second edition, Florence: Sansoni.
(1965) *Aforismi inattuali sull'arte*, Florence: Sansoni.
(1966) *Problemi della libertà*, Florence: Sansoni.
(1967) *Filosofia a società*, Florence: Sansoni.
(1968) *Galilei, Calvino, Rousseau: tre antesignani del tempo moderno*, Florence: Sansoni.
(1969) *Idee pedagogiche di Antonio Gramsci*, Brescia: La Scuola.
(1974) *Scritti per l'universita*, Florence: Sansoni.
(1981) *Una svolta di civilta*, Turin: ERI.

Secondary literature:

Editorial matter in Calabro, Gr. (ed.) (1961), *Franco Lombardi*, Turin: Edizioni di 'Filosofia'.
Harris, H. S. (1965) 'The "modernity" of Franco Lombardi', in G. L. Kline (ed.) *European Philosophy Today*, Chicago: Quadrangle.

Educated in the idealist tradition from Hegel to **Gentile**, Lombardi has arrived at his own philosophy largely in reaction to it, drawing also on ideas from Feuerbach, Marx and Kierkegaard (on the last of whom he wrote the first commentary in Italian).

In Lombardi's view absolute idealism involves a false epistemology. Such a view (he argues) includes the thesis that knowledge is the intellectual intuition of an independent reality. To attain such knowledge is to share god's view of the world, and presuppose that a purely impersonal contemplative, neutral and rational mode of thought is possible. Lombardi (following Kierkegaard) objects that there is no absolute thought, only an individual who thinks (1953, pp. 201–8), placed in a given situation which requires action and decision. Only when viewed from this personalist perspective does the real nature of human freedom become clear: it is a freedom which weighs on us ('una libertà pesante') because it involves our accepting responsibility for our own investigations into truth and for the decisions based on them.

Freedom understood in this sense is an important element in what Lombardi calls 'modernity', a notion to which he has devoted a good deal of attention. The contrary notion to the modern, in Lombardi's analysis, is not the ancient but the medieval, which last he epitomizes as involving a negative attitude to the world and the flesh, and devoted to salvation in the next life. By contrast, modernity involves: a positive attitude to the world and to the scientific investigation of it; a belief in progress; toleration; democracy and the ultimate collapse of national boundaries. The ethic which is consonant with this set of beliefs, unsurprisingly, has strong existentialist elements: the sense of burdensome freedom and responsibility already referred to; belief in the value of individuals and so egalitarianism, with self-realization as the ultimate goal.

Sources: Review of *Nascita del mondo moderno* in *Mind* 64, 256, Oct 1955, pp. 566–9.

ROBERT WILKINSON

Lonergan, Bernard

Canadian. *b:* 17 December 1904, Buckingham, Quebec. *d:* 26 November 1984, Pickering, Ontario. *Cat:* Thomist. *Ints:* Epistemology; methodology; metaphysics; philosophical theology. *Educ:* Heythrop College and Gregorian University. *Infls:* Aristotle, Aquinas and Newman. *Appts:* 1953–1965, Gregorian University; 1966–70, Regis College, Toronto; 1973–83, Boston College.

Main publications:

(1957) *Insight*, London: Longman, Green & Co.; fifth edition, *Collected Works of Bernard Lonergan*, vol. 3, Toronto: University of Toronto Press, 1992.

(1967) *Collection*, edited by F. E. Crowe, New York: Herder & Herder; second edition, *Collected Works of Bernard Lonergan*, vol. 4, Toronto: University of Toronto Press, 1988.

(1968) *Verbum: Word and Idea in Aquinas*, London: Darton, Longman & Todd.

(1974) *A Second Collection*, edited by William F. J. Ryan and Bernard J. Tyrell, London: Darton, Longman & Todd.

Secondary literature:

Crowe, Frederick E. (1992) *Lonergan*, London: Geoffrey Chapman.

Lamb, Matthew L. (ed.) (1981) *Creativity and Method*, Milwaukee: Marquette University Press.

McShane, Philip (ed.) (1971–2) *Papers from the International Lonergan Congress 1970*, 2 vols, Dublin: Gill & Macmillan (vol. 2: *Language, Truth and Meaning*).

Meynell, Hugo A. (1976) *An Introduction to the Philosophy of Bernard Lonergan*, London: Macmillan; second edition, 1991.

Tracy, David (1970) *The Achievement of Bernard Lonergan*, New York: Herder & Herder.

Bernard Lonergan was the main exponent in English of what is sometimes called 'transcendental Thomism'. This emerged from a confrontation, and a partial synthesis, of some elements of Kantian method with Thomistic realism, initiated earlier in the century by **Maréchal**. A fundamental principle in Lonergan's philosophy is his definition of being as 'the objective of the pure desire to know'. Reality, that is, has a structure which is isomorphic with the structure of knowledge. It follows that a description and a theory of knowledge is a precondition and the foundation of metaphysics. A knowledge of knowledge leads to a knowledge of what is known, and what is known is what there is.

This methodological priority of epistemology over metaphysics was strongly contested by Thomists such as **Gilson**, for whom a philosophy that began with a study of consciousness could never escape from it and arrive at the extra-mental world. Gilson pointed to Descartes and Kant as philosophers who conspicuously failed in this respect. Transcendental Thomists, however, would claim that Kant's view that we cannot know things in themselves was a kind of failure of nerve. If Kant had exploited his own critical method to the full, he would have come to realize that the very concept of knowledge is itself intelligible and possible only on the prior assumption of real objects and properties which are objects for knowledge, and which are actually known by the knowing subject.

For Lonergan, then, philosophy begins with the attempt to know what knowing is. The very possibility of knowing what knowing is is inherent in the nature of consciousness. Knowing is a conscious activity, and consciousness is an awareness immanent in cognitional acts. The knowing of which we are aware has a threefold character: empirical, intellectual and rational. As empirical, knowing is sensing, perceiving and imagining. As intellectual, knowing involves the act of understanding and the formation of concepts. As rational, knowing culminates in affirmations of what there is. These are not three types or stages of knowing, but constitute a dynamic unity. All knowing requires a process of 'insight' (hence the title of Lonergan's most famous work), which is the name he uses for the act of understanding a set of data. Insight is exemplified in Archimedes's cry 'Eureka', and in the slaveboy in Plato's *Meno*. The early chapters of *Insight* provide a detailed analysis of the activity of knowing in mathematics, the empirical sciences and common sense.

The dynamic, historically evolving, methodologically diverse character of knowing makes it plain that reality cannot be conceived of as a static universe ruled by classical laws of physics. Lonergan describes it rather as 'emergent probability', a phrase designed to indicate that the universe functions as much by statistical probabilities as by classical laws. When reality is conceived of as the knowable, as something 'proportionate' to human cognition ('proportionate being'), it can be said to have three components: 'potency' is the component that is experienced or imagined; 'form' is the component that is known by the understanding; 'act' is the component known by the judgement of reason.

These three components can themselves be of different kinds. Our understanding of things is an understanding both of their properties and relations, and of their concrete individuality: the former is 'conjugate form' and the latter is 'central form', terms which correspond with Aristotle's accidental and substantial form. Coordinate with these we can also distinguish central and conjugate potency, and central and conjugate act. Central act is existence and conjugate act is occurrence.

Lonergan also examines practical reasoning and the possibility of ethics. He defines good as

'the object of desire'. However, one of the things that we desire is knowledge, and this desire generates a second sense of good: the good of order, as instantiated in the state, the economy or the family. Good refers here to states of affairs which are rationally and purposefully designed, willed and constructed to satisfy our desires. Good as the object of rational choice presents itself as value. On the ontological level, good refers to every kind of order and, at its limit, to the intelligibility intrinsic in being. Moral choices involve four elements: sensible and imaginative representations; practical insight; practical reflection; and decision.

One of the peculiarities of human knowing is that, although we have an unrestricted desire to know, we have a limited capacity to know. Thus, 'the range of possible questions is larger than the range of possible answers'. This consideration leads Lonergan to the postulation of transcendent being, that is to say, being that is beyond us, which is 'without the domain of man's outer and inner experience'. Transcendent being, however, must be presumed to be intelligible, and this leads to the logical possibility of an unrestricted act of understanding, whose object includes transcendent as well as proportionate being. Its object would also include self-understanding (since all knowing is, by definition, conscious). Such an understanding would be one of the characteristics of God.

The affirmation of what God is, and the affirmation that God is, are different matters. Lonergan believes that many of the arguments for the existence of God are included in the general form: 'If the real is completely intelligible, God exists. But the real is completely intelligible. Therefore, God exists.' However, Lonergan does not think that this argument will persuade someone who was hitherto an agnostic or an atheist that God exists. Its function rather is, like that of St Anselm's proof, to demonstrate to those who already believe in God that their belief is rationally grounded and defensible. Lonergan is regarded by some as having one of the most powerful philosophical minds of the twentieth century, but he is not widely known outside Thomistic circles.

Sources: *Catholic Encyclopedia; RPL* 83, 1985.

HUGH BREDIN

Lopatin, Lev Mikhailovich
Russian. *b:* 1 June (13 N.S.) 1855, Moscow. *d:* 21 March 1920, Moscow. *Cat:* Idealist; neo-Leibnizian personalist. *Educ:* Graduated from University of Moscow in 1879. *Infls:* Leibniz, Lotze,

Schopenhauer and Solov'ev. *Appts:* 1883–1920, Professor of Philosophy, University of Moscow.

Main publications:

(1886–91) *Polozhitel'nye zadachi filosofii* [The Positive Tasks of Philosophy], 2 vols, Moscow.

(1911) *Filosofskie kharakteristiki i rechi* [Philosophical Characterizations and Addresses], Moscow (one essay is translated by A. Bakshy as 'The philosophy of Vladimir Soloviev', *Mind*, 25 (1916): pp. 426–60, 1916).

(1913) 'Monizm i pliuralizm', *Voprosy filosofii i psikhologii*, 6 (116) (brief translated extracts included in Louis J. Shein (ed.), *Readings in Russian Philosophical Thought*, The Hague: Mouton, pp. 158–74, 1968).

Secondary literature:

Zenkovsky, V. V. (1953) *A History of Russian Philosophy*, trans. George L. Kline, London: Routledge & Kegan Paul, vol. 2, pp. 645–57.

Lopatin, a friend from childhood of the religious philosopher **Solov'ev**, was not only a leading Russian neo-Leibnizian, but a pioneer of Russian psychology. He was President of the Moscow Psychological Society from 1899 until its suppression in 1917, and editor of *Voprosy filosofii i psikhologii* [Problems of Philosophy and Psychology]. An eccentric and unworldly figure, he perished during the famine attending the post-revolutionary civil war.

According to Lopatin's 'spiritualistic' metaphysics, every phenomenon, whether physical or psychical, is the manifestation of an inner, supratemporal, spiritual force. All material effects and properties (including extension) are secondary and derivative; matter and its laws are themselves the result of a primary creative causality. Lopatin rejected the notion of a transcendent soul; the soul is substantial, and being immanent in psychical phenomena is directly intuited in our inner experience. Despite its immanence, the soul's awareness of time shows that it is supratemporal, and therefore indestructible, since destruction is an event in time.

Lopatin steered a path between Hegel's absolute monism and the more recent metaphysical pluralism which he identified with William **James** among others. In his view, the manifest interconnectedness of things and the uniformity of nature pointed to an essential prior unity, and he advanced a vital monism recognizing 'unity in multiplicity and multiplicity in unity': that is, the

reality of both God and the multiplicity of separate beings.

Lopatin saw free human creative action as gradually establishing a moral order in the world, and saw the possibility of 'radical moral upheavals', or moral creativity, as the key to the nature of the human spirit. **Zenkovsky** accordingly characterized his philosophy as 'ethical personalism'.

COLIN CHANT

Lorenzen, Paul

German. *b:* 24 March 1915, Kiel, Germany. *Cat:* Mathematician; philosopher of mathematics and the sciences. *Ints:* Logic; philosophy of mathematics and the sciences. *Educ:* Kiel, Berlin and Göttingen. *Infls:* Kant and Hugo Dingler. *Appts:* 1956–62, Professor of Philosophy, Kiel; 1962–80, Professor of Philosophy, Erlangen; 1965–71, Visiting Professor, Austin, Texas; 1967–8, John Locke Lecturer, Oxford University; 1972–5, Visiting Professor, Boston University; from 1980, Emeritus Professor of Philosophy, Erlangen.

Main publications:

(1955) *Einführung in die operative Logik und Mathematik*, Berlin: De Gruyter.

(1958) *Formale Logik*, Berlin: De Gruyter (English translation, *Formal Logic*, trans. F. J. Crosson, Dordrecht: Reidel, 1965).

(1962) *Metamathematik*, Mannheim: Hochschultaschenbucher.

(1965) *Differential und Integral. Eine konstruktive Einführung in die klassische Analysis*, Frankfurt: Akademische Verlaggesellschaft (English translation, *Differential and Integral Calculus: A Constructive Introduction to Classical Analysis*, trans. J. Bacon, Austin: University of Texas Press, 1971).

(1965) *Logik und Grammatik*, Mannheim: Duden-Beitrage.

(1968) *Methodisches Denken*, Frankfurt: Suhrkamp.

(1969) *Normative Logic and Ethics*, Mannheim: Bibliographisches Institut.

(1973) (with O. Schremmer) *Konstrucktive Logik, Ethik und Wissenschaftstheorie*, Mannheim: Bibliographisches Institut.

(1974) *Praktische Philosophie und Konstruktive Wissenschaftstheorie*, Frankfurt: Suhrkamp.

(1978) (with K. Lorenz) *Dialogische Logik*, Darmstadt: Wissenschaftliche Buchgesellschaft.

(1983) *Elementargeometrie als Fundament der Analytischen Geometrie*, Mannhiem: Bibliographisches Institut.

(1985) *Grundbegriff technischer und politischer Kultur*, Frankfurt: Suhrkamp.

(1987) *Constructive Philosophy*, Amherst: University of Massachusetts Press (translation by Karl Richard Pavlovic of excerpts from various of Lorenzen's publications, especially from 1968 and 1974).

(1987) 'Critique of political and technical reason: the Evert William Beth Lectures of 1980', *Synthèse71: 127–218*.

Secondary literature:

Butts, R. E. and Brown J. R. (eds) (1989) *Constructivism and Science: Essays in Recent German Philosophy*, Norwell: Kluwer.

Lorenz, Kuno (ed.) (1979) *Konstructionem versus Positionen, Betrage zur Discussion um doe Konstructive Wissenschaftheorie*, Berlin: De Gruyter.

Sagal, P. T. (1987) 'Paul Lorenzen's constructivism and the recovery of philosophy', *Synthetic Philosophy* 2: 173–8.

Lorenzen is a leading exponent of 'constructivism' who follows in the tradition of Kant but at the same time acknowledges both the linguistic turn given to philosophy by **Frege**, **Russell** and **Wittgenstein** and the pragmatic turn given to it by **Peirce** and others. He has characterized his 'constructive philosophy' as being in the spirit of Kant, but making use of the tools of modern philosophy of science. He is opposed to the foundationalism of the positivists, holding that theoretical concepts are ultimately based on human practice. The decisive points of Kant for him are the primacy of 'practical reason', which is 'justified by a demonstration that our theories in logic, mathematics, and physics are instruments made by us for our technical purposes' (1987, p. ix). Together with W. Kamlah, Lorenzen founded the Erlangen School in the early 1960s. His work has been influential in the USA as well as in Germany.

Sources: Mittelstrass; NUC; PI.

STUART BROWN

Losev, Aleksei Fedorovich

Russian. *b:* 10 September (O.S.) 1893, Novocherkassk, Russia. *d:* 24 May 1988, Moscow. *Cat:* Dialectical idealist; aesthetician; classicist. *Ints:* Ancient philosophy; aesthetics; philosophy of language; philosophy of history. *Educ:* Moscow University. *Infls:* Plato, Plotinus, Hegel and V. Solov'ev. *Appts:* 1919–21, Nizhnii Novgorod University; 1921–30, State Academy of Arts and Sciences and Moscow Conservatory of Music;

1942–4, Moscow State University; 1944–88, Moscow Pedagogical Institute.

Main publications:

(1927) *Antichnyi kosmos i sovremennaia nauka* [The Ancient Cosmos and Contemporary Science], Moscow.

(1927) *Muzyka kak predmet logiki* [Music as a Subject of Logic], Moscow.

(1927) *Filosofiia imeni* [Philosophy of the Name], Moscow).

(1927) *Dialektika khudozhestvennoi formy* [The Dialectics of Artistic Form], Moscow.

(1930) *Dialektika mifa*, Moscow.

(1963–92) *Istoriia antichnoi estetiki* A History of Ancient Aesthetics], 8 vols, Moscow.

(1976) *Problemy simvola i realisticheskoe iskusstvo* [Problems of the Symbol and Realist Art], Moscow.

(1977) *Antichnaia filosofiia istorii* [Ancient Philosophy of History], Moscow.

(1978) *Estetika Vozrozhdeniia* [The Aesthetics of the Renaissance], Moscow.

(1982) *Znak. Simvol. Mif: Trudy po iazykoznaniiu* [Sign, Symbol, Myth: Works in Linguistics], Moscow.

(1990) *Vladimir Solov'ev i ego vremia* [Vladimir Solov'ev and his Times], Moscow.

All 1927–30 works (plus some other early works) are reprinted in a series of three collections:

(1993) *Bytie–imia–kosmos* [Being, Name, Cosmos], Moscow: Mysl'.

(1993) *Ocherki antichnogo simvolizma i mifologii* [Essays in Ancient Symbolism and Mythology], Moscow: Mysl'.

(1994) *Mif–chislo–sushchnost'* [Myth, Number, Essence], Moscow: Mysl'.

Secondary literature:

Alekseev, P. V. (ed.) (1993) *Filosofy Rossii xix–xx stoletii*, Moscow, pp. 110–11.

Haardt, Alexander (1993) *Husserl in Russland: Phänomenologie der Sprache und Kunst bei Gustav Spet und Aleksej Losev*, Munich: Wilhelm Fink (contains bibliography).

Skalon, D. Iu. D. Kashkarov (1983) 'A. F. Losev: k devianostoletiiu' [A. F. Losev: For his ninetieth birthday], *Novyi zhurnal* [New Journal] 150: 282–92.

Takho-Godi, A. (1989) 'Aleksei Fedorovich Losev', *Soviet Studies in Philosophy*, Fall: 30–44.

Losev gained renown with a series of eight brilliant books in ancient philosophy, aesthetics, the philosophy of language/and mythology published between 1927 and 1930. In them he employed a version of **Husserl's** phenomenological method to elaborate a dialectical metaphysics that owed more to Plato and Plotinus than to Hegel. The idealist cast of Losev's dialectical outlook was displayed in 1930 when he wrote that 'a dialectical materialism is a crying absurdity' (1930, p. 147).

That statement proved to be the last criticism of Marxist philosophy published in Stalin's Russia, and for it Losev was deprived of freedom for three years and deprived of appropriate philosophical recognition for the reaminder of his long life. For 23 years he could not publish his writings. When he was able to resume publishing upon Stalin's death in 1953, it was only on subjects more or less closely related to aesthetics and classical philology and only with the msot scrupulous attention to the shibboleths of Marxist orthodoxy. None the less, and despite his (by then) almost total blindness, Losev's ensuing output was stunning in both quantity and quality, encompassing some 27 additional books and hundreds of articles, the philosophical content and implications of which frequently went well beyond their nominal subjects. His monumental eight-volume *Istoriia antichnoi estetiki* [A History of Ancient Aesthetics] (1963–92) is a comprehensive study of Greek and Roman philosophy which established him as Russia's leading authority on the subject. He also translated the works of Plato, Aristotle, Plotinus and others into Russian.

Although Losev's post-1953 works have inspired generations of Russian students and are valued for their original scholarship, their philosophical profile is clouded by the heavy demands of Soviet censorship. Losev himself claimed publicly to have become a convert to Marxist materialism after 1930; privately, he admitted to remaining a Russian Orthodox Christian. D. Skalon contends that philosophically Losev was throughout his life a Hegelian objective idealist. Takho-Godi (Losev's widow) affirms more plausibly that Losev sought to overcome the opposition between materialism and idealism, in the spirit of Vladimir **Solov'ev**'s metaphysics of 'total-unity' (*vseedinstvo*); this suggestion is consistent with the great esteem in whcih Losev held Solov'ev's conception from his youth until the writing of his last book, a study of Solov'ev's philosophy.

Sources:

JAMES SCANLAN

Lossky, Nikolai Onufrievich
Russian. *b:* 6 December (18 O.S.) 1870, Kreslavka, Vitebsk province. *d:* 24 January 1965, Paris. *Cat:*

Religious philosopher; intuitionist; personalist. *Educ:* University of St Petersburg; postgraduate under Windelband at Strasbourg and Wilhelm Wundt at Leipzig. *Infls:* Plotinus, Leibniz, Bergson, Solov'ev and the Russian neo-Leibnizian A. A. Kozlov. *Appts:* 1907–21, taught philosophy at University of St Petersburg, Professor of Philosophy, 1916–21; 1942–5, Professor of Philosophy, University of Bratislava; 1947–50, Professor of Philosophy, St Vladimir Russian Orthodox seminary, New York.

Main publications:
(1906) *Obosnovanie intuitivizma*, St Petersburg (English translation, *The Intuitive Basis of Knowledge: An Epistemological Enquiry*, trans. Natalie Duddington, London: Macmillan, 1919).
(1917) *Mir kak organicheskoe tseloe*, Moscow (English translation, *The World as an Organic Whole*, trans. Natalie Duddington, London: Humphrey Milford, 1928).
(1927) *Svoboda voli*, Paris (English translation, *Freedom of Will*, trans. Natalie Duddington, London: Williams and Norgate, 1932).
(1931) *Tsennost' i bytie: Bog i Tsarstvo Bozhie kak osnova tsennostei*, Paris (English translation, *Value and Existence*, trans. S. S. Vinokooroff, London: George Allen & Unwin, 1935).
(1938) *Chuvstvennaia, intellektual'naia i misticheskaia intuitsiia* [Sensory, Intellectual and Mystical Intuition], Paris.
(1951) *History of Russian Philosophy*, New York: International Universities Press.

Secondary literature:
Kohanski, A. S. (1936) *Lossky's Theory of Knowledge*, Nashville: Vanderbilt University.
Zenkovsky, V. V. (1953) *A History of Russian Philosophy*, trans. George L. Kline, London: Routledge & Kegan Paul, vol. 2, pp. 657–75.

Lossky was expelled from his local gymnasium for his atheism. In 1921 he was deprived of his Chair of Philosophy at University of St Petersburg because of his religious beliefs, and in the following year was among the Russian philosophers exiled from the Soviet Union. He settled in Prague at the invitation of the statesman and historian of Russian ideas Tomás **Masaryk**, remaining in Czechoslovakia until 1945. Thereafter he lived in the United States and France.

The starting-point of Lossky's 'intuitivism' was his rejection of all causal or representational theories of knowledge: all objects of knowledge are immediately apprehended or intuited by the subject and although the subject's cognitive act of knowing is temporal, the 'epistemological coordination' between subject and object which is the necessary condition of knowing is itself outside space and time. Following **Solov'ev**, Lossky distinguished three kinds of intuition: sensory intuition of events in space and time; intellectual intuition of ideal objects, such as number and logical relations; and mystical intuition of the absolute, which is a metalogical being transcending the laws of identity, contradiction and the excluded middle.

Lossky intended his intuitivist epistemology to validate metaphysics. His own personalist 'ideal-realism' was akin to Leibniz's monadology, although he rejected the notion of a 'windowless' monad: rather, 'everything is immanent in everything'. Like **Lopatin**, Lossky avoided a pure pluralism, and attributed to the absolute both the creation of a multiplicity of 'substantival agents' and the preservation of their unity and consubstantiality. These agents exist outside of space and time, although space and time are their 'mode of activity'; and, according to his evolutionary doctrine of 'hierarchical personalism', they can achieve through the exercise of free will and by reincarnation a higher level of being. Thus a proton may eventually become an 'actual' person recognizing the existence of absolute values, and freely choosing the path to God rather than the path of egoism. Lossky appealed to religious experience and revelation in identifying the absolute with the Christian Trinity, including Christ as the God–man; his conception of Sophia as the created world-spirit was more restricted than that of **Bulgakov** and **Florensky**.

Lossky's *History of Russian Philosophy* (1951) is a valuable commentary on religious and idealist philosophers (including himself), although it is the mirror image of Soviet histories in its scant way with secular thinkers.

COLIN CHANT

Lotman, Iurii Mikhailovich

Russian-Estonian. *b:* 1922, Petrograd. *Cat:* Aesthetician; semiotician; cultural historian. *Ints:* Aesthetics; semiotics; philosophy of culture; philosophy of literature. *Educ:* Leningrad State University. *Infls:* N. S. Trubetskoi, Iu. N. Tynianov and Ferdinand de Saussure. *Appts:* Taught at Tartu (Estonia) Teachers Institute (1950–4); Tartu University (1954–93).

Main publications:

(1964) *Lektsii po struktural'noi poetike: vvedenie, teoriia stikha* [Lectures on Structural Poetics: Introduction, Theory of Verse], Tartu.

(1970) *Struktura khudozhestvennogo teksta*, Moscow (English translation, *The Structure of the Artistic Text*, trans. Ronald Vroon, University of Michigan, 1977).

(1972) *Analiz poeticheskogo teksta*, Leningrad (English translation, *Analysis of the Poetic Text*, trans. D. Barton Johnson, Ann Arbor, Michigan: Ardis, 1976).

(1973) *Semiotika kino i problemy kinoestetiki*, Tallinn (English translation, *Semiotics of Cinema*, trans. Mark E. Suino, University of Michigan, 1976).

(1990) *Universe of the Mind: A Semiotic Theory of Culture*, trans. Ann Shukman, Indiana University Press.

Secondary literature:

Koshelev, A. D. (ed.) (1994) *Iu. M. Lotman: Tartusko-moskovskaia semioticheskaia shkola* [Iu. M. Lotman and the Tartu-Moscow Semiotic School], Moscow: Gnozis (contains bibliography)

Reid, Allan (1990) *Literature as Communication and Cognition in Bakhtin and Lotman*, New York: Garland.

Shukman, Ann (1977) *Literature and Semiotics: A Study of the Writings of Yu. M. Lotman*, Amsterdam: North-Holland Publishing Company.

Lotman was the leading theoretician in the Moscow-Tartu group of semioticians who apply structural-semiotic analysis to the study of the arts (especially literature) and to culture in general. Although criticized by doctrinaire Marxist–Leninists in their homeland before the break-up of the Soviet Union, the group's work has attracted much interest in Europe and America, particularly among literary theorists.

Lotman, viewing the natural languages as 'modelling systems'—structures of signs whose meanings 'model' the world they refer to—argues that art, like myth and religion, is a 'secondary modelling system', or more complex language superimposed upon natural language. A work of art, then, is a text with multiple levels and orders of meanings—a communicative structure joining artist and public through the shared languages of a particular culture.

In his later years Lotman and his colleagues broadened their focus from the fields of literature and the other arts to the structural-semiotic study of the broader cultural context of communication. In his last theoretical monograph, *Universe of the Mind* (1990), he introduced the term 'semiosphere' as a name for the highly complex and dynamic but at the same time unified semiotic universe of a culture.

JAMES SCANLAN

Lovejoy, Arthur Oncken

American. **b:** 10 October 1873, Berlin, Germany. **d:** 30 December 1973, Baltimore. **Cat:** Critical realist; intellectual historian. **Ints:** Epistemology; history of ideas. **Educ:** University of California (Berkeley) and Harvard. **Infls:** Descartes and Locke. **Appts:** Professor, Washington University of St Louis, 1901–8; Professor, Johns Hopkins University 1910–38.

Main publications:

(1914) *Bergson and Romantic Evolutionism*, Berkeley.
(1930) *The Revolt against Dualism*, New York: W. W. Norton.
(1936) *The Great Chain of Being*, Cambridge, Mass.: Harvard University Press.
(1948) *Essays in the History of Ideas*, Baltimore: Johns Hopkins Press.
(1961) *Reflections on Human Nature*, Baltimore: Johns Hopkins Press.
(1961) *The Reason, the Understanding and Time*, Baltimore: Johns Hopkins Press.
(1963) *The Thirteen Pragmatisms*, Baltimore: Johns Hopkins Press.

For many years Lovejoy concentrated on the theory of knowledge which was being actively developed in a realist direction, and in opposition to the previously dominant idealism and pragmatism, from the publication of a realistic manifesto in 1910 by W. P. **Montague**, R. B. **Perry** and others. Lovejoy was one of a group of 'critical realists' who dissented from the excessive naivety, as they saw it, of the first wave of American realists. In his substantial *Revolt against Dualism* (1930) he deployed his impressive critical powers against all those contemporaries, above all **Russell** and **Whitehead**, who had too much identified the content of perceptual experience with its public object. He argued for dualism of two kinds: epistemological, between content sensed and the physical object that caused it, and psychophysical, between the mind and the physical world. His negative criticisms were much more powerful than his positive defences of the representative theory against the traditional objection that it made the supposed public objects of perception entirely inaccessible, indeed unintelligible. Perhaps aware of the very large disparity between his critical and his constructive abilities he turned to intellectual

history, inventing the specific form of it known as the history of ideas. It differs from traditional intellectual history in following the history of particular ideas, and in seeking them not in major works of theory but in a large mass of lesser writings. He founded and was the first editor of the *Journal of the History of Ideas*, which still flourishes, and himself wrote a masterly account of the idea of the great chain of being and also memorably on romanticism and primitivism. He was an ardent supporter of academic freedom and helped found the American Association of University Professors to defend it. Although he was born in Germany to a German mother, he was violently hostile to the German side in the First World War. Lovejoy's theory of knowledge was respectfully received but has been without influence, having failed to provide representationism with any new intellectual support. The history of ideas movement he began remains vigorous, although it has not altogether confined itself within the limits he laid down.

Sources: Passmore 1957; Edwards; Hill.

ANTHONY QUINTON

Löwith, Karl

German. **b:** 9 January 1897, Munich. **d:** 25 May 1973, Heidelberg, Germany. **Cat:** Associated with phenomenology and existentialism. **Ints:** Philosophy of history; politics; society and culture. **Educ:** Universities of Munich (1919), Freiburg, under Husserl (1920–3), and, in collaboration with Heidegger, Marburg (1924–8). **Infls:** Literary influences: Hegel, Feuerbach, Marx, Kierkegaard and Nietzsche. Personal influences: Husserl and Heidegger. **Appts:** Emigrated in 1934, becoming Rockefeller Fellow in Rome (1934–6); then Professor of Philosophy, Imperial University of Tohoku (1936–41), Hartford Theological Seminary (1941–9), New School for Social Research, New York (1949–52), University of Heidelberg (1952–64).

Main publications:

(1928) *Das Individuum in der Rolle des Mitmenschen*, Munich: Drei Masken Verlag.
(1932) 'Max Weber und Karl Marx', *Archiv für Sozialwissenschaft und Sozialpolitik* 67: 53–99, 175-214 (English translation, *Max Weber and Karl Marx*, trans. H. Fantel, T. Bottomore and W. Outhwaite, London: Allen & Unwin, 1982).
(1933) *Kierkegaard und Nietzsche*, Frankfurt am Main: V. Klostermann.
(1935) *Nietzsches Philosophie des ewigen Wiederkehr*, Berlin: Verlag die Runde.

(1941) *Von Hegel zu Nietzsche*, Zurich and Stuttgart: Europa Verlag (English translation, *From Hegel to Nietzsche*, trans. D. E. Green, London: Constable, 1965).

(1949) *Meaning in History: The Theological Implications of the Philosophy of History*, Chicago: University of Chicago Press.

(1953) *Martin Heidegger. Denker in dürftiger Zeit*, Frankfurt am Main: S. Fischer.

(1966) *Nature, History and Existentialism*, Evanston: Northwestern University Press.

(1969) *Permanence and Change: Lectures on the Philosophy of History*, Cape Town: Haum.

Secondary literature:

Brown, H. and Riedel, M. (eds) (1967) *Natur und Geschichte. Karl Löwith zum 70. Geburtstag*, Stuttgart, Berlin, Cologne and Mainz: Kohlhammer.

Habermas, J. (1963) 'Karl Löwiths stoischer Rückzug vom historischen Bewusstsein', *Merkur* 17.

Riesterer, B. P. (1969) *Karl Löwith's View of History: A Critical Appraisal of Historicism*, The Hague: Martinus Nijhoff.

Löwith's philosophy consists, in large part, of a sustained critique of Hegelian thought. His early writings, composed under the influence of and in reaction to **Heidegger**'s existential analysis, contain a view of man's existence in the world according to which man is essentially 'fellow man' (*Mitmensch*), defined by his social roles and the familiar forms of everyday existence; and the world itself is essentially, not the environmental world (*Umwelt*), but the shared human world (*Mitwelt*) constituted by the fundamental I–Thou structure.

Löwith's later thought contains a critique of historicism: modern historicism, such as that of Hegel and Marx, maintains what is, in effect, a Christian view of history as a process of salvation (*Heilsgeschehen*) but, in its secularized form, without the validating theological-metaphysical foundations. Löwith's later thought also contains an attempt to return to the pre-Christian, Greek conception of nature, and employs **Nietzsche**'s concept of the eternal recurrence to do so.

Sources: EF; NDB.

DAVID WALFORD

Lu Xun (Lu Hsun) (pen-name of Zhu Shuren)

Chinese. *b:* 1881, Shaoxing, Zhejiang Province, China. *d:* 1936, Shanghai. *Cat:* Writer and critic. *Ints:* Literature; aesthetics; social thought. *Educ:* The School of Railways and Mines, Nanjing, and Sendai Provincial Medical School, Japan. *Infls:* The Chinese classics; Chinese, Russian and other European literature; Western and Japanese aesthetics; Charles Darwin, T. E. Huxley, Nietzsche and Marxist writings. *Appts:* Posts at the Ministry of Education; 1920–6, Beijing National University and Beijing Normal University; 1926, Amoy University, Xiamen; 1927, Zhongshan University, Guangzhou.

Main publications:

(1938) *Complete Works of Lu Xun*, 20 vols, Lu Xun Quanji Publishing House.

(1951) *Diaries of Lu Xun*, Shanghai: Shanghai Publishing Company.

(1952) *Letters of Lu Xun*, 2 vols.

(1956–60) *Selected Works of Lu Xun*, 4 vols (English translation, Beijing: Foreign Languages Press).

(1959) *Brief History of Chinese Fiction* (English translation, Beijing: Foreign Languages Press).

Secondary literature:

Boorman, H. (ed.) (1970) *Biographical Dictionary of Republican China*, New York and London: Columbia University Press.

Complete Chinese Encyclopedia (1987), Philosophy Volumes, Beijing: Chinese Encyclopedia Publications.

Hsia, C. T. (1961) *A History of Modern Chinese Fiction 1917–1957*, New Haven: Yale University Press.

Zhu Shuren, who wrote as Lu Xun, was the most significant literary figure of twentieth-century China. His stylistically brilliant stories and essayswere calculated to arouse China from the apathy, self-deception and inhumanity of a corrupt and exhausted tradition and to promote the development of a free, rational and mature society. His hope for a spiritual transformation was based on his reading of philosophy as well as history and literature. With 'Diary of a madman' (1918), in the journal *New Youth*, he inaugurated Western fiction in China. From the time of the May Fourth Movement his individualism and renunciation of the past gave modernizing focus to the political and literary movements of the time. His stories condensed the ills of China into haunting images. His genius for biting humour, undeceived vision, sceptical distance, passionate anger and terse exposition provided a complex literary texture to express his moral and social sensibility.

When he turned from stories to concentrate his main literary efforts on essays after 1926, the same gifts of style, sensibility and moral courage made him China's leading commentator on contemporary affairs. His early outrage at the effects of Chinese family, language, morality, superstition and self-deceiving smugness was turned against the brutality, censorship and denial of individual rights under Guomindang rule. He was stunned by the violent Guomindang purge of Communists in 1927, and by 1929 he came to see the Communists as the only hope for Chinese renewal. Although he read Marxist writings with great intensity and aligned himself with the Party, he never became a Party member. He remained individual and undisciplined, looking for a transformation of values at the heart of renewal, arguing for individual rights and free expression. He pursued the uneasy task of retaining Nietzschean individualism within Marxist social analysis. His aesthetics rejected propaganda and slogans as art, along with art divorced from a social function. Art was directly perceived as beautiful, while conveying truth. Lu Xun's ability to explore a sick society, to capture it in powerful symbols, to write with searing honesty, gave him great moral prestige with generations of intellectuals, including philosophers. More systematic thinkers have benefited from his moral intelligence, his integrity and his social vision. Liberal critics valued these characteristics from the beginning. Communist critics were hostile and dimissive until he became an ally; after his death they praised him as a hero.

Lu Xun was also a poet, a major historian of Chinese literature, a retriever of ancient tales, a collector of stone rubbings, and a collector and promoter of woodblock printing and other popular art.

NICHOLAS BUNNIN

Luce, A(rthur) A(ston)

British. *b:* 21 August 1882, Gloucestershire. *d:* 28 June 1977, Dublin. *Cat:* Historian of philosophy; Berkeleyan philosopher. *Ints:* Berkeley; metaphysics. *Educ:* Trinity College, Dublin. *Infls:* Bergson and Berkeley. *Appts:* 1912–51, Fellow, 1942, Senior Fellow, 1946–51, Vice-Provost, 1934–49, Professor of Moral Philosophy, 1953–77, Berkeley Professor of Metaphysics, Trinity College, Dublin.

Main publications:

(1922) *Bergson's Doctrine of Intuition*, London: SPCK.

(1934) *Berkeley and Malebranche: A Study in the Origins of Berkeley's Thought*, London: Oxford University Press; reprinted, New York: Garland, 1988.

(1944) *Berkeley's Philosophical Commentaries: An editio diplomatica transcribed and edited with an introduction and notes ...*, London: Nelson.

(1945) *Berkeley's Immaterialism: A Commentary on his 'A Treatise Concerning the Principles of Human Knowledge'*, London: Nelson.

(1948–57) (ed. with T. E. Jessop) *The Works of George Berkeley, Bishop of Cloyne*, 9 vols, Edinburgh: Nelson.

(1949) *The Life of George Berkeley, Bishop of Cloyne*, London: Nelson; reprinted, London: Routledge, 1992.

(1954) *Sense without Matter; or, Direct perception*, Edinburgh: Nelson; reprinted, Westport, Conn.: Greenwood, 1973.

(1963) *The Dialectic of Immaterialism: An Account of the Making of Berkeley's Principles*, London: Hodder & Stoughton.

Secondary literature:

Berman, D. (1977) 'A bibliography of the published writings of Dr A. A. Luce', *Hermathena* 123: 11–18.

McCracken, C. J. (1983) *Malebranche and British Philosophy*, Oxford: Clarendon Press, pp. 208ff.

As well as being a philosopher and a scholar, Luce was an Anglican clergyman who became a Canon (1936) and later Precentor (1953) of St Patrick's Cathedral in Dublin. Rejecting the idealist tradition from Kant to **Bradley**, he wrote on philosophers with whose views he had an affinity. In his book on **Bergson**, for instance, he wrote: 'The Bergsonian theory... supports idealism in making mind the predominant partner in our psychophysical being. It is realist too. For according to it real persons really perceive a real world' (1922, p. 97). These were virtues also, as he saw it, in Berkeley's philosophy, a modernized version of which he defended in his *Sense without Matter* 1954. Although a contributor to contemporary philosophical debates, Luce's main influence has been as a scholar. Co-editor of the standard edition of Berkeley and author of the standard biography, Luce is noted for his contributions to understanding the early development of Berkeley's philosophy. He drew attention to the importance of the *Philosophical Commentaries* for understanding Berkeley's thought. This new research led him to propose, contrary to prevailing assumptions, that Berkeley was not exclusively to be seen as the successor of Descartes and Locke but as much indebted to Malebranche—a view now generally accepted.

Sources: Correspondence (with J. V. Luce); J. V. Luce (1988) 'The Luce perspective on Berkeley: An outline of the intellectual development of Dr A. A. Luce', *BS* 1; WW.

STUART BROWN

Lukács, Gyorgy

Hungarian. *b:* 13 April 1885, Budapest. *d:* 1971, Budapest. *Cat:* Marxist; aesthetician; metaphysician; political philosopher; literary theorist. *Ints:* Hegel. *Educ:* Universities of Berlin and Heidelberg, and the Marx–Engels Institute in Moscow. *Infls:* Marx, Hegel, Kant, Dilthey, Weber, Rosa Luxemburg, Georges Sorel and Georg Simmel. *Appts:* Professor of Aesthetics and Cultural Philosophy, University of Budapest.

Main publications:

(1911) *Die Seele und die Formen*, Berlin: Fleischel (English translation, *Soul and Form*, trans. Anna Bostock, London: Merlin Press, 1974).

(1920) *Die Theorie des Romans*, Berlin: Paul Cassirer (English translation, *The Theory of the Novel*, trans. Anna Bostock, London: Merlin Press, 1971).

(1923) *Geschichte und Klassenbewusstsein*, Berlin: Malik Verlag (English translation, *History and Class Consciousness*, trans. Rodney Livingstone, London: Merlin Press, 1971).

(1924) *Lenin: Studie über den Zusammenhang seiner Gedanken*, Vienna: Verlag der Arbeiterbuchhandlung (English translation, *Lenin: A Study on the Unity of his Thought*, trans. Nicholas Jacobs, London: NLB, 1970).

(1947) *A történelmi regény*, Budapest: Hungaria (English translation, *The Historical Novel*, trans. Hannah and Stanley Mitchell, Harmondsworth: Penguin, 1969).

(1947) *Goethe und seine Zeit*, Berne: Francke (English translation, *Goethe and his Age*, trans. Robert Anchor, London: Merlin Press, 1968).

(1947) *A polgár nyomában: a hetvenéves Thomas Mann*, Budapest: Hungaria (English translation, *Essays on Thomas Mann*, trans. Stanley Mitchell, London: Merlin Press, 1964).

(1948) *Der Junge Hegel*, Zurich and Vienna: Europa Verlag (English translation, *The Young Hegel*, trans. Rodney Livingstone, London: Merlin Press, 1975).

(1950) *Studies in European Realism*, trans. Edith Bone, London: Hillway.

(1958) *Wider den missverstanden Realismus*, Hamburg: Claasen (English translation, *The Meaning of Contemporary Realism*, trans. John and Necke Mander, London: Merlin Press, 1963).

(1963) *Die Eigenart des Aesthetischen*, Neuwied: Luchterhand.

(1976) *Zur ontologie des gesellschaftlichen seins*, Budapest: Magveto Kiado (English translation, *The Ontology of Social Being*, trans. David Fernbach, London: Merlin Press, 1978).

Secondary literature:

Arato, Andrew and Breines, Paul (1978) *The Young Lukács and the Origins of Western Marxism*, London: Seabury Press and New York: Pluto Press.

Gluck, Mary (1985) *George Lukács and his Generation, 1900–1918*, Cambridge: Mass.: Harvard University Press.

Heller, Agnes (ed.) (1983) *Lukács Reappraised*, New York: Columbia University Press.

Joos, Ernest (ed.) (1987) *George Lukács and his World: A Reassessment*, New York: Peter Lang.

Lichtheim, George (1970) *Lukács*, Collins.

Marcus, Judith and Tarr, Zoltan (eds) (1989) *George Lukács: Theory, Culture, and Politics*, New Brunswick, NJ: Transaction.

Zitta, Victor (1964) *George Lukács' Marxism: Alienation, Dialectics, Revolution. A Study in Utopia and Ideology*, The Hague: Martinus Nijhoff.

Lukács is generally regarded as one of the first theorists of note in what has come to be called 'Western' Marxism, a writer who made valuable contributions to several areas of Marxist theory, most notably perhaps in aesthetics. He is identified with a Hegelian approach to Marxism which was at odds with Communist Party orthodoxy for most of his lifetime. His earliest writings on aesthetics were tinged with the neo-Kantianism so fashionable in pre-First World War Central European intellectual circles, and he described himself as a 'subjective idealist' at this point in his career. From *The Theory of the Novel* (1920) onwards, however, the influence of Hegel begins to dominate. Lukács's mature intellectual development is very much tied up with the political fortunes of Marxism, and at various times he was an activist on behalf of the Communist Party in Hungary and Germany as well as holding Hungarian government posts during the Soviet Republic of 1919 and the uprising of 1956. During the 1930s and 1940s Lukács spent much of his time in Moscow, working at the Marx–Engels Institute and the Philosophical Institute of the Moscow Academy of Sciences, as well as editing various literary periodicals. On his return to Hungary after the Second World War he took up a Chair at the University of Budapest, although he was later expelled from the Communist Party for his part in the 1956 uprising and even exiled for a while. Lukács's most contentious work of Marxist theory is *History and Class Consciousness* (1923), whose Hegelian idealist bias, lukewarm commitment to materialism and generally anti-positivist sentiments scandalized the Russian Communist Party leadership in the 1920s. Lukács was later to reject the idealist dimension of this work, although Hegel remained a lifelong source of inspiration. It is Lukács's aesthetic writings that have probably done the most to build his reputation, particularly his works of literary criticism and literary theory. *Studies in European Realism* (1946), *The Historical Novel* (1937) and *The Meaning of Contemporary Realism* (1957) have all been highly influential studies, and represent some of the most successful defences of realism in the Marxist canon. A supporter of the official Soviet aesthetic doctrine of socialist realism, Lukács nevertheless could be severely critical of its simplistic tendencies and he developed a variant form known as 'critical realism', which judged novels less in terms of their political correctness than on their ability to make plain the socio-political forces that shaped human character in any given historical period. This led to the controversial rejection on ideological grounds of the modernist tradition in literature (Kafka and Joyce, for example) in favour of approved 'critical realists' like Thomas Mann. In late career Lukács explored the history of aesthetic theory in *The Specificity of the Aesthetic* (1963), a heavily Hegelian work centrally concerned with the issues of reflection and representation, and, finally, the ontological theories of Marx and Hegel (published posthumously in 1976. Lukács has been a highly influential figure in the Western Marxist tradition, although his dogmatic commitment to realism and dislike of modernist experimentation have drawn criticism from various quarters—most notably perhaps from the playwright Bertolt Brecht, who clashed with Lukács over the form a Marxist aesthetic should take. The impact of Lukács' brand of Hegelianized Marxism can be seen in the work of Walter **Benjamin**, the Frankfurt School, the French-Romanian theorist Lucien **Goldmann** and the American critic Frederic Jameson.

STUART SIM

Łukasiewicz, Jan

Polish. *b:* 21 January 1878, Lvov (Lemberg). *d:* 13 February 1956, Dublin. *Cat:* Logician; historian of logic. *Ints:* Logic of propositions and ancient Greek logic. *Educ:* Mathematics and Philosophy, University of Lvov. *Infls:* Puzyna and Twardowski. *Appts:* 1906–11, Lecturer (Privatdozent) in Philosophy, Lvov, 1911, received title of 'Extraordinary' Professor from Emperor Francis Joseph I; 1915–39, Professor of Philosophy, Warsaw; 1918–19, Head of Department of Higher Schools in the Polish Ministry of Education; 1922–3 and 1931–2, Rector, University of Warsaw; 1939–44, home destroyed, lived 'in wretched conditions', lectured in Polish Underground University; 1944–5, left Warsaw in face of Russian advance, eventually becoming attached to the Polish Scientific Institute in Brussels; 1946–56, Professor of Mathematical Logic, Royal Irish Academy.

Main publications:

(1906) 'Analiza i konstruckcja pojecia przyczyny' [Analysis and Construction of the Concept of Cause], *Przeglad Filozoficzny* 6: 105–79.
(1910) *O zasadzie sprzecznosci u Arystotelesa. Studyum krytyczne* [On the Principle of Contradiction in Aristotle: A Critical Study], Cracow.
(1913) *Die logischen Grundlagen der Warhrscheinlichkeitsrechnung*, Cracow.
(1920) 'O logice trójwartosœciowej' [On three-valued logic], *Ruch Filozoficzny* 5: 169–71; reprinted in S. McCall (ed.), *Polish Logic 1920–1939*, Oxford: Oxford University Press, 1967.
(1927) 'O logice Stoików' [On the logic of the Stoics'], *Przeglad Filozoficzny* 30: 278-9.
(1929) *Elementy logiki matematycznej*, Warsaw (English translation, *Elements of Mathematical Logic*, trans. O. Wojtasiewicz, Oxford: Oxford University Press, 1963).
(1934) 'Z historji logiki zdán' [From the history of the logic of propositions], *Przeglad Filozoficzny* 37: 417–37.
(1951) *Aristotle's Syllogistic from the Standpoint of Modern Formal Logic*, Oxford: Oxford University Press; second edition, 1957.
(1953) 'A system of modal logic', *The Journal of Computing Systems* 1: 111–49.
(1970) *Selected Works*, ed. L. Borkowski, Amsterdam and London: North Holland (includes bibliography).

Secondary literature:

Borkoski, L. and Slupecki, J. (1958) 'The logical works of J. Łukasiewicz', *Studia Logica* 8: 7–56.
Kotarbinski, T. (1958) 'Jan Łukasiewicz's works on the history of logic', *Studia Logica* 8: 57–62.
Prior, A. N. (1958) 'Łukasiewicz's contributions to logic', in R. Klibansky (ed.), *Philosophy in the Midcentury*, Florence: 'La Nuova Italia' Editrice.
Wójcicki, R. (ed.) (1977) *Selected Papers on Łukasiewicz Sentential Calculi*, Warsaw: Polskiej Aka-

demii Nauk (contains a bibliography of Łukasiewicz logics).

Łukasiewicz had an early interest in the concept of causation and, together with his teacher **Twardowski**, translated Hume's first *Inquiry* into Polish. He was also interested in scientific methodology, but he had been introduced to mathematical logic through Puzyna's lectures and this became his main focus and where he made his mark as one of the founders of the Warsaw school of logic, whose symbolic notation, accepted as one of the standard notations, derives from him. His main contributions were to the logic of propositions and to the history of ancient logic. In 1917 he constructed the first system of three-valued propositional calculus (including 'probable' as a value as well as 'true' and 'false'), in which he rejected the principle of bivalence ('Every proposition is either true or false'). Although the philosophical import of this development is controversial, he challenged the assumption that there are 'laws of thought'. Łukasiewicz intended that his new system would provide room for modal logic, an area to which he gave a good deal of attention in his later years.

In the history of logic he wrote a highly influential work in which he sought to interpret Aristotle's various statements of the principle of contradiction. He came to the view that Aristotle's syllogistic had been presented in the wrong way, and sought to argue that the syllogisms are not schemata of valid inferences, as textbooks assumed. He also revived interest in the logic of the Stoics, showing that their debates with the Aristotelians had been entirely misunderstood. Though he was not the first to make the claim, he established the importance of the Stoics in the history of logic as the discoverers of propositional logic.

Sources: Z. A. Jordan (1945) *The Development of Mathematical Logic and of Logical Positivism in Poland Between the Two Wars*, Oxford: OUP; Edwards; Mittelstrass; B. Sobocinski (1956) 'In Memorian Jan Łukasiewicz', *PSt* (Ireland) 6: 3–49 (with bibliography and an account of his life by Łukasiewicz).

STUART BROWN

Lunacharsky, Anatolii Vasil'evich

Russian. *b:* 11 November (23 N.S.) 1875, Poltava. *d:* 26 December 1933, Menton, France. *Cat:* Marxist. *Educ:* Studied Philosophy and Natural Science at the University of Zurich. *Infls:* Marx, Engels, Avenarius, Bogdanov and Dewey.

Main publications:

(1908–11) *Religiia i sotsializm* [Religion and Socialism], 2 vols, St Petersburg.
(1965) *On Literature and Art*, trans. Avril Pyman and Fainna Glagoleva, Moscow: Progress Publishers (selections of shorter works).
(1981) *On Education: Selected Articles and Speeches*, trans. Ruth English, Moscow: Progress Publishers (selections of shorter works).

Secondary literature:

O'Connor, T. E. (1983) *The Politics of Soviet Culture: Anatolii Lunacharskii*, Ann Arbor: UMI Research Press.

Lunacharsky became a Marxist while a gymnasium student in Kiev. He was forced to continue his education abroad, and fell under the influence of Avenarius at Zurich. Returning to Russia in 1898, he was imprisoned and eventually exiled to Siberia. He was in Western Europe from 1904 until 1917, except for a year in Russia following the 1905 Revolution, when he was again imprisoned. He sided with the Bolsheviks after the 1903 conference of the Russian Social-Democratic Labour Party, although he broke with **Lenin** over the philosophical basis of Marxism, as well as Party tactics in the wake of the 1905 Revolution. After the October Revolution, he was appointed Commissar for Enlightenment (1917–29). He actively pursued his interests in poetry, drama, aesthetics and literary criticism, and did much to reconcile the old intelligentsia to the new regime. He ultimately resigned for want of support for his educational policies; he died *en route* to take up the post of Soviet Ambassador to Spain.

Lunacharsky's early blending of empiriocriticism with Marxism was reinforced by **Bogdanov**, whom he befriended during his internal exile and whose sister he married. Lunacharsky went further than Bogdanov in his revisionism during the prerevolutionary years: his notion of 'God-building' (*bogostroitel'stvo*) portrayed socialism as a new secular religion, and saw in the development of a proletarian culture the prospect of collective immortality. Although he later renounced these views, his optimism about the perfectibility of human beings persisted in his educational theories, which were also influenced by John **Dewey**'s progressivist philosophy of education. He favoured a broad 'polytechnical' education, and insisted that such an education was necessary for the reconstruction of the social order culminating in the emergence of the new Soviet citizen.

COLIN CHANT

Lutoslawski, Wincenty

Polish. *b:* 1863, Warsaw. *d:* 1954, Cracow. *Cat:* Idealist. *Ints:* Metaphysics; politics. *Infls:* Plato, Leibniz, Gustave Teichmüller and Polish messianism. *Appts:* Taught in Italy, France, England, Switzerland and the USA before being appointed Professor in the University of Vilna (1919).

Main publications:

In languages other than Polish:
(1897) *The Origin and Growth of Plato's Logic.*
(1898) *Über die Grundvoraussetzung und die Konsequenz der individualistischen Weltanschauung.*
(1899) *Seelenmacht. Abriss einer zeitgemässen Weltanschauung.*
(1907) *Between East and West.*
(1909) *Unsterblichkeit der Seele*; and later editions.
(1910) *Der wiedergeborene Mensch.*
(1917) *L'État national.*
(1919) *La Conscience nationale.*
(1924) *The World of Souls.*
(1926) *Das Geheimnis des allgemeinen Wohlstandes.*
(1930) *The Knowledge of Reality.*
In Polish:
(1900) *Z dziedziny nysli* [The Supremacy of Thought].
(1903) *Eleusis.*
(1905) *Logika.*
(1910) *Ludzkosc Odrodzona* [Regenerated Mankind].
(1922) *Praca narodowa* [The Task of the Nation].
(1925) *Niesmiertelnosc duszy in wolnosc woli* [The Immortality of the Soul and the Freedom of the Will], third edition,.
(1926) *Tajemnica powszechnego dobrobytu, zarys teorji gospodarstwa narodowego* [The Mystery of General Well-being and Sketch for a Theory of National Economy].

Secondary literature:

(1898) Review of 1897 in *Mind* 7, 26, April: 271ff.
(1925) Review of 1924 in *International Journal of Ethics* 35, Jan: 208ff.

Lutoslawski first became known in Western Europe as a scholar of Plato. In his book of 1897 he sets out a view of the development of Plato's logic based on a careful ordering of the dialogues, the ordering itself being derived from stylometric work. The thought of Plato then becomes one of the chief influences on the formation of Lutoslawski's own philosophy, a pluralistic idealism including the doctrine of metempsychosis and culminating in the politics of messianic nationalism.

Lutoslawski distinguishes four types of worldview which in his view form a progression: materialism, idealism, pantheism and spiritualism. Beyond these, he argues, lies the highest form of moral development, which is messianism. The messianist is characterized by active love, and, since the most intimate groups of souls are what we call nations, the active love of the messianist takes the form of national consciousness. Lutoslawski's thought is optimistic, and he argues that ultimately the combined effects of human messianism and divine inspiration will free us from the effects of the Fall and, as with Plato, his work includes a vision of the utopia to come: small states will disappear; so too will big cities, rendered unnecessary by improvements in communication. Many of the offices of the state (e.g. those concerned with war and taxation) will naturally wither. Life will generally be a well-organized country life, with a notable increase in leisure time, which can be devoted to contact with the thought of others.

ROBERT WILKINSON

Luxemburg (née Luksenburg), Rosa

Polish-German. *b:* 5 March 1870, Zamosc, Poland (Russian Poland). *d:* 15 January 1919, Berlin (murdered when arrested). *Cat:* Political activist and theorist writing on Marxist social and political philosophy and philosophy of economics. *Ints:* Reform of Marxist thought. *Educ:* Zurich University, Switzerland (1890, enrolled in the Faculty of Philosophy, followed courses in natural sciences and mathematics; 1892, changed to the Faculty of Law); 1894, researched at the major Polish library in Paris; 1897, PhD, 'The development of industry in Poland'. *Appts:* Journalist: first articles on socialist issues and events published 1892; last article 1919; almost 700 articles, pamphlets, speeches, books; Cofounder of the SDKP (Social Democracy of the Kingdom of Poland), 1892–3; Coleader with Karl Liebknecht and Clara Zetkin of the International Group (Spartacists), a faction within the SPD (Social Democratic Party of Germany), 1915–17; remained within USPD (Independent Social Democratic Party of Germany) following the party split in 1917, separated as the Spartacus League in 1918; Cofounder with Karl Liebknecht of the KPD(S) (Communist Party of Germany (Spartacists)), 1919; drafted SDKPL (Social Democracy of the Kingdom of Poland and Lithuania) party programme *What Do We Want?*, 1904; drafted Spartacists programme *Leitsätze* [Guiding Principles], 1916 (used later for the Third International); helped agenda demand for women's franchise at Stuttgart Congress of

Socialist International, 1907; promoted anti-war declaration by Basel Congress of Socialist International, 1912, and denounced militarism, 1912–4. Editor of *The Workers' Cause* (*Sprawa Robotnicza*), 1894, of *Social Democratic Review* (*Przeglad Socjaldemokratyczny*) and *Red Flag* (*Czerwony Sztandar*), 1903; Associate Editor of *Vorwärts* [Forward], 1905; editor of *Die rote Fahne* [*The Red Flag*], 1918. Taught Marxian economics at the SPD Party School in Berlin, 1907–13. Periodically arrested and imprisoned for her political opinions and activities.

Main publications:

(1899) *Social Reform or Revolution. With Appendix: Militia and Militarism*, Leipzig (based on a series of articles published in 1898, 'Socialreform oder Revolution' and 'Mit einem Anhang: Miliz und Militarismus'); revised and supplemented second edition, 1908. (Criticisms of Eduard Bernstein's reformist gradualism which began the revisionist debate; promotes anti-militarism.)

(1904) 'Organisationsfragen der russischen Sozialdemokraten', *Neue Zeit* 2: 484–92, 529–35; also *Iskra*, 10 July 1904 (Russian dating), 69: 2–7 (famous polemic with Lenin; criticisms of his vanguard centralism).

(1906) *Z doby rewolucyjnej. Co dalej?* [In the revolutionary hour: what next?], Warsaw.

(1906) *Massenstreik, Partei und Gewerkschaften*, Hamburg (perhaps her most important statement on the tactical question: the dialectical role of the general strike for developing class consciousness and accelerating socialist transformation in historical change).

(1908) 'Kwestia narodowosciowa i autonomia' [The national question and autonomy] *Przeglad Socjaldemokrtyczny* 6, August, reprinted in Roza Luksemburg, *Wybor Pism*, Warsaw vol. II, pp. 114–66, Warsaw (English translation in *The National Question: Selected Writings*, ed. H. B. Davis, New York: Monthly Review Press, 1976) (renounces nationalism as regressive and promotes multinational socialism, a common theme in her writing).

(1912) 'Women's suffrage and class struggle', speech at the Second Social Democratic Women's Rally, Stuttgart, 12 May; text in *Ausgewahlte und Schriften*, vol. II, Dietz Verlag, 1951, pp. 433–41 (English translation in *Selected Political Writings*, 1971) (subordinates gender struggle to class struggle, but agrees with Charles Fourier that socialist emancipation is incomplete without women's emancipation).

(1913) *Die Akkumulation des Kapitals. Ein Beitrag zur ökonomischen Erklarung des Imperialismus*, Berlin (English translation, *The Accumulation of Capital*, trans. Agnes Schwarzschild, intro. Joan Robinson, London: Routledge & Kegan Paul, London, 1951, reprinted 1971) (a major contribution to Marxist economics analysing the inherent contradiction of capitalism which leads to its collapse and the indispensable role of proletarian struggle for the creation of socialism; a Marxist criticism of Marx).

(1916) (under pseudonym 'Junius') 'Die Krise der Sozialdemokratie', Zurich; known as *The Junius Pamphlet* (analyses the collapse of the Second International with the outbreak of the First World War in 1914; argues that the choice of Socialism or Barbarism is a world-historical choice which demands resolute action by the proletariat; an Appendix sets out guidelines for the reconstruction of the International, adopted by the Spartacus League, used later by the Third International).

(1918) 'Was will der Spartakusbund?', *Die rote Fahne* 29, 14 December.

(1921) *Die Akkumulation des Kapitals oder was die Epigonen aus der Marxschen Theorie gemacht haben. Eine Antikritik*, Leipzig (English translation, 'The accumulation of capital—anti-critique', in *Imperialism*, 1972).

(1922) *Die russische Revolution. Eine kritische Wurdigung*, ed. with intro. by Paul Levi, from Luxemburg's papers, Berlin (attacks the abrogation of political freedoms in Bolshevik Russia while applauding their historical accomplishment of seizing power).

(1925) *Einfuhrung in die Nationalokonomie*, ed. Paul Levi, Berlin (chapter 1 reprinted as *What is Economics?*, trans. T. Edwards, New York: Pioneer, 1954, reprinted by S. Wanasinghe, Ceylon: Colombo, 1968) (based on her lectures for SPD Party School in Berlin, 1907–13; argues national economies are illusory and reveals the world economy).

Collected editions:

(1960) *Collected Economic Papers*, Oxford: Blackwell.

(1961) *The Russian Revolution and Leninism or Marxism?*, ed. B. D. Wolfe, Ann Arbor: University of Michigan Press; reprinted 1970.

(1970) *Rosa Luxemburg Speaks*, ed. Mary-Alice Waters, New York: Pathfinder.

(1971) *Selected Political Writings of Rosa Luxemburg*, ed. Dick Howard, New York and London: Monthly Review Press.

(1972) *Selected Political Writings*, ed. Robert Looker, London: Jonathan Cape.

(1972) (with N. Bukharin) *Imperialism and the Accumulation of Capital*, London: K. Tarbuck.

Secondary literature:

Abraham, R. (1989) *Rosa Luxemburg: A Life for the International*, Oxford and New York: Berg (useful bibliography and chronology at end).

Basso, L. (1975) *Rosa Luxemburg: A Reappraisal*, London: Deutsch.

Bonner, S. E. (ed.) (1979) *The Letters of Rosa Luxemburg*, Boulder, Col.: Westview.

——(1981) *A Revolutionary for Our Times: Rosa Luxemburg*, London: Pluto.

Dunayevskaya, R. (1981) *Rosa Luxemburg, Women's Liberation and Marx's Philosophy of Revolution*, Atlantic Highlands, NJ: Humanities; Brighton: Harvester.

Ettinger, Elizbeta (1987) *Rosa Luxemburg. A Life*, London: Harrap.

Frölich, Paul (1904) *Rosa Luxemburg: Ideas in Action*, London: Left Book Club, reprinted and annotated, London: Pluto Press, 1972 (the standard Marxist-Leninist biography).

Geras, N. (1976) *The Legacy of Rosa Luxemburg*, London: New Left Books (philosophical and scholarly appraisal of her key theories; useful bibliography at end).

Lenin, V. I. (1966) 'Notes of a publicist', *Collected Works*, vol. 33, Moscow and London: Progress/ Lawrence; Wishart, pp. 204–11.

Lukács, G. (1968) 'The Marxism of Rosa Luxemburg', in *History and Class Consciousness*, London: Merlin.

Nettl, J. P. (1966) *Rosa Luxemburg*, 2 vols, Oxford: Oxford University Press (comprehensive bibliography of her works at the end of vol. 2: 699 entries plus collections of her works).

Stalin, J. (1933) 'Some questions regarding the history of Bolshevism' (Letter to the editors of *Proletarskaia Revoliutsiia*), in *Stalin, Leninism*, vol. 2, London: Modern Books.

Trotsky, L. (1970) 'Hands off Rosa Luxemburg' and 'Rosa Luxemburg and the 4th International', in *Rosa Luxemburg Speaks*.

——*Martyrs of the Third International: Karl Liebknecht, Rosa Luxemburg*, London: Prinkipo.

——*Political Profiles*, London: New Park.

Rosa Luxemburg's thought was developed in the crucible of committed socialist political struggle spanning some three decades of the international workers' movement in Europe. Ever at the centre of debate, she fought for an understanding of praxis which never surrenders theory to activism nor sacrifices democracy to socialism. From her early criticisms (1899) of Eduard **Bernstein**'s reformist gradualism (*Evolutionary Socialism*), which crystallized the revisionist debate, Luxemburg always rejected the idea that the objectives of revolutionary socialism could be achieved by the partial, incremental reform of bourgeois capitalism. She developed an analysis (especially in *Massenstreik*, 1906) of the dialectical role of the general strike for developing class consciousness and accelerating socialist transformation in historical change and argued that the choice of 'Socialism or Barbarism', with the inevitable collapse of capitalism, is a world-historical choice which demands resolute action by the proletariat. Her criticisms (1904; *Massenstreik*, 1906; and 1922) of **Lenin**'s theory of revolutionary vanguard centralism and Bolshevik policies after the 1917 Russian Revolution articulated her insistence that there could be no real socialism without democracy as well as no real democracy without socialism. During the 1905 Russian Revolution she developed the idea of permanent revolution: that socialism is a process of transforming political and economic relations towards ever greater democratic control by the workers themselves. Luxemburg helped give birth to, and continues to symbolize, the emancipatory tradition in Marxism as a challenging alternative to the orthodox Marx–Lenin–Stalin lineage.

PATRICIA SCALTSAS

Lyotard, Jean-François

French. **b:** 1924. **Cat:** Postmodernist; political philosopher; philosopher of language; aesthetician; culture theorist. **Educ:** University of Paris; 1971, doctorate. **Infls:** Marx, Freud, Lacan, Nietzsche and Kant. **Appts:** 1972, Professor of Philosophy, University of Paris VIII (Vincennes), 1949–59, taught at Lycées and the University of California at Irvine; founding member of the International College of Philosophy, Paris. Held posts at various universities in the USA.

Main publications:

(1954) *La Phénoménologie*, Paris: Presses Universitaires de France, 1954 (English translation, *Phenomenology*, trans. Brian Beakley, Albany, NY: SUNY Press, 1991).

(1971) *Discours, figure*, Paris: Klinckseick.

(1974) *Économie libidinale*, Paris: Minuit (English translation, *Libidinal Economy*, trans. Iain Hamilton Grant, London: Athlone Press, 1993).

(1977) *Instructions païennes*, Paris: Galilée.

(1977) *Rudiments païens: genre dissertatif*, Paris: Union générale d'éditions.

(1979) (with Jean-Loup Thebaud) *Au Juste*, Paris: Christian Bourgeois (English translation, *Just Gaming*, trans. Wlad Godzich, Manchester: Manchester University Press, 1985).

(1979) *La Condition postmoderne*, Paris: Minuit (English translation, *The Postmodern Condition*, trans. Geoffrey Bennington and Brian Massumi, Manchester: Manchester University Press, 1984).

(1983) *Le Différend*, Paris: Minuit (English translation, *The Differend*, trans. George Van Den Abbeele, Manchester: Manchester University Press, 1988).

(1984) *Tombeau de l'intellectuel et autres papiers*, Paris: Galilée.

(1988) *Peregrinations*, New York: Columbia University Press (written in English by Lyotard).

(1988) *L'inhumain*, Paris: Galilée (English translation, *The Inhuman*, trans. Geoffrey Bennington and Rachel Bowlby, Cambridge: Polity, 1991).

Secondary literature:

Bennington, Geoffrey (1988) *Lyotard: Writing the Event*, Manchester: Manchester University Press.

Callinicos, Alex (1989) *Against Postmodernism: A Marxist Perspective*, Cambridge: Polity Press.

Dews, Peter (1987) *Logics of Disintegration: Poststructuralist Thought and the Claims of Critical Theory*, London and New York: Verso.

Readings, Bill (1991) *Art and Politics: Introducing Lyotard*, London: Routledge.

Sarup, Madan (1990) *An Introductory Guide to Poststructuralism and Postmodernism*, Hemel Hempstead: Harvester.

Sim, Stuart (1992) *Beyond Aesthetics: Confrontations with Poststructuralism and Postmodernism*, Hemel Hempstead: Harvester.

Postmodernism is a sceptically inclined form of philosophy which calls into question the certainties of other discourses, and Lyotard is one of the movement's leading theorists. Although best known for his writings on postmodernism he has published widely in various areas of philosophy such as philosophy of language, political philosophy and aesthetics. His early work is in the Marxist tradition; but in common with many left-wing French intellectuals he turned sharply against Marxism in the aftermath of the 1968 'évènements', and in his highly controversial study *Économie libidinale* (1974) he staked out a provocatively post-Marxist position which rejected the basic assumptions of Marxist methodology. This line of development culminated in *The Postmodern Condition* (1979), where the notion of universal theories was dismissed out of hand, the argument being that such 'grand narratives' (for example Marxism) had lost all credibility. Against grand narrative, with its authoritarian connotations, Lyotard championed the cause of 'little narrative', essentially the narrative of individual human beings, which needed no foundational justification (Lyotard is a committed antifoundationalist). Much of his post-1968 political thinking is structured around the idea of specific campaigns to correct abuses of individual freedoms. Lyotard has become increasingly concerned with the nature and rules of judgement in his later work, where his line of argument tends to be that judgement is essentially pragmatic and specific to a discourse. In Lyotard's view discourses are incommensurable, and between any two discourses lies an unresolvable area of dispute, or 'differend'. Kant is a constant point of reference in these later writings, where Lyotard consciously seems to be trying to return to a pre-Marxist and Hegelian framework of dialectical thought. The iconoclastic sentiments of *The Postmodern Condition* struck a chord in contemporary intellectual circles and have inspired a whole generation of cultural theorists. Reaction amongst more orthodox left-wing thinkers to Lyotard's postmodernist scepticism has been predictably hostile.

STUART SIM

M

Mac Leod, Andries Hugo Donald

Belgian-Swedish. *b:* 10 August 1891, Ledeberg, Belgium. *d:* 28 March 1977, Tierp, Sweden. *Cat:* Analytical philosopher; mathematician. *Ints:* Ontology; philosopy of mind. *Educ:* After studies in Mathematics and Physics, Dr sc. at Ghent 1914. Also studied Philosophy at Uppsala University. *Infls:* Husserl and Phalén. *Appts:* Taught Mathematics and Physics in Belgium; 1939–77, residing in Sweden, where he devoted all his time to philosophical writing; 1960, Fil. Dr. *honoris causa*, Uppsala University.

Main publications:

(1927) *Sur quelques questions se présentant dans l'étude du concept de réalité*, Paris: Librairie Scientifique J. Hermann.

(1947) 'What is a true assertion?', *Theoria*.

(1960) *Beskaffenhet och innehåll av ett medvetande* [The Nature and the Content of an Act of Consciousness], Uppsala: Appelbergs.

(1964) *De psykiska företeelsernas förhållande till rum och tid* [The Relation of Mental Phenomena to Space and Time] Stockholm: Filosofiska Inst., Stockholm University (Flemish translation, *Het bewustzijn in zijn verhouding tot ruimte en tijd*, Ghent: Studia Philosophica Gandensia, 2. Suppl., 1965).

(1972) *Verklighet och negation* [Reality and Negation], Uppsala: Almqvist & Wiksell (summary in French, *Theoria*, 1974: 125–37).

Secondary literature:

Theoria (1980) 5 (obituary and bibliography).

Andries Mac Leod started as a mathematician. His first book (in French, 1922) was a comprehensive survey of non-Euclidean geometry. His mathematical training is evident in all the philosophical works, in the rigorous shaping of proofs and definitions. His philosophical method is well illustrated by the paper 'What is a true assertion?' (1947). In most of his works he deals with abstract problems related to fundamental concepts of our thinking, for example reality, identity, negation, 'now', act of consciousness and intentionality.

Husserl's *Logische Untersuchungen* influenced Mac Leod, but he was even more influenced by **Phalén**, whom he deeply admired. *The Nature and Content of an Act of Consciousness* (1960) gives a subtle analysis of problems connected with Phalén's thesis (criticized by **Segelberg**) that an act of consciousness intending AB is not composed of an act intending A and an act intending B. There are interesting differences between Mac Leod and Phalén on certain important problems, for example concerning the relation of mental phenomena to time. Mac Leod developed a nominalist theory which has certain points in common with that of Nelson **Goodman**, although historically they are quite independent of each other.

THORILD DAHLQUIST

McCloskey, Henry John

Australian. *b:* 11 July 1925, Melbourne, Australia. *Cat:* Ethical institutionist; political liberal. *Ints:* Moral philosophy; political philosophy; environmental philosophy. *Educ:* University of Melbourne (BA 1948, MA 1949, PhD 1952, LittD 178). *Infls:* W. D. Ross, J. Passmore and J. L. Mackie. *Appts:* 1953–5, Lecturer in Philosophy, University of Western Australia, Nedlands; 1955–69, Lecturer, Senior Lecturer and Reader in Philosophy, University of Melbourne, Parkville; from 1969, Professor of Philosophy, La Trobe University, Bundoora.

Main publications:

(1963) 'Mill's liberalism', *Philosophical Quarterly* 13: 143–56.

(1965) 'A critique of the ideals of liberty', *Mind* 74: 483–508.

(1965) 'Rights', *Philosophical Quarterly* 15: 115–27.

(1969) *Meta-Ethics and Normative Ethics*, The Hague: Nijhoff.

(1971) *John Stuart Mill; A Critical Study*, London: Macmillan.

(1974) *God and Evil*, The Hague: Nijhoff.

(1983) *Ecological Ethics and Politics*, Littlefield: Totowa Rowman.

Secondary literature:
Martin, R. and Nickel, J. W. (1980) 'Recent work on the concept of rights', *American Philosophical Quarterly* 11.
Parent, W. A. (1974) 'Some recent work on the concept of liberty', *American Philosophical Quarterly* 17.

According to McCloskey the desire to defend ethical cognitivism, political liberalism and human moral rights has been the chief inspiration of his philosophical writings (*Contemporary Authors* p. 343).

In 1969 he provided what one reviewer describes as 'the most comprehensive statement of an Intuitionist view that I have seen'. In part the book is a continuation of the debates concerning such issues as the relationship between fundamental moral concepts, the analysis of moral conflict and the nature of intrinsic goodness which were a feature of early twentieth-century intuitionism. Even more significant, however, were his uncompromising criticisms of non-cognitivist views of the relationship between fact and value, the speech act account of meaning and the nature of moral reasoning; criticisms which came to be widely accepted amongst philosophers in later years. McCloskey defended the intuitionist commitment to synthetic a priori moral truths, to a plurality of basic moral principles and to the possibility of conflict amongst these basic principles. Accepting such views led him into sharp conflict with utilitarians and his attacks on that view foreshadowed many of the criticisms of Mill which subsequently appeared in 1971.

McCloskey's work on political liberalism and on human rights is clearly influenced by his moral theory. Distinctive interpretations are offered of prima facie rights such as the right to life, to privacy and to freedom of expression, all of them grounded in respect for human personhood and autonomy. The importance of his work in these fields was widely recognized. Major survey articles (1974 and 1980) were devoted to lengthy and respectful examinations of his ideas. Underlying much of McCloskey's work is a commitment to liberal democracy, although he believes that no philosopher has successfully articulated the liberal ideal.

McCloskey explains that J. L. **Mackie**'s writings on the problem of evil persuaded him to change from being a committed Christian to being a philosophical atheist, a view which he defends in the book *God and Evil* (1974).

Ecological themes are prominent in McCloskey's later writings; he explores human duties to present and future generations, to the preservation of wildlife and to the care of endangered species. One reviewer commented on his 1983 book: 'It is human and liberal, philosophically tough minded and strongly committed to solving ecological problems' (S. M. Brown, *Philosophical Review* 93, 1984).

Sources: IDPP; CA 110.

H. BUNTING

McDougall, William
American. *b:* 1871, Chadderton, England. *d:* 1938, Durham, North Carolina. *Cat:* Psychologist. *Ints:* Hormic psychology; instincts; ESP. *Educ:* University of Cambridge and St Thomas's Hospital, London. *Infls:* C. S. Sherrington (with whom he worked for a while in London) and William James (especially his *Principles of Psychology*). *Appts:* Taught psychology in England and America; Fellow, St John's College, Cambridge, 1889–1904; Wilde Reader in Mental Philosophy, Oxford, 1904; Professor of Psychology first at Harvard University (1920) and then at Duke University (1927).

Main publications:
(1905) *Physiological Psychology*, London: J. M. Dent.
(1908) *An Introduction to Social Psychology*, London: Methuen & Co.
(1911) *Body and Mind: A History and Defense of Animism*, London: Methuen & Co.
(1912) *The Pagan Tribes of Borneo*, London: Macmillan.
(1912) *Psychology: The Study of Behaviour*, London: Thornton.
(1923) *An Outline of Psychology*, New York and London: Butterworth Ltd.
(1924) *Ethics and Some Modern World Problem*, New York and London: Puttnam & Sons.
(1926) *An Outline of Abnormal Psychology*, New York and London: Methuen.
(1927) *Character and the Conduct of Life*, New York and London: Methuen.
(1928) (with J. B. Watson) *The Battle of Behaviourism*, London: Kegan Paul, Trench, Trubner & Co.
(1936) *Psychoanalysis and Social Psychology*, London: Methuen.

Secondary literature:
Greenwood, M., and Smith, M. (1939–41) 'William McDougall', in *Obituary Notices of Fellows of the Royal Society* 3: 39–62, London (contains a complete bibliography).

Nicole, J. E. (1930) *Psychopathology*, New York:
Dodd, Mead & Co.; third edition, 1942, chs 15, 16,
21.

Woodworth, R. S. (1931) *Contemporary Schools of
Psychology*, New York and London: Methuen,
ch. 6.

Although widely influential in his day, William
McDougall is now remembered mainly as the
founder of hormic, or instinct-driven, psychology.
His first major work on psychology was *Physiological Psychology* (1905), in which he brought
together the ideas of **James** and Sherrington.
During the First World War he ran a medical unit
for shell-shocked soldiers which was to provide
the case material for his *Outline of Abnormal
Psychology* (1926). After the war he moved to
America, where he published a number of
polemical works of a political character. He
supported the work of J. B. Rhine on ESP and
sought experimental proof of Lamarckism.

McDougall first outlined his hormic psychology in *An Introduction to Social Psychology* in
1908. 'Hormic' is derived from the Greek *horme*,
meaning impulse. In opposition to the stimulus-
response model of behaviourism, hormic psychology takes activity to be driven by instincts. These
are innate psychophysical dispositions to behave
in certain ways. They are made up of three
elements: cognitive, affective and conative. For
example, the instinct of self-preservation comprises the cognitive 'perception of danger', the
affect of fear and a conative drive leading to flight.
Behaviour is thus to be understood as an active
striving after goals (such as self-preservation)
rather than merely a passive response to stimuli.

In normal human development the instincts
become associated with objects and socially
acquired patterns of behaviour called 'sentiments'. These include the higher instincts, such
as parental love and family feeling, which are
organized hierarchically around a master sentiment. In a mature personality the master sentiment is 'self-regard'. McDougall elaborated this
theory of personality in later publications (*An
Outline of Psychology*, 1923; *An Outline of
Abnormal Psychology*, 1926; and *Character and
the Conduct of Life*, 1927), showing how the self-
regarding sentiment was strengthened through
identification with those we admire. This resulted
in an integration of personality, an aspect of child
development which, he argued, both **Freud** and
Jung had neglected.

Although initially an experimental psychologist, McDougall came to rely increasingly on
metaphysical speculation as a substitute for
empirical research. In his early work he espoused
a form of psychoneural parallelism to explain the
coexistence of subjectivity and purposive activity
on the one hand and causality on the other.
However, in *Body and Mind* (1911) he discarded
this in favour of a cocktail of dualist-interaction-
ism, vitalism, animism and Lamarckism. Morals
emerged as an aspect of the self-regarding
sentiment, free will being the control of the
primitive instincts through the exercise of conscience. In a further elaboration of this theory he
pictured the personality as made up of monads,
some goal-seeking (and hence free), others cause-
directed (and hence determined), these being
organized hierarchically through telepathic influences under the control of a supreme monad (the
self). Despite the highly speculative nature of
much of McDougall's later work his prolific
writings and charismatic teaching inspired many
students to study psychology. His early experimental work is of lasting importance.

Sources: DNB 1931–40; Reese; Edwards.

K. W. M. FULFORD

McGilvary, Evander Bradley

American. *b:* 19 July 1864, Bangkok. *d:* September
1953. *Cat:* Realist (perspective realist). *Ints:* The-
ory of knowledge; nature of consciousness. *Educ:*
Davidson College, Princeton and University of
California. *Infls:* William James and Hegel. *Appts:*
Sage Professor of Ethics, Cornell University;
Professor of Philosophy, University of Wisconsin.

Main publications:

(1904) (ed. with others) *Studies in Philosophy*,
Berkeley: University of California Press.

(1907) 'Pure experience and reality: a re-assertion',
Philosophical Review 16: 266–84.

(1907) 'The physiological argument against realism',
Journal of Philosophy 4: 683–92.

(1911) 'Experience as pure and consciousness as
meaning', *Journal of Philosophy* 8: 511–25.

(1912) 'The relation of consciousness and object in
sense perception', *Philosophical Review* 21: 152–75.

(1931) 'The revolt against dualism', *Philosophical
Review* 40: 246–65.

(1956) *Toward a Perspective Realism*, La Salle: Open
Court.

Secondary literature:

Murphy, Arthur E. (1959) 'McGilvary's perspective
realism', *Journal of Philosophy* 56: 149–65.

Oliver, Donald E. (1938) 'The logic of perspective
realism', *Journal of Philosophy* 35: 197–208.

McGilvary tried to solve the problem of illusion and hallucinations that the direct realists could not resolve satisfactorily (see entry under **Marvin**) with his doctrine of perspective realism. According to perspective realism, the objects do not possess sensible qualities themselves. Instead sensible qualities are perceived from some perspective spatial, temporal, etc. Since all properties are relative, there would be no contradiction where the same table appears to be round and elliptical. If the perspective realist viewpoint is correct it seems that no perception could ever be erroneous!

Sources: WWW(Am).

INDIRA MAHALINGAM CARR

Mach, Ernst

Austrian. *b:* 18 February 1838, Turas, Moravia. *d:* 19 February 1916, Munich. *Cat:* Physicist; physiologist; epistemologist. *Ints:* Philosophy and history of physics. *Educ:* University of Vienna 1855–60, doctorate 1860, Habilitation 1861. *Infls:* Berkeley, Hume, Kant, R. Avenarius, H. von Helmholtz, G. Kirchhoff, G. Fechner and R. Du Bois Reymond. *Appts:* Chair of Mathematics, University of Graz, 1864–7; Chair of Physics, Charles University, Prague, 1867–95; Chair of the History and Theory of the Inductive Sciences, University of Vienna, 1895–1901.

Main publications:

(1872) *Die Geschichte und die Wurzel des Satzes von der Erhaltung der Arbeit*, Prague, J. G. Clave'sche (English translation, *The History and the Root of the Principle of the Conservation of Energy*, trans. P. E. B. Jourdain, Chicago: Open Court, 1911).

(1873) *Grundlinien der Lehre von den Bewegungsempfindungen*, Leipzig: W. Engelmann.

(1883) *Die Mechanik in ihrer Entwicklung, historisch-kritisch dargestellt*, Leipzig: F. A. Brockhaus (English translation, *The Science of Mechanics*, London: Watts & Co., 1893).

(1886) *Beiträge zur Analyse der Empfindungen*, Jena: Fischer (English translation, *The Analysis of Sensations*, trans. Williams and Waterlow, Chicago: Open Court, 1914).

(1896) *Populär-Wissenschaftliche Vorlesungen*, Leipzig: J. A. Barth (English translation, T. J. MacCormack, Chicago: Open Court, 1895).

(1896) *Die Principien der Wärmelehre historische-kritisch entwickelt*, Leipzig: J. A. Barth (English translation, *Principles of the Theory of Heat*, ed. B. McGuinness, Dordrecht: Reidel, 1986).

(1906) *Erkenntnis und Irrtum*, Leipzig: J. A. Barth.

(1910) 'Die Leitgedanken meiner naturwissenschaftlichen Erkenntnislehre und ihre Aufnahme durch die Zeitgenossen', *Scientia* 7: 2ff (*Physikalische Zeitschrift* 11: 599–606).

(1915) *Kultur und Mechanik*, Stuttgart: W. Spemann.

(1921) *Die Principien der Physikalischen Optik historisch und erkenntnis-psychologisch entwickelt*, Leipzig: J. A. Barth (English translation, *The Principles of Physical Optics*, trans. J. S. Anderson and A. F. A. Young, London: Methuen, 1926.

(1978) *Wissenschaftliche Kommunikation, die Korrespondenz Ernst Machs*, ed. J. Thiele, Kastelaun: Henn.

Secondary literature:

Adler, F. (1918) *Ernst Machs Überwindung des mechanischen Materialismus*, Vienna: Brand.

Ayer, A. J. (ed.) (1959) *Logical Positivism*, Glencoe, Ill.: Free Press of Glencoe.

Bradley, J. (1971) *Mach's Philosophy of Science*, London: Athlone Press.

Brentano, F. C. (1988) *Über Ernst Machs 'Erkenntnis und Irrtum'*, Amsterdam: Rodopi.

Dingler, H. (1924) *Die Grundgedanken der Machschen Philosophie*, Leipzig: J. A. Barth.

Haller, R. and Stadler, F. (eds) (1988) *Ernst Mach–Werk und Wirkung*, Vienna: Hölder Pichler Tempsky.

Henning, H. (1985) *Ernst Mach als Philosoph*, Leipzig: J. A. Barth.

Hentschel, K. (1988) 'Die Korrespondenz Duhem-Mach zur Modelbeladenheit von Wissenschaftsgeschichte', *Annales of Science*, 40: 73–91.

Kraft, V. (1950) *Der Wiener Kreis*, Vienna: Springer (English translation, The Vienna Circle, trans. A. Pap, New York: Philosophical Library, 1953).

Lenin, V. I. (1909) *Materialism and Empiriocriticism: Critical Comments on a Reactionary Philosophy*, Moscow: Foreign Languages Publishing House, 1952.

Mises, R. von (1938) *Ernst Mach und die Empirische Wissenschaftsauffassung*, The Hague: van Stockum & Zoon.

——(1951) *Positivism*, Cambridge, Mass.: Harvard University Press.

Musil, R. (1908) *Beiträge zur Beurteilungen der Lehren Machs*, Berlin: Wilmersdorf.

Popper, K. R. (1965) *A Note on Berkeley as a Predecessor of Mach, Conjectures and Refutations*, London: Routledge, pp. 166–74.

Schlick, M. (1938) *Gesammelte Aufsätze*, Vienna: Gerold & Co.

An anti-clerical positivist, Mach developed a thoroughgoing phenomenalist position that was widely influential through his disciples in the

Vienna Circle and beyond. Opposed to rationalist approaches to science and suspicious of misplaced rigour, he attempted to show that science was one, and based ultimately on sensations, interpreted into different subjects—physics, biology or psychology—according to the point of view or direction of the inquirer. Objects, whether living or dead, were mere bundles of sensations. In setting out these views he often adopted the then common quasi-historical mode of critical history, in which he attempted to show that the most abstract formulations of theoretical physics, with their seemingly absolutist claims to a deep knowledge of reality, actually derived from experience, and were on rigorous analysis dispensable. For Mach, theories had no other function than the economical description of phenomena, and the only test of their worth was in experience. Parts of them not reflected in experience had no meaning, although they could be vindicated by the successful realization of predictions derived from their theories. Indeed prediction played a major role in his system. Explanation was not the function of theory, but no more than the reduction of the unfamiliar to the familiar. Rejecting any notion of the a priori, he regarded scientific theory as in the highest degree provisional. His use of the history of science was widely influential in the early development of the discipline.

Sources: Edwards: J. Thiele (1963) 'Ernst Mach Bibliography', *Centaurus* 8: 189–237; J. T. Blackmore (1972) *Ernst Mach: His Work, Life and Influence*, Berkeley and London: Univ. of California Press; DSB 8: 595a–607b; Mittelstrass; NDB 1986; Metzler.

R. N. D. MARTIN

Macherey, Pierre

French. **b:** 1938. **Cat:** Marxist; literary theorist; metaphysician. **Ints:** Structural Marxism. **Educ:** École Normale Supérieure. **Infls:** Marx, Lenin, Althusser and others in the Marxist tradition. **Appts:** Lecturer in Philosophy, Paris I.

Main publications:

(1965) (with Louis Althusser, Etienne Balibar *et al.*) *Lire le Capitale* Paris: Maspero.

(1966) *Pour une théorie de la production littéraire*, Paris: Maspero (English translation, *A Theory of Literary Production*, trans. Geoffrey Wall, London: Routledge & Kegan Paul, 1978).

(1979) *Hegel ou Spinoza*, Paris: Maspero.

(1989) *Comte: la philosophie et les sciences*, Paris: Presses Universitaires de France.

(1990) *À quoi pense la littérature?: exercices de philosophie littéraire*, Paris: Presses Universitaires de France.

Secondary literature:

Eagleton, Terry (1976) *Criticism and Ideology*, London: NLB.

——(1976) *Marxism and Literary Criticism*, London: Methuen.

——(1986) *Against the Grain*, London: Verso.

A student and disciple of the structural Marxist philosopher Louis **Althusser**, Pierre Macherey is best known for his application of Althusser's theory of ideology to the field of literary studies. Literature is a form of ideological production to Macherey, and in his most important book, *A Theory of Literary Production* (1966), he argues that when 'read against the grain' literary texts will reveal the contradictions of the ideology within which they were composed. Since any ideology (capitalism, for instance) is concerned to disguise all its internal contradictions, this turns the literary text into a particularly fruitful area of study for the Marxist critic. Macherey's work has had a very considerable impact on literary theory and criticism, and the 'reading against the grain' approach that he advocates has been widely adopted, perhaps most notably in the English-speaking world by Terry Eagleton.

Sources: See secondary literature.

STUART SIM

MacIntyre, A(lasdair) C(halmers)

British. **b:** 1929, Glasgow. **Cat:** Analytic philosopher. **Ints:** Ethics; history of ethics; Aristotle; Aquinas; Confucianism. **Educ:** Universities of London and Manchester. **Infls:** Franz Steiner, Karl Polanyi and St Thomas Aquinas. **Appts:** Lecturer in Philosophy of Religion, University of Manchester, 1951–7; Lecturer in Philosophy, University of Leeds, 1957–61; Fellow of University College, Oxford, 1963–6; Professor of Sociology, University of Essex, 1966–70; University Professor of Philosophy and Political Science, University of Boston, 1972–80; W. Alton Jones Distinguished Professor of Philosophy, Vanderbilt University, 1982–8; McMahon/Hank Professor of Philosophy, University of Notre Dame, from 1988; various other positions at Oxford, Yale, Princeton, Brandeis University, Wellesley College.

Main publications:
(1953) *Marxism: An Interpretation*, London: SCMP; revised and reissued as *Marxism and Christianity*, New York: Schocken Books, 1968.
(1955) (ed. with Antony Flew) *New Essays in Philosophical Theology*, London: SCMP.
(1958) *The Unconscious*, London: Routledge & Kegan Paul.
(1959) *Difficulties in Christian Belief*, London: SCMP.
(1966) *A Short History of Ethics*, New York: Macmillan.
(1967) *Secularization and Moral Change*, London: Oxford University Press.
(1971) *Against the Self-Images of the Age*, London: Duckworth.
(1981) *After Virtue*, London: Duckworth.
(1987) 'The idea of an educated public', in G. Haydon (ed.) *Education and Values*, London University Institute of Education.
(1988) *Whose Justice? Which Rationality*, Notre Dame: Notre Dame University Press.
(1990) *First Principles, Final Ends and Contemporary Philosophical Issues*, Milwaukee: Marquette University Press.
(1990) *Three Rival Versions of Moral Enquiry*, Notre Dame: Notre Dame University Press.

Secondary literature:
Horton, J. and Mendus, S. (eds) (1993) *After MacIntyre*, Oxford: Polity Press.
MacIntyre, Alasdair, Dahl, Norman O., Baier, Annette and Schneewind, J. B. (1991) 'Book symposium' on *Whose Justice? Which Rationality?*, in *Philosophy and Phenomenological Research* 11: 149–78.

MacIntyre's first book, written when he was 23, tried to rescue both a purified Christianity and a purified Marxism for the modern world. He argued that, properly understood, Marxism, as the historical successor to Christianity, largely shares both its content and its function as an interpretation of human existence.

In 1955 *New Essays in Philosophical Theology*, which MacIntyre edited with Antony **Flew**, and which gathered together a number of essays applying the methods of conceptual analysis to specific religious issues, reinaugurated the serious study of the philosophy of religion, a subject which had been moribund in the analytical tradition for some decades.

Since the mid-1960s most of MacIntyre's work has been concerned with ethical and social theory.

In *A Short History of Ethics* (1966) he attacked the notion that moral concepts are a timeless,

unchanging, determinate set. He held rather that they are embodied in, and partially constitutive of, forms of social life, and so change as social life changes. This does not mean merely that different societies have held different things to be right or good but, much more radically, that what it means to describe something as right or good may itself change; indeed, the very idea of morality is subject to change. So, to take one central case, the peculiarly moral, Kantian sense of 'ought' that characterizes much modern ethical thought—an 'ought' that expresses obligations binding on all rational beings as such, but unable to be derived logically from any factual statements—is completely absent in, for instance, the Homeric period. It arose, according to MacIntyre, in the modern period when the social roles and ideals that had originally provided a backing for it gradually dropped away. And this development explains the peculiarly intractable nature of moral disputes in the modern world, which is not a feature of all possible moralities but of one with a certain history.

MacIntyre developed in detail this diagnosis of the problems of modern morality in *After Virtue* (1981). Its central claim is that modern morality is in deep disarray. It is, he suggested, no more than the fragments of a conceptual scheme which has lost the context which once made it intelligible, and to which have been added, as a way of attempting to cope with the breakdown of the traditional moral philosophy, such moral fictions as natural rights and utility. The attempt is a failure since, for one thing, there are no such things as natural rights or utility; and, for another, this yoking of incompatible moral traditions has largely made of morality just what **Nietzsche** and various forms of emotivism have claimed that it is: the mere expression of subjective preference with no objective criteria for deciding between them.

If morality is again to make sense for us, we must, according to MacIntyre, recapture something of the Aristotelian tradition of moral philosophy. Further, given the nature of our society and its ruling liberal individualist ideas, this will not be easy. It would entail recapturing a number of ideas that are now lost. The concept of what MacIntyre calls a *practice*—a cooperative enterprise in pursuit of goods internal to that enterprise—would be essential; this, outside of the area of games, and particularly in our participation in political life, we have all but lost. So too we should need to recapture the notion of a *whole human life*, an idea lost to us now because bureaucratic modernity has seen to it that our lives have no unity. And, third, we should need to recapture the sense that what we are is largely a matter of what we have become through our history and traditions. Without these notions, morality can make little sense for us. The choice, as MacIntyre puts it, is between Nietzsche and Aristotle.

Given this analysis, a central problem is how rationally to recommend one tradition of thought as against another. MacIntyre turned to this issue in *Whose Justice? Which Rationality?* (1988) and in his Gifford Lectures, *Three Rival Versions of Moral Enquiry* (1990). The accounts of justice that we find in Aristotle and Hume—to take what are for us two of the most central examples—are, according to MacIntyre, embedded in overall systems of thought which respectively impose their own standards of rationality on them. That being so, how may we adjudicate between them? MacIntyre argues that there can be no such thing as a rational enquiry which does not adopt the standpoint of a particular tradition; this, however, need not involve any form of relativism, since the tradition from which one reasons may itself involve an absolute conception of truth. So it is with the Thomist tradition that MacIntyre recommends in these works. And it can show itself rationally superior to both the Nietzschean tradition and the tradition of post-Enlightenment ethics that we have inherited; it can solve problems that these traditions themselves must recognize to be problems, and explain why they themselves cannot do so. If the state of modernity is characterized by lack of agreement about even the most fundamental questions, what role does this leave for the university? In 'The idea of an educated public' (1987), MacIntyre argued that the dual aim of the liberal university—to prepare students for a social role and to teach them to think for themselves—could no longer be achieved: the demise of the 'educated public', a self-conscious body of people with a common intellectual inheritance and shared standards of argument, has made it impossible. In *Three Rival Versions of Moral Enquiry* he envisages the university 'as a place of constrained disagreement, of imposed participation in conflict, in which a central responsibility of higher education would be to initiate students into conflict' (pp. 230–1). MacIntyre's work has been widely influential. Some, however, have questioned his historical interpretation; and many have not found modern moral thought to be in such comparative disarray as he suggests.

Sources: Flew; WW 1992; Becker; personal communication.

ANTHONY ELLIS

Mackenzie, John Stuart

British. **b:** 29 February 1860, Glasgow. **d:** 6 December 1935, Brockweir, near Chepstow. **Cat:** Absolute idealist and eclectic philosopher. **Ints:** Moral philosophy; social philosophy; metaphysics. **Educ:** University of Glasgow, University of Edinburgh and Trinity College, Cambridge. **Infls:** Personal influences: Edward Caird, Sir Henry Jones and J. M. E. McTaggart. Literary influences: Hegel, Meinong and Spencer. **Appts:** 1890–6, Fellow of Trinity College, Cambridge; 1895–1915, Professor of Logic and Metaphysics, University College, Cardiff.

Main publications:

(1890) *An Introduction to Social Philosophy*, Glasgow: Maclehose & Sons.
(1893) *Manual of Ethics*, Tutorial Series, London: University Correspondence College.
(1902) *Outlines of Metaphysics*, London: Macmillan.
(1917) *Elements of Constructive Philosophy*, London: Allen & Unwin.
(1918) *Outlines of Social Philosophy*, London: Allen & Unwin.
(1920) *Fundamental Problems of Life: An Essay on Citizenship as the Pursuit of Values*, London: Allen & Unwin.
(1931) *Cosmic Problems*, London: Macmillan.

Secondary literature:

Hoernlé, R. F. A. (1918) Review of *Elements of Constructive Philosophy*, in *Philosophical Review* 27: 522–31.
Laird, J. (1931) Critical Notice of *Cosmic Problems*, in *Mind* 40: 400–1.
Muirhead, J. H. (1936) 'The life and work of J. S. Mackenzie', in Mrs. Mackenzie (ed.) *John Stuart Mackenzie*, London: Williams & Norgate.

J. S. Mackenzie belonged to a generation of British idealists who found themselves challenged by other philosophies, such as empiricism, hedonism and individualism. He was at Cambridge when Hegel was still little known there and a paper by him had a decisive influence on a fellow student, **McTaggart**, then 'an ardent Spencerian' (Muirhead 1936, p. 4). His *Manual of Ethics* (1893) went into six editions and many students were introduced to idealism in moral, social and political philosophy through Mackenzie's textbooks. He had been a pupil of Edward Caird and Henry **Jones** and always claimed a close affinity with their philosophy (Muirhead 1936, p. 16). This is not to say that he added nothing of his own. He was constantly absorbing new currents of thought, including strong elements of realism,

and in his hands Caird's philosophy became 'a liberal eclecticism' (Passmore 1957, p. 54n.).
Sources: DNB 1931–40; Mrs Mackenzie (ed.) (1936) *John Stuart Mackenzie*, London: Williams & Norgate; CBP II; Passmore 1957.

STUART BROWN

McKeon, Richard P(eter)

American. **b:** 26 April 1900, Union Hill, New Jersey. **d:** 31 March 1985, Chicago, Illinois. **Cat:** Historian of philosophy. **Ints:** History of philosophy. **Educ:** Columbia University, AB and AM 1920, PhD 1928; University of Paris, 1925–8. **Infls:** Aristotle, Cicero and Dewey. **Appts:** 1925–35, Instructor to Assistant Professor of Philosophy, Columbia University; 1934–5, Visiting Professor of History, University of Chicago; 1935–85, Professor of Greek and Philosophy, University of Chicago (Professor Emeritus, 1977).

Main publications:

(1928) *The Philosophy of Spinoza: The Unity of his Thought*, New York: Longmans, Green, & Co.; reprinted, Woodbridge, CT: Ox Bow Press, 1987.
(1952) *Freedom and History: The Semantics of Philosophical Controversies and Ideological Conflicts*, New York: Noonday Press.
(1954) *Thought, Action, and Passion: Essays*, Chicago: University of Chicago Press.

Secondary literature:

Plockmann, G. K. (1990) *Richard McKeon: A Study*, Chicago: University of Chicago Press.

A master of all periods of the history of philosophy, McKeon developed a metaphilosophy focused on the methods and language of philosophy, authoring numerous erudite scholarly essays. He espoused a radical pluralism, while he sought to reach irenic standpoints to interpret dialectically philosophical disagreements. He also pursued applications of his pluralism in international relations, serving as a US delegate to UNESCO and as American Cultural Ambassador in France in 1945–7.
Sources: WW(Am); *New York Times*, 3 Apr 1985.

ANDREW RECK

Mackie, J(ohn) L(eslie)

British. **b:** 1917, Sydney, Australia. **d:** 1981, Oxford. **Cat:** Analytic philosopher. **Ints:** History of philosophy; metaphysics; ethics; philosophy of religion. **Educ:** Universities of Sydney and Oxford. **Infls:** British Empiricists. **Appts:** 1946–51, Lecturer, University of Sydney; 1951–4, Senior Lecturer, University of Sydney; 1955–9, Professor of Philosophy, University of Otago; 1959–63, Challis Professor of Philosophy, University of Sydney; 1963–7, Professor of Philosophy, University of York; 1967–81, Fellow and Praelector in Philosophy, University College, Oxford; 1978–81, University Reader; 1974, Fellow of the British Academy.

Main publications:

(1973) *Truth, Probability, and Paradox*, Oxford: Clarendon Press.
(1974) *The Cement of the Universe: A Study of Causation*, Oxford: Clarendon Press.
(1976) *Problems From Locke*, Oxford: Clarendon Press.
(1977) *Ethics: Inventing Right and Wrong*, Harmondsworth: Penguin.
(1980) *Hume's Moral Theory*, London: Routledge & Kegan Paul.
(1982) *The Miracle of Theism*, Oxford: Clarendon Press.
(1985) *Selected Papers*: vol. 1, *Logic and Knowledge*; vol. 2, *Persons and Values*, ed. Joan Mackie and Penelope Mackie, Oxford: Clarendon Press.

Secondary literature:

Honderich, Ted (ed.) (1985) *Morality and Objectivity*, London: Routledge.

Mackie's work is a consistent, uncompromising and sophisticated empiricist approach to a wide range of philosophical problems. This is nowhere more evident than in *Ethics* (1977), which, though certainly not his best, is probably Mackie's most influential book, and has largely been responsible for the widespread philosophical concern with the objectivity of ethics in the 1980s and 1990s. He argues that our everyday ethical thought is committed to the existence of objective values which simply do not exist. He thus embraces a sort of scepticism, though a scepticism mitigated by his acceptance of the need to create a code of behaviour to enable people to live together in communities, a code which he adumbrates in the second part of the book.

His positive suggestions here are much in the tradition of Hobbes and Hume; and Mackie's writing constantly draws illuminatingly, though not uncritically, on the history of philosophy. His works on Locke and Hume for example, are motivated by the belief that their arguments, when suitably reconstructed, contain more of the truth than is often recognized. *The Cement of the Universe* (1974), possibly Mackie's best book, develops a broadly Humean theory of causality, arguing that causal statements are to be understood in terms of counterfactuals. As against Hume, however, he argues that singular causal statements are conceptually prior to any generalizations. Mackie was suspicious of the technicality which is characteristic of much modern philosophy, and his writing, though no less complex than the subject demands, is always admirably clear.

Sources: *The Times*, 15 Dec 1981; John McDowell (1982) 'John Leslie Mackie', *PBA*, 76; Simon Blackburn (1982) 'A memorial address', *University College Record*; G. L. Cawkwell (1982) 'A memorial address', *University College Record*; personal communication with Penelope Mackie.

ANTHONY ELLIS

Macmurray, John

British. *b:* 16 February 1891, Maxwellton, Kincudbrightshire. *d:* 21 June 1976, Edinburgh. *Cat:* Idealist; personalist. *Ints:* Moral philosophy; metaphysics. *Educ:* University of Glasgow and Balliol College, Oxford. *Appts:* 1919–21, Lecturer in Philosophy, Manchester; 1921–2, Professor of Philosophy, Witwatersrand, Johannesburg; 1922–8, Fellow and Tutor in Philosophy, Balliol College, Oxford; 1928–44, Grote Professor of the Philosophy of Mind and Logic, London; 1944–58, Professor of Moral Philosophy, Edinburgh.

Main publications:

(1934) *Interpreting the Universe*, London: Faber & Faber.
(1935) *Reason and Emotion*, London: Faber & Faber; reprinted with introduction by J. E. Costello, Atlantic Highlands, NJ: Humanities Press, 1992.
(1939) *The Boundaries of Science: A Study in the Philosophy of Psychology*, London: Faber & Faber.
(1957) *The Self as Agent*, London: Faber & Faber; reprinted with introduction by S. M. Harrison, Atlantic Highlands, NJ: Humanities Press, 1991.
(1961) *Persons in Relation*, London: Faber & Faber; reprinted with introduction by F. G. Kirkpatrick, Atlantic Highlands, NJ: Humanities Press, 1991.

Secondary literature:

Fergusson, D. A. S. (1992) *John Macmurray in a Nutshell*, Musselburgh: Handsel Press.
Warren, Jeanne (1989) *Becoming Real: An Introduction to the Thought of John Macmurray*, York: Ebor Press.

Macmurray emerged from the First World War with the conviction, common to many of his generation, that the philosophical traditions in which he had been educated had proved inadequate to meet the crises of his age. He maintained that the most important task of philosophy was to provide an accurate account of what it was to be a person or self. One mistake made by previous systems of philosophy was to consider people to be analogous either to complex machines or to living organisms. Both accounts were inaccurate: instead, a person is to be regarded as *sui generis*.

What is essential to the self, according to Macmurray, is not the attribute of thought but that of action. The self should thus be conceived primarily as an agent. Action is not a process, but is necessarily intentioned. Furthermore, Macmurray maintained, a proper account of the universe would show that it is the intentional action of God. One reviewer, A. R. C. Duncan, acclaimed Macmurray's *Self as Agent* (1957) as a 'pioneer work of the first importance' (*Philosophy* 36 (1961): 234).

Another inaccuracy in traditional philosophy, according to Macmurray, was to consider the self in isolation from others. In his *Persons in Relation* (1961) he sought to show that full selfhood can only be achieved in a dialogical relation with at least one other person, to form a community of selves.

Sources: Macquarrie; Sell; WW; *The Newsletter of the John Macmurray Fellowship*.

STUART BROWN AND KATHRYN PLANT

Macquarrie, John

British. *b:* 27 June 1919, Renfrew, Scotland. *Cat:* Presbyterian turned Anglican philosopher-theologian. *Ints:* Existentialism. *Educ:* University of Glasgow. *Infls:* F. H. Bradley, Ian Henderson, R. Bultmann, M. Heidegger, P. Tillich, K. Rahner and John Knox (New Testament scholar). *Appts:* Army chaplain, 1945–8; St Ninian's Church, Brechin, 1948–53; Lecturer, University of Glasgow, 1953–62; Professor of Systematic Theology, Union Seminary, New York, 1962–70; Lady Margaret Professor of Divinity, University of Oxford, and Canon of Christ Church, 1970–86; FBA, 1984.

Main publications:

(1955) *An Existentialist Theology*, London: SCM Press.
(1960) *The Scope of Demythologising*, London: SCM Press.
(1963) *Twentieth Century Religious Thought*, London: SCM Press.

(1965) *Studies in Christian Existentialism*, London: SCM Press.

(1966) *Principles of Christian Theology*, London: SCM Press.

(1967) *God-Talk*, London: SCM Press.

(1967) *God and Secularity*, London: Lutterworth Press.

(1970) *Three Issues in Ethics*, London: SCM Press.

(1972) *Existentialism*, London: Hutchinson.

(1975) *Thinking About God*, London: SCM Press.

(1982) *In Search of Humanity*, London: SCM Press.

(1984) *In Search of Deity: An Essay in Dialectical Theism*, London: SCM Press (Gifford Lectures).

(1986) *Jesus Christ in Modern Thought*, London: SCM Press.

Secondary literature:

Kee, A. and Long, E. T. (eds) (1986) *Being and Truth: Essays in Honour of John Macquarrie*, London: SCM Press (includes a bibliography).

Whereas some theologians early reach a position recognizably theirs, which they proceed to elaborate and defend for the rest of their days, Macquarrie's intellectual progress has followed his developing religious experience, and this to an unusual degree. Second thoughts have led him not so much to repudiate earlier views, as to balance them with further considerations. In his autobiographical memoir, significantly entitled 'Pilgrimage in theology', he recounts his passage from commitment to F. H. **Bradley**'s suprarational absolute, which 'cohered rather well with my own somewhat pantheistic religiosity' via **Bultmann**, from whom he learned the significance of God's mighty *acts* (which the idealists had wrongly construed as symbols), and **Heidegger**, who taught him the importance, over against pure existentialism, of ontology, to a more orthodox Christian position, in which key influences were Knox and **Rahner**, and dismay at the reductionist tendencies of the so-called secular theology of the 1960s, of which his *God and Secularity* (1967) is a rebuttal. His increasing concern for the centralities of the Christian faith followed his departure from a Presbyterianism perceived as Word-bound to an Anglicanism deemed more catholic, and manifested itself in a panentheism couched in incarnational terms. His studies in quest of humanity and of deity prompted his more positive appreciation of natural theology, and led him towards a Christology: *Jesus Christ in Modern Thought* (1990).

Macquarrie has done much to introduce Bultmann and Heidegger to British readers, and his ability to master vast amounts of material and to present his findings clearly and fairly is shown to good effect in his *Twentieth Century Religious Thought* (1963), as well as in his numerous contributions to dictionaries. With his feet in both philosophical and theological soil he has been ideally equipped for the role of frontiersman, as is exemplified in his *God-Talk* (1967), in which he responds to the challenge of linguistic analysis. His practical interest emerges in, for example, *Three Issues in Ethics* (1970). He has also written on more strictly doctrinal and on ecumenical themes.

Macquarrie has not (so far) been led significantly to revise his opinion of student days that Calvin and **Barth** are 'specially intolerable'. Those who perceive this as a lamentable lacuna have been prevented from according him unmixed praise. Their hesitation is not unrelated to the more general complaint that Macquarrie's definition of theology as 'reflection upon a religious faith' is inadequate, for it wrongly makes religious experience the subject matter of theology. However, it is as impossible as it would be foolhardy to predict the final intellectual destination of a theologian whose life and works have so clearly borne witness to his own conviction that human selfhood is ever developing.

Sources: WW; Kee & Long (1986); Sell.

ALAN SELL

McTaggart, John McTaggart Ellis

British. *b:* 1866, London. *d:* 1925, London. *Cat:* Ontological idealist. *Ints:* Metaphysics. *Educ:* MA and LittD, Trinity College, Cambridge. *Infls:* Spinoza and Hegel. *Appts:* Fellow of Trinity College, Cambridge, 1891–1923; College Lecturer, 1897–1923.

Main publications:

(1896) *Studies in the Hegelian Dialectic*, Cambridge.

(1901) *Studies in Hegelian Cosmology*, Cambridge.

(1906) *Some Dogmas of Religion*, London: Arnold; second edition, 1930.

(1910) *A Commentary on Hegel's Logic*, Cambridge.

(1921–7) *The Nature of Existence*, 2 vols, Cambridge: Cambridge University Press.

(1934) *Philosophical Studies*, ed. S. V. Keeling, London: Arnold (papers of 1893–1923).

Secondary literature:

Broad, C. D. (1933–8) *Examination of McTaggart's Philosophy*, Cambridge.

Geach, P. T. (1979) *Truth, Love and Immortality*, London: Hutchinson.

McTaggart gave short, clear outlines of his thinking in two papers reprinted in *Philosophical Studies* (1934): early, in 'The further determination of the absolute' (1893), and late, in 'An ontological idealism' (1923). There was little change in his views during his lifetime, although he did move from a preference for a dialectical, Hegelian method towards a more directly deductive exposition. His final position is summed up in the two volumes of *The Nature of Existence* (1921–7), a detailed and comprehensive treatment of his idealist metaphysics, along with its ramifications for religion and the place of values.

McTaggart called himself as 'ontological idealist' ('all reality is spirit') although he did not regard this position as being open to 'rigid demonstration' (1921–7, SS432). He was also, unusually, an epistemological realist in that he said that knowledge was a true belief: 'and I should say that a belief was true when, and only when, it stands in a relation of correspondence to a fact' (1934, p. 273). Although he was impressed by Hegel, and has often been classed with **Bradley** as an English neo-Hegelian, his idiosyncratic form of idealism differed from Hegel and Bradley in crucial ways (see 1921–7, SS48, 52, 136). He accepted the real existence of separate individuals. He thought that individual truths could be fully true, and believed that truth consisted in a relation of correspondence between a belief and a fact. The starting-point for his idealism was not the dependence of an object on a knowing subject but 'the assertion that nothing exists but spirit' (SS52). He differed from Hegel and Bradley, too, in the clarity of his exposition and the modesty of its tone (see, for example, SS912). **Broad** commented unkindly that if Hegel was the prophet of the absolute and Bradley its chivalrous knight, McTaggart was its 'devoted and extremely astute family solicitor' (Introduction to second edition of *Some Dogmas of Religion*, 1906, p. xxviii). This is less than fair, not only because McTaggart's meticulous caution is more likely to appeal to modern readers than Bradley's haphazard rhetoric, but because McTaggart's Universe, 'a substance which contains all content, and of which every other substance is a part' (1921–7, SS135), is far less metaphysically charged than Bradley's Hegelian Absolute. Although McTaggart rarely acknowledged the direct debit, his nearest philosophical ancestor was not Hegel but Spinoza: both he and Spinoza aimed at the same kind of comprehensive, deductively explained metaphysical view. He felt a sympathy with the mystical strain in Part V of Spinoza's *Ethics* (see 1906,

SS247), but he also shared the reluctance of Spinoza to appeal directly to mystical experience.

The exact details of McTaggart's system will be followed by very few modern readers. There are numerous undefined terms. The reasoning, from a priori premises, is proudly deductive, allowing for only two empirical postulates: that something exists and that what is exists is differentiated (1921–7, chapter 3). There is a plurality of (spiritual) substances which together make up the Universe, but no God (SS500). McTaggart considers issues of divisibility, definition and identity to reach a conclusion that a *sui generis* relation of 'determining correspondence' must hold between wholes and parts of substances (see SS197, 202). Reality as it is has to be very different from how it seems. Space, time and physical objects are all proved to be 'unreal' (ibid., chapters 33–5). (And it is the ingenious proof of the unreality of time which remains the most widely studied part of the system.) Individual minds are substances which must be immortal (liable to metempsychosis): a point to which McTaggart attached great personal significance. Love was seen as an 'emotional quality' of souls of particular importance: an 'intense and passionate' 'species of liking' only felt by persons for each other (SS459–60). McTaggart's moral philosophy was only scantily developed. His attribution of values to states of souls and his views on the indefinability of good owe a clear debt to **Moore** (who would hardly have accepted the supporting metaphysics, including its uncompromising determinism). *The Nature of Existence* ends with Spinozistic praise of 'a timeless and endless state of love—love so direct, so intimate and so powerful that even the deepest mystic rapture gives us but the smallest foretaste of its perfection' (SS913). McTaggart's philosophy is highly individual in combining views that are often held apart: a belief in the immortality of the soul along with atheism; ontological idealism along with epistemological realism and pluralism. McTaggart is usually seen as a foil in the early development of G. E. Moore and **Russell**, who both came to differ diametrically from him after their revolt against idealism in 1898. Later readers may find that his arguments were less ridiculous that Moore and Russell portrayed them to be. His argument on the unreality of time, in particular, continues to attract some interest. Few today will accept his opinion that the 'utility of Metaphysic is to be found ... in the comfort it can give us' (1934, p. 184). He had no disciples and no successors, but he has had occasional admirers, sometimes unexpectedly; for example: 'I could not

... imagine a much more exciting and rewarding enterprise than the rational rigour combined with the satisfaction of one's deepest cravings that it seemed McTaggart offered' (M. Tanner, 'Metaphysics and music', in A. Phillips Griffiths (ed.), *The Impulse to Philosophise*, Cambridge, 1992, p. 191).

RICHARD MASON

Maeztu, Ramiro de

Spanish. *b:* 4 May 1875, Vitoria, Spain. *d:* 1936, Madrid (assassinated). *Cat:* Political philosopher. *Educ:* Instituo de Vitoria. *Infls:* Unamuno and Ortega y Gasset. *Appts:* Journalist in Bilbao, Madrid and London after travelling throughout Europe and Cuba; served as Spain's Ambassador to Argentina in 1927; born of a Basque father and a British mother, Maeztu was bilingual which afforded him numerous work opportunities in London.

Main publications:

(1899) *Hacia otra España*, Bilbao.
(1911) *Obreros e intelectuales*, Bilbao.
(1916) *Authority, Liberty and Function in the Light of the War: A Critique of Authority and Liberty as the Foundations of the Modern State and an Attempt to Base Societies on the Principle of Function*, London: G. Allen & Unwin; New York: Macmillan.
(1925) *Don Quijote, Don Juan y la Celestina*, Madrid.
(1934) *Defensa de la hispanidad*, Madrid (also Buenos Aires: Editorial Poblet, 1942).
(1962) *Autobiografía*, Madrid: Editorial Nacional.
(1966) *Los intelectuales y un epílogo para estudiantes*, Madrid: Ediciones Rialp.

In his *Authority, Liberty and Function in the Light of the War* (1916), Maeztu develops an anti-liberal political theory. He blames German culture for many of Europe's problems, including the war. Many critics have accused him of anti-German bias. *Defensa de la hispanidad* (1934) is the result of Maeztu's Catholic and nationalistic thought. His nationalism is developed in this work into an anti-rational, mystical Hispanism.

AMY A. OLIVER

Mahdi, M(uhsin) Sayyid

Iraqi. *b:* 21 June 1926, Karbala, Iraq. *Cat:* Islamic political philosopher; philosopher of religion. *Ints:* al-Farabi. *Educ:* American University of Beirut and University of Chicago, PhD 1954. *Infls:* Arnold Bergsträsser, Nabia Abbot and Leo Strauss. *Appts:* Teaching posts in University of Baghdad, University of Freiburg, University of Chicago and Harvard University.

Main publications:

(1957) *Ibn Khaldun's Philosophy of History: A Study in the Philosophic Foundation of the Sciences of Culture*, Chicago, University of Chicago Press; second edition, 1971.

(1968) (ed.) *Alfarabi's Utterances Employed in Logic (Alfz)*, Beirut: Dav El-Machreq.

(1969) *Alfarabi's Philosophy of Plato and Aristotle*, Ithaca: Cornell University Press.

(1969) (ed.) *Alfarabi's Book of Letters (Huruf)*, Beirut: Dar El-Machreq.

Mahdi has made a very distinguished contribution to the study of Islamic philosophy, and especially to Muslim political philosophy, significantly affecting the direction of the subject in the second half of this century. He has a thorough grounding in both German philosophy and the social sciences, and this helped him to produce a study of the thought of ibn Khaldun which broke new ground by widening the notion of Islamic studies itself. Ibn Khaldun's science of culture is shown to rest on the Islamic philosophical tradition, and not primarily on jurisprudence. In his pioneering work on the philosophy of al-Farabi, as an editor, translator and commentator, he described the importance of Farabi's thought as a philosopher and not just as a historical figure in Islamic culture. Mahdi's writings are characterized by exceptional clarity and profundity. Through the example of his writings and through his influence upon his many students, he has made an important impact upon the nature of contemporary Islamic philosophy.

Sources: C. Butterworth (ed.) (1992) *The Political Aspects of Islamic Philosophy: Essays in Honor of Muhsin S. Mahdi*, Cambridge, Mass.

OLIVER LEAMAN

Maihofer, Andrea

German. *b:* 1953. *Cat:* Feminist philosopher. *Ints:* Feminist ethics; feminist theory of law. *Educ:* Universities of Mainz, Tübingen and Frankfurt; PhD in Philosophy, 1987. *Infls:* Student of Jürgen Habermas in Frankfurt; feminist theory (Carol Gilligan) and feminist philosophy (Jessica Benjamin, Luce Irigaray). *Appts:* Assistant (wissenschaftliche Mitarbeiterin), Department of Social Sciences, University of Frankfurt.

Main publications:

(1988) 'Ansätze zur Kritik des moralischen Universalismus. Zur moraltheoretischen Diskussion um Gilligans Thesen zu einer "weiblichen" Moralauffassung' [Approaches to a critique of moral universalism. On the discussion of Gilligan's theses on a 'feminine' view of morality], *Feministische Studien* 6, 1: 32–52.

(1989) 'Der Ausschluß der Frauen aus den Menschenrechten' [The exclusion of women from human rights], *Neue Gesellschaft*, Frankfurter Hefte 7.

(1990) (ed. with Ute Gerhard, Mechthild Jansen, Pia Schmid and Irmgard Schultz) *Differenz und Gleichheit. Menschenrechte haben (k)ein Geschlecht* (Difference and equality. Human rights do (not) have a gender), Frankfurt am Main: Ulrike Helmer Verlag.

(1990) 'Gleichheit nur für Gleiche?' [Equality only for equals?], in *Differenz und Gleichheit*, pp. 351–67.

(1992) 'Universalismus versus Relativismus/Partikularismus?' [Universalism vs. Relativism/Particularism?], in Maja Pellikaan-Engel (ed.) *Against Patriarchal Thinking. A Future Without Discrimination?* (Proceedings of the VIth Symposium of the International Association of Women Philosophers (IAPh), Amsterdam), Amsterdam: VU University Press.

(1994) *Geschlecht als Existenzweise* [Gender as a manner of existence], Frankfurt am Main: Ulrike Helmer Verlag.

Andrea Maihofer is concerned with the roots of modern ethics in Enlightenment ideas of equality, humanity and dignity and their effects on the position of women in law and morality. She challenges the idea of universalism as a necessary basis for all modern ethics and as the sole alternative to relativism. The hegemony of the idea of identity or equality over the acceptance of difference is in itself already a feature of male-dominated thinking and has to be scrutinized and revised if equality is to mean more than mere adaptation of the female to the male norm.

Sources: Peui Kaan-Engel (ed.) (1992) *Against Patriarchal Thinking*, Amsterdam: V U Press.

URSULA STICKLER

Malcolm, Norman

American. **b:** 1911, Selden, Kansas. **d:** 1990, London. **Cat:** Analytic philosopher. **Ints:** Philosophy of language; epistemology; philosophy of mind; philosophy of religion. **Educ:** Universities of Nebraska, Harvard and Cambridge. **Infls:** G. E. Moore and Ludwig Wittgenstein. **Appts:** 1940–2,

Instructor, Princeton University; 1947–50, Assistant Professor, 1950–5, Associate Professor, 1950–64, Professor of Philosophy, 1964–78, Susan Linn Sage Professor; 1979–90, Visiting Professor, Cornell University; 1990, Fellow, King's College, London.

Main publications:

(1958) *Ludwig Wittgenstein: A Memoir*, with a biographical sketch by G. H. von Wright, Oxford: Oxford University Press; second edition, with Wittgenstein's letters to Malcolm, 1984.

(1962) *Dreaming*, London: Routledge & Kegan Paul.

(1963) *Knowledge and Certainty: Essays and Lectures*, Englewood Cliffs: Prentice-Hall.

(1971) *Problems of Mind: Descartes to Wittgenstein*, New York: Harper & Row.

(1977) *Memory and Mind*, Ithaca: Cornell University Press.

(1977) *Thought and Knowledge*, Ithaca: Cornell University Press.

(1984) (with D. M. Armstrong) *Consciousness and Causality: A Debate on the Nature of Mind*, Oxford: Basil Blackwell.

(1986) *Nothing is Hidden: Wittgenstein's Criticism of His Early Thought*, Oxford: Basil Blackwell.

(1993) *Wittgenstein: A Religious Point of View?*, London: Routledge.

(1995) *Wittgensteinian Themes, Essays 1978–1989*, ed. G. H. von Wright, Ithaca: Cornell University Press.

Secondary literature:

Putnam, Hilary, (1962) *Dreaming and depth grammar*, in R. Butler (ed.) *Analytical Philosophy, First Series*, Oxford: Basil Blackwell.

Malcolm's earliest work—and possibly some of his best—minutely analysed and rejected the argument, commonly propounded by epistemologists from Hume onwards, that no empirical judgement can be known for certain to be true since future experience may always give us reason to think it false. One of the most discussed of Malcolm's works, however, was his book *Dreaming* (1962), in which he argued that dreams are not mental experiences that take place during sleep. The idea that they are such mental experiences is an incoherent theory generated by the desire to explain a phenomenon that has no (philosophical) explanation, namely that 'sometimes when people wake up they relate stories in the past tense under the influence of an impression' (p. 87). (One reason this book was so widely discussed was that it seemed to encapsulate a sort of behaviourism that was widely thought to be unavoidable given the basically Wittgensteinian foundation to which many were attracted.)

In an influential article, Malcolm argued that one version of the ontological argument for the existence of God is in fact valid—a view almost universally rejected since Kant. His argument rested upon the idea that the reality of God's existence is to be found in the 'language games' of religious believers, and that one of those 'language games' involves the concept of a God who has 'necessary existence'.

The influence of G. E. **Moore** on Malcolm is clear in his constant attempt to recall philosophers to ordinary language; and the influence of **Wittgenstein** is clear in his underlying belief that our only access to reality, whether the reality of God or of mental phenomena such as dreams, is through human linguistic practices. The influence of both is clear in his sympathy with the deliverances of common sense, and it is on these foundations of his philosophical work that most criticism of Malcolm has focused.

Sources: Passmore 1957; personal communication with Ruth Malcolm.

ANTHONY ELLIS

Mally, Ernst

Austrian. *b:* 11 October 1879, Krainburg, Austria. *d:* 8th March 1944, Schwanburg, Austria. *Ints:* Philosophy of logic; metaphysics. *Educ:* Studied philosophy, mathematics and physics at the University of Graz. *Infls:* Meinong and Russell. *Appts:* Acquired the *Venia legendi* for philosophy at the University of Graz in 1913; succeeded Meinong in the Chair of Philosophy at Graz, 1921–41. Retired due to ill health, but continued running regular philosophical discussions at his home.

Main publications:

(1912) *Gegenstandstheoretische Grundlagen der Logik und Logistik*, Leipzig.
(1914) 'Über die Unabhängigkeit der Gegenstände vom Denken' *Zeitschrift für Philosophie und philosophische Kritik*, vol. 155: 37ff.
(1922) *Studien zur Theorie der Möglichkeit und Ähnlichkeit. Allgemeine Theorie der Verwandtschaft gegenständlicher Bestimmungen*, no. 194 in the series Sitzungsbericht der philosophisch-historischen Klasse der Akademie der Wissenschaften, Vienna.
(1926) *Grundgesetze des Sollens, Elemente der Logik des Willens*, Graz: Leuschner & Lubensky.
(1935) *Erlebnis und Wirklichkeit, Einleitung zur Philosophie der Natürlichen Weltauffassung*, Leipzig: Julius Klinkhardt.

(1938) *Anfangsgründe der Philosophie, Leitfaden für den philosophischen Einführungsunterricht an höheren Schulen*.
(1938) *Warhscheinlichkeit und Gesetz, Ein Betrag zur wahrscheinlichkeitstheoretischen Begründung der Naturwissenschaft*, Berlin: Walter de Gruyter & Co.
(1971) (ed. Karl Wolf and Paul Weingartner) *Logische Schriften*, Dordrecht: Reidel.

Secondary literature:

Mokre, Johann (1971) 'Gegenstandstheorie—Logik—Deontik', in Karl Wolf and Paul Weingartner (eds), *Logische Schriften*, Dordrecht: Reidel, pp. 16–20.
Weingartner, Paul (1971) 'Bemerkungen zu Mallys später Logik', in Karl Wolf and Paul Weingartner (eds), *Logische Schriften*, Dordrecht: Reidel, pp. 21–5.
Wolf, Karl (1968) 'Die Grazer Schule: Gegenstands-Theorie und Wertlehre', in L. Gabriel and J. Mader (eds), *Philosophie in Österreich*, Vienna: Bundesverlag, pp. 31–56.

Much of Mally's thought concerns logic and ontology. His influence on these subjects arises primarily out of his Principle of Independence and his two distinctions concerning kinds of property and modes of predication.

'There are objects of which it is true to say that there are no such objects.' To overcome this sort of paradoxical proposition, Mally introduced the principle of independence of *Sosein* (nature, essence) and *Sein* (being, existence). *Merely possible* objects such as the Golden Mountain, and *impossible* objects such as the round square, are not part of the world either concretely (like trees, which exist and are real), or abstractly (like facts and relations, which subsist and are ideal); they are nevertheless objects of thought and talk. These objects are neither real and existent, nor ideal and subsistent—they just are.

Meinong took this principle over and made it central to his theory of objects. Mally went on to reject it, though it appears in a more sophisticated and developed guise in his two fundamental distinctions.

The golden mountain neither exists nor subsists—it falls outside of either mode of *Sein* (being). To avoid the naïve principles of abstraction of object and property, Mally introduces his seminal distinction between two kinds of property that can be incorporated in an axiomatic theory of objects: *formale* properties (such as being golden, being round) and *ausserformale* properties (such as being existent, simple, determinate, impossible). Possible and impossible objects have their *formale* properties in their *Sosein* (nature) in the same way as existent and subsistent objects do. *Ausserformale* properties, on the other hand, are strictly excluded from the *Sosein* of all objects.

By contrast, Mally's second distinction (which has been called 'Mally's Heresy' depends upon two copulas: the ordinary, or 'satisfying', and the special, or 'determining', what **Russell** calls a 'propositional function'. So 'being golden and mountainous' is a determination of a possible object, the golden mountain, but it is satisfied neither by an existent nor a subsistent object. It has the property of being golden, though quite differently from the way the Statue of Athene has the property of being a statue.

Mally's paradox of thought has also been much discussed. Can a thought refer to itself? Mally takes this question to be analogous to Russell's paradox, and argues that it has no legitimate sense at all, since an affirmative answer, like its denial, would lack sense.

Sources: NDB; J. N. Findlay (1963) *Meinong's Theory of Objects and Values*, Oxford; K. Lambert (1983) *Meinong and the Principle of Independence*, Cambridge.

ANDREA CHRISTOFIDOU

Malraux, André

French. *b:* 1901, Paris. *d:* 1976, Créteil. *Cat:* Aesthetics. *Infls:* Nietzsche and contemporary absurdist and existentialist views. *Appts:* After studying Oriental languages, Malraux spent some time in China in the 1920s, a supporter of the Kuomintang, and his experiences furnished the material for a number of his major novels, notably *La Condition humaine* (1933; Prix Goncourt); he later fought against Franco in Spain and in the French Resistance; after the Second World War, he had several government appointments, notably Minister for Cultural Affairs, 1960–9.

Main publications:

(1946) *Esquisse d'une psychologie du cinéma*, Paris: Gallimard.

(1947–9) *Psychologie de l'art*, 3 vols, Geneva: Skira.

(1950) *Saturne, essai sur Goya*, Paris: NRF.

(1951) *Les Voix du silence*, Paris: NRF (English translation, *The Voices of Silence*, Stuart Gilbert, Princeton, NJ: Princeton University Press, 1953; new edition, 1978).

(1952–4) *Le Musée imaginaire de la sculpture mondiale*, 3 vols, Paris: Gallimard.

Secondary literature:

Davezac, B. (1963) 'Malraux's ideas on art and method in art criticism', *Journal of Aesthetics and Art Criticism*, 22 (Winter): 177–88.

Frohock, W. (1952) *André Malraux and the Tragic Imagination*, California: Stanford University Press.

Righter, W. (1964) *The Rhetorical Hero: An Essay on the Aesthetics of André Malraux*, London: Routledge.

Late in life André Malraux, political activist, soldier and award-winning novelist, devoted almost two decades to writing on aesthetics. With great intelligence and learning he develops a number of views which have since won wide acceptance. His views on art are not, however, isolated from the rest of the worldview which informs his novels, an outlook containing both absurdist and existentialist elements. For Malraux the universe is absurd, incommensurable with human purposes. The fact of death turns human life into a destiny, and, together with certain other forms of action, the creative act of the artist is one of humankind's central responses to this predicament.

In the course of developing his view of the place of art in the human economy, Malraux elaborates a number of theses concerning style. He dismisses the view that there can be a 'neutral style' or 'innocent eye'. All artists operate within a context, and the most important element of that context is previous art: 'Whether an artist begins to paint, write, or compose early or late in life, and however effective his first works may be, always behind them lies the studio, the cathedral, the museum, the library or the concert-hall' (1951, p. 315). Artists begin with pastiche, gradually liberating themselves from previous models as their own style develops. Genuine styles are not mannerisms, nor are they mere technical devices: a true style is born from a genuine response to the human predicament. Thus artists are not transcribers of the scheme of things, but are its rivals.

Yet, while there cannot be a styleless art, and while the history of art in the world shows that masterpieces can be produced in many styles, Malraux contends that all true works of art have something in common, namely that the nature of the creative impulse behind them is the same: 'the victory of each individual artist over his servitude, spreading like ripples on the sea of time, implements art's eternal victory over the human situation. All art is a revolt against man's fate [*L'art est un anti-destin*]' (ibid., p. 639). The creative act is one of humankind's noblest responses to the fact of mortality.

ROBERT WILKINSON

Mañach, Jorge

Cuban. **b:** 1898. **d:** 1961. **Cat:** Phenomenologist; existentialist. **Infls:** Scheler and Simmel.

Main publications:

(1928) *Indagación del choteo*, Havana; second edition, Miami: Mnemosyne, 1969.

(1950) *Martí: Apostle of Freedom*, trans. Coley Taylor, New York: Devin-Adair.

(1959) *Dewey y el pensamiento americano*, Madrid: Taurus.

(1972) *Jorge Mañach: Homenaje de la Nación Cubana*, Rio Piedras, Puerto Rico: Editorial San Juan.

(1975) *Frontiers in the Americas: A Global Perspective*, New York: Teachers' College Press.

Secondary literature:

De la Torre, Amalia (1978) *Jorge Mañach: Maestro del ensayo*, Miami: Ediciones Universal.

Mañach belonged to a generation of Cuban intellectuals who founded the review *Avance* in 1927. He is best known for his highly regarded biography of José Martí. His early work on the *choteo*, a term he defined as 'a strong urge for independence which becomes externalized in a joke which is completely destructive of authority', is a combination of phenomenology and cultural history which seeks to analyse the Cuban national essence. Mañach undertakes a 'reevaluation of things formerly considered trivial or ridiculous' and seeks to discover 'the significance of the insignificant'. Like other thinkers of the *Avance* generation Mañach initially supported Fidel Castro but was later exiled from Cuba for his criticism of the regime.

AMY A. OLIVER

Mandelbaum, Maurice (H.)

American. **b:** 9 December 1908, Chicago. **d:** 1 January 1987, Hanover, New Hampshire. **Cat:** Critical realist. **Ints:** Philosophy of history; philosophy of social science; ethics; history of modern philosophy. **Educ:** Dartmouth College, New Hampshire and Yale. **Appts:** 1934–47, Instructor, then Assistant Professor, Swarthmore College; 1947–57, Professor of Philosophy, Dartmouth College, New Hampshire; 1957–79, Professor of Philosophy, Johns Hopkins University; 1979–83,

Adjunct Professor of Philosophy, and from 1983, Professor Emeritus, Dartmouth College.

Main publications:

(1934) *The Problem of Historical Knowledge: An Answer to Relativism*, New York: Liveswith; reprinted, New York: Harper & Row, 1969.

(1942) 'Causal analysis in history', *Journal of the History of Ideas* 3: 30–50.

(1955) *The Phenomenology of Moral Experience*, Glencoe, Ill.: Free Press, reprinted, Baltimore: Johns Hopkins Press, 1969.

(1955) 'Societal facts', *British Journal of Sociology* 6: 305–17.

(1961) 'The problem of covering laws', *History and Theory* 1: 229–42.

(1964) *Philosophy, Science and Sense Perception: Historical and Critical Studies*, Baltimore: Johns Hopkins Press.

(1971) *History, Man and Reason: A Study in Nineteenth Century Thought*, Baltimore: Johns Hopkins Press.

(1977) *The Anatomy of Historical Knowledge*, Baltimore: Johns Hopkins Press.

(1984) *Philosophy, History and the Sciences: Selected Critical Essays*, Baltimore: Johns Hopkins Press.

(1987) *Purpose and Necessity in Social Theory*, Baltimore: Johns Hopkins Press.

Secondary literature:

Dray, William H. (1979) 'New departures in the theory of historiography', *Philosophy of the Social Sciences* 9: 499–507.

Lloyd, Christopher (1989) 'Realism and structuralism in historical theory: a discussion of the thought of Maurice Mandelbaum', *History and Theory* 28: 296–325.

Mandelbaum defended a form of critical realism at a time when it was no longer widely accepted. He established himself as an astute critic of a number of views that had become near orthodoxies, especially those associated with radical empiricism. A key point of departure for him was the concept of causation. He opposed the Humean orthodoxy that all events are loose and separate and that no connection is perceived between them. He maintained on the contrary that all causes and effects are linked together 'in such a way that they may be said to constitute aspects of a single ongoing process' (1977, p. 76).

His philosophy of history was informed by his epistemology and led him to a complex independent position. He rejected the view of **Hempel** that historical explanation involves general laws. According to Mandelbaum, the historian uses general assumptions but is not concerned to arrive at law-like conclusions. Mandelbaum rejected the view that there was a sharp distinction between scientific generalizations and those of common life. What makes history objective is not its covert use of social laws or conformity to the methods of natural science but the common appeal to evidence. Historians shows their creativity by the way they handle evidence and by discovering new evidence.

Mandelbaum's opposition to subjectivism and relativism was not always successful. His *Phenomenology of Moral Experience* (1955), which relied on a notion of 'moral fittingness', was criticized as an ineffective riposte. Although there was a consistent underlying tendency in his criticisms, he was at his best as a critic rather than in elaborating his own views. As well as attacking the experimental atomism of the radical empricists, Mandelbaum also rejected their view that what is true of a society is reducible to statements about the individuals who constitute it. Here and elsewhere Mandelbaum managed to see beyond false alternatives, rejecting both the radical individualism of one party and the metaphysical holism of the idealists.
Sources: CA; DAS.

STUART BROWN

Mannheim, Karl

German. *b:* 27 March 1893, Budapest. *d:* 9 January 1947, London. *Cat:* Sociologist; epistemologist. *Ints:* Sociology of knowledge; the structure of modern society; education; political sociology. *Educ:* Universities of Budapest, Berlin, Paris, Freiburg and Heidelberg. *Infls:* Literary influences: Marx, Max Weber, Dilthey, Scheler and Lukács. Personal: Sir Fred Clarke. *Appts:* 1926–30, Lecturer in Sociology, University of Heidelberg; 1930–3, Professor and Head of the Department of Sociology, University of Frankfurt; 1933–45, Lecturer in Sociology, London School of Economics; also Lecturer in the Sociology of Education, 1941–44; 1945–7, Professor of Education and Sociology, Institute of Education, University of London.

Main publications:

(1922) *Die Strukturanalyse der Erkenntnistheorie*, Berlin: Reuther & Reichard.

(1929) *Ideologie und Utopie*, Bonn: Cohen; expanded edition, *Ideology and Utopia: An Introduction to the Sociology of Knowledge*, London: Routledge, 1936.

(1935) *Mensch und Gesellschaft im Zeitalter des Umbaus*, Leiden: Sijthoff; revised edition, *Man and Society in an Age of Reconstruction*, London: Routledge, 1940.

(1952) *Essays on the Sociology of Knowledge*, ed. Paul Kecskemeti, London: Routledge.

Secondary literature:

Loader, Colin (1985) *The Intellectual Development of Karl Mannheim*, London: Cambridge University Press.

Longhurst, Brian (1989) *Karl Mannheim and the Contemporary Sociology of Knowledge*, London: Macmillan.

Simonds, A. P. (1978) *Karl Mannheim's Sociology of Knowledge*, Oxford: Clarendon Press.

Mannheim was a sociologist who achieved prominence with *Ideology and Utopia* (1929) in which he defined the nature and scope of the sociology of knowledge. He contributed also to the analysis of modern society, the sociology of education and political sociology.

Mannheim's formulation of the sociology of knowledge arose as a reaction against the *Geistephilosophie* of German idealism. Drawing from many sources, especially **Weber**'s methodology, Marxism and historicism, he argued that society determines both the form and content of cognition, with the exception of mathematics and parts of the natural sciences. Thus he regarded knowledge largely as a function of conditions that are not themselves mental but pertain to the social situation of the thinking subject, and the sociology of knowledge itself as a general method for the correct study of thought and the history of ideas.

Mannheim's central concern was with the phenomenon of ideology. He distinguished between (i) the particular, (ii) the total, and (iii) the general conceptions of ideology; that is to say, ideology as designating: (i) isolated portions of the mental experience of the other (whether a group or an individual) as distortions of their life in society; (ii) the whole of the other's thought; and (iii) the inclusion of one's own thinking within the total conception. He held that with the emergence of (iii) the theory of ideology develops into the sociology of knowledge, the task of which is to achieve a comprehensive, epistemological and historical perspective transcending the partial perspectives associated with particular social positions, an all-inclusive analysis of the social influences of thought. Mannheim also defended utopian thought, maintaining that although it (like ideology) produces distorted images of reality it nevertheless (unlike ideology) sustains the will to shape history and therewith the ability to understand it. Mannheim's great achievement was twofold. He founded the discipline of the sociology of knowledge and brought the term ideology to the attention of sociologists everywhere.

Sources: Wintle; Bullock & Woodings; Turner; WW.

STEPHEN MOLLER

Mannoury, Gerrit

Dutch. *b:*17 May 1867, Wormerveer. *d:*30 January 1956, Amsterdam. *Cat:* Philosopher of language; philosopher of mathematics; main representative of the Dutch Signific Movement. *Educ:* Autodidactic education; courses in Mathematics at the University of Amsterdam. *Infls:* F. Van Eeden, L. E. J. Brouwer and A. Heyting. *Appts:* Member of the Dutch Mathematical Society from 1895; Professor of Mathematics and its Philosophy, University of Amsterdam, 1917–37; honorary doctorate, 1946.

Main publications:

(1909) *Methodologisches und Philosophisches zur Elementar-Mathematik*, Harlem: P. Visser Azn.
(1925) *Mathesis en Mystiek. Een signifiese studie van kommunisties standpunt*, Amsterdam: Maatschappij voor goede en goedkoope lectuur.
(1934) 'Die signifische Grundlagen der Mathematik', *Erkenntnis* 4, 4: 288–309, 4, 5: 317–45.
(1938) 'Signifische Analyse der Willenssprache als Grundlage einer physikalische Sprachsynthese', Fourth International Congress for the Unity of Science, Cambridge, 1938, in: *Erkenntnis* 7: 180–8, 366–9.
(1969), 'A concise history of significs', *Methodology and Science* 2: 171–80.

Secondary literature:

Heijerman, E. (1990) 'Relativism and significs: Gerrit Mannoury on the foundations of mathematics', in H. W. Schmitz, *Essays on Significs*, Amsterdam and Philadelphia: Bejamins, pp. 247–72.
Schmitz, H. W. (1984) 'Searle ist in Mode, Mannoury nicht: Sprech- und Hörakt im niederländischen Signifik-Kreis' *Zeitschrift für Semiotik* 6, 4: pp. 445–63.

The mathematician and philosopher Mannoury was the moving force behind the Signific Movement in the Netherlands. The term 'significs' was coined by Victoria Lady Welby, whose critical ideas on the nature of language and communication were introduced in Holland after 1892 by the psychiatrist, poet and social reformer Frederik Van Eeden. In 1922 the Signific Circle was founded (G. Mannoury, L. E. J. **Brouwer**, F. Van Eeden, J. Van Ginniken), aiming at social reform through critique of language. In the 1930s more participants from a wide range of disciplines became involved in significs; there were contacts with the Vienna Circle and the Unity of Science movement, and the journal *Synthese* was founded (1936). After ten international signific conferences and the death of Mannoury, the movement evaporated in the 1960s.

Significs can be defined as 'the theory of mental associations which underlie human language acts, with the exception of theories of language in a narrower sense' (Mannoury 1934). Long before **Austin** and **Searle** developed the theory of speech acts, Mannoury developed his theory of *language acts*. These include actions of both speaker and hearer on the basis of their mutual expectations. In the performance of a language act, memory, internal experience, perception, volition and emotion of speaker and hearer interact in a complex way. 'Meaning' is thus mainly conceived in mental terms; this has been both the strength and the weakness of the theory, which was founded on an obsolete form of association psychology.

With respect to the philosophy of mathematics, Mannoury has had a vital influence on L. E. J. Brouwer, the founder of intuitionistic mathematics. In 1903 he introduced symbolic logic into the Netherlands, and in 1927 he formulated a prize question which led **Heyting** to a first formalization of intuitionistic logic.

ERIK HEIJERMAN

Mao Zedong (Mao Tse-Tung)

Chinese. *b:* 1893, Shaoshan, Xiangtang County, Hunan Province, China. *d:* 1976, Beijing. *Cat:* Marxist; political and military leader; poet. *Ints:* Social and political philosophy. *Educ:* First Normal School, Changsha, Hunan Province and briefly audited courses at University of Beijing. *Infls:* Kang Youwei, Liang Qichao, Yan Fu and Western liberal thinkers, Li Dazhao, Chen Duxiu, Marx, Lenin, Stalin, and Soviet theoreticians, Ai Siqi, and Qin Shihuang (China's first Emperor). *Appts:* Chairman, Central Executive Committee, Chinese Soviet Republic, 1931–4; Chairman, Council of People's Commissars, Chinese Soviet Republic, 1931–4; Chairman, Politburo, Chinese Communist Party, 1935–; Chairman, Standing Committee, Chinese Communist Party Politburo, 1956–76; Chairman, Revolutionary Military

Council, 1945–9; Chairman, People's Revolutionary Military Council, 1954–9; Commander in Chief, People's Liberation Army, 1945–9; Chairman, National Defence Council, 1954–9; Chairman, Chinese Communist Party Central Committee, 1943–76; Chairman, People's Government Council (Head of State), 1949–58.

Main publications:

(n.d.) *Dialectical Materialism (Lecture Notes)*, Dalian: Dazhong Bookshop.
(n.d.) *Selected Writings by Chairman Mao*, n.p.
(1960) *Comrade Mao Zedong on Marxist Philosophy (Extracts)*, Urumqi: Xinjiang Qingnian Publishing House.
(1960) *Mao Zedong's Philosophical Thought*, extracts compiled by the Department of Philosophy of Peking University).
(1960–5, 1977) *Selected Works of Mao Tse-tung*, 5 vols, Beijing: Foreign Languages Press.
(1966) *Quotations From Chairman Mao*, Beijing: People's Publishing Company.
(1967) *Selected Readings*, Beijing: Foreign Languages Press.
(1968) *Selected Readings of Mao Zedong's Writings*, 2 vols, Beijing: People's Publishing House.
(1988) *Mao Zedong's Collected Annotations on Philosophy*, Beijing: Zhongyang Wenxian Research Institute.

Secondary literature:

Boorman, H. (ed.) (1970) *Biographical Dictionary of Republican China*, New York and London: Columbia University Press.
Briere, O. (1956) *Fifty Years of Chinese Philosophy 1898–1950*, London: George Allen & Unwin Ltd.
Complete Chinese Encyclopedia (1987), Philosophy Volumes, Beijing: Chinese Encyclopedia Publications.
Louie, K. (1986) *Inheriting Tradition: Interpretations of the Classical Philosophers in Communist China 1949–1966*, Hong Kong: Oxford University Press.
Schram, S. (1966) *Mao Tse-tung*, Harmondsworth: Penguin Books.
——(1989) *The Thought of Mao Tse-tung*, Cambridge: Cambridge University Press.

After early radical activity organizing peasants and students in Hunan Province, Mao turned to Marxism under the influence of **Li Dazhao** and **Chen Duxiu**, China's first major Marxist figures. He argued from a Marxist perspective for the legitimacy of seizing power by force against Bertrand **Russell**'s reformist gradualism during Russell's visit to Hunan. Mao represented Hunan at the founding meeting of the Chinese Communist Party in 1921 and entered a busy life of organizational, educational and trade union activities. He became a member of the Communist Party's Central Committee and the Director of its Organization Department in 1923. Under Comintern policy of cooperating with the Nationalists, Mao also held important posts with the Guomindang, dealing with party organization, propaganda and the peasant movement. Mao's study of the peasantry convinced him that overthrowing the landlord class was necessary for China to secure a prosperous and independent future. He recognized the crucial revolutionary potential of China's peasant population and the importance of opening the party bureaucracy to the influence of the masses. When first articulated, these views were rejected by the Party in favour of orthodox concentration on the urban proletariat as the main focus of revolutionary activity.

During the years of Party instability following the Guomindang massacre of Communists in 1927, Mao established a base in Jiangxi Province. Together with the military strategist Zhu De, he developed theories dealing with party organization and leadership and with control of population and territory. Their guerrilla and mobile warfare and popular revolutionary mobilization evaded successive campaigns organized by Guomindang leader Jiang Jieshi (Chiang Kia-shek) to crush them. In Jiangxi, Mao also had his first experience directing a major purge of those rebelling against his authority. Mao's successful application of his theoretical position increased his political power, culminating in his elevation to party leadership in 1935 as Chairman of the Politburo.

By 1934, however, Guomindang encirclement forced Mao and his followers to embark upon the Long March which, after terrible losses, ended at Yanan, Shanaxi Province. Mao's lectures in Yanan reflected years of revolutionary experience and explored many matters, including military strategy, government, philosophy, literature and art. In all cases, he argued for the primacy of politics. His integrated military and political ideas bore fruit in the Anti-Japanese War and in renewed civil war against Jiang Jieshe and the Guomindang. Mao's victory led to the establishment of the People's Republic in 1949.

As a ruler Mao veered between the cautious and flexible pragmatism of his principal colleagues and his own utopian, voluntarist populism displayed in the establishment of the communes, the Great Leap Forward and the Cultural Revolution. He broke with the Soviet Union, which provided a model of revolution so different from his own. The humiliating failure of the Great Leap Forward threatened his position and led to the Cultural Revolution, in which Mao appealed to the populace against the Party apparatus. In the face of the resulting anarchy and violence, Mao turned to the army to restore order; but with a debilitated Party and dogmatic leadership under the Gang of Four, he spent his last years publicly revered, though in growing isolation and confusion.

In the treatment of philosophers and other intellectuals, Mao also responded to conflicting demands. Because his regime needed the cooperation of sophisticated, Western-educated figures to articulate and implement new policies, Mao included all who were not enemies in a broad front programme of New Democracy. His conception of democracy, however, was based on the doctrine of popular dictatorship, in which the party would exercise leadership through constant attention to the masses. He was contemptuous of the 'flabby liberalism' of bourgeois democracy. Mao sought to reshape the thinking of intellectuals to gain loyalty as well as consent on the model of his party rectification campaign of 1942–3. Mao provided gestures of conciliation, but also closed the universities to retrain philosophers and others in Marxist thought. He waged intense campaigns against intellectual opponents, initially the pragmatist and liberal philosopher **Hu Shi**. The relative latitude of the Hundred Flowers Campaign gave way to the harsh Anti-Rightist Campaign when Mao was angered by the depth of residual bitterness and opposition amongst intellectuals. A modest return to wider debate was swept away by the Cultural Revolution, during which distinguished figures were humiliated and physically attacked, with some hounded to death. Intellectuals were sent to the countryside, in some cases with their work of a lifetime destroyed.

Regarding the brutal side of his treatment of intellectuals, Mao compared himself with Qin Shihuang, China's rationalizing and unifying first Emperor. In other more positive ways, Mao aimed to sinify Marxism by placing it within the context of Chinese history, thought and literature, although he was hostile to Confucianism as the central ideology of China's feudal past.

Mao's own philosophical work took the form of lectures on dialectical materialism delivered in 1937 in Yanan. For the most part, these lectures were unimpressive summaries of Soviet texts, but two essays 'On practice' and 'On contradiction' were extracted and printed in revised form in 1950 and 1952. 'On practice' discusses Marxist episte-mology and the relations between theory and practice. The theme of seeking the truth from the facts derives from ancient Chinese sources and was used to combat the Moscow-educated dogmatists who challenged Mao's authority. More original was 'On contradiction', an exploration of dialectics drawn theoretically from ancient yin-yang doctrines as well as from Hegel and Marx and practically from Mao's understanding of Chinese society. The claim that contradictions would continue to arise in society even after the establishment of socialism supported Mao's doctrine of permanent revolution. His distinction between antagonistic and non-antagonistic contradictions allowed room for discussion rather than violence as a response to some controversies. His voluntarism was supported by the claim that at times superstructure, theory and relations of production took priority in determining social developments. 'On practice' and 'On contradiction' became major elements in Mao Zedong Thought, studied and emulated throughout China. Their dogmatic use undermined the doctrines of voluntarist flexibility, respect for the facts and the concrete appropriation of China's complex history within universal Marxist thought.

NICHOLAS BUNNIN

Marc-Wogau, Konrad

Swedish. *b:* 4 April 1902, Moscow. *d:* 27 October 1991, Uppsala. *Cat:* Analytical philosopher; historian of philosophy. *Ints:* Kant; epistemology; history of philosophy. *Appts:* 1946–68, Professor of Theoretical Philosophy, Uppsala University.

Main publications:

(1932) *Untersunchugen zur Raumlehre Kants*, Lund: Håkan Ohlsson.

(1936) *Inhalt und Umfang des Begriffs*, Uppsala: Humanistiska Vetenskapssamfundet.

(1938) *Vier Studien zu Kants Kritik der Urteilskraft*, Uppsala: Acta Universitatis Upsaliensis.

(1945) *Die Theorie der Sinnesdaten. Probleme der neueren Erkenntnistheorie in England*, Uppsala: Acta Universitatis Upsaliensis.

(1951) 'Kants Lehre vom analytischen Urteil', *Theoria* (English translation, 'Kant's doctrine of the analytical judgment', in *Philosophical Essays*, 1967.

(1967) *Philosophical Essays: History of Philosophy, Perception, Historical Explanation*, Lund: Library of Theoria (contains bibliography).

(1968) *Studier till Axel Hägerströms filosofi* [Studies in the Philosophy of Axel Hägerström], Falköping: Bokförlaget Prisma.

Secondary literature:
Broad, C. D. (1947) 'Professor Marc-Wogau's Theorie der Sinnesdaten', *Mind*.
——(1992) *Theoria* (obituary).

In his youth Marc-Wogau was a disciple of **Hägerström** and, especially, of **Phalén**. Their influence is evident in the writings of the 1930s, for example in his use of Phalén's dialectical method in the study of the history of philosophy, and in the interesting discussions in *Theoria* (1936–40) between the young Marc-Wogau and the old Ernst **Cassirer**. Later, however, he was more influenced by the analytical philosophers in Cambridge (**Moore**, **Russell**, W. E. Johnson and **Broad**).

Marc-Wogau made very important and comprehensive contributions in two fields: the epistemological discussion of sense data and the study of Kant. For the former his main work is *Die Theorie der Sinnesdaten* (1945). It contains a thorough scrutiny of theories of empirical knowledge in contemporary British epistemology (and in the Vienna Circle). It also presents an independent positive theory of the relation between sense-perception and physical objects. Marc-Wogau applies certain results of contemporary experimental psychology of perception, particularly concerning the phenomena of constancy in the sensations of size, shape and colour. He introduces the concept of abstractive difference and a new analysis of existence-sentences of a certain kind. He returned to the sense-data problems in several papers, including one on perceptual space and one on a theory of **Ryle**'s; a few of these papers are collected in the *Philosophical Essays* (1967).

In the first book on Kant (1932) several important themes of Kant's precritical and critical philosophy are dealt with, for example Kant's attempt to unite Newton's and Leibniz's conceptions of space, the concept of phenomenon and the Trendelenburg gap. In the second book on Kant (1938) both problems concerning teleology and the concept of organism and problems concerning the beautiful and the sublime are dealt with. It also contains an analysis of Kant's moral proof of the existence of God. In spite of its shortness, 'Kant's Lehre vom analytischen Urteil' (1951) is of great interest.

Marc-Wogau published many important works outside the above two fields, for example

on the problems of historical explanation. His interest in the history of philosophy was by no means limited to Kant: in minor writings he analysed important problems in Plato, Aristotle, Descartes, Berkeley, Fichte, Marx, **Hägerström** and others.

THORILD DAHLQUIST

Marcel, Gabriel

French. *b:* 1889, Paris. *d:* 1973, Paris. *Cat:* Neo-Socratic and theistic existentialist; playwright and musician. *Ints:* The phenomenology of the human existence; metaphysical reality; ethics. *Educ:* The Sorbonne, Paris; 1908, doctoral thesis on 'The Metaphysical Ideas of Coleridge and their Relationship to the Philosophy of Schelling'. *Infls:* Karl Jaspers and Roman Catholicism. *Appts:* 1912–40, taught intermittently at various secondary schools in Verdôme, Paris and Sens; worked for the Red Cross in the Second World War; 1929, converted to Roman Catholicism; undertook numerous European lecture tours, including the Gifford Lectures in 1949–50.

Main publications:
(1927) *Journal métaphysique* (1913–23), Paris: Gallimard (English translation, *Metaphysical Journal*, trans. Bernard Wall, Chicago: Regnery, 1952).
(1935) *Être et avoir*, Paris: Aubier (English translation, *Being and Having*, trans. Katherine Farrer, New York: Harper & Brothers, 1949).
(1945) *Homo Viator: Prolégomènes à une métaphysique de l'espérance*, Paris: Aubier (English translation, *Homo Viator: Introduction to a Metaphysic of Hope*, trans. Emma Crawford, Chicago: Regnery, 1951; reprinted, New York: Harper & Row, 1962).
(1945) *La Métaphysique de Royce*, Paris: Aubier.
(1949–50) *Le Mystère de L'être* (The Gifford Lectures) (English translation in 2 vols, *The Mystery of Being*: 1. *Reflection and Mystery* (1949); 2. *Faith and Reality* (1950), trans. G. S. Fraser and R. Hague, Chicago: Regnery).
(1955) *The Decline of Wisdom*, New York: Philosophical Library.
(1963) *The Existential Background of Human Dignity*, Cambridge: Mass.: Harvard University Press.

Secondary literature:
Gilson, Étienne (ed.) (1947) *Existentialisme chrétien: Gabriel Marcel*, Paris: Plon (essays in honour of Marcel, including his reply, 'Regard en arrière', trans. in *The Philosophy of Existence*, London: The Harvill Press, 1948).

Hammond, Julien (1992) 'Marcel's philosophy of human nature', *Dialogue* 35, 1: 1-5.

Schilpp, Paul A. (ed.) (1994) *The Philosophy of Gabriel Marcel*, La Salle: Open Court.

Troisfontaines, Roger (1953) *De l'Existence à l'Être*, 2 vols, Paris (concordance and bibliography).

Marcel's philosophy is discursive and unsystematic: the expression of a reflective exploration rather than a record of conclusions reached. His intention is to reveal a metaphysical reality and his starting-point is the human situation, the experience of being-in-the-world. The mainspring of his thought is the claim that the human person is, *au fond*, a participant in, rather than a spectator of, reality and the life of the world; a being that ultimately cannot be encompassed to become an object of thought.

Marcel described himself as Socratic and questioning rather than as an existentialist. He repudiated idealism because of the 'way in which [it] overrates the part of construction in sensual perception', and he was repelled by philosophies that deployed special terminologies or proceeded by assuming that reason, properly exerted, could achieve a total grasp of reality. 'Reality', he wrote, 'cannot be summed up.' Immediate, personal experience is the touchstone of all his enquiries, and in this he resembles the avowedly existentialist thinkers even though he emphasized personal transcendence and human relationships rather than the existential freedom and autonomy traditionally associated with existentialism. He developed a phenomenology of his own that owed nothing to **Husserl**.

Marcel distinguished two kinds of consciousness, 'first reflection' and 'second reflection'. In first reflection a person might mentally stand back from, say, a direct relationship of friendship, in order to describe and objectify it. This, according to Marcel, is to separate oneself from the relationship and to treat it as a 'problem' in need of explanation. In 'second reflection' the immediacy of the relationship is restored, but additionally there is an awareness of participation in Being: the recognition that we inhabit a 'mystery'; that it is not our prime task to separate ourselves and objectify this condition and that 'Having', that sense of owning one's body, talents, abilities, must be transformed into 'Being'.

On the basis of this analysis Marcel conducts an investigation into a range of concepts, including incarnation, fidelity, hope, faith, love and *disponibilité* (availability). In being *disponible* a person is receptive to others, is fully present and responsive to them and, through this kind of intersubjectivity, affirms a mutual participation in Being.

A summary of Marcel's ideas conveys little of his thought's philosophical penetration, which is achieved by detailed and vivid phenomenological enquiry rather than by the orderly presentation of proofs. His dramatic and other writings powerfully complement the major themes of the philosophy.

Sources: PI.

DIANÉ COLLINSON

Marchesini, Giovanni

Italian. *b:* 18 September 1868, Noventa Vicentina, Italy. *d:* 8 November 1931, Padua. *Cat:* Philosopher of positivism. *Educ:* Student of Ardigò at Padua. *Infls:* Ardigò. *Appts:* Biographer of Ardigò; 1902–, Professor, University of Padua.

Main publications:

(1898) *La crisi del positivismo e il problema filosofico*.

(1901) *Il simbolismo nella conoscenza e nella morale*.

(1902) *Il dominio dello spirito*.

(1905) *Le finzioni dell'anima*.

(1925) *La finzione nell'educazione, o la pedagogia del 'come se'*.

Marchesini's philosophy is a record of the debates about positivism in Italy at the turn of the century. His approach to positivism led to the 'theory of fictions' which on the one hand denies metaphysical validity to ethical ideals in order to constrain them within a positivistic interpretation of moral life and on the other recognizes their normative and pragmatic office in human action. He stressed the merely negative significance of the concept of the absolute and its merely symbolic character but in such a way as to reveal a commitment to what may be called 'idealistic positivism' involving the theory of fictions, which justifies the practical utility of ideals of value while asserting their lack of theoretical validity. Values are fictitious projections that help preserve us by projecting the products of the imagination on to the world. Scientific truth is a fiction in which we ideologically transform nature, as is the ethical ideal with its notion of good and duty. Calling these 'fictions' is not to deny their regulative force. Marchesini is a possible precursor of **Vaihinger**'s philosophy of the 'as if'.

COLIN LYAS

Marcus, Ruth Barcan

American. *b:* 1921, New York City. *Cat:* Logician.

Educ: New York University, BA 1941; Yale University, MA 1942, PhD 1946. *Infls:* Rudolf Carnap, Ernst Cassirer, A. N. Prior and W. V. O. Quine. *Appts:* Research Associate in Anthropology, Institute for Human Relations, Yale University, 1945–7; AAUW Fellow 1947–8; Visiting Professor, Northwestern University, 1950–7; Guggenheim Fellow, 1953–4; Assistant, then Associate Professor, Roosevelt University, Chicago, 1957–63; Professor of Philosophy, University of Illinois at Chicago, 1964–70, Head of Department, 1963–9; Fellow, University of Illinois Center for Advanced Study, 1968–9; Professor of Philosophy, Northwestern University, 1970–3; Reuben Post Halleck Professor of Philosophy, Yale University, from 1973; Fellow, Centre for Advanced Study in Behavioral Science, Stanford University, California, 1979; Fellow, Institute for Advanced Study, University of Edinburgh, 1983; Visiting Fellow, Wolfson College, Oxford, 1985, 1986: Visiting Fellow, Clare Hall, Cambridge, 1988; Fellow of the American Academy of Arts and Sciences.

Main publications:

(1946) 'A functional calculus of first order based on strict implication', *Journal of Symbolic Logic* 11: 1–16.

(1947) 'The identity of individuals in a strict functional calculus of second order', *Journal of Symbolic Logic* 12: 12–15.

(1961) 'Modalities and intensional languages', *Synthese* 13: 303–22.

(1962) 'Interpreting quantification', *Inquiry* 5: 252–9.

(1963) 'Classes and attributes in extended modal systems', *Acta Philosophica Fennica* 16: 123–36.

(1967) 'Essentialism in modal logic', *Nous* I, 1: 90–6.

(1972) 'Quantification and ontology', *Nous* VI, 3.

(1968) 'Modal logic', in R. Klibansky (ed.), *Contemporary Philosophy*, Florence: La Nuova Editrice, pp. 87–101.

(1969) 'Extensionality', *Mind* 78: 55–62.

(1976) 'Dispensing with possibilia', *Proceedings and Addresses of The American Philosophical Assocation* 44: 39–51.

(1990) 'A backward look at Quine's animadversions on modalities', in R. Barrett and R. Gibson (eds), *Perspectives on Quine*, Oxford: Blackwell, pp. 230–43.

(1993) *Modalities: Philosophical Essays*, Oxford: Oxford University Press.

Secondary literature:

Sinnott-Armstrong, W., Raffman, D. and Asher, Nicholas (eds) (1995) *Modality, Morality and*

Belief: Essays in Honor of Ruth Barcan Marcus, Cambridge: Cambridge University Press.

Ruth Marcus made major contributions to the development of modal logic. Some of the best known modal systems had already been axiomatised by C. I. **Lewis** in 1918, but it was Marcus who extended them by providing modal predicate logic. She also favoured what is known as 'substitutional' quantification over 'objectual' quantification, regarding the former as helping to resolve certain problems arising from mixing quantifiers with modal operators and with verbs of attitude like 'believes'. Controversially, she maintained that extensionality in logic was a matter of degree.

Some ten years ahead of Saul **Kripke** she put forward the theorem to the effect that all genuine identity statements, if true, were necessarily true. She also anticipated later work on the notion of direct reference, treating proper names as 'tags', as not as equivalent in meaning to descriptions. Additionally, she originated the thesis which now bears her name—the 'Barcan formula' which, informally, states that if it is possible that there is an object with a given property, then it follows that there is an object which possibly has that property. A feature of these theses, which attracted much discussion, is their prima facie commitment to essentialism, that is to say the view that entities have at least some of their properties of necessity.

Years later, evincing a freshness of response to some of the developments she had helped to stimulate, she recommended substitutional quantification as the most appropriate for the new 'Meinongian' logics (those accommodating reference to nonexistents) which had been developed by Terence Parsons and others. Throughout, however, her most distinguished opponent has been W. V. O. **Quine**, who remained convinced that modality and essentialism were suspect and had no place in any scientific account of the world. Not even Ruth Marcus escaped the charge that modal logic had been conceived in the sin of confusing use and mention, but Quine himself would be the first to acknowledge the significance and calibre of the work of this sometimes neglected philosophical logician.

Sources: WW(Am) 1994.

DENIS POLLARD

Marcuse, Herbert

German. *b:* 19 July 1898, Berlin. *d:* 30 July 1979, Munich. *Cat:* Critical theorist. *Ints:* History of philosophy; social philosophy; psychoanalytic theory. *Educ:* Philosophy at Berlin and Freiburg (doctorate 1923); further study in Freiburg, 1929–32, with Husserl and Heidegger; left after his relations with Heidegger deteriorated. *Infls:* Husserl, Heidegger, Adorno, Horkheimer, Hegel, Marx and Freud. *Appts:* Member of Institut für Sozialforschung, from 1933; exile in Geneva, New York and California; Section Head, Office of Strategic Services, 1942–50; Professor of Philosophy, Brandeis University, 1954–67; Professor of Philosophy, University of California at Santa Barbara, 1967.

Main publications:

(1928) 'Beiträge zu einer Phänomenologie des historischen Materialismus', *Philosophische Hefte*: 45–68.

(1932) *Hegels Ontologie und die Grundlegung einer Theorie der Geschichtlichkeit*, Frankfurt: V. Klostermann (English translation, *Hegel's Ontology and the Theory of Historicity*, Seyla Benhabib, Cambridge, Mass.: MIT Press, 1987).

(1936) (with Erich Fromm and Max Horkheimer) *Studien über Autorität und Familie*, Paris: F. Alcan.

(1941) *Reason and Revolution. Hegel and the Rise of Social Theory*, New York: Oxford University Press; second edition, Boston: Beacon Press, 1960.

(1955) *Eros and Civilization: A Philosophical Inquiry into Freud*, Boston: Beacon Press.

(1964) *One Dimensional Man: Studies in the Ideology of Advanced Industrial Society*, Boston: Beacon Press.

(1964) *Soviet Marxism: A Critical Analysis*, Boston: Beacon Press; new edition, Harmondsworth: Penguin, 1971.

(1965) *Kultur und Gesellschaft*, 2 vols, Frankfurt: Suhrkamp.

(1965) (with Robert P. Wolff and Barrington Moore Jr) *A Critique of Pure Tolerance*, Boston: Beacon Press.

(1968) *Negations: Essays in Critical Theory*, Boston: Beacon Press.

(1968) *Psychoanalyse und Politik*, Frankfurt: Europäische Verlagsanstalt.

(1968) (with others) *Aggression und Anpassung in der Industriegesellschaft*, Frankfurt: Suhrkamp.

(1969) *An Essay on Liberation*, Boston: Beacon Press.

(1969) *Ideen zu einer kritischen Theorie der Gesellschaft*, Frankfurt: Suhrkamp.

(1970) *Five Lectures: Psychoanalysis, Politics and Utopia*, trans. Jeremy J. Shapiro and Shierry M. Weber, Boston: Beacon Press.

(1972) *Counterrevolution and Revolt*, Boston: Beacon Press.

(1973) *Studies in Critical Philosophy*, Jois de Bres, Boston: Beacon Press.

(1975) *Zeit-Messungen. Drei Vorträge und ein Interview*, Frankfurt: Suhrkamp.

(1977) *Die Permanenz der Kunst. Wider eine bestimmte marxistische Ästhetik: Ein Essay*, Munich: Hanser.

(1978) *The Aesthetic Dimension: Towards a Critique of Marxist Aesthetics*, Boston: Beacon Press.

(1978–) *Schriften*, Frankfurt: Suhrkamp.

(1980) *Das Ende der Utopie. Vorträge und Diskussionen in Berlin 1967*, Frankfurt: Verlag Neue Kritik.

Secondary literature:

Breuer, Stefan (1977) *Die Krise der Revolutionstheorie. Negative Vergesellschaftung und Arbeitsmetaphysik bei Herbert Marcuse*, Frankfurt: Syndikat Autoren- und Verlagsgesellschaft.

Brunkhorst, Hauke and Koch, Gertrud (1987) *Herbert Marcuse zur Einführung*, Hamburg: Junius.

Claussen, Detlev (1981) *Spuren der Befreiung— Herbert Marcuse. Eine Einführung in sein politisches Denken*, Darmstadt: Luchterhand.

Habermas, Jürgen (ed.) (1968) *Antworten auf Herbert Marcuse*, Frankfurt: Suhrkamp.

——(1978) *Gespräche mit Herbert Marcuse*, Frankfurt: Suhrkamp.

Jansohn, Heinz (1971) *Herbert Marcuse: Philosophische Grundlagen seiner Gesellschaftskritik*, Bonn: Bouvier.

Katz, Barry (1982) *Herbert Marcuse and the Art of Liberation: An Intellectual Biography*, London: New Left Books.

Kellner, Douglas (1984) *Herbert Marcuse and the Crisis of Marxism*, London: Macmillan.

MacIntyre, Alasdair (1970) *Marcuse*, Glasgow: Fontana.

Mattick, Paul (1972) *Critique of Marcuse: One-Dimensional Man in Class Society*, London: Merlin.

Roth, Roland, *Rebellische Subjektivität. Herbert Marcuse und die neuen Protestbewegungen*, Frankfurt and New York: Campus.

Stark, Franz (ed.) (1971) *Revolution oder Reform. Herbert Marcuse und Karl Popper. Eine Konfrontation*, Munich: Kösel (English translation, *Reform or Revolution: A Confrontation Between Herbert Marcuse and Karl Popper*, trans. Michael Aylway and A. T. Ferguson, Chicago: New University Press, 1976).

Wolff, Kurt H. and Moore Jr, Barrington (eds) *The Critical Spirit: Essays in Honor of Herbert Marcuse*, Boston: Beacon Press.

Of the core members of the Frankfurt School, Marcuse was both the most actively political and the most concerned with a directly philosophical engagement with classical Marxism and with the phenomenology of his teachers **Husserl** and **Heidegger**. Marcuse's early work in particular is strongly marked by the attempt to fuse Marxist and phenomenological insights, a central feature of later existentialist Marxism in France and of praxis philosophy in Yugoslavia. Along with Marxism and phenomenology, the third element—already prominent in the 1930s in Marcuse's many essays in the Institute's journal, the *Zeitschrift für Sozialforschung*, and in his contribution to its joint project on authority and the family—was Freudian theory. His postwar work was dominated by a reworking of themes in Marx (especially the analysis of alienation in the 1844 manuscripts) and **Freud**, in an ambitious theory of human emancipation. Together, *Eros and Civilization* (1955) and *One Dimensional Man* (1964) made Marcuse the paradigmatic thinker of the New Left across North America and Western Europe in the late 1960s and into the 1970s—a role which surprised but did not disturb him. Although the empirical analysis in *One Dimensional Man* can be questioned, and it now appears in some ways as a left variant of the theories of industrial society prominent in the 1950s and 1960s, it remains a brilliant attempt at a philosophical diagnosis of the times.

WILLIAM OUTHWAITE

Maréchal, Joseph

Belgian. *b:* 1 July 1878, Charleroi, France. *d:* 11 December 1944, Louvain. *Cat:* Scholastic. *Ints:* Metaphysics; epistemology. *Educ:* University of Louvain. *Infls:* Pierre Rousselot, Aquinas and Kant. *Appts:* 1919–35, Professor of the History of Philosophy, Jesuit house of studies, Louvain.

Main publications:

(1922–6) *Le Point de départ de la métaphysique*:
(1922) Cahier I, *De l'antiquité à la fin du moyen âge*; third edition, Brussels: L'Edition Universelle; Paris: Desclée, 1944.
(1923) Cahier II, *Le Conflit du rationalisme et de l'empiricisme dans la philosophie moderne avant Kant*; third edition, Brussels: L'Edition Universelle; Paris: Desclée, 1944.
(1923) Cahier III, *La Critique de Kant*; third edition, Brussels: L'Edition Universelle; Paris: Alcan, 1944.
(1926) Cahier V, *Le Thomisme devant la philosophie critique*, Louvain: Museum Lessianum; Paris: Alcan.

(1947) Cahier IV, *Par delà le Kantisme*, Brussels: L'Edition Universelle; Paris: Desclée.
(1950) *Mélanges Joseph Maréchal*, 2 vols, Brussels: L'Edition Universelle.
(1950) *Mélanges Joseph Maréchal*, 2 vols, Brussels: L'Edition Universelle (includes bibliography and a number of critical studies).
Javier, Benjamin P. (1965) 'Joseph Maréchal's metaphysics of intellectual dynamism', *The Modern Schoolman* 42: 375–98.
John, Helen James (1966) *The Thomist Spectrum*, New York: Fordham University Press, pp. 139–49.
Milet, Albert (1940–5) 'Les "Cahiers" du P. Maréchal. Sources doctrinales et influences subies', *Revue Néoscolastique de Philosophie* 43: 225–51.
Van Riet, Georges (1963) *Thomistic Epistemology*, 2 vols, St Louis and London: Herder, vol. I, pp. 236–71.

Maréchal was an early exponent of what has come to be called 'transcendental Thomism': a form of neoscholastic philosophy generated by an engagement, confrontation and partial synthesis with the Kantian critique. At the heart of Maréchal's theory of knowledge is his conception of the intellect as active and dynamic, in the sense that it has a dynamic drive or tendency towards Being. This dynamism, he argued, is one of the a priori conditions of the possibility of the objective contents consciousness. The objectivity of the phenomenal object, immanent in consciousness, is possible only on the supposition that consciousness is intentional, that real being is present as an end towards which the intellect drives itself. We do, therefore, have a direct (though not an intuitive) knowledge of things in themselves. Thus, even if we begin at Kant's own starting-point, we can go beyond him, methodologically and philosophically, to the kind of metaphysics presented most completely in Aquinas, since, for Aquinas, the objectively real is the primitive datum, and mental contents are explained in terms of it. The five volumes, or *cahiers*, of Maréchal's great work constitute a remarkable history of the problem of knowledge, and the fifth *cahier* gives us his critique, from a Thomistic perspective, of the Kantian critique. A sixth *cahier*, which was to have presented his own theory of knowledge, was unfortunately never written. Maréchal did not receive universal acclaim from the Thomists of his own time, but his reputation has grown to the point where he is now regarded as one of the leading Thomists of the century.

Sources: DFN; EF.

HUGH BREDIN

Margolis, Joseph

American. **b:** 16 May 1924, Newark, New Jersey. **Cat:** Analytic philosopher; philosopher of art; philosopher of history and culture. **Ints:** Philosophy of science; aesthetics. **Educ:** Columbia University. **Infls:** C. S. Peirce, L. Wittgenstein and J. L. Austin. **Appts:** 1947–56, Instructor, and Assistant Professor (1954) in Philosophy, Long Island University; 1956–8, Assistant Professor of Philosophy, University of South Carolina; 1958–9, Visiting Assistant Professor of Philosophy, University of California, Berkeley; 1960–5, Associate Professor, Professor (1965) of Philosophy, and Senior Research Associate in Psychiatry, University of Cincinnati; 1965–7, Professor of Philosophy and Head, Department of Philosophy, University of Western Ontario; from 1968, Professor of Philosophy, and Laura H. Carnell Professor of Philosophy (1990), Temple University.

Main publications:

(1962) (ed.) *Philosophy Looks at the Arts*, New York: Charles Scribner's Sons; second edition, Philadelphia, PA: Temple University Press, 1978; third edition, 1986.

(1965) *The Language of Art and Art Criticism: Analytic Questions in Aesthetics*, Detroit, MI: Wayne State University Press.

(1966) *Psychotherapy and Morality: A Study of Two Concepts*, New York: Alfred A. Knopf.

(1971) *Values and Conduct*, Oxford and New York: Clarendon Press.

(1973) *Knowledge and Existence*, New York: Oxford University Press.

(1975) *Negativities: The Limits of Life*, Columbus, OH: Charles Merrill.

(1978) *Persons and Minds*, Boston Studies in the Philosophy of Science, Dordrecht: D. Reidel.

(1980) *Art and Philosophy*, Atlantic Highlands, NJ: Humanities Press and Hassocks: Harvester Press.

(1984) *Culture and Cultural Entities*, Dordrecht: D. Reidel.

(1986) *Pragmatism Without Foundations: Reconciling Relativism and Realism*, Oxford: Basil Blackwell.

(1987) *Science Without Unity: Reconciling the Natural and the Human Sciences*, Oxford: Basil Blackwell.

(1989) *Texts Without Referents: Reconciling Science and Narrative*, Oxford: Basil Blackwell.

(1991) *The Truth about Relativism*, Oxford: Basil Blackwell.

(1993) *The Flux of History and the Flux of Science*, Berkeley, CA: University of California Press.

Margolis's prodigious output in philosophy—with articles and reviews up to 1993 amounting to some 500 items—covers nearly all aspects of the subject. However, his principal contributions are in the philosophy of the human sciences and in aesthetics. He has developed a refined and original form of relativism, an account of cultural emergence, a distinctive metaphysics encompassing cultural phenomena from works of art to speech acts and human thought, and detailed analyses of reference, identity and intentionality. One aim of his later work has been to try to draw the best from the tradition of twentieth-century continental philosophy to enrich the conceptual resources of analytic philosophy. He is sympathetic to the historicist trend in such writers as Michel **Foucault** and Hans-Georg **Gadamer**, in particular the view that thinking itself is historical in structure, not determined by timeless categories. In aesthetics he has argued that works of art are 'physically embodied and culturally emergent entities', thereby defining a middle path between idealist and reductionist theories of art. The view reflects an earlier discussion of persons which rejects both dualism and reductive materialism. He has also argued that mutually incompatible interpretations can be true of a single work of art, this being a further consequence of his relativism. He is at pains to emphasize, however, that his relativism is 'robust', not to be equated with radical subjectivism. Not any interpretation is as good as any other. In his later work he sees interpretation itself (in the sense of hermeneutics) playing an increasingly central role in the explanation of both cultural and natural objects.

Sources: Cooper; DAS.

PETER LAMARQUE

Marias Aguilera, Julian

Spanish. **b:** 1914, Valladolid, Spain. **Cat:** Catholic ratio-vitalist. **Ints:** Metaphysics; history of philosophy. **Educ:** Studied philosophy in Madrid (1931–6) under Gaos, Zubiri and Ortega. **Infls:** Gaos, Zubiri and Ortega. **Appts:** Cofounder with Ortega of the Instituto de Humanidades (1948); many academic appointments in Spain and the USA, notably at Wellesley College, (1951–2), Harvard (1952), UCLA (1955) and Yale (1956); member of numerous philosophical bodies in Spain, USA and Latin America.

Main publications:

Nearly all the following are available in *Obras*, 8 vols, Madrid: Revista de Occidente, 1958; dates of first editions are given below:

(1941) *Historia de la filosofía.*
(1943) *Miguel de Unamuno.*
(1944) *S. Anselmo y el insensato.*
(1947) *Introducción a la filosofía.*
(1949) *El método historico de las generaciones.*
(1954) *Idea de la metafísica.*
(1954) *Biografía de la filosofía.*
(1954) *Ensayos de teoría.*
(1955) *La estructura social: teoría y método.*
(1960) *Ortega I: Circunstanca y vocación.*
(1967) *Nuevos ensayos de filosofía.*
(1970) *Antropología metafísica.*

Secondary literature:
Carpintero, Helio (1968) *Cinco aventuras españolas,*
   Madrid: *Revista de Occidente.*
Donoso, A. (1982) *Julian Marias,* Bonton: Twayne.
López-Morillas, J. (1961) *Intelectuales y espirituales,*
   Madrid: Revista de Occidente.

Although he developed and extended the ideas of his mentor, the major direction of Marias's thought is set by **Ortega**'s ratio-vitalism. This Marias attempts to blend with Catholicism, and adds to it a detailed philosophical anthropology. According to ratio-vitalism, the fundamental reality is neither matter nor mind but life, and Marias's acceptance of this colours all his thought, not least his extensive views concerning the nature of philosophy in general (and so its history) and of metaphysics in particular.

Life is a task (*quehacer*), not a datum: I must do something with my circumstances in order to survive. I must orient myself with regard to reality, and the function of philosophy is to provide that orientation with regard to what is fundamental. Accordingly, all philosophy worthy of the name is authentic, being a direct response to our condition. At the core of philosophy is metaphysics, the investigation of ultimate reality. Marias insists that existence is an interpretation of reality, not an ultimate fact. The belief in existence is a pre-theoretical belief but a belief none the less. Ontology, the study of existence, is therefore something to be accounted for by metaphysics. Further, vitalism informs Marias's attitude to Aristotelian logic, also often held to be an indispensable element of philosophy. To the vitalist such logic, with its focus on stable essences, displaces individual life from its rightful place at the focus of philosophical interest. For Marias, reality involves neither strict identities nor radical discontinuities, and any logic which regards analytic truths ('abstract predication' in Marias's terms) as the standard of knowledge will fail to do justice to its fluidity and flux. This point of view

underlies Marias's extensive writings on the history of Western philosophy.

One of the most distinctive areas of Marias's thought concerns what he calls the empirical structure of human life (*la estructura empírica de la vida humana*: cf. especially 1949; *Ensayos*, 1954; and 1955). By this he means a set of features of life midway between its definitional properties and those elements peculiar to individual lives. Into this he puts the form of the human body, its sexuality, language, our capacity for laughter, the rhythm of the generations, the length of time spent sleeping and the form of our settlements. These elements of our condition he regards as acquired and mutable, though long-lasting and so relatively stable. These Marias regards as an entirely proper area of concern for a philosopher, and once more this follows from his vitalist presuppositions: to live well I must understand my circumstances, and where elements of my circumstances are as important as these, no philosopher can ignore them.

ROBERT WILKINSON

Mariátegui, José Carlos
Peruvian. **b:** 1894. **d:** 1930. **Cat:** Marxist thinker. **Infls:** Sorel, Nietzsche, Croce, William James and Renan. **Appts:** Journalist and political organizer until his untimely death.

Main publications:
(1928) *Siete ensayos de interpretación de la realidad peruana*, new edition, Mexico: Ediciones Era, 1979.
(1957–70) *Obras completas de José Carlos Mariátegui*, 20 vols, Lima: Empresa Editora Amauta.
(1971) 'The anti-imperialist perspective', *New Left Review* 70: 67–72.
(1971) *Seven Interpretive Essays on Peruvian Reality*, trans. Marjorie Urquidi, Austin: University of Texas Press.
(1976) (ed. with Ricardo Martínez de la Torre) *Amauta: Revista mensual de doctrina, literatura, arte, polémica*, 6 vols, facsimile edition, Lima: Empresa Editora Amauta.

Secondary literature:
Liss, Sheldon B. (1984) *Marxist Thought in Latin America*, Berkeley: University of California Press.
Schutte, Ofelia (1993) *Cultural Identity and Social Liberation in Latin American Thought*, Albany: SUNY Press.
Vanden, Harry E. (1986) *National Marxism in Latin America: José Carlos Mariátegui's Thought and Politics*, Boulder: Lynne Reinner Publishers.

As the leading Latin American Marxist thinker, Mariátegui distinguished himself not only by providing the first socialist interpretation of Peruvian history, but by his creative, original and innovative brand of Indo-Hispanic socialism. His thought is distinct from traditional Marxist analyses in its unique tendency to blend other philosophical movements, such as existentialism, into socialist interpretations. Mariátegui founded the Peruvian Socialist Party in 1928.

AMY A. OLIVER

Marion, Jean-Luc

French. **b:** 1946. **Cat:** Phenomenology; postmodern theology. **Ints:** Descartes; metaphysics; phenomenology, especially of divine revelation; history of philosophy. **Educ:** École Normale Supérieure, 1967–70. **Infls:** Descartes, Nietzsche, Husserl, Heidegger, Levinas and Derrida. **Appts:** Professor of Philosophy, University of Poitiers and University of Paris X.

Main publications:

(1975) *Sur l'ontologie grise de Descartes*, Paris: Vrin.

(1977) *L'Idole et la distance*, Paris: Grasset.

(1981) *Sur la théologie blanche de Descartes: Analogie, création des vérités et fondement*, Paris: PUF.

(1982) *Dieu sans l'être: Hors texte*, Paris: Arthème Fayard (English translation, *God without Being: 'Hors Texte'*, Chicago: University of Chicago Press, 1991).

(1986) 'The essential incoherence of Descartes' definition of divinity', in Rorthy, A. (ed.), *Essays on Descartes' Meditations*, Berkeley: University of California Press, pp. 287–337.

(1986) *Sur la prisme métaphysique de Descartes*, Paris: PUF.

(1990) *Réduction et donation, Recherches sur Husserl, Heidegger et la phénomologie*, Paris: PUF.

(1991) *La Croisée du visible*, Paris: la Différence.

(1991) *Questions cartésiennes*, Paris: PUF.

Secondary literature:

Ashworth, E. J. (1981) Review of *Sur la prisme métaphysique de Descartes* (1986), in *Studia Cartesiana* (Amsterdam) 2: 219–24.

Cottingham, J. (1985) Review of *Sur la prisme métaphysique de Descartes* (1986), *Times Higher Education Supplement*, 19 November 1985.

Derrida, J. (1987) 'Comment ne pas parler', in *Psyché*, Paris: Gallimard.

Greisch, J. (1991) 'L'Herméneutique dans la "phénoménologie comme telle"', *Revue de Métaphysique et de Morale*, 96, 1, 'À propos de *Réduction et*

donation de Jean-Luc Marion', Paris: Armand Colin, pp. 43–64.

Henry, M. (1991) 'Quatre principes de la phénoménologie', *Revue de Métaphysique et de Morale* 96, 1, 'À props de *Réduction et donation* de Jean-Luc Marion', Paris: Armand Colin, pp. 3–26.

Larmore, C., Review of *Sur la prisme métaphysique de Descartes* (1986) *Journal of Philosophy* 81, 3: 156–62.

Laruelle, F. (1991) 'L'Appel et le phénomène', *Revue de Métaphysique et de Morale* 96, 1, 'À propos de *Réduction et donation* de Jean-Luc Marion', Paris: Armand Colin, pp. 27–42.

Tracy, D. (1991) Preface and introduction to *God without Being: 'Hors Texte'*.

Jean-Luc Marion has two specialist study areas, the interpretation of Descartes in the light of poststructuralist and phenomenological philosophy and the elaboration of a postmodern theology. These are brought together through a critique of Descartes's metaphysical definitions of God from the standpoint of a theology based on divine revelation. For Marion, revelation is the only possible basis for a theology in the postmodern world. Reason can only provide us with a God as 'idol' and not a God as 'icon'. Philosophy and theology must therefore move away from metaphysics and towards phenomenological experiences such as charity. Jean-Luc Marion is important in contemporary poststructuralist and phenomenological work on theology and the divine, in particular where his work crosses that of **Derrida** and **Levinas**.

Sources: Catalogues of Bibliothèque Nationale, Paris and National Library of Scotland.

JAMES WILLIAMS

Maritain, Jacques

French. **b:** 18 November 1882, Paris. **d:** 28 April 1973, Toulouse. **Cat:** Thomist. **Ints:** All areas of philosophy. **Educ:** University of Sorbonne, Collège de France and University of Heidelberg. **Infls:** Bergson, Aquinas, Charles Péguy and Léon Bloy. **Appts:** 1914–40, Institut Catholique, Paris; 1948–60, Princeton.

Main publications:

(1920) *Art et scolastique*, Paris: Librairie de L'Art Catholique; third edition, 1935 (English translation, *Art and Scholasticism*, London: Sheed & Ward; New York: Charles Scribner's Sons, 1930).

(1932) *Distinguer pour unir, ou les degrès du savoir*, Paris: Desclée de Brouwer; eighth edition, 1963 (English translation, *The Degrees of Knowledge*,

London: G. Bles; New York: Charles Scribner's
Sons, 1959).

(1934) *Sept leçons sur l'être et les premiers principes de
la raison spéculative*, Paris: Pierre Téqui (English
translation, *A Preface to Metaphysics*, London and
New York: Sheed & Ward, 1939).

(1942) *Les Droits de l'homme et la loi naturelle*, New
York: Editions de la Maison Française; Paris: Paul
Hartmann, 1947 (English translation, *The Rights
of Man and Natural Law*, New York: Charles
Scribner's Sons, 1943; London: G. Bles, 1944).

(1947) *Court Traité de l'existence et de l'existant*,
Paris: Paul Hartmann (English translation, *Ex-
istence and the Existent*, New York: Pantheon
Books, 1948).

(1947) *La Personne et le bien commun*, Paris: Desclée
de Brouwer (English translation, *The Person and
The Common Good*, New York: Charles Scribner's
Sons; London: G. Bles, 1948).

(1953) *Creative Intuition in Art and Poetry*, New
York: Pantheon Books; London: Harvill Press,
1954.

Secondary literature:

(1972) *The New Scholasticism* 46: 118–28 (bibliography, excluding articles up to 1961).

Allard, Jean-Louis (ed.) (1985) *Jacques Maritain*,
Ottawa: University of Ottawa Press.

Hudson, Deal W. and Mancini, Matthew J. (eds)
(1987) *Understanding Maritain*, Macon, Ga.:
Mercer University Press.

Knasas, John F. X. (ed.) (1988) *Jacques Maritain:
The Man and his Metaphysics*, Notre Dame, Ind.:
University of Notre Dame Press.

Phelan, Gerald B. (1937) *Jacques Maritain*, New
York: Sheed & Ward.

Redpath, Peter A. (ed.) (1992) *From Twilight to
Dawn: The Cultural Vision of Jacques Maritain*,
Notre Dame, Ind.: University of Notre Dame
Press.

Rover, Thomas Dominic (1965) *The Poetics of
Maritain*, Washington, DC: The Thomist Press.

Jacques Maritain was one of the most significant
and influential Thomistic philosophers of the first
half of the twentieth century. It is possible to
regard him as a conservative and orthodox
Thomist, more like **Garrigou-Lagrange** than like
apparently more radical transcendental Thomists
such as **Maréchal** and **Lonergan**. However, his
philosophical subtlety and insight raised him far
above his more pedestrian contemporaries, and
his genius was supported, rather than suppressed
or distorted, by the Thomistic framework within
which he worked.

Maritain's epistemology and his metaphysics
can conveniently be dealt with together. The act of
knowledge, he states, begins in the encounter
between an intellect and sensible realities. These
realities, however, are envisaged by the intellect in
one of two ways. In one way, the intellect
concentrates upon observable and measurable
phenomena; and being as such, though it is the
metaphysical foundation of phenomena, is ignored. This is the perspective adopted by the
empirical sciences. In the other way, which
Maritain calls the way of common sense, sensible
realities are either apprehended unreflectively or,
if reflectively, by a mental process of progressive
abstraction and classification, culminating in a
concept of being which has a universal extension
but little or no intension: 'being' then becomes an
empty concept. This perspective, if divested of all
connection with reality, is the starting-point of
logic and mathematics.

Common-sense knowledge, however, can also
generate an intuition of being *qua* being, and this
intuition is the beginning of metaphysics. The
object of such an intuition (which he variously
called abstractive intuition, eidetic intuition and
eidetic visualization) is being in all its richness and
plenitude, the exploration of which is a lifetime's
work. The intuition is intellectual in character,
and thus unlike Bergsonian intuition. Also, it is
not given to everyone to have it. It is, in fact, 'a
sublime and exceedingly rare mental endowment',
a 'gift bestowed upon the intellect', a kind of
intuition never experienced, for instance, by Kant.

Maritain believed that, by reflecting both
upon being, the object of the intuition, and also
upon the concept of being which the intuition
brings forth in our minds, the metaphysician can
progressively clarify and formulate various properties and principles of being. Thus he will observe
the distinctness of essence and existence. Again,
he will find that he is able to apprehend being
under different aspects. In one aspect, he sees that
being possesses the attribute of unity. In another
aspect, being as an object of thought, he sees its
truth. Being as an object of love and will possesses
goodness. In this way, the metaphysician comes to
formulate the transcendental attributes of being:
its unity, truth and goodness.

Reflection on being, and our intuitive concept
of it, also produce the first principles of reason.
Thus, being as something given to the mind, and
being as something affirmed by the mind, come
together as subject and predicate of the judgement
'being is being', the principle of identity (whose
logical counterpart is the principle of non-contradiction). This principle is not a tautology, but an
expression of the energy of existence, of the

affluence and luxury of being. The principle of sufficient reason, that 'everything which is, to the extent to which it is, possesses a sufficient reason for its being', follows from reflection on the fact that being and intellect are connatural, or made for one another. It also induces reflection on the distinction between dependent existence and existence *a se*, and thus leads us to the idea of a Divine Being.

Maritain's social and political philosophy was a response to the cataclysmic events of the 1930s and 1940s, and was in essence a defence of liberal democracy against the two extremes of totalitarianism and individualist utilitarianism. At the heart of his thinking is a distinction between the individual and the person. The concept of the individual is opposed to the concept of the universal. An individual is a instantiation of humanity in a particular living body. Since all matter has a kind of 'avidity' for being, an individual seeks an egotistical absorption of everything into itself. It also is disposed to change and dissolution. Personality, in contrast, refers to the spiritual identity of human beings. It has two characteristics: first, persons have a wholeness and independence, a possession of their own existence, such that their actions aim to perfect and realize themselves; and second, the spiritual nature of persons disposes them to be open to others and otherness, to engage in communication, love and friendship.

Both individuality and personality generate the urge to live in society, and have an influence on social organization and social justice. As individuals, we look to society for the satisfaction of our material needs. As persons, however, we seek out other people in love and friendship. It is on the latter level that Maritain explains his conception of the common good, which is one of his fundamental socio-political principles and the foundation, in his view, of true democracy. The common good is not the same as a collection of individual goods, in the utilitarian manner. Neither is it the same as the public good, if by this is meant the good of a social collective regarded as something distinct from the good of its members. The common good is, rather, the good of 'a multitude of persons', and that is to say, the good of each person individually which is, simultaneously, the good of the society of persons taken as a whole.

The good in question is the good of persons, and thus pertains to spiritual and cultural development. A necessary precondition for this is personal freedom, and this implies the progressive freeing of humanity from economic bondage and totalitarian repression. It also justifies the traditional values in social and political theory: progress, human dignity, equality, democracy and morality in public life.

Maritain's aesthetics, or rather his philosophy of art, exploits the notion of 'creative intuition'. This is a type of intuition which originates in the preconscious or unconscious mind: not the Freudian unconscious of instinct and repressed desire, but a preconscious which underlies and provides the energy for intellection. In some people, 'privileged or ill-fated', preconscious energies are productive and formative, or in short, creative.

Creative intuition is cognitive, although it is a non-conceptual or preconceptual form of knowledge. What it reveals is both the subjectivity of the artist and, simultaneously, the reality of things with which his subjectivity is connatural. Realities are grasped in their singularity rather than their essence, but their very singularity is emblematic of the universe of things to which they belong. A work of art is therefore a sign both of the universe at large and of the subjective universe of the artist. Maritain's works no longer receive the attention that they attracted during his lifetime, and his type of Thomism is not at present fashionable. It remains to be seen whether his influence can equal his stature.

Sources: DFN; EF; WWW; *RPL* 71, 1973.

HUGH BREDIN

Markovič, Mihailo

Yugoslav. *b:* 1923, Belgrade. *Cat:* Marxist social theorist; Serbian political figure. *Ints:* Social and political philosophy; philosophy of language. *Educ:* University of Belgrade and University of London. *Appts:* Taught Philosophy at the University of Belgrade from 1956 until 1975, when he was removed from his teaching position for political reasons; 1983, named Chair of the Committee for Philosophy and Social Theory of the Serbian Academy of Sciences and Arts in Belgrade; active in Yugoslav politics in the early 1990s (Vice President of the Serbian Socialist Party, 1990–2).

Main publications:

(1952) *Revizija filozofskikh osnova marksizma u Sovjetskom savezu* [The Revision of the Philosophical Foundations of Marxism in the Soviet Union], Belgrade.

(1956) *Logika* [Logic], Belgrade.

(1958) *Formalizam u savremenoj logiči* [Formalism in Contemporary Logic], Belgrade.

(1961) *Dijalektička teorija značenja*, Belgrade; second edition, 1971 (English translation, *Dialectical Theory of Meaning*, trans. D. Rouge, J. Coddington and Z. Minderovič, Dordrecht: D. Reidel, 1984).

(1967) *Humanizam i dijalektika* [Humanism and Dialectics], Belgrade.

(1968) *Dialektik der Praxis*, Frankfurt.

(1974) *The Contemporary Marx: Essays on Humanist Communism*, Nottingham: Spokesman Books.

(1974) *From Affluence to Praxis: Philosophy and Social Criticism*, University of Michigan Press.

(1982) *Democratic Socialism: Theory and Practice*, Sussex: Harvester Press.

Secondary literature:

Crocker, David A. (1983) *Praxis and Democratic Socialism: The Critical Social Theory of Markovič and Stojanovič*, Sussex: Harvester Press.

Sher, Gerson S. (1977) *Praxis: Marxist Criticism and Dissent in Socialist Yugoslavia*, Indiana University Press.

During the 1950s, Markovič's philosophical activity (which included two years of study with A. J. Ayer in London) was concentrated mainly on logic and the philosophy of language. This work culminated in 1961 in his major monograph *Dialectical Theory of Meaning*, one of the earliest attempts by a Marxist philosopher to deal in depth with the subject of meaning. Markovič rejects positivist, behaviorist and existentialist theories of meaning in favour of one based on the Marxian concept of *praxis* (practice, in the sense of free, productive activity). 'The meaning of a sign', he wrote, 'is the practice by which it is created and which its use serves' (p. 321).

Thereafter he turned to social and political philosophy and employed the concept of *praxis* in elaborating a theory of democratic socialism based on humanistic principles derived from the writings of Marx (especially the 'Economic-Philosophic Manuscripts of 1844'). In this activity he was part of a group of like-minded philosophers from Belgrade and Zagreb who gathered around the influential journal *Praxis*, published from 1964 until suppressed by the government in 1975. In that year Markovič and seven of his colleagues in the Philosophy Department at the University of Belgrade ('the Belgrade eight') were suspended indefinitely from their teaching positions because of their critical stance towards what they viewed as authoritarian and bureaucratic deformations of socialism in Yugoslavia.

Markovič's arguments for democratic socialism, elaborated principally in *From Affluence to Praxis* (1974) and *Democratic Socialism: Theory*

and Practice (1982), are premised on the conviction that only in such a system can people live a life of *praxis* in the sense of realizing their best human capacities through independent and creative, but at the same time socially oriented, action. In Markovič's view this would be a society of 'radical humanization', free of alienated labour, in which human beings are no longer treated as things. Its institutional features would include social ownership of the means of production, worker self-management and flexible central planning by democratically elected representative bodies.

Markovič's active support of the policies of the Slobodan Milosevič government in the early 1990s drew fire from critics who regarded it as inconsistent with his expressed humanistic and democratic ideals.

JAMES SCANLAN

Marquard, Odo

German. *b:* 26 February 1928, Stolp, Pommern. *Cat:* Sceptic. *Ints:* Political philosophy; hermeneutics; philosophy of history; philosophy of culture. *Educ:* 1954, doctorate awarded, University of Freiburg in Breisgau, under Max Muller; 1963, *Habilitationschrift*, University of Münster. *Infls:* Rousseau, Kant, Schelling, Marx, Kierkegaard, Heine, Heidegger, Gadamer, Plessner and Joachim Ritter. *Appts:* 1963, Assistant Professor of Philosophy, University of Münster; briefly at University of Giessen; 1993, Professor of Philosophy, University of Darmstadt.

Main publications:

(1958) *Skeptische Methode im Blick auf Kant*, Munich: Alber.

(1981) *Abschied vom Prinzipiellen*, Stuttgart: Reclams Universal Bibliothek (English translation, *Farewell to Matters of Principle*, trans. R. M. Wallace, London: Odeon, Oxford University, 1989).

(1986) *Apologie des Zufalligen*, Stuttgart: Reclams Universal Bibliothek (English translation, *In Defence of the Accidental: Philosophical Studies*, trans. R. M. Wallace, London: Odeon, Oxford University Press, 1991).

(1987) *Aesthetica und Anaesthetica: Zur Philosophie der schönen und nicht mehr schönen Kunst*, Schöningh: Paderborn.

Odo Marquard is a 'free thinker' who upholds the tradition of German philosophical scepticism which reaches back through **Nietzsche** and Kant to the nonconformist tradition of Protestant thought. As recent German political history has besmirched the term *Lebensphilosophie*, it is misleading to associate Marquard with it; and yet, like Nietzsche, he is passionately committed to the view that only 'lived problems' rather than the niceties of conceptual puzzles are worthy of philosophy. In *Farewell to Matters of Principle* (1981) he remarks, in a manner that echoes Kant and **Dilthey**, that 'one should seek ... dealing in philosophy, only with such ideas as one also thinks of during the difficult situations in life, and which, if need be, one can live with one's whole life long. ... Experience without philosophy is blind, philosophy without experience is empty: one cannot really have a philosophy without first having the experience to which it is the answer' (p. 7).

Marquard was initiated into philosophical scepticism in Joachim Ritter's heterogeneous *Collegium Philosophicum* (Munster). Ritter taught that one found one's philosophical voice by encountering alien attitudes firsthand, learning from difference. In 'In praise of polytheism' (1968), Marquard argued that freedom does not consist in having a single history or philosophy but in having many. Intellectual pluralism is freedom's sceptical defence against the prisons of monotheistic and monological metaphysics. Scepticism, he suggests, knows that conflict and contradiction are undeniably present in human beings and should be accepted rather than solved, for only in the anatagonisms of diversity can free thought arise.

Marquard's scepticism stands upon a central insight of phenomenological hermeneutics concerning our lack of disposition over prior givens. As human beings we can never achieve a principled beginning or departure from an ungrounded past but only a remaining within what one already historically was: one must 'link up'. We cannot 'spend our lives waiting for a principled permission to finally begin living' since our death comes more quickly than rational principles do (ibid., p. 17). Accordingly, Marquard emerges as a substantial opponent of critical theory: 'we must provide grounds not for our non-choices, but for our choices, for the things we can change. The burden of proof is on the one who proposes change ... Death comes too soon to permit total changes and total rational groundings' (pp. 14–15).

Scepticism is linked by Marquard to hermeneutics as the latter is a means of understanding the art of navigating oneself through the contingencies of existence (tradition), some of which require that we hold fast to them whilst others necessitate establishing a distance between oneself

and them. Marquard abandons the notion of an absolute text in favour of a pluralization of both text and reader. 'This', he argues, 'represents a separation of the powers that texts and interpretations are, so that it is now possible to say that ... hermeneutics is scepticism and scepticism today is hermeneutics' (ibid., p. 18).

Marquard's scepticism bids farewell to principled (unified) philosophy but not to a philosophical questioning which seeks a diversity of approaches and hence intellectual choice: 'real freedom ... consists in freedoms, in the plural. These come about as a result of the motleyness of what is pre-given: as a result of the fact that the plurality—the rivalry, the counterbalancing oppositions, the balance—of its powers either neutralize or limits their grip on the individual. Freedoms are the result of the separation of powers ... Scepticism's doubt is not absolute perplexity but is rather a manifold sense of the *isothenes diaphonia* (evenly balanced disagreement), the balance not only of conflicting dogmas, but also of conflicting realities (ibid., p. 17).

Sources: *Kurschners Deutscher Gelehrten-Kalender, 1992*, Berlin: de Gruyter, 1992.

NICHOLAS DAVEY

Märten, Lu (Louise Charlotte)

German. *b:* 24 September 1879, Charlottenburg, Berlin. *d:* 12 August 1970, Steglitz, Berlin. *Cat:* Aesthetician; journalist; commentator. *Ints:* The arts and social reform, especially in relation to women and democracy. *Educ:* Self-educated because of poor health when young; 1903, joined the Social Democratic Party (SDP); 1920, joined the German Communist Party (KDP). *Appts:* From 1898, worked as a journalist and writer contributing reviews, stories, and literary and art criticism to a range of publications including *Gleichheit* (Equality) and *Arbeiterinnen-Zeitung* (Women Workers' Paper).

Main publications:

(1906) *Meine Liedsprachen, Gedichte* [My Wordsong: A Poem].

(1909) *Bergarbeiter: Schauspiel in einem Akt* [Miners: A Play in One Act], Stuttgart: J. H. W. Dietz.

(1909) *Torso: Das Buch eines Kindes* [Torso: A Child's Book].

(1914) *Die wirtschaftliche Lage der Künstler* [The Economic Situation of the Artist], Munich: G. Muller.

(1919) *Ästhetik und Arbeiterschaft* [Aesthetics and the Working Classes].

(1919) *Die Künstlerin* [The Woman Artist], Munich: A. Langen.

(1924–49) *Wesen und Veränderung der Formen/ Künste: Resultate historisch-materialistischer Untersuchungen* [The Nature and Change of Forms: Results of Historical-materialist Investigations], Frankfurt: Taifun.

(1936) *Yali: Ein Buch von allem Werden* [A Book of All Becoming].

(1949) *Zur Geschichte der Frau vom Muttericht bis zur Gegenwart* [A History of Women from Matriarchy to the Present].

(1982) *Formen für den Alltag: Schriften, Aufsatze, Vorträge* [The Forms of Daily Life: Writings, Essays, Lectures], Dresden: Verlag der Künst.

Secondary literature:

May, R. (1982) 'Theorie der Formen wider Theorie der Künste?', in Lu Märten, *Formen für den Alltag*.

Plumpe, G. (1975) 'Künstform und Produktionspraxis im Blick auf Lu Märten', in *Arbeitsfeld Materialistische Literaturtheorie: Beiträge zu ihrer Gegenstandbestimmung*.

Märten's philosophical development was closely interwoven with the experience of her deprived and difficult youth: the early deaths of her parents and siblings and the poverty-stricken conditions under which she strove for intellectual and artistic self-realization. She earned a living by journalism but wrote concurrently on the theory and sociology of art. Three early books (1914, both of 1919) were followed in 1924 by her major theoretical work, which was largely ignored at the time of its publication. Thereafter, financial difficulties supervened, forcing Märten to live in seclusion while she endeavoured but failed to make money by writing film scripts. She turned to journalism again in 1945 and worked as well as a publishers' reader, at the same time resuming her writing on politics, women and aesthetics. In 1950 she withdrew from all engagement in public debate as a protest against the cultural policy of the GDR.

Märten maintained that art developed out of work but that the unity of art and work was destroyed by the division of labour in society, rendering art a 'luxury' and a 'special area'. She proposed that the concept of 'art' be abandoned and replaced by that of 'form', with the aim of propounding a comprehensive theory of the purposive-practical activity of human beings. Working within a historico-materialism, and in the belief that 'every era discovers its own method', she sought to analyse types of art and the various forms of artistic expression and to

relate them to 'being and change'. She was unsympathetic to the notion of the autonomy of art but also to contemporary communist debates that ignored formal qualities. 'It should be understood', she wrote, 'that so-called art, seen historically, is not merely content but in the first instance is form.' She urged attention to the art of film as a medium for the development of new forms and thought.

Sources: Meyer & Vahle.

DIANÉ COLLINSON

Martinetti, Piero

Italian. *b:* 21 August 1872, Canavese, Aosta, Italy. *d:* 23 March 1943, Canavese. *Cat:* Philosopher of positivism. *Infls:* Schuppe. *Appts:* Professor of Theoretical Philosophy, University of Milan, 1906–31; resigned in protest at the oath required by the fascists.

Main publications:

(1902–04) *Introduzione alla metafisica*.

(1913) *E. Kant: Commento ai Prolegomeni*; new edition, Milan: Feltrinelli, 1968.

(1923) *Brevario spirituale*.

(1926) *Saggi e discorsi*.

(1928) *La libertà*, new edition, Turin: Boringhieri, 1965 (includes bibliography).

(1934) *Gesù Cristo e il cristianesimo*.

(1936) *Il Vangelo*.

(1942) *Ragione e fede*.

(1943) *Hegel*.

Anthologies:

(1972) *Saggi filosofici e religiosi*, ed. L. Pareyson, Turin: Bottega d'Erasmo.

(1972) *Saggi e Discorsi*, ed. L. Pareyson, Rome: A. Armando.

(1976) *Scritti di metafisica e di filosofia della religione*, ed. E. Agazzi, Milan: Edizione di Comunita.

Secondary literature:

Poggi, A. (1990) *Piero Martinetti 1872–1943*, Milan: Marzorati.

Martinetti's work defends the possibility of a certain form of metaphysics. Positivists, he claims, have fallen into the vulgar habit of thinking of metaphysics as anti-scientific a priori deduction. Scientific metaphysics, however, attends to fact. It interprets the data but looks for their sense. Post-Kantian idealism is rejected and a new inductive metaphysics inaugurated. Beginning a posteriori one ascends by successive syntheses to a grasp of the absolute. In that ascent the first stage is the self as a mere sentient consciousness. There is, however, the irresistible belief that my states of consciousness are not private but continually interact with the consciousnesses of others. This gives me a glimpse of something that transcends me, and leads me to the next level, the logical level of synthesis where we use such concepts as substance and cause. The final stage is absolute unity, which is that which informs all other unities and that to which they all aspire. Of that unity we can have no concept but only an intuition by means of symbols, the most complex of all of which is language. Through language we have a glimpse, however imperfect, of absolute unity. Martnetti claims that each of the steps towards the absolute is necessitated by what has gone before, but each is a step towards liberation. One such step is morality, at which stage we realize the aspiration to see life *sub specie aeternitatis* and so participate in an impersonal vision of reality. At the level above morality comes religion, a first stage of which is myth, which pulls religion towards the sensible, and which yields art as an imperfect representation of the absolute.

COLIN LYAS

Marty (Martin), Anton (Marcus)

Swiss. *b:* 18 October 1857, Schwyz, Switzerland. *d:* 1 October 1914, Prague. *Cat:* Philosopher of language. *Ints:* Metaphysics; philosophy of mind. *Educ:* University of Würzburg. *Infls:* Brentano (his teacher). *Appts:* From 1869, Professor of Philosophy, Schwyzer Lyzeum; 1875–80, Professor of Philosophy, University of Czernowitz; 1880–1913, Professor of Philosophy, German University of Prague.

Main publications:

(1875) *Über den Ursprung der Sprache*, Würzburg: Stuber.

(1879) *Die geschichtliche Entwicklung der Farbensinnes*, Vienna: Gerold.

(1908) *Untersuchungen zur Grundlegung der allgemeinen Sprachtheorie*, Halle: Niemeyer, reprinted Hildesheim: Olms, 1976.

(1910) *Zur Sprachphilosophie. Die logische, lokalistische und andere Kasustheorien*, Halle: Niemeyer.

(1916) *Raum und Zeit*, ed. J. Eisenmeier, A. Kastil and O. Kraus, Halle: Niemeyer (posthumous).

(1916–20) *Gesammelte Schriften*, ed. J. Eisenmeier, A. Kastil and O. Kraus, Halle: Niemeyer.

(1940–50) *Nachgelassene Schriften*, ed. Otto Funke, Berne: Francke.

Secondary literature:

Kraus, Oscar (1916) *Anton Marty: sein Leben und seine Werke*, Halle.

Kuroda, S. Y. (1972) 'Anton Marty and the transformational theory of meaning', *Foundations of Language* 9: 1-36.

Mulligan, Kevin (ed.) (1990) *Mind, Meaning and Metaphysics: The Philosophy and Theory of Language of Anton Marty*, Dordrecht: Kluwer Academic.

Spinicci, Paolo (1990) *Il significato e la forma linguistica Pensiero, esperienza, linguaggio nella filosofia de Anton Marty*, Milan: Angeli.

Marty has sometimes been described as **Brentano**'s Minister for Language. Although he was sometimes critical of his former teacher and more independent than this description implies, Marty was closely associated with Brentano for forty years. Moreover his theory of language was based upon Brentano's empirical psychology and he adopted his teacher's classification of psychic phenomena. At the same time he rejected Brentano's view of mental objects. To do this he appealed to the Aristotelian distinction between objects that 'exist' (what can be asserted by a true existential judgement) and what is 'real' (what enters into causal relations). On that view mental objects such as distinctions could be said to exist without having to concede to them any reality.

Although he also wrote on the nature of space and time, Marty's philosophy of language represents his most important contribution. His new theory of grammar is comparable in some respects with the transformational grammar of **Chomsky**, and his causal theory of meaning has been compared to that of **Grice**. Although these comparisons constitute rediscoveries, Marty had some influence in his time on **Twardowski** and, through him, on the Lvov–Warsaw School.

Sources: Edwards; Mittelstrass; Burkhardt.

STUART BROWN

Marvin, Walter Taylor

American. *b:* 28 April 1872, New York. *d:* 26 May 1944. *Cat:* Direct realist–new realist. *Ints:* Epistemology; history of philosophy. *Educ:* University of Columbia, Universities of Halle and Bonn. *Infls:* William James. *Appts:* Professor of Philosophy, Rutgers University.

Main publications:

(1903) *Introductions to Systematic Philosophy*, New York (s.n.).

(1912) (with E. B. Holt) *et al The New Realism*, New York (s.n.).

(1917) *The History of European Philosophy*, New York (s.n.)

In the early part of this century realism was revived in the USA by a number of prominent philosophers. It came in a variety of guises—direct realism and indirect (dualist) realism. Marvin, a direct realist, was a member of the group known as the New Realists.

According to direct realism, material objects exist externally and independently of our sense experience, and our perception is a direct awareness of the external object. Properties such as shapes, colours and hardness are intrinsic properties and objective according to the direct realist.

Holding that shapes and colours are all intrinsic properties and objective creates problems for the direct realist. For instance, John who looks at a table from the top sees a round shape and Andrew who looks at the same table from a distance sees an elliptical shape. Could a table be both round and elliptical? Is this not self-contradictory? Marvin (like E. B. **Holt**) tried to resolve this problem by saying that the table is both elliptical and the subject perceives only one of the properties of the table, because of the nervous system, selects one of the properties from the set of properties.

Although the above solution may to some extent answer the problem posed in relation to the table, it is insufficient to cope with illusions or errors in perception. What of the rope that is perceived as a snake?

Sources: WWW(Am).

INDIRA MAHALINGAM CARR

Masaryk, Tomás Garrigue

Czech. *b:* 7 March 1850, Hodonín, Moravia. *d:* 14 September 1937, Lány, Czechoslovakia. *Cat:* Philosopher and statesman. *Ints:* Social and political philosophy; philosophy of history; Russian philosophy. *Educ:* Universities of Vienna and Leipzig. *Appts:* Taught Philosophy at Vienna from 1879 to 1881, and in 1882 was appointed Professor of Philosophy at Charles University (Prague); subsequently active in politics, he became the first President (1918–35) of the new state of Czechoslovakia.

Main publications:

(1881) *Der Selbstmord als sociale Massenerscheinung der modernen Civilisation*, Vienna (English translation, *Suicide and the Meaning of Civilization*,

trans. W. B. Weist and R. G. Batson, University of Chicago, 1970).

(1885) *Základové konkretné logiky* [Fundamentals of Concrete Logic], Prague.

(1913) *Russland und Europa*, 2 vols, Jena (English translation, *The Spirit of Russia*, trans. E. and C. Paul, 2 vols, London: Allen & Unwin, 1919).

(1925) *Světová revoluce*, Prague (English translation, *The Making of a State*, trans. H. W. Steed, London: Allen & Unwin, 1927).

(1931–5) *Hovory s T. G. Masarykem*, 3 vols, Prague (English translation, *President Masaryk Tells His Story* and *Masaryk on Thought and Life*, trans. M. and R. Weatherall, London, 1934, 1938).

Secondary literature:

Beld, A. van den (1975) *Humanity: The Political and Social Philosophy of Thomas G. Masaryk*, The Hague: Mouton (bibliography).

Novák, Josef, ed. (1988) *On Masaryk: Texts in English and German*, Amsterdam: Rodopi.

Winters, S. B., Pynsent, R. B. and Hanak, H. (eds) (1990) *T. G. Masaryk (1850–1937)*, 3 vols, London: Macmillan.

Masaryk produced a wide range of philosophical works, including early essays on Hume, a study of the classification and interrelations of the sciences (his 1885 book) and a monumental history of Russian philosophy (1913). In epistemology he subscribed to realism (he preferred the term 'concretism') and was inclined towards empiricism, though he also advanced a view of cognition as a synthesis of sense perception, reason, feelings and will. Masaryk was a confirmed theist but rejected supernatural revelation as a source of knowledge.

Masaryk's principal interest in philosophy, already evident in the 1881 study of suicide, was in its use as an instrument for the diagnosis and treatment of social ills. A believer in moral absolutes grounded in a religious perception of the world, he elaborated the humanitarian ideals that he saw as the goals of historical progress. He identified those ideals with democracy and individualism and was a stern critic of Marxism.

JAMES SCANLAN

Mascall, E(ric) L(ionel)

British. *b:* 12 December 1905, London. *d:* 14 February 1993, Seaford, England. *Cat:* Anglican theologian. *Ints:* Philosophy of religion. *Educ:* Pembroke College, Cambridge (Mathematics 1st; wrangler); Ely Theological College. *Infls:* Austin Farrer, Gregory Dix, Gabriel Hebert and

Lionel Thornton, and contacts via the Fellowship of St Alban and St Sergius. **Appts:** Senior Mathematics Master, Bablake School, Coventry, 1928–31; St Andrew's, Stockwell Green, 1932–5; St Matthew's, Westminster, 1935–7; Sub-warden, Scholae Cancelarii, Lincoln, 1937–45; Lecturer and Tutor, Christ Church, Oxford, 1945 -62; University Lecturer in Philosophy of Religion, 1948–62; Professor of Historical Theology, King's College, London, 1962–73; Honorary Canon of Truro Cathedral, 1973–84; FBA, 1974.

Main publications:

(1943) *He Who Is.*
(1949) *Existence and Analogy.*
(1957) *Words and Images.*
(1971) *The Openness of Being* (Gifford Lectures).

A mathematician by training, a priest by calling, a theologian by profession and a humorist by nature, Mascall's defence of natural theology along Thomist lines, and his critique of those who denied the meaningfulness of theological discourse (*Words and Images*, 1957), earned him considerable respect in traditional Christian circles. Elsewhere he argued for the reconcilability of science and religion, expounded the doctrines of grace, creation, the Incarnation and the Trinity, and indulged in 'critical but courteous' rebuttals of secularizing Christian radicals, Christological reductionists and others. In his ecumenical writings he typically had the Orthodox and Roman Catholics in view rather than Protestants, however orthodox and catholic. His published humour includes 'A hymn for the logical empiricists' to be sung to 'The Londonfreddy Air'; and his *Saraband: The Memoirs of E. L. Mascall* engagingly displays his interests and blind spots.
Sources: WW; *Saraband*, Leominster: Gracewing, 1992; obituary notices.

ALAN SELL

Maurras, Charles

French. **b:**1868, Martigues, France. **d:**1952, Saint-Symphorien. **Cat:** Political theorist; poet. **Ints:** Politics. **Infls:** De Maistre, Comte and P.G.F. Le Play. **Appts:** A poet strongly influenced by classicism, Maurras became a political activist after the Dreyfus case, cofounding the far-right Action française with Léon Daudet, and editing its eponymous newspaper (1908–44); imprisoned for life in 1944 for passing information to the Nazis, Maurras was released on health grounds shortly before his death in 1952.

Main publications:
Dates of first publication only are given; Maurras is most conveniently approached via his *Oeuvres capitales*, 4 vols, Paris: Flammarion, 1954.
(1901) *Anthinéa.*
(1905) *L'Avenir de l'intelligence.*
(1912) *La Politique religieuse.*
(1913) *L'Action française et la religion catholique.*
(1928) *Romantisme et révolution.*
(1931) *Méditation sur la politique de Jeanne d'Arc.*
(1931–4) *Dictionnaire politique et critique.*
(1937) *Devant l'Allemagne éternel.*
(1937) *Mes idées politiques*
(1941) *La seule France.*
(1949) *Au grand juge de France.*
(1949) *Inscription sur nos ruines.*

Secondary literature:
Capitan-Peter, C. (1972) *Charles Maurras et l'idéologie d'Action française*, Paris: Le Seuil.
McClelland, J. S. (1970) *The French Right*, London: Cape (includes some translations).
Massis, H. (1961) *Maurras et notre temps*, 2 vols, second edition, Paris: Plon.
Vandromme, P. (1966) *Maurras, l'Église de l'ordre*, Paris: Centurion.

The political writings of Maurras exhibit a comprehensive set of beliefs not uncommon on the far right. The basic assertions concern human nature. For Maurras human beings are primarily social, not individual. We are born into particular families and particular states, and so nationalism (Maurras argues) is in a profound sense the most natural of political sentiments. To claim, as Rousseau (loathed by Maurras) did, that we are individuals before we are members of society is to take the road to disaster. Believe this and we become, in his friend Barrès's terms, *déraciné* or rootless. Further, nature is deeply inegalitarian: we are born unequal in 'blood', strength and looks, and this is entirely normal and healthy. Any attempt to deny this, to level differences, is foolish in the extreme, destructive of what Maurras calls the rich and inexhaustible fields of human difference (*Mes idées politiques*, 1937). The good is the natural, and what is natural is authority, hierarchy, property, community, personal ties to the soil and hereditary ties of blood (ibid).

From this set of ideas Maurras deduces his main political recommendations. His negative views consist chiefly in a hatred of the ideals behind the French Revolution and of democratic forms of government, accompanied by an unrelenting anti-semitism (summed up in his book of 1928). Human beings are neither all equal nor all brothers, and to offer the masses political liberty encourages them to regard laws as revisable whims of those in power. Democratic states tend to become ever more centralized: if a party in power wishes to be reelected, it must constantly court and keep watch on the electorate, and to do this requires an ever greater network of officials. Further, the egalitarian aspects of modern democracies cause a general levelling down in all areas of human achievement: for example, more mediocrities are given power, inevitably make blunders, and are treated indulgently by their dim-witted peers when they do so.

Strong states are states whose political system reflects the order of nature. In the case of France, Maurras recommended the return of the monarchy and unwavering support for familiy ties and the Catholic Church (although the latter did not welcome the support of l'Action française). The function of leaders is to command, and if the power to command is attained only by electoral mandate it is not sufficiently respected and inefficiency follows. Not to make the most of inequality is madness: the gifted and powerful are indispensable to mankind. They are the energy, ornament and salvation of the world.

ROBERT WILKINSON

Mauthner, Fritz

Austrian. **b:** 22 November 1849, Königgrätz, Bohemia. **d:** 28 June 1923, Meersburg. **Cat:** Philosopher of language; writer. **Ints:** Philosophy of language; philosophy of religion; mysticism. **Educ:** Studied Law, amongst other subjects, in Prague, but did not take a degree. **Infls:** Hume. **Appts:** 1876–1905, theatre critic for *Berliner Tageblatt*; 1905–7, Freiburg; 1907–23, Meersburg, devoting himself to philosophy.

Main publications:

(1901–2) *Beiträge zu einer Kritik der Sprache*, I–III, Stuttgart; several editions and republications, including Frankfurt, Berlin and Vienna, 1982.

(1910) *Worterbuch der Philosophie. Neue Beiträge zur einer Kritik der Sprache*, I–II, Munich and Leipzig; second edition, Leipzig, 1923–4.

(1922–3) *Der Atheismus und Seine Geschichte in Abendlande*, I–IV, Stuttgart and Berlin.

(c. 1924) *Gottlose Mystik*, Dresden.

(1925) *Die Drei Bilder der Welt. Ein sprachkritischer Versuch*, Erlangen (posthumous).

Secondary literature:

Eisen, W. (1929) *Fritz Mauthners Kritik der Sprache. Eine Darstellung und Beurteilung vom Standpunkt eines kritischen Positivismus*, Vienna and Leipzig.
Kuhn, J. (1975) *Gescheiterte Sprachkritik. Fritz Mauthners Leben und Werk*, Berlin and New York: de Gruyter (with extensive bibliography).
Kappstein, T. (1926) *Fritz Mauthner. Der Mann und sein Werk*, Berlin and Leipzig.
Landauer, G. (1903) *Skepsis und Mystik. Versuche im Anschluss an Mauthners Sprachkritik*, Berlin; Cologne, 1923.
Weiler, G. (1970) *Mauthner's Critique of Language*, Cambridge: Cambridge University Press.

Mauthner did not follow a career but gained a reputation for his poetry, novels, parodies and critiques. His philosophical activity took place and drew attention mostly outside the academic sphere. He was influenced by Hume's scepticism and empiricism. On their grounds he developed his 'critique of language'. On Mauthner's view language does not reflect the world, but rather a worldview that rests on one's poor fortuitous senses. Taking language seriously, as one's means for knowing the facts of reality, was for Mauthner 'word superstition'. Since each person depicts in their own language their own worldview, language is not shared by different persons and genuine communication is impossible. The public practice of using words and sentences is of expressive, rather than descriptive powers. For Mauthner, philosophy is a critique of language, meant to show the person the way towards being mystically silent, after one's having done away with language 'before, behind and in' oneself.

Mauthner applied his critique of language most intensively to religious expressions. Accordingly, he utterly rejected theology, describing himself as a godless mystic. Some of Mauthner's views bear resemblance to certain elements of Wittgenstein's philosophy, both in the *Tractatus* (where Mauthner's method is mentioned but not adopted, in 4.0031) and in his later writings.
Sources: Edwards; NöB, 3, 1926, pp. 144–51.

ASA KASHER

Mawdudi, Sayyid Abu Al-Ala

Indian-Pakistani. **b:** 1903, Aurangabad, India. **d:** 1979. **Cat:** Islamic political thinker. **Ints:** Political philosophy; orthodox fundamentalism and religious thought. **Educ:** Educated at home, local *madrasah* and self-educated. **Infls:** Islamic thought and comtemporary Western political theory. **Appts:** Journalist and writer, and founder of

Jamati-Islami (the Islamic Association) which campaigned for the re-establishment of an Islamic world order or society.

Main publications:
(1960) *Islamic Law and Constitution*, Lahore.
(1960) *Towards Understanding Islam*, trans. K. Ahmad, Lahore.
(1961) (with others) *Studies in the Family Law of Islam*, Karachi.

Secondary literature:
Ahmad, A. (1970) *Islamic Modernism in India and Pakistan 1857–1964*, London: Oxford University Press.

Although Mawdudi started his political life as a fervent opponent of a separate Islamic state such as Pakistan, he later came to appreciate the need and desirability of such a state; yet throughout his writings he represents nationalism as a pernicious and un-Islamic idea. The basis of Islam in his view is the acknowledgement of God as the sole source of authority, and anything else such as the law of the state or the will of the people is no more than idolatry. The community, he held, needs to return to the early ideas of the Prophet and his four successors and where there is the need to incorporate new developments to take account of changing circumstances, this should be done by using reason within the context of Islam rather than using Islam within the context of reason. Islam is essentially rational, and there is no need to look beyond it to find how to adapt traditional rules to suit modern circumstances.

Mawdudi's notion of the Islamic polity is as a theocracy governed by a man who is the agent and representative of God: all will go well with the state provided that it is ruled by those who are knowledgeable in the way of the Prophet and the first four caliphs. Although human beings are weak and fragile creatures, they also represent God on earth, and they are obliged to carry out divine commands in their organization of society. There is no scope for political life outside religion, and to be a member of Islamic society one has to acknowledge and accept the perfection and finality of the *sharia*, the revealed law. Mawdudi has had an important influence upon the Islamic world, and his works have been much translated. His basic doctrine, that society should be founded on the principles of Islam and nothing else, has played an important role in intellectual life in the Islamic world.

OLIVER LEAMAN

Mayz Vallenilla, Ernesto
Venezuelan. *b:* 3 September 1925, Maracaibo, Venezuela. *Cat:* Phenomenologist. *Educ:* Doctorate, Universidad Central de Venezuela; also studied at the Universities of Göttingen and Freiburg (under Martin Heidegger at Göttingen). *Appts:* Professor at the Central University of Venezuela, then Dean of the School of Humanities; currently Professor of Philosophy, Simon Bolivar University, Caracas; founding Rector of the University, 1969–79.

Main publications:
(1949) *La idea de estructura psíquica en Dilthey*, Caracas: Universidad Central de Venezuela.
(1956) *Fenomenología del conocimiento: el problema de la constitución del objeto en la filosofía de Husserl*, Caracas: Universidad Central de Venezuela.
(1957) *El problema de América*, Mexico: UNAM; second edition, 1969; third edition, 1992.
(1960) *Ontología del conocimiento*, Caracas: Universidad Central de Venezuela.
(1965) *El problema de la nada en Kant*, Madrid: Revista de Occidente.
(1966) *Del hombre y su alienación*, Caracas: Instituto Nacional de Cultura y Bellas Artes.
(1974) *Esbozo de una crítica de la razón ténica*, Caracas: Equinoccio.
(1983) *Ratio ténica*, Caracas: Monte Avila Editores.
(1984) *El ocaso de las universidades*, Caracas: Monte Avila Editores.
(1984) *El sueño del futuro*, Caracas: Equinoccio; second edition, 1990.
(1990) *Fundamentos de la Metatécnica*, Caracas: Monte Avila Editores.

Mayz Vallenilla was instrumental in building Venezuela's most active philosophical centre at the Universidad Simón Bolívar. Much of his work focuses on contemporary continental philosophy. His phenomenological approach is evident in his original essay, *El problema de América* (1957).

AMY A. OLIVER

Mazzantini, Carlo
Italian. *b:* 1895, Reconquista, Argentina. *d:* 1971, Turin. *Cat:* Neoscholastic; personalist. *Ints:* Epistemology. *Educ:* Studied in Turin. *Infls:* Ancient and neoscholastic thought; Heidegger. *Appts:* Universities of Cagliari (1942–9), Genoa (1949–59) and Turin (1959 on).

Main publications:
(1923) *La speranza nell'immortalità*.

(1929) *La lotta per l'evidenza.*
(1930) *Realtà e intelligenza.*
(1930–2) *Le basi della teologia naturale nella filosofia tomista.*
(1935) *Il problema della verità necessarie e la sintesi a priori di Kant.*
(1942) *Il tempo.*
(1945) *Capisaldi filosofici*, Turin: Editore Gheroni.
Plus many later studies of the history of philosophy, notably:
(1949) *La filosofia nel filosofare umano, I: Storia del pensiero antico*, Turin: Marietti.
For a summary exposition, see his own:
(1944) *Linee di metafisica spritualistica come filosofia della virtualità ontologica*, in M. Sciacca (ed.), *Filosofi Italiani contemporanei*, Como: Carlo Marzorati.

Secondary literature:
Barone, F. (1985) *La Filosofia di Carlo Mazzantini*, Roma: Studium.

Mazzantini himself epitomized the main debt and direction of his philosophy in the remark: 'Nessuna salvezza per la filosofia, fuori della tradizione ellenica e scolastica' ('No salvation for philosophy, outside the Hellenic and scholastic tradition', 1944, p. 285). There is a *philosophia perennis*, and it is embodied in neoscholasticism, the only true heir of Greek thought and catholic scholasticism. Unsurprisingly, then, much of Mazzantini's philosophy is a version of catholic spiritualism cast in neoscholastic categories. For example, his proof of the immortality of the soul relies on the act—potency distinction: the soul is the form of the body. Because it is capable of action, the soul can exist without the material body (which is merely potency), and so is by nature immortal (*naturalmente immortale*). The Hellenic value placed on harmony informs Mazzantini's criticisms of other schools, notably Hegelian idealism, which preclude the harmonizing of contraries. (He was far more sympathetic to the less destructive Crocean version of idealism.)

Mazzantini departed from 'orthodox' neoscholasticism in a number of respects, but most notably in his sympathy for Heideggerian thought (as formulated in *Sein und Zeit*), and his preoccupation with time and its centrality to human experience. He analyses the present as a synthesis of the temporal and the eternal, this present being not merely a temporal point but an 'authentic present'. This present is real in virtue of the eternity derived from infinite eternity without which there would be neither time nor times.

ROBERT WILKINSON

Mead, George Herbert
American. **b:** 27 February 1863, South Hadley, Massachusetts. **d:** 26 April 1931, Chicago, Illinois. **Cat:** Pragmatist; social psychologist. **Ints:** Naturalism. **Educ:** Oberlin College, AB 1883; Harvard University, 1887–8; Universities of Leipzig and Berlin, 1888–91. **Infls:** James, Royce, Wundt and Dewey. **Appts:** 1891–4, Instructor to Assistant Professor, University of Michigan; 1894–1931, Assistant Professor to Professor, University of Chicago.

Main publications:
(1932) *The Philosophy of the Present*, ed. and intro. A. E. Murphy, and prefatory remarks by John Dewey, La Salle, Ill.: Open Court Publishing Co.
(1934) *Mind, Self and Society from the Standpoint of a Social Behaviorist*, ed. and intro. C. W. Morris, Chicago: University of Chicago Press.
(1936) *Movements of Thought in the Nineteenth Century*, ed. and intro. M. H. Moore, Chicago: University of Chicago Press.
(1938) *The Philosophy of Act*, ed. and intro. C. W. Morris, in collaboration with J. M. Brewster, A. M. Dunham, and D. L. Miller, Chicago: University of Chicago Press.
(1964) *Selected Writings*, ed. and intro. A. J. Reck, Indianapolis, Indiana: Bobbs-Merrill; reprinted, Chicago: University of Chicago Press, 1981.
(1982) *The Individual and the Social Self*, ed. and intro. D. L. Miller, Chicago: University of Chicago Press.

Secondary literature:
Cook, G. A. (1993) *George Herbert Mead: The Making of a Social Pragmatist*, Urbana and Chicago: University of Illinois Press.
Joas, H. (1985) *G. H. Mead: A Contemporary Re-examination of his Thought*, Cambridge, MA: MIT Press.
Miller, D. L. (1973) *George Hebert Mead: Self, Language, and the World*, Austin: University of Texas Press.

Ranked among American pragmatists only after **Peirce**, **James** and **Dewey**, Mead is esteemed because of his contributions to social psychology. Presented in *Mind, Self and Society* (1934), his theory of social behaviourism traces naturalistically the origin of mind to animal conduct. Central is the role of gestures, and most essentially the vocal gesture, inasmuch as it recoils as much on the organism making it as on the organism receiving. In the case of biological individuals with complex cerebral structures, such as humans, the reflexiveness of the vocal gesture gives rise to meanings or significant symbols. Mead's explanation of significant symbols is behaviouristic, and his definition of language is in terms of a social system of such symbols. On his theory, moreover, mind is tantamount to language.

Mead's theory of the individual conscious self is also behaviouristic. The self is social; its individuation arises within the social process. Fundamental to its development is its capacity to take the role of the other and ultimately the generalized other. In play an individual assumes the role of another, as, for example, a small girl playing with her doll pretends to be her mother. In a game an individual performs a role and also assumes the role of the generalized other, as, for example, in baseball when a batter takes into account all the other baseball players on the field and the rules of the game when he bats. Individuals using language or acting in society are habituated to assume such roles to share meanings and values. Indeed, the selfhood of the individual is a product of such social processes.

Mead sought to explain the categories of matter, space and time in terms of the principles of sociality advanced in his social psychology. He proposed a theory of the past as a representation from the present in *The Philosophy of the Present* (1938), and he was at work on a cosmic philosophy of the act, an objective relativism, in *The Philosophy of Act* (1938). Still he construed the speculative feat to 'see the world whole' pragmatically. Dependent on the ability of individuals to take the attitude of the generalized other, it consists in infusing their own experience and conduct with 'the most highly organized logical, ethical, and aesthetic attitudes of the community, those attitudes which involve all that organized thinking, acting, and artistic creations and appreciation imply' (1964, p. 337).

Sources: Edwards; WW(Am); obituary, *New York Times*, 27 Apr 1931.

ANDREW RECK

Mei Yibao (Mei Yi-pao)

Chinese. *b:* 1900, Tianjin, China. *Cat:* Historian of Chinese philosophy. *Ints:* Mozi. *Educ:* Qinghua University, BA 1922; Oberlin College, BA 1924; University of Chicago, PhD 1927; University of Cologne, postdoctoral studies 1927–9. *Infls:* Mozi, John Dewey and Alfred North Whitehead. *Appts:* 1928–37, academic and administrative posts, then Dean at the College of Arts and Letters, at Yenching University, Beijing; after closure by the Japanese, Yenching University moved to Chengdu, with Mei as acting President and acting

Chancellor; after the war, Professor of Philosophy at Yenching University, left in 1948 in the face of impending Communist seizure of the city; taught for a term at St John's University, Shanghai; Visiting Professor, University of Chicago, Oberlin College, and Princeton University, and others; 1955–, Professor State University of Iowa.

Main publications:

(1929) (trans.) *The Ethical and Political Philosophy of Motse*, London: Probsthain.

(1934) *Motse, the Neglected Rival of Confucius*, London: Probsthain.

(1964) (contributor to) W. De Bary *et al.*, *Sources of Chinese Tradition*, 2 vols, New York: Columbia Unversity Press.

Secondary literature:

Boorman, H. (ed.) (1970) *Biographical Dictionary of Republican China*, New York and London: Columbia University Press.

Mei's early work on Mozi provided the basis for a career first as a teacher and as a major Christian educator in China and then as an interpreter of Chinese tradition in the United States. He argued that the dominance of the Confucian tradition in China obscured a rival tradition of Mozi and his followers, which had much to offer China as it reconsidered its past. He considered Mozi's methodology, ethics, politics, economics and religion. He was attracted to Mozi's three criteria of truth and his utilitarian ethical principle of universal love. Although it would be a mistake to consider Mozi's political views as democratic, they nevertheless had an egalitarian aspect and were less rigidly hierarchical than Confucianism. Mozi's economics and religion reflected the ignorance and primitive nature of his society, yet might have developed richly had the tradition not been extinguished.

NICHOLAS BUNNIN

Meinecke, Friedrich

German. *b:* 30 October 1862, Salzwedel, Prussia. *d:* 6 February 1954, Berlin. *Cat:* Political philosopher; historian. *Ints:* German history; historical theory; political history and theory. *Educ:* University of Berlin. *Infls:* Literary influences: Kant, Goethe and Leopold von Ranke. Personal: Johann Gustav Droysen, Heinrich von Treitschke, Ernst Troeltsch and Wilhelm Dilthey. *Appts:* 1893–1935, Editor of *Historische Zeitschrift*; 1901–6, Professor of History, Strasburg; 1906–

14, Professor, Freiburg im Breisgau; 1914–28, Professor, Berlin.

Main publications:

(1908) *Weltburgertum und Nationalstaat*, Munich and Berlin: Oldenbourg.

(1924) *Die Idee der Staatsräson in der neueren Geschichte*, Munich and Berlin: Oldenbourg.

(1936) *Die Entstehung des Historismus*, 2 vols, Munich and Berlin: Oldenbourg.

Secondary literature:

Hofer, Walther (1950) *Geschichtsschreibuung und Weltanschaung: Betrachtungen zum Werk Friedrich Meineckes*, Munich: Cotta.

Hughes, H. Stuart (1979) *Consciousness and Society*, Sussex: Harvester, pp. 229–48.

After studying under the historians Johann Droysen and Heinrich von Treitschke and the philosopher-historian Wilhelm **Dilthey** at Berlin, Meinecke worked for fourteen years in the Prussian state archives. His principal interests were in the history of political ideas, the problems of European ethico-political thought and, later, in *Entstehung des Historismus* (1936), the history and theory of historiography or 'historicism'.

The fundamental question with which he grappled was whether ethics and state power could be harmonized. Having first attempted, in *Weltburgertum und Nationalstaat* (1908), to achieve a tentative rapprochement between ethics and power he then, in *Die Idee der Staatsräson* (1924), came to the regretful conclusion that the two were ultimately irreconcilable (Hughes 1979, p. 243). This change reflected his development from an admirer of Bismarck and the national power-state to a temperate liberal and democratic reformer who championed the humanist and cosmopolitan values in the German tradition.

In *Entstehung des Historismus* (1936) Meinecke traced the rise of historical thinking from Vico to Ranke. By identifying the acme of modern historicism not with Hegel or Marx but with Ranke, and in also emphasizing the importance of the conscience of the individual, he implied a clear condemnation of the whole development of German thought that had ultimately led to Hitler and Nazism.

Meinecke's stance resulted in his being removed from active teaching and also from his editorship of *Historische Zeitschrift*. However, he continued to write and publish until his death in 1954. Although not a rigorous philosopher, Meinecke was a critically minded and scrupulous historian and thinker who was recognized as having made vital contributions to his subjects.
Sources: Metzler; Edwards; Bullock & Woodings.

STEPHEN MOLLER

Meinong, Alexius (von)

Austrian. *b:* 17 July 1853, Lemberg (now Lvov). *d:* 27 November 1920. *Cat:* Metaphysician. *Ints:* Philosophy of mind; perception. *Educ:* Studied at University of Vienna, first History with subsidiary Philosophy (graduating 1874), then, via the Law School, Philosophy. *Infls:* Hume, Kant, Schopenhauer, Brentano, Carl Menger, Russell and several of his own students. *Appts:* Taught at Vienna, 1878–82, and then Graz, becoming full Professor, 1889; founded first laboratory for experimental pyschology in Austria at Graz, 1894.

Main publications:

(1877, 1882) *Hume-studien*: I, *Zur Geschichte und Kritik des modernen Nominalismus*, II, *Zur Relationstheorie*, in *Sitzungsberichte der philosophisch—historischen Klasse der Kaiserlichen Akademie der Wisenschaften*, vols 78, 101, Vienna (see 1966 for translations).

(1885) *Über philosophische Wissenschaft und ihre Propädeutik*, Vienna: A. Holder.

(1894) *Psychologisch-ethische Untersuchungen zur Werth-Theorie*, Graz: Leuschner & Lubensky.

(1896) 'Über die Bedeutung des Weberschen Gesetzes. Beiträge zur Psychologie des Vergleichens und Messens', in *Zeitschrift für Psychologie und Physiologie der Sinnesorgane* 11.

(1899) 'Über Gegenstande höherer Ordnung und deren Verhältniss zur inneren Wahrnehmung', in *Zeitschrift für Psychologie und Physiologie der Sinnesorgane*, 21.

(1902) *Über Annahmen*, Leipzig: J. A. Barth (see 1910).

(1904) 'Über Gegenstandstheorie', in A. Meinong (ed.), *Untersuchungen zur Gegenstandstheorie und Psychologie*, Leipzig: J. A. Barth (English translation, 'The theory of objects', trans. I. Levi, R. B. Terrell and R. M. Chisholm, in R. M. Chisholm (ed.), *Realism and the Background of Phenomenology*, Glencoe, Ill.: Free Press, 1960.

(1906) 'Über die Erfahrungsgrundlagen unseres Wissens', in *Abhandlungen zur Didaktik und Philosophie der Naturwissenschaften* Sonderabdruck der *Zeitschrfit für den physikalischen und chem ischen Unterricht* 1.

(1906) 'Über die Stellung der Gegenstandstheorie im System der Wissenschaften, in Zeitschrift für Philosophie und philosophische Kritik 129.

(1910) *Über Annahmen*, second edition, considerably revised, Leipzig: J. A. Barth (English translation, *On Assumptions*, trans. J. Heanue, Berkeley, Cal.: University of California Press, 1983; editor's introduction includes details of how 1910 differs from 1902).

(1915) *Über Möglichkeit und Wahrscheinlichkeit*, Leipzig: J. A. Barth.

(1917) 'Über emotionale Präsentation', in *Sitzungsberichte der Akademie der Wissenschaften in Wien*, Philosophisch-historischen Klasse 183 (English translation, *On Emotional Presentation*, trans. M.-L. Schubert Kalsi, Evanston, Ill.: Northwestern University Press, 1972).

(1918) 'Zum Erweise des allgemeinen Kausalgesetzes', in *Sitzungsbericht der Akademie der Wissenschaften in Wien*, Philophich-historischen Klasse 189.

(1920) 'Selbstdarstellung', in *Gesaumtausgabe* (1968–78), vol. 7 (partial English translation, in R. Grossman, *Meinong*, London: Routledge & Kegan Paul, 1974.

(1923) *Zur Grundlegung der allgemeinen Werttheorie* (in place of second edition of 1894), Graz: Leuschner & Lubensky.

(1966) K. F. Barber, *Meinong's Hume Studies*, University Microfilms, Michigan: Ann Arbor (translation with commentary of 1877 and parts of 1882).

Collected editions:
(1913–14) *Gesammelte Abhandlungen*, Leipzig: J. A. Barth.

(1968–78) *Alexius Meinong Gesamtausgabe*, 8 vols, Graz: Akad. Druck- und Verlagsanstalt (vol. 7 includes full bibliography).

Secondary literature:
Chisholm, R. M. (1982) *Brentano and Meinong Studies*, Amsterdam: Rodopi.

Findlay, J. N. (1933) *Meinong's Theory of Objects*, Oxford: Clarendon Press; second expanded edition, 1963.

Grazer Philosophische Studien 25–6 (1985–6) (contains several articles on Meinong).

Grossmann, R. (1974) *Meinong*, London: Routledge & Kegan Paul.

Lambert, K. (1983) *Meinong and the Principle of Independence*, Cambridge: Cambridge University Press.

Radakovic, K., Tarouca, S. and Weinhandl, F. (eds) (1952) *Meinong-Gedenkschrift*, vol. 1, Graz: 'Styria' Steirische Verlagsanstalt.

Russell, B. (1904) 'Meinong's theory of complexes and assumptions', *Mind*.

Schubert Kalsi, M. L. (1987) *Meinong's Theory of Knowledge*, Dordrecht: Nijhoff (includes biographical note and discussions of Brentano's influence on Meinong and Meinong's on Chisholm).

After his initial study of history Meinong entered philosophy via its own history, working on his own on Kant for the subsidiary subject in his first degree, and then, at **Brentano**'s suggestion, on Hume. He soon turned to pure philosophy, though in his early years combining it, as was almost inevitable then, with psychology, setting up the first Austrian experimental laboratory in psychology, in Graz, where he worked from 1882, being almost completely blind for his last fifteen years or so. His experimental work was on psychology of perception, but he gradually emancipated himself from 'psychologism', the attempt to solve philosophical problems by irrelevant empirical or introspective methods. Here as elsewhere he worked in parallel with **Frege** and **Husserl**, though apparently without any mutual influence. Nevertheless he insisted that psychology must not be abandoned altogether. Like a good phenomenologist he insisted on 'inner experiences' as a, if not the, subject matter for philosophy (1968–78, vol. 7, p. 11, written in 1920), and in 1912 wrote an article entitled 'For psychology and against psychologism in general value theory' (*Logos* III, 1912, reprinted in vol. 3 of *Alexius von Meinong Gesamtausgabe* (1968–78).

Meinong was unfortunate in living too early to be flung out of Austria by Hitler, so that he could not join the many German-speaking philosophers in exile who wrote in English. Apart from a single page in *Mind* (1879, reprinted in 1968–78, vol. 7) he wrote exclusively in German, and, despite the better fate of **Mach** and Frege, that may be partly why he has never achieved the popularity in Anglophone philosophy of Moore and Russell, with whom he has considerable philosophical kinship. Only recently, after the pioneering efforts of J. N. **Findlay** and R. M. **Chisholm** and others, have translations started appearing.

The one thing everybody knows about Meinong is that he had a jungle, providing rich nutrient for all manner of strange beasts, from the golden mountain to the round square. Recently, however, the lushness of its vegetation has come under more sceptical scrutiny (Grossman 1974; N. Griffin in *Grazer Philosophie Studien*, 1985–6). The issue is complex. Meinong does talk in a jungly sort of way, and apart from being and subsistence we are asked to accept, at various times, quasi-being, pseudo-existence and 'outside-of-being-ness' (*Aussersein*, variously translated, but often and perhaps best left untranslated). If we are to talk about something, he thinks, there must in some sense be something there to talk about. But in what sense? Every thought must have an object (*Gegenstand*), which Meinong then treats as an entity (Grossman (1974) translates *Gegenstand* as 'entity', but this seems question-begging and breaks the link with thought). Some objects are real (*wirklich*): roughly, those that are perceptible and in space and time. These also subsist (*bestehen*), but some objects merely subsist and are not real, though they still have being (*Sein*); they are higher-order objects and presuppose objects of the lowest order, which one can say 'with a grain of salt'— one of Meinong's favourite expressions—they have as parts; a stock example is the difference between red and green, although the assignment of objects in general to the different orders is a complex matter. Some objects, however, neither exist nor subsist, such as the golden mountain and the existence of the golden mountain, although we can think of them and they have properties or 'being so' (*Sosein*): the golden mountain is golden.

Meinong now faces a problem because of the principle that higher-order objects presuppose lower-order ones. But how can the perfectly good higher-order object, the nonexistence of the golden mountain, subsist if its presupposed lower-order object, the golden mountain, does not? At first he toyed with a shadowy third kind of being, or 'quasi-being', which would belong to every object, i.e. anything at all, however absurd or contradictory. 'There are objects of which it is true that there are no such objects', as he puts it with conscious paradox (1904, translation p. 83), thereby raising questions about quantification that have similarly engaged Frege, **Russell** and **Quine**. This does indeed suggest the jungle, and he later said that it betrayed the same 'prejudice in favour of the actual' (or real) that he had sought to oppose by a third alternative to existence and subsistence (1910, translation pp. 159, 170). But his main objection was that being of universal application it would have no significance, and his later solution was 'the *Aussersein* of the pure object' (1904, translation pp. 83–6). The point, in effect, is to abandon the need to specify an ontological status for the basic objects of thought. But alas! *Aussersein* itself ends up as something 'being-like' (*seinsartiges*), which does not after all apply universally: the round square has it only in a qualified way, and things even more defective, like

the paradoxical Russell class, not at all (1917, chapter 2; cf. Heanue's introduction to his translation of 1910, pp. xxx–xxxi; Griffin, in *Grazer Philosophische Studien* 1985–6, draws some interesting implications regarding modern 'paraconsistent' logic).

Meinong regards all this as a new philosophical subject, the theory of objects, an a priori science of objects in general; so far, he thinks, mathematics is the only part of this theory which has been developed. It goes beyond metaphysics, which is, or should be, an empirical science studying everything which can be known empirically (1904, translation pp. 109–10 especially). Facts about what exists can only be known empirically, whereas all other facts are knowable only a priori (1910, translation p. 61). This claim, however, to see a new rival to metaphysics has not been generally accepted.

In escaping from psychologism Meinong went beyond Brentano by distinguishing (along with **Twardowski** and Husserl but with greater insistence) the object and the content of a thought or experience (e.g. 1917, chapter 7), and also by distinguishing 'assumptions' or 'supposals' (*Annahmen*) as intermediate between judgements and ideas or representations (*Vorstellungen*)—a topic to which he devoted a whole book, although he has been accused (by C. D. **Broad** reviewing 1910 in *Mind*, 1913) of conflating assuming (or just pretending) a proposition is true with merely entertaining it (does 1910—translation p. 254—counter this?) . But judgements etc. are not the propositions or states of affairs they are of. Meinong calls these 'objectives' (*Objektive*), a rather wider term (1910, translation pp. 75–6). Objectives form a special class of objects, distinguished as essentially being positive or negative, the (in German) rather harsh term *Objekt* then being introduced for other objects. Finally he applies these various notions, or analogues of them, to develop theories of emotional and conative, as well as cognitive, mental processes and their objects, and develops an objectivist theory of values. Apart from his widespread role as an Aunt Sally of ontological profligacy, Meinong influenced the 'critical realism' of **Dawes Hicks** and others, and philosophers currently better known such as **Ryle** and Chisholm. Some of the ideas touched on in the last paragraph show a considerable kinship with, if less direct and overt influence on, the later theories of speech acts and the currently popular investigations into content. (See also Findlay, in Radakovic *et al.* (eds) 1952.) **Sources:** PI; Passmore 1957; Edwards; personal communication with Prof. P. Simons.

A. R. LACEY

Melden, A(braham) I(rving)
American. *b:* 9 February 1910, Montreal, Canada. *d:* 17 November 1991, Irvine, California. *Cat:* Analytic philosopher. *Ints:* Ethics; rights theory; action theory. *Educ:* University of California, Los Angeles, BA 1931; Brown University, MA 1932, University of California, Berkeley, PhD 1938. *Infls:* Literary influences include Moore, Wittgenstein, Ryle and A. E. Murphy; personal influences include Ralph Blake, Murphy, Arthur Smullyan, A. Sesonske and M. Black. *Appts:* Instructor, University of California, Berkeley, 1939–41; Assistant, Associate then full Professor of Philosophy, University of Washington, 1946–64; Professor of Philosophy, University of California, Irvine, 1964–77; Professor Emeritus, from 1977; recalled, 1977–82; President of the American Philosophical Association, 1962; served several years as editor of *Philosophy Research Archives* and coedited 'The Basic Problems in Philosophy' series of Wadsworth Publishing Co.

Main publications:
(1950) (ed.) *Ethical Theories*, New York (Prentice-Hall), with a Preface and Introduction 'On the nature and problems of ethics'; 2nd ed., 1955; 2nd ed., revised 1967.

(1958) (ed.) *Essays in Moral Philosophy*, Seattle: University of Washington Press, Introduction, pp. vii–xii.

(1959) *Rights and Right Conduct*, Oxford: Basil Blackwell, several reprints of sections.

(1961) *Free Action*, London: Routledge & Kegan Paul, several reprints of sections.

(1962) 'Reasons for action and matters of fact' (Presidential address), *Proceedings and Addresses of the American Philosophical Assocation* XXXV: 45–60.

(1964) (ed.) *The Theory of Practical Reason* (Carus Lectures), by Arthur E. Murphy, La Salle, Ill.: Open Court Publishing Co., with an Introduction (very illuminating), pp. ix–xviii.

(1970) (ed.) *Human Rights*, Belmont, California: Wadsworth; Introduction, pp. 1–9.

(1977) *Rights and Persons*, Oxford: Basil Blackwell, Berkeley and Los Angeles: University of California Press.

(1988) *Rights in Moral Lives. A Historical-Philosophical Essay*, Berkeley and Los Angeles: University of California Press.

Secondary literature:
Singer, M. G. (1981) 'Recent trends and future prospects in ethics', *Metaphilosophy* 12: 218–19 (contains a brief discussion of his views on moral rights).

Melden's writings on action generated intense discussion. He became noted for his discussions of rights, starting with an essay 'The concept of universal human rights', in *Language, Science, and Human Rights* (Philadelphia: University of Pennsylvania Press, 1952, pp. 167–88), which started him on a lifelong pursuit of this topic, as indicated in the titles of three of the books listed above, the first of which, *Rights and Right Conduct* (1959) also made some acute contributions to understanding moral reasoning. Rejecting any sharp distinction between *is* and *ought*, Melden argued that certain factual claims, such as 'He is your father', already imply certain judgements about how one ought to act, without the need for some universal normative major premise. A similar theme was also argued in his Presidential Address of 1962: that reasons for action are grounded in facts, which have their moral relevance built in as part of the way of life of the community in which these facts are recognized and described as they are. He later argued that rights are distinct moral entities, irreducible to duties or obligations and the notion of right conduct; are inextricably linked with human personality; and must be recognized as an essential feature of moral situations and moral discourse. Melden's work has been constantly referred to and commented on. He was awarded several fellowships and received numerous invitations to lecture around the world. He wrote in a lucid and graceful style, without recourse to unneeded technicalities, and he was an excellent editor of other people's work. However, Melden's distinctive ideas about the essential nature and character of rights, as an ineliminable feature of morality, still remain to be appreciated, discussed and appraised. A number of discussions are listed in the *Philosopher's Index*.
Sources: *PI*; K. Lambert and G. Santas (1993) memorial notice, *PAAPA* 66: 83–5; CV Oct 1989; WW(West) 1972–3; personal acquaintance.

MARCUS SINGER

Meliukhin, Serafim Timofeevich

Russian. *b:* 6 June 1927, Tambovsk province, Russia. *Cat:* Marxist. *Ints:* Dialectical materialism; cosmology; philosophy of physics. *Educ:* Moscow State University and the Institute of Philosophy of the Soviet Academy of Sciences. *Infls:* Marx and Lenin. *Appts:* From 1953, taught Philosophy at various institutions in Russia; from 1974, Head of the Department of Dialectical Materialism (now called the Department of General Theoretical Philosophy) at Moscow State University.

Main publications:

(1958) *Problema konechnogo i beskonechnogo* [The Problem of the Finite and the Infinite], Moscow.

(1960) *O dialektike razvitiia neorganicheskoi prirody* [On the Dialectics of the Development of Inorganic Nature], Moscow.

(1966) *Materiia i ee edinstve, beskonechnosti i razvitii* [Matter in Its Unity, Infinity and Development], Moscow.

(1967) *Material'noe edinstvo mira v svete sovremennoi nauki* [The Material Unity of the World in the Light of Contemporary Science], Moscow.

(1977) *Filosofskie osnovaniia estestvoznaniia* [Philosophical Foundations of the Natural Sciences], Moscow.

Secondary literature:

Alekseev. P. V. (ed.) (1993) *Filosofy Rossii xix–xx stoletii*, Moscow, pp. 120–1.

Graham, Loren R. (1972) *Science and Philosophy in the Soviet Union*, New York: Alfred A. Knopf; revised editon, *Science, Philosophy, and Human Behavior in the Soviet Union*, Columbia University Press, 1987.

Scanlan, James P. (1985) *Marxism in the USSR*, Cornell University Press.

Coming after a long period during which Soviet Marxist–Leninist philosophers had rejected certain scientific theories as 'bourgeois' and incompatible with dialectical materialism, Meliukhin's book *Problema konechnogo i beskonechnogo* (1958) reflected a new willingness to entertain Western cosmological theories such as **Einstein**'s and a desire generally to accommodate dialectical materialism to advances in the sciences. Although not ready to accept relativity theory in its entirety, Meliukhin affirmed that it supports dialectical materialism in viewing space and time as inseparable from matter.

Meliukhin's subsequent writings contain similarly undogmatic reformulations of the requirements of dialectical materialism, focusing primarily on questions of the nature of matter and the structure of the physical universe. Meliukhin asserts that the orthodox Soviet conception of materialism, based on **Lenin**'s insistence that being 'objective reality' is the only philosophically relevant property of matter, is actually a conception not of materialism but of realism; he advocates the construction of a new philosophical theory of matter in which its characteristics are derived not from the analysis of Lenin's definition but from the findings of the sciences. Before the break-up of the USSR, Meliukhin also interpreted Lenin's statement that matter is 'infinite in depth' as signifying not that the components of matter are infinitely divisible (a reading favoured by some literalists) but that there is an infinity of forms in which matter exists. Meliukhin's views were criticized by Soviet traditionalists as lacking partisan commitment to Marxism–Leninism.

Meliukhin's less conservative approach to Marxism–Leninism contributed to the partial liberalization of Soviet philosophy in the decades after Stalin's death, particularly after 1974 when he assumed the influential position of Head of the Department of Dialectical Materialism at Moscow State University (from 1974–7 he also served as Dean of the Philosophy Faculty at that institution). A significant feature of his approach wass the conviction that fields such as ethics, aesthetics and the history of philosophy should not all be subsumed under the rubric of dialectical and historical materialism, as the more partisan Marxist–Leninists had argued earlier, but should be considered separate philosophical disciplines.

JAMES SCANLAN

Mercier, Désiré Joseph

Belgian. *b:* 21 November 1851, Brabant, Belgium. *d:* 23 January 1926, Brussels. *Cat:* Scholastic. *Ints:* Thomist philosophy. *Educ:* Malines and University of Louvain. *Infls:* Aquinas and Kant. *Appts:* 1882–1906, Professor of Thomistic Philosophy, the University of Louvain; 1889–1906, President, Institut Supérieur de Philosophie, University of Louvain.

Main publications:

(1892–7) *Cours de philosophie*:

(1894) vol. I, *Logique*; seventh edition, Louvain: Uystpruyst-Dieudonné; Paris: Alcan, 1922.

(1894) vol. II, *Métaphysique générale ou ontologie*; seventh edition, Louvain: Uystpruyst-Dieudonné; Paris: Alcan, 1923.

(1892) vol. III, *Psychologie*; eleventh edition, Louvain: Uystpruyst-Dieudoneé; Paris: Alcan, 1923.

(1897) vol. IV, *Critériologie générale ou théorie générale de la certitude*; eighth edition, Louvain: Uystpruyst-Dieudonné; Paris: Alcan, 1923.

(1905) (with Désiré Nys and Maurice De Wulf) *Traité élémentaire de philosophie*, 2 vols; fifth edition, Louvain: Institut Supérieur de Philosophie; Paris: Alcan, 1920 (English translation, *A Manual of Modern Scholastic Philosophy*, 2 vols, London: Kegan Paul, Trench, Trubner and St Louis: Herder, 1926).

Secondary literature:

(1926) *Revue Néoscolastique de Philosophie* 28 (a Mercier issue, with bibliography on pp. 251–8).

De Raeymaeker, Louis (1952) *Le Cardinal Mercier et l'Institut Supérieur de Philosophie de Louvain*, Louvain: Publications Universitaires.

Gade, John A. (1934) *The Life of Cardinal Mercier*, New York: Scribners.

Van Riet, Georges (1963) *Thomistic Epistemology*, 2 vols, St Louis and London: Herder, vol. I, pp. 124–63.

Mercier was a key figure in the development of contemporary scholastic philosophy. He was the first holder of a Chair of Thomistic philosophy created at the University of Louvain in 1882. He inaugurated the Institut Supérieur de Philosophie (also at Louvain) in 1889, and founded the *Revue Néoscolastique de Philosophie* in 1894 (renamed *Revue Philosophique de Louvain* in 1946). Mercier made a sharp distinction between scholastic philosophy and theology, and strove to create a Thomistic philosophy which would engage in dialogue with other philosophical schools, and with the sciences, and which dealt with the problems of contemporary life in a contemporary language. He also encouraged scholarly study of the great medieval philosophers. The Institut Supérieur quickly attracted many distinguished scholars and philosophers, and has been a centre and powerhouse of contemporary scholasticism up to the present day. Much of Mercier's published output, and in particular his *Cours de philosophie* (1892–7), was designed for use as student texts, albeit advanced students, and is not much read nowadays. Its historical importance lies in the example it set of a Thomism which used Aquinas as an inspiration for independent thought, which was fully alive to the value of the empirical sciences (Mercier was instrumental in establishing at Louvain one of the earliest laboratories for experimental psychology), and alive also to the importance of Kant. He was most original and innovative in the field of epistemology, and his *Critériologie générale*, which deals

with the problems of certitude, is a significant work which is still worth reading. His reputation in philosophy, however, depends almost wholly upon his role as midwife of twentieth-century scholasticism.

Sources: DFN; EF; WWW; *RNP* 28, 1926.

HUGH BREDIN

Merleau-Ponty, Maurice

French. *b:* 1908, Rochefort-sur-mer, France. *d:* 1961. *Cat:* Phenomenologist. *Ints:* Epistemology; philosophy of language; aesthetics. *Educ:* After a brilliant student career at various lycées and the École Normale Supérieur (1926–30), Merleau-Ponty gained his agrégation in 1931. *Infls:* Descartes, Husserl, Sartre and empirical psychology. *Appts:* Taught in a number of lycées before the Second World War; served in the French army during the war; professorships at Lyon, the Sorbonne and finally the Collège de France; Coeditor, with Sartre and de Beauvoir, of *Les Temps Modernes*.

Main publications:

(1942) *La Structure du comportement*, Paris: PUF.

(1945) *Phénoménologie de la perception*, Paris: NRF Gallimard.

(1947) *Humanisme et terreur*, Paris: Gallimard.

(1948) *Sens et non-sens*, Paris: Nagel.

(1953) *Eloge de la philosophie*, Paris: NRF Gallimard.

(1955) *Les Aventures de la dialectique*, Paris: Gallimard.

(1960) *Signes*, Paris: NRF Gallimard.

Secondary literature:

Dillon, M. C. (1988) *Merleau-Ponty's Ontology*, Bloomington: Indiana University Press.

Edie, J. M. (1987) *Merleau-Ponty's Philosophy of Language*, Lanham: University Press of America.

Madison, G. B. (1973) *La Phénoménologie de Merleau-Ponty*, Paris: Klincksieck.

Robinet, A. (1970) *Merleau-Ponty*, Paris: PUF.

Spiegelberg, H. (1969) *The Phenomenological Movement*, vol. II, second edition, The Hague: Martinus Nijhoff.

Tilliette, X. (1970) *Merleau-Ponty*, Paris: Seghers.

Merleau-Ponty has been presented both as a phenomenologist and as an existentialist, but a study of his thought reveals the limited utility of general labels of this kind. Whilst he was the first French thinker to use the term 'phenomenology' in the title of a major work and to identify philosophy with phenomenology, he does not rely greatly on the methods of **Husserl**; and equally, although he shares many of the concerns of his friend **Sartre**, Merleau-Ponty disagrees with the latter on such fundamental issues as the extent of human freedom. He argues that experience is shot through with pre-existent meanings, largely derived from language and experienced in perception.

Merleau-Ponty arrived at these views gradually, beginning from a prolonged and extensive study of the psychology of perception. His first significant work, *La Structure du comportement* (1942) is essentially a critique of the major psychological theories of perception of the time, notably behaviourism and Gestalt theory (as put forward by **Köhler**). Merleau-Ponty denied that there is a causal relationship between the physical and the mental, and he therefore finds the behaviourist account of perception, entirely in terms of causation, unacceptable. Gestalt theory he finds not false but not developed sufficiently to do justice to the facts of perception. His general conclusion is that a new approach is needed if perception is to be properly understood.

This new approach is his version of phenomenology, and its application to perception is the subject of his second and most important work, *Phénoménologie de la perception* (1945). The fundamental premise of this work is that of the primacy of perception: our perceptual relation to the world is *sui generis*, and logically prior to the subject–object distinction. Theories of perception which deny this are rejected in the opening chapters of the work: for example, all sense-data theories are dismissed, since they attempt to reconstruct experience by using artificial abstractions which presuppose the subject–object dichotomy. By contrast Merleau-Ponty goes on to explore the phenomenal field by using a much expanded notion of Gestalt. It is argued that the elements of Gestalts are both inherently meaningful and open or indeterminate.

One of the most original features of this phenomenology is his theory of the role of the body in the world as perceived (*le monde perçu*), an area of thought he develops at much greater length than does Sartre. Merleau-Ponty contends that a number of the most fundamental features of perception are a result of our physical incarnation: our perception of space is conditioned by our bodily mode of existence; or again, we regard perceived things as constant because our body remains constant. Further, Merleau-Ponty contends that perception is a committed (*engagé*) or existential act, not one in which we are merely passive. We discover meanings in the world, and

commit ourselves, without complete logical justification, to believing in its future.

The concluding section of the work draws out some important consequences of these views, firstly concerning Cartesianism. As with Husserl, Merleau-Ponty's thought to some extent defines itself by reference to that of Descartes. Merleau-Ponty is logically bound to deny that Cartesianism is acceptable, and this he does. The Cartesian presupposition of a distinction between meditating ego and transcendent cogitata is incompatible with the thesis of the primacy of perception, and thus Merleau-Ponty classifies the cogito of the second *Meditation* as a merely 'verbal cogito'. He replaces it with a 'true cogito' of the form 'there is a phenomenon; something shows itself'. Put in metaphysical terms, the fundamental category revealed by Merleau-Ponty's philosophy is what he terms 'being-in-the-world' (*être-au-monde*). The subjective and the objective are facets of this prior, embracing structure.

This thesis conditions his analysis of time, in which he argues that the notions of time and subjectivity are mutually constitutive. Time is not a feature of the objective world, but is a dimension of subjectivity: past and future appear in our present and can only occur in a temporal being. Time is more than the form of the inner life, and more intimately related to subjectivity than is suggested by regarding it as an attribute or property of the self. To analyse time, Merleau-Ponty contends, is to gain access to the complete structure of subjectivity.

In the final pages of the *Phenomenology of Perception* Merleau-Ponty discusses the nature and limits of human freedom, a theme developed further in the political works, *Humanisme et terreur* (1947) and *Les Aventures de la dialectique* (1955). He rejects the Sartrean doctrine that we are condemned to be (absolutely) free, replacing it with his own view that we are condemned to meaning. Experience comes ready furnished with meanings, and so although we are free to make choices the field of freedom is accordingly circumscribed. These meanings are conveyed by a number of social institutions, but above all by language. As he puts it in his discussion of the cogito: 'Descartes, and a fortiori his reader, begin their meditation in what is already a universe of discourse' (*Phenomenology of Perception*, p. 401). Unsurprisingly, it was to a consideration of the role of language as a vehicle for intersubjectivity that Merleau-Ponty turned in his final years, but he did not live to work out a complete theory.

Merleau-Ponty also developed an interest in aesthetics, especially of the visual arts. This follows from his theory of the primacy of perception: he found in painting a fuller appreciation of our special perceptual relation with the world than in science or in philosophies which analyse perception in terms of the primacy of the subject–object distinction.

ROBERT WILKINSON

Meyer-Wichmann, Clara Gertrud

Dutch. *b:* 17 August 1885, Hamburg. *d:* 15 February 1922, The Hague. *Cat:* Dialectical and feminist philosopher. *Ints:* Philosophy of law. *Educ:* Law, University of Utrecht. *Infls:* Hegel and Marx. *Appts:* Civil servant at the Central Office of Statistics, 1914–21.

Main publications:

(1912) *Beschouwingen over de historische grondslagen der tegenwoordige omvorming van het strafbegrip* (Reflections about the Historical Foundations of the Actual Metamorphosis of the Concept of Penalty), Leyden: Brill.

(1920) *Inleiding tot de philosophie der samenleving* [Introduction to the Philosophy of Society], Haarlem: Bohn.

(1920) *Misdaad, straf en maatschappij* [Crime, Penalty and Society], Utrecht: Bijleveld.

(1924) *Bevrijding* [Liberation], Arnhem: Van Loghum Slaterus (posthumous).

(1936) *Vrouw en Maatschappij* [Woman and Society], Utrecht: Bijleveld (posthumous).

Meyer-Wichmann developed an anarchist theory of society, based on the principle of non-violence. Her conviction is that the ideal society cannot be reached by violent means because such means are in principle contradictory to this goal. She joined the International Anti-Militarist Movement and in 1920 founded the League of Religious Anarcho-Communists. Her view on criminal law opposes the idea of punishment: nobody, not even the state, has any right to punish other people. We need a new theory and a new practice of education, taking into account factors of heredity, environment and psychology. She started a movement for abolishing imprisonment, the so called 'abolitionism'. Instead of punishment the only need of society today is protection against 'criminals'. If society is changing, most criminality, as caused by society itself, will disappear. From her viewpoint of equality she strongly pleaded the cause of the emancipation of women.

WIM VAN DOOREN

Meyerson, Émile

Polish (naturalized French). *b:* 12 February 1859, Lublin, Poland. *d:* 4 December 1933, Paris. *Cat:* Metaphysician; epistemologist. *Ints:* Philosophy of science. *Educ:* Göttingen, Heidelberg and Berlin; Paris from 1882 (chemistry). *Infls:* H. Kopp, K. Kroman, C. Renouvier, H. Høffding and neo-Kantianism. *Appts:* Freelance scholar; Member of Royal Danish Academy, 1926.

Main publications:

(1908) *Identité et réalité*, Paris: Payot (English translation, K. Loewenberg, London: Allen & Unwin, 1930).

(1921) *De l'explication dans les sciences* 2 vols, Paris: Payot (English translation, *Explanation in the Sciences*, trans. M.-A. and D. A. Spifle, Dordrecht: Kluwer, 1991).

(1925) *La Déduction relativiste*, Paris: Payot (English translation, *The Relativistic Deduction*, trans. D. A. and M.-A. Spifle, Dordrecht: Reidel, 1985).

(1931) *Du cheminement de la pensée*, 3 vols, Paris: Alcan.

(1933) *Réel et déterminisme dans la physique quantique*, Paris: Hermann.

(1936) *Essais*, Paris: Vrin.

(1939) *Correspondance entre Harald Høffding et Émile Meyerson*, Copenhagen: E. Munksgaard.

Secondary literature:

Boas, G. (1930) *A Critical Analysis of the Philosophy of Émile Meyerson*, Baltimore: Johns Hopkins University Press.

Brunschvicg, L. (1926) 'La Philosophie d'Émile Meyerson', *Revue de Métaphysique et de Morale*, 33: 39–63.

Bull. Soc. Fr. Phil., April 1961 (various).

Denti, M. A. (1940) *Scienza e Filosofia in Meyerson*, Firenze: La Nuova Italia.

Kelly, T. R. (1937) *Explanation and Reality in the Philosophy of Émile Meyerson*, Princeton: Princeton University Press.

Lalande, A. (1922) 'L'Épistémologie de M. Meyerson, *Rev. Phil. France et de l'Étranger*, 96: 259–80.

Marcucci, S. (1962) *Émile Meyerson, Epistemologia e Filosofia*, Florence: Le Monnier.

——(1963) Review of Mourélos 1963, *Physis* 5: 199–205.

Metz, A. (1932) *Une nouvelle philosophie des sciences, le causalisme de M. Émile Meyerson*, Paris: Alcan.

——(1934) *Meyerson, une nouvelle philosophie de la connaissance*, Paris: Alcan.

Mourélos, G. (1963) *L'Épistémologie positive et la critique meyersonnienne*, Paris: PUF.

See, H. (1932) *Science et philosophie d'après la doctrine de M. E. Meyerson*, Paris: Alcan.

Wallace, W. A. (1974) *Causality and Scientific Explanation*, Ann Arbor, Michigan: University of Michigan Press.

Zahar, E. (1980) 'Einstein, Meyerson and the role of mathematics in physical discovery', *British Journal for Philosophy & Science*, 31: 1–43.

A self-taught philosopher, Meyerson became a kind of anti-positivist idealist for whom science was the product of a priori ideas in the mind of the scientist not of the conditions nature imposed, a view in Meyerson's opinion borne out by his extensive researches in the history of science which, he claimed, refuted the programme of the objective description of nature. For Meyerson the aim of scientific knowledge was the causes of the things and the identities underlying the superficial flux of the phenomena. Under the traditional regulative principle *causa aequat effectum*, variety and heterogeneity were to be reduced to homogeneity and unity. He did not, however, believe that this goal was in practice achievable. Nature resisted the endeavours of the scientist and he saw the progress of science as a tension between rationalizing tendencies leading to a sort of Parmenidean elimination of genuine change, and nature's irrationality resisting it. For example, Carnot's principle, that heat could not be completely converted into work, showed that time and change could not be eliminated from the theory of heat. His attempts to come to grips philosophically with the new quantum and relativistic physical theories (rejecting the so-called Copenhagen interpretation of the quantum theory) earned Meyerson the respect of **Einstein**. As much through his circle of acquaintance as through his writings he became influential in much modern French historiography of science, as in the work of such figures as Alexandre **Koyré** and Hélène Metzger.

Sources: DSB; Edwards; Mittelstrass.

R. N. D. MARTIN

Midgley, Mary

British. *b:* 13 September 1919, London. *Cat:* Applied ethicist; moral philosopher. *Educ:* Somerville College, Oxford, 1938–42. *Appts:* Lecturer, University of Reading, 1948–59; Lecturer, then Senior Lecturer, University of Newcastle-upon-Tyne, 1960–80.

Main publications:

(1978) *Beast and Man: The Roots of Human Nature*, Ithaca, NY: Cornell University Press.

(1981) *Heart and Mind: The Varieties of Moral Experience*, Brighton: Harvester Press.

(1983) *Animals and Why They Matter*, Athens, GA: University of Georgia Press.

(1983) (with Judith Hughes) *Women's Choices: Philosophical Problems Facing Feminism*, London: Weidenfeld & Nicolson.

(1984) *Wickedness: A Philosophical Essay*, London: Routledge & Kegan Paul.

(1985) *Evolution as Religion: Strange Hopes and Stranger Fears*, London: Methuen.

(1989) *Wisdom, Information and Wonder: What is Knowledge For?*, London: Routledge.

(1991) *Can't We Make Moral Judgements?*, New York: St. Martin's Press.

(1992) *Science as Salvation: A Modern Myth and its Meaning*, London: Routledge.

(1994) *The Ethical Primate: Humans, Freedom and Morality*, London: Routledge.

The central thesis in Midgley's philosophy is that minimalist conceptions of human nature (in science and in philosophy) are seriously misleading because of their depersonalizing and reductive explanations of what it is to be human. She argues for a broader conception of human nature formulated through knowledge gathered from many disciplines including philosophy, science, sociobiology, anthropology and ethnology.

Midgley is critical of the sociobiological positions of E. O. Wilson and Richard Dawkins for the fatalism and egoism she believes they expound. She identifies the roots of these positions in the Cartesian view of the solitary thinker, which Midgley thinks is both egocentric and anthropocentric. In *Beast and Man* (1978), she argues that human nature is influenced by both biology and culture, so that our genes and instincts in some ways shape moral life. We act according to a set of needs, but we also have the capacity to determine goods for ourselves, and to reflect on and correct our behaviour. We are responsible for virtue and vice since they are products of the conscious, reflective acts of free beings.

Midgley's critique of science is also expressed in her position that science as a religion has dangerous consequences. She argues that, for example, the 'endless-escalator model' of evolution has become a kind of secular religion. The implications of such scientific 'myths' are twofold: they lead to the dismissal of the non-human world from the moral sphere; and the futuristic fantasies of some scientific theories ignore urgent contemporary problems. Philosophy, too, makes these mistakes when it attempts to imitate science, and consequently moves away from helping us to know how to live. However, philosophy should be used to underpin and thus give a firm foundation to science through its metaphysical, epistemological and moral ideas.

Midgley argues that the proper course for both science and philosophy is to recognize the limits of so-called 'value-free' knowledge and universal truth, and to embrace a more grounded, practical morality. To achieve this, she suggests a revised account of morality that incorporates a set of noncontractual duties to others (including non-humans), and emphasises the important roles played by shared community, kinship and feelings in our moral judgements.

Sources: Personal communication.

EMILY BRADY

Mikhailovsky, Nikolai Konstantinovich

Russian. *b:* 15 November (27 N.S.) 1842, Meschovsk, Kaluga province. *d:* 28 January (10 February N.S.) 1904, St Petersburg. *Cat:* Populist. *Educ:* Studied Natural Sciences at the St Petersburg Institute of Mining Engineers; expelled in 1861 for part in student protests. *Infls:* J. S. Mill, Proudhon, Marx, V. G. Belinksy, A. I. Herzen and Lavrov. *Appts:* Editor, *Otechestvennye zapiski*, 1869–84; 1892–, editor, *Russkoe bogatstvo*.

Main publications:

(1869–70) 'Chto takoe progress?' [What is progress?], serialized in *Otechestvennye zapiski* [Notes of the Fatherland].
(1965) (ed. J. M. Edie *et al.*) *Russian Philosophy*, Chicago: Quadrangle Books, vol. 2, pp. 170–98 (translated extracts from Mikhailovsky's articles, including the above).

Secondary literature:

Billington, J. H. (1958) *Mikhailovsky and Russian Populism*, Oxford: Clarendon Press.
Walicki, A. (1969) *The Controversy over Capitalism: Studies in the Social Philosophy of the Russian Populists*, Oxford: Clarendon Press.

The noble-born Mikhailovsky edited the radical journal *Otechestvennye zapiski* from 1869 to 1884. His 'Chto takoe progress?' helped inspire the 'to the people' movement of 1873–4. From 1879 he was closely associated with the revolutionary populist group Narodnaia Volia [People's Will], and was exiled after the assassination of Alex-ander II in 1881. From 1892, having renounced revolution, he edited the liberal populist journal *Russkoe bogatstvo* [Russian Treasury].

After **Lavrov**'s emigration, Mikhailovsky became the leading theoretician of populism inside Russia. The influence of Lavrov's anthropologism is evident in his views: the centrality of the 'integral personality'; subjectivism in history and sociology; and the tension between epistemological relativism and an ethical idealism based on the subjective consciousness of freedom (in which respect Mikhailovsky exploited the dual meaning of *pravda* as 'truth' and 'justice'). Unlike Lavrov, he was especially antagonistic to the division of labour and the social and cultural divisions which sprang from it; his own anthropocentric idea of progress (explicitly opposed to **Spencer's**) involved the diminishing heterogeneity of society and the increasing heterogeneity of its members. Taking issue with Comte, he advanced a three-stage historical periodization, beginning with the 'objectively anthropocentric' outlook of primitive societies, followed by an 'eccentric' period of the suppression and fragmentation of the individual, and culminating in a 'subjectively anthropocentric period' when individual freedom is reconciled with the social solidarity exemplified in the peasant commune. Lavrov and Mikhailovsky directly influenced Viktor Chernov and the Russian Social Revolutionaries, and there are affinities in **Kropotkin** and **Tolstoy**. Negatively, they stimulated the invective of early Russian Marxists of all shades, including **Plekhanov**, **Lenin** and **Berdyaev**.

COLIN CHANT

Miki, Kiyoshi

Japanese. *b:* 1897, Hoyogo, Japan. *d:* 1945, (jail, shortly after the end of the Second World War). *Cat:* Marxist humanist. *Ints:* Philosophy of history; political philosophy. *Educ:* Kyoto University; studied in Europe with Rickert and Heidegger, 1922–5. *Infls:* Nishida and Marxism. *Appts:* 1925–7, Lecturer at Third High School, Kyoto; 1927–, Professor, Hosei University, Tokyo; arrested in 1930 and charged with breaking the Peace Preservation Law, and forced to resign his university position.

Main publications:

(1926) *Pascal niokeru Ningen no Kenkyu* [A Study of the Concept of the Human in Pascal].
(1928) *Yuibutsu Shikan to Gendai no Ishiki* [The Historical-Materialist View and the Political Awareness of our Contemporaries].

(1932) *Rekishi Tetsugaku* [Philosophy of History].
(1939) *Kosoryoku no Ronri* [Principle of the Power of
   Organization].
(1941) *Jinseiron Note* [Notes on the Fundamental
   Idea in the Philosophy of Life].
(1946–51) *Miki Kiyoshi Zenshu* [Miki's Works],
   Tokyo: Iwanami Publishing; reissued 1984–6.

One of the founders of philosophical studies in
Japan, and a cult writer among young Japanese
students of letters, Miki was a typical representative of the group of Japanese philosophers active
in the first half of the twentieth century. He
typified a pattern which combined two seemingly
contradictory strands in Japanese thought of the
time: (i) the philosophical heritage of Japan; and
(ii) Western thought, represented by the Marxism
then in vogue. Deeply influenced in his youth by
Nishida's *Zen no Kenkyu* [A Study of the Good],
Miki was involved in the Kyoto group of
philosophers. His study in Europe and meeting
there with other Japanese students like Hani Goro
enhanced his interest in Marxism. These two
aspects, the Japanese and the Western Marxist,
remain the two poles of Miki's thought until the
end of his life.

   Having started his career as a Marxist humanist, Miki took an active role in the publication of
journals such as *Shako Kagaku no Hata no Motoni*
[Under the Flag of Newly Rising Science] and
Proletarian Kagaku [Proletarian Science]. However, a change in the direction of his social
commitment emerges after his arrest in 1930.
Although in 1933 he joined Gakugei Jiyu Domei
[The Free League for Liberal Arts] and denounced the then emerging Japanese fascism, his
philosophical stance in this period was ambiva-
lent. While he clung to rationalism he did furnish
some justification for Japanese expansionism and
aggression in terms of his theory of *Toa Kyodotai*
[East Asian Community/*Gesellschaft*] and *Kosor-
yoki no Ronri* [Principle of the Power of Organiza-
tion], as **Heidegger** has been represented as doing
for the Nazis. This was partly because he was
always under close surveillance and considerable
pressure from the ruling authorities, but also
because he was inclined to believe in and admire
(like Nishida) a specifically Japanese mentality,
epitomized in the Japanese imperial house.

   Ironically, Miki was sent to the Japanese
occupied territories of the Philippines to work
for the army as a correspondent officer in 1942.
Despite his contribution to the war and the life of
the nation, his life in fascist Japan was difficult. He
was again arrested shortly before the war for
allegedly hiding a member of the communist

party. He died in jail just after the end of the war
and the release of left-wing prisoners. Hani Goro,
Japan's most prominent historian and Miki's
comrade, lamented his untimely death as a
'symbolic mistake and the shame of Japan even
after the war ended'.

                                    TOGO TSUKAHARA

Milhaud, Gaston

French. *b:* 1858, Nîmes, France. *d:* 1918, Paris. *Cat:*
Epistemologist; philosopher of science. *Infls:*
Émile Boutroux and Paul Tannery. *Appts:* Taught
in various lycées; Professor of Philosophy, University of Montpellier; 1900, Chair in the History
of Philosophy, University of Paris.

Main publications:

(1893) *Leçons sur les origines de la science grecque*,
   Paris: Alcan.
(1894) *Essai sur les conditions et les limites de la
   certitude logique*, Paris: Baillière.
(1898) *Le Rationnel*, Paris: Alcan.
(1900) *Les Philosophes géomètres de la Grèce*, Paris:
   Alcan.
(1902) *Le Positivisme et le progrès de l'esprit*, Paris:
   Alcan.
(1906) *Études sur la pensée scientifique chez les Grecs
   et chez les Modernes*, Paris: Société Française.
(1911) *Nouvelles études sur l'histoire de la pensée
   scientifique*, Paris: Alcan.

Secondary literature:

Revue d'histoire des sciences 12, 1959 (contains
   bibliography).

Milhaud came to philosophy through the study of
mathematics, and was active particularly in the
areas of the history of philosophy and epistemology, as is shown by his publications. Early in his
career he accepted that the realm of logical
necessity based on the principle of non-contradiction and found in pure mathematics provides
the only area of absolute certainty in knowledge.
Later, he added to this account the view that pure
mathematics is dependent on human thought,
which is spontaneous and creative, and thus
contains an irreducible element of contingency.

   According to Milhaud, the area of pure
mathematics is to be separated from that of the
sciences, as the latter has to have experience as one
of its components. Under the influence of Émile
Boutroux, who maintained that the various
sciences are to a greater or lesser extent not fully
deterministic and that the state of scientific
knowledge is partially dependent on the human

mind, Milhaud argued that science is not a purely empirical enquiry. Instead, although the principles of scientific investigation are suggested by experience, the selection and analysis of data and the construction of scientific theories, whilst having to be in accordance with the requirements of rationality, are primarily due to the spiritual initiative and activity of the human mind. Such features are not determined by either external or internal factors, and the mind transcends experience in its spontaneous creativity in the scientific enterprise. Scientific methodology cannot be applied to every area of human life, but is limited in scope.

The history of scientific theories does not, according to Milhaud, show a smooth transition or continuum: changes in scientific thought are revolutionary, not evolutionary. Milhaud can thus be considered as a precursor to Alexandre **Koyré** and Georges **Canguilhem**.

KATHRYN PLANT

Millas, Jorge

Chilean. *b:* 1917, Santiago, Chile. *d:* 1982. *Cat:* Vitalist. *Educ:* Studied Law at the University of Chile, and Philosophy at the University of Iowa. *Infls:* Bergson, Ortega, Enrique Molina and Clarence Finlayson. *Appts:* Visiting Professor, Columbia University and the University of Puerto Rico; professorial appointments at a variety of universities in Chile.

Main publications:

(1943) *Idea de la individualidad*.
(1970) *Ideas de la filosofía: el conocimiento*, Santiago: Editorial Universitaria.
(1977) *The Intellectual and Moral Challenge of Mass Society*, Normal, Ill.: Applied Literature Press.
(1978) *El rol de la ciencia en el desarrollo*, Santiago: Corporación de Promoción.
(1978) *La violencia y sus máscaras: dos ensayos de filosofía*, Santiago: Ediciones Aconcagua.
(1981) *Idea y defensa de la universidad*, Santiago: Editorial del Pacífico.
(1985) *Escenas inéditas de Alicia en el país de la maravillas*, Santiago: Pehuen.

Secondary literature:

Jaksic, Iván (1989) *Academic Rebels in Chile: The Role of Philosophy in Higher Education and Politics*, Albany, NY: SUNY Press.

Influenced by existentialism and anti-positivism, Millas placed the individual at the centre of his thought. His theory of individualism, which he termed *personalismo* posited that the individual is the core reality whereas all groups of which the individual may form part, such as family, nation and society, are symbolic constructs which deny the range of individual personalities. Consistent with his concern for the individual, the primary topics in Millas's philosophy are spirituality and freedom. He disdained social and political interference in the individual's existence. Millas believed that Latin America was an ideal place from which to make a universal contribution to the philosophy of the individual.

AMY A. OLIVER

Miró Quesada Cantuarias, Francisco

Peruvian. *b:* 1918, Lima. *Cat:* Neorationalist. *Ints:* Epistemology; logic; philosophy of mathematics; phenomenology; philosophy of law; political philosophy. *Educ:* Received doctorates in Mathematics and Philosophy, as well as a Law degree from the Universidad de San Marcos in Lima. *Infls:* Husserl and mathematical logic. *Appts:* Professor of Contemporary Philosophy, Universidad de San Marcos, 1939; subsequently Professor of Philosophy of Mathematics, Universidad de San Marcos; Professor of Political Science, Universidad de San Marcos; Cofounder of the Peruvian Philosophical Society, 1942.

Main publications:

(1941) *Sentido del movimiento fenomenológico*, Lima: Miranda.
(1944) *La filosofía en el Perú actual*, Buenos Aires.
(1945) *El problema de la libertad y la ciencia*, Lima: Miranda.
(1946) *Lógica*, Lima.
(1951) *Ensayos I*, Lima: Santa María.
(1956) *El filósofo europeo visto por el latinoamericano*, Mexico: Instituto Panamericano de Geografía e Historia.
(1956) *Problemas fundamentales de la lógica jurídica*, Lima: Sociedad Peruana de Filosofía.
(1958) *Iniciación lógica*, Lima: Universidad de San Marcos.
(1959) *El hombre sin teoría*, Lima: Universidad de San Marcos.
(1959) *La otra mitad del mundo*, Lima.
(1961) *Las estructuras sociales*, Lima.
(1964) *La ideología de acción popular*, Lima: Santa Rosa.
(1966) *Notas sobre la cultura latinoamericana y su destino*, Lima: Industrialgráfica.
(1969) *Humanismo y revolución*, Lima: Casa de la Cultura del Perú.

(1974) *Despertar y proyecto del filosofar latinoamericano*, Mexico: Fondo de Cultura Económica.

(1975) *La historia de las ideas en América Latina*, Tunja: Universidad Pedagógica y tenológica de Colombia.

(1976) *Las paradojas de la revolución*, Lima: Capacitación ONAMS.

(1976) *Siete temas de linguística teórica y aplicada*, Trujillo: Universidad Nacional de Trujillo.

(1977) *La universidad como generadora de autonomía nacional*, Santo Domingo: Universidad Autónoma de Santo Domingo.

(c. 1978) *Historia, problema y promesa*, Lima: Pontificia Universidad Católica del Perú.

(1978) *Impacto de la metafísica en la ideología latinoamericana*, Mexico: Universidad Autónoma.

(1979) *La filosofía de lo americano*, Mexico: Universidad Autónoma.

(1980) *Lógica I*, Lima: Prado Pastor.

(1981) *Para iniciarse en la filosofía*, Lima: Universidad de Lima.

(1981) *Proyecto y realización del filosofar latinoamericano*, Mexico: Fondo de Cultura Económica.

(1985) *La moral en la política*, Panamá: Instituto Latinoamericano de Estudios Avanzados.

(1986) *Ensayos de filosofía del derecho*, Lima: Universidad de Lima.

Secondary literature:

Gracia, Jorge J. E. (1986) *Latin American Philosophy*, New York: Prometheus, pp. 135–6.

Salazar Larrain, Arturo (1961) *Las estructuras sociales de Francisco Miró Quesada*, Lima: Empresa Gráfica T. Scheuch.

Miró Quesada views the crucial problem of philosophical anthropology not as that of the status of human essence, but rather as an epistemological problem. According to him, this is the problem of formulating an adequate theory of man. He approaches the problem of formulating such a theory by arguing that the traditional epistemological positions involved in dialectical philosophy, historicism, positivism, pragmatism and rationalism have been shown to be inadequate by scientific developments. As an alternative he uses modern logic and recent philosophical methods to describe the structure and dynamics of rational thought.

In political philosophy, Miró Quesada has sought a more rigorous foundation for politics than that provided by such contemporary philosophies as Marxism and Christian socialism. His approach involves the formulation of a character-ization of humanism which is independent of all metaphysical positions.

A. PABLO IANNONE

Misch, Georg

German. *b:* 5 April 1878, Berlin. *d:* 10 June 1965, Göttingen, Germany. *Cat:* Leading exponent of W. Dilthey's philosophy. *Ints:* Philosophy of life; phenomenology. *Educ:* Berlin. *Infls:* Dilthey. *Appts:* Dilthey's assistant, son-in-law and collaborator; Professor of Philosophy, Marburg, and from 1919, Göttingen.

Main publications:

(1930) *Lebensphilosophie und Phenomenologie* [The Philosophy of Life and Phenomenology], Bonn.

(1947) *Die Geschichte der Autobiographie* [The History of Autobiography], Göttingen.

(1947) *Vom Lebens- und Gedankenkreis Wilhelm Diltheys* [Of the Life and Thought of William Dilthey] (incorporating the important article 'Die Idee der Lebensphilosphie und die Theorie der Geistenwissenschaften' [The idea of the philosophy of life and the theory of human studies], 1924), Frankfurt.

(1993) *Der Aufbau der Logic auf dem Boden der Philosophie des Lebens* [The Development of Logic on the Basis of the Philosophy of Life] (edition of a lecture course).

Equally important is Misch's editorship of volumes II, V and VI of the *Collected Works* of W. Dilthey, initiated after his death, and his preliminary report of 117 pages, which introduces vol. V and provided the first indication of Dilthey's philosophy as a whole based on unpublished material or materials scattered in obscure journals and annual society proceedings.

Secondary literature:

Bollnow, O. F. (1982–3) *Der Aufbau der Logik auf dem Boden der Philosophie des Lebens: Die Logik Vorlesungen von Georg Misch*, in *Studien zur Hermenautik*, vol. II, Freiburg and Munich: Surkamp.

In the book on the philosophy of life and phenomenology (1930) Misch systematizes and carries forward **Dilthey**'s philosophy and contrasts it with those of **Husserl** and **Heidegger**. When Misch—as a Jew—had to leave Germany during the Nazi period a potentially fruitful debate between these philosophical positions was aborted. Misch returned to Göttingen after the war and his work on autobiography reflects Dilthey's belief in the value of this genre for the understanding of man and history. His writings and his influence on his students, O. F. **Bollnow** in particular, assured the continued and indeed increasing impact of Dilthey's philosophy.

H. P. RICKMAN

Mises, Richard von

Austrian-American. *b:* 19 April 1883, Lemberg, Germany. *d:* 14 July 1953, Boston, Massachusetts. *Cat:* Positivist; mathematician; aerodynamicist; theoretical physicist; Rilke scholar. *Ints:* Applied mathematics. *Educ:* Vienna Technical University and the Technical University in Brünn. *Infls:* Literary influences: Ernst Mach, J. Venn and Rilke. Personal: Hilda Geiringer and Abraham Wald. *Appts:* 1909–20, Professor of Applied Mathematics, University of Strasbourg, then (1919) at the Technical University in Dresden; 1920–33, Professor of Mathematics and Founder Director, Institute for Applied Mathematics, University of Berlin; 1921, Founder and Editor (until 1933) of the *Zeitschrift für angewandte Mathematik und Mechanik*; 1933–9, Professor of Mathematics and Director, Mathematical Institute, University of Istanbul; 1939–53, Associate Professor, then (1944) Gordon McKay Professor of Aerodynamics and Applied Mathematics, Harvard University.

Main publications:

(1919) 'Fundamentalsätze der Wahrscheinlichkeits-rechnung', *Mathematische Zeitschrift* 4: 1–97.
(1919) 'Grundlagen der Wahrscheinlichkeitsrech-nung', *Mathematische Zeitschrift* 5: 52–100.
(1928) *Wahrscheinlichkeit, Statistik und Wahrheit*, Berlin: Springer (English translation, *Probability, Statistics and Truth*, trans. Neyman, Scholl and Rabinowitsch, New York: MacMillan, 1939).
(1939) *Kleines Lehrbuch des Positivismus*, Berlin: Springer (English translation, *Positivism: A Study in Human Understanding*, trans. Jerry Berstein and Roger G. Newton, Cambridge: Mass.: Harvard University Press, 1951).
(1964) *Selected Papers of Richard von Mises*, 2 vols, Providence, RI: American Mathematical Society vol. 1, *Geometry, Mechanics, Analysis*, vol. 2, *Probability and Statistics; General*.

Secondary literature:

Cramér, Harald (1953) 'Richard von Mises' work in probability and statistics', *Annals of Mathematical Statistics* 24: 657–62.
Popper, Karl R. (1982) *Unended Quest: An Intellectual Autobiography*, third, revised edition, London: Fontana, pp. 84ff.

Wald, Abraham (1955) *Selected Papers in Statistics and Probability*, New York: McGraw-Hill, pp. 25–45.

Von Mises is best known for his contributions to applied mathematics, a field that he made famous and which he took to include mechanics, practical analysis, probability and statistics, and some aspects of geometry and philosophy of science. A pioneer in aerodynamics, he made fundamental advances in boundary-layer-flow theory and air-foil design. A member of the Vienna Circle, he developed his own form of 'scientific' philosophy, a conception of science in the general sense of the German *Wissenschaft* which he followed up through the various domains of thought and life in *Positivism* (1939). He was also a recognized authority on Rilke, in whose esoteric poems he found confirmation of his belief that in areas of life not yet explored by science poetry expresses the experiences of the mind.

Von Mises's principal work in mathematics concerned probability and statistics. His long-term aims were to lay the foundations of a science of probability and to develop a unified theory of probability and statistics. In *Probability* (1928) he sought a frequency theory of probability which would be as empirical as theoretical physics. He attempted to meet the objections that probability was inexact and that frequency cannot be identified with probability through the ideal concept of a 'collective' which could facilitate operations with the mathematical calculus of probabilities and fulfil the requirement of 'randomness'. In later writings he continued to restate and extend these ideas. Von Mises's contributions to applied mathematics exerted a profound, global influence. Abraham Wald and Karl **Popper** were particularly prominent in the subsequent development of his ideas.

Sources: Passmore 1957; EF.

STEPHEN MOLLER

Mitchell, Basil George

British. *b:* 9 April 1917, Bath, Somerset. *Cat:* Philosopher of religion; ethicist. *Ints:* Ethics. *Educ:* Queen's College, Oxford. *Infls:* Austin Farrer and H. H. Price. *Appts:* Naval service, 1940–6; Lecturer, Christ Church, Oxford, 1946–7; Fellow and Tutor in Philosophy, Keble College, 1947–67; Nolloth Professor of the Philosophy of the Christian Religion, and Fellow of Oriel College, 1968–84; FBA, 1983.

Main publications:

(1957) (ed.) *Faith and Logic*, London: Allen & Unwin.

(1967) *Law, Morality and Religion in a Secular Society*, London: Oxford University Press.

(1973) *The Justification of Religious Belief*, London: Macmillan.

(1980) *Morality: Religious and Secular*, London: Oxford University Press (Gifford Lectures).

(1990) *How to Play Theological Ping-Pong*, London: Hodder & Stoughton.

(1993) 'War and friendship', in Kelly James Clark (ed.), *Philosophers Who Believe*, Downer's Grove, IL: Inter Varsity Press, pp. 23–44 (autobiographical).

(1995) *Faith and Criticism*, London: Oxford University Press.

Secondary literature:

Abraham, W. J. and Holtzer, S. W. (1987) *The Rationality of Religious Belief: Essays in Honour of Basil Mitchell*, Oxford: Clarendon Press.

Ferré, F. (1962) *Language, Logic and God*, London: Eyre & Spottiswoode.

In the heyday of linguistic analysis Mitchell stoutly maintained both that such analysis was not necessarily inimical to Christian faith, and that the adumbration of worldviews was 'no part of the philosopher's business'. He participated in the 'Theology and Falsification' debate of the 1950s, granting **Flew**'s claim that the problem of evil presented real difficulties to believers, but arguing that their faith will not allow them to regard theological assertions as only 'provisional hypotheses to be discarded if experience tells against them'. In *Faith and Logic* (1957) he argued that while belief in God's grace cannot be established by empirical evidence, it has empirical application. In *The Justification of Religious Belief* (1973) his case was that since we cannot strictly know whether or not there is a God, Christian theism, *qua* worldview, must be judged according to its ability to make sense of all the available evidence. The weight Mitchell places upon personal judgement in his cumulative theistic argument has caused concern to some whose arguments have, in turn, been found to be less than compelling.

In *Law, Morality and Religion* (1967), Mitchell shows how disagreements on moral issues derive from more or less fundamentally different understandings of morality as such—not least when those disagreeing are recognizable liberals. His Gifford Lectures (1980) comprise a critique of scientific, romantic and liberal humanism, to-gether with a denial of the view that the traditional Western intuitions of conscience can be defended by entirely secular arguments, and without reference to Christian views of the human being's nature and needs.

A professional philosopher who is a Christian (as distinct from one who propounds a 'Christian philosophy'), Mitchell's patient and discerning quest of reasonableness in religion and morality has earned him the respect of a wide circle of students, colleagues and readers.

Sources: WW; Sell; personal acquaintance.

ALAN SELL

Molina Garmendia, Enrique

Chilean. *b:* 4 August 1871, La Serena, Chile. *d:* 1964. *Cat:* Social philosopher. *Educ:* Educated in Chile at the Instituto Pedagógico. *Appts:* Minister of Education; Founder, Universidad de Concepción; Editor of *Atenea*.

Main publications:

(1907) *La ciencia y el tradicionalismo*.

(1914) *Filosofía americana ensayos*.

(1925) *Por los valores espirituales*.

(1925) *Dos filósofos contemporáneos: Guyau y Bergson*; second edition, Santiago: Nascimento, 1948.

(1936) *La herencia moral de la filosofía griega*.

(1944) *Nietzsche, dionisiaco y asceta: Su vida, su ideario*.

(1947) *De lo espiritual en la vida humana*, second edition, Santiago: Nascimento.

(1951) *La filosofía en Chile en la primera mitad del siglo XX: notas y recuerdos*; second edition, Santiago: Nascimento, 1953.

(1952) *Desarrollo de Chile en la primera mitad del siglo XX*, 2 vols, Santiago: Universidad de Chile.

(1984) *Obra completa*.

Secondary literature:

Escobar, Roberto (1976) *La filosofía en Chile*, Santiago: Editorial Universal.

Jaksic, Iván (1989) *Academic Rebels in Chile: The Role of Philosophy in Higher Education and Politics*, Albany, NY: SUNY Press.

Lipp, Solomon (1975) *Three Chilean Thinkers*, Waterloo: Wilfrid Laurier Press.

Although he ostensibly freed himself from the influence of positivism, which had been dominant in Chilean philosophy, Molina was slow to shed the last vestiges of determinism and was critical of **Bergson** until as late as 1925. Gradually he shifted to an anti-positivist stance later in life and concerned himself with issues of moral responsibility and spiritual life. Molina is often considered one of the 'founders' of Latin American philosophy. He was deeply interested in education. He edited the journal *Atenea* until 1957.

AMY A. OLIVER

Mondolfo, Rodolpho

Italian. *b:* 1877, Senigallia. *d:* 1976, Buenos Aires. *Cat:* Historian of philosophy. *Ints:* Ancient Greek thought; modern European philosophy; Marxism. *Educ:* University of Florence. *Infls:* Zeller. *Appts:* Professor of the History of Philosophy, Turin (1910–14) and Bologna (1914–38); emigrated to Argentina, 1938; Professor at Córdoba and Tucumán; received many academic honours.

Main publications:

The following is a brief selection only. Mondolfo was a prolific writer, and many of his works appear in both Italian and Spanish versions. Almost invariably, whichever is the later version is extensively revised.

(1902) *Un psicologo associazionista: E. B. de Condillac.*

(1903–4) *Saggi per la storia della morale utilitaria*, 2 vols.

(1928) *Il pensiero antico. Storia della filosofia greco-romana*; eighth edition, in Spanish, 2 vols, Buenos Aires: Losada, 1980.

(1934) *L'infinito nel pensiero dei greci.*

(1944) *Rousseau y la conciencia moderna.*

(1947) *Tres filosofos del Renacimiento* (Bruno, Galileo, Campanella), Buenos Aires: Losada.

(1949) *Problemas y métodos de investigación en la historia de la filosofia*; second edition, Buenos Aires: EUDEBA, 1960.

(1955) *La comprension del sujeto humano en la cultura antigua*; second edition, Buenos Aires: Editorial universitaria, 1979.

(1960) *Marx y marxismo*, Mexico: Fondo de Cultura Economica.

(1962) *Da Ardigo a Gramsci*, Milan: Nuova Accademia.

(1977) *El humanismo de Marx*, second (augmented) edition, Mexico: Fondo de Cultura Economica.

Secondary literature:

Mondolfo has been the subject of several Festschrift volumes, notably:

Jaeger, W. (ed.) (1962) *Estudios de historia de filosofia (Homenaje a Rodolfo Mondolfo)*, Tucumán: Universidad Nacional de Tucumán.

One of the most revered of historians of philosophy in Italy and Latin America, Mondolfo maintained a prolific output during most of his long life. Three areas of thought occupied most of his work: the philosophy of ancient Greece; European thought from Hobbes to Condillac; and Marxism. Of these, his work on the first is generally held to be of the greatest importance. A principal aim of his studies of ancient philosophy is to combat the view that the Greeks conceived the universe as static and finite, and so he sought to emphasize notions of dynamism, infinity and subjectivity in the ideas of the thinkers concerned. In his works on Marxism, there is a complementary stress on the dynamic, non-determinist elements he finds in this philosophy.

A number of general convictions underlie Mondolfo's work. First, no philosophy, whatever its pretensions to the contrary, is independent of its milieu and every system is composed of beliefs which are *sub specie temporis*. Second, there is always and inevitably a subjective element in the writing of the history of philosophy, since the individual historian must attempt to relive the philosophical experience of the past. Third and importantly, Mondolfo does not accept that these two convictions entail any form of self-refuting subjectivism. There is, he argues, an element of progress in the history of philosophy, a gradual refining and clarification of the problems concerned. This he equates with what he calls 'a progressive deepening of philosophical consciousness' (*una profundización progressiva de la conciencia filosófica*; 1960 second edition, p. 31).

ROBERT WILKINSON

Monod, Jacques

French. *b:* 1910, Paris. *d:* 1976, Paris. *Cat:* Scientist; philosopher of science. *Educ:* Faculté des Sciences, Paris. *Appts:* 1954–9, Director of the Department of Cellular Biochemistry, Pasteur Institute; 1959, Professor, Faculté des Sciences; 1965, together with François Jacob and André Lwoff, awarded the Nobel Prize for Medicine.

Main publications:

(1970) *Le Hasard et la nécessité*, Paris: Éditions du Seuil (English translation, *Chance and Necessity*, London: Collins, 1972).

Secondary literature:

Azzolini, V. (1980) *Risposta a Monod: Casa e Necessità*, Turin: MEB.

According to Monod living beings have three essential characteristics: teleonomy, or being endowed with a purpose; autonomous morphogenesis, or having a structure with autonomous determinism; and invariant reproduction, or the capacity to generate beings of the same structure as themselves. There appears to be a contradiction between the third of these characteristics and Darwinian evolution, which Monod reconciles by the now commonplace solution of mutation. This happens, according to Monod, partly by chance and partly by necessity. Each of the various events which cause the mutation of a species is a link in a deterministic chain, but the coming together of the events happens purely by chance.

The last chapter of Monod's work is philosophically the most interesting. He compares biological to cultural evolution, or the 'evolution of ideas'. Ideas have never been selected because of their truth, but before the advent of modern Western science they were selected on the basis of two principles: their 'performance' and their 'spreading' value. The former is measured by such factors as the greater social cohesiveness and self-confidence which the adoption of an idea gives to a group, and the latter according to its effectiveness in explaining the place of human beings within the universe.

With the adoption of the framework within which modern Western science could operate with such spectacular success, the condition of explanation gave way to that of performance. The 'old covenant', or the various explanations of humanity's necessary place within the scheme of things, has been irretrievably broken, and modern humanity will be left in a state of anxiety and distress until a 'new covenant' can be found. Monod's suggestion of a way forward is based on the solution of the seeming paradox between the objective and value-free nature of knowledge assumed by Western science and the allegedly separate domain of the theory of values. The requirement that objectivity is a necessary and primary feature of knowledge does not come from within knowledge, but is an ethical choice. Similarly, knowledge can be chosen as the supreme value, and we can become the creators and the citizens of our own 'new world'.

KATHRYN PLANT

Montague, Richard Merett

American. **b:** 20 September 1930, Stockton, California. **d:** 7 March 1971, Los Angeles. **Cat:** Logician; philosopher of language. **Ints:** Mathematical logic; the semiotics of natural languages.

Educ: University of California, Berkeley. **Infls:** Carnap, Tarski, Frege, Gödel and A. N. Prior. **Appts:** 1955–71, Professor of Mathematical Logic, University of California, Los Angeles.

Main publications:

(1968) 'Pragmatics', in *Contemporary Philosophy: A Survey. 1: Logic and Foundations of Mathematics*, ed. R. Klibansky, Florence: La Nuova Italia Editrice.

(1969) 'On the nature of certain philosophical entities', *The Monist* 53, 2: 159-94.

(1970) 'English as a formal language', in *Linguaggi nella Società e nella Tecnica*, ed. B. Sentini *et al.*, Milan: Comunità.

(1970) 'Pragmatics and intensional logic', *Synthèse* 22: 68–94.

(1970) 'Universal grammar', *Theoria* 36: 373–98.

(1974) *Formal Philosophy: Selected Papers of Richard Montague*, ed. R. H. Thomason, New Have: Yale University Press.

Secondary literature:

Cresswell, M. J. (1973) *Logic and Languages*, London: Methuen.

Partee, Barbara Hall (1975) 'Montague grammar and transformational grammar', *Linguistic Inquiry* 6: 203–300.

Montague was a mathematical logician who became fascinated with the idea that the various 'methods' developed in mathematical logic might be successfully applied to the analysis of natural language. Convinced that there is 'no important theoretical difference between natural languages and the artificial languages of logicians', he sought 'to comprehend the syntax and semantics of both kinds of languages within a single natural and mathematically precise theory' (1974, p. 222). In pursuing this project Montague followed Carnap and Tarski by taking the definition of 'truth in a model' as the fundamental semantic redicate of the sentences of the languages he described. He recognized, however, that an outstanding difficulty was how to account for the 'indexicals' of natural languages (those expressions whose reference or denotation is determined by the context of utterance of the expressions) in an exact 'model-theory'.

Montague first dealt explicitly with this and other issues closely connected to natural languages in 'Pragmatics' (1968). He outlined a theory of pragmatic languages in terms of both extensions (associated with all expressions) relative to an 'index' (context, possible world, etc.) and intensions reinterpreted as functions connecting with each expression and index the extension that the expression has with respect to that index. He also anticipated some applications of this theory.

In 'Universal grammar' (1970), Montague devised a general theory of language (his celebrated 'Montague grammar') which presented both syntax and semantics in an algebraic form. He also introduced a formal theory of translation, maintaining that the interpretation of a sentence or a language may be induced through a translation of that sentence or that language into an already interpreted language. Finally, he presented both intensional logic and a description of English in terms of his universal or Montague grammar, suggesting that the sentences of English can be translated into intensional logic according to their syntactical structure. Montague's seminal contributions were curtailed by his untimely death (by murder) in 1971. His influence on the study of language has been immense. One important expansion of his ideas may be found in *Partee* 1975.

Sources: Passmore 1985; Bullock & Woodings.

STEPHEN MOLLER

Montague, William Pepperell

American. *b:* 24 November 1874, Chelsea, Massachusetts. *d:* 1 August 1953. *Cat:* Realist; animistic materialist. *Ints:* Epistemology; nature of consciousness. *Educ:* Harvard University. *Infls:* William James and Plato. *Appts:* Professor and Johnsonian Professor of Philosophy, University of Columbia; Carnegie Professor in International Relations to Japan, Czechoslovakia and Italy.

Main publications:

(1912) (with E. B. Holt *et al.*) *The New Realism*, New York (s.n.).

(1925) *The Ways of Knowing or the Methods of Philosophy*, London: George Allen & Unwin.

(1930) *Belief Unbound, A Promethean Religion for the Modern World*, New Haven: Yale University Press.

(1930) (with George P. Adams) *Contemporary American Philosophy* 2 vols, London: Allen & Unwin.

(1940) *The Way of Things—a Philosophy of Knowledge, Nature and Value*, New York: Prentice-Hall.

(1950) *Great Visions of Philosophy, Varieties of Speculative Thought in the West from the Greeks to Bergson*, La Salle, Ill: Open Court.

Secondary literature:
Parkhurst, Helen Huss (1954) 'The philosophic creed of William Pepperell Montague', *Journal of Philosophy* 52: 593–637.

Montague was one of the six members of the US New Realist movement in the early part of this century (the others were E. B. **Holt**, W. T. **Marvin**, R. B. **Perry**, W. B. Pitkin and E. G. Spaulding). According to the New Realists the world of objects is real and independent of our sense experience of them (see entry on Marvin).

Apart from epistemology, Montague was interested in the nature of mind and its relation to the body. According to him the soul, possessing all the attributes of mind, is a kind of energy which, though private and observable only as internal sensation, is none the less causally effective on the visible cerebral matrix.

Sources: WWW(Am).

INDIRA MAHALINGAM CARR

Moore, G(eorge) E(dward)

British. *b:* 1873, London. *d:* 1958, Cambridge, England. *Cat:* Analytic philosopher. *Ints:* Epistemology; moral philosophy. *Educ:* University of Cambridge University, 1892–6. *Infls:* J. M. E. McTaggart and Bertrand Russell. *Appts:* Lecturer in Philosophy at University of Cambridge, 1911–25, Professor of Mental Philosophy and Logic, 1925–39, University of Cambridge; Editor of *Mind*, 1921–47; Fellow of the British Academy, 1918; Order of Merit, 1951.

Main publications:

(1903) *Principia Ethica*, Cambridge: Cambridge University Press.

(1912) *Ethics*, London: Williams & Norgate.

(1922) *Philosophical Studies*, London: Routledge & Kegan Paul.

(1953) *Some Main Problems of Philosophy*, London: George Allen & Unwin.

(1959) *Philosophical Papers*, London: George Allen & Unwin.

(1962) *Commonplace Book, 1919–1953*, London: George Allen & Unwin.

(1986) *G. E. Moore: The Early Essays*, Philadelphia: Temple University Press.

(1991) *The Elements of Ethics*, Philadelphia: Temple University Press.

Secondary literature:
Ambrose, Alice and Lazerowitz, Morris (eds) (1970) *G. E. Moore: Essays in Retrospect*, London: George Allen & Unwin.

Klemke, E. D. (ed.) (1969) *Studies in the Philosophy of G. E. Moore*, Chicago: Quadrangle Books.

Schilpp, P. A. (ed.) (1968) *The Philosophy of G. E. Moore*, third edition, Open Court: La Salle.

When Moore was a student the idealism of such philosophers as **Bradley** and **Bosanquet** was dominant in British philosophy. It is no surprise, then, that Moore's earliest published work shows considerable sympathy with this movement. However, his famous 1903 paper 'The refutation of idealism' (*Mind* 12, 1903) marked a break with it, and his work over the next few years, along with that of Bertrand **Russell**, was a sustained criticism of the idealist movement. This work is often thought to put Moore squarely in the empiricist camp, and much of it is certainly an attempt to clarify an empiricist epistemology. However, the limits of this empiricism are clearly visible in his ethical work, where he held that goodness was a non-natural, irreducible property, the object of direct, non-sensory knowledge.

Much of Moore's later work was concerned with the scepticism that characterized the empiricist movement from Hume to Russell. In opposition to this, he defended the view that most of the things that we think we know we really do know. This gave rise to the popular image of Moore as the philosopher of plain common sense.

There is, however, little to sustain that image in Moore's first published book, *Principia Ethica* (1903). It defended a consequentialist theory of ethics, holding that the fundamental concept of ethics is the good, and that right actions are those which maximize the good. A popular version of such a theory is the utilitarianism of Mill and Bentham, the doctrine that marries consequentialism with hedonism, and holds that the right action is always that which maximizes happiness. Moore, however, ferociously rejected the hedonism that he found in utilitarianism and held instead that goodness is to be found in a number of different things, but preeminently in the experience of personal affection and the contemplation of beauty. (This aspect of his philosophy strongly influenced the Bloomsbury Group, of which he was a member.) He held that it is impossible to give any *argument* as to what are the ultimate goods; it is self-evident, and we know *directly*, without argument, what they are. What actions will maximize the good could not be directly known, however; this is a matter of calculation, and so Moore rejected the type of intuitionism which held that we could directly know, without argument or calculation, what are the right acts or the correct moral rules.

That 'the fundamental principles of Ethics must be self-evident' (1903, p. 143) Moore thought followed from a more basic claim: the fundamental principles of ethics cannot be inferred from any further principles; they are true, but there is no *reason why* they are true. This view was part of what was to become the most influential aspect of *Principia Ethica*: its attack on naturalism in ethics. Moore was never completely clear just what he had in mind by talking of naturalism, and he gave a number of different explanations. But we may say that it was, in a general way, any attempt to reduce evaluative notions to non-evaluative ones. The attempt to do so Moore baptized 'the Naturalistic Fallacy', and it seemed to Moore, and to many others, that it followed from his diagnosis that ethical propositions could not be inferred in any way from non-ethical ones. A concern with this issue dominated moral philosophy in the English-speaking world for more than half a century following the publication of Moore's book. Many thought that Moore's argument had captured the essential autonomy of ethics. Others, however, thought that it rendered ethics a suspect endeavour, since it seemed to put it largely beyond the pale of rational argument.

Moore's subsequent writing on ethics had nothing like the influence of *Principia Ethica*. His *Ethics* (1912) was a minute statement of utilitarianism, and an equally minute examination of some objections to it. It defends a consequentialist position, though mainly by asserting that it is self-evidently correct, a type of argument that has had little force against generations of philosophers who thought that it is self-evidently incorrect.

Once he had broken with the idealist tradition, Moore's dominating concern was to understand the nature of sense data and their relation to the material world. Outside of ethics, it is his work in this general area that was most influential. He began this in a series of lectures given in 1910–11 (*Some Main Problems of Philosophy*, 1953), and his very last works still show a concern with the problem. Roughly speaking, sense data might be thought to be identical with material objects, which would yield a theory of perception often known as direct realism; or they might be thought to be separate, mental entities which represented material objects (the representative theory of perception); or it might be that there are no material objects independent of our sense data, and that to know a proposition about a material object is merely to know that if certain conditions were satisfied then certain sense data would be experienced (phenomenalism). Moore analysed these types of theory, over and over again, in enormous detail in such articles as 'A defence of common sense' (1925; reprinted in *Philosophical Papers*, 1959) and 'Proof of an external world' (1939; reprinted in *Philosophical Papers*).

These papers, like nearly all of Moore's work, are characterized by an obsessive concern simply to be clear about just what philosophers have *meant* when they have made such typically philosophical claims as that we can never really know anything about the external world, or that time or space is unreal. The painstaking analysis in such papers gave rise to the popular view that analysis was an end in itself for Moore, but this was not so. He saw it merely as the necessary groundwork for arriving at the truth.

Moore did not arrive speedily at many philosophical truths: about the relation of sense data to external objects, for instance, he did not form a view until 1953 and even then he did no more than reject direct realism. On the question of whether we could have knowledge of the external world, however, Moore formed an opinion very early. In his 1905–6 lecture 'The nature and reality of objects of perception' (*Philosophical Studies*, 1922), Moore submitted to inordinately detailed examination the meaning of the question whether we can have any knowledge of the external world. In *Some Main Problems of Philosophy* (1953) he began to work towards an answer, one which, in one way or another, he held to for the rest of his life: surely, the claim that I know some things about the external world is more certain than any argument that might be given to show it wrong. His position found its most famous exposition on the occasion when, in a British Academy lecture ('Proof of an external world', published in *Proceedings of the British Academy* 25), he claimed to disprove the proposition that we cannot know the existence of external objects by pointing out to the audience his two hands. This typified what came to be thought of as the characteristic Moorean 'appeal to common sense'.

There has been much debate as to what force—if any—this argumentative strategy had. To some, it has seemed that Moore was doing no more than merely denying what philosophers have given *arguments* for. Others have thought that he was trying to show that such philosophical claims violated the rules of ordinary language. It is fair to say that Moore himself was never clear in his own mind just what was the force of his arguments.

Whatever their precise force, however, they had enormous influence, transforming the face of epistemology.

Moore was not a great prose stylist, once guilelessly writing an 82-word sentence in which 46 of the words are 'so' or 'and'. His writing, however, always aspired to, and usually achieved, a remarkable simplicity and clarity.

Sources: Passmore 1957; Flew; *The Times*, 25 Oct 1958, p. 10.

ANTHONY ELLIS

Morgan, Conwyn Lloyd

British. **b:** 6 February 1852, London. **d:** 6 March 1936, Hastings. **Cat:** Evolutionary philosopher and scientist. **Ints:** Nature, life and mind; scientific method. **Educ:** The School of Mines and Royal College of Science, London. **Infls:** Personal influences: T. H. Huxley and Samuel Alexander. Literary influences include Charles Darwin and Spinoza. **Appts:** 1884–1919, Professor of Geology and Zoology and (from 1910) of Psychology and Ethics at University College, Bristol; 1887–1910, Principal, then (1909) First Vice Chancellor of University of Bristol; 1889, FRS.

Main publications:

(1894) *An Introduction to Comparative Psychology*, London: Walter Scott,
(1906) *The Interpretation of Nature*, New York: Putnam's.
(1910) *Psychology for Teachers*, London: Edward Arnold.
(1912) *Instinct and Experience*, London: Methuen.
(1923) *Emergent Evolution*, London: Henry Holt.
(1926) *Life, Mind, and Spirit*, London: Henry Holt.
(1929) *Mind at the Crossways*, London: Williams & Norgate.

Secondary literature:

MacDougall, William (1929) *Modern Materialism and Emergent Evolution*, London: Macmillan.
MacKinnon, Flora, I. (1924) 'The meaning of "emergent" in Lloyd Morgan's *Emergent Evolution*, *Mind 33*: 311–5.

Morgan was a pioneer in the scientific study of comparative psychology. His researches had a Darwinian background. He held that evolution is a continuous and hierarchical, though not a 'finalistic' or 'vitalistic' process.

In his Gifford Lectures, given after his retirement in 1919 and subsequently published *Emergent Evolution* (1923) and *Life, Mind, and Spririt* (1926), he sought to elaborate the philosophical concept of 'emergence' and to lay the foundations for a scientific method capable of dealing with those higher and more complex forms of behaviour, as in the personality, whose essence had been deliberately left out of natural science in the seventeenth century. Thus his realist and purportedly 'descriptive' metaphysics, which repudiated the old mechanistic naturalism, was intended both to be in harmony with the findings of science and to lead us beyond them.

Morgan used the term 'emergent' to show that the higher orders of being are not mere 'resultants' of the lower and antecedent, and are not contained in them as an effect in its efficient cause. He argued that life has emerged from matter, and mind from life; and each of these distinct but continuous levels is not simply a modification of the lower and preceding, but something genuinely and qualitatively new, which defies interpretation in terms of the lower level from which it has developed, and therefore demands explanation according to its own principles. Finally, he maintained that God, as spirit, is the creative agency which manifests itself in the whole process of evolution. Morgan's evolutionary philosophy enjoyed a certain vogue in the twenties and thirties, and influenced A. N. **Whitehead**.

Sources: WW; Reese; Edwards; Macquarrie.

STEPHEN MOLLER

Morin, Edgar

French. **b:** 1921. **Cat:** Neo-Marxist; social philosopher. **Infls:** André Malraux and French communists of his own and the previous generation. **Appts:** Joined the Parti Communiste Français in the spring of 1942 when working for the French Resistance; expelled in 1950 after he failed to renew his membership; later his interests changed to popular culture and mass communication; various research posts in the social sciences; editor-in-chief of a Paris newspaper in the 1960s.

Main publications:

(1951) *L'Homme et la mort dans l'histoire*, Paris: Correa; revised edition, *L'Homme et la mort*, Paris: Éditions du Seuil, 1970.
(1959) *Autocritique*, Paris: Juillard.
(1969) *Introduction à une politique de l'homme*, Paris: Éditions du Seuil.
(1969) *La Rumeur d'Orléans*, Paris: Éditions du Seuil (English translation, *Rumour in Orleans*, London: Anthony Blond, 1971).
(1975) *L'Esprit du temps: Essai sur la culture de masse*, Paris: Grasset.

Secondary literature:

Caute, D. (1964) *Communism and the French Intellectuals*, London: Deutsch.

Morin joined the PCF during the same period as many other French intellectuals, partly because he thought that communism was the best vehicle for the fight against fascism and colonialism. He advocated the use of violence in the overthrow of both ideologies, and saw comradeship and political action as two of the primary virtues of the communist cause.

He acknowledged the influence of André **Malraux**, who in his opinion had fused the romantic with the realist and rationalist aspects of the communist movement, and regarded the sufferings of the Russian people at Stalingrad as a concrete symbol of the romantic element of communism.

Even after his expulsion from the PCF Morin still identified the communist cause too closely with events in the USSR under the Stalinist regime, and saw the USA, with its policies of economic and cultural colonialism, as the main antagonist of communism and the international solidarity of the proletariat. When, under Kruschev, evidence of the Stalinist atrocities became common knowledge in the West, Morin's position changed to one of believing that true communism had a progressive and self-correcting nature.

Morin was against the attempt, backed by Stalin's cultural commissar Zhdanov, to impose socialist realism on revolutionary art and literature outside the USSR. He thought that French political and cultural conditions were not suited to the constraints of realist orthodoxy, but instead could incorporate the more flexible and adventurous approach of anti-realist Marxist aesthetics.

Morin's autobiography *Autocritique* (1959) is a useful source for his own thought and the position of other French communist intellectuals from the 1940s onwards.

Morin's later interest in mass culture included a critique of contemporary sociological methodology. He regarded the abstractions of statistics and social models as being of secondary importance, and the concrete event or crisis as the primary object of study. The historical dimension of any crisis, and its capacity to change society, should not be ignored.

KATHRYN PLANT

Moritz, Manfred Süskind

Swedish. **b:** 4 June 1909, Berlin. **d:** 5 December

1990, Lund. *Cat:* Analytical moral philosopher; philosopher of law; historian of philosophy. *Ints:* Kant; philosophical logic. *Educ:* Dr. Phil., University of Berlin, 1933; Fil. Dr., University of Lund, 1951. *Infls:* Hägerström. *Appts:* 1959–73, Professor of Practical Philosophy, Lund; 1973, Jur. Dr *honoris causa*, Lund.

Main publications:

(1951) *Studien zum Pflichtbegriff in Kants kritischer Ethik*, Lund: Gleerup.

(1960) *Kants Einteilung der Imperative*, Lund: Library of Theoria.

(1960) *Über Hohfelds System der juridischen Grundbegriffe*, Lund: Library of Theoria.

(1964) 'Über die Kritik am Naturrecht', *Danish Yearbook of Philosophy*.

(1966) *Inledning i värdeteori. Värdesatsteori och värdeontologi* (Introduction to Value Theory. Theory of Value-sentences and Ontology of Value), Lund: Studentlitteratur.

(1966) 'Pflicht und Moralität. Eine Antinomie in Kants Ethik', *Kant-Studien*.

(1968) 'On second order norms: An interpretation of "ought implies can" and "is commanded implies is permitted"', *Ratio*.

(1969) 'Über konditionale imperative', *Liber Amicorum in Honour of Alf Ross*, Copenhagen: Juristforbundets Forlag.

Secondary literature:

(1969) *Logik, rätt och moral. Filosofiska studier tilläguade Manfred Moritz* [Logic, Law and Morals. Philosophical Studies Dedicated to Manfred Moritz], Lund: Student Litteratur (with a bibliography).

(1992) *Theoria*, p. 1–2 (obituary).

The *Studien* (1951) analyse several fundamental ideas of Kant's ethics, for example the doctrine of autonomy and *Achtung vor dem Gesetz* (reverence for the law), and *der Äquivalenzsatz der Verpflichtung*, a thesis which is implicit in Kant according to Moritz. His analysis of Kant breaks new ground in respect of method and, together, the works of 1951 to 1960 form the most important contribution to the study of Kant's moral philosophy in Sweden after **Hägerström**'s monumental *Kants Ethik* (1902).

Moritz insists that logical relations exist only between sentences having a truth value, and he shares Hägerström's view that ethical sentences are neither true nor false. This leads him to reject the usual interpretation of deontic logic and of the traditional concept of juridicial inferences. Many (not all) theorems of deontic logic are to be

interpreted as normative principles (second-order norms); there is a similar approach in Moritz's discussion of the principle 'ought implies can', and in his analysis of free will. In the essay of 1964, a short but illuminating paper, Moritz makes a very important distinction between two often confused senses of 'natural law'.

THORILD DAHLQUIST

Morris, Charles William

American. *b:* 23 May 1901, Denver, Colorado. *d:* 15 January 1979, Gainsville, Florida. *Cat:* Philosopher of language; empiricist; semiotician. *Ints:* Education; social psychology. *Educ:* University of Wisconsin at Madison, Northwestern University and University of Chicago. *Infls:* Personal influences include G. H. Mead and Carnap; literary influences include Peirce, Russell, Ogden and Richards, Cassirer and Bloomfield. *Appts:* 1925–30, Instructor in Philosophy, Rice University, Houston; 1931–58, Associate Professor, Lecturer then Research Professor, University of Chicago; 1958–79, Research Professor in Philosophy (until 1971), then Professor Emeritus, University of Florida.

Main publications:

(1932) *Six Theories of Mind*.

(1937) *Logical Positivism, Pragmatism, and Scientific Empiricism*, Paris: Herman et Cie.

(1938) *Foundations of the Theory of Signs* (being the *International Encyclopedia of Unified Science*, vol. 1, no. 2), Chicago: Chicago University Press.

(1939) 'Esthetics and the theory of signs', *Journal of Unified Science (Erkenntnis)* 8: 131–50.

(1943) *Paths of Life: Preface to a World Religion*, New York: Harper & Brothers.

(1946) *Signs, Language and Behavior*, New York: Prentice-Hall.

(1948) *The Open Self*, New York: Prentice Hall.

(1956) *Varieties of Human Value*, Chicago: Chicago University Press.

(1962) 'On the history of the International Encyclopedia of Unified Science', in *Logic and Language, Studies Dedicated to Rudolf Carnap*, Dordrecht: D. Reidel.

(1963) *Signification and Significance*, Cambridge, Mass.: MIT Press.

(1966) *Festival* (poems), New York: Braziller.

(1970) *The Pragmatic Movement in American Philosophy*, New York: George Braziller.

(1971) *Writings on the General Theory of Signs*, The Hague: Mouton.

(1972) (ed. with A. B. Russell and C. A. Scott) *Libraries in Secondary Schools*, London: School Library Association.

Secondary literature:
Black, Max (1947) 'The limitations of a behaviouristic semiotic', *Philosophical Review* 56: 258–72.
Eschbach, Achim (ed.) (1981) *Zeichen über Zeichen über Zeichen*, Tübingen: Gunter Narr Verlag.

A man of wide interests and sympathies, and of enormous industry, Charles Morris is known first and foremost as a semiotician (to use the term which he himself coined). Semiotic was to be the scientific study of sign- behaviour and signs of all types: 'whether in animals or men, whether normal or pathological, whether linguistic or nonlinguistic, whether personal or social'. The interdisciplinary nature of the subject he both stressed and lauded.

Semiotic was famously divided by Morris into the three main branches of syntactics, semantics and pragmatics, where syntactics is the study of the relations of signs to one another, semantics the study of the relations of signs to their significata, and pragmatics the study of the relations of signs to their users and uses. In this respect, though in few others, Morris's terminology has been widely adopted.

Following his teacher **Mead** (whose writings he helped to edit), Morris adopted a (social) behaviourist orientation, while maintaining that semiotic was in principle detachable from this orientation. He belonged to the American pragmatist tradition but had made a tour of European centres of philosophy in the early 1930s; he has been aptly described as a liaison officer between pragmatism and logical positivism. Along with **Carnap** (whose appointment to Chicago he secured) he served as subeditor of the *Encyclopedia of Unified Science*, of which Neurath was editor-in-chief.

Morris's interests encompassed education, Zen Buddhism and W. H. Sheldon's studies of human types. In education, *knowledge* of sign phenomena helped to immunize against exploitation and manipulation by signs.
Sources: Thomas Sebeok (1986) *Encyclopaedic Dictionary of Semiotic*, Amsterdam: Mouton de Gruyter; Turner; obituary, Charles Hartshorne, *Semiotica* 28: 193–4.

CLIVE BORST

Mosca, Gaetano
Italian. *b:* 1 April 1858, Palermo, Sicily. *d:* 8 November 1941, Rome. *Cat:* Political philosopher. *Appts:* Taught law at Turin, from 1896, then taught the history of politics and institutions at University of Rome, from 1924.

Main publications:
(1884) *Sulla teorica dei governi e sul governo parlementare.*
(1887) *Le costituzioni moderne.*
(1896) *Elementi di scienza politica*, fifth edition, Bari: Laterza, 1952.
(1902–3) *Il principio aristocratico ed il democractico nel passato e nell'avvenire.*
(1933) *Storia delle dottrine politiche*, sixth edition, Bari: Laterza, 1970; (English translation, *A Short History of Political Philosophy*, trans. S. Koff, New York: Crowell, 1972).
(1958) *Cio che la storia potrebbe insegnare: scritti di scienza politica*, Milan: Giuffre.
(1966) *La classe politica*, ed. and intro. N. Bobbio, Bari: Laterza (English translation, *The Ruling Class*, trans. H. Kahn, New York: McGraw-Hill, 1967).
(1971) *Il tramonto dello stato liberale*, Catania: Bonanno.

Secondary literature:
Albertoni, E. (1978) *G. Mosca*, Milan: Giuffre.
Czudnowski, M. (ed.) *Does Who Governs Matter?*, Proceedings of the Mosca Centennial, Dekalb, Ill.: Northern Illinois University Press.

Mosca maintained that, whatever the form of government, power is always held by an organized minority, a political class, which masters by stratagems that vary according to epochs and conditions (military force, wealth and the like) and from the power they have just by virtue of the fact that they are organized. However, since there is an inalienable human need not to feel governed merely by force, the political classes justify their rule by abstract principles which need to correspond to the ideas of human life that are prevalent in the society that is being governed by them. Mosca further claims that in society one can detect two opposite tendencies, the aristocratic and the democratic. The former represents the propensity to keep power in the hands of the descendants of the minority who govern; the latter represents the contrary wish to renew the government with elements that come from the governed. Alongside these tendencies stand two principles, equally contrary: the autocratic, through which the authorities transmit their orders down to those below them, and the liberal, which thinks of power as delegated from below. Within the governing minority one can distinguish two elements. One is the government properly so-called, the other is the larger sum total of all existing political forces. The whole edifice is crowned by the notion of 'judicial defence', a body of doctrine that purports to legitimize the ruling class (e.g. the divine right of kings). All this is presented as having the necessity and univers-ality of a scientific law, reflecting a positivism in Mosca's thinking. Unlike Marx, Mosca does not think of classes as necessarily conflicting. His theory has many points of contact with that of **Pareto**.

COLIN LYAS

Mothersill, Mary

American. *b:* 27 May 1923, Edmonton, Alberta. *Cat:* Analytical philosopher. *Ints:* Aesthetics; moral philosophy. *Educ:* BA, University of Toronto, 1944; PhD, Harvard, 1954. *Infls:* Arnold Isenberg and Immanuel Kant. *Appts:* Vassar, 1947–51; Columbia, 1951–3; University of Connecticut, 1953–7; University of Michigan, 1957–8; University of Chicago, 1958–61; Professor, Barnard College, Columbia University, from 1964.

Main publications:

(1952) 'Moral Philosophy and meta-ethics', *Journal of Philosophy* 49.
(1955) 'The use of normative language', *Journal of Philosophy* 52.
(1959) 'Moral knowledge', *Journal of Philosophy* 56.
(1960) 'Agents, critics and philosophers', *Mind* 69.
(1961) 'Critical reasons', *Philosophical Quarterly* 11.
(1961) '"Unique" as an aesthetic property', *Journal of Philosophy* 58.
(1965) 'Is art a language ?', *Journal of Philosophy* 62.
(1965) (ed.) *Ethics*, New York: Macmillan.
(1973) 'Notes on feminism', *Monist* 57.
(1983) 'Some notes on "What can't be said"', in Leigh S. Cauman (ed.), *How Many Questions?*, Indianapolis: Hackett.
(1984) *Beauty Restored*, Oxford: Clarendon Press; new edition, New York: Adams, Bannister, Cox, 1991.

Mary Mothersill's early writing focused on topics in ethics. Her major contribution to aesthetics is her book *Beauty Restored* (1991), in which she defends a theory of aesthetic judgement influenced by Immanuel Kant and Arnold Isenberg. She maintains that there are no laws nor general principles of taste and yet that some individual judgements of taste are nevertheless genuine. She

argues that these two features of judgements of taste are not only consistent, but also coherent. **Sources:** DAS, 1974; PI.

NIGEL WARBURTON

Mou Zongsan (Mou Tsung-san)

Chinese. *b:* 1908, Xianen County, Shandong Province, China. *Cat:* Idealist. *Ints:* Kantianism and neo-Confucian thought. *Educ:* Peking University. *Infls:* Neo-Confucian idealist philosophers, Kant, Hegel and Whitehead. *Appts:* 1945–7, Professor, Central University, Nanjing; 1947–9, Professor, Nanjing University; 1949–55, Professor, National Taiwan Normal University; 1955–60, Professor, Tsinghua University; 1960–75, Professor, University of Hong Kong; Professor, New Asia Institute of Advanced Chinese Studies, Hong Kong.

Main publications:

(n.d.) *Critique of Cognitive Mind.*
Moral Mind and Moral Creativity.
(n.d.) (1968) *The Substance of Mind and the Substance of Nature*, Taipei: Zhongshan Book Company.
(1971) *Intellectual Intuition and Chinese Philosophy*, Taipei: Commercial Press.
(1975) *Phenomena and the Thing in Itself*, Taipei: Student Bookstore.
(1985) *An Essay on the Supreme Good*, Taipei: Student Bookstore.

Secondary literature:

Briere, O. (1956) *Fifty Years of Chinese Philosophy 1898–1950*, London: George Allen & Unwin Ltd.
Republic of China Yearbook 1989 (1989) Taipei: Kwang Hwa Publishing Company.

Mou responded to the challenge of Western positivism with a synthesis of idealist neo-Confucian philosophy and German idealism, particularly that of Kant and Hegel. On the Chinese side, he derived inspiration from Mengzi and the later idealists Lu Xiangshan (twelfth century) and Wang Yangming (sixteenth century). Mou's unorthodox reading of Kant expressed his views that the mind is a substance and that individuals have intellectual intuition which actively creates its objects, claims that Kant rejected in the *Critique of Pure Reason*. Although Mou adapted Kantian themes and doctrines for his own purposes, rather than providing an accurate scholarly reading, he brought engagement and excitement to his over-riding philosophical tasks. He wished to justify Western science and democracy, but by showing that they were grounded transcendentally in human subjectivity, to leave room for the Confucian tradition. In addition to arguing that the *Critique of Pure Reason* showed how science was possible and that the *Critique of Practical Reason* showed how democracy was possible, he used his account of Chinese thought to buttress Kant's momentous claim that practical reason has priority over theoretical reason. Although he saw the grounds of subjectivity in our cognitive capacity, the priority of practical reason over theoretical reason carried with it a priority for agency, creativity and morality over cognition and science. This agency, in turn, was captured in the presentation of the subject as a free infinite mind capable of intellectual intuition. The movement from subjective origin to science and democracy was to be accomplished through self-negation and a twofold unfolding of the absolute consciousness, although the precise value of these notions is unclear. In spite of these difficulties, Mou has been a significant interpreter of Kant, first in China and then in Taiwan. His focus on science and democracy recalls **Chen Duxiu**'s earlier modernizing slogan of 'Mr Science' and 'Mr Democracy', but for Mou the achievement of these goals required cooperation with traditional Confucian idealism.

NICHOLAS BUNNIN

Mounier, Emmanuel

French. *b:* 1905, Grenoble, France. *d:* 1950, Châtenay-Malabry. *Cat:* Personalist; philosopher of religion; moral philosopher; social philosopher. *Educ:* 1924–7, studied philosophy at Grenoble and Paris. *Infls:* Influenced by Charles Péguy and Henri Bergson; personal influences include Jacques Chevalier and Jacques Maritain. *Appts:* 1931–9, taught at several lycées; 1932, founded, as a vehicle for his personalist philosophy, the journal *Esprit*, later (1941–4) banned by the Vichy government; 1939–40, military service; imprisoned in 1942 for suspected subversive activities; returned to Paris in 1944 to revive the publication of *Esprit* and to continue his writing career.

Main publications:

(1935) *Révolution personnaliste et communautaire*, Paris: Aubier.

(1936) *De la propriété capitaliste à la propriété humaine*, Paris: Desclée de Brouwer.

(1936) *Manifeste au service du personnalisme*, Paris: Aubier.

(1945) *L'Affrontement chrétien*, Neuchâtel: Baconnière.

(1946) *Liberté sous conditions*, Paris: Seuil.

(1946) *Traité du caractère*, Paris: Seuil (English translation, *The Character of Man*, London: Rockcliff, 1956).

(1947) *Qu'est-ce que le personnalisme?*, Paris: Seuil.

(1950) *Le Personnalisme*, Paris: PUF (English translation, *Personalism*, London: Routledge & Kegan Paul, 1952).

(1961–3) *Oeuvres de Mounier*, 4 vols, Paris: Seuil.

Secondary literature:

Amato, J. (1975) *Mounier and Maritain*, Alabama: University of Alabama Press (contains an extensive bibliography of articles and books by and about Mounier).

Esprit 174, December 1950, and the special edition of April 1970 (commemorative issues).

Moix, C. (1960) *La Pensée d'Emmanuel Mounier*, Paris: Seuil.

Zaza, N. (1955) *Étude critique de la notion d'engagement chez Emmanuel Mounier*, Geneva: Droz.

Emmanuel Mounier was the chief source and leading proponent of a French philosophical movement known as personalism. He asserted that, by the first half of the twentieth century, humanity was confronted by crises in all aspects of its life, including the sterile intellectual tension between idealism and materialism, and the opposing ideologies of individualism versus collectivism and capitalism versus totalitarianism. What had permitted the widening gap between these various conflicting ideologies and had rendered their resolution impossible without a radical restructuring of personal and social life was humanity's distorted image of itself, which from the Renaissance onwards had degenerated through egocentrism to egoism.

According to Mounier, the only way in which this state of crisis and impending disaster could be resisted and challenged was for human beings to recover an adequate sense of themselves as persons, with an appreciation of their inherent worth and dignity, spirituality, creativity and freedom. People are also social beings, and the ideal of social life is that of a community consisting of a network of personal relationships, in and through which everyone can find a sense of their own worth and that of others. Mounier recognized that his views in this area bore a close resemblance to those of Martin **Buber**.

Mounier's personalism had a religious dimension. One of his criticisms of contemporary Western society was that the importance given to individualism had usurped the place of a true belief in God and had implied a denial of the respect due to both the natural and the social creation. His ideal for a restructured society was a radicalized Catholicism that stressed personal, social and political rights and freedoms for all, instead of the doctrinal beliefs which, he alleged, were a dominant feature of contemporary Catholicism. His personalist ideals are said by one commentator to be nothing less than a 'search for a new Christian civilization', and a 'drive to resacralize the world' (Amato 1975, p. 124).

Mounier offered a critique of bourgeois individualism which owed much to Marx. Whilst refusing to declare allegiance to any specific French political party during the interwar years, his sympathies lay with anti-capitalism and socialism. He issued a moral indictment of bourgeois society because, he claimed, such a society had resulted in an impoverished and soulless vision of the world, a denial of people's rights and a refusal to recognize their need of a sense of intrinsic dignity. Individualism had also produced its own antitheses of collectivism and totalitarianism. He attributed to Marx the recognition of the alienation of human beings from their own nature and the products of their labour, and the exposure of the hitherto concealed value-system of bourgeois ideology.

One criticism of Mounier is that, whilst he can be credited with an awareness of the ills of contemporary society, and a recommendation of how those ills were to be cured, he did not indicate by what measures the new social and personal order was to be put in place. His injunction was to 'remake the Renaissance', with a value-system of communistic humanitarianism, but without telling us how to do so.

KATHRYN PLANT

Mudimbe, V(alentin)-Y(ves) or V(ombi) Y(oka)

Zaïrean. *b:* 8 December 1941, Likasi, Zaïre. *Cat:* Philosopher of cultural anthropology; poet and novelist. *Educ:* Studied at Université Lovanium of Kinshasa and at University of Louvain, 1962–70. *Infls:* Marx, Freud, Lévi-Strauss, Sartre, Lacan, Foucault, Althusser and Kagame. *Appts:* Taught at Louvain, Paris X, Nanterre and Kinshasa; Dean of Université Nationale du Zaïre, 1972–4; Professor, Haverford College, Pennsylvania; Professor of Romance Studies and Comparative Literature, Duke University, North Carolina.

Main publications:

(1972) *Autour de la nation*, Kinshasa/Lubumbashi: Éditions du Mont-Noir.

(1972) *Réflexions sur la vie quotidienne*, Kinshasa: Éditions du Mont-Noir.
(1973) *L'autre face du royaume*, Lausanne: L'Âge d'Homme.
(1982) *L'Odeur du Père*, Paris: Présence Africaine.
(1988) *The Invention of Africa*, Bloomington: Indiana University Press.
(1991) *Parables and Fables*, Madison: University of Wisconsin Press.
(1993) (with Kwame Anthony Appiah) 'The impact of African studies on philosophy', in Robert H. Bates, V. Y. Mudimbe and Jean, O'Barr (eds), *Africa and the Disciplines*, Chicago: University of Chicago Press.
(1994) *The Idea of Africa*, London: International African Institute.

Secondary literature:

Masolo, D. A. (1994) *African Philosophy in Search of Identity*, London: Routledge.
Mouralis, Bernard (1988) *V. Y. Mudimbe ou Le Discours, l'écart et l'écriture*, Paris: Présence Africaine (contains a full biography and shows the relation between Mudimbe's poetry, novels and philosophy).

In his early writings (1972) Mudimbe was concerned with the social sciences and with the place and function of the intellectual in independent Africa. He asks what conditions can help to build an African science that is not derived from European 'Africanism' and warns against the illusion that the history of European anthropology, from evolutionism to structuralism, and the theme of 'ethnocide' developed for instance by Jaulin, might be considered as a progressive purification of knowledge.

In *L'Odeur du Père* (1982), Mudimbe argues that the root of knowledge is in the ability of the subject to perceive itself as a subject, and not in models offered by science. This point of view is central in the two books recently written by Mudimbe in English (1988, 1991), in which he puts forward the view that Africa does not exist in and by itself, but only as an object constructed by a European or African mind.

Mudimbe's thought draws on a wide spectrum of European culture although he opposes both European 'Africanism', with its tendency to reify notions such as 'tribe', 'African tradition', 'African wisdom', etc., and the discourse of African nationalism that regards African culture as a reality that is independent of European conceptions of it. Mudimbe's eclecticism has been criticized on the grounds that is is not appropriate to the solution of essentially African problems.

Nevertheless, his readership has grown steadily, especially among young scholars who respond to the paradoxical elements in his thought.

BERNARD MOURALIS

Muirhead, John Henry

British. *b:* 28 April 1855, Glasgow. *d:* 24 May 1940, Rotherfield, Sussex. *Cat:* Idealist. *Ints:* Ethics; social philosophy; history of philosophy. *Educ:* Glasgow University and Balliol College, Oxford. *Infls:* Edward Caird and T. H. Green. *Appts:* Professor of Philosophy and Political Economy, Birmingham, 1897–1922.

Main publications:

(1892) *Elements of Ethics*, London.
(1900) *Chapters on Aristotle's Ethics*, London.
(1908) *The Service of of the State*, London.
(1915) *German Philosophy in Relation to the War*, Oxford.
(1918) (with H. J. Hetherington) *Social Purpose*, London.
(1928) *The Use of Philosophy*, London.
(1930) *Coleridge as Philosopher*, London.
(1931) *The Platonic Tradition in Anglo-Saxon Philosophy*, London.
(1932) *Rule and End in Morals*, Oxford.

Secondary literature:

Muirhead, J. H. (1942) *Recollections of a Journeyman in Philosophy*, ed. J. W. Harvey.
Robertson, C. G. and Ross, W. D. (1940) obituary in *Proceedings of the British Academy*.

Muirhead's services to philosophy were considerable, as historian of the tradition of resistance to empiricism in English-language philosophy and of Coleridge's philosophical career, as the original editor of the important 'Library of Philosophy' published by Allen & Unwin, as editor of the first two volumes of *Contemporary British Philosophy*, composed of essays surveying their work by leading figures and, in a modest way, by applying his genial, amorphous idealism to social problems. The form of idealism he had imbibed from Edward **Caird** was an accommodating affair, well suited for reconciling apparently conflicting views in some kind of eclectic harmony. This amiably undiscriminating spirit is evident in his ethical writings, which are his chief direct contribution to philosophy. Like other idealists he rejects both the greatest happiness principle and Kant's abstract conception of duty as sufficient accounts of morality in favour of the idea of self-realization, understood as embracing both particular desires

and the rational form of self-imposed law. With the passage of time, new developments were found a place, particularly the insistence of the Oxford moralists, **Prichard** and **Ross**, on the intuitive character of obligation. Muirhead's largest contribution to philosophy, in the widest sense, is his discernment of what he called the Platonic tradition, a more or less continuous, if sometimes only just detectable, stream of thought, in opposition to the dominant native empiricism. At a time when most British philosophers were indifferent to, and so ignorant of, the history of the subject, he drew attention to Cudworth, Norris and Collier, as well as to the incorporation of German philosophy into British thought in the nineteenth-century from Coleridge and Carlyle onwards.

Sources: Metz; DNB; Passmore 1957.

ANTHONY QUINTON

Mumford, Lewis

American. *b:* 19 October 1895, Flushing, Long Island. *d:* 26 January 1990, New York City. *Cat:* Social philosopher; writer; regional planner; educationalist. *Ints:* Philosophy of culture and civilization. *Educ:* City College of New York, Columbia University and the New School of Social Research. *Infls:* Personal influences: Patrick Geddes and Thorstein Veblen. Literary: Walt Whitman, Ralph Waldo Emerson and Herman Melville. *Appts:* 1920, Acting Editor of the *Sociological Review*; 1923, founding member of the Regional Planning Association of America; 1926–36, Coeditor of *The American Caravan*; 1935–7, Member of the Board of Higher Education in New York; 1938–44, Member of the American Council on Education; 1943–4, Professor of Humanities, Stanford University; 1951–72, Professor of Land and City Planning, University of Pennsylvania; 1962–5, President, Academy of Arts and Letters; 1957–60, Visiting Professor, MIT; 1961, Riba Royal Gold Medal for Architecture; 1972, National Medal for Literature; 1973–4, Visiting Professor, MIT; 1983, Benjamin Franklin Medal, RSA; 1986, National Medal of Arts.

Main publications:

(1934–52) *The Renewal of Life* series:
   (1934) 1. *Technics and Civilisation*, London: Routledge.
   (1938) 2. *The Culture of Cities*, London: Secker & Warburg.
   (1944) 3. *The Condition of Man*, London: Secker & Warburg.

(1952) 4. *The Conduct of Life*, London: Secker & Warburg.

Secondary literature:
Goist, P. D. (1972) 'Seeing things whole: a consideration of Lewis Mumford', *Journal of the American Institute of Planners* 38, 6: 379–91.
Newman, E. S. (1971) *Lewis Mumford: A Bibliography 1914–1970*, New York: Harcourt Brace.

Mumford's social philosophy was an 'organic humanism' (as he called it) that was inspired by the ideas of Patrick Geddes and the traditional American humanism of Whitman and Emerson, and thoroughly imbued with the ideal of the unification and equal cultivation of the arts, the sciences and the humanities.

A fundamental aim of his philosophy was both to offer a comprehensive interpretation of Western civilization and to show what changes in its fabric are necessary if it is to make the most of the vast powers it may now command, changes which, he held, have become imperative if it is 'to save itself from extinction' by means of the very instruments it 'too devoutly worships' (1944, Preface).

Mumford was particularly critical of what he regarded as the dominance and one-sided development of science and technology, with its corresponding displacement of the older forms of human value, art, thought and practice.

In his programme for 'renewal' Mumford called for a reorientation of the whole of contemporary culture through the promotion of an ideal of life in which all the diverse kinds of human activity, practical and theoretical, are held in a 'dynamic equilibrium' and pursued as 'a single indivisible whole' (1944, pp. 391–423). Mumford's ideas have exerted a global influence not so much in social philosophy as in regional planning and architecture.
Sources: Bullock & Woodings; DAS; WW.

STEPHEN MOLLER

Münsterberg, Hugo
German. ***b:*** 1863, Danzig, Germany. ***d:*** 1916, USA. ***Cat:*** Empiricist in psychology; idealist in philosophy. ***Ints:*** Philosophy; psychology; film. ***Educ:*** University of Leipzig, where he undertook a degree in psychology under Wilhelm Wundt, 1882–5; University of Heidelberg, 1885–7; University of Freiburg, habilitation, 1877–92. ***Infls:*** Wilhelm Wundt. ***Appts:*** 1887–92, Dozent (Lecturer) in Psychology, University of Freiburg; 1892–5, Temporary Chairman of the Department

of Philosophy, Harvard University (in those days psychology was grouped with philosophy); 1895–7, back to his old past at Freiburg; 1897–1916, Professor of Philosophy (William James alters his professorship from 'Professor of Psychology' in order for Münsterberg to assume the position).

Main publications:
(1889–92) *Beiträge zur experimentellen Psychologie* 2 vols, Freiburg: Mohr.
(1916) *The Photoplay: A Psychological Study*, D. Appleton & Co., reprinted as *The Film: A Psychological Study* (with a foreword by R. Griffiths), New York: Dover Publications, 1970.
(1933) *On the Witness Stand: Essays on Psychology and Crime*, Boston: Clark Boardman & Co.

In his main and, some would say, his only work in experimental psychology (published while he was in Freiburg), Münsterberg examined the problem of the 'fluctuations of perception'. The experiment sought to determine the responses of a subject who is asked to report his responses when faced with a weak light. The subject's responses alternated between positive (for example, 'The light is visible') and negative ('The light is not visible') replies. For Münsterberg such fluctuations to visual stimuli were caused by alterations in accommodation. Although criticized by E. Pace, J. W. Slaughter and C. E. Ferree, whose experiments contradicted his results, Münsterberg's research was recognized as significant because it opened up avenues for others.

For the duration of his stay at Harvard, he preoccupied himself with applying psychology to numerous and diverse fields, such as criminology, psychotherapy, industry and film experience. In the process he succeeded in bringing psychology to the attention of the American public.

When he tried to initiate a rapprochement between America and Germany, at a time when Americans were afraid of Germany, during the First World War, he failed and, for his pains, his American audience turned against him. He died in 1916, his dream of peace between his adopted country and his country of origin unrealized. With his death his final book on the psychology of film experience, in which he anticipated a number of contemporary ideas, was also forgotten.
Sources: E. G. Boring (1950) *A History of Experimental Psychology*, New York: Appleton-Century-Crofts; E. Hearst (1979) *The First Century of Experimental Psychology*, New Jersey: Lawrence Erlbaum Associates; T. S. Krawiec (ed.) (1972) *The Psychologists* 2 vols, Oxford: OUP; H. Münsterberg (1916) *The Photoplay: A Psychological Study*, D. Appleton & Co.,

repr. as *The Film: A Psychological Study*, New York: Dover Pubns, 1970; S. S. Stevens (ed.) (1966) *Handbook of Experimental Psychology*, London: John Wiley & Sons.

SEBASTIEN ODIARI

Murdoch, (Jean) Iris

Irish. *b:* 15 July 1919, Dublin. *Cat:* 'I might describe myself as a Wittgensteinian neo-Platonist!'. *Ints:* Moral philosophy; Plato; religion; metaphysics. *Educ:* MA, Somerville College, Oxford; Newnham College, Cambridge. *Infls:* Plato, Wittgenstein, Sartre and Weil. *Appts:* Fellow of St Anne's College, Oxford, from 1948.

Main publications:

(1953) *Sartre, Romantic Rationalist*, Cambridge: Bowes & Bowes; second edition, *Sartre, Romantic Realist*, 1980.
(1970) *The Sovereignty of Good*, London: Routledge & Kegan Paul.
(1977) *The Fire and the Sun*, Oxford.
(1986) *Acastos*, London: Chatto & Windus.
(1992) *Metaphysics as a Guide to Morals*, London: Chatto & Windus.

Secondary literature:

Begnal, K. (1987) *Iris Murdoch A Reference Guide*, Boston: G. K. Hall.

Iris Murdoch's philosophical works have been few in comparison with her many novels, although she herself might see little distinction between the genres: 'It may be that the best model for all thought is the creative imagination' (1992, p. 169). The views in almost all her philosophical writings are recapitulated and elaborated in *Metaphysics as a Guide to Morals* (1992). Ruminative in pace, discursive in style and intuitive in the flow of its arguments, this wide-ranging treatise is at the farthest point from conventional academic exposition. It must be ironic that a work written in this way might well turn out to be seen as one of the finest and most original examples of philosophy produced in twentieth-century Britain.

Murdoch has always stood apart from analytical orthodoxy. Plato has been her model and prime inspiration. *Metaphysics as a Guide to Morals* makes no effort to argue basic Platonic premises which a more cautious author would have felt some need to defend. ('A work of art is of course not a material object, though some works of art are bodied forth by material objects so as to seem to inhere in them' is asserted without argument on p. 2.) The Platonic themes she has

pursued have been largely those of the *Phaedrus* and of the *Republic*: the soul; the indispensability of metaphor; the motivation for the search for truth (Eros, to her and Plato); the reality of the good; the relations between art, truth, the good and God.

One of her starting-points has been opposition to a view of the self which she identifies in both **Sartre** and **Wittgenstein**: a view that left morality to be located only in the rightness of discrete choices, displacing goodness, character and virtue—'The agent, thin as a needle, appears in the quick flash of the choosing will' ('On "God" and "Good"', in *The Sovereignty of Good*, 1970, p. 53). She has maintained a confidence in the solidity and continuity of the self (or the *soul*, as she prefers it): 'What goes on inwardly in the soul is the essence of each man, it's what makes us individual people. The relation between that inwardness and public conduct *is morality*' ('Art and Eros: a dialogue about art', in *Acastos*, 1986, p. 31). She writes of 'our confidence in our own inner life of thought and judgment and in our real existence as individual persons capable of truth' (1992, p. 221): 'no theory can remove or explain away our moral and rational mastery of our individual being' (p. 213). This anti-existentialist confidence is realized interestingly in her fiction. One of her characters says: 'one is responsible for one's actions, and one's past does belong to one. You can't blot it out by entering a dream world and decreeing that life began yesterday. You can't make yourself into a new person overnight' (*The Black Prince*, Harmondsworth: Penguin, 1975, p. 359).

Against **Derrida** (whom she classes as a 'structuralist') she argues for a clear, strong view of truth: 'the truth, terrible, delightful, funny, whose strong lively presence we recognise in great writers' (1992, p. 215). Her argument is a transcendental one: 'We must check philosophical theories against what we know of human nature (and hold on to that phrase too) ... Language is meaningful, *ergo* useful, it performs its *essential* task, through its ability to be truthful' (p. 216).

Truth, reality and the good are linked in her work as they are in the *Republic*, except that, for her, a vision of the real is not the preserve of the mathematically educated elite, as it was Plato: 'We find out in the most minute details of our lives that the good is the real. Philosophy too can attend to such details' (p. 430). As with Plato, visual imagery is central (and also the imagery of *attention*, from Simone **Weil**): 'Looking can be a kind of intelligent reverence. Moral thinking, serious thinking, is clarification (visual image).

The good, just, man is lucid' (p. 463). We *see* reality; a truthful view of it shows us the good, and 'The sovereign Good is ... something which we all experience as a creative force' (p. 507).

Much of her thinking has been devoted to the value and danger of art. (Her interpretations of Plato on these themes are in *The Fire and the Sun* and in 'Art and Eros', in *Acastos*.) Good art, she believes, 'shows us how difficult it is to be objective by showing us how differently the world looks to an objective vision' (1970, p. 86).

Metaphysics as a Guide to Morals includes extended reflections on the value in ontological arguments. Murdoch wrote earlier that 'God was (or is) a *single perfect transcendent non-representable and necessarily real object of attention*; and ... moral philosophy should attempt to retain a central concept which has all these characteristics' ('On "God" and "Good"', in 1970, p. 55). Yet 'to speak of "religious language" as something specialised, supposed to be expressive rather than referential, is to separate religion from the truth-seeking struggle of the whole of life' (1992, p. 418).

Clarity of vision must be matched by clarity of language. To achieve this remains one of the roles of philosophy:

> We must ... preserve and cherish a strong truth-bearing everyday language, not marred or corrupted by technical discourse or scientific codes; and thereby promote the clarified objective knowledge of man and society of which we are in need as citizens, and as moral agents
>
> (p. 164).

And:

> The task of philosophy is not less but more essential now, in helping to preserve and refresh a stream of meticulous, subtle, eloquent ordinary language, free from jargon and able to deal clearly and in detail with matters of a certain degree of generality and abstraction. We cannot see the future, but must fear it intelligently
>
> (p. 211).

She writes that she has been wanting to put the argument of Plato 'into a modern context as background to moral philosophy, as a bridge between morals and religion, and as relevant to our new disturbed understanding of religious truth' (p. 511). Her thought must be unique as a creative reimagining of Plato in the late twentieth century.

RICHARD MASON

Murphy, Arthur E(dward)

American. *b:* 1 September 1901, Ithaca, New York. *d:* 11 May 1962, Austin, Texas. *Cat:* Moral philosopher; theorist of knowledge. *Ints:* Nature of philosophy; contemporary philosophy; American philosophy; philosophy in relation to culture. *Educ:* University of California, BA 1923, PhD 1925. *Infls:* Personal influences include Alexander, Lovejoy, Mead, Ralph Blake, C. J. Ducasse and M. Black; literary influences include Santayana, Peirce, Whitehead, Collingwood, Dewey, Moore, Broad and Wittgenstein. *Appts:* Instructor in Philosophy, University of California, 1926–7; University of Chicago, 1927–8; Assistant Professor of Philosophy, Cornell University, 1928–9; Associate Professor of Philosophy, University of Chicago, 1929–31; Professor of Philosophy, Brown University, 1931-9, University of Illinois, 1939–45; Cornell University, 1945–53; University of Washington, 1953–8; University of Texas, from 1958.

Main publications:

(1943) *The Uses of Reason*, New York: The Macmillan Co.
(1945) (with others) *Philosophy in American Education*, New York and London: Harper & Brothers Publishers.
(1963) *Reason and the Common Good: Selected Essays*, ed. W. H. Hay and M. G. Singer, Englewood Cliffs, NJ: Prentice-Hall, Inc. (contains bibliography).
(1965) *The Theory of Practical Reason*, ed. A. I. Melden, La Salle, Ill.: Open Court (Melden's introduction is a good guide to Murphy's thought).
(1993) 'Pragmatism and the context of rationality', ed. M. G. Singer, *Transactions of the Charles S. Peirce Society* 29, 2, 3, 4: 123–78, 331–68, 687–722.
(forthcoming) *Reason, Reality and Speculative Philosophy*, ed. M. G. Singer, Madison: University of Wisconsin Press (contains preface, memoir and introduction).

Secondary literature:

Encyclopedia of Philosophy, ed. Paul Edwards, New York: Macmillan and the Free Press, 1967, vol. 5.
Introduction to 'Pragmatism and the context of rationality ', 1993, pp. 123–41.
Kolenda, K. (1969) *In Defense of Practical Reason: A Study and Application of Arthur Murphy's Theory*, Houston: Rice University Studies.

Singer, M. G. (1985) 'Two American philosophers:
Morris Cohen and Arthur Murphy ', in M. G.
Singer (ed.), *American Philosophy*, Cambridge:
Cambridge University Press, pp. 295–329, esp. pp.
309–20.

During his lifetime Murphy enjoyed considerable
prestige amongst his American colleagues. He
coined the expression 'objective relativism' in his
first publication, in 1926, and developed the view
in papers in the next few years. Objective
relativism was stimulated by **Einstein**'s theory of
relativity and those philosophical theories, such
as **Alexander**'s and **Whitehead**'s, that arose from it.
It is the view that events rather than things
constitute the primary ontological category and
that the relations into which events enter are
essential to their nature. In one relation something
can have one set of characteristics, in another a
quite different set. This relativity extends to the
relations between events and observers and is not
subjective but objective. Hence events and things
are what they are only in their relationships; this
relativity is objective; hence objective relativism.

Murphy eventually repudiated his own brain-
child for reasons explained in *Reason and the
Common Good* (1963). Murphy had first advanced
objective relativism not as a finished philosophy
but as the basis for a research programme which
would have to 'justify itself in many fields', while
'the work in most of them has yet to be done'. On
Murphy's later diagnosis, this work was not done,
but rather objective relativism was generalized
beyond the context of its significant application
and generated paradoxes and absurdities. Objective relativism thus failed because it neglected 'the
consistent application of contextual principles',
so that 'the theory became just one of the "isms"
and has shared their fate'. Consideration of this
philosophical tendency led Murphy to develop his
method of contextual analysis.

Murphy conducted a lifelong inquiry 'into the
conditions and ... character of the application of
reason to human affairs' and attempted to
develop a philosophy that would genuinely help
to organize and harmonize facts and ideas that
human beings are inevitably confronted with by
the force of experience, in such a way that they
could deal more intelligently with common and
uncommon human problems. He called the
method he worked out contextual analysis. He
was convinced that no recipe could be laid down
in advance that would provide automatic solutions to such problems. What is needed, he said, is
a developed understanding and capacity to

provide a way of going on, for there is no final
overall solution to the problems of life.

Murphy had a way of expressing himself that
was often extraordinarily funny, and a conviction
that a sense of humour is an important part of
humane philosophizing. His sense of humour was
combined with a rare sense of irony, and he was
especially adept at thinking up amusing and
imaginative examples and parables. He also had
an uncanny knack of getting directly at the heart
of someone else's point of view and distilling the
essence of his thought. This led some of his
contemporaries to regard him as merely a critic of
others' ideas. However, although he was often
critical, it is more accurate to regard him as an
interpreter of unusual insight. Furthermore, he
was constructing a philosophy of his own out of
his studies of other philosophical ideas and of
cultural tendencies and traditions. He complained
that in contemporary philosophy 'the love of
argument has supplanted the love of wisdom', and
that too many thinkers were content to 'hitch their
wagon to a trend'. Good sense, good will and good
judgement were virtues he especially prized. As
one of his commentators remarked, the conviction that 'gives unity to Murphy's thought ... is
that good sense can be found in the common life
from which our philosophical inquiries take their
departure and hence ... it is back to this common
life ... that our philosophy must return us'.

Sources: Obituary, *PAAPA*, 36, 1963, pp. 118–19;
WWW(Am) 1961–8; Profs F. L. Will and W. H. Hay;
personal acquaintance.

MARCUS SINGER

Mveng, Engelbert

Cameroonian. *b:* 9 May 1930, Ebolowa, department of Ntem, Cameroon. *d:* 1995 *Cat:* Aesthetician; theologian; cultural politician. *Educ:* Minor
Seminary of Akono; Major Seminary of Otele;
entered the Society of Jesus in 1951 to study
Classics, Philosophy and Theology at the Catholic
University of Louvain, Belgium, at Vals Chantilly,
Fourvière, Lyon, and the Sorbonne; third cycle
Doctorate, 1964, Paris, on Christianization and
paganism according to St Augustine; Doctorat
d'État on the Greek sources of African history in
1970. *Infls:* L. S. Senghor. *Appts:* Professor, College
Libermann, 1958–60; Professor of History, Fed-
eral University in Yaounde; Director of Cultural
Affairs, Republic of Cameroon; a consultant to
UNESCO, Mveng has been active in a great
number of cultural activities including the General Secretariat of the African Society of Culture
(Paris), the first and second World Festival of

Negro Arts in Dakar (Senegal) and Lagos (Nigeria), and the Foundation Queen Elisabeth for Egyptological Studies (Belgium).

Main publications:

(1964) *L'Art de L'Afrique Noire*, Paris: Mame.

(1966) *Dossier culturel panafricain*, Paris: Présence Africaine.

(1972) *Les Sources grecques de l'histoire négro-africaine*, Paris: Présence Africaine.

An artist himself, Mveng is preoccupied by two main problems: that of artistic creation and that of an adaptation of Christianity to African cultures. His claim is that instead of adapting Christianity to the African context one should integrate African cultural structures and intuitions in an acculturated Christianity.

V. Y. MUDIMBE

N

Nabert, Jean

French. **b:** 21 July 1881, Izeaux, Dauphiné, France. **d:** 13 October 1960, Loctudy, Brittany. **Cat:** Metaphysician; moral philosopher; religious philosopher. **Ints:** Self-consciousness; ethics; the problem of evil. **Educ:** Agrégé in Philosophy, 1909. **Infls:** Descartes, Kant, Maine de Biran and J. G. Fichte. **Appts:** Professor of Philosophy, Lycées de Saint-Lô (1908–10), Brest (1910–1914) and Metz, Germany (1919–24); thereafter taught in Paris; appointed Inspector General of Philosophy in Secondary Schools in Paris, 1945.

Main publications:

(1924) *L'Expérience intériéure de la liberté*, Paris: (P.U.F.).
(1943) *Éléments pour une éthique*, Paris: PUF.
(1955) *Essai sur le mal*, Paris: PUF.
(1959) 'Le divin et Dieu', *Les Études philosophiques*: 321–32.
(1966) *Le Désir de Dieu*, Paris: Aubier (posthumous).

Secondary literature:

Baufay, Jacques (1974) *La Philosophie religieuse de Jean Nabert*, Presses Universitaires de Namur.
Leverth, Paule (1971) *Jean Nabert ou l'exigence absolue*, Paris: Seghers.

Nabert sought to develop *la tradition de la philosophie réflexive*, as represented by Descartes, Kant, Maine de Biran and J. G. Fichte. The point of departure of his philosophy was therefore an analysis of the meaning and conditions of the cogito, that is, of self-consciousness or reflective awareness.

In his *L'Expérience intérieure* (1924), he argued that consciousness is not to be considered as a 'thing' among other things nor even as a manifestation of being (*l'être*) but as activity, more precisely as founded in the activity of a subject. Thus he denied that action is reducible to consciousness and affirmed the identity of being and activity.

According to Nabert every subject is essentially divided, separated from itself and therefore dissatisfied. This dissatisfaction is an expression of *un desir d'être* that is never appeased, even in moral action. In his *Éléments pour une éthique* (1943) he traced the origin of this desire to what he called the 'affirmation originaire' of self-consciousness, maintaining that there is an intrinsic negative element within this affirmation ever preventing the subject from achieving self-reconciliation.

This position underlay Nabert's searching analysis of evil in his *Essai sur le mal* (1955). In his view evil in all its forms is unjustifiable; yet neither morality nor religion nor anything else can assure us that we will surmount it. This tragic sense of life also informed his religious philosophy, which rested on an original distinction between the idea of God and that of the divine. Nabert's philosophy has influenced a number of French thinkers, particularly Paul **Ricoeur**.
Sources: Huisman; EF.

STEPHEN MOLLER

Naess, A(rne) D(ekke) (Eide)

Norwegian. **b:** 27 January 1912, Oslo, Norway. **Cat:** Philosophical generalist; historian of philosophy. **Ints:** Early interest was epistemology and ethics; in later years aspects of environmental and peace issues. **Educ:** University of Oslo, Mag.Art. in Philosophy (with Astronomy and Mathematics), 1933; PhD in Philosophy, 1936; studied in Paris, 1931, in Vienna, 1934–5, and at the University of California, Berkeley, 1938–9. **Infls:** The logical positivists, Sextus Empiricus, Spinoza and Gandhi. **Appts:** 1939–70, Professor of Philosophy, University of Oslo.

Main publications:

(1936) *Erkenntis und wissenschaftliches Verhalten*, Oslo: Universitetsforlaget.
(1939) *Truth as Conceived by Those Who are Not Professional Philosophers*, Oslo: Univeristetsforlaget.
(1952) 'Toward a theory of interpretation and preciseness', in L. Linsky (ed.), *Semantics and the Philosophy of Language*, Urbana, Chicago and London: University of Illinois Press.
(1953) *Interpretation and Preciseness*, Oslo: Universitetsforlaget.

(1953) *Filosofiens Historie* [A History of Philosophy], 3 vols, Oslo: Universitetsforlaget.
(1968) *Scepticism*, London: Routledge & Kegan Paul; Oslo: Universitetsforlaget.
(1968) *Four Modern Philosophers: Carnpa, Wittgenstein, Heidegger, Sartre*, Chicago: University of Chicago Press.
(1969) *Hvilken verden er den virkelige?* [Which World is the Real One?], Oslo: Universistetsforlaget.
(1972) *The Pluralist and Possibilist Aspects of the Scientific Enterprise*, Oslo: Universitetsforlaget.
(1974) *økologi, samfunn og livsstil* [Ecology, Society and Lifestyle], fourth revised edition, Oslo: Universitetsforlaget.
(1992) 'How should the empirical movement be promoted today?', in E. M. Barth and Jan van Dormael (eds), *From an Empirical Point of View: The Empirical Turn in Logic*, Ghent: Communication and Cognition.

Secondary literature:
Gullvåg, I. and Wetlesen, J. (eds) (1982) *In Sceptical Wonder. Inquiries into the Philosophy of Arne Naess on the Occasion of his 70th Birthday*, Oslo: Universiteitsforlaget.

Naess's early work although quite distinctive in several respects, is similar in spirit to that of leading logical positivists. He developed a radically empiricist account of semantics, encompassing empirically satisfactory defintions of such semantic concepts as 'synonymity', 'ambiguity', 'preciseness' and 'definiteness (or depth) of (communicative) intention'. Not only are semantic theories empirically testable. When semnatic terms have gained widespread ('truth' is an example), Naess thinks it makes sense to test by questionnaire how these terms are in fact used by ordinary speakers. The core idea is that language is primarily a vehicle for communication. Hence semantics is to be viewed as a theory of interpretation.

Since conceptual schemes are mostly expressed by linguistic means, the theory of preciseness and interpretation has an immediate bearing on the possibility of deciding between or even securing intercommunicability across, competing worldviews. Naess strives hard to avoid relativism. On the other hand, he defends, in one major work, the conceptual coherence and pyschological possibility of Pyrrhonian scepticism.

Naess's early work in ethics addressed foundational issues, in an empiricist vein. In later years, he has concentrated on philosophical and, broadly speaking, political aspects of peace and environmental issues. Indeed, he has for long been a prominent participant in the Norwegian people's movement relating to the latter.

Naess has been hugely important for establishing in Norway a modern, institutionalized philosophical tradition.

Sources: Flo, Olav and Naess, Arne (1971) 'Selected ist of his philosophical writings in the English and German languages, 1936–70', *Synthese* 3, pp. 348–52; personal commmunication.

STIG RASMUSSEN

Nagel, Ernest

American. *b:* 16 November 1901, Mesto, Czechoslovakia. *d:* 10 September 1985, New York City. *Cat:* Philosophical naturalist. *Ints:* Philosophy of science. *Educ:* City College of New York, BA 1923; Columbia University, MA 1925, PhD 1930. *Infls:* Cohen, Dewey and Carnap. *Appts:* 1930 -1, Instructor, the City College of New York; 1931–66, Assistant Professor to John Dewey Professor of Philosophy, Columbia University; 1966–7, Professor of Philosophy, Rockefeller University; 1966–70, Distinguished Professor of Philosophy, Columbia University.

Main publications:
(1934) (with M. Cohen) *An Introduction to Logic and Scientific Method*, New York: Harcourt Brace.
(1939) *Principles of the Theory of Probability*, in *The International Encyclopedia of Unified Science*, vol. I, no. 6, Chicago: University of Chicago Press.
(1950) *John Stuart Mill's Philosophy of Scientific Method*, New York: Hafner.
(1954) *Sovereign Reason and Other Studies in the Philosophy of Science*, Glencoe, Ill.: Free Press.
(1957) *Logic Without Metaphysics and Other Essays in the Philosophy of Science*, Glencoe, Ill.: Free Press.
(1958) (with J. R. Newman) *Gödel's Proof*, New York: New York University Press.
(1961) *The Structure of Science: Problems in the Logic of Scientific Explanation*, New York: Harcourt, Brace & World.
(1962) (ed. with P. Suppes and A. Tarski) *International Congress for Logic, Methodology and Philosophy*, Palo Alto, CA: Stanford University Press.
(1982) *Teleology Revisited and Other Essays in the Philosophy and History of Science*, New York: Columbia University Press.

Secondary literature:
Reck, A. J. (1968) *The New American Philosophers: An Exploration of Thought Since World War II*, Baton Rouge, La.: Louisiana State University

Press; reprinted, New York: Dell Publishing Co., 1970.

Thayer, H. S. (1967) 'Nagel, Ernest', in Paul edwards (ed.) *Encyclopedia of Philosophy*, vol. 5.

The teaching of M. **Cohen** at the City College of New York attracted Nagel to philosophy. From his mentor Nagel derived a profound appreciation of logic and a sense of the primacy of the role of reason in experimental science. This early orientation favoured a realist interpretation of the theories and concepts of natural science. At Columbia University, however, experimental pragmatism prevailed under the sway of John **Dewey**, and Nagel was drawn in the direction of naturalism and empirical pragmatism. His study of formal mathematical logic, embracing investigations into probability theory and the foundations of mathematics, led him to a keen appreciation of logical empiricism. Nagel sought to equilibrate these various tendencies towards realism and pragmatism, rationalism and empiricism, philosophical analysis and systematic philosophy, within a comprehensive, sophisticated theory of scientific naturalism. Like Cohen, Nagel had a rare genius for lucid exposition of the most recondite matters in logic, mathematics and natural science. He was among the first Americans to take account of the rise of logical positivism. His article 'Impressions and appraisals of analytic philosophy in Europe', originally published in the *Journal of Philosophy* in 1936 and later reprinted in his *Logic Without Metaphysics* (1957), reviewed the works of **Wittgenstein**, **Schlick**, **Carnap** and the Polish logicians, in addition to the analytic movement at Cambridge University under G. E. **Moore** and Wittgenstein. Nagel assimilated their contributions to his own rationalism and naturalism. The naturalism to which Nagel subscribed maintains two theses. First, the executive order of nature consists of the actions and organizations of spatio-temporally located bodies that produce the occurrence of all events, qualities, processes, behaviours of individual entities, and so forth. Second, 'the manifest plurality and variety of things, of their qualities and functions, are an irreducible feature of the cosmos' (1957, p. 7). So Nagel's naturalism, bound to science as the only way to know, is not simplistically reductionist. It offers 'a generalized account of the cosmic scheme and of man's place in it, as well as a logic of inquiry' (ibid., p. 6). Nagel was a prolific author of essays and book reviews for professional journals, scientific periodicals and literary reviews. *Sovereign Reason* (1954) is a collection of sixteen articles. The titular essay is a detailed critique of Blanshard's vision of the scope and office of human reason; Nagel dissected and refuted **Blanshard**'s theory of internal relations, which allegedly culminated in an intelligible cosmos of necessarily related parts. Although a rationalist, Nagel was antipathetic to idealistic speculations that proceeded dialectically and denied the manifest reality of plurality, change, novelty and contingency. His naturalism was married not to dialectic, but to analysis and the methods of science as the avenues to knowledge.

In 'Logic without ontology', an essay originally published in V. H. Krikorian (ed.), *Naturalism and the Human Spirit* (New York: Columbia University Press, 1944) and reprinted in *Logic Without Metaphysics*, Nagel examined several interpretations of the principle of non-contradiction; he contended that they involve metaphysical assumptions incompatible with the nature of scientific knowledge. Nagel's own theory of logic is naturalistic and contextualistic. Examining the principles of logic as they operate in the specific contexts of the language of science, he concluded that they are not a priori structures of reality, nor empirical generalizations, nor mere formal tautologies, but normative rules, prescriptive for the use of language. Nagel's naturalism was not silent in matters of religion. He not only defended atheism by attacking theistic arguments as logically flawed, but advocated atheism on the moral ground that, while life is ultimately tragic, it is morally imperative that we follow the route of reason and science in order to try to solve its problems, instead of succumbing to illusions and false hopes. Nagel's major book is *The Structure of Science* (1961). It examines the logical structure of scientific explanations, their mutual relations, their functions in inquiry and their devices for systematizing knowledge. In seeking explanations scientists construct theories, of which Nagel sought to define the cognitive status. Criticizing the claims of descriptivists, instrumentalists and realists, Nagel proposed a contextualism. He found that each of the rival philosophies of the cognitive status of scientific theories was useful in different contexts of scientific investigation, the instrumentalist in the upper levels of theory and the realist at the level of empirical statements, while the descriptivist combined both philosophies in dealing with these different levels. Hence Nagel sought to resolve the conflicts by reducing the disputes to matters of language. Moreover, Nagel's treatment of the disputes over the cognitive status of scientific theories as tantamount to verbal conflicts over 'preferred modes of speech' is paradigmatic of his contextualistic, linguistic strategy in resolving philosophical disputes at large. It is reminiscent of the pragmatism of William **James**, who jocularly compared quibbles over whether we can run around a squirrel running around a tree with meaningless metaphysical disputes, and also of the logical positivism of Rudolf Carnap, for whom metaphysical disputes originate in confusions about language. In 1980 Columbia University awarded Nagel the Nicholas Murray Butler Medal for excellence in philosophy.

Sources: Obituary, *New York Times*, 22 Sep 1985; RA, 5.

ANDREW RECK

Nagel, Thomas

American. *b:* 4 July 1937, Belgrade. *Cat:* Metaphysician; ethicist; philosopher of mind. *Ints:* Metaphysics; ethics; philosopher of mind. *Educ:* Cornell University, BA 1958; University of Oxford, BPhil 1960; Harvard University, PhD 1963. *Infls:* Rawls, Wittgenstein, Chomsky, Nozick, Harman, Wiggins, Kripke, T. Clarke, Parfit, Scanlon and R. Dworkin. *Appts:* Taught at Berkeley, 1963–6, Princeton, 1966–72; Professor of Philosophy, Princeton, 1972–80; Professor of Philosophy, New York University, from 1980; Visiting Professor, Oxford, 1990.

Main publications:

(1965) 'Physicalism', *Philosophical Review*.

(1970) *The Possibility of Altruism*, Oxford: Clarendon.

(1971) 'Brain bisection and the unity of consciousness', *Synthèse*; reprinted in *Mortal Questions* (1979) (largely responsible for putting this topic on the philosophical map).

(1974) 'What is it like to be a bat?', *Philosophical Review*; reprinted in *Mortal Questions* (1979) (probably his most influential publication).

(1974) (ed. with V. Held and S. Morgenbesser) *Philosophy, Morality, and International Affairs*, New York: Oxford University Press.

(1979) *Mortal Questions*, Cambridge: Cambridge University Press (includes two new pieces, on 'Pansychism' and 'Subjective and objective').

(1980) 'The limits of objectivity', in S. McMurrin (ed.), *The Tanner Lectures on Human Values*, vol. 1, Salt Lake City, UT: Utah University Press (three lectures given at Brasenose College, Oxford, 1969, and included with others in the volume).

(1980) (ed. with M. Cohen and T. Scanlon) *Marx, Justice, and History*, Princeton, NJ: Princeton University Press.

(1986) *The View from Nowhere*, New York and Oxford: Oxford University Press.

(1987) *What Does It All Mean? A Very Short Introduction to Philosophy*, New York: Oxford University Press.

(1991) *Equality and Partiality*, Oxford: Oxford University Press.

Secondary literature:

Carlson, G. R. (1990) 'Pain and the quantum leap to agent-neutral value', *Ethics*.

Kraut, R. (1972) 'The rationality of prudence', *Philosophical Review*.

Lycan, W. G. (1987) *Consciousness*, Cambridge, Mass.: MIT Press (see chapter 7, note 4, for further references).

McCulloch, G. (1988) 'What it is like', *Philosophical Quarterly*.

Malcolm, N. (1988) 'Subjectivity', *Philosophy*.

Pugmire, D. (1989) 'Bat or Batman?', *Philosophy*.

Robins, M. H. (1988) 'The objectivity of agent-relative values', in S. H. Lee (ed.), *Inquiries into Values*, Lewistown, NY: Edwin Mullen Press.

Smith, Q. (1991) 'Concerning the absurdity of life', *Philosophy*.

Sturgeon, N. L. (1974) 'Altruism, solipsism, and the objectivity of reasons', *Philosophical Review*.

Vannoy, R. (1980) *Sex without Love: A Philosophical Exploration*, Buffalo, NY: Prometheus.

Nagel's work spans and connects two main areas, ethics and philosophy of mind. *The Possibility of Altruism* (1970) has 'possibility' in its title because not everyone is altruistic (pp. 145–6), but could as well be called 'The Rationality of Altruism'. Starting from the claim that reasons for actions are not limited to present desires, except in the trivial sense that any principle of action can be regarded as a desire *qua* leading to action, he argues that prudence, the concern for oneself, as a temporal continuant, at other times, implies that practical judgements must be 'assimilable to the standpoint of temporal neutrality ' (p. 71). To accept such a judgement is to accept a justification for what to do, not just for a *belief* about what one *should* do (pp. 65, 109). This is applied to defend rationally prudence over times and then, controversially, altruism over persons.

The View from Nowhere (1986) explores further the nature of the self, favouring a dual aspect view while rejecting all forms of reductionism, including physicalism—despite his earlier reluctant acceptance of physicalism (1965), but the change may be largely verbal. The self must be what underlies experience (1986, pp. 38, 44) and may well be the brain (p. 40), but it is the 'subjective mental properties' that must not be reducible (pp. 39–40, 48; cf. the article of 1974). The distinctive core of the work then attempts to reconcile two fundamentally different ways, subjective and objective, in which we view the world in answer to questions like 'what makes just one of billions of conscious selves me?', 'Why am I the particular person I am?', 'How, while being a conscious centre, can I conceive of the world as centreless, though containing me?' His answer (chapter 4, SS3) is that each of us is not just a centre of experiences but is also an 'objective self' which has to think of itself 'as the world soul in humble disguise'. This objective self is not a separate entity but an aspect of oneself that is the subject of an 'impersonal conception of the world ... attached to and developed from the perspective of' the person one is. These ideas are then applied in balanced discussions, from a generally realist standpoint, of values and duties and their mutual relations, among other topics, and in *Equality and Partiality* (1991) of political issues. Discussions have focused especially on the relevance of chapter 9 of *The View from Nowhere* for the double effect doctrine, and on altruism, the 1974 article, and physicalism.

Sources: PI; DAS, 7th edn, 4, 1978; personal communication.

A. R. LACEY

Nagib Mahmud, Zaki

Egyptian. *b:* 1905, near Damietta, Egypt. *d:* 9 September 1993. *Cat:* Logical positivist; theoretical philosopher. *Educ:* University of London, PhD 1947. *Appts:* Member of the editorial staff of many magazines; Professor of Philosophy, University of Kuwait.

Main publications:

(1953) *Khurafat al-Mitafiziqiyyah* [Superstitions of Metaphysics].
(1963) *Falsafah wa Fann* [Philosophy and Art].
(1967) *Wujhat Nazar* [The Standpoint of Speculation].
(1971) *Tagdid al-Fikr al-Arabi* [The Renewal of Arabic Thought].

Secondary literature:

Khoury, P. (1984) *Tradition et modernité*, Paris (contains critical references to his ideas).

Nagib Mahmud argued for the adequacy of sensible knowledge and scientific language for describing the external world. He argued that metaphysics is a myth because it is not able to give reliable answers to factual questions. He held that when philosophy is concerned with politics, education, and humanism in general, it is grounded on 'hypothesis': any thinker is free to choose the principles on which he raises his theories. Since contemporary reality is characterized by continuous change and ancient authors' assumptions are inconsistent with modernity, he favoured a reconciliation between rationalism and some of the methodological views of past thinkers such as the Mutazilites. Revival of Arabic thought needs a critical analysis of tradition; speculation must be independent of political considerations. Reason has the task of organizing the outside world from a practical (namely 'tactical') point of view, while religion must fuel the 'strategy' of renewal from an ideal point of view.

Sources: Chartier, M. (1973) 'La Rencontre Orient–Occident dans la pensée de trois philosophes egyptiens contemporaines: Hasan Hanafi, Fu'ad Zakariyya, Zaki Nagib Mahmud', in *Oriente Moderno*.

MASSIMO CAMPANINI

Nancy, Jean-Luc

French. *b:* 26 July 1940, Caudéran, Gironde, Bordeaux. *Cat:* Poststructuralist. *Ints:* History of modern philosophy; literature; aesthetics; politics; psychoanalysis; German romanticism. *Educ:* Lycée Français Charles-de-Gaulle in Baden-Baden; Lycée Louis-le-Grand, Paris; Lycée Lakanal, Sceaux; Université de Paris (Agrégé de philosophie, Doctorat d'État). *Infls:* Kant, Hegel, Nietzsche, Heidegger and Derrida. *Appts:* Maître assistant, then Maître de conférences, Université des Sciences Humaines de Strasbourg, since 1972; Chargé de cours, University of Berlin (German Federal Republic), 1973–4 and 1980–3; Chargé de conférences, École Normale Supérieure, since 1971; Visiting Professor, University of California at San Diego, 1985–7; member of the Groupe de recherche sur les théories du signe et du texte, University of Strasbourg; member of the Groupe de recherches politiques de la philosophie, École Normale Supérieure; formally a member of GREPH.

Main publications:

(1973) (with Philippe Lacoue-Labarthe) *Le Titre de la lettre*, Paris, Galilée (essays on Lacan).

(1973) *La Remarque speculative (un bon mot de Hegel)*, Paris: Galilée.

(1976) *Le Discourse de la syncope*, Paris: Aubier-Flammarion.

(1978) (with Philippe Lacoue-Labarthe) *L'Absolu littéraire*, Paris: Seuil (English translation, *The Literary Absolute*, trans., intro. and additional notes Philip Barnard and Cheryl Lester, Albany: SUNY Press, 1988).

(1979) *Ego Sum*, Paris: Flammarion.

(1981) (with Philippe Lacoue-Labarthe) *Les Fins de l'homme*, Paris: Galilée (essays on Derrida).

(1982) *Le Partage des voix*, Paris: Galilée.

(1983) *L'Imperatif catégorique*, Paris: Flammarion.

(1986) *L'Oubli de la philosophie*, Paris: Galilée.

(1986) *La Communauté désoeuvrée*, Paris: C. Bourgois (English translation, *The Inoperative Community*, trans. Peter Connor *et al.*, ed. Peter Connor, foreword Christopher Fynsk, Minneapolis: University of Minnesota Press, 1991).

(1987) *Des Lieux divins*, Mauvezin: Trans-Europ-Repress.

(1988) *L'Expérience de la liberté*, Paris: Galilée.

(1990) *Une pensée finie*, Paris: Galilée.

(1991) *Le poids d'une pensée*, Quebec: Editions Le Griffon d'argile.

(1993) *Le sens du monde*, Paris: Galilée.

(1994) *Les muses*, Paris: Galilée.

Secondary literature:
Translators' preface to the English translation of *L'Absolu littéraire*.

Nancy is a member of the influential groups of French philosophers (including Philippe **Lacoue-Labarthe**, Jean-François **Lyotard** and Jacques **Derrida**) whose project has been to interpret the works of Kant, Hegel, **Nietzsche** and **Heidegger** through a constant reference to the social and historical events of this century. His collaboration with Lacoue-Labarthe in *L'Absolu littéraire* is a seminal work on German romanticism which shows how key poststructuralist moves can be traced back to the work of Schelling and Novalis. Nancy is a key figure in the development of critical readings of deconstruction and the works of Jacques Derrida (see *Les Fins de l'homme*, 1981). In his later works (1988, 1990) Nancy reflects upon the sense of existence (as finitude, liberty, love and death) through a reading of the philosophical tradition in the context of historical and existential events.

JAMES WILLIAMS

Nasr, S(eyyed) Hossein
Iranian. *b:* April 1933, Tehran. *Cat:* Islamic philosopher; philosopher of religion, especially mysticism; historian of science. *Ints:* Shiite philosophy; mysticism. *Educ:* Early education in Tehran; studied Physics and Mathematics at MIT; MA and PhD on Islamic science, Harvard University. *Infls:* Corbin, Schuon, Mulla Sadra, Avicenna and Shiite thinkers. *Appts:* Professor at Harvard, Tehran, American University of Beirut, Princeton, Utah, Temple, and George Washington University; Dean, later Vice Chancellor, Tehran University and Chancellor, Aryamehr University; Founder and First President, Iranian Academy of Philosophy.

Main publications:
(1964) *Three Muslim Sages*, Cambridge, Mass.

(1968) *Science and Civilization in Islam*, Cambridge, Mass.

(1978) *Introduction to Islamic Cosmological Doctrines*, Boulder.

(1981) *Knowledge and the Sacred*, Edinburgh.

(1985) *Sufi Essays*, Albany: SUNY Press.

(1987) *Traditional Islam in the Modern World*, London: Routledge.

Nasr is a very prolific writer on both modern and traditional Islamic philosophy, and his training in modern Western philosophy has not prevented him from seeing the significance of *ishraqi* (illuminationist) thought. A particularly important contribution which he made to modern Iranian intellectual life was its introduction to more traditional forms of Islamic philosophy in such a way as to show its relevance. He has done much to popularize Suhrawardi's philosophy, and especially his Persian mystical narratives. Nasr has dealt with a wide range of topics, ranging from humanity and nature to cosmology, aesthetics and metaphysics. Many of his works undertake to provide a specifically Islamic response to the challenges of modernity. In general, he argues that the spiritual poverty of the West is explained through its secularization of knowledge and the loss of contact with the sacred. The identification of knowledge with scientific knowledge in a narrow sense has led the springs of sacred knowledge to dry up, and it is now necessary to turn to the East for spiritual refreshment.

Nasr regards metaphysics as the basis of Islamic philosophy, and both ontology and science are linked to a notion of pure being as the origin of existence. Religious law represents the practical side of that existence, and the Qur'an itself has to be related to the inner meaning of the aims of humanity which lie in the nature of being. Like Schuon and Corbin, Nasr sees philosophy in the Islamic world continuing after Averroes in the Shiite world through the influence of Suhrawardi and Sabzawari, with a continuing development of neo-Platonic ideas and Islamic insights into the nature of spiritual harmony and perennial philosophy which represent the progress of wisdom. This sort of wisdom is common to a variety of religions, but is perhaps most clearly portrayed in mystical and Sufi forms of thought. By showing how these disparate forms of expression are linked with more modern types of philosophy Nasr has gone a long way towards reconciling twentieth-century philosophy with earlier philosophical approaches in the Islamic world. He has not only influenced contemporary philosophy through his publications, but has been active in organizing conferences and academic institutions for the pursuit of Islamic philosophy. These have had a considerable impact in the Islamic world.

Sources: Personal communication.

OLIVER LEAMAN

Natorp, Paul

German. **b:** 24 January 1854, Düsseldorf. **d:** 17 August 1924, Marburg, Germany. **Cat:** Neo-Kantian (Marburg School); historian of philosophy; metaphysician; pedagogue. **Educ:** Classics and History at Bonn and Berlin. **Infls:** Hermann Cohen. **Appts:** Professor of Philosophy and Pedagogy, Marburg, from 1885.

Main publications:

(1882) *Descartes' Erkenntnistheorie*, Marburg: El-wert.
(1884) *Forschungen zur Geschichte des Erkenntnis-problems im Altertum*, Berlin: Hertz.
(1889) *Sozialpädagogik*, Stuttgart: Frommann.
(1903) *Platos Ideenlehre. Eine Einführung in den Idealismus*, Leipzig: Felix Meiner.
(1909) *Pestalozzi. Sein Werk und seine Ideen*, Stuttgart: Teubner.
(1910) *Die logischen Grundlagen der exakten Naturwissenschaft*, Stuttgart: Teubner.
(1911) *Die Philosophie. Ihr Problem und ihre Probleme*, Göttingen: Vandenhoeck & Ruprecht.
(1912) *Allgemeine Psychologie nach kritischer Methode*, Freiburg: J. C. B. Mohr.
(1958) *Philosophische Systematik*, Hamburg: Meiner.

Secondary literature:

Cassirer, E. (1925) 'Paul Natorp', *Kant-Studien* 30: 276–77.
Gadamer, Hans-Georg (1954–5) 'Die philosophische Bedeutung Paul Natorps', *Kant-Studien* 46: 129–34.
Holzhey, Helmut (1986) *Cohen und Natorp*, 2 vols, Basel and Stuttgart: Schwabe & Co.

Marx, W. (1964) 'Die philosophische Entwicklung Paul Natorps im Hinblick auf das System H. Cohens', *Zeitschrift für philosophische Forschung* 18: 486–500.

Ruhloff, J. (1966) 'Paul Natorps Grundlegung der Pädagogik', Freiburg (dissertation).

Saltzman, J. D. (1981) *Paul Natorp's Philosophy of Religion within the Marburg Neo-Kantian Tradition*, Hildesheim: Olms.

In his earlier works Natorp followed Hermann **Cohen**'s conception of philosophy, arguing that each philosophical discipline must be systematically grounded in an actual science or practice. However, Natorp was more interested in pedagogical theory than in jurisprudence. Accordingly, he had a tendency to de-emphasize the formal rules of the moral law, and to emphasize the moral education of individuals. Following Pestalozzi, he developed a socialist conception of education (*Sozialpädagogik*) that was based on the premise that education is always social education. Education prepares human beings for life in their community. This community is not just one of individuals externally related to one another by laws, but a truly moral community. Natorp meant to develop a critique of pedagogical reason that would analyse the conditions of the possibility of education. This theory of education transformed Kantian individualism into a form of communitarianism in which the 'organic' community assumed a life of its own. In fact, the truly 'concrete' in his theory is not the individual but the community. Although this community was at first not understood in terms of historical or ethnic association, it was, to a considerable degree, his theory of community that led him to a 'metaphysics of the German essence' and other nationalist excesses in 1914. Natorp's late philosophy constituted a move away from neo-Kantian philosophy and towards a metaphysical theory of the spirit. In moving away from Kant, he went 'back to Hegel', thus reversing the original neo-Kantian move. Natorp was one of the most important members of the Marburg School of neo-Kantianism. His writings were instrumental in spreading the views of the Marburg School to the wider public. He also influenced Edmund **Husserl** in his critique of psychologism. Such thinkers as Heinz **Heimsoeth** were also influenced by Natorp in their metaphysical interpretation of Kant, and they remained much closer to Natorp than they themselves were willing to admit.

MANFRED KUEHN

Nédoncelle, Maurice

French. *b:* 30 October 1905, Roubaix, Nord, France. *d:* 1976, Strasbourg. *Cat:* 'Personalist' philosopher. *Ints:* Philosophy of religion; aesthetics. *Educ:* Seminary Saint-Sulpice and the Sorbonne. *Infls:* John Henry Cardinal Newman, Baron von Hügel and Maine de Biran. *Appts:* Taught philosophy and theology, Nogent-sur-Marne, 1930–45; Professor of Theology and Dean, Université des Sciences Humaines de Strasbourg, 1945–76.

Main publications:

(1935) *La Pensée religieuse de Friedrich von Hügel*, Paris: Vrin.
(1942) *La Réciprocité des consciences*, Paris: Aubier.
(1943) *La Personne humaine et la nature*, Paris: PUF.
(1946) *La Philosophie religieuse de Newman*, Strasbourg: Sostrable.
(1957) *Vers une philosophie de l'amour et de la personne*, Paris: Aubier.
(1961) *Conscience et Logos. Horizons et méthode d'une philosophie personnaliste*, Paris: L'Epi.
(1970) *Le Chrétien appartient à deux mondes*, Paris: Centurion.
(1974) *Intersubjectivité et ontologie. Le défi personnaliste*, Paris: Nauwelaerts.

Secondary literature:

Liddle, V. T. (1966) 'The personalism of Maurice Nédoncelle', *Philosophical Studies*: 112–30.

Nédoncelle was a leading Catholic exponent of a type of philosophy called 'personalism', a philosophy that does not simply uphold the value of personality but contends that personal life is the active ground of the world, that the key to the problems of philosophy is found in personality and, furthermore, that reality consists of a system of persons related through God as the supreme Person. His philosophy was also much inspired by the works of Cardinal Newman and Baron von **Hügel**. Like von Hügel, he attached importance to the direct mystical apprehension of God but, also like von Hügel, he insisted on the divine transcendence.

Nédoncelle contended that the human personality 'creates itself' (*créateur de soi par soi*); but each individual person can only truly develop in unifying his or her relation with every other and with God and it is the Christ, the God–Man, who unifies our relation with God and others. Nédoncelle's personalism was that rare thing, a rigorous philosophy inspired by a devotional spirit. It represents an important strand of Catholic religious philosophy in the twentieth century, influential not only in France but also in Italy and Germany.

Sources: Huisman; EF.

STEPHEN MOLLER

Nelson, Leonard

German. *b:* 11 July 1883, Berlin. *d:* 29 November 1927, Göttingen, Germany. *Cat:* Neo-Kantian (neo-Friesian); metaphysician; moral philosopher. *Educ:* Göttingen University. *Appts:* Professor at Göttingen.

Main publications:

(1905) *Jakob Fries und seine Kritiker* (Abhandlungen der Fries'schen Schule. Neue Folge. Bd. 1, Heft 2), Göttingen: Vandenhoeck & Ruprecht, pp. 233–319.
(1908) *Über das sogenannte Erkenntnisproblem* (Abhandlungen der Fries'schen Schule. Neue Folge. Bd. 2, Heft 4), Göttingen: Vandenhoeck & Ruprecht, pp. 413–818.
(1911) *Die Unmöglichkeit der Erkenntnistheorie*, Göttingen: Vandenhoek & Ruprecht.
(1917) *Über die Grundlagen der Ethik*, vol. I, *Kritik der praktischen Vernunft*, Leipzig: Veit.
(1923) *System der philosophischen Rechtslehre und Politik*, Frankfurt/Main: Verlag öffentliches Leben.
(1948) *Drei Schriften zur kritischen Philosophie* Wolfenbüttel: Wolfenbütteler Verlagsanstalt.
(1959) *Beiträge zur Philosophie der Logik und Mathematik*, Hamburg: Meiner. (1962) *Fortschritte und Rückschritte in der Philosophie, von Hume und Kant bis Hegel und Fries*, Frankfurt/Main: Verlag öffentliches Leben.
Translations include:
——(1956) *System of Ethics*, New Haven: Yale University Press.
——(1965) *Socratic Method and Critical Philosophy; Selected Essays*, New York: Dover Publications (originally published 1949).
——(1970) *Critique of Practical Reason*, Scarsdale, NY: Leonard Nelson Foundation (originally published 1957).
——(1970) *Progress and Regress in Philosophy: From Hume and Kant to Hegel and Fries*, Oxford: Blackwell.

Secondary literature:

Falkenfeld, Hellmuth (1928) 'Leonard Nelson', *Kant-Studien* 33: 247–55.
Specht, M. and Eichler, M. (1954) *Leonard Nelson zum Gedächtnis*, Frankfurt am Main.
Westermann, C. (1969) *Recht und Pflicht bei Leonard Nelson*, Bonn: Bouvier.

Nelson was the founder of the so-called 'neo-Friesian' school. The members of this school based their approach on the thought of Jakob Friedrich Fries (1773–1843), who himself had advocated a positivistic philosophy that followed Kant, Jacobi, Schleiermacher and Ernst Platner. Nelson saw Fries as having solved Hume's problem, and thus as having perfected Kant's philosophy. His attempt to make Reinhold relevant again for the philosophical discussion of the day therefore also meant a return to Kant. Nelson believed that 'every important dispute in philosophy is a dispute about principles'. He argued that Kantian epistemology cannot provide sufficient conditions for the objective validity of our knowledge. It can only supply necessary conditions for it, and it must thus be supplemented by another approach. Nelson called this approach 'deduction', and he understood by it a descriptive psychological theory of reason. Arguing that our perceptual judgements are not only based on logical principles, but also on sensations that are immediately evident, he claimed that it was these sensations that are most basic for determining the objective validity of judgements. Since epistemology was an attempt to find a criterion for the objective validity of judgements that itself constituted a judgement, it was, he felt, an enterprise doomed from the start. Metaphysics, though not based on psychological description, must be preceded by it. The psychological deduction does not prove the basic philosophical principles, but it determines what they are. Indeed he argued that in so far as these principles are truly basic they cannot possible be proved. Just as Nelson's metaphysics proceeded by descriptive analysis, so his moral philosophy started from psychological observation. Nelson argued that our moral feeling proves that we have duties. The content of these duties was determined through another 'deduction', which was meant to determine 'the interests of pure practical reason'. He found two principles, namely (i) the categorical imperative, or the principle of balanced consideration of all interests, which stated that one should never 'act in such a way that you could not agree to your way of acting if the interests of those affected were also your own', and (ii) the principle of rational self-determination that states that everyone should pursue his own ends independently and in accordance with the true, the good, and the beautiful. He thought that there was no tension between these two principles, if the true interests of humanity were understood.

Nelson's theory, like that of Fries before him, was often accused of 'psychologism', and it remained rather controversial. However, it is not always clear whether these criticisms were motivated by philosophical or by political reasons, for Nelson was also very active in the Social Democratic movement. He not only openly advocated socialism as the best way to transform the unfair political system of Germany into a fair and just society, but he founded such political organizations as the 'Internationale Sozialistische Kampfbund'. His demands for reform extended to animal rights. Indeed he argued that the slaughter of animals constituted a form of exploitation that stood in the way of the development of a society without exploitation.

MANFRED KUEHN

Neumann, John von

Hungarian-American. **b:** 28 December 1903, Budapest. **d:** 8 February 1957, Washington, DC. **Cat:** Mathematician. **Ints:** Mathematical logic; foundations of quantum theory; game theory; computers. **Educ:** 1921–3, Universities of Budapest and Berlin; 1923–5, Federal Institute of Technology, Zurich; 1926, PhD, University of Budapest. **Infls:** David Hilbert. **Appts:** 1926–7, Rockefeller Fellow, University of Göttingen; 1927–9, Privatdozent, Berlin University; 1929–30, University of Hamburg; 1930–3, Professor of Mathematics, Princeton University; 1933–57, Professor, Institute for Advanced Study, Princeton University.

Main publications:

(1928) 'Die Axiomatisierung der Mengenlehre', *Mathematische Zeitschrift* 27: 669–752.
(1932) *Mathematische Grundlagen der Quantenmechanik*, Berlin: Springer (English translation, *Mathematical Foundations of Quantum Mechanics*, Princeton: Princeton University Press, 1955).
(1936) (with G. Birkhoff) 'The logic of quantum mechanics', *Annals of Mathematics* 37: 823–43.
(1944) (with O. Morgenstern) *Theory of Games and Economic Behavior*, Princeton: Princeton University Press.
(1958) *The Computer and the Brain*, New Haven: Yale University Press.
(1987) 'First draft of a report on the EDVAC', in W. Aspray and A. Burks (eds), *Papers of John von Neumann on Computing and Computer Theory*, Cambridge, Mass.: MIT Press.

Secondary literature:

Aspray, W. (1990) *John von Neumann and the Origins of Modern Computing*, Cambridge, Mass.: MIT Press.

Hughes, R. (1989) *The Structure and Interpretation of Quantum Mechanics*, Cambridge, Mass.: Harvard University Press.

Luce, R. D. and Raiffa, H. *Games and Decisions*, New York: John Wiley.

Quine, W. (1969) *Set Theory and Its Logic*, revised edition, Cambridge, Mass.: Harvard University Press.

Von Neumann's early work was in the foundations of mathematics. He provided the first finite axiomatization of set theory in a paper based on his doctoral dissertation. After losing confidence in **Hilbert**'s programme due to **Gödel**'s results, von Neumann returned to the mathematical foundations of quantum theory. In *Mathematical Foundations* (1932) he provides an abstract formalism that unites the **Schrödinger** and **Heisenberg** representations. His work with Birkhoff led to research in quantum logic that was highly influential for three decades. His next venture was into economics, where his book with Morgenstern, *Theory of Games and Economic Behavior* (1944), was the first rigorous presentation of game theory. The last part of his life was devoted to computers. His 'first draft' paper (1987) was the first to lay out the design of a stored programme computer, and he was instrumental in setting up two of the first operational general-purpose computers, ENIAC and EDVAC, at the University of Pennsylvania. Von Neumann's work in logic has become part of the standard literature (see **Quine** 1969). His foundational work in quantum theory serves as the basis for most contemporary work.

Sources: *Collected Papers* (1961), vols 1–6, New York: Pergamon Press.

PAUL HUMPHREYS

Neurath, Otto

Austrian. ***b:*** 10 December 1882, Vienna. ***d:*** 22 December 1945, Oxford. ***Cat:*** Logical positivist; physicalist. ***Ints:*** Theory of knowledge; philosophical method; social philosophy. ***Educ:*** Vienna and Berlin Universities. ***Infls:*** Marx. ***Appts:*** Director, Social and Economic Museum, Vienna, 1924–34.

Main publications:

(1921) *Anti-Spengler*, Munich: Callwey.
(1930) *Modern Man in the Making*, New York: Knopf.
(1931) *Empirische Soziologie*, Vienna: Springer.
(1944) *Foundations of the Social Sciences*, Chicago: University of Chicago Press.

(1973) *Empiricism and Sociology*, Dordrecht: Reidel.
(1983) *Philosophical Papers*, Dordrecht: Reidel.

Secondary literature:

Neurath, M. and Cohen, R. S. (eds) (1973) *Empiricism and Sociology*, Dordrecht: Reidel, chapter 1.

Otto Neurath had a considerably more colourful life than most philosophers. From an early age he was independent-minded to the point of eccentricity, noisy, red-bearded and combative. His philosophical writings are almost entirely confined to the 1930s. His first serious post was as professor of political economy at the Vienna Academy of Commerce. After the war, until his flight from Austria to Holland in 1934, he founded and directed socio-economic museums in Vienna. For the rest of his life he lived from hand to mouth, marketing his method of visual education through diagrams ('isotypes'). In between he had, in the chaos of postwar Bavaria, been head of central planning for the socialist government and for the brief communist government which succeeded it, and had narrowly escaped execution. His early writings were largely on economics, apart from some articles on logic, written with his second wife, the sister of Hans Hahn, and a history of the science of optics. Within the group of philosophers and philosophically-minded scientists around **Schlick** he was the chief impresario. He brought them together as the Vienna Circle and founded the periodical *Erkenntnis*, in which their views were expounded. He was the most fiercely antimetaphysical member of the Circle, hostile to the mysticism of **Wittgenstein**'s *Tractatus*. Schlick had been converted from his initial realism to phenomenalism by his exposure to Wittgenstein and **Carnap**'s *Aufbau* which reconstituted the world on a phenomenalistic basis. Neurath, along with **Popper**, converted Carnap to the view that the basis of empirical knowledge is beliefs about material objects. Also in agreement with Popper, Neurath took all empirical knowledge to be problematic and fallible, but he rejected Popper's falsification theory as a piece of pseudo-rationalism. In his view all sciences were really one and that one science was physics: the central platform of physicalism and the movement associated with it of 'unified science'. The foundation of this point of view was Neurath's conviction that science is inescapably intersubjective, a social product, not the hidden property of a host of individual consciousnesses. His own work in sociology was presented as a concrete example of the unified science he favoured (one hardly likes to say 'had in mind'). Sociology in his conception is the inheritor of history and political economy and concerns the observable behaviour of entities in space and time. His persisting respect for Marx leads him to credit him with very much that doctrine. Generally, for all his devotion to science, Neurath was not a determinist. The future is not fixed: we have to choose and the better our science the more our choices will secure us what we want. That outlook was passionately expressed in his early critique of the fatalistic mumbo-jumbo of **Spengler**. Neurath's influence was largely exercised, by way of personal contact, on his contemporaries. His writings have proved less impressive than his powerful personality.

Sources: Passmore 1957; V. Kraft (1953) *The Vienna Circle*, New York: Philosophical Library.

ANTHONY QUINTON

Nicol, Eduardo

Mexican. **b:** 18 December 1907, Barcelona. **d:** 1991, Mexico City. **Cat:** Metaphysician. **Educ:** Studied at the University of Barcelona and the National Autonomous University of Mexico. **Infls:** Vasconcelos. **Appts:** 1940–, Professor of Philosophy, National Autonomous University of Mexico.

Main publications:

(1941) *Psicología de las situaciones vitales*, Mexico: Colegio de México.
(1946) *La idea del hombre*, Mexico: Editorial Stylo.
(1953) *La vocación humana*, Mexico: Colegio de México.
(1957) *Metafisca de la expresión*, second edition, 1977.
(1961) *El problema de la filosofía hispánica*, Madrid: Editorial Tecnos.
(1980) *La reforma de la filosofía*, Mexico: Fondo de Cultura Económica.
(1982) *Crítica de la razón simbólica*, Mexico: Fondo de Cultura Económica.
(1985) *El porvenir de la filosofía*, Mexico: Fondo de Cultura Económica (first edition 1972).

Secondary literature:

González, Juliana and Sagols, Lizbeth (eds) (1990) *El ser y la expresión: homenaje a Eduardo Nicol*, Mexico: Universidad Nacional Autónoma de México.

Nicol was one of a group of Spanish philosophers exiled after the fall of Republican Spain who went to Mexico. He founded two philosophical journals, *Filosofía y letras* (1941) and *Diánoia* (1954).

With Eduardo García Maynez, Nicol founded the Centro de Estudios Filosóficos (today called the Instituto de Investigaciones Filosóficas) at the Universidad Nacional Autónoma de México. He was named Doctor *honoris causa* by the University of Barcelona in 1984. In his book of 1961, Nicol identified a paradox in José **Vasconcelos**'s concept of the 'cosmic race' by noting that *indigenismo* and negritude are racial concepts put forth as worthy of special attention at the same time as Vasconcelos holds the ideal of purging racial consciousness from society.

AMY A. OLIVER

Niebuhr, Helmut Richard

American. **b:** 3 September 1894, Wright City, Missouri. **d:** 5 July 1962, Greenfield, Massachusetts. **Cat:** Theologian. **Educ:** Elmhurst College; Eden Theological Seminary, Washington University, St Louis; University of Chicago; Yale Divinity School. **Infls:** George Herbert Mead, Karl Barth and Paul Tillich. **Appts:** Eden Theological Seminary, 1919–21 and 1927–31; Yale Divinity School, 1938–62.

Main publications:

(1929) *Moral Relativism and the Christian Ethic*, New York: Holt.
(1929) *The Social Sources of Denominationalism*, New York: Holt.
(1937) *The Kingdom of God in America*, New York: W. Hett, Clark & Co.
(1941) *The Meaning of Revelation*, New York: Macmillan.
(1951) *Christ and Culture*, New York: Harper.
(1960) *Radical Monotheism and Western Culture*, Lincoln: University of Nebraska.
(1963) *The Responsible Self: An Essay in Christian Moral Philosophy*, New York: Harper & Row.

Secondary literature:

Fadner, Donald E. (1975) *The Responsible God: A Study of the Christian Philosophy of H. Richard Neibuhr*, Missoula: Scholar's Press.

An ordained Evangelical and Reformed minster (United Church of Christ following a 1959 merger), Neibuhr combined an early interest in sociology, pragmatism and the social gospel with the existential absoluteness of neo-Orthodoxy. In consequence he held that humans, although standing within the relativities of history, are able to encounter an absolute God. Moral relativism is countered by the view that our responsibility is not to the good or the right but to something more

existentially tailored, which he called the 'fitting response' to God. In that response the world moves closer to the kingdom of God.
Sources: DAB.

WILLIAM REESE

Niebuhr, Reinhold

American. *b:* 21 June 1892, Wright City, Missouri. *d:* 1 June 1971, Stockbridge, Massachusetts. *Cat:* Neo-Orthodox social theorist and theologian. *Ints:* Ethics; political philosophy. *Educ:* Elmhurst College, Illinois; Eden Theological Seminary, St Louis; Yale University. *Infls:* Karl Barth. *Appts:* Union Theological Seminary (NYC), 1928–60, where he was first Associate Professor of Philosophy of Religion, and then Professor of Applied Christianity, and Ethics and Theology.

Main publications:

(1932) *Moral Man and Immoral Society*, New York: Scribner's.
(1935) *An Interpretation of Christian Ethics*, New York: Harper & Row.
(1937) *Beyond Tragedy: Essays on the Christian Interpretation of History*, New York: Scribner's; London: Nisbet & Co. Ltd.
(1940) *Christianity and Power Politics*, New York: Scribner's.
(1941, 1943) *The Nature and Destiny of Man*, 2 vols, New York: Scribner's (Gifford Lectures).
(1944) *The Children of Light and the Children of Darkness*, New York: Scribner's.
(1949) *Faith and History*, New York: Scribner's.
(1953) *Christian Realism and Political Problems*, New York: Scribner's.
(1958) *Pious and Secular America*, New York: Scribner's.

Secondary literature:

Harland, Gordon (1960) *The Thought of Reinhold Niebuhr*, New York: Oxford University Press.
Kegeley, Charles W. and Bretall, Robert W. (eds) (1956) *Reinhold Niebuhr: His Religious, Social and Political Thought*, New York: Macmillan (includes bibliography).
Scott Jr, Nathan A. (ed.) (1975) *The Legacy of Reinhold Niebuhr*, Chicago and London: University of Chicago Press.

The first two main emphases in Neibuhr's thought derives from his social conscience, the other from his religious sensibility. The social emphasis was actualized during his ministry in Detroit. As pastor to automobile workers he preached the Social Gospel, criticized the insensitivities of industrial management to the needs of workers, embraced pacificism and joined the Socialist party. He believed that moral progress is possible and, by implication, that the Kingdom of God can be brought forth on earth.

His religious sensibility, on the other hand, was evangelical, and presumed original sin and the relation of the soul to the transcendent God. As this emphasis came into play, he rejected the inevitability of human progress, adopted the position of 'Christian realism' and, although he did not consider himself to be a theologian, his writings helped to develop the Protestant theology of neo-Orthodoxy in which God is regarded as 'wholly other', human pride and egotism are the signs of man's fall, a demonic element suffuses all human actions and there are 'perennial moral contraindications on every level of human advance' (1938, p. 38). At the same time he felt that Karl **Barth**'s version of God's otherness gave no play to human moral responsibility. Niebuhr's mature view effects, or attempts, a balance between these two emphases, which may be viewed as two dimensions: one horizontal and in the stream of time; the other vertical, relating man to the divine. Horizontally, the self or soul is a member of society; vertically, it belongs to God. The horizontal ethic is social, committed to achieving justice. The vertical ethic is personal, committed to sacrificial love. Sin likewise has two dimensions. Its horizontal dimension is injustice. Its vertical dimension is the transcendent self's refusal to admit its creatureliness, i.e. its pride. The pride which makes a pretence of absoluteness is, on the horizontal level, the obstinate egotism leading to social injustice. Sin is finally resolved, on the vertical level, by divine mercy and forgiveness. Its resolution on the horizontal level is problematic.

We are required to engage in political activity because there are institutional changes which will do more in terms of moving towards the good society than any number of changes of heart. For example, social adjustment is needed within the framework of capitalism. But we must enter into such activity with the humility and sense of trust in God's mercy and forgiveness proper to the vertical dimension. Even so, our success on the horizontal level is necessarily partial and streaked with ambiguity. The incompatibilities of the two dimensions will be resolved only at the end of history.
Sources: Edwards; J. Bingham (1961) *Courage to Change: An Introduction to the Life and Thought of Reinhold Niebuhr*, New York: Scribner's.

WILLIAM REESE

Nielsen, Kai

Canadian (naturalized 1974). *b:* 15 May 1926, Marshall, Michigan. *Cat:* Analytic philosopher. *Ints:* Ethics; philosophy of religion; social philosophy. *Educ:* University of North Carolina and Duke University. *Appts:* 1955–7, Hamilton College; 1957–60, Amherst College, 1961–2, Harper College; 1962–70, New York University; 1970–, University of Calgary; 1975–6, City University of New York.

Main publications:

(1971) *Contemporary Critiques of Religion*, London: Macmillan.

(1973) *Ethics without God*, Buffalo: Prometheus; second edition, 1989.

(1973) *Scepticism*, London: Macmillan.

(1984) *Equality and Liberty: A Defense of Radical Egalitarianism*, Totoura, NJ: Bowman & Allenfield.

(1985) *Philosophy and Atheism*, Buffalo: Prometheus.

(1989) *God, Skepticism and Modernity*, Ottawa: University of Ottawa Press.

(1991) *After the Demise of the Tradition: Rorty, Political Theory and the Fate of Philosophy*, Boulder: Westview.

(1992) *God and the Grounding of Morality*, Ottawa: University of Ottawa Press.

(1995) *On Transforming Philosophy: A Metaphilosophical Inquiry*, Boulder: Westview.

Secondary literature:

Beehler, R., Copp, D. and Szabados, B. (eds) (1992) *On the Track of Reason: Essays in Honor of Kai Nielsen*, Boulder: Westview Press (contains bibliography extending into 1992).

Nielsen's thinking begins in ethics and extends at once to both social philosophy and philosophy of religion. His position in ethics is reminiscent of Hume, resting ultimately on moral sentiment. This 'subjective' foundation is modified by the fact that the discipline is 'rule-governed' and possesses an 'objective rationale'. In social philosophy the 'bedrock' ethical point of the unfairness in life prospects for some children is not subject to objective proof, yet it is that ethical point which commits him to a program of social equality, and to socialism. Once again, if religion were necessary for ethics, it would have a justification; but the cosmological frameworks of religious people are 'free spinning wheels', unrelated to their ethical commitments. Furthermore, religious statements are 'very, very close' to 'Ideology' statements, so close that nothing will

count for or against them. Having no function these free spinning wheels might as well be jettisoned, leaving the field to ethics.

WILLIAM REESE

Nietzsche, Friedrich

German. *b:* 15 October 1844, Rocken. *d:* 25 August 1900, Weimar, Germany. *Cat:* Post-Kantian philosopher. *Ints:* Ontology: epistemology; Greek and Christian thought; theory of values; nihilism; aesthetics; cultural theory. *Educ:* 1858–64, received a primarily classical education at the renowned Pforta school; after a brief spell at the University of Bonn, where he intended to study Philology and Theology, went to the University of Leipzig to study Philology under Ritschl. *Infls:* Ancient Greek thought, particularly Heraclitus, Plato and Socrates; Montaigne, Spinoza, Lichtenberg, La Rochefoucauld, Schopenhauer, Wagner, F. Lange, Kuno Fischer and Emerson. *Appts:* 1869–79, taught philosophy, University of Basel (increasing ill-health and disillusion with academic life prompted his resignation); 1879–, survived on a sparse pension, living ascetically and wandering restlessly, mainly between Sils Maria in the Ober-Engadine, Nice and Turin; 1889, collapsed, was taken back to Germany and died soon after.

Main publications:

The now authoratative edition of Nietzche's collected works is the *Nietzsche Werke: Kritische Gesamtansgabe* (KGW), 30 vols, ed. Giorgio Colli and Mazzino Montinari, Berlin: de Gruyter, 1967–78.

(1872) *Die Gebürt der Tragödie* (English translation, *The Birth of Tragedy*, trans. W. Kaufmann, New York: Viking Press, 1954).

(1873–6) *Unzeitgemässe Betrachtungen*; Bd I, *David Strauss, der Bekenner und Schriftsteller*, 1873; Bd 2, *Vom Nutzen und Nachteil der Historie für das Leben*, 1874; Bd 3, *Schopenhauer als Erzieher*, 1874; Bd 4, *Richard Wagner in Bayreuth*, 1876 (English translations, *Untimely Meditations*: no. 1, *David Strauss, the Confessor and Writer*; no. 2, *On the Uses and Disadvantages of History for Life*; no. 3, *Schopenhauer as Educator*; no. 4, *Richard Wagner in Bayreuth*, trans. R. J. Hollingdale, Cambridge: Cambridge University Press, 1983).

(1878–80) *Menschliches, Allzumenschliches*, Bd 1, 1878, Bd 2, *Vermischte Meinungen und Sprüche*, 1879, *Der Wanderer und sein Schatten*, 1880 (English translation, *Human All Too Human*, including 'Assorted maxims and opinions' and 'The wanderer and his shadow', trans. R. J.

Hollingdale, Cambridge: Cambridge University Press, 1986).

(1881) *Die Morgenröthe* (English translation, *Daybreak*, trans. R. J. Hollingdale, Cambridge: Cambridge University Press, 1982).

(1882) *Die fröhliche Wissenschaft*, Abt. V 343–83, 1887 (English translation, *The Gay Science*, trans. W. Kaufmann, New York: Vintage Press, 1974).

(1883–5) *Also sprach Zarathustra*, Abt. 1 & 2, 1883, Abt. 3, 1884, Abt. 4, 1885 (English translation, *Thus Spoke Zarathustra*, trans. R. J. Hollingdale, Harmondsworth: Penguin Classics, 1969).

(1886) *Jenseits von Gut und Böse* (English translation, *Beyond Good and Evil*, trans. W. Kaufmann, New York: Vintage Press, 1966).

(1887) *Zur Genealogie der Moral* (English translation, *On the Genealogy of Morals*, trans. W. Kaufmann and R. J. Hollingdale, New York: Vintage Press, 1968).

(1888) *Der Fall Wagner* (English translation, 'The case of Wagner', trans. W. Kaufmann, in *The Portable Nietzsche*, ed. W. Kaufmann, New York: Viking Press, 1954).

(1889) *Die Götzen-Dämmerung* (English translation, *The Twilight of the Idols*, trans. R. J. Hollingdale, Harmondsworth: Penguin Classics, 1968).

(1895) *Der Antichrist* (English translation, *The Anti-Christ*, trans. R. J. Hollingdale, Harmondsworth: Penguin Classics, 1968).

(1895) *Nietzsche contra Wagner* (English translation, *'Nietzsche against Wagner'*, trans. W. Kaufmann, in *The Portable Nietzsche*, ed. W. Kaufmann, New York: Viking Press, 1954*).

(1908) *Ecce Homo* (English translation, *Ecce Homo*, trans. W. Kaufmann, New York: Vintage Press, 1968).

Two of Nietzsche's important early essays, 'Philosophy in the tragic age of the Greeks' (1872–5) and 'Truth and lies in a nonmoral sense' (1873) appear in translation by D. Brezeale in *Philosophy and Truth: Selections from Nietzsche's Notebooks of the Early 1870s*, Atlantic Highlands, NJ: Humanities Press, 1979. A substantial quantity of Nietzsche's later, most philosophically provocative unpublished notes appear in the posthumous and ill-named collection *Der Wille zur Macht* (*Samtliche Werke*, Bd IX), edited by Baeumler, Stuttgart: Kröner, 1965 (English translation, *The Will to Power*, trans. W. Kaufmann and R. J. Hollingdale, London: Weidenfeld & Nicolson, 1969).

Secondary literature:

Allison, D. (ed.) (1977) *The New Nietzsche, Contemporary Styles of Interpretation*, New York: Dell Publishing Co.

Ansell Pearson, K. (1991) *Nietzsche and Modern German Philosophy*, London: Routledge.

Deleuze, G. (1983) *Nietzsche and Philosophy*, London: Althone Press.

Heidegger, M. (1979–82) *Nietzsche*, ed. and trans. D. Krell, 4 vols, New York: Harper Row.

Janz, Otto (1978) *Friederich Nietzsche*, 3 vols, Munich: Carl Hanser Verlag (probably the most reliable and scholarly biography).

Nehemas, A. (1985) *Nietzsche: Life as Literature*, Cambridge, Mass.: Harvard University Press.

Schacht, R. (1983) *Nietzsche*, London: Routledge.

Schrift, A. (1990) *Nietzsche and the Question of Interpretation*, London: Routledge.

The enigma of Friedrich Nietzsche, one of twentieth-century Europe's most influential philosophers, does not lie in the now well-documented politically motivated abuse of his writings by his sister Elizabeth Forster-Nietzsche but in the fact that his philosophy is simultaneously familiar and remote. The post-structuralist genealogical stratagems of Michel **Foucault** and **Derrida**'s dissolution of fixed meaning make Nietzsche's nihilism and perspectivism strangely familiar. Yet that familiarity is disconcerting, for Nietzsche's voice also speaks in the now unfamiliar philosophical languages of Schopenhauer, Lange, Spir and Teichmuller.

Nietzsche's notoriety rests upon such singular doctrines as the will to power, the eternal recurrence, nihilism and the announcement of God's death, iconoclastic expression, mastery of aphoristic form, and a deployment of contradiction and inconsistency which for many compromised his philosophical status. Nietzsche's reception is now an autonomous field of study and recent scholarship has come to question the 'received' view of him as an unorganized thinker, suggesting that his written *corpus* gains its coherence in its very plurality. His responses to nihilism and to art's relation to existence clearly vary but the questions to which his different responses are an answer are invariably the same.

Nietzsche's early university experiences set his lifelong philosophical preoccupations: first, interpreting Ancient Greek culture as a response to the existential problematic of finitude; second, pursuing the philosophical and cultural consequences of post-Kantian metaphysical scepticism; and third, maintaining intellectual integrity whatever the cost. His thought is an instance of a *Lebensphilosophie*: philosophy without experience is empty and experience without philosophy is blind. A combination of his knowledge of Greek thought, his discovery of Schopenhauer and a reading of the history of philosophy by Kuno Fischer established his primary philosophical *Leitmotifen*. First, reality is an endless Becoming (*Werden*). Second, as instrumentalist devices language and reason reflect the world not as it is but how our needs require us to perceive it. Third, within religion, ethical codes and scientific practice humanity has institutionalized its values, projected and mistaken them as aspects of being-in-itself. Fourth, the existential predicament is grasped as the imminent risk of having one's belief in reason as a criterion of truth and reality exploded by the unintelligibility of flux and of having, as a consequence, to stare into the presence of nihilism. And, fifth, there is the question of how one can live with a knowledge of the latter abyss. When read as a continuous response and reappraisal of thse *Leitmotifen*, the alleged inconsistencies of Nietzsche's thinking virtually vanish.

Artistenmetaphysik is the name Nietzsche gives to his first response to these *Leitmotifen* as expressed within *The Birth of Tragedy* (1872) and the *Untimely Meditations* (1873–6). Combining an assumed universal existential predicament with the hermeneutical axiom of looking at one's own through the eyes of the foreign, he contends that the relevance of Greek aesthetic practice lies in its transformation of the existential predicament without recourse to otherworldly metaphysics. The Dionysian arts of music and drama do so by ecstatically succumbing to flux, the Apollonian plastic arts by deliberately denying the actuality of becoming with the illusion of timeless beauty, and tragic drama by reconciling its audience to the horror of every open finitude with a closed and graspable image of it.

The *Artistenmetaphysik* is an inverted Platonism: metaphysical truth is vacuous whilst art as living within appearance is understood as the means of suppressing awareness of the futility of existence. Socratic reasoning is attacked for atrophying the aesthetic impulse. By positing the illusion of an intelligible world of Being, the desire to create a reality according to our needs is negated. Nietzsche was haunted by the question: what creative resources will European thought retain if the Socratic faith is rendered empty and nihilism looms?

The 'experimentalist' phase of Nietzsche's thinking—*Human All Too Human* (1878–80), *Daybreak* (1881) and *The Gay Science* (1882)—exposes the shortcomings of this aesthetic. As all illusions are temporary, Apollonian aesthetics can only exacerbate the existentialist predicament. The loss of its spell will make the return to Dionysian actuality even more painful. The *Artistenmetaphysik* entails a needlessly pessimistic view of becoming. Finitude *per se* is not the problem, but our evaluation of it. Accordingly, Nietzsche's *experimentalische Denken* criticizes religious and moral systems which alienate individuals from actuality by perpetrating the illusion of fixed truths. Art is condemned for beautifying such truths and extending their influence subsequent to the collapse of their supporting beliefs. Experimentalism quests for both historical and non-European exemplars of 'this-worldly' lifestyles which promote values affirming rather than denying the existential predicament. Yet this experimentalism requires what it criticizes, namely, the imaginative capacity to speculate about what is not seen but might be the case, an imaginative capacity which is condemned in art as capable of estranging one from actuality. In addressing this problem, *Thus Spoke Zarathustra* (1883–5) announces Nietzsche's final phase of thinking, which centres around the notions of the will to power, radical nihilism, perspectivism and the eternal recurrence. Within *Thus Spoke Zarathustra* notions of existential alienation, willing, becoming and creativity are fused into a unified monistic ontology in which artistic creativity becomes the transforming vehicle of mankind's being as a mode of becoming. Pain, suffering and contradiction are no longer seen as objections to existence but as an expression of its actual tensions. This does not rid the individual of his suffering but transforms his evaluation of it. In Nietzsche's thinking the importance of the creative individual lies in his being an embodiment of the life-transforming process which constitutes all becoming.

In subsequent writings, the will to power is developed into a Leibniz-like monadology without the latter's central organizing principle. Within this ontology of flux, inanimate and animate beings are presented as different densities of *Kraftzentren* (power centres) combining and interchanging for the sake of the greater power, i.e. unhindered activity. This account of becoming is the ground both of Nietzsche's repudiation of unchanging things and selves and of his affirmation of perspectivism: the world does not exist apart from the totality of perspectival interactions which make it up. This *Interpretationsphilosophie* operates both as critical hermeneutic and as an aesthetic prescription for the new *Weltanschauung*. If there is no absolute truth or ground, the question arises as to what values prompt a belief in their existence. The absence of meaning-in-itself is no cause for pessimism since it liberates us from the canons of culturally transmitted meaning to the end of creating our own purposes and values. The dynamic is that of having to overcome the need for received meaning (Nietzsche's definition of weakness) in order to take responsibility for legislating one's own (his definition of strength). The eternal recurrence gains its ethical force in this context for, as well as being a hypothesis about how within infinite time endless but numerical finite configurations of energy must repeat themselves, it also serves as an existential prohibition. Without taking on the creative responsibility for one's perspective one is eternally condemned to a repetition of the same disillusionment, as adopted faith after faith is broken within the vortex of the abyss. Art as the means of projecting meaning and value into existence thereby returns to pride of place within Nietzsche's analysis of the existential predicament. Despite the enormous impact of Nietzsche's thought upon European art and literature, his philosophical reception continues to be distorted by the ideological consequences of his sister's politically inspired editorial meddling and its strange legitimization by Marxist intellectuals desirous of perpetuating the myth of Nietzsche as a philosophical precursor of fascism. What is not in question, however, is that the piety of his metaphysical nihilism and his endeavour to contemplate existence without recourse to religious apologetics affects the direction of Heideggerian thought and, because of that, subsequently shapes French post-structuralism and deconstruction. In its account of disclosive meaning, hermeneutics now assumes what Nietzsche's aphoristic devices demonstrate. As words can communicate as clearly through the unsaid as through the said, the aphoristic rather than the systematic style is better suited to invoking the unstated realms of thought behind assertions. Nietzsche's major contribution to this sea-change in twentieth-century European philosophical sensibility is only now beginning to receive the acknowledgement it truly merits.

NICHOLAS DAVEY

Nishida, Kitaro

Japanese. *b:* 1870. *d:* 1945. *Cat:* Zen philosopher. *Infls:* Profoundly influenced by the Zen Buddhist canon, the negative theology of Nicholas of Cusa, French positivism, Bergson, William James, Fichte and Hegel. *Appts:* 1901, *koji* (lay Zen practitioner); Professor of Philosophy and Religion, former Imperial Kyoto University.

Main publications:

(1911) *An Inquiry into the Good* (English translation, M. Abe and C. Ives, New Haven, CT and London: Yale University Press, 1990).
(1915) *Thought and Experience*; extended in 1937.
(1917) *Intuition and Reflection in Self-consciousness* (English translation, V. H. Viglielmo, Y. Takeuchi and J. S. O'Leary, Albany: State University of New York Press, 1987).
(1923) *Art and Morality* (English translation, D. A. Dilworth and V. H. Viglielmo, Honolulu: University of Hawaii Press, 1973).
(1927) *From the Actor to the Seer.*
(1930) *The Self-consciousness of the Universal.*
(1932) *The Self-determination of Nothingness.*
(1933–4) *Fundamental Problems of Philosophy* (English translation, D. A. Dilworth, Tokyo: Sophia University, 1970).
(1933–45) *Philosophical Essays*, 3 vols.
(1945) *The Logic of the Place of Nothingness and the Religious World-view* (English translation, *Last Writings: Nothingness and the Religious World-view*, D. A. Dilworth, Honolulu: University of Hawaii Press, 1987).
(1947–53) *Complete Works*, 18 vols, Tokyo.

Secondary literature:

Collinson, D. and Wilkinson, R. (1994) *Thirty-Five Oriental Philosophers*, London: Routledge.
Nishitani, Keiji (1991) *Nishida Kitaro*, trans. J. W. Heisig and Yamamoto Seisaki, Oxford: Yale University Press.
Toratoro, Shimonura (1960) *Nishida Kitaro and Some Aspects of his Philosophical Thought*, Tokyo.
Yoshinori, Takeuchi (1982) 'The philosophy of Nishida', in Frederick Franck (ed.) *The Buddha Eye*, New York: Cross Road.
Waldenfels, Hans (1980) *Absolute Nothingness: Foundations for a Buddhist–Christian Dialogue*, trans. J. W. Heisig, New York: Paulist Press.

Kitaro Nishida is esteemed as the first modern Japanese 'philosopher' in the European sense and is primarily associated with the founding of the 'Kyoto School' of philosophy. Through his role in that school Nishida had a seminal influence upon such contemporary Japanese philosophers as Abe Masao, Yoshinori Takeuchi, Hajime **Tanabe** but particularly upon the two greatest twentieth-century disseminators of Japanese thought in the West, D. T. **Suzuki** and Keiji **Nishitani**.

Perhaps the respective courses of European and Japanese thought are now so propitiously aligned that the importance of Nishida's philosophical achievement can be appreciated outside Asia. Since the epoch-making work of **Nietzsche** and **Heidegger**, much continental European philosophy has attempted to resolve the challenge of nihilism by articulating the nature of existence and existential experience without recourse to metaphysical dogma or a philosphical language tainted by the traditional categories of metaphysics. Such an undertaking is a particularly difficult one as European thought lacks what Buddhist tradition has long possessed, namely an experimental analytic capable of theorizing nothingness. On the other hand, the situation faced by many Japanese religious thinkers after the Meiji restoration of 1868 was to capitulate to the increasing influences of European norms of thought, to become outright nationalist reactionaries or to utilize the conceptual artillery of European philosophy as a means of bringing into communicable clarity for Japanese and European readers alike the undogmatic but elusive insights of Zen philosophy. Nishida made the last path his own and offered to European philosophy a profoundly non-nihilistic Zen view of nihility rendered in Western philosophical terms.

The confrontation of Buddhist thought and Western philosophy in Nishida's work involves a characteristic conceptual and experiential transposition. Whereas Christianity and Western metaphysics might be disadvantaged by holding the absolute (God) to be above both immediate expression and experience, they have the advantage of a conceptual framework which can cognize the transcendent. Conversely, Zen philosophy is advantaged by regarding the absolute (i.e. reality 'as it is') to be amenable to immediate experience, while it lacks the conceptual artillery to grapple with that which lies beyond immediate expression. Nishida attempts a fusion of the positive aspects of both European and Zen tradition by suggesting that the Zen experiential intuition of absolute nothingness (*zettai mu*) can be conceptually articulated via Nicholas of Cusa's negative concept of God: it is never that which can be stated of it for it is always more than that; it is what it is not stated to be.

Nishida's invocation of absolute nothingness or emptiness (*sunyata*) should not be understood within the customary polarities of being and non-being, affirmation and denial. *Zettai mu* encompasses both the immanent simultaneity of all coming into being (*creatio ex nihilo*) and of all passing away. It is close to what the existential metaphysics of Nietzsche and Heidegger would render as the 'being' of all becoming. Rather than calling it Being, Nishida names the absolute 'nothingness' on the grounds that were the absolute an absolute Being, all potentialities

would be realized and the infinity of coming into being and passing away would be denied. *Zettai mu* allegedly preserves that potentiality, offering to Western thought the possibility of an existentially affirmative nihilism. It fell to Nishitani, one of Nishida's most talented successors, to work out the philosophical implications of such a mode of thought.

NICHOLAS DAVEY

Nishitani, Keiji

Japanese. **b:** 27 February 1900. **d:** 1991. **Cat:** Zen philosopher; philosopher of religion. **Educ:** Schooled in Ishikawa Prefecture and Tokyo; in 1924 graduated in Philosophy from Kyoto University. **Infls:** Meister Eckhart, Nietzsche, Dostoyevsky, Kierkegaard, Heidegger, Emerson, Carlyle, St Francis, Nishida, Sosseki, Hakuin and Takuan. **Appts:** 1926, Lecturer in Ethics and German, Kyoto Imperial College; 1928, Lecturer, Buddhist Otani University; 1935, Professor of Religion, Kyoto Imperial University; 1936–9, studied with Heidegger in Freiburg, Germany; 1955–63, Chair of Modern Philosophy, Kyoto State University.

Main publications:

(1940) *The Philosophy of Fundamental Subjectivity*, Tokyo.

(1946) *Nihilism*, Tokyo (English translation, *The Self-Overcoming of Nihilism*, trans. G. Parkes and Setsuko Aihara, Albany, NY: State University of New York Press, 1990).

(1948) *Studies in Aristotle*, Tokyo.

(1949) *God and Absolute Nothingness*, Tokyo.

(1961) *What is Religion?*, Tokyo (English translation, *Religion and Nothingness*, trans. Jan Van Bragt, London: California University Press, 1982).

(1992) 'The awakening of self in Buddhism', 'The I–thou relation in Zen Buddishm', and 'Science and Zen', in Frederick Franck (ed.) *The Buddha Eye: An Anthology of the Kyoto School*, New York: Cross Road, pp. 22–30, 47–60 and 111–37 respectively.

Secondary literature:

Parkes, Graham (ed.) (1991) *Nietzsche and Asian Thought*, Chicago: University of Chicago Press; see pp. 13, 18, 106–11, 195–9, 213 (useful on Nishitani and excellent on Japan's assimilation of German philosophy).

Van Bragt, Jan (1961) 'Introductory essay' to *Religion and Nothingness*, London: California University Press.

Waldenfels, Hans (1980) *Absolute Nothingness: Foundations for a Buddhist-Christian Dialogue*, trans. J. W. Heisig, New York: Paulist Press (contains substantial bibliography of Nishitani's published articles).

Nishitani was a leading figure in the Kyoto School of Japanese philosophy, a non-sectarian Zen Buddhist philosopher profoundly concerned with interconnecting, first, Christian and Buddhist ethics and, second, the Buddhist ontology of *sunyata* (emptiness) with European ontologies of nothingness (nihilism). A student of Martin **Heidegger** from 1936–9, significantly he attended the latter's lectures on **Nietzsche** and nihilism at Freiburg University. One of the most outstanding non-European commentators on both the mystical tradition in German theology and the works of Kierkegaard, Nietzsche and Heidegger, Nishitani was also a renowned translator into Japanese, one of his principal achievements being the translation of Schelling's *Essence of Human Freedom*.

The hermeneutic axiom 'questioning one's own from the perspective of the foreign' describes Nishitani's lifelong preoccupation with nineteenth- and twentieth-century European existentialist thought as offering a means to articulating and philosophically reappropriating the central conceptions of Zen thought. Nishitani commenced his philosophical career exclusively preoccupied with thinkers of the continental European existential and phenomenological tradition. Not until his discovery of the philosophy of Nishida did Nishitani, far from abandoning his former interests, see them as a means to reengage with the Zen tradition of religion and philosophy. Like Nishida, Nishitani focuses primarily upon the problem of nihilism and Zen's capacity to accept and yet positively transform an ontology of nothingness. Some brief contextual remarks will illuminate the circumstances appertaining to Nishitani's fusion of aspects of European with Zen philosophical tradition.

Japanese cultural tradition tends not to attribute to individualism the same value as Occidental culture. Although unusual for a Japanese, it was not personally inappropriate that after the death of his father and the onset of a serious tubercular affliction the young Nishitani should turn in his sense of hopelessness and despair to arch-European analysts of the suffering individual consciousness, namely, Nietzsche, Kierkegaard, Dostoevsky and Heidegger. And yet despite their unJapanese individualism, key elements in these thinkers made them curiously accessible to Nishitani. The aesthetical-existential dimension of Japanese tradition emphasizes the aesthetic as the meaningfully sensed and emotionally appropriated and the existential as that which affects the very substance of one's personal being. A terser summary of Nietzsche's and Heidegger's aspirations for philosophy could not be found. Their high regard for aesthetic intuitions of the meaningfully 'disclosed' irrespective of volition is clearly paralleled in the Japanese understanding of the aesthetic. Furthermore, the highly indeterminate character of the Japanese language, which lends itself to allegory and allusion, finds a curious resonance in the styles of Nietzsche and Heidegger, who more often than not convey their meaning not by the utterance of pure statements but by allowing the unspoken reservoirs of meaning behind the said to be resonated by what is said. Given such hermeneutical 'crossovers', it is perhaps not so surprising that Nietzsche's and Heidegger's examination of nihility should profoundly strike Nishitani's philosophical imagination, nor that he should be able to offer such a lucid and pertinent critique of their analysis as he does, but from the philosophical perspective of Zen Buddhism.

The underlying motif of Nishitani's thinking is religious in the special Zen sense of refusing to distinguish between the religious and philosophical quest. When Nishitani writes that religion is the existential exposure of the problematic which is contained in the usual mode of self-being, so would he equally accept Tillich's assertion that the proper role of philosophy is to advance existential interests, to existentialize humanity's mode of being. The transition from 'the usual mode of self-being' to 'fully existentialized human existence' is in Nishitani's terms the journey from the Great Doubt (*taigi*) to the Great Affirmation, from the traumatic discovery of the emptiness of self-centred being to the ecstatic insight that such a loss of (illusory) selfhood is a condition of realizing what was in fact always the case: that one is neither set apart from nor set against the universe but intertwined with *all* of its aspects.

The presuppositions of this transformative argument are eightfold. First, all things are becoming (*shojo*: perpetually coming to be and passing back into extinction) as they are nothing (*mu*) or lack an essence. Second, the world is therefore an emptiness (*sunyata*). Third, the things which make up the world must be considered not as stable identities but as fields of force or energy, the character of which perpetually change according to mutual density and proximity. Fourth, Nishitani equates this Nietzschean ontology with the Buddhist notion of 'networks of causation' (*pratitya-samutpada*), thereby linking the Sanskrit conception of *karma* (the interdependence of all things) with Nietzsche's *amor fati*. Fifth, adapting the *Heart Sutra*'s contention that the 'hindrance of ignorance' is the principal cause of suffering, Nishitani contends *pace* Nietzsche that egoistic self-preoccupation, the fictions of pyschology and the 'metaphysics of grammar' prevent us from seeing that 'self that is not a self', namely the 'original self' which has its ecstatic 'home-ground' in the interconnectedness of all those fields which constitute *sunyata*. Sixth, Nishitani then embarks upon a critique of Western technology not so much because it presupposes the fiction of the self as detached cognitive subject but because mechanistic explanation renders redundant the very subject which it supposedly serves: 'at the basis of technological thought lies the ... "dehumanization" of humanity ... With regard to a human being, the dimension out of which a "thou" confronts an "I" is completely erased'. Seventh, what Nishitani fears within the process of 'dehumanization' is the irrevocable appearance of what Nietzsche would call 'passive nihilism'. Technology's subversion of the existential 'why?' with the purposeless 'how' of mechanistic explanation suggests that the ultimate 'for-the-sake-of-which' may be for the sake of nothing at all. Western science and philosophy thus lead for Nishitani to the crisis of nihilistic despair. However, eighth, the Japanese term for crisis none the less also implies an opportunity and it is at the moment of the Great Doubt that Nishitani comes into his own.

Nietzsche's solution to passive nihilism is active nihilism. If there are no meanings in themselves, not only can the world not be condemned as meaningless (passive nihilism) but we are free to create our own meanings and perspectives (active nihilism). Nishitani correctly perceives that Nietzsche's active nihilism requires that one pass through passive nihilism. That, however, implies that active nihilism cannot fully overcome its passive forerunner since the act of creating 'new' values presupposes precisely the gulf between subject and world which sets the oppositional basis for the problem of passive nihilism in the first place.

Having exposed the *cul de sac* in the Western analysis of nihilism, Nishitani turns back via Nishida to the Zen tradition but armed with European philosophical techniques capable of rendering into reasonable and meaningful words the wordless wisdom of Zen. The result of that return is that nihilism can be made to overcome itself. For Nishitani, 'religion is an existential exposure to the problematic in the usual mode of self-being'. Within Buddhist dialectics, the Great (philosophical) Doubt can transform itself into the Great (religious) Affirmation. Returning to the concept of essenceless networks of causation, Nishitani remarks:

> On that field of emptiness, each thing comes into its own and reveals itself in a self-affirmation, each in its own possibility and *virtus* of being. The conversion to and entrance to that field means, for us men, the fundamental affirmation of the being of all things, and at the same time of our own existence. The field of emptiness is nothing but the field of the great affirmation.

One could not be more removed from Nietzsche's active nihilism than here, for whereas the latter distances the creative individual from those who cannot overcome the rancours of passive nihilism, Nishitani's position offers via 'the waters of nihilism' an ecstatic reconcilation of the 'empty' or 'purified' self with all other beings that constitute the 'field of emptiness' that is the world. Nishitani's philosophical mission is undoubtedly rendered all the more difficult because of his standing both within and without his tradition, and yet precisely because he attempts to 'question his own through the eye of the foreign' we—the European foreigner—obtain an extraordinary 'eye into our own'.

NICHOLAS DAVEY

N'Krumah, Kwame

Ghanaian. *b:* 1909, Nkroful, Gold Coast. *d:* 27 April 1972, Bucharest, Romania. *Cat:* Political philosopher. *Educ:* Primary and secondary schools at Catholic institutions and at Achimota; awarded a teaching certificate, taught in Gold Coast until 1935; Lincoln University, Pennsylvania, BA in 1939; attended MA courses in Philosophy and Pedagogy at the University of Pennsylvania, Philadelphia. *Infls:* M. Ataturk, Marcus Garvey and Karl Marx. *Appts:* 1945, Co-secretary of the Fifth Pan-African Conference in Manchester; 1947, secretary of the United Gold Coast Convention; 1949, organized his own party, the Convention People's Party; the Gold Coast became Ghana on 6 March 1957 and N'Krumah was its first President in April 1960.

Main publications:
(1961) *I Speak of Freedom*, London: Heinemann.
(1963) *Africa Must Unite*, London: Heinemann.
(1964) *Consciencism*, London: Heinemann.
(1965) *Neo-Colonialism: The Last Stage of Imperialism*, London: Heinemann.
(1967) *Ghana, The Autobiography of Kwame N'Krumah*, London: Thomas Nelson.
(1973) *Revolutionary Path*, London: Panaf Books.

An activist and a politician, N'Krumah based his action on the understanding that there is such a thing as an African social reality. This is constituted by the complementarity of a tradition, Christianity and/or Islam, and the legacy of a major aculturation brought about by colonization. The process of a political liberation that he situates between **Senghor**'s spiritualist socialism and Naher's nationalism is presented as an African practice of materialism. Its formalization in *Consciencism* (1964) has been criticized as vague and questionable.

V. Y. MUDIMBE

Noddings (née Rieth), Nel
American. *b:* 19 January 1929, Irvington, New Jersey. *Cat:* Feminist philosopher; educator. *Ints:* Philosophy of education; feminist ethics; mathematical problem-solving. *Educ:* BA, Mathematics, Montclair Stage College, 1949; MA Mathematics, Rutgers, 1964; PhD Education, Stanford, 1973. *Infls:* John Dewey, William James and Martin Buber. *Appts:* Taught mathematics at various high schools, 1949–72; Director of precollegiate education, University of Chicago, 1975–6; Assistant Professor, Pennsylvania State University at State College, 1973; from 1977, Stanford (Full Professor from 1986, Lee L. Jacks Professor of Child Education, from 1992 Associate Dean 1990–2, Acting Dean of Education 1992 -3); Phi Beta Kappa Visiting Scholar, 1989–90; Stanford Graduate School of Education Anne Roe Award, 1992; President, John Dewey Society, President, National Philosophy of Education Society, 1992; Member of Board of Directors, Center for Human Caring, School of Nursing, Denver, from 1986; Member of Advisory Board, *American Journal of Education and Educational Theory*.

Main publications:
(1984) *Caring: A Feminine Approach to Ethics and Moral Education*, Berkeley, CA: University of California Press.
(1989) *Women and Evil*, Berkeley, CA: University of California Press.

(1993) *Educating for Intelligent Belief or Unbelief* (The John Dewey Lecture), New York: Teachers College Press.

Secondary literature:
Grimshaw, J. (1986) *Feminist Philosophers: Women's Perspectives on Philosphical Traditions*, Brighton: Harvester Wheatsheaf; titled *Philosophy and Feminist Thinking*, Minneapolis: University of Minnesota Press, 1986.
Hoagland, S. L. (1991) 'Some thoughts about "caring"', in C. Card (ed.), *Feminist Ethics*, Lawrence: University Press of Kansas.
Ruddick, S. (1989) *Maternal Thinking: Toward a Politics of Peace*, Boston: Beacon.

Noddings's *Caring* (1984), along with Gilligan's *In a Different Voice* (1982), continues to spark off vigorous debate about the fundamental concepts and evaluations in ethics. Anchoring moral behaviour in the goodness of natural caring, Noddings argues that its core is a care-filled receptivity to those involved in moral situations, and hence rejects the rigidity of rule and principle to focus on the particular in human relations.
Women and Evil (1989) explores the sexism of traditional views of evil and how they served to control women. Noddings then takes up the nurturing standpoint of women to develop a morality of evil which aims to help humans live less painfully and fearfully.
Sources: PI; personal communication.

PATRICIA SCALTSAS

Northrop, F(ilmer) S(tuart) C(uckow)
American. *b:* 27 November 1893, Janeville, Wisconsin. *d:* 23 July 1992, Exeter, New Hampshire. *Cat:* Philosopher of science. *Ints:* Philosophy of law. *Educ:* Beloit College, BA 1915; Yale University, MA 1919; Harvard University, MA 1922, PhD 1924. *Infls:* Bakewell, Hocking and Whitehead. *Appts:* 1923–47, Instructor to Professor of Philosophy, Department Chair (1938–40), Master (1940–7), Silliman College; 1947–62, Sterling Professor of Philosophy and Law (Emeritus Professor, 1962), Yale University.

Main publications:
(1931) *Science and First Principles*, New York: Macmillan; reprinted, Woodbridge, CT: Ox Bow Press, 1979.
(1946) *The Meeting of East and West: An Inquiry Concerning World Understanding*, New York: Macmillan; reprinted, Woodbridge, CT: Ox Bow Press, 1979.

(1947) *The Logic of the Sciences and the Humanities*, New York: Macmillan; reprinted, Woodbridge, CT: Ox Bow Press, 1983.

Secondary literature:
Reck, A. J. (1968) *The New American Philosophers*, Baton Rouge: Louisiana State University Press; reprinted, New York: Dell Publishing Co., 1970, pp. 197–220.
Sedden, F. (1995) *An Introduction to the Philosophical Works of F. S. C. Northrop*, Lewistown, PA: Edward Mellen Press.

Originally a philosopher of science, Northrop probed the epistemological foundations of science and undertook spectulatively to extend his discoveries cosmically and culturally. *The Meeting of East and West* (1946) established his fame as an interpreter of the differences between cultures and a seeker of conflict resolutions by humanistic and scientific methods. He devoted the final decades of his career to the philosophy of law, with special focus on international law.
Sources: WW(Am); *New York Times*, 23 Jul 1992.
ANDREW RECK

Nowell-Smith, P(atrick) H(orace)
British. *b:* 1914, near Padstow, England. *Cat:* Analytic philosopher. *Ints:* Ethics; philosophy of history. *Educ:* University of Oxford and Harvard University. *Infls:* J. L. Austin and R. G. Collingwood. *Appts:* 1946–57, Fellow, Trinity College, Oxford; 1957–64, Professor of Philosophy, University of Leicester; 1964–9, University of Kent; 1969–85, Professor of Philosophy, York University, Toronto.

Main publications:
(1954) *Ethics*, Harmondsworth: Penguin Books; second edition, Oxford: Blackwell, 1957.
(1977) 'The constructionist theory of history', *History and Theory* 16.
(1982) 'Historical facts', in David Carr *et al.* (eds) *Philosophy of History and Contemporary Historiography*, Ottawa: Ottawa University Press.

Secondary literature:
Austin, J. L. (1956) 'Ifs and cans', *Proceedings of the British Academy*.
Warnock, Mary (1960) *Ethics since 1900*, Oxford: Oxford University Press.

In the style current in Oxford after the Second World War, Nowell-Smith's most important work explores the logic of ethical concepts. Basically accepting **Moore**'s account of the Naturalistic Fallacy, he held that there was a crucial distinction between describing and evaluating. He emphasized that evaluative words have a number of different functions, but their most fundamental use was in the context of choosing (either choosing oneself or advising others). His account is thus similar to that of R. M. **Hare**.

Ethics (1954) also contained influential discussions of egoism, the sense of duty and freedom of the will.
Sources: WW 1992; personal communication.
ANTHONY ELLIS

Nozick, Robert
American. *b:* 16 November 1938, Brooklyn. *Cat:* Political philosopher; epistemologist. *Ints:* Political philosophy; epistemology. *Educ:* Columbia University, BA 1959; Princeton University, AM 1961, PhD 1963, with dissertation on 'The Normative Theory of Individual Choice'. *Infls:* Locke, Rawls, Hempel, Vlastos, Morgenbesser. *Appts:* Taught at Princeton, 1962–5; Fullbright Scholar, University of Oxford, 1963–4; taught at Harvard, 1965–7, and at Rockefeller University, 1967–9; Professor of Philosophy, Harvard, 1969–85, from 1985, Arthur Kingsley Porter Professor of Philosophy; Woodrow Wilson National Fellowship, 1959–60; Fellow at Van Leer Jerusalem Foundation 1976–7; Fellow of Center for Adanced Study in Behavioral Sciences, Palo Alto, 1971–2; Rockefeller Foundation Fellowship, 1979–80; National Endowment of Humanities Fellowship, 1987–8; Fellow of American Academy of Arts and Sciences, 1984–; Honorary AM, Harvard, 1969; Honorary DHumLitt, Knox College, 1983.

Main publications:
(1968) 'Moral complications and moral structures', *Natural Law Forum*.
(1969) 'Newcomb's problem and two principles of choice', in N. Rescher (ed.), *Essays in Honour of Carl G. Hempel*, Dordrecht: Reidel (this article introduced the problem to the philosophical world).
(1974) *Anarchy, State, and Utopia*, Oxford: Blackwell (received National Book Award 1975).
(1981) *Philosophical Explanations*, Oxford: Oxford University Press (received Ralph Waldo Emerson Award 1982; as well as epistemology this book treats metaphysics, philosophy of mind and ethics).
(1989) *The Examined Life*, New York: Simon & Schuster.

(1990) (ed.) *Harvard Dissertations in Philosophy, 1930–1988* 20 vols, New York: Garland Press.

(1990) *The Normative Theory of Individual Choice*, New York: Garland Press (reprint of 1963 PhD dissertation).

(1993) *The Nature of Rationality*, Princeton, NJ: Princeton University Press.

Secondary literature:

Block, W. (1980) 'On Robert Nozick's "On Austrian methodology"', *Inquiry*.

Campbell, R. and Sowden, L. (eds) *Paradoxes of Rationality and Cooperation*, Vancouver: UBC Press (reprints 1969 article with discussions).

Capaldi, N. (1984) 'Exploring the limits of analytic philosophy: a critique of Nozick's *Philosophical Explanations*', *Interpretation*.

Corlett, J. A. (ed.) (1991) *Equality and Liberty: Analysing Rawls and Nozick*, New York: St Martin's Press, London: Macmillan.

Dancy, J. (1985) *An Introduction to Contemporary Epistemology*, Oxford: Blackwell.

Elster, J. and Moene, K. O. (eds) (1989) *Alternatives to Capitalism*, New York: Cambridge University Press.

Journal of Libertarian Studies, 1977 (has several relevant articles).

Machan, T. R. (1989) *Individuals and Their Rights*, La Salle, Ill: Open Court.

Moffatt, R. C. L. (ed.) (1978) '"Minimal government" in theory and practice', in *Personalist* (October issue, devoted to Nozick).

Narveson, J. (1988) *The Libertarian Idea*, Philadelphia: Temple University Press.

Nielsen, K. (1985) *Equality and Liberty: A Defence of Radical Egalitarianism*, Totowa, NJ: Rowman & Allanfeld.

Noonan, H. W. (1985) 'The closest continuer theory of identity', *Inquiry*.

Paul, J. (ed.) (1981) *Reading Nozick: Essays on Anarchy, State, and Utopia*, Totowa, NJ: Rowman & Littlefield.

Political Theory, 1977 (contains some relevant articles).

Sampson, G. (1978) 'Liberalism and Nozick's "minimal state"', *Mind* (cf. discussion by J. R. Danley in *Mind*, 1979).

Schaefer, D. (1984) 'Libertarianism and political philosophy: a critique of Nozick's *Anarchy, State, and Utopia*', *Interpretation*.

Wolff, J. (1991) *Robert Nozick: Property, Justice and the Minimal State*, Cambridge: Polity Press.

Nozick has made notable contributions to both political philosophy and epistemology. His most famous work, *Anarchy, State, and Utopia* (1974), propounds an extreme libertarian position. Starting from the inviolability of certain rights he claims that justice is not a matter of achieving a certain end-state nor a pattern of distribution but rests on entitlement: given certain rules of acquisition in a Lockean 'state of nature', and certain rules of transfer by contract or gift, 'whatever arises from a just situation by just steps is itself just' (p. 152). A 'minimal state' is envisaged as hypothetically developing from the state of nature, limited to 'protecting all its citizens against violence, theft, and fraud, and to the enforcement of contracts, and so on' (p. 26), and Part II claims that no further development of the state can be justified. However, an important principle of rectification is implied, and may involve some redistribution in actual societies, though without 'introduc[ing] socialism as the punishment for our sins' (p. 153), and some features are later modified (for example, see *The Examined Life* (1989), chapter 3, on inheritance). Critics have asked, inter alia, whether he succeeds in steering between anarchism and the more extensive state, whether he relies overmuch on moral behaviour, whether his doctrine of entitlement is adequately founded, especially the rules of acquisition, and whether he can avoid supplementing rights with other considerations.

In epistemology Nozick analyses knowledge in terms of 'tracking' the truth (*Philosophical Explanations*, chapter 3): one knows a truth if one believes it, would not believe it were it false, but would believe it were it true. He uses this to deal with scepticism, but it has controversial features: for example, that one can know a conjunction while not knowing (but merely believing) one of its conjuncts (p. 228).

Nozick's latest book, *The Nature of Rationality* (1993), starts by exploring the rationale of acting on principle and then introduces the notion of symbolic utility, i.e. the value of something as a symbol, a notion he had used in *The Examined Life* (pp. 286ff) to moderate some of the conclusions of *Anarchy, State, and Utopia*. As well as offering further views on Newcomb's problem (compare the 1969 article), he develops a theory of rational belief (although one might wonder whether he here satisfactorily distinguishes belief from acceptance), and emphasizes throughout the role of evolution in determining why we have the intuitions we have, especially when, as with the Euclidean nature of space, these intuitions are not strictly true (p. 105).

Sources: IWW 1993–4; WW(Am) 1992–3; PI; personal communication.

A. R. LACEY

Nuchelmans, Gabriel

Dutch. *b:* 15 May 1922, Oud-Gastel, The Netherlands. *Cat:* Philosopher of logic; philosopher of language. *Ints:* History of analytical philosophy. *Educ:* Classical Philology and Philosophy. *Infls:* Bocheński, Ayer and Popper. *Appts:* Taught Greek and Latin in secondary school, 1949–64; Ordinary Professor of Philosophy, University of Leyden, 1964–87.

Main publications:

(1950) *Philologos, philologia and philologein* Assen: Van Gorcum (dissertation).

(1965) *David Hume*, Baarn: Wereldvenster.

(1969) *Overzicht van de analytische wijsbegeerte* [Survey of Analytical Philosophy], Utrecht: Spectrum.

(1973/80/83) *Theories of the Proposition* 3 vols, Amsterdam: North Holland Publishing Co.

(1991) *Dilemmatic Arguments. Towards a History of Their Logic and Rhetoric*, Amsterdam: North Holland Publishing Co.

Nuchelmans is one of the editors of the Synthese Library and, until very recently, was a member of the editorial board of Synthese Historical Library.

He is especially interested in subjects belonging to the philosophy of logic, philosophical semantics and philosophy of language in general, both from a systematic and from a historical point of view and in particular with the purpose of showing how these viewpoints can be fruitfully connected. Some of his main activities are the study of the validity of judgements and the analysis of normative rules in language.

WIM VAN DOOREN

Nursi, B(ediuzzaman) Said

Kurdish. *b:* 1876, Nurs, Hizan, Bitlis, Turkey. *d:* 1960, Urfa. *Cat:* Theosophist and philosopher of religion. *Ints:* Islamic modernism. *Educ:* Educated in *madrasas* in Pirmis then in Hizan and finally in Dogubeyazit. He obtained a diploma (*ijazat*) at the age of fifteen in 1888. *Infls:* Islamic mystical tradition in general and Ahmad Faruqi Sirhindi, known as Imam Rabbani, in particular. *Appts:* Founder of 'Nor' movement.

Main publications:

(1976) *Belief or Unbelief: The Result of a Choice*, trans. Umit Simsek, Albany.

(1976) *Fruits from the Tree of Light*, trans. Hamid Algar, Albany: The Risele-i Nur Institute of America.

(1976) *The Miracle of Muhammed*, trans. Hamid Algar, El-Cerrito.

(1976) *Sincerity and Brotherhood*, trans. Hamid Algar, Berkeley.

(1987) *The Key to Belief*, trans. Sükran Vahide, Istanbul.

(1987) *Man and Universe*, trans. Meryem Weld, Istanbul.

(1987) *The Tongues of Reality*, trans. Sükran Vahide, Istanbul.

(1989) *The Damascus Sermon*, trans. Sükran Vahide, Istanbul.

(1992) *Belief and Man*, trans. Sükran Vahide, Istanbul.

Nursi's life was eventful. He was constantly involved in political as well as religious protest against the secularist change during the establishment of the new Turkish Republic, and was imprisoned on more than one occasion. He was among the founders of the *Ittihad-i Islami*, the Muslin Union, a movement that sought to restore the Islamic tradition and imbue it with fresh vitality.

Nursi's philosophical thought was founded on the premise that an Active Intelligence has set the pattern of the laws of nature. The manifestations of these laws are, he held, appearances that signify the presence of the Real. The regularities governing matter have their source in God, and Nature is the theophany of God, embodying what is sacred.

Nursi maintained that the world of archetypes (*alemi-i-misal*) and the world of phenomena (*alemi-i shuhud*) are cognitively different realms and that the world or archetypes, even though it is the source of the phenomenal world, cannot be analysed by means of the concepts of the phenomenal world. He propounded a theory of Illumination as a way of coming to know God and as an alternative to a severely intellectual approach to spiritual knowledge. In a similarly populist vein he concentrated on practical and personal ethics rather than ritual and convention, maintaining that a Muslim society could withstand the ills generated by Western civilization if it were nourished by Islamic spirituality.

Sources: Serif Mardin (1989) *Religion and Social Change in Modern Turkey: The Case of Bediuzzaman Said Nursi*, Albany: Albany State UP.

ADNAN ASLAN

Nussbaum, Martha C.

American. *b:* 6 May 1947, New York. *Cat:* Ancient philosopher; philosopher of literature; philosopher of ethics. *Educ:* New York University, 1964–

9; Harvard University, 1970–5. *Infls:* Aristotle and Henry James. *Appts:* Assistant, Associate, then full Professor of Philosophy and Classics, Harvard University, 1975–82; 1984–, Professor, then University Professor of Classics; and Comparative Literature, Brown University.

Main publications:

(1978) (trans. with commentary) *Aristotle's 'De Motu Animalium'*, Princeton: Princeton University Press.

(1982) (ed. with Malcolm Schofield) *Language and Logos: Studies in Ancient Greek Philosophy Presented to G. E. L. Owen*, Cambridge: Cambridge University Press.

(1986) (ed.) G. E. L. Owen, *Logic, Science and Dialectic: Collected Papers in Greek Philosophy*, Ithaca: Cornell University Press.

(1986) *The Fragility of Goodness: Luck and Ethics in Greek Tragedy and Philosophy*, Cambridge: Cambridge University Press.

(1990) *Love's Knowledge: Essays on Philosophy and Literature*, New York: Oxford University Press.

(1992) (ed. with Amelie Oksenberg Rorty) *Essays on Aristotle's 'De Anima'*, Oxford: Clarendon Press.

(1993) (ed. with Amartya Sen) *Quality of Life, WIDER Studies in Development Economics*, Oxford: Oxford University Press.

(1993) (ed. with Jacques Brunschwig) *Passions and Perceptions: Studies in Hellenistic Philosophies of Mind*, Cambridge: Cambridge University Press.

(1994) *The Therapy of Desire: Theory and Practice in Hellenistic Ethics*, Princeton: Princeton University Press.

Nussbaum has contributed significantly to contemporary philosophy through her focus on the interrelatedness of philosophy and literature. She argues that philosophical discourse should be enriched through the narratives of novels, poetry and plays. In particular, narrative articulates the complexities of moral life in more fruitful ways than the abstract theorizing characteristic of philosophy.

Her views are not merely a critique of philosophical style but they also constitute an attack on the moral foundationalism of Plato and Kant. This position is given its fullest expression in *The Fragility of Goodness* (1986), a study of moral luck through the writings of Aristotle, Plato and Greek tragedy. The contingencies of human life render some goods 'fragile', for example love, but such goods are none the less valuable for human flourishing. Recognizing this value demands a conception of practical reason that includes feeling and imagination as well as the intellect. Narratives embody this approach because they capture the particularity and contingency of human action and reveal the contextual richness of moral deliberation.

In addition to making important contributions to Aristotelian scholarship, Nussbaum has extended Aristotle's notion of the 'good' to moral issues in development economics. She defends a non-relativistic account of moral values which is informed by cultural difference but is none the less anchored in 'certain features of our common humanity'.

Sources: Discussion (several articles) of Martha Nussbaum's *The Fragility of Goodness* (1986), *PInv* 16, 1, Jan 1993; DAS, 4, 1982.

EMILY BRADY

Nygren, Anders

Swedish. *b:* 1890. *d:* 1972, Lund, Sweden. *Cat:* Theologian; philosopher of religion. *Educ:* University of Lund. *Infls:* Gustav Aulén. *Appts:* Professor, University of Lund, 1924–39; Bishop of Lund, from 1949 until his death.

Main publications:

(1923) *Filosofisk och Kristen Etik*, Lund: Gleerup.

(1930) *Eros und Agape*, Gütersloh: Bertelsmann (English translation, *Agape and Eros*, London: SPCK, 1932).

(1970) *Tro och Vetande: religionsfilosofiska och teologiska essayer*, Stockholm: Helsingfors (English translation, *Meaning and Method: Prolegomena to a Scientific Philosophy of Religion and a Scientific Theology*, Philadelphia: Fortress Press, 1972).

Secondary literature:

Macquarrie, J. (1963) *Twentieth Century Religious Thought*, London: SCM Press, chapter 20.

In his early career Nygren maintained that religions can be characterized and differentiated by their underlying *motifs*: that is, by the way each holds that communion with the Absolute is to be realized. The motif of Christianity is *agape*: a disinterested, selfless and theocentric love. Human beings cannot attain *agape* by their own efforts, but instead it is made known to us only through the Christian revelation. *Agape* is contrasted with *eros*, the motif of Hellenistic philosophy. At its highest, for example in Plato, *eros* is an intellectual love of the world of reality, or of the Forms. There is, according to Nygren, no way in which *eros* can lead to *agape*.

Nygren's position outlined above implies that

there is very little, if any, connection between philosophy and theology, but in a later publication (1970) he modified this view. He agreed with the traditional view that theology is a science, and that it must conform to the requirements of consistency and clarity. Christianity cannot stand isolated from cultural and intellectual develop-ments: if it is thought to do so it becomes meaningless in the sense that it loses any relevance to the lives of human beings. Our understanding of Christianity must not remain static but, like every other intellectual discipline, has to change and deepen.

KATHRYN PLANT

O

O'Brien, Mary

Canadian. **b:** 8 July 1926, Glasgow, Scotland. **Cat:** Philosopher and educationalist; founding member of the Feminist Party of Canada. **Ints:** Feminist theory; social and political theory. **Educ:** York University, Ontario, 1966–76. **Infls:** Marx and Hegel. **Appts:** Lecturer, Assistant, Associate, then full Professor of Sociology in Education, Ontario Institute for Studies in Education, 1976–87.

Main publications:

(1981) *The Politics of Reproduction*, London: Routledge & Kegan Paul. (1989) *Reproducing the World*, Boulder, CO: Westview Press.

O'Brien develops a feminist concept of 'reproduction' that replaces traditional social and political conceptions of history and culture. In *The Politics of Reproduction* (1981), her theory of 'reproductive consciousness' revises Marx's stages of human history. For women, childbirth constitutes a 'mediated dialectic' which establishes continuity between individual and species. By contrast, men's reproductive consciousness alienates them from species-continuity. The first stage of reproductive consciousness is the discovery of paternity in which men seek to artificially establish species-continuity through 'potency principles', that is, primogeniture, legal rights and other institutions. The result is male domination and the relegation of women to the private sphere. The second stage in the dialectic of gendered consciousness is reproductive technology, which is revolutionary in enabling women to choose parenthood. She has since argued that a third revolution, a radical transformation of the patriarchal state, is possible only by following a strategy dictated by a feminist social theory. Although her ideas have strongly influenced feminist thought, some feminists have suggested that her position leads to biological determinism. However, she claims that women's reproductive consciousness is a social phenomenon despite its natural roots.

Sources: Somer Brodribb (ed.) (1989) 'Feminist theory: the influence of Mary O'Brien', special issue of *RFR*, 19, 1, Sep; Center for Women's Studies in Education, Ontario Inst. for Studies in Education.

EMILY BRADY

O'Neill, Onora

British. **b:** 23 August 1941, Aughafatten, Northern Ireland. **Cat:** Philosopher of ethics; Kantian; political philosopher. **Educ:** Somerville College, Oxford, 1959–62; Harvard University, 1963–9. **Infls:** Kant. **Appts:** Assistant, then Associate Professor, Barnard College, Columbia University, 1970–7; Lecturer, Senior Lecturer, Reader, then Professor, University of Essex, 1977–92; 1992–, Principal of Newnham College, Cambridge.

Main publications:

(1975) *Acting on Principle*, New York: Columbia University Press.
(1978) (ed. with W. Ruddick) *Having Children: Legal and Philosophical Reflections on Parenthood*, New York: Oxford University Press.
(1986) *Faces of Hunger: an Essay on Poverty, Development and Justice*, London: George Allen & Unwin.
(1989) *Constructions of Reason: Explorations of Kant's Practical Philosophy*, Cambridge: Cambridge University Press.
(forthcoming) *Bounds of Justice*, Cambridge: Cambridge University Press.

O'Neill is concerned with developing a reading of Kant's ethical theory which counters the objection that it is too abstract and inflexible to be a practical guide for human action. She interprets Kant's critique of reason as constructivist and antifoundationalist. The authority of reason stems not from the solitary reasoner but from principles of thought and action that can be freely adopted by a community of reasoners. For Kant, then, both practical and theoretical reason rest on the categorical imperative. O'Neill views the categorical imperative as a principle of universalization applied in different situations to assess the agent's intentions, and so it is not the source of a general set of rules, but rather it tells us how to act rightly in each particular case. She argues that the categorical imperative is a useful principle for action on the grounds that the formulation of a maxim involves all facts and circumstances relevant to the agent's intentions.

O'Neill contrasts her position with the Kantian liberalism of **Rawls**. The categorical imperative includes obligations which extend beyond those connected with rights since it generates both perfect and imperfect obligations, thereby making room for virtues as well as rights. In arguing that maxims may be collectively formulated and rejected, O'Neill seeks an alternative to the position that Kant's ethics is essentially individualistic. Out of this interpretation of Kant, O'Neill develops an account of justice which combines the application of universal principles with a sensitivity to context and difference. She believes that Kantian ethics can thus be more readily applied to solving contemporary problems such as hunger and poverty.

Sources: Personal communication.

EMILY BRADY

Oakeshott, Michael Joseph

British. *b:* 11 December 1901, London. *d:* 1992, Swanage, Dorset. *Cat:* Idealist. *Ints:* Political philosophy; philosophy of history; philosophy of action. *Educ:* St George's School, Harpenden; Caius College, Cambridge, Marburg and Tübingen. *Infls:* Bradley and Burke. *Appts:* Fellow, Caius College, Cambridge, 1927–48; Professor of Political Science, LSE, London, 1951–68.

Main publications:

(1933) *Experience and its Modes*, Cambridge.
(1962) *Rationalism in Politics*, London: Methuen.
(1975) *On Human Conduct*, Oxford: Clarendon Press.
(1975) *Hobbes on Civil Association*, Oxford: Blackwell.
(1983) *On History*, Oxford: Blackwell.
(1989) *The Voice of Liberal Learning*, New Haven and London: Yale University Press.
(1993) *Religion, Politics and the Moral Life*, New Haven and London: Yale University Press.
(1993) *Morality and Politics in Modern Europe*, New Haven and London: Yale University Press.

Secondary literature:

Grant, Robert (1990) *Oakeshott*, London: Claridge Press.

Michael Oakeshott's academic employments were in History until the 1939 war and in political science after it, but his chief publication in the earlier period was a work of general philosophy and in the later on the philosophies of politics and history. *Experience and Its Modes* (1933) resembles the writings of F. H. **Bradley** in its general method and in the abstract hauteur of its approach, and is comparable in structure to **Collingwood**'s *Speculum Mentis* in distinguishing experience into various 'modes'—philosophy, history, science and practice. Of these philosophy alone is complete and free from presuppositions, rather in the manner of Plato's 'dialectic'. The others survey experience from a particular point of view: as past events in the case of history, as a system of quantities in the case of science. In each there is no sharp distinction between thought and its objects, between experiencing and what is experienced. A striking new development was the political theory expounded in the essays of the period immediately after the war, collected in *Rationalism in Politics* (1962). Their main drift is that politics should not be conceived as an exercise of technical rationality, in which, under the guidance of science, means are chosen for specifically identified ends. The knowledge required for its successful conduct is implicit knowledge-how, achieved by immersion in tradition and practical political experience. Politics does not pursue a goal, it is, rather, a task, that of maintaining, above all by way of law, a settled order in which people can most adequately pursue their own purposes. There is no one ideal pattern of public order; different societies require different constitutional tailoring. Ideologies, laying down universal prescriptions, are illusions, misconstruing the historically developed rights of a particular community as a model for general application. An ideology, as he puts it, is an abridgment of a particular form of political experience wrongly presented as a regime for all. Instrumental rationality is not wholly rejected; it properly animates what Oakeshott calls 'enterprise associations' in which people come together for the pursuit of a clearly identified common purpose, as contrasted with 'civil associations', like a family, a club and, most importantly, the state. Oakeshott is a writer of elegantly mandarin prose, in which there is no place for detailed argument with specific opponents or for the interruption of scholarly footnotes. In adding a further mode, that of poetry or imaginative literature, to his original list, he presents a new image of their relations to each other. It is that of conversation, dialogue for its own sake, as contrasted with argument, dialogue intended to achieve a definite result. Oakeshott's general philosophy has remained an object of distant, puzzled respect but his political thinking has been highly influential on a generation of political theorists, among whom may be mentioned Roger Scruton and John Gray, who are, however, by no means simply disciples. He is without doubt the most notable conservative political thinker of the second half of the twentieth century, perhaps, indeed, the most notable since Edmund Burke.

Sources: W. H. Greenleaf (1966) *Oakeshott's Philosophical Politics*; Paul Franco (1990) *The Political Philosophy of Michael Oakeshott*.

ANTHONY QUINTON

Oman, John Wood

British. *b:* 23 July 1860, Stenness, Orkney, Scotland. *d:* 17 May 1939, Cambridge, England. *Cat:* Presbyterian minister; theologian. *Ints:* Philosophy of religion. *Educ:* Edinburgh, Erlangen, Heidelberg and Neuchâtel Universities, and The United Presbyterian Theological Hall, Edinburgh. *Infls:* F. D. E. Schleiermacher and Albrecht Ritschl. *Appts:* St James, Paisley (asst.); Clayport Street Presbyterian Church, Alnwick, 1888–1907; Professor (1907–35) and Principal (1922–35), Westminster College, Cambridge; FBA, 1938.

Main publications:

(1906) *The Problem of Faith and Freedom in the Last Two Centuries*, London: Hodder & Stoughton.
(1917) *Grace and Personality*, Cambridge: Cambridge University Press.
(1931) *The Natural and the Supernatural*, Cambridge: Cambridge University Press.

Secondary literature:

Bevans, S. (1992) *John Oman and His Doctrine of God*, Cambridge: Cambridge University Press.
Healey, F. G. (1965) *Religion and Reality: The Theology of John Oman*, Edinburgh: Oliver & Boyd.

His titles suggest Oman's objective of holding together realities sometimes deemed incompatible. He locates the root of religion in our immediate sense of the supernatural. In Christianity this is conceived as the personal God who graciously discloses himself to human beings in the context of the realm of nature. The supernatural claims us, but this in such a way that as we realize personhood in relation to God, others and the created order, our freedom is enhanced, not violated. Hence Oman's opposition to authoritarianism, whether biblicist, theological or ecclesiastical. Oman's personalism was thrown into the shadows by the theology of the Word. Even his

defenders regret his relative weakness on Christology, and his failure to follow through to a fully developed doctrine of the Trinity. But that he fastened upon themes of perennial importance for theology only the most prejudiced will deny.

Sources: DNB and sources there cited; Sell.

ALAN SELL

Omel'ianovskii, Mikhail Erazmovich

Ukrainian. *b:* 19 January (O.S.) 1904, Kiev. *d:* 1 December 1979, Moscow. *Cat:* Marxist philosopher of science; academic administrator. *Ints:* Dialectical materialism; philosophy of physics. *Educ:* Institute of Red Professors in Moscow and the Institute of Physics of Moscow University. *Infls:* Marx, Engels and Lenin. *Appts:* Taught and served as an administrator at Voronezh Chemical-Technical Institute (1931–44), the Institute of Philosophy of the Soviet Academy of Sciences (1944–6 and 1955–1979) and the Institute of Philosophy of the Ukrainian Academy of Sciences (1946–55); one of the founders of the latter Institute and served as its Director, 1946–52.

Main publications:

(1947) *V. I. Lenin i fizika XX veka* [V. I. Lenin and Twentieth-Century Physics], Moscow.
(1947) *Borot'ba materiializmu proty idealizmu v suchasnii fizytsi* [The Struggle of Materialism against Idealism in Contemporary Physics], Kiev.
(1956) *Filosofskie voprosy kvantovoi mekhaniki* [Philosophical Problems of Quantum Mechanics], Moscow.
(1968) *Materialisticheskaia dialektika i metody estestvennykh nauk* [Materialist Dialectics and the Methods of the Natural Sciences], Moscow.
(1970) *Lenin i sovremennaia nauka*, Moscow (English translation, *Lenin and Modern Natural Science*, trans. S. Syrovatkin, Moscow, 1978).
(1973) *Dialektika v sovremennoi fiziki*, Moscow (English translation, *Dialectics in Modern Physics*, trans. H. C. Creighton, Moscow).
(1984) *Razvitie osnovanii fiziki XX veka i dialektika* [Dialectics and the Development of the Foundations of Twentieth-Century Physics], Moscow.

Secondary literature:

Alekseev, P. V. (ed.) (1993) *Filosofy Rossii xix-xx stoletii*, Moscow, p. 139.
Graham, Loren (1972) *Science and Philosophy in the Soviet Union*, New York: Alfred A. Knopf; revised edition, *Science, Philosophy, and Human Behavior in the Soviet Union*, Columbia University Press, 1987.

Scanlan, James P. (1985) *Marxism in the USSR*, Cornell University Press.

One of the most influential Soviet philosophers of science in the decades after the Second World War, Omel'ianovskii was a prominent figure in discussions of the relationship between dialectical materialism and modern theories in physics. His views were affected by the intensely ideological pressures of the late 1940s and 1950s, but after Khrushchev's denunciation of Stalin in 1956, Omel'ianovskii worked to liberalize dialectical materialism and facilitate communication between philosophers and scientists.

Omel'ianovskii is best known for his philosophical discussions of the principles of quantum mechanics. In his 1947 book *V. I. Lenin i fizika XX veka* [V. I. Lenin and Twentieth-Century Physics], he argued that **Heisenberg**'s indeterminacy principle and **Bohr**'s principle of complementarity, properly understood, could be accepted by a dialectical materialist, but severe criticism caused him to repudiate the principle of complementarity in a volume published later in the same year in Kiev. His 1956 book was an ambitious attempt to develop a complete dialectical materialist version of quantum theory without appeal to complementarity. In subsequent years, however, he moved in the direction of his Soviet colleague V. A. **Fock**, and in his 1973 book he accepts complementarity as compatible with materialism (relying on Fock's doctrine of 'potentialities') and as reflecting a dialectical mode of thought.

JAMES SCANLAN

Orestano, Francesco

Italian. *b:* April 1873, Alia, Palermo, Sicily. *d:* 1945. *Cat:* 'Superrealist'. *Ints:* Metaphysics; ethics. *Educ:* Studied in Palermo and Leipzig. *Infls:* Nicolai Hartmann. *Appts:* Professor of Moral Philosophy and the History of Philosophy, Palermo (1907–24), where he also taught Philosophy of Law; retired 1924; numerous official appointments, e.g. drafting educational legislation (1903–5); membership of learned societies, e.g. President of the Società Filosofica Italiana.

Main publications:

Opere complete, 18 vols, Milan: Bocca, 1939–44.
(1903) *Le idee fondamentali di F. Nietzsche nel loro progressivo svolgimento.*
(1907) *I valori umani*, 2 vols.
(1911–15) *Prolegomeni alla scienza del bene e del male*, 2 vols.
(1925) *Nuovi principî.*

(1934) *Verità dimostrate. Saggi di filosofia critica.*
(1936) (with Francesco Olgiati) *Il realismo.*
(1939) *Il nuovo realismo.*

Secondary literature:

Dollo, C. (1967) *Il pensiero filosofico di Francesco Orestano*, Padua: CEDAM.
Ottaviano, C. (1933) *Il pensiero di Francesco Orestano*, Palermo: Industrie riunite editoriali siciliane.

The theme which unifies the various aspects of Orestano's thought, and which is reflected in his self-description as 'superrealist', is his realism and complementary repudiation of the Italian idealist tradition. In his metaphysics he argues that, with one exception, the Aristotelian-Kantian apparatus of categories is provisional and revisable, the exception being the category of relation. This Orestano calls the 'category of categories' (*la categoria delle categorie*), regarding it as constitutive of all human experience. Conscious life is in essence experience of relations, and any suggested set of categories is a subset of the class of all possible relational categories. Further, he holds that the experience of relations ineludibly involves experience of a transcendent, objective world. This latter is given in experience.

An analogous realism informs his major ethical works (1907, 1911–15 and 1925). Orestano argues for a version of the interest theory of value: values are reflections of our interests and, further, they are constants derived from the entire biopsychic process we call life, which he accordingly characterizes as the 'unity of estimation' (*unità di misura*) of all values. Life itself, the precondition of interests, Orestano regards as the only absolute we experience. The absolute value of life Orestano epitomizes in his categorical imperative: so act as always to respect and promote the absolute value of life. In practice, to live the life recommended by Jesus is to do precisely this. To live in this way is to show that we can be part of a transcendent realm, and this in turn Orestano regards as ground for belief in the immortality of the soul.

ROBERT WILKINSON

Ortega y Gasset, José

Spanish. *b:* 1883, Madrid. *d:* 1955, Madrid. *Cat:* Ratio-vitalist. *Educ:* Educated at the University of Madrid and then in Germany. *Appts:* Began his career as a neo-Kantian; he began to develop his own ideas from 1910 onwards as Professor of Metaphysics at Madrid, a position he retained until forced into exile by the Civil War and the

Second World War; returned to Madrid in 1948, founding, with Julián Marías, the Institute of Humanities.

Main publications:

All in *Obras completas*, 12 vols, Madrid: Alianza/
Revista de occidente, 1983:
(1912) *Meditaciones del Quijote.*
(1921) *España invertebrada*; revised 1922 and 1934.
(1925) *La deshumanizacion del arte.*
(1930) *La rebelión de las masas.*
(1932–3) *Unas lecciones de metafisica* (published 1966).
(1935) *Historia como sistema.*
(1940) *Ideas y creencias.*
(1958) *La idea de principio en Leibniz y la evolución de la teoría deductiva* (posthumous).

Secondary literature:

Borel, J. (1959) *Raison et vie chez Ortega y Gasset*, Neuchâtel: La Baconnière.
Garagorri, P. (1970) *Introducción a Ortega*, Madrid: Alianza Editorial.
Guy, A. (1969) *Ortega y Gasset*, Paris: Seghers.
Mariàs, J. (1960) *Ortega y Gasset: circunstancia y vocación*, Madrid: Revista de Occidente.

Ortega is a figure of the first importance in the recent intellectual history of his country, both as a writer and as editor of the *Revista de Occidente*, a periodical and a series of books through which modern European ideas were transmitted to Spain. Ortega's own extensive writings range over history, politics, aesthetics and art criticism as well as the history of philosophy, metaphysics, epistemology and ethics. They are written in lucid Castilian, by a master of the language, making Ortega a considerable stylist as well as an important thinker.

After a youthful period as a neo-Kantian, Ortega began to develop his own ideas in the *Meditaciones del Quijote* (1914), and the lines of thought adumbrated there are worked out in his major philosophical works thereafter, culminating in the incomplete, posthumously published *La idea de principio en Leibniz* (1958), on which Ortega was working at the time of his death. Ortega referred to his own mature philosophy as 'ratio-vitalist', a term he uses regularly from the early 1920s onwards.

Ortega's metaphysics begins with a critique of both realism and idealism. The former takes the world or objects to be the ultimate reality, while the latter gives priority to the self. Neither view is acceptable, since there is a further category logically prior to both that of self and that of

thing, and this ultimate category is life: 'I am not my life. This, which is reality, is made up of me and of things. Things are not me and I am not things: we are mutually transcendent, but both are immanent in that absolute coexistence which is life' (1932–3, XIII). Further, although the life of an individual is given to them, each person must work unceasingly to preserve it. We are in continual danger of catastrophe, and to avoid it is our ceaseless endeavour. As he often says, 'Life is a task' ('La vida es quehacer'). Our chief asset in this struggle is reason. By 'reason' he does not mean pure intellection or a capacity for abstract thought, but more broadly, 'any intellectual action which puts us in contact with reality, by means of which we knock against the transcendent' (i.e. things; 1935, IX). This is the 'vital reason' (*razon vital*) which gives his thought its name.

This philosophy contains markedly existentialist elements. Ortega contended that the natural sciences had made no progress with regard to understanding human affairs. The reason for this is that science presupposes that nature is fixed or immutable (an assumption he refers to as the 'gigantic arbitrariness of Parmenides'), whereas human beings have no fixed nature. A human being is not a thing but a drama, and nature is merely a transitory label we fix to what we encounter in our lives: 'Man is the being who makes himself' (1935, VII). Ortega's principal ethical injunction, to live an authentic life, is grounded directly on this view. Like **Sartre**, Ortega regards human beings as condemned to be free. At each moment many possibilities are open to us, and we must choose between them. Freedom is not an activity exercised by a being with a fixed nature. To be free means to lack a constitutive identity.

Science rests on 'Eleatic' assumptions of the fixed character of nature. To deal with the affairs of human beings, who lack a fixed nature, a different sort of discipline is necessary and this is history. Life is the fundamental reality, and history is the systematic science of life. We are what has happened to us, both as individuals and as a species, and human affairs are only understandable by understanding their history. Further, history, like all knowledge, is something that we make in our struggle to survive, not a dispassionate discovery of truth. All our intellectual discoveries are elements in what Ortega calls perspectives, views of the world which ineluctibly involve an individual point of view. The only false perspective is one which claims to transcend a point of view and be absolute.

Politically, Ortega favoured a form of aristocracy, his views resting on his theories of the nature of life combined with a firm belief in natural inequalities of ability between people. Life is a struggle, and culture is insecure, needing constant attention and modification if it is not to collapse. Most human beings are incapable of the creativity and foresight needed to maintain culture, and revolutions by the masses are merely goalless protests which threaten to destroy culture. Culture is maintained by an intellectual aristocracy, who take care, however, to avoid involvement in the day-to-day activity of government, which is tedious and degrading. For the rest of the time, they should occupy themselves with what Ortega regarded as the 'exact fantasies' of philosophy, mathematics or science, games invented to allay the boredom of humdrum existence. These ideas were developed by Ortega over a long period, from *La rebelión de las masas* (1930) until his death: they are still under elaboration in this final work, *La idea de principio en Leibniz*.

ROBERT WILKINSON

Ostwald, Friedrich Wilhelm

German. **b:** 2 September 1853, Riga, Latvia. **d:** 4 April 1932, Leipzig, Germany. **Cat:** Physicist; physical chemist; philosopher of science. **Educ:** Tartu, Estonia, 1872–8; Habilitation, 1881. **Infls:** Spinoza and E. Haeckel. **Appts:** Riga Polytechnikum, 1881–7; Leipzig, 1887–1906; Founder with Van t'Hoff of the *Zeitschrift für physikalische Chemie*, 1887; Nobel Prize, 1909.

Main publications:

(ed.) (1889) *Ostwalds Klassiker der exakten Wissenschaften*, Leipzig: W. Engelmann.

(1895) *Die Überwindung des wissenschaftlichen Materialismus*, Leipzig: Veit & Co.

(1895) *Vorlesungen über Naturphilosophie*, Leipzig: Veit & Co.

(1902–) *Annalen der Naturphilosophie*, Leipzig: Veit & Co.

(1906) *Individuality and Immortality*, Boston and New York: Houghton Mifflin.

(1908) *Grundriss der Naturphilosophie*, Leipzig: Reclam.

(1909) *Die energetische Grundlagen der Kulturwissenschaften*, Leipzig: Klinckhardt.

(1910) *Die Forderung des Tages*, Leipzig: Akademische Verlagsgesellschaft.

(1911–16) *Monistische Sonntagspredigten*, 7 vols, Leipzig: Akademische (I–V), Leipzig: Unesma (VI–VII).

(1912) *Die energetische Imperativ*, Leipzig: Akademische Verlagsgesellschaft.

(1912) *Die Energie*, Leipzig: J. A. Barth.

(1913) *Die Philosophie der Werte*, Leipzig: A. Kroner.

(1914) *Arbeiten zum Monismus*, Leipzig: Unesma.

(1914) *Auguste Comte der Mann und sein Werk*, Leipzig: Unesma.

(1914) *Der Moderne Naturphilosophie*, Leipzig: Akademische.

(1926–7) *Lebenslinien*, 3 vols, Berlin: Klasing & Co.

(1929) *Die Pyramide der Wissenschaften*, Stuttgart and Berlin: J. G. Cotta'sche.

(1960) *Wissenschaft contra Gottesglaube*, ed. F. Herneck, Leipzig: Urania.

Secondary literature:

Adler, F. W. (1905) *Die Metaphysik in der Ostwaldschen Energetik*, Leipzig: OR Reisland.

Burkamp, W. (1913) *Die Entwicklung des Substanzbegriffs bei Ostwald*, Leipzig: E. Reinicke.

Capek, M. (1967) 'Ostwald, Wilhelm' in Paul Edwards (ed.) *Encyclopedia of Philosophy*, New York: Macmillan, VI: 5b–7a.

Delbos, V. (1916) *Une théorie allemande de la culture W. Ostwald*, Paris: Bloud & Gay.

Deltte, R. J. (1984) 'The energetics controversy in late 19th-century Germany: Helm, Ostwald and their critics', PhD thesis, Yale University.

Dochmann, A. (1908) *F. W. Ostwalds Energetik*, Bern: Scheitlin & Co.

Driesch, H. (1904) *Naturbegriffe und Natururteile*, Leipzig: W. Englemann.

Duhem, P. (1903) *L'Évolution de la mécanique*, Paris: Hermann.

Lenin, V. I. (1909) *Materialism and Empiriocriticism*, Moscow: Foreign Languages Publishing House.

Meyerson, E. (1908) *Identité et réalité*, Paris: Alcan.

Rey, A. (1907) *La Théorie physique chez les physiciens contemporains*, Paris: Alcan.

Rolla, A. (1908) *La Filosofia energetica*, Turin: Bocca.

Schnehen, W. von, *Energetische Weltanschauung*, Leipzig: T. Thomas.

One of the principal founders (with Svante Arrhenius and J. H. Van t' Hoff) of physical chemistry in the late nineteenth-century, with a reputation based on his work on the theory of solutions and electrolysis and on the theory and standardization of colour, Ostwald's metaphysics is an outgrowth of his scientific views. Just as in physical chemistry all that mattered were the energy relationships between different states, so in reality, on the positivist assumption that metaphysics can and should reflect one's science, matter was a redundant concept since only energy changes were experientially detectable. Thus in the eyes of Ostwald the ways were open towards a metaphysical monism in which matter was abolished and energy was the only substance. Ostwald energetically publicized his views in contributions to widely sold book series, and generalized this approach into ethics, proclaiming the 'categorical imperative' of the minimization of energy. He drew the obvious pacifist conclusion that war was evil but changed his mind on the outbreak of the First World War. While as a scientific programme energetics was popular and successful until the rise of the new atomic physics in the early years of the twentieth century, relatively few of Ostwald's scientific allies accepted his metaphysical conclusions. Although proclaimed as an anti-materialist system, it seemed to lead only to a new form of materialism. Like many other positivists he contributed extensively to the history of science. He also collaborated with **Couturat** in the international language movement.

Sources: G. Ostwald (1953) *Wilhelm Ostwald mein Vater*, Stuttgart: Berliner Union; DSB 15: 455a–469a.

R. N. D. MARTIN

Ottaviano, Carmelo

Italian. *b:* 18 January 1906, Modica, Sicily. *d:* Deceased. *Cat:* Philosopher of realism. *Educ:* Catholic University of the Sacred Heart, Milan. *Appts:* From 1939, Professor of History of Philosophy, Universities of Caglian, Naples and Catania.

Main publications:

(1942) *Metafisica dell'essere parziale*, second edition, Padua: CEDAM, 1947.
(1948) *Critica dell'idealismo*, Padua: CEDAM.
(1952) *Il problema morale come fondamento dell'problema politico*, Padua; CEDAM.
(1964) *La tragicità del reale ovvero la maliconia delle cose*, Padua; CEDAM.
(1964) *Critica di socialismo*, Padua: CEDAM.
(1968) *La legge della belezza come legge universale della natura*, Padova: CEDAM.

Ottaviano's work begins with a closely argUed criticism of the interior contradictions of idealism. The existence of the real world is demonstrated as coexisting with the self and reality is apprehended by the subjective mediation of direct contact. Finite entities in the process of becoming are shown to have to posit their existence in space and time. An examination of the negative reality of space and time reveals the way in which that leads to the sense of the tragedy of finite existence, whence theology gets involved with philosophy. God, in willing creation, forsees the gradual self-elevation of finite beings into a superior order. The supernatural is that which makes the finite finite, and liberates it from the tragic involvement with space and time by the spirItualization of the body. Given the importance of the spiritualization of the body, the incarnation should return to the centre of our speculations and Christian dogma should be given a more convincing defence. Ottaviano's work also contains an analysis of the connection between grace and free will, ethical analyses of duty and virtue and remarks on the pedagogical implications of his work.

COLIN LYAS

Otto, Rudolf

German. *b:* 25 September 1869, Peine. *d:* 6 March 1937, Marburg, Germany. *Cat:* Neo-Kantian; theologian; philosopher of religion. *Educ:* Erlangen and Göttingen. *Appts:* Professor at Göttingen (1904–14), Breslau (1914–17) and Marburg (1917–29).

Main publications:

(1907) *Naturalismus und Religion*, Tübingen: J. C. B. Mohr (English translation, *Naturalism and Religion*, London: Williams & Norgate, 1907).
(1909) *Kantisch-Fries'sche Religionsphilosophie*, Tübingen: J. C. B. Mohr (English translation, *The Philosophy of Religion*, New York: Richard Smith, 1931).
(1917) *Das Heilige, über das Irrationale in der Idee des Göttlichen und sein Verhältnis zum Rationalen*, Breslau, 25th edition, Munich: Beck, 1936 (English translation, *The Idea of the Holy, An Inquiry into the Non-rational Factor of the Divine and its Relation to the Rational*, trans. J. W. Harvey, Oxford: Oxford University Press, 1923).
(1926) *West-Östliche Mystik*, Gotha: Klotz (English translation, *Mysticism, East and West. A Comparative Analysis of the Nature of Mysticism*, New York: Macmillan, 1932).
(1932) *Sünde und Urschuld*, Munich: Beck.

Secondary literature:

Almond, Philip (1986) *Rudolf Otto: An Introduction to His Religious Philosophy*, Chapel Hill, NC: University of North Carolina Press.
Davidson, Robert F. (1947) *Rudolf Otto's Interpretation of Religion*, Princeton: Princeton University Press.

Otto is best known for his analysis of the religious. He believed that the experience of the holy was central in all of religion. Influenced both by Friedrich Schleiermacher and by Immanuel Kant, Otto argued that we must differentiate in the holy a feeling of the numinous and the schematizing concepts. The former is characterized by mystery, awe and fascination (*mysterium tremendum fascinans*). It cannot be reduced to other, non-religious feelings, but it constitutes a cognitive feeling *sui generis*. It is of something 'wholly other' than man. Numinous feelings disclose the nominous object. However, we must think of the nominous object by means of certain ideograms, or better, by certain schematizing concepts. Otto's views on the origin of the religious in the numinous was very influential especially among theologians.

MANFRED KUEHN

Ouyang Jianwu

Chinese. **b:** 1871, Yihuang, Jiangxi Province, China. **d:** 1943, Jiangjin, Sichuan Province, China. **Cat:** Buddhist reformer. **Ints:** 'Conciousness Only' Buddhism; idealist philosophy. **Educ:** Studied Song and Ming dynasty Neo-Confucianism, especially Wang Yangming, in his youth and then Buddhism with Yang Wenhui in Nanjing after the turn of the century. He travelled for a short time in Japan. **Infls:** Xuan Cang and Yang Wenhui. **Appts:** Taught at the Guangdong Guangxi Advanced Teachers' School; head of the Buddhist Scripture Printing Press upon Yang's death in 1911 and established a Buddhist Research Section; 1922, started the Chinese Academy of Inner Learning, headed a University 1924–7 to study the Marks of Existence School of Buddhism; after the outbreak of war with Japan in 1937, led followers to Sichuan, and established a branch of the Chinese Academy of Inner Learning.

Main publications:

(n.d.) *Buddha's Compassion*, Foxue Book Company.
(n.d.) *The Buddhist Law: Neither Religion Nor Philosophy*, Foxue Book Company.
(n.d.) *A Decisive Analysis of Idealism*, Foxue Book Company.
(n.d.) (ed.) *The Essential Scripture*.
(n.d.) Preface to the last fifty volumes of *On the Shrine of Yoga*.
(n.d.) *Wujing on Inner and Outer Learning (Collected Works)*.
(1921) *Selected Discussions on Consciousness Only Buddhism*, Nanjing, Institute of Inner Learning.
(1963) *On the State of Nothingness*, Taipei: Guangwen Bookstore.

Secondary literature:

Boorman, H. (1970) (ed.) *Biographical Dictionary of Republican China*, New York and London: Columbia University Press.

Briere, O. (1956) *Fifty Years of Chinese Philosophy 1898–1950*, London: George Allen & Unwin Ltd.

Chan, W. (1953) *Religious Trends in Modern China*, New York: Columbia University Press.

Complete Chinese Encyclopedia (1987), Philosophy Volumes, Beijing: Chinese Encyclopedia Publications.

Although not an original thinker, Ouyang initiated the modernization of Buddhism in China. His Buddhist studies began with the Marks of Existence and Consciousness Only Schools. The latter, propounding a rationalist and atheistic metaphysics with sophisticated analyses of consciousness, knowledge, the self and external objects, was taken from India by the monk Xuan Cang (596–664). With Ouyang's revival it proved an attractive basis for the later absorption of modern Western doctrines. Ouyang then turned to the Prajna School and the Nirvana School. Ouyang's account of the difference between Marks of Existence and Consciousness Only Buddhism led to a split into sects. He influenced Abbot Taixu, **Liang Souming** and **Xiong Shili**. **Liang Qichao** and Tang Yongtong, among others, listened to his lectures.

NICHOLAS BUNNIN

Ovink, Bernard Jan Hendrik

Dutch. **b:** 24 July 1862. **d:** 15 August 1944. **Cat:** Neo-Kantian. **Ints:** Theory of knowledge; philosophy of religion. **Educ:** Classical Philology and Philosophy, University of Utrecht. **Infls:** Personal influences included Van der Wyck and Spruyt; philosophical influences included Plato, Kant and Natorp. **Appts:** Taught Greek and Latin at secondary schools; Professor of Philosophy, University of Utrecht, 1913–32.

Main publications:

(1909) *Wijsgeerige en taalkundige verklaring van Plato's Gorgias* [Philosophical and Linguistic Explanation of Plato's Gorgias], Leyden: Brill (dissertation).

(1913) *Het kritisch idealisme* [The Critical Idealism], Utrecht: Oosthoek (Inaugural Lecture).

(1928) *De zekerheid der menschelijke kennis* [The Certainty of Human Knowledge], Zutphen: Thieme.

(1931) *Philosophische Erklärung der Platonischen Dialoge Meno und Hippias Minor*, Paris and Amsterdam.

(1938) *De filosofie en het wezen van den mensch* [Philosophy and the Essence of Man], Paris and Amsterdam.

(1940) *Philosophie und Sophistik*, 's-Gravenhage: Van Stockum.

Ovink's philosophy had its starting-point in the Marburg neo-Kantian interpretation of Kant's philosophy. Human knowledge is based on an unchangeable and irreducible a priori. There is no need for any metaphysical basis; the only task for philosophy is to analyse and to determine the logical form of all knowledge and science. Philosophy is therefore nothing more than criticism of knowledge or, in other words, self-reflection of reason. Nevertheless human reason is restricted and finite and it must be supplied by faith. Philosophy has a very modest task because human wisdom is superseded by divine wisdom. True morality is therefore based on Christian faith. His last book, on philosophy and sophistry (1940), especially, claims the value of philosophy to be no more than a critical tool. Ovink's influence was great. His pupils organized themselves into the 'Genootschap voor Critische Philosophie' [Society for Critical Philosophy] in 1923. The society continued under slightly different names until 1982.

WIM VAN DOOREN

Ovsiannikov, Mikhail Fedotovich

Russian. *b:* 21 November (O.S.) 1915, Russia. *d:* 11 August 1987, Moscow. *Cat:* Marxist aesthetician; academic administrator. *Ints:* Aesthetics; history of Western philosophy. *Educ:* Moscow Pedagogical Institute and Moscow State University. *Infls:* Hegel and Marx. *Appts:* 1960–87, Head, Department of Marxist-Leninist Aesthetics, Moscow State University; 1963–87, Head, Section of Aesthetics of the Institute of Philosophy of the Soviet Academy of Sciences; 1968–74, Dean, Philosophy Faculty, Moscow State University.

Main publications:

(1959) *Filosofiia Gegelia* [The Philosophy of Hegel], Moscow.

(1959) (with V. V. Sokolov) *Istoriia domarksistskoi zarubezhnoi filosofii* [The History of Pre-Marxist Foreign Philosophy], Moscow.

(1963) (with Z. V. Smirnova) *Ocherki istorii esteticheskikh uchenii* [Essays in the History of Aesthetic Doctrines], Moscow.

(1962–70) (ed.) *Istoriia estetiki* The History of Aesthetics], 5 vols, Moscow.

(1964) (ed. with V. A. Razumnyi) *Kratkii slovar' po estetiki* [Short Dictionary of Aesthetics], Moscow.

(1974) *Esteticheskaia teoriia K. Marksa, F. Engel'sa, V. I. Lenina* [The Aesthetic Theory of K. Marx, F. Engels and V. I. Lenin], Moscow.

(1978) *Istoriia esteticheskoi mysli* [History of Aesthetic Thought], Moscow; second edition, 1983.

Secondary literature:

Alekseev, P. V. (ed.) (1993) *Filosify Rossii xix–xx stoletii* [Russian Philosophers of the 19th–20th Centuries], Moscow, p. 136.

Scanlan, James P. (1985) *Marxism in the USSR: A Critical Survey of Current Soviet Thought*, Cornell University Press.

Swiderski, Edward M. (1979) *The Philosophical Foundations of Soviet Aesthetics*, Dordrecht: D. Reidel.

A Marxist-Leninist with broad interests in the history of thought, Ovsiannikov aided in reintroducing Western European philosophy into the Soviet Union after the years of Stalinist isolation and in establishing aesthetics as a separate philosophical discipline within the framework of Marxist philosophy in the USSR. His history of 'foreign philosophy' before Marx and his monograph on the philosophy of Hegel, both published in 1959, were among the first works of their kind to appear as a result of the post-Stalin 'thaw'.

In aesthetics his contributions included authorship and editorship of several groundbreaking works, including the first Russian-language dictionary of aesthetics, a history of aesthetic thought and a multivolume collection of Western and Russian sources in aesthetics. In keeping with his philosophical commitment to Marxism he gave special attention to the social context of art and to its ideological function of promoting the building of communism.

Because of Ovsiannikov's leadership positions at both Moscow State University and the Institute of Philosophy, the bulk of graduate study in aesthetics in the USSR took place under his aegis from the early 1960s until his death.

JAMES SCANLAN

Owen, Gwilym Ellis Lane

British. *b:* 18 May 1922, Portsmouth, England. *d:* 10 July 1982, Cambridge, England. *Cat:* Classical philosopher; philosopher of language. *Educ:* Corpus Christi College, Oxford. *Infls:* Literary influences include Russell, Werner Jaeger and Vlastos;

personal influences include Ryle. **Appts:** 1950–3, Research Fellow in Arts at the University of Durham; 1953–66, Lecturer, then Reader in Ancient Philosophy, then Professor of Ancient Philosophy at Oxford University; 1966–73, Victor S. Thomas Professor of Philosophy and the Classics at Harvard University; 1973–82, Laurence Professor of Ancient Philosophy at Cambridge University.

Main publications:

(1960) (ed. with A. Düring) *Aristotle and Plato in the Mid-Fourth Century*, Göteborg: Elanders Boktryckeri Actiebolag.

(1968) (ed.) *Aristotle on Dialectic: The Topics*, Oxford: Oxford University Press.

(1982) *Logic, Science and Dialectic* (Owen's collected papers in Greek philosophy), ed. Martha Nussbaum, London: Duckworth.

Secondary literature:

Schofield, M. and Nussbaum, M. (eds) *Language and Logos: Studies in Ancient Greek Philosophy presented to G. E. L. Owen*, Cambridge: Cambridge University Press (contains bibliography of Owen's publications).

Although he wrote no book and only a relatively modest number of published papers, G. E. L. Owen exerted through these, lectures, seminars, graduate supervision and conferences a profound influence on postwar scholarship in ancient philosophy. As well as having a central interest in both Plato and Aristotle, Owen also exercised his impressive array of erudition, insight and analytic skills on the pre-Socratics and the science of the ancient world.

Owen took a keen interest in the dating of Plato's dialogues and the works of Aristotle, and correlatively in developments in the views of these philosophers, perhaps above all in the vicissitudes of the theory of Forms. His unorthodox, and still highly controversial, contention that Plato's *Timaeus* should be classified as a middle-period rather than a late dialogue—on the grounds of its uncritical acceptance of the theory of Forms—projected Owen right to the forefront of classical scholarship, where he remained. His happy knack of simultaneous engagement with classical scholarship and live philosophical issues is illustrated by his discussions of Aristotle's conception of focal meaning, in relation to such words as 'medical', 'good', 'being' and 'exists'.

Sources: WW 1982; obituary, *The Times*, 12 Jul 1982; CA 107, 1983.

CLIVE BORST

P

Paci, Enzo

Italian. *b:* 19 December 1911, Ancona, Italy. *d:* 21 July 1976, Milan. *Cat:* Existentialist; phenomenologist; critical Marxist. *Ints:* Philosophy of man. *Educ:* University of Milan. *Infls:* Antonio Banfi, Marx, Merleau-Ponty, Husserl and Whitehead, A. N. *Appts:* 1951–7, Professor of Philosophy, University of Pavia; 1958–76, Professor of Philosophy, University of Milan.

Main publications:

(1950) *Il nullo et il problema dell'uomo*; third edition, Turin: Taylor, 1967.

(1954) *Tempo e relazione*, Turin: Taylor.

(1957) *Dall'esistenzialismo al relazionismo*, Messina and Florence: D'Anna.

(1957) *La filosofia contemporanea*, Milan: Garzanti.

(1967) *Funzione delle scienze e significato dell'uomo*; fourth edition, Milan: Il Saggiatore, 1970 (English translation, *The Function of the Sciences and the Meaning of Man*, Evanston, Ill: Northwestern University Press, 1972).

(1973) *Idee per un enciclopedia fenomenologica*, Milan: Bompiani.

Secondary literature:

(1986) *Aut Aut*, (Enzo Paci edition), Milan.

Civita, Alfredo (1983) *Bibliografia degli scritti di Enzo Paci*, Florence: La Nuova Italia.

Dallmayr, Fred R. (1973) 'Phenomenology and Marxism: A salute to Enzo Paci', in George Psathas (ed.), *Phenomenological Sociology*, New York and London: John Wiley & Sons, pp. 305–56.

Maiorca, Bruno (1987) 'Centodieci scritti di Enzo Paci (1938–1987)', *Rivista di Storia della Filosofia* 42: 747–58.

Semerari, Giuseppe (1977) 'L'opera e il pensiero di Enzo Paci', *Rivista Critica di Storia della Filosofia* 32: 78–94.

Vigorelli, Amedeo (1987) *L'esistenzialismo positivo di Enzo Paci*, Milan: Franco Angeli.

Paci's seminal work, *Tempo e relazione* (1954), sets forth a version of process philosophy which has some affinities with **Whitehead**. The universe consists, he argues, not of bounded objects in space, but of processes or events, of which objects are but the historical and temporary products. It is events, not objects, that are metaphysically primitive. Events are related to one another in a continual interweaving dialectic, which is governed and informed by a dynamic tendency to realize the values of truth, goodness and beauty. It is the relations among events which establish their identity, and this is true also of persons, who are focal points in particular networks of developing and changing processes. The 'stuff' of the universe is relation rather than substance; and time rather than space is the dimension which the universe inhabits. Paci's reputation in Italy was very high during his lifetime, but has declined since then.

Sources: DFN; EF.

HUGH BREDIN

Palmer, George Herbert

American. *b:* 19 March 1842, Boston, Masachusetts. *d:* 7 May 1933, Cambridge, Massachusetts. *Cat:* Idealist. *Ints:* Moral theory. *Educ:* Harvard; two years studying in Germany and visiting Paris were his only substantial breaks from Cambridge, Massachusetts; in 1870 he obtained a theological degree from Andover Theological Seminary. *Appts:* Instructor in Greek at Harvard in 1870; produced a translation of the *Odyssey*, but transferred to Philosophy two years later and continued to teach until 1913; built the philosophy department and served as Chairman when James, Royce, and Santayana were hired; he was, however, more a 'philosopher's philosopher' and less a public figure than James and Santayana, and his colleagues regarded him with respect; played a variety of roles in the administration of the university. He had a continuing interest in literature and wrote about George Herbert, Browning, and Shakespeare.

Main publications:

(1887) *The New Education*, Boston: Little, Brown & Co.

(1901) *The Field of Ethics*, Boston: Houghton Mifflin.

(1903) *The Nature of Goodness*, Boston: Houghton Mifflin.

(1911) *The Problem of Freedom*, Boston: Houghton Mifflin.

(1919) *Altruism: Its Nature and Varieties*, New York: Scribner.

(1930) *The Autobiography of a Philosopher*; New York: Houghton Mifflin, Greenwood Press, 1968.

The Nature of Goodness (1903), widely thought to be Palmer's best work, centres on a distinction between extrinsic and intrinsic goodness. Extrinsic goodness is goodness which a thing possesses by virtue of its ability to produce something else. Intrinsic goodness is a property which belongs to certain wholes so organized that every part is good for every other part. Like most idealist thinkers, Palmer associated the good with self-realization, but his self-realization involved a social order. He spoke of the 'conjunct self' and the 'separate self'. The conjunct self is composed of relations with other selves. It may seem that this logically implies the priority of the separate self, since there must be something to be related, but Palmer argues that the 'separate self' considered by itself is unintelligible.

He believed strongly that philosophy departments should be staffed by people who disagreed with one another and insisted on a strongly pluralistic atmosphere at Harvard—one from which he drew much of his inspiration. One can see the influence of his colleagues in his work. He is most like **Royce** in his own ethical theory, but overall much more cautious and constantly critical of wide-ranging speculations. Like **James**, he appreciated down-to-earth examples. Although both *The Nature of Goodness* and *The Field of Ethics* (1901) contain distinctions and analyses which are still useful, and Palmer continues to be remembered in American intellectual history, especially in the history of higher education, his work has attracted little critical attention from contemporary philosophers.

Sources: Edwards; WWW(Am).

LESLIE ARMOUR

Pap, Arthur

Swiss-American. *b:* 1921, Zurich. *d:* 7 September 1959, New Haven, Connecticut. *Cat:* Logical positivist. *Ints:* Philosophy of logic; philosophy of science; epistemology. *Educ:* Juilliard School, New York; Columbia University, New York. *Infls:* Carnap and Nagel. *Appts:* Lecturer, Chicago and City College, New York, 1946–9; Professor, Oregon, 1949–53; Yale, 1953–9.

Main publications:

(1946) *The A Priori in Physical Theory*, New York: King's Crown.

(1949) *Elements of Analytic Philosophy*, New York: Macmillan.

(1955) *Analytische Erkenntnislehre*, Vienna: Springer.

(1958) *Semantics and Necessary Truth*, New Haven: Yale University Press.

(1962) *Introduction to the Philosophy of Science*, Glencoe: Free Press.

Secondary literature:

Blanshard, Brand (1962) 'Epilogue', in Pap, *Introduction to the Philosophy of Science*.

Pap was perhaps the last of the logical positivists, indeed a combative and vehement one. He showed his loyalty by going to Vienna in the mid-1950s in order to reacquaint philosophers there with the persistence and progress of the school that had come into existence there but had been more or less completely obliterated in the two decades since the *Anschluss* of 1938. But while he largely confined himself to the favourite topics of the Vienna Circle, engaged himself with them in a traditionally positivistic fashion, with large recourse to the symbolism of modern formal logic, and was unwaveringly hostile to irrationalism and the supernatural, he was doggedly critical of positivist doctrines and, to the extent that he went so far as to provide an alternative to the views he rejected, espoused aprioristic or Platonistic ones. The prime example of this tormented position was his criticism of the theory that all necessary truth is analytic, set out in numerous articles and his most important book, *Semantics and Necessary Truth* (1958). In it he argued that if *analytic* meant 'reducible by definitions to a truth of logic' then *nothing can be red and green all over*, although necessary, is not analytic. If *analytic* means 'true in virtue of meaning' the thesis that all necessary truth is analytic is trivial. In the same spirit he opposed the idea that necessary truth is a matter of linguistic convention of the ground that while it is a matter of linguistic convention that the sentence, the string of words, 'all bald men are bald' expresses a necessary truth, the necessity of the proposition that the words express is not. That was to ascribe real, substantial existence to meanings, to concepts and propositions, as objects of a kind of intellectual, and so non-empirical, intuition in the manner of such anti-positivists as C. D. **Broad** and A. C. **Ewing**. In the same way he found fault with all but the most attenuated and toothless formulations of the verification principle. He attacked phenomenalism for lacking an adequate account of the conditionals about sense-data to which it proposed to reduce statements about the material world. He worried away at the regularity theory of causation on the familiar ground that it cannot distinguish mere coincidental regularities from real causal connections. On the question of probability he was critical of the frequency theory, but showed some readiness to accept **Carnap**'s version of the range theory. An interestingly typical instance of Pap's breezy destructiveness is an article in which two more or less positivistic theses are set up to destroy each other like Kilkenny cats: the nominalism that identifies qualities with the sets of their instances and the anti-substance view that there is no more to a thing than the set of its qualities.

Pap was an active disputant in his short life but the subject has to some extent moved away from the field of his main interests.

Sources: Passmore 1957; Hill.

ANTHONY QUINTON

Papanoutsos, Evangelos

Greek. **b:** 27 July 1900, Piraeus, Greece. **d:** 2 May 1982, Athens. **Cat:** Epistemologist. **Ints:** Theory of knowledge; ethics; aesthetics; philosophy of education; history of philosophy. **Educ:** Universities of Athens, Berlin, Tübingen and Paris. **Infls:** Pragmatism, Bergson, Otto, Spranger and Kant. **Appts:** Taught in secondary education (1921–31); taught in and directed many teachers' training colleges (1931–44); director and general secretary in the Ministry of Education (1944–6, 1950–3, 1963–5), where he became a pioneer of educational reform; founding member of the prestigious educational association Athenaion (1946–67); Editor of the journal *Education* (1947–61); Member of Parliament (1974–7); member of the Academy of Athens (1980–2); held an honorary doctorate in Law from the University of St Andrews (1965).

Main publications:

(1924) *The Philosophy of Henri Bergson*, Alexandria.

(1924) *Pragmatism or humanism*, Alexandria.

(1928) *The Trilogy of the Mind: Art, Ethics, Science*, Alexandria and Athens.

(1930) *On Art*, Alexandria and Athens.

(1932) *On Ethics*, Athens.

(1937) *On Science*, Athens.

(1948) 'La catharsis aristotélicienne', *Eranos* 34 (Göteberg): 77–93; 'La catharsis des passions

d'après Aristotle', Athens: Institut Français d'Athens, 1953.

(1948) *Aesthetics*, Athens: Ikaros.

(1949) *Ethics*, Athens: Ikaros.

(1954/62/73) *Theory of knowledge*, Athens (English translation from the second edition, *The Foundations of Knowledge*, trans. J. P. Anton and B. Coukis, Albany NY: SUNY Press, 1968).

(1974) *Law and Virtue*, Athens: Ekdoseis Dodone.

(1976) *Education: Our Major Problem*, Athens: Ekdoseis Dodone.

(1978) *The Crisis of our Civilisation*, Athens: Philippotes.

(1980) *Ephemera, Present and Past*, Athens: Ikaros.

(1989) *Arts and Emotion: The Aesthetics of E.P.P.*, New York: Peter Lang.

Secondary literature:

Henderson, G. P. (1983) *E. P. Papanoutsos*, Boston: Twayne Publishers.

Although a thinker with varied interests in ethics, aesthetics, philosophy of history and the history of philosophy, Papanoutsos's most important work was in epistemology. Here he advocated a form of rationalism which he described as 'critical philosophy', aiming at a synthesis of traditional dualisms and a transcendence of dogmatism and relativism.

STAVROULA TSINOREMA

Papini, Giovanno

Italian. **b:** 9 January 1881, Florence. **d:** 8 July 1956. **Cat:** Pragmatist and literary figure. **Infls:** Nietzsche, Bergson, James and F. C. S. Schiller. **Appts:** Editor of various reviews, including *Leonardo, La Voce, L'Anima, Lacoba, La Rinasata*.

Main publications:

(1906) *Il crepusculo dei filosofi*, Milan: Lombarda.

(1913) *Pragmatismo*, Milan (many editions).

(1913) *Un uomo finito*, Milan (English translation, *A Man Finished*, trans Mary Agnetti, London, Hodder & Stoughton: 1930).

(1929) *S. Agustino*, Florence.

(1932) *Gli amanti di sofia*, Florence: Vallecchi.

Secondary literature:

Gullace, G. (1962) 'The pragmatist movement in Italy', *Journal of the History of Ideas* 23: 91–106.

Prezzolini, G. (1914) *Discorso su Giovanni Papini*, Florence.

Santucci, Antonio (1963) *Il pragmatismo in Italia*, Bologna.

Sciacca, M. F. (1927) *Il secolo XX*, second edition, vol. 1, pp. 22–5.

Papini was a leading figure in the Italian reaction against positivism at the beginning of the century. He and others founded a nonconformist review (*Leonardo*) in which the advocacy of pragmatism was intermingled with a broad reformist programme in both politics and religion. Pragmatism was associated with liberation from the orthodoxies which then prevailed in the Italian academic world. Papini was a pluralist, allowing value to metaphysics but rejecting the notion of absolute metaphysical truth. In later life his interests turned increasingly in the direction of religion. Compared with Giovanni **Vailati** or Mario Calderoni, Papini does not emerge as the most rigorous or philosophically interesting of the Italian pragmatists. Nor did pragmatism, opposed by the Church and, later, by the idealists **Croce** and **Gentile**, really put down roots in Italy. However, in large measure due to the influence of Papini, it was of some importance in the period prior to the First World War.

Sources: Edwards; BLC; NUC; Ridolfi, *Vita di G. Papini*.

STUART BROWN

Pardo, Raymundo

Argentinian. *b:* 1916, Argentina. *Cat:* 'Evolutionary empiricist'. *Ints:* Epistemology. *Infls:* Aristotelian-Thomist tradition and J. S. Mill. *Appts:* Professor of Epistemology and History of Science, Universidad Nacional de la Plata, 1948–55; same post and Director of the School of Philosophy, Universidad Nacional de Rosario, from 1956.

Main publications:

(1949) *Ensayo sobre los integrantes racionales (esquema)*, Buenos Aires: Sociedad Argentina de Filosofia.

(1951) *La doctrina epistemologica*, Buenos Aires: Sociedad Argentina de Filosofia.

(1951) *Los datos de la linguistica y el caracter evolutivo de la razon*, Buenos Aires: Sociedad Argentina de Filosofia.

(1953) *Las epistemologias evolutivas de la razon en la filosofia contemporanea*, Buenos Aires: Sociedad Argentina de Filosofia.

(1954) *Del origen a la esencia del conocimiento: los datos de la ciencia y el problema del mundo exterior*, Buenos Aires: Sociedad Argentina de Filosofia (the fifth part of the essay on 'integrantes racionales').

(1965) *Ser y verdad en una teoria evolutiva: sexta parte del Ensayo sobre los integrantes racionales*, Buenos Aires: Sociedad Argentina de Filosofia.

(1973) *La ciencia y la filosofia como saber sin ser: primera seccion de la septima parte del Ensayo sobre los integrantes racionales*, Rosario, Santa Fe: Universidad Nacional de Rosario.

Pardo's thought is in essence the outcome of the application of empiricist principles (derived from Mill) to the problems of the Aristotelian–Thomist tradition. His epistemology rests on the axiom that all concepts are derived from experience, including the most abstract categories of self, reason and being. The central term announced in 1949 and used by Pardo throughout his philosophy is that of a 'rational integrant' (*integrante racional*), defined as 'everything which comes within the perceptual-apperceptive experience of a mind' (*todo aquello que cae bajo la experiencia percepto-aperceptiva de una mente*), and so close to Locke's use of the term 'idea'. Any mental content is a rational integrant in this sense, and reason, in Pardo's usage, is the conjunction of them all.

Further, as a consequence of his work on both formal and empirical science, Pardo contends that all concepts are mutable, including that of being (cf. 1965 and 1973): there can be 'knowledge without [the concept of] being' (*saber sin ser*). Another way of saying that concepts change is to say that they evolve: hence Pardo's self-description as an 'evolutionary empiricist' (cf. 1953). An obvious objection to this view is that, since it entails that the concept of truth is in principle also mutable, it is perniciously relativistic. Pardo's reply is to agree that his views entail that truth is non-absolute; but he also insists that the rational integrant 'truth' is 'characteristic' (*caracteristico*) of human thought in general.

Sources: Ferrater Mora.

ROBERT WILKINSON

Pareto, Vilfredo

Italian. *b:* 15 July 1848, Paris. *d:* 1923, Celigny. *Cat:* Economic and social philosopher. *Educ:* Educated initially as an engineer, Pareto worked initially in Turin (the family had returned to Italy in 1858), then turned to economics and sociology. *Appts:* Professor, University of Lausanne, 1892–1908; retired from teaching in 1908 and lived in Celigny (near Geneva), where he wrote his last works.

Main publications:

In *Oeuvres complètes*, Geneva: Droz, 1964–89:

(1896–7) *Cours d'économie politique*.

(1902) *Systèmes socialistes.*
(1906) *Manuale d'economia politica.*
(1916) *Trattato di sociologia generale.*
(1920) *Fatti e theorie.*

Secondary literature:

Freund, J. (1986) *Pareto*, Washington DC: Plutarch.
Mongardini, C. (1973) *V. Pareto: Dall'economica alla sociologia*, Rome: Bulzoni.
Powers, C. (1986) *V. Pareto*, Beverly Hills: Sage.
Spirito, U. (1978) *V. Pareto*, Rome: Cadmo.

The son of an exiled supporter of Mazzini, Pareto worked as an engineer and railway director until controversies about free trade lured him to economics. An inheritance allowed him to study the new mathematical economics of Walras, whom he succeeded at the University of Lausanne. He was an economist and sociologist who believed both subjects to form part of a unified social science constructed upon the inductive methodological principles of the empirical natural sciences. To economics he contributed the theory of equilibrium and the idea of the maximum efficiency of an economy as one in which it is impossible to improve one person's utility without damaging another's (Pareto optimality). He believed that the means-end rationality of economics needed supplementation by an account of non-rational action in social behaviour and by an account of political power (the theory of elites). Pareto believed a large part of human behaviour to be non-logical. The task of the social scientist is to penetrate the rationalizations (derivations) people offer in order to detect the attitudes (residues) which underlie them. Against Marx, Pareto argued that class struggle and the superstructure of a society do not have a solely economic base. In all societies there is a separation between masses and elites, social equilibrium being upheld by the renewing circulation of elites. The theory of elites is still strongly influential in social and political theory. *Systèmes socialistes* (1902) discusses various theories with brilliant élan and enormous erudition, if it does not always accurately characterize the positions of the theorists under discussion. It is, given its author's commitment to scientific objectivity, an oddly polemical work and its protests at all the feebleness and humanitarianism of the bourgeois, its deprecations of democratic and pacifist aspirations, and its belief in the inevitability of violence and the dictatorship of the minority pervade also the *Trattato di sociologia generale* (1916).

COLIN LYAS

Pareyson, Luigi

Italian. *b:* 4 February 1918, Piasco. *d:* 6 September 1991, Rapallo. *Cat:* Aesthetician. *Ints:* Existentialism; German idealism; philosophy of man. *Educ:* University of Turin. *Infls:* Augusto Guzzo, Karl Jaspers and German idealism. *Appts:* 1952–85, Professor of Philosophy and Director of the Institute of Aesthetics, University of Turin.

Main publications:

(1950) *Esistenza e persona*; fourth edition, Genoa: Il Melangolo, 1985.
(1954) *Estetica: teoria della formatività*; third edition, Florence: Sansoni, 1974.
(1961) *L'estetica e i suoi problemi*, Milan: Marzorati.
(1967) *L'esperienza artistica*; second edition, Milan: Marzorati, 1974.
(1971) *Verità e interpretazione*, Milan: Mursia.

Secondary literature:

Bredin, Hugh (1966) 'The aesthetics of Luigi Pareyson', *The British Journal of Aesthetics* 6: 193–203.
D'Acunto, Giuseppe (1985) 'Il problema dell'interpretazione in Luigi Pareyson', *Cannochiale* (Rome) 3: 71–93.
Modica, Giuseppe (1980) *Per una ontologia della libertà. Saggio sulla prospettiva filosofica di Luigi Pareyson*, Rome: Cadmo.
Zander, H. (1972) 'Ästhetische Universalität und künstlerische Autonomie. Eine Untersuchung der ästhetischen Grundbegriffe Luigi Pareysons', *Zeitschrift für Ästhetik und allgemeine Kunstwissenschaft* 17: 232–61.

Pareyson is best known in Italy and abroad as a philosopher of aesthetics. The central concept in his aesthetics is that of 'formativity' (*formatività*), which he defines as 'a way of making such that, while one makes, one invents the way of making'. Pareyson considers formativity to be a distinctive feature in all human activity, a feature which testifies to, and is a product of, the freedom and autonomy of the person. In the case of art, however, formativity is engaged in for its own sake rather than instrumentally: art, thus, is 'pure formativity'. Pareyson avoids aesthetic formalism by arguing that the artist's 'way of making', his mode of formativity, is a kind of transformation of his personality, so that content, which expresses and reflects the personality, is also an aspect of form. Pareyson's work on aesthetics was always well received, and his reputation is still high.
Sources: DFN; EF; *Dizionario generale degli autori italiani contemporanei.*

HUGH BREDIN

Parfit, D(erek) A(ntony)

British. **b:** 1942, Chengtu, West China. **Cat:**
Analytic philosopher. **Ints:** Ethics; philosophy of
mind. **Educ:** Balliol College, Oxford. **Infls:** Henry
Sidgwick. **Appts:** Since 1967, various Fellowships
at All Souls College, Oxford; 1986, Fellow of the
British Academy.

Main publications:

(1984) *Reasons and Persons*, Oxford: Clarendon
Press.

Secondary literature:

(1986) Symposium on *Reasons and Persons*, in *Ethics*
96.
Dancy, Jonathan (ed.) (forthcoming) *Reading Parfit*,
Oxford: Basil Blackwell.

In *Reasons and Persons* (1984), Parfit exhaustively
attacks the idea that the rational course of action
for an individual is always to further his own
good. In place of this he proposes a broadly
utilitarian ethic, although one that gives some
priority to benefiting those who are worse off.
These normative views rest partly upon a view of
personal identity. According to Parfit, a person's
identity over time consists merely in the various
relationships between certain psychological states
and traits, such as remembering, intending,
believing and so on. These relationships can hold
to different degrees (one remembers more of what
happened yesterday than of what happened forty
years ago), and so the continuance of one's
personal identity is also a matter of degree. Parfit
holds that, since we are less strongly psychologically connected with our more distant future
selves, it is not irrational for us to care less about
our further future. Our concern for the welfare of
others, however, should be correspondingly greater, since, given this view of personal identity, the
distinction between individual persons is correspondingly weaker.

Parfit's work is widely thought to be one of the
most significant contributions to utilitarian theory this century.

Sources: WW 1992; personal communication.

ANTHONY ELLIS

Pariente, Jean-Claude

French. **b:** 1930. **Cat:** Philosopher of language;
epistemologist. **Ints:** Theory and history of lan-
guage. **Educ:** Université de Clermont-Ferrand
(Agrégé in Philosophy). **Infls:** Condillac, Leibniz,
Henri Bergson, Wittgenstein, Ernst Cassirer and
Noam Chomsky. **Appts:** Professor of Philosophy,
Université de Clermont-Ferrand.

Main publications:

(1969) 'Bergson et Wittgenstein', *Revue internationale de Philosophie* 2–3.

(1971) 'Le rationalisme appliqué de J.-J. Rousseau',
in *Hommage à Jean Hyppolite*, Paris: PUF.

(1973) *Le Langage et l'individuel*, Paris: Colin.

(1975) 'Sur la théorie du langage à Port-Royal', in
Studia Leibnitziana 7.

(1979) 'Grammaire, logique et ponctuation', in
Textes et Documents, Société Française d'Étude du
XVIIIième Siècle, Clermont-Ferrand.

(1982) 'Sur la théorie du verbe chez Condillac', in J.
Suard (ed.), *Condillac et les problemes de langage*,
Paris: Slatkine.

Secondary literature:

Griffiths Phillips, A. (ed.) (1989) *Contemporary
French Philosophy*, Cambridge: Cambridge University Press.

Pariente is a philosopher of language and
epistemologist whose work is oriented in two
directions, the one more theoretical and the other
more historical.

In his chief work, *Le langage et l'individuel*
(1973), it is the theoretical approach that is
dominant. Here his concern is to establish that
the idea of individuality must be conceived as a
formal notion (*notion formelle*), that is to say,
defined linguistically and not as a material notion
(*notion matérielle*)—not, that is to say, in its
relation to determinate aspects of reality. In his
view, this approach allows one to conceive forms
of individuality other than those that are exemplified in ordinary objects of experience; so that
the theory of individuality will then consist in
determining for each type of 'language of knowledge' (*langage de connaissance*) the principles of
individualization with which it operates and the
forms of individuality that these sustain. In this,
Pariente's ideal objective is to determine a
scientific criterion which would apply to the
various human sciences (for example, psychology)
and assist in rendering their methods more exact.

Pariente regards his historical studies of
language (for example, the account of the
grammar and the logic of Port-Royal in his article
of 1975) as complementing his theoretical investigations by providing a perspective in which we
may better appreciate the problems arising from
our present-day grammar and logic. Pariente's

original and stimulating work is not yet widely known outside of France.
Sources: Huisman.

STEPHEN MOLLER

Passmore, John

Australian. *b:* 19 September 1914, Sydney, Australia. *Cat:* Empirical realist. *Ints:* History of philosophy; history of ideas; philosophical method. *Educ:* Sydney University. *Infls:* Anderson and Popper. *Appts:* Lecturer, Sydney University, 1935–49; Professor of Philosophy, Otago University, New Zealand, 1950–4; Reader, then Professor, Australian National University, Canberra, from 1954.

Main publications:

(1951) *Ralph Cudworth*, Cambridge: Cambridge University Press.
(1952) *Hume's Intentions*, Cambridge: Cambridge University Press.
(1957) *A Hundred Years of Philosophy*, London: Duckworth.
(1961) *Philosophical Reasoning*, London: Duckworth.
(1970) *The Perfectibility of Man*, London: Duckworth.
(1974) *Man's Responsibility for Nature*, London: Duckworth.
(1978) *Science and its Critics*, London: Duckworth.
(1980) *The Philosophy of Teaching*, London: Duckworth.
(1985) *Recent Philosophers*, London: Duckworth.
(1991) *Serious Art*, London: Duckworth.

Secondary literature:

Passmore, John (1975) 'The making of an Australian philosopher', in *Philosophers on Their Own Work*.

Passmore is the historian *par excellence* of twentieth-century philosophy, in the English-speaking world. He has always been a loyal disciple of **Anderson**, but has managed to achieve a distinguished and very productive philosophical career in the face of what has been called 'Andersonian blight', the dictatorial antagonism of Anderson to any published exposition and development of his thought by his pupils. Passmore's first books concerned philosophers of the fairly remote past. They were thoroughly scholarly, especially that on Cudworth, but they were also philosophical. Cudworth was shown to be less of an ethical rationalist than had been supposed. Hume was seen as subverting by his own findings the large intellectual aim he had set

himself: that of being the Newton of the human or social sciences. Anxious to undermine the pretensions of religion to rational justification, Hume undermined science as well, in this somewhat anticipating the verificationism of the logical positivists. Passmore's most impressive production is his *A Hundred Years of Philosophy* (1957), a magnificently thorough and underivative account of philosophy from J. S. Mill's *System of Logic* in 1843 to the date of publication. It is not, like A. J. **Ayer**'s much more lightweight potboiler on the same subject, a partisan work, but it has a point of view, revealed in its distribution of attention and occasional comments. Passmore is in favour of rationally argued, rather than prophetic or sibylline, philosophy, but applies a hospitably inclusive concept of rationality, which embraces the British idealists, **Brentano** and the phenomenological movement, American realists, new and critical, and argumentative metaphysicians of all sorts as well as the apostolic succession from **Russell** and **Moore**. The book is particularly good on the detail and philosophical implications of developments in logic. Twenty-eight years later in *Recent Philosophers* (1985) the story was brought up to date with a vengeance, only the most chic publications being considered at any length. Passmore's own philosophical position has to be extracted from the emphases of his large history, from his defence of an irreducible multiplicity of philosophical methods in his admirable *Philosophical Reasoning* (1961) and the articles, few in number, that are not about other philosophers. Like **Popper**, he affirms that there can be no mechanical method of scientific discovery. A one-world naturalism is derived from Anderson's doctrine that there is only one way of being. He thinks well of **Ryle**, but not of Oxford ordinary-language philosophy. He takes science to be the paradigm of rational thought, but discards the programmatic rigidities of logical positivism. He has written, on the margins of philosophy, about the history of the idea of human perfectibility and of the idea of concern for the well-being of nature. He has contributed to aesthetics; both in a celebrated article on its dreariness and more positively in a thorough, richly detailed but ultimately rather inconclusive study of 'serious art'. Since Passmore has propounded no definite body of doctrine he has had no clearly discernible influence. His philosophical histories, however, soon secured unquestioned authority and have retained it, without serious competition.
Sources: Grave.

ANTHONY QUINTON

Pastore, Valentino Annibale

Italian. **b:** 13 November 1868, Orbassano, Turin. **d:** 27 February 1956, Turin. **Cat:** Philosopher of science. **Appts:** Professor of Theoretical Philosophy, University of Turin.

Main publications:

(1906) *Logica formale dedotta dalla considerazione dei modelli meccanici.*
(1907) *Del nuove spirito della scienza e della filosofia.*
(1910) *Sillogismo e proporzione.*
(1911) *Dell'essere e del conoscere.*
(1913) *Il pensiero puro.*
(1921) *Il problema della causalità*, 2 vols.
(1923) *Il solipsismo.*
(1936) *La logica del poteziamento.*
(1939) *Logica sperimentale.*
(1940) *L'acrisia di Kant.*
(1946) *La filosofia di Lenin*, Milan: Bolla.
(1948) *La volontà dell'assurdo. Storia e crisi dell'esistenzialismo*, Milan: Bolla.
(1957) *La qualia*, Padua: CEDAM.

Secondary literature:

Russo, G. (1982) *Annibale Pastore*, Catania: Edizioni Greco.
Selvaggi, F. (1947) *Dalla filosofia alla tecnica*, Rome: Gregorian University.

The first, and for many years the only, Italian philosopher to wrestle with modern science and its philosophy, Pastore's work is characterized by a deep knowledge of developments in mathematics and science in the twentieth century and displays a mastery of its language and concepts. He opened Italian philosophy to a whole new range of problems: to the most advanced analyses of the concept of number and the foundations of geometry; to Russell's amalgamation of logic and mathematics; and to the theory of relativity and the new advances made in physics by **Einstein**, **Schrödinger**, **Heisenberg** and **Bohr**. For Pastore epistemology, the theory of knowledge, is, in its strictest sense, the theory of science and the problem of scientific method, a problem to which much of his writing is devoted, and a problem of immediate significance in the Italy of his day which had witnessed a surge of irrationalism and of antiscientific and antipositivist sentiment. After 1922, while still dealing with scientific knowledge, Pastore came to a conception of philosophy as the study of pure thought, a 'general logic' whose basis lies outside particular logical systems, and with Geymonat undertook the search for the process of construction of the

most elementary forms of thinking. This involved a somewhat obscure distinction between logic as logicality (the 'general logic' mentioned above) and logic as a particular system in which there is talk of a 'logical intuition of the universe'. His sense of mystery was further to motivate his study of existentialism and historical materialism.

COLIN LYAS

Patočka, Jan

Czech. **b:** 1 June 1907, Turnov. **d:** 13 March 1977, Prague. **Cat:** Phenomenologist. **Ints:** Ancient philosophy; phenomenology; hemeneutics; philosophy of science. **Educ:** DSc, PhD, Charles University of Prague, 1931; Habilitation, Charles University of Prague, 1936; 1932–3, University of Berlin, where he studied under N. Hartmann, while also working with Brock, Reichenbach and Klein; after 1933, went to Freiburg, where he studied with Husserl and Fink. **Infls:** Ancient philosophy (especially Plato and Aristotle); the transcendental phenomenology of Edmund Husserl; the existential treatment of *Dasein* and the hermeneutics of Being of Martin Heidegger; the humanism of the Moravian philosopher T. G. Masaryk. **Appts:** Dozent (Lecturer), Charles University of Prague, 1945–8; with the Communist takeover in 1948 he was banned from teaching; became an archivist, Masaryk Institute, 1948; when the latter was closed he found a clerical post in the Comenius Archive of the Pedagogic Institute; Professor of Philosophy, Charles University of Prague, 1965–70.

Main publications:

(1936) *Přirzoneý svét filosofický problém* '[The Natural World as a Philosophical Problem], Prague: UNKUČ (French translation, *Le Monde naturel comme un problème philosophique*, trans. J. Danēk *et al*, Martinus Nijhoff, 1976).
(1938) (with Ludwig Langrebe) *Edmund Husserl zum Gedächtnis*, Prague: Academia (a memorial lecture).
(1942) 'Dvoji rozum a přírode v némeckém osvícenstiví' [Two senses of reason and nature in the German Enlightenment], in *Svazky úvah a studii*, Prague: V. Petr (translated by E. Kohák in his book on Patočka).
(1953) 'Mezihra na prahu moderní vědy: Cusanus a Komenský' [An interlude at the threshold of modern science: Cusanus and Comenius] in *Vesmír* 32, 9: 322–5.
(1964) 'O filosofickém významu Aristotelova pojetí pohybu a historických výzkumu vénovaných jeno vývji' [Philosophical significance of Aristotle's

conception of movement], in *Acta universitatis Carolinae, philosophica et historica*, 1: 87–97, Prague: Universita Karlova.

(1966) *Úvod do studio Husserlovy fenomenologie* [Introduction to the study of Husserl's phenomenology], Prague: Státní Pedagogické Nakladatelství, serialized in *Filosofický časopis* 13: 5 and 6 (1965) and 14: 1, 3, 5 (1966).

(1967) 'Prirodzený svet a fenomenológia' [Natural world and phenomenology], in *Existencialismus a fenomenológica*, Bratislava: Obzor, pp. 27–71 (translated by E. Kohák in his book on Patočka).

(1972) 'La Philosophie de la crise des sciences d'après E. Husserl et sa conception d'une phénoménologie du "monde de la vie"', in *Archiwum historii, filozofii i mysli spolecznej* 18: 3–18, Warsaw (translated by E. Kohák in his book on Patočka).

(1973) 'Die Gefahren der Technisierung in der Wissenschaft bei E. Husserl und das Wesen der Technik als Gefahr bei M. Heidegger' [The dangers of technicization in science according to E. Husserl and the essence of technology as danger according to M. Heidegger], in Czech as 'Nebezpečí technizace ve vědě u E. Husserl a bytostné jádro technik jako nebezpbčí u M. Heidegger', in *Svédectvi* 16, 62: 262–72, 1980 (an interview with Patočka is included in this issue; this article is translated by E. Kohák in his book on Patočka).

(1975) 'Kacířské eseje o filosofii dějini' [Heretical essays in the philosophy of history], Prague; reprinted in Munich: Edice Arkýř, 1980 (originally circulated clandestinely; translations exist in English, Italian, French, Norwegian and German).

(forthcoming) *Jan Patočka: Ausgewählte Schriften*, (ed.) K. Nellen, Stuttgart: Klett-Cotta-Verlag (the volumes in this series are still being published; a similar objective of publishing the whole of Patočka's works has been undertaken in France).

Secondary literature:

Although the majority of Patočka's published works are now available in several European languages, no critical assessment of his philosophy has yet appeared.

In reading Patočka's work it is apparent that here is an original mind struggling with the limitations of **Husserl**'s transcendental phenomenology, while, at the same time, attempting to extend it to the sphere of the existential and the historical. In this regard, Patočka's philosophy has much in common with most post-Husserlian philosophy as represented by thinkers such as **Sartre**, **Merleau-Ponty** and **Levinas**. In his dialogue with Husserl Patočka begins by observing that a human being inhabits two worlds that interweave

into each other. First, there is the objective world of logic and mathematics, that is, of science. Second, there is the pre-objective world of common sense—what Husserl would later call *Lebenswelt*. Philosophy has the task, Patočka insists, of interrogating these two worlds in order to reveal the underlying domain of human praxis as the source of creativity. But, contrary to Husserl's idealism, philosophy does this not by reducing brute reality to consciousness but by accepting the irreducibility of reality to consciousness. Transcendental phenomenology must, it would seem, find a way to accommodate a reality that is completely other. It finds it through an alliance with **Heidegger**'s existential-historical analysis of *Dasein* and Being. Only then would philosophy be in a position to analyse the problem of how the human individual can regain itself, i.e. 'win itself', through the dialectical movement of 'self-surrender' to the world of 'objectifiable' ('Natural world and phenomenology', 1967).

Sources: Burr; E. Kohák (1978) *Idea and Experience; Edmund Husserl's Project of Phenomenology in 'Ideas I'*, London: Univ. of Chicago Press; *Jan Patočka: Philosophy and Selected Writings*, Chicago: Univ. of Chicago Press, 1989 (with bibliography); Spiegelberg.

SEBASTIEN ODIARI

Paton, Herbert James

British. *b:* 30 March 1887, Perthshire. *d:* 2 August 1969, Perth. *Cat:* Kant scholar. *Ints:* Kant; moral philosophy; philosophy of religon. *Educ:* University of Glasgow and Balliol College, Oxford. *Infls:* Personal influences include Sir Henry Jones and J. A. Smith. Literary influences: Plato, Hegel, Berkeley, Green, Edward Caird, Croce, Joachim and, after 1927, Kant. *Appts:* 1911–27, Fellow and Praelector in Classics and Philosophy, Queen's College, Oxford; 1927–37, Professor of Logic and Rhetoric, University of Glasgow; 1937–52, White's Professor of Moral Philosophy, Oxford.

Main publications:

(1927) *The Good Will: A Study of the Coherence Theory of Goodness* London: Allen & Unwin.

(1936) *Kant's Metaphysic of Experience. A Commentary on the First Half of the Kritik der reinen Vernunft*, London: Allen & Unwin.

(1947) *The Categorical Imperative: A Study in Kant's Moral Philosophy*, London: Hutchinson.

(1951) *In Defence of Reason*, London: Hutchinson.

(1955) *The Modern Predicament: A Study in the Philosophy of Religion*, London: Allen & Unwin.

Secondary literature:

Cross, R. C. (1956) 'The modern predicament', *Philosophical Quarterly* 6: 359–65.

Walsh, W. H. (1970) 'Herbert James Paton: 1887–1969', *Proceedings of the British Academy* 56: 293–308.

H. J. Paton's first book was basically a work of idealist ethics. However, he was mainly concerned to interpret the work of Kant, defending it from some of the commonly accepted criticisms of his time, especially those of **Caird**, **Prichard** and **Kemp Smith**. He helped to raise the standard of exegesis of some of Kant's most difficult texts to a new level. But he tended to explain Kant in Kantian terms and his critics sometimes complained at his lack of critical distance and failure to explain Kant to their satisfaction.

Although his reputation was primarily that of a scholar and teacher (one of his pupils was Gilbert **Ryle**), Paton retained a sympathy for idealism and metaphysics. His 1951 book was critical of the analytical philosophy that had by then established itself in Oxford. In this book he argues that 'the main work ... of philosophy is to be synoptic ... to fit our different experiences and our different theories, as far as may be, into a consistent whole' (Paton 1951, p. 13). In his *The Modern Predicament* (1955) he argues that the only ground for religious belief is religious experience rather than argumentation. Philosophy can show, in the manner of Kant's critical philosophy, that the world as science sees it does not include the whole of reality.

Sources: CBP III, pp. 337–54; WW.

STUART BROWN

Paul, George Andrew

British. *b:* 18 May 1912, Corsock, Dumfrieshire, Scotland. *d:* 4 April 1962, Coniston Water, Cumbria (sailing accident). *Cat:* Analytic philosopher. *Ints:* Perception; moral philosophy; political philosophy. *Educ:* University of St Andrews and Trinity College, Cambridge. *Infls:* Main personal influences are Wittgenstein and Moore; literary influences include Hume. *Appts:* 1939, Research Fellowship at Trinity College, Cambridge; 1939–45, Lecturer in Philosophy, University of Melbourne University; 1945–62, Fellow in Philosophy, University College, Oxford.

Main publications:

(1935) 'The analysis of sense data', *Analyse* 3: 12–20.

(1936) 'Is there a problem about sense data?', *Proceedings of the Aristotelian Society*, supplementary volume 15: 61–77.

(1938) 'Lenin's theory of perception', *Analysis* 5: 65–73.

(1938) Critical notice of L. S. Stebbing, *Philosophy and the Physicists*, *Mind* 47: 361–76.

(1947) 'The problem of guilt', *Proceedings of the Aristotelian Society*, supplementary volume 21: 209–18.

(1950) Article on Democracy, in *Chambers's Encyclopaedia*, vol. IV, London: George Newnes.

(1957) Essays on Moore and Wittgenstein, in A. J. Ayer (ed.) *Revolution in Philosophy*, London: Macmillan.

G. A. Paul wrote rather little, though his best-known article was published the same year (1936) in which he graduated from Cambridge. During the war years he was based at Melbourne University, where he promulgated the not yet published views of the post-*Tractatus* **Wittgenstein**, and where he is reported to have exerted an astonishing influence far outside the confines of his own department (a class he gave in logic one year, for instance, was attended by all the full-time staff of the history department).

The remainder of his career (with the exception of two brief spells as a Visiting Professor) was spent at University College, Oxford, where he taught moral, political and ancient philosophy, and served for ten years as its domestic bursar.

The method of philosophizing employed by Paul was very much in the British analytic tradition, but with a strong Wittgensteinian flavour. In his classic article on sense data, for example, he drew attention to the temptation to make misleading linguistic analogies: talk of sense data was more a matter of the introduction of a new notation than the discovery of new type of entity, as in the case of the fovea. Introduction of the notation was to be judged by its convenience, but did not take us further towards a correct description of reality.

He was married to the sister of F. P. **Ramsey**.

Sources: Obituary, *The Times*, 16 Apr 1962; *Bibliographica Philosophica 1934–45*; letter from Timothy Williamson; birth certificate from New Register House, Edinburgh; Grave.

CLIVE BORST

Pauler, Akos von

Hungarian. *b:* April 1876, Budapest. *d:* June 1933, Budapest. *Cat:* Systematic philosopher. *Ints:* Logic; epistemology. *Educ:* Budapest, Leipzig and the

Sorbonne. *Infls:* Bolzano, Husserl and, later on, Plato. *Appts:* Professorships of Philosophy at the Universities of Kolozsvár (1912) and Budapest (1915–33).

Main publications:
(1902) *Das Problem des Dinges an sich in der neueren Philosophie.*
(1904) *Az ismeretelméleti kategóriák problémája* [The Problem of Gnoseological Categories].
(1907) *Az etikai megismerés* [Ethical Knowledge].
(1911) *A logikai alapelvek elméletéhez* [Theory of the Principles of Logic].
(1920) *Bevezetésa filozófiába* [Principles of Philosophy] (German translation, *Grundlagen der Philosophie*, 1925).
(1925) *Logika*, German translation, *Logik*, 1925.
(1933) *Aristoteles I.*
(1938) *Metafizika.*
(1958) *Tanulmányok az idelogia köréból* [Studies in the Field of Ideology].

Secondary literature:
Blazsanyik, J. (1937) *Ein System der Metaphysik (Akos von Pauler)*, Budapest: Druck von 'Jovo Nyomdaszovetkezet'.
'Magyar filozofiai tarsasag' (1936) *Gedenkschrift für Akos von Pauler*, Berlin and Leipzig: Walter de Gruyter & Co.

Deeply impressed by Bolzano's arguments for the depsychologization of logic, Pauler's fundamental aim was to introduce the maximum possible objectivity into philosophy. Such objectivity, he argued, is achievable by using the method he called reduction, distinct from both induction and deduction. The reductive method begins from the given and works back to its ultimate presuppositions, of which philosophy is the study. (This method deeply influenced his younger compatriot von **Brandenstein**.) The subject has five major subdivisions: logic, ethics, aesthetics, metaphysics and what Pauler calls 'ideology', in effect general ontology (cf. 1920).

Pauler's logic is generously conceived, involving principles others might well call metaphysical. Thus, beyond the laws of identity, contradiction and excluded middle, it involves the 'laws' of connection (everything is connected with everything else); of classification (everything can be classified); and correlativity (there is nothing relative without an absolute). Pauler's metaphysics has a strongly Leibnizian bias: there is a plurality of substances, each being a centre of activity based on intention. Change is always and only from potency to act, and therefore all process

is towards self-realization. The principle of self-realization is the Absolute, at first differentiated from and then identified with god by Pauler. In ethics Pauler embraced a form of utilitarianism, resting on a libertarian analysis of the will.
Sources: Edwards; Ferrater Mora; DFN.

ROBERT WILKINSON

Paulsen, Friedrich
German. *b:* 16 July 1846, Langenhorn, Schleswig-Holstein, Germany. *d:* 14 August 1908, Berlin. *Cat:* Pantheistic monist. *Ints:* History of philosophy; philosophy of education. *Educ:* Universities of Erlangen, Berlin, Bonn and Kiel (1867–71). *Infls:* Aristotle, Spinoza, Kant, Schopenhauer and Eduard von Hartmann. *Appts:* *Extraordinarius* for Philosophy (1877–93) and then *Ordinarius* for Philosophy and Education (1893–1908), University of Berlin.

Main publications:
(1875) *Versuch einer Entwicklungsgeschichte der kantischen Erkenntnistheorie*, Leipzig: Fues.
(1889) *System der Ethik*, Berlin: W. Hertz (English translation, *A System of Ethics*, trans. F. Thilly, London: Kegan, Paul & Co., 1899).
(1892) *Einleitung in die Philosophie*, Berlin: W. Hertz (English translation, *Introduction to Philosophy*, trans. F. Thilly, New York: H. Holt & Co., 1911).
(1896) *Immanuel Kant. Sein Leben und seine Lehre*, Stuttgart: F. Frommann (English translation, *Immanuel Kant: His Life and Doctrine*, trans. J. E. Creighton and A. Lefevre, London: J. C. Nimmo, 1902).
(1901) *Philosophia militans*, Berlin: Reuter & Reichard.
(1905) *Zur Ethik und Politik*, 2 vols, Berlin: Verlag der deutschen Bücherei.
(1909) *Aus meinem Leben. Jugenderinnerungen*, Jena: E. Diederichs (English translation, *Friedrich Paulsen: An Autobiography*, trans. T. Lorenz, New York: Columbia University Press, 1938).

Secondary literature:
Schulte-Hubert, B. (1914) *Die Philosophie Friedrich Paulsens*, Berlin: D. Thomas.
Speck, J. (1926) *Friedrich Paulsen. Sein Leben und sein Werk*, Langensalza: J. Beltz.
Spranger, E. (ed.) (1912) *Friedrich Paulsens gesammelte pädagogische Abhandlungen*, Stuttgart: J. A. Cotta (contains bibliography).

Paulsen's two most celebrated works, the 1889 *System der Ethik* and the 1892 *Einleitung*, written in a popular style and addressed primarily to students and laymen, enjoyed immense success. Paulsen subscribes to a form of pantheism or idealist monism. His writings are inspired by a double polemic against the supernatural dualism of Christianity and the materialistic mechanism of natural science. The world is construed as an emanation of God, the All-One; matter and mind are manifestations of spirit; the laws of nature are expressions of the Divine Will. Paulsen offers a basically Kantian account of our experience and knowledge of nature. His anti-hedonistic account of morality construes the good in terms of human perfection and harmony.

Paulsen is, perhaps, better remembered today for his *Immanuel Kant* (1896) (distinctive for its view that Kant was concerned not to destroy metaphysics but to establish a new metaphysics on a moral foundation), and for his numerous and important works on the theory of education and on the history of the German universities (most of them still regarded as classics in their own right, and many of them available in English translation).

Sources: Edwards; EF; Eisler.

DAVID WALFORD

Peacocke, C(hristopher) A(rthur) B(ruce)

British. *b:* 22 May 1950, Birmingham, England. *Cat:* Analytical philosopher. *Ints:* Philosophy of mind; philosophy of language. *Educ:* University of Oxford; 1971, MA, PPE; 1974, BPhil in Philosophy; 1979, DPhil in Philosophy; scholarships to Oxford and Harvard. *Infls:* P. F. Strawson, D. Davidson, M. Dummett, J. McDowell and G. Evans. *Appts:* 1973–5, Junior Research Fellow, Queen's College, Oxford; 1975 -9, Prize Fellow, All Souls College, Oxford; 1979–85, Fellow and Tutor, New College, Oxford, and CUF Lecturer in Philosophy, Oxford University; 1985–8, Susan Stebbing Professor of Philosophy, King's College, University of London; from 1989, Waynflete Professor of Metaphysical Philosophy in the University of Oxford and Fellow of Magdalen College, Oxford; since 1975, numerous visiting positions in the UK, USA, Mexico and Australia.

Main publications:

(1979) *Holistic Explanation: Action, Space, Interpretation*, Oxford: Oxford University Press.
(1983) *Sense and Content: Experience, Thought and Their Relations*, Oxford: Oxford University Press.
(1986) *Thoughts: An Essay on Content*, Oxford: Blackwell.
(1992) *A Study of Concepts*, Cambridge: Mass.: MIT Press.

Secondary literature:

Wright, C. (1993) 'A note on two realist lines of argument', in *Realism, Meaning and Truth*, second edition, Oxford: Blackwell.

Although Christopher Peacocke's work definitely belongs within the mainstream of 'analytic' philosophy, as practised at Oxford University, his thought has at least three distinguishing characteristics. First—and most importantly—along with mainly G. **Evans** and C. McGinn, Peacocke has been instrumental in redirecting analytic philosophy away from a sole preoccupation with the analysis of language towards a more direct approach to the analysis of concepts and thoughts, or 'contents'. Thus, contrary to the views of, for example, **Frege** and **Dummett**, explanatory patterns in the philosophy of mind and action, as well as possession and attribution conditions for a thinker's mastery of concepts, admit of investigation independently of a prior resolution of problems pertaining to the philosophy of language. Second, Peacocke's thought is influenced by contemporary thinkers in the USA to an extent not paralleled in that of his leading Oxford-based predecessors. Third, particularly in later years, Peacocke has explicity striven to map interconnections between his own work and that of researchers in the cognitive sciences.

Peacocke's contributions are multifarious, influential and cover a wide area of interest—mainly the philosophy of mind, the philosophy of language and logic, the philosophy of action and the philosophy of space and time. More specifically, he argues, in reply to Dummett's anti-realist challenge to the realist conception of meaning, that the semantical realist (and adherent to classical logic) can embrace what is found in the principle that linguistic meaning is 'manifestable' and thus fully public. On a sane construction of verificationism that doctrines does not rule out realism, according to Peacocke.

Sources: Personal communication.

STIG RASMUSSEN

Peano, Giuseppe

Italian. *b:* 27 August 1858, Spinetta, Italy. *d:* 20 April 1932, Turin, Italy. *Cat:* Mathematical logician. *Ints:* Philosophy of mathematics. *Educ:* Turin University. *Infls:* K. Weierstrass, G. Cantor and current tendencies towards axiomatization in mathematics. *Appts:* Professor, Turin University, 1890–1932.

Main publications:
(1891–1906) (ed.) *Rivista di matematica* (and variant titles), 8 vols, Turin: Bocca.
(1895) (ed.) *Formulario matematico* (and variant titles); fifth edition, 1908.
(1957–9) *Opere scelte*, 3 vols, Rome: Cremonese.

Secondary literature:
Borga, M. *et al.* (1985) *I contributi fondazionali della scuola di Peano*, Milan: Franco Angeli.
Rodriguez-Consuergra, F. (1991) *The Development of Bertrand Russell's Philosophy*, Basel: Birkhauser.

Peano is a key figure in the contemporary search for axiom systems in mathematics. He is also the link between the development from the 1860s of rigorous mathematical analysis as conceived by Weierstrass and the emergence in the 1890s of 'mathematical logic' (his name in this sense). He realized that the language of analysis needed refinement in order to make explicit not only logical relationships between terms and propositions, but also the quantification ('for all' and 'there exists') over both individuals and predicates. In addition, he recognized the merits of **Cantor**'s set theory within analysis (from which in fact it had arisen in the early 1870s), and brought it under his logical umbrella. Indeed much of the notation that we still use for both logic and set theory comes from him or his many followers who became known as 'the Peanists'.

Peano also imitated Weierstrass as a leader, building up around him in Turin a remarkable coterie of followers and disciples. He gave them two organs in which to publish: the *Rivista* for papers and the various editions of the *Formulario* in which their formulations of branches of mathematics were codified (often with valuable historical references). The three principal followers were C. Burali-Forti (1861–1931), A. Padoa (1868–1937) and M. Pieri (1860–1913).

The presentation in the *Formulario* started out from arithmetic (for which Peano had produced his axiomatization in 1889) and proceeded to set theory; the subsequent coverage of mathematics included basic algebra and geometry, real and complex numbers, the calculus, the theory of curves, and vector algebra. But the Peanists were always chary of absorbing mathematics into this logic, and distinguished logical from mathematical notions in their explanations.

This was not the reaction of a young listener to Peano and his chief trio when they had papers presented on 3 August 1900 at the International Congress of Philosophy in Paris. **Russell** saw Peano's structure as The System which he had

been seeking, and under its impiration it he announced the 'logicist' thesis which they had eschewed.

Unlike Russell, Peano was wary of exploring philosophical issues in his logico-mathematics, but he was uncommonly sharp on several matters. For example, during the concern with the paradoxes of set theory in the 1900s he glimpsed the distinction between mathematical and semantic ones. His forte was definitions in mathematics (the subject of his Paris lecture); for example, the essentials of Russell's theory of denoting are in one of his pieces in the second edition (1897) of the *Formulario*.

The later editions of this work, and many of Peano's papers from the 1900s, were written in 'Latin without inflection', and from that decade on he became increasingly concerned with advocating it as an international language. But he maintained his encouragement of logic and logically minded philosophers. One of his last students was Ludovico Geymonat.

IVOR GRATTAN-GUINNESS

Pears, David Francis
British. *b:* 8 August 1921, Bedfont, Middlesex. *Cat:* Philosopher of mind. *Ints:* Hume; Russell; Wittgenstein. *Educ:* Balliol College, Oxford. *Infls:* Literary influencew include Aristotle, Hume, Russell and Wittgenstein. *Appts:* 1948–50, Research Lecturer, Christ Church, Oxford; 1950–60, Fellow, Corpus Christi College, Oxford; 1960–88, Tutor in Philosophy, Christ Church; 1972–85, Reader in Philosophy, Christ Church; 1985–8, Professor of Philosophy, then Professor Emeritus, University of Oxford.

Main publications:
(1951) 'The problem of universals', *Philosophical Quarterly* 1: 218–27.
(1953) 'Incompatibilities of colours', in A. Flew (ed.) *Logic and Language*, second series, Oxford: Blackwell.
(1957) (ed.) *The Nature of Metaphysics*, London: Macmillan.
(1963) (ed.) *David Hume: A Symposium*, London: Macmillan.
(1963) (ed.) *Freedom and the Will*, London: Macmillan.
(1963) 'Is existence a predicate?', *Aquinas Papers* 38, London: Aquinas Press.
(1967) *Bertrand Russell and the British Tradition in Philosophy*, London: Fontana.
(1971) *What is Knowledge?*, London: Allen & Unwin.
(1971) *Wittgenstein*, London: Fontana.

(1972) (ed.) *Bertrand Russell*, New York: Doubleday.

(1972) (ed.) *Russell's Logical Atomism*, London: Fontana.

(1975) *Questions in the Philosophy of Mind*, London: Duckworth.

(1979) 'A comparison between Ayer's view about the privileges of sense-datum statements and the views of Russell and Austin', in G. F. Macdonald (ed.), *Perception and Identity*, London: Macmillan.

(1980) 'Aristotle's analysis of courage' in A. O. Rorty (ed.), *Essays on Aristotle's Ethics*, Berkeley: University of California Press.

(1984) *Motivated Irrationality*, Oxford: Oxford University Press.

(1987–8) *The False Prison: A Study of the Development of Wittgenstein's Philosophy*, vols 1 and 2, Oxford: Oxford University Press.

(1990) *Hume's System: An Examination of the First Book of His Treatise*, Oxford: Oxford University Press.

(1990) 'Wittgenstein's holism', *Dialectica* 44: 165–73.

Having been Oxford-educated and primarily Oxford-based throughout his professional career, David Pears is very much an Oxford philosopher; but with a central interest in those two great Cambridge philosophers Russell and Wittgenstein, he is perhaps equally well described as an Oxbridge philosopher. He has also been a frequent visitor to the United States and has held many visiting professorships there.

Pears is responsible for some of the best scholarship in recent years on the three philosophers on whom he has concentrated his scholarly attention: David Hume, Bertrand **Russell** and Ludwig **Wittgenstein**. To professionals, university students and, in some cases, the educated public alike Pears has helped to make the thought of these three seminal thinkers exciting and accessible whilst in no way disguising difficulty and depth. In 1961 he produced, together with Brian McGuiness, a translation of Wittgenstein's *Tractatus Logico-Philosophicus*, rendering the original in more straightforward prose than the earlier translation of C. K. Ogden and correcting some of its mistakes. This was followed in 1971 by a translation of the *Prototractatus*.

Solipsism is identified as 'the dominant issue in the *Tractatus*' and Pears has provided the most extended treatment of the ins and outs of Wittgenstein's changing stance on this topic. In *The False Prison*, two 'stabilizing resources' required for possessing a language are distinguished: appeal to standard objects and appeal to the judgements of other people. The most popular interpretation of Wittgenstein's private-language argument, the so-called social or community interpretation, is found inadequate in concentrating only on the latter.

Motivated Irrationality explores the idea of acting irrationally in a motivated manner, as expressed primarily in the cases of irrational belief formation and acting against one's better judgement. It is contended that philosophers, perhaps because of their professionally cool use of reason, have tended, unlike psychologists, to exaggerate human rationality. The more recent book, on Hume, sees him as having rejected not only rationalism but also naive empiricism. The remaining more sophisticated empiricism embraces both theory of belief and theory of meaning, achieving remarkable results despite deficiencies in a method working from (private) ideas. Pears finds a kinship between the naturalism of Hume and that of Wittgenstein.

Pears lists as non-philosophical interests entomology and the visual arts. He was made a Fellow of the British Academy in 1970, and was President of L'Institut International de Philosophie from 1988 to 1991.

Sources: WW 1993; IWW 1993–4; CA 65–8, 1977.

CLIVE BORST

Pearson, Karl

British. *b:* 27 March 1857, London. *d:* 27 April 1936, Surrey. *Cat:* Scientist; philosopher of science. *Educ:* Mathematics, King's College, Cambridge; Law, Heidelberg and Berlin. *Infls:* Ernst Mach and Francis Galton. *Appts:* 1880, Fellow of King's; 1881, called to the Bar but did not practise; 1884–1911, Chair of Applied Mathematics and Mechanics, University College, London; 1896, Fellow of the Royal Society; 1911–33, newly created Chair of Eugenics, University College, London; 1901, founded with Francis Galton and W. F. R. Weldon *Biometrika*, which he edited until his death; Lecturer in Geometry at Gresham College, London.

Main publications:

(1888) *The Ethic of Freethought: A Selection of Essays and Lectures*, London: T. Fisher Unwin; republication, London: Adam and Charles Black, 1901.

(1892) *The Grammar of Science*, London: Walter Scott; second and third editions, London: Adam and Charles Black, 1900 and 1911; Everyman edition, London: J. M. Dent & Sons Ltd., 1937.

(1901) *National Life from the Standpoint of Science*, London: Adam and Charles Black; reissued with

Appendices, 1905; later published as no. XI of the *Eugenics Lectures Series*.

Secondary literature:
Lenin, V. I. (1937) *Materialism and Empirico-Criticism*, Moscow: Progress Publishers.
Morant, G. M. (1939) *A Bibliography of the Statistical and Other Writings of Karl Pearson*, London: Biometrika Office, University College.
Pearson, E. S. (1936–7) 'Karl Pearson; an appreciation of some aspects of his life and work', *Biometrika* 27 and 29.
Peirce, C. S. (1931–58) *Collected Papers*, Cambridge, Mass.: Harvard University Press (see especially volume 80).

Pearson was a founder of biometrics and modern statistical theory, establishing statistics as a discipline. He said that Spinoza was the only philosopher whose conception of the deity was compatible with scientific knowledge. In spite of this, his philosophy of science was positivist, indeed even Machian. He upheld the unity of method, based on verification. Sense-impressions form the verifiable bedrock constituting the external world that science studies. Science establishes contingent correlations between them, rendering knowledge and prediction possible. Theoretical constructs are conceptual models which enable us to describe and organize the sequence of phenomena. To regard 'force', 'mass' or 'life' as anything more is to succumb to metaphysical obscurities. The following quotation bears out the above:

> law in the scientific sense only describes in mental short-hand the sequences of our perceptions. It does not explain why those perceptions have a certain order nor why that order repeats itself; the law discovered by science introduces no element of necessity into the sequence of our sense-impressions; it merely gives a concise statement of how changes are taking place. That a certain sequence has occurred and recurred in the past is a matter of experience to which we give expression in the concept of causation; that it will continue to recur in the future is a matter of belief to which we give expression in the concept of probability.
>
> (*The Grammar of Science*, p. 99)

In spite of being an enthusiastic humanist and socialist, his studies of eugenics led him to believe that the more fertile but less able and less energetic should not be allowed to swamp the 'good' stock.

Sources: CBD; Edwards.

KEEKOK LEE

Péguy, Charles

French. *b:* 1873, Orléans, France. *d:* 1914, Villeroy (died in action). *Cat:* Socialist. *Ints:* Politics. *Educ:* Born in humble circumstances, Péguy won a scholarship to the École Normale Supérieure; began but did not complete his *agrégation de philosophie*. *Infls:* Descartes and Bergson. *Appts:* Founded the *Cahiers de la Quinzaine* (1900–14), in which nearly all his work first appeared; a notable and prolific poet as well as prose stylist, and a major figure in French cultural history of his generation.

Main publications:
All in the Pléiade *Oeuvres en prose*, 2 vols, ed. Marcel Péguy, Paris: Gallimard, 1961, and *Oeuvres en prose complètes*, 3 vols, ed. Robert Burac: Paris: Gallimard, 1992.
(1897) *De la cité socialiste*.
(1898) *Marcel, premier dialogue de la cité harmonieuse*.
(1900) *Réponse brève à Jaurès*.
(1905) *Notre Patrie*.
(1914) *Note sur M. Bergson et la philosophie bergsonienne*.
(1914) *Note conjointe sur M. Descartes et sur la philosophie cartésienne* (incomplete, written 1914, published posthumously).

Secondary literature:
Dru, A. (1956) *Péguy*, London: Harvill Press.
Servais, Y. (1953) *Charles Péguy: The Pursuit of Salvation*, Oxford: Blackwell.

Péguy began his intellectual life as an idealistic socialist (cf. 1897 and 1898), vehemently critical of those he deemed to have betrayed these ideals (cf. 1900). He argued that there is nothing unpleasant in human nature that is innate and so ineradicable, and tends towards perfectibilism. Most discord and discontent is traceable to unequal distribution of goods between human beings, real or perceived, and so, when such inequalities are eradicated, a golden age can begin. The harmonious city of socialism is characterized by an extreme collectivism: all goods are owned by the state and distributed free according to need, thus eliminating the corrosive effects of competition, including its most destructive consequence, inequality of access to goods. Once the material well-being of the city is secured, the citizens will be free to cultivate their inner lives and to devote their extensive leisure time to the major disinterested pursuits of art, science and philosophy. All thought on such matters will be subject to complete liberty of conscience. The competition to be excluded from the human condition includes that between states, and the harmonious city will adopt internationalist and entirely non-racist foreign policies.

These views did not stand the test of experience, and within a few years (cf. 1905) Péguy had become a patriotic nationalist and a Catholic, adopting beliefs in, for example, the ineluctibility of national roots and in the unique mission of France. Philosophically, the most interesting later works are the two *Notes* (1914) and in particular his argument that **Bergson**'s views (of which he was a consistent admirer) are deeply coherent with Catholicism. Péguy's root conviction about the universe was that it is various, untidy and dynamic, such that no philosophy can do it justice which seeks to impose on it a framework of fixed concepts. Nothing is given forever, and we must be ready constantly to readapt: such a readiness he regarded as the common fundamental belief both of Christianity and of Bergson's philosophy.

ROBERT WILKINSON

Peirce, Charles S(anders)

American. **b:** 10 September 1839, Cambridge, Massachusetts. **d:** 14 April 1914, Milford, Pennsylvania. **Cat:** Physicist; logician; philosopher of science; pragmatist philosopher. **Ints:** Logic; philosophy of science. **Educ:** Harvard University, BA in Physics, 1859, MA 1862, BS in Chemistry, 1863. **Infls:** Duns Scotus, Kant and Boole. **Appts:** 1861–91, Physicist and Astronomer, United States Coast and Geodetic Survey; 1864–5, Lecturer, Philosophy of Science, Harvard University; 1867–72, Assistant Director, Harvard Observatory; 1879–84, Lecturer in Logic, Johns Hopkins University.

Main publications:

(1868) 'Questions concering certain faculties claimed for man', *Journal of Speculative Philosophy* 2: 103–114; reprinted in *CP* 5: 135–55.
(1868) 'Some consequences of four incapacities', ibid. 2: 140–57; reprinted in *CP* 5: 156–89.
(1869) 'Grounds of validity of the laws of logic: further consequences of four incapacities', ibid. 2: 193–208; reprinted in *CP* 5: 190–222.
(1877) 'The fixation of belief', *Popular Science Monthly* 12: 1–15; reprinted in *CP* 5: 223–47.
(1878) 'How to make our ideas clear', ibid. 12: 286–302; reprinted in *CP* 5: 248–71.

(1878) 'The doctrine of chances', ibid. 12: 604–15; reprinted in *CP* 2: 389–414.
(1878) 'The probability of induction', ibid. 12: 705–18; reprinted in *CP* 2: 415–32.
(1878) 'The order of nature', ibid. 13: 203–17; reprinted in *CP* 6: 283–301.
(1878) 'Deduction, induction, and hypothesis', ibid. 13: 470–82; reprinted in *CP* 2: 372–88.
(1891) 'The architecture of theories', *The Monist* 1: 161–76; reprinted in *CP* 6: 11–27.
(1892) 'The doctrine of necessity examined', ibid 2: 321–37; reprinted in *CP* 6: 36–45.
(1892) 'The law of mind', ibid. 2: 533–59; reprinted in *CP* 6: 86–113.
(1892) 'Man's glassy essence', ibid. 3: 1–22; reprinted in *CP* 6: 155–75.
(1982–) *Writings of Charles S. Peirce. A Chronological Edition*, ed. Max H. Fisch, *et al.*, Bloomington: Indiana University Press.

Collections:
(1931–5) *The Collected Papers of Charles Sanders Peirce*, vols 1–6, ed. Charles Hartshorne and Paul Weiss, Cambridge, Mass.: Harvard University Press. (Cited below as *CP* followed by volume and page numbers.)
(1959) *The Collected Papers of Charles Sanders Peirce*, vols 7–8, ed. Arthur Burks, Cambridge, Mass.: Harvard University Press. (Cited below as *CP* followed by volume and page numbers.)

Secondary literature:

Feibleman, J. K. (1946) *An Introduction to Peirce's Philosophy, Interpreted as a System*, New York: Harper & Brothers.
Murphey, M. G. (1961) *The Development of Peirce's Philosophy*, Cambridge, Mass.: Harvard University Press.
Thompson, M. (1953) *The Pragmatic Philosophy of C. S. Peirce*, Chicago: University of Chicago Press.

The son of Benjamin Peirce, the most eminent American mathematician in the nineteenth century and a Harvard professor, Charles Peirce began his career as a physicist with the United States Coast and Geodetic Survey, of which his father was superintendent. As a working scientist he was a pioneer in the effort to map our galaxy, publishing in 1878 *Photometric Researches*. In the 1870s he was one of the major participants in the Metaphysical Club in Cambridge, Massachusetts. This informal group included William **James**, Oliver Wendell Holmes and Chauncey Wright, and is the alleged birthplace of American pragmatism. After his resignation from the Geodetic Survey in 1891, Peirce lived in Arisbe near Milford, Pennsylvania. Living in poverty, he wrote and occasionally lectured for the rest of his life. William James often came to his assistance, providing funds and arranging for his lectures.

A series of three articles in the *Journal of Speculative Philosophy* in 1868–9 launched Peirce as a philosopher who rejected the foundationalism, intuitionism, introspectionism and egoism prevalent in modern philosophy since Descartes. In this series of articles Peirce contended that scepticism could not be employed wholesale to beliefs in general, as Descartes had proposed, nor could it be used to establish beliefs that were absolutely certain, since every belief was fallible. Further, he denied that introspection was a means of internal observation of private mental states, and contended that all knowledge of mind is inferred from external observation. He therefore denied that the human mind has the capacity of intuition to grasp clear and distinct ideas as certain truths. Inquiry, he maintained, is a social and not a private enterprise. He also depicted thinking as essentially the interplay of signs, generalizing even that the individual human mind is but a sign. From 1877 to 1878 a series of six articles in the *Popular Science Monthly* established Peirce as a pioneer in the philosophy of science. The series is most famous for Peirce's enunciation of the principle of pragmatism, stated in the second article without use of the word, as the following rule for the clarification of ideas: 'Consider what effects, which might conceivably have practical bearings, we conceive the object of our conception to have. Then, our conception of these effects is the whole of our conception of the object' (*CP* 5: 258). When in 1898 James used the term 'pragmatism', inspiring an international philosophical movement, he cited Peirce's formula. Displeased by James's psychologizing of a logical principle, and by his transformation of a methodological rule into a metaphysics wedded to nominalism, Peirce renamed his principle 'pragmaticism'—a word 'ugly enough to be safe from kidnappers' (*CP* 5: 277). Many of Peirce's most influential ideas were presented in the *Popular Science* articles: his conception of belief as a habit of action; his conception of enquiry as the process of fixing belief; his emphasis on the scientific method as the only reliable method of fixing belief; his doctrine of fallibilism—namely, that no belief is absolutely certain; his conceptions of truth as the opinion that the unlimited community of scientific enquirers is fated to reach and of reality as the object of that opinion; his conception of natural law as statistical, and hence the doctrine of chances; his discovery of the role of

hypothesis in scientific inquiry, which he called abduction to distinguish it from induction and deduction. Peirce's philosophical investigations anticipated major developments not only in pragmatism and the philosophy of science, but also in symbolic logic and the theory of signs. His writings on formal logic, many of them posthumously published, presage the subsequent rise of symbolic logic, and his work on the theory of signs, which he named 'semiotic', remains in the forefront of current research. In his logical investigations Peirce had discovered three fundamental kinds of relations: one-term (monadic), two-term (dyadic) and three-term (triadic), all other kinds of relations being resoluble into these three, but none of the three being reducible further. Meaning, the sign-relation, he found to be a triadic relation, its three terms being the sign, the object and the interpretant. The three kinds of relations are the key to Peirce's basic set of categories: Firstness (Quality), Secondness (Relation) and Thirdness (Generality). In a series of five articles that appeared in *The Monist* in 1891–3, Peirce undertook to erect a system of metaphysics, a 'cosmogonic' philosophy, by drawing upon the principles and concepts of the sciences. Peirce argued for tychism (the doctrine of objective chance), synechism (the doctrine of continuity) and agapism (the doctrine of evolutionary love). He also identified his categories of firstness, secondness, and thirdness phenomenologically and psychologically as feeling, resistance, and conception. Drawing upon the principles and conceptions of the special sciences, he sketched a cosmogonic philosophy of evolutionary idealism. Peirce maintained that philosophy is a science. During his life he made several attempts to classify the sciences and place philosophy within the classification. The theme threading his various efforts is that the sciences be ranked according to the generality of their principles and conceptions, so that the more general be at the top of the hierarchy, those lying below being less general yet depending upon the higher for some of their general principles. Hence all sciences are divided into three classes in descending order: sciences of discovery, sciences of review and practical sciences. Philosophy is located in the sciences of discovery, which are ranked in descending order: mathematics, philosophy (coenoscopy) and the special sciences (ideoscopy). Philosophy, moreover, is subdivided in descending order as phenomenology (phaneroscopy), normative science (including ethics, esthetics, logic) and metaphysics. Peirce never completed his lifework, but he left at his death a welter of papers, which his widow sold to the Harvard University Department of Philosophy. These papers have proved to be a treasure-trove for philosophical scholars. *The Transactions of the Charles S. Peirce Society*, founded in 1964 and edited by Peter Hare and Richard S. Robin, is a journal that, in quarterly publication, presents articles and reviews on Peirce and Peirce scholarship.

Sources: DAB: Edwards; EAB.

ANDREW RECK

Penelhum, Terence Michael

British-Canadian. *b:* 26 April 1929, Bradford-on-Avon, England. *Cat:* Authority on Butler and Hume; analytical philosopher. *Ints:* Philosophy of religion; epistemology. *Educ:* University of Edinburgh, and Oriel College, Oxford. *Infls:* The traditional approach in philosophy as passed down in Edinburgh by A. E. Taylor and N. Kemp Smith; the analytical style of Ryle's Oxford. *Appts:* Lecturer to Associate Professor, University of Alberta, 1953–63; Professor of Philosophy (1963–78) and then of Religious Studies (1978–88), University of Calgary; FRS Can.

Main publications:

(1970) *Survival and Disembodied Existence*, London: Routledge & Kegan Paul.

(1971) *Religion and Rationality*, New York: Random House.

(1971) *Problems of Religious Knowledge*, London: Macmillan.

(1975) *Hume*, London: Macmillan.

(1983) *God and Skepticism*, Dordrecht: D. Reidel.

(1985) *Butler*, London: Routledge & Kegan Paul.

(1989) (ed.) *Faith*, London: Macmillan.

(1992) *David Hume: An Introduction to his Philosophical System*, West Lafayette, IN: Purdue University Press.

(1993) 'A belated return', in Kelly James Clark (ed.) *Philosophers Who Believe*, Downer's Grove: Inter Varsity Press, pp. 223–36 (autobiographical).

Secondary literature:

MacIntosh, J. J. and Meynell, H. A. (eds) (1994) *Faith, Scepticism and Rationality: A Festschrift for Terence Penelhum*, Calgary: University of Calgary Press.

Appreciative of the benefits of analytical techniques, Penelhum has consistently applied them to substantive philosophical questions, especially in epistemology and philosophy of religion. He has countered scepticism—not least that of religious

apologists (fideists) who welcome sceptical assessments of reason as leaving room for faith and commitment. An authority on **Butler** and Hume, he has provided careful and balanced evaluations of their arguments. Thus, while in no way neglecting Butler's contribution to ethics, he has elucidated his significant arguments *qua* philosopher of religion; and while not denying Hume's widely acknowledged importance for epistemology, he has brought his arguments in the fields of psychology, ethics and religion into greater prominence. In the latter part of his career Penelhum has viewed his philosophical concerns within the broader context of a department of Religious Studies.

Sources: WW(Can) 1992; personal communication.

ALAN SELL

Pepper, Stephen C(oburn)

American. *b:* 19 April 1891, Newark, New Jersey. *d:* 1 May 1972, Berkeley, California. *Cat:* Aesthetician. *Ints:* Value-theorist; metaphysician. *Educ:* Harvard University, BA 1913, MA 1914, PhD 1916. *Infls:* Santayana, G. H. Palmer, R. B. Perry, C. I. Lewis and Whitehead. *Appts:* 1916–17, Instructor, Wellesley College; 1919–72, Assistant Professor to Professor of Philosophy (Chair, Philosophy Department, 1953–8; Emeritus Professor, 1958–72), 1938–47, Assistant Dean, College of Letters and Science, 1938–52, Chairman, Art Department, University of California at Berkeley.

Main publications:

(1937) *Aesthetic Quality: A Contextualistic Theory of Beauty*, New York: Scribner's; reprinted, West Port, CT: Greenwood Press, 1970.

(1945) *The Basis of Criticism in the Arts*, Cambridge, Mass.: Harvard University Press.

(1948) *World Hypotheses: A Study in Evidence*, Berkeley and Los Angeles: University of California Press.

(1958) *The Sources of Value*, Berkeley and Los Angeles: University of California Press.

(1967) *Concept and Quality: A World Hypothesis*, La Salle, Ill.: Open Court.

Secondary literature:

Reck, A. J. (1968) *The New American Philosophers*, Baton Rouge: Louisiana State University Press, pp. 44–80; reprinted, New York: Dell Publishing Co., 1979.

More than any American philosopher of his generation, Pepper contributed to the establishment of aesthetics and philosophy of art as special fields of study. His *Aesthetic Quality* (1937) offered a pure, precise theory that defined a new type of pragmatic, or contextualist, aesthetics.

Pepper's *World Hypotheses* (1948), based on his root-metaphor theory, which originated in his aesthetics, is a theory of metaphysical systems, which he called 'world hypotheses'. According to Pepper there are four world hypotheses that are equally plausible: formism, mechanism, organicism and contextualism.

Pepper also advanced a comprehensive, empirical, naturalistic general theory of value in *The Sources of Value* (1958). Its central concepts are the notions of the purposive act and of the selective system. He came to consider the purposive act to be a new root metaphor. His *Concept and Quality* (1967) presents his own metaphysics based on this new root metaphor. He called it 'selectivism'.

Sources: WW(Am); *PAAPA*; *New York Times*, 6 May 1972.

ANDREW RECK

Perelman, Chaim

Belgian. *b:* 1912, Warsaw. *d:* 1984, Brussels. *Cat:* Philosopher of law; rhetorician. *Ints:* Ethics; politics; 'rhetoric'; philosophy of law. *Infls:* Dupréel. *Appts:* Perelman's family moved to Brussels soon after his birth; a student at the University of Brussels, Perelman was later to be appointed Professor there.

Main publications:

(1933) *De l'arbitraire dans la connaissance.*

(1945) *De la justice*, Brussels: Offices de publicité.

(1952) (with L. Olbrechts-Tyteca) *Rhétorique et philosophie: pour une théorie de l'argumentation en philosophie*, Paris: PUF.

(1958) (with L. Olbrechts-Tyteca) *Traité de l'argumentation: la nouvelle rhétorique*, 2 vols, Paris: PUF (English translation, *The New Rhetoric: A Treatise on Argumentation*, trans. J. Wilkinson and P. Weaver, University of Notre Dame Press, 1971).

(1963) *Justice et raison*, Brussels: Presses Universitaires de Bruxelles.

(1964) *Cours de logique*, seventh edition, Brussels: Presses Universitaires de Bruxelles.

(1964) *Raisonnement et démarches de l'historien*, Brussels: Université libre de Bruxelles.

(1968) *Droit, morale, et philosophie*, Paris: Librairie générale de droit et de jurisprudence.

(1969) *Les Catégories en histoire*, Brussels: Université libre de Bruxelles.

(1976) *Logique juridique. Nouvelle rhétorique*, Paris: Dalloz.

(1989) *Rhétoriques*, Brussels: Presses Universitaires de Bruxelles.

Secondary literature:

Meyer, M. (1986) *De la métaphysique à la rhétorique; essais à la mémoire de C. P.*, Brussels: Éditions de l'Université de Bruxelles (includes bibliography).

Undoubtedly the best-known Belgian philosopher of his generation, Chaim Perelman began his career with work on logic, particularly on logical paradoxes and the concept of infinity. Thereafter, he devoted his attention to two main areas: first, the analysis of basic moral and political concepts, notably justice, and second the nature and scope of philosophical argument. His conclusions concerning the former have a close and direct link with his views on the latter.

In his analysis of the concept of justice (in 1945 and its revisions), Perelman distinguishes a formal principle common to all senses of the term, that like persons be treated alike, from principles of application or material principles, which specify the relevant respects of likeness. Of these latter he picks out six: to each person the same thing; to each according to their merits; works; needs; rank, or legal entitlement. In early papers Perelman argues that the choice between these material principles is arbitrary, and cannot be resolved by reasoning. In later papers, he is less pessimistic, and the change follows from his modified conception of what counts as a respectable mode of philosophical argument.

Perelman came to believe that, in a number of areas of philosophy, the human sciences and law, the arguments used are not and cannot be reduced to either the reasoning *more geometrico* advocated by Descartes, or the inductive methods which, he held, are used in the natural sciences. Moreover, the restriction of the term 'rational' to these two types of argument has brought about a neglect of the actual processes of our thinking which oversimplifies the facts. Reason can be used not only to weigh evidence but also to induce or increase adherence to beliefs which can in the nature of things only be probable. Perelman devoted a great deal of time to the study of these modes of argument which are neither deductive nor inductive, and this study he called the 'new rhetoric' (cf. 1958).

ROBERT WILKINSON

Perry, Ralph Barton

American. *b:* 3 July 1876, Poultney, Vermont. *d:* 22 January 1957, Cambridge, Massachusetts. *Cat:* New realist and pragmatist. *Ints:* Philosophy of value theoies; American philosophy. *Educ:* Princeton and Harvard Universties. *Infls:* William James. *Appts:* Williams College, 1899–1900; Smith College, 1900–2; Harvard, 1902–46.

Main publications:

(1905) *The Approach to Philosophy*, London and New York: Longmans.

(1912) 'A realistic theory of independence', in Holt, Edwin, *et al.*, *The New Realism*, New York: Macmillan, pp. 99–151.

(1912) *Present Philosophical Tendencies: A Critical Survey of Naturalism, Idealism, and Realism*, New York: Longmans.

(1918) *The Present Conflict of Ideals: A Study of the Philosophical Background of the World War*, New York: Longmans.

(1926) *General Theory of Value*, London and New York: Longmans.

(1927) *Philosophy of the Recent Past: An Outline of European and American Philosophy since 1860*, New York and London: Scribner's.

(1931) *A Defence of Philosophy*, Cambridge, Mass.: Harvard University Press.

(1935) *The Thought and Character of William James*, 2 vols, Cambridge, Mass.: Harvard University Press.

(1938) *In the Spirit of William James*, New Haven.

(1945) *One World in the Making*, New York: Current Books, Inc.

(1948) *The Thought and Character of William James*, Cambridge, Mass.: Harvard University Press.

(1954) *Realms of Value: A Critique of Human Civilization*, Cambridge, Mass: Harvard University Press.

Secondary literature:

Kuklick, Bruce (1977) *The Rise of American Philosophy: Cambridge, Massachusetts, 1860–1930*, New Haven: Yale University Press, chapter 18.

A youthful call to the Presbyterian ministry was transformed into that of 'teacher and scholar' when Perry 'migrated' from Princeton to Harvard, trading religion for philosophy. At Harvard he chose the 'way of **James**' with its 'youthful spirit of revolt' over the more conservative way of **Royce**. From then on his 'true' religion would contain whatever 'confirms man's humanity to man' (CAP II, p. 208). Support for those confirming causes was expressed in a succession of writings, one of which (1945) is listed above. His applied philosophy was supported, in turn, by his theoretical work.

One of the leaders of the new realism, Perry argued for realism and against what he took to be its rivals: idealism, pragmatism and naturalism. His primary target was idealism, against which he argued that idealists misread the 'egocentric predicament', concluding fallaciously that since everything humans know is an idea, reality must be ideational. Against pragmatism he argued that pragmatists were so obsessed by their opposition to idealism that they overemphasized 'the standpoint of practical belief' (1912, p. 39). His argument against naturalism (in both its forms, materialism and positivism) was that it is a philosophical generalization of science, and science is not the whole of truth. The field is left, then, to realism with its principle of 'the independence of the immanent' (ibid. p. 313): things known are immanent in the knowledge relation while sustaining non-cognitive relations with each other.

The rejection of pragmatism is somewhat puzzling, unless selective, since he held that the new realists work 'within the spirit of William James' and he contrasted **Schiller**'s version of pragmatism with 'James's realism' (1935, II, p. 510). His interest theory of value was naturalistic, and compatible with both realism and pragmatism. All of this leads us to class him as both realist and pragmatist.

For Perry value is any object of any interest. Interest involves expectation, having a forward reference, 'a striving after the not-yet-attained' (1926, p. 250). Values are ranked by their interests' degrees of intensity, preference and inclusiveness. Inclusiveness implies the integration or harmonizing of interests, each person seeking to harmonize the interests of one's own specific life. When conflict appears in the interests of a group the harmonizing or organizing of interests appears as morality: 'Morality takes conflict as its point of departure and harmony of interests as its goal' (1954, p. 87). For individual and group, 'harmonious happiness' is both the norm of morality and its goal (i.e. the *summum bonum*). The norm has the advantage of being able to appeal to all persons jointly.

All successful institutions practise integration of interests for the benefit of their members and, among social forms, democracy is best adapted to the implementations of this norm. Identifying morality with democracy, Perry was able to 'do good' by defending the cause of democracy in both World Wars, lauding the moral superiority of the Western Allied cause, insisting on the compatibility (in the West) of human freedom and military conscription, and urging that since democracy 'implies international organization as a phase of its own development' (1945, p. 97), morality demands a 'league of humanity'. He therefore supported the form that league assumed at the close of each World War. He also found a strong link between democracy and science, and argued for welfare and for a regulated version of capitalism. Supporting the right of educators to refuse to testify before Congressional committees when charged with subversion, he was himself investigated by the Subversive Activities Control Board in 1954.

Sources: CAP II.

WILLIAM REESE

Peters, R(ichard) S(tanley)

British. *b:* 31 October 1919, India. *Cat:* Philosopher of psychology and philosopher of education. *Ints:* Moral philosophy. *Educ:* Queen's College, Oxford, and Birkbeck College, London. *Infls:* British analytical philosophy, Kant and Popper. *Appts:* 1949–62, Lecturer, then Reader, in Philosophy, Birkbeck College, London; 1961, Visiting Professor of Philosophy of Education, Harvard; 1962–82, Professor of Philosophy of Education, Institute of Education, University of London; from 1982, Emeritus Professor of Philosophy of Education, Institute of Education, University of London.

Main publications:

(1953) *Brett's History of Pyschology*, London: Allen & Unwin.

(1956) *Hobbes*, London: Penguin Books.

(1958) *The Concept of Motivation*, London: Routledge & Kegan Paul.

(1959) *(with S. I. Benn) Social Principles and the Democratic State, London: Allen & Unwin.*

(1966) *Ethics and Education*, London: Routledge & Kegan Paul.

(1967) (ed.) *The Concept of Education*, London: Routledge & Kegan Paul.

(1970) (with P. H. Hirst) *The Logic of Education*, London: Routledge & Kegan Paul.

(1972) (ed. with R. F. Dearden and P. H. Hirst) *Education and the Development of Reason*, London: Routledge & Kegan Paul.

(1973) (ed.) *The Philosophy of Education*, Oxford: Oxford University Press.

(1974) *Psychology and Ethical Development*, London: Allen & Unwin.

Secondary literature:

Cooper, D. E. (ed.) (1986) *Education, Values and Mind: Essays for R. S. Peters*, London: Routledge & Kegan Paul.

Peters's early work applied the techniques of contemporary conceptual analysis, with its close attention to linguistic usage, to an examination of psychological theories, both on a large historical canvas, as in *Brett's History of Psychology* (1953), and, more specifically, in the field of motivation (1958). From the early 1960s his interests as a general philosopher in psychology, ethics and social philosophy were fruitfully applied to issues in education as he took the lead in establishing British philosophy of education as a serious academic discipline. He based this firmly in the tradition of conceptual analysis, his own major contribution being on the concept of education itself. In *Ethics and Education* (1966) Peters saw education as initiation into various 'worthwhile activities', largely of an intellectual and aesthetic sort, to be pursued for their own sake. His justification of worthwhile activities, like his justification of basic moral principles such as benevolence and liberty in the same book, was in a 'transcendental' mode, Kantian in inspiration. Throughout his various writings on education in general and moral education in particular, Peters developed his own view of the enterprise as based squarely on the pursuit and application of reason—in opposition to both instrumentalist and progressivist accounts. Drawing on his early philosophical interests, he combined in his theory an account of mind and learning as socially determined, a vision of the aims and rational procedures which the educator should follow, and a picture of the principles and institutions of a liberal-democratic society in which the educational ideal was to be realized. He was cofounder of the Philosophy of Education Society of Great Britain and first editor of the *Journal of Philosophy of Education*.

Sources: M. Collits (1994) 'R. S. Peters: a man and his work', unpub. PhD thesis, Univ. of New England, Armidale, Australia.

JOHN WHITE

Petronijevic, Branislav

Serbian. *b:* 1875, Sorljaca, Serbia. *d:* 1954. *Cat:* 'Monopluralist'. *Ints:* Metaphysics. *Infls:* Spinoza, Leibniz and Hegel. *Appts:* Professor of Philosophy, Belgrade.

Main publications:

(1897) *Der ontologische Beweis für das Dasein des Absoluten.*

(1898) *Der Satz vom Grunde: Eine logische Untersuchung.*

(1900) *Prinzipien der Erkenntnislehre. Prolegomena zur absoluten Metaphysik.*

(1904–12) *Prinzipien der Metaphysik,* 2 vols.

(1907) *Die typischen Geometrien und das Unendliche.*

(1921) *L'Evolution universelle.*

(1930) *Hauptsätze der Metaphysik.*

Plus works in Serbian on Schopenhauer, Nietzsche, Spencer and Hegel.

Secondary literature:

Anthony, R. (1930) 'Résumé des travaux philosophiques et scientifiques de B. Petronijevic', *Revue Générale des Sciences Pures et Appliquées* 50: 312ff.

At the heart of Petronijevic's thought is his method, a modified version of Hegelian dialectic (developed in his book of 1904–12). He differs from Hegel in maintaining (i) that dialectic is concerned with contrary rather than contradictory concepts and (ii) that the stage of synthesis is inessential. It can either precede the antithesis, or be absent from the dialectic in those cases where the antithesis presupposes the prior being of the thesis. A synthesis is necessary only in the case where thesis and antithesis are totally mutually exclusive, and this is true for only one pair of contraries, namely One and Many. In this case, there is a synthesis, the notion of a finite class of intensive, continuous points, such that all components have a mutual tendency to separation.

Using this method, Petronijevic sought to reconcile the philosophies of Spinoza and Leibniz (hence his self-designation as a 'monopluralist'). He argues that the universe is evolving from a condition of instability towards one of absolute stability, in which there will be equilibrium in the relation between particular elements or monads and the universal substance which underlies them. This last is the subject of a special division of philosophy, beyond metaphysics, which Petronijevic called 'hypermetaphysics'.

ROBERT WILKINSON

Pfänder, Alexander

German. *b:* 7 February 1870, Iserlohn, Germany. *d:* 18 March 1941, Munich. *Cat:* Phenomenologist. *Ints:* Philosophical psychology; the human condition. *Educ:* Polytechnics of Hanover and Munich, and Munich University. *Infls:* Literary influence: Husserl. Personal: Theodor Lipps,

Wilhelm Wundt and Husserl. *Appts:* 1901–8, Lecturer, 1908 -35, Professor, Munich University.

Main publications:

(1900) *Phänomenologie des Wollens: eine psychologische Analyse,* Leipzig: Johann Ambrosius Barth (English translation, together with 'Motive und Motivation' (1911), *Phenomenology of Willing and Motivation,* trans. Herbert Spiegelberg, Evanston: Northwestern University Press, 1967).

(1904) *Einführung in die Psychologie* [Introduction to Psychology], Leipzig: Johann Ambrosius Barth.

(1911) 'Motive und Motivation', in *Münchener philosophische Abhandlungen* (Festschrift for Theodor Lipps), ed. A. Pfänder, Leipzig: Johann Ambrosius Barth (English translation, see 1900 above).

(1913–16) *Zur Psychologie der Gesinnungen* [On the Psychology of Directed Sentiments], parts I and II, Halle: Max Niemeyer.

(1921) *Logik* [Logic], Halle: Max Niemeyer.

(1933) *Die Seele des Menschen* [The Human Psyche], Halle: Max Niemeyer.

(1948) *Philosophie der Lebensziele* [Philosophy and the Goals of Life], ed. Wolfgang Trillhaas, Göttingen: Vandenhoeck & Rupprecht (posthumous).

(1973) *Ethik in kurzer Darstellung* [A Concise System of Ethics], ed. Peter Schwankl, Munich: Wilhelm Fink (posthumous).

(1973) *Philosophie auf phänomenologischer Grundlage* [Philosophy on a Phenomenological Basis], ed. Herbert Spiegelberg, Munich: Wilhelm Fink (posthumous).

Secondary literature:

Schumann, Karl (1973) *Die Dialektik der Phänomenologie I: Husserl über Pfänder,* The Hague: Martinus Nijhoff.

Spiegelberg, Herbert (1967) *The Phenomenology of Willing and Motivation,* Evanston: Northwestern University Press (contains a useful introduction and several reprinted essays, as well as the translations mentioned above).

——(1973) 'Is reduction necessary for phenomenology? Husserl's and Pfänder's replies', *Journal of the British Society for Phenomenology* 4: 3–15.

——(1974) '"Epoche" without reduction: some replies to my critics', *Journal of the British Society for Phenomenology* 5: 256–61.

——(1982) *The Phenomenological Movement,* The Hague: Martinus Nijhoff (contains a substantial section on Pfänder).

—— and Avé-Lallemant, Eberhard (1982) *Pfänder-Studien,* The Hague: Martinus Nijhoff (collection of essays and other materials on Pfänder, including

Paul Ricoeur's 'Phénoménologie de vouloir et approche par le langage ordinaire').

Pfänder originally intended to be an engineer, but was drawn to philosophy by the descriptive psychology of Theodor **Lipps**, who became his main teacher. But he grew dissatisfied with Lipps's psychologism and moved towards **Husserl**, who was then developing his phenomenology, becoming the leader of the Munich Phenomenological Circle. Husserl commissioned his *Logik*, and had high hopes of him, but when the Munich Circle refused to accept his later ideas he distanced himself.

Pfänder developed his own version of phenomenology, coming to see it as a check on all other knowledge. The method was threefold: clarification of meaning, temporary suspension of belief in the object's reality, and phenomenological verification—a probing perception through which the object may give itself 'bodily' to us. Spiegelberg argues that it is more 'presuppositionless' than Husserl's.

Pfänder's work on directed sentiments, with its analyses of 'ungenuine' feelings and its spatial metaphor of the 'central self', are especially noteworthy. In his great work on the human psyche he exhibits the meaning of human life as the creative self-unfolding of an individual nature given to each of us in germ. It contains a remarkable systematization of the fundamental types of motivation. In the posthumously published ethics there is a suggestive separation between the value-ethics and the ethics of obligation. Persistent ill-health prevented his completing it and the general philosophy.

Pfänder was a thinker of extraordinary integrity, profundity and thoroughness. His writing has great clarity, and his descriptions and apt metaphors are seasoned with dry humour.

FRANCIS DUNLOP

Phalén, Adolf Krister

Swedish. *b:* 19 January 1884, Småland, Sweden. *d:* 16 October 1931, Uppsala. *Cat:* Analytical philosopher. *Ints:* Ontology; epistemology; philosophy of mind. *Educ:* Uppsala University. *Infls:* Brentano, Husserl, Meinong, Stumpf, Herbart and Natorp; most important in this connection is Hägerström. *Appts:* 1916–31, Professor of Theoretical Philosophy, Uppsala University.

Main publications:

(1910) *Kritik av subjektivismen* [A Critique of Subjectivism], Uppsala; reprinted in 1979.

(1912) *Das Erkenntnisproblem in Hegels Philosophie. Die Erkenntniskritik als Metaphysik*, Uppsala: Berling.
(1913) *Beitrag zur Klärung des Begriffs der inneren Erfahrung*, Uppsala: Acta Universitatis Upsaliensis.
(1914) 'Hume's psychological explanation of the idea of causality', trans. Thomas Mautner, in *International Philosophical Quarterly* (original Swedish text reprinted in 1979).
(1914) *Zur Bestimmung des Begriffs des Psychischen*, Uppsala: Almqvist & Wiksell.
(1918) 'Über das Problem der Veränderung', in I. Hedenius *et al.* (eds), *Adolf Phalén in Memoriam. Philosophical Essays*, Uppsala: Almqvist & Wiksell, 1937; reprinted in (1979).
(1922) *Über die Relativität der Raum- und Zeitbestimmungen*, Uppsala: Almqvist & Wiksell.
(1924) 'Adolf Phalén', in R. Schmidt (ed.), *Die Philosophie der Gegenwart in Selbstdarstellungen*, V, Leipzig: Felix Meiner; reprinted in (1979).
(1931) 'Our common notions and their dialectic movements in the history of philosophy', in *Proceedings of the 7th International Congress of Philosophy*, Oxford; reprinted in (1979).
(1973–8) *Ur efterlämnade manuskript* [Phalén's Literary Remains], vols 1–9, ed. C. E. Sjöstedt, Stockholm: Natur och Kultur (vols 4–8 deal with the history of epistemology, vols 1–3 and 9 contain conceptual analysis).
(1979) *Mindre arbetren* [Minor Works], Lund: Bokförlaget Doxa.

Secondary literature:

Dahlquist, T. (1995) 'Adolf Phalén', *Svenskt Biografiskt Lexikon* [Swedish Biographical Dictionary] (with a bibliography.

Logical analysis of the fundamental concepts of our thinking is the main task of philosophy according to Phalén. His analyses of the concepts of reality in 1924 and change in 1918 provide good illustrations of his method of conceptual analysis. The naive concepts of common sense contain contradictions, and their dialectic is reflected in the development of philosophy (cf. 1931). The investigation of this process is an essential task of the study of the history of philosophy (Phalén's dialectical method). Several of Phalén's contributions to the study of the history of philosophy are of great interest, for example, 1912 and a posthumous book on Kant's epistemology (vol. 7 in 1971–8). Like **Hägerström** (but with independent arguments) Phalén rejects subjectivistic epistemology. According to him the idea of subject–objectivity (the idea that there is an act of consciousness identical with its own content) is absurd, but yet implied by many epistemological theories of various philosophical traditions. In his most comprehensive work, *Zur Bestimmung des Begriffs des Psychischen* (1914) several of the great problems in the philosophy of mind are dealt with, and the theories of **Bergson**, **Husserl**, **James**, **Münsterberg**, Wilhelm **Wundt** and other eminent philosophers and psychologists of Phalén's time are critically examined.

                    THORILD DAHLQUIST

Phillips, D(ewi) Z(ephaniah)

British. *b:* 1934, Swansea, Wales. *Cat:* Analytic philosopher. *Ints:* Ethics; philosophy of religion; philosophy and literature. *Educ:* Universities of Oxford and Swansea. *Infls:* Søren Kierkegaard, Simone Weil, Ludwig Wittgenstein and Rush Rhees. *Appts:* 1961, Assistant Lecturer; 1962, Lecturer, University of St Andrews; 1963, Lecturer, University College of North Wales, Bangor; 1965, Lecturer, 1967, Senior Lecturer, 1971, Professor of Philosophy, 1989, Vice Principal, University College of Swansea; 1992, Danforth Professor of Philosophy of Religion, Claremont Graduate School; other visiting appointments in USA.

Main publications:

(1965) *The Concept of Prayer*, London: Routledge & Kegan Paul.
(1970) *Death and Immortality*, London: Macmillan.
(1970) *Faith and Philosophical Enquiry*, London: Routledge & Kegan Paul.
(1970) (with M. O. Mounce) *Moral Practices*, London: Routledge & Kegan Paul.
(1971) (with Ilham Dilman) *Sense and Delusion*, London: Routledge & Kegan Paul.
(1974) *Athronyddu Am Grefydd*, Llandysul: Gwasg Gorner.
(1976) *Religion Without Explanation*, Oxford: Basil Blackwell.
(1982–) (ed.) *Philosophical Investigations*, Oxford: Basil Blackwell.
(1982) *Through a Darkening Glass: Philosophy, Literature and Cultural Change*, Oxford: Blackwell.
(1982) *Dramau Gwenlyn Parry*, Caernarfon: Gwasg Pantycelyn.
(1985) *Belief, Change and Forms of Life*, London: Macmillan.
(1986) *R. S. Thomas: Poet of the Hidden God*, Basingstoke: Macmillan.
(1988) *Faith After Foundationalism*, London: Routledge.

(1990) *From Fantasy to Faith: The Philosophy of Religion and Twentieth-Century Literature*, Basingstoke: Macmillan.
(1992) *Interventions in Ethics*, London: Macmillan.
(1992) *Wittgenstein and Religion*, London: Macmillan.

Secondary literature:

Nielsen, Kai (1967) 'Wittgensteinian fideism, *Philosophy* 42.
Sherry, P. (1972) 'Is religion a "form of life"?', *American Philosophical Quarterly* 9.

Phillips's major contribution has been in the philosophy of religion, where he has opposed the idea that religious belief involves metaphysical commitments. The reality of God, according to Phillips, is to be found in the religious believer's 'forms of life' and their 'language games'. He spelled this out in *The Concept of Prayer* (1965), where he argued that genuine prayers are not an attempt to communicate with a supernatural being, but rather ways of coming to understand, and come to terms with, oneself. Their specifically religious dimension is given by the language which the believer finds to be essential to the activity. Much of Phillips's work has been devoted to exploring and defending this general conception of religion, a conception on which the traditional attempt to find a rational justification for belief in God is radically misconceived.

In a similar way, Phillips has opposed the desire to look for a theoretical, and external, justification for *ethical* beliefs. The rationale for an ethical belief is to be found in the form of life to which it gives partial expression, and such forms of life are irreducibly diverse. Phillips's work has been extensively discussed. Its major influence has been amongst those sympathetic to a certain interpretation of **Wittgenstein**; others have generally felt that its denial of a theoretical commitment in religious and ethical beliefs is implausible.

Sources: WW 1992; personal communication.

                        ANTHONY ELLIS

Philonenko, Alexis

French. *b:* 21 May 1932. *Cat:* Historian of philosophy. *Infls:* Kant, Fichte and Hegel. *Appts:* Professor of Philosophy, University of Caen and University of Geneva; currently Professor of Philosophy, University of Rouen.

Main publications:

(1966) *La Liberté humaine dans la philosophie de Fichte*; Paris: Vrin, 1980.

(1968) *Théorie et praxis dans la pensée morale et politique de Kant et de Fichte*; third edition, Paris: Vrin, 1988.

(1980) *Schopenhauer. Une Philosophie de la tragédie*, Paris: Vrin.

(1982) *Études kantiennes*, Paris: Vrin.

(1984) *Jean-Jacques Rousseau et la pensée du malheur*, Paris: Vrin.

(1984) *L'Oeuvre de Fichte*, Paris: Vrin.

(1986) *La Théorie kantienne de l'histoire*, Paris: Vrin.

(1989) *L'École de Marbourg. Cohen-Natorp-Cassirer*, Paris: Vrin.

(1989) *L'Oeuvre de Kant*, 2 vols, Paris: Vrin.

(1990) *La Jeunesse de Feuerbach (1828–1841). Introduction à ses positions fondamentales*, Paris: Vrin.

(1990) *Le Transcendental et la pensée moderne*, Paris: PUF.

(1994) *Bergson: de la philosophie comme science religieuse*, Paris: Cerf.

Also translations of Kant, Fichte and Hegel.

In French philosophy, where history of philosophy is taken very seriously, Philonenko is widely acknowledged as the most important historian of philosophy of his generation, one of the most important now working anywhere in the world. His main field of predilection is German idealism, particularly Fichte, with additional writings on Rousseau, German neo-Kantianism, Schopenhauer and Feuerbach. He is the central figure of Fichte studies in France as well as one of the several most important students of Fitche in the world today. His studies of Fichte have done much to rescue this philosopher from Hegel's erroneous interpretation, which is widely reproduced in secondary works.

TOM ROCKMORE

Piaget, Jean

Swiss. *b:* 1896, Neuchâtel, Switzerland. *d:* 1980, Geneva. *Cat:* Developmental psychologist. *Ints:* Child development, especially cognitive; epistemology. *Educ:* University of Neuchâtel, PhD on biology of land molluscs; University of Zurich, psychology; Sorbonne University, psychology, logic, philosophy of science. *Infls:* Philosophical influences: Kant, André Lalande and Léon Brunschvieg. Psychological influence: Alfred Binet. *Appts:* 1921, Director of Studies, Institut J.-J. Rousseau (now Institut des Sciences de l'Education), Geneva (1932, Codirector); 1925, Professor of Philosophy, University of Neuchâtel; 1929, Professor of the History of Scientific Thought, University of Geneva; 1940, Professor

of Experimental Psychology, Director of the Psychological Laboratory, Geneva; 1955, Professor of Psychology, Sorbonne, and Director, Centre International de l'Epistémologie Génétique, Geneva.

Main publications:

(1924) *Le Langage et la pensée chez l'enfant*, Paris: Delachaux & Niestle (English translation, *The Language and Thought of the Child*, trans. M. Warden, London: K. Paul, Trench, Trubner & Co., 1926; second edition, trans. M. Gabain, 1932).

(1924) *Le Jugement et la raisonnement chez l'enfant*, Paris: Delachaux & Niestle (English translation, *Judgement and Reasoning in the Child*, trans. M. Warden, London: Routledge & Kegan Paul, 1928).

(1930) *The Child's Conception of Physical Causality*, trans. M. Grabin, London: Routledge & Kegan Paul (originally published 1927).

(1936) *The Origin of Intelligence in the Child*, London: Routledge & Kegan Paul, 1953; New York: International Universities Press, 1966.

(1937) *The Child's Construction of Reality*, London: Routledge & Kegan Paul, 1955; New York: Basic Books, 1954.

(1941) (with A. Szeminska) *La Genèse du nombre chez l'enfant*, Paris (English translation, *The Child's Conception of Number*, trans. C. Gattegno and F. M. Hodgson, London: Routledge & Kegan Paul, 1952).

(1941) (with Barbel Inhelder) *The Child's Construction of Quantities*, London: Routledge & Kegan Paul and New York: Basic Books, 1974.

(1974) *Experiments in Contradiction*, London: Routledge & Kegan Paul; New York: Norton.

(1974) *The Development of Thought*, London: Routledge & Kegan Paul; New York: Norton.

Secondary literature:

Boden, M. A. (1979) *Piaget*, Brighton: Harvester Press and London: Fontana Paperbacks; New York: Viking Press, 1980.

Flavell, J. H. (1963) *The Developmental Psychology of Jean Piaget*, Princeton, NJ: Van Nostrand (includes full bibliography up to 1963).

Hundert, E. M. (1989) 'The child's construction of reality', ch. 4 of *Philosophy, Psychiatry and Neuroscience*, Oxford: Clarendon Press.

Piaget's theory of cognitive development in children, genetic epistemology, has become widely influential in psychology and education. The key insight of genetic epistemology is that our cognitive abilities, in particular our grasp of basic physical concepts and logical operations, are not 'given' but acquired in a series of developmental stages through interaction with the environment. Originally a biologist, Piaget became interested in developmental psychology during his time in Paris. Extending **Binet**'s work on IQ testing, he was struck by the difficulty found by many children as old as eight in following apparently straightforward syllogisms. Children, it seemed to him, lacked certain logical capacities which as adults we take for granted. Working initially by talking with children, including his own, he went on to develop a series of ingenious experiments by which he was able to map out the stages through which these capacities are acquired.

Piaget proposed four main stages (each with a number of substages): sensorimotor, preoperational, concrete operational and formal operational. The order, though not the duration, of these stages is fixed. The sensorimotor stage lasts from birth up to about age 4. The new born-infant has no ability to organize its world. It has a number of inborn reflexes—grasping, sucking, following a moving object—through which it operates on its environment. The experiences generated by these reflex activities allow the child to build up rudimentary conceptions of space and time, of the distinction between the self and the world, and of the independent existence of objects. Piaget observed, for instance, that up to about eight months, a baby loses interest in a toy if it is hidden. The toy, he claimed, simply ceases to exist. The baby has to learn through repeated experiences that objects continue to exist even when we are not directly aware of them. At the sensorimotor stage, the child's world is a world of 'pictures emerging from nothingness at the moment of action, to return to nothingness at the moment when the action is finished' (Piaget 1937: 43).

The sensorimotor stage is followed by the preoperational stage (when language is acquired) and the 'concrete operations period', which together last up to young adolescence. During this period the child gradually ceases to depend on immediate perception and develops the capacity for logical thinking. Piaget found, for example, that a young child shown pairs of sticks of unequal length is unable to infer from the separate perceptions 'A longer than B' and 'B longer than C' that A is longer than C. Again, in a series of famous 'conservation experiments', he showed that children had to learn the principle of invariance. In one experiment the child is first shown two identical glasses with equal amounts of water in them, A and B; the water from B is then poured into a third glass, C, which is thinner, the level of the water thus ending up higher. The

child's response to this, up to about eight years, is typically to claim that the amounts of water in A and B are equal, but that there is more water in C than A.

The last developmental stage, corresponding broadly with adolescence, is the 'formal operations period'. This is the least studied of Piaget's stages. It involves the emergence of the ability for 'scientific' thinking, the key to which is the ability to isolate relevant causes. This in turn, Piaget claimed, required the ability not only for logical thinking but also for second-order reflection on one's own thought processes.

Although Piaget's work was largely observational and experimental, he read widely in philosophy as a young man and throughout his life remained actively interested in the philosophical implications of his findings. He considered himself to be concerned with the traditional problems of the theory of knowledge while at the same time regarding these as biological problems. The 'reality' with which epistemology is concerned is the environment in which organisms live. Hence the 'problem of the relation between thought and things ... becomes the problem of the relation of an organism to its environment' (Piaget 1930, p. 129). If we study this relationship not as it *is* but as it *comes to be*, we have indeed a genetic epistemology.

To the extent that he was concerned with the constructive aspects of mind, Piaget was a Kantian. He considered himself 'very close to the spirit of Kantianism' and wrote of 'The child's construction of reality'. However, where Kant posited a priori cognitive structures necessary for the organization of experience, Piaget posited inherited modes of functioning by means of which, through interaction with the environment, cognitive structures were developed. These modes of functioning were no more than the simple reflex activities of the sensorimotor stage, which, by 'generalization' and 'differentiation', led ultimately to the emergence of the power of abstraction and other high-level cognitive functions. There was also, as Hundert (1989) has pointed out, a (largely unacknowledged) Hegelian component to Piaget's thinking. In addition to 'assimilation', a Kantian construction of reality by the mind, cognitive development depended on 'accommodation', a Hegelian adaptation of the mind to reality. With the possible exception of psychoanalysis, Piaget's genetic epistemology, though still controversial, has been the single most important influence on modern developmental psychology. The dependence of cognitive development on active exploration of the environment is a cornerstone of educational theory and practice. His philosophy has been much criticized. He has been accused of the 'genetic fallacy' of confusing the (psychological) origins of logical structures with their (formal) properties. It has been said that his developmental stages are, merely, logically necessary: second-order reflection presupposes first-order reflection, for instance. Yet the empirical psychology he helped to found is philosophically significant: it gives substance to philosophical speculation (there *is* no *tabula rasa*, for instance; the concepts of 'self' and 'other' really *are*, as Kant supposed, mutually dependent); and it is anti-foundational, the a priori itself being shown to be rooted not just in experience, but, ultimately, in primitive sensorimotor reflexes.

Sources: Harré & Lamb.

K. W. M. FULFORD

Piéron, Henri

French. *b:* 1881. *d:* 1964. *Cat:* Philosopher of psychology. *Appts:* Various academic posts in psychology.

Main publications:

(1910) *L'Évolution de la mémoire*, Paris: Flammarion.

(1923) *Le Cerveau et la pensée*, Paris: Alcan (English translation, *Thought and the Brain*, London: Paul, Trench & Trubner, 1927).

(1925) *Psychologie expérimentale*, Paris: Vuibert (English translation, *Principles of Experimental Psychology*, London: Kegan Paul, Trench & Trubner, 1929.

(1936) *La Connaissance sensorielle et les problèmes de la vision*, Paris: Hermann.

(1945) *Aux sources de la connaissance*, Paris: Gallimard (English translation, *The Senses: Their Functions, Processes and Mechanisms*, London: Müller, 1952).

(1950) *Le Fonctionnement humain de la vision*, Paris: Éditions Lux.

(1952) *Les Problèmes fondamentaux de la psychophysique dans la science actuelle*, Paris: Hermann.

Henri Piéron was primarily a professional psychologist, but he realized that his work had philosophical implications in that it assumed a certain concept of human nature. He held the view that theories of human nature can be tested experimentally.

As a psychologist Piéron's area of interest was human sensory experience. He believed that the human subject was not merely the passive recipient of their sensory experiences, but that each human being constructed their own worldview through the projection of their perceptions.

Piéron's concept of the human subject was anti-essentialist. He held that the human self had no fixed and permanent essence, but was dynamic. It does have a structure, but this undergoes a process of integrated development. He thought that the differences between human beings were just as important as the similarities. He was against much of the psychological research of the nineteenth century which treated human beings as statistical abstractions. He maintained that psychology should concentrate more on the concrete individual and that psychological tests which allowed for a range of responses were more useful, because they yielded a more complex picture of the self, than those which required a simple 'yes or no' answer.

Given his position that the knowing subject constructs their own worldview, Piéron's philosophical outlook has affinities with phenomenology; and given his view that human beings are dynamic, it has affinities with the existentialism of such thinkers as Louis **Lavelle**.

KATHRYN PLANT

Piñera Llera, Huberto

Cuban. *b:* 21 June 1911, Cardenas, Cuba. *d:* 30 November 1986, Houston, Texas. *Cat:* Existentialist; anti-positivist; historian of ideas. *Educ:* Doctorate in Philosophy, National University in Havana, 1942; won the national Philosophy Prize in 1951 for his essay on 'Philosophy of life and existential philosophy'. *Appts:* Exiled in New York in 1960; taught in the Department of Spanish and Portuguese at New York University, 1961–76; after retirement, moved to Miami-Dade Community College, Biscayne College and Florida Memorial College.

Main publications:

(1957) *Historia contemporánea de las ideas en Cuba.*

(1960) *Panorama de la filosofía cubana*, Washington, DC: Pan American Union.

(1970) *El pensamiento español de los siglos XVI y XVII.*

(1975) *Filosofía y literatura: aproximaciones*, Madrid: Playor.

(1978) *Cuba en su historia*, Madrid: La Muralla.

(1980) *Introducción e historia de la filosofía*, Miami: Ediciones Universal.

(1982) *Idea, sentimiento y sensibilidad de José Martí*, Miami: Ediciones Universal.

(1989) *Sartre y su idea de la libertad*, New York: Senda Nueva de Ediciones.

Secondary literature:
Homenaje a Humberto Piñera: Estudios de literatura, Madrid: Playor.

Piñera, Estela and de la Solana, Alberto Gutiérrez (1991) *Humberto Piñera Llera: Pensador, escritor, crítico y educador*, Montclair, NJ: Senda Nueva de Ediciones.

As a historian of philosophy Piñera identified and analysed the following periods in the history of ideas in Cuba: theological philosophy, anti-scholasticism, philosophical polemic, Krausism, Enrique José **Varona** and positivism, Rafael Montoro and Hegelianism, and contemporary philosophy. Beginning as an anti-positivist, Piñera reacted against philosophical movements that tended towards what he called 'scientific reductionism' and instead favoured philosophy that grew out of existentialism and focused on the individual.

His brother is the writer Virgilio Piñera.

AMY A. OLIVER

Pines, Shlomo
Israeli, of French origin. *b:* 1908, Paris. *d:* 1986, Jerusalem. *Cat:* Historian of philosophy and science; translator. *Ints:* Comparative ancient and medieval Greek, Christian, Islamic and Jewish philosophy. *Educ:* Paris University; 1940, emigrated Palestine. *Infls:* Ancient and medieval philosophy and science. *Appts:* 1937–9, Lecturer, Institut d'Histoire des Sciences et des Techniques de l'Université de Paris; 1948–52, Official, Middle East Division, Israel Ministry for Foreign Affairs; 1952–retirement; Lecturer, then Professor, General and Jewish Philosophy; Fellow, Israel Academy of Sciences and Humanities; Israel Prize, 1968.

Main publications:
(1936) *Beiträge zur islamischen Atomlehre*, New York: Garland, 1987.
(1963) (trans.) Maimonides, *Guide for the Perplexed*, Chicago, University of Chicago Press.
(1967) 'Scholasticism after Thomas Aquinas and the teachings of Hasdai Crescas and his predecessors', *Israel Academy, Sciences and Humanities* 1, 10 (Jerusalem).
(1968) 'Spinoza's Tractatus Theologico-Politicus, Maimonides, and Kant', *Scripta Hierosolymitana* 20: 3–54.

(1973) 'Some traits of Christian theological writings in relation to Moslem Kalam and to Jewish thought', *Israel Academy of Sciences and Humanities* 5, 4 (Jerusalem).
(1979) *Collected Works of Shlomo Pines*, vol 1, Jerusalem: Magnes, vols 1–2, Leiden: Brill, 1979–86.
(1986) *Studies in Arabic Versions of Greek Texts and in Mediaeval Science*, Jerusalem: Magnes Press, and Leiden: Brill, 1986.

Secondary literature:
Idel, Moshe (ed.) (1988–90) *Sefer ha-Yovel li-Shelomoh Pines* [Jubilee Volume for Shlomo Pines], Jerusalem: Hebrew University.
Sirat, Colette (1985) *A History of Jewish Philosophy in the Middle Ages*, Cambridge: Cambridge University Press, pp. vii, 103, 124, 132–3, 139, 158, 162, 198–9, 201–3, 314, 321, 370 (bibliography, pp. 414, 416, 423–4, 426–7, 430, 441–3 and 456).

Pines was an innovator in medieval philosophical and scientific research. He analysed the atomic theories of Muslim theologians which influenced, mostly negatively, medieval Jewish philosophy. He revolutionized the academic approach to a key part of Judah Halevi's philosophy, emphasizing the Shi'ite origins of what had hitherto largely been regarded as a particularist Jewish doctrine. He was the first to research and translate Abu-l-Barakat, a medieval Jewish philosopher who converted to Islam and introduced the idea of apperception of time into medieval philosophy, opposing Aristotelian Islamic doctrines of space. Pines' translation of, as well as his perceptive introduction to, Maimonides' *Guide for the Perplexed*, made this greatest of medieval Jewish philosophical works widely accessible. Pines also found links between some of the great medieval Jewish and Christian thinkers, such as Hasdai Crescas, and the School of Duns Scotus. Pines has influenced two generations of medievalists, for example Leo Strauss, Sirat and Idel. The twentieth volume of *Iyyun* (1969) was dedicated to him.

Sources: EncJud; NUC.

IRENE LANCASTER

Plamenatz, John (Petrov)
Montenegrin (naturalized British). *b:* 16 May 1912, Cetinje, Montenegro. *d:* 19 February 1975, Oxford. *Cat:* Political philosopher. *Ints:* Marxism. *Educ:* Oriel College, Oxford. *Infls:* Hegel, Montaigne, Pascal and Rousseau. *Appts:* 1936–51, Fellow of All Souls College, Oxford; 1951–67,

Official Fellow of Nuffield College, Oxford; 1967–75, Chichele Professor of Social and Political Theory, University of Oxford.

Main publications:

(1938) *Consent, Freedom and Political Obligation*, London: Oxford University Press; second edition, 1968.

(1949) *The English Utilitarians*, Oxford: Basil Blackwell; second revised edition, 1958.

(1954) *German Marxism and Russian Communism*, London: Longman.

(1960) *On Alien Rule and Self-Government*, London: Longman.

(1963) *Man and Society*, 2 vols, London: Longman; second edition, revised by M. E. Plamenatz and R. Wokler, 1992.

(1970) *Ideology*, London: Pall Mall.

(1973) *Democracy and Illusion*, London: Longman.

(1975) *Karl Marx's Philosophy of Man*, Oxford: Clarendon.

Secondary literature:

Miller, D. and Siedentop, L. (eds) (1983) *The Nature of Political Theory*, Oxford: Clarendon.

Plamenatz practised political philosophy during a period when it was deeply unfashionable or even thought no longer to exist as a subject. His name is not associated with any distinctive theory. He developed his own views largely in the course of criticism of classic political thinkers, as in his *Man and Society* (1963), which covered ground from Machiavelli to Marx.

Plamenatz acknowledged the contribution which empirical studies and conceptual analysis could make to understanding such thinkers. But he insisted that there was something more to their views, which could not be dismissed as mere exhortation or expression of personal preferences. As a whole, their work contained a philosophy of life, a vision of how human beings are and how they should be. Plamenatz observed that there is a connection between these two things, even among theorists who believe in an is-ought dichotomy.

His interest in these thinkers was not historical but critical. He recognized that the genesis of their views would depend heavily on their social and intellectual context, but insisted that that need not be the focus of one's concerns. He was equally unconcerned with defending his particular interpretation of a given thinker: one gave the best interpretation one could, but that was not what one was bound to discuss if one's preoccupations were elsewhere. What he was most interested in was extracting a core of argument, of perennial and universal interest, which he would then attempt to restate as clearly as possible and assess for validity. The distinctiveness of Plamenatz's approach is well illustrated in his treatment of Marx, the subject of his posthumous *Karl Marx's Philosophy of Man* (1975) and discussed at length in his *German Marxism and Russian Communism* (1954), *Man and Society* (1963) and *Idealism* (1970). He pays little attention to the context in which Marx wrote or to contemporary Marx scholarship. His interest is in extracting a series of propositions from Marx's texts. He then argues that the general claim that the base of society determines the superstructure suffers from incoherence, because determiner and determined are already conceptually connected: the base cannot be specified except in terms belonging to the superstructure. Here, a plausible general thesis, whether correctly attributed to the thinker or not, is articulated and evaluated.

Sources: I. Berlin (1980) *Personal Impressions*, ed. H. Hardy, London: Hogarth Press, pp. 116–22; obituary, *The Times*, 27 Feb 1975, p. 16; WWW 1971–80; conversation with R. Wokler.

KEITH GRAHAM

Planck, Max Karl Ernst Ludwig

German. *b:* 23 April 1858, Kiel, Germany. *d:* 4 October 1947, Göttingen, Germany. *Cat:* Physicist and philosopher. *Ints:* Philosophy of science. *Educ:* Munich and Berlin; PhD, Munich, 1879. *Infls:* P. Von Jolly, Kirchhoff and Helmholtz. *Appts:* Kiel, 1885–9; Berlin, 1889–1926; Nobel Prize, 1919; Secretary of the Prussian Academy of Sciences, 1912–43; President, Kaiser Wilhelm Gesellschaft, 1930–7; Royal Society, 1926; opposed Hitler and his son was executed for his part in the July 1944 plot.

Main publications:

(1909) *Die Einheit des physikalischen Welbildes*, Leipzig: S. Hirzel.

(1910) *Die Stellung der neueren Physik zur mechanischen Naturanschauung*, Leipzig: S. Hirzel.

(1914) *Dynamische und statistische Gesetzmässigkeit*, Berlin: Norddeutsche.

(1920) *Die Entstehung und bisherige Entwicklung der Quantentheorie*, Nobel Prize speech, Braunschweig: Vieweg (English translation, *The Origin and Development of the Quantum Theory*, trans. Clarke and Silberstein, Oxford: Clarendon, 1922).

(1925) *Vom Relativen zur Absoluten*, Leipzig: S. Hirzel.

(1926) *Physikalische Gesetzlichkeit im Lichte neuerer Forschung*, Leipzig: J. A. Barth.

(1931) *Positivismus und reale Aussenwelt*, Leipzig: Akademische.
(1932) *Der Kausalbegriff in der Physik*, Leipzig: J. A. Barth.
(1933) *Where is Science Going?*, trans. J. Murphy, London: Allen & Unwin.
(1935) *Der Physik im Kampf über die Weltanschauung*, Leipzig: J. A. Barth.
(1936) *Vom Wesen der Willensfreiheit*, Leipzig: J. A. Barth.
(1936) *The Philosophy of Physics*, trans. Johnston, London: Allen & Unwin.
(1938) *Determinismus oder Indeterminismus*, Leipzig: J. A. Barth.
(1938) *Religion und Naturwissenschaft*, Leipzig: J. A. Barth.
(1938) *Wege zur physikalischen Erkenntnis*, Leipzig: S. Hirzel.
(1947) *Sinn und Grenzen der Naturwissenschaften*, Leipzig: J. A. Barth.
(1948) *Wissenschaftliche Selbstbiographie*, Leipzig: J. A. Barth (English translation, *Scientific Autobiography*, trans. F. Gaynor, London: Williams & Norgate, 1950).
(1952) *Scheinprobleme der Wissenschaft*, Leipzig: J. A. Barth.
(1964) (with others) *Vorlesungen über Thermodynamik*, eleventh edition, Berlin: de Gruyter (biography and bibliography).

Secondary literature:
Anon. (1950) 'Planck, Max', in W. Ziegenfuss and G. Jung, *Philosophenlexikon*, II: 279–82.
Giua, Michele (1945) *Storia delle Scienze ed eipistemogia, Galieo, Boyle, Planck*, Turin: Chiantore.
Schlick, M. (1959) 'Positivism and realism', in A. J. Ayer, *Logical Positivism*, Glencoe, Ill.: Free Press.
Vogel, H. (1961) *Zum philosophischen Werk Max Plancks*, Berlin: Akademie Verlag.

Planck was the ultimate founder of the quantum theory with his successful mathematization of the radiation of an ideal 'black body', on the basis that energy was radiated and absorbed in packets of a finite size depending on its frequency, a discovery to which he may have been helped by his then unfashionable belief in the fundamental truth of the second law of thermodynamics (heat does not spontaneously flow from a cold body to a hot). Planck expressed his views in occasional papers, sometimes collected together in translation only. He moved in his later career from an early positivism to a more realistic position in which he came to see the goal of physics as the true underlying unity of the world. He was particularly interested in the causality issues which quantum mechanics made particularly pressing. He separated, in a manner reminiscent of **Duhem**, ordinary common-sense experience from physical theory, and claimed that causality held strictly in the latter and not in the former. He claimed to deal with the free will problem, in a manner similar to Leibniz, by asserting that causality was only a problem if the actor knew in advance what was going to happen to him, which was not the case. An anti-positivist who saw a role for metaphysics in physics and vice versa, he believed that physical truths were not human inventions but existed independently of men's minds.

Sources: Edwards; obituary, *Obituary Notice of Fellows of the Royal Society* 6 (1948): 161–88; L. de Broglie (1948) 'Max Planck', *RQS*, 5th series, 9: 155–65; H. R. Hartmann (1953) *Max Planck als Mensch und Denker*, Thün: Ott Verlag; M. J. Klein (1962) 'Max Planck and the beginnings of the quantum theory', *AHES* I: 459–79; M. J. Klein (1963) 'Planck, entropy and quanta', *NP* I: 83–108; A. Hermann (1973) *Max Planck in Selbstzeugnissen und Bilddokumenten*, Hamburg; DSB 11: 7a–17b.

R. N. D. MARTIN

Plantinga, Alvin
American. *b:* 1932, Ann Arbor, Michigan. *Cat:* Analytic philosopher. *Ints:* Ontology; epistemology; philosophy of religion; philosophy of logic. *Educ:* Calvin College, University of Michigan and Yale University. *Infls:* W. H. Jellema, Henry Stob and Roderick Chisholm. *Appts:* 1957–8, Instructor, Yale University; 1958–63, Assistant Professor, then Associate Professor, Wayne State University; 1963–82, Associate Professor, then Professor, Calvin College; from 1982, John A. O'Brien Professor, University of Notre Dame; visiting positions at other universities.

Main publications:
(1967) *God and Other Minds*, Ithaca: Cornell University Press.
(1974) *God, Freedom and Evil*, Harper.
(1974) *The Nature of Necessity*, Oxford: Oxford University Press.
(1980) *Does God Have a Nature?*, Milwaukee: Marquette University Press.
(1983) 'Reason and belief in God', in *Faith and Rationality*, ed. A. Plantinga and N. Wolterstorff, Eerdmans.
(1992) *Warrant: The Current Debate*, New York: Oxford University Press.
(1992) *Warrant and Proper Function*, New York: Oxford University Press.

Secondary literature:

Hoitenga, D. (1991) *Faith and Reason from Plato to Plantinga*, Albany: SUNY.

McLeod, Mark S. (ed.) *Rationality and Theistic Belief: An Essay in Reformed Epistemology*, Ithaca: Cornell University Press.

Nous 2 (1993): Ernest Sosa, 'Proper functionalism and virtue epistemology'; Richard Feldman, 'Proper functionalism'; Alvin Plantinga, 'Why we need proper function'.

Phillips, D. Z. (1988) *Faith After Foundationalism*, Part 1, London: Routledge.

Tomberlin, James and van Inwagen, Peter (eds) (1985) *Alvin Plantinga*, Dordrecht: Reidel.

Plantinga's work has been characterized by the careful application of techniques of modern logic to traditional problems in epistemology, metaphysics and especially the philosophy of religion. A member of the Christian Reformed Church, he has tried to defend religious belief against the claim that it is irrational. In *God and Other Minds* (1967) he argued that belief in God was, in crucial ways, like belief in other minds. Neither can be given any ultimate rational justification, but neither needs it: they can be regarded as beliefs which are epistemologically basic, and which it is rational to accept without justification. This theory of knowledge, known as 'reformed epistemology', has been developed in detail in Plantinga's later works. More generally, he has argued that a belief is justified if it is the result of properly functioning cognitive capacities in an appropriate environment, a conception which, he holds, has its most natural home in a theistic setting.

In *The Nature of Necessity* (1974) he developed a 'quantified modal realism', a theory, derived partly from Leibniz, which explains the nature of necessity in terms of possible worlds. Much of Plantinga's work (such as his discussion of the 'problem of evil', and his defence of a version of the ontological argument, an argument which had been almost universally rejected since Kant) has been informed by this conception. Plantinga's work has been one of the major stimuli to the use of modern logical and philosophical techniques in philosophical theology, particularly in the US. He is generally regarded as one of most powerful modern philosophers of religion.

Sources: Personal communication.

ANTHONY ELLIS

Plekhanov, Georgii Valentinovich

Russian. *b:* 29 November (11 December N.S.) 1856, Gudalovka, Tambov province. *d:* 30 May 1918, Terioki, Finland. *Cat:* Marxist. *Educ:* Educated at the St Petersburg Mining Institute; expelled in 1876 for his revolutionary activities. *Infls:* Spinoza, Hegel, Feuerbach, Marx, Engels and N. G. Chernyshevsky.

Main publications:

(1883) *Sotsializm i politicheskaia bor'ba* [Socialism and the Political Struggle], Geneva.

(1884) *Nashi raznoglasiia* [Our Differences], Geneva.

(1894) *Anarchismus und Sozializmus*, Berlin (English translation, *Anarchism and Socialism*, trans. Eleanor Marx Aveling, London: Twentieth Century Press, 1895).

(1895) *K voprosu o razvitii monisticheskogo vzgliada na istoriiu*, St Petersburg (English translation, *In Defence of Materialism: The Development of the Monist View of History*, trans. Andrew Rothstein, London: Lawrence and Wishart, 1947).

(1896) *Beiträge zur Geschichte des Materialismus*, Stuttgart (English translation, *Essays in the History of Materialism*, trans. Ralph Fox, London: John Lane, 1934).

(1898) 'K voprosu o roli lichnosti v istorii', in *Nauchnoe obozrenie* [Scientific Review], 3–4 (English translation, *The Role of the Individual in History*, London: Lawrence and Wishart, 1940).

(1908) *Osnovnye voprosy marksizma*, St Petersburg; second edition, Moscow, 1928 (English translation of second edition, *Fundamental Problems of Marxism*, trans. Eden and Cedar Paul, London: Martin Lawrence, 1929).

(1974–81) *Selected Philosophical Works*, 5 vols, Moscow: Progress Publishers (main works).

Secondary literature:

Baron, S. H. (1963) *Plekhanov: The Father of Russian Marxism*, Stanford: Stanford University Press.

Steila, D. (1991) *Genesis and Development of Plekhanov's Theory of Knowledge: A Marxist between Anthropological Materialism and Physiology*, Dordrecht: Kluwer Academic Publishers.

Born into a poor noble family, Plekhanov joined the revolutionary populist movement in the 1870s, and was successively a leading member of the Zemlia i volia [Land and Freedom] and Chernyi Peredel [Black Repartition] groups. From 1880 to 1917 he lived in Western Europe, and was soon converted to Marxism. In 1883 he founded in Geneva Osvobozhdenie truda [Liberation of Labour], the first Russian Marxist group, and was active in the Second International from its inception in 1889. From 1895 on, he collaborated with **Lenin**, whose admiration for Plekhanov as a theorist survived their differences. Plekhanov voted with Lenin and the Bolsheviks at the 1903 conference of the Russian Social-Democratic Labour Party, though he subsequently moved towards the Mensheviks. He supported Russia's participation in the First World War, and condemned the Bolshevik seizure of power.

Plekhanov, who coined the term 'dialectical materialism', saw himself as a defender of Marxist orthodoxy, excoriating on one hand **Bernstein**'s gradualist revisionism, and on the other the Bolsheviks' 'subjectivist' or 'Blanquist' violation of the Marxist sequence of historical development. Although he came to see 'social man' as the maker of history, he regarded outstanding individuals as instruments of historical necessity, and equated freedom with the harnessing of reason and necessity. He attacked the 'legal' Marxists' neo-Kantian and **Bogdanov**'s empiriomonist revisions of the philosophical basis of Marxism, insisting both that material objects are knowable and that they exist independently of human experience. But his own theory of 'hieroglyphs', according to which sensations are not exact copies of objects but symbolically representative of them, was attacked by Lenin as idealist In 1905 Plekhanov disowned the term 'hieroglyph' (borrowed from the Russian physiologist I. M. Sechenov), though not the theory.

Plekhanov was a pioneer of Marxist aesthetics, emphasizing the ultimately economic origins and social function of art, but allowing an 'objective' criterion for the evaluation of an artistic work: the correspondence between its form and its idea. Works of art also have their own proper language, which distinguish them from propaganda.

COLIN CHANT

Plessner, Helmuth

German. *b:* 4 September 1892, Wiesbaden, Germany. *d:* 12 June 1985, Göttingen, Germany. *Cat:* Historian of philosophy; sociologist; cofounder of philosophical anthropology. *Ints:* Philosophy of man; philosophy of culture. *Educ:* Studied Medicine, Zoology and then Philosophy at Freiburg, Heidelberg, Berlin and Erlangen. *Infls:* Dilthey and Husserl. *Appts:* Taught in Cologne, 1920–34; left Germany and worked at Gröningen until 1951 (except when dismissed by the Nazis, 1942–5); 1951–62, Professor of Sociology, Göttingen; after retirement, Visiting Professor at the New School for Social Research in New York (1962–3).

Main publications:

(1928) *Die Stellung des Menschen im Kosmos* [Man's Place in the Universe].

(1928) *Die Stufen des Organischen und Der Mensche. Eine Einleitung in die philosophische Anthropologie* [The Stages of the Organic and Man: An Introduction to Philosophie Anthropology].

(1935) *Das Schicksal deutschen Geiste im Ausgang seiner Bürgerlichen Epoche.*

(1941) *Lachen und Weinen* [Laughing and Weeping].

(1953) *Zwischen Philosophie und Gesellschaft* [Between Philosophy and Society].

(1964) *Conditio Humana.*

(1971) *Philosophische Anthropologie* [Philosophical Anthropology].

(1980) *Gesammelte Schriften*, ed. G. Dux, Frankfurt: Suhrkamp.

Secondary literature:

Habermas, Jürgen (1953) 'Anthropologie', in Fischer Lexikon vol. II, *Philosophie*, Frankfurt: Fischer (contains bibliography).

Hammer, Felix (1967) *Die excenttrische Position des Menchen: Methode und Grundlinien der philosophischen Anthropologie Helmuth Plessners*, Bonn: Bouvier.

Rehberg, K. S. (1984) 'Das Werk Helmuth Plessners', *Kölnische Zeitschrift für Sociologie und Social Psychologie* 36.

The face of the German spirit at the end of its bourgeois stage, as historian of ideas Plessner explored the history of German nationalism and compared the philosophies of different cultures. His sociology ranged over the science, education, politics and culture of both the West and the East, pointing out, for example, the semireligious function culture played in predominantly Protestant societies.

He is best known, however, beside Max **Scheler**, as creator of philosophical anthropology as a systematic discipline dealing with the traditional philosophical question 'what is man?', and providing focus and conceptual guidance to all the disciplines dealing with man. In his idea of 'anthropology' and his recognition of the shaping influence of historical and social factors he was indebted to **Dilthey**, while he derived his phenomenological approach from **Husserl**, under whom he had studied. He shifted emphasis, however, on to man as a psychophysical unit decisively conditioned by his physiological makeup, whose greater flexibility and responsiveness to change distinguished him from other animals and gave him a unique place in the order of organic nature. The philosophical coordination of a whole range of empirical disciplines shows man both conditioned on different levels and yet shaping his own nature.

Sources: Edwards; Landgrebe.

H. P. RICKMAN

Poincaré, Jules Henri

French. **b:** 29 April 1854, Nancy, France. **d:** 17 July 1912, Paris. **Cat:** Mathematician; philosopher of mathematics; philosopher of science. **Ints:** Foundations of mathematics; scientific method. **Educ:** Educated at the École Polytechnique, Nancy, where he obtained his doctorate in 1879. **Appts:** Taught mathematical analysis, University of Caen; 1981, Professor of Mathematics, University of Paris; elected to the Académie des Sciences in 1887, and to the Académie Française in 1908; important mathematical contributions in differential equations, number theory and algebra.

Main publications:

(1902) *La Science et l'hypothèse*, Paris: E. Flammarion (English translation, *Science and Hypothesis*, New York: Dover Publications, 1952).

(1905) *La Valeur de la science*, Paris: E. Flammarion (English translation, *The Value of Science*, New Yorks: Dover Publications, 1958).

(1908) *Science et méthode*, Paris: E. Flammarion (English translation, *Science and Method*, New York: Dover Publications, 1956).

Secondary literature:

Giedymin, J. (1982) *Science and Convention: Essays on Henri Poincaré's Philosophy of Science and the Conventionalist Tradition*, Oxford: Pergamon Press (exposition and analysis of Poincaré's conventionalist views).

Together with **Einstein** and Lorenz, Poincaré was closely associated with the original development of the special theory of relativity. Though he spoke of a principle of relativity he did not formulate relativity theory in the way we understand it. There are, nevertheless, parallels between his work and that of Einstein in the first decade of the twentieth century.

In response to the discovery of non-Euclidean geometries and the subsequent rejection of an orthodox Kantian view about our knowledge of the geometry of space, Poincaré formulated a conventionalist view about the foundations of geometry. He claimed, that is, that the basic axioms of a geometry do not express experiential propositions or logical necessities about spatial entities, but are rather 'definitions in disguise' in the sense that they record decisions about how spatial terms, such as 'point', and 'straight line', are to be used. Different definitions will result in different geometries, and the choice between them will depend upon considerations of convenience and simplicity. In his *Science and Hypothesis* (1902) Poincaré developed and extended his conventionalism to cover the foundations of physics: conventional principles as well as experimental laws play an important role in the physical sciences, he argued. He resisted, though, the extreme view that all supposedly empirical scientific claims are conventional. Physical science is a factual science concerning a real mind-independent world, even though its basic principles have a conventional character.

Poincaré's view about the foundations of mathematical analysis was developed from Kant's view that our knowledge of arithmetical truths, though synthetic, is nevertheless a priori. We have, Poincaré claimed, non-empirical intuitive knowledge of the objects of mathematical analysis. Accordingly, he rejected the attempts of **Russell** and other logicists to base arithmetic on logic: their attempts to produce definitions of the integers were, he claimed, quite needless. He emphasized the role of the principle of mathematical induction, claiming that this principle is irreducible to logic. Moreover, the logical paradoxes which threatened to undermine the logicist programme were the product, he thought, of using concepts, such as that of actual infinity, which could not be properly constructed and intuited. In this respect, his views anticipated and influenced **Brouwer**'s intuitionism.

BARRY GOWER

Polak, Leo(nard)

Dutch. **b:** 6 January 1880, Steenwijk, The Netherlands. **d:** 9 December 1941, Sachsenhausen (concentration camp). **Cat:** Neo-Kantian. **Ints:** Philosophy of law; philosophy of culture; epistemology. **Educ:** Philosophy and Law, University of Amsterdam. **Infls:** Personal influences included Heymans and Van der Wyck; philosophical influences included Spinoza, Kant and Guyau. **Appts:** Lecturer in Epistemology, University of Amsterdam, 1912; Professor of Philosophy of Law, University of Leyden, 1925; Professor of Philosophy, University of Groningen, from 1928; prominent member of the Dutch League of Atheists 'De Dageraad' (the Dawn) and speaker for the Atheist Broadcasting Company.

Main publications:

(1912) *Kennisleer contra materie-realisme* [Theory of Knowledge Against Matter-realism], Amsterdam: Versluys.

(1915) *Oorlogsfilosofie* [Philosophy of War], Amsterdam: Versluys.

(1921) *De zin der vergelding I* [The Sense of Retribution I], Amsterdam: Emmering (dissertation).

(1931) *Le sens de la mort*, Paris: PUF.

(1936) *Sexuele ethiek* [Sexual Ethics], Amsterdam: Kosmos.

(1947) *De zin der vergelding II* [The Sense of Retribution II], Amsterdam: Van Oirschot (posthumous).

(1947) *Verspreide geschriften* [Collected Papers] 2 vols, Amsterdam: Van Oirschot.

Secondary literature:

Spigt, P. (ed.) (1946) *Leo Polak*, Amsterdam.

Polak considered philosophy first of all as the science of the unity of our knowledge. It is necessary and also possible to solve philosophical problems in a rational and objective way. The ratio is the common instrument of all men, situated on a higher level than all kinds of beliefs that contradict each other. The foundation of philosophy is laid by the pure subject; nature is the product of this subject. Polak's critical philosophy thus opposes all 'dogmatism' that is founded on nature.

In ethics and in philosophy of law the mind is the source of objective and unchangeable rules and norms. This autonomous position is in agreement with the Stoa and with Spinoza, leading to the sentence that 'virtue is its own reward'. Within the same tradition Polak states that freedom is causality descending from the strength of our own will, and coercion is causality in spite of our own will. The real foundation of the free personality is called 'character'. Personal death means no more than the end of subjective life; whatever is done in an objective way will remain. The meaning of death is the call to moral behaviour during lifetime.

The moral good originates from the principle of objectivity: the categorical imperative commands: 'you have to will objectively', without regarding your own subjective and personal feelings and emotions; you must act as if you were an objective person. The moral bad originates from subjective desire and leads to conflicts with other subjects and with society as a whole. The greatest evil of our time is making war. No objective argument can be found to justify it and therefore all preparation for war is criminal and moral duty is to be an anti-militarist. In his great work on criminal law Polak expounds the theory of retaliation: the only meaning of punishment can be found within the sphere of retributive justice. Punishment has no sense in the context of reconciliation or of compensation, because the only effect of punishment has to be to restore the violated (objective) order. The criminal sought pleasure in badness, and the balance has to be recovered by inflicting sorrow.

WIM VAN DOOREN

Polanyi, Michael

Hungarian-British. **b:** 12 March 1891, Budapest, Hungary. **d:** 22 February 1976. **Cat:** Philosopher-scientist. **Ints:** Philosophy of science; social philosophy; philosophy of religion. **Educ:** Medicine, Universty of Budapest; Physical Chemistry, Karlsruhe; PhD in Chemistry, Budapest. **Infls:** Bredig (in physical chemistry) and Einstein. **Appts:** Karlsruhe, Berlin Kaiser Wilhelm Institute for Fibre Chemistry, 1920 (Professor 1926); Manchester (Physical Chemistry 1933, Social Studies 1948); Merton College, Oxford, 1959–61.

Main publications:

(Omitting the scientific work.)

(1940) *The Contempt of Freedom: The Russian Experiment and After*, London: Watts.

(1946) *Science, Faith and Society*, London: Oxford University Press.

(1951) *The Logic of Liberty: Reflections and Rejoinders*, London: Routledge & Kegan Paul.

(1958) *Personal Knowledge: Towards a Post-critical Philosophy*.

(1959) *The Science of Man*, London: Routledge.

(1967) *The Tacit Dimension*, London: Routledge.

(1969) *Knowing and Being*, ed. Grene, London: Routledge.

Secondary literature:

Brennan, J. (1977) 'Polanyi's transcendence of the distinction between objectivity and subjectivity, especially as applied to the philosophy of science', *Journal of the British Phenomenological Society* 8: 141–52.

Gelwick, R. (1977) *The Way of Discovery: An Introduction to the Thought of Michael Polanyi*, New York: Oxford University Press.

Langford, T. A. and Poteat, W. H. (1968) *Intellect and Hope: Essays in the Thought of Michael Polanyi*, Durham, NC: Duke University Press.

Torrance, T. F. (1980) 'The place of Michael Polanyi in modern philosophy of science', *Ethics in Science and Medicine* 7: 57–95.

Originally a physical chemist and chemical physicist, Michael Polanyi is best known for his epistemology opposed to positivist and like scientistic views. In the manner of much continental philosophy he opposed the subject-object distinction but in other respects his views are comparable to those of **Popper** and **Duhem**. Their differing approaches can perhaps be regarded as alternative ways of dealing with the infinite regress problem. Whereas Popper deals with the unprovability of the principles of theories, by making them pure conjectures, judged solely and objectively by reports of tests, Polanyi believes that in the assessment of theories and tests the so-called 'tacit knowledge' of scientists plays an essential role. For him, tacit knowledge seems to play a rather stronger role than judgement or finesse, as in Duhem, who, however, was always clear that judgement never proved anything. Polanyi may have been above all else concerned to defend human freedom, as in his other concerns in political economy, but it is not clear how this strong view of tacit knowledge can be consistently maintained. Polanyi's approach has become popular with theologians like Torrance and Newbigin.

Sources: R. E. Innis (1977) 'Michael Polanyi in memoriam', *ZAW* 8: 22–9; 'Science and religion in the thought of Michael Polanyi', *Zygon* 17 (1982): 3–87 (various); W. Ways (1978) 'Michael Polanyi: recollections and comparisons', *JBSP* 9: 44–55; E. A. Shils (1976) 'Great citizen of the republic of science, Michael Polanyi', *Minerva* 14: 1–5; E. P. Wigner and R. A. Hodgkin (1977) *BMFRS* 23: 413–48; DSB 1971–80, 677b–678b.

R. N. D. MARTIN

Polin, Raymond

French. **b:** 1910, Briançon. **d:** 1992, Paris. **Cat:** Existentialist; moral philosopher. **Appts:** Taught at the École Normale Supérieure, 1935–8, and at various lycées, 1938–45; Professor at the Sorbonne, 1961–81; Visiting Professorships at Harvard and Yale Universities.

Main publications:

(1944) *La Création des Valeurs*, Paris: PUF.
(1945) *La Compréhension des Valeurs*, Paris: PUF.
(1948) *Du Laid, du mal, du faux*, Paris: PUF.
(1977) *La Liberté de notre temps*, Paris: Vrin.
(1984) *Le Liberalisme*, Paris: Table Ronde.

(1993) *La Création des cultures*, Paris: PUF.

Secondary literature:
Smith, C. (1964) *Contemporary French Philosophy: A Study in Norms and Values*, London: Methuen, chapter 11.

For Polin there is a radical division between the world of fact and that of value. Facts are fixed, can be known and consist of what is in some sense before us. By contrast, values are fluid, not present to us and consist of a demand for something other than what there is. They have to be created, and what is necessary to their creation is the imagination, which frees us from the actual and allows us to consider what is possible.

When a value is created it becomes fixed and present to us. It is thus no longer a value but a fact: its status is inevitably destroyed by its being brought into being. We must go on to new values in a process of endless and continuous creation.

Values, according to Polin, are not grounded in anything which can function as their guarantee or authority. Any authority for the creation of values would itself have to be guaranteed by a more fundamental authority, and there would thus be an infinite regress.

Polin contrasts values with social norms. Values are private and must be acted upon to be brought into being. If a value, once brought into being and thus having the status of a fact, is accepted by society, it is a social norm. As such, it is public and can be investigated as a historical phenomenon.

KATHRYN PLANT

Popkin, Richard Henry

American. **b:** 27 December 1923, New York. **Cat:** Historian of philosophy. **Ints:** Scepticism; seventeenth- and eighteenth-century philosophy. **Educ:** Columbia University. **Infls:** Personal influences: P. O. Kristeller, Ernest Nagel and J. H. Randall. Literary influences: Sextus Empiricus, Bayle and Hume. **Appts:** 1945–6, Fellow at Yale; 1947–60, Assistant, then Associate Professor of Philosophy, State University of Iowa; 1960–3, Professor of Philosophy, Harvey Mudd College and Claremont Graduate School; 1963–72, Professor of Philosophy, University of California, San Diego; 1973–86, Professor of Philosophy and Jewish Studies, Washington University, St Louis.

Main publications:

(1960) *The History of Scepticism from Erasmus to Descartes*, Assen: Van Gorcum.

(1979) *The History of Scepticism from Erasmus to Spinoza*, Berkeley: University of California Press.

(1992) *The Third Force in Seventeenth Century Thought*, Leiden: Brill.

Secondary literature:

Watson, R. A. and Force, J. E. (eds) (1979) *The High Road to Pyrrhonism*, San Francisco: Austin Hill Press.

—— and ——(eds) (1988) *The Sceptical Mode in Modern Philosophy: Essays in Honor of Richard H. Popkin*, Dordrecht: Nijhoff (contains bibliography).

While still a student, R. H. Popkin found in Sextus Empiricus 'a philosophical author that I could make sense of, who spoke to me' (Watson & Force 1988, p. 106). He found that Sextus and Hume provided him with 'a way of fighting back' against the doctrines his teachers would have him accept. His interest in the history of scepticism grew and culminated in his pioneering *History* (1960).

Popkin established a new context for Descartes's philosophy in the 'sceptical crisis' of the post-Reformation period. As his pupil R. A. Watson put it 'Instead of Copernicus and Galileo, the influence of Erasmus and Montaigne are found to be paramount' (Watson & Force 1988, p. xiii). Not only has Popkin contributed a new interpretation of the rise of modern philosophy, but his research has often uncovered neglected sources and his many papers have often put the received wisdom in doubt.

Sources: DAS; R. H. Popkin (1988) 'Intellectual autobiography: warts and all', in Watson & Force.

STUART BROWN

Popper, Karl Raimund

Austrian-British. *b:* 28 July 1902, Himmelhof, Vienna. *d:* 17 September 1994. *Cat:* Philosopher of science; political philosopher. *Ints:* Epistemology. *Educ:* Studied at University of Vienna and (after its foundation in 1925) the Pedagogic Institute, 1919–28 (Maturas 1922 and 1924); PhD, 'Zur Methodenfrage der Denkpsychologie', 1928); also training as cabinet-maker and teacher in Mathematics and Science (with qualifying thesis on 'Axiome, Definitionen und Postulate der Geometrie', 1929) and working as social worker and then schoolteacher. *Infls:* Hume, Kant, Fries, Laplace, K. Büchler, H. Gomperz, Bolzano, Einstein, Bohr, R. Lammer, Tarski, V. Kraft, J. Kraft, Carnap, Feigl and von Mises. *Appts:* Taught at Canterbury University College, New Zealand, 1937–46, and London School of Economics, 1947–69, holding Chair in Logic and Scientific Method from 1949; FBA 1958; knighted for services to philosophy, 1964; FRS 1976; CH 1982.

Main publications:

A number of Popper's books were conceived or written many years before they were published, and they were often revised and expanded in later editions.

(1934) *Logik der Forschung*, Vienna: Springer.

(1945) *The Open Society and Its Enemies*, London: Routledge.

(1950) 'Indeterminism in quantum physics and in classical physics', *British Journal for Philosophy of Science*.

(1957) *The Poverty of Historicism*, London: Routledge & Kegan Paul; Boston, Mass.: Beacon Press (revised version of three articles originally published separately in 1944–5).

(1959) *The Logic of Scientific Discovery*, London: Hutchinson; New York: Basic Books (translation of revised and expanded version of *Logik der Forschung* 1934).

(1959) 'The propensity interpretation of probability', *British Journal for Philosophy of Science*.

(1972) *Objective Knowledge: An Evolutionary Approach*, Oxford: Clarendon.

(1974) 'Replies to my critics', in P. A. Schilpp (ed.), *The Philosophy of Karl Popper*, La Salle, Ill.: Open Court.

(1977) (with Sir J. C. Eccles) *The Self and Its Brain: An Argument for Interactionism*, Berlin: Springer International.

(1979) *Die beiden Grundprobleme der Erkenntnistheorie*, ed. T. R. Hansen, Tübingen: J. C. B. Mohr (Paul Siebeck).

(1982) *The Open Universe: An Argument for Indeterminism*, ed. W. W. Bartley III, London: Hutchinson; Totowa, NJ: Rowman & Littlefield.

(1982) *Quantum Theory and the Schism in Physics*, ed. W. W. Bartley III, London: Hutchinson; Totowa, NJ: Roman & Littlefield.

(1983) *Realism and the Aim of Science*, ed. W. W. Bartley III, London: Hutchinson; Totowa, NJ: Rowman & Littlefield (this and the previous two titles form (with additions) volumes I, II, and III respectively of *Postscript: After Twenty Years* in proof since 1957 but never published).

(1986) *Unended Quest: An Intellectual Autobiography*, London: Fontana (extracted from P. A. Schilpp (ed.), *The Philosophy of Karl Popper*, La Salle: Open Court, 1974).

(1990) *A World of Propensities: Two New Views on Causality* and *Towards an Evolutionary Theory of Knowledge*, Bristol: Thoemmes.

Collected editions:

(1963) *Conjectures and Refutations: The Growth of Scientific Knowledge*, London: Routledge & Kegan Paul; New York: Basic Books (essays and lectures).

(1983) D. Miller (ed.) *A Pocket Popper*, London: Fontana; reprinted as *Popper Selections*, Princeton: Princeton University Press, 1985.

(1984) *Auf der Suche nach eine besseren Welt*, Munich and Zurich: Piper (English translation, *In Search of a Better World: Lectures and Essays from Thirty Years*, London and New York: Routledge, 1992).

Secondary literature:

Bambrough, R. (ed.) (1967) *Plato, Popper and Politics: Some Contributions to a Modern Controversy*, Cambridge: Heffer.

Bunge, M. (ed.) (1964) *The Critical Approach to Science and Philosophy*, Glencoe, Ill,: Free Press; London: Collier-Macmillan.

Burke, T. E. (1983) *The Philosophy of Popper*, Manchester: Manchester University Press.

Currie, G. and Musgrave, A. (eds) (1985) *Popper and the Human Sciences*, Dordrecht: Nijhoff.

De Vries, G. J. (1952) *Antisthenes Redivivus: Popper's Attack on Plato*, Amsterdam: North-Holland.

Levinson, P. (ed.) (1982) *In Pursuit of Truth: Essays on the Philosophy of Karl Popper on the Occasion of his Eightieth Birthday*, New York: Humanities Press.

Levinson, R. B. (1953) *In Defence of Plato*, Cambridge, Mass.: Harvard University Press.

Magee, B. (1973) *Popper*, London: Fontana.

——(1985) *Philosophy and the Real World: An Introduction to Popper*, La Salle, Ill.: Open Court.

O'Heart, A. (1980) *Karl Popper*, London: Routledge & Kegan Paul.

Schilpp, P. A. (ed.) (1974) *The Philosophy of Karl Popper*, La Salle, Ill.: Open Court.

Wilkins, B. T. (1978) *Has History Any Meaning? A Critique of Popper's Philosophy of History*, Hassocks: Harvester.

Williams, D. E. (1978) *Truth, Hope, and Power: The Thought of Karl Popper*, Toronto, Buffalo and London: Toronto University Press.

Popper did not become a professional philosopher until his mid-thirties, after publishing the first version of the book by which he is most well known, *Logik der Forschung* (1934), and did not seem to think much of professional philosophers in general, at least to judge by his thoughts round his ninetieth birthday (*Sunday Times*, 12 July 1992). But he had been concerned with philosophical problems at least since the age of 17, when he first raised and solved the problem of demarcating science from non-science, and this and the problem of induction occupied much of his attention over the next few years (see *Conjectures and Refutations*, 1963). His official studies, however (when he was not training to be a cabinet-maker), were in science and mathematics and in psychology, especially child psychology, which brought him to his teacher Karl Büchler, and Alfred **Adler** and Heinrich Gomperz, among others. As a Jew, however, an academic, or indeed any, career in Austria was not going to be possible for him, and after being invited to lecture in England on the strength of his book he passed via New Zealand (at a time when academic research was strangely frowned upon there: see 1986, p. 119) to his final academic home in London. An incidental interest lay in music, where he had interesting ideas on the genesis of polyphony (ibid., SS12), and has had music of his own performed recently (*Sunday Times*, 12 July 1992).

Popper's philosophy is summed up in the title of one of his books: *Conjectures and Refutations* (1963). His contact with the Vienna Circle (although he was never invited to formal membership) and with psychology as studied in Vienna, as well as a reading of Hume and Kant, convinced him that two basic, and connected, sins are psychologism and inductivism. The quest for justification of our theories seems to lead to either an infinite regress or a basis in pure experience, whether this is regarded as underlying all statements (as Fries held a century earlier) or as represented by epistemologically privileged statements, as with the Vienna Circle. But no such basis exists (*The Logic of Scientific Discovery*, 1959, SSSS25–6)—as indeed is now widely accepted. His teacher Büchler had divided language into three functions, expressive, communicative and descriptive, but Popper added a fourth: argumentative, claiming that this showed 'the priority of the study of logic over the study of subjective thought processes' (1986, p. 77)—which incidentally convinced him that there were no such things as conditioned reflexes (ibid.). Inductivism, the view that statements or theories can be given positive support inductively, raises 'Hume's problem' (see 1972, p. 85), which Popper claimed to solve, by showing that scientific theories are indeed immune to verification, or to positive confirmation, but are open to falsification. Induction itself in fact he generally regarded as not only invalid but never actually used (although *The Logic of Scientific Discovery* (pp. 52–3) seems to relax this latter claim).

Falsifiability brings us to the hub of Popper's

philosophy. Many readers at first thought that he was simply substituting falsifiability for the verifiability of the Vienna Circle as the criterion for meaningfulness. He since emphasized time and again that this was not so, and the point was taken. Falsifiability provides, by what he admitted is 'a proposal for an agreement or convention' (ibid., p. 37), a way of distinguishng empirical scientific statements from pseudoscience like astrology, or else, as he later decided, from metaphysics (1986, p. 41), which is not necessarily meaningless, for the negation of a falsifiable universal statement (like 'All swans are white') will not itself be falsifiable but is hardly meaningless. Also metaphysical statements, on this criterion, can provide a useful stimulus for science, as with atomism and the corpuscular theory of light (1963, pp. 257–8).

The proper procedure for science is to set up hypotheses designed to be as falsifiable as possible, and then test them by reference to 'basic statements', i.e. those whose form makes them potential falsifiers of the hypothesis, as 'There is a black swan here now' would, if accepted, falsify 'All swans are white'. The basic statements themselves must be falsifiable (hence the importance of adding 'here now' in the above example), and the regress that threatens is stopped when we reach ones we all *decide* to accept—we should not regard them as certain or established, as verificationists regard their basic statements. The need for decision on when to stop testing opens the way to abuse by 'conventionalist strategems', or 'immunization' as he later called it (1972, p. 30), but conventionalism can be avoided (*The Logic of Scientific Discovery*, pp. 108–9). One of the most controversial features of Popper's system is his replacement of confirmation (in the sense of positive support) by 'corroboration', which a hypothesis acquires by surviving severe tests (see ibid., p. 251, n.1): can he really avoid inductivism? Popper insisted at one point that an appraisal must be synthetic, not tautological, but he also insisted that we can never make any hypothesis more probable, in the sense of 'more likely to be true'. How then can saying that a hypothesis is corroborated go beyond saying simply that it *has* passed certain tests? Any attempt to *appraise* it *in the light of* this seems ruled out, and 'if corroborated then appraised' becomes tautological (see especially ibid., p. 251, n. 1, SSSS81–2, pp. 418–19, and 1972, p. 19, SSSS23–4 (answering **Salmon** on this—but what are we to make of 'good reason(s)' at p. 81, line 7 up, p. 91, line 1?).) Elsewhere, though in a different context, he agreed that a fresh requirement he introduced

may indeed involve 'a whiff of verificationism' (1963, p. 248, n.31).

Although for Popper we cannot show our theories to be 'likely to be true', we can show them to have 'likeness to the truth' 'verisimilitude', a notion he introduced in *Conjectures and Refutations* (1963) or shortly before, encouraged by **Tarski**'s rehabilitation, as Popper saw it, of the notion of truth (*The Logic of Scientific Discovery*, p. 274, n. 1; 1963, pp. 223–37). A falsified theory can, however, still be useful, as is Newton's.

Epistemology, Popper thought, should study not subjective acts of knowing but objective things known (1972, chapter 3), which belong to the third of the three 'worlds' he postulates, physical objects and subjective states inhabiting the other two (1986, SS38; 'Replies to my critics', 1974, SS21; *The Open Universe*, 1982, Addendum I).

Somewhat analogous to falsifiability is the 'negative utilitarianism' Popper developed in his other main work, *The Open Society and its Enemies* (1945), stressing the need to minimize evil rather than maximize good, which can lead to counterproductive utopianism. In this connection he strongly criticized Plato, Hegel and Marx, and with them the appeal to essentialism and definitions, provoking strong defences of Plato (1952, 1953), to which an Addendum to the 1962 edition of *The Open Society and its Enemies* replies. In similar vein *The Poverty of Historicism* (1957) attacks historicism, the view that there are laws or patterns in history that the social sciences should aim to predict, and which combines the 'naturalistic' approach of physical science with the 'antinaturalistic' *Verstehen* approach.

Topics omitted here include: mind and body (1977), indeterminism (1950, revised in *The Open Universe*, 1982; 1972, chapter 6); propensities (the 1959 article, included in *Philosophy and Physics*, 1974, and in 1990).

Sources: Interview by Lesley White, *Sunday Times*, News Review, 12 Jul 1992, p. 8; Edwards.

A. R. LACEY

Pos, Hendrik Josephus

Dutch. *b:* 11 July 1898, Amsterdam. *d:* 25 September 1955, Haarlem. *Cat:* Objective idealist. *Ints:* Philosophy of language; philosophy of science; philosophy of culture. *Educ:* Classical Philology, Free (Orthodox-Protestant) University at Amsterdam; Philosophy, Universities of Heidelberg and Paris (Sorbonne). *Infls:* Personal influences included Rickert, Husserl and Cassirer; philosophical influences included Descartes,

Kant and Hegel. *Appts:* Professor of General Linguistics, Free University at Amsterdam, 1923–32; left because of conflicts about religion; Professor of Philosophy, University of Amsterdam, 1932 until his death; spent most of the German occupation in prison (1940–3); a founder of the Dutch Humanist League, 1946; first President of the FISP (Fédération Internationale des Sociétés de Philosophie) and President of its Congress at Amsterdam, 1948; President of the editorial board of the *Algemeen Nederlands Tijdschrift voor Wijsbegeerte.*

Main publications:

(1922) *Zur Logik der Sprachwissenschaft*, Heidelberg: Winter (dissertation).

(1923) *Kritische Studien über philologische Methode*, Heidelberg: Winter (second dissertation).

(1932) *Het apriori in de geesteswetenschappen* [The A Priori in the Social Sciences], Amsterdam: Swets en Zeitlinger.

(1940) *Filosofie der wetenschappen* [Philosophy of Sciences], Arnhem: Van Logum Slaterus.

(1957–8) *Keur uit de verspreide geschriften* [Anthology of Collected Papers], 2 vols, Assen: Van Gorcum (posthumous).

Pos developed a linguistic theory stating the primacy of language, that grew out into a general view on the primacy of the world as a whole in an objective–idealist manner. Pos remained rationalist in a neo-Kantian way and never became an empiricist. His theory of language gave a phenomenological correction to the then prevailing theory of structuralism. Pos defended the a priori of **Husserl** against the pure descriptive attitude of the structuralists. Phenomenological reflection can show that theoretical concepts and structures are founded in time as their ground.

In his metaphysics and in his theory of knowledge Pos started with the a priori as the source of culture. The unity of all sciences is based upon self-consciousness. Philosophy is the research of reason about itself. Metaphysics is founded in self-experience and reflection upon it. In the socio-political field, too, human reason has its validity in shaping norms and maxims. Pos attacked irrational tendencies, especially Nazism, from the beginning. He defended human dignity and human rights in theory, but also in practical organizations. After the Second World War he engaged in left-wing socialism.

WIM VAN DOOREN

Post, Emil Leon

Polish-American. *b:* 11 February 1954, Augustów, Poland. *Cat:* Mathematical logician. *Educ:* 1917, BS, College of the City of New York; 1918, AM, Columbia University; 1920, PhD, Columbia University. *Infls:* Bertrand Russell and Thoraf Skolem. *Appts:* 1917–20, Lecturer in Mathematics, Columbia University; 1921, Proctor Fellow at Princeton University; 1922, Instructor, Columbia University; 1927, New York City High Schools; 1927 and 1935–54, City College of New York; 1918, Member of the American Mathematical Society.

Main publications:

(1921) 'Introduction to a general theory of propositions', *American Journal of Mathematics* 43: 163–85.
(1936) 'Finite combinatory processes—formulation I', *Journal of Symbolic Logic*, 1: 103–5.
(1943) 'Formal reductions of the general combinatorial decision problem', *American Journal of Mathematics* 65: 197–215.
(1944) 'Recursively enumerable sets of positive integers and their decision problems', *Bulletin of the American Mathematical Society* 50: 284–316.
(1946) 'A variant of a recursively unsolvable problem', *Bulletin of the American Mathematical Society* 52: 264–8.
(1946) 'Note on a conjecture of Skolem', *Journal of Symbolic Logic* 11: 73–4.
(1947) 'Recursive unsolvability of a problem of Thue', *Journal of Symbolic Logic* 12: 1–11.

Secondary literature:

Kleene, Stephen Cole (1962) *Introduction to Metamathematics*, Amsterdam: North Holland Publishing Co.
Van Heijenoort, J. (ed.) (1967) *From Frege to Godel: A Sourcebook in Mathematical Logic 1879–1931*, Cambridge, Mass.: Harvard University Press.

Emil Post's work, along with that of Jan **Łukasiewicz**, was a major contribution to the development of modern logic, and more specifically, many-valued logics. He constructed a system of many-valued logic which, following **Russell** and **Whitehead**'s *Principia Mathematica*, took negation and disjunction as primitive, but giving them a many-valued interpretation. The remaining logical connectives were then defined in terms of these two. Post also showed how many-valued logic could be used to demonstrate the independence of axioms in axiomatic systems. While having a less philosophical motivation than **Łukasiewicz**, his work none the less opened up the whole debate about the status of so-called 'classical' two-valued logic.

Two notions are particularly associated with his name: Post-completeness and Post-consistency as applied to systems of logic. Briefly, such a system is Post-complete if every well-formed formula becomes provable once we adjoin to the axioms any well-formed formula that is not provable. A system containing propositional variables is Post-consistent if no well-formed formula consisting of a single propositional variable is provable.

Sources: DSB.

DENIS POLLARD

Pound, Roscoe

American. **b:** 27 October 1870, Lincoln, Nebraska. **d:** 1 July 1964, Cambridge, Massachusetts. **Cat:** Philosopher of law; sociologist of jurisprudence; legal historian. **Educ:** University of Nebraska, AB 1888, AM 1889, PhD in Botany 1897; Harvard Law School, 1889–90; admitted to Bar, 1890. **Infls:** Literary influences include J. B. Ames, R. Stammler, J. Kohler, R. von Jhering, Darwin, James and Dewey; personal influences include J. C. Gray, C. C. Langdell, J. B. Thayer and J. H. Wigmore. **Appts:** Assistant Professor of Law, 1899–1903, Dean of Law Department, 1903–7, Professor of Law, Northwestern University, 1907–9; University of Chicago, 1909–10; Story Professor of Law, University of Nebraska, 1910–13, Carter Professor of Jurisprudence, 1913–37, Dean of Law School, 1916–36, University Professor, 1937–47, Professor Emeritus from 1947, Harvard University.

Main publications:

(1921) *The Spirit of the Common Law*, Francestown, NH: Marshall Jones Co.

(1922) *An Introduction to the Philosophy of Law*, New Haven, CT: Yale University Press; revised edition, 1954.

(1923) *Interpretations of Legal History*, Cambridge: Harvard University Press.

(1924) *Law and Morals*, Chapel Hill, NC: University of North Carolina Press.

(1942) *Administrative Law*, Pittsburgh: University of Pittsburgh Press.

(1942) *Social Control Through Law*, New Haven: Yale University Press.

(1959) *Jurisprudence*, 5 vols, St Paul: West Publishing Co.

Secondary literature:

Cohen, Morris R. (1933) 'Roscoe Pound', in *Law and the Social Order*, New York: Harcourt, Brace and Co.

Martin, Michael (1965) 'Roscoe Pound's philosophy of law', *Archiv für Rechts und Sozialphilosophie*, 51: 37–5.

Sayre, Paul (1948) *The Life of Roscoe Pound*, Iowa City: State University of Iowa.

Setaro, Franklyn C. (1942) *A Bibliography of the Writings of Roscoe Pound*, Cambridge: Harvard University Press (needs updating).

Stone, Julius (1950) *The Province and Function of Law*, Cambridge: Harvard University Press.

Wigdor, David (1974) *Roscoe Pound: Philosopher of Law*, Westport and London: Greenwood Press.

Pound is generally regarded as the outstanding American writer on jurisprudence of his time. An accomplished botanist, trained in practising scientific method, he had enormous knowledge of the history of law and of legal philosophy. He was a founder of 'sociological jurisprudence', criticized what he contemptuously labelled 'mechanical jurisprudence' in favour of 'functional jurisprudence', and stressed the importance of 'law in action' as opposed to 'law in books'. He developed and extended a theory of social interests and of law as means of social control and as existing to secure social interests. He also developed a conception of the 'jural postulates of civilized society'—the wants and claims involved in civilized society—for example, that in civilized society people must be able to assume that they will be free from random violence and intended aggression. On the basis of these postulates and his theory of social interests, Pound formulated a principle, derived from James's pragmatic ethics, that legislation and adjudication should aim at securing all social interests as far as possible and maintaining a balance or harmony among them compatible with securing all of them. Pound regarded the application and refinement of this principle as providing the basis for a 'continually more efficacious social engineering'. Despite the importance of these pragmatic and liberal elements in his thinking, and despite the influence on his thinking of neo-Hegelian, neo-Kantian and pragmatic thinkers, Pound's politics were extremely conservative. This mixture did not always make for clarity or consistency, and his immense learning often got in the way of analytic precision and clear analysis.

Sources: AmBio 1937–8; WWW(Am); WWW 1961–70; WAB 1979; Ralph A. Newman (ed.) (1962) *Essays* *in Jurisprudence in Honor of Roscoe Pound*, Indianapolis: Bobbs-Merrill Co.

MARCUS SINGER

Pradines, Maurice

French. *b:* 1874, Glovelier, Switzerland. *d:* 1958, Paris. *Cat:* Psychologist. *Ints:* Philosophy of action; epistemology; aesthetics; ethics. *Educ:* Lycée Henri IV and École Normal Supérieure; agrégé 1895. *Infls:* Blondel and Bergson. *Appts:* University of Strasbourg (1919–38); Sorbonne (1938–41); Académie Française 1949; continued to publish extensively after his retirement from teaching in 1941.

Main publications:

(1909) *Critique des conditions d'action*, 2 vols.
(1928–34) *Philosophie de la sensation*, 3 vols.
(1941) *L'Esprit de la religion*.
(1943–8) *Traité de psychologie*, 3 vols, Paris: PUF; reissued 1956 and 1958.
(1955) *L'Aventure de l'esprit dans les espèces*, Paris: Flammarion.

Secondary literature:

Grappe, A. and Guyot, R. (eds) (1976) *Maurice Pradines ou l'épopée de la raison*, Paris: Ophrys.

The fundamental belief explored throughout the work of Maurice Pradines is announced in the thesis submitted for his *agrégation*: he took seriously Goethe's remark: 'In the beginning was action.' He argues that knowing or thinking is an action, a point Kant failed to appreciate, and thus that a critique of the faculty of action must precede a critique of knowledge (cf. 1909). Again, the whole of his enormously detailed work on sensation (cf. 1928–34) rests on the assertion that sensation is not a matter of the reception of brute data, prior to processing by the mind, but rather is active and a product of *l'activité perceptive*, an activity, not a mere reception.

Pradines extended his psychological investigations into areas often not touched by such work. Thus, for example, volume II of 1943–8 contains much on the subject of aesthetics. Pradines argues that human aesthetic capacity is a mutation, a capacity which has freed itself from the exigencies of utilitarian service to the organism, and instead treats sensations playfully, endowing them with symbolic significance and arriving finally at disinterestedness. The beautiful is what we happen to find ravishing (1943–8, vol. II, p. 269).

For many years a theist, Pradines came to revise his religious beliefs late in life (cf. 1955). He came to believe that the concept of God marks only a direction, and that the task of humanity is to advance in this direction. Whoever does not advance towards God goes nowhere.

ROBERT WILKINSON

Pratt, James Bissett

American. *b:* 22 June 1875, Elmira, New York. *d:* 15 January 1944, Williamstown, Massachusetts. *Cat:* Critical realist. *Ints:* Philosophy of religion. *Educ:* Williams College, Columbia, University of Berlin and Harvard. *Infls:* Significant influences, leading him to the study of oriental religions, include Otto Pfleiderer, William James, Josiah Royce and G. H. Palmer. *Appts:* Williams College, 1905–43.

Main publications:

(1907) *Psychology of Religious Belief*, New York: Macmillan (Japanese translation, 1911).
(1909) *What is Pragmatism?*, New York: Macmillan.
(1920) 'Critical realism and the possibility of knowledge', in *Essays in Critical Realism*, New York: Macmillan.
(1920) *The Religious Consciousness: A Psychological Study*, New York: Macmillan.
(1922) *Matter and Spirit*, New York: Macmillan.
(1928) *The Pilgrimage of Buddhism*, New York: Macmillan.
(1931) *Adventures in Philosophy and Religion*, New York: Macmillan.
(1937) *Personal Realism*, New York: Macmillan.
(1939) *Naturalism*, New Haven: Yale University Press.
(1941) *Can We Keep the Faith?*, New Haven: Yale University Press.
(1949) *Reason in the Art of Living*, New York: Macmillan.
(1950) *Eternal Values in Religion*, New York: Macmillan.

Secondary literature:

Myers, Gerald E. (ed.) (1961) *Self, Religion, and Metaphysics: Essays in Memory of James Bissett Pratt*, New York: Macmillan.

Finding pragmatism inadequate, his trenchant criticisms turning on its future directedness and the instrumental status accorded by it to reason, and finding idealism less probable than realism, Pratt made common cause with the critical realists. At the end of his 1920 essay, however, Pratt pointed out that inference requires a recognition of 'the act of transcendence' (p. 216), which one takes on faith, and it is this which

takes one beyond solipsism to a real world. The recognition of transcendence led him, in a course of thought extending from his initial publication on psychology of religion through *Matter and Spirit* (which suggested a dualism of process) and *Personal Realism* (which moved 'toward some form of personalism': ibid., p. 217), into his extended analyses of the religions of India. Initially inspired by the religious writings of William **James**, and deepened by two sabbatical years spent in India, the books emerging from this endeavour were, as he said, his most extensive, and 'the undertone of the *Upanishads* has ... never been long out of hearing' (CAP, II, p. 218).
Sources: CAP II.

WILLIAM REESE

Prawitz, Dag
Swedish. *b:* 16 May 1936, Stockholm. *Cat:* Logician; philosopher of language. *Ints:* Mathematical logic. *Educ:* University of Stockholm. *Infls:* Literary influences include Brouwer, Hilbert, Gentzen, Kreisel and Dummett; personal influences include Anders Wedberg and Stig Kanger. *Appts:* Associate Professor (Docent) in Theoretical Philosophy, Stockholm University, 1965–6, and at Lund University, 1967–9; Professor of Philosophy, Oslo University, Norway, 1971–7; Professor of Theoretical Philosophy, Stockholm University, from 1977.

Main publications:
(1965) *Natural Deduction: A Proof-Theoretic Study*, Stockholm Studies in Philosophy 3, Stockholm: Stockholm University.
(1967) 'Completeness and Hauptsatz for second order logic', *Theoria* 33: 246–58.
(1968) 'Hauptsatz for higher order logic', *The Journal of Symbolic Logic* 33: 452–7.
(1972) 'Ideas and results in proof theory', in N. E. Fenstad (ed.), *Proceedings of the Second Scandinavian Logic Symposium*, Amsterdam: North-Holland.
(1973) 'Towards a foundation of a general proof theory', in P. Suppes *et al.* (eds), *Logic, Methodology and Philosophy of Science* IV, Amsterdam: North-Holland.
(1974) 'On the idea of a general proof theory', *Synthese* 27: 63–77.
(1977) 'Meaning and proofs: on the conflict between classical and intuitionistic logic', *Theoria* 48: 2–40.
(1987) 'Dummett on a theory of meaning and its impact on logic', in B. M. Taylor (ed.), *Michael Dummett: Contributions to Philosophy*, Dordrecht: Martinus Nijhoff.

Prawitz's major contributions have been within mathematical logic, especially proof theory. In connection with his proof theoretic investigations he has also been developing a theory of meaning that explains sentence meaning in terms of provability-conditions rather than truth-conditions.

The dissertation, *Natural Deduction* (1965) concerns Gentzen-style calculi of natural deduction. The main results are normal form theorems: it is proved that every proof in one of the systems under consideration (classical logic, intuitionistic logic ...) can be transformed into a proof that has an especially simple normal form. The normal form theorems are closely related to Gentzen's Hauptsatz for the corresponding sequent calculi. In 'Completeness and Hauptsatz' (1967) Prawitz proves Takeuti's conjecture that the Hauptsatz holds also for second-order predicate logic. In 'Hauptsatz' (1968) this result is extended to the simple theory of types.

STEN LINDSTRÖM

Price, Henry Habberley
British. *b:* 1899. *d:* November 1984. *Cat:* Epistemologist. *Ints:* Philosophy of mind, belief and perception. *Educ:* Educated at Winchester and New College, Oxford. *Infls:* Cook Wilson and Russell. *Appts:* Served in the RFC during the First World War; Lecturer at Liverpool University, 1922–3; Fellow of Trinity, 1924–35; Wykeham Professor of Logic and Fellow of New College, 1935–59; retired from this Chair 1959; Gifford Lecturer 1960 and Sarum Lecturer 1970–1; Visiting Professor, UCLA, 1962.

Main publications:
(1932) *Perception*.
(1940) *Hume's Theory of the External World*.
(1953) *Thinking and Experience*; second edition, London: Hutchinson, 1969.
(1953) *Some Aspects of the Conflict Between Science and Religion*, Cambridge: Cambridge University Press (Eddington Lecture).
(1969) *Belief*, London: Allen & Unwin.
(1972) *Essays in the Philosophy of Religion*, Oxford: Oxford University Press.

Secondary literature:
Burgener, R.J. (1957) 'Price's theory of the concept, *Review of Metaphysics* 11: 143–59.
Fleming, B. N. (1965) 'Price on infallibility', *Mind* 75 (April): 193–210.

Mundle, C. W. K. (1954) 'Review of *Thinking and Experience*' (1953), in *Philosophical Quarterly* 4: 156–65.

Yates, J. C. (1987) 'Disembodied existence in an objective world', *Religious Studies* 23: 531–8.

Yost, R. M. (1964) 'Price on appearing and appearances', *Journal of Philosophy* 61: 328–33.

The focus of Price's interest in his first two books (1932 and 1940) is the philosophy of perception. His overall aim in *Perception* is to use the notion of sense data to construct a non-phenomenalist theory of perception. The method used, as in Price's later works, is phenomenological, with deliberate exclusion of scientific considerations. Price argues that a relation of belonging can be established between sense data and physical objects. Unless they are hallucinatory, all sense data belong to 'families', the members of which are geometrically and qualitatively continuous. The chief member of such a family Price calls the 'standard solid' on which all other members of the family converge. Not all members of families are experienced by the same person, and so families are public. Price avoids phenomenalism by declining to identify a family with a physical object, on the grounds that the latter can resist, and can operate causally; yet he has to concede that nothing can be said about the physical object except that it has certain 'powers'. Price's thought on perception informs his fine Hume commentary (1940), a study of *Treatise* 1, iv 2. He argues that Hume was wrong to conclude that there is an insoluble contradiction between reason and the senses. The seeds of a solution can be found in Hume's concept of the imagination, which fills the gaps in sensation and makes perception of the material world possible. Price argues that Hume treats (and must treat) the imagination somewhat as the transcendental ego he is usually supposed to have dispensed with, being closer to Kant in this respect than is generally noticed.

Price next turned his attention to the philosophy of thinking, and in *Thinking and Experience* (1953) gives his analysis of the nature of concepts. He disagrees both with views which identify conceptual thought with the use of symbols and those which make concepts inspectable mental entities present to the mind in cognition. Price argues for a variety of dispositional theory. Conceptual cognition is ultimately a function of memory. The best way to understand it is to ask how concepts manifest themselves, and they do this in a number of ways: for example, in the production of images, mental or physical, of instances of the concept or in the use and understanding of words, most importantly in the readiness to use alternative verbal formulations. The root manifestation of a concept is recognition of instances of it: recognitional capacity is the essential precondition of thought and intelligent action.

A third major theme of Price's thought is his interest in religion, a theme which became more prominent in his last works. He became President of the Society for Psychical Research in 1939, and was greatly concerned to elucidate the consequences of mystical and paranormal phenomena for philosophy. Thus, for example, at the conclusion of his revised Gifford Lectures (1969), after a searching examination of occurrence and dispositional theories of belief, Price considers the implications of his arguments for propositions asserting the immortality of the soul and the existence of a transcendent god. He argues that neither type of proposition is meaningless: there is slight (if hard to interpret) evidence for immortality from the existence of paranormal phenomena (a point also made in *Aspects*, 1953), and there can also be empirical evidence for the existence of god, once latent human spiritual capacities are developed.

ROBERT WILKINSON

Prichard, Harold Arthur

British. *b:* 1871, London. *d:* 1947, Oxford. *Cat:* Realist; intuitionist. *Ints:* Epistemology; ethics. *Educ:* New College, Oxford. *Infls:* Influenced (negatively) by Hume (ethical writings) and (positively) by Cook Wilson. *Appts:* Oxford: Fellow of Hertford, 1895–8; Fellow of Trinity, 1898–1924; after an illness, appointed White's Professor of Moral Philosophy and Fellow of Corpus Christi, 1928; retired 1937; FBA 1932; revered as a teacher and regarded, with H. W. B. Joseph, as one of the leading Oxford philosophers of his generation.

Main publications:

(1909) *Kant's Theory of Knowledge*.

(1928) *Duty and Interest* (Inaugural Lecture).

(1950) *Knowledge and Perception*, London: Oxford University Press (collection of papers).

(1968) *Moral Obligation*, Oxford: Oxford University Press (collection of papers; includes 1928).

Secondary literature:

Dahl, N. O. (1986) 'Obligation and moral work: reflections on Prichard and Kant', *Philosophical Studies* 50: 369–99.

Hamlyn, D. W. (1980) 'Knowing and believing', *Philosophical Review* 55: 317–28.

Monson, J. R. and Charles, H. (1954) 'Prichard, Green and moral obligation', *Philosophical Review* 63: 74–87.

Price, H. H. (1947) 'Harold Arthur Prichard', *Proceedings of the British Academy* 33 (a good exposition of Prichard's views).

Prichard's work on epistemology, dating largely from the early part of his career, shows a profound debt to **Cook Wilson**. From him Prichard took over the thesis that knowledge is an ultimate and *sui generis*, and he objected to any epistemologies which (in his view) deny this. Thus (in 1909) he criticizes the Kantian view that knowledge can be defined in terms of synthesis; and in later papers he attacks the attempts of psychologists to try to explain it as a construction from something held to be more basic, usually sensation or feeling. Again, he objected to sense-datum theory on the ground that it embodies the claim that sensation is a form of knowledge, for example because we know we are seeing a coloured patch. Prichard argues that, strictly, there are no colours (or sounds) to have a knowledge of. The perceptual situation is best described as 'someone-seeing-a-colour/hearing-a sound'. Whilst the colour (etc.) is not identical with the seeing, it is dependent on it. Further, since knowledge is ultimate and immediate, it needs no further vindication by the further knowledge that it is knowledge. Any further attempts to furnish a criterion of knowledge, like Cartesian clarity and distinctness, are attempts to answer an improperly conceived question.

A parallel line of thought underlies Prichard's ethics, announced in his best-known paper, 'Does moral philosophy rest on a mistake?' (*Mind* 1912, reprinted in 1968). His central thesis is that the sense of obligation to do, or the rightness of, an action is absolutely underivative or immediate. We become aware of obligations by careful consideration of the situation in which we find ourselves, and understanding the situation leads us to recognize immediately its possession of the predicate of being obligatory: it is the thesis that moral properties are objects of immediate awareness which has attracted to Prichard the label of 'intuitionist' in ethics. What Prichard is denying is that our awareness of the obligatory needs vindication by any further, more general moral principle: the 'mistake' on which moral philosophy has rested, from Plato onwards, is to look for such a principle. Obligations do not need to be deduced from principles, because they are self-

evident. Prichard claims that obligations are irreducibly different and varied in nature, for example paying debts, telling the truth, overcoming timidity. Again, virtue (doing good willingly) is distinct from morality (as a sense of obligation); these are held by Prichard to be independent if coordinate forms of goods.

These views are developed largely by way of criticism of other theories in Prichard's papers. He began a full-length statement of his views in ethics (see the title essay in 1968), but did not live to complete it.

Sources: DNB.

ROBERT WILKINSON

Pringle-Pattison, Andrew Seth (born Andrew Seth; added Pringle-Pattison in 1898)

British. **b:** 20 December 1856, Edinburgh. **d:** 1 September 1931, Haining, near Selkirk. **Cat:** Personal idealist; critical realist. **Ints:** History of philosophy; epistemology; philosophy of religion. **Educ:** University of Edinburgh, University of Jena and University of Göttingen. **Infls:** Taught by Fraser and Lotze. Particularly influenced by reading of Kant, Hegel and Reid. **Appts:** 1883–7, Professor of Logic and Metaphysics, University College, Cardiff; 1887–91, Professor of Logic, Rhetoric and Metaphysics, University of St Andrews; 1891–1919, Professor of Logic and Metaphysics, University of Edinburgh.

Main publications:

(1882) *The Development from Kant to Hegel*, London: Williams & Norgate.

(1885) *Scottish Philosophy: A Comparison of the Scottish and German Answers to Hume*, Edinburgh: Blackwood.

(1887) *Hegelianism and Personality*, London: Blackwood.

(1898) *Balfour Lectures on Realism*, posthumous republication, Edinburgh and London: Blackwood, 1933.

(1917) *The Idea of God in the Light of Recent Philosophy*, Oxford: Clarendon Press.

(1922) *The Idea of Immortality*, Oxford: Clarendon Press.

(1930) *Studies in the Philosophy of Religion*, Oxford: Clarendon Press.

Secondary literature:

Baillie, J. B. (1931) 'Pringle-Pattison as a philosopher', Proceedings of the British Academy 17: 461–89.

Hallet, H. F. (1933) 'Andrew Seth Pringle-Pattison, 1856–1931', *Mind* 42: 137–49.

Merrington, E. N. (1924) 'A Scottish thinker: Andrew Seth Pringle-Pattison', *Australasian Journal of Psychology and Philosophy* 2.

Sell, A. P. F. (1995) *Philosophical Idealism and Christian Belief*, Cardiff: University of Wales Press and New York: St Martin's Press.

Tennant, F. R. (1931) Critical Notice of *Studies in the Philosophy of Religion*, *Mind* 40: 93ff.

Pringle-Pattison was attracted by Hegelianism as a young man but put off it by his own moralistic individualism, drawing more on a broadly Kantian approach. In his Balfour Lectures he identified himself as a 'critical realist' about the external world. He adopted early on the view that philosophy is the 'watchdog of knowledge'. He was sceptical about systems of philosophy and held that religion and poetry went deeper than philosophy could. None the less he did not abandon metaphysics. In his major book of 1917, he argued that 'God, or the Absolute' was the source of individuation, though not Himself an individual amongst others. He described his philosophy as 'a larger idealism' in which the dictates of morality and religion are reconciled with the findings of science. He was, however, cautious in his claims for immortality, which he made neither a condition of morality nor a central article of religion. Passmore writes that his philosophy had 'a distinct attraction for philosophers of a not too rigorous cast of mind, in search of a philosophy which would tread a comfortable *via media* between naturalism and absolutism, science and religion, the rights of personality and the demands of the community' (Passmore 1957, p. 73). Pringle-Pattison's eclectic or what he called 'larger' idealism was an example of the kind of 'normal idealism' (as the historian Metz called it) that flourished in Australia and a number of other parts of the English-speaking world.

Sources: J. B. Capper 'Andrew Seth Pringle-Pattison: 1856–1931', *PBA* 17: 447–61; DNB 1931–40; Edwards; Metz; Passmore 1957.

STUART BROWN

Prior, Arthur Norman

New Zealander. *b:* 4 December 1914, Masterton, New Zealand. *d:* 7 October 1969, Trondheim, Norway. *Cat:* Logician. *Ints:* Ethics; metaphysics. *Educ:* University of Otago, Dunedin, New Zealand. *Infls:* John Findlay, and later Łukasiewicz. *Appts:* 1937, Assistant Lecturer in Philosophy, University of Otago; 1946–9, Lecturer, 1949–52, Reader, 1953–8, Professor, Canterbury University College, New Zealand; 1959–66, Professor of Philosophy, University of Manchester; 1966–9, Fellow of Balliol College, Oxford.

Main publications:
(1949) *Logic and the Basis of Ethics*, Oxford: Clarendon Press.
(1955) *Formal Logic*, Oxford: Clarendon Press.
(1957) *Time and Modality*, Oxford: Clarendon Press.
(1968) *Papers on Time and Tense*, Oxford: Clarendon Press.
(1971) *Objects of Thought*, ed. P. T. Geach and A. J. P. Kenny, Oxford: Clarendon Press.
(1976) *Papers in Logic and Ethics*, ed. P. T. Geach and A. J. P. Kenny, London: Duckworth.
(1977) (with Kit Fine) *Worlds, Times, and Selves*, London: Duckworth.

Secondary literature:
Copeland, Jack (ed.) (1994) *Logic and Reality: Essays in Pure and Applied Logic in Memory of Arthur Prior*, Oxford: Oxford University Press.
Flo, Olav (compiler) (1976) 'A bibliography of the philosophical writings of A. N. Prior', in Prior, pp. 219–29.
Haack, Susan (1978) *Philosophy of Logics*, New York: Cambridge University Press.
Le Poidevin, R. and MacBeath, M. (eds) (1993) *The Philosophy of Time*, Oxford: Oxford University Press.

Prior's earliest significant philosophical work was in the foundations of ethics. In his first book, *Logic and the Basis of Ethics* (1949), he traced the eighteenth-century precursors of the twentieth-century critique of ethical naturalism. At that time Prior was himself a non-naturalist, although he would subsequently change his mind on this subject. He was already taking a keen interest in the logic of 'ought' statements and the notion of a special *deontic logic*.

In the 1950s his interests turned increasingly to formal logic. He entered into correspondence with **Łukasiewicz**, and became—for the rest of his life—a fervent champion of 'Polish Notation' in logic. (In Polish Notation the order of the operators disambiguates statements, without any need for parentheses.) At this period Prior contributed numerous articles to the *Journal of Symbolic Logic*, a journal he would later edit. He also developed a lifelong interest in the history of logic, writing a number of articles on ancient and medieval logicians.

Prior's greatest contribution to twentieth-century philosophy is his invention of *tense logic*. His early commitment to Calvinism had led him to think long and hard about predestination and foreknowledge; his later reflections owe more to Aristotle's conviction that the future is still open and indeterminate. In the early 1950s he saw how to develop a system of tense logic based on a formal analogy with modal logic. For 'possibly p' read 'p now or in the future'; for 'p is not possible', read 'not p now or in the future'. In 1955–6 Prior visited Oxford and delivered the fruits of these reflections as the John Locke Lectures, later published as *Time and Modality* (1957).

In the philosophy of time, Prior opposed the view (since championed by Hugh Mellor) that tense words like 'now' are token-reflexives. In his *Papers on Time and Tense* (1968) he argues for the reality of the 'flow of time', and expresses support for the metaphysical view that only the present truly exists. Likewise in the realm of modality, Prior was a committed 'actualist', claiming that modal idioms like 'possibly' and 'necessarily' are primitive, and that only *actual* objects exist.

A frequent target for Prior's critical papers was Willard Van Orman **Quine**, for whom Prior nevertheless had considerable affection and respect. In an important paper given at Helsinki in 1962 he attacked Quine's notion of referential opacity, and articulated the beginnings of what he felt was a superior account of belief-ascriptions such as 'A believes that p'. A book with the title *Objects of Thought* was left unfinished at his death but was seen through publication by Peter **Geach** and Anthony **Kenny** in 1971. Prior's influence on late twentieth-century philosophy has been extensive but diffuse. His importance lies in the number and variety of the logical tools he has added to the philosopher's toolkit. Metaphysicians concerned with the passage of time, creation, necessity and possibility, and moral philosophers concerned with determinism, deliberation, the 'openness' of the future and the deontic category of the 'to-be-done', will alike find themselves in his debt.

Sources: WWW; obituary notice, *PBA* 56, 1970.

ANDREW PYLE

Putnam, Hilary

American. *b:* 31 July 1926, Chicago, Illinois. *Cat:* Philosopher of mathematics. *Ints:* Philosophy of mind; philosophy of science; philosophy of language. *Educ:* University of Pennsylvania, BA 1948; University of California at Los Angeles, PhD (supervisor Hans Reichenbach), 1952. *Infls:* William James, C. S. Peirce, John Dewey, Rudolf Carnap and Ludwig Wittgenstein. *Appts:* Northwestern University, Princeton University; Professor of the Philosophy of Science, MIT, 1961–5;

Professor of Philosophy, Harvard University, 1965–76; Walter Beverley Pearson Professor of Mathematical Logic, 1976–; President, American Philosophical Association, 1976; President, Association of Symbolic Logic, 1980.

Main publications:
(1960) 'Minds and machines', in Sidney Hook (ed.), *Dimensions of Mind*, Albany, NY: SUNY Press.
(1967) 'Mathematics without foundations', *Journal of Philosophy* 64.
(1972) *Philosophy of Logic*, London: Allen & Unwin.
(1975) 'The meaning of meaning', in Keith Gunderson (ed.) *Language, Mind and Knowledge*, Minnesota Studies in the Philosophy of Science, vol. VII, Minneapolis: University of Minnesota Press.
(1975) *Mathematics, Matter and Method*, Philosophical Papers, vol. 1, Cambridge: Cambridge University Press.
(1975) *Mind, Language and Reality*, Philosophical Papers, vol. 2, Cambridge: Cambridge University Press.
(1978) *Meaning and the Moral Sciences*, London: Routledge.
(1980) 'Models and reality', *Journal of Symbolic Logic* 45.
(1981) *Reason, Truth and History*, Cambridge: Cambridge University Press.
(1982) *Renewing Philosophy*, Cambridge, Mass.: Harvard University Press.
(1983) *Realism and Reason*, Philosophical Papers, vol. 3, Cambridge: Cambridge University Press.
(1987) *The Many Faces of Realism*, La Salle: Open Court.
(1988) *Representation and Reality*, Cambridge, MA: MIT Press.

Secondary literature:
Clark, P. and Hale, B. (eds) (1994) *Reading Putnam*, Oxford: Basil Blackwell.

Hilary Putnam is a philosopher who manifests a unique blend of technical skill and breadth of interest. Early in his career he made significant contributions to the philosophy of mathematics and the application of logic to quantum theory. Elsewhere, his best-known writings have covered topics in the philosophy of mind, meaning and the contemporary debates about realism.

It is no surprise, therefore, that Putnam's discussions of the problems of meaning are intimately related to the positions he has taken, and frequently abandoned, on some of the central philosophical questions. He formerly espoused a form of realist position, which he later described disparagingly as 'metaphysical realism' which he characterized in terms of two basic theses: (i) that there is a determinate and mind-independent world; and (ii) that there is ultimately one 'true' theory of this world which is the goal of scientific investigation.

Where meaning is concerned, the focus of much debate has been the thesis that meaning determines reference. Putnam has contended that theories which endeavour to reduce meaning to mental states or inner processes are manifestly unsatisfactory. Deploying what has become one of the more shop-worn of philosophical fictions, he asks us to imagine two planets which differ only in the fact that one has water and the other a superficially indistinguishable fluid with fundamentally different chemical constituents. On the first planet there is an individual who speaks English; on the second planet another individual who speaks a language indistinguishable syntactically and phonetically from English. Neither of these individuals can be distinguished in terms of their utterances about the local fluid they experience: they produce identical utterances featuring the word 'water'. Putnam's point is that the word cannot mean on the lips of the first individual what it does when uttered by the second individual, because in each case there is a different fluid being referred to. So the locus of meaning cannot be 'in the mind', or if it is, it cannot determine what is being referred to in the world beyond the skull. But even granted at this point, a truth-conditional account would not be sufficient to pin down reference either. For this reason Putnam urged a shift down from the level of the sentence to the level of terms or referring expressions. So how does one fix the meaning of such terms? One familiar solution, rejected by Putnam, is the one according to which both proper names and kind terms are to be construed as abbreviated descriptions or clusters of such.

Instead, Putnam exploits the idea, due to Saul **Kripke**, of the 'rigid designator', an expression which retains the same reference in 'all possible worlds'. So a term like 'Kripke' would refer essentially to that individual, whereas the expression 'The author of *Naming and Necessity*' would not. Pursuing this approach with regard to kind terms, for example 'gold', 'copper', etc., Putnam would maintain that these 'rigidly' designate the particular metals whose fundamental constitution is the object of scientific investigation. He does, however, point out that reference can be secured by descriptions, amounting in effect to stereotypes, based on the more overt characteristics of the substances described, and this is the common currency of ordinary communication. Meaning, after all, has a social dimension and cannot be exclusively a matter of what goes on inside individual heads. As he abandoned realism, so Putnam shifted his ground on the relation between reference and meaning: the ability to understand language does not require what realism demands, namely that there is some secure 'match' between language and 'the world'. Thus has he moved to a more verificationist stance on meaning.

Of all the positions that Putnam has rejected, one of the most significant in late twentieth-century philosophy is functionalism. Formerly its leading exponent, he later considered it to be fatally flawed. Briefly, functionalism in the philosophy of mind is the thesis that psychological states, for example 'believing that snow is white', 'hoping that functionalism is true', are essentially computational states of the brain. Human psychology, therefore, is merely the software of the brain-computer. Putnam originally endeavoured to characterize functionalism in terms of **Turing** machine states, but one consequence of meaning not being in the head is that it is not possible to individuate concepts or beliefs without reference to the environment (including the social environment) of the cognitive agent. Putnam views the whole strategy of looking for some non-intentional characterization of the mental as misconceived, and the attempt to assign one kind of computational state to each kind of 'propositional attitude' as naive. Together with this goes his general rejection of a scientism which he saw as infecting philosophy, and his increasing preoccupation with normative issues. Putnam's influence may be measured in the lively debates he has conducted both against representatives of the realism he rejected on the one hand, and positions like that of Richard **Rorty**, which he regards as self-defeatingly relativistic.

Sources: See secondary literature.

DENIS POLLARD

Q

Qadir, C. A.

Pakistani. *b:* 4 November 1909. *Cat:* Eclectic; historian of Islamic philosophy. *Ints:* Science. *Infls:* Iqbal, M. M. Sharif and E. Rosenthal. *Appts:* President of the Pakistan Philosophical Congress; Professor of Philosophy, University of Punjab.

Main publications:

(1963) *The World of Philosophy,*, Lahore: Sharif Presentation Committee.

(1978) *The Islamic Philosophy of Life and its Significance*, Lahore: Progressive Publishers.

(1981) *Falsafa-i-Jideed aur Uskay Dabistan* [Modern Philosophy and its Schools], Lahore: West Pakistan Urdu Academy.

(1990) *Philosophy and Science in the Islamic World*, London: Routledge.

Secondary literature:

Irtau, G. (ed) (1987) *Beyond Conventional constructs*, Lahore: Pakistan Philosophical Congress.

Qadir combines aspects of logical positivism, conceptual analysis, existentialism and psycho-analysis in his approach to philosophy. Logical positivism, he maintains, is very useful in dealing with science but not helpful in dealing with problems relating to personal existence, where existentialism is more appropriate. Even dialectical materialism has a role to play in explaining the importance of the material modes of production. Philosophy and science are related to religious thought yet have put Islamic traditions under strain. This has led to the necessity to defend and justify Islam within the context of the world of science, a perfectly possible procedure provided that one selects the appropriate philosophical technique. The twentieth century has witnessed a great deal of progress in Islamic science and philosophy, and this can be seen to extend the tradition of Islamic philosophy and science into a new and important future role.

Sources: Qadir 1990.

OLIVER LEAMAN

Qian Mu (Ch'ien Mu)

Chinese. *b:* 1895, Wuxi, Jiangsu Province, China. *d:* 1990, Taiwan. *Cat:* Historian of Chinese philosophy. *Ints:* Traditional Chinese thought. *Educ:* Wuxi Normal School. *Infls:* Ancient Chinese philosophers and Qing dynasty textual critics. *Appts:* Professor, Yenching University, Beijing; Professor, University of Beijing; Professor, Qinghua University; Professor, Beijing Normal University; Professor, Southwest Associated University, Changsha and Kunming; Professor, Wuhan University; Professor, Sichuan University; Director, Research Institute on Chinese Culture; Professor, Yunnan University, Kunming; Professor, Jiangnan University; 1951–65, President, New Asia College, Hong Kong; Member, Academia Sinica; Member, Taiwan Central Research Institute.

Main publications:

(n.d.) *Analysis of Laozi*.

(n.d.) *Chinese Confucian Thought*, Zhongshan Book Company.

(n.d.) *Introduction to the Confucian School of Idealist Philosophy in the Song and Ming Dynasties*.

(n.d.) *Traditional Government in Imperial China*.

(1925) *Essentials of the Analects*, Shanghai: Commercial Press.

(1928) *General Discussion of Sinology*, Shanghai: Commercial Press.

(1929) *Hui Shi and Gongsun Long*, Shanghai: Commercial Press.

(1930) *Mozi*, Shanghai: Commercial Press.

(1930) 'Chronological biography of Liu Xin and Liu Xiang', *Yenching Journal*.

(1934) *Wang Shouren*, Shanghai: Commercial Press.

(1935) *Chronology of the Pre-Qin Philosophical Schools*, Shanghai: Commercial Press.

(1937) *History of Chinese Scholarship in the Last Three Hundred Years*, Shanghai: Commercial Press.

(1940) *New Studies of Zhu Xi*.

(1940) *Outline of Chinese History*, Shanghai: Commercial Press.

(1948) *Research on Mengzi*, Shanghai: Kaiming Bookstore.

Secondary literature:

Boorman, H. (ed) (1970) *Biographical Dictionary of Republican China*, New York and London: Columbia University Press.

Briere, O. (1956) *Fifty Years of Chinese Philosophy 1898–1950*, London: George Allen & Unwin Ltd.

Complete Chinese Encyclopedia (1987), Philosophy Volumes, Beijing: Chinese Encyclopedia Publications.

Dennerline, J. (1988) *Qian Mu and the World of Seven Mansions*, New York: Yale University Press.

Qian was a poor schoolteacher without higher education who rose to scholarly fame through masterly studies of Chinese intellectual history. The Commercial Press, Shanghai, China's leading academic publisher, provided crucial early support. The culmination of his career was his Presidency of New Asia College, started by traditional scholars who had fled Communist rule and now amalgamated with other colleges into the Chinese University of Hong Kong. Qian's writing covered general introductory works drawn from his school or university lectures, advanced critical surveys, and detailed studies of individual figures. His *General Discussion of Sinology* (1928) and his wartime *Outline of Chinese History* (1940) became widely used textbooks. His studies of the Confucian *Analects*, of the ancient logicians **Hui Shi** and Gongsun Long and of Mozi provided the groundwork for his general assessment of pre-Qin schools of philosophy, widely praised as the culmination of the Qing dynasty school of textual criticism. This work was followed by his *History of Chinese Scholarship in the Last Three Hundred Years* (1937) a major re-evaluation stressing the continuity between Sung and Qing neo-Confucianism. His 1930 study of the former Han dynasty scholar Liu Xin and his father Liu Xiang decisively criticized **Kang Youwei**'s claim that Liu Xin had forged the old text version of the analects. Qian thus defended the central traditions of Confucian scholarship and removed the justification Kang had found for treating Kongzi as a reformer. Qian also prepared a major study of Zhu Xi, the great twelfth-century neo-Confucian.

NICHOLAS BUNNIN

Quine, W(illard) V(an) (Orman)

American. *b:* 25 June 1908, Akron, Ohio. *Cat:* Logician. *Ints:* Philosophy of language; mathematical logic; epistemology; philosophy of science. *Educ:* Oberlin College, Ohio; Harvard University, PhD 1932; University of Oxford. *Infls:*
Rudolf Carnap, C. I. Lewis, Bertrand Russell, H. M. Sheffer and Alfred Tarski. *Appts:* 1936–78, first Instructor, then Associate Professor, Professor and eventually Peirce Professor of Philosophy at Harvard University; 1978–, Professor Emeritus, Harvard.

Main publications:

(1934) *A System of Logic*, Cambridge, Mass.: Harvard University Press.

(1940) *Mathematical Logic*, New York: Norton.

(1941) *Elementary Logic*, Boston: Ginn.

(1950) *Methods of Logic*, New York: Holt.

(1953) *From a Logical Point of View: 9 Logico-Philosophical Essays*, Cambridge, Mass.: Harvard University Press.

(1960) *Word and Object*, Cambridge, Mass.: MIT Press.

(1963) *Set Theory and Its Logic*, Cambridge, Mass.: Harvard University Press.

(1966) *The Ways of Paradox and Other Essays*, New York: Random House.

(1966) *Selected Logic Papers*, New York: Random House.

(1969) *Ontological Relativity and Other Essays*, New York: Columbia University Press.

(1970) *Philosophy of Logic*, Englewood Cliffs, NJ: Prentice-Hall; second edition, Cambridge, Mass.: Harvard University Press, 1986.

(1974) *The Roots of Reference*, La Salle, Ill.: Open Court.

(1978) (with J. S. Ullian) *The Web of Belief*, New York: Random House.

(1981) *Theories and Things*, Cambridge, Mass.: Harvard University Press.

(1987) *Quiddities: An Intermittently Philosophical Dictionary*, Cambridge, Mass.: Harvard University Press.

(1990) *Pursuit of Truth*, Cambridge, Mass.: Harvard University Press.

Secondary literature:

Barrett, R. B. and Gibson, Roger F. (eds) (1990) *Perspectives on Quine*, Oxford: Blackwell.

Davidson, D. and Hintikka, J. (eds) (1969) *Words and Objections: Essays on the Philosophy of W. V. O. Quine*, Dordrecht: Reidel.

Dilham, Ilham (1984) *Quine on Ontology, Necessity and Experience: A Philosophical Critique*, London: Macmillan.

Gibson, Roger F. (1982) *The Philosophy of W. V. Quine*, Tampa: University Presses of Florida.

—— (1988) *Enlightened Empiricism: An Examination of W. V. Quine's Theory of Knowledge*, Tampa: University of S. Florida Press.

Gochet, Paul (1986) *Ascent to Truth: A Critical Examination of Quine's Philosophy*, Munich: Munich Verlag.

Hahn, L. E. and Schilpp, P. A. (eds) (1986) *The Philosophy of W. V. Quine*, Peru, Ill.: Open Court.

Hookway, Christopher (1988) *Quine*, Cambridge: Polity Press.

Kirk, R. (1986) *Translation Determined*, Oxford University Press.

Shahan, R. W. and Swoyer, C. (eds) (1979) *Essays on the Philosophy of W. V. Quine*, Norman, Ok.: University of Oklahoma Press, and Hassocks, Sussex: Harvester (includes bibliography).

Quine's influence on analytic philosophy has been profound and wide-ranging. His early contribution to logic amounted to a substantial modification of the **Russell**–**Whitehead** system of *Principia Mathematica*, but like Russell he remained loyal to the idea of extensional two-valued logic, evincing a considerable scepticism about the very notion of alternative logics, especially those constructed to accommodate modal concepts like those of necessity and possibility.

Quine was himself influenced by logical positivism, but even while reacting to it, he preserved a strong empiricist orientation. He shared with the positivists the view that science is the only source of knowledge. There is no 'first philosophy' of the type envisaged by traditional philosophers. Espousing a broad naturalism, Quine saw philosophy as part of science, in effect as natural science's reflection on itself. He was particularly concerned with the application of this naturalistic perspective to language. In a famous paper ('Two dogmas of empiricism', in 1953) he mounted an assault on analyticity and the whole notion of 'truth by virtue of meaning'. At issue was the positivist verification principle, according to which analytic statements were characterized as those which were 'verified' by all experiences or observations. He further argued that attempts to define analyticity were circular, involving equally problematic notions like that of synonymy or sameness of meaning, and that verification could not be applied to individual statements in isolation. Quine thus embraced a holistic view in which our beliefs confronted experience, not individually, but as an entire body. Predictions which turned out to be false would entail a revision of the overall system, but this would not dictate exactly how the adjustments were to be made.

Quine, therefore, had a strong aversion to intensional notions such as those of 'meaning', 'property' or 'proposition', seeing them as having no legitimate role in a proper semantic or psychological theory. One upshot of his attack on analyticity and meaning was that there were no 'objective' relations of synonymy or sameness of meaning, and hence all translation was indeterminate. This thesis of the 'indeterminancy of translation' entails that the linguistic behaviour of language speakers is consistent with incompatible but equally coherent schemes or 'manuals' of translation that might be constructed. There is no 'fact of the matter' as to the meaning of a speaker's utterances. Given that, on Quine's view, there are no meanings or analytic truths, then there is an immediate and radical implication for philosophy itself: there is no role for philosophy as an activity exclusively or predominantly concerned with a priori theorizing about 'concepts' or 'meanings'.

Quine sought to extend his programme by naturalizing epistemology, providing a heavily behaviouristic account of the relation of beliefs and theories to sensory input. Quine appeals to the fact that we do, after all, learn language not only from the non-human world, but from other human beings, and that acquiring such language understanding is a matter of bringing one's own speech behaviour into line with that of others in one's particular language community.

Quine is also justly renowed for his discussion of ontological commitment, commenced in the seminal paper ('On what there is', in Quine 1953). Without exaggeration it can be said that this paper generated a vast secondary literature devoted to questions of ontology and reference. The question for Quine is how one determines the ontological commitments of a theory (or a person's body of beliefs about what exists). Natural language is unhelpful in this regard, since it has many different ways of expressing such commitments, i.e. there is no one readily identifiable syntactic device serving the purpose. Furthermore, speakers of natural language talk prima facie about all manner of things: their sentences contain names of nonentities, there are definite descriptive phrases which do not always have the function of referring to objects. Quine's recommendation was that ontological disputes could be clarified by resort to logic, and more specifically the device of quantification. This would mean that, in the technical thought logical idiom, ontological commitment would be expressed by means of what is standardly known as the 'existential' quantifier (informally expressed by 'There is ...' or 'There exists'). Thus someone could express their ontological commitment by saying things of the form 'There are Xs', where 'X' indicates the kinds of entity to which the person is committed. This is the basis for Quine's famous slogan that 'To be is to be the value of a bound variable' (that is, a variable bound by the existential quantifier).

Critics pointed out that there are at least some uses of 'There is' and related expressions in natural language which do not plausibly carry ontological commitment, e.g. 'there are several ways of dealing with this problem', but which, if subjected to the technical regimentation Quine recommends, would involve such commitment. Quine's indeterminacy thesis has implications for his account of ontological commitment: if there is no ultimate fact of the matter about what exactly someone is saying or what entities they are referring to in their utterances, then what a speaker if ontologically committed to becomes relativized to the particular manual or scheme of translation used to interpret their utterances.

For all the relativistic overtones of his approach, Quine has commitments of his own, not least of which is his physicalism, his view of physics as the basic science to which all other 'lesser' sciences should be in principle reducible. Despite a pronounced leaning towards nomalism, he reluctantly feels he has to countenance one category of abstract entity–sets. Science needs mathematics, and while one might dispense with many of the apparent 'entities' of mathematics such as numbers, no mathematics adequate for physical science can be sustained without sets. As always, Quine's ultimate justification for his stances is essentially pragmatic, and his own outlook represents yet another twist to the story of American pragmatism in philosophy.

Quine's views have been the focus of many debates: with Rudolf **Carnap** and Jerrold **Katz** on the notion of analyticity, and with Ruth **Marcus Barcan** and others on the question of modality and the possibility of modal logics. He had a significant influence on Donald **Davidson**, his holism has been questioned, perhaps most forcefully by Jerry **Fodor**, and despite his own logical stance, he has inspired much work on the development of logics tolerating reference to nonentities, at least some of which have put in question his coupling of the notions of existence and quantification.

Sources: Edwards; Turner; Quine, W. V. O. *The Time of My Life: An Autobiography*, Cambridge, Mass.: MIT Press, 1985.

DENIS POLLARD

Quinton, Anthony Meredith

British. *b:* 1925, Saltash, Cornwall. *Cat:* Analytic philosopher. *Educ:* Christchurch College, Oxford. *Infls:* Russell, Ryle and Ayer. *Appts:* Fellow, All

Souls, Oxford, 1949–55; Fellow, New College, Oxford, 1955–78 (Emeritus Fellow from 1980); President, Trinity College, Oxford, 1978–87 (Honorary Fellow from 1987); Fellow (1977) and Vice-President (1985–6) of British Academy; life peer, 1982.

Main publications:

(1967) (ed.) *Political Philosophy*, Oxford: Oxford University Press.
(1973) *The Nature of Things*, London: Routledge.
(1973) *Utilitarian Ethics*, London: Macmillan.
(1978) *The Politics of Imperfection*, London: Faber.
(1980) *Francis Bacon*, Oxford: Oxford University Press.
(1982) *Thoughts and Thinkers*, London: Duckworth.

Quinton's philosophy is best seen as a series of modifications to or reactions against the tradition of British philosophy that runs from the empiricists of the eighteenth century, through Mill in the nineteenth, and on to **Russell** and **Ayer** in the twentieth. Thus in epistemology he has defended a foundationalism, but one in which the basic statements are about physical objects, not sense impressions. In logic he has supported the traditional empiricist theses that all a priori truths are analytic, and that all analytic truths are true in virtue of facts about the meanings of words. In the philosophy of mind, he has supported the now widely held view that the mind is contingently identical to the brain; but he has interestingly combined this with the less common belief that if we are to individuate mental events and attribute causal powers to them, then the dualist hypothesis that such events are non-physical is not so much contingently false as incoherent. This in turn implies that *some* form of materialism is not merely true, but is the *only* coherent option. Less traditionally, he has denied that there is an unbridgeable fact/value gap, arguing that value is definable in broadly utilitarian terms, by reference to human satisfaction and suffering. In politics, he has defended a modest and humane conservatism.

More unusually for a modern analytic philosopher, he has shown (particularly in *Thoughts and Thinkers*, 1982) a range of interests and sympathies which, encompassing the Frankfurt School and Marshall McLuhan, Polish philosophy and Mortimer Adler, goes well beyond the limits of most current English-speaking philosophers.

Sources: WW 1993.

NICHOLAS EVERITT

R

Radhakrishnan, Sarvepalli

Indian. **b:** 5 September 1888, Tiruttani, near Madras. **d:** 16 April 1975. Madras. **Cat:** Idealist. **Ints:** Metaphysics; epistemology; Eastern religions; Western philosophy. **Educ:** Madras Christian College. **Infls:** Advaita Vedanta. **Appts:** 1931–6, Vice-Chancellor, Andhra University; 1936–52, Professor of Eastern Religious and Ethics, University of Oxford; 1939–48, Vice Chancellor, Benaras Hindu University; 1946–52, Head Indian delegation, UNESCO; 1949–52, Indian Ambassador to Russia; 1952–62, Vice-President of India; 1962–7, President of India.

Main publications:

(1923) *Indian Philosophy*, vol. I, London: George Allen & Unwin.
(1927) *Indian Philosophy*, vol. II, London: George Allen & Unwin.
(1927) *The Hindu View of Life*, London: George Allen & Unwin.
(1931) *An Idealist View of Life*, London: George Allen & Unwin.
(1933) *East and West in Religion*, London: George Allen & Unwin.
(1939) *Eastern Religions and Western Thought*, Oxford: Oxford University Press.
(1947) *Religion and Society*, London: George Allen & Unwin.
(1948) *The Bhagavad Gita*, London: George Allen & Unwin.
(1960) *The Brahma Sutra*, London: Allen & Unwin.

Secondary literature:

Gopal, S. (1989) *Radhakrishnan: A Biography*, New Delhi: Oxford University Press.
Schilpp, Paul Arthur (1952) *The Philosophy of Sarvepalli Radhakrishnan*, La Salle: Open Court Publishing.

Radhakrishnan's philosophy is mainly founded on Shankara's Advaita Vedanta, although he has modified it to some extent. The influence of Shankara is at its most explicit in his metaphysics. According to Radhakrishnan, the sciences are unable to provide an adequate account of reality since they cannot account for values and religious experiences. For him, the purpose, values and qualities of existence that are to be found in the world require an ontological foundation. And this foundation is provided by the Absolute, Supreme or *Brahman*, which is free from the distinctions of subject and object, beyond speech and mind, indescribable and eternal.

The problem with a philosophy that posits oneness as Reality is the nature of its relation to the world as we know it—that is, as consisting of distinct objects. For Sankara, the world of phenomena including *Ishvara* (personal aspect of Brahman or personal God) is an illusion (*maja*) or magic (*indrajala*) and therefore dismissible. Radhakrishnan, however, does not treat the world of *Ishvara* as unreal. For him, the world is real since it is a creation of the Supreme. However, unlike the Supreme which is uncreated and eternal, the world is temporal, imperfect and dependent. '*Maya*' has a standing in the world of reality ... it is not so much a veil as the dress of God' (1960, p. 157). And *Ishvara* too is an aspect of the Absolute and is not an illusion.

The comprehension of *Brahman*, according to Radhakrishnan, takes place through intuitive knowledge—the intimate fusion of the mind with reality. In intuitive knowledge, the subject becomes one with the object of knowledge. In this it differs from perception or inference, the other two modes of knowing, where the subject–object distinction persists. Since Radhakrishnan views intuition as a valid means of knowledge, he is led to hold that religion is a proper concern of philosophy rather than theology.

Religious faith and religion, according to Radhakrishnan, play important roles in man's comprehension of reality and the evolution of the divine nature in man, which in turn promote peaceful coexistence, justice and equality.

Given Radhakrishnan's views about the divine nature of mankind, it is surprising that he endorsed the caste system which decides the status of an individual in society on the basis of heredity. In *The Hindu View of Life* (1927, pp. 98–126) he regards the caste system as a singular achievement of Hinduism. Radhakrishnan seems to justify the equity of the caste system the basis of *karma*—the doctrine that the present life is based on the deeds of the past and the future life is based on the deeds of the present. This doctrine not only provides a convenient justification for the current status of an individual within society but allows for mobility in that an individual could be born in a better caste in the future by monitoring his actions closely. However, in a later work Radhakrishnan seems to have modified his views on the Hindu caste system due to its negative effects on society. In *Religion and Society* (1947, p. 132) he states: 'Caste divisions have prevented the development of homogeneity among the Hindus. To develop a degree of organic wholeness and a sense of common obligation, the caste spirit must go. We have to get rid of the innumerable castes and outcasts, with their spirit of exclusiveness, jealousy, greed and fear.' Although Radhakrishnan's philosophy owes much to Shankara's Advaita Vedanta, he has reinterpreted it in a manner to make it more relevant to contemporary life as affected by science and social progress.

INDIRA MAHALINGAM CARR

Radulescu-Motru, Constantin

Romanian. *b:* 1868, Sutoesti. *d:* 1954. *Cat:* Energetist; personalist. *Ints:* Metaphysics. *Educ:* Studied in Romania and Germany (doctorate from Leipzig). *Infls:* Wilhelm Ostwald and Wilhelm Stern. *Appts:* 1904, Professor of Philosophy, University of Bucharest; heavily involved in journal publication, and teaching and research in philosophy and psychology.

Main publications:

(1912) *Elemente de metafizica*, second, definitive edition, 1928.
(1924) *Curs de psihologie*.
(1927) *Personalismul energetic*.
(1932) *Vocatia*.
(1936) *Românismul*.
(1940) *Timp si destin*.
(1946) *Morala personalismului energetic*, Bucharest: Monitorul Oficial si Imprimeriile Statutui.

One of the most industrious and influential of early Romanian thinkers, Radulescu-Motru drew heavily on the energetism of **Ostwald** and the personalism of **Stern**. From the former, Radulescu took his central metaphysical hypothesis: that the ultimate reality is neither matter nor consciousness but energy, and the universe is the manifestation of the evolution of this energy in time. Much of the universe is understandable by means of positive science, which has as its goal complete

and non-relative knowledge. However, there is one key manifestation of cosmic energy which eludes understanding in general, positivistic laws, and that is the individual human consciousness. Alone among existents, human consciousness can be aware of the nature of the universal process and so is described by Radulescu as being 'correlated with' or 'reflecting' cosmic evolution. In human consciousness, the highest form of existent, the universal process attains self-awareness.

ROBERT WILKINSON

Rahman, Fazlur

Pakistani. *b:* 1919, Punjab. *d:* 1988, Chicago. *Cat:* Islamic philosopher; historian of philosophy. *Infls:* Avicenna, ibn Taymíyya and Islamic modernism, Simon Van Den Bergh. *Appts:* Lecturer, University of Durham, England and McGill University, Montreal; Director, Institute of Islamic Research, Karachi; Professor, University of Chicago and University of California, Los Angeles.

Main publications:

(1952) *Avicenna's Psychology*, London: Oxford University Press.
(1958) *Prophecy in Islam: Philosophy and Orthodoxy*, London: Allen & Unwin.
(1975) *The Philosophy of Mulla Sadra*, Albany: State University of New York Press.
(1979) *Islam*, Chicago: University of Chicago Press.
(1980) *Major Themes of the Qur'an*, Minneapolis: Bibliotheca Islamica.

Secondary literature:

Cragg, K. (1985) 'Fazlur Rahman of Karachi and Chicago', in *The Pen and the Faith: Eight Modern Muslim Writers and the Qur'an*, London: Allen & Unwin.
Denny, F. (1989) 'Fazlur Rahman: Muslim intellectual', *Muslim World* 74: 91–101.
——(1991) 'The legacy of Fazlur Rahman', in Y. Haddad (ed.) *The Muslims of America*, New York: Oxford University Press.

Rahman's early works dealt with important aspects of classical Islamic philosophy, and he set very high standards in the analysis of Avicenna, al-Farabi and the *falasifa* (Islamic philosophers). In his later work he concentrated more on Islamic theology and Islam itself, although he did try to show in his work on Mulla Sadra how philosophy in the Islamic world continued to flourish after its apparent decline in the eleventh century after the onslaught of al-Ghazali. In his work on the Qur'an he pointed to the unity and cohesion of the text of the book which centres on its practical ethical character. Much has changed since the original message transmitted by Muhammad, but the ethical force of the message has remained the same. It is important to reinterpret the text in such a way as to demonstrate its relevance to Muslims in modern society. Rahman criticizes Islamic philosophy for its obsession with metaphysics and its disinclination to consider ethical issues as central.

The Qur'an and the *hadith* (traditions) were misunderstood by their interpreters as rigid and immutable, whereas they in fact are products of a particular cultural and historical context, and to understand them properly one must regard them as part and parcel of a particular time. If one does this, one will be able to see how to apply them to changing circumstances. If no effort is made to relate Islam to its original context, the Muslim is left with the choice between secularism and an antiquated and rigid religious system. The Qur'an needs to be freed from its straitjacket of commentary and tradition in order for it to be fully applicable to new realities in the modern age. In the end Rahman emphasizes the importance of the *ijtihad* (independent thought) of the believer through which life can be breathed into the body of the religion.

Rahman was obliged to leave Pakistan in the late 1960s due to the furore which his views on Islamic modernism created. None the less, he has had a large impact upon the modernist movement throughout the intellectual world of Islam.

Sources: Personal communication with L. E. Goodman.

OLIVER LEAMAN

Rahner, Karl

German. *b:* 5 March 1904, Freiburg, Germany. *d:* 30 March 1984, Innsbruck, Austria. *Cat:* Roman Catholic theologian. *Ints:* Philosophy of religion. *Educ:* Feldkirch, Austria; Pullach, near Munich; Valkenburg, Netherlands; Universities of Freiburg and Innsbruck. *Infls:* Joseph Maréchal; the Catholic tradition tempered by Kant, Fichte and Hegel; Heidegger. *Appts:* Lecturer at Innsbruck, 1937–9 (faculty closed by the Nazis); pastoral work in Vienna, then teaching at Pullach until 1948, when he returned to Innsbruck; Professor, Universities of Munich (1964–7) and Münster (1967–71).

Main publications:

(1961–81) *Theological Investigations*, 20 vols, London: Darton, Longman & Todd.

(1969) *Hearers of the Word*, London: Sheed & Ward.
(1976) *Foundations of Christian Faith*, London: Darton, Longman & Todd.

Secondary literature:

Bibliographies of Rahner: Freiburg 1969, 1974, 1979, 1984.
Carr, A. E. (1979) *The Theological Method of Karl Rahner*, Atlanta: American Academy of Religion.
Gelpi, D. L. (1966) *Life and Light: A Guide to the Theology of Karl Rahner*, New York: Sheed & Ward.
Kelly, W. J. (ed.) (1980) *Theology and Discovery: Essays in Honour of Karl Rahner*, Milwaukee: Marquette University Press.
O'Donovan, Leo J. (ed.) (1980) *A World of Grace: An Introduction to the Themes and Foundations of Rahner's Theology*, New York: Crossroad.
Roberts, Louis (1967) *The Achievement of Karl Rahner*, New York: Herder & Herder.
Vorgrimler, H. (1986) *Understanding Karl Rahner: An Introduction to His Life and Thought*, London: SCM Press.

Rahner's thought turns upon the unity of such distinct yet inseparable ideas as the sacred and the secular, nature and grace, transcendence and history. The Incarnation, which reveals humanity's union with God, is the supreme instance of this unity. God is personally related to all, and this relationship establishes and facilitates, rather than thwarts or frustrates, human autonomy and freedom.

With Aquinas and Kant, Rahner holds that all human knowledge is grounded in the finite world of experience. But our human questions (a Heideggerian starting-point) at once reveal our ability to transcend that world; for we reach out from what we know partially to what may be more fully, though not yet perfectly, known (eschatology is important to Rahner); for the God who reveals himself is also, in an important sense, ever concealed.

Consistently with his recognition of difference in unity, Rahner investigates both the epistemological conditions of our reception of revelation and the historical content of revelation. He thus proceeds from a theory of knowledge to Christology, and thence to the ecclesiastical community, called to be a servant (not a clerically dominated clique) in the world. In this last connection Rahner's contribution to ecumenism, and to the Second Vatican Council, should not be overlooked.

To Hans von Balthasar's complaint that his theology was too anthropocentric, Rahner replied

that it was integral to his thought that in the Incarnation the anthropocentric and the theocentric are indissolubly united. He insisted that one cannot speak of God without at the same time speaking of humanity—and vice versa. When his pupil, the political theologian Johann Baptist Metz, charged him with underemphasizing the societal aspects of human freedom, Rahner retorted that a genuine political theology cannot proceed 'without reflection on those essential characteristics of man which transcendental theology discloses'. Others, more sceptical, have wondered how far a satisfactory case can be made for the deliverances of the dogmatic tradition, the validity of which Rahner's theology presupposes.
Sources: Obituary notices.

ALAN SELL

Ramos, Samuel
Mexican. *b:* 1897, Zitácuaro, Mexico. *d:* 1959, *Cat:* Social philosopher. *Infls:* Ortega, Scheler, Klages, Hartmann, Bergson and José Gaos.

Main publications:
(1934) *El perfil del hombre y la cultura en México*, Mexico.
(1940) *Hacia un nuevo humanismo*, Mexico.
(1943) *Historia de la filosofía en México*, Mexico: Universidad Nacional Autónoma de México.
(1950) *Filosofía de la vida artística*, Mexico.
(1962) *Profile of Man and Culture in Mexico*, trans. Peter G. Earle, Austin, Texas: University of Texas Press.
(1975–) *Obras completas*, Mexico: UNAM.

Secondary literature:
Basave Fernández de Valle, Agustín (1965) *Samuel Ramos: Trayectoria filosófica y antología de textos*, Monterrey, Mexico: Universidad de Nuevo León.
Schutte, Ofelia (1993) *Cultural Identity and Social Liberation in Latin American Thought* New York: SUNY Press.
Weinstein, Michael A. (1976) *The Polarity of Mexican Thought*, Pennsylvania State University Press.

In his classic *Profile of Man and Culture in Mexico* (1962) Ramos critically applies Adlerian psychoanalysis to the Mexican psyche. He unmasks an inferiority complex and a profound sense of alienation. In his quest for authentic expression in Mexico, Ramos relates philosophy of culture to psychology and argues for assimilation rather than imitation of external cultural influences. In this regard, he plays a key role in the development of philosophy of *lo mexicano* and makes a major contribution to cultural identity in Latin America.

AMY A. OLIVER

Ramsey, Frank Plumpton
British. *b:* 22 February 1903, Cambridge, England. *d:* 19 January 1930, Cambridge. *Cat:* Philosopher of mathematics; logician. *Educ:* 1923, graduated in Mathematics, Trinity College, Cambridge; 1924–6, Fellowship at King's College, Cambridge. *Infls:* Wittgenstein, Russell and Keynes. *Appts:* 1926–30, University Lectureship in Mathematics, University of Cambridge.

Main publications:
(1931) *The Foundations of Mathematics and Other Logical Essays*, ed. Richard B. Braithwaite, London: Routledge.
(1978) *Foundations: Essays in Philosophy, Logic, Mathematics and Economics*, ed. D. H. Mellor, London: Routledge.
(1991) *Frank Plumpton Ramsey on Truth*, ed. N. Rescher and U. Majer, Dordrecht: Kluwer.

Secondary literature:
Mellor, D. H. (1980) *Prospects for Pragmatism*, Cambridge: Cambridge University Press.
Ryle, G. (1950) *'If', 'so', and 'because'*, in M. Black (ed.), *Philosophical Analysis*, Ithaca: Cornell University Press.
Sahlin, Nils-Eric (1990) *The Philosophy of F. P. Ramsey*, Cambridge: Cambridge University Press.

Son of an eminent mathematician and President of Magdalene College, and brother of Arthur Michael who became Archbishop of Canterbury, Ramsey had a short but nevertheless outstanding career at Cambridge where he made important contributions to logic and philosophy. He wrote highly original papers on the foundations of mathematics, probability, theory of knowledge, philosophy of science and economics. His early essays, 'The foundation of mathematics' (written in 1925) and 'Mathematical logic' (written in 1926) revealed the influence of **Wittgenstein's** *Tractatus Logico-Philosophicus* and **Russell** and **Whitehead's** *Principia Mathematica*. Ramsey accepted Russell and Whitehead's logicist objective of deriving mathematics from logic, but sought to do so without collapsing into the paradoxes which Russell had tried to resolve with the theory of types. Thus Ramsey introduced a notion of 'predicative functions'—that is, truth functions which allow many arguments—which was derived from Wittgenstein.

Later papers revealed a development of Ramsey's thought towards pragmatism and intuitionism with regard to the problem of truth, although he maintained that a pragmatic theory of truth was actually a supplement to the correspondence theory, rather than a rival. Thus in 'General propositions and causality' (written in 1929) he argued that general propositions—for example 'All men are mortal'—are not strictly speaking propositions with truth functions which can be determined as either true or false. Instead, he argued, they represent the kind of proposition which it is reasonable or unreasonable to maintain. Thus to hold that 'All men are mortal' is to reasonably expect that all men we meet in the future will be mortal. General propositions do not make definite statements about objects, he maintained. Most of Ramsey's essays were published posthumously. In the Introduction to his collection of essays in 1931 **Braithwaite** said that Ramsey's premature death 'deprives Cambridge of one of its intellectual glories and contemporary philosophy of one of its profoundest thinkers'.

DAVID LAMB

Ramsey, Ian T(homas)

British. *b:* 31 January 1915, Bolton, Lancashire. *d:* 6 October 1972, London. *Cat:* Divine; logical empiricist. *Ints:* Philosophy of religion. *Educ:* Studied Mathematics, Moral Sciences and Theology at Christ's College, Cambridge (1935–9) and trained for the Anglican priesthood at Ripon College, Oxford. *Infls:* Influences include Locke, Berkeley, Butler, Russell, Bradley and Ryle. *Appts:* 1943–9, Chaplain of Christ's College, Cambridge; 1944–51, Fellow of Christ's College, Cambridge; 1951–66, Nolloth Professor of the Philosophy of the Christian Religion, University of Oxford; 1966–72, Bishop of Durham.

Main publications:

(1940–1) 'The quest for a Christian philosophy', *The Modern Churchman*, 30.

(1957) *Religious Language: An Empirical Placing of Theological Phrases*, London: SCM.

(1960) *Freedom and Immortality*, London: SCM.

(1961) (ed.) *Prospect for Metaphysics: Essays of Metaphysical Exploration*, London: Allen & Unwin.

(1964) *Models and Mystery*, London: Oxford University Press.

(1964) *Religion and Science: Conflict and Synthesis*, London: SPCK.

(1965) *Christian Discourse: Some Logical Explorations*, London: Oxford University Press.

(1971) *Words about God: The Philosophy of Religion*, London: SCM; New York: Harper & Row.

(1974) *Christian Empiricism*, London: Sheldon Press.

Secondary literature:

Gill, Jerry H. (1976) *Ian Ramsey: To Speak Responsibly of God*, London: Macmillan (includes select bibliography).

Pye, Jonathan H. (1979) *A Bibliography of the Published Work of Ian Thomas Ramsey*, Durham: Abbey House Publications.

In an early article Ramsey applauded 'the admirable and justifiable movement of **Moore** and **Russell** in favour of clarification as a function of philosophy' but thought that this conception of philosophy had been taken to 'ridiculous extremes' by the way these ideas had been developed in the logical positivism of the Vienna Circle (1940–1, p. 462). Ramsey's 'logical empiricism' is already anticipated in his programmatic statement that 'in reaching our idea of God we shall do well to take our cue from the relation of God to the world of sense-experience that idea of God as far as possible in terms of our concept of personality' (ibid., pp. 465–6). The purpose of religious language, according to Ramsey, is to bring about a 'cosmic disclosure' which prompts a total commitment on the part of the hearer. The disclosure comes about when 'the penny drops' and the hearer is enabled to anchor what is being said in personal experience. Ramsey's work has attracted a good deal of attention since the late 1950s, in America as well as in Britain. Philosophers have, however, been sharply critical of the vagueness of some of his key terms, such as 'disclosure', and of his epistemology generally. He has been criticized for giving religious discourse a suspicious immunity from criticism. R. N. **Smart** argues that, if the penny did not drop and the disclosure did not occur, Ramsey would not take this as evidence that a religious belief was false (*Philosophical Quarterly* 10 (1960): 93–4). In the light of **Flew**'s challenge that statements need to be falsifiable to have meaning, Ramsey's account of religious language seemed less than satisfactory—particularly in view of his commitment to empiricism.

Sources: DNB; David Edwards (1973) *Ian Ramsey*, London: OUP (biography); PI; obituary in *The Times*, 7 Oct 1972.

STUART BROWN

Ramsey, R. Paul

American. **b:** 10 December 1913, Mendehall, Mississippi. **d:** 1988. **Cat:** Christian moralist; just war theorist. **Ints:** Moral philosophy. **Educ:** Yale University (BD 1940, PhD 1943). **Infls:** J. Edwards and H. R. Niebuhr. **Appts:** 1937–9, Instructor in History, Millsaps College, Jackson, Mississippi; 1942–4, Assistant Professor of Christian Ethics, Garrett Theological Seminary, Illinois; 1944–82, Assistant, Associate and Full Professor of Religion, Princeton University.

Main publications:

(1950) *Basic Christian Ethics*, Scribner.
(1957) (ed.) *Jonathan Edwards: 'Freedom of the Will'*, Yale University Press.
(1957) (ed.) *Faith and Ethics: The Theology of H. R. Niebuhr*, Harper.
(1961) *War and the Christian Conscience*, Duke University Press.
(1962) *Nine Modern Moralists*, Prentice-Hall.
(1966) *Deeds and Rules in Christian Ethics*, Scribner.
(1966) 'Two concepts of general rules in Christian ethics', *Ethics* 76: 192–207.
(1968) *The Just War*, Scribner.
(1970) *Fabricated Man*, Yale University Press.
(1971) *The Patient as Person*, Yale University Press.
(1975) *Ethics of Fetal Research*, Yale University Press.
(1978) *Ethics at the Edge of Life*, Yale University Press.

Secondary literature:

Emery, S. W. (1958) 'Ethics in a theological manner', *Personalist* 39: 139–48.
Smith, D. H. and Johnson, J. T. (eds) (1974) *Love and Society: Essays in the Ethics of Paul Ramsey*, Missoula: MT Scholars Press.

Paul Ramsey viewed the Christian religion as being of fundamental importance for an understanding of the nature of morality and a central concern of his work is to describe the relationship between the two. He was particularly concerned with the implications of a Christian ethic for the social and political world.

The theoretical foundations of Ramsey's philosophy are to be found in 'Two concepts' (*Deeds and Rules in Christian Ethics*, 1966 and 'Two concepts of general rules in Christian Ethics', 1966). Working within the broad tradition of natural law theory, Ramsey sought to demonstrate that the teaching of Christ fulfilled and transformed that law. Although the command 'do what love and the Christian community command' is fundamental, Ramsey was anxious

to qualify the role of love in his ethical system. Thus he recognized the rules of justice which are independent of the basic principle; he is critical of various forms of teleological ethics; and he argues that it is not always permissible to perform the most loving action since such an action may run counter to a general practice which embodies love. These themes also emerge from his treatment of twentieth-century moral theorists (1962).

Ramsey argues that a theory of 'statecraft' forms an important part of the Christian ethic and in 1961 and 1968 he develops an account of the role of the nation state within an international community. The theory of political authority and political responsibility which he defends allows for justified conflict and violence in carefully defined circumstances. 'To "Save politics",' he writes, 'will require an effective challenge both to native American pacifism ... and to our inclination to invoke a narrow doctrine of "military necessity"' (1968, p. ix). The account, which closely follows traditional 'just-war' theory, also permits revolutionary violence in the pursuit of democratic ideals. The most important shift of emphasis between 1961 and 1968 relates to the defence in his later work of the claim that if it would be immoral to use a certain form of force it would also be immoral to threaten the use of such force.

In later years Ramsey's focus shifted to medical ethics. The definitive statement of his views within this field is *Ethics at the Edge of Life* (1978), a revision and extension of the 1975 Bampton Lectures at Columbia University which deals with issues such as abortion, euthanasia and the benign neglect of defective newborns. A notable feature of Ramsey's position is his emphasis on the value of 'early' human life. He argued that six months of babyhood might be viewed as being of as much ultimate worth as sixty years of manhood or womanhood. Ramsey writes (1987, p. xiii): 'Respect for life and the protection of life ... do not vary according to duration, achievement or productivity.'
Sources: DAP; CA 5; PI.

H. BUNTING

Rand, Ayn (Alissa)

Russian-American. **b:** 2 February 1905, St Petersburg. **d:** 6 March 1982, New York City. **Cat:** Objectivist philosopher; novelist. **Ints:** Man and society; ethics; epistemology. **Educ:** University of St Petersburg. **Infls:** Literary influences: Aristotle, Victor Hugo and Dostoevsky. Personal: Frank O'Connor. **Appts:** 1958–68, Lecturer, Nathanial

Branden Institute, NYC; 1962–76, Editor of *The Objectivist* (from 1971, called *The Ayn Rand Letter*); 1968–78, Visiting Lecturer, Yale, Princeton, Harvard, MIT, Columbia and other universities.

Main publications:
(1943) *The Fountainhead*, Indianapolis: Bobbs-Merrill.
(1957) *Atlas Shrugged*, New York: Random House.
(1965) *The Virtue of Selfishness: A New Concept of Egoism*, New York: New American Library.
(1967) *Introduction to Objectivist Epistemology*, New York: The Objectivist Inc.
(1971) *The New Left: The Anti-Industrial Revolution*, New York: New American Library.
(1982) *Philosophy: Who Needs It?*, Indianapolis: Bobbs-Merrill.

Secondary literature:
Merrill, Ronald E. (1991) *The Ideas of Ayn Rand*, Peru: Open Court.
Smith, George H. (1991) *Atheism, Ayn Rand, and other Heresies*, Buffalo: Prometheus.

As an adolescent during the Russian Revolution, Rand saw people shot in the streets and lamented the triumph of the Bolsheviks. In her studies she was antipathetic to Plato's idealism and attracted to Aristotle's rationalism. Two years after graduating with a degree in history from St Petersburg, she left Russia for the USA, where she was naturalized.

Rand became the author of two unconventional but best-selling novels, *The Fountainhead* (1943) and *Atlas Shrugged* (1957). In these, as in her other writings, she challenged prevalent philosophies of the time with her 'objectivism', a rationalist ethic of 'heroic individualism' repudiating all forms of altruism as 'collectivist' traps, incompatible with a free society. Her 'objectivist' creed was that reality exists as the 'objective absolute'; that reason is our means of grasping it; that morality is a 'rational science' with human life as its standard, self-interest as its driving force, individual happiness as its purpose and freedom as its consequence. Thus Rand proclaimed unfettered selfishness and capitalism to be the only means to the salvation of the individual and society. Rand argued her case with messianic passion and authority, winning a coterie of avid disciples.
Sources: Kersey; Ms., September 1978.

STEPHEN MOLLER

Randall, John Herman
American. *b:* 14 February 1899, Grand Rapids, Michigan. *d:* 1 December 1980, New York City. *Cat:* Historian of philosophy; naturalist metaphysician. *Ints:* History of philosophy; naturalism; metaphysics. *Educ:* Columbia University, BA 1918, MA 1919, PhD 1922. *Infls:* Woodbridge and Dewey. *Appts:* 1920–80, Instructor to Professor of Philosophy (Emeritus Professor, 1967–80), Columbia University.

Main publications:
(1926) *The Making of the Modern Mind: A Survey of the Intellectual Background of the Present Age*, Boston: Houghton Mifflin Company; revised edition, 1940; reprinted; New York: Columbia University Press, 1976.
(1958) *Nature and Historical Experience: Essays in Naturalism and the Theory of History*, New York: Columbia University Press.
(1960) *Aristotle*, New York: Columbia University Press.
(1962–5) *The Career of Philosophy*, vols 1 and 2, New York: Columbia University Press.
(1977) *Philosophy after Darwin. Chapters for the Career of Philosophy, volume III, and Other Essays*, ed. B. J. Singer, New York: Columbia University Press.

Secondary literature:
Anton J. P. (ed.) (1967) *Naturalism and Historical Understanding: Essays on the Philosophy of John Herman Randall, Jr.*, Albany: SUNY Press.

The son of an eminent Columbia University historian, Randall as a very young man established his fame as a historian of philosophy with *The Making of the Modern Mind* (1926). An exponent of philosophical naturalism, Randall synthesized the philosophies of his teachers, **Woodbridge** and **Dewey**, reinterpreting Aristotle (1960) in Deweyan terms and the naturalist's process metaphysics in terms of Aristotelian substantialism in *Nature and Historical Experience* (1958). His *Career of Philosophy* (1962–5) and the unfinished *Philosophy after Darwin* (1977) constitute scholarship of the first rank on the history of modern philosophy.
Sources: WW(Am); *New York Times*, 3 Dec 1980.

ANDREW RECK

Rashdall, Hastings
British. *b:* 24 June 1858, London. *d:* 9 February 1924, Carlisle. *Cat:* Personal idealist. *Ints:* Ethics; philosophy of religion. *Educ:* New College, Ox-

ford. *Infls:* Berkeley and Lotze. *Appts:* Fellow, Hertford College, Oxford, 1889–95: Fellow, New College, Oxford, 1895–1917.

Main publications:

(1907) *Theory of Good and Evil* 2 vols, Oxford: Oxford University Press.
(1909) *Philosophy and Religion*, London: Duckworth.
(1912) *The Problem of Evil*, Manchester.
(1914) *Is Conscience an Emotion?*, London: Duckworth.
(1930) *God and Man*, ed. H. J. Major and F. L. Cross, Oxford: Blackwell.

Secondary literature:

Webb, C. C. J. (1928) in P. E. Matheson, *Life of Hastings Rashdall*, Oxford: Oxford University Press.

Rashdall was sufficiently distinguished as an intellectual historian and as a theologian proper to have secured a lasting reputation in either of these capacities considered on its own. In the first role his main achievement was his *The Universities of Europe in the Middle Ages* (1895), still, after a century, the unsuperseded authority on the subject. In the second it was his *Idea of Atonement in Christian Theology* (1919) in which the Abelardian view that Christ's self-sacrifice is a morally stimulating example is defended. In it he adheres to the kind of general rationality which he found and admired in the medieval scholastics and to which much attention is given in his history of medieval universities. His own position was set out in an elementary but systematic way in his brilliantly clear *Philosophy and Religion* (1909). It is idealist, but the idealism is personal not absolute, the doctrine of Berkeley, not that of the Oxinian Hegel in which he had been brought up. Everything that there is is either minds or their mind-dependent contents. But finite, individual minds are not to be seen as somehow parts, or 'adjectives' of a universal mind in which they are all comprised. Even God, although the highest mind, is not infinite; he has limited himself by the creation of a plurality of finite minds, exclusive of each other and of him. What we perceive is sensations, which are mental, and the relationships in which we conceive them in thought are also the work of mind. The unity of the world which we know in experience requires a single mind to sustain and order it. Our knowledge of God is inferential, but none the worse for that, for so is our knowledge of our friends. His substantial conception of personality rules out mystic union

with God. One heterodox conclusion to which his resolute personalism led him was that the doctrine of the Trinity cannot be taken literally. If God were three persons there would be three Gods. In his down to earth way he took the Humean view that we perceive only regular succession, but added the Berkeleyan rider that we are aware of real causation in our awareness of the will. His *Theory of Good and Evil* (1907) is solider and less retrospective in its assumptions. A view much like **Moore**'s is advanced, which Rashdall named 'ideal utilitarianism'. It is utilitarian in being consequential, defining the right as that which will yield the most good; ideal in holding that pleasure or happiness, while part of the good, is not the whole of it, knowledge and virtue also good in themselves. Intuition is invoked to discover that these things are good and to judge their relative goodness. Rashdall's book is superior to Moore's in almost every respect but brevity and force: it covers a very broad range of ethical subjects (freedom and determinism, punishment, justice, among many others); it treats morality in a serious and realistic way. It lacks the analytical power of **Sidgwick**'s *Methods of Ethics*, but is less gloomily inconclusive and is fit for comparison with it. Rashdall's combative disposition brought his liberal heresies into public notice (he denied God's omnipotence, as well as his infinitude, and said Christ did not himself claim to be divine). This and his occupancy of a prominent position in the Church gave him influence, although they also attracted acrimonious criticism. Twentieth-century moral philosophy would have benefited if he and Sidgwick had received the attention given to Moore.

Sources: Metz; Passmore 1957; Edwards; DNB.

ANTHONY QUINTON

Rauh, Frédéric

French. *b:* 31 March 1861, St-Martin-le-Vinux, Isère, France. *d:* 20 February 1909, Paris. *Cat:* Moral philosopher; psychologist. *Ints:* Ethics; the nature of moral truths. *Educ:* L'École Normale Supérieure. *Infls:* Jules Lachelier, Ravaisson and Émile Boutroux. *Appts:* 1898–1901, Professor of Philosophy, Faculté des Lettres de Toulouse; 1901–9, Professor of Philosophy, Sorbonne and L'École Normale Supérieure.

Main publications:

(1890) *Essai sur le fondement métaphysique de la morale*, Paris: Alcan.
(1899) *De la méthode dans la psychologie des sentiments*, Paris: Alcan.

(1903) *L'Expérience morale*, Paris: Alcan.
(1911) *Études de morale*, ed. H. Wallon, Paris: Alcan
(posthumous).

Secondary literature:
Dantin, H. (1910) 'Frédéric Rauh: sa psychologie de
la conaissance et de l'action', *Revue de Métaphysique et de Morale*: 185–218, 318–44.
Junod, Robert (1932) 'F. Rauh. Essai de biographie
intellectuelle', PhD, University of Geneva.

Rauh's enduring preoccupation was with the
nature and ground of morality. His work, however, passed through different phases. At first, he
championed a metaphysics inspired by the 'spiritualism' of Jules **Lachelier** and Émile **Boutroux**.
Thus in his *Essai* (1890) he criticized the attempt
to ground ethics in naturalism and maintained
that the only real certitude is the Idea, the
invisible, and that therefore there can be no ethics
without metaphysics, without the search for an
absolute which is the type of every being.
Accordingly, he defined moral action as 'métaphysique en acte' (1890, pp. 4, 9).

None the less Rauh's subsequent works were
anti-metaphysical. In them he adopted an experimentalist standpoint, arguing that there is no
difference between the ways in which moral truths
and scientific truths are established and obtain
our assent. Consequently he held that we must not
attempt to deduce moral certainty from abstract
ideologies, but must assume instead the impersonal attitude of the scientist in each situation, and
put relevant ideas to the critical test by comparing
them with reality and other ideas.

Rauh stressed that morality has its source not
in passive conformity to social norms or pre-
established standards, but rather in individual
initiative and creativity. To some extent, he
prepared the way for later French philosophers,
such as Jean Grenier and Raymond **Polin**, who
stressed the primacy of choice and the creation of
values.
Sources: Benrubi; Huisman; EF.

STEPHEN MOLLER

Ravaisson-Mollien, Jean Gaspard Félix Lacher

French. **b:** 23 October 1813, Namur, Belgium. **d:**
18 May 1900, Paris. **Cat:** 'Spiritualiste' or spiritual
realist. **Ints:** Metaphysics; history of philosophy.
Educ: Studied under Schelling in Munich and
under Cousin in Paris. **Infls:** Aristotle, Maine de
Biran, Leonardo da Vinci, Secrétan and Scottish
common-sense philosophers. **Appts:** 1838–40,

University of Rennes; 1840–60, Inspector General
of Libraries; 1860–70, Inspector General in the
Department of Higher Education; from 1870,
Curator of Antiquities at the Louvre, where he
became known for his examination of the Venus
de Milo.

Main publications:
(1837–46) *Essai sur la métaphysique d'Aristote*, 2 vols,
Paris.
(1838) *De l'habitude*, Paris, reprinted in *Revue de
Métaphysique et de Morale* 2, 1894.
(1868) *La Philosophie en France au XIXe siècle*, Paris:
Imprimerie Impériale.
(1933) *Testament philosophique et fragments, pré-
cédés de la notice lue en 1904 à l'Académie des
sciences morales et politiques par Henri Bergson*, ed.
C. Devivaix, Paris: Boivin.

Secondary literature:
Bossu, L. (1872) *Galérie des métaphysiciens con-
temporains*, Louvain: Peeters.
Dopp, J. (1933) *F. Ravaisson, la formation de sa
pensée d'après des documents inédits*, Louvain:
Institut Supérieur de Philosophie.
Gunn, J. A. *Modern French Philosophy*, London: T.
Fisher Unwin, especially pp. 73–5.
Janicaud, D. (1969) 'Une généalogie du spiritualisme
Français, aux sources du Bergsonisme, Ravaisson
et la métaphysique', *Arch. Int. d'Hist. des Idées*, no.
30, The Hague: Martinus Nijhoff.

Under the the influence of Scottish common-
sense philosophy, opposed to both the eclecticism
of Cousin and to positivism, Ravaisson-Mollien
developed in 'spiritualism' a type of metaphysical
theism. Opposed to materialism he professed
opposition also to idealism, though with the
dominating role ascribed to consciousness, the
tendencies of his own work were idealistic. It was
very influential in the third quarter of the nineteenth century and was still being discussed early
in the twientieth century. **Lachelier**, Émile **Boutroux** and Henri **Bergson** are regarded as to
varying extents his disciples. He played an
important role in the founding of the *Revue de
Métaphysique et de Morale*.
Sources: Edwards; H. Bergson, in Ravaisson-Mollien
1933; É. Boutroux (1900) 'La Philosophie de Félix
Ravaisson', *RMM* 7–8: 699–716; X. Léon (1900)
RMM (supplt), Jul, 8: 1–2; L. Léger, *Académie des
Inscriptions et Belles Lettres*, 14 Jun 1901; Th. Ruyssen
(1887) *La Grande Encyclopédie, Paris, Société Anonyme
de la Grande Encyclopédie*, 28: 180b–181b; ChEnc 11:
534b–535a.

R. N. D. MARTIN

Rawls, John

American. *b:* 21 February 1921, Baltimore. *Cat:* Social contract theorist. *Ints:* Moral and political philosophy; philosophical analysis. *Educ:* Princeton University. *Infls:* Social contract theorists such as Rousseau and Hobbes. *Appts:* Assistant Professor, Cornell University; John Cowles Professor of Philosophy, Harvard, from 1976.

Main publications:

(1958) 'Justice as fairness', *Philosophical Review*, 67: 164.
(1971) *A Theory of Justice*, Cambridge, Mass.: Belknap Press and Oxford University Press.
(1993) *Political Liberalism*, New York: Columbia University Press.

Secondary literature:

Barry, Brian (1973) *The Liberal Theory of Justice: A Critical Examination of the Principal Doctrines in 'A Theory of Justice' by John Rawls*, Oxford: Clarendon Press.
Blecker, H. Gene and Smith, Elizabeth H. (1980) *John Rawls' Theory of Social Justice: An Introduction*, Athens: Ohio University Press.
Chandran, Kukathas and Pettit, Philip (1990) *Rawls: A Theory of Justice and its Critics*, Cambridge: Polity.
Daniels, Norman (ed.) (1975) *Reading Rawls: Critical Studies in Rawls' 'A Theory of Justice'*, Oxford: Blackwell.
Hart (1972–3) 'Rawls on liberty and its priority', *University of Chicago Law Review*.
Martin, Rex (1985) *Rawls and Rights*, Lawrence, Kansas: University Press of Kansas.
Pogge, Thomas (1989) *Realizing Rawls*, Ithaca, NY: Cornell University Press.
Wolff, Robert Paul (1977) *Understanding Rawls: A Reconstruction and Critique of 'A Theory of Justice'*, Princeton University Press.

In his book *A Theory of Justice* (1971) Rawls is concerned with discovering the principles which any society must have if it is to be just. In order to arrive at these principles he uses the hypothetical device of placing actors behind a veil of ignorance. Each actor in this hypothetical situation has no knowledge of his place in society, his class or social status, his psychological inclinations, his intelligence and strengths, the particulars of his rational plan of life, the economic and political situation of his society, the level of cultural attainment of his society and the generation to which he belongs (p. 137). Denial of such information to the actors, according to Rawls, will allow them to arrive at principles that are not evaluated purely on the basis of circumstances specific to the actors. The actors in the original position, however, understand political affairs, principles of economic theory, the basis of social organization and the laws of human psychology (pp. 137–8). They are also assumed to act with a sense of rational self-interest and to be capable of a sense of justice (i.e. acting on the agreed principles) (pp. 140–5).

According to Rawls the parties in the original position will arrive at the following two principles: First Principle: Each person is to have an equal right to the most extensive total system of equal liberties compatible with a similar system of liberty for all. Second Principle: Social and economic inequalities are to be arranged so that they are both: (i) to the greatest benefit of the least advantaged, consistent with the just savings principle; and (ii) attached to offices and positions open to all under conditions of fair equality of opportunity (p. 302).

According to Rawls liberty, the first principle, is to have 'lexical' priority in that the first principle must be satisfied before the second principle is considered (see Hart 1972–3, p. 534 for a critical account, and Barry 1973).

Although Rawls is correct in stressing the importance of liberty one cannot but raise others, the following questions. Will the original position always yield the two Rawlsian principles? Could it not, for instance, yield education as a basic principle? Do the actors, ignorant of their society's economic and political development, have sufficient information to arrive at the two principles? Or, do the actors agree on these principles because they happen to be just in themselves?

Sources: DAS.

INDIRA MAHALINGAM CARR

Reale, Miguel

Brazilian. *b:* 6 November 1910, São Bento do Sapucaí, São Paulo, Brazil. *Cat:* Philosopher of law. *Educ:* School of Law, University of São Paulo. *Infls:* Marx, Hegel, Heidegger and Husserl. *Appts:* From 1941, Professor of Philosophy of Law, University of São Paulo; 1949–50, Rector of the University of São Paulo.

Main publications:

(1934) *O estado moderno*.
(1935) *Formação da política burguesa*.
(1940) *Teoria do direito e do estado*.
(1976) *Filosofia em São Paulo*, second edition, São Paulo: Editorial Grijalbo.

(1979) *Teoría tridimensional do direito*, second edition, São Paulo: Saraiva.

(1980) *O homem e seus horizontes*, São Paulo: Editora Convivio.

(1982) *Filosofia do direito*; fifteenth edition, São Paulo: Saraiva, 1993.

(1982) *A filosofia na obra de Machado de Assis e 'Antologia filosofica de Machado de Assis'*, São Paulo: Livraria Pioneira Editora.

(1984) *Figuras da inteligencia brasileira*, Rio de Janeiro: Tempo Brasileiro; Fortaleza, Brazil: Universidade Federal do Ceará.

(1989) *O belo e outros valores: ensaios filosoficos*, Rio de Janeiro: Academia Brasileira de Letras.

Secondary literature:
Sturm, Fred G. (1989) 'Philosophy in Brazil today', in Jorge J. E. Gracia and Mireya Camurati (eds), *Philosophy and Literature in Latin America*, Albany, NY: SUNY Press.

In 1949 Reale founded the Brazilian Institute of Philosophy, which organized the first Brazilian Congress of Philosophy in 1950. As President of the Institute Reale founded the *Revista Brasileira de Filosofia* in 1951. As a philosopher of law he has made significant contributions with his tridimensional model of the nature and function of law. In his more recent philosophical work, Reale attempts to synthesize Marxist and Hegelian dialectics with Heideggerian and Husserlian phenomenology.

AMY A. OLIVER

Recasens-Siches, Luis
Mexican. *b:* 19 June 1903, Guatemala City (of Spanish parents). *Cat:* Philosopher of law. *Educ:* Universities of Barcelona and Madrid in the 1920s, with additional studies in Rome, Berlin and Vienna. *Appts:* Taught in Spain at Santiago de Compostela, Salamanca, Valladolid and Madrid, also in Mexico, Guatemala, El Salvador, Chile and Peru.

Main publications:
(1927) *La filosofia del derecho de Francisco Suárez*.

(1936) *Estudios de filosofia del derecho*.

(1939) *Vida humana, sociedad y derecho*.

(1940) *Fundamentos de la filosofia del derecho*.

(1948) *Latin American Legal Philosophy*, trans. Gordon Ireland, Cambridge, Mass.: Harvard University Press.

(1963) *Panorama del pensamiento jurídico en el siglo XX*, 2 vols, Mexico: Porrúa.

(1970) *Introducción al estudio del derecho*, Mexico: Porrúa.

(1973) *Nueva filosofia de la interpretación del derecho*, Mexico: Porrúa.

(1975) *Tratado general de filosofia del derecho*, Mexico: Porrúa.

(1976) *Antología, 1922–1974*, Mexico: Fondo de Cultura Económica.

Secondary literature:
Rodríguez García, Fausto E. (1980) *Estudios en honor del doctor Luis Recasens-Siches*, Mexico: Universidad Nacional Autónoma de México.

The dominant figure in modern philosophy of law in Latin America, Recasens-Siches seeks to distinguish law, which he views as form, from justice, which he views as one kind of content. He has served as co-editor of the journal *Sociologia Internationalis*, published in West Berlin, since 1964.

AMY A. OLIVER

Regan, Thomas Howard
American. *b:* 28 November 1938, Pittsburgh, Pennsylvania. *Cat:* Analytical philosopher; moral philosopher; social philosopher. *Ints:* Moral philosophy; social philosophy. *Educ:* University of Virginia. *Infls:* G. E. Moore. *Appts:* 1965–7, Assistant Professor of Philosophy, Sweet Briar College, Sweet Briar, Virginia; from 1967, Associate Professor and Professor, North Carolina State University.

Main publications:
(1972) 'A defence of Pacifism', *Canadian Journal of Philosophy* 2.

(1974) *Understanding Philosophy*, Dickenson.

(1975) (with P. Singer) *Animal Rights and Human Obligations*, Englewood-Cliffs, NJ: Prentice-Hall.

(1980) *Matters of Life and Death*, New York: Random House.

(1981) (with D. Van De Veer) *And Justice for All*, Totowa, NJ: Rowman & Littlefield.

(1982) *All Things That Dwell Therein: Essays on Animal Rights and Environmental Ethics*, University of California Press.

(1983) 'A refutation of utilitarianism', *Canadian Journal of Philosophy* 13.

(1983) *The Case for Animal Rights*, London: Routledge & Kegan Paul.

(1986) *Animal Sacrifices: Religious Perspectives On The Use of Animals in Science*, Philadelphia: Temple University Press.

(1986) *Bloomsbury's Prophet: G. E. Moore and the Development of His Moral Philosophy*, Philadelphia: Temple University Press.
(1986) (ed.) *G. E. Moore: The Early Essays*, Philadelphia: Temple University Press.
(1987) (ed.) (with D. Van de Veer) *Heath Care Ethics: An Introduction*, Philadelphia: Temple University Press.
(1988) *Animal Rights*, London: Routledge & Kegan Paul.

Secondary literature:
Narveson, J. (1987) 'On a case for animal rights', *Monist* 70.
Paske, G. H. (1988) 'Why animals have no right to life', *Australian Journal of Philosophy* 66.
Sumner, L. W. (1986) Review of *The Case for Animal Rights* (1983), *Nous* 20.

Thomas Regan has made important contributions to philosophical discussion of practical ethics, to study of the theoretical foundations of morality and to an understanding of the philosophy of G. E. **Moore**. Notable features of his work have been his arguments for the role of rights in moral theory and for the role he assigns to rights in our understanding of the moral status of animals. Regan's definitive statement of these themes was given in *The Case for Animal Rights* (1983), a book which, according to A. L. Sumner, 'has raised to a new level the quality of argument on the non-consequentialist side'.

Regan rejects both egoism and Kantian approaches to ethics on the grounds of their internal inconsistencies and their failure to accommodate our reflective intuitions. His main critical energies, however, are directed against utilitarianism. He argues in the two works of 1983 that a theory which advocates welfare maximization entails moral judgements which it would be outrageous to accept: in particular, since it would legitimize immoral forms of animal experimentation, it violates the principle that inherently valuable creatures should not be used as a mere means to the good of other creatures. Regan argues that 'the respect principle' ('we are to treat those individuals who have inherent value in ways that respect their inherent value') is the fundamental principle of morality. It entails other rights, in particular a right to equal treatment which does not permit trade-offs with considerations of utility. Within this framework Regan develops an elaborate defence of the moral status of animals. He argues that at least some animals are capable of intentional states such as beliefs, intentions and emotions. Their interests are,

therefore, a proper object of moral concern, and a contention of the book is that only a recognition of animal rights can do justice to this moral standing.

While paying tribute to the force of his arguments for animal rights, some commentators have expressed surprise at the vehemence of Regan's attack on philosophers who make welfare rather than rights the central concept in an account of the moral standing of animals.

Regan's work on G. E. Moore (1986) throws light on the formative influences on the development of Moore's ethics and suggests distinctive interpretations of central doctrines of *Principia Ethica*. In spite of the striking contrasts between the positions of Moore and Kant, Regan presents *Principia Ethica*, especially the view that moral judgements are synthetic and the view that goodness is a simple non-natural property, as developments of essentially Kantian ideas and as liberating moral theory from oppressive conservatism. Moore's controversial thesis that the only things which are intrinsically good are friendship and the appreciation of beautiful objects is presented as Moore's attempt to find meaning in life after his abandonment of religious belief. Little attention is paid to the striking contrasts which exist between Moore's consequentialism and Kant's view of the foundations of ethics.

Regan has contributed significantly to discussions of a wide range of other issues in practical ethics: to health care ethics, to business ethics and to the ethics of war and peace. Particularly influential was his argument in 1972 that standard objections to pacifism can be overcome in a deontological ethical system.
Sources: CA 104; PI.

H. BUNTING

Reichenbach, Hans
German-American. *b:* 26 September 1891, Hamburg. *d:* 9 April 1953, Los Angeles, California. *Cat:* Logical empiricist. *Ints:* Probability theory; philosophy of physics; epistemology. *Educ:* Berlin, Munich, Göttingen, Erlangen and Stuttgart. *Infls:* Russell, Einstein and Von Mises. *Appts:* Assistant Professor, Tech Hochscule, Stuttgart, 1920–6; Professor of Physics, Berlin, 1926–33; Professor of Philosophy, Istanbul, 1933–8; UCLA, 1938–53.

Main publications:
(1928) *The Philosophy of Space and Time*, New York: Dover.

(1935) *Theory of Probability*, Berkeley and Los Angeles: University of California Press.

(1938) *Experience and Prediction*, Chicago: University of Chicago Press.

(1944) *Philosophical Foundations of Quantum Mechanics*, Berkeley and Los Angeles: University of California Press.

(1947) *Elements of Symbolic Logic*, New York: Macmillan.

(1951) *The Rise of Scientific Philosophy*, Berkeley and Los Angeles: University of California Press.

(1956) *The Direction of Time*, Berkeley and Los Angeles: University of California Press.

(1959) *Modern Philosophy of Science*, London: Routledge.

(1978) *Selected Writings* 2 vols, Dordrecht: Reidel.

Secondary literature:

Reichenbach, H. (1978) 'Memories of Hans Reichenbach' in *Selected Writings* vol. 2, p. 1–90.

Reichenbach was the leader of the Berlin group allied to the larger Vienna Circle of logical positivists. By training a physicist, he was well-equipped for his early axiomatization of the theory of relativity and work on space and time, and for his later work on the philosophical interpretation of quantum mechanics. His largest contribution was in the field of probability. Here he was a resolute defender of the propositions, first, that there is only one concept of probability (as against those from Hume to **Carnap** who would distinguish probability arising from insufficient evidence from probability arising from conflicting evidence) and, second, that all probability must be interpreted in terms of frequency. With von **Mises**, he identified the probability that an A is a B with the limit of the ratios of As that are Bs to As in general in increasingly long series of As. He dealt boldly, if not always very convincingly, with the large number of problems posed by his homogenization of the concept. Do single events have probabilities? How is the notion of the limit of a series to be intelligibly applied outside the infinite series of pure mathematics to the finite series which are all that nature would seem able to provide? Above all, how can the probability of theories or hypotheses, supported to some extent by evidence but not entailed by it, be shown to be a case of the limit of ratios or frequencies? It cannot be the proportion of the predictions derivable from the theory that turn out to be true. A theory just over half of whose predictions were true would be more probable than not on that view, but would in fact be simply and certainly false. Nor can it plausibly be held that a theory is probable to

the extent that theories like it have proved to be correct to the appropriate extent. Reichenbach offered a justification of induction within the framework of his account of probability. To reason inductively is to assume that observed frequencies have a limit. If the assumption is correct, induction is bound to discover them. Reichenbach applied probability to the question of meaningfulness. Where the Viennese positivists defined it in terms of verifiability, he defined it in terms of probability or weight. He concluded that the deductive logic of the limiting cases of truth and falsity is itself a limiting case of probability logic. The theory of knowledge set out in his excellent and insufficiently noted *Experience and Prediction* (1938) argues for concrete things as an empirical basis for knowledge as against impressions. Statements about the latter are not really certain and are not 'psychologically primary'. In response to the anomalies of quantum physics he suggested that the conflict between wave and particle interpretations could be circumvented by having recourse to a three-valued logic. He also addressed himself to the problems of laws of nature ('nomic' or 'nomological' statements) which are neither simple summaries nor conjuctions nor logical necessities. He wrote an admirably forceful and combative introduction to philosophy as he understood it: *The Rise of Scientific Philosophy* (1951). Reichenbach was an influential teacher, thanks to a combination of authority and lucidity. Among his students were Adolf **Grünbaum** and Hilary **Putnam**.

Sources: Edwards; Passmore 1957; Hill.

ANTHONY QUINTON

Reid, Louis Arnaud

British. *b:* 18 February 1895, Ellon, Scotland. *d:* 26 January 1986, London. *Cat:* 'New realist'; philosopher of education. *Ints:* Epistemology; aesthetics; moral philosophy; philosophy of religion; educational theory. *Educ:* University of Edinburgh and University College of Wales, Aberystwyth. *Infls:* Literary influences: Kant, J. S. Mill and B. Bosanquet. Personal: A. E. Taylor and Dorothy. M. Emmet. *Appts:* 1919–32, Lecturer in Philosophy, University College of Wales, Aberystwyth, then (1926) University of Liverpool; 1932–47, Professor of Mental and Moral Philosophy, University of Durham, Armstrong College, Newcastle upon Tyne; 1947–62, Professor of Philosophy of Education, University of London, then Professor Emeritus (1962–86).

Main publications:

(1923) *Knowledge and Truth*, London: Macmillan.

(1931) *A Study in Aesthetics*, London: Allen & Unwin.

(1937) *Creative Morality*, London: Allen & Unwin.

(1939) *Preface to Faith*, London: Allen & Unwin.

(1944) *Rediscovery of Belief*, London: Lindsey Press.

(1961) *Ways of Knowledge and Experience*, Oxford: Oxford University Press.

(1962) *Philosophy and Education*, London: Heinemann.

(1969) *Meaning in the Arts*, New York: Humanities Press.

(1986) *Ways of Understanding and Education*, London: Heinemann.

Secondary literature:

Collingwood, R. G. (1932) Review of *A Study in Aesthetics* (1931), in *Philosophy* 7 (July): 335–7.

In *Knowledge and Truth* (1923) Reid critically reviewed the whole 'New Realist' theory of knowledge, which had begun with G. E. **Moore** (Metz, p. 538), to present his own variation of the realist doctrine that in knowledge the mind apprehends something that is 'given'. Reid stressed that knowledge is not a mere passive mirroring of reality but a dynamic activity by which we achieve contact with the objectively real. He defined truth as knowledge which is the apprehension of reality, or a part of it, as it really is. Besides theoretical experience Reid briefly considered aesthetic experience.

This prepared the way for *A Study in Aesthetics* (1931), a work largely concerned with the special problems in aesthetic, such as the relation between art and truth, art and morality, and the 'kinds' of beauty. Reid's approach implied a treatment of aesthetic as an autonomous philosophical science, not simply as a branch of the theory of perception. In subsequent works, Reid also considered moral experience and religious experience.

In *Ways of Knowledge and Experience* (1961) Reid surveyed all these various modes of experience synoptically, placing them on a single 'map'. That this mapping had explicit connections to curriculum planning reflected Reid's involvement in the philosophy of education. As first occupant of the Chair in the Philosophy of Education at London, Reid played an important role in establishing the philosophy of education as a special subject taught in British universities.

Sources: Metz; WW.

STEPHEN MOLLER

Reinach, Adolf

German. **b:** 23 December 1883, Mainz, Germany. **d:** 16 November 1917, killed in action at Diksmuide, Flanders. **Cat:** Phenomenologist. **Ints:** Philosophy of law; social philosophy; epistemology; ethics; logic; philosophy of mathematics; philosophy of religion. **Educ:** Law, Philosophy and Psychology at Munich, Berlin and Göttingen. **Infls:** Literary influences include Plato and Hume; personal influences include Edmund Husserl and Theodor Lipps. **Appts:** 1909–14, Privatdozent, University of Göttingen.

Main publications:

(1911) *Kants Auffassung des Humeschen Problems*.

(1911) *Zur Theorie des negativen Urteils*.

(1913) *Die apriorischen Grundlagen des bürgerlichen Rechtes*.

(1914) *Über Phänomenologie*.

All included in:

(1989) *Sämtliche Werke*, Textkritisiche Ausgabe in 2 Bänden, ed. Karl Schuhmann and Barry Smith, Munich: Philosophia Verlag.

Secondary literature:

Burkhardt, A. (1986) *Soziale Akte, Sprechakte und Textillokutionen. A. Reinach's Rechtsphilosophie und die moderne Linguistik*, Tübingen: Max Niemeyer Verlag.

Mulligan, K. (ed.) (1987) *Speech: Act and Sachverhalt: Reinach and the Foundations of Realist Phenomenology*, Dordrecht, Boston and Lancaster: Martinus Nijhoff.

Reinach was an outstanding exponent of the kind of realist phenomenology inspired by **Husserl's** *Logical Investigations*. This understanding of phenomenology is brilliantly artculated in a lecture delivered in 1914 in Marburg, the stronghold of neo-Kantianism. Everything has its 'what', its essence. Phenomenology is the study of essences and relations between essences. We can have a direct access to essences in a non-sensory kind of seeing or intuition (*Wesensschau*). Relations between essences are a priori. The a priori has, as such, nothing to do with how we think or even how we must think. In his study of the essence of judgement Reinach develops the notion of a state of affairs (*Sachverhalt*) as that which is believed or asserted. *Negative* states of affairs can obtain with precisely the same objectivity as positive states of affairs. In the area of the phenomenology of acts his treatment of social acts, i.e. those which essentially stand in need of being heard, is of particular interest. It anticipates later developments in the theory of speech acts.

Reinach also made significant contributions to the history of philosophy, most notably in his essay on Kant's treatment of Hume where he criticizes the customary equation of Hume's judgements concerning 'relations of ideas' with analytic judgements, thereby calling in question Kant's criticism of Hume.

Sources: K. Schuhmann and B. Smith (1987) 'Adolf Reinach: an intellectual biography', in K. Mulligan (ed.), *Speech Act and Sachverhalt: Reinach and the Foundations of Realist Phenomenology*, Dordrecht: Martinus Nijhoff.

PAUL GORNER

Ren Jiyu (Jen Chi-yu)

Chinese. **b:** 1916, Pingyuan, Shandong Province, China. **Cat:** Marxist; historian of Buddhism and other Chinese religions; historian of ancient Chinese philosophy. **Educ:** University of Beijing. **Infls:** His teacher Tang Yongtong and Marxist thinkers. **Appts:** Lecturer, Southwest Associated University; Professor, University of Beijing; Director, Institute for Research on World Religions, Chinese Academy of Social Sciences; Professor, Institute of Philosophy, Chinese Academy of Social Sciences; Director, Chinese Tibetan–Buddhist Research Institute; Deputy Director, Institute of History of Chinese Philosophy; Head, National Library, Beijing; Visiting Professor, University of Toronto.

Main publications:

(1956) *Mozi*, Shanghai: Renmin Publishing House.

(1956) (ed.) *Laozi Translated into Modern Chinese*, Beijing: Guji Publishing House.

(1957) (contributor to) *A Symposium on Problems of the Chinese Philosophy*, Beijing: Kexue Publishing House.

(1963) *Collection of Buddhist Thinking During the Han and Tang Dynasties*, Beijing: Three Bookshops United Company.

(1963) (chief editor) *A History of Chinese Philosophy*, 4 vols, Beijing: Renmin Publishing House; third edition, 1979.

(1964) *Han Fei*, Shanghai: Shanghai Renmin Publishing House.

(1973) *A Brief History of Chinese Philosophy*, Beijing: Renmin Publishing House.

(1978) *A New Translation of Laozi*, Shanghai: Shanghai Guji Publishing House.

(1983) *History of the Development of Chinese Philosophy*, Beijing: Renmin Publishing House.

(1990) *Chinese Daoist Philosophers*.

Secondary literature:

Complete Chinese Encyclopedia (1987), Philosophy Volumes, Beijing: Chinese Encyclopedia Publications.

Louie, K. (1986) *Inheriting Tradition: Interpretations of the Classical Philosophers in Communist China 1949–1966*, Hong Kong: Oxford University Press.

As a Professor at University of Beijing, Ren took part in the debates of the 1950s and 1960s about the history of Chinese philosophy and about the interpretation of major traditional figures. He is also a leading historian of Chinese religion, especially Buddhism. With the reorganization of philosophy and the reopening of at least some leading philosophy departments, scholars were obliged to adjust to an imposed Marxist methodology which gave priority to the historical circumstances and alleged class allegiances of philosophers over purely internal assessment of their thought. The main question was whether a philosopher or school was idealist and reactionary or materialist and progressive. Ren recognized the crudity and limitations of this question, alleging that it ignored a more central Chinese conflict between dialectics and metaphysics and failed to recognize benefits arising from the interaction between materialism and idealism. Ren's own employment of the distinction at times showed greater subtlety, as in his defence of Laozi and Zhuangzi as both aristocratic in class origin and materialist in their representation of the interests of ordinary people. He also recognized that because of inadequate historical knowledge the class to which a figure was assigned could turn out to be an artefact of one's scheme of historical periodization rather than a social reality. In particular the rival schemes of historical periods proposed by **Guo Moruo** and Fan Wenlan produced very different readings of class affiliation for ancient figures. Ren's evaluations of pre-Qin dynasty philosophers relied heavily on conjecture and tendentious interpretation, but nevertheless showed ingenious use of Marxist methodology. In common with many of his contemporaries he hoped to achieve insight into the past, but also used his version of the past to guide attitudes towards contemporary problems.

Ren saw Kongzi as a reactionary and idealist, but one who made important contributions to feudal culture in spite of oppressing the slaves and opposing the new social forces threatening the Zhou dynasty aristocracy. Ren saw the conflict between Confucians and legalists as inherent in their different relations to Zhou dynasty authority and not as an accidental late development, a position which later helped support Cultural Revolution attitudes towards ideological struggle. Ren had great enthusiasm for Laozi, whom he considered a progressive materialist (with remnants of idealism) and history's first natural dialectician. The *dao* for Laozi moved according to natural laws and was a precursor of natural science. Here Ren's account conflicted with the views and method of **Guang Feng** and Lin Yushi. On the basis of detailed textual study, they argued that Laozi's *dao* was timeless and absolute and hence idealist. They claimed that we must understand a system philosophically before moving on to historical analysis, whilst Ren argued that philosophical understanding must come indirectly on the basis of historical understanding. In particular, a system must not be imposed anachronistically in interpreting ancient texts. Again opposing idealist interpretations, Ren saw Zhuangzi as progressive, individualistic and proto-scientific, with explanation and metaphysics based on the natural world and material substance. Fatalism and relativism were flaws in his outlook. Ren rejected the inner chapters of the *Zhuangzi* as a Han forgery, thus denying the most plausible grounds for a contrary interpretation of Zhuangzi. Ren's view of Mozi, although valuable, was less sophisticated than these other studies. In addition to his strictly philosophical analyses, Ren produced important assessments of Chinese religion, including his history of Chinese Buddhism.

NICHOLAS BUNNIN

Renouvier, Charles Bernard

French. **b:** 1815, Montpellier, France. **d:** 1903, Pradès. **Cat:** Neo-Kantian. **Ints:** Critical philosophy; epistemology. **Educ:** École Polytechnique. **Infls:** Kant, Descartes, Antoine Cournot and Auguste Comte. **Appts:** Founded the monthly journal *L'Année philosophique* in 1867 and supported himself by his philosophical writings.

Main publications:

(1842) *Manuel de philosophie moderne*, Paris: Paulin.

(1844) *Manuel de philosophie ancienne*, Paris: Paulin.

(1854–64) *Essais de critique générale*, 4 vols, Paris: Bureau de la Critique Philosophique.

(1869) *Science de la morale*, Paris: Ladrange.

(1876) *Uchronie*, Paris: Bureau de la Critique Philosophique.

(1885–6) *Esquisse d'une classification systématique des doctrines philosophiques*, 2 vols, Paris: Bureau de la Critique Philosophique.

(1896) *Philosophie analytique de l'histoire*, Paris: Leroux.

(1903) *Le Personnalisme*, Paris: Alcan.

Secondary literature:

Hamelin, O. (1927) *Le Système de Renouvier*, Paris: Vrin.

Méry, M. (1952) *La Critique du christianisme chez Renouvier*, Paris: Vrin.

Verneaux, R. (1945) *L'Idéalisme de Renouvier*, Paris: Vrin.

Renouvier disagreed with Kant's view that there are things-in-themselves behind the phenomena of which we are aware. He asserted that the latter are all that we do and can know, and are appearances of nothing but themselves. He rejected both the extreme empiricist position that phenomena are simply given, and the extreme idealist theory that they are totally dependent on the mind which perceives them. Instead, he took a Kantian 'middle way' by maintaining that phenomena are represented through and take their form from the intersubjectively invariable categories which constitute the framework of our knowledge and judgements about the world, and which are found within the individual consciousness. Renouvier replaces Kant's original twelve categories with a list of only nine: relation, number, position, succession, becoming, quality, causation, end or purposiveness and individuality or personality. Knowledge, according to Renouvier, is a relationship between the represrenter, or individual knower, and the represented, or phenomena. All knowledge contains judgements that something is or is not the case, and Renouvier (following Descartes) considered that all judgements contain the element of will: hence, his position on knowledge is one of voluntarism.

The relation of causation can also only fully be accounted for by taking the role of the will into consideration. Phenomenal events alone explain the mechanistic aspect of this relation, but what is injected into every such event is the will, which cannot help but impose a purpose or end on to the phenomena perceived.

The phenomenal world thus presents itself to us through the mediating factor of the will. It is this element, and the view put forward by Renouvier that each phenomenon is different from and irreducible to any other, which rescues the whole scheme of things from complete determinism and introduces the considerations of freedom and chance. Both freedom of choice and the perception of events in the world are limited by the categories, and thus not completely random, but our choices and the perception of different and discrete phenomena ensure that there is no complete uniformity in the world.

Renouvier applied his theory about the lack of complete uniformity in events to history. Since history is the study of human behaviour, which is at least partly governed by choice, and of human concern with individual events irreducible one to another, it is an arena to which any alleged deterministic general laws, such as those said to have been discovered by Comte and Hegel, are inapplicable. According to Renouvier, it is incorrect to think of historical events as completely or even partially explicable by the actions of cohesive social groups considered as one agent; social groups are composed of individual people who make individual decisions.

The relationship between ethics and history is one of dependence of the latter on the former. Moral choices provide the source for historical change, and such change is to be judged by moral criteria. There is no guarantee of betterment through the historical process: societies whose members live in fellowship with each other can develop only if there are decisions reached by enlightened people who respect the individuality and autonomy of others.

Renouvier rejected the metaphysical attributes of God as unintelligible, and instead he asserted that the only meaningful conception of God was as a being endowed with moral and anthropomorphic qualities. He was hostile to the Catholic Church, which he viewed as trying to impose a uniform set of beliefs and a metaphysical God on to its adherents, and sympathetic to Protestantism, which he saw as a movement based on individual belief and conscience.

One criticism of Renouvier is his own admission that no part of his elaborate structure, and in particular his view of freedom, can be proved. Instead, he defended his theories by saying that they at least provided a consistent framework which made knowledge possible; but the satisfaction of these two requirements is not a sufficient foundation for philosophical system-building.

KATHRYN PLANT

Main publications:
(1910) *Le antimonie dello spirito.*
(1911) *Sic et Non.*
(1914) *La trascendenza.*
(1919) *Lineamenti de filosofia scettica.*
(1920) *La filosofia dell'autorità.*
(1920) *La scepsi estetica.*
(1925) *Apologia dell'ateismo.*
(1925) *Realismo.*
(1932) *Le aporie della religione.*
(1933) *La filosofia dell'assurdo.*
(1934) *Il materialismo critico.*
(1935) *Critica della morale.*
(1939) *Autobiografia intellettuale.*
(1942) *La morale come pazzia.*
(1943) *Lettere spirituali.*
(1989) *Autobiografia intellettuale*, Milan: Dall'Oglio.

Secondary literature:
Buonauti, E. (1945) *G. Rensi*, Rome: Partenia.
Giornata Rensiana (1967), Milan: Marzorati.
Morra, G. (1958) *Scetticismo e misticismo nel pensiero de G. Rensi*, Syracuse: Editrice Ciranna.

The first period of Rensi's philosophical life, up to the First World War, issued in a species of Hegelian mysticism, which, contrary to **Gentile** and **Croce**, extracted from idealism the necessity for a mystical transcendence of existence. The First World War led Rensi to believe in the irrationality of reality. There is no sovereign reason, only conflicting reasons in a chaotic world. This led to a series of works in applied scepticism. Scepticism implies atheism, but atheism is still a religion because it answers (albeit negatively) the question of supreme reality. After 1922, when absolute idealism was influential in Italy, Rensi obstinately affirmed the materialism and pessimism to which idealism was opposed. Materialism implies pessimism. It offers us evil and conflict. One form of morality, a pure folly, is disinterested recognition of evil and a protest against it. Strangely, a profound religiosity pervades even the most sceptical works, an interior sense of a mysterious force which Rensi simply called 'the voice of God in me'.

COLIN LYAS

Rensi, Giuseppe

Italian. **b:** 31 May 1871, Vilafranca Veronese, Italy. **d:** 14 February 1941, Genoa. **Cat:** Philosopher of mysticism. **Appts:** Translator of Josiah Royce; Professor at Ferrara, Florence, Messina and Genoa, until dismissed from his post in 1927 for his opposition to the Fascists.

Rescher, Nicholas

American. **b:** 1928, Hagen, Germany. **Cat:** Philosophical polymath and pragmatic idealist. **Ints:** Logic; philosophy of science; Leibniz's philosophy. **Educ:** Queen's College, New York, and Princeton University. **Infls:** German idealism and American pragmatism. **Appts:** 1957–61, Lehigh

University; 1961–, Professor of Philosophy, Research Professor of Philosophy and University Professor of Philosophy, University of Pittsburgh.

Main publications:

(1966) *Distributive Justice* New York: Bobbs-Merrill Co.

(1967) *The Philosophy of Leibniz*, Englewood Cliffs: Prentice Hall Inc.

(1973) *The Coherence Theory of Truth*, Oxford: Clarendon Press.

(1975) *A Theory of Possibility*, Oxford: Basil Blackwell.

(1977) *Methodological Pragmatism*, Oxford: Basil Blackwell.

(1978) *Scientific Progress*, Oxford: Basil Blackwell.

(1979) *Cognitive Systematization*, Oxford: Basil Blackwell.

(1979) *The Logic of Inconsistency*, Oxford: Basil Blackwell.

(1980) *Induction*, Oxford: Basil Blackwell.

(1983) *Conceptual Idealism*, Oxford: Basil Blackwell.

(1984) *The Limits of Science*, Berkeley and Los Angeles: University of California Press.

(1985) *The Strife of Systems*, Pittsburgh: University of Pittsburgh Press.

(1986) *Ongoing Journey*, Lanham, MD (autobiography).

(1987) *Ethical Idealism: A Study of the Import of Ideals*, Berkeley, CA, and London: University of California Press.

(1988) *Rationality*, Oxford: Clarendon Press.

(1992) *A System of Pragmatic Idealism, Vol. I: Human Knowledge in Idealistic Perspective*, Princeton: Princeton University Press.

(1993) *Pluralism*, Oxford: Clarendon Press.

(1993) *A System of Pragmatic Idealism Vol. II: The Validity of Values*, Princeton: Princeton University Press.

(1993) *A System of Pragmatic Idealism, vol. III: Methodological Inquiries*, Princeton: Princeton University Press.

Secondary literature:

Almeder, Robert (ed.) (1982) *Praxis and Reason: Studies in the Philosophy of Nicholas Rescher*, Washington, DC: University Press of America.

Bottani, Andrea (1989) *Veritá e Coerenza: Suggio su'll epistemologia coerentista di Nichlas Rescher*, Milan: Franco Angeli Liberi.

Coomann, Heinrich (1984) *Die Kohaerenztheorie der Wahrheit*, Frankfurt, Bern and New York: Peter Lang.

Sosa, Ernest (ed.) (1979) *The Philosophy of Nicholas Rescher*, Dordrecht: Reidel.

In his recent trilogy, *A System of Pragmatic Idealism* (1992–3), Rescher aims to combine ideas expounded in more than 50 books and 211 articles that preceded it. The result, a system of pragmatic idealism, endorses traditional idealism's emphasis on the contributions made by our subjectivity to our conception of reality, but does not lose sight of the objective constraints imposed on proper cognitive construction by our given needs and by interests that derive from our circumstances. The pragmatism defended is, moreover, an *objective* pragmatism of what works *impersonally*, rather than a *subjective* pragmatism of what works *for me* or *for us*. It is applied not only to our factual commitments but also to our value commitments. With regard to values, again, a good measure of objectivity derives from our emplacement in reality, which imposes upon us certain basic projects not constructed or freely chosen, but given. About these we cannot properly deliberate.

The third volume of the trilogy opposes the rampant nihilism of a 'post-philosophical' age. Pluralism is regarded as compatible with a philosophical search for truth. Philosophical views are of course bound to reflect differences in backgrounds of experience and reflection. Moreover, people are bound to differ constitutionally as well, in ways that will affect what they find plausible or regard as worth pursuing. Universal acceptance and consensus are hence not in the offing, and may never be realized in philosophy. But that does not entail scepticism or relativism, since equal access to the truth is not guaranteed to all by their very constitution and opportunities.

Rescher's most important contributions to philosophy have prominently involved: (i) the rehabilitation of idealism in general and the coherence theory of truth in particular; (ii) the revival and reconstruction of pragmatism; (iii) the development of inconsistency-tolerant logic; and (iv) the development of an exponential retardation theory of scientific progress.

In sheer productivity and in the vast scope of his accomplishment, Rescher has few peers in the history of philosophy. From his great energy, intellectual power and restless curiosity has come a system of philosophy unsurpassed in our century.

E. SOSA

Revel, Jean-François

French. *b:* 1924, Marseilles. *Cat:* Common-sense philosopher. *Educ:* Studied philosophy at the École Normale Supérieure. *Infls:* British empiricist tradition. *Appts:* Taught French literature in Mexico and Italy, and philosophy in Lille and Paris, 1956–61; various posts in journalism, including the literary editorship of *L'Express*.

Main publications:

(1957) *Pourquoi les philosophes?*, Paris: Pauvert.
(1962) *La Cabale des dévots*, Paris: Pauvert.
(1968) *Histoire de la philosophie occidentale*, Paris: Stock.
(1971) *Les Idées de notre temps*, Paris: Laffont.
(1988) *La Connaissance inutile*, Paris: Grasset.

Revel is not a professional philosopher, and his interests are wide-ranging. In addition to the publications listed above he has produced a history of the links between culture and cuisine; and literary and political commentaries, including one (*Ni Marx ni Jésus*, Paris: Laffont, 1971) about the prospect of a world revolution which would begin in the USA.

Revel sees his function in relation to the philosophical establishment as one of demystification: of challenging and deflating what he sees as the pseudo-intellectual self-satisfaction of much of twentieth-century French academic philosophy. He has declared himself to be totally hostile to any attempt to formulate an all-encompassing ideology or philosophical system, and has issued tirades against metaphysics, spiritualist philosophy, phenomenology, existentialism and the obscurities of structuralism and post-structuralism. Particular philosophers to have come under criticism in Revel's publications include Henri **Bergson**, Pierre **Teilhard de Chardin**, Martin **Heidegger** and Claude **Lévi-Strauss**.

The critical standpoint of Revel stems from an approach of everyday common sense in the face of philosophical obscurantism. He raises the issue of whether there is any meaning to the philosophical vocabulary used in the various grandiose systems of the thinkers whom he attacks. In addition, he maintains that many of today's worthwhile questions are to be addressed, not by philosophy, but by the various sciences. Although Revel is by no means a rigorous thinker, he can be regarded as aligning himself with the empiricism of much of the Anglo-Saxon philosophical tradition of this and previous centuries.

KATHRYN PLANT

Rey, Abel

French. *b:* 1873, Chaon-sur-Seine. *d:* 1940, Paris. *Cat:* Rationalistic positivist. *Ints:* Philosophy and history of science; epistemology; ethics. *Educ:*

L'École Normale Supérieure. *Infls:* Descartes, Auguste Comte, Henri Berr and Rignano. *Appts:* Taught philosophy at the Lycées de Bourg, Beauvais and Dijon. Professor of the History and Philosophy of Science, Sorbonne, 1919–40.

Main publications:

(1903) *Eléments de philosophie scientifique et morale*, Paris: E. Cornely.
(1907) *La Théorie de la physique chez les physiciens contemporains*, Paris: Alcan.
(1908) *La Philosophie moderne*, Paris: Flammarion.
(1911) *Leçons de psychologie et de philosophie*, Paris: E. Cornely.
(1926) *Leçons de philosophie*, Paris: F. Rieder.
(1933) *La Jeunesse de la science grecque*, Paris: La Renaissance du livre.

Secondary literature:

Benrubi, I. (1926) *Contemporary Thought of France*, trans. E. B. Dicker, London: Williams & Norgate, pp. 54–6.
Poirier, R. (1926) *Philosophes et savants français*, vol. 2, *La Philosophie de la science*, Paris: Alcan, pp. 25–9.

Rey's chief aim was to develop a 'scientific philosophy' which would withhold from philosophy any content but the results of scientific experiment. Thus he championed an 'experimentalism' or 'rationalistic positivism' which eschewed all claims to a knowledge transcending experience, to all metaphysics, and sought a general synthesis of every kind of scientific knowledge. Neither the subject nor the method of this philosophy was to differ from those of positive science. Only its standpoint would be more general: philosophy is essentially 'une critique générale'. In this respect Rey adhered to the classic rationalistic ideal. With Descartes and Comte he interpreted philosophy as the unity of human knowledge at which all separate forms of knowledge are ultimately aiming and to which they attach themselves as vital branches. Accordingly, Rey defined the philosopher as the historian of the scientific thinking of his age, whose business it is to survey all branches of science in respect of their methods and results, and then to summarize, to achieve a comprehensive, critical view of the state of experimental knowledge as a variegated whole. But he denied that philosophy can make claim to scientific precision: philosophical statements are hypothetical only. In his later period Rey adopted a less overtly anti-metaphysical approach and increasingly stressed the realistic nature of his views.

Rey's ideal of a scientific philosophy represented a distinctly French version of the general positivist programme of a unified science. **Sources:** EF.

STEPHEN MOLLER

Rhees, Rush

British. *b:* 19 March 1905, Rochester, USA. *d:* 22 May, 1989, Swansea. *Cat:* Wittgensteinian. *Ints:* Philosophy and language; mathematics and religion; moral philosophy. *Educ:* Universities of Edinburgh, Göttingen, Innsbruck and Cambridge. *Infls:* John Anderson, Alfred Kastil, G. E. Moore and L. Wittgenstein. *Appts:* Lecturer in Philosophy, University of Manchester and University College of Swansea, 1940–66; Honorary Professor of Philosophy and Fellow, University College of Swansea, 1966.

Main publications:

(1953) (ed. with G. E. Anscombe) L. Wittgenstein, *Philosophical Investigations*, Oxford: Basil Blackwell; third, revised edition, 1967.

(1956) (ed. with G. E. Anscombe and G. H. von Wright) L. Wittgenstein, *Remarks on the Foundations of Mathematics*, Oxford: Basil Blackwell; third, revised edition, 1978.

(1958) (ed.) L. Wittgenstein, *The Blue and Brown Books*, Oxford: Basil Blackwell (with an Introduction by Rhees).

(1964) (ed.) L. Wittgenstein, *Philosophische Bemerkungen*, Oxford: Basil Blackwell (English translation, 1975).

(1969) (ed.) L. Wittgenstein, *Philosophische Grammatik*, Oxford: Basil Blackwell (English translation, 1974).

(1970) *Discussions of Wittgenstein*, London: Routledge & Kegan Paul.

(1970) (ed.) L. Wittgenstein, *Eine Philosophische Betrachtung*, Frankfurt: Suhrkamp.

(1974) 'Questions on logical inference', in G. Vesey (ed.), *Understanding Wittgenstein*, Royal Institute of Philosophy Lectures 1972–3, London: Macmillan.

(1981) (ed.) L. Wittgenstein, *Personal Recollections*, Oxford: Basil Blackwell; revised edition in paperback, Oxford: Oxford University Press, 1984 (with a Postscript by Rhees).

(1990) 'Ethical reward and punishment', in R. Gaita (ed.), *Value and Understanding: Essays for Peter Winch*, London: Routledge.

Secondary literature:

Phillips, D. Z. and Winch, Peter (eds) (1989) *Wittgenstein: Attention to Particulars*, London: Macmillan (contains incomplete bibliography).

Having studied philosophy with John **Anderson** (at Edinburgh), Alfred Kastil (at Innsbruck) and G. E. **Moore** (at Cambridge), Rhees became a student and close friend of Ludwig **Wittgenstein**. Rhees himself became renowned as a teacher during his long career at University College of Swansea, where his colleagues included Peter **Winch** and his students included D. Z. **Phillips**.

As one of Wittgenstein's literary executors Rhees was responsible for editing and bringing to publication some of the most important of Wittgenstein's later writings. He was also a distinguished exponent of Wittgenstein's ideas, and his papers were influential in shaping discussion of Wittgenstein's work in the 1950s and 1960s.

Rhees followed Wittgenstein in thinking that philosophical difficulties are rooted in confusions about language, confusions about what speaking is, about what being intelligible is. And, like Wittgenstein, he emphasized the importance of reflecting upon examples to appreciate the role that expressions of language play in people's lives. Developing this theme led Rhees (in his paper 'Wittgenstein's builders' (1959), reprinted in *Discussions of Wittgenstein*, 1970) to criticize Wittgenstein's suggestion (in #2 of *Philosophical Investigations*) that a few words given as commands on a building site could constitute a whole language. Rhees argued that, in isolation from the rest of the builders' lives, the employment of such words would be like moves in a game rather than the speaking of language in which people have discussions, ask and answer questions, and so on. The nature of the internal relationship between 'the language a people speak and the life or culture they develop' is explored with great sensitivity in Rhees's remarks on religion, ethics and aesthetics collected in *Without Answers* (1969).

Sources: Obituary, *Independent*, 3 Jul 1989.

PETER LEWIS

Ribot, Théodule Armand

French. *b:* 1839, Guingamp, France. *d:* 1916, Paris. *Cat:* Psychologist; philosopher of mind. *Infls:* Herbert Spencer and Hippolyte Taine. *Appts:* Professor, Sorbonne, 1885–8; Director of the Psychology laboratory, Collège de France, 1888; founded and edited the *Revue Philosophique de la*

France et de l'Étranger; elected to the Académie des Sciences Morales, 1899.

Main publications:
(1881) *Les Maladies de la mémoire*, Paris: Baillière (English translation, *The Diseases of Memory*, New York: Fitzgerald, 1883).
(1883) *Les Maladies de la volonté*, Paris: Baillière (English translation, *The Diseases of the Will*, New York: Fitzgerald, 1884).
(1885) *Les Maladies de la personnalité*, Paris: Baillière (English translation, *The Diseases of Personality*, New York: Fitzgerald, 1887).
(1888) *La Psychologie de l'attention*, Paris: Alcan (English translation, *The Psychology of Attention*, Chicago: Open Court, 1890).
(1897) *L'Évolution des idées générales*, Paris: Alcan (English translation, *The Evolution of General Ideas*, Chicago: Open Court, 1899).
(1900) *Essai sur l'imagination créatrice*, Paris: Alcan (English translation, *Essay on the Creative Imagination*, Chicago: Open Court, 1906).
(1907) *Essai sur les passions*, Paris: Alcan (English translation, *The Psychology of the Emotions*, London: Walter Scott Publishing Co., 1911).

Secondary literature:
Dugas, L. (1924) *La Philosophie de Théodule Ribot*, Paris: Alcan.
Le Centenaire de Théodule Ribot (1939), Agen: Imprimerie Moderne, (various authors).

Ribot's professional career was centred mainly on psychology, but he fully realized from the outset that his positivist approach to psychology implied a philosophical theory of mind. He stated that the study of the mind was not to be thought of as falling within the province of metaphysics, but that it formed the subject matter of an empirical enquiry with a physiological and not a wholly introspective basis.

In his earlier publications Ribot concentrated on abnormal psychology. From a review of many clinical cases of mental diseases he declared himself to be against the general theories of speculative psychology, which insisted that such phenomena as the will and the memory were always subject to the same analysis and explanation. Instead, he maintained that such terms as 'memory' and 'will' were simplistic labels for a complex set of phenomena not all explicable in the same way.

In his later career Ribot's field of enquiry changed to the investigation of normal psychological phenomena. His approach to such phenomena was reductionist, in that he maintained that

our emotional lives are ultimately reducible to our physiological states, whether or not we are conscious of them. Subconscious mental activity is to be traced back to various motor activities, and the emotions of sentient beings are due to their needs and desires, which in turn are due to their physiological organization. The sensibility of organisms evolved before their consciousness, and emotional life before the intellect.

In *Essai sur l'imagination créatrice* (1900) Ribot attempted to discover rules by which the creative imagination works, and from which aesthetic judgements can be deduced.

KATHRYN PLANT

Rickert, Heinrich

German. *b:* 25 May 1863, Danzig, Germany. *d:* 25 July 1936, *Cat:* Neo-Kantian. *Educ:* Literature and Philosophy at Berlin, Zürich and Strasbourg. *Infls:* Richard Avenarius, Friedrich Paulsen, Max Weber and Wilhelm Windelband. *Appts:* Professor at Freiburg and Heidelberg.

Main publications:
(1888) *Die Lehre von der Definition*, Freiburg: J. C. B. Mohr.
(1892) *Der Gegenstand der Erkenntnis*, Freiburg: J. C. B. Mohr.
(1896–1902) *Die Grenzen der wissenschaftlichen Begriffsbildung. Eine logische Einleitung in der historischen Wissenschaften* 2 vols, Tübingen: J. C. B. Mohr.
(1905) *Die Probleme der Geschichtsphilosophie*, Heidelberg: C. Winter.
(1920) *Die Philosophie des Lebens*, Tübingen: J. C. B. Mohr.
(1921) *System der Philosophie* vol. 1, Tübingen: J. C. B. Mohr.
(1924) *Kant als Philosoph der Kultur*, Tübingen: J. C. B. Mohr.
(1924) *Kulturwissenschaft und Naturwissenschaft*, sixth and seventh editions, Tübingen: J. C. B. Mohr.
(1930) *Die Logik des Prädikats und das Problem der Ontologie*, Heidelberg: C. Winter.
(1934) *Grundprobleme der Philosophie. Methodologie, Ontologie, Anthropologie*, Tübingen: J. C. B. Mohr.
(1962) *Science and History: a Critique of Positivist Epistemology*, Princeton: NJ: Van Nostrand.
(1980) *The Limits of Concept Formation in Natural Science: a Logical Introduction to the Historical Sciences*, Cambridge: Cambridge University Press.
(1988) *The Limits of Concept Formation in Natural Science: a Logical Introduction to the Historical*

Sciences, trans. Guy Oakes, Cambridge, Mass.: MIT Press.

Secondary literature:
Böhm, Franz (1933) 'Die Philosophie Heinrich Rickerts', *Kant-Studien* 38: 1–18.

Faust, August (1927) *Heinrich Rickert und seine Stellung innerhalb der deutschen Philosophie der Gegenwart*, Tübingen: J. C. B. Mohr.

Oakes, Guy (1988) *Weber and Rickert: Concept Formation in the Cultural Sciences*, Cambridge, Mass.: MIT Press.

Ramming, Gustav (1948) *Karl Jaspers und Heinrich Rickert*, Bern: A. Francke.

Seidel, H. (1968) *Wert und Wirklichkeit in der Philosophie H. Rickerts*, Bonn: Bouvier.

Zocher, R. (1937) 'Heinrich Rickerts philosophische Entwicklung', *Zeitschrift für die Kulturphilosophie*.

Rickert was the most important student of **Windelband**. He elaborated more fully the latter's suggestions concerning the priority of the practical in philosophy. Also like Windelband, he was especially concerned with the problem of differentiating between the natural sciences on the one hand and the historical disciplines on the other, arguing that the fundamental distinction between them was not one of substance but one of method. However, he felt that Windelband's discussion was inadequate. He argued that it was insufficient to differentiate between 'nomothetic' and 'ideographic' method, to say that the one aimed at general laws whereas the other was concerned with the individual, and to make them mutually exclusive. The historian does not simply mean to describe historical events, but he wants to make them comprehensible. Furthermore, he argued, the historian intends to transform something that is by itself irrational into a rational account.

Rickert was as much a follower of Plato as he was a follower of Kant in his fundamentally dualistic thinking. In fact, he may have been more indebted to Plato in this respect. Thus he differentiated at the most fundamental level between a world of ultimate being (*überwirkliches Sein*) and a world of experience. The world of experience was divided again into a world of existence and a world of valuations, between that which is and that which ought to be, or between nature and culture. The world of existence consisted again of two worlds, namely a world of physics and psychology whose objects are real, and a world of mathematics whose objects are ideal. And finally he divided the world of really existing things (i.e. the world of physics and

psychology) into a world of physical being and a world of mental being.

Rickert's distinction between the world of existence and the world of valuations formed one important part of the background of his conception of science. Thus he differentiated between sciences. The other important part of the background of his conception of science is his distinction between generalizing and individualizing thinking. The natural sciences were for him generalizing and not concerned with valuations (non-cultural). History was individualizing and concerned with valuations (cultural). While these two disciplines were at the extremes, and while there were for him many in the middle that were either ideographic and non-cultural (like geology) or nomothetic and cultural (like sociology or psychology), they were for that very reason the most interesting to Rickert.

History interested him most, for he thought that value, or the 'ought', was the true object of knowledge, not being, or the 'is'. What is recognized as existent is for a Kantian, at least in part, a result of judgement, and judgements for Rickert were ultimately impossible without a transcendent norm, namely that of truth. Our judgement that something 'is' the case must always be seen against the background of this transcendent 'ought'. Furthermore, history was for him of the particular event, and he thought that 'the single event is the only thing that really happens'. Science and its laws were for him the result of human judgement and thus superimposed on what really happens. Rickert did not believe that the concern with the individual and with value led to historicism and relativism. Rather, he hoped to show that there are a number of 'transcendent cultural values' that can guide the historian in his interpretation of any event. Rickert's discussion of the difference between the natural and cultural sciences was very influential, if only because it was very controversial. Some of his main critics include R. G. **Collingwood** and Hans-Georg **Gadamer**.

MANFRED KUEHN

Ricoeur, Paul
French. *b:* 27 February 1913, Valence, Drôme, France. *Cat:* Hermeneutics. *Ints:* Phenomenology; existentialism; literary theory; Biblical studies. *Educ:* Philosophy, Universities of Rennes and Paris. *Infls:* Jaspers, Marcel, Husserl, Heidegger, Gadamer and Freud. *Appts:* Professor of Metaphysics, Universities of Paris IV and Paris X; Dean of Faculty, University of Paris X;

John Nuveen Professor Emeritus, University of Chicago.

Main publications:
(1950) *Philosophie de la volonté. I. Le volontaire et l'involontaire*, Paris: Aubier (English translation, *Freedom and Nature: The Voluntary and the Involuntary*, trans. E. V. Kohak, Evanston: Northwestern University Press).

(1955) *Histoire et vérité*, Paris: Seuil (English translation, *History and Truth*, trans. C. A. Kelbley, Evanston: Northwestern University Press, 1965).

(1960) *Philosophie de la volonté. Finitude et culpabilité. I. L'homme faillible*, Paris: Aubier (English translation, *Fallible Man*, trans. C.A. Kebley, Chicago: Henry Regnery, 1965).

(1960) *Philosophie de la volonté. Finitude et culpabilité. II. La symbolique du mal*, Paris: Aubier (English translation, *The Symbolism of Evil*, New York: Harper & Row, 1967).

(1965) *De l'interprétation. Essai sur Freud*, Paris: Seuil (English translation, *Freud and Philosophy: An Essay on Interpretation*, trans. D. Savage, New Haven: Yale University Press).

(1969) *Le Conflit des interprétations. Essais de l'herméneutique*, Paris: Seuil (English translation, *The Conflict of Interpretations: Essays in Hermeneutics*, Evanston: Northwestern University Press, 1974).

(1975) *La Métaphore vive*, Paris: Seuil (English translation, *The Rule of Metaphor: Multi-Disciplinary Studies of the Creation of Meaning in Language*, trans. R. Czerny et al., Toronto: University of Toronto Press, 1978).

(1983) *Temps et récit, Tome I*, Paris: Seuil (English translation, *Time and Narrative, Vol. I*, trans. K. McLaughlin and D. Pellauer, Chicago: University of Chicago Press, 1984).

(1984) *Temps et récit. Tome II. La Configuration dans le récit de fiction*, Paris: Seuil (English translation, *Time and Narrative, Vol. II*, trans. K. McLaughlin and D. Pellauer, Chicago: University of Chicago Press, 1988).

Secondary literature:
Bourgeois, P. (1990) *Traces of Understanding: A Profile of Heidegger's and Ricoeur's Hermeneutics*, Amsterdam: Rodopi Wurzburg.

Klemm, D. (1983) *The Hemeneutical Theory of Paul Ricoeur: A Constructive Analysis*, London and Toronto: Associated Universities Presses.

Reagan, C. (ed.) (1979) *Studies in the Philosophy of Paul Ricoeur*, Athens, OH: Ohio University Press.

Stevens, B. (1991) *On Paul Ricoeur*, London: Routledge.

——(1991) *L'Apprentissage des signes: Lecture de Paul Ricoeur*, Dordrecht: Kluwer.

The first stage in Paul Ricoeur's thought, reinforced by his study of the works of **Jaspers** in a prisoner of war camp in Germany during the Second World War, is existentialist. This existentialist basis then shifts towards phenomenology and the philosophies of **Husserl** and **Heidegger**— Ricoeur translated the first volume of Husserl's *Ideen* into French. After phenomenology, or more precisely from within phenomenology, his thought proceeds to a philosophical hermeneutics, the proper term for Ricoeur's mature philosophy. Philosophical hermeneutics studies the diverse structures through which meaning can be brought to the subject, structures such as culture, religion, society and language: it owes much to phenomenological study of experience but at the same time offers a powerful critique of the foundations of traditional phenomenology. Philosophical hemeneutics brings together two strands of hermeneutics corresponding to two of Ricoeur's main interests: Biblical interpretation and the philosophical question of textual interpretation as found in Schleiermacher, **Dilthey**, Heidegger and **Gadamer**. Here, the self-transparent autonomous sujectivity at the foundation of phenomenology is replaced by the need to interpret meaning as carried by various structures. For Ricoeur the meaning carried by structures such as texts cannot be known absolutely and thus the subject cannot claim to absolute knowledge or self-knowledge. If the central question for philosophical hermeneutics is that of meaning then its guiding principle is that the many sources of meaning cannot be reconciled into a single account or discourse. Ricoeur's work is the attentive study of these various discourses and of how they impinge on the subject and undo any attempt to bring them together into one. Ricoeur's work is important in debates on phenomenology, existentialism, hermeneutics, critical theory, deconstruction and poststructuralism. It offers a philosophy that mediates between the traditional position put forward by philosophers such as Gadamer in hermeneutics and Husserl in phenomenology and the poststructuralist critiques of those positions as encountered in the work of **Derrida** or **Lyotard** (both of whom studied with Ricoeur).

Sources: Catalogues of Bibliothèque Nationale, Paris and National Library of Scotland.

JAMES WILLIAMS

Rida, Rashid

Syrian. *b:* 1865, Tripoli, Lebanon. *d:* 1935, Cairo. *Cat:* Islamic philosopher; Islamic modernist. *Educ:* Educated locally. *Infls:* Muhammad Abduh, Jamal al-Din al-Afghani and traditionalist Islamic philosophers such as al-Ghazali and ibn Taymiyya. *Appts:* Writer and journalist; Director of a seminary in Cairo for Muslim missionaries; enthusiastic participant in Islamic politics.

Main publications:

(1923) *al-Khilafa* [The Caliphate], Cairo.
(1925) *al-Wahha-biyyu-n wal Hijaz* [The Wahhabis and the Hejaz], Cairo.
(1947) *al-Sunna wa'l shia* [Sunnism and Shi'ism], Cairo.
(1947) *al-Wahy al-muhammadi* [The Revelation of Muhammad], Cairo.

Rida fell very much under the influence of Muhammad **Abduh** and did a great deal through his journalistic writings and editorship of *al-Manar* to publicize the views of Abduh and al-Afghani throughout the Islamic world. Like his predecessors he was interested in the question why the Islamic world, which in the past was so far in advance of the Christian, had fallen into a more backward position in the twentieth century. Rida suggests that the Europeans' success is based upon their adherence to a notion of nationality and their abandonment of religion. Muslims can discover such a principle of unity and community in their religion. Rida was far more committed to a Sunni interpretation, and particularly a Hanbali version, of Islam than were his predecessors, and he regarded the Wahhabis in Arabia as coming closest to the most genuine form of Islam. The best sort of society is an Islamic community which is led by a caliph, advised by the *ulama* (religious authorities) with the result that the laws of Islam are developed to take account of modern society and its requirements.

The interesting philosophical aspects of Rida's thought occur mainly in his writings on *tafsir*, the interpretation of the Qur'an, and he brings out in an interesting fashion the role of the notion of *maslaha* (interest) in jurisprudence. If the notion of *maslaha* is important in the construction of law, then that law will have to vary as conditions vary, since what counts as being in the interest of the community and its members will alter in different circumstances. The great danger to religion is adherence to *taqlid*, to blind obedience to tradition, reliance upon which has been so disastrous in Islamic history. Those who are qualified to exercise their judgement on the nature of law, the *ulama*, should do so in the context of the circumstances of the time and not just rely on traditional practices. In this way Islam will be accompanied by rules which express the essence of the religion, and not practices which have grown up over time but which have led to stagnation and weakness. Rida played an important part in creating a particular approach to the notion of Islam in modern society. He took a more traditional path than his mentor Abduh and provided an intellectual basis for the pursuit of the Sunni interpretation of the role of positive law. Many Islamic modernists were influenced by his approach and tried to use it to combine the traditional aspects of religion with the demands of modernity.

Sources: A. Hourani (1983) *Arabic Thought in the Liberal Age 1798–1939*, Cambridge: CUP.

OLIVER LEAMAN

Riehl, Alois

Austrian. *b:* 27 April 1844, Bozen, South Tirolia. *d:* 21 November, Potsdam-Neubabelsberg. *Cat:* Neo-Kantian; historian of philosophy. *Educ:* Philosophy at Vienna, Munich, Graz and Innsbruck. *Infls:* W. von Helmholtz and Friedrich Herbart. *Appts:* Professor of Philosophy at Freiburg, Kiel, Halle and Berlin.

Main publications:

(1871) *Moral und Dogma*, Vienna: Gerold's Sohn.
(1872) *Über Begriff und Form der Philosophie*, Berlin: Duncker.
(1876–87) *Der philosophische Kritizismus und seine Bedeutung für die positive Wissenschaft* 3 vols, Leipzig: Engelmann.
(1889) *Giordano Bruno*, Leipzig: Engelmann.
(1904) *H. V. Helmholtz in seinem Verhältnis zu Kant*, Berlin: Reuther & Reichard.
(1922) *Führende Denker und Forscher*, Leipzig: Quelle & Meyer.
(1925) *Philosophische Studien aus vier Jahrzehnten*, Leipzig: Quelle & Meyer.

Secondary literature:

Maier, Heinrich (1926) 'Alois Riehl', *Kant-Studien* 31: 563–9.
Rickert, Heinrich (1924) 'Alois Riehl', *Logos* 13: 162–185.
Siegel, Carl (1932) *Alois Riehl*, Graz: Festschrift der Universität Graz.

Riehl viewed Kant as continuing the approach of Locke, Berkeley and Hume. His position may be characterized as an attempt to mediate between positivism and Kantian criticism. He advocated a realistic interpretation of Kant's thing in itself, arguing that it must be understood as an attempt to capture the 'given-ness' of things that is always bound up with experience. Riehl had a great influence on his student Richard Hönigswald, who, in opposition to the Marburg neo-Kantians, continued the realistic interpretation of Kant.

MANFRED KUEHN

Rignano, Eugenio

Italian. **b:** 31 May 1870, Livorno, Italy. **d:** 9 February 1930. **Cat:** Positivist philosopher. **Appts:** Editor of *Scientia*.

Main publications:

(Many translated into English.)

(1901) *Di un socialismo in accordo con la dottrina economica liberale.*
(1904) *La sociologia nel corso di filosofia positiva di Augusto Comte.*
(1907) *Sulla trasmissibilità dei caratteri acquisiti.*
(1912) *Essais de synthèse scientifique.*
(1920) *Psicologia del ragionamento.*
(1922) *La memoria biologica.*
(1925) *La vita nel suo aspetto finalistico.*
(1926) *Che cosa é la vita?*
(1926) *Man not a Machine.*
(1928) *Problemi della psiche.*
(1928) *Il fine dell'uomo.*

Secondary literature:

Needham, J. (1927) *Man a machine: In Answer to a Romantic and Unscientific Treatise Written by Sig. Eugenio Rignano and Entitled 'Man not a Machine*, London: Paul Trench and Trubner.

Rignano began with sociology and economics and then turned to problems in biology and psychology. He places memory at the basis of all biological phenomena, believing it to make possible all adaptation and the formation of instincts and emotions and even (following **Mach**) of reason. He distinguished constructive from intentional reasoning. The former seeks new truths and characterizes positive science; the latter seeks confirmation of what is already believed and characterizes metaphysics. Despite a scepticism about the latter activity Rignano elaborates a kind of biological metaphysics which posits a nervous energy at the foundation of life and evolution that is capable of moulding matter and directing it adaptively. Indeed, life in its entirety shows an end-directedness that would be inexplicable without this directing force, a force

which continues into moral life so as to guarantee to individuals the satisfaction of their needs in more harmonious societies.

COLIN LYAS

Rintelen, Fritz-Joachim von

German. **b:** 1898, Stettin, Germany. **d:** 1980, Mainz, Germany. **Cat:** Philosopher of value. **Ints:** European culture and values; existentialism. **Educ:** 1924, doctorate awarded by University of Munich. **Infls:** Plato, existentialism and German idealism. **Appts:** 1933, Professorship, University of Bonn; 1936, Professorship, University of Munich (suspended on political grounds in 1941); held posts at the Universities of Cordoba, Los Angeles, Chicago, Delhi and Tokyo; 1947, Member of International Institute of Philosophy.

Main publications:

(1924) *Pessimistische Religionsphilosphie der Gegenwart*, Munich: F. A. Pfeiffer.
(1930) *Die Bedeutung des philosophischen Wertproblems*, Regensburg: J. Habbel.
(1932) *Der Wertgedanke in der europäischen Geistesentwicklung: Altertum und Mittelalter*, Halle: M. Nismeyer.
(1947) *Damonie des Willens*, Mainz: F. Kupferberg.
(1951) *Philosophie der Endlichkeit als Spiegel der Gegenwart*, Meisenheim/Glan (English translation, *Beyond Existentialism*, trans. Hilda Graef, London: George Allen & Unwin, 1961).
(1968) *Der Aufstieg im Geiste*, Frankfurt: Metopen-Verlag.
(1973) *Contemporary German Philosophy and Its Background*, Bonn: Bouvier Verlag Herbert Grundmann.

Secondary literature:

Siebert, Charles (1973) 'A conversation with F. J. von Rintelen', in *Listening* 8: 125–8.
Wisser, Richard (ed.) (1960) 'Wertwirklichkeit und Sinnverstandniss. Gedanken zur Philosophie von Fritz-Joachim von Rintelen', in *Sinn und Sein: Ein Philosophisches Symposium F. J. von Rintelen gewidmet*, Tübingen.

The whole of von Rintelen's adult life coincided with a time of intellectual, political and cultural upheaval that included spectacular advances in physics as well as the development of existential ideas and the radical questioning of traditional and humane values. He opposed philosophies that subjugated the rational to the irrational as well as those that asserted unresolvable dualisms and tensions and he developed a theory of value, meaning and personality that he used in his mature philosophy to analyse and clarify the extremely complex movements of European thought that he experienced and witnessed. He conceived of human history as the endeavour to actualize an objective sphere of value through the concretization and particularization of individual values in the life and minds of human beings. His thought was a counteraction to psychologism, pessimism, subjectivity, atheism and finitude: he maintained that a secure spirituality could be restored by the recognition of the transcendent value system he propounded.

Sources: Huisman; Edwards.

DIANÉ COLLINSON

Rogers, Arthur Kenyon

American. **b:** 27 December 1868, Donellan, New Jersey. **d:** 1 November 1936, Rockport, Massachusetts. **Cat:** Epistemologist; ethicist. **Ints:** History of ethics; history of philosophy; metaphysics. **Educ:** Colby College, AB 1891; Johns Hopkins, 1891–2; Hartford School of Sociology, 1894–5; University of Chicago, PhD 1898. **Infls:** Plato, Emerson, John Burnet and A. E. Taylor. **Appts:** Instructor, Chicago Academy, 1893–4; Assistant Superintendent, Charity Organization Society, Hartford, Connecticut, 1895–6; Instructor in Philosophy and Pedagogy, Alfred University, 1899–1900; Professor of Philosophy and Education, Butler College, 1900–10; Professor of Philosophy, University of Missouri, 1910–14; Yale University, 1914–20.

Main publications:

(1899) *A Brief Introduction of Modern Philosophy*, New York: Macmillan Co.

(1901) *A Student's History of Philosophy*, New York: Macmillan; second edition, 1907, third edition, 1932.

(1920) *Essays in Critical Realism: A Co-operative Study of the Problem of Knowledge*, London: Macmillan and Co., Ltd.

(1922) *English and American Philosophy Since 1800: A Critical Survey*, New York: Macmillan.

(1922) *The Theory of Ethics*, New York: Macmillan.

(1923) *What is Truth? An Essay in the Theory of Knowledge*, New Haven: Yale University Press.

(1927) *Morals in Review*, New York: Macmillan.

(1933) *The Socratic Problem*, New Haven: Yale University Press.

(1934) *Ethics and Moral Tolerance*, New York: Macmillan.

Note: *An Introduction to Ethics*, the author's last work, edited and prepared for publication by Robert L. Calhoun, remains unpublished.

Rogers was an independent thinker who worked in a number of areas of philosophy. Although one of the critical realists, in the main he belonged to no school, but worked everything out for himself with careful attention paid to established knowledge and common sense. Good sense and balance, based on extensive scholarship, marked all of his ventures. In dealing with philosophical questions as they presented themselves to him, without attempting to fit his views into some pre-established system, he was in some ways a forerunner of what came to be called philosophical analysis, and his work was in general congruence with Sidgwick's philosophy of common sense:

> The business of philosophy is to clarify and bring into harmony ... the fundamental beliefs that are implicated in our normal human interests ... this reference to the needs of living ... furnishes the touchstone by which alone the sanity of philosophical reasonings and conclusions can be tested.

Also:

> Systems of philosophy have pretty generally hesitated to concede ... to the common sense of mankind, and I have always in consequence found myself excluded from that comforting sense of security that comes from membership in an established ... school of thought.

He held a coherence view of justification and a correspondence theory of truth, and that belief, not experience, 'is the starting-point of our cognitive contact with the world'.

> Scepticism is ... a demand for a criterion of truth, and ... has assumed an importance in philosophy ... very much out of proportion to the part which healthy doubt plays in our practical life. If in practical life we were to hesitate to act until we had absolute ... certainty, we never should begin to move at all. ... Scepticism ... assumes that philosophical truth is ... removed from the business of living [and] divorces philosophy from the rest of life ... whereas life itself is essentially a development.

This, from his first philosophical work (1899), foreshadows some of the ideas of **Dewey** and **Moore**. Thus: 'The value of knowledge ... is to be found only in the fact that it contributes, ultimately, to life; it has no use purely in itself, but is meant to be acted upon.' In ethics he held to a mild form of teleological theory combined with a theory of natural rights.

> A natural right is what a man cannot give up without violating his essential nature. It may be in accordance with justice that a few men only should possess the right to vote; it cannot possibly be just that only a few men should have the opportunity to live a satisfying life.

Rogers was highly regarded by his contemporaries and respected for his careful thinking, lack of dogmatism and fairness to opposing views. His works were reviewed favourably, some of them at length, in the major journals of the period, tended to be read and were often cited. No comprehensive studies of his philosophy have appeared and no comprehensive bibliography of his works exists. A bibliography of his papers can be compiled by consulting the comprehensive indexes of the major journals of the period.

Sources: Obituary, *PR* 36 (1937): 196; WWW 1929–40; WWW(Am) 1897–1942.

MARCUS SINGER

Roig, Arturo Andrés

Argentinian. *b:* 16 July 1922, Mendoza, Argentina. *Cat:* Historian of ideas; social and political philosopher. *Educ:* National University of Cuyo and the Sorbonne. *Appts:* Professor of the History of Argentine Thought and Culture, Universidad Nacional del Cuyo, Mendoza, Argentina.

Main publications:

(1969) *Los krausistas argentinos*, Puebla: Cajica.

(1977) *Esquemas para una historia de la filosofía ecuatoriana*; second edition, Quito: Universidad Católica, 1982.

(1981) *Filosofía, universidad y filósofos en América Latina*, Mexico: Universidad Nacional Autónoma de México.

(1981) *Teoría y crítica del pensamiento latinoamericano*, Mexico: Fondo de Cultura Económica.

(1986) 'The actual function of philosophy in Latin America', in Jorge J. E. Gracia (ed.), *Latin American Philosophy in the Twentieth Century*, Buffalo, New York: Prometheus Books.

Secondary literature:

Schutte, Ofelia (1993) *Cultural Identity and Social Liberation in Latin American Thought*, New York: SUNY Press.

Roig was forced to leave his native Argentina for political reasons and lived in Ecuador for a number of years, where he was a significant force behind renewed interest in the historiography of Ecuadorean ideas. His works offer new theoretical and historiographical categories for the study of philosophy in Latin America as well as foundational and critical perspectives on the philosophy of liberation. Borrowing from Hegel, Roig believes that authentic philosophy involves affirmation of the self as valuable, together with historical consciousness and identification with one's cultural legacy.

AMY A. OLIVER

Romero, Francisco

Spanish-Argentinian. *b:* 1891, Seville, Spain. *d:* 7 October, 1962. Buenos Aires. *Cat:* Philosopher of anthropology; philosopher of values. *Infls:* Ortega y Gasset, Korn, Scheler, Klages, Hartmann, Husserl and Garcia Morente. *Appts:* Taught in Buenos Aires; 1946–, Professor, Colegio Libre de Estudios Superiores.

Main publications:

(1938) *Filosofía de la persona y otros ensayos de filosofía*, Buenos Aires.

(1952) *Sobre la filosofía en América*, Buenos Aires: Editorial Raigal.

(1957) *Filósofos y problemas*, Buenos Aires: Losada.

(1958) *Ideas y figuras*, Buenos Aires: Losada.

(1960) *Ortega y Gasset y el problema de la jefatura espiritual, y otros ensayos*, Buenos Aires: Losada.

(1964) *Theory of Man*, trans. William F. Cooper, Berkeley: University of California Press.

(1967) *La estructura de la historia de la filosofía y otros ensayos*, Buenos Aires: Losada.

The following English translations of excerpts of the work of Francisco Romero by Willard Trask appear in Aníbal Sánchez Reulet (ed.) (1954) *Contemporary Latin American Philosophy*, Albuquerque: University of New Mexico Press:
'Person and transcendence', pp. 269–75.
'Program of a philosophy', pp. 255–69.

Secondary literature:

Ardao, Arturo, *et al.* (1983) *Francisco Romero: Maestro de la filosofía* Caracas: Sociedad Interamericana de Filosofía.

Rodríguez Alcalá, Hugo (1954) *Francisco Romero: Vida y obra*, New York: Hispanic Institute, Columbia University.

Romero's philosophy of the person stressed freedom and creativity as essential for his concept of 'transcendence'. He sought to develop a philosophy of culture taking into account the profound effect that certain cultural objects have on the person.

AMY A. OLIVER

Roretz, Karl (Oscar Ernst Albrecht)

Austrian. *b:* 24 July 1881, Horn, Lower-Austria. *d:* 17 July 1967, Vienna. *Cat:* Critical positivist; fictionalist. *Ints:* Epistemology; history of philosophy; philosophy and psychology of culture. *Educ:* Jurisprudence, Philosophy and Medicine, University of Vienna; doctoral thesis, 'Das Einfühlungsproblem in der modernen Ästhetik', 1906. *Infls:* Hans Vaihinger and Friedrich Nietzsche. *Appts:* 1922–51, Privatdozent for recent history of philosophy, University of Vienna; from 1930, Extraordinary Professor.

Main publications:

(1914) *Diderots Weltanschauung (ihre Voraussetzungen, ihre Leitmotive)*, Vienna.
(1922) *Zur Analyse von Kants Philosophie des Organischen*, Vienna.
(1927) *Die Metaphysik eine Fiktion*, Vienna and Leipzig.
(1937) *An den Quellen unseres Denkens (Studien zur Morphologie der Erkenntnis und Forschung)*, Vienna and Leipzig.
(1976) *Ziele und Wege philosophischen Denkens*, ed. Franz Austeda, Vienna: Franz Deuticke.

Secondary literature:

Austeda, Franz (1976) 'Roretz als Denker und Lehrer', in Austeda (ed.), *Karl Roretz: Ziele und Wege philosophischen Denkens*, Vienna: Franz Deuticke.

Although Roretz belonged to the positivistic tradition, he is at the same time influenced by neo-Kantianism. As an epistemologist he took an anti-dogmatic and scientific standpoint and vehemently criticized metaphysical doctrines: metaphysical concepts are inconsistent fictions (fictions in the sense of Hans **Vaihinger**). In his major work An den Quellen unseres Denkens [Sources of our thought] (1937), Roretz analyses the so-called '*Vitalbegriffe*' (vital concepts) which have their origin in volitive or evaluative attitudes.

As a philosopher and psychologist of culture he was concerned with the inner dynamics of cultural products and the analysis of mass phenomena in religion, politics and art. As a historian of philosophy he played a decisive role as a contributor to Rudolf **Eisler**'s *Wörterbuch der philosophischen Begriffe*; in 1924 Roretz edited *Geschichte der neueren Philosophie* from the posthumous manuscripts of his teacher Friedrich Jodl. Within a greater philosophical audience Roretz is rather unknown.

THOMAS BINDER

Rorty, Richard McKay

American. *b:* 4 October 1931, New York. *Cat:* Post-analytical, hermeneutical, pragmatist. *Ints:* Nature and history of philosophy; metaphysics. *Educ:* BA, Chicago, 1949; MA, Chicago, 1952; PhD, Yale, 1956. *Infls:* Dewey, Heidegger, Sellars, Wilfred S. and Wittgenstein. *Appts:* Yale, 1954–6; Wellseley, 1958–61; Princeton, 1961–82; Virginia, 1982–; many visiting appointments.

Main publications:

(1967) *The Linguistic Turn*, Chicago: University of Chicago Press.
(1979) *Philosophy and the Mirror of Nature*, Princeton: Princeton University Press.
(1982) *Consequences of Pragmatism*, Minnesota: University of Minnesota Press (papers of 1972–80).
(1989) *Contingency, Irony, and Solidarity*, Cambridge: Cambridge University Press.
(1991) *Essays on Heidegger and Others*, Cambridge: Cambridge University Press (papers of 1983–9).
(1991) *Objectivity, Relativism, and Truth*, Cambridge: Cambridge University Press (papers of 1983–9).

Secondary literature:

Hall, David L. (1993) *Richard Rorty: Prophet and Poet of the New Pragmatism*, Ithaca: SUNY Press.
Malachowski, A. R. (ed.) (1990) *Reading Rorty*, Oxford: Blackwell.
Saatkamp, H. J. (ed.) (1995) *Rorty and Pragmatism: The Philosopher Responds to His Critics*, Vanderbilt.
West, C. (1989) *The American Evasion of Philosophy*, London: Macmillan (contains a critical version of Rorty's development, chapter 5, pp. 194–210).

Rorty's first book, *The Linguistic Turn* (1967), contained a long introduction on the 'Metaphilosophical difficulties of linguistic philosophy' which signalled many of his reservations about the analytical-linguistic tradition (from which he originated), as well as revealing his interest in the nature and place of philosophy.

His large international reputation was founded by *Philosophy and the Mirror of Nature* (1979), which (like the work of **Wittgenstein**) offered a comprehensive aetiology for the problems in current philosophy. (But, unlike Wittgenstein, Rorty provides a good deal of historical analysis in support of his views.)

According to Rorty, the mind, as a subjective mirror of objective, external nature, has been a persuasive and dominating presence in Western thought, at least from the time of its most famous 'invention' by Descartes. A polarity between mind and nature, he believed, lay behind the very statement of the standard problems of epistemology. And that polarity was only restated in a variant form when the mind (regarded as a theatre for representations) was replaced, in the twentieth century, by language, and when the problems of epistemology were recast as problems of (linguistic) reference.

Rorty has always been acutely self-conscious about the nature of philosophical activity, and *Philosophy and the Mirror of Nature* included theorizing about the role and status of both past (often erroneous) and future (redirected) philosophizing as an element in its wider diagnosis. Philosophy's prestigious role as elitist cultural criticism, Rorty thought, was a consequence of the privileged terrain of the mind (later, language) as a courtroom where the philosopher could arbitrate on the acceptability of claims to knowledge (later, meaningfulness), often on the basis of 'foundationalist' theorizing, and sometimes with pretensions of being outside history. The historical dismantling of the mind removed the privileged status of philosophy. Philosophical problems had to be seen as intrinsically non-timeless, given that no one could expect to produce a finally correct, purely philosophical question and answer. What was left, Rorty thought in Part III of *Philosophy and the Mirror of Nature*, could be seen by use of **Oakeshott**'s notion of the *conversation of mankind*:

> To see keeping a conversation going as a sufficient aim of philosophy, to see wisdom as consisting in the ability to sustain a conversation, is to see human beings as generators of new descriptions rather than beings one hopes to be able to describe accurately
>
> p. 378

He pointed towards what he thought to be the less dogmatic, less problem-solving tenor of the hermeneutical tradition as a way forward. Philosophy, in any case, could be seen as a 'literary genre' (Introduction to *Consequences of Pragmatism*, 1982, p. xiv)—a thought personified by his transition at that time from a Chair in Philosophy to one in Literature (then, later, in Humanities). His view of philosophy as literature receives some incidental support from his own admirable style of writing: plain, lucid and often witty.

His work since 1979 has pursued themes initiated in *Philosophy and the Mirror of Nature*, branching into an increasingly elaborated dialogue with critics and commentators.

(1) If philosophers' truth cannot be pure and timeless it can at least have some pragmatic value. Rorty is a frank pragmatist about truth, identifying himself as clearly in the tradition of **James** and **Dewey**. This was much debated in the 1980s, with not much progress beyond the positions staked out by James and **Russell** before 1910.

(2) Rorty portrayed the representational mind as a source of problems underlying apparently opposed philosophical positions. That procedure could stand as a clear model of deconstructionist *unmasking*. He saw his own approach as post-analytical, closer to the approaches adopted in current continental European philosophy. He traced out a history of influences leading towards his thinking, from **Nietzsche** through **Heidegger**. This history has been the subject of much debate, like his history of earlier philosophy in *Philosophy and the Mirror of Nature*. His work on **Derrida** has created an obvious comparison with his own view of 'philosophy as a kind of writing'.

(3) As an anti-foundationalist, anti-essentialist work, *Philosophy and the Mirror of Nature* (like the *Philosophical Investigations* of Wittgenstein) presented a remarkably essentialist story about the origin of philosophical problems and the place of philosophy. (Rorty, though, has not yet tested his thinking against what is apparently the most extremely non-historical territory: the traditional problems in the philosophy of mathematics.) The thought that this story might be a narrowly North American and European one was put to Rorty with some force at the Inter-American Congress of Philosophy at Guadalajara in 1985. There, his notion of philosophy as *play* (a provocative extrapolation of *conversation*) was subject to sharp criticism by Latin American philosophers who had been in touch with a different European tradition of philosophy as radical political critique (see *Proceedings and Addresses* of the American Philosophical Association, vol. 59, no. 5, June 1986, pp. 747–59).

Contingency, Irony, and Solidarity (1989)

pursues the themes developed and discussed in the decade after *Philosophy and the Mirror of Nature*, but with a wider political understanding. ('We Western liberal intellectuals should accept the fact that we have to start from where we are' ('Solidarity or objectivity?' (1985), in *Objectivity, Relativism, and Truth*, 1991). Rorty's views were prominent in debates over the social and cultural position of philosophy which raged in American academe through the 1980s. He created for himself a problem of combining an estimation of any reasoned attitude as a contingent choice of language with his own professed liberal preferences. His solution was a form of conscious ('ironic') self-consciousness: 'the citizens of my liberal utopia would be people who had a sense of the contingency of their language of moral deliberation, and thus of their community' (p. 61). A way of life could not be founded on a story based on truths about the human condition (as discovered by philosophers). It might be grounded in stories, but they would be ones told in drama, in fiction or in philosophy, without pretensions to being timeless discoveries.

RICHARD MASON

Rose, Gillian

British. *b:* 20 September 1947, London. *Cat:* Sociologist; political philosopher. *Ints:* Philosophy of social, political and ethical questions; also Judaism, history and law. *Educ:* BA, University of Oxford, 1967–70; Philosophy Department, Columbia University, 1970–1; DPhil, University of Oxford, 1971–4. *Infls:* Hegel, Nietzsche, Marx, Adorno and critical theory, Kierkegaard and Levinas. *Appts:* Lecturer, Sociology, University of Sussex; 1989–, Professor of Sociology and European Thought, University of Warwick.

Main publications:

(1978) *A Melancholy Science; An Introduction to the Thought of Theodor W. Adorno*, London: Macmillan.

(1981) *Hegel Contra Sociology*, London: Athlone.

(1984) *Dialectic of Nihilism, Post-structuralism and Law*, Oxford: Blackwell.

(1992) *The Broken Middle: Out of our Ancient Society*, Oxford: Blackwell.

(1993) *Judaism and Modernity: Philosophical Essays*, Oxford: Blackwell.

Rose's work has been broadly concerned with ethical, political and methodological questions raised in (and by) the historical context of modernity, although the challenging range of

her scholarly interests makes it difficult to classify her writings. Urging further reflection on the role and direction of critical thought, problems of judging and legitimation, future communities, and issues of tradition and history, her diverse texts raise questions about authorship and gender, Judaic thought and theology, as well as legal, literary and political forms of writing. Her attempts to keep alive the possibility of critique, in disciplines such as philosophy, sociology, politics and law, issue a regenerative challenge to resignation or complacency.

Sources: WWWWE.

ALISON AINLEY

Rosenzweig, Franz

German Jew. *b:* 25 December 1886, Kassel, Germany. *d:* 12 December 1929, Frankfurt am Main. *Cat:* Religious existentialist; translator. *Ints:* Philosophies of Judaism and Chistianity; philosophy of language. *Educ:* 1905–14, Philosophy, History and Classics in various universities. *Infls:* German idealism. Personal influences: Martin Buber, Leo Baeck, Hermann Cohen, Erich Fromm, Friedrich Meinecke, Eugen Rosenstock-Huessy, Gershom Scholem and Ernst Simon. *Appts:* 1920, Cofounder, Freies Jüdisches Lehrhaus; 1922–9, taught from home after serious illness; ordained rabbi by Leo Baeck; nearly converted to Christianity, but changed his mind after experiencing Orthodox *Yom Kippur* service in Berlin, 1913; experiences in First World War led to renunciation of an academic career.

Main publications:

(1917) *Das älteste Systemprogramm des deutschen Idealismus* [The Oldest Programmatic System of German Idealism], Heidelberg: Winter.

(1920) *Hegel und der Staat* [Hegel and the State], Munich: Oldenbourg (based on prewar PhD).

(1921) *Der Stern der Erlösung*, Frankfurt: Schocken; 2nd ed. 1930, and Heidelberg: Schneider, 1954 (English translation, *The Star of Redemption*, trans. W. Hallo, New York: Holt, Rinehart & Winston, 1970; new ed., Notre Dame Press, 1985).

(1937) *Kleinere Schriften* [Shorter Writings], Berlin: Schocken.

Secondary literature:

(1988) *The Philosophy of Franz Rosenzweig* (conference), Hanover, NH: University Press of New England; Brandeis University Press.

Bergman, Samuel H. (1961) *Faith and Reason: An Introduction to Modern Jewish Thought*, Washington DC: Bnai Brith; New York: Schocken Books, 1963.

Glatzer, N. N. (ed.) (1953) *Franz Rosenzweig: His Life and Thought*, New York: Schocken, 1961.

Guttman, Julius (1964) *Philosophies of Judaism*, trans. D. W. Silverman, London: Routledge & Kegan Paul (bibliography, p. 410).

Handelman, Susan (1991) *Fragments of Redemption: Jewish Thought and Literary Theory in Benjamin, Scholem & Lévinas*, Bloomington: Indiana University Press (bibliography, pp. 365–76).

Horwitz, Rivkah (1989) 'Revelation and the Bible according to twentieth-century Jewish philosophy' in *Jewish Spirituality II* ed. A. Green, New York: Crossroad, pp. 346–70 (includes bibliography).

Juden in Kassel, 1808–1933 (1987), Kallel: Thiele & Schwartz (exhibition).

Mendes-Flohr, Paul (1987) *Philosophy of Franz Rosenzweig*, Hanover, NH: University Press of New England.

Mosès, Stéphanie (1982) *Système et Révelation: La Philosophie de Franz Rosenzweig*, Paris: Seuil (English translation, *System and Revelation*, Detroit: Wayne State University, 1992).

Rosenzweig was a precursor of existentialism. However, his attachment to Judaism was influenced by the neo-Kantian, Hermann **Cohen**. There is a correlation between Rosenzweig's views and **Heidegger**'s *Being and Time*. Rosenzweig's chef d'oeuvre, *The Star of Redemption* (1921) was, however, regarded as of primarily Jewish interest until about fifty years after Rosenzweig's death. In it, and influenced by the later Schelling, Rosenzweig opposed German idealist philosophy, and emphasised the immediate presence of God. For Rosenzweig revelation is not an historical event but God's continuous verbal relationship with humanity. Following Kant, Rosenzweig distinguished universal laws (*Gesetzen*) and 'commandments' (*Geboten*), born out of love. Later he held *halakhah* (Orthodox Jewish law) to be a channel for the commandments. Rosenzweig's anti-idealism resembled **Buber**'s, but they differed in attitude to *halakhah*. Rosenzweig held that whereas Christianity was bound by history, Judaism's unfolding relationship of God, humanity and world was biologically determined. He was influenced in this view both by the religious medieval Jewish philosopher Judah Halevi, and the modern evolutionary determinist Charles Darwin.

Sources: EncJud; Schoeps.

IRENE LANCASTER

Ross, W(illiam) D(avid)

British. *b:* 1877, Thurso. *d:* 1971, Oxford. *Cat:* Intuitionist. *Ints:* Ethics; Aristotle. *Educ:* University of Edinburgh and Balliol College, Oxford. *Infls:* G. E. Moore and H. A. Prichard. *Appts:* 1900–2, Lecturer, 1902–29, Fellow, 1924–9, Senior Tutor, 1929–47, Provost, Oriel College, Oxford; 1941–4, Vice Chancellor, Oxford University; 1927, Fellow, 1936–40, President of the British Academy; 1919, OBE; 1938, KBE.

Main publications:
(1923) *Aristotle*, London: Methuen.
(1930) *The Right and the Good*, Oxford: Clarendon Press.
(1939) *The Foundations of Ethics*, Oxford: Clarendon Press.
(1951) *Plato's Theory of Ideas*, Oxford: Clarendon Press.
(1954) *Kant's Ethical Theory; A Commentary on the Grundlegung zur Metaphysik der Sitten*, Oxford: Clarendon Press.

Secondary literature:
Hudson, W. D. (1973) *Modern Moral Philosophy*, London: Macmillan, second edition; 1983.
Warnock, G. J. (1967) *Contemporary Moral Philosophy*, London: Macmillan.

Ross held that certain ethical truths were self-evident: they could be 'intuited' by any person of educated moral sensibilities. First, we could intuit that a number of things are intrinsically good, namely knowledge, virtue and pleasure. Second, we could also intuit that certain actions are right or wrong. But unlike H. A. **Prichard**, who influenced him greatly, he did not hold that we could intuit the truth of judgements about *particular* actions unmediated by general principles. It was certain *kinds* of actions—such as keeping promises or murdering—whose rightness or wrongness we could intuit.

Although, according to Ross, we could intuit that certain kinds of action are wrong, there is, he thought, probably no kind that is *always* wrong to do, since our duties may, in certain circumstances, conflict. To deal with the problem of conflicting duties Ross held that what we intuit are *prima facie* obligations. By *prima facie* he meant, roughly, that they hold unless they conflict with other, stronger duties. However, what, more precisely, the notion of a *prima facie* duty comes to has been much debated.

Ross held that rightness was an objective property of our actions, one which, although we could intuit its presence, was indefinable.

Although it was an objective property it was one that, in some way, depended upon the presence of other properties, such as the tendency to cause pain.

In the aftermath of logical positivism, intuitionism was largely rejected. It was, and is, generally felt that Ross could give an adequate account neither of the idea of intuition nor of the action-guiding force of ethical beliefs. It is also generally felt that he failed to explain adequately how moral rightness 'depends' upon other properties.

Ross was General Editor of the important series of Oxford translations of the works of Aristotle, and he produced editions with commentaries of a number of Aristotle's works. From 1947 to 1949 he was Chairman of the Royal Commission on the Press, whose report in 1949 led to the creation of the Press Council.

Sources: Flew; Becker; *The Times*, 6 May 1971, p. 18.

ANTHONY ELLIS

Rosset, Clément
French. **b:** 1939. **Cat:** Neo-Nietzschean and Schopenhauerian. **Ints:** Philosophy of the tragic; ontology; aesthetics. **Educ:** École Normale Supérieure (Agrégé in Philosophy). **Infls:** Nietzsche, Schopenhauer, J. J. Rousseau and Martin Heidegger. **Appts:** From 1967, Maître-assistant then Professor of Philosophy, Faculté des Lettres et Sciences Humaines de Nice.

Main publications:

(1960) *La Philosophie tragique*, Paris: PUF.

(1964) *Le Monde et ses remèdes*, Paris: PUF.

(1967) *Schopenhauer, philosophe de l'absurde*, Paris: PUF.

(1969) *L'Esthétique de Schopenhauer*, Paris: P.U.F.

(1972) *Logique du pire, éléments pour une philosophie tragique*, Paris: PUF.

(1973) *L'Anti-nature, éléments pour une philosophie tragique*, Paris: PUF.

(1976) *Le Réel et son double*, Paris: Gallimard.

(1978) *Le Réel. Traité de l'idiotie*, Paris: Éditions de Minuit.

(1979) *L'Objet singulier*, Paris: Éditions de Minuit.

Secondary literature:

Favre, C. (1975) Review of *Logique du pire* (1972), in *Revue Philosophique de la France et de l'Étranger*, 165: 92–3.

Smith, Colin (1962) 'Survey of philosophy in France', *Philosophy* 37: 273–6.

Rosset has taken up themes from **Nietzsche** and Schopenhauer and developed them into a 'philosophie tragique', whose central concept is that of chance or risk (*le hasard*). According to *La Philosophie tragique* (1960), there are two attitudes to life, the moral and the tragic. By a transvaluation of values he proposes that the moral is bad and the tragic good. He sees the moral tradition of Plato, Voltaire, Hegel and Marx as perversely extolling happiness. The antithesis of this tradition, Rosset believes, is to be found in that of the tragic, as embodied, for example, in Rousseau and Beethoven. By overlooking the tragic nature of reality, he maintains, we are 'dying of happiness': of this we become aware, at least momentarily, under the 'tragic' spell of great music or poetry.

Rosset's writings of 1972 and 1973 developed this view further in terms of the concept of chance, understood as designating the fundamental, self-sufficient reality. And in his works of 1976, 1978 and 1979 he attempted to determine the attributes of chance, to formulate an ontology of chance.

Writing in an exalted style and with a sense of mission, Rosset has presented a philosophy that boldly challenges traditional philosophical assumptions and ontologies.

Sources: Huisman.

STEPHEN MOLLER

Rossi-Landi, Ferruccio
Italian. **b:** 1 March 1921, Milan. **Cat:** Philosopher of language. **Appts:** Professor of Theoretical Philosophy, University of Trieste.

Main publications:

(1968) *Il linguaggio come lavoro e come mercato*, Milan: Bompiani.

(1973) *Ideologies of Linguistic Relativity* The Hague: Mouton.

(1975) *Charles Morris e la semiotica novecentesca*, Milan: Feltrinelli.

(1977) *Linguistics and Economics*, The Hague: Mouton.

(1978) *Ideologia*, Milan: Isedi.

(1980) *Significato, communicazione e parlare comune*, Venice: Marsilio.

(1985) *Semiotica e ideologica*, Milan: Bompiani.

(1985) *Metodica filosofica e scienza dei signi*, Milan: Bompiani.

(1992) *Between signs and non-signs*: Philadelphia: Benjamins.

Secondary literature:

Ponzio, A. (1988) *Rossi-Landi e la filosofia del linguaggio*, Bari: Adriatica.

Rossi-Landi's concerns are with general semiotics, linguistic philosophy, philosophy of language and other sign systems, Marxism, ideology, and the problem of adequate communicative systems. He is one of the more notable of continental European philosophers who has sought to understand, criticize and develop what is often believed to be a characteristically Anglo-Saxon linguistic turn in philosophy. Note here, for example, the critical discussion of linguistic philosophy in *Significato, communicazione e parlare comune* (1980) and the attempt further to develop the notion of speech as social practice. How close he was to some of the important developments in linguistic philosophy is shown in *Language as Work and Trade* (the English translation of *Il linguaggio come lavoro e come mercato*, 1968) with its vivid, amusing and gently ironic first-hand picture of the day on which **Wittgenstein**'s *Philosophical Investigations* was published in Oxford. Rossi-Landi's work continues in new forms some of the pervasive themes of Italian philosophy in this century, such as the status of idealism, positivism and Marxism. Thus *Ideologies of Linguistic Relativity* (1973), treats the **Sapir–Whorf** theory of linguistic relativity not as something of merely contemporary interest but as leading back to more general problems: it treats the theory as an instance of what is substantially a neo-idealist theory, and to be criticized as such, but, and more widely, it treats the controversy about linguistic relativity as resting on a whole set of problems about language and alienation, problems acute for 'civilisations of the white race' which 'for thousands of years have been swollen with dogmatism and arrogance ... and by now are dangerous for themselves and the rest of mankind'. *Il linguaggio come lavaro e come mercato* illustrates a further strength of the best contemporary Italian philosophy, namely its power to infuse what is often in the Anglo-Saxon world left at a theoretical level with a passionate commitment to praxis. This remarkable work puts forward the outline of a Marxist semiotics which, contrary to many contemporary Marxist suspicions of semiotics as neo-capitalistic, is traced back to Marx himself and his analysis of the commodity. What is the more interesting is that this account is based on a careful and provocative deployment of the work of Wittgenstein in which that philosopher is placed within the wider framework of a critique of alienation. What begins to emerge is a new approach to Marxist theories about the relation between structure and superstructure. Hitherto there have been difficulties in explaining what mediates the two, to which

Rossi-Landi replies with the suggestion that what mediates is the totality of sign systems that now operate in every community and are immediately used, for the first time, throughout the world.

COLIN LYAS

Rotenstreich, Nathan

Israeli. *b:* 1914, Galicia, Spain. *d:* 1994. *Cat:* Philosopher and active intellectual. *Ints:* History of philosophy; philosophy of man. *Educ:* Hebrew University of Jerusalem. *Appts:* Member of Faculty from 1949, and Rector, 1965–9, Hebrew University of Jerusalem; member of the national Israel Academy of Sciences and Humanities since its inception; active member of the ruling party of Israel until 1961; endorsed the socialist and the social democratic attitudes of the regime; when an internal power struggle took place within the ruling party, was conspicuous in siding with the opponents of Ben-Gurion, one of the founding fathers of Israel and its first Prime Minister; led a group of intellectuals who argued against Ben-Gurion's positions, on moral grounds.

Main publications:

Most of Rotenstreich's books were published in Hebrew and then translated into English. They include:

(1958) *Between Past and Present*, New Haven: Yale University Press.

(1963) *Spirit and Man: An Essay on Being and Value*, The Hague: Nijhoff.

(1963) *The Recurring Pattern: Studies in Anti-Judaism in Modern Thought*, London: Weidenfeld & Nicolson.

(1965) *Basic Problems of Marx's Philosophy*, Indianapolis: Bobbs-Merrill.

(1965) *Experience and Its Systematization: Studies in Kant*, The Hague: Nijhoff; second edition, 1972.

(1966) *On the Human Subject: Studies in the Phenomenology of Ethics and Politics*, Springfield, Ill: Thomas.

(1968) *Jewish Philosophy in Modern Times: From Mendelssohn to Rosenzweig*, New York: Holt, Rinehart and Wisnton.

(1972) *Philosophy: The Concept and its Manifestations*, Dordrect.

(1974) *From Substance to Subject: Studies in Hegel*, The Hague: Nijhoff.

(1976) *Philosophy, History and Politics: Studies in Contemporary English Philosophy of History*, The Hague: Nijhoff.

(1979) *Practice and Realization: Studies in Kant's Moral Philosophy*, The Hague: Nijhoff.

(1984) *Jews and German Philosophy: The Polemics of Emancipation*, New York: Shocken Books.

(1984) *Legislation and Exposition: Critical Analysis of Differences between the Philosophy of Kant and Hegel*, Bonn: Bouvier.

(1988) *Order and Might*, Albany, NY: State University of New York.

(1989) *Alienation: The Concept and its Reception*, Leiden: E. J. Brill; first edition, 1963, Jerusalem.

(1991) *Immediacy and Its Limits: A Study in Martin Buber's Thought*, Chur, Switzerland: Harwood Academic Publishers.

Rotenstreich's philosophical works consist of (i) interpretative and critical studies of Kant, Hegel and Marx and their traditions; (ii) philosophical discussions of modern Jewish thought, both in the context of European history of ideas and in the context of the Jewish national revival in Israel; and (iii) the development of his own views (for example, in his *Spirit and Man*, 1963), in which the major role was played by a conception of the human, *sui generis* experiencing and spontaneous being.

ASA KASHER

Rougés, Alberto

Argentinian. **b:** 1880, Tucumán, Argentina. **d:** 1945, Tucumán, Argentina. **Cat:** Metaphysician. **Ints:** Phenomenology. **Educ:** Studied Law at the Universidad Nacional de Buenos Aires. **Infls:** Christian philosophy. **Appts:** Co-founder, Professor of Philosophy, 1914, member of University Council, 1914–20 and 1933–4, and Rector, 1944–5, Universidad Nacional de Tucumán. Held many public positions in education. Director of family sugar cane factory until it closed down in 1943.

Main publications:

(1905) *La lógica de la acción y su aplicación al derecho*, Buenos Aires: Las Ciencias.

(c. 1938) *Educación y tradición*, Buenos Aires: Comisión Argentina de Publicaciones e Intercambio.

(1938) *Población y vitalidad*, Buenos Aires: Comisión Argentina de Publicaciones e Intercambio.

(1943) *Las jerarquías del ser y la eternidad*, Tucumán: Universidad Nacional de Tucumán.

Secondary literature:

Pro, Diego F. (1967) *Alberto Rougés*, Tucumán: Universidad Nacional de Tucumán.

Valenti, María Eugenia (1973) 'La filosofía de Alberto Rougés', *Ensayos y estudios* November: 27–35.

In his main work, *Las jerarquías del ser y la eternidad* (1943), Rougés describes a hierarchy of being based on the various degrees in which particular beings manifest eternity, which he characterizes as an infinitely rich present. He begins by contrasting physical with spiritual reality. The physical world is instantaneous and therefore, he argues, must be described either as merely mechanistic or as merely phenomenal and without being. By contrast, he describes spiritual reality not as instantaneous but as having some duration. This is both the duration of the conserved past and that of the expected future. Such spiritual reality has various levels or degrees of eternity, and leads to a hierarchy of values. Each particular being—including each physical being—manifests a certain degree of eternity. Physical beings manifest eternity the least. The maximum degree of eternity is manifested by that being which is the closest to the divine enterprise constituted by all the hierarchies of being. This being has the highest value.

A. PABLO IANNONE

Rougier, Louis

French. **b:** 10 April 1889, Lyons, France. **Cat:** Logical empiricist. **Ints:** Epistemology; philosophy of science; criticism of metaphysics. **Infls:** Edmond Goblot and Schlick. **Appts:** Professor at Besançon, Cairo, Caen.

Main publications:

(1920) *La Philosophie géometrique d'Henri Poincaré*, Paris: Alcan.

(1920) *Les Paralogismes du rationalisme*, Paris: Alcan.

(1921) *La Structure des théories deductives*, Paris: Alcan.

(1925) *La Scolastique et le Thomisme*, Paris: Gautier-Villans.

(1955) *Traité de la connaissance*, Paris: Gautier-Villans.

(1960) *La Métaphysique et le langage*, Paris: Flammarion.

Secondary literature:

Rougier, L. (1961) 'Mon itineraire philosophie', *La revue liberale*.

Louis Rougier was not quite the only French adherent of the logical positivism of the Vienna Circle, but he was certainly the most productive and interesting. Brought up in the intellectual atmosphere of **Poincaré**'s conventionalism, he was convinced that logical systems are matters of choice, not reports of the general structure of the world. This was the centre of a general assault on rationalism, understood as the idea that there is just one single universally valid set of notions and principles, common to all minds. In his early years he wrote some lucid expositions of the new physics of relativity and quanta and of its philosophical implications. He also produced a massive critique of Thomist scolasticism, taking its central error to be the principle that there is a real distinction between essence and existence: the instrument with which Aquinas attempted to carry out the impossible feat of reconciling Aristotle and Christianity. In his later, much shorter book on metaphysics and language, this diagnosis is generalized and the errors of Greek, scholastic and German idealist philosophy are persuasively traced to idiosyncrasies of the Greek, Latin and German languages. In his magnum opus, *Traité de la connaissance* (1955), dedicated to Moritz **Schlick**, Rougier applies his logical conventionalism to a broad range of issues in epistemology and the philosophy of science. He has written scholarly works on the early anti-Christian philosopher Celsus and more popular, political and economic works of a right-wing liberal character, in defence of liberty against egalitarian and democratic excesses. In the Second World War he played an obscure and somewhat questionable part as an emissary from Pétain to Churchill. Rougier does not seem to have had any perceptible influence on the very limited and localized emergence of analytic philosophy in France, which has come about, to the extent that it has, as a result of direct study of that philosophy's Anglo-Saxon exponents.

Sources: Edwards.

ANTHONY QUINTON

Royce, Josiah

American. *b:* 10 November 1855, Grass Valley, California. *d:* 14 September 1916, Cambridge, Massachusetts. *Cat:* Absolute idealist. *Ints:* Metaphysics. *Educ:* University of California, Berkeley, AB 1875; Universities of Leipzig and Göttingen, 1875–6; Johns Hopkins University, PhD 1878. *Infls:* Kant, Fichte, Hegel, Schopenhauer, Bradley, James and Peirce. *Appts:* 1878–82, Instructor in English, University of California, Berkeley; 1882–1916, Visiting Professor to Professor of Philosophy, Harvard University.

Main publications:

(1885) *The Religious Aspect of Philosophy*, Boston: Houghton Mifflin; reprinted, New York: Dover, 1955.

(1892) *The Spirit of Modern Philosophy*, Boston: Houghton Mifflin; reprinted, New York: Dover, 1983.

(1897) *The Conception of God*, New York: Macmillan.

(1899–1900) *The World and the Individual*, 2 vols, New York: Macmillan; reprinted, Magnolia, Mass.: Peter Smith, 1983.

(1908) *The Philosophy of Loyalty*, New York: Macmillan.

(1908) *Race Questions, Provincialism, and Other American Problems*, New York: Macmillan.

(1912) *The Sources of Religious Insight*, New York: Charles Scribner's Sons.

(1913) *The Problem of Christianity*, New York: Macmillan; reprinted, Chicago: University of Chicago Press, 1968.

(1914) *War and Insurance*, New York: Macmillan.

(1916) *The Hope of the Great Community*, New York: Macmillan.

(1919) *Lectures on Modern Idealism*, New Haven, CT: Yale University Press.

Secondary literature:

Clendenning, J. (1985) *The Life and Thought of Josiah Royce*, Madison: University of Wisconsin Press.

Marcel, G. (1945) *La Métaphysique de Royce*, Paris: Gallimard (English translation, *Royce's Metaphysics*, trans. V. and G. Ringer, Chicago: University of Chicago Press, 1956).

Oppenheim, F. M. (1980) *Royce's Voyage Down Under: A Journey of the Mind*, Lexington, Kentucky: University of Kentucky Press.

Smith, J. E. (1950) *Royce's Social Infinite*, New York: Library of Liberal Arts Press.

The son of pioneer parents, Josiah Royce brought to his philosophical career as the leading American exponent of absolute idealism the flair of a Westerner. Already a Harvard University professor of philosophy, Royce published a history focused on the first decade of the Americanization of California, *California from the Conquest in 1846 to the Second Vigilance Committee in San Francisco* (Boston: Houghton Mifflin, 1886). He exposed the chicanery of General John Charles Fremont, the principal figure in the American seizure of the Mexican province. Pursuing his analysis of American character as susceptible to false ideals, Royce also published a realistic Western novel, *The Feud of Oakfield Creek* (Boston: Houghton Mifflin, 1887). The novel depicts a feud between a San Francisco millionaire against a populist settler over the possession of land. Royce's philosophical idealism dawned early in his career. Kant and Hegel were his philosophical idols, and the problems of knowledge his earliest philosophical concerns. In Germany he attended the lectures of H. Lotze, and at Johns Hopkins he studied under G. S. Morris. The first major fruition of his idealism was *The Religious Aspect of Philosophy* (1885), a work which contains a unique argument for the existence of God as the Absolute Knower. The argument proceeds from the existence of error. Since truth consists in the correspondence of a judgement to its object, and since all judgements refer to the objects they intend, no judgement could be deemed false, so that error would not exist. But error, the discrepancy of a judgement with its real object, does exist. The possibility of error requires the supposition of further judgements transcending the error. Such further judgements culminate in an all-inclusive system of thought, or the Absolute Knower. Royce's argument for the absolute from the possibility of error persuaded few thinkers, although William **James** at the time fell under its spell. Major challenges, most notably in the debate arranged by George Holmes **Howison** at the University of California in the summer of 1895, later published in *The Conception of God* (1997), confronted Royce with the objection that his absolutism swallowed up personality and moral responsibility. Royce's next approach to the absolute was *The World and the Individual* (1899–1900). Based on Royce's Gifford Lectures delivered at the University of Aberdeen, it identifies as the 'world knot' the double-barrelled question: What is an idea and how is an idea related to reality? Royce distinguished the internal meaning of an idea from its external meaning. The internal meaning is the purpose in the mind having the idea; the external meaning is the object to which the idea refers. In the first volume of *The World and the Individual* Royce distinguished four answers to the question, each generating a conception of being: realism, mysticism, critical rationalism and constructive idealism. As a result of Royce's dialectical examination, only the fourth—constructive idealism—is left standing as the sole conception that bridges the gap between idea and reality. The idealist conception regards the purpose in the individual mind as an expression of the same Will that expresses itself in the world. Idealism, according to Royce's argument, further guarantees the reality of finite individuals embraced in the Absolute Individual. To make his case Royce utilized conceptions derived from modern mathematics and mathematical logic, and in particular sought to respond to the absolutism of F. H.

Bradley, who had denied the possibility of knowledge of the absolute. Thus the first volume contains, in addition to the lectures, a supplementary essay, 'The one, the many, and the Infinite'. Hence Royce was a pioneer in the use of mathematical logic in the formulation of philosophical argumentation. Bradley's positive influence on Royce is evident in Royce's use of the term 'experience' instead of the term 'thought' in his later philosophy. Meanwhile, Royce's colleague William James, with whom he had team-taught courses, was developing his own philosophy of radical empiricism, pragmatism and pluralism, and the debates continued on home ground. In addition, younger philosophers, such as Ralph Barton **Perry**, took issue with Royce's treatment of realism, and the movement of new realism was launched. Royce entered the fray. He insisted that his own conception of ideas as purposes was a form of pragmatism, which was tenable only if it was absolute. James's reduction of absolute idealism pragmatically to signifying merely that, since the world is conceived to be perfect, we may take 'moral holidays' had irritated the morally conscientious Royce. After all, one of Royce's arguments for personal immortality had pivoted on his acceptance of the Kantian idea that the finite individual self needs all eternity to fulfil his moral obligation. But Royce retorted in kind to James's strictures. He construed James's conception of truth to mean 'truth' is equivalent to the 'expedient', and he translated the oath of the witness in the jury box in court as follows: 'I swear to tell the expedient, the whole expedient, and nothing but the expedient, so help me future experience.' And he persisted in his dismissal of realism as an epistemology, charging that it placed an unbridgeable gulf between ideas and reality. But Royce's indulgence in polemics did not deter him from constructive philosophical work. In the wake of pragmatism, his thought turned practical. In *The Philosophy of Loyalty* (1908), he grounded morality, first, in the principle of loyalty as the commitment of the individual to a cause, and, ultimately, on the principle of loyalty to loyalty. The relation of the finite individual to the absolute persisted as Royce's most crucial philosophical problem. *The Problem of Christianity* (1913), esteemed to be Royce's greatest work, was his last major attempt to solve the problem. Borrowing from Charles **Peirce** the theory of interpretation as a triadic relation, he construed interpretation to be a cognitive social process distinct from perception and conception, and designated its three terms as (i) the consciousness being interpreted, (ii) the interpreting consciousness, and (iii) the consciousness to whom the interpretation is addressed. Individuals participating in interpretation are bound together to form a community, thereby exemplifying how many finite individuals can become one community. Royce pointed to Pauline Christianity as the exemplar of the principle of the community of interpretation. As individuals have the capacity to extend themselves to embrace common events in the past and common deeds in the future as their own, they are capable of forming communities of memory and of hope. Add to this capacity the principle of loyalty, or love, shaped by the Will to Interpret, and humankind is destined to form the invisible Church, the Community of Interpretation, the Beloved Community. In a basic sense, Royce's last major work transformed the absolute into a community. Royce was intellectually and emotionally shaken by the outbreak of the First World War. He responded, hastily, to propose a visionary scheme of international insurance to safeguard nations against war. When insurance experts criticized the proposal as impractical, he offered a revision that did not allay the criticisms.

Sources: DAB; Edwards; J. Clendenning (ed.) (1970) *The Letters of Josiah Royce*, Chicago: Univ. of Chicago Press; EAB.

ANDREW RECK

Rozanov, Vasilii Vasil'evich

Russian. *b:* 20 April (O.S.) 1856, Vetluga, Russia. *d:* 5 February 1919, Sergiev Posad, Russia. *Cat:* Religious philosopher; critic; essayist;. *Ints:* Philosophy of culture; philosophy of religion; philosophical anthropology. *Educ:* Moscow University. *Infls:* Dostoevsky and Nietzsche. *Appts:* Taught in provincial secondary schools before assuming a low-level government post in St Petersburg in 1893; first won broad attention as a writer in 1891 with his critical study of Dostoevsky, entitled *Legenda o Velikom inkvizitore* [The Legend of the Grand Inquisitor]; in 1899 he retired and devoted himself exclusively to writing; in addition to his several books, he was a frequent contributor of controversial essays on philosophical, religious and political themes to the newspapers and reviews of the day, particularly those of conservative orientation.

Main publications:

(1886) *O ponimanii* [On the Understanding], Moscow.

(1899) *Religiia i kul'tura* [Religion and Culture], St Petersburg.

(1900) *Priroda i istoriia* [Nature and History], St Petersburg.

(1901) *V mire neiasnogo i nereshennogo* [In the World of the Obscure and of the Uncertain], St Petersburg.

(1911) *Liudi lunnogo sveta: metafizika khristianstva* [People of the Moonlight: The Metaphysics of Christianity], St Petersburg.

(1912) *Uedinennoe*, St Petersburg (English translation, *Solitaria*, trans. S. S. Koteliansky, London, 1927).

(1913–15) *Opavshie list'ia*, 2 vols, St Petersburg (English translation, *Fallen Leaves*, trans. S. S. Koteliansky, London, 1929).

(1917–18) *Apokalipsis nashego vremeni* [The Apocalypse of Our Times], 1–10, Sergiev Posad.

(Rozanov's writings, except for the 1886 book, have been published in Russia in various single- and two-volume editions since 1990.)

Secondary literature:

Barabanov, E. G. (1990) 'V. V. Rozanov', in V. V. Rozanov, *Religiia kul'tura*, Moscow, pp. 3–16.

Poggioli, Renato (1962) *Rozanov*, New York: Hilary House.

Stammler, Heinrich A. (1984) *Vasilij Vasil'evič Rozanov als Philosoph*, Giessen: Wilhelm Schmitz Verlag.

Zenkovsky, V. V. (1953) *A History of Russian Philosophy*, 2 vols, trans. George L. Kline, London: Routledge & Kegan Paul.

Rozanov's first and only purely philosophical book, *O ponimanii* (1886), was an attempt to reconcile scientific and religious cognition in a unified theory. His writings thereafter ranged over the whole field of contemporary culture and were prized by many not only for their controversial and original views but for the spontaneity and arresting imagery of their aphoristic style. His influence extended to many Russian writers and thinkers, including Dmitrii Merezhkovskii, Nikolai **Berdyaev**, and Pavel **Florensky**.

Rozanov's developed philosophical outlook, expressed in the books published from 1911 until his death, may be described as a form of mystical theism in which sexuality is glorified. Man is linked with the divine through his generative capacity, according to Rozanov, who called sexuality man's 'noumenal aspect', as contrasted with the merely phenomenal being of his other qualities. Without renouncing Russian Orthodoxy, Rozanov none the less criticized Christianity severely for its denial of the flesh. He favoured the religious outlook of the Old Testament, which he interpreted as accepting the 'sanctity' of biological forces.

JAMES SCANLAN

Rubel, Maximilien

Russian (French citizen from 1937). *b:* 1905, Czernowitz (then part of Austro-Hungarian Empire). *Cat:* Neo-Marxist philosopher. *Ints:* Marxist ethics; critical Marxism; political philosophy. *Educ:* Law and Philosophy in Vienna and Czernowitz; 1934, Licence des lettres, Paris; 1954, Doctorat des lettres, Sorbonne. *Infls:* Marx, Engels, Karl Krauss and Henri Lefebvre. *Appts:* Founder and editor of *Études de Marxologie*, a journal published under the auspices of the French Institute for Applied Economic Science; from 1947, affiliated with the Centre National de la Recherche Scientifique; taught at University of Paris; Visiting Professor at numerous European and North American universities.

Main publications:

(1956) *Bibliographie des oeuvres de Karl Marx*, Paris: M. Rivière.

(1960) *Karl Marx devant le bonapartisme*, The Hague: Mouton.

(1963–82) (ed.) Karl Marx, *Oeuvres*, with Introduction, Notes and Appendices, 3 vols: *Economie*, vols 1 and 2, Paris: Gallimard, 1963, 1968; and *Philosophie*, vol. 3, Paris: Gallimard, 1982.

(1974) *Marx critique du marxisme: Essais*, Paris: Payot.

(1975) (with Margaret Manale) *Marx Without Myth: A Chronological Study of his Life and Work*, Oxford: Blackwell.

(1975) *Joseph W. Stalin in Stelbstzeugnissen und Bilddokumenten*, Reinbek bei Hamburg: Rowohlt.

Secondary literature:

O'Malley, J. and Algozin, K. (1982) *Rubel on Karl Marx: Five Essays*, Cambridge: Cambridge University Press.

Rubel is notable as an intellectual revolutionary and as an authority on and rigorous scholar of Marx's thought. It was always his aim critically to examine developed forms of 'Marxism' in the light of Marx's original ideas and he regarded those ideas as germane and generative rather than as components of a finished and static system. He edited the three volumes of Marx's writings, published by Gallimard, that have become the standard French edition of Marx and he named and was virtually the first practitioner of the discipline of *marxologie*. The list of his publications on Marx contains more than eighty items.

Rubel's own ideas were radical and penetrating. He argued that an organization such as the party was itself a bourgeois formulation and maintained that the destruction of the state as the preliminary to the inauguration of a collectively managed society must be effected by the spontaneous activity of the workers rather than by any such organization.

Rubel perceived not only a scientific and descriptive element in Marx's thought but also a utopian-ethical vision that demanded realization through the activities of the class comprised of 'the most numerous and most poor, to whom Marx attributed the consciousness of this emancipatory mission' (*Etudes de Marxologie*, no. 18, April/May 1976, p. 921).

Sources: BDN.

DIANÉ COLLINSON

Rubenstein, Richard Lowell

American. *b:* 8 January 1924, New York. *Cat:* 'Death-of-God' theologian; rabbi. *Educ:* 1942–5, Hebrew Union College, Cincinatti: 1946, BA, University of Cincinnati; 1952–87, MHL, Rabbi and DHL, Jewish Theological Seminary, New York; 1955–60, STM and PhD, Harvard. *Infls:* Unitarianism, Reform and Conservative Judaism; poverty and non-religious upbringing; antisemitism; the Holocaust; death of infant son, 1950. *Appts:* 1952–4, Rabbi in Brockton; 1954–6, Natick; 1955–8, Harvard University; 1958–70, Dir. Hillel, and Jewish student chaplain, University of Pittsburgh and Carnegie Institute of Theology; 1969–70, Professor of Humanities, University of Pittsburgh; 1970–, Professor, then Distinguished Professor, of Religion, Florida State University; 1976–7, Postdoctoral Fellow, Society of Religion in Higher Education, National Humanities Institute; Fellow, Yale University; 1979, Visiting Professor, California State University; 1985, Vancouver State University; 1980–, Codirector, Institute of Humanities; 1982–91, President, Washington Institute of Values in Public Policy; 1991–, Member, Pres. Council International Religious Federation of World Peace; 1983, Member, Editorial Board, *International Journal World Peace*; 1987, advisory board, *International Journal of Unity of Science*; 1989–92, advisory board, Institute for the Study of the American Wars; editor of various journals on humanism, religions and politics; member, Rabbinical Assembly America; American Academy of Religion; Social Science Study of Religion; Soc. Bib. Lit. Int. Psychohist. Assn.

Main publications:
(1966) *After Auschwitz: Radical Theology and Contemporary Judaism*, Indianapolis: Bobbs-Merrill; rev. ed., Baltimore, MD: Johns Hopkins University, 1992.
(1968) *The Religious Imagination: A Study in Psychoanalysis and Jewish Theology*, Indianapolis, Bobbs-Merrill; Lanham, MD: University Press of America, 1985 (won Portico d'Ottavia prize for Italian translation).
(1970, 1972) *Morality and Eros*, New York: McGraw Hill.
(1975) *The Cunning of History*, New York: Harper & Row; Torch Harper Collins, 1987.
(1983) *The Age of Triage*, Boston: Beacon Press.

Secondary literature:
Hellig, J. (1993) 'Richard L. Rubenstein', in *Interpreters of Judaism in the Late Twentieth Century*, ed. S. T. Katz, Washington DC: Bnai Brith Books, pp. 249–64.

Rubenstein is a controversial theologian who attempts to understand the meaning of Jewish existence without God, whom he considers to have died at Auschwitz. However, rather than suggesting that 'God is dead', he states in *After Auschwitz* (1966) that 'we live in the time of the death of God ... The death of God is a cultural fact. We shall never know whether it is more than that.' Any transcendent meaning to Jewish destiny must, in his view, increasingly be bound up with the security of the State of Israel. He received hostile criticism in the American Jewish community and has increasingly become more interested in the philosophy of global issues.
Sources: EncJud; WW(Am) 1992–3, p. 2908.

IRENE LANCASTER

Rubinshtein, Sergei Leonidovich

Russian. *b:* 6 June (O.S.) 1889, Odessa. *d:* 11 January 1960, Moscow. *Cat:* Marxist philosopher of psychologist. *Ints:* Psychology; epistemology; dialectical materialism. *Educ:* Marburg University. *Infls:* Philosophical influences include Marx and Lenin; scientific influences include Ivan Pavlov and I. M. Sechenov. *Appts:* Taught and held administrative positions at various academic institutions in Russia, including the Institute of Philosophy of the Soviet Academy of Sciences (Head of the Psychology Section, 1945–60).

Main publications:
(1914) *Eine Studie zum Problem der Methode*, Marburg.
(1934) 'Problemy psikhologii v trudakh Karla Marksa' [Problems of Psychology in the Works of Karl Marx], *Sovetskaia psikhotekhnika*, 1: 3–20.
(1935) *Osnovy psikhologii* [Soviet Psychotechnics], Moscow.
(1940) *Osnovy obshchei psikhologii* [Principles of General Psychology], Moscow.
(1957) *Bytie i soznanie* [Being and Consciousness], Moscow.
(1958) *O myshlenii i putiakh ego issledovaniia* [On Thinking and the Ways of Investigating It], Moscow.
(1959) *Printsipy i puti razvitiia psikhologii* [The Principles and Paths of Development of Psychology], Moscow.
(1973) *Problemy obshchei psikhologii* [Problems of General Psychology], Moscow.

Secondary literature:
Alekseev, P. V. (ed.) (1993) *Filosofy Rossii xix–xx stoletii* [Russian Philosophers of the 19th–20th Centuries], Moscow, pp. 158–9.
Graham, Loren R. (1972) *Science and Philosophy in the Soviet Union*, New York: Alfred A. Knopf; revised editon, *Science, Philosophy, and Human Behavior in the Soviet Union*, Columbia University Press, 1987.

On the basis of his analysis of the writings of Marx, Rubinshtein in his 1934 article enunciated the thesis of the unity of consciousness and activity, which became the leading theoretical principle of Soviet psychology during the 1940s. It formed the foundation of the system of psychology presented in his influential textbook *Osnovy obshchei psikhologii* (1940). Rubinshtein's subsequent and similarly influential works were devoted largely to the attempt to integrate theoretically the reflex theory of Sechenov and Pavlov, **Lenin**'s epistemological theory of reflection, and the dialectical materialist ontology of Soviet Marxism. Rubinshtein found the key to the mutual adjustment of these positions in a dialectical materialist interpretation of the principle of determinism, whereby external causes operate by way of internal conditions. He argued that a proper understanding of determinism permits resolution of such problems as the place of psychic or 'ideal' phenomena in a material world, the nature of thinking and the nature of personality.

JAMES SCANLAN

Ruddick, Sara

American. *b:* 1935, USA. *Cat:* Feminist philosopher. *Ints:* Ethics; political theory; feminist theory. *Infls:* Feminism; feminist standpoint theory (Nancy Hartsock), care-ethics debate (Jean Bethke Elshtain, Carol Gilligan, Nell Noddings) and feminist theory and history of science (Sandra Harding, Evelyn Fox Keller, Genevieve Lloyd); also Virginia Held, Alison Jaggar, William Ruddick, Amelie Rorty, Elizabeth Spelman, Joyce Treblicot and Margaret Walker. Mainstream philosophy: Late Wittgensteinian thought, critical theory (Jürgen Habermas), existentialism (Jean-Paul Sartre), relativism (R. Bernstein, Richard Rorty, Peter Winch) and postmodernism (Jean-François Lyotard). *Appts:* Lecturer in Philosophy, Women's Studies and Literature, Eugene Lang College of the New School for Social Research, New York.

Main publications:

(1977) (ed. with Pamela Daniels) *Working it Out. 23 Women Writers, Artists, Scientists and Scholars Write About Their Life and Work*, New York: Pantheon.

(1980) 'Maternal thinking', *Feminist Studies*, 6, 2: 342–67.

(1983) 'Pacifying the forces—drafting women in the interest of peace', *Signs* 8, 3: 471–89.

(1984) (ed. with Carol Ascher and Louise DeSalvo) *Between Women. Biographers, Novelists, Critics, Teachers and Artists Write About Their Work on Women*, Boston and London: Beacon Press.

(1987) 'Remarks on the sexual politics of reason', in Eva Feder Kittay and Diana T. Meyers (eds) *Women and Moral Theory*, Totowa, NJ: Rowman & Littlefield.

(1989) *Maternal Thinking. Towards a Politics of Peace*, Boston, Mass.: Beacon Press, and London: The Women's Press.

Sara Ruddick is a feminist thinker who maintains that women's moral thinking is not only different from that of men but also superior in some respects. She does not explain this difference essentially, by attributing it to women's biology, but rather as deriving from a structural similarity of women's lives, experiences, traditions and practices. The advantages of women's reasoning are, she holds, the preference of preserving life and an interpersonal communication, and the acceptance and appreciation of change or growth: qualities that are necessary for successful mothering. Hence her adoption of the term 'maternal thinking' for her account of structures of thinking centred on relationships striving for peace and development and based on attentiveness, responsiveness and acceptance. For the success of this policy it is, however, necessary that men as well as women should adopt these strategies. There is, she maintains, no reason, biological or otherwise, why men should not be able to do so.

Sources: Kittay and Meyers (eds) (1987) *Women and Moral Theory*, Totowa: NJ: Rowman & Littlefield; S. Ruddick (1990) *Maternal Thinking*, London: Women's Press.

URSULA STICKLER

Russell, Bertrand Arthur William

British. *b:* 18 May 1872, Trelleck, Wales. *d:* 2 February 1970, Penrhyndeudraeth. *Cat:* Logical empiricist (with reservations). *Ints:* Mathematical logic; metaphysics; philosophy of mind; politics; philosophy of science; history of philosophy; (opposition to) religion. *Educ:* Trinity College, Cambridge, 1890–4. *Infls:* Hume, Peano, Moore and Wittgenstein. *Appts:* Fellow of Trinity College, Cambridge, 1895–1901 and 1944–70; College Lecturer, 1910–16; University of Chicago, 1938–9; University of California at Los Angeles, 1939–40; many visiting appointments.

Main publications:

The McMaster University Edition of Russell's *Collected Papers* (London: Allen & Unwin, 1983–) will be the definitive edition.

See also Werner, M. (1981) *Bertrand Russell: A Bibliography of his Writings 1895–1976*, Munich: Saur, and Blackwell, K. and Juja, H. (eds) (1995) *A Bibliography of Bertrand Russell*, London: Routledge. In particular:

(1900) *A Critical Exposition of the Philosophy of Leibniz*, Cambridge: Cambridge University Press.

(1903) *The Principles of Mathematics*, Cambridge: Cambridge University Press; second edition, 1937.

(1905) 'On denoting', in *Mind* (reprinted in many collections).

(1910) *Philosophical Essays*, London: Longmans, Green.

(1910–13) (with A. N. Whitehead) *Principia Mathematica*, Cambridge: Cambridge University Press; second edition, 1925–7.

(1912) *The Problems of Philosophy* London: Williams & Norgate.

(1913) *The Theory of Knowledge*; in *Collected Papers*, vol. VII, ed. E. R. Eames and K. Blackwell, London: Allen & Unwin, 1984 (published posthumously).

(1914) *Our Knowledge of the External World as a Field for Scientific Method in Philosophy*, London: Open Court.

(1918) *The Philosophy of Logical Atomism* (lectures), in *Monist*, 1918–19.
(1919) *Introduction to Mathematical Philosophy*, London: Allen & Unwin.
(1921) *The Analysis of Mind* London: Allen & Unwin.
(1927) *The Analysis of Matter*, London: Kegan Paul.
(1940) *An Inquiry into Meaning and Truth*, London: Allen & Unwin.
(1945) *A History of Western Philosophy*, London: Allen & Unwin.
(1948) *Human Knowledge: Its Scope and Limits*, London: Allen & Unwin.
(1959) *My Philosophical Development*, London: Allen & Unwin.
(1967–9) *Autobiography*, London: Allen & Unwin.

Secondary literature:
Ayer, A. J. (1972) *Russell*, London: Fontana/Collins.
Blackwell, K. (1985) *The Spinozistic Ethics of Bertrand Russell*, London: Allen & Unwin.
Griffin, N. (1991) *Russell's Idealist Apprenticeship*, Oxford: Clarendon Press.
Hylton, P. (1990) *Russell, Idealism and the Emergence of Analytical Philosophy*, Oxford: Clarendon Press.
Jager, R. (1972) *The Development of Bertrand Russell's Philosophy*, London: Allen & Unwin.
Kilmister, C. (1984) *Russell*, Brighton: Harvester.
Monk, R. (1995) *Phantoms of the Dusk*, London: Cape (biography, vol. 1).
Pears, D. F. (1967) *Bertrand Russell and the British Tradition in Philosophy*, London: Fontana/Collins.
Ryan, A. (1988) *Bertrand Russell: A Political Life*, Harmondsworth: Allen Lane.
Savage, C. Wade and Anderson, C. A. (eds) (1989) *Rereading Russell: Essays in Bertrand Russell's Metaphysics*, Minneapolis: University of Minnesota Press.
Schilpp, P. A. (ed.) (1944) *The Philosophy of Bertrand Russell*, Evanston and Chicago: Northwestern University Press.

Russell summed up his work, not always without some reconstructive hindsight, in *My Philosophical Development* (1959) and in his *Autobiography* (1967–9). In 1895 he formed a plan to 'write one series of books on the philosophy of the sciences from pure mathematics to physiology, and another series of books on social questions. I hoped that the two series might ultimately meet in a synthesis at once scientific and practical' (1967–9, vol. 1, p. 125). The first part of this project was achieved, but not the final synthesis: most commentators agree that there is an unbridgeable gap between his writings on metaphysical or mathematical philosophy on one side and his works on morality, education, politics and his polemics against religion on the other. This latter part of his output (see Ryan 1988 for a full discussion) has been far less highly valued by later academic critics, although the proportion of his writing remaining in print must be testimony to its continuing popularity.

His long philosophical career fell into several phases.

(1) Until 1898, he was a Hegelian idealist (see Griffin 1991), a period he repudiated entirely.

(2) Then, he wrote: 'It was towards the end of 1898 that **Moore** and I rebelled against both Kant and Hegel. Moore led the way, but I followed closely in his footsteps' (1959, p. 54). Until around 1911 he was deeply engaged in the philosophy and foundations of mathematics, espousing varying forms of strongly realist metaphysics and epistemology.

(3) In 1911 he met **Wittgenstein**, first as his teacher and soon as a colleague. He had a period of atomism allied to forms of neutral monist ontology, with an increasing interest in language.

(4) From about 1927 to 1938 he spent much time away from narrowly defined philosophy, lecturing and writing on a huge range of popular subjects.

(5) Between 1938 and about 1950 he returned to academic philosophical work, making contributions to the philosophy of science.

(6) From 1950 to his death at the age of 98 in 1970, most of his energies went on extremely active political campaigning.

Russell said that his original interest in philosophy had two sources:

On the one hand, I was anxious to discover whether philosophy would provide any defence for anything that could be called religious belief, however vague; on the other hand, I wished to persuade myself that something could be known, in pure mathematics if not elsewhere.

(1959, p. 11)

It is impossible to summarize common or continuous views in his work; but there are some assumptions that do underlie it from 1898 onwards.

(1) He never moved away from an egocentric, Cartesian stance as the starting-point for philosophical questioning, and was therefore unable to shake off the set of traditional problems associated with the reliability of 'our' knowledge of 'the external world'. Here, he ended in a familiar *cul de sac*: 'the whole of what we perceive without

inference belongs to our private world. In this respect, I agree with Berkeley. The starry heaven that we know in visual sensation is inside us. The external starry heaven that we believe in is inferred' (ibid., p. 27).

(2) He always maintained a reasoned confidence in what he was happy to collect under the title of *science*, accepting its results as data for philosophy, and preferring to clothe his philosophical writing in scientistic terminology ('analysis', 'atomism', 'incomplete symbols'). This preference may have been a reaction against the view of metaphysics as a consolatory branch of *belles lettres* which he castigated in his idealist predecessors.

(3) More important, he always maintained that philosophy, in analogy with 'science', could and should deliver substantive results: theories about what exists, what can be known, how we come to know it. This assumption in his work caused some of its most serious problems, and also set it apart in the most obvious way from both the early and the late thinking of Wittgenstein. Although he shared the early Wittgenstein's use of a language of analysis, a work such as *The Philosophy of Logical Atomism* (1918; very unlike Wittgenstein's *Tractatus*) was deeply ambiguous about the nature of the analytical enterprise, its objectives and the nature of its end-points. The status of his 'logical atoms' was entirely unclear. The whole project was presented as a 'scientific' investigation into what sort of things exist, and how the mechanism of perceptual knowledge is meant to work. Yet he understood that he was in what he himself believed to be the territories of physics and empirical psychology. Russell retained a desire for an edifice of philosophical theory which would somehow explain how the mechanism of perception related to what can be known (or, sometimes, said). Here, his roots in the traditions of British empiricism are evident (see Pears, 1967), overlaid with an apparatus of modern logic and dressed in quasi-scientific language.

Russell's important contributions to philosophy began negatively, with his rejection of the idealism he had read in **Bradley** and heard from **McTaggart** (see Hylton 1990). His study of Leibniz (1900) gave an example for later analytical-historical studies in identifying a handful of crucial tenets in Leibniz, and then diagnosing the conflicts inherent in them. The same procedure was applied by Russell (and **Moore**) against idealism. There, the crucial tenet was claimed to be the 'dogma of internal relations': all individuals are necessarily related to each other,

forming a single Whole. Russell argued for the existence of genuinely independent individuals and the entire truth of particular statements (see his *Philosophical Essays*, 1910). His leap from idealism to a world of separate facts raised problems about the ontological status of those facts, and the relations between a judging subject, a judgement and an object of judgement (see F. P. **Ramsey**, 'Facts and propositions', *Aristotelian Society Supplementary Volume*, 1927, for a clear discussion). Regardless of his difficulties, to him, pluralism was a necessary presupposition of 'analysis' (see *The Philosophy of Logical Atomism*, 1918, I).

Russell's ontological speculations were never resolved. By the time of *The Analysis of Mind* (1927) he had reached this view:

> The stuff of which the world of our experience is composed is, in my belief, neither mind nor matter, but something more primitive than either. Both mind and matter seem to be composite, and the stuff of which they are compounded lies in a sense between the two, in a sense above them both, like a common ancestor.
>
> (p. 11)

Both physics and psychology were built upon 'a neutral stuff' (p. 287). The mind itself was construed along Humeian lines, with 'a collection of events connected with each other by memory-chains' (p. 27) as a modernized version of Hume's *congeries* of ideas.

Russell's paper of 1905, 'On denoting', was the foundation of much twentieth-century philosophizing about language (F. P. Ramsey called it 'a paradigm of philosophy'). The overt question was the 'meaning' of expressions such as 'the common factor of 6 and 9' (or, more problematically, 'the integer between 2 and 3') or 'the King of France'. The question was forced on Russell by his assumption that the meaning of terms was what they stood for (following a model of naming). Such 'definite descriptions' plainly had meanings where, in some cases, they stood for nothing. The essential point of his theory, Russell wrote,

> was that although 'the golden mountain' may be grammatically the subject of a significant proposition, such a proposition when rightly analysed no longer has such a susbject. The proposition 'the golden mountain does not exist' becomes 'the propositional function "x

is golden and a mountain" is false for all values of *x*'.

(1959, p. 84)

Existence was understood in terms of truth: '"The author of *Waverley* exists" means "there is a value of *c* for which the propositional function '*x* wrote *Waverley*' is always equivalent to '*x* is *c*' is true"' (p. 85).

'On denoting' showed how a logical form could differ from obvious forms of common language. But it was not until 1918, Russell claimed later, that he first become interested in the definition of 'meaning' and in the relation of language to fact. 'Until then I had regarded language as "transparent" and had never examined what makes its relation to the non-linguistic world' (1959, p. 145). Although in his final period, after 1950, he tended to play down his earlier work on language (perhaps as a result of his scorn for what he considered as trivial, 'linguistic' philosophy), some of that work had been well ahead of its time. From 1921, for example, there is a passage that could have come from Wittgenstein twenty years later:

> Understanding words does not consist in knowing their dictionary definitions, or in being able to specify the objects to which they are appropriate. Understanding language is more like understanding cricket: it is a matter of habits, acquired in oneself and rightly presumed in others. To say that a word has a meaning is not to say that those who use the word correctly have ever thought out what the meaning is: the use of the word comes first, and the meaning is to be distilled out of it by observation and analysis. Moreover, the meaning of a word is not absolutely definite: there is always a greater or less degree of vagueness.

(The Analysis of Mind, 1921, pp. 197–8)

... and more strongly still: 'For my part, I believe that, partly by means of the study of syntax, we can arrive at considerable knowledge concerning the structure of the world' (last words of *An Inquiry into Meaning and Truth*, 1940).

Russell's reputation is most unshakeable in logic and the philosophy of mathematics. His early search for a solid base of certainty for mathematical truth led him to the view that it was grounded in logic. His *logicism* was developed independently from the earlier work of **Frege**, and was expressed in notation he had learned from Giuseppe **Peano** in 1900. *The Principles of Mathematics* (1903) and the three volumes of *Principia Mathematica* (1910–13, written with A. N. **Whitehead**) remain as treasure-stores of painstaking logical argument: the foundation for modern, systematic logic (see Kilmister 1984). But the cracks in Russell's project began to show as early as 1901, putting an end to his 'logical honeymoon', as he said (1959, p. 75). His interpretation of numbers as classes of classes was underminded by paradox: consider a class that is not a member of itself—is it a member of itself?—if yes, then no—if no, then yes. The theorizing required to avert this paradox cost Russell years of thought, and led to the development of important parts of the technical apparatus in *Principia Mathematica*. Later, after 1911, discussions with Wittgenstein convinced Russell that the logicist project was flawed in principle. He came to accept the view of the *Tractatus* that mathematical statements are vacuous tautologies, not truths about a realm of logico-mathematical entities.

In 1938, aged 66 and temporarily tired by two decades of political polemics, Russell returned to the academic teaching of philosophy. The results—*An Enquiry into Meaning and Truth* (1940) and *Human Knowledge* (1948)—contained valuable work on scientific method. He came to the view that inductive inference cannot be enough for 'science', and moved towards a surprisingly Kantian position that some 'principles of inference' must be presupposed: 'And whatever these principles of inference may be, they certainly cannot be logically deduced from facts of experience. Either, therefore, we know something independently of experience, or science is moonshine' (1948, p. 524). He ended by expressing his deeply ingrained empiricism in the broadest, most general terms:

> such inadequacies as we have seemed to find in empiricism have been discovered by strict adherence to a doctrine by which empiricist philosophy has been inspired: that all human knowledge is uncertain, inexact, and partial. To this doctrine we have not found any limitation whatever.

(ibid., closing words)

Nothing has been said here about Russell's works on morality, politics and religion. These were copious, forceful, elegant and full of wit, but he himself rarely saw them as original. He never shook off the radical, aristocratic, Victorian liberalism inherited from his parents. His attitude to religion was essentially that of an eighteenth-century rationalist.

An interesting angle on the tensions between Russell's many concerns is seen in his affection for Spinoza (see Blackwell 1985) and a Spinozistic strain that appears many times in his writing (most strikingly, at the end of *The Problems of Philosophy*, 1912). Passages such as this, on Spinoza, must have contained some element of would-be self-portraiture: 'The love of humanity is a background to all his thoughts, and prevents the coldness which his intellectualism might otherwise engender. It was through the union of the love of truth and the love of humanity, combined with an entire absence of self-seeking, that he achieved a nobility, both in life and in speculation, which has not been equalled by his predecessors or successors in the realm of philosophy' (review of Hale White and Stirling's translation of Spinoza's *Ethics*, *The Nation*, 12 November 1910, in *Collected Papers*, vol. VI, p. 254). Russell's repeated attempts at systematic philosophical theorizing maintain their interest more from the brilliance of his writing and the virtuosity of his logical talents than from the creation of any single positive set of views that could be encapsulated as *Russell's Philosophy*. (Indeed, it seems to have been fairly early in his career that he realized he was fated to change his mind so often that a lasting synthesis was unlikely.)

Russell is still the most widely read philosopher in the analytical tradition, as he might have wished: 'Philosophy proper deals with matters of interest to the general educated public, and loses much of its value if only a few professionals can understand what is said' (1948, p. 5). His popularity has had one important consequence: his writings may have brought more people to an interest in philosophy than those of anyone else in the twentieth century, and this is not negligible. He himself came to judge his political campaigning against nuclear weapons as more valuable than theoretical philosophizing. Whatever one thinks of that, the example he set for the role of an intellectual in practical affairs has been hugely influential. (Here he resembles Noam **Chomsky**, who delivered the memorial lectures on Russell in Cambridge in 1970.)

The Principles of Mathematics (finished on the last day of the nineteenth century), written at great speed, with a passion of intellectual discovery, must remain a monument to Russell's great logical gifts. His place, with Frege, as a founder and builder of modern logic, must be untouchable.

His influence as a philosopher is less clear. Versions of logical empiricism similar to Russell's varied positions remained popular in academic philosophy in the USA for some time after the influence of Wittgenstein had obliterated them in Britain. Russell's analytical, quasi-scientific approach remained the dominant style in philosophy (but regrettably without his elegance and wit).

His relationship with Wittgenstein has been much debated. From 1911 to 1913 Russell's problems became Wittgenstein's problems. The extent of his intellectual generosity towards Wittgenstein was poorly acknowledged and has not been adequately recognized.

RICHARD MASON

Ruyer, Raymond

French. *b:* 1902, Plaingaing, Vosges, France. *Cat:* Philosopher of science; metaphysician. *Ints:* Theory of values; purposeful activity; biology and evolution; consciousness. *Educ:* L'École Normale Supérieure, 1921 –24. *Infls:* Aristotle, Descartes, Leibniz, René Le Senne and Antoine Cournot. *Appts:* 1945–74, Professor of Philosophy, University of Nancy.

Main publications:

(1930) *Esquisse d'une philosophie de la structure*, Paris: Alcan.
(1930) *L'Humanité de l'avenir d'après Cournot*, Paris: Alcan.
(1937) *La Conscience et le corps*, Paris: PUF.
(1948) *Le Monde des valeurs*, Paris: Aubier.
(1952) *Philosophie de la valeur*, Paris: Armand Colin.
(1952) *Neo-finalisme*, Paris: PUF.
(1960) *Paradoxes de la conscience et limites de l'automatisme*, Paris: Albin Michel.
(1964) *L'Animal, l'homme, la fonction symbolique*, Paris: Gallimard.
(1974) *La Gnose de Princeton*, Paris: Fayard.

Secondary literature:

Vax, L. (1953) 'Introduction à la métaphysique de Raymond Ruyer', *Revue de la Métaphysique et de Morale*: 188–202.
Wiklund, R. A. (1960) 'A short introduction to the neofinalist philosophy of Raymond Ruyer', *Philosophy and Phenomenological Research*: 187–99.

Ruyer's philosophy, in some respects a revival of ideas expounded by Aristotle and Leibniz, uses the evidence provided by the sciences to construct a comprehensive conception of the universe or metaphysics.

In his first book, *Esquisse d'une philosophie de la structure* (1930), Ruyer offered an original interpretation of mechanism as form or structure. But in *La Conscience et le corps* (1937), he abandoned mechanism and presented a fresh theory, according to which every being institutes actions, acts in view of some purpose of which it is conscious, even if in some very ill-defined sense. This seeking after fulfilment of a type, he holds, is characteristic of value-seeking activity; but it is only on the human level that there arises reflective awareness of the transcendent (non-spatiotemporal) realm of values, with reference to which the phenomenal (spatiotemporal) activity of every being must be understood.

Ruyer has developed these themes in many subsequent writings, contending that in any account of value there are three aspects to be distinguished: the agent, the form and the ideal, where 'form' is understood as 'type actually realized' and 'ideal' as 'governing essence'. For instance, an artist, the agent, seeking an ideal of beauty, produces a particular form of picture. All three aspects, he maintains, are united in the idea of God, understood both as the ultimate source of all activity in the world and as the point of convergence of all values.

Though he is little known to Anglo-Saxon philosophers; Ruyer has constructed one of the most important metaphysical systems produced in France this century.

Sources: Huisman; EF.

STEPHEN MOLLER

Ryle, Gilbert

British. **b:** 19 August 1900, Brighton, England. **d:** 15 October 1976, Yorkshire (died while on holiday). **Cat:** Analytical philosopher. **Ints:** Epistemology; philosophy of mind; theory of meaning; Plato. **Educ:** Queen's College, Oxford. **Appts:** Taught at Oxford; served with the Welsh Guards; Waynflete Professor of Metaphysical Philosophy, 1945; Editor of *Mind*, 1947.

Main publications:

(1931–2) 'Systematically misleading expressions', *Proceedings of the Aristotelian Society* 32.

(1933) *John Locke on the Human Understanding*, Oxford: Oxford University Press (lecture).

(1945) *Philosophical Arguments*, Oxford: Clarendon Press (inaugural lecture).

(1949) *The Concept of Mind*, London and New York: Hutchinson.

(1954) *Dilemmas*, Cambridge: Cambridge University Press.

(1962) *A Rational Animal*, London: Athlone Press (lecture).

(1966) *Plato's Progress*, Cambridge: Cambridge University Press.

(1971) *Collected Papers*, 2 vols (vol. 1: *Critical Esssays*; vol. 2: *Collected Essays, 1929–68*), London: Hutchinson; New York: Barnes & Noble.

(1979) *On Thinking*, ed. K. Kolenda, Oxford: Blackwell; New Jersey: Rowman & Littlefield.

(1993) *Aspects of Mind*, ed. Rene Meyer, Oxford: Blackwell.

Secondary literature:

Addis, Laird and Lewis, Douglas (1968) *Moore and Ryle: Two Ontologists*, University of Iowa Press.

Kolenda, K. (ed) (1972) *Studies in Philosophy: A Symposium on Gilbert Ryle*, Houston: Rice University.

Lyons, William (1980) *Gilbert Ryle: An Introduction to His Philosophy*, Brighton: Harvester Press.

Wood, Oscar P. and Pitcher, George (eds) (1960) *Ryle: A Collection of Critical Essays*, New York, Doubleday (good bibliography and autobiographical sketch).

Ryle's earliest philosophical interests focused on problems about philosophical method: what is characteristic of the sorts of questions that philosophers ask, and how are such questions to be satisfactorily answered? These concerns led him initially to a study of the work of recent and contemporary German philosophers, such as **Meinong, Brentano, Bolzano, Husserl** and **Heidegger**, and it is with these authors that his first publications were concerned. But a distinctively Rylean answer to these problems began to emerge with the 1932 paper 'Systematically misleading expressions'. This argues that philosophical puzzles arise from a failure to notice that some expressions, often of ordinary language, are 'of such a syntactical form that [they] are improper to the fact recorded', and hence that the philosopher's job is 'the detection of the sources *in linguistic idioms* of recurrent misconceptions and absurd theories' (emphasis added). For example, just as 'Mr Baldwin is a statesman' picks out a subject and says that the subject has an attribute, so grammar would suggest that 'Mr Pickwick is a fiction' in a similar way picks out a subject and says that the subject has an attribute. But this suggestion, Ryle argues, is false. It is clear from the article that Ryle thinks that those who are misled by systematically misleading expressions are not the ordinary, unreflective users of them, but rather those (like philosophers) who theorize about them, and are hence led to postulate strange existents (like Mr Pickwick, or, more philosophically, Platonic forms, propositions, universals, etc.). What is less clear from the article is what makes an expression *non*-misleading, or 'proper' to the facts it records.

This conception of philosophy is extended, and given lengthy application, in Ryle's best-known work, *The Concept of Mind* (1949). The book is a prolonged attack on Cartesian dualism, which Ryle mockingly labels 'the official doctrine', or the dogma of the ghost in the machine. He argues that the Cartesian is guilty of a series of 'category mistakes'—in other words, that he has been misled by systematically misleading expressions. *Exactly* what a category is, is never made clear, but roughly it is a range of items of which the same sorts of things can be meaningfully asserted. Thus, in a cricket team, the bowler and the batsman belong to the same category, in that they are members of the team. But team spirit would belong to a different category, since it is not a further and ethereal member of the team but rather is a set of *relations between* the members, and relations between entities are not themselves a further entity of the same kind. Again, two citizens who pay taxes belong to the same category, but the average tax-payer belongs to a different one. Ryle argues that the Cartesian has failed to notice that our mental and physical concepts belong to different categories. Realizing that talk about the mind is not talk about a *physical* entity, the Cartesian concludes that it must be talk about a *non-physical* entity, failing to realize that it is not talk about an entity of any kind. In addition to, and perhaps as a consequence of, making this overarching category mistake, the dualist is then led into subsidiary errors of a similar kind, for example in confusing occurrences or episodes on the one hand, with dispositions, tendencies and capacities on the other.

Ryle's positive thesis, which assigns mentalistic talk to what he regards as the correct category, treats talk about the mind as talk about the way in which we behave. 'In describing the workings of a person's mind', he tells us, 'we are not describing a set of shadowy operations. We are describing the ways in which parts of his conduct are managed'. So to say that someone was painting thoughtfully would be to say *how* he was painting, not to say his painting was accompanied by a second invisible process of thinking. It is statements like this, and others with a similar content, which support the interpretation of Ryle as a logical behaviourist. But Ryle's account of specific mental concepts often falls short of his programmatic declarations. When talking about emotions and sensations, for example, he does not attempt to show that in describing someone as feeling a pang, we are 'describing the ways in which parts of his conduct are managed'. He argues instead that one can make mistakes about one's feelings and sensations because the description of them often embodies a hypothesis about what caused them (for example, a chill *of disquiet*, a tug *of commiseration*) and this hypothesis can be mistaken. This may be true, but it does not establish the official behaviourist programme. Problems about the nature of the mind, and the recurrent temptation to think of our mental life as a set of operations performed in a private 'inner' theatre, continued to preoccupy Ryle in his later writings, and some of his subsequent reflections can be found in the second volume of his *Collected Papers* (1971) and in the two posthumous collections of material *On Thinking* (1979) and *Aspects of Mind* (1993).

It was not just in the field of mind that Ryle deployed his conception of philosophical methodology. In *Dilemmas* (1954), he sought to show that other philosophical puzzles (about fatalism, about infinity, about the contrast between common sense and science, etc.) arise out of a misunderstanding of how language operates, and can be solved by getting clear about the proper logic of everyday concepts. Part of his interest in Plato (revealed in a number of articles in volume 1 of the *Collected Papers*, and in *Plato's Progress*, 1966) derived from his ability to interpret Plato as engaging in the sort of logico-linguistic analysis which Ryle himself favoured. Without in any way founding a school of 'Ryleans', Ryle was an immensely influential philosopher. With Wittgenstein and Austin, although in a very different way from each of them, he was responsible for the linguistic method of philosophizing which dominated the middle decades of the century and which was known as linguistic philosophy. Although few philosophers would now endorse the behaviourism of *The Concept of Mind*, its insistence on a priori connections between mind and behaviour would still be widely accepted—for example, by functionalists among others. Even philosophers such as D. M. **Armstrong** and D. C. **Dennett**, who would count themselves among Ryle's critics, would acknowledge the influence on them of Ryle's thinking. If Ryle's writings now seem the products of an earlier era, it is because their considerable lessons have been so thoroughly absorbed into contemporary thinking.

Sources: Edwards; DNB; Turner; WW.

NICHOLAS EVERITT

S

Salazar Bondy, Augusto

Peruvian. *b:* 1925. *d:* 1974. *Cat:* Historian of ideas.
Infls: Phenomenology, existentialism and (later)
analytic thought. *Appts:* Professor, Universidad
Mayor (San Marco).

Main publications:

(1955) *Philosophy in Peru: A Historical Study*, trans.
Elizabeth Flower, Washington, DC: Pan American
Union.

(1965) *Historia de las ideas en el Perú contemporáneo:
el proceso del pensamiento filosófico*, 2 vols, Lima:
Moncloa.

(1968) *¿Existe una filosofía de nuestra América?*;
twelfth edition, Mexico: Siglo Veintiuno Editores,
1992.

(1969) *Sentido y problema del pensamiento filosófico
hispano-americano*, Occasional Publications, no.
16, Lawrence, KS: University of Kansas Center for
Latin American Studies (with English translation
and comments by Arthur Berndtson and Fernando
Salmerón).

(1971) *Para una filosofía del valor*, Santiago de Chile:
Editorial Universitaria.

(1974) (with others) *América Latina, filosofía y
liberación. Simposio de filosofía latinoamericana*,
Buenos Aires: Editorial Bonum.

(1986) 'The meaning and problem of Hispanic
American thought', in Jorge J. E. Gracia (ed.),
*Latin American Philosophy in the Twentieth Cen-
tury*, Buffalo, NY: Prometheus Books.

Secondary literature:

Schutte, Ofelia (1993) *Cultural Identity and Social
Liberation in Latin American Thought*, Albany:
NY: SUNY Press.

Salazar Bondy's early thinking was influenced by
phenomenology and existentialism. Analytic philosophy increasingly influenced his work in the
1960s. His view of philosophy in Latin America is
unusual because he rejected the idea that Latin
America has produced authentic philosophical
traditions, and blamed imperialist domination for
this void. Although many critiqued his negation
of Latin American philosophy, Salazar Bondy

believed that underdevelopment effectively prevented philosophizing.

AMY A. OLIVER

Salmerón, Fernando

Mexican. *b:* 30 October 1925. Córdoba, Veracruz,
Mexico. *Cat:* Historian of ideas. *Educ:* Universidad Veracruzana; National Autonomous University of Mexico, where he received his doctorate
in philosophy in 1965; University of Freiburg.
Appts: Professor of Philosophy, National Autonomous University of Mexico.

Main publications:

(1959) *Las mocedades de Ortega y Gasset*; third
edition, Mexico: UNAM, 1983.

(1962) *Cuestiones educativas y páginas sobre México*;
second edition, Xalapa: Universidad Veracruzana,
1980.

(1965) *La doctrina del ser ideal en tres filósofos
contemporáneos: Husserl, Hartmann y Heidegger*,
Mexico: UNAM.

(1968) (with José Adem) *La filosofía y las matemá-
ticas: su papel en el desarrollo (dos ensayos)*,
Mexico: Ediciones Productividad.

(1971) *La filosofía y las actitudes morales*, third
edition, Mexico: Siglo Veintiuno Editores, 1986.

(1983) *La investigación en la Universidad y las
innovaciones técnicas*.

(1987) *José Gaos: Filosofía de la filosofía e historia de
la filosofía*, Mexico: Ciudad Universitaria,
UNAM.

Salmerón served as Director of the Institute for
Philosophical Research at the National Autonomous University of Mexico from 1966 to 1978.
For a history of the Institute, see Salmerón's
article 'El instituto de investigaciones filosóficas',
in *La palabra y el hombre*, 26: (1978) 3–19.

Salmerón's philosophical projects seek to
employ logic and philosophy of science to clarify
many traditional problems of ethics or epistemology. He is currently working on the papers of
José **Gaos y Gonzalez Pola**.

AMY A. OLIVER

Salmon, Wesley Charles

American. *b:* 9 August 1925, Detroit. *Cat:* Philosopher of science. *Ints:* Probability and induction; causation; explanation; space and time. *Educ:* 1947, MA, University of Chicago; 1950, PhD, UCLA. *Infls:* Hans Reichenbach. *Appts:* 1953–63, Brown University; 1963–73, Professor of Philosophy, Indiana University; 1973–81, Professor of Philosophy, University of Arizona; from 1981, Professor of Philosophy, University of Pittsburgh.

Main publications:

(1957) 'Should we attempt to justify induction?', *Philosophical Studies* 8: 33–48.

(1963) 'On vindicating induction', in H. Kyburg and E. Nagel (eds), *Induction: Some Current Issues*, Middletown, CT: Wesleyan University Press.

(1967) *The Foundations of Scientific Inference*, Pittsburgh: University of Pittsburgh Press.

(1971) *Statistical Explanation and Statistical Relevance*, Pittsburgh: University of Pittsburgh Press.

(1975) 'An encounter with David Hume', in J. Feinberg (ed.), *Reason and Responsibility*, third edition, Encino, CA: Dickenson Publishing Company.

(1975) *Space, Time and Motion: A Philosophical Introduction*, Encino, CA: Dickenson Publishing Company.

(1984) *Scientific Explanation and the Causal Structure of the World*, Princeton: Princeton University Press.

(1990) *Four Decades of Scientific Explanation*, Minneapolis: University of Minnesota Press.

Secondary literature:

Fetzer, James H. (ed.) (1988) *Probability and Causality: Essays in Honor of Wesley C. Salmon*, Dordrecht: D. Reidel.

McLaughlin, R. (ed.) (1982) *What? Where? When? Why? Essays on Induction, Space and Time*, Dordrecht: D. Reidel.

Wesley Salmon is a central defender of empiricism within the scientific tradition. A student of Hans **Reichenbach**, he has ably defended the relative frequency interpretation of probability throughout his career. Beginning in 1971, Salmon developed first a statistical then a causal account of scientific explanation that has attracted more attention than any other since **Hempel**'s deductive-nomological account, which it replaced. He has argued for induction as a legitimate part of scientific inference, defending amongst other things Reichenbach's pragmatic vindication. He has also championed the cause of scientific realism, using the principle of the common cause

as the main inference device. Within spacetime theories, he has advocated the conventionality of simultaneity relations.

PAUL HUMPHREYS

Sanchez de Zavala, Victor

Spanish. *b:* 1926, Pamplona, Spain. *Cat:* 'Linguistic praxiologist'. *Ints:* Philosophy of language: philosophy of science. *Educ:* Trained initially as an engineer, Sanchez de Zavala later studied philosophy, notably philosophy of language. *Infls:* Austin, Chomsky and other contemporary linguistic scientists. *Appts:* Responsible for introducing much Austinian thought to Spanish readers.

Main publications:

(1965) *Enseñar y aprender*, Madrid: Ediciones Peninsula.

(1972) *Hacia una epistemolgía del lenguaje*, Madrid: Alianza.

(1973) *Indiagaciones praxiológicas sobre la actividad lingüística*, Madrid: Siglo Veintiuno de España Editores.

(1974) *Semantica y sintaxis en la linguistica transformatoria*, Madrid: Alianza.

(1976) *Sobre el lenguaje de los antropoides*, Mexico: Siglo Ventiuno Editores.

(1978) *Comunicar y conocer en la actividad linguistica*, Madrid: Fundación Juan March.

(1981) *Imagen y lenguajes*, Barcelona: Fontanella.

(1982) *Funcionalismo estructural y generativismo*, Madrid: Alianza.

The fundamental intuition at the core of Sanchez's thought is that the sciences, including linguistics, form a linked whole. Attempts to compartmentalize those studies, and to treat individual disciplines or subdisciplines as autonomous, impoverish the sciences thus conceived, causing them to fail to do justice to the complexity of their subject matters. In the philosophy of science, this insight leads Sanchez to find analogies of practice in sciences such as logic and psychology, sociology and biology, biology and physics. In linguistics and the philosophy of language, which constitute Sanchez's chief area of interest, the working out of this insight informs both his negative and his positive views.

Thus, while appreciative of the degree of depth and rigour brought to linguistics by the theory of generative grammar, Sanchez deplores its tendency to treat syntax as a fundamental and autonomous feature of language. Equally, semantics taken alone is a mere subscience, dealing with an almost arbitrarily isolated aspect of language. Rather, any linguistic theory worthy of the name must be able to account for our capacity to produce and receive messages appropriate to the circumstances in which we find ourselves. Hence his own linguistic theory he labels praxiology, to stress its attention to the human context of linguistic capacities and utterances. Illocutionary utterances, he argues, can only be understood in the context of an analysis of action. The implications of praxiology are far-reaching, since for Sanchez it is language which differentiates the human from the non-human: 'La esencia humana estriba en el lenguaje' ('The essence of humanity lies in language', 1972, p. 57). Again, it is through language that we gain what understanding we have of being: 'el lenguaje es la casa del ser, y el hombre su pastor' ('language is the house of being, and humankind its guardian', ibid.). The ramifications of the philosophy of language extend through anthropology to metaphysics.

ROBERT WILKINSON

Sánchez Vázquez, Adolfo

Spanish-Mexican. *b:* 1915, Algciras, Cadiz, Spain. *Cat:* Marxist; aesthetician. *Educ:* Universidad Central, Madrid, and the National Autonomous University of Mexico; Master's Degree in Philosophy, 1955, and doctorate, 1966, the National Autonomous University of Mexico. *Appts:* Professor of Aesthetics, Marxism, and Social and Political Philosophy, the National Autonomous University of Mexico.

Main publications:

(1965) *Las ideas estéticas de Marx*, Mexico.

(1972) *Antología: textos de estética y teoría del arte*, Mexico: Universidad Nacional Autónoma de México.

(1974) *Art and Society: Essays in Marxist Aesthetics*, trans. Maro Riofrancos, New York: Monthly Review Press.

(1977) *The Philosophy of Praxis*, trans. Mike Gonzalez, London: Merlin Press and Atlantic Highlands, NJ: Humanities Press.

(1984) *Ensayos sobre arte y marxismo*, Mexico: Grijalbo.

(1985) *Adolfo Sánchez Vázquez*, Barcelona: Anthropos.

(1985) *Filosofía de la praxis*, Mexico: Grijalbo.

Secondary literature:

González, Juliana and Carlos Pereyra, and Lozano, Gabriel Vargas (eds) (1987) *Praxis y filosofía:*

Ensayos en homenaje a Adolfo Sánchez Vázquez, Mexico: Grijalbo.

Sánchez Vázquez is part of the generation of 'transplanted' philosophers who were exiled after the fall of Republican Spain. At an early age in Spain he joined the United Socialist Youth and became editor of its newspaper, *Ahora*. His philosophical work concentrates on the aesthetic ideas of Marx, the relationship between **Lenin** and art, and artistic and literary politics. Sánchez Vázquez seeks to include socialism and art in a broad conception of the person.

AMY A. OLIVER

Santayana, George (Jorge Augustin Nicolas Ruiz de S.)

Spanish. *b:* 16 December 1863, Madrid. *d:* 29 September 1952, Rome. *Cat:* Systematic philosopher. *Ints:* Metaphysics; epistemology; ethics; aesthetics; politics. *Educ:* Taken to America 1872; educated at Harvard. *Infls:* Plato, Aristotle and Spinoza. *Appts:* Member of Philosophy Department, Harvard, 1889–1912; an inheritance allowed him to relinquish his post in 1912, after which Santayana lived in Europe, based chiefly in Rome, and devoted himself to writing (he retained Spanish nationality all his life but wrote in English).

Main publications:

All published by Scribners (New York) and Constable (London). A collected edition of works up to 1940, the Triton Edition, was published by Scribners (14 volumes). A new complete works is currently being issued by the MIT Press.

(1896) *The Sense of Beauty*.

(1905–6) *The Life of Reason*, 5 vols.

(1910) *Three Philosophical Poets*.

(1913) *Winds of Doctrine*.

(1916) *Egotism in German Philosophy*.

(1923) *Scepticism and Animal Faith*.

(1927/30/38/40) *The Realms of Being*.

(1933) *Some Turns of Thought in Modern Philosophy*.

(1946) *The Idea of Christ in the Gospels*.

(1951) *Dominations and Powers*.

Secondary literature:

Ames, Van Meter (1965) *Proust and Santayana: The Aesthetic Way of Life*, New York: Russell & Russell.

Arnett, W. E. (1957) *Santayana and the Sense of Beauty*, Bloomington: Indiana University Press.

Butler, R. (1956) *The Mind of Santayana*, Chicago: Henry Regnery.

Cory, D. M. (1963) *Santanaya: The Later Years*, New York: Braziller.

Duron, J. (1949) *La Pensée de George Santayana*, Paris: Nizet.

Farré, L. (1953) *Vida y Pensamiento de Jorge Santayana*, Madrid: Verdad y Vida.

Lachs, J. (1988) *George Santayana*, Twayne Publishers.

Levinson, H. S. (1992) *Santayana: Pragmatism and the Spiritual Life*, University of North Carolina Press.

Munson, T. N. (1962) *The Essential Wisdom of George Santayana*, New York: Columbia Unversity Press.

Schilpp, P.A. (ed.) (1940) *The Philosophy of George Santayana*, Evanston and Chicago: Northwestern University Press.

Sprigge, T. L. S. (1974) *Santayana*, London: Routledge.

Santayana is usually thought of as the author of *The Sense of Beauty* (1896) and of its central thesis, that beauty is pleasure taken to be a property of an object. It is a quirk of history that the creator of the system of the *Realms of Being* (1927–40), and of its predecessor *The Life of Reason* (1905–6), should be best known for a doctrine he does not refer to after his first book. One of the reasons for the comparative neglect of Santayana's works since his death has undoubtedly been his prose style: a poet, essayist and novelist as well as a philosopher, Santayana preferred to write in a prose which is mellifluous, metaphorical and often beautiful. His reputation as a prose stylist is unassailable, but his work did not find favour with those who believed that philosophy should be written as it was by William **James** or **Russell**.

The major work of the early part of Santayana's career is *The Life of Reason* (5 volumes), an evaluative survey of human institutions from the standpoint of ethical eudaemonism: happiness is the good for humankind, and is best secured by the harmonization of our various interests by the use of reason. Santayana surveys society, religion, art and science, estimating which, if any, of the forms of these institutions exhibited in history have promoted the rational life, and sketching alternative, ideal forms. These surveys are prefaced in the first volume, *Reason in Common Sense*, by an account of the birth of reason, the process whereby the immediate flux of experience is ordered by the mind. What emerges is the 'common-sense' world picture of a universe of physical objects and minds, with a concomitant development of self-consciousness,

and a shift from instinctive action to the deliberate pursuit of ideals. Hence, Santayana says that his subject is progress. He sets out to answer the question: 'In which of its adventures would the human race, reviewing its whole experience, acknowledge a progress and a gain?' (Triton Edition, vol. III, p. 13).

The stress on progress and the dynamic reform of institutions gave this work considerable appeal in the USA, where elements of aestheticism and detachment in Santayana's earlier works had attracted adverse criticism. Interestingly, when free of the Harvard ambience (which he never liked), Santayana developed in the *Realms of Being* a system in which a refined aestheticism becomes prominent. The compatibility of this system with that of the *Life of Reason* is a central issue in Santayana studies.

Santayana prefaces the later system with *Scepticism and Animal Faith* (1923), in which its epistemological basis is set out. If knowledge is that which is beyond all doubt, then the only acceptable epistemology is a solipsism of the present moment. However, it is psychologically impossible to live by such a belief; we have an irresisitible urge ('animal faith') to believe in the independence of the external world, and therefore our worldview contains non-indubitable elements. Further, Santayana distinguishes between existence and being: to exist is to stand in external relations such that these relations are not deducible from the nature of the existent. Being is the ontological status attributable to, for example, definite qualities which do not happen to be part of the existing universe, for example a definite shade of colour. Santayana next proceeds to divide what there is into four irreducibly different categories, the four realms of being: essence, matter, truth and spirit.

An essence is a character or quality which has the ontological status of being, and the being of every essence is exhausted by its definition, not in words, 'but the character which distinguishes it from every other essence. Every essence is perfectly individual' (Triton Edition, vol. XIV, p. 19). All essences are universal and eternal, being individual, outside space and time, and standing in no external relations. The totality of all essences is the realm of essence and is infinite. Santayana insists that all essences are equally primary, although whether this can be true of the essence of pure being itself is a moot point. Some essences are manifested in existence; one mode of manifestation is to be imagined by a consciousness; another is embodiment in matter.

Matter is the only active principle among the

realms of being. It is external to consciousness, spatial, temporal and mutable: all change and all existence (as distinct from being) is grounded in matter. It is the flux of matter which determines which essences are embodied, and accordingly determines the content of the realm of truth. Spirit (i.e. consciousness) is an epiphenomenon of matter. A central concept in this philosophy of nature is that of a trope, defined as the essence or form of an event. This notion is used by Santayana to define what he calls the psyche. Denying all causal efficacy to spirit, Santayana has to find a material agent to determine the course of life and both body and spirit, and this is the psyche, 'a system of tropes, inherited or acquired, displayed by living bodies in their growth and behaviour' (Triton Edition, vol. XIV, p. 324).

Santayana held a correspondence theory of truth: propositions are true if what they assert to be the case is the case, and the sum of all true propositions is the realm of truth. Further, Santayana contends that any fact has a complete description which constitutes the truth about it. Since such a description, however, would include a specification of all the relations of the fact, any complete description of any fact would be infinite. The realm of truth is that segment of the realm of essence which happens to be illustrated in existence.

The fourth realm of being is that of spirit or consciousness. Spirit and body are not two facts incongruously juxtaposed and mysteriously related: they are realizations of the same fact in incomparable realms of being. Spirit is a moral integration and dignity accruing to a body when the latter develops a certain degree of organization and responsiveness to distant things. It is incarnate by nature, not accident, and cannot exist disembodied. Santayana sometimes defines spirit as the inner light of attention, and attention is by definition transitive. An instance of awareness Santayana calls an intuition, and the object given in intuition is an essence. When an essence is taken to be a sign of something in the external world, our knowledge of the object is symbolic. When the essence is intuited for itself, our knowledge is said to be literal. Pure intuition Santayana considers to be the natural function of spirit, to which it tends whenever it can (which is, generally, very rarely). To experience essences in pure intuition is also to experience them aesthetically, and so the spiritual and aesthetic modes of life turn out to be identical.

In many respects, Santayana's claim for the unity of his earlier and later thought is defensible: many major positions remain unchanged, notably materialism and epiphenomenalism. There is room for a contemplative ethic in both systems, though it is true that it is hardly mentioned in *The Life of Reason*, whereas it is prominent in *The Realms of Being*.

ROBERT WILKINSON

Sapir, Edward

American. *b:* 26 January 1881, Schleswig-Holstein, Germany. *d:* 4 February 1939, New Haven, Connecticut. *Cat:* Philosopher of language; anthropologist; ethnologist. *Ints:* American Indian languages and culture; linguistics. *Educ:* Columbia University. *Infls:* Personal influences: Franz Boas, Benjamin Lee Whorf and Leonard Bloomfield. Literary: Nikolai Trubetskoi and Roman Jakobson. *Appts:* 1925–31, Lecturer, University of Chicago; 1931–9, Professor in Anthropology and Linguistics, Yale.

Main publications:

(1921) *Language*, New York: Harcourt, Brace.
(1934) *Selected Writings in Language, Culture and Personality*, ed. D. G. Mandelbaum, Berkeley: California University Press.

Secondary literature:

Lucy, John A. (1992) *Grammatical Categories and Cognition: A Case Study of the Linguistic Relativity Hypothesis*, vol. 1, New York: Cambridge University Press.
Mathiot, Madeleine (ed.) (1979) *Ethnolinguistics: Boas, Sapir and Whorf Revisited*, The Hague: Mouton.
Pinxten, Rix (ed.) (1975) *Universalism vs. Relativism in Language: Proceedings of a Colloquium on the Sapir–Whorf Hypothesis*, The Hague: Mouton.

Sapir was inspired by Franz Boas at Columbia to study native American languages. After graduating he developed a special expertise in Nootka and other Indian tongues during years of fieldwork. He published papers on a wide diversity of anthropological and linguistic topics, all of which reflected his fundamental conviction of the inseparability of language and culture. According to his analysis of the conceptual role of speech, human beings are largely at the mercy of the particular language which has become the mode of expression for their society: we experience the world as we do because the language habits of our community predispose certain choices of interpretation. Language habits are acquired from and shared with others, those others who belong to the same linguistic community. But language habits and the ways of experiencing the world which go with them are shared only with some, not all, other persons. They are not the general property of all mankind: not all people share the same traditions.

Sapir's views profoundly influenced Benjamin **Whorf**, his pupil. Both men were relativists who saw no universal language, just languages. Thus according to the 'Sapir-Whorf hypothesis' (as it is called) each natural language is an attribute of a particular culture; each articulates a *Weltanschauung* radically distinct from all the others.
Sources: DAS; Bullock & Woodings; Devine.

STEPHEN MOLLER

Sartre, Jean-Paul

French. **b:** 1905, Paris. **d:** 1980, Paris. **Cat:** Existentialist. **Ints:** Phenomenology; ontology; psychology. **Educ:** École Normale Supérieure, 1924–8; research student at the Institut Français in Berlin and at Freiburg University, 1933–5. **Infls:** Literary influences: Descartes, Hegel, Husserl, Heidegger and Marx. Personal influence: Simone de Beauvoir. **Appts:** Taught philosophy at lycées in Paris and elsewhere.

Main publications:

(1936) 'La Transcendence de l'égo', in *Recherches Philosophiques* 6 (English translation, 'The transcendence of the ego', trans. F. Williams and R. Kirkpatrick, New York: Noonday Press, 1957).
(1936) *L'Imagination*, Paris: Alcan (English translation, *The Imagination*, trans. F. Williams, University of Michigan Press, 1962).
(1939) *Esquisse d'une théorie des émotions*, Paris: Hermann (English translation, *Sketch for a Theory of the Emotions*, trans. Philip Mairet, Methuen, 1962).
(1940) *L'Imaginaire: psychologie phénoménologique de l'imagination*, Paris: Gallimard (English translation, *The Psychology of Imagination*, New York: Bernard Frechtman, 1948).
(1943) *L'Être et le néant*, Paris: Gallimard (English translation, *Being and Nothingness*, trans. Hazel Barnes, London: Methuen, 1957).
(1960) *Critique de la raison dialectique*, part 1, Paris: Gallimard (English translation, *Critique of Dialectical Reason*, trans. Hazel Barnes, New York, 1964).
(1983) *Cahiers pour une morale*, Paris: Gallimard (English translation, *Notebooks for an Ethics*, trans. David Pellaner, Chicago: University of Chciago Press, 1992).

(1983) *Les Carnets de la drôle de guerre*, Paris: Gallimard (English translation, *War Diaries*, trans. Q. Hoare, London: Verso Books).
(1985) *Critique de la raison dialetique*, vol. 2 (incomplete), Paris: Gallimard.
(1989) *Vérité et existence*, Paris: Gallimard (English translation, *Truth and Existence*, trans. Ronald Aronson, Chicago: Chicago University Press, 1992).

Secondary literature:

Blackham, H. J. (1961) *Six Existentialist Thinkers*, London: Routledge & Kegan Paul.
Catalano, J. S. (1987) *Commentary on Jean-Paul Sartre's Critique of Dialectical Reason*, Chicago: University of Chicago Press.
Cranston, M. (1962) *Sartre*, Edinburgh: Oliver & Boyd.
Danto, A. C. (1975) *Sartre*, New York: Viking Press.
Howells, Christina (ed.) (1992) *The Cambridge Companion to Sartre*, Cambridge: Cambridge University Press.
Manser, A. (1967) *Sartre*, New York: Oxford University Press.
Murdoch, I. (1953) *Sartre, Romantic Rationalist*, Cambridge: Bowes & Bowes.
Warnock, M. (1972) *The Philosophy of Sartre*, London: Hutchinson.

Sartre was a leading exponent of atheistic existentialism, a novelist, playwright and critic as well as a philosopher. He was at one time a Communist, then a Marxist. In later life he developed his own style of Marxist sociology. During the Second World War he was a soldier and for nine months was a prisoner of war in Germany. After his release he worked in the Resistance Movement and when the war ended became editor of *Les Temps Moderne*. In 1964 he was awarded, but refused, the Nobel Prize for Literature. He became politically active after the 1968 May Revolt. His last major philosophical work, the *Critique of Dialectical Reason* (1960) was written, he maintained, to reconcile existentialism and Marxism. Concomitantly with his philosophical work he was producing novels, plays, criticism and political comment. His first novel, *Nausea* (1938), succeeds both as philosophy and novel. His trilogy of novels *Roads to Freedom* is regarded as a classic of twentieth-century literature.

Sartre's early work is influenced by and is also critical of **Husserl** and **Heidegger**. In *The Transcendence of the Ego* (1936) he uses a phenomenological method, derived from Husserl, to describe the structure of consciousness.

At the same time he argues against Husserl's identification of the self with transcendental consciousness. In *The Imagination*, *The Psychology of the Imagination* and *Sketch for a Theory of the Emotions* (1936, 1940, 1939) he works at the borderline between philosophy and psychology. In the last of these he criticizes the theories of **James**, Janet and Dembo, rejects **Freud**'s theory of the unconscious and develops his own view of emotion as a means of transforming the world.

Sartre's *Being and Nothingness* (1943) is a major document of existentialism. He describes it as 'an essay on phenomenological ontology'. Its primary question is: 'What is it like to be a human being?' Sartre's answer is that human reality consists of two modes of existence: of being and of nothingness. The human being exists both as an in-itself (*en-soi*), an object or thing, and as a for-itself (*pour-soi*), a consciousness. The existence of an in-itself is 'opaque to itself ... because it is filled with itself'. In contrast, the for-itself, or consciousness, has no such fullness of existence, because it is no-thing.

Sartre sometimes describes consciousness of things as a kind of nausea produced by a recognition of the contingency of their existence and the realization that this constitutes Absurdity. The realization generates a desire of the for-itself to exist with the fullness of being of an existing thing but without contingency or loss of consciousness. The desired embodying of consciousness is never possible: it can never become a thing and remain consciousness. The two regions of being are entirely distinct and the ideal of fusing them is 'an unrealizable totality which haunts the for-itself and consitutes its very being as a nothingness of being'. He says: 'It is this ideal which can be called God ... man fundamentally is the desire to be God.'

According to Sartre, consciousness, because it is nothingness, makes us aware of the possibility of choosing what we will be. This is the condition of human freedom. To perform an action a person must be able to stand back from participation in the world of existing things and so contemplate what does not exist. The choice of action is also a choice of oneself. In choosing oneself one does not choose to exist: existence is given and one has to exist in order to choose. From this analysis Sartre derives a famous slogan of existentialism: 'existence precedes and commands essence'. He maintains that there is no reason for choosing as one does. The choice is unjustified, groundless. This is the perpetual human reality.

'Bad faith' is an important concept in Sartrean existentialism. To act in bad faith is to turn away from the authentic choosing of oneself and to act in conformity with a stereotype or role. Sartre's most famous example is that of a waiter:

> Let us consider this waiter in the café. His movement is quick and forward, a little too precise, a little too rapid. He comes towards the patrons with a step a little too quick ... his voice, his eyes express an interest a little too solicitous for the order of the customer ... he gives himself the quickness and pitiless rapidity of things ... the waiter in the café plays with his condition in order to *realize* it.
>
> (1943, p. 59)

After the Second World War Sartre began a radical reconstruction of his ideas. He planned the *Critique of Dialectical Reason* (1960) in two volumes, the first to be a theoretical and abstract study, the second a treatment of history, but he completed only one volume. His aim was to establish an a priori foundation for dialectical thought which would justify Marx's transformation of the Hegelian dialectic by showing that rational human activity, or praxis, is necessarily dialectical. He saw Marxism as the dominant philosophy of the twentieth century and existentialism as one element in its structure. At the same time he criticizes Marxism's way of observing society as a whole within a dialectical framework and its neglect of the individual point of view. He therefore advocates the use of the dialectic from the agent's standpoint and argues that praxis, examined, shows itself to embody the dialectical procedures as a necessary condition of its activities: we unavoidably use it, he maintains, whenever we attempt to examine ourselves or society at large. This is the basis of the proposed interaction of Marxism and existentialism that will enable Marxism to take on 'a human dimension'.

Sartre has been criticized for the conception of total human freedom he expounded in *Being and Nothingness*, and especially for the implications of his account of the human being as a solitary individual who is detachable from historical and social contexts (see, for example, **Murdoch** 1953, chapter 7). In the *Critique* he repudiates much of that early position and admits limits to freedom.

Some of Sartre's philosophical writings have, in accordance with his wishes, been published posthumously; most significantly, *Notebooks for an Ethics* (1983), a work that goes some way to fulfilling the promise Sartre made at the end of *Being and Nothingness* to devote a subsequent work to ethical questions.

DIANÉ COLLINSON

Saussure, Ferdinand de

Swiss. *b:* 1857, Geneva. *d:* 1913, Geneva. *Cat:* Language theorist; semiotician. *Educ:* Universities of Geneva, Berlin and Leipzig. *Infls:* The neogrammarian school of linguistics. *Appts:* Teacher of languages, École Pratique des Hautes Études, Paris; Professor of Linguistics, University of Geneva.

Main publications:

(1878) *Mémoire sur le système primitif des voyelles dans les langues indo-europeennes*, Leipzig: publisher unknown.
(1916) *Cours de linguistique générale*, ed. Charles Bally, Albert Sechehaye and Albert Reidlinger, Paris: Payot (*Course in General Linguistics*, trans. Wade Baskin, London: Peter Owen, 1960).

Secondary literature:

Aarsleff, Hans (1982) *From Locke to Saussure: Essays on the Study of Language and Intellectual History*, London: Athlone Press.
Culler, Jonathan (1975) *Structuralist Poetics: Structuralism, Linguistics and the Study of Literature*, London: Routledge; Ithaca, NY: Cornell University Press.
——(1976) *Saussure*, London: Collins.
Holdcroft, David (1991) *Saussure: Signs, System, and Arbitrariness*, Cambridge: Cambridge University Press.
Koerner, E. F. K. (1973) *Ferdinand de Saussure: The Origin and Development of his Linguistic Thought in Western Studies of Language*, Braunschweig: Vieweg.
Starobinski, Jean (1979) *Words Upon Words: The Anagrams of Ferdinand de Saussure*, New Haven: Yale University Press.

Saussure is acknowledged to be the founder of modern linguistics, the thinker most responsible for reorganizing the discipline along scientific lines. Through his *Course in General Linguistics* (1916) he, had a major impact not just on linguistics but on cultural studies in general, the book providing the basis for the development of structuralism and semiology, the theory of signs. Saussure's earliest source of influence was the neogrammarian school of historical linguistics that he encountered at the University of Leipzig during his studies there, although he was ulti-

mately to react against what was essentially a philologically oriented style of linguistics. The only book published by Saussure during his life was the early neogrammarian-influenced *Mémoire* (1878), a work of comparative philology which investigated the vowel system of early Indo-European languages, but his fame rests on the *Course*, published posthumously from student notes of his University of Geneva lecture series, 1907–11. Saussure's primary concern in the *Course* is to outline a methodology for linguistics, thus establishing the nature of the linguist's object of study and placing the subject on a scientific footing. What he is searching for in his enquiry is the underlying structures of language. It is this methodological bias which marks him out from previous schools of linguistics, which in the main had treated the subject historically. The linguistic model developed by Saussure has been adopted and refined by structuralist theorists such as **Lévi-Strauss** and **Barthes**, and through their work and that of their followers has attained a powerful cultural significance. Saussure's most important insight is probably his recognition that language is a system: a self-contained and self-regulating totality with its own set of rules and procedures, or grammar. Language as a system (*langue*), the primary object of Saussure's enquiry, is differentiated from language as a set of utterances (*parole*), with chess, another self-contained, self-regulating totality, being put forward as an analogy for how *langue* operates. The heart of Saussure's linguistics is the theory of the sign, an entity consisting of a signifier (a word, whether spoken or written) and a signified (the mental image or concept lying behind a word). When signifier and signified combine in an act of understanding, the word 'dog' and the concept of 'dog' for example, they form the sign. Language for Saussure is a system of signs bound together by grammatical conventions, and it constitutes the model for all other sign-systems within the general science of semiology. When we respond to a sign within a system, as to the colour showing on a traffic light, we do so according to our understanding of the grammar of the particular system. To say that the sign is conventional is to say that it is arbitrary—one word being as good as another to describe an object, as long as there is general agreement as to its use amongst the relevant language-users—and this has been one of the most contentious notions in Saussure, since it raises the spectre of radical instability of meaning. Saussure himself was unhappy with the implications of the notion and eventually settled for the rather unsatisfactory solution of 'relative' arbitrariness instead. The arbitrariness of the sign allows it to change over time, and Saussure distinguishes between language in its synchronic and dischronic forms. The former refers to language as a static totality complete with its constant element (its grammar), the latter to language in its evolutionary phases in time where change can occur, say in the meaning of a word. Saussure further distinguishes between syntagmatic and paradigmatic relations as regards words. When words are strung together in phrases or sentences, these grammatically organized sequences are called syntagms; when words are more loosely connected (as in the 'association of ideas' mode of thinking), then they are described as being in associative (or paradigmatic) relation. Value is seen to be system-bound and function-oriented for Saussure: the value of a word is a matter of its functional relationship to other words in its sequence.

Saussure also pursued a rather curious theory in later life that Latin poets had deliberately concealed anagrams of proper names in their work, although he never managed to produce any very hard evidence for his belief and published nothing on the topic. Saussure's work has proved to be a major source of inspiration both inside and outside the field of linguistics, and the *Course* can be considered one of the landmarks of twentieth-century intellectual history, particularly in the way that it establishes the credentials of language as the crucial site for debates about culture. In this respect Saussure is one of the major sources of what has been called the 'linguistic turn' in modern intellectual enquiry. Within linguistics itself Saussure's influence lives on in the development of structural linguistics—one of the dominant trends in the discipline—from the work of **Jakobson** and the Prague School (who influenced Lévi-Strauss in their turn) down to **Chomsky** and his transformational-generative grammar. In wider cultural context Saussure's linguistic theories have provided the basis for structuralism, with the terminology and various binary oppositions of the *Course* being taken over wholesale by structuralists and semiologists. Until the advent of poststructuralism the linguistic model developed by Saussure constituted one of the most powerful and influential analytical tools available to culture theorists, and Saussure's ideas have been enthusiastically propagated in fields as diverse as anthropology (Lévi-Strauss), fashion and advertising (Barthes) and even psychoanalysis (the post-Freudian French psychoanalyst Jacques **Lacan** has argued that the unconscious is structured like a language). The standard approach adopted by the structuralist in the analysis of any cultural phenomenon is derived straight from Saussurean methodology: it is to demarcate the boundaries of the system in question, then to set about classifying the operations of the system's grammar within synchronic and diachronic perspective. Even post-structuralism, which consciously seeks to undermine the assumptions of structuralist methodology, such as the commitment to deep structures and to metaphysical essences in general, owes a considerable debt to Saussure since it is his notion of the arbitrariness of the signifier that provides one of the starting points for the post-structuralist project. Derridean deconstruction, as a case in point, relentlessly emphasizes the signifier's arbitrariness in order to back up its claim that meaning is basically unstable, thus licensing some of the wilder flights of post-structuralist fantasy. **Derrida**'s deployment of Saussure in the cause of poststructuralism has ensured that the latter figure remains a significant cultural force right through to the close of the twentieth century.

STUART SIM

Schaff, Adam

Polish. *b:* 1913. *Cat:* Marxist. *Ints:* Epistemology; philosophy of language. *Educ:* Lwow, Paris and Moscow. *Infls:* Marxism-Leninism; also developments in logic (Tarski) and linguistics (Sapir, Whorf), and Sartre. *Appts:* Professor of Marxism-Leninism, University of Warsaw (1946); Director of the Institute of Philosophy and Sociology of the Polish Academy of Sciences; Editor of the journal *Mysl Filozoficzna* [Philosophical Thought].

Main publications:

(1948) *Wstep do teorii marksizmu* [Introduction to Marxist Theory], Warsaw: Ksiazka i Wiedza.

(1950) *Narodziny i rozwój filozofii marksistowskiej* [Origins and Evolution of Marxist philosophy], Warsaw: Ksiazka i Wiedza.

(1951) *Z zagadnien marksistowskiej teorii prawdy* [Some Problems in the Marxist Theory of Truth], Warsaw: Ksiazka i Wiedza.

(1955) *Obiektywny charakter praw historii* [On the Objective Character of Laws of History], Warsaw: Panstwowe Wydawnictwo Naukowe.

(1960) *Wstep do semantyki* [Introduction to Semantics], Warsaw: Panstwowe Wydawnictwo Naukowe.

(1961) *Marksizm a egzystencializm* [Marxism and Existentialism], Warsaw: Ksiazka i Wiedza.

(1962) *Filozofia czlowieka* [Philosophy of Man], Warsaw: Ksiazka i Wiedza.

(1964) *Jezyk a poznanie* [Language and Cognition], Warsaw: Panstwowe Wydawnictwo Naukowe.

(1965) *Marksizm a jednostka ludzka* [Marxism and the Human Individual], Warsaw: Panstwowe Wydawnictwo Naukowe.

(1970) *Historia i prawda* [History and Truth], Warsaw: Ksiazka i Wiedza.

(1975) *Szkice o struckturalizmie* [Studies in Structuralism], Warsaw: Ksiazka i Wiedza.

(1975) *Humanismus, sprachphilosophie, erkenntnistheorie des marxismus*, Vienna: Europaverlag.

(1980) *Stereotypen und das mensliche Handeln*, Vienna: Europaverlag.

Secondary literature:

Skolimoski, H. (1967) *Polish Analytical Philosophy*: London: Routledge.

Regarded as one of Poland's most important Marxist philosophers, Schaff's thought is distinguished by an unusual degree of open-mindedness. He does not regard Marxism as a finished corpus of sacred writ, but as open, needing modification in the light of changing circumstance, and especially progress in science. In his career, he engaged seriously with three other traditions: Polish analysis (represented by **Tarski** and others); semantics (**Sapir** and **Whorf**); and **Sartre**'s existentialism.

Whilst critical of the views of Tarski, Schaff did come to accept that the standard Leninist theory of truth is inadequate, and attempted (cf. 1951) to elaborate a correspondence theory of truth compatible with dialectical materialism, and takes over a good deal of analytic method and vocabulary. Again Schaff considers the absence of semantics in Marxism to be a gap to be filled, and this he attempts to plug in his books of 1960 and 1964. He shows considerable sympathy for the views of Sapir and Whorf, construed not as a basis for 'linguistic relativism' but as excellent evidence for the rootedness of linguistic structures in the prevailing socio-economic conditions. His major positive assertion in *Language and Cognition* is that there are no thoughts which are not linguistic, this assertion being advanced as a synthetic proposition.

Whilst Sartre's existentialism, with its assertion of the autonomy and freedom of the individual, is incompatible with Marxism, Schaff again finds that this tradition indicates a gap in Marxism, this time in respect of philosophical anthropology, and in his book of 1965 Schaff begins the construction of a Marxist 'philosophy of man'. His argument here involves what many ideologues would regard as a debatable interpretation of Marx: economics is always a means, the end being human liberation. Throughout his life, and not just as a young man, Marx was concerned not with 'economic man' but with the well-being of fully rounded individuals. Marxism is a humanist philosophy.

ROBERT WILKINSON

Schechter, Solomon (Shneur Zalman)

American Jew. **b:** 7 December 1847, Focsani, Romania. **d:** 19 November 1915, New York. **Cat:** Rabbi; founder, Conservative Judaism movement. **Ints:** Integrating Jewish religion to German Jewish Historical School. **Educ:** Teenage Rabbinic studies, Lemberg; 1875–87, Rabbinics and Semitics, University of Vienna; 1879, Hochschule für die Wissenschaft des Judentums and University, Berlin; 1891–8, MA and DLitt, University of Cambridge, England; 1911, DLitt, Harvard. **Infls:** Rabbinic tradition and the German Historical School. **Appts:** 1890–2, Lecturer, then Reader, in Rabbinics, University of Cambridge; 1899–1901; Professor of Hebrew, University College, London; 1902–15, President, Jewish Theological Seminary of America; 1913, Founder, United Synagogue of America; recovered the Cairo *Genizah* and edited the *Jewish Quarterly Review* and the *Jewish Encyclopaedia*.

Main publications:

(1896–1924) *Studies in Judaism* 3 vols, London: A C Black, and New York: Macmillan & Co, and Philadelphia: JPSA, reprinted, New York: Freeport, 1972.

(1909) *Some Aspects of Rabbinic Theology*, New York: Macmillan, 1910, 1923, and New York: Behrman House, 1936, and Woodstock, Vermont: Jewish Lights reprint, 1993.

(1915) *Seminary Addresses and Other Papers*, Cincinnati: Ark, and New York: Arno, 1969.

Secondary literature:

Bentwich, Norman (1931) *Solomon Schechter: A Biography*, Philadelphia: JPSA, 1938, 1940, 1941.
——(ed.) (1946) *Selected Writings*, Oxford: Phaidon.

In his *Some Aspects of Rabbinic Theology* (1909) Schechter was the first to give a methodological presentation of Jewish theology. He founded the American Jewish Conservative Movement, which has remained the largest Jewish religious group in the USA and has therefore been of enormous influence. This movement stressed the 'collective conscience of Catholic Israel'. Schechter supported Zionism against some strenuous Jewish opposition. His work on the *Geniza*, including the discovery of medieval philosophical works which have still not been completely deciphered, has contributed greatly to an understanding of that period.

Sources: EncJud; WWW(Am) 1897–1942; WW(Am) 1916–7; NUC; DAB, pp. 421–3.

IRENE LANCASTER

Scheffler, Israel

American. *b:* 25 November 1923, New York. *Cat:* Analytical philosopher. *Ints:* Philosophy of education; epistemology; philosophy of science. *Educ:* Brooklyn College and University of Pennsylvania. *Infls:* Influences include Hempel and Quine. *Appts:* 1952–64, Instructor, rising to Professor of Education, 1964–92; Victor S. Thomas Professor of Education and Philosophy, 1992–, Emeritus Professor, Harvard University.

Main publications:

(1958) *Philosophy and Education*, Boston: Allyn & Bacon.

(1960) *The Language of Education*, Springfield, Illinois: Thomas.

(1963) *The Anatomy of Inquiry: Philosophical Studies in the Theory of Science*, New York: Knopf.

(1965) *Conditions of Knowledge: An Introduction to Epistemology and Education*, Chicago: Scott, Freeman.

(1967) *Science and Subjectivity*, Indianapolis: Bobbs-Merrill.

(1973) *Reason and Teaching*, London: Routledge & Kegan Paul.

(1974) *Four Pragmatists: A Critical Introduction to Peirce, James, Mead, and Dewey*, London: Routledge & Kegan Paul.

(1979) *Beyond the Letter: A Philosophical Inquiry into Ambiguity, Vagueness, and Metaphor in Language*, London: Routledge Kegan & Paul.

(1986) *Inquiries: Philosophical Studies of Language, Science, and Learning*, Indianapolis: Hackett.

(1991) *In Praise of the Cognitive Emotions*, New York: Routledge.

Secondary literature:

Elgin, Catherine (ed.) (1993) 'Festschrift in honor of Israel Scheffler', *Synthese* 94: 1 (includes critical discussions, responses and bibliography).

Meiland, J. W. (1974) 'Kuhn, Scheffler, and objectivity in science', *Philosophy of Science* 41: 179–87.

Noddings, N. (1976) '"Reasonableness" as a requirement of teaching', *Proceedings of the Philosophy of Education Society* 32: 181–6.

Scheffler associates himself with the pragmatist tradition of seeking to overcome 'inherited dualisms of knower and known, mind and body, fact and value, theory and practice, ends and means' (1986, p. 379). Like the classical pragmatists his interests have been broad, particularly in the philosophy of science and education, but including also ethics, epistemology and language, as well as ritual and social policy.

A concern to defend rationality and objectivity against their modern critics is a recurrent feature of his writings. Scheffler's defence of objectivity involves him in rejecting the 'fixed foundation' strategy commonly accepted by the positivists and other apologists for science. He seeks to hold the middle ground between such an indefensible objectivism and the subjectivism to which its critics have felt driven by offering a more plausible account of objectivity. In his *Science and Subjectivity* (1967), for instance, he argues that observation statements, though neither guaranteed nor incorrigible, provide an adequate basis for testing theories when they are taken together with the requirement of coherence. It has been claimed that Scheffler's widely discussed and influential defence of rationality in education 'has ... offered great intellectual and moral support to those who have tried to defend teachers and children from the onslaughts of the educational teleologists in the 1960s, the behaviourists in the 1970s and the reform report writers in the 1980s' (Elgin 1993, p. 25). But he is also known for his defences of objectivity in the philosophy of science against the scepticism and relativism of a variety of authors, particularly **Kuhn**.

Sources: CA; DAS; PI database; WW(Am).

STUART BROWN

Scheler, Max

German. *b:* 22 August 1874, Munich. *d:* 19 May 1928, Frankfurt. *Cat:* Phenomenologist. *Ints:* Value theory; epistemology; metaphysics; philosophy of religion; sociology of knowledge; philosophical anthropology. *Educ:* University of Jena. *Infls:* Husserl, Augustine, Pascal, Nietzsche and Bergson. *Appts:* 1899–1906, Lecturer, University of Jena; 1906–10, Lecturer, University of Munich; 1919–28, Professor of Philosophy and Sociology, University of Cologne; 1928, Professor of Philosophy, University of Frankfurt.

Main publications:

(1913) *Der Formalismus in der Ethik und die materiale Wertethik* (English translation, *Formalism in Ethics and Non-Formal Ethics of Value*, trans. M. S. Frings and R. L. Funk, Evanston: Northwestern University Press, 1973).

(1913) *Zur Phänomenologie und Theorie der Sympathiegefühle und von Liebne und Hass* (English translation, *The Nature of Sympathy*, trans. P. Heath, London: Routledge & Kegan Paul, 1954).

(1921) *Vom Ewigen im Menschen* (English translation, *On the Eternal in Man*, trans. B. Wall, London: SCM Press).

(1926) *Die Wissensformen und die Gesellschaft.*

(1928) *Die Stellung des Menschen im Kosmos.*

All included in:

(1954) *Gesammelte Werke*, Berne: A. Francke Verlag.

Secondary literature:

Frings, M. S. (1965) *Max Scheler*, Pittsburgh: Duquesne University Press.

——(ed.) (1974) *Max Scheler (1874–1928): Centennial Essays*, The Hague: Martinus Nijhoff.

Good, P. (ed.) (1975) *Max Scheler im Gegenwartsgeschehen der Philosophie*, Bern.

Perrin, R. (1991) *Max Scheler's Concept of the Person*, London: Macmillan.

The early years of Scheler's philosophical career were spent in Jena, which at that time was dominated by idealism of the neo-Kantian variety. However the study of **Husserl**'s *Logical Investigations* converted him to phenomenology, which he interpreted as essentially realist in character. In 1906 he moved to Munich and joined an already flourishing circle of phenomenologists. But in 1910 he became a private scholar, having had to resign his position in Munich for personal reasons. This situation lasted until his appointment to a Chair in Cologne in 1919. At the beginning of the First World War he wrote his *The Genius of War and the German War*, in which, like many other intellectuals including Husserl, he saw something positive in war, a kind of spiritual regeneration. After the war, however, he adopted a pacifist position. For a time he was a committed Catholic. However, he never had any time for official Church philosophy, drawing inspiration from Augustine rather than Aquinas. He later distanced himself from Catholicism and even from theism. He died at the height of his powers in 1928, shortly after his move to Frankfurt. His friend and admirer, Martin **Heidegger**, announcing his death to his own students in Marburg, described Scheler as the most powerful force in contemporary philosophy.

Scheler was not a typical academic philosopher. He was an elemental force, a kind of philosophical volcano. The sheer profusion of his ideas and the lack of any clearly defined unity makes summary difficult. For a large part of his career he described himself as a phenomenologist. What attracted him about Husserl's *Logical Investigations* was the attack on psychologism and the defence of the possibility of the intuition of essences. He was deeply hostile to the idealistic form which Husserl's phenomenology subsequently assumed. Scheler's phenomenological realism is distinctive in the epistemological priority it gives to feeling and emotion over 'theoretical' modes of consciousness. Perhaps the best example of Scheler's phenomenology at work is his *Formalism in Ethics* (1913), the work for which he will probably be best remembered. In this work he defends what would nowadays be called a form of moral realism. It is partly a negative work, designed to demonstrate the inadequacies of the most influential attempt to combat subjectivism and relativism, viz. Kantian ethics, that 'colossus of steel and bronze' as Scheler calls it. The formalism and consequent emptiness of Kantian ethics rests on a failure to distinguish between *goods* as things that are desired and aimed for and *values*. Kant is absolutely right in thinking that ethics with its unconditional requirements on conduct cannot be based on goods. But it does not follow that it cannot be based on values. It is a mistake to suppose that what is a priori concerns form only. Values are a priori and moreover exhibit a hierarchical order which is itself a priori. There is clearly some affinity here with the intuitionism of **Moore** and **Ross** (Scheler was familiar with the former). But whereas the apprehension of value is something essentially intellectual for these British intuitionists, for Scheler values are disclosed in feelings. The denial of cognitive significance to feelings, he thinks, rest on the mistaken view that feelings are simply internal occurrences, lacking intentional structure. It would be interesting to investigate, from a Schelerian perspective, how far Hume's subjectivism rests on an inadequate understanding of the nature of feeling.

Scheler also applied phenomenology to notable effect in the field of religion. In his *On the Eternal in Man* (1921), written when he was still a professing Catholic, he describes the essential structures of religious consciousness. Such phenomenological description embraces both the 'object' of such consciousness, as intended, and the various forms of religious 'act' which make up such consciousness. There can be no proof (*Beweis*) of God's existence but there can be an *Aufweis*, in the sense of a bringing to see. In his later, less phenomenological and more metaphysical, work in this area God is depicted not as a preexisting entity but as something emergent in man in the course of a cosmic struggle between spirit (*Geist*) and urge (*Drang*), the two essential attributes of the primordial ground of being (*Urgrund des Seins*).

Other features of Scheler's thought which deserve mention are:

(1) His concept of personhood. A person is not a thing or substance, not even a non-physical thing or substance. Rather a person is the 'executor', 'doer' (*Vollzieher*) of 'acts'. It does not exist as something behind its acts but *in* and *through* its acts. As such persons in their personhood can never be objectified.

(2) His treatment of the 'problem of other minds'. Rejecting both analogical inference and empathy as the basis of such knowledge, he claims that attention to the 'phenomenological facts' shows that we directly perceive the other person's joy in their laughter, their sorrow in their tears, and so on. We can only deny this on the basis of the presupposition that perception is simply a 'complex of physical sensations'.

(3) His conception of the sociology of knowledge, which investigates the connections between different kinds of knowledge and the value systems of different social groups. However, he insists that this does not amount to sociologism, which would have the same sceptical and relativistic consequences as the psychologism so effectively refuted by Husserl.

(4) His notion of philosophical anthropology. In his *Die Stellung des Menschen im Kosmos* (1928) he deals first with those elements which human beings share with animals: feeling-urge (*Gefühlsdrang*), instinct, associative memory and organically bound practical intelligence. As regards these features human beings differ from animals only in degree. The *essential* difference is that human beings have spirit (*Geist*), animals do not. It is spirit which makes human beings open to the world (*weltoffen*) in the sense that they are able to objectify things and view them as they are rather than being wholly absorbed in an 'environment' (*Umwelt*) structured by their life needs.

PAUL GORNER

Schiffer, Stephen
American. *b:* 20 February 1940, Atlantic City,

New Jersey. *Cat:* Philosopher of language; philosopher of mind. *Educ:* BA, University of Pennsylvania, 1962; DPhil, Oxford, 1970. *Infls:* H. P. Grice. *Appts:* Assistant Professor of Philosophy, University of California, Berkeley, 1967–75; Associate Professor of Philosophy, University of Southern California, 1975–83; Professor of Philosophy, University of Arizona, 1983–8; Distinguished Professor of Philosophy, CUNY Graduate Center, since 1988.

Main publications:

(1972) *Meaning*, Oxford: Clarendon Press.

(1977) 'Naming and knowing', in P. French, T. Uehling and H. Wettstein (eds), *Midwest Studies in Philosophy* 2, Minneapolis: University of Minnesota Press.

(1978) 'The basis of reference', *Erkenntnis* 13: 171–206.

(1982) 'Intention-based semantics', *Notre Dame Journal of Formal Logic* 23: 119–56.

(1987) *Remnants of Meaning*, Cambridge, Mass.: MIT Press.

(1992) 'Belief ascription', *Journal of Philosophy* 89: 499–521.

Secondary literature:

Fodor, Jerry (1989) 'Review essay: "Remnants of Meaning" by Stephen Schiffer', *Philosophy and Phenomenological Research* 50, 409–23.

Levine, Joseph (1989) 'Breaking out of the Gricean circle', *Philosophical Studies* 57: 207–16.

Stephen Schiffer is a central figure in the current debates on issues at the intersection of philosophy of language and philosophy of mind. He is a student of H. P. **Grice**, and his early work, starting with his 1972 monograph on meaning, was an elaboration of Gricean or 'intention-based' semantics. The goal of this semantics was to reduce speaker-meaning to intention, and then reduce expression-meaning to the reduced speaker-meaning. Having gradually lost confidence in the viability of this programme, Schiffer argued in *Remnants of Meaning* (1987) that intention-based semantics, as well as *any* systematic theory of meaning, is impossible. He argued that there are no suitable objects of thought for beliefs and other intentional attitudes, and thus that there can be no relational theory of thought. On his view, without such a relational theory, a compositional semantics for natural languages is impossible. His critique extends to representational theories of mind.

PETER DLUGOS

Schiller, F(erdinand) C(anning) S(cott)

British. *b:* 16 August 1864, Ottenson, near Altona, Denmark. *d:* 6 August 1937, Los Angeles. *Cat:* Pragmatist; humanist. *Ints:* Logic; evolution. *Educ:* Balliol College, University of Oxford. *Infls:* Personal influences include Stout and William James; other influences include Darwin, J. S. Mill, A. Sidgwick and Ward. *Appts:* 1893–7, Instructor in Philosophy, Cornell University; 1897–1926, Tutorial Fello, Corpus Christi College, Oxford; 1929, Professor of Philosophy, University of Southern California.

Main publications:

(1891) (under pen name 'Troglodite') *Riddles of the Sphynx: a Study in the Philosophy of Evolution*, London: Sonnenschein; second edition, 1894.

(1902) 'Axioms as postulates', in H. Sturt (ed.), *Personal Idealism: Philosophical Essays by Eight Members of the University of Oxford*, London: Macmillan.

(1903) *Humanism: Philosophical Essays*, London: Macmillan.

(1907) *Studies in Humanism*, London: Macmillan.

(1912) *Formal Logic: A Scientific and Social Problem*, London: Macmillan.

(1924) *Problems of Belief*, London: Hodder & Stoughton.

(1926) *Eugenics and Politics: Essays*, London: Constable.

(1929) *Logic for Use: An Introduction to the Voluntarist Theory of Knowledge*, London: G. Bell.

(1966) *Humanistic Pragmatism: The Philosophy of F. C. S. Schiller*, ed. R. Abel, New York: Free Press; London: Collier-Macmillan.

Secondary literature:

Abel, Reuben (1955) *The Pragmatic Humanism of F. C. S. Schiller*, New York: King's Crown Press (with bibliography).

Johnston, Maurice (1934) *Truth according to Professor Schiller*, Hinkley: S. Walker.

McKie, J. I. (1938) 'Dr. F. C. S. Schiller (1864–1937)', *Mind* 47: 135–9.

Marett, R. R. (1937) 'Ferdinand Canning Schiller, 1864–1937', 23: 538–50.

Metz, Rudolf (1938) *A Hundred Years of British Philosophy*, trans. J. W. Harvey, T. E. Jessop and H. Sturt, ed. J. H. Muirhead, London: Allen & Unwin, pp. 453–74. (Originally published in German, Heidelberg, 1934.)

Thayer, H. S. (1968) *Meaning and Action: A Critical History of Pragmatism*, Indianapolis: Bobbs-Merrill.

Winetrout, Kenneth (1917) *F. C. S. Schiller and the Dimensions of Pragmatism*, Columbus: Ohio University Press.

Schiller's first work combined evolutionary metaphysics with a personal idealism advocating the individual as the key to the riddle of the world. Although broadly within the Darwin-Spencer tradition, this book was teleological rather than mechanistic and, although humanist, it was not naturalistic. Already he was strongly anti-rationalistic, dismissing the Hegelian system as 'the most ingenious system of illusions that adorns the history of thought' (1891, p. 159). Although he shunned the word, Schiller was already inclined to the pragmatism of which he became renowned as the leading British exponent. His pragmatism was greatly reinforced by his personal association with William **James** during his time at Cornell. But Schiller was indebted to a range of British and European sources and should not be thought of simply as a disciple of James. He was part of a reaction against absolute idealism, against mechanistic psychology and against abstract inquiries generally that affected many philosophical figures in Britain around the turn of the century.

When Schiller returned to Oxford, he became the champion in Britain of the pragmatic theory of truth. He opposed abstract metaphysics and wished to see the abolition of formal logic, proposing instead that logic should be conceived as a set of fallible rules aiming to aid the search for truth. In his *Logic for Use* (1929) and elsewhere Schiller applied the Darwinian principle of natural selection to rival theories, claiming that the fittest are the ones that survive. Although pragmatism never made much impact in Britain, Schiller's persistent criticisms of **Bradley** contributed to the waning of idealism as the dominant style of philosophy in Oxford. **Sources:** DNB 1931–40; Passmore 1957.

STUART BROWN

Schlick, Friedrich Albert Moritz

German. *b:* 14 April 1882, Berlin. *d:* 22 June 1936, Vienna. *Cat:* Physicist; philosopher physics. *Ints:* Epistemology. *Educ:* Berlin 1900–4, Heidelberg 1901, Lausanne 1902; PhD in Physics, Berlin, 1904; Habilitation, Rostock, 1911 (concept of truth). *Infls:* Helmholtz, Kirchhoff, Hilbert, Mach, Planck, Poincaré and Wittgenstein. *Appts:* Rostock 1911–21, Kiel 1921; Chair of the History and Theory of the Inductive Sciences, University of Vienna, 1921–36.

Main publications:

(1917) *Raum und Zeit in der moderne Physik*, Berlin: Springer (English translation, *Space and Time in Contemporary Physics*, Oxford: Clarendon, 1920).

(1918) *Allgemeine Erkenntnislehre*, Berlin: Springer; second edition, 1925 (English translation, *General Theory of Knowledge*, Blumberg, Vienna and New York: Springer, 1974).

(1921) (ed. with P. Hertz) H. von Helmholtz, *Schriften zur Erkenntnistheorie*, Berlin: Springer.

(1922) (with M. Rubner and E. Warburg) *Helmholtz als Physiker, Physiologe und Philosoph*, Karlsruhe: C. F. Müller.

(1925) 'Naturphilosophie', in M. Dessoir (ed.) *Lehrbuch der Philosophie*, Berlin, II, 397–492.

(1927) *Vom Sinn des Lebens*, Erlangen: Palm & Enke.

(1930) *Fragen der Ethik*, Vienna: Springer (English translation, *Problems of Ethics*, trans. Rynin, New York: Prentice-Hall, 1939).

(1934) *Les Énoncés scientifiques et la réalité du monde extérieur*, Paris: Hermann.

(1935) *Sur le fondement de la connaissance*, Paris: Hermann.

(1937) *L'École de Vienne et la philosophie traditionelle, Travaux du IXe Congrès International de Philosophie*, Paris: Hermann.

(1938) *Gesammelte Augsätze*, Vienna: Gerold & Co.

(1948) *Gesetz, Kausalität und Wahrscheinlichkeit*, Vienna: Gerold & Co.

(1948), Grundzüge der Naturphilosophie, Vienna: Gerold & Co (English translation, *Philosophy of Nature*, trans. von Zeppelin, New York: Philosophical Library, 1968).

(1952) *Natur und Kultur*, ed. J. Rauscher, Vienna: Stgt Humboldt Verlag.

(1979) *Philosophical Papers*, 2 vols, ed. Mulder and van de Velde Schlick, Vienna Circle Collection no. 11, Dordrecht: Reidel.

(1986) *Die Probleme der Philosophie in ihrem Zusammenhang*, ed. Mulder *et al.*, Hamburg: Suhrkamp (English translation, *The Problems of Philosophy in their Interconnection*, trans. Heath, Vienna Circle Collection, no. 18, Dordrecht: Reidel, 1987).

Secondary literature:

Ayer, A. J. (1970) *Logical Positivism*, London: Allen & Unwin.

Gadol, E. T. (1982) *Rationality and Science*, Vienna, Springer.

Haller, R. (ed.) (1982) *Schlick und Neurath ein Symposion*, Amsterdam: Rodopi.

Johnston, W. M. (1972) *The Austrian Mind*, Berkeley: University of California Press.

Juhos, B. (1967) 'Schlick, Moritz', in Paul Edwards (ed.) *Encyclopedia of Philosophy*, New York: Macmillan, VII: 319a–324b.

Kraft, V. (1950) *Der Wiener Kreis*, Vienna: Springer (English translation, *The Vienna Circle*, trans. A. Pap, New York: Philosophical Library, 1953).

Neurath, O. (1935) *Le Développement du Cercle de Vienne et l'avenir de l'empirisme logique*, Paris: Hermann.

Passmore, J. A. (1957) *A Hundred Years of Philosophy*; second edition, London: Duckworth, 1966.

Reichenbach, H. (1951) *The Rise of the Scientific Philosophy*, Berkeley and Los Angeles: University of California Press.

Ryckman, T. A. (1991) 'Conditio sine qua non. Zuordnung in the early epistemologies of Cassirer and Schlick', *Synthèse* 88: 57–95.

Waismann, F. and McGuinness, B. (eds) (1967) *Wittgenstein und der Wiener Kreis*, Oxford: Blackwell (English translation, *Wittgenstein and the Vienna Circle*, trans. Schulte and McGuiness, Oxford: Blackwell, 1979).

Moritz Schlick was the key figure in the later development of the neo-positivist Vienna Circle. An early exponent of **Einstein**'s relativity theory he was brought, at the suggestion of Hans Hahn, from Kiel to the Vienna Chair orginally created for Ernst **Mach**. At least initially, though, his work shows no trace of the verificationist doctrines usually associated with the Vienna Circle. Schlick's approach also differed from that of his associates in that there was little of their obvious left-wing and anti-clerical politics. Schlick's anti-metaphysical programme sought a more scientific and rigorous philosophy, depending on a logical analytic approach. In this, no doubt, he was one source of the anti-historical attitude that so marked off the neo-positivists from even their hero Mach among their predecessors. In his early work the general theory of knowledge was to be modelled on the abstract sciences, particularly physics and mathematics. It was to be purely discursive, consisting of the knowledge of the relations between things, not the acquaintance with things in themselves, which he regarded as metaphysical. Such purely propositional knowledge was to be attained by conjectural systems of concepts set up as signs to represent things, to symbolize them and their mutual relations, and be verified after the fact. Truth, not rejected by Schlick but regarded as easily obtainable compared with the more valuable generality of relations, is defined by the existence of unambiguous reference to the facts. In this discursive propositional system concepts were defined implicitly by their place in the system, and theory was thought of as a kind of net giving each concept and thus object its place. It thus functioned as a classification of reality.

It is hard to assign the detailed influences behind Schlick's work. He shows acquaintance with most of the empiricists and rationalists among his predecessors, in French and English as well as in German, including the nineteenth-century positivists and neo-Kantians. His system, however, has much in common with that of **Duhem** of the early 1890s, no doubt because of their mutual dependence on nineteenth-century physicists like Kirchhoff and acquaintance with highly formalized mathematical systems. It has also, with its strongly fallibilist tendency, much that would have been more acceptable to **Popper** than the later verificationist and probabilistic theories associated with neo-positivism. Its one feature in common with later neo-positivism is its insistence that analytic a priori and synthetic a posteriori are mutually exclusive, and on the principle of contradiction. The verifiability theory of meaning was very much a later development, possibly under the influence of the Wittgenstein of the *Tractatus*. It is difficult to see how Schlick could have acquiesced in anything like the doctrine, possibly misrepresented by **Ayer**, that meaningful sentences were logical constructions out of sense data. For if sense data are genuine sensations, signs could never be logical constructions of what they signify, and if not, it remains unclear how concepts and propositions do in fact represent the actual sensations.

Sources: Metzler; H. Feigl (1937) in *Erkenntnis* 7: 393–419; P. Frank (1949) *Modern Science and its Philosophy*, Cambridge, Mass.: Harvard UP; Ziegenfuss & Jung; NöB, 19: 120–8; DSB 1975: 177a–179b (bibliography).

R. N. D. MARTIN

Schmitt, Charles Bernard

American. **b:** 4 August 1933, Louisville, Kentucky. **d:** 15 April 1986, Padua, Italy. **Cat:** Historian of philosophy and science. **Ints:** Renaissance and early modern philosophy; science; universities. **Educ:** PhD, Columbia University, 1963. **Infls:** Kristeller. **Appts:** Fordham University, New York; University of California at Los Angeles; University of Leeds, 1967–73; University of London, Warburg Insitute, 1973–86.

Main publications:

(1971) *A Critical Survey and Bibliography of Studies on Renaissance Aristotelianism*, Padua: Antenore.

(1972) *Cicero Scepticus*, The Hague: Martinus Nijhoff.

(1980) *Cesare Cremonini, un Aristotelico al Tempo di Galilei*, Venezia: Centro Tedesci du Studi Veneziani.

(1981) *Studies in Renaissance Philosophy and Science*, London: Variorum.

(1981–6) (ed.) *History of Universities*, Amersham: Avebury; Oxford: Open University Press.

(1982) (ed. with W. F. Ryan) *Pseudo-Aristotle, the Secret of Secrets, Sources and Influences*, London: Warburg Institute.

(1983) *John Case and Aristotelianism in Renaissance England*, Kingston and McGill: McGill-Queens University Press.

(1983) *Aristotle and the Renaissance*, Cambridge, Mass.: Harvard University Press.

(1984) *The Aristotelian Tradition and the Renaissance*, London: Variorum.

(1985) *Gianfrancesco Pico della Mirandola*, The Hague: Martinus Nijhoff.

(1985) (with D. Knox) *Pseudo-Aristoteles Latinus*, London: Warburg Institute.

(1986) *Pseudo-Aristotle in the Middle Ages*, London: Warburg.

(1987) (with others) *The Cambridge History of Renaissance Philosophy*, Cambridge: Cambridge University Press.

(1987) (with R. H. Popkin) *Scepticism from the Renaissance to the Enlightenment*, Wiesbaden: Harrassowitz.

(1989) *Reappraisals in Renaissance Thought*, ed. C. Webster, London: Variorum.

(1992) (with B. P. Copenhaver) *Renaissance Philosophy*, Oxford: Oxford University Press.

Secondary literature:

Henry, J. and Hutton, S. (1990) *New Perspectives on Renaissance Thought*, London: Duckworth (a collection of papers largely deriving from a memorial symposium covering most of Schmitt's interests and with a bibliography of his writings by C. Blackwell).

Popkin, R. H. (1993) 'The role of scepticism in modern philosophy reconsidered', *Journal of the History of Philosophy* 31: 501–17.

Charles Schmitt was an intellectual historian with wide interests, whose early thorough bibliographic approach to the history of philosophy in the Renaissance broadened during his time at Leeds to include the history of science and the wider historical context, as well as periods like the seventeenth century, usually regarded as falling outside the Renaissance period. His early bibliographic concern led him to examine in particular the syllabuses of Renaissance and later universities, from which he concluded (i) that Renaissance universities were not the sterile places of humanist legend, and (ii) that Aristotelianism was not the spent force it is often been alleged to have been. For him the dominant feature of the Renaissance was less the Platonizing humanism that attracted the attention of his predecessors, but Aristotelianism, which, he believed, retained its vitality until the late seventeenth century when Aristotelians ceased to listen to modern thinkers. Equally, he had drawn attention to the importance of the systematic study of the development of universities. He also came to the view that the conventional periodization of the Renaissance was too narrow. He saw a Latin-based international *res publica litterarum* lasting from the late Middle Ages to the end of the seventeenth century, when the increasing use of vernacular languages cut off from each other the intellectuals using them. He also ranks as one the most important supporters of R. H. **Popkin**'s campaign to have scepticism recognized as a serious historical phenomenon with far-reaching effects in the seventeenth century and after.

Sources: Biographical pieces in Schmitt 1987 and in Henry Hutton 1990; personal communication.

R. N. D. MARTIN

Scholem, Gershom (Gerhard)

Israeli. *b:* 5 December, 1897, Berlin. *d:* 20 February 1982, Jerusalem. *Cat:* Historian of religion; philosopher; translator; librarian. *Ints:* Jewish mysticism and messianism. *Educ:* 1915–17, Berlin; 1917–18, Jena; 1918–19, Berne; 1922, PhD, Munich; changed from Maths and Philosophy to Oriental Languages; his PhD was a translation of, and commentary on, the *Sefer ha-Bahir*, the earliest extant kabbalistic text. *Infls:* The German critico-historical tradition and Zionist philosophy. Personal influences: poets Haim Bialik and Shmuel Agnon; Martin Buber, Hermann Cohen, Judah Magnes, Walter Benjamin, Yitzhak Baer, Shmuel H. Berman, Julius Guttman, Gustav Landauer, Franz Rosenzweig and Ernst A. Simon. *Appts:* 1923–82, Head of Department of Hebraica and Judaica, University Library, Lecturer, Professor, Jewish Mysticism, Emeritus Professor and then Dean, Hebrew University, Jerusalem; 1938, 1949, Visiting Professor, Jewish Institute of Religion, New York; 1956–7, Brown University, Providence, Rhode Island; 1962–8,

Vice President and 1968–82, President, Israel National Academy of Science and Humanities; State Prize of Israel, 1958; Rothschild Prize, 1962; Honorary doctorate, Hebrew Union College and Jewish Institute of Religion, New York; 1988, exhibition, 'Gershom Shalom', Hebrew University, Jerusalem; The Gershom Scholem Centre, Hebrew University, Jerusalem, Ramat Gan.

Main publications:

(1923) *Das Buch Bahir*, Leipzig: Drugulin (based on PhD, 1922); Berlin: Schocken, 1933, Darmstadt: Wissenschaftliche Buchgesellschaft, 1970.

(1925) *Alchemie und Kabbala*, Breslau: Schatzky.

(1941) *Major Trends in Jewish Mysticism*; Jerusalem: Schocken, and New York: Schocken, 1946, London: Thames & Hudson, 1955, Schocken, 1961.

(1960) *Jewish Gnosticism, Merkabah Mysticism and Talmudic Tradition*, New York: Jewish Theological Seminary of America; new edns 1965 and 1968.

(1960) *Zur Kabbala and ihrer Symbolik*, Zurich: Rhein-Verlag (English translation, *On the Kabbalah and Its Symbolism*, trans. Ralph Mannheim, London: Routledge & Kegan Paul, and New York: Schocken, 1965, 1969).

(1962) *Ursprung und Anfänge der Kabbala*, Berlin: De Gruyter (English translation, *Origins of the Kabbala*, Princeton, NJ: Princeton University Press, 1987).

(1971) *The Messianic Idea in Judaism and Other Essays on Jewish Spirituality*; London: Allen & Unwin, and New York: Schocken, 1989.

(1974) *Kabbalah*, Jerusalem: Keter, and New York: Quadrangle.

(1976) *On Jews and Judaism in Crisis: Selected Essays*, New York: Schocken.

(1987–8) *Collected Works: Kitvei Gershom Shalom*, Jerusalem: Magnes.

Secondary literature:

Alter, R. (1991) *Necessary Angels*, Cambridge, Mass.: Harvard University Press.

Biale, David (1979) *Gershom Scholem: Kabbalah and Counter-History*, Cambridge, Mass.: Harvard University Press.

——(1993) 'Gershom Scholem' in *Interpreters of Judaism in the Late Twentieth Century*, ed. S. T. Katz, Washington, DC: Bnai Brith, pp. 265–79 (includes bibliography).

Bouganim, A. (1990) *Le Juif Égaré*, Paris: Desclée de Brouwer.

Catane, M. (1977) *Bibliografiah shel kitvei-Gershom Scholem*, Jerusalem: Magnes (includes bibliography).

Dan, Joseph (1987) *Gershom Scholem and the Mystical Dimension of Jewish History*, New York: New York University Press.

Exhibition, 'Gershom Shalom', Hebrew University, Jerusalem.

Finkelstein, N. (1992) *The Ritual of New Creation*, Albany: SUNY Press.

Handelman, Susan (1991) *Fragments of Redemption: Jewish Thought & Literary Theory in Benjamin, Scholem & Lévinas*, Bloomington: Indiana University Press (includes bibliography).

Luz, E. (1989) 'Rabbi Kook and G. Scholem: Zionism as a dialectical movement', in 'Spiritual and anti-spiritual trends in Zionism', in *Jewish Spirituality II*, ed. A. Green, New York: Crossroad, pp. 392–5.

Mendes-Flohr, Paul (1989) 'Law and sacrament: ritual observance in twentieth-century Jewish thought', in Green, ibid, pp. 320–2.

Schweid, Eliezer (1983) *Mistikah ve-Yadut lefi-Gershom Shalom*, Jerusalem: Magnes (English translation, *Judaism and Mysticism according to Gershom Scholem*, Atlanta: Scholars Press, 1985).

Urbach, E. E., Werblowsky, R. J. Z. and Wirszubski, C. (eds) (1965) *Studies in Mysticism and Religion Presented to Gershom G. Scholem on his Seventieth Birthday*, Jerusalem: Magnes.

Scholem was the originator of the modern critico-historical study of Jewish mysticism and it was he, more than anyone, who made it a respectable subject of academic study. Some of his theories on the role of Gnosticism and the importance of history in the development of mystical and messianic trends in Judaism have been challenged, especially by **Idel** (*Kabbalah, New Perspectives*, Yale 1988) who prefers a more phenomenological approach. Schweid (1983), has criticized Scholem's denigration of the Hebrew Bible, *Halakhah* (Jewish Law) and Jewish philosophy. Both Handelman (1991) and Biale (1993) have offered psychological reasons for Scholem's approach. However, in stressing a side of Judaism which had previously been rejected by scholars, Scholem performed a service of great magnitude. He has influenced literary theorists and has made Jewish ideas more accessible to the general public by his pluralistic approach.

Sources: EncJud; Schoeps.

IRENE LANCASTER

Scholz, Heinrich

German. *b:* 1884, Berlin. *d:* 1956. *Cat:* Theologian; logician. *Ints:* Philosophy of mathematics. *Educ:* Universities of Berlin and Erlangen. *Infls:* The

Platonist tradition; L. Couturat, J. Lukasiewicz, A. N. Whitehead and B. Russell. *Appts:* Professor of Systematic Theology and Philosophy of Religion, University of Breslau, 1917–19; Professor of Philosophy, University of Kiel, 1919–56.

Main publications:

(1911) *Glaube und Unglaube in der Weltgeschichte*, Leipzig.

(1921) *Die Religionsphilosophie des Als-ob*, Leipzig.

(1961) *Mathesis Universalis*, ed. H. Hermes, F. Kambartel and J. Ritter, Basel and Stuttgart (an anthology with a bibliography).

(1961) *Concise History of Logic*, New York: Philosophical Library.

Secondary literature:

Fallenstein, M. (1981) *Religion als philosophisches Problem*, Frankfurt am Main: Peter Lang.

Stock, Eberhard (1987) *Die Konzeption einer Metaphysik im Denken vom Heinrich Scholz*, Berlin: Walter de Gruyter.

Setting his face against subjectivism and existentialism—for the question of truth could not be raised if their methods were allowed—Scholz went in quest of the foundations of universal knowledge. He made extensive studies of the histories of logic, mathematics and science, and was convinced that the axiomatic method alone would yield fruitful results. He scrutinized Leibniz's doctrines of identity and possibility, wrote on classical and scholastic philosophers and, while valuing the contribution of **Carnap** and the Vienna Circle, considered that Platonism yielded stronger theoretical constructions than positivism. He developed a '**Russell**-revised Platonism' to serve as the ontological foundation of mathematics. His work was not readily accessible to 'the intelligent philosophical layman', and even most metaphysicians—perhaps chilled by Scholz's insistence that mathematical logic is indispensable to metaphysics—managed to ignore it.

Sources: Edwards.

ALAN SELL

Schrödinger, Erwin

Austrian. *b:* 12 August 1887, Vienna. *d:* 4 January 1961, Alpbach, Austria. *Cat:* Theoretical physicist. *Ints:* Atomic physics; the science of life. *Educ:* Vienna 1906–10. *Infls:* Spinoza, L. Boltzmann, F. Exner, F. Hasenöhrl, E. von Schweidler, Einstein, Planck, L. de Broglie. *Appts:* University of Vienna, 1910–4 and 1918–20; Jena, 1920; Professor, Stuttgart, 1920; Breslau, 1920; Zurich, 1920–7;

Berlin, 1927–33; Oxford, 1933–6; Graz, 1936–8; Gent, 1938–9; Dublin Institute of Advanced Studies, 1939–56; Vienna, 1956–8; Nobel Prize, 1933; Royal Society, 1949; German Order, Pour le Mérite, 1957; Austrian Medal for Arts and Sciences, 1957.

Main publications:

(1932) *Über Indeterminismus in der Physik*, Leipzig: J. A. Barth.
(1935) *Science and the Human Temperament*, London: Allen & Unwin.
(1944) *What is Life?*, Cambridge: Cambridge University Press (1992 edition includes *Mind and Matter* and *Autobiographical Sketches*).
(1951) *Naturwissenschaft und Humanismus*, Vienna: F. Deuticke (English translation, *Science and Humanism*, trans. J. Murphy, Cambridge: Cambridge University Press, 1951).
(1954) *Nature and the Greeks*, Cambridge: Cambridge University Press.
(1956) *Expanding Universes*, Cambridge: Cambridge University Press.
(1957) *Science, Theory and Man*, New York: Dover.
(1958) *Mind and Matter*, Cambridge: Cambridge University Press.
(1961) (with W. Heisenberg and M. Born) *On Modern Physics*, London: Orion Press.
(1961) *Meine Weltansicht*, Hamburg: Zsolnay (English translation, *My View of the World*, trans. Hastings, Cambridge: Cambridge University Press, 1964).
(1963) *Die Wellenmechanik*, Stuttgart: Battenberg (includes biography by Hermann and bibliography by Koch).
(1963) *Schrödinger, Einstein, Lorentz, Briefe zur Wellenmechanik*, ed. Przibram, Vienna: Springer (English translation, *Letters on Wave Mechanics*, New York: Philosophical Library, 1967).

Secondary literature:

Gribben, J. (1985) *In Search of Schrödinger's Cat*, Hounslow: Wildwood House.
Jammer, M. (1966) *The Conceptual Development of the Quantum Theory*, New York: McGraw-Hill.
Kilmister, C. W. (ed.) (1987) *Schrödinger Centenary*, Cambridge: Cambridge University Press.
Klein, M. J. (1964) 'Einstein and the wave-particle duality', *Natural Philosopher* 3: 1–49.
Moore, W. J. (1989) *Schrödinger: A Life of Thought*, Cambridge: Cambridge University Press.
Olby, R. (1971) 'Schrödinger's problem', *Journal of the History of Biology* 4: 119–48.

Schrödinger was the prime originator of the wave mechanical interpretation of the quantum theory

on the lead of Louis de **Broglie** who first suggested that matter was really a system of waves. Schrödinger saw in this the prospect of a universal wave theory of matter on the analogy of that for light. Just as the classical theory of light was at best an approximation to the more accurate wave theory, so he hoped that the new wave mechanics would turn out to be the fundamental theory of which classical mechanics was an imprecise rendering only holding good at short wavelengths. He was thus opposed to the statistical interpretation of the new quantum theory developed by Max **Born** and in sympathy with **Einstein**'s attempts to refute it. He also attempted to pursue Einstein's programme of a unified field theory including all the forces of matter. Interested in physicalistic theories of life, he saw the success of the new quantum mechanics in providing a rationale for the stability of chemical molecules, the prospect for a like explanation of life, and in this proved an inspiration to later generations of molecular biologists.

Sources: W. Heitler (1961) 'Erwin Schrödinger', *BMFRS* 7: 221–8 (bibliography); W. T. Scott (1967) *Erwin Schrödinger*, Amherst, Mass.: Univ. of Mass. Press (bibliography); DSB 1975: 217b–223b.

R. N. D. MARTIN

Schubert-Soldern, Richard von

Czech. *b:* 1852, Prague. *d:* 1935. *Cat:* Immanentist. *Ints:* Metaphysics; epistemology. *Infls:* Avenarius and Schuppe. *Appts:* Professor of Philosophy and Privatdozent in Leipzig, and later at the Gymnasium in Görz.

Main publications:

(1882) *Über Transzendenz des Objekts und des Subjekts.*
(1884) *Grundlagen einer Erkenntnistheorie.*
(1887) *Reproduktion, Gefühl und Wille.*
(1887) *Grundlagen zu einer Ethik.*
(1896) *Über den Begriff der allgemeinen Bildung.*
(1896) *Das menschliche Glück und die soziale Frage.*
(1905) *Die menschliche Erziehung.*

Secondary literature:

Lamers, R. W. T. (1990) *Richard von Schubert-Solderns Philosophie des erkenntnistheoretischen Solipsismus*, Frankfurt: Peter Lang.

Schubert-Soldern was effectively a follower of Schuppe, to whom he owed an extensive debt and whose philosophy of immanence he largely adopted, adding to it some ideas from the 'philosophy of pure experience' or empiriocriticism of Avenarius. Existence is predicable only of the contents of consciousness, and no object may be characterized as existent except in so far as it is such a content. Further, consciousness itself is not an entity of a different class from its contents, but is identical with the conjunction of contents. This entails not that only 'I' exist but rather that only my conscious contents exist (so to speak). No contents can be properly interpreted as evidence for the existence of an external world. Schubert-Soldern described this philosophy as 'gnoseological solipsism'.

ROBERT WILKINSON

Schurman, Jacob Gould

Canadian-American. **b:** 22 May 1854, Freetown, Prince Edward Island. **d:** 12 August 1942, New York. **Cat:** Idealist. **Ints:** Science; ethics; evolution; philosophy of religion. **Educ:** Prince of Wales College, Charlottetown, P.E.I., 1870–2; Acadia University, Wolfville, Nova Scotia, 1872–5; University of London, 1875–8. **Infls:** Kant. **Appts:** Professor of English Literature, Logic, and Political Economy, Acadia University, 1880; Professor of Philosophy, Dalhousie University, Halifax, 1882; Cornell University, 1885; President of Cornell University, 1892, and served until 1921, although he obtained leaves of absence to serve as first Chairman of the Philippines Commission, and as US Minister to Greece and Montenegro; after his Cornell service he became US Ambassador to China and then to Germany; founded the *Philosophical Review* in 1892.

Main publications:

(1881) *Kantian Ethics and the Ethics of Evolution*, Edinburgh and London: Williams & Norgate.

(1887) *The Ethical Import of Darwinism*, New York: Scribner's.

(1890) *Belief in God: Its Origin, Nature, and Basis*, New York: Scribner's.

(1896) *Agnosticism and Religion*, New York: Scribner's.

(1914) *The Balkan Wars, 1912–1913*, Princeton: Princeton University Press.

Secondary literature:

Armour, Leslie (1981) *The Idea of Canada and the Crisis of Community*, Ottawa: Steel Rail.

——and Trott, Elizabeth (1981) *The Faces of Reason*, Waterloo: Wilfrid Laurier University Press.

Wilson, Daniel J. (1990) *Science, Community and the Transformation of American Philosophy 1860–1930*, Chicago: University of Chicago Press.

Schurman was a metaphysical idealist, but his principal interests were in the alleged conflicts between science and religion, and in formulating a worldview based on reason and experience. His early works deal with the moral issues which various thinkers believed to have been posed by the theory of evolution. Against the social Darwinists he argued that evolution has only an indirect bearing on moral principles because moral theories cannot be based upon scientific principles. The indirect bearing of evolutionary theories arises from the fact that the application of moral theories involves factual premises and so different historical situations pose different problems in different historical contexts. The fact that the universe is evolving suggests that the conditions for ideal moral behaviour arise only at a given stage of development.

Two of Schurman's later books deal with questions of religion, which he believed could be given a rational foundation. Although he was much interested in the British idealists and his philosophy was strongly shaped by the conflicts of his time over biological evolution, Schurman's work is most strongly marked by his respect—critical though it was—for Kant. Armour and Trott (1981) have explored the relations between his philosophy and his diplomatic and educational work. Armour (1981) has made an effort to reconstruct the philosophy of history which is immanent in his *Balkan Wars* (1914). His influence on the creation of the American Philosophical Association and the professionalization of American philosophy is mentioned in Wilson (1990).

Sources: WWW(Am).

LESLIE ARMOUR

Schutz (originally Schütz or Schuetz), Alfred

Austrian. **b:** 13 April 1899, Vienna. **d:** 20 May 1959, New York City. **Cat:** Phenomenological sociologist. **Ints:** Philosophy of the social science. **Educ:** University of Vienna. **Infls:** Bergson and Husserl. **Appts:** 1920, Secretary, Union of Austrian Banks; from 1929, legal adviser, Reitler and Co. (Viennese international banking house); asked to join in the establishment of The International Phenomenological Society (1940–c. 1950) and to become an editor of the Society's journal, *Philosophy and Phenomenological Research* (1940–); Visiting Professor at the Graduate Faculty, New School for Social Research, 1943–4, Full Professor, 1952 and Chairman of the Sociology Department; his courses included the methodology of the social sciences, theory of social role, sociology of language, and self and society; it was his professional 'double-life'—as banker and phenomenologist—which led to his untimely death.

Main publications:

(1932) *Der sinnhafte Aufbau der sozialen Welt. Eine Einleitung in die verstehende Soziologie* (English translation, *The Phenomenology of the Social World*, trans. G. Walsh and F. Lehnert, Evanston: Northwestern University Press, 1967).

(1962/4/6) *Alfred Schutz Collected Papers*, The Hague: Nijhoff (vol. I, *The Problem of Social Reality*, ed. M. Natanson; vol. II, *Studies in Social Theory*, ed. A. Brodersen; Vol. III; *Studies in Phenomenological Philosophy*, ed. Ilse Schutz), The Hague: Nijhoff.

(1970) *Reflections on the Problem of Relevance*, ed. R. M. Zaner, New Haven: Yale University Press.

(1970) *On Phenomenology and Social Relations: Selected Writings of Alfred Schutz*, ed. H. R. Wagner, Chicago: University of Chicago Press.

(1973) (with Thomas Luckman) *The Structures of the Life-World* (vol. l), Evanston, Ill: Northwestern University Press (translated from *Die Strukturen der Lebenswelt*, the work on which Schutz was engaged at the time of his death; vol. 2 was published in German in 1984).

Secondary literature:

Cox, Ronald R. (1978) *Schutz's Theory of Relevance: A Phenomenological Critique*, The Hague: Nijhoff.

Embree, Lester (ed.) (1988) *Worldly Phenomenology: The Continuing Influence of Alfred Schutz on North American Human Science*, Washington DC: University Press of America.

Natanson, Maurice (ed.) (1971) *Phenomenology and Social Reality: Essays in Memory of Alfred Schutz*, The Hague: Nijhoff.

Wolff, Kurt H. and Psathas, George (1984) *Alfred Schutz: Appraisals and Developments*, The Hague: Nijhoff.

In 1932, after 12 years of research, Schutz published his main work, *Der sinnhafte Aufbau der sozialen Welt*. He dedicated a copy of the book to Edmund **Husserl**, who invited Schutz to Freiburg im Breisgau to meet his circle of phenomenologists and brought the book to the attention of his student, Aron **Gurwitsch**, saying 'He [Schutz] is a bank-executive by day and a phenomenologist by night!'. In 1935, when Schutz was planning a business trip to Paris, Husserl urged him to meet Gurwitsch. As a result they became lifelong friends and correspondents.

On 13 March 1938, while Schutz was again in Paris on business, Germany occupied Austria. Like Gurwitsch, Schutz was Jewish. He had no choice but to remain in Paris. The invasion of Prague on 15 March 1939 led to Schutz's decision to leave with his wife and two children for New York on 14 July. For most refugees visas were difficult to obtain, but Schutz's position was secure due to his banking connections. He was, however, anxious for his friends in Paris, and it was his work in aiding refugees which brought him into contact with The New School for Social Research in New York, and particularly with its Graduate Faculty of Political and Social Sciences—a 'University in Exile' for refugee scholars (established in 1933).

Schutz's main work, *Der sinnhafte Aufbau* (1932) is a critical analysis of the sociological theory of Max **Weber**. Schutz agrees with Weber that the subjective meanings of social actions can be understood only by means of rational models or 'ideal types', but his aim is to find a systematic, philosophical foundation for Weber's view. Drawing on **Bergson** and especially Husserl, Schutz argues that a subject's intended meaning is constituted in inner-consciousness and is dependent upon the project which constitutes the required action. Understanding of others is, therefore, possible by means of logical constructs—'ideal types'—fashioned from our own accumulated experience.

Between 1940 and 1959 Schutz published over 30 essays, most of which now appear in his *Collected Papers* (1962–6). These essays are an enrichment of *Der sinnhafte Aufbau* and deal with a wide variety of problems: intersubjectivity, signs and symbols, language, typification and knowledge, 'multiple realities', social action, methodology, and critical discussions of William **James**, Max **Scheler**, Jean-Paul **Sartre** and, of course, Husserl. In his 'The problem of transcendental intersubjectivity in Husserl' (*Collected Papers*, vol. III), he argues, contrary to Husserl, that even transcendental reflection depends upon intersubjectivity as a fundamental datum of the lifeworld.

Schutz had plans for a massive opus called 'The World as Taken for Granted: Toward a Phenomenology of the Natural Attitude'. The first part of this, 'Preliminary Notes on the Problem of Relevance' (written 1947–51) finally became *Reflections on the Problem of Relevance* (1970), and the rest, on which Schutz continued to work until his death, was continued by Thomas Luckmann and became *Die Strukturen der Lebenswelt* (1973). The problem of relevance concerns why some facts of experience become a topic of thought and others not, why some topics are interpreted and why some and not others motivate us to act. *Die Strukturen der Lebenswelt* concerns: the everyday lifeworld and the natural attitude; the stratifications of the lifeworld; knowledge of the lifeworld (including relevance and typicality) and knowledge and society (concerning the social stock of knowledge). Schutz's aim in this work was to bring together what was scattered in diverse publications, but his work was not complete: he left us with the unending task of a historical theory of society.

Sources: Richard Grathoff (ed.) (1989) *Philosophers in Exile. The Correspondence of Alfred Schutz and Aron Gurwitsch, 1939–1959*, Bloomington and Indianapolis: Indiana UP; Helmut Wagner (1983) *Alfred Schutz: An Intellectual Biography*, Chicago: Univ. of Chicago Press.

BARRY JONES

Schwartzmann, Félix

Chilean. *b:* 1913. *Cat:* Social philosopher. *Appts:* Professor of Sociology; taught history and philosophy of science.

Main publications:

(1950) *El sentido de lo humano en América*, Santiago: Universidad de Chile.

(1967) *Teoría de la expresión*, Santiago: Universidad de Chile.

(1992) *El libro de las revoluciones*, Santiago: Editorial Univerisitaria (extensively revised version of 1950).

Secondary literature:

Shultz, M. (1978) *La antropologia de Felix Schwartzmann*, Santiago de Chile: Editorial Universitaria.

In his work of 1950 Schwartzmann analysed the literary and philosophical writings of North and South Americans, especially Chileans, and reached the conclusion that their concept of the person is more optimistic than that which is generally put forth by European thinkers. The approach of *Teoría de la expresión* is radically different, with an emphasis on theoretical concerns without the grounding in specific cultural circumstances that he sought in his earlier work.

AMY A. OLIVER

Schwarzschild, Steven

American Jew. *b:* 5 February 1924, Frankfurt am Main. *d:* September 1989, St Louis. *Cat:* Histor-

ian of philosophy and Jewish thought; Rabbi. *Ints:* Classical and modern Jewish philosophy; modern continental philosophy; Jewish theology. *Educ:* Jewish Theological Seminary, New York; 1946–55, BHL, Rabbi, MHL, DHL, Hebrew Union College; 1948, BA, University of Cincinnati; doctorate on Philosophy of History in Nachman Krochmal and Hermann Cohen. *Infls:* Kant, Hermann Cohen and Marburg School. Personal influences include Rabbi Joseph Dov Soloveitchik and Isaac Hutner. *Appts:* 1948–9, Rabbi in rebuilt Jewish community, East and West Berlin; 1949–67, Rabbi, Fargo, North Dakota and Lynn, Mass.; 1967–89, Lecturer, then Professor of Philosophy and Judaics, University of Washington, St Louis; 1961–9, Editor, *Judaism–A Quarterly Journal*; only active rabbi for many years to hold joint membership, Reform Central Conference of American Rabbis and Conservative Rabbinical Assembly; 1973, Honorary DD, Hebrew Union College; Visiting Professor, 1975, Hebrew University, Jerusalem; 1981, Notre Dame University, USA; member of various philosophical associations.

Main publications:

(1960) *Franz Rosenzweig (1886–1929)–Guide to Reversioners*, London: Hillel.

(1981) *Roots of Jewish Nonviolence*, Nyack, NJ: Jewish Peace Fellowship.

(1990) *The Pursuit of the Ideal: Jewish Writings of Steven Schwarzchild*, ed. M. M. Kellner, Albany: SUNY Press.

Secondary literature:

Kellner, M. M. (1993) 'Steven Schwarzchild', in *Interpreters of Judaism in the Late Twentieth Century*, ed. S. T. Katz, Washington, DC: Bnai Brith, pp. 281–300 (includes bibliography).

Swarzschild was the first major thinker to write in English on S. R. Hirsch, Hermann **Cohen** and F. Rosenzweig. He criticized orthodox Marxism and the spiritual ideals of Christianity, whilst retaining an antipathy to Zionism based on his view that the Jew must be the perpetual stranger in society until the advent of the Messiah. This may be one of the reasons for his comparative public obscurity, although he has exercised enormous influence over Jewish scholars and rabbis. He has written negatively on Hegel and positively on Kant and Maimonides. He regards Judaism as a complete and self-sufficient system, and for this reason has been called the last of the medieval Jewish philosophers. Following Cohen, he attempts to align the teachings of the *Torah* (Hebrew Bible and rabbinical commentaries) with Kantian philosophy. Like A. **Heschel**, he defines Judaism not spatially but as ethical voluntarism, emphasizing *halakhah* (Jewish Law). He regards the 'spatial' approach to religion as heretical paganism or Christianity. Just as **Jabès** associates the term 'Jew' with 'writer' and **Levinas** with the 'other', Schwarzschild posits a 'Jewish' philosophical approach which can embrace any thinker or movement of which he approves, such as Kant, **Sartre** and **Wittgenstein**. However, Spinoza and Marx are regarded negatively by him for demonstrating a Christianizing tendency. Schwarzschild depicts clear differences between the two religions, emphasizing the political, this-worldly quality of the Jewish concept of the Messiah. Schwarzschild is an unusual American-Jewish thinker, because most of his ideas, although expressed with originality, stem from European, and particularly German-Jewish, thought, without much American input.

Sources: DAS, 4, 1982, p. 481.

IRENE LANCASTER

Sciacca, Michele Federico

Italian. *b:* 18 July 1908, Giarre, Catania, Sicily. *d:* 24 February 1975, Genoa. *Cat:* Spiritualist Christian philosopher. *Appts:* Cofounder of the Gallarate movement; editor of *Giornale di metafisica* and *Humanitas*. Professor of the History of Philosophy, Pavia 1938; Professor of Theoretical Philosophy, 1947, and then Philosophy, 1968, University of Genoa.

Main publications:

(1935) *Reid.*

(1936) *Linee di uno spiritualismo critico.*

(1938) *Teoria e pratica della volontà.*

(1938) *Metafisica de Platone.*

(1941) *Il secolo XX*, 2 vols.

(1944) *Il problema di Dio e della religione nella filosofia attuale.*

(1956) *L'uomo, questo squilibrato.*

(1956) *Atto e Essere.*

(1956) *Morte e immortalità*

(1959) *Filosofia e metafisica.*

(1960–) *Opere Complete*, Milan: Marzorati.

(1965) *La libertà e il tempo.*

(1967) *L'Intériorité objective*, revised edition.

(1968) *Filosofia e antifilosofia.*

Secondary literature:

Antonelli, M. and Schiavone, M. (eds) (1959) *Studi in onore di M. F. Sciacca*, Milan: Marzorati.

Ottonello, P. (1969) *Bibliografia di M. F. Sciacca da 1931–1968*, Milan: Marzorati.

——(1978) *M. F. Sciacca*, Milan: Marzorati.

Sciacca took from **Gentile** the notion that concrete being is act not fact and, influenced by Plato, Augustine and **Blondel**, he arrived at the notion of the philosophy of 'integration' in which all forms of being and existence are grounded in the subject. Sciacca, having affirmed the primacy of existence, now seeks critically to recover the nature of being. He denies the existentialist contention that existence can be a nothingness and asserts its concrete reality in its search for its proper nature, which he calls 'objective interiority'. Any attempt to found our existence on ourselves alone is doomed to failure. We must posit ourselves with reference to what transcends us and the immanent ground of our being is a transcendent God. The consequences of this for human action and for future life are explored in *Morte e immortalità* (1956) and *La libertà e il tempo* (1965).

COLIN LYAS

Searle, J(ohn) R(ogers)

American. *b:* 1932, Denver. *Cat:* Analytic philosopher. *Ints:* Philosophy of language; philosophy of mind. *Educ:* Universities of Wisconsin and Oxford. *Infls:* Gottlob Frege, Ludwig Wittgenstein and J. L. Austin. *Appts:* 1959, Assistant Professor, 1964, Associate Professor, 1967, Professor, University of California, Berkeley; visiting positions in Britain, Italy, Germany, Canada, Brazil, Norway and the USA; 1977, Member of the American Academy of Arts and Sciences.

Main publications:

(1958) 'Proper names', *Mind* 68.

(1964) 'How to derive "ought" from "is"', *Philosophical Review* 73.

(1969) *Speech Acts*, Cambridge: Cambridge University Press.

(1978) 'Prima facie obligations', in Joseph Raz (ed.), *Practical Reasoning*, Oxford: Oxford University Press.

(1979) *Expression and Meaning*, Cambridge: Cambridge University Press.

(1980) 'Minds, brains, and programs', *The Behavioral and Brain Sciences* 3.

(1983) *Intentionality*, Cambridge: Cambridge University Press.

(1984) *Minds, Brains and Science: The 1984 Reith Lectures*, London: British Broadcasting Corporation.

(1985) (with Daniel Vanderveken) *Foundations of Illocutionary Logic*, Cambridge: Cambridge University Press.

(1992) *The Rediscovery of the Mind*, Cambridge, Mass.: MIT Press.

Secondary literature:

Lepore, Ernest and van Gulick, Robert (eds) (1991) *John Searle and His Critics*, Oxford: Basil Blackwell.

Parret, Herman and Vershueren, Jef (eds) (1992) *Searle on Conversation*, Amsterdam Press and John Benjamins.

Searle has tried to develop a comprehensive theory of language and the mind. Following **Austin**, he held that all speech consists of 'speech acts' and speech acts have different levels. Uttering a sentence—referring and predicating— Searle called a 'propositional act'. But in performing a propositional act one may thereby perform a further act: *in* uttering it one may be, for instance, commanding, apologizing, or whatever. Such further acts Searle called 'illocutionary acts'. Much of Searle's early work was devoted to clarifying the notions of propositional and illocutionary acts, and classifying the various sorts of illocutionary act.

A speech act is an action, and much of Searle's more recent work has been an attempt to forge an account of the mental—in particular to give an account of intentionality. His account places intentionality within the area of the biological: according to Searle, the mind is caused by and realized in the physical structure of the brain. Although he favours a naturalistic account he has resisted popular reductionist theories. Most famously, he has argued against the fashionable attempt to understand the mind as a computer program: in his famous 'Chinese room' argument, he argued that computer programs are specified in purely syntactical terms, and thus cannot capture the semantic dimension that is essential to many mental phenomena.

One of Searle's earliest, and most famous, articles ('How to derive "ought" from "is"') already used some of the techniques of speech-act theory, arguing that such linguistic practices as promising enabled one to derive, by normal logical means, evaluative conclusions form factual premises. Searle's work has, from the beginning, engendered considerable controver-

sy—in the case of his rejection of computer models of the mind, from outside of the philosophical community. The conception of speech acts, however, has become part of common philosophical thought.

Sources: Personal communication.

ANTHONY ELLIS

Segelberg, Ivar Torstensson

Swedish. *b:* 10 January 1914, Härnösand, Sweden. *d:* 20 July 1987, Gothenburg. *Cat:* Analytical philosopher; phenomenologist. *Ints:* Ontology; philosophy of mind. *Educ:* Universities of Uppsala and Gothenburg. *Infls:* Husserl, Broad, Phalén and Russell. *Appts:* 1951–80, Professor of Theoretical Philosophy, University of Gothenburg.

Main publications:

(1945) *Zenons paradoxer. En fenomenologisk studie* [The Paradoxes of Zeno: A Phenomenological Study], Stockholm: Natur och Kultur (English translation, H. Hochberg and K. Mulligan, in preparation).

(1947) *Begreppet egenskap* [The Concept of Property], Stockholm: Svenska Tryckeriaktiebolaget (English translation, by H. Hochberg and K. Mulligan, forthcoming).

(1951) 'The intentionality of gladness', *Theoria*.

(1953) *Studier över medvetandet och jagidén* [Studies of Consciousness and the Idea of Self], Stockholm: Svenska Tryckeraktiebolaget (English translation, by H. Hochberg and K. Mulligan, forthcoming).

(1963) 'Some reflections on incompatible qualities', in *Philosophical Essays Dedicated to Gunnar Aspelin*, Lund: Gleerup.

Secondary literature:

Hochberg, H. (1991) 'Ivar Selgelberg', *Handbook of Metaphysics and Ontology*, ed. H. Burkhardt and B. Smith, Vienna: Philosophia Verlag.

Wedberg, A. (1980) 'Sweden', *Handbook of World Philosophy: Contemporary Developments Since 1945*, ed. John R. Burr, London: Aldwych Press.

In *The Paradoxes of Zeno* (1945) Segelberg presents several distinctions and phenomenological considerations which are of great interest not only in connection with Zeno's paradoxes but also in many other contexts, for example the distinction between a collection and a complex unity, the classification of relations and the analysis of the naive conception of motion. *The Concept of Property* (1947) contains a new theory of the phenomenal quality relation and a detailed criticism of alternative theories. In the essay of

1951 the intentionality of an emotion is analysed, and all attempts to define this type of intentionality in causal terms are rejected. In *Studies of Conciousness* (1953) problems concerning the general structure of mental acts and the identity of the self are examined. 'Some reflections on incompatible qualities' (1963) tries to show that the incompatibility of phenomenal colours is a special case of a general law which is neither a law of formal logic nor a natural law; the epistemological status of this law is discussed.

Segelberg has been called 'perhaps Sweden's most original postwar philosopher (**Wedberg**, 1980). He was inspired by **Husserl** (especially *Logische Untersuchungen*) and by **Broad** (especially *Mind and its Place in Nature*) and, to a lesser degree, by **Phalén** (especially *Über die Relativität der Raum- und Zeitbestimmungen*); later also by G. **Bergmann**.

Throughout his life Segelberg's philosophical reflection was stimulated by **Russell**'s distinction between knowledge by acquaintance and knowledge by description. He was a very good amateur botanist, and he combined his philosophical and botanical interests in an unfinished work on the biological concept of species. Segelberg did not publish very much, but he was an inspiring teacher.

THORILD DAHLQUIST

Segerstedt, Torgny

Swedish. *b:* 11 August 1908, Mellerud, Sweden. *Cat:* Theorist of knowledge; moral philosopher; sociologist; historian of philosophy. *Ints:* History of philosophy. *Infls:* G. H. Mead and Ernst Cassirer; later Margenau, Braithwaite. *Appts:* 1938–47, Professor of Practical Philosophy, 1947–48, Professor of Sociology, 1955–78, Rector Magnificus, Uppsala University; from 1975, Member of the Swedish Academy.

Main publications:

(1934) *Value and Reality in Bradley's Philosophy*, Lund: Gleerup (dissertation).
(1935) *The Problem of Knowledge in Scottish Philosophy: Reid—Stewart—Hamilton—Ferrier*, Lund: Acta Universitatis Lundensis.
(1937) *Moral sense-skolan och dess inflytande på svensk filosofi* [The Moral Sense School and its Influence on Swedish Philosophy], Lund: Acta Universitatis Lundensis.
(1938) *Verklighet och värde. Inledning till en socialpsykologisk värdeteori* [Reality and Value: Introduction to a Social-psychological Theory of Value], Lund: Glerup.

(1938) *Frihet och människovärde* [Freedom and Human Dignity], Lund: Gleerup.
(1944) *Ordens makt. En studie i språkets psykologi* [The Power of Words; A Study in the Psychology of Language], Lund; second edition, Uppsala: Argos, 1968 (German translation, *Die Macht des Wortes. Eine Sprachsoziologie*, New York: European Sociology Series, 1975).
(1966) *The Nature of Social Reality: An Essay in the Epistemology of Empirical Sociology*, Stockholm: Svenska Bokförlaget Bonniers.
(1986–92) *Svenska Akademien i sin samtid. En idéhistorisk studie* [The Swedish Academy in its Time. A Study in the History of Ideas] I–III, Stockholm: Norstedts.

Secondary literature:
(1978) *Universitet i utveckling: Uppsala Universitet under Torgny T. Segerstedts rektorat 1955–78* [University in Development: Uppsala University under the Presidency of Torgny T. Segerstedt 1955–78], Acta Universitatis Upsaliensis (contains a bibliography).

Among the philosophers who influenced Segerstedt's early philosophical views are G. H. **Mead** and Ernst **Cassirer**. Behaviourist social psychology affected his views on the mechanisms of language, for example in *The Power of Words* (1944). In *Reality and Value* (1938) Segerstedt maintains a relativistic epistemology according to which truth is relative be a community of language, and urges that immediate experience of reality coincides with immediate experience of value. In *The Nature of Social Reality* (1966) he examines 'which theoretical assumptions must be held, if sociology is to be possible as a social science'. According to Segerstedt the concept of a social group is 'a theoretical construct, not a result of induction, but a general model'. He combines his sociologically oriented theory of knowledge and valuation with an individualistic humanism in ethics, often referring to Kant's principle of personality and doctrine of the *Würde* (dignity) of man.

An important part of Segerstedt's research considers the history of philosophy and the history of ideas. Some of his early writings (for example, those of 1934 and 1935), deal with British philosophy and some with French philosophy (Rousseau and **Meyerson**). None the less most of his works in these fields concern Swedish themes, for example *The Moral Sense School* (1937), his books on the history of academic freedom, and his momnumental work (1986–92) on the Swedish history of ideas as mirrored in the Swedish Academy during the years 1786–1936.

THORILD DAHLQUIST

Sellars, Roy Wood
American. *b:* 9 July 1880, Egmondville, Ontario, Canada. *d:* 5 September 1973, Ann Arbor, Michigan. *Cat:* Critical realist; physical realist. *Ints:* Epistemology; epistemology; social philosophy. *Educ:* University of Michigan, AB 1903, PhD 1908. *Infls:* Wenley, Lloyd, James and G. E. Moore. *Appts:* 1903–73, Assistant Professor to Professor of Philosophy (Emeritus Professor from 1956), University of Michigan.

Main publications:
(1916) *Critical Realism*, Chicago: Rand McNally & Co.
(1916) *The Next Step in Democracy*, New York: Macmillan Co.
(1917) *The Essentials of Logic*, New York: Houghton Mifflin Co.
(1917) *The Essentials of Philosophy*, New York: Macmillan Company; reprinted, New York: AMS Press, 1974.
(1918) *The Next Step in Religion*, New York: Macmillan Co.; reprinted, New York: AMS Press, 1974.
(1920) 'Knowledge and its categories', in *Essays in Critical Realism*, New York: Macmillan Co., pp. 187–229.
(1922) *Evolutionary Naturalism*, Chicago: Open Court Publishing.
(1926) *The Principles and Problems of Philosophy*, New York: Macmillan Co.
(1928) *Religion Coming of Age*, New York: Macmillan Co.; reprinted, New York: AMS Press, 1974.
(1932) *The Philosophy of Physical Realism*, New York: Macmillan Co.
(1949) (with V. J. Mc Gill and M. Farber) *Philosophy for the Future: Quest of Modern Materialism*, New York: Macmillan Co.
(1969) *Reflections on American Philosophy from Within*, South Bend, IN: University of Notre Dame Press.
(1970) *The Principles, Perspectives, and Problems of Philosophy. An Exploration in Depth*, Champlain, NY: Pageant Publishing Co.
(1970) *Social Patterns and Political Horizons*, Nashville, TN: Aurora Publishers.

Secondary literature:
Delaney, C. F. (1969) *Mind and Nature: A Study of the Naturalistic Philosophy of Cohen, Woodbridge,*

and Sellars, South Bend, IN: University of Notre Dame Press, pp. 145–208.
Melchert, N. P. (1968) *Realism, Materialism, and the Mind: The Philosophy of Roy Wood Sellars,* Springfield, Ill.: Charles C. Thomas.
Reck, A. J. (1964) *Recent American Philosophy*, New York: Pantheon, pp. 208–42.
Warren, W. P. (1975) *Roy Wood Sellars*, New York: Twayne Publishers.

Among the first philosophers to criticize the new realists for failing to explain error because they had not distinguished sharply enough cognitive mental states from objects known, Sellars was a leading figure in the movement of critical realism. His standpoint was that of the plain man, one who believes there exists a natural world. Knowlege of this world, according to the critical realists, consists of (i) immediate apprehension of data, and (ii) the employment of these data as the basis of indirect knowledge of the world. In regard to the status of the immediate data, some critical realists, like **Santayana**, affirmed that they are essences. Sellars, however, maintained that they are mere psychological events. *The Philosophy of Physical Realism* (1932) presents Sellars' most complete statement of his critical realist epistemology and the materialist metaphysics he espoused. Life and mind he regarded as emergents that had evolved with processes of matter but remain substantially material, spatio-temporal systems.

Sellars' ventures into social and religious philosophy were too radical for the American mainstream. He maintained that socialism is the next step in democracy, promising to secure 'an economic organization of society which will give the maximum possible at any one time of justice and liberty' (*The Next Step in Democracy*, 1916, p. 9). In religion Sellars' materialistic naturalism rejected the idea of God and the idea of human immortality. He defined the spiritual 'as an expression of human life as it develops in society' (1928, p. 243). Sellars was a leading naturalistic humanist. In 1933 he published a humanist manifesto in *The New Humanist*, and in 1973 he was a signatory to the humanist manifesto published in the *New York Times* (26 August).
Sources: Edwards; *PAAPA* 17, pp. 231–2; WW(Am).

ANDREW RECK

Sellars, Wilfrid Stalker
American. *b:* 20 May 1912, Ann Arbor, Michigan. *d:* 2 July 1989, Pittsburgh, Pennsylvania. *Cat:*

Analytic philosopher. *Ints:* Analytic philosophy; metaphysics; philosophy of science. *Educ:* Rhodes Scholar, University of Oxford. *Appts:* University of Iowa, 1938–43; University of Minnesota, 1946–59; promoted to Professor 1951, Chair 1952–9; Yale University, 1959–63; from 1963, University Professor of Philosophy and Research Professor of the Philosophy of Science, University of Pittsburgh; 1950, with Herbert Feigl, founded *Philosophical Studies*, the first scholarly journal explicitly devoted to analytic philosophy, edited jointly until 1971 and by Sellars alone for a further three years.

Main publications:

(1963) *Science, Perception and Reality*, London and New York: Routledge & Kegan Paul; reissued, Atascadero, CA: Ridgeview, 1991.

(1967) *Philosophical Perspectives* Springfield, Ill.: Charles C. Thomas; reissued in 2 vols, Atascadero, CA: Ridgeview, 1977.

(1968) *Science and Metaphysics: Variations on Kantian Themes*, The John Locke Lectures for 1965–6, London and New York: Routledge & Kegan Paul; reissued, Atascadero, CA: Ridgeview, 1992 (including complete bibliography).

(1974) *Essays in Philosophy and Its History*, Dordrecht: D. Reidel.

(1980) *Naturalism and Ontology*, The John Dewey Lectures for 1973–4, Atascadero, CA: Ridgeview.

(1981) *Pure Pragmatics and Possible Worlds*, ed. and intro. J. F. Sicha, Atascadero, CA: Ridgeview (a retrospective collection of early essays, including a comprehensive bibliography).

(1981) 'Foundations for a metaphysics of pure process', The Paul Carus Lectures for 1977–8, *The Monist* 64: 3–90.

(1989) *The Metaphysics of Epistemology: Lectures by Wilfrid Sellars*, ed. Pedro V. Amaral, Atascadero, CA: Ridgeview (posthumous).

Secondary literature:

Castañeda, Hector-Neri (ed.) (1975) *Action, Knowledge, and Reality: Critical Studies in Honor of Wilfrid Sellars*, Indianapolis, IN: Bobbs-Merrill (contains Sellars' intellectual autobiography).

Delaney, C. F., *et al.* (1977) *The Synoptic Vision: Essays on the Philosophy of Wilfrid Sellars*, Notre Dame, IN: University of Notre Dame Press.

Pitt, Joseph C. (ed.) (1978) *The Philosophy of Wilfrid Sellars: Queries and Extensions*, Dordrecht, D. Reidel.

Seibt, Johanna (1990) *Properties as Processes: A Synoptic Study of Wilfrid Sellars' Nominalism*, Atascadero, CA: Ridgeview.

Sellars' published work includes significant contributions to metaphysics and epistemology, to the philosophies of mind, language and science, and to moral philosophy and the theory of action, as well as to our understanding and appreciation of great historical figures from Plato to Kant. His writings are complex and conscientiously dialectical and synthesizing, typically undercutting accepted dichotomies and attempting to mediate conflicting intuitions.

Advancing a comprehensive critique of the 'myth of the given', Sellars became a leading contributor to the ongoing Anglo-American critique of 'the Cartesian concept of mind' and the correlative shift of semantic attention from the categories of thought to those of public language. He saw philosophy as challenged to achieve a synthesis of the *manifest image*, the focal concern of 'perennial philosophy', and the *scientific image*, still in the process of emerging from the fruits of theoretical reasoning, into a single synoptic vision. His own sketch of a synthesis was Kantian in spirit, but thoroughgoingly naturalistic and nominalistic. A sophisticated theory of *conceptual roles*, concretely instantiated in the conducts of representers and transmissible by modes of cultural inheritance, formed the basis for Sellars' treatment of both categorial ontological idioms and mentalistic intentional contexts. His own ontology combined a robust scientific realism with a form of linguistic nominalism which treated traditional categorial discourse as the classificatory discourse of a functional metalanguage transposed into the 'material mode of speech'. His account of intentional contexts was marked by psychological nominalism the denial that any sort of commerce with abstract entities is an essential ingredient of mental acts, and his own alternative 'verbal behaviourism' constituted the original version of *functionalism* in the contemporary philosophy of mind.

JAY F. ROSENBERG

Senghor, Léopold Sédar

Senegalese. *b:* 9 October 1906, Joal, Senegal. *Cat:* Philosopher of cultures and languages; politician. *Educ:* Libermann College and the Lycée van Vollenhoven; Baccalaureate, 1928; Lycée Louis-le-Grand, Paris, and École Normale Supérieure, Paris, Licence in 1931 and DES (equivalent of MA) with a thesis on 'Exoticism in Baudelaire', 1935; awarded an agrégation de grammaire. *Infls:* Paul Claudel, Frobenius, Karl Marx and Pierre Teilhard de Chardin. *Appts:* Successively taught at

Lycée Descartes in Tours, Marcellin Berthelot in St Maur-des-Fossés, and at the Colonial Institute of African Languages and Civilizations in Paris.

Main publications:

The complete works of Léopold Sédar Senghor have been published since 1964 under the title *Liberté* by Éditions du Seuil.

A socialist politician, Senghor was the elected representative of Senegal to the French Parliament. He was a member of the French government between 1955 and 1957. In 1959 he was elected President of the Federal Assembly of the Mali Federation of Senegal and Sudan. Less than a year later, with the dissolution of the Federation, Senghor became the first President of Senegal. He resigned from this position in 1980 and was elected, shortly thereafter, to the French Academy.

Senghor was one of the founders, together with Aimé Cesaire, Alioune Diop and Léon Damas, of the Negritude Movement, an organization that has often been reduced to a caricature and in which emotion is assimilated to blackness and reason to the Greek tradition. Senghor's thought is more complex. It is a reflection on life and force, in complementary realms: nature, animals, human beings and ancestors. In this hierarchy, emotion is conceptualized as a step in consciousness. The African universe would be the typical illustration of a general law of interaction between vital forces animating these realms and, from this viewpoint, Senghor's thesis seems to reduce the Negro to the feminine. The Negro's reason would differ from white reason in that it is supposed to be intuitive and communicative, while Greek reason would be analytical and utilitarian.

Negritude is the experience of being and living in communion in a natural, social and spiritual harmony. It also implies some basic political positions, namely that colonization depersonalized Africans and therefore the end of colonization is a condition for a possible self-fulfilment. Thus Negritude is simultaneously an existential paradigm and a political project. It also implies that among the methods for liberation, socialism seems the most reasonable. For Senghor, Marxist socialism is only a method. He clearly dissociates Marxism as humanism from Marxism as a theory of knowledge.

Marxism as humanism presents a clear analysis of alienation and opposes the fact that human beings under capitalism would be simply a means of production. We are socialist, according to Senghor, because we believe in ther usefulness of Marx's and Engels' analysis of societies. However, Senghor views Marxism's theory of knowledge as problematic, particularly in its ambition to reduce all social movements to class struggle and negative religion.

The process from Negritude to Marxism leads to what Senghor considers the last step: universal civilization. From the first step of living in communion with nature and arriving at complex social organizations, Senghor believes that there is a natural law, which is one of harmony, in the development and elaboration of evolving things and humans towards a unitary universe.

V. Y. MUDIMBE

Serres, Michel

French. *b:* 1930, South of France. *Cat:* Philosopher of science; epistemologist; mariner. *Appts:* Professor, History of Science, Sorbonne (Paris I).

Main publications:

(1966) 'Établissement, par nombres et figures de l'harmonie préetablie', in *Revue of International Philosophy* 20: 216–27.

(1967) 'Analyse symbolique et methode structurale/2', *Revue Philosophique de France* 4: 157.

(1967) 'Le Retour de la nef', *Les Études Philosophiques* 22: 251–64.

(1968) 'L'Évidence, la vision et la tact', *Les Études Philosophiques* 2: 191–6.

(1969) *Hermés I: La Communication*, Paris: Minuit.

(1971) *Genèse: Récits métaphysiques*, Paris: Grasset.

(1974) *Hermés III: La Traduction*, Paris: Minuit.

(1975) *Esthétiques sur Carpaccio*, Paris: Hermann.

(1975) *Feux et signaux de brume: Zola*, Paris: Grasset.

(1977) *La Naissance de la physique dans le texte de Lucrèce: Fleuves et turbulences*, Paris: Minuit.

(1977) *Hermés IV: La Distribution*, Paris: Minuit.

(1980) *Hermés V: Le Passage du Nord-Ouest*, Paris: Minuit (*Hermés: Literature, Science and Philosophy*, ed. Josue V. Harari and David F. Bell, Baltimore: Johns Hopkins University Press, 1982: translation of selections from *Hermés I–V*).

(1980) *Le Parasite*, Paris: Grasset (English translation, *The Parasite*, trans. with notes Lawrence R. Schehr, Baltimore: Johns Hopkins University Press, 1982).

(1982) *Le Systéme de Leibniz et ses modèles mathématiques* 2 vols, republished in 1 volume, Paris: PUF.

(1983) *Rome: Le Livre des fondations*, Paris: Grasset.

(1983) *Détachment apologue*, Paris: Flammarion.

(1985) *Les Cinq Sens*, Paris: Seuil.

(1987) 'L'Anthropologie des sciences: Un programme pour la philosophie?' *Philosopiques* 14: 147–71.

(1992) 'The natural contract', trans. F. McCarren, *Critical Inquiry* 19, 1: 1–21.

Secondary literature:

(1979) 'Interférence et turbulences ', *Critique* 380 (contains essays on Serres by Shoshana Felman, René Girard, Pierre Pachet, Claud Mouchard and others).

Descombes, Vincent (1980) *Modern French Philosophy*, trans. L. Scott-Fox and J. L. Harding, Cambridge: Cambridge University Press, pp. 85–92.

Latour, Bruno (1987) 'The Enlightenment without the critique: a word on Michel Serres' philosophy', *Philosophy* 21: 83–97.

Mortley, Raoul (ed.) (1991) *French Philosophers in Conversation: Levinas, Schneider, Serres, Irigaray, Le Doeuff, Derrida*, New York: Routledge.

Serres' work is encyclopedic in scope and presents a radical challenge to established views on epistemology and the philosophy of science: all kinds of data inform and contribute towards an holistic philosophy calling into question the delimitation of science and knowledge away from a broad interpretation of the senses and communication. The main orientation being to produce a theory of human relations and institutions, Serres began with a study of Leibniz. Certain themes defined there remain prevalent throughout his work, notably those of *combination, communication* and *invention*. In the *Hermés* series (1969–77) Serres deals with the relationship between communication, translation and interference. He analyses the fundamental systems at work in a text and shows that such systems are analogous to those at work in other seemingly unrelated texts. In *La Distribution* (1977) Serres goes on to ask radical questions about origins, the roots of language and our notions of space and time. Serre's later work pushes this radical question of the foundation of epistemology into a rethinking of the senses and their relation to preset interferences, both between senses and between pre-existing structures and the senses. For example, in *Le Parasite* (1980) Serres shows that there is a fundamental parasitical component at the root of all major human institutions and disciplines—society, economy, the major sciences and the hard sciences. Thus a drift away from science and towards the senses marks Serres work as a whole. This move towards the senses and to their poetic literary presentation can be seen best in the later books, notably in *Les Cinq Sens* (1985).

JAMES WILLIAMS

Sertillanges, Antonin-Dalmace (also known as Antonin Gilbert)

French. *b:* 17 November 1863, Clermont-Ferrand, France. *d:* 26 July 1948, Sallanches. *Cat:* Medievalist. *Ints:* Thomistic philosophy, both medieval and contemporary. *Educ:* Dominican houses of study in Corsica and Spain. *Infls:* Aquinas and Bergson. *Appts:* 1900–18, Professor of Moral Philosophy, Institut Catholique, Paris.

Main publications:

(1910) *Saint Thomas d'Aquin*, 2 vols; fourth edition, Paris: Alcan, 1925.

(1914) *La Philosophie morale de saint Thomas d'Aquin*; second edition, Paris: Alcan, 1922.

(1939–41) *Le Christianisme et la philosophies*, 2 vols, Paris: Aubier.

(1945) *L'Idée de création et ses retentissements en philosophie*, Paris: Aubier.

(1948–51) *Le Problème du mal*, 2 vols, Paris: Aubier.

Secondary literature:

Piolanti, Antonio (1988) 'P. Antonin-Dalmace Sertillanges O.P. Un tomista da non dimenticare', *Doctor Communis* (Rome) 41: 79–90.

Pradines, Maurice (1951) *Notice sur la vie et les oeuvres du R. P. Antoine Sertillanges, 1863–1948*, Paris: Firmin Didot.

Schmölz, Franz-Martin (1987–8) 'Antonin-Dalmace Sertillanges (1863–1948)', in Emerich Coreth (ed.), *Christliche Philosophie im katholischen Denken des 19. und 20. Jahrhunderts*, 2 vols, Graz, Vienna and Cologne: Verlag Styria, vol. II, pp. 485–92.

Sertillanges is known as much for his works of theology and spirituality as for his strictly philosophical writings, and he is sometimes dismissed, quite wrongly, as a Catholic apologist. In fact he was a very independent and open-minded exponent of Thomistic philosophy. Like many French thinkers of his generation he was strongly influenced by **Bergson**, with whom he was closely associated and on whom he wrote a number of books. His studies of Aquinas are models of enlightened scholarship and thought, and it is upon these that his high reputation still depends.

Sources: DFN; EF; *Dizionario universale della letteratura contemporanea*.

HUGH BREDIN

Sevenhuijsen, Selma

Dutch. *b:* 23 August 1948, Haarlem, The Netherlands. *Cat:* Feminist philosopher. *Ints:* Women and the welfare state; motherhood and reproductive politics; the history and theory of women and family law; feminism and political theory; especially liberal political theory; women, ethics and moral theory; history of feminism and children's interests. *Educ:* 1966–76, Political Science and Political Theory and History in Amsterdam, PhD with a dissertation on the order of fatherhood. *Infls:* Feminist philosophers: Seyla Benhabib, Lorraine Code, Nancy Fraser, Sandra Harding, Alison Jaggar, Evelyn Fox Keller, Genevieve Lloyd, Carol Pateman, Val Plumwood, Adrienne Rich, Carol Smart and Iris M. Young. The protagonists of the 'care as political issue' debate: Jean B. Elshtain, Carol Gilligan, Virginia Held and Sara Ruddick. Political philosophers: Hannah Arendt, Michel Foucault and Joan Tronto. *Appts:* 1979–89, Lecturer in Political Science, University of Amsterdam; since 1989; Professor/Chair of Comparative Women's Studies, Social Faculty, University of Utrecht; Director of an interdisciplinary research programme on 'Gender and Morality as Social Practice'.

Main publications:

(1985) 'Feminism, illegitimacy and affiliation law in the Netherlands', Paper for the Summer Symposium on the Legal History of the American Family, Legal History Programme, University of Madison.

(1986) 'Fatherhood and the political theory of rights: theoretical perspectives on feminism', *International Journal of the Sociology of Law* 14, 3–4: 329–40.

(1987) *De orde van het vaderschap. Politieke debatten over huwelijk, ongehuwd moederschap en afstamming in Nederland 1879–1900* [The Order of Fatherhood. Political Debates on Filiation, Unwed Motherhood and Marriage in the Netherlands], Amsterdam: Stichting Beheer IISG.

(1988) 'Gelijkheid en rechtvaardigheid. Feminisme en de politieke theorie van John Rawls' [Equality and justice], *Recht en Kritiek* 15, 2: 137–60.

(1988) 'Vrouwelijkheid als bron van politieke wijsheid. Amerikaanse politieke filosopen over het moederschap' [Motherhood as a source of political wisdom], *Amsterdams Sociologisch Tijdschrift* 15, 2: 208–34.

(1989) (ed. with Carol Smart) *Child Custody and the Politics of Gender*, London: Routledge.

(1989) *The Portrait on the Wall. International Trends in Gender Politics and Child Custody after Divorce*, London: Institute of Education.

(1991) (ed. with Elizabeth Meehan) *Equality Politics and Gender*, London: Sage (collection of essays from European Consortium of Political Research Workshop on Equality Principles and Gender Politics: Theories, Programmes and Practices, 1989).

(1991) 'The morality of feminism', *Hypatia*, 6, 2: 173–91.

(1992) 'Mothers as citizens: feminism, educational theory and the reform of Dutch family law 1870–1910', in Carol Smart (ed.) *Regulating Womanhood. Historical essays on Marriage, Motherhood and Sexuality*, London: Routledge.

(1993) 'Paradoxes of gender. Ethical and epistemological perspectives on care in feminist political theory', *Acta Politica* 2: 131–48.

Selma Sevenhuijsen's work is an example of concrete historical investigation of the legal and social situation of women and the philosophical insight to be won with the application of a critical feminist perspective. Her research into concepts such as family and fatherhood reveals underlying patriarchal presumptions in moral and political philosophy but does not neglect to point out the pitfalls of a 'romantic' admiration of women's qualities on the other hand.

Selma Sevenhuijsen's work concentrates on feminist philosophy and feminist politics: the ethics and politics of care, reproductive technology and health care policies. She investigates traditional moral and political concept, such as equality, justice, autonomy and their gender dimensions. She describes her philosophical attitude as 'a moderate version of postmodernism'.

Sources: Conversations with Selma Sevenhuijsen.

URSULA STICKLER

Shariati, A(li)

Iranian. *b:* 19 June 1933, Khorasan, Iran. *d:* June 1977, England. *Cat:* Islamic revolutionary philosopher. *Ints:* Shi'ite philosophy and revolutionary change. *Educ:* Mashhad Teachers College, Mashhad University and Sorbonne University, Paris. *Infls:* Louis Massignon, Frantz Fanon and Jean-Paul Sartre, Muhammad Abduh and Iqbal. *Appts:* Taught at Mashhad University and the Husainiya Irshad, Tehran.

Main publications:

(1969) *Islamshenasi* (Islamology), Mashhad: Ins Press.

(1972) *Shahadat* (Martyrdom), Tehran: Hosayyiehad Ershad Press.

(1975) *Jabre-e tarikhi* (Historical Determinism),
  Tehran.
(1975) *Tamaddon va tajaddod* (Civilization and
  Modernization), Islam Student Association Press.
(1979) *On the Sociology of Islam*, Berkeley: Mizan
  Press.
(1980) *From Where Shall We Begin?*, Houston: Book
  Distribution Press.
(1980) *Marxism and other Western Fallacies*, Berkeley: Mizan Press.

Secondary literature:
Abrahamian, E. (1989) *Radical Islam: The Iranian
  Mojahedin*, London: I. B. Tauris.
Mortimer, E. (1982) *Faith and Power*, London: Faber
  & Faber.

Although he had a traditional religious upbringing in provincial Iran, Shariati went to Paris for
graduate study and was heavily influenced by the
radical ideas of French culture and anti-colonial-
ism. He was in frequent conflict with the Pahlavi
authorities on his return to Iran and could only
broadcast his views in clandestine ways. He was a
modernist who argued that it is only acceptable to
retain religious beliefs if these are associated with
the ideology of liberation. He argued in many of
his works that the Shi'ite version of Islam places
the emphasis upon the idea of justice. He criticized
the quietist tendency in some Shi'ite theology, and
he interprets Islam as political. His thought
should be distinguished from that of Khomeini,
in that the latter insisted on strong authority in the
people with legal authority. Shariati suggests that
it is possible for anyone to grasp the essential
progressive nature of Islam if they read the Qur'an
in the right way.

Shariati's views should be sharply differentiated from Marxism. On his view there is a
dialectical development of human history but it
is structured by God's will, the desire of human
beings to reach a higher state of consciousness
and the class struggle as symbolized by the story
of Cain and Abel, where Cain represents the
powerful who rule and Abel the ruled or the
masses. In the beginning society was formed of
equal and free individuals who later became
differentiated into classes in conflict with each
other. This leads to two sorts of religion, one for
the oppressors and one for the oppressed. God
has sent the Prophet to establish a community
that would permanently struggle to achieve
social justice, human cooperation and a classless
society with public and common ownership of
the means of production. Although Shariati's
ideas sometimes seem rather confused, they

came to have great political significance in Iran
in the 1970s and 1980s, combining as they do
some aspects of Marxism with Shi'ism in ways
attractive to a prerevolutionary climate. His
basic thesis that people in the Third World have
first to regain their cultural heritage before they
can overthrow imperialism and become modern
is highly suggestive, and the power of his rhetoric
and the force of his personality came to hold
sway over large numbers of Iranian intellectuals.
He was a truly modern philosopher in the sense
that he was prepared to consider arguments and
ideas as parts of his general ideology no matter
where they originated, an unusual feature in a
paradigmatically Islamic thinker.

OLIVER LEAMAN

Shen Youding (Shen Yu-ting)

Chinese. *b:* 1908, Shanghai. *d:* 1992, Beijing. *Cat:*
Logician; historian of Chinese logic. *Ints:* Philo-
sophy; mathematical logic. *Educ:* Qinghua Uni-
versity; Harvard University in the USA;
Heidelberg and Freiburg Universities in Ger-
many; pursued research in Britain. *Infls:* Jin
Yuelin. *Appts:* Professor of Philosophy, Southwest
Associated University, Qinghua University and
University of Beijing; Research Professor, Insti-
tute of Philosophy, the Chinese Academy of
Sciences (later Chinese Academy of Social
Sciences).

Main publications:
(1953) 'A contrary view on the category of all
  categories that have roots'.
(1955) 'Two semantic paradoxes', *Journal of Symbolic Logic*.
(1957) *Cardinal Mathematical Calculations*.
(1957) 'Elementary calculus'.
(1962) 'The Moist canon on number', *Guangming
  Daily*.
(1963) 'The "Essay on Marks of Things" punctuated
  and explained', *Guangming Daily*.
(1979) 'Inquiry into Gongsun Long'.
(1980) *Logic in Mozi*.
(1981) 'Parts which do not rely on the classifier', *Pure
  Logical Calculations*.

Secondary literature:
Complete Chinese Encyclopedia (1987), Philosophy
  Volumes, Beijing: Chinese Encyclopedia Publica-
  tions.

Shen was a powerful logician and a sensitive
historian of Chinese logic, especially that which
appeared in Moist texts. He had wide interests in

Chinese and Western philosophy, with good Greek and a close understanding of **Wittgenstein**'s *Tractatus*. He was a student of **Jin Yuelin** and a teacher of **Wang Hao**. As a student, he was **Quine**'s contemporary at Harvard. He published little, but his writings and lecture courses all had impact. His work on the *Moist Canon* provided a precise and systematic reconstruction of Moist logic and corrected earlier textual misunderstandings. In his work on Western logic, Shen discussed such topics as semantic paradox, strict implication, quantification and the logical structure of language. Colleagues and students considered Shen a philosopher and logician of genius.

NICHOLAS BUNNIN

Shestov, Lev (pseudonym of Lev Isaakovich Shvartsman)

Russian. *b:* 31 January 1866, Kiev. *d:* 20 November 1938, Paris. *Cat:* Religious existentialist; irrationalist. *Educ:* Universities of Moscow and Kiev. *Infls:* Pascal, Dostoevsky and Nietzsche. *Appts:* Taught Philosophy at Kiev University and Simferopol' University (1919–20) and at the University of Paris (1922–37).

Main publications:

(1903) *Dostoevskii i Nitsshe*, St Petersburg (English translation by Spencer Roberts, in Shestov, *Dostoevsky, Tolstoy, and Nietzsche*, Ohio University Press, 1969).

(1905) *Apofeoz bespochvennosti*, St Petersburg (English translation, *All Things Are Possible*, trans. S. S. Koteliansky, London and New York, 1920).

(1923) *Vlast' kliuchei (Potestas clavium)*, Berlin (English translation, *Potestas Clavium*, trans. Bernard Martin, Ohio University Press, 1968).

(1929) *Na vesiakh Iova*, Paris (English translation, *In Job's Balances*, trans. Camilla Coventry and C. A. Macartney, London, 1932).

(1939) *Kirgegard i ekzistentsial'naia filosofiia*, Paris (English translation, *Kierkegaard and Existential Philosophy*, trans. Elinor Hewitt, Ohio University Press, 1968; originally published in French in 1936).

(1951) *Afiny i Ierusalim*, Paris (English translation, *Athens and Jerusalem*, trans. Bernard Martin, Ohio University Press, 1966; published in French and German in 1938).

(1993) *Sochineniia v 2-kh tomakh* [Works in Two Volumes] 2 vols, Moscow.

Secondary literature:

Kline, George L. (1968) *Religious and Anti-Religious Thought in Russia*, University of Chicago Press.

Wernham, J. C. S. (1968) *Two Russian Thinkers: An Essay in Berdyaev and Shestov*, University of Toronto Press.

Zenkovsky, V. V. (1953) *A History of Russian Philosophy*, 2 vols, trans. George L. Kline, London: Routledge & Kegan Paul.

Shestov's writing was a prolonged attack on the rationalism that he believed had poisoned traditional philosophy, from the ancient Greeks to Edmund **Husserl** (who called Shestov his 'friend and antipode'). By 'rationalism' Shestov meant the belief in an orderly universe marked by necessary laws and eternal truths discoverable by human reason. Among the evils of rationalism he counted its blindness to what is individual, contingent and mysterious in human existence; its destruction of freedom and morality through the worship of necessity; and its limitation of the power of God by positing truths that even God cannot change.

Like Kierkegaard, whose work he came to know only late in life, Shestov finds the affirmation of freedom and moral value in an irrational leap of faith, to the acceptance of a God bound by no human requirements. Shestov's irrationalism extends to the point of denying the principle of noncontradiction: he contends that God can undo an event that has already occurred. Shestov believed in the possibility of creating a non-rationalistic Christian philosophy based on the Old and New Testaments, but his own writing remained unsystematic and aphoristic.

JAMES SCANLAN

Shoemaker, Sydney

American. *b:* 29 September 1931, Boise, Idaho. *Cat:* Philosopher of mind; metaphysician. *Ints:* Philosophy of mind; metaphysics. *Educ:* Studied at Reed College, Portland, Oregon, BA 1953; Fullbright Scholar, Edinburgh University, 1953–4; Cornell University, 1954–7, PhD 1958; elected to Phi Beta Kappa, 1953. *Infls:* Locke, Wittgenstein, Malcolm, Putnam, Armstrong, D. Lewis and Davidson. *Appts:* Taught at Ohio State University, 1957–60, Harvard (Santayana Fellow), 1960–1, Cornell, 1961–7, Rockefeller Institute, New York, 1967–70; Professor of Philosophy at Cornell, from 1970; Susan Linn Sage Professor, Cornell, from 1978; Visiting Professor at Columbia, 1968, Calgary, 1969, and

Harvard, 1970; John Locke Lecturer, University of Oxford, 1972; Fellow of Center for Advanced Study in Behavioural Sciences, Stanford, 1973–4; National Endowment for Humanities Fellowship, 1980–81; Guggenheim Fellow and Fellow at National Humanities Center, 1987 –8; Vice-President, Eastern Division, American Philosophical Association, 1992–3, President, 1993–4; Editor, *Philosophical Review*, intermittently from 1964; General Editor, Cambridge Studies in Philosophy, 1982–90.

Main publications:
(1963) *Self-Knowledge and Self-Identity*, Ithaca, NY: Cornell University Press.
(1969) 'Time without change', *Journal of Philosophy*, reprinted in *Identity, Cause, and Mind* (1984), and in R. Le Poidevin and M. MacBeath (eds), *The Philosophy of Time*, Oxford: Oxford University Press, (outside his main area but influential).
(1970) 'Persons and their pasts', *American Philosophical Quarterly*, reprinted in *Identity, Cause, and Mind* (1984) (for 'quasi-remembering').
(1983) (ed. with C. Ginet) *Knowledge and Mind: Philosophical Essays*, New York: Oxford University Press (essays in honour of N. Malcolm, including one by Shoemaker reprinted in *Identity, Cause, and Mind*, 1984).
(1984) *Identity, Cause, and Mind: Philosophical Essays*, Cambridge: Cambridge University Press (reprinted articles, including those of 1969 and 1970, forming his most important work; Introduction contains brief philosophical autobiography, showing his changes of view after 1963).
(1984) (with R. Swinburne) *Personal Identity*, Oxford: Blackwell.

Secondary literature:
Lycan, W. G. (1971) 'Williams and Stroud on Shoemaker's sceptic', *Analysis*.
Miri, M. (1973) 'Memory and personal identity', *Mind*.
Penelhum, T. (1959) 'Personal identity, memory, and survival', *Journal of Philosophy* (criticizes article by Shoemaker in same volume).
Rosenberg, A. (1984) 'Mackie and Shoemaker on dispositional properties', *Midwest Studies in Philosophy* 9.
Schumacher, J. A. (1976) 'Memory unchained again', *Analysis* 36.
Swinburne, R. G. (1980) 'Properties, casaution, and projectibility', in L. J. Cohen and M. Hesse (eds), *Applications of Inductive Logic*, Oxford: Oxford University Press (discussion of article by Shoemaker in same volume, followed by Shoemaker's reply and further discussions).

Walton, K. (1973) 'Shoemaker and personal identity', *Personalist*.
Williams, B. A. O. (1968) 'Knowledge and meaning in the philosophy of mind', *Philosophical Review*.
Zemach, E. (1969) 'Personal identity without criteria', *Australasian Journal of Philosophy*.

Initially, in *Self-Knowledge and Self-Identity* (1963), Shoemaker appealed to criteria, especially bodily identity, for analysing personal identity, while insisting that we know ourselves without criteria (and using throughout the idea that an expression only makes sense in a context if its negation also makes sense there). Later, however, he gave primacy to psychological continuity over bodily identity and, discussing the possibility of 'fission' in 'Persons and their pasts' (1970), introduced 'quasi-remembering', where the previous experience that memory involves need not be that of the rememberer. But he then abandoned the emphasis on criteria (as inviting confusion between what personal identity is and how we know it) and concentrated instead on the functionalism for which he has been most influential: mental states are defined by how they function, i.e. by their causes and effects on behaviour. He has argued, controversially, that functionalism can tolerate qualia (the qualitative aspects of experience—the 'redness' of red), that it is impossible that qualia should be absent from a creature behaving exactly like one in which they were present (there are no 'zombies'), but that your qualia and mine could in principle differ in behaviourally undetectable ways.
Sources: IWW 1993–4; WW(Am) 1991–2; *PI*; personal communication.

A. R. LACEY

Shpet, Gustav Gustavovich
Russian. *b:* 26 March (O.S.) 1879, Kiev. *d:* 16 November 1937, Siberia. *Cat:* Phenomenologist. *Ints:* Philosophy of language; aesthetics; philosophy of history; history of philosophy. *Educ:* Universties of Kiev, Göttingen and Moscow. *Infls:* Hegel, V. S. Solov'ev, Husserl and W. von Humboldt. *Appts:* Taught Philosophy at Moscow University, 1910–21; during the 1920s he held administrative positions in various scholarly institutes and organizations in Moscow.

Main publications:
(1914) *Iavlenie i smysl'*, Moscow (English translation, *Appearance and Sense*, trans. Thomas Nemeth, Dordrecht: Kluwer Academic Publishers,

1991; the introductory materials contain appreciations).

(1916) *Istoriia kak problema logiki* [History as a Problem in Logic], Moscow.

(1922) *Ocherk razvitiia russkoi filosofii* [An Essay in the Development of Russian Philosophy], Petrograd.

(1922–3) *Esteticheskie fragmenty*, [Aesthetic Fragments], 3 vols, Petrograd.

(1927) *Vnutrennaia forma slova* [The Inner Form of the World], Moscow.

(1927) *Vvedenie v etnicheskuiu psikhologiiu* [Introduction to Ethnic Philosophy], Moscow.

(1989) *Sochineniia* [Works], Moscow.

(forthcoming) *Hermeneutics and Its Problems*, ed. George L. Kline, trans. Erika Freiberger-Sheikholesami, Indiana University Press (the introductory materials contain appreciations of Shpet's thoughts).

Secondary literature:
Haardt, Alexander (1993) *Husserl in Russland: Phänomenologie der Sprache und Kunst bei Gustav Spet und Aleksej Losev*, Munich: Wilhelm Fink Verlag contains bibliography.

Study with **Husserl** at Göttingen in 1912–13 led to Shpet's first book, *Appearance and Sense*, a sympathetic exposition of the German philosopher's doctrine. Shpet was not an orthodox Husserlian, however, for his outlook was coloured by the ontological and realist tendencies of Russian philosophy and he approached phenomenology less as an analysis of transcendental subjectivity than as a reconstruction of reality as a living, concrete whole. He sought, moreover, to complete that reconstruction by attending to two elements neglected by Husserl—social being, and signs and the 'hermeneutical acts' of consciousness by which signs are interpreted. Shpet emphasized the social character of consciousness and language, postulating a form of collective consciousness within which communication takes place.

Shpet developed these themes in a series of further books, all completed within the period 1916–27, addressed to problems in history, aesthetics, social psychology, literature and the general science of hermeneutics. On the strength of this work he is considered a pioneer in the development of semiotic studies in Russia. During the same period he also produced substantial works in the history of Russian philosophy.

Shpet's non-Marxist philosophical orientation cost him his professorship at Moscow University in 1921, and after 1927 he was no longer able to publish in philosophy. In 1935 he was exiled to Siberia; convicted there on fabricated charges of anti-Soviet activity, he was executed in 1937.

JAMES SCANLAN

Sibley, F(rank) N(oel)
British. *b:* 28 February 1923, London. *Cat:* Aesthetician; analytic philosopher. *Ints:* Aesthetics. *Educ:* University College, Oxford. *Infls:* Oxford philosophy of the 1950s, particularly Gilbert Ryle and J. L. Austin. *Appts:* 1949–53, Assistant Professor, Yale University; 1953–5, Assistant Professor, University of Iowa; 1955–6, Visiting Lecturer in Philosophy, University of Michigan; 1956–64, Assistant Professor and Associate Professor, Cornell University; 1964–85, Professor of Philosophy, University of Lancaster; from 1985, Emeritus Professor.

Main publications:
(1955) 'Seeking, scrutinizing and seeing', *Mind* 64: 455–78.

(1959) 'Aesthetic concepts', *Philosophical Review* 68: 421–50.

(1959) 'Aesthetics and the look of things', *Journal of Philosophy* 56: 905–15.

(1965) 'Aesthetic and non-aesthetic', *Philosophical Review* 74: 135–59.

(1967–8) 'Colours', *Proceedings of the Aristotelian Society* 68: 145–66.

(1968) 'Objectivity and aesthetics', *Proceedings of the Aristotelian Society* supplementary volume 42: 31–54.

(1970) 'Ryle and thinking', in O. Wood and G. Pitcher (eds), *Ryle: A Collection of Critical Essays*, New York: Doubleday.

(1971) (ed.) *Perception: A Philosophical Symposium*, London: Methuen.

(1974) 'Particularity, art and evaluation', *Proceedings of the Aristotelian Society* supplementary volume 48: 1–21.

(1983) 'General criteria and reasons in aesthetics', in J. Fisher (ed.), *Essays on Aesthetics: Perspectives on the Work of Monroe C Beardsley*, Philadelphia, PA: Temple University Press.

(1985) 'Originality and value', *British Journal of Aesthetics* 25: 169–84.

(1993) 'Making music our own', in Michael Krausz (ed.), *The Interpretation of Music*, Oxford: Clarendon Press.

Secondary literature:

Beardsley, Monroe (1982) *The Aesthetic Point of View*, Ithaca, NY: Cornell University Press.

Cohen, Ted (1973) 'Aesthetic and non-aesthetic', *Theoria* 39.

Margolis, Joseph (1965) *Language of Art and Art Criticism*, Detroit: Wayne State University Press.

Meager, Ruby (1970) 'Aesthetic concepts', *British Journal of Aesthetics* 10.

In spite of a relatively small published output, Sibley is generally regarded as a key figure in postwar analytic aesthetics. His analysis of aesthetic concepts, for example, both introduced to the philosophical community some distinctive logical features of an aesthetic vocabulary and established a certain style and rigour in modern debates in aesthetics. Sibley argued that aesthetic concepts such as 'graceful' or 'balanced' were distinct from, and not reducible to, non-aesthetic concepts such as 'square' or 'red', and required a discrimination of 'taste' for their application. The former 'emerged', but were not logically derivable, from the latter. In later work he showed how this had deep consequences for the kinds of support available for critical judgements. Sibley's work in aesthetics developed from a more general interest in problems of perception, to which he also made significant contributions.

Sources: Cooper.

PETER LAMARQUE

Simmel, Georg

German. *b:* 1 March 1858, Berlin. *d:* 29 March 1918, Strasbourg. *Cat:* Idealist; philosopher of history, culture and society. *Educ:* University of Berlin, 1877–84. *Infls:* Kant, Hegel, Schopenhauer and Nietzsche; personal friend of Max Weber, Rickert, Husserl, von Harnack and Rilke. *Appts:* *Privatdozent* (1884–1900) and then *Extraordinarius* (1900–14) for Philosophy, University of Berlin; *Ordinarius* for Philosophy, University of Strasbourg (1914–18).

Main publications:

(1890) *Über die soziale Differenzierung*, Leipzig: Duncker & Humblot.

(1892) *Die Probleme der Geschichtsphilosophie*, Leipzig: Duncker & Humblot (English translation, *The Problems of the Philosophy of History: An Epistemological Essay*, trans. G. Oakes, New York: Free Press, 1977).

(1892–3) *Einleitung in die Moralwissenschaft*, 2 vols, Berlin: W. Hertz.

(1906) *Die Religion*, Frankfurt am Main: Rütten & Loening (English translation, *Sociology of Religion*, trans. C. Rosenthal, New York: Ayer, 1959).

(1907) *Schopenhauer und Nietzsche*, Leipzig: Duncker & Humblot (English translation, *Schopenhauer and Nietzsche*, trans. H. Loiskandl, *et al.*, Amherst: University of Massachusetts Press, 1986).

(1908) *Soziologie*, Leipzig (partial translations by K. H. Wolff, *The Sociology of Georg Simmel*, New York: Free Press of Glencoe, and London: Collier-Macmillan, 1964; and by K. H. Wolff and R. Bendix, *Conflict: The Web of Group Affiliations*, New York: Free Press of Glencoe, 1964).

(1910) *Hauptprobleme der Philosophie*, Leipzig: G. J. Göschen.

(1917) *Grundfragen der Soziologie*, Berlin: G. J. Göschen.

(1988–) *Gesammelte Werke*, 24 vols, Frankfurt am Main: Suhrkamp/KNO.

Secondary literature:

Gassen, K. and Landmann, M. (eds) (1958) *Buch des Dankes an Georg Simmel*, Berlin: Duncker & Humblot.

Spykman, N. J. (1925) *The Social Theory of Georg Simmel*, Chicago: University Press of Chicago.

Weingartner, R. H. (1962) *Experience and Culture: The Philosophy of Georg Simmel*, Middletown, CT: Wesleyan University Press.

Wolff, K. H. (ed.) (1959) *Georg Simmel 1858–1918*, Columbus, Ohio: Ohio State University Press.

Simmel's importance as philosopher (and also as sociologist) only came to be recognized after his death. He was, in fact, a highly original, fertile and influential thinker, who foreshadowed developments in phenomenology and exisentialism, and was one of the founders of modern sociology.

Simmel's early thought involved a relativistic, pragmatist, evolutionary adaptation of the Kantian a priori. His later philosophy (from about 1900 onwards) was more metaphysical in character and involved postulating the existence of a 'realm of ideal contents', the criterion of objective evaluation. Simmel foreshadowed certain phenomenological existentialist ideas (particularly those of **Jaspers**) by maintaining that consciousness and the subject–object distinction presupposes and arises within the 'gap' between need and its satisfaction; that life (his starting-point) could only be lived, not conceptually known, and that it involved production; and that the origin of culture (philosophy, science, art, religion and morality) was to be attributed to

man's transcending the praxis of ordinary life and acting freely, for the sake of form alone.
Sources: Edwards; EF; Eisler.

DAVID WALFORD

Simon, Akiva E(rnst)
Israeli. **b:** 15 March 1899, Berlin. **d:** 18 August 1988, Jerusalem. **Cat:** Philosopher of education. **Ints:** Jewish and general history of education; application of educational theory; Jewish texts as a source of educational inspiration. **Educ:** PhD, Heidelberg University, 1923. **Infls:** Rosenzweig and Buber. **Appts:** 1923–8, Coeditor with Martin Buber, *Der Jude*, Lecturer, Freies Jüdisches Lehrhaus, Frankfurt; 1933, Cofounder, Institute for Adult Jewish Education, Frankfurt; 1939–88, Senior Lecturer, Associate, Professor, Codirector, Director, and then Emeritus Professor, School of Education, Hebrew University, Jerusalem; Visiting Professor, Jewish Theological Seminary, New York, and University of Judaism, Los Angeles; Corresponding Member, German Academy for Language and Literature, 1977; Israel Prize for Education, 1967; Dr Honoris Causa, Jewish Theological Seminary, 1969 and Hebrew Union College, 1980.

Main publications:
(1928) *Ranke und Hegel*, Munich: R. Oldenbourg.
(1934) *Aufbau im Untergang* [Reconstruction in Destruction], Tübingen: Mohr.
(1965) *Brücken, Gesammelte Aufsätze* [Bridges, Collected Essays], Heidelberg: Schneider.
(1980) *Entscheidung zum Judentum. Essays und Vorträge* [To Decide for Judaism], Frankfurt: Surhkamp.
(1982) *Ha'im od Yehudim anachnu?* [Do We Still Live as Jews?], Tel Aviv.
(1983) *Ha-Z'chut le-Chanech—ha-Chova le-Chanech* [The Right to Educate—The Duty to Educate], Tel Aviv.
(1985) *Va'adim, Tsematim, Netivim* [Aims, Junctures, Paths: The Thinking of Martin Buber], Tel Aviv: Sfriat Poalim.

Secondary literature:
Büler, M. (1986) *Erziehung zur Tradition—Erziehung zu Widerstand: Ernst Simon und die jüdische Erwachsenbildung in Deutschland* [Education for Tradition—Education for Opposition: Ernst Simon and Jewish Adult Education in Germany], Berlin: Selbstverlag.
Frankenstein, C. and Sarel, B. (eds) (1980) *Festschrift zum 80. Geburtstag E. Simons*, Jerusalem.

Simon, an ardent Zionist, emigrated to Palestine in 1928, but was invited to return to Germany in 1933 to contribute to Martin **Buber**'s work in Jewish Adult Education. He was a religious humanist whose philosophy of education, influenced by **Buber**, fired his quest for a peaceful solution to the Jewish–Arab problem, including a binational state in Palestine. His educational interests were wide and encompassed religion, the Hebrew language, psychology, psychoanalysis and contemporary political problems. He combined a scholarly thoroughness, typical of a sound German education, with the compassion and humanity of an enlightened upbringing, enhanced by his own experiences of Nazi Germany. His emphasis on the *Torah*, or Jewish teaching and tradition, as the link between God and humanity was influenced by Franz **Rosenzweig** and permeated his entire oeuvre and conduct.
Sources: EncJud; Schoeps; personal communication; Prof. Uriel Simon, Bar Ilan Univ.

IRENE LANCASTER

Singer, Marcus George
American. **b:** 4 January 1926, New York City. **Cat:** Anglo-American philosopher. **Ints:** Moral philosophy; philosophy of law; history of philosophy. **Educ:** University of Illinois, AB 1948, and Cornell University, PhD 1952. **Infls:** Personal influences: A. R. Turquette, Frederick Will, Max Black, Gregory Vlastos and Arthur Murphy. Literary influences: Kant, J. S. Mill, Sidgwick, Peirce, William James, John Dewey and Morris R. Cohen. **Appts:** Assistant in Philosophy 1948–9, Instructor, 1949–51, Cornell; Instructor, Assistant, Associate, full and Emeritus Professor, 1952–, University of Wisconsin; Visiting Fellow, 1962–3, Honorary Research Fellow 1984–5, Birkbeck College, University of London; Visiting Fellow, 1977, 1984–5, University of Warwick; Director, public lecture series on American Philosophy, 1984–5, Royal Institute of Philosophy, London; various visiting teaching appointments in the USA.

Main publications:
(1961) *Generalization in Ethics*, New York: Alfred A. Knopf.
(1977) (ed.) *Morals and Values*, New York: Scribner's.
(1977) 'The principle of consequences reconsidered', *Philosophical Studies*.
(1985) 'Universalizability and the generalization principle', in Nelson T. Potter and Mark Timmons (eds), *Morality and Universality*, Dordrecht and Boston: Reidel.

(1985) (ed.) *American Philosophy*, Cambridge: Cambridge University Press.

(1986) 'The ideal of a rational morality', *Proceedings of the American Philosophical Association*.

Secondary literature:
Nakhnikian, George (1964) 'Generalization in ethics', *The Review of Metaphysics*.

Verdi, J. J. (1977) 'In defence of Marcus Singer', *Personalist*.

Singer's main philosophical influence lies in his attempt to provide a basis for distinguishing and establishing authentic moral *reasons*. In *Generalization in Ethics* (1961), Singer argued that, when properly used and qualified, the 'generalization argument'—i.e. if everyone were to do *x*, the consequences would be disastrous (or undesirable); therefore no one ought to do *x*—is a valid form of moral reasoning. His discussion attempted to elucidate the components of this argument and ascertain its conditions of validity. In the ensuing years Singer has sought to distinguish his position on 'generalization' both from various forms of utilitarianism and from the views of those (for example, R. M. **Hare** and Alan **Gewirth**) who focus on the consideration of 'universalizability' in ethics.

Sources: WW(Am) 1992–3.

WILLIAM LANGENFUS

Singer, Peter Albert David

Australian. *b:* 6 July 1946, Melbourne, Australia. *Cat:* Analytical philosopher; moral philosopher. *Ints:* Applied ethics; utilitarianism; animal welfare; sociobiology; political philosophy. *Educ:* University of Melbourne and University College, Oxford. *Infls:* J. S. Mill and K. Marx. *Appts:* 1971–3, Radcliffe Lecturer in Philosophy, University College Oxford; 1973–4, Visiting Assistant Professor of Philosophy, New York University; 1974–6, Senior Lecturer in Philosophy, La Trobe University; from 1977, Professor of Philosophy, Monash University.

Main publications:
(1973) 'The triviality of the debate over "is ought" and the definition of "Moral"', *American Philosophical Quarterly* 10.

(1973) *Democracy and Disobedience*, Oxford: Clarendon.

(1975) (ed.) *Animal Rights and Human Obligations*, Englewood Cliffs, NJ: Prentice-Hall.

(1975) *Animal Liberation: A New Ethics for our Treatment of Animals*, New York: Random House.

(1979) *Practical Ethics*, Cambridge: Cambridge University Press.

(1980) *Marx*, Oxford: Oxford University Press.

(1981) *The Expanding Circle*, Oxford: Clarendon Press.

(1982) (ed.) (with W. Walters) *Test Tube Babies*, Oxford: Oxford University Press.

(1983) *Hegel*, Oxford: Oxford University Press.

(1985) (with D. Wells) *Making Babies: The New Science and Ethics of Conception*, New York: C. Scribner's.

(1991) (ed.) *A Companion to Ethics*, Oxford: Blackwell.

Secondary literature:
Fox, M. (1978) 'Animal liberation: a critique', *Ethics* 88.

Lockwood, M. (1979) 'Singer on killing and the preference for life', *Inquiry* 22.

Steinbock, B. (1978) 'Speciesism and the idea of equality', in *Philosophy* 53.

Peter Singer is a prolific philosopher whose views on controversial moral issues and on the nature of ethics have had a significant impact on the development of late twentieth-century moral philosophy.

In an influential article (1973) Singer challenged the preeminence of metaethics in twentieth-century moral philosophy. He argued that the 'is ought' question and the definition of 'morality' are marginal terminological issues, best settled by stipulation so that moral philosophy can 'move on to consider more important issues'. Prominent amongst those 'more important things' were racial, species and gender discrimination; political disobedience and violence; animal welfare; abortion, euthanasia, and infanticide. Singer's treatment of them combined philosophical passion with a remarkably lucid argumentative style.

Democracy and Disobedience (1973) examined the justification for disobeying the law in a democratic society. Singer rejected traditional justifications for both obedience and disobedience, and argued that democratic decisions should be obeyed only because they represent a fair compromise between competing interests and because democratic participation entails prior consent to agreed decisions.

Singer consistently attacked conventional ways of treating animals; he argued against their being sacrificed for the pleasures of human palates and against their being used in scientific experimentation. Central to *Animal Liberation* (1975), wrote Singer, 'is the claim that to discriminate against beings solely on account of their species is a form of prejudice, immoral and indefensible in the same way that discrimination on the basis of race is immoral and indefensible'. Even if vegetarianism fails as a large-scale concern, none the less commitment on the part of individuals can decrease the demand for meat production and decrease also the amount of pain suffered.

Practical Ethics (1979) quickly achieved the status of a classic. It proclaimed the importance of applied ethics; it defended a radical utilitarian approach to a wide range of important moral issues; it was one of those rare books that engaged specialist and beginner alike. However, although R. G. Frey described it as 'one of the best general discussions of practical ethics that I have come across', he was voicing the sentiment of many when he expressed doubts about the theoretical adequacy of the book. Singer devoted only one sketchy chapter to normative ethics and his attempt to combine utilitarianism with a form of egalitarianism, his 'deduction' of utilitarianism from the universalizability of moral judgements and his blending of classical and preference versions of utilitarianism all attracted widespread criticism.

The book also challenged conventional morality. For example, Singer's view of personhood entailed that the lives of higher animals are of as much or greater value than the lives of some humans and that euthanasia, abortion and infanticide could be justified on utilitarian grounds. Not surprisingly, these views have provoked popular as well as philosophical criticism. A common view is that whilst Singer has demonstrated the independence of practical ethics from metaethics his work has also demonstrated the fundamental dependence of practical ethics upon normative ethics.

Singer's later work (1981) draws upon the ideas of sociobiologists to explain aspects of human nature and to construct an associated account of the foundations of ethics. As such it can be seen as an attempt to provide the theoretical depth which was missing in some of his earlier work.

Sources: CA 8; *PI*.

H. BUNTING

Skinner, B(urrhus) F(rederick)

American. *b:* 1904, Susquehanna, Pennsylvania. *d:* 1990, Cambridge, Massachusetts. *Cat:* Behaviourist psychologist. *Educ:* Hamilton College and Harvard University. *Infls:* I. P. Pavlov, J. B.

Watson and Bertrand Russell. *Appts:* 1936, University of Minnesota; 1944, University of Indiana; 1948, Harvard University (1957, Edgar Pierce Professor).

Main publications:
(1938) *The Behavior of Organism: An Experimental Analysis*, New York: Appleton-Century-Crofts.
(1948) *Walden Two*, London: Macmillan.
(1953) *Science and Human Behavior*, London: Macmillan.
(1957) *Verbal Behavior*, Englewood Cliffs: Prentice-Hall.
(1968) *The Technology of Teaching*, New York: Appleton-Century-Crofts.
(1969) *Contingencies of Reinforcement: A Theoretical Analysis*, New York: Appleton-Century-Crofts.
(1971) *Beyond Freedom and Dignity*, New York: Knopf.
(1974) *About Behaviorism*, New York: Knopf.
(1976) *Particulars of My Life*, New York: Knopf.
(1978) *Reflections on Behaviorism and Society*, Englewood Cliffs: Prentice-Hall.
(1979) *The Shaping of a Behaviorist: Part Two of an Autobiography*, New York: Knopf.
(1983) *A Matter of Consequences: Part Three of an Autobiography*, New York: Knopf.
(1987) *Upon Further Reflection*, Englewood Cliffs: Prentice-Hall.

Secondary literature:
Chomsky, Noam (1971) 'The case against B. F. Skinner', *New York Review of Books*, 30 December.
Sagal, Paul T. (1981) *Skinner's Philosophy*, Washington, DC: University Press of America.

Skinner's most important work has been in empirical psychology. He eschewed, for the purposes of psychology, any concern with unobservables, whether mental or physical, and held that psychology should study directly patterns of behaviour. In particular, he concentrated on the responses of organisms to external stimuli which, by 'punishing' or 'rewarding' behaviour, processes which he called positive and negative reinforcement, build up the patterns of behaviour which are the basis of psychological laws. Most of his experimental work was done with pigeons and rats in what are often referred to as 'Skinner Boxes', but he also attempted to apply his techniques to the study of human behaviour.

Skinner wrote a considerable amount of somewhat amateurish philosophy, most famously in his novel *Walden Two* (1948), and most systematically in *Beyond Freedom and Dignity* (1971).

He held that mental states, including the having of intentions and purposes, were at most epiphenomenal, a by-product of the patterns of behaviour to which we mistakenly think they give rise.

Since all patterns of behaviour, according to Skinner, are the product of past reinforcement, there is no such thing as freedom if this is thought of as freedom from all external control. Properly understood, the desire for freedom is simply the desire that our behaviour be produced by positive (i.e. pleasant) reinforcers rather than aversive ones. This desire is one that Skinner thought we should respect. He held that society could not avoid control but that it should try to move away from punishment as a mode of social control, and that it should be practicable to design a world in which positive reinforcement would make punishable behaviour nonexistent. This may seem to threaten man's dignity, but that is a concept that Skinner deals with dismissively. He held that the intentional design of a culture, and the control of human behaviour that it implies, are essential if the human species is to continue to develop. Outside of academic psychology, Skinner's main influence has been in the field of education. He was a pioneer in the development of programmed instruction for use with so-called 'teaching machines'.

Sources: *The Times*, 20 Aug 1990, p. 10.

ANTHONY ELLIS

Skjervheim, Hans

Norwegian. *b:* 1928. *Cat:* Philosophy of the social sciences. *Ints:* Hermeneutics. *Educ:* Studied in Oslo, Norway and Germany. *Infls:* Dilthey and the German hermeneutic tradition. *Appts:* 1969, Professor of Philosophy, University of Bergen 1974–5; Professor of Philosophy, Roskilde University Centre, Denmark; from 1975, Professor of Philosophy, University of Bergen.

Main publications:

(1959) *Objectivism and the Study of Man*, Oslo: Universitetsforlaget.

(1964) *Vitskapen om mennesket og den filosofiske refleksjon* [The Science of Man and the Philosophical Reflection], Oslo: Tanum.

(1968) *Det liberale dilemma* [The Liberal Dilemma], Oslo: Tanum.

(1973) *Ideologi-analyse, dialektikk, sosiologi* [Analysis of Ideology, Dialectics, Sociology], Oslo: Pax.

(1976) *Deltakar og tilskodar og andre essays* [Participant and Spectator and Other Essays], in the series Idé og tauke, Oslo: Tanum-Noali.

(1992) *Filosofi og dømmekraft* [Philosophy and Judgement], in the series Det blå bibliotek, Oslo: Universitetsforlaget.

During his years of study in Oslo in the 1950s Skjervheim took up criticism of what he saw as positivistic tendencies in the so-called Oslo School of philosophers and social scientists, influenced by Arne **Naess**. His *Objectivism and the Study of Man* (1959) may be seen as the antithesis to Naess's *Erkenntnis und wissenschaftliches Verhalten* (Cognition and Scientific Behaviour, 1936). It was an attempt to 'rehabilitate the Diltheyan view that the transcendental problems of social and historical science are essentially different from the parallel problems with respect to natural science' (1959, p. 3). Hence his aim was to demonstrate the indefensibility of the unity of science doctrine of the logical empiricists, which may also be regarded as the underlying tenet of Naess's *Erkenntnis*. Skjervheim saw this doctrine as one expression of a general philosophical standpoint that he called 'objectivism': a naturalistic approach where everything is treated as an object in the world, or as relations between objects in the world. The objectivist ideal of science is monistic: it seeks an all-embracing science comprising nature as well as man, society and culture, based on physics. He regarded **Carnap** as the clearest spokesman for this view.

Skjervheim contrasted objectivism to subjectvism, whose central notion is intentionality. Subjectivism holds that the categories of meaning and intentionality are presupposed by the humanistic sciences in a way which sets them apart from the natural sciences, and that the humanistic disciplines must make use of methods of understanding and interpretation in a way which distinguishes them from natural sciences. According to subjectivism, meaning or intentionality is a fundamental category that cannot be reduced to anything else. Skjervheim quotes **Jaspers**'s remark that intentionality is an 'Urphänomen'. Skjervheim claimed, in accord with **Dilthey**, **Weber** and others, that meaning is given in experience meanings must belong to the given (1959, p. 33). Since meaning is fundamental and given, there is, according to subjectivism, no need for a *theory* of meaning. Rather, meanings belong to the epistemological basis for any empirical theory (ibid., p. 44).

Objectivism, on the other hand, as applied to man and society, is faced with the task of accounting for intentionality, meaning and communication on a naturalistic basis: a theory of meaning on a physicalistic basis must be provided. Meaning must be reduced to, or explained in, physicalistic terms for things, relationships and processes in the physical world. Objectivists, such as Naess in *Erkenntnis*, have usually sought such an account in terms of behaviour, taking behaviour to be describable in physicalistic terms. But Skjervheim objects that a theory of meaning in terms of behaviour will not involve a reduction of meaning to physical phenomena and processes. Behaviour is in itself meaningful; there is no neutral description of behaviour independent of understanding and interpretation, taking the agent's intention into account. Skjervheim concludes that the sciences of man must always take account of the intentions of the agents. In the interpretation of behaviour, the observer and the observed must share a common frame of understanding and meaning. Here, he is in accord with the Verstehen-tradition. In his view, the task of the sciences of man is understanding, not prediction and control. But the social scientist, like any scientist, contributes to reshaping our behavioural environment. He does this not by treating fellow humans as objects, or considering society as a fact from the outside, but by 'participating in that great dialogue among men which results in reshaping ... the "world" in which we live'. But this 'is to participate in defining reality, or defining that which we ought to accept' (ibid., pp. 75–6). A later work in the same vein is *Participant and Spectator* (1978). Skjervheim has been strongly influenced by the German hermeneutic tradition, phenomenology and existentialism. He stands as a mediator of these continental traditions to a postwar Norwegian intellectual milieu that had been strongly influenced by Naess's early views, analytic philosophy and American pragmatism and social science. He has had a considerable influence on younger philosophers in Norway.

I. GULLVÅG

Smart, J(ohn) J(amieson) C(arswell)

British-Australian. *b:* 16 September 1920, Cambridge, England. *Cat:* Materialist; utilitarian philosopher. *Ints:* Metaphysics; philosophy of mind; ethics. *Educ:* University of Glasgow and University of Oxford. *Infls:* Influences include C. A. Campbell, C. B. Martin, U. T. Place, Quine and Ryle. *Appts:* 1948–50, Junior Research Fellow, Corpus Christi College, Oxford; 1950–72, Hughes

Professor of Philosophy, University of Adelaide (Emeritus Professor since 1972); 1972–76, Reader in Philosophy, La Trobe University, Melbourne; 1976–85, Professor of Philosophy, Institute of Advanced Studies, Australian National University, Canberra (Emeritus Professor since 1985).

Main publications:

(1961) *An Outline of a System of Utilitarian Ethics*, Melbourne: Melbourne University Press.
(1963) *Philosophy and Scientific Realism*, New York: Humanities Press.
(1968) *Between Science and Philosophy: An Introduction to the Philosophy of Science*, New York: Random House.
(1973) (with B. O. A. Williams) *Utilitarianism: For and Against*, London: Cambridge University Press.
(1984) *Ethics, Persuasion and Truth*, Boston: Routledge & Kegan Paul.
(1987) *Essays, Metaphysical and Moral: Selected Philosophical Essays*, Oxford: Blackwell.
(1989) *Our Place in the Universe, Oxford: Blackwell.*

Secondary literature:

Pettit, P. *et al.* (eds) (1987) *Metaphysics and Morality: Essays in Honour of J. J. C. Smart*, New York: Blackwell.

Reacting against the idealist ethos of his undergraduate studies of philosophy, 'Jack' Smart was first tempted by behaviourism and what he called 'the second hand Wittgensteinianism' of Oxford. He came to the materialist theory of mind partly through dissatisfaction with behaviourism and partly through the influence of **Place**, who was a colleague at Adelaide. Smart defines materialism as 'the theory that there is nothing in the world over and above those entities which are postulated by physics (or, of course, those entities which will be postulated by future and more adequate physical theories)' (1987, p. 203). In accordance with that view he denied that there were 'irreducible psychical entities' and claimed that mental states were to be identified with states of the brain. This view has been developed also by others, such as D. M. **Armstrong**, and Smart has refined and modified his original claim in the light of criticism.

Smart came to abandon his earlier belief in philosophy as an autonomous a priori discipline and to admit considerations of 'scientific plausibility' as relevant to philosophical argumentation. This made him sympathetic to **Quine**'s rejection of the analytic–synthetic distinction and made it possible for him to embrace materialism as a metaphysical position. A noncognitivist in his meta-ethics, Smart has sought to defend a form of hedonistic act-utilitarianism against modern critics.

Sources: J. J. C. Smart (1975) 'My semantic ascents and descents', in C. J. Botembo and S. J. Odell (eds) *The Owl of Minerva: Philosophers on Philosophy*, New York: McGraw-Hill; WW(Aus) 1992.

STUART BROWN

Smart, (Roderick) Ninian

British. *b:* 6 May 1927, Cambridge, England. *Cat:* Philosopher and phenomenologist of religion. *Ints:* Philosophy of mathematics. *Educ:* Queen's College, Oxford. *Infls:* J. L. Austin, R. C. Zaehner, R. Rorty and P. Tedesco. *Appts:* Assistant Lecturer in Philosophy, University College of Wales, Aberystwyth, 1952–5); Visiting Lecturer in the History and Philosophy of Religion, King's College, London, 1956–61; H. G. Wood Professor of Theology, University of Birmingham, 1961–7; Professor of Religious Studies, University of Lancaster, 1967–88; J. F. Rowny Professor of Religious Studies, University of California at Santa Barbara, from 1976.

Main publications:

(1958) *Reasons and Faiths*, London: Routledge & Kegan Paul.

(1962) *A Dialogue of Religions*, London: SCM Press.

(1964) *Doctrine and Argument in Indian Philosophy*, London: Allen & Unwin.

(1964) *Philosophers and Religious Truth*, London: SCM Press.

(1969) *The Religious Experience of Mankind*, New York: Scribner's.

(1970) *Philosophy of Religion*, New York: Random House.

(1973) *The Phenomenon of Religion*, London: Macmillan.

(1979) *The Phenomenon of Christianity*, London: Collins.

(1982) *Beyond Ideology*, London: Collins.

(1983) *World Views*, London: Macmillan.

(1986) *Religion and the Western Mind*, London: Macmillan.

(1991) (with S. Konstantine) *A Christian Systematic Theology in World Context*, Minneapolis: Fortress Press.

Secondary literature:

Masefield, P. and Wiebe, D. (eds) (1995) *Aspects of Religion. Essays in Honour of Ninian Stuart*, New York: Peter Lang.

Through his worldwide lecturing, his pioneering work—notably the creation of the Department of Religious Studies at University of Lancaster—and his many books, Smart has shown himself one of the most catholic of writers on religion, in terms of both content and personal openness to traditions other than his own (the Anglican). Subjects as diverse as philosophy, Pali and Particular Baptists fall within his purview. Marxism and humanism are welcomed to the domain of religious studies. He has contributed to the discussion of the place and nature of religious education. He maintains throughout the distinction between theology and religious studies—the latter being deemed less value-laden than the former.

Smart has explored many of the traditional problems in the philosophy of the Christian religion, upholding the importance of intellectual enquiry and conceptual analysis over against what he perceives as tendencies towards opacity and anti-intellectualism in existentialism. He has accorded F. R. **Tennant** a fresh hearing on the problem of evil, and has rejected the implicit irrationalism of the Wittgensteinians. He has welcomed Otto's analysis of religious experience for its attention to non-European religious expressions, and has himself increasingly turned his attention to the phenomenology of religion, the requirments of which are, in his view, empathy with and the close analysis of one's own and other traditions. Such work is necessary because revelations and religious experiences are many and different. We make a serious mistake if we do not remind believers that the experiences in which faith is rooted are then interpreted, and that interpretations are properly open to scrutiny. Conversely, we cannot adequately engage in the philosophical anlysis of religious assertions if we close our ears to the dialogue of religions.

In his widely used book *The Religious Experience of Mankind* (1969) Smart ranged widely over the world's religions, classifying the dimensions of religion thus: the ritual, the mythological, the doctrinal, the ethical, the social and the experiential. In *The Phenomenon of Christianity* (1979) he turned his attention in greater detail to his own tradition, and taught the salutary lesson that Christianity is no one thing, but 'a kaleidoscope of different lived interpretations of the meaning of faith'—a thesis which he illustrated from history, geography, doctrine and philosophy. Smart has done as much as any living scholar to remove religious blinkers and to foster inner- and inter-religious dialogue of a kind marked by empathy, careful phenomenological analysis and integrity—which last entails not least the acknowledgement of intractable religious *differences*.

Sources: WW; WW(Rel); personal communication.

ALAN SELL

Smith, John Alexander

British. *b:* 1863, Dingall, Scotland. *d:* 19 December 1939, Oxford. *Cat:* Idealist. *Ints:* Aristotle; metaphysics; history; aesthetics. *Educ:* University of Edinburgh and Balliol College Oxford, 1884–7. *Infls:* Personal influences: R. L. Nettleship and Edward Caird. Literary: Aristotle, Kant, John Grote, Benedetto Croce and Giovanni Gentile. *Appts:* 1886–91, Lecturer in Greek, University of Edinburgh; 1891–1909, Tutor in Philosophy, Balliol College, Oxford; 1910–35, Waynflete Professor of Moral and Metaphysical Philosophy, Oxford.

Main publications:

(1913–14) 'On feeling', *Proceedings of the Aristotelian Society* 14: 49–75.

(1919–20) 'The philosophy of Giovanni Gentile', *Proceedings of the Aristotelian Society* 20: 63–78.

(1924) *The Nature of Art: An Open Letter to the Professor of Poetry in the University of Oxford*, Oxford: Clarendon Press.

(1924) 'Philosophy as the development of the notion and reality of self-consciousness', in J. H. Muirhead (ed.), *Contemporary British Philosophy*, second series, London: Allen and Unwin, pp. 225–44.

(1924–5) 'The issue between monism and pluralism', *Proceedings of the Aristotelian Society* 25: 41–60.

Secondary literature:

Patrick, James (1985) *The Magdalen Metaphysicals: Idealism and Orthodoxy at Oxford 1901–1945*, Atlanta: Mercer University Press.

Smith's first interests were in philological and literary studies. He was a noted Aristotelian scholar and polymath. From 1891 to 1910, his philosophy gradually developed from a **Cook Wilsonian** realism to an idealism which owed much to his discovery of the writings of Benedetto **Croce** and Giovanni **Gentile**, whose doctrines he eventually appropriated to his own needs and ends (1924, pp. 228–34).

Smith attempted to occupy a middle position between the idealism offered by F. H. **Bradley** and Bernard **Bosanquet** and that offered by Croce and Gentile. He maintained that 'all reality is history' but a 'timeless history, an event which occupies the whole of Time', engendered by 'Spirit' and manifesting itself most freely and fully in 'Self-Consciousness' (1924, pp. 241–4). A much respected teacher, Smith passed on the legacy of his idealism to his successor in the Waynflete Chair, R. G. **Collingwood**.

Sources: DNB; Metz.

STEPHEN MOLLER

Smith, John E(dwin)

American. *b:* 27 May 1921, Brooklyn, New York. *Cat:* Pragmatist; historian of American philosophy. *Ints:* Philosophy of religion and American philosophy. *Educ:* Union Theological Seminary and Columbia. *Appts:* 1945–6, Vassar College; 1946–52, Barnard College; 1952–91, Yale University.

Main publications:

(1950) *Royce's Social Infinite*, New York: Liberal Arts Press.

(1961) *Reason and God: Encounters of Philosophy with Religion*, New Haven and London: Yale University Press.

(1963) *The Spirit of American Philosophy*, New York: Oxford University Press; revised edition, 1982.

(1965) *Philosophy of Religion*, New York: Macmillan.

(1968) *Experience and God*, New York: Oxford University Press.

(1968) *Religion and Empiricism*, Milwaukee: Marquette University Press.

(1970) *Themes in American Philosophy*, New York: Harper & Row.

(1973) *The Analogy of Experience: An Approach to Understanding Religious Truth*, New York: Harper & Row.

(1978) *Purpose and Thought: The Meaning of Pragmatism*, New Haven: Yale University Press.

(1992) *America's Philosophical Vision*, Chicago: University of Chicago Press.

(1992) *Jonathan Edwards: Puritan, Preacher, Philosopher*, Notre Dame: University of Notre Dame.

(1994) *Quasi-Religions: Humanism, Marxism and Nationalism*, Basingstoke: Macmillan.

Secondary literature:

(1995) 'Four essays on *America's Philosophical Vision*, and Smith's response' *Transactions of the Peirce Society*, Winter (including bibliography, 1945–95).

Colapietro, Vincent (1993) 'America's philosophical vision–John E. Smith', *International Philosophical Quarterly* 33: 355–64.

Reck, Andrew T. (1986) 'John E. Smith as interpreter of American philosophy', *Transactions of the Peirce Society* 22: 239–56.

From the start of his career Smith has combined an interest in American pragmatism with one no less intense in philosophy of religion. The unity of these interests was first reflected in his early selection of Royce for book-length analysis, noting in successive lines of his Preface the unheralded importance of **Royce**'s interpretation of Christianity and Royce's intellectual debt to Charles **Peirce**. Throughout his work that double interest continues, one of these topics almost invariably leading to the other. When writing of pragmatism, its treatment of philosophy of religion is included; when writing of religion the pragmatic approach is often featured. In this regard, while supportive of all the pragmatists, Smith often adverted to Royce as providing the appropriate balance of individuality and community, along with the generality of purpose necessary to a religious consideration of the ground and purpose of human existence. Beyond this, he smoothes out occasional rough edges in the various approaches of the pragmatists, and relates their concerns to contemporary issues in philosophy.

WILLIAM REESE

Smuts, Jan Christian

South African. *b:* 25 May 1870, Riebeck West, Cape Colony. *d:* 11 September 1950, Irene, Transvaal. *Cat:* Philosopher of evolution; soldier; statesman. *Ints:* 'Holism'. *Educ:* Victoria College of Stellenbosch and Christ's College, Cambridge, where he studied Law. *Infls:* Literary influences: Leibniz, Walt Whitman and A. N. Whitehead. Personal: Sibella Kriege and Louis Botha. *Appts:* 1919–24, Prime Minister of South Africa (again 1939–48); 1930, FRS; 1931–4, Rector of University of St Andrews; 1936–50, Chancellor of Cape Town University; 1948–50, Chancellor of University of Cambridge.

Main publications:

(1926) *Holism and Evolution*, London: Macmillan & Co.

Secondary literature:

McDougall, William (1928) 'The confusion of the concept', *Journal of Philosophical Studies* 3: 440–2.
Morgan, C. Lloyd (1927) Review of *Holism and Evolution* (1926), in *Journal of Philosophical Studies* 2: 93–7.

Williams, Basil (1946) *Botha, Smuts and South Africa*, London: Hodder & Stoughton.)

As an undergraduate at Cambridge the subject of personality greatly interested Smuts and he wrote a short work on 'Walt Whitman: a study of the evolution of personality'. This study and a sequel, 'An inquiry into the whole' (1910), were never published. When, in 1924, a change of government released him from the burdens of office, he made a fresh start with his study of wholes and 'holism' in nature which resulted in *Holism and Evolution* (1926).

Smuts's thesis is that 'holism' or 'whole-making' is a primordial factor underlying the creative evolution of the universe. The history of nature advances through a linked hierarchy of four principal phases of increasing complexity and integration, namely, matter, life, mind and personality, each phase emerging as a clearer and fuller embodiment of 'wholeness' than its predecessor. He argues that this evolution is not the product of an immanent teleology; rather, it is possible only on the assumption of the 'holistic factor' operative throughout as a *vera causa*, productive of genuine novelty. The appeal of an evolutionary philosophy such as that of Smuts may have diminished, but the ideas of wholes and wholeness have gained wide currency in many different disciplines.
Sources: Edwards; WW.

STEPHEN MOLLER

Soloveitchik, Joseph Dov

American Jew. *b:* 27 March 1903, Pruzhan, Poland. *d:* 8 April 1993, Boston, Massachusetts. *Cat:* Orthodox Rabbi; philosopher. *Ints:* Neo-Kantian; existentialisism; epistemology; phenomenology; philosophy of science; philosophy of *halakhah* (Jewish Law). *Educ:* Talmud (Code of Jewish Law) by severe Brisker Litvak method; 1920–5, private secular studies, Warsaw; 1925–31, Philosophy, Logic, Epistemology, Metaphysics and PhD on H. Cohen, University of Berlin. *Infls:* Maimonides, Kant, H. Cohen and Joseph Maier, sociologist of *halakhah*. Personal influences included strictly Orthodox *Talmudic*, anti-philosophical upbringing. *Appts:* 1932, Chief Rabbi, Boston; founder, first New England Jewish day school; lectured informally to postgraduate *Talmudic* students; 1941–82, chief *Talmudist* and Professor of Jewish Philosophy, Graduate School, Yeshiva University, New York; 1952, Chairman, *Halakhah* (Practice of Jewish Law), Commission of the Rabbinical Council of America; 1946–92,

Hononary President, Mizrachi (Religious Zionists of America); declined Chief Rabbinate of Tel Aviv, 1935; Israel, 1959; and Great Britain, 1964.

Main publications:

(1932) *Das Reine Denken und die Seinskonstituierung bei Hermann Cohen* [Pure Thought and the Consituting of Being in Hermann Cohen], Berlin: Reuther Reichard (based on PhD).

(1944) *Ish ha-Halakhah, Galui ve-Nistar* [Halakhic Man, Revealed and Hidden], Jerusalem: Orot (English translation, *Halakhic Man*, Philadelphia: JPSA, 1983).

(1944) *The Halachic Mind: An Essay on Jewish Tradition and Modern Thought*, Ardmore, PA, and New York: Seth Press, 1986.

(1965) 'The lonely man of faith', *Tradition*, Summer: 5–67; New York: Doubleday, 1992.

Secondary literature:

Borowitz, Eugene, (1983) 'A theology of modern orthodoxy: Rabbi Joseph B. Soloveitchik', in *Choices in Modern Jewish Thought*, New York: Behrman House.

Hartman, David (1985) *A Living Covenant*, New York: Free Press; and London: Collier Macmillan.

Kaplan, L. (1988) 'Rabbi Joseph B. Soloveitchik's philosophy of halakhah', in *Jewish Law Annual* 7, ed. B. S. Jackson, New York, pp. 139–97.

Kolitz, Z. (1993) *Confrontation: The Existential Thought of Rabbi J. B. Soloveitchik*, Hoboken, NJ: Ktav.

Mozeson, L. M. (1991) *Echoes of the Song of the Nightingale*, West New York, NJ: Shaare Zedek.

Noveck, S. (ed.) (1963) *Great Jewish Thinkers of the Twentieth Century*, New York: Bnai Brith, pp. 281–97.

Ravitsky, A. (1986) 'Rabbi J. B. Soloveitchik on human knowledge: between Maimonidean and neo-Kantian philosophy', *Modern Judaism*, 6, 2: 157–88.

Singer, D. (1993) 'Joseph Soloveitchik', in *Interpreters of Judaism in the Late Twentieth Century*, ed. S. T. Katz, Washington, DC: B'nai B'rith, pp. 325–42.

——and Sokol, M. (1982) 'Joseph Soloveitchik: lonely man of faith', *Modern Judaism*, 2, 3: 227–72.

Soloveitchik's philosophy is an attempt to reconcile his strict and systematic intellectual *Talmudic* upbringing with the fruits of his secular philosophical studies, in order to constitute his ideal prototype of the 'halakhic man'. He sees the *halakhah* (Jewish Law) as an exact system, comparable to physics. *Halakhic Man* (1944) was the first attempt to adumbrate a specifically

spiritual role for Jewish Law, by combining the intellectual and religious side of man in neo-Kantian fashion. In 'The lonely man of faith' (1965) Soloveitchik replaces neo-Kantianism with an existential model, positing two 'Adams', based on the two versions of the creation story in *Genesis* 1 and 2. 'Majestic' Adam is creative and assertive, wishing to dominate nature, whereas 'covenantal' Adam is passive and submissive. These two types reside within every Jew, and are both divinely sanctioned. This view impacts on environmental issues, as Soloveitchik finds divine sanction for humanity's secular role in dominating and subduing the world. Soloveitchik also describes the existential 'loneliness' of the individual which can be assuaged only by the covenantal relationship with God. In apparent contrast to **Buber**, he advocates the relationship with God as the only way to relate to ones fellow, rather than the other way round.

In other works Soloveitchik discusses the idea of *devekut* (cleaving to God) through a combination of knowledge and love, as well as the philosophical link between the Holocaust and the establishment of the State of Israel. In his later work he describes three rather than two 'Adams', and appears undecided as to whether he prefers the intellectual-assertive or the religious-submissive type of behaviour.

Soloveitchik is regarded as the spiritual leader of modern Jewish Orthodoxy, especially in America. He advised on contemporary issues, such as the definition of a Jew for the purposes of emigration to, or marriage in, Israel, and the vexed status of women in Jewish Law. In most cases, and based largely on his unusual Kantian and existential approach to *halakhah* in decision-making, he tended to the side of liberalism, thereby becoming an unlikely ally of reformist elements within Orthodoxy and incurring the wrath of hard-liners. He valued the saving of lives alone the retention of land in the West Bank. However, he regarded inter-faith dialogue between Jews and Christians as 'utterly absurd', because he viewed the two religions as totally distinct entities. His view on Christianity has become the established view of all segments of Orthodox Judaism, although Soloveitchik has participated with Christian groups in the study of social problems which affect both communities. By lecturing for over four decades at Yeshiva University, a post in which he succeeded his father, and by remaining singularly modest and unassuming, Soloveitchik wielded tremendous intellectual and personal influence on American Jewish Orthodoxy, and on the wider world. He is regarded by many as the greatest Orthodox thinker of the century and opened up the philosophical study of Jewish Law and its implications for politics and sociology to much-needed debate.

Sources: EncJud; NUC; Schoeps, 1992; obituary, *The Times*, 21 Apr 1993.

IRENE LANCASTER

Solov'ev (also Soloviev, Solovyev, etc.), Vladimir Sergeevich

Russian. *b:* 16 January (28 N.S.) 1853, Moscow. *d:* 31 July (13 August N.S.) 1900, Uzkoe, near Moscow. *Cat:* Religious philosopher; poet; mystic. *Educ:* University of Moscow and Moscow Theological Academy. *Infls:* Plato, Nicholas of Cusa, Böhme, Spinoza, Kant, Schopenhauer, Hartmann, Hegel, Schelling, Fedorov and the slavophile I. V. Kireevsky. *Appts:* Taught at the Universities of Moscow and St Petersburg; ceased in 1882 following his public call for the pardon of the assassins of Alexander II.

Main publications:

(1874) *Krizis zapadnoi filosofii: protiv pozitivistov* [The Crisis of Western Philosophy: Against the Positivists], Moscow.

(1877–81) *Chteniia o bogochelovechestve*, in *Pravoslavnoe obozrenie* [Orthodox Review] (English translation, *Lectures on Godmanhood*, trans. Peter P. Zouboff, London: Dennis Dobson, 1948).

(1880) *Kritika otvlechennykh nachal* [The Critique of Abstract Principles], Moscow.

(1897) *Opravdanie dobra: nravstvennaia filosofiia*, Moscow (English translation, *The Justification of the Good: An Essay on Moral Philosophy*, trans. Natalie Duddington, Constable, 1918).

(1950) (arranged by S. L. Frank) *A Solovyov Anthology*, trans. Natalie Duddington, London: SCM Press.

Secondary literature:

Copleston, F. C. (1986) *Philosophy in Russia: From Herzen to Berdyaev*, Tunbridge Wells and Notre Dame: Search Press and University of Notre Dame Press, ch. 9.

Lossky, N. O. (1952) *History of Russian Philosophy*, London: George Allen & Unwin, ch. 8.

Sutton, J. (1988) *The Religious Philosophy of Vladimir Solovyov: Towards a Reassessment*, Basingstoke: Macmillan.

Zenkovsky, V. V. (1953) *A History of Russian Philosophy*, trans. George L. Kline, London: Routledge & Kegan Paul, vol. 2, ch. 16.

Son of an eminent historian of Russia, Solov'ev was not only a philosopher and mystic, but also a noted poet and controversial writer on ecclesiastical politics who in the 1880s advocated the reunion of the Catholic and Orthodox Churches under the Pope and the Tsar. An eccentric and ascetic personality, Solov'ev experienced visions, most notably of a woman he took to be Sophia, the personification of divine wisdom (one such vision occurred in 1875 in the British Museum library). Sophia, sometimes defined as the 'eternal feminine', inspired his best-known poetry, and is one of the most influential concepts in his religious philosophy (see, for example, **Bulgakov** and **Florensky**); it is, however, one of the most ambiguous, and some commentators accord it secondary importance in Solov'ev's metaphysics.

Despite the fantastic and mystical elements in his writings, Solov'ev should be remembered as the first systematic Russian philosopher. Although his work demands careful periodization, it can be characterized overall as an attempt to synthesize science, German idealism and Christianity by reference to the ultimate metaphysical category of total-unity (*vseyedintsvo*). His debt to Hegel and Schelling is evident in his choice of concepts and his taste for triads (for example, the three hypostases of his absolute metaphysical entity are correlated with the Christian Trinity, and then with truth, beauty and goodness, and so on); and also in his vision of a fallen world of particularity seeking to regain its original unity. He was nevertheless critical of the one-sidedness of Western empiricism and rationalism, and saw Hegelian objective idealism as displaying the limitations of the latter. Solov'ev's goal was 'integral knowledge'; reason and experience were necessary but not sufficient, and knowledge of the absolute was only possible through 'mystical intuition'.

In typically Russian fashion, Solov'ev sought a moral and social significance from his synthetic philosophy: nothing less than the progressive transfiguration of the world through love, and the spiritual regeneration of humanity, captured in the notion of Godmanhood (*bogochelovechestvo*). He rejected the radicalism of the intelligentsia (having himself embraced the nihilism of the 1860s in his adolescent years), and regarded socialism as taking to extremes the one-sided vew of humanity inherent in capitalism. But he was no reactionary, and shocked religious conservatives in the 1890s by giving credit to the intelligentsia for their concern with human brotherhood, a concern improperly neglected by the Church.

COLIN CHANT

Sommers, Frederic Tamler

American. *b:* 1 January 1923, New York City. *Cat:* Logician; ontologist. *Ints:* Semantics (especially formal and logical); arithmetical logic. *Educ:* Columbia University. *Infls:* Literary Influence: Aristotle, Leibniz and Russell. Personal: Ernest Nagel and Christina Hoff. *Appts:* 1955–63, Assistant Professor of Philosophy, Columbia University, then (1961) City College of the City University of New York; from 1963, Associate Professor, then (1966) Professor of Philosophy, Brandeis University.

Main publications:

(1963) 'Types and ontology', *Philosophical Review* 72: 327–62.
(1964) 'A program for coherence', *Philosophical Review* 73: 522–7.
(1965) 'Predicability', in Max Black (ed.), *Philosophy in America*, London: Allen & Unwin.
(1967) 'On a Fregean dogma', in Imre Lakatos (ed.), *Problems in the Philosophy of Mathematics*, Amsterdam: North Holland.
(1970) 'The calculus of terms', *Mind* 79: 1–39.
(1982) *The Logic of Natural Language*, Oxford: Oxford University Press.

Secondary literature:

Angelelli, Ignacio (1982) 'Predication: new and old', *Critica* 40: 121–5.
Englebretsen, G. (1981) *Three Logicians*, The Netherlands: Van Gorcum.
Nelson, John D. (1964) 'On Sommers' reinstatement of Russell's ontological program', *Philosophical Review* 73: 517–21.

Sommers has always thought of his work as an 'Aristotelian development' (1963, p. 362). In the 1950s and early 1960s his interests were focused upon the logical constraints on linguistic competence (sense-nonsense constraints) and how they are embodied in natural language. In a remarkable paper, he sought to reinstate 'the old Russell programme for an ontology which is defined by a logically correct (or corrected) language', maintaining that 'linguistic structures and ontological structures are isomorphic' and that 'all languages have the same ontological structure in an important sense' (1963, pp. 327, 350–1, 352).

In the late 1960s Sommers started work on the logical syntax of natural languages, in

opposition to current logic which uses a syntax of an artificial language. Thus he controversially proclaims the truth of 'term logic', where terms are the fundamental units (as against 'sentential logic', where sentences are the fundamental units) and seeks to vindicate and restore the pre-Fregean traditional theory of predication. His main thesis is that, contrary to what is now commonly believed by logicians, singular and general statements do not differ in logical form. In other words, both singular and general statements can be viewed as categoricals, as sentences predicating a predicate of a subject.

Sommers' plan to rehabilitate traditional logic (in effect, an extension of the Aristotelian syllogistic into a universal logic) in the face of the diversity of modern logic has been criticized as 'retrogressive' by Angelelli (1982). But it has been defended by Englebretsen (1981).

Sources: Passmore 1985; CA 113, pp. 460–1.

STEPHEN MOLLER

Sorel, Georges

French. *b:* 1847, Cherbourg, France. *d:* 1922, Boulogne-sur-Seine. *Cat:* Social and political philosopher. *Educ:* Trained as an engineer at the École Polytechnique. *Infls:* Karl Marx, Giambattista Vico and Benedetto Croce. *Appts:* Worked for the Department of Roads and Bridges in metropolitan France and Algeria; retired at 45 and devoted the rest of his life to writing a number of books on various aspects of philosophy, the best-known of which are on social and political theory.

Main publications:

(1889) *Contribution à l'étude profane de la Bible*, Paris: Ghio.
(1902) *Essai sur l'Église et l'État*, Paris: Suresnes.
(1903) *Saggi di critica del marxismo*, Milan: Sandron.
(1907) *Les Préoccupations métaphysiques des physiciens modernes*, Paris: Suresnes.
(1908) *La Décomposition du marxisme*, Paris: Rivière (English translation in the appendix of I. L. Horowitz, *Radicalism and the Revolt against Reason: The Social Theories of Georges Sorel*, London: Routledge & Kegan Paul, 1964).
(1908) *Les Illusions du progrès*, Paris: Rivière.
(1908) *Réflexions sur la violence*, Paris: Libraire des Pages Libres (English translation, *Reflections on Violence*, London: Allen & Unwin, 1915).
(1919) *Matériaux d'une théorie du prolétariat*, Paris: Rivière.
(1921) *De l'utilité du pragmatisme*, Paris: Rivière.
(1935) *D'Aristote à Marx*, Paris: Rivière.

(1987) *From Georges Sorel*, New Brunswick and London: Transaction Books (selection in English).

Secondary literature:
Cahiers Georges Sorel, Société d'Études Soréliennes, Paris (nos. 1–5 of this journal contain a bibliography).
Jennings, J. (1985) *Georges Sorel: The Character and Development of his Thought*, London: Macmillan.
Vernon, R. (1978) *Commitment and Change: Georges Sorel and the Idea of Revolution*, Toronto: University of Toronto Press.

Georges Sorel made contributions to many areas of philosophy, including the philosophy of science. He maintained that physical scientists do not take as their subject matter 'natural nature', or the way in which the world works, but 'artificial nature', in the form of their own experiments and models. The latter is a 'closed world', as it does not reproduce the indeterministic and entropic conditions found in 'natural nature' but yields deterministic laws. Sorel saw himself as a pragmatist: physical laws and hypotheses are not put forward as general truths about the world, but as conventions which are found useful by the scientific community. Any advances made in the physical sciences are inapplicable to the biological sciences, which are far less amenable to reduction to 'artificial nature', and thus far less deterministic.

Sorel's best-known views are in the areas of social theory, violence and myth. His social theory reflects the distinction previously made between 'natural' and 'artificial' nature, as he maintained that there are at work in all societies degenerative forces which threaten a relapse into social chaos, and that social theory should not take as its subject matter a fixed and permanent 'social essence' or one unique, ideal social structure, but should instead pay attention to the distinctive features of particular societies.

According to Sorel violence is not always destructive. The violent confrontation of a decadent and degenerate society is usually the only means by which a new social order can be established. Violence can also serve as a means of rejecting those lukewarm fellow-travellers of a rising social movement who wish to compromise its principles, and of reaffirming those principles among true followers of the movement. Sorel pointed out that both French republicanism and Christianity had, at the beginning, adopted violent methods to ensure their establishment.

The preservation of the purity of an ideology can also be aided by the retention of an alternative or 'schismatic' language or terminology. Sorel cited the case of Christianity's continued use of Biblical language as one reason why the Church, even after its acceptance by Rome, still retained an ideology independent of that of the Roman Empire.

From his study of the use of myth in various historical movements Sorel formed the view that myth had a social function: it was the expression of a concrete vision of the future from which inspiration could be drawn, but which would be realized only if the ideals embodied in the myth became the aspirations of all humanity.

KATHRYN PLANT

Sorley, W(illiam) R(itchie)

British. *b:* 4 November 1855, Selkirk, Scotland. *d:* 28 July 1935, Cambridge, England. *Cat:* Idealist. *Ints:* Ethics; history of philosophy. *Educ:* Edinburgh and Trinity College, Cambridge. *Infls:* Lotze, Rickert and Windelband. *Appts:* Fellow of Trinity College, Cambridge, 1883–8; Professor of Logic and Philosophy, Cardiff, 1888–94; Professor of Moral Philosophy, Cambridge, 1900–33.

Main publications:
(1885) *The Ethics of Naturalism*.
(1904) *Recent Tendencies in Ethics*.
(1911) *The Moral Life and Moral Worth*.
(1918) *Moral Values and the Idea of God*, Cambridge.
(1920) *History of English Philosophy*, Cambridge: Cambridge University Press.

Secondary literature:
Tennant, F. R. (1936) Obituary Notice in *Pro. Brit. Acad.*

Sorley taught in Cambridge for the first third of the century at a time when Bertrand **Russell** and G. E. **Moore** were comprehensively supplanting the kind of idealism he practised. But he was not wholly isolated since his professorial colleague, James **Ward**, was also an idealist of sorts and a theist. Under the influence of the Baden school of neo-Kantians (**Windelband** and **Rickert**) he derived their distinction of natural science as affirming general laws from history and the human sciences as describing individual persons and texts from a metaphysical dualism of existence and value. Both of these independent realms are objects of experience. Both are present in and constitutive of persons. God, the ultimate source of the world's unity, is also personal. Evil is present in the created world because of God's decision to limit himself by according freedom and independence to finite minds. Sorley argues to the existence of God on moral grounds. Moral self-realization is incomplete unless unified by faith in God. Moral agents conceive an ideal goodness which they cannot attain but whose recognized validity implies its realization in God. Sorley came at the end of the practice of his style of philosophy and would seem to have left no disciples and to have had little influence, although his views have some affinity with those of A. E. **Taylor**. His admirable, learned and judicious *History of English Philosophy* (1920) has lasted much better than his original contributions to philosophy.

Sources: Metz; Passmore 1957.

ANTHONY QUINTON

Sosa, Ernest

American. **b:** 17 June 1940, Cardenas, Cuba. **Cat:** Analytical philosopher. **Ints:** Epistemology; metaphysics; philosophy of mind. **Educ:** BA, University of Miami, Coral Gables, Florida; PhD, University of Pittsburgh, Pittsburgh, Pennsylvania. **Infls:** Roderick Chisholm and a host of historical figures: Plato, Aristotle, Descartes, Frege, Russell, Moore and Wittgenstein. **Appts:** Taught at University of Western Ontario, and, since 1964, at Brown University, where he succeeded Roderick Chisholm as the Romeo Elton Professor of Natural Theology; visited at the Universities of Pittsburgh, Miami, Michigan and Texas, at the National University of Mexico, and at Harvard University; Editor of *Philosophy and Phenomenological Research*; General Editor of *Cambridge Studies in Philosophy* (Cambridge University Press) and *Great Debates in Philosophy* (Blackwell).

Main publications:

(1970) 'Propositional attitudes de dicto and de re', *Journal of Philosophy* 67.

(1980) 'The raft and the pyramid: coherence versus foundations in the theory of knowledge', *Midwest Studies in Philosophy* 5.

(1987) 'Subjects among other things: persons and other beings', *Philosophical Perspectives* 1.

(1987) *'Serious philosophy and freedom of spririt',* *Journal of Philosophy 84.*

(1990) 'Surviving matters', *Noûs* 24.

(1991) *Knowledge in Perspective*, Cambridge: Cambridge University Press.

(1993) 'Putnam's pragmatic realism', *Journal of Philosophy* 90.

(1993) 'The truth of modest realism', *Philosophical Issues* 4.

(1993) 'Epistemology, realism, and truth', *Philosophical Perspectives* 7.

(1994) 'Philosophical scepticism and externalist epistemology', *Proceedings of the Aristotelian Society.*

(1994) 'Reply to Foley and Fumerton', *Philosophical Issues* 5.

(1995) 'Perspectives in virtue epistemology: reply to Bonjour and Dancy', *Philosophical Studies* 78.

Secondary literature:

Much of Sosa's work in Spanish has been collected by Carlos Pereda and Margarita Valdes, of the Instituto de Investigaciones Filosoficas, National University of Mexico, in *Conocimiento y Virtud Intelectual.*

Bonjour, Laurence (1995) 'Sosa on knowledge, justification, and aptness', *Philosophical Studies* 78.

Dancy, Jonathan (1995) 'Supervenience, virtues, and consequences: a commentary on *Knowledge in Perspective* by Ernest Sosa', *Philosophical Studies* 78.

Foley, Richard (1994) 'Sosa's epistemology', *Philosophical Issues* 5.

Fumerton, Richard (1994) 'Sosa's epistemology', *Philosophical Issues* 5.

Sosa's writings in epistemology, metaphysics and the philosophy of mind have been widely influential among analytical philosophers. He is perhaps best known for advancing 'virtue perspectivism', a doctrine with roots in coherentist and foundationalist epistemological traditions usually assumed to be at odds. According to Sosa, whether a belief constitutes reflective knowledge depends not merely on how it was produced—its foundational ancestry—but also on the believer's perspective on his own circumstances as knower. To accommodate the apparent capacity of non-reflective agents for knowledge, Sosa distinguishes 'animal' and 'reflective' knowledge in a way analogous to Descartes's distinction between *cognitionem* and *scientia*. Only reflective knowledge depends straightforwardly on the believer's perspective. In either case, however, only beliefs produced by truth-conducive intellectual virtues are candidates for knowledge.

In other writings, Sosa has defended a modified Fregean position according to which a thinker's reference to an object is always mediated by sense, although sense can be either Fregean and absolute or quasi-Fregean and perspectival. In the latter case, reference is determined only with the aid of context. Such a conception forgoes the need to postulate any special *de re* relation between thinkers and the objects of their thoughts, explaining away considerations adduced in behalf of such a special relation within the confines of the modified Fregean position.

Sosa's views on personal identity reflect a broadly Aristotelian conception of persons, a conception he has undertaken to defend against the charge that it implies that one's survival cannot matter rationally even to oneself. In recent years Sosa has published articles defending objectivity, 'modest realism' and the reality of knowledge against the ascendant scepticism, relativism and anti-realism of our times. He has been active internationally, a frequent speaker at conferences and a plenary speaker at international congresses.

JOHN HEIL

Spann, O(thmar)

Austrian. *b:* 10 October 1878, Altmannsdorf (near Vienna). *d:* 8 July 1950, Neustift (Burgenland). *Cat:* Philosopher of economics and sociology. *Ints:* Economics; social philosophy; philosophy of history; philosophy of religion. *Educ:* Universities of Vienna, Zurich, Bern and Tübingen. *Infls:* Plato, Aristotle, Thomas Aquinas and German idealism. *Appts:* 1907, Habilitation, German Technical University of Brünn (Brno); 1909, Professor of Political Economy, German Technical University of Brünn; 1919, Professor of Economy and Sociology, University of Vienna; 1938, removed from his Chair at the University of Vienna by the National Socialists, imprisonment; 1945, retirement.

Main publications:

(1911) *Die Haupttheorien der Volkswirtschaftslehre auf dogmengeschichtlicher [lehrgeschichtlicher] Grundlage*, Leipzig: Quelle & Meyer (Gesamtausgabe vol. 2) (English translations, *The History of Economics*, New York, 1930, 1972; *Types of Economic Theory*, London, 1930).

(1914) *Kurzgefasstes System der Gesellschaftslehre*, Berlin: Guttentag, later editions published under the title *Gesellschaftslehre*, Leipzig: Quelle & Meyer (*Gesamtausgabe* vol. 4).

(1921) *Der wahre Staat. Vorlesungen über Abbruch und Neubau der Gesellschaft*, Leipzig: Quelle & Meyer (*Gesamtausgabe* vol. 5).

(1924) *Kategorienlehre*, Jena: Fischer (*Gesamtausgabe* vol. 9).

(1928) *Der Schöpfungsgang des Geistes. Die Wiederherstellung des Idealismus auf allen Gebieten der Philosophie*, Jena: Fischer (*Gesamtausgabe* vol. 10).

(1932) *Geschichtsphilosophie*, Jena: Fischer (*Gesamtausgabe* vol. 12).

(1933) *Philosophenspiegel. Die Hauptlehren der Philosopohie begrifflich und lehrgeschichtlich dargestellt*, Leipzig: Quelle & Meyer (*Gesamtausgabe* vol. 13).

(1935) *Erkenne Dich selbst. Eine Geistesphilosophie als Lehre vom Menschen und seiner Weltstellung*, Jena: Fischer (*Gesamtausgabe* vol. 14).

(1937) *Naturphilosophie*, Jena: Fischer (*Gesamtausgabe* vol. 15).

(1947) *Religionsphilosophie auf geschichtlicher Grundlage*, Vienna: Gallus (*Gesamtausgabe*, vol. 16).

(1963–79) *Gesamtausgabe*, ed. W. Heinrich *et al.*, 21 vols, Graz: Akademische Druck- und Verlagsanstalt.

Secondary literature:

Becher, W. (1985) *Der Blick aufs Ganze. Das Weltbild Othmar Spanns*, Munich: Universitas.

Bernsdorf, W. (1980) 'Spann, Othmar', *Internationales Soziologenlexikon*, vol. 1, Stuttgart: Enke, pp. 404–5.

Heinrich, W. (ed.) (1979) 'Othmar Spann–Leben und Werk, Graz: Akademische Druck- und Verlagsanstalt (*Gesamtausgabe* vol. 21).

Johnston, W. M. (1972) *The Austrian Mind: An Intellectual and Social History 1848–1938*, Berkeley: University of California Press, pp. 311–15.

Pichler, J. H. (ed.) (1988) *Othmar Spann oder Die Welt als Ganzes*, Vienna: Böhlau.

Rieber, A. (1971) *Vom Positivismus zum Universalismus*, Berlin: Duncker & Humbolt.

Siegfried, K.-J. (1974) *Universalismus und Faschismus*, Vienna: Europaverlag.

According to Spann sociological facts generally need to be regarded as spiritual (*geistige*) phenomena. Therefore no empirical methods may be applied in the social sciences, but only such methods may be used which are well suited to what the humanities are dealing with.

Following Adam Müller's concept of society, Spann uses the categories of 'whole' and 'part' as an analogy for the basic relationship between individual and society, stating that the 'whole' must always be given precedence over the individual part. The interaction between the individual members and the subordinate community has to be understood in the sense of a spiritual mutuality (for which Spann coined the artificial term *Gezweiung*), from which all social phenomena can be derived according to a certain hierarchy. Thus society with its course of history would mean that there is a deployed spirit (*ausgegliederter Geist*) which ultimately manifests itself in the system of the 'true state'.

As a consequence Spann applies the metaphysical principle of universalism to the various fields of the humanities, especially to the philosophy of history, natural philosophy and the philosophy of religion. Those are also the domains on which the work of the late Spann was centred. Spann's doctrines, which are marked by a strict rejection of any kind of experimental, quantifying or causal-mechanistic methods of examination, were severely criticized even when he was still alive. Nevertheless, his book *Die Haupttheorien der Volkswirtschaftslehre* (1911) was one of the most widespread publications among economic literature (the 28th edition came out in 1969). The 'fight over O. Spann', which also dealt with his fascist ideas, has now lost its topicality. Even years later some supporters of his school were among the Austrian economists, such as the scholars W. Andreae, J. Baxa and W. Heinrich. The tradition of Spann's holistic philosophy is being continued by the Society for Holistic Research in connection with the journal *Zeitschrift für Ganzheitsforschung*, Vienna.

Sources: Edwards.

REINHARD FABIAN

Sparshott, Francis Edward
Canadian (naturalized 1970). **b:** 19 May 1926, Chatham, England. **Cat:** Aesthetician. **Educ:** BA, MA, Corpus Christi College, Oxford. **Infls:** Plato and Joseph Margolis. **Appts:** University of Toronto, 1950–5; Assistant Professor, Victoria College, University of Toronto; 1955–62; Associate Professor, 1958–9, Professor 1964–91 (University Professor 1982), Northwestern University, Evanston, Illinois; Visiting Professor, University of Illinois, Urbana, 1966.

Main publications:
(1958) *An Enquiry into Goodness and Related Concepts: with some Remarks on the Nature and Scope of Such Enquiries*, Chicago: University of Chicago Press.

(1963) *The Structure of Aesthetics*, Toronto: University of Toronto Press.

(1966) 'Socrates and Thrasymachus', *Monist*.

(1967) *The Concept of Criticism: An Essay*, Oxford: Clarendon Press.

(1970) 'Disputed evaluations', *American Philosophical Quarterly* 4.

(1971) 'Basic film aesthetics', *Journal of Aesthetic Education*.

(1972) *Looking for Philosophy*, Montreal: McGill-Queen's Press.

(1982) *The Theory of the Arts*, Princeton: Princeton University Press.

(1988) *Off the Ground: First Steps to a Philosophical Consideration of Dance*, Princeton: Princeton University Press.

Francis Sparshott is a prolific writer both on general topics in aesthetics and on the aesthetics of particular art forms such as dance and film. His major books on aesthetics, *The Structure of Aesthetics* (1963), *The Concept of Criticism* (1967) and *The Theory of the Arts* (1982), combine to form a comprehensive survey of the major topics in aesthetics.

Sources: DAS, 1974; *PI*; WW(Can); WW(Am), 48th edn.

NIGEL WARBURTON

Spencer, Herbert
British. **b:** 27 April 1820, Derby. **d:** 8 December 1903, Brighton. **Cat:** Evolutionary naturalist; systematic philosopher. **Ints:** Metaphysics; ethics; political theory. **Appts:** No formal higher educaiton, and never held a university position; left school at 16, and worked as a schoolteacher, a railway engineer and a journalist, before settling in London to earn a living from his writings; self-taught, learning from such friends as Lewes, George Eliot, Huxley, Tyndall and Chapman.

Main publications:
Spencer's main work is his ten-volume *System of Synthetic Philosophy*, published by Williams & Norgate of London, and appearing in the following order:

(1862) *First Principles*, 1 vol.

(1864–7) *Principles of Biology*, 2 vols.

(1870–2) *Principles of Psychology*, 2 vols.

(1876–96) *Principles of Sociology*, 3 vols.

(1892–3) *Principles of Ethics*, 2 vols.

Other important works include:

(1861) *On Education*, London: Williams & Norgate.

(1879) *The Data of Ethics*, London: Williams & Norgate.

(1884) *Man versus the State*, London: Williams & Norgate.

(1904) *Autobiography*, London: Williams & Norgate.

Secondary literature:

Dewey, John (1904) 'The philosophical work of Spencer', *Philosophical Review* 13: 159–75.

Duncan, David (1908) *The Life and Letters of Herbert Spencer*, London: Methuen.

Elliot, H. (1917) *Herbert Spencer*, London: Constable.

Hudson, W. H. (1908) *Herbert Spencer*, London: Constable.

James, William (1911) *Memoirs and Studies*, New York: Longmans Green & Co.

Pringle-Pattison, A. S. (1904) 'The life and philosophy of Herbert Spencer', *Quarterly Review* 200: 240–67.

Royce, Josiah (1904) *Herbert Spencer: An Estimate and a Review*, New York: Fox, Duffield, & Co.

Rumney, J. (1934) *Herbert Spencer's Sociology*, London: Williams & Norgate (contains complete bibliography).

Ward, James (1899) *Agnosticism and Naturalism*, 2 vols, London: Adam & Charles Black.

More recent literature includes:

Peel, J. D. Y. (1971) *Herbert Spencer: The Evolution of a Sociologist*, London: Heinemann.

Taylor, M. W. (1922) *Man versus the State: Herbert Spencer and Late Victorian Individualism*, Oxford: Clarendon.

Turner, J. H. (1985) *Herbert Spencer: A Renewed Appreciation*, Beverley Hills: Sage.

Wiltshire, David (1978) *The Social and Political Thought of Herbert Spencer*, Oxford: Oxford University Press.

Spencer's place in a dictionary of twentieth-century philosophers must be somewhat debatable. His philosophy was largely the product of the Victorian period; by the time of his death in 1903 much of it was already out of date. He was, however, enormously widely read and discussed: his works went into numerous editions and were translated into many languages. His major work is the ten-volume *System of Synthetic Philosophy* (1862–93), which provides a synoptic overview of the best scientific knowledge of his age.

In *First Principles* (1862), Spencer sought to reconcile science with religion by positing the existence of 'the Unknowable', behind the phenomenal universe of the natural sciences, maintaining that science concerns itself with the knowable, religion with the unknowable. This doctrine played no further part in Spencer's system, and deserved the gibe of F. H. **Bradley**: 'Mr Spencer's attitude towards the unknowable seems a proposal to take something for God simply because we do not know what the devil it can be'.

If the natural sciences provide all our knowledge of the phenomenal world, and the noumenal world is unknowable, what role is left for philosophy? Spencer answers that the various special sciences provide only partial syntheses of sensory knowledge: philosophy can provide higher abstractions and hence more general principles. Philosophy is thus the culmination of scientific enquiry, the systematic ordering and unification of the results of the special sciences.

On the subject of a priori knowledge Spencer attempted a compromise between rationalism and empiricism. There are, he admits, some truths of which the negations are *inconceivable* (e.g. 'two straight lines cannot enclose a space') and which thus seem a priori valid. What is a priori to the individual is, however, not so for the race: our geometrical 'intuitions' are a sort of racial memory, the legacy of the experience of generations of ancestors. This is, in the final analysis, not so much a compromise between empiricism and rationalism as an empiricst *explanation* of why some propositions seem rationally self-evident to us.

The core of Spencer's whole philosophy is the doctrine of evolution.

'Evolution' is an integration of matter and concomitant dissipation of motion; during which the matter passes from an indefinite, incoherent homogeneity to a definite coherent heterogeneity; and during which the retained motion undergoes a parallel transformation'
(1862, p. 396).

Apart from an essay on the nebular hypothesis of Kant and Laplace, Spencer had little to say about the inorganic world; his system begins with biology. He was committed to some version of the theory of evolution before the publication of Darwin's *Origin of Species* in 1859, although he had doubts about the sufficiency of the Darwinian mechanism of natural selection. The popular phrase 'survival of the fittest', and the development of the political ideology known as 'social Darwinism', are both due to Spencer rather than Darwin.

In psychology and sociology Spencer's method was synthetic: he would amass empirical data before deriving significant abstractions and generalizations. He thus belongs, with Auguste Comte, among the pioneers of empirical sociology, seeing social development as a necessary part of the cosmic evolutionary process, and subject to the same basic law. The degree of differentiation and specialization within a society is a measure of its degree of evolution.

This philosophical sociology led Spencer directly to political conclusions. The highest form of society, he argued, is one which allows most individual freedom, i.e. the liberal free-market society of Victorian capitalism. In *Man versus the State* (1884) and elsewhere, he insisted that the only proper role for the state was protection of its citizens against external aggression and internal disorder, and warned of an impending tyranny if the state were to overstep those limits.

Spencer's system culminated in the *Principles of Ethics* (1892–3), in which, once again, he tried to trace the effects of the law of evolution. Concerning the foundations of ethics he held that moral intuitions are the products of a sort of racial memory, justified by their grounding in the evolution of the race. (Races with certain moral intuitions survived and prospered at the expense of others). Here Spencer thought (erroneously) that Darwin's 'survival of the fittest' justified his own extreme individualism. His evolutionary naturalism, with its tendency to equate 'more highly evolved' with 'more valuable', was of course one of G. E. **Moore's** primary targets in his *Principia Ethica*.

Spencer's influence was vast and enduring. Metz speaks of an 'evolutionary-naturalist' *school* in British philosophy (Lewes, Stephen, Clifford, Tyndall, **Pearson**, Huxley), and traces its substantial debts to Spencer. Even though Spencer's system has not survived, his 'principles' are dismissed as obscure or question-begging, and his voluminous works gather dust in our libraries, many of his fundamental ideas remain potent. Tracing our metaphysical and moral 'intuitions' to their evolutionary origins is taken seriously by philosophers like Michael Ruse and biologists like Richard Dawkins. The idea of a natural order of 'progress' from one form of society to another is hotly debated by social theorists. Liberal individualism and social Darwinism have proved very popular among the 'libertarian right' in England and in the USA.

Sources: DNB; Metz; Passmore 1957; EncBrit.

ANDREW PYLE

Spengler, Oswald

German. *b:* 29 May 1880, Blankenburg, Harz, Germany. *d:* 8 May 1936, Munich. *Cat:* Philosopher of history. *Ints:* Theories of universal history. *Educ:* Munich, Berlin, Halle; PhD 1904. *Infls:* Goethe, Hegel, Schelling and Dilthey. *Appts:* Private scholar, Munich, from 1904.

Main publications:

(1904) *Heraklit eine Studie*, Halle: Kaemmerer.
(1904) *Der metaphysische Grundgedanke der Heraklitschen Philosophie*, Halle: Kamemmerer.
(1918–22) *Der Untergang des Abendlandes, Umrisse einer Morphologie der Weltgeschichte*, Munich: C. H. Beck (English translation, *The Decline of the West*, trans. Atkinson, London: Allen & Unwin, 1928).
(1921) *Pessimismus?*, Berlin: G. Stilke.
(1924) *Neubau des Deutschen Reiches*, Munich: Beck.
(1926) *Preussentum und Sozialismus*, Munich: C. H. Beck.
(1933) *Mensch und Technik*, Munich: C. H. Beck (English translaition, *Man and Technics*, London: Allen & Unwin, 1963).
(1933) *Politische Schriften*, Munich: C. H. Beck.
(1933) *Jahre der Entscheidung*, Munich: C. H. Beck (English translation, *The Hour of Decision*, trans. Atkinson, New York: Knopf, 1934).
(1937) *Reden und Aufsätze*, Munich: C. H. Beck.
(1963) *Briefe 1913–36*, ed. Koltanek, Munich: C. H. Beck (English translation, *The Spengler Letters 1913–36*, ed. Helps, London: Allen & Unwin, 1966).
(1985) *Briefwechsel zwischen Oswald Spengler und Wolfgang E. Groeger*, ed. Z. Werner, Hamburg: H. Buske.

Secondary literature:

Adorno, T. W. (1955) *Prismen*, Berlin: Suhrkamp.
Baltzer, A. (1959) *Oswald Spenglers Bedeutung für die Gegenwart*, Neheim-Hüsten: E. Nicklaus.
Collingwood, R. G. (1927) 'Oswald Spengler and the theory of historical cycles', *Antiquity* 1: 311–25, 435–46.
Düren, W. (1940) *Meine Unterredung mit Oswald Spengler*, Bonn: Röhrscheid.
Fauvel, J. (1981) 'Physics and society', in *Modern Physics and Problems of Knowledge* (Block IV of *Science and Belief from Darwin to Einstein*), Milton Keynes: Open University Press.
Forman, P. (1971) *Weimar culture, causality and quantum theory, Historical Studies in the Physical Sciences* 3: 1–115.
Gauhe, E. (1937) *Spengler und die Romantik*, Berlin: Junker & Dünnhaupt.
Haering, T. L. (1921) *Struktur der Weltgeschichte*, Tübingen: J. C. B. Mohr.
Heller, E. (1952) *The Disinherited Mind*, Cambridge: Bowes & Bowes.
Hughes, H. S. (1952) *Oswald Spengler*, New York: Scribners.

Neurath, O. (1921) *Antispengler*, Munich: Callwey.

Schoeps, H. J. (1953) *Vorläufer Spenglers*, Leiden: E. J. Brill.

Schroeter, M. (1922) *Der Streit um Spengler*, Munich: C. H. Beck.

——(1949) *Die Metaphysik des Untergangs*, Munich: Leibniz-Verlag.

——(1965) *Spengler-Studien*, Munich: C. H. Beck.

Stutz, E. (1959) *Oswald Spengler als politischer Denker*, Bern: C. H. Beck.

Spengler was an advocate of a cyclical view of history on the basis of a quasi-biological interpretation of the rise, maturity and decline of cultures. History was the story of the rise, maturity and decline of independent cultures between which there could be no genuine communication of cultural artefacts—he seems to have accepted the relativism that results from this position, although perhaps not faced up to the damaging consequences for his own historicist enterprise. For him there was no overall rationality governing the development and succession of cultures and, despite the biological model, their growth was not wholly determined. In his 'morphology', every aspect of a culture was bound by analogies to every other including its political and religious systems, and in its system of analogies Western culture was quite separate both from its Hellenistic predecessor and from its semitic contemporary. He believed in the pre-eminent role of Germany in the history of Western culture but rejected Nazism. In his own time his work may have been influential as much for the low value it assigned technical scientific knowledge in comparison with intuitive philosophical knowledge, as for the headline story of Western decline, although in his opinion the best that could be done at the present stage of cultural development was to concern oneself with such matters. Spengler was suspicious of such materialistic notions as causality, preferring to talk of the destinies of the cultures of his morphology. The vogue for his work in early Weimar Germany has been seen by Paul Forman as one source of the rise of quantum mechanics in physics.

Sources: Edwards; A. M. Koktanek (1968) *Oswald Spengler in seiner Zeit*, Munich: C. H. Beck; Brockhaus 17.

R. N. D. MARTIN

Spiegelberg, Herbert

German (naturalized American in 1944). *b:* 18 May 1904, Strasbourg. *d:* 6 September 1990, St

Louis, Missouri. *Cat:* Phenomenological philosopher. *Ints:* Philosophical history; philosophy of ethics. *Educ:* Heidelberg, 1922–4; Freiburg, 1924–5; PhD, Munich, 1928. *Infls:* Alexander Pfänder and Edmund Husserl. *Appts:* 1938–41, Research Associate, Swarthmore College; 1941–63, member of faculty, Lawrence College (subsequently Lawrence University); 1954–63, Ingraham Professor of Philosophy and Chairman of the Department of Philosophy; 1963–71, Professor of Philosophy, Washington University, St Louis; from 1971, Professor Emeritus.

Main publications:

(1930) 'Über das Wesen der Idee. Eine Ontologische Untersuchung' (Munich dissertation), *Jahrbuck für Philosophie und Phänomenologische Forschung* 11.

(1935) *Antirelativismus. Kritik des Relativismus und Skeptizismus der Werte und des Sollens*, Zurich: Max Niehans.

(1935) *Gesetz und Sittengesetz. Strukturanalytische und historische Vorstudien zu einer gesetzesfreien Ethik* (Munich Habilitationsschrift), Zurich: Max Niehans.

(1960) *The Phenomenological Movement: A Historical Introduction* 2 vols, Boston: Nijhoff; second edition, 1969, third, enlarged edition, 1982.

(1963) *Alexander Pfänders Phänomenologie*, The Hague: Nijhoff.

(1972) *Phenomenology in Psychology and Psychiatry. A Historical Introduction*, Evanston, Ill.: Northwestern University Press.

(1975) *Doing Phenomenology: Essays on and in Phenomenology*, Dordrecht: Kluwer.

(1981) *The Context of the Phenomenological Movement: Comparative and Historical Studies*, The Hague: Nijhoff.

(1982) (ed. with E. Avé-Lallemant) *Pfänder-Studien*, Dordrecht: Kluwer.

(1986) *Steppingstones Toward an Ethics for Fellow Existers: Essays 1944–83*, Dordrecht: Nijhoff.

Secondary literature:

Bossert, Phil (ed.) (1975) *Phenomenological Perspectives: Historical and Systematic Essays in Honour of Herbert Spiegelberg*, The Hague: Nijhoff.

Hamrick, William S.(ed.) (1985) *Phenomenology in Practice and Theory*, The Hague: Nijhoff.

——*et al.* (eds) (1990) 'The Philosophy of Herbert Spiegelberg' *Journal of the British Society for Phenomenology* 21 (January).

Spiegelberg's work comprises historical studies within phenomenology; the theory and *practice* of phenomenology and, perhaps above all, extensive studies in the philosophy of ethics. He was also a scholar and translator of the work of the Munich phenomenologist, Alexander **Pfänder**, who was perhaps his main philosophical influence.

His reputation as the 'historian of phenomenology' was secured by his extraordinarily influential work, *The Phenomenological Movement* (1960). It contains detailed expositions of method, principles and terminology and histories of **Husserl**, the Göttingen, Freiburg and Munich phenomenological circles and of subsequent developments in Germany, France and worldwide. *The Context of the Phenomenological Movement* (1981) is a collection of 15 articles from 1936–73 containing further information on the historical and philosophical connections between Husserl, **Brentan**, **Peirce**, Pfänder, **Austin**, **James** and **Wittgenstein**.

Phenomenology in Psychology and Psychiatry (1972) is a general account of how phenomenology has been applied by psychologists and psychiatrists in Europe and North America, and a detailed account of the work of ten of the leading figures in the field. *Doing Phenomenology* (1975), a collection of essays of 1940–70, is not only a redeployment of the descriptive and eidetic methods of his Munich dissertation, it also answers the need of actually *doing* phenomenology rather than just talking about it.

In 1935 he published two important ethical works: *Antirelativismus*—a critique of the relativism and scepticism of values and of moral obligations, and his (380-page) *Gesetz und Sittengesetz*—structural-analytical and historical preliminary studies towards a law-free ethics. The latter was complemented by *Sollen und Dürfen* [Ought and May]—a philosophical foundation of ethical rights and duties. His *Steppingstones* (1986) is a collection of 16 articles arranged in a thematic progression. Roughly, the 'steppingstones' are: the discovery of self, the transposal of self and other, human dignity and equality, and global ethics.

Sources: Correspondence with Prof. Hamrick.

BARRY JONES

Spirito, Ugo

Italian. *b:* 9 September 1896, Arezzo, Italy. *d:* 28 April 1979, Rome. *Cat:* Philosopher in the tradition of Gentile; a leader of the new Hegelian left in Italy. *Appts:* Professor of Economics, University of Pisa, 1932–5; Professor of Philosophy, Universities of Messina, 1935–6, Genoa 1936–8, and Rome, from 1938.

Main publications:

(1921) *Il pragmatismo nella filosofia contemporanea.*
(1930) *L'idealismo italiano e i suoi critici.*
(1930) *La critica della'economia liberale.*
(1932) *I fondamenti dell'economia corporativa.*
(1933) *Capitalismo e corporativismo.*
(1936) *Scienza e filosofia.*
(1937) *La via come ricerca.*
(1939) *Dalla economia liberale al corporativismo.*
(1941) *La vita come arte.*
(1948) *Il problematicismo.*
(1950–) *Opere complete*, Florence: Sansoni.
(1953) *La vita come amore.*
(1958) *Cristeanismo e communismo.*
(1963) *Critica alla democrazia.*
(1964) *Critica dell'estetica.*
(1964) *Nuovo umanesimo.*
(1965) *Il comunismo.*
(1966) *Dal mito alla scienza.*
(1969) *Giovanni Gentile.*
(1971) *Storia della mia ricerca.*
(1973) *Due falsi scienza: la socilogia et la psicoanalisi.*
(1977) *Memorie di un incosciente.*

Secondary literature:

Lizzio, M. (1968) *Marxismo e metafisica*, Catania: Bonanno.
Stefano, L. di (1980) *Ugo Spirito*, Rome: Volpe.
Tamassia, F. (ed.) (1986) *Le opere di Ugo Spirito: Bibliografia*, Rome: Fondazione: Ugo Spirito.

Spirito's philosophy has at its core the thesis of the identity of philosophy and science. The distinction between philosophy as knowledge of the universal and science as knowledge of the particular is rejected and is replaced by the notion of a process that moves from the particular to the universal and vice versa, in which the identity of philosophy and science consists, and in which the absolute unity of traditional metaphysics is construed as the ideal limit sought but never attained by science. Because of the obscurity of this final goal Spirito adopted a 'problematist view' of philosophy which recognizes and exposes any contradictory quest for total truth. The elaboration of this philosophy took Spirito into the notion of life as love. Rather than claiming to know the whole truth we recognize instead that each point of the universe has its own centre, what Spirito calls omnicentrism. Spirito notes the mutliplicity of philosophical views in the modern world, but notes also the unifying force of science and technology. Spirito develops his thought in two directions. On the one hand he shows the evolution of a collective, anti-individualistic society founded on the commonly agreed values of science which will transcend idiosyncratic ideologies. That pushes us towards corporativism. On the other hand there is the individuality implicit in the notion of science as ever self-critical and hypothetical.

COLIN LYAS

Spivak, Gayatri Chakravorty

Indian. *b:* 24 February 1942, Calcutta. *Cat:* Spivak resists categorization, but is concerned with the critique of humanism. *Ints:* Deconstruction. *Educ:* BA 1959, University of Calcutta; PhD 1967, Comparative Literature, Cornell University. *Infls:* Marx, Derrida, Mahasweta Devi and Ranajit Guha. *Appts:* Andrew W. Mellon Professor of English, 1986–91, Adjunct Professor, Department of Philosophy, University of Pittsburgh, 1987–91; Professor, then Avalon Professor in the Humanities, from 1991; Adjunct Professor, Department of Philosophy, Columbia University, from 1991.

Main publications:

(1976) (trans. and critical preface to) Jacques Derrida, *Of Grammatology*, Baltimore: Johns Hopkins.
(1988) 'Deconstructing historiography', 'Scattered speculations on the question of value' and other essays, in *In Other Worlds: Essays in Cultural Politics*, London: Routledge.
(1993) 'More on power/knowledge', 'Limits and openings of Marx in Derrida' and 'Not virgin enough to say that (s)he occupies the place of the other', in *Outside in the Teaching Machine*, London: Routledge.
(1993) *The Post-Colonial Critic: Interviews, Strategies, Dialogues*, ed. Sarah Harasym, London: Routledge.
(1995) *The Spivak Reader*, ed. Donna Landry and Gerald McLean, London: Routledge.

Spivak first came to prominence with her lengthy and now seminal introductory essay to **Derrida** (1976). Her commitment to deconstruction is interdisciplinary, extending into literary, political and cultural fields, as well as philosophy; and she has been deeply influential in the development of recent Anglo-American academic feminism. Concerned always with the marginalization of the 'Other'—whether it be in sexual, racial, colonial or gender paradigms—Spivak cautions against the excesses of poststructuralism which would reify and dematerialize lived experience. Despite a sure and often startling performance of abstract high theory, Spivak emphasizes the 'usefulness' of

deconstruction, stressing always that the aim is not to destroy the constructs that are addressed—truth, essence, masculinity and so on—but to negotiate with them. Although there can be 'no absolute justification in *any* position', there are nevertheless necesary fictions, and responsibility rests in the self-reflexive awareness of the limits of such closures. Spivak thus sees deconstruction as a positive force, opening up multiple possibilities of displacement, but directed also towards politically strategic (albeit provisional) realignments. As with other theorists of deconstruction, her project is finally an ethical one.

Sources: Personal communication.

MARGRIT SHILDRICK

Spranger, (Franz Ernst) Eduard

German. *b:* 27 June 1882, near Berlin. *d:* 17 September 1963, Tübingen. *Cat:* Neo-Hegelian; educational theorist; social philosopher. *Ints:* Psychology; social philosophy. *Educ:* Universities of Leipzig, Berlin and Tübingen. *Infls:* Influences include Dilthey, Hegel and Weber. *Appts:* 1911–20, Professor of Philosophy, Leipzig; 1920–46, Professor of Philosophy and Pedagogy, Berlin; 1946 (until retirement), Professor of Philosophy, Tübingen.

Main publications:

(1909) *Wilhelm von Humboldt und die Humanitätsidee*, Berlin: Reuther & Reichard.
(1910) *Wilhelm von Humboldt und die Reform des Bildungswesens*, Berlin: Reuther & Reichard.
(1914) *Lebensformen; geisteswissenschaftliche Psychologie und Ethik der Personlichkeit*, Halle: Niemeyer (trans. J. W. Pigors, *Types of Men: the Psychology of Ethics and Personality*, Halle: Niemeyer, 1928).
(1924) *Psychologie des Jugendalters*, Leipzig: Quelle & Meyer.
(1942) *Goethes Weltanschauung. Reden und Aufsätze*, Leipzig and Wiesbaden: Insel.
(1947) *Die Magie der Seele*, Tübingen: Mohr.

Secondary literature:

Baehr, H. W. (ed.) (1957) *Erziehung sur Menschlichkeit–Festschrift für Eduard Spranger zum 75. Geburtstag*, Tübingen.
Neu, Theodore (1958) *Bibliographie Eduard Spranger*, Tübingen.
Wenke, Hans (ed.) (1957) *Eduard Spranger, Bildnis eines geistigen Menschen unserer Zeit*, Heidelberg.

Spranger began as a pupil and follower of **Dilthey** but his attempt to develop the notion of *verstehen* in psychology and to give an account of the human sciences (*Geisteswissenschaften*) generally led him to a Hegelian position.

His main work, *Lebensformen* (1914), distinguished six forms of value and six corresponding types of personality in modern culture—truth (theoretical), utility (economic), beauty (aesthetic), love (social), power (political) and the vital totality of value (religious). Spranger was prominent as a humanist and for taking a stand on cultural values. In philosophy he was a major influence in the 1920s on the German neo-Hegelian revival.

Sources: Edwards; NUC.

STUART BROWN

Stace, Walter Terence

British. *b:* 17 November 1886 London. *d:* 2 August 1967, Princeton, New Jersey. *Cat:* Empiricist; phenomenalist. *Ints:* Epistemology; metaphysics; ethics, philosophy of religion; mysticism. *Educ:* Trinity College, Dublin. *Infls:* Moore, Russell and H. S. Macran. *Appts:* Professor, Princeton, 1932–55.

Main publications:

(1920) *Critical History of Greek Philosophy*, London: Macmillan.

(1924) *The Philosophy of Hegel*, London: Macmillan.

(1929) *The Meaning of Beauty*, London: Grant Richards.

(1932) *Theory of Knowledge and Existence*, Oxford: Clarendon Press.

(1937) *The Concept of Morals*, London: Macmillan.

(1940) *The Nature of the World*, Princeton: Princeton University Press.

(1942) *The Destiny of Western Man*, New York: Reynal & Hitchcock.

(1953) *Time and Eternity*, Princeton: Princeton University Press.

(1953) *Religion and Modern Mind*, London: Macmillan.

(1960) *Mysticism and Philosophy*, Philadelphia: Lippincott.

Secondary literature:

Price, H. H. (1932) 'Mr Stace's theory of the external world', *Mind*.

Smith, J. W. (1967) in Paul Edwards (ed.) *Encyclopedia of Philosophy*; New York: Macmillan & Co.

The most conspicuous feature of Stace as a philosopher is the superb clarity and lucidity of his writing, an attribute accompanied, in his case, by a certain simple-mindedness. His style reflects his admiration for **Moore** but it is better than Moore's because less cluttered and repetitious. Stace did not become a professional philosopher until his mid-forties, after a career in the Ceylon civil service where he rose to be Mayor of Colombo. During that career he wrote some books, most notably an encyclopedic survey of the philosophy of Hegel. In 1934 he published a famous article in *Mind* called 'Refutation of realism', arguing that there could be no valid argument of any kind from the private impressions with which alone we are directly acquainted to anything beyond or outside them.

He is said to have claimed that the article was a kind of joke, but its central thesis is embodied in his main epistemological work, *Theory of Knowledge and Existence* (1932), where, however, he avoided its apparently solipsistic implications. He maintained that most of the constituents of the common-sense and scientific pictures of the world are hypothetical constructions, taking **Russell**'s 'supreme maxim of scientific philosophizing' to its uttermost limit. As elements of the construction, he allowed himself to draw on the sense-experiences of other minds to assist in the construction of an objective world. The exercise, fortified by this bold assumption which appears to leap over the fact that our knowledge of other minds requires antecedent knowledge of the bodies through which they are manifested, is carried through with great perseverance. *The Nature of the World* (1940), which Stace subtitled 'an essay in phenomenalistic metaphysics', pursues the ontological consequences of his epistemic reductions. The ultimate elements of the world are 'cells', bipolar entities consisting of an act of consciousness and a datum. Both acts and data are abstractions, incapable of independent existence. Only those pulses of consciousness that enter into the history of persons actually exist. In a chapter on God Stace dismisses all proofs of his existence and says that it can be justified only on the basis of mystical experience. That theme was developed in the last three books, all on religion. His unappetizing conclusion is that the testimony of mystics is none the worse for being intrinsically self-contradictory. In ethics Stace defended a sensible kind of utilitarianism, disentangling happiness from pleasure. Stace's writings received some attention from H. H. **Price** and A. J. **Ayer**, and some *Mind* articles of the 1930s critical of positivism from a traditionally empiricist standpoint aroused discussion.

ANTHONY QUINTON

Stalnaker, R(obert Culp)

American. *b:* 22 January 1940, Princeton, New Jersey. *Cat:* Philosopher of language; philosopher of mind. *Ints:* Philosophical logic; pragmatics; intensional logic. *Educ:* Wesleyan University and Princeton. *Infls:* S. A. Kripke and Richmond Thomason. *Appts:* 1965–8, Instructor, then Assistant, Yale; 1968–71, Associate Professor, University of Illinois, Urbana; 1971–89, Associate Professor, then Professor of Philosophy, Cornell; since 1994, Professor of Philosophy, Massachusetts Institute of Technology.

Main publications:

(1968) 'A theory of conditionals', in N. Rescher (ed.) *Studies in Logical Theory*, Oxford, Blackwell (APQ Monograph 2); reprinted in E. Sosa (ed.), *Causation and Conditionals*, Oxford: Oxford University Press, 1975, and in F. Jackson (ed.) *Conditionals*, Oxford: Oxford University Press, 1991.
(1970) (with R. Thomasen) 'A semantic analysis of conditional logic', *Theoria* 36.
(1970) 'Probability and conditionals', *Philosophy of Science* 37.
(1972) 'Pragmatics', in G. Harman and D. Davidson (eds), *Semantics of Natural Language*, Dordrecht: Reidel.
(1973) 'Presuppositions', *Journal of Philosophical Logic* 2.
(1978) 'Assertion', in P. Cole (ed.), *Syntax and Semantics 9: Pragmatics*, New York: Academic.
(1981) 'Indexical Belief', *Synthese* 49.
(1984) *Inquiry*, Cambridge, Mass.: MIT Press.

Secondary literature:

Hardegree, G. M. (1974) 'The conditional in quantum logic', *Synthese* 29.
Lewis, D. (1973) *Counterfactuals*, Oxford: Blackwell, especially pp. 77–83.
Salmon, N. (1986) *Frege's Puzzle*, Cambridge, Mass.: MIT Press, pp. 168–9.
Thomason, R. (1970) 'Decidability in the logic of conditionals', in A. R. Anderson, R. B. Marcus and R. Martin (eds), *The Logical Enterprise*, New Haven and London: Yale University Press.
Van Fraassen, B. C. (1974) 'Hidden vairables in conditional logic', *Theoria* 40.

Along with R. Thomason, Stalnaker invented the idea that a strong conditional (e.g. a counterfactual) is to count as true in a world *i*, if and only if its consequent is true in the possible world 'nearest' (most similar) to *i*, where the antecedent of the conditional is true. The world i may be the actual world. This semantic analysis accounts for the fact that unlike, for example, the material conditional, counterfactuals are not subject to such logical rules as transitivity, strengthening the antecedent and contraposition. Stalnaker devised a propositional conditional logic on the basis of this idea and later, with Thomason, a first-order conditional logic, which they proved to be sound and complete. Thomason proved the propositional part of the logic to be effectively decidable and presented a natural deduction version of the logic. David **Lewis**, who developed similar ideas independently, has shown that Stalnaker's conditional logic is a special case within a cluster of such logics; and G. Hardegree was able to prove that the Stalnaker conditional is formally identical to the conditional in quantum logic.

Among Stalnaker's numerous other contributions to studies in the semantics and pragmatics of natural language is an attempt to develop an account of 'that'-clauses which vindicates the idea of identifying a proposition with the set of possible worlds in which it is true.

Sources: DAP; DAS.

STIG RASMUSSEN

Stammler, Rudolf

German. *b:* 19 February 1856, Alsfeld, Germany. *d:* 25 April 1938, Wernigerode, Germany. *Cat:* Neo-Kantian; philosopher of law. *Ints:* Marxism. *Educ:* Giessen and Leipzig Universities. *Infls:* Hermann Cohen and Paul Natorp. *Appts:* Professor in Berlin from 1916.

Main publications:

(1896) *Wirtschaft und Recht nach der materilistischen Geschichtsauffassung*, Leipzig: Veit.
(1902) *Die Lehre vom richtigen Recht*, Berlin: Guttentag (English translation, *The Theory of Justice*, trans. Isaac Husik, New York: Macmillan, 1925).
(1922) *Lehrbuch der Rechtsphilosophie*, Berlin: Walter de Gruyter.
(1925) *Rechtsphilosophische Abhandlungen und Vorträge*, Charlottenburg: R. Heise.

Secondary literature:

Breuer, Isaac (1912) *Der Rechtsbegriff auf der Grundlage der Stammlerschen Soziaiphilosophie*, Würzburg: Leibig.

Stammler tried to apply Kant's critical philosophy to jurisprudence. Influenced by the Marburg School, he advocated a philosophy of right in which the ideal of a community of autonomous historical human beings that are related to one another in one organic whole was central. This 'social ideal' was for him a task that must be pursued by moral beings. It formed for him the foundation of right law and a society in which the interests of free individuals are realized without negating their autonomy as moral beings. Stammler was highly critical of Marxism and its materialistic view of historical processes.

Stammler was one of the most important philosophers of law of the Weimar republic. However, he was influential not only in Germany, but also other European countries and the USA. Max **Weber** vehemently rejected Stammler's criticism of Marxism.

MANFRED KUEHN

Stebbing, Lizzie Susan

British. *b:* 2 December 1885, Wimbledon. *Cat:* Logician; philosopher of science. *Ints:* Logic; philosophy of science. *Educ:* Studied at Girton (Historical Tripos I 1906, II 1907, Moral Sciences Tripos II 1908); MA, London, 1912; DLit, London, 1931. *Infls:* Bradley, Whitehead, Moore, Russell, Broad, W. E. Johnson, Carnap, E. A. Burtt, Dingle and W. Wilson. *Appts:* Taught at University of Cambridge, 1911–24, King's College, London, 1913–15, Westfield College, London, 1914–20, Bedford College, London, 1915–20 (part-time), 1920–43 (full-time); Professor of Philosophy at Bedford College, London, 1933; Visiting Professor at Columbia University, 1931–2; Fellow of Royal Historical Society, 1916.

Main publications:

(1914) *Pragmatism and French Voluntarism*, Cambridge: Cambridge University Press.
(1929) 'Realism and modern physics', *Proceedings of the Aristotelian Society*, supplementary vol. 9.
(1930) *A Modern Introduction to Logic*, London: Methuen, revised and expanded, 1933.
(1934) *Logic in Practice*, London: Methuen, revised by C. W. K. Mundle, 1954.
(1936) (with C. D. Lewis) *Imagination and Thinking*, London: British Institute of Adult Education, Life and Leisure Pamphlets 4.
(1937) *Philosophy and the Physicists*, Harmondsworth: Penguin.
(1939) *Thinking to Some Purpose*, Harmondsworth: Penguin.
(1941) *Ideals and Illusions*, London: Watts.
(1943) *A Modern Elementary Logic*, London: Methuen, revised by C. W. K. Mundle, 1952.

Secondary literature:

Hannay, A. H. (ed.) (1948) *Philosophical Studies*, London: Allen and Unwin (essays in her honour, although only two of them, by Laird and Ewing, are primarily on her work; includes appreciation by John Wisdom, and bibliography).
Magg, P. (1946) 'Homage to Susan Stebbing', *Personalist* (biographical and personal reminiscences).

Stebbing represents a generally realist approach to philosophy, although in the case of perception the realism is indirect: we perceive the sun indirectly by seeing a sensum directly (1929). Her first book, *Pragmatism and French Voluntarism* (1914), attacks the pragmatists on the nature of truth and the French voluntarists for assimilating the knower and the known. She came to philosophy via **Bradley**'s *Appearance and Reality*, but her main interests lay in logic and philosophy of science. She made a pioneering and widely acclaimed attempt to combine in an introductory textbook (1930) the traditional syllogistic logic (treated partly for its own sake but partly for university syllabus reasons) with modern developments due to **Russell** and others; this involved some epistemology and metaphysics, on which she also wrote various articles.

Philosophy and the Physicists (1937) fiercely attacks the physicists **Jeans** and (especially) **Eddington** for misunderstanding the enterprise that science is about in a way that leads them to idealist conclusions. Eddington in particular is accused of what amounts to confusing the construction by the mind of a scientific theory with its construction of the world itself, and in the famous 'two worlds' passage (pp. 47–8) of treating alternative accounts of something as though they were accounts of two parallel things. Eddington's use of the indeterminacies of quantum physics to defend free will is rejected as irrelevant because of the minute amounts involved, and Stebbing develops a compatibilist view emphasizing the agent rather than a mere passive series of causally related events.

Later Stebbing turned briefly to ethics and politics, in *Ideals and Illusions* (1941) defending liberal values based on reflection against *Realpolitik* and both totalitarian and otherworldly ideologies, but some, thought not all, reviewers were lukewarm (see Hannay 1948, p. 20).
Sources: PI: WWW 1941–50.

A. R. LACEY

Stefanini, Luigi

Italian. *b:* 3 November 1891, Treviso, Italy. *d:* 16 January 1956, Padua. *Cat:* Personalist philosopher. *Appts:* Professor of Theoretical Philosophy,

University of Messina, 1936–40; Professor of History of Philosophy, University of Padua, 1940–56; Cofounder of the Gallarate movement; Founder of *Rivista di estetica.*

Main publications:
(1913) *Saggio sulla filosofia di M. Blondel.*
(1930) *Idealismo cristiano.*
(1932–5) *Platone,* 2 vols.
(1936) *Immaginismo comme problema filosofica.*
(1939) *Problem: auttuali dell'arte.*
(1949) *Metafisica della forma,* Padua: Liviana.
(1950) *Metafisica della persona,* Padua: Liviana.
(1952) *Esistenzialismo ateo ed esistenzialismo teistico,* Padua: Liviana.
(1953) *La mia prospettiva filosofica,* Brescia: Morceliana.
(1955) *Trattato di estetica.*
(1970) *Il corporativismo,* Florence: Sansoni.
(1979) *Personalismo sociale,* Rome: Studium.
(1979) *Personalismo filosofica,* Rome: Studium.

Secondary literature:
Gregoretti, P. (1983) *Persona ed essere,* Trieste: Universita di Trieste.
Scritti in onore di Luigi Stefanini (1960), Padua: Liviana.

The central thrust of Stefanini's work is a sustained development of the notion, rooted in a French Augustinianism, which we might call 'imagism', the notion that we are created in the image of God and that our proper vocation is to confirm to our eternal exemplar. This is investigated through the investigation of Christian idealism, Christian spiritualism, and personalism. For Stefanini Christian idealism treats the self as created and not, as with **Gentile**, self-creating. His Christian spiritualism rejects existentialism and phenomenology as dividing the existential from the transcendent and lays stress on the self as existence which utters itself in the word that alludes to and depends on the absolute. Finally, in the investigation of personalism, **Spirito**'s notion of 'imagism' finds its mature form. The self cannot sustain itself without transcendence and realizes itself in relation to the transcendent.

COLIN LYAS

Stegmüller, Wolfgang
Austrian-German. *b:* 3 June 1923, Natters, Austria. *d:* 1 June 1991, Munich. *Cat:* Philosopher of science; analytical philosopher. *Educ:* Innsbruck University, DPhil 1945, Habilitation 1949. *Infls:* Rudolf Carnap and Carl Gustav

Hempel. *Appts:* 1954–56, Assistant, then Titular Professor of Philosophy, Innsbruck University; 1958–90, Professor of Philosophy, Munich University, and Chairman of the University's Institute for Philosophy, Logic, and Philosophy of Science; 1966, Corresponding Member of the Austrian Academy (Österreichische Akademie der Wissenschaften); 1967, Member of the Bavarian Academy (Bayerische Akademie der Wissenschaften).

Main publications:
(1952) *Hauptströmungen der Gegenwartsphilosophie,* Vienna and Stuttgart: Kröner, 1960: made into 4 volumes (first edition of vol. 4, 1989; eighth edition of vol. 2, 1987) (English translation, *Main Currents in Contemporary German, British, and American Philosophy,* Dordrecht, 1969).
(1954) *Metaphysik-Wissenschaft-Skepsis,* Vienna: Sammlung Die Universität; second edition, Vienna: Springer, 1969.
(1957) *Das Wahrheitsproblem und die Idee der Semantik,* Vienna: Springer.
(1969–86) *Probleme und Resultate der Wissenschaftstheorie und Analytischen Philosophie,* 4 vols, Berlin, Heidelberg and New York: Springer (English translation of vol. 2, part 2, *The Structure and Dynamics of Theories,* New York: Springer, 1976).
(1977) *Collected Papers on Epistemology, Philosophy of Science and History of Philosophy,* 2 vols, Dordrecht: Reidel.
(1979) *The Structuralist View of Theories: A Possible Analogue of the Bourbaki Programme in Physical Science,* Berlin, Heidelberg and New York: Springer.

Secondary literature:
Feyerabend, P. K. (1977) 'Changing patterns of reconstruction', *The British Journal for the Philosophy of Science,* 28.
Hempel, C. G., Putnam, H. and Essler, W. K. (eds) (1983) *Methodology, Epistemology, and Philosophy of Science: Essays in Honour of Wolfgang Stegmüller on the Occasion of his 60th Birthday, 3 June 1983,* Dordrecht: Reidel.
Kuhn, T. S. (1976) 'Theory-change as structure-change', *Erkenntnis* 10.
Müller-Ponholzer, A. and Molz, E. (eds) (1992) 'Die Schriften von Wolfgang Stegmüller', *Erkenntnis* 36.

Stegmüller played a very important role in the revival of interest in analytic philosophy and philosophy of science in Germany, Austria and Switzerland after the Second World War. His *Hauptströmungen der Gegenwartsphilosophie*

(1952, 4 volumes)—the most widespread and comprehensive work on contemporary philosophy in the German-speaking world—shows Stegmüller's ability to interpret and clearly reconstruct philosophical positions, some of them by philosophers with widely different philosophical backgrounds like **Brentano**, **Husserl**, **Scheler**, **Heidegger**, **Wittgenstein**, **Carnap**, **Putnam**, **Kripke** and **Mackie**.

Stegmüller's extensive writings on the philosophy of science have had a great influence not only on philosophers but also on scientists. He is especially noted for promoting and thoroughly researching the so-called non-statement or structuralist view of scientific theories, originally put forward by J. D. Sneed. According to Sneed scientific theories are not sets of statements but mathematical structures with intended applications. Using the structuralist framework, Stegmüller was continually trying to solve the problem of theoretical concepts and to close the gap between systematic and historical (**Kuhn**, **Feyerabend**) accounts of scientific progress.

KLAUS PUHL

Stein (Sister Teresa Benedicta), Edith

German. **b:** 1891, Breslau (then German empire, now Wroclaw, Poland). **d:** 1942, Auschwitz concentration camp. **Cat:** Phenomenologist; theologian. **Ints:** Husserlian phenomenology; Thomism; Catholic mystical theology. **Educ:** University of Breslau, 1911; Universities of Göttingen and Freiburg, 1913–18. **Infls:** Husserl, St Thomas Aquinas, Roman Ingarden, Adolp Reinach and Wilhelm Dilthey. **Appts:** 1913–18, Personal Assistant to Edmund Husserl; 1922–9, teacher of German, Dominican School, Speyer; 1927–32, lecture tours in Europe; 1932–3, Lectureship in Philosophy, University of Münster; 1933, entered Carmelite convent.

Main publications:

(1917) *Zum Problem der Einfühling* [On the Problem of Empathy]; trans. Waltraud Stein, foreword by Erwin Strauss, The Hague: Nijhoff, 1964.

(1956) *Writings of Edith Stein* ed., trans. and intro. Hilde Graef, Westminster: Newman Press (part IV for philosophy).

(1950) *Endliches und Ewiges Sein* [Finite and Eternal Being], Louvain: Nauwelaerts & Herder.

Secondary literature:

Collins, James (1942) 'Edith Stein and the advance of phenomenology', *Thought* 17.

Graef, Hilde (1956) *Scholar and the Cross: The Life and Work of Edith Stein*, Westminster: Newman Press.

Herbstrith, Waltraud (1985) *Edith Stein: A Biography*, San Francisco: Harper & Row.

Edith Stein's philosophical work falls into two parts, the earlier phenomenology which took its impetus from her years as personal assistant to Husserl, responsible for the editing and transcription of his notes, and her later, Thomist writings, undertaken after her conversion to Roman Catholicism in 1922.

Her 1917 examined empathy as 'a particular form of the act of knowing' and as a fundamental capacity of pure consciousness. It led her to the analysis of the concept of a person, a task that dominated much of her subsequent work. She was a member of the Munich Circle, a group that did much to propagate Husserlian thought. Her conversion to Roman Catholicism, her translation of Aquinas's *Questiones Disputate Veritate* and her intensive study of his thought resulted in her acceptance of tenets of faith and Aristotelian ontological categories as a basis for philosophical investigation. This was regarded by Roman **Ingarden** as 'a tragic finale' to her philosophical development and a failure to preserve Husserlian objectivity. Edith Stein's philosophical reputation, particularly in respect of her work in phenomenology, has been overshadowed by the story of her martyrdom at Auschwitz.

Sources: Kersey.

DIANÉ COLLINSON

Steiner, Rudolf

Austrian. **b:** 27 February 1861, Kraljevec (then Austria). **d:** 30 March 1925, Dornach, Switzerland. **Cat:** Theosopher. **Ints:** Philosophy of education; religion. **Educ:** Technical University of Vienna. **Infls:** Personal influence: Schroer. Philosophical influence: Goethe and Kant. **Appts:** 1886–93, Editor, Goethe Archive, Weimar; 1897–1904, Editor, *Magazine for Literature*, Berlin; 1902–9, General Secretary, German Theosophical Society; 1909–25, Director, World Theosophical Society.

Main publications:

(1963) *Knowledge of Higher Worlds*, trans. G. Metaxa, rev. B. S. Osmond and C. Davy.

(1979) *Occult Science*, trans. G. and M. Adams.

(1989) *Theosophy*, trans. M. Cotterell and A. P. Shepherd.

(1992) *The Philosophy of Spritual Activity*, second edition, trans. R. Stebbing.

Secondary literature:
Aeppli, W. (1986) *Rudolf Steiner: Education and the Developing Child*, Bristol: Rudolf Steiner Press.
Davy, J. (1975) *Rudolf Steiner: A Sketch of his life and work*, Bristol: Rudolf Steiner Press.
Easton, S. C. (1975) *Man and World in the Light of Anthroposophy*, Bristol: Rudolf Steiner Press.
Flew, A. (ed.) (1979) *A Dictionary of Philosophy*, London: Pan.
Hutchins, E. (1984) *Introduction to the Mystery Plays of Rudolf Steiner*, Bristol: Rudolf Steiner Press.
Lauer, H. E. (1981) *Aggression and Repression in the Individual and Society*, Bristol: Rudolf Steiner Press.

The underlying principle in all of Steiner's writings is 'anthroposophy', or 'wisdom about man', which for Steiner signifies 'awareness of one's humanity'. He was dedicated to a belief that humanity's most important task is to cultivate its evolving spiritual perceptions.

There were three stages to his work. From 1900 to 1909 he developed a 'science of the spirit' based on the reappraisal of the human consciousness of Christ. From 1910 to 1917 he applied this new approach to diverse areas of scientific, artistic, educational and medical life, working from the new Anthroposophical Centre (the Goetheanum) in Dornach. From 1917 until his death this work was consolidated with emphasis on the need to bring spiritual knowledge into daily activity, and to invoke the support of the twin concepts of *karma* (volitional action) and what Steiner called the 'Christ impulse'.

Such wide-ranging work required philosophical (or anthroposophical) forays into many different areas. Primarily an esoteric, religious philosophy, Steiner's ideas begin and end with the assertion that Christ's resurrection 'marked the central upward turning point in human evolution', and that all spiritual activity is directed towards understanding and, ultimately, knowledge (the 'Christ impulse'). He held that illness is potentially positive, and connected to the whole person; and that agriculture and husbandry must be understood in both physical and cosmic terms. The arts, he maintained, have suffered from their separation from science and religion: art takes scientific forms, and the connection with religion is in the realm of the artistic manifestation of 'spiritual realities ex-

perienced before birth'. His educational theories, practised in Waldorf Schools, posit three seven-year cycles: willing ('natural expression' in activity); feeling (the development of the 'imaginative, rhythmical and emotional faculties'); and 'clear, informed, integrated thinking'. Steiner was hugely influential in his own lifetime, and since his death his doctrines have been kept alive by the proselytizing zeal of converted philanthropic interests. Intellectually, his work suffers from all the drawbacks of thinly disguised, though well-argued, esoteric, 'mystical' preaching. His ideas are of the kind that are apt to fuel the continuing debate about where the borders of philosophy lie.

DAVID SPOONER

Stern, Louis William

German. *b:* 29 April 1871, Berlin. *d:* 28 March 1938, Durham, North Carolina. *Cat:* Critical personalist; psychologist. *Ints:* Theory of personality and individuality; teleo-mechanics. *Educ:* University of Berlin. *Infls:* Literary: Aristotle, Leibniz and Gustav Fechner. Personal: Hermann Ebbinghaus and Clara Stern. *Appts:* 1897–1916, Instructor, then (1907) Associate Professor of Philosophy and Psychology, University of Breslau; 1916 -18, Professor, Colonial Institute and Lecture Fund, Hamburg; 1919–33, cofounder of, and Professor of Psychology at, the Hamburg Institute; 1934–8, Professor of Psychology, Duke University, Durham, NC.

Main publications:
(1906–24) *Person und Sache*, 3 vols, Leipzig: Barth.
(1915) *Vorgedanken zur Weltanschauung*, Leipzig: Barth.
(1930) *Studien zur Personwissenschaft*, Leipzig: Barth.
(1932) *Personalistik als Wissenschaft*, Leipzig: Barth.
(1935) *Allgemeine Psychologie auf personalistischen Grundlage*, The Hague: Nijhoff (English translation, *General Psychology from the Personalistic Standpoint*, trans. H. D. Spoer, New York: Macmillan, 1938).

Secondary literature:
Macleod, R. B. (1938) 'William Stern', *The Psychological Review*: 347–53.

Stern was both philosopher and psychologist. Although best known for his devising of the Intelligence Quotient in 1912, he also made pioneering studies of the perception of change and of childhood and children's language. He founded the Berlin Institute for Applied Psychology in 1906 and the *Journal for Applied Psychology* in 1907, and helped to establish Hamburg University in 1916. In 1933 he was forced to flee Nazi Germany and emigrated to the USA.

Stern's philosophy, reflecting his differential psychology, was concerned above all with personal being. Rejecting dualistic and naturalistic as well as idealistic, vitalistic and theistic approaches, he held that the individual person must be understood as a unique totality, striving towards goals, self-contained and self-determining, yet open to the surrounding world and formative of mutually inclusive relations with others. Stern elaborated this view in terms of a hierarchical theory of 'teleo-mechanism', according to which the world of 'things' or mechanical uniformities is at once derivative from and included as part of the purposive activities of supervenient personal beings. While Stern enjoyed considerable reputation as a psychologist, his philosophy of personal being, largely at odds with prevailing trends, has been overlooked.

Sources: Edwards; Metzler; DFN; Devine.

STEPHEN MOLLER

Stevenson, C(harles) L(eslie)

American. *b:* 1908, Cincinnati. *d:* 1979, Bennington, Vermont. *Cat:* Analytic philosopher. *Ints:* Ethics; philosophy of language. *Educ:* Yale University and University of Cambridge. *Infls:* Hume and Moore G. E. *Appts:* 1937–1944, Assistant Professor, Yale University; 1946–77, Associate Professor and Professor, University of Michigan; 1977–9, Professor, Bennington College.

Main publications:

(1944) *Ethics and Language*, New Haven: Yale University Press.
(1963) *Facts and Values: Studies in Ethical Analysis*, New Haven: Yale University Press.

Secondary literature:

Hudson, W. D. (1983) *Modern Moral Philosophy*, London: Macmillan; second edition, 1983.
Warnock, G. J. (1967) *Contemporary Moral Philosophy*, London: Macmillan.

Stevenson held that ethical judgements do not primarily state facts. Instead they have two other functions: they express the speaker's emotions or attitudes; and they seek to influence the attitudes of those addressed. This theory, the 'emotive theory of ethics' (or 'emotivism') was extremely influential from the 1940s to the 1960s, especially in Britain. The theory of ethical judgements was backed by a more general theory of signs. Stevenson held that the meaning of a sign was a dispositional property to cause certain psychological reactions in the hearer. The *descriptive* meaning of a sign was its disposition to cause *cognitive* psychological states, such as beliefs. But many signs also had *emotive* meaning: the disposition to cause *affective* states, such as desires and emotions. It is, according to Stevenson, this emotive meaning that is central to ethical utterances. According to what Stevenson called his first pattern of analysis, 'This is wrong' means, roughly, 'I disapprove of this; do so as well'.

Ethical terms may also have descriptive meaning. This descriptive meaning, however, is rarely firmly fixed; and this is one of the things that makes ethical argument possible. The word 'justice', for instance, evokes positive emotions in nearly everyone, but there is considerable disagreement as to what counts as, say, a just distribution of wealth. This makes possible Stevenson's more complicated 'second pattern of analysis'. Ethical disputants typically agree about the emotive meaning of an ethical term, but disagree about its descriptive meaning; and ethical argument often consists, according to Stevenson, in 'persuasively redefining' ethical terms.

Stevenson's theory is a form of non-naturalism. He did not agree with **Moore**'s view that ethical judgements must always be synthetic, since he accepted that the descriptive meaning of an ethical term could be exhaustively defined in naturalistic terms. But such a definition would, obviously, leave untouched the *emotive* meaning of the term, and no definition of the descriptive meaning of the term could rationally require one to take any particular attitude towards it.

Many objected to Stevenson's theory on the ground that it could not give an adequate account of the place of reason in ethics. It was also objected that it placed too much emphasis on what was merely one function of ethical language, and was unable to give an adequate account of others (such as merely wondering to oneself what one ought to do). More fundamentally, it has been objected that Stevenson never gave any clear account of the distinction between emotive meaning and descriptive meaning.

Sources: *New York Times*, 19 Mar 1979.

ANTHONY ELLIS

Stöhr, Adolf

Austrian. *b:* 24 February 1855, St Pölten, Austria. *d:* 10 February 1921, Vienna. *Cat:* Positivistic philosopher; experimental pyschologist. *Ints:* Philosophy of language; philosophy of science; psychology. *Educ:* Finished school in Vienna 1873; studied first at the Faculty of Law, and then Classical and Modern Philology, Chemistry and Botany; attended lectures at the Medical Faculty, and later turned to Philosophy; received his PhD, with *summa cum laude* in 1880. *Appts:* Lecturer in Theoretical Philosophy, 1885–1901; 1901, Associate Professor; 1911, Full Professor of Philosophy for Inductive Sciences, in succession to the Chair of Mach and Boltzmann.

Main publications:

(1883) *Vom Geiste. Eine Kritik der Existenz des mentalen Bewußtseins,* Vienna.
(1884) *Analyse der reinen Naturwissenschaft Kants,* Vienna.
(1889) *Umriß einer Theorie der Namen,* Leipzig and Vienna.
(1898) *Algebra der Gammatik,* Leipzig.
(1907) *Philosophie der unbelebten Materie,* Leipzig.
(1910) *Lehrbuch der Logic in psychologisierender Darstellung,* Leipzig.
(1911) *Psychologie der Aussage,* Berlin.
(1917) *Psychologie. Tatsachen, Probleme und Hypothesen,* Vienna and Leipzig.
(1974) *Philosophische Konstruktionen und Reflexionen,* Vienna: Deuticke.

The basis of Stöhr's 'psychologisierende Logik' is the distinction between the form of thinking (*Denkform*) and the form of language (*Sprachform*). When mixing up these two forms, our thinking turns into a 'glossomorphic' form. The reason for the glossomorphic use of language is grounded in a shortness of vocabulary which makes the use of metaphor necessary. Stöhr's language resulted in a distinction between philosophy as sciences and metaphysics, which aims at becoming a science but is doomed to fail. Metaphysics, a field between science and arts, may thus satisfy the need to construct all-comprising pictures of worlds. There exist 'I-worlds' and uncountable 'Thou-worlds'. Stöhr warns that the psychological 'I' may be confused by a fiction of a mental subject.
Sources: EncJud.

RUDOLF HALLER

Stojanovič, Svetozar

Yugoslav. *b:* 1931, Yugoslavia. *Cat:* Marxist social theorist. *Ints:* Social and political philosophy; ethics. *Educ:* University of Belgrade. *Appts:* Taught at the University of Belgrade from 1964 (Chair of Department of Philosophy and Sociology, 1971–3); suspended from teaching for political reasons in 1975, along with the seven other members of the Belgrade 'Praxis' group; from 1981, Professor in the Centre for Philosophy and Social Theory at the University of Belgrade; from 1989, frequent Visiting Professor at the University of Kansas.

Main publications:

(1964) *Savremena metaetika* [Contemporary Metaethics], Belgrade.
(1969) *Izmedu ideala i stvarnosti,* Belgrade (English translation, *Between Ideals and Reality: A Critique of Socialism and Its Future,* trans. Gerson Sher, Oxford University Press, 1973).
(1978) *Geschichte und Parteibewusstsein,* Munich (English translation, *In Search of Democracy in Socialism: History and Party Consciousness,* trans. Gerson Sher, Buffalo, NY: Prometheus Books, 1981).
(1988) *Perestroika: From Marxism and Bolshevism to Gorbachev,* Buffalo, NY: Prometheus Books.
(1995) *What Has Happened to Communism and Marxism?,* University of Kansas Press.

Secondary literature:

Crocker, David A. (1983) *Praxis and Democratic Socialism: The Critical Social Theory of Markovič and Stojanovič,* Sussex: Harvester Press.
Sher, Gerson S. (1977) *Praxis: Marxist Criticism and Dissent in Socialist Yugoslavia,* Indiana University Press.

Stojanovič's early interest in analytic ethics of the Anglo-American variety, expressed in his first book, *Savremena metaetika* (1964), gave way by the late 1960s to the sympathetic but critical development of Marxist social theory that has occupied him ever since. His interest in Marxism has a strong ethical component, inasmuch as his attachment is to Marx's humanistic ideals rather than to communism as a social structure.

Stojanovič believes that major corrections are needed in classical Marxist social theory. One such correction, originally proposed in his book *Between Ideals and Reality* (1969), is the addition of what he calls 'statism' to Marx's social typology. Stojanovič regards the Soviet Union, for example, as representing a type of social structure not accommodated in Marxist theory—a socio-*political* rather than socio-*economic* formation, or one in which a class rules through a monopoly on political power rather than economic ownership, creating a new type of class oppression. A second needed correction is the introduction of a distinction between a ruling class and a dominant class. Stojanovič argues that Marx failed to recognize that the bourgeoisie is the first class in history that can dominate society without ruling it. Capitalism was thus a new form of class society—one that permits the broad development of democratic institutions while at the same time the bourgeoisie retains its dominance. Stojanovič elaborates the distinction between ruling and dominant classes in his book *Perestroika* (1988), arguing that many of Marx's theoretical weaknesses can be traced to overlooking it.

Stojanovič's positive social ideal is a society in which no class either rules or is dominant—a democratic socialist society, which he thinks can evolve from democratic capitalism. He calls it 'socialism with a civil and bourgeois face' (1988, p. 139), meaning a society in which democratic planning and public ownership of major economic facilities are combined with private ownership of 'non-strategic productive means', market competition, and production for profit by private, cooperative and self-managed public enterprises. In his 1995 book, examining the disintegration of Yugoslavia and the collapse of Communist statism, he ascribes only a 'regulative-critical' rather than a 'constructive-operative' significance to Marx's ideas and advocates a 'post-Marxist' programme of global cooperation to avert an apocalyptic end to the human species.

JAMES SCANLAN

Stout, G(eorge) F(rederick)

British. *b:* 6 January 1860, South Shields. *d:* 18 August 1944, Sydney. *Cat:* Psychologist; philosopher of mind. *Ints:* Epistemology; philosophy of mind. *Educ:* St John's College, Cambridge. *Infls:* Personal influences include James Ward and Henry Sidgwick. Literary influences: Plato, Spinoza, Locke, Berkeley, Kant, Herbart and Brentano. *Appts:* 1884–96, Fellow of St John's College, Cambridge; 1891–1920, Editor of *Mind*; Wilde Reader in Mental Philosophy at Oxford; 1903–36, Professor of Logic and Metaphysics, St Andrews.

Main publications:

(1896) *Analytic Psychology*, 2 vols, London: Unwin.
(1899) *A Manual of Psychology*, London: University Tutorial Press.
(1930) *Studies in Philosophy and Psychology*, London: Macmillan.

(1931) *Mind and Matter*, Cambridge: Cambridge University Press.
(1952) *God and Nature*, ed. A. K. Stout, Cambridge: Cambridge University Press.

Secondary literature:

Broad, C. D. (1932) Review of *Mind and Matter* in *Mind* 41: 113ff.
Mabbot, J. D. (1953) Critical Notice of *God and Nature*, in *Mind* 62: 523–35.
Mace, C. A. (1945) 'George Frederick Stout, 1860–1944', *Proceedings of the British Academy* 31: 307–16.
——(1967) 'Stout, George Frederick', in Paul Edwards (ed.) *Encyclopedia of Philosophy*, New York: Macmillan, 8: 22–4.
Passmore, J. A. (1952) Memoir, in A. K. Stout (ed.) *God and Nature*, Cambridge: Cambridge University Press (with bibliography).

Stout absorbed the essentials of the system of his teacher, James **Ward**, but transformed and extended them into an original system of his own. He claimed this combined idealism and realism as well as rationalism and empiricism. He acknowledged indebtedness to various sources and sought to come to terms with the analytical philosophy of the younger Cambridge philosophers, **Russell**, **Moore** and **Wittgenstein**. Among Stout's central ideas were that thought always implies something real in what is thought about; that, instead of thinking of mind and body as separate substances, it is better to think of a dualism of attributes combined in a single entity, the embodied self; and that conative activity is involved in all human processes, even in those of cognition. Stout's influence was limited, partly because of the emergence of behavioural psychology and partly because of the reaction amongst philosophers against speculative systems. However, his collaborator, C. A. Mace, wrote of him: 'There is probably no philosopher who in his own thinking so smoothly made the transition from the prevailing idealism of the late nineteenth century to the prevailing critical, non-speculative philosophy of the mid-twentieth century. Something of the idealist tradition is preserved in his sophisticated defense of philosophical animism, but more important are his detailed contributions to the transition from the philosophy of mind of the nineteenth century to that of the twentieth' (Mace 1967, p. 24).
Sources: DNB 1941–50; Passmore, 1957.

STUART BROWN

Strawson, Peter Frederick

British. **b:** 23 November 1919, London. **Cat:** Analytical philosopher of logic and language. **Ints:** Epistemology; metaphysics. **Educ:** St John's College, Oxford. **Infls:** Analytical and Oxford philosophy, in particular H. P. Grice. **Appts:** 1946, Assistant Lecturer in Philosophy, University College of North Wales; John Locke Scholar, University of Oxford; 1947–68, Lecturer in Philosophy (1947), Praelector (1948), Fellow (1948–68), Honorary Fellow (1979) of University College, Oxford; 1960, Fellow of the British Academy; 1966–87, Reader (1966–8), then Waynflete Professor of Metaphysical Philosophy (1968–87), University of Oxford; 1968–87, Fellow, then Honorary Fellow (1989), Magdalen College, Oxford; 1971, Honorary Member, American Academy of Arts and Sciences; 1977, Knighted; 1990, Member, Academia Europaea; several visiting appointments in the USA and Europe.

Main publications:

(1952) *Introduction to Logical Theory*, London: Methuen.

(1959) *Individuals: An Essay in Descriptive Metaphysics*, London: Methuen; new edition, London: Routledge, 1990.

(1966) *The Bounds of Sense: An Essay on Kant's 'Critique of Pure Reason'*; new edition, London: Routledge, 1990.

(1971) *Logico-Linguistic Papers*, London: Methuen.

(1974) *Freedom and Resentment, and Other Essays*, London: Methuen.

(1974) *Subject and Predicate in Logic and Grammar*, London: Methuen.

(1985) *Scepticism and Naturalism: Some Varieties. The Woodbridge Lectures 1983*, London: Methuen.

(1992) *Analysis and Metaphysics: An Introduction to Philosophy*, Oxford: Oxford University Press.

Secondary literature:

Corvi, Roberta (1979) *La filosofia di P. F. Strawson*, Scienze Filosofiche 24, Milan: Vita e Penserio.

Van Straaten, Z. (ed.) (1980) *Philosophical Subjects: Essays Presented to P. F. Strawson*, Oxford: Clarendon Press (includes select bibliography of Strawson's work to 1980).

The influence of analytical and ordinary language philosophy account for Strawson's interest in language, thought and their 'objects'. This interest appears already in 'Truth' (*Analysis*, 1949), which attacks the semantic theory of truth: 'true' does not describe semantic or other properties; rather, 'true' and 'false' are performative or expressive—to say a sentence is 'true' is to express agreement with it. This article prompted his controversy with J. L. **Austin**, a defender of the correspondence theory of truth: explaining truth as correspondence between statements and facts fails, argues Strawson, since facts are not something statements name or refer to—'facts are what statements (when true) state' (1971, p. 196).

Strawson's 1950 article 'On referring' (collected in 1971) attacks **Russell**'s 'theory of definite descriptions'. For Russell, a sentence such as 'The King of France is wise' is false, since, when analysed, it contains an assertion of existence (namely, 'There is a King of France'). Russell's analysis, Strawson argues, compounds the notions of referring to something and asserting its existence—'to refer is not to assert' (p. 15)—though in referring to something one may 'imply' (in the special sense Strawson reserves for this word) that it exists. Strawson argues that Russell fails to distinguish sentences (or expressions), their use and their utterance. Whereas for Russell a sentence is true, false or meaningless, Strawson maintains that a sentence is significant in virtue of conventions governing its use, irrespective of whether the sentence, when uttered, is about something. A sentence such as that concerning the King of France is meaningful but, if not used to refer to something, the question of its truth or falsity does not arise.

Interest in the relation between formal logic and ordinary language continues in *Introduction to Logical Theory* (1952), which partly aims 'to bring out some points of contrast and of contact between the behaviour of words in ordinary speech and the behaviour of symbols in a logical system' (p. iv). Formal logicians cannot, Strawson argues, give the exact, systematic logic of expressions of everyday speech, 'for these expressions have no exact and systematic logic' (p. 57). Formal logic is an 'idealized abstraction' revealing certain structural traits of ordinary language but omitting others. The notion of a gap between formal logic and ordinary language has drawn criticism (for example, **Quine** in *Mind*, 1953), but it motivates Strawson's criticisms of the formal semantics popularized by Donald **Davidson** (see 'On understanding the structure of one's language', in *Freedom and Resentment*, 1974).

Strawson's concerns also appear in *Individuals* (1959), the subtitle of which, however, marks a new interest in 'descriptive metaphysics'. This enterprise differs from 'revisionary metaphysics', in that while 'descriptive metaphysics is content to describe the actual structure of our thought about the world, revisionary metaphysics is concerned to produce a better structure' (p. 9), and from conceptual analysis in its scope and generality, since its aims 'to lay bare the most general features of our conceptual structure'. The book's first part maintains that material bodies are the basic particulars to which we refer and of which we predicate qualities, kinds, etc. Chapter 3, 'Persons', argues for the primitiveness of the concept of a person, 'a type of entity such that *both* predicates ascribing states of consciousness *and* predicates ascribing corporeal characteristics ... are equally applicable to a single individual of that single type' (p. 102). Making states of consciousness secondary in relation to the concept of a person enables Strawson to avoid traditional difficulties concerning the mind–body problem. The book's second part examines the distinction between logico-grammatical subjects and their predicates. Reflection on two traditional criteria for this distinction allows Strawson to view particulars as paradigm logical subjects and thus to explain 'the traditional, persistent link in our philosophy between the particular–universal distinction and the subject–predicate (reference–predication) distinction' (p. 188). In arguing that a subject expression presupposes some empirical fact identifying a particular, Strawson comes to regard particulars as 'complete' and universals as 'incomplete', thus giving added depth to **Frege**'s notion of 'saturated' and 'unsaturated' sentence constituents.

The conclusions reached in *Individuals* form the basis for later works, notably *The Bounds of Sense* (1966) and *Subject and Predicate* (1974), but also underpin Strawson's examination of scepticism and naturalism in 1985, where he rejects philosophical scepticism and reductive naturalism by appeal to certain traits in ordinary ways of thinking and speaking. Certain essays in *Freedom and Resentment*, however, show Strawson's work in other areas of philosophy (notably ethics and aesthetics); and in his most recent publication (1992, published in France in 1985), based on introductory courses taught at Oxford, he examines the nature of philosophical practice (which turns out to be largely his own). In this work, he distances himself from ordinary language philosophy and reductive analytical philosophy, regarding philosophy as the attempt to understand the relations between concepts, an attempt that, while broadly 'analytical', does not

aim to reduce such concepts to others more simple.
Sources: P. F. Strawson (1988) 'Ma philosophie: son développement, son thème central et sa nature générale', *RTP* 120: 437–52; WW; IWW; Burkhardt; Edwards.

STUART LEGGATT

Strong, Charles Augustus
American. *b:* 28 November 1862, Haverhill, Massachusetts. *d:* 23 January 1940. *Cat:* Realist–critical realism. *Ints:* Epistemology; nature of consciousness. *Educ:* University of Rochester, Harvard. *Appts:* Associate Professor, University of Chicago; Professor of Psychology, University of Columbia.

Main publications:
(1903) *Why the Mind has a Body*, New York: Macmillan.
(1918) *The Origin of Consciousness*, London: Macmillan.
(1923) *A Theory of Knowledge*, New York: Macmillan.

Strong was a member of a group known as the critical realists. According to critical realism, items of information about the external objects we perceive are not part of the objects. Instead they are 'character complexes' which are taken to be characters of the external objects at the moment of perception. Where the perception is erroneous these characters are not part of the external object and in non-erroneous perception they are. But what are these 'character complexes'? Are they contents of sensory experience? According to Strong the 'character complex' is not a content of sensory experience but a logical entity or essence.

Although critical realism resolves to some extent the problems relating to erroneous perception by suggesting that the data in perception are generated by and are not part of the external object, the nature of the 'character complex' as explained by Strong is less than clear.
Sources: WWW(Am).

INDIRA MAHALINGAM CARR

Struve, Petr Berngardovich
Russian. *b:* 26 January (7 February N.S.) 1870, Perm'. *d:* 26 February 1944, Paris. *Cat:* Marxist, then idealist. *Educ:* Graduated in Law at University of St Petersburg in 1895. *Infls:* Marx, Engels, Kant, Fichte and Riehl. *Appts:* 1890s,

editor of *Novoe slovo* and *Nachalo*; 1901–5, editor, *Osvobozhdenie*; 1907, Deputy, Constitutional Democrat Party; editor; *Russkaia mysl'*; 1907–17, taught Economics at St Petersburg Polytechnical Institute.

Main publications:

(1894) *Kriticheskie zametki k voprosu ob ekonomicheskoi istorii Rossii* [Critical Remarks on the Question of the Economic History of Russia], St Petersburg.

(1902) *Na raznye temy, 1893–1901 gg.: sbornik statei* [On Various Themes 1893–1901: A Collection of Articles], St Petersburg.

(1909) 'Intelligentsiia i revolutsiia', in *Vekhi: sbornik statei o russkoi intelligentsii*, Moscow (English translation, *Landmarks*, trans. Marian Schwartz, New York: Karz Howard, 1977).

(1911) *Patriotica: politika, kul'tura, religiia, sotsializm*, St Petersburg.

Secondary literature:

Kindersley, R. (1962) *The First Russian Revisionists: a Study of 'Legal Marxism' in Russia*, Oxford: Clarendon Press.

Pipes, R. E. (1970) *Struve: Liberal on the Left, 1870–1905*, Cambridge, Mass.: Harvard University Press.

——(1980) *Struve: Liberal on the Right, 1905–1944*, Cambridge, Mass.: Harvard University Press.

The son of the Governor of Perm' province, and a member of an originally German family which produced a dynasty of Russian astronomers, Struve was an economic historian as well as a philosopher. He edited the Marxist journals *Novoe slovo* [New Word] and *Nachalo* [Beginning] in the late 1890s, and in 1898 drafted the manifesto of the Russian Social-Democratic Labour Party. By 1901, his revisionism led **Lenin** and other 'orthodox' Marxists to expel him from the Social-Democratic movement, and he involved himself in liberal politics. While in Germany from 1901 to 1905, he edited the illegal liberal journal *Osvobozhdenie* [Liberation]. After the 1905 Revolution, he led the right wing of the Constitutional Democrat Party, becoming a deputy at the Second Duma in 1907; he also edited *Russkaia mysl'* [Russian Thought]. He actively opposed the October Revolution of 1917 as a member of the White movement, and emigrated to Western Europe after its defeat.

Struve's *Kriticheskie zametki* (1894) was the *locus classicus* of 'legal' Marxism. This was a gradualist, evolutionary version of Marxism, subscribed to by a number of Russian economics

professors, and tolerated by the autocracy because it insisted against the dangerous populists that Russia could not bypass the capitalist economic stage of development (a welcome view during the state-led industrial spurt of the 1890s). The populists accused all Russian Marxists of being apologists for the bourgeoisie, and were vindicated in Struve's case. A revisionist from his earliest Marxist publications, he came to accept capitalism and liberal values in themselves, rather than as preconditions of socialism.

Among Struve's revisionist stances was his advocacy of a neo-Kantian philosophical basis for Marxism ('critical Marxism'). Struve looked to Kant for a justification of continuous change rather than change by leaps, and sought to distinguish between an empirical realm of historical necessity and an ideal, free realm of values; he therefore rejected the causal dependence of the 'superstructure' of ideas on the economic base. He quickly moved to transcendent idealism on the basis of the critical philosophy, and contributed to the symposium *Problems of Idealism* (1903), along with **Berdyaev**, **Bulgakov** and S. L. **Frank**. These four ex-Marxists also contributed to the controversial collection *Landmarks* (1909); Struve in particular decried the Russian intelligentsia's maximalist irreligiosity and hostility to the state, and called for a radical reexamination of its worldview and a refocussing of its efforts on political education.

COLIN CHANT

Stumpf, Karl

German. *b:* 1848, Wiesenthied, near Würzburg, Bavaria. *d:* 1936. *Cat:* Empiricist; disciple of Brentano's Act School of psychology. *Ints:* Metaphysics; the relation between phenomenology and psychology; music. *Educ:* University of Würzburg; PhD, 1868 and Habilitation, 1870, University of Göttingen. *Infls:* At the University of Würzburg, Stumpf was attracted to Franz Brentano, for whom the methodology of the *naturwissenschaft* was characteristic of the philosophical method. Later, at the University of Göttingen, he came under the influence of the philosopher/psychologist Rudulph Hermann Lotze (1817–81), who taught him epistemology. Stumpf's ideas of spatial representation owed a great deal to K. E. K. Hering (1834–1918). Later Edmund Husserl (Stumpf's student in the 1880s) had an impact on Stumpf's application of phenomenology to psychology. *Appts:* Professor of Philosophy, University of Würzburg, 1873; Professor of Philosophy, University of Prague, 1879; Professor of Philosophy, University of Halle, 1884; Professor of Philosophy, University of Munich, 1889; Professor of Philosophy, University of Berlin, 1894.

Main publications:

(1883–90) *Tonpsychologie* 2 vols, Leipzig: Herzel (English translation of extract from vol. II, in Benjamin Rand (ed.), *Modern Classical Psychologists*, Boston: Houghton Mifflin, 1912, pp. 619–23).

(1906) *Erscheinungen und psychische Funktionen* (*Abhandlungen der Berliner Akademie*, 1907, no. 4, 40 pp).

(1906) *Zur Einteilung der Wissenschaften* (*Abhandlungen der Berliner Akademie*, 1907, no. 5, 94 pp).

(1924) *Selbstdarstellung* in R. Schmidt (ed.), *Philosophie der Gegenwart*, V, Leipzig: Felix Meiner, pp. 205–65 (contains bibliography) (English translation in C. Murchison (ed.), *A History of Psychology in Autobiography*, vol. 1, trans. T. Hodge & S. Langer, New York: Russell & Russell, 1961, pp. 389–443).

Stumpf's influence on the evolution of psychology in general was somewhat limited because his principal interests centred on the psychology of tone and music. Indeed most of his writings relate to that specific field. His systematic works have enhanced the understanding of tone-combinations, and the science of psychophysics in particular. His importance stems from his introduction of phenomenology to the field of psychology.

Stumpf interprets phenomenology as a propaedeutic of science (*Vorwissenschaft*), including psychology. Specifically, he held that phenomenology descriptively treats primary and secondary phenomena, or acts—echoing **Brentano** rather than **Husserl**. Primary phenomena are what are immediately present to the senses (*Sinneserscheinungen*). Secondary phenomena are the images of the primary phenomena. Given that these phenomena do not causally depend on themselves, phenomenology should limit itself to analysing the nature, relations and the structural laws of their being, while leaving psychology (and other sciences) to investigate the non-phenomenal elements these phenomena depend on. The advantages of this programme of what has been called Stumpf's 'experimental phenomenology' are that for the first time it opened up the possibility: (i) of studying phenomena that are not covered by psychology or the physical sciences; (ii) of analysing neutral

phenomena that are the basis of the sciences; and (iii) of exploring these neutral domains in a systematic manner. Some of Stumpf's influence on psychology manifested itself through his students, Wolfgang **Köhler** and Kurt **Koffka**, the Gestaltists.

Sources: E. G. Boring (1950) *A History of Experimental Psychology*, New York: Appleton-Century-Crofts; E. Hearst (1979) *The First Century of Experimental Psychology*, New Jersey: Lawrence Erlbaum Associates; T. S. Krawiec (ed.) (1972) *The Psychologists*, 2 vols, Oxford: OUP; S. S. Stevens (ed.) (1966) *Handbook of Experimental Psychology*, London: John Wiley & Sons.

SEBASTIEN ODIARI

Sturzo, Luigi

Italian. *b:* 26 November 1871, Caltagirone, Sicily. *d:* 8 August 1959, Rome. *Cat:* Social and political philosopher. *Appts:* Founded the Italian Popular Party, 1919; exposed the deficiencies of fascism in 1926; exiled in 1924; Life Senator for his role in the creation of the Italian Republic, 1952.

Main publications:

(1950) *Del metodo sociologico.*

(1954) *Opera Omnia*, Bologna: Zanichelli (all the volumes below have been translated into English).

  La società sua natura e leggi (vol. 1).

  La comunità internazionale e il diritto di guerra (vol. 2).

  La società: Sociologica storistica (vol. 3).

  Chiesa e Stato (vols 4–6).

  La vera vita (vol. 7).

Secondary literature:

Carra, A. (1972) *Fondamenti sociali ed azione politica in Luigi Sturzo*, Catania: Bonanno.

Santo, B. (1979) *Luigi Sturzo oggi*, Catania: Centro di Luigi Sturzo.

Walsh, J. and Quick, J. (1953) 'A Sturzo bibliography', *Thought* 28: 202–8.

Sturzo's sociological investigations are historical and experimental and involve the historicist conception of sociology as the science of society with a 'concrete dialectic', a notion which bears the influence of Augustine, Leibniz, Vico and **Blondel**. Man, bound to time and history, is at once free and conditioned, individual and social, not a fixed essence but a singular history and a projection of collective purposes, the institutionalization of which may lead to conflicts of interests between social groups. The most powerful antidote to a conflict of interests is the involvement of the divine in human events, an involvement which motivates human progress, yielding an optimistic vision of mankind moving, albeit with occasional backward steps, to a greater socialization.

COLIN LYAS

Su Shaozhi (Su Shao-chih)

Chinese. *b:* 1925, Beijing. *Cat:* Marxist philosophy and economics. *Ints:* Economic and political thought. *Educ:* Chongqing University and Nankai University, Tianjin. *Infls:* Marx and many other Western theorists. *Appts:* Associate Professor, Fudan University, Shanghai; Editor, Theoretical Department, *People's Daily* newspaper; Vice-Director and Director, 1982–7, Institute of Marxism, Leninism and Mao Zedong Thought, Chinese Academy of Social Sciences.

Main publications:

(1982) *Democracy and Socialism in China*, Discussion between Su and M. Barrett Brown, W. Brus, J. Eaton and A. Hegedus.
(1983) (co-author) *Marxism in China*, Nottingham: Spokesman.
(1983) *Developing Marxism under Contemporary Conditions*.
(1983) *Democratisation and Reform*, Nottingham: Spokesman.
(1985) *Socialism in the Eastern Bloc*.
(1989) *China's Present Situation and the Necessity of Developing the Political Reform*, Copenhagen: University of Copenhagen.

With the return of relative flexibility and moderation after the fall of the Gang of Four, Su began to examine institutional requirements for the rapid development of productive forces in China. This, rather than class struggle, he understood to be the essence of socialist policy. He used the common slogans of 'seeking truth from facts' and of 'using practice as the criterion of truth' to oppose a return to policy based on political dogma and bureaucratic convenience. His economic proposals for ownership reform to dilute the role of state-owned enterprises, distribution reform, a reduced emphasis on heavy industry to improve incentives, and market reform to complement centralized planning led him to consider the political background of economic reform. He argued for reduced concentration of power in the bureaucracy, for openness to the experience of other countries, and for the separation of government, enterprise management and politics. He called for moribund democratic structures to be given new life in politics and enterprises, using

Chen Duxiu's call for 'science and democracy' to propose a new understanding of socialist democratic centralism. He claimed that without democracy, there could be neither socialism nor modernization. Su's proposals for political reform grew in urgency and he was removed from his highly influential post as Director of the Institute of Marxism, Leninism and **Mao Zedong** Thought in 1987, although he remained a member of the Institute. In many respects Su's thought moved from a Marxist to a post-Marxist perspective. Along with the eminent physicist Professor Fang Lizhi, Su provided an intellectual basis for the pro-democracy movement of 1989. After the movement was crushed, Su taught in the USA. His arguments for greater democracy in China continue to have influence, partly because they emerged as a requirement for economic success. His growing radicalism has inspired many to seek a deeper understanding of democracy than offered by Su in his own programmatic work.

NICHOLAS BUNNIN

Sumner, William Graham

American. *b:* 30 October 1840, Paterson, New Jersey. *d:* 12 April, 1910, Englewood, New Jersey. *Cat:* Social philosopher; political economist. *Ints:* Social science; political economy; cultural anthropology. *Educ:* Yale University, Universities of Geneva, Göttingen and Oxford. *Infls:* Literary influences: Herbert Spencer, H. T. Buckle, Julius Lippert and E. B. Tylor. *Appts:* 1872–1909, Professor of Political and Social Science, Yale.

Main publications:

(1906) *Folkways: A Study of the Sociological Importance of Usages, Manners, Customs, Mores, and Moral*, New York: Dover (reprinted 1959).
(1927) (with Albert G. Keller) *The Science of Society*, 4 vols, New Haven: Yale University Press.

Secondary literature:

Davie, Maurice R. (1963) *William Graham Sumner: An Essay of Commentary and Selections*, New York: Crowell.
Starr, Harris E. (1925) *William Graham Sumner*, New York: Holt.

After graduating from Yale in 1863 Sumner studied in Europe, returning to a tutorship at Yale in 1866. In 1867 he became an Episcopalian clergyman. In 1872 he gave up his ministry for a Professorship in Economics at Yale and achieved renown for his championing of individualism and laissez-faire.

After 1890 Sumner's interests shifted from

economics to sociology. Inspired by the writings of **Spencer** and Lippert, he began to collect ethnographical materials and to develop an inductive 'science of society'. These researches issued in his epochal *Folkways* (1906).

Central to Sumner's sociology was his identification of the fundamental social forces with 'folkways', group habits and the prereflective human means of adjustment to the conditions of life that cluster to form social institutions. Sumner argued that folkways become 'mores' when they 'include a judgement that they are conducive to societal welfare, and when they exert a coercion on the individual to conform to them' (1927, vol. 1, p. 34). Thus mores are fewer than folkways and when laid down by society they become morals or actions which humans think they must perform because socially important. Sumner held that both folkways and mores develop through the often unconscious variations in their observance that are then imitated. In *The Science of Society* (1927) he elaborated a theory of the unilinear evolution of all mankind's social institutions. As an economist, Sumner was merely a publicist for social Darwinism, but as a sociologist he was a brilliant innovator. Indeed he was one of the founding fathers of American sociology.

Sources: Edwards.

STEPHEN MOLLER

Sun Zhongshan (Sun Chung-shan or Sun Yat-sen)

Chinese. *b:* 1866, Cuiheng, Guangdong Province, China. *d:* 1925, Beijing. *Cat:* Social and political thinker; statesman. *Educ:* The Medical Schools of Pok Chai Hospital, Guangzhou and Alice Memorial Hospital, Hong Kong. *Infls:* Western socialist political thinkers, including Henry George and Marx; also Darwin, Christianity and neo-Confucianism. *Appts:* 1905–12, leader of the Tongmenghui [Revolutionary Alliance]; 1911, leader of the Republican Revolution; 1912, first President of the Republic of China; 1912–25, leader of the Guomindang [Nationalist Party].

Main publications:

(1917–19) *Principles of National Reconstruction*, Zhengzhong Book Company.
(1924) *Fundamentals of National Reconstruction*, Shanghai: Commercial Press.
(1928) *Three Principles of the People* or *Trimedism*, Shanghai: Commercial Press.
(1957) *Collected Works of Sun Zhongshan*, revised edition, 6 vols, Taipei.

(1957) *Selected Works of Sun Zhongshan*, 2 vols, Beijing.

Secondary literature:
Boorman, H. (ed.) (1970) *Biographical Dictionary of Republican China*, New York and London: Columbia University Press.
Briere, O. (1956) *Fifty Years of Chinese Philosophy 1898–1950*, London: George Allen & Unwin Ltd.
Complete Chinese Encyclopedia (1987), Philosophy Volumes, Beijing: Chinese Encyclopedia Publications.
Martin, B. (1970) *Strange Vigor: A Biography of Sun Yat-sen*, Port Washington, NY: Kennikat Press

In the face of successive humiliations for China in the 1880s, Sun concluded that only the overthrow of the Qing Dynasty and the foundation of a Chinese republic would permit national renewal. For nearly two decades he organized open and clandestine revolutionary organizations and abortive uprisings. 'Zhongshan', the Chinese translation of his Japanese cover name, became the name by which he was universally known. In exile he travelled endlessly to raise funds and to maintain his political organization among overseas Chinese, while seeking support from Western statesmen. A possible alliance with **Kang Youwei**, the leading figure in the 1898 Hundred Days Reform, failed because Sun's republican and Kang's monarchist views proved irreconcilable. Kang became a bitter rival but, despite repeated setbacks, the republican cause gained ascendancy. In 1911 successful internal military revolts led to the formation of a Republic with Sun as its first President, although he soon gave way to the military leader Yuan Shikai in an attempt to consolidate republican rule and to end instability. Sun was involved in continuing political conflict until the end of his life in his attempt to establish stable national rule as a basis for national reconstruction. In 1921 a rump parliament in Guangzhou returned him to a disputed presidency for a year, but his most lasting legacy from this period derives from his party reorganization and his writing.

Sun's dismay over the lack of investment and political support from the Western democracies led him to turn to the new Soviet authorities for advice and collaboration. He reorganized his political organization, the Guomindang, on Leninist lines, with power concentrated in the leadership, strict discipline and ideological control. Against objections from some supporters, he agreed to cooperation with the Chinese Communist Party, with individual Communists eligible to join the Guomindang. Earlier on he established a politically committed and highly trained military force under Jiang Jieshi (Chiang Kai-shek) as a basis for enforcing unified rule in China. These activities provided the different grounds for his later veneration in both the Republic and the People's Republic.

Sun's main political programme, contained in *Three Principles of the People* (1928), centred on nationalism, democracy and the people's livelihood. His notion of nationalism began with his early oppositon to Qing Dynasty rule, but later encompassed his hostility to imperialist domination. He initially proposed a three-stage development of democracy in China, starting with military government guided by a revolutionary party, followed by a period of local democracy under political tutelege, and culminating in popular political rights under a full constitutional democracy. This period could lead to a time of Confucian great harmony, with universal peace based on the virtue of humanity. Sun's conception of democracy was initially drawn from the USA, but he later added examination and control branches of government, derived from Chinese traditional practice. Under Soviet influence he came to emphasize the importance of a tightly disciplined revolutionary party in the first two stages of his programme to achieve democracy. Regarding people's livelihood Sun proposed an eclectic programme drawn from Henry George and other socialist theorists and adapted to Chinese conditions. He rejected Marx's theories of class struggle and surplus value and thought Marxist theory unsuitable for China. He also proposed large-scale economic and social developments to transform China into a modern socialist state, but continuing instability and the impossibility of gaining sufficient foreign investment thwarted his plans.

Much of Sun's political thinking had Western inspiration, but failure to achieve his revolutionary programme led to some traditional philosophical reflection. In 'Psychological reconstruction' in *Principles of National Reconstruction*, (1917–19), he accepted the doctrine of the sixteenth-century neo-Confucian idealist Wang Yangming that knowledge and action are one. He rejected the claim that revolution failed because 'knowing is easy, but doing is difficult'; rather, he claimed, knowing is difficult and doing is easy. If a revolutionary party with unified leadership could provide knowledge for the people then popular revolutionary action would be easy. Instilling appropriate attitudes to overcome ignorance thus became a central

revolutionary task. His views about knowledge and action deserve critical attention at both political and philosophical levels.

NICHOLAS BUNNIN

Suzuki, Daisetsu Teitaro

Japanese. *b:* 18 October 1870, Kanazawa, Japan. *d:* 12 July 1966, Tokyo. *Cat:* Zen Buddhist. *Educ:* Kanazawa, Tokyo Semmon Gakko (Waseda University) and Tokyo Imperial University. *Infls:* Literary influences include Congshen of Zhao-Zhou (778–897), Bankei Yotaku (1622–93), Shinran (1173–1262); personal influences incude Shaku Soyen, Nishida Kitaro. *Appts:* Professor, Gakushu-in, 1919–21; Lecturer, Tokyo Imperial University, 1910–16; Professor, Otani University, 1921–60.

Main publications:

Works in English include:

(1907) *Outlines of Mahayana Buddhism*, London: Luzac & Co.

(1927) *Essays in Zen Buddhism*; Second Series 1933, Third Series 1934, London: Luzac & Co.

(1947) *The Essence of Buddhism*, London: The Buddhist Society.

(1949) *The Zen Doctrine of No-Mind* London: Rider & Co.

(1959) *Zen and Japanese Culture*, New York: Pantheon Books.

(1970) *Shin Buddhism*, London: The Buddhist Society.

Secondary literature:

Fromm, E. (1967) 'Memories of Dr. Suzuki', *The Eastern Buddhist*, New Series II.

Switzer, A. I. (1985) *D. T. Suzuki*, London: The Buddhist Society.

Although Zen is only one of the many sects of Buddhism, in the West it is almost a byword for Buddhism in general. This is the result of Suzuki's effort to teach Buddhism to the West through Zen, which is philosophically great interest. At the foundation of Suzuki's activities in propagating Buddhism, which continued until he was 96 years old, was his original interpretation of Buddhism. Since the birth of Buddhism in the fifth century BC there have been several radical theoretical leaps. Mahayana Buddhism came into existence in the first century BC and the sects of Sino-Japanese Mahayana, Zen, Pure-Land and Shin Buddhism in the sixth, twelfth and thirteenth centuries AD respectively. Each leap was the original creation of an individual, and Suzuki is another such.

From a philosophical point of view, at the core of Mahayana Buddhism is the question of the relation between the subject and objects. Through its long history the Mahayana has maintained the philosophical bent which is evident in its asking such a question. Suzuki made this inclination clear in terms of contemporary thought with unprecedented subtlety. However, he does not elucidate the meaning of Buddhism, particularly the Mahayana tradition, by borrowing Western philosophical terminology. Rather, Suzuki's originality lies in his finding in Buddhism answers to universal philosophical questions. Such an explanation of Mahayana thought as stated below is only possible under the influence of Suzuki.

The intuition running through the history of Mahayana Buddhism is the oneness of the contradictory. An aspect of this intuition is that the knower and the known are one. This amounts to knowing without an object. The meaning of the subject has changed, as has that of the object. The self as the subject that knows the object and the object known are both illusions. The world that appears after one abandons illusion is called Emptiness.

Suzuki was well aware that the fundamental intuition stated above has a bearing on the basic problems of philosophy. The existence of other minds, the nature of time and space and the relation of good and evil, for example, are questions the meaning of which will change fundamentally in the light of this intuition. Taking innumerable examples from Shin-Buddhism, which he regarded as the zenith of the Mahayana tradition, from Chinese and Japanese Zen, etc., Suzuki describes how this transformation takes place. At the same time he calls attention to Chinese and Japanese artistic activities in general, seeing them as the expression of Mahayana, particularly Zen, thought. There is a reason for this emphasis on art. Scepticism about language is fundamental to Mahayana, especially to Zen, as is emphasized by Suzuki. For, by employing language solely as a means for description, we tend to reinforce the differentiation between the subject and its object. One of the most powerful Zen masters, Congshen of Zhao-Zhou (778–897) who greatly influenced Suzuki, once said, when asked about the essence of Buddhism: 'The cedar tree in the courtyard'. Zen does not reject language. On the contrary, Zen tries to use language as a living force. But for one who is used to thinking of

language as exclusively descriptive, Zen seems to be forbidding. It is art, especially visual art, that gives us a glimpse of Mahayana.

Suzuki constantly tries to make us aware of the limitations of syllogistic thinking which, according to him, is based on the subject–object distinction. He was a prolific writer with a distinctive style, and his style reflects his vision of logic in which syllogism is merely a part. Suzuki in his later years expressed this logic thus: 'Non-A is not A, therefore A.'

REISHI TAYAMA

Swabey, Marie Collins

American. **b:** 8 December 1880, Kansas City. **d:** 3 March 1966, San José, California. **Cat:** Social philosopher. **Ints:** Political and social philosophy; metaphysics. **Educ:** Wellesley College, 1913; MA, University of Kansas, 1914; PhD, Cornell University, 1919. **Infls:** Darwin, Arnold Toynbee and Ernst Cassirer. **Appts:** Instructor in Philosophy, Wellesley College, 1919–20: Instructor in Philosophy and eventually Professor Emeritus, New York University, 1924–56.

Main publications:

(1920) *Some Modern Conceptions of Natural Law*, New York: Longmans, Green & Co.
(1930) *Logic and Nature*, New York: New York University Press; reprinted 1953.
(1937) *Theory of the Democratic State*, Harvard University Press.
(1954) *The Judgement of History*, New York: Philosophical Library.
(1961) *Comic Laughter: A Philosophical Essay*, New Haven: Yale University Press.

Swabey's broad concern in all her work was to examine and justify the rational foundations of social structures. In *Logic and Nature* (1930) she argues that metaphysics is grounded on logical foundations. In *The Judgement of History* (1954) she rejects historical relativism and argues a case for the existence of moral absolutes.

Her *Comic Laughter* (1961) is an acute conceptual analysis in which she carefully distinguishes comic from other kinds of laughter and discusses irony, satire, nonsense, incongruity, the tragic, the sublime and the ridiculous. She eschews biological and psychological explanations of comic laughter, dismissing **Bergson**'s view that it is 'the mechanical encrusted upon the living' as belonging with psychological theories, and pursues a philosophical and logical enquiry which, she maintains, not only yields 'a logical moment of truth' but also provides 'an inkling, as it were, of the hang of things, sometimes even a hint of cosmic beneficence'. All her writing reveals her conviction concerning the existence of an ultimate and ideal harmony that supports the multifariousness of mundane living.

Sources: Kersey; WWW(Am) 1968, p. 920.

DIANÉ COLLINSON

Swinburne, R(ichard) G(ranville)

British. *b:* 1934, Smethwick, England. *Cat:* Analytic philosopher. *Ints:* Philosophy of science; philosophy of religion. *Educ:* University of Oxford. *Appts:* 1963–9, Lecturer in Philosophy, University of Hull (Senior Lecturer, 1969–72); 1972–85, Professor of Philosophy, University of Keele; 1985 to present, Nolloth Professor of the Christian Religion, University of Oxford.

Main publications:

(1968) *Space and Time*, London: Macmillan; second edition, 1981.
(1971) *The Concept of Miracle*, London: Macmillan.
(1973) *An Introduction to Confirmation Theory*, London: Methuen.
(1977) *The Coherence of Theism*, Oxford: Clarendon Press; second edition, 1993.
(1979) *The Existence of God*, Oxford: Clarendon Press; second edition, 1991.
(1983) *Faith and Reason*, Oxford: Clarendon Press.
(1984) (with Sydney Shoemaker) *Personal Identity*, Oxford: Basil Blackwell.
(1986) *The Evolution of the Soul*, Oxford: Clarendon Press.
(1989) *Responsibility and Atonement*, Oxford: Clarendon Press.
(1991) *Revelation*, Oxford: Clarendon Press.

Secondary literature:

Mackie, J. L. (1982) *The Miracle of Theism*, Oxford: Clarendon Press, chs 5, 7, 8.
McNaughton, David (1992) 'Reparation and atonement', *Religious Studies*, 28.
Padgett, Alan (ed.) (1944) *Reason and the Christian Religion*, Oxford: Oxford University Press.

Swinburne's early publications were mainly in the philosophy of science, but his most important work has been in the philosophy of religion. He has been a major figure in a movement, more influential in the USA than in the UK, that has resuscitated philosophical theology with an injection of sophisticated modern philosophical techniques and doctrines. His first substantial contribution was a trilogy on belief in God. In the first volume, *The Coherence of Theism* (1977), he argues that the notion of an eternal, omnipotent, omniscient and benevolent God is a coherent one. The second, *The Existence of God* (1979), argues that, although no argument can make the existence of God certain, a number of arguments from experience do, taken together, render it more probable than not that there is a God. (The argument here is heavily influenced by his views on confirmation theory.) In the third volume, *Faith and Reason* (1983), he discusses the relevance of such probability judgements to religious faith.

Responsibility and Atonement (1989) and *Revelation* (1991) are the first two volumes of a projected tetralogy on the philosophy of Christian doctrine.

In his Gifford Lectures (1986), subsequently published as *The Evolution of the Soul* (1986), he argues for a philosophy of mind that is broadly sympathetic to Cartesian dualism: mental states are states of the soul, which is a separate substance from the body.

Sources: WW 1992; personal communication.

ANTHONY ELLIS

Szasz, Thomas Stephen

Hungarian-American. *b:* 1920, Budapest, Hungary. *Cat:* Psychiatrist; psychoanalyst. *Ints:* Concept of mental illness; abuses of psychiatry; ethical, political and medico-legal aspects of psychiatry. *Educ:* University of Cincinnati, BA(-Hons) Physics, 1941; MD, 1944 (year prize); medical training posts in Boston, Cincinnati and Chicago; trained in psychiatry at the University of Chicago Clinic, and in psychoanalysis at the Chicago Institute for Psychoanalysis. *Infls:* Spinoza, Wittgenstein and J. S. Mill; also dramatists—Shakespeare, Molière and Ibsen. *Appts:* Taught psychiatry at The Upstate University of New York, Syracuse; Professor of Psychiatry, 1956; Emeritus Professor, 1990; private practice in psychotherapy; has held a number of honorary academic appointments and received many awards.

Main publications:

A synthesis of his views is given in *Insanity: The Idea and its Consequences*, New York: John Wiley, 1987. A clear summary statement of his central philosophical claims is to be found in 'The myth of mental illness', *American Psychologist* 15 (1960): 113–18.

(1957) *Pain and Pleasure: a Study of Bodily Feelings*, New York: Basic Books; second edition, 1975; with a new Preface, Syracuse: Syracuse University Press, 1988.

(1961) *The Myth of Mental Illness: Foundations of a Theory of Personal Conduct*, New York: Hoeber-Harper; revised edition, New York: Harper & Row, 1974.

(1963) *Law, Liberty and Psychiatry: An Inquiry into the Social Uses of Mental Health Practises*, New York: Macmillan.

(1965) *The Ethics of Psychoanalysis: The Theory and Method of Autonomous Psychotherapy*, New York: Basic Books; with a new Preface, New York: Basic Books/Harper Colophon, 1974; with a new Preface, Syracuse: Syracuse University Press, 1988.

(1965) *Psychiatric Justice*, New York: Macmillan; with a new Afterword, Syracuse: Syracuse University Press, 1988.

(1970) *Ideology and Insanity: Essays on the Psychiatric Dehumanization of Man*, Garden City, NY: Doubleday Anchor; with a new Preface, Syracuse: Syracuse University Press, 1991.

(1970) *The Manufacture of Madness: A Comparative Study of the Inquisition and the Mental Health Movement*, New York: Harper & Row.

(1973) (ed., Preface, Introduction and Epilogue) *The Age of Madness: the History of Involuntary Mental Hospitalization Presented in Selected Texts*, Garden City, NY: Doubleday Anchor.

(1976) *Ceremonial Chemistry: The Ritual Persecution of Drug Addicts and Pushers*, Garden City, NY: Doubleday Anchor; with a new Preface, Holmes Beach, FL: Learning Publications, 1985.

(1978) *The Myth of Psychotherapy: Mental Healing as Religion, Rhetoric and Repression*, Garden City, NY: Doubleday Anchor; with a new Preface, Syracuse: Syracuse University Press, 1988.

(1980) *Sex by Prescription*, Garden City, NY: Doubleday Anchor (UK edition, *Sex: Facts, Frauds and Follies*, Oxford: Basil Blackwell, 1981); with a new Preface, Syracuse: Syracuse University Press, 1990

(1994) *Cruel Compassion: Psychiatric Control of Society's Unwanted*, New York: John Wiley & Sons.

Secondary literature:

Fulford, K. W. M. (1989) *Moral Theory and Medical Practice*, Cambridge: Cambridge University Press (develops a reconciliation of the theories of Szasz and his opponents); reprinted 1995.

Roth, M. (1976) 'Schizophrenia and the theories of Thomas Szasz', *British Journal of Psychiatry*, 129: 317–26 (criticisms of Szasz's analysis of the concept of mental illness).

——and Kroll, J. (1986) *The Reality of Mental Illness*, Cambridge: Cambridge University Press.

Smirnoff, A. Y. U. and Snow, E. (1993) 'Concepts of disease and the abuse of psychiatry in the USSR', *British Journal of Psychiatry*, 162: 801–10.

Thomas Szasz was one of the main catalysts of the social and intellectual movement in the 1960s and 1970s which has become known as 'anti-psychiatry'. His central thesis is that psychiatry is an illegitimate extension of physical medicine. The concepts of illness and disease as used in physical medicine are, he argues, biological concepts, based on objective norms of bodily functioning. The concept of mental illness on the other hand is a moral and legal concept defined by norms which are social-evaluative in nature. To extend physical medicine in this way is not only misleading but positively harmful. It results in the twin evils of psychiatric *oppression*, involuntary 'treatment' of people who may be distressed, deviant, even delinquent, but not really ill; and psychiatric *dependence*, passive reliance on 'therapy' instead of facing up to life's problems and tackling them for what they are in an open and direct way. Szasz has developed this thesis in a number of detailed studies of different areas of psychiatric thought and practice, historical and modern. In his clinical work he follows his own precept, offering, through psychotherapy, improved understanding as a basis for independent action. Szasz's radical stance has provoked often impassioned denunciations by psychiatrists (Roth 1976). However, the institutionalized abuse of psychiatry in some countries, and the sporadic occurrences of such abuses elsewhere, show the extent to which psychiatric patients remain vulnerable in the ways he identified (Fulford, Smirnoff and Snow 1993). His sceptical analysis has served as the spur to the development of a far more sophisticated understanding of the concepts not only of mental but also of physical disorder (Roth and Kroll 1986), and through this to improvements in practice (Fulford 1989).

Sources: CB, 1975; CA: Bullock & Woodings; Corsini; *Psychlit* journal articles (Silver Platter); UCDCL; personal communication.

K. W. M. FULFORD

T

Tagore, Rabindranath

Indian. *b:* 7 May 1861, Calcutta. *d:* 7 August 1941, Calcutta. *Cat:* Poet. *Ints:* Metaphysics; epistemology; social and political thought; aesthetics. *Educ:* Studied Law in England, 1878–80. *Infls:* Advaita Vedanta, Vaishnavism and natural scientists such as Thomas Huxley, Jean Lamarck and Charles Darwin. *Appts:* Founded Visvabharati, a university at Satiniketan, near Bolpur, West Bengal; Nobel Prize for Literature, 1913.

Main publications:

(1913) *Sadhana: The Realisation of Life*, London: Macmillan & Co.
(1921) *Nationalism*, London: Macmillan & Co.
(1941) *Crisis in Civilisation*, Calcutta: Visva-Bharati.
(1959) *Personality*, London: Macmillan & Co.

Secondary literature:

Radhakrishnan, Sarvepalli (1918) *The Philosophy of Rabindranath Tagore*, London: Macmillan & Co.
Nehru, Jawaharlal (1931) *The Golden Book of Tagore*, Calcutta: Golden Book Committee.
Tagore, R. (1953) *The Religion of an Artist*, Calcutta: Visva-Bharati.

Tagore's philosophy is a curious mixture of idealism, spiritualism and materialism. This is a consequence of various influences, from the ideas contained in Advaita Vedanta and the Vaishnavite teachings on *bhakti* (love for personal God) to the views of natural scientists such as Thomas Huxley, Jean Lamarck and Charles Darwin.

Tagore, in the true spirit of Vedantism, accepted *Brahman*—that which is devoid of subject–object distinction, qualityless, eternal and indescribable—as the absolute truth. He also accepted that nature and the entire world of distinct objects exist objectively and that all the objects and phenomena of nature and the laws by which their existence is governed are knowable.

According to Tagore, perception—the mode through which man acquires knowledge of the world, the laws of nature and the truth—is of three kinds. The first is intellectual perception. Here the intellect interprets sense-data on the basis of their reliability and strength. The second is perception related to practical activity. This kind of perception allows man to acquire knowledge of the behaviour of the various objects around him and the laws of nature so that it can be usefully employed by him for his own ends. The third is perception of the emotions. Here man cognizes not only his own soul but his soul in others.

Unlike Vedanta, which concerned itself solely with man's spiritual well-being, Tagore regarded man's social well-being as important. He was appalled by the social conditions of the Indian people and recommended reforms in areas such as agriculture, education, health care and social structure. Tagore had a great impact on the Indian nationalist movement with his poems, plays and other literary works. According to Jawaharlal Nehru (1931, pp. 182–5):

> [He] was a beacon of light to all of us, ever pointing to the finer and nobler aspects of life and never allowing us to fall into the ruts which kill individuals as well as nations. Nationalism, especially when it urges us to fight for freedom, is noble and life-giving. But often it becomes a narrow creed, and limits and encompasses its votaries and makes them forget the many-sidedness of life. But Rabindranath Tagore has given to our nationalism the outlook of internationalism and has enriched it with art and music and the magic of his words, so that it has become the full-blooded emblem of India's awakened spirit.

INDIRA MAHALINGAM CARR

Taha, Mahmud

Sudanese. *b:* 1908, village of the Blue Nile province. *d:* 18 January 1985. Khartum (hanged by Nimeyri's regime). *Cat:* Islamic jurist and reformer. *Educ:* Self-taught; studied religious sciences and especially sufism (al-Hallag, al-Ghazali and Ibn 'Arabi) in his thirties, after a long involvement in the practical problems of agriculture. *Appts:* Nationalist; fought against British occupation in his youth, imprisoned in

1940 for the first time; after the Independence of Sudan (1956), founded a political party, The Republican Brothers (*Al-Ikhwan al-Gumhuriyyun*) and strongly opposed all the dictatorial regimes of his country; his religious ideas were condemned by al-Azhar's *ulama*.

Main publications:
(1947) *Ar-Risalah ath-Thaniyah fil Islam* [The Second Mission of Islam], Omdurman.

Secondary literature:
Renaud, P. (1985) article in *Comprendre*.

Taha emphasized the need to renew Islamic legislation, whilst maintaining its grounding in traditional law (*shariah*), in order to make it an effective tool in rebuilding Muslim Society. He rejected a literal interpretation of the rules and penalties prescribed by the *shariah* and argued that Muhammad regulated Muslim life by law when he was living in Medina but, as a prophet sent to all men, delivered a noble ethical perspective, far higher than mere social legislation. This noble perspective, whose aim is the sincere worship of God (*ibadat*) is included in the Meccan chapters of the Koran and was later codified in the *sunnah* (the customary practice of Muhammad). The *sunnah* is the basis of Modern Islam, the Islam of eschatology (*al-Islam al-Akhir*), addressed to all humanity. The second mission of Islam, according to Taha, leads to a threefold equality: in economics by socialism; in politics by democracy; in society by the suppression of any discrimination.
Sources: 'Dossier des études arabes', Pontifical Inst. of Arabic Studies, 1986, 70–1.

MASSIMO CAMPANINI

Taixu (T'ai-hsu)
Chinese. *b:* 1890, Haining, Zhejianag Province, China. *d:* 1947, Shanghai. *Cat:* Buddhist monk and reformer. *Ints:* Consciousness Only school of Buddhism. *Educ:* Received Buddhist instruction at the Tiantong Temple near Ningbo, with further study under Yang Wenhui. *Infls:* Various schools of Buddhism, Zhang Binglin and Yan Fu; reformist, anarchist and socialist thought. *Appts:* Head of Wuchang Buddhist Institute; Founder of World Buddhist Association; Founder of many other Buddhist organizations.

Main publications:
(n.d.) *Essentials of Buddhism*, Foxue Book Company.

(n.d.) *New Theory of Idealism*, Foxue Book Company.
(n.d.) (ed.) *The Sound of the Tide*.
(n.d.) *Writings of the Buddhist Teacher Taixu*, 3 vols, Foxue Book Company.
(1928) *Lectures on Buddhism*, Paris.
(1930) *Origins of the Most Eminent Buddhist Sects*, Hankou: Xinchi Publishers.
(1931) *Influence of Buddhism on Chinese Culture*, Xian: Chinese Buddhist Society.
(1932) *Philosophy*, Shanghai: Foxue Book Company.
(1932) *Taixu's Discourses*, 3 vols, Shanghai: Zhonghua Book Company.
(1932) *A View of the History of Liberty*.
(1938) *Studies of Consciousness Only Buddhism*, Shanghai: Commercial Press.
(1940) *The A.B.C. of Buddhism*.
(1940) *Essential Discourse of the Buddhist Patriarchs*.
(1940) *The True Theory of Reality*, Zhonghua Book Company.
(1945) *Regulations for the Reformation of the Order*, Foxue Book Company.

Secondary literature:
Boorman, H. (ed.) (1970) *Biographical Dictionary of Republican China*, New York and London: Columbia University Press.
Briere, O. (1956) *Fifty Years of Chinese Philosophy 1898–1950*, London: George Allen & Unwin Ltd.
Chan, W. (1953) *Religious Trends in Modern China*, New York: Columbia University Press.
Complete Chinese Encyclopedia (1987), Philosophy Volumes, Beijing: Chinese Encyclopedia Publications.

'Taixu', the Buddhist term for the great void, was the chosen name of China's most eminent modernizing reformer of Buddhist doctrines, monastic order and lay practice. Taixu was influenced by the ideas of political and social reform in China and saw Buddhism and socialism as compatible expressions of the same universal viewpoint. His Buddhism followed the idealist Consciousness Only school and formed an atheistic rational system open to Western philosophy and science rather than a religious faith. He sought to renew decadent Buddhism through education, by diverting income from religious property to social welfare and by encouraging the intelligent examination of religious texts among monks and within lay discussion groups among educated urban Chinese. He gained a dominant position in spite of criticism by the leaders of religious 'free land' Buddhism and the rivalry of **Ouyang Jianwu** for leadership of the Consciousness Only school. Through travel, writing and organizational skill he spread his activities to Tibetan Lamaism and to the renovation or establishment of Buddhism elsewhere in the world.

Taixu's great cultivation gave new life to Buddhist doctrines through rational assessment and defence. His idealist system centred on traditional Buddhist themes of consciousness and illumination, but used modern scientific and philosophical theories, including those of **Einstein**, to argue for his metaphysical and epistemological claims. He contrasted the world of appearances with the true reality of the mind and of laws known by the mind: although distracted by external appearances one could pursue knowledge by a path of virtue to illumination, the perfect state of which was attained by the Buddha. All men were capable of illumination, but this required arduous discipline through instruction, thought or contemplative practice. The principles of illumination were the traditional doctrines of the eternity of flux of being, the origin of being in consciousness, the negation of the self and the negation of the objective existence of the universe. He argued that God was not necessary to support human virtue and enlightenment and that it was a superstitious error to worship the Buddha. He claimed that his version of Buddhism, with its rejection of dogma and superstition, provided an understanding of liberty superior to the ideologies of the time.

NICHOLAS BUNNIN

Taketani, Mitsuo

Japanese. **b:** 1911, Fukuoka, Japan. **Cat:** Marxist; nuclear physicist. **Ints:** Philosophy of science; environmentalism. **Educ:** Physics at Kyoto University. **Infls:** Marx. **Appts:** Twice arrested by the authorities for involvement in Marxist organizations; unable to obtain a substantive post until after the Second World War; 1953–, Rikkyo University, Tokyo.

Main publications:

(1946) *Benshoho no Shomondai* [Several Problems Concerning Dialectics], revised edition, Tokyo: Keiso Publishing, 1966.

(1949) *Kagaku Tetsugaku Geijutsu* [Science, Philosophy, Art], Tokyo: Soryusha.

(1968) *Taketani Mitsuo Chosakushu* [Taketani's Works], Tokyo: Keiso Publishing.

(1976–) *Taketani Mitsuo Gendai Ronshu*, [Taketani's Works on Contemporary Issues], Tokyo: Keiso Publishing.

(1979) *Tokken no Jinken* [Privilege and Human Rights], Tokyo: Keiso Publishing.

(1981) *Gendai Gijutsu no Kozo* [Structure of Today's Technology], Tokyo: Gitjutsu to Ningen Publishing.

(1982) *Kagakusha no Shakaiteki Sekinin* [Social Responsibility for Scientists], Tokyo: Keiso Publishing.

Before obtaining a post at Rikkyo University, Tokyo, in 1953, Taketani's life, both as physicist and philosopher, had been difficult. After the Second World War, however, his influence grew greatly. His interest in debates about the uses of technology and involvement in the anti-nuclear peace movement as a nuclear physicist marked an epoch in the postwar philosophical world in Japan. He also became actively engaged in a number of environmental movements in the 1970s, and has forcibly accused fellow scientists of the violation of both nature and human rights.

TOGO TSUKAHARA

Tan Sitong (T'an Ssu-t'ung)

Chinese. **b:** 1865, Liuyang, Hunan Province, China. **d:** 1898, Beijing. **Cat:** Confucian syncretism. **Ints:** Philosophy of humanity. **Educ:** Studied the Chinese classics. **Infls:** The neo-Confucian materialists Zhang Zai (eleventh century) and Wang Fuzhi (seventeenth century) and the neo-Confucian idealists Lu Xiangshan (twelfth century) and Wang Yangming (early sixteenth century); Kang Youwei, Liang Qichao, Confucian, Buddhist and Christian thinkers, and Western science. **Appts:** Work promoting new learning and modern education in Hunan Province; Secretary to the Grand Council supervising reforms during the Hundred Days Reform of 1898.

Main publications:

(1954) *Complete Works of Tan Sitong*, Beijing: Three Bookstores United Company.

(1958) *Philosophy of Humanity*, Shanghai: Zhonghua Book Company.

Secondary literature:

Briere, O. (1956) *Fifty Years of Chinese Philosophy 1898–1950*, London: George Allen & Unwin Ltd.

Chan, S. *T'an Ssu-t'ung: An Annotated Bibliography*.

Chan, W. (1963) *A Source Book in Chinese Philosophy*, Princeton: Princeton University Press.

Complete Chinese Encyclopedia, Philosophy Volumes, Beijing: Chinese Encyclopedia Publications.

Tan adapted Confucian thought to modern circumstances. Under the influence of **Kang Youwei** and **Liang Qichao** he progressed from efforts to modernize education to more comprehensive reformist activities. In 1898 he was appointed one of four Secretaries to the Grand Council overseeing reforms for the Emperor. With the empress dowager's coup Tan was arrested and executed. He is the most prominent martyr of the Hundred Days Reform.

Tan's major work, *Philosophy of Humanity* (1958), focused on the central Confucian virtue of *ren* (humanity) and was strongly influenced by the utopian thought of Kang Youwei. After previously seeing *qi* or material principle as metaphysically basic, Tan came to regard *ren* as functionally identified with ether, the imperceivable, universal and indestructable element basic to all reality. He thus tried to bring together Confucian thought and a scientific account of the natural world. His identification of moral and natural reality led to the claim that *ren* should be realized not only for human well-being, but also for the welfare of the universe. His vision was one of Confucian great unity and Moist universal love, abolishing all social divisions of class, sex and nation. He showed hostility to unreformed Confucian moral practices, and attempted to relate his views to Buddhism and Christianity as well as to Confucian tradition. His understanding of Western science and thought was limited and his syncretism often clumsy, but his attempt to provide an intellectual basis for modernizing reform within the Confucian tradition had influence in this century, especially in view of his martyrdom.

NICHOLAS BUNNIN

Tanabe, Hajime

Japanese. *b:* 3 February 1885, Tokyo, Japan. *d:* 29 April 1962. *Cat:* Philosopher of science. *Ints:* Kyoto school of philosophy. *Educ:* Department of Mathematics and Department of Philosophy, Tokyo Imperial University. *Infls:* Heidegger, Husserl, Hermann Cohen, Max Planck, Jules Poincaré, Nishida Kitar and Hatano Seiichi. *Appts:* Assistant Professor of Philosophy of Science at Thoku Imperial University, 1913–19; Professor of Philosophy, Kyoto Imperial University, 1919–45; visiting scholar, Universities of Berlin and Freiburg, 1922–4.

Main publications:

(1915) *Saikin no shizen-kagaku* [Contemporary Natural Science], Iwanami Shoten.

(1918) *Kagaku gairon* [Introduction to Science], Iwanami Shoten.
(1924) *Kanto no mokutekiron* [Kant's Teleology], Iwanami Shoten.
(1932) *Hegeru-tetsugaku to benshoho* [Hegelian Philosophy and Dialectics], Iwanami Shoten.
(1933) *Tetsugaku tsuron* [An Outline of Philosophy], Iwanami Shoten.
(1937) *Tetsugaku to kagaku to no aida* [Between Philosophy and Science], Iwanami Shoten.
(1946) *Zange-do toshite no tetsugaku*, Iwanami Shoten (English translation, *Philosophy as Metanoetics*, trans. Y. Tareuchi, V. Vilielmo and J. Heisig, Los Angeles and Berkeley: University of California Press, 1986).
(1946) *Shu no ronri no benshoho* [Dialectic of the Logic of the Species], Akitaya.
(1947) *Jitsuzon to ai to jissen* [Existence, Love and Praxis], Tokyo: Chikuma Shobo.
(1948) *Kirisutokyo no bensho* [The Dialectic of Christianity], Tokyo: Chikuma Shobo.
(1949) *Tetsugaku nyumon* [An Introduction to Philosophy], 5 vols, Tokyo: Chikuma Shobo.
(1963–4) *Tanabe Hajime zenshu* [The Complete Works of Tanabe Hajime], 15 vols, Tokyo: Chikuma Shobo.

Secondary literature:

Philosophical Studies of Japan (several articles).
Piovesana, Gino K. (1968) *Recent Japanese Philosophical Thought, 1862–1962*, Tokyo: Sophia University Press (republished in New York: St John's University Press, 1969).
Unno and Heisig (eds) (1990) *The Religious Philosophy of Tanabe Hajime: the Metanoetic Imperative*, Berkeley: Asian Humanities Press.

Although remembered as a philosopher of considerable versatility, Tanabe's interest in philosophy was founded upon a thorough background in mathematics and the natural sciences and a consequent search for an approach to the sciences based on philosophical principles. The result was a constant stress on the need for practical application in the study of philosophy.

Tanabe's early focus on neo-Kantian philosophy was more a reflection of the prevailing trend of the times than of a deep-rooted affinity and, particularly following his return to Kyoto in 1927 after a period of study of phenomenology in Germany, there is increasing evidence in his writings of a move away from German idealism towards the study of dialectics. In particular, influenced by **Nishida**'s focus on 'absolute nothingness', Tanabe came to stress the concept of an 'absolute dialectic', developing this into his own philosophical system based on the theory known as the 'logic of the species' (*shu no ronri* 1946) in which 'the species' represented the nation as a historical mediating force between the individual and mankind.

Defeat in the Pacific War, which happened to coincide with Tanabe's retirement from Kyoto Imperial University, exercised a profound influence on the direction of his research, subsequent publications evidencing a heightened political awareness and a greater urgency in his advocacy of peaceful reform and democracy for Japan. At the same time, there is evidence of criticism of his own earlier philosophical methodology for its tendency to make absolutes of what he called 'species' and a move away from Buddhism to an increasingly Christian perspective, as suggested by the author's self-categorization as a '*werden-der Christ*'. Tanabe's contribution to the emergence of an acknowledged school of philosophical thought in Japan is hard to exaggerate, this being duly recognized in 1951 with the conferment of the prestigious Order of Cultural Merit for his work.

Sources: *Kodansha Encyclopedia of Japan*; Edwards; EncBrit; *Cambridge Encyclopedia of Japan*.

MARK WILLIAMS

Tang Junyi (T'ang Chun-i)

Chinese. *b:* 1909, Yibin, Sichuan, China. *d:* 1978, Hong Kong. *Cat:* Hegelian idealist. *Ints:* Comparative philosophy; ethics; the self and spiritual values. *Educ:* Nanjing Central University. *Infls:* Hegel and the idealist Confucians Mengzi, Lu Xiangshan (twelfth century) and Wang Yangming (sixteenth century). *Appts:* Professor, Nanjing Central University; Professor and Dean, New Asia College, Hong Kong.

Main publications:

(n.d.) *Matter, Mind and Human Life*.

(n.d.) *The Reconstruction of Humanistic Spirit*.

(1934) *Comparative Studies in the Philosophies and Thought of China and the Occident*, Shanghai: Zhengzhong Book Company.

(1944) *Construction of the Moral Self*, Commercial Press.

(1958) *The Meaning of Culture and the Rationality of Morality*, 2 vols.

(1976) *The Spiritual Value of Chinese Culture*.

(1977) *The Existence of Life and the Realm of Spirit*, 2 vols, Taipei: Student Book Store.

(1977) *The Fundamentals of Chinese Philosophy*, 7 vols, Taipei: Student Book Store.

Secondary literature:

Briere, O. (1956) *Fifty Years of Chinese Philosophy 1898–1950*, London: George Allen & Unwin Ltd.

Complete Chinese Encyclopedia (1987), Philosophy Volumes, Beijing: Chinese Encyclopedia Publications.

Republic of China Yearbook 1989 (1989) Taipei: Kwang Hwa Publishing Company.

Using a method derived from Hegel's *Phenomenology of Spirit*, Tang Junyi ordered and assessed human moral experience as autonomous spiritual development. His approach was hostile both to materialism in metaphysics and to utilitarianism in ethics. His phenomenology encompassed post-Hegelian European developments, including Nietzschean thought, scholarly and aesthetic moral sensibility, and human ideals derived from Hindu mysticism and Chinese Confucianism. Between the origin of morality in individual instinct and its final realization, Tang discerned several stages in the development of the moral self, each with its own characteristics. The study of spirit, morality and the self were for him aspects of the same developmental investigation. At each stage Tang presented an ideal representation of the person attaining that stage. The perfect person, again presented in an ideal description, was the ultimate goal of his system, and his Hegelian–Confucian syncretism emerged with his choice of a Confucian ideal, displaying the virtue of humanity, as the culmination of his Hegelian journey. Through his examination of the structure and development of human subjectivity, Tang offered a Western metaphysical underpinning for the idealist Confucian tradition. His account of the self and spirit also attempted to provide a transcendental basis for science, the humanities and religion. In his later writings he followed Hegel in shifting attention from the individual self to a broader concern for culture. He was concerned to explore the values of Chinese culture, but also to understand the plurality of cultures in a way allowing coexistence. The culmination of Tang's work was a major history of Chinese philosophy.

NICHOLAS BUNNIN

Tang Yongtong (T'ang Yung-t'ung)

Chinese. *b:* 1893, Huangmei, Hubei Province, China. *d:* 1964, Beijing. *Cat:* Buddhist. *Ints:* Neodaoist mysticism; Indian philosophy. *Educ:* Studied with Ouyang Jianwn; at Qinghua University, Beijing; at Hamline and Harvard Universities in the USA. *Infls:* Ouyang Jianwu. *Appts:* Professor at Southeast University (now Nanjing University), Nankai University, University of Beijing (Dean of Humanities) and the Southwest Associated University; 1947, lectured at the University of California, elected an Academician and Fellow of the Chinese Academy of Sciences; 1949–, Chairman of the Board, then Vice President of University of Beijing; held positions in the People's Consultative Conference and the National People's Congress.

Main publications:

(n.d.) *Manuscript of the History of Buddhism in the Sui and Tang Dynasties*.

(n.d.) *Selected Academic Papers of Tang Yongtong* (including 'Preliminary treatise on the metaphysical schools of the Wei and Jin Periods, 220–420', 'Selected manuscripts of the past', 'Notes on recovery' and 'A brief history of philosophy in India').

(1934) *The History of Buddhism in the Han, Weig, Jin, and Southern and Northern Dynasties*, Shanghai: Commercial Press.

(1957) *Drafts of Essays on Wei-Jin Metaphysics*, Beijing: Renmin Publishing House.

(1962) *Miscellaneous Drafts of Yesterday*, Beijing: Renmin Publishing House.

(1962) (with Ren Jiyu) *A Brief Discussion of the Social and Political Ideas of the Metaphysical Schools of the Wei-Jin Period*, Shanghai: Shanghai Remin Publishing House.

Secondary literature:

Boorman, H. (1970) *Biographical Dictionary of Republican China*, New York and London: Columbia University Press.

Complete Chinese Encyclopedia (1987), Philosophy Volumes, Beijing: Chinese Encyclopedia Publications.

Tang Yongtong was an outstanding student of ancient philosophy, specializing in the history of Chinese Buddhism, Indian philosophy and gnosticism. Early work on Aristotle contributed to his lifelong interest in comparative methodology and provided the basis for his well-regarded history of Western philosophy, in which he also focused on rationalism and empiricism. His historical insights and philological skills provided the basis for a critical approach to ancient materials. Tang's detailed textual mastery complemented a capacity to ask original questions about the history and doctrines of Buddhism. The aspect of his history most directly significant for philosophy is his examination of the metaphysics of daoism and Buddhism, although his ability to clarify and

place many central concepts has also been widely appreciated.

NICHOLAS BUNNIN

Tarde, Gabriel

French. *b:* 12 March 1842, Sarlat, Dordogne, France. *d:* 13 May 1904, Paris. *Cat:* Social philosopher; criminologist; psychologist. *Ints:* Social laws; social imitation. *Educ:* L'École Normale Supérieure. *Infls:* Auguste Comte, Antoine Augustin Cournot and Émile Boutroux. *Appts:* 1881–1900, Directeur du Service de la Statistique au Ministère de la Justice; 1900–4, Professor of Sociology, Collège de France.

Main publications:

(1890) *Les Lois de l'imitation*, Paris: Alcan.
(1890) *La Philosophie pénale*, Lyon: A. Stork.
(1894) *La Logique sociale*, Paris: Alcan.
(1897) *L'Opposition universelle: essai d'une théorie des contraires*, Paris: Alcan.
(1898) *Études de psychologie sociale*, Paris: Alcan.
(1898) *Les Lois sociales: esquisse d'une sociologie*, Paris: Alcan.
(1901) *L'Opinion et la foule*, Paris: Alcan.

Secondary literature:

Benrubi, I. (1926) *Contemporary Thought of France*, trans. E. B. Dicker, London: Williams & Norgate, pp. 92–4.

Matagrin, A. (1909) *La Philosophie sociale de Gabriel Tarde*, Paris: Alcan.

Tarde's sociology grew out of his work as a criminologist engaged in the study of deviant behaviour. Loosely attached to the school of Antoine Cournot, he developed a psychological as against a purely biological or mechanical conception of scientific sociology.

Tarde's enduring aim was to reduce all social facts to the phenomenon of imitation, in which an act, a feeling or an idea tends to be transmitted from one person to another. By maintaining in a novel way that the starting-point of imitation is invention, an essentially individual and non-social fact, he called into question the generally accepted notion that fundamental social facts are constituted by an interdependence, based on coordination without imitation. Thus for Tarde the sociologist's task is to determine how imitation occurs and is modified under circumstances of every kind, in short to establish the 'laws of imitation'. According to him, from such laws we may infer that humanity is advancing towards an ever growing unity and equality. These views, which were explicitly opposed to those of Émile **Durkheim** in particular, aroused much debate. Tarde was one of the most brilliant early representatives of the 'École du milieu social', which stands opposed, in the field of criminology, to the biological school.

Sources: Huisman; EF.

STEPHEN MOLLER

Tarozzi, Guiseppe

Italian. *b:* 24 March 1866, Turin. *d:* 20 July 1958, Padua. *Cat:* Positivist. *Ints:* Philosophy of man. *Educ:* University of Padua. *Infls:* Roberto Ardigò. *Appts:* 1902–6, Professor of Philosophy, University of Palermo; 1906–36, Professor of Philosophy, University of Bologna.

Main publications:

(1930) *L'esistenza e l'anima*, Bari: Laterza.

(1936) *La libertà umana e la critica al determinismo*, Bologna: Zanichelli.

(1936) *La ricerca filosofica*, Naples: Rondinella.

(1951) *L'infinito e il divino*, Bologna: Cappelli.

Secondary literature:

Garin, Eugenio (1966) *Storia della filosofia italiana*, 3 vols, Turin: Einaudi, vol. III, pp. 1273–6.

Sciacca, Michele (1964) *Philosophical Trends in the Contemporary World*, Notre Dame, Ind.: University of Notre Dame Press, p. 51.

Tarozzi is remembered for simultaneously defending positivism and rejecting determinism. He insisted that a close inspection of the facts of experience revealed that every fact is singular and therefore unrepeatable. Causality, whether universal or otherwise, is a notion whose intelligibility presupposes that the singularity of facts is ignored in favour of their membership of classes: causal laws represent the behaviour of these classes. While this is a methodological necessity for the sciences, reality itself need not be thought of as deterministic. Tarozzi thus exploits the positivist emphasis on the facts of experience in his rejection of the determinism which is often associated with positivism. At the beginning of the century idealism became the dominant philosophy in Italy, and Tarozzi is regarded as the last Italian positivist of note.

Sources: EF; *Dizionario generale degli autori italiani contemporanei*; *Dizionario universale della letteratura contemporanea*.

HUGH BREDIN

Tarski, Alfred

Polish-American. *b:* 14 January 1902, Warsaw. *d:* 26 October 1983, Berkeley, California. *Cat:* Mathematician; logician; philosopher. *Ints:* The theory of truth; philosophy of language; logic; semantics; foundations of mathematics. *Educ:* University of Warsaw, PhD 1926 (supervised by Stanislaw Lesniewski). *Infls:* Lvov-Warsaw School, Stanislaw Lesniewski, Jan Łukasiewicz. *Appts:* 1922–5, Instructor in Logic, Polish Pedagological Institute, Fical, Warsaw; 1925–39, Docent, and Adjunct Professor of Mathematics and Logic, University of Warsaw; 1939–41, Research Associate in Mathematics, Harvard University; 1941–2, Member, Institute for Advanced Study, Princeton; 1939–68, Lecturer, Associate Professor, then Professor (1946) at the University of California, Berkeley; 1968–83, Professor Emeritus, University of California, Berkeley.

Main publications:

(1933) *Projeci prwady w Jezykach nauk dedukcyjnych* [The Concept of Truth in the Languages of Deductive Sciences], Warsaw.

(1935) *O logice matematycanaj i metodsie dedukcjnaj*, Lvov (translated and expanded as *Introduction to Logic and the Methodology of Deductive Sciences*, New York: Oxford University Press, 1941).

(1935–6) 'Der Wahrheitsbegriff in den formalisierten Sprachen', *Studia Philosophica* 1: 261–405.

(1944) 'The semantic conception of truth and the foundations of semantics', *Journal of Philosophy and Phenomenological Research* 4: 341–75.

(1953) (with Andrzej Mostowski and Raphael M. Robinson) *Undecidable Theories*, Amsterdam: North-Holland.

(1956) (ed. and trans. J. H. Woodger) *Logic, Semantics, Metamathematics: Papers from 1923 to 1938*, Oxford: Clarendon Press.

(1973) (with R. M. Montague and D. S. Scott) *An Axiomatic Approach to Set Theory*, Amsterdam: North-Holland.

(1981) (ed. S. R. Grant and R. N. Mackenzie) *The Collected Works of Alfred Tarski*, 4 vols, University of California Press.

Secondary literature:

Barwise, J. and Etchemendy, J. (1987) *The Liar: An Essay on Truth and Circularity*, Oxford: Oxford University Press.

Black, Max (1948) 'The semantic definition of truth', *Analysis* 8: 49–63.

Carnap, Rudolf (1934) *Logical Syntax of Language*, Vienna, London: Kegan Paul and New York: Harcourt Brace, 1937.

Church, Alonzo (1979) 'A comparison of Russell's resolution of the semantical antinomies with that of Tarski', *Journal of Symbolic Logic* 41: 747–60.

Field, Hartry (1972) 'Tarski's theory of truth', *Journal of Philosophy* 69(13): 347–75.

Jordan, Zbigniew (1967) 'The development of mathematical logic in Poland between the two wars', in Storrs MacCall (ed.), *Polish Logic 1920–39*, Oxford: Clarendon Press.

Luschei, Eugene C. (1962) *The Logical Systems of Lesniewski*, Amsterdam: North-Holland.

Popper, Karl R. (1972) 'Philosophical comments on Tarski's theory of truth', in *Objective Knowledge: An Evolutionary Approach*, Oxford: Clarendon Press.

Quine, W. V. (1966) 'On an application of Tarski's theory of truth', in *Selected Logic Papers*, New York: Random House.

Wolenski, Jan (1993) 'Tarski as a philosopher', in Coniglione, F. (ed.) *Polish Scientific Philosophy*, Amsterdam: Rodopi.

Alfred Tarski made major contributions to logic and mathematical theory. Whle his own interests were predominantly mathematical, his work on metalogic and semantics has had the most direct impact on the development of analytical philosophy, although his earlier contributions on set theory are of interest to more logically orientated philosophers, as is his work on the concept of logical consequences which anticipated by more than a decade similar, but less well-known work by Karl **Popper** on deductive inference.

His most thorough exploration of the semantic issues was in his monograph-length paper (The Concept of Truth in Formalized Languages, first published in German, 1935–6). As the title implies, Tarski saw his task as one of providing a satisfactory account of truth for the specialized idioms of science and mathematics. The elements of Tarski's strategy were a) to characterize what he called adequacy conditions—the minimal conditions that should be met by any adequate theory of truth, and b) to provide a definition of truth which meets those conditions. The aim was to supply a definition of the term 'true sentence' which was both materially adequate and formally correct. He noted that although the notion of a true sentence in colloquial language seemed quite clear and intelligible, he considered that all previous attempts to characterize exactly what this really meant had been fruitless and vague. While owning himself to be puzzled by traditional disputes, he none the less thought that he was determining the core sense of the 'classical' or

'correspondence' notion, as opposed to other well-established notions, including the pragmatist notion of truth as utility.

For Tarski, any acceptable definition of truth should have as a consequence all instances of his T-schema: 'S is true if, and only if, p', for which one concrete example might be 'Snow is white' is true if, and only if, snow is white'. It is important to emphasize that Tarski's schema is not itself intended as a definition—that is the point of calling it a material adequacy condition—it serves to fix the extension of the predicate '... is true', the things to which it applies, namely the sentences of the given language. As regards formal correctness, this condition is intended to avoid the notorious paradoxes and antinomies, of which the Liar paradox is among the best known. These anomalies arises when i) a language contains its own semantics, i.e. the means of referring to its own expressions, and ii) when the standard logical laws apply. Tarski regarded i) as a conspicuous feature of natural languages, and in large measure it explains his pessimism about the possibility of applying formal methods to informal, as contrasted with formal, languages. Given that abandoning logical law was unthinkable, Tarski introduced his distinction between object-language and metalanguage. By this means, he hoped to neutralize the antinomies. Thus, for a given language L, the prima facie paradoxical sentence 'This sentence is false in L' could not itself be a sentence of the object-language L, but only of its metalanguage L*. Moreover, for adequate discussion of semantics, the meta-language needed to be richer in expressive resources than the language it was used to discuss.

Tarski's reason for thinking that instances of the T-schema give only 'partial' definitions of truth is this: that only the totality of such T-sentences for a language could provide a complete definition, and given that the number of sentences in a language is potentially infinite, no such totality of T-sentences could be delivered. Tarski also required that no semantic terms (e.g. 'true') should be taken as primitive. In this he was influenced by his commitment to physicalism which could no more tolerate irreducible semantic concepts than it could tolerate irreducible mentalistic ones.

Tarski's theories have had a mixed reception among philosophers. From a technical point of view, Tarski's strategy only works for sentences whose logical forms can be represented in first-order logic, i.e. for sentences whose truth-values are determined by the truth-values of atomic sentences. But there are many meaningful sentences which do not readily lend themselves to such formalization, such as counterfactual conditionals and sentences involving modal notions like those of necessity and possibility.

Karl Popper enthusiastically embraced Tarski's work on truth as rehabilitating the traditional correspondence theory. Others have regarded his adequacy condition as a best neutral and at worse irrelevant to the debate concerning the merits of the correspondence notion as against those of the coherentists and the pragmatists. One complaint has been that Tarski's theory supplies no *criterion* of truth, although it was never part of his intention to provide such a criterion. Despite Tarski's own scepticism about the possibility of applying his formal methods to natural languages, there have been comprehensive attempts to exploit his ideas in providing theories of meaning for natural languages, of which two of the more notable examples are provided by the work of Donald **Davidson** and Richard **Montague**. Additionally, Hartry **Field** contributed amendments to the theory with a view to fulfilling Tarski's own physicalist aims. The debate between proponents of truth-conditional semantics and more informal approaches to the issue of meaning in natural languages owes a considerable debt to Tarski's pioneering work.

Sources: Edwards; Steven Givant (1986) 'Bibliography of Alfred Tarski', *JSL* 5: 913–41; Turner; Jan Wolenski (1989) *Logic and Philosophy in the Lvov-Warsaw School*, Norwell: Kluwer.

DENIS POLLARD

Tatarkiewicz, Wladyslaw

Polish. **b:** 1886, Warsaw. **d:** 1981. **Cat:** Value theorist; historian of philosophy. **Ints:** Aesthetics; ethics; history of philosophy, especially in Poland. **Educ:** Sent down from Warsaw University after involvement in nationalist student politics, Tatarkiewicz studied in Switzerland, France and Germany (doctoral studies on Aristotle at Marburg, concluded in 1910). **Infls:** Aristotle. **Appts:** First major appointment was as Professor at Lvov; then moved (1915) to Warsaw University, where he was Professor until his death, creating an international reputation as an aesthetician and historian of philosophy; a member of many international and national learned societies.

Main publications:

A highly selective list from a voluminous output:
(1910) *Die Disposition der aristotelischen Prinzipien*.

(1919) *O bezwzglednosci dobra* [On the Intransigence of Good].
(1927) *O szczesciu* (On Happiness) (English translation, *Analysis of Happiness*, The Hague: Nijhoff, 1976).
(1931) *Les trois morales d'Aristote*.
(1931) *Historia filozofii* [History of Philosophy], 2 vols.
(1960–8) *Historia estetyki*, 3 vols (English translation, *History of Aesthetics*, The Hague: Mouton, 1970–4).
(1975) *Dzieje szesciu pojec*, Warsaw: PWN (English translation, *A History of Six Ideas: An Essay in Aesthetics*, The Hague: Nijhoff, 1980).

Secondary literature:

Jaworski, Marek (1975) *Wladyslaw Tatarkiewicz*, Warsaw: Wydawn Interpress.

One of the most important Polish philosophers of this period, Tatarkiewicz derived from his doctoral work on Aristotle a lifelong interest in value theory, initially focused on moral value, but later expanded to the area of the aesthetic. In his ethical studies, Tatarkiewicz addresses the issues of the mode of being of values, their hierarchy and the possibility of their reduction. His conclusions include the thesis that good and evil are designations for features which are objective or, as he puts it, 'intransigent' properties (hence 1919).

After the Second World War Tatarkiewicz produced a number of works of international stature on the history of Western aesthetics and the analysis of aesthetic concepts (notably 1960–8 and 1975). These concepts, he argues, exhibit a number of properties which make study of them especially demanding: (i) the initial concepts from the ancient world have been overlaid by notions from later periods, producing a blurring of sense akin to that generated by successive exposures on a single photographic plate; (ii) the concepts in aesthetic discourse have entered the field from an unusually varied set of backgrounds—e.g. philosophy, criticism, artists, and common speech—and this has produced a high number of different meanings for a given term; and (iii) many aesthetic concepts are concerned with emotional matters, and are unusually resistant to scholarly treatment. The area of aesthetics, he concludes, is densely tangled, and moreover exhibits a considerable degree of conceptual instability—there is no key concept in the field of discourse which has survived without real change.

Tatarkiewicz's other main area of significant achievement is in the history of philosophy, including that of his native country. He discerns two major tendencies in philosophical thought: (i) a maximalist approach, within which philosophers attempt systematic accounts of the whole *rerum natura*; and (ii) a minimalist approach, in which the task of the philosopher is to scrutinize the foundations of knowledge. Underlying all Tatarkiewicz's work in the history of thought is the bedrock conviction that the subject is irreducibly untidy, complex and tangled: the world of human achievement is hardly less various than the world of nature, and attempts to impose tidy schemata on either will result in simplistic falsification.

ROBERT WILKINSON

Tawney, Richard

British. *b:* 30 November 1880, Calcutta, India. *d:* 16 January, 1962. London. *Cat:* Christian socialist; social and political philosopher. *Ints:* Social and political philosophy. *Educ:* Balliol College, Oxford. *Infls:* T. H. Green, C. Gore, M. Weber and W. Temple. *Appts:* 1913–15, Director of the Ratan Tata Foundation, London School of Economics; 1915–16, served in the ranks of the infantry; 1918–31, Reader in Economic History, London School of Economics; 1931–49, Professor of Economic History, London School of Economics.

Main publications:

(1912) *The Agrarian Problem in the Sixteenth Century* London: Longman's, Green & Co.

(1921) *The Acquisitive Society*, London: G. Bell & Sons.

(1925) (ed.) Thomas Wilson, *A Discourse Upon Usury*, London: G. Bell & Sons.

(1926) *Religion and the Rise of Capitalism*, London: John Murray.

(1931) *Equality*, London: George Allen & Unwin.

(1953) *The Attack and Other Papers*, London: George Allen & Unwin.

(1964) *The Radical Tradition*, ed. G. Hinder, London: George Allen & Unwin.

(1978) *History and Society: Essays by R. H. Tawney*, ed. J. M. Winter, London: Routledge & Kegan Paul.

Secondary literature:

Hasley, A. H. (1976) 'R. H. Tawney', in *Traditions of Social Policy*, Oxford: Blackwell.

MacIntyre, A. (1971) 'The socialism of R. H. Tawney', in *Against The Self-Images of the Age*, London: Duckworth.

Winter, J. M. (1972) 'A bibliography of the published writings of R. H. Tawney', *Economic History Review*.

A reformer and social philosopher, Tawney was concerned to describe the structure of a just economic order and to advocate the changes of British institutional life which reconstruction in accordance with his principles would require. The driving impulses behind his work were a radical Christian socialism, a concern for social injustice and a deep-seated hatred of capitalism. His ideas have greatly influenced socialist thought in Britain throughout the twentieth-century. In writing of him: 'A scholar, a saint, a social reformer, R. H. Tawney is loved and respected by all who know him', Beatrice Webb spoke for many later writers. According to R. H. S. Wright (1987) Tawney's work was 'Crossman's bible'; for Tony Benn there is 'none greater' in the socialist tradition.

Tawney is notable for his stress on the importance of values; an emphasis which distinguished him from many of his socialist contemporaries. He did not question the importance of a scientific understanding of society but he rejected a socialism premised on deterministic laws of social change; he did not deny the relevance of data-collecting to policy but he accused the Webbs of failing to see the limitations of such an approach. Marxists and the social policy school had failed, alike, to see the crucial importance of values to the socialist vision. To the task of describing those values he devoted himself. Modern society, he argued, 'was sick through the absence of a moral idea'.

The imagery of social sickness and health was central to his work: it occupied a central place in *The Acquisitive Society* (1921). Influenced by the idealist derivation of rights from functions he argued that the central defect of capitalism was that it creates an acquisitive society in which economic relations are defined by reference to the absolute rights of individuals, irrespective of the function which those rights serve. Such a society corrupts those whom it benefits economically and destroys the dignity of those who suffer under it. By contrast, a functional society links rights to social purposes; industry, therefore, ceases to serve the exclusive interests of owners and promotes instead the interests of all who labour in it.

Equality, which Tawney (1931) viewed as being centrally concerned with fellowship and social integration, played a central role in his socialism. His approach to liberty differs, therefore, from that of traditional liberals who saw equality merely as part of a theory of distributive justice. Tawney argued that equality before the law, equality of opportunity and even equality of wealth and income were worthless unless accompanied by a transformation of social context. For this reason he argued that equality must be grounded in the equal worth of every person and the social unity which stems from recognition of mutual solidarity. Nor did he see equality as inimical to freedom: freedom, he argued, involves an expansion of human capacities rather than a removal of restrictions. In a reconstituted society, therefore, equality would not necessarily entail identity of treatment. Although Tawney's work continues to inspire Fabian socialists, Hasley's (1976) cautious remarks about the 'precarious position' of 'the Tawney heritage' aptly define his philosophical standing.

Sources: Sills; Bullock & Stallybrass.

H. BUNTING

Taylor, Alfred Edward

British. **b:** 22 December 1869, Oundle, Northamptonshire. **d:** 31 October 1945, Edinburgh. **Cat:** Theistic idealist. **Ints:** Metaphysics; ethics; religion; history of philosophy. **Educ:** New College, Oxford. **Infls:** Bradley. **Appts:** Lecturer, Merton College, Oxford, 1891–8; Lecturer, Manchester, 1898–1903; Professor of Logic and Metaphysics, McGill, Montreal, 1903–8; Professor of Moral Philosophy, St Andrews, 1908–24; Professor of Moral Philosophy, Edinburgh, 1923–41.

Main publications:

(1901) *The Problem of Conduct*, London.
(1903) *Elements of Metaphysics*, London: Methuen.
(1926) *Plato: the Man and his Work*, London: Methuen.
(1930) *The Faith of a Moralist*, London: Macmillan.
(1934) *Philosophical Studies*, London: Macmillan.
(1945) *Does God Exist?*, London: Macmillan.

Secondary literature:

Ross, W. D. (1945) obituary in *Proceeding s of the British Academy*.
Sell, A. P. F. (1995) *Philosophical Idealism and Christian Belief*, Cardiff: University of Wales Press and New York: St Martin's Press.

Taylor had the unique, but perhaps rather overwhelming, privilege of close personal contact with the generally reclusive F. H. **Bradley** during his twenties, when he was at Bradley's college in Oxford. His first two books revealed that influence in apparently opposed ways. *The Problem of Conduct* (1901) is Bradleyan only in its scepticism. It maintains that ethics is independent of metaphysics and can be carried on only in an empirical, descriptive way. In opposition to Hegelianism he gives an account of the psychology of moral feeling that is continuous with eighteenth-century British doctrines of the moral sense. He holds that there is an irresoluble conflict between the self and society as moral ends, described in rather exalted terms as a conflict between personal culture and social service. The most that can be achieved is a compromise; there is no evident moral progress. His *Elements of Metaphysics*, two years later, is a presentation of Bradleyan idealism in the orderly style of a textbook or manual. After a long period of work on the history of philosophy—most notably on Plato, who turned out to be closer to Christianity than might have been supposed—he returned to ethics in a very different spirit from that to be found in his first book. In *The Faith of a Moralist* (1930) and some lesser subsequent books he argued that morality presupposes religion. The true good we cannot but conceive as eternal and infinite. We cannot achieve the moral end of self-perfection without grace, which Taylor calls the 'initiative' of God. Nothing finite can be truly satisfying (an echo of Bradley's critique of the notion that pleasure can be an ultimate end of conduct). Immortality is required as a condition of the self-perfection we are called on to aim at. In heaven, where there is no sin or inclination to it, we can still be actively good. The God presupposed by morality as the guarantor of freedom, effective agency and immortality is an incomplete, formal conception. It calls out for, but does not prescribe a particular form of, revelation of divine personality. Taylor's commitment to literal Christianity ruled out any such ideas as that time is unreal or that the finite individual personality is an insubstantial entity, a mere modification, or appearance, of the absolute as it was for Bradley. Taylor's influence was exercised almost wholly through his historical works which were much discussed and respected.

Sources: Metz; Copleston; Passmore 1957.

ANTHONY QUINTON

Taylor, Charles Margrave

Canadian. **b:** 15 November 1931. **Cat:** Postanalytical. **Ints:** The self; language; political philosophy. **Educ:** BA, McGill University, 1952; BA, University of Oxford, 1955; MA and DPhil, University of Oxford, 1961. **Infls:** Hegel and contemporaries; Heidegger. **Appts:** Fellow of All Souls' College, Oxford, 1956–61; McGill University, 1961–76; University of Oxford, Professor of Social and Political Theory, 1976–81; McGill University, Professor of Political Science, 1982–.

Main publications:

(1964) *The Explanation of Behaviour*, London: Routledge & Kegan Paul.

(1975) *Hegel*, Cambridge: Cambridge University Press.

(1979) *Hegel and Modern Society*, Cambridge: Cambridge University Press ('largely a condensation' of *Hegel*).

(1985) *Philosophical Papers*, 2 vols, Cambridge: Cambridge University Press.

(1989) *Sources of the Self*, Cambridge: Cambridge University Press.

(1991) *The Ethics of Authenticity*, Harvard: Harvard University Press.

(1992) *Multiculturalism and 'The Politics of Recognition'*, Princeton: Princeton University Press.

Secondary literature:

Tully, J. (ed.) (1994) *Philosophy in an Age of Pluralism*, Cambridge: Cambridge University Press.

Taylor himself provides the best summary of his interests (up to 1985) in the Introduction to his *Philosophical Papers*. His later large-scale study, *Sources of the Self* (1989), was foreshadowed there, but his central interest has not changed otherwise: he calls it 'philosophical anthropology' (1985, p. 1). What he has opposed has also remained constant: 'a certain vision of man, an associationist psychology, utilitarian ethics, atomistic politics of social engineering, and ultimately a mechanistic science of man' (1975, p. 539). He has always wanted to argue against the 'understanding of human life and action implicit in an influential family of theories in the sciences of man. The common feature of this family is the ambition to model the study of man on the natural sciences' (1985, p. 1).

A start was made in his early, anti-behaviourist *The Explanation of Behaviour* (1964). The project has been continued with persuasive consistency throughout Taylor's work, to the extent that he has succeeded in staking out and mapping the claims of what are now well-recognized, opposed positions on the philosophical battleground.

His principal themes have been: the self and modern identity; theories of language and of the mind; atomism in society and political theory; the inescapability of history and morality. He has wanted to tie these together into a view of the person as defined by its social location, understandable in terms of its past and its moral framework. He has seen human freedom as the capacity of people to create their own categories within the contexts inherited through history.

Taylor ascribes the origin of his view of the person (through **Heidegger**) to Hegel—'Human beings are self-interpreting animals' ('Self-interpreting animals', in 1985, vol. 1, p. 45)—although his defence for this view will strike many as far clearer than those of his predecessors. A characteristic line of argument he has used is to consider what he takes to be a concept in common use—his usual example is *shame*—and to show how its nature determines what is taken to be human, and how such an essentially reflexive, self-determining notion eludes any form of behaviourism. Properties like *being shameful* he sees as 'subject-referring': they can only exist in a world in which there are subjects of experience, because 'they concern in some way the life of the subject *qua* subject'. They 'do not fit into an objectivist's view of the world. This allows for an account of things in terms of objective properties, and then also perhaps for a subjective reaction to or view of things on the part of the subject. Emotions like shame do not fit into either slot' (ibid., pp. 54–5).

Because the person defines him or herself, any definition must depend on the language in which it is framed, as well as on the moral values embodied in it by its use over time. Subjectivity must be 'situated'—a view seen by Taylor in Hegel: 'Subjectivity was necessarily situated in life, in nature, and in a setting of social practices and institutions' (1975, p. 567; 1979, p. 164). *Sources of the Self* (1989) aimed to retrieve the historical and moral frameworks and to argue that they cannot be eliminated: 'My self-understanding necessarily has temporal depth and incorporates narrative' (p. 50). What we are is how we see ourselves, which must depend on how we (and our ancestors) have seen ourselves, the languages we have used, the history of the concepts that have been used, the values that have been contained in them.

Taylor's understanding of politics is grounded in a rejection of 'atomism': this, he thinks, 'represents a view about human nature and the human condition which (among other things) makes a doctrine of the primacy of rights plausible'. Atomism 'affirms the self-sufficiency of man alone or, if you prefer, of the individual', against the Aristotelian view of man as an inescapably social animal (1985, vol. 2, p. 189).

His philosophy of language links together the centrality of representation and the type of objectivized mechanism (seen in cognitive psychology) which he most dislikes. These are both rejected wholesale in favour of what he sees as expressivist accounts originating, for example, from Herder, Humboldt and Hamann, through Heidegger, with Wittgenstein as a later adherent (see ibid., vol. 1, Part III).

Taylor's thinking (like that of Alastair **MacIntyre**) roots present identity in concepts and frameworks inherited from the past. No explicit case is made against the possibility of critical, would-be-external examination of a present view of the self. Nor is there a determinate account of just *whose* view it is meant to be. Since any crisis in conceptions of self may well originate from alternative pictures presented by the natural sciences and from blurred and overlapping cultural inheritances, these could be serious shortcomings. Taylor ends *Sources of the Self* with an appeal to the hope which he finds 'implicit in Judaeo-Christian theism' (p. 521), although nothing in the book lends that any metaphysical support. Further treatment is promised.

RICHARD MASON

Taylor, Richard

American. *b:* 5 November 1919, Charlotte, Michigan. *Cat:* Analytic philosopher. *Ints:* Metaphysics; philosophy of religion. *Educ:* University of Illinois, Oberlin College and Brown University. *Infls:* Fichte, Schopenhauer, C. J. Ducasse and Roderick Chisholm. *Appts:* 1951–2, 1953–63, Brown University; 1953, Swarthmore College; 1963–6, Columbia University; 1966–86, University of Rochester; sometime Resident Philosopher, Hartwick College, since 1989.

Main publications:

(1963) *Metaphysics*, Englewood Cliffs, NJ: Prentice Hall; revised editions, 1974, 1983.

(1966) *Action and Purpose*, Englewood Cliffs, NJ: Prentice Hall.

(1970) *Good and Evil*, New York: Macmillan.

(1973) *Freedom, Anarchy and the Law*, New York: St Martin's Press; second edition, Englewood Cliffs, NJ: Prentice Hall, 1982.

(1973) *With Heart and Mind*, New York: St Martin's Press.

(1982) *Having Love Affairs*, Buffalo: Prometheus.

(1985) *Ethics, Faith and Reason*, Englewood Cliffs, NJ: Prentice-Hall, Inc.

Secondary literature:

Van Inwagen, Peter (ed.) (1980) *Time and Cause: Essays Presented to Richard Taylor*, Dordrecht: Reidel (bibliography to 1978).

Although Taylor is usually assigned a place among analytic philosophers, as a result of his approach to such topics as time, causality (including backwards causation), action and purpose, from the beginning he looked with favour on at least one version of the argument from design, held humans to be not very much like machines and, while not demonstrating that they can do otherwise, he believed he had 'destroyed all the familiar philosophical arguments purporting to show that they cannot' (1966, p. 264). His later view, still less encumbered, which he has called 'serious philosophy' and *philosophia perennis*, separates him from the usual sense given to 'analytic philosophy'. Perhaps the perennial philosophy fills up the gaps left by analytic philosophy. The meaning of life is now said to be found in the will to live, and in the activities engendered by that will. Still later, its meaning 'is not to *do* but simply to *be*'. We are invited, at least by indirection, to turn from the cold reality of intellect to an obvious but unsayable knowledge that God, whose creation we are and whom we should love with absolute love, exists. 'Nature, God and the self—which is both an illusion and the only thing there is—never begin, never cease' (1973, p. 118).

In the second edition of *Freedom, Anarchy, and the Law* (1982) he placed himself within the 'libertarian framework' of social philosophy, while cautioning that there are no natural rights to life and property, and that the foundation of rights is utilitarian.

Sources: Personal communication.

WILLIAM REESE

Teilhard de Chardin, Pierre

French. *b:* 1 May 1881, Orcines, Puy de Dôme, France. *d:* 10 April 1955, New York. *Cat:* Geologist; palaeontologist; metaphysician; speculative theologian. *Ints:* Biological evolution; origins of man; spiritual understanding of evolution. *Educ:* 1898–1905, Jesuit schools at Aix en Provence and in Jersey; 1908–12, Hastings Jesuit House; 1912–20, the Sorbonne (PhD 1922). *Infls:* M. Boule, H. Bergson, E. Le Roy, V. I. Vernadsky. *Appts:* 1905–8, Jesuit College, Cairo; 1920–6, Institut Catholique de Paris (Geology); 1926–38, various posts in China; 1950, Académie des Sciences; 1951–5, Wenner-Gren Foundation for Anthropological Research, New York.

Main publications:

(1953) *Paléontologie humaine*, Paris: Gauthier-Villars.

(1955) *Le Phénomène humain*, Paris: Seuil (English translation, *The Phenomenon of Man*, trans. Wall, London: Collins, 1959).

(1956) *L'Apparition de l'homme*, Paris: Seuil.

(1956) *Le Groupe zoologique humain*, Paris: A. Michel.

(1957) *Le Milieu divin*, Paris: Seuil (English translation, *Le Milieu Divin*, London: Collins, 1960).

(1957) *La Vision du Passé*, Paris: Seuil (English translation, *The Vision of the Past*, trans. Cohen, London: Collins, 1966).

(1959) *L'Avenir de l'homme*, Paris: Seuil (English translation, *The Future of Man*, trans. Denny, London: Collins, 1964).

(1961) *Hymne de l'universe*, Paris: Seuil (English translation, *Hymn of the Universe*, trans. Bartholomew: London: Collins, 1965).

(1962) *L'Énergie humaine*, Paris: Seuil (English translation, *Human Energy*, trans. Cohen, London: Collins, 1969).

(1963) *L'Activation de l'Énergie*, Paris: Seuil.

(1963) *La Place de l'homme dans la nature*, Paris: Seuil.

(1965) *Science et Christ*, Paris: Seuil.

(1966) *Je m'explique*, Paris: Seuil (English translation, *Let Me Explain*, trans. Hague, London: Collins, 1974).

(1969) *Comment je crois*, Paris: Seuil.

Secondary literature:

Baudry, G. H. (1971) *Ce que croyait Teilhard*, Tours: Mame.

Carles, J. and Deupleix, A. (1991) *Teilhard de Chardin*, Paris: Seuil (contains bibliography).

Corte, N. (1957) *La Vie et l'âme du Père Teilhard de Chardin* (English translation, *Pierre Teilhard de Chardin*, trans. Jarret-Kerr, London: Burns & Oates, 1960).

Crespy, G. (1961) *La Pensée théologique de Teilhard de Chardin*, Paris: Éditions Universitaires.

Cuenot, C. (1958) *Pierre Teilhard de Chardin—les grandes étapes de son évolution*, Paris: Plon.

——(1968) *Nouveau Lexique, Teilhard de Chardin*, Paris: Seuil.

——(1972) *Ce que Teilhard a vraiment dit*, Paris: Stock.

De Lubac, H. (1962) *La Pensée religieuse du Père Teilhard de Chardin*, Paris: Aubier (English translation, *The Religion of Teilhard de Chardin*, London: Collins, 1967).

Hanson, A. T. (ed.) (1970) *Teilhard Reassessed*, London: Darton Longman & Todd.

Lukas, M. and E. (1977) *Teilhard*, Garden City, NY: Doubleday.

Mooney, C. F. (1966) *Teilhard de Chardin and the Mystery of Christ*, London: Collins.

Philippe de la Trinité (1968) *Teilhard de Chardin, Étude critique*, Paris: La Table Ronde.

Speaight, R. (1967) *Teilhard de Chardin*, London: Collins.

A palaeontologist, Teilhard de Chardin developed an optimistic evolutionary theistic metaphysics in cooperation with Édouard le Roy, in which matter, life, mind and spirit are seen as stages in each of which there is a parallel increase in complexity and consciousness, pointing ultimately to a final 'planetization' or ultra-human convergence of all the peoples of the world. As the universe evolves materially there is a movement towards higher levels of consciousness, through the emergence of life on earth and the emergence of rational self-consciousness in man. The last stage means that man can now share in the direction of evolution. How far this represented commentary after the fact rather than a serious neo-Lamarckian alternative to the modern 'synthetic theory' interpretation of evolution is unclear. With its pantheistic and indeed deistic flavour this was theologically suspect and indeed damaging to his teaching career—it was the reason why for most of his life he was refused permission to teach and had to work outside France. Most of his work was only published after his death, whereupon it enjoyed startling public success, even in Catholic countries where it may have succeeded in smoothing the path to the acceptance of evolutionary theories by Catholics.

Sources: Obituary, *ASCR*, 240: 1673–77; J. Carles (1964) *Teilhard de Chardin, sa vie, son oeuvre*, Paris: PUF; C. Cuénot (1965) *Pierre Teilhard de Chardin: A Biographical Study*, trans. V. Collimore, London: Burns & Oates; J. E. Jarque (1970) *Bibliographie générale ... jusqu'à la fin Décembre 1969*, Fribourg: Édition Univers; T. A. Edwards; G. H. Baudry (1972) *Pierre Teilhard de Chardin Bibliographie 1881–1972*, Lille: Facultés Catholiques; DSB 1976: 274b–277b (bibliographie raisonnée); S. J. Gould (1980) 'The Piltdown conspiracy', *NH* 89: 8–28; 'Piltdown in letters', *NH* 90 (1981): 12–30; M. and E. Lukas (1983) 'The haunting', *Antiquity* 57: 7–11.

R. N. D. MARTIN

Tempels, Placide Frans

Belgian. *b:* 18 February 1906, Berlaar, Belgium. *d:* 1978, Belgium. *Cat:* Theorist of acculturation, Christian conversion, ethnology and Evangelization. *Educ:* Franciscan Novice, 1924; studied Philosophy and Theology, Thielt, 1924–30, ordained in the Roman Catholic Priesthood, 15 August 1930. *Infls:* Thomas Aquinas, Bergson and Lucien Lévy-Bruhl. *Appts:* Roman Catholic missionary in the Belgian Congo, Katanga, 1933–62.

Main publications:

(1945) *La Philosophie bantoue*, Elisabethville: Lovania (English translation, *Bantu Philosophy*, Paris: Présence Africaine, 1959).

(1962) *Notre rencontre I*, Léopoldville: Centre d'Etudes.

Secondary literature:

De Craemer, Willy (1977) *The Jamaa and the Church*, Oxford: Clarendon.

A Thomist by education, Tempels was a disciple of **Lévy-Bruhl** in the 1930s. He was convinced of the usefulness of distinguishing prelogical from logical mentalities, conceiving a conversion from the first to the second stage as an objective of missionizing and civilizing Africa. In the mid 1940s, while doing ethnographic work in Kabondo-Dianda, he experienced a spiritual rupture. He rejected Lévy-Bruhl's ideas and began to work on his Bantu philosophy. His book (1945) became a best seller almost immediately. Its main thesis is that all human conduct depends on a general system of principles and that there should accordingly be reason to find out and study the fundamentals of Bantu beliefs and behaviour, and their essential philosophical system. For Tempels this philosophy is an ontology which signifies an equation between being and force and which would result in a hierarchy of all beings and things, from those less animated by the vital force to those having a perfect vitality. Animal, human, ancestral and divine are dimensions in the exchange and interaction of forces which can be reinforced or diminished. Tempels believed that his Bantu-ontology could be an introduction to the anthropologies of all primitive people in general and the best way of Christianizing pagans. In 1953 Tempels, as a pastor of a parish in Ruwe (near Kolwezi, Belgian Congo) and a professor of religion, initiated a movement called *Jamaa* or Family which celebrates and emphasizes the concepts of life, love and fecundity. He was expelled from the Congo by the Catholic hierarchy and died in an ecclesiastical prison in Belgium in 1978.

V. Y. MUDIMBE

Temple, William

British. *b:* 15 October 1881, Exeter. *d:* 26 October 1944, Westgate-on-Sea. *Cat:* Divine, idealist. *Ints:* Philosophy of religion. *Educ:* Balliol College, Oxford. *Infls:* Personal influences: Edward Caird. Literary influences: Plato, Kant and, later, Whitehead. *Appts:* 1904–10, Fellow and Lecturer in Philosophy, Queen's College, Oxford; 1920–9, Bishop of Manchester; 1929–42, Archbishop of York; 1942–4, Archbishop of Canterbury.

Main publications:

(1910) *The Faith and Modern Thought*, London: Macmillan.
(1917) *Mens Creatrix*, London: Macmillan.
(1924) *Christus Veritas*, London: Macmillan.
(1934) *Nature, Man and God*, London: Macmillan.

Secondary literature:

Emmet, Dorothy (1948) ' William Temple, the philosopher', in F. A. Iremonger (ed.) *William Temple, Archbishop of Canterbury: His Life and Letters*, London: Oxford University Press.
Padget, J. F. (1974) *The Christian Philosophy of William Temple*, The Hague: Nijhoff.
Temple, C. O. (1961) *William Temple's Philosophy of Religion*, London: Seabury Press.
Thomas, O. C. (1961) *William Temple's Philosophy of Religion*, London: SPCK.

Temple, following **Caird**, began by looking on philosophy as the search for a unifying spiritual principle that would provide a synthesis of different or even opposed ways of thinking. Towards the end of his life, however, he seems to have moved increasingly far from idealism. In a letter to Dorothy **Emmet** he insisted that 'we must completely get away from ... the notion that the world as it now exists is a rational whole ... the world as we see it is strictly unintelligible' (Iremonger 1948, p. 537).

His last philosophical work follows the trend towards a more realistic epistemology. 'My contention is that in cognition the subject–object relation is ultimate, and neither term is in any degree reducible to the other' (1934, p. 126). In this work he postulates a hierarchy of being— matter, life, intelligence, spirit. Beginning from natural phenomena we trace the evolutionary process up to the emergence of spirit and then turn back and interpret the whole process in

terms of spirit. Temple called this philosophy 'dialectical idealism'.
Sources: DNB 1941–50.

STUART BROWN

Tennant, Frederick Robert

British. *b:* 1 September 1866, Burslem, Staffordshire. *d:* 9 September 1957, Cambridge, England. *Cat:* Empiricist. *Ints:* Philosophy of religion; philosophy of mind. *Educ:* Caius College, Cambridge (natural science). *Infls:* James Ward. *Appts:* Fellow, Trinity College, Cambridge, 1913–57.

Main publications:

(1912) *The Concept of Sin*, Cambridge: Cambridge University Press.
(1925) *Miracle and its Presuppositions*, Cambridge: Cambridge University Press.
(1928–30) *Philosophical Theology* 2 vols, Cambridge: Cambridge University Press.
(1932) *Philosophy of the Sciences*, Cambridge: Cambridge University Press.
(1943) *The Nature of Belief*, London: Centenary Press.

Secondary literature:

Broad, C. D. (1957) obituary in *Proceedings of the British Academy*.

Tennant became a professional philosopher of religion after some years of teaching science at his old school and, after ordination in 1894, two decades as a parish priest. His attitude to religion was unwaveringly intellectualist. Theology for him was a continuation of philosophy. Religious belief requires rational justification which must appeal to ordinary perceptual and, to some extent, moral experience. Religious experience (and, a fortiori, mystical experience, about which he was highly sceptical) could lend only supplementary support. His rational temper was revealed in his early writing about sin. Defining it, reasonably enough, as wrongdoing accompanied by awareness of its being wrong, he concluded that original sin is impossible. New-born infants are incapable of sinning, although they have instinctive tendencies which may, in due time, lead to it. Nor can sinfulness be inherited, especially not from Adam and Eve, who are mythical. The first, and much longer, volume of his chief work (1928–30) sets out the philosophical preliminaries to his theology, drawn largely from the philosophical psychology of his teacher James **Ward**. An examination of the constitutive elements of the mind yields the conclusion that there must be a pure, substantial ego to hold them together. It is not an object of direct acquaintance, but reflection shows that it is active. Value-judgements involve feeling, but are not on that account subjective. Induction requires faith in the 'reasonableness of the universe'. Religious experience can be explained without God. Reason alone cannot establish human survival of death. In his second volume he turns to the existence of God and argues that the only good argument for it is the argument from design, which he states very fully, adding to the usual varieties of adaptation in nature the fact of the beauty of nature and the objectivity of morals. Like Hobbes, but more reverently, he takes the attribution of infinity and perfection to God to be merely honorific. Moral evil is a consequence of man's having freedom of choice; physical evil is required by the lawfulness of nature. Tennant had some influence among thoughtful Christians but did not, like his comparably unorthodox contemporary **Rashdall**, get embroiled in controversy or come to general public notice. In his unworldly intellectualism he is a fine representative of the honourable kind of abstract lucidity often found in Cambridge, for example in **McTaggart** and **Moore**.
Sources: Edwards; DNB.

ANTHONY QUINTON

Thomson, Judith Jarvis

American. *b:* 1929, New York City. *Cat:* Analytic philosopher. *Ints:* Rights; philosophy of law; moral philosophy; philosophy of action. *Educ:* BA, Barnard College, Columbia University; BA, MA, University of Cambridge; PhD, Columbia University. *Appts:* MIT, since 1964.

Main publications:

As Judith Jarvis:

(1961) 'Notes on Strawson's logic ', *Mind*, 70.
(1961) 'Ethics and *Ethics and the Moral Life*', *Journal of Philosophy* 58, February.

As Judith Jarvis Thomson:

(1964) (with James Thomson) 'How not to derive "ought" from "is"', *Philosophical Review* 73.
(1966) 'Grue', *Journal of Philosophy* 63.
(1968) (ed. with Gerald Dowkin) *Ethics*, Sources in Contemporary Philosophy, Harper & Row.
(1971) 'A defense of abortion', *Philosophy and Public Affairs* 1; reprinted in Peter Singer (ed.), *Applied Ethics*, Oxford: Oxford University Press, 1986.
(1973) 'Preferential hiring', *Philosophy and Public Affairs* 2.

(1973) 'Rights and deaths', *Philosophy and Public Affairs* 2.

(1976) 'Killing, letting die, and the Trolley Problem ', *Monist* 59.

(1977) *Acts and Other Events*, Ithaca and London: Cornell University Press.

(1984) 'Remarks on causation and liability', *Philosophy and Public Affairs* 13.

(1985) 'The Trolley Problem', *The Yale Law Journal* 94.

(1986) *Rights, Restitution, and Risk: Essays in Moral Theory*, ed. William Parent, Cambridge, Mass. and London: Harvard University Press.

(1987) (ed.) *On Being and Saying: Essays for Richard Cartwright*, Cambridge, Mass.: MIT Press.

(1990) *The Realm of Rights*, Cambridge, Mass.: Harvard University Press.

Secondary literature:

Finnis, John (1973) 'The rights and wrongs of abortion', *Philosophy and Public Affairs* 2.

Hursthouse, Rosalind (1987) 'Women's rights and wrongs', chapter 5 of *Beginning Lives*, Oxford: Blackwell.

Judith Jarvis Thomson has made a major contribution to the philosophy of rights and in particular to questions about when it is morally permissible to infringe another's right to life. Her most famous essay, 'A defense of abortion' (1971), demonstrated by means of an ingenious thought experiment that even if we were to concede that a foetus has rights, in many cases these would be outweighed by the rights of a woman to decide what happens in and to her body. This essay has been the starting-point for most subsequent discussion of the morality of abortion. Her treatment of the Trolley Problem pinpointed essential differences between deflecting a danger onto a different target, thereby causing one death rather than five, and, for instance, forcing someone to sacrifice their life so that they can be an organ donor for five patients who would otherwise die. In *The Realm of Rights* (1990) she has further developed themes dealt with in the collection of her essays *Rights, Restitution and Risk* (1986). Her work is characterized by imaginative use of both hypothetical and real cases.

Sources: PI.

NIGEL WARBURTON

Tillich, Paul

German. *b:* 20 August 1886, Starzeddel, Prussia. *d:* 22 October 1965, Chicago, Illinois. *Cat:* Ex-istentialist; theologian. *Ints:* Philosophy of religion. *Educ:* Universities of Berlin, Tübingen, Breslau and Halle-Wittenberg. *Infls:* Schelling and Martin Heidegger. *Appts:* University of Berlin, Privatdozent 1919–24; Universities of Marburg, Dresden and Leipzig, 1925–9; Professor of Philosophy, Frankfurt, 1929–33; Union Theological Seminary, 1933–55; Harvard, 1955–62; University of Chicago, 1962–5; ordained into the Evangelical Lutheran Church of the province of Brandenburg, 1912.

Main publications:

(1932) *The Religious Situation*, New York: Holt.

(1936) *The Interpretation of History*, New York: Scribners.

(1948) *The Protestant Era*, Chicago: Chicago University Press.

(1948) *The Shaking of the Foundations*, New York: Scribners.

(1951–63) *Systematic Theology*, 3 vols, Chicago: University of Chicago Press.

(1952) *The Courage To Be*, New Haven: Yale University Press.

(1954) *Love, Power, and Justice*, New York: Oxford University Press.

(1957) *Dynamics of Faith*, New York: Harper.

(1959) *Theology of Culture*, New York: Oxford University Press.

(1962) *Morality and Beyond*, New York: Harper & Row.

(1963) *Christianity and the Encounter of the World Religions*, New York: Columbia University Press.

(1965) *Ultimate Concern*, ed. D. M. Brown, New York: Harper & Row.

Secondary literature:

Alston, William P. (1961) 'Tillich's conception of a religious symbol', in Sidney Hook (ed.), *Religious Experience and Truth*, New York: SUNY Press.

Kegley, C. W. and Bretall, R. W. (eds) (1956) *The Theology of Paul Tillich*, New York: Macmillan (includes bibliography).

McKelway, A. J. (1964) *The Systematic Theology of Paul Tillich*, Richmond, Va.: John Knox Press.

Scharlemann, Robert P. (1969) *Reflection and Doubt in the Thought of Paul Tillich*, New Haven: Yale University Press.

Tillich burst onto the American scene in a time of contradictions, as a dialectical thinker wishing to do justice to basic but opposing points of view valid within a certain context but not assimilable to each other. His genius lay in bringing the opposed positions into juxtaposition so that they might enrich each other while remaining themselves. His witness was such that his European publications in article form were quickly translated and made into books which exercised wide influence in the American theological scene, and beyond.

He worked with four oppositions: (i) that between neo-Orthodoxy and Christian liberalism, where his religious existentialism added social relevance to the former and depth to the latter; (ii) Protestantism and Catholicism, where he endorsed the Protestant principle (forbidding identification of the divine with any human creation), while producing a system intelligible to Thomistically inclined scholars; (iii) philosophy and theology, where the former posed questions whose most fruitful answers were to be found in a theological 'method of correlation', bringing finite and infinite perspectives together; (iv) bourgeois capitalism and the Marxist challenge, where he said 'yes' to the 'prophetic, humanistic and realistic elements' in Marx and 'no' to the negative elements in the Soviet system (1936, section 11, part 1).

Exploring the 'symbolic' character of religious expression, Tillich argued that symbols point to the ultimate and 'participate' in the reality they signify. They also have life histories, coming into being, developing, becoming enfeebled, dying and being replaced by other symbols. 'Being itself' he believed to be a literal expression, apparently because it was, in his view, a self-validating concept.

Tillich defined religion as the object of ultimate concern. Movement from anxiety to courage is one of the routes to the ultimate. On this theme (1952) he discussed four stages of courage, which recapitulated stages of culture. The 'courage to be as a part' gives way to individuality, the 'courage to be as oneself'. This stage of life, and of the world, gives way to meaninglessness and the 'courage of despair'. Despair gives way to the 'courage to accept acceptance' and ordinary theism to 'the God above the God of theism'.

Sources: Reese.

WILLIAM REESE

Tolstoy, Leo (Lev Nikolaevich Tolstoi)

Russian. *b:* 25 August (9 September N.S.) 1828, Iasnaia Poliana estate, Tula province. *d:* 7 November (20 N.S.) 1910, Astapovo railway station, Lipetsk province. *Cat:* Religious philosopher; novelist. *Educ:* Studied at the University of Kazan', 1844–7, without graduating. *Infls:* Rousseau, Stendhal, de Maistre and Schopenhauer.

Main publications:
(n.d.) *V chem moia vera?*, Geneva (English translation, *What I Believe*, trans. Constantine Popoff, London: Elliot Stock, 1885).
(1884) *Ispoved'* [A Confession], Geneva (English translation, *My Confession and The Spirit of Christ's Teaching*, London: Walter Scott, 1877).
(1891) *O zhizni* Geneva (English translation, *Life*, trans. Isabel F. Hapgood, New York: T. Y. Crowell, 1888).
(1898) *Chto takoe iskusstvo?*, Moscow, (English translation, *What Is Art?*, Aylmer Maude, London: Brotherhood Publishing Co).
(1928–37) *Tolstoy Centenary Edition*, 21 vols, Oxford and London: Oxford University Press (Tolstoy's main works).

Secondary literature:
Berlin, I. (1953) *The Hedgehog and the Fox: An Essay on Tolstoy's View of History*, London: Weidenfeld & Nicolson.
Diffey, T. J. (1985) *Tolstoy's 'What Is Art?'*, London: Croom Helm.
Murphy, D. (1992) *Tolstoy and Education*, Dublin: Irish Academic Press.
Šilbajoris, R. (1991) *Tolstoy's Aesthetics and his Art*, Columbus, Ohio: Slavica.

After military service and his first literary efforts during the 1850s, Tolstoy devoted himself between 1859 and 1862 to a school for peasant children on his estate, after which he named his short-lived pedagogical journal *Iasnaia Poliana*. A period of epochal literary creativity between 1863 and 1876, including the writing of *War and Peace* and *Anna Karenina*, ended in deep personal crisis, precipitating the rejection of his literary achievements and aristocratic privileges, and the elaboration during the 1880s of his religious and social teachings. In the 1890s he organized relief for famine-stricken peasants and supported persecuted religious minorities; his estate became the object of pilgrimages. His rejection of established political and ecclesiastical authority led in 1901 to his excommunication by the Russian Orthodox Church, and to the exile of his followers.

Having contemplated suicide during his spiritual crisis, Tolstoy found in the instinctive religious belief of the peasants a way out of Schopenhauer's pessimism about the meaning of life. He went on to reject most Christian doctrine; his religious anarchism was based on the ethical content of Christianity, which he generalized as 'the law of love'. In accordance with this law, he not only repudiated the organized violence and coercion of the state (unlike Rousseau, the hero of his adolescence), but also the violence of warfare, patriotism, capital punishment, private property and political revolution. His principle of non-violent resistance to evil by force influenced his correspondent **Gandhi**, as well as his Russian disciples.

A persistent theme of Tolstoy's theoretical writings was the rejection of individualism. In *Life* (1891) he advanced an impersonalist metaphysics invoking the notion of a 'reasonable consciousness' transcending individuality, time and space. In the Epilogue to *War and Peace*, he denied the power of individuals like Napoleon to move nations, either *per se* or as expressions of some general historical goal; the task of historians is to uncover the laws governing events, the multiple causes of which included acts of human free will. In *What is Art?* (1898) he rejected the identification of artistic worth with beauty, if this amounts to no more than individual pleasure. The purpose of art is to convey feelings, and genuine art is that which conveys the religious consciousness of its time. All 'high art' since the Renaissance stood condemned by this criterion.

COLIN CHANT

Topcu, Nurettin

Turkish. *b:* 1909, Istanbul. *d:* 1975, Istanbul. *Cat:* Bergsonian 'spiritual idealist'. *Ints:* Sufism; ethics; metaphysics. *Educ:* Studied at Lycée Bordeaux, Strasbourg and at Sorbonne University, 1928–34. *Infls:* Henri Bergson and Maurice Blondel. *Appts:* Philosophy teacher at Galatasaray Lycée in Istanbul in 1934, and at Ataturk Lycée in Izmir in 1935; taught philosophy and sociology in various colleges in Istanbul, including Robert College in the 1940s and 1950s.

Main publications:

(1934) *Conformisme et Révolte*, Paris.

(1959) *Garb in Ilmi Zihniyeti ve Ahlak Gorusu* (Knowledge and Ethics in the Western Mind), Istanbul.

(1960) *Komunizme Kars Yeni Nizam* [A New Order Against Communism], Istanbul.

(1960) *Turkiye'nin Maarif Davas* [Turkey's Problem of Education], Istanbul.

(1961) *Ahlak Nizam* [Ethical Order], Istanbul.

(1965) *Varolmak* [Becoming] Istanbul.

(1968) *Bergson*, Instanbul.

(1968) *Iradenin Davas* [The Problem of the Will], Istanbul.

(1968) *Islam ve Insan* [Islam and Man], Instanbul.

(1970) *Kultur ve Medeniyyet* [Culture and Civilization], Istanbul.

(1974) *Mevlana and Tasavvuf* [Rúmi and Sufism], Istanbul.

(1978) *Milliyyetciligimizin Esaslar* [The Fundamentals of our Nationalism], Istanbul.

Topcu returned to Turkey in 1934 after studying at the Sorbonne. In 1939, while he was a high-school teacher in Izmir, he started publishing a journal called *Haraket* [Action]. In the 1940s he was associated with a Sufi circle led by Sheikh Abdul Aziz Bekkini.

Topcu places humankind at the centre of his philosophy and sought to introduce a new approach to the concept of reality, one that was consonant with his Islamic background. He held that the real cannot be sought in the region of the accidental but in that of the immutable, the essential and the eternal. In the quest for the real the positivist sciences, he said, are useless, since they deal with accidents. They fragment being in an attempt to understand it and fail to realize that reality as a whole cannot be found in parts of reality. He insisted that only mystical experience, which is capable of comprehending being as a whole, is able to provide an apprehension of the real.

Topcu claims that the basis of every civilization is a dynamic mystical passion. For him, only mysticism (more precisely, mystical life) and faith are able to resuscitate religion from its static and unproductive state. He regards the human being not as an alien portion of being, but as a being who contains the entirety of existence. He sees in Surfism not only the reactualization of the ethical tenets of Islam but also a philosophical strand of Islamic life and thought. Topcu played a significant role in the revival of Islamic-Turkish culture in Turkey. He was founder of a 'communitarian nationalist' movement and his philosophical thought became a source of inspiration for middle-class right-wing intellectuals in Turkey.

Sources: Suleyman Seyfi Ogun (1992) *Turkiye'de Cemmatc Milliyyetcilik ve Nurettin Topcu* [Communitarian Nationalism in Turkey and Nurettin Topcu], Istanbul: Dergah Yayinlari.

ADNAN ASLAN

Tosaka, Jun

Japanese. *b:* 27 September 1900, Tokyo. *d:* 9 August 1945, Nagano. *Cat:* Materialist. *Ints:* Marxist philosophy; philosophy of science. *Educ:* Dai-ichi High School, Tokyo, and Kyoto University (graduated 1924). **Infls:** Kant, Hegel, Windelband, Marx and contemporary philosophy of science. **Appts:** Professor of Philosophy, Otani College, 1929–31; Lecturer in Philosophy, Hosei University, 1931–5; frequently in trouble for his opposition to militarism, and died in prison.

Main publications:

See his *Collected Works*, 8 vols, Tokyo: Ito-Shoten Publishing Co., 1946–8; and his *Complete Works*, 5 vols, Keiso Publishing Co., 1966–7.
(1924) *The Process of the Formation of Physical Space–Kant's Theory of Space.*
(1926) *On Space as Category.*
(1927) *On Space as Character: The Outline of Theory.*
(1928) *Analysis of the Concept of Space.*
(1930) *Logic of Ideology.*
(1933) *Philosophy of Technology.*
(1934) *Lecture on Modern Philosophy.*
(1934) *Theory of Japanese Ideology.*
(1937) *The Theory of Knowledge.*
(1938) *The Relationship between Criticism and the Theory of Knowledge.*
(1941) *The Concept of Technology and Science.*

Secondary literature:

Kawamura Mitsuo (1959) *The Theory of Tosaka Jun's Learning-between the Ideological and the Logical*, Nagoya: Essays on the Tenth Anniversary of Nagoya University.
Kozai Yoshishige *et al.* (1972) *Tosaka Jun's Humanity, Thought and Works* (a discussion meeting), Tokyo: Gendai to Shiso, vol. 8.
Niijima, S., Mori, K., Honma, K., *et al.* (1948) *Research on Tosaka Jun* Tokyo: Studies on Materialism, vol. 4.
Ogawa Haruhisa (1973) *Tosaka Jun and Today*, Tokyo: Gendai to Shiso, vol. 12.
Oka Kunio (1948) *Tosaka Jun as Materialist*, Riso, vol. 184.

Tosaka's starting-point as a thinker was the academism of the Kyoto School of philosophy, represented by **Nishida** Kitaro and **Tanabe** Hajime, but the process of his philosophical development was destined to cause him to part from this school. In his earlier essays, through thinking deeply about space, he departed from Kantian and neo-Kantian views and came to adopt a materialist position.

In 1927 he published an essay, *On Space as Character*, with the subtitle *The Outline of Theory*. The key concept in this work is that of character. It means that this standpoint is based

not on intuition or understanding but on the commonsense things in our daily life.

Thus he writes: When people live ordinarily, in conformity to convention, not to scientific thinking, they discover Nature as what they can just depend on. For people the concept of Nature will be nothing else than their dependence on reality. This is the motive by which Nature as common sense is brought into existence: thus this is the first step in the character of this concept. The concept of Matter will be understood frequently and also justly as such a character of Nature, that is, materialistically.

Further, he pays attention to the way in which its method affects the character of science. This he discussed in *Analysis of the Concept of Space* (1928), as follows:

> The relation of the mutual implication between Method and Object is not a partial condition like a thing that is subsumed and understood by means of one established category, if possible; rather it must belong to the radical relation that unifically conditions the understanding of all categories. Hence now, independently of the concept of interaction or *Gemeinschaft*, it is necessary for this mutual implication to be analyzed.

In order to complete this theory of science based on his materialism, Tosaka needed to make the structure of mutual implication as one process of cognition clear, replacing the question 'Does the category of space belong to either actual existence or to intuition?' with the question concerning mutual implication between method and object; but he died before this work could be completed.
Sources: Nakaoka Tetsuro (1976) *Tosaka Jun shu*, Tokyo: Cikuma-shobo.

KIYOHIKO FUJIMOTO

Toulmin, S(tephen) E(delston)

British. **b:** 1922, London. **Cat:** Analytic philosopher. **Ints:** History of ideas; ethics; philosophy of science. **Educ:** University of Cambridge. **Infls:** Ludwig Wittgenstein and John Wisdom. **Appts:** 1947–51, Fellow, King's College, Cambridge; 1949–55, Lecturer in the Philosophy of Science, Oxford; 1955–9, Professor of Philosophy, University of Leeds; 1960–4, Director, Nuffield Foundation for the History of Ideas; 1965–9, Professor of Philosophy, Brandeis University; 1969–72, Professor of Philosophy, Michigan State University; 1972–3, Provost, Crown College,

University of California, Santa Cruz; 1973–86, Professor in Committee on Social Thought, University of Chicago; from 1986, Avalon Professor of Humanities, Northwestern University; visiting positions in the USA, Australia and Israel.

Main publications:

(1950) *An Examination of the Place of Reason in Ethics*, Cambridge: Cambridge University Press.

(1953) *The Philosophy of Science: An Introduction*, London: Hutchinson.

(1958) *The Uses of Argument*, Cambridge: Cambridge University Press.

(1961) *Foresight and Understanding*, London: Hutchinson.

(1961–5) (with June Goodfield) *The Ancestry of Science*: vol. 1, *The Fabric of the Heavens*; vol. 2, *The Architecture of Matter*; vol. 3, *The Discovery of Time*, London: Hutchinson.

(1972) *Human Understanding, Volume 1*, Oxford: Clarendon Press.

(1973) (with Allan Janik) *Wittgenstein's Vienna*, London: Weidenfeld & Nicholson.

(1976) *Knowing and Acting*, London: Collier Macmillan.

(1982) *The Return to Cosmology*, Berkeley: University of California Press.

(1988) (with Albert Jonsen) *The Abuse of Casuistry* Berkeley: University of California Press.

(1989) *Cosmopolis*, New York: Free Press.

Secondary literature:

Cooley, J. C. (1959) 'Toulmin's revolution in logic', *Journal of Philosophy*.

Toulmin's wide-ranging work has been unified by his opposition to a conception of reasoning that takes the traditional deductive syllogism as its paradigm. This theme, developed in detail in *The Uses of Argument* (1958), was already present in *Reason in Ethics* (1950), where he argued that reasoning in ethics, as in other fields, could be understood only by relating it to its specific function, the harmonization of behaviour in a community. *The Philosophy of Science* (1953) announced another theme that has been central to Toulmin's work: the need for a more thoroughly historical, contextual approach to the study of science.

Both themes are central in Toulmin's later work. *The Abuse of Casuistry* (1988) recommends a return to casuistry in ethics, a method of reasoning which focuses on the the details of particular cases rather than on the application of general principles according to narrow logical

criteria. In *Cosmopolis* (1989) he argues that the diverse manifestations of 'modernity'—whose development can be understood only against the background of the social and political ends which thought, particularly scientific thought, has served—are held together by a mistaken conception of rationality derived from the seventeenth century. The way forward requires recapturing the essentials of an earlier, 'humanist' conception. Toulmin's early work was highly influential in a climate sympathetic to broadly Wittgensteinian ideas. His later work has been less influential amongst philosophers, though more influential in some other areas of the humanities.

Sources: WW(Am) 1990–1; WW, 1992; personal communication.

ANTHONY ELLIS

Touraine, Alain Louis Jules François

French. *b:* 3 August 1925, Hermanville. *Cat:* Sociologist; neo-Marxist. *Ints:* Post-industrial society; social structures and social movements. *Educ:* L'École Normale Supérieure. *Infls:* Marx, Max Weber, Tonnies and Simmel. *Appts:* 1950–7, Member of research staff, Le Centre de la Recherche Scientifique, Paris; 1958–, Acting Director, then (1960) Director of Studies, École Pratique des Hautes Études; 1966–9, Professor, Faculté des Lettres de Paris-Nanterre; 1970–80, Founder and Director, Centre d'Étude des Mouvements Sociaux; from 1980, Founder and Director of Le Centre d'Analyse et d'Intervention Sociologiques.

Main publications:

(1965) *Sociologie de l'action*, Paris: Seuil.

(1969) *La Société post-industrielle*, Paris: Denoëls (English translation, *The Post-Industrial Society*, trans. L. F. S. Mayhew, New York: Random House, 1971).

(1973) *Production de la société*, Paris: Seuil (English translation, *The Self-Production of Society*, trans. Derek Coltman, Chicago: University of Chicago Press, 1977).

(1978) *Sociologie permanente*: vol. 1, *Le Voix et le regard*, vol. 2 (with F. Dubet, Z. Hegedus, and M. Wieviorka), *Lutte étudiante*, Paris: Seuil.

(1984) *Le Retour de l'acteur*, Paris: Fayard.

Secondary literature:

Ansart, Pierre (1990) *Les sociologies contemporaines*, Paris: Seuil.

Durand, Jean-Pierre and Weil, Robert (1989) *Sociologie contemporaines*, Paris: Vigot.

Eder, Klaus (1982) 'A new social movement?', *Telos* 52: 5–20.

Touraine is one of the foremost theoreticians of contemporary French sociology. For many years he developed theories of social structure, but in his more recent writings (1984) few conventional Marxist structural–functional ideas remain and the emphasis is on social movements.

Touraine's understanding of social movements connects with his view of 'post-industrial society', a term which he has made famous. According to him, technical rationality formerly helped society to produce (the industrial society). Today, however, it also enables society to command its own social organization and reproduction. Thus 'post-industrial' societies are marked by what Touraine calls 'historicity', a power in which knowledge of social processes is used to reshape social conditions. Control of this power, he holds, has accrued to a new technocratic elite that is steering the entire social order towards the perfectly programmed society, an 'impoverishing homogeneity' (1984, p. 38).

Touraine recognizes that this control can be countered only by social groups capable of initiating lines of protest which generate new social movements, such as the student movement in the 1960s and the environmental movement of today, that are quite different from the old forms of class conflict. It is these movements, and their connections to the forces against which they are ranged, that Touraine has been concerned to study, thereby offering a critique of technical, bureaucratic ideology. Although critical opinion on his work varies it is generally acknowledged that Touraine has done much to advance basic sociological analysis.

Sources: CA 85–8, pp. 591–2.

STEPHEN MOLLER

Toynbee, Arnold Joseph

British. **b:** 14 April 1889, London. **d:** 22 October 1975, York. **Cat:** Historian and philosopher of history. **Educ:** Balliol College, Oxford, 1907–11. **Infls:** Personal influences include Veronica Boulter. Literary: H. T. Buckle and Oswald Spengler. **Appts:** 1912–15, Tutor, Balliol College, Oxford; 1919 -24, Professor of Byzantine and Modern Greek Language, Literature and History, London University; 1925–55, Director of Studies in the Royal Institute of International Affairs, Chatham House, London.

Main publications:

(1934–61) *A Study of History*, 12 vols, London: Oxford University Press: vols 1–3, 1934; vols 4–6, 1939; vols 7–10, 1954; vols. 11–12, 1961.
(1956) *An Historian's Approach to Religion*, London: Oxford University Press.

Secondary literature:

Dray, W. H. (1961) 'Toynbee's search for historical laws', *History and Theory* 1: 32–54.
Montague, Ashley (ed.) (1956) *Toynbee and History: Critical Essays and Reviews*, Boston: Porter Sargent.
Walsh, W. H. (1963) 'Toynbee reconsidered', *Philosophy* 1: 71–8.

Toynbee began as a Greek and Latin scholar and soon developed a thorough knowledge of Greek literature and history. His output was prodigious. Although he was a professed agnostic, a strong religious interest pervaded his writings.

Toynbee's monumental *Study of History* (1934–61) presents a large-scale analysis of the nature of 'civilizations' and the processes which lead to their integration, fossilization and transformation. What he purports to show is that some twenty-six civilizations, conceived as self-contained units, exemplify certain similar patterns in their development. He claims to have arrived at this scheme 'scientifically', by way of inductive generalization.

Toynbee's interpretation, which is one of the most obvious examples of what is sometimes called 'speculative philosophy of history', was met with severe criticism from professional historians. Toynbee, however, was widely read by the general public. The outstanding achievement of his work, despite its evident methodological flaws, is that it provided a useful corrective to single-track conceptions of history and initiated stimulating comparisons between civilizations.

Sources: Edwards; WW; DNB; Macquarrie; Bullock & Woodings.

STEPHEN MOLLER

Troeltsch, Ernst

German. **b:** 17 February 1865, Augsburg, Germany. **d:** 1 February 1923. **Cat:** Lutheran theologian. **Ints:** Social philosophy. **Educ:** Universities of Erlangen, Göttingen and Berlin. **Infls:** A. Ritschl, W. Windelband, H. Rickert and W. Dilthey. **Appts:** Assistant Pastor in Munich; Lecturer in Theology, Göttingen, 1891–2; Extraordinary Professor,

University of Bonn, 1892–4; Professor of Philosophy, University of Berlin, 1915–23.

Main publications:

(1891) *Vernunft und Offenbarung bei Johann Gerhard
und Melanchthon*, Göttingen.

(1905) *Psychologie und Erkenntnistheorie in der
Religionswissenschaft*, Tübingen.

(1911) *Die Bedeutung der Geschichtlichkeit Jesu für
den Glauben*, Tübingen.

(1912) *Protestantism and Progress*, London: Williams & Norgate.

(1915) *Augustin, die christliche Antike und das
Mittelalter*, Munich.

(1923) *Christian Thought: Its History and Application*, London: University of London Press.

(1924) *Der Historismus und seine Überwindung*,
Berlin.

(1924) *Spektator-Briefe, Aufsätze über die deutsche
Revolution und die Weltpolitik 1918–1922*, Tübingen.

(1925) *Deutscher Geist und Westeuropa*, Tübingen.

(1931) *The Social Teaching of the Christian Churches*,
London: Allen & Unwin.

(1972) *The Absoluteness of Christianity and the
History of Religions*, London: SCM Press.

Secondary literature:

Alberca, I. E. (1961) *Die Gewinnung theologischer
Normen aus der Geschichte der Religion bei E.
Troeltsch*, Munich.

Bodenstein, W. (1959) *Neige des Historismus, Ernst
Troeltschs Entwicklungsgang*, Gütersolh.

Clayton, J. P. (ed.) (1976) *Ernst Troeltsch and the
Future of Theology*, Cambridge: Cambridge University Press.

Graf, F. W. and Ruddies, H. (1982) *Ernst Troeltsch
Bibliographie*, Tübingen: Mohr.

Köhler, W. E. (1941) *Ernst Troeltsch*, Tübingen.

Reist, B. A. (1966) *Toward a Theology of Involvement:
The Thought of Ernst Troeltsch*, London: SCM
Press.

Rubanowice, R. J. (1982) *Crisis in Consciousness:
The Thought of Ernst Troeltsch*, Tallahassee:
University Presses of Florida.

Vermeil, E. (1922) *La Pensée religieuse d'Ernst
Troeltsch*, Paris.

A leading member of the 'History of Religions'
school, Troeltsch's writings bear upon the disciplines of theology, history, philosophy and
sociology, all of which have to face the fact of
the clash between absolute religious or moral
values and historical relativities. Modestly confessing his inability finally to resolve matters,
Troeltsch nevertheless clearly exhibited the nature

of the problem and suggested, for example, that
while (with Kant) the laws of morality are
permanent, we are only aware of morality as it
has developed and been expressed under the
impress of, and modified by, historical, social and
political forces. Hence the tension between values
and norms which are held to transcend history,
and our need to understand what actually
presents itself to us in history. Regarding the
latter, we must seek to make a concrete historical
occurrence 'as intelligible as if it were part of our
own experience'.

In Christianity the problem takes the form:
how can we hold together the absolute claims of
revelation and the diverse ways in which the
religion has actually developed into churches,
sects and mystical types? Even among the
churches there are distinct differences, as
Troeltsch showed in his comparison of the
Lutheran and Calvinist traditions—both of
them products of the Reformation, yet differing
significantly in doctrine, ethos and polity. Again,
since the primary facts of history are inherently
uncertain, the findings of historians must be
deemed provisional only, and revisable in the
light of fresh evidence. It follows that no specific
set of historical facts—those, for example,
concerning Jesus—can be taken as final in the
sense of non-supersedable. It is conceivable that
Christianity may lose its status as the supreme
world religion. It may, *pro tem*, be final for those
of the West 'because we have nothing else', but
'other racial groups ... may experience their
contact with the divine in a quite different way'.
Further, since all historical events are of the
same order, we have no option but to assess
particular historical probabilities by analogy
with our personal experience and knowledge of
occurrences elsewhere. There can be no interventions of a transcendent divine, and the
supernatural is excluded.

It is important to observe that for all his
emphasis upon the historico-social conditioning
of religious ideas, Troeltsch repudiates the
Marxist view that religion is but a perverted
product of such conditioning. Rather, religious
convictions derive from the autonomous religious consciousness. This is consistent with his
determination, for all his indebtedness to group
theories of personality and his studies of family,
state and Church, not to submerge the individual in the corporate. This is clearly exemplified
in his political thought.

Active in politics, Troeltsch became convinced that the root cause of the First World
War lay in a deficient political philosophy which

emerged in the wake of the Romantic glorification of the state. His remedy (very different from that of the 'dialectical theologians') was the elevation of the Enlightenment emphasis upon the importance and rights of the individual, and of groups of individuals ordering their corporate life democratically. Troeltsch's cautionary words of 1911 were nothing short of prophetic:

> Let us jealously preserve that principle of freedom which draws its strength from a religious metaphysic; otherwise the cause of freedom and personality may well be lost in the very moment when we are boasting most loudly of our allegiance to it, and of our progress in this direction.

Troeltsch's exclusion of the supernatural, his openness to religious experience in the broadest sense and his willingness to conceive of the demotion of Christianity sparked criticism from some quarters. It has been pointed out that his use of analogy may be countered by the construction of other analogies. The concept of group personality has been subjected to criticism since his day, and his method of categorizing expressions of Christianity as church, state, mystical has been questioned.

Although such thinkers as F. von **Hügel** and C. C. J. **Webb** have heeded Troeltsch's ideas, to many British philosophers and theologians he has been a ray of light (sometimes weak), or a cloud (occasionally threatening), of which they were more or less aware, but which never quite reached their shore (although see Clayton 1976).
Sources: Obituary notices.

ALAN SELL

Troilo, Erminio

Italian. *b:* 8 July 1874, Archi. *d:* 19 December 1968, Padua. *Cat:* Philosopher of absolute realism. *Infls:* Ardigò. *Appts:* Professor of Theoretical Philosophy, Universities of Palermo, 1915–20, and Padua, from 1920.

Main publications:

(1907–13) *La filosofia di Giordano Bruno*, 2 vols.
(1908) *Necessità d'integrazione del positivismo*.
(1910) *Il momento critico del positivismo*.
(1912) *Il positivismo e i diritti dello spirito*.
(1926) *Roberto Ardigò*.
(1927–32) *Studi di Benedetto Spinoza*.
(1932) *Ripensando la logica di Hegel*.
(Also numerous works on the history of philosophy.)

Secondary literature:

Gentile, M. (1969) *Erminio Troilo*, Rome: Accademia Nazionale dei Lincei.

After subjecting positivism to a critical revision Troilo reached, around 1920, a fully metaphysical position, a journey also mediated by reflection on Bruno and Spinoza. He called this position 'absolute realism'. Philosophy was conceived as a way of illuminating life and teaching us how to live. In addition, picking up a theme that goes back to Parmenides, he thought it impossible to think and be outside of Being. The absolute unity and fecund plasticity of Being are, for Troilo, the foundation of all immanence and transcendence, the foundation of immanence because nothing is outside Being, and the foundation of transcendence because the ontological reality of Being guarantees the reality of individual beings and unites them into a fundamental relationship. He was opposed to idealism (although he shared its monism) and equally to any transcendent creationism. Like Spinoza's his philosophical speculations are animated by a sense of religion, which accounts for his respectful attitude to Christian faith.

COLIN LYAS

Tronti, Mario

Italian. *b:* 21 July 1931, Rome. *Cat:* Political philosopher.

Main publications:

(1970) *Piano capitalistico e classe operaio*, Milan: Sapere.
(1971) *Operai e capitale*, Turin: Einaudi.
(1975) *Hegel politico*, Rome: Instituto della Enciclopedia Italiana.
(1977) *Stato e rivoluzione in Inghilterra*, Milane: Il saggitore.
(1977) *Sul autonomia del politico*, Milan: Feltrinelli.
(1980) *Soggetti, crisi, potere*, Bologna: Cappelli.
(1980) *Il tempo della politica*, Rome: Editori Muniti.
(1992) *Con le spalle al futuro*, Rome: Editori Muniti.

Tronti was a militant involved with leftist minority groups, an involvement which ended in 1967 with his return to the PCI (Italian Communist Party). His earlier 'laborist' positions were the basis for the discussion and organization of political groups to the left of the PCI. His initial Marxism, close to **Della Volpe**'s, was radicalized in the 1960s and the political analysis of working classes became a theoretical problem, solved by radicalizing the interpretation of Marx's theory of labour value as found in the *Grundrisse*. The working class determines the development of capital and the factory is the centre of revolutionary social dynamics. During the 1960s and 1970s he queried his ideas of a 'monotheistic' causal account of capital, of the factory–society relationship and the relevance of Marxist instruments to a grasp of the importance of the political to the modern world. This led to the theory of the autonomy of the political, and to the claim that the movement of the working class and of women and youth had to be traced within and against capitalist development and within and against the state.

COLIN LYAS

Trotsky, Leon (pen-name of Lev Davidovich Bronshtein)

Russian. *b:* 26 October (7 November N.S.) 1879, Ianovka, Ukraine. *d:* 21 August 1940, Mexico City (assassinated by Soviet agent). *Cat:* Marxist. *Educ:* Studied at the University of Odessa, without graduating. *Infls:* Marx, Engels and the Russian Marxist Alexander Parvus.

Main publications:

(1906) *Nasha revoliutsiia* [Our Revolution], St Petersburg.

(1920) *Terrorizm i kommunizm*, Petrograd (English translation, *The Defence of Terrorism (Terrorism and Communism): A Reply to Karl Kautsky*, London: George Allen & Unwin, 1921).

(1923) *Literatura i revoliutsiia*, Moscow (English translation, *Literature and Revolution*, trans. Rose Strunsky, London: George Allen and Unwin, 1925).

(1924) *Novyi kurs*, Moscow (English translation, *The New Course*, trans. Max Shachtman, New York: International Publishing Co., 1943).

(1930) *Moia zhizn': opyt avtobiografii*, 2 vols, Berlin (English translation, *My Life: An Attempt at an Autobiogaphy*, New York: Charles Scribner's Sons, 1930).

(1930) *Permanentnaia revoliutsiia*, Berlin (English translation, *The Permanent Revolution*, trans. Max Shachtman, New York: Pioneer Publishers, 1931).

(1931–3) *Istoriia russkoi revoliutsii*, 2 vols, Berlin (English translation, *The History of the Russian Revolution*, trans. Max Eastman, New York: Simon & Schuster, 1932).

Secondary literature:

Deutscher, I. (1954) *The Prophet Armed: Trotsky 1879–1921*, London: Oxford University Press.

——(1959) *The Prophet Unarmed: Trotsky 1921–1929*, London: Oxford University Press.

——(1963) *The Prophet Outcast: Trotsky 1929–1940*, London, Oxford University Press.

Knei-Paz, B. (1978) *The Social and Political Thought of Leon Trotsky*, Oxford: Clarendon Press.

Mandel, E. (1979) *Trotsky: A Study in the Dynamic of his Thought*, London: NLB.

Born into a family of Jewish colonists, Trotsky was a populist before embracing Marxism and joining a workers' organization in South Russia when a student. In 1902 he escaped consequent Siberian exile, and joined **Lenin** and other revolutionary émigrés in Western Europe. He broke with Lenin at the decisive 1903 conference of the Russian Social-Democratic Labour Party and thereafter was closer to the Mensheviks. He returned to Russia to play a leading role in the 1905 Revolution, and again escaped to Western Europe from subsequent internal exile. He denounced Russia's involvement in the First World War, and, having returned to Russia after the February Revolution, mended his differences with Lenin, organized the Bolshevik seizure of power in St Petersburg and, as commander of the Red Army, helped defend it during the civil war. Having been outmanoeuvred by Stalin after Lenin's death, he was expelled from the Party in 1927, and eventually exiled abroad in 1929. In 1938 he and his followers founded the Fourth International, two years before his death at the hands of Soviet agents in Mexico.

Although committed to its fundamentals, Trotsky regarded Marxism as a method of analysis rather than a finished body of absolute truths. His distinctive contribution to Marxist theory, his theory of uninterrupted or 'permanent' revolution, stressed the peculiarities of the Russian historical situation. Russia, and other 'backward' countries, could not simply recapitulate the Western European historical process, since that very process impinges upon, and forces, their own. Trotsky generalized this perception as the universal laws of uneven and combined development, his prime application of the Marxian dialectic. In the Russian case, the result was the coexistence of archaic and highly modern cultural, economic and social forms, notably the development of a proletariat before a bourgeoisie. Russia could in consequence bypass a lengthy and separate capitalist stage of development and go straight to a dictatorship of the proletariat; but the lack of capitalist development also meant that it was impossible to build socialism in one country alone against a hostile external environment (this was the crux of his fatal disagreement with Stalin). However, according to Trotsky, the increasingly international nature of the capitalist system entailed that revolution in a backward country would disturb the equilibrium of the system and accelerate the process of world revolution.

Lenin came to accept Trotsky's analysis of the peculiar ripeness for revolution of the Russian situation, and for a while after 1917 Trotsky accommodated Lenin's views on strict party discipline, or 'revolutionary centralism'. In general, however, Trotsky believed in the self-organization of the working class, based on the workers' soviet and a multi-party system. He decried the counter-revolutionary nature of the 'Thermidor' of Stalinist 'bureaucratism', explaining it as a manifestation of the retrogressive aspects of a society in transition from capitalism to socialism.

Trotsky was much less concerned with purely philosophical problems than, for example, **Bogdanov**, **Plekhanov** or Lenin. His extensive writings on literature exhibit a tension between respect for artistic autonomy and the universality of great art, and a Marxist emphasis on the social origins and functions of art. He was only peripherally involved in the 1920s debates on the philosophy of science, most notably through a speech on the Russian chemist Mendeleyev, in which he charted a course between mechanistic reductionism and the autonomy of individual sciences. If anything, his intervention favoured the mechanists; he was nevertheless, for political reasons, bracketed with the disgraced Deborinites as a 'Menshevizing idealist'.

COLIN CHANT

Tugarinov, Vasilii Petrovich

Russian. *b:* 29 December (O.S.) 1898, Tver province, Russia. *d:* 1978, Leningrad. *Cat:* Marxist dialectical materialist. *Ints:* Dialectical materialism; historical materialism; value theory. *Educ:* Moscow State University and the Communist Academy. *Appts:* Taught Philosophy at various institutions of higher learning from 1939; from 1951, Professor of Philosophy at Leningrad University (Dean of the Philosophy Faculty, 1951–60).

Main publications:

(1954) *Zakony ob"ektivnogo mira, ikh poznanie i ispol'zovanie* [The Laws of the Objective World, Their Cognition and Utilization], Leningrad.

(1955) *O prirode soznaniia* [On the Nature of Consciousness], Leningrad.
(1956) *Sootnoshenie kategorii dialekticheskogo materializma* [The Interrelationship of the Categories of Dialectical Materialism], Leningrad.
(1956) *Zakony prirody i obshchestva* [The Laws of Nature and Society], Moscow.
(1958) *Sootnoshenie kategorii istoricheskogo materializma* [The Interrelationship of the Categories of Historical Materialism], Leningrad.
(1960) *O tsennostiakh zhizni i kul'tury* [On the Values of Life and Culture], Leningrad.
(1968) *Teoriia tsennostei v marksizme* [The Theory of Values in Marxism], Leningrad.
(1971) *Filosofiia soznaniia* [Philosophy of Consciousness], Moscow.

Secondary literature:
Alekseev, P. V. (ed.) (1993) *Filosofy Rossii xix–xx stoletii* [Russian Philosophers of the 19th–20th Centuries], Moscow, pp. 187–8.
Scanlan, James P. (1985) *Marxism in the USSR: A Critical Survey of Current Soviet Thought*, Ithaca, NY; Cornell University Press.

A confirmed Marxist–Leninist, Tugarinov did pioneering work in the elaboration of dialectical materialism as a philosophical system in the Soviet Union after Stalin's death in 1953. On a wide range of issues Tugarinov was one of the first Soviet philosophers to go beyond the simplistic dogmatism of the Stalin era to the construction of articulated and coherent philosophical theories consistent with the Marxist worldview.

These issues included the nature of matter, on which Tugarinov defended a substantialist thesis over the objections of Engels and **Lenin**; the theoretical structure of dialectical materialism and historical materialism as systems of categories; the character, role and cognizability of laws in both nature and history; and the nature of the 'social being' that, for Marx, determines social consciousness. On the last question, Tugarinov's identification of social being with human life activity gave impetus to a new approach to historical materialism that focused on practical activity rather than on the relation between forces and relations of production. Tugarinov's 1960 book *O tsennostiakh zhizni i kul'tury* [On the Values of Life and Culture] was the first Soviet work to pose the problem of investigating values philosophically, and it initiated the development of Soviet value theory, to which Tugarinov contributed with his 1968 book as well. Tugarinov argued that a Marxist axiology must avoid both subjectivism and absolutism; that could be accomplished, he thought, by analysing evaluational attitudes as derivative from cognitive attitudes.

JAMES SCANLAN

Tugendhat, Ernst

German. *b:* 8 March 1930, Büenn, Czechoslovakia. *Cat:* Analytic philosopher (with background in German philosophy). *Ints:* Philosophy of language; phenomenology; metaphysics; ethics; ancient philosophy. *Educ:* Stanford University and Freiburg University. *Infls:* Personal influences include Heidegger; literary influences include Frege, G. H. Mead and Wittgenstein. *Appts:* 1960–6, Assistant, University of Tübingen; 1966–75, Professor of Philosophy, University of Heidelberg; 1976–80, Member of the Max Planck Institute, Starnberg; 1980–92, Professor of Philosophy, Freie Universität, Berlin; 1992–, Visiting Professor, Universidad Catolica de Chile, Santiago.

Main publications:

(1958) *Tai Kata Tinos: Eine Untersuchung zu Struktur und Ursprung Aristotelischer Grundbegriffe*, Freiberg/Munich: Karl Alber.
(1967) *Der Wahrheitsbegriff bei Husserl und Heidegger*, Berlin: Habilitationschrift.
(1970) 'The meaning of "Bedeutung" in Frege', *Analysis* 30: 177–89.
(1976) *Vorlesungen zur Einführung in der Sprachanalytische Philosophie*, Frankfurt: Suhrkamp (English translation, *Traditional and Analytic Philosophy*, Cambridge: Cambridge University Press,1982).
(1984) *Probleme Der Ethik*, Stuttgart: Reclam.
(1986) *Nachdenken über die Atomkriegsgefahr und Warum man sie nicht sieht*, Berlin: Rotbuch.
(1986) *Self-Consciousness and Self-Determination*, Cambridge, Mass.: MIT Press (translation of *Selbstbewusstsein und Selbsbestimmung*, 1979; Frankfurt, Suhrkamp).
(1992) *Philosophische Aufsätze*, Frankfurt: Suhrkamp.
(1992) *Ethik und Politik*, Frankfurt: Suhrkamp.
(1993) *Vorlesungen über Ethik*, Frankfurt: Suhrkamp.

Secondary literature:

Lütterfield, Wilhelm (1982) *Bin ich nur öffentliche Person? E. Tugendhat's Idealismuskritik*, Vienna: Anton Haim Meisenheim.

The writings of Ernst Tugendhat have done much to familiarize the German-speaking world with Anglo-American philosophy. Although convinced of its methodological fruitfulness he maintained that analytic/linguistic philosophy had lost sight of its roots and of fundamental metaphysical issues. On the other hand, he argued that while continental philosophy had remained in touch with such issues, it stood in need of the superior analytic tools possessed by English-speaking philosophers. After studying classical philology at Stanford Tugendhat transferred to Freiburg in order to hear Heidegger; in 1966 a stay at the University of Michigan oriented him to linguistic analysis.

One major theme in Tugendhat's work has been to stress the centrality of language and of the merits of a semantics based on the sentence as opposed to the name/object relation. **Frege** he interpreted accordingly. Similarly, in his important book on the twin concepts of self-consciousness and self-determination, self-knowledge is treated as propositional, while self-determination is seen to depend upon the communicative use of language and the availability of social roles. Tugendhat regards the contribution of **Heidegger** as indispensable although giving insufficient weight to language and the social dimension. While **Habermas** was influenced by *Selbstbewusstsein und Selbsbestimmung*, Tugendhat has in recent years been a prominent critic of the former's discourse ethics.
Sources: WW(Eur) 1985; Wer 25, 1986/7; brief letter from Tugendhat; Nida.

CLIVE BORST

Turing, A(lan) M(athison)

British. *b:* 23 June 1912, London. *d:* 7 June 1954, Wilmslow, Cheshire. *Cat:* Mathematician; pioneer of computing theory. *Ints:* Logic; artificial intelligence; philosophy of mind. *Educ:* King's College, Cambridge and Princeton University. *Infls:* Alonzo Church. *Appts:* 1933–6, Fellow of King's College, London, Cambridge; 1939–45, served official for British Foreign Office, actually involved in highly secret code-cracking operation at Bletchley Park, which resulted in the award of an OBE in 1946; 1945–8, National Physical Laboratory, working on the design and construction of an 'automatic computing engine'; 1948–54, Reader at the University of Manchester and Assistant Director, Manchester Automatic Digital Machine Publications.

Main publications:

(1937) 'On Computable Numbers with an Application to the *Entscheidungsproblem*', *Proceedings of the London Mathematical Society, vol. 42 (1937) pp. 230–65.*

(1937) 'Compatibility and x-definability', *Journal of Symbolic Logic* (1937) pp. 153–63.

(1939) *Systems of Logic Based on Ordinals*, London: C. F. Hodgson and Son 1947 Lecture: 'The Automatic Computing Machine, given in London, 20 Feb., 1947; typescript held at King's College, Cambridge.

(1950) 'Computing machinery and intelligence', *Mind* 59: 433–60.

(1990) (ed. D. C. Ince) *Collected Works of A. M. Turing: Morphogenesis,; 1992: Mechanical Intelligence*, New York: Elsevier Series and Amsterdam: North Holland Publishing Co.

Secondary literature:

(1977) *Report on the Papers of Alan Mathison Turing OBE, FRS (1912–1954)* London, Royal Commission on Historical Manuscripts.

Atton, J. Supplementary Catalogue of Papers and Correspondence of Alan Mathison Turing FRS (1912–1954): London, Contemporary Scientific Archives Centre, 1985.

Boone, W. W. Review of Turing 1950, *Journal of Symbolic Logic*, vol. 17, 1952, pp. 74–6.

Church, A. (1936) 'A Note on the Entscheidung Problem', in *Journal of Symbolic Logic*, vol. 1, pp. 40–44; addendum 101–2.

Hodges, Andrew (1983) *Alan Turing: The Enigma of Intelligence*, London: Hutchinson.

Hoffstadter, Douglas R. and Dennett, Daniel (1981) (eds) 'The Turing test: A coffee house conversation' in *The Mind's Eye*, Basic Books, 1981; Penguin, 1982, pp. 69–95. (Original title: 'Metamagical themes: A coffee house conversation on the Turing test to determine if a machine can think', *Scientific American*, 1981, pp. 15–36.

Mays, W. (1953) 'Can machines think?', *Philosophy* 27: 148–62.

Though his life was cut short and he published relatively little, A. M. Turing made important contributions to mathematical logic and to computer science and provoked much discussion amongst philosophers with his suggestion that a machine could satisfy all the requirements of being a mind. His important 1937 paper was concerned with the question whether a mechanical process could be devised for deciding whether a statement A, or not-A, or neither, was provable within a given system. His negative conclusion, reached also by others, had implications for the philosophy of logic and mathematics. But more influential was his postulation of a hypothetical machine, subsequently known as a 'Turing Machine', which would do the calculations. This machine was a forerunner of the modern digital computer. Turing was led to consider that such a machine might be able to peform any operation of which the human mind was capable. He was led in his 1950 paper to propose a criterion whether a person at the end of a data-link could tell the difference between the output of a machine and the output of a human being using the same communications process.

Sources: *BMFRS* 1955 (with bibliography); PI; Turner.

STUART BROWN

Turró, Ramón

Spanish. *b:* 1854, Malgrat, near Gerona, Spain. *d:* 1926, Barcelona. *Cat:* Radical empiricist; psychobiologist; literary and political journalist. *Ints:* Philosophy of science; epistemology. *Educ:* University of Barcelona. *Infls:* Bernard, Brown-Séquard, Helmholtz, Kant, Pasteur and Pavlov. *Appts:* 1900–14, Researcher, University of Barcelona Faculty of Medicine; 1914–26, Researcher, later Director, Municipal Laboratory of Barcelona; 1923–6, Founder, Catalan Philosophy Society.

Main publications:

(1912) *Els orígens del coneixement: la fam*, Barcelona.

(1912) *Criterología de J. Balmes*, Barcelona.

(1925) *Diàlegs sobre filosofia de l'estética i de la ciéncia*, Barcelona.

Secondary literature:

Aróstegui, A. (1950) 'La filosofía critica de R. Turró', *Revista de Filosofía*, Madrid.

Guy, A. (1955) 'L'intuition trophique selon R. Turró', in *Vie et pensée*, Paris, pp. 119–24.

——(1983) *Histoire de la philosophie espagnole*, Toulouse: Association des Publications de l'Université de Toulouse-Le Mirail.

Tusquets, J. (1926) 'L'obra filósofica de R. Turró, *Criterion*, chapter 6.

Turró has been described as a 'radical empiricist', and this can be seen to be clearly based on his emphasis on strict inductive observation and experimentation. This was in the main reaction to the cavalier disregard for established methodologies and the critical analysis of accepted dogma practised by his teacher, Professor José Letamendi. This stress on induction led to his best known work, *Els orígens del coneixement: la fam* [The Origins of Knowledge: Hunger] (1912), in which, within a positivist framework opposed to the idealism of Kantian epistemology, he sought to explain the appearance and constitutive factors of natural certainty, and of the complex problem of knowledge, whose origins, he argued, lay in the experience of hunger, not an 'amorphous necessity' but a sum of 'elective tendencies' which select from nature the most appropriate elements which would lead to the reconstitution of the organism. This process begins with a 'trophic disquiet' which grasps only vaguely the danger to the organism that hunger represents.

The 'trophic reflex' then motivates and guides the reparative organs. However, when the organs' reserves have been exhausted, pure hunger appears, which this time is felt consciously, altering the 'trophic intuition' which, aware of alimentary needs and the precise quantities required, organizes itself around the 'trophic experience', the experience of a series of reparative drives. Above all, Turró maintained, this is a logical process, carried out upon sensorially imposed data. His methodological coherence was well received, especially amongst psycho-biologists such as Clara Davis and D. Katz, and A. Aróstegui labelled his system 'a metaphysics of substance'. The renowned Spanish philosopher Miguel de **Unamuno**, in his Prologue to the Castillian translation of Turró's major work, joked 'I eat, therefore I am'.

DAVID SPOONER

Twardowski, Kazimierz

Austrian, of Polish descent. *b:* 1866, Vienna. *d:* 1938. *Cat:* Descriptive empiricist; philosophical reformer. *Ints:* Philosophical psychology and epistemology. *Educ:* Philosophy, University of Vienna. *Infls:* Franz Brentano. *Appts:* 1894–5, Lecturer at Vienna; 1895–1930, Professor of Philosophy, University of Lvov.

Main publications:

(1892) *Idee und Perzeption*, Vienna.
(1894) *Zur Lehre vom Inhalt und Gegenstand der Vorstellungen* (English translation, *On the Content and Object of Presentations*, trans. R. Grossman, The Hague: Martinus Nijhoff, 1977).
(1898) *Wyobrazenia i pojecia* [Images and Concepts], Lvov.
(1900) 'O tak zwanych prawdach wzgeldnych' [On so-called relative truths] *Ksiega Pamiatkowa Uniwersytetu Lwowskiego* Lvov (German translation, 'Über sogenannte relative Wahrheiten', *Archiv für Systematische Philosophie* 8, 4: 415–47, 1902).
(1901) *Zasadnicze pojecia dydaktyki i logiki*, Lvov.

(1903) 'Über begriffliche Vorstellungen' [On conceptual presentations], *Beilage zum XVI Jahresbericht der Philosophischen Gesellschaft an der Universität zu Wien*, Leipzig.
(1910) *O filzofji średniowiecznej.*
(1910) *O metodzie psychologji*, Lvov.
(1911) *O czynnościach i wytworach*, Cracow.
(1913) *O psychologji, jej przedmiocie, zadaniach i metodzie*, Lvov.
(1927) *Rozprawy i artykuly filozoficzne*, Lvov.
(1965) *Wybrane pisma filozoficzne* [Selected Philosophical Papers], ed. T. Czezowski, Warsaw.

Secondary literature:

(1948) 'Tribute to Kazimierz Twardowski on the 10th anniversary of his death', *Journal of Philosophy* 57: 209–15.
Czezowski, T. (1948) 'Kazimierz Twardowski as Teacher', *Studia Philosophica* 3: 13–17.
Findlay, J. N. (1938) *Meinong's Theory of Objects*, London.
Ingarden, R. (1948) 'The scientific activity of Kazimierz Twardowski', *Studia Philosophica* 3: 17–30.
Jordan, Z. A. (1963) *Philosophy and Ideology*, Dordrecht (contains bibliography).
Krzywicki-Herburt, G. (1967) 'Twardowski, Kazimierz', in Paul Edwards (ed.) *Encyclopedia of Philosophy*, vol. 8, London: Collier Macmillan, pp. 166–7.

At the turn of the century Twardowski's emphasis on a new, intellectually responsible mode of inquiry contributed to the transformation of European philosophy and had a decisive influence on the intellectual and cultural life of Poland. He was opposed to nebulous speculation and destructive skepticism, and wanted to make philosophy more scientific through the clarification of its problems, a rigorous analytical methodology and the elimination of conceptual obscurities. He believed that the radical (non-experimental) empiricism of **Brentano**'s 'descriptive psychology' could be the basis of this new, scientific philosophy.

However, he needed to go beyond Brentano, and in his *Zur Lehre vom Inhalt und Gegenstand der Vorstellungen* (1894) he argued that, whereas a mental act and its content form a single unity (which Brentano had called a 'psychological phenomenon'), the *object* of a mental act is invariably *extraneous* to that act and its inherent content. This analysis, which not only led Twardowski to his general theory of the objects of thought but also contributed to the demise of psychologism in logic and philosophy, influenced

Alexius **Meinong**, Edmund **Husserl** and to some extent Moritz **Schlick**, and through them much of early twentieth-century philosophy.

Later Twardowski formulated a non-psychologistic and non-Platonizing account of logic based upon the distinction between mental acts and their products, extended this to a general theory and clarification of the sciences and repeatedly examined the various methodological issues of psychology. He was critical of reductive materialism, defended introspection as a source of knowledge and presented a lucid critique of relativism in his influential 'O tak zwanych prawdach wzglednych' [On so-called relative truths] (1900).

As a teacher, Twardowski transformed Polish philosophy and endowed it with a distinct style. He organized the teaching of philosophy, initiated regular philosophical meetings, founded the first Polish psychological laboratory (1901), the Polish Philosophical Society (1904), and in 1911 the quarterly journal, *Ruch Filozoficzny*, which he edited until his death and which is still published by the Polskie Towarzystwo Filozoficzne-Warszawa. In 1935 he became the chief editor of *Studia Philosophica*, a periodical publishing works of Polish philosophers in foreign languages. He was also the editor of a number of series of original works and translations, many of them inspired by him, such as Wladyslaw Witwicki's acclaimed translations of Plato. At the turn of the century Twardowski's emphasis on a new, intellectually responsible mode of inquiry contributed to the transformation of European philosophy and had a decisive influence on the intellectual and cultural life of Poland. As Twardowski devoted more and more time to his educational activities, his own work was bound to suffer; and to a degree this accounts for why his students tended to pursue their own independent lines of inquiry. For example, his best known students, Jan **Łukasiewicz**, Stanislaw **Leśniewski**, Kazimierz **Ajdukiewicz** and Tadeusz **Kotarbiński** differed from Twardowski methodologically in their emphasis on the philosophical relevance of symbolic logic, and both Leśniewski's 'ontology' and Kotarbiński's 'reism' were reactions to what was seen as Platonism in Twardowski's general theory of objects. However, his influence—not unlike that of G. E. **Moore**—was due less to his specific doctrines than his emphasis on free and responsible inquiry. His students never ceased to thank him for that as also for his personal example.

Sources: Bibliography in *Ruch Filozoficzny* 14 (1938): 14–39, compiled by D. Gromska.

BARRY JONES

Tymieniecka, Anna Teresa

Polish-American. *b:* 1923, Marianowo, Poland. *Cat:* Phenomenologist. *Ints:* Metaphysics of the creative act; imagination; the human sciences; social ethics. *Educ:* 1946, University of Cracow; 1951, the Sorbonne; 1952, University of Fribourg (PhD). *Infls:* Edmund Husserl, Roman Ingarden, Alfred Tarski and S. C. Pepper. *Appts:* 1957, Assistant Professor, Pennsylvania State University; 1961–6, Associate Scholar, Radcliffe Institute for Independent Study; 1972–3, Professor of Philosophy, St John's University, Jamaica; from 1975, President and Roman Ingarden Professor of Philosophy, The World Institute for Advanced Phenomenological Research and Learning; Editor, *Analecta Husserliana: The Yearbook of Phenomenological Research*.

Main publications:

(1960) *Phenomenology and Science in Contemporary European Thought*, New York: Farrar, Straus & Giroux.

(1966) *Leibniz' Cosmological Synthesis*, Netherlands: Royal Van Gorcum; New York: Humanities Press, 1965.

(1966) *Why is There Something Rather than Nothing? Prolegomena to the Phenomenology of Cosmic Creation*, New York: Royal Van Gorcum/Humanities Press.

(1972) *Eros et Logos: Introduction à la phénoménologie de l'expérience créatice*, Louvain: Nauweleerts.

(1982) (ed. and with others) *The Philosophical Reflection of Man in Literature*, Boston: Reidel.

(1988) *Logos and Life: Creative Experience and the Critique of Reason*, Dordretch: Kluwer.

(1989) *Logos and Life: Book 2, The Three Movements of the Soul: The Spontaneous and the Creative in Man's Self-Interpretation of the Sacred*, Dordrecht: Kluwer Academic Publishers.

(1994) *Logos and Life: Book 3, The Passions of the Soul and the Elements in the Onto-Poiesis of Culture)*, Dordrecht: Kluwer Academic Publishers.

Numerous monographs and papers by Tymieniecka are published in *Analecta Husserliana: The Yearbook of Phenomenological Research*, vos 1–46, Dordrecht: Kluwer Academic Publishers.

Secondary literature:

Kaelin, Eugene F. and Schrag, Calvin O. (eds)
American Phenomenology, Dordrecht: Kluwer
Academic Publishing.

Spiegelberg, H. (1969) *The Phenomenological
Movement*, 2 vols, The Hague: Nijhoff.

Tymieniecka came to phenomenology through
Husserl and **Ingarden**. She dedicated herself to
furthering its practice and study, at first by a
thorough allegiance to the ideas of her teachers
and later through theories of her own that led her
to a standpoint she has called 'the Phenomenology of Life and of the Human Condition in the
Unity-of-Everything-There-Is-Alive'.

Always taking the human condition as a
starting-point, the pursuit of her own ideas led
Tymieniecka to proclaim the supreme importance of creative activity in human life. Accordingly, her phenomenological enquiries are largely
focused on the personal experience of creativity
and its relationship to cosmic principles and
dynamic structures. She rejected the Husserlian
notion of 'transcendental consciousness', maintaining instead that 'initial spontaneity' is a
principle of movement and 'creative imagination' the principle responsible for the renewal of
structural types in a constitution. From this
basis she developed 'a metaphysics of the
creative act', a poetics in which, in her second
work of 1966, she explored what she has
described as 'self-individualizing becoming',
vigorously opposing deconstructionist analyses
of literature and asserting the primacy of the
'life-significance' of literary works.

In the later decades of the twentieth century
Tymieniecka has worked to produce a reconstruction of philosophy that has sought to
realize Husserl's dream of phenomenology as a
mathesis universalis. She has taken the Husserlian question of the origin of sense as central and
has posited the human creative function as the
unifying factor that not only bestows meaning
but also reveals moral sense as the foundation of
intersubjectivity, as that which mediates communication and as that which is, *au fond*, the
source of the unity of the 'multiple rationalities'
of all branches of knowledge. She has rejected an
earlier and Leibnizian ontological universalism
in favour of a thesis of 'concrete becoming', a
phenomenology of actual existence.

Tymieniecka's founding and continuing support of The International Husserl and Phenomenological Research Society (1969), The
International Society for Phenomenology and
Literature (1974), The International Society for
Phenomenology and the Human Sciences (1976)
and her founding and presidency of the World
Institute for Advanced Phenomenological Research and Learning in Belmont, Massachusetts
(1975–6) have done much to advance phenomenology. Its dissemination owes a good deal to
the yearbook, *Analecta Husserliana*, also
founded by Tymieniecka, in 1968, which she
has edited and to which she has contributed
unflaggingly.

Sources: Correspondence with Louis Houthakker;
Huisman.

DIANÉ COLLINSON

U

Uexküll, Jakob Johann Baron von

Estonian-German. *b:* 8 September 1864, Keblas (Estland). *d:* 25 July 1944, Capri. *Cat:* Philosopher and methodologist of biology; zoologist. *Ints:* Animal behaviour; physiology; morphology; environment. *Educ:* Universities of Dorpat (Tartu) and Heidelberg. *Infls:* Literary influences: Kant, Goethe, Leibniz, Mendel and Cuvier. Personal: G. Kriszat and Hans Driesch. *Appts:* 1925–40, Honorary Professor and, from 1926, Director of the Institut für Umweltforschung, University of Hamburg.

Main publications:

(1909) *Umwelt und Innerwelt*, Berlin: J. Springer; second edition, 1921.

(1920) *Theoretische Biologie*, Berlin: J. Springer (English translation, *Theoretical Biology*, trans. D. L. Mackinnon, New York: Harcourt, 1926).

(1930) *Die Lebenslehre*, Potsdam: Muller & Kiepenheuer.

Secondary literature:

Cassirer, Ernst (1944) *An Essay on Man*, New Haven: Yale University Press, pp. 23ff.

——(1950) *The Problem of Knowledge: Philosophy, Science and History Since Hegel*, New Haven: Yale University Press, pp. 199–203.

Schubert-Soldern, R. (1962) *Mechanism and Vitalism: Philosophical Aspects of Biology*, London: Burns & Oats, pp. 175 ff.

Uexküll was primarily an anatomist, whose thinking was influenced by vitalism, by Cuvier's concept of 'anatomical type' and by Kant's transcendental philosophy. Although he held biology to be 'a purely natural science' (1930, 9), he nevertheless drew metaphysical conclusions and advanced a speculative theory of immaterial 'formal structure' (*Bauplan*) based on the pure relationships of geometry and stereometry.

Uexküll regarded life as irreducible to physico-chemical terms. According to him, every organism is a complex whole of interacting functions, whose nature may be inferred from its vital 'form' or 'stucture'. However, he stressed that the organism cannot be conceived in isolation from its environment (*Umwelt*). What constitutes the specific nature of an organism is the way in which, by virtue of its 'form', it receives stimuli from its world and transmutes them within itself. So every animal, including man, is perfectly fitted (*eingepasst*) to its environment.

Thus Uexküll repudiated the Darwinian idea of adaptation to environment: it is rather the 'form' of the animal which 'creates' the environment by its activity. This view presented an ingenious revision of the principles of biology by extending Kant's transcendentalism to animals. But its appeal to an immaterial vital 'form' as the key to biological science appears chimerical to the perspective of present-day biology. Uexküll's biological scheme greatly impressed Ernst **Cassirer**, who made use of it for a characterization of the human world (Cassirer 1944, p. 24).

Sources: Edwards; Brockhaus.

STEPHEN MOLLER

Ulken, H(ilmi) Ziya

Turkish. *b:* 1901, Istanbul. *d:* 5 June 1973, Istanbul. *Cat:* Muslim eclectic philosopher. *Ints:* Islamic philosophy; ethics. *Educ:* Istanbul University, 1918–21. *Infls:* Jalal al-din Rumi, Spinoza and Max Scheler. *Appts:* Geography teacher in high school; Professor of Philosophy, Istanbul University, 1944–71.

Main publications:

(1928) *Felsefe Desleri* [Lectures on Philosophy], Istanbul.

(1931) *Ask Ahlak* [The Ethic of Love], Istanbul.

(1941) *Mant Tarihi* [The History of Logic], Istanbul.

(1946) *Ahlak* [Ethics], Istanbul.

(1946) *Islam Dusuncesi* [Islamic Thought], Istanbul.

(1951) *Tarihi Maddecilige Reddiye* [The Refutation of Historical Materialism], Istanbul.

(1953) *La Pensée de l'Islam*, Istanbul.

(1954) *Les Opuscules d'Avicenne*, Istanbul.

(1957) *Islam Felsefesi Tarihi* [The History of Islamic Philosophy], Istanbul.

(1957–8) *Felsefeye Giris* [An Introduction to Philosophy], 2 vols, Ankara.

(1966) *Islam Felsefesi* [Islamic Philosophy], Istanbul.
(1967) *Humanisme des cultures*, Ankara.
(1968) *Varlk ve Olus* [Being and Becoming], Ankara.

Ulken, like his contemporaries, wanted to construct 'an original Turkish philosophy' through the synthesis of Western philosophy with Islamic thought in order to match the intellectual needs of the newly established Turkish Republic. He was thoroughly eclectic: intellectually at home with both Western and Islamic philosophy. Ulken played an important role in the revival of philosophical studies in Turkey. Many of his works were extensively used as textbooks in philosophy departments in the universities. His ideas exerted a powerful influence on philosophy in post-1960 Turkey.

Sources: Dr Eyyub Sanay (1986) *Hilmi Siya Ulken*, Ankara: Kultur ve Turizm Bakanligi Yaynlar.

ADNAN ASLAN

Unamuno y Jugo, Miguel de

Spanish. **b:** 1864, Bilbao, Spain. **d:** 1935, Salamanca. **Cat:** Analyst of the human condition. **Ints:** Epistemology; ethics. **Infls:** Pascal and Kirkegaard. **Appts:** Spent almost all of his adult life, from 1891 onwards, at the University of Salamanca, first as Professor of Greek and then as Rector; this way of life was punctuated by six years of political exile (1924–30), enforced by the government of Primo de Rivera as a result of Unamuno's republicanism.

Main publications:

All in *Obras completas*, 16 vols, Madrid: Aguado, 1950–9:

(1895) *En torno al casticismo.*
(1905) *Vida de Don Quijote y Sancho.*
(1910) *Mi religión y otros ensayos breves.*
(1912) *Contra esta y aquello.*
(1913) *Del sentimiento trágico de la vida.*
(1931) *La agonía del Christianismo.*

Secondary literature:

Ferrater Mora, José (1957) *Unamuno, bosquejo de una filosofia*, second edition, Buenos Aires: Editorial Sudamericana.
Huertas-Jourda, José (1963) *The Existentialism of M. de Unamuno*, Gainsville: University of Florida Press.
Lacey, A. (1967) *Miguel de Unamuno: The Rhetoric of Existence*, The Hague: Mouton.
Marías, Julián (1943) *Miguel de Unamuno*, Madrid: Espasa-Calpe.

Meyer, François (1955) *L'ontologie de M. de Unamuno*, Paris: PUF.
Oromí, Miguel (1943) *El pensamiento filosófico de Miguel de Unamuno*, Madrid: Espasa-Calpe.
Rudd, Margaret Thomas (1963) *The Lone Heretic*, Austin: University of Texas Press.

Unamuno was perhaps not a philosopher in the sense in which **Russell** or **Wittgenstein** were, and was not concerned with either the construction of systems or the analysis of technical problems. Yet his thought, though unsystematic, has a reach and penetration which make it impossible not to classify it as philosophical. It centres around a number of profound themes: immortality, religion, the role of reason, human nature and the human predicament, and how to live in a world in which reason does not appear to cohere with or satisfy the deepest of human needs. Unamuno was also concerned with some specifically Spanish themes: the nature of the Spanish character, the place of Spain in Europe and the right form of government for his country. These concerns are expressed not only in Unamuno's primarily religious or philosophical works, but also in poetry and novels.

The basis of Unamuno's thought is his view of human nature and the human predicament. He objects strongly to the conception of human nature espoused by academic philosophers, a conception which overemphasizes our rationality and the value of reason while at the same time ignoring the most important aspects of our situation. For Unamuno, a human being is not an entity whose primary and distinctively valuable attribute is the capacity for rational thought but rather an individual of flesh and blood (*de carne y hueso*, literally of flesh and bone), faced with the fact of mortality and agonizing internal conflicts—this stress on individuality, concreteness and *angst* is one of a number of elements in Unamuno's outlook which make it more akin to existentialism than any other. Consonant with this basic premise is his repeated attack on rationalism, especially in its scientific form. For reasons which will become clear, he regards reason as the faculty which leads us to despair, and rationalism falsifies the human condition by failing to deal adequately with our deepest needs. His attack on what he termed 'wretched logic' (*la cochina logica*) begins in his *Vida de Don Quijote y Sancho* (1905) and is a major theme of his most important philosophical work, *Del sentimiento trágico de la vida* (1912).

Reason leads us to despair, Unamuno argues, principally because its conclusions contradict the deepest of all human desires, the hunger for personal immortality (*el hambre de la inmortalidad personal*). Above all things, human beings wish to continue to be themselves indefinitely, though without the experience of pain. Moreover, our wish is not for an immortality of angelic contemplation or merging with an absolute but for the resurrection of the body, and for a life of perpetual action. The whole tendency of rational investigation is to indicate that this deepest of wishes is in fact frustrated, and there is therefore a profound tension at the heart of the human condition: 'to live is one thing and to understand is another ... there is between them such an opposition that we can say that everything vital is anti-rational and everything rational anti-vital. And this is the basis of the tragic sense of life' (1913, ch. 2). Our deepest wish is to live forever, whilst our reason tells us we are faced with annihilation. This painful contradiction is the tragic sense of life, and never leaves us: human consciousness, Unamuno concludes, is therefore best characterized as a lifelong illness.

Granted that we have no belief in personal immortality, how is it appropriate for us to behave in this condition? Unamuno argues that an authentic life is possible, a life informed by adherence to an ideal based on a passage in Senancour's novel *Obermann* (1804): if annihilation is what is reserved for us, let us make it an injustice. We must strive to become fully ourselves, to make ourselves irreplaceable. We must fight destiny, even if we know we have no hope of victory, in a Quixotic manner. Our only 'practical solace' (*consuelo práctico*) for having been born is work—Unamuno notes that Adam and Eve were set to work *before* the Fall—and so in practical terms we must seek full personal realization and irreplaceability via our work. We must so work as to leave our mark on others, to dominate them: 'The true religious morality is at bottom aggressive, invasive' (1913, ch. 11) This 'domination', however, is not to be thought of as a crude political ascendancy or attaining of worldly power, but rather a making of ourselves unforgettable, and this can often be done as well passively as actively.

In the course of elaborating this outlook Unamuno develops a number of other ideas of philosophical interest. As might be expected, granted his view of human nature and the place of reason in it, Unamuno has an appropriate philosophy of belief. Our fundamental attitudes to life are not the consequence of rationally worked out beliefs, but spring instead from

features of the personality which are not rational: 'It is not our ideas which make us optimists or pessimists, but our optimism or pessimism, derived as much from physiological or perhaps pathological origins, which makes our ideas' (1913, ch. 1). The tragic sense (*sentimiento*) of life is no exception: it is universal and prerational, though it can be corroborated by rational beliefs. Further, Unamuno's outlook leads him to a particular conception of the activity of philosophizing itself. Philosophy is not a detached, rational pastime nor an academic or scholastic discipline, but a way of coping with the human predicament: we live first, then philosophize (*primum vivere, deinde philosophari*). We philosophise either to resign ourselves to life, or to find some finality in it, or to amuse ourselves and distract ourselves from our griefs.

ROBERT WILKINSON

Urban, Wilbur M(arshall)

American. **b:** 27 March 1873, Mount Joy, Pennsylvania. **d:** 16 October 1952, New Haven, Connecticut. **Cat:** Idealist. **Ints:** Metaphysician; philosophy of value; philosopher of language. **Educ:** Princeton University BA 1895; the Universities of Jena, Leipzig, Munich and Graz (PhD, Leipzig, 1897). **Infls:** J. M. Baldwin, O. Liebmann, Wundt, Nietzsche, Meinong, Husserl and Rickert. **Appts:** 1897–8, Reader in Philosophy, Princeton; 1898–1902, Professor of Philosophy and Psychology, Ursinus College, Pennsylvania; 1902–20, Professor of Philosophy, Trinity College, Connecticut; 1920–30, Stone Professor of Philosophy, Dartmouth College, New Hampshire; 1931–52, Professor and Chair, Department of Philosophy (Emeritus Professor from 1941), Yale.

Main publications:

(1897) *A History of the Principle of Sufficient Reason*, Philadelphia: privately printed; reprinted as volume I, *Princeton Contributions to Philosophy*, ed. A. T. Ormond, 1898.

(1909) *Valuation: Its Nature and Laws*, London and New York: Swan Sonnenschein and Co., Ltd and Macmillan Co.; reprinted, New York: AMS Press, 1974.

(1929) *The Intelligible World*, New York: Macmillan Co.; reprinted New York: AMS Press, 1974.

(1930) *Fundamentals of Ethics*, New York: Henry Holt & Co.

(1930) 'Metaphysics and value', in G. P. Adams (ed.), *Contemporary American Philosophy*, New York:

Macmillan Co., vol. 2, pp. 355–81; reprinted, New York: Russell & Russell, Inc., 1962.

(1939) *Language and Reality*, London and New York: Macmillan Co.; reprinted, New York: AMS Press, 1974.

(1949) *Beyond Realism and Idealism*, London: George Allen & Unwin, Ltd.

(1951) *Humanity and Deity*, London: George Allen & Unwin, Ltd.

Secondary literature:

Reck, A. J. (1964) *Recent American Philosophy*, New York: Pantheon, pp. 154–80.

——(1995) 'W. M. Urban's philosophy of history', *Transactions of the Charles S. Peirce Society*, vol 31 (summer).

Shibles, W. A. (1971) *An Analysis of Metaphor in the Light of W. M. Urban's Theories*, The Hague: Mouton.

Smith, J. E. (1953) 'Beyond realism and idealism: an appreciation of W. M. Urban (1873–1952)', *Review of Metaphysics*, 6, 3 (March): 337–50.

The study of **Nietzsche**'s *Genealogy of Morals* shook Urban as a young student in Germany to undertake what he deemed to be his great philosophical enterprise in the study and defence of values. He considered values central to philosophy, and speculative philosophy to be indispensable to civilization. More than any philosopher of his generation, Urban shifted the argument for idealism from epistemology to the field of values.

Urban sought early to formulate a general theory of value and valuation. Drawing upon the psychology of his time, *Valuation* (1909) offers a phenomenology of values. It is the first work in English in the field which he himself named 'axiology'. He next went on to realize his intention of elaborating the value-motif and the value-centric predicament in several branches of philosophy.

The Intelligible World (1929) is a defence of *philosophia perennis* by the use of self-referential argument against the naturalisms spawned in the wake of the First World War. It provides the clearest, most cogent and comprehensive statement of Urban's metaphysical idealism.

As analytic philosophers in the 1930s assaulted traditional philosophy and the objectivity of values, Urban concentrated on the philosophy of language. He was 'concerned with the evaluation of language as a bearer of meaning, as a medium of communication and as a sign or symbol of reality' (1939, p. 37). Stressing the codependence of meaning and

value, he located meanings conveyed by language within a speech community united by common orientation towards values.

When the disputes between idealism and realism threatened to exhaust philosophy, Urban sought to reconcile the two philosophical types by appealing to values in meeting the separate minimal demands of each. While the realist insists that knowledge, to be true, must refer to reality beyond it, the idealist holds that meaning and value are inseparable. Urban's idealistic philosophy is constructed along realistic lines in that he maintains that being, meaning and value are necessarily related to each other.

Humanity and Deity (1951) carries the value-centric approach into the field of rational theology, in opposition to atheistic naturalists and religious existentialists. Urban approached the concept of God by means of the traditional concepts of human value. He declared: 'Humanity and Deity' like the inside and the outside of the curve, like the mountain and the valley, are apart from each other unthinkable' (1951, p. 49).

At the time of his death Urban left unpublished a book-length manuscript of studies in the philosophy of history.

Sources: Blau, pp. 302–12; W. M. Urban, 'God and the historians, and other studies in the philosophy of history', *MA*, Yale Univ. Library, New Haven, CT; WW(Am).

ANDREW RECK

Urmson, J(ames) O(pie)

British. *b:* 1915, Yorkshire. *Cat:* Analytic philosopher. *Ints:* Philosophy of language; ethics; history of philosophy; aesthetics. *Educ:* University of Oxford. *Infls:* J. L. Austin. *Appts:* 1939–45, Fellow, Magdalen College, Oxford; 1945–55, Student, Christ Church, Oxford; 1955–9, Professor, University of St Andrews; 1959–78, Fellow, Corpus Christi College, Oxford; 1975–80, Professor, Stanford University; visiting positions in the USA.

Main publications:

(1956) *Philosophical Analysis*, Oxford: Clarendon Press.

(1960) (ed.) *The Concise Encyclopedia of Western Philosophy and Philosophers*, London: Hutchinson.

(1968) *The Emotive Theory of Ethics*, London: Hutchinson.

(1982) *Berkeley*, Oxford: Oxford University Press.

(1988) *Aristotle's Ethics*, Oxford: Blackwell.

(1990) *The Greek Philosophical Vocabulary*, London: Duckworth.

(1992) (trans.) Simplicius of Cilicia, *Corollaries on Place and Time*, Ithaca: Cornell University Press.

Secondary literature:

Dancy, Jonathan *et al.* (eds) (1988) *Human Agency: Language, Duty and Value*, Stanford: Stanford University Press.

Urmson has written influentially in many areas of philosophy. *Philosophical Analysis* (1956) became a standard account of British analytical philosophy between the two World Wars. His *Emotive Theory of Ethics* (1968) criticized and developed the emotivism of C. L. **Stevenson**, using in part distinctions derived from **Austin** (whose posthumous work Urmson played a major role in publishing). His introduction to Aristotle's ethics helped consolidate the place of Aristotle in contemporary ethical studies. He has also produced influential work in aesthetics.

Sources: WW 1992.

ANTHONY ELLIS

V

Vaihinger, Hans

German. *b:* 25 September 1852, Nehren. *d:* 17 December 1933, Halle, Germany. *Cat:* 'As-If' philosopher; metaphysician; Kant philologist. *Educ:* Theology, Philosophy and Classics at Tübingen, Leipzig and Berlin. *Infls:* Hermann Avenarius, Eduard von Hartmann, Friedrich A. Lange and Friedrich Nietzsche. *Appts:* Lecturer in Strasbourg; Professor at Halle.

Main publications:

(1876) *Hartmann, Dühring und Lange*, Iserlohn: Baedeker.
(1881–92) *Kommentar zu Kants Kritik der reinen Vernunft* 2 vols, Stuttgart: W. Spemann.
(1902) *Nietzsche als Philosoph*, Berlin: Reuther & Reichard.
(1911) *Die Philosophie des Als Ob*, Leipzig: Meiner (English translation, *The Philosophy of 'As If'*, trans. C. K. Ogden, London: Routledge & Kegan Paul.
(1924) *Pessimismus und Optimismus*, Leipzig: Rothschild.

Secondary literature:

Del-Negro, Walter (1934) 'Hans Vaihingers philosophisches Werk mit besonderer Berücksichtigung seiner Kantforschung', *Kant-Studien* 39: 316–327.
Von Noorden, H. (1953) 'Der Wahrheitsbegriff in Vaihinger's Philosophie des Als Obs', *Zeitschrift für philosophische Forschung* 8.

Vaihinger is perhaps best known for his fictionalism, or his philosophy of 'as if'. He endorsed the principle that an 'idea whose theoretical untruth or incorrectness, and therewith its falsity, is admitted, is not for that reason practically valueless and useless; for such an idea, in spite of its theoretical nullity, may have great practical importance'. Thought was, he believed, always in the service of the biological struggle for existence. It was therefore a merely biological function for him. Yet thought has for him a tendency to formulate problems which it cannot possibly solve, such as the question of the meaning of life. This problem cannot be answered (because it is a meaningless question). We can only show its psychological sources. Yet, some of the answers that have been given to this question, while clearly false, are just as clearly quite useful. Thus the fiction of a higher spirit that created and rules the world has been quite satisfying to many. Even mathematics and science rely on fictions that are self-contradictory (such as the concepts of the infinitely small and the atom). They are employed because they have proved themselves to be eminently fruitful. Moral values and ideals especially serve 'life'. Even if they are irrational, we should employ them. We must act 'as if' they were true because they have biological utility.

Vaihinger himself contrasted his principle with the pragmatic principle that truth in theory is proved by what is useful in practice, admitting that there is a similarity in practice, although the two are diametrically opposed in principle. Vaihinger was most deeply influenced by the pessimism, irrationalism, and voluntarism in Schopenhauer, although he also cites Hume and John Stuart Mill as important for his early development. When he got to know Nietzsche's works relatively late in life (1898), he found him to be a kindred spirit and fully endorsed his works. Vaihinger rejected the labels of 'scepticism' and 'agnosticism' for his theory, claiming that 'relativism' would be a more appropriate term for it. Vaihinger's work as a Kant scholar was perhaps more important than his fictionalism. His commentary on Kant's *Critique of Pure Reason* is still a standard work of Kant scholarship. His theory of the composition of the *Prolegomena* (*Blattversetzungshypothese*) is today accepted as essentially correct by most, and his 'patchwork theory' of the first *Critique* has been found compelling by Norman **Kemp Smith** and others. As a cofounder of both the Kant Society and of *Kant-Studien*, he had a great influence on the direction it took towards neo-Kantianism. Another journal he founded, the *Annalen der Philosophie*, was more concerned with the spread of his own fictionalism.

MANFRED KUEHN

Vailati, Giovanni

Italian. *b:* 24 April 1863, Crema, Italy. *d:* 14 May 1909, Rome. *Cat:* Logician; epistemologist. *Ints:* History of philosophy; history of science. *Educ:* Studied Engineering at the University of Turin. *Infls:* G. Peano, V. Volterra, C. S. Peirce, E. Mach, G. W. Leibniz, C. Brentano, G. E. Moore and B. Russell. *Appts:* Lecturer, History of Mechanics, Turin University, 1896–9, thereafter freelance writer; associated with the editorial committee of *Revista di Filosofia*.

Main publications:

(1911) *Scritti*, ed. Calderoni, Leipzig: J. A. Barth (contains bibliography by O. Premoli).

(1911) *Il Pragmatismo*, ed. Papini, Lanciano: Carabba; republished, Florence: Valecchi, 1943.

(1919) *Gli Strumenti della Conoscenza*, ed. Calderoni, Lanciano: Carabba.

(1957) *Il Metodo della Filosofia*, ed. F. Rossi Landi, Bari: Laterza (contains bibliography).

(1959) *Scritti di Metodologia e di analisi del linguaggio*, ed. Sciacca, Milan: G. Principato.

(1962) 'Cinque Lettere di Giovanni Vailati a Ernst Mach', ed. L. Caferio, *Riv. Crit. Stor. Fil.* 17: 68–74.

(1971) *Epistolario 1891–1909*, ed. Lanaro, Turin: G. Enaudi.

(1978) 'Lettere di Giovanni Vailati a Bernardino Varisco', ed. F. Fomenti, *Riv. Crit. Stor. Fil.* 33: 326–40.

(1987) *Scritti*, 3 vols, ed. Quaranta, Sala Bolgnese: Arnaldo Forni (a different from that edited by Calderoni; contains bibliography).

Secondary literature:

Binanti, L. (1979) *Giovanni Vailati Filosofia e Scienza*, L'Aquila: Japadre (contains bibliography).

Garin, E. (1955) *Cronache di Filosofia Italiana*, Bari: Laterza. *Riv. Crit. Stor. Fil.* 18, Vailati Centenary Issue, 1963 (various).

Rossi-Landi, F. (1957–8) 'Materiali per lo studio di Vailati', *Riv. Crit. Stor. Fil.* 12: 468–85, 12: 82–108 (contains bibliography).

——(1967) 'Vailati, Giovanni' in Paul Edwards (ed.) *Encyclopedia of Philosophy*, New York: Macmillan, vol. 8, pp. 224b–226a.

Vailati was an Italian pragmatist of the period in which nineteenth-century positivism was giving way to the neo-idealism of **Croce** and **Gentile**, which he opposed. He adopted a logical-analytical approach to the study of language, including that of science. Opposed to systems, he proposed that philosophy should be a neutral analytical discipline treating opinions as facts to be understood and verified. In the wide-ranging historical work with which his career began, he shows openness to external factors while adhering to the method of the philosophical historian in the manner common at the time as in **Mach** and **Duhem**. Subjects studied included the metaphysics of Aristotle, the history of mechanics, and Saccheri and the origins of non-Euclidean geometry. He believed that scientists and philosophers should cooperate, rather than ignore or attempt to dominate each other. Vailati suffered an eclipse after his death (among philosophers, though less so among historians of science) due to the fragmentary nature of his output and the rise of idealism, but he has attracted more interest from the 1950s, particularly with the centenary of his birth.

Sources: DSB 1976: 550b–551b.

R. N. D. MARTIN

Valéry, Paul

French. *b:* 1871, Sète, France. *d:* 1945, Paris. *Cat:* Introspectionist; sceptic. *Educ:* Law at Montpellier. *Infls:* Descartes. *Appts:* Valéry abandoned his early vocation for poetry in 1892, and took an administrative job (which he kept until 1922) which allowed him ample time for personal study; he returned to poetry in 1917 (*La Jeune Parque* and later *Charmes*, 1922), and spent the years after 1922 as one of France's most celebrated men of letters, although producing only prose works in this period.

Main publications:

All now in the 2-volume Pléiade edition of Valéry's *Oeuvres*, ed. Jean Hytier, Paris: Gallimard, 1987 and 1988:

(1894–1945) *Cahiers*, ed. Judith Robinson-Valéry, 2 vols, Paris: Gallimard, Pléiade, 1973.

(1895) *Introduction à la méthode de Léonard de Vinci* (with *Note et digression*, added 1919).

(1896) *La Soirée avec M. Teste* (plus eight other works, from 1924 on, concerning this character, collectively republished as *M. Teste*, Paris: Gallimard, 1946).

(1923) *Eupalinos ou l'architecte*.

(1932) *Discours de l'histoire*.

Secondary literature:

Bourbon-Busset, J. de (1964) *Paul Valéry ou la mystique sans Dieu*, Paris: Plon.

Robinson, J. (1963) *L'Analyse de l'esprit dans les Cahiers de Valéry*, Paris: Corti.

Valéry might at first seem an odd choice for inclusion in the present work. He professed himself ill at ease in philosophy, regarded professional philosophical debate as a word-game and claimed that 'All metaphysics results from bad use of words' (*Cahiers*, I, p. 481). Yet Valéry could not ignore philosophical concerns: as a young man he was torn by two contrary impulses, one towards poetry, the other towards attaining an understanding of the world of mathematical clarity and all possible minuteness. For the sake of the latter this major poet abandoned poetry for twenty years, devoting himself to a scrupulous examination of consciousness and its contents which was to last throughout his life and is the subject of the extensive *Cahiers*. His intellectual heroes, both historical and fictional—Leonardo, Monsieur Teste and Eupalinos—have all attained absolute clarity concerning the nature and limitations of consciousness.

What emerges from Valéry's lengthy records of introspection is a species of scepticism reminiscent by turns of Montaigne, Descartes or Hume. Whatever the variety and extent of thought or perception, all mental activity is marked by its origin: it is always, obviously or not, the thought of a limited self: 'Even our most 'profound' thought is bound by unbreakable conditions which render all thought 'superficial'' (1919). We live in a hall of mirrors, forever trapped by our limitations. We like to speak of 'inspiration' or 'genius' or 'profundity', believing that by their means we penetrate to reality, but, scrupulously examined, these terms turn out to be mere place-markers for ignorance, signs marking the location of unexplored areas. The limit of human attainment is seen in the intellect of a Leonardo, who combines creativity with absolute clarity: for Valéry, Leonardo's exceptionality resides in the extreme exactness of his powers of conceptual discrimination, not in any ill-defined power to penetrate to we-know-not-what.

The same sceptical suspicion of grandiose claims underlies Valéry's views on the nature of history, views which were the occasion for heated debate. History is not a science, but largely a matter of inspiration and invention ('est surtout Muse', 1932). Not only is historical evidence always incomplete, but it is coloured by the interests and limitations of the historian. History is the study of events which do not repeat themselves, and to seek to draw from it lessons or prophecies is pointless. It is rather one of the most dangerous products of intellectual chemistry: its usual effect is to cause nations to become fixated on old wounds or old dreams of grandeur or persecution. In fact history permits us to foresee nothing. It teaches us only the value of a general preparedness, which allows up to cope better with the unpredictable future.

What Valéry hated in philosophy was not the subject itself, but only that style of philosophical thought which pays insufficient heed to its epistemological foundations and loses itself in cloudy claims to knowledge of ultimate things.

ROBERT WILKINSON

Van Fraassen, Bastiaan Cornelius

American (formerly Canadian citizen). *b:* 5 April 1941, Goes, The Netherlands. *Cat:* Philosopher of science; logician; semanticist. *Ints:* Philosopical logic; philosophy of time and space. *Educ:* University of Alberta, Canada, and University of Pittsburg. *Infls:* Personal influences include Grünbaum, Sellars, Margenau, Leonard and Putnam; literary influences include Russell and Reichenbach. *Appts:* 1966–9, Assistant Professor then Associate Professor, Yale University; 1969–81, Associate then full Professor, University of Toronto; 1976–82, Professor, University of Southern California; 1982–, Professor of Philosophy, Princeton University.

Main publications:

(1969) *An Introduction to the Philosophy of Time and Space*, New York: Random House; second edition, New York: Columbia University Press, 1985.

(1971) *Formal Semantics and Logic*, New York: Macmillan.

(1972) (with K. Lambert) *Derivation and Counterexample: an Introduction to Philosophical Logic*, Encino, California: Dickinson.

(1978) 'Essence and existence', in N. Rescher (ed.), *Studies in Ontology*, Oxford: Blackwell.

(1980) *The Scientific Image*, Oxford: Oxford University Press.

(1981) (ed. with E. Beltrametti) *Current Issues in Quantum Logic*, New York: Plenum.

(1982) 'The Charybdis of realism: epistemological implications of Bell's inequality', *Synthese* 5: 25–38.

(1985) 'Empiricism in the philosophy of science', in P. M. Churchland and C. A. Hooker (eds), *Images of Science: Essays on Realism and Empiricism, with a Reply by Bas C. van Fraassen*, Chicago: Chicago University Press.

(1989) *Laws and Symmetry*, Oxford: Oxford University Press.

(1991) *Quantum Mechanics: An Empiricist View*, Oxford: Oxford University Press.

Secondary literature:
(1993) *Philosophy and Phenomenological Research*
53: 411–44 (author summary, reviews, and reply to
reviews of *Laws and Symmetry*).

Philosophical Logic (1971–7), and joint editor of
the *Journal of Symbolic Logic* (1983–9).
Sources: WW(Am), supplt to 44th edn, 1987–8; IWW
1993–4; DAS, 8, 1982.

CLIVE BORST

Bas van Fraassen is one of the leading contemporary philosophers of science and his 'constructive empiricism' is probably the best known and
most closely argued defence of an anti-realist
stance on the nature of science. While recognizing
the collapse of the logical positivist programme,
his strongly empiricist and antimetaphysical
convictions lead him to reject the obvious realist
alternative. Scientific theories aim to be true only
to the extent of being empirically adequate, of
saving the phenomena. The theoretical content is
such only that it *could* constitute a true description
of reality.

Van Fraassen indeed recognizes a double
underdetermination: that of theory by observational data, and in the interpretation of any
theory. An interpretation (of, for example,
quantum mechanics) tells us what the world
could be like according to the theory. A central
contention is rejection of the currently popular
'inference to the best explanation'. Moreover, the
very idea of laws of nature is dismissed as
philosophically indefensible and outdated, its
place being partly taken by the idea of symmetry.
In *Quantum Mechanics*—originally to have been
part of *Laws and Symmetry*— he defends 'the
Copenhagen variant of the modal interpretation'. Real indeterminism is accepted.

From the time of his doctoral dissertation
under Adolf **Grünbaum**, van Fraassen has been
keenly interested in the philosophy of time and
space. Another theme has been the nature of
scientific explanation; and what he termed his
'pragmatic' account of this in *The Scientific
Image* has been widely discussed. Drawing on
erotetic logic (the logic of questions), he
conceives of an explanation as answering a
question of the form: why did A happen rather
than X (where X is a member of the contrast-
class)?

Apart from philosophy of science, van
Fraassen is best known for an expertise in logic,
metalogic and semantics; and he advocates a
semantic conception of scientific theories whereby a theory is conceived as a family of models.
He was, early on, one of the main advocates of
free logic, allowing for singular terms, like
'Pegasus', which nevertheless do not refer. Van
Fraasen was editor-in-chief of the *Journal of*

Van Steenberghen, Fernand

Belgian. *b:* 13 February 1904, Sin-Josse-ten
Noorde. *Cat:* Scholastic. *Ints:* Modern Thomism;
history of medieval philosophy. *Educ:* University
of Louvain. *Infls:* Aquinas, Aristotle and De Wulf.
Appts: 1939–74, Professor of the History of
Medieval Philosophy, University of Louvain.

Main publications:
(1945) *Epistémologie*; fourth edition, Louvain: Editions de l'Institut Supérieur de Philosophie, 1966
(English translation, *Epistemology*, New York:
Wagner, 1970).
(1946) *Aristote en occident*, Louvain: Editions de
L'Institut Supérieur de Philosophie (English
translation, *Aristotle in the West*, Louvain: Nauwelaerts, 1954).
(1946) *Ontologie*; fourth edition, Louvain: Editions
de l'Institut Supérieur de Philosophie, 1966 (English translation, *Ontology*, New York: Wagner,
1970).
(1955) *The Philosophical Movement in the Thirteenth
Century*, Edinburgh: Nelson.
(1961) *Dieu caché*, Louvain: Publications Universitaires (English translation, *Hidden God*, Louvain:
Publications Universitaires; St Louis: Herder,
1966).
(1966) *La philosophie au XIIIe siècle*, Louvain:
Publications Universitaires; Paris: Béatrice-Nau-
welaerts.
(1980) *Thomas Aquinas and Radical Aristotelianism*,
Washington, DC: Catholic University of America
Press.
(1989) *Philosophie fondamentale*, Longueil, Quebec:
Le Préambule.

Secondary literature:
Elders, Léon (1983) 'Le Problème de l'existence de
Dieu dans les Steenberghen', *Divus Thomas* (Pia-
cenza) 86: 171–87.
Pirard, Regnier (1974) 'Hommage à M. le professeur
F. Van Steenberghen', *Revue Philosophique de
Louvain* 72: 435–8.
Salmon, Elizabeth G. (1954) 'What is being?', *Review
of Metaphysics* 7: 613–31.
Tognolo, Antonio (1967) 'L'epistemologia di F. Van
Steenberghen', in Carlo Giacon (ed.), *Posizione e
criterio del discorso filosofico*, Bologna: Patròn, pp.
79–97.

Van Steenberghen's *Epistemology* (1945) and *Ontology* (1946) were standard student texts in Louvain and elsewhere in the middle decades of the century, and represent a Thomism enlarged by its sympathy with Husserlian phenomenology. His most interesting work is *Dieu caché* (1961), a brilliant and penetrating critique of Aquinas's 'five ways' and other proofs of the existence of God. His medieval studies are of permanent value, not least his two-volume work on Siger of Brabant. He engaged in a long controversy with **Gilson** about the possibility of 'Christian philosophy', a phrase which Van Steenberghen regards with the utmost distrust.

Van Steenberghen's reputation as a historian of thirteenth-century philosophy is unsurpassed.
Sources: DFN; EF.

HUGH BREDIN

Varisco, Bernardino
Italian. *b:* 20 April 1850, Chiara, Brescia, Italy. *d:* 21 October 1933. *Cat:* Positivist, later metaphysican. *Appts:* Professor of Theoretical Philosophy, University of Rome, 1906–25.

Main publications:
(1901) *Scienza e opinioni.*
(1905) *La conscenza.*
(1910) *I massimi problemi.*
(1910) *Consci te stessi.*
(1928) *Sommario di filosofia.*
(1939) *Dall'uomo a Dio.*

Secondary literature:
Calogero, G. (1950) *La filosofia di Bernardo Varisco*, Messina: G. D'Anna.
Dallo, C. (1967) *Momenti e problemi dello spiritualismo*, Padua: CEDAM.
Librizzi, C. (1942) *Il pensiero di B. Varisco*, Padua: CEDAM.

Varisco is a philosopher whose work falls into two stages, the positivistic and the metaphysical. The first phase begins with the primary, given fact of a multiplicity of conscious subjects, each, in the style of Leibniz, with its own perspective on the world. Conscious life shades off in unbroken gradations into unconscious life and into the inanimate, the assertion of such an unbroken gradation manifesting a commitment to an equally Leibnizian panpsychism. Varisco's move to the University of Rome in 1906 saw the start of his new, metaphysical directions of thought which sought to reconcile the scientific and religious ways of understanding. His problem, to which his answer is decidedly obscure, is how to move from the set of assertions about the plurality of subjects so categorically affirmed in his first stage of philosophy, to assertions about the unitary reality of the universe which he seems to suppose to be required in religion. The answer appears to be an appeal to something called 'being', which is present in every individual act of thought by which objects are apprehended by subjects. This Being is then identified with a universal subject which is thinking itself in all particular subjects and in all the particular objects of the world. Being thus conceived is, as he admits, a somewhat abstract notion which falls short of most people's understanding of a personal God. At the final stage of his life's work (see the posthumously published *Dall'uomo a Dio*, 1939) he arrives at a more full-blown theism, arguing that God limits himself in the act of creating men who can freely cooperate creatively with him. He believes this to be not merely a view supportive of a religious attitude to life but one that is especially congenial to Christianity.

COLIN LYAS

Varona, Enrique José
Cuban. *b:* 13 April, 1949, Camagüey, Cuba. *d:* 1933. Havana. *Cat:* Positivist; educator; social and political philosopher. *Educ:* Doctorate, University of Havana. *Infls:* Spencer, Comte, Ward, Durkheim, Darwin, Huxley, Bain and Wundt. *Appts:* 1898–1917, Professor of Logic, Ethics, Psychology and Sociology, University of Havana; Secretary of Education in the Cabinet of General Leonard Wood, and reorganized the University of Havana; elected Vice President of Cuba and held that post under General Mario García Mendocal, 1913–7.

Main publications:
(1880) *Conferencias filosóficas, 1a serie: Lógica*, Havana.
(1888) *Conferencias filosóficas, 2a serie: Psicología*, Havana.
(1888) *Conferencias filosóficas, 3a serie: Moral*, Havana.
(1902) *Nociones de lógica*, Havana.
(1907) *El caso de Nietzsche.*
The two following English translations of excerpts of the work of Varona by Willard Trask appear in Aníbal Sánchez Reulet (ed.) (1954) *Contemporary Latin American Philosophy*, Albuquerque: University of New Mexico Press:
'Aphorisms', pp. 16–22.

'The sentiment of solidarity as the foundation of ethics', pp. 3–16.

Secondary literature:
Guadarrama, Pablo and Oropeza, Edel Tussel (1986) *El pensamiento filosófico de Enrique José Varona*, Havana: Editorial Ciencias Sociales.
Vitier, Medardo (1937) *José Varona*, Havana.

Despite his active political career Varona was one of the most prolific Latin American philosophers of the twentieth century, leaving nearly 2,000 published works at the time of his death. He is considered one of the most important positivist thinkers in Latin America.

AMY A. OLIVER

Vasconcelos, José
Mexican. **b:** 1882, Oaxaca, Mexico. **d:** 1959, Mexico City. **Cat:** Aesthetic monist. **Ints:** Metaphysics; ethics; politics. **Infls:** Pythagoras, Plotinus, Schopenhauer and Bergson. **Appts:** Following an education as a lawyer, Vasconcelos joined Caso and others as a founder of the Atheneum of Youth (Ateneo de la Juventud), the group from which a Mexican school of philosophy was to emerge; an active participant in the political struggles of 1910 and thereafter, Vasconcelos was several times exiled, but returned to become Minister of Education and President of the National University; he ceased to be active in politics after an unsuccessful candidature for the Presidency in 1929; his last important post (1939 onwards) was as Director of the National Library.

Main publications:
All in *Obras completas*, 4 vols, Mexico Libreros Mexicanos Unidos, 1957–61.
(1916) *Pitágoras: una teoría del ritmo.*
(1918) *El monismo estetico.*
(1932) *Etica.*
(1936) *Estética.*
(1945) *Logica organica.*
(1952) *Todología: filosofia de la coordinación.*

Secondary literature:
Betancourt, R. F. (1986) 'La filosofia de José Vasconcelos: exposición y valoración', *Logos* (Mexico) 14 (May–Aug): 27–81.
Ferraro, J. (1979) 'Progress through the cosmic race: a Mexican philosophy of history', *International Philosophical Quarterly* 19 (1979): 427–42.
Patino, J. R. (1984) 'Axiologia de José Vasconcelos', *Logos* (Mexico) 12 (May-Aug.): 87–102.

Weinstein, M. E. (1976) *The Polarity of Mexican Thought*, Pennsylvania and London: Pennsylvania State University Press.

Together with his contemporary **Caso**, Vasconcelos is one of the founders of Mexican philosophy and, as with Caso, his thought is best understood as a reaction to Comtean positivism. Vasconcelos drew from **Bergson** the conviction that the order of things is libertarian, and concluded that the deductive and inductive logics on which positivism relied were unable to articulate the forms of free creativity which he discerned as the essential operations of consciousness. At the heart of Vasconcelos's thought is what he terms 'organic logic' (*logica organica*), his attempt to articulate the principles of thought. This logic, however, is only part of his philosophy, which, unlike Caso's, aims to be comprehensive, systematic and prophetic: in his first significant work (on Pythagoras) he claims that the philosopher must interpret the whole of the order of things, akin to an artist working on the vastest of scales, and he never deviated from this view.

The root assumption behind Vasconcelos's organic logic is that the fundamental act of consciousness is cognition not of individual items but of 'wholes' (*conjuntos*), and so organic logic is the elaboration of the principles which govern this act. Further, consciousness derives its unity from the pursuit of purposes. The wholes are greater than the sum of their parts because the wholes are invested with meaning as a result of being realizations of purposes. Purposiveness involves the subordination of both reason and emotion to imagination, the faculty which envisions goals or purposes. The most perfect form of the act of creating wholes is the creative aesthetic act of the artist, who fuses heterogeneous elements into wholes—according to the principles of rhythm, harmony and melody. It is these aesthetic principles, held by Vasconcelos to be a description of the nature of human experience, which he advances as the principles of organic logic: hence the standard description of his philosophy as aesthetic monism.

These principles are applied by Vasconcelos in ethics and politics, on both of which he wrote extensively. The ideal human act is one which is both an end in itself and in which each element is both a means to and a constituent of that end. Analogously, the ideal community is one where the principle of mutual respect and appreciation would be not only a means to permit easy conduct of relations but also an end constitutive of the community. Such a community does not yet exist, but Vasconcelos prophesied in his work setting out his utopia that it would come about. In *La Raza cosmica* (1925; *Obras completas*, vol. 2), his central concern is with racial relations. Generally speaking, history shows that the dominant race or races (presently those involved in Western technocracy) seek to keep themselves racially pure, in order to maintain their advantages over the less developed. However, such a procedure will become otiose when material progress and ease of communication have unified the world. Vasconcelos foresaw and advocated the coming of a global society in which racial fusion would be the norm. The resultant new race, the 'cosmic race' (*raza cosmica*), would emerge from Latin America, the continent most advanced towards racial fusion. The cosmic race will live in an aesthetic society, in which actions will be judged according to their beauty and consequent happiness engendered.

ROBERT WILKINSON

Vassallo, Angel

Argentinian. *b:* 1902, Buenos Aires. *d:* 1978. *Cat:* Metaphysician. *Ints:* Metaphysics; ethics. *Infls:* German idealism, mysticism and Blondel. *Appts:* Professorships in the Universidades del Litoral, La Plata and Buenos Aires; Professor of Theory of Knowledge, Instituto del Profesorado Secundario, Buenos Aires.

Main publications:

(1938) *Cuatro lecciones sobre metafisica.*

(1938) *Nuevos prolegomenos a la metafisica*; second edition, Buenos Aires: Losada, 1945.

(1939) *Elogio de la vigilia*; second, enlarged edition, Buenos Aires: Emece, 1950.

(1940) (with F. Romero and L. Aznar) *Alejandro Korn.*

(1945) *Que es filosofia? O de una sabiduría heroica*; third, revised edition, Buenos Aires: Losada, 1963.

(1945) *Ensayo sobre la ética de Kant y la metafisica de Hegel*, Buenos Aires: Pucara.

(1957) *El problema moral*; fourth edition, Buenos Aires: Catalogos, 1994.

(1968) *Retablo de la filosofia moderna: figuras y fervores*, second edition, Buenos Aires: Catalogos.

Secondary literature:

Gonzalo Casas, Manuel (1942) *Tres irrupciones metafisicas en el pensamiento de Angel Vassallo*, Argentina: Traverso de San Francisco.

The foundation of Vassallo's thought is to be found in his analysis of consciousness. He regarded as false both the thesis that consciousness is a self-contained realm of concepts reflecting a correlative, intelligible reality, and the idealist analysis of being as an infinite subject. The essential property of human consciousness, he asserts, is its finitude: life is a property of concrete subjects. Yet, while in essence finite, human consciousness contains within itself an urge to participate in a transcendent infinite. (There is an obvious and acknowledged similarity between this view and **Blondel**'s assertion that finite, human action points by its very nature from the phenomenal towards the supraphenomenal.) Further, this impulse towards the transcendent is the key to authenticity: the more fully we approximate to the transcendent, the more fully is our life realized.

Granted this identification of authenticity and transcendence, it will be clear that, for Vassallo, the distinction between ethics and metaphysics is unreal. Much of Vassallo's thought is devoted to an analysis of our finite mode of being, and to exploring the possibility of our attaining a full and complete wisdom, of which philosophical thought is one aspect.

Sources: DFN; Ferrater Mora.

ROBERT WILKINSON

Vattimo, Gianni

Italian. *b:* 1936, Turin. *Cat:* Hermeneutic ontologist; aesthetician. *Educ:* Vattimo took his philosophy doctorate under Luigi Pareyson at the University of Turin in the late 1950s; in the 1960s he undertook postdoctoral study at the University of Heidelberg with Hans-Georg Gadamer and Karl Lowith. *Infls:* Kant, Hegel, Adorno, Walter Benjamin, Ernst Bloch, Heidegger, Gadamer, E. Gombrich, Kuhn, Arnold Gehlen, Jacques Lacan, Gilles Deleuze, Michel Foucault, Jean Baudrillard and Lyotard. *Appts:* Succeeded Pareyson as Professor of Aesthetics in the University of Turin; since 1982, Professor of Theoretical Philosophy, University of Turin.

Main publications:

(1961) *Il conetto di fare in Aristotle.*

(1963) *Essere, stoira e linguaggio in Heidegger.*

(1967) *Poesia e ontologia.*

(1968) *Schleiermacher, filosofo dell'interpretazione.*

(1971) *Introduzione a Heiddeger*, Laterza.

(1974) *Il soggetto e la maschere*, Bompiani.

(1981) *Al di la del soggetto: Nietzsche, Heidegger, et l'ermeneutica*, Feltrinelli.

(1981) *Le avventure della differenza*, Turin: Garzanti Editore (English translation, *The Adventure of Difference*, trans. C. Blamires, Oxford: Polity, 1993).

(1983) *Il pensiero debole*, Feltrinelli.

(1985) *Introduzione a Nietzsche*.

(1989) *La societa trasparente*, Turin: Garzanti Editore (English translation, *The Transparent Society*, trans. David Webb, Oxford: Polity, 1992).

(1989) *La fine della modernita* (English translation, *The End of Modernity*, trans. R. N. Snyder, Oxford: Polity Press, 1988).

(1993) 'The truth of hermeneutics', in H. J. Silverman (ed.) *Questioning Foundations: Truth, Subjectivity and Culture*, Continental Philosophy V, London: Routledge, 1993).

Secondary literature:

Very little secondary reading on Vattimo in English is available. J. R. Snyder's introductory essay in his own translation of Vattimo's *The End of Modernity*, as cited above, is particularly commendable.

Vattimo is a philosopher in the post-Heideggerian vein who is much concerned with the problems of nihilism, hermeneutic ontology, aesthetics and postmodern thought. His work is characterized by an attempt to utilize and radicalize **Nietzsche**'s philosophy in order to articulate what 'postmodern' thinking might entail. The attempt to articulate the nature of what postmodern thought entails is dominated by the pivotal notions 'accomplished nihilism' (*il nichilista compiuto*) and 'weak (in the sense of modest) philosophizing' (*il pensiero debole*), both of which derive their sense from his effort to face up to and follow out rather than transcend the implications of Nietzsche's radical nihilism and its exposure of systematic rationalist philosophy as a 'strong' instance of the will to power.

Vattimo's thinking found its individual tenor in the late 1960s when, under the influence of French post-structuralist readings of **Nietzsche** and **Heidegger**, he began to question the hitherto dominant existentialist and neo-Marxist Gramscian strands of postwar Italian philosophy. Adopting Heidegger's 1946 'Letter on humanism' and Nietzsche's philosophical critique of European nihilism, Vattimo contended that with the death of God philosophical humanism loses its principal *raison d'être*, and that with the affirmation of endless becoming as actuality all fixed and progressivist truths are exposed as groundless fictions. In consequence, instead of a philosophy of identity with its unification of Being and history, Vattimo proceeded to affirm a style of thought which gave preeminence to difference and a hermeneutic ontology.

His philosophy of difference argues that there is no world which is outside of interpretation. What constitutes our world is a plethora of subjective and intersubjective interpretations. The only world which can be known is that of difference, the world constituted by different interpretations. The infinite interpretability of reality as articulated by both Nietzsche and **Derrida** promotes what Vattimo describes as a hermeneutic ontology, a world in which an individual confronts neither fixed truths nor things but only yet more interpretive choices. Hermeneutic ontology 'is nothing other than the interpretation of our condition or situation since Being is nothing apart from its event' (*The End of Modernity*, p. 3).

Vattimo suggests that postmodernity constitutes not so much a discernible historical epoch but a reflective awareness of the singular if not monological horizon of post-Cartesian European thought. Vattimo's philosophy of difference refuses closure and effectively pluralizes history. Postmodern thought is grasped as nihilistic in the sense of denying substantive truths; but insofar as it demonstrates that previous universal claims to meaningfulness are but the particular claims of specific individuals, it allows individuals and individual groups to reappropriate universally proclaimed truths as their singular truths. European history can no longer be proclaimed world history and yet the exposure of its not being world history makes European history more discernibly European, that is, not African or Chinese history. *Il pensiero debole* reflects Nietzsche's notion of a 'modest philosophy' spurning the arrogance of universal answers. It is metaphysically but not existentially nihilistic, as it insists that questions of meaning and value can only be raised regionally, and never definitively.

Postmodern thinking represents an accomplished nihilism in a threefold sense. First, *il pensiero debole* involves embracing the transition from denouncing universalizing and totalizing philosophical perspectives to affirming them on a regional basis. Second, such a transition involves an ironic revaluation (*Umwertung*) of philosophical tradition which recognizes that although its key terms and universalistic pursuits are defunct, it is the pursuit and critique of 'truth' which has uncovered the radical pluralism within hermeneutic ontology. Third, the substantive devaluation of rationalist and metaphysical philosophy does not render its language completely redundant. It retains what Vattimo terms a fictive value. The redundancy of the rationalist pursuit of meaning-in-itself does not leave empty the question of what is meaningful for us. Vattimo's nihilism demonstrates that because rationalist or modernist pretensions to truth always were the perspectival projections of a singular group, we are free to experiment with, project and negotiate with a number of philosophical perspectives provided we remember, in a philosophically accomplished manner, their 'fictive' or 'modest' status. Vattimo looks primarily to aesthetic experience for that reminder.

Following Heidegger, Vattimo maintains that the primary value of aesthetic experience is that if offers experiential endorsement of a philosophy of difference. An appreciation of great art reveals an 'ontology of decline', a revelation of the 'fallen' and therefore different nature of past meanings and values. Yet the 'trace' of such meanings keeps the questions and problematics they addressed open, allowing the contemporary world not to be closed off from them but to venture its own perspective upon them. Of greatest importance for Vattimo, finally, is how aesthetic consciousness—understood as the radical disruption of ordinary expectancies—epitomizes the human experience of morality. Aesthetic experience reminds us not only of the fragility of reason's attempt to render the world intelligible but also of how the world can suddenly and inexplicably present itself as different to the expected. Aesthetic consciousness therefore embraces an insight into both the *Abgrund* of mortality and the possibilities of creative otherness within a world of difference.

NICHOLAS DAVEY

Vaz Ferreira, Carlos

Uruguayan. **b:** 15 October 1972, Montevideo, Uruguay. **d:** 3 January 1958, Montevideo. **Cat:** Moral philosopher; social philosopher. **Appts:** At age 25, awarded Chair (*cátedra*) in Philosophy, University of Montevideo, following a university-wide competition; law degree in 1903; a public educator *par excellence* and involved with primary, secondary and higher education throughout his life; among his most important appointments at the University of Montevideo were Professor of Philosophy of Law, 1924–9; Rector, 1929–30, 1935–8, 1938–43; Dean of Arts and Sciences, 1952–5, 1955–8.

Main publications:

Vaz Ferreira's complete works were published by the University Press of Montevideo in 19 volumes in 1957 and in 25 volumes in 1963. Among these, his main writings were:

(1905) *Ideas y observaciones.*
(1908) *Conocimiento y acción.*
(1909) *Moral para intelectuales.*
(1910) *Lógica viva.*
(1933) *Sobre el feminismo.*
(1936) *¿Cuál es el signo moral de la inquietud humana?.*
(1938) *Fermentario.*
(1940) *La actual crisis del mundo desde el punto de vista racional.*
(1957) *Los problemas de la libertad y los del determinismo*: Buenos Aires: Coni Hermanos.

Secondary literature:

(1956) *La filosofía en el Uruguay en el siglo XX*, Mexico: Fondo de Cultura Económica.
Ardao, Arturo (1971) *Etapas de la inteligencia uruguaya*, Montevideo: Universidad de la República.
Zum Felde, Alberto, *Proceso intelectual del Uruguay*, 4 vols, Montevideo: University of Montevideo Press.

One of Latin America's most influential social philosophers in the early twentieth century, Vaz Ferreira distinguishes 'factual' issues from 'normative' issues and develops a moral and social philosophy based on both. For example, in his work on feminism, first published in 1933 but written between 1914 and 1921, Vaz Ferreira analyses 'factual' differences between the sexes such as physical strength, the effects of pregnancy and childbirth, and historical achievements of men and women, and then speculates about 'normative' issues such as the political and civil rights of women, the social life of women and the organization of the family within society. Vaz Ferreira's philosophical method stimulates reflection, well ahead of his time, on topics such as the equitable division of household tasks, divorce, artificial insemination and abortion.

AMY A. OLIVER

Venn, John

British. **b:** 1834, Hull, Yorkshire. **d:** 1923, Cambridge, England. **Cat:** Logician. **Ints:** Deductive and inductive logic; theory of probability. **Educ:** Caius College, Cambridge. **Infls:** George Boole. **Appts:** Fellow of Gonville and Caius College, Cambridge, 1857, and taught logic 1862–1892;

1858, ordained into the Church of England; 1883, took advantage of the Clerical Disabilities Act to retire from holy orders; 1883, Fellow of the Royal Society; from around 1890, devoted himself increasingly to college history; became President of his college in 1903.

Main publications:

(1866) *The Logic of Chance*, London and Cambridge: Macmillan; second edition, 1876; third editon, 1888.

(1881) *Symbolic Logic*, London: Macmillan; second edition, 1894.

(1889) *The Principles of Empirical or Inductive Logic*, London and New York: Macmillan.

Secondary literature:

Keynes, J. M. (1921) *A Treatise on Probability* London: Macmillan.

Lewis, C. I. (1960) *A Survey of Symbolic Logic*, New York: Dover.

Venns's *Logic of Chance* (1866) was one of the earliest sustained accounts of the frequency theory of probability, since defended by von **Mises** and **Reichenbach**. Only the frequency theory, Venn argues, can capture that range of uses of 'probable' for which probability is something objective and measurable. His *Symbolic Logic* (1881) is largely derived from Boole, although the use of diagrams to illustrate the relations between sets has since become associated with Venn's name. The later work, *Inductive Logic* (1889), is largely a critical commentary on Mill. Mill's famous methods, Venn argues, will only be applicable where the possible causes for a given effect are (i) finite in number, and (ii) already known, which will only rarely be the case. This line of criticism earned Venn a reputation as a sceptic about induction.

Sources: DNB; WWW; Metz; Passmore 1957.

ANDREW PYLE

Vernadsky, Vladimir Ivanovich

Russian. *b:* 28 February (12 March N.S.) 1863, St Petersburg. *d:* 6 January 1945, Moscow. *Cat:* Philosopher of science. *Educ:* Graduated in Physics and Mathematics at University of St Petersburg in 1885. *Infls:* Fedorov and Le Roy. *Appts:* 1890–8, lecturer in Mineralogy and Crystallography; 1898–1911, Professor of Mineralogy, University of Moscow; 1915–17, 1926–30, Chair of Commission for the Study of the Natural Productive Forces of Russia (KEPS); 1922–39, Director of Radium Institute; 1927–45, Director of the Biogeochemical Laboratory of the Soviet Academy of Sciences.

Main publications:

(1922) *Ocherki i rechi* [Essays and Speeches], Petrograd.

(1988) *Filosofskie mysli naturalista* [Philosophical Thoughts of a Naturalist], Moscow.

Secondary literature:

Bailes, K. E. (1990) *Science and Russian Culture in an Age of Revolutions: V. I. Vernadsky and his Scientific School, 1863–1945*, Bloomington: Indiana University Press.

Vucinich, A. (1991) 'The struggle for the freedom of science in the Soviet Union: V. I. Vernadsky', *Minerva* 29: 476–86.

Born into a noble family, and son of a well-known liberal economist, Vernadsky joined a liberal student circle, and went on to become a prominent *zemstvo* liberal. He cofounded (with **Struve** among others) Soiuz Osvobozhdeniia [Union of Liberation] in 1903, and the Constitutional Democratic Party in 1905. He served on the State Council from 1906 to 1911, in which year he resigned his chair at the University of Moscow in protest against government interference. He was briefly Assistant Minister for Education in the Kerensky government. Unlike many non-Marxist scholars (including his son George, who became an eminent émigré historian of Russia), he opted to remain in the new Soviet Union.

First and foremost a scientist, Vernadsky was the founder of biogeochemistry, the study of the chemical composition and distribution of living matter. In the early 1900s he was the leading exponent in Russia of a 'scientific worldview'. His position was more subtle than the uncompromising positivism of the Russian nihilists: although insisting on the reality of the world, he stressed the dubitability of most current scientific knowledge, and its nourishment by philosophical and religious ideas. He also linked both the nature and the development of science with democratic institutions.

Vernadsky went on to develop a holistic worldview. Extrapolating from his scientific work on the exchange of matter between living and inert structures, he emphasized the 'biosphere' as a new geological stratum of living matter, and then, following **Le Roy**, added the 'noosphere' as a new stratum dominated by freely thinking humanity, radically changing the biosphere in its own interests. These ideas are now seen as anticipating some features of contemporary environmentalism.

After the Revolution, Vernadsky resisted the encroachment of dialectical materialism on natural science, and in particular the appointment of Deborin and others to the Academy of Sciences in 1929. He engaged in a debate with **Deborin** in the early 1930s, during which he asserted his own 'philosophical scepticism' in the face of charges of eclecticism and sympathy with religion and idealism. In the Stalinist era, Vernadsky was generally pilloried for advancing a vitalist variant of idealism, although after Stalin's death **Kedrov** and others revived his philosophical ideas, attempting to demonstrate their compatibility with dialectical materialism. Although many of his writings were published for the first time, they were heavily censored. It was not until *perestroika* that his *Philosophical Thoughts of a Naturalist* (1988) was issued without cuts, and his assertion of the superiority of scientific knowledge to dialectical materialism made unambiguous.

COLIN CHANT

Villoro Toranzo, Luis

Mexican. *b:* 3 November 1922, Barcelona (of Mexican parents). *Cat:* Historian of ideas. *Educ:* MA and Doctorate in Philosophy, Universidad Nacional Autónoma de México; postgraduate study at the Sorbonne and at the Ludwigsuniversität in Munich. *Appts:* Taught at the Universidad Nacional Autónoma de México and the Universidad Autónoma Metropolitana/Iztapalapa; President of the Asociación Filosófica de México; Mexico's Ambassador to UNESCO.

Main publications:

(1950) *Los grandes momentos del indigenismo en México*, Mexico: El Colegio de Mexico.
(1961) *La crítica del positivismo básico a la metafisica.*
(1963) *La idea y el ente en la filosofia de Descartes*, Mexico City: UNAM.
(1975) *Estudios sobre Husserl*, Mexico: Universidad Nacional Autónoma de México.
(1982) *Creer, saber, conocer*, Mexico: Siglo Veintiuno Editores.
(1983) *El proceso ideológico de la revolución de independencia*, Mexico: Universidad Nacional Autónoma de México.
(1985) *El concepto de la ideologia y otros ensayos*, Mexico: Fondo de Cultura Económica.
(1989) *Sahagun; or, The Limits of the Discovery of the Other*, 1992 Lecture Series Working Papers, no. 2, College Park, Maryland.

In the 1950s Villoro was a member of the Hyperion group, a philosophical circle that discussed Mexican identity. Villoro has held editorial positions with several journals including *Revista de la Universidad de México, El espectador* and *Crítica: revista hispanoamericana de filosofia*. He has translated works of **Husserl**, **Marcel** and others into Spanish. His books of 1950, 1983 and 1985 are perhaps the most significant. In *Creer, saber, conocer* (1982), he tries to solve the problem of scepticism, defending a conception of knowledge as an objectively justified belief.

AMY A. OLIVER

Virasoro, Miguel Angel

Argentinian. *b:* April 1900, Santa Fé, Argentina. *d:* 1966, Buenos Aires. *Cat:* 'Dialectical existentialist'. *Ints:* Metaphysics. *Educ:* Initially a student of Law at La Plata, Virasoro switched to Philosophy. *Infls:* Hegel, Fichte, Gentile and Scheler.. *Appts:* Taught Modern and Contemporary Philosophy at the University of Buenos Aires (1939–55), then at Cordoba, Bahía Blanca and Mendoza; regarded as one of the most distinguished Argentine thinkers of his generation.

Main publications:

(1928) *Una teoría del yo como cultura.*
(1932) *La logica de Hegel.*
(1942) *La libertad, la existencia y el ser.*
(1964) *Para una nueva idea del hombre y de la antropologia filosófica*, Tucuman: Universidad Nacional de Tucuman.
(1965) *La intuición metafisica*, Buenos Aires: Ediciones C. Lohle.

Secondary literature:

Arteta, E. N. (1945) *La libertad, la existencia y la dialéctica: En torno de la filosofia de Miguel Angel Virasoro* Universidad (Santa Fé) iv, 18: 81–162.

The overriding aim of Virasoro's philosophy is to synthesize the two currents of thought he regarded as fundamental, Hegelianism and existentialism. Existence has a dialectical character, manifest not only in its evolution but also in the bedrock metaphysical intuition (cf. 1965) by which we are aware of it. Our root experience of existence is of a finitude which at the same time reveals itself as absolute, as 'infinite anxiety' (*ansiedad infinita*). Anxiety is to be distinguished from angst (*angustia*): whilst the latter is purely negative, anxiety has a positive aspect, connoting a hunger for existence, the immanent impulse and invariable process of self-creation. Existence is anxiety, whilst Being is satiety (*saciedad*), and the ultimate substance of existence is freedom (cf. 1942). Existence emerges from nothingness and chooses being; it is a free realization of itself, manifesting itself in the historical destiny of mankind. The most fundamental of all disciplines, therefore, is what Virasoro calls philosophical anthropology (cf. 1964), the study of this destiny.

ROBERT WILKINSON

Vivekananda, (Datta, Narendranath)
Indian. *b:* 12 January 1863, Calcutta. *d:* 4 July 1902, Calcutta. *Cat:* Neo-Vedantist. *Ints:* Metaphysics; social philosophy. *Educ:* Studied Law in Calcutta, 1878–84; appointed Ramakrishna's successor in 1886. *Infls:* Influenced by Ramakrishna Paramahamsa, the ideas of the liberal reformist movement—the Brahmo Samaj—of which he was a member while a student at college and Advaita Vedanta. *Appts:* Founded the Ramakrishna Mission (religious order) near Calcutta, May 1897.

Main publications:
(1924) *The Complete Works of Swami Vivekananda*, 6 vols, Mayavati, Almora: Advaita Ashrama (containing his major works *Bhakti Yoga, Jnana Yoga, Karma Yoga, Raja Yoga, Inspired Talks* and *Chicago Addresses*).
(1946) *On India and Her Problems*, Mayavati, Almora: Advaita Ashrama
(1953) Swami Nikhilananda, *Vivekananda: The Yogas and Other Works*, New York: Ramakrishna–Vivekananda Centre (also containing the above-mentioned works of Vivekananda).

Secondary literature:
Isherwood, Christopher (1986) *Ramakrishna and His Disciples*, Vedanta Society of California.
Nikhilananda, Swami (1953) *Vivekananda: A Life*, New York: Ramakrishna–Vivekananda Centre.
Vivekananda (1957) *My Life and Mission*, Calcutta.
Williams, George M. (1974) *The Quest for Meaning of Swami Vivekananda*, California: New Horizons Press.

Vivekananda can be regarded as a modern exponent of Advaita Vedanta. According to Vivekananda *Brahman*, which is non-dual, eternal, qualityless, indescribable and beyond space and time, is Reality. Positing a non-dual *Brahman* as Reality, as he recognized, raises difficulties in explaining the existence of a universe with its natural phenomena and objects that are distinct

and finite. In other words, how does the infinite *Brahman* become the finite universe? According to Vivekananda *Brahman* or the Absolute becomes the universe by coming through time (*kala*), space (*desa*) and causation (*nimitta*). 'Time, space and causation are like the glass through which the Absolute is seen, and when It is seen on the lower side it appears as the universe' (*Complete Works*, vol. II, p. 130). At this juncture, it is natural to ask the question as to why the infinite *Brahman* should become finite. To this, according to Vivekananda, there is no answer since the question posed does not make sense. It is nonsensical since it requires the application of concepts to *Brahman* that are inapplicable to it.

According to Vivekananda the ultimate goal for all individuals is awareness of *Brahman*. And this realization is possible through different forms of discipline (*yoga*) which reflect the different dominant tendencies, like reason and emotions, that are found in individuals. These are *jnana yoga, bhakti yoga, karma yoga*, and *raja yoga*.

In *jnana yoga* realization is achieved through the knowledge (*jnana*) that the phenomenal world—a product of ignorance (*avidya*)—is unreal. In *bhakti yoga* realization is achieved through love and selfless devotion (*bhakti*) to a personal God (*Ishvara*)—the relative aspect of *Brahman*. *Karma yoga* brings about realization through selfless action (*karma*). In other words it is doing good for good rather than doing good with selfish motives:

> Although a man has not studied a single system of philosophy, although he does not believe in any God, and never has believed, although he has not prayed even once in his whole life, if the simple power of good actions has brought him to that state where he is ready to give up his life and all else for others, he has arrived at the same point to which the religious man will come through his prayers and the philosopher through his knowledge. (1924, vol. I, p. 84)

Realization through *raja yoga* takes place through direct awareness of *Brahman* brought about by a number of ethical, physical and psychical exercises.

Vivekananda considered himself to be a socialist. Although there were a number of reforms taking place in areas like child marriage and widow remarriage at the time in India, he perceived these as peripheral. He regarded the improvement of the conditions of the masses to be the main task.

> Remember that the nation lives in the cottage. But, alas, nobody ever did anything for them. Our modern reformers are very busy about widow remarriage. Of course, I am a sympathiser in every reform, but the fate of the nation does not depend upon the number of husbands their widows get, but upon the conditions of the masses. (1946, p. 72)

He felt that social reform could take place only if the lower classes themselves supported it. The way the lower classes could be aroused was through religion and education. According to him, religion was an important tool for social reform in India since the 'Hindu man drinks religiously sleeps religiously marries religiously and robs religiously' (1957, p. 3).

It would not be trite to say that Vivekananda was responsible for bringing Vedantism to the West and popularizing it within India. And, without doubt, he also played a major role in raising Indian national consciousness.

INDIRA MAHALINGAM CARR

Vlastos, Gregory

American. **b:** 27 July 1907, Istanbul (Greek/Scottish parentage; emigrated to America, 1925). **d:** 12 October 1991, Berkeley, California. **Cat:** Historian of Greek philosophy. **Ints:** Political philosophy; philosophy of religion. **Educ:** Robert College, Istanbul, Chicago Theological Seminary and Harvard University. **Infls:** Analytic school (A. N. Whitehead and Max Black), Anglo-American liberal political tradition and Christian socialism. **Appts:** 1931–48, Lecturer, Associate Professor, then full Professor of Philosophy, Queen's University, Ontario, Canada; 1948–55, Professor of Philosophy, Cornell; 1955–76, Stuart Professor of Philosophy, Princeton; 1977–87, Mills Professor of Philosophy, University of California at Berkeley; numerous visiting appointments in the USA and Europe;, received many honorary degrees.

Main publications:

(1937) 'Organic categories in Whitehead', *Journal of Philosophy* 34: 253–63; reprinted in G. L. Kline, *Whitehead: Essays in His Philosophy*, Englewood Cliffs, NJ: Prentice-Hall, 1963.
(1942) 'The religious foundations of democracy: fraternity and liberty; fraternity and equality', *Journal of Religion* 22: 1–19, 137–55.

(1953) 'Isonomia', *American Journal of Philosophy* 74: 337–66.
(1954) 'The third man argument in the *Parmenides*', *Philosophical Review* 63: 319–49; reprinted, with addenda, in R. E. Allen (ed.) *Studies in Plato's Metaphysics*, London, 1965, and in the Bobbs-Merrill Reprint Series in Philosophy, PHIL.
(1962) 'Justice and equality', in R. Brandt (ed.) *Social Justice*, Englewood Cliffs, NJ: Prentice-Hall; reprinted in J. Feinberg, *Moral Concepts*, Oxford Readings in Philosophy, Oxford: Oxford University Press, 1969, and in J. Waldron, *Theories of Rights*, Oxford Readings in Philosophy, Oxford: Oxford University Press, 1984.
(1973) *Platonic Studies*, Princeton, NJ: Princeton University Press; reprinted 1981.
(1975) *Plato's Universe*, Oxford: Oxford University Press.
(1983) 'The Socratic Elenchus', *Oxford Studies in Ancient Philosophy* 1: 27–58.
(1991) *Socrates: Ironist and Moral Philosopher*, Cambridge: Cambridge University Press.
(1994) *Socratic Studies*, ed. M. Burnyeat, Cambridge: Cambridge University Press.

Secondary literature:

Kahn, C. H. (1992) 'Vlastos' Socrates', *Phronesis* 37: 233–58.
Lee, E. N., Mourelatos, A. P. D. and Rorty, R. M. (eds) (1973) *Exegesis and Argument: Studies in Greek Philosophy presented to Gregory Vlastos*, *Phronesis*, Supp. 1 (contains complete bibliography on Greek philosophy and selection of other writings, up to 1973).

Vlastos is important for work in two related fields. First, he examined the religious and ethical foundations of democracy, for example in his 1942 article and especially in his analytically presented 1962 article (based on a critique of Plato). He argued strongly for a theory of social justice based upon recognition of equal worth of individuals (and gave frequent active support to causes of the liberal left). Second, his major contribution lay in pioneering the application of contemporary analytic philosophical techniques to the exegesis of Plato, notably in his 1954 article, a detailed examination of the apparent self-predication of Plato's Forms in *Parmenides*, a study which sparked off many other contributions and to which Vlastos himself frequently returned. In the later part of his career he worked extensively on Socrates and developed an argument (culminating in *Socrates*, 1991) for a distinct Socratic philosophy within Plato's early dialogues. Perhaps more than any of his contemporaries, Vlastos combined analytic rigour with classical scholarship and a strong historical sense, the latter notably in his 1953 article and numerous other contributions to pre-Socratic and Greek historical thought (see bibliography in Lee *et al.* 1973). He is also significant as a teacher of a distinguished generation of American scholars of Greek philosophy.

Sources: A. A. Long, obituary, *Independent*, 23 Oct 1991; M. Burnyeat, obituary, *Phronesis* 37, 2, 1992; A. P. D. Mourelatos, obituary, *Gnomon* 65, 4: 378–82, 1993; in preparation, D. W. Graham (ed.) *Miscellaneous Papers*, 2 vols.

CHRIS EMLYN-JONES

Voegelin, Eric Herman Wilhelm

German-American. *b:* 3 January 1901, Cologne, Germany. *d:* 19 January 1985, Stanford, California. *Cat:* Political philosopher; philosopher of history. *Ints:* Man; society; civilization. *Educ:* University of Vienna. *Infls:* Literary influences: Plato, Karl Krauss and Max Weber. Personal: Alfred Schutz. *Appts:* 1923–38, Assistant, Privatdozent (1928), then Associate Professor (1929), Law Faculty, University of Vienna; 1943–58, Associate Professor, Professor (1946), then Boyd Professor (1952) of Government, Louisiana State University; 1958–69, Professor of Political Science, University of Munich; 1969–85, Senior Research Fellow, Hoover Institution, Stanford.

Main publications:

(1956–1988) *Order and History*, 5 vols, Baton Rouge: Louisiana State University Press:
1. *Israel and Revelation*, 1956.
2. *The World of the Polis*, 1957.
3. *Plato and Aristotle*, 1957.
4. *The Ecumenic Age*, 1974.
5. *In Search of Order*, 1988.

(1966) *Anamnesis: Zur Theorie der Geschichte und Politik*, Munich: Piper (English translation, *Anamnesis*, trans. and ed. by Gerhard Niemeyer, Indiana: University of Notre Dame Press, 1978).

Secondary literature:

Sandoz, Ellis (ed.) (1982) *Eric Voegelin's Thought: A Critical Appraisal*, North Carolina: Duke University Press.
Webb, Eugene (1982) *Eric Voegelin, Philosopher of History*, Seattle: University of Washington Press.

Forced out of his post at Vienna after the Nazi annexation of Austria in 1936, Voegelin fled to Switzerland and then emigrated to the USA in 1938.

His researches, unbound by disciplinary conventions, extended to political science, comparative religions, history, archaeology, ethnology, law, literary criticism and philosophy. He devoted his life's work to an analysis of the nature and sources of order and disorder in human existence. His search for understanding unfolded in a long series of writings, including his monumental *Order and History* (1956–88), which reflected his antipathy to the claims of ideological fanaticism. Voegelin sought the 'true being' of man and society through a comprehensive philosophy of human existence which would transcend what he called the 'immanentist' limits of modern thought. His philosophy aimed to renew both man's sense of his rootedness in historical process and his awareness of his 'openness' towards the transcendent reality of 'God'. Voegelin is considered by some to be one of the most penetrating and challenging political philosophers of our century. His writings became particularly popular among the dissidents of Central Europe in the decades preceding the collapse of Communism.

Sources: DAS; Sills 18.

STEPHEN MOLLER

Volkelt, Johannes

German. *b:* 21 July 1848, Bielitz-Biala, Silesia. *d:* 8 May 1930, Leipzig, Germany. *Cat:* Neo-Kantian; metaphysician. *Ints:* Aesthetics. *Infls:* Hegel, Schopenhauer and Eduard von Hartmann.

Main publications:

(1886) *Erfahrung und Denken*, Hamburg and Leipzig: Voss.
(1905–14) *System der Ästhetik* 3 vols, Munich: Beck.
(1918) *Gewissheit und Wahrheit*, Munich: Beck.
(1925) *Phänomenologie und Metaphysik der Zeit*, Munich: Beck.
(1928) *Das Problem der Individualität*, Munich: Beck.

Secondary literature:

Neumann, Thomas (1978) *Gewissheit und Skepsis. Untersuchungen zur Philosophie Johannes Volkelts*, Amsterdam: Rodopi.

Volkelt at first was himself a speculative metaphysician. However, after a sceptical period, he came to advocate a critical metaphysics which was based on the acceptance of an extra-subjective reality, namely what he called the 'trans-subjective minimum'. Together with **Liebmann**, he is sometimes counted among the metaphysical directions of neo-Kantianism. His interpretetation of time and individuality is a good example of his critical-realistic metaphysics. He was also important for his systematic treatment of aesthetics.

MANFRED KUEHN

Volsky, Stanislav (pen-name of Andrei Vladimirovich Sokolov)

Russian. *b:* 1880, Moscow. *d:* c. 1936, Soviet Gulag. *Cat:* Nietzschean Marxist. *Ints:* Ethics; social and political philosophy. *Educ:* Studied at Moscow University, from which he was expelled for radical activities in 1899. *Infls:* Literary influences include Marx and Nietzsche; personal influences include A. A. Bogdanov and A. V. Lunacharsky. *Appts:* Political activist, journalist; until 1927 held minor posts in Gosplan and other Soviet agencies; from *c.* 1930 worked as a translator.

Main publications:

(1906) *K voprosu o natsionalizatsi zemli* [On the Question of the Nationalization of Land], St Petersburg.

(1906) *Sotsializm i russkaia obshchina* [Socialism and the Russian Village Commune], St Petersburg.

(1909) *Filosofiia bor'by: Opyt postroeniia etiki marksizma* [The Philosophy of Struggle: An Essay in Marxist Ethics], Moscow.

(1917) *Sotsial'naia revoliutsiia na Zapade i v Rossii* [The Social Revolution in the West and in Russia], Moscow: Studencheskoe izdatel'stvo.

(1919) *Teoriia i praktika anarkhizma* [The Theory and Practice of Anarchism], third edition, Moscow: Gosudarstvennoe izdatel'stvo.

(1920) *Dans le royaume de la famine et de la haine. La Russie bolchéviste*, Paris.

(*c.* 1928) *Foma Kampanella* [Tommaso Campanella], Moscow and Leningrad: Gosudarstvennoe izdatel'stvo.

Secondary literature:

Anon. (1929) 'Vol'skii', in *Bol'shaia sovetskaia entsiklopediia* [Great Soviet Encyclopedia] (first edition), vol. 13, cols 66–7.

Kline, George L. (1979) 'The Nietzschean Marxism of Stanislav Volsky', in Anthony M. Mlikotin (ed.), *Western Philosopical Systems in Russian Literature*, Los Angeles: University of Southern California Press, pp. 177–95.

Like the other Russian 'Nietzschean Marxists' of the early twentieth century (**Bogdanov**, **Lunacharsky** and V. A. Bazarov) Volsky saw that, despite differences on other points (such as egalitarianism versus elitism), Marx and **Nietszche** shared a powerful future orientation and a conviction that the just society (Marx) and the highest possible culture (Nietzsche) both stand 'beyond (bourgeois-Christian) good and evil'. According to Volsky, individuals in the distant future, under socialism, will be 'freed from the numbing pattern of coercive norms' and the 'idea of duty', the 'inevitable companion of bourgeois society' (1909, p. 272), and will become free, creative, passionate and proud. 'Struggle', he insisted, 'is the joy of existence' and 'socialism is freedom of struggle' (pp. 306, 302). Developing Nietzsche's insight that 'enemy' means not scoundrel but adversary, Volsky celebrated the cultural *agon* of 'friend-enemies', free and fervent defenders of opposed cultural values and ideals. But he saw clearly that in **Lenin**'s Russia of 1917–20 there was neither freedom nor the joy of cultural creativity but only dull submission to brutal repression.

GEORGE KLINE

von Wright, G(eorg) H(enrik)

Finnish. *b:* 1916, Helsinki. *Cat:* Analytical philosopher. *Ints:* Ethics; philosophy of mind; logic; epistemology. *Educ:* Universities of Helsinki and Cambridge. *Infls:* Eino Kaila, G. E. Moore and Ludwig Wittgenstein. *Appts:* 1946–61, Professor of Philosophy, Helsinki University; 1948–51, Professor of Philosophy, University of Cambridge; 1961–86, Research Professor, Academy of Finland; 1965–77, Andrew D. White Professor-at-Large, Cornell University.

Main publications:

(1951) *A Treatise on Induction and Probability*, London: Routledge & Kegan Paul.

(1957) *The Logical Problem of Induction*, Oxford: Basil Blackwell; second edition, 1965 (first published as volume III in the series *Acta Philosophica Fennica*, 1941).

(1957) *Logical Studies*, London: Routledge & Kegan Paul.

(1963) *Norm and Action: A Logical Enquiry*, London: Routledge & Kegan Paul.

(1963) *The Varieties of Goodness*, London: Routledge & Kegan Paul.

(1968) *An Essay in Deontic Logic and the General Theory of Action*, Amsterdam: North-Holland Publishing Co.

(1971) *Explanation and Understanding*, Ithaca: Cornell University Press.

(1974) *Causality and Determinism*, New York: Columbia University Press.

(1982) *Wittgenstein*, Minneapolis: University of Minnesota Press.

(1983–4) *Philosophical Papers of G. H. von Wright*, vol. 1, *Practical Reason*; vol. 2, *Philosophical Logic*, vol. 3, *Truth, Knowledge, and Modality*, Oxford: Basil Blackwell.

Secondary literature:

Schilpp, P. A. and Hahn, L. E. (eds) (1989) *The Philosophy of Georg Henrik von Wright*, La Salle: Open Court.

Von Wright's first important work concerned the 'problem of induction'. Philosophers have been troubled by the thought that we can have no reason to think that our past or present experience is a reliable guide to the future, and this thought has been a major part of philosophical scepticism about knowledge. Von Wright argued that there was no real problem of induction. That it is impossible to guarantee that the future will be, in certain respects, like the past was, he claimed, a disguised tautology, a claim about language usage, and thus free of all sceptical implications.

In 1949 he conceived of the idea of a general theory of modality, having branches such as epistemic logic (the study of the formal properties of such terms as 'know' and 'believe') and deontic logic (the study of the formal properties of normative concepts). In particular, with an article in *Mind* in 1951, he initiated a major research programme in deontic logic and he has continued to contribute to this important area, as in, for instance, the first of the two series of Gifford Lectures he delivered in 1959 and 1960 (subsequently published as *Norm and Action*, 1963).

Probably von Wright's major influence has been in the area of ethics and action. In the first series of Gifford Lectures (subsequently published as *The Varieties of Goodness*, 1963) he argued that a correct ethical theory must be broadly teleological, based upon the notion of individual human welfare. Although his theory had affinities with utilitarianism, he gave a central place to the idea of the virtues—a conception which had been much neglected in analytical ethics for a considerable time.

Since **Wittgenstein**'s death, von Wright has been one of the three executors of his unpublished writings. 'Wittgenstein influenced my intellectual development more than anyone else could have done ... I was not able to follow him very well in my own work ... because his *style* of thought is so different from my own' (1982, p. 11). Most of von Wright's work is characterized

by painstaking clarification and analysis of concepts.

Sources: Personal communication.

ANTHONY ELLIS

Vuillemin, Jules

French. *b:* 1920. *Cat:* Historian of philosophy; epistemologist. *Ints:* Theories of science and mathematics; metaphysics; Kant and the Kantian heritage. *Educ:* University of Strasbourg. *Infls:* Martial Gueroult, Marx, Søren Kierkegaard, Kant, Hermann Cohen, Bertrand Russell, Rudolf Carnap and Nelson Goodman. *Appts:* Taught philosophy at the Faculté des Lettres de Clermond-Ferrand; since 1962, Professor of Philosophie de la Connaissance, Collège de France (successor to Maurice Merleau-Ponty).

Main publications:

(1948) *Essai sur la signification de la mort*, Paris: PUF.
(1954) *L'Héritage kantien et la révolution copernicienne, Fichte, Cohen, Heidegger*, Paris: PUF.
(1955) *Physique et métaphysique kantiennes*, Paris: PUF.
(1967) *De la logique a la théologie, cinq études sur Aristotle*, Paris: Flammarion.
(1968) *Leçons sur la première philosophie de Russell*, Paris: Armand Colin.
(1971) *La Logique et le monde sensible, étude sur les théories contemporaines de l'abstraction*, Paris: Flammarion.

Secondary literature:

Jolivert, Jean (1973) Review of *La Logique et le monde sensible* (1971), *Revue Philosophique de la France et de l'Étranger* 163: 379–83.

A disciple of Martial **Gueroult**, Vuillemin is one of the foremost French historians of philosophy and epistemologists. A prolific writer, his studies cover a wide range of topics. His early writings were inspired by Marxism and existentialism. But his philosophy soon took a different turn, finding a fresh point of departure in the tradition of critical Kantianism. This led him to take up the critical project of Kant anew, for the present day, integrating it with the lessons of the analytical movement in philosophy (Bertrand **Russell**, G. E. **Moore**, Rudolph **Carnap**, also Nelson **Goodman**). Thus the guiding aim of Vuillemin's interrogation of the history of philosophy, evident in his *L'Héritage kantien* (1954) and in all his subsequent writings, is to show how the philosophy (or metaphysics) and the science of a particular period are engaged on a cooperative task, that there is symbiosis of the two: the scientist is assured by the philosopher that the world really is what he assumes it to be; the philosopher is assured by the scientist that his a priori theories are vindicated by every appeal to the facts. In pursuing this ambitious objective, Vuillemin has produced works that are widely praised for their great precision and rigour.

Sources: Huisman.

STEPHEN MOLLER

Vvedensky, Aleksandr Ivanovich

Russian. *b:* 1856, Tambov province. *d:* 7 March 1925, Leningrad. *Cat:* Neo-Kantian. *Educ:* Studied Mathematics at the Universities of Moscow and St Petersburg; changed to Philosophy at St Petersburg, studying under Vladislavlev, the first Russian translator of Kant's *Critique of Pure Reason*. *Infls:* Hume and Kant. *Appts:* From 1890, Professor of Philosophy, University of St Petersburg.

Main publications:

(1888) *Opyt postroeniia teorii materii na printsipakh kriticheskoi filosofii* [Attempt at the Construction of a Theory of Matter on the Principles of Critical Philosophy], St Petersburg.
(1901) *Filosofskie ocherki* [Philosophical Essays], St Petersburg.
(1912) *Logika kak chast' teorii poznaniia* [Logic as a Part of the Theory of Knowledge], St Petersburg.
(1914) *Psikhologiia bez vsiakoi metafiziki* [Psychology without any Metaphysics], St Petersburg.

(1973) (ed. Louis J. Shein) *Readings in Russian Philosophical Thought: Logic and Aesthetics*, The Hague: Mouton (includes brief translated extracts from *Logic as a Part of the Theory of Knowledge*, second revised edition, St Petersburg, 1912).

Secondary literature:

Zenkovsky, V. V. (1953) *A History of Russian Philosophy*, trans. George L. Kline, London: Routledge & Kegan Paul, vol. 2, pp. 678–87.

Vvedensky was the foremost Russian neo-Kantian. The defining characteristic of his 'logicist' version of the critical philosophy was his insistence that the law of contradiction is only necessary or 'natural' for phenomena or 'representations', whereas it is 'normative' only for thought; he concluded that a priori knowledge, or science, is necessarily limited to phenomena. In this way he felt that he was giving a 'new and easy proof of philosophical criticism'. But Vvedensky found it intolerable to be imprisoned in the world of phenomena, and looked to philosophy for a complete worldview. Although things in themselves are inaccessible to a priori cognition, their existence may be inferred from the 'a posteriori elements' of experience. He also allowed undemonstrated faith, associated with the 'moral sense', as a way other than knowledge of excluding doubt; but although he agreed with Kant that practical reason leads to faith in the existence of God, the immortality of the soul and freedom of the will, he believed that it also requires faith in the existence of other minds.

COLIN CHANT

W

Wahl, Jean

French. **b:** 1888, Marseilles. **d:** 1974, Paris. **Cat:** Existentialist; poet. **Ints:** Phenomenology; dialectics; metaphysics; anti-Hegelianism. **Educ:** Passed his agrégation in 1910. **Infls:** Kierkegaard, Hegel, Heidegger, Jaspers, Marcel and Nietzsche. **Appts:** Professor of Philosophy, Sorbonne; created Collège Philosophique; Director of *Revue de Métaphysique et de Morale*; President of the Société Française de Philosophie.

Main publications:

(1929) *Le Malheur de la conscience dans la philosophie de Hegel*, Paris: Rieder.
(1948) *The Philosopher's Way*, New York: Oxford University Press.
(1951) *La Pensée de l'existence*, Paris: Flammarion.
(1953) *Traité de métaphysique*, Paris: Payot.
(1959) *Les Philosophes de l'existence*, Paris: Armand Colin (English translation, *Philosophers of Existence: An Introduction to the Basic Thought of Kierkegaard, Jaspers, Marcel, Sartre*, London: Routledge & Kegan Paul, 1969).
(1962) *Tableau de la philosophie française*, Paris: Gallimard.
(1964) *L'Expérience métaphysique*, Paris: Flammarion.

Secondary literature:

Alquié, F. (1954) 'Jean Wahl et le philosophie', *Critique*, June 1954.
Levinas, E. (1976) 'Jean Wahl sans avoir ni être', in *Jean Wahl et Gabriel Marcel*, Paris: Beauchesne.
Ricoeur, P. (1976) 'Entre Gabriel Marcel et Jean Wahl', in *Jean Wahl et Gabriel Marcel*, Paris: Beauchesne.

The importance of Jean Wahl to twentieth-century French philosophy is mainly as a teacher. His lectures at the Sorbonne were influential in disseminating existentialist and Hegelian thought. Wahl's philosophy concentrates on the opposition of Kierkegaard and Hegel and his existentialism is presented in opposition to Hegelian dialectics. This approach came to form the critical aspects of the reception of Hegel by French philosophers in the 1930s and beyond (his lectures on **Bergson, Nietzsche, Husserl** and **Heidegger** were collected together and published by the Sorbonne in *Cours*, Paris: Centre de Documentation Universitaire, 1961). The influence of Wahl's teaching was reinforced by the many important professional positions he held and by his efforts to disseminate philosophy outside academic spheres, notably through the Collège Philosophique.

Sources: Catalogue of Bibliothèque Nationale, Paris.

JAMES WILLIAMS

Waismann, Friedrich

Austrian. **b:** 1896, Vienna. **d:** 1959, Oxford. **Cat:** Linguistic philosopher. **Ints:** Philosophy of mathematics; philosophy of science; philosophy of language; philosophical methodology. **Educ:** University of Vienna. **Infls:** Ludwig Wittgenstein. **Appts:** 1937–8, Lecturer, University of Cambridge; 1946–8, Lecturer in the Philosophy of Science and Mathematics, University of Oxford; 1948–50, Senior Lecturer in the Philosophy of Mathematics, University of Oxford; 1950–5, Reader in the Philosophy of Mathematics, University of Oxford; 1955–9, Reader in the Philosophy of Science, University of Oxford.

Main publications:

(1936) *Einführung in das mathematisches Denken*, Vienna: Springer (English translation, *Introduction to Mathematical Thinking*, New York: Ungar, 1951).
(1945) 'Verifiability', *Proceedings of the Aristotelian Society*, Supplementary Volume.
(1949–52) 'Analytic-synthetic', *Analysis* 10.2, 11.2, 11.3, 11.6, 13.1, 13.4.
(1965) *The Principles of Linguistic Philosophy*, ed. Rom Harré, London: Macmillan.
(1968) *How I See Philosophy*, ed. Rom Harré, London: Macmillan.
(1977) *Philosophical Papers*, ed. Brian McGuinness, Dordrecht: Reidel.
(1979) *Wittgenstein and the Vienna Circle*, ed. Brian McGuinness, trans. Joachim Schulte and Brian McGuinness, Oxford: Blackwell.

(1982) *Lectures on the Philosophy of Mathematics*, ed. Wolfgang Grassl, Amsterdam: Rodopi.

As a member of the Vienna Circle Waismann worked closely with **Wittgenstein** on a book expounding the latter's ideas (a version of which was subsequently published as *The Principles of Linguistic Philosophy*, 1965). In 1935, Wittgenstein broke off the collaboration, but Waismann's subsequent work continued to be heavily influenced by his views.

Waismann is largely remembered as the expositor of Wittgenstein's views. Some of his own developments of these views, however, were important. Perhaps the most influential was that of the 'open texture' of language: although there may be perfectly good rules for the use of our concepts, these cover only the usual circumstances and there are imaginable circumstances in which we should not know whether they applied. This phenomenon, which Waismann considered a virtue of language rather than a vice, had important implications. It led to the thesis that even empirical statements could not be completely verifiable by observation, and supported his view that there could be no rigid demarcation between analytic and synthetic statements.

Sources: *The Times*, 6 Nov 1959; Stuart Hampshire, 'Friedrich Waismann', *PBA*, 1960; Passmore 1957; Anthony Quinton (1977) 'Introduction' to Waismann's *Philosophical Papers*; Oxford Univ. Calendar; Cambridge Univ. Dept of Manuscripts and Univ. Archives; personal communication with Gordon Baker and Brian McGuiness.

ANTHONY ELLIS

Waldenfels, Bernhard

German. *b:* 17 March 1934, Essen, Germany. *Cat:* Phenomenological philosopher. *Ints:* Social theorist. *Educ:* Bonn, Innsbruck and Munich (1954–60); the Sorbonne, 1960–2. *Infls:* Helmut Kuhn and Kurt von Fritz. *Appts:* 1968–76, Lecturer, then Associate Professor, Munich; since 1976, Professor Ordinarius in Philosophy (especially practical philosophy), Ruhr University; 1970–76, Cofounder and Vice President of the German Society for Phenomenological Research; Coeditor of *Phänomenologie und Marxismus* 4 vols, 1977–9), of omnibus volumes on Gurwitsch and Schutz (1983), Merleau-Ponty (1986) and Foucault (1991), and of the journal *Philosophische Rundschau*.

Main publications:

(1961) *Das sokratische Fragen* [The Socratic Questions], Munich dissertation, Meisenheim: Verlag: A. Hain.

(1971) *Das Zwischenreich des Dialogs* [The Mid-realm of Dialogue. Social-philosophical Investigations in Connection with Edmund Husserl] (Munich Habilitationsschrift), The Hague: Martinus Nijhoff.

(1980) *Der Spielraum des Verhaltens* [The Play-space of Behaviour], Frankfurt: Suhrkamp.

(1983) *Phänomenologie in Frankreich* [Phenomenology in France], Frankfurt: Suhrkamp.

(1985) *In den Netzen der Lebenswel* [In the Web of the Lifeworld], Frankfurt: Suhrkamp.

(1987) *Ordnung im Zwielicht* [Order at Twilight], Frankfurt: Suhrkamp.

(1990) *Der Stachel des Fremden* [The Thorn of the Strange], Frankfurt: Suhrkamp.

(1992) *Einführung in die Phänomenologie* [Introduction to Phenomenology], Munich: W. Fink.

Editor and translator of several of Merleau-Ponty's works.

Waldenfels' philosophy is at the boundary of modernism and post-modernism. His main influences are Husserlian 'lifeworld' phenomenology, **Merleau-Ponty**'s philosophy of 'chiasm' and 'incarnate meaning' and, more recently, French poststructuralism and posthermeneutics. In his 'The Mid-realm of Dialogue' (1971) he takes his departure from a 'bipolar event'—the 'equiprimordiality' of self and other—in which dialogue functions as a living medium. 'The Play-space of Behaviour' (1980) is influenced by Merleau-Ponty, structural linguistics and semiotics. It concerns a 'space' or 'free play' where inside and outside interpenetrate and which forestalls both the retreat into pure consciousness and the reduction to physical mechanisms. French phenomenology encompasses major variants on the Husserlian original, and in his *Phenomenology in France* (1983) Waldenfels traces these developments particularly in the work of **Sartre**, Merleau-Ponty, **Levinas** and **Ricoeur**. In his 'In the Web of the Lifeworld' (1985), he resists Husserl's view of the lifeworld with its 'forced unity', and argues instead that the impact of 'brute being' forces us to view the lifeworld as an unfinished order with room for otherness and the uncanny. His 'Order at Twilight' (1987) is an elegant and pensive study of the threshold between nature and culture, and his 'The Thorn of the Strange' (1990) concerns the question of a suitable response to 'otherness'—the 'thorn' or 'prickle in the flesh' which causes us to overstep the bounds of the personal and collective order. His most recent book, 'Introduction to Phenomenology' (1992) is an overview of the various branches of phenomenology in Europe and the USA.

Sources: Personal communication; Fred Dallmayr (1989) 'On Bernhard Waldenfels', *SR* 56, 3 (Autumn).

BARRY JONES

Wang Dianji (Wang Tien-chi)

Chinese. *b:* 1900, Hubei Province, China. *d:* 1979, Beijing. *Cat:* Logician; historian of Chinese and Western formal logic. *Educ:* University of Beijing and in France. *Infls:* Jin Yuelin. *Appts:* Lecturer, University of Beijing, Peking Normal School, Shengyang Dongbei University, Sichuan University, and other universities; Professor, University of Beijing; Professor, Beijing Normal University; Research Professor, Institute of Philosophy, Chinese Academy of Social Sciences.

Main publications:

(1927) *On Logic and Mathematical Logic.*
(1937) *Modern Logic.*
(1961–) *Investigations of Historical Materials of Chinese Logical Thought*, 4 vols.
(1979) *A History of Chinese Logical Thought.*
History of Western Logic.

Secondary literature:

Briere, O. (1956) *Fifty Years of Chinese Philosophy 1898–1950*, London: George Allen & Unwin Ltd.

Wang was an important contributor to the development of mathematical logic in China. His work on Chinese logical thought provided a comprehensive and sophisticated history of the field. *Modern Logic* (1937) dealt systematically with modern developments in logic, criticized classical logic and discussed the likely future pattern of logical thought. He also wrote on the history of mathematics and on the history of inductive logic and scientific method.

NICHOLAS BUNNIN

Wang Guowei (Wang Ku-wei)

Chinese. *b:* 1877, Haining, Zhejiang Province, China. *d:* 1927, Beijing. *Cat:* German idealist; historian of ancient China; archaeologist; literary historian, critic and poet. *Ints:* Metaphysics; epistemology; aesthetics. *Educ:* Studied Chinese classics; Japanese and European languages in Shanghai; physics in Tokyo; ancient historical materials in Kyoto. *Infls:* Kant, Schiller, Schopenhauer and Nietzsche. *Appts:* Teacher of ethics and psychology, Nantung Normal School; Officer, Board of Education; Professor, private university, Shanghai; Adviser, Graduate School in Chinese Studies, University of Beijing; Tutor, staff of deposed Emperor Puyi; Professor of Sinological Studies, Qinghua University.

Main publications:

(1905) *Essays of Jingan.*
(1923) *Guantang Anthology.*
(1940) *Collected Works of the Late Wang Guowei of Haining*, 48 vols, Shanghai: Shangwu Yin Book Company.
(1976) *The Complete Works of Wang Guowei*, 25 vols, Taipei: Datong Book Company.
(1984) *The Complete Works of Wang Guowei: Correspondence*, Beijing: Zhonghua Book Company.

Secondary literature:

Bonner, J. (1986) *Wang Kuo-wei: An Intellectual Biography*, London: Harvard University Press.
Boorman, H. (ed.) (1970) *Biographical Dictionary of Republican China*, New York and London: Columbia University Press.
Briere, O. (1956) *Fifty Years of Chinese Philosophy 1898–1950*, London: George Allen & Unwin Ltd.
Complete Chinese Encyclopedia (1987), Philosophy Volumes, Beijing: Chinese Encyclopedia Publications.
Fung, Y. L. (1966) *A Short History of Chinese Philosophy*, New York: The Free Press.

Considered to be among the most brilliant and original Chinese scholars of this century, Wang Guowei made important contributions to a wide range of fields. He gave up his early interest in philosophy and literature at the age of 30 to concentrate on ancient Chinese history and archaeology. His work deciphering inscriptions on oracle bones, tortoise shells and bamboo strips transformed the study of Shang history. His examination of the history of Chinese script showed a mastery of Qing textual criticism and modern historiographic and archaeological method. His studies of the Chinese novel *The Dream of the Red Chamber*, poetry (especially the *ci* form) and Yuan drama were critically revolutionary. Unlike other early Chinese admirers of Western thought, Wang had a deep understanding of the works he studied. His philosophical interests centred on German idealism, especially Kant, Schiller, Schopenhauer and **Nietzsche**. Wang used his studies of foreign philosophy to analyse basic Chinese philosophical concepts and to form a theory of aesthetics to use in his critical writings.

Three essays are worth examining: 'Discussing nature', 'Analysing reason' and 'The origin of life'. Wang took up Kantian themes in his account of *xing* (nature), but argued that nature was beyond experience and unknowable. His discussion of *li* (reason or principle) distinguished a broad unchanging notion and a narrow notion of *li* within nature, neither of which was contained in the world of experience. He saw life as having an origin in the natural world, but also as orientated towards a human ideal. He claimed that life was controlled by outside forces and that free will was illusory. In sum, he held the pessimistic view that unreal concepts controlled mankind.

Wang's early enthusiasm for Kant gave way to a deeper attachment to Schopenhauer. He argued that Kant's treatment of *noumena* led to scepticism, which could be overcome only through Schopenhauer's account of time, intuition, reason and will. He claimed that Schopenhauer used Kantian epistemology to form a coherent system of metaphysics, ethics and aesthetics.

Wang integrated the aesthetic ideas of Kant, Schiller, Schopenhauer and Nietzsche into traditional Chinese theories of art. Beauty, he claimed, gave pleasure without serving any external function, although he accepted Schopenhauer's view that art relieved mankind from pain. He explored Kant's account of genius and saw literature as the free creative play of genius. He discussed the complex relationship between natural and artistic beauty, arguing that, although they had the same form, judging natural beauty differed from judging artistic beauty. Natural beauty has to be mediated through artistic beauty to reach its completion, and something naturally unbeautiful can be seen as beautiful through art. The aesthetic ideal of classical elegance is accidental and acquired through experience rather than necessary and universal. Its achievement depends partly on genius but also on cultivation and practice.

Wang's decision to give up philosophy derived from a tension between the grand metaphysical, ethical and aesthetic systems which he loved and the more modest claims of positivism, hedonism and empiricism which he thought worthy of belief. The scrupulous sense of method and justification which governed his later historical and archaeological work extinguished his desire to carry on with the philosophical work which gave him gratification. Wang, a committed royalist, drowned himself in Kunming Lake at the Summer Palace when political events in 1927 seemed in his eyes to threaten humiliation.

NICHOLAS BUNNIN

Wang Hao (Wang Hao)

Chinese-American. *b:* 1921, Jinan, Shandgon Province, China. *d:* 1995. *Cat:* Philosopher and mathematician. *Ints:* Philosophy of mathematics; logic; metaphysics and epistemology. *Educ:* Southwest Associated University; Qinghua University; Harvard University; University of Zurich. *Infls:* His teachers Jin Yuelin and Wang Dianji, as well as Kurt Gödel, Bertrand Russell, Ludwig Wittgenstein and W. V. O. Quine. *Appts:* Professor, Harvard University; Professor, Rockefeller University; 1955–6, John Locke Lecturer, University of Oxford; Visitor, Institute for Advanced Studies, Princeton.

Main publications:

(1962) *A Survey of Mathematical Logic.*
(1974) *From Mathematics to Philosophy*, London: Routledge.
(1986) *Beyond Analytic Philosophy: Doing Justice to What We Know*, Cambridge, Mass.: MIT Press (Bradford Books).
(1987) *Reflections on Kurt Gödel*, Cambridge. Mass.: MIT Press.

Secondary literature:

Complete Chinese Encyclopedia (1987), Philosophy Volumes, Beijing: Chinese Encyclopedia Publications.

Wang Hao's studies in China led to doctoral work at Harvard and a career in mathematics and philosophy in the USA. His main philosophical writings have drawn on deep mathematical and logical understanding, but also show distinctively philosophical interests and abilities. In his philosophy of mathematics Wang sought to anchor mathematical knowledge in intuitive truths, known to us through reflective thinking going beyond the immediately obvious. Our intuitive knowledge is prior to any particular theory and is the ground for checking our philosophical claims. He invented the terms 'substantial factualism' and 'phenomenography' to name different versions of his view. Because positivism ignored our intuitive knowledge it was empty and artificial. Linguistic philosophy was unsystematic and too concerned with arbitrary demands for clarity and the facts of language instead of the rich resources of our intuitive knowledge.

In *From Mathematics to Philosophy* (1974),

Wang used the notion of substantial factualism to hold together comments on a wide variety of mathematical concepts and their implications for philosophy. His main discussions consider the relationship between mathematical logic and the philosophy of mathematics, Russellian logic, logical truth, the concept of set, logicism and the nature of mathematics, necessity, analyticity and apriority, mathematics and computers, minds and machines, and the relation of the pursuit of knowledge to human life.

In *Beyond Analytic Philosophy* (1986), Wang contributed to the current self-examination of the analytic tradition in philosophy. He argued that the central viewpoints of **Carnap** and **Quine** were deficient because they abjured direct intuition of abstract objects, thus impoverishing mathematical understanding. Allowing such Gödelian intuition would do justice to what we know and provide a radical reorientation for philosophy. Because mathematical knowledge is there intuitively, philosophy would become a matter of perspicuous ordering rather than of creativity or discovery. It would provide a worldview rather than specialist knowledge. Wang ambitiously proposed a philosophy drawing on many Eastern and Western influences. His friendship with Kurt **Gödel** led to the *Reflections* (1987) publicizing and exploring Gödel's philosophical views, many of which profoundly influenced his own central philosophical programme.

NICHOLAS BUNNIN

Ward, James

British. *b:* 27 January 1843, Liverpool, England. *d:* 4 March 1925, Cambridge, England. *Cat:* Theistic idealist. *Ints:* Philosophy of mind; metaphysics. *Educ:* Berlin, Göttingen and Cambridge. *Infls:* Lotze. *Appts:* Fellow of Trinity College, Cambridge, 1875–1925; Professor of Mental Philosophy and Logic, Cambridge.

Main publications:

(1899) *Naturalism and Agnosticism*, Cambridge.
(1911) *The Realm of Ends*, Cambridge.
(1918) *Psychological Principles*, Cambridge.
(1923) *A Study of Kant*, Cambridge.

Secondary literature:

Murray, A. H. (1937) *The Philosophy of James Ward*.
Sorley, W. R. and Hicks, G. D. (1925) in *Mind*.

Ward came to philosophy comparatively late. After a Congregationalist upbringing, he became a Unitarian minister. Then, after study in Cambridge, he spent some time in Germany working on biology and psychology and responding to the influence of Lotze, above all, but also that of **Wundt** and **Brentano**. For a long time he concentrated on psychology, of an introspective and more or less philosophical kind, and did not venture in philosophy proper until halfway through his career. The ideas of his *Psychological Principles* of 1918 had been set out to widespread acclaim in his article on psychology in the *Encyclopaedia Britannica* in 1886. His criticism of traditional British associationism was much more effective and well aimed than the polemical generalities of **Green** and **Bradley**. We need only to attend to what is going on in our minds to realize that the contents of our consciousnesses are not clearly distinct and demarcated mental atoms. What is present to consciousness is a continuum, exhibiting variations of quality, but not an aggregation of bits and pieces. Furthermore, the mind is active in experience, not merely receptive of what is presented to it. Consciousness is always attentive and selective. The mind in all its aspects is 'conative' or positively active. This conclusion led Ward to insist on the reality of the self as active subject, not a mere related flow of experiences. The metaphysical speculations of the later part of Ward's career have evoked less interest and attention. On the one hand he developed a familiar critical theme of the idealism of his age about the abstractness, and, therefore, only partial or limited truth, of the findings of the natural sciences. Useful rules of thumb for certain kinds of practice, they do not represent the real character of the world. Ward suggests that to learn about the concrete we should turn to history, but he has nothing much to say about history. Its main virtue is that it deals with the minds of individual persons. The world, he contends, consists of minds, of some sort or other, some above us, others, perhaps more numerous, below. His 'spiritual pluralism' is very different from that of **McTaggart**. For McTaggart matter is an illusion; for Ward it is rudimentary mind. The main reason given for Ward's panpsychist speculation is the principle of continuity. He finds purposiveness everywhere in the world. Everywhere ends are pursued, and, therefore, values operative. Ward's psychological ideas were extremely influential so long as the subject continued to use introspection as its principal method. The chief continuator of his work in this area was G. F. **Stout**. Another follower was F. R. **Tennant**, who made use of his theory of the self in developing his own account of the soul in his comprehensive philosophy of religion. It is interesting to reflect that Ward was Bertrand **Russell**'s main tutor in philosophy. His marginal comments to Russell's undergraduate essays (see *Collected Papers*, vol. 1) are thoroughly sensible and conventional.

Sources: Metz; Copleston; Passmore 1957.

ANTHONY QUINTON

Warnock, H(elen) M(ary)

British. *b:* 14 April 1924, Winchester. *Cat:* Philosophy of ethics; philosopher of education; philosopher of mind. *Educ:* St Swithun's, Winchester, and Lady Margaret Hall, Oxford. *Infls:* Personal influence: family, past and present. Philosophical influence: J. L. Austin. *Appts:* 1949–66, Fellow and Tutor in Philosophy, St Hugh's College, Oxford; 1966–72, Headmistress of Oxford High School; 1972–6; Talbot Research Fellow, Lady Margaret Hall, Oxford; 1976–84, Senior Research Fellow, St Hugh's College, Oxford (Honorary Fellowship awarded 1985); 1985–92, Mistress of Girton College, Cambridge; from 1992, Life Fellow, Girton College, Cambridge.

Main publications:

(1960) *Ethics since 1900*, Oxford: Oxford University Press.

(1965) *The Philosophy of Sartre*, London: Hutchinson.

(1966) *Existentialist Ethics*, London: Macmillan.

(1970) *Existentialism*, Oxford: Oxford University Press.

(1976) *Imagination*, London: Faber & Faber.

(1977) *Schools of Thought*, London: Faber & Faber.

(1977) (with T. Devlin) *What Must We Teach?*, London: Temple Smith.

(1979) *Education: A Way Forward*, Oxford: Blackwell.

(1985) *A Question of Life*, Oxford: Blackwell.

(1987) *Memory*, London: Faber & Faber.

(1988) *A Common Policy for Education*, Oxford: Oxford University Press.

(1989) *Universities: Knowing Our Minds*, London: Chatto & Windus.

(1992) *The Uses of Philosophy*, Oxford: Blackwell.

(1994) *Imagination and Time*, Oxford: Blackwell.

(1995) (ed.) *Women Philosophers*, London: Everyman.

In the latter half of the twentieth century Warnock has been widely influential in the formulation of policy in education, environmental issues, animal experimentation and human fertilization, having chaired government committees dealing with these matters.

Her early writings are concerned with ethics and existentialism or, more precisely, ethics *in* existentialism. Critical of the Marxist tendency (at one time exhibited by **Sartre**) dogmatically to subsume the individual under a collectivity, she maintained that what had suffered above all else was the status of philosophy itself, and that the salvaging of both philosophy and existentialism was bound up with the resuscitation of the social person as against the 'subjective anti-scientific dogmatism' (1979, p. 140) of much metaphysics.

Her work in the philosophy of education shows a similar anti-theoretical stance. In *Schools of Thought* (1977) she argued that the Socratic question about the possibility of teaching virtue is intimately related not only to moral but also to political questions; that there are no educational criteria devoid of moral and political constituents; and that to attempt to conceptualize an educational good without regard to its political resonances is to misunderstand its moral aspects and the vinculations that morality has with political expediency. What she sees as decisive in setting the curriculum content are 'the twin values of work and the expanding imagination'.

Her claim that there must exist some specialized forum for reflection on what should be taught was taken up in *Universities: Knowing Our Minds* (1989) where she argued that an intellectual elite is a necessary element in society and that it should not be dictated to from outside but must be free to declare its views without restraint. In *Imagination* (1976) she traced the development of that concept, concluding that its cultivation should be the highest goal of an enlightened education. Warnock is primarily a moral philosopher working in the fields of education and medical ethics. Her ability to show the relationships between theory and practice, and to demonstrate the value of practical reasoning and philosophical thinking in general, has rendered her work important and influential.

Sources: WW 1995.

DAVID SPOONER

Watkins, John William Neville

British. *b:* 31 July 1924, Woking, Surrey. *Cat:* Social political and philosopher; philosopher of science. *Educ:* Royal Naval College, Dartmouth (1938–41), London School of Economics and Yale University. *Infls:* Predominant personal influence is Popper, but also Lakatos; literary influences include Hempel, Collingwood, Hayek and Dawkins. **Appts:** 1950–8, Assistant Lecturer, then Lecturer in Political Science, 1958–66, Reader in History of Philosophy, 1966–89, Professor of Philosophy, London School of Economics and Political Science, University of London; 1972–5, President of the British Society for the Philosophy of Science.

Main publications:

(1957) 'Historical explanation in the social sciences', *British Journal for the Philosophy of Science* 8: 104–17.

(1965) *Hobbes's System of Ideas*, London: Hutchinson; second edition, 1973.

(1970) 'Imperfect rationality', in R. Borger and F. Cioffi (eds), *Explanation in the Behavioural Sciences*, Cambridge: Cambridge University Press.

(1975) 'Three views concerning human freedom', in R. S. Peters (ed.), *Nature and Conduct*, London: Macmillan.

(1977) 'My LSE', in Joan Abse (ed.), *My LSE*, London: Robson Books.

(1983) *Tre Saggi su 'Scienza e Metafisica'*, Rome: Borla.

(1984) *Science and Scepticism*, London: Hutchinson; Princeton: Princeton University Press.

(1987) 'A new view of scientific rationality', in J. C. Pitt and P. Marcello (eds) *Rational Changes in Science*, Dordrecht: D. Reidel.

(1991) 'Scientific rationality and the problem of induction: responses to criticisms', *British Journal for the Philosophy of Science* 42: 343–68.

(1992) 'Destroyer action, Ile de Batz, 9 June 1944', *The Mariner's Mirror* 78: 307–25.

Secondary literature:

D'Agostini, F. and Jarvie, I. C. (eds) (1988) *Freedom and Rationality*, Dordrecht: D. Reidel (contains bibliography of publications of Watkins).

After distinguished service in the Royal Navy (1941–6), for which he was decorated with the DSC, J. W. N. Watkins spent the whole of his professional career at the London School of Economics. Initially concentrating on social and political philosophy, in later years his contribution has been at least as notable in the philosophy of science, where he has put up a spirited defence of critical rationalism as against rationality-scepticism.

Describing himself as a neo-Popperian, Watkins, like **Popper**, eschews the use of inductive reasoning, holding that rational theory choice can be based upon (degree of) corroboration.

But he provides a lesser aim for science than Popper: not increasing verisimilitude or truthlikeness, for an acceptable scientific theory need only be possibly true.

A concern with issues of choice and rationality has been a unifying theme in Watkins's work. His early discussions of methodological individualism were influential; and he has also advocated negative utilitarianism (minimizing misery) and indeterminism. His book on Hobbes, which stressed the political theory as an outcome of Hobbes's materialist metaphysics and philosophy of language, was widely acclaimed.

Watkins gave several talks on the BBC which were printed in *The Listener*. He was co-editor of the *British Journal for the Philosophy of Science*, 1974–9. He is now at work on a further book, on human freedom.

Sources: CA FR 21–4; brief letter from Watkins and CV.

CLIVE BORST

Watson, John

British-Canadian. **b:** 25 February 1847, Glasgow. **d:** 17 January 1939. Kingston, Ontario. **Cat:** Idealist. **Ints:** History of philosophy; philosophy of religion. **Educ:** University of Glasgow, graduating in 1872. **Infls:** John Caird and Edward Caird. **Appts:** Professor of Logic, Metaphysics, and Ethics at Queen's University, Kingston, 1872; 1901, Vice Principal of the university; his entire career was spent there, although he was a Visiting Professor at the University of California, Berkeley, in 1895–6 and a Gifford Lecturer at the University of Glasgow in 1910–12; a strong influence on Canadian protestantism, he played an important role in the founding of the United Church of Canada, but never, in fact, joined it.

Main publications:

(1872) *The Relation of Philosophy to Science*, Inaugural Lecture, Queen's University, Kingston, Canada, 16 October 1872; reprinted in Douglas Rabb (ed.), *Religion and Science in Early Canada*, Kingston, Ontario: Frye, 1988.

(1881) *Kant and his English Critics*, Glasgow: J. Maclehose.

(1882) *Schelling's Transcendental Idealism*, Chicago: S. C. Briggs.

(1894) *Hedonistic Theories; from Aristippes to Spencer*, London: Maclehose.

(1895) *Comte, Mill and Spencer: An Outline of Philosophy*, Glasgow: Maclehose; fourth edition,

1908 (subsequent editions appeared simply as *Outline of Philosophy*).

(1896) *Christianity and Idealism*, New York: Macmillan.

(1899) *Philo and the New Testament*, Kingston, Ontario: W. Bailie.

(1907) *The Philosophical Basis of Religion*, Glasgow: Maclehose.

(1908) *The Philosophy of Kant Explained*, Glasgow: Maclehose.

(1910–12) *The Interpretation of Religious Experience*, 2 vols, Glasgow.

(1919) *The State in Peace and War*, Glasgow: Maclehose.

Secondary literature:

Armour, Leslie and Trott, Elizabeth (1981) *The Faces of Reason*, Waterloo: Wilfrid Laurier University Press.

Rabb, Douglas (ed.) (1988) *Religion and Science in Early Canada*, Kingston, Ontario: Frye.

Watson was a major figure in the development of Canadian idealism. He was strongly influenced by John and Edward **Caird**, although he was less strongly attached than Edward Caird to a literal evolutionism in the philosophy of religion. His idealism was more historically oriented than that of his English contemporaries **Bradley** and **Bosanquet**. He conceived God as essentially a community which could find expression in a worldly political order. The most constant theme running through his work is the reunion of God and a man in a single community, and his whole philosophy could be seen as a celebration of man's escape from the shadow of Calvinist predestinarianism—a shadow which the Caird brothers did so much to lift in Scotland. But his main technical interests were always in the theory of knowledge and, more precisely, in the passage from Kantian phenomenalism to a picture of reality which would do justice to the demands of science and to his own passion for the close analysis of experience. His inaugural lecture at Queen's on science and philosophy thus foreshadows his career over the more than half a century that he remained in Kingston. His study of Kant began early and lasted all his life.

He took very seriously the philosopher's duty to the public, and his *State in Peace and War* (1919) advocates a kind of world order which is influenced by his understanding of Canadian political federalism and which is meant to provide rational underpinning for a society whose fragmentation has been regularly predicted. He strove to reach an understanding with

philosophers in Quebec and philosophers in Quebec admired his understanding of the philosphy of Aquinas though they disliked his Hegelianism. His vision of a pluralistic society had much in common with that in Louis Lachance's *Religion et nationalisme*. His *Christianity and Idealism* (1896) was written in response to an invitation to lecture at the University of California during the debate between Josiah **Royce** and his successor there, George Holmes **Howison**. Howison wrote a preface to the book suggesting that Watson's position was well received by the California philosophers. Two chapters are devoted to Watson in Armour and Trott (1981) and there is a discussion of his work in Rabb (1988).

Sources: CanBio.

LESLIE ARMOUR

Watson, John Broadus

American. *b:* 1878, Greenville, South Carolina. *d:* 1958, Woodberry, Connecticut. *Cat:* Psychologist. *Ints:* Behaviourist psychology. *Educ:* Furma (Baptist) College, Greenville; majored in Psychology, with Philosophy and Neurology; PhD, University of Chicago, 1903. *Infls:* Dilthey and Parlor. *Appts:* Assistant and Instructor in Psychology, University of Chicago, 1903–8; Professor of Experimental and Comparative Psychology, Johns Hopkins University, 1908–20. Subsequently, various appointments in the advertising industry.

Main publications:

(1913) 'Psychology as the behaviourist views it', *Psychological Review* 20: 158–77.

(1914) *Behaviour: An Introduction to Comparative Psychology*, New York: H. Holt & Co.

(1919) *Psychology from the Standpoint of a Behaviourist*, Philadelphia: Lippincott.

Secondary literature:

Cohen, D. and J. B. Watson (1979) *The Founder of Behaviourism*, London and Boston: Routledge & Kegan Paul.

Robinson, D. N. (1976) *An Intellectual History of Psychology*, New York: Macmillan.

J. B. Watson was the founder of behaviourism, the view that scientific psychology should be concerned solely with the publicly available data of behaviour, whether human or animal, rather than with speculation about subjective experience and hidden mental mechanisms. Born into a prosperous farming family, he showed exceptional ability from an early age (he was the youngest person ever to be awarded a PhD). By the time of his appointment as Professor at the Johns Hopkins University, his work had already started to attract attention. He set out a first version of his behaviourism in an article in the *Psychological Review* (1913), but it was not until 1914, with the publication of his first major book, *Behaviour: An Introduction to Comparative Psychology*, that he gained wide recognition. He elaborated his position in *Psychology from the Standpoint of a Behaviourist* (1919), showing how behaviourism could be applied to complex human activities as well as to the simpler behaviour of animals kept under laboratory conditions.

In 1920 Watson divorced his wife and married one of his students. In the ensuing scandal he resigned his Chair and started a new career in advertising. Apart from new editions of *Behaviourism*, in which he adopted ever more dogmatic positions, and a number of popular books on psychology (including *The Psychological Care of Infant and Child*, 1928, written jointly with his wife), he did no new academic work of substance after this time.

Watson reacted against introspectionist elements inherent in the then dominant schools of human psychology, derived from Titchener and **Wundt**, and the functionalism of animal psychology. He sought to establish a purely objective approach to psychology, based only on publicly verifiable data, modelled on the natural sciences, reducible ultimately to physiology, and allowing no distinction (other than on a scale of complexity) between human beings and animals. There would be no place in such a psychology for mentalistic concepts such as sensations, purposes, understanding, meaning and, not least, consciousness itself.

Watson was a radical. This was his strength. Each of his major themes had been anticipated by one or other of his contemporaries, but he was able to mould them into a coherent theory and to show their potential applications to a wide range of practical problems. His radicalism was also his weakness. In his later work, as clear-sighted conviction turned to dogmatism, he produced a number of extreme ideas which did little to advance the behaviourist programme. He moved from a balanced view of the interaction of heredity and upbringing on development (including human development) to an uncompromising environmentalism. Emotions became patterns of internal bodily adjustments, instincts patterns of outward activity, thought itself no more than 'implicit laryngeal activity' (a theory he later repudiated). He argued that children

should be brought up, not with affection and regard, but in a stimulus-response environment with a minimum of emotional contamination. Watson's influence waned quite rapidly during his lifetime and he was often treated with hostility and derision by his peers. He remains none the less one of the seminal figures of twentieth-century psychology. His early work helped to shape the experimental and theoretical basis of the subject, and behaviourism, revived during the postwar period through the work of B. F. **Skinner** and others, has become the source of important advances in clinical psychology.

Sources: Edwards; Goldenson; Harré & Lamb.

K. W. M. FULFORD

Watsuji, Tetsuro

Japanese. *b:* 1 March 1889, Himeji, Japan. *d:* 16 December 1960, Tokyo. *Cat:* Philosopher of ethics; historian of Japanese ethics and culture. *Educ:* Tokyo Imperial University. *Infls:* Literary influences include Nietzsche, Kierkegaard, Heidegger and Dogen; personal influences include Soseki Natsume, Inazo Nitobe and Kitaro Nishida. *Appts:* Associate Professor of Ethics, 1925–31, Professor of Ethics, Kyoto Imperial University, 1931–4; Professor of Ethics, Tokyo Imperial University, 1934–45; Professor of Ethics, Tokyo University, 1945–9; President of the Japanese Society of Ethics, 1950–60.

Main publications:

(1913) *Niiche* [Nietzsche], Tokyo: Uchidarokakuho.

(1915) *Zeren Kierukegooru* [Søren Kierkegaard], Tokyo: Uchidarokakuho.

(1919) *Koji Junrei* [A Pilgrimage of Old Temples], Tokyo: Iwanami-Shoten.

(1926) *Genshi Kirisuto Kyo no Bunka Shiteki Igi* [The Meaning of the Cultural History of Primitive Christianity], Tokyo: Iwanami-Shoten.

(1926) *Nihon Seishin Shi Kenkyu* [An Inquiry into the History of the Japanese Spirit], Tokyo: Iwanami-Shoten.

(1927) *Genshi Bukkyo no Jissen Tetsugaku* [Practical Philosophy of Primitive Buddhism], Tokyo: Iwanami-Shoten.

(1934) *Ningen no Gaku toshite no Rinrigaku* [Ethics as a Science of the Human Being], Tokyo: Iwanami-Shoten.

(1935) *Fudo—Ningengakuteki Kosatsu* [Natural Features—an Antrhopological Consideration], Tokyo: Iwanami-Shoten.

(1937) *Men to Persona* [Mask and Persona], Tokyo: Iwanami-Shoten.

(1937) *Rinrigaku, Jo Kan* [Ethics, Book 1], Tokyo:
Iwanami-Shoten.
(1942) *Ringrigaku, Chu Kan* [Ethics, Book 2], Tokyo:
Iwanami-Shoten.
(1943) *Sonno Shiso to Sono Dento* [Royalism and its
Tradition], Tokyo: Iwanami-Shoten.
(1948) *Porisuteki Ningen no Rinrigaku* [The Ethics of
the Human Being in the City-state], Tokyo:
Hakujitsu-Shoin.
(1949) *Ringrigaku, Ge Kan* [Ethics, Book 3], Tokyo:
Iwanami-Shoten.
(1952) *Nihon rinri Shiso Shi. Jo/Ge Kan* [History of
Japanese Ethical Thought, Books 1/2], Tokyo:
Iwanami-Shoten.
(1961–3) *Watsuji Tetsuro Zenshu 1–20 Kan* [Com-
plete Works of Watsuji Tetsuro, vols 1–20], Tokyo:
Iwanami-Shoten.

Secondary literature:
Karaki, J. (1963) *Watsuji Tetsuro*, Tokyo: Chikuma-
Shobo.
Komaki, O. (1986) *Watsuji Tetsuro*, Tokyo: Shimizu-
Shoin.
Kosaka, M. (1964) *Nishida Kitaro to Watsuji Tetsuro*,
Tokyo: Shincho-Sha.
Sakabe, M. (1986) *Watsuji Tetsuro*, Tokyo: Iwanami-
Shoten.
Yuasa, Y. (1984) *Watsuji Tetsuro—Kindai Nihon
Tetsugaku no Unmei* [Watsuji Tetsuro—The Des-
tiny of Modern Japanese Philosophy], Kyoto:
Mineruva-Shobo.

We cannot see in Watsuji a sharp tension between,
on the one hand, nation or society and, on the
other, the individual, a tension which afflicts
Japanese thinkers from the beginning to the
middle of the Meiji era. Some critics claim, for
example, that we can find no dark aspects in his
biography, that as a philosopher he is a kind of
aesthete who contemplates beauty. However, in
Practical Philosophy of Primitive Buddhism (1927)
he does not regard true Buddhistic recognition
(*Gedatsu*) as being simply contemplation (*theoria*)
or a practice that contrasts with *theoria*. Rather,
he regards it as a conversion of one's life, *tout
court*. And he regards a recognition of Truth as
indistinguishable from a realization of Good, and
thinks that people in general must realize the
integrity of Truth and Good. He considers both
Buddhism and Kierkegaard's thought as practical
philosophies, and studies **Nietzsche** and Kierkegaard from the viewpoint of self-realization. As
the path to discovery of one's proper self, Watsuji
engages with them and other thinkers. Conversely,
along this path of discovery, he seems to become
more conscious of himself as a Japanese person.

Already in *A Pilgrimage of Old Temples*
(1919) he relates the *fudo* (natural features) of
ancient Japan to the character of its people.
During his travels in Europe this relationship
between the *fudo* and human existence becomes
clearer to him. He comes to the word *fudo* as a
general designation for such natural aspects as
the climate, the seasons and the geological and
geographical features of a region. However, *fudo*
is different from the Greek conception of nature
and any objective conception of nature as
studied in the natural sciences. Rather, *fudo* can
be roughly characterized as akin to a place
wherein we ourselves are founded in roles within
the human lifeworld, *aida-gara* (*Verhältnis*) in
Japanese. The character of *fudo* constitutes but
one mode of human existence. Watsuji's theory
of *fudo* tends towards a spatial construal of
human existence, unlike Heidegger's temporal
conception.

In *Ethics as a Science of the Human Being*
(1934) Watsuji aims to go beyond such polarities
as subject-object, theory-practice, action-con-
templation, etc., by means of the concept of
aida-gara, which he thinks is derivable only from
a hermeneutical analysis of the Japanese concepts of human being (*Ningen*) and existence
(*Sonzai*). Reflecting the influence of **Nishida**,
Watsuji thinks that *aida-gara* existence consists
in the unity in absolute negation of the whole
and the individual. This kind of existence is
construed as continuous creative action. Watsuji
finds the fundamental structure of human
existence in subjective spatiality.

In *History of Japanese Ethical Thought* (1952)
Watsuji provides analyses of what we can call the
Zeitgeist of the peoples of ancient, medieval and
modern Japan. However, these analyses seem
lacking in any political dimension. Rather, they
provide, as it were, crystalline cultural portraits
which, Watsuji thinks, represent universal aspects of ethics, aspects which are merely
manifested in their respective times.

KINYA MASUGATA

Webb, C(lement) C(harles) J(ulian)
British. **b:** 25 June 1865, London. **d:** 5 October
1954, Aylesbury. **Cat:** Personal idealist. **Ints:**
History of philosophy; philosophy of religion.
Educ: Christ Church, Oxford. **Infls:** Personal
influences: Green, Cook Wilson, Joseph, Prichard
and von Hügel. Literary influences: Kant, Green,
Lotze, Otto and Plato. **Appts:** 1880–1922, Fellow
of Magdalen College, Oxford; 1920–30, Oriel
Professor of the Philosophy of Religion, Oxford.

Main publications:

(1911) *Problems in the Relations of God and Man*, London: James Nisbet.

(1915) *Studies in the History of Natural Theology*, Oxford: Clarendon Press.

(1919) *God and Personality*, Aberdeen: University Studies.

(1920) *Divine Personality and Human Life*, Oxford: Clarendon Press.

Secondary literature:

Anon. (1945) Bibliography, in C. C. J. Webb, *Religious Experience*, London: Oxford University Press.

Ross, W. D. (1955) 'Clement Charles Julian Webb, 1865–1954', *Proceedings of the British Academy* 41: 339–47.

Sell, A. P. F. (1988) *The Philosophy of Religion 1875– 1980*, London: Croom Helm.

——(1995) *Philosophical Idealism and Christian Belief*, Cardiff: University of Wales Press and New York: St Martin's Press.

Although sometimes described as a 'personal idealist', Webb was an eclectic philosopher, responding to and drawing on a wide range of ancient and modern writers. He took from his teacher, **Cook Wilson**, a realism 'for which spirit is no less real than matter'. None the less he was closer to the absolute idealists than his friend Hastings **Rashdall**. He took up the controversy about individuality and personality in the first of his series of Gifford Lectures. He maintained (in *God and Personality*, 1919) that God cannot be finite but He is none the less personal. Webb was a prolific writer and capable of prodigious scholarship (as he proved with his editions of the writings of John of Salisbury). His skill and care in attending to the thoughts of others was valued by his pupils, including W. D. **Ross**. But his written work has been less influential.

Sources: DNB 1951–60; CBP II.

STUART BROWN

Weber, Max

German. *b:* 21 April 1864, Erfurt, Thuringia, Germany. *d:* 14 June 1920, Munich. *Cat:* Neo-Kantian; sociologist; social philosopher; philosopher of the social sciences. *Ints:* Philosophy of social science. *Educ:* Heidelberg, Berlin and Göttingen. *Infls:* Literary influences include Kant, Hegel and Dilthey; main personal influence, Wilhelm Rickert. *Appts:* Professor of Economics, Freiburg, 1894–6, Heidelberg, 1896–7; prolonged ill health prevented a full academic career; made 'Honorarprofessor' at Heidelberg, 1903; associate editor of *Archiv für Sozialwissenschaft und Sozialpolitik*, from 1903; Professor of Sociology, Vienna, 1918; Professor of Economics, Munich, 1919–20.

Main publications:

(1930) *The Protestant Ethic and the Spirit of Capitalism*, trans. Talcott Parsons, London: George Allen & Unwin; reissued, New York: Charles Scribner's Sons, 1958.

(1947) *From Max Weber*, trans. H. H. Gerth and C. Wright Mills, New York: Oxford University Press.

(1949) *On the Methodology of the Social Sciences*, trans. and ed. E. A. Shils and H. A. Finch, Glencoe, Ill: The Free Press.

(1978) *Weber: Selections*, ed. W. G. Runciman and trans. Eric Matthews, Cambridge: Cambridge University Press.

Secondary literature:

Hughes, H. Stuart (1958) *Consciousness and Society*, London: McGibbon & Kee, chapter 8.

Reinhard, Bendix (1966) *Max Weber: An Intellectual Portrait*, London: Methuen (contains bibliography).

Weber was not primarily a philosopher. The most philosophically interesting part of Weber's work is found in his reflections on the methods of the social sciences. He wanted the social sciences to be relevant to political and social issues, but thought it an ethical duty of the social scientist (as a scientist) to be 'value-free'. Science could tell us the most effective means to a given end but could not settle for us which ends we should choose. Choice of ends was a matter for a personal commitment, which a serious person must necessarily make, but there was a wide range of possible internally consistent value-systems between which to choose.

The distinctive feature of the *social* sciences was that they dealt with human behaviour to the extent that it is seen by the agent as having a meaning involving relations to others. The task of social science is to understand this meaning, with a view to formulating general laws of social behaviour (*verstehende Soziologie* or interpretative sociology). Explanations in social science must be adequate both at the level of meaning and at the causal level. To grasp the meaning of an action is not necessarily to share the agent's values; nor does the possibility of such 'understanding' (*Verstehen*) imply that the action is rational. It is possible, however, to construct 'ideal types' of perfectly rational behaviour, which can be fully understood, and less rational actions can then be understood as approximations to the ideal.

Weber also had a vision of the development of Western capitalist society which could be described as a philosophy of history. He saw it as becoming more and more 'disenchanted' and concerned with rationality in a purely 'means-end' sense. The causes of this development did not, as in Marxism, lie in economics and technology, but in ideas and beliefs ultimately derived from Calvinist theology and ethics.

ERIC MATTHEWS

Wedberg, Anders Erik Otto

Swedish. *b:* 30 March 1913, Stockholm. *d:* 20 February 1978, Danderyd, Sweden. *Cat:* Analytical philsopher; historian of philosophy. *Ints:* Logic; philosophy of law. *Educ:* Universities of Uppsala and Stockholm. *Infls:* Russell, Frege, Carnap, Naess and Phalén. *Appts:* 1949–76, Professor of Theoretical Philosophy, Stockholm University.

Main publications:

(1937) 'Bertrand Russell's empiricism', in I. Hedenius *et al.* (eds), *Adolf Phalén in Memoriam: Philosophical Essays*, Uppsala: Almqvist & Wiksell.

(1937) *Den logiska strukturen hos Boströms filosofi. En studie i klassisk metafysik* [The Logical Structure of the Philosophy of Boström: A Study in Classical Metaphysics], Uppsala: Almqvist & Wiksell.

(1944) 'The logical construction of the world: a critical analysis of Rudolf Carnap's *Der logische Aufbau der Welt*', *Theoria*.

(1951) 'Some problems in the logical analysis of legal science', *Theoria*; reprinted in *Contemporary Scandinavian Philosophy*, Baltimore and London: The Johns Hopkins Press, 1972.

(1955) *Plato's Philosophy of Mathematics*, Uppsala: Almqvist & Wiksell; reprinted, Westport, CT: Greenwood Press Publishers, 1977 (Japanese translation, 1975).

(1968) *Philosophical Papers* I, Stockholm: Philosophical Institute of Stockholm University.

(1972–3) 'How Carnap built the world in 1928', *Synthese*; reprinted in J. Hintikka (ed.), *Rudolf Carnap, Logical Empiricist*, Dordrecht: Reidel, 1975.

(1982–4) *A History of Philosophy*, 3 vols, Oxford: Clarendon Press (English version of a work in Swedish of 1958–66; the chapters on Ryle, Austin, Naess, Hägerström and Phalén are omitted in the English version).

Secondary literature:
Theoria 1978 (obituary and bibliography).

Anders Wedberg's contribution to philosophy is a large number of logical and semantic analyses. In several of them mathematical logic is used. Most of these analyses deal with arguments in modern or earlier philosophy, but Wedberg has also elucidated fundamental ideas in other theoretical fields: legal science, linguistics and the theory of measurement. He has also dealt, further, with Aristotelian syllogistic, deontic logic and the foundations of mathematics. A few of these analyses are collected in *Philosophical Papers* (1968). The critical talent is outstanding in Wedberg's work: brilliant examples are his two studies of **Carnap**'s *Aufbau*, published in 1944 and 1972–3. There are also ingenious constructive suggestions in Wedberg's writings, for example in the paper of 1951, one of the most weighty contributions to the development of the Scandinavian realism of law after **Hägerström**.

Anders Wedberg's philosophical reflection was to a high degree stimulated by the work of Bertrand **Russell**. In questions of method Wedberg was influenced by the logical empiricists, but he never embraced their general theses. In a short period of his youth, during which he published the early writings on Russell and Boström 1937), he was an adherent of the Uppsala school of conceptual analysis (**Phalén**, Hägerström). In contrast to the logical empiricists, this school had a deep interest in the history of philosophy, an interest that Wedberg retained all his life. With *Plato's Philosophy of Mathematics* (1955) and *A History of Philosophy* (1982–4) he made important contributions to the study of the history of theoretical philosophy. A much discussed detail in the former is the thesis that there is a fundamental antinomy in Plato's theory of ideas. As a historian of philosophy Wedberg was an innovator as regards method, especially in his precision technique. Two distinctive features of *A History of Philosophy* are the illuminating comparisons of certain ideas in ancient philosophy with certain ideas in modern mathematical logic and the great attention paid to Bolzano and **Frege**.

THORILD DAHLQUIST

Weil, Eric

French. *b:* 1904. *d:* 1977. *Cat:* Moral and political

philosopher. **Infls:** Alexandre Kojève. **Appts:** Various academic posts, including a Professorship at the University of Lille.

Main publications:

(1950) *Hegel et l'état*, Paris: Vrin.
(1950) *Logique de la philosophie*, Paris: Vrin.
(1969) *Philosophie morale*, Paris: Vrin.
(1970) *Essais et conférences*, Paris: Plon.
(1970) *Problèmes kantiens*, Paris: Vrin.
(1984) *Philosophie politique*, Paris: Vrin.

Secondary literature:

The University of Lille has established the Centre de Recherche Eric Weil, which in 1987 published the *Cahiers Eric Weil*: this work contains an extensive bibliography.

Eric Weil's philosophical development was influenced by a revival of Hegelian studies in France during the interwar period. Broadly, there are two interpretations of Hegel's political philosophy. The first is that which presents Hegel as a reactionary: with his theory of the state, he simply wished to endorse the political status quo of contemporary Prussian absolutism. His political thought is also, on this view, regarded as the forerunner of German imperialism and National Socialism. The second interpretation of Hegel is that of a philosopher whose works are in the mainstream of Western political thought. According to this view, Hegel was a moderate reformist and a theorist of the modern constitutional state. This view was pioneered in the latter half of the twentieth century by three Hegelian scholars: T. M. Knox, Joachim Ritter and Eric Weil. It is due to their work that the first interpretation has now been superseded by the second.

Weil, following Hegel, considers the use and development of reason to be crucial to progress in ethics and politics. Reason leads to freedom and happiness, whereas the failure to develop its use accounts for the climate of despondency, confusion and lack of direction in postwar Western European societies.

KATHRYN PLANT

Weil, Simone

French. **b:** 1909, Paris. **d:** 1943, near Ashford, Kent, England. **Cat:** Moral and social philosopher; philosopher of religion. **Educ:** Collège Henri IV and École Normale Supérieure. **Infls:** Plato, Pythagoras and the Stoics, and Eastern philosophy; personal influences include Emile Chartier ('Alain') and the Dominican priest Father J. M. Perrin. **Appts:** After having received her agrégation, taught at different lycées; 1934–5, worked in a Renault factory in Paris, and for a short time in 1936 was in an anarchist brigade in the Spanish Civil War; came to London to join the Free French in 1942; contracted tuberculosis and, refusing to eat more than her compatriots under the Nazi occupation, died in a nursing home.

Main publications:

(1947) *La Pesanteur et la Grâce*, Paris: Plon (English translation, *Gravity and Grace*, London: Ark Paperbacks, 1987).
(1950) *L'Attente de Dieu*, Paris: Gallimard (English translation, *Waiting on God*, London: Routledge & Kegan Paul, 1951).
(1950) *L'Enracinement*, Paris: Gallimard (English translation, *The Need for Roots*, London: Ark Paperbacks, 1987).
(1951) *La Condition ouvrière*, Paris: Gallimard.
(1951) *Lettre à un religieux*, Paris: Gallimard.
(1955) *Oppression et liberté*, Paris: Gallimard (English translation, *Oppression and Liberty*, London: Ark Paperbacks, 1988).
(1988) *Oeuvres Complètes*, 4 vols, Paris: Gallimard.

Secondary literature:

Kempfner, G. (1960) *La Philosophie mystique de Simone Weil*, Paris: La Colombe.
McClellan, D. (1989) *Simone Weil: Utopian Pessimist*, London: Macmillan.
Winch, P. (1989) *Simone Weil: The Just Balance*, Cambridge: Cambridge University Press.

Simone Weil's work was wide-ranging and diffuse, but concentrated on two central areas: moral and social issues, and the religious life. In the former she embarked on a quest for a programme of social justice and enquired into the nature and possibility of human freedom. In the latter she was concerned with the spiritual, religious and mystical elements which, she believed, were interwoven with this earthly life.

The two facets of Weil's philosophy were linked by her conception of humanity. She considered that our situation in the universe is twofold: we have an inner sense of freedom and the belief that humanity is basically good, but these are constantly threatened with encroachment and annihilation from outside by the forces of necessity found in the natural laws which govern the universe.

The freedom and goodness of humanity are also under threat from immersion in a collectivist society. Human beings may believe that they will gain a sense of security from being a part of such a society, but the reality is that their individuality will be distorted or destroyed. Weil detected a strong collectivist and universalist tendency in contemporary society, but it is not a modern phenomenon: collectivism can also be found in various historical periods, including that of the Roman Empire, which Weil referred to as the 'great beast'.

In *La Condition ouvrière* (1951) she stated that modern industrial organizations in particular have an exploitative capitalist social structure which puts profit and production before human beings, and thus depersonalizes and dehumanizes them. Although she recognized that there can be no abolition of industrial organizations, she recommended that work must be reorganized, not as a bureaucratic 'hierarchy of functions' with its inevitable division of labour, but as an industrial democracy with workers having full consultation about their own working lives and conditions. Crucially Weil thought that such restructuring, in order to be complete, would have to be shot through with spiritual values and the workers' awareness of their own dignity and sense of responsibility towards each other.

The theme of responsibility and duty towards others is also taken up in *L'Enracinement* (1950). Weil considered that people cannot claim rights, but have rights conferred on them. They are, purely because of their status as human beings, the objects of the eternal and unconditional duties binding on all human agents. In this work, she developed the theme that people need to feel rooted in a community, for which the state is no substitute. If there is no cohesive social group to which people belong, as is the case with many industrial workers, there is a sense of dislocation and loss. Nevertheless, to have a sense of community does not fully satisfy human needs: people also have to be rooted in the spiritual realm.

Spiritual growth reaches its completion in what Weil regarded as the only true loss of self, that of the one-pointedness of mystical experience in which the self is emptied and becomes transparent to God. This state is attainable through rigorous spiritual self-discipline, like that outlined by St John of the Cross and prefigured or reflected in certain non-Christian philosophies, such as that of Plato and many varieties of Eastern thought.

KATHRYN PLANT

Weinstein, Michael A.

American. *b:* 24 August 1942, New York. *Cat:* Political philosopher. *Educ:* Williams College, New York University and Case Western Reserve University, from which he received his PhD in 1967. *Appts:* Taught a year at Virginia Polytechnic Institute; 1968–, Purdue University, presently Professor of Political Theory, and has served on doctoral committees in political science, philosophy, and American studies; 1979, Milward Simpson Professor of Political Science at the University of Wyoming; both the Guggenheim and Rockefeller Foundations have awarded him major Fellowships.

Main publications:
(1976) *The Polarity of Mexican Thought*, University Park: Pennsylvania State University Press.
(1977) *The Tragic Sense of Political Life*, Columbia: University of South Carolina Press.
(1978) *Meaning and Appreciation: Time and Modern Political Life*, West Lafayette, Indiana: Purdue University Press.
(1979) *The Structure of Human Life: A Vitalist Ontology*, New York: New York University Press.
(1982) *The Wilderness and the City: American Classical Philosophy as a Moral Quest*, Amherst: University of Massachusetts Press.
(1984) *Unity and Variety in the Philosophy of Samuel Alexander*, West Lafayette, Indiana: Purdue University Pres.
(1985) *Finite Perfection: Reflections on Virtue*, Amherst: University of Massachusetts Press.
(1993) (with Deena Weinstein) *Postmodern(ized) Simmel*, London: Routledge.
(1994) *Data Trash: A Theory of the Virtual Class*, St Martin's Press.
(1995) *Culture/Flesh: A Postcivilized Meditation*, Savage, M.D. Rowman & Littlefield.

Weinstein's work has been characterized by a continuing reference to the situation of the critical person, inevitably immersed in both the traditions of Western philosophy and the decentring themes of twentieth-century intellectual life. With a self-described intellectual origin in the socio-cultural criticism of the 1960s, Weinstein has developed powerful syntheses of classical American and contemporary European thought. Originally attracted to Jamesian radical empiricism and existentialism (**Heidegger**), some of Weinstein's later work incorporated a 'sociology of knowledge' understood to include a healthy respect for Freudian and various other psycho-social critiques of individualism. A dimension of this respect for self-critiquing perspective has been numerous powerful essays which examine contemporary American social science and academic 'professionalism'. Noteworthy for a North American philosopher has been a respect for Hispanic thought, particularly Latin American anti-positivism and such Iberians as **Orgega y Gasset** and, as a book title of 1977 reveals, Miguel de **Unamuno**.

More recently, in essays on philosophy and political values, and in innumerable reviews of photography displays in the Chicago area, Weinstein has explored the 'postmodern' with obvious openness, and made clearer a persistent vision of the self-critical individual equipped with a kind of 'vitalist' psycho-physical anchoring, a sense of human life which seeks to critique comprehensively and avoid reductive descriptions of the subjective and relativistic, take account of death and embrace a broad possibility of appreciation and expression of the human condition as found in particular lives.

AMY A. OLIVER

Weiss, Paul

American. **b:** 19 May 1901, New York City. **Cat:** Metaphysician. **Educ:** City College of New York, BBS 1927; Harvard University, AM 1928, PhD 1929. **Infls:** Whitehead and Peirce. **Appts:** 1931–45, Assistant Professor to Professor of Philosophy, Bryn Mawr College; 1945–69, Professor of Philosophy, Yale University (Emeritus Professor from 1969); from 1969, Heffer Professor of Philosophy, Catholic University of America.

Main publications:

(1931–5) (ed. with C. Hartshorne) *Collected Papers of Charles Sanders Peirce*, 6 vols, Cambridge, MA: Harvard University Press.

(1938) *Reality*, Princeton: Princeton University Press; reprinted, Carbondale: Southern Illinois University Press, 1967.

(1958) *Modes of Being*, Carbondale: Southern Illinois University Press.

(1977) *First Considerations: An Examination of Philosophical Evidence*, Carbondale: Southern Illinois University Press.

Secondary literature:

(1995) *Being and Other Realities*, La Salle, Ill.: Open Court.

Hahn, L. E. (ed.) (1995) *The Philosophy of Paul Weiss*, La Salle, Ill.: Open Court, The Library of Living Philosophers.

Krettek, T. (ed.) (1987) *Creativity and Common Sense. Essays in Honour of Paul Weiss*, Albany: SUNY Press.

Founding first editor of the *Review of Metaphysics*, Weiss began his career as a logician. *Reality* (1938) presents a metaphysical theory restricted to actuality. Cognizant that it was inadequate for ethics, Weiss went on to present a theory of man and morality that requires additional ontological realms. *Modes of Being* (1958) is his systematic modal ontology, positing four modes of being: actuality, ideality, existence and God. In subsequent decades Weiss has traced the ramifications of his ontology in all the fields of human experience, such as art, religion, science, politics, law and history. His latest works constitute a postmodal metaphysics, with actualities juxtaposed to finalities (the revised modalities) and a pervasive principle of creativity, termed the 'dunamis'.

Sources: I. C. Lieb (1961) *Experience, Existence, and the Good: Essays in Honor of Paul Weiss*, Carbondale: Southern Illinois UP; WW(Am).

ANDREW RECK

Weitz, Morris

American. **b:** 24 July 1916, Detroit, Michigan. **d:** 1987. **Cat:** Aesthetics; philosophy in literature; analytic philosophy. **Educ:** BA, Wayne State University, 1938; PhD, University of Michigan, 1943. **Infls:** Wittgenstein. **Appts:** University of Washington, 1944–5; Vassar College, 1945–8; Ohio State University, 1954–69; Professor, Brandeis University, from 1969.

Main publications:

(1950) *Philosophy of the Arts*, Harvard: Harvard University Press; new edition, New York: Russell & Russell, 1964.

(1953) 'Oxford philosophy', *Philosophical Review* 62.

(1956) 'The role of theory in aesthetics', *Journal of Aesthetics and Art Criticism* 15; reprinted in Weitz (ed.), *Problems in Aesthetics: An Introductory Book of Readings*, New York: Macmillan, 1959; second edition, 1970.

(1963) *Philosophy in Literature: Shakespeare, Voltaire, Tolstoy and Proust*, Wayne State University Press.

(1964) *Hamlet and the Philosophy of Literary Criticism*, Chicago: Chicago University Press; reissued London: Faber, 1972.

(1977) *The Opening Mind: A Philosophical Study of Humanistic Concepts*, Chicago and London: University of Chicago Press.

(1988) *Theories of Concepts: A History of the Major Philosophical Tradition*, London: Routledge (includes complete bibliography).

Secondary literature:

Abrams, M. H. (1972) 'What's the use of theorizing about the arts?', in M. W. Bloomfield (ed.), *In Search of Literary Theory*, Ithaca.

Mandelbaum, Maurice (1965) 'Family resemblances and generalization concerning the arts', *American Philosophical Quarterly* 2, 3; reprinted in Weitz (ed.), *Problems in Aesthetics: An Introductory Book of Readings*, New York: Macmillan, 1959; second edition, 1970.

Weitz wrote extensively on the basic concepts of literary criticism and art history. He also investigated philosophical ideas expressed in literature. In 'The role of theory in aesthetics' (1956) he argued that generalizations about the nature of art, particularly those that assumed that art could be defined in terms of necessary and sufficient conditions, involved a logically vain attempt to define what could not be defined and foreclosed on artistic creativity. These claims stirred **Mandelbaum** and others to defend the attempt to find a definition of art, although Weitz continued to maintain his view that such an attempt was misguided. Weitz's later writings, particularly *The Opening Mind* (1977), expanded his account of open concepts, a notion derived from **Wittgenstein**'s writings on family resemblance terms, and investigated the history of theories of concepts.

Sources: DAS, 6th edn; *PI*; complete bibliography (excl. book reviews) in Weitz 1988.

NIGEL WARBURTON

Wellmer, Albrecht

German. *b:* 9 July 1939. *Cat:* Social philosopher; critical theorist. *Ints:* Philosophy of science; moral philosophy; political philosophy. *Infls:* Critical theory, especially Adorno and Habermas. *Appts:* Professor of Philosophy, University of Konstanz; Professor of Philosophy, Free University of Berlin.

Main publications:

(1967) *Methodologie als Erkenntnistheorie: Zur Wissenschaftslehre Karl R. Poppers*, Frankfurt: Suhrkamp.

(1969) *Kritische Gesellschaftstheorie und Positivismus* (English translation, *Critical Theory of Society*, trans. John Cumming, New York: Seabury, 1974).

(1977) 'Kommunikation und Emanzipation. Überlegungen zur "Sprachkritischen Wende" der kritischen Theorie', in Urs Jaeggi and Axel Honneth (eds), *Theorien des Historischen Materialismus*, Frankfurt: Suhrkamp.

(1985) *Zur Dialektik von Moderne und Postmoderne. Vernunftkritik nach Adorno*, Frankfurt: Suhrkamp.

(1986) *Ethik und Dialog. Elemente des moralischen Urteils bei Kant und in der Diskursethik*, Frankfurt: Suhrkamp.

(1986) (ed. with Axel Honneth) *Die Frankfurter Schule und die Folgen*, Berlin: De Gruyter.

(1988) 'Intersubjectivity and reason', in Lars Hertzberg and Juhani Piatarinen (eds), *Perspectives on Human Conduct*, Leiden: E. J. Brill.

(1991) *The Persistence of Modernity: Aesthetics, Ethics and Postmodernism*, trans. David Midgley, Cambridge: Polity.

(1993) *Endspiele: die unversöhnliche Moderne. Essays und Vorträge*, Frankfurt: Suhrkamp.

Secondary literature:

Adorno, Theodor *et al.* (1976) *The Positivist Dispute in German Sociology*, trans. Glyn Adey and David Frisby, London: Heinemann.

Wellmer's early work carried forward the critique of positivism developed in the 'Positivism Dispute' of the early 1960s, (Adorno *et al.* 1976). His *Critical Theory of Society* (1969) remains an exceptionally valuable discussion of critical theory. Like **Habermas** and **Apel** he has since worked more substantially in moral philosophy and on the relations between discourse ethics and social theory, paying particular attention to the challenge of 'postmodern' theory.

WILLIAM OUTHWAITE

Wertheimer, Max

Czech-American. *b:* 15 April 1880, Prague. *d:* 12 October 1943, New Rochelle, New York. *Cat:* Psychologist; social philosopher; musician. *Ints:* The structure of wholes; truth; educational theory. *Educ:* Charles University, Prague, and the Universities of Berlin and Würzburg. *Infls:* Literary influences include Spinoza, Kant and L. E. J. Brouwer. Personal: Einstein, Carl Stumpf, O. Külpe, Kurt Koffka and Wolfgang Köhler. *Appts:* 1912–18, Lecturer in Psychology, University of Frankfurt; 1918–33, Lecturer then, (1921) Professor of Psychology, University of Berlin; 1934–43, Professor of Psychology and Philosophy, New School for Social Research, New York.

Main publications:

(1945) *Productive Thinking*, New York: Harper (posthumous); enlarged edition, ed. Michael Wertheimer, 1959.

(1970) *Wertheimer's Seminars Revisited: Problem Solving and Thinking*, reconstructed by A. S. and E. H. Luchins, 3 vols. Albany: State University of New York, Faculty Student Association (posthumous).

(1978) *Revisiting Wertheimer's Seminars: Value, Social Influences and Power, Problems in Social Psychology*, reconstructed by A. S. and E. H. Luchins, 3 vols, Lewisburg, PA: Bucknell University Press (posthumous).

Secondary literature:

Köhler, Wolfgang (1944) 'Max Wertheimer: 1880–1943', *Psychological Review* 51: 143-6.

Watson, Robert I. (1963) *The Great Psychologists: From Aristotle to Freud*, Philadelphia: Lippincott, pp. 403–22.

Wertheimer is famous as the originator of Gestalt psychology, which attempts to examine psychological phenomena as 'structural wholes'; that is, not as aggregates in which the parts are added, but as integral unities arising from the interrelations of their parts.

His philosophy, which came to the fore only after he had moved to America in 1933, reflected his Gestalt theory. In his *Productive Thinking* (1945) he distinguished between the laws of logic and the laws of thought, between habitual, imitative behaviour and creative, productive acts of thinking. Thus he criticized the current educational emphasis on traditional logic, arguing that important problem-solving processes such as grouping and reorganization, which deal with problems as structural wholes, were not recognized in logic. For Wertheimer truth was a function not of individual details but of the entire systematic structure of experience where all is relevant to all. Wertheimer's Gestalt theory has had an enormously stimulating influence not only on psychology but also on philosophy, especially the philosophy of perception and aesthetics.

Sources: EF.

STEPHEN MOLLER

Westermarck, Edward Alexander

Swedish-Finnish. *b:* 20 November 1862, Helsinki. *d:* 3 September 1939, London. *Cat:* Anthropologist; moral philosopher. *Ints:* Sociology of morals. *Educ:* University of Helsinki. *Infls:* J. S. Mill and Spencer. *Appts:* 1903–7, Lecturer in Sociology, London School of Economics; 1906–18, Professor of Practical Philosophy, University of Helsinki; 1907–30, Professor of Sociology, London School of Economics.

Main publications:

(1891) *The History of Human Marriage*, London: Macmillan.

(1906–8) *The Origin and Development of the Moral Ideas*, 2 vols, London and New York: Macmillan.

(1926) *A Short History of Marriage*, London and New York: Macmillan.

(1932) *Early Beliefs and their Social Influence*, London: Macmillan.

(1932) *Ethical Relativity*, London: Kegan Paul.

Secondary literature:

Acta Philosophica Fennica (1982) (issue devoted to the life and work of Westermarck; includes bibliography and critical appreciations).

Mackie, J. L. (1967) 'Westermarck' in Paul Edwards (ed.) *Encyclopedia of Philosophy*, New York: Macmillan, vol. 8, pp. 284–6.

Westermarck's first major book, *The Origin and Development of the Moral Ideas* (1906–08), took him many years to produce and in it his subjectivist view of ethics is already presupposed. He argued that, since there are no objective moral truths, the task of a scientific ethics is 'to investigate the moral consciousness as a fact'. Accordingly he made a comparative and historical survey of the varying attitudes and practices of different human societies on such topics as homicide, blood revenge, charity and slavery.

Westermarck's subjectivism was criticized by G. E. **Moore** amongst others and he replied to his critics in his main philosophical work, *Ethical Relativity* (1932). He sought to show that those philosophical theories which sought to provide an underpinning for an objectivist ethics, such as utilitarianism and evolutionary ethics, failed to provide a suitable defence for their fundamental principles. Subjectivist and relativist views in ethics, though widely popular, have been extensively criticized by philosophers. 'Nevertheless', in the opinion of J. L. **Mackie**, 'some contemporary philosophers believe that Westermarck's views on ethics are substantially correct and that he made an important contribution to the development and defense of views of this kind' (1967, p. 286).

Sources: Westermarck (1929) *Memories of My Life*, London: Allen & Unwin.

STUART BROWN

Weyl, Hermann

German. *b:* 9 November 1885, Elmshorn, Hamburg. *d:* 8 December 1955, Zürich. *Cat:* Mathematician; philosopher of mathematics; philosopher of science. *Ints:* Mathematical logic. *Educ:* Göttingen (doctorate 1908) (Hilbert). *Infls:* David Hilbert, Minkowski, Eckehart, Einstein, Fichte, Husserl, Kant, Felix Klein, Leibniz, Russell and Zermelo. *Appts:* 1908-13, Göttingen; 1913–30, Zurich; 1930–3, Göttingen; 1933–51, Princeton.

Main publications:

(1918) *Raum–Zeit–Materie, Vorlesungen über allgemeinen Relativitäts-theorie*, Berlin: Springer.
(1921) *Space–Time–Matter*, trans. Brose, New York: Dutton.
(1924) *Was ist die Materie?, Zwei Aufsätze zur Naturphilosophie*, Berlin.
(1927) *Philosophie der Mathematik und Naturwissenschaft*, Munich: R. Oldenbourg.
(1932) *The Open World: Three Lectures on the Metaphysical Implications of Science*, New Haven: Yale University Press.
(1934) *Mind and Nature*, Philadelphia: Philadelphia University Press.
(1949) *Philosophy of Mathematics and Natural Science*, Princeton: Princeton University Press.
(1952) *Symmetry*, Princeton: Princeton University Press (contains bibliography).

Secondary literature:

Besswanger, P. (1966) 'Hermann Weyl and mathematical texts', *Ratio* 8: 25–43.
Rosen, N. (1982) 'Weyl's geometry and physics', *Foundations of Physics* 12: 213–48.
Speiser, D. (1971) 'La nouvelle édition de *Raum–Zeit–Materie* de Hermann Weyl', *Revue des Questions Scientifiques* 32: 387–84.
Vizgen, V. P. (1984) 'Einstein, Hilbert, Weyl, Genesis des Programms der einheitlichen geometrischen Feldtheorie', *Zeitschrift für Geschichte der Naturwissenschaft, Technik und Medizin*.

A mathematician with wide interests in mathematics and its philosophy, Weyl was an early contributor to the construction of the general theory of relativity. He brought to his philosophical interests wide philosophical reading and was unable to accept the view that arbitrary postulation was all in the foundation of mathematics, being notably opposed to the axiom of choice in mathematical logic. He was a marked advocate of mathematical intuitionism, otherwise associated with L. **Brouwer**.

Sources: M. H. A. Newman *et al.* (1958) *BMMRS* 3: 305–23; C. Chevalley (1957) 'Hermann Weyl (1885–1955)' *Enseignement, mathématique*, 2e série, 3, 157–87; DSB 1976: 281a–285b.

R. N. D. MARTIN

Whitehead, A(lfred) N(orth)

British. *b:* 15 February 1861, Ramsgate, England. *d:* 30 December 1947, Cambridge, Massachusetts. *Cat:* Mathematician; philosopher of science; process metaphysician. *Ints:* Philosophy of science. *Educ:* Trinity College, Cambridge, BA 1884, DSc 1905. *Infls:* Maxwell, Boole and Russell. *Appts:* 1884–1910, Fellow, Assistant Lecturer to Senior Lecturer, University of Cambridge; 1911–18, Lecturer in Applied Mathematics and Mechanics, University College, London; 1918–24, Chief Professor of Mathematics, Imperial College of Science and Technology, London, and Dean of the Faculty of Science, University of London (1918–22); 1924–37, Professor of Philosophy, Harvard; 1931, elected Fellow of the British Academy; 1945, awarded the Order of Merit by the British Crown.

Main publications:

(1910–13) (with Bertrand Russell) *Principia Mathematica*, 3 vols, Cambridge: Cambridge University Press.
(1919) *An Enquiry Concerning the Principles of Natural Knowledge*; second edition, Cambridge: Cambridge University Press, 1925.
(1920) *The Concept of Nature*, Cambridge: Cambridge University Press.
(1922) *The Principle of Relativity, with Applications to Physical Science*, Cambridge: Cambridge University Press.
(1925) *Science and the Modern World*, New York: Macmillan Co.; reprinted, New York: The Free Press, 1967.
(1926) *Religion in the Making*, New York: Macmillan Co.
(1927) *Symbolism: Its Meaning and Effect*, New York: Macmillan Co.; reprinted, New York: Fordham University Press, 1985.
(1928) *The Aims of Education and Other Essays*, New York: Macmillan Co.; reprinted, New York: The Free Press, 1967.
(1929) *The Function of Reason*, Princeton, NJ: Princeton University Press; reprinted, Boston: Beacon Press, 1958.
(1929) *Process and Reality: An Essay in Cosmology*, New York: Macmillan Co.; reprinted corrected edition, ed. D. R. Griffin and D. W. Sherburne, New York: The Free Press, 1967.

(1933) *Adventures of Ideas*, New York: Macmillan Co.; reprinted, New York: The Free Press, 1967.
(1934) *Nature and Life*, Chicago: University of Chicago Press.
(1938) *Modes of Thought*, New York: Macmillan Co.

Secondary literature:
Lowe, V. (1962) *Understanding Whitehead*, Baltimore: Johns Hopkins University Press.
——(1985) *Alfred North Whitehead: The Man and His Work, Vol. I: 1861–1910*, Baltimore: Johns Hopkins University Press.
——(1990) *Alfred North Whitehead: The Man and His Work, Vol. II: 1910–1947*, ed. J. B. Schneewind, Baltimore: Johns Hopkins University Press.
Schilpp, P. A. (ed.) (1941) *The Philosophy of Alfred North Whitehead*, Evanston: Northwestern University Press; second edition, New York: Tudor Publishing Co., 1951.
Sherburne, D. W. (1966) *A Key to Whitehead's 'Process and Reality'*, New York: Macmillan; reprinted, Chicago: University of Chicago Press, 1981.

Whitehead first achieved eminence in the field of mathematics. His fellowship dissertation was devoted to Maxwell's *Treatise on Electricity and Magnetism*. Becoming engrossed in the investigation of the various systems of symbolic reasoning allied to ordinary algebra, such as Hamilton's quaternions, Grassman's calculus of extension and Boole's symbolic logic, he authored (1898) *A Treatise on Universal Algebra, with Applications*, vol. 1 (Cambridge University Press). In 1903 he was elected a Fellow of the Royal Society in London. He next published (1903) *The Axioms of Projective Geometry* (Cambridge University Press) and (1907) *The Axioms of Descriptive Geometry* (Cambridge University Press).

Meanwhile, Whitehead had come to accept the logicist thesis that the foundations of mathematics rested in logic, a thesis favoured by Bertrand **Russell**, his former student at Cambridge who had switched to philosophy. In 1901 Whitehead and Russell began their famous collaboration, the former serving as the mathematician, the latter as the philosopher, to produce *Principia Mathematica*. Whitehead was to prepare a fourth volume on geometry, but never did so. The new matter in the second edition (1925) is solely Russell's. After resigning his lectureship at Cambridge and moving to London, Whitehead produced a popular, introductory text for the Home University Library of Modern Knowledge, *An Introduction to Mathematics* (London: Williams & Norgate, 1911). He

also delivered several addresses and wrote numerous papers on education, published in *The Organisation of Thought, Educational and Scientific* (London: Williams & Norgate, 1917) and *The Rhythm of Education* (London: Christophers, 1922). This phase of his work culminated in *The Aims of Education and Other Essays* (1928). In London Whitehead's focus shifted to the philosophy of science. This shift, which allied him with the neo-realists G. E. **Moore**, C. D. **Broad**, T. P. Nunn and Bertrand Russell, also led to his philosophical break with Russell.

Whitehead's contributions to the philosophy of science, or of nature, are contained in several remarkable books. *An Enquiry Concerning the Principles of Natural Knowledge* (1919) unleashed Whitehead's realism. *The Concept of Nature* (1920) decried the bifurcation of nature into mind and nature, and, having adopted a realistic stance, portrayed nature as consisting of the passage of events, to be understood in terms of objects, including what Whitehead called 'eternal objects', recurrent universals akin to Plato's forms or Santayana's essences. In this work Whitehead also unveiled his method of extensive abstraction, a method to explain how mathematical entities such as points and lines are abstracted from concrete experience. *The Principle of Relativity, with Applications to Physical Science* (1922) was Whitehead's endeavour to offer a theory alternative to Einstein's. At Harvard Whitehead's philosophy took a speculative turn. In *Science and the Modern World* (1925) he showed how the categorial presuppositions formulated by the philosopher-scientists of the seventeenth century exhibited a cosmology which the romantic poets of the nineteenth century had rebelled against because of its devaluation of nature, and which the scientific discoveries of the late nineteenth and early twentieth centuries were overthrowing. Whitehead suggested nothing less than a revolution in philosophical cosmology, an overhaul of the basic categories of thought. *Science and the Modern World* was a popular success. It elucidated then arcane scientific theories such as relativity and quantum mechanics, associating these scientific notions with a whole range of human values, in history, literature, religion and civilization. It also introduced philosophical phrases that caught on in process philosophy, such as the fallacy of misplaced concreteness, the fallacy of simple location and the conception of God as the principle of concretion. *Religion in the Making* (1926) defined religion as that which the individual does in his own solitude to appreciate the novelty and to assuage the loss that incessant change or process entails. It further advanced process theology when it underscored the dynamic quality of religion as itself caught up in change. *Symbolism: Its Meaning and Effect* (1927) presented Whitehead's theory of conceptual meaning and of perceptual knowledge. This epistemology repudiated the theories of the contemporary heirs of David Hume. It recognized two sorts of perception, perception in the mode of presentational immediacy and perception in the mode of causal efficacy. Ready to present a new system of philosophy, Whitehead seized the opportunity to do so in the Gifford Lectures he delivered at Edinburgh in 1928. The result was the most famous system of speculative philosophy in the English language in the twentieth century—*Process and Reality* (1929). Defining speculative philosophy as the endeavour to frame a consistent and coherent system of categories which would be comprehensive enough to interpret every item of experience, Whitehead proposed such a system, subject to subsequent revision. Among its nine categories of existence are the categories of actual entities, eternal objects, prehensions and nexus. An actual entity is an occasion of experience, identical with the simplest quantum event; it feels—i.e. prehends—all its past negatively and positively. It is lured, concresces or completes itself, then perishes, to be prehended by its successors. Ingredient in its constitution are eternal objects which ingress or are prehended by it. Actual entities form societies, or nexus; the human person, for example, is a society. Distinct from the categories of existence is the category of the ultimate: it is creativity, the one, and the many. Creativity is, however, not God: it is neither an actual entity nor a society of actualities, but rather the surge of activity or novelty, of flux ongoing in all actual entities. The idea of God is a notion derivative from the categories, categorial obligations and categorial explanations advanced by Whitehead. As the first accident of creativity, God, in his primordial and in his consequent natures, is the actual entity that guarantees the order of cosmos. *Process and Reality* has been grandly appreciated by some American philosophers, such as, F. S. C. **Northrop**, Paul **Weiss** and Charles **Hartshorne**, although others, like W. V. O. **Quine**, are more disposed to continue in the vein of the earlier works. Still it has endured as the mainspring of process theology. Noteworthy among Whitehead's last books is *Adventures of Ideas* (1933). It presents his philosophy of civilization, stressing the primary, creative role of general ideas. It also offers easy access to Whitehead's mature philosophy.

Sources: DNB 1941–50; Edwards.

ANDREW RECK

Whorf, Benjamin Lee

American. *b:* 24 April 1897, Winthrop, Massachusetts. *d:* 26 July 1941, Wethersfield, Connecticut. *Cat:* Philosopher of language; social anthropologist. *Ints:* Metalinguistics; thought; culture. *Educ:* Massachusetts Institute of Technology. *Infls:* Edward Sapir. *Appts:* Whorf held no academic posts. He pursued the career of fire prevention officer.

Main publications:

(1952) *Collected Papers on Metalinguistics*, Washington: Foreign Service Institute, Department of State (posthumous).
(1956) *Language, Thought, and Reality: Selected Writings of Benjamin Lee Whorf*, ed. and intro. John B. Carrol, Massachusetts: MIT Press (posthumous).

Secondary literature:

Hoijer, H. (ed.) (1954) *Language in Culture, American Anthropologist* 56, Memoir no. 79.
——(1992) *Grammatical Categories and Cognition: A Case Study of the Linguistic Relativity Hypothesis* vol. 1, New York: Cambridge University Press.
Rollins, P. C. (1979) *Benjamin Lee Whorf: Lost Generation Theories of Mind, Language and Religion*, Ann Arbor: Michigan University Microfilms International.

Whorf's views were formed under the guidance of Edward **Sapir** and through his own studies of Maya and Hopi Indian languages. He offered the hypothesis (also called the 'Sapir–Whorf' hypothesis') that the belief that the cognitive processes of all human beings possess a universal structure which operates prior to and independently of linguistic communication is erroneous. He held that the linguistic patterns themselves profoundly influence what we perceive in the world and how we think about it. Since these patterns vary widely, the modes of thinking and perceiving in groups utilizing different languages will result in basically different worldviews. Thus Whorf introduced 'a new principle of relativity', according to which all observers are not led by the same physical evidence to the same *Weltanschauung* (1952, p. 21).

Whorf exemplified this principle especially by

contrasting Indo-European languages to Hopi. Whereas the former, he noted, have parts of speech, separable subject and predicate and emphasize time, Hopi does not, but rather signifies an event as a whole and without temporal distinctions. This, he maintained, means that the Hopi *Weltanschauung* is quite different from our own, though 'equally valid' (1952, p. 67). The Whorfian hypothesis of the linguistic relativity of the categories of cognition is embedded in a powerful current of contemporary thought. But Whorf's hypothesis has been changed over time through its iterations in various disciplines and studies: for example, where Whorf focused on the influence of language on thought, later iterations frequently focus on language determining thought.

Sources: DAS; Bullock & Woodings.

STEPHEN MOLLER

Wiesel, Elie (Eliezer)

Transylvanian Jew. *b:* 30 September 1928, Sighet, Transylvania. *Cat:* Author; journalist; existentialist; philosopher of Holocaust. *Ints:* The Holocaust; world peace. *Educ:* Hasidic and general until deportation to Auschwitz and Buchenwald from the age of fifteen; 1946–7, *Talmud* (Code of Jewish Law) with Rabbi Mordechai Shushani (Levinas's teacher) Paris; 1948–51, French Literature, Philosophy and Pyschology, Sorbonne and University of Paris. *Infls:* Hasidism; experiences of concentration camps; extermination of his entire family; Hebrew literature; psychology; Rabbi M. Shushani, Camus, Dostoevsky, A. Malraux, Nietzsche, Sartre, Mauriac and Kafka. *Appts:* On liberation from Buchenwald, Wiesel was sent to France with other child survivors (the British prevented him and many others from settling in Palestine); and he worked as camp counsellor, choir director, tutor and translator; 1949, Foreign Correspondent, *Yedi'ot Acharonot* (Israeli newspaper); 1957, journalist, *Jewish Daily Forward* (Yiddish newspaper); journalist for Israeli, French and American newspapers;. DLitt (hon.), 1967, Jewish Theological Seminary, New York; 1975, Marquette University; 1987, University of Paris; 1964, Prize for Universalité de la Langue Française; LHD (hon.), 1968, Hebrew Union College; 1973, Yeshiva University; 1974, Boston University; 1980, Brandeis University; PhD (hon.), Universities of Bar Ilan, 1973; Haifa, 1986; and Ben Gurion, the Negev, 1988; various honorary LLDs and HHDs; Dr, Humane Letters; Distinguished Professor of Judaic Studies, City College, New York, 1972–6; Professor of Religious Studies, and then Philosophy, Boston, 1976–; Visiting Scholar, Human Sciences, Yale University, 1982–3 and many others; Chair, US President's Commission on Holocaust, 1979; Chair, US Holocaust Memorial Council, 1980; on various educational and humanitarian boards; Fellow, Jewish Academy Arts and Sciences; various literary prizes, France; books translated into many languages, including Dutch, Japanese and Norwegian; Distinguished Foreign-Born American Award and other awards in Israel, France, Norway, USA, Italy and Brazil; Nobel Peace Prize, Oslo 1986; Artists and Writers for Peace in the Middle East Award, 1987; Elie Wiesel Chair in Holocaust Studies and Elie Wiesel Award for Holocaust Research, Haifa University, 1987; Ellis Island Medal of Honor, 1992; First Primo Levi Award, 1992; Légion d'Honneur, France; US Congressional Gold Medal of Achievement at nationally televised White House ceremony, 1985; 1995, helped organize joint 50th anniversary commemoration by the worldwide Jewish community and the Polish government at Auschwitz concentration camp.

Main publications:

(1956) *Un di Velt Hot Geshvign* [And the World Remained Silent] Buenos Aires, (French translation, *La Nuit*, Minuit, 1958, 1973, 1975; English translation, *Night*, trans. S. Rodway, New York: Hill & Wang, 1960, 1972; Avon, 1970; London: Fontana/Collins, 1972; Harmondsworth, Middlesex: Penguin, 1981).

(1960) *L'Aube*, Paris: Seuil (English translation, *Dawn*, trans. F. Renaye, New York: Hill & Wang, 1961, 1970, 1972; Toronto: Bantam Books, 1982).

(1961) *Le Jour*, Paris: Seuil (English translation, *Day*, 1961; all three as *The Night Trilogy, or Night, Day, The Accident*, New York: Hall & Wang, 1972, 1985, 1987; London: Robson, 1974; *Night, Dawn, Day*, New York: Aronson, Bnai Brith, 1985, 1987).

(1966) *Les Juifs du Silence*, Paris: Seuil (English translation, *The Jews of Silence*, New York: Holt, Rinehart & Winston, 1966; London: Vallentine Mitchell, 1968, 1973; New York: Schocken, 1987).

(1966) *Le Chant des Morts* [The Song of the Dead], Paris: Seuil (English translation, *Legends of our Time*, trans. S. Donadio, New York: Holt, Rinehart & Winston, 1968; Schocken, 1982).

(1966) *Le Mendiant de Jérusalem*, Paris: Seuil, 1966, (English translation, *A Beggar in Jerusalem*, trans. L. Edelman and E. Wiesel, New York: Schocken, 1970; 1985).

(1970) *One Generation After*, trans. L. Edelman and E. Wiesel, New York: Random House, 1970; Avon,

1972; Schocken, 1982; Bibliophile Library, 1986 (original in French, *Entre Deux Soleils*).

(1972) *Souls on Fire*, trans. Marion Wiesel, London: Weidenfeld & Nicolson; New York: Summit, 1984; Northvale, NJ: Aronson, 1993 (original in French, *Célébration Hassidique*).

(1979) *A Jew Today*, trans. Marion Wiesel, New York: Vintage.

(1979) *The Trial of God*; New York: Random House; Schocken, 1986.

(1983) *The Golem*, New York: Summit.

(1988) (with A. H. Friedlander) *The Six Days of Destruction*, Oxford: Pergamon, and Mahwah, NJ.

(1990) (with P. de Saint-Cheron) *Evil and Exile*, Notre Dame: University of Notre Dame Press.

Secondary literature:

Berenbaum, M. (1979) *The Vision of the Void: Theological Reflections on the Works of Elie Wiesel*, Middletown, Conn.: Wesleyan University Press.

Berger, A. L. (1993) 'Elie Wiesel', in *Interpreters of Judaism in the Late Twentieth Century*, ed. S. T. Katz, Washington, DC: Bnai Brith, pp. 369–91 (includes bibliography).

Brown, R. Mc. (1983) *Elie Wiesel: Messenger to All Humanity*; Notre Dame: University of Notre Dame Press, 1989; revised 1990 .

Engel, V. (1989) *Fou de Dieu ou Dieu des Fous*, Brussels: de Boeck.

Fine, E. S. (1982) *Legacy of Night: The Literary Universe of Elie Wiesel*, Albany: SUNY Press.

Friedman, M. S. (1987) *Abraham Joshua Heschel and Elie Wiesel, You Are My Witness*, New York: Farrar, Straus, Giroux.

Frost, C. J. (1985) *Religious Melancholy or Psychological Depression?*, Lanham, MD: University Press of America.

Rittner, C. (1990) *Elie Wiesel: Between Memory and Hope*, New York: New York University Press.

Walker, G. B. (1988) *Elie Wiesel: A Challenge to Theology*, Jefferson, NC: McFarland.

Wiesel is most famous for his existential philosophy of the Holocaust, written in novel form. Only his first novel, written in Yiddish, describes his own experiences. He has discussed the role played by Christianity in the Holocaust, the continual Holocaust denial and the increasing rise of anti-semitism, especially in the wake of the 'democratization' of eastern Europe. He is rare in being regarded as a member of both the Jewish mystical, and the French existential, traditions. He has become almost an icon in some European countries, and has, more than any other thinker, influenced post-Holocaust theology and philosophy.

Wiesel has challenged Orthodox Judaism by declaring the Holocaust to be a more significant occurrence in Jewish and world history even than God's revelation to the Jews at Mount Sinai. He particularly emphasizes the role of silence in the Holocaust and accuses God of breaking His covenant with the Jewish people. Basing himself on the Lurianic Kabbalah of the sixteenth century Galilean town of Sfat, Wiesel construes evil as contained within the divine. It is up to humanity to assist God in repairing the world, a concept known as *tikkun*. Wiesel rebukes Richard **Rubenstein** for asserting that God is dead, and points out that this is not the view taken by Holocaust survivors. Like the biblical Job, Wiesel believes in God but is sceptical of divine justice. He nevertheless asserts that the survival of Judaism transcends even the need for a just deity.

Wiesel regards his writing as a dialogue with himself, with the reader and with God. He says that since the Holocaust it is impossible for there to be art for art's sake. Everything must be written with the Holocaust as its background. He stresses the importance of memory as a device for transformation and for preventing another Holocaust (just as the early rabbis had emphasized the importance of memorizing texts as a means of grounding themselves in Jewish tradition). Despite speaking on behalf of other victims of atrocities, such as the Tibetans, the Burmese and the Bosnians, Wiesel constantly reiterates the uniqueness of the Holocaust. Wiesel's ideas have powerfully influenced Jewish and Christian post-Holocaust theology and other philosopher-rabbis, for example, Irving Greenberg and Emil **Fackenheim**. Ironically, by stressing the Jewish rather than universal aspects of the Holocaust, Wiesel has only helped the ecumenical movement, as much by his character as his writings. He is regarded by many non-Jews as the world's chief spokesman for the Holocaust and even for the Jewish people, as was recognized when he was awarded the Nobel Peace Prize in 1986. More recently he acted as mediator between the Jewish community and the Polish government regarding the format for commemorating the 50th anniversary of the Holocaust in Poland, 1995.

Sources: EncJud; Schoeps; WW(Fr) 1992–3, p. 1669; WW(Am) 1992–3, p. 3567; NUC.

IRENE LANCASTER

Wiggins, David

British. *b:* 8 March 1933, London. *Cat:* Metaphysician; philosopher of mind; ethicist. **Ints:** Metaphysics; philosophy of language; ethics. **Educ:** Oxford University, BA 1955, MA 1958. **Infls:** Heraclitus, Aristotle, Leibniz, Hume, Frege, Peirce, Tarski, P. Strawson, B. Williams, J. L. Austin, Putnam, Kripke, R. Cartwright, McDowell and G. Evans. **Appts:** Assistant Principal, Colonial Office, London, 1957–9; lecturer at University of Oxford, 1959; Fellow of New College, Oxford, 1960–7; Professor of Philosophy at Bedford College, University of London, 1967–80; Fellow of University College, Oxford, 1980–9; Professor of Philosophy at Birkbeck College, University of London, 1989–94; Wykeham Professor of Logic, New College, Oxford, from 1994; Visiting Fellow at Princeton, 1958–9 and 1980; Visiting Professor at Stanford, 1964–5 and 1985–6, at Harvard, 1968 and 1972, at All Souls, Oxford, 1973, and at New York University Law School, 1988; FBA, 1978; Fellow of Center for Advanced Study in Behavioral Sciences, Stanford University, 1985–6; Member of Institut International de Philosophie; Foreign Honorary Member of American Academy of Arts and Sciences, 1992.

Main publications:

(1967) *Identity and Spatio-Temporal Continuity*, Oxford: Blackwell.

(1976) 'Truth, invention and the meaning of life', *Proceedings of the British Academy*, London (reprinted with some changes in *Needs, Values, and Truth*, 1987).

(1980) *Sameness and Substance*, Oxford: Blackwell.

(1987) *Needs, Values, and Truth: Essays in the Philosophy of Value*, Oxford: Blackwell; significantly revised edition, 1991.

Secondary literature:

De Paul, M. R. (1990) Critical Notice of Wiggins' *Needs, Values and Truth* (1987), *Mind*.

Forbes, G. (1983) 'Wiggins on sets and essence', *Mind* (Review of Wiggins 1980).

Noonan, H. (1976) 'Wiggins on identity', *Mind*.

Shoemaker, S. (1970) 'Wiggins on identity', *Philosophical Review* (review of Wiggins 1967).

Williams, S. G. and Lovibond, S. M. (eds) (1990) *Essays on David Wiggins's Work*, with *Replies*, Oxford: Blackwell.

Wright, C. (1993) *Realism, Meaning and Truth*, second edition, Oxford: Blackwell (includes a comment on *Needs, Values, and Truth*).

Wiggins's two main books, published in 1967 and 1980, focus on problems concerning identity—and indeed illustrate this, since the latter started by revising the former but kept only half a chapter. Starting from an Aristotelian distinction between the 'is' of identity and the 'is' of constitution, he insists on two theses which go together, despite often being taken to clash, and which have both proved controversial. First, identity is absolute, not relative, i.e. (where *a* and *b* are *f*-things and at least one is a *g*-thing) *a* cannot be the same *f*-thing as *b* while not being the same *g*-thing as *b*. But, second, *a* and *b* cannot simply be the same, without there being some kind *f* such that they are the same *f*-thing.

A substance must have some sortal property (a property that answers the question *what is this substance?*), obeying certain restrictions, which applies to it throughout its history (1980, p. 59), and the implications of this are discussed for natural kind terms, artifacts, works of art, and persons. The later chapters of *Sameness and Substance* develop a moderate essentialism, on the basis of argument not presupposing modal logic (and foundational, the author claims, of something resembling the Kripkean treatment of individuals in modal logic). According to Wiggins moderate essentialism which individuals belong essentially to some kind or species. Individual essences are dispensed with, however, even though the necessity of identity is vindicated. Wiggins defends his view of identity and individualism against certain constrasting extreme positions of simple realism and outright conceptualism. He bases the concept of a person on an objective view of human beings as animals, partly rescuing Locke's use of memory from Butler's charge of circularity by making memory one but only one ingredient in what identifies persons. Persons are conscious continuants, conscious of their states as continuants. They are things in nature, i.e. animals, but animals that interpret one another in the light of 'norms of rationality and reciprocity.

Needs, Values, and Truth (1987) contains one of the few systematic treatments in analytical philosophy of the idea of a need as it figures in moral and political argument, and explores many other themes relating philosophy with metaphysics and the philosophy of language. But it is perhaps most noted for developing a kind of pluralism concerning values which is cognitivist, objectivist *and* (in a sense explicated by reference to Hume's moral philosophy) subjectivist (p. 346). Wiggins deprecates the term 'moral realism' (pp. 330–1); he relies on a view of truth

which owes something to both **Peirce** and **Tarski** and rejects the correspondence theory.
Sources: WW 1992–3; IWW 1993–4; personal communication.

A. R. LACEY

Wild, John D(aniel)
American. *b:* 10 April 1902, Chicago, Illinois. *d:* 22 October 1972, New Haven, Connecticut. *Cat:* Realist; existentialist. *Ints:* Ethics. *Educ:* University of Chicago, PhB 1923, PhD 1926; Harvard University, MA 1925. *Infls:* Plato, Aristotle, Kierkegaard and Husserl. *Appts:* 1927–61, Instructor to Professor of Philosophy, Harvard University; 1961–3, Professor and Chair, Department of Philosophy, Northwestern University; 1963–72, Professor of Philosophy (Emeritus Professor 1969), Yale University.

Main publications:
(1946) *Plato's Theory of Man: An Introduction to the Realist Philosophy of Culture*, Cambridge, Mass.: Harvard University Press.

(1948) *Introduction to Realistic Philosophy*, New York: Harper; reprinted, Lanham, Maryland: University Press of America, 1984.

(1955) *The Challenge of Existentialism*, Bloomington: Indiana University Press; reprinted, Westport, CT: Greenwood, 1979.

(1959) *Human Freedom and Social Order: An Essay in Christian Philosophy*, Durham, NC: Duke University Press.

(1963) *Existence and the World of Freedom*, Englewood Cliffs, NJ: Prentice Hall.

Secondary literature:
Rome, S. and B. (eds) (1964) *Philosophical Interrogations*, New York: Holt, Rinehart & Winston, pp. 119–78.

Wild began his career as a philosophical scholar whose mind was early seared by the religious and moral concerns of Kierkegaard. His first systematic response was to advocate a return to reason by the restoration of the philosophical realism of Plato and Aristotle. *The Challenge of Existentialism* (1955) marks the beginning of his second response in published form, promoting the acceptance of phenomenological and existentialist thought in the English-speaking world.
Sources: WW(Am); *New York Times*, 25 Oct 1972.

ANDREW RECK

Wilkes, Kathleen
British. *b:* 23 June 1946, Berkshire, England. *Cat:* Philosopher of mind; philosopher of science. *Ints:* Empirical psychology; psychoanalysis; ancient philosophy; epistemology. *Educ:* St Hughes College, University of Oxford; PhD, Princeton, 1974. *Infls:* Aristotle, Thomas Nagel and Richard Rorty. *Appts:* Tutor, St Hilda's College, Oxford, since 1973.

Main publications:
(1978) *Physicalism*, Atlantic Highlands, NJ: Humanities Press.
(1981) 'Functionalism, psychology, and the philosophy of mind', *Philosophical Topics* 12: 147–68.
(1984) 'Pragmatics in science and theory in common sense', *Inquiry* 27: 339–62.
(1984) 'Is consciousness important?', *British Journal of the Philosophy of Science* 35: 223–43.
(1986) 'Nemo psychologus nisi physiologus', *Inquiry* 29: 168–85.
(1988) *Real People: Personal Identity without Thought Experiments*, Oxford: Clarendon Press.
(1988) 'Freud's metapsychology', *Proceedings of the Aristotelian Society Supplement*, 62: 117–37.
(1991) 'The relationship between scientific psychology and common-sense psychology', *Synthese*, 15–39.

Secondary literature:
Malcolm, Norman (1979–80) '"Functionalism" in philosophy of psychology', *Proceedings of the Aristotelian Society* 80: 211–30.

Kathleen Wilkes has taken a broadly empirical and interdisciplinary approach to issues in the philosophy of mind and psychology. She has been a consistent defender of physicalism and functionalism, and has argued against the exclusive pursuit of the 'top-down' approach taken by philosophical psychologists such as **Fodor**. She has argued that functionalism, once properly construed and informed by empirical data, can unify psychology and neurophysiology. Wilkes has also argued in 'Pragmatics' (1984), (1986) and (1991) that, contrary to the assumptions of eliminative materialists and philosophical psychologists alike, folk psychology is not a protoscientific theory and thus does not compete with, and is not replaceable by, some future neuroscience. Her limited defences of Freud place him squarely in the physicalist tradition.

Wilkes's work on personal identity is collected in her 1988 monograph, *Real People*. She has argued that the highly speculative thought experiments that have been so characteristic of analytic approaches to personal identity are unhelpful, and has instead focused on real-life problems for the notion of personhood: cerebral commissurotomy, multiple personality disorder, foetuses, and children born with severe mental and physical impairments. In this work, and throughout her career generally, Wilkes has argued for an Aristotelian perspective on mind and person.

PETER DLUGOS

Williams, Bernard Arthur Owen

British. *b:* 1929, Essex. *Cat:* Analytic philosopher. *Ints:* Ethics; philosophical psychology; Descartes. *Educ:* Balliol College, Oxford. *Infls:* Personal influences include Gilbert Ryle; literary influences include Nietzsche's critique of morality. *Appts:* 1951–4, Fellow, All Souls, Oxford; 1954–9, New College, Oxford; 1959–67, Lecturer then Professor of Philosophy, Bedford College, London; 1967–87, Knightbridge Professor of Philosophy, Fellow then Provost of Kings College, Cambridge; Visiting positions in Ghana, USA and Australia; 1979, Chairmanship of Committee on Obscenity and Film Censorship; 1988, Monroe Deutsch Professor of Philosophy, University of California, Berkeley; 1990, White's Professor of Moral Philosophy, Fellow of Corpus Christi College, Oxford; 1993, Committee on Social Justice.

Main publications:

(1966) (ed. with A. C. Montefiore) *British Analytical Philosophy*, London: Routledge.
(1973) *Morality: An Introduction to Ethics*, Harmondsworth: Penguin.
(1973) *Problems of the Self*, Cambridge: Cambridge University Press.
(1973) (with J. J. C. Smart) *Utilitarianism: For and Against*, Cambridge: Cambridge University Press.
(1978) *Descartes: The Project of Pure Enquiry*, Harmondsworth, Penguin.
(1981) *Moral Luck*, Cambridge University Press.
(1982) (ed. with Amartya Sen) *Utilitarianism and Beyond*, Cambridge: Cambridge University Press.
(1985) *Ethics and the Limits of Philosophy*, Cambridge, Mass.: Harvard University Press.
(1993) *Shame and Necessity*, Berkeley: University of California Press.

Secondary literature:

Altham, J. and Harrison, R. (eds) (1995) *World, Mind and Ethics: Essays on the Moral Philosophy of Bernard Williams*, Cambridge: Cambridge University Press.

Statman, Daniel (1993) *Moral Luck*, New York: SUNY Press.

Williams argues for what he calls an absolute conception of reality: a conception of the world as it is, independent of the peculiarities of human perceptual experience, that explains and justifies the perceptual judgements we make. He holds that in ethics there is no such Archimedean point, neither for philosophical reflection about ethics nor for personal moral deliberation: there is no foundation for ethics in any position other than the diverse and irreducible considerations of ethical deliberation. Yet he rejects subjectivist theories of ethics on the grounds that moral claims are experienced objectively as constraints or demands, and that moral attitudes admit of support and attack by reason. At the same time he makes trenchant criticisms of those accounts of rationality in moral thought which abstract from the empirical conditions of ethical experience in favour of some impartial, universalistic or contractual basis for ethics. Both Kantian and utilitarian positions are rejected as based on inadequate accounts of ethical agency, denying the role of personal relations and commitment in moral deliberation and seeking to eliminate risk and conflict from moral thought. Shame or regret for what one has done are moral attitudes essential to a conception of moral agency. In particular, Williams (1985) rejects what he describes as the 'peculiar institution' of modern morality centered on notions of rights, obligations and duty misleadingly contrasted with self-interest.

In his significant contributions to the debate on personal identity, Williams views the self as an essentially embodied and socially located being, constituted through reflective responsibility for past actions and a concern for its future states. In his account of practical reason he argues for the plurality, mutual irreducibility and incommensurability of goods, maintaining that the possibility of conflict, particularly conflict between moral and other values such as scientific enquiry or creative activity, cannot be eliminated from rational, practical thought. Practical deliberation is essentially first personal, though not thereby necessarily egoistic.

In *Shame and Necessity* (1993), Williams combines an insistence that there is a continuity between Ancient Greek thought, as manifested through Homer and tragic drama, and modern ethical thinking, with his views on political and social thought. He maintains a qualified allegiance to enlightenment ideals of modernity in which personal and social values can be subjected to reflective critique, although only from positions within the lived experience of the social world. Critical discussion of Williams's work has focused particularly on personal identity, on the relations between utilitarianism and integrity, and on his claim (1981, ch. 8) that a reason for action must be internal to the agent's beliefs and perspective.

Sources: WW 1993.

CAROLYN WILDE

Williams, Donald Cary

American. **b:** 1899,. **Cat:** Empirical realist. **Ints:** Epistemology; metaphysics; induction and probability. **Infls:** R. B. Perry. **Appts:** Professor, University of California, Los Angeles, and then Harvard University.

Main publications:

(1947) *The Ground of Induction*, Cambridge, Mass.: Harvard University Press.
(1966) *Principles of Empirical Realism*, Springfield, Ill.: Thornes.

Secondary literature:

Campbell, Keith (1976) *Metaphysics*, Encino, Cal.: Dickenson.

Donald C. Williams has been described as a member of the second generation of the American new realists. It was in the spirit of that school that he produced a connected series of articles in the mid-1930s, collectively called 'Realism as an inductive hypothesis'. This aimed at the refutation of all forms of epistemological subjectivism, whether phenomenalist, pragmatist or positivist. A priori arguments for subjectivism were accused of committing a fallacy of misplacing modifiers, for example, confusing the defensible proposition that everything we know is an object of consciousness with the indefensible thesis that we know that everything is an object of consciousness. Inductive arguments for scepticism are argued to entail solipsism if they are consistent, which their opponents then seek to evade by various shifts. Williams believes that we have direct knowledge of material things, and not merely of mental representations of them, and that the mind is part of the nature of which it is aware. Two important articles about time and our awareness of it have been much admired. What particularly brought him to notice was his well-argued defence of induction. Since most of the reasonably large samples of a population closely resemble the population from which they are drawn in their composition, we can validly infer, without certainty but often with quite high probability, from the character of the sample to that of the population. Variants of this argument were elaborated by R. F. Harrod and J. L. **Mackie**. It has been widely criticized for the allegedly illegitimate assumption that all the formally distinct samples from a population have an equal probability of being selected. An interesting later development was Williams's theory of tropes, in pursuit of maximum ontological economy. A trope is an instantiation of a property at a specific place and time, which may be extended in both domains: this instance of redness here, now, for example. A concrete particular is a set of spatio-temporally coincident tropes: a universal is a set of tropes that are similar to one another. Williams always tackles the large problems he addresses in a colourfully entertaining style. William's justification of induction is still very much alive, notably in the work of D. C. Stove, for all the criticism to which it has been subjected. His theory of tropes or abstract particulars has been worked out in detail by Keith Campbell in such a way as to make clear its explanatory power.

Sources: Passmore 1957; Hill, pp. 112–6.

ANTHONY QUINTON

Winch, Peter Guy

British. **b:** 14 January 1926, London. **Cat:** Philosopher of the social sciences. **Ints:** Ethics; philosophy of action; philosophy of religion. **Educ:** St Edmunds Hall, Oxford. **Infls:** Main literary influence is Wittgenstein, but also Simone Weil; personal influences include Rush Rhees. **Appts:** 1951–64, Assistant Lecturer, then Lecturer, then Senior Lecturer, University of Wales, Swansea; 1964–7, Reader in Philosophy, Birkbeck College, University of London; 1967–84, Professor of Philosophy, King's College, London; 1985–, Professor of Philosophy, University of Illinois, Urbana/Champaign.

Main publications:

(1958) *The Idea of a Social Science and its Relation to Philosophy*, London: Routledge & Kegan Paul; second edition, 1990.
(1964) 'Understanding primitive society', *American Philosophical Quarterly* 1: 307–24.
(1966) 'Can a good man be harmed?', *Proceedings of the Aristotelian Society* 66: 55–70.
(1968) 'Moral integrity', Inaugural Lecture, King's College, University of London.

(1969) (ed.) *Studies in the Philosophy of Wittgenstein*, London: Routledge & Kegan Paul.

(1972) *Ethics and Action* (collected essays to 1971), London: Routledge & Kegan Paul.

(1980) (trans.) L. Wittgenstein, *Culture and Value*, Oxford: Blackwell (translation of *Vermischte Bermerkungen*).

(1982) 'Ceasing to exist', Lecture to the British Academy (reprinted in 1987).

(1987) *Trying to Make Sense* (further essays, since 1972) Oxford: Blackwell.

(1989) *Simone Weil: The Just Balance*, Cambridge: Cambridge University Press.

(1989) (ed. with D. Z. Phillips) *Wittgenstein: Attention to Particulars, Essays in Honour of Rush Rhees*, Basingstoke: Macmillan.

(1990) (ed. with Ian Maclean and Alan Montefiore) *The Political Responsibility of Intellectuals*, Basingstoke: Macmillan.

(1992) 'Persuasion', in P. French, T. Ühling and K. Wettstein (eds) *Midwest Studies in Philosophy* XVII, Notre Dame: Notre Dame University Press.

(1993) (ed.) Norman Malcolm, *Wittgenstein: A Religious Point of View* (with a response by Peter Winch), Oxford: Blackwell.

Secondary literature:

Gaita, R. (ed.) (1990) *Value and Understanding*, Essays for Peter Winch, London: Routledge (contains bibliography of Winch's publications).

Several features in the philosophical orientation of Peter Winch have their primary roots in some central themes in the later **Wittgenstein**: the concentration on concrete examples, the attention to particulars and the mistrust of generalizing, the investigation of diverse forms of life and the relations between language, reality and social institutions. Again following Wittgenstein but of much broader base is the recurrent concern with understanding as such and its limits, making sense or failing despite appearances to so. In contrast to Wittgenstein himself, however, Winch frequently takes his examples and illustrations from literary sources.

What has attracted most attention has undoubtedly been his early work on the type or types of understanding appropriate to social phenomena, whether those of our own or of other cultures. His first book—which was translated into several European languages—stressed the kinship between social studies and philosophy and the inappropriateness or misleadingness of the application of the methods of the natural sciences. Understanding the life and institutions of a primitive society requires an appreciation of its own concepts, including that of rationality, in turn integrally related to its own language and modes of life. Hence, in order to understand an alien culture it may be necessary to extend the concepts we already possess.

Winch has himself drawn attention to the continuity in treatment and subject matter of the various concepts he has investigated, whether those of ethics, religion, action or human nature and human life in general. He has also, particularly in recent years, contributed to the direct elucidation of Wittgenstein's thought.

From 1965–71 Winch edited the journal *Analysis*.

Sources: IWW 1993–4; CA FR 29–32, 1978.

CLIVE BORST

Windelband, Wilhelm

German. *b:* 11 May 1848, Potsdam. *d:* 22 October 1915, Heidelberg, Germany. *Cat:* Neo-Kantian; historian of philosophy. *Educ:* First Medicine and Natural Sciences, then History and Philosophy at Berlin and Göttingen. *Infls:* Rudolf Hermann, Lotze and Otto Liebmann. *Appts:* Professor first at Zürich, then at Freiburg and later at Strassburg and Heidelberg.

Main publications:

(1870) *Die Lehren vom Zufall*, Berlin: Henschel.

(1873) *Über die Gewißheit der Erkenntnis*, Berlin: Henschel.

(1878–80) *Geschichte der neueren Philosophie*, 2 vols, Leipzig: Breitkopf & Hätzel.

(1888) *Geschichte der abendländischen Philosophie im Altertum*, Munich: Beck.

(1892) *Lehrbuch der Geschichte der Philosophie*, Tübingen: J. C. B. Mohr (English translation, *A History of Philosophy*, trans. J. H. Tufts, 2 vols, New York: Macmillan, 1901).

(1900) *Platon*, Stuttgart: Frommann.

(1904) *Über Willensfreiheit*, Tübingen: J. C. B. Mohr.

(1924) *Präludien: Aufsätze und Reden zur Philosophie und ihrer Geschichte*, fifth edition, Tübingen: J. C. B. Mohr.

Secondary literature:

Daniels, C. (1929) *Das Geltungsproblem in Windelbands Philosophie*, Berlin.

Rickert, Heinrich (1915) *Wilhelm Windelband*, Tübingen: J. C. B. Mohr.

Windelband understood philosophy as a science of universally valid values. He offered a methodology of science in which he contrasted the natural sciences and the sciences of culture, claiming that in the natural sciences we are seeking universal laws, while in cultural or historical studies we are seeking to understand individual facts. Kant was important to him mainly because he saw him as having re-established the unity of science and philosophy. However, he criticized Kant for not having done sufficient justice to the historical sciences. His motto was 'to understand Kant is to go beyond Kant'. His conception of a universal normative consciousness that makes valuing fundamental to the historical sciences is clearly inspired by Kant. However, it also owes a great deal to Kant's idealistic successors. In his later years Windelband openly pleaded for a greater emphasis on Hegel. Windelband laid the foundation for the Baden or Southwest German School of neo-Kantianism. He was its most important member. Heinrich **Rickert** was his most important student.

MANFRED KUEHN

Wisdom, A(rthur) J(ohn) T(errence)

British. *b:* 1904, London. *d:* 1993, Cambridge, England. *Cat:* Analytic philosopher. *Ints:* Philosophy of mind; philosophical methodology. *Educ:* University of Cambridge. *Infls:* J. E. McTaggart, G. E. Moore and Ludwig Wittgenstein. *Appts:* 1929–34, Lecturer, University of St Andrews; 1934–68, Fellow of Trinity College, Cambridge (1934–52, Lecturer in Moral Sciences, 1952–68, Professor of Philosophy); 1968–72, Professor of Philosophy, University of Oregon.

Main publications:

(1931) *Interpretation and Analysis*, London: K. Paul, Trench, Trubner.
(1934) *Problems of Mind and Matter*, Cambridge: University of Cambridge Press; reprint with a new Preface, 1963.
(1952) *Other Minds*, Oxford: Basil Blackwell.
(1955) *Philosophy and Psychoanalysis*, Oxford: Basil Blackwell.
(1965) *Paradox and Discovery*, Oxford: Basil Blackwell.
(1969) *Logical Constructions*, ed. Judith Jarvis Thomson, New York: Random House.
(1991) *Proof and Explanation: The Virginia Lectures*, ed. Stephen F. Barker, Lanham: University Press of America.

Secondary literature:

Bambrough, Renford (ed.) (1974) *Wisdom: Twelve Essays*, Rowman & Littlefield.
Dilman, Ilham (ed.) (1984) *Philosophy and Life: Essays on John Wisdom*, The Hague: Nijhoff.

Gasking, D. A. T. (1957) 'The philosophy of John Wisdom, I and II', *Australasian Journal of Philosophy*.

Strongly influenced by the early **Wittgenstein**'s 'picture theory of language', Wisdom's earliest work was an attempt to clarify the nature of logical analysis. This had been a central preoccupation of the empiricist tradition since Jeremy Bentham, and, in the 1920s and 1930s, was a dominant concern of those who had been influenced by **Russell**, **Moore** and Wittgenstein. The idea was that some concepts are 'logical constructions' out of other, more fundamental ones. So, for instance, statements about nations should be analysable into statements about the individuals that compose them; and statements about material objects, it was hoped, would be analysable into statements about sense data. Wisdom held that analysis was the essence of philosophy, whose aim was therefore not to arrive at new facts but to furnish a better understanding of those that we already know.

The obsession with logical analysis began to wane, partly owing to the difficulty of actually producing any satisfactory analyses, and in the mid-1930s Wisdom came under the influence of the 'later' philosophy that Wittgenstein was beginning to develop in Cambridge. One of the first fruits of this influence was Wisdom's 1936 article 'Philosophical perplexity' (*Proceedings of the Aristotelian Society* 16, 1936). By now he had arrived at the view that philosophical theories are, in a certain way, verbal: they are disguised recommendations that we use language in certain ways. For example, the sort of scepticism that holds that we can never know for certain any proposition about material objects, when properly understood, can be seen simply to recommend that we should always preface any statement about material objects with 'probably'. But philosophical theories are not *merely* verbal: they may also express insight into the similarities and differences between the logics of various sorts of statement, similarities and differences which may be concealed by ordinary language. Scepticism draws our attention, for instance, to a likeness shared by all statements about material objects: though circumstances may, in particular cases, make it senseless to doubt their truth, nothing in the nature of the statements themselves guarantees their truth. It also draws our attention to the difference between statements about material objects and statements about our sensations: statements about our own sensations are simply not susceptible of error in the way in which statements about material objects are. Philosophical theories thus illuminate 'the ultimate structure of facts' by illuminating the logical structures of different areas of our thought.

Although the influence of Wittgenstein is clear here, Wisdom thought, rightly or wrongly, that Wittgenstein was prone to regard philosophical theories as *merely* the product of linguistic confusion. Wisdom held that they could also give expression to linguistic penetration.

Wisdom's most extended treatment of a particular philosophical topic was given to the problem of other minds, in a series of articles published in *Mind* from 1940 to 1943. Even here, however, the dominating concern is with the question how philosophers can come to say such things as that we can never know what another person thinks, and what insights such theories may embody, however confusedly.

In his later writing Wisdom came more and more to emphasize the role of *particular cases* in reasoning. Decisions in such areas as aesthetics, morality and the law he thought cannot be determined by general principles; we must simply look in detail at the particular case, determine how similar it is to other cases and decide it accordingly. This procedure could not be determined by general principles for, first, we do not have any such principles and, second, if we did they would have in any case to be underwritten by their conformity to convincing particular cases. This, he held, was true of reasoning in general.

This conception is present already in his highly influential article 'Gods', published in *Proceedings of the Aristotelian Society* in 1944. Though a dispute about the existence of God is not a dispute that can be settled by experimental means, nor by pure logic, it is, he argued, amenable to rational dispute, in much the same way that disputes about beauty, for instance, are amenable to rational dispute. Wisdom's work was highly influential, especially in Cambridge, until the 1970s, when the more systematic approach to philosophy that was developing, particularly in Oxford, began to become dominant. Thereafter his writings were to a large extent ignored. This neglect may have been fostered in part by his prose style, which, apparently representing directly his slightly convoluted manner of speech, is, though often witty, not easy to read. J. O. **Urmson** called him 'something of a landmark in the history of philosophy' (*Philosophical Analysis*, Oxford: Clarendon Press, 1956, p. 173).

Sources: Passmore 1957; Flew; WW 1992.

ANTHONY ELLIS

Wittgenstein, Ludwig Josef Johann

Austrian (naturalized British in 1939). *b:* 26 April 1889, Vienna. *d:* 29 April 1951, Cambridge, England. *Cat:* Logical atomist (developed form); later, *sui generis*. *Ints:* Language; philosophy of mind; logic; philosophy of mathematics; nature of philosophy. *Educ:* Technische Hochschule, Charlottenburg, 1906–8; University of Manchester, 1908–11; Trinity College, Cambridge 1911–13. *Infls:* In *Culture and Value* he listed Boltzmann, Hertz, Schopenhauer, Frege, Russell, Kraus, Loos, Weininger, Spengler and Sraffa; Brouwer might be added. *Appts:* Fellow of Trinity College, Cambridge, 1930–6; Professor of Philosophy and Fellow of Trinity College, Cambridge, 1939–47.

Main publications:

(1921) *Logisch-Philosophische Abhandlung* (the only major work published in his lifetime), in *Annalen der Naturphilosophie* vol. 14 (English translation, *Tractatus Logico-Philosophicus*, trans. D. F. Pears and B. F. McGuinness, London: Routledge & Kegan Paul, 1961).

Wittgenstein's principal works (with dates of composition), include:

(1914–16) *Notebooks 1914–16*; ed. G. E. M. Anscombe and G. H. von Wright, trans. G. E. M. Anscombe, Oxford: Blackwell, 1961.

(1929) 'A lecture on ethics'; in *Philosophical Review* 74, 1965 (in Klagge and Nordmann 1993).

(before 1933) 'Philosophy', sections 86–93 of the so-called *Big Typescript* (in Klagge and Nordmann 1993).

(1933–5) *The Blue and Brown Books*; Oxford: Blackwell, 1958.

(1931–48) 'Bemerkungen über Frazers *Golden Bough*'; ed. R. Rhees, in *Synthese* 17, 1967 (in Klagge and Nordmann 1993.

(1937–44) *Bermerkungen über die Grundlagen der Mathematik* (English translation, *Remarks on the Foundations of Mathematics*, ed. G. H. von Wright, R. Rhees and G. E. M. Anscombe, trans. G. E. M. Anscombe, Oxford: Blackwell, 1956).

(1938 and 1942–6) *Lectures and Conversations on Aesthetics, Psychology and Religious Belief*; ed. C. Barrett, Oxford: Blackwell, 1966.

(to 1949) *Philosophische Untersuchungen* (English translation, *Philosophical Investigations*, ed. G. E.

M. Anscombe and R. Rhees, trans. G. E. M. Anscombe, Oxford: Blackwell, 1953).

(1949–51) *Über Gewissheit* (English translation, *On Certainity*, ed. G. E. M. Anscombe and G. H. von Wright, trans. G. E. M. Anscombe and D. Paul, Oxford: Blackwell, 1969).

(1914–51) *Vermischte Bermerkungen* (English translation, *Culture and Value*, ed. G. H. von Wright, trans. P. Winch, Oxford: Blackwell, 1980).

Other publications consist of correspondence, lecture notes by students and manuscripts by Wittgenstein varying in length from short notes to fully finished typescripts. Several important short writings are collected in J. Klagge and A. Nordmann (eds) (1993) *Ludwig Wittgenstein: Philosophical Occasions 1912–1951*, Indianapolis and Cambridge: Hackett.

Secondary literature:

Principal biographies in English:

McGuinness, B. F. (1988) *Wittgenstein: A Life*, vol. 1, London: Duckworth (to 1922).

Malcolm, N. (1958) *Ludwig Wittgenstein: A Memoir with a Biographical Sketch by George Henrik von Wright*, Oxford.

Monk, R. (1990) *Ludwig Wittgenstein: The Duty of Genius*, London: Cape.

Bibliographies:

Frongia, G. and McGuinness, B. F. (eds) (1990)*Wittgenstein: A Bibliographical Guide*, Oxford: Blackwell.

Shanker, V. A. and Shanker, S. G. (1986) *Ludwig Wittgenstein: Critical Assessments*, vol. 5, *A Wittgenstein Bibliography*, London: Croom Helm (lists 5,868 items).

Selected monographs and commentaries:

Anscombe, G. E. M. (1959) *An Introduction to Wittgenstein's Tractatus*, London: Hutchinson.

Black, M. (1964) *A Companion to Wittgenstein's Tractatus*, Cambridge.

Hacker, P. M. S. (1972) *Insight and Illusion*, Oxford; revised 1986.

——and Baker, G. P. (1980, 1986; 1990, 1995) *Wittgenstein: An Analytical Commentary on the Philosophical Investigations*: vol. 1, *Meaning and Understanding*; vol. 2, *Rules, Grammar and Necessity*; vol. 3, *Meaning and Mind*; vol. 4, *Mind and Will*, Oxford: Blackwell.

Hallett, G. (1977) *A Companion to Wittgenstein's Philosophical Investigations*, Ithaca, NY: Cornell University Press.

Kenny, A. (1973) *Wittgenstein*, Harmondsworth: Penguin.

Kerr, F. (1986) *Theology after Wittgenstein*, Oxford: Blackwell.

Kripke, S. A. (1982) *Wittgenstein on Rules and Private Language*, Oxford: Blackwell.

McGinn, C. (1984) *Wittgenstein on Meaning*, Oxford: Blackwell.

Malcolm, N. (1986) *Nothing is Hidden*, Oxford: Blackwell.

Pears, D. F. (1987–8) *The False Prison* , 2 vols, Oxford.

Wright, C. (1980) *Wittgenstein on the Philosophy of Mathematics*, London: Duckworth.

There are many collections of papers, including:

Block, I. (ed.) (1981) *Perspectives on the Philosophy of Wittgenstein*, Oxford: Blackwell.

Pitcher, G. (ed.) (1968) *Wittgenstein: The Philosophical Investigations*, London: Macmillan (contains many initial reviews and important early papers on Wittgenstein).

Phillips Griffiths, A. (ed.) (1991) *Wittgenstein: Centenary Essays*, Royal Institute of Philosophy Lectures vol. 28 (1989–90), Cambridge.

Shanker, V. A. and S. G. (eds) (1986) *Ludwig Wittgenstein: Critical Assessments*, 5 vols, London: Croom Helm.

Vesey, G. (ed.) (1974) *Understanding Wittgenstein*, Royal Institute of Philosophy Lectures vol. 7 (1972–3), London: Macmillan.

Wittgenstein has been the most influential twentieth-century philosopher in the English-speaking world. Interpretations of his work vary radically on almost every point, to the extent that it would be misleading to suggest that any neutral account can be given. Some knowledge of his life is needed to form a view of the two phases of his work—represented by his two masterpieces, the *Tractatus Logico-Philosophicus* and the *Philosophical Investigations*—and of the relationship between them. Opinions differ on the continuity or discontinuity of his development, from commentators who see a complete volte-face to those who detect enduring interests and attitudes.

In his youth Wittgenstein studied for six years as an engineer. He worked briefly, in the late 1920s, as an architect. Perhaps as a result, a practical, almost mechanical, approach to philosophy can sometimes be seen in his work, even in writing as abstract as his *Remarks on the Foundations of Mathematics* (see I, SS 119, 122; III, SS 21, 49, 51; V, S 51).

In 1911 he went to Trinity College, Cambridge, to study with **Russell**, on the advice of **Frege**. The themes which took life in his notebooks soon afterwards included some which had preoccupied Russell for many years: the nature and ingredients of a proposition; its relation to objects; logical truth. There was also a concern with the will, the self and the place of value which Wittgenstein may have brought from his early reading of Schopenhauer.

The *Tractatus Logico-Philosophicus* was composed during the Great War while Wittgenstein was serving in the Austrian army. (Few classics of philosophy could have been written in worse conditions.) He wrote of it in a letter to Ludwig von Ficker (1919): 'My work consists of two parts: of the one presented here, plus all that I have *not* written. And it is precisely this second part that is the important one. My book draws limits to the sphere of the ethical from the inside as it were' (P. Engelmann, *Letters from Ludwig Wittgenstein with a Memoir*, Oxford: Blackwell, 1967, p. 143). Despite the Russellian logical skeleton of the work—of great technical interest to later Anglo-American commentators—Wittgenstein's emphasis on the ethical aims of the *Tractatus* must be taken seriously. He believed (and continued to believe at least up to his 'Lecture on ethics' in 1929) that value stood outside what he thought of as 'the world': 'If there is any value that does have value, it must lie outside the whole sphere of what happens and is the case' (6.41).

He needed to fit together 'what happens and is the case' with what *can* be said about it, and to set that apart from what *cannot* be said—about 'the sense of the world' (6.41) and about 'the will in so far as it is the subject of ethical attributes' (6.423). *Saying* is possible. Saying—language—consists of 'the totality of propositions' (4.001). And 'only propositions have sense' (3.31). But: 'If the world had no substance, then whether a proposition had sense would depend on whether another proposition was true. In that case we could not sketch out any picture of the world (true or false)' (2.0211–12). But 'we' *can* do this... so the world does have a substance ... The argument is a Kantian, transcendental one, leading to a world of objects, pictured in language. 'A proposition is a picture of reality' (4.01/4.021) and 'The totality of true propositions is the whole of natural science ...' (4.11).

Wittgenstein relied on strong dichotomy: on one side was language consisting of articulated (3.141) propositions, in which everything sayable depended on (without necessarily being reducible to) the fact that elementary propositions can picture states of affairs; on the other side were the realms of the will, ethics and the mystical. Here, nothing could be *said*, though something

might be *shown*. Logic and mathematics, which could not be seen as presenting facts about the world, were diagnosed as tautologies—the limiting case of the combination of signs (4.466). They were not—like attempts to *say*something about value or ethics—nonsensical (*unsinnig*). But they were empty of sense (*sinnlos*) because they *said* nothing. The contrast was between what was *said* and what was *shown*: 'Logical so-called propositions *show* [the] logical properties of language and therefore of [the] Universe, but *say* nothing' (*Notebooks 1914–16*, p. 107). Logic was 'not a body of doctrine but a mirror-image of the world' (6.13).

These views embodied radical implications for philosophy. It could not be a 'body of doctrine' or aim at 'philosophical propositions'. It could be an activity of elucidation—'the logical clarification of thoughts' (4.112). And what was written in the *Tractatus* might well be elucidatory, but would have to be recognized as nonsensical itself: purporting to *say* what could only be *shown*. 'What we cannot speak about we must pass over in silence' (7).

After the *Tractatus* Wittgenstein underwent a decade of mental turmoil when he worked in rural Austria as an elementary teacher and as a gardener. He returned to philosophy in the late 1920s during the time when he was helping to design a house for his sister in Vienna. In 1928 he attended a lecture by **Brouwer** (on Mathematics, Science and Language). He joined discussions of the Vienna Circle. In 1929 he went back to Cambridge, where he was awarded a PhD for the *Tractatus* and where he began the teaching which was to have an enormous influence on philosophy during and after the rest of his life.

Wittgenstein was never a logical positivist. But the frequent misidentification of the 'objects' in the *Tractatus* with items of elementary experience may have led his thoughts towards the connections between linguistic sense and the empiricist notion of 'inner' mental experiences. This theme was central to much of his subsequent work. A less evident but equally significant breaking-point came in his early view of necessity as tautological. The crux appeared very early as a concern: 'A point cannot be red and green at the same time: at first sight there seems no need for this to be a logical impossibility' (*Notebooks 1914–16*, 16 August 1916; see also *Tractatus* 6.3751). Further thought on this in the 1930s led to a new understanding of modality.

A view of meaning was needed in Wittgenstein's early thinking to sustain his view of what was unsayable. In his middle and later years meaning moved to the centre of his interests in its own right. The *Blue Book* (1933–4) opened with the question 'What is the meaning of a word?' In the *Tractatus* (3.203) he had written: 'A name means an object. The object is its meaning ...'. This single, direct, essentialist link between language and reality was denied later, or diminished to a special case. Wittgenstein's attention moved towards the meaningfulness of gestures, questions, orders, proposals, guesses, greetings, wishes and so on. He catalogued cases where precision and determinacy were irrelevant to meaningfulness, and where the senses of common terms (for example, 'game') could be conveyed successfully when they could not be found to stand for anything in common. His interest in meaning in social contexts has often been seen as a form of holism—sense would be determined by an indefinitely wide range of linguistic, social and cultural conditions ('use in language', *Philosophical Investigations* I, S43). But more probably, having held an extremely clear-cut theory of meaning, he now wanted to deny that *any* theory could cover the sufficient or necessary conditions for meaning or meaningfulness. (See Anscombe, 'A theory of language?', in Block 1981.)

The most important area where this was applied was where words had been thought to stand for mental objects: 'red' somehow stands for my inner impression of redness; 'toothache' gets its sense for me because I have used it to stand for an ache in my tooth. Part I of the *Philosophical Investigations* is preoccupied with this theme. It comes to a focus in the passages known as the 'private language arguments' (SS242–309; or wider—see **Kripke** on this point). One strand in these arguments is a suggestion that an understanding of the sense of any term cannot depend on personal acquaintance with its reference (what it stands for). Someone who has never had toothache (seasickness, a hangover) uses 'seasickness' just as intelligibly as someone who has. Its meaning 'for' the user of the word, which seems essential, 'drops out of consideration as irrelevant' (I, S293). What matters is that the word is used in accordance with the rules of language, which have to be social, 'public', not 'private' inside the language-user. Otherwise the word could have no 'function' (S260). Its use could have no 'criterion of correctness': 'whatever is going to seem right to me is right. That only means that here we can't talk about "right"' (S 258). 'The meaning of a word is not the experience (*Die Bedeutung ist nicht das Erlebnis*)

one has in hearing or saying it, and the sense (*Sinn*) of a sentence is not a complex of such experiences' (ibid., II, p. vi).

This thinking was fatal to an empiricist account of meaning, where words acquired their meanings by standing for mental contents (ideas, sense data, impressions). The whole view of language as a 'vehicle of thought' (I, S329) changed radically. So did central elements in any philosophical psychology, such as the self and the will. The latter half of the *Philosophical Investigations*, Part I, and subsequent lectures in the 1940s worked through the consequences and ramifications.

Wittgenstein's *Remarks on the Foundations of Mathematics* is an incomplete and unrevised text which must be read with reservations. In it he stresses the need for practical use as a touchstone for mathematical theorizing: 'What can the concept "non-denumerable" be used for?', for instance (on Cantor, I, Appendix II, S2). He may have been influenced by Brouwer, and some have read him as a mathematical intuitionist, although the psychological basis of intuitionism cannot have appealed to him.

His work has had much influence in social anthropology, social theory and the philosophy of religion (Leach, **Winch**, D. Z. **Phillips**). The denial of clear foundations for meaning in the form of determinate links between language and reality could be widened from language to social or religious practice. A search for justifications in terms of objective, factual truth might be replaced by legitimation in terms of social or cultural use.

Wittgenstein himself was extremely averse to any form of theorizing—linguistic, social, mathematical and so: 'We can only *describe* and say, human life is like that' ('Remarks on Frazer', in Klagge and Nordmann 1993, p. 121). This applied equally in philosophy, although it is undeniable that he did present his own aetiology, diagnosis and prescription for philosophical problems. It should be enough to describe the actual use of language. 'Philosophical problems arise when language *goes on holiday*' (*Philosophical Investigations* I, S38). Like Kant, he believed that people have tendencies to think (speak) in ways which lead to erroneous, illusory or misleading questions. The answer, he believed, was to see the normal uses of language perspicuously, to get a clear oversight (*Übersicht*). The aim was '*complete* clarity. But this means that the philosophical problems *completely* disappear' (I, S133).

Wittgenstein's final period, in Part II of the

Philosophical Investigations, in *On Certainty* and in his lectures of the 1940s, showed a new balance among his interests. His dislike of philosophical theory and his views on the philosophy of mind focused into a dislike of 'scientific' psychology. He had said earlier that 'What we are supplying are really remarks on the natural history of human beings' (I, S415). *On Certainty* applied this in the theory of knowledge. Epistemological *certainty* could have its origins neither in theoretical foundations (as in classical empiricism) nor in unsupported, intuitive common sense (as asserted by G. E. **Moore**). Instead, doubt, certainty, justification, evidence, knowledge and so on were associated with actual social practice, and that appeared to provide some kind of legitimation: 'Our knowledge forms an enormous system. And only within this system has a particular bit the value we give it' (S410); 'I would like to reserve the expression "I know" for the cases in which it is used in normal linguistic exchange' (S260). *On Certainty* is an unrevised text, dating from the last months of Wittgenstein's life. He might well have repudiated the appearance of unsophisticated holism and relativism that can be read into some of its less cautious passages.

Wittgenstein regarded his later philosophy as intrinsically unsystematic. His philosophical style was highly individual: aphoristic, full of questions, suggestions, jokes, snatches of dialogue, arguments with himself. Wittgenstein's writings, in terms of the volume of commentary on them, have had an immense influence. His work was at the centre of philosophical attention in the English-speaking world through at least the 1950s and 1960s, with its main school of study at Oxford. (It was also the subject of lurid debate, as, for example, engendered by **Gellner**'s *Words and Things* (1959).)

Wittgenstein advised his own students to give up philosophy and take up something useful instead, such as medicine or carpentry. To the extent that few did this (though some did) his successful influence may have been slight. He was equally unsuccessful in convincing his successors against the value of explanatory theory. Attempts to discover theories of meaning (or even reference) have continued unabated, in the face of the plain implication of the *Philosophical Investigations* that there can be no suffcient conditions for making sense. The growth of cognitive psychology and social theory also show how his thinking may have been disregarded.

There could be no single verdict on Wittgenstein. The *Tractatus*—as he probably intended it—stands at one pole of a certain type of metaphysics, presenting a clear, dogmatic account of what can be said and why. Some strands in his later thought appealed to writers associated with postmodernism: metaphysical explanation and justification were abolished, to be replaced only by a clear view of how things are, how language is used, how culture and society operate.

RICHARD MASON

Wollheim, Richard (Arthur)

British. *b:* 5 May 1923, London. *Cat:* Philosopher of mind; aesthetician. *Ints:* Psychoanalysis; political philosophy. *Educ:* Balliol College, Oxford. *Infls:* Hume, Freud and Wittgenstein. *Appts:* 1949–63, Assistant Lecturer, then Lecturer (1951), then Reader (1960) in Philosophy, University College London; 1963–85, Grote Professor of Philosophy of Mind and Logic, University of London; 1982–5, Professor of Philosophy, Columbia University; 1985–, Mills Professor, University of California, Berkeley; 1989–, Professor of Philosophy and the Humanities, University of California, Davis.

Main publications:
(1959) *F. H. Bradley*, Harmondsworth: Penguin; revised edition, 1969.
(1962) (ed.) F. H. Bradley, *Ethical Studies*, London: Oxford University Press.
(1963) (ed.) *Hume on Religion*, London: Collins.
(1968) *Art and its Objects*, Harmondsworth: Penguin; second edition with supplementary essays, Cambridge: Cambridge University Press, 1980.
(1969) (ed.) F. H. Bradley, *Appearance and Reality*, London: Oxford University Press.
(1971) *Freud*, London: Fontana.
(1973) *On Art and the Mind*, London: Allen Lane.
(1974) (ed.) *Freud: A Collection of Critical Essays*, New York: Anchor Press.
(1975) (ed.) J. S. Mill *Three Essays*, Oxford: Oxford University Press.
(1982) (ed. with J. Hopkins) *Philosophical Essays on Freud*, Cambridge: Cambridge University Press.
(1984) *The Thread of Life*, Cambridge, Mass.: Harvard University Press.
(1987) *Painting as an Art*, London: Thames & Hudson.
(1993) *The Mind and its Depths*, Cambridge, Mass.: Harvard University Press.

Secondary literature:
Hopkins, J. and Savile, A. (eds) (1992) *Psychoanalysis, Mind and Art*, Oxford: Blackwell.

Wollheim has written challenging essays in political philosophy but is best known for his work in aesthetics and philosophy of mind. His ideas exhibit unity, and in both of the latter areas he introduces psychoanalytical (specifically Kleinian) notions. Projection is perhaps the most crucial. Here we avoid anxiety by ascribing our own state, or something associated with it, to another person or thing. We manage anger, say, by perceiving another as angry with us, or sadness by perceiving a painting or landscape as sad.

In aesthetics, he has sponsored successive versions of the thesis that pictorial representation is best understood in terms of *seeing in*, according to which we attend both to the marks on a flat surface present to the eyes and to the experience of things not so present but caused by things which are (cf. *Art and its Objects*, (1968 and, *Painting as an Art*, 1987). Painting as an art is to be understood psychologically, by ineliminable reference to the artist's intentions: these must relate together in a particular way and cause particular experiences in an informed spectator. Wollheim resists the assimilation of art to language, codes and conventions, despite exploiting the analogy of art as a form of life.

The Thread of Life (1984) is an attempt to produce a philosophy of mind appropriate to psychoanalytical theory. Just as the status of paintings is to be understood by a consideration of the activity of painting, so the process of living is seen as prior both to a life itself and to the person. It is understood as taking place against the background of unconscious fantasies arising from unresolved conflicts buried in the past. Narrowly conceived morality, based on obligation, is held to derive from introjection, to be punitive and to involve the creation of a superego alien to the subject. It is contrasted with value, which is held to derive from projection and is associated with the promotion of love. Wollheim himself advocates a broadly conceived morality which is an amalgam of obligation and goodness. Many contributors to Hopkins and Savile (1992) testify to Wollheim's influential and inspirational role as head of the radical Philosophy Department at University College London in its zenith.

Sources: Cooper; WW; personal communication.

KEITH GRAHAM

Woodbridge, Frederick James Eugéne

American. *b:* 26 March 1867, Windsor, Ontario. *d:* 1 June 1940. *Cat:* Naturalist; realist. *Ints:* Metaphysics. *Educ:* Amherst College, University of

Berlin. *Infls:* Aristotle and Santayana. *Appts:* Professor of Philosophy, University of Columbia; Roosevelt Professor in Berlin; editor, *Journal of Philosophy.*

Main publications:

(1916) *The Purpose of History*, New York: Columbia University Press.

(1926) *The Realm of Mind: An Essay in Metaphysics*, New York: Columbia University Press.

(1929) *Contrasts in Education*, New York: Columbia University Press.

(1930) *Hobbes Selections*, London: Charles Scribner's Sons.

(1937) *Nature and Mind*, New York: Columbia University Press.

(1965) *Aristotle's Vision of Nature*, ed. and intro. J. H. Randall, New York: Columbia University Press.

Secondary literature:

Costello, Harry T. (1944) 'The naturalism of Frederick J. E. Woodbridge' in Y. H. Krikorian (ed.) *Naturalism and the Human Spirit*, New York, pp. 295–318.

For Woodbridge, naturalism was an attitude and not a doctrine. As a naturalist in this sense, he held that nature provides us with all the materials for investigation and that mind and life are products of nature. As a realist he maintained that consciousness was not a source of the objective world; instead it presupposed the existence of the objective world.

Sources: WWW(Am).

INDIRA MAHALINGAM CARR

Wright, Crispin (James Garth)

British. *b:* 21 December 1942, Bagshot, Surrey. *Cat:* Analytical anti-realist. *Ints:* Philosophy of mathematics; logic; philosophy of language. *Educ:* Trinity College, Cambridge, BA 1964, MA, PhD 1968; Christ Church, Oxford, BPhil 1969, DLitt 1988. *Infls:* Personal influence includes Dummett; literary influence includes Frege and Wittgenstein. *Appts:* Junior Research Fellow, Trinity College, Oxford, 1967–9; Prize Fellow, All Souls, Oxford, 1969–71; Lecturer, Balliol College, Oxford, 1969–70; Lecturer, University College, London, 1970–1; Research Fellow, All Souls College, Oxford, 1971–8; Professor of Logic and Metaphysics, University of St Andrews, 1978–87; Professor of Philosophy, (1992), Nelson Professor, University of Michigan.

Main publications:

(1980) *Wittgenstein on the Foundations of Mathematics*, London: Duckworth, and Cambridge, Mass.: Harvard University Press.

(1983) *Frege's Conception of Numbers as Objects*, Aberdeen University Press and Humanities Press.

(1986) *Realism: Meaning and Truth*, Oxford: Blackwell; expanded second edition, 1992.

(1993) *Truth and Objectivity*, Cambridge, Mass.: Harvard University Press.

(1993) *Realism: Rules and Objectivity*, Oxford: Blackwell.

Whatever topic Wright addresses, the lynchpin of his work, following the lead of **Dummett**, is the 'Realism/Anti-Realism' dispute. Wright painstakingly explores the nature and implications of adopting intuitionist logic and anti-realist semantics and has succeeded in sharpening the debate in many ways. He has not confined his attention to technical semantical and logical issues, but, going beyond attention to global realism and global anti-realism, has explored the past, other minds, etc., in the light of this overarching approach.

Meaning, for Wright, must respect quasi-verificationist constraints: the notion of truth deployed in a theory of meaning should not and cannot transcend possible evidence. Whilst addressing similar issues to those Dummett considers, Wright is suspicious of semantic monism (a theory of meaning using a single key-concept such as truth or assertability) and of seeing the Principle of Bivalence as crucial to acceptance/rejection of realism.

In the philosophy of mathematics Wright broke with Dummett's reading of **Frege** and gave some defence of Frege's 'Platonism' whilst rejecting his 'realism', doctrines Dummett tied together. Wright has succeeded in helping Dummett force philosophers to reconsider their perhaps unthinking realism and to shift the axis of attention to metaphysics in a semantical direction. His work, notwithstanding the difficulty of the subject matter, has increasingly attracted high approbation.

Sources: WW 1993; Univ. of St Andrews Philosophy Dept.

ANDREW WRIGHT

Wundt, Wilhelm Max

German. *b:* 1832, Mannheim, Germany. *d:* 1920, Grossbothen, near Munich. *Cat:* Psychologist; physiologist. *Ints:* Introspective and psychophysical research in psychology; history of psychology; anthropology; logic; philosophy of science and ethics. *Educ:* Studied Medicine at the Universities of Tübingen, Heidelberg and Berlin. *Infls:* Leibniz, Schopenhauer and Hegel. *Appts:* Privatdozent, Helmholtz Physiological Institute, Heidelberg, 1857; Professor of Inductive Philosophy, Leipzig, 1875.

Main publications:

(1880–3) *Logik*, 2 vols, Stuttgart: F. Enke; fourth and fifth editions, 3 vols, 1919–24.

(1863) *Vorlesungen über die Menschen und Tier-Seele*, 2 vols, Leipzig (English translation, *Lectures on Human and Animal Psychology*, trans. J. G. Greighton and E. B. Titchener, London: S. Sonnenschein, 1896).

(1874) *Grundzüge der physiologischen Psychologie*, Leipzig: W. Engelmann (English translation, *Principles of Physiological Psychology*, trans. E. B. Titchener, New York: Macmillan & Co, 1904).

(1889) *System der Philosophie*, Leipzig: W. Engelmann.

(1915) *Die Nationen und ihre Philosophie*, Leipzig: A. Kröner.

(1916) *Leibniz*, Leipzig: A. Kröner.

(1917–26) *Völkerpsychologie*, first to fourth editions, 10 vols, Leipzig: A. Kröner.

(1920) *Erlebtes und Erkanntes, Selbstbiographie* (autobiography), Stuttgart: A. Kröner.

(1926) *Wilhelm Wundts Werk, ein Verzeichnis Seiner Sämtlichen Schriften*, ed. Eleonore Wundt, Munich: C. H. Beck (contains complete bibliography).

A Wilhelm Wundt archive, established by his daughter in his house at Grossbothen, was transferred to the Psychological Institute of the University of Leipzig on her death and is administered by the Institute.

Secondary literature:

Boring, E. G. (1950) *A History of Experimental Psychology*, second edition, New York: Prentice Hall, pp. 318–47.

Bringmann, W. G. and Scheerer, E. (eds) (1980) *Psychological Research, Wundt Centennial Issue*, 42: 1–189.

——and Tweney, R. D. (eds) (1980) *Wundt Studies: A Centennial Collection*, Toronto: Hogrefe.

Nef, Willi (1923) *Die Philosophie Wilhelm Wundts*, Leipzig: Fehrische Buchhandlung.

Peters, R. S. (ed.) (1953) *Brett's History of Psychology*, London: Allen & Unwin, pp. 479–88.

Robinson, D. N. (1982) *Towards a Science of Human Nature: Essays on the Psychologies of Hegel, Mill, Wundt and James*, Columbia: Columbia University Press.

Wilhelm Wundt is widely acknowledged as the founder of experimental psychology. He is believed to have formed many of his philosophical ideas in his early twenties, during a long convalescence from a serious illness. As a young man in Heidelberg he worked at the Physiological Institute on sense perception and related problems. This led directly to his recognition of the need for a scientific psychology rooted in physiology. After his appointment as Professor of Inductive Philosophy at Leipzig he founded the Institut für Experimentelle Psychologie (in 1879), thereby establishing the prototype for modern departments of experimental psychology.

Wundt believed that conscious processes should be investigated both by experiment and by introspection. Experimental methods, he held, created the conditions under which introspection could yield exact data and knowledge of causal relations. However, this approach was most fruitful for relatively simple mental activities, like perception. At this level simple associationism could be helpful; though it is necessary to postulate a 'principle of creative resultants' to explain how perception comes to involve more than the mere addition of stimuli. The cultural world could not be understood in these terms, however. This world, a world of motives, purposes and reasons, was better investigated through anthropological work on such phenomena as myth and custom. Wundt's two main psychological works reflect this divide, the *Physiologische Psychologie* (1874), and the *Völkerpsychologie* [Anthropological Psychology] (1917–26).

As a philosopher Wundt would have studied logic and philosophy as part of his scientific training, but he was otherwise largely self-taught. He had wide-ranging interests: ethics (he defended the idea of absolute values of which we could have a priori knowledge, yet which could be expressed differently in different cultural environments); the philosophy of science (although drawn to idealism, and opposed to sensationalism, he espoused some aspects of positivism while insisting on the non-reducibility of culture and art); and the mind-brain problem (following Leibniz, acknowledged in a biography, he believed in psychophysical parallelism). He held that logic, as a theory of the form of synthetic thought, underpinned the methodologies of all sciences. However, psychology was the link between scientific and cultural knowledge and hence 'preparatory' to philosophy. Wundt was a prolific writer (his life's output of published work has been estimated at 53,000 pages) and an inspiring teacher whose students founded laboratories for experimental psychology in many parts of the world. Emil Kraepelin, whose nosology of psychiatric disorders remains the basis of modern classifications, worked with him in Leipzig. The tension in his work between positivism and idealism sometimes led him into inconsistency, and his hopes for unifying science through psychology as a basis for philosophy have not been realized. The contrasting aspects of human experience with which he was concerned—mind and culture, cause and volition, subjective and objective knowledge—remain unreconciled in the psychology he helped to establish.

Sources: Reese; Goldenson.

K. W. M. FULFORD

X

Xenopol, Alexandru Dimitrie

Romanian. *b:* 1847, Iasy, Romania. *d:* 1920. *Cat:* Historian; philosopher of history. *Ints:* Philosophy of history. *Infls:* Influenced by other participants in the debate on the nature of history current at his time, e.g. Gervinus, Ottokar Lorenz, Hermann Paul and many others. *Appts:* Professor, University of Iasy (from 1883).

Main publications:

(1908) *La théorie de l'histoire* (an expanded version, translated by Xenopol of *Principiile fundamentale ale istoriei*, 1891).
(1901) *L'hypothèse dans l'histoire.*
(1908) *L'histoire, est-elle une science?*
Plus substantial works on Romanian history.

Secondary literature:

Botez, O. (1928) *Alexandru Xenopol*, Bucharest: Tip. Ion C. Vacarescu.
Saveri Varanno, F. (1931) *Il problema della storia in Xenopol*, Gubbio: Oderisi.

Xenopol, who wrote in French as well as Romanian, was a well-known historian of his generation in Europe.The goal of Xenopol's philosophy of history is to show that history is a science, but of a kind distinct from natural science. He divides changes into two classes, repetitions and successions. A repetition is a change in which the recurring elements are more similar to one another than dissimilar; a succession is a sequence in which the dissimilarity of its elements outweighs their similarity (1908, p. 365). Natural science studies repetitious change; history studies successive change. Xenopol argues further that to each of these major modes of change corresponds a type of causality. Causality of repetition is such that the cause is always concomitant with the effect; in causality of succession the cause always precedes the effect. Causality of repetition manifests itself as a law of natural science; causality of succession as what Xenopol calls a historical series.

A series is a succession of diverse phenomena, the result of the causal interaction of the multifarious and constantly changing forces at work in history. A historical series is unique, and this has an important corollary for what type of 'laws' are possible in the science of history. The laws of natural science, which pertain to repetitious change, can predict precisely what phenomena will recur when given conditions obtain. Historical laws, which pertain to successive change, cannot in principle predict the exact nature of future historical events, but only the direction or tendency which events will have, granted the historical conditions obtaining.

ROBERT WILKINSON

Xie Youwei (Hsieh Yu-wei)

Chinese. *b:* Mei County, Guandong Province, China. *d:* 1976, Taiwan. *Cat:* Idealist. *Ints:* Contemporary philosophy; ethics; philosophy of psychology; history and civilization. *Educ:* Dongwu University and Harvard University. *Infls:* Royce and Bradley. *Appts:* Professor, Zejian University; Professor, Nanjing Central University; Director, Institute of Philosophy, Chinese Academy of Culture, Taiwan; Professor, Chinese University of Hong Kong.

Main publications:

(n.d.) *Elements of Ethics*, Zhengzhong Book Company.
(n.d.) *Philosophy and Psychology*, Zhengzhong Book Company.
(n.d.) *The Spirit of Chinese Culture.*
(1941) *Critiques of Famous Contemporary Philosophical Works*, Chongqing, Shengli.
(1953) *Mankind and Culture.*
(1955) *Talking About Philosophy.*
(1963) *History of Western Philosophy.*
(1969) *Collection of Essays on Chinese and Western Philosophy.*
(trans.) F. H. Bradley, *Ethical Studies.*
(trans.) J. Royce, *Philosophy of Loyalty.*

Secondary literature:

Briere, O. (1956) *Fifty Years of Chinese Philosophy 1898–1950*, London: George Allen & Unwin Ltd.

Xie was an acute critic of early twentieth-century philosophy under the neo-Hegelian influence of **Royce** and **Bradley**. His philosophical interests were accompanied by work in psychology, history and culture. Xie translated Royce's *Philosophy of Loyalty* and Bradley's *Ethical Studies* but, unlike many neo-Hegelians, did not develop a personal system of philosophy. Instead, he wrote critical essays on a variety of thinkers, including **Xiong Shili**, **He Lin**, Zhang Shizhao, **Dewey**, **Price**, **Hume**, **Adler**, **Whitehead**, **Croce**, **Alexander** and **Tagore**. In common with many Chinese philosophers he tried to establish the essential characteristics of Chinese and Western thought in order to understand the different patterns of historical development and as a guide for the future. He saw ancient Chinese philosophy as idealistic, practical, proceeding by intuitive affirmation rather than proof, and religious in attitude. Modern Chinese philosophy was also idealistic, but was theoretical as well as practical, rational as well as intuitive, and philosophical in attitude. Modern Western thought was idealist: it identified the religious and the human, rejected dualism and matter, gave prominence to questions of value, and placed thought in its historical setting. It also emphasized careful analysis within the context of scientific method and mathematical logic. The idealism and rationality of modern Chinese thought provided a basis for absorbing other features from the West. In his moral thinking Xie shared neo-Hegelian hostility to utilitarianism, but tried to reconcile the western theories of Royce and Bradley with Confucian doctrines. Moral life centred on the self and the problems of self-realization. Self-realization, in turn, was the achievement of an ideal self, which he considered one's true self in contrast to the merely empirical self. Self-realization placed one in harmony with nature, morality and law because, on his account, natural, moral and judicial law originated with the ideal self. To respect the law in one's practice was to respect the nature of one's ideal self. Because freedom was a matter of knowing one's nature and following it in practice, the Hegelian theme of freedom as self-realization and the Confucian theme of harmony were united. Confucian thought was placed within a Western metaphysical context, gaining whatever strength such an incorporation could provide.

NICHOLAS BUNNIN

Xiong Shili (Hsung Shih-li)

Chinese. **b:** 1885, Huanggang, Hubei Province, China. **d:** 1968, **Cat:** Confucian–Buddhist idealist.

Educ: Studied Consciousness Only Buddhism with Ouyang Jianwu at the Institute of Buddhism, Nanjing. **Infls:** *Book of Changes*, Consciousness Only Buddhism, idealist neo-Confucianism of Lu Xiangshan (twelfth century) and Wang Yangming (sixteenth century), and Western philosophers including Bergson. **Appts:** Teacher of new Consciousness Only thought at University of Beijing; Fuxing Academy, Loshan; teacher, National Zhejiang University; Professor, University of Beijing.

Main publications:

(n.d.) *Notes on Higher Buddhist Logic*.
(n.d.) *Refutation of Consciousness Only*.
(1932, 1940–4) *The New Theory of Consciousness Only*, classical Chinese edition and vernacular Chinese edition, 3 vols, Shanghai: Commercial Press.
(1935–47) *The Essence of Shili*, 4 vols, Beijing: Peking University.
(1937) *Comprehensive Explication of the Buddhist Theory of Philosophy*, Beijing: Peking University.
(1944) *Essentials of Studying the Classics*, Shanghai: Zhengzhong Publishing House.
(1956) *The Original The Original Confucianism*, Shanghai: Longmen United Bookstore.
(1959) *An Essay Illuminating the Mind*, Shanghai, Longmen United Bookstore.
(1961) *Elaborating the Principle of Heaven and Earth*, Hong Kong.

Secondary literature:

Boorman, H. (ed.) (1970) *Biographical Dictionary of Republican China*, New York and London: Columbia University Press.
Briere, O. (1963) *Fifty Years of Chinese Philosophy 1898–1950*, London: George Allen & Unwin Ltd.
Chan, W. (1963) *A Source Book in Chinese Philosophy*, Princeton: Princeton University Press.
Complete Chinese Encyclopedia (1987), Philosophy Volumes, Beijing: Chinese Encyclopedia Publications.
Munro, D. C. (n.d.) *Humanism in Modern China: Fung Yu-lan and Hsiung Shih-li*, Ann Arbor: University of Michigan Press.

Xiong was one of the most powerful and original Chinese metaphysical thinkers of this century. After early republican revolutionary activity, he turned to scholarship, studying Consciousness Only Buddhism with **Ouyang Jianwu**. His dissatisfaction with Consciousness Only doctrines led him to create his own system, expressed systematically in *The New Theory of Consciousness Only* (1932). His views drew on the *Book of*

Changes and on the revival in China of Consciousness Only Buddhism and idealist neo-Confucianism. He also showed the influence of **Bergson** and other Western philosophers.

The central notion of Xiong's metaphysics is that of original substance: a perpetually evolving absolute, eternal reality, capable of instantaneous change in endless closing and opening, producing and reproducing. His original substance replaces the Consciousness Only school's notion of consciousness as the most fundamental philosophical concept. Because there could be no original substance without movement and no movement without original substance, movement and original substance were identified. Evolving original substance is the only reality, but it is unknowable in itself. Xiong provides room for other entities, such as spirit, mind and matter, by seeing them as manifestations or functions of the underlying substance and by adopting the Confucian identification of substance and function. He saw spirit (as world soul) as more basic than matter, but considered them to be two aspects of a substantial whole. Spirit, as a manifestation of underlying reality, was the ground for both subjectivity and the objective world. Because Xiong did not allow individual identity to spirit, he thought that his system avoided idealism and materialism without embracing pantheism. We can provisionally see matter as resulting from the integration produced by the closing motion of substance, and mind as resulting from the self-determination produced by the opening motion, although both mind and matter lack the unqualified reality of original substance. Material force, as function, is seen as united with principle, as substance and function, thus underlining the unity of the material world and underlying substance. Individual minds are part of original mind, identified with the Confucian virtue of *ren* (humanity), and are capable of pure rational knowledge and love of goodness. The mind and the will refer to substance, while consciousness, the central notion of the Consciousness Only school, refers to function, thus meriting a less fundamental status in our philosophical thought. With great intellectual power, Xiong criticized Buddhist and idealist neo-Confucian thought, providing a new formulation of their themes and a new metaphysical basis for their doctrines. Aside from his ingenuity in adapting traditional views, Xiong displayed a broad vision and an admirable capacity for argument. Before

Liberation, his work attracted a school of disciples.

NICHOLAS BUNNIN

Xirau (Palau), Joaquim

Catalan. **b:** 1894, Figueras, Spain. **d:** 1946, Mexico. **Cat:** Phenomenologist. **Ints:** Metaphysics; epistemology; philosophy of value. **Educ:** University of Barcelona (Licenciado 1917). **Infls:** Scheler, Garcia Morente and Ortega. **Appts:** Professor at Salamanca (1927) and Barcelona (1928); taught at Cambridge (UK), 1929; Dean of Faculty of Letters, Barcelona (1933); Professor at the Casa de España and UNAM (Mexico), 1939; influenced, among others, Ferrater Mora.

Main publications:

(1921) *Leibniz: Las condiciones de la verdad eterna.*
(1923) *Rousseau y las ideas políticas modernas.*
(1927) *Descartes y el idealismo subjetivista moderno.*
(1927) *El sentido de la verdad.*
(1929) *La teoría de los valores en relación con la Etica y el Derecho.*
(1930) *El sentit de la vida i el problema dels valors.*
(1936) *L'amor i la percepció dels valors.*
(1940) *Amor y mundo.*
(1942) *Lo fugaz y lo eterno.*
(1946) *Vida y obra de Ramón Llull: Filosofía y Mística*, Mexico: Orion.
(1953) *Sentido de la presencia*, Mexico: Fondo de Cultura Económica.
The volume of *Obras* (Mexico: UNAM, 1953) contains 1940, 1942 and 1946 plus articles and translations from English, French and German.

Secondary literature:

Abellán, J. L. (1967) *Filosofía española en America, 1936–1966* Madrid: Guadarrama.
Johnson, J. W. (1946) 'Método y fines de la filosofia de J. Xirau', *Cuadernos Americanas*, July–Aug.
Lopez Quintas, A. (1970) *Filosofía Española Contemporanea*, Madrid: BAC.

From his extensive studies in the history of Western philosophy, Xirau derived the belief that there is at the heart of modern thought a pernicious rupture between being and value, with the latter being relegated (generally) to the status of the subjective or regarded in some degree less 'real' than being. This rupture he attributed to the influence of positive science, with its tendencies to intellectualism, mechanism and reductionism. Xirau argued that positive science has its limits, and is entirely inadequate to deal with matters of the spirit. He set out to restore value to its rightful place in the scheme of things, relying not a little on the techniques of phenomenology in general and **Scheler** in particular.

The analysis of perception common in positivist philosophies Xirau regarded as importantly incomplete. Ratiocination on sense data is not the only high road to truth, and is indeed only partially revelatory of being-as-is. There is another and richer mode of perception, which springs from the attitude to the world Xirau calls love (cf. the key texts of 1936 and 1940). By this he does not mean a romantic, personal attachment but a true openness to the plenitude of being, an attitude to all there is which manifests itself as a superabundance of spiritual life and accurate perception of the value of things and experiences. Loving perception penetrates to being-as-is, and what is revealed is a reality with two co-ultimate facets, namely being and value. By comparison, the mode of perception which underlies utilitarian, pragmatist and relativist theories of truth is partial. Truth is to be attained not via science, but via love.

ROBERT WILKINSON

Y

Yamuni Tabush, Vera

Mexican. *b:* 30 May 1917, San José, Costa Rica (of Lebanese parents). Mexican citizen 1949. *Cat:* Historian of ideas. *Educ:* MA, Philosophy, Universidad Nacional Autónoma de México, 1949, doctorate in 1954; postgraduate study in Paris, Algiers and Lebanon. *Appts:* Universidad Nacional Autónoma de México.

Main publications:

(1951) *Conceptos e imágenes en pensadores de lengua española*, Mexico: Fondo de Cultura Económica.
(1980) *José Gaos: el hombre y su pensamiento*, Mexico: Universidad Nacional Autónoma de México.
(1989) *José Gaos: su filosofía*, Mexico: Universidad Nacional Autónoma de México.

In addition to her professorial duties Yamuni earned a medical degree in 1973. She is currently a full-time Professor of Philosophy and a practising physician. She is a leading authority on the thought of one of the most influential figures in twentieth-century philosophy in Mexico, José **Gaos** (1900–69), with whom she studied. Yamuni's work on Gaos analyses his role as a 'transplanted' Spanish philosopher who was exiled after the fall of Republican Spain, his concept of the person, his interpretation of the history of philosophy and his metaphysics. In addition to her books Yamuni has published more than forty articles on philosophy, the role of women in society and the Arab world.

AMY A. OLIVER

Yan Fu (Yen Fu)

Chinese. *b:* 1854, Fuzhou, Fujian Province, China. *d:* 1921, Fuzhou. *Cat:* Philosophy translator and commentator. *Ints:* Social thought; logic. *Educ:* Studied at School of Navigation, Majiang Naval Academy, Fuzhou; Greenwich Naval College (1877–9). *Infls:* Herbert Spencer, Adam Smith and John Stuart Mill. *Appts:* Chancellor, Beiyang Naval Academy, Tianjin; Director of Translation Bureau, Imperial University, Beijing; Chief Editor, Bureau of Terminology; Chancellor, University of Beijing.

Main publications:

Translations with notes and commentaries of:
(1897) Thomas Huxley, *Evolution and Ethics and Other Essays*, chapters 1–2, Shanghai: Commercial Press.
(1900) Adam Smith, *Wealth of Nations*, Shanghai: South Ocean Publishers.
(1900) John Stuart Mill, *On Liberty*, Shanghai: Commercial Press.
(1903) Herbert Spencer, *Study of Sociology*.
(1904) Edward Jenks, *A History of Politics*.
(1904) Montesquieu, *Esprit des Lois*.
(1905) (half of) John Stuart Mill, *A System of Logic*, Shanghai: Commercial Press.
(1909) (adaptation) William Jevons, *Lessons in Logic*.

Secondary literature:

Boorman, H. (ed.) (1970) *Biographical Dictionary of Republican China*, New York and London: Columbia University Press.
Briere, O. (1956) *Fifty Years of Chinese Philosophy 1898–1950*, London: George Allen & Unwin Ltd.
Complete Chinese Encyclopedia (1987), Philosophy Volumes, Beijing: Chinese Encyclopedia Publications.
Fung, Y. (1948) *A Short History of Chinese Philosophy*, New York: The Free Press.
Schwartz, B. (1964) *In Search of Wealth and Power: Yen Fu and the West*, Cambridge, Mass.: Harvard University Press.

After training in English at Naval College in Fuzhou, Yen was sent to Greenwich Naval College in England, where he supplemented his naval studies with readings in sociology, economics, politics and philosophy to discover the source of Western power. Under **Spencer**'s influence, he argued that Social Darwinism provided the best framework for understanding Western strength and for shaping Chinese policy to achieve the wealth and power needed to overcome foreign dominance. Although he saw democratic politics as necessary to his programme, his evolutionary perspective led to extreme caution in moving away from China's despotic political tradition. He proposed that a first stage of political reform should be under the guidance of an educated elite. Although he attacked conservatives who thought that no change was necessary, he believed that the Chinese population was not ready to exercise democratic rights and that premature reform would lead only to chaos. He criticized the reformers **Kang Youwei** and **Liang Qichao**, the revolutionary **Sun Zhonghan** and the May Fourth Movement. With some misgivings, he supported Yuan Shikai, who appointed him to become Chancellor of the University of Beijing and allowed his name to be used in Yuan's attempt to become Emperor. He had previously supported the proposal to make Confucianism the state religion, and at the end of his life he rejected Westernization in favour of a return to Chinese traditions.

In his earlier and more optimistic stage, Yan considered education to be at the heart of a programme to strengthen China. He translated a series of important Western works into Chinese. He accompanied the translations, written in a pure classical style, with extensive notes and commentaries pointing out the relevance of each text for Chinese circumstances. His enthusiasm for Spencer led him to see the individualism of Mill's *On Liberty* and Smith's *Wealth of Nations* mainly as a means of advancement in the struggle for existence. In writing for a Chinese audience, Yan drew comparisons between the Western writers and familiar Chinese texts. He thus made the authors more intelligible and more acceptable. His interest in logic derived from his assessment that the discipline was the foundation of Western knowledge, a view perhaps encouraged by the lack of a formal logic tradition in China. Yan's translations and commentaries were immensely popular and influential in China. Figures as diverse as Liang Qichao, **Lu Xun**, **Hu Shi** and **Mao Zedong** acknowledged his influence. More than anyone, he promoted the attractions of Western learning based on clear, intelligible and stylish translations. Although his period as Chancellor of the University of Beijing is perhaps undervalued, his achievements were overshadowed by those of his brilliant successor **Cai Yuanbei**.

NICHOLAS BUNNIN

Yates, Frances Amelia

British. *b:* 28 November 1899, Southsea, England. *d:* 29 September 1981, Surbiton, England. *Cat:* Historian of philosophy and culture. *Ints:* Giordano Bruno and the Renaissance; the 'occult' sciences. *Educ:* University College, London. *Infls:* Personal influences: Fritz Saxl, Gertrude Bing, E. H. Gombrich, Dorothea Waley Singer and R. W. Yates. Literary influences: E. Garin and P. O. Kristeller. *Appts:* 1944–67, Lecturer in Renaissance Culture and Editor of Publications, then (1956) Reader in the History of the Renaissance, then (1967) Honorary Fellow, Warburg Institute, University of London; 1967, FBA; 1970, Ford Lecturer, University of Oxford; 1972, OBE; 1977, DBE.

Main publications:

(1947) *The French Academies of the Sixteenth Century*, London: Warburg Institute.

(1964) *Giordano Bruno and the Hermetic Tradition*, London: Routledge & Kegan Paul.

(1966) *The Art of Memory*, London: Routledge & Kegan Paul.

(1972) *The Rosicrucian Enlightenment*, London: Routledge & Kegan Paul.

(1975) *Astrea: The Imperial Theme in the Sixteenth Century*, London: Routledge & Kegan Paul.

Secondary literature:

Hillgarth, J. N. and Trapp, J. B. (eds) (1982) *Frances A. Yates, 1899–1981*, Warburg Institute memorial booklet.

The interest that formed the nucleus from which Yates's researches radiated was the nature and significance of Giordano Bruno's writings and life. As early as 1936 she had planned to translate Bruno's *Cena de le Ceneri*. Through word of this, she came to be introduced to the circles of the Warburg Institute.

In a succession of original inter-disciplinary writings, Yates explored the cultural and intellectual life of the Renaissance. Her *French Academies* (1947) traced the interrelationships between the philosophical, artistic, religious, and political activities fostered by the academies established by the courtiers of the King of France.

Her monumental *Giordano Bruno* (1964) emphasized the importance of the influence of 'hermeticism' (an arcane complex of neo-Platonic philosophy, associated 'occult' sciences and aesthetics) in the Italian Renaissance. She contended that the dissemination of hermeticism throughout Europe by its chief proponent, the itinerant Bruno, was central to the development of the arts, the sciences and the imperial politics of the sixteenth century.

In her *Art of Memory* (1966) she showed how the 'art of memory', inherited and recorded by the Romans, was revived, in occult form, at the Renaissance (particularly by Bruno) and penetrated the arts and sciences of Europe, including the Shakespearian theatre. Yates's pioneering studies have vastly increased our understanding of Renaissance philosophy and culture and, implicitly, of the development from 'magical' to 'scientific' rationality.

Sources: Kersey; DNB; Bullock & Woodings.

STEPHEN MOLLER

Yazdi, M(ehdi) Hairi

Iranian. *b:* 1923, Qum. *Cat:* Islamic philosopher; historian of philosophy; philosopher of religion. *Ints:* Mysticism. *Educ:* Studied at Qum, Mashhad and Tehran Universities, and later at University of Michigan and University of Toronto. *Infls:* Mulla Sadra, Nasr al-Din Tu-i, ibn Sina and twentieth-century Western philosophers. *Appts:* Taught at Harvard, Georgetown, McGill and Oxford Universities and later at Tehran University.

Main publications:

(1960) *Ilm-i kulli* [Universal Knowledge], Tehran.
(1969) *Kawishhayi aql-i nazari* [Investigations of Pure Reason], Tehran: Tehran University Press.
(1981) *Hiram-i hasti* [The Pyramid of Existence], Tehran: Iranian Centre for the Study of Civilization.
(1982) *Kawishhayi aql-i amali* [Investigations of Practical Reason], Ethran: Cultural Studies & Research Institute.
(1992) *The Principles of Epistemology in Islamic Philosophy: Knowledge by Presence*, Albany: SUNY.

Although Mehdi Hairi had a traditional religious education in Iran and became interested in a wide range of philosophical traditions, especially those stemming from Persian thinkers of the ishraqi school of mystics. He is far from parochial in his scope, combining a wide range of medieval and modern Islamic philosophy with current philosophy as practised in the West. His work on religion is characterized by a concern with an analytic approach, and even when considering difficult aspects of mysticism he uses an approach more normal among the medieval Islamic philosophers and contemporary Western philosophers than among the Shi'ite Persian religious authorities. Through his students and his writings Hairi has come to have a considerable influence on Islamic philosophers. He has demonstrated how it is possible to employ a variety of philosophical techniques when dealing with important theoretical and practical topics, and in particular how useful Western philosophy can be in combination with Islamic philosophy. This has not always endeared him to the religious authorities, and many of those influenced by him are prudent to be reticent about that influence, but many modern figures in Islamic philosophy find his work very helpful in dealing with a range of philosophical problems.

Sources: Foreword by Seyyed Hossein Nast, in Yazdi 1992; personal communication.

OLIVER LEAMAN

Yolton, John William

American. *b:* 10 November 1921, Birmingham, Alabama. *Cat:* Historian of philosophy. *Ints:* The philosophy of Locke; seventeenth- and eighteenth-century philosophy; philosophy of science. *Educ:* Universities of Cincinnati, California (Berkeley) and Balliol College, Oxford. *Infls:* Literary influences: Locke, Dewey and Russell. Personal: Jean S. Yolton. *Appts:* 1952–3, Visiting Lecturer in Philosophy, Johns Hopkins University; 1953–7, Assistant Professor of Philosophy and Bicentennial Preceptor, Princeton University; 1957 -61, Associate Professor of Philosophy at Kenyon College, Gambier, Ohio; 1961–3, Professor of Philosophy, University of Maryland; 1963–78, Professor of Philosophy, York University, Ontario; from 1978, Professor of Philosophy and Dean of Rutgers College, Rutgers University, New Jersey.

Main publications:

(1956) *John Locke and the Way of Ideas*, Oxford: Clarendon Press.
(1960) *The Philosophy of Science of A. S. Eddington*, The Hague: Nijhoff.
(1967) *Metaphysical Analysis*, Toronto: University of Toronto Press.
(1970) *John Locke and the Compass of Human Understanding*, Cambridge: Cambridge University Press.
(1971) *Locke and Education*, New York: Random House.
(1983) *Thinking Matter: Materialism in Eighteenth-Century Britain*, Minneapolis: University of Minnesota Press.
(1985) *John Locke : A Study of His Thought*, Oxford: Blackwell.

(1992) *Locke and French Materialism*, Oxford: Blackwell.
(1993) *A Locke Dictionary*, Oxford: Blackwell.

Secondary literature:

Agassi, Joseph (1986) Review of *Thinking Matter* (1983), in *Philosophy of the Social Sciences* 16: 526–8.
Kitely, Murray, (1970) Review of *Metaphysical Analysis* (1967), in *Philosophical Review* 79: 139–42.
Odegard, Douglas (1972) Review of *John Locke and the Compass of Human Understanding* (1970), in *Philosophical Review* 81: 250–3.
Rogers, G. A. J. (1993) Review of *Locke and French Materialism* (1992), in *Philosophical Books* 34, 2: 85–7.

Yolton is one of the foremost authorities on seventeenth- and eighteenth-century philosophy and on Locke in particular, although he has also written on other topics, including the philosophy of science and metaphysics.

Yolton's approach is typified by *John Locke and the Way of Ideas* (1956). In a thorough, exact and highly technical way, he showed how Locke's *Essay Concerning Human Understanding* marked the beginning of the empirical tradition in British philosophy. Arguing that Locke's chief purpose in the *Essay* was practical, Yolton also demonstrated how Locke's philosophical doctrines were very often directly related to the burning moral and religious issues of the day.

Yolton's many subsequent writings are augmentations of his initial book, offering detailed studies of Locke's place in science and religion, of his relation to his contemporaries, and of his lesser known works on economics, education and theology.

Yolton's highly acclaimed corpus represents one of the fullest explorations of Locke's philosophy ever undertaken.
Sources: CA FR 37–40, p. 643.

STEPHEN MOLLER

Yu Guangyuan (Yu Kuang-yuan)

Chinese. *b:* 1915, Shanghai. *Cat:* Marxist; philosopher of science; philosopher of social sciences; economist. *Ints:* Economics. *Educ:* Physics at Qinghua University, Beijing. *Infls:* Marxist thinkers. *Appts:* Professor, University of Beijing; Vice-President of the Chinese Academy of Social Sciences; Chairman of the Chinese Society of the Dialectics of Nature; Chief Editor, *Newsletter of Research on the Dialectics of Nature*; Chief Editor, *Encyclopedia of Dialectics of Nature*; Vice-Chairman, Editorial Board, *The Chinese Encyclopedia*; held many important party and governmental advisory posts in Yanan and, after 1949, in Beijing, dealing with science, technology, economics and planning.

Main publications:

(1956) *Studying Marxist–Leninist Philosophy.*
(1979) *Questions on the Objective Nature of Law.*
(1980–81) *Study on the Place of Socialism in Political Economy*, 2 vols.
(1981) *How to Conduct Investigations and Research.*
(1981) *On the Study of Social Science.*
(1982) *Theses, Lectures and Notes on Philosophy (1950–1966).*
(co-translator) Friedrich Engels, *Dialectics of Nature.*

Secondary literature:

Complete Chinese Encyclopedia (1987), Philosophy Volumes, Beijing: Chinese Encyclopedia Publications.

Yu's wide-ranging abilities allowed him to pursue an economics career as well as to study philosophy of science (under the title dialectics of nature) since the 1930s. He organized two major research programmes in dialectics of nature before and after the Cultural Revolution (1956–67 and 1978–85). As a result, philosophy of science became established as the best developed area of Western philosophy in China. His discussion of the methodology of research and the philosophy of the social sciences have also had an impact.

Yu has shown a bold independence of analysis many times in his career and has frequently drawn criticism. He argued against a Stalinist view of philosophy in 1956. He proposed an advanced commodity interpretation of the Chinese economy against the view that the notion of commodity should be applied solely to capitalist economic systems. After the Cultural Revolution, he supported the introduction of policies of reform and was the first to argue that politics as well as economics should be publicly discussed.

NICHOLAS BUNNIN

Z

Zamboni, Giuseppe

Italian. **b:** 2 August 1875, Verona. **d:** 8 August 1950, Verona. **Cat:** Philosopher of knowledge; philosopher of religion. **Educ:** University of Padua. **Appts:** Professor of Criteriology and Gnoseology, Universita Cattolica del Sacro Cuure, Milan, 1921–31; Visiting Professorships at Padua, 1935–6, 1941–2.

Main publications:

(1923) *La gnoseologia dell'atto come fondamento della filosfia dell'essere.*
(1924) *Introduzione al corso di gnoselogia pura.*
(1935) *Verso la filosofia*, 3 vols.
(1940) *La persona umana*, second edition, Milan: Vita e pensiero, 1983.
(1951) *La dottrina della coscienza immediata*, Verona: Tipografia veronese.

Secondary literature:

Giulietti, G. (1965) *La filosofia del profundo in Husserl e in Zamboni*, Treviso: Libreria Editrice Canova.
Guidi, S. del (1982) *Autobiografia etica di G. Zamboni*, Bologna: EDB.
Marcolungo, F. (1975) *Scienza e filosofia in G. Zamboni*, Padua: Antenove.

Zamboni's philosophy lies within, although it has important differences from, the vast apparatus of neoscholasticism. The aim of all his meditations was to solve the problem of the immediate foundations of all our knowledge. He distinguishes a field of experience that is sensory and rooted in feeling and a field of experience that is supersensible and intellectual. The first consists of sense data, feelings and images of both of these, all of which appear as objects to the perceiver. The second consists of experiences of the self, the experience of assent and dissent and the acts of abstraction and analysis. The experience of the self is central, being the sole experience of substance. The experience of the self is the basis of the distinction between the I and the not-I and is the necessary condition for the abstraction of concepts and universalization. Zamboni appropriates and analyses the Thomistic notion of substance as *actus essendi* or existential energy on the basis of which he can defend the doctrine of creation. Zamboni also applies his method to the analysis of aesthetics and ethics.

COLIN LYAS

Zambrano, María

Spanish. **b:** 1907, Vélez-Málaga, Spain. **d:** 1991, Madrid. **Cat:** Ratio-vialist; existentialist. **Ints:** Philosophy of literature; philosophy of religion. **Educ:** University of Madrid. **Infls:** Bergson, Ortega y Gasset and Unamuno. **Appts:** Professor of Philosophy, 1939, Universidad de Morelia (Mexico); 1941–53, Professor, Universidad and Instituto de Altos Estudios, Havana; lived in Rome (1953–4) and then Jura (from 1964) devoted to study.

Main publications:

(1939) *Pensamiento y poesía en la vida española*, Mexico.
(1939) *Filosofia y poesia*, Mexico.
(1944) *El pensamiento vivo de Séneca*, Buenos Aires.
(1955) *El hombre y lo divino*, Mexico: FCE.
(1965) *El sueño creador*, Mexico: Veracruzana.
(1965) *España, sueño y verdad*; second edition, Barcelona: EDHASA, 1982.
(1967) *La tumba de Antígona*, Mexico: Siglo Veintiuno.
(1982) *Dos fragmentos sobre el amor*, Málaga: Begar.

Secondary literature:

(1987) 'María Zambrano: Pensadora de la Aurora', *Anthropos* 70–1 (various authors).
Abellán, J. L. (1967) *Filosofia española en América*, Madrid: Ediciones Guadarrama, pp. 166–89.
Aranguren, J. L. (1966) *Los sueños de M. Zambrano*, Madrid: Revista de Occidente.
——et al. (1982) *María Zambrano o la Metafisica recuperada*, Málaga.
Guy, A. (1956) *Les Philosophes espagnols d'hier et d'aujourd'hui*, Toulouse: Association des Publications de l'Université de Toulouse-Le Mirail, pp. 207–10.

There are three primary preoccupations in the work of María Zambrano and all can be traced ineluctably to her status first as understudy to **Ortega y Gasset** in the University of Madrid, and secondly to that of her active Republicanism and later exile. The first, chronologically, is her elaboration of the notion of 'poetic reason', that faculty allowing the spirit to penetrate *secundum quid* in the essence of things by virtue of the recognition of coexistence. This forms part of Zambrano's search for a new type of knowledge able to penetrate the mysteries of the soul and which would bring in its train a reform of our spiritual procedures, a central feature of this being reason's acceptance of distant or even hostile forms of knowing.

Second, and due to this notion, ancient Greek and Roman philosophy can be substantially reinterpreted. In a primary stage of animism confusion and lack of things rules. The second stage of development brings an appearance of things in slow configuration, displaying 'certain uniformity', together with the slow dawning of their resistance to being. This assumed, the establishment of logic and dialectic takes place, reflecting now though on things—concepts—rather than on things themselves. This signifies a marking of distances, of the constitution of ethics as the arbiter of rational conduct. At this moment, given the deconstruction of the world, solitude takes over, the absence of gods/God forms a vacuum in which being realizes itself as a mere thing. Christianity is ready to fill the void created by such disquiet. Seneca's 'mediatory reason' provides the palliative to this situation, whilst Ortega's theory of generations fills the narrative space between the extinction of one faith and the wait for the next. The search for the sacred, explained dialectically in the framework of the characteristic dimensions of time: whilst modern paganism celebrates the yet-to-be where everything is predictable, authentic religious liberation will open up the future, the unpredictable, domain of infinite hope, and in this way being passes from the sacred to the sacrifice, and from the sacrifice to the divine.

Third, a phenomenological-existentialist streak describes all the imaginable disturbed states experienced by being, as well as their remedies, prime amongst them being the access to hope. The archetypal figures in this inverted *Huis clos* being Antigone, pure conscience and radiant piety. Zambrano's work, particularly those aspects to do with ethics and religion, have influenced a whole generation of moral philosophers, mainly her contemporaries, such as Aranguren, **Ferrater Mora** and Savater.

DAVID SPOONER

Zapffe, P(eter) W(essel)

Norwegian. *b:* 1899, Tromsø. *d:* 1990, Asker, Norway. *Cat:* Existential philosopher; poet, novelist, essayist, dramatist and humorist; literary critic; methodologist. *Ints:* Metaphysics. *Educ:* Studied and practised Law for a number of years before returning to the University of Oslo to study Philosophy; PhD, Oslo, 1941.

Main publications:

(1933) 'Den siste Messias' [The Last Messiah], *Janus* 9.
(1941) *Om det tragiske* [On the Tragic], Oslo: Gyldendal; reprinted in 1983, Oslo: Aventura.
(1951) *Den fortapte sønn* [The Prodigal Son], Oslo: Gyldendal.
(1961) *Indføring i litteraer dramaturgi* (Introduction to Literary Theory of Drama).
(1965) *Den logiske sandkasse* [The Logical Sandbox, Oslo: Universitetsforlaget.
(1971) *Lyksalig pinsefest* [Blessed Whitsun Feast], Oslo: Gyldendal.
(1985) *Rikets hemmelighet* [The Secret of the Kingdom], Oslo: Aventura.

Secondary literature:

Fløistad, Guttorm (1969) 'Innledning', in G. Fløistad (ed.) *Peter Wessell Zapffe*.
Nilsen, Lars (1988) *Pessimisme som filosofisk posisjon*.

In his versatility Zapffe may be compared to and perhaps surpasses **Sartre**. His main philosophical work is the monumental book *Om det tragiske* [On the Tragic] (1941). One of the author's goals in this work is to clarify and determine what he calls the structure of the tragic phenomenon or the objectively tragic. The basic for his proposed definition of the tragic is a comprehensive analysis of the human field of interest, especially the part which is marked by defeat and doom. The general definition arrived at in this way may be put as follows: the objectively tragic is characterized by a course of events where the individual is struck by a catastrophe as a consequence of greatness in its unfolding of abilities and interests.

However, Zapffe's errand is not merely to explicate and define the tragic. His deeper aim is to 'illuminate the only necessary and eternally burning problem, *what it means to be human*'. His account has the force of a general philosophy of human existence and the conditions of its realization. Man has a need for meaning in the specific parts of life. The question of meaning here is the question 'to what end?', 'for what purpose?'. Actions may be meaningful or meaningless. If one continues to ask for meaning or purpose, one ends up asking 'to what end?' in relation to one's life as a whole. What is the meaning of life? When posing this question, Zapffe seeks an answer that satisfies man's metaphysical need. He claims that man has a fundamental need for a *moral world order*, where everything has plan and meaning, where suffering, if it is necessary, is applied after an economic principle, where the destinies are adequate to the needs, in short, where everything occurs *justly* according to each individual's evaluation, or according to an evaluation to which everybody can ascend by their own means. Thus, he formulates man's metaphysical need as a quest for a just world order. This quest must not be conflated with the need for a loving god and a life after one's bodily death. The religious feeling is a *means*, and in his view an illusory means, to satisfy the metaphysical quest which, as human conditions are, cannot be satisfied.

Zapffe considers the metaphysical need for a moral world order as the essential mark of the human being. Man's metaphysical need is a surplus endowment that finds no adequate answer in reality. Thus, a discrepancy arises between the most essential need of man and the world in which he finds himself. In this conflict man can experience the tragic in his own form of existence. And this experience may be stronger the more he seeks to realize his need for meaning and justice. An increasing demand is met by a correspondingly categorical veto. In this sense man is doomed to fail, to suffer an irremediable defeat in the utmost realization of his nature. The reception of Zapffe's philosophy has been somewhat mixed. In Norway some have felt that his writings on Jesus and his discussion of the problem of evil are offensive to Christian beliefs. However, there has been a growing recognition of him as a major existential philosopher. Arne **Naess**'s words herald this recognition: 'P. W. Zapffe has a unique position in Nordic philosophy of life. He has in his main work, *Om det tragiske*, created a philosophical structure that takes up for clarifying analysis a series of the central questions of our time, and he does it with an originality and intensity of involvement reminiscent of Søren Kierkegaard'.

Sources: Guttorm, Fløistad, 'Zapffe, Peter Wessel', in *Norsk biografisk leksikon*.

I. GULLVÅG

Zaragüeta y Bengoechea, Juan
Spanish (of Basque origin). *b:* 1883, Orio (near San Sebastian), Spain. *d:* 1974. *Cat:* Neo-Thomist; systematic thinker. *Ints:* Value theory. *Educ:* After early theological training in Saragossa, Zaragüeta studied Philosophy at Louvain (1905–8). *Infls:* The neo-Thomism of Louvain and Ortega. *Appts:* Returning to Spain, he assumed the Chair of Philosophy at the Seminario Conciliar in Madrid (1908–17), and later occupied chairs of Religion and Moral Philosophy, of Law and Economics, of Pedagogy and of Rational Psychology at some of the most distinguished Spanish academic institutions; retired from teaching in 1953; remained a member of many learned societies in Spain and abroad.

Main publications:

(1920) *Contribución del lenguaje a la filosofía de las valores* (address on admission to the Real Academia de Ciencias Morales y Políticas).

(1941) *La intuición en la filosofía de Henri Bergson*, Madrid: Espasa-Calpe.

(1947) (with García Morente) *Fundamentos de filosofía e historia de los sistemas filosóficos*, Madrid: Espasa-Calpe.

(1950) *Filosofía y vida: I: La vida mental (descripción)*, Madrid: CSIC.

(1952) *Filosofía y vida: II: Problemas y métodos*, Madrid: CSIC.

(1954) *Filosofía y vida: III: Soluciones*, Madrid: CSIC.

(1963) *Estudios filosóficos*, Madrid: Instituto de Filosofía 'Luis Vives'.

(1968) *Curso de filosofía*, 3 vols, Madrid: Gredos.

Secondary literature:

Alvarez de Linea, A. (1953) 'En la jubilación de D. Juan Zaragüeta. Su vida, sus obras, su concepción filosófica', *Revista de Filosofía* 12: 177–89.

Escobar, L. (1951) 'Filósofos de España. Doctor Juan Zaragüeta y Bengoechea', *Logos I* (Mexico) 3: 109–21.

López de Munáin, R. (1956) 'Una nueva exposición de la filosofía como ciencia de la totalidad', *Verdad y Vida* 14: 203–50.

One of the most eminent and revered Spanish academics of his day, Zaragüeta's thought is a blend of Louvainian neo-Thomism with a discreet version of the ratio-vitalism of **García Morente** and **Ortega y Gasset**. Zaragüeta was also an appreciative though far from uncritical student of **Bergson**, and was greatly interested in the psychological sciences in his period. Further, he was one of the first of his countrymen to highlight the importance of careful linguistic studies to philosophy. Whilst Zaragüeta accepted neo-Thomism as the *philosophia perennis*, he did not regard it as unmodifiable in the light of recent discoveries. He quoted with approval Cardinal Mercier's principle: *vetera novis augere et perficere*.

All these traits are manifested in his magnum opus, the three-volume *Filosofía y vida*, a work of immense scope reminiscent of the *summa* of the scholastic tradition. The first volume is a phenomenological description of mental life, individual and social, focusing on the objects of consciousness, conscious activity and the subject of consciousness, the self-identical 'I'. The work ends with an analysis of the synthetic process of human life in terms of three basic categories: quantity, quality and vivacity. Volume II sets out what Zaragüeta characterizes as the 'vital problems' arising from the processes of conceptualization and the making of judgements, both theoretical and practical, and suggests methodologies appropriate to their solution. The final volume contains Zaragüeta's solutions to the problems he has discussed in the earlier books, and he outlines his own ideas on biology, history, cosmology and the relation of man and god. Philosophy itself emerges as the culmination of science, with at its heart a metaphysics aspiring to knowledge of the transcendent.

A subject to which Zaragüeta returns often is the theory of value. He contends that value is distinct from being, and, when it occurs, adds something to the latter. The relation of value to being is 'la condición del adjetivo respecto al sustantivo' ('the condition of the adjective with respect to the noun', from 'Being and value', an essay in 1963). He argues that valuation is a special act of consciousness (*la función estimativa*) distinct from cognition, and that evaluative modes of thought have their own unique logic: for example, the intensity of occurrence of a moral quality can affect its nature, the same not being true (he argues) of non-evaluative qualities. The judgements made as a result of evaluations are truth-functional. He is careful to stress that to consider values as discrete from

being is only possible by means of abstraction. Our life experience is of an evaluated reality.

ROBERT WILKINSON

Zea, Leopoldo

Mexican. **b:** 30 June 1912, Mexico City. **Cat:** Philosopher of history. **Educ:** National Autonomous University of Mexico; Master's Degree 1943, Doctoral Degree 1944. **Appts:** Professor Emeritus, National Autonomous University of Mexico; Director, Center for Latin American Studies (CCYDEL); Editor, journal *Cuadernos americanos*; author of more than fifty books on Latin American intellectual history, many of which have been translated into English, French, Italian, Russian and other languages; honorary degrees throughout Europe and Latin America; awarded the Gabriela Mistral Prize by the Organization of American States, 1986.

Main publications:
(1963) *The Latin American Mind*, trans. James H. Abbott and Lowell Dunham, Norman, OK: University of Oklahoma Press.
(1969) *Latin America and the World*, trans. Frances K. Hendricks and Beatrice Berler, Norman, OK: University of Oklahoma Press.
(1974) *Positivism in Mexico*, trans. Josephine H. Schultze, Austin, Texas: University of Texas Press.
(1978) *Filosofía de la historia americana*, Mexico: Fondo de Cultura Económica.
(1988) *Discurso desde la marginación y la barbarie*, Barcelona: Anthropos.
(1992) *The Role of the Americas in History*, trans. Sonja Karsen, ed. with an introduction by Amy A. Oliver, Savage, Maryland: Rowman & Littlefield.

Secondary literature:
Medin, Tzvi (1986) *Leopoldo Zea: Ideología, historia y filosofía de América Latina*, Mexico City: Universidad Nacional Autónoma de México.
Schutte, Ofelia (1993) *Cultural Identity and Social Liberation in Latin American Thought*, Albany: SUNY Press.

In his early works on positivism in Mexico, Zea demonstrates that while positivism was promoted as an 'objective' and 'scientific' doctrine which could most efficiently manage society, from the beginning certain members of the middle class reaped the benefits of the positivistic administration of Porfirio Díaz at the expense of the rest of the middle class and society. In addition to being a seminal contribution to the intellectual history of nineteenth-century Latin America, this emphasis on Mexican thought as it affected the nation socially and politically marks Zea's conviction that all philosophy arises from concrete individuals with particular historical circumstances and that 'universal' truths are then suspect. Zea seeks truth in values such as equality, tolerance and respect for the individual as he continues to question that which is considered 'universal'.

AMY A. OLIVER

Zeller, Eduard Gottlob

German. **b:** 22 January 1814, Kleinbottwar, Württemberg. **d:** 19 March 1908, Stuttgart. **Cat:** Historian of philosophy; theologian. **Ints:** History of ancient philosophy and of early Christianity. **Educ:** Doctorate, Tübingen, 1836; Berlin. **Infls:** F. C. Baur (son-in-law and pupil), D. F. Strauss (near contemporary at Tübingen), Kant, Schleiermacher and Hegel. **Appts:** Professor of Theology, Bern, 1847; Professor of Philosophy, Marburg 1849; Heidelberg, 1862; Berlin, 1872–95.

Main publications:

(1839) *Platonische Studien*, Tübingen: C. F. Osiander.

(1839–) (joint editor from vol. 5 onwards) A. F. von Pauly, *Real-Encyclopädie der Alterthumswissenschaft*, Stuttgart: J. B. Metzler.

(1845–52, 1920–3) *Die Philosophie der Griechen in ihrer geschichtliche Entwicklung*, 5 vols, Tübingen: L. F. Fues.

(1853) *Das theologische System Zwinglis*, Tübingen: Fues.

(1865–84) *Vorträge und Abhandlungen*, 3 vols, Leipzig: Fues.

(1873) *Geschichte der deutschen Philosophie seit Leibni*, Munich: R. Oldenbourg.

(1873) *D. F. Strauss in seinem Leben und seinen Schriften geschildert*, Bonn: E. Strauss.

(1883) *Grundriss der griecheschen Philosophie*, Leipzig: Fues Verlag R. Reisland.

(1910–11) *Kleine Schriften*, 3 vols, ed. O. Leuze, H. Diels and K. Holl, Berlin: Georg Reimer (chronological bibliography in vol. III, pp. 513–58).

(1942–57) (ed.) *Theologische Jahrbücher*.

Secondary literature:

Merz, J. T. (1896–1914) *A History of European Thought in the Nineteenth Century*, 4 vols, Edinburgh: Blackwood (see vol. III, pp. 71–4 and 296, and vol. IV, pp. 339–40 and 343–4).

Zeller argued for the decisive influence of ancient philosophy on the origins of Christianity as well as on its later development, and upheld a theological

programme in which unfettered reason alone would count. He separated what he called philosophy of religion from history of religion. He rejected the radical reductionism, typical of the young Hegelians, of religion into feeling or will or wish-fulfillment, for a more balanced approach. When later excluded from theological Chairs by the polemical atmosphere surrounding the 'higher criticism', Zeller moved into the history of ancient philosophy in which his work was characterized by a dominating interest in the internal systematic understanding of his subject, and philological rigour. He later withdrew his initial attempt to dispute Plato's authorship of the *Laws*. He objected to what he saw as Hegel's confusion of history and logic, and from 1862 on abandoned his early Hegelianism and became a major factor in the rise of neo-Kantianism, although opposing the idealism of many neo-Kantians, and argued for a rehabilitation of systematic philosophy with some positivistic overtones. In his later career Zeller extended his interests from ancient philosophy to modern.

Sources: H. Diels, in Zeller, 1910–11, vol. 3, pp. 465–511; W. Dilthey, *Neue Freie Presse*, Vienna, no. 15670, 5 Apr 1908, repr. in W. Dilthey (1970) *Gesammelte Schriften*, Göttingen: Vandenhoeck & Ruprecht, vol. 15, pp. 267–78.

R. N. D. MARTIN

Zenkovsky (Zen'kovskii), Vasilii Vasil'evich

Russian. **b:** 4 July (O.S.) 1881, Proskurov, Russia. **d:** 5 August 1962, Paris. **Cat:** Religious idealist. **Ints:** Philosophy of religion; philosophy of psychology; history of Russian philosophy. **Educ:** Kiev University. **Infls:** Vladimir Solov'ev, L. M. Lopatin and Sergei Bulgakov. **Appts:** 1915–19, Professor of Psychology, University of Kiev; 1920–3, Professor of Theology and Philosophy, University of Belgrade; 1923–6, Director, Institute of Pedagogy, Prague; 1926–62, Professor of Philosophy, Russian Orthodox Institute, Paris; 1942, ordained to the Russian Orthodox priesthood.

Main publications:

(1914) *Problema psikhicheskoi prichinnosti* [The Problem of Psychic Causality], Kiev.

(1926) *Russkie mysliteli i Evropa* [Russian Thinkers and Euorpe], Paris.

(1934) *Problema vospitaniia v svete khristianskoi antropologii* [The Problem of Education in the Light of Christian Anthropology], Paris.

(1948–50) *Istoriia russkoi filosofii*, 2 vols (English translation, *History of Russian Philosophy*, trans.

George L. Kline, 2 vols, London: Routledge &
Kegan Paul, 1953).
(1957) *Apologetika* [Apology], Paris.
(1961–4) *Osnovy khristianskoi filosofii* [Principles of
Christian Philosophy] 2 vols, Frankfurt.

Secondary literature:
Alekseev, P. V. (ed.) (1993) *Filosofy Rossii xix–xx
stoletii* [Russian Philosophers of the 19th and 20th
Centuries], Moscow, pp. 69–70.
Lossky, N. O. (1952) *History of Russian Philosophy*,
London: George Allen & Unwin.
Zernov, Nicolas (1963) *The Russian Religious
Renaissance of the Twentieth Century*, New York:
Harper & Row.

In his principal philosophical writings Zenkovsky
developed a Christian metaphysics that incorporates aspects of Sergei **Bulgakov**'s doctrine of
Sophia. He devoted special attention to the nature
of the human soul, the character and justification
of religious experience and the relation between
God and the created world.

According to Zenkovsky, at the pinnacle of
the soul's hierarchical structure is the capacity to
make contact with a reality that transcends the
subject. At one level this reality may present
itself in mystical experience as an ineffable all-
embracing unity; the person who searches no
deeper may espouse pantheism. Beyond that
limited form of contact with the divine, however—which is actually contact with 'passive
Sophia', or the created aspect of the world—is
the possibility of knowing a personal Divine
Being through revelation; this is the higher,
theistic form of religious experience, or contact
with the Divine Sophia—God himself. Zenkovsky's doctrine of creation includes the controversial thesis that time exists in God, rather than
beginning in the created world—a thesis he
believes is necessary in order to answer the
question of what existed *before* created time.
Zenkovsky's religious philosophy was influential
chiefly within Russian émigré and Eastern
Orthodox Christian communities, but he
achieved broader renown for his authoritative
two-volume history of Russian philosophy. The
work helped to keep non-Marxist Russian
philosophical traditions alive even in the Soviet
Union, where a limited edition for circulation
among approved scholars was issued in 1956.

JAMES SCANLAN

Zhang Binglin (Chang Ping-lin)
Chinese. *b:* 1868, Yuhang, Zhejiang Province,
China. *d:* 1936, Suzhou. *Cat:* Historian of ancient
Chinese philosophy; anti-Qing dynasty political
leader. *Ints:* Textual criticism and philological
studies, Zhuangzi, Buddhism and old text Confucianism. *Educ:* Studied the Chinese classics in
Yuhang and the classics, philology and history
with Yu Yue in Hangzhou. *Infls:* Zhuangzi, anti-
Manchu scholars, Yu Yue and ancient philolo-
gists. *Appts:* 1896–8, staff member, *Current Affairs
Journal*; 1898, staff member of Zhang Zhidong
(Governor General of Hubei and Hunan Pro-
vinces); 1902–3, teacher of sinological studies,
Patriotic Society school, Shanghai; 1906–8, Editor, the Tongmenghui journal *Minbao* (Tokyo);
1906–8, Leader, Restoration Society revolutionary party and other political groups; posts under
Sun Zhongshan and Yuan Shikai; Editor, the
journal *Huaguo*; Head, Zhangshi guoxue jiang
yansuo private school, Suzhou; Editor, magazine
Zhiyan.

Main publications:
(n.d.) *Answers to Questions on Philology*.
(n.d.) *Discussions of Chinese Classics*, Zhonghua
Book Company.
(n.d.) *Interpretation of Jiwulun*.
(n.d.) *Interpretation of Zhuangzi*.
(n.d.) *Literature and History*.
(n.d.) *Liu Zizheng's Views on the Zuozhuan*.
(n.d.) *New Dialects*.
(n.d.) *Notes on the Spring and Autumn Annals and on
Zuo's Commentary*.
(n.d.) *A Study of the Radicals in the Shuowen*.
(1906–11) articles in *Classical Studies Academic
Journal*.
(1914) *Revised Views*.
(1914) *Selected Works of Zhang Taiyan*.
(1917–19) *Zhang's Works*, 24 vols.
(1933) *Second Series of Zhang's Works*.
(1939) *Catalogue of the Writings of Taiyan*.
(1939) *Third Series of Zhang's Works*, 3 vols.

Secondary literature:
Boorman, H. (ed.) (1970) *Biographical Dictionary of
Republican China* New York and London: Co-
lumbia University Press.
Briere, O. (1956) *Fifty Years of Chinese Philosophy
1898–1950*, London: George Allen & Unwin Ltd.
Complete Chinese Encyclopedia (1987), Philosophy
Volumes, Beijing: Chinese Encyclopedia Publica-
tions.
Weber, J. (1986) *Politics im Leben des Gelehrten
Cheng Ping-lin 1869–1936*, Hamburg: MOAG.

Zhang Binglin, who was also known as Zhang
Taiyan, was a major political figure acting to

overthrow the Qing dynasty and an outstanding commentator on the Confucian classics and other ancient Chinese philosophy. He also developed his own philosophical system. His early political collaboration with **Liang Qichao** and **Kang Youwei** in the late 1890s ended over his rejection of Kang's devotion to maintaining the monarchy. In 1900 Zhang cut off his queue to display his unwillingness to cooperate with monarchists seeking reform within the framework of the Qing dynasty. Several times he was forced to seek safety in Taiwan and Japan, where he instigated the formation of anti-Manchu patriotic organizations imbued with a sense of Chinese history and a devotion to anti-Qing revolution. Upon his return to Shanghai in 1902 Zhang joined **Cai Yuanbei** and others in radical educational projects, which also provided a focus for secret revolutionary work. In this period he taught sinological studies at the Patriotic Society school. His anti-Qing articles in the newspaper *Subao* led to imprisonment in Shanghai, after which he returned to Japan to edit the journal *Minbao* for Sun Zhongshan's revolutionary party Tongmenghui. Zhang's growing discontent with Sun led to an unsuccessful attempt to remove Sun as head of the Tongmenghui. In 1910 Zhang was elected head of a rival revolutionary party, the Guangfuhui, or Restoration Society. After the 1911 revolution Zhang resigned from the Tongmenghui and formed parties and groupings challenging the Tongmenghui and its successor, the Guomindang, in the unstable politics of early Republican China. Zhang served China's first Presidents, **Sun Zhongshan** and Yuan Shikai, but conflict with Yuan led to his house arrest from 1913 until Yuan's death in 1916. Zhang lectured abroad to overseas Chinese. Upon his return unsuccessful missions for Sun's Guangzhou government led to Zhang's retirement from political life in 1918.

Zhang's great strength as a scholar grew out of his training with Yu Yue in philology and textual criticism. Zhuangzi's views and daoist suspicion of civilization and the state led to early opposition to Confucianism, but he later became a leading commentator on the Confucian classics, supporting the traditional old text school of interpretation against Kang Youwei's advocacy of new text interpretation. He was especially devoted to *Zuo's Commentary on the Spring and Autumn Annals*. His interest in Buddhist writings led to influential studies comparing the daoist writings of Laozi and Zhuangzi with the Buddhist text *Jushe Weilun*. Buddhist, daoist and Western idealism influenced his mature systematic philosophy. He held that a single underchanging hidden principle underlies all perception and that subjective perceptions require no objective world to explain them. His analysis of perception, influenced by Kant, combined categories derived from rational thought and empirical representations. Although Zhang wrote several superb works in philology and linguistics, the most important for philosophical study is his *Discussions of Chinese Classics*, showing how linguistic knowledge is crucial to understanding classical texts. He used Indian, Western and ancient Chinese logic to develop a sophisticated theory of names. He was also interested in ancient Chinese legal and ethical codes as central to Chinese culture, with a special concern for rites of mourning. Zhang wrote traditional prose and poetry of great distinction. He strenuously opposed the vernacular movement begun by **Hu Shi**, but by the end of his life this movement had displaced Zhang's own style from the centre of literary life.

NICHOLAS BUNNIN

Zhang Dainian (Chang Tai-nien)

Chinese. **b:** 1909, Hebei Province, China. **Cat:** Historian of Chinese philosophy. **Educ:** Beijing Normal University. **Infls:** British analytical philosophy and logic; Marx and Engels. **Appts:** Professor, Qinghua University; Professor, University of Beijing; President, Society for the Study of the History of Chinese Philosophy.

Main publications:

(1956) *Zhang Zai: Eleventh Century Chinese Materialist Philosopher*, Wuhan: Hubei Renmin Publishing House.

(1957) 'History of Chinese philosophical problems', in *Chinese Philosophical Compendium: A Short History of Chinese Materialist Thought*, Beijing: Zhongguo Qingnian Publishing House.

(1957) *A Preliminary Study of the Laws for the Development of Chinese Ethical Thought*, Beijing: Koxue Publishing House.

(1957) (contributor to) *Symposium on Problems of the History of Chinese Philosophy*, Beijing: Kexue Publishing House.

(1989) *A Discussion of the Essential Categories of Ancient Chinese Philosophical Thought*.

Secondary literature:

Chan, W. T. (1967) *Chinese Philosophy, 1949–1963: An Annotated Bibliography of Mainland China Publications*, Honolulu: East–West Center Press.

Complete Chinese Encyclopedia (1987), Philosophy Volumes, Beijing: Chinese Encyclopedia Publications.

Louie, K. (1986) *Inheriting Tradition: Interpretations of the Classical Philosophers in Communist China 1949–1966*, Hong Kong: Oxford University Press.

As a widely respected philosopher in China's leading department of philosophy, Zhang Dainian took part in debates in the 1950s concerning the value of continuing the study of traditional Chinese philosophy under Communist rule. At a time of intellectual reorganization under tight ideological control inspired by the Soviet figure A. A. Zhdanov, he argued that ancient Chinese thought could be studied by Marxist methods because, contrary to received opinion, it had many features in common with Western thought. In particular, he sought to legitimate such study by tracing a progressive materialist pattern in Chinese philosophy. Rather than rejecting the whole Chinese intellectual and moral past, he argued that scientific and democratic views of past philosophers could be retained. He also argued that traditional moral ideas could be accepted, at least those which, although retained throughout class-divided history, had their origin in primitive classless society. His general programme and his detailed analysis of such ancient figures as Mozi and Xunzi contained distortions and confusions in response to the extreme pressures of the times, but his work also displayed subtle and persuasive argument. Zhang's cautious defence of traditional thought within a Marxist perspective helped to allow Marxist and non-Marxist colleagues alike to continue work on traditional thought after the crucial exchanges of the 1957 *Symposium on Chinese Philosophy.*

NICHOLAS BUNNIN

Zhang Dongsun (Chang Tung-sun)

Chinese. *b:* 1886, Suzhou district, Jiangsu Province, China. *d:* 1972, Beijing. *Cat:* Neo-Kantian. *Ints:* Theory of knowledge and sociology. *Educ:* Studied Buddhism and Western philosophy in Tokyo, Japan and received an imperial degree on the basis of his foreign education. *Infls:* Kant, Hume, John Dewey, Bertrand Russell, C. I. Lewis, Wilhelm Wundt and Liang Qichao. *Appts:* Leading member, Progressive Party; member, Liang Qichao's research clique; 1916, Secretary General, Parliament; Editor of *China Times* and other newspapers and journals; 1925–30, Professor of Philosophy and Dean, College of Arts, Guanghua University, Shanghai; 1925–30, President, China Institute, Wusong; 1930–51, Professor of Philosophy, Yenching University, Beijing; leading member, National Socialist Party; leading member, China Democratic League.

Main publications:
(1929) *Collected Essays on New Philosophy*, Shanghai: Commercial Press.
(1930) *Moral Philosophy*, Shanghai: Zhonghua Book Company.
(1931) *Philosophy*, Shanghai: Shi Jie Book Company.
(1934) *Modern Philosophy*, Shanghai: Shi Jie Book Company.
Philosophy of Value, Shanghai: Shi Jie Book Company.
(1934) *On the Theory of Knowledge*, Shanghai: Shi Jie Book Company.
(1934) (ed.) *The Debate on Dialectical Materialism*, Minyu Book Company.
Psychoanalysis, Shanghai: Shi Jie Book Company.
(1946) *Knowledge and Culture*, Chongqing and Shanghai: Commercial Press.
(1946) *Reason and Democracy*, Chongqing and Shanghai: Commercial Press.
(1946) *Thought and Democracy*, Chongqing and Shanghai: Commercial Press.
(1947) *Democracy and Socialism*, Shanghai: Guancha Company.
Translator of Bergson, *Matter and Memory* & *Creative Evolution* and Plato, *Six Dialogues.*

Secondary literature:
Boorman, H. (ed.) (1970) *Biographical Dictionary of Republican China*, New York and London: Columbia University Press.
Briere, O. (1956 *Fifty Years of Chinese Philosophy 1898–1950*, London: George Allen & Unwin Ltd.
Chan, W. T. (1963) *A Source Book in Chinese Philosophy*, Princeton: Princeton University Press.
Complete Chinese Encyclopedia (1987), Philosophy Volumes, Beijing: Chinese Encyclopedia Publications.

Zhang Dongsun was a major commentator on Western philosophy, who developed his own neo-Kantian system of epistemology and metaphysics. After wartime imprisonment by the Japanese he argued that sociology rather than metaphysics was the key to understanding knowledge. In politics, he was influenced by Western constitutional theory and the principles of **Liang Qichao**. In the 1920s and 1930s he sought to find a middle way between nationalist and Communist rule. After the Second World War he sought an intellectual rapprochement with Marxism, but was none the less excluded by the new authorities from the faculty of Yenching University.

After the 1911 revolution Zhang edited and contributed to journals seeking to determine a constitutional basis for republican politics. He supported the 1913 attempt to designate Confucianism China's state religion and took part in Liang Qichao's 1916 'research clique', serving as Secretary General of Parliament. The failure of Parliament to establish reforms led Zhang to become Editor of the independent Shanghai newspaper *China Times*, where he was a major progressive commentator on Chinese affairs. He also sought to enrich Chinese intellectual life by introducing the young to the central concepts of Western philosophical thought. Although involved in the earliest stages of introducing Marxism to China, Zhang came into conflict with the party leaders by arguing that capitalism was necessary to achieve China's industrial development and by rejecting the application of Marx's concept of class struggle to China. Zhang was a major figure in the 1923 'science versus philosophy' debate, in which he supported the view of his friend Zhang Junmei (Carsun Chang) that the categories of science were inadequate for many central aspects of human experience. His assessment of the crude understanding of his opponents provided the setting for his own account of idealist epistemology and of the place of philosophy in scientific knowledge. With Zhang Junmei and other contributors to the journal *National Renaissance*, he founded the democratic National Socialist Party in 1934. He continued to oppose Marxism, notably through editing *The Debate on Dialectical Materialism* (1934). Zhang emerged from his wartime imprisonment by the Japanese to become a leading figure in the China Democratic League, a further attempt to mediate between the Communists and nationalists. Zhang's growing sympathy for Marxism led to a break with Zhang Junmei and to prominent activity in the early days of the People's Republic. In 1952, after a campaign of criticism related to his independent attitude towards ideological reform among Chinese academics, Zhang was removed from his academic and other posts.

Zhang's academic career began in 1925, but his most important work, dealing with knowledge, appeared after 1930 when he became a Professor at Yenching University, Beijing. Although deeply influenced by Kant, Zhang rejected Kantian dualism, according to which phenomena were produced by sensations ordered by mentally imposed categories. As an alternative source of order he proposed an 'epistemological pluralism', with Kantian phenomena produced by combinations of four mutually dependent but irreducible elements of knowledge: order, category, postulate and concept. His reliance on structures and laws to constitute the external world and his denial of sensation led to a vehement rejection of the concept of substance. Without substance, the universe was a construct, with the process of construction partly ascribable to nature and partly to our cognitive activity. Consciousness itself was also a construct derived from an underlying synthesis. Knowledge, even apparently direct perceptual knowledge, included interpretation, and Zhang rejected any absolute distinction between direct acquaintance and recognition under a concept. He saw sensations, perceptions, concepts and the categories as different products of a single integrative synthesis. Concepts were seen as signs having a normative role; the entry of concepts into the conceptual world in which all concepts were related allowed the strongest concepts to shape the others. Concepts were also regulated by the demand that they not conflict with perceptions. In his later work Zhang sought a sociological rather than a philosophical explanation of why some concepts played the role of categories. Zhang's structuralism, influenced by mathematical formulae as paradigms of knowledge, perhaps prepared the way to his rejection of metaphysics in favour of sociology during his incarceration by the Japanese. After the war his books dealt with society, democracy and socialism. He argued that socialism and democracy were synonymous and that intellectuals were obliged to guide society towards democratization and the eventual disappearance of the state.

NICHOLAS BUNNIN

Zhang Shenfu (Chang Shen-fu)

Chinese. *b:* 1893, Xiaoduokou, Hebei Province, China. *d:* 1986, Beijing. *Cat:* Analytical philosophy; mathematical logic; Marxism; Confucianism. *Ints:* Philosophy of Bertrand Russell; dialectical materialism; logical positivism. *Educ:* Studied in Paris at the Sorbonne (informally) and in Göttingen, at the Mathematical Institute (informally). *Infls:* Bertrand Russell and Marx. *Appts:* Posts at Guangzhou University, Jinan University, People's University and University of Peking; 1921, Professor, Qinghua University, Beijing; 1930s, a founder of the Chinese Communist Party; 1946–8, a leader of the Democratic League.

Main publications:
(1927) (translator) Wittgenstein, *Tractatus Logico-Philosophicus*, in *Philosophical Review*.
(1931) *Thought as Such*, Shanghai.
(1989) *Collection of Papers on Russell's Philosophy*, Beijing: Educational Science Publishing Company (papers on dialectical materialism, logical positivism, science, feminism, sexual freedom, and politics).

Secondary literature:
Briere, O. (1956) *Fifty Years of Chinese Philosophy, 1898–1950*, London: George Allen & Unwin Ltd.
Schwarcz (1992) *Time for Telling the Truth is Running Out: Conversations with Zhang Shenfu*, New Haven: Yale University Press.

Zhang Shenfu, who was trained in mathematics and philosophy, was the principal early transmitter and interpreter of Bertrand **Russell**'s philosophy in China. He thus introduced analytical philosophy as a rival to German idealism, **Dewey**'s pragmatism and the philosophy of **Bergson**. Although the Russellian approach never came to dominate professional philosophy in China, Zhang provided the basis for the studies of Chinese philosophers closest to the main Anglo-American tradition. In his own work, he attempted to integrate Russell's philosophy with dialectical materialism and in the 1930s became interested in logical positivism. His 1927 translation of the *Tractatus Logico-Philosophicus* in the journal *Philosophical Review* introduced Wittgenstein to China. Zhang's Chinese title for the *Tractatus*, *Treatise on Names and Reason*, indicates that the work deals with linguistics and logic. Zhang was also drawn to Russell's social views, including his attitudes toward feminism and sexual freedom, and to the work of **Freud**.

Zhang had some philosophical influence in the 1930s, but never achieved the great prominence of his younger brother **Zhang Dainian**. He left academic life for politics. After his role in the Chinese Communist Party as a founder and as chief party representative in France and Germany, Zhang resigned in 1925 on the grounds of personal as well as ideological disputes. In any case, his free, exploratory thought, stressing self-liberation over social organization, came into conflict with Leninist party discipline. As a Communist, he is best known for introducing Zhou Enlai into the Party. Zhang later became a leader of the Democratic League, which sought to find a means of reconciling the Communist Party and the Guomindang to avoid further civil war, but was expelled in 1948.

NICHOLAS BUNNIN

Zhao Jibin (Chao Chi-pin)
Chinese. *b:* 1905, Nehuang, Henan Province, China. *d:* 1982, Beijing. *Cat:* Marxist historian of Chinese philosophy. *Educ:* Studied on his own without formal higher education. *Appts:* Professor at Fudan, Northeast, Dongwu and Shandong Universities; Fellow, Institute of History, the Chinese Academy of Social Sciences; President of various teachers' colleges; Adviser, Philosophy Teaching and Research Section, the Chinese Communist Party Higher School.

Main publications:
(n.d.) *Outline of the History of Chinese Philosophy.*
(1950) *A Brief History of the Theory of Chinese Knowledge and Action.*
(1950) *Chinese Philosophical Thought.*
(1950) *On the Essentials of Philosophy.*
(1950) *A Critique of Ancient Confucian Philosophy*, Shanghai: Zhonghua Book Company.
(1957) (with Hou Wailu and Du Guoxiang) *A General History of Chinese Thought*, 6 vols, Beijing: Renmin Publishing House.
(1962) *A New Exploration of the Analects*, Beijing: Renmin Publishing House.
(1963) *A Record of Knowledge Acquired through Hard Work*, 2 vols, Beijing: Renmin Publishing House.

Secondary literature:
Chan, W. T. (1967 *Chinese Philosophy, 1949–1963: An Annotated Bibliography of Mainland China Publications*, Honolulu: East–West Center Press.
Complete Chinese Encyclopedia (1987), Philosophy Volumes, Beijing: Chinese Encyclopedia Publications.
Louie, K. (1986) *Inheriting Tradition: Interpretations of the Classical Philosophers in Communist China 1949–1966*, Hong Kong: Oxford University Press.

Zhao was a prolific and influential historian of Chinese philosophy who wrote from a radical Marxist perspective. From the 1940s he argued that Kongzi belonged to the declining Zhou dynasty slave-owning class, whose interests he tried to protect. Unlike many holding the same view, Zhao supported his position by means of sophisticated textual study and philological analysis. His understanding of *ren* in the Confucian *Analects* as 'slave owners' rather than 'men' and his argument that benevolence was secondary to a return to Zhou rites in Confucian values sharply challenged the view that Kongzi was a humane proponent of universal morality rather than a reactionary defender of class interests. Again employing a close textual examination, he contrasted Mozi, seen by him as a common man committed to hard work and human creativity and the transmission of tradition, with Kongzi, who was committed only to transmit Zhou values. In the 1960s Zhao's textual analysis was joined by the historical studies of radical anti-Confucian figures like **Guang Feng**. Although their views received only moderate support at the time, they contained impressive arguments which were enforced upon all intellectuals by the Cultural Revolution and the Anti-Confucian Campaign.

NICHOLAS BUNNIN

Zheng Xin (Cheng Hsin)

Chinese. *b:* 1905, Lujiang, Anhui Province, China. *d:* 1974. *Cat:* Kantian. *Educ:* Nankai University, Berlin University, Germany, and Yale University, USA. *Infls:* Kant and the neo-Kantian Bruno Bauch. *Appts:* Professor, University of Beijing; Chairman, Department of Philosophy, University of Beijing; Member, Research Institute of Philosophy, Chinese Academy of Science; Vice-Chairman, Chinese Society of Philosophy.

Main publications:

(1936) *Truth and Reality.*
(1946) *Description of Kantianism*, Shanghai: Commercial Press.
(1950) *Critique of Kant's Philosophy.*
(1957) 'Liberate idealism', in *A Symposium on the Problems of the History of Chinese Philosophy*, Beijing: Kexue Publishing House.

Secondary literature:

Briere, O. (1956) *Fifty Years of Chinese Philosophy 1898–1950*, London: George Allen & Unwin Ltd.
Complete Chinese Encyclopedia (1987), Philosophy Volumes, Beijing: Chinese Encyclopedia Publications.

After his studies in Germany and the USA, Zheng brought serious western Kantian scholarship to China under the influence of the neo-Kantian Bruno **Bauch**. His study of the *Critique of Pure Reason*, especially in *Description of Kantianism* (1946), showed a high level of scholarly and philosophical sophistication. In the 1950s, however, the importance of Hegel for Marx's thinking and the hostility of Engels towards Kant led to a rejection of Kantian studies in favour of work on

Hegel among those able to pursue serious work on German classical philosophy, a shift which undervalued the studies of Kantian philosophers like Zheng. Nevertheless, his work continued to influence his own students at Peking University.

In his cogent 1956 article 'Liberate idealism' Zheng provided a measured defence of idealism, claiming that many Chinese philosophers were materialist in public and in politics while idealists in private and in academic study. He argued that idealism in history was not a simple error and that systems of idealist thought, containing components of different worth, required scholarly care in their analysis and evaluation. He argued against rejecting idealism as a whole and, on that basis, argued for maintaining the study of idealism in China. Although his views seemed modest, they challenged a methodology adapted from Zhdanov which provided no standpoint from which piecemeal assessment could be made.

NICHOLAS BUNNIN

Zhu Guangqian (Chu Kuang-ch'ien)

Chinese. *b:* 1879, Tongcheng, Anhui Province, China. *d:* 1986, Beijing. *Cat:* Aesthetics; psychology. *Educ:* Hong Kong University, Universities of Edinburgh and London in the UK, Universities of Paris and Strasbourg in France. *Infls:* Croce. *Appts:* Professor, Department of Western Languages, Peking University, Sichuan University and Wuhan University; Honorary President, Chinese Academy of Aesthetics.

Main publications:

——*Abnormal Psychology*, Shanghai, Commercial Press.
——*Collected Essays on Aesthetic Criticism.*
——*Discussing Literature.*
——*A History of Western Aesthetics.*
——*Letters on Aesthetics.*
——*The Psychology of Literary Art*, Beijing, Beibing Bookstore.
——*Twelve Letters to the Young.*
——(trans.) Croce, *Aesthetics.*
(1932) *A Discussion of Poetry.*
(1932) *On Beauty*, Kaiming Bookstore.
(1936) *The Psychology of Tragedy.*
(1948) *A Critical Study of Croce's Philosophy*, Zhengzhong Book Company.
(1948) *On Poetry*, Zhengzhong Bookstore.

Secondary literature:

Briere, O. (1956) *Fifty Years of Chinese Philosophy 1898–1950*, London: George Allen & Unwin Ltd.

Complete Chinese Encyclopedia (1987) Philosophy Volumes, Beijing: Chinese Encyclopedia Publications.

Zhu Guangqian was widely read in aesthetics, but gave his greatest devotion to the works of **Croce**. He saw life as a work of art, with a perfect life a full expression of personality governed by demanding aesthetic principles of composition. His aestheticism placed the value of beauty higher than those of truth and goodness. Beauty could be found in intellectual products, such as philosophical systems, as well as in life and works of art. These scholarly systems could be doubted while being loved, with such delight making men free and happy.

In his early analysis of aesthetic perception, Zhu held that the perception of beauty differed from perception in science. Aesthetic perception was not conceptual and was not related to practical concerns; rather, it was determined by the contemplation and appreciation of solitary images. From 1950 he offered a different analysis, which brought together subjective and objective points of view. Beauty was conditioned by objectivity, but the subjective recognition of the effect of emotions allowed an object to become an image or emblem of itself. With this subjectively grounded reflexivity came beauty. After 1960 Zhu emphasized a Marxist practical point of view, uniting the objective and the subjective in the practical.

NICHOLAS BUNNIN

Zhu Qianzhi (Chu Ch'ien-chih)

Chinese. *b:* 1899, Fuzhou, Fujian Province, China. *d:* 1972, Beijing. *Cat:* Historian of philosophy. *Educ:* Peking University and in Japan. *Infls:* Hegel and Japanese philosophy. *Appts:* Jinan University and Zhongshan University, Guangzhou, Professor and Head of Philosophy Department, Peking University; Professor, World Religion Reseach Institute, Chinese Academy of Social Sciences.

Main publications:

(n.d.) *Hegel and Comtism*, Minzhi Book Company.
(n.d.) *Hegel's Philosophy of History*, Shanghai: Commercial Press.
(1921) *Philosophy of Revolution*.
(1921) *Philosophy of Zhou Yi, Uniting All Under Communism, Revolution of the People and the Unification of the World, History of the Exchange of Chinese and Western Culture.*
(1924) *Sentimentalist's View of the Universe and Human Life*, Taidong Library.

(1956) *Li Zhi, Pioneer of Anti-Feudalistic Thought in Sixteenth Century China*, Wuhan Hubei People's Publishing House.
(1958) *The Zhu Xi School in Japan*, Beijing: Three Bookstore United Company.
(1958) *The History of Japanese Philosophy: Exegesis of Laozi*, Shanghai: Longmen United Bookstore.
(1962) *The Classical School and the Wang Yangming School in Japan*, Shanghai, Remin Publishing House.

Secondary literature:

Briere, O. (1956) *Fifty years of Chinese Philosophy, 1898–1950*, London: George Allen & Unwin Ltd.
Chan, W. T. (1967) *Chinese Philosophy, 1949–1963: An Annotated Bibliography of Mainland China Publications*, Honolulu: East–West Center Press.
Complete Chinese Encyclopedia (1987) Philosophy Volumes, Beijing: Chinese Encyclopedia Publications.

Zhu Qianzhi was a figure of comprehensive scholarly knowledge. He took part in the May Fourth Movement as a student at Peking University and formed an early enthusiasm for socialist revolutionary thought. He also cultivated an interest in Hegel, which shaped his concern for cultural influence.

His mature work was devoted to the history of philosophy, particulary the influence of Chinese philosophy in the West and in Japan, the influence of Western culture in China, and the history of Japanese philosophy. In a famous study, he examined how missionaries interpreted Chinese philosophy and culture to the West and how Western culture had influence on China. He later wrote about European interpretations of Confucius in the seventeenth and eighteenth centuries. He was an authority on cultural relations between China and Japan, and his work is highly appreciated by Japanese scholars. He examined the response in Japan to the great twelfth-century neo-Confucian synthesis of Zhu Xi and to the sixteenth century neo-Confucian idealism of Wang Yangming. These philosophers dominated Chinese philosophy to modern times and have continuing influence in attempts to revive neo-Confucian philosophy. Zhu's studies recognise the great importance of Chinese thinkers for Japanese philosophy. His painstaking study of Laozi is highly regarded.

NICHOLAS BUNNIN

Ziff, P(aul)

American. *b:* 22 October 1920, New York. *Cat:*

Analytical philosopher. *Ints:* Philosophy of language; aesthetics; philosophy of mind; epistemology. *Educ:* Received a BFA in Painting and a PhD in Philosophy, both from Cornell University. *Infls:* Jeremy Bentham amd J. L. Austin. *Appts:* 1953–9, Instructor, then Assistant Professor, Harvard University; 1958, Instructor, Princeton University; 1959–64, Assistant, then Associate Professor, University of Pennsylvania; 1964–8, Professor, University of Wisconsin at Madison; 1966, Visiting Professor, University of Calgary; 1968–70, Professor, University of Illinois at Chicago Circle; 1970–90, William Rand Kenan Jr Professor, University of North Carolina.

Main publications:

(1960) *Semantic Analysis*, Ithaca, NY: Cornell University Press.

(1962) *J. M. Hanson*, Ithaca, NY: Cornell University Press.

(1966) *Philosophic Turnings*, Ithaca, NY: Cornell University Press (Italian translation in 1969).

(1972) *Understanding Understanding*, Ithaca, NY: Cornell University Press.

(1984) *Antiaesthetics: An Appreciation of the Cow with the Subtile Nose*, Dordrecht: D. Reidel.

(1984) *Epistemic Analysis: A Coherence Theory of Knowledge*, Dordrecht: D. Reidel.

Secondary literature:

Jamieson, D. (ed.) (1994) *Language, Art, and Mind: Essays in Appreciation and Analysis, in Honor of Paul Ziff*, Dordrecht: Kluwer.

Educated in the Wittgensteinian milieu of Cornell in the late 1940s and deeply influenced by interactions with J. L. **Austin** in Harvard and Oxford in the mid-1950s, Ziff was one of the early American practitioners of British-style analytic philosophy. However, unlike most British philosophers of that period, Ziff viewed science as important and relevant in addressing philosophical problems. His *Semantic Analysis* (1960) was a rigorous attempt to develop an empirical program for semantics, and involved bringing together the linguistic philosophy of Austin with the linguistics of **Harris** and **Chomsky**. The first draft of *Epistemic Analysis* (1984) was composed in the early 1960s and, although much revised, it bears the mark of his attempt to bring the methods of *Semantic Analysis* to bear on problems of knowledge. During the late 1950s and 1960s he published a series of influential papers exploring the relations between mind and behaviour. His 1965 *Journal of Philosophy* paper, 'The simplicity of other minds', is an early statement of an 'inference to the best explanation' approach to the problem of other minds. During the late 1960s and 1970s Ziff increasingly turned his attention away from semantics towards questions about the pragmatics of language use. Some of this work is included in *Understanding Understanding* (1972).

Ziff trained as a painter before studying philosophy, and has been a practising artist throughout his career. His dissertation was on **Collingwood**'s aesthetic theory, and his work in aesthetics has been characterized by close attention both to works of art and to acts of aesthetic appreciation. Some of his early work in aesthetics is collected in *Philosophical Turnings* (1966) but his most ambitious contribution is *Antiaesthetics* (1984). There are unified themes in Ziff's work, but he was more of a problem-oriented than a systematic philosopher. For that reason, as well as others, he has few followers. His most important contribution was his role in the development of analytic philosophy in America, particularly his bringing together the methods of J. L. Austin with the scientific concerns of American analytic philosophy. His contributions to aesthetics during a period in which this field was considered marginal by many philosophers will be remembered, and he will also be viewed as a forerunner in the development of serious concern with the pragmatics of language use.

DALE JAMIESON

Zong Baihua (Tsiung Pai-hua)

Chinese. *b:* 1897, Changshu, Jiangsu Province, China. *d:* 1986, Beijing. *Cat:* Syncretist of Chinese and Western Aesthetics; poet. *Ints:* Kant; Goethe; daoism; *Book of Changes. Educ:* Shanghai Tongji University; Universities of Frankfurt and Berlin, Germany (1920–25). *Infls:* Kant, Goethe and Chinese aesthetics. *Appts:* Professor, Southeast University, Suzhou, Jiangsu Province; Professor, Central University; Professor, Nanjing University; 1949–52, Professor, University of Beijing; Consultant, Chinese National Society of Aesthetics.

Main publications:

(n.d.) *Concerning the Meaning of Art.*

(n.d.) *A Walk with Aesthetics.*

(1987) *Art and the I Ching.*

(1987) *A General Discussion of the Origin and Development of Chinese Art.*

Translator of Kant, *Critique of Judgment.*

Secondary literature:
Complete Chinese Encyclopedia (1987), Philosophy
  Volumes, Beijing: Chinese Encyclopedia Publica-
  tions.

Zong was an outstanding Chinese poet of the
1920s who also developed a compelling aesthetic
theory. As a poet he helped to originate contemporary Chinese poetry. In the 1920s he was a
leader of the Young People's China society, to
which **Mao Zedong** also belonged. Zong employed the austere contrasts of fulfilment and
emptiness and of the limited and unlimited to
structure his account of aesthetics. He was deeply
influenced by his studies in Germany and was
especially drawn to the works of Goethe. His work
on Kant encouraged his own high level of
abstraction in his aesthetic thinking. He saw
similarities between the notion of fulfilment and
Goethe's spirit of progression, but also saw in
Goethe's writings the deep aesthetic understanding which can arise from emptiness. In Goethe, he
criticized the tragic Faustian movement from the
limited to seek the unlimited.

His account of Chinese artistic spirit also
stressed fulfilment and emptiness, but in Chinese
art he saw a capacity to unite the limited and the
unlimited. In this regard he was particularly
interested in the aesthetics of the metaphysical
school of the Wei and Jin dynasties (AD 220–
420). He returned repeatedly to consider the
problem of the relationship between aesthetic
conception and space in Chinese art. He saw
space in Chinese art as representing a unity
between limited men and limitless nature and
traced this conception of men, space, nature and
the universe to philosophical sources in daoism
and the *Book of Changes*.

NICHOLAS BUNNIN

Zubiri Apalátegui, Xavier

Spanish (of Basque origin). *b:* 1898, San Sebastian, Spain. *d:* 1983. *Cat:* Neo-Thomist. *Ints:*
Metaphysics; philosophy of religion. *Educ:* Zubiri
studied under Ortega and Zaragüeta at Madrid
(1918–20), and then went on to neo-Thomist and
theological studies at Louvain and the Gregorian
University in Rome (1919–21). *Infls:* Louvainian
neo-Thomism, Ortega and existentialism. *Appts:*
He continued his studies after assuming the Chair
of the History of Philosophy at Madrid (1926),
going on to pursue Mathematics, Biology, Physics
(under de Broglie and Schrödinger), Classics with
Jaeger and Phenomenology with Husserl and
Heidegger; returning from France (where he

studied oriental languages) after the Spanish Civil
War, Zubiri took the Chair of the History of
Philosophy at Barcelona (1940–2), thereafter
devoting himself to giving private courses and
the translation of scientific and philosophical
works.

Main publications:
(1942) *Naturaleza, Historia, Dios*, Madrid: Editora
  Nacional; fifth, augmented editon, 1963.
(1962) *Sobre la esencia*, Madrid: Sociedad de
  Estudios y Publicaciones.
(1963) *Cinco lecciones de Filosofía*, Madrid: Sociedad de Estudios y Publicaciones.

Secondary literature:
After 1962 only:
Babolin, A. (1972) 'Il pensiero religioso de Xavier
  Zubiri nella critica d'oggi', *Aquinas*, 15: 7–24.
Lazcano, R. (1993) *Panorama bibliographico de
  Xavier Zubiri*, Madrid: Ed. Revista Augustin.
Lopez-Quintas, A. (1986) 'El llegado intelectual de
  Xavier Zubiri', *Pensamiento* 42 (Jan -Mar): 103–8.
Rovaletti, M. L. (1985) *Hombre y realidad: homenaje
  a Xavier Zubiri*, Buenos Aires: University of
  Buenos Aires Press.

A man of the most extensive erudition and a
philosophical doyen to his contemporaries, Zubiri, like his teacher Zaragüeta, was a neo-
Thomist scrupulous to acquaint himself with
current developments in philosophy, science and
other areas. His philosophy is in essence a
reasoned defence of neo-Thomism against certain
modern forms of philosophy. Zubiri was in no
hurry to publish, and the major works of 1942 and
1962 each set out ideas long considered, developed in lecture courses delivered over many years.
Philosophy (he notes in 1942) is not merely an
occupation, even the best of occupations, but a
fundamental mode of intellectual existence, and
to be treated with respect.

The central idea underlying *Naturaleza*
(1942) is that modern humankind, misled by
the three great deviations from truth of positivism, pragmatism and historicism, is spiritually
adrift, unaware of the true nature of reality and
its own place in it, a condition he calls
desligación (literally, the condition in which
binding ties have broken; being un-anchored).
The reality of our condition is that we exist in
god. We are blinded to this by science, which
fastens only on those aspects of things which
enable us to exercise power over them. Contrary
to the claims of existentialism we have a nature.
We do not just find ourselves in the world but

are implanted in it, and our life is a mission. We can escape the pitfalls of science and come to grasp the true nature of things. Behind the phenomena studied in science is an overarching support Zubiri calls divinity (*deidad*). To grasp this is to be aware of things from within (*por dentro*).

In the course of elaborating the views in *Naturaleza*, Zubiri felt he needed to elaborate a first philosophy, and this he did in his next major work (1962), in which he sets out his metaphysics. Essence and reality are here interdefined. The essence of a thing is that which is within a given thing and in virtue of which it is what it is. The real is that which acts on itself or others in virtue of its own proper characteristics; reality is thus made to reside not in origin (natural or artificial) but in power to act in virtue of essence. Real things are to be contrasted with things experienced (*cosas-sentido*): these have concepts but not essences; for example, a table, whose formal definition is in terms of human purposes, is in this sense not real. Further, reality is to be distinguished from being. Reality is primarily something in itself (*de suyo*); being is a moment of reality.

Human beings have a substantive mode of being. Our condition is characterized by a radical concern or restlessness (*inquietud*: Zubiri consistently notes that he does not mean what existentialists mean by *angst*) to realize our substantive conditions by our actions in time. In each of our actions we are bound to the ultimate, and the ultimate is the reality of god. To be aware of this is to be in the condition of *religación*, a state of spiritual wholeness in which we know the true nature of things and our place, and theirs, in god.

ROBERT WILKINSON

GUIDE TO SCHOOLS AND MOVEMENTS

This contains short descriptions and bibliographies concerning the major schools of philosophy mentioned in the main entries. Names in bold indicate that there are individual entries for these philosophers. The **Category Index** (p. 909–917) and the **Index of Interests** (p. 918–924) list those philosophers connected with particular schools and movements.

Absolute Idealism

A form of **idealism** that stems from Schelling and Hegel and which includes **Hegelianism**, though it was developed outside Germany as much with reference to native philosophical controversy as to Hegel. Forms of absolute idealism were developed in England by **Bradley, Joachim** and **Bosanquet** and, in America, by **Royce, Calkins** and **Blanshard**. Absolute idealism regards the world of sense as only partially real. Human knowledge, or what passes as such, is highly fragmentary and partial. True knowledge is of propositions that perfectly cohere with one another. Whatever is real is an aspect of the eternal consciousness or Absolute Spirit. Absolute idealism had some tendency to pantheism and collectivism and was opposed by those wishing to emphasize individual persons in metaphysics (**personalists**) and in politics.

Bibliography

Cunningham, G. Watts (1993) *The Idealistic Argument in Recent British and American Philosophy*, Freeport, NY: Books for Libraries Press.

Joachim, H. H. (1906) *The Nature of Truth*, Oxford.

Metz, Rudolf (1938) *A Hundred Years of British Philosophy*, trans. J. W. Harvey, T. E. Jessop and H. Sturt, ed. J. H. Muirhead, London: Allen & Unwin. (Originally published in German, Heidelberg, 1934.)

Quinton, A. M. (1971–2) 'Absolute Idealism', *Proceedings of the British Academy* 57.

Randall Jr, John Herman (1967) 'F. H. Bradley and the working-out of absolute idealism', *Journal of the History of Philosophy* 5: 245–67.

Robinson, Daniel S. (1951) 'Philosophy today: absolute idealism', *Personalist* 32: 125–36.

Sprigge, T. L. S. (1983) *The Vindication of Absolute Idealism*, Edinburgh: Edinburgh University Press.

STUART BROWN

Analytical Philosophy

Analytical philosophers are those who believe that the main, or the only, task for philosophy is the 'analysis' of concepts and that philosophy should not attempt, or can attempt only with qualifications, to be 'synthetic', i.e. to make statements about the nature of reality. Though the modern analytical movement has tended to be opposed to traditional metaphysics, analysis has been conceived as a part of philosophy at least since Socrates. The modern movement began with **Frege**'s analytical work on the nature of mathematics and is characterized initially by an emphasis on logical analysis. **Russell**'s theory of descriptions, which sought to show how a referring expression like 'the present King of France' could have meaning even though no such person exists, was taken to be a paradigm of logical analysis. Among the other leading early figures were **Moore** and the early **Wittgenstein**. The **Vienna Circle**, especially **Carnap**, was influenced by this phase of analytical philosophy and in turn influenced it, for instance, through A. J. **Ayer**. Though Cambridge and Vienna are commonly regarded as the birthplaces, Justus **Hartnack** has claimed that analytical philosophy originated, largely independently, in **Uppsala**. Poland also developed its own tradition of analytical philosophy, associated with **Twardowski** and the **Lvov-Warsaw** Circle.

Analytical philosophy has developed in a number of ways. One development was through the influence of the later Wittgenstein, who, after his return to philosophy in the late 1920s, became increasingly doubtful about the practice of reductive analysis. Strictly speaking, he rejected analysis, but his later **linguistic philosophy** is commonly regarded as a development within the same tradition rather than a repudiation of it. Analytical philosophy took root in the highly pluralistic culture of America and, in so doing, was itself affected by other movements such as **pragmatism** and, as a result, became more diverse. Because of these and other developments, many of the tenets characteristic of early analytic philosophy have been questioned from within the tradition. Some, like **Quine**, have attacked the analytic-synthetic distinction. **Strawson**, though he sought to defend it, was willing to engage in what he termed 'descriptive metaphysics'. The place of logic in philosophy is no longer agreed. Many analytical philosophers since the 1970s have had broader sympathies with traditions, both present and past, to which their predecessors had been hostile.

A further broadening influence on analytical philosophy has been a burgeoning of interest in areas of philosophy which had previously been neglected. Whereas logic, language, epistemology and philosophy of science had seemed to be central areas, since the 1950s analytical philosophers have been working, for instance, in such areas as the following: aesthetics (**Sibley, Wollheim** and others), ethics (**Stevenson, Hare, Foot** and others), philosophy of education (**Hirst** and **Peters**), philosophy of history (**Dray**), philosophy of law (**Dworkin** and **Hart**), philosophy of religion (**Alston, Mitchell** and **Swinburne**, amongst others), philosophy of the social sciences (**Winch**) and political philosophy (G. A. **Cohen**).

Philosophy in the English-speaking world, as well as in Scandinavia, has remained broadly within this tradition, and its influence has continued to increase elsewhere. It has been introduced in Spanish, for instance, by **Ferrater Mora**, in German by **Tugendhat** and, in Portuguese by **Hegenberg**. In France commentary on Wittgenstein has been given by Jacques **Bouveresse** and on **Davidson** and **Dennett** by Pascal **Engel**.

Select Bibliography

Ammerman, Robert (ed.) (1965) *Classics of Analytic Philosophy*, New York: McGraw-Hill.

Antiseri, Dario (1975) *Filisofia Analitica: l'analisi del linguaggio nella Cambridge-Oxford Philosophy*, Rome: Citta Nuova.

Corrado, Michael (1975) *The Analytic Tradition in Philosophy. Background and Issues*, Chicago: American Library Association. (Contains bibliography.)

Ferrater Mora, José (1974) *Cambio de marcha in filosofia* [Shifting Gear in Philosophy], Madrid: Alianza Editorial.

Hartnack, Justus (1967) 'Scandinavian philosophy' in Paul Edwards (ed.) *Encyclopedia of Philosophy*, New York: Macmillan & Co.

Hylton, Peter Russell (1990) *Idealism and the Emergence of Analytic Philosophy*, Oxford: Clarendon Press.

Pap, Arthur (1949) *Elements of Analytic Philosophy*, New York: Macmillan.

Passmore, John (1988) *Recent Philosophers*, London: Duckworth.

Skolimowski, Henryk (1967) *Polish Analytical Philosophy. A Survey and Comparison with British Analytical Philosophy*, London: Routledge & Kegan Paul.

Urmson, J. O. (1956) *Philosophical Analysis*, Oxford: Oxford University Press.

Weitz, Morris (ed.) (1966) *Twentieth Century Philosophy: The Analytic Tradition*, New York: Free Press.

Williams, Bernard and Montefiore, Alan (1965) *British Analytical Philosophy*, London: Routledge & Kegan Paul.

STUART BROWN

Comtean Positivism

A movement that pursued the ideals and practices of the positivism inspired by Auguste Comte (1798–1875). According to Comte, the history of the sciences must pass through theological and metaphysical stages before arriving at the 'positive' stage, when scientists abandon claims to absolute truth in favour of the empirical study of the 'relations of succession and resemblance' between phenomena. The French Revolution, according to Comte, had taken French society from a theological to a metaphysical stage. What was needed was a positive sociology which, because properly scientific, would command consent and lead to a better society. Later on, Comte made positivism into a kind of secular religion, with holy days, a calendar of 'saints' and a catechism. Positivist Societies assembled in quasi-churches and engaged in a secular analogue of worship, a cult of reason.

Comte's positivism was very influential in France and in the twentieth century **Lévy-Bruhl** wrote an enthusiastic book about Comte. By the 1920s, however, according to Benrubi, French philosophy was more marked by reactions against an 'empiric positivism' (Benrubi, p. 13). Comte had a number of admirers in England, including J. S. Mill. A London Positivist Society was founded in 1877 though, from 1898–1916—most of the life of the movement in England—there were two independent Positivist groups in England. According to Metz, they 'displayed their greatest strength and vigour of growth' in the eighties and nineties. 'At the turn of the century a rapid process of decay set in which nothing could arrest, and under which the whole movement languished and slowly died away', (Metz p. 181). One of the groups, led by Frederic **Harrison**, remained more active and its journal *The Positivist Review* was published until 1925.

A number of Italian philosophers were influenced by Comtean positivism, including **Ardigò, Marchesini, Martinetti, Rignano** and **Varisco**. It was also influential in Latin America in the nineteenth century but, when its application failed to deliver political or economic improvements, there were reactions against it in the early twentieth century, which were an important starting-point for much original philosophical thought, notably with **Caso** and **Vasconcelas** in Mexico.

Bibliography
Benrubi, Isaac (1926) *Contemporary Thought of France*, trans. Ernest B. Dicker, London: Williams & Norgate.

Bridges, J. H. (ed.) (1915) *Illustrations of Positivism: A Selection of Articles from the 'Positivist Review' in Science, Philosophy, Religion and Politics*, London: Watts.

Charlton, D. G. (1963) *Secular Religions in France 1815–1870*, London: Oxford University Press.

Kent, W. (1932) *London for Heretics*, London: Watts. (Originally published in German, Heidelberg, 1934.)

Metz, Rudolf (1938) *A Hundred Years of Philosophy*, trans. J. W. Harvey, T. E Jessop and H. Sturt, ed. J. H. Muirhead, London: Allen & Unwin. (Originally published in German, Heidelberg, 1934.)

STUART BROWN AND ROBERT WILKINSON

Critical Realism

This label was adopted by an influential group of American realists in 1920 to distinguish themselves from the **new realists** of a decade before. The group included D. **Drake**, A. O. **Lovejoy**, J. B. **Pratt**, A. K. **Rogers**, G. **Santayana**, R. W. **Sellars** and C. A. **Strong**. They opposed what they took to be the 'naive' realism of the new realists, who believed that physical objects were perceived directly. According to the critical realists the mind directly perceives only ideas or sense-data. They thus returned to the epistemological dualism of Descartes. Some, but not all, also accepted an ontological dualism of mind and body.

Outside America, **Dawes Hicks** adopted the term 'critical realism' to characterize his own position. (See also **Realism**.)

Bibliography
Primary:
Drake, D. and others (1920) *Essays in Critical Realism*, New York: Garden Press.

Kurtz, Paul (1967) *American Philosophy in the Twentieth Century: A Sourcebook*, New York: Macmillan.

Sellars, R. W. (1932) *A Philosophy of Physical Realism*, New York: Macmillan.

Secondary:
Harlow, V. E. (1931) *A Bibliography and Genetic Study of American Realism*, Oklahoma City: Harlow.

Montague, William. P. (1937) 'The story of American realism', *Philosophy* 12: 140–50, 155–61.

Passmore, John (1957) *A Hundred Years of Philosophy*, London: Duckworth, ch. 12.

STUART BROWN

Empiricism

Broadly, the doctrine that all knowledge of the world is based upon sense-experience. Empiricism has been particularly favoured in the twentieth century by both **Pragmatists** and **Logical Positivists**. William **James** referred to his theory of knowledge as 'radical empiricism' and both A. J. **Ayer** and Herbert **Feigl** styled their view 'logical empiricism'. Although empiricism was very influential in the first half of the century, especially amongst philosophers of science and those who were sceptical about the possibility of metaphysics, it later became subject to radical criticism from philosophers such as **Quine**, **Wittgenstein** and **Feyerabend**.

Bibliography
Anderson, John (1962) *Studies in Empirical Philosophy*, Sydney: Angus & Robertson.

Ayer, A. J. (1940) *Foundations of Empirical Knowledge*, London: Macmillan.

Feyerabend, Paul K. (1965) 'Problems of empiricism', in R. G. Colodny (ed.) *Beyond the Edge of Certainty*, Englewood Cliffs, NJ: Prentice-Hall.

Jørgenson, Jørgen (1951) *The Development of Logical Empiricism*, Chicago: University of Chicago Press.

Morick, Harold (ed.) (1972) *Challenges of Empiricism*, Belmont, CA: Wadsworth, and London: Methuen, 1980.

Quine, W. Van O. (1936) 'Two dogmas of empiricism', in *From a Logical Point of View*, London: Gollancz; second edition 1946.

STUART BROWN

Evolutionary Philosophers

Not so much a school as a variety of philosophers who have given evolution, particularly Darwin's theory, a central place in their system. These have sometimes been **naturalistic**, as was **Haeckel**'s, and sometimes agnostic, as was **Spencer**'s. But others have sought to accommodate Darwin's scientific work within a metaphysical or evaluative framework that was more sympathetic to religion. Some, like C. Lloyd **Morgan**, interpreted the idea of evolution in a non-mechanistic and non-reductionist way, leaving room for theism. Others, like **Teilhard de Chardin**, have accommodated evolution within a pantheistic system.

Bibliography
Primary:
Boodin, John Elof (1923) *Cosmic Evolution.*
Bergson, Henri (1907) *L'Evolution creatrice*, Paris.
Goudge, Thomas A. (1961) *The Ascent of Life: A Philosophical Study of Evolution*, London: Allen & Unwin.
Hobhouse, L. T. (1901) *Mind in Evolution*, London.
Morgan, C. Lloyd (1923) *Emergent Evolution*, London.
Noble, E. (1926) *Purposive Evolution*, London.
Sellars, Roy Wood (1922) *Evolutionary Naturalism*, Chicago: Open Court.
Secondary:
Dotterer, Ray H. (1950) 'Early philosophies of evolution', in V. T. A. Ferm (ed.) *A History of Philosophical Systems*, Freeport, NY: Books for Libraries Press, pp. 365–73.
MacDougall, W. (1923) *Modern Materialism and Emergent Evolution*, London, 1923.
Stow, Persons (ed.) (1950) *Evolutionary Thought in America*, New Haven, CT: Yale University Press.

STUART BROWN

Existentialism

The term 'existentialism' is usually taken to refer to a broad movement, of which **Heidegger** and **Sartre** are often regarded as the two main exponents. Other thinkers frequently labelled 'existentialist' are Kierkegaard, **Jaspers**, **Marcel**, **Buber** and, in her earlier writings, Simone de **Beauvoir**. It has also been claimed that such temporally remote figures as St Augustine and Pascal are amongst the intellectual ancestors of existentialism. The movement reached its zenith in the immediate postwar period in France, but began to decline by the 1960s.

A general concern of existentialism is to give an account of what it is like to exist as a human being in the world. There is no complete unanimity on what this account must contain: both the atheism of Sartre and the religious thought of Marcel and Buber are incorporated within existentialist thought. Nevertheless, certain more explicit features of this bald statement can be formulated. Epistemologically, it is denied that there can be an absolutely objective description of the world as it is without the intervention of human interests and actions. The world is a 'given' and there is no epistemological scepticism

about its existence; it has to be described in relation to ourselves. There is no fixed essence to which beings have to conform in order to qualify as human beings; we are what we decide to be. Human consciousness has a different mode of being from that of physical objects. A human being exists not only as a thing (a body) but also as 'no-thing'; that is, as a consciousness, or emptiness, that is the condition for choosing what one will do and be. We cannot choose whether or not to choose; even if we think we can refuse to make a choice, that in itself is a choice.

The issues of freedom and choice are of crucial importance in existentialism. Sartre thinks that authentic choices are completely undetermined. If we act to fulfil the requirements of a social role— if, for example, a waiter carries out what he thinks are the pre-set duties of his job, or unrequited lovers behave as they think they ought to do— then we are guilty of choosing in bad faith. If we make our decisions merely by reference to an external moral code or set of procedures, then we are, similarly, not arriving at authentic choices. Buber disagrees with Sartre over what it is to choose: he maintains that values which have been discovered, not invented, can be adopted for one's life (Cooper 1990: 173).

Many existentialists consider that there are two approaches to the world. For Sartre, we can erroneously consider ourselves to be determined objects, no different in the way we exist from the fixed, familiar, solid physical objects that surround us. When we become aware that our existence is not like that of physical objects, we are thereby dislocated from the material world and slide into an authentic perspective which is fluid and *angst*-ridden. For Buber, there is no feeling of *angst* or dislocation. Any of our experiences are capable of transporting us from the humdrum, everyday, causally-governed I-It world-perspective in which only part of our being is engaged, to the atemporal and acausal I-Thou world of freedom, dialogue and the reclamation of the wholeness of our human existence.

It is often claimed that existentialism is concerned with key or crisis experiences. Existentialist themes are thus suitable for inclusion in literary works, as has happened with Sartre's philosophical novel *La Nausée* and with many of his plays, including *Les Mains Sales*.

According to David Cooper (1990: viii), existentialism has had an influence on later philosophers such as Richard **Rorty**. It is in the mainstream of twentieth-century philosophical thought and contributes significantly to the replacement of the Cartesian inheritance which has dominated philosophy for the last three centuries.

Bibliography

Primary:

The primary sources for existentialism are to be found under the individual headings of the various existentialist thinkers. Publication details of Sartre's novel and play are as follows:

Sartre, J.-P. (1938) *La Nausée*, Paris: Gallimard (English translation, *Nausea*, London: Penguin, 1976).

—— (1948) *Les Mains Sales*, Paris: Gallimard (English translation, *Crime Passionnel*, London: Methuen, 1961).

Secondary:

Cooper, David E. (1990) *Existentialism*, Oxford: Blackwell.

Kaufmann, W. (ed.) (1975) *Existentialism from Dostoievsky to Sartre*, New York: New American Library.

Macquarrie, J. (1973) *Existentialism: An Introduction, Guide and Assessment*, London: Penguin.

Olafson, F. A. (1967) *Principles and Persons: An Ethical Interpretation of Existentialism*, Baltimore: Johns Hopkins University Press.

Solomon, R. C. (1972) *From Rationalism to Existentialism*, New York: University Press of America.

—— (1987) *From Hegel to Existentialism*, Oxford: Oxford University Press.

Sprigge, T. L. S. (1984) *Theories of Existence*, London: Penguin.

Warnock, M. (1970) *Existentialism*, Oxford: Oxford University Press.

KATHRYN PLANT

Frankfurt School

This term was initially used to refer to the 'Critical Theorists' associated with the Institut für Sozialforschung [Institute for Social Research], after it was re-established in Frankfurt am Main after the Second World War; it has now come to be used to cover 'critical theory' as a whole, from its beginnings in the 1920s to its present state as a dispersed but still active philosophical tradition.

The Institut für Sozialforschung was established as a private foundation in 1923 to develop interdisciplinary Marxist research, and when Max **Horkheimer** succeeded the historian Carl Grünberg as Director in 1930 he inaugurated the conception of a distinctive 'critical theory'. The Institute provided a base or looser forms of support for many of the most brilliant neo-Marxist thinkers of the twentieth century.

Although the rise of Nazism meant that it had to move, first to Geneva and Paris, and then, in 1934, to New York, its work survived all these vicissitudes and its journal, the *Zeitschrift für Sozialforschung*, published from 1932 to 1941 (the last three parts in English), remains one of the richest intellectual documents of the period.

As well as Max Horkheimer, Theodor **Adorno** and Herbert **Marcuse**, those associated with the Institute included Walter **Benjamin**, the historian Franz Borkenau, Horkheimer's close associate the economist Friedrich Pollock and two other economists, Henryk Grossman and Arkady Gurland, the psychologists Bruno Bettelheim and Erich Fromm, the political and legal theorists Otto Kirchheimer and Franz Neumann, the Sinologist Karl Wittfogel and the literary theorist Leo Lowenthal. Felix J. Weil, the founder of the Institute, also published two literature surveys in the journal, whose articles and book reviews spanned an enormous range of material.

The distinctive Frankfurt School perspective is, however, essentially that of Adorno, Horkheimer and Marcuse. It is a flexible neo-Marxism oriented around an increasingly negative philosophy of history epitomized by Adorno and Horkheimer's *Dialectic of Enlightenment*, which they wrote at the height of the Second World War, arguing that the Enlightenment critique of myth and domination itself contributes to new forms of domination. Helmut Dubiel has aptly characterized their perspective as a response to three critical challenges: those of fascism, Stalinism and managerial capitalism, whose perceived similarities and apparent invincibility pushed the Frankfurt thinkers into a position of permanent and increasingly desperate opposition.

A second generation of postwar critical theorists, notably Jürgen **Habermas**, Karl-Otto **Apel**, Albrecht **Wellmer** and, for a time, Alfred Schmidt, pursued the perspectives of the Frankfurt School in a more orthodox academic context, aiming to integrate the individual social sciences with philosophy in a constructive synthesis closer to the original intentions of Critical Theory than to its postwar development. More recently, a number of philosophers and sociologists who worked with Habermas in the 1970s such as Claus Offe, Axel **Honneth**, and Klaus Eder are continuing the project of critical theory into the nineties.

Bibliography

Primary:

The Institute's collective publications include the following (as well as various histories listed in Jay 1973).

(1936) *Studien über Autorität und Familie*, Paris: Felix Alcan.

(1956) *Soziologische Exkurse*, Frankfurt: Europäische Verlagsanstalt (English translation, *Aspects of Sociology*, trans. John Viertel, London: Heinemann, 1973).

Secondary:

Bottomore, Tom (1984) *The Frankfurt School*, London: Tavistock.

Dubiel, Helmut (1978) *Wissenschaftsorganisation und politische Erfahrung. Studien zur frühen Kritischen Theorie*, Frankfurt: Suhrkamp (English translation, *Science and Politics. Studies in the Development of Critical Theory*, Cambridge, Mass.: MIT Press, 1985).

Held, David (1980) *Introduction to Critical Theory: Horkheimer to Habermas*, London: Hutchinson.

Honneth, Axel and Wellmer, Albrecht (eds) (1986) *Die Frankfurter Schule und die Folgen*, Berlin: De Gruyter.

Jay, Martin (1973) *The Dialectical Imagination. A History of the Frankfurt School and the Institute of Social Research*, 1923–1950, London: Heinemann. (Includes substantial bibliography.)

Wiggershaus, Rolf (1987) *Die Frankfurter Schule*, Munich: Hanser (English translation, *The Frankfurt School*, trans. Michel Robertson, Cambridge: Polity, 1993).

WILLIAM OUTHWAITE

Hegelianism

A form of **absolute idealism**, associated with the influence of the German philosopher, G. W. F. Hegel (1770–1831). Hegelianism was important throughout the Western World in the nineteenth century and its influence was carried into the twentieth century — for instance, by Edward **Caird** in Britain and W. T. **Harris** in America. Hegelians elsewhere included **Bolland** in the Netherlands. Native forms of absolute idealism, more tenuously linked to Hegel, were developed in England by **Bradley** and **Bosanquet**, in Italy by **Croce** and **Gentile** and, in America, by **Royce** and **Blanshard**. Though Hegel was a *bête noire* to analytical philosophers and his influence in the English-speaking world was very low in the middle decades of the century, study of his work has burgeoned since the 1970s.

Bibliography

De Guibert, Bernard (1949) 'Hegelianism in France', *Modern Schoolman* 26: 173–7.

Findlay, J. N. (1956) 'Some merits of Hegelianism', *Proceedings of the Aristotelian Society* 56: 1–24.

Haldar, H. (1927) *Neo-Hegelianism*, London.

Levy, Heinrich (1927) *Die Hegel-Renaissance in der deutschen Philosophie*, Charlottenburg.

McTaggart, John Ellis (1901) *Studies in Hegelian Cosmology*, Cambridge.

Metz, Rudolf (1938) *A Hundred Years of British Philosophy*, trans. J. W. Harvey, T. E. Jessop and H. Sturt, ed. J. H. Muirhead, London: Allen & Unwin. (Originally published in German, Heidelberg, 1934.)

STUART BROWN

Hermeneutics

Hermeneutics, the art and methodology of interpretation originated in Ancient Greece, became an adjunct to theology under Christianity and achieved prominence in the last century as a methodology of the human studies which challenged the predominance of positivism. Recently it became fashionable among Western intellectuals, particularly because it figured in the philosophies of **Heidegger** and **Gadamer**.

Interpreting the law, religious texts and literature is as old as the investigation of nature. Because life and liberty can depend on getting the law right, salvation on correctly reading the divine message, and cultural coherence on reasonable agreement about literature, hermeneutics arose to meet the need for methodical and veridical interpretation. The primary subject matter of hermeneutics are texts but by the nineteenth century — mainly through the work of Schleiermacher and **Dilthey** — meaningful phenomena such as speech, physical expressions, actions, rituals or conventions, were included as text-like because in them human experience is interpreted and communicated. So their study–unlike that of mute nature–requires a hermeneutic approach. Understanding a person's worries or the institutions of a society is more like interpreting a poem or legal text than like explaining chemical changes.

The range of hermeneutics has been further extended — first in Dilthey's Philosophy of life, and more recently in contemporary, continental philosophy — by stressing that interpretation is a pervasive and characteristic feature of human life which finds its systematic consummation as a Hermeneutic Philosophy.

The traditional, but continually refined methodology of interpretation starts by recognizing as its aim the grasping of the meaning of individual entities. The relation between parts and whole, both the internal structure of a text (or something text-like) and its wider context become focal, resulting in the Hermeneutic Circle in which the meaning of the parts determine that of the whole, while the latter, in turn, determines the former (a sentence and its words, a poet's whole output and one of his poems, are examples). As a consequence there is here no fixed starting point for cognition and this has been treated as a challenge to the search for certain foundations associated with traditional epistemology.

This does not, however, dispense with epistemological issues. Even if certainty eludes us, as it does in other cognitive enterprises, and there are, notoriously, subjective elements in much interpreting, truth, or at least a distinction between better and worse, remains the goal. To ground such judgements requires spelling out the presuppositions of a hermeneutic approach.

One is that there are common, basic features of humanity. There would be no basis for interpretation if we could not assume — in spite of variety and historical change — that others purposively are capable of reasoning and emotionally respond much like us.

The second presupposition is Vico's principle that man can understand what man has made. The two presuppositions are, obviously, interdependent. A common nature makes the human world familiar and our capacity to decode its manifestations confirms and defines the range of that communality.

Hermeneutics as the methodical exploration of meaning is distinct from other forms of cognition and uses presuppositions and processes all of its own; this does not exclude, however, sharing some presuppositions and procedures with other cognitive approaches.

Bibliography

Dilthey, W. (1976) 'The development of hermeneutics', in H. P. Rickman (ed.) *Dilthey: Selected Writings*, Cambridge: Cambridge University Press. (The original German version appeared in vol. 5 of his Collected Works.)

Gadamer, H. G. (1975) *Truth and Method*, trans. Terren Bruden and John Cumming, London: Sheed & Ward.

Habermas, Jürgen (1968) *Knowledge and Human Interest*, trans. J. Shapiro Heinmann, Evanston, Ill.: Northwestern University Press.

Palmer, R. E. (1969) *Hermeneutics*, Evanston, Ill.: Northwestern University Press.

Ricoeur, Paul (1981) *Hermeneutics and the Human Sciences*, ed. and trans. John B. Thompson, Cambridge: Cambridge University Press.

H. P. RICKMAN

Idealism

In the late seventeenth century the term 'idealist' was used by Leibniz to refer to a philosopher who gave priority to the human mind, who attached a lesser importance to the senses and who opposed **materialism**. He referred to Plato as 'the greatest of the idealists', associating the Greek philosopher with doubts about the existence of a material world. This last aspect impressed Kant, and as a result of his influence, idealism came to be most commonly contrasted with **realism**. Kant sought to mediate and, in his way, overcome the dispute between realists and idealists. But he acknowledged his was a form of idealism (as well as a form of realism) and he greatly influenced the German idealist tradition which, especially through Hegel, held a dominant position in Western philosophy at the beginning of the twentieth century.

Hegelianism was represented in the early twentieth century by Edward **Caird** in Britain and W. T. **Harris** in America. Native forms of **absolute idealism** were developed in England by **Bradley** and **Bosanquet** and, in America, by **Royce**. Absolute idealism was, however, being opposed from the beginning of the century and indeed before by **pragmatism**, **personalism** (or personal idealism) and **realism**. The influence of idealism waned considerably during the first half of the century, though there were indications of a revival in the 1980s and 1990s.

Bibliography
Primary:
Foster, John (1982) *The Case for Idealism*, London: Routledge & Kegan Paul.
Rescher, Nicholas (1982) *Conceptual Idealism*, Washington, DC: University Press of America.
Sprigge, T. L. S. (1983) *The Vindication of Absolute Idealism*, Edinburgh: Edinburgh University Press.
Walker, R. C. S. (1989) *The Coherence Theory of Truth: Realism, Anti-Realism, Idealism*, London: Routledge.
Secondary:
Coates, P. and Hutto, D. (eds) (forthcoming) *Current Issues in Idealism*, Bristol: Thoemmes Press.
Cunningham, G. Watts (1933) *The Idealistic Argument in Recent British and American Philosophy*, Freeport, NY: Books for Libraries Press.
Dasgupta, Surendranath (1962) *Indian Idealism*, Cambridge: Cambridge University Press.
Ewing, A. C. (1945) *Idealism: A Critical Survey*, London: Methuen.
Howie, John and Burford, Thomas (eds) (1975) *Contemporary Studies in Philosophical Idealism*, Boston, Mass.: Stark & Co.
Metz, Rudolf (1938) *A Hundred Years of British*

Philosophy, trans. J. W. Harvey, T. E. Jessop and H. Sturt, ed. J. H. Muirhead, London: Allen & Unwin. (Originally published in German, Heidelberg, 1934.)

Milne, Alan (1962) *The Social Philosophy of English Idealism*, London: Allen & Unwin.

Muirhead, J. H. (1931) *The Platonic Tradition in Anglo-Saxon Philosophy. Studies in the History of Idealism in England and America*, London: Allen & Unwin.

Quinton, A. M. (1971–2) 'Absolute idealism', *Proceedings of the British Academy* 57.

Vesey, Godfrey (ed.) (1982) *Idealism. Past and Present*, Cambridge: Cambridge University Press.

STUART BROWN

Intuitionism

In mathematics intuitionism names a system propounded by L. E. J. **Brouwer** (1881–1966) that identifies truth with being known to be true. Its claim is that in mathematics a statement is true only if there is proof of it and that a mathematical entity exists only if a constructive existence proof can be given for it. According to Brouwer, mathematics is not reducible to logic in the way propounded by **Frege** and **Russell**. Mathematical intuitionism rejects the law of double negation, the law of the excluded middle and classical *reductio*.

In ethics intuitionism is the view that moral truths are known by intuition, that is, known directly rather than inferred. G. E. **Moore** (1873–1958) was a major proponent of this view, holding that goodness was a non-natural and non-analysable property that could be apprehended by a faculty of 'intuition'.

Bibliography

Dummett, Michael (1977) *Elements of Intuitionism*, Oxford: Oxford University Press.

Heyting, A. (1966) *Intuitionism*, second edition, Amsterdam: North-Holland.

Hudson, W. D. (1967) *Ethical Intuitionism*, London: Macmillan.

Parkinson, G. H. R. (1988) *An Encyclopaedia of Philosophy*, London: Routledge.

DIANÉ COLLINSON

Legal Positivism

The term 'positivism' is used in a special sense in connection with the law, for instance to deny that there are any rights (such as supposed 'natural rights') except those granted by the 'positive' laws of particular countries. Legal positivism goes back at least to the eighteenth century and is associated, for instance, with Jeremy Bentham. It is represented in the twentieth century by, amongst others, Hans **Kelsen**. Although legal positivists are not necessarily positivists in a broader sense, legal positivism is a consequence of **Logical Positivism** insofar as statements about 'natural rights' can be regarded as metaphysical and therefore, on that doctrine, meaningless. Some of those associated with logical positivism, such as the founder of the **Uppsala School**, Axel **Hägerström**, are known also for being legal positivists.

Bibliography

Detmold, M. J. (1984) *The Unity of Law and Morality: A Refutation of Legal Positivism*, London: Routledge & Kegan Paul.

MacCormick, Neil (1986) *An Institutional Theory of Law: New Approaches to Legal Positivism*, Dordrecht: Reidel.

Shuman, Samuel I. (1963) *Legal Positivism: Its Scope and Limitations*, Detroit: Wayne State University Press.

STUART BROWN

Linguistic Philosophy

Influenced in varying degree by the later **Wittgenstein**, a number of mostly Oxford or Cambridge philosophers, including **Ryle**, **Austin** and **Wisdom** began to practice philosophy as though its problems could be solved, or dissolved, through careful attention to details of language. Ryle's influential *Concept of Mind* sought to show, by looking at mental verbs, adverbs and adjectives, how the Cartesian 'ghost in the machine' was a myth. Austin drew attention to some of the other uses of language than to state facts. Wisdom sought to develop an idea of Wittgenstein's that philosophy was in some respects like psychotherapy. Linguistic philosophy has been influential throughout the English-speaking world, for instance, in the work of **Bouwsma** and **Searle** in America, and Scandinavia, through the work of von **Wright** and **Hartnack** and others.

Linguistic philosophy may be regarded as a development within **analytical philosophy**, which also focuses on language. But those who are usually called 'linguistic philosophers' reject the idea of a logical language and stress the study of ordinary language.

Bibliography

Chappell, V. C. (ed.) (1964) *Ordinary Language*, Englewood Cliffs, NJ: Prentice-Hall, 1964.

Rorty, Richard (ed.) (1967) *The Linguistic Turn: Recent Essays in Philosophical Method*, Chicago: Chicago University Press. (Contains good bibliography.)

Waismann, Friedrich (ed. Rom Harré) (1965) *The Principles of Linguistic Philosophy*, London: Macmillan.

STUART BROWN

Logical Positivism

The term 'Logical Positivism' was used originally to refer to the standpoint of a group of philosophers, scientists and philosophers who became known as the **Vienna Circle**. The chief tenets of logical positivism were that: (1) the only genuine propositions (that are strictly true or false about the world) are those that are verifiable by the methods of science; (2) the supposed propositions of ethics, metaphysics and theology are not verifiable and so are not strictly 'meaningful'; (3) the propositions of logic and mathematics are meaningful but their truth is discovered by analysis and not by experiment or observation; (4) the business of philosophy is not to engage in metaphysics or other attempted assertions about what is the case–it is, rather, to engage in analysis.

Although logical positivism belongs within the broad movement known as **positivism** and can be thought of as having precursors in the eighteenth century Enlightenment and in the nineteenth century movement associated with Comte, it is a distinctively twentieth century development, reflecting a new emphasis on logic and language. It is presaged in **Wittgenstein**'s *Tractatus Logico-Philosophicus* (1921) but properly derives from the **Vienna Circle** and associated groups in Berlin (to which **Hempel** and von **Mises** were attached), **Lvov** and **Uppsala**. It became one of the most influential movements in philosophy in the middle decades of the century. After the rise of Nazism, many of the leading figures of the movement, including **Carnap** and Hempel, emigrated to the United States. Logical positivism was also influential in Scandinavia, in Sweden as the legacy of the Uppsala School, in Finland through the advocacy of **Kaila** and in Denmark because of **Jørgensen**. In England the movement had one of its most eloquent representatives in A. J. **Ayer**, whose critique of ethical and religious propositions continued to influence philosophical debate long after the Second World War, as in the writings by R. M. **Hare** on ethics and in the critique by A. G. N. **Flew** of theological assertions.

Although logical positivism was very influential it had never been free of difficulties. It had never been possible to state the all-important principle of verifiability accurately enough so that it drew the line between the propositions of science, on the one hand, and those of metaphysics etc. on the other, in the 'right' place. The credibility of the principle was undermined by repeated failure to draw this line satisfactorily or to explain the status of the principle itself. Leading philosophers who had at one time been sympathetic to logical positivism moved to new positions. W. Van O. **Quine**, for instance, argued that the distinction between analytic and synthetic propositions assumed in much empiricist writing was not tenable. In the 1960s there was a broad reaction against scientism in the West. The scientistic orientation of the logical positivists had been repugnant to some philosophers such as Wittgenstein all along. By the late 1960s logical positivism was no longer directly influential in Western intellectual culture, though it had influenced the development of **analytical philosophy**.

Bibliography
Primary:

Ayer, A. J. (1936) *Language, Truth and Logic*, London: Gollancz; second edition 1946.

—— (ed.) (1959) *Logical Positivism*, Glencoe, Ill.: Free Press, and London: Allen & Unwin. (This work has an extensive bibliography.)

Feigl, H. and Blumberg, A. (1931) 'Logical positivism, a new movement in European philosophy', *Journal of Philosophy*.

Reichenbach, Hans (1951) *The Rise of Scientific Philosophy*, Berkeley and Los Angeles: University of California Press.

Secondary:

Coffa, J. Alberto (1991) *The Sematic Tradition from Kant to Carnap: To the Vienna Station*, Cambridge: Cambridge University Press.

Friedman, Michael (1991) 'The re-evaluation of logical positivism', *Journal of Philosophy* 10.

Gower, Barry (ed.) (1987) *Logical Positivism in Perspective*, Totowa: Barnes & Noble.

Hanfling, Oswald (1981) *Logical Positivism*, Oxford: Blackwell.

Quine, W. Van O. (1936) 'Two dogmas of empiricism', in *From a Logical Point of View*, London: Gollancz; second edition 1946.

Jørgenson, Jørgen (1951) *The Development of Logical Empiricism*, Chicago: University of Chicago Press (Encyclopedia of Unified Science Series).

Rescher, Nicholas (ed.) (1985) *The Heritage of Logical Positivism*, New York: Lanham.

STUART BROWN

Lvov-Warsaw School

Also known as 'the Warsaw Circle', this school of logical analysis had affinities with the **Vienna Circle**. Though they developed independently there were many contacts between the two groups. But, according to Z. Jordan, other philosophers such as **Russell**, **Frege**, Hume, Leibniz, Mill, Spencer, Bolzano, **Bretano**, **James**, **Poincaré**, Duhem, **Mach**, **Hilbert**, **Einstein**, **Husserl**, **Bridgman**, **Whitehead** and **Weyl** were 'equally influential' (Jordan 1945, p. 32). The School's central preoccupation was with logic and language. They sought in a logical language 'a more perfect medium than ordinary speech'. Negatively they distrusted 'abstract speculation of an illusive and deceptive clarity'. Some, like **Ajdukiewicz**, were closer to **Logical Positivism**, but others, like **Kotarbiski**, **Łukasiewicz** and **Tarski**, though favouring logic without metaphysics, held less extreme views than the **Vienna Circle**. In general the Polish philosophers avoided the ambitious programmatic ventures of the Austrians.

Bibliography

Coniglione, Francesco (ed.) (1993) *Philosophy and Determinism in Polish Scientific Philosophy*, Amsterdam: Rodopi.

Jordan, Z. (1945) *On the Development of Mathematical Logic and of Logical Positivism in Poland between the Two Wars*, London: Oxford University Press.

Skolimowski, Henryk (1967) *Polish Analytical Philosophy: A Survey and Comparison with British Analytical Philosophy*, New York: Humanities Press.

Woleenski, Jan (1984) *Logic and Philosophy in the Lvov-Warsaw School*, Dordrecht: Kluwer Academic.

STUART BROWN

Marxism

Although probably best known as a socio-political theory (the source of Communism, for example), Marxism is at base a philosophical theory whose roots lie in **Hegelian** idealism and its notion of the dialectic. Whereas Hegel postulated a 'World Spirit' gradually attaining self-realization through a process of dialectical progression, the Marxist dialectic is firmly located at the material level—thus the concept of dialectical materialism on which Marxism is structured. When applied to history by Marx (see *The Communist Manifesto*) the theory of dialectical materialism yields a picture of class struggle being waged over time, with each form of society (or 'thesis') generating its own contradiction (or 'antithesis'), until a new synthesis is achieved, setting off the dialectical process on yet another cycle. From such a perspective medieval society is superseded by bourgeois society, which in its turn is to be superseded by a new, classless, socialist society — the 'dictatorship of the proletariat', where the working class takes over control of society's means of production, thereby extending the cycle of class struggle.

Marx saw society as consisting of an economic base and cultural superstructure, with the base as dominant. The nature of a society's cultural superstructure (its various institutions, legal, political, educational, and so forth) was held to be largely determined by the nature of its economic base and the means of production this entailed. Marx explores the nature of the economic base of a capitalist society, and the type of social being that proceeds from it, in his major work, *Capital*. The main impact of capitalist economics, it is contended, is to alienate workers from their labour, a phenomenon later referred to by Marxist theorists as reification—the transformation of labour and worker into commodities to be bought and sold on the open market. Marx thus bequeaths to his followers a philosophical theory which has a definite socio-political agenda —to change the world, rather than merely to interpret it.

In the twentieth century Marxism has been an extremely influential theory, not just politically (as in the establishment of several Marxist political systems such as the USSR and the Chinese People's Republic), but also philosophically and aesthetically. There have been various schools within Marxism, among the most important of which have been the Soviet and the Western; the former (**Lenin**, Stalin *et al.*) primarily concerned with the practical political issue of constructing a new socialist state, and the latter (**Lukács**, the **Frankfurt School** *et al.*) generally characterized as more interested in aesthetic and academic philosophical matters. (Maoism represents yet another variant, an adaptation of Marxist thought to the very different social conditions of a peasant-dominated Eastern society.) Marxism's impact on aesthetic debate has been considerable, with the controversy between supporters of realism and modernism mirroring a longer-running historical debate about the proper social role of art and the artist.

In the late twentieth century the decline of Marxism as an international political force has severely eroded its philosophical and aesthetic authority. For **postmodernists**, for example, Marxism has become a paradigm case of an outmoded 'grand narrative', or universal theory.

Bibliography

Anderson, Perry (1976) *Considerations on Western Marxism*, London: NLB.

McLellan, David (1973) *Karl Marx: His Life and Thought*, Basingstoke: Macmillan.

Marx, Karl (1867) *Das Kapital*, Hamburg: Meissner & Behre (English translation, *Capital*, vol. I, trans. Eden and Cedar Paul, London: Dent, 1960).

—— and Engels, Friedrich (1848) *Manifest der Kommunistischen Partei*, London: Communist League (English translation, *The Communist Manifesto*, ed. Frederic L. Bender, New York and London: Norton, 1988).

STUART SIM

Materialism

In metaphysics, the view that the world is fundamentally material and that mental phenomena are a function of or are reducible to physical phenomena. Materialism and **idealism** are diametrically opposed in metaphysics and there is a long history to this opposition in Chinese and Indian philosophy, as well as in European. **Marxism** involves what is known as 'dialectical materialism', which has been influential not only in the former Soviet Union and in China, but also, though to a much lesser degree, in Japan and Latin America. Materialists in the western world characteristically adopt what they term 'scientific **realism**'. Philosophical materialism has had influential advocates in both the United States (R. W. **Sellars**) and Australia (J. J. C. **Smart** and D. M. **Armstrong**) and is now vigorously debated in books and journals throughout the English-speaking world.

Bibliography

Armstrong, D. M. (1968) *A Materialist Theory of Mind*, London: Routledge & Kegan Paul; second edition, 1993.

Bunge, Mario (1981) *Scientific Materialism*, Dordrecht: Reidel.

Churchland, Paul M. (1981) 'Eliminative materialism and propositional attitudes', *Journal of Philosophy* 78: 67–90.

Feyerabend, Paul K. (1963) 'Materialism and the mind-body problem', *Review of Metaphysics* 17: 49–66.

Lund, David H. (1994) *Perception, Mind and Personal Identity: A Critique of Materialism*, Lanham, MD: University Press of America.

McGill, V. J., Farber and Sellars (1949) *Philosophy for the Future: The Quest of Modern Materialism*, New York.

McGinn, Colin (1980) 'Philosophical materialism', *Synthese* 44: 173–206.

Madell, Geoffrey (1988) *Mind and Materialism*, Edinburgh: Edinburgh University Press.

O'Connor, John (ed.) (1969) *Modern Materialism: Readings on Mind-Body Identity*, New York: Harcourt, Brace & World.

Robinson, Howard (1982) *Matter and Sense: A Critique of Contemporary Materialism*, Cambridge: Cambridge University Press.

Sellars, R. W. (1950) 'The new materialism', in V. T. A. Ferm (ed.) *A History of Philosophical Systems*, Freeport, NY: Books for Libraries Press, pp. 418–28.

Smart, J. J. C. (1963) *Philosophy and Scientific Realism*, New York: Humanities Press.

STUART BROWN

Munich Circle

The Munich Circle (based at the University of Munich) marks a significant moment in the development of phenomenology in the first half of the twentieth century. The origin of the circle owed much to Theodor **Lipps** (1851–1914), for the early members of the circle were his students who had been holding regular meetings (since 1901) for the purposes of discussing his (Lipps's) descriptive psychology–see his *Grundtatsachen des Seelebens* (1883). The group called itself Akademisch-Psychologischer Verein, and it was at one of its meetings that Lipps chose to defend his psychologism against **Husserl**'s recent onslaught on it in *Logische Untersuchungen* (1901). Husserl had argued that, contrary to Lipps's claim, psychologism could not act as a foundation for logic; for to suggest that the psychology of knowledge can furnish such a foundation is to leave open the avenue to scepticism and, with it, the destruction of knowledge, and of any sense of truth and falsehood. Despite his vigorous defence of his position, Lipps was horrified to witness the speed with which his students progressively embraced the new discipline of **phenomenology**, especially in its Husserlian formulation in the *Logische Untersuchungen*, in addition to their interest in Husserlian aesthetics and the general issue of value. What was clear to these students, but opaque to Lipps, was that here was a radical approach to the question of the foundation of science which did not depend on psychologism, **positivism** or **naturalism**.

Intoxicated by Husserl's new discipline of phenomenology, the members of the circle began to travel between Munich and Göttingen, where Husserl was teaching at the time. This meant that some members of the Munich Circle were also members of the Göttingen Circle.

The members of the Munich Circle whose energy and scholarship solidified the phenomenological approach to philosophy in the following years were: Adolf **Reinach** (before his departure for Göttingen, where he founded another phenomenological circle), Theodor Conrad, Moritz **Geiger**, Aloys Fischer, August Gallinger, Ernst von Aster, Hans Cornelius, Dietrich von Hildebrand and, from 1906, Max **Scheler**. Those who belonged to the Munich and the Göttingen Circles were: Wilhelm Schapp, Kurt Stavenhagen, Hedwig **Conrad-Martius**, Dietrich von Hildebrand, Jean Hering, Edith **Stein**, Fritz Kaufmann, Alexander **Koyré** and Roman **Ingarden**.

Select Bibliography

Boring, E. G. (1950) *A History of Experimental Psychology*, second edition, New York: Appleton-Century-Crofts.

Geiger, Moritz (1913) 'Beiträge zur Phänomenologie des ästhetischen Genusses', *Jahrbuch für Philosophie und Phänomenologische Forschung* 1, Halle: Niemeyer, pp. 567–684.

Ingarden, Roman (1957) 'Über die gegenwärtigen Aufgaben der Phänomenologie' *Archivio di Filosofia*, pp. 229–42.

Spiegelberg, A. (1971) *The Phenomenological Movement: A Historical Introduction*, The Hague: Martinus Nijhoff.

SEBASTIEN ODIARI

Naturalism

This term has many meanings and there are not only different kinds of naturalism — ethical, epistemological and aesthetic, for instance — but varieties within these. None the less, when the term is used out of context and without qualification, it most commonly refers to a perspective according to which it is not necessary to invoke any supernatural causes in order to explain phenomena. **Materialism** is one form of naturalism, but a naturalist need not be a materialist. **Santayana** was a major influence on American naturalism in the early twentieth century, for instance on Morris **Cohen** and **Woodbridge**; **Dewey**, R. W. **Sellars**, Ernest **Nagel** and Sidney **Hook** were also leading naturalists.

Ethical naturalism is another common form of naturalism, according to which actions that are right or wrong are so in virtue of possessing some (natural) property. **Utilitarianism** is one kind of naturalistic ethics.

Bibliography

Fenner, D. E. W. (1993) 'Varieties of aesthetic naturalism', *American Philosophical Quarterly* 30: 353–62.

Ferm, Vergilius (1950) 'Varieties of naturalism', in V. T. A. Ferm (ed.) *A History of Philosophical Systems*, Freeport, NY: Books for Libraries Press, pp. 429–41.

Franklin, R. L. (1973) 'Recent work on ethical naturalism', *American Philosophical Quarterly* 7: 55–95.

Krikorian, Y. H. (ed.) (1944) *Naturalism and the Human Spirit*, New York: Columbia University Press.

Kurtz, Paul (1990) *Philosophical Essays in Pragmatic Naturalism*, Buffalo, NY: Prometheus.

Munro, James (1960) '"Naturalism" in philosophy and aesthetics', *Journal of Aesthetics and Art Criticism* 19: 133–8.

Pettit, Philip (1992) 'The nature of naturalism—II', *Proceedings of the Aristotelian Society, Supplementary Volume* 66: 245–66.

Pratt, J. B. (1939) *Naturalism*, New Haven, CT: Yale University Press.

Scott, Jr, Robert B. (1980) 'Five types of ethical naturalism', *American Philosophical Quarterly* 17: 261–70

Sellars, R. W. (1970) 'Realism, naturalism and humanism', in G. P. Adams and W. P. Montague (eds), *Contemporary American Philosophy*, vol. 2, 1930.

Stroud, Barry (1977) 'Transcendental arguments and epistemological naturalism', *Philosophical Studies* 31: 105–15.

Wagner, S. J. and Warner, R. (eds) (1993) *Naturalism: A Critical Appraisal*, Notre Dame: Notre Dame University Press.

STUART BROWN

Neo-Kantians

The so-called 'Neo-Kantians' did not so much form one unified movement as they represented many, often quite different, reactions to the philosophical positions prevalent in Germany around the middle of the nineteenth century, and especially to Hegelian Idealism and the many different forms of **Naturalism**, Monism and **Materialism** found in Büchner, **Haeckel**, Vogt and others. During this period, characterized by an 'anarchy of conviction' (**Dilthey**), the 'return to Kant' seemed to be a promising strategy to many. Yet, there appears to be no clearly identifiable philosophical tendency common to all. The term *Neukantianismus* has been in use since about 1875. Though it was at that time not unusual to talk of *Jungkantianer* (young Kantians) or of a 'new criticism', the characterization of the new approach to philosophy as 'neo-Kantianism' took hold.

Otto **Liebmann**, who formulated the motto 'Back to Kant' in 1865, is usually regarded as the first representative of this movement. Others who were important for the beginnings of Neo-Kantianism were Eduard **Zeller** (1814–1908), Hermann von Helmholtz (1821–94), and Friedrich Albert Lange (1828–75), who are sometimes taken to characterize the 'early' or 'physiological' Neo-Kantianism. Their view is contrasted with the 'metaphysical' or 'realistic' views of Liebmann, Alois **Riehl** (1844–1924), Enrich **Adickes** (1866–1928), Friedrich **Paulsen** (1864–1908), and Max Wundt (1879–1963), for instance. A late representative of this persuasion is Heinz **Heimsoeth** (1886–1975). The two most important philosophical traditions identifiable within Neo-Kantianism are the so-called 'Marburg School' and the 'Southwest German', 'Baden' or 'Heidelberg School'. Also important was the so-called 'Göttingen' or 'Neo-Friesian' school.

The most important philosophers of the Marburg school were Hermann **Cohen** (1842–1918), Paul **Natorp** (1854–1924), and Ernst **Cassirer** (1874–1945). Also significant were Rudolf **Stammler** (1856–1938), Karl Vorländer (1860–1928), and Arthur Buchenau (1879–1946). Cohen's and Natorp's thought was close to the metaphysical school, but Cohen placed a greater emphasis on 'the fact of science' and epistemological considerations. Indeed, philosophy for him was nothing but a 'theory of the principles of science and therewith of all culture'. Opposed to any form of Psychologism, Cohen opted for a very Platonic interpretation of Kant. Cassirer, who was Natorp's most important student, placed more emphasis on culture than his teachers. In doing so, he came close to the views of the Baden school. The philosophers of this form of Neo-Kantianism had placed greater emphasis on the investigation of values and their role in the humanities from the very beginning. The most important members of this school were Wilhelm **Windelband** (1848–1915) and Heinrich **Rickert** (1863–1936). Others were Jonas **Cohn** (1869–1947), Emil Lask (1875–1915) and Bruno **Bauch** (1877–1942). The Göttingen school was characterized by the thought of Leonard **Nelson** (1882–1927) who, to a large extent, followed Jakob Friedrich Fries (1773–1843). Reacting

especially to the Marburg school, Nelson placed greater emphasis on psychology, while at the same time denying that he was advocating Psychologism. Nelson was not as influential as his colleagues in Marburg and Baden, though Rudolf Otto (1869–1937) was to some extent indebted to him.

Bibliography

Adair-Toteff, Christopher (1994) 'The neo-Kantian Raum controversy', *British Journal of the History of Philosophy* 2: 131–48.

Beck, Lewis White (1967) 'Neo-Kantianism', in Paul Edwards (ed.) *The Encyclopedia of Philosophy*, New York: Macmillan.

Dussort, Henri (1963) *L'école de Marbourg*, Paris: Presses universitaires de France.

Finnis, J. M. (1987) 'Legal enforcement of "Duties of oneself": Kant vs. Neo-Kantians', *Columbia Law Review* 87: 433ff.

Köhnke, Klaus-Christian (1992) *The Rise of Neo-Kantianism: German Academic Philosophy between Idealism and Positivism*, New York: Cambridge University Press. (Originally published in German as *Entstehung und Aufstieg des Neukantianismus*, Frankfurt am Main: Suhrkamp, 1986.)

Lehmann, Gerhard (1963) 'Kant im Spätidealismus und die Anfänge der neukantischen Bewegung', *Zeitschrift für philosophische Forschung* 23: 438–56.

Ollig, Hans-Ludwig (ed.) (1982) *Neukantianismus. Texte der Marburger und der Südwestdeutschen Schule, ihre Vorläufer und Kritiker*, Stuttgart: Reclam Verlag.

—— (ed.) (1987) *Materialien zur Neukantianismus-Diskussion*, Darmstadt: Wissenschaftliche Buchgesellschaft.

Piché, Claude (1991) 'Kants dritte Kritik und die Genese des badischen Neukantianismus', *Akten des siebenten internationalen Kant-Kongresses, kurfürstliches Schloss zu Mainz, 1990*, II(2), ed. Gerhard Funke, Bonn and Berlin: Bouvier Verlag, pp. 615–28.

Willey, Th. E. (1978) *Back to Kant. The Revival of Kantianism in German Social and Historic Thought, 1860–1914*, Detroit.

MANFRED KUEHN

Neoscholasticism

The name given to a philosophical movement which began in the middle of the nineteenth century and which, though it has tended to focus narrowly on the thought of Thomas Aquinas, can be regarded as a revival and continuation of scholastic philosophy in general. Scholasticism, as it came to be called during the Renaissance, originated in the Aristotelian revival of the twelfth century, and flourished in the thirteenth and fourteenth centuries. After a period in the doldrums it was revived in the sixteenth and seventeenth centuries by Cajetan, John of St Thomas, and Francisco Suárez, in what is known as the 'second scholasticism'. It then declined once more, and was virtually moribund until a revival of interest in Thomas Aquinas took place within the Catholic Church in the early and mid-nineteenth century. Despite initial hostility within that Church, important centres of a revived scholasticism had been established in Rome and Louvain by the end of the century, and a number of influential journals consolidated the revival. Initially, in Louvain at any rate, neoscholastics were committed to a belief in a *philosophia perennis*, and to the view that, in the entire history of European thought, Aquinas had come closest to expounding such a philosophy. However, study of the sometimes radical differences among the great medieval philosophers showed that the quest for a *philosophia perennis* was not part of the scholastic tradition, and throughout the present century neoscholasticism itself has manifested substantial internal divisions. What all neoscholastics share is, firstly, a commitment to some form of realism, both epistemological and, in particular, the objective reality of values; secondly, a commitment to metaphysics as the foundational philosophical science; and thirdly, a belief that earlier scholastic philosophers approached philosophical issues in broadly the right kind of way. The dominant trend in neoscholasticism at present is 'transcendental Thomism', which derives from a confrontation and partial synthesis of some elements of Thomism with Kant (Bernard **Lonergan**, Emerich Coreth, Joseph **Maréchal**) and **Heidegger** (Johannes Lotz).

Bibliography

John, Helen James (1966) *The Thomist Spectrum*, New York: Fordham University Press.

McCool, Gerald A. (1989) *Nineteenth-Century Scholasticism*, New York: Fordham University Press.

—— (1989) *From Unity to Pluralism*, New York: Fordham University Press.

Van Riet, Georges (1965) *Thomistic Epistemology*, 2 vols, St Louis and London: Herder.

HUGH BREDIN

New Realism

The 'New Realists' were a group of six American philosophers (E. B. **Holt**, W. T. **Marvin**, W. P. **Montague**, R. B. **Perry**, W. T. Pitkin and E. G. Spaulding) who produced a series of programmatic articles in 1910 and shortly thereafter. In these articles they opposed the idealist doctrine of internal relations. They asserted the independence of the known from the knower in the case of at least some objects—physical things, minds or mathematical entities. To avoid either an idealistic or a materialist theory of the mind, some—particularly Holt—adopted a neutral monism.

In England, **Moore** and **Russell** have a good deal in common with these New Realists, as had **Alexander**, and are sometimes grouped with them. (See also **Critical Realism** and **Realism**.)

Bibliography

Primary:

Holt, Edwin B. *et al.* (1910) 'The program and first platform of six realists', *Journal of Philosophy, Psychology and Scientific Methods* 7: 393–401.

—— (1912) *The New Realism: Cooperative Studies in Philosophy*, New York: Macmillan.

Secondary:

Boman, L. (1955) *Criticism and Construction in the Philosophy of the American New Realism*, Stockholm: Alquist & Wittsell.

Metz, Rudolf (1938) *A Hundred Years of British Philosophy*, trans. J. W. Harvey, T. E. Jessop and H. Sturt, ed. J. H. Muirhead, London: Allen & Unwin, pp. 530–704. (Originally published in German, Heidelberg, 1934.)

Passmore, John (1957) *A Hundred Years of Philosophy*, London: Duckworth, ch. 11.

STUART BROWN

Personalism

The term has its origins in the nineteenth century in the view of Schleiermacher and others that God is a person and not as conceived in systems of pantheism and **Absolute Idealism**. Its use in the earlier part of the twentieth century, when a number of philosophers claimed the title, is more focused on individual human persons as fundamental and irreducible realities. **Maritain, Mounier** and **Stefanini** defended a Christian or Catholic 'personalism' against naturalistic and **materialistic** philosophies. For similar reasons some absolute idealists, including **Caird, Calkins** and Green are associated with personalism. But, to a large extent, those who called themselves 'personalists' were reacting against the then prevalent tradition of absolute idealism. Many were themselves inclined to **idealism**, such as **Brightman, Carr, Howison, Rashdall** and **Webb**, and rejected the tendency of **Hegelian** idealism to monism and pantheism, which they took to deny ultimate reality to individual persons. But some personalists were **realists**, as were **Pringle-Pattison** and **Pratt**. The **pragmatist Schiller** adopted the word for himself. **Macmurray**'s personalism was partly a reaction to broader cultural influences which tended to depersonalize people as well as to mechanistic and reductionist trends in philosophy. The same is true to a large extent of the Mexican personalist, Antonio **Caso**.

Personalism under Howison and **Bowne**, became an established school at the University of Boston, as it did also at the University of Southern California. The journal *The Personalist* was founded in 1919 but was renamed *The Pacific Philosophical Quarterly* in 1980.

Bibliography
Primary:
Bowne, Borden Parker (1908) *Personalism*, Norwood, Mass.: Plimpton Press.

Knudson, A. C. (1949) *The Philosophy of Personalism*, Boston, Mass.: Boston University Press.

Macmurray, J. (1961) *Persons in Relation*, London: Faber.

Sturt, H. (ed.) (1902) *Personal Idealism*, London: Macmillan.

Secondary:
Brightman, E. S. (1950) 'Personalism (including personal idealism)', in V. T. A. Ferm (ed.) *A History of Philosophical Systems*, Freeport, NY: Books for Libraries Press.

Deats, Paul and Robb, Carol (1986) *The Boston Personalist Tradition in Philosophy, Social Ethics, and Theology*, Macon, GA: Mercer University Press.

Lavely, John H. (1967) 'Personalism', in Paul Edwards (ed.) *Encyclopedia of Philosophy*, New York: Macmillan & Co.

Metz, Rudolf (1938) *A Hundred Years of British Philosophy*, trans. J. W. Harvey, T. E. Jessop and H. Sturt, ed. J. H. Muirhead, London: Allen & Unwin, pp. 380–98. (Originally published in German, Heidelberg, 1934.)

Passmore, John (1957) *A Hundred Years of Philosophy*, London: Duckworth, ch. 4.

STUART BROWN

Phenomenology

What unites the various things that have been called phenomenology is more a matter of family resemblance than doctrines held in common. The following kinds of phenomenology may be distinguished.

Realist phenomenology
This owed its inspiration to **Husserl**'s *Logical Investigations*. It is characterized by a rich ontology which rejects the **empiricist** restriction of what there is to the physical and the mental. There are physical entities and mental entities but there are also numbers, states of affairs, logical laws, institutions, works of art and so on. Following the slogan 'To the things themselves!' entities of all ontological types are to be taken as they present themselves to consciousness and not as some theory or system says they must be. Everything has its 'what', its essence. Phenomenology is the study of essences and relations between essences by means of a kind of non-sensory seeing or intuition (*Wesensschau*). The truths which such phenomenology lays bare are a priori. The a priori is not merely formal but can pertain to literally anything, e.g. there are a priori truths about sensation. Moreover the *necessity* which characterizes a priori truths has nothing to do with how we think or even how we must think but is purely objective. Although considerable emphasis is given to the intentionality of consciousness—its being 'of' or 'about' something, its directedness-toward something—and intentional experiences constitute much of the subject-matter of phenomenology, this is not because it is thought that somehow things other than consciousness depend for their existence and character on consciousness. Rather the failure to recognize intentionality is blamed for attempts to reduce material objects to sensations, logic to psychology, values to feelings.

Transcendental phenomenology
Despite having been the inspiration for realist phenomenology Husserl's phenomenology developed into a form of **idealism**. For transcendental phenomenology consciousness or subjectivity is the exclusive theme. Objects of consciousness figure in phenomenological description but as purely intentional objects, i.e. objects *qua* objects of consciousness. From motives which are partly Cartesian and partly Kantian a procedure is adopted for arriving at *pure* consciousness. This is not an item in the world but that for which there is a world. The operation which enables the phenomenologist to enter the transcendental dimension of pure consciousness is the phenomenological or transcendental reduction. This is a way of *reflecting* on consciousness, as opposed to being absorbed by the world and items in the

world, which involves the suspending or putting out of action of all beliefs regarding the real existence and real nature of all objects of consciousness (including the world as a whole). Intentionality is no longer conceived as the way in which a conscious subject relates itself to a pre-existing reality but as the medium in which what counts as real is constituted. Transcendental phenomenology is the description of the essential structures of the constitution (constituting) of the world in transcendental subjectivity.

Hermeneutic phenomenology
This is how **Heidegger** describes his own form of phenomenology. Phenomenology is the method of ontology, the study of the Being (*Sein*) of beings (what is, *Seiendes*). A necessary preliminary to the question of the meaning of Being as such is the ontology of the being which asks the question about Being. To say that Being is the proper subject-matter of phenomenology suggests that Heidegger is engaged in something totally different from transcendental phenomenology, for which the subject-matter is transcendental consciousness. However the difference is not as great as it first seems. Being is not some great abstraction but that which makes it possible for beings to show themselves or be encountered. *Dasein* (Heidegger's term for human being) is unique inasmuch as its Being involves an understanding of Being, that of itself and that of what is not itself. Phenomenology is hermeneutic in the sense that it consists in the *interpretation*, the conceptual unfolding (*Auslegung*) of *Dasein*'s understanding of Being. The being with the understanding of Being is not a transcendental ego outside the world but a being whose Being is Being-in-the-world. However this is not a crude reverting to pre-Kantian naiveté. *Dasein* is not in the world in the sense of one thing being located in a much bigger thing. It is not a *subject* which unlike the transcendental subject is not outside the world. Rather the conception of *Dasein* as Being-in-the-world represents an attempt to overcome the subject-object dichotomy. What Heidegger means by 'world' is a structure of significance. This is not something over and against *Dasein* but part and parcel of what *Dasein* is. Reversing the customary order, theoretical modes of intentionality, comportment to beings, are seen as grounded in practical modes. Being-in-the-world is not itself an instance of intentionality, but a condition of the possibility of intentionality.

Existential phenomenology
This is best exemplified by **Merleau-Ponty**. To-

wards the end of his philosophical career Husserl introduced the idea of the *Lebenswelt* (life-world), the world of lived experience. The properties and structures attributed by the natural sciences to the 'objective' world are themselves the product of a process of idealization and mathematization of 'life-wordly' structures. The task of philosophy is not to down-grade the life-world as 'mere appearance' but to remove from it the 'garment of ideas' which science has thrown over it. Largely through the influence of Merleau-Ponty many phenomenologists came to see the description of the life-world and the exposure of the 'prejudice' of the idea of an objective world of wholly determinate entities as phenomenology's principal task. What makes such phenomenology existential as opposed to transcendental is that the consciousness of the life-world it seeks to describe is that of the concrete, situated, historical, engaged body-subject in the world rather than that of a transcendental ego. It involves a 'reduction' in the sense of the suspension or putting out of action of the objective sciences but not a genuinely transcendental reduction. Unlike Husserl, Merleau-Ponty does not see the laying bare of the life-world as merely a stage on the way to world-constituting transcendental subjectivity.

Bibliography
Primary:
Husserl, E. (1990) *Logische Untersuchungen*, Halle; second edition, 1913 (English translation, *Logical Investigations*, trans. J. N. Findlay, London: Routledge & Kegan Paul, 1970).
——(1913) *Ideen zu einer reinen Phänomenologie und phänomenologischen Philosophie*, Halle (English translation, *Ideas: General Introduction to Pure Phenomenology*, trans. W. R. Boyce Gibson, London: Allen & Unwin, 1958).
——(1949) *Cartesianische Meditationen*, The Hague (English translation, *Cartesian Meditations*, trans. Dorion Cairns, The Hague: Martinus Nijhoff, 1969).
——(1962) *Die Krisis der europäischen Wissenschaften und die transzendentale Phänomenologie*, The Hague (English translation, *The Crisis of European Sciences and Transcendental Phenomenology*, trans. David Carr, Evanston: Northwestern University Press, 1970).
Heidegger, M. (1927) *Sein und Zeit*, Halle (English translation, *Being and Time*, trans. John Macquarrie and Edward Robinson, Oxford: Basil Blackwell, 1962).
——(1976) *Grundprobleme der Phänomenologie*, Frankfurt (English translation, *The Basic Pro-*

blems of Phenomenology, trans. Albert Hofstadter, Bloomington: Indiana University Press, 1982).

—— (1979) *Prolegomena zur Geschichte des Zeitbegriffs*, Frankfurt (English translation, *History of the Concept of Time Prolegomena*, trans. Theodore Kisiel, Bloomington: Indiana University Press, 1985).

Merleau-Ponty, M. (1945) *Phénoménologie de la Perception*, Paris (English translation, *Phenomenology of Perception*, trans. Colin Smith, London: Routledge & Kegan Paul, 1962).

Secondary:

Howard. M., Howarth, J. and Keat, R. (1991) *Understanding Phenomenology*, Oxford: Basil Blackwell.

Pivcevic, E. (1970) *Husserl and Phenomenology*, London: Hutchinson University Library.

Spiegelberg, H. (1960) *The Phenomenological Movement*, The Hague.

PAUL GORNER

Philosophical Anthropology

This movement can be traced back to the eighteenth century—particularly to Kant—and it has precursors in the early part of the twentieth century, including **Dilthey** and **Husserl**. It flourished in Germany in the 1920s and 1930s, when Max **Scheler** and Helmut **Plessner** were key figures. It has since spread elsewhere and has attracted attention in the English-speaking world. The movement can be characterized as a reaction against the overly scientistic, mechanistic or reductionist studies of human nature characteristic of Darwinian, Freudian and other approaches. Modern science is often seen by those who associate themselves with philosophical anthropology as in a state of crisis (sometimes as reflecting a crisis in Modern European society). With its emphasis on not treating humans as mere scientific objects but as free beings, it has affinities with certain other movements, such as **Existentialism** and **Phenomenology**. Amongst those most commonly associated with philosophical anthropology are Ludwig **Binswanger**, Martin **Buber**, Ernst **Cassirer**, Arnold **Gehlen**, R. D. Lang, Michael **Polanyi** and Werner Sombart. But the breath of the movement makes a consensus about its history unlikely. It has been developed in a number of discipline areas, including biology, psychology and theology, in different ways. Those who describe themselves as engaging in 'philosophical anthropology' define themselves in various ways and they construct and associate themselves with different histories.

Bibliography

Primary:

Agassi, Joseph (1977) *Towards a Rational Philosophical Anthropology*, The Hague: Martinus Nijhoff.

Cassirer, Ernst (1963) *An Essay on Man*, New Haven, CT: Yale University Press.

Haeffner, G. (trans. E. Watkins) (1990) *The Human Situation: A Philosophical Anthropology*, Notre Dame: Notre Dame University Press.

Holbrook, David (1988) *Further Studies in Philosophical Anthropology*, Aldershot: Avebury.

Landmann, Michael (1955) *Philosophische Anthropologie*, Berlin (English translation, *Philosophical Anthropology*, trans. D. J. Parent, Philadelphia: Westminster Press, 1974).

Rescher, Nicholas (1990) *Human Interests: Reflections on Philosophical Anthropology*, Stanford: Stanford University Press.

Secondary:

Lenfers, Dietmar (1989) *The Marvel of Human Being: A Student Manual of Philosophical Anthropology*, Dublin: Dominican.

Pappe, H. O. (1961) 'On philosophical anthropology', *Australasian Journal of Philosophy* 39: 47–64.

—— (1967) 'Philosophical anthropology', in Paul Edwards (ed.) *Encyclopedia of Philosophy*, New York: Macmillan & Co.

Wein, H. (1957) 'Trends in philosophical anthropology in post-war Germany', *Philosophy of Science*: 46–56.

STUART BROWN

Positivism

Broadly, any view that accords to science a monopoly of knowledge about the universe. Positivism is characteristically anti-metaphysical and commonly anti-religious. The term was introduced by Claude-Henri Saint-Simon (1760–1825) and popularized by his follower, Auguste Comte (1789–1857). **Comtean Positivism** was not only a philosophy but a substitute religion–a religion of humanity, with its equivalents of churches and worship. It was less professionally academic than the **Logical Positivism** of the **Vienna Circle**, some of whose members rejected the term 'positivism' because of its associations with the older movement and preferred the phrase 'logical **empiricism**'. Against this, however, one member, Victor **Kraft**, argued in favour of accepting the label 'positivist': 'The Vienna Circle shares with traditional positivism, after all, the restriction of all positive knowledge.'

Bibliography
Frankel, Charles (1950) 'Positivism', in V. T. A. Ferm (ed.) *A History of Philosophical Systems*, Freeport, NY: Books for Libraries Press, pp. 329–39.

Kolakowski, Leszek (1968) *Positivist Philosophy from Hume to the Vienna Circle*, trans. N. Guterman, New York: Doubleday, and Harmondsworth: Penguin Books, 1972.

Kraft, Victor (1953) *The Vienna Circle: The Origin of Neo-Positivism*, trans. A. Pap, New York: Philosophical Library.

STUART BROWN

Post-Marxism

Post-Marxism can be defined in two main ways: first, as an attempt to reformulate Marxist thought in the light of recent theoretical and social developments that challenge many of the assumptions and categories of classical **Marxism**; secondly, as a *rejection* of Marxist doctrine in favour of one or other of these recent theoretical developments. One way of signalling the difference is Ernesto Laclau and Chantal Mouffe's distinction between being 'post-*Marxist*' or '*post*-Marxist'. To be the former is, with Laclau and Mouffe, to be committed to finding space within Marxism for a whole new range of social protest movements—feminism, anti-institutional ecology, ethnic, national, and sexual minorities, for example—as well as for the techniques of **poststructuralism** and **postmodernism**. It is also to challenge the validity of many classical Marxist assumptions such as the central position of the working class in bringing about social change, and the notions of hegemony and historical necessity. The new Marxism aims at a pluralistic approach to politics.

Post-Marxism, on the other hand, implies a definite break with, and move beyond, the Marxist cause and its concerns. A case in point would be the many French intellectuals whose faith in Marxist theory was shaken by the actions of the French Communist Party during the 1968 Paris *événements*, when the Party was widely felt to have colluded with the state in defusing a revolutionary situation. Thinkers such as Jean-François **Lyotard** and Jean **Baudrillard** subsequently rejected Marxism, turning instead to postmodernism in its various guises. *Post*-Marxism is more of an attitude—of disillusionment in the main—towards Marxism than a specific system of thought in its own right.

Bibliography
Laclau, Ernesto and Mouffe, Chantal (1985) *Hege-mony and Socialist Strategy: Towards a Radical Democratic Politics*, London: Verso.

—— and —— (1987) 'Post-Marxism without apologies', *New Left Review*, 166.

Lyotard, Jean-François (1974) *Economie libidinale*, Paris: Minuit (English translation, *Libidinal Economy*, trans. Iain Hamilton Grant, London: Athlone Press, 1993).

Smart, Barry (1992) *Modern Conditions, Postmodern Controversies*, London: Routledge.

STUART SIM

Postmodernism

Postmodernism is a movement which began in the 1970s. Its chief exponents include Jean-François **Lyotard**, Jean **Baudrillard**, Gilles **Deleuze** and Félix **Guattari**. It is found in philosophy, culture and the arts, and claims **Nietzsche** amongst its philosophical ancestors.

Whilst no clear definition of postmodernism can be given, it includes an examination of the social and cultural tendencies which have dominated advanced capitalist societies since the late 1950s and is characterized by dislocation and fragmentation; a concern with images, the superficial and the ephemeral; and a rejection of the traditional philosophical search for an underlying unity, reality, order and coherence to all phenomena. The movement is a successor to and a critique of **modernism**, a term which Lyotard (1979, 1984, p. xxiii) uses 'to designate any science that ... make[s] an explicit appeal to some grand narrative'. Such narratives are alleged to be comprehensive accounts of a teleological process which will ultimately realize some hitherto idealized state of affairs. The two accounts for which Lyotard reserves his main attack are that of emancipation, which stems from the Enlightenment and the French Revolution, and that of speculation, which stems from the **Hegelian** tradition and its ideal of the complete synthesis of knowledge. All grand narratives and the consensual collusion or acquiescence upon which they were founded have collapsed, and the question of justification or 'legitimization' of any enterprise which was permitted by their assumption has once more become acute.

Lyotard maintains that due to the computerization of the past three decades, the nature of knowledge itself has changed. Any information which cannot be rendered into a form suitable for being stored in a databank is marginalized. Knowledge is legitimized not by an appeal to its truth, or its ability to represent accurately what is objectively the case. Instead, there is an appeal to its efficiency: minimization of input or maximization of output or both are the goals to be achieved.

To replace grand narratives there are language-games, which are relative, restricted and incommensurable. Each language-game is governed by its own set of rules and is played by those who contract in, whether implicitly or explicitly. There is no self-legitimation of language-games, which are arbitrary and thus replaceable. They are always placed against an opponent, whether other people or language as it is traditionally used.

Postmodernism also advocates the view that time is dislocated. On the 'grand narrative' approach, time is regarded as a constant, uniform, objective, one-directional flow which is split into past, present and future. The present is considered as the link between past and future, and the temporal process is reflected in the tenses of verbs. According to postmodernism, there is no objective reality governing the structure of language: what is traditionally thought of as being in the past or the future can be recalled or inscribed into what is traditionally regarded as the present. With the rejection of 'grand narrative' time, there is a temporal fragmentation into a series of perpetual and dislocated presents which are not to be contrasted with the past or the future.

Novels which 'play' with the temporal process, such as James Joyce's *Finnegans Wake*, are in this respect to be regarded as postmodern, as are all avant-garde works of art which are presentations of dislocated or fragmented time, space or meaning, whether or not they are from the postwar period. A play such as Samuel Beckett's *Waiting for Godot* is held to be a repudiation of the modernist expectation that there is any overall, comprehensive meaning to be found within the text itself, or to be legitimately provided by any unregenerately modernist member of the audience. The avant-garde is on the margins of art, and is kept there by those who collude in or create the arbitrary rules of art criticism. The view that there is no objective reality behind the series of ephemeral images which are presented to us reaches its most extreme in statements such as Baudrillard's, that the Gulf War did not take place; instead, the West was confronted with fragmentary television images which presented, but did not represent, American 'smart bombs' taking out Iraqi emplacements.

Some aspects of the postmodernist programme are of more interest or use than others. The avant-garde in art can lead the audience, viewer or critic to think about and possibly to revise the expectations or principles on which their approach to art is based, but not all consensually founded beliefs are arbitrary and replaceable, and emancipation and the relief of suffering are worthy goals even if they can never be fully realized.

Select Bibliography
Primary:
Lyotard, J.-F. (1979) *La Condition Postmoderne*, Paris: Editions de Minuit (English translation, *The Postmodern Condition*, trans. G. Bennington and B. Massumi, Manchester: Manchester University Press, 1984).

Secondary:
Fekete, J. (ed.) (1987) *Life after Postmodernism: Essays on Value and Culture*, Manchester: Manchester University Press.
Jameson, F. (1990) *Postmodernism, or the Cultural Logic of Late Capitalism*, Durham, NC: Duke University Press.
Norris, C. (1990) *What's Wrong with Postmodernism? Critical Theory and the Ends of Postmodernism*, Baltimore: Johns Hopkins University Press.
Sarup, M. (1988) *An Introductory Guide to Post-structuralism and Postmodernism*, Hemel Hempstead: Harvester Wheatsheaf.
Silverman, H. J. (ed.) (1990) *Postmodernism—Philosophy and the Arts*, London: Routledge.
—— and Welton, D. (eds) (1988) *Postmodernism and Continental Philosophy*, Albany: State University of New York Press.

KATHRYN PLANT

Post-structuralism

Post-structuralism is a movement within philosophical and literary criticism. It emerged from and was hostile to **structuralism**, which laid claim to scientific objectivity, detachment and comprehensiveness. Its main exponents are Jacques **Derrida**, Jacques **Lacan**, Julia **Kristeva**, Jean-François **Lyotard** and, in his later writings, Roland **Barthes**. It has trends in common with **postmodernism** and includes deconstruction within its scope. It began in France in the late 1960s, quickly spreading to other parts of Europe and North America.

As a movement, it is characterized by being anti-traditional, anti-metaphysical and anti-ideological. At its most philosophically respectable, it claims that many or all philosophical writings in the Western tradition inadvertently undermine themselves by not being able to sustain the assumptions on which they are based. One example of this is found in Derrida's critique of **Lévi-Strauss**, where Derrida claims that there is an underlying contradiction between the assertions that the taboo on incest is natural, but nevertheless has to be enforced by social sanctions. Another illustration comes from Rousseau's *Emile*: it is asserted that the psychological nature of women is different from that of men, but that women should not (not cannot) follow the same interests and occupations as men.

According to post-structuralist thought, there is no stability of meaning or, in Derrida's terminology, no 'metaphysics of presence' in language. This position goes against the view of **Saussure** that the meanings of words can be anchored down by those of other words which occur in the same sentence or phrase. The post-structuralist argument is that a word cannot be thus fixed in meaning, because that of other words is equally unstable.

Allied to this position is the broad view that the meaning of a literary text is also indeterminate. This assertion can be understood in one of two ways: that instead of there being just one definitive and authoritative interpretation of a literary work, there can be multiple meanings; or that a text can take any interpretation whatsoever. The more moderate claim can be useful because it allows new approaches in literary criticism.

Post-structuralism casts doubt upon the status of the subject as a persisting entity, as such an entity would be a fixed and permanent structure.

Advantage is taken by some of the North American post-structuralists, and by Derrida himself, of the inclusion of word-association by Saussure in his work on linguistics. Such association escapes from the allegedly public nature and rule-governedness of language, and is held up as a prime example of liberation and creativity. Derrida's article 'Shibboleth' (Hartman and Budick (eds) 1986) contains the word-associations 'shibboleth', 'circumcision', 'anniversaries', 'rings' 'constellations', and is interspersed with words in German; no doubt to take advantage of the Saussurean assertion that the division between natural languages is not clear-cut but arbitrary.

What is most useful in the post-structuralist programme are the secondary commentaries on the works of previous thinkers and the new perspectives on literary texts. If these aspects alone were retained from post-structuralism, it would become a less radical and more respectable philosophical and literary movement.

Select Bibliography
Derrida, J. (1986) 'Shibboleth', in G. Hartman and S. Budick (eds) *Midrash and Literature*, New Haven: Yale University Press.

Dews, P. (1987) *Logics of Disintegration: Post-Structuralist Thought and the Claims of Critical Theory*, London: Verso.

Easthope, A. (1988) *British Post-Structuralism*, London: Routledge.

Merquior, J. (1986) *From Prague to Paris: A Critique of Structuralist and Post-Structuralist Thought*, London: Verso.

Sarup, M. (1988) *An Introductory Guide to Post-structuralism and Postmodernism*, Hemel Hempstead: Harvester Wheatsheaf.

Weedon, C. (1987) *Feminist Practice and Post-Structuralist Theory*, Oxford: Blackwell.

KATHRYN PLANT

Pragmatism

Pragmatism originated in the 1860s out of discussions among a number of thinkers in science, mathematics, law, psychology, and philosophy, all influenced by Darwin's theory of evolution, aiming at attaining a scientific philosophy in which questions could be settled as decisively as in the sciences. The term 'pragmatic' was adopted from Kant's *Critique of Pure Reason*, where it is used to designate a type of judgement about which there can be no objective certainty but about which one is practically certain, as shown by one's willingness to bet on it. **Peirce** credited the British psychologist and philosopher Alexander Bain with the key definition of belief as 'that on which one is prepared to act'. Although pragmatism is not a philosophy of opportunism and is not incompatible with adhering to certain principles, it is centrally concerned with what 'works' for the purposes at hand, and the idea of the practical is central to the pragmatic philosophy, even though pragmatism's conception of the practical is itself a disputed matter.

One thinker, otherwise little known, who played an important role in the development of pragmatism was Chauncey Wright, a scientist and mathematician who constantly emphasized the importance of the Darwinian theory and attempted in his brief life to work out an evolutionary account of consciousness. The actual founder of pragmatism was Charles Sanders Peirce. Peirce conceived of pragmatism as a method for the clarification of ideas, and used it to clarify the ideas of meaning, truth, and reality. Peirce thought of inquiry as originating in doubt, uncertainty, an unsatisfactory feeling from which we struggle to free ourselves, which in turn stimulates inquiry or thought, aimed at eliminating the irritation of doubt by producing in its place belief, which Peirce characterized as a satisfactory feeling marked in our natures as a habit of action. To have a belief is to have a habit of acting in a certain way under certain conditions. The idea is that the meaning of an abstract conception is to be found in our conception of its practical or sensible effects under various hypothetical conditions. Peirce arrived at his conception of truth by applying the pragmatic criterion; thus he held that the truth is that opinion upon which inquiry converges if carried on long enough, so that the truth is the opinion fated to be accepted as the ultimate outcome of inquiry. Thus, instead of defining inquiry as a process aiming at truth, Peirce defined truth as the outcome of inquiry, inquiry carried on in a certain way and with certain safeguards, such as those that characterize scientific procedures. Reality, he claimed, is what it is independently of what anyone thinks about it, so reality is the object of a true belief.

Peirce's conception was adopted and modified by William **James**. Applying the pragmatic theory of meaning to the concept of truth, James was led to the view that the truth of an idea is to be found in its working; it is true if it satisfies, is verifiable and verified in experience. Peirce was bothered by this modification of his original idea, and re-named his doctrine 'pragmatic*is*m', a term 'ugly enough to be safe from kidnappers'. What troubled Peirce was that James appeared to allow subjective elements into the equation: if believing that a certain idea is true would lead one to act in a way different from the way one would behave if one believed it false, then on James's view the idea would be said to have meaning, for it makes a difference in conduct and concrete life. For Peirce this importation of belief into the criterion of meaning was not applicable in the requisite way to scientific inquiry. On James's view, since reality is malleable and subject to change in accordance with human desires, so therefore is truth. This Peirce could not accept. However, while Peirce's writings were generally ignored, James's treatment of it made pragmatism famous as well as controversial.

James made pragmatism famous. John **Dewey** applied it to all areas of life, especially though not solely to education. Dewey held that an idea is true if it satisfies the conditions of the problem it was developed to solve. Dewey conceived of all ideas as hypotheses, tentative solutions to problems, true to the extent that they satisfy the conditions of the problem. Dewey's model of inquiry is the biological one of what an organism does when it is hungry: hunger is a dissatisfied state from which the organism struggles to free itself by engaging in food seeking activities; the activity of finding and eating food satisfies the conditions of the problem, and thinking, on Dewey's view, arises only out of problematic or indeterminate situations. Although the indeterminate situation becomes determinate through inquiry, determinacy is not a permanent condition; the solution of one problem leads to new problems, and the meaning of life, knowing, and inquiry are to be found in action. Dewey generalized this model to cover social and moral problems as well as scientific inquiry. On Dewey's view, called 'instrumentalism', all social thinking is a form of social inquiry involving experimentation, which requires active modification of the environment. The situation consisting in the organism in constant interaction with the environment changes as the relation between the organism and the environment changes, and the aim is to exercise intelligent control over the indeterminate situation to bring it to a satisfactory termination. Thus ideas, thinking, mind are instrumental to reconstruction of the indeterminate situation, and inquiry and knowing occur for the sake of adaptation to and modification of the environment. Dewey came to hold that the traditional problems of epistemology and large numbers of other traditional philosophical questions arise out of confusions generated by tradition, failure to question unexamined presuppositions, and failure to take adequate account of the biological basis of human life.

Both James and Dewey held that mind developed in the process of evolution as a means of enabling creatures who developed minds to adapt to and modify their environments. George Herbert **Mead** held views very like Dewey's. However, he carried this evolutionist and pragmatic view of mind further than the other pragmatists, and developed an original theory of the origin of language and intelligence and the self out of the interactions among different organisms and the gestures in which they engage in this interaction. This led to an original and very difficult metaphysics and a theory of social psychology remarkable for its originality and fruitfulness.

C. I. **Lewis** developed a 'conceptualistic pragmatism', a pragmatic theory of the a priori. Whereas Dewey regarded the distinction between analytic and empirical truths as an 'untenable dualism' merely marking the different roles each play in inquiry, Lewis advanced the idea that a priori ideas can be justified and modified on pragmatic grounds. It is the a priori element in knowledge, Lewis held, which is pragmatic, not the empirical. F. C. S. **Schiller** had quite a different perspective, not that of a logician. Though not one of the originators of pragmatism, he was a British ally very sympathetic to some ideas of William James, especially James's idea of the will to believe. He called his philosophy humanism, and it has come to be called pragmatic humanism. He played an important role in British philosophy as a critic of the absolute idealism of **Bradley** and **Bosanquet**, a role enhanced by his special rhetorical gifts.

All told, the most important pragmatists were Peirce, James, and Dewey. In recent years some of their key ideas have been accepted, modified, and applied in different ways by such contemporary philosophers as W. V. O. **Quine**, Donald **Davidson**, and Richard **Rorty**. So, after a period of desuetude in the middle part of the twentieth century, pragmatism, in a somewhat different guise, is very much alive and again at the centre of philosophical discussion.

Bibliography

Abel, Reuben (1966) *Humanistic Pragmatism: The Philosophy of F. C. S. Schiller*, New York: The Free Press.

Dewey, John (1920) *Reconstruction in Philosophy*, Boston, Mass.: The Beacon Press, revised edition, 1948.

Fisch, Max H. (1986) *Peirce, Semeiotic, and Pragmatism*, Bloomington: Indiana University Press.

James, William (1907) *Pragmatism*, New York: Longmans, Green and Co.

—— (1909) *The Meaning of Truth: A Sequel to 'Pragmatism'*, New York: Longmans, Green and Co.

Madden, Edward H. (1963) *Chauncey Wright and the Foundations of Pragmatism*, Seattle: University of Washington Press.

Mead, George Herbert (1934) *Mind, Self and Society*, Chicago: University of Chicago Press.

—— (1964) *Selected Writings*, ed. Andrew J. Reck, Chicago: University of Chicago Press.

Murphy, Arthur E. (1993) 'Pragmatism and the context of rationality', *Transactions of the C. S. Peirce Society* 29(2, 3 and 4): 123–78, 331–68, 687–722.

Peirce, C. S. (1934) *Collected Papers*, vol. V, *Pragmatism and Pragmaticism*, Cambridge, Mass.: Harvard University Press.

Sleeper, Ralph W. (1986) *The Necessity of Pragmatism*, New Haven, CT: Yale University Press.

Thayer, H. S. (1981) *Meaning and Action: A Critical History of Pragmatism*, Indianapolis: Hackett Publishing Company, second edition.

—— (ed.) (1982) *Pragmatism: The Classic Writings*, Indianapolis: Hackett Publishing Company.

Wiener, Philip P. (1949) *Evolution and the Founders of Pragmatism*, Cambridge, Mass.: Harvard University Press.

MARCUS SINGER

Process Philosophy

A metaphysical philosophy that postulates process rather than substance as fundamental. This movement has been dominated by **Whitehead**, though **Hartshorne** has also been influential in the latter part of the century. The journal *Process Studies* was founded in 1971.

Bibliography

Brown, Delwin, *et al.* (eds) (1971) *Process Philosophy and Christian Thought*, Indianapolis: Bobbs-Merrill.

Lucas, George (1989) *The Rehabilitation of Whitehead: An Analytic and Historical Assessment of the Process of Philosophy*, Albany, NY: SUNY Press.

Moreland, J. P. (1988) 'An enduring self: the Achilles' heel of process philosophy', *Process Studies* 17: 193–9.

Neville, Robert C. (1974) *The Cosmology of Freedom*, New Haven, CT: Yale University Press.

—— (1987) 'Contributions and limitations of process philosophy', *Process Studies* 16: 283–98.

Reck, Andrew J. (1975) 'Process philosophy, a categorical analysis', *Tulane Studies in Philosophy* 24: 58–91

Sibley, Jack R. and Gunter, Pete A. Y. (eds) (1978) *Process Philosophy: Basic Writings*, Washington, DC: University Press of America.

STUART BROWN

Realism

Controversies connected with 'realism' are deeply embedded in philosophy and, in the West, date back at least to Plato and Aristotle, each of whom was a prototype for one kind of realist. Plato opposed the view that moral values are dependent on social convention and his theory of forms represents one kind of moral realism. Plato's 'realism' has tended to be associated with belief in the existence of abstract entities generally and especially about mathematical objects. Realism in mathematics has been a common, though controversial position, and was espoused by **Frege**, amongst others.

Although a realist about abstract objects, Plato tended to deny the reality of the objects of the senses and, for this reason, is associated with **idealism**. In this respect Aristotle differed from him and Aristotle's realism about the objects of the senses remains hugely influential, for instance, in the Scholastic tradition. Even when **absolute idealism** dominated in British and American universities, early in the twentieth century, Aristotle always provided an alternative. Twentieth-century realism has not only these connections with the distant past but also with other realisms, such as that of the Scottish Common Sense School. It is thus a word of great historical complexity and no general statement can do justice to the choice of the term 'realist' by twentieth-century philosophers as a whole. Realism has been opposed not only to idealism, but to subjectivism, relativism, constructivism and phenomenalism. The opposition to idealism, however, was of particular importance earlier in the century.

The realist revolt against absolute idealism dates back at least to **Russell** and **Moore** in the 1890s. It was characterized by an espousal of pluralism, external relations, a correspondence theory of truth and a belief in realities independent of a mind. In America there were different schools of realism such as **New Realism** and **Critical Realism** and these terms are also extended to thinkers with similar views elsewhere.

Among the persistent problems about realism has been, how to accommodate it within an **empiricist** epistemology. Those who have favoured an empiricist epistemology of science have been inclined to deny the reality of theoretical entities. Against this there have been those who have called themselves 'scientific realists', such as W. **Sellars**, who have wished to assert the reality of all the entities spoken of in science, including those that are not observable.

Many philosophers in the 1980s and 1990s, reacting against a previously common subjectivism in ethics or various forms of pervasive relativism, have sought to defend ethical realism.

Bibliography

Primary:

Bhaskar, Roy (1975) *A Realist Theory of Science*, Leeds: Leeds Books.

Devitt, Michael (1984) *Realism and Truth*, Oxford: Blackwell.

Moore, G. E. (1903) 'The refutation of idealism', *Mind* New Series 7.

Putnam, Hilary (1982) 'Three kinds of scientific realism', *Philosophical Quarterly* 32: 195–200.

Wild, John (1948) *Introduction to Realistic Philosophy*, New York: Harper & Bros.

Wright, Crispin (1992) *Truth and Objectivity*, Cambridge, Mass.: Harvard University Press.

Secondary:

Bowman, Lars (1955) *Criticism and Construction in the Philosophy of American New Realism*, Stockholm: Almqvist & Wiksell.

—— (1967) 'British and American realism, 1900–1930', *Monist* 51: 159–304.

Dummett, Michael (1982) 'Realism', *Synthese* 52: 55–112.

Feyerabend, Paul (1964) 'Realism and instrumentalism', in Mario Bunge (ed.) *The Critical Approach to Science and Philosophy*, New York: Free Press.

Harlow, Victor (1931) *A Bibliography and Genetic Study of American Realism*, Oklahoma City: Harlow Publishing Co.

Passmore, John (1985) *Recent Philosophers*, London: Duckworth, ch. 5.

Perry, Ralph Barton (1926) *Philosophy of the Recent Past*, part V, New York: Scribner's.

Schneider, Herbert (1946) *A History of American Philosophy*, New York: Columbia University Press, pp. 571–2.

—— (1964) *Sources of Contemporary Realism in America*, Indiana: Bobbs-Merrill.

STUART BROWN

Semiology

Semiology, or 'the science of signs', is largely derived from the work of the linguist Ferdinand de **Saussure**, one of the major sources of inspiration behind **structuralism**, a movement that can fairly claim to be the home of semiological analysis. For Saussure, language was a system and, crucially, a system of conventionally-agreed signs that elicited a predictable response from the individual. The study of language was essentially the study of the relations between its various signs, that is, of the internal grammar of the linguistic system. Language became the model for how all sign systems worked, with Saussure predicting the development of a more general discipline called 'semiology' (after the Greek word for sign, *semeion*) that would study such systems.

Semiological analysis is a matter of analysing the grammatical relations between signs within a given system. Claude **Lévi-Strauss** thus treats a group of South American Indian myths as a self-contained system, where the signs in question are manipulated around in each individual myth in the manner of variations on a theme. The group in effect constitutes a genre with its own common underlying grammar.

Roland **Barthes**' work contains some of the most sustained examples of semiological analysis in the structuralist literature, with its detailed researches into such phenomena as advertising and fashion. In each case Barthes's concern is to identify the semiological codes involved in the system and how the audience responds to these. Literature and film equally go to make up sign systems for structuralist analysis, with the analyst setting out to identify and describe the grammar applying within an individual text, or across literary or cinematic genres (detective thrillers, westerns, etc.).

Bibliography

Barthes, Roland (1957) *Mythologies*, Paris: Seuil (English translation, *Mythologies*, trans. Annette Lavers, London: Jonathan Cape, 1972).

Culler, Jonathan (1983) *Structuralist Poetics: Structuralism, Linguistics and the Study of Literature*, London: Routledge & Kegan Paul.

Lévi-Strauss, Claude (1964) *Mythologiques I: Le cru et le cuit*, Paris: Plon (English translation, *The Raw and the Cooked: Introduction to a Science of Mythology, I*, trans. John and Doreen Weightman, New York: Harper & Row, 1969).

Saussure, Ferdinand de (1916) *Cours de linguistique générale*, ed. Charles Bally, Albert Sechehaye and Albert Reidlinger, Paris: Payot (English translation, *Course in General Linguistics*, trans. Wade Baskin, London: Peter Owen, 1960).

STUART SIM

Structuralism

Structuralism is a methodology originally used in the social sciences and later adapted to the treatment of literary texts and, more broadly, all artworks. Its first major exponent was Ferdinand de **Saussure**, whose theoretical work in linguistics is the common ancestor of all later structuralist analyses. Saussure himself gave the impetus to later structuralist work by his statement that all aspects of social life could be treated by the methodology that he had adopted for linguistics.

The structuralist approach is what Saussure calls 'static' or 'synchronic': that is, it is ahistorical. It takes a cross-section of its subject-matter and provides an analysis of the way in which all parts of a self-regulating system function together to form a consistent and coherent whole. Such elements have meaning or significance or function only by comparison with other elements, and from their place within the total system. For Saussure, the meaning of a word, or what he calls a 'sign', is partly determined by contrast with the other words in the context of which it occurs. Structuralist methodology is also intended to be purely descriptive: it takes as its raw data only

actually-occurring social phenomena, which it does not evaluate or judge.

One important distinction made by Saussure was that between the deeper level of *langue*, or the rules and procedures operative within a natural language, and the surface level of *parole*, or the strings of words generated within and limited by those rules and procedures. A two-tier division was similarly adopted by later comparative structuralists: **Lévi-Strauss**, for example, thought that particular myths were exemplifications of a deeper underlying structure or pattern common to all myths, and claimed that his discoveries in this area could be used for a further structuralist study of how all human minds operate. Structuralism links all individual examples of social phenomena to their underlying structure, and this means that their authors or origins are not taken into consideration in any way.

If used properly, structuralist analyses can be useful, although limited. One criticism levelled against the methodology is that it simply assumes that the phenomena studies are coherent wholes: neither in Lévi-Strauss's treatment of myth, nor in Edmund Leach's study of Genesis, is there any attempt to disprove the competing hypothesis that the subject-matter is a loose collection of narrative from different sources. Another objection is that, by the improper use of the methodology, what is alleged to be the underlying structure of particular exemplifications is simply imposed and not discovered.

Structuralism has had a powerful influence on many disciplines throughout most of the twentieth century, but in the last three decades it has been displaced by **post-structuralism**, its hostile descendant.

Bibliography

Works on structuralism by individual authors include:

Barthes, R. (1990) *S/Z*, trans. R. Miller, Oxford: Blackwell.

Leach, E. (1969) *Genesis as Myth*, London: Jonathan Cape.

Lévi-Strauss, C. (1969) *The Raw and the Cooked*, London: Jonathan Cape.

Saussure, F. de (1974) *Course in General Linguistics*, London: Fontana.

General works on structuralism include:

Piaget, J. (1971) *Structuralism*, London: Routledge.

Sturrock, J. (ed.) (1979) *Structuralism and Since*, Oxford: Oxford University Press.

KATHRYN PLANT

Uppsala School

The Uppsala School was, according to **Wedberg**, 'the first unequivocally naturalistic academic school in philosophy' in Sweden. Academic philosophy there had previously been strongly idealistic. The new positivistic movement was founded by Axel **Hägerström** and Adolf **Phalén** and flourished in the period 1910–40. Justus **Hartnack** has claimed that **analytical philosophy** can be said to have originated, largely independently, in three places: Cambridge, Uppsala and Vienna. The Uppsala School shared with the **Vienna Circle** a strong bias against metaphysics, as well as the view that moral utterances have no truth value. It shared with the Cambridge analysts such as **Moore** and **Russell** both their emphasis on conceptual analysis and a strong commitment to **realism** in reaction to the previously dominant **idealism**.

The Uppsala School was in some respects continued in the period after the Second World War by Konrad **Marc-Wogau**, Ingemar **Hedenius** and others. These, however, were more influenced by the Vienna Circle and by Anglo-American analytical philosophy than by Hägerström and Phalén.

Bibliography

Hartnack, Justus (1967) 'Scandinavian philosophy', in Paul Edwards (ed.) *Encyclopedia of Philosophy*, New York: Macmillan & Co.

Sandin, Robert T. (1962) 'The founding of the Uppsala School', *Journal of the History of Ideas* 23: 496–512.

Wedberg, Anders (1980) 'Sweden', in John R. Burr (ed.) *Handbook of World Philosophy: Contemporary Developments Since 1945*, London: Aldwych Press, pp. 173–90.

STUART BROWN

Utilitarianism

Utilitarianism is a normative ethical doctrine springing from largely nineteenth-century foundations and deriving from the view that happiness is the greatest good. It judges the morality of acts by their consequences. The best known version of the Principle of Utility is that formulated by John Stuart Mill (1806–73): 'The creed which accepts as the foundation of morals, Utility, or the greatest Happiness Principle holds that actions are right in proportion as they tend to promote happiness, wrong in their proportion as they tend to produce the reverse of happiness' (*Utilitarianism*, ch. 1).

Jeremy Bentham (1748–1832) is widely regarded as the founder of modern Utilitarianism although its general principle was enunciated earlier by Helvetius, Hutcheson and Hume. Bentham maintained that only pleasure is intrinsically good and pain intrinsically bad, and that the amount of pleasure or pain produced is the determining factor in judging the morality of an action.

J. S. Mill refined Bentham's morally vulnerable claim that it is the *quantity* of pleasure or pain that counts by distinguishing between 'higher' and 'lower' pleasures, but in allowing that some pleasures are better than others this doctrine invited the criticism that in cases of two actions producing equal amounts of pleasure something other than pleasure determines their moral values. Mill also placed emphasis on personal liberty and the individual conscience rather than on the mechanical calculation of pleasures and the social and legislative sanctions favoured by Bentham. A significant flaw in Mill's defence of happiness as the supreme good is his failure effectively to meet the criticism that there is a general conviction that on many occasions the bringing about of a just state of affairs over-rides the aim of creating the maximum of happiness.

Utilitarian doctrine was criticized and developed by Henry Sidgwick (1833–1900) who in *The Methods of Ethics* (1874) rejected psychological hedonism and argued that moral principles may be known intuitively. G. E. **Moore**, in chapter 3 of his *Principia Ethica* (1903), likewise rejected psychological hedonism and also argued that Utilitarianism was guilty of committing the naturalistic fallacy, that is, of deducing moral judgements from statements of fact. His own view was that good is a non-natural property that is known intuitively and that an action is right if its consequences would be better than any other alternative and possible action.

In the latter half of the twentieth century much discussion has focused on the relative merits of rule-utilitarianism, which holds that right actions are those that conform to rules general observance of which would maximize happiness, and act-utilitarianism, which holds that the right action is the particular one that maximizes happiness in a situation. Both forms of utilitarianism are vulnerable to the criticism that they do not adequately satisfy intuited principles concerning justice and equity. Another influential view is that developed by J. J. C. **Smart** who has argued that there is no proof of the truth or falsity of utilitarianism but that it embodies a certain attitude that is apt to appeal to the generality of people and that offers guidance for the conduct of the moral life. A comparable approach has been elaborated by R. M. **Hare**, resulting in a doctrine of 'preference utilitarianism' that avoids many of the difficulties connected with the estimation of pleasures and pains and in which the morally right act is the one that provides people with what they would prefer to have and prevents them from having what they prefer not to have.

Utilitarianism has been stringently criticized by Bernard **Williams** who has maintained that it disregards the kind of significance life actually has for mature persons who, he points out, shape their lives meaningfully by means of projects the importance of which is not recognized by a doctrine that seeks simply to satisfy as many preferences as possible, taking no account of their differing values.

Bibliography
Primary:
Bentham, Jeremy (1789) *Introduction to the Principles of Morals and Legislation*, London.
Mill, J. S. (1861) *Utilitarianism*, London.
Moore, G. E. (1903) *Principia Ethica*, Cambridge: Cambridge University Press.
Sidgwick. H. (1874) *The Methods of Ethics*, London: Macmillan.
Warnock, M. (ed.) (1962) *Utilitarianism*, London: Fontana/Collins. (Contains Mill's *Utilitarianism*, his *On Liberty*, and the first five chapters of Bentham's *Introduction to the Principles of Morals and Legislation*.)
Secondary:
Hare, R. M. (1981) *Moral Thinking*, Oxford: Clarendon Press.
Lyons, D. (1965) *The Forms and Limits of Utilitarianism*, Oxford: Oxford University Press.
Quinton, A. (1973) *Utilitarian Ethics*, London: Macmillan.
Sen, A. K. and Williams, B. A. O. (eds) (1982) *Utilitarianism and Beyond*, Cambridge: Cambridge University Press.
Smart, J. J. C. and Williams, B. A. O. (1973) *Utilitarianism: For and Against*, Cambridge: Cambridge University Press.

DIANÉ COLLINSON

Vienna Circle

The name adopted by a group of **Logical Positivists** in Vienna who were led by Moritz **Schlick**. The leading philosophers in the group were Rudolf **Carnap**, Otto **Neurath**, Herbert **Feigl**, Friedrich **Waismann**, Edgar Zilsel and Victor **Kraft**. Amongst the prominent scientists and mathematicians were Phillip **Frank**, Karl Menger, Kurt **Gödel** and Hans Hahn. Both Ludwig

Wittgenstein and Karl **Popper** knew members of the Circle, though they distanced themselves from its ideas. A. J. **Ayer** was associated with the Circle as a young man and became one of the most able advocates of its point of view in the English-speaking world. The group published a manifesto in 1929 stating its 'scientific outlook' (*wissenschaftliche Weltauffassung*). It also organized an international congress in Prague, followed by others in the 1930s at Königsberg, Copenhagen, Prague, Paris and Cambridge. By these means alliances were formed with similar groups in Berlin, **Uppsala** and Warsaw (see **Lvov-Warsaw School**). The Vienna Circle had fellow-travellers throughout the world, particularly in the USA (Ernest **Nagel**, Charles **Morris** and W. V. O. **Quine**) and in Britain (Susan **Stebbing** and Richard **Braithwaite**). Its international influence was consolidated through editorial control of the journal *Erkenntnis*, which Carnap and Hans **Reichenbach** made the principal publication of the Logical Positivism movement.

The Circle was broken up by the rise of Nazism in the German-speaking world. Its influence remained none the less considerable in other countries. In the USA, where Carnap had emigrated, an ambitious series of brochures entitled the *International Encyclopedia of Unified Science* was planned. This series was eventually completed, though some of the numbers in it (**Kuhn**'s *Structure of Scientific Revolutions*, for instance) were remote in spirit from logical positivism. In the English-speaking world generally the influence of the Vienna Circle was considerable, though diluted, because of the way logical positivism affected **Analytical Philosophy**. In Scandinavia the influence has also continued, particularly through the **Uppsala School**.

Bibliography
Ayer, A. J. (1956) 'The Vienna Circle', in Gilbert Ryle, *et al. The Revolution in Philosophy*, London: Macmillan.
—— (1959) 'History of the Logical Positivism movement', in A. J. Ayer (ed.) *Logical Positivism*, Glencoe, Ill.: Free Press, and London: Allen & Unwin, pp. 3–10.
Kraft, Victor (1950) *Der Wiener Kreis, Der Ursprung des Neopositivismus*, Vienna (English translation, *The Vienna Circle: The Origin of Neo-Positivism*, trans. A. Pap, New York: Philosophical Library, 1953).
Neurath, Otto (1935) *Le développment du Cercle de Vienne et l'avenir de l'empiricisme logique*, Paris: Hermann.
——Carnap, R. and Hahn, H. (1929) *Wissenschaf-*

tliche Weltauffassung: Der Wiener Kreis, Vienna: Wolf.

Smith, Barry (1987) 'Austrian origins of logical positivism', in Barry Gower (ed.) *Logical Positivism in Perspective*, Totowa, NJ: Barnes & Noble.

Übel, Thomas E. (ed.) (1991) *Rediscovering the Forgotten Vienna Circle*, Dordrecht: Kluwer Academic Publishers.

STUART BROWN

Vitalism

This term and some close variants have been used to describe some quite different types of philosophy in the twentieth century.

One of the major types of usage is in the philosophy of biology, where vitalism is used to denote the view that life is a property of organisms which is irreducible to physio-chemical processes, a view held, for example, by **Driesch** and von **Uexküll**. These thinkers maintain that, whilst there are close links between the organic and inorganic properties of organisms, no reduction of the former to the latter is possible. Organisms exhibit principles or modes of being entirely distinct in kind from the non-organic. Vitalism in this sense is to be differentiated from the views of biologists like J. S. **Haldane** and von **Bertalanffy**, who preferred to think of themselves as 'organicists', maintaining that many organic processes can be reduced to inorganic ones, but denying that the inorganic can be identified with the mechanical.

The second important usage of this term is in the compound 'ratio-vitalism', adopted by **Ortega y Gasset** to describe his own philosophy, and consequently very influential in the Hispanic language communities. Ortega differentiates his view from the usage in the philosophy of biology described above; from epistemologies which regard knowledge as a biological process (e.g. Avenarius); and from epistemologies claiming the possibility of a non-rational grasp of ultimate reality (e.g. **Bergson**). Ratio-vitalism is the view that (a) reason is the only means to knowledge, but (b) insists that reason must be regarded as a property of a living subject, thinking the system in question.

Bibliography

Edwards, Paul (ed.) (1967) *Encyclopedia of Philosophy*, New York: Macmillan & Co.

Ferrater Mora, José (1984) *Diccionario de Filosofia*, Madrid: Alianza Editorial, fifth edition.

Nagel, E. (1961) *The Structure of Science*, London: Routledge & Kegan Paul.

Ortega y Gasset, José (1924) *Ni vitalismo ni racionalismo*, also in *Obras Completas* III.

Schlick, M. (1949) *Philosophy of Nature*, New York: Philosophical Library.

Toulmin, S. and Goodfield, J. (1962) *The Architecture of Matter*, London: Hutchinson.

ROBERT WILKINSON

NATIONALITY INDEX

The nationality for each entrant is given; those of dual nationality are listed under one or the other but not both, i.e. Lévi-Strauss is listed under Belgian-French. Changes of citizenship are also given where known.

Catalan
Xirau

Chilean
Echeverría
Giannini
Millas
Molina Garmendia
Schwartzmann

Chinese
Ai Siqi
Cai Yi
Cai Yuanbei
Chan Wing-tsit
Chen Duxiu
Fang Dongmei
Feng Youlan
Gao Heng
Guang Feng
Guo Moruo
He Lin
Hong Qian
Hou Wailu
Hu Shi
Jin Yuelin
Kang Youwei
Li Dazhao
Li Shizen
Li Zehou
Liang Qichao
Liang Souming
Liu Jie
Lu Xun
Mao Zedong
Mei Yibao
Mou Zongsan
Ouyang Jianwu
Qian Mu
Ren Jiyu
Shen Youding
Su Shaozhi
Sun Zhongshan
Taixu
Tan Sitong
Tang Junyi
Tang Yongtong
Wang Dianji
Wang Guowei
Xie Youwei
Xiong Shili
Yan Fu
Yu Guangyuan
Zhang Binglin
Zhang Dainian
Zhang Dongsun
Zhang Shenfu
Zhao Jibin
Zheng Xin
Zhu Guangqian
Zhu Qianzhi
Zong Baihua

Chinese-American
Wang Hao

Colombian
Belaünde

Cuban
Mañach
Piñera Llera
Varona

Czech
Kol'man
Körner (later British)
Kosík
Masaryk
Patočka
Schubert-Soldern

Czech-American
Wertheimer

Czech-German
Kautsky

Danish
Bohr
Hartnack
Høffding
Jørgensen

Dominican Republic
Henríquez Ureña

Dutch
Beerling
Beth
Bierens de Haan
Bolland
Brouwer
Bruggen
De Vogel
Delfgaauw
Dèr Mouw
Dooyeweerd
Heymans
Heyting
Hollak
Hubbeling
Loen
Mannoury
Meyer-Wichmann
Nuchelmans
Ovink
Polak
Pos
Sevenhuijsen

Egyptian
Abd al-Raziq
Abduh
Amin
Al Aqqad
Fuad
Hanafi
Khalid
Nagib Mahmud

Estonian-German
Uexküll

Finnish
Kaila
von Wright

French
Alain
Alquié
Aron
Bachelard, G.
Balibar
Barbusse
Barthes
Bataille
Baudrillard
Beauvoir
Berger
Bergson
Binet
Blondel
Bourdieu
Boutroux
Bouveresse
Bréhier
Broglie
Brunschvicg
Camus
Canguilhem
Castoriadis (originally
    Greek)
Cavaillès
Corbin
Courtine
Couturat
Dagognet
Deleuze
Descombes
Ducasse (naturalized US
    citizen, 1910)
Dufrenne
Duhem
Duméry
Dunan
Durkheim
Engel
Éspinas
Foucault
Fougeyrollas
Fouillée
Garrigou-Lagrange
Gaultier
Gilson
Goblot
Gouhier
Guattari
Gueroult
Gurvitch (of Russian
    origin)
Hamelin
Hannequin
Herbrand
Hyppolite

Jabès (born Egypt of
    Italian-Jewish parents)
Jankélévitch
Jaurès
Kofman
Koyré
Laberthonnière
Lacan
Lachelier
Lacoue-Labarthe
Lalande
Lavelle
Le Doeuff
Le Roy
Le Senne
Lefebvre
Lefort
Léon
Levinas
Lévy-Bruhl
Loisy
Lyotard
Macherey
Malraux
Marcel
Marion
Maritain
Maurras
Merleau-Ponty
Milhaud
Monod
Morin
Mounier
Nabert
Nancy
Nédoncelle
Pariente
Péguy
Philonenko
Piéron
Poincaré
Polin
Pradines
Rauh
Ravaisson-Mollien
Renouvier
Revel
Rey
Ribot
Ricoeur
Rosset
Rougier
Ruyer
Sartre
Serres
Sertillanges
Sorel
Tarde
Teilhard de Chardin
Touraine
Valéry
Vuillemin
Wahl
Weil, E.
Weil, S.

French-Romanian
Goldmann

Georgian
Bakradze

German
Adickes
Adorno
Apel
Bauch
Becker
Benjamin
Bernstein
Bloch
Bollnow
Born
Bultmann
Bühler
Cantor (born Russia)
Carnap
Cassirer
Cohen, H. (German Jew)
Cohn
Conrad-Martius
Dessoir
Deussen
Dilthey
Driesch
Duhring
Eucken
Fischer
Frank, M.
Frege
Gadamer
Gehlen
Geiger
Geyser
Habermas
Haeckel
Hartmann, E. von
Hartmann, N.
Havemann
Heidegger
Heimsoeth
Heisenberg
Hilbert
Hoernlé (born British
  South African)
Honneth
Horkheimer
Husserl
Jaspers
Klages
Klinger
Korsch
Külpe
Landgrebe
Liebert
Liebmann
Lipps
Lorenzen
Löwith
Maihofer
Mannheim

Marcuse
Marquard
Märten
Meinecke
Misch
Münsterberg
Natorp
Nelson
Nietzsche
Ostwald
Otto
Paulsen
Pfänder
Planck
Plessner
Rahner
Reinach
Rickert
Rintelen
Rosenzweig (German
  Jew)
Scheler
Schlick
Scholz
Simmel
Spengler
Spiegelberg (naturalized
  American, 1944)
Spranger
Stammler
Stein
Stern
Stumpf
Tillich
Troeltsch
Tugendhat
Vaihinger
Volkelt
Waldenfels
Weber
Wellmer
Weyl
Windelband
Wundt
Zeller

German-American
Arendt (emigrated to
  USA, 1941)
Grünbaum
Hempel
Koffka
Köhler
Kristeller (moved to
  USA, 1939)
Lewin
Loeb
Reichenbach
Voegelin

German-Austrian
Brentano

**German-Swiss-
American**
Einstein

Ghanaian
N'Krumah

Greek
Androutsos
Axelos
Boreas
Georgoulis
Papanoutsos

Guatemalan-American
Castañeda

Guinean
Cabral

Hungarian
Brandenstein
Heller
Juhos
Lakatos
Lukács
Pauler

Hungarian-American
Neumann
Szasz

Hungarian-British
Kolnai
Polanyi

Indian
Ali
Aurobindo
Chatterjee
Gandhi
Iqbal
Radhakrishnan
Spivak
Tagore
Vivekananda

Indian-Pakistani
Mawdudi

Iranian
Nasr
Shariati
Yazdi

Iraqi
Mahdi

Irish
Coffey
Murdoch

Israeli
Bar-Hillel (born Austria)

Bergman (born
  Czechoslovakia)
Buber (of Austrian
  origin)
Idel (born in Romania)
Leibowitz (born Latvia)
Pines (of French origin)
Rotenstreich
Scholem (born
  Germany)
Simon (born Germany)

Italian
Abbagnano
Aliotta
Ardigò
Banfi
Bonatelli
Buonaiuti
Calogero
Carabellese
Carbonara
Carlini
Castelli-Gattinara di
  Zubiena
Cavarero
Colorni
Corradi Fiumara
Croce
Del Vecchio
Della Volpe
Eco
Fabro
Galli
Gentile
Gramsci
Guardini
Guzzo
La Via
Labriola
Levi (of Spanish-Jewish
  ancestry)
Lombardi
Marchesini
Martinetti
Mazzantini
Mondolfo
Mosca
Orestano
Ottaviano
Paci
Papini
Pareto
Pareyson
Pastore
Peano
Rensi
Rignano
Rossi-Landi
Sciacca
Spirito
Stefanini
Sturzo
Tarozzi
Troilo

Tronti
Vailati
Varisco
Vattimo
Zamboni

Japanese
Hatano
Kaneko
Miki
Nishida
Nishitani
Suzuki
Taketani
Tanabe
Tosaka
Watsuji

Kurdish
Nursi

Latvia
Kook (immigrant to pre-
    mandate Palestine)

Lithuanian
Gurwitsch (became
    German 1930, and
    American 1946)

Livonian-German
Keyserling

Martinican (French)
Fanon

Mexican
Caso
Larroyo
Nicol
Ramos
Recasens-Siches
Salmerón
Vasconcelos
Villoro Toranzo
Yamuni Tabush
Zea

Montenegrin
Plamenatz (naturalized
    British)

Moroccan
Lahbabi
Laroui

New Zealander
Baier, A. C.
Bennett
Harré
Prior

Norwegian
Føllesdal
Naess

Skjervheim
Zapffe

Pakistani
Qadir
Rahman

Peruvian
Delgado Espinosa
Deústua
Iberico y Rodriguez
Mariátegui
Miró Quesada Cantuarias
Salazar Bondy

Polish
Ajdukiewicz
Bocheński
Chwistek
Golaszewska
Ingarden
Kotarbiński
Leśniewski
Łukasiewicz
Lutoslawski
Meyerson (naturalized
    French)
Schaff
Tatarkiewicz

Polish-American
Post
Tarski
Tymieniecka

Polish-British
Kolakowski
Lewy

Polish-German
Luxemburg

Portugese
Barreto
Coimbra

Romanian
Cioran
Radulescu-Motru
Xenopol

Russian
Akselrod, P. B.
Aksel'rod (Ortodoks)
Aleksandrov, A. D.
Aleksandrov, G. F.
Andreas-Salomé
Asmus
Berdyaev
Bogdanov
Bukharin
Bulgakov
Chicherin
Deborin
Drobnitskii

Fedorov
Florensky
Fock
Frank, S. L.
Frolov
Ilyenkov
Kareev
Kedrov
Kollontai
Kopnin
Kovalevsky
Kropotkin
Lapshin
Lavrov
Lenin
Lopatin
Losev
Lossky
Lunacharsky
Meliukhin
Mikhailovsky
Ovsiannikov
Plekhanov
Rozanov
Rubel (became French
    citizen, 1937)
Rubinshtein
Shestov
Shpet
Solov'ev
Struve
Tolstoy
Trotsky
Tugarinov
Vernadsky
Volsky
Vvedensky
Zenkovsky

Russian-American
Jakobson
Rand

Russian-Estonian
Lotman

Russian-French
Kojève

Rwandan
Kagame

Senegalese
Senghor

Serbian
Petronijevic

South African
Degenaar
Smuts

South African-British
Findlay

Spanish
Amor Ruibal
D'Ors y Rovira
Ferrater Mora
Gaos y Gonzalez Pola
García Morente
Giner de los Rios
Laín Entralgo
Maeztu
Marias Aguilera
Ortega y Gasset
Sanchez de Zavala
Santayana
Turró
Unamuno y Jugo
Zambrano
Zaragüeta y Bengoechea
    (of Basque origin)
Zubiri Apalátegui (of
    Basque origin)

Spanish-Argentinian
Romero

Spanish-Mexican
Sánchez Vázquez

Sudanese
Taha

Swedish
Boodin
Hägerström
Hedenius
Kanger
Marc-Wogau
Moritz
Nygren
Phalén
Prawitz
Segelberg
Segerstedt
Wedberg

Swedish-Finnish
Westermarck

Swiss
Bachelard, S.
Barth
Binswanger
Brunner
Gourd (naturalized 1876)
Hersch
Jauch
Jung
Marty
Piaget
Saussure

Swiss-American
Pap

Syrian
Al-Azm
Rida

Tibetan
Gyatso

Transylvanian
Wiesel (Jew from
 Romania/Hungary)

Turkish
Izmirli
Topcu
Ulken

Ukrainian
Ahad ha-Am (Ukrainian
 Jew)
Omel'ianovskii

Uruguayan
Ardao
Vaz Ferreira

Uruguayan-Mexican
Lapoujade

Venezuelan
Mayz Vallenilla

Yugoslav
Markovič
Stojanovič

Yugoslav-Croatian
Ivekovič

Zaïrian
Mudimbe

CATEGORY INDEX

This index is linked to the *Cat:* field in the main entry, and reflects the main 'types' of philosopher, i.e. the main philosophical subject area of an entrant's work. An entrant may be (and often is) listed under more than one category.

Utilitarianism
Mach
Smart, J. J. C.

Value theory
Dupréel
Frondizi
Joad
Lewis, C. I.
Rintelen
Tatarkiewicz

Vitalism
Marias Aguilera
Millas
Ortega y Gasset
Zambrano

Western philosophy
Cai Yuanbei

Wittgenstein
Findlay

Writer
Bell
Kolakowski
Mauthner

INDEX OF INTERESTS

This index is linked to the *Ints:* field in the main entry, and gives the special area(s) of interest for each philosopher.

INDEX OF INFLUENCES

This is an index of influences on twentieth-century philosophers. It is drawn almost entirely from what contributors have provided under the heading **Influences** in the context of particular entries and should be used in conjunction with other indexes, in particular the **Category Index**. Many of those categorized as 'Marxist' philosophers are not also listed here as influenced by Marx, since it was judged repetitious. Often those listed as *influenced* by a particular tradition would be said to *belong* to another tradition.

INDEX OF PEOPLE

This index consist of those persons mentioned in the accounts given of the thought and reception, who were of some significance to the entrant. They may be influences on the entrant, admirers, critics (hostile or otherwise), persons influenced by the entrant, etc. and may or may not work or have worked in the field of philosophy (for instance, some are writers).

INDEX OF SUBJECTS

Lists subjects (branches of philosophy, theology, literature, etc.) mentioned in the text paragraphs of an entry as being of some significance to the entrant.

Marburg School: Cassirer; Cohen, H.; Natorp; Stammler
Marxism: Adorno; Banfi; Bulgakov; Carbonara; Croce; Della Volpe Frank, S. L.; Habermas; Hook; Horkheimer; Ingenieros; Kovalevsky; Laroui; Liang Qichao; MacIntyre; Mannheim; Marcuse; Rossi-Landi; Sartre; Tronti; Vuillemin Weber; Zhang Dongsun
Marxism - Leninism: Aksel'rod (Ortodoks)
materialism: Armstrong; Chen Duxiu; Guang Feng; Lenin; Mounier Ren Jiyu; Rensi
metaphysics: Guardini
methodological individualism: Watkins
modernism: Buonaiuti; Castelli-Gattinara di Zubiena
Moism: Mei Yibao
Moscow Linguistic Circle: Jakobson
Moscow-Tartu: Lotman
Munich Phenomenological Circle: Pfänder
mysticism: Bergson; Danto; Tang Junyi; Topcu

naturalism: Anderson; Fraser; Hare; Moore; Nagel, E.; Pears; Perry
Nazism: Meinecke
negative utilitarianism: Watkins
neo-Confucianism: Chan Wing-tsit; Fang Dongmei; Qian Mu
neo-Kantianism: Banfi; Philonenko; Zeller
neo-Platonism: De Wulf; Florensky
neo-positivism: Schlick
neoscholasticism: Zamboni
neo-vitalism: Driesch
New Criticism: Beardsley
New Culture Movement: Li Dazhao
New Realism: James; Marvin; Montague, W. P.; Perry; Royce
nihilism: Solov'ev
nominalism: Armstrong; Chwistek
normal idealism: Pringle-Pattison

objective idealism: Solov'ev
ontology: Hartmann, N.

panentheism: Hartshorne
peripateticism: Corbin
permanent revolution: Mao Zedong
personal idealism: Schiller
personalism: Giner de los Rios; Lopatin; Nédoncelle
Petofi Circle: Kosík
phenomenalism: Moore

phenomenology: Brentano; Gibson; Guardini; Hyppolite; Kosík Mañach; Marcuse; Reale; Salazar Bondy; Skjervheim; Tanabe; Tang Junyi; Van Steenberghen
philosophy of action: Austin
philosophy of culture: Li Shizen; Ramos
philosophy of education: Lunacharsky
philosophy of history: Croce; Weber
philosophy of law: Kenny
philosophy of life: Li Shizen
philosophy of mind: Brentano; Donnellan
philosophy of religion: Kojève
philosophy of science: Aliotta
philosophy of war: Kenny
Platonism: De Raeymaeker; Hartmann, N.
pluralism: Berlin; James; McKeon; Papini; Russell
political philosophy: Wollheim
populism: Kovalevsky; Lenin; Mao Zedong
positivism: Alberini; Ardao; Bonatelli; Cruz Costa; Del Vecchio Gadamer; Grene; Habermas; Henríquez Ureña; Ingenieros; Korn; Lavrov; Léon Mosca; Mou Zongsan; Papini; Piñera Llera; Planck; Troilo; Vernadsky; Wang Hao Zea
postmodernism: Gellner; Haraway
pragmatism: Baillie; Dewey; Hook; Morris; Nagel, E.; Perry; Scheffler Zhang Shenfu
Prague Linguistic Circle: Jakobson
prescriptivism: Hare
private-language argument: Pears
process philosophy: Hartshorne; Paci
psychoanalysis: Brentano; Qadir; Ramos
psychologism: Popper
psychology: Chomsky
psychology of perception: Dretske; Meinong

quantum mechanics: Kaila; Planck
quantum theory: Schrödinger

radical empiricism: James
rationalism: Castelli-Gattinara di Zubiena; Colorni; Feyerabend Pears; Solov'ev; Spencer; Stout; Tang Yongtong; Watkins
realism: Aliotta; Armstrong; Castelli-Gattinara di Zubiena; Chwistek Cornman; Jin Yuelin; Lenin; Lewis, H. D.; Mackenzie; Moore; Perry; Salmon; Stout Troilo

Reconstructionism: Kaplan, M. M.
relativism: Gellner; Hesse
reliabilism: Alston
revisionism: Bogdanov; Lunacharsky; Plekhanov; Struve
right-wing Hegelianism: Chicherin
romanticism: Guo Moruo

sarvodaya: Gandhi
satyagraha: Gandhi
scepticism: Cornman; Hu Shi; Mackie; Nozick; Peirce; Rensi; Wisdom
scholasticism: Coffey; Kenny
school of Sainte-Beuve: Bachelard
secularism: Fuad
semantics: Morris
semiotics: Rossi-Landi
sense-datum theory: Jackson
Signific Movement: Mannoury
social Darwinism: Sumner; Yan Fu
socialism: Berdyaev; Chen Duxiu; Fuad; Hook; Kollontai; Kovalevsky Labriola; Lavrov; Lenin; Liang Qichao; Lunacharsky; Mao Zedong; Mariátegui Mounier; Nielsen; Sánchez Vázquez; Sellars, R. W.; Solov'ev; Struve; Su Shaozhi Taixu; Trotsky; Zhang Dongsun
sociology: Della Volpe
sociology of knowledge: Mannheim
solipsism: Pears
Spinozism: Farrer
spiritual realism: Jones
spiritualism: Ardao
Stoics: Łukasiewicz
structural anthropology: Fougeyrollas
structuralism: Mudimbe
subjective idealism: Jones; Lenin
Sufism: Corbin
symbolic logic: Peirce
symbolism: Langer
syntactics: Morris

theology: De Vogel; Kenny; Mercier; Ottaviano; Sertillanges
theosophy: Corbin
Thomism: Buonaiuti; Copleston; De Raeymaeker; Duhem; Farrer Garrigou-Lagrange; Gilson
totalitarianism: Arendt

unity of science: Mannoury
utilitarian theory: Parfit
utilitarianism: Brandt; Hare; Hedenius; Moore; Popper

verificationism: Dummett; Hong Qian
Vienna Circle: Ayer; Bergmann; Feigl; Frank, P.; Jørgensen